Table of Contents

How to Use This Price Guide

Information used in this price guide was obtained from various manufacturers, publishers, producers, retailers and other secondary market sources.

Because secondary market prices can vary from region to region—and even within a given locale—values listed in this price guide are just that: *guides* to help collectors, insurance agents, appraisers and others determine the "going" or "asking" price. These values reflect the most often asked-for or sold-for prices. This guide is not published to determine exact pricing information on collectibles and should not be taken as such.

YR	NAME	LIMIT	ISSUE	TREND
① SCHMID			③	
② LOWELL DAVIS			L. DAVIS FARM SET	
85	MAIN HOUSE	CL	42.50	125.00
④	⑤	⑥	⑦	⑧

How to Read the Price Guide

① Manufacturer or Publisher

② Artist

③ Series

④ Year of Production or Publication

⑤ Name of Piece

⑥ Edition Size or Status of Piece

⑦ Issue price

⑧ Trend price at time of this publication

1999

COLLECTOR'S
mart magazine

Price Guide to
LIMITED EDITION
COLLECTIBLES

Edited by Mary L. Sieber
and the staff of
COLLECTOR'S
mart magazine

Published by

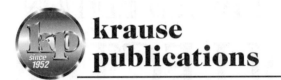 **krause
publications**

700 E. State Street • Iola, WI 54990-0001
Telephone: 715/445-2214

Please call or write for our free catalog.
Our toll-free number to place an order or obtain a free catalog is 800-258-0929
or please use our regular business telephone 715-445-2214
for editorial comment and further information.

Library of Congress Catalog Number: 95-077317
ISBN: 0-87341-646-5
Printed in the United States of America

Cover Photograph Credits:

Front cover: Garcia Beanie Baby by Ty Inc. Oakbrook, Ill.; *Premiere Gene* doll courtesy
Ashton-Drake Galleries, Niles, Ill.; *Street By the Park* print by P. Buckley Moss, courtesy
The Moss Portfolio, Mathews, VA.; *Four Calling Birds* blown-glass ornament courtesy
Christopher Radko, Elmsford, N.Y.; and *Bibbity, Bobbity Boo* figurine courtesy Walt Disney
Classics Collection/Walt Disney Art Editions, Burbank, Calif.

Back cover: Lights of Home plate by Terry Redlin, courtesy Hadley Collection,
Bloomington, Minn.; *Centenary Swan* crystal figurine by Swarovski Consumer Goods
Ltd., Cranston, R. I.; and Harmony Kingdom's *Red Rose* box figurine courtesy Harmony
Ball Co., Columbus, Ohio.

These abbreviations will be used to indicate edition size or status of a piece:

CL = Closed

FD = Firing Days
(limited to a certain number of firing days)

OP = Open

RT = Retired

SO = Sold Out

ST = Set
(two or more items issued together with one price)

SU = Suspended

TL = Time Limited

UD = Undisclosed

YR = Year of issue
(limited to calendar year of issue)

DS = Discontinued

* = Unknown

N/A = Not Available

TW = Temporarily Withdrawn

Collectibles are listed alphabetically by category (bells, cottages, dolls, etc.); alphabetically by company (Anri, Cybis, etc.); alphabetically by series name; chronologically by year of issue; and alphabetically by title within each issue year.

Note: Price ranges may reflect various demands in the market from one geographic location to another; the condition of the collectible; specific markings found on the piece; and/or changes that occurred while the piece was in production.

Introduction

Welcome to the fourth edition of the *Collector's mart magazine Price Guide to Limited Edition Collectibles*. We've taken the information from our third edition, studied it, added to it, and updated it to create an incredible resource of nearly 60,000 prices that covers the broad spectrum of limited edition collectibles.

Our goal for the *Price Guide to Limited Edition Collectibles* is a simple one: to provide a guide listing thousands of secondary market prices covering the gamut of limited edition collectibles including bells, cottages, dolls, figurines, ornaments, plates, prints and steins. The term "secondary market" may be confusing to collectors, but simply put, it is the market collectibles enter after they have left the original, primary point of retail sales. It exists because a buyer is searching for an item no longer available through regular retail distribution channels. Secondary market transactions are represented by sales between individual collectors as well as dealers who may or may not be involved with primary retail selling.

To arrive at what we consider a fair trend price—or the average price at which a collectible is currently trading hands—we employ a panel of limited edition collectibles experts as well as comb secondary market newsletters and auction results; work with secondary market dealers and exchange specialists; monitor the manufacturers of limited edition collectibles; and listen to our readers, many of whom know as much about their collectible of choice as any expert. Please keep in mind this book is simply a guide to be used in conjunction with every other bit of information you may be able to obtain to determine a realistic value for your collectible. In the end, enthusiasts like you, who actually purchase collectibles on the secondary market, determine the values of those collectibles.

We've divided this book into categories that make it easy for you to find the information relevant to the items you collect: bells, cottages, dolls and plush, figurines, ornaments, plates, prints and steins. An introduction precedes each section and summarizes many of the trends occurring in today's marketplace.

Items within the listings are arranged alphabetically, first by company name, then by series name, and then by the artist's last name. They are further organized chronologically by the year in which the collectible was issued, then alphabetically by the title of the piece. Folios at the top of each page mark each section and make flipping through the book quick and easy. Two indexes at the back of the book help you locate items for which you may not have the necessary information.

Special thanks go to the distinguished group of secondary market specialists and collectibles experts who helped us with this edition. Within their respective fields, these experts have provided us with prices and trends, filled in missing information and prepared overviews of the various categories. Those individuals are:

- Dean Genth, Miller's Hallmark and Gift Galleries, Eaton, Xenia and Cincinnati, Ohio. Expert on M.I. Hummel, Swarovski crystal and Precious Moments figurines.

- Ken Armke, Jean Jackson and Melanie Moss, OHI Exchange, New Braunfels, Texas. Experts on Anheuser-Busch steins, David Winter cottages, Department 56 cottages, Lilliput Lane cottages and Harbour Lights lighthouses.

- Matthew Rothman, Lighthouse Trading Co., Limerick, Pa. Expert on Harbour Lights and Cheryl Spencer Collin lighthouses and Forma Vitrum architectural structures.

- Don Newton of The Willows, Elk Grove, Calif. Expert on prints by Thomas Kinkade, Dennis Patrick Lewan and Jack Terry as well as figurines by Shelia's Inc., FJ Designs/Cat's Meow and JP Editions.

- Kay Laubauch, Shickshinny, Pa. Expert on David Winter cottages.

- Dee Brandt, Classic Endeavors, Greenback, Tenn. Expert on Walt Disney Classics Collection figurines, Harbour Lights lighthouses and Forma Vitrum architectural structures.

- Melanie J. Benham, Glitter, Raleigh, N.C. Expert on glass ornaments by Christopher Radko, Kurt S. Adler Inc. (Polonaise Collection) and Patricia Breen.

- Connie DeAngelo, Gifts, Glass & Much, Much More, Allentown, Pa. Expert on Fenton Art Glass.

- Charles and Sharon Bragg, B & B Shop, Lima, Ohio. Experts on Fenton Art Glass.

- Charlotte M. Rush, Tyler, Texas. Expert on Lowell Davis figurines.

- Peggy Whiteneck, East Randolph, Vt. Expert on Lladr— figurines and ornaments.

- Susan K. Elliott, Worldwide Association of Gift and Collectible Retailers (NALED), Dallas. Expert on plates and plate history.

- Jay Brown, Gallery One, Mentor, Ohio. Expert on prints, especially those released by The Greenwich Workshop and Mill Pond Press.

- Richard Rogers, Ruby's Dolls, Mahopac, N.Y. Expert on Annalee Mobilitee dolls.

- Teresa Reyes, Bronx, N.Y. Expert on Swarovski crystal.

- Clara Johnson Scroggins, Tampa, Fla. Expert on ornaments.

- Betty Hodges, Mission, Kan. Expert on dolls.

- Rick and Terri Peters, independent brokers and publishers of Pictorial Treasures, Pawhuska, Okla. Expert on Thomas Kinkade prints as well as prints by other major artists.

- Robert Zschack, Clifton, N.J. Expert on Gregory Perillo plates.

We'd also like to acknowledge those of you who wrote or called with information and suggestions. Thanks, too, to Daisy Cain, associate editor of Collector's mart, and the Krause Publications book production department for their invaluable assistance.

— Mary L. Sieber

Even with all the information we've gleaned through our market experts and by studying auction reports and exchange service publications, we constantly strive for more accurate prices. That's where you can help. If you have information you feel will benefit this book, please send it our way so we may update our records. Send information to:

Collector's mart Price Guide to Limited Edition Collectibles
700 E. State St.
Iola, WI 54990-0001
Attn. Mary Sieber

Bells

Bellsizations long gone. They are steeped in mystery, surrounded by legends of special powers ranging from thwarting demons to invoking curses and lifting spells.

In general, bells were most often used as a signal, marking significant points of ritual, calling to worship, tolling the hours, announcing events and helping communities to rejoice, mourn or send warning. Their power was at one time extremely significant to many religions. Bells have also been treasured as patriotic symbols and war trophies.

Most cultures today have turned these utilitarian objects into works of art with respect to shape, materials and ornamentation. Created of porcelain, wood, metal, china, crystal and other materials, the melodious chimers are a double joy for collectors because they are both lovely to hear and see.

The hobby of collecting limited edition bells rocketed to its zenith in the 1970s, especially during the United States' Bicentennial when a multitude of special bells were produced to commemorate the historic occasion. Unfortunately, the bell market became saturated, and as a result the hobby settled into a quieter pastime.

Today, many special Bicentennial bells, as well as Lladró porcelain bells, Waterford crystal bells and Jan Hagara Christmas bells, which are no longer produced, remain popular and do well on the secondary market. Bells produced by Pairpoint still rank high on collectors' lists as well.

Today's popular bell manufacturers include Fenton Art Glass, Goebel Inc., Enesco Corp., Fort Inc., Seymour Mann and Roman Inc., among others.

BELLS

YR NAME	LIMIT	ISSUE	TREND

ANRI
J. FERRANDIZ   ANRI WOODEN CHRISTMAS BELLS

76 CHRISTMAS	YR	6.00	52.00
77 CHRISTMAS	YR	7.00	42.00
78 CHRISTMAS	YR	10.00	42.00
79 CHRISTMAS	YR	13.00	30.00
80 CHRISTMAS KING, THE	YR	17.50	18.00
81 LIGHTING THE WAY	YR	18.50	20.00
82 CARING	YR	18.50	19.00
83 BEHOLD	YR	18.50	19.00
85 NATURE'S DREAM	YR	18.50	20.00

J. FERRANDIZ   JUAN FERRANDIZ MUSICAL CHRISTMAS BELLS

76 CHRISTMAS	YR	25.00	82.00
77 CHRISTMAS	YR	25.00	82.00
78 CHRISTMAS	YR	35.00	77.00
79 CHRISTMAS	YR	47.50	62.00
80 LITTLE DRUMMER BOY	YR	60.00	65.00
81 GOOD SHEPHERD BOY, THE	YR	63.00	65.00
82 SPREADING THE WORD	YR	63.00	65.00
83 COMPANIONS	YR	63.00	65.00
84 WITH LOVE	YR	55.00	57.00

ARTAFFECTS
R. SAUBER   BELLS

87 MOTHERHOOD BELL	*	25.00	26.00
87 NEWBORN BELL	*	25.00	26.00
87 SWEET SIXTEEN BELL	*	25.00	26.00
87 WEDDING BELL, THE (GOLD)	*	25.00	26.00
87 WEDDING BELL, THE (SILVER)	*	25.00	26.00
87 WEDDING BELL, THE (WHITE)	*	25.00	26.00

R. SAUBER   BRIDE BELLES FIGURINE BELLS

88 CAROLINE	*	27.50	28.00
88 ELIZABETH	*	27.50	28.00
88 EMILY	*	27.50	28.00
88 GROOM	*	27.50	28.00
88 JACQUELINE	*	27.50	28.00
88 LAURA	*	27.50	28.00
88 MEREDITH	*	27.50	28.00
88 REBECCA	*	27.50	28.00
88 SARAH	*	27.50	28.00

G. PERILLO   INDIAN BRAVE ANNUAL BELL

89 CHRISTMAS POW-WOW	YR	24.50	33.00
90 INDIAN BRAVE	YR	24.50	25.00
91 INDIAN BRAVE	YR	24.50	25.00

G. PERILLO   INDIAN PRINCESS ANNUAL BELL

89 LITTLE PRINCESS, THE	YR	24.50	31.00
90 INDIAN PRINCESS	YR	24.50	25.00

ARTISTS OF THE WORLD
T. DEGRAZIA   DEGRAZIA BELLS

80 FESTIVAL OF LIGHTS	5000	40.00	90.00
80 LOS NINOS	7500	40.00	90.00

BING & GRONDAHL
E. JENSEN   ANNUAL CHRISTMAS BELL

83 CHRISTMAS IN THE OLD TOWN	YR	45.00	46.00
84 CHRISTMAS LETTER, THE	YR	45.00	46.00
85 CHRISTMAS EVE AT THE FARMHOUSE	YR	45.00	46.00
86 SILENT NIGHT, HOLY NIGHT	YR	45.00	46.00
87 SNOWMAN'S CHRISTMAS EVE, THE	YR	47.50	48.00
88 OLD POET'S CHRISTMAS, THE	YR	49.50	50.00
89 CHRISTMAS ANCHORAGE	YR	52.00	53.00
90 CHANGING OF THE GUARDS	YR	55.00	56.00
91 COPENHAGEN STOCK EXCHANGE AT XMAS, THE	YR	59.50	60.00

J. NIELSEN   ANNUAL CHRISTMAS BELL

98 CHRISTMAS	YR	65.00	65.00

J. STEENSEN   ANNUAL CHRISTMAS BELL

92 CHRISTMAS AT THE RECTORY	YR	62.50	63.00
93 FATHER CHRISTMAS IN COPENHAGEN	YR	62.50	63.00

H. THELANDER   ANNUAL CHRISTMAS BELL

80 CHRISTMAS IN THE WOODS	YR	39.50	40.00
81 CHRISTMAS PEACE	YR	42.50	43.00
82 CHRISTMAS TREE, THE	YR	45.00	46.00

J. WOODSON   CHRISTMAS IN AMERICA BELL

88 CHRISTMAS EVE IN WILLIAMSBURG	YR	27.50	105.00
89 CHRISTMAS EVE AT THE WHITE HOUSE	YR	29.00	77.00
90 CHRISTMAS EVE AT THE CAPITOL	YR	30.00	31.00
91 INDEPENDENCE HALL	YR	35.00	36.00
92 CHRISTMAS IN SAN FRANCISCO	YR	37.50	38.00
93 COMING HOME FOR CHRISTMAS	YR	37.50	38.00

YR NAME	LIMIT	ISSUE	TREND

BRADFORD EDITIONS
*
HEAVEN'S LITTLE HELPERS BELL COLLECTION

97 BUNCH OF LOVE	120-DAY	20.00	20.00

C.U.I./CAROLINA COLLECTION
J. HARRIS
STERLING CLASSIC

91 BARN OWL	RT	100.00	103.00
91 CAMBERWELL BEAUTY	RT	100.00	103.00
91 CLOUDED YELLOW	RT	100.00	103.00
91 KINGFISHER	RT	100.00	103.00
91 LARGE BLUE	RT	100.00	100.00
91 MOUSE	RT	100.00	100.00
91 PEACOCK	RT	100.00	100.00
91 SMALL TORTOISESHELL	RT	100.00	100.00
91 SWALLOWTAIL	RT	100.00	100.00

CROWN & ROSE
J. BERGDAHL
12 DAYS OF CHRISTMAS

82 FIVE GOLDEN RINGS	7500	75.00	80.00
83 SIX GEESE A' LAYING	7500	75.00	80.00
84 SEVEN SWANS A' SWIMMING	7500	78.00	80.00

M. DINKEL
12 DAYS OF CHRISTMAS

78 PARTRIDGE IN A PEAR TREE	7500	50.00	300.00
79 TWO TURTLEDOVES	7500	55.00	80.00
80 THREE FRENCH HENS	7500	60.00	85.00

J. SPOUSE
12 DAYS OF CHRISTMAS

81 FOUR CALLING BIRDS	7500	70.00	80.00

DANBURY MINT
ROCKWELL INSPIRED
THE NORMAN ROCKWELL COMMEMORATIVE BELL

79 TRIPLE SELF-PORTRAIT	*	29.50	35.00

ROCKWELL INSPIRED
THE WONDERFUL WORLD OF NORMAN ROCKWELL

79 BABY-SITTER	*	27.50	30.00
79 BACK TO SCHOOL	*	27.50	30.00
79 BATTER UP	*	27.50	30.00
79 FRIEND IN NEED	*	27.50	30.00
79 GRAMPS AT THE REINS	*	27.50	30.00
79 GRANDPA'S GIRL	*	27.50	30.00
79 LEAPFROG	*	27.50	30.00
79 PUPPY IN THE POCKET	*	27.50	30.00

ROCKWELL INSPIRED
VARIOUS

75 DOCTOR AND DOLL	*	27.50	55.00
76 DISCOVERY, THE	*	27.50	45.00
76 FREEDOM FROM WANT	*	27.50	45.00
76 GRANDPA SNOWMAN	*	27.50	45.00
76 NO SWIMMING	*	27.50	45.00
76 SAYING GRACE	*	27.50	45.00
77 KNUCKLES DOWN	*	27.50	40.00
77 PUPPY LOVE	*	27.50	40.00
77 REMEDY, THE	*	27.50	40.00
77 RUNAWAY, THE	*	27.50	40.00
77 SANTA'S MAIL	*	27.50	40.00
77 TOM SAWYER	*	27.50	40.00

DAVE GROSSMAN CREATIONS
ROCKWELL INSPIRED
NORMAN ROCKWELL COLLECTION

75 FACES OF CHRISTMAS NRB-75	RT	12.50	37.00
76 BEN FRANKLIN (BICENTENNIAL)	RT	12.50	27.00
76 DRUM FOR TOMMY NRB-76	RT	12.00	32.00
80 LEAPFROG NRB-90	RT	50.00	58.00

DEPARTMENT 56
*
HERITAGE VILLAGE

96 CHRISTMAS BELLS	YR	35.00	35.00

ENESCO CORP.
P. HILLMAN
CHERISHED TEDDIES CHRISTMAS

92 ANGEL BEAR	*	20.00	65.00

*
FROM BARBIE WITH LOVE

96 HERE COMES THE BRIDE FI BELL 174734	YR	40.00	40.00
96 SWIRLED BELL W/HEART HANDLE 162272	*	12.50	13.00

KINKA
KINKA BELLS

89 EASTER...FILLED W/HOPE & BLESSINGS 116610	OP	22.50	23.00
89 YOUR LOVE IS SPECIAL TO ME 116580	OP	22.50	23.00
90 CHRISTMAS IS A TIME OF LOVE 119962	YR	25.00	25.00
91 LIFE IS ONE JOYOUS STEP/ANOTHER 121320	YR	22.50	23.00
91 MAY THE GLOW OF GOD'S LOVE 120596	YR	22.50	23.00

M. ATTWELL
MEMORIES OF YESTERDAY

90 HERE COMES BRIDE/GOD BLESS HER 523100	OP	25.00	26.00

S. BUTCHER
PRECIOUS MOMENTS ANNUAL BELLS

80 LET THE HEAVENS REJOICE E-5622	YR	17.00	210.00
82 I'LL PLAY MY DRUM FOR HIM E-2358	YR	17.00	60.00
83 SURROUNDED WITH JOY E-0522	YR	18.00	55.00
84 WISHING YOU A MERRY CHRISTMAS E-5393	YR	19.00	50.00
85 GOD SENT HIS LOVE 15873	YR	19.00	40.00

YR	NAME	LIMIT	ISSUE	TREND
85	WISHING YOU A COZY CHRISTMAS 102318	YR	20.00	40.00
86	LOVE IS THE BEST GIFT OF ALL 109835	YR	22.50	35.00
88	OH HOLY NIGHT 522821	YR	25.00	40.00
88	TIME TO WISH/MERRY CHRISTMAS 115304	YR	25.00	40.00
89	ONCE UPON A HOLY NIGHT 523828	YR	25.00	35.00
90	MAY YOUR CHRISTMAS BE MERRY 524182	YR	25.00	35.00
92	BUT THE GREATEST OF THESE/LOVE 527726	YR	25.00	30.00
S. BUTCHER			**PRECIOUS MOMENTS COLLECTION**	
92	WISHING YOU/SWEETEST CHRISTMAS 530174	YR	25.00	32.00
S. BUTCHER			**PRECIOUS MOMENTS VARIOUS BELLS**	
80	GOD UNDERSTANDS E-5211	RT	17.00	55.00
80	JESUS IS BORN E-5623	SU	17.00	45.00
80	JESUS LOVES ME E-5208	SU	17.00	53.00
80	JESUS LOVES ME E-5209	SU	15.00	50.00
80	PRAYER CHANGES THINGS E-5210	SU	18.00	47.00
80	WE HAVE SEEN HIS STAR E-5620	SU	17.00	45.00
81	LORD BLESS YOU AND KEEP YOU, THE E-7175	SU	17.00	40.00
81	LORD BLESS YOU AND KEEP YOU, THE E-7176	SU	17.00	48.00
81	MOTHER SEW DEAR E-7181	SU	17.00	43.00
81	PURR-FECT GRANDMA, THE E-7183	SU	17.00	45.00
82	LORD BLESS YOU AND KEEP YOU, THE E-7179	SU	22.50	43.00

FENTON ART GLASS

YR	NAME	LIMIT	ISSUE	TREND
*	BELL 7668LT 6-1/2" CHRISTMAS MORN	*	*	28.00
80	BELL 7564BD	*	*	25.00
80	BELL 7564JA	*	*	25.00
80	BELL 9462BD BASKETWEAVE	*	*	36.00
81	BELL 7562VB STAR	*	*	55.00
81	BELL 7563VY STAR CRIMPED	*	*	50.00
81	BELL 7564FN MOTHER'S DAY	*	*	30.00
81	BELL 7564SS	*	*	30.00
81	BELL 8265BO LILY OF VALLEY	*	*	32.00
81	BELL 9462CD BASKETWEAVE	*	*	30.00
81	BELL 9462DR BASKETWEAVE	*	*	30.00
81	BELL 9462SF	*	*	30.00
81	BELL 9463FL NATIVITY	*	*	40.00
81	BELL 9463FT NATIVITY	*	*	40.00
81	BELL 9463TB NATIVITY	*	*	40.00
81	BELL 9463TG NATIVITY	*	*	35.00
81	BELL 9463VE NATIVITY	*	*	25.00
82	BELL 7564BA	*	*	22.00
82	BELL 7564IN IRIS	*	*	35.00
82	BELL 7564KP	*	*	35.00
82	BELL 7564NA MOTHER'S DAY	*	*	35.00
82	BELL 7564VI	*	*	35.00
82	BELL 9660FG CRAFTSMAN	*	*	30.00
83	BELL 1760TE MINI TEDDY BEAR	*	*	19.00
83	BELL 1760TE PETITE TEDDY	*	*	20.00
83	BELL 1760WC WINTER CHAPEL	*	*	35.00
83	BELL 7564 SCHALLER, IA	*	*	48.00
83	BELL 7564FD WILDFLOWERS	*	*	30.00
83	BELL 7564RQ MOTHER'S DAY	*	*	30.00
83	BELL 7564TT	*	*	30.00
83	BELL 7564XA BUDWEISER CLYDESDALES	*	*	75.00
83	BELL 9667KT BLUE BIRD CC	*	*	65.00
83	BELL G1665HG	*	*	24.00
84	BELL 1760FA	*	*	35.00
84	BELL 1773RK	*	*	25.00
84	BELL 3645PO	*	*	100.00
84	BELL 7564PM PRECIOUS PANDA	*	*	25.00
84	BELL 9662VE GIRL	*	*	25.00
84	BELL 9662VP GIRL	*	*	45.00
85	BELL 1760CL PETITE CLOWN	*	*	25.00
85	BELL 1760F4 MINI	*	*	25.00
85	BELL 1760HQ PETITE HOBBYHORSE	*	*	25.00
85	BELL 7564F8	*	*	25.00
85	BELL 7667WP XMAS FANTASY	*	*	25.00
85	BELL 7668K2 SUMMER FUN 6-1/2"	*	*	35.00
85	BELL 7668K3 BACK TO SCHOOL 6-1/2"	*	*	35.00
85	BELL 7668K4 WINTER WONDER 6-1/2"	*	*	35.00
85	BELL 7668K5 THANKSGIVING 6-1/2"	*	*	35.00
85	BELL 7668K6 XMAS CHEER 6-1/2"	*	*	35.00
85	BELL 7673SM SNOWMAN	*	*	47.00
85	BELL 7674SM SNOWMAN	*	*	30.00
85	BELL 9663NK GARDEN OF EDEN	*	*	35.00
85	BELL HARRY NORTHWOOD/GOOD LUCK	*	*	65.00
85	BELL V1774V3 BARNYARD PIGS	*	*	24.00
85	BELL V1774V4 BARNYARD LAMP	*	*	24.00
85	BELL V1774V5 BARNYARD GOOSE	*	*	24.00
86	BELL 1760HW	*	*	24.00
86	BELL 6665UO 7-1/2"	*	*	28.00
86	BELL 6665UO REFLECTIONS	*	*	22.00
86	BELL 7662EW PETITE 4-1/2"	*	*	22.00
86	BELL 7662WQ PETITE 4-1/2"	*	*	22.00

YR	NAME	LIMIT	ISSUE	TREND
86	BELL 7668EW 6-1/2"	*	*	35.00
86	BELL 8361NK BARRED OWL	*	*	35.00
86	BELL 8466DK FABERGE	*	*	35.00
86	BELL 9066BR WHITTON	*	*	50.00
86	BELL 9665PW BEAUTY	*	*	35.00
86	BELL V1760FX PETITE 4-1/2"	*	*	18.00
86	BELL V1774FX OVAL 6-1/2"	*	*	28.00
87	BELL 1760PN PETITE CHILDHOOD	*	*	18.00
87	BELL 3067MI HOBNAIL	*	*	15.00
87	BELL 7662FS PETITE	*	*	18.00
87	BELL 7668FS 6-1/2"	*	*	30.00
87	BELL 9665OO BEAUTY	*	*	18.00
87	BELL 9667CA AURORA	*	*	18.00
88	BELL 1760RD PETITE	*	*	18.00
88	BELL 7662HL PETITE	*	*	18.00
88	BELL 7662VC PETITE	*	*	18.00
88	BELL 7668 BEE-BALM 6-1/2"	*	*	25.00
88	BELL 7668 COLUMBINE 6-1/2"	*	*	25.00
88	BELL 7668 JACOB'S LADDER 6-1/2"	*	*	32.00
88	BELL 7668 LILAC MARIPOSA 6-1/2"	*	*	32.00
88	BELL 7668 PASTURE THIMBLE 6-1/2"	*	*	28.00
88	BELL 7668 RED CLOVER 6-1/2"	*	*	28.00
88	BELL 7668BD BIRDS OF WINTER 6-1/2"	*	*	30.00
88	BELL 7668VC 6-1/2"	*	*	30.00
88	BELL 7669ML MUSICAL	*	*	45.00
88	BELL 7669VZ MUSICAL XMAS	*	*	45.00
88	BELL 9761OC CROSS HANDLE	*	*	25.00
88	BELL C7562JQ CRESTED	*	*	40.00
88	BELL C7662EQ PETITE	*	*	22.00
88	BELL C7667EQ	*	*	40.00
88	BELL C7668QC MUSICAL XMAS 6-1/2"	*	*	45.00
88	BELL EDWARD MUHLEMAN/GOOD LUCK	*	*	50.00
89	BELL 1760CX PETITE CHILDHOOD	5000	*	20.00
89	BELL 8267MP MEDALLION	*	*	29.00
89	BELL 9761VE CROSS	*	*	20.00
89	BELL 9763RU PETITE HEART	*	*	18.00
89	BELL C1773UQ MOTHER'S DAY	*	*	25.00
90	BELL 6761ES PAISLEY 7"	*	*	36.00
90	BELL 7662AF PETITE	*	*	19.00
90	BELL 7662FH PETITE	*	*	22.00
90	BELL 7667BL	*	*	42.00
90	BELL 7667NB	*	*	42.00
90	BELL 7668SN MOTHER'S DAY 6-1/2"	*	*	45.00
90	BELL 9266ES BOW & DRAPE 4-1/2"	*	*	22.00
90	BELL 9266LX BOW & DRAPE 4-1/2"	*	*	17.00
90	BELL 9266SR BOW & DRAPE 4-1/2"	*	*	15.00
90	BELL 9266TL BOW & DRAPE 4-1/2"	*	*	22.00
90	BELL 9268TL BOW & DRAPE 6"	*	*	30.00
90	BELL 9462FH BASKETWEAVE	*	*	30.00
90	BELL 9560LX TEMPLE	*	*	38.00
90	BELL 9560RE TEMPLE	*	*	45.00
90	BELL 9560RN TEMPLE	*	*	37.00
90	BELL C7666KP COPPER ROSE	*	*	42.00
90	BELL C7668MN MOTHER'S DAY 6-1/2"	*	*	38.00
90	BELL C7668UW THANKSGIVING 6-1/2"	*	*	38.00
90	BELL C7668VD VALENTINE'S DAY 6-1/2"	*	*	45.00
90	BELL C7668XA XMAS BLUE BORDER 6-1/2"	*	*	40.00
90	BELL C7668XA XMAS GREEN BORDER 6-1/2"	*	*	40.00
90	BELL C7668XA XMAS ROSES & PINE 6-1/2"	*	*	40.00
90	BELL C9268ET EASTER	*	*	45.00
90	BELL C9560GZ TEMPLE	*	*	40.00

PETITE ARTIST SERIES

YR	NAME	LIMIT	ISSUE	TREND
87	BELL 1760SF	*	*	18.00
89	BELL 1760AC	5000	*	20.00

90TH ANNIVERSARY

YR	NAME	LIMIT	ISSUE	TREND
95	BELL 9667JE 7"	OP	35.00	38.00

D. JOHNSON
BIRDS OF WINTER ED. I

YR	NAME	LIMIT	ISSUE	TREND
87	BELL 7668BC 6-1/2"	4500	29.50	40.00

D. JOHNSON
BIRDS OF WINTER ED. II

| 88 | BELL 7667BD 6-1/2" | 4500 | 29.50 | 45.00 |

D. JOHNSON
BIRDS OF WINTER ED. III

| 90 | BELL 7667BL 6-1/2" | 4500 | 29.50 | 40.00 |

D. JOHNSON
BIRDS OF WINTER ED. IV

| 90 | BELL 7667NB 6-1/2" | 4500 | 29.50 | 40.00 |

F. BURTON
CHRISTMAS AT HOME ED. I

| 90 | BELL 7668HD 6-1/2" | 3500 | 39.00 | 65.00 |

F. BURTON
CHRISTMAS AT HOME ED. II

| 90 | BELL 7668HJ 6-1/2" | 3500 | 35.00 | 45.00 |

F. BURTON
CHRISTMAS AT HOME ED. III

| 92 | BELL 7668HQ 6-1/2" | 3500 | 39.00 | 45.00 |

F. BURTON
CHRISTMAS AT HOME ED. IV

| 93 | BELL 7668HT | 3500 | 39.50 | 40.00 |

M. DICKINSON
CHRISTMAS CLASSICS ED. I

| 78 | BELL 7466CV CHRISTMAS MORN | * | 25.00 | 40.00 |

YR	NAME	LIMIT	ISSUE	TREND
	K. CUNNINGHAM	**CHRISTMAS CLASSICS ED. II**		
79	BELL 7466NC NATURE'S CHRISTMAS	*	30.00	40.00
	D. JOHNSON	**CHRISTMAS CLASSICS ED. III**		
80	BELL 7466GH 6-1/2" GOING HOME	*	32.50	50.00
	D. JOHNSON	**CHRISTMAS CLASSICS ED. IV**		
81	BELL 7466AC 6-1/2"	*	35.00	35.00
	R. SPINDLER	**CHRISTMAS CLASSICS ED. V**		
82	BELL 7466OC 6-1/2"	*	35.00	35.00
	D. JOHNSON	**CHRISTMAS FANTASY ED. I**		
83	BELL 7667AI 6-1/2"	7500	35.00	40.00
	D. JOHNSON	**CHRISTMAS FANTASY ED. II**		
84	BELL 7667GE 6-1/2"	7500	37.50	38.00
	D. JOHNSON	**CHRISTMAS FANTASY ED. III**		
85	BELL 7667WP 6-1/2"	7500	37.50	65.00
	L. EVERSON	**CHRISTMAS FANTASY ED. IV**		
87	BELL 7667CV 6-1/2"	CL	37.50	38.00
	L. PIPER	**CHRISTMAS LIMITED EDITIONS**		
86	BELL 7667XS 6"	5000	35.00	65.00
	M. REYNOLDS	**CHRISTMAS LIMITED EDITIONS**		
92	BELL 7463ZW WINTER ON TWILIGHT BLUE 6-1/2"	2500	29.50	40.00
93	BELL 7463SD MANGER SCENE ON RUBY 6-1/2"	2500	39.50	40.00
93	BELL 7463TV REINDEER ON BLUE 6-1/2"	2500	30.00	30.00
93	BELL 7465GQ FLORAL ON GRN/MUSICAL 6-1/2"	2500	39.50	45.00
94	BELL 7463VG MAGNOLIA ON GOLD 6-1/2"	1000	35.00	35.00
94	BELL 7463VP ANGEL ON IVORY 6-1/2"	1000	39.00	40.00
94	BELL 7465VK PARTRIDGE ON RUBY-MTNS. 6-1/2"	1000	48.50	49.00
95	BELL 2967TH BOW & HOLLY ON IVORY 6-1/2"	900	39.50	40.00
95	BELL 7463TP CHICKADEE ON GOLD 6-1/2"	900	39.50	40.00
95	BELL 7667TQ ICED POINSETTIA ON RUBY 5-1/2"	900	45.00	45.00
96	BELL 2967AC 6-1/2"	2000	39.50	40.00
96	BELL 5144AV 6"	2000	39.50	40.00
96	BELL 6662CH HOLLY BERRIES ON GOLD IRID. 6-1/2"	1500	39.50	40.00
96	BELL 7668QP PARTRIDGE ON SPRUCE 6-1/2"	1500	35.00	35.00
	R. SPINDLER	**CHRISTMAS LIMITED EDITIONS**		
96	BELL 7768QV MOONLIT ON RUBY 6-1/2"	1500	45.00	45.00
96	BELL 9463N7 NATIVITY SCENE 6-1/2"	1500	49.00	48.00
	F. BURTON	**CHRISTMAS STAR "OUR HOME IS BLESSED"**		
95	BELL 7668VT 6-1/2"	2500	45.00	45.00
	F. BURTON	**CHRISTMAS STAR "SILENT NIGHT"**		
94	BELL 7463VS 6"	2500	45.00	45.00
	F. BURTON	**CHRISTMAS STAR ED. III**		
96	BELL 7463SN 6-1/2"	2500	48.00	60.00
	*	**CLYDESDALE**		
83	BELL 7564XA	*	9.25	65.00
	*	**CONNOISSEUR COLLECTION**		
83	BELL 9660WI CRAFTSMEN	3500	25.00	65.00
84	BELL 9163UR	3500	25.00	55.00
	D. BARBOUR	**CONNOISSEUR COLLECTION**		
86	BELL 7666SB	2500	60.00	140.00
	L. EVERSON	**CONNOISSEUR COLLECTION**		
83	BELL 7562UF	2000	50.00	95.00
85	BELL 7666EB 6-1/2"	2500	55.00	100.00
88	BELL 7666ZW 7"	4000	45.00	85.00
89	BELL 9667KT 7"	3500	50.00	75.00
	M. REYNOLDS	**CONNOISSEUR COLLECTION**		
91	BELL 6761UZ 7"	2000	50.00	50.00
	F. BURTON	**DESIGNER BELLS**		
96	BELL 4568EB 6-1/2"	2500	60.00	60.00
	K. PLAUCHE	**DESIGNER BELLS**		
96	BELL 7667HW 5-1/2"	2500	50.00	50.00
	M. REYNOLDS	**DESIGNER BELLS**		
96	BELL 4564IN 6"	2500	60.00	60.00
96	VANITY SET 7199WB 4 PC	1500	250.00	250.00
	R. SPINDLER	**DESIGNER BELLS**		
96	BELL 7562PP 7"	2500	55.00	55.00
	FINN	**DOWN HOME**		
83	BELL 7455FV	1000	65.00	65.00
	F. BURTON	**FAMILY SIGNATURE SERIES**		
98	DON FENTON ROYAL PURPLE BELL, 6 1/2"	TL	99.00	99.00
	*	**HISTORIC COLLECTION**		
93	BELL 3645RN 5 1/2"	OP	25.00	30.00
	*	**HISTORICAL COLLECTION**		
89	BELL 3645XC	*	17.50	20.00
90	BELL 8265BX 6" LILY OF THE VALLEY	*	16.50	30.00
91	BELL 9065DT 5-1/2"	*	25.00	25.00
91	BELL 9560BO TEMPLBELLS 6-3/4"	*	17.50	22.00
92	BELL 3567XV 6"	*	19.50	22.00
92	BELL 9667GF 7" AURORA	*	29.00	35.00
93	BELL 3645RV 5-1/2"	OP	17.50	25.00
94	BELL 9667SS 7"	OP	25.00	25.00
94	BELL 9667ST 7"	*	35.00	35.00
94	BELL 9667ST AURORA 7"	OP	25.00	25.00

YR	NAME	LIMIT	ISSUE	TREND
M. DICKINSON			**LIGHTHOUSE POINT**	
83	BELL 7466LT	1000	65.00	65.00
*			**LOVES ME, LOVES ME NOT**	
94	BELL, 6" 7463RY	TL	49.00	55.00
M. REYNOLDS			**MARY GREGORY**	
93	BELL 7463RQ RUBY 6"	CL	49.00	49.00
94	BELL 7463RY RUBY 6"	CL	49.00	55.00
95	BELL 7463RG 6-1/2"	CL	49.00	55.00
*			**MOTHER'S DAY SERIES**	
80	BELL 7564NB NEWBORN	*	*	25.00
*			**PETITE ARTIST**	
82	BELL 1760TC	*	*	18.00
83	BELL 1760WC	*	*	20.00
M. DICKINSON			**SMOKE 'N CINDERS**	
84	BELL, 7667TL	1250	*	85.00
M. DICKINSON			**SMOKE'N CINDERS**	
84	BELL 7667TL DESIGNER	1250	*	90.00
M. REYNOLDS			**VALENTINE'S DAY**	
92	BELL 7668XB 6"	CL	35.00	35.00

GOEBEL INC.

YR	NAME	LIMIT	ISSUE	TREND
M.I. HUMMEL			**M.I. HUMMEL ANNUAL BELLS**	
78	LET'S SING HUM-700	CL	50.00	88.00
79	FAREWELL HUM-701	CL	70.00	63.00
80	THOUGHTFUL HUM-702	CL	85.00	63.00
81	IN TUNE HUM-703	CL	85.00	88.00
82	SHE LOVES ME HUM-704	CL	85.00	113.00
83	KNIT ONE HUM-705	CL	90.00	113.00
84	MOUNTAINEER HUM-706	CL	90.00	113.00
85	ANNIVERSARY BELL HUM-730	CL	*	1750.00
85	SWEET SONG HUM-707	CL	90.00	113.00
86	SING ALONG HUM-708	CL	100.00	175.00
87	WITH LOVING GREETINGS HUM-709	CL	110.00	200.00
88	BUSY STUDENT HUM-710	CL	120.00	175.00
89	LATEST NEWS HUM-711	CL	135.00	175.00
90	WHAT'S NEW? HUM-712	CL	140.00	175.00
91	FAVORITE PET HUM-713	CL	150.00	175.00
92	WHISTLER'S DUET HUM-714	CL	160.00	200.00
95	FESTIVAL HARMONY W/FLUTE	CL	55.00	55.00
M.I. HUMMEL			**M.I. HUMMEL CHRISTMAS BELLS**	
89	CHRISTMAS BELL HUM-775	CL	35.00	65.00
90	CHRISTMAS BELL HUM-776	CL	37.50	65.00
91	CHRISTMAS BELL HUM-777	45	39.50	65.00
92	CHRISTMAS BELL HUM-778	CL	45.00	65.00
93	CHRISTMAS BELL HUM-779	CL	50.00	55.00
93	CHRISTMAS BELL HUM-780	CL	50.00	55.00
94	CHRISTMAS BELL HUM-781	OP	55.00	55.00
96	CHRISTMAS BELL HUM 782	OP	65.00	65.00
98	ECHOES OF JOY HUM 784	*	*	70.00

GORHAM

YR	NAME	LIMIT	ISSUE	TREND
CURRIER & IVES			**CURRIER & IVES MINI BELLS**	
76	CHRISTMAS SLEIGH RIDE	YR	9.95	38.00
77	AMERICAN HOMESTEAD	YR	9.95	27.00
78	YULE LOGS	YR	12.95	21.00
79	SLEIGH RIDE	YR	14.95	20.00
80	CHRISTMAS IN THE COUNTRY	YR	14.95	21.00
81	CHRISTMAS TREE	YR	14.95	18.00
82	CHRISTMAS VISITATION	YR	16.50	18.00
83	WINTER WONDERLAND	YR	16.50	18.00
84	HITCHING UP	YR	16.50	18.00
85	SKATERS' HOLIDAY	YR	17.50	18.00
86	CENTRAL PARK IN WINTER	YR	17.50	18.00
87	EARLY WINTER	YR	19.00	20.00
N. ROCKWELL			**MINI BELLS**	
81	TINY TIM	YR	19.75	20.00
82	PLANNING CHRISTMAS VISIT	YR	20.00	20.00
N. ROCKWELL			**VARIOUS**	
75	SANTA'S HELPERS	YR	19.50	32.00
75	SWEET SONG SO YOUNG	YR	19.50	52.00
75	TAVERN SIGN PAINTER	YR	19.50	32.00
76	FLOWERS IN TENDER BLOOM	YR	19.50	42.00
76	SNOW SCULPTURE	YR	19.50	48.00
77	CHILLING CHORE (CHRISTMAS)	YR	19.50	36.00
77	FONDLY DO WE REMEMBER	YR	19.50	58.00
78	GAILY SHARING VINTAGE TIMES	YR	22.50	23.00
78	GAY BLADES (CHRISTMAS)	YR	22.50	23.00
79	A BOY MEETS HIS DOG (CHRISTMAS)	YR	24.50	32.00
79	BEGUILING BUTTERCUP	YR	24.50	27.00
80	CHILLY RECEPTION (CHRISTMAS)	YR	27.50	28.00
80	FLYING HIGH	YR	27.50	28.00
81	SKI SKILLS (CHRISTMAS)	YR	27.50	28.00
81	SWEET SERENADE	YR	27.50	28.00
82	COAL SEASON'S COMING	YR	29.50	30.00

YR	NAME	LIMIT	ISSUE	TREND
82	YOUNG MAN'S FANCY	YR	29.50	30.00
83	CHRISTMAS MEDLEY	YR	29.50	30.00
83	MILKMAID, THE	YR	29.50	30.00
84	MARRIAGE LICENSE	OP	32.50	33.00
84	TINY TIM	YR	29.50	30.00
84	YARN SPINNER	5000	32.50	33.00
84	YOUNG LOVE	YR	29.50	30.00
85	YULETIDE REFLECTIONS	5000	32.50	33.00
86	HOME FOR THE HOLIDAYS	5000	32.50	33.00
86	ON TOP OF THE WORLD	5000	32.50	33.00
87	ARTIST, THE	5000	32.50	33.00
87	MERRY CHRISTMAS GRANDMA	5000	32.50	33.00
88	HOMECOMING, THE	15000	37.50	38.00

GREENWICH WORKSHOP
J. CHRISTENSEN

98	1998 MRS. CLAUS BELL	OP	59.00	59.00

HALLMARK
R. CHAD

		DICKENS CAROLER BELL		
90	MR. ASHBOURNE 1ST ED. 2175QX505-6	YR	21.75	38.00
91	MRS. BEAUMONT 2175QX503-9	YR	21.75	38.00
92	LORD CHADWICK 3RD EDITION 2175QX455-4	YR	21.75	38.00
93	LADY DAPHNE 4TH ED. 2175QX550-5	YR	21.75	33.00

HAMILTON GIFTS
M. HUMPHREY

			BELLS	
92	HOLLIES 996095	OP	22.50	23.00
92	SARAH 999385	OP	22.50	23.00
92	SUSANNA 999377	OP	22.50	23.00

HAMPSHIRE PEWTER CO.
*

		TWELVE DAYS OF CHRISTMAS		
93	PARTRIDGE IN A PEAR TREE	500	65.00	70.00
94	TWO TURTLEDOVES	500	65.00	70.00

JAN HAGARA COLLECTABLES
J. HAGARA

		VICTORIAN CHILDREN		
86	BETSY	TL	25.00	75.00
86	JENNY	TL	25.00	75.00
86	JILL	YR	35.00	100.00
86	JIMMY	TL	25.00	75.00
86	JODY	TL	25.00	75.00
86	LISA	TL	25.00	75.00
86	LYDIA	TL	25.00	75.00
87	HOLLY	YR	35.00	40.00
88	MARIE	YR	35.00	35.00

KAISER
K. BAUER

		KAISER CHRISTMAS BELLS		
80	SLEIGH RIDE AT CHRISTMAS	15000	60.00	65.00
81	SNOWMAN	15000	60.00	65.00

N. PETER

		KAISER CHRISTMAS BELLS		
79	ESKIMO CHRISTMAS	15000	60.00	65.00

T. SCHOENER

		KAISER CHRISTMAS BELLS		
78	NATIVITY, THE	15000	60.00	65.00

K. BAUER

		KAISER TREE ORNAMENT BELLS		
79	CAROLERS, THE	YR	27.50	45.00
80	HOLIDAY SNOWMAN	YR	30.00	45.00
81	CHRISTMAS AT HOME	YR	30.00	45.00
82	CHRISTMAS IN THE CITY	YR	30.00	45.00

KIRK STIEFF
*

			BELL	
92	SANTA'S WORKSHOP CHRISTMAS BELL	3000	40.00	40.00

K. STIEFF

		CHRISTMAS BELLS		
90	SILVER BELLS	YR	29.00	29.00
91	HERALD ANGEL	YR	29.00	29.00

K. STIEFF

		MUSICAL BELLS		
77	ANNUAL BELL 1977	CL	17.95	80.00
78	ANNUAL BELL 1978	CL	17.95	75.00
79	ANNUAL BELL 1979	CL	17.95	55.00
80	ANNUAL BELL 1980	CL	19.95	55.00
81	ANNUAL BELL 1981	CL	19.95	70.00
82	ANNUAL BELL 1982	CL	19.95	80.00
83	ANNUAL BELL 1983	CL	19.95	55.00
84	ANNUAL BELL 1984	CL	19.95	45.00
85	ANNUAL BELL 1985	CL	19.95	45.00
86	ANNUAL BELL 1986	CL	19.95	45.00
87	ANNUAL BELL 1987	CL	19.95	35.00
88	ANNUAL BELL 1988	CL	22.50	40.00
89	ANNUAL BELL 1989	CL	25.00	28.00
90	ANNUAL BELL 1990	CL	27.00	28.00
91	ANNUAL BELL 1991	CL	28.00	30.00
92	ANNUAL BELL 1992	YR	30.00	30.00

YR	NAME	LIMIT	ISSUE	TREND
	D. BACORN			
86	NUTCRACKER	OP	29.95	30.00
87	CLARA	OP	29.95	30.00

LANCE CORP.

P.W. BASTON — HUDSON PEWTER BICENTENNIAL BELLS

YR	NAME	LIMIT	ISSUE	TREND
74	BENJAMIN FRANKLIN	CL	*	90.00
74	GEORGE WASHINGTON	CL	*	90.00
74	JAMES MADISON	CL	*	90.00
74	JOHN ADAMS	CL	*	90.00
74	THOMAS JEFFERSON	CL	*	90.00

LENOX CHINA/CRYSTAL COLLECTION

* — ANNUAL CRYSTAL CHRISTMAS BELLS

YR	NAME	LIMIT	ISSUE	TREND
81	PARTRIDGE IN A PEAR TREE	15000	55.00	56.00
82	HOLY FAMILY	15000	55.00	56.00
83	THREE WISE MEN	15000	55.00	56.00
84	DOVE	15000	57.00	58.00
85	SANTA CLAUS	15000	57.00	58.00
86	DASHING THROUGH THE SNOW	15000	64.00	65.00
87	HERALDING ANGEL	15000	76.00	77.00
91	CELESTIAL HARPIST	15000	75.00	80.00
*				**BIRD BELLS**
91	BLUEBIRD	OP	57.00	58.00
91	CHICKADEE	OP	57.00	58.00
91	HUMMINGBIRD	OP	57.00	58.00
92	ROBIN	OP	57.00	58.00
*				**CAROUSEL BELL**
92	CAROUSEL HORSE	OP	45.00	47.00
*				**SONGS OF CHRISTMAS**
91	WE WISH YOU A MERRY CHRISTMAS	YR	49.00	50.00
92	DECK THE HALLS	YR	53.00	55.00

LINCOLN MINT BELLS

N. ROCKWELL — LINCOLN BELLS

YR	NAME	LIMIT	ISSUE	TREND
75	DOWNHILL DARING	*	25.00	70.00

LLADRO

YR	NAME	LIMIT	ISSUE	TREND
91	SPRING BELL L7613M	YR	35.00	35.00
92	SUMMER BELL L7614M	YR	*	35.00
93	AUTUMN BELL L7615M	YR	*	35.00
94	WINTER BELL L7616M	YR	*	35.00
*				**ANNUAL CHRISTMAS BELLS**
87	CHRISTMAS BELL L5458M	YR	29.50	80.00
88	CHRISTMAS BELL L5525M	YR	32.50	35.00
89	CHRISTMAS BELL L5616M	YR	32.50	100.00
90	CHRISTMAS BELL L5641M	YR	35.00	65.00
91	CHRISTMAS BELL L5803M	YR	37.50	45.00
92	CHRISTMAS BELL L5913M	YR	37.50	45.00
93	CHRISTMAS BELL L6010M	YR	*	45.00
94	CHRISTMAS BELL L6139M	YR	*	65.00
95	CHRISTMAS BELL L6206M	YR	*	55.00
96	CHRISTMAS BELL L6297M	YR	*	50.00
*				**LIMITED EDITION BELL**
94	1994 ETERNAL LOVE BELL 7542M	RT	95.00	95.00

MUSEUM COLLECTIONS INC.

N. ROCKWELL — COLLECTORS BELLS

YR	NAME	LIMIT	ISSUE	TREND
82	25TH ANNIVERSARY	OP	45.00	48.00
82	50TH ANNIVERSARY	OP	45.00	48.00
82	FOR A GOOD BOY	OP	45.00	48.00
82	WEDDING/ANNIVERSARY	OP	45.00	48.00

PICKARD

* — CHRISTMAS CAROL BELL SERIES

YR	NAME	LIMIT	ISSUE	TREND
77	FIRST NOEL, THE	3000	75.00	78.00
78	O LITTLE TOWN OF BETHLEHEM	3000	75.00	78.00
79	SILENT NIGHT	3000	80.00	83.00
80	HARK! THE HERALD ANGELS SING	3000	80.00	83.00

RECO INTERNATIONAL

J. MCCLELLAND — JOYOUS MOMENTS

YR	NAME	LIMIT	ISSUE	TREND
80	I LOVE YOU	5000	25.00	26.00
81	SEA ECHOES	5000	25.00	26.00
82	TALK TO ME	5000	25.00	26.00
	S. KUCK			**RECO BELL COLLECTION**
88	CHARITY	OP	15.00	17.00
88	GRACE	OP	15.00	17.00
88	PEACE	OP	15.00	17.00
	S. KUCK			**SPECIAL OCCASIONS-WEDDING**
89	WEDDING, THE	OP	15.00	17.00
	C. MICARELLI			**SPECIAL OCCASIONS-WEDDING**
91	FROM THIS DAY FORWARD	OP	15.00	17.00
91	TO HAVE AND TO HOLD	OP	15.00	17.00

YR NAME	LIMIT	ISSUE	TREND

REED & BARTON
*

NOEL MUSICAL BELLS

YR NAME	LIMIT	ISSUE	TREND
80 1980 BELL	YR	20.00	53.00
81 1981 BELL	YR	22.50	48.00
82 1982 BELL	YR	22.50	38.00
83 1983 BELL	YR	22.50	48.00
84 1984 BELL	YR	22.50	51.00
85 1985 BELL	YR	25.00	41.00
86 1986 BELL	YR	25.00	36.00
87 1987 BELL	YR	25.00	35.00
88 1988 BELL	YR	25.00	28.00
89 1989 BELL	YR	25.00	28.00
90 1990 BELL	YR	27.50	28.00
91 1991 BELL	YR	30.00	31.00
92 1992 BELL	YR	30.00	31.00

*

YULETIDE BELLS

YR NAME	LIMIT	ISSUE	TREND
81 YULETIDE HOLIDAY	YR	14.00	15.00
82 LITTLE SHEPHERD	YR	14.00	15.00
83 PERFECT ANGEL	YR	15.00	16.00
84 DRUMMER BOY	YR	15.00	16.00
85 CAROLER	YR	16.50	18.00
86 NIGHT BEFORE CHRISTMAS	YR	16.50	17.00
87 JOLLY ST. NICK	YR	16.50	18.00
88 CHRISTMAS MORNING	YR	16.50	18.00
89 BELL RINGER, THE	YR	16.50	18.00
90 WREATH BEARER, THE	YR	18.50	18.00
91 A SPECIAL GIFT	YR	22.50	23.00
92 MY SPECIAL FRIEND	YR	22.50	23.00

RIVER SHORE
N. ROCKWELL

NORMAN ROCKWELL SINGLE ISSUES

YR NAME	LIMIT	ISSUE	TREND
81 GRANDPA'S GUARDIAN	7000	45.00	47.00
81 SPRING FLOWERS	347	175.00	180.00

N. ROCKWELL

ROCKWELL CHILDREN SERIES I

YR NAME	LIMIT	ISSUE	TREND
77 FIRST DAY OF SCHOOL	7500	30.00	80.00
77 FLOWERS FOR MOTHER	7500	30.00	65.00
77 FOOTBALL HERO	7500	30.00	80.00
77 SCHOOL PLAY	7500	30.00	80.00

N. ROCKWELL

ROCKWELL CHILDREN SERIES II

YR NAME	LIMIT	ISSUE	TREND
78 DRESSING UP	15000	35.00	53.00
78 FIVE CENTS A GLASS	15000	35.00	42.00
78 FUTURE ALL AMERICAN	15000	35.00	55.00
78 GARDEN GIRL	15000	35.00	42.00

ROMAN INC.
I. SPENCER

ANNUAL NATIVITY BELLS

YR NAME	LIMIT	ISSUE	TREND
90 NATIVITY	YR	15.00	16.00
91 FLIGHT INTO EGYPT	YR	15.00	16.00
92 GLORIA IN EXCELSIS DEO	YR	15.00	16.00
93 THREE KINGS OF ORIENT	YR	15.00	16.00

F. HOOK

FRANCES HOOK BELLS

YR NAME	LIMIT	ISSUE	TREND
85 BEACH BUDDIES	15000	25.00	30.00
86 SOUNDS OF THE SEA	15000	25.00	30.00
87 BEAR HUG	15000	25.00	30.00

R. FERRUZZI

THE MASTERPIECE COLLECTION

YR NAME	LIMIT	ISSUE	TREND
82 MADONNA OF THE STREETS	OP	25.00	26.00

F. LIPPE

THE MASTERPIECE COLLECTION

YR NAME	LIMIT	ISSUE	TREND
79 ADORATION	OP	20.00	22.00

P. MIGNARD

THE MASTERPIECE COLLECTION

YR NAME	LIMIT	ISSUE	TREND
80 MADONNA WITH GRAPES	OP	25.00	26.00

G. NOTTI

THE MASTERPIECE COLLECTION

YR NAME	LIMIT	ISSUE	TREND
81 HOLY FAMILY, THE	OP	25.00	26.00

ROYAL COPENHAGEN
S. VESTERGAARD

CHRISTMAS

YR NAME	LIMIT	ISSUE	TREND
92 QUEEN'S CARRIAGE, THE	YR	69.50	70.00
93 CHRISTMAS GUESTS	YR	69.50	70.00
98 CHRISTMAS	YR	65.00	65.00

SAMSONS STUDIOS
S. BUTCHER

MCCOONS COUNTY

YR NAME	LIMIT	ISSUE	TREND
* "5 O'CLOCK MAN" WITH POLKA DOT TIE	RT	15.00	50.00
* BREAK TIME	RT	15.00	50.00
* CHOW TIME- COWBOY	RT	15.00	70.00
* DINNER TIME	RT	15.00	50.00
* GET UP- WOMAN WITH CURLERS	RT	15.00	125.00
* LUNCH TIME	RT	15.00	50.00

SANDSTONE CREATIONS
T. DEGRAZIA

A FANTASY EDITION

YR NAME	LIMIT	ISSUE	TREND
* PARTY TIME	7500	40.00	40.00
* WEE THREE	7500	40.00	40.00
80 LITTLE PRAYER	7500	40.00	40.00
81 FLOWER VENDOR	7500	40.00	40.00

YR	NAME	LIMIT	ISSUE	TREND

SCHMID
L. DAVIS — DAVIS BELLS

YR	NAME	LIMIT	ISSUE	TREND
91	BLOSSOM	OP	75.00	75.00
91	CARUSO	OP	75.00	75.00
91	KATE	OP	75.00	75.00
91	OLE BLUE & LEAD	OP	75.00	75.00
91	WILBUR	OP	75.00	75.00
91	WILLY	OP	75.00	75.00

*
DISNEY ANNUALS

YR	NAME	LIMIT	ISSUE	TREND
85	SNOW BIZ	10000	16.50	17.00
86	TREE FOR TWO	10000	16.50	17.00
87	MERRY MOUSE MEDLEY	10000	17.50	18.00
88	WARM WINTER RIDE	10000	19.50	20.00
89	MERRY MICKEY CLAUS	10000	23.00	23.00
90	HOLLY JOLLY CHRISTMAS	10000	26.50	27.00
91	MICKEY & MINNIE'S ROCKIN' CHRISTMAS	10000	26.50	27.00

L. DAVIS — LOWELL DAVIS MINI BELL

YR	NAME	LIMIT	ISSUE	TREND
92	NEW DAY	YR	10.00	10.00

M.I. HUMMEL — M.I. HUMMEL CHRISTMAS BELLS

YR	NAME	LIMIT	ISSUE	TREND
72	ANGEL WITH FLUTE	YR	20.00	80.00
73	NATIVITY	YR	15.00	82.00
74	GUARDIAN ANGEL, THE	YR	17.50	47.00
75	CHRISTMAS CHILD, THE	YR	22.50	47.00
76	SACRED JOURNEY	YR	22.50	26.00
77	HERALD ANGEL	YR	22.50	52.00
78	HEAVENLY TRIO	YR	27.50	42.00
79	STARLIGHT ANGEL	YR	38.00	47.00
80	PARADE INTO TOYLAND	YR	45.00	58.00
81	A TIME TO REMEMBER	YR	45.00	55.00
82	ANGELIC PROCESSION	YR	45.00	52.00
83	ANGELIC MESSENGER	YR	45.00	58.00
84	A GIFT FROM HEAVEN	YR	45.00	75.00
85	HEAVENLY LIGHT	YR	45.00	80.00
86	TELL THE HEAVENS	YR	45.00	47.00
87	ANGELIC GIFTS	YR	47.50	48.00
88	CHEERFUL CHERUBS	YR	52.50	53.00
89	ANGELIC MUSICIAN	YR	53.00	53.00
90	ANGEL'S LIGHT	YR	53.00	53.00
91	MESSAGE FROM ABOVE	1500	58.00	58.00
92	SWEET BLESSINGS	5000	65.00	65.00

M.I. HUMMEL — M.I. HUMMEL MOTHER'S DAY BELLS

YR	NAME	LIMIT	ISSUE	TREND
76	DEVOTION FOR MOTHERS	YR	22.50	57.00
77	MOONLIGHT RETURN	YR	22.50	47.00
78	AFTERNOON STROLL	YR	27.50	47.00
79	CHERUB'S GIFT	YR	38.00	47.00
80	MOTHER'S LITTLE HELPER	YR	45.00	47.00
81	PLAYTIME	YR	45.00	47.00
82	FLOWER BASKET, THE	YR	45.00	47.00
83	SPRING BOUQUET	YR	45.00	47.00
84	A JOY TO SHARE	YR	45.00	47.00

C. SCHULZ — PEANUTS ANNUAL BELLS

YR	NAME	LIMIT	ISSUE	TREND
79	A SPECIAL LETTER	10000	15.00	30.00
80	WAITING FOR SANTA	10000	15.00	28.00
81	MISSION FOR MOM	10000	17.50	25.00
82	PERFECT PERFORMANCE	10000	18.50	20.00
83	PEANUTS IN CONCERT	10000	12.50	15.00
84	SNOOPY & THE BEAGLE SCOUTS	10000	12.50	15.00

C. SCHULZ — PEANUTS CHRISTMAS BELLS

YR	NAME	LIMIT	ISSUE	TREND
75	WOODSTOCK, SANTA CLAUS	YR	10.00	25.00
76	WOODSTOCK'S CHRISTMAS	YR	10.00	25.00
77	DECK THE DOGHOUSE	YR	10.00	20.00
78	FILLING THE STOCKING	YR	13.00	15.00

C. SCHULZ — PEANUTS MOTHER'S DAY BELLS

YR	NAME	LIMIT	ISSUE	TREND
73	MOM?	YR	5.00	15.00
74	SNOOPY/WOODSTOCK/PARADE	YR	5.00	15.00
76	LINUS AND SNOOPY	YR	10.00	15.00
77	DEAR MOM	YR	10.00	15.00
78	THOUGHTS THAT COUNT	YR	13.00	15.00

C. SCHULZ — PEANUTS SPECIAL EDITION BELL

YR	NAME	LIMIT	ISSUE	TREND
76	BICENTENNIAL	YR	10.00	20.00

L. DAVIS — RFD BELL

YR	NAME	LIMIT	ISSUE	TREND
79	BLOSSOM	RT	65.00	65.00
79	CARUSO	RT	65.00	65.00
79	KATE	RT	65.00	65.00
79	OLE BLUE & LEAD	RT	65.00	65.00
79	WILBUR	RT	65.00	65.00
80	WILLY	RT	65.00	65.00

SEYMOUR MANN
BERNINI — CONNOISSEUR BELL COLLECTION

YR	NAME	LIMIT	ISSUE	TREND
96	BUTTERFLY/LILY CLT 332	OP	15.00	15.00
96	HUMMING BIRDS/MORNING GLORY CLT 322	OP	15.00	15.00
96	ROSES/FORGET ME NOT CLT 342	OP	15.00	15.00

YR	NAME	LIMIT	ISSUE	TREND

STUDIOS OF HARRY SMITH
H. SMITH

CHRISTMAS TREE ORNAMENTS

YR	NAME	LIMIT	ISSUE	TREND
95	CANTERBURY BELL	150	195.00	195.00

TOWLE SILVERSMITHS
*

SILVERPLATED CHRISTMAS BALL BELL

YR	NAME	LIMIT	ISSUE	TREND
79	1979 BALL BELL	10000	14.50	15.00
80	1980 BALL BELL	10000	20.00	20.00
81	1981 BALL BELL	10000	20.00	20.00
82	1982 BALL BELL	5000	24.00	24.00
83	1983 BALL BELL	3500	25.00	25.00
84	1984 BALL BELL	4000	20.00	20.00
85	1985 BALL BELL	4500	25.00	25.00
86	1986 BALL BELL	2500	32.00	32.00

*

SILVERPLATED CHRISTMAS BELL

YR	NAME	LIMIT	ISSUE	TREND
80	1980 SILVERPLATED BELL	10000	17.50	18.00
81	1981 SILVERPLATED BELL	5000	20.00	20.00
82	1982 SILVERPLATED BELL	5000	24.00	24.00
83	1983 SILVERPLATED BELL	3500	24.00	24.00
84	1984 SILVERPLATED BELL	5000	20.00	20.00
85	1985 SILVERPLATED BELL	4500	30.00	30.00
86	1986 SILVERPLATED BELL	4500	30.00	30.00
87	1987 SILVERPLATED BELL	4500	30.00	30.00
88	1988 SILVERPLATED BELL	2500	32.00	32.00
89	1989 SILVERPLATED BELL	4500	34.00	34.00
91	1991 SILVERPLATED BELL	*	20.00	20.00

*

SILVERPLATED CHRISTMAS MUSICAL BELL

YR	NAME	LIMIT	ISSUE	TREND
81	1981 MUSICAL BELL	20000	27.50	28.00
82	1982 MUSICAL BELL	10000	27.50	28.00
83	1983 MUSICAL BELL	2500	27.50	28.00
84	1984 MUSICAL BELL	4500	25.00	25.00
85	1985 MUSICAL BELL	4000	30.00	30.00
86	1986 MUSICAL BELL	4000	32.00	32.00
87	1987 MUSICAL BELL	4000	32.00	32.00
88	1988 MUSICAL BELL	3500	34.00	34.00
89	1989 MUSICAL BELL	4000	35.00	35.00
90	1990 MUSICAL BELL	*	27.50	28.00
91	1991 MUSICAL BELL	*	27.50	28.00

WATERFORD WEDGWOOD USA
*

NEW YEAR BELLS

YR	NAME	LIMIT	ISSUE	TREND
79	PENGUINS	YR	40.00	40.00
80	POLAR BEARS	YR	50.00	50.00
81	MOOSE	YR	55.00	55.00
82	FUR SEALS	YR	60.00	60.00
83	IBEX	YR	64.00	64.00
84	PUFFIN	YR	64.00	64.00
85	ERMINE	YR	64.00	64.00

Cottages

Ken Armke

One of the most popular limited edition collectibles today is the miniature architectural structure, more commonly referred to as the "cottage." The giants in the industry—Department 56, David Winter and Lilliput Lane—still rank among collectors as their favorite collectibles lines.

The genre has expanded in the last few years to include lighthouses, which have taken a considerable jump in popularity. The lighthouse companies casting the brightest beacon today include Harbour Lights, George Z. Lefton Co., Forma Vitrum and Spencer Collin Lighthouses.

Whether composed of traditional cottages, lighthouses or a combination of both, many individual collections harbor items of substantial value in today's secondary marketplace.

When The Grange, a David Winter creation, was retired by John Hine Studios in 1989 due to production problems, the impact was astounding. Within a single month of its retirement the cottage doubled in value, then tripled, then climbed to more than seven times its retail issue price.

One of many examples from the Department 56 line, Norman Church could be bought for as little as $40 prior to its retirement in 1987. In today's secondary market, it is seldom offered for under $3,000.

It's no wonder, then, that the collectibles secondary market offers an investment lure; there are lots of collectors out there searching for The Grange or Norman Church at a ground-floor price.

The question: Are opportunities such as these still available today?

The answer: Possibly.

Be aware, though, that the collectibles secondary market is much more akin to, say, the commodities market than it is to a state lottery. Lottery winnings are generally due totally to luck. Secondary market success, on the other hand, demands that luck be accompanied by a great deal of knowledge and information.

How does one gain knowledge and information? In all the customary ways, such as gleaning the information provided by this publication, and through the experience of buying and collecting for pleasure rather than for potential profit.

KEN ARMKE SR., president of OHI Exchange, initiated one of the first comprehensive secondary market exchanges covering architectural miniatures. His company has since become a primary source for cottages available on the secondary market.

COTTAGES

YR	NAME	LIMIT	ISSUE	TREND
	AMAZEE GIFTS			
	S. MEYERS	**CENTURY CLASSICS CENTURY LIGHTS**		
95	ADMIRALTY HEAD, WA	3995	66.00	66.00
95	BARNEGAT, NJ	10000	58.00	58.00
95	BOSTON HARBOR, MA	3475	58.00	58.00
95	BUFFALO, NY	3475	54.00	54.00
95	BURROWS ISLAND, WA	2995	66.00	66.00
95	CAPE BLANCO, OR	RT	58.00	58.00
95	CAPE HATTERAS, NC	10000	58.00	58.00
95	CHARLOTTE-GENESEE, NY	3475	40.00	40.00
95	COQUILLE RIVER, OR	2995	66.00	66.00
95	DIAMOND HEAD, HI	10000	54.00	54.00
95	FORT GRATIOT, MI	3475	58.00	58.00
95	GREAT POINT, MA	2475	58.00	58.00
95	HILTON HEAD, SC	10000	54.00	54.00
95	HOLLAND, MI	4975	66.00	66.00
95	MARBLEHEAD, OH	7500	54.00	54.00
95	MONTAUK POINT, NY	3475	54.00	54.00
95	NEW POINT, MA	RT	40.00	40.00
95	NORTH HEAD, WA	2995	58.00	58.00
95	OLD POINT LOMA, CA	4550	66.00	66.00
95	PLYMOUTH, MA	3475	58.00	58.00
95	PONCE DE LEON, FL	3475	54.00	54.00
95	SAND POINT, MI	3475	66.00	66.00
95	TYBEE ISLAND, GA	3475	58.00	58.00
95	UMPQUA, OR	2995	58.00	58.00
96	ASSATEAGUE, VA	4975	62.00	62.00
96	BLOCK ISLAND, RI	4896	86.00	86.00
96	CAPE MAY, NJ	4995	58.00	58.00
96	CHICAGO HARBOR, IL	4250	66.00	66.00
96	EAST QUODDY HEAD, CANADA	2475	58.00	58.00
96	JUPITER INLET, FL	7500	58.00	58.00
96	LORAIN LIGHT, OH	3195	66.00	66.00
96	NAUSET BEACH, MA	4995	56.00	56.00
96	OCRACOKE ISLAND LIGHT, NC	3975	54.00	54.00
96	PORT ISABEL, TX	3975	58.00	58.00
96	ROSE ISLAND, RI	4111	68.00	68.00
96	SANDY HOOK, NJ	4995	58.00	58.00
96	SPLIT ROCK, MN	4449	66.00	66.00
96	ST. AUGUSTINE, FL	10000	62.00	62.00
96	ST. GEORGE REEF, CA	4500	62.00	62.00
96	ST. SIMMONS, GA	3975	58.00	58.00
96	WEST QUODDY HEAD, ME	4995	66.00	66.00
96	YAQUIRA HEAD, OR	4500	60.00	60.00
	S. MEYERS	**CENTURY CLASSICS CENTURYVILLE**		
94	CATHEDRAL	RT	70.00	70.00
94	CENTURYVILLE B&O	3250	56.00	56.00
94	CRANES EYE POINT	RT	50.00	55.00
94	FOGGY POINT	RT	50.00	50.00
94	GOTHIC CHURCH	3436	60.00	60.00
94	MR. JOHN JOHNSON	2960	50.00	50.00
94	MR. LYLE E. WILSON	2960	50.00	50.00
94	MS. HILDA GRANT	RT	50.00	55.00
94	MS. MARY THOMPSON	2342	50.00	50.00
94	RICHARD AND JAN SMITH	2960	50.00	50.00
94	SCHOOLHOUSE	RT	56.00	56.00
94	VILLAGE CHURCH	3250	60.00	60.00
95	BED & BREAKFAST	1975	56.00	56.00
95	FIRE STATION	1975	60.00	60.00
95	LAWRENCE KEITH	1975	64.00	64.00
95	MRS. MARY WILLIAM	1975	60.00	60.00
95	SHIP ISLAND MISS	RT	48.00	48.00
95	SWEET SHOPPE	1975	56.00	56.00
	S. MEYERS	**CENTURY CLASSICS EVERGREEN VILLAGE**		
94	CANDYMAKER'S	2475	36.00	36.00
94	CARPENTER'S	2475	36.00	36.00
94	COBBLER'S	2475	36.00	36.00
94	COTTAGE POINT	RT	36.00	36.00
94	EVERGREEN CHURCH	RT	50.00	50.00
94	TRAIN CONDUCTOR'S	2475	36.00	36.00
	BAND CREATIONS			
	RICHARDS/PENFIELD	**AMERICA'S COVERED BRIDGES**		
95	BILLIE CREEK, PARKE COUNTY, IN	OP	29.95	30.00
95	BRIDGE AT THE GREEN, BENNINGTON COUNTY, VT	OP	29.95	30.00
95	BUNKER HILL, CATAWBA COUNTY, NC	OP	29.95	30.00
95	BURFORDVILLE, CAPE GIRADEAI COUNTY, MO	OP	29.95	40.00
95	CEDAR CREEK, OZAUKEE COUNTY, WI	OP	29.95	30.00
95	CHISELVILLE, BENNINGTON COUNTY, VT	OP	29.95	30.00
95	ELDER'S MILL, OCONEE COUNTY, GA	OP	29.95	30.00
95	ELIZABETHTON, CARTER COUNTY, TN	OP	29.95	30.00

YR	NAME	LIMIT	ISSUE	TREND
95	FALLASBURG, KENT COUNTY, MI	OP	29.95	30.00
95	GILLILAND, ETOWAH COUNTY, AL	OP	29.95	30.00
95	HUMPBACK, ALLEGHENY COUNTY, VA	OP	29.95	30.00
95	KNOX , CHESTER COUNTY, PA	OP	29.95	30.00
95	NARROWS, PARKE COUNTY, IN	OP	29.95	30.00
95	OLD BLENHEIM, SCHOHARIE COUNTY, NY	OP	29.95	40.00
95	PHILIPPI, BARBOUR COUNTY, WV	OP	29.95	40.00
95	ROBERTS, PREBLE COUNTY, OH	OP	29.95	30.00
95	ROBYVILLE, PENOBSCOT COUNTY, ME	OP	29.95	30.00
95	ROSEMAN, MADISON COUNTY, IA	OP	29.95	30.00
95	SHIMENAK, LINN COUNTY, OR	OP	29.95	30.00
95	THOMPSON MILL, SHELLY COUNTY, IL	OP	29.95	30.00
95	WAWONA, MARIPOSA COUNTY, CA	OP	29.95	30.00
95	ZUMBROTA, GOODHUE COUNTY, MN	OP	29.95	30.00
96	BRIDGTON COVERED BRIDGE, INDIANA	OP	29.95	30.00
96	KNOEBEL'S GROVE AMUSEMENT PARK, PENNSYLVANIA	OP	29.95	30.00
96	OLINS COVERED BRIDGE, OHIO	OP	29.95	30.00
RICHARDS/PENFIELD	**AMERICA'S FARMLAND COLL.- AMERICA'S COUNTRY BARNS**			
96	PENNSYLVANIA DUTCH BARN	OP	29.95	30.00
RICHARDS/PENFIELD	**BEST FRIENDS - RIVER SONG**			
95	BRICK HOUSE	OP	19.95	20.00
95	CHURCH	OP	19.95	20.00
95	GINGERBREAD HOUSE	OP	19.95	20.00
95	STUCCO HOUSE	OP	19.95	20.00
95	WOOD HOUSE	OP	19.95	20.00

BRANDYWINE WOODCRAFTS

YR	NAME	LIMIT	ISSUE	TREND
M. WHITING				**ACCESSORIES**
94	ELM TREE W/BENCHES	OP	16.00	16.00
94	LAMP W/BARBER POLE	OP	11.00	11.00
M. WHITING				**COUNTRY LANE I**
95	BERRY FARM	OP	30.00	30.00
95	COUNTRY SCHOOL	OP	30.00	30.00
95	DAIRY FARM	OP	30.00	30.00
95	FARM HOUSE	OP	30.00	30.00
95	GENERAL STORE, THE	OP	30.00	30.00
95	SCHOOL	OP	30.00	30.00
M. WHITING				**COUNTRY LANE II**
95	ANTIQUES & CRAFTS	OP	30.00	30.00
95	BASKETMAKER	OP	30.00	30.00
95	COUNTRY CHURCH	OP	30.00	30.00
95	FISHING LODGE	OP	30.00	30.00
95	HERB FARM	OP	30.00	30.00
95	OLDE MILL	OP	30.00	30.00
95	SPINNERS & WEAVERS	OP	30.00	30.00
M. WHITING				**COUNTRY LANE III**
96	COUNTRY AIRFIELD	OP	30.00	30.00
96	COUNTRY CLUB	OP	30.00	30.00
96	OLD ORCHARD	OP	30.00	30.00
96	POST OFFICE	OP	30.00	30.00
96	STATE FAIR	OP	30.00	30.00
96	VOLUNTEER FIREHOUSE	OP	30.00	30.00
M. WHITING				**CUSTOM COLLECTION**
94	SMITHFIELD CLERK'S OFFICE	OP	9.00	9.00
M. WHITING				**HOMETOWN VI**
93	COUNTRY CHURCH	RT	24.00	30.00
93	DINER	RT	24.00	30.00
93	GENERAL STORE	RT	24.00	30.00
93	PUBLIC SCHOOL	RT	24.00	30.00
93	TRAIN STATION	RT	24.00	30.00
M. WHITING				**HOMETOWN VII**
93	CANDY SHOP	OP	24.00	24.00
93	DRESS SHOP	OP	24.00	24.00
93	FLOWER SHOP	OP	24.00	24.00
93	PET SHOP	OP	24.00	24.00
93	POST OFFICE	OP	24.00	24.00
93	QUILT SHOP	OP	24.00	24.00
M. WHITING				**HOMETOWN VIII**
94	BARBER SHOP	OP	28.00	28.00
94	COUNTRY DOCTOR	OP	28.00	28.00
94	COUNTRY STORE	OP	28.00	28.00
94	FIRE COMPANY	OP	28.00	28.00
94	SEWING SHOP	OP	26.00	26.00
M. WHITING				**HOMETOWN IX**
94	BED & BREAKFAST	OP	29.00	29.00
94	CAFE/DELI	OP	29.00	29.00
94	HOMETOWN BANK	OP	29.00	29.00
94	HOMETOWN GAZETTE	OP	29.00	29.00
94	TEDDYS & TOYS	OP	29.00	29.00
M. WHITING				**HOMETOWN X**
95	BRICK CHURCH	OP	29.00	29.00
95	DOLL SHOPPE, THE	OP	29.00	29.00
95	GENERAL HOSPITAL	OP	29.00	29.00
95	GIFT BOX, THE	OP	29.00	29.00

YR	NAME	LIMIT	ISSUE	TREND
95	POLICE STATION	OP	29.00	29.00
M. WHITING				**HOMETOWN XI**
95	ANTIQUES	YR	29.00	29.00
95	CHURCH II	YR	29.00	29.00
95	GROCER	YR	29.00	29.00
95	PHARMACY	YR	29.00	29.00
95	SCHOOL II	YR	29.00	29.00
M. WHITING				**HOMETOWN XII**
96	BRIDAL & DRESS SHOPPE	YR	29.00	29.00
96	COUNTRY LANE SIGN	YR	20.00	20.00
96	FIVE & DIME	YR	29.00	29.00
96	HOMETOWN SIGN	YR	22.00	22.00
96	HOMETOWN THEATER	YR	29.00	29.00
96	POST OFFICE	YR	29.00	29.00
96	TRAVEL AGENCY	YR	29.00	29.00
M. WHITING				**NORTH POLE COLLECTION**
93	CANDY CANE FACTORY	OP	24.00	24.00
93	ELF CLUB	OP	24.00	24.00
93	TEDDY BEAR FACTORY	OP	24.00	24.00
93	TOWN CHRISTMAS TREE	OP	20.00	25.00
94	POST OFFICE	OP	25.00	25.00
94	TOWN HALL	OP	25.00	30.00
M. WHITING				**TREASURED TIMES**
94	HALLOWEEN HOUSE	750	32.00	32.00
94	HAPPY BIRTHDAY HOUSE	750	32.00	32.00
94	MOTHER'S DAY HOUSE	750	32.00	32.00
94	NEW BABY BOY HOUSE	750	32.00	32.00
94	NEW BABY GIRL HOUSE	750	32.00	32.00
94	VALENTINE'S DAY HOUSE	750	32.00	32.00
M. WHITING				**WILLIAMSBURG COLLECTION**
93	CAMPBELL'S TAVERN	OP	28.00	28.00
93	KINGS ARM TAVERN	OP	25.00	25.00
M. WHITING				**YORKTOWN COLLECTION**
93	DIGGES HOUSE	OP	22.00	27.00

CAVANAGH GROUP

			COCA-COLA BRAND TOWN SQUARE COLLECTION	
*				
92	CANDLER'S DRUGS	CL	40.00	60.00
92	DEE'S BOARDING HOUSE	CL	40.00	450.00
92	DICK'S LUNCHEONETTE	CL	40.00	60.00
92	GILBERT'S GROCERY	CL	40.00	75.00
92	HOWARD OIL	CL	40.00	145.00
92	TRAIN DEPOT	CL	40.00	275.00
93	CITY HALL	CL	40.00	80.00
93	EXTRA! EXTRA!	CL	7.00	13.00
93	GONE FISHING	CL	11.00	15.00
93	JACOB'S PHARMACY	CL	25.00	450.00
93	MOONEY'S ANTIQUE BARN	CL	40.00	75.00
93	OCCIER PAT	CL	7.00	10.00
93	OLD NUMBER SEVEN	CL	15.00	15.00
93	ROUTE 93 COVERED BRIDGE	CL	20.00	40.00
93	SODA JERK	CL	7.00	12.00
93	STREET VENDOR	CL	11.00	17.00
93	T. TAYLOR'S EMPORIUM	CL	40.00	65.00
93	TICK TOCK DINER,THE	CL	40.00	60.00
94	CHECKER PLAYERS	CL	15.00	15.00
94	CROWLEY CAB CO.	CL	11.00	15.00
94	FLYING "A" SERVICE STATION	CL	40.00	40.00
94	HOMEWARD BOUND	CL	8.00	8.00
94	MCMAHON'S GENERAL STORE	CL	40.00	40.00
94	PLAZA DRUGS	CL	20.00	40.00
94	SLEDDERS	CL	11.00	11.00
94	SLEIGH RIDE	CL	15.00	15.00
94	STATION #14 FIREHOUSE	CL	40.00	40.00
94	STRAND THEATRE	CL	40.00	40.00
94	TOWN GAZEBO	CL	20.00	30.00
95	BOYS WITH SNOWBALLS	CL	11.00	11.00
95	COCA-COLA BOTTLING WORKS	CL	40.00	50.00
95	GRIST MILL	CL	40.00	40.00
95	JENNY'S SWEET SHOPPE	CL	40.00	40.00
95	LIGHTHOUSE POINT SNACK BAR	CL	40.00	40.00
95	LUNCH WAGON	CL	15.00	15.00
96	CARLSON'S GENERAL STORE	OP	40.00	40.00
96	CHANDLER'S SKI RESORT	RT	40.00	40.00
96	CLARA'S CHRISTMAS SHOP	RT	40.00	40.00
96	COOPER'S TREE FARM	OP	20.00	20.00
96	DIAMOND SERVICE STATION	RT	40.00	40.00
96	SCOOTER'S DRIVE IN	OP	40.00	40.00
96	TOWN BARBER SHOP	OP	40.00	40.00
96	WALTON'S 5 & 10	OP	40.00	40.00
97	CENTRAL HIGH	OP	40.00	40.00
97	DEW DROP INN	OP	40.00	40.00
97	FIVE AND DIME	OP	40.00	40.00
97	MRS. MURPHY'S CHOWDER HOUSE	OP	40.00	40.00
97	SOUTH STATION	OP	40.00	40.00

YR NAME	LIMIT	ISSUE	TREND

CREATIVE CRAFTSMEN
M. FENLEY — VINTAGE VILLAGE

YR NAME	LIMIT	ISSUE	TREND
95 OLD WINDMILL, THE	500	96.00	96.00
95 PRAIRIE CHURCH	500	145.00	145.00
96 BILLY'S LITTLE COTTAGE	300	50.00	50.00

DAVE GROSSMAN CREATIONS
* — GONE WITH THE WIND

YR NAME	LIMIT	ISSUE	TREND
95 ATLANTA	RT	15.00	15.00
95 BELLE'S PLACE	RT	15.00	15.00
95 FEDERAL TAIL	RT	15.00	15.00
95 PITTYPAT HOUSE	RT	15.00	15.00
95 TARA	RT	15.00	15.00
95 TWELVE OAKS	RT	15.00	15.00

* — MOUSEHOLE COLLECTION

YR NAME	LIMIT	ISSUE	TREND
94 19TH HOLE GOLF HOUSE	RT	30.00	30.00
94 ANN HALFWAY COTTAGE	RT	30.00	30.00
94 COURT HOUSE	RT	30.00	30.00
94 LEIGHTON HOUSE	RT	30.00	30.00
94 ST. MICKIE MOUSE CHURCH	RT	30.00	30.00

DAVID WINTER COTTAGES/ENESCO CORP.
D. WINTER — CHAPELS & CHURCHES COLLECTION

YR NAME	LIMIT	ISSUE	TREND
98 ST. CHRISTOPHER'S CHURCH	OP	110.00	110.00
98 THORNHILL CHAPEL	OP	90.00	90.00

D. WINTER — COLLECTOR'S GUILD/REDEMPTION PIECES

YR NAME	LIMIT	ISSUE	TREND
97 ABBOTS	YR	75.00	75.00
97 GAMEKEEPER	YR	85.00	85.00
97 SEXTONS	YR	*	N/A
98 CHARCOAL BURNER'S, THE	YR	85.00	85.00
98 COPPICER'S COTTAGE, THE	YR	90.00	90.00
98 MISTLETOE COTTAGE	YR	*	N/A

D. WINTER — ENGLISH VILLAGE COLLECTION

YR NAME	LIMIT	ISSUE	TREND
97 CAT & PIPE INN	RT	55.00	50.00
97 CHANDLERY, THE	RT	55.00	50.00
97 CHURCH & VESTRY	RT	55.00	50.00
97 CONSTABULARY, THE	RT	55.00	50.00
97 CRYSTAL COTTAGE	RT	55.00	50.00
97 ENGINE HOUSE	RT	55.00	50.00
97 GLEBE COTTAGE	RT	55.00	50.00
97 HALL	RT	55.00	50.00
97 ONE ACRE COTTAGE	RT	55.00	50.00
97 POST OFFICE	RT	55.00	50.00
97 QUACKS COTTAGE	RT	55.00	50.00
97 RECTORY	RT	55.00	50.00
97 SEMINARY, THE	RT	55.00	50.00
97 SMITHY	RT	55.00	50.00
97 TANNERY	RT	55.00	50.00

D. WINTER — FOREST OF DEAN COLLECTION

YR NAME	LIMIT	ISSUE	TREND
97 ABBEY RUINS	OP	55.00	50.00
97 ARTIST'S STUDIO, THE	OP	55.00	50.00
97 CITADEL, THE	OP	55.00	50.00
97 FOREST OF DEAN MINE	OP	55.00	50.00
97 OBSERVATORY, THE	OP	55.00	50.00
97 SAWMILL, THE	OP	55.00	50.00

D. WINTER — GENERAL RANGE

YR NAME	LIMIT	ISSUE	TREND
97 HEREWARD THE WAKE'S CASTLE	3500	175.00	158.00
97 MILESTONE COTTAGE	OP	130.00	117.00
97 ST. GEORGE AND THE DRAGON	OP	150.00	135.00
98 TOM'S YARD	5000	130.00	130.00

D. WINTER — HAUNTED HOUSE COLLECTION

YR NAME	LIMIT	ISSUE	TREND
98 HOUSE OF USHER	YR	175.00	175.00

D. WINTER — MYSTICAL CASTLES OF BRITAIN

YR NAME	LIMIT	ISSUE	TREND
98 HALIDON HILL	OP	130.00	117.00
98 HOTSPUR'S KEEP, THE	OP	110.00	99.00
98 MYTON TOWER	OP	130.00	117.00
98 WITCHES' CASTLE, THE	4250	175.00	158.00

D. WINTER — OLIVER TWIST CHRISTMAS COLLECTION

YR NAME	LIMIT	ISSUE	TREND
97 MR. BUMBLES	RT	110.00	99.00
98 MR. FANG-THE MAGISTRATE'S HOME	YR	110.00	110.00

D. WINTER — PILGRIM'S WAY COLLECTION

YR NAME	LIMIT	ISSUE	TREND
97 ALCHEMIST'S COTTAGE, THE	OP	50.00	45.00
97 BRICKIES, THE	OP	50.00	45.00
97 DINGLE, THE	OP	50.00	45.00
97 FALCONRY, THE	OP	50.00	45.00
97 SERF'S COTTAGE, THE	OP	50.00	45.00
97 ST. JOSEPH'S COTTAGE	OP	50.00	45.00
98 GRISELDA'S COTTAGE	OP	90.00	90.00
98 MARQUIS WALTER'S MANOR	5000	150.00	150.00

D. WINTER — PUBS & TAVERNS OF ENGLAND

YR NAME	LIMIT	ISSUE	TREND
98 BIRD CAGE, THE	OP	100.00	100.00
98 GOOD INTENT, THE	OP	100.00	100.00
98 HOP PICKERS, THE	OP	130.00	130.00
98 TICKLED TROUT, THE	4500	150.00	150.00

YR	NAME	LIMIT	ISSUE	TREND
D. WINTER		**SEASIDE BOARDWALK COLLECTION**		
97	FISHERMAN'S SHANTY	OP	110.00	99.00
97	HARBOURMASTER'S WATCH TOWER	OP	125.00	113.00
97	JOLLY ROGER TAVERN	OP	199.00	179.00
97	LODGING & SEA BATHING	OP	180.00	162.00
97	TRINITY LIGHTHOUSE	OP	150.00	150.00
97	WATERFRONT MARKET	OP	125.00	113.00
D. WINTER		**SHERWOOD FOREST COLLECTION**		
97	FRIAR TUCK'S SANCTUM	OP	50.00	45.00
97	KING RICHARD'S BOWER	OP	50.00	45.00
97	LITTLE JOHN'S RIVERLOFT	OP	50.00	45.00
97	LOXLEY CASTLE	OP	150.00	135.00
97	MAID MARIAN'S RETREAT	OP	50.00	45.00
97	MUCH'S MILL	OP	50.00	45.00
97	SHERWOOD DIORAMA	OP	40.00	36.00
97	WILL SCARLETT'S DEN	OP	50.00	45.00
D. WINTER		**SOUTH DOWNS COLLECTION**		
97	PARISH SCHOOL HOUSE, THE	RT	55.00	50.00
97	SUNDAY SCHOOL	RT	55.00	50.00
D. WINTER		**SPECIAL EVENT**		
97	SUFFOLK GARDEN (TOUR)	YR	60.00	60.00
98	TRUFFLEMAN'S HOUSE, THE	YR	75.00	75.00

DAVID WINTER COTTAGES/JOHN HINE STUDIOS

YR	NAME	LIMIT	ISSUE	TREND
D. WINTER		**BRITISH TRADITIONS**		
90	BLOSSOM COTTAGE (MAY)	RT	59.00	88.00
90	BOAT HOUSE, THE (MARCH)	RT	38.00	68.00
90	BULL & BUSH, THE (DECEMBER)	RT	38.00	57.00
90	BURN'S READING ROOM (JANUARY)	RT	31.00	66.00
90	GROUSE MOOR LODGE (AUGUST)	RT	48.00	75.00
90	GUY FAWKES (NOVEMBER)	RT	31.00	49.00
90	HARVEST BARN (OCTOBER)	RT	31.00	56.00
90	KNIGHT'S CASTLE (JUNE)	RT	59.00	89.00
90	PUDDING COTTAGE (APRIL)	RT	78.00	91.00
90	ST. ANNE'S WELL (JULY)	RT	48.00	82.00
90	STAFFORDSHIRE VICARAGE (SEPTEMBER)	RT	48.00	69.00
90	STONECUTTERS COTTAGE (FEBRUARY)	RT	48.00	64.00
D. WINTER		**CAMEOS COLLECTION**		
92	BARLEY MALT KILN	RT	12.50	20.00
92	BROOKLET BRIDGE	RT	12.50	20.00
92	DIORAMA-BRIGHT	RT	30.00	54.00
92	DIORAMA-LIGHT	RT	52.00	26.00
92	GREENWOOD WAGON	RT	12.50	20.00
92	LYCH GATE	RT	12.50	43.00
92	MARKET DAY	RT	12.50	33.00
92	ONE MAN JAIL	RT	12.50	20.00
92	PENNY WISHING WELL	RT	12.50	33.00
92	POTTING SHED, THE	RT	12.50	30.00
92	POULTRY ARK	RT	12.50	20.00
92	PRIVY, THE	RT	12.50	20.00
92	SADDLE STEPS	RT	12.50	20.00
92	WELSH PIG PEN	RT	12.50	20.00
D. WINTER		**CASTLE COLLECTION**		
93	CASTLE COTTAGE OF WARWICK, THE-CARNIVAL EVENT	4000	160.00	406.00
94	GUARDIAN CASTLE	8490	*	375.00
94	GUARDIAN CASTLE, THE (PREM. ED.)	RT	*	494.00
94	KINGMAKER'S CASTLE, THE	7150	225.00	336.00
94	KINGMAKER'S CASTLE, THE (CARNIVAL EVENT)	2750	395.00	463.00
95	BISHOPSGATE	RT	175.00	165.00
95	BISHOPSGATE (PREM. ED.)	3500	225.00	194.00
95	CASTLE TOWER OF WINDSOR (CARNIVAL)	RT	435.00	525.00
95	CASTLE WALL, THE	RT	65.00	83.00
95	GUARDIAN GATE, THE	RT	150.00	129.00
95	GUARDIAN GATE, THE (PREM. ED.)	RT	199.00	153.00
96	CHRISTMAS CASTLE	2950	160.00	305.00
96	ROCHESTER CASTLE	2500	150.00	215.00
96	ROCHESTER CASTLE (CARNIVAL W/SNOW)	1000	569.00	650.00
96	ST. GEORGE'S CASTLE	RT	130.00	235.00
D. WINTER		**CELEBRATION COTTAGES COLLECTION**		
94	CELEBRATION CHAPEL	RT	75.00	75.00
94	CELEBRATON CHAPEL (PREM. ED.)	3500	150.00	119.00
94	SPRING HOLLOW	RT	65.00	71.00
94	SPRING HOLLOW (PREM. ED.)	3500	125.00	95.00
94	SWEETHEART HAVEN	RT	60.00	63.00
94	SWEETHEART HAVEN (PREM. ED.)	3500	115.00	97.00
95	MOTHER'S COTTAGE	RT	65.00	65.00
95	MOTHER'S COTTAGE (PREM. ED.)	3500	90.00	100.00
95	STORK COTTAGE/BOY	RT	65.00	93.00
95	STORK COTTAGE/GIRL	RT	65.00	108.00
D. WINTER		**CENTRE OF THE VILLAGE**		
80	LITTLE MARKET	RT	29.00	62.00
80	MARKET STREET	RT	49.00	98.00
80	ROSE COTTAGE	RT	29.00	68.00
80	WINE MERCHANT, THE	RT	29.00	80.00
80	WINE MERCHANT, THE (OLD STYLE)	RT	29.00	N/A

O'Donovan's Castle *is an impressive issue created by David Winter for John Hine Studios.*

Bill Job's Thompson's Drug, *a 1994 release by Forma Vitrum as part of the Vitreville collection, is retired.*

Stonington Harbor, CT, *a Harbour Lights Collector's Society Exclusive piece for 1996, has increased in value since its retirement.*

Haunted House, *a 1996 piece by David Winter for John Hine Studios, is limited to an edition of 4,900.*

Cape Canaveral, FL, *a retired piece from Harbour Lights' Southeast Region collection, has increased in value.*

The Fishing Lodge, *an open edition piece from Marlene Whiting's Country Lane II collection for Brandywine Collectibles, brings to life the rustic charm of a stay in the country.*

YR	NAME	LIMIT	ISSUE	TREND
82	IVY COTTAGE	RT	22.00	57.00
82	VILLAGE SHOP, THE	OP	22.00	61.00
83	BAKEHOUSE, THE	RT	32.00	78.00
83	GREEN DRAGON INN, THE	RT	32.00	51.00
84	CHAPEL, THE	RT	49.00	98.00
84	PARSONAGE, THE	RT	390.00	515.00
84	SPINNER'S COTTAGE	RT	29.00	56.00
85	COOPER'S COTTAGE, THE	RT	58.00	89.00
D. WINTER		**COLLECTORS GUILD EXCLUSIVE**		
87	QUEEN ELIZABETH SLEPT HERE	RT	183.00	392.00
87	ROBIN HOOD'S HIDEAWAY	RT	54.00	232.00
87	VILLAGE SCENE, THE	RT	*	232.00
88	BLACK BESS INN	RT	60.00	132.00
88	PAVILION, THE	RT	52.00	144.00
89	COAL SHED, THE	RT	112.00	146.00
89	HOME GUARD	RT	105.00	136.00
90	COBBLER, THE	RT	40.00	64.00
90	PLUCKED DUCKS, THE	RT	*	66.00
90	POTTERY, THE	RT	40.00	58.00
91	PERSHORE MILL	RT	*	69.00
91	TOMFOOL'S COTTAGE	RT	100.00	133.00
91	WILL O' THE WISP	RT	120.00	118.00
92	BEEKEEPER'S, THE	RT	65.00	84.00
92	CANDLEMAKER'S, THE	RT	65.00	79.00
92	IRISH WATER MILL	RT	*	82.00
92	PATRICK'S WATER MILL	RT	*	124.00
93	ON THE RIVERBANK	RT	*	68.00
93	SWAN UPPING COTTAGE	RT	69.00	86.00
93	THAMESIDE	RT	79.00	97.00
94	15 LAWNSIDE ROAD	RT	*	55.00
94	ASHE COTTAGE	RT	62.00	76.00
94	WHILEAWAY COTTAGE	RT	70.00	86.00
95	BUTTERCUP COTTAGE	RT	60.00	100.00
95	FLOWER SHOP, THE	RT	150.00	217.00
95	FRIENDSHIP COTTAGE	RT	45.00	107.00
95	GARDENER'S COTTAGE	RT	*	93.00
96	MODEL DAIRY, THE	RT	*	70.00
96	PLOUGH FARMSTEAD	RT	125.00	185.00
96	PUNCH STABLES	RT	150.00	213.00
D. WINTER		**CURRENT PIECES**		
91	CASTLE IN THE AIR	RT	675.00	751.00
91	INGLENOOK COTTAGE	RT	60.00	76.00
91	MOONLIGHT HAVEN	RT	120.00	174.00
91	WEAVER'S LODGINGS, THE	RT	65.00	85.00
96	GOLF CLUBHOUSE	RT	165.00	243.00
97	ABBEY RUINS, THE	RT	45.00	173.00
97	CITADEL, THE	RT	45.00	160.00
97	FOREST OF DEAN	RT	45.00	185.00
D. WINTER		**DAVID WINTER RETIRED PIECES**		
80	COACHING INN, THE	RT	165.00	2450.00
80	DOVE COTTAGE	RT	60.00	2375.00
80	FORGE, THE	RT	60.00	1525.00
80	LITTLE FORGE	RT	27.00	N/A
80	LITTLE MILL	RT	40.00	N/A
80	LITTLE MILL-REMODELED	RT	40.00	1150.00
80	MILL HOUSE	RT	50.00	2300.00
80	MILL HOUSE-REMODELED '83	RT	50.00	2033.00
80	QUAYSIDE	RT	52.00	1250.00
80	THREE DUCKS INN	RT	60.00	1700.00
81	CASTLE KEEP	RT	30.00	1600.00
81	CHINCHESTER CROSS	RT	50.00	3850.00
81	CORNISH COTTAGE	RT	30.00	678.00
81	DOUBLE OAST	RT	60.00	3600.00
81	OLD CURIOSITY SHOP, THE	RT	40.00	2130.00
81	PROVENCAL ONE (FRENCH MKT.)	RT	*	6000.00
81	PROVENCAL TINY A (FRENCH MKT.)	RT	*	N/A
81	PROVENCAL TINY B (FRENCH MKT.)	RT	*	N/A
81	PROVENCAL TWO (FRENCH MKT.)	RT	*	N/A
81	ST. PAUL'S CATHEDRAL	RT	40.00	1500.00
81	TYTHE BARN	RT	40.00	1157.00
82	BLACKSMITH'S COTTAGE	RT	22.00	387.00
82	CORNISH TIN MINE	RT	22.00	77.00
82	FAIRYTALE CASTLE	RT	115.40	353.00
82	HOUSE ON TOP, THE	RT	93.00	254.00
82	MINER'S COTTAGE	RT	22.00	203.00
82	MOORLAND COTTAGE	RT	22.00	228.00
82	SABRINA'S COTTAGE	RT	30.00	2938.00
82	WM. SHAKESPEARE'S BIRTHPLACE (LARGE)	RT	60.00	1575.00
83	ALMS HOUS, THE	RT	60.00	414.00
83	COTTON MILL, THE	RT	42.00	483.00
83	HAYBARN, THE	RT	22.00	255.00
83	WOODCUTTER'S COTTAGE	RT	87.00	288.00
84	HOUSE OF THE MASTER MASON	RT	75.00	234.00
85	HERMIT'S HUMBLE HOME	RT	87.00	205.00
85	SUFFOLK HOUSE	RT	49.00	82.00

YR	NAME	LIMIT	ISSUE	TREND
88	CROFTER'S COTTAGE	RT	51.00	101.00
91	PRINTERS AND THE BOOKBINDERS, THE (BOOKENDS)	RT	120.00	102.00
92	AUDREY'S TEA ROOM	RT	90.00	127.00
92	AUDREY'S TEA SHOP	RT	90.00	192.00
95	WELCOME HOME COTTAGE	RT	99.00	108.00
95	WELCOME HOME COTTAGE-MILITARY	RT	99.00	152.00

D. WINTER   **DICKENS CHRISTMAS CAROL COLLECTION**

YR	NAME	LIMIT	ISSUE	TREND
87	EBENEZER SCROOGE'S COUNTING HOUSE	RT	97.00	232.00
88	HOGMANAY (CHRISTMAS IN SCOTLAND...)	RT	100.00	137.00
89	A CHRISTMAS CAROL	RT	135.00	144.00
90	MR. FEZZIWIG'S EMPORIUM	RT	135.00	109.00
91	FRED'S HOME	RT	145.00	128.00
92	SCROOGE'S SCHOOL	RT	160.00	154.00
93	OLD JOE'S BEETLING SHOP	RT	175.00	182.00
94	SCROOGE FAMILY HOME, THE	RT	175.00	175.00
94	SCROOGE FAMILY HOME, THE (PREM. ED.)	RT	230.00	225.00
94	UP ON THE HOUSE TOP (STAFF GIFT)	RT	*	60.00
95	MISS BELLE'S COTTAGE	RT	185.00	198.00
95	MISS BELLE'S COTTAGE (PREM. ED.)	2200	235.00	273.00
96	TINY TIM	RT	150.00	263.00
96	TINY TIM-PREMIER EDITION	2200	180.00	253.00

D. WINTER   **DISNEYANA**

YR	NAME	LIMIT	ISSUE	TREND
92	CINDERELLA CASTLE	500	250.00	1528.00
93	SLEEPING BEAUTY CASTLE	500	250.00	813.00
94	EURO DISNEY CASTLE	500	250.00	463.00

D. WINTER   **ENGLISH VILLAGE COLLECTION**

YR	NAME	LIMIT	ISSUE	TREND
94	CAT & PIPE INN, THE	RT	53.00	62.00
94	CHANDLERY, THE	RT	53.00	54.00
94	CHURCH AND VESTRY, THE	RT	57.00	63.00
94	CONSTABULARY, THE	RT	60.00	65.00
94	CRYSTAL COTTAGE	RT	53.00	54.00
94	ENGINE HOUSE, THE (BRN. DR. GEN. VISION)	RT	55.00	62.00
94	ENGINE HOUSE, THE (RD. DR. DISNEY EXCLUSIVE)	RT	55.00	N/A
94	GLEBE COTTAGE	RT	53.00	59.00
94	HALL, THE	RT	55.00	62.00
94	ONE ACRE COTTAGE	RT	55.00	54.00
94	POST OFFICE, THE	RT	53.00	65.00
94	QUACK'S COTTAGE	RT	57.00	54.00
94	RECTORY, THE	RT	55.00	54.00
94	SEMINARY, THE	RT	57.00	82.00
94	SMITHY, THE	RT	50.00	53.00
94	TANNERY, THE	RT	50.00	50.00

D. WINTER   **GARDEN COTTAGES OF ENGLAND**

YR	NAME	LIMIT	ISSUE	TREND
95	SPENCER HALL GARDENS	4300	395.00	379.00
95	SPENCER HALL GARDENS (PREM. ED.)	2200	495.00	455.00
95	WILLOW GARDENS	4300	250.00	220.00
95	WILLOW GARDENS (PREM. ED.)	2200	299.00	280.00
96	PARK, THE	RT	300.00	300.00
97	PARK, THE-PREMIER EDITION	RT	400.00	518.00

D. WINTER   **HEART OF ENGLAND**

YR	NAME	LIMIT	ISSUE	TREND
85	APOTHECARY SHOP, THE	RT	24.00	54.00
85	BLACKFRIARS GRANGE	RT	24.00	79.00
85	CRAFTSMAN COTTAGES	RT	24.00	58.00
85	HOGS HEAD TAVERN, THE	RT	24.00	83.00
85	MEADOWBANK COTTAGES	RT	24.00	53.00
85	SCHOOLHOUSE, THE	RT	24.00	63.00
85	SHIREHALL	RT	24.00	73.00
85	ST. GEORGE'S CHURCH	RT	24.00	71.00
85	VICARAGE, THE	RT	24.00	92.00
85	YEOMAN'S FARMHOUSE	RT	24.00	45.00
88	WINDMILL, THE	RT	38.00	83.00

D. WINTER   **IN THE COUNTRY**

YR	NAME	LIMIT	ISSUE	TREND
82	BROOKSIDE HAMLET	RT	75.00	85.00
82	DROVER'S COTTAGE	RT	22.00	43.00
83	BOTHY, THE	RT	32.00	151.00
83	FISHERMAN'S WHARF	RT	32.00	118.00
83	PILGRIM'S REST	RT	49.00	150.00
84	SNOW COTTAGE	RT	75.00	104.00
84	TOLLKEEPER'S COTTAGE	RT	87.00	127.00
86	THERE WAS A CROOKED HOUSE	RT	97.00	234.00
87	JOHN BENBOW'S FARMHOUSE	RT	78.00	89.00
96	LOVER'S TRYST	RT	125.00	188.00
96	THERE WAS A NARROW HOUSE	RT	115.00	168.00

D. WINTER   **IRISH COLLECTION**

YR	NAME	LIMIT	ISSUE	TREND
92	FOGARTYS	RT	75.00	100.00
92	IRISH ROUND TOWER	RT	65.00	85.00
92	MURPHYS	RT	100.00	95.00
92	O'DONOVAN'S CASTLE	RT	145.00	241.00
92	ONLY A SPAN APART	RT	80.00	92.00
92	SECRET SHEBEEN	RT	70.00	76.00

D. WINTER   **LANDOWNERS COLLECTION**

YR	NAME	LIMIT	ISSUE	TREND
81	TUDOR MANOR HOUSE	RT	49.00	84.00
81	TUDOR MANOR HOUSE (OLD STYLE)	RT	49.00	N/A
82	DOWER HOUSE, THE	RT	22.00	46.00

YR	NAME	LIMIT	ISSUE	TREND
84	CASTLE GATE	RT	154.90	261.00
85	SQUIRES HALL	RT	93.00	90.00
86	FALSTAFF'S MANOR	RT	242.00	305.00
88	GRANGE, THE	RT	120.00	1071.00
D. WINTER			**MASTERPIECE COLLECTION**	
96	GUINEVERE'S CASTLE	4300	299.00	475.00
96	GUINEVERE'S CASTLE (PREM. ED.)	2200	350.00	625.00
96	HAUNTED HOUSE	4900	325.00	350.00
96	WRECKERS COTTAGE	RT	225.00	225.00
D. WINTER			**MIDLANDS COLLECTION**	
88	BOTTLE KILN	RT	78.00	100.00
88	COAL MINER'S ROW	RT	90.00	144.00
88	DERBYSHIRE COTTON MILL	RT	65.00	235.00
88	GUNSMITHS	RT	78.00	88.00
88	LACEMAKER'S	RT	120.00	129.00
88	LOCK KEEPERS COTTAGE	RT	65.00	84.00
D. WINTER			**NEW SHERWOOD FOREST COLLECTION**	
95	DIORAMA	RT	100.00	70.00
95	FRIAR TUCK'S SANCTUM	RT	45.00	35.00
95	KING RICHARD'S BOWER	RT	45.00	60.00
95	LITTLE JOHN'S RIVERLOFT	RT	45.00	63.00
95	LOXLEY CASTLE	RT	150.00	170.00
95	MAID MARIAN'S RETREAT	RT	50.00	125.00
95	MUCH'S MILL	RT	45.00	50.00
95	WILL SCARLETT'S DEN	RT	50.00	49.00
D. WINTER			**PORRIDGE POT ALLEY COLLECTION**	
95	COB'S BAKERY	RT	125.00	101.00
95	COB'S BAKERY (PREM. ED.)	3500	165.00	122.00
95	PORRIDGE POT ARCH	RT	50.00	113.00
95	SWEET DREAMS	RT	79.00	76.00
95	SWEET DREAMS (PREM. ED.)	3500	99.00	95.00
95	TARTAN TEAHOUSE	RT	99.00	95.00
95	TARTAN TEAHOUSE (PREM. ED.)	3500	129.00	123.00
D. WINTER			**REGIONS COLLECTION**	
81	SINGLE OAST	RT	22.00	59.00
81	STRATFORD HOUSE	RT	75.00	139.00
81	TRIPLE OAST	RT	60.00	134.00
81	TRIPLE OAST (OLD STYLE)	RT	60.00	N/A
82	COTSWOLD COTTAGE	RT	22.00	48.00
82	COTSWOLD VILLAGE	RT	60.00	136.00
82	SUSSEX COTTAGE	RT	22.00	77.00
83	HERTFORD COURT (ERIC)	RT	87.00	118.00
85	KENT COTTAGE	RT	49.00	113.00
D. WINTER			**SCOTTISH COLLECTION**	
82	OLD DISTILLERY, THE	RT	312.20	804.00
89	GATEKEEPER'S	RT	65.00	141.00
89	GATEKEEPERS COLOURWAY	1000	*	401.00
89	GILLIE'S COTTAGE	RT	65.00	98.00
89	HOUSE ON THE LOCH, THE	RT	65.00	117.00
89	MACBETH'S CASTLE	RT	200.00	284.00
89	OLD DISTILLERY (RE-RELEASED)	RT	450.00	618.00
89	SCOTTISH CROFTER (REMOLDED)	OP	42.00	88.00
89	SCOTTISH CROFTERS	RT	42.00	69.00
D. WINTER			**SEASIDE BOARDWALK**	
95	BARNACLE THEATRE	RT	175.00	188.00
95	DOCK ACCESSORY (INCLUDED WITH EACH PIECE)	RT	*	N/A
95	FISHERMAN'S SHANTY	RT	110.00	143.00
95	HARBOUR MASTER'S WATCH-HOUSE	RT	125.00	119.00
95	JOLLY ROGER TAVERN	RT	199.00	245.00
95	LODGINGS & SEA BATHING	RT	165.00	158.00
95	WATERFRONT MARKET	RT	125.00	131.00
96	TRINITY LIGHTHOUSE	RT	135.00	225.00
D. WINTER			**SHIRES COLLECTION**	
93	BERKSHIRE MILKING BYRE	RT	38.00	48.00
93	BUCKINGHAMSHIRE BULL PEN	RT	38.00	48.00
93	CHESHIRE KENNELS	RT	36.00	57.00
93	DERBYSHIRE DOVECOTE	RT	36.00	54.00
93	GLOUCESTERSHIRE GREENHOUSE	RT	40.00	54.00
93	HAMPSHIRE HUTCHES	RT	34.00	45.00
93	LANCASHIRE DONKEY SHED	RT	38.00	51.00
93	OXFORDSHIRE GOAT YARD	RT	32.00	47.00
93	SHROPSHIRE PIG SHELTER	RT	32.00	47.00
93	STAFFORDSHIRE STABLES	RT	36.00	51.00
93	WILTSHIRE WATERWHEEL	RT	34.00	55.00
93	YORKSHIRE SHEEPFOLD	RT	38.00	54.00
D. WINTER			**SOUTH DOWNS COLLECTION**	
96	ELFIN COTTAGE	RT	60.00	91.00
96	PARISH SCHOOL, THE	RT	45.00	97.00
97	SUNDAY SCHOOL CHAPEL, THE	RT	60.00	198.00
D. WINTER			**SPECIAL EVENTS**	
88	WINTERS HILL (JIM'LL FIX-IT)	250	375.00	3500.00
90	CARTWRIGHTS COTTAGE	RT	45.00	78.00
92	BIRTHSTONE WISHING WELL	RT	40.00	68.00
92	MAD BARON FOURTHRITE'S FOLLY	18854	275.00	234.00

YR	NAME	LIMIT	ISSUE	TREND
93	ARCHES THRICE	RT	150.00	160.00
93	HORATIO PERNICKETY'S AMOROUS INTENT	9990	350.00	289.00
93	PLUM COTTAGE	4500	50.00	186.00
94	BIRTHDAY COTTAGE (ARCHES THWONCE)	RT	55.00	73.00
94	QUINDENE MANOR	3000	695.00	720.00
94	QUINDENE MANOR-PREM. ED.	1500	850.00	820.00
94	WINTER ARCH	RT	25.00	76.00
94	WISHING FALLS COTTAGE	RT	65.00	68.00
95	GRUMBLEWEED'S POTTING SHED	RT	99.00	168.00
95	NEWTOWN MILLHOUSE	4500	195.00	176.00
95	WHISPERS COTTAGE	RT	99.00	132.00
96	CHRISTMAS TOYSHOP, THE (MUSICAL GLOBE)	1500	50.00	138.00
96	DERBY ARMS, THE (DW APPEARANCE)	RT	60.00	113.00
96	PRIMROSE COTTAGE (PAINTER EVENT)	RT	65.00	116.00

D. WINTER **TINY SERIES**

YR	NAME	LIMIT	ISSUE	TREND
80	ANN HATHAWAY'S COTTAGE	RT	*	613.00
80	COTSWOLD FARMHOUSE	RT	*	613.00
80	CROWN INN	RT	*	613.00
80	ST. NICHOLAS' CHURCH	RT	*	632.00
80	SULGRAVE MANOR	RT	*	613.00
80	WM. SHAKESPEARE'S BIRTHPLACE	RT	*	597.00

D. WINTER **VILLAGE COLLECTION**

YR	NAME	LIMIT	ISSUE	TREND
81	VILLAGE, THE	RT	362.00	536.00
81	VILLAGE, THE (OLD STYLE)	RT	362.00	N/A

D. WINTER **WELSH COLLECTION**

YR	NAME	LIMIT	ISSUE	TREND
93	A BIT OF NONSENSE	RT	52.00	71.00
93	PEN-Y-CRAIG	RT	88.00	91.00
93	TYDDYN SIRIOL	RT	88.00	102.00
93	Y DDRAIGG GOCH	RT	88.00	80.00

D. WINTER **WEST COUNTRY**

YR	NAME	LIMIT	ISSUE	TREND
86	DEVONCOMBE	RT	73.00	103.00
86	SMUGGLER'S CREEK	RT	390.00	516.00
86	TAMAR COTTAGE	RT	46.00	85.00
87	DEVON CREAMERY	RT	63.00	120.00
87	ORCHARD COTTAGE	RT	92.00	109.00
88	CORNISH ENGINE HOUSE	RT	120.00	153.00
88	CORNISH HARBOUR	RT	120.00	165.00

D. WINTER **WINTERVILLE COLLECTION**

YR	NAME	LIMIT	ISSUE	TREND
94	CLOCKHOUSE, THE	RT	165.00	166.00
94	CLOCKHOUSE, THE (PREM. ED.)	RT	215.00	178.00
94	TOYMAKER, THE	RT	135.00	125.00
94	TOYMAKER, THE (PREM. ED.)	3500	175.00	181.00
95	ST. STEPHEN'S	5750	150.00	175.00
95	ST. STEPHEN'S (PREM. ED.)	1750	195.00	182.00
95	YE MERRY GENTLEMEN'S LODGINGS	5750	125.00	123.00
95	YE MERRY GENTLEMEN'S LODGINGS (PREM. ED.)	1750	170.00	160.00
96	AT HOME WITH COMFORT AND JOY	5750	110.00	130.00
96	AT HOME WITH COMFORT AND JOY-PREMIER EDITION	1750	145.00	173.00

DEPARTMENT 56

* **ALPINE VILLAGE**

YR	NAME	LIMIT	ISSUE	TREND
86	ALPINE VILLAGE 6540-4 (SET OF 5)	RT	150.00	150.00
86	APOTEHEKE 6540-4	RT	37.00	52.00
86	BESSON BIERKELLER 6540-4	RT	37.00	40.00
86	E. STAUBR BAECKER 6540-4	RT	37.00	37.00
86	GASTHOF EISL 6540-4	RT	37.00	40.00
86	MILCH-KASE 6540-4	RT	37.00	52.00
87	ALPINE CHURCH 6541-2	RT	32.00	221.00
87	JOSEF ENGEL FARMHOUSE 5952-8	RT	33.00	1122.00
88	GRIST MILL 5953-6	RT	45.00	45.00
90	BAHNOF 5615-4	RT	42.00	95.00
91	ST. NIKOLAUS KIRCHE 5617-0	OP	38.00	38.00
92	GATE HOUSE 5530-1, SELECT OPEN HOUSE	RT	23.00	35.00
92	KUKUCK UHREN 5618-9, ALPINE SHOPS	OP	38.00	38.00
92	METTERNICHE WURST 5618-9, ALPINE SHOPS	RT	38.00	38.00
93	CLIMB EVERY MOUNTAIN 5613-8, (SET OF 4)	OP	28.00	28.00
93	SPORT LADEN 5612-0	OP	50.00	50.00
94	BAKERY & CHOCOLATE SHOP 5614-6	OP	38.00	38.00
94	POLKA FEST 5607-3, (SET OF 3)	OP	30.00	30.00
95	ALPEN HORN PLAYER AT ALPINE SIGN 5618-2	OP	20.00	20.00
95	KAMM HAUS 5617-1	OP	*	42.00
96	DANUBE MUSIC PUBLISHER #56173	OP	55.00	55.00
98	SPIELZEUG LADEN	*	65.00	65.00

* **BACHMAN'S**

YR	NAME	LIMIT	ISSUE	TREND
87	HOME TOWN BOARDING HOUSE 670-0	SU	34.00	275.00
87	HOME TOWN CHURCH 671-8	SU	40.00	390.00
88	HOME TOWN DRUGSTORE 672-6	SU	40.00	675.00

* **CHRISTMAS IN THE CITY**

YR	NAME	LIMIT	ISSUE	TREND
87	BAKERY 6512-9	RT	38.00	117.00
87	CATHEDRAL, THE 5962-5	RT	60.00	293.00
87	CHRISTMAS IN THE CITY 6512-9 (SET OF 3)	RT	112.00	585.00
87	CHRISTMAS IN THE CITY SIGN 5960-9	RT	6.00	18.00
87	PALACE THEATRE 5963-3	RT	45.00	813.00
87	SUTTON PLACE BROWNSTONES 5961-7	RT	80.00	862.00
87	TOWER RESTAURANT 6512-9	RT	38.00	225.00

YR	NAME	LIMIT	ISSUE	TREND
87	TOY SHOP & PET STORE 6512-9	RT	38.00	277.00
87	VEHICLES 5964-1, (SET OF 3)	OP	22.00	22.00
88	CHOCOLATE SHOPPE, THE 5968-4	RT	40.00	157.00
88	CITY HALL 5969-2	RT	65.00	146.00
88	HANK'S MARKET 5970-6	RT	40.00	88.00
88	VARIETY STORE 5972-2	RT	45.00	175.00
89	5607 PARK AVENUE TOWNHOUSE 5977-3	RT	48.00	91.00
89	5609 PARK AVENUE TOWNHOUSE 5978-1	RT	48.00	105.00
89	BOULEVARD 5516-6	RT	25.00	40.00
89	DOROTHY'S DRESS SHOP 5974-9	RT	70.00	524.00
89	MAILBOX/FIRE HYDRANT 5517-4, RD, WH & BL	RT	6.00	18.00
89	RITZ HOTEL 5973-0	RT	55.00	85.00
89	TOWN SQUARE GAZEBO 5513-1	OP	19.00	19.00
89	UTILITIES SET 5512-3	OP	12.50	13.00
89	WROUGHT IRON FENCE EXTENSION SET 5515-8	OP	12.00	12.00
89	WROUGHT IRON GATE W/FENCE 5514-0	OP	15.00	15.00
90	'TIS THE SEASON 5539-5	RT	12.95	28.00
90	BUSY SIDEWALKS 5535-2, (SET OF 4)	RT	28.00	46.00
90	DOCTOR'S OFFICE, THE 5544-1	RT	60.00	78.00
90	MAILBOX/FIRE HYDRANT 5517-4, RED & GREEN	OP	6.00	18.00
90	RED BRICK FIRE STATION 5536-0	RT	55.00	85.00
90	REST YE MERRY GENTLEMEN 5540-9	OP	12.95	13.00
90	SUBWAY ENTRANCE 5541-7	OP	15.00	15.00
90	WONG'S IN CHINATOWN 5537-9	RT	55.00	82.00
91	ALL SAINTS CORNER CHURCH 5542-5	OP	105.00	105.00
91	ARTS ACADEMY 5543-3	RT	45.00	88.00
91	DOCTOR'S OFFICE 5544-1	RT	60.00	78.00
91	HOLLYDALE'S DEPARTMENT STORE 5534-4	RT	85.00	85.00
91	LITTLE ITALY- RISTORANTE	RT	52.00	91.00
91	ST. MARK'S CHURCH 5549-2	RT	120.00	2080.00
92	CITY CLOCKWORKS 5531-0, UPTOWN SHOPPE	RT	56.00	50.00
92	HABERBASHERY 5531-0, UPTOWN SHOPPE	RT	40.00	40.00
92	MUSIC EMPORIUM 5531-0, UPTOWN SHOPPE	RT	54.00	54.00
92	UPTOWN SHOPPES #5531-0	RT	*	N/A
93	POTTERS TEA SELLER 5880-7	RT	45.00	50.00
93	SPRING STREET COFFEE HOUSE	RT	45.00	55.00
93	WEST VILLAGE SHOPS #5880-7	RT	*	N/A
94	BROKERAGE HOUSE 5881-5	RT	*	N/A
94	CHAMBER ORCHESTRA 5884-0, (SET OF 4)	OP	*	N/A
94	CITY BROKERAGE HOUSE 5881-5	OP	48.00	48.00
94	FIRST METROPOLITAN BANK 5882-3	RT	60.00	60.00
94	HERITAGE MUSEUM OF ART 5883-1	OP	96.00	96.00
94	HOLIDAY FIELD TRIP 5885-8, (SET OF 3)	RT	*	28.00
95	BRIGHTON SCHOOL 5887-6	OP	*	52.00
95	BROWN STONES ON THE SQ. 5887-7 (SET OF 2)	OP	*	90.00
95	CHOIR BOYS ALL IN A ROW 5889-2	OP	20.00	20.00
95	HOLY NAME CHURCH 5887-5	OP	96.00	96.00
95	IVY TERRACE APARTMENTS 5887-4	RT	60.00	60.00
95	KEY TO THE CITY AT CHRISTMAS CITY SIGN 5889-3	OP	20.00	20.00
95	ONE MAN BAND & DANCING DOG 5889-1 (SET OF 2)	OP	18.00	18.00
95	VILLAGE EXPRESS VAN-CANADA OM216	OP	45.00	45.00
95	YES, VIRIGINA 5889-0, (SET OF 2)	OP	12.50	13.00
96	CAFE CAPRICE FRENCH RESTAURANT	OP	45.00	45.00
96	GRAND CENTRAL RAILWAY STATION	OP	90.00	90.00
96	WASHINGTON STREET POST OFFICE	OP	52.00	52.00
97	CAFE CAPRISE FRENCH RESTAURANT 58882	*	*	N/A
97	GRAND CENTRAL RAILWAY STATION 58881	*	*	N/A
98	CAPITOL, THE	*	110.00	110.00
98	JOHNSON'S GROCERY & DELI	*	60.00	60.00
98	RIVERSIDE ROW SHOPS	*	52.00	52.00
*				**DICKENS' VILLAGE**
84	ABEL BEESLEY BUTCHER 6515-3	RT	25.00	140.00
84	BEAN AND SON SMITHY SHOP 6515-3	RT	25.00	221.00
84	CANDLE SHOP 6515-3	RT	25.00	183.00
84	CROWNTREE INN 6515-3	RT	25.00	329.00
84	GOLDEN SWAN BAKER 6515-3	RT	25.00	176.00
84	GREEN GROCER 6515-3	RT	25.00	195.00
84	JONES & CO. BRUSH/BASKET SHOP 6515-3	RT	25.00	342.00
84	ORIGINAL SHOPS, THE 6515-3 (SET OF 7)	RT	175.00	975.00
85	DICKENS' COTTAGES 6518-8 (SET OF 3)	RT	75.00	1300.00
85	DICKENS' VILLAGE CHURCH (DARK CARAMEL) 6516-1	RT	35.00	163.00
85	DICKENS' VILLAGE CHURCH (GREEN) 6516-1	RT	35.00	460.00
85	DICKENS' VILLAGE CHURCH (LT. CREAM) 6516-1	RT	35.00	199.00
85	DICKENS' VILLAGE CHURCH (TAN/FLESH) 6516-1	RT	35.00	124.00
85	DICKENS' VILLAGE MILL 6519-6	RT	35.00	5168.00
85	STONE COTTAGE (SPLIT PEA GREEN) 6518-8	RT	25.00	375.00
85	STONE COTTAGE (TAN) 6518-8	RT	25.00	660.00
85	STONE COTTAGE (TAN/GREEN) 6518-8	RT	25.00	390.00
85	THATCHED COTTAGE 6518-8	RT	25.00	173.00
85	TUDOR COTTAGE 6518-8	RT	25.00	350.00
85	VILLAGE CHURCH (CREAM-YELLOW) 6516-1	RT	35.00	199.00
86	BLYTHE POND MILL HOUSE 6508-0	RT	37.00	244.00
86	BY THE POND MILL HOUSE 6508-0	RT	37.00	124.00
86	CHADBURY STATION & TRAIN 6528-5	RT	65.00	335.00
86	CHRISTMAS/COTTAGES 6500-5 (SET OF 3)	OP	75.00	137.00

Ship Inn *was created by the artists of Lilliput Lane.*

One Acre Cottage *from 1994 was one of 15 new pieces from John Hine Studios to celebrate the 15th anniversary of David Winter Cottages.*

Carolina Lighthouse, *part of the Coastal Classics collection by Bill Job for Forma Vitrum, is an open edition.*

The Old Vicarage at Christmas *is one of the few Lilliput Lane cottages to be designed with snow.*

Honeysuckle Cottage, *introduced in 1992, was the Lilliput Lane 10th anniversary special.*

Home Sweet Home *is the creation of artist Ray Day. The piece is produced by Lilliput Lane.*

YR	NAME	LIMIT	ISSUE	TREND
86	COTTAGE OF BOB CRATCHIT & TINY TIM 6500-5	RT	30.00	131.00
86	COTTAGE TOY SHOP 6507-2	RT	27.00	296.00
86	DICKENS' LANE SHOPS 6507-2 (SET OF 3)	RT	80.00	748.00
86	FEZZIWIG'S WAREHOUSE 6500-5	RT	30.00	53.00
86	NORMAN CHURCH 6502-1	3500	40.00	2925.00
86	SCROOGE & MARLEY COUNTING HOUSE	RT	30.00	88.00
86	THOMAS KERSEY COFFEE HOUSE 6507-2	RT	27.00	166.00
86	TUTTLE'S PUB 6507-2	RT	27.00	212.00
87	BARLEY BREE FARMHOUSE & BARN 5900-5 (SET OF 2)	RT	60.00	410.00
87	BRICK ABBEY 6549-8	RT	33.00	368.00
87	CHESTERTON MANOR HOUSE 6568-4	RT	45.00	1625.00
87	DICKENS' VILLAGE SIGN 6569-2	RT	6.00	15.00
87	DOVER COACH/ORIGINAL 6590-0	RT	18.00	72.00
87	KENILWORTH CASTLE 5916-1	RT	70.00	634.00
87	NEW ENGLAND VILLAGE SIGN 6532-3	RT	6.00	18.00
87	OLD CURIOSITY SHOP 5905-6	OP	40.00	75.00
87	OX SLED/BLUE 5901-1	RT	20.00	137.00
87	OX SLED/TAN 5901-1	RT	20.00	270.00
88	BOOTER AND COBBLER 5924-2	RT	32.00	131.00
88	C.F. PUBLIC HOUSE 5904-8	RT	35.00	748.00
88	COBBLESTONE SHOPS 5924-2 (SET OF 3)	RT	95.00	479.00
88	COUNTING HOUSE & SILAS THIMBLRTON BARRISTER 5902-1	RT	32.00	59.00
88	GEORGE WEETON WATCHMAKER 5926-9	RT	33.00	49.00
88	IVY GLEN CHURCH 5927-7	RT	35.00	69.00
88	MERCHANT SHOPS 5926-9 (SET OF 5)	RT	150.00	244.00
88	MERMAID FISH SHOPPE 5926-9	RT	33.00	72.00
88	NIC(K)OLAS NICKLEBY COTTAGE 5925-0	RT	36.00	131.00
88	NICHOLAS NICKLEBY	RT	36.00	72.00
88	NICHOLAS NICKLEBY 5925-0 (SET OF 2)	RT	72.00	165.00
88	NICHOLAS NICKLEBY CHARACTER 5929-3, SET OF FOUR	RT	20.00	34.00
88	T. WELLS FRUIT & SPICE SHOP 5924-2	RT	32.00	88.00
88	WACKFORD SQUEERS BOARDING SCHOOL 5925-0	RT	36.00	88.00
88	WALPOLE TAILORS 5926-9	RT	33.00	24.00
88	WHITE HORSE BAKERY 5926-9	RT	33.00	56.00
88	WOOL SHOP, THE 5924-2	RT	32.00	209.00
89	BETSEY TROTWOOD'S COTTAGE 5550-6	RT	42.00	66.00
89	CHRISTMAS MORNING 5588-3 (SET OF 3)	OP	18.00	18.00
89	COBLES POLICE STATION 5583-2	RT	38.00	124.00
89	DAVID COPPERFIELD 5550-6 (SET OF 3)	RT	125.00	244.00
89	FLAT OF EBENEZER SCROOGE, THE 5587-5	OP	38.00	82.00
89	GREEN GATE 5586-7	RT	65.00	234.00
89	KINGS ROAD CAB 5581-6	OP	30.00	30.00
89	KNOTTINGHILL CHURCH 5582-4	RT	52.00	69.00
89	MR. WICKFIELD SOLICITOR 5550-6	RT	42.00	85.00
89	PEGGOTTY'S SEASIDE COTTAGE (GREEN) 5550-6	RT	42.00	62.00
89	PEGGOTTY'S SEASIDE COTTAGE (TAN) 5550-6	RT	42.00	108.00
89	ROYAL COACH 5578-6	RT	55.00	75.00
89	RUTH MARION 5585-9	RT	65.00	316.00
89	RUTH MARION 5589-9 (PROOF)	RT	65.00	446.00
89	THEATRE ROYAL 5584-0	RT	45.00	85.00
89	TOWN SQUARE GAZEBO 5513-1	OP	19.00	19.00
89	VICTORIA STATION 5574-3	OP	110.00	110.00
90	BISHOP'S OAST HOUSE 5567-0	RT	45.00	82.00
90	C.H. WATT PHYSICIAN #55691	RT	*	35.00
90	FLYING SCOT TRAIN, THE 5573-5 (SET OF 4)	OP	50.00	50.00
90	HOLIDAY TRAVELERS 5571-9, (SET OF 3"	OP	25.00	25.00
90	KINGS ROAD 5568-9 (SET OF 2)	RT	72.00	104.00
90	TUTBURY PRINTER 5569-0	RT	40.00	52.00
90	VICTORIA STATION TRAIN PLATFORM 5575-1	OP	22.00	22.00
91	ASHBURY INN 5555-7	RT	60.00	62.00
91	BROWNLOW'S HOUSE 5553-0	RT	38.00	78.00
91	FAGIN'S HIDE-A-WAY 5552-2	RT	72.00	75.00
91	MAYLIE'S COTTAGE 5553-0	RT	38.00	75.00
91	NEPHEW FRED'S FLAT 5557-3	RT	36.00	59.00
91	OLIVER TWIST 5553-0 (SET OF 2)	RT	75.00	111.00
92	CROWN & CRICKET INN 5750-9	RT	100.00	134.00
92	HEMBLETON PEWTERER 5800-9	RT	72.00	92.00
92	KING'S ROAD POST OFFICE 5801-7	OP	45.00	45.00
92	LIONHEAD BRIDGE 5864-5	OP	22.00	22.00
92	OLD MICHAELCHURCH 5562-0	RT	46.00	62.00
92	YANKEE JUD BELL CASTING 5643-0	RT	44.00	44.00
93	A. BIELER FARM 5648-0 SET OF 2	RT	92.00	92.00
93	BOARDING & LODGING SCHOOL 5819-2 #18	RT	48.00	108.00
93	BRINGING FLEECES TO MILL, 5819-0 (SET OF 2)	OP	35.00	35.00
93	BUMPSTEAD NYE CLOAKS & TREACLE 5808-4	RT	38.00	38.00
93	C. BRADFORD WHEELWRIGHT & SON 5818-1, (SET OF 2)	RT	24.00	24.00
93	DASHING THRU THE SNOW 5820-3	OP	33.00	33.00
93	GREAT DENTON MILL 5812-2	RT	50.00	50.00
93	KINGFORD BREW HOUSE 5811-4	RT	45.00	59.00
93	LOMAS LIMITED MOLASSES & TREACLE 5808-6	RT	38.00	38.00
93	PIED BULL INN, THE 5751-7	RT	100.00	136.00
93	PUMP LANE SHOPPES 5808-4 SET OF 3	RT	112.00	143.00
93	VISIONS OF CHRISTMAS PAST 5817-3, (SET OF 3)	OP	28.00	39.00
93	W.M. WHEATCAKES & PUDDINGS 5808-7	RT	38.00	40.00
94	BOARDING & LODGING SCHOOL 5809-2	YR	48.00	108.00

YR	NAME	LIMIT	ISSUE	TREND
94	BOARDING & LODGING SCHOOL 5810-6	OP	48.00	72.00
94	CHELSEA MARKET CURIOSITY 5827-0, (SET OF 2)	OP	28.00	28.00
94	CHELSEA MARKET MISTLETOE 5826-2, (SET OF 2)	OP	25.00	25.00
94	CHRISTMAS CAROL HOLIDAY TRIMMING SET 5831-9 S/21	OP	65.00	65.00
94	DEDLOCK ARMS 5752-5	RT	100.00	127.00
94	GIGGELSWICK MUTTON & HAM 5822-0	RT	48.00	48.00
94	HATHER HARNESS 5823-8	RT	48.00	48.00
94	PEACEFUL GLOW ON CHRISTMAS EVE 5830-8, (SET OF 3)	OP	30.00	30.00
94	PORTOBELLO COTTAGES 5824-6, (SET OF 3)	OP	120.00	120.00
94	PORTOBELLO RD, PEDDLER, SET OF THREE	OP	28.00	28.00
94	POSTERN/10TH ANNIVERSARY PC 9871-0	RT	18.00	30.00
94	VICTORIAN WROUGHT IRON FENCE & GATE 5252-3	OP	15.00	15.00
94	WHITTLESBOURNE CHURCH 5821-1	OP	85.00	85.00
94	WINTER SLEIGHRIDE 5825-4	OP	18.00	18.00
95	BLENHAM STREET BANK 5833-0	OP	60.00	60.00
95	BRICKSTON ROAD WATCHMEN 5839-0, (SET OF 2)	OP	25.00	25.00
95	CHELSEA MARKET HAT, MUNGER & CART 5839-2	OP	*	N/A
95	CHOP SHOP, THE	RT	35.00	35.00
95	DURSLEY MANOR 5832-9	OP	50.00	50.00
95	J.D. NICHOLS TOY SHOP 5832-8	OP	48.00	48.00
95	MALTINGS, THE 5833-5	OP	50.00	50.00
95	PARTRIDGE/PEAR TREE, 12 DAYS OF CHRISTMAS 5835-1	OP	35.00	35.00
95	PEA PUDDLEWICK SPECTACLE SHOP	OP	35.00	35.00
95	SIR JOHN FALLSTAFF INN	RT	100.00	111.00
95	START A TRADITION SET DV STARTER SET 5832-7	RT	85.00	85.00
95	TALLY HO 5839-1, (SET OF 5)	OP	25.00	25.00
95	TWO TURTLEDOVES-12 DAYS OF CHRISTMAS 5836-0	OP	33.00	33.00
95	VILLAGE DUDDEN CROSS CHURCH, THE 5834-3	OP	45.00	45.00
95	WRENBURY BAKER	RT	35.00	35.00
95	WRENBURY SHOPS 5833-1, (SET OF 3)	OP	100.00	100.00
96	BUTTER TUB BARN #58338	OP	48.00	48.00
96	BUTTER TUB FARMOUSE #58337	OP	40.00	40.00
96	CHRISTMAS CAROL COTTAGE REVISITED #58339	OP	60.00	60.00
96	CHRISTMAS CAROL COTTAGE, THE	OP	60.00	60.00
96	GRAPES INN, THE #5753-4	RT	*	153.00
96	MELANCHOLY TAVERN,THE	OP	45.00	45.00
96	MULBERRIE COURT	OP	90.00	90.00
96	OLE COMDEN TOWN CHURCH,THE	OP	55.00	55.00
96	QUILLY'S ANTIQUES	OP	46.00	46.00
96	RAMSFORD PALACE #58336	RT	*	514.00
96	RAMSFORD PALACE- SET OF 17	27500	175.00	175.00
97	GAD'S HILL PLACE 57535	RT	98.00	98.00
97	MELANCHOLY TAVERN 58346	*	45.00	45.00
97	MULBERRIE COURT 58345	*	90.00	90.00
97	NETTIE QUINN PUPPETS & MARIONETTES 58344	*	50.00	50.00
97	OLDE CAMDEN TOWN CHURCH 58346	*	55.00	55.00
97	QUILLY'S ANTIQUES 58348	*	*	N/A
98	MANCHESTER SQUARE (SET OF 25)	*	250.00	250.00
*	**DISNEY PARKS VILLAGE**			
87	AUTOMOBILES #5964-1	RT	*	N/A
88	VILLAGE EXPRESS TRAIN #5980-3	RT	*	208.00
92	VILLAGE EXPRESS VAN #5865-3	RT	*	34.00
93	C. BRADFORD, WHEELWRIGHT & SON #5818-1	RT	*	34.00
93	KNIFE GRINDER #5649-9	RT	*	49.00
93	PLAYING IN THE SNOW SET #5556-5	RT	*	34.00
93	VISION OF A CHRISTMAS PAST #5817-3	RT	*	39.00
94	DISNEY PARKS FAMILY #5354-6	RT	*	46.00
94	DISNEYLAND FIRE DEPARTMENT #105 #5352-0	RT	*	59.00
94	MICKEY & MINNIE #5353-8	RT	*	34.00
94	MICKEY'S CHRISTMAS CAROL #5350-3	RT	*	189.00
94	OLD WORLD ANTIQUES GATE #5355-4	RT	*	21.00
94	OLDE WORLD ANTIQUES SHOPS #5351-1	RT	*	117.00
95	BALLOON SELLER #5353-9	RT	*	69.00
95	SILVERSMITH #5352-1	RT	*	358.00
95	TINKERBELL'S TREASURES #5352-2	RT	*	228.00
96	CHRISTMAS BELLS #98711	RT	*	52.00
*	**HERITAGE VILLAGE COLLECTION**			
90	TOWN CRIER & CHIMNEY SWEEP 5569-7, (SET OF 2)	OP	15.00	15.00
91	BRINGING HOME THE YULE LOG 5558-1, (SET OF 3)	OP	28.00	28.00
91	HOLIDAY COACH 5561-1	OP	70.00	70.00
91	POULTRY MARKET 5559-0, (SET OF 3)	RT	32.00	46.00
92	CHURCHYARD GATE & FENCE 5806-8, (SET OF 3)	OP	15.00	15.00
92	CHURCHYARD GATE & FENCE 5807-6, (SET OF 4)	OP	16.00	16.00
94	BROWNING COTTAGE 58249	RT	*	N/A
94	COBB COTTAGE 58248	RT	*	N/A
94	MR. & MRS. PICKLE 58247	RT	*	N/A
95	DUDDEN CROSS CHURCH 5834-3	RT	*	N/A
97	TOWER OF LONDON (SET OF 5) 58500	RT	*	N/A
*	**HERITAGE VILLAGE COLLECTION ACCESSORIES**			
84	CAROLERS 6526-9 (SET OF 3)	RT	10.00	98.00
85	VILLAGE TRAIN 6527-7 (SET OF 3) BRIGHTON	RT	12.50	390.00
86	CHRISTMAS CAROL FIGS. 6501-3 (SET OF 3)	RT	12.50	79.00
86	COVERED WOODEN BRIDGE 6531-5	RT	10.00	46.00
86	LIGHTED TREE W/CHILDREN & LADDER 6510-2	RT	35.00	267.00
86	NEW ENGLAND WINTER SET 6532-3 (SET OF 5)	RT	18.00	35.00

YR	NAME	LIMIT	ISSUE	TREND
86	SLEIGHRIDE 6511-0	RT	20.00	62.00
87	BLACKSMITH 5934-0 (SET OF 3)	RT	20.00	75.00
87	CITY PEOPLE 5965-0 (SET OF 5)	RT	28.00	59.00
87	DOVER COACH 6590-0	RT	18.00	72.00
87	FARM PEOPLE & ANIMALS 5901-3 (SET OF 5)	RT	24.00	75.00
87	MAPLE SUGARING SHED 6589-7 (SET OF 3)	RT	19.00	316.00
87	OX SLED 5951-1	RT	20.00	101.00
87	SHOPKEEPERS 5966-8 (SET OF 4)	RT	15.00	36.00
87	SILO & HAY SHED, 5950-1 (SET OF 2)	RT	18.00	179.00
87	SKATING POND 6545-5	RT	24.00	69.00
87	STONE BRIDGE 6546-3	RT	12.00	56.00
87	VILLAGE WELL & HOLY CROSS 6547-1 (SET OF 2)	RT	13.00	124.00
88	CHILDE POND & SKATERS 5903-0 (SET OF 4)	RT	30.00	88.00
88	CITY BUS & MILK TRUCK 5983-8 (SET OF 2)	RT	15.00	30.00
88	CITY NEWSSTAND 5971-4 (SET OF 4)	RT	25.00	53.00
88	FEZZIWIG AND FRIENDS 5928-5 (SET OF 3)	RT	12.50	56.00
88	NICHOLAS NICKLEBY 5929-3 (SET OF 4)	RT	20.00	34.00
88	ONE HORSE OPEN SLEIGH 5982-0	RT	20.00	34.00
88	SALVATION ARMY BAND 5985-4 (SET OF 6)	RT	24.00	78.00
88	VILLAGE HARVEST PEOPLE 5941-2 (SET OF 4)	RT	28.00	67.00
88	VILLAGE TRAIN TRESTLE 5981-1	RT	17.00	56.00
88	WOODCUTTER AND SON 5986 (SET OF 2)	RT	10.00	62.00
89	CENTRAL PARK CARRIAGE 5979-0	OP	30.00	30.00
89	CONSTABLES 5579-4 (SET OF 3)	RT	18.00	46.00
89	FARM ANIMALS 5945-5 (SET OF 4)	RT	15.00	26.00
89	HERITAGE VILLAGE SIGN W/SNOWMAN 5572-7	RT	10.00	21.00
89	ORGAN GRINDER 5957-9 (SET OF 3)	RT	21.00	34.00
89	RIVER STREET ICE HOUSE CART 5959-5	RT	20.00	56.00
90	CAROLERS ON THE DOORSTEP 5570-0, (SET OF 4)	OP	25.00	37.00
91	COME INTO THE INN 5560-3, (SET OF 3)	RT	22.00	33.00
92	CHURCH YARD 5563-8	RT	15.00	39.00
92	GATE HOUSE 5530-1	RT	23.00	52.00
*		**LITTLE TOWN OF BETHLEHEM**		
87	LITTLE TOWN/BETHLEHEM 5975-7 (SET OF 12)	OP	150.00	150.00
*		**MEADOWLAND**		
79	ASPEN TREES 5052-6	RT	16.00	32.00
79	COUNTRYSIDE CHURCH 5051-8	RT	25.00	100.00
79	SHEEP 5053-4	RT	12.00	24.00
79	THATCHED COTTAGE 5050-0	RT	30.00	260.00
*		**NEW ENGLAND VILLAGE**		
86	APOTHECARY SHOP 6530-7	RT	25.00	134.00
86	BRICK TOWN HALL 6530-7	RT	25.00	179.00
86	GENERAL STORE 6530-7	RT	25.00	374.00
86	JACOB ADAMS FARMHOUSE & BARN 6538-2	RT	65.00	488.00
86	LIVERY STABLE & BOOT SHOP 6530-7	RT	25.00	212.00
86	NATHANIEL BINGHAM FABRICS 6530-7	RT	25.00	156.00
86	NEW ENGLAND 6530-7 (ORIGINAL SET OF 7)	RT	170.00	1040.00
86	RED SCHOOLHOUSE 6530-7	RT	25.00	364.00
86	STEEPLE CHURCH 6530-7	RT	25.00	124.00
86	STEEPLE CHURCH 6539-0	RT	30.00	91.00
87	CRAGGY COVE LIGHTHOUSE 5930-7	RT	45.00	79.00
87	SMYTHE WOOLEN MILL 6543-1	RT	42.00	1203.00
87	TIMBER KNOLL LOG CABIN 6544-7	RT	38.00	176.00
87	VILLAGE EXPRESS ELECTRIC TRAIN/BLACK 5997-8	RT	90.00	265.00
87	WESTON TRAIN STATION 5931-5	RT	42.00	325.00
88	ADA'S BED & BOARDING HOUSE 2ND 5940-4	RT	36.00	144.00
88	ADA'S BED & BOARDING HOUSE 3RD 5940-4	RT	36.00	144.00
88	ADA'S BED & BOARDING HOUSE 5940-4 1ST	RT	36.00	144.00
88	ANNE SHAW TOYS 5939-0	RT	27.00	150.00
88	BEN'S BARBERSHOP 5939-0	RT	27.00	88.00
88	CHERRY LANE SHOPS 5939-0 (SET OF 3)	RT	80.00	423.00
88	OLD NORTH CHURCH 5932-3	OP	45.00	82.00
88	OTIS HAYES BUTCHER SHOP 5939-0	RT	27.00	85.00
88	RED COVERED BRIDGE 5987-0	RT	17.00	30.00
88	VILLAGE EXPRESS ELECTRIC TRAIN SET 5980-3	OP	100.00	100.00
89	BERKSHIRE HOUSE (ORIG BLUE) 5942-0	RT	40.00	137.00
89	BERKSHIRE HOUSE/TEAL 5942-0	RT	40.00	134.00
89	HV PROMOTIONAL EARTHENWARE SIGN 9953-8	RT	5.00	20.00
89	JANNES MULLET AMISH BARN 5944-7	RT	48.00	104.00
89	JANNES MULLET AMISH FARM HOUSE 5943-9	RT	32.00	143.00
89	MAILBOX/FIRE HYDRANT 5517-4 RED,WH & BL	RT	6.00	18.00
90	AMISH FAMILY 5948-0, (SET OF 3)	RT	20.00	34.00
90	AMISH FAMILY 5948-0, SET OF 3 W/MOUSTACHE	RT	20.00	59.00
90	CAPTAIN'S COTTAGE 5947-1	RT	42.00	56.00
90	ICHABOD CRAIN'S COTTAGE 5954-4	RT	32.00	59.00
90	MAILBOX & FIRE HYDRANT, RED & GREEN 5517-4	RT	6.00	18.00
90	SHINGLE CREEK HOUSE 5946-3	RT	40.00	43.00
90	SLEEPY HOLLOW CHURCH 5955-2	RT	36.00	53.00
90	SLEEPY HOLLOW SCHOOL 5954-4	RT	32.00	101.00
90	SLEEPY HOLLOW SCHOOL 5954-4 (SET OF 3)	RT	96.00	176.00
90	VAN TASSEL MANOR 5954-4	RT	32.00	59.00
91	MCGREBE-CUTTERS & SLEIGHS 5640-5	RT	48.00	56.00
92	BLUEBIRD SEED & BULB 5642-1	OP	48.00	65.00
92	STONEY BROOK TOWN HALL 5644-8	RT	42.00	40.00
92	YANKEE JUD BELL CASTING	RT	44.00	56.00

YR	NAME	LIMIT	ISSUE	TREND
93	A. BIELER BARN 5648-9	OP	50.00	50.00
93	A. BIELER FARMHOUSE 5648-9	OP	42.00	42.00
93	BLUE STAR ICE CO. 5647-2	RT	45.00	45.00
93	PENNSYLVANIA DUTCH BARN #56482	RT	*	N/A
93	PENNSYLVANIA DUTCH FARMHOUSE #56481	RT	*	66.00
94	ARLINGTON FALLS CHURCH 5651-0	RT	40.00	40.00
94	CAPE KEAG FISH CANNERY 5652-9	OP	48.00	48.00
94	OLD MAN & THE SEA, THE 5655-3 (SET OF 3)	OP	25.00	25.00
94	OVER THE RIVER & THROUGH THE WOODS 5654-5,SET OF 3	OP	35.00	35.00
94	PIGEONHEAD LIGHTHOUSE 5653-7	OP	50.00	50.00
94	TWO RIVERS BRIDGE 5656-1	OP	35.00	35.00
95	CHOWDER HOUSE 5657-1	OP	*	40.00
95	FARM ANIMALS 5658-8, (SET OF 8)	OP	33.00	33.00
95	FRESH PAINT FOR THE N.E. SIGN 5659-2	OP	20.00	20.00
95	HARVEST PUMPKIN WAGON 5659-1	OP	45.00	45.00
95	JEREMIAH BREWSTER HOUSE 56568	RT	*	N/A
95	LOBSTER TRAPPER 5658-9, (SET OF 4)	OP	35.00	35.00
95	LUMBERJACKS 5659-0, (SET OF 2)	OP	30.00	30.00
95	PIERCE BOAT WORKS 5657-3	OP	*	55.00
95	THOMAS T. JULIAN HOUSE 56569	RT	*	N/A
95	WOODBRIDGE POST OFFICE 5657-2	OP	40.00	40.00
96	APPLE VALLEY SCHOOL	OP	35.00	35.00
96	BOBWHITE COTTAGE	OP	50.00	48.00
96	J. HUDSON STOVEWORKS	OP	60.00	60.00
97	BOBWHITE COTTAGE 56576	*	50.00	50.00
97	J. HUDSON STOVE WORKS 56574	*	60.00	60.00
97	NAVIGATIONAL CHARTS & MAPS 56575	*	*	N/A
98	EAST WILLET POTTERY	*	45.00	45.00
98	SEMPLE'S SMOKEHOUSE	*	45.00	45.00
98	STEEN'S MAPLE HOUSE (SMOKING HOUSE)	*	60.00	60.00
*	**NORTH POLE COLLECTION**			
90	ELF BUNKHOUSE 5601-6	RT	40.00	59.00
90	NORTH POLE 5601-4 (SET OF 2)	RT	70.00	104.00
90	REINDEER BARN 5601-4	OP	40.00	40.00
90	SANTA'S WORKSHOP 5600-6	RT	72.00	446.00
90	TRIMMING THE NORTH POLE 5608-1	RT	10.00	46.00
91	NEENEE'S DOLLS & TOYS 5620-0	RT	38.00	62.00
91	NORTH POLE SHOPS 5621-9 (SET OF 2)	RT	75.00	75.00
91	ORLEY'S BELL & HARNESS SUPPLY 5621-9	RT	38.00	75.00
91	RIMPY'S BAKERY 5621-9	RT	38.00	79.00
91	TASSY'S MITTENS/HASSEL'S WOOLIES 5622-7	RT	50.00	95.00
92	ELFIE'S SLEDS & SKATES 5625-1	RT	48.00	60.00
92	OBBIE'S BOOKS & LETRINKA'S CANDY 5624-3	RT	70.00	70.00
92	POST OFFICE 5623-5	OP	45.00	50.00
93	NORTH POLE CHAPEL 5626-0	OP	45.00	45.00
93	NORTH POLE EXPRESS DEPOT 5627-8	OP	48.00	48.00
93	NORTH POLE GATE 5632-4	OP	33.00	33.00
93	SANTA'S LOOKOUT TOWER 5629-4	OP	45.00	45.00
93	SANTA'S WOODWORKS 5628-6	RT	42.00	65.00
93	SING A SONG FOR SANTA 5631-6, (SET OF 3)	OP	28.00	28.00
93	WOODSMAN ELVES 5630-8, (SET OF 3)	RT	30.00	69.00
94	BEARD BARBER SHOP 5634-0	RT	28.00	28.00
94	DOLLS & SANTA'S BEAR WORKS 5635-9, (SET OF 3)	OP	96.00	96.00
94	ELFIN SNOW CONE WORKS 5633-2	RT	40.00	40.00
94	LAST MINUTE DELIVERY	OP	*	35.00
94	NORTH POLE DOLLS & SANTA'S BEAR WORKS 5635-9	RT	*	N/A
94	SNOW CONE ELVES 5637-5, (SET OF 4)	OP	30.00	30.00
95	BUSY ELF SCULPTS THE N. POLE SIGN 5636-6	OP	20.00	20.00
95	CHARTING SANTA'S COURSE 5636-4, (SET OF 2)	OP	25.00	25.00
95	ELFIN FORGE & ASSEMBLY SHOP 5638-4	OP	65.00	65.00
95	ELVES' TRADE SCHOOL 5638-7	OP	*	50.00
95	I'LL NEED MORE TOYS 5636-5, (SET OF 2)	OP	25.00	25.00
95	SANTA'S ROOMING HOUSE 5638-6	OP	*	50.00
95	TIN SOLDIER SHOP 5638-3	RT	42.00	42.00
95	WEATHER & TIME OBSERVATORY 5638-5	OP	50.00	50.00
96	HALL OF RECORDS	OP	50.00	50.00
96	POPCORN & CRANBERRY HOUSE #56388	RT	45.00	45.00
96	ROUTE 1 NORTH POLE, HOME OF MR. & MRS. CLAUS	OP	110.00	110.00
96	SANTA'S BELL REPAIR #56389	OP	45.00	45.00
96	START A TRADITION SET #56390	RT	85.00	176.00
97	CHRISTMAS BREAD BAKERS 56393	*	*	N/A
97	HALL OF RECORDS 56392	*	50.00	50.00
97	ROUTE 1 NORTH POLE 56391	*	110.00	110.00
98	ELSIE'S GINGERBREAD (SMOKING HOUSE)	YR	65.00	65.00
98	GLASS ORNAMENT WORKS	*	60.00	60.00
98	MRS. CLAUS' GREENHOUSE	*	68.00	68.00
98	SANTA'S LIGHT SHOP	*	*	N/A
*	**ORIGINAL SNOW VILLAGE COLLECTION**			
76	COUNTRY CHURCH 5004-7	RT	18.00	475.00
76	GABLED COTTAGE 5002-1	RT	20.00	335.00
76	INN, THE- 5003-9	RT	20.00	488.00
76	MOUNTAIN LODGE 5001-3	RT	20.00	481.00
76	SMALL CHALET 5006-2	RT	15.00	544.00
76	STEEPLE CHURCH 5005-4	RT	25.00	790.00
77	MANSION DK. GREEN 5008-8	RT	30.00	683.00

YR	NAME	LIMIT	ISSUE	TREND
77	MANSION TEEL	RT	30.00	440.00
77	STONE CHURCH, 10 IN. 5009-6	RT	35.00	550.00
77	VICTORIAN HOUSE 5007-0	RT	30.00	511.00
78	CAPE COD 5013-8	RT	20.00	400.00
78	GENERAL STORE, TAN 5012-0	RT	25.00	566.00
78	GENERAL STORE, WHITE 5012-0	RT	25.00	450.00
78	HOMESTEAD 5011-2	RT	30.00	257.00
78	NANTUCKET 5014-6	RT	25.00	293.00
78	SKATING RINK & DUCK POND 5015-3 (SET)	RT	16.00	715.00
78	SMALL DOUBLE TREES W/BLUE BIRDS 5016-1	RT	13.50	165.00
78	SMALL DOUBLE TREES W/RED BIRDS 5016-1	RT	13.50	56.00
79	ADOBE HOUSE 5066-6	RT	18.00	2795.00
79	BROWNSTONE 5056-7	RT	36.00	520.00
79	COUNTRYSIDE CHURCH 5058-3	RT	28.00	319.00
79	GIANT TREES 5065-8	RT	20.00	267.00
79	KNOB HILL, GOLD 5055-9	RT	30.00	407.00
79	KNOB HILL, GRAY 5055-9	RT	30.00	145.00
79	LOG CABIN 5057-5	RT	22.00	634.00
79	MEADOWLAND COUNTRYSIDE CHURCH 5051-8	RT	25.00	700.00
79	MEADOWLAND THATCHED COTTAGE 5050-0	RT	30.00	600.00
79	MISSION CHURCH 5062-5	RT	30.00	1170.00
79	MOBILE HOME 5063-3	RT	18.00	2100.00
79	SCHOOL HOUSE 5060-9	RT	30.00	446.00
79	STONE CHURCH, 8.5 IN. 5059-1	RT	22.00	1073.00
79	TUDOR HOUSE	RT	25.00	441.00
79	VICTORIAN 5054-2	RT	30.00	449.00
80	CATHEDRAL CHURCH 5067-4	RT	36.00	2990.00
80	COLONIAL FARM HOUSE 5070-9	RT	30.00	312.00
80	STONE MILL HOUSE 5068-2	RT	30.00	556.00
80	TOWN CHURCH 5071-7	RT	33.00	397.00
80	TRAIN STATION W/3 TRAIN CARS, 6 HOLES 5085-6	RT	100.00	455.00
80	TRAIN STATION WITH 3 CARS , 8 HOLES 5085-6	RT	100.00	300.00
81	BAKERY 5077-6	RT	30.00	238.00
81	BARN 5074-1	RT	32.00	462.00
81	CORNER STORE 5076-8	RT	30.00	257.00
81	ENGLISH CHURCH 5078-4	RT	30.00	314.00
81	ENGLISH COTTAGE 5073-3	RT	25.00	293.00
81	LARGE SINGLE TREE 5080-6	RT	17.00	62.00
81	WOODEN CLAPBOARD 5072-5	RT	32.00	267.00
82	BANK 5024-5	RT	32.00	611.00
82	CARRIAGE HOUSE 5021-0	RT	28.00	378.00
82	CENTENNIAL HOUSE 5020-2	RT	32.00	449.00
82	FLOWER SHOP 5082-2	RT	25.00	527.00
82	GABLED HOUSE 5081-4	RT	30.00	540.00
82	NEW STONE CHURCH 5083-0	RT	32.00	468.00
82	PIONEER CHURCH 5022-9	RT	30.00	400.00
82	SKATING POND 5017-2	RT	25.00	410.00
82	STREET CAR 5019-9	RT	16.00	390.00
82	SWISS CHALET 5023-7	RT	28.00	595.00
83	CHATEAU 5084-9	RT	35.00	605.00
83	ENGLISH TUDOR 5033-4	RT	30.00	257.00
83	FIRE STATION 5032-6	RT	32.00	650.00
83	GINGERBREAD HOUSE 5025-3	RT	24.00	478.00
83	GOTHIC CHURCH 5028-8	RT	36.00	338.00
83	GOVERNOR'S MANSION 5003-2	RT	32.00	390.00
83	GROCERY 5001-6	RT	35.00	303.00
83	PARSONAGE 5029-6	RT	35.00	475.00
83	TOWN HALL 5000-8	RT	32.00	355.00
83	TURN OF THE CENTURY 5004-0	RT	36.00	325.00
83	VICTORIAN COTTAGE 5002-4	RT	35.00	442.00
83	VILLAGE CHURCH 5026-1	RT	30.00	360.00
83	WOODEN CHURCH 5031-8	RT	30.00	416.00
84	BAYPORT 5015-6	RT	30.00	310.00
84	CONGREGATIONAL CHURCH 5034-2	RT	28.00	600.00
84	DELTA HOUSE 5012-1	RT	32.00	381.00
84	GALENA HOUSE 5009-1	RT	32.00	436.00
84	HAVERSHAM HOUSE 5008-3	RT	37.00	222.00
84	MAIN STREET HOUSE 5005-9	RT	27.00	250.00
84	NEW SCHOOL HOUSE 5037-7	RT	35.00	235.00
84	PARISH CHURCH 5039-3	RT	32.00	342.00
84	RIVER ROAD HOUSE 5010-5	RT	36.00	251.00
84	SCOTTIE W/TREE 5038-5	RT	3.00	240.00
84	STRATFORD HOUSE 5007-5	RT	28.00	175.00
84	SUMMIT HOUSE 5036-9	RT	28.00	501.00
84	TRINITY CHURCH 5035-0	RT	32.00	429.00
85	CHURCH OF THE OPEN DOOR 5048-2	RT	34.00	137.00
85	DEPOT AND TRAIN WITH TWO TRAINS 5051-2	RT	65.00	221.00
85	DUPLEX 5050-4	RT	35.00	182.00
85	PLANTATION HOUSE 5047-4-6	RT	37.00	125.00
85	RIDGEWOOD 5052-0	RT	35.00	215.00
85	SPRUCE PLACE 50499-0	RT	33.00	296.00
85	STUCCO BUNGALOW 2045-8	RT	30.00	410.00
85	WILLIAMSBURG HOUSE 5046-6	RT	37.00	137.00
86	2101 MAPLE 5043-1	RT	32.00	374.00
86	ALL SAINTS CHURCH 5070-9	RT	38.00	75.00

Ruth Marion Scotch Woolens *was limited to 17,500 pieces and is part of Department 56's Dickens' Village.*

Ada's Bed and Boarding House, *from Department 56's New England Village, was issued in several colors before it was retired in 1991.*

New England Village's Timber Knoll Log Cabin was closed by Department 56 in 1990.

Cobles Police Station *was not embraced by Department 56 collectors who chose to believe that no crime existed in their miniature town. The piece was issued in 1990 and retired in 1991.*

Old Joe's Beetling Shop *was designed by David Winter for John Hine Studios for Christmas 1993. Issued for $175, the secondary market value of the retired piece has risen.*

Members of the Lilliput Lane Collectors' Club in 1992 could purchase Forget-Me-Not *by David Tate for $130.*

YR	NAME	LIMIT	ISSUE	TREND
86	APOTHECARY 5076-8	RT	34.00	173.00
86	BAKERY 5077-6	RT	35.00	150.00
86	BEACON HILL HOUSE 5065-2	RT	31.00	176.00
86	CARRIAGE HOUSE 5071-7	RT	29.00	137.00
86	HIGHLAND PARK HOUSE 5063-6	RT	35.00	169.00
86	LINCOLN PARK DUPLEX 5060-1	RT	33.00	153.00
86	MICKEY'S DINER 5078-4	RT	22.00	832.00
86	PACIFIC HEIGHTS HOUSE 5066-0	RT	33.00	130.00
86	RAMSEY HILL HOUSE 5067-9	RT	36.00	143.00
86	SAINT JAMES CHURCH 5068-7	RT	37.00	208.00
86	SONOMA HOUSE 5062-8	RT	33.00	163.00
86	TOY SHOP 5073-3	RT	36.00	127.00
86	TWIN PEAKS 5042-3	RT	32.00	566.00
86	WAVERLY PLACE 5041-5	RT	35.00	407.00
87	CATHEDRAL CHURCH 5019-9	RT	50.00	124.00
87	CUMBERLAND HOUSE 5024-5	RT	42.00	88.00
87	FARM HOUSE 5089-0	RT	40.00	127.00
87	FIRE STATION NO. 2 5091-1	RT	40.00	254.00
87	JEFFERSON SCHOOL 5082-2	OP	36.00	221.00
87	LIGHTHOUSE 5030-0	RT	36.00	637.00
87	RED BARN 5081-4	RT	38.00	166.00
87	SNOW VILLAGE FACTORY 5013-0	RT	45.00	153.00
87	SNOW VILLAGE RESORT LODGE 5092-0	RT	55.00	160.00
87	SPRINGFIELD HOUSE 5027-0	RT	40.00	88.00
87	ST. ANTHONY HOTEL & POST OFFICE 5006-7	RT	40.00	182.00
88	COBBLESTONE ANTIQUE SHOP 5123-3	RT	36.00	98.00
88	CORNER CAFE 5124-1	RT	37.00	134.00
88	HOME SWEET HOME/HOUSE & WINDMILL 5126-8	RT	60.00	140.00
88	JOHN DEERE WATER TOWER 5133-0	RT	20.00	683.00
88	KENWOOD HOUSE 5054-7	RT	50.00	153.00
88	MAPLE RIDGE INN 5121-7	RT	55.00	88.00
88	PALOS VERDES 5141-1	RT	38.00	75.00
88	REDEEMER CHURCH 5127-6	RT	42.00	65.00
88	SERVICE STATION 5128-4	RT	38.00	358.00
88	SINGLE CAR GARAGE 5125-0	RT	22.00	82.00
88	STONEHURST HOUSE 5140-3	OP	38.00	52.00
88	VILLAGE MARKET 5044-0	RT	39.00	130.00
88	VILLAGE STATION AND TRAIN 5122-5	RT	65.00	108.00
89	COLONIAL CHURCH 5119-5	RT	60.00	117.00
89	COURTHOUSE 5144-6	RT	65.00	208.00
89	CRACK THE WHIP #5171-3	RT	*	25.00
89	DOCTOR'S HOUSE 5143-8	RT	56.00	127.00
89	J. YOUNG'S GRANARY 5149-7	RT	45.00	115.00
89	JINGLE BELLE HOUSEBOAT 5114-4	RT	42.00	176.00
89	NORTH CREEK COTTAGE 5120-9	RT	45.00	88.00
89	PARAMOUNT THEATER 5142-0	RT	42.00	176.00
89	PINEWOOD LOG CABIN 5150-0	RT	38.00	69.00
89	VILLAGE WARMING HOUSE 5145-4	RT	42.00	72.00
90	56 FLAVORS ICE CREAM PARLOR 5151-9	RT	42.00	127.00
90	A HOME FOR THE HOLIDAYS #5165-9	RT	*	16.00
90	MAINSTREET HARDWARE STORE 5153-5	RT	42.00	91.00
90	MORNINGSIDE HOUSE 5152-7	RT	45.00	98.00
90	PRAIRIE HOUSE 5156-0	RT	42.00	95.00
90	QUEEN ANNE VICTORIAN 5157-8	RT	48.00	48.00
90	SPANISH MISSION CHURCH 5155-1	RT	42.00	117.00
90	VILLAGE REALTY 5154-3	RT	42.00	78.00
91	CHRISTMAS SHOP, THE 5097-0	RT	38.00	38.00
91	DOUBLE BUNGALOW 5407-0	RT	45.00	66.00
91	FINKLEA'S FINERY: COSTUME SHOP 5405-4	RT	45.00	85.00
91	GOTHIC FARMHOUSE 5404-6	RT	48.00	48.00
91	HONEYMOONER MOTEL 5401-1	RT	42.00	88.00
91	JACK'S CORNER BARBER SHOP 5406-2	RT	42.00	111.00
91	OAK GROVE TUDOR 5400-3	RT	42.00	78.00
91	SOUTHERN COLONIAL 5403-8	RT	48.00	108.00
91	VILLAGE GREENHOUSE 5402-0	RT	35.00	53.00
92	AIRPORT #5439-9	RT	*	104.00
92	AL'S TV SHOP	RT	40.00	65.00
92	CHRISTMAS PUPPIES #5432-1	RT	*	30.00
92	CRAFTSMAN COTTAGE	RT	55.00	85.00
92	GOOD SHEPHERD CHAPEL & CHURCH SCHOOL #5424-0	RT	*	98.00
92	GRANDMA'S COTTAGE 5420-8	RT	42.00	42.00
92	HARTFORD HOUSE	RT	55.00	85.00
92	POST OFFICE 5422-4	OP	35.00	55.00
92	PRINT SHOP & VILLAGE NEWS 5425-9	RT	38.00	72.00
92	SPIRIT OF SNOW VILLAGE AIRPLANE #5440-2	RT	*	33.00
92	ST. LUKE'S CHURCH 5421-6	RT	45.00	88.00
92	VILLAGE POST OFFICE	RT	35.00	38.00
92	VILLAGE STATION 5438-0	RT	65.00	75.00
92	VILLAGE VET & PET SHOP	RT	32.00	45.00
93	CHRISTMAS AT THE FARM #5450-0	RT	*	16.00
93	DAIRY BARN 5446-1	RT	55.00	55.00
93	DINAH'S DRIVE-IN 5447-0	RT	45.00	45.00
93	HUNTING LODGE 5445-3	RT	50.00	50.00
93	MOUNT OLIVET CHURCH 5442-9	RT	65.00	85.00
93	NANTUCKET RENOVATION 5441-0	YR	55.00	59.00

YR	NAME	LIMIT	ISSUE	TREND
93	PINT-SIZE PONY RIDES #5453-4	RT	*	37.00
93	SNOWY HILLS HOSPITAL 5448-8	RT	48.00	48.00
93	SPIRIT OF SNOW VILLAGE AIRPLANE #5458-5	RT	*	13.00
93	VILLAGE NEWS DELIVERY #5459-3	RT	*	21.00
93	VILLAGE PUBLIC LIBRARY 5443-7	RT	55.00	55.00
93	WOODBURY HOUSE 5444-5	RT	45.00	59.00
94	FISHERMAN'S NOOK CABINS (SET/2) 5461-5	OP	50.00	50.00
94	FISHERMAN'S NOOK RESORT 5460-7	OP	75.00	75.00
94	FISHERMAN'S NOOK TROUT CABIN 5461-5	OP	*	N/A
94	CARMEL COTTAGE 5466-6	RT	*	N/A
94	COCA-COLA BRAND BOTTLING PLANT 5469-0	RT	*	N/A
94	FEDERAL HOUSE 5465-8	RT	*	N/A
94	MARVEL'S BEAUTY SALON 5470-4	RT	*	N/A
94	ORIGINAL SNOW VILLAGE STARTER SET, THE	OP	49.99	50.00
95	BEACON HILL VICTORIAN 5485-7	*	60.00	60.00
95	BOWLING ALLEY 5485-8	*	42.00	42.00
95	CHRISTMAS COVE LIGHTHOUSE 5483-6	*	60.00	60.00
95	COCA-COLA BRAND DRUGSTORE 5484-4	*	55.00	55.00
95	DUTCH COLONIAL #5485-6	RT	*	59.00
95	HOLLY BROTHERS' GARAGE 5485-4	*	48.00	48.00
95	PEPPERMINT PORCH DAY CARE 5485-2	RT	45.00	45.00
95	PISA PIZZA PALACE 5485-1	*	35.00	35.00
95	RYMAN AUDITORIUM 5485-5	RT	75.00	75.00
95	SNOW CARNIVAL ICE PALACE 5485-0	*	95.00	95.00
95	STARBUCK'S COFFEE 5485-9	*	48.00	48.00
95	VILLAGE POLICE STATION 5485-3	*	48.00	48.00
96	BIRCH RUN SKI CHALET	OP	60.00	60.00
96	BOULDER SPRINGS HOUSE #54873	RT	60.00	60.00
96	CHRISTMAS LAKE HIGH SCHOOL	OP	52.00	52.00
96	HARLEY-DAVISON MOTORCYCLE SHOP	OP	65.00	65.00
96	NICK'S TREE FARM #54871 -SET OF 10	*	40.00	40.00
96	REINDEER BUS DEPOT #54874	RT	42.00	42.00
96	ROCKABILLY RECORDS	OP	45.00	45.00
96	ROSITA'S CANTINA	OP	50.00	50.00
96	SANTA COMES TO TOWN #5486-2	RT	*	N/A
96	SECRET GARDEN FLORIST, THE	OP	50.00	50.00
96	SINGLE VICTORIAN	OP	55.00	55.00
96	SMOKY MOUNTAIN RETREAT #54872	*	65.00	65.00
96	TREETOP TREE HOUSE	OP	35.00	35.00
98	BRANDON BUNGALOW, THE	*	55.00	55.00
98	CHRISTMAS BARN DANCE	*	65.00	65.00
98	FARM HOUSE	*	50.00	50.00
98	GRACIE'S DRY GOODS & GENERAL STORE (SET OF 2)	*	70.00	70.00
98	HERSHEY'S CHOCOLATE SHOP	*	55.00	55.00
98	ITALIANATE VILLA	*	55.00	55.00
98	LINDEN HILLS COUNTRY CLUB (SET OF 2)	*	60.00	60.00
98	MCDONALD'S	*	65.00	65.00
98	ROLLERAMA ROLLER RINK	*	56.00	56.00
*	**ORIGINAL SNOW VILLAGE COLLECTION ACCESSORIES**			
79	CAROLERS 5064-1	RT	12.00	160.00
80	CERAMIC CAR 5069-0	RT	5.00	62.00
81	CERAMIC SLEIGH 5079-2	RT	5.00	59.00
82	SNOWMAN WITH BROOM 5018-0	RT	3.00	15.00
83	MONKS-A-CAROLING 6459-9	RT	6.00	65.00
84	MONKS-A-CAROLING 5040-7	RT	6.00	39.00
84	SCOTTIE WITH TREE 5038-5	RT	3.00	115.00
85	FAMILY MOM/KIDS, GOOSE/GIRL 5057-1	RT	11.00	34.00
85	SANTA/MAILBOX 5059-8	RT	11.00	34.00
85	SINGING NUNS 5053-9	RT	6.00	150.00
85	SNOW KIDS SLED & SKIS 5056-3	RT	11.00	46.00
86	GIRL/SNOWMAN BOY 5095-4	RT	11.00	59.00
86	KIDS AROUND THE TREE 5094-6	RT	15.00	34.00
86	SHOPPING GIRLS WITH PACKAGES 5096-2	RT	11.00	39.00
87	3 NUNS WITH SONGBOOKS	RT	6.00	189.00
87	CAROLING FAMILY 5105-5 (SET OF 3)	RT	25.00	32.00
87	CHILDREN IN BAND 5104-7	RT	15.00	30.00
87	CHRISTMAS CHILDREN 5107-1 (SET OF 4)	RT	20.00	39.00
87	FOR SALE SIGN 5108-0	RT	3.50	21.00
87	PRAYING MONKS 5103-9	RT	6.00	52.00
87	SNOW KIDS 5113-6 (SET OF 4)	RT	20.00	34.00
88	APPLE GIRL/NEWSPAPER BOY 5129-2	RT	11.00	36.00
88	HAYRIDE 5117-9	RT	30.00	82.00
88	SCHOOL BUS/SNOW PLOW 5137-3 (SET OF 2)	RT	16.00	82.00
88	SCHOOL CHILDREN 5118-7 (SET OF 3)	RT	15.00	25.00
88	SISAL TREE LOT 8183-3	RT	45.00	108.00
88	WATER TOWER 5133-0	RT	20.00	189.00
88	WOODSMAN AND BOY 5130-6 (SET OF 2)	RT	13.00	34.00
88	WOODY STATION WAGON 5136-5	RT	6.50	43.00
89	CALLING ALL CARS 5174-8 (SET OF 2)	CL	15.00	75.00
89	KIDS TREE HOUSE 5168-3	CL	25.00	72.00
89	MAILBOX 5179-9	RT	3.50	21.00
89	SKATE FASTER MOM 5170-5	CL	13.00	36.00
89	SPECIAL DELIVERY 5148-9 (SET OF 2)	RT	16.00	72.00
89	STATUE OF MARK TWAIN 5173-0	CL	15.00	42.00
89	THROUGH THE WOODS 5172-1 (SET OF 2)	CL	18.00	23.00

YR	NAME	LIMIT	ISSUE	TREND
*			**VILLAGE CCP MINIATURES**	
86	CHURCH 6564-1	CL	23.00	112.00
86	ESTATE 6564-1	CL	23.00	200.00
86	VICTORIAN MINIATURES 6563-3 (SET OF 5)	CL	65.00	N/A
86	VICTORIAN MINIATURES 6564-1 (SET OF 2)	CL	45.00	300.00
86	WILLIAMSBURG HOUSE, BLUE 6566-8	CL	10.00	60.00
86	WILLIAMSBURG HOUSE, BROWN BRICK 6566-8	CL	10.00	40.00
86	WILLIAMSBURG HOUSE, BROWN CLPBD 6566-8	CL	10.00	40.00
86	WILLIAMSBURG HOUSE, RED 6566-8	CL	10.00	60.00
86	WILLIAMSBURG HOUSE, WHITE 6566-8	CL	10.00	40.00
86	WILLIAMSBURG SNOWHOUSE 6566-8 (SET OF 6)	CL	60.00	500.00
87	ABEL BEESLEY BUTCHER 6558-7	CL	12.00	39.00
87	BARLEY BREE FARMHOUSE 6562-5	CL	15.00	52.00
87	BEAN AND SON SMITHY SHOP 6558-7	CL	12.00	39.00
87	BLYTHE POND MILL HOUSE 6560-9	CL	16.00	40.00
87	BRICK ABBEY 6562-5	CL	15.00	105.00
87	CANDLE SHOP 6558-7	CL	12.00	46.00
87	CHESTERTON MANOR HOUSE 6562-5	CL	15.00	143.00
87	CHRISTMAS CAROL 6561-7 (SET OF 3)	CL	30.00	189.00
87	COTTAGE OF BOB CRATCHIT/TINY TIM 6561-7	CL	10.00	26.00
87	COTTAGE TOY SHOP 6591-9	CL	10.00	46.00
87	CROWNTREE INN 6558-7	CL	12.00	39.00
87	DICKENS VILLAGE CHURCH 6560-9	CL	16.00	40.00
87	DICKENS' CHADBURY STATION & TRAIN 6592-7	CL	28.00	59.00
87	DICKENS' COTTAGES 6559-5 (SET OF 3)	CL	30.00	175.00
87	DICKENS' LANE SHOPS 6591-9 (SET OF 3)	CL	30.00	153.00
87	DICKENS' VILLAGE 6558-7 (SET OF 7)	CL	72.00	345.00
87	DICKENS' VILLAGE 6560-9 (SET OF 3)	CL	48.00	N/A
87	DICKENS' VILLAGE 6562-5 (SET OF 4)	CL	60.00	N/A
87	FEZZIWIG'S WAREHOUSE 6561-7	CL	10.00	55.00
87	GOLDEN SWAN BAKER 6558-7	CL	12.00	43.00
87	GREEN GROCER 6558-7	CL	12.00	39.00
87	JONES & CO BRUSH & BASKET SHOP 6558-7	CL	12.00	40.00
87	LITTLE TOWN/BETHLEHEM 5976-5 (SET OF 12)	CL	85.00	293.00
87	NORMAN CHURCH 6560-9	CL	16.00	163.00
87	OLD CURIOSITY SHOP, THE 6562-5	CL	15.00	59.00
87	SCROOGE & MARLEY'S COUNTINGHOUSE 6561-7	CL	10.00	46.00
87	STONE COTTAGE 6559-5	CL	10.00	169.00
87	THATCHED COTTAGE 6559-5	CL	10.00	135.00
87	THOMAS KERSEY COFFEE HOUSE 6591-9	CL	10.00	59.00
87	TUDOR COTTAGE 6559-5	CL	10.00	125.00
87	TUTTLE'S PUB 6591-9	CL	10.00	39.00
88	APOTHECARY SHOP 5935-8	CL	10.50	21.00
88	BRICK TOWN HALL 5935-8	CL	10.50	255.00
88	CRAGGY COVE LIGHTHOUSE 5937-4	CL	14.50	124.00
88	DICKENS' KENILWORTH CASTLE 6565-0	CL	30.00	160.00
88	GENERAL STORE 5935-8	CL	10.50	50.00
88	JACOB ADAMS BARN 5937-4	CL	14.50	46.00
88	JACOB ADAMS FARMHOUSE 5937-4	CL	14.50	46.00
88	LIVERY STABLE & BOOT SHOP 5935-8	CL	10.50	34.00
88	MAPLE SUGARING SHED 5937-4	CL	14.50	40.00
88	NATHANIEL BINGHAM FABRICS 5935-8	CL	10.50	59.00
88	NEW ENGLAND VILLAGE 5935-8 (SET OF 7)	CL	72.00	300.00
88	NEW ENGLAND VILLAGE 5937-4 (SET OF 6)	CL	85.00	N/A
88	RED SCHOOLHOUSE 5935-8	CL	10.50	98.00
88	SMYTHE WOLLEN MILL 5937-4	CL	14.50	189.00
88	STEEPLE CHURCH 5935-8	CL	10.50	80.00
88	TIMBER KNOLL LOG CABIN 5937-4	CL	14.50	36.00

DIFFERENT DRUMMER STUDIOS

*			**COLLECTOR'S CLUB MEMBERSHIP**	
95	BOSTON COMMUNITY CHURCH	*	*	N/A
95	FRANKFORT METHODIST CHURCH	*	*	N/A
95	VINCENNES CATHEDRAL	*	*	N/A
96	GINGERBREAD HOUSE	OP	*	N/A
M. NENNI			**DOOR COUNTY**	
95	AL JOHNSON'S RESTAURANT	OP	12.50	13.00
95	CUPOLA HOUSE	OP	12.50	13.00
95	GILL'S ROCK	OP	12.50	13.00
95	ICE CREAM FACTORY	OP	12.50	13.00
M. NENNI			**HISTORIC HOME SERIES V**	
95	CULBERTSON MANSION OF NEW ALBANY, IN	OP	12.50	13.00
95	ELLER HOUSE OF FISHERS, IN	OP	12.50	13.00
95	PINK LADY OF LOUISVILLE, KY	OP	12.50	13.00
*			**HISTORIC HOME SERIES VI**	
96	CRAIG HOUSE	OP	12.50	13.00
96	MY OLD KENTUCKY HOME	OP	12.50	13.00
*			**HISTORIC LIGHTHOUSE**	
96	ASSATEAQUE LIGHTHOUSE	OP	12.50	13.00
96	GRAND HAVEN LIGHTHOUSE	OP	12.50	13.00
96	HOLLAND LIGHTHOUSE	OP	12.50	13.00
96	MACKINAC POINT LIGHTHOUSE	OP	12.50	13.00
96	MISSION POINT LIGHTHOUSE	OP	12.50	13.00
96	ROUND ISLAND LIGHTHOUSE	OP	12.50	13.00

YR	NAME	LIMIT	ISSUE	TREND
*			**MACKINAC ISLAND**	
96	CHIPPEWA HOTEL	OP	12.50	13.00
96	WINDERMERE HOTEL	OP	12.50	13.00
M. NENNI			**MACKINAC ISLAND**	
95	BAY VIEW BED-BREAKFAST	OP	12.50	13.00
95	INN ON MACKINAC	OP	12.50	13.00
M. NENNI			**MAPLE STREET**	
95	DR. HUTCHING'S OFFICE OF MADISON, IN	OP	12.50	13.00
95	HOB NOB RESTAURANT OF NASHVILLE, IN	OP	12.50	13.00
95	MOTHER OF SORROWS CHURCH OF PENINSULA, OH	OP	12.50	13.00
95	WOODSTOCK OPERA HOUSE OF WOODSTOCK, IL	OP	12.50	13.00
*			**SANTA TOWN**	
96	MRS. CLAUS CONFECTIONARY	OP	13.50	14.00
96	SNOW FACTORY	OP	13.50	14.00
M. NENNI			**SANTA TOWN**	
95	ANGEL SHOP	OP	13.50	14.00
95	REINDEER STABLE	OP	13.50	14.00
95	SANTA'S HOUSE	OP	13.50	14.00
95	SANTA'S WORKSHOP	OP	13.50	14.00
95	SLEIGH SHED	OP	13.50	14.00

ENESCO CORP.

YR	NAME	LIMIT	ISSUE	TREND
*			**ENGLISH COTTAGES**	
*	CARRICK HOUSE	RT	*	N/A
*	CULLODEN COTTAGE	RT	*	N/A
*	EILEAN DONAN CASTLE	RT	*	N/A
*	ERIKSAY CROFT	RT	*	N/A
*	FISHERMAN'S BOTHY	RT	*	N/A
*	INVERLOCHIE HAME	RT	*	N/A
*	MAIR HAVEN	RT	*	N/A
*	UGLY HOUSE	RT	*	N/A
97	FIRST SNOW AT BLUEBELL	RT	250.00	250.00
97	HARVEST HOME	RT	250.00	250.00
97	HESTERCOMBE GARDEN	RT	350.00	350.00
97	SCOTNEY CASTLE GARDEN	RT	300.00	300.00
S. BUTCHER			**PRECIOUS MOMENTS**	
88	THERE'S A CHRISTIAN WELCOME HERE 523011	OP	45.00	80.00
S. BUTCHER		**PRECIOUS MOMENTS SUGAR TOWN**		
92	'94 SUGAR TOWN HOUSE- CL. SET	OP	189.00	200.00
92	LIGHTED CHAPEL 529621	OP	85.00	90.00

ERTL COLLECTIBLES

YR	NAME	LIMIT	ISSUE	TREND
L. DAVIS		**AMERICAN COUNTRY BARN SERIES**		
*	CAMBREL ROOFED BANK BARN	RT	50.00	50.00
*	ROUND BARN	RT	50.00	50.00
*	VICTORIAN BARN	RT	50.00	50.00
*	WESTERN LOG BARN	RT	50.00	50.00
97	ARCH ROOFED STONE BARN	YR	55.00	55.00
97	WESTERN PRAIRIE BARN	YR	55.00	55.00
98	CROSS-GAMBREL ROOFED BARN	YR	55.00	55.00
98	GLACIAL ROCK BARN	YR	55.00	55.00
98	ITALIANATE BARN	YR	55.00	55.00
98	OCTAGON BARN	YR	55.00	55.00
98	SHAKER ROUND STONE BARN	YR	55.00	55.00
L. DAVIS		**AMERICAN COUNTRY SIGNATURE SERIES**		
*	GEORGE WASHINGTON'S BARN AT MT. VERNON	YR	70.00	70.00
98	FRANK LLOYD WRIGHT MIDWAY BARN	YR	75.00	75.00
L. DAVIS			**FARM COUNTRY CHRISTMAS**	
97	BARN	OP	95.00	95.00
97	CAT & BIRD HOUSE	OP	25.00	25.00
97	CHICKEN HOUSE	OP	60.00	60.00
97	DINNERBELL	OP	25.00	25.00
97	FARM HOUSE	OP	85.00	85.00
97	GARAGE	OP	65.00	65.00
97	GEESE	OP	35.00	35.00
97	MAILBOX	OP	25.00	25.00
97	SILO	OP	65.00	65.00
97	SMOKEHOUSE	OP	70.00	70.00

FJ DESIGNS/CAT'S MEOW

YR	NAME	LIMIT	ISSUE	TREND
F. JONES			**ACCESSORIES**	
83	5" HEDGE	RT	3.00	40.00
83	5" IRON FENCE	RT	3.00	40.00
83	8" HEDGE	RT	3.25	45.00
83	8" IRON FENCE	RT	3.25	57.00
83	8" PICKET FENCE	RT	3.25	40.00
83	IRON GATE	RT	3.00	65.00
83	LILAC BUSHES	RT	3.00	300.00
85	CHERRY TREE	RT	4.00	45.00
85	CHRISTMAS PINE TREE	RT	4.00	40.00
85	CHRISTMAS TREE WITH RED BOWS	RT	3.00	150.00
85	FALL TREE	RT	4.00	30.00
85	PINE TREE	RT	4.00	30.00
85	POPLAR TREE	RT	4.00	45.00
85	SUMMER TREE	RT	4.00	35.00

YR	NAME	LIMIT	ISSUE	TREND
86	BLUE SPRUCE	RT	4.00	7.00
86	CABLE CAR	RT	4.00	15.00
86	CAROLERS	RT	4.00	16.00
86	CHICKENS	RT	3.25	18.00
86	COWS	RT	4.00	20.00
86	DAIRY WAGON	RT	4.00	16.00
86	DUCKS	RT	3.25	16.00
86	FJ REAL ESTATE SIGN	RT	3.00	24.00
86	HORSE & CARRIAGE	RT	4.00	15.00
86	ICE WAGON	RT	4.00	17.00
86	LIBERTY ST. SIGN	RT	3.25	15.00
86	MARKET ST. SIGN	RT	3.25	16.00
86	TOURING CAR	RT	4.00	15.00
86	WELLS, FARGO WAGON	RT	4.00	15.00
86	WISHING WELL	RT	3.25	23.00
87	5" PICKET FENCE	RT	3.00	18.00
87	BAND STAND	RT	6.50	18.00
87	BUTCH AND T.J.	RT	4.00	15.00
87	CHARLIE & CO.	RT	4.00	14.00
87	FJ EXPRESS	RT	4.00	18.00
87	HORSE & SLEIGH	RT	4.00	10.00
87	NANNY HOUSE	RT	4.00	10.00
87	RAILROAD SIGN	RT	3.00	16.00
87	WINDMILL	RT	3.25	12.00
87	WOODEN GATE	RT	3.00	17.00
88	COLONIAL BREAD WAGON	RT	4.00	13.00
88	FLOWER POTS	RT	4.00	12.00
88	GAS LIGHT	RT	4.00	12.00
88	MAIL WAGON	RT	4.00	10.00
88	MAIN ST. SIGN	RT	3.25	12.00
88	PONY EXPRESS RIDER	RT	4.00	13.00
88	SKIPJACK	RT	6.50	15.00
88	STREET CLOCK	RT	4.00	10.00
88	TELEPHONE BOOTH	RT	4.00	12.00
88	U.S. FLAG	TL	4.50	5.00
89	ADA BELLE	RT	4.00	11.00
89	CLOTHESLINE	RT	4.00	9.00
89	HARRY'S HOTDOGS	RT	4.00	9.00
89	PASSENGER TRAIN CAR	RT	4.00	9.00
89	PUMPKIN WAGON	RT	3.25	9.00
89	QUAKER OATS TRAIN CAR	RT	4.00	9.00
89	ROSE TRELLIS	RT	3.25	9.00
89	RUDY & ALDINE	RT	4.00	8.00
89	SNOWMEN	RT	4.00	9.00
89	TAD & TONI	RT	4.00	9.00
90	1909 FRANKLIN LIMOUSINE	RT	4.00	7.00
90	1913 PEERLESS TOURING CAR	RT	4.00	7.00
90	1914 FIRE PUMPER	RT	4.00	7.00
90	5" WROUGHT IRON FENCE	RT	3.00	6.00
90	AMISH BUGGY	RT	4.00	8.00
90	BUS STOP	RT	4.00	7.00
90	CHRISTMAS SPRUCE	RT	4.00	5.00
90	CHRISTMAS TREE LOT	RT	4.00	7.00
90	EUGENE	RT	4.00	7.00
90	GERSTENSLAGER BUGGY	RT	4.00	7.00
90	LITTLE RED CABOOSE	RT	4.00	8.00
90	RED MAPLE TREE	RT	4.00	8.00
90	SANTA & REINDEER	RT	4.00	7.00
90	TULIP TREE	RT	4.00	12.00
90	VETERINARY WAGON	RT	4.00	7.00
90	VICTORIAN OUTHOUSE	RT	4.00	7.00
90	WATKINS WAGON	RT	4.00	7.00
91	AMISH GARDEN	TL	4.00	5.00
91	BARNYARD	TL	4.00	5.00
91	CHESSIE HOPPER CAR	TL	4.00	5.00
91	CONCERT IN THE PARK	TL	4.00	5.00
91	JACK THE POSTMAN	TL	3.25	5.00
91	MARBLE GAME	RT	4.00	5.00
91	MARTIN HOUSE	TL	3.25	5.00
91	ON VACATION	TL	4.00	5.00
91	POPCORN WAGON	TL	4.00	5.00
91	SCAREY HARRY (SCARECROW)	TL	4.00	5.00
91	SCHOOL BUS	TL	4.00	5.00
91	SKI PARTY	TL	4.00	5.00
91	USMC WAR MEMORIAL	TL	6.50	7.00
91	VILLAGE ENTRACE SIGN	TL	6.50	7.00
94	SALVATION ARMY BAND	TL	4.50	5.00
96	SMUCKER TRAIN CAR	RT	5.00	85.00
98	COTTAGE GARDEN	OP	14.00	14.00
98	DOMINIC & HIS FLYING CATS	OP	14.00	14.00
98	FEASTING	OP	14.00	14.00
98	FLOWERS FOR SALE	OP	11.00	11.00
98	GARAGE SALE SIGN	OP	14.00	14.00
98	HAWTHORN TREE	OP	11.00	11.00
98	LANDS END MARINA	OP	14.00	14.00

Forma Vitrum's Trinity Church,
*limited to 7,000 pieces, has been
retired. It is from Bill Job's
Vitreville Collection.*

Key West, FL *from the Southeast Region
collection by Harbour Lights, has more than
tripled in value. Originally offered in 1993, it
has since been retired.*

*A retired piece from Bill Job's Vitreville
Collection,* The Country Church *has
increased in value since it was released
in 1993 by Forma Vitrum.*

Yaquina Bay Lighthouse, *part of
Michael Morris' "Oregon Coast"
series produced by Genesis Designs,
is limited to an edition of 3,000.*

YR	NAME	LIMIT	ISSUE	TREND
98	LITTLE MISS MUFFET	OP	11.00	11.00
98	MAYFLOWER II	OP	11.00	11.00
98	MILITIA MUSTER	OP	14.00	14.00
98	SILVER FIR	OP	10.00	10.00
98	SOUTHERNMOST POINT MARKER	OP	14.00	14.00
98	SWINGSET	OP	14.00	14.00
98	THREE LITTLE KITTENS	OP	11.00	11.00
98	WISTERIA	OP	14.00	14.00
F. JONES				**AMERICAN BARNS**
92	BANK BARN	OP	8.50	9.00
92	CRIB BARN	OP	8.50	9.00
92	OHIO BARN	OP	8.50	9.00
92	VERMONT BARN	OP	8.50	9.00
F. JONES				**AMISH LIFE SERIES**
98	AMISH CLOTHESLINE	OP	14.00	14.00
98	BAKING DAY	OP	14.00	14.00
98	DAWDY HAUS	OP	11.00	11.00
98	HOME FROM SCHOOL	OP	14.00	14.00
98	LEVI MILLER HOME	OP	11.00	11.00
98	MAPLE GROVE SCHOOL	OP	11.00	11.00
98	MILLER BARN	OP	11.00	11.00
98	PRODUCE FOR SALE	OP	14.00	14.00
F. JONES				**ANNUAL EDITIONS COLLECTION**
98	BLACK DOG TAVERN	*	11.00	11.00
98	CHATEAU MONTELENA	*	11.00	11.00
98	CLOWNS	*	11.00	11.00
98	CORNISH/WINDSOR BRIDGE	*	11.00	11.00
98	FATHER FLANAGAN'S HOME	*	11.00	11.00
98	MARK TWAIN BOYHOOD HOME	*	11.00	11.00
98	OAK ALLEY PLANTATION	*	11.00	11.00
98	SILVER BUSH	*	11.00	11.00
F. JONES				**BIBLICAL THEMES**
98	MOSES & THE TEN COMMANDMENTS	OP	11.00	11.00
98	SERMON ON THE MOUNT	OP	11.00	11.00
F. JONES				**BLACK HERITAGE SERIES**
94	MARTIN LUTHER KING BIRTHPLACE	RT	8.00	50.00
F. JONES				**CHIPPEWA LAKE AMUSEMENT PARK**
93	BALLROOM	OP	4.50	5.00
93	BATH HOUSE	OP	4.50	5.00
93	MIDWAY	OP	4.50	5.00
93	PAVILION	OP	4.50	5.00
F. JONES				**CHRISTMAS '83 WILLIAMSBURG**
83	CHRISTMAS '83 WILLIAMSBURG SET	RT	24.00	3500.00
83	CHRISTMAS CHURCH	RT	6.00	450.00
83	FEDERAL HOUSE	RT	6.00	450.00
83	GARRISON HOUSE	RT	6.00	450.00
83	GEORGIAN HOUSE	RT	6.00	450.00
F. JONES				**CHRISTMAS '84 NANTUCKET**
84	CHRISTMAS '84 NANTUCKET SET	RT	26.00	1600.00
84	CHRISTMAS SHOP	RT	6.50	250.00
84	POWELL HOUSE	RT	6.50	350.00
84	SHAW HOUSE	RT	6.50	350.00
84	WINTHROP HOUSE	RT	6.50	250.00
F. JONES				**CHRISTMAS '85 OHIO WESTERN RESERVE**
85	BELLEVUE HOUSE	RT	7.00	250.00
85	CHRISTMAS '85 OHIO WESTERN RESERVE SET	RT	27.00	1000.00
85	GATES MILLS CHURCH	RT	7.00	250.00
85	OLMSTEAD HOUSE	RT	7.00	250.00
85	WESTERN RESERVE ACADEMY	RT	7.00	250.00
F. JONES				**CHRISTMAS '86 SAVANNAH**
86	CHRISTMAS '86 SAVANNAH SET	RT	29.00	900.00
86	J.J. DALE ROW HOUSE	RT	7.25	150.00
86	LAFAYETTE SQUARE HOUSE	RT	7.25	145.00
86	LIBERTY INN	RT	7.25	200.00
86	SIMON MIRAULT COTTAGE	RT	7.25	200.00
F. JONES				**CHRISTMAS '87 MAINE**
87	CAPPY'S CHOWDER HOUSE	RT	7.75	250.00
87	CAPTAIN'S HOUSE	RT	7.75	250.00
87	CHRISTMAS '87 MAINE SET	RT	31.00	925.00
87	DAMARISCOTTA CHURCH	RT	7.75	250.00
87	PORTLAND HEAD LIGHTHOUSE	RT	7.75	250.00
F. JONES				**CHRISTMAS '88 PHILADELPHIA**
88	CHRISTMAS '88 PHILADELPHIA SET	RT	31.00	613.00
88	ELFRETH'S ALLEY	RT	7.75	175.00
88	GRAFF HOUSE	RT	7.75	175.00
88	HEAD HOUSE	RT	7.75	175.00
88	HILL-PHYSICK-KEITH HOUSE	RT	7.75	175.00
F. JONES				**CHRISTMAS '89 IN NEW ENGLAND**
89	CHRISTMAS '89 IN NEW ENGLAND SET	RT	32.00	350.00
89	HUNTER HOUSE	RT	8.00	100.00
89	OLD SOUTH MEETING HOUSE	RT	8.00	100.00
89	SHELDON'S TAVERN	RT	8.00	125.00
89	VERMONT COUNTRY STORE, THE	RT	8.00	100.00

YR	NAME	LIMIT	ISSUE	TREND
F. JONES		**CHRISTMAS '90 COLONIAL VIRGINIA**		
90	CHRISTMAS '90 COLONIAL VIRGINIA SET	RT	32.00	500.00
90	DULANY HOUSE	RT	8.00	75.00
90	RISING SUN TAVERN	RT	8.00	85.00
90	SHIRLEY PLANTATION	RT	8.00	70.00
90	ST. JOHN'S CHURCH	RT	8.00	100.00
90	ST. JOHN'S CHURCH (BLUE)	RT	8.00	175.00
F. JONES		**CHRISTMAS '91 ROCKY MOUNTAIN**		
91	CHRISTMAS '91 ROCKY MOUNTAIN SET	RT	33.00	185.00
91	FIRST PRESBYTERIAN CHURCH	RT	8.20	55.00
91	TABOR HOUSE	RT	8.20	65.00
91	WESTERN HOTEL	RT	8.20	40.00
91	WHELLER-STALLARD HOUSE	RT	8.20	40.00
F. JONES		**CHRISTMAS '92 HOMETOWN**		
92	AUGUST IMGARD HOUSE	RT	8.50	50.00
92	CHRISTMAS '92 HOMETOWN SET	RT	34.00	250.00
92	HOWEY HOUSE	RT	8.50	50.00
92	OVERHOLT HOUSE	RT	8.50	50.00
92	WAYNE CO. COURTHOUSE	RT	8.50	50.00
F. JONES		**CHRISTMAS '93 ST. CHARLES**		
93	CHRISTMAS '93 ST. CHARLES SET	RT	36.00	80.00
93	LEWIS & CLARK CENTER	RT	9.00	20.00
93	NEWBILL-MCELHINEY HOUSE	RT	9.00	20.00
93	ST. PETER'S CATHOLIC CHURCH	RT	9.00	20.00
93	STONE ROW	RT	9.00	20.00
F. JONES		**CHRISTMAS '94 NEW ORLEANS**		
94	BEAUREGARD-KEYES HOUSE	RT	10.00	17.00
94	CHRISTMAS '94 NEW ORLEANS SET	RT	40.00	50.00
94	GALLIER HOUSE	RT	10.00	17.00
94	HERMANN-GRIMA HOUSE	RT	10.00	17.00
94	ST. PATRICK'S CHURCH	RT	10.00	17.00
F. JONES		**CHRISTMAS '95 NEW YORK SERIES**		
95	CHRISTMAS '95 NEW YORK SERIES SET	RT	40.00	55.00
95	CLEMENT C. MOORE HOUSE	RT	10.00	13.00
95	FRAUNCES TAVERN	RT	10.00	13.00
95	FULTON MARKET	RT	10.00	13.00
95	ST. MARKS IN THE BOWERY	RT	10.00	13.00
F. JONES		**CHRISTMAS '96 ATLANTA SERIES**		
96	CALLANWOLDE	YR	11.00	11.00
96	FIRST BAPTIST CHURCH	YR	11.00	11.00
96	FOX THEATRE	YR	11.00	11.00
96	MARGARET MITCHELL HOUSE	YR	11.00	11.00
F. JONES		**CIRCUS SERIES**		
95	SIDESHOW	RT	10.00	13.00
96	FERRIS WHEEL	YR	10.00	10.00
F. JONES		**COLLECTOR CLUB 19TH CENTURY MASTER BUILDERS**		
93	ALEXANDER JACKSON DAVIS	RT	10.25	25.00
93	ANDREW JACKSON DOWNING	RT	10.25	25.00
93	COLLECTOR CLUB 19TH CENTURY MASTER BUILDERS SET	RT	41.00	100.00
93	HENRY HOBSON RICHARDSON	RT	10.25	25.00
93	SAMUEL SLOAN	RT	10.25	25.00
F. JONES		**COLLECTOR CLUB A CHRISTMAS CAROL**		
98	CHRISTMAS PRESENT, PAST, FUTURE SET OF 3	*	20.00	20.00
F. JONES		**COLLECTOR CLUB AMERICAN HOLIDAY SERIES**		
96	AND TO ALL A GOODNIGHT	YR	11.00	11.00
96	BOO TO YOU	YR	11.00	11.00
96	EASTER'S ON ITS WAY	YR	11.00	11.00
96	LET FREEDOM RING	YR	11.00	11.00
F. JONES		**COLLECTOR CLUB AMERICAN SONGWRITERS**		
91	ANNA WARNER HOUSE	RT	9.25	80.00
91	BENJAMIN R. HANBY HOUSE	RT	9.25	80.00
91	COLLECTOR CLUB AMERICAN SONGWRITERS SET	RT	37.00	350.00
91	OSCAR HAMMERSTEIN HOUSE	RT	9.25	80.00
91	STEPHEN FOSTER HOME	RT	9.25	80.00
F. JONES		**COLLECTOR CLUB FAMOUS AUTHORS**		
89	COLLECTOR CLUB FAMOUS AUTHORS SET	RT	35.00	800.00
89	HARRIET BEECHER STOWE	RT	8.75	200.00
89	HERMAN MELVILLE'S ARROWHEAD	RT	8.75	200.00
89	LONGFELLOW HOUSE	RT	8.75	200.00
89	ORCHARD HOUSE	RT	8.75	200.00
F. JONES		**COLLECTOR CLUB GIFT HOUSES**		
89	BETSY ROSS HOUSE	RT	*	200.00
90	AMELIA EARHART	RT	*	100.00
91	LIMBERLOST CABIN	RT	*	50.00
92	ABIGAIL ADAMS BIRTHPLACE	RT	*	50.00
93	PEARL S. BUCK HOUSE	RT	*	50.00
94	LILLIAN GISH	RT	*	30.00
95	ELEANOR ROOSEVELT	RT	*	N/A
96	MOTHER'S DAY CHURCH	YR	*	N/A
98	ELIZABETH CADY STANTON HOUSE	*	11.00	11.00
F. JONES		**COLLECTOR CLUB GREAT INVENTORS**		
90	COLLECTOR CLUB GREAT INVENTORS SET	RT	37.00	450.00
90	FORD MOTOR CO.	RT	9.25	100.00
90	SETH THOMAS CLOCK CO.	RT	9.25	75.00

YR	NAME	LIMIT	ISSUE	TREND
90	THOMAS EDISON	RT	9.25	100.00
90	WRIGHT CYCLE CO.	RT	9.25	100.00
F. JONES		**COLLECTOR CLUB LITTLE TOWN ON THE PRAIRIE**		
98	INGALLS FAMILY	*	7.00	7.00
F. JONES		**COLLECTOR CLUB MT. RUSHMORE PRESIDENTIAL SERIES**		
95	COLLECTOR CLUB MT. RUSHMORE PRESIDENTIAL SERIES SE	RT	48.00	48.00
95	GEORGE WASHINGTON BIRTHPLACE	RT	12.00	12.00
95	METAMORA COURTHOUSE	RT	12.00	12.00
95	THEODORE ROOSEVELT BIRTHPLACE	RT	12.00	12.00
95	TUCKAHOE PLANTATION	RT	12.00	12.00
F. JONES		**COLLECTOR CLUB ROUTE 66**		
98	BOOTS MOTEL-ROUTE 66	*	14.00	14.00
F. JONES		**COLLECTOR CLUB SIGNERS OF THE DECLARATION**		
92	COLLECTOR CLUB SIGNERS OF THE DECLARATION SET	RT	39.00	250.00
92	GEORGE CLYMER HOME	RT	9.75	50.00
92	JOHN WITHERSPOON HOME	RT	9.75	50.00
92	JOSIAH BARTLETT HOME	RT	9.75	50.00
92	STEPHEN HOPKINS HOME	RT	9.75	50.00
F. JONES		**COLLECTOR CLUB WILLIAMSBURG MERCHANTS**		
94	COLLECTOR CLUB WILLIAMSBURG MERCHANTS SET	RT	45.00	75.00
94	CRAIG JEWELER	RT	11.15	15.00
94	EAST CARLTON WIGMAKER	RT	11.15	15.00
94	J. GEDDY SILVERSMITH	RT	11.15	15.00
94	M. HUNTER MILLINERY	RT	11.15	15.00
F. JONES		**COLONIAL LIGHTHOUSE SERIES**		
98	BEAVERTAIL LIGHTHOUSE	OP	11.00	11.00
98	BOSTON LIGHT	OP	11.00	11.00
98	BRANT POINT LIGHTHOUSE	OP	11.00	11.00
98	COLONIAL LIGHTHOUSE BOXED SET	*	50.00	50.00
98	NEW LONDON HARBOR LIGHT	OP	11.00	11.00
F. JONES		**COVERED BRIDGE SERIES**		
95	CREAMERY BRIDGE	RT	10.00	13.00
96	KENNEDY BRIDGE	YR	10.00	10.00
F. JONES		**DICKENS CHRISTMAS CAROL SERIES**		
98	CRATCHIT'S HOUSE	OP	12.00	12.00
98	FEZZIWIG'S WAREHOUSE	OP	12.00	12.00
98	SCROOGE & MARLEY	OP	12.00	12.00
98	SCROOGE'S FLAT	OP	12.00	12.00
F. JONES		**DISCUS THROWER**		
96	DISCUS THROWER	6000	10.00	10.00
F. JONES		**FALL**		
86	GOLDEN LAMB BUTTERY	RT	8.00	50.00
86	GRIMM'S FARMHOUSE	RT	8.00	45.00
86	MAIL POUCH BARN	RT	8.00	50.00
86	VOLLANT MILLS	RT	8.00	50.00
F. JONES		**GREAT AMERICANS SERIES**		
96	DANIEL BOONE HOME	YR	10.00	10.00
F. JONES		**GREEN GABLES SERIES**		
96	GREEN GABLES HOUSE	YR	10.00	10.00
F. JONES		**HAGERSTOWN**		
88	HAGERSTOWN SET	RT	32.00	100.00
88	J. HAGER HOUSE	RT	8.00	25.00
88	MILLER HOUSE	RT	8.00	25.00
88	WOMAN'S CLUB	RT	8.00	25.00
88	YULE CUPBOARD	RT	8.00	25.00
F. JONES		**HISTORIC SALEM SERIES**		
98	HAWKE'S HOUSE	OP	11.00	11.00
98	HOUSE OF SEVEN GABLES	OP	11.00	11.00
98	SALEM WITCH MUSEUM	OP	11.00	11.00
98	U.S. CUSTOM HOUSE	OP	11.00	11.00
F. JONES		**KEY WEST SERIES**		
98	AUDOBON HOUSE	OP	11.00	11.00
98	KEY WEST LIGHTHOUSE	OP	11.00	11.00
98	PINK HOUSE	OP	11.00	11.00
98	SOUTHERNMOST HOME	OP	11.00	11.00
F. JONES		**LIBERTY ST.**		
88	COUNTY COURTHOUSE	RT	8.00	25.00
88	GRAF PRINTING CO.	RT	8.00	25.00
88	WILTON RAILWAY DEPOT	RT	8.00	25.00
88	Z. JONES BASKETMAKER	RT	8.00	30.00
F. JONES		**LIFE CELEBRATIONS COLLECTION**		
98	GREETINGS FROM BOY	OP	11.00	11.00
98	GREETINGS FROM GIRL	OP	11.00	11.00
98	HAPPY BIRTHDAY CAKE	OP	11.00	11.00
98	ST. FRANCIS GARDEN GREETING	OP	11.00	11.00
98	WEDDING COUPLE	OP	11.00	11.00
F. JONES		**LIGHTHOUSE**		
90	ADMIRALTY HEAD	RT	8.00	11.00
90	CAPE HATTERAS LIGHTHOUSE	RT	8.00	16.00
90	SANDY HOOK LIGHTHOUSE	RT	8.00	11.00
90	SPLIT ROCK LIGHTHOUSE	RT	8.00	16.00
F. JONES		**LIMITED EDITION PROMOTIONAL ITEMS**		
90	FYRCREST FARM HOMESTEAD	RT	10.00	125.00

YR	NAME	LIMIT	ISSUE	TREND
92	GLEN PINE	RT	10.00	27.00
93	CONVENTION MUSEUM	RT	13.00	13.00
93	FJ FACTORY	OP	13.00	13.00
93	FJ FACTORY/GOLD CAT EDITION	RT	13.00	490.00
93	NATIVITY CAT ON THE FENCE	RT	20.00	30.00
94	FJ FACTORY/5 YEAR BANNER	RT	10.00	18.00
94	FJ FACTORY/HOME BANNER	RT	10.00	10.00
F. JONES		**LITTLE TOWN ON THE PRAIRIE SERIES**		
98	BREWSTER SCHOOL	OP	12.00	12.00
98	DESMET FIRST CONGREGATIONAL CHURCH	OP	12.00	12.00
98	PA & MA INGALLS HOME	OP	12.00	12.00
98	SURVEYOR'S HOUSE	OP	12.00	12.00
F. JONES				**MAIN ST.**
87	FRANKLIN LIBRARY	RT	8.00	25.00
87	GARDEN THEATRE	RT	8.00	25.00
87	HISTORICAL MUSEUM	RT	8.00	35.00
87	MAIN ST. SET	RT	32.00	110.00
87	TELEGRAPH/POST OFFICE	RT	8.00	35.00
F. JONES		**MARK TWAIN'S HANNIBAL SERIES**		
95	BECKY THATCHER HOUSE	RT	10.00	13.00
96	HICKORY STICK	YR	10.00	10.00
F. JONES				**MARKET ST.**
89	SCHUMACHER MILLS	RT	8.00	24.00
89	SEVILLE HARDWARE STORE	RT	8.00	24.00
89	WEST INDIA GOODS STORE	RT	8.00	24.00
89	YEANKEE CANDLE COMPANY	RT	8.00	24.00
F. JONES		**MARTHA'S VINEYARD SERIES**		
95	JOHN COFFIN HOUSE	RT	10.00	13.00
96	WEST CHOP LIGHTHOUSE	YR	10.00	10.00
F. JONES				**MISCELLANEOUS**
85	PENCIL HOLDER	RT	4.00	210.00
85	RECIPE HOLDER	RT	4.00	250.00
86	SCHOOL DESK-BLUE	RT	12.00	N/A
86	SCHOOL DESK-RED	RT	12.00	175.00
F. JONES				**NANTUCKET**
87	JARED COFFIN HOUSE	RE	8.00	35.00
87	MARIA MITCHELL HOUSE	RT	8.00	35.00
87	NANTUCKET ATHENEUM	RT	8.00	35.00
87	NANTUCKET SET	RT	32.00	85.00
87	UNITARIAN CHURCH	RT	8.00	35.00
F. JONES		**NATIONAL TREASURES SERIES**		
98	JEFFERSON MEMORIAL	OP	12.00	12.00
98	LINCOLN MEMORIAL	OP	12.00	12.00
98	STATUE OF LIBERTY	OP	12.00	12.00
98	WASHINGTON MONUMENT	OP	12.00	12.00
F. JONES				**NAUTICAL**
87	H & E SHIPS CHANDLERY	RT	8.00	32.00
87	LORAIN LIGHTHOUSE	RT	8.00	32.00
87	MONHEGAN BOAT LANDING	RT	8.00	32.00
87	NAUTICAL SET	RT	32.00	105.00
87	YACHT CLUB	RT	8.00	32.00
F. JONES		**NEIGHBORHOOD EVENT SERIES**		
95	BIRELY PLACE	RT	13.00	18.00
95	PETER SEITZ TAVERN & STAGECOACH	RT	13.00	18.00
96	BAILEY-GOMBERT HOUSE	YR	13.00	13.00
96	SEA CHIMES	YR	13.00	13.00
F. JONES				**OHIO AMISH**
91	ADA MAE'S QUILT BARN	TL	8.00	10.00
91	BROWN SCHOOL	TL	8.00	10.00
91	ELI'S HARNESS SHOP	TL	8.00	10.00
91	JONAS TROYER HOME	TL	8.00	10.00
F. JONES				**PAINTED LADIES**
88	ANDREWS HOTEL	RT	8.00	24.00
88	LADY AMANDA	RT	8.00	24.00
88	LADY ELIZABETH	RT	8.00	24.00
88	LADY IRIS	RT	8.00	24.00
88	PAINTED LADIES SET	RT	32.00	60.00
F. JONES		**PLYMOUTH PLANTATION SERIES**		
98	FRANCIS COOK HOME	OP	12.00	12.00
98	JOHN ALDEN HOME	OP	12.00	12.00
98	MYLES STANDISH HOME	OP	12.00	12.00
98	PLYMOUTH PLANTATION BOXED SET	*	40.00	40.00
98	SAMUEL FULLER HOME	OP	12.00	12.00
F. JONES		**POSTAGE STAMP LIGHTHOUSE SERIES**		
96	POSTAGE STAMP LIGHTHOUSE SERIES SET	RT	75.00	75.00
F. JONES				**ROSCOE VILLAGE**
86	CANAL COMPANY	RT	8.00	55.00
86	JACKSON TWP. HALL	RT	8.00	55.00
86	OLD WAREHOUSE RESTAURANT	RT	8.00	55.00
86	ROSCOE GENERAL STORE	RT	8.00	55.00
86	ROSCOE VILLAGE SET	RT	32.00	150.00
F. JONES				**ROUTE 66 COLLECTION**
98	ROUTE 66 COLLECTION BOXED SET	*	100.00	100.00

YR NAME	LIMIT	ISSUE	TREND
F. JONES	**ROUTE 66 COLLECTION SERIES XVI**		
98 ARCADIA ROUND BARN	OP	11.00	11.00
98 BLUE SWALLOW MOTEL	OP	11.00	11.00
98 CORAL COURT	OP	11.00	11.00
98 JACKRABBIT BILLBOARD	OP	14.00	14.00
98 ROUTE 66 SHIELD	OP	14.00	14.00
98 SANTA MONICA PIER	OP	11.00	11.00
98 SNOW CAP	OP	11.00	11.00
98 U-DROP INN	OP	11.00	11.00
98 WIGWAM VILLAGE	OP	11.00	11.00
98 WIL ROGERS MOTOR COURT SIGN	OP	14.00	14.00
98 WILL ROGERS HOTEL	OP	11.00	11.00
F. JONES			**SERIES 01**
83 ANTIQUE SHOP	RT	8.00	113.00
83 APOTHECARY	RT	8.00	113.00
83 BARBERSHOP	RT	8.00	100.00
83 BOOK STORE	RT	8.00	90.00
83 CHERRY TREE INN	RT	8.00	N/A
83 FEDERAL HOUSE	RT	8.00	90.00
83 FLORIST SHOP	RT	8.00	90.00
83 GARRISON HOUSE	RT	8.00	125.00
83 RED WHALE INN	RT	8.00	N/A
83 SCHOOL	RT	8.00	100.00
83 SERIES 01 SET OF 12 WITH INN	RT	96.00	1150.00
83 SERIES 01 SET OF 14 WITH 3 INNS	RT	112.00	2500.00
83 SWEETSHOP	RT	8.00	125.00
83 TOY SHOPPE	RT	8.00	125.00
83 VICTORIAN HOUSE	RT	8.00	90.00
83 WAYSIDE INN	RT	8.00	N/A
F. JONES			**SERIES 02**
84 ATTORNEY/BANK	RT	8.00	125.00
84 BROCKE HOUSE	RT	8.00	125.00
84 CHURCH	RT	8.00	125.00
84 EATON HOUSE	RT	8.00	165.00
84 GRANDINERE HOUSE	RT	8.00	125.00
84 MILLINERY/QUILT	RT	8.00	175.00
84 MUSIC SHOP	RT	8.00	150.00
84 S & T CLOTHIERS	RT	8.00	165.00
84 SERIES 02 SET	RT	96.00	750.00
84 TOBACCONIST/SHOEMAKER	RT	8.00	125.00
84 TOWN HALL	RT	8.00	150.00
F. JONES			**SERIES 03**
85 ALLEN COE HOUSE	RT	8.00	60.00
85 CONNECTICUT AVE. FIREHOUSE	RT	8.00	60.00
85 DRY GOODS STORE	RT	8.00	65.00
85 EDINBURGH TIMES	RT	8.00	60.00
85 FINE JEWELERS	RT	8.00	45.00
85 HOBART-HARLEY HOUSE	RT	8.00	65.00
85 KALORAMA GUEST HOUSE	RT	8.00	45.00
85 MAIN ST. CARRIAGE SHOP	RT	8.00	65.00
85 OPERA HOUSE	RT	8.00	65.00
85 RISTORANTE	RT	8.00	65.00
85 SERIES 03 SET	RT	80.00	575.00
F. JONES			**SERIES 04**
86 BENNINGTON-HULL HOUSE	RT	8.00	50.00
86 CHAGRIN FALLS POPCORN SHOP	RT	8.00	50.00
86 CHEPACHET UNION CHURCH	RT	8.00	50.00
86 JOHN BELVILLE HOUSE	RT	8.00	50.00
86 JONES BROS. TEA CO.	RT	8.00	50.00
86 LITTLE HOUSE GIFTABLES	RT	8.00	50.00
86 O'MALLEY'S LIVERY STABLE	RT	8.00	50.00
86 SERIES 04 SET	RT	80.00	500.00
86 VANDENBERG HOUSE	RT	8.00	50.00
86 VILLAGE CLOCK SHOP	RT	8.00	50.00
86 WESTBROOK HOUSE	RT	8.00	50.00
F. JONES			**SERIES 05**
87 AMISH OAK/DIXIE SHOE	RT	8.00	25.00
87 ARCHITECT/TAILOR	RT	8.00	35.00
87 CONGRUITY TAVERN	RT	8.00	35.00
87 CREOLE HOUSE	RT	8.00	35.00
87 DENTIST/PHYSICIAN	RT	8.00	35.00
87 M. WASHINGTON HOUSE	RT	8.00	35.00
87 MARKETHOUSE	RT	8.00	35.00
87 MURRAY HOTEL	RT	8.00	35.00
87 POLICE DEPARTMENT	RT	8.00	35.00
87 SERIES 05 SET	RT	80.00	350.00
87 SOUTHPORT BANK	RT	8.00	35.00
F. JONES			**SERIES 06**
88 BURTON LANCASTER HOUSE	RT	8.00	24.00
88 CITY HOSPITAL	RT	8.00	24.00
88 FIRST BAPTIST CHURCH	RT	8.00	24.00
88 FISH/MEAT MARKET	RT	8.00	24.00
88 LINCOLN SCHOOL	RT	8.00	24.00
88 NEW MASTERS GALLERY	RT	8.00	24.00
88 OHLIGER HOUSE	RT	8.00	24.00

Department 56's Smythe Woolen Mill, *from the New England Village, was issued in 1987 and is limited to 7,500 pieces.*

Berkshire House *was added to the Department 56 New England Village line in 1989.*

Nathaniel Bingham Fabrics, *also referred to as the Post Office because the mail came into and went out of the shop, was a 1986 New England Village issue from Department 56.*

From Shelia's Inc.'s "Key West" series, Shelia Thompson's Shotgun Sister *architectural facade retails for $17.*

Department 56 issued the General Store *with their original set of seven New England Village pieces.*

The Brick Town Hall *was an original issue packaged with the set of seven starter New England Village pieces manufacturerd by Department 56.*

YR	NAME	LIMIT	ISSUE	TREND
88	PRUYN HOUSE	RT	8.00	24.00
88	SERIES 06 SET	RT	80.00	250.00
88	STIFFENBODY FUNERAL HOME	RT	8.00	24.00
88	WILLIAMS & SONS	RT	8.00	24.00
F. JONES				**SERIES 07**
89	BLACK CAT ANTIQUES	RT	8.00	16.00
89	HAIRDRESSING PARLOR	RT	8.00	19.00
89	HANDCRAFTED TOYS	RT	8.00	19.00
89	JUSTICE OF THE PEACE	RT	8.00	19.00
89	OCTAGONAL SCHOOL	RT	8.00	19.00
89	OLD FRANKLIN BOOK SHOP	RT	8.00	19.00
89	THORPE HOUSE BED & BREAKFAST	RT	8.00	19.00
89	VILLAGE TINSMITH	RT	8.00	19.00
89	WILLIAMS APOTHECARY	RT	8.00	19.00
89	WINKLER BAKERY	RT	8.00	19.00
F. JONES				**SERIES 08**
90	FJ REALTY COMPANY	RT	8.00	15.00
90	GLOBE CORNER BOOKSTORE	RT	8.00	15.00
90	HABERDASHERS	RT	8.00	15.00
90	MEDINA FIRE DEPARTMENT	RT	8.00	15.00
90	NELL'S STEMS & STITCHES	RT	8.00	15.00
90	NOAH'S ARK VETERINARY	RT	8.00	15.00
90	PICCADILLI PIPE & TOBACCO	RT	8.00	15.00
90	PURITAN HOUSE	RT	8.00	15.00
90	VICTORIA'S PARLOUR	RT	8.00	15.00
90	WALLDORFF FURNITURE	RT	8.00	15.00
F. JONES				**SERIES 09**
91	ALL SAINTS CHAPEL	TL	8.00	10.00
91	AMERICAN RED CROSS	TL	8.00	10.00
91	CENTRAL CITY OPERA HOUSE	TL	8.00	10.00
91	CITY HALL	TL	8.00	10.00
91	CPA/LAW OFFICE	TL	8.00	10.00
91	GOV. SNYDER MANSION	TL	8.00	10.00
91	JEWELER/OPTOMETRIST	TL	8.00	10.00
91	SPANKY'S HARDWARE CO.	TL	8.00	10.00
91	TREBLE CLEF,THE	TL	8.00	10.00
F. JONES				**SERIES 10**
92	CITY NEWS	OP	8.50	9.00
92	FUDGE KITCHEN	OP	8.50	9.00
92	GRAND HAVEN	OP	8.50	9.00
92	HENYAN'S ATHLETIC SHOP	OP	8.50	9.00
92	LEPPERT'S 5 & 10 CENT	OP	8.50	9.00
92	MADELINE'S DRESS SHOP	OP	8.50	9.00
92	OWL AND THE PUSSYCAT	OP	8.50	9.00
92	PICKLES PUB	OP	8.50	9.00
92	PURE GAS STATION	OP	8.50	9.00
92	UNITED CHURCH OF ACWORTH	OP	8.50	9.00
F. JONES				**SERIES 11**
93	BARBERSHOP/GALLERY	OP	4.50	5.00
93	HADDONFIELD BANK	OP	4.50	5.00
93	IMMANUEL CHURCH	OP	4.50	5.00
93	JOHANN SINGER BOOTS & SHOES	OP	4.50	5.00
93	PET SHOP/GIFT SHOP	OP	4.50	5.00
93	POLICE-TROOP C	OP	4.50	5.00
93	SHRIMPLIN & JONES PRODUCE	OP	4.50	5.00
93	STONES RESTAURANT	OP	4.50	5.00
93	U.S. ARMED FORCES	OP	4.50	5.00
93	U.S. POST OFFICE	OP	4.50	5.00
F. JONES				**SMITHSONIAN CASTLE**
96	SMITHSONIAN CASTLE	RT	15.00	15.00
F. JONES				**SOUTHERN BELLES SERIES**
96	AUBURN	YR	10.00	10.00
F. JONES				**SPECIAL ITEM**
94	SMOKEY BEAR WITH 50TH STAMP	RT	8.00	10.00
95	SMOKEY BEAR	RT	9.00	13.00
F. JONES				**TRADESMEN**
88	BUCKEYE CANDY & TOBACCO	RT	8.00	24.00
88	C.O. WHEEL COPMANY	RT	8.00	24.00
88	HERMANNHOF WINERY	RT	8.00	24.00
88	JENNEY GRIST MILL	RT	8.00	35.00
F. JONES				**WASHINGTON**
91	NATIONAL ARCHIVES	TL	8.00	10.00
91	U.S. CAPITOL	TL	8.00	10.00
91	U.S. SUPREME COURT	TL	8.00	10.00
91	WHITE HOUSE	TL	8.00	10.00
F. JONES				**WILD WEST**
89	DRINK'EM UP SALOON	RT	8.00	24.00
89	F.C. ZIMMERMANN'S GUN SHOP	RT	8.00	24.00
89	MARHSAL'S OFFICE	RT	8.00	24.00
89	WELLS, FARGO & CO.	RT	8.00	24.00
F. JONES				**WINE COUNTRY SERIES**
96	CHARLES KRUG WINERY	YR	10.00	10.00

YR	NAME	LIMIT	ISSUE	TREND

FORMA VITRUM

B. JOB — **BED & BREAKFAST**

YR	NAME	LIMIT	ISSUE	TREND
95	BROOKVIEW BED & BREAKFAST 11303	RT	295.00	580.00
96	EDGEWATER INN 11305	RT	310.00	350.00
97	BAVARIAN LODGE	1500	225.00	225.00

B. JOB — **CHRISTMAS**

YR	NAME	LIMIT	ISSUE	TREND
94	GINGERBREAD HOUSE 19111	RT	100.00	180.00
95	CONFECTIONER'S COTTAGE 41101	RT	100.00	130.00
96	LOLLIPOP SHOPPE 41102	RT	110.00	120.00
97	PEPPERMINT PLACE 41103	RT	110.00	110.00

B. JOB — **COASTAL CLASSICS**

YR	NAME	LIMIT	ISSUE	TREND
94	CAROLINA 21103	OP	65.00	65.00
94	MAINE 21102	OP	50.00	50.00
94	MICHIGAN 21101	OP	50.00	50.00
95	BAYSIDE BEACON 21013	OP	65.00	65.00
95	LOOKOUT POINT 21012	OP	60.00	60.00
95	PATRIOTS POINT 29010	OP	70.00	70.00
95	SAILORS KNOLL 21011	OP	65.00	65.00
96	CAPE HOPE 21014	OP	100.00	100.00
96	COZY COTTAGE 21500	OP	70.00	70.00

B. JOB — **COASTAL HERITAGE**

YR	NAME	LIMIT	ISSUE	TREND
95	CAPE NEDDICK, ME 25002	RT	140.00	170.00
95	MARBLEHEAD, OH 25201	RT	75.00	90.00
95	NORTH HEAD, WA 25302	1995	100.00	100.00
95	OLD POINT LOMA, CA 25301	1995	100.00	100.00
95	PORTLAND HEAD, ME 25003	RT	140.00	170.00
95	SANDY HOOK, NJ 25001	3759	140.00	140.00
95	ST. SIMONS, GA 25101	1995	120.00	120.00
96	CAPE HATTERAS, NC 25102	3867	120.00	120.00
96	FIRE ISLAND, NY 25005	2996	150.00	150.00
96	NEW LONDON, CT 25004	2996	145.00	145.00
96	PEGGY'S COVE, NS 25501	2500	75.00	75.00
96	PIGEON POINT, CA 25303	2996	125.00	125.00
96	SPLIT ROCK, MN 25202	2996	130.00	130.00
96	ST. AUGUSTINE, FL 25103	2996	130.00	130.00
97	CAPE LOOKOUT, NC 25105	1997	80.00	80.00
97	JUPITER, FL 25104	1997	80.00	80.00
97	WEST QUODDY HEAD, ME 25007	1997	140.00	140.00
98	HARBOR TOWN HILTON HEAD, SC	2998	80.00	80.00
98	SE BLOCK ISLAND, RI	998	160.00	160.00

B. JOB — **COCA-COLA THROUGH THE DECADES**

YR	NAME	LIMIT	ISSUE	TREND
97	CORNER DRUG	5000	145.00	145.00
97	SAM'S GROCERY	5000	85.00	85.00
97	TOWN CINEMA	5000	145.00	145.00
98	BARBER SHOP	*	*	N/A
98	GAS STATION	*	*	N/A
98	MERCANTILE COMPANY	*	*	N/A
98	SANDY SHOAL LIGHTHOUSE	*	*	N/A

B. JOB — **DISNEY LIGHTED VILLAGE**

YR	NAME	LIMIT	ISSUE	TREND
97	DWARF'S COTTAGE SNOW WHITE	1937	215.00	215.00
98	BELL'S COTTAGE	*	*	N/A
98	GEPETTO'S TOY SHOP	*	*	N/A

B. JOB — **VITREVILLE**

YR	NAME	LIMIT	ISSUE	TREND
93	BAVARIAN CHAPEL 11503	RT	90.00	128.00
93	BREADMAN'S BAKERY 11301	RT	70.00	85.00
93	CANDLEMAKER'S DELIGHT 11801	RT	60.00	72.00
93	CANDYMAKER'S COTTAGE 11102	RT	65.00	100.00
93	COUNTRY CHURCH 11502	RT	105.00	120.00
93	PILLARS OF FAITH 11504	RT	90.00	108.00
93	ROOFER'S ROOST 11203	RT	74.00	90.00
93	TAILOR'S TOWNHOUSE 11204	RT	94.00	94.00
94	MAPLEWOOD ELEMENTARY SCHOOL 11401	OP	100.00	100.00
94	THOMPSON'S DRUG 11302	RT	140.00	150.00
94	TRINITY CHURCH 11511	RT	130.00	156.00
94	VITREVILLE POST OFFICE 11402	RT	90.00	108.00
95	FIRE STATION 11403	OP	100.00	100.00
95	MAYOR'S MANOR MUSICAL 11205	OP	85.00	85.00
95	MILLER'S MILL (MUSICAL) 11304	OP	115.00	115.00
96	KRAMER BUILDING 11404	OP	100.00	100.00
97	BREADMAN'S BAKERY-RENOVATION 11301R	RT	85.00	180.00
97	KLAUS CLOCK SHOPPE 11307	OP	75.00	75.00
97	WILDWOOD CHAPEL 11505	OP	60.00	60.00
98	FARAH'S FLOWER SHOP	OP	80.00	80.00
98	JESSIE'S BARBER SHOP	OP	45.00	45.00
98	WHITE STONE CHAPEL	1250	85.00	85.00

B. JOB — **WOODLAND VILLAGE**

YR	NAME	LIMIT	ISSUE	TREND
93	BADGER HOUSE 31003	RT	85.00	108.00
93	CHIPMUNK HOUSE 31005	RT	85.00	102.00
93	OWL HOUSE 31004	RT	85.00	102.00
93	RACCOON HOUSE 31002	RT	85.00	102.00
94	RABBIT HOUSE 31001	RT	94.00	115.00

YR NAME	LIMIT	ISSUE	TREND
GENESIS DESIGNS			
M. MORRIS		**BETHLEHEM VILLAGE**	
92 BETHLEHEM STABLE	3000	75.00	72.00
92 MARKETPLACE	3000	70.00	66.00
92 PEASANT HOUSE	3000	50.00	46.00
M. MORRIS		**CASCADES**	
93 ALMOST PARADISE - CENTRAL	3000	50.00	47.00
M. MORRIS		**CENTRAL OREGON**	
93 MT. BACHELOR SKIER	OP	30.00	26.00
M. MORRIS		**COLUMBIA RIVER**	
93 MULTNOMAH FALLS LODGE - 1925	3000	70.00	58.00
M. MORRIS		**JESUS' WORLD**	
92 EMPTY TOMB	3000	75.00	72.00
M. MORRIS		**NATIONAL PARK**	
97 AHWAHNEE HOTEL YOSEMITE	YR	110.00	110.00
97 WINTER AHWAHNEE	YR	110.00	110.00
M. MORRIS		**NORTHWEST**	
94 TIMBERLINE LODGE - 1938	3000	74.00	68.00
94 WINTER TIMBERLINE LODGE - 1938	3000	74.00	68.00
95 CRATER LAKE LODGE	3000	78.00	74.00
96 OLD FAITHFUL INN - YELLOWSTONE	3000	96.00	90.00
97 SNOQUALMIE TRAIN STATION	3000	70.00	70.00
98 PILOT BUTTE INN	3000	84.00	84.00
M. MORRIS		**OREGON COAST**	
92 HECETA HEAD LIGHTHOUSE	RT	38.00	37.00
94 HECETA HEAD LIGHTHOUSE	RT	70.00	60.00
94 LIGHTKEEPER'S COTTAGE	3000	70.00	60.00
95 COQUILLE RIVER LIGHTHOUSE	3000	60.00	60.00
96 CAPE ARAGO III LIGHTHOUSE	3000	60.00	60.00
96 TILLAMOOK ROCK LIGHTHOUSE	3000	70.00	70.00
96 UMPQUA RIVER LIGHTHOUSE	3000	60.00	60.00
96 YAQUINA BAY LIGHTHOUSE	3000	70.00	60.00
97 CAPE BLANCO LIGHTHOUSE	3000	60.00	60.00
97 CAPE MEARES	3000	70.00	70.00
97 YAQUINA HEAD LIGHTHOUSE	3000	70.00	70.00
M. MORRIS		**PATRIARCHS, THE**	
92 NOAH'S ARK	3000	50.00	47.00
93 ABRAHAM AT THE OAKS	3000	60.00	60.00
M. MORRIS		**WASHINGTON COAST**	
97 CAPE DISAPPOINTMENT	3000	70.00	70.00
97 GRAYS HARBOR LIGHTHOUSE	3000	70.00	60.00
97 NORTH HEAD LIGHTHOUSE	3000	70.00	70.00
98 ADMIRALTY HEAD LIGHTHOUSE	3000	70.00	70.00
98 CAPE FLATTERY LIGHTHOUSE	3000	70.00	70.00
98 DESTRUCTION ISLAND LIGHTHOUSE	3000	70.00	70.00
98 MUKILTEO LIGHTHOUSE	3000	70.00	70.00
98 NEW DUNGENESS LIGHTHOUSE	3000	70.00	70.00
M. MORRIS		**WILDLIFE**	
95 REX NANOOK	OP	80.00	78.00
GOEBEL INC.			
M.I. HUMMEL		**BAVARIAN VILLAGE COLLECTION**	
96 ANGEL'S DUET	*	50.00	50.00
96 BENCH & PINE TREE, THE/SET	*	25.00	25.00
96 CHRISTMAS MAIL	*	50.00	50.00
96 COMPANY'S COMING	*	50.00	50.00
96 SLED & PINE TREE, THE/SET	*	25.00	25.00
96 VILLAGE BAKERY, THE	*	50.00	50.00
96 VILLAGE BRIDGE, THE	*	25.00	25.00
96 WINTER'S COMFORT	*	50.00	50.00
96 WISHING WELL, THE	*	25.00	25.00
HADLEY COMPANIES			
T. REDLIN		**HOMESTEAD COLLECTION**	
95 COMFORTS OF HOME	45 DAYS	90.00	90.00
96 EVENING WITH FRIENDS	45 DAYS	90.00	90.00
HARBOUR LIGHTS			
B. YOUNGER			
98 CAPE FLORIDA, FL	10000	78.00	78.00
98 CHICAGO HARBOR, IL	10000	73.00	73.00
98 EXECUTION ROCK, NY	10000	78.00	78.00
98 FAULKNER'S ISLAND, CT	10000	70.00	70.00
98 HORTON POINT, NY	10000	75.00	75.00
98 LORAIN, OH	10000	75.00	75.00
98 OLD SAYBROOK, CT	10000	69.00	69.00
B. YOUNGER		**CHESAPEAKE SERIES**	
96 CONCORD, MD 186	9500	66.00	66.00
96 SANDY POINT, MD 167	9500	70.00	70.00
96 SHARP'S ISLAND, MD 185	RT	70.00	70.00
96 THOMAS POINT 181	RT	99.00	189.00
97 DRUM POINT, MD 180	RT	99.00	160.00
B. YOUNGER		**CHRISTMAS ANNUALS**	
95 CHRISTMAS 1995 - BIG BAY POINT, MI 700	RT	75.00	640.00

YR	NAME	LIMIT	ISSUE	TREND
96	CHRISTMAS 1996 COLCHESTER, VT 701	RT	75.00	100.00
97	CHRISTMAS 1997 WHITE SHOAL, MI	RT	*	100.00
B. YOUNGER				**EVENT PIECE**
96	SUNKEN ROCK, NY 602	RT	25.00	56.00
97	EDGARTOWN, MA 603	YR	35.00	80.00
B. YOUNGER				**GREAT LAKES REGION**
91	FORT NIAGARA, NY 113	RT	60.00	128.00
91	SAND ISLAND, WI 112	RT	60.00	103.00
92	BUFFALO, NY 122	RT	60.00	147.00
92	CANA ISLAND, WI 119	RT	60.00	126.00
92	GROSSE POINT, IL 120	RT	60.00	130.00
92	MARBLEHEAD, OH 121	RT	50.00	127.00
92	MICHIGAN CITY, IN 123	RT	60.00	123.00
92	OLD MACKINAC POINT, MI 118	RT	65.00	174.00
92	SPLIT ROCK, MI 124	RT	60.00	2700.00
92	SPLIT ROCK, MN 124	RT	60.00	129.00
94	HOLLAND (BIG RED), MI 142	RT	60.00	182.00
95	ROUND ISLAND, MI 153	9500	85.00	66.00
95	SELKIRK, NY 157	9500	75.00	75.00
95	TAWAS PT., MI 152	RT	75.00	120.00
95	WIND POINT, WI 154	9500	78.00	78.00
96	CHARLOTTE-GENESEE, NY 165	9500	77.00	77.00
97	GRAND TRAVERSE, MI 191	9500	80.00	80.00
97	PRESQUE ISLE, PA 201	9500	75.00	75.00
B. YOUNGER			**GREAT LIGHTHOUSES OF THE WORLD**	
94	CAPE HATTERAS, NC 401	OP	50.00	50.00
95	BOSTON HARBOR, MA 402	OP	50.00	50.00
95	PORTLAND HEAD, ME 404	OP	50.00	50.00
95	SOUTHEAST BLOCK ISLAND, RI 403	OP	50.00	50.00
96	SANDY HOOK, NJ 418	OP	50.00	50.00
97	BARNEGAT, NJ 414	OP	45.00	45.00
97	CAPE NEDDICK, ME 410	OP	50.00	50.00
97	HILTON HEAD, SC 415	OP	50.00	50.00
97	MONTAUK, NY 405	OP	55.00	55.00
97	NEW LONDON LEDGE, CT	OP	55.00	55.00
97	POINT LOMA, CA, 409	OP	50.00	50.00
97	PONCE DE LEON, FL 408	OP	55.00	55.00
97	ST. AUGUSTINE, FL 411	OP	45.00	45.00
97	ST. SIMONS, GA 416	OP	50.00	50.00
B. YOUNGER				**GULF COAST REGION**
95	BILOXI, MS 149	RT	60.00	90.00
95	BOLIVAR, TX 146	RT	70.00	90.00
95	NEW CANAL, LA 148	RT	65.00	90.00
95	PENSACOLA, FL 150	RT	80.00	80.00
95	PORT ISABEL, TX 147	RT	65.00	65.00
97	MIDDLE BAY, AL 187	RT	99.00	145.00
B. YOUNGER		**HARBOUR LIGHTS COLLECTOR'S SOCIETY**		
95	POINT FERMIN, CA 501	RT	80.00	174.00
96	SPYGLASS COLLECTION, CT 503	*	*	32.00
96	STONINGTON HARBOUR, CT 502	RT	70.00	100.00
97	AMELIA ISLAND, FL	*	*	0.00
97	PORT SANILAC, MI 506	*	80.00	80.00
B. YOUNGER				**INTERNATIONAL SERIES**
96	PEGGY'S COVE, NOVA SCOTIA 169	9500	68.00	68.00
97	HOOK HEAD, IRELAND 198	9500	71.00	71.00
97	LA JUMENT, FRANCE 192	RT	68.00	68.00
97	LONGSHIPS, UK 193	9500	68.00	68.00
97	MACQUARIE, AUSTRALIA 197	9500	68.00	68.00
B. YOUNGER				**LADY LIGHTKEEPERS**
96	CHATHAM, MA 172	9500	70.00	70.00
96	IDA LEWIS, RI 174	9500	70.00	70.00
96	MATINICUS, ME 173	9500	77.00	77.00
96	POINT PINOS, CA 170	9500	70.00	70.00
96	SAUGERTIES, NY 171	9500	75.00	75.00
B. YOUNGER				**NORTHEAST REGION**
91	BOSTON HARBOR, MA 117	RT	60.00	165.00
91	CASTLE HILL, RI 116	RT	60.00	100.00
91	GREAT CAPTAIN'S ISLAND, CT 114	RT	60.00	100.00
91	SANDY HOOK, NJ 104	RT	60.00	250.00
91	WEST QUODDY HEAD, ME 103	RT	60.00	150.00
92	MINOT'S LEDGE, MA 131 BLUE WATER	*	60.00	130.00
92	MINOT'S LEDGE, MA 131 GREEN WATER	RT	60.00	180.00
92	NAUSET, MA 126	RT	66.00	175.00
92	NEW LONDON LEDGE, CT 129 BLUE WATER	RT	66.00	157.00
92	NEW LONDON LEDGE, CT 129 GREEN WATER	RT	66.00	185.00
92	PORTLAND BREAKWATER, ME 130	RT	60.00	125.00
92	PORTLAND HEAD, ME 125	RT	66.00	600.00
92	SOUTHEAST BLOCK ISLAND, RI 128	RT	71.00	270.00
92	WHALEBACK, NH 127	RT	60.00	120.00
94	BARNEGAT, NJ 139	RT	60.00	195.00
94	CAPE NEDDICK (NUBBLE), ME 141	RT	66.00	189.00
94	MONTAUK, NY 143	RT	85.00	213.00
95	BRANT POINT, MA 162	9500	66.00	100.00
95	HIGHLAND, MA 161 NO S	RT	75.00	125.00

YR	NAME	LIMIT	ISSUE	TREND
95	HIGHLANDS, MA 161-VARIATION	*	75.00	80.00
96	CAPE MAY, NJ 168	RT	75.00	115.00
96	FIRE ISLAND, NY 176	RT	70.00	98.00
96	PEMAQUID, ME 164	RT	90.00	100.00
96	SCITUATE, MA 166	9500	77.00	100.00
97	BEAVERTAIL, RI 188	9500	80.00	80.00
97	JEFFREY'S HOOK, NY 195	9500	66.00	66.00

B. YOUNGER   **REUNION PIECES**

YR	NAME	LIMIT	ISSUE	TREND
97	NEW POINT LOMA 604	RT	70.00	880.00
97	NEW POINT LOMA 605	*	*	450.00

B. YOUNGER   **SOUTHEAST REGION**

YR	NAME	LIMIT	ISSUE	TREND
91	CAPE HATTERAS, NC 102 MOLD ONE	RT	60.00	4950.00
92	CAPE HATTERAS, NC 102R MOLD TWO	RT	60.00	808.00
93	HILTON HEAD, SC 136	RT	60.00	525.00
93	KEY WEST, FL 134	RT	60.00	363.00
93	OCRACOKE, NC 135	RT	60.00	285.00
93	PONCE DE LEON, FL 132	RT	60.00	310.00
93	ST. AUGUSTINE, FL 138	RT	71.00	520.00
93	ST. SIMONS, GA 137	RT	66.00	367.00
93	TYBEE, GA 133	RT	60.00	258.00
94	ASSATEAGUE, VA 145 MOLD ONE	RT	69.00	350.00
94	ASSATEAGUE, VA 145 MOLD TWO	RT	69.00	163.00
95	CURRITUCK, NC 158	RT	80.00	172.00
95	JUPITER, FL 151	RT	77.00	179.00
96	BALD HEAD, NC 155	RT	75.00	100.00
96	BODIE, NC 159	RT	77.00	115.00
96	CAPE CANAVERAL, FL 163	RT	80.00	133.00
96	CAPE LOOKOUT, NC 175	RT	64.00	175.00
97	CAPE HENRY, VA 196	RT	82.00	82.00
97	MORRIS ISLAND, SC NOW 190	RT	65.00	65.00
97	MORRIS ISLAND, SC THEN 189	RT	85.00	85.00
97	SANIBEL ISLAND, FL	RT	120.00	145.00

B. YOUNGER   **SPECIAL EDITIONS**

YR	NAME	LIMIT	ISSUE	TREND
95	LEGACY LIGHT 600 (RED)	RT	65.00	150.00
95	LEGACY LIGHT 601 (BLUE)	RT	65.00	65.00
98	ROOSEVELT, NY	*	30.00	30.00

B. YOUNGER   **STAMP SERIES**

YR	NAME	LIMIT	ISSUE	TREND
95	MARBLEHEAD, OH 413	OP	50.00	50.00
95	SPECTACLE REEF, MI 182 (410)	RT	60.00	60.00
95	SPLIT ROCK, MN 412	OP	60.00	60.00
95	ST. JOSEPH, MI 183 (411)	RT	60.00	60.00
95	THIRTY MILE POINT, NY 184 (414)	RT	62.00	62.00

B. YOUNGER   **WESTERN REGION**

YR	NAME	LIMIT	ISSUE	TREND
91	ADMIRALITY HEAD, WA 101 MISSPELLED	RT	60.00	132.00
91	ADMIRALTY HEAD, WA 101	RT	60.00	182.00
91	BURROWS ISLAND, OR 108 WRONG STATE	RT	60.00	1195.00
91	BURROWS ISLAND, WA 108	RT	60.00	340.00
91	CAPE BLANCO, OR 109	RT	60.00	100.00
91	COQUILLE RIVER, OR 111	RT	60.00	2725.00
91	NORTH HEAD, WA 106	RT	60.00	110.00
91	OLD POINT LOMA, CA 105	RT	60.00	159.00
91	ST. GEORGE'S REEF, CA 115	RT	60.00	137.00
91	UMPQUA RIVER, OR 107	RT	60.00	112.00
91	YAQUINA HEAD, WA 110	5500	60.00	104.00
94	DIAMOND HEAD, HI 140	RT	60.00	151.00
94	HECETA HEAD, OR 144	RT	60.00	110.00
95	POINT ARENA, CA 156	RT	60.00	187.00
96	ALCATRAZ, CA 177 (407)	RT	77.00	169.00
96	CAPE MEARES, OR 160	9500	68.00	100.00
96	MUKILTEO, WA 178 (417)	9500	55.00	100.00

HAWTHORNE

*

ANNE OF GREEN GABLES

YR	NAME	LIMIT	ISSUE	TREND
*	GREEN GABLES W/ANNE 79151	*	49.95	50.00

*

BEACONS OF FREEDOM/ILLUMINATED

YR	NAME	LIMIT	ISSUE	TREND
95	PORTLAND HEAD LIGHTHOUSE 79181	*	40.00	40.00
95	WEST QUODDY HEAD LIGHTHOUSE 79182	*	40.00	40.00

K./H. LEVAN   **CHESTNUT HILL STATION**

YR	NAME	LIMIT	ISSUE	TREND
93	CHESTNUT HILL DEPOT 78253	CL	30.00	30.00
93	PARKSIDE CAFE 78252	CL	30.00	30.00
93	WISHING WELL COTTAGE 78251	CL	30.00	30.00
94	BICYCLE SHOP 78254	CL	30.00	30.00

*

CHRISTMAS IN BEDFORD FALLS/ILLUMINATED

YR	NAME	LIMIT	ISSUE	TREND
*	BAILY BROS. BUILDING & LOAN 79392	*	40.00	40.00
95	OLD GRANVILLE PLACE, THE 79391	*	40.00	40.00

*

COLONIAL CHRISTMAS/ILLUMINATED

YR	NAME	LIMIT	ISSUE	TREND
*	BRUTON PARISH CHURCH, THE 79463	*	40.00	40.00
95	MARGARET HUNTER'S SHOP 79462	*	40.00	40.00
95	MARKET SQUARE TAVERN/FREE SIGN 79461	*	40.00	40.00

K./H. LEVAN   **CONCORD: HOMETOWN OF AMERICA LITERATURE**

YR	NAME	LIMIT	ISSUE	TREND
91	HAWTHORNE'S WAYSIDE RETREAT 78221	CL	40.00	40.00
92	EMERSON'S OLD MANSE 78222	CL	40.00	40.00
93	ALCOTT'S ORCHARD HOUSE 78223	CL	40.00	40.00

There are three versions of the Steeple Church (New England Village). The first were issued by Department 56 in 1986.

Ben's Barber Shop *was issued along with* Otis Hayes Butcher Shop *and* Anne Shaw Toys *in a set designed for the New England Village produced by Department 56.*

Released by Department 56, Santa's Lookout Tower is a member of the North Pole Collection and retails for $45.

The Counting House & Silas Thimbleton Barrister *(Dickens' Village) was only issued from 1988-90. Department 56 retired the piece after only two years.*

YR	NAME	LIMIT	ISSUE	TREND
*			**CONNIE LAYTON'S VICTORIANA**	
95	MAY COTTAGE 78971	*	29.95	30.00
*			**CURRIER & IVES SUMMER**	
95	AMERICAN HOMESTEAD SUMMER 78731	*	30.00	30.00
95	HOME ON THE MISSISSIPPI 78732	*	30.00	30.00
*			**CURRIER & IVES: THE ART OF AMERICA**	
94	AMERICAN HOMESTEAD WINTER 78281	*	30.00	30.00
95	A COLD MORNING 78288	*	30.00	30.00
95	EARLY WINTER 78286	*	30.00	30.00
95	FEEDING THE CHICKENS 78283	*	30.00	30.00
95	OLD GRIST MILL, THE 78284	*	30.00	30.00
95	SNOW STORM 78282	*	30.00	30.00
95	WINTER EVENING 78285	*	30.00	30.00
95	WINTER MOONLIGHT 78287	*	30.00	30.00
	K./H. LEVAN		**GONE WITH THE WIND**	
92	TARA...SCARLETT'S PRIDE 78171	CL	40.00	40.00
92	TWELVE OAKS...THE ROMANCE 78172	CL	40.00	40.00
93	AGAINST HER WILL 78174	CL	43.00	43.00
93	MESSAGE FOR CAPT. BUTLER 78175	CL	43.00	43.00
93	RHETT'S RETURN 78173	CL	40.00	40.00
93	TARA 79421	CL	40.00	40.00
94	ALONE 78178	CL	46.00	46.00
94	ATLANTA CHURCH 79423	CL	40.00	40.00
94	HOPE FOR A NEW TOMORROW 78176	CL	43.00	43.00
94	I HAVE DONE ENOUGH 78180	CL	46.00	46.00
94	KENNEDY STORE 79424		40.00	40.00
94	RED HORSE SALOON 79425		40.00	40.00
94	SWEPT AWAY 78177	CL	46.00	46.00
94	TAKE ME TO TARA 78179	CL	46.00	46.00
94	TWELVE OAKS 79422	*	40.00	40.00
95	ASHLEY'S SAFE 78183	CL	46.00	46.00
95	BUTLER'S MANSION 79426	*	40.00	40.00
95	DIGNITY AND RESPECT 78182	CL	46.00	46.00
95	REVENGE ON SHANTY TOWN 78181	*	46.00	46.00
*			**GONE WITH THE WIND ACCESSORIES**	
95	BARBEQUE, THE 91253	*	25.00	25.00
95	BUTLERS, THE 91255	*	25.00	25.00
95	HELPING THE WOUNDED 91250	*	25.00	25.00
95	O'HARAS, THE 91252	*	25.00	25.00
95	RHETT & SCARLETT 91254	*	25.00	25.00
95	SCARLETT & ASHLEY 91251	*	25.00	25.00
*			**GONE WITH THE WIND LIMITED EDITION COLLECTION**	
97	RHETT & SCARLETT POSTER SCENE	*	80.00	80.00
*			**GONE WITH THE WIND MINIATURES**	
*	ASHLEY'S SAFE/TRAIN STATION	*	30.00	30.00
*	MESSAGE FOR CAPT. BUTLER/HOPE 78663	*	30.00	30.00
*	REVENGE/DIGNITY & RESPECT 78666	*	30.00	30.00
*	RHETT'S RETURN/AGAINST HER WILL 78662	*	30.00	30.00
*	SPRINGHOUSE/CARRIAGE HOUSE 78668	*	30.00	30.00
*	SWEPT AWAY/ALONE 78664	*	30.00	30.00
*	TAKE ME TO TARA/DONE ENOUGH 78665	*	30.00	30.00
*	TARA MILL/STABLE 78669	*	30.00	30.00
95	SCARLETT'S PRIDE/ROMANCE 78661	*	29.95	30.00
	K./H. LEVAN		**GONE WITH THE WIND SPECIAL EDITIONS**	
94	BURNING OF ATLANTA 78185	10000	79.95	80.00
95	BUTLER MANSION, THE 78186	10000	80.00	80.00
*			**HAWTHORNE MINIATURE NATIVITY**	
95	NATIVITY 91010	*	40.00	40.00
95	PALM TREES 91018	*	25.00	25.00
95	SITTING CAMELS, BLESSED BEASTS/MARY'S DONKEY 91017	*	25.00	25.00
95	STABLE KEEPER & STANDING CAMEL 91016	*	25.00	25.00
*			**HELEN STEINER RICE ACCESSORIES**	
95	BOY W/LANTERN 91301	*	20.00	20.00
95	GIRL SNOWANGEL 91302	*	20.00	20.00
95	LAMPS 91303	*	20.00	20.00
*			**HELEN STEINER RICE: WINDOWS OF GOLD**	
94	INSPIRATION POINT LIGHTHOUSE 79541	*	35.00	35.00
94	PEACE ON FAITH 79542	*	40.00	40.00
94	WINTERS WARMTH 79543	*	40.00	40.00
*			**HERSHEY, PA: AN AMERICAN DREAM COME TRUE**	
95	BIRTHPLACE OF MILTON HERSHEY 78951	CL	30.00	30.00
95	DERRY CHURCH SCHOOL 78952	*	30.00	30.00
	T. KINKADE		**HOME FOR THE HOLIDAYS COLLECTION**	
97	EVENING CAROLERS	*	30.00	30.00
*			**HOMETOWN AMERICA**	
92	EVERGREEN COTTAGE 83601	*	34.95	35.00
93	EVERGREEN VALLEY SCHOOL 83602	CL	34.95	35.00
93	VILLAGE BAKERY, THE 83603	CL	37.95	38.00
94	EVERGREEN GENERAL STORE 83606	*	39.95	40.00
94	EVERGREEN VALLEY CHURCH 83605	*	38.00	38.00
94	WOODCUTTER'S REST 83604	*	38.00	38.00
95	WAITING FOR SANTA 83607	*	40.00	40.00
*			**HUMMEL ACCESSORIES**	
95	LARGE TREE/SLED 91312	*	25.00	25.00

YR	NAME	LIMIT	ISSUE	TREND
95	SMALL TREE/BENCH 91313	*	25.00	25.00
95	VILLAGE BRIDGE 91310	*	25.00	25.00
95	WISHING WELL 91311	*	25.00	25.00
*				
	HUMMEL'S BAVARIAN CHRISTMAS			
*	ALL ABOARD 79287		50.00	50.00
*	LITTLE BOOTMAKER 79288		50.00	50.00
*	OFF FOR THE HOLIDAYS 79286		50.00	50.00
94	ANGEL'S DUET 79281		50.00	50.00
94	BAKERY, THE 79282		50.00	50.00
95	COMPANY'S COMING 79283		50.00	50.00
95	POST OFFICE 79285		50.00	50.00
95	WINTER'S COMFORT 79284		50.00	50.00
	K./H. LEVAN			
	INSIDE GONE WITH THE WIND			
*	WILKES LIBRARY 78582		40.00	40.00
94	PRIDE AND PASSION 78581		40.00	40.00
	KINKADE'S HOME FOR THE HOLIDAYS			
*	MOONLIT VILLAGE CHURCH 78022		30.00	30.00
*	VICTORIAN CHRISTMAS 78021		30.00	30.00
	T. KINKADE			
	LAMPLIGHT VILLAGE COLLECTION			
96	KINKADE'S COTTAGE 78321		30.00	30.00
97	LAMPLIGHT INN		30.00	30.00
	LAS VEGAS			
*	FLAMINGO, THE 79091	*	49.95	50.00
*	HARRAH'S 79092		50.00	50.00
	R. BROUILETTE			
	LOST VICTORIANS OF OLD SAN FRANCISCO			
91	GRANDE DAME OF NOB HILL 78111	CL	35.00	35.00
92	EMPRESS OF RUSSIAN HILL 78112	CL	35.00	35.00
93	PRINCESS OF PACIFIC HEIGHTS 78113	CL	35.00	35.00
	MARTY BELL'S MARTHA'S VINEYARD			
*	SUMMERLAND 79891	*	39.95	40.00
	MAYBERRY			
94	COURTHOUSE, THE 79721	*	40.00	40.00
94	FLOYD'S BARBER SHOP 79722	*	40.00	40.00
94	MAYBERRY METHODIST CHURCH 79725	*	40.00	40.00
94	POST OFFICE 79726	*	40.00	40.00
94	TAYLOR HOME, THE 79724	*	40.00	40.00
94	WALLY'S FILLING STATION 79723	*	40.00	40.00
	MAYBERRY ACCESSORIES			
95	ANDY & BARNEY 91350	*	22.00	22.00
95	AUNT BEE & OPIE 91351	*	22.00	22.00
95	PATROL CAR & GAS PUMPS 91352	*	22.00	22.00
	MCMEMORIES			
95	MCDONALD'S RESTAURANT 31901	*	39.95	40.00
	NORTH POLE ACCESSORIES			
94	GETTING READY FOR CHRISTMAS 91203	*	24.00	24.00
94	LETTERS FOR SANTA SET 91202	*	24.00	24.00
94	SANTA'S HELPER'S SET 91200	CL	24.00	24.00
94	SWEET DELIGHTS SET 91201	*	24.00	24.00
95	COOKIES FOR KIDDIES 91204	*	24.00	24.00
	G. HOOVER			
	P.O. #1, NORTH POLE			
94	SANTA'S POST OFFICE 79102	*	40.00	40.00
94	SANTA'S TOY SHOPPE W/SIGN 79101	*	40.00	40.00
95	SANTA'S CANDY SHOP 79103	*	40.00	40.00
95	SANTA'S GIFT WRAP CENTRAL 79104	CL	40.00	40.00
	K./H. LEVAN			
	PEACEABLE KINGDOM			
93	SQUIRE BOONE'S HOMESTEAD 78561		35.00	35.00
94	WHITE HOUSE INN 48562		35.00	35.00
	C. WYSOCKI			
	PEPPERCRICKET GROVE			
*	BUDZEN'S ROADSIDE FOOD STORE 78784		50.00	50.00
95	EVENING SLED RIDE 78783	*	50.00	50.00
95	PEPPERCRICKET FARM 78781	*	50.00	50.00
95	VIRGINIA'S NEST 78782	*	50.00	50.00
98	FIREHOUSE NO. 2	*	50.00	50.00
	REMEMBERING MAIN STREET			
98	FANNIE MAY CANDIES	*	40.00	40.00
	ROCKWELL'S FOUR FREEDOMS/ILLUMINATED			
*	DOCTOR'S COUNTRY HOME 79947	*	40.00	40.00
*	FREEDOM FROM WANT: THE FARMHOUSE 79944	*	40.00	40.00
*	FREEDOM IS KNOWLEDGE: THE LIBRARY 79945	*	40.00	40.00
*	SCHOOL, THE 79946	*	40.00	40.00
94	FREEDOM FROM FEAR: THE ROCKWELL HOMESTEAD 79942	*	40.00	40.00
94	FREEDOM OF WORSHIP: ARLINGTON CHURCH 79941	*	40.00	40.00
95	FREEDOM OF SPEECH: TOWN HALL 79943	*	40.00	40.00
	ROCKWELL'S HEART OF STOCKBRIDGE/ILLUMINATED			
95	BELL TOWER 79235	*	40.00	40.00
95	CHURCH ON THE GREEN 79234	*	40.00	40.00
95	FIREHOUSE 79233	*	40.00	40.00
95	ROCKWELL'S HOME 79231	*	40.00	40.00
95	ROCKWELL'S STUDIO 79232	*	40.00	40.00
	ROCKWELL'S HOME FOR THE HOLIDAYS			
92	BRINGING HOME THE TREE 78122	CL	35.00	35.00
92	BRINGING HOME THE TREE 82292	CL	35.00	35.00
92	CAROLERS IN THE CHURCHYARD 78123	*	38.00	38.00

YR	NAME	LIMIT	ISSUE	TREND
92	CAROLERS IN THE CHURCHYARD 82293	CL	38.00	38.00
92	CHRISTMAS EVE AT THE STUDIO 78121	CL	35.00	35.00
92	CHRISTMAS EVE AT THE STUDIO 82291	CL	34.95	35.00
93	A ROOM AT THE INN 78127	*	40.00	40.00
93	A ROOM AT THE INN 82297	*	40.00	40.00
93	LETTERS TO SANTA 78128	*	40.00	40.00
93	LETTERS TO SANTA 82298	*	40.00	40.00
93	OVER THE RIVER 78125	CL	38.00	38.00
93	OVER THE RIVER 82295	CL	38.00	38.00
93	SCHOOL'S OUT 78126	CL	40.00	40.00
93	SCHOOL'S OUT 82296	CL	38.00	38.00
93	THREE-DAY PASS 78124	*	38.00	38.00
93	THREE-DAY PASS 82294	*	38.00	38.00
94	A GOLDEN MEMORY 78131	CL	42.00	42.00
94	A WHITE CHRISTMAS 78129	CL	42.00	42.00
94	A WHITE CHRISTMAS 82299	CL	42.00	42.00
94	LATE FOR THE DANCE 78130	*	42.00	42.00
94	LATE FOR THE DANCE 82300	*	42.00	42.00
95	A GOLDEN MEMORY 82301	CL	42.00	42.00
95	READY & WAITING 78132	CL	42.00	42.00
95	READY & WAITING 82302	CL	42.00	42.00
*	**ROCKWELL'S HOMETOWN COLLECTION**			
*	BELL TOWER, THE 82283	CL	36.95	37.00
90	ROCKWELL'S RESIDENCE 82281	CL	34.95	35.00
91	CHURCH ON THE GREEN, THE 82285	CL	39.95	40.00
91	FIRE HOUSE, THE 82284	CL	36.95	37.00
91	GREY STONE CHURCH 82282	CL	34.95	35.00
92	BERKSHIRE PLAYHOUSE 82288	CL	43.00	43.00
92	CITIZEN'S HALL 82287	CL	42.95	43.00
92	MISSION HOUSE, THE 82289	CL	43.00	43.00
92	OLD CORNER HOUSE, THE 82290	CL	43.00	43.00
92	TOWNE HALL 82286	CL	40.00	40.00
93	PARSONAGE COTTAGE 82207	CL	43.00	43.00
93	PLAIN SCHOOL 82206	CL	43.00	43.00
93	TRAIN STATION 82208	CL	43.00	43.00
94	OLD RECTORY 82209	CL	43.00	43.00
*	**ROCKWELL'S MAIN STREET**			
93	ANTIQUE SHOP 79843	*	30.00	30.00
93	BANK, THE 79845	*	30.00	30.00
93	COUNTRY STORE, THE 79842	*	30.00	30.00
93	LIBRARY, THE 79846	*	30.00	30.00
93	RED LION INN, THE 79847	*	30.00	30.00
93	ROCKWELL'S STUDIO 79841	*	30.00	30.00
93	STOCKBRIDGE SIGN 79840	CL	10.00	10.00
93	TOWN OFFICES, THE 79844	*	30.00	30.00
*	**ROCKWELL'S NEIGHBORHOOD**			
94	FIDO'S NEW HOME 78482	*	30.00	30.00
94	LEMONADE STAND, THE 78481	*	30.00	30.00
94	SIDEWALK SPEEDSTER 78483	*	30.00	30.00
*	**ROCKWELL'S SEASONS IN STOCKBRIDGE**			
*	COUNTRY STORE/ROCKWELL STUDIO 78823	*	30.00	30.00
*	FIREHOUSE/OLD CORNER HOUSE 78822	*	30.00	30.00
95	ROCKWELL RESIDENCE/ANTIQUE SHOP 78821	*	29.95	30.00
*	**SPRINGTIME ON MAIN STREET**			
93	ROCKWELL'S STUDIO 78381	*	29.95	30.00
K./H. LEVAN			**STONEFIELD VALLEY**	
92	CHURCH IN THE GLEN 78444	CL	38.00	38.00
92	MEADOWBROOK SCHOOL 78442	CL	35.00	35.00
92	SPRINGBRIDGE COTTAGE 78441	CL	35.00	35.00
92	WEAVER'S COTTAGE 78443	CL	38.00	38.00
93	FERRYMAN'S COTTAGE 78447	CL	40.00	40.00
93	HILLSIDE COTTAGE 78446	CL	40.00	40.00
93	PARSON'S COTTAGE 78445	CL	38.00	38.00
93	VALLEY VIEW FARM 78448	CL	40.00	40.00
K./H. LEVAN		**STROLLING THROUGH COLONIAL AMERICA**		
91	EASTBROOK CHURCH 78004	CL	38.00	38.00
91	HIGGIN'S GRIST MILL 78003	CL	38.00	38.00
91	JEFFERSON'S ORDINAIRE 78001	CL	35.00	35.00
91	MILLRACE STORE 78002	CL	35.00	35.00
92	CAPT. LEE'S GRAMMAR SCHOOL 78006	CL	40.00	40.00
92	COURTHOUSE ON THE GREEN 78005	CL	38.00	38.00
92	EVERETT'S JOINER SHOP 78008	CL	40.00	40.00
92	VILLAGE SMITHY, THE 78007	CL	40.00	40.00
K./H. LEVAN			**SUNSET COVE**	
94	WATERCOLOR COTTAGE 78051	*	35.00	35.00
95	ARTISTS DELIGHT 78052	*	35.00	35.00
K./H. LEVAN		**TARA: THE ONLY THING WORTH FIGHTING FOR**		
93	A DREAM REMEMBERED 78621	*	30.00	30.00
94	CARRIAGE HOUSE 78623	*	30.00	30.00
94	KITCHEN AND GATEWAY 78624	CL	30.00	30.00
94	MILL, THE 78625	*	30.00	30.00
94	SPRINGHOUSE AND HIDEAWAY 78622	CL	30.00	30.00
95	STABLE, THE 78626	*	30.00	30.00

YR	NAME	LIMIT	ISSUE	TREND
*			**THATCHER'S CROSSING**	
93	CHAPEL CROSSING 78763	CL	30.00	30.00
93	MIDSUMMER'S COTTAGE 78762	CL	30.00	30.00
93	ROSE ARBOUR COTTAGE 78761	CL	30.00	30.00
94	WOODCUTTER'S COTTAGE 78764	CL	30.00	30.00
*		**THOMAS KINKADE'S CANDLELIGHT COTTAGES**		
92	OLDE PORTERFIELD TEA ROOM 78151	*	25.00	24.90
93	CHANDLER'S COTTAGE 78152	*	25.00	24.90
93	MERRITT'S COTTAGE 78154	*	28.00	28.00
93	SWANBROOKE COTTAGE 78153	*	25.00	25.00
94	CANDLELIT COTTAGE 78157	*	30.00	30.00
94	SEASIDE COTTAGE 78155	*	28.00	28.00
94	SWEETHEART COTTAGE 78156	*	30.00	30.00
95	CEDAR NOOK COTTAGE 78158	*	30.00	30.00
*		**THOMAS KINKADE'S CANDLELIGHT COTTAGES/ILLUMINATED**		
93	CHANDLER'S COTTAGE 79002	CL	30.00	30.00
93	OLD PORTERFIELD TEA ROOM 79001	CL	30.00	30.00
*			**THOMAS KINKADE'S CHRISTMAS MEMORIES**	
95	HOME BEFORE CHRISTMAS 78876	*	35.00	35.00
95	HOME TO GRANDMA'S 78872	*	35.00	35.00
95	HOMESPUN HOLIDAY 78875	*	35.00	35.00
95	OLD PORTERFIELD GIFT & SHOPPE 78871	*	35.00	35.00
95	SILENT NIGHT 78873	*	35.00	35.00
95	STONEHEARTH HUTCH 78877	*	35.00	35.00
95	WARMTH OF HOME 78874	*	35.00	35.00
*			**THOMAS KINKADE'S ENCHANTED CHRISTMAS**	
*	COTTAGE BY THE SEA 78876	*	30.00	30.00
*	SWEETHEARTS COTTAGE 78885	*	30.00	30.00
95	HEATHER'S HUTCH 78884	*	30.00	30.00
95	JULIANNE'S COTTAGE 78882	*	30.00	30.00
95	MCKENNA'S COTTAGE 78881	*	30.00	30.00
95	MILLER'S COTTAGE 78883	*	30.00	30.00
*			**THOMAS KINKADE'S LAMPLIGHT LANE**	
95	KINKADE'S COTTAGE 79051	*	50.00	50.00
*		**THOMAS KINKADE'S ST. NICHOLAS CIRCLE/ILLUMINATED**		
93	TOWN HALL 79681	*	40.00	40.00
94	EVERGREEN APOTHECARY 79687	CL	40.00	40.00
94	FIREHOUSE, THE 79686	CL	40.00	40.00
94	HOLLY HOUSE INN 79688	CL	40.00	40.00
94	KRINGLE BROS. 79684	CL	40.00	40.00
94	MRS. C'S BAKERY 79685	CL	40.00	40.00
94	NOEL CHAPEL 79682	*	40.00	40.00
94	S.C. TOYMAKER 79683	*	40.00	40.00
K./H. LEVAN			**VICTORIA GROVE**	
92	LILAC COTTAGE 78331	CL	35.00	35.00
92	ROSE HAVEN 78332	CL	35.00	35.00
93	CHERRY BLOSSOM 78333	CL	35.00	35.00
*			**VILLAGE ACCESSORIES**	
94	BRINGING HOME THE TREE SET 91000	*	22.00	22.00
94	CHRISTMAS SHOPPING SET 91002	*	22.00	22.00
94	DECORATING THE TREE SET 91006	*	22.00	22.00
94	GREETINGS & GAMES SET 91001	*	22.00	22.00
94	NORMAN ROCKWELL & TRIO OF CAROLLERS 91003	*	22.00	22.00
94	OLD FASHIONED STREET LIGHTS SET 91700	*	22.00	22.00
94	ROARING ROADSTERS SET 91500	*	22.00	22.00
94	SHOPKEEPER & TRAVELERS SET	*	22.00	22.00
94	SKATING POND, THE 91007	*	24.00	24.00
94	SLIPPING & SLIDING SET	*	22.00	22.00
94	SNOW COVERED EVERGREENS SET 91600	*	22.00	22.00
94	VILLAGE VEHICLES SET 91502	*	22.00	22.00
94	VINTAGE V-8S SET 91502	*	22.00	22.00
95	AUTUMN TREES 91022	*	30.00	30.00
95	BACKYARD BARBEQUE 91019	*	22.00	22.00
95	COUNTRY FARMSTAND 91020	*	30.00	30.00
95	EARLY MORNING DELIVERY 91013	*	22.00	22.00
95	FIRE DRILL 91025	*	24.00	24.00
95	HOLIDAY MAIL 91011	*	22.00	22.00
95	LAST DAY OF SCHOOL BEFORE CHRISTMAS 91012	*	22.00	22.00
95	LAUNDRY DAY 91024	*	22.00	22.00
95	OUT FOR A STROLL 91015	*	22.00	22.00
95	PICKING OUT A PUMPKIN 91021	*	40.00	40.00
95	REFRESHMENTS 91014	*	22.00	22.00
95	SIDEWALK SELLERS 91009	*	22.00	22.00
95	SNOWMAN & TREE SET 91008	*	22.00	22.00
95	SUMMER TREES 91023	*	22.00	22.00
96	VILLAGE CLOCK 91701	*	22.00	22.00
*		**WELCOME TO MAYBERRY COLLECTION**		
97	MAYBERRY HOTEL	*	40.00	40.00
98	MAYBERRY SCHOOLHOUSE	*	40.00	40.00
*			**WIZARD OF OZ**	
95	JOURNEY BEGINS, THE 78891	*	149.50	150.00
*		**WYSOCKI SMALL TOWN CHRISTMAS**		
95	YE VERY OLDE FRUITCAKE SHOPPE 79121	*	39.95	40.00

YR	NAME	LIMIT	ISSUE	TREND
	C. WYSOCKI	**WYSOCKI'S SEASIDE COVE COLLECTION**		
97	BEACH BUMS	*	50.00	50.00

JAN'S ORIGINALS

YR	NAME	LIMIT	ISSUE	TREND
	J. BENSON	**CHARLESTON, SOUTH CAROLINA SERIES**		
94	CHARLESTON HORSE CARRIAGE CO.	200	20.00	20.00
94	DOCK STREET THEATRE	200	48.00	48.00
94	GAZEBO AT THE BATTERY	200	20.00	20.00
94	PINEAPPLE FOUNTAIN	200	20.00	20.00
95	CHARLESTON OLD FIREHOUSE	200	50.00	50.00
95	CITADEL CHAPEL, THE	200	52.00	52.00
95	PORGY & BESS CATFISH ROW	200	50.00	50.00
	J. BENSON		**SIGNATURE SERIES**	
92	CITADEL BARRACKS, THE	200	50.00	50.00
92	ST. PHILIP'S CHURCH	200	48.00	60.00
92	SWAN HOUSE, THE	200	52.00	60.00
93	COLLEGE OF CHARLESTON	200	50.00	50.00
93	MIDDLETON PLANTATION	200	50.00	50.00
93	NO. 2 MEETING ST. INN	200	48.00	48.00
93	PINK HOUSE, THE	200	42.00	42.00
93	RAINBOW ROW	RT	65.00	200.00
93	ST. MICHAEL'S CHURCH	200	48.00	48.00
94	HOUSE OF CHARLESTON	200	48.00	48.00
94	MARKET HALL	200	48.00	48.00
94	MORRIS ISLAND LIGHTHOUSE	200	46.00	46.00
94	RUTLEDGE HOUSE, THE	200	48.00	48.00
94	WREN'S NEST, THE	200	52.00	52.00
95	ADVENT EPISCOPAL CHURCH	200	48.00	48.00
95	FIRST BAPTIST CHURCH	200	50.00	50.00
95	HUNTER HOUSE, THE	200	52.00	52.00
95	LIGHTHOUSE ON LITTLE CUMBERLAND ISLAND	200	46.00	46.00
95	LITTLE CUMBERLAND LIGHTHOUSE	200	48.00	48.00
95	MARIETTA COBB MUSEUM OF ART	200	50.00	50.00
95	MORGAN COUNTY COURTHOUSE	200	56.00	56.00
95	OLD CARTOW CO. COURTHOUSE	200	52.00	52.00
95	OLD U.S. POST OFFICE (BARTOW)	200	48.00	48.00
95	OLD WEST CHEROKEE HIGH SCHOOL	200	52.00	52.00
95	ST. MARY'S CATHOLIC CHURCH	200	46.00	46.00
95	STILESBOROUGH ACADEMY	200	48.00	48.00
95	TABERNACLE BAPTIST CHURCH	200	50.00	50.00
95	TRINITY UNITED METHODIST CHURCH	200	52.00	52.00
95	UHARLEE COVERED BRIDGE	200	52.00	52.00
96	ALTOONA DUMP	200	54.00	54.00
96	CARTERSVILLE FIRE STATION NO. 1	200	50.00	50.00
96	FIRST METHODIST CHURCH-MADISON	200	52.00	52.00
96	MADISON BAPTIST CHURCH	200	50.00	50.00
96	MADISON PRESBYTERIAN CHURCH	200	48.00	48.00
96	ROBIN NEST	200	52.00	52.00
96	SKYLINE OF ATLANTA	200	70.00	70.00
97	AMELIA ISLAND LIGHTHOUSE	200	46.00	46.00
97	HILTON HEAD LIGHTHOUSE	200	46.00	46.00
97	LIGHTHOUSE TYBEE ISLAND	200	46.00	46.00
97	ST. SIMON'S LIGHTHOUSE	200	46.00	46.00
	J. BENSON		**SOUTH CAROLINA SERIES**	
94	FIRST BAPTIST CHURCH OF BATESBURG	500	48.00	48.00
94	L. B. HAYNES CHAPEL	200	48.00	48.00
94	ST. JOHN'S UNITED METHODIST CHURCH	200	48.00	48.00
94	UNITED METHODIST CHURCH, LEESVILLE	200	48.00	48.00
95	PRESBYTERIAN CHURCH, LEESVILLE/BATESBURG	200	48.00	48.00

JEFFREY SCOTT CO.

YR	NAME	LIMIT	ISSUE	TREND
	*		**LIGHTHOUSE POINT**	
94	ADMIRALTY HEAD	15000	50.00	55.00
94	BOSTON HARBOR	15000	40.00	44.00
94	CAPE HATTERAS	15000	40.00	50.00
94	CHICAGO HARBOR	15000	40.00	46.00
94	KEY WEST	15000	45.00	47.00
94	OLD MACKINAC POINT	15000	45.00	49.00
94	POINT VICENTE	15000	40.00	44.00
94	PORTLAND BREAKWATER	15000	40.00	40.00
94	SPLIT ROCK	15000	45.00	49.00
94	ST. AUGUSTINE	15000	50.00	52.00
94	ST. SIMONS	15000	50.00	55.00
94	WEST QUODDY HEAD	15000	45.00	48.00

JOHN HINE STUDIOS LTD.

YR	NAME	LIMIT	ISSUE	TREND
	M. WIDEMAN		**AMERICAN COLLECTION**	
89	BAND STAND	RT	90.00	100.00
89	BARBER SHOP	RT	40.00	44.00
89	BLOCKHOUSE, THE	RT	25.00	35.00
89	CAJUN COTTAGE	RT	50.00	70.00
89	CALIFORNIA WINERY	RT	180.00	230.00
89	CHERRY HILL SCHOOL	RT	45.00	70.00
89	COLONIAL WELLHOUSE	RT	15.00	32.00
89	DOG HOUSE	RT	10.00	30.00

YR	NAME	LIMIT	ISSUE	TREND
89	FORTY-NINER CABIN	RT	50.00	70.00
89	GARCONNIERE	RT	25.00	42.00
89	GINGERBREAD HOUSE, THE	RT	60.00	75.00
89	HACIENDA	RT	51.00	56.00
89	HAUNTED HOUSE	RT	100.00	110.00
89	HAWAIIAN GRASS HUT	RT	45.00	50.00
89	KING WILLIAM TAVERN	RT	99.00	168.00
89	KISSING BRIDGE, THE	RT	50.00	58.00
89	LOG CABIN, THE	RT	45.00	58.00
89	MAPLE SUGAR SHACK, THE	RT	50.00	58.00
89	MISSION, THE	RT	99.00	110.00
89	NEW ENGLAND CHURCH, THE	RT	79.00	96.00
89	NEW ENGLAND LIGHTHOUSE	RT	99.00	125.00
89	OCTAGONAL HOUSE	RT	40.00	55.00
89	OLD MILL, THE	RT	100.00	115.00
89	OPERA HOUSE, THE	RT	89.00	100.00
89	OUT HOUSE, THE	RT	15.00	24.00
89	OXBOW SALOON	RT	90.00	125.00
89	PACIFIC LIGHTHOUSE, THE	RT	89.00	105.00
89	PLANTATION HOUSE	RT	119.00	168.00
89	PRAIRIE FORGE	RT	65.00	90.00
89	RAILHEAD INN	RT	250.00	295.00
89	RIVER BELL, THE	RT	99.00	110.00
89	SEASIDE COTTAGE	RT	225.00	275.00
89	SIERRA MINE	RT	120.00	150.00
89	SOD HOUSE	RT	40.00	55.00
89	STAR COTTAGE	RT	30.00	45.00
89	SWEETHEART COTTAGE	RT	45.00	70.00
89	TOBACCONIST	RT	45.00	48.00
89	TOWN HALL	RT	129.00	125.00
89	TREE HOUSE	RT	45.00	50.00
89	WISTERIA	RT	15.00	28.00
91	CHURCH IN THE DALE	RT	130.00	144.00
91	DESERT STORM TENT	RT	75.00	75.00
91	FIRE STATION	RT	160.00	176.00
91	JOE'S SERVICE STATION	RT	90.00	100.00
91	MILK HOUSE	RT	20.00	22.00
91	MO AT WORK	RT	35.00	35.00
91	MOE'S DINER	RT	100.00	300.00
91	PAUL REVERE'S HOUSE	RT	90.00	90.00
92	GRAIN ELEVATOR	RT	110.00	110.00
92	NEWSSTAND	RT	30.00	30.00
92	TELEPHONE BOOTH	RT	16.00	16.00
92	TOPPER'S DRIVE-IN	RT	120.00	120.00
92	VILLAGE MERCANTILE	RT	60.00	60.00

M. COOPER — GREAT BRITISH PUBS

YR	NAME	LIMIT	ISSUE	TREND
89	BELL, THE	RT	80.00	104.00
89	BLACK SWAN	RT	80.00	78.00
89	BLUE BELL	RT	58.00	58.00
89	COACH & HORSES	RT	80.00	80.00
89	CROWN INN, THE	RT	80.00	117.00
89	DICKENS INN	RT	100.00	100.00
89	DIRTY DUCK	RT	25.00	25.00
89	EAGLE, THE	RT	35.00	35.00
89	FALKLAND ARMS	RT	25.00	25.00
89	FALSTAFF, THE	RT	35.00	35.00
89	FEATHERS, THE	RT	200.00	200.00
89	GEORGE & PILGRIMS	RT	25.00	25.00
89	GEORGE SOMERSET	RT	100.00	100.00
89	GEORGE, THE	RT	58.00	58.00
89	GREEN MAN, THE	RT	*	80.00
89	GRENADIER	RT	25.00	25.00
89	HAWKESHEAD	RT	25.00	900.00
89	JAMAICA INN	RT	40.00	40.00
89	KING'S ARMS	RT	28.00	28.00
89	LION, THE	RT	58.00	58.00
89	LYGON ARMS	RT	35.00	35.00
89	MONTAGUE ARMS	RT	58.00	78.00
89	OLD BRIDGE HOUSE	RT	38.00	38.00
89	OLD BULL INN	RT	88.00	88.00
89	PLOUGH, THE	RT	28.00	28.00
89	SHERLOCK HOLMES	RT	100.00	98.00
89	SMITH'S ARMS	RT	28.00	28.00
89	SUFFOLK BULL	RT	35.00	35.00
89	SWAN, THE	RT	35.00	35.00
89	WHEATSHEAF	RT	35.00	35.00
89	WHITE HORSE	RT	40.00	40.00
89	WHITE TOWER	RT	35.00	35.00
89	YE GRAPES	RT	88.00	105.00
89	YE OLD SPOTTED HORSE	RT	80.00	150.00

C. LAWRENCE — MUSHROOMS

YR	NAME	LIMIT	ISSUE	TREND
89	COBBLERS, THE	2500	265.00	320.00
89	CONSTABLES, THE	2500	200.00	200.00
89	ELDERS OF MUSHROOM, THE	2500	175.00	200.00
89	GIFT SHOP, THE	2500	350.00	475.00

YR	NAME	LIMIT	ISSUE	TREND
89	MINISTRY, THE	2500	185.00	245.00
89	MUSH HOSPITAL FOR MALINGERERS, THE	2500	250.00	325.00
89	PRINCESS PALACE, THE	750	600.00	840.00
89	ROYAL BANK OF MUSHLAND	2500	235.00	295.00

J. HERBERT — **SHOEMAKER'S DREAM**

YR	NAME	LIMIT	ISSUE	TREND
91	BABY BOOTY (BLUE)	OP	45.00	45.00
91	BABY BOOTY (PINK)	OP	45.00	45.00
91	CASTLE BOOT	OP	55.00	55.00
91	CHAPEL, THE	OP	55.00	55.00
91	CLOCKTOWER BOOT, THE	OP	60.00	60.00
91	CROOKED BOOT, THE	OP	35.00	35.00
91	GATE LODGE, THE	OP	65.00	65.00
91	JESTER BOOT, THE	OP	29.00	29.00
91	RIVER SHOE COTTAGE	OP	55.00	55.00
91	ROSIE'S COTTAGE	OP	40.00	40.00
91	SHOEMAKER'S PALACE	OP	50.00	50.00
91	TAVERN BOOT	OP	55.00	55.00
91	WATERMILL BOOT	OP	60.00	60.00
91	WINDMILL BOOT	OP	65.00	65.00
92	CHRISTMAS BOOT	OP	55.00	55.00
92	CLOWN BOOT	OP	45.00	45.00
92	GOLF SHOE, THE	OP	35.00	35.00
92	SPORTS SHOE, THE	OP	35.00	35.00
92	UPSIDE DOWN BOOT	OP	45.00	45.00
92	WISHING WELL SHOE	OP	32.00	32.00

JP EDITIONS
*

ASPECT OF WINDSOR

YR	NAME	LIMIT	ISSUE	TREND
92	NORMAN GATE	100	270.00	2000.00
93	MARBECK'S	100	330.00	1500.00
93	SALISBURY TOWER	100	300.00	1500.00
94	CURFEW TOWER	100	315.00	1500.00

P. GATES — **CASTLES OF ENGLAND**

92	HEVER CASTLE	250	350.00	900.00
92	SCOTNEY CASTLE	250	350.00	1100.00

P. GATES — **CASTLES OF GREAT BRITAIN**

94	GRAIGIEVAR CASTLE	400	390.00	410.00

P. GATES — **CASTLES OF WALES**

94	CALDICOT CASTLE	400	380.00	400.00
94	CASTELL COCH	400	420.00	550.00

P. GATES — **GATE HOUSE COLLECTION**

93	GUILDFORD LODGE	400	420.00	440.00

GATES OF WARWICK

92	EAST GATE	100	210.00	2000.00
92	NORTH GATE	100	280.00	2000.00
92	SOUTH GATE	100	295.00	2000.00
93	WEST GATE	100	350.00	2100.00

P. GATES — **GREAT ENGLISH HOMES**

94	GAINSBOROUGH HALL	450	420.00	500.00

P. GATES — **UNIVERSITY BUILDINGS**

92	RADCLIFFE CAMERA	250	295.00	875.00
93	GATE OF HONOUR	250	295.00	600.00

LILLIPUT LANE LTD.
*

A YEAR IN AN ENGLISH GARDEN COLLECTION

YR	NAME	LIMIT	ISSUE	TREND
94	AUTUMN HUES	RT	85.00	85.00
94	WINTER WONDER	RT	85.00	85.00
95	SPRING GLORY	RT	120.00	85.00
95	SUMMER IMPRESSIONS	RT	120.00	85.00

* — **ALLEGIANCE COLLECTION**

97	HOME OF THE BRAVE	*	80.00	80.00
97	I PLEDGE ALLEGIANCE	*	80.00	80.00
97	IN REMEMBRANCE	*	80.00	80.00
97	ONE NATION UNDER GOD	*	80.00	80.00

R. DAY — **ALLEGIANCE COLLECTION**

98	BY DAWN'S EARLY LIGHT	OP	70.00	70.00
98	FOURTH OF JULY	1776	70.00	70.00
98	I'LL BE HOME FOR CHRISTMAS	OP	75.00	75.00
98	STARS & STRIPES FOREVER	OP	75.00	75.00

D. TATE — **AMERICAN COLLECTION**

84	ADOBE CHURCH	RT	23.00	1040.00
84	ADOBE VILLAGE	RT	60.00	1950.00
84	CAPE COD	RT	23.00	650.00
84	COUNTRY CHURCH	RT	95.00	88.00
84	COVERED BRIDGE	RT	23.00	2000.00
84	FORGE BARN	RT	23.00	650.00
84	GENERAL STORE	RT	23.00	675.00
84	GRIST MILL	RT	23.00	500.00
84	LIGHTHOUSE	RT	23.00	975.00
84	LOG CABIN	RT	23.00	910.00
84	MIDWEST BARN	RT	23.00	374.00
84	SAN FRANCISCO HOUSE	RT	23.00	910.00
84	WALLACE STATION	RT	23.00	910.00

YR NAME	LIMIT	ISSUE	TREND
R. DAY		**AMERICAN LANDMARKS**	
89 COUNTRYSIDE BARN	RT	75.00	88.00
89 FALLS MILL	RT	130.00	131.00
89 MAIL POUCH BARN	RT	75.00	108.00
90 COUNTRY CHURCH	RT	83.00	95.00
90 COVERED MEMORIES	RT	110.00	134.00
90 GREAT POINT LIGHT	OP	50.00	82.00
90 HOMETOWN DEPOT	RT	68.00	82.00
90 PEPSI COLA BARN	RT	87.00	215.00
90 PIONEER BARN	RT	30.00	59.00
90 RIVERSIDE CHAPEL	RT	83.00	111.00
90 ROADSIDE COOLERS	RT	75.00	105.00
90 SIGN OF THE TIMES	RT	34.00	43.00
91 FIRE HOUSE 1	RT	100.00	85.00
91 RAMBLING ROSE	RT	60.00	60.00
91 SCHOOL DAYS	RT	75.00	60.00
91 VICTORIANA	RT	295.00	345.00
92 16.9 CENTS PER GALLON	OP	150.00	150.00
92 GOLD MINERS' CLAIM	RT	110.00	110.00
92 HOME SWEET HOME	RT	120.00	95.00
92 SMALL TOWN LIBRARY	RT	130.00	130.00
92 WINNIE'S PLACE	RT	395.00	446.00
93 SEE ROCK CITY	RT	35.00	35.00
93 SHAVE AND A HAIRCUT	RT	95.00	95.00
93 SIMPLY AMISH	RT	110.00	110.00
94 BIRDSONG, THE	RT	85.00	117.00
94 FRESH BREAD	*	95.00	95.00
94 HARVEST MILL	3500	395.00	390.00
94 HOLY NIGHT	*	170.00	170.00
94 SPRING VICTORIAN	RT	170.00	170.00
95 AFTERNOON TEA	RT	495.00	495.00
98 LOBSTER AT THE PIER	OP	90.00	90.00
98 SEEK AND FIND	OP	80.00	80.00
R. DAY		**AN AMERICAN JOURNEY**	
98 DAY DREAMS	OP	75.00	75.00
98 DOG DAYS OF SUMMER	OP	55.00	55.00
98 LACE HOUSE	OP	85.00	85.00
98 MORNING HAS BROKEN	OP	85.00	85.00
98 SAFE HARBOR	1783	75.00	75.00
98 VICTORIAN ELEGANCE	OP	130.00	130.00
*		**ANNIVERSARY SPECIAL**	
92 HONEYSUCKLE COTTAGE 1992	RT	195.00	124.00
93 COTMAN COTTAGE	RT	220.00	186.00
94 WATERMEADOWS	RT	189.00	156.00
95 GERTRUDE'S GARDEN	RT	192.00	192.00
96 CRUCK END	OP	130.00	130.00
97 SUMMER DAYS	*	165.00	165.00
98 SHADES OF SUMMER	YR	170.00	170.00
*		**BLAISE HAMLET CLASSICS**	
93 CIRCULAR COTTAGE	RT	95.00	140.00
93 DIAL COTTAGE	RT	95.00	140.00
93 DIAMOND COTTAGE	RT	95.00	140.00
93 DOUBLE COTTAGE	RT	95.00	163.00
93 JASMINE COTTAGE	RT	95.00	137.00
93 OAK COTTAGE	RT	95.00	150.00
93 ROSE COTTAGE	RT	95.00	195.00
93 SWEET BRIAR COTTAGE	RT	95.00	147.00
93 VINE COTTAGE	RT	95.00	147.00
D. TATE		**BLAISE HAMLET COLLECTION**	
89 CIRCULAR COTTAGE	RT	110.00	135.00
89 DIAMOND COTTAGE	RT	110.00	135.00
89 OAK COTTAGE	RT	110.00	135.00
90 DIAL COTTAGE	RT	110.00	135.00
90 SWEET BRIAR COTTAGE	RT	110.00	135.00
90 VINE COTTAGE	RT	110.00	128.00
91 DOUBLE COTTAGE	RT	200.00	200.00
91 JASMINE COTTAGE	RT	140.00	140.00
91 ROSE COTTAGE	RT	140.00	189.00
*		**BRITISH COLLECTION**	
98 BOWBEAMS	OP	180.00	180.00
98 BWTHYN BACH GWYN	OP	35.00	35.00
98 COWSLIP COTTAGE	OP	120.00	120.00
98 GOLDEN MEMORIES	OP	90.00	90.00
98 HUBBLE BUBBLE	OP	35.00	35.00
98 LADY JANE'S COTTAGE	OP	35.00	35.00
98 MEDWAY MANOR	OP	120.00	120.00
98 NIGHTINGALE COTTAGE	OP	25.00	25.00
98 OLD FORGE, THE	OP	55.00	55.00
98 PARSON'S RETREAT	OP	90.00	90.00
98 PASTURES NEW	OP	350.00	350.00
98 PINEAPPLE HOUSE, THE	OP	60.00	60.00
98 PUDDLE DUCK	OP	80.00	80.00
98 SCOTCH MIST	OP	70.00	70.00
98 STONEMASON, THE	OP	120.00	120.00
98 TUPPENY BUN	OP	35.00	35.00

YR	NAME	LIMIT	ISSUE	TREND
*			**CHRISTMAS COLLECTION**	
92	CRANBERRY COTTAGE	RT	47.00	59.00
92	HOLLYTREE HOUSE	RT	47.00	52.00
93	GINGERBREAD SHOP, THE	RT	35.00	35.00
93	PARTRIDGE COTTAGE	RT	35.00	35.00
93	ST. JOSEPH'S CHURCH	RT	50.00	108.00
94	RING O BELLS	RT	35.00	35.00
94	ST. JOSEPH'S SCHOOL	RT	35.00	117.00
94	VICARAGE, THE	RT	35.00	134.00
D. TATE			**CHRISTMAS COLLECTION**	
92	CHESTNUT COTTAGE	RT	47.00	52.00
*			**CHRISTMAS IN AMERICA**	
96	HOME FOR THE HOLIDAY	2596	495.00	455.00
97	LET HEAVEN AND NATURE SING	*	158.00	158.00
97	TO GRANDMOTHER'S HOUSE WE GO	*	158.00	158.00
*			**CHRISTMAS LODGE**	
92	HIGHLAND LODGE	RT	180.00	195.00
93	EAMONT LODGE	RT	185.00	208.00
94	SNOWDON LODGE	RT	175.00	179.00
95	KERRY LODGE	RT	160.00	160.00
*			**CHRISTMAS SPECIAL**	
96	ST. STEPHEN'S CHURCH/1ST SERIES	OP	100.00	100.00
97	CHRISTMAS PARTY	*	150.00	150.00
98	FROSTY MORNING	YR	150.00	150.00
*			**COCA-COLA COUNTRY**	
96	A CHERRY COKE-JUST THE PRESCRIPTION	*	100.00	100.00
96	COUNTRY FRESH PICKINS	*	160.00	160.00
96	FILL'ER UP AND CHECK THE OIL	*	130.00	130.00
96	HAZARDS OF THE ROAD	*	55.00	55.00
96	HOOK, LINE AND SINKER	*	100.00	100.00
96	WE'VE GOT IT (OR THEY DON'T MAKE IT)	*	100.00	100.00
97	COUNTRY CANVAS	*	16.00	16.00
97	MMMM...JUST LIKE HOME	*	130.00	130.00
97	OH BY GOSH, BY GOLLY	*	90.00	90.00
97	SATURDAY NIGHT JIVE	*	100.00	100.00
97	THE LUNCH LINE	*	42.00	42.00
97	WET YOUR WHISTLE	*	42.00	42.00
R. DAY			**COCA-COLA COUNTRY**	
98	MILK FOR MOM & A COKE FOR ME	OP	95.00	95.00
98	THEY DON'T MAKE 'EM LIKE THEY USED TO	OP	70.00	70.00
D. SIMPSON			**COUNTRYSIDE SCENE PLAQUES**	
89	BOTTLE KILN	RT	50.00	50.00
89	CORNISH TIN MINE	RT	50.00	50.00
89	COUNTRY INN	RT	50.00	50.00
89	CUMBRIAN FARMHOUSE	RT	50.00	50.00
89	LIGHTHOUSE	RT	50.00	50.00
89	NORFOLK WINDMILL	RT	50.00	50.00
89	OASTHOUSE	RT	50.00	50.00
89	OLD SMITTY	RT	50.00	50.00
89	PARISH CHURCH	RT	50.00	50.00
89	POST OFFICE	RT	50.00	50.00
89	VILLAGE SCHOOL	RT	50.00	50.00
89	WATERMILL	RT	50.00	78.00
*			**DISNEYANA CONVENTION**	
95	BO-PEEP TEA ROOMS	RT	85.00	85.00
95	KENDAL TEA HOUSE	*	85.00	85.00
95	NEW FOREST TEAS	*	120.00	120.00
96	SWALESDALE TEAS	*	85.00	85.00
D. TATE			**DUTCH COLLECTION**	
91	AAN DE AMSTEL	RT	79.00	60.00
91	BEGIJNHOF	RT	55.00	35.00
91	BLOEMENMARKT	RT	79.00	60.00
91	DE BRANDERIJ	RT	73.00	55.00
91	DE DIAMANTAIR	RT	79.00	60.00
91	DE PEPERMOLEN	RT	55.00	35.00
91	DE WOLHANDELAAR	RT	73.00	55.00
91	DE ZIJDEWEVER	RT	79.00	60.00
91	REMBRANT VAN RIJN	RT	120.00	85.00
91	ROZENGRACHT	RT	73.00	50.00
*			**ENGLISH COTTAGES**	
87	CLOCKMAKERS COTTAGE	RT	40.00	260.00
87	STREET SCENE #1	RT	40.00	350.00
87	STREET SCENE #10	RT	45.00	290.00
87	STREET SCENE #2	RT	45.00	350.00
87	STREET SCENE #3	RT	45.00	350.00
87	STREET SCENE #4	RT	45.00	290.00
87	STREET SCENE #5	RT	40.00	290.00
87	STREET SCENE #6	RT	40.00	290.00
87	STREET SCENE #7	RT	40.00	290.00
87	STREET SCENE #8	RT	40.00	290.00
87	STREET SCENE #9	RT	45.00	98.00
88	BROCKBANK	RT	58.00	88.00
92	CLEY-NEXT-THE-SEA	RT	725.00	637.00
92	WHEYSIDE COTTAGE	RT	47.00	35.00

YR	NAME	LIMIT	ISSUE	TREND
93	BIRDLIP BOTTOM	RT	50.00	50.00
93	CATS COOMBE COTTAGE	RT	95.00	98.00
93	FOXGLOVE FIELDS	RT	85.00	98.00
93	JUNK AND DISORDERLY	RT	110.00	110.00
93	MARIGOLD MEADOW	RT	80.00	80.00
93	OLD MOTHER HUBBARD	RT	120.00	120.00
93	PURBECK STORES	RT	35.00	35.00
93	STOCKLEBECK MILL	RT	195.00	195.00
93	STRADLING PRIORY	RT	85.00	111.00
93	TITWILLOW COTTAGE	RT	45.00	45.00
94	APPLEJACK COTTAGE	*	35.00	35.00
94	CAMOMILE LAWN	RT	90.00	98.00
94	CREEL COTTAGE	RT	35.00	52.00
94	ELM COTTAGE	RT	50.00	50.00
94	LEONORA'S SECRET	RT	350.00	605.00
94	ORCHARD FARM COTTAGE	RT	110.00	110.00
94	SAFFRON HOUSE	RT	170.00	170.00
94	SPRING GATE COTTAGE	RT	95.00	95.00
94	SUNNYSIDE	RT	35.00	35.00
94	SWEET PEA COTTAGE	RT	35.00	35.00
94	TEA CADDY COTTAGE	RT	60.00	60.00
94	TIRED TIMBERS	RT	60.00	60.00
94	TWO HOOTS	RT	55.00	55.00
94	WATERSIDE MILL	*	50.00	65.00
95	BUTTON DOWN	RT	30.00	30.00
95	CHERRY BLOSSOM	RT	128.00	95.00
95	CHIPPING COOMBE	RT	525.00	553.00
95	DUCKDOWN COTTAGE	RT	95.00	70.00
95	LADYBIRD COTTAGE	RT	35.00	35.00
95	LARKRISE	RT	45.00	45.00
95	LAZY DAYS	RT	60.00	60.00
95	LITTLE HAY	*	50.00	50.00
95	LITTLE SMITHY	RT	60.00	60.00
95	MILESTONE COTTAGE	RT	35.00	35.00
95	PENNY'S POST	RT	50.00	50.00
95	PIPIT TELL	RT	64.00	50.00
95	RUSTLINGS, THE	RT	128.00	95.00
95	TRANQUILITY	RT	425.00	520.00
96	ANCHOR, THE	*	85.00	85.00
96	BIRCHWOOD COTTAGE	RT	55.00	55.00
96	BLUE BOAR	OP	85.00	85.00
96	BLUEBELL FARM	RT	250.00	250.00
96	BOXWOOD COTTAGE		30.00	30.00
96	CALENDAR COTTAGE	*	55.00	55.00
96	CHALK DOWN	*	35.00	35.00
96	CRADLE COTTAGE	OP	100.00	100.00
96	CRISPIN COTTAGE	*	50.00	50.00
96	DALESMAN, THE	RT	95.00	95.00
96	FIDDLER'S FOLLY	*	35.00	35.00
96	FLOWERPOTS	*	55.00	55.00
96	FRY DAYS	*	70.00	70.00
96	FUCHSIA COTTAGE	OP	30.00	30.00
96	GOSSIP GATE	OP	170.00	170.00
96	GULLIVER'S GATE	RT	35.00	65.00
96	HARRIET COTTAGE	*	85.00	85.00
96	HONEY POT COTTAGE	OP	60.00	60.00
96	LITTLE LUPINS	OP	40.00	40.00
96	LOXDALE COTTAGE	OP	35.00	35.00
96	POTTER'S BECK	*	35.00	35.00
96	RAILWAY COTTAGE	OP	60.00	60.00
96	REFLECTIONS OF JADE	RT	350.00	350.00
96	ROSEMARY COTTAGE	OP	70.00	70.00
96	SORE PAWS	*	70.00	70.00
96	SPINDLES, THE	RT	85.00	85.00
96	ST. JOHN THE BAPTIST	RT	75.00	75.00
96	WINDY RIDGE	RT	50.00	50.00
97	APPLEBY EAST	*	70.00	70.00
97	BEST FRIENDS	*	25.00	25.00
97	GOLDEN YEARS	*	25.00	25.00
97	GRANNY'S BONNET	*	25.00	25.00
97	OUT OF THE STORM	RT	1,250.00	1250.00
97	ROSE BOUQUET	*	25.00	25.00
97	SWEET WILLIAM	RT	25.00	25.00
97	WALTON LODGE	*	*	
97	YORKVALE COTTAGE	*	56.00	56.00
M. ADKINSON			**ENGLISH COTTAGES**	
87	FOUR SEASONS	OP	70.00	75.00
87	SADDLERS INN	RT	50.00	59.00
87	SECRET GARDEN	RT	145.00	196.00
D. HALL			**ENGLISH COTTAGES**	
86	COBBLERS COTTAGE	RT	42.00	69.00
C. HANNENBERGER			**ENGLISH COTTAGES**	
88	SHIP INN	RT	210.00	241.00
T. RAINE			**ENGLISH COTTAGES**	
86	TUDOR COURT	RT	260.00	273.00

YR	NAME	LIMIT	ISSUE	TREND
87	BEACON HEIGHTS	RT	125.00	134.00
87	GABLES, THE	RT	145.00	143.00
D. TATE			**ENGLISH COTTAGES**	
*	BURNSIDE COTTAGE	RT	30.00	520.00
82	ACORN COTTAGE	RT	40.00	52.00
82	APRIL COTTAGE	RT	*	56.00
82	BRIDGE HOUSE	RT	15.95	114.00
82	DALE HOUSE (MINI)	RT	25.00	1105.00
82	DRAPERS	RT	15.95	325.00
82	HONEYSUCKLE	RT	45.00	124.00
82	LAKESIDE HOUSE	RT	40.00	1040.00
82	OAK LODGE	RT	40.00	98.00
82	OLD MINE	RT	15.95	2500.00
82	STONE COTTAGE	RT	40.00	325.00
82	SUSSEX MILL	RT	25.00	585.00
83	ANNE HATHAWAY'S MOLD I	RT	40.00	65.00
83	CASTLE STREET	RT	130.00	416.00
83	COACH HOUSE (MINI)	RT	100.00	1170.00
83	COOPERS	RT	15.00	375.00
83	HOLLY COTTAGE	RT	43.00	62.00
83	MILLERS	RT	15.00	130.00
83	MINERS COTTAGE	RT	15.00	650.00
83	OLD POST OFFICE, THE	RT	35.00	780.00
83	RED LION INN	RT	125.00	335.00
83	THATCHERS REST	RT	185.00	225.00
83	TOLL HOUSE	RT	15.00	130.00
83	TROUTBECK FARM	RT	125.00	325.00
83	TUCK SHOP	RT	35.00	748.00
83	WARWICK HALL	RT	185.00	1999.00
83	WILLIAM SHAKESPEARE'S BIRTHPLACE	RT	130.00	147.00
83	WOODCUTTERS	RT	15.00	117.00
84	CLIBURN SCHOOL	RT	23.00	7150.00
84	DALE FARM	RT	30.00	975.00
84	DOVE COTTAGE	RT	35.00	79.00
84	OLD SCHOOL HOUSE	RT	25.00	1170.00
84	TINTAGEL	RT	40.00	195.00
85	BERMUDA COTTAGE	RT	29.00	325.00
85	BRONTE PARSONAGE	RT	72.00	124.00
85	CLARE COTTAGE	RT	30.00	50.00
85	FISHERMANS COTTAGE	RT	30.00	79.00
85	KENTISH OAST HOUSE	RT	55.00	65.00
85	MORETON MANOR	RT	55.00	79.00
85	OLD CURIOSITY SHOP, THE	RT	63.00	143.00
85	OSTLERS KEEP	RT	55.00	85.00
85	SAWREY GILL	RT	30.00	52.00
85	ST. MARY'S	RT	40.00	104.00
85	WATERMILL	RT	40.00	72.00
86	BAY VIEW	RT	40.00	91.00
86	DALE HEAD	RT	75.00	88.00
86	FARRIERS	RT	40.00	56.00
86	GULLIVER	RT	65.00	845.00
86	SCROLL ON THE WALL	RT	55.00	130.00
86	SEVEN DWARF'S COTTAGE	RT	*	975.00
86	SPRING BANK	RT	42.00	69.00
86	THREE FEATHERS	RT	115.00	176.00
87	CLOVER COTTAGE	RT	28.00	39.00
87	HOLME DYKE	RT	50.00	69.00
87	INGLEWOOD	RT	28.00	36.00
87	IZAAK WALTON'S COTTAGE	RT	75.00	108.00
87	KEEPERS LODGE	RT	75.00	98.00
87	MAGPIE COTTAGE	RT	70.00	53.00
87	RIVERVIEW	RT	28.00	50.00
87	RYDAL VIEW	RT	220.00	264.00
87	STONEYBECK	RT	45.00	52.00
87	SUMMER HAZE	OP	90.00	117.00
87	TANNER'S COTTAGE	RT	28.00	56.00
87	WEALDEN HOUSE	RT	125.00	163.00
88	BREDON HOUSE	RT	145.00	163.00
88	BROOKBANK	RT	58.00	60.00
88	CROWN INN	RT	120.00	140.00
88	PARGETTER'S RETREAT	RT	75.00	72.00
88	RISING SUN	RT	58.00	72.00
88	ROYAL OAK INN	RT	145.00	208.00
88	SAXON COTTAGE	RT	245.00	205.00
88	SMALLEST INN	RT	43.00	75.00
88	ST. MARK'S CHURCH	RT	75.00	111.00
88	SWAN INN	RT	120.00	163.00
88	SWIFT HOLLOW	RT	75.00	62.00
89	ANNE HATHAWAY'S COTTAGE II	RT	130.00	124.00
89	ASH NOOK	RT	48.00	88.00
89	BEEHIVE COTTAGE	RT	73.00	101.00
89	BRIARY, THE	RT	48.00	85.00
89	BUTTERWICK	RT	53.00	39.00
89	CHILTERN MILL	RT	88.00	104.00
89	CHINE COT	RT	36.00	39.00

Kenilworth Castle (*Dickens'*
Village) *was available for $40 to*
collectors who were purchasing
$100 worth of Department 56
merchandise.

Crater Lake Lodge *by*
Michael Morris of
Genesis Designs was
issued in 1995 as part of
the "Great Lodges of
America" series.

Produced by Hawthorne,
Ye Very Olde Fruitcake
Shoppe *from the Wysocki*
Small Town Christmas
Collection is 3-1/4 inches
high and retails for $39.95.

C. Fletcher Public House (*Dickens'*
Village) *was the fourth limited edition to be*
produced by Department 56.

YR	NAME	LIMIT	ISSUE	TREND
89	FIVEWAYS	RT	43.00	65.00
89	GREENSTED CHURCH	RT	73.00	111.00
89	HELMERE	RT	65.00	72.00
89	MAYFLOWER HOUSE	RT	88.00	195.00
89	ST. LAWRENCE CHURCH	RT	110.00	85.00
89	ST. PETER'S COVE	RT	1,375.00	1235.00
89	TANGLEWOOD LODGE	RT	97.00	117.00
89	TITMOUSE COTTAGE	RT	93.00	131.00
89	VICTORIA COTTAGE	RT	53.00	34.00
89	WIGHT COTTAGE	RT	53.00	78.00
89	WILLIAM SHAKESPEARE'S BIRTHPLACE	OP	130.00	111.00
90	BRAMBLE COTTAGE	RT	55.00	78.00
90	BUTTERCUP COTTAGE	RT	40.00	56.00
90	CHERRY COTTAGE	RT	34.00	46.00
90	CONVENT IN THE WOODS	RT	175.00	231.00
90	KING'S ARMS, THE	OP	450.00	472.00
90	MRS. PINKERTON'S POST OFFICE	RT	73.00	72.00
90	OLDE YORK TOLL	RT	83.00	156.00
90	OTTER REACH	RT	34.00	56.00
90	PERIWINKLE COTTAGE	RT	165.00	208.00
90	ROBIN'S GATE	RT	34.00	39.00
90	ROWAN LODGE	RT	50.00	91.00
90	RUNSWICK HOUSE	RT	63.00	55.00
90	STRAWBERRY COTTAGE	RT	36.00	35.00
90	SULGRAVE MANOR	RT	120.00	150.00
91	ANNE OF CLEVES	RT	250.00	250.00
91	ARMADA HOUSE	RT	175.00	163.00
91	BRIDGE HOUSE 1991	OP	25.00	20.00
91	CHATSWORTH VIEW	RT	250.00	325.00
91	DAISY COTTAGE	RT	38.00	30.00
91	DOVETAILS	RT	90.00	95.00
91	FARTHING LODGE	RT	38.00	46.00
91	FLOWER SELLERS, THE	RT	110.00	114.00
91	HOPCROFT COTTAGE	RT	120.00	111.00
91	JOHN BARLEYCORN COTTAGE	RT	130.00	111.00
91	LACE LANE	RT	90.00	111.00
91	LAPWORTH LOCK	RT	83.00	98.00
91	MICKLEGATE ANTIQUES	RT	90.00	80.00
91	MOONLIGHT COVE	RT	83.00	78.00
91	OLD SHOP AT BIGNOR	RT	215.00	195.00
91	PARADISE LODGE	RT	130.00	127.00
91	PEAR TREE HOUSE	RT	83.00	98.00
91	PRIEST'S HOUSE, THE	RT	180.00	293.00
91	PRIMROSE HILL	RT	47.00	130.00
91	SAXHAM ST. EDMUNDS	RT	1,550.00	1463.00
91	TILLERS GREEN	RT	60.00	60.00
91	VILLAGE SCHOOL	RT	120.00	120.00
91	WELLINGTON LODGE	RT	55.00	65.00
91	WITHAM DELPH	RT	110.00	98.00
92	BOW COTTAGE	RT	128.00	137.00
92	CHOCOLATE HOUSE, THE	RT	130.00	104.00
92	DERWENT-LE-DALE	OP	75.00	75.00
92	FINCHINGFIELDS	RT	90.00	78.00
92	GRANNY SMITH'S	RT	60.00	45.00
92	GRANTCHESTER MEADOWS	RT	275.00	195.00
92	HIGH GHYLL FARM	RT	360.00	325.00
92	HONEYSUCKLE COTTAGE (10TH ANNIVERSARY)	YR	195.00	179.00
92	NUTSHELL, THE	RT	75.00	65.00
92	OAKWOOD SMITHY	RT	450.00	300.00
92	PIXIE HOUSE	RT	55.00	55.00
92	PUFFIN ROW	RT	127.50	95.00
92	RUSTIC ROOF HOUSE	RT	110.00	80.00
92	WEDDING BELLS	OP	75.00	52.00
*		**ENGLISH TEA ROOM COLLECTION**		
95	BARGATE COTTAGE TEA ROOM	OP	160.00	120.00
95	GRANDMA BATTY'S TEA ROOM	OP	120.00	90.00
*		**FOUNDER'S CHOICE**		
96	ALMONRY, THE	RT	275.00	275.00
D. TATE		**FRAMED ENGLISH PLAQUES**		
90	ASHDOWN HALL	RT	60.00	60.00
90	BATTLEVIEW	RT	60.00	60.00
90	CAT SLIDE COTTAGE	RT	60.00	60.00
90	COOMBE COT	RT	60.00	60.00
90	FELL VIEW	RT	60.00	60.00
90	FLINT FIELDS	RT	60.00	60.00
90	HUNTINGTON HOUSE	RT	60.00	60.00
90	JUBILEE LODGE	RT	60.00	60.00
90	STOWSIDE	RT	60.00	60.00
90	TREVAN COVE	RT	60.00	60.00
D. TATE		**FRAMED IRISH PLAQUES**		
90	BALLYTEAG HOUSE	RT	60.00	60.00
90	CROCKUNA CROFT	RT	60.00	60.00
90	PEARSES COTTAGES	RT	60.00	60.00
90	SHANNONS BANK	RT	60.00	60.00

YR	NAME	LIMIT	ISSUE	TREND
D. TATE		**FRAMED SCOTTISH PLAQUES**		
90	BARRA BLACK HOUSE	RT	60.00	60.00
90	FIFE NESS	RT	60.00	60.00
90	KYLE POINT	RT	60.00	60.00
90	PRESTON OAT MILL	RT	60.00	60.00
D. TATE		**FRENCH COLLECTION**		
91	L'AUBERGE D'ARMORIQUE	RT	220.00	170.00
91	LA BERGERIE DU PERIGORD	RT	230.00	170.00
91	LA CABANE DYE GARDIAN	RT	55.00	45.00
91	LA CHAUMIERE DU VERGER	RT	120.00	95.00
91	LA MASELLE DE NADAILLAC	RT	130.00	95.00
91	LA PORTE SCHOENENBERG	RT	75.00	60.00
91	LE MANOIR DE CHAMPFLEURI	RT	265.00	156.00
91	LE MAS DU VIGNERON	RT	120.00	85.00
91	LE PETITE MONTMARTRE	RT	130.00	95.00
91	LOCMARIA	RT	65.00	50.00
D. TATE		**GERMAN COLLECTION**		
87	DAS GEBIRGSKIRCHLEIN	RT	120.00	120.00
87	HAUS IM RHEINLAND	RT	220.00	189.00
87	JAGHUTTE	RT	83.00	72.00
87	MEERSBURGER WEINSTUBE	RT	83.00	104.00
87	MOSELHAUS	RT	140.00	150.00
87	NURMBERGER BURGERHAUS	RT	140.00	104.00
87	SCHWARZWALDHAUS	RT	140.00	120.00
88	DAS RATHAUS	RT	140.00	140.00
88	DER FAMILIENSCHREIN	RT	53.00	90.00
88	DIE KLEINEBACKEREI	RT	68.00	101.00
92	ALTE SCHMIEDE	RT	175.00	120.00
92	DER BUCHERWURM	RT	140.00	100.00
92	ROSENGARTENHAUS	RT	120.00	90.00
92	STRANDVOGTHAUS	RT	120.00	90.00
*		**HISTORIC CASTLES OF BRITAIN**		
94	BODIAM	RT	95.00	95.00
94	CASTELL COCH	RT	120.00	120.00
94	STOKESAY	RT	85.00	85.00
95	PENKHILL CASTLE	RT	115.00	115.00
D. TATE		**IRISH COTTAGES**		
87	DONEGAL COTTAGE	RT	29.00	25.00
89	BALLYKERNE CROFT	RT	75.00	95.00
89	HEGARTY'S HOME	RT	68.00	88.00
89	KENNEDY HOMESTEAD	RT	34.00	98.00
89	KILMORE QUAY	RT	68.00	111.00
89	LIMERICK HOUSE	RT	110.00	124.00
89	MAGILLIGANS	RT	34.00	30.00
89	O'LACEY'S STORE	RT	68.00	60.00
89	PAT COHEN'S BAR	RT	110.00	144.00
89	QUIET COTTAGE	RT	73.00	114.00
89	ST. COLUMBA'S SCHOOL	RT	48.00	59.00
89	ST. KEVIN'S SCHOOL	RT	55.00	91.00
89	ST. PATRICK'S CHURCH	RT	185.00	248.00
89	THOOR BALLYLEE	RT	105.00	199.00
D. SIMPSON		**LAKELAND BRIDGE PLAQUES**		
89	AIRA FORCE	RT	35.00	35.00
89	ASHNESS BRIDGE	RT	35.00	35.00
89	BIRKS BRIDGE	RT	35.00	35.00
89	BRIDGE HOUSE	RT	35.00	60.00
89	HARTSOP PACKHORSE	RT	35.00	35.00
89	STOCKLEY BRIDGE	RT	35.00	35.00
*		**LAKELAND CHRISTMAS**		
95	LANGDALE COTTAGE	RT	48.00	48.00
95	PATTERDALE COTTAGE	RT	35.00	35.00
95	RYDAL COTTAGE	*	35.00	35.00
96	ALL SAINTS WATERMILLOCK	OP	50.00	50.00
96	BORROWDALE SCHOOL	OP	35.00	35.00
96	MILLBECK COTTAGE	OP	35.00	35.00
*		**LILLIPUT LANE COLLECTORS CLUB**		
93	CURLEW COTTAGE	RT	18.95	182.00
93	HEAVEN LEA COTTAGE	RT	150.00	134.00
94	WOODMAN'S RETREAT	RT	135.00	176.00
95	PORLOCK DOWN	RT	135.00	135.00
95	THIMBLE COTTAGE	RT	*	34.00
96	MEADOWSWEET COTTAGE	OP	110.00	110.00
96	WINNOWS	*	23.00	23.00
97	HAMPTON MANOR	*	100.00	100.00
98	KILN COTTAGE	YR	*	N/A
98	POTTERY, THE	YR	170.00	170.00
D. TATE		**LILLIPUT LANE COLLECTORS CLUB**		
86	CRENDON MANOR	RT	285.00	1300.00
86	PACKHORSE BRIDGE	RT	*	634.00
87	LITTLE LOST DOG	RT	*	699.00
87	YEW TREE FARM	RT	160.00	205.00
88	WISHING WELL	RT	*	91.00
89	WENLOCK RISE	RT	175.00	209.00
90	BRIDLE WAY	RT	100.00	121.00

YR	NAME	LIMIT	ISSUE	TREND
90	COSY CORNER	RT	*	69.00
90	DOVECOT, THE	RT	50.00	75.00
90	LAVENDER COTTAGE	RT	50.00	69.00
91	GARDENERS COTTAGE	RT	120.00	111.00
91	PUDDLEBROOK	RT	*	31.00
91	WREN COTTAGE	RT	13.95	78.00
92	FORGET-ME-NOT	RT	130.00	140.00
92	PUSSY WILLOW	RT	*	29.00
D. SIMPSON			**LONDON PLAQUES**	
89	BIG BEN	RT	40.00	40.00
89	BUCKINGHAM PALACE	RT	40.00	40.00
89	PICCADILLY CIRCUS	RT	40.00	40.00
89	TOWER BRIDGE	RT	40.00	40.00
89	TOWER OF LONDON	RT	40.00	40.00
89	TRAFALGAR SQUARE	RT	40.00	40.00
D. TATE		**ORIGINAL CHRISTMAS COLLECTION**		
88	DEER PARK HALL	RT	120.00	104.00
89	ST. NICHOLAS CHURCH	RT	130.00	117.00
90	YULETIDE INN	RT	145.00	104.00
91	OLD VICARAGE AT CHRISTMAS, THE	RT	180.00	124.00
*			**SCOTTISH COLLECTION**	
93	EDZELL SUMMER HOUSE	RT	70.00	95.00
94	LADYBANK LODGE	RT	60.00	60.00
95	AMISFIELD	RT	50.00	50.00
D. TATE			**SCOTTISH COLLECTION**	
82	CROFT, THE (WITHOUT SHEEP)	RT	29.00	1040.00
84	CROFT, THE (RENOVATED)	RT	36.00	91.00
85	BURNS COTTAGE	RT	35.00	114.00
85	PRESTON MILL	RT	45.00	50.00
87	EAST NEUK	RT	29.00	47.00
87	PRESTON MILL (RENOVATED)	OP	63.00	72.50
89	BLAIR ATHOLL	RT	275.00	312.00
89	CARRICK HOUSE	OP	48.00	35.00
89	CLAYPOTTS CASTLE	RT	72.50	88.00
89	CRAIGIEVAR CASTLE	RT	185.00	650.00
89	CULLODEN COTTAGE	OP	36.00	35.00
89	INVERLOCHIE HAME	OP	48.00	40.00
89	JOHN KNOX HOUSE	RT	68.00	117.00
89	KENMORE COTTAGE	OP	87.00	92.00
89	STOCKWELL TENEMENT	RT	63.00	70.00
90	CAWDOR CASTLE	RT	295.00	416.00
90	ELLEAN DONAN	OP	145.00	195.00
90	FISHERMANS BOTHY	OP	36.00	35.00
90	GLENLOCHIE LODGE	RT	110.00	124.00
90	HEBRIDEAN HAME	RT	55.00	85.00
90	KINLOCHNESS	OP	79.00	111.00
90	KIRKBRAE COTTAGE	RT	55.00	88.00
92	CULROSS HOUSE	RT	90.00	91.00
92	DUART CASTLE	RT	450.00	670.00
92	ERISKAY CROFT	OP	50.00	40.00
92	MAIR HAVEN	OP	47.00	35.00
A. YARRINGTON			**SCOTTISH COLLECTION**	
85	7 ST. ANDREWS SQUARE	RT	15.95	124.00
*		**SPECIAL EVENT PIECES**		
92	PLOUGHMAN'S COTTAGE	RT	75.00	108.00
93	ABERFORD GATE	RT	95.00	135.00
94	LEAGRAVE COTTAGE	RT	75.00	98.00
95	VANBRUGH LODGE	RT	60.00	60.00
96	AMBERLY ROSE	RT	45.00	45.00
97	DORMHOUSE COTTAGE	*	60.00	60.00
98	COMFORT COTTAGE	YR	50.00	50.00
D. TATE		**SPECIAL EVENT PIECES**		
89	COMMEMORATIVE MEDALLION-1989 SOUTH BEND	CL	*	105.00
90	ROWAN LODGE 1990-SOUTH BEND	RT	50.00	452.00
91	GAMEKEEPERS COTTAGE-1991 SOUTH BEND	RT	75.00	452.00
92	ASHBERRY COTTAGE-1992 SOUTH BEND	RT	*	309.00
*		**STUDLEY ROYAL COLLECTION**		
94	BANQUETING HOUSE, THE	RT	65.00	72.00
94	OCTAGON TOWER	RT	85.00	92.00
94	ST. MARY'S CHURCH	RT	115.00	104.00
94	TEMPLE OF PIETY	RT	95.00	101.00
95	FOUNTAIN'S ABBEY	RT	395.00	407.00
*			**TEA ROOMS COLLECTION**	
98	STRAWBERRY TEAS	OP	100.00	100.00
D. TATE			**UNFRAMED PLAQUES**	
89	LARGE LOWER BROCKHAMPTON	RT	120.00	120.00
89	LARGE SOMERSET SPRINGTIME	RT	130.00	130.00
89	MEDIUM COBBLE COMBE COTTAGE	RT	68.00	68.00
89	MEDIUM WISHING WELL	RT	75.00	75.00
89	SMALL STONEY WALL LEA	RT	48.00	48.00
89	SMALL WOODSIDE FARM	RT	48.00	48.00
*		**VICTORIAN SHOPS COLLECTION**		
97	APOTHECARY	*	90.00	90.00
97	BOOK SHOP	*	75.00	75.00

YR	NAME	LIMIT	ISSUE	TREND
97	HABERDASHERY	*	90.00	90.00
97	HOROLOGISH	*	75.00	75.00
97	PAWNBROKER	*	75.00	75.00
97	TAILOR	*	90.00	90.00
*			VILLAGE SHOPS COLLECTION	
92	PENNY SWEETS	RT	80.00	80.00
93	GREENGROCERS VAN	RT	16.00	37.00
93	JONES THE BUTCHER	RT	80.00	80.00
93	JONES THE BUTCHER VAN	*	16.00	16.00
93	PENNY SWEETS VAN	RT	16.00	91.00
94	TOY SHOP	*	80.00	80.00
95	BAKER'S SHOP, THE	*	85.00	85.00
95	CHINA SHOP	*	85.00	85.00
95	TOY SHOP VAN	*	16.00	16.00
96	BAKER'S SHOP VAN	OP	16.00	16.00
96	CHINA SHOP VAN	OP	16.00	16.00
D. TATE			VILLAGE SHOPS COLLECTION	
92	GREENGROCERS, THE	RT	120.00	80.00
*			WELSH COLLECTION	
92	ST. GOVAN'S CHAPEL	OP	75.00	75.00
D. TATE			WELSH COLLECTION	
84	HERMITAGE	RT	30.00	82.00
86	BRECON BACH	RT	42.00	65.00
87	RENOVATED HERMITAGE	RT	43.00	55.00
91	BRO DAWEL	RT	38.00	30.00
91	TUDOR MERCHANT	RT	90.00	70.00
91	UGLY HOUSE	OP	55.00	50.00

MCMEMORIES
*			MCMEMORIES SCULPTURES	
97	YOU DESERVE A BREAK TODAY	*	40.00	40.00

MICHAEL'S LTD.
B. BAKER

YR	NAME	LIMIT	ISSUE	TREND
			DEJA VU COLLECTION	
93	AMERICAN CLASSIC	500	99.00	110.00
93	JAMES RIVER PLANTATION	500	108.00	120.00
94	HILL TOP MANSION	1200	100.00	110.00
94	PAINTED LADIES	1200	125.00	135.00
94	WHITE POINT	700	97.00	105.00

MIDWEST OF CANNON FALLS

YR	NAME	LIMIT	ISSUE	TREND
*			COTTONTAIL LANE COLLECTION	
92	CONFECTIONARY SHOP/LIGHTED 06335-5	RT	43.00	43.00
92	FLOWER SHOP/LIGHTED 06333-9	RT	43.00	43.00
92	SPRINGTIME COTTAGE/LIGHTED	RT	43.00	43.00
92	VICTORIAN HOUSE/LIGHTED 06332-1	RT	43.00	43.00
93	BAKER/LIGHTED 01396-0	RT	43.00	43.00
93	CHURCH/LIGHTED 01385-4	RT	42.00	42.00
93	COTTONTAIL INN/LIGHTED 01394-6	RT	43.00	43.00
93	PAINTING STUDIO/LIGHTED 01395-5	RT	43.00	43.00
93	ROSE COTTAGE/LIGHTED 01386-1	RT	43.00	43.00
93	SCHOOLHOUSE/LIGHTED 01378-6	RT	43.00	43.00
94	BED & BREAKFAST/LIGHTED 00337-4	RT	43.00	43.00
94	CHAPEL/LIGHTED 00331-2	RT	43.00	43.00
94	GENERAL STORE/LIGHTED 00340-4	RT	43.00	43.00
94	PORCELAIN LIGHTED GARDEN VALLEY CHAPEL	RT	43.00	275.00
94	TRAIN STATION/LIGHTED 00330-5	RT	43.00	43.00
95	BOUTIQUE & BEAUTY SHOP/LIGHTED 12301-0	RT	45.00	45.00
95	CAFE/LIGHTED 12303-4	RT	45.00	45.00
95	ROSEBUD MANOR/LIGHTED 12304-1	RT	45.00	45.00
95	TOWN HALL/LIGHTED 12300-3	RT	45.00	45.00
96	BANDSHELL/LIGHTED 15753-4	RT	50.00	50.00
96	BUNGALOW/LIGHTED 15752-7	RT	45.00	45.00
96	CATHEDRAL/LIGHTED 12302-7	RT	47.00	47.00
96	FIRE STATION W/FIGURINES/LIGHTED 15830-2	RT	90.00	90.00
96	TOWN GARDEN SHOPPE/LIGHTED 12751-0	RT	45.00	45.00
*			CREEPY HOLLOW COLLECTION	
92	DR. FRANKENSTEIN'S HOUSE/LIGHTED 01621-3	RT	40.00	40.00
92	DRACULA'S CASTLE/LIGHTED 01627-5	RT	40.00	40.00
92	MUMMY'S MORTUARY/LIGHTED 01641-1	RT	40.00	40.00
92	WITCHES COVE/LIGHTED 01665-7	RT	40.00	40.00
93	BLOOD BANK/LIGHTED 08548-6	OP	40.00	40.00
93	HAUNTED HOTEL/LIGHTED 08549-1	OP	40.00	40.00
93	SHOPPE OF HORRORS/LIGHTED 08550-9	RT	40.00	40.00
94	CAULDRON CAFE/LIGHTED 10649-5	OP	40.00	40.00
94	MEDICASL GHOUL SCHOOL/LIGHTED 10651-8	OP	40.00	40.00
94	PHANTOM'S OPERA/LIGHTED 10650-1	OP	40.00	40.00
95	BEWITCHING BELFRY/LIGHTED 13355-2	OP	50.00	50.00
95	FUNERAL PARLOR 13356-9	OP	50.00	50.00
95	SKELETON CINEMA/LIGHTED 13354-5	CL	50.00	50.00
96	CASTLE/LIGHTED 16959-9	CL	50.00	50.00
96	GYPSY WAGON/LIGHTED 16663-5	OP	45.00	45.00
96	JACK-O-LANT-INN 16665-9	OP	45.00	45.00
96	SCHOOL HOUSE/LIGHTED 1662-8	OP	45.00	45.00
98	TRAIN DEPOT	3500	45.00	45.00

YR	NAME	LIMIT	ISSUE	TREND

PACIFIC RIM
P. SEBERN
BRISTOL TOWNSHIP

YR	NAME	LIMIT	ISSUE	TREND
90	BEDFORD MANOR	CL	30.00	30.00
90	BLACK SWAN MILLINERY	CL	30.00	30.00
90	BRISTOL BOOKS	CL	35.00	35.00
90	COVENTRY HOUSE	RT	30.00	30.00
90	GEO. STRAITH GROCER	CL	25.00	25.00
90	HIGH GATE MILL	RT	40.00	40.00
90	IRON HORSE LIVERY	RT	30.00	35.00
90	MAPS & CHARTS	CL	25.00	25.00
90	QUEEN'S ROAD CHURCH	CL	40.00	40.00
90	SILVERSMITH	RT	30.00	30.00
90	SOUTHWICK CHURCH	RT	30.00	30.00
90	TRINITY CHURCH	RT	30.00	35.00
90	VIOLIN SHOP	CL	30.00	30.00
90	WEXFORD MANOR	CL	25.00	25.00
91	BRIDGESTONE CHURCH	RT	30.00	35.00
91	ELMSTONE HOUSE	RT	30.00	35.00
91	FLOWER SHOP	RT	30.00	30.00
91	HARDWICKE HOUSE	RT	30.00	35.00
91	KILBY COTTAGE	RT	30.00	35.00
91	PEGGLESWORTH INN	RT	40.00	40.00
93	CHESTERFIELD HOUSE	CL	30.00	30.00
93	FOXDOWN MANOR	CL	30.00	30.00
94	SHOTWICK INN & SURGERY	CL	35.00	35.00
94	SURREY ROAD CHURCH	CL	40.00	40.00
95	KING'S GATE SCHOOL	CL	30.00	30.00

P. SEBERN
BRISTOL WATERFRONT

YR	NAME	LIMIT	ISSUE	TREND
92	ADMIRALTY SHIPPING	CL	30.00	30.00
92	AVON FISH CO.	CL	30.00	30.00
92	CHANDLER	CL	30.00	30.00
92	CUSTOMS HOUSE	CL	40.00	40.00
92	HAWKE EXPORTS	CL	40.00	40.00
92	QUARTER DECK INN	CL	40.00	40.00
92	REGENT WAREHOUSE	CL	40.00	40.00
93	BRISTOL POINT LIGHTHOUSE	CL	45.00	45.00
93	LOWER QUAY CHAPEL	CL	40.00	40.00
93	RUSTY KNIGHT INN	CL	35.00	35.00
94	BRISTOL TATTLER	RT	40.00	40.00
94	PORTSHEAD LIGHTHOUSE	CL	30.00	30.00
95	BRISTOL CHANNEL LIGHTHOUSE	CL	30.00	30.00

POSSIBLE DREAMS
*
CRINKLE CLAUS

YR	NAME	LIMIT	ISSUE	TREND
98	CRINKLE CANDY STORE	*	62.00	62.00
98	CRINKLE FIRE STATION	*	62.00	62.00
98	CRINKLE POLICE STATION	*	62.00	62.00
98	CRINKLE POST OFFICE	*	62.00	62.00
98	CRINKLE TOY SHOP	*	62.00	62.00

ROMAN INC.
E. SIMONETTI
FONTANINI HEIRLOOM NATIVITIES 2.5-IN. VILLAGE

YR	NAME	LIMIT	ISSUE	TREND
96	6-PC. NATIVITY VILLAGE WITH LIGHTED BASE	OP	270.00	270.00
96	BLUE KING'S TENT	OP	17.50	18.00
96	INN	OP	30.00	30.00
96	SHEPHERD'S CAMP	OP	30.00	30.00
96	STABLE	OP	30.00	30.00
96	TOWN BUILDING	OP	25.00	25.00
96	TOWN STORE	OP	25.00	25.00
97	GOLD KING'S TENT	OP	23.00	23.00
97	MARKETPLACE	OP	33.00	33.00
97	POTTERY SHOP	OP	33.00	33.00
97	PURPLE KING'S TENT	OP	23.00	23.00
97	STABLE (REVISED)	OP	33.00	33.00
97	TOWN GATE	OP	33.00	33.00
98	CARPENTER'S SHO[	OP	33.00	33.00
98	CORRAL	OP	33.00	33.00
98	POULTRY SHOP	OP	33.00	33.00

E. SIMONETTI
FONTANINI HEIRLOOM NATIVITIES 5-IN. VILLAGE

YR	NAME	LIMIT	ISSUE	TREND
96	BAKERY	OP	80.00	80.00
96	BLUE KING'S TENT	OP	50.00	50.00
96	INN	OP	85.00	85.00
96	SHEPHERD'S CAMP	OP	80.00	80.00
96	STABLE	OP	75.00	75.00
97	GOLD KING'S TENT	OP	65.00	65.00
97	MARKETPLACE	OP	90.00	90.00
97	POTTERY SHOP	OP	90.00	90.00
97	PURPLE KING'S TENT	OP	65.00	65.00
97	TOWN GATE	OP	90.00	90.00
98	CARPENTER'S SHOP	OP	90.00	90.00
98	CORRAL	OP	95.00	95.00
98	POULTRY SHOP	OP	90.00	90.00

E. SIMONETTI
FONTANINI HEIRLOOM NATIVITIES 7.5-IN. VILLAGE

YR	NAME	LIMIT	ISSUE	TREND
97	INN	OP	55.00	55.00
97	LIGHTED STABLE	OP	75.00	75.00

Biloxi Light, MS *was issued in 1995 by Harbour Lights as part of their Great Coast Region series. Limited to 5,500, the piece retailed for $60.*

Audrey's Tea Room *was only issued for a limited time due to the mold being broken in a highway accident. The piece was created by David Winter for John Hine Studios.*

Clown Boot *makes an impressive residence for those tiny enough to enjoy it. This piece by Jon Herbert also makes an equally impressive collectible (John Hine Studios).*

The Great Coast Region series from Harbour Lights added Pensacola, FL *in 1995. The edition was limited to 9,500 pieces.*

YR	NAME	LIMIT	ISSUE	TREND
97	TOWN BUILDING	OP	65.00	65.00
97	TOWN GATE	OP	40.00	40.00
97	WORK SHOP	OP	65.00	65.00
98	FISH MARKET	OP	120.00	120.00
98	GOLD KING'S TENT	OP	110.00	110.00
98	PURPLE KING'S TENT	OP	95.00	95.00

SHELIA'S COLLECTIBLES

S. THOMPSON				ACCESSORIES
94	AMISH QUILT LINE	1500	18.00	35.00
94	FORMAL GARDEN	1500	18.00	30.00
94	SUNRISE AT 80 MEETING	1500	18.00	30.00
94	VICTORIAN ARBOR	1500	18.00	35.00
95	FLOWER GARDEN	OP	13.00	13.00
95	REAL ESTATE SIGN	OP	12.00	12.00
95	WISTERIA ARBOR	OP	12.00	12.00
96	AUTUMN TREE	OP	14.00	14.00
96	BARBER GAZEBO	OP	13.00	13.00
96	GRAZING COWS	OP	12.00	12.00
96	SAILBOAT	OP	12.00	12.00
96	SPRING TREE	OP	14.00	14.00
96	SUMMERTIME PICKET FENCE	OP	12.00	12.00
96	TROPICAL PALM TREE	OP	14.00	14.00

S. THOMPSON				AMERICAN BARNS
94	PENNSYLVANIA DUTCH BARN	OP	18.00	18.00
94	ROCK CITY BARN	OP	18.00	18.00
95	CASEY BARN	RT	19.00	19.00
95	MAIL POUCH BARN	OP	19.00	19.00

S. THOMPSON				AMERICAN GOTHIC
93	GOTHIC REVIVAL COTTAGE	2500	20.00	20.00
93	MELE HOUSE	2500	20.00	20.00
93	PERKINS HOUSE	2500	20.00	20.00
93	ROSE ARBOR	2500	14.00	15.00
93	ROSELAND COTTAGE	2500	20.00	20.00

S. THOMPSON				AMISH VILLAGE
93	AMISH BARN	RT	17.00	17.00
93	AMISH BUGGY	RT	12.00	12.00
93	AMISH HOME	RT	17.00	17.00
93	AMISH SCHOOL	RT	15.00	15.00
93	COVERED BRIDGE	RT	16.00	16.00

S. THOMPSON				ARTIST CHOICE
95	BANTA HOUSE	RT	24.00	24.00
95	GREENMAN HOUSE	RT	24.00	24.00
95	RILEY-CUTLER	RT	24.00	24.00
95	WELLER HOUSE	RT	24.00	24.00

S. THOMPSON				ATLANTA
95	FOX THEATRE	OP	19.00	19.00
95	HAMMONDS HOUSE	RT	18.00	18.00
95	SWAN HOUSE	OP	18.00	18.00
95	TULLIE SMITH HOUSE	RT	18.00	18.00
95	VICTORIAN PLAYHOUSE	RT	17.00	17.00
95	WREN'S NEST	OP	19.00	19.00

S. THOMPSON				CHARLESTON
93	ASHE HOUSE	RT	16.00	16.00
93	CITADEL	RT	16.00	16.00
93	CITY HALL	1300	15.00	50.00
93	COLLEGE OF CHARLESTON	OP	16.00	16.00
93	DRAYTON HOUSE	OP	18.00	18.00
93	JOHN RUTLEDGE HOME	RT	16.00	16.00
93	SINGLE SIDE PORCH	RT	16.00	16.00
95	BOONE HALL PLANTATION	OP	18.00	18.00
95	MAGNOLIA PARLOR HOUSE	OP	19.00	19.00
95	O'DONNELLS FOLLY	OP	18.00	18.00

S. THOMPSON				CHARLESTON BATTERY
96	22 S. BATTERY	OP	19.00	19.00
96	24 S. BATTERY	OP	19.00	19.00
96	26 S. BATTERY	OP	19.00	19.00
96	28 S. BATTERY	OP	19.00	19.00

S. THOMPSON		CHARLESTON CHURCHES & PUBLIC BUILDINGS		
96	HUGENOT CHURCH	OP	19.00	19.00

S. THOMPSON				CHARLESTON HOUSE II
96	SOTTILE HOUSE	OP	19.00	19.00

S. THOMPSON			COLLECTIBLE ACCESSORIES	
93	APPLE TREE	RT	12.00	12.00
93	DOGWOOD TREE	RT	12.00	12.00

S. THOMPSON				COLLECTORS SOCIETY
93	ANNE PEACOCK HOUSE	*	16.00	16.00
93	SUSAN B. ANTHONY	*	*	70.00
94	IVY GREEN	*	*	N/A
94	SEASVIEW COTTAGE	*	17.00	17.00

S. THOMPSON				GALVESTON
95	BEISSNER HOUSE	OP	19.00	19.00
95	DANCING PAVILLION	OP	19.00	19.00
95	FRENKEL HOME	OP	19.00	19.00

YR NAME	LIMIT	ISSUE	TREND
95 REYMERSHOFFER	OP	19.00	19.00
S. THOMPSON		**GHOST HOUSE SERIES**	
94 INSIDE-OUTSIDE HOUSE	RT	18.00	18.00
94 PIRATE'S HOUSE	RT	18.00	18.00
95 GAFFOS HOUSE	OP	19.00	19.00
95 RED CASTLE	OP	19.00	19.00
S. THOMPSON		**GONE WITH THE WIND**	
95 AUNT PITTY POT'S	OP	24.00	24.00
95 GENERAL STORE	OP	24.00	24.00
95 LOEW'S GRAND	RT	24.00	24.00
95 TARA	OP	24.00	24.00
95 TWELVE OAKS	OP	24.00	24.00
96 SILHOUETTE	OP	16.00	16.00
S. THOMPSON		**INVENTOR SERIES**	
93 FORD MOTOR COMPANY	OP	17.00	17.00
93 MENLO PARK LABORATORY	OP	16.00	16.00
93 NOAH WEBSTER HOUSE	OP	15.00	15.00
93 WRIGHT CYCLE SHOP	OP	17.00	17.00
S. THOMPSON		**JAZZY NEW ORLEANS**	
94 BEAUREGARD KEYS	OP	18.00	18.00
94 GALLIER HOUSE	OP	18.00	18.00
94 LABRANCHE BUILD	OP	18.00	18.00
94 LEPRETRE HOUSE	OP	18.00	18.00
S. THOMPSON		**KEY WEST**	
95 ARTIST HOUSE	OP	19.00	19.00
95 EYEBROW HOUSE	OP	18.00	18.00
95 HEMINGWAY HOUSE	OP	19.00	19.00
95 ILLINGSWORTH	OP	19.00	19.00
95 SHOTGUN HOUSE	RT	17.00	17.00
95 SHOTGUN SISTER	RT	17.00	17.00
95 SOUTHERNMOST	OP	18.00	18.00
S. THOMPSON		**LADIES BY THE SEA**	
96 ABBEY II	OP	19.00	19.00
96 CENTENNIAL COTTAGE	OP	19.00	19.00
96 HALL COTTAGE	OP	19.00	19.00
96 HEART BLOSSOM	OP	19.00	19.00
S. THOMPSON		**LIGHTHOUSES**	
93 ASSATEAGUE ISLAND LIGHT	OP	17.00	17.00
93 CHARLESTON LIGHT	OP	15.00	15.00
93 NEW LONDON LEDGE LIGHT	OP	17.00	17.00
93 ROUND ISLAND LIGHT	OP	17.00	17.00
93 THOMAS POINT LIGHT	OP	17.00	17.00
95 CAPE HATTERAS LIGHT	OP	18.00	18.00
S. THOMPSON		**MACKINAC**	
96 AMBERG COTTAGE	OP	19.00	19.00
96 ANNE COTTAGE	OP	19.00	19.00
96 REARICK COTTAGE	OP	19.00	19.00
96 WINDERMERE HOTEL	OP	19.00	19.00
S. THOMPSON		**MAIL ORDER VICTORIANS**	
94 BREHAUT HOUSE	3300	24.00	24.00
94 GOELLER HOUSE	3300	24.00	24.00
94 HENDERSON HOUSE	3300	24.00	24.00
94 TROTMAN HOUSE	3300	24.00	24.00
S. THOMPSON		**MARTHA'S VINEYARD**	
93 ALICE'S WONDERLAND	OP	16.00	16.00
93 CAMPGROUND COTTAGE	OP	16.00	16.00
93 GINGERBREAD COTTAGE	RT	16.00	16.00
93 WOOD VALENTINE	OP	16.00	16.00
95 BLUE COTTAGE	OP	18.00	18.00
95 TRAILS END	OP	18.00	18.00
95 WHITE COTTAGE	OP	18.00	18.00
S. THOMPSON		**OLD FASHIONED CHRISTMAS**	
94 CONWAY SCENIC RAILROAD STATION	RT	18.00	18.00
94 DWIGHT HOUSE	OP	18.00	18.00
94 GENERAL MERCHANDISE	RT	18.00	18.00
94 OLD FIRST CHURCH	RT	18.00	18.00
95 CHRISTMAS INN	RT	19.00	19.00
95 TOWN SQUARE TREE	RT	18.00	18.00
S. THOMPSON		**PAINTED LADIES III**	
93 GREEN STOCKTON	OP	16.00	16.00
93 LINDA LEE	OP	16.00	16.00
93 PINK STOCKTON	OP	16.00	16.00
93 TAN STOCKTON	OP	16.00	16.00
95 STEINER COTTAGE	OP	18.00	18.00
96 CREAM STOCKTON	OP	19.00	19.00
S. THOMPSON		**PANORAMIC LIGHTS**	
96 JEFFRY HOOK	OP	19.00	19.00
96 NEW CANAL LIGHT	OP	19.00	19.00
96 QUADDY HEAD	OP	19.00	19.00
96 SPLIT ROCK LIGHTHOUSE	OP	19.00	19.00
S. THOMPSON		**PLANTATIONS**	
95 FARLEY	RT	18.00	18.00
95 LONGWOOD	OP	19.00	19.00

YR	NAME	LIMIT	ISSUE	TREND
95	MERRY SHERWOOD	OP	18.00	18.00
95	SAN FRANCISCO	OP	19.00	19.00
S. THOMPSON				**RAINBOW ROW**
93	AURORA RAINBOW ROW	OP	13.00	13.00
93	BLUE RAINBOW ROW	OP	13.00	13.00
93	CREAM RAINBOW ROW	OP	13.00	13.00
93	GRAY RAINBOW ROW	OP	13.00	13.00
93	GREEN RAINBOW ROW	OP	13.00	13.00
93	LAVENDER RAINBOW ROW	OP	13.00	13.00
93	OFF-WHITE RAINBOW ROW	OP	13.00	13.00
93	PINK RAINBOW ROW	OP	13.00	13.00
93	YELLOW RAINBOW ROW	OP	13.00	13.00
S. THOMPSON				**SAN FRANCISCO**
95	BRANDYWINE	OP	19.00	19.00
95	ECLECTIC BLUE	OP	19.00	19.00
95	EDWARDIAN GREEN	OP	19.00	19.00
95	QUEEN ROSE	OP	19.00	19.00
S. THOMPSON				**SAVANNAH**
93	CHESTNUT HOUSE	OP	18.00	18.00
93	OWENS THOMAS HOUSE	OP	16.00	16.00
96	ASENDORF HOUSE	OP	19.00	19.00
S. THOMPSON				**SHOW PIECE**
95	BALDWIN HOUSE	RT	20.00	20.00
96	WINNIE WATSON	OP	*	N/A
S. THOMPSON				**SOUTH CAROLINA LADIES**
96	CINNAMON HILL	OP	19.00	19.00
96	DAVIS-JOHNSEY	OP	19.00	19.00
96	INMAN HOUSE	OP	19.00	19.00
96	MONTGOMERY HOUSE	OP	19.00	19.00
S. THOMPSON				**VICTORIAN SPRINGTIME**
93	HEFFRON HOUSE	RT	17.00	17.00
93	JACOBSEN HOUSE	RT	17.00	17.00
93	RALSTON HOUSE	RT	17.00	17.00
93	SESSIONS HOUSE	RT	17.00	17.00
95	DRAGON HOUSE	RT	19.00	19.00
95	E.B. HALL	RT	19.00	19.00
95	GIBNEY HOME	RT	19.00	19.00
95	RAY HOME	RT	19.00	19.00
95	VICTORIA	RT	19.00	19.00
96	CLARK HOUSE	OP	19.00	19.00
96	GOODWILL	OP	19.00	19.00
96	QUEEN ANNE	OP	19.00	19.00
96	SHEPARD HOUSE	OP	19.00	19.00
96	URFER HOUSE	OP	19.00	19.00
S. THOMPSON				**WEST COAST LIGHTHOUSES**
95	EAST BROTHER LIGHTHOUSE	OP	19.00	19.00
95	MUKILTEO LIGHT	OP	18.00	18.00
95	PAINT FERMIN	OP	18.00	18.00
95	YAQUINA LIGHT	OP	18.00	18.00
S. THOMPSON				**WILLIAMSBURG**
95	CAPTIOL	OP	18.00	18.00
95	RALEIGH TAVERN	OP	18.00	18.00

SJS DESIGNS

S. STENTIFORD				**IVY ROSE COLLECTION**
93	IVY POINT LIGHTHOUSE	2000	27.00	32.00
93	MELMACKER'S LOBSTER POT CAFE	2000	27.00	32.00
93	PERIWINKLE COTTAGE, THE	2000	27.00	32.00
93	SEAFLOWER INN, THE	2000	32.00	38.00
93	VALERIE ELIZABETH'S BEACH HOUSE	2000	25.00	30.00
94	ANTIQUES BARN	2000	28.00	33.00
94	AUNTIE GEN'S	2000	27.00	32.00
94	DARRELL'S COTTAGE	2000	27.00	32.00
94	DOROTHEA'S HOUSE	2000	29.00	34.00
94	FARMER'S MARKET, T HE	2000	27.00	33.00
94	GOG'S ANIMAL BARN	2000	30.00	35.00
94	INA'S FARMHOUSE	2000	30.00	35.00
94	LINDA IRENE'S	2000	28.00	33.00
94	MARY ELLEN'S	2000	27.00	32.00
94	MISS MARGARET'S	2000	29.00	34.00
94	POLICE STATION	2000	24.00	29.00
94	SUNFLOWER COTTAGE, THE	2000	25.00	30.00
94	TOWN PHARMACY	2000	28.00	33.00

SPENCER COLLIN LIGHTHOUSES

C. SPENCER COLLIN				
*	ADMIRALTY HEAD LIGHTHOUSE	RT	112.00	112.00
*	AMERICAN SHOAL	RT	92.00	92.00
*	CHRISTMAS EVE	OP	82.00	82.00
*	EGGROCK LIGHTHOUSE	RT	94.00	94.00
*	HIGHLAND CAPE COD	RT	96.00	96.00
*	PORTLAND HEAD LIGHTHOUSE	RT	82.00	82.00
*	ROCK OF AGES LIGHTHOUSE	RT	60.00	60.00
*	RUDOLPH'S LIGHT	OP	64.00	64.00
84	PORTSMOUTH LIGHTHOUSE	CL	18.00	18.00

YR	NAME	LIMIT	ISSUE	TREND
93	ANNISQUAM HARBOR LIGHTHOUSE	2000	46.00	46.00
93	CAPE MAY LIGHTHOUSE	OP	79.00	79.00
93	FORT GRATIOT LIGHTHOUSE	2000	52.00	52.00
93	JUPITER INLET LIGHTHOUSE	2000	84.00	84.00
93	MARSHALL POINT LIGHTHOUSE	2000	46.00	46.00
93	NEW LONDON LEDGE LIGHTHOUSE	2000	120.00	120.00
93	PEGGY'S POINT LIGHTHOUSE	OP	38.00	38.00
93	PONCE INLET LIGHTHOUSE	2000	86.00	86.00
93	SAND ISLAND LIGHTHOUSE	OP	66.00	66.00
93	SPLIT ROCK LIGHTHOUSE	OP	110.00	110.00
93	ST. SIMONS ISLAND LIGHTHOUSE	2000	116.00	116.00
94	POINT ISABEL LIGHTHOUSE	2000	52.00	52.00
97	BOONE ISLAND	*	80.00	80.00
97	HILLSBORO	*	80.00	80.00
97	SAN FRANCISCO LIGHTHOUSE WATERGLOBE	*	40.00	40.00
98	ABSECON LIGHTHOUSE	*	90.00	90.00
98	SAN FRANCISCO LIGHTSHIP	*	120.00	120.00

C. SPENCER COLLIN   **ADMIRAL'S LIGHTS/FLAG QUARTER SERIES**

YR	NAME	LIMIT	ISSUE	TREND
94	ALKI POINT LIGHTHOUSE	3000	70.00	70.00
94	DIAMOND HEAD LIGHTHOUSE	3000	124.00	124.00
94	HOSPITAL POINT LIGHTHOUSE	3000	68.00	68.00
94	YERBA BUENA LIGHTHOUSE	3000	90.00	90.00

C. SPENCER COLLIN   **COMMEMORATIVE STAMP SERIES**

YR	NAME	LIMIT	ISSUE	TREND
89	CAPE HATTERAS LIGHTHOUSE	RT	70.00	250.00

C. SPENCER COLLIN   **TRADEMARK SERIES**

YR	NAME	LIMIT	ISSUE	TREND
94	10TH ANNIVERSARY LIGHTHOUSE	CL	100.00	100.00

WALT DISNEY CLASSICS COLLECTION

*   **ENCHANTED PLACES**

YR	NAME	LIMIT	ISSUE	TREND
95	SEVEN DWARF'S COTTAGE	OP	180.00	180.00
95	SEVEN DWARFS' JEWEL MINE	OP	190.00	190.00
95	WHITE RABBIT'S COTTAGE	OP	175.00	175.00
95	WOODCUTTER'S COTTAGE	OP	170.00	170.00
96	BEAST'S CASTLE	OP	245.00	245.00
96	CAPTAIN HOOK SHIP	OP	475.00	475.00
96	CINDERELLA'S COACH	OP	265.00	265.00
96	FIDDLER PIG'S STICK HOUSE	OP	85.00	85.00
96	FIFER PIG'S STRAW HOUSE	OP	85.00	85.00
96	GEPETTO'S TOY SHOP	OP	150.00	150.00
96	GRANDPA'S HOUSE	OP	125.00	125.00
96	PRACTICAL PIG'S BRICK HOUSE	OP	115.00	115.00

WB STUDIOS

J. TAYLOR

YR	NAME	LIMIT	ISSUE	TREND
75	STEEPLE CHURCH	RT	146.00	146.00
78	MEETING HOUSE	RT	224.00	224.00
78	RAINBOW CHURCH	RT	394.00	394.00
79	MANSION	RT	372.00	372.00
80	CHRISTMAS CARD	RT	174.00	174.00
80	FROG CREEK BRIDGE	RT	170.00	170.00
83	TIFFANY	RT	276.00	276.00
85	SCENTED GARDEN HOUSE	RT	146.00	146.00
86	HISTORIC STONE GATE	RT	168.00	168.00
87	TERRACE MANOR	RT	144.00	144.00
92	GREENHOUSE WITH WALKWAY	2000	490.00	490.00
93	ESTATE HOUSE	1000	900.00	900.00
94	RAMBLING ROSE	500	660.00	660.00
95	NATURE CENTER LODGE FURNISHED	500	390.00	390.00
96	ANTIQUESANTA TREASURE HOUSE FURNISHED	500	450.00	450.00
97	REVISED TERRACE MANOR	2500	190.00	190.00

R. KAY   **LIGHTED SNOWHOUSE**

YR	NAME	LIMIT	ISSUE	TREND
93	ESTATE HOUSE	1000	900.00	1000.00

J. TAYLOR   **LIGHTED SNOWHOUSE**

YR	NAME	LIMIT	ISSUE	TREND
92	GREENHOUSE W/WALKWAY	2000	490.00	525.00
94	RAMBLING ROSE	500	660.00	700.00

Dolls & Plush

Betty Hodges

Doll collecting has exploded in the collectibles arena, ranking second in popularity among hobbyists in the United States. There are more dolls available today than ever before. They abound in the marketplace in such a variety of genre that one can scarcely ignore them.

As with all buying, your own personal tastes play an important role in collecting. There are unknown factors behind every doll purchase. Why one doll appeals to you and another does not goes back to some dim reference point. Sometimes there is a special feeling connected with a certain doll, and before you know it, you've acquired it!

Childhood dolls are often the start of a collection. Collectors will go out of their way to acquire a doll they fondly remember from their early years. But no matter how you start collecting, the doll industry continues to proliferate, allowing you to add new creations to your collection at any given time.

No one can guess which dolls produced today will increase in value tomorrow. Through the years, some contemporary dolls have become quite valuable while others have not. The dolls of the early 1900s remain very desirable. Many of these dolls were played with sparingly. It is often said that Sunday afternoon was the only time children were allowed to handle these dolls.

Despite the era in which they grew up, many collectors feel their childhood dolls are as sacrosanct as the ones made decades earlier. These dolls are quite different from their older cousins but still have the same allure. Bakelite dolls made in the 1930s were abundant, but unfortunately have not worn well. Dolls composed of wood and cloth show the timeworn caress of the little hands that played with them.

Limited edition dolls are a new factor in the equation. Putting a production limit on the number of dolls made adds to their desirability. The doll that catches your eye may not be available for very long. This initial limit on the supply can increase the demand for the doll, oftentimes making it more valuable over the years.

Today's dolls have myriad diverse characteristics. The collector's desire to add more dolls to his or her collection grows, and makers fall over themselves to accommodate that desire.

There are two definite audiences for dolls produced today–children and adults. The number of dolls bought and kept by adults is unprecedented in today's doll world. These dolls are genuine collectibles, which will be cherished. They retain their beauty indefinitely.

Keep accurate records when you acquire your dolls; include the producer's name and the exact outfit the doll is wearing. Take pictures of each doll. Should you ever decide to sell your collection, these details will be essential.

Your personal taste is the key to your collection. Do you know which dolls will become valuable? Probably not, but this should not reduce the enjoyment you get from this hobby.

BETTY HODGES has 25 years of experience in the doll market. A consultant to doll artists, she has supervised dealer booths in international toy and trade markets and writes the "Doll Collecting Today" column in Collector's mart *magazine.*

DOLLS & PLUSH

YR NAME	LIMIT	ISSUE	TREND
ANNALEE MOBILITEE			
A. THORNDIKE			
* 3 IN. WYNKEN, BLYNKEN & NOD	RT	68.00	100.00
* 7 IN. SWEETHEART GIRL	RT	27.50	35.00
50 10 IN. BOY & GIRL SKIERS	*	15.00	2500.00
50 10 IN. FROGMAN (GIRL DIVER)	*	10.00	3800.00
50 10 IN. GIRL GOLFER	*	*	650.00
50 20 IN. BOY & GIRL CALYPSO DANCERS	*	*	2000.00
50 9 IN. CHOIR BOY	*	*	1000.00
53 GIRL WATER-SKIER	*	10.00	2500.00
54 10 IN. COUNTRY GIRL	*	8.95	2000.00
54 10 IN. ELF	*	*	300.00
54 10 IN. SAKS FIFTH AVE. SKIER	50	9.95	2000.00
54 26 IN. BEAN NOSE SANTA	*	20.00	750.00
54 5 IN. SNO-BUNNY CHILD	*	2.95	300.00
54 8 IN. BOY SKIER	*	5.50	1000.00
55 10 IN. BOY SWIMMER	*	*	1500.00
55 7 IN. BOY SKIER	*	*	1000.00
56 10 IN. BABY ANGEL	*	5.50	600.00
56 10 IN. FISHING GIRL	*	*	900.00
56 10 IN. WATER SKIER-GIRL	*	9.95	2500.00
56 12 IN. SANTA WITH BEAN NOSE	*	20.00	1000.00
56 7 IN. BABY ANGEL WITH FEATHER HAIR	*	3.95	250.00
57 10 IN. BOY & GIRL IN BOAT	*	17.50	2000.00
57 10 IN. BOY BUILDING BOAT	*	*	1000.00
57 10 IN. BOY SKIER	*	16.00	2500.00
57 10 IN. BOY SQUARE DANCER	*	9.95	900.00
57 10 IN. BOY WITH STRAW HAT	*	*	525.00
57 10 IN. CASUALTY SKI GROUP	*	35.00	3150.00
57 10 IN. CASUALTY TOBOGGAN GROUP	*	35.00	1250.00
57 10 IN. EASTER HOLIDAY DOLL	*	10.00	1500.00
57 10 IN. FOURTH OF JULY DOLL	*	10.00	1500.00
57 10 IN. GIRL SKIER	*	*	2500.00
57 10 IN. GIRL SQUARE DANCER	*	9.95	900.00
57 10 IN. HOLLY ELF	*	*	1600.00
57 10 IN. MR. HOLLY ELF	*	*	1650.00
57 10 IN. SKIER	*	15.00	2500.00
57 10 IN. SKIER WITH LEG IN CAST	*	35.00	2000.00
57 10 IN. THANKSGIVING DOLL	*	*	1500.00
57 10 IN. VALENTINE DOLL	*	10.00	1500.00
57 9 IN. ELF WITH MUSICAL INSTRUMENT	*	3.50	1000.00
58 10 IN. SPRING DOLL	*	10.00	2000.00
59 10 IN. ARCHITECT	*	7.00	100.00
59 10 IN. BOY & GIRL IN FISHING BOAT	*	17.00	1000.00
59 10 IN. BOY & GIRL ON BIKE	*	17.00	1000.00
59 10 IN. BOY GOLFER	*	10.00	800.00
59 10 IN. BOY SKIER	*	*	1000.00
59 10 IN. BOY SQUARE DANCER	*	10.00	900.00
59 10 IN. DENTIST	*	10.00	2000.00
59 10 IN. ELF WITH INSTRUMENT	*	3.50	2000.00
59 10 IN. FOOTBALL PLAYER	*	10.00	1500.00
59 10 IN. GIRL SKIER	*	*	2500.00
59 10 IN. GIRL SQUARE DANCER	*	10.00	900.00
59 10 IN. GIRL SWIMMER	*	*	1500.00
59 10 IN. GREEN WOODSPRITE	*	6.95	300.00
59 10 IN. TEXAS OIL MAN	*	16.00	4000.00
59 7 IN. GIRL SKIER	*	*	1000.00
59 7 IN. SANTA WITH FUR TRIM SUIT	*	2.95	300.00
60 10 IN. BATHING GIRL	*	3.95	1250.00
60 10 IN. GIRL SKIER	*	*	1250.00
60 12 IN. BIG ANGEL ON CLOUD	*	9.95	400.00
60 33 IN. BOY & GIRL ON TANDEM BIKE	*	*	4000.00
60 5 IN. ELF	*	*	250.00
60 7 IN. BABY ANGEL	*	*	300.00
60 7 IN. BABY ANGEL W/BLUE WINGS	*	*	300.00
60 7 IN. BABY ANGEL WITH STAR ON LEG	*	*	300.00
60 7 IN. BABY IN STOCKING	*	*	300.00
60 7 IN. BABY WITH BOW	*	1.50	300.00
60 7 IN. BABY WITH PINK BOW	*	*	300.00
60 7 IN. MR. AND MRS. TUCKERED	*	*	500.00
62 10 IN. STEEPLE (BOY)	*	9.00	900.00
62 5 IN. ELF W/FEATHER HAIR	*	9.00	300.00
63 10 IN. CHRISTMAS ELF W/TINSEL	*	*	200.00
63 10 IN. ELF SKIER	*	*	375.00
63 10 IN. GIRL WATER-SKIER	*	7.50	1000.00
63 10 IN. WHITE WOODSPRITE	*	*	300.00
63 10 IN. YELLOW WOODSPRITE	*	*	275.00
63 18 IN. FRIAR	*	*	400.00
63 18 IN. FRIAR BOTTLE COVER	*	3.00	350.00
63 22 IN. BELLHOP (RED)	*	*	1000.00
63 24 IN. WOODSPRITE	*	5.45	500.00

YR	NAME	LIMIT	ISSUE	TREND
63	5 IN. BABY	*	*	300.00
63	5 IN. BABY WITH ANGEL HALO	*	2.00	300.00
63	5 IN. BABY WITH SANTA HAT	*	2.50	300.00
63	5 IN. CHRISTMAS ELF	*	3.00	250.00
63	7 IN. BABY ANGEL ON CLOUD	*	2.45	300.00
63	7 IN. SATURDAY NIGHT BABY	*	2.95	350.00
64	10 IN. GENDARME	*	4.00	1000.00
64	10 IN. IMP SKIER	*	4.00	400.00
64	10 IN. MONK (GREEN)	*	3.00	350.00
64	10 IN. MONK WITH CAP	*	3.00	350.00
64	12 IN. GEORGE & SHEILA-BRIDE/GROOM MOUSE	*	12.95	600.00
64	18 IN. P.J. BOY	*	7.00	450.00
64	18 IN. WOODSPRITE	*	6.00	500.00
64	22 IN. WOODSPRITE	*	5.95	600.00
64	7 IN. ANGEL IN A BLANKET	*	2.45	300.00
64	7 IN. BRIDE & GROOM MICE	*	2.75	500.00
64	7 IN. CHRISTMAS MOUSE	*	3.95	300.00
64	7 IN. SAT. NITE ANGEL W/BLANKET	*	2.95	350.00
65	10 IN. BACK TO SCHOOL, BOY & GIRL	*	19.90	1000.00
65	10 IN. FISHING BOY	*	7.95	900.00
65	10 IN. FISHING GIRL	*	9.95	900.00
65	10 IN. MONK WITH CHRISTMAS TREE PLANTING	*	3.00	300.00
65	10 IN. REINDEER	*	4.95	500.00
65	12 IN. NIPSY-TIPSY HARE	*	7.50	1000.00
65	12 IN. SANTA	*	5.00	125.00
65	18 IN. SANTA	*	9.00	175.00
65	26 IN. MRS. SANTA WITH APRON	*	15.00	800.00
65	5 IN. GREEN GNOME	*	*	200.00
65	7 IN. DRESDEN CHINA BABIES, TWO	*	*	400.00
65	7 IN. DUMB BUNNY	*	3.95	300.00
65	7 IN. EEK, PEEK, SQUEEK MOUSE	*	3.95	200.00
65	7 IN. LAWYER MOUSE	*	6.95	200.00
65	7 IN. MR. AND MRS. SANTA	*	5.95	200.00
66	10 IN. CENTRAL GAS CO. ELF	*	*	175.00
66	10 IN. GO-GO BOY & GIRL	*	3.95	550.00
66	10 IN. GO-GO BOY DANCER	*	10.00	350.00
66	29 IN. MR. OUTDOOR SANTA	*	17.00	350.00
66	5 IN. NEW HAMPTON SCHOOL BABY	300	*	225.00
66	7 IN. ANGEL/ WHITE WINGS	*	*	225.00
66	7 IN. MOUSE WITH CANDLE	*	*	175.00
66	7 IN. YUM YUM BUNNY	*	3.95	400.00
67	10 IN. ELF WITH ROUND BOX	*	2.50	350.00
67	10 IN. ELF WITH SKIS	48	3.00	300.00
67	10 IN. MONK	*	*	200.00
67	10 IN. SURFER BOY	*	4.95	350.00
67	10 IN. SURFER BOY	*	9.95	350.00
67	10 IN. SURFER GIRL	*	9.95	350.00
67	10 IN. WORKSHOP ELF	*	*	200.00
67	12 IN. FANCY NANCY CAT CHRISTMAS	*	6.95	200.00
67	12 IN. GNOME W/PJ SUIT	*	*	400.00
67	12 IN. LAURA MAY CAT	*	6.95	400.00
67	12 IN. YUM YUM BUNNY	*	9.95	500.00
67	18 IN. MONK W/PLANT	*	7.50	250.00
67	18 IN. NUN	296	8.00	300.00
67	36 IN. CHRISTMAS CAT	*	12.00	500.00
67	7 IN. CONDUCTOR MOUSE	*	3.95	300.00
67	7 IN. GARDEN CLUB BABY	*	2.95	350.00
67	7 IN. GNOME W/PJ SUIT	*	2.50	200.00
67	7 IN. MIGUEL THE MOUSE	*	3.95	200.00
67	7 IN. MR. SANTA MOUSE	*	3.95	150.00
67	7 IN. MRS. HOLLY MOUSE	*	3.95	150.00
67	7 IN. SANTA MOUSE	*	2.00	150.00
67	7 IN. SANTA WITH TOY BAG	*	3.95	150.00
68	10 IN. BOY WITH BEACH BALL	*	5.95	400.00
68	12 IN. ICE PACK CAT	*	6.95	400.00
68	12 IN. TESSIE TAR CAT	*	6.95	400.00
68	18 IN. MR. INDOOR SANTA	*	7.50	200.00
68	18 IN. MRS. INDOOR SANTA	*	7.50	200.00
68	29 IN. MR. SANTA WITH VEST & SACK	*	16.00	200.00
68	36 IN. RED NOSED REINDEER	*	*	300.00
68	5 IN. BABY ANGEL ON CLOUD	*	2.95	200.00
68	5 IN. BABY IN SANTA CAP	*	2.00	200.00
68	5 IN. BABY IN SANTA HAT	*	3.00	200.00
68	6 IN. MYRTLE TURTLE	*	3.95	500.00
68	7 IN. BABY I'M READING	*	*	300.00
68	7 IN. BABY VAIN JANE	*	2.50	300.00
68	7 IN. FAT FANNY	*	5.95	400.00
68	7 IN. MR. & MRS. SANTA TUCKERED	*	3.00	200.00
68	7 IN. MR. HOLLY MOUSE	*	3.95	200.00
68	7 IN. NIGHTSHIRT BOY MOUSE	*	3.95	200.00
69	10 IN. BRIDE & GROOM FROGS COURTIN'	*	7.95	450.00
69	10 IN. NUN ON SKIS	1551	4.50	300.00
69	10 IN. REINDEER WITH RED NOSE	*	4.95	125.00
69	10 IN. WHITE ELF WITH PRESENTS	*	*	175.00
69	12 IN. NIGHTSHIRT MOUSE	*	*	200.00

YR	NAME	LIMIT	ISSUE	TREND
69	18 IN. SANTA KID	*	7.45	350.00
69	22 IN. GO-GO GIRL DANCER	*	10.00	450.00
69	25 IN. COUNTRY BOY & GIRL (PAIR)	69	7.00	750.00
69	4 IN. PIG-BUBBLE TIME W/CHAMPAGNE GLASS	*	4.95	300.00
69	42 IN. FROG	30	30.00	700.00
69	7 IN. BUNNY W/OVERSIZED CARROT	*	4.95	225.00
69	7 IN. CHRISTMAS BABY ON 3 HOT BOXES	*	3.00	225.00
70	10 IN. CASUALTY ELF	991	2.25	350.00
70	10 IN. CHOIR BOY	3517	4.50	150.00
70	10 IN. CHOIR GIRL	7245	5.00	150.00
70	10 IN. CLOWN	2362	4.00	175.00
70	10 IN. ELF SKIER	597	*	250.00
70	10 IN. MONK WITH SKIS	406	4.00	250.00
70	10 IN. REINDEER WITH HAT	144	5.00	125.00
70	10 IN. XMAS MUSHROOM-7 IN. SANTA & DEER	*	11.00	450.00
70	14 IN. SPRING MUSHROOM	*	*	450.00
70	18 IN. BUNNY W/BUTTERFLY	258	10.95	225.00
70	18 IN. CLOWN	542	5.00	350.00
70	18 IN. GIRL BUNNY WITH EGG	1727	16.00	200.00
70	18 IN. PATCHWORK KID	496	7.50	300.00
70	29 IN. GIRL BUNNY	*	22.00	300.00
70	7 IN. ARCHITECT MOUSE	205	3.95	225.00
70	7 IN. BLUE MONKEY	293	*	400.00
70	7 IN. BOXING MOUSE	321	3.95	250.00
70	7 IN. BUNNY W/BUTTERFLY	1264	4.95	75.00
70	7 IN. CARPENTER MOUSE	307	3.95	75.00
70	7 IN. MONKEY	293	4.95	350.00
70	7 IN. NIGHTSHIRT GIRL MOUSE	*	3.95	75.00
70	7 IN. PLUMBER MOUSE	196	3.95	350.00
70	7 IN. PROFESSOR MOUSE	248	3.95	150.00
70	7 IN. SANTA WITH XMAS MUSHROOM	*	7.00	200.00
70	7 IN. SHERIFF MOUSE	11	3.95	150.00
70	7 IN. TREASURE BABY	*	3.95	200.00
70	7 IN. YELLOW BUNNY	*	3.95	150.00
71	10 IN. BRIDE & GROOM FROGS ON BIKE	13	17.50	650.00
71	10 IN. CHOIR BOY	904	3.95	163.00
71	10 IN. CHOIR GIRL	925	3.95	163.00
71	10 IN. CLOWN	708	2.00	163.00
71	10 IN. ELF SKIER	*	*	200.00
71	10 IN. FROG W/INSTRUMENT	233	3.95	163.00
71	10 IN. NUN ON SKIS	617	4.00	275.00
71	10 IN. RED NOSED REINDEER	1588	4.95	108.00
71	18 IN. CHOIR GIRL	424	7.95	175.00
71	18 IN. FROG W/BASS VIOLA	224	11.95	750.00
71	18 IN. MRS. SANTA WITH CARDHOLDER	1563	8.00	108.00
71	18 IN. PETER BUNNY	219	10.95	300.00
71	18 IN. SANTA FUR KID	1191	7.95	300.00
71	29 IN. SNOWMAN WITH BROOM	1075	20.00	300.00
71	30 IN. WHITE BUNNY WITH CARROT	172	*	300.00
71	36 IN. REINDEER WITH TWO GNOMES	624	38.00	450.00
71	5 IN. GNOME WITH CANDLE	*	3.00	350.00
71	7 IN. ANGEL WITH PAPER WINGS	608	3.00	200.00
71	7 IN. ARTIST MOUSE	422	3.95	100.00
71	7 IN. BABY BUNTING IN BASKET	195	3.95	100.00
71	7 IN. BASEBALL MOUSE	553	4.00	75.00
71	7 IN. CHEF MOUSE	*	*	75.00
71	7 IN. MOUSE WITH INNER TUBE	267	4.00	100.00
71	7 IN. MR. & MRS. SANTA WITH BASKET	3403	5.95	100.00
71	7 IN. SKI MOUSE	1326	3.95	100.00
71	7 IN. SNOWMAN	1917	3.95	125.00
71	7 IN. THREE GNOMES W/LARGE CANDLE	80	11.95	700.00
71	7 IN. YELLOW KITTEN	103	4.50	300.00
72	10 IN. DONKEY	861	5.95	300.00
72	10 IN. ROBIN HOOD ELF	*	2.50	125.00
72	12 IN. CAT WITH MOUSE	*	13.00	150.00
72	16 IN. ELEPHANT	230	12.95	500.00
72	18 IN. LEPRECHAUN	1372	*	400.00
72	18 IN. MR. SANTA WITH SACK	850	*	100.00
72	29 IN. EASTER PARADE MOM BUNNY	508	35.00	300.00
72	29 IN. SANTA WITH CARDHOLDER SACK	686	25.00	125.00
72	30 IN. BOY BUNNY	237	25.00	300.00
72	30 IN. ELECTION DONKEY	120	24.00	700.00
72	30 IN. GIRL BUNNY	223	25.00	300.00
72	36 IN. ELECTION ELEPHANT	113	*	700.00
72	7 IN. BALLERINA BUNNY	4700	4.00	100.00
72	7 IN. BAR-BE-QUE MOUSE	907	3.95	75.00
72	7 IN. BUNNY (WITH BANDANA)	1615	3.95	75.00
72	7 IN. CHRISTMAS MOUSE	2793	3.95	75.00
72	7 IN. DIAPER MOUSE, IT'S A BOY	2293	4.50	100.00
72	7 IN. DIAPER MOUSE, IT'S A GIRL	2293	4.50	100.00
72	7 IN. GIRL GOLFER MOUSE	*	3.95	75.00
72	7 IN. HOUSEWIFE MOUSE	1768	3.95	75.00
72	7 IN. MR. & MRS. TUCKERED	1187	6.50	125.00
72	7 IN. MRS. SANTA WITH APRON AND CAP	8867	5.50	75.00
72	7 IN. PREGNANT MOUSE	820	5.50	75.00

YR	NAME	LIMIT	ISSUE	TREND
72	7 IN. SANTA WITH MUSHROOM	540	*	200.00
72	7 IN. YACHTSMAN MOUSE	1130	3.95	120.00
73	12 IN. GIRL NIGHTSHIRT MONKEY	*	7.50	300.00
73	12 IN. NIGHTSHIRT MOUSE	122	7.50	125.00
73	18 IN. MRS. SANTA	3700	7.00	100.00
73	18 IN. MRS. SANTA WITH CARDHOLDER	3900	15.00	100.00
73	7 IN. BUNNY ON BOX	795	5.50	100.00
73	7 IN. CHRISTMAS PANDA	1094	8.95	200.00
73	7 IN. FIREMAN MOUSE	557	4.50	108.00
73	7 IN. FOOTBALL MOUSE	944	4.50	75.00
73	7 IN. GOLFER MOUSE	*	5.00	75.00
73	7 IN. MR. & MRS. SANTA-WICKER LOVESEAT	3973	10.95	125.00
73	7 IN. PAINTER MOUSE	*	4.50	100.00
73	7 IN. SANTA MAILMAN	3276	5.00	100.00
73	7 IN. SKIING MOUSE	2774	4.00	100.00
73	7 IN. WAITER MOUSE	*	4.00	100.00
73	7 IN. WHITE BUNNY	1600	5.50	75.00
74	10 IN. LAD & LASS	453	*	300.00
74	10 IN. WILLIE WOG GOIN' FISHING	*	5.50	200.00
74	12 IN. RETIRED GRANDMA MOUSE	1135	13.50	125.00
74	12 IN. RETIRED GRANDPA MOUSE	1103	13.50	125.00
74	22 IN. WORKSHOP ELF	1404	10.45	150.00
74	22 IN. WORKSHOP ELF WITH APRON	1404	10.95	150.00
74	29 IN. MRS. SANTA WITH CARDHOLDER	*	29.00	125.00
74	7 IN. ARTIST MOUSE	397	5.50	75.00
74	7 IN. BLACK SANTA	1157	5.50	400.00
74	7 IN. CARPENTER MOUSE	551	5.50	75.00
74	7 IN. COWBOY MOUSE	394	5.50	108.00
74	7 IN. DOCTOR MOUSE	720	5.50	75.00
74	7 IN. HOCKEY MOUSE	687	7.95	108.00
74	7 IN. HUNTER MOUSE W/BIRD	690	5.50	125.00
74	7 IN. HUNTER MOUSE WITH DEER	1282	11.50	150.00
74	7 IN. PAINTER MOUSE	*	4.00	125.00
74	7 IN. PREGNANT MOUSE	820	*	75.00
74	7 IN. SANTA IN SKI BOB	704	4.95	250.00
74	7 IN. SEAMSTRESS MOUSE	387	4.00	75.00
74	7 IN. SECRETARY MOUSE	364	4.00	150.00
74	7 IN. VACATION MOUSE	*	*	108.00
75	10 IN. CAROLER BOY	*	*	150.00
75	10 IN. LAD & LASS	162	12.00	200.00
75	10 IN. LAD ON BICYCLE	453	6.00	200.00
75	10 IN. LASS	558	6.00	150.00
75	10 IN. RED NOSED REINDEER	4854	*	75.00
75	18 IN. HORSE	221	17.00	200.00
75	18 IN. LAD	206	11.95	200.00
75	18 IN. LAD & LASS ON BIKE	206	24.00	300.00
75	18 IN. LASS	224	11.95	200.00
75	18 IN. MRS. SANTA WITH PLUM PUDDING	*	12.00	125.00
75	25 IN. LASS WITH BASKET OF FLOWERS	92	29.00	400.00
75	5 IN. BABY DUCK	1333	4.00	108.00
75	7 IN. BEAUTICIAN MOUSE	1349	4.00	108.00
75	7 IN. BICYCLIST MOUSE	1561	5.50	108.00
75	7 IN. BOUQUET GIRL MOUSE	*	3.95	108.00
75	7 IN. CHRISTMAS MOUSE IN SANTA'S MITTEN	3959	5.95	75.00
75	7 IN. FISHERMAN MOUSE	1343	5.50	75.00
75	7 IN. GOIN' FISHIN' MOUSE	4507	5.95	75.00
75	7 IN. HOUSEWIFE MOUSE	1632	5.50	75.00
75	7 IN. PREGNANT MOUSE	879	5.50	75.00
75	7 IN. RETIRED GRANDPA MOUSE	793	5.50	75.00
75	7 IN. SKI MOUSE	5219	5.50	75.00
75	7 IN. TWO IN TENT MICE	914	*	75.00
76	10 IN. BOY IN TIRE SWING	358	6.95	125.00
76	10 IN. CLOWN	2285	5.50	175.00
76	10 IN. COUNTRY GIRL IN TIRE SWING	357	*	150.00
76	10 IN. DONKEY	1202	5.95	250.00
76	10 IN. DRUMMER BOY	*	6.00	150.00
76	10 IN. ELEPHANT	1223	5.95	250.00
76	10 IN. GIRL IN TIRE SWING	357	6.95	150.00
76	10 IN. LASS W/PLANTER BASKET	313	6.95	150.00
76	10 IN. SCARECROW	2341	5.95	150.00
76	10 IN. UNCLE SAM	1095	5.95	300.00
76	10 IN. VOTE DONKEY	1202	5.95	250.00
76	12 IN. COLONIAL BOY & GIRL MOUSE	*	26.90	250.00
76	12 IN. COLONIAL BOY MOUSE	838	13.50	150.00
76	12 IN. COLONIAL GIRL MOUSE	691	13.50	150.00
76	12 IN. GIRL MOUSE WITH PLUM PUDDING	1482	13.50	150.00
76	15 IN. ROOSTER	485	13.50	400.00
76	18 IN. CHOIR BOY	*	*	175.00
76	18 IN. CLOWN	916	13.50	350.00
76	18 IN. DRUMMER BOY	402	13.50	250.00
76	18 IN. EASTER PARADE BOY BUNNY	791	13.50	150.00
76	18 IN. ELEPHANT	285	17.00	500.00
76	18 IN. GIRL BUNNY WITH EGG	789	13.50	150.00
76	18 IN. SCARECROW	916	13.50	250.00
76	18 IN. UNCLE SAM	245	17.00	450.00

YR	NAME	LIMIT	ISSUE	TREND
76	18 IN. VOTE 76 DONKEY	285	17.00	500.00
76	18 IN. YANKEE DOODLE DANDY	153	*	350.00
76	25 IN. YANKEE DOODLE DANDY/30 IN. HORSE	41	78.00	900.00
76	30 IN. CLOWN	466	30.00	500.00
76	36 IN. ELECTION DONKEY	119	*	650.00
76	36 IN. HORSE	27	48.00	450.00
76	42 IN. SCARECROW	134	62.00	750.00
76	7 IN. BIRTHDAY GIRL MOUSE	732	5.50	75.00
76	7 IN. CARD PLAYING GIRL MOUSE	2878	5.95	75.00
76	7 IN. COLONIAL BOY MOUSE	5457	*	75.00
76	7 IN. COLONIAL GIRL MOUSE	5457	5.50	75.00
76	7 IN. GARDENER MOUSE	1255	5.50	75.00
76	7 IN. MISTLETOE ANGEL	17540	6.00	75.00
76	7 IN. MR. HOLLY MOUSE	2774	5.50	75.00
76	7 IN. MRS. HOLLY MOUSE	3078	5.50	75.00
76	7 IN. NURSE MOUSE	5164	5.95	75.00
76	8 IN. ELECTION ELEPHANT	1223	*	350.00
76	8 IN. ROOSTER	1094	5.50	250.00
76	8 IN. WHITE DUCK	3265	4.95	75.00
77	10 IN. CLOWN	4784	6.00	150.00
77	10 IN. SCARECROW	4879	5.95	150.00
77	15 IN. PURPLE ROOSTER	548	5.48	400.00
77	18 IN. CLOWN	2343	13.50	350.00
77	18 IN. EASTER PARADE BOY BUNNY	1567	13.50	150.00
77	18 IN. SCARECROW	*	13.50	250.00
77	18 IN. WHITE ELF	2600	*	100.00
77	22 IN. JACK FROST ELF	2600	11.95	125.00
77	29 IN. EASTER PARADE POP BUNNY	477	35.00	300.00
77	29 IN. MECHANICAL SEE-SAW BUNNY	*	300.00	900.00
77	29 IN. MRS. SANTA MOUSE WITH MUFF	571	50.00	300.00
77	29 IN. POP BUNNY WITH BASKET	*	11.50	300.00
77	7 IN. BASEBALL MOUSE	1634	6.00	750.00
77	7 IN. BEAUTICIAN MOUSE	1521	5.50	108.00
77	7 IN. BINGO MOUSE	1221	6.00	125.00
77	7 IN. BUNNY W/EGG	2442	5.95	75.00
77	7 IN. BUNNY WITH BUTTERFLY	2721	6.00	75.00
77	7 IN. DIET TIME MOUSE	1478	6.00	125.00
77	7 IN. GROOM MOUSE	1211	6.95	75.00
77	7 IN. HOBO MOUSE	1004	5.95	125.00
77	7 IN. MR. NIGHTSHIRT MOUSE	309	50.00	75.00
77	7 IN. SWEETHEART MOUSE	3323	5.50	75.00
77	7 IN. VACATIONER MOUSE	1040	6.00	75.00
77	8 IN. DRUMMER BOY	6522	6.00	75.00
77	8 IN. ROOSTER	1642	6.00	250.00
78	10 IN. BOY PILGRIM	3465	7.00	125.00
78	10 IN. CLOWN	4020	6.50	150.00
78	10 IN. SNOWMAN	9701	6.95	80.00
78	12 IN. CHRISTMAS GNOME	10140	*	125.00
78	12 IN. GNOME	10140	9.50	150.00
78	18 IN. CANDY GIRL	1333	15.00	250.00
78	18 IN. CLOWN	4000	14.00	300.00
78	18 IN. REINDEER	5134	9.00	150.00
78	18 IN. SNOWMAN	3971	80.00	150.00
78	29 IN. CAROLER MOUSE	658	50.00	350.00
78	29 IN. E.P. MOM & POP BUNNIES (PAIR)	529	37.00	450.00
78	36 IN. REINDEER WITH SADDLEBAGS	594	58.00	150.00
78	7 IN. AIRPLANE PILOT MOUSE	2308	6.95	75.00
78	7 IN. ARTIST BUNNY	4217	7.50	125.00
78	7 IN. BUNNIES WITH BASKET	2253	*	100.00
78	7 IN. C.B. MOUSE	2396	6.95	75.00
78	7 IN. DOCTOR MOUSE	2028	6.95	75.00
78	7 IN. DOCTOR MOUSE	816	6.95	75.00
78	7 IN. FIREMAN MOUSE	*	6.95	75.00
78	7 IN. GARDENER MOUSE	*	7.00	75.00
78	7 IN. GIRL GOLFER MOUSE	2215	6.95	75.00
78	7 IN. GROOM MOUSE	2952	9.50	75.00
78	7 IN. GROOM MOUSE	*	14.50	75.00
78	7 IN. NIGHTSHIRT MOUSE	6444	7.95	75.00
78	7 IN. POLICEMAN MOUSE	RT	7.00	100.00
78	7 IN. SANTA WITH DEER AND TREE	5813	18.50	125.00
78	7 IN. SKATEBOARD MOUSE	3733	7.95	125.00
78	7 IN. TEACHER MOUSE	2249	5.50	75.00
78	7 IN. TREE TOP ANGEL WITH WREATH	8613	6.50	75.00
79	10 IN. BOY FROG	5642	8.50	125.00
79	10 IN. SNOWMAN	12888	7.95	80.00
79	12 IN. MRS. SANTA MOUSE	7210	*	100.00
79	12 IN. NIGHTSHIRT MOUSE WITH CANDLE	5739	16.00	100.00
79	12 IN. SANTA MOUSE	*	*	100.00
79	14 IN. FATHER PIG	1500	19.00	150.00
79	14 IN. MOM PIG	1807	19.00	150.00
79	18 IN. ARTIST BUNNY	1064	16.00	200.00
79	18 IN. GIRL FROG	2338	19.00	200.00
79	18 IN. GNOME	9048	17.00	200.00
79	18 IN. MR. SANTA WITH CARDHOLDER	*	*	100.00
79	29 IN. E.P. MOM BUNNY	662	43.00	200.00

YR	NAME	LIMIT	ISSUE	TREND
79	29 IN. GNOME	1762	48.00	400.00
79	29 IN. MOTORIZED MR. & MRS. SANTA	136	400.00	500.00
79	29 IN. SNOWMAN	917	43.00	200.00
79	7 IN. BOY GOLFER MOUSE	2743	7.95	75.00
79	7 IN. C.B. MOUSE	1039	7.95	75.00
79	7 IN. C.B. SANTA	2206	7.95	75.00
79	7 IN. CARPENTER MOUSE	2024	6.95	75.00
79	7 IN. CHIMNEY SWEEP MOUSE	6331	7.95	75.00
79	7 IN. FIREMAN MOUSE	1773	6.95	75.00
79	7 IN. FISHING MOUSE	3053	7.95	75.00
79	7 IN. GARDENER MOUSE	1939	7.95	75.00
79	7 IN. GIRL GOLFER MOUSE	2316	7.95	75.00
79	7 IN. MRS. SANTA MOUSE WITH HOLLY	*	7.95	75.00
79	7 IN. PREGNANT MOUSE	1856	7.95	75.00
79	7 IN. QUILTING MOUSE	213	*	75.00
79	7 IN. SANTA MOUSE	12649	7.95	75.00
79	7 IN. SANTA WITH MISTLETOE	*	7.95	75.00
79	7 IN. SKATEBOARD MOUSE	1821	6.00	150.00
79	7 IN. SWIMMER MOUSE	3640	9.50	100.00
80	10 IN. BOY FROG	4185	9.50	100.00
80	10 IN. BOY ON RAFT	1087	29.00	150.00
80	10 IN. BRIDE FROG	1653	15.00	150.00
80	10 IN. CLOWN	8136	12.50	108.00
80	10 IN. GIRL FROG	421	9.50	100.00
80	10 IN. GROOM FROG	1611	15.00	150.00
80	10 IN. SANTA FROG	7631	9.95	150.00
80	18 IN. BOY FROG	1285	23.00	150.00
80	18 IN. C.G. BUNNY W/BASKET	3964	20.00	100.00
80	18 IN. CLOWN	3192	25.00	150.00
80	18 IN. CLOWN WITH BALLOON	3192	25.00	125.00
80	18 IN. SANTA FROG	2126	25.00	175.00
80	4 FT. CLOWN	224	150.00	400.00
80	4 IN. PIG	1615	8.50	75.00
80	42 IN. CLOWN WITH STAND	224	85.00	400.00
80	42 IN. FROG	202	90.00	400.00
80	42 IN. SANTA FROG	206	100.00	500.00
80	7 IN. BABY IN BASSINETTE	*	*	75.00
80	7 IN. BACKPACKER MOUSE	1008	9.95	75.00
80	7 IN. BALLERINA BUNNY	*	8.95	75.00
80	7 IN. BRIDE & GROOM MICE	2418	9.50	100.00
80	7 IN. CARD PLAYING GIRL MOUSE	1826	9.50	75.00
80	7 IN. DISCO BOY MOUSE	363	9.50	75.00
80	7 IN. DISCO GIRL MOUSE	*	9.50	75.00
80	7 IN. FISHING MOUSE	*	7.50	75.00
80	7 IN. GNOME	13238	9.50	75.00
80	7 IN. GREENTHUMB MOUSE	1869	9.50	75.00
80	7 IN. MOUSE WITH CHIMNEY	4452	*	75.00
80	7 IN. PILOT MOUSE	2011	9.95	75.00
80	7 IN. SANTA WITH STOCKING	17665	9.95	40.00
80	7 IN. SKATING MOUSE	3369	10.95	75.00
80	7 IN. VOLLEYBALL MOUSE	915	9.50	100.00
81	10 IN. BALLOONING SANTA	1737	40.00	150.00
81	10 IN. BOY ON RAFT	*	*	150.00
81	10 IN. BRIDE FROG	1239	15.00	150.00
81	10 IN. CLOWN	6479	9.95	108.00
81	10 IN. ELF ON BUTTERFLY	1625	25.00	125.00
81	10 IN. GROOM FROG	2061	15.00	150.00
81	10 IN. JACK FROST WITH SNOWFLAKE	5950	32.00	75.00
81	12 IN. BOY MONKEY WITH TRAPEZE	1800	24.00	250.00
81	12 IN. GIRL MONKEY WITH TRAPEZE	857	24.00	250.00
81	12 IN. SANTA MONKEY	1800	24.00	250.00
81	12 IN. WITCH MOUSE ON BROOM	1049	35.00	125.00
81	14 IN. DRAGON WITH BUSHBOY	1257	29.00	250.00
81	18 IN. BOY ON SLED	*	12.50	125.00
81	18 IN. BUTTERFLY WITH ELF	2517	28.00	125.00
81	18 IN. CAT W/7 IN. MOUSE & MISTLETOE	10999	47.00	100.00
81	18 IN. CAT W/MOUSE & MISTLETOE	18995	47.00	100.00
81	18 IN. CLOWN	2742	25.00	125.00
81	18 IN. COUNTRY BOY BUNNY WITH CARROT	1998	24.00	100.00
81	18 IN. ESCORT FOX	*	28.50	350.00
81	18 IN. FOXY LADY	*	28.50	350.00
81	18 IN. GIRL FROG	666	24.00	175.00
81	18 IN. MONK W/JUG	494	*	163.00
81	29 IN. DRAGON WITH BUSHBOY	75	63.95	750.00
81	3 IN. PIG	3435	7.95	75.00
81	4 IN. PIG	3194	7.95	75.00
81	5 IN. MINIATURE REINDEER	9080	11.50	50.00
81	7 IN. AIRPLANE PILOT MOUSE	1910	9.95	75.00
81	7 IN. BACKPACKER MOUSE	1008	9.95	75.00
81	7 IN. BASEBALL MOUSE	2380	*	50.00
81	7 IN. CARD PLAYING GIRL MOUSE	863	9.95	50.00
81	7 IN. COUNTRY BUNNIES	7940	*	50.00
81	7 IN. CROSS-COUNTRY SKI SANTA	5180	10.95	60.00
81	7 IN. ESCORT FOX	*	12.50	175.00
81	7 IN. FOXY LADY	*	12.50	175.00

YR	NAME	LIMIT	ISSUE	TREND
81	7 IN. I'M LATE BUNNY	*	*	300.00
81	7 IN. ICESKATER MOUSE	1429	9.95	75.00
81	7 IN. JOGGER MOUSE	1783	9.95	75.00
81	7 IN. MONKEY WITH BANANA TRAPEZE	3075	*	100.00
81	7 IN. NAUGHTY ANGEL	12359	10.95	75.00
81	7 IN. NURSE MOUSE	3222	11.95	75.00
81	7 IN. SANTA MONKEY	4606	10.00	100.00
81	7 IN. SANTA WITH MISTLETOE	*	10.50	75.00
81	7 IN. SANTA WITH POT BELLY	*	11.95	75.00
81	7 IN. WITCH MOUSE ON BROOM WITH MOON	1585+	25.00	100.00
81	7 IN. WOODCHOPPER MOUSE	2121	11.00	75.00
81	8 IN. BOY BBQ PIG	1159	11.95	100.00
81	8 IN. BOY BBQ PIG	4072	10.50	100.00
81	8 IN. GIRL BBQ BUNNY	2596	9.95	100.00
81	8 IN. GIRL BBQ PIG (PAIR)	3854	10.50	200.00
82	10 IN. ELF ON BUTTERFLY	882	*	140.00
82	10 IN. JACK FROST WITH SNOWFLAKE	2289	13.50	75.00
82	10 IN. MONK	6968	12.95	75.00
82	12 IN. BOY SKUNK	935	28.00	150.00
82	12 IN. DUCK WITH KERCHIEF	5861	27.00	75.00
82	12 IN. GIRL SKUNK	936	28.00	150.00
82	12 IN. NIGHTSHIRT MOUSE	2319	26.00	75.00
82	12 IN. PILGRIM BOY MOUSE	2151	28.00	75.00
82	12 IN. PILGRIM GIRL MOUSE	2017	28.00	75.00
82	12 IN. SKUNK WITH SNOWBALL	1304	*	250.00
82	18 IN. GIRL P.J. KID	5389	25.50	75.00
82	18 IN. SANTA FOX	1499	30.00	250.00
82	22 IN. CHRISTMAS GIRAFFE WITH ELF	448	44.00	350.00
82	22 IN. SUN	838	*	200.00
82	4 FT. BOY BUNNY	186	190.00	500.00
82	5 IN. DRAGON WITH BUSHBOY	1066	18.00	200.00
82	5 IN. MRS. SANTA WITH GIFT BOX	7566	10.95	50.00
82	5 IN. SANTA WITH DEER	3072	20.00	75.00
82	7 IN. ANGEL WITH TEARDROP	3092	12.95	45.00
82	7 IN. BALLERINA BUNNY	4179	9.95	45.00
82	7 IN. BRIDE MOUSE	3681	10.95	45.00
82	7 IN. CHEERLEADER MOUSE	3441	10.95	45.00
82	7 IN. COWBOY MOUSE	3776	29.00	45.00
82	7 IN. EASTER PARADE BOY BUNNY	RT	11.95	45.00
82	7 IN. FOOTBALL MOUSE	2164	10.50	45.00
82	7 IN. GIRL TENNIS MOUSE	2443	10.95	45.00
82	7 IN. GRADUATE BOY MOUSE	4971	12.00	45.00
82	7 IN. GRADUATE GIRL MOUSE	3563	10.95	45.00
82	7 IN. GROOM MOUSE	3406	10.95	40.00
82	7 IN. I'M A 10 BABY	2159	12.95	50.00
82	7 IN. MOUSE WITH STRAWBERRY	*	11.95	45.00
82	7 IN. MRS. A.M. MOUSE	2184	11.95	45.00
82	7 IN. SANTA FOX	3726	12.95	100.00
82	7 IN. SANTA FOX W/BAG	3622	12.95	100.00
82	7 IN. SANTA WREATH CENTERPIECE	1150	*	50.00
82	7 IN. SWEETHEART MOUSE	4110	11.00	50.00
82	7 IN. WINDSURFER MOUSE	4114	14.00	100.00
82	7 IN. WITCH MOUSE ON BROOM	2798	12.95	50.00
82	7 IN. WOODCHOPPER MOUSE	1910	11.95	50.00
82	8 IN. BALLERINA PIG	1058	12.95	100.00
82	8 IN. BOY BBQ PIG	1044	11.95	100.00
83	10 IN. BALLOONING ELVES	7395	60.00	200.00
83	10 IN. WORKSHOP ELF	*	*	50.00
83	12 IN. BRIDE MOUSE	854	32.00	40.00
83	12 IN. GROOM MOUSE	826	32.00	45.00
83	16 IN. MONK WITH JUG	*	28.00	150.00
83	18 IN. CLASSIC SNOWMAN #7525	SU	*	75.00
83	18 IN. FAWN	1444	33.00	150.00
83	18 IN. GINGERBREAD MAN	5027	29.00	100.00
83	18 IN. SCARECROW	2300	29.00	150.00
83	18 IN. SCARECROW	3896	33.00	150.00
83	18 IN. SCARECROW	3150	33.00	150.00
83	22 IN. SUN	*	*	150.00
83	24 IN. STORK WITH BABY	858	37.00	150.00
83	29 IN. EASTER PARADE GIRL BUNNY	*	71.95	125.00
83	5 IN. BUNNY ON MUSIC BOX	*	30.00	100.00
83	5 IN. COUNTRY GIRL BUNNY	5163	*	100.00
83	5 IN. DRAGON WITH WINGS & BABY	199	22.50	400.00
83	5 IN. E.P. BOY DUCK	5133	*	50.00
83	5 IN. E.P. GIRL DUCK	5577	*	50.00
83	5 IN. FLOPPY-EAR BOY BUNNY WITH BASKET	*	11.50	100.00
83	5 IN. SWEETHEART DUCK	1530	*	40.00
83	7 IN. CHEERLEADER MOUSE	2025	11.95	50.00
83	7 IN. CLASSIC SNOWMAN #7705	SU	*	40.00
83	7 IN. COUNTRY BOY BUNNY WITH BUTTERFLY	*	12.50	50.00
83	7 IN. COWBOY MOUSE	1794	12.95	50.00
83	7 IN. COWGIRL MOUSE	1517	12.95	50.00
83	7 IN. E.P. BOY BUNNY	*	12.50	50.00
83	7 IN. E.P. GIRL BUNNY	RT	12.50	50.00
83	7 IN. EQUESTRIAN MOUSE	*	12.95	100.00

YR	NAME	LIMIT	ISSUE	TREND
83	7 IN. FISHING BOY	*	12.95	50.00
83	7 IN. QUILTING MOUSE	2786	11.95	50.00
83	7 IN. SNOWMAN	15980	12.95	40.00
83	7 IN. WINDSURFER MOUSE	2352	14.00	100.00
83	ANGEL MAKING MUSIC #7110	SU	*	50.00
84	10 IN. AEROBIC DANCER	4875	18.00	50.00
84	10 IN. CLOWN	6383	14.00	50.00
84	10 IN. DOWNHILL SKIER	3535	32.00	100.00
84	10 IN. GINGERBREAD MAN	4615	16.00	50.00
84	10 IN. SCARECROW	3008	16.00	75.00
84	12 IN. DEVIL MOUSE	1118	30.00	150.00
84	16 IN. MONK WITH JUG	1767	35.00	150.00
84	18 IN. AEROBIC DANCER	622	36.00	100.00
84	18 IN. BOB CRATCHET	1819	50.00	100.00
84	18 IN. BOY ON SLED	2205	30.00	100.00
84	18 IN. CANDY BOY	1350	30.00	100.00
84	18 IN. CANDY GIRL	1333	30.00	100.00
84	18 IN. CLOWN	*	33.00	100.00
84	18 IN. COUNTRY GIRL BUNNY WITH BASKET	1481	32.00	100.00
84	18 IN. FAWN WITH WREATH	1444	33.00	150.00
84	18 IN. GIRL ON SLED	2328	30.00	100.00
84	18 IN. MARTHA CRATCHET	1751	36.00	100.00
84	18 IN. MONK WITH JUG	1821	35.00	150.00
84	30 IN MRS. SANTA W/CARDHOLDER APRON #6015	SU	*	125.00
84	30 IN. CLOWN	387	70.00	150.00
84	30 IN. MONK	432	79.00	400.00
84	30 IN. SNOWGIRL	685	80.00	300.00
84	30 IN. SNOWGIRL AND BOY	685	80.00	500.00
84	30 IN. SNOWMAN	956	80.00	300.00
84	32 IN. MONK WITH GARLAND	416	79.00	600.00
84	4 IN. SNOWMAN	*	170.00	500.00
84	5 IN. COUNTRY BUNNIES WITH BASKET	1110	*	90.00
84	5 IN. DUCK IN SANTA HAT	2371	12.95	40
84	5 IN. GIRL BUNNY	2594	11.50	100.00
84	5 IN. PILOT DUCKLING	4396	15.00	50.00
84	7 IN. ANGEL MOUSE	2093	15.00	40.00
84	7 IN. ANGEL ON STAR	772	33.00	40.00
84	7 IN. BASEBALL KID	2079	13.00	40.00
84	7 IN. BOWLING MOUSE	1472	14.00	40.00
84	7 IN. BOY WITH FIRECRACKER	1893	20.00	100.00
84	7 IN. COUNTRY BUNNIES WITH BASKET	2345	26.00	40.00
84	7 IN. COUNTRY GIRL WITH BASKET	715	17.00	40.00
84	7 IN. CUPID IN HEART	2445	33.00	40.00
84	7 IN. CUPID KID	6808	15.00	40.00
84	7 IN. DEVIL MOUSE	3571	14.00	40.00
84	7 IN. E.P. BOY BUNNY	5989	12.95	40.00
84	7 IN. HOCKEY PLAYER MOUSE	1525	5.50	40.00
84	7 IN. JOGGER KID	*	18.00	40.00
84	7 IN. MOUSE WITH STRAWBERRY	1776	11.95	40.00
84	7 IN. MOUSE WITH WREATH	*	12.95	40.00
84	7 IN. MRS. RETIRED MOUSE	1356	14.00	40.00
84	7 IN. NAUGHTY ANGEL	4528	15.00	40.00
84	7 IN. NIGHTSHIRT MOUSE	*	11.95	40.00
84	7 IN. SANTA ON A MOON	*	*	100.00
84	7 IN. SNOWBALL MOUSE #7740	SU	*	40.00
84	7 IN. TEACHER MOUSE	3150	14.00	40.00
84	7 IN. TEACHER MOUSE, GIRL	5064	14.00	40.00
84	7 IN. TWO BUNNIES WITH BUSHEL BASKET	2339	26.00	40.00
84	7 IN. VALENTINE BUNNY	5602	14.00	40.00
84	8 IN. MONK WITH JUG	3502	18.00	50.00
84	JOHNNY APPLESEED #627	1500	80.00	400.00
84	ROBIN HOOD	1500	80.00	350.00
85	10 IN. BRIDE	318	*	75.00
85	10 IN. CROSS COUNTRY SKIER	1150	*	100.00
85	10 IN. GROOM	264	*	75.00
85	10 IN. PANDA WITH TOY BAG	1904	20.00	45.00
85	10 IN. PENGUIN #178	3000	30.00	100.00
85	10 IN. REINDEER WITH BELL	6398	14.00	40.00
85	10 IN. SCARECROW	2930	16.00	60.00
85	12 IN. DUCK WITH RAINCOAT	*	*	60.00
85	12 IN. INDIAN BOY MOUSE	*	34.50	60.00
85	12 IN. JAZZ CAT	2622	*	100.00
85	12 IN. KID W/SLED	4707	31.50	75.00
85	12 IN. NAUGHTY ANGEL	1393	37.00	75.00
85	15 IN. JAZZ CAT	2622	32.00	60.00
85	18 IN. CHRISTMAS PANDA	2207	44.00	100.00
85	18 IN. CLOWN	2275	37.00	100.00
85	18 IN. CLOWN WITH BALLOON	1485	37.00	100.00
85	18 IN. COUNTRY BOY BUNNY W/WATERING CAN	2355	47.00	75.00
85	18 IN. VALENTINE CAT WITH HEART	2129	35.00	150.00
85	7 IN. BASEBALL KID	1221	17.00	40.00
85	7 IN. BIRTHDAY GIRL	1017	19.00	40.00
85	7 IN. BOY BUNNY WITH CARROT	3273	15.00	40.00
85	7 IN. BOY GOLFER MOUSE	2099	15.00	40.00
85	7 IN. BRIDE & GROOM MICE	2963	14.00	40.00

YR	NAME	LIMIT	ISSUE	TREND
85	7 IN. DRESS-UP BOY	1174	19.00	40.00
85	7 IN. DRESS-UP GIRL	1536	19.00	40.00
85	7 IN. GET-WELL MOUSE	1425	15.00	40.00
85	7 IN. GIRL TENNIS MOUSE	1947	15.00	40.00
85	7 IN. GRADUATE GIRL MOUSE	2884	14.00	40.00
85	7 IN. GRADUATION MOUSE	1999	14.00	40.00
85	7 IN. HAPPY BIRTHDAY BOY	937	19.00	40.00
85	7 IN. HIKER MOUSE	1781	14.00	50.00
85	7 IN. HOCKEY PLAYER KID	1578	19.00	40.00
85	7 IN. JOGGER KID	654	18.00	40.00
85	7 IN. KID WITH KITE	1084	18.00	40.00
85	7 IN. LOGO KID	3562	*	200.00
85	7 IN. VALENTINE BUNNY	5602	14.00	40.00
85	ANNIE OAKLEY #185	1500	95.00	300.00
85	CHRISTMAS TREE SKIRT	1332	25.00	100.00
86	10 IN. CHRISTMAS PANDA W/TOY BAG	4397	19.00	50.00
86	10 IN. CLOWN	3897	15.50	50.00
86	10 IN. KITTEN W/YARN & BASKET	3917	28.00	50.00
86	10 IN. UNICORN, #268	3000	36.50	100.00
86	12 IN. NAUGHTY ANGEL WITH SLINGSHOT	*	37.00	75.00
86	18 IN. COUNTRY BOY BUNNY W/WHEELBARROW	1224	47.00	75.00
86	18 IN. COUNTRY GIRL BUNNY W/FLOWERS	1205	42.00	75.00
86	18 IN. MRS. VICTORIAN SANTA	2000	*	75.00
86	18 IN. VALENTINE CAT	*	*	150.00
86	30 IN. BOY BUNNY WITH WHEELBARROW	252	119.50	125.00
86	5 IN. DUCK WITH RAINCOAT	5029	*	40.00
86	7 IN. BIRTHDAY GIRL MOUSE	3724	15.00	40.00
86	7 IN. BOATING MOUSE	2320	17.00	40.00
86	7 IN. BOY BUNNY WITH CARROT	2949	15.50	40.00
86	7 IN. BUNNY WITH EGG	2233	17.00	40.00
86	7 IN. CUPID IN HOT AIR BALLOON	391	54.95	100.00
86	7 IN. INDIAN GIRL MOUSE WITH PAPOOSE	6992	25.00	40.00
86	7 IN. LOGO KID	6271	*	175.00
86	7 IN. MOUSE WITH WHEELBARROW	2037	17.00	40.00
86	7 IN. SKIING KID	8057	18.45	40.00
86	7 IN. SWEETHEART MOUSE	6271	12.95	40.00
86	7 IN. TENNIS MOUSE	1947	16.00	40.00
86	7 IN. VALENTINE BUNNY	*	14.50	40.00
86	7 IN. VICTORIAN SANTA W/SLEIGH & DEER	6820	44.00	75.00
86	7 IN. WITCH MOUSE IN PUMPKIN BALLOON	868	77.95	150.00
86	BALLOONING CLOWN	2700	17.00	150.00
86	MARK TWAIN #467	2500	119.50	200.00
87	10 IN. BRIDE & GROOM CAT	727	*	200.00
87	10 IN. CLOWN	*	18.00	40.00
87	10 IN. COLLECTOR SANTA TRIMMING TREE	*	130.00	100.00
87	10 IN. HUCK FINN, #690	1200	102.95	125.00
87	12 IN. DUCK ON SLED	300	*	200.00
87	18 IN. BOTTLECOVER MONK	718	30.00	150.00
87	18 IN. CHEF SANTA #5632	SU	*	75.00
87	18 IN. MR. VICTORIAN SANTA	2150	58.00	75.00
87	18 IN. VICTORIAN COUNTRY BOY BUNNY	1394	50.00	75.00
87	18 IN. VICTORIAN COUNTRY GIRL BUNNY-PAIR	1492	50.00	150.00
87	18 IN. WORKSHOP SANTA	980	*	75.00
87	24 IN. CHRISTMAS GOOSE WITH BASKET	*	54.95	100.00
87	3 IN. BABY WITCH	*	14.00	50.00
87	3 IN. BRIDE & GROOM	1250	39.00	100.00
87	3 IN. CUPID IN HEART BALLOON	1715	39.00	100.00
87	30 IN. MR. VICTORIAN SANTA	450	150.00	150.00
87	30 IN. MRS. VICTORIAN SANTA	425	150.00	150.00
87	5 IN. MONK	*	14.00	50.00
87	7 IN. BABY MOUSE	2500	14.00	40.00
87	7 IN. BABY W/BLANKET & SWEATER	7836	22.00	40.00
87	7 IN. BARBEQUE MOUSE	1798	18.00	40.00
87	7 IN. BICYCLIST BOY MOUSE	1507	20.00	40.00
87	7 IN. BOY GRADUATE	2034	*	40.00
87	7 IN. BRIDE MOUSE	1801	14.50	40.00
87	7 IN. GIRL GRADUATE	2438	20.00	40.00
87	7 IN. GROOM MOUSE	1800	14.50	40.00
87	7 IN. INDIAN BOY	*	20.00	40.00
87	7 IN. KANGAROO	3000	37.50	100.00
87	7 IN. LOGO KID	11000	*	150.00
87	7 IN. VICTORIAN MR. & MRS. SANTA	*	24.00	100.00
87	BEN FRANKLIN #1776	2500	119.50	175.00
87	CARROT	2503	9.95	200.00
88	10 IN. EASTER PARADE BOY PIG	3005	24.50	40.00
88	10 IN. EASTER PARADE GIRL PIG (PAIR)	3400	24.50	40.00
88	10 IN. STORK W/3 IN. BABY	500	50.00	100.00
88	18 IN. COUNTRY MOM BUNNY W/BABY	1800	68.95	75.00
88	30 IN. VICTORIAN MRS. SANTA WITH TRAY	*	119.95	150.00
88	5 IN. OWL	3000	37.50	100.00
88	7 IN. BUNNIES ON MUSIC BOX MAYPOLE	5602	14.00	150.00
88	7 IN. BUNNY WITH SLED	3050	22.00	40.00
88	7 IN. LOGO KID	*	*	100.00
88	SHERLOCK HOLMES #391	2500	119.50	175.00
89	10 IN. MERLIN	3565	70.00	100.00

YR	NAME	LIMIT	ISSUE	TREND
89	12 IN. TRICK OR TREAT MOUSE	*	40.00	60.00
89	7 IN. BUSINESS MAN MOUSE	5085	22.00	40.00
89	7 IN. KNITTING MOUSE	5115	20.00	35.00
89	7 IN. LOGO KID	*	*	75.00
89	7 IN. POLAR BEAR CUB	3000	37.50	100.00
89	7 IN. SWEETHEART MOUSE	*	17.00	35.00
89	7 IN. TACKY TOURIST MOUSE	5116	*	35.00
89	ABRAHAM LINCOLN	2500	119.50	150.00
90	18 IN. STRAWBERRY BUNNY	2365	60.00	60.00
90	30 IN. CLOWN WITH STAND	530	100.00	100.00
90	30 IN. STRAWBERRY BUNNY	582	135.95	100.00
90	7 IN. ARTIST MOUSE	7285	*	35.00
90	7 IN. CHICKEN	3000	37.50	40.00
90	7 IN. LOGO KID	*	*	40.00
90	7 IN. MAUI MOUSE	7220	*	35.00
90	7 IN. SAILOR MOUSE	6838	24.00	35.00
90	BETSY ROSS	2500	119.50	150.00
91	10 IN. ANNALEE COLLECTOR DOLL	588	149.95	150.00
91	10 IN. AVIATOR FROG (WWI)	2110	20.00	40.00
91	10 IN. BEAR IN NIGHTSHIRT	2774	33.00	40.00
91	10 IN. BEAR IN VELOUR SANTA SUIT	3711	33.00	40.00
91	10 IN. BEAR W/SNOWBALL, KNIT HAT	3121	30.00	40.00
91	10 IN. BLACK CAT	6267	22.00	40.00
91	10 IN. BOB CRATCHET & 5 IN. TINY TIM	639	100.00	60.00
91	10 IN. BRIDE BEAR	2977	40.00	40.00
91	10 IN. CHRISTMAS ELF	16567	16.00	20.00
91	10 IN. CHRISTOPHER COLUMBUS	1132	119.50	150.00
91	10 IN. CONDUCTOR DOLL (MUSIC)	383	129.50	300.00
91	10 IN. COUNTRY BOY BUNNY	1844	43.00	40.00
91	10 IN. COUNTRY GIRL BUNNY	2044	35.00	40.00
91	10 IN. DOE	6541	21.00	35.00
91	10 IN. EASTER PARADE BOY BUNNY	4195	38.00	40.00
91	10 IN. EASTER PARADE GIRL BUNNY	5101	39.00	40.00
91	10 IN. GINGERBREAD BOY	10453	22.45	40.00
91	10 IN. GIRL W/BASKET	3592	38.00	40.00
91	10 IN. GROOM BEAR	2745	40.00	40.00
91	10 IN. HOBO CLOWN	2368	25.45	40.00
91	10 IN. HUSKIE W/5 IN. PUPPY	2860	54.95	60.00
91	10 IN. INDIAN MAN	2719	33.00	60.00
91	10 IN. INDIAN WOMAN	2779	33.00	60.00
91	10 IN. KITTEN ON SLED	3810	36.00	40.00
91	10 IN. KITTEN W/KNIT MITTENS	4124	34.00	40.00
91	10 IN. LARGE PUMPKIN	1872	49.00	80.00
91	10 IN. MAN SKATER	4881	46.00	80.00
91	10 IN. MARTHA CRATCHET W/PLUM	2136	60.00	60.00
91	10 IN. MUSIC CONDUCTOR DOLL	*	139.50	300.00
91	10 IN. NATIVITY ANGEL	2112	60.00	80.00
91	10 IN. NATIVITY SET	658	149.95	125.00
91	10 IN. PILGRIM MAN W/BASKET	2374	45.00	60.00
91	10 IN. PILGRIM WOMAN W/TURKEY	2502	45.00	60.00
91	10 IN. REINDEER W/CAP & BELL	10300	22.45	40.00
91	10 IN. SANTA FEEDING REINDEER	2618	80.00	100.00
91	10 IN. SANTA ON ROCKING HORSE	2398	50.00	100.00
91	10 IN. SANTA PIG	2685	32.00	50.00
91	10 IN. SANTA PLAYING W/TRAIN	1525	50.00	100.00
91	10 IN. SANTA W/REINDEER GOLFING	2462	80.00	100.00
91	10 IN. SCROOGE	592	90.00	100.00
91	10 IN. SHEPHERD BOY & LAMB	591	90.00	100.00
91	10 IN. SKATING BUNNY	6027	44.00	40.00
91	10 IN. SNOWY OWL	3163	26.00	40.00
91	10 IN. SPRING ELF	4060	16.00	35.00
91	10 IN. SUMMER SANTA	1926	60.00	50.00
91	10 IN. THE SPIRIT OF '76	1080	175.00	300.00
91	10 IN. TWO WISE MEN W/BRASS	476	109.95	150.00
91	10 IN. VICTORY SKI DOLL	1192	50.00	50.00
91	10 IN. WISE MAN W/CAMEL	650	109.95	150.00
91	10 IN. WOMAN SKATER	4975	46.00	75.00
91	10 IN.TINSEL ELF	17070	20.45	40.00
91	12 IN. BASKET COUPLE	2028	96.95	100.00
91	12 IN. BAT	3113	30.00	75.00
91	12 IN. CHRISTMAS SWAN	674	63.95	75.00
91	12 IN. DRUMMER BOY	3298	40.00	50.00
91	12 IN. EASTER DUCK W/WATERING	1407	50.00	50.00
91	12 IN. PILGRIM BOY MOUSE	1980	43.00	50.00
91	12 IN. PILGRIM GIRL MOUSE	1978	43.00	50.00
91	12 IN. PJ KID W/BLONDE HAIR	2726	30.00	40.00
91	12 IN. PJ KID W/BROWN HAIR	2307	30.00	40.00
91	12 IN. SANTA DUCK	1187	54.00	40.00
91	12 IN. SANTA W/POTBELLIED STOVE	5887	60.00	50.00
91	12 IN. SANTA'S HELPER PAINTING	5274	36.00	50.00
91	12 IN. SANTA'S POSTMAN	6980	36.00	50.00
91	12 IN. SCARECROW	2330	41.00	50.00
91	12 IN. SPIDER	5194	33.00	100.00
91	12 IN. SPRING SWAN	615	50.00	50.00
91	12 IN. TREE TOP ANGEL	2589	43.00	50.00

YR	NAME	LIMIT	ISSUE	TREND
91	12 IN. TUCKERED COUPLE	2574	90.00	75.00
91	12 IN. VELOUR MRS. SANTA	3677	50.00	60.00
91	12 IN. VELOUR SANTA W/TOYBAG	3517	50.00	75.00
91	15 IN. HOBO CLOWN	1295	48.00	75.00
91	18 IN. ANGLE W/INSTRUMENT	1009	56.00	100.00
91	18 IN. BUNNY KID W/BUNNY	2859	50.00	100.00
91	18 IN. CHEF SANTA	4511	47.00	75.00
91	18 IN. CHOIR BOY	3120	57.95	75.00
91	18 IN. CHOIR GIRL	2188	57.95	75.00
91	18 IN. DAY-AFTER-CHRISTMAS SANTA	2263	80.00	75.00
91	18 IN. EASTER PARADE BOY BUNNY	2056	63.00	75.00
91	18 IN. EASTER PARADE GIRL BUNNY	2254	63.00	75.00
91	18 IN. GINGERBREAD BOY	3966	51.00	75.00
91	18 IN. MRS. SANTA W/PRESENTS	5497	50.00	75.00
91	18 IN. MRS. SANTA W/TRAY	5143	50.00	75.00
91	18 IN. NAUGHTY KID	547	74.95	75.00
91	18 IN. PJ KID	1307	40.00	60.00
91	18 IN. PJ KID HANGING STOCKING	1396	47.00	60.00
91	18 IN. PJ KID IN 2 FT. STOCKING	RT	61.95	75.00
91	18 IN. PUMPKIN COSTUME KID	1317	75.00	150.00
91	18 IN. REINDEER W/CHRISTMAS	4053	52.95	75.00
91	18 IN. SANTA W/CARDHOLDER	8056	60.00	75.00
91	18 IN. SANTA W/GIFT LIST	6334	44.00	75.00
91	18 IN. SANTA W/STOCKING	4466	48.00	75.00
91	18 IN. SNOWMAN W/BROOM	4218	44.00	75.00
91	18 IN. SNOWY OWL	965	65.95	75.00
91	18 IN. THORNY THE GHOST	1270	52.00	100.00
91	18 IN. TRICK OR TREAT BUNNY KID	625	50.00	100.00
91	18 IN. WITCH	2033	63.95	100.00
91	22 IN. CHRISTMAS STOCKING	4993	18.45	100.00
91	22 IN. RED CHRISTMAS ELF	3679	35.00	50.00
91	3 IN. WATER BABY IN POND LILY	3720	15.00	50.00
91	30 IN. MR. & MRS. TUCKERED	644	291.45	200.00
91	30 IN. MRS. SANTA W/CARDHOLDER	1483	119.95	140.00
91	30 IN. SANTA W/LIGHTED TREE	509	190.00	140.00
91	30 IN. VELOUR MRS. SANTA W/MUFF	755	160.45	140.00
91	30 IN. VELOUR SANTA W/PIPE & BAG	1221	160.45	140.00
91	36 IN. REINDEER (ANIMATED)	134	339.95	350.00
91	36 IN. REINDEER W/CARDHOLDER	879	148.45	150.00
91	5 IN. ANGEL	9844	23.00	40.00
91	5 IN. BABY SWAN	3168	14.00	35.00
91	5 IN. CHRISTMAS DRAGON	4125	24.00	35.00
91	5 IN. DUCK ON FLEXIBLE FLYER	3822	26.00	35.00
91	5 IN. EASTER PARADE BOY DUCK	4261	22.00	35.00
91	5 IN. EASTER PARADE GIRL DUCK	5105	24.00	35.00
91	5 IN. ELF (WORKSHOP)	16359	13.45	15.00
91	5 IN. FAWN	13027	14.45	15.00
91	5 IN. FLUFFY YELLOW CHICK	6979	16.00	20.00
91	5 IN. LAMB	4302	16.00	20.00
91	5 IN. LEPRECHAUN	6384	16.00	30.00
91	5 IN. SAILOR DUCK	2241	22.00	20.00
91	5 IN. SPRING LAMB	6709	17.00	20.00
91	5 IN. TRIM-A-TREE ELF	10108	12.95	20.00
91	5 IN. WINTER DUCK IN INNER TUBE	2.992	24.00	30.00
91	7 IN. ANGEL ON SLED W/CLOUD	2313	30.00	30.00
91	7 IN. ANGEL W/MUSICAL INSTRUMENT	5879	20.00	30.00
91	7 IN. BAKER MOUSE	6895	26.00	30.00
91	7 IN. BEN FRANKLIN MOUSE	5029	30.00	30.00
91	7 IN. BUNNY KID	3827	23.45	30.00
91	7 IN. CAROLLER BOY	510	23.00	30.00
91	7 IN. CAROLLER BOY MOUSE W/MUSIC	7281	15.45	30.00
91	7 IN. CAROLLER GIRL	5134	23.00	30.00
91	7 IN. CHRISTMAS GNOME	15503	18.00	30.00
91	7 IN. COUNTRY BOY BUNNY	SU	20.45	30.00
91	7 IN. COUNTRY GIRL BUNNY	SU	20.45	30.00
91	7 IN. DESERT STORM MOUSE	37475	30.00	30.00
91	7 IN. DISNEY COLLECTION	300	80.00	300.00
91	7 IN. DRAGON KID	1116	32.00	50.00
91	7 IN. DUMMMER BOY	7031	22.45	50.00
91	7 IN. EARTH DAY MOUSE	5863	30.00	30.00
91	7 IN. EASTER PARADE BOY	7043	21.00	30.00
91	7 IN. EASTER PARADE DRESS-UP BOY	*	27.45	30.00
91	7 IN. EASTER PARADE GIRL	9120	19.00	30.00
91	7 IN. FLYING ANGEL W/MISTLETOE	6003	19.00	30.00
91	7 IN. GHOST KID W/PUMPKIN	1982	24.45	50.00
91	7 IN. GNOME W/MUSHROOM	5007	30.00	50.00
91	7 IN. INDIAN BOY	3371	30.00	50.00
91	7 IN. INDIAN GIRL	2777	23.00	50.00
91	7 IN. LOGO KID	26516	19.50	60.00
91	7 IN. MOUSE IN BOX	5526	20.00	30.00
91	7 IN. MOUSE IN SANTA'S HAT	9742	18.00	30.00
91	7 IN. MOUSE W/CANDY CANE	5206	18.00	30.00
91	7 IN. MOUSE W/CHRISTMAS STOCKING	6543	18.00	30.00
91	7 IN. MOUSE W/MAILBAG	14546	26.00	30.00
91	7 IN. MOUSE W/PRESENTS	8075	18.00	30.00

"Hush My Baby" sings the chubby-cheeked Suzy created by artist Bette Ball. Suzy is from the "Victoria Ashlea Originals" collection by Goebel.

Mattel's first Bob Mackie Barbie doll, Gold Barbie has greatly increased in value since its release in 1990.

Justin from the Moments to Remember Collection by Yolanda Bello for Ashton-Drake Galleries, has increased in value since its 1991 release.

Limited to 1,000, Teacher's Pet from Good-Kruger Dolls was issued in 1991 for $199.

Lee Middleton pays tribute to the season of joy with her 1991 Christmas Angel.

YR	NAME	LIMIT	ISSUE	TREND
91	7 IN. MOUSE W/SNOWBALL	6805	18.00	30.00
91	7 IN. MOUSE W/TENNIS RACQUET	5674	22.00	30.00
91	7 IN. MR. TUCKERED MOUSE	12413	20.00	30.00
91	7 IN. MRS. SANTA HANGING MERRY	11769	28.00	30.00
91	7 IN. MRS. SANTA W/PRESENTS	8060	26.45	30.00
91	7 IN. MRS. TUCKERED MOUSE	13266	20.00	30.00
91	7 IN. PILGRIM KIDS W/BASKET	2672	53.95	50.00
91	7 IN. PILGRIM MICE SET W/BASKET	2721	43.00	50.00
91	7 IN. PUMPKIN KID	3517	27.45	50.00
91	7 IN. RED CROSS NURSE MOUSE	8305	30.00	50.00
91	7 IN. RITZ SNOWMAN	10309	27.00	30.00
91	7 IN. SANTA BRINGING HOME	8604	28.00	30.00
91	7 IN. SANTA IN TUB W/RUBBER DUCKY	5373	34.00	50.00
91	7 IN. SANTA W/GIFTLIST & TOY BAG	8886	22.45	30.00
91	7 IN. SANTA W/MAILBAG & LETTERS	12156	28.00	30.00
91	7 IN. SANTA W/SLEIGH	3407	40.00	30.00
91	7 IN. SECRETARY MOUSE	6394	30.00	30.00
91	7 IN. SHERIFF MOUSE (D.S.)	1191	50.00	75.00
91	7 IN. SKELETON COSTUME KID	2596	24.45	50.00
91	7 IN. SLEDDING MOUSE	5950	21.00	30.00
91	7 IN. SNOWMAN W/PIPE	7401	24.00	30.00
91	7 IN. SWEETHEART BOY MOUSE	7865	20.00	30.00
91	7 IN. SWEETHEART GIRL MOUSE	7865	19.00	30.00
91	7 IN. TRICK OR TREAT BUNNY KID	2187	26.00	50.00
91	7 IN. TWO IN A TENT MICE	*	35.00	30.00
91	7 IN. VELOUR MRS. SANTA W/COAT	5808	27.45	30.00
91	7 IN. VELOUR SANTA W/COAT & PIPE	*	27.45	30.00
91	7 IN. VIDEO MOUSE	4978	26.00	30.00
91	7 IN. WAITER MOUSE	4573	26.00	30.00
91	7 IN. WITCH KID	3311	27.45	30.00
91	7 IN. WORKSHOP MOUSE	12536	22.00	30.00
91	7 IN. WORKSHOP SANTA	3872	27.00	30.00
91	DESERT MOUSE HEAD PIN	9141	7.95	30.00
91	LARGE TURKEY	1132	57.95	75.00
91	RED CROSS NURSE MOUSE HEAD	8572	7.95	30.00
91	SANTA W/PRESENTS	7863	23.00	30.00
91	SMALL TURKEY	2586	35.00	50.00
91	SMALL TURKEY W/7 IN. INDIAN GIRL	1658	58.00	75.00
92	10 IN. ANNALEE BASEBALL PLAYER	5760	30.00	60.00
92	10 IN. ANNALEE PITCHER	1283	36.00	60.00
92	10 IN. BEAR IN NIGHTSHIRT	3434	34.00	40.00
92	10 IN. BEAR IN VELOUR SANTA SUIT	3938	33.00	40.00
92	10 IN. BEAR W/SNOWBALL, KNIT HAT	3826	30.00	40.00
92	10 IN. BLACK CAT	4101	26.00	40.00
92	10 IN. CHRISTMAS ELF	18130	16.00	20.00
92	10 IN. CHRISTMAS EVE BOB	1681	70.00	75.00
92	10 IN. CHRISTMAS EVE SCROOGE	1722	60.00	60.00
92	10 IN. COUNTRY BOY BUNNY	2395	35.00	40.00
92	10 IN. COUNTRY GIRL BUNNY	2577	35.00	40.00
92	10 IN. DOE	2096	21.00	30.00
92	10 IN. EASTER PARADE BOY BUNNY	3902	39.00	40.00
92	10 IN. EASTER PARADE GIRL BUNNY	4832	39.00	40.00
92	10 IN. FATHER TIME	1796	54.95	75.00
92	10 IN. FISHING SANTA IN BOAT	1582	100.00	100.00
92	10 IN. FROG IN BOAT	3231	32.00	40.00
92	10 IN. GINGERBREAD BOY	7361	22.45	35.00
92	10 IN. INDIAN MAN	1834	34.45	60.00
92	10 IN. INDIAN WOMAN	1816	33.00	60.00
92	10 IN. JACOB MARLEY	672	90.00	90.00
92	10 IN. KITTEN W/KNIT MITTENS	4004	34.00	40.00
92	10 IN. MAN SKATER	2688	46.00	55.00
92	10 IN. MARTHA CRATCHET W/PLUM	784	60.00	60.00
92	10 IN. MRS. BEAR IN NIGHTSHIRT	4661	39.00	40.00
92	10 IN. PILGRIM MAN W/BASKET	1803	45.00	45.00
92	10 IN. PILGRIM WOMAN W/TURKEY	1904	45.00	45.00
92	10 IN. REINDEER W/CAP & BELL	10650	23.00	25.00
92	10 IN. SANTA AT WORKBENCH	2209	70.00	70.00
92	10 IN. SAVING SANTA	1605	60.00	60.00
92	10 IN. SNOW QUEEN	4390	39.00	40.00
92	10 IN. SNOWY OWL	2634	26.00	30.00
92	10 IN. TENNIS SANTA	2115	50.00	50.00
92	10 IN. TINSEL, THE ELF	9967	20.45	25.00
92	10 IN. UNCLE SAM FOLK HERO	1034	88.00	150.00
92	10 IN. WOMAN SKATER	2754	46.00	45.00
92	12 IN. BASKET COUPLE	1	600.00	75.00
92	12 IN. BAT	2107	32.00	75.00
92	12 IN. CHEF SANTA	3353	45.00	60.00
92	12 IN. DRUMMER BOY	3316	40.00	40.00
92	12 IN. MRS. SANTA W/POINSETTA	3463	50.00	50.00
92	12 IN. PILGRIM BOY MOUSE	1449	43.00	45.00
92	12 IN. PILGRIM GIRL MOUSE	1474	43.00	45.00
92	12 IN. PJ BOY	7526	30.00	30.00
92	12 IN. PJ GIRL	7903	30.00	30.00
92	12 IN. SANTA W/POTBELLIED STOVE	1818	61.95	65.00
92	12 IN. SANTA'S PAINTING HELPER	2737	39.00	40.00

YR	NAME	LIMIT	ISSUE	TREND
92	12 IN. SANTA'S POSTMAN	3650	40.00	40.00
92	12 IN. SCARECROW	1873	42.00	45.00
92	12 IN. SNOWMAN	5457	42.00	45.00
92	12 IN. SPIDER	3461	39.00	100.00
92	12 IN. TALL NORTH POLE W/SNOW	2511	8.95	9.00
92	12 IN. TUCKERED COUPLE	1827	90.00	90.00
92	12 IN. VELOUR MRS. SANTA	2160	50.00	50.00
92	12 IN. VELOUR SANTA W/TOYBAG	2284	50.00	50.00
92	18 IN. BUNNY KID W/BUNNY	2117	50.00	50.00
92	18 IN. CHEF SANTA	5314	48.00	50.00
92	18 IN. COUNTRY BOY BUNNY	SU	54.95	60.00
92	18 IN. EASTER PARADE BOY BUNNY	1695	66.00	70.00
92	18 IN. EASTER PARADE GIRL BUNNY	1918	66.00	70.00
92	18 IN. GINGERBREAD BOY	2969	51.00	55.00
92	18 IN. GIRL BUNNY W/FLOWERS	1501	54.95	70.00
92	18 IN. MRS. SANTA W/POINSETTA	6790	53.95	55.00
92	18 IN. MRS. SANTA W/PRESENTS	4314	52.95	55.00
92	18 IN. REINDEER W/CHRISTMAS	3441	52.95	55.00
92	18 IN. REINDEER W/NORTH POLE	2755	63.95	65.00
92	18 IN. SANTA W/BANNER	6871	52.95	55.00
92	18 IN. SANTA W/CARDHOLDER	4260	60.00	60.00
92	18 IN. SANTA W/GIFT LIST	4447	46.00	40.00
92	18 IN. SANTA W/STOCKING	3859	50.00	50.00
92	18 IN. SANTA W/TRAY	3955	52.95	55.00
92	18 IN. SNOWMAN W/BROOM	4405	47.00	50.00
92	18 IN. SNOWY OWL	740	65.95	60.00
92	18 IN. WITCH	1369	63.95	75.00
92	18 IN. WITCH W/STAND	2760	65.95	75.00
92	22 IN. CHRISTMAS STOCKING	6128	18.45	30.00
92	22 IN. RED CHRISTMAS ELF	4066	35.00	40.00
92	30 IN. MRS. SANTA W/CARDHOLDER	1380	119.95	125.00
92	30 IN. OUTDOOR SANTA	1724	100.00	125.00
92	30 IN. SANTA W/BANNER	1654	119.95	125.00
92	30 IN. SANTA W/NORTH POLE	1674	109.95	125.00
92	30 IN. VELOUR MRS. SANTA W/MUFF	576	160.45	160.00
92	30 IN. VELOUR SANTA W/PIPE & BAG	548	160.45	160.00
92	32 IN. STOCKING W/REMOVABLE	2052	28.00	30.00
92	36 IN. REINDEER W/CARDHOLDER	1219	148.45	150.00
92	5 IN. ANGEL	7967	23.00	25.00
92	5 IN. CHRISTMAS DRAGON	3132	24.00	25.00
92	5 IN. CHRISTMAS LAMB	10104	20.00	25.00
92	5 IN. DUCK ON FLEXIBLE FLYER	3124	26.00	25.00
92	5 IN. EASTER PARADE BOY DUCK	3370	22.00	25.00
92	5 IN. EASTER PARADE GIRL DUCK	4468	24.00	25.00
92	5 IN. ELF (WORKSHOP)	13825	13.45	20.00
92	5 IN. EQUESTRIENNE W/ HORSE	1063	74.95	70.00
92	5 IN. FAWN	10939	14.45	25.00
92	5 IN. FLUFFY YELLOW CHICK	4342	18.00	25.00
92	5 IN. LEPRECHAUN	4705	16.00	25.00
92	5 IN. RAINCOAT DUCK	5397	27.00	25.00
92	5 IN. SPRING LAMB	5053	18.00	25.00
92	5 IN. TRIM-A-TREE ELF	11985	12.95	20.00
92	7 IN. ANGEL ON MOON	2885	40.00	40.00
92	7 IN. ANGEL W/MUSICAL INSTRUMENT	6347	20.00	20.00
92	7 IN. ARTIST BUNNY W/BRUSH	5346	21.00	25.00
92	7 IN. BABY NEW YEAR	6254	27.00	45.00
92	7 IN. BALLERINA KID	4553	28.00	45.00
92	7 IN. BALLERINA ON MUSIC BOX	2718	42.00	45.00
92	7 IN. BEACH KID W/BOAT	3817	30.00	45.00
92	7 IN. BIRTHDAY GIRL MOUSE	*	24.00	25.00
92	7 IN. BIRTHDAY MOUSE	9592	24.00	25.00
92	7 IN. BRIDE BUNNY	5929	23.00	25.00
92	7 IN. BUNNY IN SLEEPER-GREEN	6338	20.00	25.00
92	7 IN. BUNNY IN SLEEPER-YELLOW	6338	20.00	25.00
92	7 IN. CAROLLER BOY	4606	23.00	25.00
92	7 IN. CAROLLER GIRL	4913	23.00	25.00
92	7 IN. CAROLLER MOUSE W/BIG HAT	18789	20.00	25.00
92	7 IN. CAROLLING MOUSE #7754	SU	*	25.00
92	7 IN. CHAMPAGNE MOUSE IN GLASS	9553	26.00	25.00
92	7 IN. CHEF SANTA #5045	11297	29.00	30.00
92	7 IN. CHRISTMAS GNOME	9102	19.00	25.00
92	7 IN. COUNTRY BOY BUNNY	3993	20.45	25.00
92	7 IN. COUNTRY GIRL BUNNY	3937	20.45	25.00
92	7 IN. DESERT STORM MOUSE	3114	30.00	35.00
92	7 IN. DEVIL KID	6076	24.00	45.00
92	7 IN. DISNEY COLLECTION	300	60.00	350.00
92	7 IN. DRACULA KID	5637	26.00	45.00
92	7 IN. DRUMMER BOY	7297	22.45	25.00
92	7 IN. EASTER PARADE BOY BUNNY	6668	21.00	25.00
92	7 IN. EASTER PARADE GIRL BUNNY	9314	21.00	25.00
92	7 IN. FISHING MOUSE	6145	32.00	25.00
92	7 IN. FLYING ANGEL W/MISTLETOE	6457	19.00	25.00
92	7 IN. GNOME W/MUSHROOM	1691	36.00	45.00
92	7 IN. GOLFER MOUSE	7435	27.00	25.00
92	7 IN. GREEN THUMB MOUSE	5995	26.00	25.00

YR	NAME	LIMIT	ISSUE	TREND
92	7 IN. GROOM BUNNY	5578	23.00	25.00
92	7 IN. INDIAN BOY	2315	30.00	45.00
92	7 IN. INDIAN GIRL	2297	23.00	45.00
92	7 IN. KID W/KITE	3850	30.00	45.00
92	7 IN. LADY BUG KID	4970	30.00	45.00
92	7 IN. LOGO KID	17524	25.00	50.00
92	7 IN. MOUSE IN BOX	4994	20.00	25.00
92	7 IN. MOUSE IN CORNUCOPIA	7833	23.00	25.00
92	7 IN. MOUSE IN SANTA'S HAT	10941	18.00	25.00
92	7 IN. MOUSE ON CHEESE	14923	26.00	25.00
92	7 IN. MOUSE W/MAILBAG	8000	26.00	25.00
92	7 IN. MOUSE W/NORTH POLE	10089	22.00	25.00
92	7 IN. MOUSE W/PRESENTS	*	18.00	25.00
92	7 IN. MOUSE W/SNOWBALL	7095	18.00	25.00
92	7 IN. MOUSE W/TENNIS RACQUET	4110	22.00	25.00
92	7 IN. MR. TUCKERED MOUSE	7533	20.00	25.00
92	7 IN. MRS. SANTA CANDLEHOLDER	9595	26.00	25.00
92	7 IN. MRS. SANTA HANGING MERRY	6411	28.00	25.00
92	7 IN. MRS. SANTA W/POINSETTA	11484	30.00	25.00
92	7 IN. MRS. SANTA W/PRESENTS	7124	28.00	25.00
92	7 IN. MRS. TUCKERED MOUSE	8321	20.00	25.00
92	7 IN. PILGRIM KID W/BASKET	2303	53.95	25.00
92	7 IN. PILGRIM MICE SET W/BASKET	2364	43.00	45.00
92	7 IN. PIRATE KID	5412	24.00	45.00
92	7 IN. PUMPKIN KID	3619	27.45	45.00
92	7 IN. RED CROSS NURSE MOUSE	*	30.00	40.00
92	7 IN. RITZ SNOWMAN	6037	27.00	40.00
92	7 IN. SANTA BRINGING HOME	5921	28.00	25.00
92	7 IN. SANTA CARDHOLDER	9831	26.00	25.00
92	7 IN. SANTA IN CHIMNEY	8119	34.00	25.00
92	7 IN. SANTA ON MOON	4157	47.00	45.00
92	7 IN. SANTA SKUNK	6753	28.00	25.00
92	7 IN. SANTA W/GIFT LIST & TOY BAG	7815	24.00	25.00
92	7 IN. SANTA W/MAILBAG & LETTERS	7493	28.00	25.00
92	7 IN. SANTA W/PRESENTS	6594	24.00	25.00
92	7 IN. SCARECROW KID	4595	28.00	45.00
92	7 IN. SHERIFF MOUSE (D.S.)	283	50.00	70.00
92	7 IN. SKATEBOARD KID	3894	30.00	45.00
92	7 IN. SLEDDING MOUSE	6247	21.00	25.00
92	7 IN. SNOWMAN W/PIPE	7779	24.00	25.00
92	7 IN. SPRING CHICKEN W/BOAT	2753	35.00	35.00
92	7 IN. SPRING SKUNK	1590	23.00	25.00
92	7 IN. SWEETHEART BOY MOUSE	5723	20.00	25.00
92	7 IN. SWEETHEART GIRL MOUSE	6522	19.00	25.00
92	7 IN. TWO IN A TENT MICE	2910	35.00	25.00
92	7 IN. VELOUR MRS. SANTA W/COAT	5289	27.45	25.00
92	7 IN. VELOUR SANTA W/COAT & PIPE	5140	27.45	25.00
92	7 IN. WITCH KID	3592	28.00	45.00
92	7 IN. WORKSHOP MOUSE	6618	22.00	25.00
92	DESERT MOUSE HEAD PIN	991	8.95	25.00
92	LARGE FLOWER	2526	19.00	20.00
92	LARGE PUMPKIN	2469	49.00	60.00
92	MINI SANTA WREATH	2140	24.00	25.00
92	NURSE MOUSE HEAD PIN	1615	8.95	30.00
92	PINK FLOWER PICK	6611	5.95	10.00
92	RED CROSS NURSE MOUSE HEAD	*	8.95	25.00
92	SAILOR KID W/BOAT	*	*	35.00
92	SKATING BUNNY	4005	44.00	35.00
92	SUN HEAD FLORAL PLANTER PICK	5419	5.95	10.00
92	SUN MAGNET	7133	6.45	9.00
92	SUN PIN	6395	5.95	10.00
92	YELLOW FLOWER PICK	6165	5.95	10.00
93	10 IN. ANGEL BEAR	OP	33.00	35.00
93	10 IN. BEAR IN NIGHTSHIRT W/CANDLE	OP	34.00	35.00
93	10 IN. CATCHER	OP	38.50	55.00
93	10 IN. CHRISTA MCAULIFFE/SKATER	OP	36.00	35.00
93	10 IN. CHRISTMAS ELF	OP	16.00	15.00
93	10 IN. CHRISTMAS EVE BOB CRATCHET	OP	70.00	70.00
93	10 IN. CHRISTMAS EVE SCROOGE	OP	60.00	60.00
93	10 IN. COUNTRY BOY BUNNY W/VEG.	OP	35.00	35.00
93	10 IN. COUNTRY GIRL BUNNY W/VEG.	OP	35.00	35.00
93	10 IN. DOCTOR BEAR	YR	36.00	40.00
93	10 IN. DOE	OP	21.00	25.00
93	10 IN. EASTER PARADE BOY BUNNY	5139	39.00	40.00
93	10 IN. EASTER PARADE GIRL BUNNY	6590	39.00	40.00
93	10 IN. FARMER W/ROOSTER	1	1,000.00	1000.00
93	10 IN. FATHER TIME	OP	54.95	60.00
93	10 IN. FROG IN BOAT	OP	36.00	40.00
93	10 IN. GARDENING SUMMER SANTA	OP	70.00	70.00
93	10 IN. GINGERBREAD BOY	OP	22.45	30.00
93	10 IN. HEADLESS HORSEMAN W/PUMPKIN/HORSE	OP	56.95	60.00
93	10 IN. KITTEN W/ORNAMENT	OP	34.00	35.00
93	10 IN. MRS. BEAR IN NIGHTSHIRT W/CANDLE	OP	39.00	35.00
93	10 IN. MRS. SKATING SANTA	OP	50.00	50.00
93	10 IN. PONY EXPRESS RIDER	OP	98.00	100.00

YR	NAME	LIMIT	ISSUE	TREND
93	10 IN. SANTA W/FIREPLACE AND 3 IN. CHILD	OP	90.00	100.00
93	10 IN. SANTA W/TOBOGGAN	OP	60.00	60.00
93	10 IN. SANTA'S HELPER BEAR	OP	34.00	40.00
93	10 IN. SKATING PENGUIN	OP	35.00	40.00
93	10 IN. SKATING SANTA	OP	50.00	50.00
93	10 IN. SNOW QUEEN TREE TOPPER	OP	30.00	25.00
93	10 IN. SNOWY OWL	OP	26.00	25.00
93	10 IN. ST. NICK TREE TOP	OP	30.00	25.00
93	10 IN. TOBOGGAN SANTA	OP	60.00	60.00
93	10 IN. WINTER ELF	OP	17.00	20.00
93	12 IN. BOY PILGRIM W/BASKET	OP	45.00	45.00
93	12 IN. CHEF SANTA	OP	45.00	50.00
93	12 IN. DRUMMER BOY	OP	40.00	35.00
93	12 IN. GIRL PILGRIM W/PIE	OP	45.00	45.00
93	12 IN. INDIAN BOY	RT	36.00	40.00
93	12 IN. MRS. SANTA W/POINSETTIA	OP	50.00	50.00
93	12 IN. PJ BOY	OP	30.00	30.00
93	12 IN. PJ GIRL	OP	30.00	30.00
93	12 IN. SANTA IN CHIMNEY	OP	70.00	70.00
93	12 IN. SANTA'S POSTMAN W/CDHLDR MAILBAG	OP	41.00	41.00
93	12 IN. SCARECROW	OP	42.00	42.00
93	12 IN. SNOWMAN	OP	42.00	42.00
93	12 IN. TUCKERED COUPLE	OP	90.00	90.00
93	14 IN. GRAPEVINE WREATH W/7 IN. E.P.GIRL BUNNY	OP	32.00	32.00
93	14 IN. LG. USABLE PUMPKIN W/TOP	OP	50.00	50.00
93	14 IN. WREATH W/ WINTER ELF	OP	26.00	26.00
93	18 IN. CHEF SANTA	OP	48.00	48.00
93	18 IN. COUNTRY BOY BUNNY W/VEG.	OP	54.95	55.00
93	18 IN. COUNTRY GIRL BUNNY W/VEG.	OP	54.95	55.00
93	18 IN. EASTER PARADE BOY BUNNY	OP	66.00	66.00
93	18 IN. EASTER PARADE GIRL BUNNY	OP	66.00	66.00
93	18 IN. MAN SKATER (BRN. HAIR)	OP	45.00	45.00
93	18 IN. MRS. OUTDOOR SANTA	OP	50.00	50.00
93	18 IN. MRS. SANTA W/POINSETTA	OP	53.95	54.00
93	18 IN. REINDEER W/CHRISTMAS SADDLEBAGS	OP	52.95	53.00
93	18 IN. SANTA IN SLEIGH	OP	74.95	75.00
93	18 IN. SANTA ON TOBOGGAN	OP	70.00	70.00
93	18 IN. SANTA W/BANNER	OP	52.95	53.00
93	18 IN. SANTA W/GIFT LIST & TOYBAG	OP	46.00	46.00
93	18 IN. SANTA W/LIGHTS	5441	54.95	55.00
93	18 IN. SNOWMAN W/BROOM	OP	48.00	48.00
93	18 IN. VICTORIAN MRS. SANTA	OP	64.95	65.00
93	18 IN. VICTORIAN SANTA	OP	64.95	65.00
93	18 IN. WITCH W/STAND	OP	65.95	66.00
93	18 IN. WOMAN SKATER (BLONDE)	OP	45.00	45.00
93	22 IN. CHRISTMAS ELF	OP	35.00	35.00
93	22 IN. CHRISTMAS STOCKING	OP	18.45	19.00
93	3 IN. BABY JESUS IN MANGER/BLONDE	OP	17.00	17.00
93	3 IN. FISHING SANTA IN BOAT	OP	25.00	25.00
93	3 IN. SANTA PIN IN CARD	OP	17.00	17.00
93	30 IN. MRS. SANTA W/CARDHOLDER	OP	200.00	115.00
93	30 IN. SANTA W/NORTH POLE	OP	129.95	130.00
93	30 IN. WITCH KID	OP	149.95	150.00
93	36 IN. REINDEER W/CDHLDR SADDLEBAGS	OP	148.45	149.00
93	5 IN. BABY JESUS IN MANGER W/BABY	OP	26.00	26.00
93	5 IN. BLACK CHRISTMAS LAMB	OP	20.00	20.00
93	5 IN. CHRISTMAS LAMB WHITE FLEECE	OP	20.00	20.00
93	5 IN. DUCK ON FLEXIBLE FLYER SLED	2923	26.00	26.00
93	5 IN. EASTER PARADE BOY DUCK	OP	22.00	22.00
93	5 IN. EASTER PARADE GIRL DUCK	OP	24.00	24.00
93	5 IN. ELF	OP	13.45	14.00
93	5 IN. FAWN	OP	15.00	15.00
93	5 IN. LEPRECHAUN W/POT 'O GOLD	8775	16.00	16.00
93	5 IN. RAINCOAT DUCK	OP	22.45	23.00
93	5 IN. TRIM-A-TREE ELF	OP	12.95	13.00
93	7 IN. ANGEL (BLACK HAIR)	OP	23.00	23.00
93	7 IN. ANGEL (BLONDE HAIR)	OP	23.00	23.00
93	7 IN. ANGEL (BROWN HAIR)	OP	23.00	23.00
93	7 IN. ANGEL MOUSE	OP	22.00	22.00
93	7 IN. ANGEL W/MUSICAL INSTRUMENT	OP	20.00	20.00
93	7 IN. ARAB BOY	YR	36.00	36.00
93	7 IN. ARTIST BUNNY W/BRUSH & PALETTE	OP	21.00	21.00
93	7 IN. BABY NEW YEAR (BLONDE)	4127	27.00	27.00
93	7 IN. BALLERINA KID (BLONDE)	OP	28.00	28.00
93	7 IN. BALLERINA ON MUSIC BOX	OP	42.00	42.00
93	7 IN. BAR MITZVAH BOY	YR	28.00	28.00
93	7 IN. BASEBALL MOUSE	6291	26.00	30.00
93	7 IN. BASKETBALL BOY	YR	26.00	550.00
93	7 IN. BEDTIME KID	YR	26.00	450.00
93	7 IN. BIRTHDAY GIRL MOUSE	OP	24.00	24.00
93	7 IN. BIRTHDAY MOUSE	5550	24.00	24.00
93	7 IN. BOY BUILDING SNOWMAN	OP	22.00	48.00
93	7 IN. BOY BUNNY W/ VEGETABLE	5200	20.45	21.00
93	7 IN. BRIDE BUNNY	4529	23.00	23.00
93	7 IN. BUNNY IN SLIPPER/GREEN	2550	20.00	20.00

YR	NAME	LIMIT	ISSUE	TREND
93	7 IN. BUNNY IN SLIPPER/YELLOW	OP	20.00	20.00
93	7 IN. BUTTERFLY KID	OP	28.00	30.00
93	7 IN. CAROLLER MOUSE W/BIG HAT & TREE	OP	20.00	20.00
93	7 IN. CHAMPAGNE MOUSE	6985	26.00	26.00
93	7 IN. CHEF SANTA	OP	29.00	29.00
93	7 IN. CHOIR BOY	OP	26.00	26.00
93	7 IN. CHOIR GIRL	OP	26.00	26.00
93	7 IN. CHRISTMAS GNOME	OP	19.00	19.00
93	7 IN. COUNTRY GIRL BUNNY W/VEG.	5621	20.45	21.00
93	7 IN. DEVIL KID	OP	24.00	24.00
93	7 IN. DRACULA KID	OP	26.00	26.00
93	7 IN. DRUMMER BOY	OP	22.45	23.00
93	7 IN. EASTER PARADE BOY BUNNY	OP	21.00	21.00
93	7 IN. EASTER PARADE GIRL BUNNY	OP	21.00	21.00
93	7 IN. FACTORY IN THE WOODS MOUSE	8226	30.00	35.00
93	7 IN. FIREMAN MOUSE	YR	26.00	30.00
93	7 IN. FISHING BOY	YR	30.00	30.00
93	7 IN. FLOWER KID/YELLOW	OP	28.00	28.00
93	7 IN. FLYING ANGEL W/MISTLETOE	OP	19.00	19.00
93	7 IN. FREE-STANDING SANTA #5005	SU	*	N/A
93	7 IN. GHOST MOUSE	7803	26.00	26.00
93	7 IN. GIRL EATING TURKEY	OP	39.00	75.00
93	7 IN. GROOM BUNNY	3887	23.00	23.00
93	7 IN. HOT SHOT BUSINESSMAN KID	YR	37.00	40.00
93	7 IN. INDIAN BOY (BLACK HAIR)	OP	30.00	30.00
93	7 IN. INDIAN GIRL (BLK. PONYTAILS)	OP	23.00	23.00
93	7 IN. JUMP ROPE GIRL	YR	26.00	30.00
93	7 IN. LADY BUG KID	OP	30.00	30.00
93	7 IN. LOGO KID (DOLL SOCIETY)	OP	27.50	28.00
93	7 IN. MOUSE IN CORNUCOPIA	OP	24.00	24.00
93	7 IN. MOUSE IN SANTA'S HAT	OP	18.00	18.00
93	7 IN. MOUSE ON CHEESE	OP	27.00	27.00
93	7 IN. MOUSE W/MAILBAG & LETTERS	OP	26.00	26.00
93	7 IN. MOUSE W/NORTH POLE	OP	22.00	22.00
93	7 IN. MOUSE W/SNOWBALL	OP	18.00	18.00
93	7 IN. MR. TUCKERED MOUSE	7059	20.00	20.00
93	7 IN. MRS. SANTA CANDLEHOLDER	OP	26.00	26.00
93	7 IN. MRS. SANTA HANGING "MERRY XMAS" SIGN	OP	28.00	28.00
93	7 IN. MRS. SANTA W/POINSETTIA	OP	30.00	30.00
93	7 IN. MRS. SANTA W/PRESENTS	OP	28.00	28.00
93	7 IN. MRS. TUCKERED MOUSE	OP	20.00	20.00
93	7 IN. PILGRIM BOY HUGGING FAWN	OP	41.00	41.00
93	7 IN. PILGRIM GIRL W/PIE	OP	26.00	26.00
93	7 IN. PILGRIM MICE SET W/BASKET	OP	47.00	47.00
93	7 IN. PINK FLOWER KID	OP	26.00	26.00
93	7 IN. PIRATE KID	OP	24.00	24.00
93	7 IN. RITZ SNOWMAN	RT	27.00	27.00
93	7 IN. SANTA BRINGING HOME CHRISTMAS TREE	OP	28.00	28.00
93	7 IN. SANTA CANDLEHOLDER	OP	26.00	26.00
93	7 IN. SANTA IN CHIMNEY	OP	35.00	35.00
93	7 IN. SANTA SKIING #5242	SU	28.00	28.00
93	7 IN. SANTA SKUNK	OP	28.00	28.00
93	7 IN. SANTA W/DOVE	1	1,250.00	1250.00
93	7 IN. SANTA W/LIGHTS	OP	30.00	30.00
93	7 IN. SANTA W/MAILBAG & LETTERS	OP	28.00	30.00
93	7 IN. SANTA W/PRESENTS	6996	24.00	24.00
93	7 IN. SANTA W/SLEIGH	OP	40.00	40.00
93	7 IN. SCARECROW KID	OP	28.00	28.00
93	7 IN. SNOWMAN (MRS. RITZ)	OP	26.00	26.00
93	7 IN. SNOWMAN ON TOBOGGAN	RT	30.00	30.00
93	7 IN. SNOWMAN W/PIPE	OP	24.00	24.00
93	7 IN. SPRING CHICKEN W/BOAT	OP	35.00	35.00
93	7 IN. SPRING ROOSTER	OP	35.00	35.00
93	7 IN. SPRING SKUNK	OP	23.00	23.00
93	7 IN. ST. PATRICK'S DAY MOUSE	OP	26.00	26.00
93	7 IN. SWEETHEART BOY MOUSE	OP	20.00	20.00
93	7 IN. SWEETHEART GIRL MOUSE	OP	19.00	19.00
93	7 IN. VICTORIAN MRS. SANTA	OP	30.00	30.00
93	7 IN. VICTORIAN SANTA	OP	30.00	30.00
93	7 IN. VICTORIAN SANTA IN SLEIGH	OP	50.00	50.00
93	7 IN. WHITE MOUSE IN SLIPPER	RT	25.00	25.00
93	7 IN. WHITE MOUSE ON TOBOGGAN	OP	30.00	30.00
93	7 IN. WHITE MOUSE W/PRESENT	OP	22.00	22.00
93	7 IN. WHITE SKATING MOUSE	OP	25.00	25.00
93	7 IN. WITCH MOUSE	OP	26.00	26.00
93	7 IN. WIZARD MOUSE	OP	28.00	28.00
93	7 IN. YELLOW FLOWER KID	OP	26.00	26.00
93	8 IN. BOY TURKEY	OP	35.00	35.00
93	8 IN. GIRL TURKEY	OP	35.00	35.00
93	BLUE FLOWER PICK	OP	7.95	8.00
93	CHRISTMAS CHICKEN	OP	35.00	35.00
93	LARGE FLOWER W/FACE	OP	21.00	23.00
93	SANTA NAPKIN RINGS SET OF 4	OP	40.00	40.00
93	SM. CHRISTMAS DOVE	OP	26.00	28.00
93	SUN PIN	OP	5.95	6.00

YR	NAME	LIMIT	ISSUE	TREND
94	10 IN. ANGEL BEAR	3377	34.50	35.00
94	10 IN. BALLERINA BEAR	1	1,100.00	1050.00
94	10 IN. BASKETBALL PLAYER, BLACK	2012	32.00	32.00
94	10 IN. BASKETBALL PLAYER, WHITE	3699	32.00	32.00
94	10 IN. BOSTON BRUINS HOCKEY PLAYER	OP	48.00	48.00
94	10 IN. CATCHER	3440	38.50	39.00
94	10 IN. COUNTRY GIRL BEAR	1	925.00	925.00
94	10 IN. DOE	4319	22.00	22.00
94	10 IN. EASTER PARADE BOY BUNNY	SU	40.00	40.00
94	10 IN. EASTER PARADE GIRL BUNNY	SU	40.00	40.00
94	10 IN. EASTER PARADE SHOPPER OSTRICH	2368	33.50	38.00
94	10 IN. GINGERBREAD BOY	5182	23.50	24.00
94	10 IN. GREEN CHRISTMAS ELF	6719	17.00	17.00
94	10 IN. HEADLESS HORSEMAN W/PUMPKIN	1593	56.95	57.00
94	10 IN. HOBO CLOWN	6826	31.00	31.00
94	10 IN. KITTEN W/ORNAMENT	RT	35.00	35.00
94	10 IN. LG. FLOWER W/FACE	1807	21.00	21.00
94	10 IN. MRS. SANTA "LAST MENDING"	5751	48.00	48.00
94	10 IN. OLD WORLD CAROLLER MAN	5549	28.00	28.00
94	10 IN. OLD WORLD CAROLLER WOMAN	5595	28.00	28.00
94	10 IN. OLD WORLD SANTA W/SKIS	4331	50.00	50.00
94	10 IN. OLD WORLD SKATERS ON MUSIC BOX	1660	119.95	120.00
94	10 IN. RED CHRISTMAS ELF	9079	17.00	17.00
94	10 IN. RED COAT	1000	80.00	80.00
94	10 IN. REINDEER W/CAP & BELL	10319	24.00	24.00
94	10 IN. SKATING PENGUIN	RT	35.00	35.00
94	10 IN. SOCCER PLAYER	5751	35.00	35.00
94	10 IN. TREE TOP ANGEL #7274	SU	30.00	30.00
94	10 IN. WHITE CHRISTMAS ELF	RT	17.00	17.00
94	10 IN. WHITE ST. NICHOLAS	5560	44.00	44.00
94	10 IN. WINDOW SHOPPER OSTRICH	RT	38.00	38.00
94	10 IN. WINTER ELF	8504	17.50	18.00
94	12 IN. BEAN NOSE SANTA	OP	119.50	120.00
94	12 IN. BOY PILGRIM W/BASKET	2132	46.00	46.00
94	12 IN. CHEF SANTA	1519	46.00	46.00
94	12 IN. DEVIL KID	2610	40.00	40.00
94	12 IN. DRUMMER BOY	3792	40.00	40.00
94	12 IN. GIRL CAT KID	3176	36.00	36.00
94	12 IN. GIRL PILGRIM W/PIE	2140	46.00	46.00
94	12 IN. GIRL SCARECROW	3978	48.00	48.00
94	12 IN. MRS. SANTA CARDHOLDER	4443	40.00	40.00
94	12 IN. NORTH POLE W/RED RIBBON WRAP	1561	9.50	10.00
94	12 IN. SANTA IN CHIMNEY	668	70.00	70.00
94	14 IN. GRAPEVINE WREATH W/GIRL BUNNY	2505	35.00	35.00
94	14 IN. LG. USABLE PUMPKIN W/TOP	2486	50.00	50.00
94	17 IN. TEEPEE	1838	38.00	38.00
94	18 IN. CHEF SANTA	2888	50.00	50.00
94	18 IN. COUNTRY BOY BUNNY W/HOE	1260	56.95	57.00
94	18 IN. COUNTRY GIRL BUNNY W/BASKET	1549	56.95	57.00
94	18 IN. EASTER PARADE BOY BUNNY	2019	66.00	66.00
94	18 IN. EASTER PARADE GIRL BUNNY	2299	66.00	66.00
94	18 IN. HO HO HO SANTA #5504	SU	*	N/A
94	18 IN. INDOOR SANTA W/LIGHTS	3785	56.95	57.00
94	18 IN. MR. FUR SANTA ON STAND	4546	46.00	46.00
94	18 IN. MR. OLD WORLD SANTA	OP	52.00	52.00
94	18 IN. MRS. OLD WORLD SANTA	5278	50.00	50.00
94	18 IN. MRS. OUTDOOR SANTA	3614	50.00	50.00
94	18 IN. MRS. SANTA CARDHOLDER	4312	52.95	53.00
94	18 IN. MRS. SANTA W/POINSETTIA	2992	55.95	56.00
94	18 IN. MUSICAL MRS. SANTA	1498	60.00	60.00
94	18 IN. MUSICAL SANTA/GIFT LIST	1316	60.00	60.00
94	18 IN. OLD WORLD REINDEER W/BELLS	5201	60.00	60.00
94	18 IN. PJ KID W/2 XMAS STOCKINGS	2428	60.00	60.00
94	18 IN. REINDEER W/CHRISTMAS SADDLEBAGS	3235	54.95	55.00
94	18 IN. SANTA IN SLEIGH	1140	77.95	78.00
94	18 IN. SANTA ON TOBOGGAN	1499	70.00	70.00
94	18 IN. SANTA W/CARDHOLDER SACK	4899	54.95	55.00
94	18 IN. SNOWMAN W/BROOM	4092	50.00	50.00
94	18 IN. WITCH	1823	67.95	68.00
94	22 IN. CHRISTMAS ELF, BLACK HAIR	3606	35.00	35.00
94	22 IN. CHRISTMAS STOCKING	6796	19.00	19.00
94	24 IN. TURKEY	1116	100.00	100.00
94	3 IN. BABY JESUS IN MANGER	RT	17.50	18.00
94	3 IN. FISHING SANTA IN BOAT	3048	25.00	25.00
94	3 IN. SPRING PIXIE PICK CHIL	3557	10.95	11.00
94	3 IN. SUN PICK PAINTED SUN FACE	1883	5.95	6.00
94	3 IN. SUN PIN	7346	5.95	6.00
94	30 IN. COUNTRY GIRL BUNNY W/BASKET	722	119.95	120.00
94	30 IN. MR. OLD WORLD SANTA	1453	124.95	125.00
94	30 IN. MRS. OLD WORLD SANTA	1410	124.95	125.00
94	30 IN. MRS. SANTA W/CDHLDR SKIRT	1141	119.95	120.00
94	30 IN. OUTDOOR SANTA W/TOY BAG	1019	125.95	126.00
94	30 IN. SANTA W/CARDHOLDER SACK	1148	119.95	120.00
94	30 IN. SANTA W/NORTH POLE SUIT	643	131.95	132.00
94	30 IN. SNOWMAN	1782	119.95	120.00

YR	NAME	LIMIT	ISSUE	TREND
94	30 IN. WITCH KID	722	149.95	150.00
94	36 IN. REINDEER W/CDHLDR SADDLEBAGS	902	154.50	155.00
94	4 FT. QUILTED TREE SKIRT #7990	SU	25.00	25.00
94	5 IN. BABY JESUS IN MANGER	1726	27.00	27.00
94	5 IN. BLACK CHRISTMAS LAMB	4713	20.00	20.00
94	5 IN. CHRISTMAS LAMB/WHITE #7424	SU	20.00	20.00
94	5 IN. DUCK/FLEXIBLE FLYER SLED	3186	27.00	27.00
94	5 IN. EASTER PARADE BOY DUCK	3678	23.00	23.00
94	5 IN. EASTER PARADE GIRL DUCK	4697	25.00	25.00
94	5 IN. ELF (WORKSHOP)	9416	14.00	14.00
94	5 IN. FAWN	8700	15.00	15.00
94	5 IN. GOLD FALL ELF	6153	14.50	15.00
94	5 IN. GREEN CHRISTMAS ELF	8834	14.00	14.00
94	5 IN. GREEN SPRING ELF	3261	14.00	14.00
94	5 IN. HALLOWEEN ELF, BLACK #3000	RT	15.00	15.00
94	5 IN. HALLOWEEN ELF, ORANGE #3001	RT	15.00	15.00
94	5 IN. LEPRECHAUN W/POT 'O GOLD	7410	18.00	18.00
94	5 IN. OLD WORLD CAROLLER BOY	7611	20.00	20.00
94	5 IN. OLD WORLD CAROLLER GIRL	7817	20.00	20.00
94	5 IN. OLD WORLD SANTA W/9 IN. WREATH	2330	33.00	33.00
94	5 IN. ORANGE FALL ELF	6280	14.50	15.00
94	5 IN. RAINCOAT DUCK	2410	28.00	28.00
94	5 IN. RED CHRISTMAS ELF	11911	14.00	14.00
94	5 IN. SPRING ELF W/6 IN. WREATH	1704	18.00	18.00
94	5 IN. WHITE CHRISTMAS ELF	RT	14.00	14.00
94	5 IN. WINTER ELF	10769	14.00	14.00
94	5 IN. YELLOW SPRING ELF	3932	14.00	14.00
94	7 IN. ANGEL MOUSE	10343	23.00	23.00
94	7 IN. ANGEL W/MUSICAL INSTRUMENT	4302	21.00	21.00
94	7 IN. ANGEL/BLACK HAIR	2877	24.00	24.00
94	7 IN. ANGEL/BLONDE HAIR	4584	24.00	24.00
94	7 IN. ANGEL/BROWN HAIR	3362	24.00	24.00
94	7 IN. ARTIST BUNNY W/BRUSH/PALETTE	4303	22.00	22.00
94	7 IN. AUCTION TIMES MOUSE	5962	30.00	30.00
94	7 IN. BABY BUNNY W/BOTTLE	6588	20.00	20.00
94	7 IN. BIRTHDAY GIRL MOUSE	3777	24.00	24.00
94	7 IN. BRIDE MOUSE	4674	23.00	400.00
94	7 IN. BUTTERFLY KID, BLACK BODY	2226	29.00	29.00
94	7 IN. CANDY KISS KID	1	2,250.00	2200.00
94	7 IN. CHAMPAGNE MOUSE	6360	27.00	27.00
94	7 IN. CHEERLEADER GIRL	4568	27.00	28.00
94	7 IN. CHEF SANTA	5618	30.00	30.00
94	7 IN. CHOIR BOY	2873	27.00	27.00
94	7 IN. CHOIR BOY W/BLACK EYE	2912	27.00	27.00
94	7 IN. CHOIR GIRL, BLONDE HAIR	3424	27.00	27.00
94	7 IN. CHRISTA MCAULIFFE SNOWBD KID	OP	40.00	40.00
94	7 IN. CLOWN MOUSE	1	1,050.00	1025.00
94	7 IN. COCKTAIL MOUSE	1	1,100.00	1050.00
94	7 IN. COUNTRY BOY BUNNY W/HOE	4842	21.50	22.00
94	7 IN. COUNTRY GIRL BUNNY W/BASKET	6083	21.50	22.00
94	7 IN. DRACULA KID, BLACK HAIR	2126	27.00	27.00
94	7 IN. DRUMMER BOY	6817	24.00	24.00
94	7 IN. EASTER PARADE BOY BUNNY	9937	22.00	22.00
94	7 IN. EASTER PARADE GIRL BUNNY	13186	22.00	22.00
94	7 IN. FLYING ANGEL #7113	SU	20.00	20.00
94	7 IN. FOOTBALL MOUSE	5998	30.00	30.00
94	7 IN. GHOST MOUSE	4698	27.00	27.00
94	7 IN. GIRL BLDG A SNOWMAN	13459	24.00	24.00
94	7 IN. GIRL W/TEDDY BEAR	4712	27.00	27.00
94	7 IN. GRADUATION BOY MOUSE	3769	23.00	23.00
94	7 IN. GROOM MOUSE	OP	23.00	23.00
94	7 IN. HABITAT MOUSE	5011	30.00	30.00
94	7 IN. HERSHEY KID	9698	37.50	38.00
94	7 IN. HOT SHOT BUSINESS GIRL	OP	*	675.00
94	7 IN. INDIAN BOY, BLACK HAIR	2848	31.00	31.00
94	7 IN. INDIAN GIRL, BLACK PONYTAILS	2892	23.00	23.00
94	7 IN. JAIL HOUSE MOUSE	3309	26.00	26.00
94	7 IN. LARGE CABBAGE	778	15.00	15.00
94	7 IN. LOGO KID (DOLL SOCIETY)	OP	27.50	28.00
94	7 IN. MARBLES KID/RED TANK TOP	OP	27.50	28.00
94	7 IN. MISSISSIPPI LEVEE MOUSE	3012	30.00	30.00
94	7 IN. MOUSE IN CORNUCOPIA	6467	25.00	25.00
94	7 IN. MOUSE IN SANTA'S HAT	11641	18.50	19.00
94	7 IN. MOUSE W/SNOWBALL	8745	18.50	19.00
94	7 IN. MR. OLD WORLD SANTA	9620	28.00	28.00
94	7 IN. MRS. OLD WORLD SANTA	9439	28.00	28.00
94	7 IN. MRS. SANTA CARDHOLDER	4443	40.00	40.00
94	7 IN. MRS. SANTA W/FUR TRIM	8848	22.50	23.00
94	7 IN. MRS. SANTA W/POINSETTIA	5397	31.00	31.00
94	7 IN. MRS. SANTA W/PRESENTS	5923	29.00	29.00
94	7 IN. NAUGHTY ANGEL	8380	23.00	23.00
94	7 IN. PILGRIM BOY HUGGING FAWN	2004	42.00	42.00
94	7 IN. PILGRIM GIRL W/PIE BLONDE HAIR	2984	27.00	27.00
94	7 IN. PILGRIM MICE SET W/BSKT	2873	47.00	47.00
94	7 IN. POLICEMAN MOUSE	4788	28.00	28.00

YR	NAME	LIMIT	ISSUE	TREND
94	7 IN. RITZ SNOWMAN	4903	28.00	28.00
94	7 IN. SANTA IN CHIMNEY	3255	36.00	36.00
94	7 IN. SANTA W/DOVE	1	1,250.00	1200.00
94	7 IN. SANTA W/LIGHTS	4678	31.00	31.00
94	7 IN. SANTA W/PRESENTS	5586	25.00	25.00
94	7 IN. SANTA W/RD. FUR TRIM SUIT	8922	20.00	20.00
94	7 IN. SANTA W/SLEIGH	3301	40.00	40.00
94	7 IN. SANTA W/SNOWSHOES & TREE	8582	29.00	29.00
94	7 IN. SANTA W/TREE & SLED	8865	29.00	29.00
94	7 IN. SCOTTISH LAD	3995	30.00	28.00
94	7 IN. SMALL CHRISTMAS DOVE	RT	27.00	27.00
94	7 IN. SNOWMAN (MRS. RITZ)	5344	27.00	27.00
94	7 IN. SNOWMAN W/PIPE	6179	26.00	26.00
94	7 IN. ST. PATRICK'S DAY MOUSE	4746	27.00	27.00
94	7 IN. SWEETHEART BOY MOUSE	4424	20.00	20.00
94	7 IN. THANKSGIVING BOY	1881	40.00	38.00
94	7 IN. VALENTINE GIRL KID W/CARD	6220	25.00	28.00
94	7 IN. VICTORIAN SANTA IN SLEIGH	1179	50.00	50.00
94	7 IN. WHITE MOUSE IN SLIPPER	5838	26.00	26.00
94	7 IN. WHITE MOUSE ON TOBOGGAN	RT	30.00	30.00
94	7 IN. WHITE MOUSE W/PRESENT	8170	23.00	23.00
94	7 IN. WHITE SKATING MOUSE	11452	26.00	26.00
94	7 IN. WITCH MOUSE	RT	27.00	27.00
94	7 IN. WIZARD MOUSE	3892	29.00	29.00
94	7 IN. YELLOW FLOWER KID	OP	29.00	29.00
94	7 IN. YELLOW FLOWER KID, BLONDE	2303	27.00	27.00
94	8 IN. BOY TURKEY	2852	35.00	35.00
94	8 IN. EAR OF CORN	1342	9.95	10.00
94	8 IN. GIRL TURKEY	2174	35.00	35.00
94	SET OF 3 LG. PEA PODS & CARROTS	1377	15.00	15.00
94	SET OF 3 RD. TOMATOES 2 IN.	805	9.95	10.00
94	SMALL PEA PODS & CARROTS (3)	1342	12.50	13.00
94	TREE TOP STAR W/ 3 IN. ANGEL	6424	21.00	28.00
95	10 IN. BOSTON BRUINS HOCKEY PLAYER	OP	48.00	48.00
95	10 IN. CANADIAN MOUNTIE	OP	74.95	75.00
95	10 IN. CANADIAN MOUNTIE W/HORSE	OP	129.50	130.00
95	10 IN. CHRISTMAS ELF #7358	SU	*	N/A
95	10 IN. COLLECTOR, MR. NASHVILLE SANTA	OP	45.00	45.00
95	10 IN. COLLECTOR, MR. SANTA W/WEE HELPERS	OP	74.95	75.00
95	10 IN. COLLECTOR, MRS. NASHVILLE SANTA	OP	45.00	45.00
95	10 IN. DOE	OP	22.50	23.00
95	10 IN. EASTER PARADE BOY BUNNY	OP	41.00	41.00
95	10 IN. EASTER PARADE GIRL BUNNY	OP	41.00	41.00
95	10 IN. FROG ON LILY PAD	OP	24.00	24.00
95	10 IN. GREEN CHRISTMAS ELF	OP	17.50	18.00
95	10 IN. INDIAN MAN	OP	43.00	43.00
95	10 IN. INDIAN WOMAN	OP	43.00	43.00
95	10 IN. KITTEN W/ORNAMENT	OP	36.00	36.00
95	10 IN. LARGE FLOWER W/FACE	OP	21.00	21.00
95	10 IN. OLD WORLD CAROLLER MAN	OP	29.00	29.00
95	10 IN. OLD WORLD CAROLLER WOMAN	OP	29.00	29.00
95	10 IN. RED CHRISTMAS ELF	OP	17.50	18.00
95	10 IN. RED TREE TOP ANGEL	OP	38.00	38.00
95	10 IN. REDCOAT W/CANNON	1000	80.00	80.00
95	10 IN. REINDEER	OP	24.00	24.00
95	10 IN. REINDEER W/7 IN. SANTA	OP	48.00	48.00
95	10 IN. REINDEER W/CAP & BELL	OP	25.00	25.00
95	10 IN. SKATING PENGUIN	OP	36.00	36.00
95	10 IN. TREE TOP ANGEL	OP	36.00	36.00
95	10 IN. VALENTINE GIRL BEAR	SU	36.00	36.00
95	10 IN. WHITE CHRISTMAS ELF	OP	17.50	18.00
95	10 IN. WHITE ST. NICHOLAS	OP	45.00	45.00
95	10 IN. WINDOW SHOPPER OSTRICH	OP	39.00	39.00
95	10 IN. WINTER ELF	OP	18.00	18.00
95	12 IN. BOY PILGRIM W/BASKET	OP	47.00	47.00
95	12 IN. CACTUS SET	RT	18.00	18.00
95	12 IN. CAROUSEL HORSE	OP	60.00	60.00
95	12 IN. CHEF SANTA	OP	47.00	47.00
95	12 IN. DRUMMER BOY	OP	40.00	40.00
95	12 IN. GIRL CAT KID	OP	37.00	37.00
95	12 IN. GIRL PILGRIM W/PIE	OP	47.00	47.00
95	12 IN. GIRL SCARECROW	OP	49.00	49.00
95	12 IN. MR. INDOOR SANTA W/TREE TOP STAR	OP	50.00	50.00
95	12 IN. MRS. INDOOR SANTA W/GARLAND	OP	45.00	45.00
95	12 IN. MRS. SANTA CARDHOLDER	OP	44.00	44.00
95	12 IN. NORTH POLE	OP	9.95	10.00
95	12 IN. OLD WORLD ST. NICHOLAS	OP	54.95	55.00
95	12 IN. ROSE & IVY ARBOR	OP	50.00	50.00
95	12 IN. SANTA IN CHIMNEY	OP	71.95	72.00
95	14 IN. LARGE USABLE PUMPKIN W/REMOVABLE TOP	OP	50.00	50.00
95	17 IN. TEEPEE #9026	RT	38.00	38.00
95	18 IN. CHEF SANTA	OP	52.00	52.00
95	18 IN. COUNTRY BOY BUNNY W/APPLE	OP	68.00	68.00
95	18 IN. COUNTRY GIRL BUNNY W/APPLE	OP	68.00	68.00
95	18 IN. EASTER PARADE BOY BUNNY	OP	68.00	68.00

YR	NAME	LIMIT	ISSUE	TREND
95	18 IN. EASTER PARADE GIRL BUNNY	OP	68.00	68.00
95	18 IN. INDOOR SANTA W/LIGHTS	OP	64.00	64.00
95	18 IN. MR. FUR SANTA ON STAND	OP	47.00	47.00
95	18 IN. MR. INDOOR SANTA W/TREE TOP STAR	OP	60.00	60.00
95	18 IN. MR. OLD WORLD SANTA	OP	52.95	53.00
95	18 IN. MRS. INDOOR SANTA W/GARLAND	OP	54.95	55.00
95	18 IN. MRS. OLD WORLD SANTA	OP	51.00	51.00
95	18 IN. MRS. OUTDOOR SANTA	OP	51.00	51.00
95	18 IN. MRS. SANTA CARDHOLDER	OP	53.95	54.00
95	18 IN. MUSICAL SANTA W/GIFT LIST	OP	61.95	62.00
95	18 IN. OLD WORLD REINDEER W/BELLS	OP	61.95	62.00
95	18 IN. PJ KID IN 2-FT. STOCKING	OP	61.95	62.00
95	18 IN. REINDEER W/CHRISTMAS SADDLEBAGS	OP	55.95	56.00
95	18 IN. REINDEER W/SANTA	OP	90.00	90.00
95	18 IN. SANTA ON TOBOGGAN	OP	74.00	74.00
95	18 IN. SANTA W/CARDHOLDER SACK	OP	60.00	60.00
95	18 IN. SANTA W/GIFT LIST & TOYBAG	OP	50.00	50.00
95	18 IN. SNOWMAN W/BROOM	OP	52.00	52.00
95	18 IN. WITCH W/STAND	OP	70.00	70.00
95	2 IN. PUMPKIN W/FACE 9028	RT	6.95	7.00
95	2 IN. RED TOMATOES SET OF THREE	OP	12.95	13.00
95	21 IN. SANTA HUGGING REINDEER #6605	SU	*	N/A
95	22 IN. CHRISTMAS STOCKING	OP	19.50	20.00
95	22 IN. GREEN CHRISTMAS ELF	OP	36.00	36.00
95	22 IN. RED CHRISTMAS ELF	OP	36.00	36.00
95	3 IN. BABY JESUS IN MANGER	OP	18.00	18.00
95	3 IN. CHRISTMAS MORN' ITSIE VIGNETTE	OP	68.00	68.00
95	3 IN. MUSICAL BALLOONING KIDS	OP	55.95	56.00
95	3 IN. SPRING PIXIE PICK	OP	11.50	12.00
95	3 IN. SUN PIN	OP	5.95	6.00
95	3 IN. SWEETHEART ITSIE BOY MOUSE	OP	20.00	20.00
95	3 IN. SWEETHEART ITSIE GIRL MOUSE	OP	15.00	15.00
95	3 IN. WITCH W/BROOM	OP	18.00	18.00
95	3 IN. WITCH W/HALLOWEEN MOON	OP	45.00	45.00
95	30 IN. COUNTRY BOY BUNNY W/APPLES	OP	124.95	125.00
95	30 IN. MR. OLD WORLD SANTA	OP	124.95	125.00
95	30 IN. MRS. OLD WORLD SANTA	OP	125.00	125.00
95	30 IN. MRS. SANTA W/CARDHOLDER APRON	OP	119.95	120.00
95	30 IN. OUTDOOR SANTA W/TOY BAG	OP	137.95	138.00
95	30 IN. SANTA W/CARDHOLDER SACK	OP	119.95	120.00
95	30 IN. SANTA W/NORTH POLE	OP	137.95	138.00
95	30 IN. SNOWMAN	OP	119.95	120.00
95	30 IN. WITCH KID	OP	149.95	150.00
95	36 IN. REINDEER W/CARDHOLDER SADDLEBAGS	OP	154.50	155.00
95	4 FT. TREE SKIRT	OP	30.00	30.00
95	5 IN. ANGEL W/CHRISTMAS MOON	OP	45.00	45.00
95	5 IN. ANGEL W/MISTLETOE	OP	16.50	17.00
95	5 IN. BABY JESUS IN MANGER W/HAY	OP	27.50	28.00
95	5 IN. BLACK CHRISTMAS LAMB	OP	20.50	21.00
95	5 IN. BOUDOIR BABY W/BLANKET	OP	20.00	20.00
95	5 IN. CACTUS SET	OP	18.00	18.00
95	5 IN. EASTER PARADE BOY DUCK	OP	23.50	24.00
95	5 IN. EASTER PARADE GIRL DUCK	OP	25.50	26.00
95	5 IN. ELK WORKSHOP	OP	14.50	15.00
95	5 IN. FAWN	OP	15.50	16.00
95	5 IN. GOLD FALL ELF W/LEAF	OP	15.00	15.00
95	5 IN. GREEN CHRISTMAS ELF	OP	14.50	15.00
95	5 IN. GREEN SPRING ELF	OP	14.50	15.00
95	5 IN. HALLOWEEN ELF/BLACK	OP	15.50	16.00
95	5 IN. HALLOWEEN ELF/ORANGE	OP	15.50	16.00
95	5 IN. LEPRECHAUN W/POT 'O GOLD	OP	20.00	20.00
95	5 IN. OLD WORLD CAROLLER BOY	OP	20.50	21.00
95	5 IN. OLD WORLD CAROLLER GIRL	OP	20.50	21.00
95	5 IN. OLD WORLD SANTA W/9 IN. WREATH #4550	RT	34.00	34.00
95	5 IN. ORANGE FALL ELF W/LEAF	OP	15.00	15.00
95	5 IN. PIXIE PICCOLO PLAYER	OP	30.00	30.00
95	5 IN. RED CHRISTMAS ELF	OP	14.50	15.00
95	5 IN. SAILOR DUCK	OP	25.50	26.00
95	5 IN. WHITE CHRISTMAS ELF	OP	14.50	15.00
95	5 IN. WHITE CHRISTMAS LAMB	OP	20.50	21.00
95	5 IN. WINTER ELF	OP	14.50	15.00
95	5 IN. YELLOW SPRING ELF	OP	14.50	15.00
95	7 IN. ANGEL MOUSE	OP	23.50	24.00
95	7 IN. ANGEL W/HARP	OP	27.00	27.00
95	7 IN. ANGEL W/MUSICAL INSTRUMENT	OP	21.50	22.00
95	7 IN. ANGEL/BLACK HAIR	OP	24.50	25.00
95	7 IN. ANGEL/BLONDE HAIR	OP	24.50	25.00
95	7 IN. ANGEL/BROWN HAIR	OP	24.50	25.00
95	7 IN. ARTIST BUNNY W/BRUSH & PALETTE	OP	22.50	23.00
95	7 IN. BABY BUNNY W/BABY BOTTLE	OP	20.50	21.00
95	7 IN. BICYCLIST BOY MOUSE	OP	26.00	26.00
95	7 IN. BIRTHDAY GIRL MOUSE	OP	24.50	25.00
95	7 IN. BRIDE MOUSE	OP	23.50	24.00
95	7 IN. CALIFORNIA MUDSLIDE MOUSE	OP	30.00	30.00
95	7 IN. CAROLLER MOUSE W/BIG HAT & TREE	OP	21.50	22.00

YR	NAME	LIMIT	ISSUE	TREND
95	7 IN. CHAMPAGNE MOUSE IN GLASS	OP	27.50	28.00
95	7 IN. CHEF MOUSE	RT	27.50	28.00
95	7 IN. CHEF SANTA	OP	30.50	31.00
95	7 IN. CHOIR BOY	OP	27.50	28.00
95	7 IN. CHOIR BOY W/BLACK EYE	OP	27.50	28.00
95	7 IN. CHOIR GIRL	OP	27.50	28.00
95	7 IN. CHRISTMAS PARTY GIRL MOUSE #7736	RT	19.00	19.00
95	7 IN. COUNTRY BOY BUNNY W/APPLE	OP	22.00	22.00
95	7 IN. COUNTRY GIRL BUNNY W/APPLE	OP	22.00	22.00
95	7 IN. DOWN THROUGH THE CHIMNEY MOUSE #7729	SU	*	N/A
95	7 IN. DRUMMER BOY	OP	24.50	25.00
95	7 IN. EASTER BUNNY KID W/BASKET	OP	22.50	23.00
95	7 IN. FLYING ANGEL	OP	22.00	22.00
95	7 IN. GARDEN CLUB MOUSE	RT	25.00	23.00
95	7 IN. GHOST MOUSE	OP	27.50	28.00
95	7 IN. GIRL BUILDING A SNOWMAN	OP	25.00	25.00
95	7 IN. GRADUATION BOY MOUSE	OP	24.50	25.00
95	7 IN. GRADUATION GIRL MOUSE	OP	24.50	25.00
95	7 IN. GROOM MOUSE	OP	23.50	24.00
95	7 IN. GYPSY GIRL KID #3035	RT	32.00	32.00
95	7 IN. HABITAT MOUSE	RT	30.50	31.00
95	7 IN. HERSHEY KID	RT	38.50	67.00
95	7 IN. HOCKEY KID	OP	31.00	31.00
95	7 IN. HOLLY GIRL MOUSE #7711	RT	19.00	19.00
95	7 IN. HOUSEWIFE MOUSE	OP	26.00	26.00
95	7 IN. INDIAN BOY KID #3154	RT	30.00	30.00
95	7 IN. INDIAN BOY KID W/SPEAR	OP	30.00	30.00
95	7 IN. INDIAN GIRL KID W/BEADS	OP	30.00	30.00
95	7 IN. JOSEPH CHILD	OP	29.00	29.00
95	7 IN. LARGE CABBAGE	OP	18.00	18.00
95	7 IN. LOGO KID/DOLL SOCIETY	OP	30.00	30.00
95	7 IN. MARBLES KID	OP	27.50	28.00
95	7 IN. MARY CHILD W/DOLL	OP	29.00	29.00
95	7 IN. MOTORCYCLE MOUSE "MIKEY THE BIKEY"	OP	31.00	31.00
95	7 IN. MOUSE IN CORNUCOPIA	OP	25.50	26.00
95	7 IN. MOUSE IN SANTA'S HAT	OP	19.00	19.00
95	7 IN. MOUSE KID #3037	RT	22.50	23.00
95	7 IN. MOUSE W/SNOWBALL	OP	19.00	19.00
95	7 IN. MR. & MRS. INDOOR SANTA W/TREE	OP	70.00	70.00
95	7 IN. MR. OLD WORLD SANTA	OP	29.00	29.00
95	7 IN. MRS. SANTA W/FUR TRIM	OP	24.00	25.00
95	7 IN. MRS. SANTA W/PRESENTS	OP	31.00	31.00
95	7 IN. NASHVILLE BOY	OP	31.50	32.00
95	7 IN. NASHVILLE GIRL	OP	30.00	30.00
95	7 IN. NAUGHT ANGEL W/BLACK EYE	OP	26.00	26.00
95	7 IN. PILGRIM BOY HUGGING FAWN	OP	43.00	43.00
95	7 IN. PILGRIM GIRL W/PIE	OP	28.00	28.00
95	7 IN. PILGRIM MICE SET W/BASKET	OP	48.00	48.00
95	7 IN. PJ KID ON ROCKING HORSE #7232	SU	30.00	30.00
95	7 IN. SANTA	OP	20.50	21.00
95	7 IN. SANTA HUGGING REINDEER #6510	SU	48.00	48.00
95	7 IN. SANTA MOUSE IN CHIMNEY	OP	35.00	35.00
95	7 IN. SANTA SKIING	OP	30.00	30.00
95	7 IN. SANTA W/LIGHTS	OP	32.00	32.00
95	7 IN. SANTA W/NORTH POLE	OP	36.00	36.00
95	7 IN. SANTA W/PRESENTS	OP	28.00	28.00
95	7 IN. SANTA W/SLEIGH	OP	40.00	40.00
95	7 IN. SANTA W/SNOWSHOES & TREE	OP	30.00	30.00
95	7 IN. SANTA, INDOOR	OP	20.00	20.00
95	7 IN. SHEPHERD CHILD W/LAMB	OP	40.00	40.00
95	7 IN. SMALL CHRISTMAS DOVE	OP	27.50	28.00
95	7 IN. SNOWMAN ON TOBOGGAN	OP	31.00	31.00
95	7 IN. SNOWMAN W/PIPE	OP	26.50	27.00
95	7 IN. SNOWWOMAN/MRS. RITZ	OP	27.50	28.00
95	7 IN. SOUTH AMERICAN GIRL	YR	32.00	32.00
95	7 IN. ST. PATRICK'S DAY MOUSE	OP	27.00	37.00
95	7 IN. SWEETHEART BOY MOUSE	OP	21.00	21.00
95	7 IN. SWEETHEART GIRL MOUSE	OP	21.00	21.00
95	7 IN. SWISS ALPS BOY	YR	32.00	32.00
95	7 IN. TREE TOP STAR W/3 IN. ANGEL	OP	21.50	22.00
95	7 IN. TREETOP MOUSE IN CHIMNEY	OP	35.00	35.00
95	7 IN. VALENTINE GIRL W/CARD	OP	27.00	27.00
95	7 IN. WHITE MOUSE IN SLIPPER	OP	26.50	27.00
95	7 IN. WHITE MOUSE ON TOBOGGAN W/PRESENT	OP	31.00	31.00
95	7 IN. WHITE SKATING MOUSE	OP	26.50	27.00
95	7 IN. WITCH MOUSE 3009	RT	27.50	28.00
95	7 IN. WIZARD MOUSE	OP	29.50	30.00
95	8 IN. BOY TURKEY	OP	35.50	36.00
95	8 IN. EAR OF CORN	OP	12.95	13.00
95	8 IN. EASTER PARADE BOY BUNNY	OP	28.00	28.00
95	8 IN. EASTER PARADE GIRL BUNNY	OP	28.00	28.00
95	8 IN. GIRL TURKEY	OP	35.50	36.00
95	LARGE PEA PODS & CARROTS SET OF THREE	OP	16.00	16.00
95	WYNKEN, BLYNKEN & NOD	OP	63.00	63.00
96	10 IN. BABY CAKES BEAR	OP	38.00	38.00

YR	NAME	LIMIT	ISSUE	TREND
96	10 IN. CANDY BASKET ELVES #2992	RT	42.00	42.00
96	10 IN. CAROLLING BOY BEAR	OP	42.00	42.00
96	10 IN. CAROLLING GIRL BEAR	OP	42.00	42.00
96	10 IN. CAROLLING REINDEER	OP	25.00	25.00
96	10 IN. COUNTRY BOY BEAR	SU	44.00	44.00
96	10 IN. COUNTRY BUMPKIN SCARECROW	OP	38.00	38.00
96	10 IN. COUNTRY GIRL BEAR	SU	42.00	42.00
96	10 IN. DOE	OP	22.50	23.00
96	10 IN. EASTER PARADE BOY BEAR	RT	42.00	42.00
96	10 IN. EASTER PARADE GIRL BEAR	RT	42.00	42.00
96	10 IN. FLYING WITCH	OP	38.00	38.00
96	10 IN. GHOST OF CHRISTMAS FUTURE #5457	RT	29.50	30.00
96	10 IN. GHOST OF CHRISTMAS PAST #5455	RT	40.00	40.00
96	10 IN. GREEN CHRISTMAS ELF	OP	17.50	18.00
96	10 IN. HOOK, LINE AND SANTA	OP	45.00	45.00
96	10 IN. INDIAN MAN	OP	43.00	43.00
96	10 IN. INDIAN WOMAN	OP	43.00	43.00
96	10 IN. JESTER & FRIEND	OP	34.00	34.00
96	10 IN. JOSEPH	OP	37.50	38.00
96	10 IN. LEAPIN' FROG	SU	18.00	18.00
96	10 IN. LOVER BOY BEAR	RT	40.00	40.00
96	10 IN. MARY HOLDING BABY JESUS	OP	39.50	40.00
96	10 IN. MR. FARMER	RT	35.00	35.00
96	10 IN. MR. SCROOGE #5467	RT	37.50	38.00
96	10 IN. MRS. FARMER	RT	35.00	35.00
96	10 IN. OLD TYME CAROLLING MAN	OP	39.00	39.00
96	10 IN. OLD TYME CAROLLING WOMAN	OP	39.00	39.00
96	10 IN. OLD WORLD TREE TOP ANGEL #7276	RT	47.00	47.00
96	10 IN. PILGRIM MAN	OP	45.00	45.00
96	10 IN. PILGRIM WOMAN	OP	40.00	40.00
96	10 IN. PUMPKIN PATCH ELF	OP	24.00	24.00
96	10 IN. PUPPIES FOR CHRISTMAS SANTA	OP	80.00	80.00
96	10 IN. RED CHRISTMAS ELF	OP	17.50	18.00
96	10 IN. REINDEER	OP	24.00	24.00
96	10 IN. TREE TOP ANGEL	OP	41.00	41.00
96	10 IN. TRICK OR TREAT ELF	OP	21.00	21.00
96	10 IN. WANDERING ST. NICHOLAS #5393	RT	49.00	49.00
96	10 IN. WINTER ELF	OP	18.00	18.00
96	10 IN. WISE MAN BEARING FRANKINCENSE	OP	44.00	44.00
96	10 IN. WISE MAN BEARING GOLD	OP	44.00	44.00
96	10 IN. WISE MAN BEARING MYRRH	OP	44.00	44.00
96	10 IN. WOMAN GOLFER	RT	44.00	44.00
96	10 IN. WOMAN TENNIS PLAYER	RT	44.00	44.00
96	10 IN. WOODLAND SANTA & REINDEER 5392	RT	66.00	66.00
96	12 IN. BROWN HORSE	RT	35.50	36.00
96	12 IN. CACTUS SET	OP	6.00	6.00
96	12 IN. CAROLLING MRS. SANTA #5496	SU	46.00	46.00
96	12 IN. CAROLLING SANTA #5497	SU	56.00	56.00
96	12 IN. CAROUSEL HORSE	OP	*	N/A
96	12 IN. CAROUSEL HORSE #2	RT	68.00	68.00
96	12 IN. CHRISTMAS EVE MRS. SANTA	OP	60.00	60.00
96	12 IN. CHRISTMAS EVE SANTA	OP	60.00	60.00
96	12 IN. DRUMMER BOY	OP	45.00	45.00
96	12 IN. MOTHER DUCK	RT	50.00	50.00
96	12 IN. NORTH POLE	OP	10.50	11.00
96	12 IN. OLDE WORLD ST. NICHOLAS #5450	RT	63.00	63.00
96	12 IN. ROSE & IVY ARBOR	RT	50.00	50.00
96	12 IN. STREET LAMP	OP	14.00	14.00
96	12 IN. TOMMY TURKEY #3162	RT	76.00	76.00
96	12 IN. WORKSHOP SANTA	OP	54.00	54.00
96	15 IN. HAUNTED TREE	OP	45.00	45.00
96	17 IN. TEEPEE	OP	38.00	38.00
96	18 IN. BEARY CHRISTMAS STOCKING	RT	78.00	78.00
96	18 IN. CHEF SANTA	OP	61.00	61.00
96	18 IN. COUNTRY BOY BUNNY	OP	68.00	68.00
96	18 IN. COUNTRY GIRL BUNNY	SU	68.00	68.00
96	18 IN. EASTER PARADE BOY BUNNY	OP	68.00	68.00
96	18 IN. EASTER PARADE GIRL BUNNY	OP	37.50	38.00
96	18 IN. MR. FUR SANTA ON STAND	OP	50.00	50.00
96	18 IN. MRS. OUTDOOR SANTA	OP	53.00	53.00
96	18 IN. MRS. SANTA HANGING CRANBERRIES & POPCORN	SU	60.00	60.00
96	18 IN. MUSICAL CAROLLING SANTA	OP	58.00	58.00
96	18 IN. OLD WORLD MRS. SANTA/LAMB #5653	RT	84.00	84.00
96	18 IN. OLD WORLD SANTA #5652	RT	76.00	76.00
96	18 IN. PUTTING ON THE RITZ SNOWMAN #7527	SU	65.00	65.00
96	18 IN. REINDEER W/CHRISTMAS SADDLEBAGS	OP	60.00	60.00
96	18 IN. REINDEER W/VELOUR SANTA	OP	104.00	104.00
96	18 IN. SANTA W/GIFT LIST & TOYBAG	OP	54.00	54.00
96	18 IN. SNOWMAN W/BROOM	OP	55.00	55.00
96	18 IN. SUNFLOWER	RT	23.50	24.00
96	18 IN. TUCKERED MRS. SANTA & PJ KID	OP	95.00	95.00
96	18 IN. TUCKERED SANTA & PJ KID	OP	92.00	92.00
96	18 IN. WITCHY BREW	OP	83.00	83.00
96	2 IN. PUMPKIN W/FACE	OP	7.00	7.00
96	2 IN. RED TOMATOES SET OF THREE	RT	13.50	14.00

YR	NAME	LIMIT	ISSUE	TREND
96	22 IN. CHRISTMAS STOCKING	OP	19.50	20.00
96	22 IN. GREEN CHRISTMAS ELF	OP	39.50	40.00
96	22 IN. RED CHRISTMAS ELF	OP	39.50	40.00
96	24 IN. COUNTRY CATTAIL	RT	26.00	26.00
96	25 IN. SUNFLOWER	RT	26.00	26.00
96	29 IN. BUTTERFLY PIN	RT	15.00	14.00
96	3 IN. BIRTHDAY MOUSE	SU	21.00	21.00
96	3 IN. BRIDE MOUSE	RT	24.00	24.00
96	3 IN. BUTTERFLY PICK	RT	15.00	15.00
96	3 IN. CANOEING INDIAN KIDS	OP	40.00	40.00
96	3 IN. CAROLLING BOY #8036	SU	18.00	18.00
96	3 IN. CAROLLING GIRL #8034	SU	18.00	18.00
96	3 IN. COMPUTER MOUSE	RT	21.50	22.00
96	3 IN. EASTER BUNNY	SU	19.50	20.00
96	3 IN. FROGGIE	SU	13.50	14.00
96	3 IN. GHOST MOUSE	RT	20.00	20.00
96	3 IN. GROOM MOUSE	OP	22.00	22.00
96	3 IN. HERSHEY BOY MOUSE	SU	23.00	23.00
96	3 IN. HERSHEY GIRL MOUSE	RT	23.00	23.00
96	3 IN. HIKER MOUSE	RT	25.00	25.00
96	3 IN. INDIAN BOY ITSIE SERIES	OP	20.00	20.00
96	3 IN. INDIAN GIRL	OP	20.00	20.00
96	3 IN. LADYBUG PICK	OP	15.00	15.00
96	3 IN. MAILMAN MOUSE	RT	22.00	22.00
96	3 IN. MATCHBOX MICE	OP	34.00	34.00
96	3 IN. MUSICAL BALLOONING BEARS	RT	60.00	60.00
96	3 IN. NURSE MOUSE	SU	21.50	22.00
96	3 IN. PILGRIM BOY	OP	22.00	22.00
96	3 IN. PILGRIM GIRL ITSIE SERIES	OP	22.00	22.00
96	3 IN. SLEIGH RIDE SANTA	OP	23.50	24.00
96	3 IN. TEACHER MOUSE	OP	20.00	20.00
96	3 IN. WITCH W/BROOM	OP	19.00	19.00
96	3 IN. WITCH W/HALLOWEEN MOON	OP	45.00	45.00
96	3 IN. WIZARD MOUSE 2999	RT	24.00	24.00
96	3 IN. YELLOW DUCKLING	SU	21.00	21.00
96	30 IN. CHRISTMAS ELF/RED	OP	67.00	67.00
96	30 IN. DECK THE HALLS SANTA	OP	169.50	170.00
96	30 IN. MRS. SANTA W/CARDHOLDER APRON	OP	126.00	126.00
96	30 IN. OLD WORLD MRS. SANTA #6253	RT	152.00	152.00
96	30 IN. OLD WORLD SANTA #6252	RT	160.00	160.00
96	30 IN. SHOPPING MRS. SANTA #6212	SU	156.50	157.00
96	30 IN. SKELETON KID #3019	RT	123.00	123.00
96	30 IN. SUNDAY MORNING SANTA #6011	SU	125.00	125.00
96	36 IN. OLD WORLD REINDEER #6751	SU	146.00	146.00
96	4 FT. TREE SKIRT	OP	33.00	33.00
96	4 IN. ANGEL W/MISTLETOE	OP	18.00	18.00
96	4 IN. PUPPY PRESENT	OP	19.00	19.00
96	4 IN. STREET LAMP	OP	8.00	8.00
96	5 IN. ANGEL CENTERPIECE	OP	31.00	31.00
96	5 IN. BLACK CHRISTMAS LAMB	OP	17.50	18.00
96	5 IN. BLANKET BABY BOY	RT	20.00	20.00
96	5 IN. BLANKET BABY GIRL	RT	20.00	20.00
96	5 IN. CACTUS SET	OP	23.50	24.00
96	5 IN. ELF CENTERPIECE #7346	SU	27.00	27.00
96	5 IN. ELF WORKSHOP	OP	*	N/A
96	5 IN. FAWN	OP	16.50	17.00
96	5 IN. GREEN CHRISTMAS ELF	OP	15.00	15.00
96	5 IN. HALLOWEEN ELF/BLACK	OP	15.00	15.00
96	5 IN. HALLOWEEN ELF/ORANGE	OP	15.00	15.00
96	5 IN. HOLLY BERRY ANGEL	OP	22.00	22.00
96	5 IN. LEPRECHAUN W/POT 'O GOLD	RT	22.00	22.00
96	5 IN. OLD WORLD SANTA W/9 IN. WREATH	OP	34.00	34.00
96	5 IN. PIXIE PICCOLO PLAYER	RT	30.00	30.00
96	5 IN. RED CHRISTMAS ELF	OP	15.00	15.00
96	5 IN. SAILOR DUCK	RT	27.50	28.00
96	5 IN. TEEPEE	OP	20.00	20.00
96	5 IN. WHITE CHRISTMAS LAMB	OP	17.50	18.00
96	5 IN. WINTER ELF	OP	15.00	15.00
96	5 IN. WOOLY LAMB #5424	SU	17.00	17.00
96	5 IN. YELLOW DUCK	SU	22.00	22.00
96	7 IN. ANGEL CENTERPIECE #7177	SU	*	N/A
96	7 IN. ANGEL MOUSE	OP	23.50	24.00
96	7 IN. ANGEL W/HARP	OP	27.00	27.00
96	7 IN. ANGEL W/MUSICAL INSTRUMENT	OP	21.50	22.00
96	7 IN. ANGEL/BLONDE HAIR	OP	24.50	25.00
96	7 IN. BAKER KID	RT	31.00	31.00
96	7 IN. BANANA KID 3065	RT	27.50	28.00
96	7 IN. BICYCLIST BOY MOUSE	RT	28.00	28.00
96	7 IN. CAROLLER MOUSE W/BIG HAT & TREE	OP	24.00	24.00
96	7 IN. CAROLLING SNOWMAN	OP	29.50	30.00
96	7 IN. CHEF MOUSE	OP	27.50	28.00
96	7 IN. CHEF SANTA	OP	30.00	30.00
96	7 IN. CHRISTMAS PARTY GIRL MOUSE	OP	19.50	20.00
96	7 IN. COUNTRY BOY BUNNY	OP	24.50	25.00
96	7 IN. COUNTRY GIRL BUNNY	OP	23.00	23.00

YR	NAME	LIMIT	ISSUE	TREND
96	7 IN. COUNTRY GIRL MOUSE	SU	26.00	26.00
96	7 IN. DRUMMER BOY	OP	29.00	29.00
96	7 IN. EASTER BUNNY KID W/BASKET	RT	24.50	25.00
96	7 IN. HERSHEY KID	RT	40.00	39.00
96	7 IN. LETTER TO SANTA MOUSE	OP	23.00	23.00
96	7 IN. MAKING FRIENDS SNOWMAN	OP	28.00	28.00
96	7 IN. MOONBEAM SANTA MOBILE	OP	46.00	46.00
96	7 IN. MOUSE KID	OP	26.00	26.00
96	7 IN. MOUSE W/SNOWBALL	OP	19.50	20.00
96	7 IN. MR. & MRS. SANTA EXCHANGING GIFTS	OP	57.00	57.00
96	7 IN. NAUGHTY ANGEL W/BLACK EYE	OP	28.00	28.00
96	7 IN. NEW YEAR'S MOUSE #8205	SU	20.00	20.00
96	7 IN. OLD WORLD MRS. SANTA #5152	RT	32.00	32.00
96	7 IN. OLD WORLD SANTA #5153	RT	40.00	40.00
96	7 IN. PILGRIM BOY MOUSE	OP	26.00	26.00
96	7 IN. PILGRIM GIRL MOUSE	OP	24.00	24.00
96	7 IN. PJ KID ON ROCKING HORSE	OP	30.00	30.00
96	7 IN. POWDER PUFF BABY	RT	21.00	21.00
96	7 IN. SAINT PATRICK'S DAY KID	OP	31.00	31.00
96	7 IN. SANTA	OP	22.00	22.00
96	7 IN. SANTA CENTERPIECE #5245	RT	35.00	35.00
96	7 IN. SANTA HUGGING REINDEER	OP	51.00	51.00
96	7 IN. SANTA MOUSE IN CHIMNEY	OP	36.50	37.00
96	7 IN. SANTA SKIING	OP	30.00	30.00
96	7 IN. SHOPPING MRS. SANTA	OP	36.50	37.00
96	7 IN. SHOPPING SANTA	OP	36.50	37.00
96	7 IN. SLEIGH RIDE SANTA COUPLE	OP	84.00	84.00
96	7 IN. SNOWBALL FIGHT KID #7233	SU	30.50	31.00
96	7 IN. SNOWBALL W/PIPE	OP	30.00	30.00
96	7 IN. SPIDER KID 3064	RT	27.50	28.00
96	7 IN. SWEETHEART BOY	RT	32.50	33.00
96	7 IN. SWEETHEART BOY MOUSE	OP	21.00	21.00
96	7 IN. SWEETHEART GIRL MOUSE	OP	*	N/A
96	7 IN. TRIM TIME SANTA	OP	33.00	33.00
96	7 IN. TUCKERED BOY MOUSE	OP	22.50	23.00
96	7 IN. TUCKERED GIRL MOUSE	OP	22.50	23.00
96	7 IN. VALENTINE GIRL KID W/CARD	OP	27.50	28.00
96	7 IN. WHITE SKATING MOUSE	OP	28.50	29.00
96	7 IN. WITCH KID	OP	32.00	32.00
96	7 IN. WITCH MOUSE	OP	28.00	28.00
96	8 IN. CORN STALK	OP	12.00	12.00
96	8 IN. EAR OF CORN	RT	13.00	13.00
96	8 IN. FLOWERING LILY PAD	SU	10.00	10.00
96	CRECHE FOR NATIVITY	OP	40.00	40.00
96	LARGE PEA PODS & CARROTS SET OF THREE	RT	23.00	23.00
96	MOONBEAM SANTA MOBILE #5200	SU	*	N/A
96	SCROOGE'S BED	OP	44.00	44.00
96	WYNKEN, BLYNKEN & NOD	OP	68.00	68.00
97	10 IN. AUTUMN ANGEL	RT	*	N/A
97	10 IN. BLUE SANTA	RT	*	N/A
97	10 IN. CAROLLING BOY BEAR	RT	*	N/A
97	10 IN. CAROLLING GIRL BEAR	RT	*	N/A
97	10 IN. CAROLLING REINDEER	SU	*	N/A
97	10 IN. COUNTRY BUMPKIN SCARECROW	SU	*	N/A
97	10 IN. FLYING WITCH	SU	*	N/A
97	10 IN. FROSTY ELF	SU	*	N/A
97	10 IN. HOOK, LINE & SANTA	RT	*	N/A
97	10 IN. MEDICINE MAN	SU	*	N/A
97	10 IN. MYSTICAL SANTA	RT	*	N/A
97	10 IN. OLD TYME CAROLLING MAN	RT	*	N/A
97	10 IN. OLD TYME CAROLLING WOMAN	RT	*	N/A
97	10 IN. PUPPIES FOR CHRISTMAS SANTA	RT	*	N/A
97	10 IN. TRICK OR TREAT ELF	SU	*	N/A
97	12 IN. CHRISTMAS EVE MRS. SANTA	SU	*	N/A
97	12 IN. CHRISTMAS EVE SANTA	SU	*	N/A
97	12 IN. DRUMMER BOY	SU	*	N/A
97	12 IN. WORKSHOP SANTA	SU	*	N/A
97	15 IN. HAUNTED TREE	RT	*	N/A
97	18 IN. CATCH OF THE DAY SANTA	RT	*	N/A
97	18 IN. MRS. SANTA W/DOVE	RT	*	N/A
97	18 IN. REINDEER	SU	*	N/A
97	18 IN. SANTA HANGING ORNAMENT	SU	*	N/A
97	18 IN. TUCKERED MRS. SANTA & PJ KIDS	SU	*	N/A
97	18 IN. TUCKERED SANTA & PJ KIDS	SU	*	N/A
97	18 IN. VINEYARD MONK	SU	*	N/A
97	18 IN. WITCHY BREW	SU	*	N/A
97	22 IN. CHRISTMAS ELF, GREEN	SU	*	N/A
97	22 IN. JUST-A-JESTER	RT	*	N/A
97	22 IN. PEEK-A-BOO STOCKING	SU	*	N/A
97	3 IN. CANOEING INDIAN KIDS	RT	*	N/A
97	3 IN. INDIAN BOY	SU	*	N/A
97	3 IN. INDIAN GIRL	SU	*	N/A
97	3 IN. MATCHBOX MICE	RT	*	N/A
97	3 IN. MONK WITH CASK	SU	*	N/A
97	3 IN. PILGRIM BOY	SU	*	N/A

YR	NAME	LIMIT	ISSUE	TREND
97	3 IN. PILGRIM GIRL	SU	*	N/A
97	3 IN. SLEIGH RIDE SANTA	SU	*	N/A
97	3 IN. SWEET SURPRISE MOUSE	RT	*	N/A
97	3 IN. WITCH KID	SU	*	N/A
97	30 IN. AUTUMN JESTER	RT	*	N/A
97	30 IN. CHRISTMAS ELF, RED	SU	*	N/A
97	30 IN. DECK THE HALLS SANTA	SU	*	N/A
97	30 IN. FINISHING TOUCH SANTA	SU	*	N/A
97	30 IN. MRS. LAST MINUTE WRAPPING	SU	*	N/A
97	30 IN. MRS. SANTA & SQUEAK	SU	*	N/A
97	4 IN. PUPPY PRESENT	RT	*	N/A
97	5 IN. FROSTY ELF	SU	*	N/A
97	5 IN. HOLLY BERRY ANGEL	SU	*	N/A
97	5 IN. MISTLETOE ANGEL	SU	*	N/A
97	5 IN. WORKSHOP ELF	SU	*	N/A
97	7 IN. BABY NEW YEAR KID	SU	*	N/A
97	7 IN. CAROLLING SNOWMAN	SU	*	N/A
97	7 IN. HEARTH & HOME SANTA	RT	*	N/A
97	7 IN. HOLIDAY BASKET COUPLE	SU	*	N/A
97	7 IN. HOSTESS MOUSE	RT	*	N/A
97	7 IN. ICE FISHING KID	RT	*	N/A
97	7 IN. LETTER TO SANTA MOUSE	SU	*	N/A
97	7 IN. NAUGHTY ANGEL	SU	*	N/A
97	7 IN. SANTA MOUSE ON SWAG	RT	*	N/A
97	7 IN. SANTA'S TOUCH	SU	*	N/A
97	7 IN. SHOPPING MRS. SANTA	SU	*	N/A
97	7 IN. SHOPPING SANTA	SU	*	N/A
97	7 IN. SKATING GIRL MOUSE	SU	*	N/A
97	7 IN. SLEIGH RIDE SANTA COUPLE	SU	*	N/A
97	7 IN. SWASHBUCKLER BOY	RT	*	N/A
97	7 IN. TAGS	RT	*	N/A
97	7 IN. TATTERS	RT	*	N/A
97	7 IN. TRIM TIME SANTA	RT	*	N/A
97	7 IN. TUCKERED BOY MOUSE	RT	*	N/A
97	7 IN. TUCKERED GIRL MOUSE	RT	*	N/A
97	7 IN. WITCH KID	SU	*	N/A
97	7 IN. WIZ KID	RT	*	N/A
97	CORN STALK WITH PUMPKIN	SU	*	N/A
97	SMALL TEE PEE	SU	*	N/A
98	10 IN. HARVEST ANGEL	5000	*	N/A
98	10 IN. VICTOR BUNNY	3500	55.00	55.00
98	10 IN. VICTORIA BUNNY	3500	55.00	55.00
98	10 IN. WANDA THE WITCH	5000	*	N/A
98	3 IN. LITTLE NIBBLES	3500	40.00	40.00
98	7 IN. SPORTS ENTHUSIAST	3500	55.00	55.00

A. THORNDIKE — **DICKENS SERIES**

YR	NAME	LIMIT	ISSUE	TREND
96	10 IN. GHOST OF CHRISTMAS PRESENT	RT	*	N/A
96	10 IN. MR. SCROOGE'S BED	RT	*	N/A

ANRI
*

DISNEY DOLLS

YR	NAME	LIMIT	ISSUE	TREND
89	MICKEY MOUSE, 14 IN.	2500	850.00	895.00
89	MINNIE MOUSE, 14 IN.	2500	850.00	895.00
89	PINOCCHIO, 14 IN.	2500	850.00	895.00
90	DAISY DUCK, 14 IN.	2500	895.00	895.00
90	DONALD DUCK, 14 IN.	2500	895.00	895.00

J. FERRANDIZ — **FERRANDIZ DOLLS**

YR	NAME	LIMIT	ISSUE	TREND
89	GABRIEL, 14 IN.	1000	550.00	575.00
89	MARIA, 14 IN.	1000	550.00	575.00
90	MARGARITE, 14 IN.	CL	575.00	725.00
90	PHILIPE, 14 IN.	CL	575.00	675.00
91	CARMEN, 14 IN.	1000	730.00	730.00
91	FERNANDO, 14 IN.	1000	730.00	730.00
91	JUANITA, 7 IN.	1500	300.00	300.00
91	MIGUEL, 7 IN.	1500	300.00	300.00

S. KAY — **SARAH KAY DOLLS**

YR	NAME	LIMIT	ISSUE	TREND
88	BRIDE AND GROOM MATCHING SETS	*	1,300.00	1350.00
88	BRIDE TO LOVE AND TO CHERISH	750	750.00	775.00
88	CHARLOTTE (BLUE)	1000	550.00	575.00
88	EMILY, 14 IN.	750	500.00	500.00
88	GROOM WITH THIS RING DOLL	750	550.00	575.00
88	JENNIFER, 14 IN.	750	500.00	500.00
88	KATHERINE, 14 IN.	750	500.00	500.00
88	MARTHA, 14 IN.	750	500.00	500.00
88	RACHAEL, 14 IN.	750	500.00	500.00
88	REBECCA, 14 IN.	750	500.00	500.00
88	VICTORIA, 14 IN.	750	500.00	500.00
89	ELEANOR (FLORAL)	1000	550.00	575.00
89	ELIZABETH (PATCHWORK)	1000	550.00	575.00
89	HELEN (BROWN)	1000	550.00	575.00
89	HENRY	1000	550.00	575.00
89	MARY (RED)	1000	550.00	575.00
90	CHRISTINA, 14 IN.	1000	575.00	725.00
90	FAITH, 14 IN.	CL	575.00	675.00
90	POLLY, 14 IN.	CL	575.00	675.00

YR	NAME	LIMIT	ISSUE	TREND
90	SOPHIE, 14 IN.	CL	575.00	650.00
91	ANNIE, 7 IN.	1500	300.00	300.00
91	JANINE, 14 IN.	1500	750.00	750.00
91	JESSICA, 7 IN.	1500	300.00	300.00
91	JULIE, 7 IN.	1500	300.00	300.00
91	MICHELLE, 7 IN.	1500	300.00	300.00
91	PATRICIA, 14 IN.	1500	730.00	730.00
91	PEGGY, 7 IN.	1500	300.00	300.00
91	SUSAN, 7 IN.	1500	300.00	300.00

ARTAFFECTS
G. PERILLO | | | | ART DOLL COLLECTION

86	MORNING STAR, 17 1/2 IN.	1000	250.00	250.00
88	SUNFLOWER, 12 IN.	2500	175.00	175.00
90	LITTLE DOVE, 12 IN.	5000	175.00	175.00
90	STRAIGHT ARROW, 12 IN.	5000	175.00	175.00

G. PERILLO | | | | CHILDREN OF THE PLAINS

92	BRAVE AND FREE	OP	111.00	111.00
93	BIRD SONG	OP	111.00	111.00
93	GENTLE SHEPHERD	OP	111.00	111.00
93	SONG OF SIOUX	OP	111.00	111.00
94	CACTUS FLOWER	OP	111.00	111.00
94	LITTLE FRIEND	OP	111.00	111.00
94	PATHFINDER	OP	111.00	111.00
94	PRINCESS OF THE SUN	OP	111.00	111.00

* | | | | COUNTRY MUSICIANS COLLECTION

94	DANNY	OP	118.00	118.00

* | | | | RUFFLES AND RHYMES DOLL COLLECTION

93	LITTLE BO PEEP (15 IN.)	OP	89.00	89.00
94	LITTLE BO PEEP	OP	107.00	107.00

G. PERILLO | | | | SINGLE ISSUE

94	LITTLE BREEZE	OP	114.00	114.00

ASHTON-DRAKE GALLERIES
T. TOMESCU

97	ETERNAL LOVE	*	133.00	133.00

S. BILOTTO | | | | A CENTURY OF BEAUTIFUL BRIDES

97	1900S KATHERINE	TL	63.00	63.00

J. MCCLELLAND | | | | A CHILDREN'S CIRCUS

90	TOMMY THE CLOWN	RT	78.00	78.00
91	JOHNNIE THE STRONGMAN	RT	83.00	83.00
91	KATIE THE TIGHTROPE WALKER	RT	78.00	78.00
92	MAGGIE THE ANIMAL TRAINER	RT	83.00	83.00

C. MCCLURE | | | | A JOY FOREVER COLLECTION

97	VICTORIAN HARMONY	TL	130.00	130.00

T. MENZENBACH | | | | A MOTHER'S WORK IS NEVER DONE

95	DON'T FOREGET TO WASH BEHIND YOUR EARS	TL	60.00	60.00
96	A KISS WILL MAKE IT BETTER	TL	60.00	60.00
96	WHO MADE THIS MESS?	TL	60.00	60.00

J. GOOD-KRUGER | | | | ALL I WISH FOR YOU

94	I WISH YOU LOVE	RT	50.00	50.00
95	I WISH YOU FAITH	TL	50.00	50.00
95	I WISH YOU HAPPINESS	TL	50.00	50.00
95	I WISH YOU WISDOM	TL	50.00	50.00
96	I WISH YOU CHARITY	TL	50.00	50.00
96	I WISH YOU LUCK	TL	50.00	50.00

Y. BELLO | | | | AMERICA THE BEAUTIFUL

96	BILLY	RT	50.00	50.00
96	BOBBY	RT	50.00	50.00

J. KOVACIK | | | | AMERICAN DREAM

94	HOPE	RT	80.00	80.00
94	PATIENCE	RT	80.00	80.00

J. GOOD-KRUGER | | | | AMISH BLESSINGS

90	REBECCAH	RT	68.00	125.00
91	ADAM	RT	75.00	165.00
91	RACHEL	RT	69.00	125.00
92	ELI	RT	80.00	95.00
92	RUTH	RT	75.00	125.00
93	SARAH	RT	80.00	125.00

J. IBAROLLE | | | | AMISH INSPIRATIONS

94	ETHAN	RT	70.00	70.00
94	MARY	RT	70.00	70.00
96	ANNA	YR	74.95	75.00
96	SETH	RT	74.95	75.00

J. KOVACIK | | | | ANNE OF GREEN GABLES

95	ANNE SHIRLEY	CL	70.00	70.00
96	DIANA BARRY	TL	70.00	70.00
96	GILBERT BLYTHE	TL	70.00	70.00
96	JOSIE PYE	TL	70.00	70.00

D. EFFNER | | | | AS CUTE AS CAN BE

93	SUGAR PLUM	RT	50.00	100.00
94	ANGEL FACE	RT	50.00	75.00
94	PUPPY LOVE	RT	50.00	75.00
95	PATTY CAKE	TL	50.00	50.00

The first edition Legend of the
Poinsettia from 1992 was inspired by the
Mexican tale of the miracle of the
poinsettia. Wendy Lawton created this
14-inch porcelain doll that was
distributed in a limited edition of 750 by
the LawtonDoll Co.

Jessica, by Gorham Dolls, plays the tune
"My Favorite Things." The doll has
increased in value since its 1986 release.

A musical piece by Gorham Dolls,
Meredith plays the tune "We've Only Just
Begun."

Terry, by doll designer Bette Ball, is music to the
hearts of collectors. She plays the tune "Fly Me
to the Moon." Produced by Goebel.

YR	NAME	LIMIT	ISSUE	TREND
K. BARRY-HIPPENSTEEL			**BABY BOOK TREASURES**	
90	ELIZABETH'S HOMECOMING	RT	58.00	58.00
91	CATHERINE'S CHRISTENING	RT	58.00	58.00
91	CHRISTOPHER'S FIRST SMILE	RT	63.00	63.00
J. GOOD-KRUGER			**BABY TALK**	
94	ALL GONE	RT	50.00	85.00
94	BYE, BYE!	RT	50.00	55.00
94	NIGHT, NIGHT	RT	50.00	50.00
K. BARRY-HIPPENSTEEL			**BABY'S WORLD OF WONDER**	
96	ANDREW	TL	60.00	60.00
96	SARAH	TL	60.00	60.00
97	JASON	TL	60.00	60.00
97	KIRSTEN	*	70.00	70.00
P. BOMAR			**BALLET RECITAL**	
96	CHLOE	TL	70.00	70.00
96	HEIDI	TL	70.00	70.00
96	KYLIE	TL	70.00	70.00
T. TOMESCU			**BARELY YOURS**	
94	CUTE AS A BUTTON	RT	70.00	125.00
94	SNUG AS A BUG IN A RUG	RT	75.00	75.00
96	CLEAN AS A WHISTLE	RT	75.00	75.00
96	COOL AS A CUCUMBER	RT	75.00	75.00
96	GOOD AS GOLD	RT	75.00	75.00
96	PRETTY AS A PICTURE	RT	75.00	75.00
C. JACKSON			**BEACH BABIES**	
96	CARLY	TL	80.00	80.00
96	KYLE	TL	80.00	80.00
97	KELLIE	TL	80.00	80.00
G. RADEMANN			**BEAUTIFUL DREAMERS**	
92	KATRINA	CL	89.00	125.00
92	NICOLETTE	CL	90.00	90.00
93	BRIGITTE	CL	94.00	94.00
93	GABRIELLE	CL	94.00	94.00
93	ISABELLA	CL	94.00	94.00
B. HANSON			**BEAUTY AND GRACE**	
97	ISABELLA	TL	100.00	100.00
B. DEVAL			**BLESSED ARE THE CHILDREN**	
96	BLESSED ARE THE PEACEMAKERS	TL	70.00	70.00
96	BLESSED ARE THE PURE OF HEART	TL	70.00	70.00
S. FREEMAN			**BLOSSOMING BELLES**	
97	YELLOW ROSE	*	*	N/A
K. BARRY-HIPPENSTEEL			**BORN TO BE FAMOUS**	
89	LITTLE SHERLOCK	RT	87.00	87.00
90	LITTLE FLORENCE NIGHTINGALE	RT	87.00	87.00
91	LITTLE DAVY CROCKETT	RT	92.00	92.00
92	LITTLE CHRISTOPHER COLUMBUS	RT	95.00	95.00
A. BROWN			**BOYS AND BEARS**	
96	CODY AND THE CUDDLE BEAR	TL	63.00	63.00
97	NICKY AND NAPTIME BEAR	TL	63.00	63.00
97	SAMMY AND SHARING BEAR	TL	63.00	63.00
J. SINGER			**BOYS WILL BE BOYS**	
93	FIRE'S OUT (BOBBY)	CL	70.00	75.00
*			**CALENDAR BABIES**	
95	APRIL SHOWERS	OP	25.00	25.00
95	BACK TO SCHOOL	OP	25.00	25.00
95	CUPID	OP	25.00	25.00
95	HAPPY HAUNTING	OP	25.00	25.00
95	JOLLY SANTA	OP	25.00	25.00
95	JUNE BRIDE	OP	25.00	25.00
95	LEPRECHAUN	OP	25.00	25.00
95	MAY FLOWERS	OP	25.00	25.00
95	NEW YEAR	OP	25.00	25.00
95	SUN & FUN	OP	25.00	25.00
95	THANKSGIVING TURKEY	OP	25.00	25.00
95	UNCLE SAM	OP	25.00	25.00
M. TRETTER			**CAUGHT IN THE ACT**	
92	STEVIE (CATCH ME IF YOU CAN)	CL	50.00	155.00
93	KELLY (DON'T I LOOK PRETTY?)	CL	50.00	95.00
94	BECKY (KLEENEX BOX)	RT	60.00	60.00
94	MIKEY (LOOK IT FLOATS)	CL	55.00	65.00
94	NICKIE (COOKIE JAR)	RT	60.00	60.00
94	SANDY	RT	60.00	60.00
S. FREEMAN			**CHARMING DISCOVERIES**	
97	CYNTHIA	TL	90.00	90.00
J. SINGER			**CHILD'S GARDEN OF VERSES**	
91	LAND OF NOD, THE	CL	79.00	80.00
93	MY SHIP & I	CL	85.00	85.00
93	MY TOY SOLDIERS	CL	80.00	80.00
93	PICTURE BOOKS IN WINTER	CL	85.00	85.00
M. SIRKO			**CHILDREN OF CHRISTMAS**	
94	LITTLE ANGEL	CL	80.00	80.00
94	LITTLE DRUMMER BOY	CL	80.00	80.00

YR	NAME	LIMIT	ISSUE	TREND
95	O CHRISTMAS TREE	CL	80.00	80.00
95	SUGAR PLUM FAIRY	CL	80.00	80.00
Y. BELLO		**CHILDREN OF MOTHER GOOSE**		
87	LITTLE BO PEEP	RT	58.00	130.00
87	MARY HAD A LITTLE LAMB	RT	58.00	125.00
88	LITTLE JACK HORNER	RT	63.00	95.00
89	MISS MUFFET	RT	63.00	100.00
M. SEVERINO		**CHILDREN OF THE SUN**		
93	DESERT STAR	RT	70.00	75.00
93	LITTLE FLOWER	RT	70.00	75.00
Y. BELLO		**CHRISTMAS MEMORIES**		
94	CHRISTOPHER	RT	60.00	120.00
94	JOSHUA	RT	60.00	120.00
94	STEPHANIE	RT	60.00	120.00
C. MCCLURE		**CINDY'S PLAYHOUSE PALS**		
89	MEAGAN	RT	87.00	87.00
89	SHELLY	RT	87.00	87.00
90	RYAN	RT	89.00	89.00
91	SAMANTHA	RT	89.00	89.00
E. WILLIAMS		**CLASSIC BRIDES OF THE CENTURY**		
90	FLORA, THE 1900S BRIDE	RT	145.00	145.00
91	JENNIFER, THE 1980S BRIDE	RT	149.00	149.00
93	KATHLEEN, THE 1930S BRIDE	CL	150.00	150.00
M. TRETTER		**COUNTRY SWEETHEARTS**		
96	MILLIE	TL	63.00	63.00
K. BARRY-HIPPENSTEEL		**CUDDLE CHUMS**		
95	HEATHER	CL	60.00	60.00
95	JEFFREY	CL	60.00	60.00
A. TSALKIHN		**DAY IN THE LIFE OF EMILY ANN**		
96	BREAKTIME	TL	83.00	83.00
K. BARRY-HIPPENSTEEL		**DAYS OF THE WEEK**		
94	MONDAY	RT	50.00	50.00
95	FRIDAY	RT	50.00	50.00
95	SATURDAY	RT	50.00	50.00
95	SUNDAY	RT	50.00	50.00
95	THURSDAY	RT	50.00	50.00
95	TUESDAY	RT	50.00	50.00
95	WEDNESDAY	RT	50.00	50.00
M. TRETTER		**DECORATING THE TREE**		
96	MELISSA	TL	60.00	60.00
96	PATRICK	TL	60.00	60.00
96	RYAN	TL	60.00	60.00
96	TRISHA	TL	60.00	60.00
B. DEVAL		**DEVAL FAIRYTALES**		
96	CINDERELLA	TL	93.00	93.00
96	RAPUNZEL	TL	93.00	93.00
97	PRINCESS AND THE FROG, THE	TL	95.00	95.00
97	SLEEPING BEAUTY	TL	95.00	95.00
*		**DIANA, THE PEOPLE'S PRINCESS**		
97	DIANA, THE PRICESS OF WALES	TL	133.00	133.00
D. EFFNER		**DIANNA EFFNER'S CLASSIC COLLECTION**		
95	HILARY	RT	80.00	80.00
96	EMILY	TL	80.00	80.00
96	WILLOW	TL	80.00	80.00
D. EFFNER		**DIANNA EFFNER'S FAVORITE LITTLE GIRLS**		
97	SCHOOLGIRL JENNY	*	80.00	80.00
D. EFFNER		**DIANNA EFFNER'S MOTHER GOOSE**		
90	MARY QUITE CONTRARY	CL	78.00	200.00
91	LITTLE GIRL W/THE CURL, GOOD	CL	79.00	200.00
91	LITTLE GIRL W/THE CURL, HORRID	CL	79.00	250.00
92	LITTLE BOY BLUE	RT	85.00	85.00
93	CURLY LOCKS	RT	90.00	120.00
93	SNIPS & SNAILS	CL	85.00	135.00
93	SUGAR & SPICE	CL	90.00	115.00
P. COFFER		**DOWN THE GARDEN PATH**		
91	ANGELICA	CL	85.00	85.00
91	ROSEMARY	CL	79.00	85.00
93	AMANDA BY THE SHORE	CL	90.00	140.00
L. DI LEO		**ELVIS: LIFETIME OF A LEGEND**		
92	'68 COMEBACK	CL	100.00	100.00
94	KING OF LAS VEGAS	RT	100.00	100.00
A. TSALKIHN		**EMILY ANNE'S BUSY DAY**		
97	CALLING GRANDMA	TL	83.00	83.00
97	ENJOYING A SNACK	TL	83.00	83.00
G. RADEMANN		**EUROPEAN FAIRYTALES**		
95	LITTLE RED RIDING HOOD	RT	80.00	100.00
95	SNOW WHITE	RT	80.00	80.00
M. TRETTER		**FAMILY TIES**		
94	WELCOME HOME BABY BROTHER	RT	80.00	80.00
95	HAPPILY EVER AFTER	RT	90.00	90.00
95	KISS AND MAKE IT BETTER	RT	90.00	90.00
L. DI LEO		**FATHER'S TOUCH**		
93	2 A.M. FEEDING	CL	100.00	105.00

YR	NAME	LIMIT	ISSUE	TREND
T. TOMESCU		**FIRST DAY AT WALT DISNEY WORLD**		
97	DISNEY WORLD BOY	*	100.00	100.00
97	DISNEY WORLD GIRL	*	100.00	100.00
T. TOMESCU		**FLURRY OF ACTIVITY**		
96	MAKING SNOWFLAKES	TL	73.00	73.00
97	MAKING ICICLES	TL	73.00	73.00
97	MAKING SUNSHINE	*	73.00	73.00
C. MCCLURE		**FOREVER STARTS TODAY**		
97	ANGELICA	*	200.00	200.00
T. MENZENBACH		**FROM THE HEART**		
92	CAROLIN	CL	7999	110.00
92	ERIK	CL	80.00	130.00
P. TUMMINIO		**FROM THIS DAY FORWARD**		
94	ELIZABETH	RT	90.00	90.00
95	BETH	RT	90.00	90.00
95	BETTY	RT	90.00	90.00
95	LISA	RT	90.00	90.00
D. RICHARDSON		**GARDEN OF INNOCENCE**		
97	KINDNESS	TL	93.00	93.00
B. HANSON		**GARDEN OF INSPIRATIONS**		
94	DAISY CHAIN	RT	70.00	70.00
94	GATHERING VIOLETS	RT	70.00	70.00
96	GARDEN PRAYER	RT	75.00	75.00
96	HEART'S BOUQUET	RT	75.00	75.00
M. ODOM		**GENE**		
95	PREMIERE (BLONDE)	RT	70.00	120.00
96	MONACO (BRUNETTE)	RT	70.00	70.00
96	RED VENUS (RED HEAD)	RT	70.00	70.00
M. ODOM		**GENE-SHARE THE DREAM**		
97	BIRD OF PARADISE	OP	80.00	80.00
97	ICED COFFEE	OP	80.00	80.00
97	WHITE HYACINTH	OP	80.00	80.00
J. GOOD-KRUGER		**GENTLE JOYS**		
97	FILLING EACH DAY WITH HUGS AND KISSES	TL	50.00	50.00
M. GIRARD-KASSIS		**GIFTS FOR MOMMY**		
97	MERRY CHRISTMAS	TL	63.00	63.00
S. FREEMAN		**GINGHAM & BOWS**		
95	GWENDOLYN	TL	70.00	70.00
96	ASHLEIGH	TL	70.00	70.00
96	BRIDGET	TL	70.00	70.00
96	MALLORY	TL	70.00	70.00
W. LAWTON		**GIRLS OF CLASSIC LITERATURE**		
95	POLLYANNA	TL	80.00	80.00
96	LAURA INGALLS	TL	80.00	80.00
96	REBECCA OF SUNNYBROOK FARM	TL	80.00	80.00
B. CONNER		**GOD HEARS THE CHILDREN**		
95	NOW I LAY ME DOWN	TL	80.00	80.00
96	ALL CREATURES GREAT & SMALL	TL	80.00	80.00
96	GOD IS GREAT, GOD IS GOOD	TL	80.00	80.00
96	WE GIVE THANKS FOR THINGS WE HAVE	TL	80.00	80.00
C. HANFORD		**GONE WITH THE WIND**		
96	SCARLETT	*	90.00	90.00
B. MADEJA		**GROWING UP LIKE WILDFLOWERS**		
96	ANNIE	TL	50.00	50.00
96	BONNIE	TL	50.00	50.00
K. BARRY-HIPPENSTEEL		**GROWING YOUNG MINDS**		
91	ALEX	CL	79.00	89.00
S. GUSTAFSON		**GUSTAFSON'S FAIRY TALES**		
93	GOLDILOCKS AND THE THREE BEARS	CL	135.00	135.00
J. GOOD-KRUGER		**HAPPINESS IS HOMEMADE**		
97	HUGS MADE BY HAND	TL	73.00	73.00
K. BARRY-HIPPENSTEEL		**HAPPINESS IS...**		
91	PATRICIA (MY FIRST TOOTH)	CL	69.00	110.00
92	CRYSTAL (FEEDING MYSELF)	CL	70.00	105.00
93	BRITTANY (BLOWING KISSES)	CL	70.00	105.00
93	JOY (MY FIRST CHRISTMAS)	CL	70.00	100.00
94	CANDY CANE (HOLLY)	RT	70.00	70.00
94	PATRICK (MY FIRST PLAYMATE)	RT	70.00	70.00
K. BARRY-HIPPENSTEEL		**HAPPY THOUGHTS**		
94	BUBBLE UP WITH JOY	*	60.00	65.00
94	LAUGHTER IS THE BEST MEDICINE	RT	60.00	60.00
L. DUNSMORE		**HATS OFF TO THE SEASONS**		
97	SPRINGTIME ROBIN	*	83.00	83.00
C. MCCLURE		**HEAVENLY INSPIRATIONS**		
92	EVERY CLOUD HAS A SILVER LINING	CL	60.00	85.00
93	WISH UPON A STAR	CL	60.00	80.00
94	LUCK AT THE END OF RAINBOW	RT	65.00	65.00
94	PENNIES FROM HEAVEN	RT	70.00	75.00
94	SUNSHINE ANGEL	RT	70.00	70.00
94	SWEET DREAMS	RT	65.00	65.00
J. IBAROLTE		**HEIRLOOM BABY COLLECTION**		
97	BLONDE BOY	*	100.00	100.00
97	BLONDE GIRL	*	100.00	100.00

YR	NAME	LIMIT	ISSUE	TREND
J. LUNDY				
	HERITAGE OF AMERICAN QUILTING			
94	ELEANOR	RT	80.00	80.00
96	ABIGAIL	RT	80.00	80.00
96	LOUISA	RT	85.00	85.00
96	RUTH ANNE	RT	85.00	85.00
D. EFFNER				
	HEROINES FROM THE FAIRY TALE FOREST			
88	LITTLE RED RIDING HOOD	RT	68.00	240.00
89	GOLDILOCKS	RT	68.00	90.00
90	SNOW WHITE	RT	73.00	175.00
91	RAPUNZEL	RT	79.00	165.00
93	CINDERELLA (BALLGOWN)	RT	80.00	175.00
93	CINDERELLA (RAGS)	CL	80.00	175.00
H. HUNT				
	HOLLY HUNT'S BONNET BABIES			
91	GRANDMA'S LITTLE GIRL (MISSY)	CL	69.00	70.00
92	SUSIE (SOMEBODY LOVES ME)	CL	69.00	100.00
K. BARRY-HIPPENSTEEL				
	HOW LITTLE WAS I?			
96	CLAIRE	YR	60.00	60.00
S. BRYER				
	HOW LITTLE WAS I?			
95	BRITTANY	RT	60.00	60.00
K. BARRY-HIPPENSTEEL				
	I WANT MOMMY			
93	TIMMY (MOMMY I'M SLEEPY)	CL	60.00	155.00
93	TOMMY (MOMMY I'M SORRY)	CL	60.00	125.00
94	TAMMY (UP MOMMY)	RT	65.00	95.00
M. TRETTER				
	I'D RATHER BE FISHIN'			
97	FISHIN' BUDDIES	TL	73.00	73.00
97	HOOKED ON FISHIN'	TL	73.00	73.00
98	FISH STORY	TL	73.00	73.00
K. BARRY-HIPPENSTEEL				
	I'M JUST LITTLE			
96	I'M A LITTLE ANGEL	RT	50.00	50.00
96	I'M A LITTLE CUTIE	TL	50.00	50.00
96	I'M A LITTLE DEVIL	RT	50.00	50.00
K. BARRY-HIPPENSTEEL				
	INTERNATIONAL FESTIVAL OF TOYS AND TOTS			
89	CHEN, A LITTLE BOY FROM CHINA	CL	78.00	105.00
89	NATASHA	RT	78.00	78.00
90	MOLLY	RT	83.00	83.00
91	HANS	RT	88.00	88.00
92	MIKI, ESKIMO	RT	88.00	88.00
F. WICK				
	INTERNATIONAL SPIRIT OF CHRISTMAS			
89	AMERICAN SANTA	CL	125.00	125.00
C. MCCLURE				
	JOY FOREVER			
96	VICTORIAN SERENITY	TL	130.00	130.00
97	VICTORIAN BLISS	TL	130.00	130.00
97	VICTORIAN PEACE	TL	130.00	130.00
K. BARRY-HIPPENSTEEL				
	JOYS OF SUMMER			
93	LITTLE SQUIRT	CL	50.00	65.00
93	TICKLES	CL	50.00	170.00
94	HAVIN' A BALL	RT	55.00	65.00
94	LIL' SCOOP	RT	55.00	95.00
94	YUMMY	RT	55.00	65.00
T. TOMESCU				
	JUST BEFORE BEDTIME			
97	TUCK ME IN, MOMMY	*	63.00	63.00
A. BROWN				
	JUST CAUGHT NAPPING			
96	ASLEEP IN THE SADDLE	TL	70.00	70.00
96	OATMEAL DREAMS	TL	70.00	70.00
97	DOG TIRED	TL	70.00	70.00
97	PRIVATE, KEEP OUT	TL	70.00	70.00
B. BAMBINA				
	JUST LIKE ME			
96	AMBER	YR	60.00	60.00
96	CARMEN	YR	60.00	60.00
96	TIFFANY	YR	60.00	60.00
Y. BELLO				
	KEEPSAKE VINYL COLLECTION			
96	CHRISTY	*	40.00	40.00
P. RYAN BROOKS				
	KING AND I			
91	SHALL WE DANCE	RT	175.00	400.00
G. RADEMANN				
	LANGUAGE OF FLOWERS COLLECTION			
97	A ROSE IS LOVE	*	*	N/A
97	CALLA LILIES FOR INNOCENCE	*	73.00	73.00
W. HANSON				
	LASTING TRADITIONS			
93	SOMETHING OLD	CL	70.00	75.00
94	FINISHING TOUCH	RT	70.00	70.00
94	HER TRADITIONAL GARTER	RT	85.00	85.00
94	MOTHER'S PEARLS	RT	85.00	85.00
W. LAWTON				
	LAWTON'S NURSERY RHYMES			
94	LITTLE BO PEEP	RT	80.00	125.00
94	LITTLE MISS MUFFET	RT	80.00	80.00
94	MARY HAD A LITTLE LAMB	RT	85.00	85.00
94	MARY, MARY QUITE CONTRARY	RT	85.00	85.00
E. SHELTON				
	LEGENDS OF BASEBALL			
96	TY COBB	RT	80.00	80.00
T. TOMESCU				
	LEGENDS OF BASEBALL			
94	BABE RUTH	RT	80.00	80.00
94	LOU GEHRIG	RT	80.00	80.00

YR	NAME	LIMIT	ISSUE	TREND
	K. BARRY-HIPPENSTEEL		LET'S PLAY MOTHER GOOSE	
94	COW JUMPED OVER THE MOON	CL	70.00	70.00
94	HICKORY, DICKORY, DOCK	CL	70.00	95.00
	R. MATTINGLY		LIFE'S LITTLE BLESSINGS	
97	CHARITY IS A BLESSING	TL	83.00	83.00
	G. RADEMANN		LITTLE BITS	
93	LOVE	CL	40.00	45.00
93	SUNSHINE	CL	40.00	45.00
94	INNOCENCE	CL	40.00	40.00
94	TENDERNESS	CL	40.00	40.00
	K. BARRY-HIPPENSTEEL		LITTLE GYMNAST	
96	LITTLE GYMNAST	TL	60.00	60.00
	M. SEVERINO		LITTLE HANDFULS	
93	ABBY	RT	40.00	45.00
93	JOSIE	RT	40.00	45.00
93	RICKY	RT	40.00	45.00
	J. IBAROLLE		LITTLE HOUSE ON THE PRAIRIE	
92	LAURA INGALLS	CL	80.00	95.00
93	ALMANZO	CL	85.00	100.00
93	MARY INGALLS	CL	80.00	350.00
93	NELLIE OLSON	CL	85.00	110.00
94	CARRIE	CL	85.00	80.00
94	MA INGALLS	CL	85.00	90.00
94	PA INGALLS	CL	85.00	90.00
96	BABY GRACE	CL	70.00	70.00
	J. WOLF		LITTLE LACY SLEEPYHEADS	
96	JACQUELINE	TL	100.00	100.00
	C. MCCLURE		LITTLE PERFORMERS	
97	JOELLE	TL	95.00	95.00
97	LAUREN	TL	95.00	95.00
	W. LAWTON		LITTLE WOMEN	
94	AMY	CL	60.00	65.00
94	BETH	CL	60.00	65.00
94	JO	CL	60.00	65.00
94	MEG	CL	60.00	65.00
96	MARMEE	CL	60.00	65.00
	W. LAWTON		LITTLE WOMEN AT CHRISTMAS	
97	MEG, JO, BETH, AMY, MARMEE (SET OF 5)	*	200.00	200.00
	M. ATTWELL		LITTLE WORDS OF WISDOM	
94	FRIEND IN NEED IS A FRIEND INDEED, A	CL	60.00	65.00
95	TOMORROW IS ANOTHER DAY	CL	60.00	65.00
96	BEAUTY IS IN THE EYE OF THE BEHOLDER	CL	60.00	60.00
	L. DI LEO		LOOK AT ME	
93	ROSE MARIE	CL	50.00	55.00
94	ANN MARIE	CL	50.00	50.00
94	LISA MARIE	CL	55.00	55.00
	T. MENZENBACH		LOTS OF LOVE	
93	HANNAH NEEDS A HUG	CL	50.00	95.00
93	KAITLYN	CL	50.00	95.00
94	NICOLE	CL	55.00	55.00
95	FELICIA	CL	55.00	55.00
	D. ORTEGA		LOVE, MARRIAGE, BABY CARRIAGE TEDDY BEAR	
97	CARRIE	*	50.00	50.00
	C. MCCLURE		LUCKY CHARMERS	
95	LUCKY STAR	TL	70.00	70.00
96	BIT O' LUCK	TL	70.00	70.00
	B. DEVAL		MADONNA & CHILD	
96	MADONNA & CHILD	TL	100.00	100.00
	K. BARRY-HIPPENSTEEL		MAGIC MOMENTS	
96	BIRTHDAY BOY	TL	70.00	70.00
96	HAPPY ANNIVERSARY	*	50.00	50.00
96	HAPPY BIRTHDAY	*	40.00	40.00
	Y. BELLO		MAGICAL MOMENTS OF SUMMER	
95	WHITNEY	TL	60.00	60.00
96	DANA	*	60.00	60.00
96	ZOE	TL	60.00	60.00
	M. TRETTER		MAINSTREET SATURDAY MORNING	
94	KENNY	CL	70.00	70.00
96	BETTY	CL	70.00	70.00
96	DONNY	CL	70.00	70.00
	J. LICERTZ		MCMEMORIES 40TH ANNIVERSARY ICONS COLLECTION	
96	SPEEDEE	*	60.00	60.00
	D. EFFNER		MCMEMORIES MCDONALDS & ME COLLECTION	
96	YOU DESERVE A BREAK TODAY	*	60.00	60.00
	M. GIRARD-KASSIS		MEMORIES OF A VICTORIAN CHILDHOOD	
97	LYDIA	*	83.00	83.00
97	PAIGE	*	83.00	83.00
98	OLIVIA	*	83.00	83.00
	T. TOMESCU		MESSAGES OF HOPE	
86	BEHOLD, I STAND AT THE DOOR	CL	130.00	130.00
86	GOOD SHEPHERD, THE	CL	130.00	130.00
94	LET THE LITTLE CHILDREN COME TO ME	CL	130.00	130.00
96	OUR FATHER	TL	130.00	130.00

YR	NAME	LIMIT	ISSUE	TREND
Y. BELLO			**MIRACLE OF LIFE**	
96	BEAUTIFUL NEWBORN	TL	50.00	50.00
96	HER VERY FIRST SMILE	TL	50.00	50.00
96	WATCH HER CRAWL	TL	50.00	50.00
W. LAWTON			**MIRACLE OF LIFE**	
96	SHE'S SITTING PRETTY	TL	50.00	50.00
T. TOMESCU			**MIRACLES OF JESUS**	
96	MULTIPLYING THE LOAVES	TL	100.00	100.00
96	WATER INTO WINE	TL	100.00	100.00
97	WALKING ON WATER	TL	100.00	100.00
Y. BELLO			**MOMENTS TO REMEMBER**	
91	JUSTIN	CL	75.00	80.00
92	JILL	CL	80.00	115.00
93	BRANDON (RING BEARER)	CL	80.00	85.00
93	SUZANNE (FLOWER GIRL)	CL	80.00	85.00
A. CRANSHAW			**MOMMY CAN YOU FIX IT?**	
97	EDGAR	*	50.00	50.00
M. HOLSTAD			**MOMMY, CAN I KEEP IT?**	
96	BELINDA'S NEW KITTY	*	50.00	50.00
B. BAMBINA			**MORNING GLORIES**	
96	DEW DROP	TL	50.00	50.00
96	ROSEBUD	TL	50.00	50.00
J. GOODYEAR			**MY CLOSEST FRIENDS**	
92	BOO BEAR (EVIE)	CL	79.00	140.00
92	ME/BLANKIE (STEFFIE)	CL	79.00	95.00
92	MY BEARY BEST FRIEND	CL	80.00	80.00
92	MY SECRET PAL (ROBBIE)	CL	85.00	90.00
P. RYAN BROOKS			**MY FAIR LADY**	
91	ELIZA AT ASCOT	CL	125.00	400.00
J. SINGER			**MY HEART BELONGS TO DADDY**	
92	PEANUT	CL	50.00	95.00
92	PUMPKIN	CL	50.00	60.00
94	PRINCESS	CL	60.00	60.00
K. BARRY-HIPPENSTEEL			**MY LITTLE BALLERINA**	
94	MY LITTLE BALLERINA	CL	60.00	60.00
J. KOVACIK			**MY SECRET GARDEN**	
86	COLIN	CL	70.00	70.00
86	DICKON	CL	70.00	75.00
86	MARTHA	CL	70.00	75.00
94	MARY LENNOX	CL	70.00	70.00
S. HOUSLEY			**NATURALLY PLAYFUL COLLECTION**	
97	PEEK-A-BOO BUNNY	TL	83.00	83.00
C. MCCLURE			**NOSTALGIC TOYS**	
96	AMELIA	TL	80.00	80.00
96	CHARLOTTE	TL	80.00	80.00
J. WOLF			**NURSERY NEWBORNS**	
94	IT'S A BOY	CL	80.00	90.00
94	IT'S A GIRL	CL	80.00	90.00
J. GOOD-KRUGER		**OH HOLY NIGHT NATIVITY COLLECTION**		
94	HOLY FAMILY, THE	CL	130.00	130.00
95	ANGEL	CL	60.00	60.00
95	BLUE KING, THE	CL	60.00	60.00
95	KNEELING KING, THE	CL	60.00	60.00
95	SHEPHERD WITH LAMB	CL	60.00	60.00
95	SHEPHERD WITH PIPES	CL	60.00	60.00
95	STANDING KING, THE- PURPLE	CL	60.00	60.00
Y. BELLO		**ONLY AT GRANDMA & GRANDPA'S COLLECTION**		
96	I'LL FINISH THE STORY	TL	90.00	90.00
96	TEDDY MAKES THREE	*	100.00	100.00
P. BOMAR			**OUR OWN BALLET RECITAL**	
96	CHLOE	TL	70.00	70.00
J. IBAROLLE			**PASSPORTS TO FRIENDSHIP**	
95	SERENA	TL	80.00	80.00
96	ASHA	TL	80.00	80.00
96	KALO	TL	80.00	80.00
96	LILIANA	TL	80.00	80.00
J. GOOD-KRUGER			**PATCHWORK OF LOVE**	
96	FAMILY PRIDE	TL	60.00	60.00
96	FONDEST MEMORIES	TL	60.00	60.00
96	HARD WORK PAYS OFF	TL	60.00	60.00
96	LOVE ONE ANOTHER	TL	60.00	60.00
96	SIMPLICITY IS BEST	TL	60.00	60.00
96	WARMTH OF HEART	TL	60.00	60.00
J. GOODYEAR			**PEEK-A-BOO**	
93	WHERE'S JAMIE?	CL	70.00	75.00
B. BAMBINA			**PERFECT PAIRS**	
95	AMBER	CL	60.00	60.00
95	CARMEN	CL	60.00	60.00
95	TIFFANY	CL	60.00	60.00
96	SUSIE	TL	60.00	60.00
Y. BELLO			**PETTING ZOO**	
96	ANDY	CL	60.00	60.00
96	CORY W/BUNNY	CL	60.00	60.00

YR NAME	LIMIT	ISSUE	TREND
96 KENDRA	CL	60.00	60.00
96 MADDIE W/CHICK	CL	60.00	60.00
S. KREY		**POLLY'S TEA PARTY**	
90 POLLY	CL	78.00	125.00
91 LIZZIE	CL	79.00	79.00
92 ANNIE	CL	83.00	83.00
A. BROWN		**POTPOURRI BABIES**	
96 BUBBLE TROUBLE	TL	50.00	80.00
S. KUCK	**PRECIOUS MEMORIES OF MOTHERHOOD**		
89 LOVING STEPS	CL	125.00	140.00
90 LULLABY	CL	125.00	125.00
91 EXPECTANT MOMENTS	CL	149.00	200.00
92 BEDTIME	CL	150.00	150.00
S. HOUSELY		**PRECIOUS PAPOOSES**	
95 SLEEPING BEAR	CL	80.00	80.00
96 BRIGHT FEATHER	TL	80.00	80.00
96 CLOUD CHASER	TL	80.00	80.00
96 SWIFT FOX	TL	80.00	80.00
J. GOODYEAR		**PRETTY IN PASTELS**	
94 PRECIOUS IN PINK	CL	80.00	55.00
R. MILLER		**QUILTED ANGEL BABIES**	
97 ANGEL OF LOVE	*	73.00	73.00
97 ANGEL OF LUCK	*	73.00	73.00
Y. BELLO		**RAINBOW OF LOVE**	
95 BABY BLUE SKY W/BASKET	CL	60.00	60.00
95 BABY GREEN EARTH	CL	60.00	60.00
95 BABY YELLOW SUNSHINE	CL	60.00	65.00
96 BABY ORANGE SUNSET	CL	60.00	60.00
96 BABY PINK FLOWER	CL	60.00	60.00
96 BABY PURPLE MOUNTAIN	CL	60.00	60.00
ROCKWELL- INSPIRED		**ROCKWELL CHRISTMAS**	
93 MERRY CHRISTMAS GRANDMA	CL	60.00	63.00
J. IBAROLLE		**SEASONS OF JOY**	
97 NICHOLAS, THE WINTER BABY	TL	83.00	83.00
98 KIMBERLY	*	75.00	75.00
K. BARRY-HIPPENSTEEL		**SENSE OF DISCOVERY**	
93 SWEETIE	CL	60.00	65.00
G. RADEMANN		**SENSE OF SECURITY**	
96 AMY	TL	63.00	63.00
S. BILOTTO		**SHE WALKS IN BEAUTY**	
96 WINTER ROMANCE	TL	93.00	93.00
97 SUMMER DREAM	TL	93.00	93.00
C. MCCLURE		**SIBLINGS THROUGH TIME**	
96 ALEXANDRA	CL	70.00	70.00
96 GRACIE	CL	60.00	60.00
J. GOOD-KRUGER		**SIMPLE GIFTS**	
96 ROLY POLY HARVEST	TL	50.00	50.00
97 CUDDLY COMPANIONS	TL	50.00	50.00
97 NAPTIME AT NOON	TL	50.00	50.00
97 PAPA'S LITTLE HELPER	TL	50.00	50.00
J. LUNDY	**SIMPLE PLEASURES, SPECIAL DAYS**		
96 ADELINE	TL	80.00	80.00
96 ELIZA	TL	80.00	80.00
96 GRETCHEN	TL	80.00	80.00
96 MOLLY	TL	80.00	80.00
T. TOMESCU		**SNOW BABIES**	
95 BENEATH THE MISTLETOE	CL	70.00	70.00
96 CATCH OF THE DAY	TL	75.00	75.00
96 FOLLOW THE LEADER	CL	75.00	75.00
96 LEARNING TO FLY	TL	75.00	75.00
96 SLIP SLIDIN'	TL	75.00	75.00
96 SNOW BABY EXPRESS	CL	75.00	75.00
K. BARRY-HIPPENSTEEL		**SOMEONE TO WATCH OVER ME**	
94 ANGEL LULLABY	CL	25.00	30.00
94 ANGEL NIGHT-NIGHT	CL	25.00	30.00
95 BABY SWEET DREAMS W/BASKET	CL	70.00	70.00
96 ANGEL SLEEPYHEAD	CL	25.00	25.00
96 ANGEL STARDUST	CL	25.00	25.00
96 ANGEL TUCK-ME-IN	CL	25.00	25.00
M. TRETTER		**SOOO BIG**	
93 JIMMY	CL	60.00	65.00
94 KIMMY	CL	60.00	60.00
Y. BELLO		**SPECIAL EDITION TOUR 1993**	
93 MIGUEL	CL	70.00	70.00
93 ROSA	CL	70.00	70.00
Y. BELLO		**SPICE OF LIFE**	
97 CINDY	TL	63.00	63.00
97 MEGAN	TL	63.00	63.00
T. TOMESCU		**TALES FROM THE NURSERY**	
97 BABY BO PEEP	*	83.00	83.00
L. TIERNEY		**TENDER MOMENTS**	
96 TENDER CARE	CL	50.00	50.00

YR	NAME	LIMIT	ISSUE	TREND
96	TENDER HEART	CL	50.00	50.00
96	TENDER LOVE	CL	50.00	50.00
J. IBAROLLE		**THEY'RE ALL PRECIOUS IN HIS SIGHT**		
97	NAOMI	TL	73.00	73.00
S. KREY		**TOGETHER FOREVER**		
94	COURTNEY	CL	60.00	65.00
94	KIM	CL	60.00	65.00
94	KIRSTEN	CL	60.00	65.00
M. GIRARD-KASSIS		**TOO CUTE TO RESIST**		
97	ALLY	TL	63.00	63.00
K. BARRY-HIPPENSTEEL		**TOO MUCH TO HANDLE**		
93	JULIE (FLOWERS FOR MOMMY)	CL	60.00	65.00
93	KEVIN (CLEAN HANDS)	CL	60.00	145.00
M. TRETTER		**TREASURED TOGETHERNESS**		
94	TENDER TOUCH	CL	100.00	100.00
94	TOUCH OF LOVE	CL	100.00	100.00
K. BARRY-HIPPENSTEEL		**TUMBLING TOTS**		
93	ROLY POLY POLLY	CL	70.00	75.00
94	HANDSTAND HARRY	CL	70.00	70.00
T. TOMESCU		**TWINKLE TOES**		
97	LITTLE CARNATION	TL	73.00	73.00
P. BOMAR		**UNDER HER WINGS**		
95	GUARDIAN ANGEL	TL	80.00	80.00
K. BARRY-HIPPENSTEEL		**VICTORIAN DREAMERS**		
96	ROCK-A-BYE/GOOD NIGHT	CL	50.00	50.00
96	VICTORIAN STORYTIME	CL	50.00	50.00
C. LAYTON		**VICTORIAN LACE**		
93	ALICIA	CL	80.00	150.00
94	COLLEEN	CL	80.00	80.00
94	OLIVIA	CL	80.00	80.00
C. MCCLURE		**VICTORIAN NURSERY HEIRLOOM**		
94	VICTORIAN LULLABY	CL	80.00	80.00
96	VICTORIAN BUNNY BUGGY	CL	140.00	140.00
96	VICTORIAN HIGHCHAIR	CL	129.95	130.00
96	VICTORIAN PLAYTIME	CL	140.00	140.00
B. DEVAL		**VISIONS OF OUR LADY**		
96	OUR LADY OF GRACE	TL	100.00	100.00
96	OUR LADY OF LOURDES	TL	100.00	100.00
Y. BELLO		**WATCHING BABY GROW**		
97	BABY BOY'S FIRST TOOTH	*	50.00	50.00
97	BABY GIRL'S FIRST TOOTH	*	50.00	50.00
D. EFFNER		**WHAT LITTLE GIRLS ARE MADE OF**		
94	PEACHES AND CREAM	CL	70.00	90.00
95	LAVENDER AND LACE	CL	70.00	70.00
95	SUNSHINE AND LOLLIPOPS	CL	70.00	70.00
T. TOMESCU		**WHERE DO BABIES COME FROM?**		
96	FRESH FROM THE PATCH	TL	80.00	80.00
96	JUST HATCHED	TL	80.00	80.00
96	SPECIAL DELIVERY	TL	80.00	80.00
97	HANDLE WITH CARE	TL	80.00	80.00
M. TRETTER		**WINTER MAGIC**		
97	BRADLEY WITH SNOWMAN	*	65.00	65.00
97	LINDSEY	*	65.00	65.00
97	PAMELA	*	65.00	65.00
97	TYLER	*	65.00	65.00
K. BARRY-HIPPENSTEEL		**WINTER WONDERLAND**		
94	ANNIE	CL	60.00	60.00
94	BOBBY	CL	60.00	60.00
S. SHERWOOD		**WINTERFEST**		
91	BRIAN	CL	89.00	125.00
92	MICHELLE	CL	90.00	160.00
93	BRADLEY	CL	90.00	90.00
M. TRETTER		**WISHFUL THINKING**		
93	DANNY (PET SHOP)	CL	80.00	85.00
M. TRETTER		**WIZARD OF OZ MINIATURES**		
97	LION	*	43.00	43.00
98	DOROTHY AND TOTO	*	43.00	43.00
98	SCARECROW	*	43.00	43.00
98	TIN MAN	*	43.00	43.00
M. TRETTER		**WONDERFUL WIZARD OF OZ**		
94	COWARDLY LION	CL	80.00	80.00
94	DOROTHY & TOTO	CL	80.00	90.00
94	SCARECROW	CL	80.00	80.00
94	TIN MAN	CL	80.00	80.00
G. RADEMANN		**WREATHED IN BEAUTY**		
96	WINTER ELEGANCE	TL	90.00	90.00
97	AUTUMN HARMONY	*	100.00	100.00
97	SUMMER SWEETNESS	*	100.00	100.00
AKERS/GIRARDI		**YEAR BOOK MEMORIES**		
91	PEGGY SUE	CL	87.00	95.00
93	GOING STEADY (PATTY JO)	CL	90.00	90.00
93	PROM QUEEN (BETTY JEAN)	CL	92.00	92.00

YR	NAME	LIMIT	ISSUE	TREND
Y. BELLO		**YOLANDA'S HEAVEN SCENT BABIES**		
93	CARNATION	CL	55.00	60.00
93	CHERRY BLOSSOM	CL	55.00	60.00
93	DAISY ANNE	CL	50.00	55.00
93	LILY	CL	55.00	60.00
93	MEAGAN ROSE	CL	50.00	100.00
93	MORNING GLORY	CL	50.00	55.00
Y. BELLO		**YOLANDA'S LULLABY BABIES**		
91	CHRISTY (ROCK-A-BYE)	CL	69.00	75.00
92	JOEY (TWINKLE, TWINKLE)	CL	69.00	75.00
93	AMY (BRAHMS LULLABY)	CL	75.00	80.00
93	EDDIE (TEDDY BEAR LULLABY)	CL	75.00	75.00
93	JACOB (SILENT NIGHT)	CL	75.00	80.00
Y. BELLO		**YOLANDA'S PICTURE PERFECT BABIES**		
85	JASON	CL	48.00	600.00
86	HEATHER	CL	48.00	250.00
87	JENNIFER	CL	58.00	250.00
87	MATTHEW	CL	58.00	195.00
87	SARAH	CL	58.00	110.00
88	AMANDA	CL	63.00	125.00
89	JESSICA	CL	63.00	80.00
90	LISA	CL	63.00	105.00
90	MICHAEL	CL	63.00	155.00
91	DANIELLE	CL	69.00	135.00
91	EMILY	CL	63.00	125.00
Y. BELLO		**YOLANDA'S PLAYTIME BABIES**		
93	LINDSEY	CL	60.00	63.00
93	SHAWNA	CL	60.00	63.00
93	TODD	CL	60.00	63.00
Y. BELLO		**YOLANDA'S PRECIOUS PLAYMATES**		
92	DAVID	CL	70.00	185.00
93	PAUL	CL	70.00	135.00
94	JOHNNY	CL	70.00	70.00
J.W. SMITH			**YOUNG LOVE**	
93	FIRST KISS	CL	120.00	125.00
M. STAUBER		**YOUR HEART'S DESIRE**		
91	JULIA	CL	99.00	130.00

ATTIC BABIES
M. MASCHINO
M. MASCHINO

YR	NAME	LIMIT	ISSUE	TREND
87	BESSIE JO	RT	33.00	38.00
87	BETH SUE	RT	30.00	35.00
87	COUNTRY CLYDE	RT	30.00	35.00
87	DIRTY HARRY	RT	30.00	35.00
87	HAROLD	RT	30.00	35.00
87	JACOB	RT	30.00	35.00
87	JENNY LOU	RT	37.00	40.00
87	MAGGIE MAE	RT	30.00	33.00
87	MISS PATTY PAT	RT	30.00	100.00
87	MUSLIN BUNNY	RT	10.00	15.00
87	MUSLIN TEDDY	RT	10.00	15.00
87	RACHEL	RT	30.00	35.00
87	RAGGEDY KITTY	RT	30.00	35.00
87	RAGGEDY SANTY	RT	75.00	205.00
87	ROSE ANN	RT	40.00	45.00
87	SALLY FRANCIS	RT	40.00	65.00
87	SARA	RT	40.00	90.00
87	TODDY SUE	RT	30.00	90.00
88	BUNNIFER	RT	40.00	45.00
88	FESTER CHESTER	RT	40.00	45.00
88	HANNAH LOU	RT	40.00	45.00
88	LAZY DAISY	RT	40.00	45.00
88	LAZY LIZA JANE	RT	48.00	53.00
88	LITTLE DOVE	RT	40.00	45.00
88	MOLLY BEA	RT	40.00	85.00
88	MOOSEY MATILDA	RT	40.00	85.00
88	NAUGHTY NELLIE	RT	33.00	90.00
88	RAGGEDY SAM	RT	60.00	120.00
88	RAGGEDY SANTY	RT	90.00	95.00
88	ROTTEN WILBER	RT	37.00	145.00
88	RUFUS	RT	36.00	85.00
88	SILLY WILLIE	RT	40.00	80.00
88	SPRING SANTA	RT	50.00	55.00
88	SWEET WILLIAM	RT	40.00	155.00
88	WACKY JACKIE	RT	40.00	45.00
89	ANNIE FANNIE	RT	45.00	50.00
89	COTTON PICKIN' NINNY	RT	50.00	95.00
89	HEAVENLY HEATHER	RT	60.00	65.00
89	HEFFY CHEFFY	RT	77.00	80.00
89	JOLLY JIM	RT	32.00	35.00
89	MS. WADDLES	RT	50.00	55.00
89	OLD TYME SANTY	RT	80.00	85.00
89	PRISSY MISSY	RT	33.00	35.00
89	RAMMY SAMMY	RT	45.00	50.00

YR	NAME	LIMIT	ISSUE	TREND
89	SKITTY KITTY	RT	45.00	145.00
89	WOOD DOLL-MEDIUM	RT	33.00	38.00
89	WOOD DOLL-SMALL	RT	25.00	30.00
90	DUCKIE DINKLE	RT	97.00	100.00
90	FRANNIE FARKLE	RT	130.00	135.00
90	FRIZZY LIZZY	RT	97.00	100.00
90	HAPPY HUCK	RT	50.00	55.00
90	IVAN IVIE	RT	130.00	135.00
90	LAMPSIE DIVIE IVIE	RT	130.00	135.00
90	PHYLBERT FARKLE	RT	130.00	230.00
90	SALIE OLLIE OTIS	RT	130.00	135.00
90	YANKEE DOODLE DEBBIE	RT	100.00	155.00
90	ZITTY ZELDA	RT	90.00	180.00
91	MAIZIE MAE	RT	30.00	35.00
91	MANDI MAE	RT	30.00	35.00
91	MEMSIE MAE	RT	30.00	35.00
91	MR. RAGGEDY CLAUS	RT	70.00	125.00
91	MRS. RAGGEDY CLAUS	RT	70.00	125.00
91	PIPPY PAT	RT	50.00	55.00
91	WINKIE BINKIE	RT	55.00	60.00
92	CANDY APPLEBEE	RT	16.00	20.00
92	CHRISTOPHER COLUMBUS	RT	80.00	85.00
92	OLD ST. NICK	RT	96.00	135.00
92	PUMPKIN PATTY	RT	80.00	85.00
92	SCARY LARRY SCARECROW	RT	80.00	85.00
92	TEENY WEENY ANGEL	RT	10.00	15.00
92	WITCHY WANDA	RT	80.00	85.00
93	HAPPY PAPPY CLAUS	RT	75.00	80.00
93	ITTY BITTY SANTA	RT	7.00	9.00
93	JAMMY MAMMY CLAUS	RT	70.00	75.00
93	MERRY OLE FARLEY FAGAN DOOBERRY	RT	133.00	135.00
93	MR. KNO MO SNO	RT	53.00	55.00
93	OLD ST. KNICKERBOCKER	RT	80.00	85.00
94	NATTIE FAE TUCKER	RT	65.00	70.00
M. MASCHINO		**ATTIC BABIES COLLECTORS CLUB**		
92	BURTIE BUZBEE, SNL	RT	40.00	45.00
93	ISSIE B. RUEBOTTOM, SNL	RT	35.00	40.00
94	SUNFLOWER FLOSSIE, SNL	RT	42.00	47.00
M. MASCHINO		**BAGGIE COLLECTION**		
91	AMERICANA BAGGIE BEAR	RT	20.00	25.00
91	AMERICANA BAGGIE GIRL	RT	20.00	25.00
91	AMERICANA BAGGIE RABBIT	RT	20.00	25.00
91	AMERICANA BAGGIE SANTA	RT	20.00	25.00
91	CHRISTMAS BAGGIE BEAR	RT	20.00	25.00
91	CHRISTMAS BAGGIE GIRL	RT	20.00	25.00
91	CHRISTMAS BAGGIE RABBIT	RT	20.00	25.00
91	CHRISTMAS BAGGIE SANTA	RT	20.00	25.00
91	COUNTRY BAGGIE BEAR	RT	20.00	25.00
91	COUNTRY BAGGIE GIRL	RT	20.00	25.00
91	COUNTRY BAGGIE RABBIT	RT	20.00	25.00
M. MASCHINO		**FIRST EDITION**		
90	RAGGEDY OLE CHRIS CRINGLE	RT	190.00	265.00
92	AMERICANA RAGGEDY SANTA	RT	87.00	90.00
M. MASCHINO		**SECOND EDITION**		
90	RAGGEDY OLE CHRIS CRINGLE	RT	190.00	195.00
92	AMERICANA RAGGEDY SANTA	RT	90.00	95.00
M. MASCHINO		**TOUR BABIES**		
93	TOUR BABY 1993	RT	20.00	25.00
94	TOUR BABY 1994	RT	25.00	25.00
M. MASCHINO		**VALENTINE COLLECTION**		
93	VALENTINE BEAR-BOY	RT	40.00	45.00
93	VALENTINE BEAR-GIRL	RT	40.00	45.00
94	HERWIN HEAPS O HUGS	RT	40.00	45.00
94	LOTTIE LOTS-A-LOVE	RT	40.00	45.00

AVONLEA TRADITIONS INC.

*			**ANNE OF GREEN GABLES**	
89	ARRIVING AT THE STATION	OP	260.00	260.00
90	DIANA BARRY	OP	260.00	260.00
90	PUFFED SLEEVES	OP	260.00	260.00
90	SCHOOL DAYS	OP	260.00	260.00
97	90TH ANNIVERSARY EDITION	990	120.00	120.00
97	LIMITED EDITION	5000	60.00	60.00
98	10TH ANNIVERSARY	2000	60.00	60.00

BOYDS COLLECTION LTD.

G. LOWENTHAL			**ANIMAL MENAGERIE**	
*	APHRODITE 5339	RT	*	N/A
*	ERIN O'PIGG	RT	*	N/A
G. LOWENTHAL			**ARCHIVE SERIES**	
*	ADDINGTON 5701-05	RT	*	N/A
*	BERTHA UTTERBUG 5758	RT	*	N/A
*	HEATH II	RT	*	N/A
*	MACMILLAN	RT	*	N/A
*	RALEIGH	RT	*	N/A

YR	NAME	LIMIT	ISSUE	TREND
*	THATCHER 5706	RT	*	N/A
*	WELLINGTON	RT	*	N/A
*	WILSON	RT	*	N/A
	G. LOWENTHAL		**ARTIST SERIES**	
*	EDGAR 5864-07	*	*	N/A
*	ELVIS 5859	RT	*	N/A
*	FARNSWORTH JR 5870-08	*	*	N/A
*	FARNSWORTH SR 5875-08	*	*	N/A
*	HIGGINS 5877-06	*	*	N/A
*	HIGGY 5876-03	*	*	N/A
	G. LOWENTHAL		**BEARS IN THE ATTIC**	
*	JETHRO 5630	RT	*	N/A
*	REVA 5630-02	RT	*	N/A
	G. LOWENTHAL		**BUBBA BEARS**	
*	BILLY RAY	RT	*	N/A
*	BOBBIE JO	RT	*	N/A
*	BUBBA	RT	*	N/A
*	ELLY MAE	RT	*	N/A
	G. LOWENTHAL		**CHOIR BEARS**	
*	GABRIEL 5825	RT	*	N/A
*	JOHN	RT	*	N/A
*	JOSHUA 5826	RT	*	N/A
*	SEBASTIAN	RT	*	N/A
	G. LOWENTHAL		**CLINTON'S CABINET**	
*	FEDERICO	RT	*	N/A
*	GEORGE	RT	*	N/A
*	VINCENT	RT	*	N/A
	G. LOWENTHAL		**FLATTIES**	
*	BRAYBURN	RT	*	N/A
*	ELMORE FLATSKI	RT	*	N/A
*	HADLEY FLATSKI	RT	*	N/A
*	LENORA FLATSTEIN	RT	*	N/A
*	NEWTON	RT	*	N/A
	G. LOWENTHAL		**FLOPPIES**	
*	ARNO-W-LD	RT	*	N/A
*	CHIPPER	RT	*	N/A
*	HESTER	RT	*	N/A
*	KIP	RT	*	N/A
*	WALKER	RT	*	N/A
	G. LOWENTHAL		**J.B. BEAN & ASSOCIATES**	
*	ALBERT B. BEAN	RT	*	N/A
*	BETTY BISCUIT	RT	*	N/A
*	DUFUS BEAR 5112	RT	*	N/A
*	J.B. BEAN	RT	*	N/A
*	LOUIE B. BEAN	RT	*	N/A
*	MISTLE	RT	*	N/A
*	OTIS B. BEAN 5107	RT	*	N/A
*	RALPH POOCHSTEIN	RT	*	N/A
*	TOE	RT	*	N/A
	G. LOWENTHAL		**NORTHERN LIGHTS**	
*	BEATRICE VHMOOSE	RT	*	N/A
*	MAYNARD VHMOOSE	RT	*	N/A
*	MURGATROYD II VHMOOSE	RT	*	N/A
*	NADIA VON HINDENMOOSE 5542-01	RT	*	N/A
	G. LOWENTHAL		**SNOWBEARS**	
*	SINKIN II	RT	*	N/A
*	TINKIN II	RT	*	N/A
	G. LOWENTHAL		**T.J.'S BEST DRESSED**	
*	ALASTAIR & CAMILLA 98042	*	*	N/A
*	ARLO 9141	*	*	N/A
*	AUBERGINE 9107	*	*	N/A
*	AUNTIE IOLA	RT	*	N/A
*	BAAAH'B	RT	*	N/A
*	BAILEY & MATTHEW 9224	*	*	N/A
*	BAILEY 9199-05	*	*	N/A
*	BIG BOY	RT	*	N/A
*	BRUCE	RT	*	N/A
*	CALVIN ELLIS	RT	*	N/A
*	CLAIRE	RT	*	N/A
*	COLLEEN O'BRUIN	RT	*	N/A
*	CORNWALLIS	RT	*	N/A
*	EDDIE BEANBERGER	RT	*	N/A
*	EDEN II	RT	*	N/A
*	EDMUND IN DENIM ROMPER & HEART SWEATER #9175-06	*	*	N/A
*	EDMUND IN NAUTICAL SWEATER & HAT 9175-03	*	*	N/A
*	EDMUND IN SWEATER/PLAID PANTS 9175-05	*	*	N/A
*	EMILY BABBIT 9150-05	*	*	N/A
*	EMMA 9101	*	*	N/A
*	FEDERICO HARES	RT	*	N/A
*	FETA 91075	*	*	N/A
*	FITZGERALD O'BRUIN	RT	*	N/A
*	GERALDO	RT	*	N/A
*	GUNNAR 9123	*	*	N/A
*	HARRISON	RT	*	N/A

YR	NAME	LIMIT	ISSUE	TREND
*	HERMINE GRISSLIN	RT	*	N/A
*	LAS	RT	*	N/A
*	LIZZIE MCBEE	RT	*	N/A
*	MARLENA 9154	*	*	N/A
*	MATTHEW	RT	*	N/A
*	MICHELLINE 91815	*	*	N/A
*	NELLIE	RT	*	N/A
*	NICHOLAS	RT	*	N/A
*	OPHELIA	RT	*	N/A
*	PETER	RT	*	N/A
*	PHILOMENA	RT	*	N/A
*	PUCK 9172	*	*	N/A
*	STEWART RAREBIT #9116	*	*	N/A
*	SVEN 9122	*	*	N/A
*	TEDDY BEANBERGER	RT	*	N/A
*	TYLER SUMMERFIELD	RT	*	N/A
*	WALTON	RT	*	N/A
*	WILLA BRUIN	RT	*	N/A

BRADFORD EDITIONS
T. CATHEY

64	18 IN. P.J. GIRL	*	7.00	450.00

BRADFORD EXCHANGE
L. DUNSMORE

HATS OFF TO THE SEASONS

97	CHRISTMAS CAROL	*	*	N/A

CAVANAGH GROUP
H. SUNDBLOM

COCA-COLA BRAND HERITAGE COLLECTION

97	HOSPITALITY	3000	200.00	200.00

DADDY'S LONG LEGS
K. GERMANY

ANGELS

94	GLORY	RT	118.00	275.00
94	HOPE	RT	118.00	300.00
94	KARA	RT	76.00	235.00
94	PRECIOUS	RT	76.00	225.00
95	DEMETRIA	1	2,500.00	11000.00
96	KEISHA	OP	80.00	80.00
96	MONICA	OP	150.00	150.00

K. GERMANY

ANIMALS

90	ABIGAIL COW, BLUE	RT	62.00	180.00
90	ABIGAIL COW, RED	RT	68.00	200.00
90	CAT IN JUMP SUIT	RT	60.00	675.00
90	GOAT-BOY	RT	62.00	700.00
90	GOAT-GIRL	RT	62.00	700.00
90	HUGH HOOFNER	RT	68.00	210.00
90	MAMIE THE PIG, GREEN	RT	68.00	575.00
90	PIG BOY	RT	58.00	675.00
90	RACCOON	RT	66.00	800.00
90	RACHAEL RABBIT	RT	15.00	185.00
90	ROBBY RABBIT	RT	44.00	550.00
90	ROSE RABBIT	RT	54.00	750.00
90	ROXANNE RABBIT	RT	52.00	540.00
90	RUDY RABBIT	RT	54.00	750.00
90	WEDDING RABBITS	RT	240.00	3300.00
91	KITTY KAT	RT	78.00	535.00
91	MAMIE THE PIG, BLUE	RT	84.00	575.00

K. GERMANY

ARTS & THEATER

90	MIME	RT	58.00	1500.00
90	WITCH HAZEL	RT	86.00	265.00
92	BABE BOUCHARD	OP	98.00	100.00
94	MARGO	RT	126.00	180.00

K. GERMANY

BABIES & TODDLERS

91	BABY JESSE	OP	18.00	20.00
95	ANNIE LEE WITH BLANKET	RT	150.00	335.00
95	ANNIE LEE WITHOUT BLANKET	RT	150.00	275.00
96	BUNNY	RT	80.00	180.00
97	BABY HANNAH	OP	80.00	80.00

K. GERMANY

CHILDREN AROUND THE WORLD

95	LIZABETH	OP	76.00	76.00
95	SU	OP	76.00	76.00
96	STARR	OP	80.00	80.00
96	TERESA	OP	80.00	80.00
97	SALLY	OP	84.00	84.00

K. GERMANY

CLOWNS

93	CECIL	OP	98.00	98.00
94	PEANUT	OP	76.00	80.00
95	SUGAR	RT	120.00	550.00
96	BUTTONS	RT	80.00	125.00
97	CRICKET	OP	94.00	94.00

K. GERMANY

COMMUNITY & FAMILY

90	SOFIE	RT	44.00	425.00
91	JUNIOR WITH HAT AND BANJO	OP	54.00	54.00
91	OMA GREEN	OP	90.00	90.00

YR	NAME	LIMIT	ISSUE	TREND
92	BESSIE	RT	94.00	145.00
92	DOC MOSES	RT	98.00	340.00
92	EZRA	OP	90.00	90.00
92	GRACIE	RT	94.00	145.00
92	JASMINE	RT	90.00	280.00
92	NURSE GARNET	RT	90.00	325.00
93	ABE	RT	94.00	155.00
93	BILLYE	RT	98.00	235.00
93	ESTHER	RT	158.00	365.00
93	JACKIE	RT	98.00	185.00
93	JUDGE	RT	98.00	245.00
93	SAM	RT	94.00	155.00
93	SLATS	RT	98.00	215.00
94	AUNT FANNIE	RT	90.00	125.00
94	CHARLES LOUIS	RT	90.00	125.00
94	MAXINE	RT	90.00	125.00
94	UNCLE LEON	RT	90.00	125.00
95	CAMILLE	RT	184.00	215.00
96	EARL & ELLA	RT	196.00	650.00

K. GERMANY — COSTUME PARTY

YR	NAME	LIMIT	ISSUE	TREND
94	TICKER	RT	76.00	220.00
94	WENDY	RT	80.00	200.00
95	GRETCHEN	RT	80.00	145.00
95	PISTOL	RT	80.00	160.00
96	GIGI	RT	90.00	100.00
97	BOOTS	RT	90.00	90.00

K. GERMANY — CULTURAL

YR	NAME	LIMIT	ISSUE	TREND
90	NETTIE	OP	70.00	95.00
90	TOBIAS	OP	72.00	90.00
95	KENYA	OP	98.00	100.00
97	AMANI	OP	104.00	104.00

K. GERMANY — DADDY'S LONG LEGS MEMBERS EDITIONS

YR	NAME	LIMIT	ISSUE	TREND
93	FAITH	RT	65.00	375.00
94	BUBBY WITH HEART BLANKET	RT	65.00	310.00
94	BUBBY WITH STAR BLANKET	RT	65.00	265.00
94	SISSY	RT	65.00	310.00
95	BULL BISHOP	RT	65.00	140.00
95	CHERRY	RT	65.00	135.00
95	JOY (ANGEL)	CL	*	N/A
96	CARRIE (ANGEL)	CL	*	N/A
96	JACK	RT	65.00	115.00
96	JILL	RT	65.00	115.00
97	BABY JESUS	YR	*	N/A
97	JOSEPH	YR	65.00	65.00
97	MARY	YR	65.00	65.00

K. GERMANY — OLD WEST

YR	NAME	LIMIT	ISSUE	TREND
90	COWBOY BUCK	RT	78.00	325.00
90	INDIAN (1ST EDITION)	RT	78.00	875.00
90	MISS LILLY	RT	78.00	325.00
91	INDIAN (2ND EDITION)	RT	*	275.00
91	STILL RIVER	1452	98.00	275.00
92	LUCKY THE GAMBLER	RT	90.00	550.00
96	SWEET SAVANNAH	2000	260.00	290.00
96	WILDWOOD WILL	RT	290.00	650.00
97	PROUD EAGLE	1500	290.00	290.00

K. GERMANY — OLD WOMAN WHO LIVED IN A SHOE

YR	NAME	LIMIT	ISSUE	TREND
96	LOUIE	OP	98.00	98.00
96	WILLIAM	OP	80.00	80.00
97	HANNAH	OP	80.00	80.00

K. GERMANY — PATRIOTIC

YR	NAME	LIMIT	ISSUE	TREND
91	UNCLE SAM (WHITE)	RT	150.00	1375.00
92	JEREMIAH	RT	90.00	280.00
95	UNCLE SAM (BLACK)	RT	120.00	120.00

K. GERMANY — SANTA CLAUS

YR	NAME	LIMIT	ISSUE	TREND
90	SANTA (WHITE)	RT	64.00	1800.00
90	SANTA RED VELVET	RT	180.00	1900.00
90	SANTA TAPESTRY	RT	180.00	1900.00
91	SANTA (BLACK)	RT	98.00	475.00
91	SANTA (WHITE)	RT	98.00	475.00
92	SANTA (BLACK)	RT	158.00	415.00
92	SANTA (WHITE)	RT	158.00	440.00
92	SANTA SPECIAL EDITION	RT	158.00	440.00
93	SANTA (BLACK)	RT	178.00	335.00
94	ODESSA CLAUS, 1ST EDITION	RT	144.00	240.00
94	TUBBIN' SANTA	RT	150.00	285.00
95	ODESSA CLAUS, 2ND EDITION	OP	144.00	144.00
95	SANTA (BLACK)	RT	160.00	215.00
95	SANTA (WHITE)	RT	160.00	215.00
96	SANTA (BLACK)	RT	200.00	200.00

K. GERMANY — SCHOOLHOUSE DAYS

YR	NAME	LIMIT	ISSUE	TREND
91	DAPHNE	RT	72.00	265.00
91	IRIS	RT	90.00	350.00
92	CHOO CHOO	RT	56.00	130.00
92	JOSIE	RT	56.00	135.00

YR	NAME	LIMIT	ISSUE	TREND
92	KATY	RT	64.00	105.00
92	MICAH	RT	64.00	105.00
93	EMILY	RT	80.00	225.00
93	LUCY	RT	64.00	130.00
93	PHOEBE	RT	64.00	130.00
93	PRISCILLA	RT	70.00	380.00
93	TIMOTHY	RT	76.00	400.00
94	JANE	RT	70.00	165.00
94	JULIE	OP	76.00	76.00
95	MARCUS	RT	76.00	145.00
95	MOLLY	RT	76.00	150.00
95	SKEETER	OP	80.00	80.00

K. GERMANY | | | | **STORYBOOK**

YR	NAME	LIMIT	ISSUE	TREND
94	LITTLE RED RIDING HOOD	RT	80.00	280.00
95	MARY AND HER LAMB	RT	80.00	175.00
96	LITTLE MS. MUFFET	1117	90.00	245.00

K. GERMANY | | | | **SUNDAY SCHOOL & CHURCH**

YR	NAME	LIMIT	ISSUE	TREND
91	JUNIOR	OP	54.00	70.00
91	MS. HATTIE	OP	90.00	95.00
91	REV. JOHNSON	OP	86.00	95.00
92	SISTER MARY KATHLEEN	RT	98.00	285.00
93	CASSIE	RT	70.00	125.00
93	POLLY	RT	70.00	125.00
93	RUTH	OP	94.00	94.00
93	SISTER CARTER	RT	94.00	165.00

K. GERMANY | | | | **WEDDING PARTY**

YR	NAME	LIMIT	ISSUE	TREND
92	JAMES & OLIVIA (SET)	CL	250.00	640.00
92	JAMES THE GROOM	RT	125.00	350.00
92	OLIVIA THE BRIDE	RT	125.00	350.00
94	MAGGIE, FLOWER GIRL	RT	98.00	150.00
94	VICTORIA BRIDE	RT	178.00	287.00
96	JOSHUA, RINGBEARER	2500	98.00	98.00
96	MAURICE THE GROOM	2500	118.00	118.00

DEPARTMENT 56
*

				HERITAGE VILLAGE DOLL COLLECTION
87	CHRISTMAS CAROL DOLLS 1000-6 (SET OF 4)	250	1,500.00	1500.00
87	CHRISTMAS CAROL DOLLS 5907-2 (SET OF 4)	OP	250.00	250.00
88	CHRISTMAS CAROL DOLLS 1001-4 (SET OF 4)	350	800.00	800.00
88	MR. & MRS. FEZZIWIG 5594-8 (SET OF 2)	OP	172.00	172.00

*

				SNOWBABIES DOLLS
88	ALISON & DUNCAN 7730-5	RT	200.00	750.00

DIANNA EFFNER PORCELAIN DOLLS
E. CHEN

YR	NAME	LIMIT	ISSUE	TREND
94	BENJAMIN	25	325.00	350.00
94	HEATHER	25	350.00	375.00

D. EFFNER

YR	NAME	LIMIT	ISSUE	TREND
93	BEDTIME JENNY	50	375.00	400.00
93	BIRTHDAY JENNY	50	375.00	400.00
93	DOLLY	50	95.00	110.00
93	EVERYDAY JENNY	CL	375.00	400.00
93	TINY (BOY OR GIRL)	50	250.00	275.00
94	KAYLA	50	450.00	475.00

L. WILSON

YR	NAME	LIMIT	ISSUE	TREND
93	SHEN	50	475.00	500.00

DOLLS BY JERRI
J. MCCLOUD | | | | **DOLLS BY JERRI**

YR	NAME	LIMIT	ISSUE	TREND
*	BOY	1000	350.00	395.00
*	DENISE	1000	380.00	475.00
*	GINA	1000	350.00	400.00
*	GOLDILOCKS	1000	370.00	525.00
*	JAMIE	800	380.00	450.00
*	LAURA	1000	350.00	200.00
*	LITTLE BO PEEP	1000	340.00	425.00
*	LITTLE MISS MUFFET	1000	340.00	425.00
*	MEGAN	750	420.00	550.00
*	MEREDITH	750	430.00	575.00
*	UNCLE REMUS	500	290.00	450.00
82	BABY DAVID	538	290.00	2000.00
84	CLARA	1000	320.00	1500.00
84	EMILY	1000	330.00	1250.00
85	BRIDE	1000	350.00	400.00
85	CANDY	1000	340.00	2000.00
85	MISS NANNY	1000	160.00	300.00
85	SCOTTY	1000	340.00	800.00
85	UNCLE JOE	1000	160.00	300.00
86	ALFALFA	1000	350.00	350.00
86	ALLISON	1000	350.00	500.00
86	AMBER	1000	350.00	800.00
86	ANNABELLE	300	600.00	600.00
86	ASHLEY	1000	350.00	450.00
86	AUDREY	300	550.00	550.00
86	BRIDGETTE	300	500.00	500.00

YR	NAME	LIMIT	ISSUE	TREND
86	CANE	1000	350.00	1200.00
86	CHARLOTTE	1000	330.00	450.00
86	CLOWN-DAVID, 3 YEARS OLD	1000	340.00	450.00
86	DANIELLE	1000	350.00	500.00
86	DAVID, 2 YEARS OLD	1000	330.00	550.00
86	DAVID-MAGICIAN	1000	350.00	500.00
86	ELIZABETH	1000	340.00	340.00
86	FOOL, THE	1000	350.00	350.00
86	HELEN JEAN	1000	350.00	500.00
86	JACQUELINE	300	500.00	500.00
86	JOY	1000	350.00	350.00
86	LUCIANNA	300	500.00	500.00
86	MARY BETH	1000	350.00	350.00
86	NOBODY	1000	350.00	500.00
86	PRINCESS AND THE UNICORN	1000	370.00	425.00
86	SAMANTHA	1000	350.00	500.00
86	SOMEBODY	1000	350.00	550.00
86	TAMMY	1000	350.00	900.00
86	YVONNE	300	500.00	500.00
88	HOLLY	1000	350.00	825.00
89	GOOSE GIRL, GUILD	CL	300.00	600.00
89	LAURA LEE	1000	370.00	550.00

DYNASTY DOLL

G. HOYT — ANNA COLLECTION

YR	NAME	LIMIT	ISSUE	TREND
92	COMMUNION GIRL	RT	125.00	130.00

* — ANNUAL

89	AMBER	RT	90.00	95.00
90	MARCELLA	RT	90.00	95.00
91	BUTTERFLY PRINCESS	RT	110.00	115.00
93	ARIEL	RT	120.00	125.00

H. TERTSAKIAN — ANNUAL

| 93 | ANNUAL BRIDE | RT | 190.00 | 195.00 |
| 94 | ANNUAL BRIDE | * | 200.00 | 205.00 |

K. HENDERSON — BALLERINA SERIES

| 93 | TINA BALLERINA | RT | 175.00 | 180.00 |

L. PO NAN — BALLERINA SERIES

| 91 | MASHA-NUTCRACKER | RT | 190.00 | 195.00 |

* — CHRISTMAS

87	MERRIE	RT	60.00	65.00
88	NOEL	RT	80.00	85.00
90	FAITH	RT	110.00	115.00
91	JOY	RT	125.00	130.00
93	GENEVIEVE	RT	164.00	169.00
94	GLORIA '94	5000	170.00	175.00

R. LEE — CLOWNS

94	BOO-BOO	5000	95.00	100.00
94	DANDY	5000	95.00	100.00
94	MUNCHIE	5000	95.00	100.00
94	PRISSY	5000	95.00	100.00
94	REGINALD	5000	95.00	100.00

* — DYNASTY COLLECTION

91	LANA	OP	85.00	90.00
93	AMANDA	3000	195.00	200.00
93	ANGELA	1500	195.00	200.00
93	NICOLE	RT	135.00	140.00
93	PATRICIA	OP	160.00	165.00
93	SHANNON	1500	195.00	200.00
94	AMY	1500	175.00	180.00
94	CHRISTINA	3500	200.00	205.00
94	LAURELYN	2000	180.00	185.00
94	REBECCA	1500	175.00	180.00

M. COHEN — DYNASTY COLLECTION

93	KADYROSE	OP	145.00	150.00
93	KATY	RT	135.00	140.00
93	TAMI	7500	190.00	195.00
93	TORY	7500	190.00	195.00

K. HENDERSON — DYNASTY COLLECTION

| 93 | JULIE | RT | 175.00 | 180.00 |

G. HOYT — DYNASTY COLLECTION

| 93 | CARLEY | OP | 120.00 | 125.00 |
| 94 | AMELIA | 1500 | 170.00 | 185.00 |

S. KELSEY — DYNASTY COLLECTION

| 94 | GABRIELLE | 1500 | 180.00 | 185.00 |
| 94 | KELSEY | 1500 | 225.00 | 230.00 |

G. TEPPER — DYNASTY COLLECTION

| 93 | HEATHER | RT | 160.00 | 165.00 |
| 93 | JULIET | RT | 160.00 | 165.00 |

H. TERTSAKIAN — DYNASTY COLLECTION

93	ANTOINETTE	5000	190.00	195.00
93	CATHERINE	5000	190.00	195.00
93	MEGAN	3500	150.00	155.00

* — INDIAN COLLECTION

| 92 | POCAHONTAS | RT | 95.00 | 110.00 |

Braelyn *by Elke Hutchens was limited to 400 in 1991. Issued at $595 by Elke's Originals Ltd., the doll fetches up to $,1500 on the secondary market.*

The first release in Yolanda's Picture-Perfect Babies, Jason *is now the most valuable doll in the collection. Released by The Edwin M. Knowles China Co. in 1985 for $48, he is now worth over $1,000.*

Julie Good-Kruger's distinctive style is apparent in Daydreams, *a 1990 issue limited to 1,000 signed and numbered dolls.*

Danielle *from the Yolanda's Picture-Perfect Babies Collection by Yolanda Bello, was released in 1991 for $69. Produced by Edwin M. Knowles China Co.*

YR	NAME	LIMIT	ISSUE	TREND
93	SITTING CLOUD	OP	100.00	105.00
94	CHIEF EAGLE'S WING	3500	165.00	170.00
94	SPRING WINDS AND LITTLE WOLF	3500	120.00	125.00
U. BRAUSER			**UTA BRAUSER'S CITY KIDS**	
93	JAMAAL	5000	220.00	225.00
93	KADEEM	3500	195.00	200.00
93	MIRAMBI	5000	190.00	195.00
93	RICKIA	3500	170.00	175.00
93	TISHA	3500	170.00	175.00
H. TERTSAKIAN			**VICTORIANS**	
94	BEVERLY	1500	195.00	200.00
94	DANIELLE	2500	195.00	200.00
94	MARGARET	1500	195.00	200.00
94	WINIFRED	1500	195.00	200.00

EDNA HIBEL STUDIOS

YR	NAME	LIMIT	ISSUE	TREND
E. HIBEL			**CHILD'S FANTASY**	
85	JENNY'S LADY JENNIFER	CL	395.00	1300.00
M. HOLCOMBE			**CHILD'S FANTASY**	
87	WENDY'S LADY GWENDOLYN	CL	495.00	900.00
88	SAMI'S LADY SAMANTHA	CL	495.00	630.00
E. HIBEL			**GRANDMA'S ATTIC**	
87	ALICE	CL	129.00	380.00
88	MARTHA	CL	139.00	400.00
M. HOLCOMBE			**GRANDMA'S ATTIC**	
89	MELANIE	CL	139.00	180.00
89	SASSEE'S LADY SMITH	CL	495.00	640.00
91	KATIE	CL	139.00	150.00
E. HIBEL			**WAX DOLL COLLECTION**	
86	WAX DOLL	12	2,500.00	3400.00

EDWIN M. KNOWLES

YR	NAME	LIMIT	ISSUE	TREND
J. GOOD-KRUGER			**AMISH BLESSINGS**	
90	REBECCAH	TL	68.00	68.00
91	RACHEL	CL	69.00	69.00
91	RACHEL AT PRAYER	TL	69.00	69.00
92	ELI	YR	80.00	80.00
92	RUTH	YR	75.00	75.00
K. BARRY-HIPPENSTEEL			**BABY BOOK TREASURES**	
90	ELIZABETH'S HOMECOMING	CL	58.00	80.00
91	CATHERINE'S CHRISTENING	TL	58.00	58.00
91	CHRISTOPHER'S FIRST SMILE	TL	63.00	63.00
K. BARRY-HIPPENSTEEL			**BORN TO BE FAMOUS**	
90	FLORENCE NIGHTINGALE	TL	87.00	87.00
90	LITTLE SHERLOCK	CL	87.00	110.00
91	LITTLE DAVY CROCKETT	CL	92.00	92.00
92	LITTLE CHRISTOPHER COLUMBUS	YR	95.00	95.00
Y. BELLO			**CHILDREN OF MOTHER GOOSE**	
87	LITTLE BO PEEP	CL	58.00	250.00
87	MARY HAD A LITTLE LAMB	CL	58.00	250.00
88	LITTLE JACK HORNER	CL	63.00	150.00
89	MISS MUFFET	CL	63.00	85.00
C. MCCLURE			**CINDY'S PLAYHOUSE PETS**	
88	MEAGAN	TL	87.00	175.00
89	RYAN	TL	83.00	83.00
89	SHELLY	TL	87.00	87.00
91	SAMANTHA	TL	89.00	89.00
D. EFFNER			**HEROINES FROM THE FAIRY TALE FORESTS**	
88	LITTLE RED RIDING HOOD	CL	68.00	175.00
89	GOLDILOCKS	CL	68.00	80.00
90	SNOW WHITE	TL	73.00	73.00
91	RAPUNZEL	TL	79.00	79.00
92	CINDERELLA	CL	79.00	79.00
K. BARRY-HIPPENSTEEL			**INTERNATIONAL FESTIVAL OF TOYS AND TOTS**	
88	CHEN, A LITTLE BOY OF CHINA	CL	78.00	250.00
89	NATASHA	CL	78.00	100.00
90	MOLLY	TL	83.00	83.00
91	HANS	TL	83.00	83.00
M. TRETTER			**LITTLEST CLOWNS**	
91	BUBBLES	TL	65.00	65.00
91	SMOOCH	CL	69.00	69.00
91	SPARKLES	TL	63.00	63.00
92	DAISY	TL	70.00	70.00
FANGEL INSPIRED			**MAUDE FANGEL'S COVER BABIES**	
90	BENJAMIN'S BALL	TL	73.00	73.00
90	PEEK-A-BOO PETER	TL	73.00	73.00
J. GOODYEAR			**MY CLOSEST FRIEND**	
91	BOO BEAR 'N ME	TL	78.00	78.00
91	ME AND MY BLANKIE	TL	79.00	79.00
STEVENS/ SIEGEL			**PARADE OF AMERICAN FASHION**	
87	GLAMOUR OF THE GIBSON GIRL, THE	CL	77.00	210.00
87	SOUTHERN BELLE, THE	CL	77.00	185.00
90	VICTORIAN LADY	TL	82.00	82.00
91	ROMANTIC LADY	TL	85.00	85.00

YR	NAME	LIMIT	ISSUE	TREND
	S. KREY		**POLLY'S TEA PARTY**	
90	POLLY	TL	78.00	78.00
91	LIZZIE	TL	79.00	79.00
92	ANNIE	TL	83.00	83.00
	M. OLDENBURG		**YESTERDAY'S DREAMS**	
90	ANDY	TL	68.00	68.00
91	JANEY	TL	69.00	69.00
	Y. BELLO		**YOLANDA'S PICTURE-PERFECT BABIES**	
85	JASON	CL	48.00	675.00
86	HEATHER	CL	48.00	250.00
87	JENNIFER	CL	58.00	250.00
88	AMANDA	CL	63.00	195.00
88	MATTHEW	CL	58.00	110.00
89	JESSICA	TL	63.00	100.00
89	SARAH	CL	58.00	110.00
90	LISA	TL	63.00	125.00
90	MICHAEL	TL	63.00	155.00
91	DANIELLE	TL	69.00	135.00
91	EMILY	TL	63.00	125.00

ELKE'S ORIGINALS
E. HUTCHENS

YR	NAME	LIMIT	ISSUE	TREND
89	ANNABELLE	250	575.00	1550.00
90	AUBRA	250	575.00	950.00
90	AURORA	250	595.00	950.00
90	KRICKET	500	575.00	525.00
90	LITTLE LIEBCHEN	250	475.00	1000.00
90	VICTORIA	500	645.00	650.00
91	ALICIA	250	595.00	625.00
91	BELINDA	400	595.00	825.00
91	BRAELYN	400	595.00	1500.00
91	BRIANNA	400	595.00	1000.00
92	BETHANY	400	595.00	825.00
92	CECILIA	435	635.00	775.00
92	CHARLES	435	635.00	550.00
92	CHERIE	435	635.00	925.00
92	CLARISSA	435	635.00	850.00
93	DAPHNE	435	675.00	625.00
93	DEIDRE	435	675.00	625.00
93	DESIREE	435	675.00	625.00

ENESCO CORP.
KINKA

YR	NAME	LIMIT	ISSUE	TREND
			KINKA LIMITED EDITION DOLL	
91	WISHING YOU CLOUDLESS SKIES 408573	2500	120.00	120.00
	M. ATTWELL		**MEMORIES OF YESTERDAY**	
90	HILARY JACK-IN-THE-BOX 376027	3750	175.00	175.00
90	HILARY, 11 IN. 376019	2500	100.00	100.00
	S. BUTCHER		**PRECIOUS MOMENTS DOLLS**	
81	DEBBIE, 18 IN. E-6214G	SU	150.00	240.00
81	MIKEY, 18 IN. E-6214B	SU	150.00	230.00
82	CUBBY, 18 IN. E-7267B	5000	200.00	545.00
82	TAMMY, 18 IN. E-7267G	5000	300.00	545.00
83	KATIE LYNNE, 16 IN. E-0539	SU	165.00	190.00
83	MOTHER SEW DEAR, 18 IN. E-2850	RT	350.00	250.00
84	AARON, 12 IN. 12424	SU	135.00	155.00
84	KRISTY, 12 IN. E-2851	SU	150.00	190.00
84	MOTHER SEW DEAR, 16 IN. E-2850	RT	350.00	380.00
84	TIMMY, 12 IN. E-5397	OP	125.00	180.00
85	BETHANY, 12 IN. 12432	SU	135.00	155.00
85	BONG BONG, 13 IN. 100455	12000	150.00	255.00
85	P.D., 7 IN. 12475	SU	50.00	80.00
85	TRISH, 7 IN. 12483	SU	50.00	55.00
86	CANDY, 13 IN. 100463	12000	150.00	355.00
86	CONNIE, 12 IN. 102253	7500	160.00	245.00
87	ANGIE, THE ANGEL OF MERCY 12491	12500	160.00	255.00
90	AUTUMN'S PRAISE 408808	YR	150.00	155.00
90	SUMMER'S JOY 408794	YR	150.00	155.00
90	VOICE OF SPRING, THE- 408786	YR	150.00	155.00
90	WINTER'S SONG 408816	YR	150.00	155.00
91	EYES OF THE LORD ARE UPON YOU, THE 429570	SU	65.00	70.00
91	EYES OF THE LORD ARE UPON YOU, THE 429589	SU	65.00	70.00
91	MAY YOU/OLD FASHIONED CHRISTMAS 417785	YR	150.00	155.00
91	YOU HAVE TOUCHED SO MANY HEARTS 427527	YR	90.00	95.00
	S. BUTCHER		**PRECIOUS MOMENTS JACK-IN-THE BOXES**	
90	AUTUMN'S PRAISE 408751	YR	200.00	205.00
90	SUMMER'S JOY 408743	YR	200.00	205.00
90	VOICE OF SPRING 408735	YR	200.00	205.00
90	WINTER'S SONG 408778	YR	200.00	205.00
91	MAY YOU/OLD FASHIONED CHRISTMAS 417777	YR	200.00	200.00
91	YOU HAVE TOUCHED SO MANY HEARTS 422282	YR	175.00	175.00

ERTL COLLECTIBLES
F. HOERLEIN

YR	NAME	LIMIT	ISSUE	TREND
			LEMUT COLLECTION I	
97	BUSTER SLEEPWEAR	OP	24.00	24.00
97	CHER SLEEPWEAR	OP	24.00	24.00

YR	NAME	LIMIT	ISSUE	TREND
97	FIFI FORMAL GOWN	OP	75.00	75.00
97	FIFI SKATING OUTFIT	OP	60.00	60.00
97	FIFI SLEEPWEAR	OP	65.00	65.00
97	FIFI UNDRESSED	OP	33.00	33.00
97	LEMUTT BLACK TIE	OP	75.00	75.00
97	LEMUTT SKIWEAR	OP	70.00	70.00
97	LEMUTT SLEEPWEAR	OP	65.00	65.00
97	LEMUTT UNDRESSED	OP	33.00	33.00

FENTON ART GLASS
M. REYNOLDS — VALENTINE'S DAY

YR	NAME	LIMIT	ISSUE	TREND
95	DOLL 5228YB 7"	2500	49.00	50.00
96	DOLL 5228WB W/MUSICAL WD. BASE	2500	55.00	55.00

FITZ & FLOYD
M. COLLINS — BLOOMERS FLOPPY FOLKS

YR	NAME	LIMIT	ISSUE	TREND
92	BLOOMER	OP	50.00	55.00
92	PEONY	OP	50.00	55.00

V. BALCOU — CHRISTMAS FLOPPY FOLKS

YR	NAME	LIMIT	ISSUE	TREND
93	SANTA CLAUS	OP	65.00	70.00
93	SANTA'S HELPER	OP	65.00	70.00
93	SANTA'S REINDEER	OP	65.00	70.00

R. HAVINS — DINOSAUR FLOPPY FOLKS

YR	NAME	LIMIT	ISSUE	TREND
94	JUNIOR SAURUS	OP	55.00	60.00
94	MAMA SAURUS	OP	55.00	60.00
94	PAPA SAURUS	OP	55.00	60.00

R. HAVINS — HALLOWEEN HOEDOWN FLOPPY FOLKS

YR	NAME	LIMIT	ISSUE	TREND
92	DRAC-IN-THE BOX	RT	60.00	65.00
92	HALLOWEEN KAT	OP	50.00	55.00
92	HAZEL WITCH	OP	50.00	55.00
92	PUMPKIN PATCH	OP	50.00	55.00
92	WANDA WITCH	OP	50.00	55.00

R. HAVINS — WONDERLAND FLOPPY FOLKS

YR	NAME	LIMIT	ISSUE	TREND
93	CHESHIRE CAT, THE	3000	60.00	65.00
93	MAD HATTER, THE	3000	60.00	65.00
93	WHITE RABBIT, THE	3000	60.00	65.00

GANZ
C. THAMMAVONGSA — COWTOWN/CHRISTMAS COLLECTION

YR	NAME	LIMIT	ISSUE	TREND
94	BUFFALO BILL CODY	OP	20.00	20.00
94	OLD MOODONALD	OP	20.00	20.00
94	SANTA COWS	OP	25.00	25.00

* — LITTLE CHEESERS/PICNIC COLLECTION

YR	NAME	LIMIT	ISSUE	TREND
92	SWEET CICELY	OP	85.00	90.00

GEORGETOWN COLLECTION INC.
L. MASON — AMERICAN DIARY DOLLS

YR	NAME	LIMIT	ISSUE	TREND
90	JENNIE COOPER	100-DAY	129.25	129.00
91	BRIDGET QUINN	100-DAY	129.25	129.00
91	CHRISTINA MEROVINA	100-DAY	129.25	129.00
91	MANY STARS	100-DAY	129.25	129.00
92	RACHEL WILLIAMS	100-DAY	129.25	129.00
92	TULU	100-DAY	129.25	129.00
93	SARAH TURNER	100-DAY	130.00	135.00

T. DEHETRE — BABY KISSES

YR	NAME	LIMIT	ISSUE	TREND
92	MICHELLE	100-DAY	118.60	119.00

C. THEROUX — CHILDREN OF THE GREAT SPIRIT

YR	NAME	LIMIT	ISSUE	TREND
93	BUFFALO CHILD	100-DAY	140.00	150.00
93	WINTER BABY	100-DAY	160.00	165.00
94	GOLDEN FLOWER	100-DAY	130.00	135.00

B. DEVAL — FAERIE PRINCESS

YR	NAME	LIMIT	ISSUE	TREND
89	FAERIE PRINCESS	CL	248.00	250.00

S. SKILLE — FARAWAY FRIENDS

YR	NAME	LIMIT	ISSUE	TREND
93	KRISTIN	100-DAY	140.00	145.00
94	DARA	100-DAY	140.00	145.00

L. MASON — GEORGETOWN COLLECTION

YR	NAME	LIMIT	ISSUE	TREND
93	QUICK FOX	100-DAY	138.95	139.00

J. GALPERIN — HEARTS IN SONG

YR	NAME	LIMIT	ISSUE	TREND
92	GRACE	100-DAY	149.60	150.00
93	MICHAEL	100-DAY	150.00	155.00

V. WALKER — KINDERGARTEN KIDS

YR	NAME	LIMIT	ISSUE	TREND
92	NIKKI	100-DAY	129.60	130.00

T. DEHETRE — LET'S PLAY

YR	NAME	LIMIT	ISSUE	TREND
92	EENTSY WEENTSY WILLIE	100-DAY	118.60	119.00
92	PEEK-A-BOO BECKIE	100-DAY	118.60	119.00

L. MASON — LINDA'S LITTLE LADIES

YR	NAME	LIMIT	ISSUE	TREND
93	SHANNON'S HOLIDAY	100-DAY	170.00	170.00

B. DEVAL — LITTLE LOVES

YR	NAME	LIMIT	ISSUE	TREND
88	EMMA	CL	139.20	150.00
89	KATIE	CL	139.20	139.00
89	MEGAN	CL	138.00	165.00
90	LAURA	CL	139.20	139.00

P. THOMPSON — MISS ASHLEY

YR	NAME	LIMIT	ISSUE	TREND
89	MISS ASHLEY	CL	228.00	230.00

YR	NAME	LIMIT	ISSUE	TREND
T. DEHETRE			**NURSERY BABIES**	
90	BABY BUNTING	CL	118.20	140.00
90	PATTY CAKE	CL	118.20	118.00
91	DIDDLE, DIDDLE	CL	118.20	118.00
91	LITTLE GIRL	100-DAY	118.20	118.00
91	ROCK-A-BYE BABY	100-DAY	118.20	118.00
91	THIS LITTLE PIGGY	100-DAY	118.20	118.00
A. TIMMERMAN			**PORTRAITS OF PERFECTION**	
93	APPLE DUMPLING	CL	149.60	150.00
93	PEACHES & CREAM	100-DAY	149.60	150.00
93	SWEET STRAWBERRY	100-DAY	149.60	150.00
94	BLACKBERRY BLOSSOM	100-DAY	149.60	150.00
B. DEVAL			**RUSSIAN FAIRY TALES DOLLS**	
93	VASILISA	100-DAY	190.00	195.00
B. DEVAL			**SMALL WONDERS**	
90	COREY	100-DAY	98.00	125.00
91	ABBEY	CL	98.00	120.00
92	SARAH	100-DAY	98.00	115.00
L. MASON			**SUGAR & SPICE**	
91	LITTLE SWEETHEART	100-DAY	118.25	118.00
91	RED HOT PEPPER	100-DAY	118.25	118.00
92	LITTLE SUNSHINE	100-DAY	141.10	141.00
P. COFFER			**TANSIE**	
88	TANSIE	CL	81.00	85.00
L. MASON			**VICTORIAN INNOCENCE**	
94	ANNABELLE	CL	130.00	135.00

GOEBEL INC.

YR	NAME	LIMIT	ISSUE	TREND
B. BALL				
93	ANGEL SWEETIE	1000	50.00	50.00
93	BILLIE BUMPS	500	150.00	150.00
93	CORY	1000	135.00	135.00
93	DOLLY DINGLE	1000	115.00	115.00
96	BROTHER MURPHY	2000	125.00	125.00
B. BALL			**80TH ANNIVERSARY ISSUE**	
93	DAISY DUMPLING	500	124.50	125.00
93	DIMPLES DUMPLING	500	150.00	150.00
93	DOLLY DINGLE	500	155.00	155.00
93	SNUGGLES SNOOKS	1500	65.00	65.00
93	TICKLEY TINGLE	500	129.00	129.00
B. BALL			**AMERICANA SERIES**	
93	CLARA	1000	235.00	235.00
93	RITA	500	475.00	475.00
93	ROSEMARIE	1000	220.00	220.00
B. BALL			**ANNUAL TREE TOP ANGEL**	
93	TREE TOP ANGEL-6TH	1000	70.00	70.00
B. BALL			**BEST DRESSED TODDLER**	
93	BUFFY	1000	245.00	245.00
93	JOSEPHINE	1000	160.00	160.00
K. KENNEDY			**BIRTHSTONE DOLLS**	
94	APRIL/DIAMOND	2500	29.50	30.00
94	AUGUST/PERIDOT	2500	29.50	30.00
94	DECEMBER/ZIRCON	2500	29.50	30.00
94	FEBRUARY/AMETHYST	2500	29.50	30.00
94	JANUARY/GARNET	2500	29.50	30.00
94	JULY/RUBY	2500	29.50	30.00
94	JUNE/LIGHT AMETHYST	2500	29.50	30.00
94	MARCH/AQUAMARINE	2500	29.50	30.00
94	MAY/EMERALD	2500	29.50	30.00
94	NOVEMBER/TOPAZ	2500	29.50	30.00
94	OCTOBER/ROSE STONE	2500	29.50	30.00
94	SEPTEMBER/SAPPHIRE	2500	29.50	30.00
B. BALL/TIMBERLAKE			**BOB TIMBERLAKE COLLECTIBLE DOLLS**	
96	ABBY LIZ	2000	195.00	195.00
96	ANN	2000	195.00	195.00
96	CARTER	2000	195.00	195.00
96	KATE	2000	195.00	195.00
K. KENNEDY			**CHERUBS COLLECTION**	
94	CHEERY CHERUB	500	169.50	169.50
B. BALL/TIMBERLAKE			**CINDY GUYER ROMANCE DOLLS**	
96	MACKENZIE	1000	225.00	225.00
B. BALL			**DOLLY DINGLE DOLLS**	
94	DOLLY DINGLE'S TRIP AROUND THE WORLD	500	129.00	129.00
96	MELVIS BUMPS	1000	99.00	99.00
B. BALL			**FOUR SEASONS**	
94	BARBARA	500	299.25	299.25
B. BALL			**HOLIDAY DOLLS**	
94	CANDY CORN	2000	89.00	89.00
94	SANTA CLAWS	500	145.00	145.00
B. BALL			**INVITATION TO A PARTY**	
94	VANESSA	1000	124.50	125.00
M.I. HUMMEL			**M.I. HUMMEL DOLLS**	
*	ANDERL 1718	CL	*	150.00

YR	NAME	LIMIT	ISSUE	TREND
*	BABY 1101 A-H	CL	*	150.00
*	BABY 1102 A-H	CL	*	150.00
*	BERTL 1503	CL	*	175.00
*	BERTL 1603	CL	*	175.00
*	BERTL 1703	CL	*	175.00
*	BRIEFTRAGER 1720	CL	*	175.00
*	CHRISTL 1715	CL	*	150.00
*	FELIX 1608	CL	*	175.00
*	FELIX 1708	CL	*	175.00
*	FRANZL 1812	CL	*	150.00
*	GANSELIESL 1717	CL	*	175.00
*	GRETEL 1501	CL	*	200.00
*	GRETEL 1601	CL	*	175.00
*	GRETEL 1701	CL	*	175.00
*	HANSEL 1504	CL	*	200.00
*	HANSEL 1604	CL	*	175.00
*	HANSEL 1704	CL	*	175.00
*	JACKAL 1714	CL	*	150.00
*	JACKAL 1806	CL	*	125.00
*	KONDITOR 1723	CL	*	175.00
*	MARIANDL 1713	CL	*	150.00
*	MARIANDL 1805	CL	*	125.00
*	MAX 1506	CL	*	200.00
*	MAX 1606	CL	*	175.00
*	MAX 1706	CL	*	175.00
*	MIRZL 1811	CL	*	150.00
*	NACHWACHTER 1719	CL	*	175.00
*	PETERLE 1710	CL	*	150.00
*	PETERLE 1810	CL	*	150.00
*	PUPPENMETTERCHEN 1725	CL	*	175.00
*	RADI-BUB 1724	CL	*	175.00
*	ROSL 1709	CL	*	150.00
*	ROSL 1801	CL	*	125.00
*	ROSL 1809	CL	*	150.00
*	RUDI 1802	CL	*	125.00
*	SCHORSCHL 1716	CL	*	150.00
*	SCHUSTERBUB	CL	*	175.00
*	SEPPL 1502	CL	*	200.00
*	SEPPL 1602	CL	*	175.00
*	SEPPL 1702	CL	*	175.00
*	SEPPL 1804	CL	*	125.00
*	SKIHASERL 1722	CL	*	175.00
*	STRICKLIESL 1505	CL	*	200.00
*	STRICKLIESL 1605	CL	*	175.00
*	STRICKLIESL 1705	CL	*	175.00
*	VRONI 1803	CL	*	125.00
*	WANDERBUB 1507	CL	*	200.00
*	WANDERBUB 1607	CL	*	175.00
*	WANDERBUB 1707	CL	*	175.00
64	CHIMNEY SWEEP 1908	CL	55.00	115.00
64	FOR FATHER 1917	CL	55.00	125.00
64	GOOSE GIRL 1914	CL	55.00	125.00
64	GRETEL 1901	CL	55.00	160.00
64	HANSEL 1902	CL	55.00	160.00
64	LITTLE KNITTER 1905	CL	55.00	125.00
64	LOST STOCKING 1926	CL	55.00	125.00
64	MERRY WANDERER 1906	CL	55.00	125.00
64	MERRY WANDERER 1925	CL	55.00	125.00
64	ON SECRET PATH 1928	CL	55.00	85.00
64	ROSA-BLUE BABY 1904/B	CL	45.00	95.00
64	ROSA-PINK BABY 1904/P	CL	45.00	95.00
64	SCHOOL BOY 1910	CL	55.00	130.00
64	SCHOOL GIRL 1909	CL	55.00	130.00
64	VISITING AN INVALID 1927	CL	55.00	130.00
84	BIRTHDAY SERENADE/BOY	CL	225.00	275.00
84	BIRTHDAY SERENADE/GIRL	CL	225.00	275.00
84	ON HOLIDAY	CL	225.00	275.00
84	POSTMAN	CL	225.00	275.00
85	CARNIVAL	CL	225.00	275.00
85	EASTER GREETINGS	CL	225.00	275.00
85	LOST SHEEP	CL	225.00	275.00
85	SIGNS OF SPRING	CL	225.00	275.00
B. BALL			**MUSEUM COLLECTION**	
94	MASAKO	500	145.00	145.00
B. BALL			**NANA'S DARLINGS**	
94	COLLEEN	1000	195.00	195.00
94	MONIQUE	1000	195.00	195.00
B. BALL			**PARTY TIME**	
93	SCARLETT	1000	259.50	260.00
B. BALL			**PERFECT PETS**	
93	BOBBI SOCKS	1000	119.25	120.00
93	LIL' HONEYSUCKLE	500	124.50	125.00
93	PENNY PUSS	1000	200.00	200.00
93	SNOWFLAKE	250	129.00	129.00

YR	NAME	LIMIT	ISSUE	TREND
93	WHISPURR	1000	150.00	150.00
94	CATSANOVA	500	129.00	129.00
K. KENNEDY				**RED HEADS**
93	GINGER MUFFIN	500	220.00	220.00
94	CARROT TOP	500	129.00	129.00
94	SHARON & DARREN O'HAIR	500	99.00	99.00
K. KENNEDY				**SITTING PRETTY**
94	SOMMER	500	139.50	140.00
B. BALL				**STERLING SERIES**
93	TAYLOR	1000	215.00	215.00
K. KENNEDY				**STOLEN KISSES**
93	KISSES	500	225.00	225.00
B. BALL				**SWEET ROMANTICS**
94	DEIDRE	500	179.50	179.50
K. KENNEDY				**TINY TOT CLOWNS**
94	BETH	2000	45.00	45.00
94	JULIE	2000	45.00	45.00
94	KAYLEE	2000	45.00	45.00
94	LESLIE	2000	45.00	45.00
94	NADINE	2000	45.00	45.00
94	SHANNON	2000	45.00	45.00
B. BALL				**U.S. HISTORICAL**
96	MARY	2000	185.00	185.00
K. KENNEDY		**VICTORIA ASHLEA BIRTHSTONE DOLLS**		
90	APRIL BIRTHSTONE DOLL-912253	CL	25.00	25.00
90	AUGUST BIRTHSTONE DOLL-912257	CL	25.00	25.00
90	DECEMBER BIRTHSTONE DOLL-912261	CL	25.00	25.00
90	FEBRUARY BIRTHSTONE DOLL-912251	CL	25.00	25.00
90	JANUARY BIRTHSTONE DOLL-912250	CL	25.00	25.00
90	JULY BIRTHSTONE DOLL-912256	CL	25.00	25.00
90	JUNE BIRTHSTONE DOLL-912255	CL	25.00	25.00
90	MARCH BIRTHSTONE DOLL-912252	CL	25.00	25.00
90	MAY BIRTHSTONE DOLL-912254	CL	25.00	25.00
90	NOVEMBER BIRTHSTONE DOLL-912260	CL	25.00	25.00
90	OCTOBER BIRTHSTONE DOLL-912259	CL	25.00	25.00
90	SEPTEMBER BIRTHSTONE DOLL-912258	CL	25.00	25.00
93	APRIL DIAMOND-912397	2500	29.50	30.00
93	AUGUST PERIDOT-912401	2500	29.50	30.00
93	DECEMBER ZIRCON-912405	2500	29.50	30.00
93	FEBRUARY AMETHYST-912395	2500	29.50	30.00
93	JANUARY GARNET-912394	2500	29.50	30.00
93	JULY RUBY-912400	2500	29.50	30.00
93	JUNE LT. AMETHYST-912399	2500	29.50	30.00
93	MARCH AQUAMARINE-912396	2500	29.50	30.00
93	MAY EMERALD-912398	2500	29.50	30.00
93	NOVEMBER TOPAZ-912404	2500	29.50	30.00
93	OCTOBER ROSESTONE-912403	2500	29.50	30.00
93	SEPTEMBER SAPPHIRE-912402	2500	29.50	30.00
95	APRIL DIAMOND-912474	2500	29.50	30.00
95	AUGUST PERIDOT-912478	2500	29.50	30.00
95	DECEMBER ZIRCON-912482	2500	29.50	30.00
95	FEBRUARY AMETHYST-912472	2500	29.50	30.00
95	JANUARY GARNET-912471	2500	29.50	30.00
95	JULY RUBY-912477	2500	29.50	30.00
95	JUNE LT. AMETHYST-912476	2500	29.50	30.00
95	MARCH AQUAMARINE-912473	2500	29.50	30.00
95	MAY EMERALD-912475	2500	29.50	30.00
95	NOVEMBER TOPAZ-912481	2500	29.50	30.00
95	OCTOBER ROSESTONE-912480	2500	29.50	30.00
95	SEPTEMBER SAPPHIRE-912479	2500	29.50	30.00
B. BALL		**VICTORIA ASHLEA ORIGINALS**		
*	CHARITY-912244	CL	70.00	70.00
82	CHARLEEN-912094	CL	65.00	65.00
82	CLOWN JOLLY-912181	CL	70.00	75.00
82	HOLLY-901233	CL	160.00	200.00
82	MARIE-901231	CL	95.00	100.00
82	TRUDY-901232	CL	100.00	100.00
83	DEBORAH-901107	CL	220.00	400.00
84	AMELIA-933006	CL	100.00	100.00
84	BARBARA-901108	CL	57.00	110.00
84	CLAUDE-901032	CL	110.00	225.00
84	CLAUDETTE-901033	CL	110.00	225.00
84	CLOWN-901136	CL	90.00	120.00
84	DIANA-901119	CL	55.00	135.00
84	HENRI-901035	CL	100.00	205.00
84	HENRIETTA-901036	CL	100.00	200.00
84	JAMIE-912061	CL	65.00	100.00
84	JEANNIE-901062	CL	200.00	550.00
84	LAURA-901106	CL	300.00	575.00
84	SABINA-901155	CL	75.00	N/A
84	SHEILA-912060	CL	75.00	135.00
84	STEPHANIE-933012	CL	115.00	115.00
84	TOBIE-912023	CL	30.00	30.00
84	VICTORIA-901068	CL	200.00	1500.00

YR	NAME	LIMIT	ISSUE	TREND
85	ADELE-901172	CL	145.00	275.00
85	CHAUNCEY-912085	CL	75.00	110.00
85	CLAIRE-901158	CL	115.00	160.00
85	CLOWN CASEY-912078	CL	40.00	40.00
85	CLOWN CHRISTIE-912084	CL	60.00	90.00
85	CLOWN JODY-912079	CL	100.00	150.00
85	DOROTHY-901157	CL	130.00	275.00
85	GARNET-901183	CL	160.00	295.00
85	LYNN-912144	CL	90.00	135.00
85	MARY-912126	CL	60.00	90.00
85	MICHELLE-912066	CL	100.00	225.00
85	MILLIE-912135	CL	70.00	125.00
85	PHYLLIS-912067	CL	60.00	60.00
85	ROSALIND-912087	CL	145.00	225.00
85	ROXANNE-901174	CL	155.00	275.00
86	ASHLEY-912147	CL	125.00	125.00
86	BABY BROCK BEIGE DRESS-912103	CL	60.00	60.00
86	BABY COURTNEY-912124	CL	120.00	120.00
86	BABY LAUREN PINK-912086	CL	120.00	120.00
86	CAT/KITTY CHEERFUL GR DR-901179	2500	60.00	60.00
86	CLOWN CALYPSO-912104	CL	70.00	70.00
86	CLOWN CAT CADWALADER-912132	CL	55.00	55.00
86	CLOWN CHRISTABEL-912095	CL	100.00	150.00
86	CLOWN CLARABELLA-912096	CL	80.00	80.00
86	CLOWN CLARISSA-912123	CL	75.00	110.00
86	CLOWN CYD-912093	CL	70.00	70.00
86	CLOWN KITTEN CLEO-912133	CL	50.00	50.00
86	CLOWN LOLLIPOP-912127	CL	125.00	225.00
86	GINA-901176	CL	300.00	300.00
86	GIRL FROG FREDA-912105	CL	20.00	20.00
86	GOOGLEY GERMAN ASTRID-912109	CL	60.00	60.00
86	PATTY ARCTIC FLOWER PRINT-901185	CL	140.00	140.00
86	PEPPER RUST DR/APPR-901184	CL	125.00	200.00
87	ALICE-901212	CL	95.00	135.00
87	AMANDA POUTY-901209	CL	150.00	215.00
87	BABY DOLL-912184	CL	75.00	75.00
87	BABY LINDSAY-912190	CL	80.00	80.00
87	BONNIE POUTY-901207	CL	100.00	100.00
87	BRIDE ALLISON-901218	CL	180.00	180.00
87	CAROLINE-912191	CL	80.00	80.00
87	CATANOVA-901227	CL	75.00	75.00
87	CATLIN-901228	CL	260.00	260.00
87	CHRISTINE-912168	CL	75.00	75.00
87	CLEMENTINE-901226	CL	75.00	75.00
87	CLOWN CHAMPAGNE-912180	CL	95.00	95.00
87	DOMINIQUE-901219	CL	170.00	225.00
87	DOREEN-912198	CL	75.00	75.00
87	JACQUELINE-912192	CL	80.00	80.00
87	JESSICA-912195	CL	120.00	135.00
87	JOY-912155	CL	50.00	50.00
87	JULIA-912174	CL	80.00	80.00
87	KITTLE CAT-912167	CL	55.00	55.00
87	KITTY CUDDLES-901201	CL	65.00	65.00
87	LILLIAN-901199	CL	85.00	100.00
87	MEGAN-912148	CL	70.00	70.00
87	MICHELLE-901222	CL	90.00	90.00
87	NICOLE-901225	CL	575.00	575.00
87	NOEL-912170	CL	125.00	125.00
87	SARAH-901220	CL	350.00	350.00
87	SOPHIA-912173	CL	40.00	40.00
87	SUZANNE-901201	CL	85.00	100.00
87	TASHA-901221	CL	115.00	130.00
87	TIFFANY POUTY-901211	CL	120.00	160.00
88	AMANDA-912246	CL	180.00	180.00
88	ANGELICA-912204	CL	150.00	150.00
88	ANNE-912213	CL	130.00	150.00
88	APRIL-901239	CL	225.00	225.00
88	ASHLEY-901235	CL	110.00	110.00
88	BABY DARYL-912200	CL	85.00	85.00
88	BABY JENNIFER-912210	CL	75.00	75.00
88	BABY KATIE-912222	CL	70.00	70.00
88	BERNICE-901245	CL	90.00	90.00
88	BETTY DOLL-912220	CL	90.00	90.00
88	BRANDON-901234	CL	90.00	90.00
88	BRITTANY-912207	CL	130.00	145.00
88	CAMPBELL KID/BOY-758701	CL	13.80	14.00
88	CAMPBELL KID/GIRL-758700	CL	13.80	14.00
88	CAT MAUDE-901247	CL	85.00	85.00
88	CATHERINE-901242	CL	240.00	240.00
88	CHRISTINA-901229	CL	350.00	400.00
88	CLOWN COTTON CANDY-912199	CL	67.00	67.00
88	CRYSTAL-912226	CL	75.00	75.00
88	DIANA-912218	CL	270.00	270.00
88	ELIZABETH-901214	CL	90.00	90.00
88	ELLEN-901246	CL	100.00	100.00

YR	NAME	LIMIT	ISSUE	TREND
88	ERIN-901241	CL	170.00	170.00
88	HEATHER-912247	CL	135.00	150.00
88	JENNIFER-901248	CL	150.00	150.00
88	JENNIFER-912221	CL	80.00	80.00
88	JESSE-912231	CL	110.00	115.00
88	KAREN-912205	CL	200.00	250.00
88	LAURA-912225	CL	135.00	135.00
88	LAUREN-912212	CL	110.00	110.00
88	MARITTA SPANISH-912224	CL	140.00	140.00
88	MELISSA-901230	CL	110.00	115.00
88	MELISSA-912208	CL	125.00	125.00
88	PAULETTE-901244	CL	90.00	90.00
88	POLLY-912206	CL	100.00	125.00
88	RENAE-912245	CL	120.00	120.00
88	SARAH W/PILLOW-912219	CL	105.00	105.00
88	STEPHANIE-912238	CL	200.00	200.00
88	SUSAN-901242	CL	100.00	100.00
88	WHITNEY BLK-912232	CL	63.00	65.00
89	ALEXA-912214	CL	195.00	195.00
89	ALEXANDRIA-912273	CL	275.00	275.00
89	ASHLEA-901250	CL	550.00	550.00
89	DIANA BRIDE-912277	CL	180.00	180.00
89	HOLLY-901254	CL	180.00	180.00
89	HOPE BABY W/PILLOW-912292	CL	110.00	110.00
89	JINGLES-912271	CL	60.00	60.00
89	LICORICE-912290	CL	75.00	75.00
89	LINDSEY-901263	CL	100.00	100.00
89	LISA-912275	CL	160.00	160.00
89	LONI-912276	CL	125.00	130.00
89	MARGOT-912269	CL	110.00	110.00
89	MARIA-912265	CL	90.00	90.00
89	MEGAN-901260	CL	120.00	120.00
89	MERRY-912249	CL	200.00	200.00
89	MISSY-912283	CL	100.00	120.00
89	NANCY-912266	CL	110.00	110.00
89	SARA-912279	CL	175.00	175.00
89	SIGRID-912282	CL	145.00	145.00
89	SUZANNE-912286	CL	120.00	120.00
89	SUZY-912295	CL	110.00	110.00
89	TAMMY-912264	CL	110.00	110.00
89	TERRY-912281	CL	125.00	135.00
89	VALERIE-901255	CL	175.00	175.00
89	VANESSA-912272	CL	110.00	110.00
90	AMY-901262	CL	110.00	110.00
90	ANNABELLE-912278	CL	200.00	200.00
90	BETTINA-912310	CL	100.00	110.00
90	EMILY-912303	CL	150.00	150.00
90	FLUFFER-912293	CL	135.00	140.00
90	HEATHER-912322	CL	150.00	150.00
90	HEIDI-901266	2000	150.00	150.00
90	HELGA-912337	CL	325.00	325.00
90	JILLIAN-912323	CL	150.00	150.00
90	JUSTINE-901256	CL	200.00	200.00
90	KELLY-912331	CL	95.00	95.00
90	KIMBERLY-912341	1000	140.00	150.00
90	MATTHEW-901251	CL	100.00	100.00
90	MRS. KATZ-912301	CL	140.00	150.00
90	PAMELA-912302	CL	95.00	95.00
90	PAULA-912316	CL	100.00	100.00
90	PRISCILLA-912300	CL	185.00	190.00
90	REBECCA-901258	CL	250.00	250.00
90	ROBIN-912321	CL	160.00	165.00
90	SAMANTHA-912314	CL	185.00	190.00
90	SHEENA-912338	CL	115.00	115.00
90	STEPHANIE-912312	CL	150.00	150.00
90	SUSIE-912328	CL	115.00	120.00
90	TRACIE-912315	CL	125.00	125.00
92	ALICIA-912388	500	135.00	140.00
92	ALLISON-912358	CL	160.00	170.00
92	ANGELICA-912339	1000	145.00	150.00
92	ASHLEY-911004	CL	99.00	110.00
92	BETSY-912390	500	150.00	150.00
92	CINDY-912384	1000	185.00	195.00
92	HILARY-912353	CL	130.00	140.00
92	HOLLY BELLE-912380	500	125.00	125.00
92	KELLI-912361	1000	160.00	170.00
92	MARJORIE-912357	CL	135.00	140.00
92	TAMIKA-912382	500	185.00	190.00
92	TRUDIE-912391	500	135.00	140.00
93	AMANDA-912409	2000	40.00	45.00
93	JESSICA-912410	2000	40.00	45.00
93	KATIE-912412	2000	40.00	45.00
93	LAUREN-912413	2000	40.00	45.00
93	NICOLE-912411	2000	40.00	45.00
93	SARAH-912408	2000	40.00	45.00

YR	NAME	LIMIT	ISSUE	TREND
K. KENNEDY			**VICTORIA ASHLEA ORIGINALS**	
88	GOLDILOCKS-912234	CL	65.00	65.00
88	MOLLY-912211	CL	75.00	75.00
88	MORGAN-912239	CL	75.00	75.00
88	SANDY-901240	CL	115.00	115.00
88	SNOW WHITE-912235	CL	65.00	65.00
89	CANDACE-912288	CL	70.00	70.00
89	CLAUDIA-901257	CL	225.00	225.00
89	GINNY-912287	CL	140.00	140.00
89	JIMMY W/PILLOW-912291	CL	165.00	165.00
89	JOY-912290	CL	110.00	110.00
89	KRISTIN-912285	CL	90.00	95.00
89	MARISSA-901252	CL	225.00	225.00
89	MELANIE-912284	CL	135.00	135.00
89	PINKY CLOWN-912268	CL	70.00	75.00
90	ALICE-912296	CL	65.00	65.00
90	AMIE-912313	CL	150.00	150.00
90	ANGELA-912324	CL	130.00	135.00
90	ANNETTE-912333	CL	85.00	85.00
90	BARYSHNICAT-912298	CL	25.00	25.00
90	BRANDY-912304	CL	150.00	150.00
90	CAROLYN-901261	CL	200.00	200.00
90	DEBRA-912319	CL	120.00	120.00
90	GIGI-912306	CL	150.00	150.00
90	HELENE-901249	CL	160.00	160.00
90	JACQUELINE-912329	CL	136.00	142.00
90	JOANNE-912307	CL	165.00	165.00
90	JULIA-912334	CL	85.00	85.00
90	MARSHMALLOW-912294	CL	75.00	75.00
90	MELINDA-912309	CL	70.00	70.00
90	MONICA-912336	CL	100.00	110.00
90	MONIQUE-912335	CL	85.00	85.00
90	PENNY-912325	CL	130.00	130.00
90	SHERI-912305	CL	115.00	115.00
90	TASHA-912299	CL	25.00	25.00
90	TIFFANY-912326	CL	180.00	180.00
92	BRITTANY-912365	CL	140.00	150.00
92	CAROL-912387	1000	140.00	145.00
92	CASSANDRA-912355	1000	165.00	170.00
92	DENISE-912345	CL	145.00	155.00
92	DOTTIE-912393	1000	160.00	165.00
92	IRIS-912389	500	165.00	170.00
92	JENNY-912374	CL	150.00	155.00
92	KRIS-912345	CL	160.00	165.00
92	LAUREN-912363	1000	190.00	200.00
92	MARGARET-912354	1000	150.00	155.00
92	MICHELLE-912381	CL	175.00	180.00
92	NOELLE-912360	1000	165.00	175.00
92	SHERISE-912383	CL	145.00	150.00
92	SUSAN-912346	1000	325.00	325.00
92	TONI-912367	CL	120.00	125.00
92	TULIP-912385	500	145.00	150.00
92	WENDY-912330	1000	125.00	135.00
93	BETH-912430	2000	45.00	50.00
93	JULIE-912435	2000	45.00	50.00
93	KAYLEE-912433	2000	45.00	50.00
93	LESLIE-912432	2000	45.00	50.00
93	NADINE-912431	2000	45.00	50.00
93	SHANNON-912434	2000	45.00	50.00
K. KENNEDY		**VICTORIA ASHLEA ORIGINALS TINY TOT CLOWNS**		
94	DANIELLE	2000	45.00	50.00
94	LINDSEY	2000	45.00	50.00
94	LISA	2000	45.00	50.00
94	MARIE	2000	45.00	50.00
94	MEGAN	2000	45.00	50.00
94	STACY	2000	45.00	50.00
K. KENNEDY		**VICTORIA ASHLEA ORIGINALS TINY TOT SCHOOL GIRLS**		
94	ANDREA-12456	2000	48.00	50.00
94	CHRISTIN-912450	2000	48.00	50.00
94	MONIQUE-912455	2000	48.00	50.00
94	PATRICIA-912453	2000	48.00	50.00
94	SHAWAN-912449	2000	48.00	50.00
94	SUSAN-12457	2000	48.00	50.00

GOOD-KRUGER DOLLS

J. GOOD-KRUGER			**LIMITED EDITION**	
90	ALICE	RT	250.00	275.00
90	ANNIE-ROSE	RT	219.00	475.00
90	CHRISTMAS COOKIE	RT	199.00	200.00
90	COZY	RT	179.00	325.00
90	DAYDREAM	RT	199.00	375.00
90	SUE-LYNN	RT	240.00	305.00
91	JOHNNY-LYNN	RT	240.00	505.00
91	MOPPETT	RT	179.00	280.00
91	TEACHERS PET	RT	199.00	255.00

YR	NAME	LIMIT	ISSUE	TREND
91	VICTORIAN CHRISTMAS	RT	219.00	280.00
92	ANNE	RT	240.00	505.00
J. GOOD-KRUGER		**LIMITED EDITION/PORCELAIN**		
92	JEEPERS CREEPERS	RT	725.00	805.00

GORHAM

YR	NAME	LIMIT	ISSUE	TREND
B. PORT		**BEVERLY PORT DESIGNER COLLECTION**		
87	CHRISTOPHER PAUL BEARKIN, 10 IN.	CL	95.00	525.00
87	KRISTOBEAR KRINGLE, 17 IN.	CL	200.00	475.00
87	MOLLY MELINDA BEARKIN, 10 IN.	CL	95.00	325.00
87	SILVER BELL, 17 IN.	CL	175.00	775.00
87	TEDWARD JONATHAN BEARKIN, 10 IN.	CL	95.00	325.00
87	TEDWINA KIMELINA BEARKIN, 10 IN.	CL	95.00	325.00
88	AMAZING CALLIOPE MERRIWEATHER, THE 17 IN.	CL	275.00	1175.00
88	BAERY MAB, 9 1/2 IN.	CL	110.00	325.00
88	HOLLYBEARY KRINGLE, 15 IN.	CL	350.00	475.00
88	MISS EMILY, 18 IN.	CL	350.00	625.00
88	T.R., 28 1/2 IN.	CL	400.00	575.00
88	THEODORE B. BEAR, 14 IN.	CL	175.00	525.00
M. SIRKO		**BONNET BABIES**		
93	CHELSEA'S BONNET	CL	95.00	100.00
B. GERARDI		**BONNETS & BOWS**		
88	ALICIA	CL	385.00	900.00
88	ALLESSANDRA	CL	195.00	450.00
88	ANNEMARIE	CL	195.00	450.00
88	BELINDA	CL	195.00	450.00
88	BETHANY	CL	385.00	1350.00
88	BETTINA	CL	285.00	520.00
88	ELLIE	CL	285.00	520.00
88	FRANCIE	CL	625.00	925.00
88	JESSE	CL	525.00	825.00
88	LISETTE	CL	285.00	520.00
D. VALENZA		**BRIDE DOLLS**		
93	SUSANNAH'S WEDDING DAY	9500	295.00	295.00
C. SHAFER		**CAROUSEL DOLLS**		
93	RIBBONS AND ROSES	CL	119.00	120.00
L. DI LEO		**CELEBRATIONS OF CHILDHOOD**		
92	HAPPY BIRTHDAY AMY	CL	160.00	160.00
D. VALENZA		**CHILDHOOD MEMORIES**		
91	AMANDA	CL	98.00	155.00
91	JENNIFER	CL	98.00	155.00
91	JESSICA-ANNE'S PLAYTIME	CL	98.00	155.00
91	KIMBERLY	CL	98.00	155.00
S. STONE AIKEN		**CHILDREN OF CHRISTMAS**		
89	CLARA, 16 IN.	CL	325.00	675.00
90	NATALIE, 16 IN.	1500	350.00	455.00
91	EMILY, 16 IN.	1500	375.00	480.00
92	VIRGINIA	1500	375.00	425.00
S. STONE AIKEN		**CHRISTMAS TRADITIONS**		
93	TRIMMING THE TREE	2500	295.00	300.00
S. STONE AIKEN		**CHRISTMAS TREASURES**		
93	CHRISSY	CL	150.00	150.00
S. STONE AIKEN		**DAYDREAMER DOLLS**		
92	HEATHER'S DAYDREAM	CL	119.00	120.00
R./L. SCHRUBBE		**DAYS OF THE WEEK**		
92	FRIDAY'S CHILD	CL	98.00	100.00
92	MONDAY'S CHILD	CL	98.00	100.00
92	SATURDAY'S CHILD	CL	98.00	100.00
92	SUNDAY'S CHILD	CL	98.00	100.00
92	THURSDAY'S CHILD	CL	98.00	100.00
92	TUESDAY'S CHILD	CL	98.00	100.00
92	WEDNESDAY'S CHILD	CL	98.00	100.00
J. PILALLIS		**DOLLIE AND ME**		
91	DOLLIE'S FIRST STEPS	CL	160.00	160.00
GORHAM		**DOLLS OF THE MONTH**		
91	MISS APRIL	CL	79.00	130.00
91	MISS AUGUST	CL	79.00	130.00
91	MISS DECEMBER	CL	79.00	130.00
91	MISS FEBRUARY	CL	79.00	130.00
91	MISS JANUARY	CL	79.00	130.00
91	MISS JULY	CL	79.00	130.00
91	MISS JUNE	CL	79.00	130.00
91	MISS MARCH	CL	79.00	130.00
91	MISS MAY	CL	79.00	130.00
91	MISS NOVEMBER	CL	79.00	130.00
91	MISS OCTOBER	CL	79.00	130.00
91	MISS SEPTEMBER	CL	79.00	130.00
S. NAPPO		**FRIENDSHIP DOLLS**		
91	ANGELA-THE ITALIAN TRAVELER	CL	98.00	98.00
L. O'CONNOR		**FRIENDSHIP DOLLS**		
91	MEAGAN-THE IRISH TRAVELER	CL	98.00	98.00
P. SEAMAN		**FRIENDSHIP DOLLS**		
91	PEGGY-THE AMERICAN TRAVELER	CL	98.00	98.00

YR	NAME	LIMIT	ISSUE	TREND
S. UEKI			**FRIENDSHIP DOLLS**	
91	KINUKO-THE JAPANESE TRAVELER	CL	98.00	98.00
YOUNG/GERARDI			**GIFT OF DREAMS**	
91	CHRISTINA (CHRISTMAS)	CL	695.00	695.00
91	ELIZABETH	CL	495.00	495.00
91	KATHERINE	CL	495.00	495.00
91	MELISSA	CL	495.00	495.00
91	SAMANTHA	CL	495.00	495.00
S. STONE AIKEN			**GIFTS OF THE GARDEN**	
91	ALISA	CL	125.00	205.00
91	DEBORAH	CL	125.00	205.00
91	HOLLY (CHRISTMAS)	CL	150.00	205.00
91	IRENE	CL	125.00	205.00
91	JOELLE (CHRISTMAS)	CL	150.00	205.00
91	LAUREN	CL	125.00	205.00
91	MARIA	CL	125.00	205.00
91	PRISCILLA	CL	125.00	205.00
91	VALERIE	CL	125.00	205.00
AIKEN/MATTHEWS		**GORHAM BABY DOLL COLLECTION**		
87	CHRISTENING DAY	CL	245.00	300.00
87	LESLIE	CL	245.00	330.00
87	MATTHEW	CL	245.00	290.00
*			**GORHAM DOLLS**	
82	BABY IN WHITE DRESS, 18 IN.	CL	250.00	375.00
82	M. ANTON, 12 IN.	CL	125.00	175.00
82	MLLE. MARSELLA, 12 IN.	CL	125.00	275.00
82	MLLE. YVONNE, 12 IN.	CL	125.00	375.00
S. STONE AIKEN			**GORHAM DOLLS**	
81	ALEXANDRIA, 18 IN.	CL	250.00	575.00
81	CECILE, 16 IN.	CL	200.00	825.00
81	CHRISTINA, 16 IN.	CL	200.00	450.00
81	CHRISTOPHER, 19 IN.	CL	250.00	850.00
81	DANIELLE, 14 IN.	CL	150.00	340.00
81	ELENA, 14 IN.	CL	150.00	700.00
81	JILLIAN, 16 IN.	CL	200.00	425.00
81	MELINDA, 14 IN.	CL	150.00	340.00
81	ROSEMOND, 18 IN.	CL	250.00	705.00
81	STEPHANIE, 18 IN.	CL	250.00	1875.00
82	BABY IN APRICOT DRESS, 16 IN.	CL	175.00	355.00
82	BABY IN BLUE DRESS, 12 IN.	CL	150.00	365.00
82	BENJAMIN, 18 IN.	CL	200.00	580.00
82	CORRINE, 21 IN.	CL	250.00	500.00
82	ELLICE, 18 IN.	CL	200.00	590.00
82	JEREMY, 23 IN.	CL	300.00	790.00
82	KRISTIN, 23 IN.	CL	300.00	640.00
82	MELANIE, 23 IN.	CL	300.00	675.00
82	MLLE. JEANETTE, 12 IN.	CL	125.00	200.00
82	MLLE. LUCILLE, 12 IN.	CL	125.00	375.00
82	MLLE. MONIQUE, 12 IN.	CL	125.00	275.00
83	JENNIFER, 19 IN. BRIDAL DOLL	CL	325.00	775.00
85	ALEXANDER, 19 IN.	CL	275.00	450.00
85	AMELIA, 19 IN.	CL	275.00	390.00
85	GABRIELLE, 19 IN.	CL	225.00	415.00
85	LINDA, 19 IN.	CL	275.00	440.00
85	NANETTE, 19 IN.	CL	275.00	375.00
85	ODETTE, 19 IN.	CL	250.00	465.00
86	ALISSA	CL	245.00	350.00
86	EMILY, 14 IN.	CL	175.00	400.00
86	FLEUR, 19 IN.	CL	300.00	450.00
86	JESSICA	CL	195.00	325.00
86	JULIA, 16 IN.	CL	225.00	400.00
86	LAUREN, 14 IN.	CL	175.00	425.00
86	MEREDITH	CL	295.00	390.00
87	JULIET	CL	325.00	425.00
*			**HOLLY HOBBIE**	
83	BLUE GIRL, 14 IN.	CL	80.00	325.00
83	BLUE GIRL, 18 IN.	CL	115.00	395.00
83	CHRISTMAS MORNING, 14 IN.	CL	80.00	275.00
83	HEATHER, 14 IN.	CL	80.00	275.00
83	LITTLE AMY, 14 IN.	CL	80.00	275.00
83	ROBBIE, 14 IN.	CL	80.00	275.00
83	SUNDAY'S BEST, 18 IN.	CL	115.00	350.00
83	SWEET VALENTINE, 16 IN.	CL	100.00	350.00
83	YESTERDAY'S MEMORIES, 18 IN.	CL	125.00	450.00
*		**HOLLY HOBBIE CHILDHOOD MEMORIES**		
85	BEST FRIENDS	CL	45.00	125.00
85	CHRISTMAS WISHES	CL	45.00	125.00
85	FIRST DAY OF SCHOOL	CL	45.00	125.00
85	MOTHER'S HELPER	CL	45.00	125.00
*		**HOLLY HOBBIE FOR ALL SEASONS**		
84	FALL HOLLY, 12 IN.	CL	43.00	200.00
84	SPRING HOLLY, 12 IN.	CL	43.00	200.00
84	SUMMER HOLLY, 12 IN.	CL	43.00	200.00
84	WINTER HOLLY, 12 IN.	CL	43.00	200.00

YR NAME	LIMIT	ISSUE	TREND
R. TONNER	**IMAGINARY PEOPLE**		
93 MELINDA, THE TOOTH FAIRY	2900	95.00	100.00
R. TONNER	**INTERNATIONAL BABIES**		
93 NATALIA'S MATRIOSHKA	CL	95.00	100.00
B. GERARDI	**JOYFUL YEARS**		
89 KATRINA	CL	295.00	380.00
89 WILLIAM	CL	295.00	380.00
KEZI	**KEZI DOLL FOR ALL SEASONS**		
85 ADRIENNE, 16 IN.	CL	135.00	500.00
85 AMBER, 16 IN.	CL	135.00	500.00
85 ARIEL, 16 IN.	CL	135.00	500.00
85 AUBREY, 16 IN.	CL	135.00	500.00
KEZI	**KEZI GOLDEN GIFTS**		
84 CHARITY, 16 IN.	CL	85.00	185.00
84 FAITH, 18 IN.	CL	95.00	210.00
84 FELICITY, 18 IN.	CL	95.00	200.00
84 GRACE, 16 IN.	CL	85.00	175.00
84 HOPE, 16 IN.	CL	85.00	210.00
84 MERRIE, 16 IN.	CL	85.00	185.00
84 PATIENCE, 18 IN.	CL	95.00	175.00
84 PRUDENCE, 18 IN.	CL	85.00	175.00
R./L. SCHRUBBE	**KIDS WITH STUFFED TOYS**		
93 TARA AND TEDDY	OP	119.00	119.00
S. STONE AIKEN	**LEGENDARY HEROINES**		
91 GUINEVERE	1500	245.00	245.00
91 JANE EYRE	1500	245.00	245.00
91 JULIET	1500	245.00	245.00
91 LARA	1500	245.00	245.00
S. STONE AIKEN	**LES BELLES BEBES COLLECTION**		
91 CHERIE	CL	375.00	475.00
91 DESIREE	1500	375.00	445.00
93 CAMILLE	1500	375.00	425.00
S. STONE AIKEN	**LIMITED EDITION DOLLS**		
82 ALLISON, 19 IN.	CL	300.00	4250.00
83 ASHLEY, 19 IN.	CL	350.00	1000.00
84 HOLLY (CHRISTMAS), 19 IN.	CL	300.00	825.00
84 NICOLE, 19 IN.	CL	350.00	800.00
85 JOY (CHRISTMAS), 19 IN.	CL	350.00	625.00
85 LYDIA, 19 IN.	CL	550.00	1300.00
86 NOEL (CHRISTMAS), 19 IN.	CL	400.00	700.00
87 JACQUELINE, 19 IN.	CL	500.00	715.00
87 MERRIE (CHRISTMAS), 19 IN.	CL	500.00	700.00
88 ANDREW, 19 IN.	CL	475.00	740.00
88 CHRISTA (CHRISTMAS), 19 IN.	CL	550.00	1200.00
90 AMEY (10TH ANNIVERSARY EDITION)	CL	650.00	925.00
S. STONE AIKEN	**LIMITED EDITION SISTER SET**		
88 KATELIN/KATHLEEN SET	CL	550.00	875.00
S. STONE AIKEN	**LITTLE WOMEN**		
83 AMY, 16 IN.	CL	225.00	575.00
83 BETH, 16 IN.	CL	225.00	575.00
83 JO, 19 IN.	CL	275.00	675.00
83 MEG, 19 IN.	CL	275.00	695.00
L. DI LEO	**LITTLEST ANGEL DOLLS**		
92 MERRIEL	CL	50.00	50.00
R. TONNER	**NATURE'S BOUNTY**		
93 JAMIE'S FRUITFUL HARVEST	CL	95.00	100.00
L. GORDON	**PILLOW BABY DOLLS**		
93 ON THE MOVE	CL	39.00	40.00
93 SITTING PRETTY	CL	39.00	40.00
93 TICKLING TOES	CL	39.00	40.00
R. TONNER	**PORTRAIT PERFECT VICTORIAN DOLLS**		
93 PRETTY IN PEACH	2900	119.00	120.00
S. STONE AIKEN	**PRECIOUS AS PEARLS**		
86 COLETTE	CL	400.00	1400.00
87 CHARLOTTE	CL	425.00	625.00
88 CHLOE	CL	525.00	725.00
89 CASSANDRA	CL	525.00	900.00
R. SCHRUBBE	**PUPPY LOVE DOLLS**		
92 KATIE AND KYLE	CL	119.00	120.00
B. GERARDI	**SMALL WONDERS**		
88 MADELINE	CL	365.00	370.00
88 MARGUERITE	CL	425.00	430.00
88 PATINA	CL	265.00	265.00
S. STONE AIKEN	**SOUTHERN BELLES**		
85 AMANDA, 19 IN.	CL	300.00	950.00
86 VERONICA, 19 IN.	CL	325.00	750.00
87 RACHEL, 19 IN.	CL	375.00	825.00
88 CASSIE, 19 IN.	CL	500.00	675.00
E. WORRELL	**SPECIAL MOMENTS**		
91 BABY'S FIRST CHRISTMAS	CL	135.00	220.00
92 BABY'S CHRISTENING	OP	135.00	135.00
92 BABY'S FIRST BIRTHDAY	OP	135.00	135.00
92 BABY'S FIRST STEPS	CL	135.00	175.00

YR	NAME	LIMIT	ISSUE	TREND
R. SCHRUBBE			**SPORTING KIDS**	
93	UP AT BAT	CL	50.00	50.00
M. MURPHY			**TENDER HEARTS**	
93	SAYING GRACE	CL	119.00	120.00
L. DI LEO			**TIMES TO TREASURE**	
90	STORYTIME	CL	195.00	200.00
91	BEDTIME	CL	195.00	200.00
92	STORYTIME	OP	195.00	195.00
93	CRADLETIME	OP	195.00	195.00
93	PLAYTIME	CL	195.00	200.00
P. VALENTINE			**VALENTINE LADIES**	
87	ANABELLA	CL	145.00	395.00
87	ELIZABETH	CL	145.00	450.00
87	JANE	CL	145.00	350.00
87	LEE ANN	CL	145.00	325.00
87	MARIANNA	CL	160.00	400.00
87	PATRICE	CL	145.00	325.00
87	REBECCA	CL	145.00	325.00
87	ROSANNE	CL	145.00	325.00
87	SYLVIA	CL	160.00	350.00
88	FELICIA	CL	225.00	400.00
88	JUDITH ANNE	CL	195.00	325.00
88	MARIA THERESA	CL	225.00	275.00
88	PRISCILLA	CL	195.00	325.00
89	JULIANNA	CL	225.00	275.00
89	ROSE	CL	225.00	275.00
B. GERARDI			**VICTORIAN CAMEO COLLECTION**	
90	VICTORIA	1500	375.00	375.00
91	ALEXANDRA	CL	375.00	375.00
S. STONE AIKEN			**VICTORIAN CHILDREN**	
92	SARA'S TEA TIME	1000	495.00	550.00
93	CATCHING BUTTERFLIES	1000	495.00	495.00
E. WOODHOUSE			**VICTORIAN COLLECTION**	
92	VICTORIA'S JUBILEE	YR	295.00	295.00
J. PILLALIS			**VICTORIAN FLOWER GIRLS**	
93	ROSE	CL	95.00	100.00

GUND INC.
*

96	MAJOR BEARKIN	700	**MOHAIR COLLECTION**	
			250.00	250.00
R.S. RAIFFE			**SIGNATURE COLLECTION**	
93	ANNIE ARCTIC	600	220.00	220.00
93	GOLD DUST	650	180.00	180.00
93	SWEET THING	500	150.00	150.00
93	THREAD BEAR	650	150.00	150.00
93	WEE WILLIE	750	100.00	100.00
94	AZURINE	700	180.00	180.00
94	BLACK MAGIC	700	180.00	180.00
94	HARRY HEARTTHROB	850	150.00	150.00
94	ROCKAFELLA	600	300.00	300.00
95	BEARNARD	350	180.00	180.00
95	BLACKBEARD	350	300.00	300.00
95	DUNBEARY	350	300.00	300.00
95	GULLIVER	250	400.00	400.00
95	O'BEARIGAN	450	140.00	140.00
95	PEANUT BUTTER	400	180.00	180.00
96	BEARBUSHKA	500	200.00	200.00
96	HUGH MONGUS	310	400.00	400.00
96	LITTLE BEAR BLUE	450	250.00	250.00
96	PAWTHORNE	540	150.00	150.00
96	SOMETHING'S BRUIN	425	350.00	350.00

H & G STUDIOS

B. BURKE			**BIRTHDAY PARTY**	
90	SUZIE	500	695.00	695.00
B. BURKE			**BRENDA BURKE DOLLS**	
89	ADELAINE	25	1,795.00	3600.00
89	ALEXANDRA	125	995.00	2000.00
89	ALICIA	125	895.00	1800.00
89	AMANDA	25	1,995.00	6000.00
89	ANGELICA	50	1,495.00	3000.00
89	ARABELLE	500	695.00	1400.00
89	BEATRICE	85	2,395.00	2395.00
89	BETHANY	45	2,995.00	2995.00
89	BRITTANY	75	2,695.00	2695.00
90	BELINDA	12	3,695.00	3695.00
91	CHARLOTTE	20	2,395.00	2395.00
91	CLARISSA	15	3,595.00	3595.00
91	SLEIGH RIDE	20	3,695.00	3695.00
91	TENDER LOVE	25	3,295.00	3295.00
92	DOROTHEA	500	395.00	400.00
93	GIOVANNA	1	7,800.00	7800.00
93	MELISSA	1	7,750.00	7750.00

YR	NAME	LIMIT	ISSUE	TREND
	B. BURKE		**CHILDHOOD MEMORIES**	
89	EARLY DAYS	95	2,595.00	2595.00
91	PLAYTIME	35	2,795.00	2795.00
	B. BURKE		**DANCING THROUGH THE AGES**	
90	MINUET	95	2,495.00	2495.00
	B. BURKE		**THE FOUR SEASONS**	
90	SPRING	125	1,995.00	1995.00

HALLMARK

YR	NAME	LIMIT	ISSUE	TREND
	E. HIBEL		**GRANDMA'S ATTIC**	
89	MELANIE	CL	139.00	180.00
91	KATIE	CL	139.00	150.00
	M. ENGELBREIT		**MARY ENGELBREIT'S FRIENDSHIP GARDEN**	
93	JOSEPHINE 6000QHG5003 PORCELAIN DOLL	12500	60.00	60.00
93	LOUISA 6500QHG5002 PORCELAIN DOLL	12500	65.00	70.00
93	MARGARET 6000QHG5001 PORCELAIN DOLL	12500	60.00	60.00
	J. GREENE		**VICTORIAN MEMORIES**	
92	ABIGAIL 1QHG1019	4500	125.00	130.00
92	ABNER 1QHG1018	4500	110.00	110.00
92	ALICE 1QHG1020	4500	125.00	130.00
92	EMMA/2500QHG1016 MINIATURE DOLL	9500	25.00	30.00
92	KATHERINE 1QHG1017	1200	150.00	150.00
92	OLIVIA 1QHG1021	4500	125.00	130.00
93	BABY DOLL BEATRICE 2000QHG1029	RT	20.00	25.00
93	HANNAH 1QHG1030	2500	130.00	130.00

HAMILTON COLLECTION

YR	NAME	LIMIT	ISSUE	TREND
*			**ANTIQUE DOLL COLLECTION**	
90	COLETTE	OP	195.00	195.00
	B. VAN BOXEL		**A CHILD'S MENAGERIE**	
93	BECKY	OP	69.00	70.00
93	CARRIE	OP	69.00	70.00
94	MANDY	OP	69.00	70.00
	A. WILLIAMS		**ABBIE WILLIAMS DOLL COLLECTION**	
92	MOLLY	CL	155.00	205.00
*			**ANNUAL CONNOISSEUR DOLL**	
92	LARA	7450	295.00	300.00
*			**ANTIQUE DOLL COLLECTION**	
89	NICOLE	CL	195.00	195.00
91	KATRINA	OP	195.00	195.00
91	LISETTE	OP	195.00	230.00
	B. PARKER		**BABY PORTRAIT DOLLS**	
91	MELISSA	CL	135.00	180.00
92	BETHANY	OP	135.00	140.00
92	JENNA	CL	135.00	200.00
93	MINDY	OP	135.00	140.00
	C. HEATH ORANGE		**BELLES OF THE COUNTRYSIDE**	
92	ERIN	OP	135.00	140.00
92	ROSE	OP	135.00	140.00
93	LORNA	OP	135.00	140.00
94	GWYN	OP	135.00	140.00
	B.P. GUTMANN		**BESSIE PEASE GUTMANN DOLL COLLECTION**	
89	HE WON'T BITE	CL	135.00	135.00
89	LOVE IS BLIND	CL	135.00	165.00
91	FIRST DANCING LESSON	OP	195.00	200.00
91	GOOD MORNING	OP	195.00	200.00
91	LOVE AT FIRST SIGHT	OP	195.00	200.00
91	VIRGINIA	OP	135.00	135.00
	C. MARSCHNER		**BEST BUDDIES**	
94	JODIE	OP	69.00	70.00
*			**BOEHM DOLLS**	
94	ELENA	OP	155.00	160.00
	BOEHM		**BRIDAL ELEGANCE**	
94	CAMILLE	OP	195.00	200.00
*			**BRIDE DOLLS**	
91	PORTRAIT OF INNOCENCE	OP	195.00	200.00
92	PORTRAIT OF LOVELINESS	OP	195.00	200.00
	P. RYAN BROOKS		**BROOKS WOODEN DOLLS**	
93	ARE YOU THE EASTER BUNNY?	15000	135.00	140.00
93	WAITING FOR SANTA	15000	135.00	140.00
94	BE MY VALENTINE	OP	135.00	140.00
	C. MATHER		**CATHERINE MATHER DOLLS**	
93	JUSTINE	15000	155.00	160.00
	C. WOODIE		**CENTRAL PARK SKATERS**	
91	CENTRAL PARK SKATERS	OP	245.00	250.00
*			**CHILDREN TO CHERISH**	
91	A GIFT OF BEAUTY	OP	135.00	140.00
91	A GIFT OF INNOCENCE	YR	135.00	140.00
	C.M. ROLFE		**CINDY MARSCHNER ROLFE DOLLS**	
93	JULIE	OP	95.00	100.00
93	KAYLA	OP	95.00	100.00
93	SHANNON	OP	95.00	100.00
94	JANEY	OP	95.00	100.00

YR	NAME	LIMIT	ISSUE	TREND
C.W. DEREK		CONNIE WALSER DEREK BABY DOLLS		
90	JESSICA	CL	155.00	250.00
91	AMANDA	OP	155.00	160.00
91	ANDREW	OP	155.00	155.00
91	SARA	CL	155.00	185.00
92	SAMANTHA	OP	155.00	160.00
C.W. DEREK		CONNIE WALSER DEREK BABY DOLLS II		
92	BETH	OP	95.00	100.00
92	STEPHANIE	OP	95.00	100.00
C.W. DEREK		CONNIE WALSER DEREK DOLLS		
92	BABY JESSICA	OP	75.00	80.00
93	BABY SARA	OP	75.00	80.00
M. SNYDER		DADDY'S LITTLE GIRL		
92	LINDSAY	OP	95.00	100.00
93	CASSIE	OP	95.00	100.00
93	DANA	OP	95.00	100.00
C.W. DEREK		DEREK TODDLERS		
94	JESSIE	OP	79.00	80.00
A. BERWICK		DOLLS BY AUTUMN BERWICK		
93	LAURA	OP	135.00	140.00
K. MCKEE		DOLLS BY KAY MCKEE		
92	ROBIN	OP	135.00	140.00
92	SHY VIOLET	CL	135.00	205.00
93	KATIE DID IT!	OP	135.00	140.00
93	RYAN	OP	135.00	140.00
A. ELEKFY		DOLLS OF AMERICA'S COLONIAL HERITAGE		
86	KATRINA	OP	55.00	60.00
86	NICOLE	OP	55.00	60.00
87	COLLEEN	OP	55.00	60.00
87	MARIA	OP	55.00	60.00
87	PRISCILLA	OP	55.00	60.00
88	GRETCHEN	OP	55.00	60.00
E. CAMPBELL		ELAINE CAMPBELL DOLLS		
94	EMMA	OP	95.00	100.00
*		FIRST RECITAL		
93	HILLARY	OP	135.00	140.00
94	OLIVIA	OP	135.00	140.00
H. KISH		HELEN KISH II DOLLS		
92	VANESSA	OP	135.00	140.00
H. KISH		HELEN KISH III DOLLS		
94	JORDAN	OP	95.00	100.00
U. LEPP		HOLIDAY CAROLLERS		
92	JOY	OP	155.00	160.00
93	NOEL	OP	155.00	160.00
*		I LOVE LUCY/PORCELAIN		
90	LUCY	CL	95.00	225.00
91	RICKY	CL	95.00	280.00
92	QUEEN OF THE GYPSIES	CL	95.00	165.00
92	VITAMEATAVEGAMIN	CL	95.00	125.00
*		I LOVE LUCY/VINYL		
88	ETHEL	CL	40.00	185.00
88	FRED	CL	40.00	140.00
90	LUCY	CL	40.00	140.00
91	RICKY	CL	40.00	160.00
92	QUEEN OF THE GYPSIES	OP	40.00	45.00
92	VITAMEATAVEGAMIN	OP	40.00	45.00
L. COBABE		I'M SO PROUD DOLL COLLECTION		
92	CHRISTINA	OP	95.00	100.00
93	JILL	OP	95.00	100.00
94	SHELLY	OP	95.00	100.00
94	TAMMY	OP	95.00	100.00
C. WOODIE		INTERNATIONAL CHILDREN		
91	ANASTASIA	OP	50.00	50.00
91	ANGELINA	OP	50.00	50.00
91	MIKO	CL	50.00	55.00
92	LIAN	OP	50.00	50.00
92	LISA	OP	50.00	50.00
92	MONIQUE	OP	50.00	50.00
J. ZIDJUNAS		JANE ZIDJUNAS PARTY DOLLS		
91	KELLY	OP	135.00	140.00
92	KATIE	OP	135.00	140.00
93	MEREDITH	OP	135.00	140.00
J. ZIDJUNAS		JANE ZIDJUNAS TODDLER DOLLS		
91	JENNIFER	OP	135.00	135.00
91	MEGAN	OP	135.00	160.00
92	AMY	OP	135.00	140.00
92	KIMBERLY	OP	135.00	140.00
J. WILSON		JEANNE WILSON DOLLS		
94	PRISCILLA	OP	155.00	160.00
C. JOHNSTON		JOHNSTON COWGIRLS		
94	SAVANNAH	OP	79.00	80.00
*		JOIN THE PARADE		
92	BETSY	OP	50.00	50.00

Miss Muffet *was the third issue in the Children of Mother Goose collection from the Edwin M. Knowles China Co. Crafted by Yolanda Bello, the doll sold for $63 in 1990 when the edition closed.*

Bride Bunny *and* Groom Bunny, *each released in 1993 by Annalee Mobilitee Dolls Inc., celebrate their blessed union.*

A porcelain doll by Jan Hagara, May *is dressed in pink from her wide-brimmed hat to her lacy pantaloons.*

Rose, Who is Love *was the first issue in the Romantic Flower Maidens collection by the W.S. George China Co. The M. Roderick work was issued in 1988 for $87.*

YR	NAME	LIMIT	ISSUE	TREND
94	PEGGY	OP	55.00	60.00
94	SANDY	OP	55.00	60.00
J. GROBBEN				
	JOKE GROBBEN DOLLS			
92	HEATHER	OP	69.00	70.00
93	BRIANNA	OP	69.00	70.00
93	KATHLEEN	OP	69.00	70.00
94	BRIDGET	OP	69.00	70.00
H. KISH				
	JUST LIKE MOM			
91	ASHLEY	CL	135.00	230.00
92	ELIZABETH	OP	135.00	140.00
92	HANNAH	OP	135.00	140.00
93	MARGARET	OP	135.00	140.00
K. MCKEE				
	KAY MCKEE KLOWNS			
93	DREAMER, THE	15000	155.00	160.00
S. KUCK				
	KUCK FAIRY			
94	TOOTH FAIRY	OP	135.00	140.00
L. COBABE				
	LAURA COBABE DOLLS			
92	AMBER	OP	195.00	200.00
92	BROOKE	OP	195.00	200.00
L. COBABE				
	LAURA COBABE DOLLS II			
93	KRISTEN	OP	75.00	80.00
L. COBABE				
	LAURA COBABE TALL DOLLS			
94	CASSANDRA	OP	195.00	200.00
94	TAYLOR	OP	195.00	200.00
S./J. HOFFMANN				
	LITTLE RASCALS			
92	SPANKY	OP	75.00	80.00
93	ALFALFA	OP	75.00	80.00
94	BUCKWHEAT	OP	75.00	80.00
94	DARLA	OP	75.00	80.00
94	STYMIE	OP	75.00	80.00
J. ESTEBAN				
	LITTLEST MEMBERS OF THE WEDDING			
93	MATTHEW & MELANIE	OP	195.00	200.00
M.H. BOGART				
	MAUD HUMPHREY BOGART DOLL COLLECTION			
89	PLAYING BRIDE	CL	135.00	155.00
90	FIRST LESSON, THE	CL	135.00	150.00
90	FIRST PARTY	CL	135.00	140.00
91	LITTLE CAPTIVE	OP	135.00	140.00
91	SEAMSTRESS	CL	135.00	150.00
92	KITTY'S BATH	OP	135.00	140.00
92	PLAYING BRIDESMAID	CL	195.00	230.00
B. PARKER				
	PARKER-LEVI TODDLERS			
92	COURTNEY	OP	135.00	140.00
92	MELODY	OP	135.00	140.00
P. PARKINS				
	PARKINS PORTRAITS			
93	KELSEY	OP	79.00	80.00
93	LAUREN	OP	79.00	80.00
94	CASSIDY	OP	79.00	80.00
94	MORGAN	OP	79.00	80.00
P. PARKINS				
	PARKINS TREASURES			
92	DOROTHY	CL	55.00	60.00
92	TIFFANY	CL	55.00	60.00
93	CHARLOTTE	OP	55.00	60.00
93	CYNTHIA	OP	55.00	60.00
P. PARKINS				
	PHYLLIS PARKINS DOLLS			
92	SWAN PRINCESS	9850	195.00	200.00
J. ESTEBAN				
	PICNIC IN THE PARK			
91	REBECCA	OP	155.00	160.00
92	EMILY	OP	155.00	160.00
92	VICTORIA	OP	155.00	160.00
93	BENJAMIN	OP	155.00	160.00
*				
	PROUD INDIAN NATION			
92	NAVAJO LITTLE ONE	CL	95.00	180.00
93	AUTUMN TREAT	OP	95.00	100.00
93	DRESSED UP FOR THE POW WOW	OP	95.00	100.00
94	OUT WITH MAMA'S FLOCK	OP	95.00	100.00
*				
	ROYAL BEAUTY DOLLS			
91	CHEN MAI	OP	195.00	200.00
*				
	RUSSIAN CZARRA DOLLS			
91	ALEXANDRA	CL	295.00	350.00
S. KUCK				
	SANDRA KUCK DOLLS			
93	A KISS GOODNIGHT	OP	79.00	80.00
94	TEACHING TEDDY	OP	79.00	80.00
C.W. DEREK				
	SANTA'S LITTLE HELPER			
92	NICHOLAS	OP	155.00	160.00
93	HOPE	OP	155.00	160.00
T. MURAKAMI				
	SONGS OF THE SEASONS HAKATA DOLL COLLECTION			
85	AUTUMN SONG MAIDEN	9800	75.00	80.00
85	SPRING SONG MAIDEN	9800	75.00	80.00
85	SUMMER SONG MAIDEN	9800	75.00	80.00
85	WINTER SONG MAIDEN	9800	75.00	80.00
E. DAUB				
	STAR TREK DOLL COLLECTION			
88	CAPTAIN KIRK	CL	75.00	125.00
88	MR. SPOCK	CL	75.00	155.00

YR	NAME	LIMIT	ISSUE	TREND
89	DR. MCCOY	CL	75.00	125.00
89	SCOTTY	CL	75.00	125.00
90	CHEKOV	CL	75.00	125.00
90	SULU	CL	75.00	125.00
91	UHURA	CL	75.00	125.00
L. DI LEO				**STORYBOOK DOLLS**
91	ALICE IN WONDERLAND	OP	75.00	80.00
V. TURNER		**THROUGH THE EYES OF VIRGINIA TURNER**		
92	DANIELLE	OP	95.00	100.00
92	MICHELLE	CL	95.00	130.00
93	WENDY	OP	95.00	100.00
94	DAWN	OP	95.00	100.00
D. SCHURIG		**TODDLER DAYS DOLL COLLECTION**		
92	ERICA	OP	95.00	100.00
93	DARLENE	OP	95.00	100.00
94	KAREN	OP	95.00	100.00
V. TURNER				**TREASURED TODDLERS**
92	WHITNEY	OP	95.00	100.00
93	NATALIE	OP	95.00	100.00
C.W. DEREK				**VICTORIAN TREASURES**
92	KATHERINE	OP	155.00	160.00
93	MADELINE	OP	155.00	160.00
*				**WOODEN DOLLS**
91	GRETCHEN	9850	225.00	280.00
91	HEIDI	9850	225.00	225.00
D. SCHURIG				**YEAR ROUND FUN**
92	ALLISON	OP	95.00	100.00
93	CHRISTY	OP	95.00	100.00
93	PAULA	OP	95.00	100.00
94	KAYLIE	OP	95.00	100.00
D. ZOLAN				**ZOLAN DOLLS**
91	A CHRISTMAS PRAYER	CL	95.00	255.00
92	QUIET TIME	OP	95.00	100.00
92	RAINY DAY PALS	OP	95.00	100.00
92	WINTER ANGEL	OP	95.00	100.00
93	FOR YOU	OP	95.00	100.00
93	THINKER, THE	OP	95.00	100.00
*				**ZOLAN DOUBLE DOLLS**
93	FIRST KISS	OP	135.00	140.00

HAMILTON GIFTS

M.H. BOGART		**MAUD HUMPHREY BOGART PORCELAIN DOLLS**		
91	MY FIRST PARTY H5686	OP	135.00	135.00
91	PLAYING BRIDE H5618	OP	135.00	135.00
91	SARAH H5617	OP	37.00	37.00
91	SUSANNA H5648	OP	37.00	37.00

JAN HAGARA COLLECTABLES

J. HAGARA				
95	ADDIE WITH PRINCESS 23 IN.	85	2,000.00	2000.00
95	JOSEPH BLUE 12 IN.	150	250.00	250.00
95	JOSEPH PINK 12 IN.	150	250.00	250.00
95	JUNE 12 IN.	300	250.00	235.00
95	KELTON 8 IN.	300	300.00	235.00
95	MAY 12 IN.	300	250.00	250.00
J. HAGARA				**PHILLIPS COUSINS**
95	DEBRA 15 IN.	250	425.00	400.00
J. HAGARA				**VICTORIAN CHILDREN**
*	ADRIANNE	*	*	198.00
*	AMANDA	*	*	250.00
*	AMY	*	*	125.00
*	ANN MARIE	*	*	350.00
*	ASHLEY	*	*	125.00
*	BONNIE	*	*	450.00
*	CLARA	*	*	475.00
*	CRISTINA	*	*	100.00
*	DACY	*	*	490.00
*	JESSICA	*	*	650.00
*	JIMMY	*	*	200.00
*	JODY	*	*	450.00
*	MATTIE	*	*	550.00
*	MEG	*	*	245.00
*	MICHAEL	*	*	650.00
*	PAIGE	*	*	1200.00
*	SHARICE	*	*	200.00
*	SHELDON	*	*	490.00
*	SHELLEY	*	*	475.00
*	TINA	*	*	420.00
*	TRACY	*	*	135.00

JAN MCLEAN ORIGINALS

J. MCLEAN		**FLOWERS OF THE HEART COLLECTION**		
90	PANSY	100	2,200.00	2700.00
90	POPPY	100	2,200.00	2800.00

YR	NAME	LIMIT	ISSUE	TREND
91	MARIGOLD	100	2,400.00	2700.00
91	PRIMROSE	100	2,500.00	2900.00
J. MCLEAN			**JAN MCLEAN ORIGINALS**	
90	PHOEBE I	25	2,700.00	3600.00
91	LUCREZIA	15	6,000.00	6000.00

JOHANNES ZOOK ORIGINALS
J. ZOOK

YR	NAME	LIMIT	ISSUE	TREND
93	ADRIANNE	500	198.00	240.00
93	ALYSSA	500	204.00	286.00
93	ANGEL GABRIEL	1000	250.00	303.00
93	BREANNA	500	190.00	230.00
93	BROOKE	1000	170.00	206.00
93	CALVIN CLOWN	500	198.00	240.00
93	CANDY CANE	*	164.00	198.00
93	CHRISTMAS CAROL	500	226.00	273.00
93	CLAIRE	1000	194.00	235.00
93	CODY	1000	194.00	235.00
93	COLLETTE	500	198.00	240.00
93	DEANNE	100	170.00	206.00
93	DENISE	250	198.00	240.00
93	DIANNA	100	170.00	206.00
93	FRANCESCA	250	220.00	266.00
93	JASMINE	250	252.00	305.00
93	JOEY	500	198.00	240.00
93	KANIKA	1000	220.00	266.00
93	LITTLE MISS MUFFET	500	188.00	227.00
93	MARISSA	1000	170.00	206.00
93	MEREDITH	500	216.00	261.00
93	MONIKA	500	198.00	240.00
93	ROCKY	500	172.00	208.00
93	ROXANNE	500	172.00	208.00
93	SISSY	500	272.00	329.00
93	TOOTH FAIRY	500	198.00	240.00
93	VALERIE	500	240.00	290.00
94	ANALISSA	350	210.00	231.00
94	ANNETTE	100	230.00	253.00
94	ANNIE	25	148.00	163.00
94	ATHENA	500	198.00	218.00
94	BABY ELF	250	198.00	218.00
94	CHERRY	100	114.00	125.00
94	CHRISTMAS NOELLE	500	224.00	246.00
94	COOKIE	350	170.00	187.00
94	CORY	350	170.00	187.00
94	COWBOY	25	172.00	189.00
94	CYNTHIA	100	194.00	213.00
94	DANIEL BOONE	500	250.00	275.00
94	DANIELLE	500	188.00	207.00
94	EMMY	500	220.00	242.00
94	GOOD NIGHT KISS	500	158.00	174.00
94	GWEN	125	198.00	218.00
94	KAREEM	500	198.00	218.00
94	KATRINA	500	198.00	218.00
94	KAYLA	1000	198.00	218.00
94	LITTLE FEATHER	100	280.00	308.00
94	MELINDA	1000	190.00	209.00
94	MERCEDES	1000	218.00	240.00
94	NURSE BETTE	500	184.00	202.00
94	POLLYANNA	500	198.00	218.00
94	SHARON	1000	190.00	209.00
94	SHAYNA	1000	190.00	209.00
94	SHELLY	100	198.00	218.00
94	SOPHIE	500	198.00	218.00
94	STARR	25	150.00	165.00
94	TRISHA	500	198.00	218.00
95	ANGIE	RT	190.00	190.00
95	BETHANY	RT	210.00	210.00
95	BRENT	RT	230.00	230.00
95	CAROLYN	RT	210.00	210.00
95	CELESTE	RT	230.00	230.00
95	CHRISTINA	RT	398.00	398.00
95	CHRISTMAS TWINS/SET	RT	430.00	430.00
95	DESIREE	RT	198.00	198.00
95	GIANNA	RT	250.00	250.00
95	JAKE	RT	230.00	230.00
95	JARED	RT	198.00	198.00
95	KORTINEE ROSE	RT	218.00	218.00
95	LESLIE	RT	198.00	198.00
95	LIL DEVIL	RT	200.00	200.00
95	LIZZY	RT	198.00	198.00
95	MARY JO	RT	190.00	190.00
95	MYCELLE	RT	170.00	170.00
95	NANCY MAY	RT	190.00	190.00
95	NATALIE & NATHAN/SET	RT	398.00	398.00
95	NICHOLETTE	RT	210.00	210.00

YR	NAME	LIMIT	ISSUE	TREND
95	PAIGE	RT	210.00	210.00
95	PAMELA SUE	RT	210.00	210.00
95	PENNY	RT	240.00	240.00
95	PRESTON	RT	290.00	290.00
95	SCARECROW	RT	290.00	290.00
95	SIERRA	RT	210.00	210.00
95	SNOW BONNY	RT	198.00	198.00
95	TREVOR	RT	180.00	180.00
96	ARIEL	RT	212.00	212.00
96	AUSTIN	RT	394.00	394.00
96	BRANDON & BREA/SET	RT	374.00	374.00
96	BRENNAN	RT	190.00	190.00
96	CHRIS	RT	198.00	198.00
96	CHRISTMAS BELLE	RT	308.00	308.00
96	CORJASHON	RT	190.00	190.00
96	DOTTIE	RT	198.00	198.00
96	GINA	RT	220.00	220.00
96	HALEY	500	234.00	234.00
96	JAMAL	250	216.00	216.00
96	JANEA	500	224.00	224.00
96	JUAN	500	190.00	190.00
96	KATY	500	198.00	198.00
96	KEIKO	500	190.00	190.00
96	KEITH	250	212.00	212.00
96	KELSEY	1000	270.00	270.00
96	KEVIN	1000	246.00	246.00
96	LABRETT	500	212.00	212.00
96	LEXUS	150	346.00	370.00
96	LINDA	250	202.00	202.00
96	MAGGIE	250	214.00	214.00
96	MARIKO	500	212.00	212.00
96	PHOENIX	1000	256.00	256.00
96	SCOTTIE	500	170.00	170.00
96	SHASTIN	500	212.00	212.00
96	TOMMY	500	206.00	206.00
98	ANGELO	350	190.00	190.00
98	BECCA	350	198.00	198.00
98	CHELSEA	250	194.00	194.00
98	CHRISTMAS HOPE	350	278.00	278.00
98	DYLAN	250	260.00	260.00
98	JOHANNA	500	298.00	298.00
98	LADONNA	350	216.00	216.00
98	LUCY	CL	184.00	184.00
98	MADISON	250	218.00	218.00
98	MEGAN	350	210.00	210.00
98	PATTI	350	192.00	192.00
98	ROXANNE	250	204.00	204.00
98	SASHA	350	224.00	224.00
98	SHELBY	500	256.00	256.00
98	TIN MAN	200	198.00	198.00

J. ZOOK   **AMISH SERIES**

YR	NAME	LIMIT	ISSUE	TREND
93	JACOB	500	158.00	191.00
94	GRACE	500	220.00	242.00
95	RUTH	RT	190.00	190.00
96	DAVID	RT	164.00	164.00
98	IAN	250	192.00	192.00

J. ZOOK   **CAREER SERIES**

YR	NAME	LIMIT	ISSUE	TREND
94	FIREMAN GREG	250	224.00	224.00
95	POLICEMAN GABE	RT	230.00	230.00
96	TEACHER LADY	500	284.00	284.00
98	CHEF PAT	350	208.00	208.00

J. ZOOK   **CHILDREN OF THE NATION**

YR	NAME	LIMIT	ISSUE	TREND
94	AMERICA	500	188.00	207.00
95	NANOOK OF THE NORTH	RT	220.00	220.00
96	PIA	1000	210.00	210.00
98	KIRSTEN	500	272.00	272.00

J. ZOOK   **EXCLUSIVE FOR IDEX**

YR	NAME	LIMIT	ISSUE	TREND
96	ANNABETH	50	198.00	198.00

J. ZOOK   **EXCLUSIVE FOR SHOW**

YR	NAME	LIMIT	ISSUE	TREND
95	CHERISH	RT	165.00	165.00
95	KATARINA	RT	230.00	230.00

J. ZOOK   **EXCLUSIVE FOR STORE**

YR	NAME	LIMIT	ISSUE	TREND
95	BABY DARLING	RT	199.00	199.00
95	BABY DEAR	RT	199.00	199.00
95	BABY PRECIOUS	RT	199.00	199.00
95	SCARLETT	RT	199.00	199.00

J. ZOOK   **EXCLUSIVE FOR TOY FAIR**

YR	NAME	LIMIT	ISSUE	TREND
95	ROSEMARY	RT	240.00	240.00
96	CHANTEL	250	270.00	270.00

J. ZOOK   **FLOWER SERIES**

YR	NAME	LIMIT	ISSUE	TREND
95	SUNFLOWER	RT	220.00	220.00
96	PANSY	1000	274.00	271.00
98	TULIP	150	206.00	206.00

YR NAME	LIMIT	ISSUE	TREND
J. ZOOK		**HALLOWEEN SERIES**	
93 TOMMY TURTLE	150	300.00	363.00
94 DONNIE DINOSAUR	150	250.00	275.00
94 HERBIE HOLSTEIN	150	250.00	275.00
J. ZOOK		**STORYBOOK SERIES**	
93 LITTLE RED RIDING HOOD	1000	244.00	295.00
94 GOLDILOCKS & BABY BEAR	350	254.00	279.00
95 CINDERELLA	RT	270.00	270.00
96 HEIDI	1000	254.00	254.00
98 JACK	350	188.00	188.00
98 JILL	350	208.00	208.00

KAISER
*

90 AMANDA, 17 IN.	1000	74.00	82.00
90 AMY, 19 IN.	1000	98.00	106.00
90 ANN, 24 IN.	1000	128.00	138.00
90 ASHLEY, 19 IN.	1000	98.00	106.00
90 ELIZABETH, 19 IN.	1000	98.00	106.00
90 HEATHER, 22 IN.	1000	116.00	126.00
90 JENNIFER, 22 IN.	1000	116.00	126.00
90 JESSICA, 22 IN.	1000	116.00	126.00
90 JILL, 24 IN.	1000	128.00	138.00
90 KELLY, 19 IN.	1000	98.00	106.00
90 KRISTY, 24 IN.	1000	128.00	138.00
90 LAURA, 24 IN.	1000	128.00	138.00
90 NEWBORN/CHRISTENING DRESS, 17 IN.	1000	74.00	82.00
90 NICOLE, 17 IN.	1000	74.00	82.00
90 SARAH, 22 IN.	1000	116.00	126.00
90 SUSAN, 17 IN.	1000	74.00	82.00

KURT S. ADLER INC.

J. MOSTROM		**FLEUR-DE-LIS**	
97 ALEXANDRIA IN PLUM	OP	20.00	20.00
97 BARBARA WITH MUFF	OP	30.00	30.00
97 BONNIE IN RIBBONS	OP	21.00	21.00
97 CAROLLING JANE WITH BOOK	OP	22.00	22.00
97 CELESTE THE GARDEN ANGEL	OP	45.00	45.00
97 CHARLOTTE WITH HAT & CAPE	OP	22.00	22.00
97 GEORGE WITH BOX	OP	22.00	22.00
97 JENNY LIND	OP	28.00	28.00
97 JONATHAN WITH HORN	OP	22.00	22.00
97 KATHRYN WITH CAPE	OP	22.00	22.00
97 LILAC FAIRY	OP	22.00	22.00
97 LILY FAIRY	OP	22.00	22.00
97 MARISSA IN MAUVE	OP	20.00	20.00
97 MELISSA IN LACE	OP	21.00	21.00
97 REBECCA BURGUNDY SKATER	OP	32.00	32.00
97 ROSE FAIRY	OP	22.00	22.00
97 SANDRA WITH BOX	OP	22.00	22.00
J. MOSTROM		**ROYAL HERITAGE COLLECTION**	
* EDMUND	RT	32.00	32.00
* PAULINE	RT	32.00	32.00
93 ANASTASIA J5746	3000	125.00	125.00
93 GOOD KING WENCESLAS W2928	2000	130.00	130.00
93 MEDIEVAL KING OF CHRISTMAS W2981	RT	390.00	400.00
94 NICHOLAS ON SKATES J5750	3000	120.00	120.00
94 SASHA ON SKATES J5749	3000	130.00	130.00
J. MOSTROM		**SMALL WONDERS**	
95 AMERICA-HOLLIE BLUE W3162	OP	30.00	30.00
95 AMERICA-TEXAS TYLER W3162	OP	30.00	30.00
95 IRELAND-CATHLEEN W3082	OP	28.00	28.00
95 IRELAND-MICHAEL W3082	OP	28.00	28.00
95 KWANZA-MUFARO W3161	OP	28.00	28.00
95 KWANZA-SHANI W3161	OP	28.00	28.00
J. MOSTROM		**WHEN I GROW UP**	
95 DR. BROWN W3079	OP	27.00	27.00
95 FREDDY THE FIREMAN W3163	OP	28.00	28.00
95 MELISSA THE TEACHER W3081	OP	28.00	28.00
95 NURSE NANCY W3079	OP	27.00	27.00
95 SCOTT THE GOLFER W3080	OP	28.00	28.00

L.L. KNICKERBOCKER CO. INC.

M. COSTA			
92 DIANA/BLOWING DANDELIONS C11246	1500	117.00	117.00
A. JACKSON			
93 ALYSSA/GIRL ON SWING C1974	2500	158.00	158.00
M. OSMOND			
97 MARIE OSMOND DOLL CARE KIT	OP	45.00	45.00
J. ANTONELLI		**ANGEL**	
97 ANGELA	20000	39.00	39.00
L. DE MENT		**ANGEL**	
97 FAITH	YR	119.00	119.00

YR NAME	LIMIT	ISSUE	TREND
B. KING			ANGEL
97 ANGEL HEART	20000	59.00	59.00
97 BAMBINA	20000	29.00	29.00
B. WHEELER			ANGEL
97 ROSETA- ANGEL ORNAMENT	20000	49.00	49.00
*		ANNETTE FUNICELLO BEARS	
95 MARY LOU	5000	26.00	26.00
95 SILVER LINING	5000	29.00	29.00
L. APPLEBERRY		ANNETTE FUNICELLO BEARS	
96 EMMY	2500	50.00	50.00
96 PEACH FUZZ	2500	29.00	29.00
C. BLACK		ANNETTE FUNICELLO BEARS	
95 GRAPE SUZETTE	2500	35.00	35.00
95 TIZZIE TEA CUP	3000	45.00	45.00
96 CHUBS	1500	59.00	59.00
96 SHELLY	2500	39.00	39.00
96 STRAWBERRY JAM	2500	39.00	39.00
G. BUTTITTA		ANNETTE FUNICELLO BEARS	
95 CELESTE	YR	119.00	119.00
96 MITZI	500	49.00	49.00
96 PRECIOUS & BAILEY	2500	46.00	46.00
96 VIRGINIA	1500	49.00	49.00
K. CLARKE		ANNETTE FUNICELLO BEARS	
95 DOLLY	2500	49.00	49.00
95 RUDY	3000	25.00	25.00
95 SHARON	2500	47.00	47.00
96 BAD HAIR BEAR	3000	39.00	39.00
96 KAREN	1500	46.25	47.00
96 NIKKI	2500	50.00	50.00
L. DEMERIT		ANNETTE FUNICELLO BEARS	
96 FAITH	YR	119.00	119.00
J. HAUGHEY		ANNETTE FUNICELLO BEARS	
96 CHERYL ANN	2500	59.00	59.00
96 JILL ANGEL	20000	20.00	20.00
L. HENRY		ANNETTE FUNICELLO BEARS	
96 CONTRARY MARY	1500	49.00	49.00
B. KING		ANNETTE FUNICELLO BEARS	
95 3RD ANNIVERSARY	3000	44.00	44.00
95 CARMELLA	2500	46.00	46.00
95 GABRIELLE	20000	39.00	39.00
95 ROSIE	5000	35.00	35.00
96 4TH ANNIVERSARY	400	44.00	44.00
96 ANGEL HEART	2000	59.00	59.00
96 BAMBINA	20000	29.00	29.00
E. KISLINGBURY		ANNETTE FUNICELLO BEARS	
96 SAILOR SAM	1500	49.00	49.00
96 WINDY	2500	39.00	39.00
C. ORLANDO		ANNETTE FUNICELLO BEARS	
95 JOEY & JOANNE	1500	50.00	50.00
H. STODDARD		ANNETTE FUNICELLO BEARS	
96 PEACHES & CREAM	2500	59.00	59.00
S. SWENSON		ANNETTE FUNICELLO BEARS	
96 OZZIE	2000	44.00	44.00
*			ANNIVERSARY
95 JOY	YR	40.00	40.00
95 NUTMEG	YR	60.00	60.00
95 ROSIE	YR	30.00	30.00
K. CROOPER			ANNIVERSARY
97 75TH ANNIVERSARY HOUSE	TL	125.00	125.00
J. HAUGHEY			ANNIVERSARY
97 SHAGGY	TL	25.00	25.00
97 SQUEAKY	TL	30.00	30.00
L. HENRY			ANNIVERSARY
97 CINNAMON	TL	37.00	37.00
B. KING			ANNIVERSARY
97 PIPPI	TL	37.00	37.00
B. MCCONNELL			ANNIVERSARY
97 MERRY	TL	50.00	50.00
L. SPEIGAL			ANNIVERSARY
97 BLUE BEARY	TL	50.00	50.00
C. ORLANDO			BEACH PARTY
94 DEDE C15004	10000	29.00	29.00
*			BEAN BAG
94 HOLLYWOOD STAR C12880	5000	30.00	30.00
A. FUNICELLO			BEAN BAG
93 CLEMENTINE C4735	2500	26.00	26.00
E. KISLINGBURY			BEAN BAG
97 CHLOE	5000	39.00	39.00
G. BUTTITTA		BEAR BUDDIES	
97 PRECIOUS & BAILEY	2500	46.00	46.00
C. FIRMAGE		BEAR BUDDIES	
97 GINGER & SPICE	3000	69.00	69.00

YR	NAME	LIMIT	ISSUE	TREND
97	MOMMY & ME	3000	59.00	59.00
97	OLIVIA & OLLIE	3000	69.00	69.00

C. ORLANDO · BEAR BUDDIES

YR	NAME	LIMIT	ISSUE	TREND
94	PUPPY LUV C15006	2500	46.25	47.00

J. HAUGHEY · BEARS ON PARADE

YR	NAME	LIMIT	ISSUE	TREND
*	CLOWN #2 C9658	5000	80.00	80.00
*	LITTLE MAJORETTE C9659	YR	40.00	40.00
*	POM POM GIRL C9657	5000	60.00	60.00
92	MARINE C11513	604	48.00	48.00
92	NAVY C11512	604	48.00	48.00
93	ARMY C4756	2500	48.00	48.00
94	AIR FORCE C8146	2500	52.00	52.00

B. MCCONNELL · BEARS ON PARADE

YR	NAME	LIMIT	ISSUE	TREND
*	APRIL C9661-765	YR	50.00	50.00
*	AUGUST C9661-769	YR	50.00	50.00
*	DECEMBER C9661-773	YR	50.00	50.00
*	FEBRUARY C9661-763	YR	50.00	50.00
*	JANUARY C9661-762	YR	50.00	50.00
*	JULY C9661-768	YR	50.00	50.00
*	JUNE C9661-767	YR	50.00	50.00
*	LITTLE LADY/LILAC C9673	YR	80.00	80.00
*	MARCH C9661-764	YR	50.00	50.00
*	MAY C9661-766	YR	50.00	49.50
*	NOVEMBER C9661-772	YR	50.00	50.00
*	OCTOBER C9661-771	YR	50.00	50.00
*	SEPTEMBER C9661-770	YR	50.00	50.00

L. HENRY · BEAUTY BUG BALL

YR	NAME	LIMIT	ISSUE	TREND
97	LADY BUG	7500	90.00	90.00
97	MADAME BUTTERFLY	7500	90.00	90.00
97	QUEEN BEE	7500	90.00	90.00
97	SIR STINK BUG	7500	90.00	90.00

M. NICOLE · BEST FRIENDS

YR	NAME	LIMIT	ISSUE	TREND
92	ERIN/GIRL W/BUNNY C9635	2500	178.50	179.00
92	GEORGIA/GIRL W/KITTEN C9637	2500	179.00	179.00
92	HILLARY/GIRL W/DUCKS C9636	2500	178.50	179.00

J. MOWRY · CHILDREN OF THE WORLD

YR	NAME	LIMIT	ISSUE	TREND
94	TOMIKA/ESKIMO C13710	2500	198.50	200.00
95	BONNIE JEAN C15218	2500	124.00	124.00

J. ARNETT · CHRISTMAS

YR	NAME	LIMIT	ISSUE	TREND
94	FATHER CHRISTMAS '94 C13427	1000	313.00	313.00

C. BELLSMITH · CHRISTMAS

YR	NAME	LIMIT	ISSUE	TREND
94	BRYANNA C14515	7500	149.25	150.00

R. SCHMIDT · CHRISTMAS

YR	NAME	LIMIT	ISSUE	TREND
92	BRYANNA/GREEN VELVET C11240	1000	183.00	183.00

C. SHAFER · CHRISTMAS

YR	NAME	LIMIT	ISSUE	TREND
97	SARAFINA SNOWFLAKE	11000	178.00	178.00

D. STEWART · CHRISTMAS

YR	NAME	LIMIT	ISSUE	TREND
93	HOLLY/BEAN BAG/MUSIC C2086	2500	114.00	114.00

B. STOEHR · CHRISTMAS

YR	NAME	LIMIT	ISSUE	TREND
97	MINI JINGLES & BELLE	2500	69.00	69.00

C. WAUGH · CHRISTMAS

YR	NAME	LIMIT	ISSUE	TREND
94	KRIS-XMAS C8329	2500	89.00	89.00

B. MCCONNELL · CIRCUS

YR	NAME	LIMIT	ISSUE	TREND
93	TRIXI-ELEPHANT C4755	2500	70.00	70.00

V. DEFILIPPO · CLASSICAL BEAUTIES

YR	NAME	LIMIT	ISSUE	TREND
93	JULIA C11395	2500	169.00	169.00
93	PRISCILLIA/DRESSED IN PEACH C11385	2500	147.00	147.00
95	NATALIE C14829	2500	154.00	154.00

P. PARKINS · CLASSICS

YR	NAME	LIMIT	ISSUE	TREND
93	ALESIA/BLACK BRIDE USA C11384	250	590.00	590.00

C. ROBINSON · CLASSICS

YR	NAME	LIMIT	ISSUE	TREND
95	LAUREN C15216	500	436.00	436.00

* · COFFEE CLUB

YR	NAME	LIMIT	ISSUE	TREND
94	HOLLYWOOD STAR C15002	OP	22.00	22.00

C. ROBINSON · COLLECTIBLES

YR	NAME	LIMIT	ISSUE	TREND
95	MORGAN C15904	1500	155.00	155.00

D. STEWART · COLLECTIBLES

YR	NAME	LIMIT	ISSUE	TREND
94	BUNNY LOVE C10941	2500	46.00	46.00
94	BUNNY LOVE CHRISTMAS C14642	2500	54.00	54.00
94	TUSH/CRAWLING BABY C10944	2500	77.00	77.00
95	BUNNY LOVE 1995 C15893	8000	41.00	41.00
95	SOME BUNNY LOVES YOU C15226	2500	45.00	45.00

G. LANGFORD · COUNTRY

YR	NAME	LIMIT	ISSUE	TREND
94	COWBOY GLEN C8147	2500	127.00	127.00

M. NICOLE · COUNTRY GIRL

YR	NAME	LIMIT	ISSUE	TREND
92	SARAH/DRESSED IN BLUE C9639	2500	159.00	159.00
92	SARITA/DRESSED IN PURPLE C9638	2500	159.00	159.00

A. FUNICELLO · CUTE & CUDDLY

YR	NAME	LIMIT	ISSUE	TREND
93	TAMMY C12199	2000	40.00	40.00

G. LANGFORD · CUTE & CUDDLY

YR	NAME	LIMIT	ISSUE	TREND
94	NOELLE C8188	2500	40.00	40.00

YR	NAME	LIMIT	ISSUE	TREND
C. WAUGH			**CUTE & CUDDLY**	
94	KASEY C8150	2500	69.00	69.00
C. BELLSMITH			**DEAR TO MY HEART**	
92	OZEANNA/GERMAN ORIGIN C10414	2500	120.00	120.00
M. NICOLE			**DEAR TO MY HEART**	
92	BRETA/DRESSED IN PEACH C9633	2500	115.00	115.00
92	GERRI/DRESSED IN MINT GRN. C9634	2500	115.00	115.00
92	TAMMY/DRESSED IN MAUVE C9632	2500	115.00	115.00
*			**ELEGANCE**	
94	JOHNNY C12882	1500	108.50	109.00
B. MCCONNELL			**ELEGANCE**	
*	CYNTHIA C9686	2500	150.00	150.00
J. OPENSHAW			**FAIRY TALE**	
94	ALICE IN WONDERLAND C13706	5000	150.00	150.00
B. STOEHR			**FAIRY TALE**	
93	SNOW WHITE C11397	5000	177.50	178.00
B. MCCONNELL			**FAMILY HELPERS**	
*	JOSIE/MAMA IN KITCHEN C9687	2500	150.00	150.00
C. SHAFER			**FASHION DESIGNER**	
97	KATE	500	249.00	249.00
C. BLACK			**FLAVORITE**	
97	STRAWBERRY JAM	2500	39.00	39.00
C. WAUGH			**FLAVORITE**	
94	CAROL C12881	1500	75.00	75.00
V. DEFILIPPO			**FOUR SEASONS**	
93	AMBER/FALL C11380	2500	188.00	188.00
B. MCCONNELL			**FOUR SEASONS**	
*	DAISY C9694	2500	109.50	110.00
C. ROBINSON			**FOUR SEASONS**	
94	SUZANNE 13882	1500	95.00	95.00
D. STEWART			**FOUR SEASONS SMALL WONDERS**	
94	SMALL WONDERS C12860	4000	56.00	56.00
95	WINTER WONDER C15224	4000	61.00	61.00
B. FINLINSON			**GREETING CARDS**	
95	EASTER C15753	YR	25.00	25.00
95	VALENTINE C15225	YR	25.00	25.00
D. STEWART			**GREETING CARDS**	
93	CHRISTMAS '93 C6483	YR	25.00	25.00
93	MOTHER'S DAY '93/DRESSED IN PINK C11945	20000	25.00	25.00
94	ALL OCCASION '94 C10943	YR	25.00	25.00
94	CHRISTMAS '94 C14645	YR	28.50	29.00
94	VALENTINE '94 C10942	YR	25.00	25.00
95	MOTHER'S DAY '95 C15754	YR	25.00	25.00
M. YOKEE			**GREETING CARDS**	
94	LIANA C12862	2500	150.00	150.00
*			**HARLEQUIN**	
94	HARLEY C12886	1500	99.00	99.00
B. MCCONNELL			**HARLEQUIN**	
*	HARLEQUIN C9691	2500	139.50	140.00
*	HARLEQUIN C9692	2500	100.00	100.00
STEWART/GRIFFITH			**HAT BOX**	
93	VIRGINIA MARIE/BRIDE C11902	3000	135.00	135.00
*			**HERMANN FACTORY**	
*	FATHER C9683	1000	229.50	230.00
D. CRYSTAL			**I CAN DREAM**	
94	PLAYING MOMMY C13714	YR	47.00	47.00
V. DEFILIPPO			**INJURED**	
92	CHELSEA/HURT LEG C11250	5000	92.00	92.00
92	DOTTIE/CHICKEN POX C11252	5000	89.00	89.00
93	MACIE/HOSPITAL GOWN C11381	5000	88.00	88.00
93	SAVANNAH/SNIFFLES C11907	5000	93.00	96.00
M. NICOLE			**INJURED**	
92	MCKENSIE/WOUNDED FINGER C9631	5000	88.00	88.00
B. STOEHR			**JESSICA'S BEST FRIENDS**	
94	ANGELICA XMAS C14644	5000	228.00	228.00
94	ANGELICA/LAVENDER DRESS C13201	5000	199.50	200.00
C. BELLSMITH			**LARGE TRUNK**	
92	TRICIA/TRAVEL THEME C10405	2500	277.00	277.00
B. MACKIE			**LEGENDARY BEAUTIES**	
95	SPRING	10000	299.50	300.00
96	AUTUMN	10000	300.00	300.00
*			**MARIE OSMOND FINE PORCELAIN**	
95	A CHILD'S SONG	1995	25.00	25.00
95	COLLECTOR CARD	10000	12.00	12.00
C. BELLSMITH			**MARIE OSMOND FINE PORCELAIN**	
95	GOLDILOCKS	1994	48.00	48.00
95	PRINCESS AND THE PEA	1995	50.00	50.00
96	BEAUTY AND THE BEAST	1996	49.00	49.00
96	THUMBELINA	1995	49.00	48.00
D. CRYSTAL			**MARIE OSMOND FINE PORCELAIN**	
96	PLAYING DOCTOR	1996	*	N/A

YR	NAME	LIMIT	ISSUE	TREND
V. DEFILLPPO		MARIE OSMOND FINE PORCELAIN		
95	NATALIE	2500	154.00	154.00
B. FILINSON		MARIE OSMOND FINE PORCELAIN		
95	BIRTHDAY	1995	25.00	25.00
95	CONNIE	3000	44.00	44.00
95	EASTER	1995	25.00	25.00
95	VALENTINE '95	1995	25.00	25.00
96	AMANDA	3000	45.00	45.00
96	AMY KATHLYN	5000	213.00	213.00
96	BRUHILDA	5000	45.00	45.00
96	HANNAH	300	55.00	55.00
96	KAREN	2500	*	N/A
96	LYDIA	3000	*	N/A
96	VALENTINE	1996	25.00	25.00
L. HATCH		MARIE OSMOND FINE PORCELAIN		
96	CINDERELLA	5000	15.00	N/A
L. HENRY		MARIE OSMOND FINE PORCELAIN		
95	BLOSSOM BUNNY	5000	117.50	118.00
95	KELLY	5000	79.00	79.00
95	KRISTI	5000	117.00	117.00
95	SANTA BUNNY	5000	156.00	156.00
96	ALEXANDRA	1500	168.00	168.00
96	FUZZY BABY & HARIET	5000	*	N/A
96	JULIENNE RABBIT	5000	124.00	124.00
96	QUEEN BEE	7500	91.00	91.00
96	TATIANA	1500	*	N/A
J. MOWRY		MARIE OSMOND FINE PORCELAIN		
95	BONNIE JEAN	2500	124.00	124.00
95	SPRING	5000	219.00	219.00
95	USHA	2500	142.00	142.00
96	RAPUNZEL	5000	170.00	170.00
96	SUNFLOWER	3000	39.00	39.00
M. OSMOND		MARIE OSMOND FINE PORCELAIN		
95	OLIVE MAY	20000	180.00	180.00
95	STORYBOOK CASSETTE	1995	17.00	17.00
96	DAISY	7500	249.00	249.00
96	DARLA	30	140.00	140.00
96	DENISE	1996	*	N/A
96	GEORGETTE	2500	170.00	170.00
96	I LOVE YOU BEARY MUCH	20000	193.00	193.00
96	MARTA	5000	98.00	98.00
96	MOTHER'S DAY GREETING CARD	50000	*	N/A
96	NIKKI	3000	42.00	42.00
96	WENDY	3000	*	N/A
C. ROBINSON		MARIE OSMOND FINE PORCELAIN		
95	GRANDMA KIT	500	456.00	456.00
95	LAUREN	500	436.00	436.00
95	MORGAN	1500	155.00	155.00
95	SOPHIA	2500	140.00	140.00
96	AUDREY	500	496.00	496.00
96	BABY RENEE	5000	200.00	200.00
96	MISTY ROSE	5000	46.00	46.00
96	MORGAN 1996	1500	156.00	156.00
96	ROSA LEIGH	1500	155.00	155.00
SCHMIDT/BELLSMITH		MARIE OSMOND FINE PORCELAIN		
95	BRYANNA '95	3500	179.00	179.00
C. SHAFER		MARIE OSMOND FINE PORCELAIN		
96	CISSY	2500	136.00	136.00
96	FAITH	2500	150.00	150.00
96	SHELBY	5000	*	N/A
SHAFER/TURNER		MARIE OSMOND FINE PORCELAIN		
95	GENNE	2500	342.00	342.00
D. STEWART		MARIE OSMOND FINE PORCELAIN		
95	BUNNY LOVE '95	8000	11.00	11.00
95	CHRISTMAS '95	1995	225.00	25.00
95	FALLIN LEAVER	4000	58.00	58.00
95	FIRST KISS	2500	137.00	137.00
95	MILLY	3000	55.00	55.00
95	MOTHER'S DAY '95	1995	25.00	25.00
95	POINSETTIA	3000	41.00	41.00
95	SOME BUNNY LOVES U	2500	45.00	45.00
95	SUMMERY DAYS	4000	63.00	63.00
95	WINTER WONDER	4000	61.00	61.00
96	BUNNY LOVE CHERUB	5000	45.00	45.00
96	TEA CUP TREASURES	3000	60.00	60.00
B. STOEHR		MARIE OSMOND FINE PORCELAIN		
95	ASHLEY	5000	195.50	196.00
95	BABY BEVERLY	5000	178.00	178.00
95	JINGLES & BELLE	15000	93.00	93.00
95	MOLLY	5000	134.50	135.00
95	POLLY PUMPKIN	3000	47.00	47.00
95	TREE TOP ANGEL	2500	186.00	186.00
95	WATCH CASE DOLL	1995	67.00	67.00
96	ANGELICA'S	5000	180.00	180.00

YR	NAME	LIMIT	ISSUE	TREND
96	BABY MARIE	5000	*	N/A
96	BABY MARIE - VINYL	2500	198.00	198.00
96	HANSEL & GRETYL	5000	206.00	206.00
96	MINDY	2000	234.00	234.00
96	MIRACLE ROSIE & RAGS	15000	121.00	121.00
96	STEPHEN	5000	235.00	235.00
96	STITCHIN STACY	5000	113.00	113.00
M. YOKEE		**MARIE OSMOND FINE PORCELAIN**		
96	CHRISSY	5000	175.00	175.00
96	KIM	5000	163.00	163.00
C. BELLSMITH			**MIRACLE CHILDREN**	
92	FRENDA/NEEDLEPOINT C10409	YR	92.00	92.00
92	GINA/HALLOWEEN CAT C10411	YR	88.00	88.00
93	FAITH/FLYING A KITE C1988	YR	77.00	77.00
94	BECKY/DADDY'S GIRL/BASEBALL C12857	YR	76.00	76.00
94	CAITLIN & BENTLY/GIRL W/DOG C12856	YR	79.00	79.00
S. BLACKALL			**MIRACLE CHILDREN**	
92	MARILYN/PLAYING DRESS-UP C11251	YR	84.00	84.00
93	AARON/GROOM C11364	YR	76.00	76.00
93	CODY/PLAYING PIRATE C11379	YR	80.00	80.00
L. HATCH			**MIRACLE CHILDREN**	
97	CARRIE	5000	79.00	79.00
L. HENRY			**MIRACLE CHILDREN**	
94	CELESTE/DRESSED LIKE AN ANGEL C14641	YR	82.00	82.00
HENRY/FINLINSON			**MIRACLE CHILDREN**	
94	TRACI/DEAF-SIGNING C13113	20000	82.00	82.00
M. NICOLE			**MIRACLE CHILDREN**	
92	BETTY/BAKING A CAKE C10413	YR	70.00	70.00
92	COURTNIE/CLOWN BABY C9627	YR	70.00	70.00
92	DANIELLE/LITTLE BALLERINA C9626	YR	70.00	70.00
92	LINDA/NO WINDOWS C10412	YR	74.00	74.00
92	PIERRE/LITTLE PICASSO C9629	YR	70.00	70.00
92	SHANNON/LITTLE NURSE C9628	YR	70.00	70.00
92	SHAWN/BORN TO SHOP C9630	YR	70.00	70.00
M. OSMOND			**MIRACLE CHILDREN**	
97	BUBBLES	500	75.00	75.00
97	FAITH	2500	149.00	149.00
D. STEWART			**MIRACLE CHILDREN**	
93	ANNIE/GIRL ON BIKE C11911	YR	75.00	75.00
93	FLORA/WEDDING THEME C11910	YR	80.00	80.00
93	MEKEL/PICNIC W/TEDDY C11909	YR	85.00	85.00
94	MOTHER'S DAY '94 C12863	YR	25.00	25.00
94	TINA/GIRL PLAYING C13711	YR	116.50	116.50
B. STOEHR			**MIRACLE CHILDREN**	
97	DOTTIE ANNE	5000	79.00	79.00
D. STEWART			**MOTHER CHILD**	
94	VIRGINIA & JORDAN C13735	3000	179.00	179.00
S. & R. FOSKEY			**MUSICAL**	
94	JOLLY C12883	2500	54.00	54.00
M. NICOLE			**MUSICAL**	
92	EMILY/MUSICAL SEWING C9640	2500	110.00	110.00
*			**NEW GENERATION**	
96	ANGELIQUE	5000	69.00	69.00
96	NICK	2500	75.00	75.00
97	CHRISTOPHER COLUMBUS	5000	30.00	30.00
J. ANTONELLI			**NEW GENERATION**	
97	ROSALEE	2500	69.00	69.00
L. APPLEBEARY			**NEW GENERATION**	
97	ANGELIQUE	5000	69.00	69.00
97	BEA	2500	49.00	49.00
K. CLARKE			**NEW GENERATION**	
97	JOY	5000	40.00	40.00
L. DE MENT			**NEW GENERATION**	
97	BAMBOO	2500	59.00	59.00
97	COTTONTAIL CLAIRE	2500	49.00	49.00
97	PRUDENCE	3000	46.00	46.00
J. HAUGHEY			**NEW GENERATION**	
97	PATCHES	5000	89.00	89.00
97	ROSIE	5000	30.00	30.00
L. HENRY			**NEW GENERATION**	
97	EDGAR	2500	49.00	49.00
97	HONEY	3500	69.00	69.00
97	NUTMEG	2500	60.00	60.00
E. KISLINGBURY			**NEW GENERATION**	
97	ALEXANDER	5000	39.00	39.00
KNICKERBOCKER			**NEW GENERATION**	
97	GULLIVER	5000	25.00	25.00
97	NICK	2500	75.00	75.00
C. ORLANDO			**NEW GENERATION**	
97	BUZZ	2500	30.00	30.00
L. SPEIGAL			**NEW GENERATION**	
97	MULLBEARY	5000	46.00	46.00

YR	NAME	LIMIT	ISSUE	TREND
H. STODDARD			**NEW GENERATION**	
97	GALA	2500	52.00	52.00
*				**NOSTALGIC**
94	THORNEY C12887	2500	70.00	70.00
K. CLARKE			**NOSTALGIC**	
94	LITTLE JOE 13877	3000	49.00	49.00
S. FOSKEY			**NOSTALGIC**	
*	BERNIE C9676	2500	60.00	60.00
*	BROWNIE C9678	2500	129.50	130.00
*	MOLLIE C9677	2500	70.00	70.00
A. FUNICELLO			**NOSTALGIC**	
94	DAPPER DAN C8194	1500	72.00	72.00
J. HAUGHEY			**NOSTALGIC**	
94	HEINZ 13878	2500	100.00	100.00
B. KING			**NOSTALGIC**	
97	HEATHER	5000	69.00	69.00
D. STEWART			**PETITE AMOUR**	
93	GOLDIE/GIRL W/BEAR C11905	3000	49.00	49.00
94	ANITA C12858	3000	41.00	41.00
94	CHRISTMAS DARLINGS '94 C13428	4000	152.00	152.00
B. STOEHR			**PETITE AMOUR**	
94	GRETL C13200	3000	51.00	51.00
C. BELLSMITH			**PICTURE DAY**	
93	CAMILLE/DRESSED IN PINK C10406	2500	216.00	216.00
93	CAROLINE/DRESSED IN RED VELVET C10407	2500	220.00	220.00
L. HENRY			**PICTURE DAY**	
94	LITTLE RED RIDING HOOD C12861	5000	199.50	200.00
*				**POP UP BOOKS**
96	CHRISTOPHER COLUMBUS	5000	30.00	30.00
*				**RAGGEDY ANN & ANDY**
96	RAGGEDY ANN & ANDY 12 IN. PORCELAIN	2500	80.00	80.00
96	RAGGEDY ANN & ANDY 6 IN. RAG	2500	30.00	30.00
C. WAUGH			**RUSSIAN**	
*	ARTYOM/BABY C9681	5000	40.00	40.00
*	MIKHAIL/BROTHER C9679	5000	70.00	70.00
*	POLINA/SISTER C9680	5000	70.00	70.00
94	DMITRI C8281	2500	44.00	44.00
J. MITCHELL			**SCRAPBOOK**	
*	BALLERINA C9695	2500	145.00	145.00
*	LET IN SNOW SNOWMAN C9698	5000	90.00	90.00
*	LET IT SNOW ANNETTE C9697	5000	145.00	145.00
*	MASQUERADE C9696	5000	145.00	145.00
*	SADDLING UP C9700	5000	80.00	80.00
*	WESTERN ROUND UP C9699	5000	145.00	145.00
D. STEWART			**SMALL TRUNK**	
93	VANESSA C11386	2500	198.00	198.00
M. COSTA			**SOMEWHERE IN TIME**	
97	RAIMI	2500	300.00	300.00
L. HATCH			**SOMEWHERE IN TIME**	
97	ELSIE	2500	450.00	450.00
J. HOLLENBRANDS			**SOMEWHERE IN TIME**	
94	ELEANOR C14755	2500	212.00	212.00
*				**SPECIAL**
94	PEANUT BUTTER C15724	800	70.00	70.00
K. CLARKE			**SPECIAL**	
94	MARION C15005	1500	46.25	47.00
A. FUNICELLO			**SPECIAL**	
93	NO NO NANNETTE C4736	2500	62.00	62.00
J. HAUGHEY			**SPECIAL**	
94	TAPESTRY BEAR PURSE 13881	1500	57.00	57.00
B. KING			**SPECIAL**	
94	GUARDIAN ANGEL BEAR C14282	10000	29.25	30.00
94	I LOVE YOU 14143	10000	40.00	40.00
97	DEARDRA	3000	52.00	52.00
B. MCCONNELL			**SPECIAL**	
*	ANETTE MOUSKEBEAR C9674	7500	80.00	80.00
*	BOBBY MOUSKEBEAR C9675	7500	80.00	80.00
*	HUGO W/JUNGLE BELLS C9690	2500	149.00	149.00
*	SKIPPER C9689	2500	149.00	149.00
94	NO NO NANETTE C4736	2500	62.00	62.00
J. MITCHELL			**SPECIAL**	
94	MIKEY C8214	1000	71.00	71.00
C. WAUGH			**SPECIAL**	
94	MEL C12885	2500	67.00	67.00
C. BELLSMITH			**STORY BOOK**	
93	JULIETTE/MAGIC FERRIS WHEEL C10404	2500	121.50	122.00
94	LITTLE BO PEEP C13708	YR	50.00	50.00
94	LITTLE RED RIDING HOOD C13199	YR	48.00	48.00
97	SANTA CLAUS IS COMING TO TOWN	5000	68.00	68.00
H. STODDARD			**SUMMER**	
97	PEACHES & CREAM	2500	59.00	59.00

YR NAME	LIMIT	ISSUE	TREND
*			SWEATER
94 JOSHUA 13879	2500	41.00	41.00
A. FUNICELLO			SWEATER
92 GINNY C11515	604	40.00	40.00
S. HARRELL			SWEATER
97 MATTHEW	2500	59.00	59.00
G. LANGFORD			SWEATER
93 LITTLE NICK-XMAS C4728	5000	55.00	55.00
B. MCCONNELL			SWEATER
* JESSICA/BABY C9685	2500	40.00	40.00
* UNCLE TEDDY C9684	2500	129.50	130.00
92 JESSICA C9685	2500	40.00	40.00
D. STEWART		SWEET DREAMS	
93 OLIVIA/BABY ON PILLOW C11904	2500	93.00	93.00
94 SWEET DREAMS BABY/ON MOON C12859	2500	90.00	90.00
G. LANGFORD		SWEET PRESERVES	
94 SWEET GINA C8324	2500	138.50	139.00
B. MCCONNELL		SWEET PRESERVES	
* FLORA C9693	2500	119.50	120.00
*			T-SHIRT
94 AF T-SHIRT A22433	*	22.00	22.00
*	TEDDY BEAR PICNIC/HERMANN FACTORY		
* MUSICAL C9682	1000	299.50	299.50
V. DEFILIPPO			TODDLER
92 JESSICA/1ST BIRTHDAY C10415	2500	249.00	249.00
92 RACHAEL/MARIE'S DAUGHTER C11254	2500	219.00	219.00
93 JESSICA/CHRISTMAS C6508	5000	249.00	500.00
J. HOLLEBRANDS			TODDLER
93 DEBBIE/DONNY'S DAUGHTER C11244	2500	262.00	262.00
M. OSMOND			TODDLER
97 DAISY	7500	249.00	249.00
97 PEEK-A-BOO	5000	299.00	299.00
B. STOEHR			TODDLER
95 ASHLEY C15217	2500	195.50	196.00
97 BABY MARIE VINYL	2500	198.00	198.00
97 SUNSHINE & HAPPINESS	7500	159.00	159.00
A. JACKSON			TWINS
93 NATHAN/BOY IN AQUA C11382	2000	104.00	104.00
93 NICOLE/GIRL IN AQUA C11383	2000	137.00	137.00
M. NICOLE			TWINS
92 ANDY & SON/COUNTRY C9641	2500	190.00	190.00
D. STEWART			TWINS
93 JENNY & JASON/CABBAGE PATCH C11430	5000	172.50	172.50
B. STOEHR			TWINS
94 MOPSY C13202	5000	104.00	104.00
94 RAGS C13202	5000	104.00	104.00
C. WAUGH			VALENTINE
92 CANDI C11511	604	75.00	75.00
B. MCCONNELL			VARSITY
* SWEATER GIRL C9688	2500	79.00	79.00
L. HENRY		VELVETEEN RABBIT	
92 VELVET/WHITE PLUSH FUR C11245	5000	121.50	122.00
93 ROBBIE RABBIT C11363	5000	150.00	150.00
94 HARELOOM BUNNY C10940	5000	125.50	124.00
94 ROSEMARIE RABBIT/BRIDE W/MASK C13198	20000	150.00	150.00
95 BLOSSOM BUNNY C15739	5000	117.75	118.00
97 HEAVENLY HARE	5000	160.00	160.00
G. BUTTITTA			VICTORIAN
97 VIRGINIA	1500	49.00	49.00
L. DE MENT			VICTORIAN
97 MISS KITTY	5000	69.00	69.00

LADIE & FRIENDS

	LIMIT	ISSUE	TREND
B./P. WISBER		1997 SPECIAL EVENT EDITION	
96 LITTLE AMANDA HIGH	YR	36.00	36.00
B. WISBER		CHRISTMAS CONCERT	
90 CLAIRE VALENTINE 1262	OP	56.00	60.00
92 JUDITH HIGH 1292	OP	70.00	74.00
93 JAMES VALENTINE 1310	OP	60.00	63.00
93 STEPHANIE BOWMAN 1309	OP	74.00	77.00
B. WISBER		CHRISTMAS PAGEANT	
85 CHRISTMAS WOOLY LAMB 1133	CL	11.00	40.00
85 EARTH ANGEL 1122	CL	30.00	100.00
85 JOSEPH & DONKEY 1119	OP	30.00	40.00
85 MARY & BABY JESUS 1118	OP	30.00	40.00
85 NOEL ANGEL 1ST EDITION 1126	CL	30.00	100.00
85 ON ANGEL 1121	CL	30.00	100.00
85 PEACE ANGEL 1ST EDITION 1120	CL	30.00	100.00
85 WISEMAN #1 1123	OP	30.00	40.00
85 WISEMAN #2 1124	OP	30.00	40.00
85 WISEMAN #3 1125	OP	30.00	40.00
85 WOODEN CRECHE 1132	OP	28.00	33.00
86 SHEPHERD 1193	OP	32.00	40.00

YR	NAME	LIMIT	ISSUE	TREND
89	NOEL ANGEL 2ND EDITION 1126	OP	48.00	52.00
89	PEACE ANGEL 2ND EDITION 1120	OP	48.00	52.00

B. WISBER | | **GRUMMELS OF LOG HOLLOW** |

YR	NAME	LIMIT	ISSUE	TREND
86	AUNT GERTIE GRUMMEL 1171	CL	34.00	90.00
86	AUNT HILDA GRUMMEL 1174	CL	34.00	90.00
86	AUNT POLLY GRUMMEL 1169	CL	34.00	90.00
86	COUSIN LOTTIE GRUMMEL 1170	CL	36.00	90.00
86	COUSIN MIRANDA GRUMMEL 1165	CL	47.00	90.00
86	GRANDMA GRUMMEL 1173	CL	45.00	90.00
86	GRANDPA GRUMMEL 1176	CL	36.00	175.00
86	MA GRUMMEL 1167	CL	36.00	90.00
86	PA GRUMMEL 1172	CL	34.00	90.00
86	S-GRUMMELS, THE- BOY/GIRL 1196	CL	15.00	40.00
86	SISTER NORA GRUMMEL 1177	CL	34.00	90.00
86	TEDDY BEAR BED 1168	CL	15.00	90.00
86	UNCLE HOLLIS GRUMMEL 1166	CL	34.00	90.00
86	WASHLINE 1175	CL	15.00	90.00

B. WISBER | | **LITTLE ONES** |

YR	NAME	LIMIT	ISSUE	TREND
85	BLACK BOY 1ST EDITION 1130	CL	15.00	55.00
85	BLACK GIRL 1ST EDITION 1130	CL	15.00	55.00
85	LITTLE ONE 1ST EDITION 1130	CL	15.00	55.00
85	WHITE BOY 1ST EDITION 1130	CL	15.00	55.00
85	WHITE GIRL 1ST EDITION 1130	CL	15.00	55.00
89	BLACK BOY 2ND EDITION 1130I	CL	20.00	25.00
89	BLACK GIRL/COUNTRY 2ND EDITION 1130G	CL	20.00	25.00
89	BLACK GIRL/PASTELS 2ND EDITION 1130E	CL	20.00	25.00
89	LITTLE ONE (WHITE) 2ND EDITION 1130H	CL	20.00	23.00
89	LITTLE ONE (WHITE) COUNTRY COLOR 2ND EDITION 1130F	CL	20.00	23.00
89	WHITE BOY 2ND EDITION 1130H	CL	20.00	25.00
89	WHITE GIRL/COUNTRY 2ND EDITION 1130F	CL	20.00	25.00
89	WHITE GIRL/PASTELS 2ND EDITION 1130D	CL	20.00	25.00
92	BOY W/EASTER FLOWERS 1306	OP	30.00	32.00
92	BOY W/SLED 1289	OP	30.00	30.00
92	CLOWN 1290	OP	32.00	32.00
92	GIRL READING 1286	CL	36.00	39.00
92	GIRL W/APPLES 1277	OP	26.00	29.00
92	GIRL W/BEACH BUCKET 1275	OP	26.00	29.00
92	GIRL W/BIRTHDAY GIFT 1279	OP	26.00	29.00
92	GIRL W/CHRISTMAS LIGHTS 1287	OP	34.00	37.00
92	GIRL W/EASTER EGGS 1276	OP	26.00	29.00
92	GIRL W/EASTER FLOWERS 1296	OP	34.00	36.00
92	GIRL W/KITTEN & MILK 1280	CL	32.00	35.00
92	GIRL W/KITTEN & YARN 1278	CL	34.00	37.00
92	GIRL W/SNOWMAN 1288	OP	36.00	39.00
92	GIRL W/VALENTINE 1291	OP	30.00	33.00
93	4TH OF JULY BOY 1307	OP	28.00	30.00
93	4TH OF JULY GIRL 1298	OP	30.00	32.00
93	BALLERINA 1321	OP	40.00	42.00
93	BUNNY 1297	OP	36.00	38.00
93	GIRL PICNICKING 1320	OP	34.00	36.00
93	GIRL W/MOP 1300	OP	36.00	38.00
93	GIRL W/SPINNING WHEEL 1299	OP	36.00	38.00
93	GIRL W/VIOLIN 1319	OP	28.00	30.00
94	BOY DYEING EGGS 1327	OP	30.00	32.00
94	BOY W/PUMPKIN 1341	OP	29.00	31.00
94	GIRL DYEING EGGS 1326	OP	30.00	32.00
94	GIRL W/LAUNDRY BASKET 1338	OP	38.00	40.00
94	GIRL W/PUPPY IN TUB 1339	OP	43.00	45.00
94	GIRL W/WAGON 1340	OP	42.00	44.00
94	NURSE 1328	OP	40.00	42.00
94	TEACHER 1329	OP	38.00	40.00
95	BASKETWEAVER 1363	OP	48.00	49.00
95	JUNE FETE BOY 1350	CL	33.00	33.00
95	JUNE FETE GIRL 1349	CL	33.00	33.00
96	BLACK GIRL ROLLERSKATING 1377	OP	40.00	40.00
96	BOY BASEBALL	*	44.00	44.00
96	BRIDE 1374	OP	42.00	42.00
96	GIRL BASEBALL	*	44.00	44.00
96	GIRL WITH SUNFLOWER 1373	OP	37.00	37.00
96	GROOM 1375	OP	23.50	24.00
96	HOT SUMMER DAY	*	53.00	53.00
96	WHITE GIRL ROLLERSKATING 1376	OP	40.00	40.00

B. WISBER | | **LITTLE ONES AT CHRISTMAS** |

YR	NAME	LIMIT	ISSUE	TREND
90	BLACK GIRL W/BASKET OF GREENS 1263	OP	22.00	27.00
90	WHITE GIRL W/COOKIE 1264	OP	22.00	27.00
90	WHITE GIRL W/GIFT 1266	OP	22.00	27.00
90	WHITE GIRL W/TREE GARLAND 1265	OP	22.00	27.00
91	BLACK BOY W/SANTA PHOTO 1273A	OP	24.00	30.00
91	BLACK GIRL W/SANTA PHOTO 1272A	OP	24.00	30.00
91	WHITE BOY W/SANTA PHOTO 1273	OP	24.00	30.00
91	WHITE GIRL W/SANTA PHOTO 1272	OP	24.00	29.00
93	BOY PEEKING 1314	OP	22.00	24.00
93	BOY PEEKING W/TREE 1313	OP	60.00	63.00
93	GIRL PEEKING 1316	OP	22.00	24.00
93	GIRL PEEKING W/TREE 1315	OP	60.00	63.00

YR	NAME	LIMIT	ISSUE	TREND
93	GIRL W/BAKING TABLE 1317	OP	38.00	40.00
93	GIRL W/NOTE FOR SANTA 1318	OP	36.00	38.00
94	GIRL W/GREENS ON TABLE 1337	OP	46.00	48.00

B. WISBER   **LITTLE ONES AT CHRISTMAS-NATIVITY**

YR	NAME	LIMIT	ISSUE	TREND
95	DONKEY 1362	OP	17.00	18.00
95	LITTLE ANGEL 1359	OP	36.00	37.00
95	LITTLE JOSEPH 1358	OP	31.00	32.00
95	LITTLE MARY WITH BABY IN MANGER 1357	OP	33.00	34.00
95	LITTLE SHEPHERD WITH LAMB 1360	OP	45.00	46.00
95	S' CRECHE 1361	OP	24.00	25.00

B. WISBER   **LIZZIE HIGH DOLLS**

YR	NAME	LIMIT	ISSUE	TREND
85	AMANDA HIGH 1ST EDITION 1111	CL	30.00	100.00
85	BENJAMIN BOWMAN 1129	CL	30.00	100.00
85	BENJAMIN BOWMAN/SANTA 1134	OP	30.00	42.00
85	CHRISTIAN BOWMAN 1110	CL	30.00	100.00
85	CORA HIGH 1115	CL	30.00	110.00
85	ELIZABETH SWEETLAND 1ST EDITION 1109	CL	30.00	100.00
85	EMMA HIGH 1103	CL	30.00	100.00
85	ESTHER DUNN 1ST EDITION 1127	CL	45.00	45.00
85	FLOSSIE HIGH 1ST EDITION 1128	CL	45.00	130.00
85	HANNAH BROWN 1131	CL	45.00	130.00
85	IDA VALENTINE 1116	CL	30.00	100.00
85	KATRINA VALENTINE 1135	CL	30.00	100.00
85	LIZZIE HIGH 1100	CL	30.00	45.00
85	LOUELLA VALENTINE 1112	CL	30.00	100.00
85	LUTHER BOWMAN 1ST EDITION 1108	CL	30.00	100.00
85	MARTIN BOWMAN 1117	CL	30.00	65.00
85	MARY VALENTINE 1105	CL	30.00	100.00
85	NATHAN BOWMAN 1354	OP	70.00	72.00
85	NETTIE BROWN 1ST EDITION 1102	CL	30.00	100.00
85	NETTIE BROWN/CHRISTMAS 1114	CL	30.00	100.00
85	PETER VALENTINE 1113	CL	30.00	90.00
85	REBECCA BOWMAN 1ST EDITION 1104	CL	30.00	100.00
85	RUSSELL DUNN 1107	CL	30.00	100.00
85	SABRINA VALENTINE 1ST EDITION 1101	CL	30.00	100.00
85	WENDEL BOWMAN 1ST EDITION 1106	CL	30.00	100.00
86	ALICE VALENTINE 1148	CL	32.00	100.00
86	ANDREW BROWN 1157	CL	45.00	130.00
86	ANNIE BOWMAN 1ST EDITION 1150	CL	32.00	100.00
86	CARRIE HIGH 1ST EDITION 1190	CL	45.00	100.00
86	CASSIE YOCUM 1ST EDITION 1179	CL	36.00	100.00
86	CHRISTOPHER HIGH 1182	CL	34.00	70.00
86	DAVID YOCUM 1195	CL	33.00	37.00
86	DELIA VALENTINE 1153	CL	32.00	100.00
86	DORA VALENTINE 1ST EDITION 1152	CL	30.00	100.00
86	EDWARD BOWMAN 1ST EDITION 1158	CL	45.00	130.00
86	EMILY BOWMAN 1ST EDITION 1185	CL	34.00	100.00
86	GRACE VALENTINE 1ST EDITION 1146	CL	32.00	100.00
86	JENNY VALENTINE 1181	CL	34.00	110.00
86	JEREMY BOWMAN 1192	CL	36.00	80.00
86	JILLIAN BOWMAN 1180	CL	34.00	110.00
86	JULIET VALENTINE 1ST EDITION 1147	CL	32.00	100.00
86	KARL VALENTINE 1ST EDITION 1161	CL	30.00	100.00
86	KATIE BOWMAN 1178	CL	36.00	80.00
86	LITTLE GHOSTS 1197	OP	15.00	20.00
86	MADALEINE VALENTINE 1ST EDITION 1187	CL	34.00	90.00
86	MAGGIE HIGH 1160	CL	30.00	100.00
86	MARIE VALENTINE 1ST EDITION 1184	CL	47.00	125.00
86	MARISA VALENTINE 1194A	OP	33.00	40.00
86	MARISA VALENTINE W/BROTHER PETEY 1194	OP	45.00	50.00
86	MARLAND VALENTINE 1183	CL	33.00	100.00
86	MARTHA HIGH 1151	CL	32.00	100.00
86	MATTHEW YOCUM 1186	CL	33.00	100.00
86	MOLLY YOCUM 1ST EDITION 1189	CL	34.00	100.00
86	RACHEL BOWMAN 1ST EDITION 1188	CL	34.00	100.00
86	SADIE VALENTINE 1163	CL	45.00	50.00
86	SALLY BOWMAN 1155	CL	32.00	110.00
86	SARA VALENTINE 1154	CL	32.00	55.00
86	SOPHIE VALENTINE 1164	CL	45.00	130.00
86	SUSANNA BOWMAN 1149	CL	45.00	130.00
86	THOMAS BOWMAN 1159	CL	30.00	100.00
86	TILLIE BROWN 1156	CL	32.00	100.00
86	WILLIAM VALENTINE 1191	CL	36.00	80.00
86	WILLIE BOWMAN 1162	CL	30.00	60.00
87	ABIGAIL BOWMAN 1199	CL	40.00	90.00
87	ADDIE HIGH 1202	OP	37.00	43.00
87	AMY BOWMAN 1201	CL	37.00	80.00
87	BRIDGET BOWMAN 1222	CL	40.00	95.00
87	CAT ON CHAIR 1217	CL	16.00	40.00
87	CHARLES BOWMAN 1ST EDITION 1221	CL	34.00	100.00
87	FLOWER GIRL, THE 1204	CL	17.00	25.00
87	GRETCHEN HIGH 1216	CL	40.00	45.00
87	IMOGENE BOWMAN 1206	CL	37.00	80.00
87	JOHANNA VALENTINE 1198	CL	37.00	100.00
87	KATIE AND BARNEY 1219	CL	38.00	43.00

YR	NAME	LIMIT	ISSUE	TREND
87	LAURA VALENTINE 1223	CL	36.00	80.00
87	LITTLE WITCH 1225	OP	17.00	24.00
87	MARGARET BOWMAN 1213	OP	35.00	43.00
87	MELANIE BOWMAN 1ST EDITION 1220	CL	36.00	130.00
87	NAOMI VALENTINE 1200	CL	40.00	90.00
87	OLIVIA HIGH 1205	OP	37.00	43.00
87	PATSY BOWMAN 1214	CL	50.00	53.00
87	PENELOPE HIGH 1208	CL	40.00	400.00
87	PRISCILLA HIGH 1226	CL	56.00	62.00
87	RAMONA BROWN 1215	CL	40.00	50.00
87	REBECCA'S MOTHER 1207	CL	37.00	55.00
87	SANTA CLAUS/SITTING 1224	CL	50.00	60.00
87	WEDDING, THE BRIDE 1203	CL	37.00	50.00
87	WEDDING, THE GROOM 1203A	CL	34.00	37.00
88	ALLISON BOWMAN 1229	CL	56.00	63.00
88	BESS HIGH 1241	OP	45.00	50.00
88	BETSY VALENTINE 1245	OP	42.00	46.00
88	DAPHNE BOWMAN 1235	CL	38.00	40.00
88	EUNICE HIGH 1240	CL	56.00	60.00
88	HATTIE BOWMAN 1239	OP	40.00	46.00
88	JACOB HIGH 1230	CL	44.00	50.00
88	JANIE VALENTINE 1231	OP	37.00	37.00
88	KINCH BOWMAN 1237	CL	47.00	50.00
88	MARY ELLEN VALENTINE 1236	OP	40.00	45.00
88	MEGAN VALENTINE 1227	CL	44.00	95.00
88	NETTIE BROWN 2ND EDITION 1102	CL	36.00	40.00
88	PAULINE BOWMAN 1228	CL	44.00	50.00
88	PHOEBE HIGH 1246	CL	48.00	90.00
88	RUTH ANNE BOWMAN 1232	CL	44.00	90.00
88	SABRINA VALENTINE 2ND EDITION 1101	CL	40.00	44.00
88	SAMANTHA BOWMAN 1238	CL	47.00	50.00
89	AMELIA HIGH 1248	OP	45.00	50.00
89	CARRIE HIGH 2ND EDITION 1190	OP	46.00	50.00
89	EMMY LOU VALENTINE 1251	OP	45.00	49.00
89	FLOSSIE HIGH 2ND EDITION 1128	CL	54.00	59.00
89	JASON HIGH 1254A	CL	20.00	25.00
89	JASON HIGH W/MOTHER 1254	CL	58.00	64.00
89	JESSICA HIGH 1253A	CL	20.00	25.00
89	JESSICA HIGH W/MOTHER 1253	CL	58.00	63.00
89	JOHANN BOWMAN 1250	CL	40.00	40.00
89	LUCY BOWMAN 1255	OP	45.00	50.00
89	MADALEINE VALENTINE 2ND EDITION 1187	OP	37.00	40.00
89	MIRIAM HIGH 1256	CL	46.00	50.00
89	MOLLY YOCUM 2ND EDITION 1189	OP	39.00	43.00
89	MRS. CLAUS 1258	OP	42.00	46.00
89	PEGGY BOWMAN 1252	CL	58.00	70.00
89	RACHEL BOWMAN 2ND EDITION 1188	OP	34.00	39.00
89	REBECCA BOWMAN 2ND EDITION 1104	CL	56.00	62.00
89	SANTA W/TUB 1257	OP	58.00	64.00
89	VANESSA HIGH 1247	OP	45.00	50.00
89	VICTORIA BOWMAN 1249	CL	40.00	44.00
90	ALBERT VALENTINE 1260	CL	42.00	45.00
90	AMANDA HIGH 2ND EDITION 1111	OP	54.00	60.00
90	EMILY BOWMAN 2ND EDITION 1185	OP	48.00	51.00
90	GRACE VALENTINE 2ND EDITION 1146	OP	48.00	51.00
90	JULIET VALENTINE 2ND EDITION 1147	CL	48.00	52.00
90	MARLENE VALENTINE 1259	CL	48.00	50.00
90	NANCY BOWMAN 1261	OP	48.00	52.00
91	ANNABELLE BOWMAN 1267	CL	68.00	72.00
91	BARBARA HELEN 1274	OP	58.00	62.00
91	CYNTHIA HIGH 1127A	CL	60.00	62.00
91	DEPARTMENT STORE SANTA, THE 1270	OP	76.00	80.00
91	ELIZABETH SWEETLAND 2ND EDITION 1109	CL	56.00	60.00
91	ESTHER DUNN 2ND EDITION 1127	CL	60.00	62.00
91	MICHAEL BOWMAN 1268	OP	52.00	55.00
91	SANTA'S HELPER 1271	OP	52.00	52.00
91	TRUDY VALENTINE 1269	CL	64.00	68.00
92	ASHLEY BOWMAN 1304	CL	48.00	50.00
92	CAROL ANNE BOWMAN 1282	CL	70.00	140.00
92	CASSIE YOCUM 2ND EDITION 1179	OP	80.00	83.00
92	CHARLES BOWMAN 2ND EDITION 1221	CL	46.00	48.00
92	DORA VALENTINE 2ND EDITION 1152	CL	48.00	50.00
92	EDWIN BOWMAN 1281	CL	70.00	70.00
92	FRANCIS BOWMAN 1305	CL	48.00	50.00
92	JOANIE VALENTINE 1295	OP	48.00	48.00
92	JOSEPH VALENTINE 1283	CL	62.00	65.00
92	KATHRYN BOWMAN 1285	CL	140.00	500.00
92	MARIE VALENTINE 2ND EDITION 1184	OP	68.00	70.00
92	MELANIE BOWMAN 2ND EDITION 1220	CL	46.00	46.00
92	NATALIE VALENTINE 1284	CL	62.00	65.00
92	TIMOTHY BOWMAN 1294	OP	56.00	60.00
92	WENDEL BOWMAN 2ND EDITION 1106	OP	60.00	64.00
92	WENDY BOWMAN 1293	OP	78.00	82.00
93	ANNIE BOWMAN 2ND EDITION 1150	OP	68.00	70.00
93	CHRISTMAS TREE W/CATS 1293A	OP	42.00	44.00

Dressed for a day at play, Tish—a Store Exclusive by the Lawton Doll Co.—is a closed edition that has increased in value since its 1991 release.

Based on the classic orchestral tale by Prokofiev, Peter and the Wolf was issued in 1992 by the Lawton Doll Co as the first edition in their Childhood Classics II collection. Limited to 750 dolls, it retailed at $495.

Limited to 1,001, John, a 12-inch Naber Kid, was released in 1996 for a retail price of $150.

The Childhood Classics II collection from the Lawton Doll Co. offered this Tom Sawyer doll in 1993. The edition size was 500.

YR	NAME	LIMIT	ISSUE	TREND
93	JUSTINE VALENTINE 1302	OP	84.00	87.00
93	LUTHER BOWMAN 2ND EDITION 1108	OP	60.00	63.00
93	MOMMY 1312	OP	48.00	48.00
93	PEARL BOWMAN 1303	OP	56.00	59.00
93	PENNY VALENTINE 1308	OP	60.00	63.00
93	SANTA CLAUS 1311	OP	48.00	48.00
94	BONNIE VALENTINE 1323	OP	35.00	37.00
94	CHRISTINE BOWMAN 1332	OP	62.00	65.00
94	EDWARD BOWMAN 2ND EDITION 1158	OP	76.00	79.00
94	ELSIE BOWMAN 1325	OP	64.00	67.00
94	GILBERT HIGH 1335	OP	65.00	68.00
94	GWENDOLYN HIGH 1342	OP	56.00	59.00
94	JAMIE BOWMAN 1324	OP	35.00	35.00
94	JOSIE VALENTINE 1322	OP	76.00	76.00
94	KARL VALENTINE 2ND EDITION 1161	OP	54.00	57.00
94	MARISA VALENTINE 1333	OP	58.00	61.00
94	MINNIE VALENTINE 1336	OP	64.00	67.00
94	PRUDENCE VALENTINE 1331	CL	180.00	180.00
94	SHIRLEY BOWMAN 1334	OP	63.00	66.00
95	ALICE VALENTINE 2ND EDITION 1148	OP	56.00	58.00
95	EDWINA HIGH 1343	OP	56.00	58.00
95	JILLIAN BOWMAN 2ND EDITION 1180	OP	90.00	92.00
95	LEONA HIGH 1355	OP	68.00	70.00
95	LYDIA BOWMAN 1347	CL	54.00	55.00
95	MATTIE DUNN 1344	OP	56.00	58.00
95	PETER VALENTINE 2ND EDITION 1113	OP	55.00	57.00
95	REGINA BOWMAN 1353	OP	70.00	72.00
95	ROBERT BOWMAN 1348	CL	64.00	66.00
95	ST. NICHOLAS 1356	OP	98.00	101.00
96	BETH BOWMAN 2ND EDITION	OP	28.50	29.00
96	CECELIA BROWN (ALONE) 1366A	OP	27.50	28.00
96	CECELIA BROWN (W/MOTHER) 1366	OP	101.00	101.00
96	CHARLOTTE HIGH 1370	OP	74.00	74.00
96	DANIEL BROWN (ALONE) 1367A	OP	27.50	28.00
96	DANIEL BROWN (WITH MOTHER) 1367	OP	101.00	101.00
96	DARLA HIGH	OP	60.00	60.00
96	DARLENE BOWMAN 1368	CL	78.00	78.00
96	DELIA VALENTINE 2ND EDITION	OP	66.00	66.00
96	LIZZIE HIGH 2ND EDITION 1100	OP	92.00	92.00
96	LOTTIE BOWMAN	OP	97.00	97.00
96	LOUIS BOWMAN	OP	28.50	29.00
96	MAISIE BOWMAN	OP	58.00	58.00
96	MATILDA HIGH	OP	60.00	60.00
96	MELODY VALENTINE	OP	67.00	67.00
96	NICHOLAS VALENTINE (ALONE) 1365A	OP	27.50	28.00
96	NICHOLAS VALENTINE (WITH MOTHER) 1365	CL	101.00	101.00
96	SALLY BOWMAN 2ND EDITION 1155	OP	76.00	76.00
96	SHANNON FITZPATRICK	OP	59.00	59.00
96	SOPHIE VALENTINE (ALONE) 1164A	OP	27.50	28.00
96	SOPHIE VALENTINE (WITH MOTHER) 2ND EDITION 1164	OP	101.00	101.00
96	SUSANNA BOWMAN 2ND EDITION	OP	50.00	50.00
96	THOMAS BOWMAN 2ND EDITION	OP	60.00	60.00
96	TUCKER BOWMAN 1369	CL	78.00	78.00

B. WISBER — **LIZZIE HIGH SOCIETY**

YR	NAME	LIMIT	ISSUE	TREND
93	AUDREY HIGH 1301	CL	59.00	300.00
93	BECKY HIGH 1330	CL	96.00	275.00
94	CHLOE VALENTINE	CL	79.00	79.00
96	DOTTIE BOWMAN	YR	78.00	78.00
96	ELLIE BOWMAN	YR	62.00	62.00

B. WISBER — **PAWTUCKETS OF SWEET BRIAR LANE**

YR	NAME	LIMIT	ISSUE	TREND
86	AUNT LILLIAN PAWTUCKET 1ST EDITION 1141	CL	32.00	115.00
86	AUNT MINNIE PAWTUCKET 1ST EDITION 1136	CL	45.00	130.00
86	BROTHER NOAH PAWTUCKET 1140	CL	32.00	115.00
86	BUNNIES, THE/BOY 1ST ED. 1145	CL	15.00	25.00
86	BUNNIES, THE/GIRL 1ST ED. 1145	CL	15.00	55.00
86	COUSIN CLARA PAWTUCKET 1ST EDITION 1144	CL	32.00	115.00
86	GRAMMY PAWTUCKET 1ST EDITION 1137	CL	32.00	115.00
86	MAMA PAWTUCKET 1ST EDITION 1142	CL	34.00	115.00
86	PAPPY PAWTUCKET 1143	CL	32.00	115.00
86	SISTER FLORA PAWTUCKET 1139	CL	32.00	115.00
86	UNCLE HARLEY PAWTUCKET 1ST EDITION 1138	CL	32.00	115.00
87	AUNT MABEL PAWTUCKET 212	CL	45.00	135.00
87	BUNNY BED 1218	CL	16.00	115.00
87	COUSIN ALBERTA PAWTUCKET 1210	CL	36.00	115.00
87	COUSIN ISABEL PAWTUCKET 1209	CL	36.00	115.00
87	SISTER CLEMMIE PAWTUCKET 1211	CL	34.00	115.00
88	COUSIN JED PAWTUCKET 1234	CL	34.00	115.00
88	COUSIN WINNIE PAWTUCKET 1233	CL	49.00	115.00
93	AUNT MINNIE PAWTUCKET 2ND EDITION 1136	OP	72.00	75.00
93	FLOSSIE PAWTUCKET 1136A	OP	33.00	35.00
94	AUNT LILLIAN PAWTUCKET 2ND EDITION 1141	OP	58.00	58.00
94	BUNNIES, THE/BOY 2ND ED. 1145A	OP	33.00	33.00
94	BUNNIES, THE/GIRL 2ND ED. 1145	OP	33.00	33.00
94	GRAMMY PAWTUCKET 2ND EDITION 1137	OP	68.00	71.00
94	MAMA PAWTUCKET 2ND EDITION 1142	OP	86.00	89.00

YR	NAME	LIMIT	ISSUE	TREND
94	PAWTUCKET BUNNY HUTCH 1141A	OP	38.00	40.00
94	UNCLE HARLEY PAWTUCKET 2ND EDITION 1138	OP	74.00	77.00
95	BUNNIES FEMALE W/LAUNDRY 1211A,THE	OP	33.00	34.00
95	LITTLE LIZZIE HIGH ANNIVERSARY SPECIAL EVENT	YR	40.00	40.00
95	LIZZIE HIGH 10TH ANNIVERSARY SIGN. ED. 1100A	YR	90.00	90.00
95	PAWTUCKET WASH LINE 1211B	OP	20.00	21.00
95	SISTER CLEMMIE PAWTUCKET 2ND EDITION 1211	OP	60.00	62.00
96	COUSIN CLARA PAWTUCKET 2ND EDITION	*	84.00	84.00
96	LITTLE REBECCA BOWMAN 1996 SPECIAL EVENT 1372	YR	37.00	37.00
96	SISTER FLORA PAWTUCKET 2ND EDITION 1139	OP	64.00	64.00

B. WISBER — **THANKSGIVING PLAY**

YR	NAME	LIMIT	ISSUE	TREND
88	INDIAN SQUAW 1244	CL	36.00	40.00
88	PILGRIM BOY 1242	CL	40.00	45.00
88	PILGRIM GIRL 1243	CL	48.00	51.00

LAWTON DOLL CO.

W. LAWTON — **A CHILD'S GARDEN OF VERSES COLLECTION**

YR	NAME	LIMIT	ISSUE	TREND
97	MY SHIP AND I	500	695.00	695.00
97	PICTURE BOOKS IN WINTER	500	695.00	695.00

W. LAWTON — **CENTERPIECES**

YR	NAME	LIMIT	ISSUE	TREND
92	LOTTA ON STAGE	CL	*	N/A
93	LITTLE COLONEL II	CL	*	N/A
95	ALICE CENTERPIECE	CL	*	N/A

W. LAWTON — **CHERISHED CUSTOMS**

YR	NAME	LIMIT	ISSUE	TREND
90	BLESSING, THE/MEXICO	CL	395.00	950.00
90	GIRL'S DAY/JAPAN	CL	395.00	500.00
90	HIGH TEA/GREAT BRITAIN	CL	395.00	500.00
90	MIDSOMMAR/SWEDEN	CL	395.00	395.00
91	FROLIC/AMISH	CL	395.00	395.00
91	NDEKO/ZAIRE	CL	395.00	700.00
92	CARNIVAL/BRAZIL	CL	425.00	425.00
92	CRADLEBOARD/NAVAJO	CL	425.00	425.00
92	PASCHA/UKRAINE	CL	495.00	550.00
93	NALAUQATAQ/ESKIMO	CL	395.00	395.00
93	TOPENG KLANA/JAVA	CL	495.00	550.00
94	KWANZAA/AFRICA	CL	425.00	425.00
95	PIPING THE HAGGIS	CL	495.00	495.00

W. LAWTON — **CHILDHOOD CLASSICS**

YR	NAME	LIMIT	ISSUE	TREND
83	ALICE IN WONDERLAND	CL	225.00	2750.00
84	HEIDI	CL	325.00	750.00
85	HANS BRINKER	CL	325.00	1350.00
86	ANNE OF GREEN GABLES	CL	325.00	2250.00
86	LAURA INGALLS	CL	325.00	650.00
86	POLLYANNA	CL	325.00	1300.00
87	JUST DAVID	CL	325.00	900.00
87	MARY LENNOX	CL	325.00	500.00
87	POLLY PEPPER	CL	325.00	475.00
88	LITTLE EVA	CL	350.00	500.00
88	REBECCA OF SUNNYBROOK FARM	CL	350.00	600.00
88	TOPSY	CL	350.00	600.00
89	HONEY BUNCH	CL	350.00	500.00
89	LITTLE PRINCESS	CL	395.00	800.00
90	MARY FRANCES	CL	350.00	370.00
90	POOR LITTLE MATCH GIRL	CL	350.00	550.00
91	BOBBSEY TWINS, THE/FLOSSIE	CL	365.00	725.00
91	BOBBSEY TWINS, THE/FREDDIE	CL	365.00	600.00
91	HIAWATHA	CL	395.00	450.00
91	LITTLE BLACK SAMBO	CL	395.00	530.00
98	MARCELLA AND HER RAGGEDY FAMILY	1000	795.00	795.00

W. LAWTON — **CHILDHOOD CLASSICS II**

YR	NAME	LIMIT	ISSUE	TREND
92	MARIGOLD GARDEN	CL	450.00	450.00
92	OLIVER TWIST	CL	450.00	450.00
92	PETER AND THE WOLF	CL	495.00	525.00
93	TOM SAWYER	CL	395.00	395.00
93	VELVETEEN RABBIT, THE	CL	395.00	395.00
94	GIRL OF THE LIMBERLOST	CL	425.00	425.00
95	LITTLE LORD FAUNTLEROY	CL	450.00	450.00
96	PHOEBE PREBLE AND HITTY	CL	595.00	595.00
97	LITTLE ORPHAN ANNIE	500	450.00	450.00

W. LAWTON — **CHILDREN'S HOUR**

YR	NAME	LIMIT	ISSUE	TREND
91	EDITH WITH GOLDEN HAIR	CL	395.00	395.00
91	GRAVE ALICE	CL	395.00	395.00
91	LAUGHING ALLEGRA	CL	395.00	395.00

W. LAWTON — **CHILDREN'S LITERATURE**

YR	NAME	LIMIT	ISSUE	TREND
98	FANTASTIC DRAWINGS OF DANIELLE	750	750.00	750.00
98	MIRETTE ON THE HIGH WIRE	750	650.00	650.00

W. LAWTON — **CHRISTMAS COLLECTION**

YR	NAME	LIMIT	ISSUE	TREND
97	VICTORIAN CHRISTMAS	350	595.00	595.00
98	YES, VIRGINIA	350	450.00	450.00

W. LAWTON — **CHRISTMAS DOLL**

YR	NAME	LIMIT	ISSUE	TREND
88	CHRISTMAS JOY	CL	325.00	715.00
89	NOEL	CL	325.00	450.00
90	CHRISTMAS ANGEL	CL	325.00	325.00

YR	NAME	LIMIT	ISSUE	TREND
91	YULETIDE CAROLE	CL	395.00	395.00
96	BIRDS' CHRISTMAS CAROL, THE	CL	450.00	450.00
W. LAWTON			**CHRISTMAS LEGENDS**	
92	LEGEND OF THE POINSETTIA, THE	CL	395.00	395.00
93	LITTLE DRUMMER BOY, THE	CL	595.00	595.00
94	SANTA LUCIA	CL	425.00	425.00
95	NUTCRACKER, THE	CL	595.00	615.00
W. LAWTON			**CLASSIC CHILDREN COLLECTION**	
97	PRIM N PROPER	350	595.00	595.00
98	FLEURETTE 'F' FIFI	350	595.00	595.00
W. LAWTON			**CLASSIC LITERATURE**	
96	SCARLET LETTER, THE	CL	1,495.00	1495.00
W. LAWTON			**CLASSIC PLAYTHINGS**	
93	PATRICIA AND HER PATSY	CL	595.00	600.00
94	KATIE AND HER KEWPIE	CL	595.00	595.00
95	BESSIE AND HER BYE LO BABY	CL	595.00	650.00
96	KATHERINE AND HER KATHE KRUSE DOLL	CL	795.00	795.00
97	GLYNNIS AND HER GOOGLIE	750	595.00	595.00
97	GRACIE AND HER GOLLIWOGG	750	595.00	595.00
98	PETRA AND PINOCCHIO	750	595.00	595.00
W. LAWTON			**CLASSIC PLAYTHINGS II**	
96	HENRIETTE AND HER HILDA	CL	1,395.00	1395.00
W. LAWTON			**COLLECTORS GUILD**	
98	BABY BOUTIQUE BLUE	YR	495.00	495.00
98	BABY BOUTIQUE PINK	YR	495.00	495.00
W. LAWTON			**CONNOISSEUR COLLECTION**	
98	MERRY WIDOW IN THREE ACTS	150	1,995.00	1995.00
W. LAWTON			**EARLY AMERICAN PORTRAIT**	
94	ABIGAIL AND JANE AUGUSTA	CL	995.00	1500.00
95	CARRIE AND SOPHIA GRACE	CL	1,250.00	1250.00
W. LAWTON			**FABRIC OF AMERICA**	
96	ZUDIE'S COVERLET	CL	895.00	895.00
97	BOBBIN LACE	350	895.00	895.00
W. LAWTON			**FOLKTALES AND FAIRY STORIES**	
92	LITTLE EMPEROR'S NIGHTINGALE, THE	CL	425.00	500.00
92	LITTLE RED RIDING HOOD	CL	450.00	600.00
92	SWAN PRINCESS	CL	495.00	495.00
92	WILLIAM TELL, THE YOUNGER	CL	395.00	395.00
93	GOLDILOCKS AND BABY BEAR	CL	595.00	640.00
93	SNOW WHITE	CL	395.00	395.00
94	LITTLE GRETEL	CL	395.00	400.00
95	RAPUNZEL	CL	450.00	475.00
W. LAWTON			**FUN WITH DICK AND JANE**	
96	DICK	CL	495.00	495.00
96	JANE	CL	495.00	495.00
W. LAWTON			**GENTLE PURSUITS**	
94	EMILY AND HER DIARY	CL	795.00	795.00
95	EUGENIA'S LITERARY SALON	CL	795.00	795.00
W. LAWTON			**GRAND TOUR**	
94	SPRINGTIME IN PARIS	CL	895.00	1250.00
95	AFRICAN SAFARI	CL	995.00	1000.00
W. LAWTON			**GUILD DOLLS**	
89	BAA BAA BLACK SHEEP	CL	395.00	750.00
90	LAVENDER BLUE	CL	395.00	425.00
91	TO MARKET, TO MARKET	CL	495.00	500.00
92	LITTLE BOY BLUE	CL	395.00	425.00
93	LAWTON LOGO DOLL	CL	350.00	525.00
94	WEE HANDFUL	CL	250.00	325.00
95	UNIQUELY YOURS	CL	395.00	500.00
96	TEDDY AND ME	CL	450.00	450.00
97	LAWTON TRAVEL DOLL, THE	*	695.00	695.00
W. LAWTON			**LANGUAGE OF FLOWERS**	
98	DAISY	350	395.00	395.00
98	VIOLET	350	395.00	395.00
W. LAWTON			**LITTLE LUXURIES**	
97	BLACK CAT LANTERN	*	30.00	30.00
97	CHECKERS SET	*	70.00	70.00
97	FATHER CHRISTMAS TREE AND VICTORIAN ORNAMENTS	*	110.00	110.00
97	JACK O'LANTERN	*	30.00	30.00
97	PHOTOGRAPH ALBUM	*	65.00	65.00
97	SEWING BOX	*	100.00	100.00
97	STEREOSCOPE	*	125.00	125.00
97	TATTING BOX	*	100.00	100.00
97	TINY BYE LO BABY	*	225.00	225.00
97	TINY HILDA	*	295.00	295.00
97	WALNUT LAP DESK	*	110.00	110.00
W. LAWTON			**LITTLE WOMEN**	
88	AMY	CL	395.00	395.00
88	BETH	CL	395.00	395.00
88	JO	CL	395.00	395.00
88	MEG	CL	395.00	395.00
W. LAWTON			**MEMORIES & MELODIES**	
93	APPLE BLOSSOM TIME	CL	295.00	325.00

YR	NAME	LIMIT	ISSUE	TREND
93	IN THE GOOD OL' SUMMERTIME	CL	295.00	295.00
93	LYDA ROSE	CL	295.00	295.00
93	SCARLET RIBBONS	CL	295.00	320.00
94	LET ME CALL YOU SWEETHEART	CL	295.00	295.00
95	EASTER PARADE	CL	295.00	295.00
W. LAWTON			**MERELY ME COLLECTION**	
97	JUST JENNY	250	495.00	495.00
97	SIMPLY SARAH	250	495.00	495.00
W. LAWTON			**NEWCOMER COLLECTION**	
87	ELLIN ELIZABETH, EYES CLOSED	CL	325.00	1000.00
87	ELLIN ELIZABETH, EYES OPEN	CL	335.00	1200.00
W. LAWTON			**ONE-OF-A-KIND**	
89	AMELIA	CL	1,400.00	1100.00
90	GOLDILOCKS AND BABY BEAR	CL	*	N/A
91	FELICITY MINDS THE QUINTS	CL	*	N/A
92	LITTLE MISS MUFFET	CL	3,900.00	3900.00
93	CURLY LOCKS, CURLY LOCKS	CL	5,700.00	5700.00
93	JACK AND THE BEANSTALK	CL	2,500.00	2500.00
94	SARA CREWE ARRIVES AT MISS MINCHIN'S	CL	11,000.00	11000.00
95	ERRANDS FOR GRANDMOTHER	CL	4,600.00	4600.00
W. LAWTON			**PLAYTHINGS PAST**	
89	EDWARD AND DOBBIN	CL	395.00	500.00
89	ELIZABETH AND BABY	CL	395.00	500.00
89	VICTORIA AND TEDDY	CL	395.00	400.00
W. LAWTON			**POETRY COLLECTION**	
94	AT AUNTY'S HOUSE	CL	795.00	800.00
95	LUCY GRAY	CL	795.00	800.00
W. LAWTON			**ROYALTY COLLECTION**	
98	GRAND DUCHESS ANASTASIA NICHOLAIEVNA	250	795.00	795.00
W. LAWTON			**SEASONS**	
88	AMBER AUTUMN	CL	325.00	500.00
89	SUMMER ROSE	CL	325.00	400.00
90	CRYSTAL WINTER	CL	325.00	325.00
91	SPRING BLOSSOM	CL	325.00	375.00
W. LAWTON			**SMALL WONDERS**	
93	JAFRY	CL	150.00	150.00
93	JAMILLA	CL	150.00	150.00
93	MEGHAN	CL	150.00	150.00
93	MICHAEL	CL	150.00	150.00
W. LAWTON			**SPECIAL EDITION**	
88	MARCELLA AND RAGGEDY ANN	CL	395.00	1025.00
93	FLORA MCFLIMSEY	CL	895.00	1200.00
94	MARY CHILTON	CL	395.00	750.00
95	THROUGH THE LOOKING GLASS	CL	495.00	495.00
W. LAWTON			**SPECIAL OCCASION**	
88	NANTHY	CL	325.00	550.00
89	FIRST DAY OF SCHOOL	CL	325.00	550.00
90	1ST BIRTHDAY	CL	295.00	375.00
W. LAWTON			**STORE EXCLUSIVE**	
89	MAIN STREET, USA	CL	350.00	450.00
90	GARDEN SONG MARTA	CL	395.00	395.00
90	LIBERTY SQUARE	CL	350.00	350.00
90	LITTLE COLONEL	CL	395.00	395.00
91	TISH	CL	395.00	600.00
92	KAREN	CL	395.00	395.00
93	A GOOFY LITTLE KID	CL	395.00	395.00
93	BRITA/TEA PARTY	CL	395.00	395.00
93	KELLYN	CL	395.00	395.00
94	KITTY	CL	425.00	425.00
94	MELISSA AND HER MICKEY	CL	495.00	495.00
94	MORGAN	CL	425.00	475.00
95	CHRISTOPHER ROBIN & WINNIE THE POOH	CL	495.00	495.00
95	JOSEPHINE	CL	*	N/A
W. LAWTON			**SUGAR 'N' SPICE**	
86	JASON	CL	250.00	1200.00
86	JESSICA	CL	250.00	1200.00
86	KERSTEN	CL	250.00	650.00
86	KIMBERLY	CL	250.00	725.00
87	GINGER	CL	275.00	330.00
87	MARIE	CL	275.00	475.00
W. LAWTON			**TIMELESS BALLADS**	
87	ANNABEL LEE	CL	495.00	500.00
87	HIGHLAND MARY	CL	495.00	750.00
87	YOUNG CHARLOTTE	CL	495.00	850.00
88	SHE WALKS IN BEAUTY	CL	550.00	700.00
W. LAWTON			**TREASURED TALES**	
94	DREAMER, THE	CL	395.00	395.00
W. LAWTON			**TRIBUTE TO JUNE AMOS GRAMMER**	
96	JUNE AMOS AND MARY ANNE	CL	1,395.00	1395.00
96	JUNE AMOS AND MARY ANNE (AUTOGRAPHED BK. ED.)	CL	1,495.00	1495.00
W. LAWTON			**WEE BITS**	
88	WEE BIT O' HEAVEN	CL	295.00	475.00
88	WEE BIT O' SUNSHINE	CL	295.00	475.00
88	WEE BIT O' WOE	CL	295.00	475.00

YR	NAME	LIMIT	ISSUE	TREND
89	WEE BIT O' BLISS	CL	295.00	360.00
89	WEE BIT O' WONDER	CL	295.00	375.00

LENOX CHINA/CRYSTAL COLLECTION

BOLSHOI NUTCRACKER DOLLS

YR	NAME	LIMIT	ISSUE	TREND
*				
91	CLARA	OP	195.00	195.00

BONNET BABY DOLLS

YR	NAME	LIMIT	ISSUE	TREND
*				
92	EASTER BONNET	OP	95.00	95.00

CHILDREN OF THE WORLD

YR	NAME	LIMIT	ISSUE	TREND
*				
89	HANNAH/THE LITTLE DUTCH MAIDEN	OP	119.00	119.00
90	HEATHER/LITTLE HIGHLANDER	OP	119.00	119.00
90	SCOTTISH/ LASS	OP	119.00	119.00
91	AMMA/AFRICAN GIRL	OP	119.00	119.00
91	SAKURA/JAPANESE GIRL	OP	119.00	119.00
92	GRETCHEN/GERMAN DOLL	OP	119.00	120.00

CHILDREN WITH TOYS DOLLS

YR	NAME	LIMIT	ISSUE	TREND
*				
91	TEA FOR TEDDY	OP	136.00	136.00

J. GRAMMER

CHINA DOLLS - CLOTH BODIES

YR	NAME	LIMIT	ISSUE	TREND
85	AMY, 14 IN.	CL	250.00	995.00
85	ANNABELLE, 14 IN.	CL	250.00	995.00
85	ELIZABETH, 14 IN.	CL	250.00	995.00
85	JENNIFER, 14 IN.	CL	250.00	995.00
85	MIRANDA, 14 IN	CL	250.00	995.00
85	SARAH, 14 IN.	CL	250.00	995.00

COUNTRY DECOR DOLLS

YR	NAME	LIMIT	ISSUE	TREND
*				
91	MOLLY	OP	150.00	150.00

P. THOMPSON

ELLIS ISLAND DOLLS

YR	NAME	LIMIT	ISSUE	TREND
91	MEGAN	CL	150.00	150.00
91	STEFAN	CL	150.00	150.00
92	ANGELINA	CL	150.00	150.00
92	ANNA	CL	152.00	152.00
92	CATHERINE	CL	152.00	152.00

FIRST COLLECTOR DOLL

YR	NAME	LIMIT	ISSUE	TREND
*				
92	LAUREN	OP	152.00	152.00

INSPIRATIONAL DOLL

YR	NAME	LIMIT	ISSUE	TREND
*				
92	BLESSED ARE THE PEACEMAKERS	OP	119.00	120.00

J. GRAMMER

INTERNATIONAL BABY DOLL

YR	NAME	LIMIT	ISSUE	TREND
92	NATALIA/RUSSIAN BABY	OP	119.00	120.00

J. GRAMMER

LENOX CHINA DOLLS

YR	NAME	LIMIT	ISSUE	TREND
84	ABIGAIL, 20 IN.	CL	425.00	2000.00
84	AMANDA, 16 IN.	CL	385.00	1700.00
84	JESSICA, 20 IN.	CL	450.00	1900.00
84	MAGGIE, 16 IN.	CL	375.00	1700.00
84	MARYANNE, 20 IN.	CL	425.00	2000.00
84	MELISSA, 16 IN.	CL	450.00	3100.00
84	REBECCA, 16 IN.	CL	375.00	1700.00
84	SAMANTHA, 16 IN.	CL	500.00	2800.00

LENOX VICTORIAN DOLLS

YR	NAME	LIMIT	ISSUE	TREND
*				
89	VICTORIAN BRIDE, THE	OP	295.00	295.00
90	CHRISTMAS DOLL, ELIZABETH	OP	195.00	195.00
91	VICTORIAN CHRISTENING DOLL	OP	295.00	295.00
92	LADY AT GALA	OP	295.00	300.00

LITTLE WOMEN

YR	NAME	LIMIT	ISSUE	TREND
*				
92	AMY, THE INSPIRING ARTIST	OP	152.00	152.00

MUSICAL BABY DOLLS

YR	NAME	LIMIT	ISSUE	TREND
*				
91	PATRICK'S LULLABYE	OP	95.00	95.00

NUTCRACKER DOLL

YR	NAME	LIMIT	ISSUE	TREND
*				
92	SUGARPLUM	OP	195.00	200.00
93	NUTCRACKER	OP	195.00	200.00

PRIMA BALLERINA COLLECTION

YR	NAME	LIMIT	ISSUE	TREND
*				
92	ODETTE/QUEEN OF THE SWANS	CL	195.00	200.00
93	SLEEPING BEAUTY	OP	195.00	195.00

A. LESTER

SIBLING DOLLS

YR	NAME	LIMIT	ISSUE	TREND
91	SKATING LESSON	OP	195.00	195.00

LINDA LEE SUTTON ORIGINALS

L.L. SUTTON

YR	NAME	LIMIT	ISSUE	TREND
86	LITTLE DAVID	2	395.00	395.00
86	LITTLE NUBBINS	99	350.00	350.00
87	CRYSTAL	5	235.00	235.00
87	JESSICA FAITH AWAKE	75	495.00	495.00
87	JESSICA FAITH NAPTIME	50	495.00	495.00
87	MARY CHRISTMAS	75	725.00	725.00
88	AT THE BALL GAME	75	365.00	365.00
88	THE TWINS, ERNIE & EXIE	40 SETS	980.00	980.00
88	THOMAS FIRST HAIRCUT	125	595.00	800.00
89	ELIZABETH	100	595.00	800.00
89	LINDA LEE JUST ME AND MY BEAR	125	495.00	495.00
90	ALL-SMILES	40	595.00	595.00
90	ROSE-A-LEE	35	625.00	800.00
91	CINDERELLA CINDERS	20	650.00	650.00
91	CINDERELLA'S BALL GOWN	20	825.00	825.00
91	CINDERELLA'S WEDDING	20	850.00	850.00
91	LITTLE RED ROSE IN CRADLE BOARD	20	1,200.00	1200.00

YR	NAME	LIMIT	ISSUE	TREND
91	POMP IN CRADLE BOARD	20	1,200.00	1200.00
92	CORKY OF COON HOLLOW	50	595.00	595.00
92	HEATHER	10	285.00	285.00
92	PUPPY LUV	25	675.00	675.00
93	LACIE MARIE	25	650.00	650.00
93	LOIS MARIE	15	795.00	795.00
93	MISS SADIE	30	1,195.00	1195.00
94	CREEK MARY	20	1,195.00	1195.00
94	FALL BROOKE	5	1,550.00	1600.00
94	GARDEN BALLET BLUE BELL	5	475.00	475.00
94	GARDEN BALLET ROSE	5	475.00	475.00
94	GARDEN BALLEY LILLY	5	475.00	475.00
94	SOPHIE	50	695.00	715.00
94	SPRING BROOKE	5	1,550.00	1600.00
94	SUMMER BROOKE	5	1,550.00	1600.00
94	WINTER BROOKE	20	1,550.00	1575.00
95	BRITTANY	20	625.00	625.00
95	CHELSEA CHERUB & HER HEAVENLY WARDROBE	25	895.00	895.00
95	HEATHER "N" HARE	20	625.00	625.00
95	LITTLE RED ROSE TODDLER	20	495.00	495.00
95	PAIGE	10	625.00	625.00
95	SOENG MIN & HER WARDROBE	25	889.00	889.00
96	GOOSE GIRL	10	595.00	595.00
96	IWA (EE-VAH)	20	495.00	495.00
96	LADIES IN WHITE (3)	5 SETS	3,250.00	3250.00
96	MOTHER MAY I	5	495.00	495.00
96	RAINBOW'S PROMISE	20	895.00	895.00
96	SODA POP WITH LOVE	20	895.00	895.00
97	CHEN LING & PANDORA	20	498.00	498.00
97	GOLDILOCKS LET'S DANCE BABY BEAR	25	550.00	550.00
97	IVIES ENGLISH GARDEN	1	1,950.00	1950.00
97	KAIV & POLAR FRIEND	10	650.00	650.00
97	TEDDIE & TEDDIE FRIEND	15	498.00	498.00
97	TOMORROW'S WASH DAY	20	650.00	650.00
97	TUESDAY	10	625.00	625.00
98	BIRD WATCHER TWINS	7 SETS	995.00	995.00
98	BONNIE BONNET CHRISTENING BABY	10	695.00	695.00
98	BREEZIE	20	895.00	895.00
98	CRICKET	15	595.00	595.00
98	HANSEL & GRETEL	10 SETS	995.00	995.00
98	HANSEL & GRETEL'S PAINTED CHALET	10	195.00	195.00
98	KOKO ON ICE	10	550.00	550.00
98	KOKO'S PAINTED IGLOO	10	195.00	195.00
98	LITTLE GOLFER	10	575.00	575.00

MATTEL

*				
*	PARISIENNE BARBIE	*	*	110.00
90	HAPPY BIRTHDAY BARBIE	*	*	39.00
91	BIRTHDAY SURPRISE BARBIE	*	*	39.00

			35TH ANNIVERSARY DOLL	
*				
94	BLONDE BARBIE	RT	40.00	45.00
94	BRUNETTE BARBIE	RT	40.00	80.00
94	GIFT PACK BARBIE	RT	79.97	150.00

B. MACKIE **BOB MACKIE BARBIE DOLL**

*	SILK AND FLAMES BARBIE	*	*	195.00
90	GOLD BARBIE 5405	RT	144.00	800.00
91	PLATINUM BARBIE 2703	RT	153.00	250.00
91	STARLIGHT SPLENDOR BARBIE 2704	RT	135.00	850.00
92	EMPRESS BRIDE BARBIE 4247	RT	232.00	900.00
92	NEPTUNE FANTASY BARBIE 4248	RT	160.00	800.00
93	MASQUERADE	RT	175.00	900.00
94	QUEEN OF HEARTS	RT	175.00	700.00

C. SPENCER **GOLDEN JUBILEE**

94	GOLDEN JUBILEE	RT	325.00	1000.00

			HOLIDAY BARBIES	
*				
88	HOLIDAY BARBIE	RT	25.00	700.00
89	HOLIDAY BARBIE	RT	35.00	250.00
90	HOLIDAY BARBIE	RT	*	200.00
91	HOLIDAY BARBIE	RT	*	190.00
92	HOLIDAY BARBIE	RT	*	150.00
93	HOLIDAY BARBIE	RT	*	140.00
94	HOLIDAY BARBIE	RT	45.00	175.00
95	HOLIDAY BARBIE	RT	45.00	100.00

			NOSTALGIC PORCELAIN BARBIE DOLLS	
*				
89	WEDDING DAY BARBIE 2641	RT	198.00	600.00
90	SOLO IN THE SPOTLIGHT 7613	RT	198.00	300.00
90	SOPHISTICATED LADY 5313	RT	198.00	240.00

			WINTER PRINCESS COLLECTION	
*				
93	WINTER PRINCESS	RT	60.00	550.00
94	EVERGREEN PRINCESS	RT	60.00	150.00
94	EVERGREEN PRINCESS (RED HAIR)	RT	60.00	400.00
95	PEPPERMINT PRINCESS	RT	60.00	80.00

YR NAME	LIMIT	ISSUE	TREND

MCMEMORIES
Y. BELLO

	HAPPY MEALS WORLD OF IMAGINATION		
97 MCDONALD'S OLD WEST DOLL	*	65.00	65.00

Y. BELLO

	MCDONALD'S TREATS FOR TOTS		
98 NATHAN PICKS A PICKLE	*	60.00	60.00

MIDDLETON DOLL CO.
L. MIDDLETON

		BIRTHDAY BABIES	
92 FALL	RT	170.00	170.00
92 SPRING	3000	170.00	170.00
92 SUMMER	RT	160.00	160.00
92 WINTER	RT	180.00	180.00

L. MIDDLETON

		CHRISTMAS ANGEL COLLECTION	
87 CHRISTMAS ANGEL 1987	RT	130.00	550.00
88 CHRISTMAS ANGEL 1988	RT	130.00	275.00
89 CHRISTMAS ANGEL 1989	RT	150.00	220.00
90 CHRISTMAS ANGEL 1990	RT	150.00	200.00
91 CHRISTMAS ANGEL 1991	RT	180.00	220.00
92 CHRISTMAS ANGEL 1992	5000	190.00	190.00
93 CHRISTMAS ANGEL 1993/GIRL	4000	190.00	190.00
93 CHRISTMAS ANGEL 1993/SET	RT	390.00	500.00
94 CHRISTMAS ANGEL 1994	5000	190.00	190.00
95 CHRISTMAS ANGEL 1995 (WHITE OR BLACK)	CL	190.00	190.00
96 CHRISTMAS ANGEL 1996	2000	250.00	250.00

L. MIDDLETON

		CLUB	
98 BYE BABY BLESSED HOMECOMING	RT	175.00	175.00
98 BYE BABY TO GRANDMOTHER'S HOUSE WE GO	TL	*	N/A

L. MIDDLETON

		FIFTIES SERIES	
96 ANGEL KISSES EARTH ANGEL	CL	130.00	130.00
96 ANGEL KISSES SPLISH SPLASH	CL	130.00	130.00
96 LITTLE ANGEL LEADER OF THE PACK	CL	130.00	130.00
96 POLLY ESTHER CAR HOP	CL	130.00	130.00
96 POLLY ESTHER PEGGY SUE	CL	130.00	130.00

L. MIDDLETON

		FIRST COLLECTIBLES	
90 DAY DREAMER (AWAKE)	RT	42.00	60.00
90 SWEETEST LITTLE DREAMER (ASLEEP)	RT	40.00	60.00
91 DAY DREAMER SUNSHINE	RT	49.00	49.00
91 TEENIE	RT	59.00	59.00

L. MIDDLETON

		FIRST MOMENTS SERIES	
84 FIRST MOMENTS (SLEEPING)	RT	69.00	310.00
86 FIRST MOMENTS (BLUE EYES)	RT	120.00	150.00
86 FIRST MOMENTS (BROWN EYES)	RT	120.00	150.00
87 FIRST MOMENTS BOY	RT	130.00	160.00
87 FIRST MOMENTS CHRISTENING (ASLEEP)	RT	160.00	245.00
87 FIRST MOMENTS CHRISTENING (AWAKE)	RT	160.00	180.00
90 FIRST MOMENTS (TWIN BOY)	RT	180.00	180.00
90 FIRST MOMENTS (TWIN GIRL)	RT	180.00	180.00
90 FIRST MOMENTS SWEETNESS	CL	180.00	180.00
92 FIRST MOMENTS AWAKE (BLUE)	RT	170.00	170.00
92 FIRST MOMENTS AWAKE (PINK)	RT	170.00	170.00
93 FIRST MOMENTS HEIRLOOM	CL	190.00	190.00
94 SWEETNESS (NEWBORN)	RT	190.00	190.00

R. O'NEILL

		KEWPIE SERIES	
97 ALMOST ANGELIC	OP	42.00	42.00
97 BREEZY	OP	42.00	42.00
97 BUDDY	OP	52.00	52.00
97 ROSEBUD	OP	52.00	52.00

L. MIDDLETON

		LIMITED EDITION PORCELAIN	
86 DEAR ONE	CL	450.00	450.00
88 BABY GRACE	RT	500.00	625.00
88 CHERISH, FIRST EDITION	RT	350.00	540.00
88 DEVAN	RT	500.00	500.00
88 DEVAN II	100	500.00	500.00
88 MY LEE II	100	500.00	500.00
88 SINCERITY, FIRST EDITION	RT	330.00	475.00
89 MY LEE	RT	500.00	645.00
91 JOHANNA	RT	500.00	500.00
91 MOLLY ROSE	RT	500.00	500.00
94 BLOSSOM	CL	500.00	550.00
94 BRIDE, THE	200	1,390.00	1490.00
94 TENDERNESS PETITE PIERROT	CL	500.00	500.00
95 ELISE- 1860S CIVIL WAR	CL	1,790.00	1790.00
95 TENDERNESS BABY CLOWN	CL	590.00	590.00

L. MIDDLETON

		LIMITED EDITION VINYL	
81 LITTLE ANGEL-KINGDOM (HAND-PAINTED)	RT	40.00	300.00
85 LITTLE ANGEL-KING II (HAND-PAINTED)	RT	40.00	200.00
89 ANGEL FANCY	RT	120.00	200.00
90 ANGEL LOCKS	RT	140.00	150.00
90 FOREVER CHERISH	RT	170.00	195.00
90 MISSY (BUTTERCUP)	5000	160.00	195.00
90 SINCERITY (APPLES & SPICE)	RT	250.00	250.00
91 BABY GRACE	RT	190.00	245.00
91 BUBBA BATBOY	RT	190.00	190.00
91 DEAR ONE (SUNDAY BEST)	RT	140.00	140.00

YR	NAME	LIMIT	ISSUE	TREND
91	DEVAN DELIGHTFUL	RT	170.00	300.00
91	JOHANNA	RT	190.00	245.00
91	MY LEE CANDY CANE	RT	170.00	300.00
91	SINCERITY (PEACHES & CREAM)	RT	250.00	250.00
92	BETH	CL	160.00	160.00
92	COTTONTOP CHERISH	RT	180.00	190.00
92	GRACIE MAE/BLONDE HAIR	OP	250.00	250.00
92	GRACIE MAE/BROWN HAIR	RT	250.00	250.00
92	MOLLY ROSE	CL	196.00	196.00
92	SERENITY (BERRIES & BOWS)	RT	250.00	250.00
92	SINCERITY (PETALS & PLUMS)	RT	250.00	250.00
93	AMANDA SPRINGTIME	2000	180.00	220.00
93	GRACIE MAE (RED VELVET)	CL	250.00	250.00
93	PATTY	CL	49.00	49.00
94	BELOVED HAPPY BIRTHDAY BLUE	CL	220.00	245.00
94	BELOVED HAPPY BIRTHDAY PINK	CL	220.00	245.00
94	JOEY (NEWBORN)	CL	180.00	190.00
94	JOHANNA (NEWBORN)	2000	180.00	180.00
95	ANGEL KISSES BELLY DANCER	CL	139.00	139.00
95	BETH FLAPPER	CL	119.00	119.00
95	BETHIE BOWS	CL	150.00	150.00
95	BETHIE BUTTONS	CL	150.00	150.00
95	BRIDE	CL	250.00	250.00
95	GORDON/GROWING UP	CL	220.00	220.00
95	GRACE/GROWING UP	CL	220.00	220.00
95	LITTLE ANGEL BALLERINA	1000	119.00	119.00
95	LITTLE BLESSINGS BLESSED EVENT	CL	190.00	190.00
95	LITTLE BLESSINGS/AWAKE BOY	CL	180.00	180.00
95	LITTLE BLESSINGS/AWAKE GIRL	CL	180.00	180.00
95	LITTLE BLESSINGS/SLEEPING BOY	CL	180.00	180.00
95	LITTLE BLESSINGS/SLEEPING GIRL	CL	180.00	180.00
95	SWEETNESS NEWBORN	RT	190.00	190.00
98	ALL DOLLED UP	5000	180.00	180.00
98	BO PEEP	2000	170.00	170.00
98	CAT NAP	2000	170.00	170.00
98	COUNTRY COZY	2500	170.00	170.00
98	LITTLE BOY BLUE	2000	170.00	170.00
98	LITTLE PLAYMATE	2000	170.00	170.00
98	LOVING TRIBUTE	*	220.00	220.00
98	MARY MARY	2000	170.00	170.00
98	PATTY CAKE	2000	170.00	170.00
98	PROUD HERITAGE BOY	2000	164.00	164.00
98	PROUD HERITAGE GIRL	2000	164.00	164.00
98	QUIET AS A MOUSE	*	180.00	180.00
98	SANTA'S LITTLE HELPER BOY	*	180.00	180.00
98	SANTA'S LITTLE HELPER GIRL	*	180.00	180.00
98	SLUMBER KISSES	1000	170.00	170.00
98	SOFTLY SLEEPING	2000	164.00	164.00
98	STARRY NIGHT	1500	170.00	170.00
98	WEE WILLIE WINKIE	2000	170.00	170.00
L. MIDDLETON			**LITTLEST BALLET COMPANY**	
88	APRIL (DRESSED IN PINK)	7500	100.00	110.00
88	JEANNIE (DRESSED IN WHITE)	7500	100.00	110.00
88	LISA (BLACK LEOTARD)	7500	100.00	110.00
88	MELANIE (DRESSED IN BLUE)	7500	100.00	110.00
89	APRIL (IN LEOTARD)	7500	100.00	110.00
89	JEANNIE (IN LEOTARD)	7500	100.00	110.00
89	MELANIE (IN LEOTARD)	7500	100.00	110.00
L. HENRY			**MY OWN BABY**	
97	NEWBORN TAYLOR BEAR	OP	120.00	120.00
L. MIDDLETON			**MY OWN BABY**	
96	FIRST BORN MY OWN BABY BOY	OP	120.00	120.00
96	FIRST BORN MY OWN BABY BOY (DARK)	OP	120.00	120.00
96	FIRST BORN MY OWN BABY GIRL	OP	120.00	120.00
96	FIRST BORN MY OWN BABY GIRL (DARK)	OP	120.00	120.00
96	LITTLE BLESSINGS MY OWN BABY AWAKE BOY	OP	120.00	120.00
96	LITTLE BLESSINGS MY OWN BABY AWAKE GIRL	OP	120.00	120.00
96	LITTLE BLESSINGS MY OWN BABY BOY	OP	120.00	120.00
96	LITTLE BLESSINGS MY OWN BABY GIRL	OP	120.00	120.00
96	LITTLE LOVE MY OWN BABY BOY	OP	120.00	120.00
96	LITTLE LOVE MY OWN BABY GIRL	OP	120.00	120.00
97	FIRST BORN AWAKE MY OWN BABY BOY	OP	120.00	120.00
97	FIRST BORN AWAKE MY OWN BABY GIRL	OP	120.00	120.00
97	FIRST MOMENTS AWAKE MY OWN BABY BOY	CL	120.00	120.00
97	FIRST MOMENTS AWAKE MY OWN BABY GIRL	CL	120.00	120.00
97	FIRST MOMENTS MY OWN BABY BOY	OP	120.00	120.00
97	FIRST MOMENTS MY OWN BABY GIRL	CL	120.00	120.00
L. MIDDLETON			**PORCELAIN BEARS & BUNNY**	
93	BABY BUSTER	RT	230.00	230.00
93	BUSTER BEAR	RT	250.00	250.00
93	BYE BABY BUNTING	RT	270.00	270.00
L. MIDDLETON			**PORCELAIN COLLECTOR**	
92	BELOVED & BE'BE'	RT	590.00	590.00
92	SENCERITY II - COUNTRY FAIR	RT	500.00	500.00
93	CHERISH - LILAC & LACE	RT	500.00	500.00

YR	NAME	LIMIT	ISSUE	TREND
R. SCHICK			**REVA SCHICK SERIES**	
98	ANGEL LOVE	2000	180.00	180.00
98	BABY MINE	2000	164.00	164.00
98	FINE & FRILLY	2000	174.00	174.00
98	FOREVER FRIEND BOY	1500	170.00	170.00
98	FOREVER FRIEND BOY/GIRL	2500	170.00	170.00
98	HEARTS & FLOWERS	2000	170.00	170.00
98	IN THE PINK	2000	180.00	180.00
98	OOPS A DAISY	2000	174.00	174.00
98	SNOW BABY	1000	170.00	170.00
98	STAR STRUCK	2000	170.00	170.00
98	SUGAR PLUM	2000	170.00	170.00
98	YESTERDAY'S DREAM BOY	1500	184.00	184.00
98	YESTERDAY'S DREAM GIRL	2500	184.00	184.00
L. MIDDLETON			**ROMPER SERIES**	
96	FIRST BORN DARK ROMPER BOY	2000	160.00	160.00
96	FIRST BORN DARK ROMPER GIRL	CL	160.00	160.00
96	FIRST BORN ROMPER BOY	CL	160.00	160.00
96	FIRST BORN ROMPER GIRL	CL	160.00	160.00
96	LITTLE LOVE TWIN BOY	CL	160.00	160.00
96	LITTLE LOVE TWIN GIRL	CL	160.00	160.00
R. O'NEILL			**SCOOTLES**	
98	SCOOTLES	*	50.00	50.00
L. MIDDLETON			**VINYL COLLECTORS SERIES**	
82	SWEET DREAMS	RT	39.00	39.00
85	ANGEL FACE	RT	90.00	150.00
86	BUBBA CHUBBS	RT	100.00	280.00
86	DEAR ONE-FIRST EDITION	RT	90.00	245.00
86	LITTLE ANGEL-THIRD EDITION	RT	90.00	110.00
87	AMANDA-FIRST EDITION	RT	140.00	300.00
87	MISSY	RT	100.00	185.00
88	BUBBA CHUBBS RAILROADER	RT	140.00	175.00
88	CHERISH	RT	160.00	245.00
88	SINCERITY-LIMITED FIRST EDITION	RT	160.00	225.00
89	DEVAN	RT	170.00	200.00
89	MY LEE	RT	170.00	280.00
89	SINCERITY-SCHOOLGIRL	RT	180.00	300.00
92	LITTLE ANGEL/BOY	RT	130.00	145.00
92	LITTLE ANGEL/GIRL	RT	130.00	145.00
92	POLLY ESTHER	CL	160.00	160.00
93	ECHO	RT	180.00	180.00
94	ANGEL KISSES BOY	CL	98.00	100.00
94	ANGEL KISSES GIRL	CL	98.00	98.00
94	BRIDE (RUBY SLIPPER)	CL	250.00	250.00
94	COUNTRY BOY	RT	118.00	118.00
94	COUNTRY BOY (DARK)	RT	118.00	120.00
94	COUNTRY GIRL	RT	118.00	118.00
94	COUNTRY GIRL (DARK)	RT	118.00	120.00
94	TOWN BOY	RT	118.00	118.00
94	TOWN BOY (DARK)	RT	118.00	118.00
94	TOWN GIRL	RT	118.00	118.00
94	TOWN GIRL (DARK)	RT	118.00	118.00
95	ECHO LITTLE EAGLE	CL	180.00	180.00
95	FIRST BORN MY BABY BOY	CL	160.00	160.00
95	FIRST BORN NEWBORN TWIN BOY	CL	160.00	160.00
95	FIRST BORN NEWBORN TWIN GIRL	CL	160.00	160.00
95	FIRST MOMENTS LULLABY TIME	1000	180.00	180.00
95	HERSHEY KISSES/GOLD	RT	100.00	125.00
95	HERSHEY KISSES/SILVER	RT	200.00	200.00
95	LITTLE BLESSINGS PRETTY IN PINK	CL	190.00	190.00
95	LITTLE LOVE VIOLETS	CL	160.00	160.00
95	POLLY ESTHER HERSHEY COUNTRY	RT	130.00	145.00
95	POLLY ESTHER SOCK HOP	CL	119.00	119.00
95	TENDERNESS FRENCH BE BE	CL	220.00	220.00
96	BELOVED BEDTIME STORY	CL	170.00	170.00
96	BELOVED GOOD FRIENDS	1500	180.00	180.00
96	BITSY SISTER	CL	130.00	130.00
96	BUBBA CHUBBS/BUBBA THE CHUBBS-KID	1000	196.00	196.00
96	CHERISH HUG-A-BUG	5000	170.00	170.00
96	ECHO ALL DRESSED UP	CL	180.00	180.00
96	FIRST BORN SO SNUGGLY	1000	170.00	170.00
96	FIRST BORN WEE ONE	5000	170.00	170.00
96	FIRST MOMENTS CHRISTENING	1000	238.00	238.00
96	FIRST MOMENTS TOOT SWEET	5000	170.00	170.00
96	GRACE FRESH AS A DAISY	300	176.00	176.00
96	HERSHEY KISSES/GREEN	RT	200.00	200.00
96	HERSHEY KISSES/RED	RT	200.00	200.00
96	HERSHEY'S BAKER GIRL	CL	130.00	130.00
96	HERSHEY'S CAKE KIDS SET (2)	CL	220.00	220.00
96	HERSHEY'S CHOCOLATE SOLDIER	CL	130.00	130.00
96	JOEY GO BYE BYE	1000	190.00	190.00
96	LITTLE BLESSINGS CUDDLE UP	CL	180.00	180.00
96	LITTLE BLESSINGS NEWBORN TWINS AWAKE BOY	CL	180.00	180.00
96	LITTLE BLESSINGS NEWBORN TWINS AWAKE GIRL	CL	180.00	180.00
96	LITTLE BLESSINGS NEWBORN TWINS SLEEPING BOY	CL	180.00	180.00

YR	NAME	LIMIT	ISSUE	TREND
96	LITTLE BLESSINGS NEWBORN TWINS SLEEPING GIRL	CL	180.00	180.00
96	LITTLE LOVE CUDDLE BUMPS	5000	170.00	170.00
96	LITTLE LOVE SUCH A GOOD BOY	CL	160.00	160.00
96	MOLLY ROSE - GOOD FRIENDS	CL	180.00	180.00
96	MY DARLING BOY	2000	170.00	170.00
96	MY DARLING GIRL	2000	170.00	170.00
96	PRETTY BABY SISTER	CL	170.00	170.00
96	TENDERNESS SO BRAVE	CL	170.00	170.00
96	YOUNG LADY BRIDE IN WHITE SATIN	CL	250.00	250.00
97	BELOVED SUNBEAMS AND FLOWERS	2500	170.00	170.00
97	CHERISH LITTLE GUY	2500	170.00	170.00
97	DEVAN HAPPY BIRTHDAY	2500	170.00	170.00
97	FIRST BORN AWAKE BEAUTY	CL	180.00	180.00
97	FIRST BORN AWAKE BERRY SWEET	CL	170.00	170.00
97	FIRST BORN BERRY SWEET	2500	170.00	170.00
97	HONEY LOVE AWAKE BOY	5000	170.00	170.00
97	HONEY LOVE AWAKE DARK BOY	2000	170.00	170.00
97	HONEY LOVE AWAKE DARK GIRL	CL	170.00	170.00
97	HONEY LOVE AWAKE GIRL	CL	170.00	170.00
97	HONEY LOVE DARK SLEEPING BOY	2000	170.00	170.00
97	HONEY LOVE DARK SLEEPING GIRL	2000	170.00	170.00
97	HONEY LOVE SLEEPING BOY	5000	170.00	170.00
97	HONEY LOVE SLEEPING GIRL	5000	170.00	170.00
97	LITTLE ANGEL WISH FINDERS STAR BRIGHT	CL	120.00	120.00
97	LITTLE ANGEL WISH FINDERS TWINKLE TWINKLE	CL	120.00	120.00
97	LITTLE BLESSINGS SHIPS AHOY	2500	170.00	170.00
97	LITTLE LOVE PEEK A BOO BOY	2500	170.00	170.00
97	LITTLE LOVE PEEK A BOO GIRL	2500	170.00	170.00
98	HONEY LOVE ASLEEP BOY (DARK)	OP	120.00	120.00
98	HONEY LOVE ASLEEP GIRL	OP	120.00	120.00
98	HONEY LOVE AWAKE BOY (DARK)	OP	120.00	120.00
98	HONEY LOVE AWAKE GIRL	OP	120.00	120.00

L. MIDDLETON   **WISE PENNY COLLECTION**

YR	NAME	LIMIT	ISSUE	TREND
93	ASHLEY/BLONDE HAIR	RT	120.00	120.00
93	ASHLEY/BROWN HAIR	RT	120.00	120.00
93	BABY DEVAN	RT	140.00	140.00
93	GORDON	RT	140.00	140.00
93	GRACE	RT	140.00	195.00
93	JENNIFER/PEACH DRESS	RT	140.00	140.00
93	JENNIFER/PRINT DRESS	RT	140.00	140.00
93	MERRY	RT	140.00	140.00
93	MOLLY JO	RT	140.00	140.00

MIDWEST OF CANNON FALLS

S. HALE   **FOLK ART GALLERY COLLECTION**

YR	NAME	LIMIT	ISSUE	TREND
94	BEWITCHING BELINDA 11425-4	OP	40.00	40.00
94	GARDENING GIRL 11426-1	OP	45.00	45.00
94	HEARTFELT ANGEL 11422-3	OP	37.00	37.00
94	HEARTFELT ANGEL 11423-0	OP	20.00	20.00
94	SANTA GONE FISHING 12029-3	OP	65.00	65.00
94	SANTA OF CHRISTMAS PAST 12057-6	OP	130.00	130.00
94	SITTING SANTA 11424-7	OP	30.00	30.00

NABER KIDS

H. NABER

YR	NAME	LIMIT	ISSUE	TREND
95	AL	RT	360.00	500.00
95	ALMA	1001	128.00	150.00
95	ANGEL	SO	128.00	300.00
95	BABY B. JOHN	DS	99.00	175.00
95	BABY B. RACHEL	DS	99.00	175.00
95	BABY B. SANDY	DS	99.00	175.00
95	BILL	1001	128.00	150.00
95	BONNI B.	1001	128.00	150.00
95	CHARI	SO	1,500.00	1800.00
95	CRYSTEL	OP	1,500.00	1800.00
95	DANNY	1001	128.00	150.00
95	EMMA	1001	128.00	150.00
95	FORGET-ME-NOT	1001	128.00	150.00
95	GILBERT	1001	128.00	150.00
95	GRETCHEN	1001	128.00	150.00
95	JAMES THE BUTLER	1001	79.00	150.00
95	KOOKY	SO	128.00	250.00
95	LESLI MARIE	1001	128.00	150.00
95	LOUI	1001	128.00	150.00
95	MELVIN	1001	128.00	150.00
95	MYSTIK	1001	128.00	150.00
95	POLLI	1001	128.00	150.00
95	THERESA	1001	128.00	150.00
95	TOBI	1001	128.00	150.00
95	WOLFGANG	1001	128.00	150.00
96	DAVID	1001	100.00	150.00
96	JOHN	1001	150.00	150.00
96	LACEY	1001	150.00	150.00
96	LIBBI	1001	150.00	150.00
96	MARGI	1001	100.00	150.00
96	MIMI	1001	150.00	150.00

YR	NAME	LIMIT	ISSUE	TREND
96	MO	1001	150.00	150.00
96	MONTI	1001	150.00	150.00
96	PAT	1001	150.00	150.00
96	RACHEL	1001	150.00	150.00
96	SANDY	1001	150.00	150.00
96	STEVI	1001	150.00	150.00
96	TED	*	150.00	150.00
96	TRACY	1001	150.00	150.00

H. NABER — **NABER KIDS CLUB ONLY**

YR	NAME	LIMIT	ISSUE	TREND
95	BABY B. BEE	*	99.00	175.00

H. NABER — **NABER KIDS EXCLUSIVE**

YR	NAME	LIMIT	ISSUE	TREND
96	JONI	1001	150.00	150.00

NAHRGANG COLLECTION

J. NAHRGANG — **PORCELAIN DOLL SERIES**

YR	NAME	LIMIT	ISSUE	TREND
89	PALMER	250	270.00	270.00
90	ALICIA	250	330.00	330.00
90	GRANT (TAKE ME OUT TO THE BALL GAME)	500	390.00	390.00
90	KARISSA	500	350.00	395.00
90	KARMAN (GYPSY)	250	350.00	395.00
90	KASEY	250	450.00	450.00
90	KELSEY	250	350.00	350.00
90	MAGGIE	500	295.00	295.00
91	ANNA MARIE	250	390.00	390.00
91	AUBRY	250	390.00	390.00
91	CARSON	250	350.00	350.00
91	ERIN	250	295.00	295.00
91	HOLLY	175	295.00	295.00
91	LAURA	250	450.00	450.00
91	MCKINSEY	250	350.00	350.00
91	RAE	250	350.00	390.00
91	SOPHIE	250	450.00	450.00
92	ALEXIS	250	390.00	390.00
92	ANNIE SULLIVAN	25	895.00	895.00
92	BROOKE	250	390.00	390.00
92	DOLLY MADISON	100	395.00	395.00
92	FLORENCE NIGHTINGALE	100	395.00	395.00
92	HARRIET TUBMAN	100	395.00	395.00
92	KATIE	250	295.00	295.00
92	MOLLY PITCHER	100	395.00	395.00
92	POCAHONTAS	100	395.00	395.00
92	TAYLOR	250	395.00	395.00

J. NAHRGANG — **VINYL DOLL SERIES**

YR	NAME	LIMIT	ISSUE	TREND
90	KARMAN (GYPSY)	2000	190.00	190.00
91	ALEXIS	500	250.00	250.00
91	ANGELA	500	190.00	190.00
91	ANN MARIE	500	225.00	225.00
91	AUBRY	2000	225.00	225.00
91	BEATRIX	500	250.00	250.00
91	BROOKE	500	250.00	250.00
91	CHELSEA	250	190.00	190.00
91	LAURA	1000	250.00	250.00
91	MOLLY	500	190.00	190.00
91	POLLY	250	225.00	225.00
91	VANESSA	250	250.00	250.00
92	DOLLY MADISON	500	199.00	199.00
92	FLORENCE NIGHTINGALE	500	199.00	199.00
92	HARRIET TUBMAN	500	199.00	199.00
92	MOLLY PITCHER	500	199.00	199.00
92	POCAHONTAS	500	199.00	199.00

ORIGINAL APPALACHIAN ARTWORKS

X. ROBERTS

YR	NAME	LIMIT	ISSUE	TREND
95	GRACELAND ELVIS	500	300.00	300.00
95	NEWBORN	1042	195.00	195.00
95	SKITTS MOUNTAIN	192	210.00	210.00
96	NEWBORN	1710	195.00	195.00

X. ROBERTS — **ANNIVERSARY BLUE**

YR	NAME	LIMIT	ISSUE	TREND
98	AUTUMN SCHOLAR	300	395.00	395.00
98	SPRING SASS	300	395.00	395.00
98	SUMMER MISCHIEF	300	395.00	395.00
98	WINTER SNUGGLES	300	395.00	395.00

X. ROBERTS — **BABYLAND**

YR	NAME	LIMIT	ISSUE	TREND
95	DELTA	200	230.00	230.00
96	MARLENE	200	230.00	230.00
97	HAYLEY	200	220.00	220.00

X. ROBERTS — **CABBAGE PATCH KIDS**

YR	NAME	LIMIT	ISSUE	TREND
82	AMY	CL	125.00	600.00
82	BILLIE	CL	125.00	550.00
82	BOBBIE	CL	125.00	550.00
82	DOROTHY	CL	125.00	550.00
82	GILDA	CL	125.00	2000.00
82	MARILYN	CL	125.00	550.00
82	OTIS	CL	125.00	550.00
82	REBECCA	CL	125.00	550.00

YR	NAME	LIMIT	ISSUE	TREND
82	SYBIL	CL	125.00	550.00
82	TYLER	2500	125.00	2750.00
83	ANDRE/MADEIRA	CL	250.00	1250.00
84	DADDY'S DARLINS'-KITTEN	CL	300.00	460.00
84	DADDY'S DARLINS'-PRINCESS	CL	300.00	460.00
84	DADDY'S DARLINS'-PUN'KIN	CL	300.00	460.00
84	DADDY'S DARLINS'-TOOTSIE	CL	300.00	460.00
88	TIGER'S EYE-VALENTINE'S DAY	CL	150.00	300.00
89	TIGER'S EYE-MOTHER'S DAY	CL	150.00	250.00
90	JOY	500	250.00	575.00
93	HAPPILY EVER AFTER BRIDE	CL	230.00	340.00
93	HAPPILY EVER AFTER GROOM	CL	230.00	340.00
93	LITTLE PEOPLE/GIRL 27 IN.	CL	325.00	800.00
93	PREEMIE	CL	175.00	285.00
93	UNICOI BALLERINA	200	200.00	310.00
93	UNICOI KIDS	1500	195.00	325.00
94	LITTLE PEOPLE/BOY 27 IN.	CL	325.00	425.00
94	MTN. LAUREL BABY SIDNEY & LANIER	100	390.00	490.00
94	MTN. LAUREL EASTER	200	225.00	325.00
94	MTN. LAUREL IRISH BOYS	100	210.00	310.00
94	MTN. LAUREL IRISH GIRLS	200	210.00	310.00
94	MTN. LAUREL KIDS	CL	195.00	310.00
94	MTN. LAUREL MYSTERIOUS BARRY	CL	225.00	325.00
94	MTN. LAUREL NORMA JEAN	CL	225.00	225.00
94	NEWBORN FORM MOBILE PATCH	CL	198.00	300.00
X. ROBERTS		**CABBAGE PATCH KIDS CIRCUS PARADE**		
87	BIG TOP CLOWN-BABY CAKES	2000	180.00	475.00
89	HAPPY HOBO-BASHFUL BILLY	1000	180.00	330.00
91	MITZI	1000	220.00	220.00
X. ROBERTS		**CABBAGE PATCH KIDS INTERNATIONAL**		
83	AMERICAN INDIAN	CL	150.00	1300.00
83	ORIENTAL	CL	150.00	1350.00
X. ROBERTS		**CALIFORNIA COLLECTORS CLUB**		
95	BUCKY	105	220.00	220.00
X. ROBERTS				**CAREER**
95	NURSE	83	210.00	210.00
X. ROBERTS		**CHRISTMAS COLLECTION**		
79	X CHRISTMAS PAIR	CL	300.00	3500.00
80	NICHOLAS/NOEL	CL	400.00	3000.00
82	BABY RUDY/CHRISTY NICOLE	CL	400.00	2000.00
83	HOLLY/BERRY	CL	400.00	1300.00
84	CAROLE/CHRIS	CL	400.00	975.00
85	BABY SANDY/CLAUDE	CL	400.00	600.00
86	HILLARY/NIGEL	CL	400.00	400.00
87	KATRINA/MISHA	CL	500.00	500.00
88	KELLY/KANE	CL	500.00	500.00
89	JOY	CL	250.00	600.00
90	KRYSTINA	CL	250.00	250.00
91	NICK	CL	275.00	275.00
92	CHRISTY CLAUS	CL	285.00	285.00
93	RUDOLPH	CL	275.00	275.00
94	NATALIE	500	275.00	275.00
95	TREENA	500	275.00	275.00
96	SAMMY	500	275.00	275.00
97	MELODY	300	295.00	295.00
98	GINGER	300	315.00	315.00
X. ROBERTS		**COLLECTORS CLUB EDITIONS**		
87	BABY OTIS	CL	250.00	550.00
89	ANNA RUBY	CL	250.00	425.00
90	LEE ANN	CL	250.00	400.00
91	RICHARD RUSSELL	CL	250.00	425.00
92	BABY DODD	CL	250.00	350.00
93	PATTI W/CABBAGE BUD BOUTONNIER	CL	280.00	300.00
95	ROSIE	322	275.00	275.00
97	ROBERT LONDON	*	275.00	275.00
X. ROBERTS				**CONVENTION BABY**
89	ASHLEY	CL	150.00	600.00
90	BRADLEY	CL	175.00	425.00
91	CAROLINE	CL	200.00	400.00
92	DUKE	CL	225.00	350.00
93	ELLEN	CL	225.00	310.00
94	JUSTIN	CL	238.50	239.00
94	MTN. LAUREL JUSTIN	200	225.00	325.00
X. ROBERTS				**HAPPILY EVER AFTER**
93	BRIDE	CL	230.00	275.00
93	GROOM	CL	230.00	275.00
X. ROBERTS				**JINGLING JESTER**
97	JACQUELINE	500	275.00	275.00
X. ROBERTS				**LITTLE PEOPLE**
78	A BLUE	CL	150.00	4000.00
78	B RED	CL	125.00	4100.00
78	C BURGUNDY	CL	100.00	2000.00
78	E BRONZE	CL	125.00	875.00
78	HELEN, BLUE	CL	150.00	6000.00

YR	NAME	LIMIT	ISSUE	TREND
79	D PURPLE	CL	100.00	2300.00
80	CELEBRITY	CL	200.00	600.00
80	GRAND EDITION	CL	1,000.00	1000.00
80	NOEL	2500	200.00	700.00
80	SP, PREEMIE	CL	100.00	550.00
80	U UNSIGNED	CL	125.00	400.00
81	NEW "EARS"	CL	125.00	200.00
81	PR II PREEMIE	CL	130.00	250.00
81	STANDING EDITION	CL	300.00	350.00
82	BABY RUDY	1000	200.00	850.00
82	CHRISTY NICOLE	1000	200.00	800.00
82	PE, NEW 'EARS PREEMIE	CL	140.00	375.00
82	U UNSIGNED	CL	125.00	450.00
84	DADDY'S DARLINS' SET OF FOUR	CL	1,600.00	2250.00
93	LITTLE PEOPLE EDITION/STANDING 27 IN.	CL	300.00	450.00
93	UNICOI EDITION	CL	210.00	280.00
96	LITTLE PEOPLE '96 (GIRLS)	300	375.00	375.00
97	LITTLE PEOPLE	300	395.00	395.00
X. ROBERTS				**MT. YONAH**
95	FIFI POCKET BABY	200	250.00	250.00
95	SP. FASHIONS: EASTER	200	215.00	215.00
95	SP. FASHIONS: VALENTINE	200	200.00	200.00
X. ROBERTS				**NACOOCHEE VALLEY**
96	EASTER	200	215.00	215.00
96	GINA (SPROUT)	200	275.00	275.00
96	HALLOWEEN	200	210.00	210.00
96	VALENTINE	100	210.00	210.00
X. ROBERTS				**OLYMPIKIDS**
95	BASKETBALL BOY	199	275.00	275.00
95	GYMNASTICS BOY	241	275.00	275.00
95	ROWING GIRL	205	275.00	275.00
95	SOCCER BOY	162	275.00	275.00
95	SOCCER GIRL	140	275.00	275.00
95	TRACK & FIELD GIRL	422	275.00	275.00
95	WEIGHTLIFTING BOY	158	275.00	275.00
96	BASEBALL BOY	159	275.00	275.00
96	BASKETBALL GIRL	302	275.00	275.00
96	CYCLIST BOY	126	275.00	275.00
96	EQUESTRIAN GIRL	350	275.00	275.00
96	SOFTBALL GIRL	140	275.00	275.00
X. ROBERTS				**PORCELAIN FRIENDS**
94	ANGELICA	CL	160.00	260.00
94	KAREN LEE	CL	150.00	250.00
94	KASSIS LOU	CL	150.00	250.00
94	KATIE LYN	CL	150.00	250.00
X. ROBERTS				**PORCELAIN PIERROT**
95	SHARRI STARR	198	160.00	160.00
X. ROBERTS				**SAUTEE VALLEY**
97	HANNAH	200	275.00	275.00

ORIGINALS BY BEVERLY STOEHR

		LIMIT	ISSUE	TREND
B. STOEHR				**BABY SERIES**
94	AMANDA	10	1,000.00	1100.00
94	KATIE BABY	10	400.00	425.00
B. STOEHR				**CHILDREN OF MEMORIES**
94	BARBARA	50	495.00	525.00
94	JUDY	10	595.00	625.00
94	SARA	50	495.00	525.00

PEGGY MULHOLLAND INC.

		LIMIT	ISSUE	TREND
B. GERARDI				**CHRISTINA DOLL COLLECTION**
93	CHRISTINA	500	499.00	499.00
93	EMILY	500	499.00	499.00
93	MICHAEL	500	499.00	499.00
93	ROSE	500	499.00	499.00
93	SARAH	500	499.00	499.00
B. GERARDI				**SWEETMMM'S**
93	LILI	RT	130.00	140.00
93	LIZABETH	RT	130.00	140.00
93	MARGARET	RT	130.00	140.00
93	MISSY	RT	130.00	140.00
93	PETER	RT	130.00	140.00
93	ROSEBUD	RT	130.00	140.00
93	SAMANTHA	RT	130.00	140.00
93	TIFFANY	RT	130.00	140.00
94	ANGEL	2-YR	130.00	130.00
94	PRINCESS ORIANA	500	150.00	150.00
95	BUTTONS	1000	159.00	159.00
95	GEORGETTE	1000	159.00	159.00
95	PJ	OP	159.00	159.00
95	THEODORE	1000	159.00	159.00
B. GERARDI				**SWEETMMM'S FIRST PARTY**
94	SUZY	500	150.00	150.00

YR	NAME	LIMIT	ISSUE	TREND
B. GERARDI		**SWEETMMM'S FIRST VIOLIN LESSON**		
95	DOROTHY	1000	179.00	179.00
B. GERARDI		**SWEETMMM'S ROCK A BYE BABY**		
94	BABY BLUE EYES	500	150.00	150.00
94	BABY BROWN EYES	500	150.00	150.00

PRINCETON GALLERY

YR	NAME	LIMIT	ISSUE	TREND
*		**BEST FRIENDS DOLLS**		
91	SHARING SECRETS	OP	78.00	78.00
*		**CHILDHOOD SONGS DOLLS**		
91	IT'S RAINING, IT'S POURING	OP	78.00	78.00
*		**DRESS UP DOLLS**		
91	GRANDMA'S ATTIC	OP	95.00	95.00
*		**FABRIQUE SANTA**		
91	CHRISTMAS DREAM	OP	76.00	76.00
*		**IMAGINARY PEOPLE**		
92	MELINDA, TOOTH FAIRY	OP	95.00	95.00
*		**LITTLE LADIES OF VICTORIAN ENGLAND**		
90	VICTORIA ANNE	OP	59.00	59.00
91	ABIGAIL	OP	59.00	59.00
91	VALERIE	OP	59.00	59.00
92	CAROLINE	OP	59.00	59.00
92	HEATHER	OP	59.00	59.00
93	BEVERLY	OP	59.00	59.00
*		**ROCK-N-ROLL DOLLS**		
93	YELLOW DOT BIKINI	OP	95.00	95.00
M. SIRKO		**ROCK-N-ROLL DOLLS**		
91	CINDY AT THE HOP	OP	95.00	95.00
92	CHANTILLY LACE	OP	95.00	95.00
*		**SANTA DOLL**		
91	CHECKING HIS LIST	OP	119.00	119.00
M. SIRKO		**TERRIBLE TWOS DOLLS**		
91	ONE MAN BAND	OP	95.00	95.00

RECO INTERNATIONAL

YR	NAME	LIMIT	ISSUE	TREND
S. KUCK		**CHILDHOOD DOLL COLLECTION**		
94	A KISS GOODNIGHT	OP	79.00	85.00
94	TEACHING TEDDY HIS PRAYERS	OP	79.00	85.00
95	READING WITH TEDDY	OP	79.00	79.00
J. MCCLELLAND		**CHILDREN'S CIRCUS DOLL COLLECTION**		
91	JOHNNY THE STRONGMAN	YR	83.00	83.00
91	KATIE THE TIGHTROPE WALKER	YR	78.00	78.00
91	TOMMY THE CLOWN	YR	78.00	78.00
92	MAGGIE THE ANIMAL TRAINER	YR	83.00	83.00
S. KUCK		**PRECIOUS MEMORIES OF MOTHERHOOD**		
90	LOVING STEPS	RT	125.00	175.00
90	LULLABY	YR	125.00	125.00
92	EXPECTANT MOMENTS	RT	149.00	149.00
93	BEDTIME	RT	149.00	149.00
*		**TENDER MOMENTS DOLLS**		
90	KATHY	OP	40.00	47.00
90	KELLI	OP	73.00	73.00
90	KIM	OP	40.00	43.00
90	KRISTI	OP	47.00	50.00
91	CANDI	OP	106.00	106.00
91	CARRIE	OP	30.00	30.00
91	CASEY	OP	80.00	80.00
91	CHRISTINE	OP	85.00	85.00
91	CONNIE	OP	80.00	80.00
91	CORINNE	OP	79.00	79.00
91	KERRI	OP	64.00	64.00
91	TANYA	OP	45.00	45.00
91	TINA	OP	73.00	73.00
91	TONI	OP	47.00	47.00

RHODES STUDIO

YR	NAME	LIMIT	ISSUE	TREND
ROCKWELL INSPIRED		**A NORMAN ROCKWELL CHRISTMAS**		
90	SCOTTY PLAYS SANTA	CL	48.00	48.00
91	SCOTTY GETS HIS TREE	CL	59.00	59.00

ROMAN INC.

YR	NAME	LIMIT	ISSUE	TREND
E. WILLIAMS		**A CHRISTMAS DREAM**		
90	CAROLE	5000	125.00	125.00
90	CHELSEA	5000	125.00	125.00
E. WILLIAMS		**ABBIE WILLIAMS COLLECTION**		
91	MOLLY	5000	155.00	155.00
E. WILLIAMS		**CLASSIC BRIDES OF THE CENTURY**		
90	FLORA, THE 1900'S BRIDE	CL	145.00	145.00
91	JENNIFER, THE 1980'S BRIDE	CL	149.00	149.00
92	CATHLEEN, THE 1990'S BRIDE	TL	149.95	150.00
93	KATHLEEN, THE 1930'S BRIDE	YR	149.00	149.00
E. WILLIAMS		**ELLEN WILLIAMS DOLLS**		
89	NOELLE	5000	125.00	125.00
89	REBECCA	7500	195.00	195.00

YR	NAME	LIMIT	ISSUE	TREND
*		TYROLEAN TREASURES: SOFT BODY, HUMAN HAIR		
90	ANDREW	2000	575.00	575.00
90	ELLAN	2000	575.00	575.00
90	ERIKA	2000	575.00	575.00
90	MARISA	2000	575.00	575.00
90	MATTHEW	2000	575.00	575.00
90	SARAH	2000	575.00	575.00
*		TYROLEAN TREASURES: WOOD BODY, MOVABLE JOINT		
90	ANN	2000	650.00	650.00
90	DAVID	2000	650.00	650.00
90	KARIN	2000	650.00	650.00
90	LISA	2000	650.00	650.00
90	MELISSA	2000	650.00	650.00
90	MONICA	2000	650.00	650.00
90	NADIA	2000	650.00	650.00
90	SUSIE	2000	650.00	650.00
90	TINA	2000	650.00	650.00
90	VERENA	2000	650.00	650.00

SALLY-LYNNE DOLLS
S. BEATTY

YR	NAME	LIMIT	ISSUE	TREND
		FRENCH REPLICAS		
85	ANNABELLE, 30 IN.	CL	950.00	2900.00
85	CANDICE, 30 IN.	100	950.00	2200.00
85	CHARLES, 30 IN.	100	1,050.00	2200.00
85	VICTORIA, 30 IN.	100	1,050.00	2900.00
86	VICTORIA AT CHRISTMAS, 30 IN.	CL	2,500.00	4100.00

SAMSONS STUDIOS
S. BUTCHER

YR	NAME	LIMIT	ISSUE	TREND
		PRECIOUS MOMENTS SOFT SCULPTURE DOLLS		
85	DONNY 4566	*	24.00	60.00
85	HEATHER 4562	*	24.00	60.00
85	PEGGY 4565	*	24.00	60.00
85	RUTHIE 4570 ORIGINAL	*	24.00	70.00
86	GWEN 1845	*	24.00	75.00
86	KATIE 5605	*	24.00	65.00
86	SNOWFLAKE 5379	*	34.00	80.00
86	TERRIE 5488	*	24.00	75.00

SANDY DOLLS INC.
S. DY

YR	NAME	LIMIT	ISSUE	TREND
		COLLECTOR ANGELS		
95	CELESTE	CL	175.00	175.00

S. DY

YR	NAME	LIMIT	ISSUE	TREND
		LIMITED EDITION ANGELS		
95	TIFFANY	RT	195.00	195.00

R. TEJADA

YR	NAME	LIMIT	ISSUE	TREND
		LIMITED EDITION ANGELS		
96	ANGENI SPIRIT ANGEL	500	175.00	175.00

R. TEJADA

YR	NAME	LIMIT	ISSUE	TREND
		NATIVE AMERICAN		
94	MORNING MIST	RT	25.00	25.00
94	SILVER STAR	RT	25.00	25.00

S. DY

YR	NAME	LIMIT	ISSUE	TREND
		SANDRA		
94	SANDRA AUTUMN	1500	50.00	60.00
94	SANDRA WINTER	1500	60.00	65.00

S. DY

YR	NAME	LIMIT	ISSUE	TREND
		SANDY CLOWNS		
94	JESTER	1000	75.00	80.00
94	JUJU	1000	60.00	65.00

S. SCHULTZ

YR	NAME	LIMIT	ISSUE	TREND
		SARAH'S GANG		
96	BUDDY	OP	25.00	25.00
96	KATIE	OP	25.00	25.00
96	TILLIE	OP	25.00	25.00
96	WILLIE	OP	25.00	25.00
97	MARIA	OP	25.00	25.00
97	MIGUEL	OP	25.00	25.00
97	SAMMY	OP	25.00	25.00
97	SHINA	OP	25.00	25.00

R. TEJADA

YR	NAME	LIMIT	ISSUE	TREND
		SWEET SPIRIT BABY		
96	LITTLE BLOSSOM--CHEROKEE IN FRONT	RT	65.00	65.00
96	LITTLE MOONBEAM	SO	85.00	85.00
97	LITTLE BEAR'S TRACK	2500	85.00	85.00
97	LITTLE RAINDROP	2500	85.00	85.00
97	LITTLE SALA	2500	85.00	85.00
98	LITTLE BEAR'S TRACK	2500	85.00	85.00
98	LITTLE SALA	2500	85.00	85.00

R. TEJADA

YR	NAME	LIMIT	ISSUE	TREND
		TRADITIONS		
94	GENTLE DOVE--WISHRAM WEDDING CEREMONY	3500	100.00	110.00
94	GREY OWL--HUNKPAPA SIOUX CHIEF	3500	250.00	275.00
94	MEADOW FLOWER--CHEROKEE PRINCESS	3500	85.00	95.00
94	SPRING WATER W/LITTLE SCOUT	3500	115.00	125.00
94	WAR CLOUD--OGLALA SIOUX CHIEF	3500	115.00	125.00
95	BRIGHT SKY--APACHE PUBERTY	3500	100.00	100.00
95	HUNTING WOLF--CROW WARRIOR	3500	100.00	100.00
95	LADY REBECCA, POWHATAN PRINCESS POCAHONTAS	3500	160.00	160.00
95	MOUNTAIN SHADOW--YAKIMA PRINCESS	3500	100.00	100.00
95	POCAHONTAS--POWHATAN PRINCESS	3500	85.00	85.00
95	PRINCESS BLUEBIRD	1000	295.00	295.00
96	WHITE MOON--BLACKFOOT NATION	3500	75.00	75.00

An older, maroon version of Patti the platypus, one of Ty Inc.'s famous Beanie Babies, is worth up to $500. The newer version, pictured here, is worth issue price.

Cecelia by Elke Hutchens of Elke's Originals Ltd. was limited to just 435 when she was issued in 1992 for $635.

Produced by the Lawton Doll Co., Goldilocks and Baby Bear, from the Folktales and Fairy Stories collection, has increased in value since its 1993 release.

Watch your step, little one! Loving Steps is the first issue in Sandra Kuck's "Precious Memories of Motherhood" collection. The doll is produced by Reco.

YR	NAME	LIMIT	ISSUE	TREND
	R. TEJADA		**WARRIOR & PRINCESS**	
94	FALLING SNOW--NEZ PERCE PRINCESS	5000	37.50	40.00
94	LAUGHING BROOK--COMANCHE PRINCESS	5000	37.50	40.00
94	ROARING RIVER--MOHAWK WARRIOR	5000	37.50	40.00
94	SHINING CLOUD--COMANCHE PRINCESS	RT	37.50	40.00
94	SOARING HAWK--COMANCHE WARRIOR	RT	37.50	40.00
94	SWIFT ELK--IROQUOIS WARRIOR	5000	37.50	40.00
94	WHITE EAGLE--APACHE WARRIOR	5000	37.50	40.00
95	BEAR'S TRACK--FOX WARRIOR	5000	37.50	38.00
95	GROWLING BEAR	5000	37.50	38.00
95	HOWLING DOG--CHEYENNE WARRIOR	5000	37.50	38.00
95	LITTLE OTTER--HUPA PRINCESS	5000	37.50	38.00
95	POCAHONTAS--POWHATAN PRINCESS	RT	37.50	38.00
95	SWAYING REED--OJIBWA PRINCESS	5000	37.50	38.00
96	LEAPING WATER--APACHE PRINCESS	5000	37.50	38.00
96	RADIANT DOVE	5000	37.50	38.00
96	WIND RIDER	5000	37.50	38.00
96	WISE BUFFALO	5000	37.50	38.00
97	EVENING STAR	5000	37.50	38.00
97	FLYING FALCON	5000	37.50	38.00
97	GRACEFUL SONG	5000	37.50	38.00
97	WHITE STONE	5000	37.50	38.00

SARAH'S ATTIC
S. SCHULTZ

YR	NAME	LIMIT	ISSUE	TREND
*	OPIE CLOTH DOLL	500	90.00	200.00
*	PEACE ANGEL CLOTH DOLL	500	50.00	200.00
*	POLLY CLOTH DOLL	500	90.00	200.00
97	BURLEY BEAR	100	130.00	130.00
97	HAZEL W/ BIBLE	100	280.00	280.00
97	PATTY COUNTRY DOLL	100	170.00	170.00
97	SASSY COUNTRY DOLL	100	170.00	170.00
97	TIMMERY DOLL	100	350.00	350.00
	S. SCHULTZ		**BEARY ADORABLES COLLECTION**	
91	CHRISTMAS BETTY BEAR	1000	160.00	160.00
	S. SCHULTZ		**HEIRLOOMS FROM THE ATTIC**	
86	AMIE AMISH DOLL	CL	40.00	40.00
86	BETSY BOO DOLL	CL	40.00	40.00
86	BILLY BEAR	CL	80.00	80.00
86	BROWNIE BEAR	CL	36.00	36.00
86	BUFFY BEAR	CL	80.00	80.00
86	CHARITY WHITE ANGEL	CL	34.00	34.00
86	CUPCAKE DOLL	CL	32.00	32.00
86	HOLLY BLACK ANGEL	RT	34.00	180.00
86	HOPE BLACK ANGEL	CL	34.00	34.00
86	JENNIE WHITE ANGEL DOLL	CL	52.00	52.00
86	JENNIE WHITE DOLL	CL	44.00	44.00
86	JUDITH ANN BLACK DOLL	CL	34.00	34.00
86	KATIE DOLL	RT	32.00	32.00
86	LOUISA MAY BLACK COTH DOLL	CL	120.00	120.00
86	MAGGIE CLOTH DOLL	RT	70.00	125.00
86	MATT CLOTH DOLL	RT	70.00	125.00
86	NELLIE DOLL	RT	32.00	32.00
86	PETER DOLL	CL	140.00	140.00
86	PRISCILLA DOLL	CL	140.00	310.00
86	SADIE BLACK DOLL	CL	70.00	120.00
86	SPIKE DOLL	RT	32.00	32.00
86	TRAPP THE CAT	CL	36.00	36.00
86	TWINKIE DOLL	CL	32.00	32.00
86	WHIMPY DOLL	CL	32.00	32.00
87	BENJI BEAR	CL	25.00	25.00
87	LEROY BLACK RAG DOLL	CL	54.00	54.00
87	LUCY BLACK RAG DOLL	CL	54.00	54.00
87	MOLLY SMALL 5 PIECE DOLL	CL	36.00	36.00
87	PATCHES WHITE RAG DOLL	CL	54.00	54.00
87	POLLY WHITE RAG DOLL	CL	54.00	54.00
87	ROXIE RABBIT	CL	32.00	32.00
87	SUNSHINE 5 PIECE DOLL	CL	79.00	79.00
87	TESS RAG DOLL	CL	140.00	140.00
87	TILLIE RAG DOLL	CL	32.00	32.00
87	WILLIE RAG DOLL	CL	32.00	32.00
88	ALBERT	CL	20.00	20.00
88	ASHLEE	CL	20.00	20.00
88	COUNTRY GIRL	CL	26.00	26.00
88	DAISY	CL	20.00	20.00
88	DAVID	CL	20.00	20.00
88	LILY BLACK DOLL	CL	90.00	90.00
88	MAYBELLE CLOTH BUNNY	CL	46.00	46.00
88	MELVILLE CLOTH BUNNY	CL	46.00	46.00
88	MICHAEL 5 PIECE DOLL	CL	44.00	44.00
88	MRS. CLAUS 5 PIECE DOLL	RT	120.00	120.00
88	SANTA 5 PIECE DOLL	RT	120.00	120.00
88	SMILEY CLOWN	CL	126.00	126.00
88	VICTORIAN BOY	CL	24.00	24.00
88	VICTORIAN GIRL	CL	24.00	24.00

YR	NAME	LIMIT	ISSUE	TREND
89	BECKY	RT	120.00	120.00
89	BEVERLY JANE BLACK DRESS	RT	160.00	160.00
89	BEVERLY JANE-RED DRESS	RT	160.00	160.00
89	BEVERLY JANE-SUNDAY'S BEST	RT	160.00	160.00
89	BOBBY	RT	120.00	120.00
89	FREEDOM CLOWN	RT	150.00	150.00
89	GLORY ANGEL	CL	50.00	225.00
89	GREEN BEVERLY JANE	RT	160.00	160.00
89	HARMONY CLOWN	RT	150.00	150.00
89	HOLLY ANGEL	CL	50.00	225.00
89	HOPE ANGEL	CL	50.00	225.00
89	JOY ANGEL	CL	50.00	225.00
89	LIBERTY ANGEL	CL	50.00	225.00
89	MEGAN DOLL	CL	70.00	70.00
89	NOEL-CHRISTMAS CLOWN	RT	120.00	120.00
89	PEACE ANGEL	CL	50.00	225.00
89	SCOTT DOLL	RT	70.00	100.00
89	SPIRIT OF AMERICA SANTA	RT	150.00	210.00
89	VICTOR	CL	120.00	120.00
89	VICTORIA	RT	120.00	120.00
90	AMERICANA BEAR	CL	160.00	160.00
90	AMERICANA HICKORY	RT	150.00	160.00
90	AMERICANA SASSAFRAS	RT	150.00	160.00
90	BEACHTIME HICKORY	RT	140.00	165.00
90	BEACHTIME SASSAFRAS	RT	140.00	165.00
90	BETTY BEAR SUNDAY	CL	160.00	160.00
90	BETTY BEAR-CHRISTMAS	CL	160.00	160.00
90	PLAYTIME HICKORY	RT	140.00	165.00
90	PLAYTIME SASSAFRAS	RT	140.00	165.00
90	SCHOOL DAYS HICKORY	RT	140.00	160.00
90	SCHOOL DAYS SASSAFRAS	RT	140.00	160.00
90	SUNDAY'S BEST HICKORY	RT	150.00	200.00
90	SUNDAY'S BEST SASSAFRAS	RT	150.00	165.00
90	SWEET DREAMS HICKORY	RT	140.00	165.00
90	SWEET DREAMS SASSAFRAS	RT	140.00	200.00
90	TEDDY BEAR SUNDAY	CL	160.00	160.00
90	TEDDY SCHOOL BEAR	CL	160.00	160.00
91	ALL CLOTH ADORA ANGEL	RT	90.00	190.00
91	ALL CLOTH ENOS ANGEL	RT	90.00	190.00
91	ALL CLOTH MUFFIN BLACK DOLL	CL	90.00	90.00
91	ALL CLOTH OPIE WHITE DOLL	CL	90.00	90.00
91	ALL CLOTH POLLY WHITE DOLL	CL	90.00	90.00
91	ALL CLOTH PUFFIN BLACK DOLL	CL	90.00	90.00
91	CHRISTMAS HICKORY	RT	150.00	160.00
91	CHRISTMAS SASSAFRAS	RT	150.00	160.00
91	CHRISTMAS TEDDY BEAR	CL	160.00	160.00
91	ENOS	RT	90.00	190.00
91	SPRINGTIME HICKORY	RT	150.00	175.00
91	SPRINGTIME SASSAFRAS	RT	150.00	200.00
92	ANGELLE GUARDIAN ANGEL	CL	170.00	170.00
92	COUNTRY EDIE	RT	170.00	170.00
92	COUNTRY EMILY	RT	250.00	250.00
92	COUNTRY EMMA	RT	160.00	160.00
92	COUNTRY HILARY	RT	200.00	200.00
92	HARPSTER W/BANJO	CL	250.00	250.00
92	KIAH GUARDIAN ANGEL	RT	170.00	170.00
92	PEACE ON EARTH SANTA	RT	175.00	325.00
92	PLAYTIME EDIE	RT	170.00	170.00
92	PLAYTIME EMMA	RT	160.00	160.00
92	SPRINGTIME BETTY BEAR	CL	160.00	160.00
92	SPRINGTIME TEDDY BEAR	CL	160.00	160.00
92	VICTORIAN EDIE	RT	170.00	170.00
92	VICTORIAN EMILY	RT	250.00	250.00
92	VICTORIAN HILARY	RT	200.00	200.00
92	WHOOPIE	CL	200.00	200.00
92	WOOSTER	CL	160.00	160.00
93	GRANNY QUILTING LADY	RT	130.00	130.00
93	JACK BOY	500	130.00	130.00
93	LILLA QUILTING LADY	CL	130.00	130.00
93	MILLIE QUILTING LADY	CL	130.00	130.00
93	SALLY BOOBA	500	130.00	130.00
94	STAR BLACK DOLL	500	120.00	120.00
94	TILLIE/CLOWN	1000	120.00	120.00
94	TWINKLE/WHITE ANGEL	500	120.00	120.00
94	WILLIE/CLOWN	1000	120.00	120.00
95	BABY DOLL/4341	RT	300.00	300.00
95	LABOR OF LOVE/4338	150	300.00	300.00
95	LABOR OF LOVE/4339	150	300.00	300.00
95	OLIVIA/4340	150	300.00	300.00
95	TILLIE/4337	RT	300.00	300.00
95	WILLIE/4336	150	300.00	300.00

S. SCHULTZ — **LITTLE CHARMERS COLLECTION**

YR	NAME	LIMIT	ISSUE	TREND
89	RED BEVERLY JANE	RT	160.00	160.00
89	SUNDAY'S BEST-BEVERLY JANE	RT	160.00	160.00
91	VICTORIAN EMMA	RT	160.00	160.00

YR	NAME	LIMIT	ISSUE	TREND
S. SCHULTZ			**SNUGGABLE HUGGABLES**	
96	AMERICANA POSIE/1900	100	130.00	130.00
96	HALLOWEEN POSIE/1902	100	130.00	130.00
96	POPPER W/JUMPSUIT/1904	100	90.00	90.00
96	POPPER W/PINAFORE/1903	100	90.00	90.00
96	SPRING POSIE/1901	100	130.00	130.00
S. SCHULTZ			**SPIRIT OF CHRISTMAS COLLECTION**	
89	FATHER CHRISTMAS DOLL	500	150.00	150.00

SCHMID

YR	NAME	LIMIT	ISSUE	TREND
J. AMOS GRAMMER			**JUNE AMOS GRAMMER**	
80	LEIGH ANN	1000	195.00	210.00
88	ROSAMUND	750	225.00	225.00
89	KATIE	1000	180.00	180.00
89	VANESSA	1000	180.00	210.00
90	JESTER LOVE	1000	195.00	210.00
90	MEGAN	750	380.00	380.00
91	HEATHER	1000	210.00	210.00
91	LAUREN	1000	280.00	280.00
91	MITSUKO	1000	210.00	210.00

SEYMOUR MANN

YR	NAME	LIMIT	ISSUE	TREND
J. WHITE			**CHRISTMAS COLLECTION**	
90	CUPID CPD-6	OP	13.50	14.00
90	DOLL TREE TOPPER OM-124	RT	85.00	85.00
90	HAT W/STREAMERS OM-118	RT	20.00	20.00
90	HEARTFACE OM-119	RT	12.00	12.00
90	LACE BALL OM-120	RT	10.00	10.00
90	TASSEL OM-118	RT	7.50	8.00
91	ELVES W/MALL CJ-454	OP	30.00	30.00
91	FLAT SANTA CJ-115	OP	7.50	8.00
91	SANTAS, SET OF 8 CJ-12	OP	60.00	60.00
P. APRILE			**CONNOISSEUR DOLL COLLECTION**	
92	BRIDE & FLOWER GIRL PAC-6	5000	800.00	800.00
92	OLIVIA PAC-12	5000	300.00	300.00
92	VIOLETTA PAC-18	5000	185.00	185.00
P. KOLESAR			**CONNOISSEUR DOLL COLLECTION**	
92	LITTLE TURTLE INDIAN PK-110	5000	150.00	150.00
92	REVAN ESKIMO PK-106	5000	130.00	130.00
E. MANN			**CONNOISSEUR DOLL COLLECTION**	
84	MISS DEBUTANTE DEBI	CL	75.00	200.00
85	CHRISTMAS CHEER-124	RT	40.00	110.00
85	WENDY-C120	CL	45.00	160.00
86	CAMELOT FAIRY-C84	RT	75.00	235.00
87	ALICIA-YK-4215	CL	90.00	90.00
87	AUDRINA-YK200	CL	85.00	150.00
87	CYNTHIA DOM-211	RT	85.00	85.00
87	DAWN-C185	RT	75.00	190.00
87	LINDA-C190	RT	60.00	125.00
87	MARCY-YK122	RT	55.00	110.00
87	NIRMALA YK-210	RT	50.00	65.00
87	RAPUNZEL-C158	RT	95.00	190.00
87	SABRINA-C208	RT	65.00	100.00
87	SAILORETTE-DOM217	RT	70.00	160.00
87	VIVIAN C-201P	RT	80.00	80.00
88	ASHLEY-C-278	CL	80.00	80.00
88	BRITTANY-TK-5	RT	120.00	120.00
88	CISSIE-DOM263	RT	65.00	140.00
88	CRYING COURTNEY PS75	RT	115.00	115.00
88	CYNTHIA-DOM-211	RT	85.00	85.00
88	DOLL OLIVER FH-392	RT	100.00	100.00
88	EMILY YK-243V	RT	70.00	70.00
88	FRANCES-C-233	CL	80.00	140.00
88	GISELLE ON GOOSE-FH176	RT	105.00	230.00
88	JESSICA-DOM-267	RT	90.00	90.00
88	JOANNE CRY BABY PS-50	CL	100.00	100.00
88	JOLIE-C231	RT	65.00	160.00
88	JULIE-C245A	RT	65.00	170.00
88	JULIETTE BRIDE MUSICAL C246L TM	RT	150.00	150.00
88	KIRSTEN-PS-40G	RT	70.00	70.00
88	LIONEL-FH206B	RT	50.00	125.00
88	LUCINDA-DOM-293	RT	90.00	90.00
88	MICHELLE & MARCEL-YK176	RT	70.00	160.00
88	PAULINE YK-230	RT	90.00	90.00
88	SABRINA C208	RT	65.00	100.00
88	SISTER AGNES C250	RT	75.00	75.00
88	SISTER IGNATIUS NOTRE DAME FH184	RT	75.00	75.00
88	SISTER TERESA FH187	RT	80.00	80.00
88	TRACY-C-3006	RT	95.00	160.00
88	VIVIAN-C201P	RT	80.00	80.00
89	AMBER-DOM-281A	CL	85.00	85.00
89	BETTY-PS27G	CL	65.00	130.00
89	BRETT-PS27B	RT	65.00	130.00
89	BRITTANY-TK-4	RT	150.00	150.00
89	CRYING COURTNEY PS-75	RT	115.00	115.00

YR	NAME	LIMIT	ISSUE	TREND
89	DAPHNE ECRU/MINT GREEN C3025	CL	85.00	85.00
89	ELISABETH OM-32	RT	120.00	120.00
89	ELIZABETH-C-246P	RT	150.00	210.00
89	EMILY-PS-48	RT	110.00	110.00
89	FRANCES-C233	CL	80.00	130.00
89	HAPPY BIRTHDAY-C3012	RT	80.00	130.00
89	HEIDI-260	RT	50.00	100.00
89	JAQUELINE-DOLL-254M	RT	85.00	85.00
89	JOANNE CRY BABY PS-50	2500	100.00	100.00
89	KAYOKO-PS24	RT	75.00	180.00
89	KIRSTEN PS-40G	RT	70.00	70.00
89	LING-LING-PS-87G	RT	90.00	90.00
89	LIZ-YK-269	RT	70.00	110.00
89	LUCINDA DOM-293	RT	90.00	90.00
89	MAI-LING-PS-79	RT	100.00	100.00
89	MARCEY YK-4005	RT	90.00	90.00
89	MARGARET-245	RT	100.00	160.00
89	MAUREEN-PS-84	RT	90.00	90.00
89	MEIMEI-PS22	RT	75.00	230.00
89	MELISSA-LL-794	RT	95.00	95.00
89	MISS KIM-PS25	RT	75.00	180.00
89	PATRICIA/PATRICK-215GBB	RT	105.00	140.00
89	PAULA PS-56	RT	75.00	75.00
89	PAULINE BONAPARTE OM-68	RT	120.00	120.00
89	RAMONA PS-31B	RT	80.00	80.00
89	REBECCA PS-34V	RT	45.00	45.00
89	ROSIE-290M	RT	55.00	90.00
89	SISTER MARY-C-249	RT	75.00	130.00
89	SUNNY PS-59V	RT	71.00	75.00
89	SUZIE-PS-32	RT	80.00	80.00
89	TATIANA PINK BALLERINA OM-60	RT	120.00	120.00
89	TERRI-PS-104	RT	85.00	85.00
89	WENDY-PS-51	RT	105.00	105.00
90	ANABELLE-C-3080	2500	85.00	85.00
90	ANGEL-DOM-335	2500	105.00	105.00
90	ANGELA-C-3084	2500	105.00	105.00
90	ANGELA-C-3084M	2500	115.00	115.00
90	ANITA-FH-277G	2500	65.00	65.00
90	ASHLEY-FH-325	2500	75.00	75.00
90	AUDREY-YK-4089	3500	125.00	125.00
90	BABY BETTY-YK-4087	3500	125.00	125.00
90	BABY JATE-WB-19	CL	85.00	85.00
90	BABY NELLY-PS-163	CL	95.00	95.00
90	BABY SUNSHINE-C-3055	CL	90.00	90.00
90	BETH-YK-4099A/B	2500	125.00	125.00
90	BETTINA-TR-4	2500	125.00	125.00
90	BEVERLY-DOLL-335	2500	110.00	110.00
90	BILLIE-YK-4056V	CL	65.00	65.00
90	CAITLIN YK-4051V	CL	90.00	90.00
90	CAITLIN-DOLL-11PH	RT	60.00	60.00
90	CAROLE-YK-4085W	RT	125.00	125.00
90	CHARLENE-YK-4112	RT	90.00	90.00
90	CHIN FA-C-3061	RT	95.00	95.00
90	CHINOOK-WB-24	RT	85.00	85.00
90	CHRISTIE WB-2	RT	75.00	75.00
90	DAISY-EP-6	RT	90.00	90.00
90	DAPHNE ECRU-C-3025	CL	85.00	85.00
90	DIANE-FH-275	RT	90.00	90.00
90	DIANNA-TK-31	RT	175.00	175.00
90	DOMINO-C-3050	RT	145.00	145.00
90	DOROTHY-TR-10	RT	135.00	135.00
90	DORRI-DOLL-16PH	RT	85.00	85.00
90	EILEEN-FH-367	RT	100.00	100.00
90	FELICIA-TR-9	RT	115.00	115.00
90	FRANCESCA-C-3021	RT	100.00	190.00
90	GERRI YK-4094	RT	95.00	95.00
90	GINNY-YK-4119	RT	100.00	100.00
90	HOPE YK-4118	RT	90.00	90.00
90	HYACINTH-DOLL-15PH	RT	85.00	85.00
90	INDIAN DOLL FH-296	RT	60.00	60.00
90	INDIAN DOLL-FH-295	CL	60.00	60.00
90	JANETTE-DOLL-385	RT	85.00	85.00
90	JILLIAN DOLL-41PH	RT	90.00	90.00
90	JOANNE-TR-12	RT	175.00	175.00
90	JULIE-WB-35	RT	70.00	70.00
90	KAREN-PS-198	RT	150.00	150.00
90	KATE-C-3060	RT	95.00	95.00
90	KATHY W/BEAR TE1	RT	70.00	70.00
90	KIKI-EP-4	RT	100.00	100.00
90	LAURA DOLL-25PH	RT	55.00	55.00
90	LAUREN-SP-300	RT	85.00	85.00
90	LAVENDER BLUE-YK-4024	RT	95.00	140.00
90	LIEN WHA-YK-4092	RT	100.00	100.00
90	LING-LING DOLL	RT	50.00	50.00
90	LISA BEIGE ACCORDION PLEAT YK-4093	RT	125.00	125.00

YR	NAME	LIMIT	ISSUE	TREND
90	LISA-FH-379	RT	100.00	100.00
90	LISA-YK-4093	CL	125.00	135.00
90	LIZA C-3053	CL	100.00	100.00
90	LOLA-SP-79	RT	105.00	105.00
90	LORETTA-FH-321	RT	90.00	90.00
90	LORI WB-72BM	RT	75.00	75.00
90	MADAME DU POMPADOUR-C-3088	RT	250.00	250.00
90	MAGGIE-PS-151P	RT	90.00	90.00
90	MAGGIE-WB-51	RT	105.00	105.00
90	MARIA-YK-4116	RT	85.00	85.00
90	MELANIE-YK-4115	RT	80.00	80.00
90	MELISSA-DOLL-390	RT	75.00	75.00
90	MERRY WIDOW-C-3040	RT	145.00	145.00
90	MERRY WIDOW-C-3040M	RT	140.00	140.00
90	NANOOK-WB-23	RT	75.00	75.00
90	NATASHA-PS-102	RT	100.00	100.00
90	ODESSA-FH-362	RT	65.00	65.00
90	PING-LING DOLL 363RV	RT	50.00	50.00
90	POLLY DOLL-22PH	RT	90.00	90.00
90	PRINCESS RED FEATHER PS-189	RT	90.00	90.00
90	PRINCESS-FH-268B	RT	75.00	75.00
90	PRISCILLA-WB-50	RT	105.00	105.00
90	SABRINA-C3050	RT	105.00	105.00
90	SALLY-WB-20	RT	95.00	95.00
90	SHIRLEY-WB-37	RT	65.00	65.00
90	SISTER MARY-WB-15	RT	70.00	70.00
90	SOPHIE-OM-1	RT	65.00	65.00
90	STACY-TR-5	RT	105.00	105.00
90	SUE CHUEN C-3061G	RT	95.00	95.00
90	SUNNY-FH-331	RT	70.00	70.00
90	SUSAN DOLL 364MC	RT	75.00	75.00
90	TANIA-DOLL376-P	RT	65.00	65.00
90	TINA-DOLL-371	CL	85.00	85.00
90	TINA-WB-32	RT	65.00	65.00
90	TOMMY-C-3064	RT	75.00	75.00
90	WENDY-TE-3	RT	75.00	75.00
90	WILMA-PS-174	RT	75.00	75.00
90	YEN YEN-YK-4091	RT	95.00	95.00
91	ABBY C3145	CL	100.00	100.00
91	ABIGAIL-EP-3	RT	100.00	100.00
91	ABIGAL-WB-72WM	CL	75.00	75.00
91	ALEXIS-EP32	CL	220.00	220.00
91	ALICIA YK-4215	3500	90.00	90.00
91	AMANDA TOAST-OM-182	CL	260.00	260.00
91	AMANDA TR-96	2500	135.00	135.00
91	AMELIA-TR-47	CL	105.00	115.00
91	AMY-C-3147	CL	135.00	145.00
91	ANN TR-52	2500	135.00	135.00
91	ANNETTE TR-59	2500	130.00	130.00
91	ANNIE YK-4214	CL	145.00	145.00
91	ANTOINETTE FH-452	2600	100.00	100.00
91	ARABELLA-C-3163	CL	135.00	145.00
91	ARIEL-EP-33	CL	175.00	175.00
91	AUDREY-FH-455	2500	125.00	125.00
91	AURORA-OM-181	2500	260.00	260.00
91	AZURE-AM-15	2500	175.00	175.00
91	BABBY ELLIE ECRU MUSICAL 402E	2500	27.50	28.00
91	BABY BETH-DOLL-406P	2500	27.50	28.00
91	BABY BONNIE W/WALKER MUSIC DOLL-409	2500	40.00	40.00
91	BABY BONNIE-SP-341	CL	55.00	55.00
91	BABY BRENT-EP-15	RT	85.00	85.00
91	BABY CARRIE-DOLL-402P	2500	27.50	28.00
91	BABY ELLIE 17	2500	65.00	65.00
91	BABY GLORIA BLACK BABY-PS-289	CL	75.00	75.00
91	BABY JOHN-PS-498	CL	85.00	85.00
91	BABY LINDA-DOLL-406E	2500	27.50	28.00
91	BABY SUE-DOLL-402B	2500	27.50	28.00
91	BELINDA C-3164	RT	150.00	150.00
91	BERNETTA-EP-40	CL	115.00	125.00
91	BETSY-AM-6	RT	105.00	105.00
91	BETTINA YK-4144	3500	105.00	105.00
91	BLAINE-TR-61	CL	115.00	115.00
91	BLYTHE-CH-15V	CL	135.00	135.00
91	BO-PEEP W/LAMB-C-3128	CL	105.00	105.00
91	BRIDGET-SP-379	2500	105.00	105.00
91	BROOKE-FH-461	2500	115.00	115.00
91	BRYNA-AM-100B	2500	70.00	70.00
91	CAMELLIA FH-457	2500	100.00	100.00
91	CAROLINE LL-838	2500	110.00	110.00
91	CAROLINE LL-905	2500	110.00	110.00
91	CHERYL TR-49	2500	120.00	120.00
91	CHIN CHIN YK-4211	CL	85.00	85.00
91	CHRISTINA-PS-261	RT	115.00	115.00
91	CINDY LOU-FH-464	2500	85.00	85.00
91	CISSY EP-56	RT	95.00	95.00

YR	NAME	LIMIT	ISSUE	TREND
91	CLARE-DOLL 465	RT	100.00	100.00
91	CLAUDINE C-3146	RT	95.00	95.00
91	COLETTE-WB-7	RT	65.00	65.00
91	COLLEEN YK-4163	RT	120.00	120.00
91	COOKIE GU-6	RT	110.00	110.00
91	COURTNEY-LL-859	RT	150.00	150.00
91	CREOLE-AM-17	RT	160.00	160.00
91	CRYSTAL YK-4237	RT	125.00	125.00
91	DANIELLE-AM-5	RT	125.00	125.00
91	DARCY EP-47	RT	110.00	110.00
91	DARCY FH-451	RT	105.00	105.00
91	DARLA C-3122	RT	110.00	110.00
91	DARLENE DOLL-444	RT	75.00	75.00
91	DAWN C-3135	RT	130.00	130.00
91	DENISE-LL-852	RT	105.00	105.00
91	DEPHINE-SP-308	RT	135.00	135.00
91	DESIREE LL-898	RT	120.00	120.00
91	DUANANE-SP-366	RT	85.00	85.00
91	DULCIE-YK-4131V	RT	100.00	100.00
91	DWAYNE C-3123	RT	120.00	120.00
91	EDIE YK-4177	RT	115.00	115.00
91	ELISABETH & LISA C-3095	RT	195.00	195.00
91	ELISE-PS-259	RT	105.00	105.00
91	ELIZABETH AM-32	RT	105.00	105.00
91	EMMALINE BEIGE/LILAC OM-197	RT	300.00	300.00
91	EMMALINE OM-191	RT	300.00	300.00
91	EMMY-C-3099	RT	125.00	125.00
91	ERIN-DOLL-4PH	RT	60.00	60.00
91	EVALINA C-3124	RT	135.00	135.00
91	FIFI AM-100F	RT	70.00	70.00
91	FLEURETTE PS-286	RT	75.00	75.00
91	FLORA TR-46	RT	125.00	125.00
91	FRANCESCA-AM-14	RT	175.00	175.00
91	GEORGIA YK-4143	RT	150.00	150.00
91	GEORGIA-YK-4131	CL	100.00	100.00
91	GIGI-C-3107	RT	135.00	135.00
91	GINGER LL-907	RT	115.00	115.00
91	GLORIA AM-100G	RT	70.00	70.00
91	GLORIA YK-4166	RT	105.00	105.00
91	GRETCHEN DOLL-446	RT	45.00	45.00
91	GRETEL DOLL-434	RT	60.00	60.00
91	HANSEL & GRETEL DOLL-448V	RT	60.00	60.00
91	HELENE AM-29	RT	150.00	150.00
91	HOLLY CH-6	RT	100.00	100.00
91	HONEY BUNNY-WB-9	RT	70.00	70.00
91	HONEY FH-401	RT	100.00	100.00
91	HOPE FH-434	RT	90.00	90.00
91	INDIRA-AM-4	RT	125.00	125.00
91	IRIS TR-58	RT	120.00	120.00
91	IVY PS-307	RT	75.00	75.00
91	JANE-PS-243L	RT	115.00	115.00
91	JANICE OM-194	RT	300.00	300.00
91	JESSICA-FH-423	RT	95.00	95.00
91	JOY-EP-23V	RT	130.00	130.00
91	JOYCE AM-100J	RT	35.00	35.00
91	JULIA-C-3102	RT	135.00	135.00
91	JULIETTE OM-192	RT	300.00	300.00
91	KAREN-EP-24	RT	115.00	115.00
91	KARMELA EP-57	RT	120.00	120.00
91	KELLY-AM-8	RT	125.00	125.00
91	KERRY-FH-396	RT	100.00	100.00
91	KIM AM-100K	RT	70.00	70.00
91	KINESHA SP-402	RT	110.00	110.00
91	KRISTI-FH-402	RT	100.00	100.00
91	KYLA YK-4137	RT	95.00	95.00
91	LAURA-WB-110P	RT	85.00	85.00
91	LEIGH DOLL-457	RT	95.00	95.00
91	LEILA-AM-2	RT	125.00	125.00
91	LENORE LL-911	RT	105.00	105.00
91	LENORE-YK-4218	3500	135.00	135.00
91	LIBBY-EP-18	RT	85.00	85.00
91	LILA FH-404	RT	100.00	100.00
91	LILA-AM-10	RT	125.00	125.00
91	LINDSEY C-3127	RT	135.00	135.00
91	LINETTA C-3166	RT	135.00	135.00
91	LISA AM-100L	RT	70.00	70.00
91	LITTLE BOY BLUE C-3159	RT	100.00	100.00
91	LIZ C-3150	RT	100.00	100.00
91	LIZA YK-4226	RT	35.00	35.00
91	LOLA-SP-363	RT	90.00	90.00
91	LONI-FH-448	2500	100.00	100.00
91	LORI EP-52	RT	95.00	95.00
91	LORI FH-446	RT	100.00	100.00
91	LOUISE LL-908	RT	105.00	105.00
91	LUCY-LL-853	RT	80.00	80.00

YR	NAME	LIMIT	ISSUE	TREND
91	MADELEINE-C-3106	RT	95.00	95.00
91	MARCY TR-55	RT	135.00	135.00
91	MARIEL C-3119	RT	125.00	125.00
91	MAUDE AM-100M	RT	70.00	70.00
91	MELISSA CH-3	RT	110.00	110.00
91	MELISSA LL-901	RT	135.00	135.00
91	MELISSA-AM-9	RT	120.00	120.00
91	MEREDITH FH-391-P	RT	95.00	95.00
91	MERYL FH-463	RT	95.00	95.00
91	MICHAEL W/SCHOOL BOOKS FH-439B	RT	95.00	95.00
91	MICHELLE EP36	RT	95.00	95.00
91	MICHELLE W/SCHOOL BOOKS FH-439G	RT	95.00	95.00
91	MIRANDA-DOLL-9PH	RT	75.00	75.00
91	MISSY DOLL-464	RT	70.00	70.00
91	MISSY PS-258	RT	90.00	90.00
91	MON YUN W/PARASOL TR-33	RT	115.00	115.00
91	NANCY W/RABBIT EP-31	RT	165.00	165.00
91	NANCY WB-73	RT	65.00	65.00
91	NELLIE-EP-1B	RT	75.00	75.00
91	NICOLE-AM-12	RT	135.00	135.00
91	NOELLE PS-239V	RT	95.00	95.00
91	PATTI DOLL-440	RT	65.00	65.00
91	PATTY-YK-4221	RT	125.00	125.00
91	PEPPER PS-277	RT	130.00	130.00
91	PIA-PS-246L	RT	115.00	115.00
91	PRINCESS SUMMER WINDS FH-427	RT	120.00	120.00
91	PRISSY WHITE/BLUE-C-3140	RT	100.00	100.00
91	RAPUNZEL C-3157	RT	150.00	150.00
91	RED WING AM-30	RT	165.00	165.00
91	ROBIN AM-22	RT	120.00	120.00
91	ROSALIND-C-3090	RT	150.00	150.00
91	SAMANTHA GU-3	RT	100.00	100.00
91	SANDRA-DOLL-6PHE	RT	65.00	65.00
91	SCARLETT FH-399	RT	100.00	100.00
91	SCARLETT FH-436	RT	135.00	135.00
91	SHAKA-SP-401	2500	110.00	110.00
91	SHARON BLUE-EP-34	CL	120.00	120.00
91	SHARON C-3237	2500	95.00	95.00
91	SHAU CHEN GU-2	RT	85.00	85.00
91	SHELLEY CH-1	RT	110.00	110.00
91	SOPHIE TR-53	RT	135.00	135.00
91	STACY DOLL-6PH	RT	65.00	65.00
91	STEPHANIE FH-467	RT	95.00	95.00
91	STEPHANIE PINK & WHITE-OM-196	RT	300.00	300.00
91	STEPHANIE-AM-11	RT	105.00	105.00
91	SUMMER AM-33	RT	200.00	200.00
91	SYBIL BEIGE-C-3131	CL	135.00	135.00
91	SYBIL PINK-12PHMC	RT	75.00	75.00
91	TAMARA OM-187	RT	135.00	135.00
91	TERRI TR-62	RT	75.00	75.00
91	TESSA AM-19	CL	135.00	135.00
91	TINA-AM-16	RT	130.00	130.00
91	VANESSA AM-34	RT	90.00	90.00
91	VICKI-C-3101	RT	200.00	200.00
91	VIOLET EP-41	RT	135.00	135.00
91	VIOLET OM-186	RT	270.00	270.00
91	VIRGINIA SP-359	YR	120.00	120.00
91	WAH-CHING/ORIENTAL TODDLER-YK-4175	RT	110.00	110.00
92	ALICE JNC-4013	OP	90.00	90.00
92	AMY-OM-06	2500	150.00	150.00
92	BETH-OM-05	CL	135.00	135.00
92	BETTE-OM-01	2500	115.00	115.00
92	CHARLOTTE-FH-484	2500	115.00	115.00
92	CHELSEA-IND-397	OP	85.00	85.00
92	CORDELIA OM-09	RT	250.00	250.00
92	DEBBIE-JNC-4006	RT	90.00	90.00
92	DEIDRE FH-473	RT	115.00	115.00
92	DEIDRE-YK-4083	CL	95.00	95.00
92	DONA FH-494	RT	100.00	100.00
92	EUGENIE OM-225	RT	300.00	300.00
92	GISELLE OM-02	RT	90.00	90.00
92	JAN OM-012	RT	135.00	135.00
92	JANET FH-496	RT	120.00	120.00
92	JET FH-478	RT	115.00	115.00
92	JODIE-FH-495	2500	115.00	115.00
92	JULIETTE OM-08	2500	175.00	175.00
92	LAURA OM-010	RT	250.00	250.00
92	LAURIE JNC-4004	RT	90.00	90.00
92	LYDIA-OM-226	RT	250.00	250.00
92	MAGGIE FH-505	RT	125.00	125.00
92	MELISSA OM-03	RT	135.00	135.00
92	NANCY JNC-4001	RT	90.00	90.00
92	SALLY FH-492	RT	105.00	105.00
92	SAPPHIRES OM-223	RT	250.00	250.00
92	SARA ANN FH-474	RT	115.00	115.00

YR	NAME	LIMIT	ISSUE	TREND
92	SCARLETT FH-471	RT	120.00	120.00
92	SONJA FH-486	RT	125.00	125.00
92	SUE JNC-4003	RT	90.00	90.00
92	TIFFANY OM-014	RT	150.00	150.00
92	TRINA OM-011	RT	165.00	165.00
92	VIOLETTE FH-503	RT	120.00	120.00
92	YVETTE OM-015	RT	150.00	150.00
93	ADRIENNE-C-3162	CL	135.00	135.00
93	ANTONIA-OM-227	RT	350.00	350.00
93	ARLENE SP-421	CL	100.00	100.00
93	BLAINE-C-3167	CL	100.00	100.00
93	CAMILLE-OM-230	2500	250.00	250.00
93	CINNAMON JNC-4014	RT	90.00	90.00
93	CLARE FH-497	RT	100.00	100.00
93	CLOTHILDE FH-469	RT	125.00	125.00
93	DONNA DOLL-447	RT	85.00	85.00
93	ELLEN YK-4223	RT	150.00	150.00
93	GENA OM-229	RT	250.00	250.00
93	HAPPY FH-479	RT	105.00	105.00
93	HEDY FH-449	RT	95.00	95.00
93	IRIS FH-483	RT	95.00	95.00
93	JAN DRESS UP OM-12	RT	135.00	135.00
93	JAN-OM-12	2500	135.00	135.00
93	JILLIAN SP-428	RT	165.00	165.00
93	JULIETTE OM-8	RT	175.00	175.00
93	KENDRA FH-481	RT	115.00	115.00
93	KIT SP-426	RT	55.00	55.00
93	LINDA SP-435	RT	95.00	95.00
93	LYNN FH-498	RT	120.00	120.00
93	MARIAH LL-909	RT	135.00	135.00
93	NINA YK-4232	RT	135.00	135.00
93	OONA TR-57	RT	135.00	135.00
93	REBECCA C-3177	RT	135.00	135.00
93	SARETTA-SP-423	2500	100.00	100.00
93	SHAKA TR-45	RT	100.00	100.00
93	SUZIE SP-422	RT	164.00	170.00
94	ABBY-YK-4533	3500	135.00	135.00
94	ADAK-PS-412	2500	150.00	150.00
94	ALICE-GU-32	2500	150.00	150.00
94	ALICE-IND-508	2500	115.00	115.00
94	ALLY-FH-556	2500	115.00	115.00
94	ALYSSA-C-3201	RT	110.00	110.00
94	ALYSSA-PP-1	2500	275.00	275.00
94	AMY-OC-43M	2500	115.00	115.00
94	ANGEL-LL-956	2500	90.00	90.00
94	ANGEL-SP-460	2500	140.00	140.00
94	ANGELICA-FH-291E	2500	85.00	85.00
94	ANGELICA-FH-291S	2500	85.00	85.00
94	ANGELICA-FH-291WG	2500	85.00	85.00
94	ANGELO-OC-57	2500	135.00	135.00
94	ANTONIA-OM-42	2500	150.00	150.00
94	ARILENE-LL-940	2500	90.00	90.00
94	ATANAK-PS-414	2500	150.00	150.00
94	BABY BELLE-C-3193	2500	150.00	150.00
94	BABY SCARLETT-C-3194	2500	115.00	115.00
94	BLAIR YK-4532	3500	150.00	150.00
94	BOBBI NM-30	2500	135.00	135.00
94	BRANDY YK-4537	3500	165.00	165.00
94	BRONWYN IND-517	2500	140.00	140.00
94	CACTUS FLOWER INDIAN LL-944	2500	105.00	105.00
94	CALLIE-TR-76	2500	140.00	140.00
94	CALYPSO-LL-942	2500	150.00	150.00
94	CARMEN-PS-408	2500	150.00	150.00
94	CASEY-C-3197	2500	140.00	140.00
94	CATHY GU-41	RT	140.00	140.00
94	CHRIS FH-561	2500	85.00	85.00
94	CHRISSIE FH-562	2500	85.00	85.00
94	CINDY OC-58	2500	140.00	140.00
94	CLARA IND-516	2500	140.00	140.00
94	CLARA IND-524	2500	150.00	150.00
94	CLARA-IND-518	2500	140.00	140.00
94	CLAUDETTE-TR-81	2500	150.00	150.00
94	COPPER-YK-4546C	3500	150.00	150.00
94	CORA-FH-565	2500	140.00	140.00
94	CORY-FH-564	2500	115.00	115.00
94	DALLAS-PS-403	2500	150.00	150.00
94	DARYL-LL-947	RT	150.00	150.00
94	DEE-LL-948	2500	110.00	110.00
94	DELILAH-C-3195	2500	150.00	150.00
94	FAITH-IND-522	2500	135.00	135.00
94	FAITH-OC-60	2500	115.00	115.00
94	FLORA-FH-583	2500	115.00	115.00
94	FLORETTE-INC-519	2500	140.00	140.00
94	GARDINER-PS-405	2500	150.00	150.00
94	GEORGIA IND-510	2500	220.00	220.00

YR	NAME	LIMIT	ISSUE	TREND
94	GEORGIA SP-456	2500	115.00	115.00
94	HATTY/MATTY-IND-514	2500	165.00	165.00
94	HEATHER-YK-4531	3500	165.00	165.00
94	HONEY-LL-945	2500	150.00	150.00
94	HYACINTH-LL-941	2500	90.00	90.00
94	INDIAN-IND-520	2500	115.00	115.00
94	IVY-C-3203	RT	85.00	85.00
94	JACQUELINE-C-3202	RT	150.00	150.00
94	JAN-FH-584R	2500	115.00	115.00
94	JANIS-FH-584B	2500	115.00	115.00
94	JENNY-OC-36M	2500	115.00	115.00
94	JILLIAN-C-3196	2500	150.00	150.00
94	JO-YK-4539	3500	150.00	150.00
94	JORDAN-SP-455	2500	150.00	150.00
94	KATE-OC-55	2500	150.00	150.00
94	KATIE-IND-511	2500	110.00	110.00
94	KELLY-YK-4536	3500	150.00	150.00
94	KEVIN YK-4543	3500	140.00	140.00
94	KEVIN-MS-25	2500	150.00	150.00
94	KIT-YK-4547	3500	115.00	115.00
94	KITTEN-IND-512	2500	110.00	110.00
94	LADY CAROLINE-LL-938	2500	120.00	120.00
94	LADY CAROLINE-LL-939	2500	120.00	120.00
94	LAUGHING WATERS-PS-410	2500	150.00	150.00
94	LAUREN-SP-458	2500	125.00	125.00
94	LINDSAY-SP-462	2500	150.00	150.00
94	LITTLE RED RIDING HOOD-FH-557	RT	140.00	140.00
94	LORETTA SP-457	2500	140.00	140.00
94	LUCINDA-PS-406	2500	150.00	150.00
94	MAGNOLIA FH-558	2500	150.00	150.00
94	MAIDEN-PS-409	2500	150.00	150.00
94	MANDY YK-4548	3500	115.00	115.00
94	MARGARET-C-3204	2500	150.00	150.00
94	MARIA GU-35	2500	115.00	115.00
94	MARY ANN-TR-79	2500	125.00	125.00
94	MARY JO-FH-552	RT	150.00	150.00
94	MARY LOU FH-565	2500	135.00	135.00
94	MARY-OC-56	2500	135.00	135.00
94	MEGAN C-3192	2500	150.00	150.00
94	MISS ELIZABETH SP-459	2500	150.00	150.00
94	MISSY-FH-567	2500	140.00	140.00
94	MORNING DEW INDIAN PS-404	2500	150.00	150.00
94	MUSICAL DOLL-OC-45M	2500	140.00	140.00
94	NATALIE PP-2	2500	275.00	275.00
94	NIKKI SP-461	2500	150.00	150.00
94	NIKKI-PS-401	2500	150.00	150.00
94	NOEL-MS-27	2500	150.00	150.00
94	NOELLE-C-3199	2500	195.00	195.00
94	NOELLE-MS-28	2500	150.00	150.00
94	ODETTA IND-521	2500	140.00	140.00
94	ORIANA-IND-515	2500	140.00	140.00
94	PAIGE GU-33	2500	150.00	150.00
94	PAMELA-LL-949	RT	115.00	115.00
94	PANAMA OM-43	2500	195.00	195.00
94	PATTY-GU-34	2500	115.00	115.00
94	PAYSON YK-4541	3500	135.00	135.00
94	PAYTON-PS-407	2500	150.00	150.00
94	PEARL IND-523	2500	275.00	275.00
94	PEGEEN-C-3205	RT	150.00	150.00
94	PEGGY TR-75	2500	185.00	185.00
94	PETULA-C-3191	2500	140.00	140.00
94	PRINCESS FOXFIRE PS-411	2500	150.00	150.00
94	PRINCESS MOONRISE-YK-4542	3500	140.00	140.00
94	PRINCESS SNOW FLOWER PS-402	2500	150.00	150.00
94	PRISCILLA-YK-4538	3500	135.00	135.00
94	REBECCA C-3177	2500	135.00	135.00
94	REGINA-OM-41	2500	150.00	150.00
94	RITA FH-553	2500	115.00	115.00
94	ROBBY-NM-29	2500	135.00	135.00
94	SARETTA SP-423	2500	100.00	100.00
94	SHAKA-TR-45	2500	100.00	100.00
94	SISTER SUZIE-IND-509	2500	95.00	95.00
94	SOUTHERN BELLE FH-570	2500	140.00	140.00
94	SPARKLE-OM-40	2500	150.00	150.00
94	STEPHIE OC-41M	2500	115.00	115.00
94	SUE SWEL TR-73	2500	110.00	110.00
94	SUGAR PLUM FAIRY OM-39	2500	150.00	150.00
94	SUZANNE LL-943	2500	105.00	105.00
94	SUZIE-GU-38	2500	135.00	135.00
94	SUZIE-SP-422	2500	164.00	165.00
94	TAFFEY TR-80	2500	150.00	150.00
94	TALLULAH-OM-44	2500	275.00	275.00
94	TERESA C-3198	RT	110.00	110.00
94	TIFFANY OC-44M	2500	140.00	140.00
94	TIPPI LL-946	RT	110.00	110.00

YR	NAME	LIMIT	ISSUE	TREND
94	TODD YK-4540	3500	45.00	45.00
94	TOPAZ TR-74	RT	195.00	195.00
94	TRIXIE TR-77	2500	110.00	110.00
94	VIRGINIA-TR-78	2500	195.00	195.00
94	WENDY MS-26	2500	150.00	150.00
95	BRENDA DOLL 551	2500	60.00	60.00
95	BRIANNA GU-300B	2500	30.00	30.00
95	BRIE C-3230	2500	30.00	30.00
95	BRIE CD-1631OC	2500	30.00	30.00
95	BRIE OM-89W	2500	125.00	125.00
95	BRITT OC077	2500	40.00	40.00
95	BRITTANY DOLL 558	2500	35.00	35.00
95	BRUGUNDY ANGEL FH-291D	2500	75.00	75.00
95	BRYNA DOLL 555	2500	35.00	35.00
95	BUNNY TR-97	2500	85.00	85.00
95	CAITLIN LL-997	2500	115.00	115.00
95	CANDICE TR-94	RT	135.00	135.00
95	CARMEL TR-93	2500	125.00	125.00
95	CAROLOTTA OM-80	2500	175.00	175.00
95	CARRIE C-3231	2500	30.00	30.00
95	CATHERINE RDK-231	2500	30.00	30.00
95	CECILY DOLL 552	RT	60.00	60.00
95	CELENE FH-618	2500	120.00	120.00
95	CELESTINE LL-982	2500	100.00	100.00
95	CHELSEA DOLL 560	2500	35.00	35.00
95	CHERRY FH-616	2500	100.00	100.00
95	CHRISTMAS KITTEN IND-530	2500	100.00	100.00
95	CLANCY GU-54	2500	80.00	80.00
95	CODY FH-629	2500	120.00	120.00
95	CYNTHIA GU-300C	2500	30.00	30.00
95	DANIELLE MER-808	2500	65.00	65.00
95	DANIELLE PS-432	2500	100.00	100.00
95	DARCY FH-636	2500	80.00	80.00
95	DARCY LL-986	2500	110.00	110.00
95	DARLA LL-988	2500	100.00	100.00
95	DENISE LL-994	2500	105.00	105.00
95	DIANA RDK-221A	2500	35.00	35.00
95	DIANE PS-444	2500	110.00	110.00
95	DINAH OC-79	2500	40.00	40.00
95	DONNA GU-300D	2500	30.00	30.00
95	DULCIE FH-622	2500	110.00	110.00
95	ELAINE CD-02210	2500	50.00	50.00
95	ELEANOR C16669	2500	35.00	35.00
95	ELIZABETH DOLL 553	2500	35.00	35.00
95	ELLIE FH-621	2500	125.00	125.00
95	EMMA DOLL-559	2500	35.00	35.00
95	EMMA GU-300E	2500	30.00	30.00
95	EMMY IND-533	2500	85.00	85.00
95	ERIN RDK-223	2500	30.00	30.00
95	FAWN C-3228	2500	55.00	55.00
95	FELICIA TR-9	2500	30.00	30.00
95	FLEUR C16415	2500	30.00	30.00
95	GEORGIA IND-528	2500	125.00	125.00
95	GINNIE FH-619	2500	110.00	110.00
95	GOLD ANGEL FH-511G	2500	85.00	85.00
95	GREEN ANGEL FH-511C	2500	85.00	85.00
95	GRETCHEN FH-620	2500	120.00	120.00
95	GUARDIAN ANGEL OM-91	2500	200.00	200.00
95	GUARDIAN ANGEL TR-98	2500	85.00	85.00
95	HAPPY RDK-238	2500	25.00	25.00
95	HEATHER LL-991	2500	115.00	115.00
95	HEATHER PS-436	2500	115.00	115.00
95	HOLLY CD-16526	2500	30.00	30.00
95	HYACINTH C-3227	2500	130.00	130.00
95	IRENE GU-56	2500	85.00	85.00
95	IRINA RDK-237	2500	35.00	35.00
95	IVANA RDK-233	2500	35.00	35.00
95	JAMAICA LL-989	2500	75.00	75.00
95	JENNIFER PS-446	2500	145.00	145.00
95	JENNY CD-16673B	2500	35.00	35.00
95	JERRI PS-434	2500	100.00	100.00
95	JESSICA RDK-225	2500	30.00	30.00
95	JEWEL TR-100	2500	110.00	110.00
95	JOELLA CD-16779	2500	35.00	35.00
95	JOY CS-1450A	2500	35.00	35.00
95	JOY TR-99	2500	85.00	85.00
95	JULIA C-3234	2500	100.00	100.00
95	JULIA RDK-222	2500	35.00	35.00
95	JUNE CD-2212	2500	50.00	50.00
95	KARYN RDK-224	2500	35.00	35.00
95	KELSEY DOLL 561	2500	35.00	35.00
95	KIMMIE CS-15816	2500	30.00	30.00
95	KITTY IND-527	2500	40.00	40.00
95	LENORE FH-617	2500	120.00	120.00
95	LENORE RDK-229	2500	50.00	50.00

YR	NAME	LIMIT	ISSUE	TREND
95	LESLIE LL-983	2500	105.00	105.00
95	LESLIE MER-809	2500	65.00	65.00
95	LILA GU-55	2500	55.00	55.00
95	LILI CD-16888	2500	30.00	30.00
95	LILY FH-630	RT	120.00	120.00
95	LINDSAY PS-442	2500	175.00	175.00
95	LISETTE LL-993	2500	105.00	105.00
95	LITTLE BOBBY RDK-235	2500	25.00	25.00
95	LITTLE LISA OM-86	RT	125.00	125.00
95	LITTLE LORI RDK-228	2500	20.00	20.00
95	LITTLE LOU RDK-227	2500	20.00	20.00
95	LITTLE MARY RDK-234	2500	25.00	25.00
95	LITTLE PATTY PS-429	2500	50.00	50.00
95	LUCIE MER-607	2500	65.00	65.00
95	LYNN LL-995	2500	105.00	105.00
95	MAE PS-431	2500	70.00	70.00
95	MAGGIE IND-532	2500	80.00	80.00
95	MARIA PS-437	2500	125.00	125.00
95	MARIELLE PS-443	2500	175.00	175.00
95	MARTINA RDK-232	2500	35.00	35.00
95	MARY ANN FH-633	2500	110.00	110.00
95	MARY ELIZABETH OC-51	2500	50.00	50.00
95	MAXINE C-3225	RT	125.00	125.00
95	MC KENZIE LL-987	2500	100.00	100.00
95	MEGAN RDK-220	2500	30.00	30.00
95	MEREDITH MER-806	2500	65.00	65.00
95	MERRI MER-810	2500	65.00	65.00
95	MINDI PS-441	2500	125.00	125.00
95	MINDY LL-990	2500	75.00	75.00
95	MIRANDA C16456B	2500	30.00	30.00
95	MIRANDA TR-91	2500	135.00	135.00
95	MONICA TR-95	2500	135.00	135.00
95	NANCY FH-615	2500	100.00	100.00
95	NATASHA TR-90	RT	125.00	125.00
95	NORMAN C-3226	2500	135.00	135.00
95	OUR FIRST SKATES RDK-226/BG	2500	50.00	50.00
95	PAIGE IND-529	2500	80.00	80.00
95	PAN PAN GU-52	2500	60.00	60.00
95	PATTY C-3220	2500	60.00	60.00
95	PAULETTE PS-430	2500	80.00	80.00
95	PAULINE PS-440	2500	65.00	65.00
95	PEACHES IND-531	2500	80.00	80.00
95	RAINIE LL-984	2500	125.00	125.00
95	ROBIN C-3236	2500	60.00	60.00
95	RUSTY CS-1450B	2500	35.00	35.00
95	SARAH C-3214	RT	110.00	110.00
95	SASHA GU-57	2500	75.00	75.00
95	SHIMMERING CAROLINE LL-992	2500	115.00	115.00
95	SLEEPING BEAUTY OM-88	2500	115.00	115.00
95	SOPHIA PS-445	2500	125.00	125.00
95	SOUTHERN BELLE BRIDE FH-637	2500	160.00	160.00
95	STACY FH-634	2500	110.00	110.00
95	STACY OC-75	2500	40.00	40.00
95	SUZANNE DOLL 554	2500	35.00	35.00
95	SUZIE OC-80	2500	50.00	50.00
95	SWEET PEA LL-981	2500	90.00	90.00
95	SYLVIE CD-16634B	2500	35.00	35.00
95	TABITHA C-3233	2500	50.00	50.00
95	TERRI OM-78	2500	150.00	150.00
95	TINA OM-79	2500	150.00	150.00
95	TOBEY C-3232	2500	50.00	50.00
95	WEL LIN GU-44	2500	70.00	70.00
95	WENDY FH-626	2500	200.00	200.00
95	WINNIE LL-965	2500	75.00	75.00
95	WINTER WONDERLAND RDK-301	2500	35.00	35.00
95	WOODLAND SPRITE OM-90	2500	100.00	100.00
95	YELENA RDK-236	2500	35.00	35.00

H. PAYNE — CONNOISSEUR DOLL COLLECTION

YR	NAME	LIMIT	ISSUE	TREND
92	LITTLE MATCH GIRL HP-205	5000	150.00	150.00
92	POLLY HP-208	5000	120.00	120.00

M. SEVERINO — CONNOISSEUR DOLL COLLECTION

YR	NAME	LIMIT	ISSUE	TREND
92	MEGAN MS-12	5000	125.00	125.00

P. APRILE — SIGNATURE DOLL SERIES

YR	NAME	LIMIT	ISSUE	TREND
91	PAULETTE-PAC-2	5000	250.00	250.00
91	PAULETTE-PAC-4	5000	250.00	250.00
92	ALEXANDRIA-PAC-19	5000	300.00	300.00
92	CASSANDRA-PAC-8	CL	450.00	450.00
92	CASSIE FLOWER GIRL-PAC-9	CL	175.00	175.00
92	CELINE-PAC-11	5000	165.00	165.00
92	CLARISSA-PAC-3	5000	165.00	165.00
92	CYNTHIA-PAC-10	RT	165.00	165.00
92	EUGENIE BRIDE-PAC-1	5000	165.00	165.00
92	EVENING STAR-PAC-5	RT	500.00	500.00
92	MELANIE PAC-14	RT	300.00	300.00
92	NADIA PAC-18	RT	175.00	175.00

YR	NAME	LIMIT	ISSUE	TREND
92	PAVLOVA PAC-17	RT	145.00	145.00
92	VANESSA PAC-15	RT	300.00	300.00
92	VIOLETTA PAC-16	RT	165.00	165.00
95	AMELIA PAC-28	5000	130.00	130.00
95	BRIE PPA-26	5000	180.00	180.00
95	IMAN PPA-24	5000	110.00	110.00
S. BILOTTO			**SIGNATURE DOLL SERIES**	
91	PRECIOUS BABY-SB-100	5000	250.00	250.00
91	PRECIOUS PARTY TIME-SB-102	5000	250.00	250.00
91	PRECIOUS SPRING TIME-SB-104	CL	250.00	250.00
M.A. BYERLY			**SIGNATURE DOLL SERIES**	
91	DOZY ELF WITH FEATHERBED-MAB-100	RT	110.00	110.00
91	DUBY ELF WITH FEATHERBED-MAB-103	RT	110.00	110.00
91	DUDLEY ELF WITH FEATHERBED-MAB-101	RT	110.00	110.00
91	DUFFY ELF WITH FEATHERBED-MAB-102	RT	110.00	110.00
E. DALI			**SIGNATURE DOLL SERIES**	
95	CARA DALI-1	5000	400.00	400.00
95	PATRICIA DALI-3	5000	280.00	280.00
95	STACY DALI-2	5000	360.00	360.00
K. FITZPATRICK			**SIGNATURE DOLL SERIES**	
95	AMANDA KSFA-1	5000	175.00	175.00
95	HAPPY JFC-100	5000	120.00	120.00
J. GRAMMER			**SIGNATURE DOLL SERIES**	
94	SIS JAG-110	RT	110.00	110.00
94	TEX-JAG-114	5000	110.00	110.00
94	TRACY JAG-111	5000	150.00	150.00
94	TREVOR-JAG-112	5000	115.00	115.00
H. KAHL-HYLAND			**SIGNATURE DOLL SERIES**	
93	GRACE-HKH-2	5000	250.00	250.00
93	HELENE-HKH-1	5000	250.00	250.00
93	REILLY-HKH-3	5000	260.00	260.00
95	AMY ROSE HKHF-200	5000	125.00	125.00
95	BRAD HKH-15	5000	85.00	85.00
95	LAUREL HKH-17R	5000	110.00	110.00
95	LAUREN HKH-202	5000	150.00	150.00
95	LUCY HKH-14	RT	105.00	105.00
95	NATASHA HKH-17P	5000	110.00	110.00
95	NIKKI HKHF-20	5000	125.00	125.00
95	SUZIE HKH-16	5000	100.00	100.00
P. KOLESAR			**SIGNATURE DOLL SERIES**	
91	BRIDGETTE-PK-104	RT	120.00	120.00
91	CLAIR ANN-PK-252	5000	100.00	100.00
91	ENOC-PK-100	5000	100.00	100.00
91	SHUN LEE-PK-102	CL	120.00	120.00
91	SPARKLE-PK-250	5000	100.00	100.00
91	SUSAN MARIE-PK-103	RT	120.00	120.00
91	SWEET PEA-PK-251	CL	100.00	100.00
92	BABY CAKES CRUMBS-PK-CRUMBS	5000	17.50	18.00
92	BABY CAKES CRUMBS-PK-CRUMBS/B	5000	17.50	18.00
92	BABY CAKES CRUMBS/BLACK-PK-CRUMBS/B	5000	17.50	18.00
92	LITTLE TURTLE INDIAN-PK-110	RT	150.00	150.00
92	RAVEN ESKIMO-PK-106	RT	130.00	130.00
G. MCNEIL			**SIGNATURE DOLL SERIES**	
95	ELEANORE GMNA-100	5000	225.00	225.00
95	HOLLY GMN-202	5000	150.00	150.00
H. PAYNE			**SIGNATURE DOLL SERIES**	
92	CREOLE BLACK-HP-202	RT	250.00	250.00
92	DARLA-HP-204	5000	250.00	250.00
92	DULCIE-HP-200	RT	250.00	250.00
92	DUSTIN-HP-201	RT	250.00	250.00
92	POLLY-HP-206	5000	120.00	120.00
92	SPANKY-HP-25	RT	250.00	250.00
P. PHILLIPS			**SIGNATURE DOLL SERIES**	
95	ADAK PPA-21	5000	110.00	110.00
95	ALAIN PPA-19	2500	100.00	100.00
95	CASEY PPA-23	5000	85.00	85.00
95	LATISHA PPA-25	5000	110.00	110.00
95	LENA PPA-20	5000	120.00	120.00
95	SHAO LING PPA-22	5000	110.00	110.00
L. RANDOLPH			**SIGNATURE DOLL SERIES**	
95	GINNY LR-2	5000	360.00	360.00
95	LENORE LRC-100	500	140.00	140.00
95	MEREDITH LR-3	5000	375.00	375.00
95	TAMMY LR-4	5000	325.00	325.00
95	TIFFANY LR-1	5000	370.00	370.00
M. SEVERINO			**SIGNATURE DOLL SERIES**	
91	ALICE-MS-7	RT	120.00	120.00
91	AMBER-MS-1	RT	95.00	95.00
91	BECKY-MS-2	RT	95.00	95.00
91	BIANCA-PK-101	RT	120.00	120.00
91	DADDY'S LITTLE DARLING-MS-8	RT	165.00	165.00
91	MIKEY-MS-3	RT	95.00	95.00
91	MOMMY'S RAYS OF SUNSHINE-MS-9	5000	165.00	165.00
91	STEPHIE-MS-6	RT	125.00	125.00

YR	NAME	LIMIT	ISSUE	TREND
91	SU LIN-MS-5	RT	105.00	105.00
91	YAWNING KATE-MS-4	RT	105.00	105.00
92	ABIGAIL-MS-11	RT	125.00	125.00
92	ADORA-MS-14	5000	300.00	300.00
92	CODY MS-19	RT	120.00	120.00
92	KATE-MS-15	RT	190.00	190.00
92	REBECCA BEIGE BONNET MS-17B	5000	175.00	175.00
92	RUBY-MS-18	5000	135.00	135.00
92	SALLY-MS-25	RT	110.00	110.00
92	STACY-MS-24	RT	110.00	110.00
92	VICTORIA W/ BLANKET-MS-10	RT	110.00	110.00
93	BONNETT BABY-MS-17W	5000	175.00	175.00

SPORTS IMPRESSIONS
*
PORCELAIN DOLLS

90	DON MATTINGLY	1990	150.00	150.00
90	MICKEY MANTLE	1956	150.00	150.00

SUSAN WAKEEN DOLL CO. INC.
S. WAKEEN **THE LITTLEST BALLET CO.**

85	CYNTHIA	375	198.00	350.00
85	JEANNE	375	198.00	800.00
85	JENNIFER	250	750.00	750.00
85	PATTY	375	198.00	450.00
87	ELIZABETH	250	425.00	1000.00
87	MARIE ANN	50	100.00	1000.00

THE COLLECTABLES
D. EFFNER

89	WELCOME HOME	1000	330.00	680.00
90	LIZBETH ANN	1000	420.00	425.00

P. PARKINS

86	TATIANA	CL	270.00	680.00
87	STORYTIME BY SARAH JANE	CL	330.00	530.00
87	TASHA	CL	290.00	530.00
89	MICHELLE	250	270.00	455.00
90	BASSINET BABY	2000	130.00	430.00
90	DANIELLE	1000	400.00	480.00
90	IN YOUR EASTER BONNET	1000	350.00	355.00
91	ADRIANNA	CL	1,350.00	1355.00
91	BETHANY	CL	450.00	455.00
91	KELSIE	500	320.00	325.00
91	LAUREN	300	490.00	495.00
91	NATASHA	CL	510.00	515.00
91	YVETTE	300	580.00	585.00
92	KARLIE	500	380.00	380.00
92	MARISSA	300	350.00	350.00
92	MARTY	250	190.00	195.00
92	MATIA	250	190.00	195.00
92	MISSY	OP	59.00	60.00
92	MOLLY	450	350.00	355.00
92	SHELLEY	300	450.00	455.00
93	AMBER	500	330.00	335.00
93	HALEY	500	330.00	335.00
93	LITTLE DUMPLING (BLACK)	500	190.00	195.00
93	LITTLE DUMPLING (WHITE)	500	190.00	195.00
93	MAGGIE	500	330.00	335.00
93	MOLLY	450	350.00	400.00
94	AFTERNOON DELIGHT	500	410.00	415.00
94	AMBER HISPANIC	500	345.00	345.00
94	MADISON	250	350.00	355.00
94	MADISON SAILOR	250	370.00	375.00
94	MORGAN	250	395.00	395.00
94	MORGAN CHRISTMAS	500	390.00	410.00
94	MORGAN IN RED	250	395.00	395.00
94	SUGAR PLUM FAIRY	500	250.00	255.00
95	A MOTHER'S LOVE	450	770.00	770.00
95	ALEXUS	150	550.00	570.00
95	BRIANNA	SO	590.00	625.00
95	CHRISTINE	350	390.00	390.00
95	MY LITTLE ANGEL BOY	SO	450.00	450.00
95	MY LITTLE ANGEL GIRL	SO	450.00	450.00

P. PARKINS **ANGELS SERIES**

92	ANGEL ON MY SHOULDER	CL	530.00	535.00
93	MY GUARDIAN ANGEL	500	590.00	595.00
94	GUARDING THE WAY	RT	950.00	955.00

P. PARKINS **BUTTERFLY BABIES**

89	BELINDA	CL	270.00	380.00
90	WILLOW	CL	240.00	380.00
92	LATICIA	CL	320.00	325.00

D. EFFNER **CHERISHED MEMORIES**

88	TEA TIME	CL	380.00	455.00

P. PARKINS **CHERISHED MEMORIES**

86	AMY AND ANDREW	CL	220.00	330.00
88	BRITTANY	CL	240.00	305.00

YR	NAME	LIMIT	ISSUE	TREND
88	HEATHER	CL	280.00	325.00
88	JENNIFER	CL	380.00	550.00
88	LEIGH ANN AND LELAND	CL	250.00	275.00
89	GENERATIONS	CL	480.00	505.00
89	TWINKLES	CL	170.00	280.00
90	CASSANDRA	CL	500.00	555.00
P. PARKINS			**COLLECTOR'S CLUB**	
91	MANDY	CL	360.00	365.00
92	KALLIE	CL	410.00	415.00
92	MOMMY AND ME	CL	810.00	815.00
94	KRYSTAL	YR	385.00	385.00
P. PARKINS			**ENCHANTED CHILDREN**	
90	KARA	CL	550.00	555.00
90	KATLIN	CL	550.00	555.00
90	KRISTIN	400	550.00	655.00
90	TIFFY	500	370.00	505.00
P. PARKINS			**FAIRY**	
88	TABATHA	1500	370.00	425.00
P. PARKINS			**LIMITED EDITION VINYL DOLLS**	
92	ANNIE	2500	190.00	190.00
92	BRENDA (BLUE DRESS)	2500	180.00	180.00
92	BRENDA (CHRISTMAS)	250	240.00	240.00
92	BRENDA (SPRING)	250	240.00	240.00
92	BRENT	2500	190.00	190.00
92	JENNY AND JEREMY (PUPPY LOVE)	2500	180.00	180.00
92	JESSICA	2500	190.00	190.00
D. EFFNER			**MOTHER'S LITTLE TREASURES**	
85	1ST EDITION	CL	380.00	705.00
90	2ND EDITION	CL	440.00	600.00
P. PARKINS			**SMALL ANGELS SERIES**	
94	EARTH ANGEL	500	195.00	200.00
P. PARKINS			**TINY TREASURES**	
91	HOLLY	1000	150.00	150.00
91	LITTLE GIRL	1000	140.00	140.00
91	TODDLER BOY	1000	130.00	130.00
91	TODDLER GIRL	1000	130.00	130.00
91	VICTORIAN BOY	1000	150.00	150.00
91	VICTORIAN GIRL	1000	150.00	150.00
92	NICOLAUS	500	160.00	160.00
92	NICOLE	500	180.00	180.00
92	TOMMIE	1000	160.00	160.00
92	TORI	1000	170.00	170.00
D. EFFNER			**YESTERDAY'S CHILD**	
82	CLEO	CL	180.00	255.00
82	COLUMBINE	CL	180.00	255.00
82	JASON AND JESSICA	CL	150.00	305.00
83	CHAD AND CHARITY	CL	190.00	195.00
83	NOEL	CL	190.00	245.00
84	KEVIN AND KARISSA	CL	190.00	275.00
84	REBECCA	CL	250.00	275.00
86	ASHLEY	CL	220.00	280.00
86	TODD AND TIFFANY	CL	220.00	255.00

TIMELESS CREATIONS

YR	NAME	LIMIT	ISSUE	TREND
A. HIMSTEDT			**BAREFOOT CHILDREN**	
87	BASTIAN	CL	329.00	750.00
87	BECKUS	CL	329.00	1800.00
87	ELLEN	CL	329.00	880.00
87	FATOU	CL	329.00	975.00
87	FATOU (CORNROLL)	CL	329.00	650.00
87	KATHE	CL	329.00	850.00
87	LISA	CL	329.00	850.00
87	PAULA	CL	329.00	825.00
A. HIMSTEDT			**BLESSED ARE THE CHILDREN**	
88	FREDERRICKE	CL	499.00	1800.00
88	KASIMIR	CL	499.00	1900.00
88	MAKIMURA	CL	499.00	1125.00
88	MALIN	CL	499.00	1610.00
88	MICHIKO	CL	499.00	1200.00
A. HIMSTEDT			**FACES OF FRIENDSHIP**	
91	LILIANE/NETHERLANDS	2-YR	598.00	750.00
91	NEBLINA/SWITZERLAND	2-YR	598.00	710.00
91	SHIREEM/BALI	2-YR	598.00	630.00
A. HIMSTEDT			**FIENE AND THE BAREFOOT BABIES**	
90	ANNCHEN/GERMAN BABY GIRL	2-YR	498.00	815.00
90	FIENE/BELGIAN GIRL	2-YR	598.00	950.00
90	MO/AMERICAN BABY BOY	2-YR	498.00	650.00
90	TAKI/JAPANESE BABY GIRL	2-YR	498.00	1000.00
A. HIMSTEDT			**HEARTLAND**	
88	TIMI	CL	329.00	600.00
88	TONI	CL	329.00	580.00
A. HIMSTEDT			**IMAGES OF CHILDHOOD**	
93	KIMA/GREENLAND	2-YR	599.00	600.00

YR	NAME	LIMIT	ISSUE	TREND
93	LONA/CALIFORNIA	2-YR	599.00	675.00
93	TARA/GERMANY	2-YR	599.00	605.00
A. HIMSTEDT			**REFLECTION OF YOUTH**	
89	ADRIENNE/FRANCE	CL	558.00	900.00
89	AYOKA/AFRICA	CL	558.00	1100.00
89	JANKA/HUNGARY	CL	558.00	1050.00
89	KAI/GERMAN	CL	558.00	850.00
A. HIMSTEDT			**SUMMER DREAMS**	
92	ENZO	2-YR	599.00	510.00
92	JULE	2-YR	599.00	700.00
92	PEMBA	2-YR	599.00	530.00
92	SANGA	2-YR	599.00	625.00

TUJAYS ARTIST DOLLS
BOSWORTH/MIKO

YR	NAME	LIMIT	ISSUE	TREND
86	ANINA	20	595.00	925.00
86	HENRY VIII	10	650.00	800.00
87	AMANDA	20	595.00	950.00
87	ANNE BOLEYN	10	550.00	700.00
87	ASHLEY	20	525.00	925.00
87	KATHERINE	20	675.00	1000.00
87	KATHERINE OF ARAGON	10	550.00	750.00
87	SOPHIE	20	475.00	875.00
88	ALTHEA	7	595.00	1000.00
88	ELIZABETH	25	395.00	595.00
88	MELISSA	25	325.00	350.00
88	SARAH	25	395.00	475.00
89	ALETA	20	575.00	825.00
89	CHARLOTTE	20	675.00	950.00
89	ESTELLE	20	575.00	850.00
89	HENRIETTA	20	575.00	800.00
90	GEORGETTE	100	475.00	740.00
90	LUCILLE	20	695.00	950.00
91	ABIGAIL	100	750.00	750.00
91	GENEVIEVE	10	975.00	975.00
91	JENNIFER	100	615.00	615.00
91	NATALIE	100	525.00	525.00
91	PHYLLIS	100	595.00	595.00
91	REBECCA	100	615.00	615.00
91	STEPHANIE	20	990.00	990.00

TY INC.
*

YR	NAME	LIMIT	ISSUE	TREND
*				**BEANIE BABIES**
*	BATTY THE BAT	*	*	12.00
*	BRITANNIA THE BEAR (EUROPEAN VERSION)	*	*	165.00
*	BRUNO THE TERRIER	*	*	8.00
*	CORAL THE FISH (NEW TAG)	RT	5.00	125.00
*	ERIN THE BEAR	*	*	250.00
*	HISSY THE SNAKE	*	*	8.00
*	IGGY THE IGUANA	*	*	7.00
*	POUNCE THE CAT	*	*	7.00
*	PRANCE THE CAT	*	*	7.00
*	PRINCESS THE BEAR	*	*	300.00
*	PUFFER THE PUFFIN	*	*	7.00
*	RAINBOW THE CHAMELEON	*	*	7.00
*	SMOOCHY THE FROG	*	*	7.00
*	SNOWBALL THE SNOWMAN	RT	*	N/A
*	SPINNER THE SPIDER	*	*	12.00
*	SPOOK THE GHOST (OLD TAG, NOT "SPOOKY")	CL	5.00	280.00
*	SPUNKY THE COCKER SPANIEL	*	*	7.00
*	STRETCH THE OSTRICH	*	*	7.00
*	STRUT THE ROOSTER	*	*	10.00
94	ALLY THE ALLIGATOR (OLD TAG)	RT	5.00	45.00
94	BLACKIE THE BEAR (OLD TAG)	CL	5.00	32.00
94	BONES THE DOG (NEW TAG)	OP	5.00	7.00
94	BONES THE DOG (OLD TAG)	CL	5.00	55.00
94	BROWNIE THE BEAR	RT	5.00	50.00
94	CHOCOLATE THE MOOSE (OLD TAG)	CL	5.00	65.00
94	CUBBIE THE BEAR (NEW TAG)	OP	5.00	20.00
94	CUBBIE THE BEAR (OLD TAG)	RT	5.00	60.00
94	DAISY THE COW (NEW TAG)	OP	5.00	7.00
94	DAISY THE COW (OLD TAG)	CL	5.00	40.00
94	FLASH THE DOLPHIN (NEW TAG)	OP	5.00	7.00
94	FLASH THE DOLPHIN (OLD TAG)	RT	5.00	110.00
94	GOLDIE THE GOLDFISH (OLD TAG)	RT	5.00	55.00
94	HAPPY THE HIPPO (GRAY)	RT	5.00	425.00
94	HUMPHREY THE CAMEL	RT	5.00	2100.00
94	INKY THE OCTOPUS (OLD TAG, TAN)	CL	5.00	240.00
94	LEGS THE FROG (NEW TAG)	OP	5.00	7.00
94	LEGS THE FROG (OLD TAG)	RT	5.00	45.00
94	LUCKY THE LADYBUG (OLD TAG, 7 SPOTS GLUED ON)	RT	5.00	95.00
94	MYSTIC THE UNICORN (OLD TAG, COARSE YARN MANE)	CL	5.00	18.00
94	NIP THE CAT (OLD TAG, WHITE FACE, BELLY)	RT	5.00	200.00
94	PATTI THE PLATYPUS (OLD TAG, PURPLE)	CL	5.00	35.00
94	PEKING THE PANDA	RT	5.00	1000.00

YR	NAME	LIMIT	ISSUE	TREND
94	PINCHERS THE LOBSTER (NEW TAG, RED)	OP	5.00	8.00
94	PINCHERS THE LOBSTER (OLD TAG, ORANGE)	CL	5.00	110.00
94	PINCHERS THE LOBSTER (OLD TAG, RED)	RT	5.00	40.00
94	QUACKERS THE DUCK (OLD TAG, W/O WINGS)	RT	5.00	1300.00
94	QUACKERS THE DUCK (OLD TAG, WITH WINGS)	RT	5.00	45.00
94	SEAMORE THE SEAL (NEW TAG)	RT	5.00	140.00
94	SEAMORE THE SEAL (OLD TAG)	RT	5.00	170.00
94	SLITHER THE SNAKE	RT	5.00	1750.00
94	SPEEDY THE TURTLE (NEW TAG)	RT	5.00	25.00
94	SPEEDY THE TURTLE (OLD TAG)	RT	5.00	40.00
94	SPLASH THE WHALE (NEW TAG)	RT	5.00	125.00
94	SPLASH THE WHALE (OLD TAG)	RT	5.00	150.00
94	SPOT THE DOG (NEW TAG, WITH SPOT)	RT	5.00	30.00
94	SPOT THE DOG (OLD TAG, W/O SPOT)	RT	5.00	1000.00
94	SPOT THE DOG (OLD TAG, WITH SPOT)	RT	5.00	40.00
94	SQUEALER THE PIG	CL	5.00	30.00
94	TEDDY THE BEAR (BROWN, NEW FACE)	RT	5.00	120.00
94	TEDDY THE BEAR (BROWN, OLD FACE)	RT	5.00	2300.00
94	TEDDY THE CRANBERRY BEAR (NEW FACE)	RT	5.00	1400.00
94	TEDDY THE CRANBERRY BEAR (OLD FACE)	RT	5.00	1650.00
94	TEDDY THE JADE BEAR (NEW FACE)	RT	5.00	1400.00
94	TEDDY THE JADE BEAR (OLD FACE)	RT	5.00	1500.00
94	TEDDY THE MAGENTA BEAR (NEW FACE)	RT	5.00	1400.00
94	TEDDY THE MAGENTA BEAR (OLD FACE)	RT	5.00	1500.00
94	TEDDY THE TEAL BEAR (NEW FACE)	RT	5.00	1400.00
94	TEDDY THE TEAL BEAR (OLD FACE)	RT	5.00	1500.00
94	TEDDY THE VIOLET BEAR (NEW FACE)	RT	5.00	1400.00
94	TEDDY THE VIOLET BEAR (OLD FACE)	RT	5.00	1500.00
94	TRAP THE MOUSE	RT	5.00	1400.00
94	VALENTINO THE BEAR (OLD TAG)	OP	5.00	30.00
94	WEB THE SPIDER	RT	5.00	850.00
94	ZIP THE CAT (NEW TAG, WHITE PAWS)	OP	5.00	8.00
94	ZIP THE CAT (OLD TAG, ALL BLACK, NO WHITE)	RT	5.00	1000.00
94	ZIP THE CAT (OLD TAG, WHITE FACE & BELLY)	RT	5.00	200.00
95	BESSIE THE COW (NEW TAG)	RT	5.00	45.00
95	BESSIE THE COW (OLD TAG)	RT	5.00	50.00
95	BLACKIE THE BEAR (NEW TAG)	OP	5.00	7.00
95	BONGO THE MONKEY (NEW TAG, BODY COLORED TAIL)	OP	5.00	7.00
95	BONGO THE MONKEY (NEW TAG, FACE COLORED TAIL)	OP	5.00	7.00
95	BONGO THE MONKEY (OLD TAG, BODY COLORED TAIL)	RT	5.00	100.00
95	BRONTY THE BRONTOSAURUS	RT	5.00	850.00
95	BUBBLES THE FISH (NEW TAG)	RT	5.00	125.00
95	BUBBLES THE FISH (OLD TAG)	RT	5.00	125.00
95	BUCKY THE BEAVER (OLD TAG)	OP	5.00	40.00
95	BUMBLE THE BEE (NEW TAG)	RT	5.00	500.00
95	BUMBLE THE BEE (OLD TAG)	RT	5.00	600.00
95	CAW THE CROW	RT	5.00	575.00
95	CHILLY THE POLAR BEAR	RT	5.00	1300.00
95	CORAL THE FISH (OLD TAG)	RT	5.00	150.00
95	DERBY THE HORSE (NEW TAG, COARSE YARN)	OP	5.00	7.00
95	DERBY THE HORSE (OLD TAG, FINE YARN)	CL	5.00	1100.00
95	DIGGER THE CRAB (NEW TAG, RED)	RT	5.00	95.00
95	DIGGER THE CRAB (OLD TAG, ORANGE)	RT	5.00	450.00
95	DIGGER THE CRAB (OLD TAG, RED)	CL	5.00	90.00
95	FLUTTER THE BUTTERFLY	RT	5.00	750.00
95	GARCIA THE BEAR (OLD TAG)	RT	5.00	170.00
95	GOLDIE THE GOLDFISH (NEW TAG)	RT	5.00	30.00
95	GRUNT THE RAZORBACK (OLD TAG)	RT	5.00	190.00
95	HAPPY THE HIPPO (LAVENDER)	OP	5.00	7.00
95	HOOT THE OWL (OLD TAG)	RT	5.00	50.00
95	INCH THE WORM (OLD TAG, FELT ANTENNAS)	RT	5.00	125.00
95	INKY THE OCTOPUS (NEW TAG, PINK)	OP	5.00	8.00
95	INKY THE OCTOPUS (OLD TAG, GRAY)	CL	5.00	195.00
95	INKY THE OCTOPUS (OLD TAG, PINK)	CL	5.00	18.00
95	KIWI THE TOUCAN	RT	5.00	150.00
95	LIZZY THE LIZARD (OLD TAG, TIE-DYE)	RT	5.00	650.00
95	MAGIC THE DRAGON (OLD TAG, LIGHT PINK STITCHING)	RT	5.00	60.00
95	MANNY THE MANATEE (OLD TAG)	RT	5.00	150.00
95	MYSTIC THE UNICORN (OLD TAG, FINE YARN MANE)	RT	5.00	125.00
95	NANA THE BROWN MONKEY	CL	5.00	100.00
95	NIP THE CAT (OLD TAG, ALL GOLD, NO WHITE)	RT	5.00	500.00
95	NIP THE CAT (OLD TAG, WHITE PAWS)	RT	5.00	35.00
95	PATTI THE PLATYPUS (OLD TAG, MAGENTA)	RT	5.00	575.00
95	PEANUT THE ELEPHANT (OLD TAG, DARK BLUE)	RT	5.00	3250.00
95	PEANUT THE ELEPHANT (OLD TAG, LIGHT BLUE)	CL	5.00	20.00
95	PINKY THE FLAMINGO	CL	5.00	40.00
95	QUACKERS THE DUCK (NEW TAG, WITH WINGS)	OP	5.00	8.00
95	RADAR THE BAT (OLD TAG)	RT	5.00	140.00
95	REX THE TYRANNASAURUS	RT	5.00	680.00
95	RINGO THE RACCOON (OLD TAG)	CL	5.00	32.00
95	SPOOKY THE GHOST (OLD TAG)	RT	5.00	35.00
95	STEG THE STEGOSAURUS	RT	5.00	300.00
95	STING THE MANTA RAY	RT	5.00	200.00
95	STINKY THE SKUNK (NEW TAG)	OP	5.00	8.00
95	STINKY THE SKUNK (OLD TAG)	CL	5.00	27.00

YR	NAME	LIMIT	ISSUE	TREND
95	STRIPES THE TIGER (DARK GOLD)	RT	5.00	150.00
95	STRIPES THE TIGER (FUZZY BELLY, NARROW STRIPES)	CL	5.00	75.00
95	STRIPES THE TIGER (LIGHT GOLD, FEWER STRIPES)	OP	5.00	225.00
95	TABASCO THE BULL	RT	5.00	200.00
95	TANK THE ARMADILLO (OLD TAG, 7 RIDGES)	RT	5.00	100.00
95	TUSK THE WALRUS	RT	5.00	160.00
95	TWIGS THE GIRAFFE (OLD TAG)	CL	5.00	37.00
95	VALENTINO THE BEAR (NEW TAG)	OP	5.00	25.00
95	VELVET THE PANTHER (NEW TAG)	RT	5.00	25.00
95	VELVET THE PANTHER (OLD TAG)	RT	5.00	25.00
95	WADDLE THE PENGUIN (NEW TAG)	OP	5.00	8.00
95	WADDLE THE PENGUIN (OLD TAG)	CL	5.00	30.00
95	ZIGGY THE ZEBRA (NEW TAG)	OP	5.00	8.00
95	ZIGGY THE ZEBRA (OLD TAG)	CL	5.00	25.00
95	ZIP THE CAT (OLD TAG, WHITE PAWS)	CL	5.00	15.00
96	ALLY THE ALLIGATOR (NEW TAG)	RT	5.00	35.00
96	BONGO THE MONKEY (OLD TAG, FACE COLORED TAIL)	CL	5.00	65.00
96	BUCKY THE BEAVER (NEW TAG)	RT	5.00	15.00
96	CHOPS THE LAMB (NEW TAG)	RT	5.00	110.00
96	CHOPS THE LAMB (OLD TAG)	RT	5.00	125.00
96	CONGO THE GORILLA	OP	5.00	7.00
96	CURLY THE BEAR	OP	5.00	10.00
96	DERBY THE HORSE (OLD TAG, COARSE YARN)	CL	5.00	50.00
96	EARS THE BUNNY (NEW TAG)	OP	5.00	8.00
96	EARS THE BUNNY (OLD TAG)	CL	5.00	18.00
96	FLIP THE CAT (NEW TAG)	OP	5.00	40.00
96	FLIP THE CAT (OLD TAG)	RT	5.00	25.00
96	FRECKLES THE LEOPARD	OP	5.00	8.00
96	GARCIA THE BEAR (NEW TAG)	RT	5.00	160.00
96	GRUNT THE RAZORBACK (NEW TAG)	RT	5.00	185.00
96	HOOT THE OWL (NEW TAG)	RT	5.00	38.00
96	INCH THE WORM (NEW TAG, FELT ANTENNAS)	CL	5.00	65.00
96	INCH THE WORM (NEW TAG, YARN ANTENNAS)	OP	5.00	8.00
96	LEFTY THE DONKEY	RT	5.00	270.00
96	LIBEARTY THE BEAR (WITH FLAG)	RT	5.00	325.00
96	LIBEARTY THE BEAR (WITHOUT FLAG)	RT	5.00	440.00
96	LIZZY THE LIZARD (NEW TAG, BLUE & YELLOW)	RT	5.00	18.00
96	LIZZY THE LIZARD (OLD TAG, BLUE & YELLOW)	RT	5.00	40.00
96	LUCKY THE LADYBUG (21 SPOTS IN FABRIC)	CL	5.00	7.00
96	LUCKY THE LADYBUG (NEW TAG, 11 SPOTS IN FABRIC)	OP	5.00	8.00
96	MAGIC THE DRAGON (NEW TAG, LIGHT PINK STITCHING)	CL	5.00	35.00
96	MAGIC THE DRAGON (NEW TAG, REG. PINK STITCHING)	RT	5.00	190.00
96	MANNY THE MANATEE (NEW TAG)	RT	5.00	145.00
96	MAPLE THE BEAR (CANADIAN DISTRIBUTION ONLY)	RT	5.00	295.00
96	MYSTIC THE UNICORN (NEW TAG, COARSE MANE)	CL	5.00	25.00
96	NIP THE CAT (NEW TAG, WHITE PAWS)	RT	5.00	18.00
96	PATTI THE PLATYPUS (NEW TAG, PURPLE)	OP	5.00	8.00
96	PEANUT THE ELEPHANT (NEW TAG, LIGHT BLUE)	OP	5.00	8.00
96	PRIDE THE BEAR	CL	5.00	270.00
96	RADAR THE BAT (NEW TAG)	RT	5.00	120.00
96	RIGHTY THE ELEPHANT (WITH FLAG)	RT	5.00	100.00
96	RIGHTY THE ELEPHANT (WITHOUT FLAG)	RT	5.00	275.00
96	RINGO THE RACCOON (NEW TAG)	OP	5.00	7.00
96	ROVER THE DOG	OP	5.00	7.00
96	SCOOP THE PELICAN	OP	5.00	7.00
96	SCOTTIE THE TERRIER	OP	5.00	7.00
96	SEAWEED THE OTTER (NEW TAG)	OP	5.00	8.00
96	SEAWEED THE OTTER (OLD TAG)	CL	5.00	30.00
96	SLY THE FOX (NEW TAG, BROWN BELLY)	CL	5.00	75.00
96	SLY THE FOX (NEW TAG, WHITE BELLY)	OP	5.00	8.00
96	SLY THE FOX (OLD TAG, BROWN BELLY)	RT	5.00	75.00
96	SNORT THE BULL	OP	5.00	7.00
96	SPARKY THE DALMATIAN	RT	5.00	100.00
96	SPIKE THE RHINO	OP	5.00	7.00
96	SPOOKY THE GHOST (NEW TAG)	RT	5.00	25.00
96	TANK THE ARMADILLO (NEW TAG, 9 RIDGES)	RT	5.00	100.00
96	TANK THE ARMADILLO (NEW TAG, 9 RIDGES, NO SHELL)	RT	5.00	90.00
96	TWIGS THE GIRAFFE (NEW TAG)	OP	5.00	8.00
96	WEENIE THE DACHSHUND (NEW TAG)	OP	5.00	8.00
96	WEENIE THE DACHSHUND (OLD TAG)	CL	5.00	35.00
96	WRINKLES THE BULLDOG	OP	5.00	7.00
97	BALDY THE EAGLE	OP	5.00	7.00
97	BERNIE THE ST. BERNARD	OP	5.00	7.00
97	BLIZZARD THE SNOW TIGER	OP	5.00	10.00
97	CHIP THE CALICO CAT	OP	5.00	7.00
97	CHOCOLATE THE MOOSE (PROMOTIONAL PIECE)	OP	5.00	8.00
97	CLAUDE THE TIE-DYE CRAB	OP	5.00	8.00
97	CRUNCH THE SHARK	OP	5.00	8.00
97	DOBY THE DOBERMAN	OP	5.00	7.00
97	DOODLE THE ROOSTER	OP	5.00	35.00
97	DOTTY THE DALMATIAN	OP	5.00	7.00
97	ECHO THE DOLPHIN	OP	5.00	7.00
97	FLEECE THE LAMB	OP	5.00	7.00
97	FLOPPITY THE BUNNY	OP	5.00	7.00
97	GRACIE THE SWAN	OP	5.00	8.00

YR	NAME	LIMIT	ISSUE	TREND
97	HIPPITY THE BUNNY	OP	5.00	8.00
97	HOPPITY THE BUNNY	OP	5.00	8.00
97	JOLLY THE WALRUS	OP	*	7.00
97	MEL THE KOALA	OP	5.00	10.00
97	NANOOK THE HUSKY	OP	5.00	10.00
97	NUTS THE SQUIRREL	OP	5.00	7.00
97	PEACE THE TIE-DYE BEAR	OP	5.00	35.00
97	POUCH THE KANGAROO	OP	5.00	9.00
97	PUGSLY THE PUG DOG	OP	5.00	7.00
97	ROARY THE LION	OP	5.00	7.00
97	SNIP THE CAT	OP	5.00	8.00
97	TEDDY	RT	*	N/A
97	TUFFY THE TERRIER	OP	5.00	7.00
97	WAVES THE WHALE	OP	5.00	7.00

VICTORIAN TRADITION
K. GLEASON — **CLASSICS COLLECTION**

93	OLIVER TWIST	50	795.00	795.00

K. GLEASON — **LAND OF FAERYE TALES & NURSERY RHYMES**

93	RED RIDING HOOD	50	795.00	795.00
95	MISS MUFFET	50	795.00	795.00

K. GLEASON — **LIFE IS FUN!**

94	2ND CHILDHOOD	20	995.00	995.00
95	MISS AMERICA	50	795.00	795.00

K. GLEASON — **NORTHERN REALM OF FAERYE**

94	BUTTONWILLOW	20	795.00	795.00
94	PTARMINI	20	795.00	795.00
94	SPRUCE	20	795.00	795.00

K. GLEASON — **PEOPLE OF THE COVENANT**

94	NOAH'S WIFE	50	795.00	795.00

K. GLEASON — **THE ALASKANS**

94	LADY DIVINE	75	795.00	795.00

W.S. GEORGE
P. RYAN BROOKS — **MY FAIR LADY**

91	ELIZA AT ASCOT	CL	125.00	150.00

M. RODERICK — **ROMANTIC FLOWER MAIDENS**

88	ROSE, WHO IS LOVE	CL	87.00	135.00
89	DAISY	CL	87.00	87.00
90	LILY	TL	92.00	160.00
90	VIOLET	TL	92.00	92.00

R. AKERS/ S. GIRARDI — **STEPPING OUT**

91	MILLIE	TL	99.00	99.00

P. RYAN BROOKS — **THE KING & I**

91	SHALL WE DANCE?	CL	175.00	175.00

R. AKERS/ S. GIRARDI — **YEAR BOOK MEMORIES**

91	PEGGY SUE	TL	87.00	87.00

Figurines

Dean A. Genth
(with Lladró expert Peggy Whiteneck)

"Secondary market" is often a confusing term for novice collectors. Secondary market is not an outlet for "seconds" or "rejects." It is, however, the market for collectibles after they have left the original, primary point of retail sales.

The primary market for collectibles is represented by the many authorized dealers that retail the various lines of collectibles. Secondary market transactions are represented by sales between individual collectors as well as dealers who may or may not be involved with primary retail selling.

Collectors often wonder how the prices are determined for figurines on the secondary market. In our free market society, the answer is quite simple—supply and demand. It is the buyer/collector who really determines the secondary market price.

Price guides and books that list secondary market prices generally track selling prices from a geographical cross-section of dealers, swap and sell event results, as well as auction results. Oftentimes these collectibles price guides list current market prices as well as other pertinent information regarding each figurine or item.

Selling items on the secondary market can be easily accomplished if the price requested is fair and the choice of dispersal is to the owner's liking. Once the selling price is determined, the seller must decide upon which method of selling will be employed. The seller can choose to sell directly to other collectors by advertising in the local classifieds or in one of the many collectibles publications such as Collector's mart magazine.

Other collectors often choose to dispose of an entire collection quickly by selling to a reputable or well-known secondary market dealer. Many secondary market dealers are experts in certain areas of collectibles and are prepared to buy large collections for their inventories.

Sometimes collectors opt to have their large collections auctioned to the highest bidders. This method assures that dispersal will be quick and almost effortless on the part of the seller. Auction prices can vary widely from time to time and locale to locale. The prices, when averaged from several auctions, usually represent what is considered to be "fair market value."

A replacement value quotation on the secondary market represents the price a buyer can expect to pay for a figurine or other collectible if that purchase must be made fairly soon. Sometimes certain items are not readily available on the secondary market, thus driving up the price of the item.

Collectors must also determine whether they will sell to a dealer at wholesale price levels or attempt to advertise with the possibility of achieving closer to retail prices. Time availability and financial resources are considerations when undertaking the task of selling to other collectors at near-retail prices on the secondary market.

Always remember that secondary markets exist because a buyer is searching for an item no longer available through regular retail distribution channels. Many reputable secondary market dealers are in business to assist you with both selling and buying figurines.

The Lladró sections of this price guide have been completely revised for accuracy of serial numbering, dating and pricing. Several new items and categories have been added to the Lladró figurines section.

We have priced matte versions of Lladró above their glazed counterparts if they've been retired several years earlier than the glazed versions of the same figurine. The company's decision in 1991 to retire much of its matte corpus has introduced a scarcity factor that enhances the desirability of matte figurines.

We believe this revised Lladró section is one of the most reliable guides available today. Collectors should be aware, however, that prices on Lladró remain volatile and may vary widely from place to place.

Dealer and appraiser DEAN A. GENTH is a secondary market expert on Precious Moments, Swarovski Silver Crystal and M.I. Hummel. He serves as special consultant for The No. 1 Price Guide to M.I. Hummel and owns Miller's Hallmark and Gift Gallery in Eaton, Xenia and Cincinnati, Ohio.

Lladró aficionado PEGGY WHITENECK updated our entire Lladró figurine and ornament sections.

FIGURINES

YR	NAME	LIMIT	ISSUE	TREND

ADOLF SEHRING STUDIO
A. SEHRING
YR	NAME	LIMIT	ISSUE	TREND
82	BORN TO RUN	30	4,000.00	4000.00
82	SCRATCHING FOAL	40	2,000.00	2000.00
83	DAYDREAMS	45	3,000.00	3000.00
83	VANITY	45	3,000.00	3000.00
83	WALKING PROUD	40	3,000.00	3000.00
84	BOY WITH FROG	54	3,000.00	3000.00
93	LILY PADS	20	20,000.00	20000.00
93	TENDERNESS	49	7,000.00	7000.00
95	NUDE	58	10,000.00	10000.00
95	POCAHONTAS	115	6,400.00	6400.00

ADRIAN TARON & SONS
S. ROSAS — HOLIDAY
YR	NAME	LIMIT	ISSUE	TREND
96	HERR SCHNEEMANN	20000	40.00	40.00
96	KRISS KRINGLE	20000	40.00	40.00

S. ROSAS — NUTCRACKER SUITE MINIS
YR	NAME	LIMIT	ISSUE	TREND
97	NUTCRACKER PRINCE	25000	45.00	45.00

TARON/STEINBACH — STEINBACH NUTCRACKERS/ALICE IN WONDERLAND
YR	NAME	LIMIT	ISSUE	TREND
97	MAD HATTER	10000	230.00	230.00
98	WHITE RABBIT	10000	21.00	21.00
98	WHITE RABBIT	10000	230.00	230.00

S. ROSAS — STEINBACH NUTCRACKERS/ALICE IN WONDERLAND
YR	NAME	LIMIT	ISSUE	TREND
97	MAD HATTER	7500	230.00	230.00
98	TWEEDLE DUM & TWEEDLE DEE	10000	22.00	22.00

TARON/STEINBACH — STEINBACH NUTCRACKERS/NURSERY RHYMES
YR	NAME	LIMIT	ISSUE	TREND
97	HUMPTY DUMPTY	10000	180.00	180.00
98	HUMPTY DUMPTY	20000	55.00	55.00
98	OLD KING COLE	10000	230.00	230.00
98	OLD KING COLE	10000	210.00	210.00

S. ROSAS — STEINBACH NUTCRACKERS/NURSERY RHYMES
YR	NAME	LIMIT	ISSUE	TREND
97	HUMPTY DUMPTY	10000	210.00	210.00
98	OLD KING COLE	10000	22.00	22.00
98	THREE MEN IN A TUB	10000	22.00	22.00

TARON/STEINBACH — STEINBACH NUTCRACKERS/NUTCRACKER SUITE
YR	NAME	LIMIT	ISSUE	TREND
92	HERR DROSSELMEYER	CL	170.00	1500.00
93	MOUSE KING	CL	190.00	950.00
94	NUTCRACKER PRINCE	10000	210.00	210.00
95	CLARA	10000	220.00	220.00
96	SUGAR PLUM	10000	220.00	220.00
98	CLARA	20000	55.00	55.00
98	TOY SOLDIER	10000	230.00	230.00

S. ROSAS — STEINBACH NUTCRACKERS/NUTCRACKER SUITE
YR	NAME	LIMIT	ISSUE	TREND
95	TCHAIKOVSKY'S CLARA	10000	220.00	220.00
96	SUGAR PLUM FAIRY	10000	230.00	230.00

TARON/STEINBACH — STEINBACH NUTCRACKERS/WISEMEN SERIES
YR	NAME	LIMIT	ISSUE	TREND
95	CASPAR	10000	220.00	220.00
96	MELCHIOR	10000	220.00	220.00
97	BALTHASAR	10000	230.00	230.00

S. ROSAS — STEINBACH NUTCRACKERS/WISEMEN SERIES
YR	NAME	LIMIT	ISSUE	TREND
95	MELCHIOR "WISEMAN"	10000	220.00	220.00
96	BALTHASAR	10000	230.00	230.00

S. ROSAS — TARON COLLECTION
YR	NAME	LIMIT	ISSUE	TREND
97	HERR DROSSELMEYER	6000	215.00	215.00
97	THREE WISEMEN	10000	135.00	135.00
98	JOURNEY TO BETHLEHEM	2000	100.00	100.00

AMERICAN ARTISTS
F. STONE
YR	NAME	LIMIT	ISSUE	TREND
*	TRIPLE CROWN BOWL	*	395.00	395.00
*	TRIPLE CROWN VASE/SIGNED	*	250.00	250.00
*	TRIPLE CROWN VASE/UNSIGNED	*	195.00	195.00

F. STONE — FRED STONE FIGURINES
YR	NAME	LIMIT	ISSUE	TREND
85	BLACK STALLION, THE (PORCELAIN)	*	125.00	200.00
85	BLACK STALLION, THE (BRONZE)	*	150.00	160.00
86	ARABIAN MARE & FOAL	*	150.00	185.00
86	TRANQUILITY	*	175.00	225.00
87	REARING BLACK STALLION (BRONZE)	*	175.00	185.00
87	REARING BLACK STALLION (PORCELAIN)	*	150.00	160.00

AMERICAST INC.
K. WINDRIX — THE COMMANDERS
YR	NAME	LIMIT	ISSUE	TREND
94	GEORGE A. CUSTER	500	195.00	200.00
94	JAMES LONGSTREET	500	195.00	200.00
94	JOSHUA L. CHAMBERLAIN	500	195.00	200.00
94	ROBERT E. LEE	5000	195.00	200.00
94	ULYSSES S. GRANT	5000	195.00	200.00
95	J.E.B. STUART	500	195.00	200.00
95	STONEWALL JACKSON	500	195.00	200.00
95	WILLIAM T. SHERMAN	500	195.00	200.00

YR NAME	LIMIT	ISSUE	TREND
ANHEUSER-BUSCH INC.			
*			
94 BUDDIES N4575	7500	65.00	65.00
95 HORSEPLAY F1	7500	65.00	65.00
96 BUDWEISER FROGS	OP	30.00	30.00
M. URDAHL			
96 SOMETHING'S BREWING	7500	65.00	65.00
ANNA-PERENNA			
P. BUCKLEY MOSS			
95 PARTRIDGE IN A PEAR TREE	OP	28.00	28.00
ANRI			
U. BERNARDI		**BERNARDI REFLECTIONS**	
94 MASTER CARVER 4 IN.	500	350.00	350.00
94 MASTER CARVER 6 IN.	250	600.00	600.00
W. & C. HALLETT		**CELESTIAL MESSENGERS**	
95 ANGEL OF CHARITY	250	375.00	375.00
96 ANGEL OF FAITH	250	375.00	375.00
96 ANGEL OF HOPE	250	375.00	375.00
J. FERRANDIZ		**CHILDREN OF THE WORLD**	
98 KAREEM	OP	285.00	285.00
98 KEISHA	OP	285.00	285.00
L. GAITHER		**CHRISTMAS EVE SERIES**	
95 GETTING READY	500	500.00	500.00
95 HITCHING PRANCER	500	500.00	500.00
98 MR. FIRST GIFT OF CHRISTMAS	500	325.00	325.00
98 MRS. FIRST GIFT OF CHRISTMAS	500	325.00	325.00
*		**CLUB ANRI**	
88 MAESTRO MICKEY, 4 1/2 IN.	CL	170.00	180.00
89 DIVA MINNIE, 4 1/2 IN.	CL	190.00	195.00
90 DAPPER DONALD, 4 IN.	CL	199.00	200.00
91 DAISY DUCK, 4 1/2 IN.	TL	250.00	255.00
J. FERRANDIZ		**CLUB ANRI**	
83 WELCOME, 4 IN.	CL	110.00	400.00
84 MY FRIEND, 4 IN.	CL	110.00	405.00
85 HARVEST TIME, 4 IN.	CL	125.00	280.00
86 CELEBRATION MARCH, 5 IN.	CL	165.00	260.00
86 HARVEST'S HELPER, 4 IN.	CL	135.00	255.00
87 WILL YOU BE MINE, 4 IN.	CL	135.00	240.00
88 FOREVER YOURS, 4 IN.	CL	170.00	255.00
89 TWENTY YEARS OF LOVE, 4 IN.	CL	190.00	195.00
89 YOU ARE MY SUNSHINE, 4 IN.	YR	220.00	220.00
91 WITH ALL MY HEART, 4 IN.	YR	250.00	255.00
92 YOU ARE MY ALL, 4 IN.	YR	260.00	260.00
93 TRULY YOURS	YR	290.00	290.00
94 DAPPER 'N DEAR	YR	250.00	250.00
94 SWEET 'N SHY 4 IN.	YR	250.00	250.00
S. KAY		**CLUB ANRI**	
84 APPLE OF MY EYE, 4 1/2 IN.	CL	135.00	400.00
85 DAD'S HELPER, 4 1/2 IN.	CL	135.00	385.00
86 MAKE A WISH, 4 IN.	CL	165.00	385.00
86 ROMANTIC NOTIONS, 4 IN.	CL	135.00	240.00
87 A YOUNG MAN'S FANCY, 4 IN.	CL	135.00	215.00
88 I'VE GOT A SECRET, 4 IN.	CL	170.00	210.00
89 I'LL NEVER TELL, 4 IN.	CL	190.00	195.00
90 A LITTLE BASHFUL, 4 IN.	YR	220.00	225.00
91 KISS ME, 4 IN.	*	250.00	255.00
92 GIFT OF LOVE	YR	*	N/A
92 MY PRESENT FOR YOU, 4 IN.	YR	270.00	270.00
93 JUST FOR YOU	YR	*	N/A
93 SWEET THOUGHTS	YR	300.00	300.00
94 SNUGGLE UP 4 IN.	YR	300.00	300.00
*		**COLLECTORS SOCIETY**	
95 ANRI ARTIST TREE HOUSE	YR	695.00	695.00
J. FERRANDIZ		**COLLECTORS SOCIETY**	
95 SEALED WITH A KISS	YR	275.00	275.00
96 ON CLOUD NINE	YR	275.00	275.00
S. HALLETT		**COLLECTORS SOCIETY**	
95 ON MY OWN 4 IN.	YR	175.00	175.00
S. KAY		**COLLECTORS SOCIETY**	
96 HELPING MOTHER	150	595.00	595.00
96 SWEET TOOTH 4 IN.	YR	200.00	199.50
97 READ ME A STORY	TL	395.00	395.00
98 LITTLE LEAGUER	YR	295.00	295.00
J. FERRANDIZ		**COLLECTORS SOCIETY GOLD LEAF**	
96 LITTLE GARDENER	150	595.00	595.00
97 TALKING TO THE ANIMALS	150	595.00	595.00
FLAVIO		**COLLECTORS SOCIETY GOLD LEAF**	
97 LA MODERNA	150	815.00	815.00
S. KAY		**COLLECTORS SOCIETY GOLD LEAF**	
97 BALLERINA	150	595.00	595.00

YR	NAME	LIMIT	ISSUE	TREND
GRANGET				**DECORATIVE**
98	DOLPHIN WITH YOUNG	OP	450.00	450.00
98	LIONESS	OP	595.00	595.00
*			**DISNEY WOODCARVINGS**	
87	DONALD DUCK, 4 IN.	CL	150.00	200.00
87	GOOFY, 4 IN. 656005	CL	150.00	250.00
87	MICKEY AND MINNIE, 6 IN. (MATCHING NUM.)	CL	625.00	1000.00
87	MICKEY MOUSE, 4 IN.	CL	150.00	290.00
87	MINNIE MOUSE, 4 IN.	CL	150.00	275.00
87	PINOCCHIO, 4 IN.	CL	150.00	425.00
88	DONALD DUCK, 1 3/4 IN.	CL	80.00	140.00
88	DONALD DUCK, 4 IN.	CL	180.00	265.00
88	DONALD DUCK, 6 IN.	CL	350.00	500.00
88	GOOFY, 1 3/4 IN.	CL	80.00	150.00
88	GOOFY, 4 IN. 656015	CL	180.00	250.00
88	GOOFY, 6 IN. 656103	CL	350.00	575.00
88	MICKEY MOUSE, 1 3/4 IN.	CL	80.00	250.00
88	MICKEY MOUSE, 4 IN.	CL	180.00	275.00
88	MICKEY SORCERER'S APPRENTICE, 2 IN.	CL	80.00	350.00
88	MICKEY SORCERER'S APPRENTICE, 4 IN.	CL	180.00	240.00
88	MICKEY SORCERER'S APPRENTICE, 6 IN.	CL	350.00	650.00
88	PINOCCHIO, 1 3/4 IN.	CL	80.00	250.00
88	PINOCCHIO, 4 IN.	CL	180.00	200.00
88	PLUTO, 1 3/4 IN.	CL	80.00	130.00
88	PLUTO, 4 IN.	CL	180.00	275.00
89	DAISY, 4 IN.	CL	190.00	275.00
89	DONALD, 4 IN.	CL	190.00	275.00
89	GOOFY, 4 IN. 656022	CL	190.00	250.00
89	MICKEY & MINNIE, 6 IN. (SET)	CL	700.00	850.00
89	MICKEY AND MINNIE, 20 IN. (MATCHED SET)	CL	7,000.00	7100.00
89	MICKEY, 10 IN.	CL	700.00	900.00
89	MICKEY, 20 IN.	CL	3,500.00	3505.00
89	MICKEY, 4 IN.	CL	190.00	350.00
89	MINI DAISY, 2 IN.	CL	85.00	125.00
89	MINI DONALD, 2 IN.	CL	85.00	175.00
89	MINI GOOFY, 2 IN.	CL	85.00	190.00
89	MINI MICKEY, 2 IN.	CL	85.00	190.00
89	MINI MINNIE, 2 IN.	CL	85.00	190.00
89	MINI PLUTO, 2 IN.	CL	85.00	125.00
89	MINNIE, 10 IN.	CL	700.00	875.00
89	MINNIE, 20 IN.	CL	3,500.00	3505.00
89	MINNIE, 4 IN.	CL	190.00	325.00
89	PINOCCHIO, 10 IN.	CL	700.00	950.00
89	PINOCCHIO, 2 IN.	CL	85.00	90.00
89	PINOCCHIO, 20 IN.	CL	3,500.00	3505.00
89	PINOCCHIO, 4 IN.	CL	190.00	200.00
89	PINOCCHIO, 6 IN.	CL	350.00	450.00
89	PLUTO, 4 IN.	CL	190.00	275.00
89	PLUTO, 6 IN.	CL	350.00	460.00
90	CHEF GOOFY, 2 1/2 IN.	CL	125.00	175.00
90	CHEF GOOFY, 5 IN.	CL	265.00	290.00
90	DONALD AND DAISY, 6 IN. (MATCHED SET)	CL	700.00	755.00
90	MICKEY MOUSE, 2 IN.	CL	100.00	165.00
90	MICKEY MOUSE, 4 IN.	CL	199.00	290.00
90	MINNIE MOUSE, 2 IN.	CL	100.00	150.00
90	MINNIE MOUSE, 4 IN.	CL	199.00	250.00
90	SORCERER'S APPRENTICE 16 IN.	100	3,500.00	3500.00
90	SORCERER'S APPRENTICE 2 IN.	CL	125.00	625.00
90	SORCERER'S APPRENTICE 4 IN.	CL	265.00	450.00
90	SORCERER'S APPRENTICE 6 IN.	1000	475.00	750.00
90	SORCERER'S APPRENTICE 8 IN.	350	790.00	850.00
91	BELL BOY DONALD, 4 IN.	CL	250.00	255.00
91	BELL BOY DONALD, 6 IN.	CL	400.00	525.00
91	MICKEY SKATING, 2 IN.	CL	120.00	275.00
91	MICKEY SKATING, 4 IN.	CL	250.00	275.00
91	MINNIE SKATING, 2 IN.	CL	120.00	145.00
91	MINNIE SKATING, 4 IN.	CL	250.00	355.00
J. FERRANDIZ				**FERRANDIZ BOY & GIRL**
76	COWBOY, 6 IN.	CL	75.00	555.00
76	HARVEST GIRL, 6 IN.	CL	75.00	605.00
77	LEADING THE WAY, 6 IN.	CL	100.00	340.00
77	TRACKER, 6 IN.	CL	100.00	375.00
78	BASKET OF JOY, 6 IN.	CL	140.00	405.00
78	PEACE PIPE, 6 IN.	CL	140.00	390.00
79	FIRST BLOSSOM, 6 IN.	CL	135.00	365.00
79	HAPPY STRUMMER, 6 IN.	CL	160.00	400.00
80	FRIENDS, 6 IN.	CL	200.00	330.00
80	MELODY FOR TWO, 6 IN.	CL	200.00	340.00
81	MERRY MELODY, 6 IN.	CL	210.00	330.00
81	TINY SOUNDS, 6 IN.	CL	210.00	330.00
82	GUIDING LIGHT, 6 IN.	CL	225.00	305.00
82	TO MARKET, 6 IN.	CL	220.00	300.00
83	ADMIRATION, 6 IN.	CL	220.00	300.00
83	BEWILDERED, 6 IN.	CL	196.00	300.00
84	FRIENDLY FACES, 3 IN.	CL	93.00	100.00

YR	NAME	LIMIT	ISSUE	TREND
84	FRIENDLY FACES, 6 IN.	CL	210.00	265.00
84	WANDERER'S RETURN, 3 IN.	CL	93.00	120.00
84	WANDERER'S RETURN, 6 IN.	CL	196.00	235.00
85	PEACEFUL FRIENDS, 3 IN.	CL	120.00	125.00
85	PEACEFUL FRIENDS, 6 IN.	CL	250.00	300.00
85	TENDER LOVE, 3 IN.	CL	100.00	115.00
85	TENDER LOVE, 6 IN.	CL	225.00	240.00
86	GOLDEN SHEAVES, 3 IN.	CL	125.00	130.00
86	GOLDEN SHEAVES, 6 IN.	CL	245.00	250.00
86	SEASON'S BOUNTY, 3 IN.	CL	125.00	130.00
86	SEASON'S BOUNTY, 6 IN.	CL	245.00	250.00
87	DEAR SWEETHEART, 6 IN.	CL	250.00	140.00
87	FOR MY SWEETHEART, 3 IN.	CL	130.00	135.00
87	FOR MY SWEETHEART, 6 IN.	CL	250.00	255.00
88	EXTRA, EXTRA!, 6 IN.	CL	320.00	325.00
88	SUNNY SKIES, 3 IN.	CL	145.00	150.00
88	SUNNY SKIES, 6 IN.	CL	320.00	325.00
89	BAKER BOY, 3 IN.	CL	170.00	175.00
89	BAKER BOY, 6 IN.	CL	340.00	345.00
89	PASTRY GIRL, 3 IN.	CL	170.00	175.00
89	PASTRY GIRL, 6 IN.	CL	340.00	345.00
90	ALPINE FRIEND, 3 IN.	CL	225.00	350.00
90	ALPINE FRIEND, 6 IN.	1500	450.00	600.00
90	ALPINE MUSIC, 3 IN.	CL	225.00	230.00
90	ALPINE MUSIC, 6 IN.	1500	450.00	600.00
91	CATALONIAN BOY, 3 IN.	CL	228.00	230.00
91	CATALONIAN BOY, 6 IN.	CL	500.00	505.00
91	CATALONIAN GIRL, 3 IN.	CL	228.00	230.00
91	CATALONIAN GIRL, 6 IN.	CL	500.00	505.00
92	MAY I, TOO?, 3 INCHES	1000	230.00	235.00
92	MAY I, TOO?, 6 INCHES	1000	440.00	445.00
92	WASTE NOT, WANT NOT, 3 INCHES	1000	190.00	195.00
92	WASTE NOT, WANT NOT, 6 INCHES	1000	430.00	435.00

J. FERRANDIZ   FERRANDIZ MATCHING NUMBER WOODCARVINGS

YR	NAME	LIMIT	ISSUE	TREND
87	DEAR SWEETHEART, 3 IN.	CL	130.00	130.00
88	BON APPETIT, 3 IN. (SET)	*	*	N/A
88	BON APPETIT, 6 IN. (SET)	*	*	N/A
88	EXTRA, EXTRA!, 3 IN.	CL	315.00	320.00
88	EXTRA, EXTRA!, 6 IN.	CL	665.00	670.00
88	PICNIC FOR TWO, 3 IN.	CL	390.00	395.00
88	PICNIC FOR TWO, 6 IN.	CL	845.00	850.00
88	SUNNY SKIES, 3 IN. (SET)	*	*	N/A
88	SUNNY SKIES, 6 IN. (SET)	*	*	N/A
89	BAKER/PASTRY, 3 IN.	CL	340.00	345.00
89	BAKER/PASTRY, 6 IN.	CL	680.00	685.00
89	DEAR SWEETHEART, 6 IN. (SET)	*	*	N/A
90	ALPINE MUSIC/FRIEND, 3 IN.	CL	450.00	455.00
90	ALPINE MUSIC/FRIEND, 6 IN.	CL	900.00	905.00
91	CATALONIAN BOY/GIRL, 3 IN.	CL	455.00	460.00
91	CATALONIAN BOY/GIRL, 6 IN.	CL	1,000.00	950.00

J. FERRANDIZ   FERRANDIZ MESSAGE COLLECTION

YR	NAME	LIMIT	ISSUE	TREND
89	GOD'S MIRACLE, 4 1/2 IN.	CL	300.00	305.00
89	GOD'S PRECIOUS GIFT, 4 1/2 IN.	CL	300.00	305.00
89	HE GUIDES US, 4 1/2 IN.	CL	300.00	305.00
89	HE IS THE LIGHT, 4 1/2 IN.	CL	300.00	305.00
89	HE IS THE LIGHT, 9 IN.	CL	600.00	575.00
89	HEAVEN SENT, 4 1/2 IN.	CL	300.00	305.00
89	LIGHT FROM WITHIN, 4 1/2 IN.	CL	300.00	305.00
89	LOVE KNOWS NO BOUNDS, 4 1/2 IN.	CL	300.00	305.00
89	LOVE SO POWERFUL, 4 1/2 IN.	CL	300.00	305.00
90	CHRISTMAS CARILLON, 4 1/2 IN.	CL	299.00	300.00
90	COUNT YOUR BLESSINGS, 4 1/2 IN.	CL	300.00	305.00
90	GOD'S CREATION, 4 1/2 IN.	CL	300.00	315.00

J. FERRANDIZ   FERRANDIZ MINI NATIVITY SET

YR	NAME	LIMIT	ISSUE	TREND
84	INFANT, 1 1/2 IN. (SET)	CL	*	N/A
84	JOSEPH, 1 1/2 IN. (SET)	CL	*	N/A
84	LEADING THE WAY, 1 1/2 IN. (SET)	CL	*	N/A
84	MARY, 1 1/2 IN.	CL	300.00	545.00
84	OX DONKEY, 1 1/2 IN. (SET)	CL	*	N/A
84	SHEEP KNEELING, 1 1/2 IN. (SET)	CL	*	N/A
84	SHEEP STANDING, 1 1/2 IN. (SET)	CL	*	N/A
85	BABY CAMEL, 1 1/2 IN.	CL	45.00	55.00
85	CAMEL GUIDE, 1 1/2 IN.	CL	45.00	55.00
85	CAMEL, 1 1/2 IN.	CL	45.00	55.00
85	HARMONY, 1 1/2 IN.	CL	45.00	55.00
85	REST, 1 1/2 IN.	CL	45.00	55.00
85	REVERENCE, 1 1/2 IN.	CL	45.00	55.00
85	SMALL TALK, 1 1/2 IN.	CL	45.00	55.00
85	THANKSGIVING, 1 1/2 IN.	CL	45.00	55.00
86	ANGEL, 1 1/2 IN.	CL	45.00	55.00
86	BALTHAZAR, 1 1/2 IN.	CL	45.00	55.00
86	CASPAR, 1 1/2 IN.	CL	45.00	55.00
86	FREE RIDE & MINI LAMB, 1 1/2 IN.	CL	45.00	55.00
86	HIKER, THE-1 1/2 IN.	CL	45.00	55.00
86	MELCHIOR, 1 1/2 IN.	CL	45.00	55.00

YR	NAME	LIMIT	ISSUE	TREND
86	STAR STRUCK, 1 1/2 IN.	CL	45.00	55.00
86	STRAY, THE-1 1/2 IN.	CL	45.00	55.00
86	WEARY TRAVELLER, 1 1/2 IN.	CL	45.00	55.00
88	DEVOTION, 1 1/2 IN.	CL	53.00	55.00
88	JOLLY GIFT, 1 1/2 IN.	CL	53.00	55.00
88	LONG JOURNEY, 1 1/2 IN.	CL	53.00	55.00
88	SWEET DREAMS, 1 1/2 IN.	CL	53.00	55.00
88	SWEET INSPIRATION, 1 1/2 IN.	CL	53.00	55.00

J. FERRANDIZ — FERRANDIZ SHEPHERDS OF THE YEAR

YR	NAME	LIMIT	ISSUE	TREND
77	FRIENDSHIPS, 3 IN.	YR	54.00	335.00
77	FRIENDSHIPS, 6 IN.	YR	110.00	650.00
78	SPREADING THE WORD, 3 IN.	YR	115.00	265.00
78	SPREADING THE WORD, 6 IN.	CL	271.00	575.00
79	DRUMMER BOY, 3 IN.	YR	80.00	240.00
79	DRUMMER BOY, 6 IN.	YR	220.00	430.00
80	FREEDOM BOUND, 3 IN.	YR	90.00	200.00
80	FREEDOM BOUND, 6 IN.	YR	225.00	395.00
81	JOLLY PIPER, 6 IN.	2250	225.00	405.00
82	COMPANIONS, 6 IN.	2250	220.00	285.00
83	GOOD SAMARITAN, 6 IN.	2250	220.00	315.00
84	DEVOTION, 3 IN.	CL	83.00	120.00
84	DEVOTION, 6 IN.	CL	180.00	230.00

J. FERRANDIZ — FERRANDIZ WOODCARVINGS

YR	NAME	LIMIT	ISSUE	TREND
69	ANGEL SUGAR HEART, 6 IN.	CL	25.00	2525.00
69	GOOD SHEPHERD, THE-3 IN.	CL	12.50	120.00
69	GOOD SHEPHERD, THE-6 IN.	CL	25.00	245.00
69	HEAVENLY GARDENER, 6 IN.	CL	25.00	2025.00
69	HEAVENLY QUINTET, 6 IN.	CL	25.00	2025.00
69	LOVE LETTER, 3 IN.	CL	12.50	155.00
69	LOVE LETTER, 6 IN.	CL	25.00	255.00
69	LOVE'S MESSENGER, 6 IN.	CL	25.00	2025.00
69	QUINTET, THE 3 IN.	CL	12.50	165.00
69	QUINTET, THE 6 IN.	CL	25.00	400.00
69	SUGAR HEART, 3 IN.	CL	12.50	455.00
69	SUGAR HEART, 6 IN.	CL	25.00	530.00
69	TALKING TO THE ANIMALS, 3 IN.	CL	12.50	135.00
69	TALKING TO THE ANIMALS, 6 IN.	CL	45.00	260.00
70	ARTIST, 3 IN.	CL	30.00	200.00
70	ARTIST, 6 IN.	CL	25.00	355.00
70	DUET, 3 IN.	CL	36.00	175.00
70	DUET, 6 IN.	CL	*	365.00
71	GOOD SHEPHERD, THE-10 IN.	CL	90.00	95.00
71	QUINTET,THE- 10 IN.	CL	100.00	725.00
71	TALKING TO THE ANIMALS, 10 IN.	CL	90.00	550.00
73	GIRL IN THE EGG, 3 IN.	CL	30.00	135.00
73	GIRL IN THE EGG, 6 IN.	CL	60.00	275.00
73	GIRL WITH DOVE, 3 IN.	CL	30.00	115.00
73	GIRL WITH DOVE, 6 IN.	CL	50.00	200.00
73	HAPPY WANDERER, 10 IN.	CL	120.00	500.00
73	NATURE GIRL, 3 IN.	CL	30.00	35.00
73	NATURE GIRL, 6 IN.	CL	60.00	275.00
73	SPRING ARRIVALS, 3 IN.	OP	30.00	160.00
73	SPRING ARRIVALS, 6 IN.	OP	50.00	350.00
73	SWEEPER, 3 IN.	CL	35.00	135.00
73	SWEEPER, 6 IN.	CL	75.00	430.00
73	TRUMPETER, 3 IN.	CL	69.00	115.00
73	TRUMPETER, 6 IN.	CL	120.00	250.00
74	BOUQUET, THE 3 IN.	CL	35.00	180.00
74	BOUQUET, THE 6 IN.	CL	75.00	330.00
74	FLIGHT INTO EGYPT, 3 IN.	CL	35.00	135.00
74	FLIGHT INTO EGYPT, 6 IN.	CL	70.00	500.00
74	GREETINGS, 3 IN.	CL	30.00	305.00
74	GREETINGS, 6 IN.	CL	55.00	480.00
74	HAPPY WANDERER, 3 IN.	CL	40.00	105.00
74	HAPPY WANDERER, 6 IN.	CL	70.00	200.00
74	HELPING HANDS, 3 IN.	CL	30.00	355.00
74	HELPING HANDS, 6 IN.	CL	55.00	710.00
74	LITTLE MOTHER 3 IN.	CL	136.00	300.00
74	LITTLE MOTHER, 6 IN.	CL	85.00	290.00
74	NEW FRIENDS, 3 IN.	CL	30.00	280.00
74	NEW FRIENDS, 6 IN.	CL	55.00	500.00
74	ROMEO, 3 IN.	CL	50.00	230.00
74	ROMEO, 6 IN.	CL	85.00	380.00
74	SPRING OUTING, 3 IN.	CL	30.00	630.00
74	SPRING OUTING, 6 IN.	CL	55.00	910.00
74	TENDER MOMENTS, 3 IN.	CL	30.00	380.00
74	TENDER MOMENTS, 6 IN.	CL	55.00	580.00
75	CHERUB, 2 IN.	CL	32.00	95.00
75	CHERUB, 4 IN.	CL	32.00	280.00
75	COURTING, 3 IN.	CL	70.00	240.00
75	COURTING, 6 IN.	CL	150.00	455.00
75	GIFT, THE 3 IN.	CL	40.00	200.00
75	GIFT, THE 6 IN.	CL	70.00	300.00
75	GOING HOME, 3 IN.	CL	40.00	160.00
75	GOING HOME, 6 IN.	CL	70.00	300.00

YR	NAME	LIMIT	ISSUE	TREND
75	HOLY FAMILY, 3 IN.	CL	75.00	250.00
75	HOLY FAMILY, 6 IN.	CL	200.00	670.00
75	INSPECTOR, 3 IN.	CL	40.00	230.00
75	INSPECTOR, 6 IN.	CL	80.00	380.00
75	LOVE GIFT, 3 IN.	CL	40.00	165.00
75	LOVE GIFT, 6 IN.	CL	70.00	300.00
75	MOTHER & CHILD, 3 IN.	CL	45.00	150.00
75	MOTHER & CHILD, 6 IN.	CL	90.00	300.00
75	SUMMERTIME, 3 IN.	CL	35.00	45.00
75	SUMMERTIME, 6 IN.	CL	70.00	265.00
75	WANDERLUST, 6 IN.	CL	70.00	455.00
76	CATCH A FALLING STAR, 3 IN.	CL	35.00	155.00
76	CATCH A FALLING STAR, 6 IN.	CL	75.00	255.00
76	COWBOY, 3 IN.	CL	35.00	155.00
76	FLOWER GIRL, 3 IN.	CL	40.00	45.00
76	FLOWER GIRL, 6 IN.	CL	90.00	310.00
76	GARDENER, 3 IN.	CL	32.00	200.00
76	GARDENER, 6 IN.	CL	65.00	325.00
76	GIRL W/ROOSTER, 3 IN.	CL	33.00	180.00
76	GIRL W/ROOSTER, 6 IN.	CL	60.00	280.00
76	LETTER, THE 3 IN.	CL	40.00	45.00
76	LETTER, THE 6 IN.	CL	90.00	600.00
76	SHARING, 3 IN.	CL	33.00	135.00
76	SHARING, 6 IN.	CL	75.00	250.00
76	WANDERLUST, 3 IN.	CL	33.00	130.00
77	BLESSING, THE 3 IN.	CL	45.00	155.00
77	BLESSING, THE 6 IN.	CL	125.00	255.00
77	HURDY GURDY, 3 IN.	CL	53.00	155.00
77	HURDY GURDY, 6 IN.	CL	112.00	395.00
77	JOURNEY, 3 IN.	CL	68.00	180.00
77	JOURNEY, 6 IN.	CL	120.00	405.00
77	LEADING THE WAY, 3 IN.	CL	63.00	125.00
77	NIGHT NIGHT, 3 IN.	CL	45.00	125.00
77	NIGHT NIGHT, 6 IN.	CL	68.00	280.00
77	POOR BOY, 3 IN.	CL	50.00	100.00
77	POOR BOY, 6 IN.	CL	125.00	200.00
77	PROUD MOTHER, 3 IN.	CL	53.00	155.00
77	PROUD MOTHER, 6 IN.	CL	130.00	355.00
77	RIDING THRU THE RAIN, 10 IN.	OP	400.00	1200.00
77	RIDING THRU THE RAIN, 5 IN.	OP	145.00	475.00
77	TRACKER, 3 IN.	CL	70.00	165.00
78	BASKET OF JOY, 3 IN.	CL	65.00	125.00
78	HARVEST GIRL, 3 IN.	CL	75.00	130.00
78	SPREADING THE WORD, 3 IN.	CL	115.00	195.00
78	SPREADING THE WORD, 6 IN.	CL	270.00	500.00
78	SPRING DANCE, 12 IN.	CL	950.00	1775.00
78	SPRING DANCE, 24 IN.	CL	48.00	6250.00
79	FIRST BLOSSOM, 3 IN.	CL	70.00	100.00
79	HAPPY STRUMMER, 3 IN.	CL	75.00	110.00
79	HE'S MY BROTHER, 3 IN.	CL	70.00	135.00
79	HE'S MY BROTHER, 6 IN.	CL	155.00	245.00
79	HIGH RIDING, 3 IN.	CL	145.00	205.00
79	HIGH RIDING, 6 IN.	CL	340.00	480.00
79	PEACE PIPE, 3 IN.	CL	85.00	120.00
79	STITCH IN TIME, 3 IN.	CL	75.00	130.00
79	STITCH IN TIME, 6 IN.	CL	150.00	240.00
80	DRUMMER BOY, 3 IN.	CL	130.00	205.00
80	DRUMMER BOY, 6 IN.	CL	300.00	405.00
80	SPRING ARRIVALS, 10 IN.	OP	435.00	775.00
80	SPRING ARRIVALS, 20 IN.	250	2,000.00	3375.00
80	TRUMPETER, 10 IN.	CL	500.00	510.00
80	UMPAPA, 4 IN.	CL	125.00	145.00
81	JOLLY PIPER, 3 IN.	CL	100.00	125.00
81	MERRY MELODY, 3 IN.	CL	90.00	120.00
81	MUSICAL BASKET, 3 IN.	CL	90.00	120.00
81	MUSICAL BASKET, 6 IN.	CL	200.00	230.00
81	STEPPING OUT, 3 IN.	CL	95.00	135.00
81	STEPPING OUT, 6 IN.	CL	220.00	280.00
81	SWEET ARRIVAL (BLUE), 3 IN.	CL	105.00	120.00
81	SWEET ARRIVAL (BLUE), 6 IN.	CL	225.00	265.00
81	SWEET ARRIVAL (PINK), 3 IN.	CL	105.00	110.00
81	SWEET ARRIVAL (PINK), 6 IN.	CL	225.00	230.00
81	SWEET DREAMS, 3 IN.	CL	100.00	145.00
81	TINY SOUNDS, 3 IN.	CL	90.00	110.00
82	BAGPIPE, 3 IN.	CL	80.00	100.00
82	BAGPIPE, 6 IN.	CL	175.00	195.00
82	BUNDLE OF JOY, 3 IN.	CL	100.00	305.00
82	BUNDLE OF JOY, 6 IN.	CL	225.00	325.00
82	CHAMPION, THE 3 IN.	CL	98.00	120.00
82	CHAMPION, THE 6 IN.	CL	220.00	260.00
82	CIRCUS SERENADE, 3 IN.	CL	100.00	165.00
82	CIRCUS SERENADE, 6 IN.	CL	220.00	225.00
82	CLARINET, 3 IN.	CL	80.00	105.00
82	CLARINET, 6 IN.	CL	175.00	205.00
82	COMPANIONS, 3 IN.	CL	95.00	120.00

YR	NAME	LIMIT	ISSUE	TREND
82	ENCORE, 3 IN.	CL	100.00	115.00
82	ENCORE, 6 IN.	CL	225.00	240.00
82	FLUTE, 3 IN.	CL	80.00	100.00
82	FLUTE, 6 IN.	CL	175.00	195.00
82	GOOD LIFE, THE 3 IN.	CL	100.00	205.00
82	GOOD LIFE, THE 6 IN.	CL	225.00	300.00
82	GUIDING LIGHT, 3 IN.	CL	100.00	125.00
82	GUITAR, 3 IN.	CL	80.00	100.00
82	GUITAR, 6 IN.	CL	175.00	195.00
82	HARMONICA, 3 IN.	CL	80.00	100.00
82	HARMONICA, 6 IN.	CL	175.00	195.00
82	HITCHHIKER, 3 IN.	CL	98.00	100.00
82	HITCHHIKER, 6 IN.	CL	125.00	230.00
82	LIGHTING THE WAY, 3 IN.	CL	105.00	145.00
82	LIGHTING THE WAY, 6 IN.	CL	225.00	300.00
82	PLAY IT AGAIN, 3 IN.	CL	100.00	120.00
82	PLAY IT AGAIN, 6 IN.	CL	250.00	260.00
82	STAR BRIGHT, 3 IN.	CL	110.00	130.00
82	STAR BRIGHT, 6 IN.	CL	250.00	300.00
82	SURPRISE, 3 IN.	CL	100.00	155.00
82	SURPRISE, 6 IN.	CL	225.00	330.00
82	SWEET DREAMS, 6 IN.	CL	225.00	335.00
82	SWEET MELODY, 3 IN.	CL	80.00	100.00
82	SWEET MELODY, 6 IN.	CL	198.00	210.00
82	TO MARKET, 3 IN.	CL	95.00	120.00
82	VIOLIN, 3 IN.	CL	80.00	100.00
82	VIOLIN, 6 IN.	CL	175.00	200.00
83	COWBOY, 20 IN.	CL	2,100.00	2125.00
83	EDELWEISS, 3 IN.	OP	95.00	200.00
83	EDELWEISS, 6 IN.	OP	220.00	485.00
83	GOLDEN BLOSSOM, 10 IN	OP	500.00	975.00
83	GOLDEN BLOSSOM, 20 IN	OP	3,300.00	5400.00
83	GOLDEN BLOSSOM, 3 IN.	OP	95.00	200.00
83	GOLDEN BLOSSOM, 6 IN.	OP	220.00	475.00
83	LOVE MESSAGE, 3 IN.	CL	105.00	155.00
83	LOVE MESSAGE, 6 IN.	CL	240.00	370.00
83	PEACE PIPE, 10 IN.	CL	460.00	505.00
84	BIRD'S EYE VIEW, 3 IN.	CL	88.00	130.00
84	BIRD'S EYE VIEW, 6 IN.	CL	216.00	705.00
84	COWBOY, 10 IN.	CL	370.00	505.00
84	HIGH HOPES, 3 IN.	CL	81.00	95.00
84	HIGH HOPES, 6 IN.	CL	170.00	265.00
84	PEACE PIPE, 20 IN.	CL	2,200.00	3475.00
84	SHIPMATES, 3 IN.	CL	81.00	120.00
84	SHIPMATES, 6 IN.	CL	170.00	250.00
84	TRUMPETER, 20 IN.	CL	2,350.00	3000.00
85	BUTTERFLY BOY, 3 IN.	CL	95.00	145.00
85	BUTTERFLY BOY, 6 IN.	CL	220.00	325.00
86	A MUSICAL RIDE, 4 IN.	RT	165.00	240.00
86	A MUSICAL RIDE, 8 IN.	RT	395.00	560.00
86	EDELWEISS, 10 IN.	OP	500.00	975.00
86	EDELWEISS, 20 IN.	250	3,300.00	5400.00
86	GOD'S LITTLE HELPER, 2 IN.	CL	170.00	260.00
86	GOD'S LITTLE HELPER, 4 IN.	CL	425.00	555.00
86	GOLDEN BLOSSOM, 40 IN.	CL	8,300.00	13000.00
86	SWISS BOY, 3 IN.	CL	122.00	175.00
86	SWISS BOY, 6 IN.	CL	245.00	400.00
86	SWISS GIRL, 3 IN.	CL	122.00	190.00
86	SWISS GIRL, 6 IN.	CL	245.00	305.00
87	AMONG FRIENDS, 3 IN.	CL	125.00	150.00
87	AMONG FRIENDS, 6 IN.	CL	245.00	295.00
87	BLACK FOREST BOY, 3 IN.	CL	125.00	150.00
87	BLACK FOREST BOY, 6 IN.	CL	250.00	300.00
87	BLACK FOREST GIRL, 3 IN.	CL	125.00	150.00
87	BLACK FOREST GIRL, 6 IN.	CL	250.00	325.00
87	HEAVENLY CONCERT, 2 IN.	CL	200.00	205.00
87	HEAVENLY CONCERT, 4 IN.	CL	450.00	555.00
87	NATURE'S WONDER, 3 IN.	CL	125.00	150.00
87	NATURE'S WONDER, 6 IN.	CL	245.00	290.00
87	SERENITY, 3 IN.	CL	125.00	150.00
87	SERENITY, 6 IN.	CL	245.00	295.00
88	ABRACADABRA, 3 IN.	CL	145.00	175.00
88	ABRACADABRA, 6 IN.	CL	315.00	355.00
88	BON APPETIT, 3 IN.	500	175.00	200.00
88	BON APPETIT, 6 IN.	500	395.00	440.00
88	PEACE MAKER, 3 IN.	CL	180.00	200.00
88	PEACE MAKER, 6 IN.	CL	360.00	405.00
88	PICNIC FOR TWO, 3 IN.	CL	190.00	210.00
88	PICNIC FOR TWO, 6 IN.	CL	425.00	475.00
88	WINTER MEMORIES, 3 IN.	CL	180.00	200.00
88	WINTER MEMORIES, 6 IN.	CL	398.00	445.00
89	MEXICAN BOY, 3 IN.	CL	170.00	180.00
89	MEXICAN BOY, 6 IN.	CL	340.00	355.00
89	MEXICAN GIRL, 3 IN.	CL	170.00	180.00
89	MEXICAN GIRL, 6 IN.	CL	340.00	355.00

From United Design's "Legend of Santa Claus" series, 1986's Santa with Pups by S. Bradford has more than doubled in value.

Hunted for centuries for its fur, the beaver joined Swarovski's "Endangered Species" series in 1992 with Mother Beaver, shown, and two pieces depicting her babies.

From Maruri USA's Graceful Reflections collection, Mute Swan with Baby was released in 1991.

Yield Not to Temptation by Sam Butcher, from Enesco's Precious Moments Collection, has increased in value since its 1989 release.

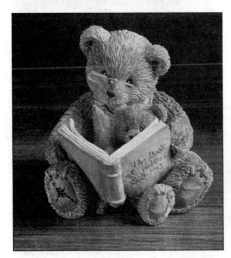

A 1993 Cherished Teddy that was released by Enesco Corp. to commemorate the 90th anniversary of the teddy bear, The Book of Teddies 1903-1993 features the bears Teddy and Roosevelt, and has increased significantly in value.

From the Clown Figurines by John McClelland collection produced by Reco International, Mr. One Note was released in 1987 as an edition of 9,500.

YR	NAME	LIMIT	ISSUE	TREND
89	SWISS BOY, 3 IN.	CL	180.00	185.00
89	SWISS BOY, 6 IN.	CL	380.00	385.00
89	SWISS GIRL, 3 IN.	CL	200.00	205.00
89	SWISS GIRL, 6 IN.	CL	470.00	475.00
92	MADONNA WITH CHILD, 3 INCHES	1000	190.00	195.00
92	MADONNA WITH CHILD, 6 INCHES	1000	370.00	375.00
92	PASCAL LAMB, 3 INCHES	1000	210.00	215.00
92	PASCAL LAMB, 6 INCHES	1000	460.00	465.00
93	CHRISTMAS TIME, 5 IN.	750	360.00	400.00
93	HOLIDAY GREETINGS, 3 IN.	1000	200.00	205.00
93	HOLIDAY GREETINGS, 6 IN.	1000	450.00	455.00
93	LOTS OF GIFTS, 3 IN.	1000	200.00	205.00
93	LOTS OF GIFTS, 6 IN.	1000	450.00	455.00
93	SANTA AND TEDDY, 5 IN.	750	360.00	375.00
94	DONKEY DRIVER, 3 IN.	OP	160.00	165.00
94	DONKEY DRIVER, 6 IN.	OP	360.00	365.00
94	DONKEY, 3 IN.	OP	200.00	205.00
94	DONKEY, 6 IN.	OP	450.00	455.00
94	SANTA RESTING ON BAG, 5 IN.	OP	400.00	405.00
95	HOMEWARD BOUND 3 IN.	OP	155.00	155.00
95	HOMEWARD BOUND 6 IN.	OP	410.00	410.00
95	TENDER CARE 3 IN.	OP	125.00	125.00
95	TENDER CARE 6 IN.	OP	275.00	300.00
W. & C. HALLETT				**HEAVENLY ANGELS**
95	ANGEL OF KINDNESS - NATURAL	250	225.00	225.00
95	ANGEL OF KINDNESS - PAINTED	250	350.00	350.00
95	ANGEL OF LOVE - PAINTED	250	350.00	350.00
95	ANGEL OF MERCY - NATURAL	250	225.00	225.00
95	ANGEL OF MERCY - PAINTED	250	350.00	350.00
95	ANGEL OF PEACE - NATURAL	250	225.00	225.00
95	ANGEL OF PEACE - PAINTED	250	350.00	350.00
96	ANGEL OF LOVE - NATURAL	250	225.00	225.00
J. FERRANDIZ				**LIMITED EDITION COUPLES**
85	FIRST KISS, 8 IN.	CL	590.00	955.00
85	SPRINGTIME STROLL, 8 IN.	CL	590.00	955.00
86	A TENDER TOUCH, 8 IN.	CL	590.00	855.00
86	MY HEART IS YOURS, 8 IN.	CL	590.00	855.00
87	HEART TO HEART, 8 IN.	CL	590.00	855.00
88	A LOVING HAND, 8 IN.	CL	795.00	855.00
J. FERRANDIZ				**MEMORIAL**
98	PEACEFUL LOVE, 10 IN.	OP	950.00	950.00
98	PEACEFUL LOVE, 20 IN.	250	4,500.00	4500.00
98	PEACEFUL LOVE, 3 IN.	OP	225.00	225.00
98	PEACEFUL LOVE, 40 IN.	12	11,500.00	11500.00
98	PEACEFUL LOVE, 6 IN.	OP	450.00	450.00
*				**MICKEY MOUSE THROUGH THE AGES**
90	STEAMBOAT WILLIE, 4 IN.	CL	295.00	525.00
91	MAD DOG, THE-4 IN.	CL	500.00	550.00
U. BERNARDI				**REFLECTIONS**
95	LEARNING THE SKILLS 4 IN.	500	275.00	275.00
95	LEARNING THE SKILLS 6 IN.	250	550.00	550.00
95	PLANNING THE TOUR 4 IN.	500	250.00	440.00
95	PLANNING THE TOUR 6 IN.	250	450.00	300.00
*				**RELIGIOUS**
98	ANGEL WITH FLUTE, GOLD	OP	610.00	610.00
98	ANGEL WITH FLUTE, PAINTED	OP	610.00	610.00
L. GAITHER				**RELIGIOUS**
98	MOSES	OP	995.00	995.00
S. KAY				**SANTA SERIES**
98	UP ON THE ROOFTOP	250	695.00	695.00
98	UP ON THE ROOFTOP	500	395.00	395.00
S. KAY				**SARAH KAY 10TH ANNIVERSARY**
93	CHRISTMAS BASKET, 4 IN.	1000	310.00	295.00
93	CHRISTMAS BASKET, 6 IN.	1000	600.00	585.00
93	INNOCENCE, 4 IN.	1000	345.00	320.00
93	INNOCENCE, 6 IN.	1000	630.00	635.00
93	JOY TO THE WORLD, 4 IN.	1000	310.00	295.00
93	JOY TO THE WORLD, 6 IN.	1000	600.00	585.00
93	MR. SANTA, 4 IN.	750	375.00	395.00
93	MR. SANTA, 6 IN.	750	695.00	735.00
93	MRS. SANTA, 4 IN.	750	375.00	395.00
93	MRS. SANTA, 6 IN.	750	695.00	735.00
93	MY FAVORITE DOLL, 4 IN.	1000	315.00	320.00
93	MY FAVORITE DOLL, 6 IN.	1000	630.00	635.00
S. KAY				**SARAH KAY FIGURINES**
83	BEDTIME, 1 1/2 IN.	CL	45.00	115.00
83	BEDTIME, 4 IN.	CL	95.00	235.00
83	BEDTIME, 6 IN.	CL	195.00	440.00
83	FEEDING THE CHICKENS, 1 1/2 IN.	CL	45.00	115.00
83	FEEDING THE CHICKENS, 4 IN.	CL	95.00	250.00
83	FEEDING THE CHICKENS, 6 IN.	CL	195.00	475.00
83	FROM THE GARDEN, 1 1/2 IN.	CL	45.00	115.00
83	FROM THE GARDEN, 4 IN.	CL	95.00	240.00
83	FROM THE GARDEN, 6 IN.	CL	195.00	455.00

YR	NAME	LIMIT	ISSUE	TREND
83	HELPING MOTHER, 1 1/2 IN.	CL	45.00	115.00
83	HELPING MOTHER, 4 IN.	CL	95.00	305.00
83	HELPING MOTHER, 6 IN.	CL	210.00	500.00
83	MORNING CHORES, 1 1/2 IN.	CL	45.00	115.00
83	MORNING CHORES, 4 IN.	CL	95.00	305.00
83	MORNING CHORES, 6 IN.	CL	210.00	505.00
83	PLAYTIME, 1 1/2 IN.	CL	45.00	115.00
83	PLAYTIME, 4 IN.	CL	95.00	250.00
83	PLAYTIME, 6 IN.	CL	195.00	500.00
83	SWEEPING, 1 1/2 IN.	CL	45.00	115.00
83	SWEEPING, 4 IN.	CL	95.00	235.00
83	SWEEPING, 6 IN.	CL	195.00	450.00
83	WAITING FOR MOTHER, 1 1/2 IN.	CL	45.00	115.00
83	WAITING FOR MOTHER, 11 IN.	CL	495.00	800.00
83	WAITING FOR MOTHER, 4 IN.	CL	95.00	235.00
83	WAITING FOR MOTHER, 6 IN.	CL	195.00	450.00
83	WAKE UP KISS, 6 IN.	CL	210.00	555.00
84	DAYDREAMING, 1 1/2 IN.	CL	45.00	130.00
84	DAYDREAMING, 4 IN.	CL	95.00	240.00
84	DAYDREAMING, 6 IN.	CL	195.00	450.00
84	FINDING R WAY, 1 1/2 IN.	CL	45.00	140.00
84	FINDING R WAY, 4 IN.	CL	95.00	250.00
84	FINDING R WAY, 6 IN.	CL	210.00	500.00
84	FLOWERS FOR YOU, 1 1/2 IN.	CL	45.00	130.00
84	FLOWERS FOR YOU, 4 IN.	CL	95.00	250.00
84	FLOWERS FOR YOU, 6 IN.	CL	195.00	450.00
84	OFF TO SCHOOL, 1 1/2 IN.	CL	45.00	130.00
84	OFF TO SCHOOL, 11 IN.	750	*	880.00
84	OFF TO SCHOOL, 20 IN.	100	*	4150.00
84	OFF TO SCHOOL, 4 IN.	4000	95.00	240.00
84	OFF TO SCHOOL, 6 IN.	4000	195.00	450.00
84	SPECIAL DELIVERY, 1 1/2 IN.	CL	45.00	130.00
84	SPECIAL DELIVERY, 4 IN.	CL	95.00	195.00
84	SPECIAL DELIVERY, 6 IN.	CL	195.00	335.00
84	TAG ALONG, 1 1/2 IN.	CL	45.00	135.00
84	TAG ALONG, 4 IN.	CL	95.00	230.00
84	TAG ALONG, 6 IN.	CL	195.00	295.00
84	WAKE UP KISS, 1 1/2 IN.	CL	45.00	555.00
84	WAKE UP KISS, 4 IN.	CL	95.00	190.00
84	WATCHFUL EYE, 1 1/2 IN.	CL	45.00	130.00
84	WATCHFUL EYE, 4 IN.	CL	95.00	240.00
84	WATCHFUL EYE, 6 IN.	CL	195.00	450.00
85	A SPECIAL DAY, 4 IN.	CL	95.00	195.00
85	A SPECIAL DAY, 6 IN.	CL	195.00	330.00
85	AFTERNOON TEA, 11 IN.	CL	650.00	775.00
85	AFTERNOON TEA, 20 IN.	CL	3,100.00	3525.00
85	AFTERNOON TEA, 4 IN.	CL	95.00	190.00
85	AFTERNOON TEA, 6 IN.	CL	195.00	350.00
85	EVERY GOOD BOY DESERVES FAVOR	4000	95.00	185.00
85	GIDDYAP!, 4 IN.	CL	95.00	250.00
85	GIDDYAP!, 6 IN.	CL	195.00	330.00
85	NIGHTIE NIGHT, 4 IN.	CL	95.00	190.00
85	NIGHTIE NIGHT, 6 IN.	CL	195.00	330.00
85	TIS THE SEASON, 4 IN.	CL	95.00	255.00
85	TIS THE SEASON, 6 IN.	CL	210.00	430.00
85	YULETIDE CHEER, 4 IN.	CL	95.00	250.00
85	YULETIDE CHEER, 6 IN.	CL	210.00	440.00
86	ALWAYS BY MY SIDE, 1 1/2 IN.	CL	45.00	100.00
86	ALWAYS BY MY SIDE, 4 IN.	CL	95.00	200.00
86	ALWAYS BY MY SIDE, 6 IN.	CL	195.00	380.00
86	BUNNY HUG, 1 1/2 IN.	CL	45.00	90.00
86	BUNNY HUG, 4 IN.	CL	95.00	175.00
86	BUNNY HUG, 6 IN.	CL	210.00	400.00
86	FINISHING TOUCH, 1 1/2 IN.	CL	45.00	90.00
86	FINISHING TOUCH, 4 IN.	CL	95.00	175.00
86	FINISHING TOUCH, 6 IN.	CL	195.00	315.00
86	GOOD AS NEW, 1 1/2 IN.	CL	45.00	95.00
86	GOOD AS NEW, 4 IN.	4000	95.00	290.00
86	GOOD AS NEW, 6 IN.	4000	195.00	500.00
86	OUR PUPPY, 1 1/2 IN.	CL	45.00	95.00
86	OUR PUPPY, 4 IN.	CL	95.00	190.00
86	OUR PUPPY, 6 IN.	CL	210.00	360.00
86	SWEET TREAT, 1 1/2 IN.	CL	45.00	90.00
86	SWEET TREAT, 4 IN.	CL	95.00	175.00
86	SWEET TREAT, 6 IN.	CL	195.00	315.00
86	TO LOVE AND CHERISH, 1 1/2 IN.	CL	45.00	90.00
86	TO LOVE AND CHERISH, 11 IN.	CL	*	670.00
86	TO LOVE AND CHERISH, 20 IN.	CL	*	3625.00
86	TO LOVE AND CHERISH, 4 IN.	CL	95.00	175.00
86	TO LOVE AND CHERISH, 6 IN.	CL	195.00	315.00
86	WITH THIS RING, 1 1/2 IN.	CL	45.00	90.00
86	WITH THIS RING, 11 IN.	CL	*	670.00
86	WITH THIS RING, 20 IN.	CL	*	3625.00
86	WITH THIS RING, 4 IN.	CL	95.00	175.00
86	WITH THIS RING, 6 IN.	CL	195.00	315.00

YR	NAME	LIMIT	ISSUE	TREND
87	A LOVING SPOONFUL, 1 1/2 IN.	CL	50.00	95.00
87	A LOVING SPOONFUL, 4 IN.	4000	150.00	295.00
87	A LOVING SPOONFUL, 6 IN.	4000	295.00	545.00
87	ALL ABOARD, 1 1/2 IN.	CL	50.00	95.00
87	ALL ABOARD, 4 IN.	CL	130.00	190.00
87	ALL ABOARD, 6 IN.	CL	265.00	360.00
87	ALL MINE, 1 1/2 IN.	CL	50.00	100.00
87	ALL MINE, 4 IN.	CL	130.00	230.00
87	ALL MINE, 6 IN.	CL	245.00	470.00
87	CUDDLES, 1 1/2 IN.	CL	50.00	100.00
87	CUDDLES, 4 IN.	CL	130.00	230.00
87	CUDDLES, 6 IN.	CL	245.00	470.00
87	LET'S PLAY, 1 1/2 IN.	CL	50.00	95.00
87	LET'S PLAY, 4 IN.	CL	130.00	190.00
87	LET'S PLAY, 6 IN.	CL	265.00	360.00
87	LITTLE NANNY, 1 1/2 IN.	CL	50.00	95.00
87	LITTLE NANNY, 4 IN.	CL	150.00	205.00
87	LITTLE NANNY, 6 IN.	CL	295.00	405.00
87	MY LITTLE BROTHER, 1 1/2 IN.	CL	70.00	95.00
87	MY LITTLE BROTHER, 4 IN.	CL	195.00	230.00
87	MY LITTLE BROTHER, 6 IN.	CL	375.00	455.00
88	GINGER SNAP, 1 1/2 IN.	CL	70.00	95.00
88	GINGER SNAP, 4 IN.	CL	150.00	190.00
88	GINGER SNAP, 6 IN.	CL	300.00	360.00
88	HIDDEN TREASURES, 1 1/2 IN.	CL	70.00	95.00
88	HIDDEN TREASURES, 4 IN.	CL	150.00	190.00
88	HIDDEN TREASURES, 6 IN.	CL	300.00	360.00
88	NEW HOME, 1 1/2 IN.	CL	70.00	95.00
88	NEW HOME, 4 IN.	CL	185.00	245.00
88	NEW HOME, 6 IN.	CL	365.00	515.00
88	PENNY FOR YOUR THOUGHTS, 1 1/2 IN.	CL	70.00	95.00
88	PENNY FOR YOUR THOUGHTS, 4 IN.	2000	185.00	265.00
88	PENNY FOR YOUR THOUGHTS, 6 IN.	CL	365.00	550.00
88	PURRFECT DAY, 1 1/2 IN.	CL	70.00	95.00
88	PURRFECT DAY, 4 IN.	CL	184.00	220.00
88	PURRFECT DAY, 6 IN.	CL	265.00	460.00
88	SCHOOL MARM 6 IN.	500	398.00	398.00
89	CHERISH, 1 1/2 IN.	CL	80.00	100.00
89	CHERISH, 4 IN.	2000	199.00	295.00
89	CHERISH, 6 IN.	2000	398.00	565.00
89	FIRST SCHOOL DAY, 1 1/2 IN.	CL	85.00	100.00
89	FIRST SCHOOL DAY, 4 IN.	2000	290.00	355.00
89	FIRST SCHOOL DAY, 6 IN.	2000	550.00	640.00
89	FISHERBOY, 1 1/2 IN.	CL	85.00	100.00
89	FISHERBOY, 4 IN.	2000	220.00	245.00
89	FISHERBOY, 6 IN.	CL	440.00	480.00
89	GARDEN PARTY, 1 1/2 IN.	CL	85.00	100.00
89	GARDEN PARTY, 4 IN.	2000	220.00	245.00
89	GARDEN PARTY, 6 IN.	CL	440.00	480.00
89	HOUSE CALL, 1 1/2 IN.	CL	85.00	100.00
89	HOUSE CALL, 4 IN.	CL	190.00	200.00
89	HOUSE CALL, 6 IN.	CL	390.00	395.00
89	TAKE ME ALONG, 1 1/2 IN.	CL	85.00	100.00
89	TAKE ME ALONG, 4 IN.	2000	220.00	290.00
89	TAKE ME ALONG, 6 IN.	1000	440.00	550.00
89	YEARLY CHECK-UP, 1 1/2 IN.	CL	85.00	100.00
89	YEARLY CHECK-UP, 4 IN.	CL	190.00	200.00
89	YEARLY CHECK-UP, 6 IN.	CL	390.00	395.00
90	BATTER UP, 1 1/2 IN.	CL	90.00	100.00
90	BATTER UP, 4 IN.	2000	220.00	270.00
90	BATTER UP, 6 IN.	2000	440.00	510.00
90	HOLIDAY CHEER, 1 1/2 IN.	CL	90.00	100.00
90	HOLIDAY CHEER, 4 IN.	2000	225.00	310.00
90	HOLIDAY CHEER, 6 IN.	1000	450.00	615.00
90	SEASONS GREETINGS, 1 1/2 IN.	CL	90.00	100.00
90	SEASONS GREETINGS, 4 IN.	2000	225.00	310.00
90	SEASONS GREETINGS, 6 IN.	1000	450.00	615.00
90	SHOOTIN' HOOPS, 1 1/2 IN.	CL	90.00	100.00
90	SHOOTIN' HOOPS, 4 IN.	2000	220.00	230.00
90	SHOOTIN' HOOPS, 6 IN.	2000	440.00	455.00
90	SPRING FEVER, 1 1/2 IN.	CL	90.00	100.00
90	SPRING FEVER, 4 IN.	2000	225.00	310.00
90	SPRING FEVER, 6 IN.	2000	450.00	615.00
90	TENDER LOVING CARE, 1 1/2 IN.	CL	90.00	100.00
90	TENDER LOVING CARE, 4 IN.	CL	220.00	245.00
90	TENDER LOVING CARE, 6 IN.	CL	440.00	480.00
91	DRESS UP, 1 1/2 IN.	3750	110.00	115.00
91	DRESS UP, 4 IN.	2000	270.00	275.00
91	DRESS UP, 6 IN.	2000	550.00	540.00
91	FIGURE EIGHT, 1 1/2 IN.	3750	110.00	115.00
91	FIGURE EIGHT, 4 IN.	2000	270.00	370.00
91	FIGURE EIGHT, 6 IN.	2000	550.00	665.00
91	FORE!!, 1 1/2 IN.	3750	110.00	120.00
91	FORE!!, 4 IN.	2000	270.00	330.00
91	FORE!!, 6 IN.	2000	550.00	585.00

YR	NAME	LIMIT	ISSUE	TREND
91	SEASON'S JOY, 1 1/2 IN.	3750	110.00	120.00
91	SEASON'S JOY, 4 IN.	2000	270.00	345.00
91	SEASON'S JOY, 6 IN.	1000	550.00	700.00
91	TOUCH DOWN, 1 1/2 IN.	3750	110.00	115.00
91	TOUCH DOWN, 4 IN.	2000	270.00	300.00
91	TOUCH DOWN, 6 IN.	2000	550.00	555.00
91	WINTER SURPRISE, 1 1/2 IN.	3750	110.00	575.00
91	WINTER SURPRISE, 4 IN.	2000	270.00	275.00
91	WINTER SURPRISE, 6 IN.	1000	550.00	540.00
92	FREE SKATING, 1 1/2 IN.	3750	110.00	115.00
92	FREE SKATING, 4 IN.	1000	310.00	315.00
92	FREE SKATING, 6 IN.	1000	590.00	625.00
92	MERRY CHRISTMAS, 1 1/2 IN.	3750	110.00	115.00
92	MERRY CHRISTMAS, 4 IN.	1000	350.00	355.00
92	MERRY CHRISTMAS, 6 IN.	1000	580.00	585.00
92	RAINDROPS, 1 1/2 IN.	3750	110.00	115.00
92	RAINDROPS, 4 IN.	1000	350.00	355.00
92	RAINDROPS, 6 IN.	1000	640.00	645.00
92	TAKE ME ALONG 11 IN.	400	950.00	950.00
92	TAKE ME ALONG 20 IN.	100	4,550.00	4550.00
92	TULIPS FOR MOTHER, 1 1/2 IN.	3750	110.00	115.00
92	TULIPS FOR MOTHER, 4 IN.	1000	310.00	315.00
92	TULIPS FOR MOTHER, 6 IN.	1000	590.00	625.00
92	WINTER CHEER, 4 IN.	2000	300.00	305.00
92	WINTER CHEER, 6 IN.	1000	580.00	585.00
93	INNOCENCE 4 IN.	1000	345.00	300.00
93	INNOCENCE 6 IN.	1000	630.00	630.00
93	JOY TO THE WORLD 4 IN.	1000	310.00	300.00
93	JOY TO THE WORLD 6 IN.	1000	600.00	600.00
93	MR. SANTA 4 IN.	750	375.00	400.00
93	MR. SANTA 6 IN.	750	695.00	725.00
93	MRS. SANTA 4 IN.	750	375.00	400.00
93	MRS. SANTA 6 IN.	750	695.00	725.00
93	MY FAVORITE DOLL 4 IN.	1000	315.00	315.00
93	MY FAVORITE DOLL 6 IN.	1000	600.00	600.00
93	TEN ROSES FOR YOU 4 IN.	1000	290.00	290.00
93	TEN ROSES FOR YOU 6 IN.	1000	525.00	525.00
94	BUBBLES & BOWS, 4 IN.	1000	300.00	305.00
94	BUBBLES & BOWS, 6 IN.	1000	600.00	605.00
94	CHRISTMAS WONDER, 4 IN.	1000	370.00	375.00
94	CHRISTMAS WONDER, 6 IN.	1000	700.00	705.00
94	CLOWNING AROUND, 4 IN.	1000	300.00	305.00
94	CLOWNING AROUND, 6 IN.	1000	550.00	555.00
94	JOLLY PAIR, 4 IN.	1000	350.00	355.00
94	JOLLY PAIR, 6 IN.	1000	650.00	655.00
94	LITTLE CHIMNEY SWEEP, 4 IN.	1000	300.00	305.00
94	LITTLE CHIMNEY SWEEP, 6 IN.	1000	600.00	605.00
98	COFFEE BREAK, 4 IN.	2000	295.00	295.00
98	COFFEE BREAK, 6 IN.	1000	575.00	575.00
98	HAVING FUN, 4 IN.	2000	295.00	295.00
98	HAVING FUN, 6 IN.	1000	575.00	575.00
S. KAY			**SARAH KAY MINI SANTAS**	
91	JOLLY SANTA, 1 1/2 IN.	CL	110.00	115.00
91	JOLLY ST. NICK, 1 1/2 IN.	CL	110.00	115.00
91	KRIS KRINGLE, 1 1/2 IN.	CL	110.00	115.00
91	SARAH KAY SANTA, 1 1/2 IN.	CL	110.00	115.00
92	A FRIEND TO ALL 1 1/2 IN.	2500	110.00	110.00
92	FATHER CHRISTMAS 1 1/2 IN.	2500	110.00	110.00
S. KAY			**SARAH KAY SANTAS**	
88	JOLLY SANTA, 12 IN.	CL	1,300.00	1305.00
88	JOLLY SANTA, 4 IN.	CL	235.00	325.00
88	JOLLY SANTA, 6 IN.	CL	480.00	605.00
88	JOLLY ST. NICK, 4 IN.	CL	199.00	425.00
88	JOLLY ST. NICK, 6 IN.	CL	398.00	855.00
89	SANTA, 4 IN.	CL	235.00	355.00
89	SANTA, 6 IN.	CL	480.00	485.00
89	SARAH KAY SANTA, 4 IN.	750	275.00	275.00
89	SARAH KAY SANTA, 6 IN.	750	550.00	550.00
90	KRIS KRINGLE SANTA, 4 IN.	CL	275.00	355.00
90	KRIS KRINGLE SANTA, 6 IN.	CL	550.00	555.00
91	A FRIEND TO ALL, 4 IN.	750	300.00	305.00
91	A FRIEND TO ALL, 6 IN.	750	590.00	595.00
92	FATHER CHRISTMAS, 4 IN.	750	350.00	355.00
92	FATHER CHRISTMAS, 6 IN.	750	590.00	595.00
95	CHECKING IT TWICE 4 IN.	500	250.00	25.00
95	CHECKING IT TWICE 6 IN.	250	395.00	395.00
96	WORKSHOP SANTA 4 IN.	500	295.00	295.00
96	WORKSHOP SANTA 6 IN.	250	495.00	500.00
S. KAY			**SARAH KAY'S FIRST CHRISTMAS**	
94	SARAH KAY'S FIRST CHRISTMAS, 4 IN.	500	350.00	355.00
94	SARAH KAY'S FIRST CHRISTMAS, 6 IN.	250	600.00	605.00
95	FIRST XMAS STOCKING 4 IN.	500	250.00	250.00
95	FIRST XMAS STOCKING 6 IN.	250	395.00	395.00
96	ALL I WANT FOR CHRISTMAS 4 IN.	500	325.00	325.00
96	ALL I WANT FOR CHRISTMAS 6 IN.	250	550.00	550.00

YR	NAME	LIMIT	ISSUE	TREND
97	CHRISTMAS PUPPY 4 IN.	500	375.00	375.00
97	CHRISTMAS PUPPY 6 IN.	250	625.00	625.00
S. KAY			**SCHOOL DAYS**	
95	I KNOW, I KNOW 4 IN.	500	250.00	250.00
95	I KNOW, I KNOW 6 IN.	250	395.00	445.00
96	HEAD OF THE CLASS 4 IN.	500	295.00	295.00
96	HEAD OF THE CLASS 6 IN.	250	495.00	495.00
97	HOMEWORK 4 IN.	500	315.00	315.00
97	HOMEWORK 6 IN.	250	520.00	520.00
98	STRAIGHT A'S, 4 IN.	500	375.00	375.00
98	STRAIGHT A'S, 6 IN.	250	650.00	650.00
S. KAY			**TRIBUTE TO MOTHER**	
95	MOM'S JOY 5"	RT	298.00	297.50
96	SWEETS FOR MY SWEET 4 IN.	250	399.00	399.00
97	STORYTIME 5 1/2 IN.	250	650.00	650.00
98	DON'T FORGET	250	650.00	650.00

ARDLEIGH-ELLIOTT

YR	NAME	LIMIT	ISSUE	TREND
L. LIU			**BASKET BOUQUETS**	
96	MAGNOLIAS MUSIC BOX	*	30.00	30.00
96	PANSIES MUSIC BOX	*	30.00	30.00
96	ROSES "MY FAVORITE THINGS" MUSIC BOX	OP	30.00	30.00
D. BROOKS		**HEAVEN'S LITTLE SWEETHEARTS**		
97	AN ANGEL'S KINDNESS BOX	*	35.00	35.00
98	AN ANGEL'S CARING	*	35.00	35.00
98	AN ANGEL'S LOVE	*	35.00	35.00
*		**LEGENDARY LOVE OF SCARLETT AND RHETT**		
97	I'M GOING TO DANCE AND DANCE MUSICAL FIGURINE	*	40.00	40.00
97	SAY YOU'RE GOING TO MARRY ME MUSICAL FIGURINE	*	40.00	40.00
97	WHAT I WANT FOR BONNIE MUSICAL FIGURINE	*	40.00	40.00
L. LIU			**LENA LIU'S FLORAL CAMEOS**	
97	REMEMBRANCE	*	40.00	40.00
L. LIU		**LENA LIU'S FLORAL GREETINGS**		
97	CIRCLE OF LOVE MUSIC BOX	*	*	N/A
B.P. GUTMANN		**LOVE'S HEAVENLY MESSENGER**		
97	SWEET SLUMBER	*	35.00	35.00
L. BOGLE			**NATIVE BEAUTY**	
97	PROMISE, THE, BOX	*	*	N/A
98	AFTERGLOW	*	35.00	35.00
98	WHITE FEATHER	*	35.00	35.00
*		**THE WONDERFUL WIZARD OF OZ**		
96	WE'RE OFF TO SEE THE WIZARD MUSIC BOX	OP	40.00	40.00

ARMANI

YR	NAME	LIMIT	ISSUE	TREND
G. ARMANI		**ANNUAL MOTHER'S DAY**		
98	MOTHER'S BOUQUET 799C	YR	175.00	175.00
G. ARMANI			**CAPODIMONTE**	
76	COUNTRY GIRL (LITTLE SHEPHERDESS) 3153	RT	48.00	275.00
77	NAPOLEON 464C	RT	250.00	500.00
78	ORGAN GRINDER 3323	RT	140.00	350.00
80	OLD DRUNK (RICHARD'S NIGHT OUT) 3243	RT	130.00	240.00
95	YOUNG HEARTS 679C	1500	900.00	900.00
97	GALLANT APPROACH 146C	750	1,250.00	1250.00
97	VENETIAN NIGHT 125C	975	2,000.00	2000.00
98	SANTA CLAUS 346C	*	400.00	400.00
G. ARMANI			**CLOWNS**	
84	CLOWN WITH DOG 653E	RT	135.00	170.00
91	BUST OF CLOWN (FIDDLER CLOWN) 725E	5000	500.00	500.00
G. ARMANI			**COMMEMORATIVE**	
92	DISCOVERY OF AMERICA-COLUMBUS 867C	RT	400.00	525.00
93	1993 MOTHER'S DAY PLAQUE 899C	RT	100.00	225.00
94	1994 MOTHER'S DAY PLAQUE 254C	RT	100.00	225.00
95	1995 MOTHER'S DAY PLAQUE 538C	RT	125.00	240.00
96	1996 MOTHER'S DAY PLAQUE 341C	RT	150.00	150.00
97	1997 MOTHER'S DAY FIGURINE MOTHER'S ANGEL 155C	YR	175.00	175.00
G. ARMANI			**DISNEYANA**	
92	CINDERELLA 783C	RT	500.00	4000.00
93	SNOW WHITE 199C	RT	750.00	1900.00
94	ARIEL 505C	RT	750.00	2675.00
95	BEAUTY AND THE BEAST 543C	RT	975.00	1475.00
96	JASMINE & RAJAH	RT	800.00	1225.00
97	CINDERELLA & THE PRINCE 107C	RT	825.00	825.00
G. ARMANI		**FIGURINE OF THE YEAR**		
93	LADY WITH BAG 2149E	RT	350.00	350.00
96	LADY JANE 390C	RT	200.00	200.00
97	APRIL 121C	YR	250.00	250.00
98	VIOLET 756C	*	250.00	250.00
G. ARMANI			**FLORENCE/DISNEY**	
95	JIMINY CRICKET SPECIAL BACKSTAMP 379C	RT	300.00	300.00
96	JIMINY CRICKET 379C	OP	300.00	300.00
96	PINOCCHIO & FIGARO 464C	OP	500.00	550.00
96	SLEEPING BEAUTY (BRIAR ROSE) 106C	OP	650.00	650.00
97	TINKERBELL 108C	OP	425.00	425.00

YR	NAME	LIMIT	ISSUE	TREND
	G. ARMANI		**FLORENTINE GARDENS**	
92	ABUNDANCE 870C	RT	600.00	900.00
92	DAWN 874C	RT	500.00	795.00
92	TWILIGHT 872C	RT	560.00	795.00
92	VANITY 871C	RT	585.00	1138.00
93	AURORA-LADY WITH DOVES 884C	7500	370.00	370.00
93	FREEDOM 906C	RT	850.00	1295.00
93	LIBERTY 903C	RT	750.00	1050.00
93	LILACS & ROSES 882C	7500	410.00	410.00
93	LOVERS 191C	RT	450.00	800.00
93	WIND SONG 904C	5000	520.00	520.00
94	AMBROSIA 482C	5000	435.00	435.00
94	ANGELICA 484C	5000	575.00	575.00
94	EMBRACE 480C	RT	1,450.00	3350.00
94	SUMMERTIME 485C	5000	650.00	650.00
95	AQUARIUS 426C	5000	600.00	600.00
95	GEMINI 427C	5000	600.00	600.00
95	VIRGO 425C	5000	600.00	600.00
96	EBONY 372C	5000	550.00	550.00
97	ARTEMIS 126C	5000	1,750.00	1750.00
97	BACCHUS & ARIANNA 419C	5000	1,500.00	1500.00
97	LEO 149C	5000	650.00	650.00
97	PISCES 171C	5000	650.00	650.00
97	TAURUS 170C	5000	650.00	650.00
98	APHRODITE 230C	3000	1,350.00	1350.00
98	CAPRICORN 699C	5000	*	N/A
98	FLORA 173C	5000	600.00	600.00
98	FLORA 173F	*	450.00	450.00
98	GOLDEN NECTAR 212C	1500	2,000.00	2000.00
98	GOLDEN NECTAR 212F	*	1,350.00	1350.00
98	POMONA 174C	5000	550.00	550.00
98	POMONA 174F	*	400.00	400.00
98	SAGITTARIUS 698C	5000	*	N/A
	G. ARMANI		**FOUR SEASONS**	
90	LADY ON SEASHORE (SUMMER) 540C	OP	440.00	440.00
90	LADY WITH BICYCLE (SPRING) 539C	OP	550.00	550.00
90	LADY WITH ICE SKATES (WINTER) 542C	OP	400.00	400.00
90	LADY WITH UMBRELLA (FALL) 541C	OP	475.00	475.00
98	AUTUMN WIND 763C	*	400.00	400.00
98	AUTUMN WIND 763F	*	275.00	275.00
98	MAY TIME 761C	*	400.00	400.00
98	MAY TIME 761F	*	275.00	275.00
98	SUMMER BREEZE 762C	*	400.00	400.00
98	SUMMER BREEZE 762F	*	265.00	265.00
98	WINTER CHILL 764C	*	400.00	400.00
98	WINTER CHILL 764F	*	205.00	205.00
	G. ARMANI		**G. ARMANI SOCIETY EVENT**	
90	PALS (BOY WITH DOG) 407S	RT	200.00	600.00
92	SPRINGTIME 961C	RT	250.00	500.00
93	LOVING ARMS 880E	RT	250.00	510.00
94	DAISY 202E	RT	250.00	450.00
95	IRIS 628E	RT	250.00	413.00
96	ROSE 678C	RT	250.00	375.00
97	MARIANNE 135C	YR	275.00	275.00
98	VICTORIA 525C	*	275.00	275.00
	G. ARMANI		**G. ARMANI SOCIETY MEMBERS ONLY FIGURINES**	
90	AWAKENING 591C	RT	138.00	1425.00
90	MY FINE FEATHERED FRIENDS 122S	RT	175.00	550.00
91	PEACE & HARMONY 824C	RT	300.00	725.00
91	RUFFLES 745E	RT	139.00	525.00
92	ASCENT 866C	RT	195.00	688.00
92	JULIE 293P	RT	90.00	225.00
92	JULIETTE 294P	RT	90.00	280.00
93	LADY ROSE 197C	RT	125.00	350.00
93	VENUS 881E	RT	225.00	550.00
94	AQUARIUS 248C	RT	125.00	350.00
94	FLORA 212C	RT	225.00	425.00
94	HARLEQUIN 490C	RT	300.00	500.00
95	MELODY 656C	RT	250.00	375.00
95	SCARLETTE 698C	RT	200.00	360.00
96	ALLEGRA 345C	RT	250.00	338.00
96	ARIANNA 400C	RT	125.00	175.00
97	IT'S MINE 136C	YR	200.00	200.00
97	SABRINA 110C	YR	275.00	275.00
98	BETH 519C	*	115.00	115.00
98	BETH-BONUS 519C	*	115.00	115.00
98	LUCIA 755C	*	325.00	325.00
98	LUCIA-REDEMPTION 755C	*	325.00	325.00
98	VICTORIA 525C	*	275.00	275.00
	G. ARMANI		**GALLERIA COLLECTION**	
93	LEDA AND THE SWAN 1012T	RT	550.00	595.00
93	LEDA AND THE SWAN 1012T (USA)	RT	550.00	550.00
93	SEA WAVE 1006T	RT	500.00	500.00
93	SEA WAVE 1006T (USA)	RT	500.00	500.00
93	SPRING HERALD 1009T	RT	500.00	595.00

YR	NAME	LIMIT	ISSUE	TREND
93	SPRING HERALD 1009T (USA)	RT	500.00	500.00
93	SPRING WATER 1007T	RT	500.00	595.00
93	SPRING WATER 1007T (USA)	RT	500.00	500.00
93	ZEPHYR 1010T	RT	500.00	595.00
93	ZEPHYR 1010T (USA)	RT	500.00	500.00
95	GRACE 1029T	1000	465.00	465.00
95	JOY 1028T	1000	465.00	465.00
95	PEARL 1019T	1000	550.00	550.00
96	EROS 406T	1500	750.00	750.00

G. ARMANI **GOLDEN AGE**

YR	NAME	LIMIT	ISSUE	TREND
96	FRAGRANCE 340C	3000	500.00	500.00
96	PROMENADE 339C	3000	600.00	600.00
96	SOIREE 338C	3000	600.00	600.00
96	SPRING MORNING 337C	3000	600.00	650.00
97	MORNING RIDE 147C	5000	770.00	770.00
98	LACEY 645C	3000	*	N/A
98	REVERIE 646C	3000	*	N/A

G. ARMANI **GULLIVER'S WORLD**

YR	NAME	LIMIT	ISSUE	TREND
94	BARREL 659T	1000	225.00	300.00
94	COWBOY 657T	RT	125.00	225.00
94	GETTING CLEAN 661T	1000	130.00	150.00
94	RAY OF MOON 658T	1000	100.00	100.00
94	SERENADE 660T	RT	200.00	235.00

G. ARMANI **IMPRESSIONS**

YR	NAME	LIMIT	ISSUE	TREND
90	BITTERSWEET 528C	RT	400.00	430.00
90	BITTERSWEET 528P	RT	275.00	600.00
90	MASQUERADE 527C	RT	400.00	430.00
90	MASQUERADE 527P	RT	300.00	600.00
90	MYSTERY 523C	RT	370.00	490.00

G. ARMANI **MASTERWORKS**

YR	NAME	LIMIT	ISSUE	TREND
95	AURORA 680C	RT	3,500.00	5000.00
98	CIRCLE OF JOY 760C	1500	2,750.00	2750.00

G. ARMANI **MOONLIGHT MASQUERADE**

YR	NAME	LIMIT	ISSUE	TREND
90	QUEEN OF HEARTS 744C	RT	450.00	450.00
91	LADY CLOWN WITH CANE 742C	RT	390.00	390.00
91	LADY CLOWN WITH DOLL 743C	RT	410.00	410.00
91	LADY HARLEQUIN 740C	RT	450.00	450.00
91	LADY PIERROT 741C	RT	390.00	390.00

G. ARMANI **MY FAIR LADIES**

YR	NAME	LIMIT	ISSUE	TREND
*	BRIEF ENCOUNTER 167C	5000	350.00	350.00
*	CHARM 197C	3000	850.00	850.00
*	IN THE MOOD 164C	5000	425.00	425.00
*	MYSTICAL FOUNTAIN 159C	3000	900.00	900.00
*	NELLIE 196C	5000	335.00	335.00
*	OPAL 758C	5000	450.00	450.00
*	STARLIGHT 150C	1500	*	N/A
87	LADY WITH PEACOCK 385C	RT	380.00	3200.00
87	LADY WITH PEACOCK 385F	RT	230.00	290.00
87	LADY WITH PEACOCK 385P	RT	300.00	400.00
88	FLAMENCO DANCER 389C	RT	400.00	600.00
88	LADY WITH BOOK 384C	RT	300.00	300.00
88	LADY WITH FAN 387C	RT	300.00	300.00
88	LADY WITH GREAT DANE 429C	RT	385.00	1125.00
88	LADY WITH MIRROR 386C	RT	300.00	1900.00
88	LADY WITH MUFF 388C	5000	250.00	250.00
88	MATERNITY (MOTHER & CHILD) 405C	RT	415.00	425.00
89	LADY WITH PARROT 616C	RT	460.00	1275.00
89	TWO CAN-CAN DANCERS 516C	RT	880.00	1720.00
90	CAN CAN DANCER 589P	RT	460.00	465.00
93	ELEGANCE 195C	5000	525.00	525.00
93	FASCINATION 192C	5000	500.00	500.00
93	LADY WITH UMBRELLA 196C	5000	370.00	450.00
93	MAHOGANY 194C	RT	500.00	1675.00
93	MORNING ROSE 193C	5000	450.00	450.00
95	AT EASE 634C	5000	650.00	650.00
95	ISADORA 633C	5000	920.00	920.00
96	GEORGIA 414C	5000	550.00	550.00
96	GRACE 383C	5000	475.00	475.00
96	IN LOVE 382C	5000	450.00	450.00
96	LARA 415C	5000	450.00	450.00
97	GARDEN DELIGHT 157C	3000	1,000.00	1000.00
97	SWANS LAKE 158C	3000	900.00	900.00
98	BRIEF ENCOUNTER 167C	5000	400.00	400.00
98	BRIEF ENCOUNTER 167F	*	230.00	230.00
98	CARMEN 520C	*	225.00	225.00
98	CARMEN 520F	*	155.00	155.00
98	CHARM 197C	3000	850.00	850.00
98	CHARM 197F	*	500.00	500.00
98	HOLLY 191C	*	300.00	300.00
98	HOLLY 191F	*	170.00	170.00
98	IN THE MOOD 164C	5000	400.00	400.00
98	IN THE MOOD 164F	*	265.00	265.00
98	MOONLIGHT 151C	1500	*	N/A
98	MYSTICAL FOUNTAIN 159C	3000	900.00	900.00
98	MYSTICAL FOUNTAIN 159F	*	630.00	630.00

YR	NAME	LIMIT	ISSUE	TREND
98	OPAL 758C	5000	450.00	450.00
98	OPAL 758F	*	315.00	315.00
G. ARMANI			**PEARLS OF THE ORIENT**	
90	ORIENTAL LADY WITH FAN 610C	RT	500.00	500.00
90	ORIENTAL LADY WITH IRIS 613C	RT	475.00	475.00
90	ORIENTAL LADY WITH PARROT 611C	RT	500.00	500.00
90	ORIENTAL LADY WITH SUNSHADE 612C	RT	550.00	550.00
G. ARMANI			**PREMIERE BALLERINAS**	
89	BALLERINA 508C	RT	470.00	530.00
89	BALLERINA WITH DRAPE 504C	RT	500.00	1200.00
89	FLYING BALLERINA 503C	RT	440.00	1400.00
89	FLYING DANCERS 518C	RT	780.00	880.00
89	KNEELING BALLERINA 517C	RT	340.00	415.00
89	TWO DANCERS 515C	RT	670.00	775.00
91	DANCER WITH PEACOCK 727C	RT	460.00	460.00
G. ARMANI			**RELIGIOUS**	
83	CHOIR BOYS 900	RT	400.00	550.00
87	CRUCIFIX 1158C	RT	155.00	160.00
87	CRUCIFIX 790C	15000	160.00	250.00
91	CRUCIFIX PLAQUE 711C	RT	265.00	285.00
93	CRUCIFIX 786C	7500	285.00	315.00
94	ASSUMPTION, THE 697C	5000	650.00	650.00
94	CHRIST CHILD (NATIVITY) 1020C	1000	175.00	175.00
94	DONKEY (NATIVITY) 1027C	1000	185.00	185.00
94	LA PIETA 802C	5000	950.00	950.00
94	MADONNA (NATIVITY) 1022C	1000	365.00	365.00
94	MAGI KING-GOLD (NATIVITY) 1023C	1000	600.00	600.00
94	MAGI KING-INCENSE (NATIVITY) 1024C	1000	600.00	600.00
94	MAGI KING-MYRRH (NATIVITY)	1000	450.00	450.00
94	OX (NATIVITY) 1026C	1000	300.00	300.00
94	RENAISSANCE CRUCIFIX 1017T	5000	265.00	265.00
94	ST. JOSEPH (NATIVITY) 1021C	1000	500.00	500.00
95	CRUCIFIXION, THE 780C	5000	500.00	500.00
95	HOLY FAMILY 788C	5000	1,000.00	1000.00
95	MOSES 606C	RT	365.00	400.00
G. ARMANI			**SEASONS**	
98	AUTUMN'S BREEZE 319C	*	300.00	300.00
98	AUTUMN'S BREEZE 319F	*	175.00	175.00
98	FALLING LEAVES 234C	*	400.00	400.00
98	FALLING LEAVES 234F	*	300.00	300.00
98	LOVE IN BLOOM 232C	*	400.00	400.00
98	LOVE IN BLOOM 232F	*	325.00	325.00
98	SNOWFLAKES 235C	*	400.00	400.00
98	SNOWFLAKES 235F	*	300.00	300.00
98	SPRING TIME 317C	*	300.00	300.00
98	SPRING TIME 317F	*	200.00	200.00
98	SUMMER MELODY 318C	*	300.00	300.00
98	SUMMER MELODY 318F	*	195.00	195.00
98	SUNSHINE 233C	*	400.00	400.00
98	SUNSHINE 233F	*	400.00	300.00
98	WINTER FUN 320C	*	300.00	300.00
98	WINTER FUN 320F	*	185.00	185.00
G. ARMANI			**SIENA COLLECTION**	
93	BACK FROM THE FIELDS 1002T	RT	400.00	500.00
93	ENCOUNTERING 1003T	RT	350.00	650.00
93	FRESH FRUITS 1001T	RT	155.00	400.00
93	HAPPY FIDDLER 1005T	RT	225.00	295.00
93	MOTHER'S HAND 1008T	2500	250.00	285.00
93	SOFT KISS 1000T	RT	155.00	350.00
93	SOUND THE TRUMPET 1004T	RT	225.00	275.00
94	COUNTRY BOY WITH MUSHROOMS 1014T	2500	135.00	135.00
G. ARMANI			**SPECIAL EVENTS**	
91	CARRYING THE BRIDE 813C	7500	400.00	400.00
91	JUST MARRIED 827C	5000	100.00	100.00
91	WEDDING COUPLE 814C	7500	600.00	600.00
91	WEDDING COUPLE 815C	7500	500.00	500.00
93	BRIDE & GROOM ON A GIG 902C	2500	1,000.00	1000.00
94	BLACK MATERNITY 502C	3000	535.00	535.00
94	PERFECT LOVE 652C	3000	1,200.00	1200.00
94	WEDDING WALTZ (BLACK) 501C	3000	750.00	750.00
94	WEDDING WALTZ (WHITE) 493C	3000	750.00	750.00
95	TENDERNESS 418C	5000	950.00	950.00
95	TOMORROW'S DREAMS 336C	5000	700.00	700.00
G. ARMANI			**SPECIAL RELEASES**	
89	EVE 590T	RT	250.00	725.00
92	COUPLE IN CAR 862C	RT	1,000.00	1000.00
92	GIRL IN CAR 861C	RT	900.00	1250.00
92	LADY WITH DOVE (DOVE DANCER) 858E	RT	320.00	320.00
93	DOCTOR IN CAR 848C	RT	800.00	825.00
G. ARMANI			**SPECIAL TIMES**	
82	CARD PLAYERS-CHEATERS 3280	OP	400.00	850.00
82	GIRL WITH CHICKS 5122	RT	95.00	495.00
82	GIRL WITH SHEEP DOG 5117	OP	100.00	180.00
82	KISSING KIDS 5138	OP	125.00	225.00

YR	NAME	LIMIT	ISSUE	TREND
82	SLEDDING 5111	OP	115.00	200.00
82	SOCCER BOY 5199	OP	75.00	150.00
G. ARMANI				**VALENTINE**
83	HOOPLA 107E	RT	190.00	200.00
G. ARMANI				**VANITY FAIR**
92	BEAUTY AT THE MIRROR 850P	RT	300.00	300.00
92	BEAUTY WITH PERFUME 853P	RT	330.00	370.00
G. ARMANI				**VIA VENETO**
*	CUDDLE UP 322C	3000	*	N/A
*	FREE SPIRIT 321C	3000	*	N/A
*	POETRY 231C	5000	600.00	600.00
*	ROMAN HOLIDAY 271C	3000	1,500.00	1500.00
94	ALESSANDRA 648C	5000	355.00	400.00
94	MARINA 649C	5000	450.00	530.00
94	NICOLE 651C	5000	500.00	695.00
94	VALENTINA 647C	5000	400.00	440.00
97	BLACK ORCHID 444C	5000	*	N/A
97	SUMMER STROLL 431C	5000	650.00	650.00
97	TIGER LILY 244C	5000	*	N/A
97	WHITNEY 432C	5000	750.00	750.00
98	POETRY 231C	5000	600.00	600.00
98	POETRY 231F	*	400.00	400.00
98	ROMAN HOLIDAY 271C	3000	1,500.00	1500.00
98	ROMAN HOLIDAY 271F	*	900.00	900.00
G. ARMANI				**WEDDING**
84	WEDDING 5132	OP	175.00	225.00
89	BRIDE AND GROOM 475P	OP	280.00	295.00
89	WEDDING 407C	OP	535.00	575.00
G. ARMANI				**WILDLIFE**
*	BRILLIANCE 586S	1500	850.00	850.00
*	CRYSTAL MORNING 597S	1500	900.00	900.00
*	GARDEN DELIGHT 734S	1500	500.00	500.00
*	MORNING CALL 742S	3000	465.00	465.00
*	MORNING MIST 737S	3000	335.00	335.00
*	ON GUARD 605S	3000	475.00	475.00
*	WILD COLOURS 727S	3000	450.00	450.00
*	WINTER'S END 583S	1500	900.00	900.00
82	SNOW BIRD 5548	OP	100.00	100.00
83	EAGLE BIRD OF PREY 3213	OP	210.00	210.00
83	ROYAL EAGLE WITH BABIES 3553	OP	215.00	215.00
89	BIRD OF PARADISE 454S	5000	475.00	475.00
89	PEACOCK 455S	5000	620.00	620.00
89	PEACOCK 458S	5000	650.00	650.00
90	FLYING EAGLE 970S	RT	620.00	650.00
90	THREE DOVES 996S	5000	690.00	690.00
91	BIRD OF PARADISE 718S	RT	500.00	500.00
91	FLAMINGO 713S	5000	430.00	430.00
91	FLYING DUCK 839S	3000	470.00	470.00
91	GREAT ARGUS PHEASANT 717S	RT	625.00	625.00
91	LARGE OWL 842S	5000	520.00	520.00
91	SWAN 714S	5000	550.00	550.00
93	GALLOPING HORSE 905S	7500	465.00	465.00
93	RAMPANT HORSE 907S	7500	550.00	550.00
93	RUNNING HORSE 909S	7500	515.00	515.00
93	VASE WITH DOVES 204S	RT	375.00	375.00
93	VASE WITH PARROT 736S	RT	460.00	560.00
93	VASE WITH PEACOCK 735S	3000	450.00	450.00
94	ELEGANCE IN NATURE (HERONS) 226S	3000	1,000.00	1000.00
94	FALCONER 224S	3000	1,000.00	1000.00
94	RUNNING FREE 972S	3000	850.00	850.00
95	COMPANIONS 302S	3000	900.00	900.00
95	FEED US! 305S	1500	950.00	950.00
95	HUNT (FALCON) 290S	3000	850.00	850.00
95	LONE WOLF 285S	3000	550.00	550.00
95	MIDNIGHT 284S	3000	600.00	600.00
95	NIGHT VIGIL 306S	3000	650.00	650.00
95	NOCTURNE 976C	1500	1,000.00	1000.00
95	PROUD WATCH 278S	1500	700.00	700.00
95	SILENT WATCH 291S	1500	700.00	700.00
95	VANTAGE POINT 270S	3000	600.00	600.00
95	WILD HEARTS 282S	3000	2,000.00	2000.00
95	WISDOM 281S	3000	1,250.00	1250.00
97	ALERT (IRISH SETTERS) 550S	975	900.00	900.00
97	COLLIE 304S	975	500.00	500.00
97	DALMATIAN 552S	975	600.00	600.00
97	EARLY DAYS (DEER) 557S	975	1,200.00	1200.00
97	FIRST DAYS (MARE & FOAL) 564S	1500	800.00	800.00
97	MONARCH (STAG) 555S	1500	1,200.00	1200.00
97	MOTHER'S TOUCH (ELEPHANTS) 579S	3000	700.00	700.00
97	NATURE'S COLORS (PHEASANT) 582S	1500	1,350.00	1350.00
97	NATURE'S DANCE (HERONS) 576S	750	1,750.00	1750.00
97	PLEASE PLAY (COCKER SPANIELS) 312S	975	600.00	600.00
97	POINTER 554S	975	700.00	700.00
97	ROYAL COUPLE (AFGHAN HOUNDS) 310S	975	850.00	850.00
97	SHEPHERD 307S	975	450.00	450.00

YR	NAME	LIMIT	ISSUE	TREND
97	SKY WATCH (FLYING EAGLE) 559S	3000	1,200.00	1200.00
97	STANDING TALL (HERON) 577S	1500	800.00	800.00
97	TRUMPETING (ELEPHANT) 578S	3000	850.00	850.00
98	BACK TO THE BARN 591S	3000	*	N/A
98	BASKET OF FUN 729S	*	265.00	265.00
98	BONDING 744S	3000	450.00	450.00
98	BRILLIANCE 586S	1500	850.00	850.00
98	CRYSTAL MORNING 597S	1500	900.00	900.00
98	DANGEROUS GAME 740S	*	185.00	185.00
98	DESCENT 604S	3000	500.00	500.00
98	EARLY ARRIVALS 593S	1500	*	N/A
98	EASY LIFE 730S	*	160.00	160.00
98	EVER WATCHFUL 602S	3000	*	N/A
98	GARDEN DELIGHT 734S	1500	500.00	500.00
98	MOON FLIGHT 603S	3000	*	N/A
98	MORNING CALL 742S	3000	465.00	465.00
98	MORNING MIST 737S	3000	335.00	335.00
98	MOTHER'S CARE 587S	*	400.00	400.00
98	ODD FELLOWS 728S	*	200.00	200.00
98	ON GUARD 605S	3000	475.00	475.00
98	ON WATCH 589S	3000	*	N/A
98	PEACOCK'S PRIDE 733S	1500	*	N/A
98	PLAY MATES 741S	*	265.00	265.00
98	SILENT FLIGHT 592S	3000	*	N/A
98	SOUND OF AFRICA 743S	*	250.00	250.00
98	SPRING ORCHESTRA 584S	975	*	N/A
98	STALLIONS 572S	1500	1,100.00	1100.00
98	SUMMER SONG 585S	1500	*	N/A
98	TROPICAL GOSSIP 726S	3000	*	N/A
98	TROPICAL SPLENDOR 288S	1500	1,750.00	1750.00
98	WILD COLORS 727S	3000	450.00	450.00
98	WINTER'S END 583S	1500	900.00	900.00
98	YORKIES 731S	*	170.00	170.00

ARMSTRONG'S

A. D'ESTREHAN — CERAMIC PLAQUE

YR	NAME	LIMIT	ISSUE	TREND
85	FLAMBOROUGH HEAD	500	195.00	195.00
85	FLAMBOROUGH HEAD (ARTIST'S PROOF)	50	295.00	295.00

L. DE WINNE — CERAMIC PLAQUE

88	KATRINA	500	195.00	195.00

M. PAREDES — CERAMIC PLAQUE

85	MOTHER'S PRIDE	400	195.00	195.00
85	MOTHER'S PRIDE (ARTIST'S PROOF)	50	295.00	295.00
85	STAMP COLLECTOR, THE	400	195.00	195.00
85	STAMP COLLECTOR, THE- (ARTIST'S PROOF)	50	295.00	295.00

W. LANTZ — HAPPY ART

82	WOODY'S TRIPLE SELF-PORTRAIT	5000	95.00	300.00

* — PRO AUTOGRAPHED CERAMIC BASEBALL CARD PLAQUE

85	BRETT, GARVEY, JACKSON, ROSE, SEAVER,	1000	150.00	150.00

* — PRO CLASSIC CERAMIC BASEBALL CARD PLAQUES

85	GEORGE BRETT, 2 1/2 X 3 1/2 IN.	OP	10.00	10.00
85	PETE ROSE, 2 1/2 X 3 1/2 IN.	OP	10.00	10.00
85	REGGIE JACKSON, 2 1/2 X 3 1/2 IN.	OP	10.00	10.00
85	STEVE GARVEY, 2 1/2 X 3 1/2 IN.	OP	10.00	10.00
85	TOM SEAVER, 2 1/2 X 3 1/2 IN.	OP	10.00	10.00

R. LEE/ R. SKELTON — RED SKELTON COLLECTION

84	CAPTAIN FREDDIE	7500	85.00	150.00
84	FREDDIE THE TORCHBEARER	7500	110.00	190.00

R. SKELTON — RED SKELTON COLLECTION

81	CLEM KADIDDLEHOPPER	7500	75.00	75.00
81	FREDDIE IN THE BATHTUB	7500	80.00	80.00
81	FREDDIE IN THE GREEN	7500	80.00	80.00
81	FREDDIE THE FREELOADER	7500	70.00	70.00
81	JR. THE MEAN WIDDLE KID	7500	75.00	150.00
81	SAN FERNANDO RED	7500	75.00	150.00
81	SHERIFF DEADEYE	7500	75.00	75.00

ARTAFFECTS

G. PERILLO — CHIEFTAINS

83	CRAZY HORSE	5000	65.00	200.00
83	GERONIMO	5000	65.00	140.00
83	JOSEPH	5000	65.00	250.00
83	RED CLOUD	5000	65.00	275.00
83	SITTING BULL	5000	65.00	500.00

G. PERILLO — CHILD LIFE

83	SIESTA	2500	65.00	75.00
83	SWEET DREAMS	1500	65.00	N/A

A. TOBEY — CHRISTIAN COLLECTION

87	BRING TO ME THE CHILDREN	OP	65.00	100.00
88	HEALER, THE	OP	65.00	65.00

G. PERILLO — GREAT CHIEFTAINS

91	CHIEF JOSEPH	5000	195.00	195.00
91	COCHISE	5000	195.00	195.00
91	CRAZY HORSE (CLUB PIECE)	CL	195.00	240.00

YR	NAME	LIMIT	ISSUE	TREND
91	GERONIMO	5000	195.00	195.00
91	RED CLOUD	5000	195.00	195.00
91	SITTING BULL	5000	195.00	195.00
*				**HEAVENLY BLESSINGS**
85	BEDDY BYE	OP	15.00	19.00
85	BUBBLES	OP	15.00	19.00
85	DAY DREAMS	OP	15.00	19.00
85	FIRST STEP	OP	15.00	19.00
85	HAPPY BIRTHDAY	OP	15.00	19.00
85	HEAVEN SCENT	OP	15.00	19.00
85	JUST UP	OP	15.00	19.00
85	LISTEN!	OP	15.00	19.00
85	RACE YOU!	OP	15.00	19.00
85	SEE!	OP	15.00	19.00
85	SO SOFT	OP	15.00	19.00
85	YUM, YUM!	OP	15.00	19.00
G. PERILLO				**LITTLE INDIANS**
82	BLUE SPRUCE	10000	50.00	75.00
82	TENDER LOVE	10000	65.00	39.00
82	WHITE RABBIT	10000	50.00	39.00
G. PERILLO				**MUSICAL FIGURINES**
89	A BOY'S PRAYER	*	45.00	65.00
89	A GIRL'S PRAYER	*	45.00	65.00
R. SAUBER				**MUSICAL FIGURINES**
84	WEDDING, THE	OP	65.00	70.00
86	ANNIVERSARY, THE	OP	65.00	70.00
87	FATHERHOOD	OP	65.00	70.00
87	HOME SWEET HOME	OP	65.00	70.00
87	MOTHERHOOD	OP	65.00	70.00
87	NEWBORN	OP	65.00	70.00
87	SWEET SIXTEEN	OP	65.00	70.00
G. PERILLO			**PERILLO COLLECTOR CLUB PIECE**	
83	APACHE BRAVE	CL	50.00	145.00
G. PERILLO			**PRIDE OF AMERICA'S INDIANS**	
88	BRAVE AND FREE	10-DAY	50.00	145.00
89	DARK EYED FRIENDS	10-DAY	45.00	75.00
89	KINDRED SPIRITS	10-DAY	45.00	50.00
89	LOYAL ALLIANCE	10-DAY	45.00	75.00
89	NOBLE COMPANIONS	10-DAY	45.00	50.00
89	PEACEFUL COMRADES	10-DAY	45.00	50.00
39	SMALL & WISE	10-DAY	45.00	50.00
89	WINTER SCOUTS	10-DAY	45.00	50.00
G. PERILLO				**PROFESSIONALS**
80	BALLERINA'S DILEMMA	10000	65.00	75.00
80	BIG LEAGUER, THE	10000	65.00	150.00
81	QUARTERBACK, THE	10000	65.00	91.00
82	MAJOR LEAGUER	10000	65.00	98.00
82	RODEO JOE	10000	65.00	39.00
83	HOCKEY PLAYER	10000	65.00	125.00
MAGO			**REFLECTIONS OF YOUTH**	
88	JULIA	*	30.00	70.00
89	JESSICA	14-DAY	30.00	60.00
89	SEBASTIAN	14-DAY	30.00	40.00
G. PERILLO				**SAGEBRUSH KIDS**
85	BLUE BIRD	OP	20.00	25.00
85	BOOTS	OP	20.00	25.00
85	DRESSING UP	OP	20.00	25.00
85	FAVORITE KACHINA	OP	20.00	25.00
85	HAIL TO THE CHIEF	OP	20.00	25.00
85	MESSAGE OF JOY	OP	20.00	25.00
85	OUCH!	CL	20.00	25.00
85	ROOM FOR TWO?	OP	20.00	25.00
85	STAY AWHILE	OP	20.00	25.00
85	TAKE ONE	CL	20.00	25.00
86	COUNTRY MUSIC	OP	20.00	25.00
86	DEPUTIES	OP	20.00	25.00
86	FINISHING TOUCHES	OP	20.00	25.00
86	HIDING PLACE, THE	OP	20.00	25.00
86	LONG WAIT, THE	OP	20.00	25.00
86	PRACTICE MAKES PERFECT	OP	20.00	25.00
86	PRAIRIE PLAYERS	OP	20.00	25.00
86	WESTWARD HO!	OP	20.00	25.00
87	JUST PICKED	OP	20.00	25.00
87	MY PAPOOSE	OP	20.00	25.00
87	PLAYING HOUSE	OP	20.00	25.00
87	ROW, ROW	OP	20.00	25.00
87	SMALL TALK	OP	20.00	25.00
87	WAGON TRAIN	OP	20.00	25.00
89	HARMONY	OP	38.00	38.00
89	MELODY	OP	38.00	38.00
89	SANTA'S LULLABY	OP	45.00	45.00
90	EASTER OFFERING	OP	28.00	28.00
90	HOW DO I LOVE THEE?	OP	38.00	38.00
90	JUST MARRIED	OP	45.00	45.00

YR	NAME	LIMIT	ISSUE	TREND
91	BABY BRONC	OP	28.00	28.00
91	HEAVENLY PROTECTOR	OP	75.00	75.00
91	JUST BAKED	OP	28.00	28.00
91	LITTLE WARRIORS	OP	28.00	28.00
91	LOVIN' SPOONFUL	OP	28.00	28.00
91	OUT OF THE RAIN (UMBRELLA GIRL)	OP	95.00	95.00
91	SAFE AND DRY (UMBRELLA BOY)	OP	95.00	95.00
91	TEDDY TOO?	OP	28.00	28.00
91	TOY TOTEM	OP	28.00	28.00
G. PERILLO			**SAGEBRUSH KIDS BANKS**	
90	BUCKAROO BANK	OP	40.00	40.00
90	PERILLO'S PIGGY BANK	OP	40.00	40.00
90	WAMPUM WIG-WAM BANK	OP	40.00	40.00
G. PERILLO		**SAGEBRUSH KIDS CHRISTMAS CARAVAN**		
87	COMPLETE SET	OP	165.00	255.00
87	GOLD, FRANKINCENSE & PRESENTS	OP	35.00	35.00
87	LEADING THE WAY	OP	90.00	120.00
87	SINGING PRAISES	OP	45.00	50.00
87	SLEEPY SENTINELS	OP	45.00	50.00
G. PERILLO			**SAGEBRUSH KIDS NATIVITY**	
86	4 PIECE SET	OP	50.00	65.00
86	BACKDROP DOVE	OP	18.00	22.00
86	BACKDROP POTTERY	OP	18.00	22.00
86	CHRIST CHILD	OP	12.50	14.00
86	COW	OP	12.00	14.00
86	DONKEY	OP	12.00	14.00
86	GOAT	OP	8.00	10.00
86	JOSEPH	OP	18.00	19.50
86	KING WITH CORN	OP	18.00	23.00
86	KING WITH JEWELRY	OP	18.00	23.00
86	KING WITH POTTERY	OP	18.00	23.00
86	LAMB	OP	6.00	8.00
86	MARY	OP	18.00	19.50
86	SHEPHERD KNEELING	OP	18.00	23.00
86	SHEPHERD WITH LAMB	OP	18.00	23.00
86	TEE PEE	OP	18.00	23.00
89	BUFFALO	OP	18.00	18.00
89	CACTUS	OP	25.00	25.00
89	PIG	OP	15.00	16.00
89	RACCOON	OP	12.50	13.00
G. PERILLO			**SAGEBRUSH KIDS WEDDING PARTY**	
90	BRIDE	OP	25.00	25.00
90	CHIEF	OP	25.00	25.00
90	DONKEY	OP	23.00	23.00
90	FLOWER GIRL	OP	23.00	23.00
90	GROOM	OP	25.00	25.00
90	RING BEARER	OP	23.00	23.00
90	WEDDING BACKDROP	OP	28.00	28.00
90	WEDDING PARTY OF 7	OP	165.00	165.00
G. PERILLO		**SAGEBRUSH KIDS-FLIGHT INTO EGYPT**		
90	MARY W/BABY, JOSEPH & DONKEY (3 PC SET)	OP	65.00	65.00
G. PERILLO		**SAGEBRUSH KIDS-SPECIAL ISSUE**		
91	ONE NATION UNDER GOD	5000	195.00	195.00
C. ROEDA			**SIMPLE WONDERS**	
91	BABY JESUS	*	35.00	35.00
91	BABY JESUS (BLACK)	*	35.00	35.00
91	BRIDE	*	55.00	55.00
91	FOREVER FRIENDS	*	40.00	40.00
91	GROOM	*	45.00	45.00
91	I LOVE EWE	*	38.00	38.00
91	JOSEPH	*	45.00	45.00
91	JOSEPH (BLACK)	*	45.00	45.00
91	LIGHTING THE WAY	*	40.00	40.00
91	LITTLEST ANGEL, THE	*	30.00	30.00
91	LITTLEST ANGEL, THE (BLACK)	*	30.00	30.00
91	MADE WITH LOVE	*	50.00	50.00
91	MARY	*	40.00	40.00
91	MARY (BLACK)	*	40.00	40.00
91	MOMMY'S BEST	*	50.00	50.00
91	OFF TO SCHOOL	*	50.00	50.00
91	PLAYING HOOKEY	*	50.00	50.00
91	SHEEP DOG	*	15.00	16.00
91	SONG OF JOY	*	40.00	40.00
91	STAR LIGHT STAR BRIGHT	*	35.00	35.00
92	A PERFECT FIT	*	45.00	45.00
92	CATCH THE SPIRIT (WISECHILD)	*	35.00	35.00
92	FALLEN ANGEL	*	35.00	35.00
92	FOLLOWING THE STAR (WISECHILD)	*	45.00	45.00
92	LIL' DUMPLIN	*	25.00	25.00
92	LIL' DUMPLIN (BLACK)	*	25.00	25.00
92	LITTLE BIG SHOT	*	35.00	35.00
92	POCKETFUL OF LOVE	*	35.00	35.00
92	POCKETFUL OF LOVE (BLACK)	*	35.00	35.00
92	RAINBOW PATROL	*	40.00	40.00
92	TEN PENNY SERENADE	*	45.00	45.00

YR NAME	LIMIT	ISSUE	TREND
92 TEN PENNY SERENADE (BLACK)	*	45.00	45.00
92 THIS TOO SHALL PASS	*	35.00	35.00
92 THREE BEARS, THE	*	45.00	45.00
92 TRICK OR TREAT	*	40.00	40.00
92 WITH OPEN ARMS (WISECHILD)	*	40.00	40.00

G. PERILLO — SINGLE ISSUE

YR NAME	LIMIT	ISSUE	TREND
84 BABYSITTER MUSICAL FIGURE	2500	65.00	90.00

G. PERILLO — SPECIAL ISSUE

YR NAME	LIMIT	ISSUE	TREND
82 PEACEABLE KINGDOM, THE	950	750.00	800.00
84 APACHE BOY BUST	CL	40.00	75.00
84 APACHE GIRL BUST	CL	40.00	75.00
84 PAPOOSE	325	500.00	525.00
85 LOVERS	CL	70.00	125.00

G. PERILLO — STORYBOOK COLLECTION

YR NAME	LIMIT	ISSUE	TREND
80 LITTLE RED RIDINGHOOD	10000	65.00	90.00
81 CINDERELLA	10000	65.00	90.00
82 GOLDILOCKS & THE THREE BEARS	10000	80.00	110.00
82 HANSEL & GRETEL	10000	80.00	100.00

G. PERILLO — THE PRINCESSES

YR NAME	LIMIT	ISSUE	TREND
84 LILY OF THE MOHAWKS	1500	65.00	155.00
84 MINNEHAHA	1500	65.00	42.00
84 POCAHONTAS	1500	65.00	60.00
84 SACAJAWEA	1500	65.00	125.00

G. PERILLO — TRIBAL PONIES

YR NAME	LIMIT	ISSUE	TREND
84 ARAPAHO	1500	65.00	200.00
84 COMANCHE	1500	65.00	200.00
84 CROW	1500	65.00	200.00

G. PERILLO — WAR PONY

YR NAME	LIMIT	ISSUE	TREND
83 APACHE WAR PONY	495	150.00	200.00
83 NEZ PERCE PONY	495	150.00	200.00
83 SIOUX WAR PONY	495	150.00	200.00

G. PERILLO — WILDLIFE FIGURINES

YR NAME	LIMIT	ISSUE	TREND
91 BALD EAGLE	OP	65.00	65.00
91 BIGHORN SHEEP	OP	75.00	75.00
91 BUFFALO	OP	75.00	75.00
91 MOUNTAIN LION	OP	75.00	75.00
91 MUSTANG	OP	85.00	85.00
91 POLAR BEAR	OP	65.00	65.00
91 TIMBER WOLF	OP	85.00	85.00
91 WHITE-TAILED DEER	OP	95.00	95.00

ARTISTS OF THE WORLD

T. DEGRAZIA — ANNUAL CHRISTMAS

YR NAME	LIMIT	ISSUE	TREND
93 FIESTA ANGELS	YR	295.00	315.00
94 LITTLEST ANGEL	YR	165.00	175.00
98 CHRISTMAS ANGEL OF LIGHT	1998	145.00	145.00

T. DEGRAZIA — DEGRAZIA FIGURINES

YR NAME	LIMIT	ISSUE	TREND
84 DISPLAY PLAQUE	CL	45.00	95.00
84 FLOWER BOY	OP	65.00	110.00
84 FLOWER GIRL	OP	65.00	110.00
84 MY FIRST HORSE	OP	65.00	110.00
84 SUNFLOWER BOY	CL	65.00	300.00
84 WHITE DOVE	OP	45.00	80.00
84 WONDERING	CL	85.00	155.00
85 JESUS	OP	25.00	55.00
85 JOSEPH	OP	55.00	90.00
85 LITTLE MADONNA	OP	80.00	125.00
85 MARY	OP	55.00	80.00
85 NATIVITY SET (3 PIECES)	OP	135.00	195.00
85 PIMA DRUMMER BOY	CL	65.00	110.00
86 BLUE BOY, THE	OP	79.00	95.00
86 FESTIVAL LIGHTS	OP	75.00	95.00
86 MERRY LITTLE INDIAN	12500	175.00	245.00
87 LOVE ME	OP	95.00	110.00
87 WEE THREE	CL	180.00	195.00
88 BEAUTIFUL BURDEN	CL	175.00	195.00
88 CHRISTMAS PRAYER ANGEL	CL	70.00	80.00
88 FLOWER BOY PLAQUE	CL	80.00	80.00
88 LOS NINOS	5000	595.00	645.00
88 MERRILY, MERRILY, MERRILY	CL	95.00	130.00
89 LOS NINOS (ARTIST'S EDITION)	48	695.00	695.00
89 MY BEAUTIFUL ROCKING HORSE	OP	225.00	245.00
89 MY FIRST ARROW	OP	95.00	110.00
89 TWO LITTLE LAMBS	OP	70.00	80.00
90 ALONE	OP	395.00	475.00
90 BIGGEST DRUM	YR	110.00	125.00
90 CRUCIFIXION	YR	295.00	295.00
90 DESERT HARVEST	5000	135.00	145.00
90 EL BURRITO	OP	60.00	75.00
90 NAVAJO BOY	YR	110.00	125.00
90 SUNFLOWER GIRL	OP	95.00	95.00
93 FLOWERS FOR MOTHER	*	145.00	150.00
93 LITTLE MEDICINE MAN	*	175.00	185.00
93 MOTHER SILENTLY PRAYS	3500	345.00	380.00
93 SADDLE UP	5000	195.00	215.00

YR	NAME	LIMIT	ISSUE	TREND
94	BEARING GIFT	*	145.00	150.00
94	FESTIVE FLOWERS	*	145.00	150.00
94	FIESTA FLOWERS	3500	197.50	210.00
94	LOVING MOTHER	3500	165.00	175.00
94	PEDRO	*	145.00	150.00
94	RIO GRANDE DANCER	*	98.00	100.00
94	SAGUARO DANCE	2500	495.00	510.00
94	SPRING BLOSSOMS	5000	170.00	180.00
95	APACHE MOTHER	3500	195.00	195.00
95	BETHLEHEM BOUND	1995	195.00	195.00
95	FLORAL HARVEST	*	185.00	185.00
95	LITTLE FARM BOY	*	165.00	165.00
95	LITTLE HELPER	3500	185.00	185.00
95	LITTLE HOPI GIRL	*	110.00	110.00
95	LITTLE NAVAJO MUSIC MAN	950	175.00	175.00
95	MY BLUE BALLOON	*	115.00	115.00
95	PIMA INDIAN DRUMMER BOY/NATIVITY	*	135.00	135.00
95	WEDDING PARTY	*	175.00	175.00
95	WEDDING PARTY CHILDREN	*	75.00	75.00
98	ADORING MOTHER	2500	185.00	185.00
98	DESERT INDIAN BOY	OP	165.00	165.00
98	LITTLE MUSIC MAKER-PLATINUM	950	165.00	165.00
98	PUEBLO SANDPAINTER	950	295.00	295.00
98	YOUNG NAVAJO PEACEMAKER	OP	145.00	145.00

R. OLSZEWSKI DEGRAZIA: GOEBEL MINIATURES

YR	NAME	LIMIT	ISSUE	TREND
85	FLOWER BOY 502-P	SU	85.00	165.00
85	FLOWER GIRL 501-P	SU	85.00	165.00
85	MY FIRST HORSE 503-P	SU	85.00	155.00
85	SUNFLOWER BOY 551-P	SU	93.00	145.00
85	WHITE DOVE 504-P	SU	80.00	135.00
85	WONDERING 505-P	SU	93.00	150.00
86	FESTIVAL OF LIGHTS 507-P	SU	85.00	225.00
86	LITTLE MADONNA 552-P	SU	93.00	200.00
86	PIMA DRUMMER BOY 506-P	SU	85.00	250.00
87	MERRY LITTLE INDIAN 508-P	CL	95.00	295.00
88	ADOBE DISPLAY 948-D	SU	45.00	85.00
89	BEAUTIFUL BURDEN 554-P	SU	110.00	175.00
90	ADOBE HACIENDA DISPLAY (LARGE) 958-D	SU	85.00	150.00
90	CHAPEL DISPLAY 971-D	SU	95.00	115.00
91	MY BEAUTIFUL ROCKING HORSE 555-P	SU	110.00	185.00

T. DEGRAZIA NATIVITY

YR	NAME	LIMIT	ISSUE	TREND
93	BALTHAZAR	*	135.00	145.00
93	EL TORO	*	95.00	99.00
93	GUSPAR	*	135.00	145.00
93	MELCHIOR	*	135.00	145.00
98	MY GUARDIAN ANGEL	OP	145.00	145.00

T. DEGRAZIA SIGNATURE EDITION

YR	NAME	LIMIT	ISSUE	TREND
98	FLOWER BOY	950	100.00	100.00
98	TINY TREASURE	950	100.00	100.00

T. DEGRAZIA VILLAGE COLLECTION

YR	NAME	LIMIT	ISSUE	TREND
93	LET'S COMPROMISE	*	65.00	75.00
93	PEACE PIPE	*	65.00	75.00
93	THREE FEATHERS	*	65.00	75.00
93	WATER WAGON	CL	295.00	325.00
98	DEVOTED LOVE	OP	75.00	75.00

ASHTON-DRAKE GALLERIES
*

THE UPSTAIRS DOWNSTAIRS BEARS

YR	NAME	LIMIT	ISSUE	TREND
94	HENRIETTA'S TEA PARTY	5600	65.00	75.00

AVONLEA TRADITIONS INC.
*

ANNE OF GREEN GABLES

YR	NAME	LIMIT	ISSUE	TREND
90	ARRIVING AT THE STATION	OP	50.00	50.00
94	A SOLEMN VOW AND PROMISE	OP	120.00	120.00
94	CARROTS! CARROTS!	OP	95.00	95.00
94	PERCHED ON THE WOODPILE	OP	120.00	120.00

BANBERRY DESIGNS INC.
L. GRUSS LUCKYPHANTS

YR	NAME	LIMIT	ISSUE	TREND
94	LAIRD	RT	9.50	10.00
94	LANGLY	RT	9.00	9.00
94	LENNY	RT	9.50	10.00
94	LEON	RT	8.50	9.00
94	LLOYD & LYNELLE	RT	10.00	10.00
95	LINUS	RT	14.00	14.00
97	GARDEN PARTY	5000	28.00	28.00

BAND CREATIONS
*

ANGELS OF THE MONTH

YR	NAME	LIMIT	ISSUE	TREND
95	APRIL ANGEL	RT	10.00	10.00
95	AUGUST ANGEL	RT	10.00	10.00
95	DECEMBER ANGEL	RT	10.00	10.00
95	FEBRUARY ANGEL	RT	10.00	10.00
95	JANUARY ANGEL	RT	10.00	10.00
95	JULY ANGEL	RT	10.00	10.00

YR	NAME	LIMIT	ISSUE	TREND
95	JUNE ANGEL	RT	10.00	10.00
95	MARCH ANGEL	RT	10.00	10.00
95	MAY ANGEL	RT	10.00	10.00
95	NOVEMBER ANGEL	RT	10.00	10.00
95	OCTOBER ANGEL	RT	10.00	10.00
95	SEPTEMBER ANGEL	RT	10.00	10.00
PENFIELD/RICHARDS				**BEST FRIENDS**
98	DREAM MAKER ANGEL	*	20.00	20.00
PENFIELD/RICHARDS		**BEST FRIENDS COFFEE, TEA, MY FRIENDS & ME**		
98	AFTERNOON SPICE STRAWBERRY SHORTCAKE	*	30.00	30.00
98	BLACKBERRY BETTY	*	20.00	20.00
98	CHAMOMILE CONFETTI	*	20.00	20.00
98	GRANNY GREEN TEA	*	20.00	20.00
98	HOT SUMMER NIGHT	*	20.00	20.00
98	JASMINE	*	20.00	20.00
98	LONG ISLAND TEA	*	20.00	20.00
98	LUSCIOUS LATTE MOCHA CREAM DELIGHT	*	30.00	30.00
98	MADAME SASSAFRAS	*	20.00	20.00
98	PASSION FLOWER HINGED BOX	*	20.00	20.00
98	SATURDAY SUNRISE	*	20.00	20.00
98	TROPICAL TWISTER	*	20.00	20.00
98	WILD BLUEBERRY	*	20.00	20.00
RICHARDS/PENFIELD		**BEST FRIENDS-A STAR IS BORN**		
95	BASEBALL BOY	OP	6.00	6.00
95	BASEBALL GIRL	OP	6.00	6.00
95	BASKETBALL BOY	OP	6.00	6.00
95	BASKETBALL GIRL	OP	6.00	6.00
95	CHEERLEADER GIRL	OP	6.00	6.00
95	FOOTBALL BOY	OP	6.00	6.00
95	GOLFER BOY	OP	6.00	6.00
95	GOLFER GIRL	OP	6.00	6.00
95	HOCKEY BOY	OP	6.00	6.00
95	SOCCER BOY	OP	6.00	6.00
95	SOCCER GIRL	OP	6.00	6.00
95	SWIMMER BOY	OP	6.00	6.00
95	SWIMMER GIRL	OP	6.00	6.00
96	BIKER BOY	OP	6.00	6.00
96	BIKER GIRL	OP	6.00	6.00
96	FISHER BOY	OP	6.00	6.00
96	FISHER GIRL	OP	6.00	6.00
96	SKIER BOY	OP	6.00	6.00
96	SKIER GIRL	OP	6.00	6.00
96	TENNIS BOY	OP	6.00	6.00
96	TENNIS GIRL	OP	6.00	6.00
RICHARDS/PENFIELD		**BEST FRIENDS-ANGEL WISHES**		
94	ANNIVERSARY	OP	12.00	12.00
94	BEST WISHES	OP	12.00	12.00
94	BRIDE AND GROOM	OP	12.00	12.00
94	CONGRATULATIONS	OP	12.00	12.00
94	CREATE A WISH	OP	12.00	12.00
94	GET WELL	OP	12.00	12.00
94	GOOD LUCK	OP	12.00	12.00
94	HAPPY BIRTHDAY	OP	12.00	12.00
94	INSPIRATIONAL	OP	12.00	12.00
94	NEW BABY	OP	12.00	12.00
RICHARDS/PENFIELD		**BEST FRIENDS-CELEBRATE AROUND THE WORLD**		
96	AROUND THE WORLD TREE	OP	20.00	20.00
96	BRITISH TREE	OP	20.00	20.00
96	ENGLAND SANTA	OP	12.00	20.00
96	GERMANY TREE	OP	20.00	20.00
96	MEXICO SANTA	OP	12.00	12.00
96	NORWAY SANTA	OP	12.00	12.00
96	RUSSIA SANTA	OP	12.00	12.00
96	SCANDINAVIAN TREE	OP	20.00	20.00
96	UNITED STATES TREE	OP	20.00	20.00
96	UNITED STATES/BLACK SANTA	OP	12.00	12.00
96	UNITED STATES/WHITE SANTA	OP	12.00	12.00
RICHARDS/PENFIELD		**BEST FRIENDS-CHRISTMAS PAGEANT**		
96	ANGEL-PEACE/JOY	OP	6.00	6.00
96	BENCH	OP	4.00	4.00
96	BOY W/STAR	OP	6.00	6.00
96	CHRISTMAS PAGEANT/10 PC SET	OP	60.00	60.00
96	DONKEY	OP	4.00	4.00
96	GIRL W/TREE	OP	6.00	6.00
96	JOSEPH	OP	6.00	6.00
96	MARY AND BABY JESUS	OP	6.00	6.00
96	SHEEP	OP	4.00	4.00
96	SIGN	OP	4.00	4.00
96	STAGE	OP	14.00	14.00
RICHARDS/PENFIELD		**BEST FRIENDS-FIRST FRIENDS BEGIN AT CHILDHOOD**		
93	A WAGON FULL OF FUN/2 PC SET	OP	15.00	15.00
93	CASTLES IN THE SAND/4 PC SET	OP	16.00	16.00
93	CHECKING IT TWICE/2 PC SET	OP	15.00	15.00
93	DAD'S BEST PAL	OP	15.00	15.00
93	FEATHERED FRIENDS	OP	13.00	13.00

YR	NAME	LIMIT	ISSUE	TREND
93	FISHING FRIENDS	OP	18.00	18.00
93	GRANDMA'S FAVORITE	OP	15.00	15.00
93	MY "BEARY" BEST FRIEND	OP	12.00	12.00
93	MY BEST FRIEND/2 PC SET	OP	24.00	24.00
93	OH SO PRETTY	OP	14.00	15.00
93	PURR-FIT FRIENDS	OP	12.00	12.00
93	QUIET TIME	OP	15.00	15.00
93	RAINBOW OF FRIENDS	RT	24.00	24.00
93	SANTA'S FIRST VISIT	OP	15.00	15.00
93	SANTA'S SURPRISE	OP	14.00	15.00
93	SHARING IS CARING	OP	12.00	12.00
RICHARDS/PENFIELD		**BEST FRIENDS-HAPPY HEARTS**		
96	A GUIDING STAR	OP	35.00	35.00
96	ANGELS IN THE SNOW	OP	35.00	35.00
96	BEST FRIENDS	OP	35.00	35.00
96	JUST MARRIED	OP	35.00	35.00
96	MAKING NEW FRIENDS	OP	35.00	35.00
96	THANKSGIVING FRIENDS	OP	35.00	35.00
RICHARDS/PENFIELD		**BEST FRIENDS-HEAVENLY HELPERS**		
96	CHILDCARE	OP	12.00	12.00
96	EMERGENCY MEDICAL TEAM	OP	12.00	12.00
96	FIREMAN	OP	12.00	12.00
96	NURSE	OP	12.00	12.00
96	POLICEMAN	OP	12.00	12.00
96	TEACHER	OP	12.00	12.00
96	VOLUNTEER	OP	12.00	12.00
RICHARDS/PENFIELD		**BEST FRIENDS-NOAH'S ARK**		
95	ANIMALS/SET OF 10	OP	20.00	20.00
95	NOAH'S ARK & RAFT	OP	42.00	42.00
RICHARDS/PENFIELD		**BEST FRIENDS-O JOYFUL NIGHT NATIVITY**		
94	ANGEL ON STABLE/WALL	OP	16.00	16.00
94	CAMEL AND DONKEY/SET OF 2	OP	8.00	8.00
94	HOLY FAMILY (JOSEPH, MARY & JESUS)	OP	16.00	16.00
94	SHEPHERD BOY	OP	8.00	8.00
94	THREE KINGS/SET OF THREE	OP	24.00	22.00
95	CAMEL STANDING	OP	6.00	6.00
95	SHEPHERD W/SHEEP/SET OF 7	OP	8.00	8.00
RICHARDS/PENFIELD		**BEST FRIENDS-RAINBOW OF FRIENDS**		
96	RAINBOW OF FRIENDS	OP	24.00	24.00
96	RAINBOW OF FRIENDS MUSIC BOX	OP	18.00	18.00
RICHARDS/PENFIELD		**BEST FRIENDS-RIVER SONG**		
93	CAROLERS/SET OF 5	OP	30.00	30.00
94	THREE CAROLERS/ASSORTED	OP	22.00	22.00
95	DOUBLE ANGELS	OP	8.00	8.00
95	SKATERS SITTING/SET OF 2	OP	12.00	12.00
95	SKATERS STANDING/SET OF 2	OP	12.00	12.00
95	SNOWBALL FIGHT/SET OF 3	OP	15.00	15.00
95	SNOWMEN/SET OF 3	OP	12.95	13.00
RICHARDS/PENFIELD		**BEST FRIENDS-WINTER WONDERLAND**		
94	3 ASSORTED WHITE TREES & 3 PRESENTS	OP	18.00	18.00
94	ACCESSORIES: RABBITS, TEDDIES, PRESENTS/SET OF 3	OP	4.00	4.00
94	MR. SANTA	OP	9.00	9.00
94	MRS. SANTA	OP	9.00	9.00
94	REINDEER/SET OF 2/STANDING & SITTING	OP	10.00	10.00
T. MADSEW		**DEER ONES**		
98	DEER GANG	*	30.00	30.00
98	DEER TREATS	*	15.00	15.00
98	DEER-O-LEERS	*	45.00	45.00
98	HEARTH & HOME	*	40.00	40.00
98	LICKETY-SPLIT	*	6.00	6.00
98	RUB-A-DUB DEER	*	16.50	17.00
98	SWING ON A STAR	*	8.50	9.00
98	TINY BUBBLES	*	20.00	20.00
*		**TUXEDOS IN THE SNOW**		
98	BLIND DATE	*	25.00	25.00
98	DECK THE TOWN	*	25.00	25.00
98	ICY TONES	*	25.00	25.00
98	PEPPERMINT DELIGHT	*	25.00	25.00
98	TASTE TEST	*	25.00	25.00
98	TUBING SURPRISE	*	25.00	25.00

BILL VERNON STUDIOS

YR	NAME	LIMIT	ISSUE	TREND
B. VERNON		**EVOLUTION**		
95	CLOUD DANCER	OP	65.00	65.00
95	FINAL FLIGHT	OP	130.00	130.00
95	MYSTIC SPIRIT	OP	50.00	50.00
95	NIGHT SPIRIT	OP	125.00	125.00
95	PRAIRIE THUNDER	OP	110.00	110.00
95	RESTLESS SOULS	OP	50.00	50.00
95	THREE BEARS	OP	95.00	95.00
95	THREE WOLF	OP	60.00	60.00
95	TRANSFORMATION, THE	OP	195.00	195.00
95	TREE KEEPER	OP	50.00	50.00
95	WATER WALTZ	5000	80.00	80.00

YR	NAME	LIMIT	ISSUE	TREND
95	WHITE FEATHER	OP	90.00	90.00
95	WIND RUNNER	OP	40.00	40.00

BING & GRONDAHL
S. BECKETT

98	TEDDY BEAR VICTOR	5000	30.00	30.00
98	TEDDY BEAR VICTORIA	5000	30.00	30.00

P. LANGELUND

98	MOTHER'S DAY	5000	98.00	98.00

J. NIELSEN

98	ANNUAL EGG	5000	30.00	30.00

AL. THERKELSEN

98	BROWN BEAR	5000	98.00	98.00

BOEHM STUDIOS
*

ANIMAL SCULPTURES

YR	NAME	LIMIT	ISSUE	TREND
52	HUNTER	250	600.00	1400.00
57	POLO PLAYER	100	850.00	4600.00
69	ADIOS	130	1,500.00	1900.00
71	BOBCATS	200	1,600.00	1990.00
71	FOXES	200	1,800.00	2350.00
71	RACCOONS	200	1,600.00	2100.00
72	RED SQUIRRELS	100	2,600.00	2770.00
73	NYALA ANTELOPE	100	4,700.00	6560.00
75	GIANT PANDA	100	3,800.00	6890.00
75	PUMA	50	5,700.00	6560.00
76	AMERICAN MUSTANGS	75	3,700.00	5660.00
76	OTTER	75	1,100.00	1500.00
77	AFRICAN ELEPHANT	50	9,500.00	14630.00
78	BLACK RHINOCEROS	50	9,500.00	9920.00
78	CAMEL & CALF	50	3,500.00	3700.00
78	GORILLA	50	3,800.00	4550.00
78	SNOW LEOPARD	75	3,500.00	4670.00
78	THOROUGHBRED W/JOCKEY	25	2,600.00	2785.00
79	BENGEL TIGER 500-13	12	25,000.00	26525.00
79	FALLOW DEER	30	7,500.00	7500.00
79	HUNTER CHASE	20	4,000.00	4085.00
79	YOUNG & FREE FAWNS	160	1,875.00	2050.00
80	ARABIAN ORYX, PAIR 50015	60	3,800.00	4130.00
80	ASIAN LION	100	1,500.00	1645.00
80	CHEETAH	100	2,700.00	3000.00
81	APPALOOSA HORSE 40193	75	975.00	1070.00
81	JAGUAR 50020	100	2,900.00	3300.00
81	POLAR BEAR W/CUBS 40188	65	1,800.00	1875.00
82	BUFFALO 50022	100	1,625.00	1625.00
82	GREATER KUDU 50023	75	7,500.00	7500.00
82	POLO PLAYS ON PINTO 55005	50	3,500.00	3500.00
83	ARABIAN STALLION/PRANCING 55007	200	1,500.00	1560.00
83	ARABIAN STALLION/REARING 55006	200	1,500.00	1560.00
84	WHITE-TAILED BUCK 50026	200	1,375.00	1650.00
85	ELEPHANT/WHITE BISQUE 200-44B	200	495.00	570.00
*				**BIRD SCULPTURES**
51	WOOD THRUSH	2	375.00	N/A
52	MALLARDS, PAIR	500	650.00	1745.00
53	BOBWHITE QUAIL, PAIR	750	400.00	2500.00
54	GOLDEN PHEASANT, BISQUE	7	200.00	11375.00
54	GOLDEN PHEASANT, DECORATED	7	350.00	19235.00
54	RINGED-NECKED PHEASANTS, PAIR	500	650.00	1800.00
54	WOODCOCK	500	300.00	2050.00
55	CARDINALS, PAIR	500	550.00	3650.00
56	BLACK-TAILED BANTAMS, PAIR	57	350.00	4800.00
56	CEDAR WAXWINGS, PAIR	100	600.00	7835.00
56	GOLDEN-CROWNED KINGLETS	500	400.00	2320.00
56	SONG SPARROWS, PAIR	50	2,000.00	38450.00
57	AMERICAN EAGLE, LARGE	31	225.00	11150.00
57	AMERICAN EAGLE, SMALL	76	225.00	9220.00
57	CALIFORNIA QUAIL, PAIR	500	400.00	2730.00
57	CAROLINA WRENS	100	750.00	5400.00
57	CERULEAN WARBLERS	100	800.00	4935.00
57	DOWNY WOODPECKERS	500	450.00	1750.00
57	INDIGO BUNTING WITH CHEROKEE ROSE	CL	250.00	675.00
57	MEADOWLARK	750	350.00	3175.00
57	RED-WINGED BLACKBIRDS, PAIR	100	700.00	5590.00
58	AMERICAN REDSTARTS	500	350.00	2000.00
58	BLACK-THROATED BLUE WARBLER	500	400.00	1775.00
58	MOURNING DOVES	500	550.00	1475.00
58	NONPAREIL BUNTINGS	750	250.00	1165.00
59	EASTERN BLUEBIRDS, PAIR	100	1,800.00	12200.00
60	RUFFLED GROUSE, PAIR	250	950.00	5075.00
61	GOLDFINCHES	500	400.00	1830.00
61	MOCKINGBIRDS, PAIR	500	650.00	3970.00
61	SUGARBIRDS	100	2,500.00	14900.00
62	BLUE JAYS, PAIR	250	2,000.00	12300.00
62	LESSER PRAIRIE CHICKENS, PAIR	300	1,200.00	2390.00
62	PTARMIGAN, PAIR	350	800.00	3450.00

YR	NAME	LIMIT	ISSUE	TREND
63	MEARN'S QUAIL, PAIR	350	950.00	3635.00
63	MOUNTAIN BLUEBIRDS	300	1,900.00	5475.00
63	TOWHEE	500	350.00	2430.00
64	BOBOLINK	500	550.00	1520.00
64	KILLDEER, PAIR	300	1,750.00	5160.00
64	ROBIN (DAFFODILS)	500	600.00	5650.00
65	CATBIRD	500	900.00	2075.00
65	FLEDGLING GREAT HORNED OWL	750	350.00	1590.00
65	PARULA WARBLERS	400	1,500.00	3370.00
65	TUFTED TITMICE	500	600.00	2040.00
65	VARIED BUNTINGS	300	2,200.00	4935.00
66	GREEN JAYS, PAIR	400	1,850.00	4120.00
66	RUFOUS HUMMINGBIRDS	500	850.00	2350.00
66	WOOD THRUSHES, PAIR	400	4,200.00	8285.00
67	BLUE GROSBEAK	750	1,050.00	1530.00
67	CRESTED FLYCATCHER	500	1,650.00	3000.00
67	FLEDGLING CANADA WARBLER	750	550.00	2200.00
67	IVORY-BILLED WOODPECKERS 474	4	*	N/A
67	NORTHERN WATER THRUSH	500	800.00	1420.00
68	COMMON TERN	500	1,400.00	6040.00
68	KESTRALS, PAIR	460	2,300.00	3150.00
68	MERGANSERS, PAIR	440	2,200.00	2975.00
68	ROADRUNNER	500	2,600.00	3680.00
69	BLACK-HEADED GROSBEAK	675	1,250.00	1535.00
69	VERDINS	575	1,150.00	1565.00
69	WESTERN BLUEBIRDS	300	5,500.00	7020.00
69	YOUNG AMERICAN EAGLE	850	700.00	1520.00
70	ORCHARD ORIOLES	550	1,750.00	2300.00
70	OVEN-BIRD	450	1,400.00	1790.00
70	SLATE-COLORED JUNCO	500	1,600.00	2240.00
71	FLICKER	250	2,400.00	2770.00
71	LITTLE OWL	350	700.00	1375.00
71	MUTE SWANS, LIFE-SIZE, PAIR	3	*	N/A
71	MUTE SWANS, PAIR	400	4,000.00	7820.00
71	NUTHATCH	350	650.00	1130.00
71	WESTERN MEADOWLARK	350	1,425.00	1725.00
71	WINTER ROBIN	225	1,150.00	1420.00
72	BARN OWL	350	3,600.00	5400.00
72	BLACK GROUSE	175	2,800.00	3100.00
72	BROWN PELICAN	100	10,500.00	14400.00
72	CACTUS WREN	225	3,000.00	3400.00
72	EUROPEAN GOLDFINCH	250	1,150.00	1400.00
72	GOLDCREST	500	650.00	1200.00
72	SNOW BUNTINGS	350	2,400.00	2700.00
72	TREE CREEPERS	200	3,200.00	3200.00
72	YELLOW-BELLIED SAPSUCKER	250	2,700.00	3200.00
73	BLACKBIRDS, PAIR	75	5,400.00	6470.00
73	BLUE TITS	300	3,000.00	3255.00
73	BROWN THRASHER	260	1,850.00	1925.00
73	EVERGLADES KITES	50	5,800.00	7340.00
73	GREEN WOODPECKERS	50	4,200.00	4890.00
73	HORNED LARKS	200	3,800.00	4435.00
73	LAPWING	100	2,600.00	3000.00
73	LAZULI BUNTINGS	250	1,800.00	2450.00
73	LONG TAIL TITS	200	2,600.00	2900.00
73	PEREGRINE FALCON	350	4,400.00	5470.00
73	SCREECH OWL	500	850.00	1495.00
73	YELLOWHAMMERS	350	3,300.00	4175.00
73	YOUNG AMERICAN EAGLE, INAUGURAL	100	1,500.00	2125.00
74	CHAFFINCH	125	2,000.00	2525.00
74	CRESTED TIT	400	1,150.00	1300.00
74	HOODED WARBLER	100	2,400.00	3020.00
74	LARK SPARROW	150	2,100.00	2325.00
74	MYRTLE WARBLERS	210	1,850.00	2105.00
74	PURPLE MARTINS	50	6,700.00	9150.00
74	RUBY-THROATED HUMMINGBIRD	200	1,900.00	2825.00
74	SONG THRUSHES	100	2,800.00	3590.00
74	STONECHATS	150	2,200.00	2550.00
74	SWALLOWS	125	3,400.00	4320.00
74	VARIED THRUSH	300	2,500.00	3100.00
74	YELLOW-BILLIED CUCKOO	150	2,800.00	3055.00
74	YELLOW-HEADED BLACKBIRD	75	3,200.00	3600.00
75	EASTERN KINGBIRD	100	3,500.00	4275.00
75	PEKIN ROBINS	100	7,000.00	9675.00
75	RED-BILLED BLUE MAGPIE	100	4,600.00	6225.00
75	YOUNG AND SPIRITED, 1976	1121	950.00	1600.00
76	BLACK-THROATED BLUE WARBLER	200	900.00	1165.00
76	CHICKADEES 400-61	400	1,450.00	1550.00
76	EAGLE OF FREEDOM I	15	35,000.00	51375.00
76	EAGLE OF FREEDOM II 400-70	200	7,200.00	7360.00
76	KINGFISHERS	200	1,900.00	2200.00
76	RIVOLI'S HUMMINGBIRD	350	950.00	1530.00
77	CAPE MAY WARBLER	400	825.00	990.00
77	CARDINALS	200	3,500.00	4095.00
77	EASTERN BLUEBIRD 400-51	300	2,300.00	2620.00

YR	NAME	LIMIT	ISSUE	TREND
77	FLEDGLING BROWN THRASHERS	400	500.00	680.00
77	ROBIN (NEST)	350	1,650.00	2080.00
77	RUFFED GROUSE/PAIR 400-65	100	4,400.00	4480.00
77	SCARLET TANAGER	4	1,800.00	4275.00
77	SCISSOR-TAILED FLYCATCHER	100	3,200.00	3650.00
78	CANADA GEESE, PAIR	100	4,200.00	4200.00
78	MOCKINGBIRDS	*	2,200.00	3045.00
78	SISKENS 100-25	250	2,100.00	2400.00
79	AVOCET	175	1,200.00	1345.00
79	CALLIOPE HUMMINGBIRD 40104	200	900.00	1115.00
79	COSTA'S HUMMINGBIRD 40103	200	1,050.00	1200.00
79	DOWNY WOODPECKER 40116	300	950.00	1000.00
79	GREY WAGTAIL	150	1,050.00	1375.00
79	LEAST TURN	350	1,275.00	3045.00
79	PRINCE RUDOLPH'S BLUE BIRD OF PARADISE 40101	10	35,000.00	37200.00
79	RACQUET-TAIL HUMMINGBIRD 40105	310	1,500.00	1960.00
79	RED-BREASTED NUTHATCH 40118	200	800.00	920.00
79	SCOPS OWL	300	975.00	1400.00
80	AMERICAN AVOCET 40134	300	1,400.00	1650.00
80	AMERICAN REDSTART 40138	225	850.00	1090.00
80	AMERICAN WILD TURKEY 40154	75	1,800.00	2010.00
80	AMERICAN WILD TURKEY/LIFE SIZE 40115	25	15,000.00	16940.00
80	ARCTIC TERN 40135	350	1,400.00	2050.00
80	BROWN PELICAN 40161	90	2,800.00	2860.00
80	CEDAR WAXWING 40117	325	950.00	1030.00
80	CRIMSON TOPAZ HUMMINGBIRD 40113	310	1,400.00	1640.00
80	KIRTLAND'S WARBLE 40169	130	750.00	885.00
80	PHEASANT 40133	100	2,100.00	2170.00
80	SCREECH OWL	350	2,100.00	3125.00
80	YELLOW WARBLER 40137	200	950.00	1060.00
81	AMERICAN BALD EAGLE 40185	655	1,200.00	1325.00
81	BLUE JAY W/WILD RASPBERRIES 40190	350	1,950.00	2400.00
81	BOREAL OWL 40172	200	1,750.00	1870.00
81	LEAST SANDPIPERS 40136	350	2,100.00	2540.00
81	MOCKINGBIRD'S NEST W/BLUEBONNET 10033	55	1,300.00	1360.00
81	MOURNING DOVE 40189	300	2,200.00	2320.00
81	NORTHERN ORIOLE 40194	100	1,750.00	1900.00
81	OSPREY 10031	25	17,000.00	21060.00
81	OSPREY 10037	100	4,350.00	4700.00
81	PEREGRINE FALCON W/YOUNG 40171	105	1,850.00	2010.00
81	ROBIN'S NEST W/WILD ROSE 10030	90	1,300.00	1375.00
81	ROSE-BREASTED GROSBEAK 10032	165	1,850.00	1875.00
81	WOOD DUCKS 40192	90	3,400.00	3550.00
82	AMERICAN EAGLE/COMMEMORATIVE 40215	250	950.00	1150.00
82	AMERICAN EAGLE/SYMBOL OF FREEDOM 40200	35	16,500.00	18550.00
82	BLACK-EARED BUSHFIT/FEMALE 10038	100	975.00	1040.00
82	BLACK-EARED BUSHFIT/MALE 10039	100	975.00	1040.00
82	BLUE JAY W/MORNING GLORIES 40218	300	975.00	1190.00
82	BLUE THROATED HUMMINGBIRD 10040	300	1,100.00	1430.00
82	GREAT WHITE EGRET 40214	50	11,500.00	15050.00
82	GREEN JAYS/PAIR 40198	65	3,900.00	3900.00
82	KILLDEER 40213	125	1,075.00	1085.00
82	MUTE SWANS/PAIR 40219	115	5,800.00	6345.00
82	ROADRUNNER 40199	150	2,100.00	2315.00
82	WREN 1036	50	1,700.00	1940.00
82	YELLOW-SHAFTED FLICKER 40220	175	1,450.00	1490.00
83	ANNA'S HUMMINGBIRD 10048	300	1,100.00	1935.00
83	CATBIRD 40246	111	1,250.00	1250.00
83	DOVE OF PEACE 40236	709	750.00	1475.00
83	DOVES W/CHERRY BLOSSOMS/PR 10049	150	7,500.00	10600.00
83	EGRET/NATIONAL AUDUBON SOCIETY 40221	1029	1,200.00	1575.00
83	FORSTER'S TERN/CRESTING 40224	300	1,850.00	2070.00
83	FORSTER'S TERN/ON THE WIND 40223	300	1,850.00	2070.00
83	GOLDEN EAGLE 10046	25	32,000.00	36075.00
83	GOLDFINCH 40245	136	1,200.00	1200.00
83	GREAT EGRET	YR	1,200.00	2400.00
83	ROYAL TERNS 10047	75	4,300.00	4845.00
83	TOWHEE 40244	75	975.00	1040.00
84	BLACKBURNIAN WARBLER	125	925.00	965.00
84	LONG-EARED OWL 10052	12	6,000.00	6250.00
84	MAGNOLIA WARBLER 40258	246	1,100.00	1100.00
84	PELICAN 40259	93	1,200.00	1230.00
84	PILEATED WOODPECKERS 40250	50	2,900.00	2915.00
84	WHOOPING CRANE	647	1,800.00	2025.00
85	CONDOR 10057	2	75,000.00	87710.00
85	PARULA WARBLERS 40270	100	2,450.00	2460.00
85	RACQUET-TAILED HUMMINGBIRD 10053	350	2,100.00	2500.00
85	SCARLET TANGER 40267	125	2,100.00	2120.00
85	SOARING EAGLE/BISQUE 40276B	304	950.00	955.00
85	SOARING EAGLE/GILDED 40276G	35	5,000.00	5280.00
85	TRUMPETER SWAN	500	1,500.00	1625.00
86	GANNET 40287	30	4,300.00	4300.00
86	SANDHILL CRANE 40286	205	1,650.00	1660.00
87	CALLIOPE HUMMINGBIRD 40319	500	575.00	595.00
87	FLAMINGO W/YOUNG 40316	225	1,500.00	1520.00

Sweep All Your Worries Away, *from Enesco Corp.'s Precious Moments Collection, illustrates the "out of sight, out of mind" attitude.*

Her tear-drop shaped eyes focused on a delicate butterfly, the girl in Sam Butcher's figurine We Are God's Workmanship, *produced by Enesco Corp., treasures a small friend.*

Time Heals *is an open edition piece from Sam Butcher's Precious Moments collection, produced by Enesco Corp.*

This precious mother-to-be—from the Precious Moments collection by Enesco Corp.—understands that The Good Lord Always Delivers.

YR	NAME	LIMIT	ISSUE	TREND
*				**FIGURINES**
77	BEVERLY SILLS	100	950.00	1000.00
77	JEROME HINES	12	825.00	1000.00
86	AMANDA W/PARASOL 10269	27	750.00	750.00
86	ARIA 67003	100	875.00	875.00
86	AURORA 67001	100	875.00	875.00
86	CELESTE 6702	100	875.00	875.00
86	DEVINA 67000	100	875.00	875.00
86	JO/SKATING 10267	26	750.00	750.00
86	MATTINA 67004	100	875.00	875.00
86	MEG W/BASKET 10268	26	625.00	625.00
*				**FISH SCULPTURES**
83	TROPICAL FISH	150	2,700.00	2700.00
*				**FLORAL SCULPTURES**
71	DAISIES	350	600.00	1045.00
71	SWAN CENTERPIECE	135	1,950.00	2925.00
71	SWEET VIBURNUM	35	650.00	1395.00
72	CHRYSANTHEMUMS	350	1,100.00	2030.00
73	DOGWOOD	250	625.00	1025.00
73	STEPTOCALYX POEPPIGII	50	3,400.00	4485.00
74	DEBUTANTE CAMELIA	500	625.00	850.00
74	DOUBLE PEONY	275	575.00	995.00
74	GENTIANS	350	425.00	725.00
74	WATERLILY	350	400.00	725.00
75	EMMETT BARNES CAMELLIA	425	550.00	760.00
75	MAGNOLIA GRANDIFLORA 300-12	750	650.00	1525.00
76	ORCHID CACTUS	100	650.00	1025.00
76	QUEEN OF THE NIGHT CACTUS	125	650.00	975.00
76	ROSE, SUPREME PEACE	250	850.00	1745.00
76	ROSE, SUPREME YELLOW	250	850.00	1725.00
76	SWAN LAKE CAMELLIA	750	825.00	1790.00
78	DOUBLE CLEMATIS CENTERPIECE	150	1,500.00	1775.00
78	EDWARD BOEHM CAMELLIA 300-23	500	850.00	950.00
78	HELEN BOEHM CAMELLIA	500	600.00	1100.00
78	HELEN BOEHM DAYLILY	175	975.00	1140.00
78	HELEN BOEHM IRIS	175	975.00	1175.00
78	PINK LOTUS 300-21	175	975.00	1050.00
78	RHODODENDRON CENTERPIECE	350	1,150.00	1900.00
78	ROSE, BLUE MOON	500	650.00	900.00
78	ROSE, PASCALI 300-24	500	950.00	1520.00
78	ROSE, TROPICANA	500	475.00	1075.00
78	SPANISH IRIS	500	600.00	750.00
78	WATSONII MAGNOLIA	250	575.00	675.00
79	CACTUS DAHLIA	300	800.00	960.00
79	GRAND FLORAL CENTERPIECE	15	7,500.00	8755.00
79	HONEYSUCKLE	200	900.00	1050.00
80	BEGONIA/PINK 30041	500	1,250.00	1465.00
80	BLUEBONNETS 30050	160	650.00	765.00
80	CAPRICE IRIS/PINK 30049	235	650.00	720.00
80	MAGNOLIA GRANDIFLORA 300-47	350	1,650.00	1930.00
80	MISS INDIANA IRIS/BLUE 30049	235	650.00	705.00
80	ORCHID/PINK 30036	175	725.00	775.00
80	ORCHID/YELLOW 30037	130	725.00	775.00
80	PARROT TULIPS 30042	300	850.00	1000.00
80	ROSE, ALEC'S RED	500	1,050.00	1390.00
80	ROSE/ELIZABETH OF GLAMIS 30046	500	1,650.00	1965.00
80	ROSE/PEACH 30038	350	1,800.00	2060.00
80	TREE PEONY 30043	325	1,400.00	1480.00
81	DAISY, WHITE	75	975.00	995.00
81	DOGWOOD 30045	510	875.00	950.00
81	JULIA HAMITER CAMELLIA 30061	300	675.00	740.00
81	NANCY REAGAN CAMELLIA 30076	600	650.00	825.00
81	POINSETTIA 30055	200	1,100.00	1225.00
81	POPPIES 30058	325	1,150.00	1260.00
81	RHODODENDRON 30064	275	825.00	895.00
81	ROSE GRACE DE MONACO 30071	350	1,650.00	1935.00
81	ROSE/ANNENBERG 30051	200	1,450.00	1490.00
81	ROSE/GRANDPA DICKSON 30069	225	1,200.00	1425.00
81	ROSE/JUST JOEY 30052	240	1,050.00	1050.00
81	ROSE/LADY HELEN 30070	325	1,350.00	1515.00
81	ROSE/NANCY REAGAN 35027	1200	800.00	920.00
81	ROSE/PRINCE CHARLES & LADY DIANA CENTERPIECE 30065	100	4,800.00	6325.00
81	ROSE/PRINCE CHARLES & LADY DIANA FLORAL 30068	600	750.00	845.00
81	ROSE/TROPICANA IN CONCH SHELL 30060	150	1,100.00	1100.00
81	ROSE/YELLOW IN SHELL 30059	300	1,100.00	1150.00
82	DOUBLE PEONY 30078	110	1,525.00	1630.00
82	MAGNOLIA CENTERPIECE 30101	15	6,800.00	6975.00
82	MARIGOLDS 30072	150	1,275.00	1275.00
82	PONTIFF IRIS 30097	200	3,000.00	3825.00
82	ROSE/JEHAN SADAT 30080	200	875.00	1025.00
82	ROSE/MOUNTBATTEN 30094	50	1,525.00	1660.00
82	ROSE/PASCALI 30093	250	1,500.00	1700.00
82	ROSE/PRINCESS MARGARET 30095	350	950.00	1165.00
82	ROSE/QUEEN ELIZABETH 30091	350	1,450.00	1780.00
82	ROSE/ROYAL BLESSING 30099	500	1,350.00	1710.00

YR	NAME	LIMIT	ISSUE	TREND
82	ROYAL BOUQUET 30092	125	1,500.00	1680.00
82	SCABIOUS W/JAPONICA 30090	50	1,550.00	1570.00
82	TIGER LILIES/ORANGE 30077	350	1,225.00	1265.00
82	TULIPS 30089	180	1,050.00	1085.00
83	CHRYSANTHEMUM 30105	75	1,250.00	1460.00
83	EMPRESS CAMELLIA/WHITE 30109	350	1,025.00	1045.00
83	ROSE/YANKEE DOODLE 30108	450	650.00	695.00
83	SPRING CENTERPIECE 30110	100	1,125.00	1190.00
84	LADY'S SLIPPER ORCHID 30112	76	575.00	575.00
84	MARY HEATLEY BEGONIA 30111	200	1,100.00	1120.00
84	ORCHID CENTERPIECE/ASSORTED 30016	150	2,600.00	2645.00
84	ORCHID CENTERPIECE/PINK 30115	350	2,100.00	2485.00
84	ORCHID, CYMBIDIUM 30114	160	575.00	620.00
84	ORCHID, ODONTOGLOSSUM 30113	100	575.00	605.00
85	CHRYSANTHEMUM PETAL CAMELLIA 30125	500	575.00	595.00
85	EMMETT BARNES CAMELLIA 30120	275	625.00	630.00
85	KAMA PUA HIBISCUS/ORANGE 30128	122	1,600.00	1610.00
85	PEONIES/WHITE 30118	100	1,650.00	1650.00
85	RHODODENDRON/PINK, YELLOW 30122	125	1,850.00	1885.00
85	ROSE/DUET 30130	200	1,525.00	1540.00
85	ROSE/HELEN BOEHM 30121	360	1,475.00	1480.00
85	SEMINOLE HIBISCUS/PINK 30129	100	1,800.00	1810.00
86	CHERRIES JUBILEE CAMELLIA 10388	250	625.00	625.00
86	GLOBE OF LIGHT PEONY 10372	125	475.00	500.00
86	ICARIAN PEONY CENTERPIECE 30119	33	2,800.00	2860.00
86	ROSE CENTERPIECE/YELLOW 10370	25	5,500.00	5620.00

BOYDS COLLECTION LTD.
G. LOWENTHAL

BEARSTONE COLLECTION

YR	NAME		ISSUE	TREND
93	ARTHUR WITH GREEN SCARF	RT	10.50	95.00
93	ARTHUR WITH RED SCARF 2003	RT	14.20	100.00
93	BAILEY BEAR WITH SUITCASE 2000 REVISED	OP	14.20	55.00
93	BAILEY IN THE ORCHARD 2006	RT	14.20	190.00
93	BAILY BEAR WITH SUITCASE 2000 (ROUGH)	RT	14.20	400.00
93	BYRON & CHEDDA WITH CATMINT 2010	RT	14.20	125.00
93	CHRISTIAN BY THE SEA	OP	14.20	110.00
93	DAPHNE HARE & MAISY EWE 2011	RT	14.20	125.00
93	FATHER CHRISBEAR AND SON 2008	RT	15.00	350.00
93	GRENVILLE AND NEVILLE THE SIGN 2099	OP	15.75	125.00
93	GRENVILLE WITH GREEN SCARF 2003-04	RT	10.50	375.00
93	GRENVILLE WITH RED SCARF 2003-08	TL	10.50	130.00
93	MORIARTY 2005	RT	13.75	110.00
93	NEVILLE THE BEDTIME BEAR 2002	RT	14.20	100.00
93	SIMONE DE BEARVOIRE AND HER MOM 2001	RT	14.20	220.00
93	VICTORIA THE LADY 2004	OP	18.40	225.00
93	WILSON WITH LOVE SONNET 2007	RT	12.60	500.00
94	AGATHA AND SHELLY SCAREDY CAT 2245	CL	16.25	75.00
94	BAILEY & EMILY FOREVER FRIENDS 2018	RT	34.00	120.00
94	BAILEY & WIXIE TO HAVE AND TO HOLD 2017	OP	15.75	150.00
94	BAILEY AT THE BEACH 2020-09	RT	15.75	140.00
94	BAILEY'S BIRTHDAY 2014	OP	16.00	175.00
94	BESSIE THE SANTA COW 2239	RT	15.75	85.00
94	CELESTE THE ANGEL RABBIT 2230	OP	16.25	295.00
94	CHARLOTTE & BEBE 2229	RT	15.75	100.00
94	CHRISTMAS BIG/LITTLE PIG 2256	RT	32.00	90.00
94	CLARA THE NURSE 2231	CL	16.25	300.00
94	CLARENCE ANGEL BEAR 2029-11	RT	12.60	100.00
94	COOKIE THE SANTA CAT 2237	RT	15.25	75.00
94	DAPHNE THE READER HARE 2226	OP	14.20	115.00
94	EDMUND & BAILEY GATHERING HOLLY 2240	CL	25.00	160.00
94	ELGIN THE ELF BEAR 2236	CL	14.20	75.00
94	ELLIOT & SNOWBEARY 2242	CL	15.25	90.00
94	ELLIOT & THE TREE 2241	CL	16.25	175.00
94	GRENVILLE AND BEATRICE, BEST FRIENDS 2016	RT	26.00	350.00
94	GRENVILLE THE GRADUATE 2233	RT	16.25	100.00
94	GRENVILLE THE SANTA BEAR 2030	RT	14.20	475.00
94	HOMER ON THE PLATE 2218	OP	15.75	85.00
94	HOPE...ANGEL BEAR W/WREATH 2501	RT	*	N/A
94	JULIETTE ANGEL BEAR 2029-10	RT	12.60	100.00
94	JUSTINA AND M. HARRISON 2015	OP	26.00	100.00
94	KNUTE & THE GRIDIRON 2245	CL	16.25	75.00
94	KRINGLE & BAILEY WITH LIST 2235	CL	14.20	90.00
94	MANHEIM THE ECO-MOOSE 2243	OP	15.50	75.00
94	MAYNARD THE SANTA MOOSE 2238	CL	15.50	75.00
94	SEBASTIAN'S PRAYER 2227	RT	16.25	92.00
94	SHERLOCK & WATSON IN DISGUISE 2019	RT	15.75	115.00
94	TED AND TEDDY 2223	RT	15.75	115.00
94	WILSON AT THE BEACH 2020-06	RT	15.75	100.00
94	WILSON THE PERFESSER 2222	RT	16.25	90.00
95	AMELIA'S ENTERPRISE 2258	CL	16.25	75.00
95	ANGELICA THE GUARDIAN 2266	CL	19.00	70.00
95	BAILEY THE BAKER WITH SWEETIE PIE 2254	CL	12.60	80.00
95	BAILEY THE CHEERLEADER 2268	CL	16.25	50.00
95	BAILEY THE HONEYBEAR 2260	CL	16.25	90.00
95	COOKIE CATBERG KNITTIN' KITTEN 2250	RT	19.00	65.00
95	DAPHNE & ELOISE WOMEN'S WORK 2251	CL	18.00	70.00

YR	NAME	LIMIT	ISSUE	TREND
95	ELF BEAR WITH LIST	*	32.00	300.00
95	EMMA THE WITCHY BEAR 2269	CL	17.50	70.00
95	GRENVILLE & KNUTE FOOTBALL BUDDIES 2255	CL	20.00	65.00
95	GRENVILLE THE STORYTELLER 2265	YR	49.00	90.00
95	HOPALONG THE DEPUTY 2247	CL	14.20	60.00
95	LEFTY ON THE MOUND 2056 (BC)	OP	15.00	75.00
95	MISS BRUIN & BAILEY THE LESSON 2259	CL	16.25	125.00
95	OTIS TAXTIME 2262	CL	16.25	65.00
95	OTIS THE FISHERMAN 2249-06	CL	15.75	65.00
95	SIMONE & BAILEY HELPING HANDS 2267	CL	26.00	60.00
95	STAGE, THE 2425	OP	35.00	35.00
95	UNION JACK LOVE LETTERS 2263	CL	19.00	70.00
95	WILSON THE WONDERFUL WIZARD OF WUZ 2261	CL	15.25	50.00
96	BAILEY HEART'S DESIRE 2272	OP	15.00	40.00
96	ELLIOT THE HERO 2280	OP	17.00	70.00
96	EMMA & BAILEY AFTERNOON TEA 2277	OP	18.00	65.00
96	EWELL & WALTON MANITOBA MOOSELMEN 2228 (CN)	12000	18.00	50.00
96	GRENVILLE & BEATRICE TRUE LOVE 2274	OP	36.00	36.00
96	GRENVILLE WITH MATTHEW & BAILEY 2281	OP	35.00	90.00
96	JUSTINA MESSAGE BEARER 2273	OP	16.00	16.00
96	KRINGLE & COMPANY 2283	OP	18.00	45.00
96	KRINGLE & COMPANY 2283-01	*	18.00	50.00
96	M. HARRISON'S BIRTHDAY 2275	OP	17.00	17.00
96	MOMMA MCBEAR 2282	OP	15.00	50.00
96	MS. GRIZ (BLUE) MONDAY MORNING 2276	OP	34.00	85.00
96	MS. GRIZ (PINK) MONDAY MORNING 2276	OP	34.00	34.00
96	MS. GRIZ...SATURDAY NIGHT 2284	OP	15.00	50.00
96	NOAH & CO. ARK BUILDERS 2278	YR	61.00	120.00
96	SIR EDMUND PERSISTENCE 2279	OP	21.00	95.00

G. LOWENTHAL — **BEARSTONE COLLECTION HOLIDAY PAGEANT**

YR	NAME	LIMIT	ISSUE	TREND
95	BALDWIN AS THE CHILD 2403	OP	15.00	40.00
95	NEVILLE AS JOSEPH 2401	OP	15.00	30.00
95	THERESA AS MARY 2402	*	15.00	30.00
96	HEATH AS CASPER 2405	*	15.00	25.00
96	RALEIGH AS BALTHAZAR 2406	*	15.00	30.00
96	THATCHER & EDEN 2407	*	18.00	25.00
96	WILSON AS MELCHOIR 2404	*	15.00	25.00

G. LOWENTHAL — **BEARSTONE COLLECTION SHOE BOX BEARS**

YR	NAME	LIMIT	ISSUE	TREND
96	AUGUSTUS GUS GRIZBERG 3200	*	19.00	40.00
96	GLADYS GRIZBERG 3201-01	*	15.00	30.00
96	THADDEUS BUD GRIZBERG 25700	*	10.00	25.00

G. LOWENTHAL — **DOLLSTONE COLLECTION**

YR	NAME	LIMIT	ISSUE	TREND
95	KATHERINE WITH AMANDA & EDMUND KIND HEARTS 3505	RT	20.00	140.00
95	MEGAN WITH ELLIOT & ANNIE CHRISTMAS CAROL 3504	RT	20.00	270.00
95	VICTORIA WITH SAMANTHA VICTORIAN LADIES 3502	RT	20.00	75.00
96	ANNE THE MASTERPIECE	OP	24.00	35.00
96	ASHLEY WITH CHRISTIE DRESS UP 3506	OP	21.00	65.00
96	BETSY WITH EDMUND...THE PATRIOTS 3503	OP	20.00	40.00
96	BETSY WITH EDMUND...WITH UNION JACK BC3503-1	OP	25.00	65.00
96	CANDICE WITH MATTHEW GATHERING APPLES 3514	OP	19.00	45.00
96	CHRISTY WITH NICOLE...SKATERS GCC EXCLUSIVE 3516	OP	26.00	60.00
96	COURTNEY WITH PHOEBE GCC EXCLUSIVE 3512-01	*	28.00	160.00
96	COURTNEY WITH PHOEBE...OVER THE RIVER 3512	CL	25.00	40.00
96	EMILY WITH KATHLEEN AND OTIS...THE FUTURE 3508	OP	30.00	80.00
96	JEAN WITH ELLIOT & DEBBIE THE BAKERS 3510	OP	20.00	45.00
96	JENNIFER WITH PRISCILLA THE DOLL IN THE ATTIC 3500	RT	21.00	125.00
96	KAREN WITH WILSON & ELOISE MOTHER'S PRESENT 3515	*	26.00	70.00
96	MALLORY WITH PATSY & JB HALLOWEEN 3517	RT	27.00	150.00
96	MEGAN WITH ELLIOT CHRISTMAS CAROL 2720	YR	39.00	60.00
96	MICHELLE WITH DAISY...READING IS FUN 3511	OP	18.00	50.00
96	PATRICIA WITH MOLLY ATTIC TREASURES 3501	OP	14.00	150.00
96	REBECCA WITH ELLIOT...BIRTHDAY! 3509	OP	21.00	70.00
96	SARAH & HEATHER WITH ELLIOT, DOLLY & AMELIA 3507	RT	46.00	75.00

G. LOWENTHAL — **FAERIE COLLECTION**

YR	NAME	LIMIT	ISSUE	TREND
96	FIXIT SANTA'S FAERIE	*	18.00	18.00

G. LOWENTHAL — **FOLKSTONE COLLECTION**

YR	NAME	LIMIT	ISSUE	TREND
94	ANGEL OF FREEDOM 2820	RT	16.00	75.00
94	ANGEL OF LOVE 2821	RT	17.00	80.00
94	ANGEL OF PEACE 2822	RT	17.00	75.00
94	BEATRICE/BIRTHDAY ANGEL 2825	RT	20.00	65.00
94	CHILLY & SON 2811	RT	17.00	50.00
94	ELMER BEEN FARMIN' LONG? 2851	OP	18.00	40.00
94	FLORENCE KITCHEN ANGEL 2824	RT	20.00	65.00
94	IDA & BESSIE THE GARDENERS 2852	OP	18.00	40.00
94	JILL LANGUAGE OF LOVE 2842	RT	18.00	65.00
94	JINGLE MOOSE 2830	RT	17.00	85.00
94	JINGLES & SON WITH WREATH 2812	RT	18.00	18.00
94	LIZZIE THE SHOPPING ANGEL 2827	RT	20.00	50.00
94	MINERVA THE BASEBALL ANGEL 2826	RT	20.00	50.00
94	MYRTLE BELIEVE 2840	OP	18.00	50.00
94	NICHOLAI 2800	RT	17.00	73.00
94	NICHOLAS WITH BOOK 2802	RT	18.00	18.00
94	NICHOLAS WITH TREE 2800	RT	18.00	23.00
94	NICK ON ICE 3001	RT	50.00	85.00
94	NIKKI WITH CANDLE 2801	RT	17.00	75.00

YR	NAME	LIMIT	ISSUE	TREND
94	OCEANA OCEAN ANGEL 2823	OP	17.00	70.00
94	PETER THE WHOPPER 2841	RT	18.00	50.00
94	RUFUS HOE DOWN 2850	OP	18.00	40.00
94	SANTA'S CHALLENGE 3002	RT	32.00	90.00
94	SANTA'S FLIGHT PLAN 3000	RT	32.00	85.00
94	WINDY WITH BOOK 2810	RT	17.00	85.00
95	ABIGAIL PEACEABLE KINGDOM 2829	OP	19.00	50.00
95	BEATRICE THE GIFTGIVER 2836	OP	18.00	50.00
95	BOOWINKLE VONHINDEN MOOSE 2831	OP	18.00	60.00
95	ERNEST HEMMINGMOOSE THE HUNTER 2835	OP	18.00	55.00
95	ESMERALDA THE WONDERFUL WITCH 2860	OP	18.00	40.00
95	ICABOD MOOSELMAN THE PILGRIM 2833	OP	18.00	40.00
95	JEAN CLAUDE & JACQUES 2815	OP	17.00	50.00
95	JEAN CLAUDE & JACQUES THE SKIERS 2710	OP	17.00	17.00
95	NANICK OF THE NORTH 2804	OP	18.00	50.00
95	NORTHBOUND WILLIE 2814	RT	17.00	50.00
95	PRUDENCE MOOSELMAID THE PILGRIM 2834	OP	18.00	40.00
95	SANTA'S FLIGHT PLAN WATERBALL	RT	37.00	60.00
95	SERAPHINA WITH JACOB & RACHEL 2828	OP	20.00	50.00
95	SIEGFRIED AND EGON THE SIGN 2899	OP	19.00	50.00
95	SLIK NICK 2803	OP	18.00	50.00
96	ALVIN T. MACBARKER DOG FACE 2872	RT	19.00	70.00
96	ATHENA THE WEDDING ANGEL	OP	19.00	50.00
96	BERNIE 2873	OP	18.00	45.00
96	BETTY COCKER 2870	OP	19.00	70.00
96	BUSTER GOES A COURTIN' 2844	OP	19.00	50.00
96	COSMOS THE GARDENING ANGEL	OP	19.00	50.00
96	EGON THE SKIER 2837	OP	18.00	50.00
96	ELMO TEX BEEFCAKE 2853	RT	19.00	40.00
96	FLORA & AMELIA THE GARDENERS 2843	OP	19.00	50.00
96	FLORA, AMELIA & ELOISE TEA PARTY 2846	OP	19.00	50.00
96	G.M.'S CHOICE ETHEREAL 28203-06	7200	19.00	125.00
96	ILLUMINA ANGEL OF LIGHT 28203	OP	19.00	50.00
96	LORETTA MOOSTEIN 2854	OP	19.00	40.00
96	NANICK & SIGFRIEND 2807	10,000	33.00	125.00
96	NANNY 2817	OP	18.00	40.00
96	NICKNOAH 2806	OP	18.00	40.00
96	NO-NO NICK 2805	OP	18.00	40.00
96	ROBIN 2816	OP	18.00	40.00
96	SERENITY THE MOTHER'S ANGEL 28204	OP	19.00	50.00
96	SPARKY MCPLUG 2871	OP	19.00	45.00
96	TOO LOOSE LAPIN 2845	OP	19.00	50.00

G. LOWENTHAL — FOLKSTONE COLLECTION GCC EXCLUSIVE

YR	NAME	LIMIT	ISSUE	TREND
96	ST. NICK 2808	*	20.00	40.00

G. LOWENTHAL — LOYAL ORDER OF FRIENDS OF BOYDS CLUB

YR	NAME	LIMIT	ISSUE	TREND
96	UNCLE ELLIOT...THE HEAD BEAN WANTS YOU!	*	30.00	30.00

G. LOWENTHAL — MUSICAL WATERGLOBES

YR	NAME	LIMIT	ISSUE	TREND
94	GRENVILLE THE SANTA BEAR 2700	RT	38.00	38.00
95	ANGELICIA THE GUARDIAN ANGEL 2702	OP	37.00	37.00
95	ELLIOT & THE TREE 2704	OP	35.00	35.00
96	NOAH & CO. 2706	6144	51.00	51.00
96	SIMONE & BAILEY 2705	OP	35.00	45.00

G. LOWENTHAL — SANTA & FRIENDS COLLECTION

YR	NAME	LIMIT	ISSUE	TREND
95	SANTA...DECEMBER 26	RT	32.00	100.00
96	SANTA'S HOBBY...THE BEARMAKER	*	35.00	50.00

BRADFORD EDITIONS

*

FAIRYTALE PRINCESS BELL JAR COLLECTION

YR	NAME	LIMIT	ISSUE	TREND
97	CINDERELLA BELL JAR	120-DAYS	30.00	30.00

T. JOHNSON — SOMEONE TO WATCH OVER ME BELL JAR COLLECTION

YR	NAME	LIMIT	ISSUE	TREND
97	FAITHFUL CARE	*	30.00	30.00

BRIERCROFT

B. FARLOW — INTERNATIONAL GIFTGIVERS

YR	NAME	LIMIT	ISSUE	TREND
95	CZECHOSLOVAKIAN	5000	*	60.00
95	IRISH FATHER CHRISTMAS	5000	*	60.00
95	NORWEGIAN NISSE	5000	*	60.00
96	CHRISTKINDEL-AUSTRIA	5000	*	60.00
96	DANISH JULEMAND	5000	*	60.00
96	SAMICHLOUS-SWITZERLAND	5000	*	60.00

B. FARLOW — INTERNATIONAL SANTAS

YR	NAME	LIMIT	ISSUE	TREND
93	AMERICAN '40S BABY BOOMER	5000	27.00	45.00
93	ITALIAN BABBO NATALIE	5000	27.00	45.00
93	SANTA'S PUP	5000	5.00	9.00
93	SWEDISH TOMTEN & YULEBOCK	5000	27.00	45.00
94	AMERICAN '40S BABY BOOMER-BLACK	5000	27.00	45.00
94	BANJO SANTA (W/ORNAMENT)	5000	16.00	30.00
94	BELGIAN ST. NICHOLAS (W/ORNAMENT)	5000	6.00	10.00
94	DUTCH SINTER KLAAS	5000	27.00	45.00
94	DUTCH SINTER KLAAS (W/ORNAMENT)	5000	6.00	10.00
94	FRENCH PERE NOEL (W/ORNAMENT)	5000	6.00	10.00
94	MARIACHI SANTA	5000	27.00	45.00
94	POLISH GIFT GIVER	5000	27.00	45.00
94	POLISH GIFT GIVER (W/ORNAMENT)	5000	6.00	10.00
94	RUSSIAN RATHER CHRISTMAS (W/ORNAMENT)	5000	6.00	10.00

YR	NAME	LIMIT	ISSUE	TREND
94	SPANISH GIFT GIVER	5000	27.00	45.00
94	SPANISH GIFT GIVER (W/ORNAMENT)	5000	6.00	10.00
94	SPOTTED PUP (W/ORNAMENT)	5000	6.00	10.00
94	U.S. '40S BABY BOOMER (W/ORNAMENT)	5000	6.00	10.00
94	U.S. '40S BABY BOOMER-BLACK (W/ORNAMENT)	5000	6.00	10.00

B. FARLOW — **MALE ANGELS**

YR	NAME	LIMIT	ISSUE	TREND
94	ANGEL AT THE TOMB	5000	25.00	39.00
94	COMMANDER ANGEL	5000	25.00	39.00
94	GABRIEL ANGEL	5000	25.00	39.00

B. FARLOW — **NATIVITY**

YR	NAME	LIMIT	ISSUE	TREND
93	INNKEEPER	5000	24.00	37.00
93	INNKEEPER'S WIFE	5000	24.00	37.00
94	EWE & NURSING LAMB	5000	12.50	24.00
94	EWE & SLEEPING LAMB	5000	12.50	24.00
94	GROUP OF SHEEP	5000	24.00	36.00
94	NATIVITY ANGEL	5000	27.00	45.00
94	SHEPHERD BOY WITH LAMB	5000	15.00	28.00
94	THRESHING FLOOR ANGEL	5000	25.00	39.00

B. FARLOW — **SMALL NISSE**

YR	NAME	LIMIT	ISSUE	TREND
95	BALD SANTA	5000	*	47.00
96	CAKE LADY	5000	*	20.00
96	COFFEEBREAK LADY	5000	*	20.00
96	COFFEEBREAK MAN	5000	*	20.00
96	DANCING LADY	5000	*	20.00
96	LUKE'S GOSPEL NATIVITY/SMALL 5 PCS	5000	*	150.00
96	READING MAN	5000	*	20.00
96	VICTORIAN SANTA	5000	*	47.00

BYERS' CHOICE LTD.

J. BYERS — **ACCESSORIES**

YR	NAME	LIMIT	ISSUE	TREND
98	DOOR	*	52.00	52.00

J. BYERS — **CAROLERS**

YR	NAME	LIMIT	ISSUE	TREND
82	VICTORIAN ADULT CAROLER (1ST VERSION)	CL	32.00	350.00
82	VICTORIAN CHILD CAROLER (1ST VERSION)	CL	32.00	375.00
83	VICTORIAN ADULT CAROLER (2ND VERSION)	OP	35.00	48.00
83	VICTORIAN CHILD CAROLER (2ND VERSION)	CL	33.00	350.00
86	SINGING DOGS	OP	13.00	13.00
86	TRADITIONAL GRANDPARENTS	OP	35.00	45.00
88	CHILDREN WITH SKATES	OP	40.00	46.00
88	SINGING CATS	OP	13.50	15.00
88	VICTORIAN GRANDPARENT CAROLERS	OP	40.00	48.00
91	ADULT SKATERS	CL	50.00	100.00
91	TODDLER ON SLED W/DOG	CL	30.00	140.00
92	CHILDREN SKATERS	OP	50.00	50.00
92	LIL' DICKENS-SHOVEL	CL	17.00	35.00
92	LIL' DICKENS-SLED	OP	17.00	17.00
92	LIL' DICKENS-SNOWBALL (LG)	CL	17.00	35.00

J. BYERS — **CHILDREN OF THE WORLD**

YR	NAME	LIMIT	ISSUE	TREND
92	DUTCH BOY	CL	50.00	240.00
92	DUTCH GIRL	CL	50.00	240.00
93	BAVARIAN BOY	CL	50.00	195.00
94	IRISH GIRL	CL	50.00	155.00

J. BYERS — **CHRISTMAS FIGURINES**

YR	NAME	LIMIT	ISSUE	TREND
98	BELSNICKLE	*	64.00	64.00
98	SEATED SANTA WITH TODDLER	*	90.00	90.00

J. BYERS — **COUNTRY CHRISTMAS STORE EXCLUSIVE**

YR	NAME	LIMIT	ISSUE	TREND
88	TOYMAKER	600	59.00	875.00

J. BYERS — **CRIES OF LONDON**

YR	NAME	LIMIT	ISSUE	TREND
91	LADY WITH APPLES	CL	80.00	1025.00
92	CRY OF LONDON-BAKER	CL	62.00	165.00
93	CHESTNUT ROASTER	CL	64.00	240.00
94	FLOWER VENDOR	CL	64.00	150.00
95	DOLLMAKER	CL	64.00	64.00
95	GIRL HOLDING DOLL	CL	48.00	48.00
98	CANDLESTICK MAKER	*	72.00	72.00
98	CHILDREN HOLDING CANDLES	*	48.00	48.00

J. BYERS — **DICKENS SERIES**

YR	NAME	LIMIT	ISSUE	TREND
83	SCROOGE (1ST EDITION)	CL	36.00	1350.00
84	MRS. CRATCHET (1ST EDITION)	CL	38.00	800.00
84	SCROOGE (2ND EDITION)	OP	38.00	50.00
85	MR. FEZZIWIG (1ST EDITION)	CL	43.00	600.00
85	MRS. CRATCHIT (2ND EDITION)	OP	39.00	50.00
85	MRS. FEZZIWIG (1ST EDITION)	CL	43.00	675.00
86	MARLEY'S GHOST (1ST EDITION)	CL	40.00	375.00
86	MR. FEZZIWIG (2ND EDITION)	CL	43.00	475.00
86	MRS. FEZZIWIG (2ND EDITION)	CL	43.00	500.00
87	MARLEY'S GHOST (2ND EDITION)	CL	42.00	260.00
87	SPIRIT OF CHRISTMAS PAST (1ST EDITION)	CL	42.00	350.00
88	SPIRIT OF CHRISTMAS PAST (2ND EDITION)	CL	46.00	325.00
88	SPIRIT OF CHRISTMAS PRESENT (1ST ED.)	CL	44.00	350.00
89	SPIRIT OF CHRISTMAS FUTURE (1ST EDITION)	CL	46.00	300.00
89	SPIRIT OF CHRISTMAS PRESENT (2ND ED.)	CL	48.00	300.00
90	BOB CRATCHET & TINY TIM	CL	84.00	225.00
90	SPIRIT OF CHRISTMAS FUTURE (2ND EDITION)	CL	48.00	310.00

YR	NAME	LIMIT	ISSUE	TREND
91	BOB CRATCHIT & TINY TIM (2ND EDITION)	OP	86.00	86.00
91	HAPPY SCROOGE (1ST EDITION)	CL	50.00	240.00
92	HAPPY SCROOGE (2ND EDITION)	CL	50.00	225.00
J. BYERS				**DISPLAY FIGURES**
81	DISPLAY LADY	CL	*	2000.00
81	DISPLAY MAN	CL	*	2000.00
82	DISPLAY DRUMMER BOY (1ST VERSION)	CL	96.00	1000.00
82	DISPLAY SANTA	CL	96.00	600.00
83	DISPLAY CAROLERS	CL	200.00	500.00
84	DISPLAY WORKING SANTA	CL	260.00	500.00
85	DISPLAY CHILDREN	CL	140.00	1300.00
85	DISPLAY DRUMMER BOY (2ND VERSION)	CL	160.00	500.00
85	DISPLAY OLD WORLD SANTA	CL	260.00	500.00
86	DISPLAY ADULTS	CL	170.00	250.00
87	DISPLAY MECHANICAL BOY W/DRUM	CL	*	700.00
87	DISPLAY MECHANICAL GIRL W/BELL	CL	*	610.00
90	DISPLAY SANTA-BAYBERRY	CL	250.00	450.00
90	DISPLAY SANTA-RED	CL	250.00	440.00
J. BYERS				**LIL' DICKENS**
98	ASSORTED TODDLERS	*	20.00	20.00
98	TODDLER WITH CAT	*	36.00	36.00
98	TODDLER WITH DOG	*	36.00	36.00
J. BYERS				**MUSICIANS**
83	VIOLIN PLAYER MAN	CL	38.00	800.00
85	HORN PLAYER	CL	38.00	750.00
85	HORN PLAYER, CHUBBY FACE	CL	37.00	900.00
86	VICTORIAN GIRL WITH VIOLIN	CL	39.00	350.00
89	MUSICIAN WITH CLARINET	CL	44.00	525.00
90	MUSICIAN WITH MANDOLIN	CL	46.00	230.00
91	BOY WITH MANDOLIN	1000	48.00	225.00
91	MUSICIAN WITH ACCORDIAN	CL	48.00	240.00
92	MUSICIAN WITH FRENCH HORN	CL	52.00	130.00
J. BYERS				**NATIVITY**
87	ANGEL-GREAT STAR (BLONDE)	CL	40.00	220.00
87	ANGEL-GREAT STAR (BRUNETTE)	CL	40.00	185.00
87	ANGEL-GREAT STAR (RED HEAD)	CL	40.00	225.00
87	BLACK ANGEL	CL	36.00	245.00
88	SHEPHERDS	CL	37.00	115.00
89	KING BALTHAZAR	CL	40.00	300.00
89	KING GASPAR	CL	40.00	125.00
89	KING MELCHIOR	CL	40.00	125.00
90	HOLY FAMILY	CL	90.00	300.00
J. BYERS				**NUTCRACKER**
93	MARIE 1ST ED.	CL	52.00	160.00
94	FRITZ 1ST ED.	CL	56.00	130.00
94	MARIE 2ND ED.	OP	53.00	53.00
95	FRITZ 2ND ED.	OP	57.00	57.00
95	LOUISE PLAYING PIANO 1ST ED.	CL	82.00	82.00
98	PRINCE	*	68.00	68.00
J. BYERS				**SALVATION ARMY**
92	WOMAN W/KETTLE 2ND ED.	OP	64.00	64.00
93	WOMAN W/TAMBOURINE	CL	58.00	58.00
94	MAN W/CORONET	OP	54.00	54.00
95	GIRL W/WAR CRY	OP	55.00	55.00
98	MAN WITH TUBA	*	58.00	58.00
J. BYERS				**SANTAS**
78	OLD WORLD SANTA	CL	33.00	610.00
78	VELVET SANTA	CL	*	300.00
82	SANTA IN SLEIGH (1ST VERSION)	CL	46.00	800.00
83	WORKING SANTA	CL	38.00	130.00
84	MRS. CLAUS	CL	38.00	250.00
84	SANTA IN SLEIGH (2ND VERSION)	CL	70.00	700.00
84	VIOLIN PLAYER MAN (1ST & 2ND VERSION)	CL	38.00	1500.00
86	MRS. CLAUS ON ROCKER	CL	73.00	625.00
86	VICTORIAN SANTA	CL	39.00	300.00
87	VELVET MRS. CLAUS	OP	44.00	44.00
88	KNECHT RUPRECHT	CL	38.00	175.00
88	SAINT NICHOLAS	OP	44.00	135.00
89	RUSSIAN SANTA	CL	85.00	470.00
90	WEIHNACHTSMANN	CL	56.00	200.00
91	FATHER CHRISTMAS	CL	48.00	115.00
92	MRS. CLAUS (2ND EDITION)	CL	50.00	115.00
92	WORKING SANTA (2ND EDITION)	OP	52.00	100.00
93	SKATING SANTA	CL	60.00	100.00
94	VELVET SANTA W/STOCKING	OP	47.00	50.00
J. BYERS				**SNOW GOOSE EXCLUSIVE**
88	MAN WITH GOOSE	600	60.00	350.00
J. BYERS				**SPECIAL CHARACTERS**
81	THANKSGIVING LADY (CLAY HANDS)	CL	*	2000.00
81	THANKSGIVING MAN (CLAY HANDS)	CL	*	2000.00
82	CHOIR CHILDREN, BOY AND GIRL	CL	32.00	600.00
82	CONDUCTOR	CL	32.00	120.00
82	DRUMMER BOY	CL	34.00	140.00
82	EASTER BOY	CL	32.00	500.00

YR	NAME	LIMIT	ISSUE	TREND
82	EASTER GIRL	CL	32.00	500.00
82	ICABOD	CL	33.00	1165.00
82	LEPRECHAUNS	CL	34.00	1750.00
82	VALENTINE BOY	CL	32.00	450.00
82	VALENTINE GIRL	CL	32.00	450.00
83	BOY ON ROCKING HORSE	300	85.00	2700.00
83	VICTORIAN CHILD	OP	33.00	48.00
84	CHIMNEY SWEEP	CL	36.00	1350.00
85	PAJAMA CHILDREN	CL	35.00	290.00
87	BOY ON SLED	CL	50.00	350.00
87	CAROLER WITH LAMP	CL	40.00	210.00
87	MOTHER'S DAY	225	94.00	360.00
88	ANGEL TREE TOP	100	*	325.00
88	MOTHER HOLDING BABY	CL	40.00	175.00
88	MOTHER'S DAY (DAUGHTER)	CL	125.00	450.00
88	MOTHER'S DAY (SON)	CL	125.00	500.00
89	GIRL WITH HOOP	CL	44.00	160.00
89	MOTHER'S DAY (WITH CARRIAGE)	3000	75.00	430.00
89	NEWSBOY WITH BIKE	CL	78.00	215.00
90	GIRL ON ROCKING HORSE	CL	70.00	100.00
90	PARSON	CL	44.00	130.00
90	POSTMAN	CL	45.00	150.00
91	BOY WITH TREE	CL	49.00	130.00
91	CHIMNEY SWEEP (CHILD)	OP	50.00	120.00
92	SALVATION ARMY-WOMAN WITH KETTLE 1ST	CL	64.00	175.00
92	TEACHER	CL	48.00	120.00
92	VICTORIAN MOTHER WITH TODDLER	CL	60.00	190.00
93	LAMPLIGHTER	OP	48.00	48.00
93	SCHOOL KIDS	CL	48.00	100.00
94	BOY W/GOOSE	CL	50.00	50.00
94	SANDWICH BOARD MAN W/RED BOARD	CL	52.00	90.00
94	SANDWICH BOARD MAN W/WHITE BOARD	OP	52.00	52.00
95	COUPLE IN SLEIGH	CL	110.00	110.00
95	SHOPPER/MAN	CL	56.00	56.00
95	SHOPPER/WOMAN	CL	56.00	56.00

J. BYERS — **SPECIALTY FIGURINES**

YR	NAME	LIMIT	ISSUE	TREND
98	CHILDREN WITH TOYS	*	57.00	57.00
98	CHILDREN WITH TREATS	*	58.00	58.00
98	INDIAN CHILDREN	*	53.50	54.00
98	MAN WITH BICYCLE	*	82.00	82.00
98	NURSE	*	60.00	60.00
98	PHOTOGRAPHER	*	70.00	70.00
98	SEATED VICTORIAN WOMAN	*	70.00	70.00
98	WOMAN SELLING CANDLES	*	66.00	66.00

J. BYERS — **STACY'S GIFTS & COLLECTIBLES EXCLUSIVES**

YR	NAME	LIMIT	ISSUE	TREND
87	SANTA IN ROCKING CHAIR WITH BOY	100	130.00	550.00
87	SANTA IN ROCKING CHAIR WITH GIRL	100	130.00	450.00

J. BYERS — **WAYSIDE COUNTRY STORE EXCLUSIVES**

YR	NAME	LIMIT	ISSUE	TREND
86	COLONIAL LAMPLIGHTER	600	46.00	900.00
87	COLONIAL WATCHMAN	600	49.00	690.00
88	COLONIAL LADY	600	49.00	550.00

J. BYERS — **WOODSTOCK INN EXCLUSIVES**

YR	NAME	LIMIT	ISSUE	TREND
87	SKIER BOY	200	40.00	300.00
87	SKIER GIRL	200	40.00	300.00
88	SUGARIN KIDS	CL	41.00	300.00
88	WOODSTOCK LADY	CL	41.00	355.00
88	WOODSTOCK MAN	CL	41.00	355.00

CAIRN STUDIO LTD.
*

YR	NAME	LIMIT	ISSUE	TREND
*	WORLD WAR II SOLDIER 328	*	*	450.00

T. CLARK — **ACORN COLLECTION**

YR	NAME	LIMIT	ISSUE	TREND
81	EL & EM 151	RT	5.00	30.00
81	EL KIM 152	RT	6.00	30.00
81	ELF 162	RT	7.00	30.00
81	ELK 154	RT	7.00	30.00
81	ELLA 153	RT	7.00	35.00
81	ELMER 155	RT	6.00	35.00
81	ELVA 157	RT	8.50	30.00
81	ELWOOD 156	RT	8.50	35.00

T. CLARK — **COLLECTOR SOCIETY ARTWORK SERIES**

YR	NAME	LIMIT	ISSUE	TREND
83	RORIE 48	RT	35.00	500.00
84	ERNEST 1030	RT	35.00	260.00
85	KILMER 1126	RT	55.00	300.00
87	HITCH 2018	RT	48.00	275.00

T. CLARK — **ESKIMOS**

YR	NAME	LIMIT	ISSUE	TREND
81	KANUK 165	RT	29.00	165.00
81	KEEGLOO 158	RT	33.00	375.00
81	KLONDIKE 166	RT	31.00	180.00

T. CLARK — **GNOMES & WOODSPIRITS**

YR	NAME	LIMIT	ISSUE	TREND
78	AMANDA 108	RT	35.00	4000.00
78	BESSIE 107	RT	35.00	4000.00
78	CALLIE 51	RT	28.00	5000.00
78	ETHAN 106	RT	35.00	2100.00
78	HAMP 105	RT	35.00	2100.00

YR	NAME	LIMIT	ISSUE	TREND
78	HAP 101	RT	35.00	1000.00
78	IVY 114	RT	35.00	3000.00
78	OBIE 104	RT	40.00	1600.00
78	PHINEAS 103	RT	35.00	1350.00
78	REUBEN 102	RT	43.00	850.00
78	SILAS 109	RT	35.00	4000.00
78	VANYA 42	RT	35.00	5000.00
79	ABNER 10	RT	35.00	750.00
79	DAISY & ERIC 116	RT	38.00	800.00
79	HUGH ROBERT 7	RT	45.00	1200.00
79	IRVIN 9	RT	35.00	1100.00
79	LUM 18	RT	35.00	1400.00
79	MODE 8	RT	35.00	1025.00
79	MOM 4	RT	35.00	140.00
79	NAOMI 19	RT	35.00	2100.00
79	OAKIE 3	RT	40.00	400.00
79	ROSCOE 6	RT	35.00	3000.00
79	SIMEON 2	RT	35.00	1385.00
79	STUMPY 5	RT	35.00	24.00
79	WIZARD 110	RT	38.00	960.00
79	XEROX 50	RT	15.00	8000.00
80	AHAB 120	RT	33.00	550.00
80	ARNOLD 124	RT	19.00	550.00
80	CALEB 129	RT	22.00	225.00
80	CHALMERS 15	RT	28.00	265.00
80	CHASE I 14	RT	28.00	400.00
80	CHASE II 128	RT	35.00	600.00
80	DEWEY 13	RT	25.00	650.00
80	DUSTY 122	RT	35.00	3600.00
80	FETZER 112	RT	25.00	750.00
80	GERBER 127	RT	30.00	525.00
80	IGOR 23	RT	31.00	375.00
80	JASON 113	RT	20.00	610.00
80	JEREMIAH 119	RT	30.00	550.00
80	KATIE 125	RT	43.00	1200.00
80	LUCKY 115	RT	17.50	450.00
80	MARTIN 111	RT	28.00	425.00
80	MCMAN 21	RT	28.00	775.00
80	MCNEIL 11	RT	25.00	210.00
80	MEG 12	RT	25.00	165.00
80	NORTON 16	RT	33.00	400.00
80	O.J. 130	RT	28.00	200.00
80	OLIN 17	RT	25.00	1300.00
80	PATRICK 117	RT	19.00	800.00
80	POPS 22	RT	29.00	210.00
80	ROCKY 132	RT	33.00	260.00
80	SEAN 131	RT	28.00	275.00
80	SHAW 126	RT	23.00	450.00
80	SHELLY 123	RT	19.00	725.00
80	STARR 133	RT	33.00	550.00
80	WINK 24	RT	25.00	325.00
81	BABY JESUS 37	RT	10.00	125.00
81	BART 134	RT	28.00	285.00
81	BICK 188	RT	35.00	1150.00
81	CAL 142	RT	45.00	1425.00
81	CARDINAL 26	RT	19.00	N/A
81	DAFFY 140	RT	35.00	250.00
81	GNOME CROSSING SIGN 984	RT	39.00	150.00
81	HANS 139	RT	35.00	250.00
81	HOWDY 138	RT	35.00	235.00
81	JACKSON 149	RT	25.00	300.00
81	LENNON 135	RT	35.00	2000.00
81	LIEF 159	RT	31.00	225.00
81	PALMER 25	RT	35.00	300.00
81	PATCH 146	RT	33.00	200.00
81	RUMPKIN 160	RT	28.00	180.00
81	SANDY 93	RT	31.00	130.00
81	SECRET 190	RT	30.00	325.00
81	SOL 163	RT	35.00	200.00
81	SUNNY 150	RT	35.00	600.00
81	SWIFTY 96	RT	16.50	150.00
81	TEX 41	RT	28.00	1950.00
82	BANBURY 30	RT	25.00	215.00
82	BOOTS 31	RT	35.00	150.00
82	EGGBERT 194	RT	31.00	150.00
82	LUCKY II 198	RT	25.00	475.00
82	MICHAEL 195	RT	28.00	245.00
82	MRS. WINK 32	RT	28.00	80.00
82	NEMO 193	RT	29.00	160.00
82	TOM CLARK CREATIONS SIGN 994	RT	*	50.00
83	ABEDNEGO 1014	RT	35.00	120.00
83	BLARNEY 1004	RT	33.00	90.00
83	BUZZY 68	RT	15.00	60.00
83	CHEESE 189	RT	25.00	230.00
83	CHEF 98	RT	13.00	50.00

YR	NAME	LIMIT	ISSUE	TREND
83	CINDY 92	RT	35.00	225.00
83	CURTIS 94	RT	45.00	90.00
83	FRANKLIN 28	RT	65.00	200.00
83	GARLENA 97	RT	13.00	60.00
83	GUS 89	RT	27.00	140.00
83	HAZEL WITCH 1003	RT	45.00	175.00
83	HEATHER & JAN 77	RT	48.00	200.00
83	HYKE 27	RT	90.00	250.00
83	JUAN 70	RT	36.00	150.00
83	JULIE 85	RT	27.00	100.00
83	KERNEL 75	RT	50.00	140.00
83	MARTHA & JAY 73	RT	65.00	150.00
83	MESHACH 1013	RT	35.00	75.00
83	NICK O' TIME 1010	RT	31.00	325.00
83	PAPA & PRINCESS 69	RT	45.00	125.00
83	PARSLEY, SAGE, THYME 1001	RT	110.00	200.00
83	PLENTY 33	RT	33.00	115.00
83	SATURDAY 90	RT	25.00	70.00
83	SHADRACH 1012	RT	35.00	75.00
83	SKIPPER 1005	RT	38.00	110.00
83	SMOKEY 95	RT	40.00	90.00
83	SOUTH BEND 43	RT	19.00	110.00
83	SPUD 34	RT	28.00	75.00
83	STU 71	RT	40.00	65.00
83	TEDDY 81	RT	25.00	N/A
83	WILBUR 1006	RT	34.00	90.00
83	WINK TOO 88	RT	28.00	75.00
83	WIZ, THE- 87	RT	35.00	85.00
83	WOODY & CHANE 1015	RT	65.00	150.00
84	7-UP 1070	RT	500.00	1800.00
84	ACE OF SPADES 1035	RT	25.00	87.00
84	ANAHEIM 1025	RT	22.00	81.00
84	BEN 1069	RT	48.00	N/A
84	BONNIE 1051	RT	25.00	N/A
84	BUBBLES 1062	RT	15.00	40.00
84	BUTCH, WICK & BISCUIT 1056	RT	70.00	175.00
84	C.D. 1050	RT	33.00	N/A
84	CLAMENTINE 1064	RT	30.00	75.00
84	COLETTE 1028	RT	22.00	45.00
84	D.G. 1031	RT	33.00	210.00
84	DOUG 1045	RT	25.00	N/A
84	EENIE 1021	RT	28.00	65.00
84	ELIZABETH 1017	RT	25.00	45.00
84	FATHER TIME 1008	RT	34.00	80.00
84	GATOR 1032	RT	25.00	185.00
84	GEORGIA 1044	RT	31.00	95.00
84	GNOME OF ZURICH 1007	RT	34.00	125.00
84	GOODFOOT 1063	RT	30.00	125.00
84	HAL 1072	RT	40.00	N/A
84	HAPPY 1061	RT	35.00	N/A
84	HENSON 1059	RT	33.00	65.00
84	HOGAN 1033	RT	35.00	60.00
84	HOMER 1058	RT	33.00	N/A
84	JACK B. NIMBLE 1055	RT	30.00	75.00
84	JACK OF DIAMONDS 1038	RT	25.00	65.00
84	JACKIE B. QUICK 1065	RT	33.00	75.00
84	JOHNNY 1052	RT	25.00	N/A
84	KEN 1026	RT	45.00	110.00
84	KING OF CLUBS 1036	RT	25.00	65.00
84	LANCE 1042	RT	28.00	75.00
84	MABEL 1016	RT	68.00	175.00
84	MADRE 1068	RT	20.00	N/A
84	MCEVER 1067	RT	29.00	60.00
84	MEENIE 1022	RT	28.00	65.00
84	MELCHIOR 1060	RT	40.00	N/A
84	MINIE 1023	RT	25.00	50.00
84	MOE 1024	RT	25.00	60.00
84	MOM TOO 1020	RT	40.00	60.00
84	MUGMON 1011	RT	25.00	N/A
84	N.O. EVELS, THE 1053	RT	70.00	N/A
84	NEWT 1043	RT	28.00	60.00
84	NOEL 1066	RT	55.00	125.00
84	O'NEAL 1019	RT	25.00	45.00
84	PADRE 80	RT	19.00	N/A
84	PAWLEY 1047	RT	31.00	N/A
84	PEANUT 1041	RT	28.00	60.00
84	QUEEN OF HEARTS 1037	RT	25.00	65.00
84	SANTA III 1054	RT	75.00	210.00
84	SHAKESPEARE 1039	RT	73.00	200.00
84	SHEN 1040	RT	60.00	130.00
84	SHORTY 1046	RT	33.00	N/A
84	SORGHUM OF GLADE VALLEY 1057	RT	35.00	85.00
84	THISTLE 1029	RT	80.00	100.00
84	TIM & RANDY 1009	RT	40.00	100.00
84	TOPSIE-TURVIE 1034	RT	38.00	140.00

YR	NAME	LIMIT	ISSUE	TREND
84	VALENTINE (VAL) 1018	RT	30.00	N/A
84	WINKIN, BLINKIN & NOD 1071	RT	65.00	150.00
84	YULE 1048	RT	55.00	140.00
85	JINGLE "E" 1124	RT	15.00	27.00
85	JINGLE "G" 1122	RT	15.00	27.00
85	JINGLE "I" 1120	RT	15.00	22.00
85	JINGLE "J" 1119	RT	15.00	27.00
85	JINGLE "L" 1123	RT	15.00	27.00
85	JINGLE "N" 1121	RT	15.00	27.00
85	LILIBET 1079	RT	17.50	80.00
85	MERRILL & LYNCH 1117	RT	60.00	140.00
86	ALPHA 2014	RT	79.00	N/A
86	BUTTON 1092	RT	30.00	N/A
86	CHIP 1094	RT	38.00	N/A
86	HOLDER 1105	RT	38.00	N/A
86	JULIUS 1097	RT	40.00	N/A
86	MOORE OR LES 1093	RT	65.00	140.00
86	PAR 1096	RT	45.00	N/A
86	RACHEL 1088	RT	65.00	N/A
86	SAMMY 1098	RT	35.00	N/A
86	UNCLE WHIT 1083	RT	65.00	N/A
87	'TWAS THE NIGHT 1130	RT	700.00	N/A
87	CASPAR 1150	RT	45.00	N/A
87	ED 2022	RT	*	140.00
87	TELLY 1189	RT	*	300.00
88	BALTHAZAR 5012	RT	35.00	N/A
88	BROTHER, SIS & DAD 1181	RT	100.00	N/A
88	EUREKA 1115	RT	70.00	N/A
88	PEDRO 1158	RT	35.00	N/A
89	ROSEMARY 1002	RT	65.00	165.00

T. CLARK   **MINIATURES**

YR	NAME	LIMIT	ISSUE	TREND
83	BIRDIE 78	RT	*	100.00
83	EDDIE 83	RT	15.00	45.00
83	FREDDY 79	RT	17.50	100.00
83	JEFF 74	RT	17.00	50.00
83	JENNIE 84	RT	17.00	125.00
83	JOSHUA 82	RT	25.00	100.00
83	POKEY 86	RT	19.00	65.00

T. CLARK   **MOUNTAINEERS**

YR	NAME	LIMIT	ISSUE	TREND
81	APPLE ANNIE 169	RT	48.00	310.00
81	JEREMIAH SALLIE 168	RT	65.00	420.00
81	NELLIE 164	RT	55.00	700.00
82	ENOCH 186	RT	80.00	175.00
82	MATTIE 184	RT	68.00	300.00
82	NATH 185	RT	65.00	400.00

T. CLARK   **NATIVITY**

YR	NAME	LIMIT	ISSUE	TREND
81	INNKEEPER 171	RT	38.00	150.00
81	JOSEPH I 36	RT	35.00	200.00
81	MARY I 35	RT	35.00	175.00
82	ANGEL 196	RT	35.00	120.00
82	SHEPHERD 197	RT	38.00	85.00
83	HERDSMAN 72	RT	33.00	120.00

T. CLARK   **SEA CAPTAINS & SAILORS**

YR	NAME	LIMIT	ISSUE	TREND
81	ABRAHAM 173	RT	65.00	225.00
81	ABRAHAM LAMP 174	RT	80.00	280.00
81	JOCK 172	RT	40.00	175.00
82	PYRATE 181	RT	75.00	780.00
82	SVEN 180	RT	55.00	280.00

T. CLARK   **SPECIAL CHARACTERS**

YR	NAME	LIMIT	ISSUE	TREND
80	SANTA I 121	RT	55.00	330.00
81	HATTIE 137	RT	55.00	250.00
81	LAWRENCE 136	RT	55.00	140.00
81	SLEUTH 179	RT	65.00	500.00
81	ST. FRANCIS 167	RT	50.00	150.00
81	ST. NICK 141	RT	40.00	600.00
82	BELLE KRINGLE 199	RT	55.00	250.00
82	DANIEL BOONE 182	RT	75.00	700.00
82	DANIEL BOONE LAMP 192	RT	85.00	1000.00
83	SANTA II 76	RT	55.00	200.00

T. CLARK   **SPECIAL COMMISSION**

YR	NAME	LIMIT	ISSUE	TREND
78	RUBENSTEIN 39	RT	*	5000.00
80	HARRIS 118	RT	45.00	1200.00
81	ADAM 300	RT	*	210.00
81	FROSTY 304	RT	*	150.00
81	NEY 143	RT	35.00	125.00
81	OLLIE 303	RT	*	140.00
81	SMILEY 301	RT	*	120.00
81	STUCK 302	RT	*	125.00
82	GORDY 40	RT	*	750.00
83	BO SCHEMBECHLER 45	RT	58.00	220.00
83	COTTON 46	RT	*	220.00
83	D.C. 99	RT	*	100.00
83	HAMLET 47	RT	58.00	135.00
83	PA PAW 49	RT	*	600.00
83	WEST VIRGINIA MOUNTAINEER 91	RT	59.00	330.00

YR	NAME	LIMIT	ISSUE	TREND
T. CLARK			**SPECIAL PROMOTIONAL**	
82	UNCLE SAM 83	RT	80.00	250.00
T. CLARK			**THE WIND IN THE WILLOWS**	
82	BADGER 177	RT	40.00	140.00
82	MOLE 176	RT	33.00	90.00
82	RATTY 175	RT	31.00	100.00
82	TOAD I 147	RT	50.00	550.00
82	TOAD II 148	RT	35.00	130.00
T. CLARK			**TRUE BUILDERS OF AMERICA**	
83	DR. GREY 321	RT	120.00	3800.00
83	MISS MARY 320	RT	*	900.00
83	NEWSPAPER BOY 325	RT	120.00	625.00
84	AVIATOR 326	RT	150.00	450.00
84	PARSON PATTERSON 324	RT	150.00	340.00
84	RAILROAD CONDUCTOR 322	RT	120.00	285.00
87	BLACKSMITH 332	RT	150.00	320.00
T. CLARK			**WESTERN**	
83	COWBOY 306	RT	60.00	140.00
83	INDIAN 307	RT	60.00	150.00

CAST ART

YR	NAME	LIMIT	ISSUE	TREND
K. HAYNES			**DREAMSICLES**	
*	BORN THIS DAY	RT	*	N/A
*	SANTA'S LITTLE HELPER	RT	*	N/A
*	SUGARFOOT	RT	*	N/A
*	TINY DANCER	RT	*	N/A
*	WISHFUL THINKING	RT	*	N/A
92	1995 ICE COMMEMORATIVE, THE	RT	35.00	165.00
92	BEST PALS	RT	15.00	45.00
92	CHERUB FOR ALL SEASONS	RT	23.00	85.00
92	DANCE BALLERINA DANCE	RT	37.00	75.00
93	BY THE SILVERY MOON	RT	100.00	300.00
93	FINISHING TOUCHES, THE	RT	85.00	165.00
93	FLYING LESSON, THE	RT	80.00	1000.00
93	FOREVER FRIENDS	RT	15.00	45.00
93	TEETER TOTS	RT	100.00	250.00
94	CUDDLE BLANKET	RT	6.50	14.00
94	EAGER TO PLEASE	RT	6.50	15.00
94	HOLIDAY ON ICE	RT	85.00	140.00
94	I CAN READ	RT	6.50	14.00
94	RECITAL, THE	RT	135.00	240.00
94	SUCKING MY THUMB	RT	6.50	15.00
94	SURPRISE GIFT	RT	6.50	15.00
94	UP ALL NIGHT	RT	6.50	12.00
97	CUTIE PIE	12,500	42.00	42.00
97	HAPPY LANDINGS	RT	88.00	88.00
97	SLEIGH BELLS RING	RT	48.00	48.00
98	HANDMADE WITH LOVE	10000	78.00	78.00
K. HAYNES		**DREAMSICLES AMERICAN CANCER SOCIETY SYMBOL OF SUPPORT**		
96	DAFFODIL DAYS	RT	15.00	15.00
98	WE ARE WINNING	OP	17.00	17.00
K. HAYNES			**DREAMSICLES ANIMALS**	
91	BUNNY HOP	RT	20.00	28.00
91	CARNATION	RT	16.00	30.00
91	DAIRY DELIGHT	RT	28.00	35.00
91	DIMPLES	RT	6.00	12.00
91	GATHERING FLOWERS	RT	18.00	30.00
91	HAMBONE	RT	10.00	18.00
91	HAMLET	RT	10.00	18.00
91	HEY DIDDLE DIDDLE	RT	16.00	25.00
91	HONEY BUN	RT	6.00	12.00
91	PIGLET	RT	10.00	18.00
91	PIGMALION	RT	6.00	12.00
91	PIGTAILS	RT	6.00	12.00
91	SOAP BOX BUNNY	RT	15.00	25.00
91	SWEET CREAM	RT	29.00	45.00
91	TINY BUNNY	RT	7.00	14.00
91	TRICK OR TREAT	RT	11.00	15.00
92	HELGA	RT	8.00	8.00
92	SARGE	RT	8.00	12.00
92	SIR HAREOLD	RT	39.00	60.00
93	PAL JOEY	RT	13.50	14.00
94	HENNIETTA	RT	28.00	35.00
K. HAYNES			**DREAMSICLES CALENDAR**	
94	AMONG FRIENDS	RT	24.00	55.00
94	AUTUMN LEAVES	RT	24.00	55.00
94	HOLIDAY MAGIC	RT	24.00	55.00
94	LOVE IN BLOOM	RT	24.00	55.00
94	NATURE'S BOUNTY	RT	24.00	55.00
94	NOW GIVE THANKS	RT	24.00	55.00
94	POOL PALS	RT	24.00	55.00
94	RIDE LIKE THE WIND	RT	24.00	55.00
94	SCHOOL DAYS	RT	24.00	55.00
94	SPECIAL DELIVERY	RT	24.00	55.00

YR	NAME	LIMIT	ISSUE	TREND
94	SPRINGTIME FROLIC	RT	24.00	55.00
94	WINTER WONDERLAND	RT	24.00	55.00
K. HAYNES			**DREAMSICLES CHRISTMAS**	
91	CHERUB & CHILD	RT	14.00	42.00
91	FOREVER YOURS	RT	44.00	65.00
91	HEAVENLY DREAMER	RT	10.50	15.00
91	MISCHIEF MAKER	RT	10.00	10.00
91	SANTA BUNNY	RT	32.00	40.00
91	SANTA'S ELF	RT	19.00	19.00
91	SITTING PRETTY	RT	9.50	14.00
91	WILDFLOWER	RT	10.00	12.00
92	A CHILD'S PRAYER	RT	7.00	15.00
92	BABY LOVE	RT	7.00	25.00
92	BLUEBIRD ON MY SHOULDER	RT	19.00	30.00
92	BUNDLE OF JOY	RT	7.00	14.00
92	CAROLER-CENTER SCROLL	RT	19.00	38.00
92	CAROLER-LEFT SCROLL	RT	19.00	38.00
92	CAROLER-RIGHT SCROLL	RT	19.00	38.00
92	DREAM A LITTLE DREAM	RT	7.00	15.00
92	LIFE IS GOOD	RT	10.00	10.00
92	LITTLE DARLIN'	RT	7.00	14.00
92	LITTLEST ANGEL	RT	7.00	14.00
93	LITTLE DICKENS	RT	24.00	35.00
93	LONG FELLOW	RT	24.00	35.00
93	ME AND MY SHADOW	RT	19.00	19.00
93	MISS MORNINGSTAR	RT	25.00	25.00
93	SWEET DREAMS	RT	29.00	70.00
94	HERE'S LOOKING AT YOU	RT	25.00	30.00
94	SIDE BY SIDE	RT	32.00	32.00
96	HOMEWARD BOUND	RT	78.00	100.00
97	TIME TO DASH	YR	78.00	78.00
98	ALL ABOARD!	YR	78.00	78.00
K. HAYNES			**DREAMSICLES COLLECTORS CLUB**	
93	A STAR IS BORN	RT	30.00	120.00
93	DAYDREAM BELIEVER	RT	30.00	80.00
94	JOIN THE FUN	RT	*	45.00
94	MAKIN' A LIST	RT	48.00	85.00
96	BEE-FRIENDED	YR	25.00	25.00
96	HEAVENLY FLOWERS	RT	25.00	40.00
96	STAR SHOWER	RT	*	40.00
97	EDITOR'S CHOICE NEWSLETTER PARTICIPATION GIFT	*	*	N/A
97	FIRST BLUSH	12500	50.00	50.00
97	FREE SPIRIT	RT	*	N/A
97	GOLDEN HALO "GOOD SAMARITAN" AWARD	*	*	N/A
97	PEACEABLE KINGDOM	OP	14.75	15.00
97	SWEET TOOTH	OP	20.00	20.00
98	LET'S GET TOGETHER	YR	*	N/A
K. HAYNES			**DREAMSICLES DAY EVENT FIGURINES**	
96	GLAD TIDINGS	RT	15.00	50.00
96	TIME TO RETIRE	RT	15.00	28.00
97	GOLDEN RULE, THE	YR	19.00	19.00
98	DAY OF FUN, A	YR	18.00	18.00
K. HAYNES			**DREAMSICLES HEAVENLY CLASSICS**	
96	BUNDLES OF LOVE	RT	78.00	1400.00
HAYNES/HACKETT			**DREAMSICLES HEAVENLY CLASSICS**	
96	HEAVEN'S GATE	RT	118.00	150.00
97	DREAMBOAT	RT	90.00	90.00
97	MAKING MEMORIES	SU	97.00	97.00
K. HAYNES			**DREAMSICLES KIDS**	
97	ANTICIPATION	OP	30.00	30.00
K. HAYNES			**DREAMSICLES LIMITED EDITION**	
96	CHILD IS BORN, A	10000	95.00	120.00
K. HAYNES			**DREAMSICLES SPECIAL EDITION**	
96	CAROUSEL RIDE- MUSICAL	OP	150.00	150.00
K. HAYNES			**GIFT TO CORONA CITIZENS**	
96	CORONA CENTENNIAL PIECE	250	*	210.00

CAVANAGH GROUP
*

			COCA-COLA BRAND HERITAGE COLLECTION	
94	SANTA AT THE LAMPPOST	OP	50.00	50.00
94	SINGLE POLAR BEAR ON ICE	OP	40.00	40.00
94	SINGLE POLAR BEAR ON ICE SNOWGLOBE	CL	40.00	40.00
95	ALWAYS	CL	30.00	30.00
95	ELAINE	CL	100.00	100.00
95	GIRL ON SWING	CL	100.00	100.00
95	PLAYING WITH DAD	CL	40.00	40.00
96	COCA-COLA STAND	OP	45.00	45.00
96	COOL BREAK	OP	40.00	45.00
96	DECORATING THE TREE	CL	45.00	45.00
96	GONE FISHING	OP	60.00	60.00
96	HOLLYWOOD SNOWGLOBE	OP	50.00	50.00
96	REFRESHING TREAT	CL	45.00	45.00
96	SANTA WITH POLAR BEAR SNOWGLOBE	OP	50.00	50.00
96	SAY UNCLE SNOWGLOBE	CL	50.00	50.00

YR	NAME	LIMIT	ISSUE	TREND
N. ROCKWELL		COCA-COLA BRAND HERITAGE COLLECTION		
95	BOY AT WELL	CL	60.00	60.00
95	BOY FISHING	CL	60.00	60.00
96	REFRESHING BREAK	OP	60.00	60.00
S. STEARMAN		COCA-COLA BRAND HERITAGE COLLECTION		
95	HOMECOMING,THE	CL	125.00	125.00
H. SUNDBLOM		COCA-COLA BRAND HERITAGE COLLECTION		
94	DEAR SANTA, PLEASE PAUSE HERE	CL	80.00	85.00
94	EIGHT POLAR BEARS ON WOOD	5000	100.00	100.00
94	EXTRA BRIGHT REFRESHMENT SNOWGLOBE	CL	50.00	60.00
94	GOOD BOYS AND GIRLS	CL	80.00	80.00
94	GOOD BOYS AND GIRLS SNOWGLOBE	CL	45.00	45.00
94	SANTA AT HIS DESK	CL	80.00	80.00
94	SANTA AT HIS DESK SNOWGLOBE	CL	45.00	45.00
94	SANTA AT THE FIREPLACE	CL	80.00	80.00
94	SANTA AT THE LAMPPOST SNOWGLOBE	CL	50.00	50.00
94	TWO POLAR BEARS ON ICE	OP	30.00	30.00
95	HOSPITALITY	5000	35.00	35.00
96	BUSY MAN'S PAUSE	OP	80.00	80.00
96	FOR ME	OP	40.00	40.00
*		COCA-COLA BRAND HERITAGE COLLECTION MUSICALS		
94	CALENDAR GIRL 1916	CL	60.00	60.00
94	EIGHT POLAR BEARS ON WOOD	10000	150.00	150.00
94	HILDA CLARK 1901	CL	60.00	60.00
94	HILDA CLARK 1903	CL	60.00	60.00
94	SANTA'S SODA SHOP	OP	50.00	50.00
95	ALWAYS	CL	50.00	50.00
H. SUNDBLOM		COCA-COLA BRAND HERITAGE COLLECTION MUSICALS		
93	DEAR SANTA, PLEASE PAUSE HERE	CL	50.00	100.00
94	GOOD BOYS AND GIRLS	CL	100.00	100.00
94	SANTA AT HIS DESK	CL	100.00	100.00
94	SANTA AT THE FIREPLACE	CL	100.00	100.00
94	TWO POLAR BEARS ON ICE	CL	45.00	45.00
95	SSSHHH!	OP	35.00	55.00
95	THEY REMEMBERED ME	5000	50.00	50.00
97	TIME TO SHARE	5000	100.00	100.00
*		COCA-COLA BRAND NORTH POLE BOTTLING WORKS		
95	ALL IN A DAYS WORK	CL	50.00	50.00
95	AN ELF'S FAVORITE CHORE	CL	30.00	30.00
95	CHECKING HIS LIST	CL	30.00	30.00
95	FILLING OPERATIONS	CL	45.00	45.00
95	FRONT OFFICE	CL	50.00	50.00
95	KITCHEN CORNER	CL	55.00	55.00
95	MAINTENANCE MISCHIEF	CL	25.00	25.00
95	MAKING THE SECRET SYRUP	CL	30.00	30.00
95	PIPE MAINTENANCE	OP	20.00	20.00
95	QUALITY CONTROL	CL	30.00	30.00
95	RESTOCKING THE VENDING MACHINE	OP	30.00	30.00
95	SANTA AT HIS DESK	OP	30.00	30.00
95	SANTA'S OFFICE	OP	50.00	50.00
95	TAKING A BREAK	OP	20.00	20.00
95	TOP SECRET	CL	30.00	30.00
95	VAULT, THE	OP	25.00	25.00
96	AN ARTIST'S TOUCH	CL	25.00	25.00
96	ART DEPARTMENT	CL	50.00	50.00
96	BIG AMBITIONS	CL	25.00	25.00
96	DELIVERY FOR MRS. CLAUS	CL	25.00	25.00
96	ELF IN TRAINING	CL	25.00	25.00
96	OOPS!	CL	25.00	25.00
96	ORDER DEPARTMENT	CL	55.00	55.00
96	PRECIOUS CARGO	CL	25.00	25.00
96	SHIPPING DEPARTMENT	CL	55.00	55.00
96	SPECIAL DELIVERY	CL	25.00	25.00
96	STROKE OF GENIUS	CL	25.00	25.00
*		COCA-COLA BRAND POLAR BEAR COLLECTION		
95	ALWAYS	OP	30.00	30.00
96	COCA-COLA STAND	OP	45.00	45.00
96	COOL BREAK	OP	40.00	40.00
96	DECORATING THE TREE	OP	45.00	45.00
96	PLAYING WITH DAD	OP	40.00	40.00
96	REFRESHING TREAT	OP	45.00	45.00
*		COCA-COLA BRAND POLAR BEAR COLLECTION MUSICALS		
95	ALWAYS	OP	50.00	50.00
H. SUNDBLOM		COCA-COLA BRAND SANTA ANIMATION		
91	SSSHHH!	CL	100.00	325.00
92	SANTA'S PAUSE FOR REFRESHMENT	CL	100.00	225.00
93	TRIMMING THE TREE	CL	100.00	195.00
95	SANTA AT THE LAMPPOST	CL	110.00	110.00
*		COCA-COLA BRAND TOWN SQUARE COLLECTION		
92	AFTER SAKTING	CL	8.00	10.00
92	BRINGING IT HOME	CL	8.00	17.00
92	COCA-COLA AD CAR	CL	9.00	25.00
92	COCA-COLA DELIVERY TRUCK	CL	15.00	27.00
92	DELIVERY MAN	CL	8.00	15.00

YR	NAME	LIMIT	ISSUE	TREND
92	GIL THE GROCER	CL	8.00	13.00
92	HORSE-DRAWN WAGON	CL	12.00	40.00
92	THIRSTY THE SNOWMAN	CL	9.00	20.00
*		**COCA-COLA POLAR BEAR CUBS**		
96	BALANCING ACT	OP	16.00	16.00
96	BEAR CUB CLUB, THE	OP	20.00	20.00
96	BEARING GIFTS OF LOVE AND FRIENDSHIP	1000	30.00	30.00
96	BIG CATCH, THE	OP	15.00	15.00
96	CHRISTMAS WISH	OP	10.00	10.00
96	ENJOY	OP	12.00	12.00
96	FRIENDS ARE FOREVER	OP	16.00	16.00
96	GIVING IS BETTER THAN RECEIVING	OP	12.00	12.00
96	GOOD FRIENDS ALWAYS STICK TOGETHER	OP	16.00	16.00
96	HELPING HAND	OP	20.00	20.00
96	I'M NOT SLEEPY...REALLY	OP	10.00	10.00
96	IT'S MY TURN TO HIDE	OP	12.00	12.00
96	LOOK WHAT I CAN DO	OP	12.00	12.00
96	PATIENCE IS A VIRTUE	OP	16.00	16.00
96	RIDE'EM COWBOY	OP	20.00	20.00
96	SKATING RINK ROMANCE	OP	16.00	16.00
96	SNOWDAY ADVENTURES	OP	12.00	12.00
96	SWEET DREAMS	OP	12.00	12.00
96	THANKS FOR THE LIFT	OP	20.00	20.00
96	THERE'S NOTHING LIKE A FRIEND	OP	16.00	16.00
96	TO GRANDMOTHER'S HOUSE WE GO	OP	12.00	12.00
96	WHO SAYS GIRLS CAN'T THROW	OP	16.00	16.00
97	CARING IS A SPECIAL GIFT	OP	16.00	16.00
97	EVERYBODY NEEDS A FRIEND	OP	12.00	12.00
97	FIRE CHIEF	OP	16.00	16.00
97	FRIENDS DOUBLE THE JOY	OP	30.00	30.00
97	FRIENDSHIP IS A HIDDEN TREASURE	OP	20.00	20.00
97	FRIENDSHIP IS THE BEST GIFT	OP	16.00	16.00
97	FRIENDSHIP IS THE PERFECT MEDICINE	OP	20.00	20.00
97	FRIENDSHIP MAKES LIFE BEARABLE	OP	16.00	16.00
97	GRADUATION DAY	OP	12.00	12.00
97	HAPPY BIRTHDAY	OP	12.00	12.00
97	I CAN'T BEAR TO SEE YOU SICK	OP	20.00	20.00
97	I GET A KICK OUT OF YOU	OP	16.00	16.00
97	ICE SKATING SNOWGLOBE	OP	45.00	45.00
97	JUST FOR YOU	OP	16.00	16.00
97	JUST LIKE MY DAD	OP	16.00	16.00
97	LITTLE BOYS ARE BEST	OP	16.00	16.00
97	LITTLE GIRLS ARE SPECIAL	OP	16.00	16.00
97	LOVE BEARS ALL THINGS	OP	12.00	12.00
97	LUCKY O'BEAR AND MCPUFFIN	OP	16.00	16.00
97	POLAR BEAR CUB SIGN	OP	16.00	16.00
97	SEEDS OF FRIENDSHIP GROW WITH CARING	OP	16.00	16.00
97	SLED RACING SNOWGLOBE	OP	35.00	35.00
97	THANKS FOR ALL YOU TAUGHT ME	OP	16.00	16.00
97	VISITS WITH YOU ARE SPECIAL	OP	20.00	20.00
97	WE DID IT	OP	20.00	20.00
97	WITH ALL MY HEART	OP	16.00	16.00
97	YOU'RE THE GREATEST	OP	20.00	20.00
*		**COCA-COLA POLAR BEAR CUBS MUSICALS**		
97	DAD SHOWED ME HOW	OPO	35.00	35.00

CHARLES SADEK IMPORT CO.

YR	NAME	LIMIT	ISSUE	TREND
73	BLUEBIRD	RT	132.00	N/A
74	OWL	RT	95.00	N/A
74	SWANS	RT	240.00	N/A
75	BLUE JAY GROUP	RT	150.00	N/A
75	HUMMINGBIRD GROUP	RT	450.00	N/A
77	INDIGO BUNTING	RT	90.00	N/A
77	LAZULI BUNTING	RT	90.00	N/A
77	ROBIN GROUP	RT	750.00	N/A
77	SCARLET TARANGER	RT	90.00	N/A
81	QUAIL COVEY	RT	275.00	N/A
84	EAGLE FAMILY	RT	190.00	N/A
86	HUMMINGBIRD GROUP	RT	240.00	N/A
87	BLUEBIRD FAMILY	RT	300.00	N/A
88	ROBIN FAMILY	RT	300.00	N/A
90	LION FAMILY	RT	300.00	N/A
92	FLYCATCHER	RT	400.00	N/A
94	DIAMOND DOVES	RT	275.00	N/A

CHARMING TAILS
D. GRIFF

YR	NAME	LIMIT	ISSUE	TREND
93	MOUSE WITH APPLE CANDLEHOLDER-PEEKING	RT	14.00	70.00
93	MOUSE WITH APPLE CANDLEHOLDER-SLEEPING	RT	14.00	70.00
94	CHESTNUT CHAPEL	RT	45.00	75.00
94	JAWBREAKERS MUSICAL WATERGLOBE	RT	40.00	80.00
94	MINI SURPRISE WATERGLOBE	RT	22.00	55.00
94	MOUSE ON CHEESE WATERGLOBE	RT	44.00	44.00
94	MOUSE ON RUBBER DUCK WATERGLOBE	RT	44.00	125.00
94	MOUSE ON VINE BASKET	RT	55.00	55.00
94	OLD COB MILL	SO	45.00	65.00

YR	NAME	LIMIT	ISSUE	TREND
94	ROCKING MICE MUSICAL	RT	65.00	200.00
94	SAILING AWAY WATERGLOBE	RT	50.00	95.00
94	SHARING THE WARMTH	RT	40.00	80.00
94	SWEET DREAMS WATERGLOBE	RT	40.00	40.00
94	TOGETHER AT CHRISTMAS WATERGLOBE	RT	30.00	65.00
94	TRIMMING THE TREE WATERGLOBE	RT	45.00	120.00
95	CARROT POST OFFICE	RT	45.00	70.00
95	PUMPKIN PLAYTIME MUSICAL	RT	35.00	75.00
95	UNDERWATER EXPLORER WATERGLOBE	RT	45.00	100.00
95	UP, UP AND AWAY MUSICAL	RT	70.00	160.00
96	CANDY APPLE CANDY STORE	9000	45.00	75.00
96	SENDING A LITTLE SNOW YOUR WAY	RT	15.00	15.00
97	LOVE DOESN'T COME WITH INSTRUCTIONS	15000	19.00	125.00
98	EVEN THE UPS AND DOWNS ARE FUN	*	16.50	17.00
98	IT'S YOUR MOVE	*	17.00	17.00
98	PICTURE PERFECT	*	18.50	19.00
98	STEADY WINS THE RACE 1998 LIMITED EDITION	*	20.00	20.00
98	THERE'S NO US WITHOUT U	*	19.50	20.00

D. GRIFF — AUTUMN HARVEST

YR	NAME	LIMIT	ISSUE	TREND
93	CAPS OFF TO YOU	RT	10.00	28.00
93	CORNFIELD FEAST	RT	15.00	90.00
93	FALL FROLICKING	RT	13.00	50.00
93	GOURD SLIDE	RT	16.00	40.00
93	MOUSE CANDLEHOLDER	RT	13.00	90.00
94	FROSTING PUMPKINS	RT	16.00	38.00
94	JUMPIN' JACK O' LANTERNS	RT	16.00	30.00
94	MOUSE ON LEAF CANDLEHOLDER	RT	17.00	85.00
94	OPEN PUMPKIN	RT	15.00	68.00
94	PAINTING LEAVES	RT	16.00	38.00
94	PEAR CANDLEHOLDER	RT	14.00	50.00
94	PUMPKIN SLIDE	RT	15.00	55.00
94	PUMPKIN VOTIVE	RT	14.00	50.00
94	STUMP CANDLEHOLDERS	RT	20.00	100.00
95	CANDY CORN VAMPIRE	RT	18.00	38.00
95	GARDEN NAPTIME	RT	18.00	30.00
95	HORN OF PLENTY	RT	20.00	33.00
95	LET'S GET CRACKIN'	RT	20.00	30.00
95	PUMPKIN PIE	RT	16.00	35.00
95	REGINALD'S HIDEAWAY	RT	14.00	15.00
96	PICKIN' TIME	RT	16.00	19.00
98	BOOOO!	*	18.00	18.00
98	JACK O'LANTERN JALOPY	*	18.00	18.00
98	PUMPKIN'S FIRST PUMPKIN	*	18.00	18.00
98	STACK O'LANTERNS	*	18.00	18.00
98	TURKEY WITH DRESSING	*	18.00	18.00
CL	HARVEST FRUIT	RT	16.00	45.00

D. GRIFF — DECK THE HALLS

YR	NAME	LIMIT	ISSUE	TREND
98	AIR MAIL TO SANTA	*	13.00	13.00
98	BUNDLE OF JOY-BABY'S FIRST CHRISTMAS	*	13.00	13.00
98	HEADING FOR THE SLOPES	*	13.00	13.00
98	OUR FIRST CHRISTMAS TOGETHER	*	13.00	13.00
98	PINE CONE PREDICAMENT-ANNUAL	*	13.00	13.00
98	SKI JUMPER	*	13.00	13.00
98	TRICYCLE BUILT FROM TREATS	*	13.00	13.00

D. GRIFF — EASTER BASKET

YR	NAME	LIMIT	ISSUE	TREND
93	ANIMALS IN EGGS	RT	11.00	40.00
93	DUCKLING IN EGG WITH MOUSE	RT	15.00	165.00
94	JELLY BEAN FEAST	RT	14.00	30.00
94	PEEK-A-BOO	RT	12.00	35.00
94	WANNA PLAY?	SO	15.00	125.00
95	BINKEY'S BOUNCING BUNDLE	SO	18.00	45.00
95	LOOK OUT BELOW	RT	20.00	30.00
95	WANT A BITE?	RT	18.00	28.00
98	CHICKIE BACK RIDE	*	15.00	15.00
98	PAINT BY PAWS	*	16.00	16.00

D. GRIFF — EVENT PIECES

YR	NAME	LIMIT	ISSUE	TREND
96	TAKE ME HOME	CL	17.00	50.00

D. GRIFF — EVERYDAY SERIES

YR	NAME	LIMIT	ISSUE	TREND
93	BINKEY IN A LILY	RT	16.00	40.00
93	HIDE AND SEEK	RT	14.00	140.00
93	KING OF THE MUSHROOM	RT	16.00	40.00
93	LOVE MICE	RT	15.00	80.00
93	MOUSE ON A GRASSHOPPER	RT	15.00	160.00
93	MOUSE ON DRAGONFLY	RT	17.00	275.00
93	RABBIT DAFFODIL CANDLEHOLDER	RT	14.00	160.00
93	SPRING FLOWERS	RT	16.00	45.00
93	TWO PEAS IN A POD	RT	14.00	35.00
94	AFTER LUNCH SNOOZE	RT	15.00	25.00
94	BINKEY GROWING CARROTS	RT	15.00	50.00
94	BINKEY'S NEW PAL	RT	14.00	35.00
94	BUNNY WITH CARROT CANDLEHOLDER	RT	12.00	85.00
94	BUTTERFLY SMELLING ZINNIA	RT	15.00	65.00
94	CAN I KEEP HIM?	SO	13.00	285.00
94	CHAUNCEY GROWING TOMATOES	RT	15.00	50.00
94	DUCKLING VOTIVE	RT	12.00	30.00

YR	NAME	LIMIT	ISSUE	TREND
94	GET WELL SOON	RT	15.00	30.00
94	HOPE YOU'RE FEELING BETTER	RT	15.00	30.00
94	HOW DO YOU MEASURE LOVE	RT	15.00	38.00
94	IT'S NOT THE SAME WITHOUT YOU	RT	15.00	25.00
94	MACKENZIE GROWING BEANS	RT	15.00	45.00
94	MENDER OF BROKEN HEARTS	RT	15.00	40.00
94	SLUMBER PARTY	RT	16.00	40.00
94	THANKS FOR BEING THERE	CL	15.00	30.00
95	BINKEY'S FIRST CAKE	RT	16.00	35.00
95	FEEDING TIME	RT	16.00	40.00
95	HELLO SWEET PEA	CL	12.00	12.00
95	I'M BERRY HAPPY	RT	15.00	28.00
95	MOUSE IN STRAWBERRY	RT	12.00	50.00
95	ONE FOR ME	RT	16.00	40.00
95	ONE FOR YOU	RT	16.00	33.00
95	PICKING PEPPERS	RT	12.00	25.00
95	SURROUNDED BY FRIENDS	RT	16.00	33.00
95	TUGGIN' TWOSOME	SO	18.00	40.00
95	WHY HELLO THERE	RT	14.00	20.00
95	YOU ARE NOT ALONE	RT	20.00	45.00
96	FRAGILE, HANDLE WITH CARE	15000	19.00	19.00
96	LOVE BLOOMS	RT	16.00	45.00
96	TAKE TIME TO REFLECT	RT	16.00	20.00
96	TRAINING WINGS	RT	16.00	20.00

D. GRIFF — LAZY DAYS OF SUMMER

YR	NAME	LIMIT	ISSUE	TREND
98	CAMPING OUT	*	18.50	19.00
98	COME ON IN-THE WATER'S FINE!	*	18.00	18.00
98	DAY AT THE LAKE, A	*	18.50	19.00
98	STEWART'S DAY IN THE SUN	*	17.00	17.00
98	TOASTING MARSHMALLOWS	*	20.00	20.00

D. GRIFF — SQUASHVILLE SERIES

YR	NAME	LIMIT	ISSUE	TREND
93	MOUSE ON STAR TREETOP	RT	14.00	50.00
94	HOT DOGGIN'	RT	20.00	40.00
94	LADY BUG EXPRESS	RT	18.00	130.00
94	MACKENZIE AND MAXINE CAROLING	RT	18.00	55.00
94	MACKENZIE BUILDING A SNOWMOUSE	SO	18.00	100.00
94	MOUSE CANDLE CLIMBER	RT	8.00	40.00
94	MOUSE CARD HOLDER	RT	13.00	40.00
94	MOUSE IN TREE HOLE CANDLEHOLDER	RT	17.00	80.00
94	MOUSE ON BASKET	RT	50.00	50.00
94	MOUSE ON VINE CANDLEHOLDER	RT	55.00	55.00
94	MOUSE ON VINE WREATH	RT	55.00	55.00
94	PYRAMID WITH MICE CANDLEHOLDER	RT	40.00	40.00
95	BINKEY'S 1995 ICE SCULPTURE	SO	20.00	40.00
95	MAIL MOUSE	RT	12.00	30.00
95	PEAR TAXI	RT	16.00	38.00
95	SLEIGH RIDE	SO	16.00	70.00
96	AIRMAIL	CL	16.00	16.00
96	ALL I CAN GIVE YOU IS ME	RT	15.00	35.00
96	ALL SNUG IN THEIR BEDS WATERGLOBE	RT	30.00	50.00
96	BABY'S FIRST CHRISTMAS WATERGLOBE	RT	28.00	50.00
96	BINKEY IN A BED OF FLOWERS	RT	15.00	35.00
96	EXTRA! EXTRA!	RT	14.00	25.00
96	JINGLE BELLS	RT	15.00	25.00
96	MY NEW TOY	RT	14.00	20.00
96	OOPS! DID I DO THAT?	RT	14.00	25.00
96	PEEKING AT PRESENTS	RT	13.00	19.00
96	REGINALD'S NEWSSTAND	RT	20.00	20.00
96	SNACK FOR THE REINDEER	RT	13.00	38.00
96	TESTING THE LIGHTS	RT	14.00	20.00
96	WAITING FOR CHRISTMAS	14000	16.00	38.00
97	ALL THE TRIMMINGS	YR	15.00	15.00
97	BABY'S FIRST CHRISTMAS	YR	19.00	19.00
98	DASHING THROUGH THE SNOW	*	16.50	17.00
98	MERRY CHRISTMAS FROM OUR HOUSE TO YOUR HOUSE	*	23.00	23.00
98	PLEASE, JUST ONE MORE	*	16.50	17.00
98	REGINALD'S CHOO-CHOO RIDE	*	19.00	19.00
98	TEAM IGLOO 1998 LIMITED EDITION	*	23.00	23.00
98	WHO PUT THAT TREE THERE?	*	16.50	17.00

D. GRIFF — WEDDING

YR	NAME	LIMIT	ISSUE	TREND
98	ALTAR OF LOVE, THE	*	24.00	24.00
98	BEST...BUNNY, THE	*	16.00	16.00
98	GET-AWAY CAR, THE	*	22.00	22.00
98	HERE COMES THE BRIDE	*	17.00	17.00
98	MAID OF HONOR	*	16.00	16.00
98	MY HEART'S ALL AFLUTTER (GROOM)	*	17.00	17.00
98	RING BEARER, THE	*	16.00	16.00
98	TOGETHER FOREVER	*	25.00	25.00
98	WEDDING DAY BLOSSOMS	*	16.00	16.00

CHRISTIAN ULBRICHT USA

C. ULBRICHT

YR	NAME	LIMIT	ISSUE	TREND
97	EAGLE DANCER	3000	240.00	240.00
98	ANGEL	2500	230.00	230.00
98	LAWYER	2500	222.00	222.00

YR	NAME	LIMIT	ISSUE	TREND
98	MR. SNOWMAN	2500	154.00	154.00
98	MRS. SNOWMAN	2500	154.00	154.00
98	SANTA IN CANOE	2500	230.00	230.00
98	SANTA W/SHORT ROBE	2500	222.00	222.00
98	SANTA WITH LONG ROBE	2500	222.00	222.00
98	SUMMER WONDERLAND	3000	230.00	230.00
98	WHITE BUFFALO	3000	240.00	240.00
C. ULBRICHT		**DICKENS CHRISTMAS CAROL**		
96	SCROOGE	5000	228.00	228.00
97	BOB CRATCHIT & TINY TIM	5000	236.00	236.00
98	MRS. CRATCHIT	5000	230.00	230.00
C. ULBRICHT		**GREAT AMERICAN INVENTORS**		
96	THOMAS EDISON	1500	270.00	270.00
97	HENRY FORD	1500	260.00	260.00
98	ALEXANDER GRAHAM BELL	1500	250.00	250.00
C. ULBRICHT		**NUTCRACKER BALLET**		
96	CLARA	5000	219.00	219.00
96	HERR DROSSELMEYER	5000	228.00	228.00
96	MOUSE KING	5000	228.00	228.00
96	PRINCE	5000	219.00	219.00
98	TOY SOLDIER	5000	238.00	238.00
C. ULBRICHT		**PLAYS OF SHAKESPEARE**		
97	JULIET	5000	230.00	230.00
97	SHAKESPEARE	5000	236.00	236.00
98	ROMEO	5000	236.00	236.00
C. ULBRICHT		**THREE MUSKETEERS**		
96	PORTOS	5000	200.00	200.00
C. ULBRICHT		**THREE WISEMEN**		
96	CASPAR	5000	209.00	209.00
C. ULBRICHT		**WIZARD OF OZ**		
97	TIN WOODMAN	5000	230.00	230.00
98	COWARDLY LION	5000	240.00	240.00
98	DOROTHY	5000	230.00	230.00

CHUST COUNTRY

T. NEIFFER		**PIGEON CREEK COLLECTIBLES**		
96	GRAMPY & ME	OP	160.00	160.00
96	OLD FAITHFUL AND OLD GLORY	OP	140.00	140.00

CONSTANCE COLLECTION

C. GUERRA		**ANNUAL SANTA CLAUS BY CONSTANCE**		
91	TEDDY CLAUS	YR	90.00	90.00
92	REACH FOR THE STARS SANTA	YR	90.00	90.00
C. GUERRA		**FRIENDS & FAMILY COLLECTION**		
92	A MOMENT W/MARGO	2500	55.00	55.00
92	ANNETTE & CHRISTIAN	2500	48.00	48.00
92	BUTTERCUPS	2500	35.00	35.00
92	CHELSEA'S EASTER	2500	37.00	37.00
92	CHRISTOPHER	2500	37.00	37.00
92	COVERED WITH LOVE	2500	60.00	60.00
92	ELIZABETH AND PHILLIP	2500	55.00	55.00
92	FIRST LOVE	2500	57.00	57.00
92	FOREVER FRIENDS	2500	51.00	51.00
92	GRANDPOPS ANGEL	2500	51.00	51.00
92	LITTLE SIS	2500	48.00	48.00
92	LOVES TENDER TOUCH	2500	33.00	33.00
92	MICHELLI BELLE	2500	31.00	31.00
92	MISSY	2500	31.00	31.00
92	MOTHER'S DAY BOUQUET	2500	42.00	42.00
92	ONE ON ONE FATHER/SON	2500	55.00	55.00
92	PARTY PAMMY	2500	31.00	31.00
92	PILLOW TALK	2500	42.00	42.00
92	PITZ AND SARA	2500	48.00	48.00
92	RACHEL'S BLUE BIRD	2500	42.00	42.00
92	SPECIAL SISTERS	2500	51.00	51.00
92	TIMEOUT TO LOVE	2500	37.00	37.00
92	TOGETHERNESS	2500	49.00	49.00
C. GUERRA		**HEAVEN SENT**		
92	ALLELUIA	2500	45.00	45.00
92	CHRISTENING DAY	2500	55.00	55.00
92	ENDURING FAITH	2500	55.00	55.00
92	LOVE IS PATIENT	2500	49.00	49.00
C. GUERRA		**KITTY KAT KLUB**		
90	KASSANDRA KITTY	1500	30.00	30.00
90	KATRINA	1500	30.00	30.00
90	KLARA KITTY	1500	30.00	30.00
90	KLARENCE KITTY	1500	30.00	30.00
90	KLAUDIUS KITTY	1500	30.00	30.00
90	KOCKEY KITTY	1500	30.00	30.00
90	KONRAD KITTY	1500	30.00	30.00
90	KOQUETTE KITTY	1500	30.00	30.00
C. GUERRA		**SANTA CLAUS BY CONSTANCE**		
86	JOLLY ST. NICK	4000	72.00	72.00
86	VICTORIAN SANTA	4000	90.00	90.00

YR	NAME	LIMIT	ISSUE	TREND
86	VICTORIAN SANTA WITH BEAR	4000	80.00	80.00
87	ANIMAL SANTA	4000	78.00	78.00
88	AMERICAN TRADITIONAL SANTA	4000	90.00	90.00
88	MIDNIGHT VISIT	4000	112.00	112.00
88	SAINT NICHOLAS OF MYRA	4000	90.00	90.00
88	SANTAS DELIVERY	4000	90.00	90.00
89	COBBLESTONE SANTA	4000	112.00	112.00
89	KITTY CHRISTMAS	4000	112.00	112.00
89	SANTA WITH BOY	1000	90.00	90.00
89	SANTA WITH DEER	4000	112.00	112.00
89	SANTA WITH GIRL	1000	90.00	90.00
89	SANTA WITH LAMB	4000	112.00	112.00
89	SANTA'S SLEIGH	1000	190.00	190.00
89	SIBERIAN SANTA	1000	190.00	190.00
89	THOMAS NAST SANTA	4000	112.00	112.00
90	CANDY CANE SANTA	1000	124.00	124.00
90	ELF SANTA	1000	298.00	298.00
90	HUNT SANTA	1000	158.00	158.00
90	KITTY CLAUS	1000	78.00	78.00
90	ROCKINGHORSE SANTA	1000	124.00	124.00
91	FIRST CHRISTMAS	1000	79.00	79.00
91	FIRST FROST	1000	250.00	250.00
91	HEAVENLY BLESSING	1000	79.00	79.00
91	LITTLE BOY'S SANTA	1000	95.00	95.00
91	SANTA'S DANCE	1000	95.00	95.00
91	SANTA'S DAY OFF	1000	90.00	90.00
91	SANTA'S GIRL	1000	95.00	95.00
92	HUSH! HUSH! SANTA	2500	60.00	60.00
92	PEACE ON EARTH	2500	64.00	64.00
92	TEST RUN SANTA	2500	79.00	79.00
92	TOUCH UP SANTA	2500	64.00	64.00

C. GUERRA   **SEASONAL SANTA**

YR	NAME	LIMIT	ISSUE	TREND
92	BASES LOADED	2500	90.00	90.00
92	FISHING DAY FUN	2500	90.00	90.00
92	FRESH POWDER FUN	2500	72.00	72.00
92	LOST BALL SANTA	2500	90.00	90.00
92	SPRING SERENITY	2500	112.00	112.00

C. GUERRA   **TENDER TOTS**

YR	NAME	LIMIT	ISSUE	TREND
92	BABY BUNS	2500	31.00	31.00
92	BABY'S BLOCKS	2500	37.00	37.00
92	BABY'S FIRST ABC'S	2500	37.00	37.00
92	FIRST CRAWL	2500	37.00	37.00
92	FIRST DAY HOME (BOY)	2500	35.00	35.00
92	FIRST DAY HOME (GIRL)	2500	35.00	35.00
92	FIRST WORDS	2500	37.00	37.00
92	NIGHT-NIGHT	2500	31.00	31.00
92	PLAYMATES	2500	33.00	33.00
92	SUGARPLUM DARLINGS	2500	37.00	37.00
92	TOYLAND	2500	37.00	37.00

C. GUERRA   **THE BRIAR PATCH**

YR	NAME	LIMIT	ISSUE	TREND
90	BARBARA BUNNY	1500	30.00	30.00
90	BARTHOLEMUE BUNNY	1500	30.00	30.00
90	BENEDICT BUNNY	1500	30.00	30.00
90	BERNARD BUNNY	1500	30.00	30.00
90	BERNICE BUNNY	1500	30.00	30.00
90	BERTRUM BUNNY	1500	30.00	30.00
90	BETSEY BUNNY	1500	30.00	30.00
90	BIRTHA BUNNY	1500	30.00	30.00
90	BLOSSUM BUNNY	1500	30.00	30.00
90	BONNIE BUNNY	1500	30.00	30.00
90	BRAIDA BUNNY	1500	30.00	30.00
90	BROTHERLY BUNNY	1500	30.00	30.00
90	BROWNIE BUNNY	1500	30.00	30.00
90	BUSTER BUNNY	1500	30.00	30.00
92	BUNNY'S BASKET	2500	22.00	22.00
92	GRANDFATHER BUN	2500	22.00	22.00
92	GRANDMOTHER BUNNY	2500	22.00	22.00
92	LOVE BUN	2500	22.00	22.00
92	MOTHER WITH TWINS	2500	22.00	22.00
92	NEW MAMMA BUNNY	2500	22.00	22.00
92	NUMBER ONE BUN	2500	22.00	22.00
92	PAPPA BUNNY	2500	22.00	22.00
92	PONDERING BUN	2500	22.00	22.00
92	PROUD PAPPA BUNNY	2500	22.00	22.00
92	WOODLAND BUNNY	2500	32.00	32.00

C. GUERRA   **THE GOLDEN AMERICANS**

YR	NAME	LIMIT	ISSUE	TREND
91	ANDRES AND SAM	1500	37.00	37.00
91	BELINDA	1500	31.00	31.00
91	BLESSED WITH LOVE	1500	55.00	55.00
91	DADDY'S DARLING	1500	48.00	48.00
91	EFFIE AND COMPANY	1500	31.00	31.00
91	EMMA AND NICKIE	1500	37.00	37.00
91	ENDLESS LOVE	1500	48.00	48.00
91	FELICIA & FLUFF	1500	37.00	37.00
91	FROZEN FRIENDS	1500	42.00	42.00

YR	NAME	LIMIT	ISSUE	TREND
91	GILBERT	1500	31.00	31.00
91	GLORYA	1500	75.00	75.00
91	GRANDMAS LOVE	1500	65.00	65.00
91	HANNAH AND KITTY	1500	42.00	42.00
91	INTO THE LIGHT	1500	31.00	31.00
91	LEARNING TO BRAID	1500	42.00	42.00
91	LETTIE THE DOLLMAKER	1500	48.00	48.00
91	MISSING YOU	1500	37.00	37.00
91	NEW PUPS	1500	31.00	31.00
91	PARTY TIME PALS	1500	55.00	55.00
91	PENNY PINCHER	1500	48.00	48.00
91	PLAY TIME	1500	31.00	31.00
91	PRAYING PALS	1500	31.00	31.00
91	PREACHER MAN	1500	31.00	31.00
91	PUDDLES	1500	37.00	37.00
91	PUPPY LOVE	1500	37.00	37.00
91	RUBY RAE AND TOM-TOM	1500	37.00	37.00
91	SCHOOL DAZE	1500	31.00	31.00
91	SUNDAY MORNING	1500	75.00	75.00
91	SWEET ASSURANCE	1500	48.00	48.00
91	SWEET DREAMS	1500	37.00	37.00
92	ANNELLE	2500	37.00	37.00
92	BALLA RENA	2500	31.00	31.00
92	BESTEST FRIENDS	2500	31.00	31.00
92	BUNNY LOVE	2500	31.00	31.00
92	CHRIS MISS	2500	31.00	31.00
92	CHURCH LADY ELLIE	2500	37.00	37.00
92	CHURCH LADY ETHEL	2500	37.00	37.00
92	CHURCH LADY PEARLE	2500	37.00	37.00
92	DUTCHIE	2500	31.00	31.00
92	FIRST POSITION	2500	31.00	31.00
92	FREE KICK DICK	2500	31.00	31.00
92	JOY BOY	2500	31.00	31.00
92	LITTLE CHASE	2500	31.00	31.00
92	LITTLE MAGIC	2500	31.00	31.00
92	LOVING EWE	2500	31.00	31.00
92	LOVING EWE TOO!	2500	33.00	33.00
92	MANDAS NABBIT	2500	31.00	31.00
92	P.S. I LOVE YOU	2500	42.00	42.00
92	PREPPIE GREGORY	2500	37.00	37.00
92	PREPPIE WINTHROP	2500	31.00	31.00
92	PRIMA DONA	2500	31.00	31.00
92	PUPPY LOVING	2500	37.00	37.00
92	QUARTERBACK JACK	2500	31.00	31.00
92	SCHOOL GIRL SAL	2500	31.00	31.00
92	SCHOOL GIRL SUE	2500	31.00	31.00
92	THERE YOU ARE!	2500	48.00	48.00
92	TOO MUCH HOMEWORK	2500	48.00	48.00
92	VALENTINE OF MINE	2500	31.00	31.00
92	VICTORY	2500	31.00	31.00

C. GUERRA VICTORIANA COLLECTION

YR	NAME	LIMIT	ISSUE	TREND
91	FRITZ	1500	37.00	37.00
91	JULIA	1500	37.00	37.00
91	PENELOPE	1500	37.00	37.00
91	ROSIE	1500	37.00	37.00
91	VICTORIA	1500	37.00	37.00

COUNTRY ARTISTS
*

YR	NAME	LIMIT	ISSUE	TREND
93	FREEDOM OF THE SEAS	RT	325.00	325.00

D. IVEY

YR	NAME	LIMIT	ISSUE	TREND
94	LORD OF THE SKIES	RT	795.00	795.00
94	SPIRIT OF FREEDOM	1500	750.00	750.00
95	GRACEFUL FLIGHT	950	695.00	695.00
95	VISIONS OF DAWN	250	2,700.00	2700.00

B. PRICE

YR	NAME	LIMIT	ISSUE	TREND
94	GUARDIAN OF THE HERD	RT	695.00	695.00
94	SUMMER DREAMS	RT	395.00	395.00
96	BROKEN DREAMS	850	375.00	375.00
96	CHALLENGE, THE	850	325.00	325.00
96	EVER PATIENT	850	375.00	375.00
96	FAMILY ADVENTURE	850	375.00	375.00
96	RESTFUL DAYS	850	750.00	750.00

R. SEFTON

YR	NAME	LIMIT	ISSUE	TREND
94	COMING HOME	RT	395.00	395.00
95	STALLIONS OF THE CAMARGUE	950	795.00	795.00
96	A TRIAL OF STRENGTH	850	750.00	750.00
96	SPIRIT OF THE PLAINS	850	850.00	850.00

K. SHERWIN

YR	NAME	LIMIT	ISSUE	TREND
94	LAST FURROW, THE	RT	395.00	395.00
95	WINTER HOLT	1500	750.00	750.00
96	AFTER THE STORM	850	450.00	450.00
96	FIRST LIGHT	850	450.00	450.00
96	SPRING OF LIFE	850	295.00	295.00

The 1995 Collectors Society Member Edition for the Swarovski Collectors Society, Inspiration Africa—The Lion *is worth between $400 and $900.*

Swarovski's 1987 Collectors Society Annual Edition, The Love Birds/ Togetherness *by Max Schreck, has skyrocketed in price.*

The 1990 Swarovski Collectors Society Annual Edition, The Dolphins' *value has soared on the secondary market to more than six times its original price of $225.*

Inspiration Africa—The Kudu *was the 1994 Collectors Society Member Edition for the Swarovski Collector's Society.*

A 1988 addition to Enesco's Memories of Yesterday line, Hush *by Mable Lucie Attwell has been retired.*

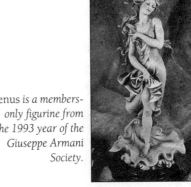

Venus *is a members-only figurine from the 1993 year of the Giuseppe Armani Society.*

YR	NAME	LIMIT	ISSUE	TREND
S. LANGFORD			**BALD EAGLE COLLECTION**	
95	BALD EAGLE LANDING	OP	128.00	135.00
95	BALD EAGLE SOARING	OP	63.00	74.00
95	HIDDEN SANCTUARY	2500	289.00	289.00
95	SPIRIT OF FREEDOM	1500	750.00	765.00
D. IVEY			**BIG CAT COLLECTION**	
95	CHEETAH	OP	198.00	205.00
95	COUGAR	OP	182.50	195.00
95	LEOPARD	OP	198.00	205.00
95	SNOW LEOPARD	OP	189.00	200.00
95	TIGER	OP	215.00	220.00
*			**BIRDS**	
98	AWAKE AT DAWN	850	295.00	295.00
D. IVEY			**BIRDS**	
98	MAJESTIC GRACE	850	425.00	425.00
98	VIEWS OF THE RIVER	850	850.00	850.00
B. PRICE			**BIRDS**	
98	WOODLAND GLADE	850	650.00	650.00
K. SHERWIN			**GRAYWOLF COLLECTION**	
92	DAWN CHORUS	OP	375.00	400.00
92	FIRST ICE OF WINTER	RT	450.00	475.00
92	HIGH GROUND	OP	225.00	250.00
92	LARGE HOWLING WOLF	OP	150.00	165.00
92	MEDIUM HOWLING WOLF	OP	95.00	105.00
92	MOTHER & CUB	OP	175.00	195.00
92	RUNNING FREE	OP	175.00	195.00
92	SMALL HOWLING WOLF	OP	49.00	55.00
92	WOLF CUBS	OP	135.00	145.00
92	WOLF KISS	OP	250.00	275.00
92	WOLF PAIR	OP	225.00	250.00
95	UNTAMED WILDERNESS	3500	450.00	450.00
S. LANGFORD			**KINGDOM OF THE EAGLE**	
98	COMMAND OF THE WATER	YR	135.00	135.00
K. SHERWIN			**KINGDOM OF THE EAGLE**	
98	DIFFICULT CROSSING, A	950	425.00	425.00
R. SEFTON			**NATIVE AMERICAN**	
98	STRENGTH OF THE SPIRIT	500	1,300.00	1300.00
K. SHERWIN			**NATIVE AMERICAN**	
98	LITTLE SPIRIT	950	340.00	340.00
R. SEFTON			**NATURE TRAIL**	
98	SHELTERED SECLUSION	850	325.00	325.00
D. IVEY			**OWLS**	
98	HERALD OF SPRING	2500	325.00	325.00
B. PRICE			**PAWPRINTS/TUSKERS**	
98	FUN & GAMES	3500	75.00	75.00
B. PRICE			**PENGUIN COLLECTION**	
95	MINIATURE PENGUIN	OP	25.00	28.00
95	MOTHER & CHICKS	OP	110.00	120.00
95	PENGUIN CHICK SLIDING	OP	53.00	55.00
95	PENGUIN CHICKS GROUP	OP	75.00	80.00
95	PENGUIN CHICKS KISSING	OP	58.00	62.00
95	PENGUIN FAMILY	OP	169.00	180.00
D. IVEY			**WILDLIFE COLLECTION**	
97	NEW ARRIVALS	850	385.00	385.00
97	REMOTE HEIGHTS	850	385.00	385.00
K. SHERWIN			**WILDLIFE COLLECTION**	
97	AN EARLY THAW	950	375.00	375.00
97	WARRIOR'S GIFT, THE	950	325.00	325.00

CREART

F. CONTRERAS			**AFRICAN WILDLIFE**	
93	CAPE BUFFALO	1500	418.00	418.00
94	NUMA LION'S HEAD	2500	418.00	418.00
E. MARTINEZ			**AFRICAN WILDLIFE**	
94	GRUMBLER CAPE BUFFALO	1500	498.00	498.00
V. PEREZ			**AFRICAN WILDLIFE**	
93	TRAVIESO	1500	198.00	198.00
F. CONTRERAS			**AMERICAN WILDLIFE**	
93	AMERICAN SYMBOL EAGLE	1500	246.00	246.00
93	RED FOX, THE	1500	199.00	199.00
93	WILD AMERICAN BISON	1500	338.00	338.00
C. ESTEVEZ			**AMERICAN WILDLIFE**	
94	CATAMOUNTAIN	2500	118.00	118.00
94	OUT OF THE DEN PUMA	1500	130.00	130.00
94	PUFFINS	1500	258.00	258.00
E. MARTINEZ			**AMERICAN WILDLIFE**	
93	BUENOS DIAS JACK RABBIT	1500	218.00	218.00
93	HOWLING COYOTE	1500	199.00	199.00
94	FREEDOM EAGLE	1500	500.00	500.00
B. NELSON			**AMERICAN WILDLIFE**	
94	AMBUSHING PUMA	1950	150.00	150.00
94	BRIEFLY REST PUMAS	1950	250.00	250.00
94	RED-TAILED HAWK	1950	130.00	130.00

YR NAME	LIMIT	ISSUE	TREND
V. PEREZ		**AMERICAN WILDLIFE**	
93 SCENT OF HONEY BEAR	1500	398.00	398.00
93 WHITE BLIZZARD WOLF	1500	275.00	275.00
94 OVER THE TOP PUMA	1500	398.00	398.00
94 SINGING TO THE MOON I WOLF	1500	398.00	398.00
94 SINGING TO THE MOON II WOLF	1500	358.00	358.00
J. ROBISON		**BIRDS OF PREY**	
94 GYRFALCON	450	1,300.00	1300.00
94 VIGILANT EAGLE	650	780.00	780.00
F. CONTRERAS		**NATURE'S CARE**	
93 DOE & FAWNS	2500	99.00	99.00
93 EAGLE & EAGLET	2500	99.00	99.00
93 GORILLA & BABY	2500	99.00	99.00
93 LIONESS & CUBS	2500	99.00	99.00
93 WOLF & PUPS	2500	99.00	99.00
C. ESTEVEZ		**NATURE'S CARE**	
93 OTTERS	2500	99.00	99.00
E. MARTINEZ		**NATURE'S CARE**	
93 JACK RABBIT & YOUNG	2500	99.00	99.00
V. PEREZ		**NATURE'S CARE**	
93 GRIZZLY & CUBS	2500	99.00	99.00
93 PENGUIN AND CHICKS	2500	99.00	99.00

CRYSTAL WORLD
*

	LIMIT	ISSUE	TREND
		ALL GOD'S CREATURES	
97 ALLIGATOR	*	100.00	100.00
97 BUFFALO	*	350.00	350.00
97 GIANT SEA TURTLE	*	250.00	250.00
97 JUNIOR	*	110.00	110.00
97 MAMA ELEPHANT	*	250.00	250.00
97 PROUD PEACOCK	*	150.00	150.00
N. MULARGIA		**ALL GOD'S CREATURES**	
97 MAJESTIC BALD EAGLE	*	1,100.00	1100.00
N. MULARGIA		**ANIMAL FRIENDS COLLECTION**	
86 MINI BUTTERFLY	CL	15.00	18.00
86 MINI DACHSHUND	CL	15.00	18.00
86 MINI FROG MUSHROOM	CL	15.00	18.00
86 MINI KOALA	CL	15.00	18.00
86 MINI MOUSE	CL	15.00	18.00
86 MINI RABBIT	CL	15.00	18.00
86 MINI SWAN	OP	15.00	15.00
93 PIG	CL	50.00	50.00
94 OWLS	OP	53.00	53.00
95 WILBUR IN LOVE	OP	90.00	90.00
R. NAKAI		**ANIMAL FRIENDS COLLECTION**	
83 ALLIGATOR	CL	46.00	55.00
83 LARGE MOUSE	CL	36.00	42.00
83 LARGE PIG	CL	50.00	60.00
83 LARGE RABBIT	CL	50.00	60.00
83 LARGE TURTLE	CL	56.00	65.00
83 MEDIUM MOUSE	CL	28.00	33.00
83 MEDIUM PIG	CL	32.00	38.00
83 MEDIUM TURTLE	CL	38.00	45.00
83 MOUSE STANDING	CL	34.00	41.00
83 SMALL ELEPHANT	CL	40.00	48.00
83 SMALL MOUSE	CL	20.00	24.00
83 SMALL PIG	CL	22.00	26.00
83 SMALL RABBIT	CL	28.00	35.00
83 SMALL TURTLE	CL	28.00	35.00
84 BEAVER	CL	30.00	36.00
84 BUTTERFLY	CL	50.00	60.00
84 DACHSHUND	CL	28.00	33.00
84 DOG	CL	28.00	33.00
84 EXTRA LARGE PEACOCK	CL	420.00	500.00
84 LARGE HIPPO	CL	50.00	60.00
84 LARGE KANGAROO	CL	50.00	60.00
84 LARGE KOALA BEAR	CL	69.00	85.00
84 LARGE PEACOCK	CL	147.00	177.00
84 MINI TURTLE	CL	18.00	22.00
84 PEACOCK	CL	50.00	60.00
84 PENGUIN	CL	34.00	41.00
84 POODLE	CL	30.00	36.00
84 PORCUPINE	CL	42.00	50.00
84 SMALL HIPPO	CL	30.00	35.00
84 SMALL KANGAROO	CL	34.00	40.00
84 SMALL KOALA	CL	28.00	32.00
84 SMALL PEACOCK	CL	37.00	44.00
85 LARGE ELEPHANT	CL	54.00	65.00
85 LARGE LION	CL	60.00	72.00
85 RACOON	CL	50.00	60.00
85 SMALL LION	CL	36.00	43.00
85 SQUIRREL	CL	30.00	36.00
86 UNICORN	CL	110.00	132.00
87 LARGE CIRCUS PUPPY	CL	50.00	60.00

YR	NAME	LIMIT	ISSUE	TREND
87	LARGE PANDA	CL	45.00	54.00
87	LARGE PLAYFUL PUP	CL	85.00	102.00
87	LARGE POODLE	CL	64.00	76.00
87	LARGE RABBIT W/CARROT	CL	55.00	66.00
87	LARGE SNOWBUNNY	CL	45.00	54.00
87	MOTHER KOALA AND CUB	CL	55.00	64.00
87	PENGUIN ON CUBE	CL	30.00	36.00
87	POSING PENGUIN	CL	85.00	102.00
87	RHINOCEROS	CL	55.00	66.00
87	SMALL CIRCUS PUPPY	CL	28.00	33.00
87	SMALL PANDA	OP	58.00	58.00
87	SMALL PLAYFUL PUP	CL	32.00	32.00
87	SMALL POODLE	CL	35.00	42.00
87	SMALL RABBIT W/CARROT	CL	32.00	36.00
87	SMALL RACOON	CL	30.00	36.00
87	SMALL SNOWBUNNY	CL	25.00	30.00
87	WALRUS	CL	70.00	84.00
89	MINI RAINBOW DOG	CL	25.00	30.00
89	MINI RAINBOW OWL	CL	25.00	30.00
89	MINI RAINBOW PENGUIN	CL	25.00	30.00
89	MINI RAINBOW SQUIRREL	CL	25.00	30.00
91	SPIKE	CL	50.00	60.00
91	SPOT	CL	50.00	60.00
93	TURTLE	CL	65.00	65.00
94	CHEESE MOUSE	OP	53.00	53.00
94	SEAL	CL	46.00	46.00
95	TEA TIME	OP	50.00	50.00

T. SUZUKI — **ANIMAL FRIENDS COLLECTION**

YR	NAME	LIMIT	ISSUE	TREND
90	BABY DINOSAUR	CL	50.00	60.00
90	BARNEY DOG	CL	32.00	38.00
90	BETSY BUNNY	CL	32.00	38.00
90	CLARA COW	CL	32.00	38.00
90	GEORGIE GIRAFFE	CL	32.00	38.00
90	HENRY HIPPO	CL	32.00	38.00
90	JUMBO ELEPHANT	OP	32.00	32.00
90	MIKEY MONKEY	CL	32.00	38.00
90	PUPPY LOVE	CL	45.00	54.00
92	TRUMPETING ELEPHANT	CL	50.00	50.00
93	PLAYFUL SEAL	OP	42.00	42.00
93	PUPPY-GRAM	OP	70.00	70.00
94	MOZART	OP	48.00	48.00
94	PLAYFUL PUP	OP	53.00	53.00
94	SWEETIE	OP	28.00	28.00
94	WILBUR THE PIG	OP	48.00	48.00
95	FIDO THE DOG	CL	27.00	27.00
95	FRISKY FIDO	CL	27.00	27.00
95	LING LING	OP	53.00	53.00
95	PERCY PIGLET	OP	19.00	19.00

N. MULARGIA — **BIRD COLLECTION**

YR	NAME	LIMIT	ISSUE	TREND
86	BIRD BATH	CL	54.00	65.00

R. NAKAI — **BIRD COLLECTION**

YR	NAME	LIMIT	ISSUE	TREND
83	LARGE OWL	CL	44.00	54.00
83	MEDIUM OWL	CL	50.00	60.00
83	MINI OWL	CL	20.00	25.00
83	SMALL OWL	CL	22.00	26.00
84	BIRD FAMILY	CL	22.00	26.00
84	LOVE BIRDS	CL	44.00	54.00
85	EXTRA LARGE PARROT	CL	300.00	360.00
85	SMALL PARROT	CL	100.00	120.00
87	LARGE PARROT	CL	130.00	160.00
91	PARROT COUPLE	CL	90.00	108.00

T. SUZUKI — **BIRD COLLECTION**

YR	NAME	LIMIT	ISSUE	TREND
90	OLLIE OWL	CL	32.00	37.00
90	SMALL WISE OWL	CL	40.00	48.00
90	TREE TOP OWLS	CL	96.00	105.00
90	WISE OWLS	CL	55.00	65.00

N. MULARGIA — **BY THE BEAUTIFUL SEA COLLECTION**

YR	NAME	LIMIT	ISSUE	TREND
87	PALM TREE	CL	160.00	190.00
93	HARBOR LIGHTHOUSE	OP	75.00	75.00

R. NAKAI — **BY THE BEAUTIFUL SEA COLLECTION**

YR	NAME	LIMIT	ISSUE	TREND
83	LARGE CRAB	CL	20.00	24.00
83	LARGE OYSTER	CL	30.00	36.00
83	MINI OYSTER	CL	12.00	15.00
83	SMALL CRAB	CL	28.00	33.00
83	SMALL OYSTER	CL	18.00	22.00
84	FISH	CL	36.00	43.00
88	DANCING DOLPHIN	CL	130.00	156.00
88	ISLAND PARADISE	CL	90.00	108.00
88	LARGE LIGHTHOUSE	CL	150.00	180.00
88	SMALL DOLPHIN	CL	55.00	65.00
88	SMALL ISLAND PARADISE	CL	50.00	60.00
88	SMALL LIGHTHOUSE	OP	80.00	80.00
91	BEAVER	CL	47.00	47.00
91	PENGUIN ON CUBE	CL	40.00	40.00
92	TROPICAL FISH	CL	95.00	95.00

YR	NAME	LIMIT	ISSUE	TREND
92	TUXEDO PENGUIN	CL	75.00	75.00
93	EXTRA LARGE OYSTER W/PEARL	CL	75.00	75.00
93	SAILBOAT	OP	100.00	100.00
94	SEAL	CL	47.00	47.00
96	FREDDY FROG	OP	30.00	30.00
96	FRIEDA FROG	OP	37.00	37.00
96	PELICAN	OP	65.00	65.00
96	PENGUIN ON CUBE	OP	48.00	48.00
T. SUZUKI		**BY THE BEAUTIFUL SEA COLLECTION**		
88	HATCHING SEA TURTLE	OP	45.00	45.00
92	BABY SEAL	OP	21.00	21.00
92	CUTE CRAB	OP	27.00	27.00
92	PLAYFUL DOLPHINS	CL	60.00	60.00
92	SEASIDE PELICAN	CL	55.00	55.00
92	WHALES, THE	CL	60.00	72.00
93	PLAYFUL SEAL	OP	45.00	45.00
94	OSCAR OTTER	OP	105.00	105.00
N. MULARGIA		**BY THE LAKE COLLECTION**		
86	LOVE SWANS	OP	83.00	83.00
96	LARGE LOVE SWANS	OP	252.00	252.00
R. NAKAI		**BY THE LAKE COLLECTION**		
83	LARGE FROG	CL	30.00	36.00
83	MINI FROG	CL	14.00	17.00
83	SMALL FROG	CL	26.00	32.00
83	SMALL SWAN	CL	28.00	34.00
84	DUCK	CL	30.00	36.00
84	FROG & MUSHROOM	CL	46.00	55.00
85	BUTTERFLY CATERPILLAR	CL	40.00	48.00
85	BUTTERFLY ON DAISY	CL	30.00	36.00
85	SMALL SWAN	CL	45.00	45.00
87	KING SWAN	CL	110.00	132.00
87	LARGE SWAN	CL	100.00	100.00
87	MEDIUM SWAN	OP	63.00	63.00
87	MINI SWAN	OP	28.00	28.00
87	SMALL SWAN	OP	32.00	32.00
90	DUCK FAMILY	CL	70.00	84.00
T. SUZUKI		**BY THE LAKE COLLECTION**		
90	SWAN FAMILY	CL	70.00	84.00
A. KATO		**CASTLES AND LEGENDS**		
91	MAJESTIC CASTLE	OP	390.00	390.00
N. MULARGIA		**CASTLES AND LEGENDS**		
90	I LOVE YOU UNICORN	CL	58.00	70.00
90	PEGASUS	CL	50.00	60.00
90	RAINBOW UNICORN	OP	50.00	50.00
90	UNICORN	CL	38.00	45.00
92	MINI FANTASY CASTLE	OP	40.00	40.00
95	LARGE FANTASY COACH	OP	368.00	368.00
95	MEDIUM FANTASY COACH	OP	158.00	158.00
95	MINI MOUSE CASTLE	OP	52.00	52.00
95	SMALL FANTASY COACH	OP	100.00	100.00
95	SMALL MOUSE COACH	OP	95.00	95.00
R. NAKAI		**CASTLES AND LEGENDS**		
87	ICE CASTLE	CL	150.00	180.00
87	RAINBOW CASTLE	OP	150.00	150.00
88	IMPERIAL CASTLE	OP	320.00	320.00
88	MYSTIC CASTLE	OP	90.00	90.00
88	SMALL ICE CASTLE	CL	90.00	108.00
89	DRAGON BABY	CL	80.00	96.00
89	MAGIC FAIRY	CL	40.00	48.00
89	MINI RAINBOW CASTLE	OP	60.00	60.00
89	STAR FAIRY	CL	65.00	78.00
89	STARLIGHT CASTLE	CL	155.00	185.00
89	UNICORN & FRIEND	CL	100.00	120.00
91	CASTLE IN THE SKY	CL	150.00	180.00
92	SMALL FANTASY CASTLE	OP	85.00	85.00
93	LARGE FANTASY CASTLE	OP	230.00	230.00
93	MEDIUM FANTASY CASTLE	OP	130.00	130.00
94	CASTLE RAINBOW RAINBOW MT. BS.	OP	1,575.00	1575.00
94	CASTLE ROYALE/CLEAR MOUNTAIN BS.	OP	130.00	130.00
95	TREASURE CASTLE	OP	63.00	63.00
96	EMERALD CASTLE	OP	105.00	105.00
T. SUZUKI		**CELEBRATION OF LIFE COLLECTION**		
97	BABY BOY CARRIAGE	*	50.00	50.00
97	BABY GIRL CARRIAGE	*	50.00	50.00
N. MULARGIA		**CLOWN COLLECTION**		
92	BABY CLOWN	CL	30.00	36.00
92	FLOWER CLOWN	CL	70.00	84.00
96	BO-BO THE CLOWN	OP	53.00	53.00
R. NAKAI		**CLOWN COLLECTION**		
85	ACROBATIC CLOWN	CL	50.00	60.00
85	BASEBALL CLOWN	CL	54.00	64.00
85	CLOWN ON UNICYCLE	CL	54.00	64.00
85	GOLF CLOWN	CL	54.00	65.00
85	JUGGLER	CL	54.00	65.00

YR	NAME	LIMIT	ISSUE	TREND
85	LARGE CLOWN	CL	42.00	50.00
85	LARGE JACK IN THE BOX	CL	64.00	77.00
85	SMALL CLOWN	CL	30.00	36.00
85	SMALL JACK IN THE BOX	CL	24.00	29.00
85	TENNIS CLOWN	CL	54.00	65.00
J. MAKOTO		**CRYSTAL CONCERTO COLLECTION**		
97	CLARINET	*	225.00	225.00
N. MULARGIA		**DECORATIVE ITEM COLLECTION**		
94	SAN FRANCISCO DOME PAPERWEIGHT	CL	75.00	75.00
96	FABULOUS FIFTIES JUKEBOX	OP	79.00	79.00
R. NAKAI		**DECORATIVE ITEM COLLECTION**		
87	STATUE OF LIBERTY	OP	65.00	65.00
87	STATUE OF LIBERTY, THE	OP	365.00	365.00
88	EMPIRE STATE BLDG.	CL	120.00	120.00
88	NATIVITY PAPERWEIGHT	CL	100.00	120.00
90	LIBERTY ISLAND	OP	95.00	95.00
90	MANHATTAN ISLAND	OP	275.00	275.00
91	POLAR BEAR PAPERWEIGHT	OP	98.00	98.00
91	WORLD TRADE CENTER	CL	168.00	168.00
92	HEART CLOCK PAPERWEIGHT	CL	100.00	100.00
92	MANHATTAN REFLECTIONS	OP	95.00	95.00
92	NIAGARA FALLS PAPERWEIGHT	OP	85.00	85.00
92	TWIN TOWERS	OP	137.00	137.00
93	DIAMOND 100MM	OP	525.00	525.00
93	DIAMOND 50MM	OP	70.00	70.00
93	DIAMOND 75MM	OP	285.00	285.00
93	MANATEE PAPERWEIGHT	OP	125.00	125.00
93	MANHATTAN ISLAND	OP	105.00	105.00
94	NY SKYLINE CLOCK PAPERWEIGHT	CL	158.00	158.00
94	WASHINGTON DC CITYSCAPE PAPERWEIGHT	OP	105.00	105.00
94	WASHINGTON DC SKYLINE CLOCK PAPERWEIGHT	CL	158.00	158.00
94	WASHINGTON VIETNAM MEMORIAL PAPERWEIGHT	CL	105.00	105.00
95	BOSTON "CITYSCAPE" PAPERWEIGHT	OP	105.00	105.00
95	MED. BOSTON SKYLINE PAPERWEIGHT	OP	80.00	80.00
95	MED. CHICAGO SKYLINE CLOCK PAPERWEIGHT	CL	158.00	158.00
95	MED. PHILADELPHIA SKYLINE PAPERWEIGHT	OP	80.00	80.00
95	PHILADELPHIA CITYSCAPE PAPERWEIGHT	OP	105.00	105.00
95	SAN FRANCISCO SKYLINE CLOCK PAPERWEIGHT	CL	158.00	158.00
96	CRYSTAL EGG AND STAND	OP	83.00	83.00
96	DIAMOND 40MM	OP	48.00	48.00
I. NAKAMURA		**DECORATIVE ITEM COLLECTION**		
89	CHICAGO SKYLINE PAPERWEIGHT	OP	150.00	150.00
89	SAN FRANCISCO SKYLINE PAPERWEIGHT	OP	150.00	150.00
89	WASHINGTON SKYLINE PAPERWEIGHT	OP	150.00	150.00
90	BASEBALL PAPERWEIGHT	CL	170.00	195.00
90	FISHING PAPERWEIGHT	CL	170.00	195.00
90	GOLFING PAPERWEIGHT	CL	170.00	195.00
90	TENNIS PAPERWEIGHT	CL	170.00	190.00
91	DALLAS SKYLINE PAPERWEIGHT	OP	180.00	180.00
93	SMALL SAN FRANCISCO SKYLINE PAPERWEIGHT	OP	45.00	45.00
G. VEITH		**DECORATIVE ITEM COLLECTION**		
88	EMPIRE STATE BLDG.	CL	120.00	120.00
88	NY SKYLINE PAPERWEIGHT	OP	100.00	100.00
92	SMALL NY PAPERWEIGHT	OP	45.00	45.00
94	MED. NY SKYLINE PAPERWEIGHT	OP	80.00	80.00
94	MED. SAN FRANCISCO SKYLINE PAPERWEIGHT	OP	80.00	80.00
94	MED. WASH. DC SKYLINE PAPERWEIGHT	OP	80.00	80.00
94	NY "CITYSCAPE" PAPERWEIGHT	OP	105.00	105.00
94	NY DOME PAPERWEIGHT	CL	75.00	75.00
94	SAN FRANCISCO CITYSCAPE PAPERWEIGHT	OP	105.00	105.00
94	WASHINGTON DC DOME PAPERWEIGHT	CL	75.00	75.00
R. NAKAI		**FRUIT COLLECTION**		
85	LARGE APPLE	OP	44.00	44.00
85	MEDIUM APPLE	OP	30.00	30.00
85	PEAR	CL	30.00	36.00
85	SMALL APPLE	OP	15.00	15.00
85	STRAWBERRIES	CL	28.00	33.00
87	MINI APPLE	OP	15.00	15.00
91	LARGE PINEAPPLE	CL	42.00	50.00
91	MEDIUM PINEAPPLE	CL	27.00	33.00
91	SMALL PINEAPPLE	CL	16.00	19.00
93	MEDIUM APPLE W/RED HEART	OP	37.00	37.00
93	SMALL APPLE W/RED HEART	OP	21.00	21.00
96	PINEAPPLE	OP	53.00	53.00
R. NAKAI		**GAMBLER COLLECTION**		
91	LUCKY 7	CL	50.00	60.00
91	MINI SLOT MACHINE	OP	30.00	30.00
91	SMALL DICE	OP	27.00	27.00
92	MINI ROLLING DICE	OP	32.00	32.00
93	LARGE ROLLING DICE	OP	60.00	60.00
93	MEDIUM ROLLING DICE	OP	48.00	48.00
93	SMALL ROLLING DICE	CL	40.00	40.00
94	LUCKY ROLL	OP	95.00	95.00
94	SUPER SLOT	OP	295.00	295.00
97	LUCKY DIE	*	69.00	69.00

YR	NAME	LIMIT	ISSUE	TREND
T. SUZUKI			**GAMBLER COLLECTION**	
91	LARGE SLOT MACHINE	OP	83.00	83.00
91	SMALL SLOT MACHINE	OP	70.00	70.00
N. MULARGIA			**HOLIDAY TREASURE COLLECTION**	
86	NATIVITY	OP	150.00	150.00
R. NAKAI			**HOLIDAY TREASURE COLLECTION**	
85	LARGE ANGEL	CL	30.00	30.00
85	LARGE CHRISTMAS TREE	OP	126.00	126.00
85	MINI ANGEL	CL	16.00	19.00
85	MINI CHRISTMAS TREE	CL	10.00	12.00
85	SMALL CHRISTMAS TREE	OP	50.00	50.00
87	LARGE RAINBOW CHRISTMAS TREE	CL	40.00	40.00
87	SMALL RAINBOW CHRISTMAS TREE	CL	25.00	25.00
90	TRUMPETING ANGEL	CL	60.00	72.00
94	CATHEDRAL W/RAINBOW BASE	OP	104.00	104.00
94	COUNTRY CHURCH	OP	53.00	53.00
94	COUNTRY CHURCH W/RAINBOW BASE	OP	63.00	63.00
94	EXTRA LARGE CHRISTMAS TREE	OP	315.00	315.00
94	MINI ANGEL	CL	25.00	25.00
94	SNOWMAN	CL	38.00	45.00
95	HAPPY BIRTHDAY CAKE	OP	63.00	63.00
95	LARGE ANGEL	OP	53.00	53.00
96	FROSTY	OP	41.00	41.00
T. SUZUKI			**HOLIDAY TREASURE COLLECTION**	
91	HOLY ANGEL BLOWING A TRUMPET	OP	38.00	38.00
91	HOLY ANGEL HOLDING A CANDLE	OP	38.00	38.00
91	HOLY ANGEL PLAYING A HARP	OP	38.00	38.00
91	SMALL NATIVITY	OP	85.00	85.00
97	ANGEL WITH HEART	*	30.00	30.00
R. NAKAI			**IMAGINATION COLLECTION**	
97	FROG PRINCE	*	55.00	55.00
T. SUZUKI			**IMAGINATION COLLECTION**	
98	WISHIN' AND A HOPPIN'	*	95.00	95.00
*			**IT'S RAINING CATS AND DOGS**	
97	SPARKIE	*	50.00	50.00
T. SUZUKI			**IT'S RAINING CATS AND DOGS**	
98	COFFEE BREAK	*	50.00	50.00
98	GLAMOUR PUSS	*	70.00	70.00
A. KATO			**KITTY LAND COLLECTION**	
92	SEE SAW PALS	OP	40.00	40.00
C. KIDO			**KITTY LAND COLLECTION**	
92	KITTEN IN BASKET	OP	35.00	35.00
R. NAKAI			**KITTY LAND COLLECTION**	
84	CAT	CL	36.00	42.00
87	LARGE CAT W/BALL	CL	70.00	84.00
87	SMALL CAT W/BALL	CL	32.00	38.00
89	RAINBOW MINI CAT	CL	25.00	30.00
90	MOONLIGHT CATS	CL	100.00	120.00
91	ROCKABYE KITTY	OP	80.00	80.00
T. SUZUKI			**KITTY LAND COLLECTION**	
90	CAT N MOUSE	CL	45.00	45.00
90	CURIOUS CAT, THE	OP	45.00	45.00
91	CALAMITY KITTY	OP	60.00	60.00
91	HELLO BIRDIE	OP	65.00	65.00
91	KITTY W/BUTTERFLY	OP	60.00	60.00
91	KITTY W/HEART	OP	27.00	27.00
91	LARGE CURIOUS CAT	OP	90.00	90.00
91	PEEKABOO KITTIES	OP	65.00	65.00
91	STROLLING KITTIES	CL	65.00	72.00
92	COUNTRY CAT	OP	60.00	60.00
92	PLAYFUL KITTY	OP	32.00	32.00
93	KITTY KARE	OP	70.00	70.00
93	LARGE PLAYFUL KITTY	CL	50.00	50.00
93	PINKY	CL	50.00	50.00
95	MOONLIGHT KITTIES	OP	83.00	83.00
N. MULARGIA			**LIMITED EDITION COLLECTION**	
86	CRUCIFIX	CL	300.00	360.00
92	SANTA MARIA	CL	1,000.00	1200.00
93	RIVERBOAT	350	570.00	600.00
93	VICTORIAN HOUSE	CL	190.00	190.00
96	MERRY-GO-AROUND	750	280.00	280.00
R. NAKAI			**LIMITED EDITION COLLECTION**	
85	EXTRA LG. EMPIRE STATE BLDG.	CL	1,000.00	1200.00
87	LG. EMPIRE STATE BLDG.	2000	650.00	650.00
89	DREAM CASTLE	500	9,000.00	9000.00
89	GRAND CASTLE	CL	2,500.00	2500.00
91	ELLIS ISLAND	CL	450.00	540.00
92	WHITE HOUSE, THE	CL	3,000.00	3600.00
93	ENCHANTED CASTLE	750	800.00	850.00
94	INDEPENDENCE HALL	750	370.00	370.00
96	EMPIRE STATE BLDG., THE	475	1,315.00	1315.00
T. SUZUKI			**LIMITED EDITION COLLECTION**	
86	AIRPLANE	CL	400.00	480.00
86	EIFFEL TOWER, THE	2000	1,000.00	1000.00

YR	NAME	LIMIT	ISSUE	TREND
87	LG. US CAPITOL BLDG.	CL	1,000.00	1200.00
87	TAJ MAHAL	2000	2,000.00	2000.00
88	SMALL EIFFEL TOWER	2000	500.00	500.00
89	SPACE SHUTTLE LAUNCH	CL	900.00	1080.00
90	TOWER BRIDGE	CL	600.00	720.00
91	CRUISE SHIP	1000	2,000.00	2000.00
93	COUNTRY GRISTMILL	1250	340.00	340.00
95	CLASSIC MOTORCYCLE	950	420.00	520.00
G. VEITH		**LIMITED EDITION COLLECTION**		
87	MANHATTANSCAPE	CL	1,000.00	1200.00
A. KATO		**NEW YORK COLLECTION**		
92	LARGE CONTEMP. EMPIRE STATE BLDG.	CL	475.00	475.00
N. MULARGIA		**NEW YORK COLLECTION**		
87	SMALL STATUE OF LIBERTY	OP	50.00	50.00
89	LIBERTY ISLAND	OP	75.00	75.00
93	HOLIDAY EMPIRE STATE BLDG.	OP	205.00	205.00
93	SMALL MANHATTAN ISLAND	OP	105.00	105.00
R. NAKAI		**NEW YORK COLLECTION**		
85	STATUE OF LIBERTY, THE	OP	250.00	250.00
87	MED. EMPIRE STATE BLDG.	OP	250.00	250.00
87	MED. STATUE OF LIBERTY	OP	120.00	120.00
87	SMALL EMPIRE STATE BLDG.	OP	120.00	120.00
90	MANHATTAN ISLAND	OP	240.00	240.00
91	MINI EMPIRE STATE BLDG.	OP	60.00	60.00
91	WORLD TRADE CENTER BLDG.	OP	170.00	170.00
92	MED. CONTEMP. EMPIRE STATE BLDG.	OP	170.00	170.00
92	MINI EMPIRE STATE BLDG. W/WINDOWS	OP	74.00	74.00
92	MINI STATUE OF LIBERTY	OP	50.00	50.00
92	SMALL CONTEMP. EMPIRE ST. BLDG. MV	CL	95.00	95.00
92	SMALL CONTEMP. EMPIRE STATE BLDG.	CL	95.00	95.00
92	SMALL TWIN TOWERS	OP	130.00	130.00
93	SMALL RAINBOW CONTEMP. EMPIRE	OP	95.00	95.00
95	CHRYSLER BLDG.	OP	275.00	275.00
N. MULARGIA		**RELIGIOUS MOMENT COLLECTION**		
87	CROSS ON MOUNTAIN	CL	30.00	36.00
87	CRUCIFIX	CL	50.00	60.00
87	CRUCIFIX ON MOUNTAIN	CL	40.00	48.00
87	SMALL CROSS	CL	40.00	48.00
88	LARGE CROSS ON MOUNTAIN	CL	85.00	100.00
92	CROSS W/ROSE	CL	30.00	30.00
95	CROSS	OP	32.00	32.00
R. NAKAI		**RELIGIOUS MOMENT COLLECTION**		
87	FACE OF CHRIST	CL	35.00	42.00
87	STAR OF DAVID	CL	40.00	48.00
I. NAKAMURA		**RELIGIOUS MOMENT COLLECTION**		
92	PEACE ON EARTH	CL	95.00	95.00
T. SUZUKI		**RELIGIOUS MOMENT COLLECTION**		
87	CHURCH	CL	40.00	40.00
R. NAKAI		**SEASIDE MEMORIES COLLECTION**		
97	COASTAL LIGHTHOUSE	*	80.00	80.00
T. SUZUKI		**SEASIDE MEMORIES COLLECTION**		
98	LOBSTER	*	125.00	125.00
N. MULARGIA		**SPRING PARADE COLLECTION**		
89	WEDDING COUPLE	OP	75.00	75.00
92	CANDLEHOLDER	CL	125.00	125.00
92	HALF DZ. FLOWER ARRANGEMENT	CL	20.00	20.00
92	HAPPY HEART	CL	25.00	25.00
92	LONG STEM ROSE	OP	35.00	35.00
92	LOVING HEARTS	OP	35.00	35.00
92	MINI WEDDING COUPLE	OP	30.00	30.00
92	WATERFRONT VILLAGE	OP	190.00	190.00
94	RAINBOW ROSE	OP	82.00	82.00
95	DESERT CACTUS	OP	48.00	48.00
95	MEDIUM WEDDING COUPLE	OP	63.00	63.00
96	AMERICAN BEAUTY ROSE	OP	53.00	53.00
R. NAKAI		**SPRING PARADE COLLECTION**		
85	FLOWER BASKET	CL	50.00	60.00
85	WEDDING COUPLE	OP	38.00	38.00
87	RED ROSE	OP	35.00	35.00
87	WHITE ROSE	CL	35.00	42.00
89	LARGE WINDMILL	CL	160.00	190.00
89	SMALL WINDMILL	CL	90.00	108.00
89	SPRING CHICK	OP	50.00	50.00
90	CROCUS	CL	45.00	54.00
91	MINI WINDMILL	CL	63.00	75.00
91	RAINBOW MINI BUTTERFLY	OP	27.00	27.00
94	ENCHANTED ROSE, THE	OP	126.00	126.00
94	LONG STEM ROSE IN VASE	OP	82.00	82.00
95	PINK ROSE	OP	53.00	53.00
95	PINK ROSE IN VASE	OP	41.00	41.00
95	SPRING BUTTERFLY	OP	62.00	62.00
96	SMALL ROSE BOUQUET	OP	45.00	45.00
96	WATER LILY, MEDIUM, AB	OP	210.00	210.00

YR	NAME	LIMIT	ISSUE	TREND
I. NAKAMURA			**SPRING PARADE COLLECTION**	
90	AFRICAN VIOLET	OP	32.00	32.00
90	HYACINTH	OP	50.00	50.00
90	ROSE BASKET	CL	52.00	61.00
92	BARREL CACTUS	CL	45.00	45.00
92	FLOWERING CACTUS	CL	58.00	58.00
93	SONGBIRDS	OP	90.00	90.00
T. SUZUKI			**SPRING PARADE COLLECTION**	
91	BLOSSOM BUNNY	OP	42.00	42.00
91	BUNNIES ON ICE	CL	58.00	58.00
91	BUNNY BUDDY W/CARROT	OP	32.00	32.00
91	CHEEP CHEEP	OP	35.00	35.00
92	CUTE BUNNY	CL	38.00	38.00
92	HUMMINGBIRD	OP	58.00	58.00
92	MINI HUMMINGBIRD	OP	29.00	29.00
92	SPRING FLOWERS	OP	40.00	40.00
97	WATER LILY, SMALL, AB	*	105.00	105.00
S, YAMADA			**SPRING PARADE COLLECTION**	
97	SPRING BLOSSOMS	*	90.00	90.00
*			**TEDDYLAND COLLECTION**	
97	BATTER'S UP	*	60.00	60.00
R. KIDO			**TEDDYLAND COLLECTION**	
91	PLAYGROUND TEDDY	CL	90.00	108.00
N. MULARGIA			**TEDDYLAND COLLECTION**	
86	MINI TEDDY	CL	15.00	18.00
87	BEACH TEDDIES	OP	60.00	60.00
87	LOVING TEDDIES	OP	75.00	75.00
87	SAILING TEDDIES	OP	100.00	100.00
87	TEETER TOTTER TEDDIES	CL	65.00	77.00
88	I LOVE YOU TEDDY	OP	50.00	50.00
88	LARGE BOUQUET TEDDY	CL	50.00	60.00
88	SMALL BOUQUET TEDDY	OP	35.00	35.00
88	TEDDIES AT EIGHT	OP	100.00	100.00
88	TEDDY FAMILY	CL	50.00	60.00
88	TOURING TEDDIES	OP	90.00	90.00
88	WINTER TEDDIES	CL	90.00	108.00
89	SHIPWRECK TEDDIES	CL	100.00	120.00
90	MOUNTAINEER TEDDY	CL	80.00	96.00
90	RAINBOW TEDDIES	CL	95.00	112.00
90	ROCKING HORSE TEDDY	CL	80.00	96.00
90	SMALL LOVING TEDDIES	OP	60.00	60.00
91	SWINGING TEDDY	OP	100.00	100.00
92	ICE CREAM TEDDIES	OP	55.00	55.00
92	PATRIOTIC TEDDY	OP	30.00	30.00
92	SMALL BEACH TEDDIES	OP	55.00	55.00
93	BLACK JACK TEDDIES	OP	97.00	97.00
94	I LOVE YOU TEDDY COUPLE	OP	95.00	95.00
95	COMPUBEAR	OP	63.00	63.00
97	UP AND AWAY	*	79.00	79.00
R. NAKAI			**TEDDYLAND COLLECTION**	
83	LARGE TEDDY BEAR	CL	68.00	75.00
83	MEDIUM TEDDY BEAR	CL	44.00	53.00
83	SMALL TEDDY BEAR	CL	28.00	35.00
85	MOTHER AND CUB	CL	64.00	77.00
87	SKATEBOARD TEDDY	CL	30.00	36.00
87	SKIING TEDDY	OP	50.00	50.00
87	SURFING TEDDY	CL	45.00	54.00
87	TEDDY BEAR CHRISTMAS	OP	100.00	100.00
88	LARGE SURFING TEDDY	CL	80.00	96.00
88	TEDDIES W/HEART	OP	45.00	45.00
89	GOLFING TEDDIES	OP	100.00	100.00
89	HAPPY BIRTHDAY TEDDY	OP	50.00	50.00
89	RAINBOW MINI BEAR	CL	25.00	30.00
89	SPEEDBOAT TEDDIES	OP	90.00	90.00
89	TEDDY W/BALLOON	CL	70.00	84.00
89	VANITY TEDDY	CL	100.00	120.00
89	WINDSURFING TEDDY	CL	85.00	102.00
91	LUCK OF THE IRISH	CL	60.00	72.00
91	SMALL TEDDY W/RED HEART	OP	42.00	42.00
91	TRIM A TREE TEDDY	CL	50.00	50.00
94	TEDDY BEAR	OP	63.00	63.00
94	TEDDY BEAR W/RAINBOW BASE	OP	75.00	75.00
95	GET WELL TEDDY	CL	48.00	48.00
95	I LOVE YOU TEDDY W/LG. HEART	OP	48.00	48.00
96	CUDDLY BEAR	OP	48.00	48.00
H. SERINO			**TEDDYLAND COLLECTION**	
91	SCHOOL BEARS	CL	75.00	90.00
T. SUZUKI			**TEDDYLAND COLLECTION**	
90	BARON VON TEDDY	CL	60.00	72.00
90	CHOO CHOO TEDDY	CL	100.00	120.00
90	STORYTIME TEDDIES	OP	70.00	70.00
90	TRICYCLE TEDDY	CL	40.00	48.00
91	CHRISTMAS WREATH TEDDY	CL	70.00	84.00
91	GUMBALL TEDDY	CL	63.00	63.00

YR	NAME	LIMIT	ISSUE	TREND
91	HEART BEAR	OP	27.00	27.00
91	HIGH CHAIR TEDDY	CL	75.00	90.00
91	MERRY CHRISTMAS TEDDY	OP	55.00	55.00
91	MY FAVORITE PICTURE	OP	45.00	45.00
91	PLAY IT AGAIN TED	OP	65.00	65.00
91	SANTA BEAR CHRISTMAS	OP	70.00	70.00
91	SANTA BEAR SLEIGHRIDE	OP	70.00	70.00
91	SCUBA BEAR	CL	65.00	78.00
92	BILLIARD BUDDIES	OP	70.00	70.00
92	SINGING BABY BEAR	OP	55.00	55.00
93	FLOWER TEDDY	OP	50.00	50.00
95	BABY BEAR'S CHRISTMAS	OP	48.00	48.00
95	FLY A KITE TEDDY	OP	41.00	41.00
95	TEDDY'S SELF PORTRAIT	OP	53.00	53.00
97	JACKPOT TEDDY	*	63.00	63.00
97	TEE-SHOT TEDDY	*	45.00	45.00
98	BROADWAY TED	*	45.00	45.00
98	MYSTIC TEDDY	*	70.00	70.00
*			**VOYAGE COLLECTION**	
97	MEDIUM CRUISE SHIP	*	550.00	550.00
97	SCHOONER	*	60.00	60.00
97	TRUCKIN'	*	260.00	260.00
N. MULARGIA			**VOYAGE COLLECTION**	
91	RAINBOW EXPRESS, THE	CL	125.00	150.00
91	SCHOONER	CL	95.00	95.00
92	SAILING SHIP	OP	38.00	38.00
93	EXPRESS TRAIN	CL	95.00	114.00
95	MINI CRUISE SHIP	OP	105.00	105.00
R. NAKAI			**VOYAGE COLLECTION**	
84	CLASSIC CAR	CL	160.00	192.00
84	LIMOUSINE	CL	46.00	55.00
84	PICKUP TRUCK	CL	38.00	48.00
84	TRACTOR TRAILER	CL	40.00	48.00
90	SQUARE RIGGER	OP	250.00	250.00
93	LARGE SAN FRANCISCO CABLE CAR	OP	59.00	59.00
93	SMALL SAN FRANCISCO CABLE CAR	OP	40.00	40.00
94	BERMUDA RIG SAILBOAT	OP	105.00	105.00
94	MAINSAIL SAILBOAT	OP	230.00	230.00
94	SMALL RIVERBOAT	OP	210.00	210.00
94	SPINMAKER SAILBOAT	OP	265.00	265.00
95	AMISH BUGGY	OP	160.00	160.00
95	AMISH BUGGY W/WOOD BASE	OP	190.00	190.00
95	TALL SHIP	OP	395.00	395.00
T. SUZUKI			**VOYAGE COLLECTION**	
84	SPORTS CAR	CL	140.00	170.00
84	TOURING CAR	CL	140.00	170.00
90	LARGE TRAIN SET	CL	480.00	575.00
90	ORBITING SPACE SHUTTLE	OP	300.00	300.00
90	SMALL AIRPLANE	CL	200.00	240.00
90	SMALL SPACE SHUTTLE LAUNCH	CL	265.00	265.00
90	SMALL TRAIN SET	OP	100.00	100.00
91	LARGE CABLE CAR	OP	130.00	130.00
91	SMALL CABLE CAR	OP	70.00	70.00
91	SMALL ORBITING SPACE SHUTTLE	OP	90.00	90.00
92	FIRE ENGINE	OP	100.00	100.00
92	MINI BI-PLANE	OP	65.00	65.00
92	MINI CABLE CAR	CL	40.00	40.00
94	SMALL CRUISE SHIP	OP	575.00	575.00
96	SMALL CLASSIC MOTORCYCLE	OP	210.00	210.00
97	GRAND CABLE CAR	*	50.00	50.00
N. MULARGIA			**WONDERS OF THE WORLD COLLECTION**	
86	SMALL SPACE NEEDLE	CL	50.00	50.00
93	SMALL CAPITOL BLDG.	OP	100.00	100.00
94	SMALL WHITE HOUSE W/OCT. MIRROR	OP	185.00	185.00
R. NAKAI			**WONDERS OF THE WORLD COLLECTION**	
86	LARGE SPACE NEEDLE	CL	160.00	160.00
86	TAJ MAHAL	OP	1,050.00	1050.00
87	US CAPITOL BLDG.	OP	250.00	250.00
93	SEARS TOWER	OP	150.00	150.00
95	LIBERTY BELL, THE	OP	160.00	160.00
95	MEDIUM TAJ MAHAL	OP	790.00	790.00
95	SMALL TAJ MAHAL	OP	215.00	215.00
T. SUZUKI			**WONDERS OF THE WORLD COLLECTION**	
90	LE PETIT EIFFEL	OP	240.00	240.00
91	CHICAGO WATER TOWER W/BASE	OP	300.00	300.00
91	CHICAGO WATER TOWER W/O BASE	CL	280.00	280.00
97	CAPITOL HILL	350	1,350.00	1350.00

CYBIS

			ANIMAL KINGDOM	
*	BULL	100	150.00	4500.00
61	HORSE	100	150.00	2000.00
65	RACCOON, RAFFLES	CL	110.00	365.00
65	SQUIRREL, MR. FLUFFY TAIL	CL	90.00	345.00
66	THOROUGHBRED	350	425.00	1450.00

YR	NAME	LIMIT	ISSUE	TREND
67	KITTEN, BLUE RIBBON	CL	95.00	500.00
68	BEAR	CL	85.00	400.00
68	BUFFALO	CL	115.00	180.00
68	ELEPHANT	100	600.00	5000.00
68	SNAIL, SIR ESCARGOT	CL	50.00	290.00
68	STALLION	350	475.00	845.00
69	COLTS, DARBY & JOAN	CL	295.00	475.00
70	DEER MOUSE IN CLOVER	CL	65.00	160.00
71	AMERICAN BULLFROG	CL	250.00	600.00
71	APPALOOSA COLT	CL	150.00	300.00
71	NASHUA	100	2,000.00	3000.00
72	PINTO COLT	CL	175.00	250.00
75	AMERICAN WHITE BUFFALO	250	1,250.00	4000.00
75	KITTEN, TABITHA	CL	90.00	150.00
75	KITTEN, TOPAZ	CL	90.00	150.00
76	BUNNY, MUFFET	CL	85.00	140.00
76	CHIPMUNK WITH BLOODROOT	225	625.00	675.00
76	PRAIRIE DOG	CL	245.00	345.00
77	BUNNY PAT-A-CAKE	CL	90.00	145.00
78	DORMOUSE MAXIMILLIAN	CL	250.00	275.00
78	DORMOUSE MAXINE	CL	195.00	225.00
78	PINKY BUNNY/CARROT	200	200.00	265.00
80	ARCTIC WHITE FOX	100	4,500.00	4700.00
80	SQUIRREL, HIGHRISE	400	475.00	525.00
81	BEAVERS, EGBERT & BREWSTER	400	285.00	335.00
82	DALL SHEEP	50	*	4250.00
84	AUSTRALIAN SULPHER CRESTED COCKATOO	25	9,850.00	9850.00
84	CHANTILLY, KITTEN	OP	175.00	210.00
85	BAXTER & DOYLE	400	450.00	450.00
85	BEAGLES, BRANIGAN & CLANCY	OP	375.00	600.00
85	BUNNY, SNOWFLAKE	OP	65.00	75.00
85	ELEPHANT, WILLOUGHBY	OP	195.00	245.00
85	MONDAY, RHINOCEROS	OP	85.00	145.00
86	DAPPLE GREY FOAL	OP	195.00	225.00
86	HUEY, THE HARMONIOUS HARE	OP	175.00	275.00
86	MICK, THE MELODIOUS MUTT	OP	175.00	275.00
86	WHITE-TAILED DEER	50	9,500.00	11500.00
*				**BIBLICAL**
*	HOLYWATER FONT, HOLY GHOST	CL	15.00	150.00
56	HOLY CHILD OF PRAGUE	10	1,500.00	75000.00
57	MADONNA, HOUSE OF GOLD	8	125.00	4025.00
60	EXODUS	50	350.00	2600.00
60	FLIGHT INTO EGYPT	50	175.00	2525.00
60	MADONNA LACE AND ROSE	OP	15.00	300.00
60	PROPHET, THE	50	250.00	3550.00
63	MOSES THE GREAT LAWGIVER	750	250.00	5550.00
64	NATIVITY, MARY	OP	*	350.00
64	ST. PETER	500	*	1275.00
76	NOAH	500	975.00	3025.00
84	CHRIST CHILD WITH LAMB	OP	*	290.00
84	NATIVITY, ANGEL, COLOR	OP	395.00	600.00
84	NATIVITY, CAMEL, COLOR	OP	625.00	850.00
84	NATIVITY, JOSEPH	OP	*	350.00
84	NATIVITY, SHEPHERD, COLOR	OP	395.00	500.00
85	NATIVITY, COW, COLOR	OP	175.00	200.00
85	NATIVITY, COW, WHITE	OP	125.00	250.00
85	NATIVITY, DONKEY, COLOR	OP	195.00	250.00
85	NATIVITY, DONKEY, WHITE	OP	130.00	175.00
85	NATIVITY, LAMB, COLOR	OP	150.00	200.00
85	NATIVITY, LAMB, WHITE	OP	115.00	150.00
*				**BIRDS & FLOWERS**
*	BIRDS & FLOWERS	250	500.00	4550.00
*	BUTTERFLY W/DOGWOOD	200	*	375.00
*	SANDPIPERS	400	700.00	1450.00
*	SKYLARKS	350	330.00	1750.00
57	TURTLEDOVES	500	350.00	4950.00
59	HUMMINGBIRD	CL	95.00	1000.00
60	BLUE-HEADED VIRIO (BUILDING NEST)	CL	60.00	1150.00
60	BLUE-HEADED VIRIO W/LILAC	275	1,200.00	2250.00
60	PHEASANT	150	750.00	5050.00
61	BLUE-GREY GNATCATCHERS (PAIR)	200	400.00	2550.00
61	GOLDEN CLARION LILY	100	250.00	4550.00
62	DUCKLING (BABY BROTHER)	CL	35.00	140.00
62	SPARROW ON LOG	CL	35.00	475.00
63	IRIS	250	500.00	4550.00
63	MAGNOLIA	CL	350.00	1000.00
64	DAHLIA YELLOW	350	450.00	1850.00
64	GREAT WHITE HERON	350	850.00	3700.00
65	CHRISTMAS ROSE	500	250.00	750.00
68	CALLA LILY	500	750.00	1750.00
68	NARCISSUS	500	350.00	550.00
68	WOOD DUCK	500	325.00	800.00
69	CLEMATIS W/HOUSE WREN	350	1,300.00	1450.00
70	DUTCH CROCUS	350	550.00	775.00
70	MUSHROOM W/BUTTERFLY	CL	225.00	475.00

YR	NAME	LIMIT	ISSUE	TREND
71	LITTLE BLUE HERON	500	425.00	1500.00
72	AMERICAN CRESTED IRIS	400	975.00	1200.00
72	AUTUMN DOGWOOD W/CHICKADEES	350	1,100.00	1250.00
72	PANSIES W/CHINA MAID	1000	275.00	360.00
74	GOLDEN WINGED WARBLER	200	1,075.00	1200.00
75	GREAT HORNED OWL (COLOR)	50	3,250.00	7550.00
75	GREAT HORNED OWL (WHITE)	150	1,950.00	4450.00
75	PANSIES W/CHINOLINA LADY	750	295.00	425.00
76	AMERICAN WHITE TURKEY	75	1,450.00	1650.00
76	AMERICAN WILD TURKEY	75	1,950.00	2250.00
76	COLONIAL BASKET	100	2,750.00	5550.00
76	CONSTANCY FLOWER BASKET	CL	345.00	425.00
76	DEVOTION FLOWER BASKET	CL	345.00	450.00
76	FELICITY FLOWER BASKET	CL	325.00	350.00
76	MAJESTY FLOWER BASKET	CL	345.00	425.00
77	APPLE BLOSSOMS	400	350.00	600.00
77	CLEMATIS	CL	210.00	350.00
77	DUCKLING (BUTTERCUP & DAFFODIL)	CL	165.00	300.00
77	HERMIT THRUSH	150	1,450.00	1500.00
77	KRESTREL	175	1,875.00	2000.00
78	KINGLETS ON PYRACANTHA	175	900.00	1150.00
78	NESTLING BLUEBIRDS	CL	235.00	260.00
80	YELLOW CONDESA ROSE	CL	*	255.00
80	YELLOW ROSE	CL	80.00	440.00
82	SPRING BOUQUET	200	750.00	1000.00
85	AMERICAN BALD EAGLE	300	2,900.00	3600.00
85	SCREECH OWL & SIBLINGS	100	3,250.00	4000.00
*				**CAROUSEL-CIRCUS**
73	CAROUSEL GOAT	325	875.00	1700.00
73	CAROUSEL HORSE	325	925.00	7550.00
74	LION	325	1,025.00	1325.00
74	TIGER	325	925.00	1475.00
75	BARNABY, BEAR	CL	165.00	315.00
75	BICENTENNIAL HORSE TICONDEROGA	350	925.00	4050.00
75	BOSUN, MONKEY	CL	195.00	400.00
76	FUNNY FACE, CHILD HEAD/HOLLY	CL	325.00	750.00
76	PERFORMING PONY, POPPY	1000	325.00	1250.00
76	SEBASTIAN, SEAL	CL	195.00	225.00
77	DANDY, DANCING DOG	CL	145.00	300.00
81	BEAR, BERNHARD	325	1,125.00	1175.00
81	BULL, PLUTUS	325	1,125.00	2100.00
81	FROLLO	1000	750.00	850.00
81	PONY	750	975.00	1000.00
82	GIRAFFE	750	*	1800.00
84	PHINEAS, CIRCUS ELEPHANT	OP	325.00	450.00
85	CAROUSEL UNICORN	325	1,275.00	2700.00
85	CIRCUS RIDER EQUESTRIENNE EXTRAORDINAIRE	150	2,275.00	3550.00
85	JUMBLES AND FRIEND	750	675.00	750.00
85	VALENTINE	OP	335.00	400.00
86	PIERRE, THE PERFORMING POODLE	OP	225.00	300.00
*				**CHILDREN OF THE WORLD**
72	ESKIMO CHILD HEAD	CL	165.00	425.00
75	INDIAN BOY HEAD	CL	425.00	925.00
75	INDIAN GIRL HEAD	CL	325.00	925.00
77	JEREMY	CL	315.00	500.00
78	JASON	CL	285.00	370.00
78	JENNIFER	CL	325.00	400.00
79	JESSICA	CL	325.00	500.00
*				**CHILDREN TO CHERISH**
*	FIRST BOUQUET	250	150.00	325.00
57	THUMBELINA	CL	45.00	525.00
58	PETER PAN	CL	80.00	1000.00
59	TINKERBELL	CL	95.00	1500.00
60	BALLERINA, RED SHOES	CL	75.00	1250.00
62	HEIDI, COLOR	CL	165.00	575.00
62	HEIDI, WHITE	CL	165.00	575.00
63	BALLERINA ON CUE	CL	150.00	675.00
63	SPRINGTIME	CL	45.00	775.00
64	ALICE IN WONDERLAND	CL	50.00	850.00
64	REBECCA	CL	110.00	350.00
66	FIRST FLIGHT	CL	50.00	500.00
68	BABY BUST	239	375.00	1050.00
68	BALLERINA, LITTLE PRINCESS	CL	125.00	725.00
71	POLLYANNA	CL	195.00	575.00
72	RAPUNZEL, PINK	1000	425.00	1100.00
73	GOLDILOCKS	CL	145.00	500.00
73	LITTLE RED RIDING HOOD	CL	110.00	465.00
74	GRETEL	CL	260.00	420.00
74	HANSEL	CL	270.00	525.00
74	MARY, MARY	500	475.00	750.00
75	RAPUNZEL, APRICOT	1500	475.00	1200.00
75	RAPUNZEL, LILAC	1000	675.00	1000.00
75	WENDY WITH FLOWERS	*	250.00	425.00
75	YANKEE DOODLE DANDY	CL	275.00	350.00
76	ELIZABETH ANN	CL	195.00	275.00

YR	NAME	LIMIT	ISSUE	TREND
76	MELISSA	OP	285.00	425.00
77	BOYS PLAYING MARBLES	CL	285.00	400.00
78	ALICE (SEATED)	CL	350.00	540.00
78	ALLEGRA	CL	310.00	375.00
78	EDITH	CL	310.00	350.00
78	LISA AND LYNETTE	CL	395.00	470.00
78	LITTLE BOY BLUE	CL	425.00	525.00
80	LITTLE MISS MUFFET	CL	335.00	400.00
81	FLEURETTE	1000	725.00	1100.00
82	ROBIN	1000	475.00	900.00
82	SLEEPING BEAUTY	750	695.00	1500.00
84	CHOIRBOY, THE	OP	325.00	350.00
84	JACK IN THE BEANSTALK	750	575.00	600.00
84	LITTLE CHAMP	OP	325.00	400.00
84	MICHAEL	OP	235.00	375.00
85	BALLERINA, RECITAL	OP	275.00	300.00
85	BALLERINA, SWANILDA	OP	450.00	700.00
85	BETH	OP	235.00	300.00
85	CLARA	OP	395.00	400.00
85	FELECIA	OP	425.00	550.00
85	FIGURE EIGHT	750	625.00	800.00
85	JODY	OP	235.00	300.00
85	MARGUERITE	OP	425.00	550.00
85	RECITAL	OP	275.00	300.00
85	VANESSA	OP	425.00	550.00
86	CLARISSA	OP	165.00	200.00
86	ENCORE, FIGURE SKATER	750	625.00	670.00
86	KITRI	OP	450.00	575.00
86	LULLABY, BLUE	OP	125.00	175.00
86	LULLABY, IVORY	OP	125.00	175.00
86	LULLABY, PINK	OP	125.00	175.00
87	PANDORA BLUE	CL	265.00	350.00
*				**COMMEMORATIVE**
67	COLUMBIA	200	1,000.00	2500.00
67	CONDUCTOR'S HANDS	250	250.00	1500.00
69	APOLLO II MOON MISSION	111	1,500.00	2500.00
71	CREE INDIAN	100	2,500.00	5500.00
72	CHESS SET	10	30,000.00	60000.00
75	GEORGE WASHINGTON BUST	CL	275.00	350.00
77	OCEANIA	200	1,250.00	1500.00
80	BRIDE, THE	100	6,500.00	10500.00
81	ARION, DOLPHIN RIDER	1000	575.00	1200.00
81	KATERI TAKAKWITHA	100	2,875.00	3000.00
81	PHOENIX	100	950.00	1000.00
84	1984 CYBIS HOLIDAY	OP	145.00	150.00
84	CREE INDIAN, MAGIC BOY	200	4,250.00	5000.00
85	HOLIDAY ORNAMENT	OP	75.00	100.00
85	LIBERTY	100	1,875.00	4000.00
86	1986 COMMEMORATIVE EGG	OP	365.00	375.00
86	LITTLE MISS LIBERTY	OP	295.00	350.00
*			**EVERYONE'S FUN TIME (LIMNETTES)**	
72	COUNTRY FAIR	500	125.00	200.00
72	POND, THE	500	125.00	200.00
72	SEASHORE, THE	500	125.00	200.00
72	WINDY DAY	500	125.00	200.00
*				**FANTASIA**
69	UNICORN	500	1,250.00	3800.00
74	CYBELE	500	675.00	675.00
74	FANTASIA	500	675.00	800.00
77	SEA KING'S STEED, OCEANIA	200	1,250.00	1500.00
77	UNICORNS, GAMBOL AND FROLIC	1000	425.00	2300.00
78	SATIN HORSE HEAD	500	1,100.00	2850.00
78	SHARMAINE, SEA NYMPH	250	1,450.00	1650.00
80	PEGASUS	500	1,450.00	3800.00
80	PEGASUS, FREE SPIRIT	1000	675.00	775.00
81	DESIREE, WHITE DEER	400	575.00	600.00
81	PRINCE BROCADE UNICORN	500	2,200.00	2650.00
82	THERON	350	675.00	850.00
84	FLIGHT AND FANCY	1000	975.00	1175.00
85	DORE'	1000	575.00	1100.00
*				**LAND OF CHEMERIC**
77	MARIGOLD	CL	185.00	525.00
77	QUEEN TITANIA	750	725.00	2500.00
77	TIFFIN	CL	175.00	525.00
79	PIP, ELFIN PLAYER	1000	450.00	675.00
81	MELODY	1000	725.00	800.00
85	OBERON	750	825.00	850.00
*			**NORTH AMERICAN INDIAN**	
69	BLACKFEET, BEAVERHEAD MEDICINE MAN	500	2,000.00	2800.00
69	DAKOTA, MINNEHAHA LAUGHING WATER	500	1,500.00	2500.00
69	ONONDAGA, HIAWATHA	500	1,500.00	2450.00
71	SHOSHONE, SACAJAWEA	500	2,250.00	2800.00
73	ESKIMO MOTHER	200	1,875.00	2700.00
73	IRIQUOIS, AT THE COUNCIL FIRE	500	4,250.00	5000.00
74	APACHE, CHATO	350	1,950.00	3300.00

YR	NAME	LIMIT	ISSUE	TREND
77	CROW DANCER	200	3,875.00	8500.00
79	GREAT SPIRIT, WANKAN TANKA	200	3,500.00	4200.00
82	CHOCTAW, TASCULUSA	200	2,475.00	4100.00
85	YAQUI, DEER DANCER	200	2,095.00	2800.00
*			**PORTRAITS IN PORCELAIN**	
65	BEATRICE	700	225.00	1800.00
65	JULIET	800	175.00	4000.00
67	FOLK SINGER	283	300.00	900.00
67	GUINEVERE	800	250.00	2350.00
68	HAMLET	500	350.00	2000.00
68	SCARLETT	500	450.00	4000.00
69	OPHELIA	800	750.00	4400.00
71	ELEANOR OF AQUITAINE	750	875.00	4250.00
72	KWAN YIN	350	1,250.00	2000.00
73	BALLET-PRINCE FLORIMOND	200	975.00	1100.00
73	BALLET-PRINCESS AURORA	200	1,125.00	1500.00
73	PORTIA	750	825.00	3800.00
74	QUEEN ESTHER	750	925.00	1800.00
75	LADY MACBETH	750	850.00	1300.00
76	ABIGAIL ADAMS	600	875.00	1300.00
76	PRISCILLA	500	825.00	1500.00
78	GOOD QUEEN ANNE	350	975.00	1500.00
79	BERENGARIA	500	1,450.00	3500.00
79	NEFERTITI	500	2,100.00	3000.00
81	JANE EYRE	500	975.00	1500.00
82	DESDEMONA	500	1,850.00	4000.00
82	LADY GODIVA	200	1,875.00	3200.00
82	PERSEPHONE	200	3,250.00	5200.00
84	BATHSHEBA	500	1,975.00	3300.00
85	KING ARTHUR	350	2,350.00	3400.00
85	KING DAVID	350	1,475.00	2200.00
85	PAGLIACCI	OP	325.00	350.00
85	ROMEO AND JULIET	300	2,200.00	3400.00
85	TRISTAN AND ISOLDE	200	2,200.00	2200.00
86	CARMEN	500	1,675.00	2000.00
*			**SPORT SCENES**	
80	JOGGER, FEMALE	CL	345.00	450.00
80	JOGGER, MALE	CL	395.00	500.00
*		**THE WONDERFUL SEASONS (LIMNETTES)**		
72	AUTUMN	500	125.00	200.00
72	SPRING	500	125.00	200.00
72	SUMMER	500	125.00	200.00
72	WINTER	500	125.00	200.00
*			**THEATRE OF PORCELAIN**	
78	COURT JESTER	250	1,450.00	1800.00
80	HARLEQUIN	250	1,575.00	1900.00
81	COLUMBINE	250	2,250.00	2300.00
81	PUCK	250	2,300.00	2500.00
*		**WHEN BELLS ARE RINGING (LIMNETTES)**		
72	EASTER EGG HUNT	500	125.00	200.00
72	INDEPENDENCE CELEBRATION	500	125.00	200.00
72	MERRY CHRISTMAS	500	125.00	200.00
72	SABBATH MORNING	500	125.00	200.00

DADDY'S LONG LEGS
K. GERMANY

YR	NAME	LIMIT	ISSUE	TREND
			COUNTY FAIR	
97	COUNTY FAIR SET	3000	175.00	175.00
97	KELLY	3000	35.00	35.00
97	NELL	3000	35.00	35.00
97	NICK	3000	35.00	35.00
97	PENNY	3000	35.00	35.00
97	PETE	3000	35.00	35.00

K. GERMANY

YR	NAME	LIMIT	ISSUE	TREND
		NURSERY RHYME CHARACTERS		
96	CURLY-LOCKS	3000	19.00	19.00
96	LITTLE BO PEEP	3000	19.00	19.00
96	LITTLE BOY BLUE	3000	17.00	17.00
96	MARY, MARY	3000	19.00	19.00
96	OLD KING COLE	3000	25.00	25.00
96	OLD MOTHER HUBBARD	3000	25.00	25.00
96	TO MARKET	3000	19.00	19.00

DANBURY MINT
N. ROCKWELL

YR	NAME	LIMIT	ISSUE	TREND
		ROCKWELL FIGURINES		
80	BOY ON STILTS	CL	55.00	60.00
80	CAUGHT IN THE ACT	CL	55.00	75.00
80	GRAMPS AT THE REINS	CL	55.00	75.00
80	GRANDPA SNOWMAN	CL	55.00	60.00
80	TRICK OR TREAT	CL	55.00	60.00
80	YOUNG LOVE	CL	55.00	125.00

DAVE GROSSMAN CREATIONS
*

YR	NAME	LIMIT	ISSUE	TREND
93	AFTER THE PROM	7500	75.00	85.00
93	GONE FISHING	1500	65.00	75.00
93	MISSED	7500	110.00	120.00

YR	NAME	LIMIT	ISSUE	TREND
94	ALMOST GROWN UP	7500	75.00	85.00
94	BABY'S FIRST STEP	7500	100.00	110.00
94	BED TIME	7500	100.00	110.00
94	BRIDE & GROOM	7500	100.00	110.00
94	FOR A GOOD BOY	7500	100.00	110.00
94	LITTLE MOTHER	7500	75.00	85.00
ROCKWELL INSPIRED		**AMERICAN ROCKWELL SERIES**		
81	BREAKING HOME TIES NRV-300	RT	2,000.00	2300.00
82	LINCOLN NRV-301	RT	300.00	375.00
82	THANKSGIVING NRV-302	RT	2,500.00	2650.00
ROCKWELL INSPIRED		**BOY SCOUT SERIES**		
81	CAN'T WAIT BSA-01	RT	30.00	50.00
81	GOOD FRIENDS BSA-04	RT	58.00	65.00
81	GOOD TURN BSA-05	RT	65.00	100.00
81	PHYSICALLY STRONG BSA-03	RT	56.00	60.00
81	SCOUT IS HELPFUL BSA-02	RT	38.00	45.00
81	SCOUT MEMORIES BSA-06	RT	65.00	70.00
82	GUIDING HAND BSA-07	RT	58.00	60.00
83	TOMORROW'S LEADER BSA-08	RT	45.00	55.00
*		**EMMETT KELLY**		
87	BIG GAME HUNTER	RT	38.00	38.00
89	CHOOSING SIDES	RT	55.00	55.00
91	ARTFUL DODGER	RT	35.00	35.00
91	EMMETT AT BAT	RT	35.00	35.00
91	I LOVE YOU	RT	80.00	80.00
92	SPOTLIGHT	RT	80.00	80.00
92	WALL STREET	RT	125.00	125.00
96	FIRE FIGHTER	*	45.00	45.00
96	SELF-PORTRAIT	RT	100.00	100.00
97	MISSED	*	50.00	50.00
97	MYSTERY SPOTLIGHT	*	40.00	40.00
97	OFF TO THE RACES	*	85.00	85.00
98	100TH BIRTHDAY	RT	50.00	50.00
B. LEIGHTON-JONES		**EMMETT KELLY CIRCUS COLLECTION**		
92	CHRISTMAS TUNES	15000	40.00	40.00
92	EMMETT AT THE ORGAN	15000	50.00	50.00
92	EMMETT AT WORK	15000	45.00	45.00
92	EMMETT THE CADDY	15000	45.00	45.00
92	LOOK AT THE BIRDIE	15000	40.00	40.00
*		**EMMETT KELLY GALLERY COLLECTION**		
96	A DOG'S LIFE	RT	100.00	100.00
96	SPOTLIGHT	RT	80.00	80.00
96	WALL STREET	RT	90.00	90.00
B. LEIGHTON-JONES		**EMMETT KELLY ORIGINAL CIRCUS COLLECTION**		
93	CHRISTMAS TUNES	5000	100.00	115.00
93	DEAR EMMETT	15000	45.00	140.00
93	HARD TIMES	15000	45.00	50.00
93	LION TAMER, THE	15500	55.00	65.00
93	SUNDAY DRIVER	15000	55.00	65.00
93	WALL STREET	5000	120.00	135.00
94	EMMETT THE CADDY	5000	125.00	145.00
94	HOLIDAY SKATER	15000	110.00	125.00
94	I'VE GOT IT	15000	90.00	110.00
94	PARENTHOOD	15000	110.00	125.00
94	STUCK ON BOWLING	15000	90.00	100.00
*		**GONE WITH THE WIND**		
92	MAMMY MINI BRONZE	RT	50.00	50.00
92	MR. O'HARA MINI BRONZE	RT	50.00	50.00
92	MRS. O'HARA MINI BRONZE	RT	50.00	50.00
92	PORK MINI BRONZE	RT	50.00	50.00
92	SCARLETT GREEN DRESS	TL	70.00	70.00
92	SCARLETT WHITE DRESS MINI BRONZE	RT	50.00	50.00
93	ASHLEY MINI BRONZE	RT	50.00	50.00
93	CHARLES HAMILTON MINI BRONZE	RT	50.00	50.00
93	RHETT GWW-12	RT	70.00	80.00
93	RHETT MINI BRONZE	RT	50.00	50.00
93	SCARLETT BBQ DRESS MINI BRONZE	RT	50.00	50.00
93	SUELLEN MINI BRONZE	RT	50.00	50.00
93	TARA DISPLAY	RT	90.00	90.00
93	TWELVE OAKS DISPLAY	RT	90.00	90.00
94	ASHLEY	OP	40.00	50.00
94	ATLANTA PITTYPAT HOUSE DISPLAY	RT	90.00	90.00
94	AUNT PITTYPAT HAMILTON MINI BRONZE	RT	50.00	50.00
94	BELLE WATLING MINI BRONZE	RT	50.00	50.00
94	GERALD O'HARA	RT	70.00	80.00
94	PRISSY MINI BRONZE	RT	50.00	50.00
94	RHETT	OP	40.00	45.00
94	RHETT WHITE SUIT MINI BRONZE	RT	50.00	50.00
94	SCARLETT	OP	40.00	45.00
94	SCARLETT BBQ DRESS	RT	70.00	80.00
94	SCARLETT IVORY DRESS MINI BRONZE	RT	50.00	50.00
96	ATLANTA SCENE 3	*	75.00	75.00
96	RHETT BLACK TUXEDO	*	70.00	70.00
96	SCARLETT & RHETT STROLLING MUSICAL WATERGLOBE	RE	55.00	55.00
96	SCARLETT BLUE DRESS	*	70.00	70.00

YR	NAME	LIMIT	ISSUE	TREND
96	TARA SCENE 1	*	75.00	75.00
96	TWELVE OAKS SCENE 2	*	75.00	75.00
97	ATLANTA BURNING WATERGLOBE	*	50.00	50.00
97	BONNIE	*	50.00	50.00
97	KISS, THE	*	100.00	100.00
97	RHETT TUXEDO	*	85.00	85.00
97	SCARLETT & RHETT	*	65.00	65.00
97	SCARLETT ATLANTA DRESS	*	70.00	70.00
97	SCARLETT BBQ DRESS	*	80.00	80.00
97	SCARLETT BBQ DRESS	*	50.00	50.00
98	SCARLETT & RHETT	*	90.00	90.00
*	**GONE WITH THE WIND/SCARLETT AND HER BEAUS**			
95	KISS, THE	RT	150.00	150.00
95	KISS, THE (ARTIST PROOF)	RT	180.00	180.00
96	WEDDING	750	150.00	150.00
96	WEDDING (ARTIST PROOF)	RT	180.00	180.00
97	SCARLETT & ASHLEY	750	150.00	150.00
97	SCARLETT & ASHLEY (ARTIST PROOF)	75	180.00	180.00
ROCKWELL INSPIRED			**HUCK FINN SERIES**	
79	SECRET, THE- HF-01	RT	110.00	130.00
80	LISTENING HF-02	RT	110.00	120.00
80	NO KINGS HF-03	RT	110.00	110.00
80	SNAKE ESCAPES HF-04	RT	110.00	110.00
ROCKWELL INSPIRED			**LARGE LIMITED EDITIONS**	
74	DOCTOR AND DOLL NR-100	RT	300.00	1600.00
74	SEE AMERICA FIRST NR-103	RT	100.00	300.00
75	BASEBALL NR-102	RT	125.00	450.00
75	NO SWIMMING NR-101	RT	150.00	450.00
79	LEAPFROG NR-104	RT	440.00	600.00
81	DREAMS OF LONG AGO NR-105	RT	500.00	750.00
82	CIRCUS NR-106	RT	500.00	550.00
84	MARBLE PLAYERS NR-107	RT	500.00	500.00
*			**MINIATURE BRONZE SERIES**	
93	SCENE II-TWELVE OAKS	5000	340.00	375.00
93	WIZARD OF OZ	5000	290.00	325.00
B. LEIGHTON-JONES			**MINIATURE BRONZE SERIES**	
94	ATLANTA	*	340.00	365.00
*			**MOUSEHOLE COLLECTION**	
94	ANNIE HALFWAY	RT	15.00	15.00
94	CHRISTMAS TRIO	RT	35.00	35.00
94	DIGGER OUTBACK DIGGER	RT	15.00	15.00
94	DOC HOLIDAY DR. GOLFER	RT	16.00	16.00
94	HARRY & SALLY HARMONY BRIDE & GROOM	RT	20.00	20.00
94	HICKORY DICKORY BOOKKEEPER	RT	16.00	16.00
94	HONEY BUNCH & DAPPER VALENTINE	RT	30.00	30.00
94	HORATIO HOLIMOUSE MINISTER	RT	15.00	15.00
94	JULIA SMILES COOK	RT	16.00	16.00
94	LORD FREDERICK MOUSE LEIGHTON R.A. R.A.	RT	18.00	18.00
94	MIC MOUSEPIECE LAWYER	RT	16.00	16.00
94	MILLIE MINIMAL & TINY TIM	RT	24.00	24.00
94	MINNIE LITTLE MAID	RT	16.00	16.00
94	MORRIS MINOR CAR	RT	30.00	30.00
94	PERCIVAL PLOD POLICEMAN	RT	16.00	16.00
94	SCOTTY MCMOUSTER	RT	16.00	16.00
94	SHORT JOHN SILVER	RT	16.00	16.00
94	SMUDGE BRIGHTLY LIGHTHOUSE	RT	30.00	30.00
94	STITTON CHEESE BUTLER	RT	16.00	16.00
94	THOMAS T. CADDIE	RT	15.00	15.00
94	WEE WILLIE CHURCH MOUSE	RT	16.00	16.00
94	WILEY R. TREADMILL JUDGE	RT	16.00	16.00
94	WILL MOUSEPEARE	RT	15.00	15.00
E. ROBERTS			**NATIVE AMERICAN SERIES**	
91	LONE WOLF	7500	55.00	55.00
92	TORTOISE LADY	7500	60.00	60.00
ROCKWELL INSPIRED			**NORMAN ROCKWELL COLLECTION**	
73	BACK TO SCHOOL NR-02	RT	20.00	35.00
73	CAROLLER NR-03	RT	23.00	35.00
73	DAYDREAMER NR-04	RT	23.00	50.00
73	DOCTOR & DOLL NR-12	RT	65.00	150.00
73	LAZYBONES NR-08	RT	30.00	300.00
73	LEAPFROG NR-09	RT	50.00	550.00
73	LOVE LETTER NR-06	RT	25.00	60.00
73	LOVERS NR-07	RT	45.00	66.00
73	MARBLE PLAYERS NR-11	RT	60.00	450.00
73	NO SWIMMING NR-05	RT	25.00	50.00
73	REDHEAD NR-01	RT	20.00	200.00
73	SCHOOLMASTER NR-10	RT	55.00	225.00
74	BASEBALL NR-16	RT	45.00	120.00
74	FRIENDS IN NEED NR-13	RT	45.00	96.00
74	SEE AMERICA FIRST NR-17	RT	50.00	85.00
74	SPRINGTIME '33 NR-14	RT	30.00	45.00
74	TAKE YOUR MEDICINE NR-18	RT	50.00	95.00
75	BARBERSHOP QUARTET NR-23	RT	100.00	1400.00
75	BIG MOMENT NR-21	RT	60.00	120.00

YR	NAME	LIMIT	ISSUE	TREND
75	CIRCUS NR-22	RT	55.00	100.00
75	DISCOVERY NR-20	RT	55.00	160.00
76	DRUM FOR TOMMY NRC-24	RT	40.00	80.00
77	PALS NR-25	RT	60.00	75.00
77	SPRINGTIME '35 NR-19	RT	50.00	55.00
78	AT THE DOCTOR NR-29	RT	108.00	160.00
78	FIRST DAY OF SCHOOL NR-27	RT	100.00	135.00
78	MAGIC POTION NR-28	RT	84.00	100.00
78	YOUNG DOCTOR NRD-26	RT	100.00	100.00
79	BACK FROM CAMP NR-33	RT	96.00	110.00
79	DREAMS OF LONG AGO NR-31	RT	100.00	160.00
79	GRANDPA'S BALLERINA NR-32	RT	100.00	110.00
79	TEACHER'S PET NRA-30	RT	35.00	80.00
80	EXASPERATED NANNY NR-35	RT	96.00	96.00
80	HANDKERCHIEF NR-36	RT	110.00	110.00
80	SANTA'S GOOD BOYS NR-37	RT	90.00	90.00
80	TOSS, THE- NR-34	RT	110.00	110.00
81	SPIRIT OF EDUCATION NR-38	RT	96.00	110.00
82	A VISIT WITH ROCKWELL NR-40	RT	120.00	120.00
82	AMERICAN MOTHER NRG-42	RT	100.00	110.00
82	CROQUET NR-41	RT	100.00	110.00
83	COUNTRY CRITIC NR-43	RT	75.00	75.00
83	GRADUATE NR-44	RT	30.00	35.00
83	SCOTTY'S SURPRISE NRS-20	RT	25.00	25.00
84	SCOTTY'S HOME PLATE NR-46	RT	30.00	40.00
86	RED CROSS NR-47	RT	67.00	75.00
87	YOUNG LOVE NR-48	RT	70.00	70.00
88	WEDDING MARCH NR-49	RT	110.00	110.00
92	CHOOSIN UP	7500	110.00	110.00
ROCKWELL INSPIRED		**NORMAN ROCKWELL COLLECTION MINIATURES**		
79	BACK TO SCHOOL NR-202	RT	18.00	25.00
79	CAROLLER NR-203	RT	20.00	25.00
79	DAYDREAMER NR-04	RT	20.00	30.00
79	DOCTOR AND DOLL NR-212	RT	40.00	40.00
79	LAZYBONES NR-208	RT	22.00	30.00
79	LEAPFROG NR-209	RT	32.00	32.00
79	LOVE LETTER NR-206	RT	26.00	30.00
79	LOVERS NR-207	RT	28.00	30.00
79	MARBLE PLAYERS NR-211	RT	36.00	38.00
79	NO SWIMMING NR-205	RT	22.00	30.00
79	REDHEAD NR-201	RT	18.00	48.00
79	SCHOOLMASTER NR-210	RT	34.00	40.00
80	BASEBALL NR-216	RT	40.00	50.00
80	FRIENDS IN NEED NR-213	RT	30.00	40.00
80	SEE AMERICA FIRST NR-217	RT	28.00	35.00
80	SPRINGTIME '33 NR-214	RT	24.00	80.00
80	SUMMERTIME '33 NR-215	RT	22.00	25.00
80	TAKE YOUR MEDICINE NR-218	RT	36.00	40.00
82	BARBERSHOP QUARTET NR-223	RT	40.00	50.00
82	BIG MOMENT NR-221	RT	36.00	40.00
82	CIRCUS NR-222	RT	35.00	40.00
82	DISCOVERY NR-220	RT	35.00	45.00
82	DRUM FOR TOMMY NRC-224	RT	25.00	30.00
82	SPRINGTIME '35 NR-219	RT	24.00	30.00
83	SANTA ON THE TRAIN NR-245	RT	35.00	55.00
84	AT THE DOCTOR'S NR-229	RT	35.00	35.00
84	DREAMS OF LONG AGO NR-231	RT	30.00	30.00
84	FIRST DAY OF SCHOOL NR-227	RT	35.00	35.00
84	MAGIC POTION NR-228	RT	30.00	40.00
84	PALS NR-225	RT	25.00	25.00
84	YOUNG DOCTOR NRD-226	RT	30.00	50.00
ROCKWELL INSPIRED		**ROCKWELL CLUB SERIES**		
81	YOUNG ARTISTS RCC-01	RT	96.00	105.00
82	DIARY RCC-02	RT	35.00	50.00
83	RUNAWAY PANTS RCC-03	RT	65.00	75.00
84	GONE FISHING RCC-04	RT	30.00	55.00
ROCKWELL INSPIRED		**TOM SAWYER MINIATURES**		
83	FIRST SMOKE TSM-02	RT	40.00	45.00
83	LOST IN CAVE TSM-05	RT	40.00	45.00
83	TAKE YOUR MEDICINE TSM-04	RT	40.00	45.00
83	WHITEWASHING THE FENCE TSM-01	RT	40.00	50.00
ROCKWELL INSPIRED		**TOM SAWYER SERIES**		
75	WHITEWASHING THE FENCE TS-01	RT	60.00	200.00
76	FIRST SMOKE TS-02	RT	60.00	200.00
77	TAKE YOUR MEDICINE TS-03	RT	63.00	170.00
78	LOST IN CAVE TS-04	RT	70.00	145.00
*		**WIZARD OF OZ**		
93	DOROTHY MINI BRONZE	RT	50.00	50.00
93	LION MINI BRONZE	RT	50.00	50.00
93	SCARECROW MINI BRONZE	RT	50.00	50.00
93	TIN MAN MINI BRONZE	RT	50.00	50.00
93	YELLOW BRICK ROAD	RT	90.00	90.00
95	EMERALD CITY MUSICAL	RT	85.00	85.00
95	WITCH'S CASTLE MUSICAL	*	85.00	85.00
96	COWARDLY LION	5000	20.00	20.00

YR	NAME	LIMIT	ISSUE	TREND
96	COWARDLY LION MUSICAL	*	35.00	35.00
96	DOROTHY	5000	20.00	20.00
96	DOROTHY MUSICAL	*	35.00	35.00
96	DOROTHY/MUNCHKIN WATERGLOBE	*	55.00	55.00
96	GOOD WITCH	5000	32.00	32.00
96	GOOD WITCH MUSICAL	*	35.00	35.00
96	MAYOR	5000	20.00	20.00
96	MORTICIAN	5000	20.00	20.00
96	OZ FIGURINE SET	RT	177.00	177.00
96	SCARECROW	5000	20.00	20.00
96	SCARECROW MUSICAL	*	35.00	35.00
96	TIN MAN	5000	20.00	20.00
96	TIN MAN MUSICAL	*	35.00	35.00
96	WICKED WITCH	5000	25.00	25.00
96	WICKED WITCH MUSICAL	*	35.00	35.00
96	WICKED WITCH MUSICAL	*	75.00	75.00
97	APPLE TREE WATERGLOBE	*	40.00	40.00
97	DOROTHY & MUNCHKIN MUSICAL	*	75.00	75.00
97	EMERALD CITY LIGHTED WATERGLOBE	*	60.00	60.00
97	FLYING MONKEY	5000	16.00	16.00
97	OZ FIGURINE SET (3 PC)	RT	48.00	48.00
97	RUBY SLIPPERS WATERGLOBE	*	40.00	40.00
97	WINKIE CASTLE GUARD	5000	16.00	16.00
97	WITCH'S CASTLE WATERGLOBE	*	40.00	40.00
97	WITCH'S CRYSTAL BALL LIGHTED WATERGLOBE	*	50.00	50.00
97	WIZARD	5000	16.00	16.00

DEPARTMENT 56

ALPINE VILLAGE
*

YR	NAME	LIMIT	ISSUE	TREND
86	ALPINE VILLAGERS 6542-0, (SET OF 3)	RT	13.00	26.00
87	ALPINE VILLAGE SIGN 6571-4	RT	6.00	11.00
89	FARM ANIMALS 5945-5, (SET OF 4)	RT	15.00	45.00
90	TOY PEDDLER 5616-2, (SET OF 3)	OP	22.00	22.00
92	BUYING BAKERS BREAD 5619-7, (SET OF 2)	RT	20.00	22.00

CHRISTMAS IN THE CITY
*

YR	NAME	LIMIT	ISSUE	TREND
87	CITY PEOPLE 5965-0, (SET OF 5)	RT	28.00	50.00
89	POPCORN VENDOR 5958-7, (SET OF 3)	RT	22.00	22.00
89	RIVER STREET ICE HOUSE CART 5959-5	RT	20.00	45.00
91	ALL AROUND THE TOWN 5545-0, (SET OF 2)	RT	18.00	17.00
91	CAROLING THRU THE CITY 5548-4, (SET OF 3)	OP	28.00	28.00
91	CITY FIRE DEPT.- FIRE TRUCK	RT	18.00	20.00
91	FIRE BRIGADE, THE 5546-8, (SET OF 2)	RT	20.00	22.00
91	MARKET DAY 5641-3, (SET OF 3)	RT	35.00	30.00
91	SKATING PARTY 5523-9, (SET OF 3)	OP	28.00	28.00
92	DON'T DROP THE PRESENTS 5532-8, (SET OF 2)	RT	25.00	25.00
92	VILLAGE EXPRESS VAN 5865-3, GREEN	OP	25.00	25.00
92	VILLAGE EXPRESS VAN 9951-1, BLACK	RT	25.00	105.00
92	WELCOME HOME, 5533-6, (SET OF 2)	RT	28.00	28.00
93	CHRISTMAS AT THE PARK 5866-1, (SET OF 3)	OP	28.00	28.00
93	PLAYING IN THE SNOW 5556-5, (SET OF 3)	OP	25.00	25.00
93	STREET MUSICIANS 5564-6, (SET OF 3)	OP	45.00	45.00
93	TOWN TREE 5565-4, (SET OF 5)	OP	45.00	45.00
93	TOWN TREE TRIMMERS 5566-2, (SET OF 4)	OP	33.00	33.00
94	HOT DOG VENDOR 5886-6, (SET OF 3)	RT	*	N/A
94	VILLAGE EXPRESS VAN-BACHMAN'S 729-3	RT	23.00	70.00
94	VILLAGE EXPRESS VAN-BRONNER'S 737-4	RT	23.00	45.00
94	VILLAGE EXPRESS VAN-CHRISTMAS DOVE 730-7	RT	25.00	50.00
94	VILLAGE EXPRESS VAN-CHRISTMAS PLACE 732-3	RT	25.00	75.00
94	VILLAGE EXPRESS VAN-EUROPEAN IMPORTS 739-0	RT	23.00	40.00
94	VILLAGE EXPRESS VAN-FORTUNOFF'S 735-8	RT	23.00	125.00
94	VILLAGE EXPRESS VAN-LOCK,STOCK.. 731-5	RT	23.00	120.00
94	VILLAGE EXPRESS VAN-LTD. ED. 733-1	RT	25.00	115.00
94	VILLAGE EXPRESS VAN-N. POLE CITY 736-6	RT	25.00	50.00
94	VILLAGE EXPRESS VAN-ROBERTS CHRISTMAS WNDLD 734-0	RT	23.00	50.00
94	VILLAGE EXPRESS VAN-STAT'S 741-2	RT	23.00	40.00
94	VILLAGE EXPRESS VAN-THE LEMON TREE 721-8	RT	30.00	45.00
94	VILLAGE EXPRESS VAN-WILLIAM GLEN 738-2	RT	23.00	50.00
94	VILLAGE EXPRESS VAN-WINDSOR SHOPPE 740-4	RT	25.00	45.00
94	VILLAGE STREET CAR 5240-0 MOTORIZED	OP	65.00	65.00

CHRISTMAS IN THE CITY - PROMOTIONAL
*

YR	NAME	LIMIT	ISSUE	TREND
92	VILLAGE EXPRESS VAN 9977-5, GOLD	RT	*	960.00

DICKENS' HINGED BOXES
*

YR	NAME	LIMIT	ISSUE	TREND
98	BAH, HUMBUG!	*	15.00	15.00
98	GOD BLESS US, EVERYONE!	*	15.00	15.00
98	SPIRIT OF CHRISTMAS	*	15.00	15.00

DICKENS' VILLAGE
*

YR	NAME	LIMIT	ISSUE	TREND
84	ORIGINAL CAROLERS, SET OF THREE WHITE POST	RT	10.00	95.00
86	CHRISTMAS CAROL CHARS 6501-3, SET OF THREE	RT	12.50	100.00
88	POULTERER 5926-9	RT	33.00	50.00
89	CHRISTMAS SPIRITS FIGURES 5589-1 (SET OF 4)	OP	28.00	28.00
89	DAVID COPPERFIELD CHARS 5551-4, (SET OF 5)	RT	33.00	30.00
89	LAMPLIGHTER 5577-8, (SET OF 2)	OP	9.00	9.00
90	C.H. WATT PHYSICIAN 5568-9	OP	40.00	40.00
91	OLIVER TWIST CHARACTERS 554-9, (SET OF 3)	RT	35.00	30.00
92	BIRD SELLER, THE 5803-3 (SET OF 3)	RT	25.00	30.00

YR	NAME	LIMIT	ISSUE	TREND
92	OLD PUPPETEER, THE 5802-5 (SET OF 3)	RT	32.00	33.00
92	VILLAGE STREET PEDDLERS 5804-1, (SET OF 2)	RT	16.00	13.00
93	CHELSEA LANE SHOPPERS 5816-5, (SET OF 4)	OP	30.00	30.00
93	CHELSEA MARKET FISH MONGERS 5814-9, (SET OF 2)	OP	25.00	25.00
93	CHELSEA MARKET FLOWER MONGERS 5815-7, (SET OF 2)	OP	28.00	28.00
93	CHELSEA MARKET FRUIT MONGERS 5813-0, (SET OF 2)	OP	25.00	25.00
94	THATCHER 5829-7, (SET OF 3)	OP	35.00	35.00
95	COBBLER AND CLOCK PEDDLER 5839-4, (SET OF 2)	OP	25.00	25.00
95	FIVE GOLDEN RINGS 5838-1, (SET OF 2)	OP	28.00	28.00
95	FOUR CALLING BIRDS 5837-9, (SET OF 2)	OP	*	N/A
95	SIX GEESE A LAYING 5838-2, (SET OF 2)	OP	*	N/A
95	THREE FRENCH HENS 5837-8, (SET OF 3)	OP	33.00	33.00
95	YE OLDE LAMP LIGHTER, DICKENS' VILLAGE SIGN 5839-3	OP	20.00	20.00
96	NETTIE QUINN PUPPETS & MARIONETTES	OP	50.00	50.00
*		DICKENS' VILLAGE SIGNATURE SERIES		
97	GAD'S HILL PLACE	YR	98.00	98.00
*		HERITAGE VILLAGE		
86	PORCELAIN TREES 6537-4, (SET OF 2)	RT	14.00	30.00
87	CITY WORKERS 5967-6 (SET OF 4)	RT	15.00	30.00
88	SNOW CHILDREN 5938-2, (SET OF 3)	RT	17.00	20.00
89	VIOLET VENDOR/CAROLERS/CHESTNUT,5580-8 SET OF 3	RT	23.00	30.00
96	12 DAYS OF DICKENS' VILLAGE, 7 SWANS A SWIMMING	OP	28.00	27.00
96	12 DAYS OF DICKENS' VILLAGE, 8 MAIDS A MILKING	OP	25.00	25.00
96	CAROLING WITH THE CRATCHIT FAMILY- SET OF 3	OP	38.00	38.00
96	CHRISTMAS BAZAAR...HANDMADE QUILTS -SET OF 2	OP	25.00	25.00
96	CHRISTMAS BAZAAR...WOOLENS & PRESERVES -SET OF 2	OP	25.00	25.00
96	CHRISTMAS CAROL, A- READING/ C.DICKENS- 5 PC	OP	45.00	45.00
96	CHRISTMAS CAROL, A- READING/ C.DICKENS- 8 PC	OP	75.00	75.00
96	CITY TAXI	OP	12.50	12.00
96	ELVES ON ICE- SET OF 4	OP	7.50	8.00
96	END OF THE LINE -SET OF 2	OP	28.00	28.00
96	FAMILY TREE, THE	OP	18.00	18.00
96	FEZZIWIG DELIVERY WAGON, THE	OP	33.00	32.00
96	GINGERBREAD VENDOR -SET OF 2	OP	23.00	22.00
96	GOING HOME FOR THE HOLIDAYS -SET OF 3	OP	28.00	28.00
96	HOLIDAY DELIVERIES	OP	47.00	16.00
96	NEW POTBELLIED STOVE FOR CHRISTMAS, A -SET OF 2	OP	35.00	35.00
96	NORTH POLE EXPRESS	OP	38.00	38.00
96	NUTCRACKER VENDOR & CART	OP	25.00	25.00
96	RED CHRISTMAS SULKY	OP	30.00	30.00
96	TENDING THE NEW CALVES- SET OF 3	OP	30.00	30.00
96	VILLAGE ANIMATED ACCESSORY TRACK	OP	65.00	65.00
96	VILLAGE ANIMATED SKI MOUNTAIN	OP	75.00	75.00
96	YEOMEN OF THE GUARD- SET OF 5	OP	30.00	30.00
*		NEW ENGLAND VILLAGE		
90	'TIS THE SEASON 5539-5	RT	12.50	13.00
90	AMISH BUGGY 5949-8	RT	22.00	50.00
90	REST YE MERRY GENTLEMEN 5540-9	RT	12.50	13.00
90	SLEEPY HOLLOW CHARACTERS 5956-0 (SET OF 3)	RT	28.00	45.00
91	MARKET DAY, 5641-3, (SET OF 3)	OP	35.00	30.00
91	SKATING PARTY 5523-9, (SET OF 3)	OP	28.00	28.00
92	HARVEST SEED CART 5645-6, (SET OF 3)	RT	28.00	28.00
92	TOWN TINKER 5646-4, (SET OF 2)	RT	24.00	30.00
92	VILLAGE PINE TREE, LG. 5218-3	OP	12.50	13.00
92	VILLAGE PINE TREE, SM. 5219-1	OP	10.00	10.00
93	BLUE STAR ICE HARVESTERS 5650-2, (SET OF 2)	OP	28.00	28.00
93	KNIFE GRINDER 5649-9, (SET OF 2)	OP	23.00	23.00
95	J. BREWSTER 5657-0 (BREWSTER BAY COTTAGES)	OP	45.00	45.00
95	T.T. JULIAN 5657-0 (BREWSTER BAY COTAGES)	OP	45.00	45.00
96	NAVIGATIONAL CHARTS & MAPS	OP	48.00	48.00
*		NORTH POLE COLLECTION		
*	CHRISTMAS CAROL REVISITED HOLIDAY TRIMMING SET	RT	*	N/A
90	SANTA & MRS. CLAUS 5609-0, (SET OF 2)	OP	15.00	15.00
90	SANTA'S LITTLE HELPERS 5610-3, (SET OF 3)	RT	28.00	50.00
90	SLEIGH & EIGHT TINY REINDEER 5611-1, (SET OF 5)	OP	42.00	42.00
91	BAKER'S ELVES 5603-0, (SET OF 3)	RT	28.00	28.00
91	TOYMAKER ELVES 5602-2, (SET OF 3)	RT	28.00	25.00
92	CHURCHYARD FENCE EXTENSIONS 5807-6	RT	*	N/A
92	CHURCHYARD GATE & FENCE 5806-8	RT	*	N/A
92	LETTERS FOR SANTA 5604-9, (SET OF 3)	RT	30.00	50.00
92	LIONHEAD BRIDGE 5864-5	RT	*	N/A
92	TESTING THE TOYS 5605-7, (SET OF 2)	OP	16.50	17.00
92	VILLAGE PORCELAIN PINE LARGE 5218-3	RT	*	N/A
92	VILLAGE PORCELAIN PINE SMALL 5219-1	RT	*	N/A
93	BLUE STAR ICE HARVESTERS 5650-2	RT	*	N/A
93	CHELSEA MARKET FISH MONGER & CART 5814-9	RT	*	N/A
93	CHELSEA MARKET FRUIT MONGER & CART 5813-0	RT	*	N/A
93	STREET MUSICIANS 5564-6	RT	*	N/A
94	HOT DOG VENDOR 5886-6	RT	*	N/A
94	SNOW CONE ELVES 5637-5	RT	*	N/A
94	THATCHERS 5829-7	RT	*	N/A
94	TWO RIVERS BRIDGE 5656-1	RT	*	N/A
94	VILLAGE PORCELAIN PINE TREES 5251-5	RT	*	N/A
95	CHARTING SANTA'S COURSE 56364	RT	*	N/A
95	COBBLER & CLOCK PEDDLER 58394	RT	*	N/A

YR	NAME	LIMIT	ISSUE	TREND
96	A CHRISTMAS CAROL READING BY DICKENS 58404	RT	*	N/A
96	CHRISTMAS BREAD BAKERS	OP	55.00	55.00
96	YEOMEN OF THE GUARD 58397	RT	*	N/A
97	HOLLY & IVY, THE "HOMES FOR THE HOLIDAYS"	RT	*	N/A

ORIGINAL SNOW VILLAGE

*

YR	NAME	LIMIT	ISSUE	TREND
92	VILLAGE USED CAR LOT 5428-3	RT	*	N/A
93	A HERD OF HOLIDAY HEIFERS 5455-0	RT	*	N/A
93	SAFETY PATROL 5449-6	RT	*	N/A
93	TOUR THE VILLAGE 5452-6	RT	*	N/A
94	COCA-COLA BRAND BILLBOARD 5481-0	RT	*	N/A
94	FEEDING THE BIRDS 5473-9	RT	*	N/A
94	MUSH! 5474-7	RT	*	N/A
94	SANTA COMES TO TOWN	RT	30.00	33.00
95	FROSTY PLAYTIME 54860	RT	*	N/A
95	GRAND OLE OPRY CAROLERS 54867	RT	*	N/A
96	A RIDE ON THE REINDEER LINES 54875	RT	*	N/A
96	CAROL THROUGH THE SNOW	OP	15.00	15.00
96	HARLEY-DAVIDSON FAT BOY & SOFTAIL	OP	16.50	16.00
96	HARLEY-DAVIDSON HOLIDAY, A -SET OF 2	OP	23.00	22.00
96	HARLEY-DAVIDSON SIGN	OP	18.00	18.00
96	HEADING FOR THE HILLS -2 ASSORTED	OP	8.50	9.00
96	HOLIDAY HOOPS -SET OF 3	OP	20.00	20.00
96	MEN AT WORK -SET OF 5	OP	28.00	28.00
96	MOVING DAY -SET OF 3	OP	33.00	32.00
96	NICK'S TREE FARM- SET OF 10	OP	40.00	40.00
96	ON THE ROAD AGAIN -SET OF 2	OP	20.00	20.00
96	RIDE ON THE REINDEER LINES, A- SET OF 3	OP	35.00	35.00
96	SANTA COMES TO TOWN, 1996, 1997	RT	35.00	35.00
96	SMOKEY MOUNTAIN RETREAT	OP	65.00	65.00
96	TERRY'S TOWING -SET OF 2	OP	20.00	20.00
96	VILLAGE ANIMATED ACCESSORY TRACK	OP	65.00	65.00
96	VILLAGE ANIMATED SKI MOUNTIAN	OP	75.00	75.00
96	VILLAGE WATERFALL	OP	65.00	65.00

PIERRO/KIRCHNER

SNOWBABIES

YR	NAME	LIMIT	ISSUE	TREND
*	FROSTY FOREST 79634	*	20.00	20.00
*	I'LL PLAY A CHRISTMAS TUNE 68801	*	16.00	16.00
*	LET'S GO SKATING 68608	*	17.00	17.00
86	BEST FRIENDS 7958-8	RT	12.00	115.00
86	CATCH A FALLING STAR WATERGLOBE	CL	18.00	550.00
86	CLIMBING ON SNOWBALL 7965-0	RT	15.00	100.00
86	GIVE ME A PUSH 7955-3	RT	12.00	60.00
86	HANGING PAIR 7966-9	RT	15.00	150.00
86	HOLD ON TIGHT 7956-1	OP	12.00	14.00
86	I'M MAKING SNOWBALLS 7962-6	RT	12.00	35.00
86	SNOWBABY NITE LITE 7959-6	CL	15.00	325.00
86	SNOWBABY PICTURE FRAME 7970-7 (SET OF 2)	RT	15.00	550.00
86	SNOWBABY STANDING WATERGLOBE	CL	8.00	350.00
87	CLIMBING ON TREE 7971-5 (SET OF 2)	RT	25.00	800.00
87	DON'T FALL OFF 7968-5	RT	12.50	100.00
87	DOWN THE HILL WE GO 7960-0	OP	20.00	22.00
87	SNOWBABIES RIDING SLEDS WATERGLOBE	CL	40.00	675.00
87	SNOWBABY WITH WINGS WATERGLOBE	CL	20.00	450.00
87	TUMBLING IN THE SNOW 7957-0 (SET OF 5)	RT	35.00	90.00
87	WHEN YOU WISH UPON A STAR MUSIC BOX	CL	30.00	40.00
87	WINTER SURPRISE 7974-0	RT	15.00	40.00
88	ARE THESE MINE? 7977-4	OP	10.00	13.00
88	FROSTY FROLIC 7981-2	4800	35.00	900.00
88	POLAR EXPRESS 7978-2	RT	22.00	80.00
88	TINY TRIO 7979-0 (SET OF 3)	RT	20.00	160.00
89	ALL FALL DOWN 7984-7 (SET OF 4)	RT	36.00	55.00
89	FINDING FALLEN STARS 7985-5	6000	33.00	175.00
89	FROSTY FUN 7983-9	RT	28.00	55.00
89	HELPFUL FRIENDS 7982-0	RT	30.00	40.00
89	ICY IGLOO 7987-1	OP	38.00	38.00
89	LET IT SNOW WATERGLOBE 7992-8	CL	25.00	35.00
89	PENGUIN PARADE 7986-3	RT	25.00	35.00
90	A SPECIAL DELIVERY 7948-0	CL	13.50	20.00
90	ALL TIRED OUT WATERGLOBE	CL	55.00	60.00
90	I WILL PUT UP THE TREE 6800-4	RT	22.00	24.00
90	PLAYING GAMES IS FUN 7947-2	RT	30.00	45.00
90	READ ME A STORY 7945-6	OP	25.00	25.00
90	TWINKLE LITTLE STARS 7942-1 (SET OF 2)	RT	38.00	45.00
90	WE WILL MAKE IT SHINE 7946-4	RT	45.00	50.00
90	WHO ARE YOU? 7949-9	RT	33.00	110.00
90	WISHING ON A STAR 7943-0	RT	20.00	35.00
91	CAN I HELP TOO? 6806-3	18500	48.00	60.00
91	DANCING TO A TUNE 6808-0 (SET OF 3)	RT	30.00	30.00
91	FISHING FOR DREAMS 6809-8	CL	28.00	35.00
91	I MADE THIS JUST FOR YOU 6802-0	OP	14.50	15.00
91	IS THAT FOR ME? 6803-9 (SET OF 2)	RT	30.00	30.00
91	PEEK-A-BOO WATERGLOBE 7938-3	CL	50.00	75.00
91	PLAY ME A TUNE WATERGLOBE	CL	50.00	50.00
91	POLAR SIGN 6804-7	RT	20.00	20.00
91	THIS IS WHERE WE LIVE 6805-5	CL	55.00	60.00
91	WAITING FOR CHRISTMAS 6807-1	RT	28.00	30.00

The first M.I. Hummel tree topper ever created, Goebel's Heavenly Angel *can spend the off-season on her polished wooden base.*

Produced by Goebel, the little fellow in M.I. Hummel's figurine A Free Flight *is ready to take off on a flight of fancy.*

Limited to an edition of 5,000, Los Niños, *one of Ted DeGrazia's works that was produced by Goebel, has increased in value since its 1988 release.*

Depending on the incision mark, M. I. Hummel's Stormy *Weather from 1985 can be valued at anywhere from $330 to $1,200.*

King of the Mountain *porcelain figurine from Schmid's Lowell Davis Collection was released in 1993 at a retail price of $500.*

YR	NAME	LIMIT	ISSUE	TREND
91	WHY DON'T YOU TALK TO ME 6801-2	OP	22.00	24.00
92	FISHING FOR DREAMS WATERGLOBE	CL	33.00	50.00
92	HELP ME, I'M STUCK 6817-9	CL	33.00	45.00
92	I NEED A HUG 6813-6	OP	20.00	20.00
92	JOIN THE PARADE 6824-1	CL	38.00	45.00
92	JUST ONE LITTLE CANDLE 6823-3	OP	15.00	15.00
92	LET'S GO SKIING 6815-2	CL	15.00	16.00
92	LOOK WHAT I CAN DO! #6819-5	RT	17.00	20.00
92	OVER THE MILKY WAY	RT	32.00	40.00
92	READ ME A STORY WATERGLOBE 6831-4	RT	33.00	33.00
92	SHALL I PLAY FOR YOU? 6820-9	OP	17.00	17.00
92	STARRY PINES 6829-2	OP	18.00	18.00
92	STARS IN A ROW, TIC-TAC-TOE	RT	33.00	40.00
92	THIS WILL CHEER YOU UP 6816-0	RT	30.00	40.00
92	WAIT FOR ME 6812-8	CL	48.00	55.00
92	WINKEN, BLINKEN, AND NOD 6814-4	OP	60.00	65.00
92	YOU CAN'T FIND ME! #6818-7	RT	*	45.00
92	YOU DIDN'T FORGET ME 6821-7	OP	33.00	33.00
93	BABY'S FIRST SMILE 6846-2	OP	30.00	30.00
93	CAN I OPEN IT NOW? 6838-1	CL	15.00	35.00
93	CROSSING STARRY SKIES 6834-9	RT	35.00	35.00
93	I FOUND YOUR MITTENS! 6836-5	RT	30.00	30.00
93	I'LL TEACH YOU A TRICK 6835-7	RT	24.00	24.00
93	I'M MAKING AN ICE SCULPTURE! 6842-0	RT	30.00	38.00
93	LET'S ALL CHIME IN! 6845-4 SET OF 2	RT	38.00	45.00
93	LOOK WHAT I FOUND 6833-0	RT	45.00	45.00
93	NOW I LAY ME DOWN TO SLEEP 6839-0	OP	13.50	14.00
93	SO MUCH WORK TO DO! 6837-3	OP	18.00	22.00
93	SOMEWHERE IN DREAMLAND 6840-3	RT	85.00	95.00
93	SOMEWHERE IN DREAMLAND, 1 SNOWFLAKE	CL	85.00	125.00
93	WE MAKE A GREAT PAIR 6843-8	OP	30.00	33.00
93	WHERE DID HE GO? 6841-1	OP	35.00	35.00
93	WHISTLE WHILE YOU WORK MUSIC BOX	CL	33.00	42.00
93	WILL IT SNOW TODAY? 6844-6	RT	45.00	60.00
94	BRINGING STARRY PINES 6862-4	RT	35.00	35.00
94	I'M RIGHT BEHIND YOU! 6852-7	OP	60.00	60.00
94	JACK FROST, A TOUCH OF WINTER'S MAGIC 6854-3	OP	90.00	90.00
94	LIFT ME HIGHER, I CAN'T REACH 6863-2	OP	75.00	75.00
94	LOOK WHAT I FOUND WATERGLOBE 68721	RT	33.00	33.00
94	MICKEY'S NEW FRIEND 714-5	RT	60.00	575.00
94	PENNIES FROM HEAVEN 6864-0	OP	18.00	18.00
94	PLANTING STARRY PINES #6870-5	RT	33.00	33.00
94	STRINGING FALLEN STARS 6861-6	OP	25.00	25.00
94	THERE'S ANOTHER ONE! 6853-5	OP	24.00	24.00
94	WE'LL PLANT THE STARRY PINES 6865-9	RT	38.00	38.00
94	WHERE DID YOU COME FROM? 6856-0	RT	40.00	40.00
95	A STAR IN THE BOX 68803	CL	18.00	25.00
95	ARE YOU ON MY LIST? 6875-6	OP	25.00	25.00
95	FROSTY PINES 76687	OP	13.00	13.00
95	I CAN'T FIND HIM 68800	OP	38.00	38.00
95	I FOUND THE BIGGEST STAR OF ALL! 6874-8	OP	16.00	16.00
95	I SEE YOU! 6878-0	OP	28.00	28.00
95	I'LL HUG YOU GOODNIGHT WATERGLOBE	OP	33.00	33.00
95	MUSH 68805	OP	48.00	48.00
95	PARADE OF PENGUINS 68804	OP	15.00	15.00
95	PLAY ME A TUNE MUSIC BOX 68809	OP	38.00	38.00
95	RING THE BELLS, IT'S CHRISTMAS 6876-4	OP	40.00	40.00
95	SKATE WITH ME WATERGLOBE	OP	33.00	33.00
95	SNOWBABIES ANIMATED SKATING POND 7668-6	OP	60.00	60.00
95	WE'RE BUILDING AN ICY IGLOO 68802	OP	70.00	70.00
95	WHAT SHALL WE DO TODAY? 6877-2	RT	33.00	33.00
96	A LITTLE NIGHT LIGHT	OP	33.00	32.00
96	CLIMB EVERY MOUNTAIN	RT	75.00	100.00
96	DISPLAY YOUR FAVORITE SNOWBABY LAMP	OP	45.00	45.00
96	FIVE-PART HARMONY	OP	33.00	33.00
96	I'M SO SLEEPY	RT	16.00	16.00
96	IT'S A GRAND OLD FLAG	OP	25.00	25.00
96	IT'S SNOWING!	OP	16.50	16.00
96	JACK FROST SLEIGHRIDE THROUGH THE STARS- SET OF 3	OP	110.00	110.00
96	LITTLE NIGHT LIGHT, A- LAMP	OP	75.00	75.00
96	MOONBEAMS- NIGHT LIGHT	OP	20.00	20.00
96	NOW I LAY ME DOWN TO SLEEP- WATERGLOBE, MUSIC BOX	OP	33.00	32.00
96	ONCE UPON A TIME- SET OF 2	OP	25.00	25.00
96	ONCE UPON A TIME...- MUSIC BOX	OP	30.00	30.00
96	PRACTICE MAKES PERFECT- WATERGLOBE, MUSIC BOX	OP	33.00	32.00
96	SLIDING THROUGH THE MILKY WAY- MUSIC BOX	OP	38.00	37.00
96	SNOWBABY DISPLAY SLED	OP	45.00	45.00
96	STARGAZING- SET OF 9	OP	40.00	40.00
96	THERE'S NO PLACE LIKE HOME 68820	OP	16.50	16.00
96	WHEN THE BOUGH BREAKS	OP	30.00	30.00
96	WHICH WAY IS UP? 68812	RT	30.00	30.00
96	WITH HUGS & KISSES-SET OF 2	OP	33.00	33.00
96	YOU ARE MY LUCKY STAR- SET OF 2	OP	35.00	35.00
96	YOU NEED WINGS TOO!	OP	25.00	25.00
96	YOU'RE MY SNOWBABY- PICTURE FRAME	OP	15.00	15.00

YR	NAME	LIMIT	ISSUE	TREND
97	LET'S GO SEE JACK FROST 68850	RT	*	N/A
97	ROCK-A-BYE BABY HINGED BOX 68848	RT	*	N/A
98	ALL WE NEED IS LOVE (MOTHER'S DAY 1998 EVENT PIECE	*	33.00	33.00
98	CANDLE LIGHT...SEASON BRIGHT TREE TOPPER	*	20.00	20.00
98	CANDLELIGHT TREES (SET OF 3)	*	25.00	25.00
98	DID HE SEE YOU? MOVING MUSICAL	*	38.00	38.00
98	HEIGH-HO WATERGLOBE/MUSIC BOX	*	33.00	33.00
98	HEIGH-HO, HEIGH-HO, TO FROLIC LAND WE GO	*	48.00	48.00
98	I LOVE YOU HINGED BOX (MOTHER'S DAY EVENT PIECE)	*	15.00	15.00
98	I'M THE STAR ATOP YOUR TREE! TREE TOPPER	*	20.00	20.00
98	JINGLE BELL	*	16.00	16.00
98	JINGLE BELL WATERGLOBE/MUSIC BOX	*	33.00	33.00
98	MOON BEAMS WATERGLOBE/MUSIC BOX	*	33.00	33.00
98	ONE FOR YOU, ONE FOR ME	*	28.00	28.00
98	POLAR EXPRESS HINGED BOX	*	15.00	15.00
98	SHIP O' DREAMS (SET OF 2)	*	135.00	135.00
98	STARLIGHT SERENADE	*	25.00	25.00
98	SWEET DREAMS HINGED BOX	*	15.00	15.00
98	THANK YOU	*	33.00	33.00
98	WHISTLE WHILE YOU WORK	*	33.00	33.00

PIERRO/KIRCHNER **SNOWBABIES PEWTER MINIATURES**

YR	NAME	LIMIT	ISSUE	TREND
*	A STAR-IN-THE-BOX #76698	*	7.50	8.00
*	CLIMB EVERY MOUNTAIN SET OF 5 #76702	*	27.50	28.00
*	COLLECTOR'S SIGN #76201	*	7.00	7.00
*	DOWN THE HILL WE GO! SET OF 2 #76066	*	14.00	14.00
*	FIVE-PART HARMONY SET OF 2 #76710	*	22.00	22.00
*	FROSTY FOREST SET OF 2 #76120	*	12.00	12.00
*	HOLD ON TIGHT! #76007	*	7.00	7.00
*	I FOUND THE BIGGEST STAR OF ALL #76690	*	7.00	7.00
*	I SEE YOU! SET OF 2 #76694	*	18.00	18.00
*	I'LL PLAY A CHRISTMAS TUNE #76696	*	7.50	8.00
*	I'M MAKING SNOWBALLS! #76023	*	7.00	7.00
*	I'M SO SLEEPY #76700	*	7.00	7.00
*	IT'S A GRAND OLD FLAG #76705	*	11.00	11.00
*	IT'S SNOWING #76706	*	7.00	7.00
*	JUST ONE LITTLE CANDLE #76449	*	7.00	7.00
*	LET'S ALL CHIME IN! SET OF 2 #76554	*	20.00	20.00
*	LET'S GO SKATING #76643	*	7.00	7.00
*	LET'S GO SKIING! #76368	*	7.00	7.00
*	MUSH! SET OF 2 #76699	*	25.00	25.00
*	NOW I LAY ME DOWN TO SLEEP #76570	*	7.00	7.00
*	RING THE BELLS...IT'S CHRISTMAS! #76692	*	20.00	20.00
*	SHALL I PLAY FOR YOU? #76422	*	7.00	7.00
*	STRINGING FALLEN STARS#76651	*	8.00	8.00
*	THERE'S NO PLACE LIKE HOME #76708	*	7.50	8.00
*	WE'RE BUILDING AN ICY IGLOO SET OF 3 #76697	*	27.50	28.00
*	WHAT SHALL WE DO TODAY? SET OF 2 #76693	*	17.00	17.00
*	WHEN THE BOUGH BREAKS #76707	*	18.00	18.00
*	WHERE DID HE GO? SET OF 4 #76546	*	20.00	20.00
*	WHICH WAY'S UP? SET OF 2 #76701	*	13.50	14.00
*	WHY DON'T YOU TALK TO ME? SET OF 2 #76252	*	12.00	12.00
*	WILL IT SNOW TODAY? SET OF 5 #76538	*	23.00	23.00
*	WINKEN, BLINKEN & NOD SET OF 3 #76589	*	27.50	28.00
*	WITH HUGS & KISSES SET OF 2 #76704	*	15.00	15.00
*	YOU NEED WINGS TOO SET OF 2 #76709	*	11.00	11.00
*	YOU'RE MY LUCKY STAR SET OF 2 #76703	*	20.00	20.00
89	ALL FALL DOWN #7617-1	CL	25.00	45.00
89	ARE ALL THESE MINE? #7605-8	CL	7.00	15.00
89	BEST FRIENDS #7604-0	CL	10.00	15.00
89	DON'T FALL OFF #7603-1	CL	7.00	15.00
89	FINDING FALLEN STARS #7618-0	CL	13.00	30.00
89	FROSTY FROLIC #7613-9	CL	24.00	30.00
89	FROSTY FUN SET OF 2 #76112	RT	14.00	14.00
89	GIVE ME A PUSH! #7601-5	CL	7.00	10.00
89	HELPFUL FRIENDS #7608-2	CL	14.00	25.00
89	ICY IGLOO WITH TREE #7610-4	CL	8.00	20.00
89	PENGUIN PARADE #7616-3	CL	13.00	30.00
89	POLAR EXPRESS #7609-0	CL	14.00	30.00
89	TINY TRIO #7615-5	CL	18.00	35.00
89	TUMBLING IN THE SNOW #7614-7	CL	30.00	60.00
89	WINTER SURPRISE #7607-4	CL	14.00	20.00
90	A SPECIAL DELIVERY #7624-4	CL	7.00	18.00
90	PLAYING GAMES IS FUN! #7623-6	CL	14.00	30.00
90	READ ME A STORY #76228	RT	11.00	11.00
90	TWINKLE LITTLE STARS #7621-0	CL	15.00	25.00
91	DANCING TO A TUNE #7630-9	CL	18.00	25.00
91	FROSTY FROLIC MUSIC BOX #7634-1	CL	110.00	115.00
91	I MADE THIS JUST FOR YOU #7628-7	CL	7.00	15.00
91	I'LL PUT UP THE TREE #7627-9	RT	9.00	9.00
91	IS THAT FOR ME? #7631-7	CL	13.00	25.00
91	WAITING FOR CHRISTMAS #7629-5	CL	13.00	20.00
91	WISHING ON A STAR #7626-0	CL	10.00	20.00
92	HELP ME, I'M STUCK SET OF 2 #76384	RT	15.00	15.00
92	I NEED A HUG #76406	RT	10.00	10.00
92	JOIN THE PARADE	RT	23.00	30.00

YR	NAME	LIMIT	ISSUE	TREND
92	THIS WILL CHEER YOU UP #7639-2	CL	14.00	20.00
92	WAIT FOR ME! #7641-4	RT	23.00	30.00
92	WINKEN, BLINKEN, AND NOD #7658-9	OP	28.00	28.00
92	YOU CAN'T FIND ME! 3#7637-6	RT	23.00	23.00
92	YOU DIDN'T FORGET ME #7643-0	CL	18.00	22.00
93	CAN I OPEN IT NOW? MUSIC BOX	CL	20.00	35.00
93	FROSTY FUN MUSIC BOX	CL	20.00	25.00
93	PENGUIN PARADE MINI MUSIC BOX #7645-5	CL	20.00	30.00
93	PLAY ME A TUNE MINI MUSIC BOX #7651-1	CL	20.00	28.00
93	READING A STORY MINI MUSIC BOX #7649-0	CL	20.00	25.00
93	SOMEWHERE IN DREAMLAND SET OF 5 #76562	RT	30.00	30.00
93	WE MAKE A GREAT PAIR #76520	RT	13.50	14.00
94	BRINGING STARRY PINES SET OF 2 #76660	RT	18.00	18.00
94	I'M RIGHT BEHIND YOU SET OF 5 #76627	RT	27.50	28.00
94	LIFT ME HIGHER, I CAN'T REACH! SET OF 5 #76678	RT	25.00	25.00
94	THERE'S ANOTHER ONE #76619	RT	10.00	10.00
94	WE'LL PLANT THE STARRY PINES SET OF 4 #76635	RT	22.00	22.00
95	ARE YOU ON MY LIST? SET OF 2 #76691	RT	9.00	9.00
98	BEST LITTLE STAR	*	6.50	7.00
98	HEIGH-HO, HEIGH-HO, TO FROLIC LAND WE GO!	*	23.00	23.00
98	JACK FROST...A TOUCH OF WINTER'S MAGIC (SET OF 3)	*	28.00	28.00
98	JINGLE BELL	*	7.00	7.00
98	STARLIGHT SERENADE	*	12.00	12.00
98	THANK YOU (SET OF 3)	*	20.00	20.00
98	WHISTLE WHILE YOU WORK	*	18.00	18.00
98	WISH UPON A FALLING STAR (SET OF 4)	*	25.00	25.00

WINTER SILHOUETTE

YR	NAME	LIMIT	ISSUE	TREND
88	SKATING CHILDREN 7773-9	RT	*	N/A
89	PUTTING UP THE TREE 7789-5	RT	*	N/A
91	ANGEL CANDLE HOLDER 7794-1	RT	*	N/A
91	BEDTIME STORIES 7792-5	RT	*	N/A
91	CAROLING BELLS 7798-4	RT	*	N/A
91	HANGING THE ORNAMENTS 7793-3	RT	*	N/A
91	SANTA'S REINDEER 7796-8	RT	*	N/A
92	CHRISTMAS PRESENTS 7805-0	RT	*	N/A
92	MARIONETTE PERFORMANCE 7807-7	RT	*	N/A
93	A BRIGHT STAR ON CHRISTMAS EVE 7843-3	RT	*	N/A
93	A CHRISTMAS KISS 7845-0	RT	*	N/A
93	SANTA LUCIA 7844-1	RT	*	N/A
94	CAT NAP SANTA 7855-7	RT	*	N/A
94	MANTELPIECE SANTA 7854-9	RT	*	N/A
95	FINISHING TOUCHES SANTA 78559	RT	*	N/A
95	KNEELING ANGEL WITH MANDOLIN 78585	RT	*	N/A
95	NAUGHTY OR NICE? SANTA WATERGLOBE MUSIC BOX 7859-0	RT	*	N/A
95	STANDING ANGEL WITH HORN 78584	RT	*	N/A
98	CHRISTMAS PAGEANT ANGELS (SET OF 4)	*	45.00	45.00
98	CLARA & THE NUTCRACKER	*	20.00	20.00
98	LETTER TO SANTA	*	38.00	38.00
98	LITTLE DRUMMER BOY (SET OF 3)	*	45.00	45.00
98	NATIVITY WATERGLOBE/MUSIC BOX	*	33.00	33.00
98	OVER THE RIVER & THROUGH THE WOODS (SET OF 2)	*	65.00	65.00
98	TELL US ABOUT THE OLDEN DAYS, GRANDPA	*	55.00	55.00

DUNCAN ROYALE

1990 & 1991 SPECIAL EVENT PIECE

YR	NAME	LIMIT	ISSUE	TREND
*	NAST & MUSIC	5000	80.00	90.00

D. APHESSETCHE

CALENDAR SECRETS

YR	NAME	LIMIT	ISSUE	TREND
90	APRIL	5000	350.00	370.00
90	AUGUST	5000	300.00	300.00
90	DECEMBER	5000	410.00	410.00
90	FEBRUARY	5000	370.00	370.00
90	JANUARY	5000	260.00	260.00
90	JULY	5000	280.00	280.00
90	JUNE	5000	410.00	410.00
90	MARCH	5000	280.00	350.00
90	MAY	5000	370.00	390.00
90	NOVEMBER	5000	410.00	410.00
90	OCTOBER	5000	350.00	350.00
90	SEPTEMBER	5000	300.00	300.00

CHRISTMAS IMAGES

YR	NAME	LIMIT	ISSUE	TREND
91	CAROLERS, THE	10000	120.00	120.00
91	CHRISTMAS PAGEANT, THE	10000	175.00	175.00
92	ARE YOU REALLY SANTA?	10000	*	N/A
92	CHRISTMAS ANGEL, THE	10000	*	N/A
92	MIDNIGHT WATCH, THE	10000	*	N/A
92	SNEAKING A PEEK	10000	*	N/A

COLLECTORS CLUB

YR	NAME	LIMIT	ISSUE	TREND
91	MUSICAL NAST	CL	80.00	95.00
91	TODAY'S NAST	RT	80.00	125.00
94	WINTER SANTA	RT	125.00	125.00
95	SANTA'S GIFT	YR	100.00	100.00

EARLY AMERICAN

YR	NAME	LIMIT	ISSUE	TREND
91	ACCOUNTANT	10000	170.00	170.00
91	BANKER	10000	150.00	150.00
91	CHIROPRACTOR	10000	150.00	150.00

YR	NAME	LIMIT	ISSUE	TREND
91	DENTIST	10000	150.00	150.00
91	DOCTOR	10000	150.00	150.00
91	FIREMAN	10000	150.00	150.00
91	HOMEMAKER	10000	150.00	150.00
91	LAWYER	10000	170.00	170.00
91	NURSE	10000	150.00	150.00
91	PHARMACIST	10000	150.00	150.00
91	POLICEMAN	10000	150.00	150.00
91	SALESMAN	10000	150.00	150.00
91	SECRETARY	10000	150.00	150.00
91	SET OF 15	10000	2,290.00	2290.00
91	STOREKEEPER	10000	150.00	150.00
91	TEACHER	10000	150.00	150.00

* **EBONY COLLECTION**

90	BANJO MAN	5000	80.00	80.00
90	FIDDLER, THE	5000	90.00	90.00
90	HARMONICA MAN	5000	80.00	80.00
91	FEMALE GOSPEL SINGER	5000	90.00	90.00
91	JUG MAN	5000	90.00	90.00
91	MALE GOSPEL SINGER	5000	90.00	90.00
91	PREACHER	5000	90.00	90.00
91	SPOONS	5000	90.00	90.00
92	A LITTLE MAGIC	5000	80.00	80.00
92	JUG TOTTER	5000	90.00	90.00
93	EBONY ANGEL	5000	170.00	170.00

* **EBONY COLLECTION/BUCKWHEAT**

92	BASS	5000	90.00	90.00
92	BONGO	5000	90.00	90.00
92	JAZZMAN SET	5000	500.00	500.00
92	O'TAY	5000	70.00	90.00
92	PAINTER	5000	80.00	90.00
92	PETEE & FRIEND	5000	90.00	90.00
92	PIANO	5000	130.00	130.00
92	SAX	5000	90.00	90.00
92	SMILE FOR THE CAMERA	5000	80.00	90.00
92	TRUMPET	5000	90.00	90.00

S. BUONAIUTO **EBONY COLLECTION/FRIENDS & FAMILY**

94	AGNES	5000	100.00	100.00
94	DADDY	5000	120.00	120.00
94	LUNCHTIME	5000	100.00	100.00
94	MILLIE	5000	100.00	100.00
94	MOMMY & ME	5000	125.00	125.00

S. BUONAIUTO **EBONY COLLECTION/JUBILEE DANCERS**

93	BLISS	5000	200.00	200.00
93	FALLANA	5000	100.00	100.00
93	KESHIA	5000	100.00	100.00
93	LAMAR	5000	100.00	100.00
93	LOTTIE	5000	125.00	125.00
93	WILFRED	5000	100.00	100.00

P. APSIT **GREATEST GIFT...LOVE**

88	ANNUNCIATION, MARBLE	5000	270.00	270.00
88	ANNUNCIATION, PAINTED PORCELAIN	5000	270.00	270.00
88	CRUCIFIXION MARBLE	5000	300.00	300.00
88	CRUCIFIXION, PAINTED PORCELAIN	5000	300.00	300.00
88	NATIVITY, MARBLE	5000	500.00	500.00
88	NATIVITY, PAINTED PORCELAIN	5000	500.00	500.00

P. APSIT **HISTORY OF CLASSIC ENTERTAINERS**

87	AMERICAN	RT	160.00	350.00
87	AUGUSTE	RT	220.00	350.00
87	GRECO-ROMAN	RT	180.00	350.00
87	GROTESQUE	RT	230.00	350.00
87	HARLEQUIN	RT	250.00	350.00
87	JESTER	RT	410.00	725.00
87	PANTALONE	RT	270.00	350.00
87	PIERROT	RT	180.00	270.00
87	PULCINELLA	RT	220.00	350.00
87	RUSSIAN	RT	190.00	350.00
87	SLAPSTICK	RT	250.00	350.00
87	UNCLE SAM	RT	160.00	300.00

P. APSIT **HISTORY OF CLASSIC ENTERTAINERS II**

88	BOB HOPE	RT	250.00	275.00
88	FESTE	RT	250.00	275.00
88	GOLIARD	RT	200.00	275.00
88	MIME	RT	200.00	275.00
88	MOUNTEBANK	RT	270.00	275.00
88	PEDROLINO	RT	200.00	275.00
88	SIGNATURE PIECE	RT	50.00	275.00
88	TARTAGLIA	RT	200.00	275.00
88	THOMASSI	RT	200.00	275.00
88	TOUCHSTONE	RT	200.00	275.00
88	TRAMP	RT	200.00	275.00
88	WHITE FACE	RT	250.00	275.00
88	ZANNI	RT	200.00	275.00

YR	NAME	LIMIT	ISSUE	TREND
P. APSIT		HISTORY OF CLASSIC ENTERTAINERS-SPECIAL RELEASES		
88	SIGNATURE PIECE	RT	50.00	50.00
90	BOB HOPE, 18 IN. (SET)	RT	1,500.00	1750.00
90	BOB HOPE, 6 IN. PORCELAIN	6000	130.00	130.00
90	MIME, 18 IN.	RT	1,500.00	1500.00
P. APSIT		**HISTORY OF SANTA CLAUS**		
89	KRIS KRINGLE, 18 IN.	1000	1,500.00	1500.00
89	MEDIEVAL, 18 IN.	1000	1,500.00	1400.00
89	NAST, 18 IN.	1000	1,500.00	1500.00
89	RUSSIAN, 18 IN.	1000	1,500.00	1500.00
89	SODA POP, 18 IN.	1000	1,500.00	1500.00
89	ST. NICHOLAS, 18 IN.	1000	1,500.00	1500.00
P. APSIT		**HISTORY OF SANTA CLAUS I**		
83	BLACK PETER	RT	145.00	380.00
83	CIVIL WAR	10000	145.00	300.00
83	DEDT MOROZ	RT	145.00	300.00
83	KRIS KRINGLE	RT	165.00	450.00
83	MEDIEVAL	RT	220.00	1100.00
83	NAST	RT	90.00	1200.00
83	PIONEER	RT	145.00	2200.00
83	RUSSIAN	RT	145.00	350.00
83	SODA POP	RT	145.00	600.00
83	ST. NICHOLAS	RT	175.00	1100.00
83	VICTORIAN	RT	120.00	500.00
83	WASSAIL	RT	90.00	350.00
87	BLACK PETER, 8 IN. WOOD	RT	450.00	350.00
87	CIVIL WAR, 8 IN. WOOD	500	450.00	450.00
87	DEDT MOROZ, 8 IN. WOOD	RT	450.00	450.00
87	KRIS KRINGLE, 8 IN. WOOD	500	450.00	450.00
87	MEDIEVAL, 8 IN. WOOD	500	450.00	450.00
87	NAST, 8 IN. WOOD	RT	450.00	450.00
87	PIONEER, 8 IN. WOOD	RT	450.00	450.00
87	RUSSIAN, 8 IN. WOOD	RT	450.00	450.00
87	SODA POP, 8 IN. WOOD	RT	450.00	450.00
87	ST. NICHOLAS, 8 IN. WOOD	500	450.00	450.00
87	VICTORIAN, 8 IN. WOOD	RT	450.00	450.00
87	WASSAIL, 8 IN. WOOD	RT	450.00	450.00
88	BLACK PETE, 6 IN. PORCELAIN	6000	40.00	80.00
88	CIVIL WAR, 6 IN. PORCELAIN	6000	40.00	80.00
88	DEDT MOROZ, 6 IN. PORCELAIN	6000	40.00	80.00
88	KRIS KRINGLE, 6 IN. PORCELAIN	6000	40.00	80.00
88	MEDIEVAL, 6 IN. PORCELAIN	6000	40.00	80.00
88	NAST, 6 IN. PORCELAIN	6000	40.00	80.00
88	PIONEER, 6 IN. PORCELAIN	6000	40.00	80.00
88	RUSSIAN, 6 IN. PORCELAIN	6000	40.00	80.00
88	SODA POP, 6 IN. PORCELAIN	6000	40.00	80.00
88	ST. NICHOLAS, 6 IN. PORCELAIN	6000	40.00	80.00
88	VICTORIAN, 6 IN. PORCELAIN	6000	40.00	80.00
88	WASSAIL, 6 IN. PORCELAIN	6000	40.00	80.00
P. APSIT		**HISTORY OF SANTA CLAUS II**		
86	ALSACE ANGEL	10000	250.00	300.00
86	BABOUSKA	10000	170.00	200.00
86	BAVARIAN	10000	250.00	300.00
86	BEFANA	10000	200.00	250.00
86	FRAU HOLDA	10000	160.00	180.00
86	LORD OF MISRULE	10000	160.00	200.00
86	MAGI, THE	10000	350.00	400.00
86	MONGOLIAN/ASIAN	10000	240.00	300.00
86	ODIN	10000	200.00	250.00
86	PIXIE, THE	10000	140.00	175.00
86	SIR CHRISTMAS	10000	150.00	175.00
86	ST. LUCIA	10000	180.00	250.00
88	ALSACE ANGEL, 6 IN. PORCELAIN	6000	80.00	90.00
88	BABOUSKA, 6 IN. PORCELAIN	6000	70.00	80.00
88	BAVARIAN, 6 IN. PORCELAIN	6000	90.00	100.00
88	BEFANA, 6 IN. PORCELAIN	6000	70.00	80.00
88	FRAU HOLDA, 6 IN. PORCELAIN	6000	50.00	80.00
88	LORD OF MISRULE, 6 IN. PORCELAIN	6000	60.00	80.00
88	MAGI, 6 IN. PORCELAIN	6000	130.00	150.00
88	MONGOLIAN/ASIAN, 6 IN. PORCELAIN	6000	80.00	90.00
88	ODIN, 6 IN. PORCELAIN	6000	80.00	90.00
88	PIXIE, 6 IN. PORCELAIN	6000	50.00	80.00
88	SIR CHRISTMAS, 6 IN. PORCELAIN	6000	60.00	80.00
88	ST. LUCIA, 6 IN. PORCELAIN	6000	70.00	80.00
*		**HISTORY OF SANTA CLAUS III**		
90	DRUID	RT	250.00	250.00
90	JULENISSE	10000	200.00	200.00
90	ST. BASIL	10000	300.00	300.00
90	STAR MAN	10000	300.00	300.00
90	UKKO	RT	250.00	250.00
91	GRANDFATHER FROST & SNOW MAIDEN	10000	400.00	400.00
91	HOTEISHO	10000	200.00	200.00
91	JUDAH MACCACBEE	10000	250.00	250.00
91	KNICKERBOCKER	10000	300.00	300.00
91	SAMICHLAUS	10000	350.00	350.00

YR	NAME	LIMIT	ISSUE	TREND
*		**HISTORY OF SANTA CLAUS-SPECIAL RELEASES**		
91	SIGNATURE PIECE	OP	50.00	50.00
92	NAST & SLEIGH	5000	500.00	500.00
*		**SANTA 1ST SERIES-PAINTED PEWTER**		
86	BLACK PETER	500	30.00	30.00
86	CIVIL WAR	500	30.00	30.00
86	DEDT MOROZ	500	30.00	30.00
86	KRIS KRINGLE	500	30.00	30.00
86	MEDIEVAL	500	30.00	30.00
86	NAST	500	30.00	30.00
86	PIONEER	500	30.00	30.00
86	RUSSIAN	500	30.00	30.00
86	SET OF 12	500	360.00	425.00
86	SODA POP	500	30.00	30.00
86	ST. NICHOLAS	500	30.00	30.00
86	VICTORIAN	500	30.00	30.00
86	WASSAIL	500	30.00	30.00
*		**SANTA 2ND SERIES-PAINTED PEWTER**		
88	ALSACE ANGEL	500	30.00	30.00
88	BABOUSKA	500	30.00	30.00
88	BAVARIAN	500	30.00	30.00
88	BEFANA	500	30.00	30.00
88	FRAU HOLDA	500	30.00	30.00
88	LORD OF MISRULE	500	30.00	30.00
88	MAGI	500	30.00	30.00
88	MONGOLIAN	500	30.00	30.00
88	ODIN	500	30.00	30.00
88	PIXIE	500	30.00	30.00
88	SET OF 12	500	360.00	425.00
88	SIR CHRISTMAS	500	30.00	30.00
88	ST. LUCIA	500	30.00	30.00
*		**WOODLAND FAIRIES**		
88	ALMOND BLOSSOM	RT	70.00	70.00
88	APPLE	RT	70.00	70.00
88	CALLA LILY	RT	70.00	70.00
88	CHERRY	10000	70.00	70.00
88	CHESTNUT	10000	70.00	70.00
88	CHRISTMAS TREE	RT	70.00	70.00
88	ELM	10000	70.00	70.00
88	LIME TREE	RT	70.00	70.00
88	MULBERRY	10000	70.00	70.00
88	PEAR BLOSSOM	RT	70.00	70.00
88	PINE TREE	10000	70.00	70.00
88	POPLAR	10000	70.00	70.00
88	SYCAMORE	RT	70.00	70.00

EGGSPRESSIONS

YR	NAME	LIMIT	ISSUE	TREND
*				**EGGSHELL**
93	AMERICA'S PRIDE	OP	140.00	140.00
93	ANGELICA	OP	50.00	50.00
93	APPLE BLOSSOM BOUQUET	OP	62.00	62.00
93	BELLS	OP	55.00	55.00
93	BILL & COO	OP	55.00	55.00
93	BIRTH DAY! DEC	OP	40.00	40.00
93	BIRTH DAY! - APR	OP	40.00	40.00
93	BIRTH DAY! - AUG	OP	40.00	40.00
93	BIRTH DAY! - FEB	OP	40.00	40.00
93	BIRTH DAY! - JAN	OP	40.00	40.00
93	BIRTH DAY! - JUL	OP	40.00	40.00
93	BIRTH DAY! - JUN	OP	40.00	40.00
93	BIRTH DAY! - MAR	OP	40.00	40.00
93	BIRTH DAY! - MAY	OP	40.00	40.00
93	BIRTH DAY! - NOV	OP	40.00	40.00
93	BIRTH DAY! - OCT	OP	40.00	40.00
93	BIRTH DAY! - SEP	OP	40.00	40.00
93	BLUE BIRDS HAPPINESS	OP	79.00	79.00
93	BLUSH	OP	105.00	105.00
93	BRR RABBIT	OP	140.00	140.00
93	BUTTERCUP	OP	85.00	85.00
93	BUTTERFLY WINGS	OP	50.00	50.00
93	CANDYLAND	OP	100.00	100.00
93	CARDINALS	OP	70.00	70.00
93	CHOO-CHOO CHRISTMAS	OP	130.00	130.00
93	CHRISTMAS CURIOSITY	OP	110.00	110.00
93	COLOURS	OP	55.00	55.00
93	DAYTIME DEN	OP	125.00	125.00
93	DEAR ONE	OP	100.00	100.00
93	DOGWOOD	OP	50.00	50.00
93	DRUMMER BOY	OP	100.00	100.00
93	EBONY	OP	105.00	105.00
93	ELEGANT CHOICE	OP	167.00	167.00
93	FAMILY OUTING	OP	100.00	100.00
93	FANTAZIA	OP	50.00	50.00
93	GABRIELA	OP	45.00	45.00
93	GOLDEN CRYSTAL	OP	125.00	125.00

YR	NAME	LIMIT	ISSUE	TREND
93	IN TUNE	OP	130.00	130.00
93	ISADORA	OP	130.00	130.00
93	KACHINA	OP	130.00	130.00
93	KEWPIE DOLL	OP	110.00	110.00
93	KRIS KRINGLE	OP	45.00	45.00
93	LARA	OP	115.00	115.00
93	LOBO	OP	85.00	85.00
93	LOVE DUET	OP	140.00	140.00
93	LOVE IN FLIGHT	OP	100.00	100.00
93	MARCELLA	OP	45.00	45.00
93	MARIA	OP	115.00	115.00
93	MCGREGOR'S GARDEN	OP	105.00	105.00
93	MIDAS	OP	105.00	105.00
93	MINT JULEP	OP	100.00	100.00
93	MISS ELLIE	OP	45.00	45.00
93	MISTY ROSE	OP	45.00	45.00
93	OH, NUTS	OP	100.00	100.00
93	PEARL	OP	100.00	100.00
93	PETER	OP	45.00	45.00
93	PETUNIA	OP	45.00	45.00
93	POINSETTIA	OP	60.00	60.00
93	ROMANTIQUE	OP	75.00	75.00
93	SANTA'S WORKSHOP	125	130.00	130.00
93	SECRET GARDEN	OP	158.00	158.00
93	SERENA	OP	140.00	140.00
93	SILVER JEWELS	OP	105.00	105.00
93	SKYE	OP	100.00	100.00
93	SLUMBERING STEGGY	OP	85.00	85.00
93	SNOWFLAKE	OP	50.00	50.00
93	STAR PRANCER	OP	140.00	140.00
93	STORYTELLER	OP	130.00	130.00
93	SUMMER ROSE	OP	45.00	45.00
93	TABITHA	OP	40.00	40.00
93	TANNENBAUM	OP	55.00	55.00
93	TINY TREASURES	OP	110.00	110.00
93	TOGETHERNESS	OP	100.00	100.00
93	TRYKE	OP	90.00	90.00
93	VELVET PRINCESS	OP	170.00	170.00
93	WAITING	OP	100.00	100.00
93	WARRIOR'S PRIDE	OP	85.00	85.00
93	WELCOME CANDLE	OP	63.00	63.00
93	WINTER COLT	OP	105.00	105.00
93	WINTER COLT (STAND)	OP	105.00	105.00
93	WINTER HAVEN	OP	105.00	105.00
93	WINTER SONG	OP	115.00	115.00
93	WINTER WONDERLAND	OP	105.00	105.00
93	YELLOW ROSE	OP	105.00	105.00
94	ABSOLUTELY AMETHYST	OP	100.00	100.00
94	ANGEL BUNNY	250	220.00	220.00
94	ANGEL OF HOPE	250	130.00	130.00
94	ANGEL OF LOVE	250	110.00	110.00
94	BEARY BLUE CHRISTMAS	250	100.00	100.00
94	BEARY PINK CHRISTMAS	250	100.00	100.00
94	CAROLING MICE	250	120.00	120.00
94	CHICKS & BUNNIES	OP	88.00	88.00
94	CHRISTMAS JOY	250	105.00	105.00
94	ETERNITY	250	170.00	170.00
94	FROSTY'S CHEER	500	64.00	64.00
94	GOLDEN HARMONY	250	160.00	160.00
94	GRANDMA'S GOODIES	OP	99.00	99.00
94	HARVEST FAIRY	OP	95.00	95.00
94	HOIDAY MEMORIES	250	190.00	190.00
94	JESSICA	125	240.00	240.00
94	LAVENDER LOVE	250	130.00	130.00
94	LOVE BIRDS	250	120.00	120.00
94	MAKING SPIRITS BRIGHT	25	300.00	300.00
94	MOTHER'S PRIDE	250	120.00	120.00
94	OH, HOLY NIGHT	250	160.00	160.00
94	OLD ST. NICKOLAS	500	64.00	64.00
94	PASSION	25	500.00	500.00
94	PASTEL & PEARLS	OP	112.00	112.00
94	PRE-SCHOOL PLAY	OP	108.00	108.00
94	PRISTINE PEARLS	OP	90.00	90.00
94	PURR-FECT HUG	RT	150.00	150.00
94	ROSE MARIE	OP	49.00	49.00
94	SANTA'S LITTLE ELVES	250	130.00	130.00
94	SANTA'S LITTLE SWEETHEART	100	100.00	100.00
94	SERENADE	250	120.00	120.00
94	SERENITY	250	115.00	115.00
94	SKIP A LONG	250	120.00	120.00
94	SPRING MELODY	250	130.00	130.00
94	SWEET DREAMS	OP	100.00	100.00
94	TEDDY BEAR SING ALONG	250	115.00	115.00
94	WEDDING IN WHITE	250	160.00	160.00
95	ANDREA	250	80.00	80.00

YR	NAME	LIMIT	ISSUE	TREND
95	ANGEL DIVINE	250	120.00	120.00
95	CABBAGE PATCH	250	105.00	105.00
95	COO	250	115.00	115.00
95	JAMIE	250	80.00	80.00
95	TARA	250	80.00	80.00

EMI

P. APSIT — EMMETT KELLY JR.

YR	NAME	LIMIT	ISSUE	TREND
94	THINKING OF YOU	2500	640.00	670.00

R. HARRIS — MASTERWORKS

YR	NAME	LIMIT	ISSUE	TREND
94	CATTLE DRIFTING BEFORE THE STORM	500	1,300.00	1400.00
94	UNKNOWN EXPLORERS	500	1,100.00	1125.00

T. KNAPP — MASTERWORKS

YR	NAME	LIMIT	ISSUE	TREND
94	COW-BOY	500	930.00	950.00
94	LUMBER CAMP AT NIGHT	500	590.00	620.00

ENDURANCE

P. SZEILER — ART OF SPORT, THE- BASEBALL

YR	NAME	LIMIT	ISSUE	TREND
96	CAL RIPKEN, JR.	4500	190.00	190.00
96	CAL RIPKEN, JR. (HAND SIGNED)	500	400.00	400.00

J. BAILEY — ART OF SPORT, THE- BOXING

YR	NAME	LIMIT	ISSUE	TREND
91	JOHN L. SULLIVAN VS. JIM CORBITT	RT	500.00	1400.00

K. FALLON — ART OF SPORT, THE- BOXING

YR	NAME	LIMIT	ISSUE	TREND
90	MUHAMMAD ALI VS. SONNY LISTON	7500	380.00	380.00

D. LOVATT — ART OF SPORT, THE- BOXING

YR	NAME	LIMIT	ISSUE	TREND
89	BOB FITZSIMMONS	RT	180.00	300
89	JAMES J. CORDETT	RT	180.00	300
89	JOHN L. SULLIVAN	RT	180.00	300.00
90	JACK DEMPSEY	RT	180.00	300
90	JACK JOHNSON	RT	180.00	300
90	JESS WILLARD	RT	180.00	300
90	TOMMY BURNS	RT	180.00	300
91	GENE TUNNEY	RT	180.00	300
91	JACK SHARKEY	RT	180.00	300
91	MAX BAER	RT	180.00	300
91	MAX SCHMELING	RT	180.00	300
91	PRIMO CAMERA	RT	180.00	300
92	JAMES J. BRADDOCK	RT	180.00	300
92	JOE LOUIS	RT	180.00	300

T. POTTS — ART OF SPORT, THE- BOXING

YR	NAME	LIMIT	ISSUE	TREND
94	FRANK BRUNO	5000	180.00	180.00
95	NIGEL BENN	5000	180.00	180.00
96	THOMAS HEARNS	5000	180.00	180.00
97	JAKE LA MOTTA (HAND SIGNED)	1950	280.00	280.00

P. SZEILER — ART OF SPORT, THE- BOXING

YR	NAME	LIMIT	ISSUE	TREND
89	MUHAMMAD ALI BRONZE	RT	190.00	300.00
92	FANTASY FIGHT JACK DEMPSEY	OP	180.00	180.00
92	FANTASY FIGHT JACK JOHNSON	OP	180.00	180.00
92	FANTASY FIGHT JOE LOUIS	OP	180.00	180.00
92	FANTASY FIGHT MIKE TYSON	OP	180.00	180.00
92	FANTASY FIGHT MUHAMMAD ALI	RT	180.00	250.00
92	FANTASY FIGHT ROCKY MARCIANO	OP	180.00	180.00
92	JOE LOUIS VS. SCHMELING	RT	500.00	1400.00
92	ROCKY MARCIANO VS. JERSEY JOE WALCOTT	RT	500.00	1400.00
93	HENRY COOPER	5000	180.00	180.00
93	HENRY COOPER VS. CASSIUS CLAY	RT	500.00	1900.00
93	MIKE TYSON 1 POSE	5000	190.00	190.00
93	MUHAMMAD ALI	5000	190.00	190.00
93	ROCKY MARCIANO	5000	180.00	180.00
93	SUGAR RAY ROBINSON	5000	180.00	180.00
93	THE LONG COUNT J. DEMPSEY G. TUNNEY REF D. BARRY	1000	480.00	480.00
94	LENOX LEWIS	500	180.00	180.00
94	MARVIN HAGLER	5000	180.00	180.00
95	EVANDER HOLYFIELD	5000	180.00	180.00
95	JOE FRAZIER	5000	190.00	190.00
95	MIKE TYSON 2 STANCE	2000	190.00	190.00
95	NASEEM HAMMED	5000	180.00	180.00
95	ROBERTO DURAN	5000	180.00	180.00
96	BUTTER BEAN (HAND SIGNED)	500	230.00	230.00
96	BUTTER BEAN (UNSIGNED)	4500	180.00	180.00
96	EVANDER HOLYFIELD BRONZE	OP	180.00	180.00
96	FANTASY FIGHT JOHN L. SULLIVAN	OP	180.00	180.00
96	MIKE TYSON 1 BRONZE	OP	190.00	190.00
96	SUGAR RAY LEONARD	5000	180.00	180.00

T. POTTS — ART OF SPORT, THE- CELEBRITY

YR	NAME	LIMIT	ISSUE	TREND
96	THREE TENORS, THE PAVAROTTI, CARRERAS & DOMINGO	10000	250.00	250.00

P. SZEILER — ART OF SPORT, THE- CELEBRITY

YR	NAME	LIMIT	ISSUE	TREND
93	ELVIS PRESLEY	7500	190.00	190.00
95	GEORGE ADAMSON	5000	180.00	180.00
95	JOHN F. KENNEDY	5000	180.00	180.00
95	POPE JOHN PAUL II	10000	180.00	180.00

T. POTTS — ART OF SPORT, THE- GOLFING

YR	NAME	LIMIT	ISSUE	TREND
96	JACK NICKLAUS	CL	190.00	190.00

YR	NAME	LIMIT	ISSUE	TREND
P. SZEILER		ART OF SPORT, THE- GOLFING		
92	BEN HOGAN	2500	180.00	180.00
92	WALTER HAGEN	2500	180.00	180.00
93	BOBBY JONES	2500	180.00	180.00
94	GENE SARAZEN	2500	180.00	180.00
94	HARRY VARDON	2500	180.00	180.00
94	OLD TOM MORRIS	2500	180.00	180.00
95	SEVE BALLESTEROS	2500	180.00	180.00
96	GARY PLAYER	2500	180.00	180.00
96	GREG NORMAN	2500	190.00	190.00
96	LAURA DAVIES	2500	180.00	180.00
96	NICK FALDO	2500	180.00	180.00
96	TOM WATSON	2500	180.00	180.00
P. WARD		ART OF SPORT, THE- GOLFING		
93	ARNOLD PALMER	CL	190.00	190.00
93	SIR HENRY COTTON	2500	180.00	180.00
T. POTTS		ART OF SPORT, THE- JOCKEYS		
96	FRANKIE DETTORI	5000	180.00	180.00
P. SZEILER		ART OF SPORT, THE- JOCKEYS		
95	LESTER PIGGOTT	5000	180.00	180.00
T. POTTS		ART OF SPORT, THE- MOTOR RACING		
96	AYRTON SENNA	7500	180.00	180.00
96	COLIN CHAPMAN	2500	180.00	180.00
96	JACKIE STEWART	2500	180.00	180.00
96	JAMES HUNT	2500	180.00	180.00
96	STIRLING MOSS	2500	180.00	180.00
P. SZEILER		ART OF SPORT, THE- MOTOR RACING		
93	SIR JACK BRABHAM	2500	180.00	180.00
94	ALAIN PROST	2500	180.00	180.00
94	MICHAEL SCHUMACHER	2500	180.00	180.00
95	ALFRED NEUBAUR	2500	180.00	180.00
95	DAMON HILL	2500	180.00	180.00
95	ENZO FERRARI	2500	180.00	180.00
95	GERHARD BERGER	2500	180.00	180.00
95	GILLES VILLENVUE	2500	180.00	180.00
95	JEAN ALESI	2500	180.00	180.00
95	NIKI LAUDA	2500	180.00	180.00
96	CARL FOGARTY	5000	180.00	180.00
96	JIM CLARK	2500	180.00	180.00
96	NIGEL MANSELL	2500	180.00	180.00
P. WARD		ART OF SPORT, THE- MOTOR RACING		
92	JUAN FANGIO	2500	180.00	180.00
T. POTTS		ART OF SPORT, THE- SOCCER		
96	ALAN SHEARER	5000	180.00	180.00
96	BOBBY MOORE	2500	180.00	180.00
96	DUNCAN EDWARDS	5000	180.00	180.00
96	ERIC CANTONA	5000	180.00	180.00
96	GEORGE BEST	5000	180.00	180.00
P. SZEILER		ART OF SPORT, THE- TRACK AND FIELD		
94	SIR ROGER BANNISTER	1500	180.00	180.00

ENESCO CORP.

YR	NAME	LIMIT	ISSUE	TREND
L. RIGG				
95	BIRD SCULPTURES	2000	60.00	60.00
95	NATHAN & SHAWNIE - BOY/GIRL INDIANS	2000	60.00	60.00
95	THOMAS & BETH - BOY/GIRL W/SONGBOOK	2000	60.00	60.00
*		BALLERINA SERIES		
91	LIFE IS ONE JOYOUS STEP 121207	YR	20.00	20.00
91	LIFE IS ONE JOYOUS STEP 121274	OP	25.00	25.00
91	YOU ARE VERY SPECIAL TO ME 121215	OP	40.00	40.00
*		BARBIE GLAMOUR COLLECTION		
94	SOLO IN THE SPOTLIGHT 1960	7500	100.00	100.00
94	SOME ENCHANTED EVENING 1960	7500	100.00	100.00
94	WEDDING ON THE CHURCH STEPS 1959	7500	100.00	100.00
P. HILLMAN		CALICO KITTENS		
*	TRUE LOVE- MUSICAL	RT	*	N/A
94	EXTRA SPECIAL	RT	15.00	15.00
94	HAND KNITTED WITH LOVE	RT	*	N/A
94	HOME SWEET HOME	RT	15.00	15.00
94	LOVE	RT	15.00	15.00
94	NOTHING IS SWEETER THAN MOM	RT	13.50	14.00
94	PURR-FECT FRIENDS	RT	15.00	15.00
94	SEW HAPPY IT'S YOUR BIRTHDAY	RT	*	N/A
94	TEA AND YOU HIT THE SPOT	RT	*	N/A
94	THINKING OF YOU	RT	15.00	15.00
94	YOU ALWAYS TOP OFF MY DAYS	RT	*	N/A
94	YOU AND ME	RT	15.00	15.00
94	YOUR FRIENDSHIP IS MY SILVER LINING	RT	*	N/A
95	ALL ABOUT ANGELS	5000	25.00	25.00
95	BUTTONED UP WITH LOVE	RT	13.50	14.00
95	GRANDMA'S ARE SEW FULL OF LOVE	RT	13.50	14.00
95	HARK - A HERALD ANGEL	*	17.50	18.00
95	HATS OFF TO A PERFECT FRIENDSHIP	RT	20.00	20.00
95	OUR FRIENDSHIP IS A QUILT OF LOVE	RT	*	N/A

YR	NAME	LIMIT	ISSUE	TREND
95	STITCH IN TIME SAVES NINE, A	3000	35.00	35.00
95	YOUR PATCHWORK CHARM SHOWS THROUGH	RT	17.50	18.00
96	HEY DIDDLE, DIDDLE THE CAT & THE FIDDLE	7500	20.00	20.00
96	I'VE BEEN A GOOD KITTY	*	17.50	18.00
96	WE WISH YOU A MERRY CHRISTMAS	*	17.50	18.00
96	YOU'VE EARNED YOUR WINGS	5000	35.00	35.00
97	PUSSY CAT AND THE QUEEN	5000	25.00	25.00
P. HILLMAN	**CALICO KITTENS 1993 CHRISTMAS INTRODUCTION**			
93	TUNE: WE WISH YOU A MERRY CHRISTMAS	RT	50.00	50.00
P. HILLMAN	**CALICO KITTENS 1994 CHRISTMAS INTRODUCTION**			
94	JOY TO THE WORLD	RT	23.00	23.00
94	LOVING GIFT, A	RT	23.00	23.00
94	PEACE ON EARTH	RT	23.00	23.00
94	YOU'RE A SPECIAL AUNT- 6 PC	RT	12.00	12.00
94	YOU'RE A SPECIAL FRIEND- 6 PC	RT	12.00	12.00
94	YOU'RE A SPECIAL GRANDMA- 6 PC	RT	12.00	12.00
94	YOU'RE A SPECIAL MOM- 6 PC	RT	12.00	12.00
94	YOU'RE A SPECIAL NIECE- 6 PC	RT	12.00	12.00
94	YOU'RE A SPECIAL SISTER- 6 PC	RT	12.00	12.00
P. HILLMAN	**CALICO KITTENS 1997 CHRISTMAS INTRODUCTION**			
97	DASH OF LOVE MAKES YOU SWEETER, A- DATED	YR	17.50	18.00
97	FRIENDSHIP IS HEAVENLY	5000	20.00	20.00
97	TUNE: O' TANNENBAUM- MUSICAL	OP	35.00	35.00
P. HILLMAN	**CALICO KITTENS A LITTLE BIRD TOLD ME**			
97	LITTLE BIRD TOLD ME YOU'RE TWEET, A	OP	20.00	20.00
97	YOU'RE MY FEATHERED FRIEND FOREVER	OP	20.00	20.00
97	YOU'RE THE CAT'S MEOW	OP	25.00	25.00
P. HILLMAN	**CALICO KITTENS APRIL SHOWERS**			
96	APRIL SHOWERS	*	17.50	18.00
96	FRIENDSHIP GROWS WHEN SHARED	*	15.00	15.00
96	I'M HOOKED ON YOU	*	17.50	18.00
96	KITE TAILS 155497	*	17.50	18.00
P. HILLMAN	**CALICO KITTENS COZY KITTEN**			
97	ALL WRAPPED UP IN WARMTH	OP	16.50	17.00
97	FRIENDSHIP COVERS THE HOLIDAYS	OP	16.50	17.00
97	HATS OFF TO FRIENDSHIP	OP	16.50	17.00
97	PURR-FECT FIT, A	OP	16.50	17.00
97	YOU HOLD THE STRINGS TO MY HEART	OP	16.50	17.00
P. HILLMAN	**CALICO KITTENS HALLOWEEN**			
95	GOBBLIN' UP THE FUN	*	15.00	15.00
95	I'M BEWITCHED WITH FRIENDSHIP	*	15.00	15.00
96	WE'VE CARVED A PERFECT FRIENDSHIP	*	13.50	14.00
96	YOU'RE THE BEST IN THE FIELD	*	13.50	14.00
P. HILLMAN	**CALICO KITTENS HOLIDAY HARMONY**			
95	FIRST NOEL, THE	*	17.50	18.00
95	I'LL BE HOME FOR CHRISTMAS	*	17.50	18.00
95	JOLLY OLD ST. NICHOLAS	*	17.50	18.00
95	OH, TANNENBAUM	*	17.50	18.00
95	SILENT NIGHT	*	17.50	18.00
95	SILVER BELLS	*	23.00	23.00
95	WINTER WONDERLAND	*	17.50	18.00
P. HILLMAN	**CALICO KITTENS ITTY BITTY KITTIES**			
*	APRIL SHOWERS	*	7.00	7.00
*	I LOVE MY KITTY	*	7.00	7.00
*	I LOVE SPRING	*	7.00	7.00
*	TO MY KITTY	*	7.00	7.00
96	CONGRATULATIONS	*	7.50	8.00
96	GET WELL	*	7.50	8.00
96	GRADUATION	*	7.50	8.00
96	HAPPY BIRTHDAY	*	7.50	8.00
96	I LOVE YOU	*	7.50	8.00
96	MY LITTLE SWEET TART	*	7.00	7.00
96	NEW BABY	*	7.50	8.00
96	YOU ARE MY SUNSHINE	*	7.00	7.00
P. HILLMAN	**CALICO KITTENS ITTY BITTY KITTIES CAT'S GOT YOUR TONGUE**			
97	ALLEY CAT- MINI	OP	7.50	8.00
97	CAT TAILS- MINI	OP	7.50	8.00
97	COOL CAT- MINI	OP	7.50	8.00
97	FAT CAT- MINI	OP	7.50	8.00
97	HOUSE CAT- MINI	OP	7.50	8.00
97	TOP CAT- MINI	OP	7.50	8.00
P. HILLMAN	**CALICO KITTENS ITTY BITTY KITTIES PURR-FECT PAIRS**			
97	BEST FRIENDS- MINI	OP	14.00	14.00
97	MOM AND ME- MINI	OP	14.00	14.00
97	TRUE LOVE	OP	14.00	14.00
P. HILLMAN	**CALICO KITTENS KITTY CAPERS**			
96	HATS OFF TO THE HOLIDAYS	*	12.50	13.00
96	I'M ALL YOURS	*	12.50	13.00
96	NOT PURR-FECT, JUST PURR-FECTLY HAPPY	*	12.50	13.00
96	WRAPPED UP IN YOU	*	15.00	15.00
96	YOU BRIGHTEN MY HOLIDAYS	*	15.00	15.00
P. HILLMAN	**CALICO KITTENS MY HEART BELONGS TO KITTY**			
96	FOR THE ONE I LOVE	*	17.50	18.00
96	HOPE ALL YOUR DREAMS COME TRUE	*	20.00	20.00

YR	NAME	LIMIT	ISSUE	TREND
96	MY FUNNY VALENTINE	*	17.50	20.00
96	SWEETS FOR THE SWEET	*	20.00	20.00
P. HILLMAN			**CALICO KITTENS NATIVITY**	
93	I'LL BRING A SPECIAL GIFT FOR YOU- 3 PC	RT	55.00	55.00
93	PURR-FECT ANGEL FROM ABOVE, A	RT	15.00	15.00
93	SHARING A SPECIAL GIFT OF LOVE- 2 PC	RT	35.00	35.00
94	FRIENDS COME FROM AFAR	RT	17.50	18.00
P. HILLMAN			**CALICO KITTENS PICKS OF THE LITTER**	
96	HELLO, LITTLE ONE	*	17.50	18.00
96	LITTLE LITTER OF BLESSINGS, A	*	15.00	15.00
96	NEW KIT ON THE BLOCK	*	12.50	15.00
96	OUR FRIENDSHIP IS SQUEEKY CLEAN	*	15.00	15.00
96	TUMMY FULL OF LOVE FOR YOU	*	12.50	13.00
96	WAGON OUR TAILS FOR YOU	*	17.50	18.00
P. HILLMAN			**CALICO KITTENS PURR-FECT PERSONALITIES**	
95	ALWAYS THINKING OF YOU	*	14.50	15.00
95	AN EXPECTED TREAT	*	14.50	15.00
95	BLUE WITHOUT YOU	*	17.50	18.00
95	FISHING FOR A FRIEND	*	14.50	15.00
95	FRIENDSHIP HAS MANY RICHES	*	17.50	18.00
95	GOOD AS NEW	*	14.50	15.00
95	GREAT SCOT WE'RE THE BEST OF FRIENDS	*	17.50	18.00
95	I'M LOST WITHOUT YOU	*	14.50	15.00
95	IT'S NO MYSTERY WE'RE FRIENDS	*	17.50	18.00
95	MY FAVORITE COMPANION	*	14.50	15.00
95	PLAYFUL AFTERNOON, A	*	14.50	15.00
95	PURR-FECT PAIR, A 112445	RT	14.50	15.00
95	SWEET DREAMS	*	14.50	15.00
95	WE'RE INSEP-PURR-ABLE FRIENDS	*	17.50	18.00
95	YOU'RE MY ALL AMERICAN FRIEND	*	17.50	18.00
96	I'D NEVER DESERT YOU	*	17.50	18.00
96	TRIED AND TRUE FOR THE RED, WHITE & BLUE	*	17.50	18.00
P. HILLMAN			**CALICO KITTENS SCAREDY CAT**	
97	CARVING A SEASON OF SMILES	OP	13.50	14.00
97	MUMMY MISCHIEF	OP	13.50	14.00
97	OUR FRIENDSHIP IS A MAGICAL SPELL	OP	13.50	14.00
97	YOU CAN ALWAYS SPOT A FRIEND	OP	13.50	14.00
P. HILLMAN			**CALICO KITTENS SPRING & EASTER**	
*	HAPPY SPRING	*	11.00	11.00
*	PURR-FECT FRIEND	*	11.00	11.00
95	EGGSTRA SPECIAL	*	11.00	11.00
95	FRIENDSHIP IS THE BEST BLESSING	*	20.00	20.00
95	FURRY AND FEATHERED FRIENDS	*	20.00	20.00
95	LOVE BLOOMS FUR-EVER	*	17.50	18.00
95	YOU MAKE LIFE COLORFUL	*	25.00	25.00
P. HILLMAN			**CALICO KITTENS ST. PATRICK'S DAY ADDITION**	
97	FISHIN' FOR GOOD LUCK	OP	15.00	15.00
P. HILLMAN			**CALICO KITTENS THE CAT'S OUT OF THE BAG**	
97	FRIENDSHIP LETS THE CAT OUT OF THE BAG	OP	17.50	18.00
97	I'M SENDING YOU A BAG FULL OF LOVE	OP	17.50	18.00
97	OUR FRIENDSHIP IS OUT OF THE BAG	OP	17.50	18.00
P. HILLMAN			**CALICO KITTENS VALENTINES**	
*	SEW IN LOVE	RT	11.00	11.00
*	SEW SWEET	*	11.00	11.00
95	BE MINE	*	11.00	11.00
95	LOVE POURS FROM MY HEART	*	23.00	23.00
95	MY LOVE BLOSSOMS FOR YOU	*	15.00	15.00
95	PAWS-ITIVELY IN LOVE	*	25.00	25.00
95	YOU MAKE IT ALL BETTER	*	15.00	15.00
P. HILLMAN			**CALICO KITTENS WELCOME HOME A LITTER OF LOVE**	
97	ALWAYS PAWS FOR PLAYTIME	OP	17.50	18.00
97	CAT NAP DREAMS	OP	13.50	14.00
97	I'M ALL WRAPPED UP OVER YOU	OP	15.00	15.00
97	SCRATCHIN' TO FIND A FRIEND LIKE YOU	OP	17.50	18.00
97	YOU'RE A LUCKY CATCH	OP	15.00	15.00
97	YOU'RE THE CHEF'S MEOW	OP	15.00	15.00
L. RIGG			**CHAPEAU NOELLE**	
94	BEAR W/HAND MIRROR - JOAN	2000	30.00	30.00
94	BEAR W/TEA SET - LINDA	2000	30.00	30.00
94	BRIDE BEAR - DIANE	2000	30.00	30.00
94	HISTORY OF HATS- 6 PC	30000	15.00	15.00
94	MRS. SANTA - BEAR W/COOKIES	2000	30.00	30.00
94	SANTA - BEAR W/LIST/PEN	2000	30.00	30.00
95	ALLISON- BEAR PAINTING	2000	30.00	30.00
95	BEAR WITH FLOWERS- MINI 4 PC	20000	15.00	15.00
95	JULIET - BEAR HOLDING DOVE	2000	30.00	30.00
95	MARY LOUISE/FRANCES - ANGEL H/O	5000	12.50	13.00
95	ROMEO - BEAR HOLDING ROSE	2000	30.00	30.00
95	SANTA/MRS. SANTA H/O	5000	12.50	13.00
95	SUSIE- BEAR W/BASKET	2000	30.00	30.00
95	THOMAS & BETH - CAROLERS H/O	5000	12.50	13.00
97	BEAR WITH PANSY	2000	30.00	30.00
97	BEAR WITH SUNFLOWER	2000	30.00	30.00

YR	NAME	LIMIT	ISSUE	TREND
				CHERISHED TEDDIES
P. HILLMAN				
92	ANNA	OP	23.00	40.00
92	BEAR IN STOCKING HAT MUSICAL WATERBALL	*	60.00	80.00
92	BENJI	RT	13.50	40.00
92	BETH	RT	17.50	40.00
92	BETH AND BLOSSOM W/ BUTTERFLY- MUSICAL	RT	50.00	100.00
92	CAMILLE	RT	20.00	30.00
92	CHRISTOPHER	OP	50.00	50.00
92	COUPLE IN BASKET WITH UMBRELLA MUSICAL	OP	60.00	60.00
92	FRIEND ALWAYS KNOWS WHEN YOU NEED A HUG, A	RT	20.00	20.00
92	FRIENDS ARE NEVER FAR APART	RT	50.00	50.00
92	FRIENDSHIP WEATHERS ALL STORMS	RT	20.00	20.00
92	JACKI	*	10.00	15.00
92	JASMINE	SU	23.00	40.00
92	JEREMY	RT	15.00	50.00
92	JOSHUA	OP	20.00	40.00
92	KAREN	*	10.00	50.00
92	KATIE	RT	20.00	40.00
92	MANDY	RT	15.00	50.00
92	NATHANIEL AND NELLIE	RT	30.00	40.00
92	RICHARD	OP	55.00	55.00
92	SARA	OP	10.00	30.00
92	THEADORE, SAMANTHA, TYLER	RT	20.00	20.00
92	THEADORE, SAMANTHA, TYLER (9 IN.)	OP	130.00	140.00
92	TUNE: LET ME BE YOUR TEDDY BEAR	RT	60.00	60.00
92	YESTERDAY'S MEMORIES ARE TODAY'S TREASURES	RT	30.00	30.00
92	ZACHARY	RT	30.00	45.00
93	BABY IN CRADLE MUSICAL	OP	60.00	60.00
93	BOOK OF TEDDIES 1903-1993, THE	YR	20.00	150.00
93	BOY PRAYING MUSICAL	RT	38.00	38.00
93	CHUGGIN' ALONG, SAIL WITH ME, WE'RE GOING PLACES	RT	17.50	18.00
93	FREDA AND TINA	OP	35.00	65.00
93	FRIENDS LIKE YOU ARE PRECIOUS AND TRUE	RT	30.00	30.00
93	GIRL PRAYING MUSICAL	RT	38.00	38.00
93	HARRISON	RT	15.00	40.00
93	JONATHAN	RT	15.00	40.00
93	LOVE SURROUNDS OUR FRIENDSHIP	RT	15.00	15.00
93	PATRICE	OP	19.00	32.00
93	PATRICK	OP	19.00	32.00
93	PRISCILLA	RT	15.00	180.00
93	PRISCILLA ANN	YR	24.00	70.00
93	ROBBIE AND RACHEL	OP	28.00	28.00
93	TEDDY ROOSEVELT	OP	20.00	20.00
93	THOMAS	RT	15.00	28.00
93	TRACIE AND NICOLE	OP	35.00	55.00
94	BABY BOY JOINTED MUSICAL	SU	60.00	60.00
94	BABY GIRL JOINTED MUSICAL	SU	60.00	60.00
94	BEAR AS BUNNY MUSICAL	RT	60.00	60.00
94	BEAR HOLDING HARP MUSICAL	RT	45.00	45.00
94	BEAR WITH GOOSE- MUSICAL	RT	45.00	45.00
94	BEAR WITH HORSE MUSICAL	OP	150.00	150.00
94	BEAR WITH TOY CHEST MUSICAL	OP	45.00	45.00
94	BEARS OF A FEATHER STAY TOGETHER	RT	15.00	15.00
94	BETH AND BLOSSOM ON ROCKING HORSE- MUSICAL	RT	*	50.00
94	BETSEY	OP	12.50	13.00
94	BETTY	OP	19.00	19.00
94	BILLY	OP	12.50	35.00
94	BOBBIE	OP	12.50	13.00
94	BOY AND GIRL IN LAUNDRY BASKET MUSICAL	RT	60.00	60.00
94	BRIDE AND GROOM MUSICAL	OP	50.00	50.00
94	GIVING THANKS FOR FRIENDS	RT	17.50	18.00
94	HAPPINESS IS HOMEMADE	RT	17.50	18.00
94	INGRID	YR	20.00	45.00
94	LITTLE FAIR FEATHER FRIEND	RT	15.00	15.00
94	NEAR & DEAR FOR CHRISTMAS	RT	22.50	45.00
94	PRISCILLA, GRETA	OP	50.00	50.00
94	THAT'S WHAT FRIENDS ARE FOR	RT	23.00	23.00
94	TUNE: LOVE MAKES THE WORLD GO ROUND	RT	40.00	40.00
94	TUNE: WIND BENEATH MY WINGS	RT	45.00	45.00
95	ABC & 123, YOU'RE A FRIEND TO ME!	*	15.00	15.00
95	ALLISON AND ALEXANDRIA	OP	25.00	40.00
95	BEST IS YET TO COME, THE/BOY	*	12.50	13.00
95	BEST IS YET TO COME, THE/GIRL	*	12.50	13.00
95	CAN I BE YOUR FOOTBALL HERO?	*	15.00	15.00
95	CUP FULL OF CHEER, A	OP	20.00	20.00
95	CUP FULL OF FRIENDSHIP, A	OP	20.00	20.00
95	DOROTHY, MILLIE AND CHRISTY	RT	*	N/A
95	FRIENDSHIP KEEPS ME ON MY TOES	*	15.00	15.00
95	FRIENDSHIP MAKES IT ALL BETTER/LAURA	*	15.00	15.00
95	GIRL BEAR ON OTTOMAN- MUSICAL	OP	55.00	55.00
95	HERE'S SOME CHEER TO LAST THE YEAR	YR	17.50	18.00
95	KISS THE HURT AND MAKE IT WELL	*	15.00	15.00
95	LET'S HEAR IT FOR FRIENDSHIP!	*	15.00	15.00
95	LOVE ME TENDER	OP	12.50	13.00
95	LOVE ME TRUE	OP	12.50	13.00

YR	NAME	LIMIT	ISSUE	TREND
95	MY PRAYER IS FOR YOU, CHRISTIAN	OP	19.00	19.00
95	MY PRAYER IS FOR YOU, CHRISTINE	OP	19.00	19.00
95	NICKOLAS	YR	20.00	35.00
95	OUR HEARTS BELONG TO YOU/PRISCILLA & GRETA	19950	50.00	50.00
95	PRISCILLA AND GRETA- INTERNATIONAL	*	50.00	120.00
95	TAKE ME TO YOUR HEART	OP	12.50	13.00
95	TRUNK FULL OF BEAR HUGS	*	23.00	23.00
95	TWO FRIENDS MEAN TWICE THE LOVE	*	25.00	25.00
95	WE'RE BEARY GOOD PALS	OP	25.00	25.00
95	WE'RE IN THIS TOGETHER	OP	25.00	25.00
96	RESIN EGG	OP	8.50	10.00
96	TWO BOYS W/LANTERN	*	50.00	50.00
96	WISHING YOU A COZY CHRISTMAS	*	25.00	25.00
97	AN AUTUMN BREEZE BLOWS BLESSINGS TO PLEASE	OP	25.00	25.00
97	CAN'T BEAR TO SEE YOU UNDER THE WEATHER	OP	15.00	15.00
97	CUP FULL OF JOY	OP	25.00	25.00
97	CUP FULL OF LOVE	OP	25.00	25.00
97	CUP FULL OF PEACE	OP	25.00	25.00
97	EASTER EGG- DATED	YR	10.00	10.00
97	I'M BATTY OVER YOU	OP	17.50	18.00
97	LILIES BLOOM WITH PETALS OF HOPE	YR	15.00	15.00
97	MOTHER'S HEART IS FULL OF LOVE, A	OP	25.00	25.00
97	OUR FRIENDSHIP WILL NEVER BE EXTINCT	OP	17.50	18.00
97	RINGING IN THE NEW YEAR WITH CHEER	OP	15.00	15.00
97	STRIKE UP THE BAND & GIVE 5 CHERISHED YEARS A HAND	YR	75.00	75.00
97	THERE'S NO ROSE SWEETER...& WHEREFORE ART THOU...	YR	60.00	60.00
97	THIS CALLS FOR A CELEBRATION	OP	15.00	15.00
97	YOU GROW MORE DEAR WITH EACH PASSING YEAR	OP	25.00	25.00
97	YOU'RE A BEAR'S BEST FRIEND	OP	20.00	20.00
97	YOU'RE MY SHOOTING STAR	OP	17.50	18.00
98	RICH-ALWAYS PAWS FOR HOLIDAY TREATS	YR	22.50	23.00
98	SEGRID, JUSTAF & INGMAR-SPIRIT OF CHRISTMAS GROWS	YR	45.00	45.00
98	VERONICA-YOU MAKE HAPPINESS BLOOM	*	15.00	15.00

P. HILLMAN   CHERISHED TEDDIES ACROSS THE SEAS

YR	NAME	LIMIT	ISSUE	TREND
96	FROM RUSSIA WITH LOVE	OP	17.50	18.00
96	I FOUND AN AMIGO IN YOU	OP	17.50	18.00
96	LOVE FANS A BEAUTIFUL FRIENDSHIP	OP	17.50	18.00
96	OUR FRIENDSHIP IS BON APPETIT	OP	17.50	18.00
96	OUR FRIENDSHIP IS FROM SEA TO SHINING SEA	OP	17.50	18.00
96	OUR FRIENDSHIP KNOWS NO BOUNDARIES	OP	17.50	18.00
96	OUR FRIENDSHIP SPANS MANY MILES	OP	17.50	18.00
96	OUR LOVE IS IN THE HIGHLANDS	OP	17.50	18.00
96	RIDING ACROSS THE GREAT WHITE NORTH	OP	17.50	18.00
96	TULIPS BLOSSOM W/FRIENDSHIP	OP	17.50	18.00
96	YOU MAKE EVERYDAY A FIESTA	OP	17.50	18.00
96	YOU'RE A JOLLY OL' CHAP!	OP	17.50	18.00
96	YOU'RE THE JEWEL OF MY HEART	OP	17.50	18.00
96	YOU'RE THE SWEDISH OF THEM ALL	OP	17.50	18.00
97	I'M LOST DOWN UNDER WITHOUT YOU	OP	17.50	18.00
97	LIKE GRAPES ON A VINE OUR FRIENDSHIP IS DIVINE	OP	17.50	18.00

P. HILLMAN   CHERISHED TEDDIES ADOPTION CENTER

YR	NAME	LIMIT	ISSUE	TREND
96	IN GRANDMOTHER'S ATTIC	19960	55.00	55.00
96	YOU MAKE WISHES COME TRUE	YR	17.50	18.00
97	WE'RE THREE OF A KIND	YR	35.00	35.00
98	MIKE-I'M SWEET ON YOU	*	15.00	15.00
98	PENNY, CHANDLER, BOOTS-WE'RE INSEPARABLE	25000	25.00	25.00

P. HILLMAN   CHERISHED TEDDIES ANGELS

YR	NAME	LIMIT	ISSUE	TREND
96	HARK THE HERALD ANGELS SING	*	20.00	20.00
97	GLORY TO THE NEWBORN KING	YR	20.00	20.00
98	ANGELA-PEACE ON EARTH AND MERCY MILD	YR	20.00	20.00

P. HILLMAN   CHERISHED TEDDIES AVON EXCLUSIVE

YR	NAME	LIMIT	ISSUE	TREND
98	JANET-YOU'RE SWEET AS A ROSE	*	9.00	9.00

P. HILLMAN   CHERISHED TEDDIES BLOSSOMS OF FRIENDSHIP

YR	NAME	LIMIT	ISSUE	TREND
97	EVERYTHING'S COMING UP ROSES	OP	15.00	15.00
97	LOVE STEMS FROM OUR FRIENDSHIP	OP	15.00	15.00
97	YOU'RE THE BEST PICK OF THE BUNCH	OP	15.00	15.00

P. HILLMAN   CHERISHED TEDDIES BY THE SEA, BY THE SEA

YR	NAME	LIMIT	ISSUE	TREND
97	EVERYTHING PAILS IN COMPARISON TO FRIENDS	OP	20.00	20.00
97	I'M YOUR BATHING BEAUTY	OP	35.00	35.00
97	READY TO MAKE A SPLASH	OP	17.50	18.00
97	THERE'S ROOM IN MY SAND CASTLE FOR YOU	OP	20.00	20.00
97	UNDERNEATH IT ALL WE'RE FOREVER FRIENDS	OP	25.00	25.00

P. HILLMAN   CHERISHED TEDDIES CHERISHED SEASONS

YR	NAME	LIMIT	ISSUE	TREND
97	AUTUMN BRINGS A SEASON OF THANKSGIVING	OP	20.00	20.00
97	SPRING BRINGS A SEASON OF BEAUTY	OP	20.00	20.00
97	SUMMER BRINGS A SEASON OF WARMTH	OP	23.00	23.00
97	WINTER BRINGS A SEASON OF JOY	OP	25.00	25.00

P. HILLMAN   CHERISHED TEDDIES CHRISTMAS

YR	NAME	LIMIT	ISSUE	TREND
92	BEAR ON ROCKING REINDEER/MUSICAL	SU	60.00	85.00
92	BEAR ON ROCKING REINDEER/MUSICAL WATERBALL	*	60.00	70.00
92	BETH AND BLOSSOM ON REINDEER	RT	23.00	30.00
92	CHARLIE, SPIRIT OF FRIENDS	RT	45.00	45.00
92	DOUGLAS	RT	20.00	65.00
92	JACOB	OP	23.00	30.00

YR	NAME	LIMIT	ISSUE	TREND
92	STEVEN	OP	20.00	35.00
92	THEADORE, SAMANTHA, TYLER	OP	20.00	20.00
93	ALICE	YR	17.50	100.00
93	ALICE (9 IN.)	SU	100.00	145.00
93	BEAR PLAYING WITH TRAIN MUSICAL	OP	40.00	40.00
93	CAROLYN	RT	23.00	35.00
93	FAMILY ON TOBOGGAN	*	170.00	195.00
93	GIRL WITH MUFF MUSICAL WATERBALL	*	50.00	75.00
93	HANS	SU	20.00	80.00
93	JOINTED BEAR CHRISTMAS MUSICAL	SU	60.00	75.00
93	MARY	OP	25.00	40.00
93	THEADORE, SAMANTHA, TYLER	SU	160.00	200.00
94	BEAR ON ROCKING HORSE MUSICAL	OP	165.00	165.00
94	BOY AND GIRL IN SLEIGH MUSICAL	OP	100.00	100.00
94	ERIC	OP	23.00	45.00
94	NILS	OP	23.00	30.00
94	SONJA	OP	20.00	35.00
95	HUGS OF LOVE & FRIENDSHIP	OP	20.00	20.00

P. HILLMAN   **CHERISHED TEDDIES CLUB**

YR	NAME	LIMIT	ISSUE	TREND
95	CUB E. BEAR	YR	17.50	35.00
95	HILARY HUGABEAR	YR	17.50	40.00
95	MAYOR WILSON T. BEARY	YR	20.00	60.00

P. HILLMAN   **CHERISHED TEDDIES CLUB MEMBERS ONLY**

YR	NAME	LIMIT	ISSUE	TREND
96	EMILY E. CLAIRE	*	17.50	18.00
96	KURTIS D. CLAW CT961	*	17.50	65.00
97	GIRL & BOY DOUBLE FIGURINE	YR	17.50	18.00
97	GIRL WITH HAT/ PURSE/ PACKAGE	YR	17.50	18.00
98	DR. DARLENE MAKEBETTER (ORANGE BAG)	*	*	N/A
98	LELA NIGHTINGALE	*	15.00	15.00
98	MAILBOX, LAMPS, WATER FOUNTAIN	*	17.50	18.00
98	WADE WEATHERSBEE	*	13.50	14.00

P. HILLMAN   **CHERISHED TEDDIES CLUB SYMBOL OF MEMBERSHIP**

YR	NAME	LIMIT	ISSUE	TREND
96	R. HARRISON HARTFORD- YELLOW PENCIL	*	*	N/A
97	CONDUCTOR WITH GREEN SUITCASE	YR	20.00	20.00
97	CONDUCTOR WITH RED SUITCASE	YR	20.00	20.00

P. HILLMAN   **CHERISHED TEDDIES CUSTOMER APPRECIATION**

YR	NAME	LIMIT	ISSUE	TREND
93	CUSTOMER APPRECIATION	YR	23.00	65.00

P. HILLMAN   **CHERISHED TEDDIES DICKENS VILLAGE**

YR	NAME	LIMIT	ISSUE	TREND
94	BEAR CRATCHIT	SU	17.50	18.00
94	EBEARNEZER SCROOGE	SU	17.50	25.00
94	GABRIEL, GARLAND, GLORIA	SU	55.00	55.00
94	JACOB BEARLY	SU	17.50	18.00
94	MRS. CRATCHIT	SU	19.00	19.00
94	TINY TED-BEAR	SU	10.00	10.00

P. HILLMAN   **CHERISHED TEDDIES DOWN STRAWBERRY LANE**

YR	NAME	LIMIT	ISSUE	TREND
96	BUNNY MINI	SU	3.50	4.00
96	COZY TEA FOR TWO/THELMA	OP	23.00	23.00
96	DASH OF LOVE SWEETENS ANY DAY!, A	OP	15.00	15.00
96	LOVE GROWS IN MY HEART	OP	15.00	15.00
96	YOU'RE BERRY SPECIAL TO ME	OP	15.00	15.00
96	YOU'RE MY BERRY BEST FRIEND!	OP	15.00	15.00
97	I PICKED THE BEARY BEST FOR YOU	YR	25.00	25.00

P. HILLMAN   **CHERISHED TEDDIES EASTER**

YR	NAME	LIMIT	ISSUE	TREND
93	ABIGAIL	SU	16.00	35.00
93	CHARITY	RT	20.00	100.00
93	CHELSEA	RT	15.00	250.00
93	DAISY	RT	15.00	800.00
93	HEIDI AND DAVID	SU	25.00	45.00
93	HENRIETTA	SU	23.00	85.00
93	MOLLY	RT	30.00	40.00
94	BECKY	SU	20.00	40.00
94	BESSIE	SU	15.00	105.00
94	COURTNEY	RT	15.00	60.00
94	FAITH	SU	20.00	50.00
94	GIRL WITH BLUE BONNET AND CHICK MINI	*	7.00	7.00
94	GIRL WITH DAISY HEADBAND MINI	*	7.00	7.00
94	GIRL WITH WHITE HAT MINI	*	7.00	7.00
94	HENRY	SU	20.00	45.00

P. HILLMAN   **CHERISHED TEDDIES EASTER/SPRING**

YR	NAME	LIMIT	ISSUE	TREND
96	BLESSINGS BLOOM WHEN YOU ARE NEAR	*	15.00	20.00
96	LOVE KEEPS ME AFLOAT	*	13.50	20.00

P. HILLMAN   **CHERISHED TEDDIES EASTER/SPRING RAINBOW LANE**

YR	NAME	LIMIT	ISSUE	TREND
95	BUNNY	OP	13.50	35.00
95	DONALD	OP	20.00	25.00
95	GAIL	OP	20.00	20.00
95	HOPE	OP	20.00	40.00
95	JENNIFER	OP	23.00	40.00
95	LISA	OP	20.00	30.00
95	MELISSA	OP	20.00	30.00
95	PETER	OP	17.50	20.00

P. HILLMAN   **CHERISHED TEDDIES ENGAGEMENT PARTY 1996**

YR	NAME	LIMIT	ISSUE	TREND
95	PARK BENCH W/2 BEARS	*	12.50	50.00

P. HILLMAN   **CHERISHED TEDDIES EVENT**

YR	NAME	LIMIT	ISSUE	TREND
97	BEARY HAPPY WISHES	YR	17.50	18.00

YR	NAME	LIMIT	ISSUE	TREND
97	PICTURE PERFECT FRIENDSHIP, A	YR	15.00	15.00
97	YOU'RE A HONEY OF A FRIEND	YR	15.00	15.00
98	HUMPHREY-JUST THE BEAR FACTS, MA'AM	*	15.00	15.00
98	LANCE-COME FLY WITH ME	*	20.00	20.00

P. HILLMAN — CHERISHED TEDDIES FALL HARVEST

YR	NAME	LIMIT	ISSUE	TREND
95	FALLING FOR YOU/PAT	OP	23.00	23.00
96	YOU'RE MY LITTLE PUMPKIN	*	23.00	23.00

P. HILLMAN — CHERISHED TEDDIES FOUNDERS DAY EVENT 1995

YR	NAME	LIMIT	ISSUE	TREND
95	TOWN TATTLER SIGNAGE	*	6.00	10.00

P. HILLMAN — CHERISHED TEDDIES FREQUENT BUYER PROGRAM

YR	NAME	LIMIT	ISSUE	TREND
97	AMELIA-YOU MAKE ME SMILE	*	35.00	35.00
97	BENNY-LET'S RIDE THROUGH LIFE TOGETHER	*	17.50	18.00
97	MARY JANE-MY FAVORITE THINGS	*	50.00	50.00

P. HILLMAN — CHERISHED TEDDIES GCC EARLY INTRO

YR	NAME	LIMIT	ISSUE	TREND
96	MOTHER'S HEART IS FULL OF LOVE, A	RT	25.00	25.00

P. HILLMAN — CHERISHED TEDDIES GRADUATION

YR	NAME	LIMIT	ISSUE	TREND
95	BOY GRADUATE	OP	12.50	13.00
95	GIRL GRADUATE	OP	12.50	13.00

P. HILLMAN — CHERISHED TEDDIES HALLOWEEN

YR	NAME	LIMIT	ISSUE	TREND
93	BRENDA	SU	15.00	15.00
93	BUCKEY	SU	15.00	15.00
93	CONNIE	RT	15.00	20.00
93	GARY	OP	19.00	25.00
93	GRETEL	OP	19.00	20.00
93	MILES	OP	17.00	30.00
93	PRUDENCE	OP	17.00	40.00
94	BREANNA	OP	15.00	30.00
94	STACIE	OP	19.00	19.00
94	TAYLOR	OP	15.00	25.00
95	"BEE" MY FRIEND	OP	15.00	15.00
95	BEARY SCARY HALLOWEEN HOUSE	OP	20.00	20.00
95	FUTURE "BEARETH" ALL THINGS, THE	OP	19.00	19.00
96	YOU HAVE A SPECIAL PLACE IN MY HEART		19.00	19.00
96	YOU'RE THE CAT'S MEOW	*	15.00	15.00

P. HILLMAN — CHERISHED TEDDIES HOLIDAY DANGLING

YR	NAME	LIMIT	ISSUE	TREND
95	STRING OF GOOD TIDINGS, A	OP	20.00	20.00
96	AN OLD FASHIONED NOEL TO YOU/NOEL	SU	15.00	15.00
96	CATCHIN THE HOLIDAY SPIRIT	OP	15.00	15.00
96	DROPPING YOU A HOLIDAY GREETING	OP	20.00	20.00
96	STRIKING UP ANOTHER YEAR	YR	17.50	18.00
96	TOY SOLDIER- DATED	YR	12.50	13.00
96	YOU ALWAYS BRING JOY	OP	15.00	15.00

P. HILLMAN — CHERISHED TEDDIES LAPLANDERS

YR	NAME	LIMIT	ISSUE	TREND
95	WARM HEARTED FRIENDS	OP	17.50	18.00
96	FEEL THE PEACE/HOLD THE JOY/SHARE...	YR	50.00	50.00
96	FRIENDS ARE ALWAYS PULLING FOR YOU	*	23.00	23.00
97	ALL PATHS LEAD TO KINDNESS & FRIENDSHIP	YR	55.00	55.00

P. HILLMAN — CHERISHED TEDDIES LITTLE SPARKLES

YR	NAME	LIMIT	ISSUE	TREND
97	APRIL	OP	7.50	8.00
97	AUGUST	OP	7.50	8.00
97	DECEMBER	OP	7.50	8.00
97	FEBRUARY	OP	7.50	8.00
97	JANUARY	OP	7.50	8.00
97	JULY	OP	7.50	8.00
97	JUNE	OP	7.50	8.00
97	MARCH	OP	7.50	8.00
97	MAY	OP	7.50	8.00
97	NOVEMBER	OP	7.50	8.00
97	OCTOBER	OP	7.50	8.00
97	SEPTEMBER	OP	7.50	8.00

P. HILLMAN — CHERISHED TEDDIES LOVE LETTERS FROM TEDDIE

YR	NAME	LIMIT	ISSUE	TREND
97	BEAR WITH HEART DANGLING BLOCKS- MINI	OP	7.50	8.00
97	BEAR WITH I LOVE BEARS BLOCKS- MINI	OP	7.50	8.00
97	BEAR WITH I LOVE HUGS BLOCKS- MINI	OP	7.50	8.00
97	BEAR WITH I LOVE YOU BLOCKS- MINI	OP	7.50	8.00

P. HILLMAN — CHERISHED TEDDIES MESSENGERS OF THE HEART

YR	NAME	LIMIT	ISSUE	TREND
95	BOY AND GIRL CUPID	*	25.00	40.00
95	BOY AND GIRL CUPID (1 OF 2)	*	19.00	27.00
95	BOY AND GIRL CUPID (2 OF 2)	*	19.00	27.00
95	BOY BEAR CUPID	SU	17.50	22.00
95	CUPID BABY BOY ON PILLOW	SU	13.50	20.00
95	CUPID BABY GIRL ON PILLOW	SU	13.50	20.00
95	CUPID BOY SITTING (1 OF 2)	*	13.50	27.00
95	CUPID BOY SITTING (2 OF 2)	*	13.50	27.00
95	GIRL BEAR CUPID	SU	15.00	30.00
95	GIRL CUPID (1 OF 2)- BE MINE	*	15.00	27.00
95	GIRL CUPID (2 OF 2)- LOVE	*	15.00	30.00

P. HILLMAN — CHERISHED TEDDIES MONTHLY FRIENDS TO CHERISH

YR	NAME	LIMIT	ISSUE	TREND
95	BE MINE/PHOEBE-FEBRUARY	OP	15.00	20.00
95	DAY AT THE PARK, A-JULY	OP	15.00	15.00
95	FRIENDSHIP IS IN BLOOM- MAY	OP	15.00	15.00
95	FRIENDSHIP IS IN THE AIR- MARCH 914770	OP	15.00	15.00
95	HAPPY HOLIDAYS, FRIEND/DENISE- DECEMBER	OP	15.00	15.00
95	NEW YEAR W/OLD FRIENDS, A	OP	15.00	15.00

YR	NAME	LIMIT	ISSUE	TREND
95	PLANTING THE SEED OF FRIENDSHIP- JUNE	OP	15.00	15.00
95	SCHOOL DAYS/SETH- SEPTEMBER	OP	15.00	15.00
95	SHOWERS OF FRIENDSHIP- APRIL	OP	15.00	30.00
95	SMOOTH SMILING/ARTHUR- AUGUST	OP	15.00	55.00
95	SWEET TREATS- OCTOBER	OP	15.00	15.00
95	THANKS FOR FRIENDS- NOVEMBER	OP	15.00	15.00
P. HILLMAN		**CHERISHED TEDDIES NATIVITY**		
92	ANGIE	OP	15.00	15.00
92	CRECHE WITH COVERLET- 2 PC	OP	50.00	45.00
92	MARIA WITH BABY JOSH	OP	35.00	50.00
92	SAMMY	OP	17.50	45.00
92	THREE KINGS- 3 PC	OP	55.00	150.00
93	MINI NATIVITY IN CRECHE	*	33.00	100.00
93	NATIVITY COLLECTOR SET	OP	100.00	190.00
93	NATIVITY MUSICAL	SU	60.00	80.00
93	NATIVITY WITH CRECHE- MUSICAL	*	85.00	100.00
94	RONNIE	OP	13.50	20.00
95	AN ANGEL TO WATCH OVER YOU/CELESTE	OP	20.00	20.00
P. HILLMAN		**CHERISHED TEDDIES NUTCRACKER SUITE**		
97	FUNCTIONAL NUTCRACKER- WOOD	OP	90.00	90.00
97	MOUSE KING,HERR DROSSELMEYER,CLARA, PRINCE-COL SET	YR	70.00	70.00
97	TUNE: DANCE OF THE SUGARPLUM FAIRY	OP	45.00	45.00
P. HILLMAN		**CHERISHED TEDDIES ONCE UPON A TEDDY**		
94	FATHER	OP	13.50	14.00
94	JACK AND JILL	OP	30.00	30.00
94	LITTLE BO PEEP	OP	23.00	23.00
94	LITTLE JACK HORNER	OP	20.00	20.00
94	LITTLE MISS MUFFET	OP	20.00	20.00
94	MARY, MARY QUITE CONTRARY	OP	23.00	23.00
94	TOM THE PIPER	OP	20.00	20.00
P. HILLMAN		**CHERISHED TEDDIES OUR CHERISHED FAMILY**		
94	MOTHER	*	20.00	40.00
94	OLDER DAUGHTER	OP	10.00	10.00
94	OLDER SON	OP	10.00	10.00
94	OUR CHERISHED FAMILY- GIFT SET	*	85.00	140.00
94	YOUNG DAUGHTER	OP	9.00	9.00
94	YOUNG SON	OP	9.00	9.00
P. HILLMAN		**CHERISHED TEDDIES SANTA CLAUS**		
97	UP ON THE ROOFTOP	YR	23.00	23.00
98	LITTLE HOLIDAY R&R, A	YR	22.50	23.00
P. HILLMAN		**CHERISHED TEDDIES SANTA EXPRESS**		
96	ALL ABOARD THE SANTA EXPRESS	OP	23.00	23.00
96	FIRST CLASS DELIVERY FOR YOU, A	OP	17.50	18.00
96	FRIENDSHIP IS ..PERFECT END..HOLIDAYS	OP	23.00	23.00
96	HE KNOWS IF YOU'VE BEEN BAD OR GOOD	OP	17.50	18.00
96	ROLLING ALONG W/FRIENDS & SMILES	OP	17.50	18.00
97	HEADING INTO THE HOLIDAYS WITH DEER FRIENDS	OP	17.50	18.00
97	HO, HO, HO... TO THE HOLIDAYS WE GO	SU	17.50	18.00
97	THIS TRAIN IS BOUND FOR HOLIDAY SURPRISES	OP	17.50	18.00
P. HILLMAN		**CHERISHED TEDDIES SANTA'S WORKSHOP**		
95	BUILDING A STURDY FRIENDSHIP, YULE	OP	23.00	23.00
95	CUP OF HOMEMADE LOVE, A	OP	19.00	19.00
95	HANDSEWN HOLIDAYS	OP	20.00	20.00
95	PAINTING YOUR HOLIDAYS W/LOVE	OP	23.00	23.00
95	YOU'RE AT THE TOP OF MY LIST	YR	20.00	20.00
96	BEARER OF GOOD TIDINGS, KLAUS	YR	20.00	20.00
P. HILLMAN		**CHERISHED TEDDIES ST. PATRICK'S DAY**		
94	KATHLEEN	OP	12.50	20.00
94	SEAN	OP	12.50	25.00
95	KEVIN	RT	12.50	30.00
95	MAUREEN	RT	12.50	30.00
97	RYAN-I'M GREEN WITH ENVY FOR YOU	OP	20.00	20.00
P. HILLMAN		**CHERISHED TEDDIES SWEETHEART BALL**		
95	JACK AND JILL	OP	35.00	35.00
96	LOVE UNVEILS A HAPPY HEART	OP	17.50	18.00
96	MY HEART WISHES FOR YOU	OP	20.00	20.00
96	SWEETHEARTS FOREVER/CRAIG & CHERI	OP	25.00	25.00
96	WON'T YOU BE MY SWEETHEART?	OP	17.50	18.00
96	YOU STEAL MY HEART AWAY	OP	17.50	18.00
96	YOU'RE THE HERO OF MY HEART	OP	20.00	20.00
98	YOU'RE THE QUEEN/KING OF MY HEART	TL	65.00	65.00
P. HILLMAN		**CHERISHED TEDDIES T IS FOR TEDDIES**		
95	BEAR W/ "A" BLOCK	OP	5.00	5.00
95	BEAR W/ "B" BLOCK	OP	5.00	5.00
95	BEAR W/ "C" BLOCK	OP	5.00	5.00
95	BEAR W/ "D" BLOCK	OP	5.00	5.00
95	BEAR W/ "E" BLOCK	OP	5.00	5.00
95	BEAR W/ "F" BLOCK	OP	5.00	5.00
95	BEAR W/ "G" BLOCK	OP	5.00	5.00
95	BEAR W/ "H" BLOCK	OP	5.00	5.00
95	BEAR W/ "I" BLOCK	OP	5.00	5.00
95	BEAR W/ "J" BLOCK	OP	5.00	5.00
95	BEAR W/ "K" BLOCK	OP	5.00	5.00
95	BEAR W/ "L" BLOCK	OP	5.00	5.00

YR	NAME	LIMIT	ISSUE	TREND
95	BEAR W/ "M" BLOCK	OP	5.00	5.00
95	BEAR W/ "N" BLOCK	OP	5.00	5.00
95	BEAR W/ "O" BLOCK	OP	5.00	5.00
95	BEAR W/ "P" BLOCK	OP	5.00	5.00
95	BEAR W/ "Q" BLOCK	OP	5.00	5.00
95	BEAR W/ "R" BLOCK	OP	5.00	5.00
95	BEAR W/ "S" BLOCK	OP	5.00	5.00
95	BEAR W/ "T" BLOCK	OP	5.00	5.00
95	BEAR W/ "U" BLOCK	OP	5.00	5.00
95	BEAR W/ "V" BLOCK	OP	5.00	5.00
95	BEAR W/ "W" BLOCK	OP	5.00	5.00
95	BEAR W/ "X" BLOCK	OP	5.00	5.00
95	BEAR W/ "Y" BLOCK	OP	5.00	5.00
95	BEAR W/ "Z" BLOCK	OP	5.00	5.00
P. HILLMAN		**CHERISHED TEDDIES THANKSGIVING**		
94	JEDEDIAH	RT	17.50	18.00
94	PATIENCE	RT	17.50	18.00
94	PHOEBE	OP	13.50	35.00
94	THANKSGIVING QUILT	OP	12.00	12.00
94	WILLIE	RT	15.00	35.00
94	WINONA	RT	15.00	25.00
94	WYATT	OP	15.00	15.00
94	WYLIE	*	15.00	26.00
P. HILLMAN		**CHERISHED TEDDIES THROUGH THE YEARS**		
93	AGE 1	OP	13.50	14.00
93	AGE 2	OP	13.50	14.00
93	AGE 3	OP	15.00	15.00
93	AGE 4	OP	15.00	15.00
93	AGE 5	OP	15.00	15.00
93	AGE 6	OP	16.50	17.00
93	BABY	OP	16.50	17.00
P. HILLMAN		**CHERISHED TEDDIES UNDER THE BIG TOP**		
96	BRUNO	OP	17.50	20.00
96	CIRCUS ELEPHANT WITH BEAR	OP	23.00	23.00
96	CLOWN ON BALL MUSICAL	OP	40.00	40.00
96	SEAL OF FRIENDSHIP	OP	10.00	10.00
96	YOU TAKE CENTER RING W/ME	OP	17.50	24.00
96	YOU'RE THE TOPS W/ME	OP	17.50	18.00
97	FRIENDS ARE BEAR ESSENTIALS	OP	20.00	20.00
97	FRIENDSHIP KEEPS YOU POPPING	OP	17.50	18.00
97	JUST CLOWNING AROUND	OP	17.50	18.00
97	LOVE IS A BEAR NECESSITY	OP	17.50	18.00
97	YOU'RE MY MANE ATTRACTION	OP	12.50	13.00
P. HILLMAN		**CHERISHED TEDDIES UP IN THE ATTIC**		
98	KAITLYN-OLD TREASURES, NEW MEMORIES	YR	50.00	50.00
P. HILLMAN		**CHERISHED TEDDIES VALENTINE**		
93	AMY W/LAVENDER BOW	OP	13.50	45.00
93	MARIE	OP	20.00	30.00
93	MICHAEL AND MICHELLE	SU	30.00	50.00
93	TIMOTHY	RT	15.00	25.00
94	ELIZABETH AND ASHLEY	RT	25.00	65.00
94	KELLY	SU	15.00	30.00
94	NANCY	RT	15.00	100.00
94	OLIVER AND OLIVIA	SU	25.00	40.00
94	VICTORIA	SU	16.50	70.00
P. HILLMAN		**CHERISHED TEDDIES VALENTINE MINI**		
94	HUGS AND KISSES	*	7.00	7.00
94	LOVE YA	*	7.00	7.00
94	YOU'RE PURR-FECT	*	7.00	7.00
P. HILLMAN		**CHERISHED TEDDIES WE BEAR THANKS**		
96	BEAR IN MIND, YOU'RE SPECIAL, DINA	RT	15.00	15.00
96	BEAR IN MIND, YOU'RE SPECIAL, JOHN	RT	15.00	15.00
96	GIVING THANKS FOR OUR FAMILY/BARBARA	RT	12.50	13.00
96	SUITED UP FOR THE HOLIDAYS	RT	12.50	13.00
96	TABLE WITH FOOD/DOG	RT	30.00	30.00
P. HILLMAN		**CHERISHED TEDDIES WINTER BEAR FESTIVAL**		
97	FRIENDSHIP NEVER MELTS AWAY	OP	30.00	30.00
97	GOING MY WAY FOR THE HOLIDAYS	OP	25.00	25.00
97	I'M HEAD OVER SKIS FOR YOU	OP	20.00	20.00
97	IT'S A HOLIDAY ON ICE	OP	20.00	20.00
97	SKATING ON HOLIDAY JOY	OP	20.00	20.00
97	SNOW FUN WHEN YOU'RE NOT AROUND	OP	19.00	19.00
97	TUNE: LET IT SNOW	OP	45.00	45.00
97	TUNE: WHITE CHRISTMAS	OP	45.00	45.00
97	WALKING IN A WINTER WONDERLAND	OP	30.00	30.00
L. RIGG		**FOUR SEASONS**		
95	CAROL - WINTER ICE SKATER	2000	30.00	30.00
95	DENISE - SPRING IN APRON	2000	30.00	30.00
95	EMILY - SUMMER SAILOR SUIT	2000	30.00	30.00
95	MELISSA- FALL W/CORNUCOPIA	2000	30.00	30.00
*		**FROM BARBIE WITH LOVE**		
95	BALLERINA, 1961 PVC 113875	*	5.00	5.00
95	BARBIE BUST PORTRAIT PORCELAIN 125601	*	15.00	15.00
95	BRIDE 1963 MUSICAL 113905	7500	100.00	100.00

YR	NAME	LIMIT	ISSUE	TREND
95	ENCHANTED EVENING, 1960 PVC 133396	*	5.00	5.00
95	GRADUATION, 1963 PVC 113867	*	5.00	5.00
95	HAPPY HOLIDAYS 1988 BARBIE 154199	YR	30.00	100.00
95	MAGNIFICENCE 1965 143111	7500	100.00	100.00
95	MIDNIGHT BLUE 1965 MUSICAL 113891	7500	100.00	100.00
95	ORIGINAL SWIMSUIT, 1959 RESIN 113700	*	30.00	30.00
95	PICNIC, 1959 RESIN 113727	*	30.00	30.00
95	POODLE PARADE, 1965 RESIN 113719	*	30.00	30.00
95	SENIOR PROM 1963 MUSICAL 125776	RT	100.00	100.00
95	SENIOR PROM, 1963 PORCELAIN 124370	*	100.00	100.00
95	SOPHISTICATED LADY '63 MUSICAL 113883	7500	100.00	100.00
95	SUBURBAN SHOPPER, 1959 RESIN 113751	*	30.00	30.00
95	WEDDING DAY, 1959 PVC 113859	*	5.00	5.00
96	ARABIAN NIGHTS, 1964 RESIN 171026	*	35.00	35.00
96	BARBIE/SCARLETT O'HARA-GRN VELVET/MUSICAL 171107	7500	50.00	50.00
96	CINDERELLA, 1964 RESIN 170992	*	35.00	35.00
96	ENCHANTED EVENING, 1960 MUSICAL 185787	2500	100.00	100.00
96	GUINEVERE, 1964 RESIN 171018	*	35.00	35.00
96	HAPPY HOLIDAY BARBIE, 1989 MUSICAL 188832	YR	100.00	100.00
96	HERE COMES THE BRIDE MUSICAL/PORCELAIN 170976	7500	100.00	100.00
96	HOLIDAY DANCE 1965 , MUSCIAL 188786	7500	100.00	100.00
96	QUEEN OF HEARTS BARBIE PORCELAIN 157651	5000	125.00	125.00
96	RED RIDING HOOD, 1964 RESIN 171034	*	35.00	35.00

K. WICKL — GNOMES

YR	NAME	LIMIT	ISSUE	TREND
93	SIGFRIED & SOPHIA	1000	70.00	70.00
94	HUBERT & HENRIETTA	2000	80.00	80.00
94	LOTHAR	1994	100.00	100.00
95	ALBERT, RESIN 127434	*	7.50	8.00
95	ALBERT, RESIN 146129	*	7.50	8.00
95	ANDREAS AND AVA , RESIN 146099	*	50.00	50.00
95	BRINA & BORG, RESIN 127191	*	25.00	25.00
95	CATRINA AND CHARLES, RESIN 146358	*	25.00	25.00
95	ETHAN, RESIN 127450	*	5.50	6.00
95	ETHAN, RESIN 146145	*	7.50	8.00
95	FERDINAND 146072	15	300.00	300.00
95	FERDINAND, RESIN 153257	*	8.50	9.00
95	GOBBY & LOU, RESIN 127183	*	25.00	25.00
95	GUSTAV, RESIN 146064	*	20.00	20.00
95	JOHANN'S DANCE SCHOOL 127493	2000	55.00	55.00
95	JOSHUA, RESIN 127485	*	5.50	6.00
95	JULIA , RESIN 146110	*	7.50	8.00
95	JULIA, RESIN 127442	*	7.50	8.00
95	KATY, RESIN 127477	*	5.50	6.00
95	LOREN AND LINDA, RESIN 146056	*	40.00	40.00
95	LOREN, RESIN 127213	*	25.00	25.00
95	LOUIS, RESIN 146102	*	30.00	30.00
95	MAGGIE, RESIN 127469	*	5.50	6.00
95	MAGGIE, RESIN 146137	*	7.50	8.00
95	NEWBORNS, RESIN 146153	*	7.50	8.00
95	OMA, RESIN 127426	*	7.50	8.00
95	OPA, RESIN 127221	*	7.50	8.00
95	PETER, RESIN 153265	*	7.50	8.00
95	PURDY AND PIPPEN, RESIN 153281	*	7.50	8.00
95	SIDNEY, RESIN 127167	*	25.00	25.00

S. BUTCHER — GROWING IN GOD'S GARDEN OF LOVE

YR	NAME	LIMIT	ISSUE	TREND
96	SOME PLANT, SOME WATER, BUT GOD..INCREASE 176958	OP	38.00	38.00
96	SOWING SEEDS OF KINDNESS 163856	OP	38.00	38.00

S. BUTCHER — GROWING IN GRACE

YR	NAME	LIMIT	ISSUE	TREND
95	AGE 1-BABY WITH CAKE 136190	OP	25.00	25.00
95	AGE 2-GIRL WITH BLOCKS 136212	OP	25.00	25.00
95	AGE 3-GIRL WITH FLOWERS 136220	OP	25.00	25.00
95	AGE 4-GIRL WITH DOLL 136239	OP	28.00	28.00
95	AGE 5-GIRL WITH LUNCH BOX 136247	OP	28.00	28.00
95	AGE 6-GIRL ON BICYCLE 136255	OP	30.00	30.00
95	IT'S A GIRL-ANGEL W/INFANT ANNOUNCEMENT 136204	OP	23.00	23.00
95	SWEET SIXTEEN-GIRL HOLDING 16 ROSES 136263	OP	40.00	40.00
96	AGE 10-GIRL BOWLING 183873	OP	38.00	38.00
96	AGE 7-GIRL DRESSED AS NURSE 163740	OP	33.00	33.00
96	AGE 8-GIRL SHOOTING MARBLES 163759	OP	33.00	33.00
96	AGE 9-GIRL WITH CHARM BRACELET 183865	OP	30.00	30.00

L. RIGG — HISTORY OF HATS

YR	NAME	LIMIT	ISSUE	TREND
95	PETITE COLLECTION - 6 ASST. PREPACK	30000	15.00	15.00

KINKA — KINKA

YR	NAME	LIMIT	ISSUE	TREND
88	BABIES ARE DREAMS YOU CAN CUDDLE 117552	OP	38.00	40.00
88	BABIES ARE DREAMS YOU CAN CUDDLE 117560	OP	45.00	50.00
88	FOR YOU...JUST BECAUSE 117781	OP	38.00	40.00
88	JUST FOR YOU ON THIS SPECIAL DAY 117501	OP	23.00	25.00
88	KEEP THE WARM GLOW OF THE SEASON 117455	OP	38.00	38.00
88	LOVE TO YOU 117757	OP	38.00	40.00
88	MAY YOUR LIFE BE FILLED WITH 117498	OP	38.00	40.00
88	THINKING OF YOU 117749	OP	38.00	38.00
88	THINKING OF YOU...NOW & ALWAYS 117528	OP	23.00	25.00
88	WISHING YOU CLOUDLESS SKIES 117471	OP	38.00	40.00
88	WISHING YOU JOY, HAPPINESS 117536	OP	40.00	45.00
88	WISHING YOU JOY, HAPPINESS 117544	OP	50.00	55.00

YR	NAME	LIMIT	ISSUE	TREND
88	YOU ARE SPECIAL TO ME 117773	OP	38.00	40.00
88	YOUR FRIENDSHIP & THOUGHTFULNESS 117463	OP	38.00	40.00
88	YOUR FRIENDSHIP WILL BE 117765	OP	38.00	40.00
89	A BOUQUET OF FLOWERS FOR YOU 119024	OP	30.00	30.00
89	BABIES ARE CHRISTMAS DREAMS 117722	YR	15.00	16.00
89	BABIES ARE CHRISTMAS DREAMS 118540	YR	15.00	16.00
89	CHRISTMAS IS A TIME TO GATHER 117676	OP	55.00	55.00
89	EASTER IS A TIME FILLED WITH 116629	OP	50.00	50.00
89	GATHER YOUR CHRISTMAS DREAMS 117862	OP	55.00	55.00
89	GATHER YOUR DREAMS AND WISHES 119032	OP	30.00	30.00
89	HAPPY 25TH ANNIVERSARY 119121	OP	75.00	75.00
89	HAPPY 40TH ANNIVERSARY 119148	OP	75.00	75.00
89	HAPPY 50TH ANNIVERSARY 119156	OP	75.00	75.00
89	IT'S THE TIME FOR CHRISTMAS 117889	OP	50.00	50.00
89	IT'S TIME FOR CHRISTMAS 117846	OP	38.00	38.00
89	JUST FOR YOU 119083	OP	30.00	30.00
89	KEEP ME IN YOUR DREAMS 119695	OP	50.00	50.00
89	KEEP THE SPIRIT 119113	OP	30.00	30.00
89	KEEP THE TRUE LIGHT OF CHRISTMAS 117684	OP	25.00	25.00
89	LOVE TO YOU 120391	OP	120.00	120.00
89	LOVE TO YOU AT THIS SPECIAL TIME 118877	OP	45.00	45.00
89	LOVE TO YOU AT THIS SPECIAL TIME 118885	OP	50.00	50.00
89	MAY APRIL SHOWERS BRING 118958	OP	30.00	30.00
89	MAY GOD'S LOVE BLESS YOUR BABY 118842	OP	45.00	45.00
89	MAY THE GLOW OF GOD'S LOVE 116661	OP	50.00	50.00
89	MAY THE GLOW OF GOD'S LOVE 116688	OP	20.00	20.00
89	MAY THE LOVE IN YOUR HEARTS 116572	OP	15.00	16.00
89	MAY THIS DAY TOUCH YOUR HEART 119105	OP	30.00	30.00
89	MAY THIS SPECIAL SEASON 118559	YR	25.00	25.00
89	MAY YOUR DAYS BE FILLED WITH LOVE 118915	OP	30.00	30.00
89	NATIVITY SCENE (3 WISE MEN) 118192	OP	45.00	45.00
89	NATIVITY SCENE (SET OF 9) 118214	OP	115.00	115.00
89	NATIVITY SCENE (SHEPHERD) 118206	OP	30.00	30.00
89	NATIVITY SCENE 118184	OP	40.00	40.00
89	REJOICE IN GOD'S PROMISE OF LOVE 116637	OP	38.00	38.00
89	REMEMBER THE DREAMS 118966	OP	75.00	75.00
89	THINKING OF YOU & WISHING 119016	OP	24.00	30.00
89	WILL YOU STOP AND COUNT THE STARS 117838	OP	38.00	38.00
89	WILL YOU STOP AND COUNT THE STARS 117870	OP	50.00	50.00
89	WISH ON THE CHRISTMAS STAR 117854	OP	38.00	38.00
89	WISH ON THE CHRISTMAS STAR 117897	OP	50.00	50.00
89	WISHING YOU CLOUDLESS SKIES 408565	2500	170.00	170.00
89	WISHING YOU EVERY HAPPINESS 117730	OP	25.00	25.00
89	WISHING YOU LOVE AND HAPPINESS 116556	OP	50.00	50.00
89	WISHING YOU LOVE AND HAPPINESS 116564	OP	38.00	38.00
89	WISHING YOU PINK ROSES 119075	OP	30.00	30.00
89	WISHING YOU SPECIAL BLESSINGS 116653	OP	17.50	18.00
89	WISHING YOU SPECIAL MOMENTS 119091	OP	30.00	30.00
89	WISHING YOUR BABY 118834	OP	17.50	18.00
89	YOU BRING JOY INTO MY LIFE 119296	OP	15.00	16.00
89	YOU'RE A DOLL 118931	OP	30.00	30.00
90	CHRISTMAS FILLS YOUR HEART 119725	OP	15.00	16.00
90	CHRISTMAS IS A GIFT FROM GOD 119849	OP	12.50	13.00
90	CHRISTMAS IS A TIME OF LOVE 119822	OP	30.00	30.00
90	CHRISTMAS IS A TIME TO SHARE 119830	OP	19.00	19.00
90	CHRISTMAS IS A TIME TO SHARE 119938	OP	10.00	10.00
90	MAY THIS CHRISTMAS DAY 119865	OP	40.00	40.00
90	MAY YOUR HEART BE FILLED 119911	OP	65.00	65.00
90	MAY YOUR STOCKING BE FILLED 119857	OP	23.00	23.00
90	SOUND OF LOVE IS FELT, THE- 119881	OP	25.00	25.00
90	SWEET MUSIC & BEAUTIFUL MEMORIES 119873	OP	25.00	25.00
90	WISHING YOU GENTLE MOMENTS 119946	OP	17.50	118.00
91	BABIES ARE THE GREATEST GIFT/GOD 121266	OP	25.00	25.00
91	BABIES TOUCH YOUR HEART 118788	OP	55.00	55.00
91	KEEP THE SPECIAL MEMORIES 122777	OP	75.00	75.00
91	MAY GOD'S LOVE FILL YOUR HEART 120553	OP	50.00	50.00
91	MAY GOD'S LOVE FILL YOUR LIFE 120561	OP	45.00	45.00
91	MAY THE BLESSINGS OF EASTER BRING 120529	OP	25.00	25.00
91	MAY THIS SPECIAL SEASON REAWAKEN 122688	OP	60.00	60.00
91	MAY YOUR LIFE BE FILLED WITH 121312	OP	120.00	120.00
91	MAY YOUR LIFE TOGETHER BE FILLED 121398	OP	23.00	23.00
91	MEMORIES ARE MADE OF SIMPLE JOYS 122653	OP	60.00	60.00
91	MUSIC AND MEMORIES FILL THIS 119873	OP	27.00	27.00
91	PLEASE FEEL BETTER SOON 121258	OP	23.00	23.00
91	REJOICE IN GOD'S LOVE 120537	OP	23.00	23.00
91	SPRING IS A TIME OF LOVE 120588	OP	19.00	19.00
91	WARM WISHES TO SOMEONE SPECIAL 122726	OP	60.00	60.00
91	WISHING YOU GENTLE HUGS 120510	OP	25.00	25.00
91	WISHING YOU GOD'S BLESSINGS 120545	OP	23.00	23.00
91	WITH LOVE TO MY SPECIAL ONE 120502	OP	45.00	45.00
92	CHRISTMAS IS A SPECIAL GIFT 117692	OP	16.75	17.00
92	CHRISTMAS IS A TIME OF LOVE 119962	OP	13.50	14.00
92	CHRISTMAS IS A TIME TO BELIEVE 122718	OP	13.75	14.00
92	CHRISTMAS IS A TIME TO SHARE 117676	OP	28.00	28.00
92	CHRISTMAS IS PEACE, LOVE 118184	OP	23.00	23.00

Crossroads *from Goebel poses the question, "Which way to turn?" for these little Hummel travelers.*

Armani's Lady With Peacock *sold for $4,500 at the Armani Auction at Walt Disney World in 1996.*

Kurt S. Adler Inc.'s Steinbach Nutcrackers appear in every garb. This one is the Sheriff of Nottingham, *the third nutcracker in the "Tales of Sherwood Forest" series.*

In 1993, Kurt S. Adler Inc. released Merlin *by P. Manck as part of their Fabriche Camelot collection.*

YR	NAME	LIMIT	ISSUE	TREND
92	CHRISTMAS IS PEACE, LOVE 118214	OP	60.00	60.00
92	I'M WRAPPING UP ALL MY DREAMS 119717	OP	30.00	30.00
92	IT'S THE SEASON OF SHARING 125342	OP	16.25	17.00
92	IT'S TIME FOR CHRISTMAS 117889	OP	25.00	25.00
92	JOIN IN THE CHORUS 125318	OP	10.00	10.00
92	MAY CHRISTMAS BLESS YOU W/GIFTS 118192	OP	23.00	23.00
92	MAY CHRISTMAS BRING YOU ALL/JOY 120413	OP	20.00	20.00
92	MAY GOD'S SPECIAL BLESSINGS 123145	OP	33.00	33.00
92	MAY THIS SPECIAL SEASON 118559	OP	15.00	16.00
92	MAY THIS SPECIAL SEASON 122688	OP	30.00	30.00
92	MAY YOU SHARE A NEW YEAR 119733	OP	11.25	12.00
92	MAY YOUR DAYS BE FILLED WITH LOVE 123188	OP	60.00	60.00
92	MEMORIES ARE MADE OF SIMPLE JOYS 122653	OP	30.00	30.00
92	MY FAVORITE THINGS 125334	OP	15.00	16.00
92	REJOICE IN GOD'S LOVE 121789	OP	38.00	38.00
92	SANTA'S LITTLE HELPER 125326	OP	16.25	17.00
92	THREE PIECE CHRISTMAS COLLECTION 118176	OP	57.00	57.00
92	WARM WISHES TO SOMEONE SPECIAL 122726	OP	30.00	30.00
92	WISH ON THE CHRISTMAS STAR 117897	OP	25.00	25.00
92	WISHING YOU MANY MOMENTS OF LOVE 123137	OP	30.00	30.00
92	WISHING YOU SPECIAL BLESSINGS 117609	OP	12.50	13.00
92	WONDER OF THIS SPECIAL SEASON, THE- 118206	OP	15.00	16.00

L. RIGG | | | | **LUCY & ME**

YR	NAME	LIMIT	ISSUE	TREND
86	BRIDE/GROOM WITH TOP HAT	*	14.00	14.00
94	DIANE	2000	30.00	33.00
94	DRESSED AS FLOWER BOX- 4 PC	*	10.00	10.00
94	JOAN	2000	30.00	33.00
94	LINDA	2000	30.00	33.00
94	MIZPAH FRIENDS- 2 PC	*	20.00	20.00
95	15TH ANNIVERSARY	1993	10.00	10.00
95	ALISON	2000	30.00	30.00
95	BABY/CRADLE- MINI ACTION MUSICAL	*	35.00	35.00
95	BEAR W/COLLECTION OF LUCY & ME FIGS	2000	30.00	30.00
95	BEAR WITH POUNDING BLOCK TOY	*	10.00	10.00
95	BRIDE/GROOM- DOUBLE	*	20.00	20.00
95	DRESSED AS AUTO MECHANIC	*	10.00	10.00
95	DRESSED AS BABY POWDER	*	10.00	10.00
95	DRESSED AS CARTON OF POPCORN	*	10.00	10.00
95	DRESSED AS DIAPER BOX	*	10.00	10.00
95	DRESSED AS HIKING SCOUT	*	10.00	10.00
95	DRESSED AS HOT DOG	*	10.00	10.00
95	DRESSED AS PEANUT BUTTER SANDWICH	*	10.00	10.00
95	DRESSED AS REAL ESTATE AGENT	*	10.00	10.00
95	DRESSED AS RECYCLE BEAR	*	10.00	10.00
95	DRESSED AS SCOUT SLEEPING	*	10.00	10.00
95	DRESSED AS SCOUT WITH COOKIES	*	10.00	10.00
95	DRESSED AS SCOUT WITH SMORES	*	10.00	10.00
95	FOUR SEASONS	2000	30.00	30.00
95	MRS. SANTA CLAUS	2000	30.00	30.00
95	ROMEO & JULIET	2000	30.00	30.00
95	SANTA CLAUS	2000	30.00	30.00
95	SUSIE	2000	30.00	30.00
95	WEARING WOW/MOM SHIRT-DOUBLE	*	20.00	20.00
96	BEAR CROSS STITCHING	*	10.00	10.00
96	BEAR HOLDING PHOTO FRAME	*	10.00	10.00
96	BEAR PAINTING	*	10.00	10.00
96	BEAR QUILTING	*	10.00	10.00
96	BEAR SEWING	*	10.00	10.00
96	BEAR WITH TRAVEL BROCHURES	*	10.00	10.00
96	BEARS STANDING IN LINE	2000	30.00	30.00
96	COUPLE ON COUCH- MUSICAL	*	40.00	40.00
96	DRESSED AS ANNIVERSARY INVITATION	*	10.00	10.00
96	DRESSED AS BABY SHOWER INVITATION	*	10.00	10.00
96	DRESSED AS BATH SALTS	*	10.00	10.00
96	DRESSED AS BATHROBE	*	10.00	10.00
96	DRESSED AS BIRTHDAY INVITATION	*	10.00	10.00
96	DRESSED AS BRIDAL INVITATION	*	10.00	10.00
96	DRESSED AS CAMERA	*	10.00	10.00
96	DRESSED AS CELEBRATION INVITATION	*	10.00	10.00
96	DRESSED AS CHOCOLATE STRAWBERRY	*	10.00	10.00
96	DRESSED AS COSMETIC BAG	*	10.00	10.00
96	DRESSED AS CREDIT CARD	*	10.00	10.00
96	DRESSED AS DUSTING POWDER	*	10.00	10.00
96	DRESSED AS GRADUATION	*	10.00	10.00
96	DRESSED AS HANDMIRROR	*	10.00	10.00
96	DRESSED AS MAPLE SYRUP TIN	*	10.00	10.00
96	DRESSED AS NAILPOLISH BOTTLE	*	10.00	10.00
96	DRESSED AS POSTCARD	*	10.00	10.00
96	DRESSED AS PRETZEL	*	10.00	10.00
96	DRESSED AS SUGAR WAFER- 3 PC	*	10.00	10.00
96	DRESSED AS SUITCASE	*	10.00	10.00
96	DRESSED AS VEGETABLE CRATE- 4 PC	*	10.00	10.00
96	HOLDING LOCKET/KEY- 2 PC	*	20.00	20.00
96	PARTY BACKER CARD	*	10.00	10.00
96	SPA BACKER CARD	*	10.00	10.00

YR	NAME	LIMIT	ISSUE	TREND
96	SUMMER VACATION BACKER CARD	*	10.00	10.00
97	ANGEL WITH BANNER- DATED	YR	10.00	10.00
97	ANGEL WITH WAND	*	10.00	10.00
97	BEAR AS SHEPHERD/DRUMMER- 2 PC	*	10.00	10.00
97	BEAR DRESSED AS KING- 3 PC	*	30.00	30.00
97	BEARS SLEDDING- 3 PC	*	12.50	13.00
97	CHRISTMAS PAGEANT MUG	*	8.00	8.00
97	DRESSED AS DEVIL BOBBING APPLES	*	10.00	10.00
97	DRESSED AS SNOWMAN	*	10.00	10.00
97	HALLOWEEN- 2 PC	*	10.00	10.00
97	NATIVITY PAGEANT- 2 PC	*	20.00	20.00
M. RHYNER-NADIG			**MARY'S MOO MOOS**	
94	AN UN-EGGSPECTED PLEASURE 628840	RT	*	N/A
94	BUTTER CREAM WISHES 627747	RT	*	N/A
94	COOKIES ARE FOR SHARING 627739	RT	*	N/A
94	CREAM OF THE CROP 628859	RT	*	N/A
94	I'M LUCKY TO KNOW YOU 627755	RT	*	N/A
94	MERRY CHRISTMOOS 651702	RT	*	N/A
94	ONCE UPON A MIDNIGHT STEER 651680	RT	*	N/A
94	OUTSTANDING IN YOUR OWN FIELD 627720	RT	*	N/A
94	PASTURE BEDTIME 627763	RT	*	N/A
94	SHUCKS, YOU'RE SWEET 627712	RT	*	N/A
94	YOU ARE THE APPLE OF MY EYE 628867	RT	*	N/A
M. RHYNER-NADIG		**MARY'S MOO MOOS 97 HALLOWEEN**		
97	ALL WRAPPED UP IN MOO	OP	15.00	15.00
97	COVERED MUSIC BOX- 3 PC	OP	20.00	20.00
97	I VANT TO DRINK MY MILK	OP	15.00	15.00
97	LAPEL PINS- 3 PC	OP	5.00	5.00
97	MOO STEER ME IN THE RIGHT DIRECTION	OP	15.00	15.00
M. RHYNER-NADIG		**MARY'S MOO MOOS AMER. DIABETES DED.**		
97	WATCHING OVER MOO NOW AND HEIFER	7200	65.00	65.00
M. RHYNER-NADIG		**MARY'S MOO MOOS BARN UNTO US**		
96	AW, STUCK! THIS IS ALL I HAVE FOR HIM	OP	16.50	17.00
96	BARN UNTO US	OP	6.00	6.00
96	HAY! WE HAVE PLENTY OF ROOM	OP	13.50	13.00
96	HERD IT FROM AN ANGEL	OP	16.50	17.00
96	I WOOD BUILD SOMETHING FOR HIM	OP	16.50	16.00
96	IS HE REALLY A KING MOO-MY?	OP	16.50	17.00
96	STACKED IN OUR FAVOR	OP	16.50	17.00
96	WEE, WEE, WEE, FOLLOWED THE STAR	OP	13.50	14.00
96	YOU BRING SUNSHINE TO OUR LIVES	OP	13.50	14.00
M. RHYNER-NADIG		**MARY'S MOO MOOS BE MOO TO YOUR SCHOOL**		
97	BLACK/YELLOW	OP	7.50	8.00
97	BLUE/WHITE	OP	7.50	8.00
97	BLUE/YELLOW	OP	7.50	8.00
97	GREEN/WHITE	OP	7.50	8.00
97	GREEN/YELLOW	OP	7.50	8.00
97	ORANGE/YELLOW	OP	7.50	8.00
97	PURPLE/WHITE	OP	7.50	8.00
97	PURPLE/YELLOW	OP	7.50	8.00
97	RED/WHITE	OP	7.50	8.00
97	RED/YELLOW	OP	7.50	8.00
M. RHYNER-NADIG		**MARY'S MOO MOOS BOO MOOS**		
96	I CAST MY SPELL ON MOO!	OP	13.50	14.00
96	LIFE IS A MOOSQUERADE	RT	13.50	14.00
96	MUSICAL STUMP	OP	12.50	15.00
96	PEEK-A-MOO!	OP	13.50	14.00
96	WHO-O-O ARE MOOO-O-O?	OP	13.50	14.00
M. RHYNER-NADIG		**MARY'S MOO MOOS BRANDED WITH LOVE**		
97	CLOCK	OP	40.00	40.00
97	COVERED BOX	OP	20.00	20.00
97	LAPEL PINS- 2 PC	OP	4.00	4.00
97	MOO CARVED A PLACE IN MY HEART	RT	13.50	14.00
97	PENCIL CUP	OP	25.00	25.00
97	PHOTOFRAME	OP	25.00	25.00
97	WHITTLE LOVE GOES A LONG WAY, A	OP	15.00	15.00
M. RHYNER-NADIG		**MARY'S MOO MOOS COUNTRY WEDDING**		
96	BEST BULL	OP	13.50	14.00
96	FLOUR GIRL	OP	10.00	10.00
96	GROOMS BULL	OP	13.50	14.00
96	I'LL NEVER LOVE AN UDDER	OP	15.00	15.00
96	MILK MAID	OP	13.50	14.00
96	MILK MAID OF HONOR	OP	13.50	14.00
96	RING BEARER	OP	10.00	10.00
M. RHYNER-NADIG		**MARY'S MOO MOOS COUNTRY WEDDING MUSICAL**		
96	WEDDING MARCH	OP	100.00	100.00
M. RHYNER-NADIG		**MARY'S MOO MOOS DATED 1997**		
97	IT'S BUTTER TO GIVE THAN TO RECEIVE	YR	16.50	17.00
M. RHYNER-NADIG		**MARY'S MOO MOOS MOO IN THE BOX**		
96	HOOFY HOLIDAYS	OP	12.50	12.00
96	I LOVE MOO!	OP	12.50	12.00
96	MOOEY CHRISTMAS	OP	12.50	13.00

YR	NAME	LIMIT	ISSUE	TREND
M. RHYNER-NADIG		**MARY'S MOO MOOS MOOEY CHRISTMAS**		
96	WHEEE ARE MOOVIN!	OP	170.00	170.00
96	WHEEE ARE MOOVIN!/DATED	YR	12.50	13.00
M. RHYNER-NADIG		**MARY'S MOO MOOS MOOS OF THE MONTH**		
97	AMERICOW THE BEAUTIFUL	OP	17.50	18.00
97	CORN BEEF & CABBAGE	OP	17.50	18.00
97	I'M JUST A COW WHO CAN'T SAY NO	OP	17.50	18.00
97	I'M SO LUCKY YOU'RE MY DUCKY	OP	17.50	18.00
97	I'M TEMPTING MOO	OP	17.50	18.00
97	KISS MOO	OP	17.50	18.00
97	MAKING THE GRADE	OP	17.50	18.00
97	MAY THE SUN ALWAYS SHINE ON MOO	OP	17.50	18.00
97	MOO & ME BY THE SEA	OP	17.50	18.00
97	MOO AUTUMN BE IN PICTURES	OP	17.50	18.00
97	MOOING THE LAWN	OP	17.50	18.00
97	SKI MOO LATER	OP	17.50	18.00
M. RHYNER-NADIG		**MARY'S MOO MOOS MOOSENGERS OF LOVE**		
96	HAY! I LOVE YOU	OP	6.75	7.00
96	HOLSTEIN YOU CLOSE	OP	6.25	7.00
96	I LOVE YOU DAIRY MUCH	OP	6.25	7.00
M. RHYNER-NADIG		**MARY'S MOO MOOS SLEIGHBULLS RING...**		
97	I'M DREAMING OF A WHITE CHRISTMOOS-MUSICAL	OP	20.00	20.00
97	JINGLE BULLS	OP	30.00	30.00
97	SILENT NIGHT, HOLY COW- MUSICAL	OP	20.00	20.00
97	WE WISH YOU A MERRY CHRISTMAS- MUSICAL	OP	25.00	25.00
M. RHYNER-NADIG		**MARY'S MOO MOOS SOWING THE SEEDS**		
97	HOE DO YOU DO	OP	17.50	18.00
97	I DIG MOO	OP	17.50	18.00
97	MOO MOOS IN POTS- 4 PC	OP	8.00	8.00
97	OUR LOVE IS GROWING	OP	20.00	20.00
97	SEED WALL HANGING	OP	25.00	25.00
97	SOWING THE SEEDS OF FRIENDSHIP	OP	13.50	14.00
97	TROWEL PLANT STICKS- 2 PC	OP	7.50	8.00
97	TROWEL PLAQUE- 2 PC	OP	20.00	20.00
97	WIND CHIME	OP	30.00	30.00
M. RHYNER-NADIG		**MARY'S MOO MOOS SPRING IS IN THE AIR**		
96	ALL A-BUZZ OVER YOU	OP	6.75	7.00
96	I'M MOOVIN INTO SPRING	OP	10.00	10.00
96	SPRING IS IN THE AIR	OP	7.50	8.00
96	TAKE ME OUT TO THE BULL GAME	OP	6.75	7.00
M. ATTWELL		**MEMORIES OF YESTERDAY**		
88	ANYWAY, FIDO LOVES ME 114588	OP	30.00	33.00
88	CAN I KEEP HER MOMMY? 114545	OP	25.00	28.00
88	DEAR SANTA 115002	OP	50.00	75.00
88	GOOD MORNING, MR. SNOWMAN 115401	OP	75.00	85.00
88	HANG ON TO YOUR LUCK! 114510	OP	25.00	28.00
88	HE KNOWS IF YOU'VE BEEN BAD/GOOD 115355	OP	40.00	45.00
88	HOW 'BOUT A LITTLE KISS? 114987	RT	25.00	28.00
88	HOW DO YOU SPELL S-O-R-R-Y? 114529	RT	25.00	40.00
88	HUSH! 114553	RT	45.00	70.00
88	I HOPE SANTA IS HOME 115010	OP	30.00	50.00
88	I PRAY THE LORD MY SOUL TO KEEP 523259	OP	25.00	47.00
88	IF YOU CAN'T BE GOOD, BE CAREFUL 114596	OP	50.00	55.00
88	IS IT REALLY SANTA? 115347	RT	50.00	65.00
88	IT HURTS WHEN FIDO HURTS 114561	OP	30.00	33.00
88	IT'S THE THOUGHT THAT COUNTS 115029	OP	25.00	28.00
88	MOMMY, I TEARED IT 114480	OP	25.00	28.00
88	MOMMY, I TEARED IT 523488	10000	25.00	310.00
88	MOMMY, I TEARED IT, 9 IN. 115924	CL	85.00	145.00
88	NOW HE CAN BE YOUR FRIEND, TOO! 115363	OP	45.00	50.00
88	NOW I LAY ME DOWN TO SLEEP 114499	RT	20.00	45.00
88	SPECIAL DELIVERY 114979	RT	30.00	45.00
88	WAITING FOR SANTA 114995	OP	40.00	55.00
88	WE WISH YOU A MERRY CHRISTMAS 115371	OP	70.00	75.00
88	WE'S HAPPY! HOW'S YOURSELF? 114502	RT	40.00	45.00
88	WELCOME SANTA 114960	OP	45.00	60.00
88	WHAT WILL I GROW UP TO BE? 114537	OP	40.00	45.00
89	AS GOOD AS HIS MOTHER EVER MADE 522392	9600	33.00	150.00
89	BLOW WIND, BLOW 520012	OP	40.00	40.00
89	DADDY, I COULD NEVER FILL/SHOES 520187	OP	30.00	30.00
89	FOR FIDO AND ME 522457	OP	70.00	70.00
89	HERE COMES THE BRIDE AND GROOM 520896	OP	50.00	50.00
89	HERE COMES THE BRIDE, 9 IN. 520527	CL	95.00	95.00
89	I'SE SPOKEN FOR 520071	RT	30.00	30.00
89	JOY TO YOU AT CHRISTMAS 522449	RT	45.00	45.00
89	KNITTING YOU A WARM & COZY WINTER 522414	OP	38.00	38.00
89	LET'S BE NICE LIKE WE WAS BEFORE 520047	OP	50.00	50.00
89	LONG AND SHORT OF IT, THE- 522384	OP	33.00	33.00
89	MUST FEED THEM OVER CHRISTMAS 522406	RT	39.00	39.00
89	SHOULD I...? 520209	OP	50.00	50.00
89	THIS ONE'S FOR YOU DEAR 520195	OP	50.00	50.00
89	WE'S HAPPY! HOW'S YOURSELF? 520616	RT	70.00	70.00
90	A DASH OF SOMETHING W/SOMETHING 524727	RT	55.00	55.00
90	A LAPFUL OF LUCK 524689	OP	15.00	30.00
90	A LAPFUL OF LUCK 525014	5000	30.00	30.00

YR	NAME	LIMIT	ISSUE	TREND
90	COLLECTION SIGN 513156	OP	7.00	7.00
90	GOT TO GET HOME FOR THE HOLIDAYS 524751	OP	100.00	100.00
90	GREATEST TREASURE THE WORLD, THE- 524808	OP	50.00	50.00
90	HE HASN'T FORGOTTEN ME 523267	OP	30.00	32.00
90	HERE COMES THE BRIDE AND GROOM 520136	OP	80.00	80.00
90	HOLD IT! YOU'RE JUST SWELL 520020	OP	50.00	50.00
90	HOPING TO SEE YOU SOON 524824	SU	30.00	30.00
90	HUSH-A-BYE BABY 524778	OP	80.00	80.00
90	I'M NOT AS BACKWARD AS I LOOKS 523240	RT	33.00	33.00
90	I'SE BEEN PAINTING 524700	OP	38.00	38.00
90	KISS THE PLACE AND MAKE IT WELL 520039	OP	50.00	50.00
90	LET ME BE YOUR GUARDIAN ANGEL 524670	OP	33.00	33.00
90	LUCK AT LAST! HE LOVES ME 520217	OP	35.00	35.00
90	NOT A CREATURE WAS STIRRIN' 524697	OP	45.00	45.00
90	TIME FOR BED, 9 IN. 523275	TL	95.00	95.00
90	WHERE'S MUVVER? 520101	OP	30.00	30.00
91	COULD YOU LOVE ME FOR MYSELF? 525618	OP	30.00	30.00
91	FRIENDSHIP HAS NO BOUNDARIES 525545	YR	30.00	30.00
91	GIVE IT YOUR BEST SHOT 525561	OP	35.00	35.00
91	GOOD MORNING, LITTLE BOO-BOO 525766	RT	40.00	40.00
91	HE LOVES ME, 9 IN. 525022	TL	100.00	100.00
91	I MUST BE SOMEBODY'S DARLING 522635	OP	30.00	30.00
91	I'M AS COMFY AS CAN BE 525480	OP	50.00	50.00
91	JUST THINKING 'BOUT YOU 523461	OP	70.00	70.00
91	OPENING PRESENTS IS MUCH FUN! 524735	OP	38.00	38.00
91	PULL YOURSELVES TOGETHER GIRLS 522783	OP	30.00	30.00
91	S'NO USE LOOKIN' BACK NOW! 527203	OP	75.00	75.00
91	SITTING PRETTY 522708	OP	40.00	40.00
91	THEM DISHES NEARLY DONE 524611	OP	50.00	50.00
91	TYING THE KNOT 522678	OP	60.00	60.00
91	WE ALL LOVES A CUDDLE 524832	OP	30.00	30.00
91	WE BELONG TOGETHER S-0001	OP	30.00	40.00
91	WELCOME TO YOUR NEW HOME M4911	YR	*	40.00
91	WHEREVER I AM/I'M DREAMING OF YOU 522686	OP	40.00	40.00
91	WHO EVER TOLD MOTHER/TWINS? 520063	OP	34.00	34.00
91	WHY DON'T YOU SING ALONG? 522600	OP	55.00	55.00
91	WISHFUL THINKING 522597	OP	45.00	45.00
92	A KISS FROM FIDO 523119	OP	35.00	35.00
92	A WHOLE BUNCH OF LOVE FOR YOU 522732	RT	40.00	40.00
92	HURRY UP FOR THE LAST TRAIN 525863	OP	40.00	40.00
92	I PRAY THE LORD MY SOUL TO KEEP 525596	OP	65.00	65.00
92	I'M HOPIN' YOU'RE MISSING ME TOO 525499	OP	55.00	55.00
92	I'SE SO HAPPY YOU CALLED 526401	TL	100.00	100.00
92	I'SE SUCH A GOOD LITTLE GIRL 522759	OP	30.00	30.00
92	NOW BE A GOOD DOG FIDO 524581	OP	45.00	45.00
92	SEND ALL LIFE'S LITTLE WORRIES 527505	RT	30.00	30.00
92	TIME FOR BED 527076	OP	30.00	30.00
92	YOU'LL ALWAYS BE MY HERO 524743	RT	50.00	50.00
93	HULLO! DID YOU COME BY UNDERGROUND?	500	40.00	40.00
93	I'M ALWAYS LOOKING OUT FOR YOU	OP	55.00	55.00
93	LITTLE MISS MUFFET	18000	50.00	50.00
93	MARY HAD A LITTLE LAMB	18000	45.00	45.00
93	MARY, MARY QUITE CONTRARY	18000	45.00	45.00
93	MOTHER GOOSE	18000	50.00	50.00
93	NOW I'M THE FAIREST OF THEM ALL	OP	35.00	35.00
93	SIMPLE SIMON	18000	35.00	35.00
94	A LITTLE LOVE SONG-FOR YOU!	OP	35.00	35.00
94	DAYS OF THE WEEK SET	1994	250.00	250.00
94	THANK GOD FOR FIDO	OP	30.00	30.00
94	TWEEDLE DUM & TWEEDLE DEE	10000	25.00	25.00
94	WOT'S ALL THIS TALK ABOUT LOVE?	OP	28.00	28.00
95	A LITTLE HELP FROM FAIRYLAND	1995	55.00	55.00
95	BOO-BOO'S BAND SET OF FIVE	OP	12.50	13.00
95	DEAR OLD DEAR, WISH YOU WERE HERE	5000	38.00	38.00
95	I COMFORT FIDO & HE COMFORTS ME	5000	50.00	50.00
95	JOIN ME FOR A LITTLE SONG	5000	50.00	50.00
95	SHARING THE COMMON THREAD OF LOVE	OP	100.00	100.00
95	WON'T YOU SKATE WITH ME	5000	35.00	35.00
95	WRAPPED IN LOVE & HAPPINESS	OP	35.00	35.00
96	A MOO ADDITION TO OUR FAMILY	7300	60.00	60.00
96	BASKET FULL OF LOVE, A	OP	50.00	50.00
96	GOD BLESS OUR FUTURE	5000	45.00	45.00
96	HOW GOOD OF GOD TO MAKE US ALL	5000	50.00	50.00
96	JUST LIKE DADDY	7500	28.00	28.00
96	JUST LONGING TO SEE YOU	7500	28.00	28.00
96	LOVING YOU ONE STITCH AT A TIME	5000	50.00	50.00
96	PUT YOUR BEST FOOT FORWARD	5000	50.00	50.00
96	WE ARE ALL HIS CHILDREN	OP	28.00	28.00
96	WE'D DO ANYTHING FOR YOU, DEAR	5000	38.00	38.00
96	WE'RE IN TROUBLE NOW!	7500	38.00	38.00
96	WHENEVER I GET A MOMENT-I THINK OF YOU	7500	38.00	38.00
96	YOU WARM MY HEART	7500	35.00	35.00
97	ALICE IN WONDERLAND	3000	150.00	150.00
97	BRINGING GIFTS OF FRIENDSHIP TO SHARE!	5000	38.00	38.00
97	DREAMS ARE SWEETER WITH FRIENDS	5000	38.00	38.00

YR	NAME	LIMIT	ISSUE	TREND
97	HOPING TO SEE YOU SOON (COVERED BOX)	OP	25.00	25.00
97	HOW 'BOUT A LITTLE KISS (COVERED BOX)	OP	25.00	25.00
97	I KNOW YOU CAN DO IT!	5000	35.00	35.00
97	I PRAY THE LORD MY SOUL TO KEEP (COVERED BOX)	OP	25.00	25.00
97	IN THE HANDS OF A GUARDIAN ANGEL	5000	50.00	50.00
97	LET ME BE YOUR GUARDIAN ANGEL (COVERED BOX)	OP	25.00	25.00
97	LET YOUR LIGHT SHINE	5000	30.00	30.00
97	MAY I HAVE THIS DANCE?	5000	50.00	50.00
97	NOW DO YOU LOVE ME OR DO YOU DON'T	OP	20.00	20.00
97	NOW I LAY ME DOWN TO SLEEP	RT	25.00	25.00
97	ROSES ARE RED- VIOLETS ARE BLUE	OP	20.00	20.00
97	THERE'S ALWAYS A RAINBOW	5000	38.00	38.00
97	TIME FOR BED	OP	25.00	25.00
97	YOU'RE MY BOUQUET OF BLESSINGS	5000	30.00	30.00
97	YOU'RE NICE	OP	20.00	20.00
M. ATTWELL	**MEMORIES OF YESTERDAY 10TH ANNIVERSARY COMMISSION**			
97	MEETING SPECIAL FRIENDS ALONG THE WAY	YR	85.00	85.00
97	MEETING SPECIAL FRIENDS ALONG THE WAY- BOX	YR	10.00	10.00
M. ATTWELL	**MEMORIES OF YESTERDAY A LOVING WISH**			
96	YOU ARE MY SHINING STAR	OP	25.00	25.00
96	YOU BRIGHTEN MY DAYS	OP	25.00	25.00
M. ATTWELL	**MEMORIES OF YESTERDAY COMFORTING THOUGHTS**			
95	YOU'RE MY SUNSHINE ON A RAINY DAY	OP	38.00	38.00
97	YOU MAKE MY HEART FEEL GLAD	OP	30.00	30.00
M. ATTWELL	**MEMORIES OF YESTERDAY EVENT ONLY**			
96	A SWEET TREAT FOR YOU	YR	30.00	30.00
97	MOMMY, I TEARED IT	YR	28.00	28.00
M. ATTWELL	**MEMORIES OF YESTERDAY FRIENDSHIP**			
96	I LOVE YOU THIS MUCH!	OP	25.00	25.00
96	I MISS YOU	OP	25.00	25.00
96	THINKING OF YOU	OP	25.00	25.00
96	YOU AND ME	OP	23.00	23.00
M. ATTWELL	**MEMORIES OF YESTERDAY HERITAGE**			
96	I DO LIKE MY HOLIDAY CREWS	1996	100.00	100.00
96	PETER PAN COLLECTOR'S SET	1000	150.00	150.00
96	TUCKING MY DEARS ALL SAFE AWAY	YR	50.00	50.00
97	EVERY STITCH IS SEWN WITH KINDNESS	YR	50.00	50.00
97	WE'RE GOING TO BE GREAT FRIENDS	YR	50.00	50.00
M. ATTWELL	**MEMORIES OF YESTERDAY NATIVITY PAGEANT**			
95	INNKEEPER	OP	28.00	28.00
96	SHEPHERD	OP	28.00	28.00
M. ATTWELL	**MEMORIES OF YESTERDAY PETER PAN**			
96	JOHN	OP	30.00	30.00
96	MICHAEL	OP	30.00	30.00
96	PETER PAN	OP	25.00	25.00
96	TINKERBELL	OP	20.00	20.00
96	WENDY	OP	25.00	25.00
M. ATTWELL	**MEMORIES OF YESTERDAY SOCIETY**			
96	FORGET-ME-NOT	OP	*	N/A
96	PEACE HEAVENLY PEACE	OP	30.00	30.00
96	YOU'VE GOT MY VOTE	OP	40.00	40.00
97	HOLDING ONTO CHILDHOOD MEMORIES	YR	*	N/A
97	WE TAKE CARE OF ONE ANOTHER	YR	45.00	45.00
97	YOU MEAN THE WORLD TO ME	YR	40.00	40.00
M. ATTWELL	**MEMORIES OF YESTERDAY SYMBOL OF MEMBERSHIP**			
93	I'M THE GIRL FOR YOU	OP	*	N/A
94	BLOWING A KISS TO A DEAR I MISS	OP	*	N/A
95	TIME TO CELEBRATE	OP	*	N/A
M. ATTWELL	**MEMORIES OF YESTERDAY WHEN I GROW UP**			
96	BUSINESSMAN	OP	25.00	25.00
96	BUSINESSWOMAN	OP	25.00	25.00
S. BUTCHER				**NOAH'S ARK**
95	CONGRATULATIONS, YOU EARNED YOUR STRIPES 127609	OP	15.00	15.00
96	I'D GOAT ANYWHERE WITH YOU 163694	OP	10.00	10.00
P. FAGAN				**PENNYWHISTLE LANE**
94	TRUNK OF TEDDIES	1000	60.00	60.00
S. BUTCHER				**PRECIOUS MOMENTS**
*	DOME W/KIDS ON CLOUD FIGURINE E7350	*	*	800.00
76	HE CARETH FOR YOU E1377B	SU	9.00	125.00
76	PRAISE THE LORD ANYHOW E1374B	RT	8.00	100.00
76	PRAYER CHANGES THINGS E1375B	SU	11.00	195.00
77	BOY & GIRL ON SEESAW E1375A	RT	11.00	125.00
77	HE LEADETH ME E1377A	SU	9.00	250.00
77	JESUS IS THE ANSWER E1381R	OP	55.00	60.00
77	LOVE IS KIND E1379A	SU	8.00	115.00
77	O HOW I LOVE JESUS E1380B	RT	8.00	110.00
78	JESUS IS BORN E2012	SU	12.00	115.00
78	UNTO US A CHILD IS BORN E2013	SU	12.00	115.00
78	WISHING YOU A SEASON FILLED W/JOY E-2805	RT	20.00	100.00
79	BE NOT WEARY IN WELL DOING E-3111	RT	14.00	140.00
79	BLESSED ARE THE PEACEMAKERS E-3107	RT	13.00	100.00
79	BUT LOVE GOES ON FOREVER E-3115	OP	16.50	70.00
79	CHRISTMAS IS A TIME TO SHARE E-2802	SU	20.00	100.00
79	COME LET US ADORE HIM E-2011	RT	10.00	300.00

YR	NAME	LIMIT	ISSUE	TREND
79	CROWN HIM LORD OF ALL E-2803	SU	20.00	85.00
79	EGGS OVER EASY E3118	RT	12.00	105.00
79	GOD LOVETH A CHEERFUL GIVER E-1378	RT	9.50	1150.00
79	GOD UNDERSTANDS E-1379B	SU	8.00	115.00
79	GOD'S SPEED E-3112	RT	14.00	85.00
79	HAND THAT ROCKS THE FUTURE, THE- E-3108	SU	13.00	120.00
79	HE CARETH FOR YOU E-1377B	SU	9.00	110.00
79	HE LEADETH ME E-1377A	SU	9.00	110.00
79	HE WATCHES OVER US ALL E-3105	SU	11.00	75.00
79	HIS BURDEN IS LIGHT E-1380G	RT	17.00	125.00
79	IT'S WHAT'S INSIDE THAT COUNTS E-3119	SU	13.00	110.00
79	JESUS IS BORN E-2012	SU	12.00	140.00
79	JESUS IS BORN E-2801	SU	37.00	315.00
79	JESUS IS THE ANSWER E-1381	SU	11.50	140.00
79	JESUS IS THE LIGHT E-1373G	RT	15.00	95.00
79	JESUS LOVES ME E-1372B	OP	7.00	100.00
79	JESUS LOVES ME E-1372G	OP	7.00	100.00
79	LORD BLESS YOU AND KEEP YOU, THE- E-3114	OP	16.00	75.00
79	LOVE IS KIND E-1379A	SU	8.00	115.00
79	LOVE LIFTED ME E-1375A	OP	11.00	110.00
79	LOVE ONE ANOTHER E-1376	OP	10.00	85.00
79	LOVING IS SHARING E-3110B	RT	13.00	100.00
79	LOVING IS SHARING E-3110G	OP	13.00	100.00
79	MAKE A JOYFUL NOISE E-1374G	OP	8.00	135.00
79	MOTHER SEW DEAR E-3106	OP	13.00	100.00
79	NATIVITY SET OF 9 PCS. E2800	OP	70.00	175.00
79	O, HOW I LOVE JESUS E-1380B	RT	17.00	110.00
79	PEACE ON EARTH E-2804	SU	20.00	165.00
79	PRAISE THE LORD ANYHOW E-1374B	RT	17.00	100.00
79	PRAYER CHANGES THINGS E-1375B	SU	11.00	175.00
79	PURR-FECT GRANDMA , THE-E-3109	OP	13.00	100.00
79	SMILE, GOD LOVES YOU E-1373B	RT	7.00	100.00
79	THEE I LOVE E-3116	RT	16.50	80.00
79	THOU ART MINE E-3113	OP	16.00	50.00
79	TO THEE W/LOVE E3120	SU	13.00	80.00
79	UNTO US A CHILD IS BORN E-2013	SU	12.00	115.00
79	WALKING BY FAITH E-3117	OP	35.00	100.00
79	WE HAVE SEEN HIS STAR E-2010	SU	8.00	100.00
80	BEAR YE ONE ANOTHER'S BURDENS E-5200	SU	20.00	80.00
80	BLESSED ARE THE PURE IN HEART E-3104	SU	9.00	40.00
80	COME LET US ADORE HIM E-5619	SU	10.00	40.00
80	COW WITH BELL FIGURINE E-5638	OP	16.00	40.00
80	DONKEY FIGURINE E-5621	OP	6.00	25.00
80	GOD IS LOVE E-5213	SU	17.00	75.00
80	HEAVENLY LIGHT, THE- E-5637	OP	15.00	60.00
80	ISN'T HE WONDERFUL E-5639	SU	12.00	60.00
80	ISN'T HE WONDERFUL E-5640	SU	12.00	67.00
80	LET NOT THE SUN GO DOWN...WRATH E-5203	SU	23.00	165.00
80	LORD BLESS YOU AND KEEP YOU, THE- E-4720	SU	14.00	40.00
80	LORD BLESS YOU AND KEEP YOU, THE- E-4721	OP	14.00	55.00
80	LOVE CANNOT BREAK/TRUE FRIENDSHIP E-4722	SU	23.00	155.00
80	LOVE LIFTED ME E-5201	SU	25.00	100.00
80	MY GUARDIAN ANGEL E-5207	SU	35.00	190.00
80	NATIVITY WALL E-5644 (SET OF 2)	OP	60.00	160.00
80	PEACE AMID THE STORM E-4723	SU	23.00	100.00
80	PRAYER CHANGES THINGS E-5214	SU	35.00	130.00
80	REJOICE O EARTH E-5636	OP	15.00	45.00
80	REJOICING WITH YOU E-4724	OP	25.00	55.00
80	SILENT KNIGHT E5642	SU	55.00	215.00
80	THANK YOU FOR COMING TO MY AIDE E-5202	SU	23.00	150.00
80	THEY FOLLOWED THE STAR E-5624	OP	130.00	260.00
80	THEY FOLLOWED THE STAR E-5641	SU	75.00	195.00
80	TO A SPECIAL DAD E-5212	OP	20.00	55.00
80	WEE THREE KINGS E-5635	OP	40.00	100.00
81	BLESS THIS HOUSE E-7164	SU	45.00	200.00
81	BUT LOVE GOES ON FOREVER E-0001	YR	*	175.00
81	BUT LOVES GOES ON FOREVER E6118	SU	16.00	60.00
81	FORGIVING IS FORGETTING E-9252	SU	38.00	75.00
81	GOD IS LOVE, DEAR VALENTINE E-7153	SU	16.00	45.00
81	GOD IS LOVE, DEAR VALENTINE E-7154	SU	16.00	40.00
81	GOD IS WATCHING OVER YOU E-7163	SU	28.00	95.00
81	HIS SHEEP AM I E-7161	SU	25.00	90.00
81	I BELIEVE IN MIRACLES E-7156	SU	17.00	115.00
81	LET THE WHOLE WORLD KNOW E-7165	SU	35.00	95.00
81	LORD GIVE ME PATIENCE E-7159	SU	25.00	55.00
81	LOVE BEARETH ALL THINGS E-7158	OP	25.00	60.00
81	LOVE IS SHARING E-7162	SU	25.00	165.00
81	PEACE ON EARTH E-4725	SU	25.00	80.00
81	PERFECT GRANDPA , THE-E-7160	SU	25.00	70.00
81	THANKING HIM FOR YOU E-7155	SU	16.00	53.00
81	THERE IS JOY IN SERVING JESUS E-7157	RT	17.00	60.00
82	3 MINI NATIVITY HOUSES/PALM TREE E-2387	OP	45.00	100.00
82	ANIMAL COLLECTION, BUNNY E-9267C	SU	6.50	25.00
82	ANIMAL COLLECTION, DOG E-9267B	SU	6.50	25.00
82	ANIMAL COLLECTION, KITTY W/BOW E-9267D	SU	6.50	25.00

YR	NAME	LIMIT	ISSUE	TREND
82	ANIMAL COLLECTION, LAMB W/BIRD E-9267E	SU	6.50	25.00
82	ANIMAL COLLECTION, PIG W/PATCHES E-9267F	SU	6.50	25.00
82	ANIMAL COLLECTION, TEDDY BEAR E-9267A	SU	6.50	25.00
82	BLESS YOU TWO E-9255	OP	21.00	42.00
82	BUNDLES OF JOY E-2374	RT	28.00	100.00
82	BUT LOVE GOES ON FOREVER PLAQUE E-0102	YR	*	100.00
82	CAMEL E2363	OP	20.00	45.00
82	CHRISTMAS JOY FROM HEAD TO TOE E2361	SU	25.00	65.00
82	COME LET US ADORE HIM E-2395 (SET OF 11)	OP	80.00	150.00
82	DROPPING IN FOR CHRISTMAS E-2350	OP	30.00	100.00
82	DROPPING OVER FOR CHRISTMAS E-2375	RT	30.00	100.00
82	END IS IN SIGHT, THE E-9253	SU	25.00	110.00
82	ESPECIALLY FOR EWE E-9282C	SU	8.00	33.00
82	FIRST NOEL, THE- E-2365	SU	16.00	70.00
82	FIRST NOEL, THE-E-2366	SU	16.00	70.00
82	GOAT FIGURINE E2364	SU	10.00	50.00
82	HOW CAN 2 WALK TOGETHER...AGREE E-9263	SU	35.00	140.00
82	I'LL PLAY MY DRUM FOR HIM E-2356	SU	30.00	95.00
82	I'LL PLAY MY DRUM FOR HIM E-2360	OP	16.00	35.00
82	I'LL PLAY MY DRUM FOR HIM E2355	SU	45.00	165.00
82	IF GOD BE FOR US...AGAINST US E-9285	SU	28.00	60.00
82	JESUS LOVES ME E-9278	OP	9.00	24.00
82	JESUS LOVES ME E-9279	OP	9.00	27.00
82	JOY TO THE WORLD E2343	SU	9.00	45.00
82	JOY TO THE WORLD E2344	SU	20.00	85.00
82	LET HEAVEN AND NATURE SING E2346	SU	50.00	145.00
82	LET HEAVEN AND NATURE SING E2347	15000	40.00	45.00
82	LOVE IS PATIENT E-9251	SU	35.00	85.00
82	MAY YOUR CHRISTMAS BE COZY E2345	SU	23.00	75.00
82	MAY YOUR CHRISTMAS BE WARM E-2348	SU	30.00	110.00
82	NOBODY'S PERFECT E-9268	RT	21.00	645.00
82	O COME ALL YE FAITHFUL E2352	SU	45.00	150.00
82	O COME ALL YE FAITHFUL E2353	RT	28.00	80.00
82	OUR FIRST CHRISTMAS TOGETHER E-2377	SU	35.00	85.00
82	PEACE ON EARTH E-9287	SU	38.00	125.00
82	PRAISE THE LORD ANYHOW E9254	RT	35.00	125.00
82	SEEK YE THE LORD E-9261	SU	21.00	50.00
82	SEEK YE THE LORD E-9262	SU	21.00	65.00
82	SENDING YOU A RAINBOW E-9288	SU	23.00	95.00
82	SHARING OUR JOY TOGETHER E-2834	SU	25.00	53.00
82	TASTE & SEE THAT THE LORD IS GOOD E-9274	RT	23.00	160.00
82	TELL ME THE STORY OF JESUS E-2349	SU	30.00	110.00
82	TO SOME BUNNY SPECIAL E-9282A	SU	8.00	35.00
82	TRUST IN THE LORD E-9289	SU	20.00	70.00
82	WE ARE GOD'S WORKMANSHIP E-9258	OP	19.00	40.00
82	WE'RE IN IT TOGETHER E-9259	SU	24.00	60.00
82	YOU HAVE TOUCHED SO MANY HEARTS 527661	SU	35.00	38.00
82	YOU HAVE TOUCHED SO MANY HEARTS E-2821	SU	25.00	45.00
82	YOU'RE WORTH YOUR WEIGHT IN GOLD E-9282B	SU	8.00	35.00
83	BABY FIGURINES E-2852	SU	12.00	23.00
83	BLESSINGS FROM MY HOUSE TO YOURS E-0503	SU	27.00	75.00
83	BRINGING GOD'S BLESSING TO YOU E-0509	SU	35.00	75.00
83	CHRISTMASTIME IS FOR SHARING E-0504	RT	37.00	90.00
83	GOD BLESS THIS BRIDE E-2832	OP	35.00	55.00
83	GOD HAS SENT HIS SON E-0507	SU	33.00	80.00
83	GOD'S PROMISES ARE SURE E-9260	SU	30.00	75.00
83	HE UPHOLDETH THOSE WHO FALL E-0526	SU	29.00	110.00
83	I GET A KICK OUT OF YOU E-2827	SU	50.00	145.00
83	IT'S A PERFECT BOY E-0512	SU	19.00	47.00
83	JESUS IS THE LIGHT THAT SHINES E-0502	SU	23.00	70.00
83	LOVE IS KIND E2847	15000	40.00	45.00
83	MAY YOUR BIRTHDAY BE A BLESSING E-2826	SU	38.00	100.00
83	ONWARD CHRISTIAN SOLDIERS E-0523	OP	24.00	75.00
83	PRAISE THE LORD ANYHOW E-9254	RT	35.00	90.00
83	PRECIOUS MEMORIES E-2828	OP	45.00	70.00
83	PREPARE YE THE WAY OF THE LORD E-0508	SU	75.00	135.00
83	PRESS ON E-9265	OP	40.00	90.00
83	SHARING OUR SEASON TOGETHER E-0501	SU	50.00	145.00
83	SURROUNDED WITH JOY E-0507	RT	35.00	75.00
83	THIS IS YOUR DAY TO SHINE E-2822	RT	38.00	120.00
83	TO A VERY SPECIAL MOM E-2824	OP	28.00	45.00
83	TO A VERY SPECIAL SISTER E-2825	OP	38.00	65.00
83	TO GOD BE THE GLORY E-2823	SU	40.00	85.00
83	TUBBY'S FIRST CHRISTMAS E-0511	SU	12.00	35.00
83	YOU CAN'T RUN AWAY FROM GOD E-0525	RT	29.00	125.00
84	A MONARCH IS BORN E-5380	SU	33.00	80.00
84	AUTUMN'S PRAISE MUSICAL 408751	LE	200.00	165.00
84	CLOWN BALANCING BALL 12238A	SU	13.50	20.00
84	CLOWN BENDING OVER BALL 12238C	SU	13.50	20.00
84	CLOWN HOLDING BALLOON 12238B	SU	13.50	20.00
84	CLOWN HOLDING FLOWER POT 12238D	SU	13.50	20.00
84	FOR GOD SO LOVED THE WORLD E-5382	SU	70.00	140.00
84	GET INTO THE HABIT OF PRAYER 12203	SU	19.00	47.00
84	GOD BLESS OUR HOME 12319	OP	40.00	70.00
84	GOD BLESS OUR YEARS TOGETHER 12440	CL	175.00	325.00

YR	NAME	LIMIT	ISSUE	TREND
84	GOD SENDS THE GIFT OF HIS LOVE E-6613	SU	23.00	85.00
84	HIS NAME IS JESUS E-5381	SU	45.00	95.00
84	I'LL PLAY MY DRUM FOR HIM E-5384	OP	10.00	24.00
84	I'M SENDING YOU A WHITE CHRISTMAS E-2829	OP	38.00	65.00
84	ISN'T HE PRECIOUS? E-5379	OP	20.00	40.00
84	IT IS BETTER TO GIVE...TO RECEIVE 12297	SU	19.00	85.00
84	JOY TO THE WORLD E-5378	SU	18.00	42.00
84	LORD, KEEP MY LIFE IN TUNE 12165	SU	38.00	85.00
84	LOVE IS KIND E5377	RT	28.00	85.00
84	LOVE NEVER FAILS 12300	OP	25.00	45.00
84	MAY YOUR CHRISTMAS BE BLESSED E-5376	SU	38.00	70.00
84	OH WORSHIP THE LORD E-5385	SU	10.00	45.00
84	OH WORSHIP THE LORD E-5386	SU	10.00	55.00
84	PART OF ME WANTS TO BE GOOD 12149	SU	19.00	65.00
84	SEEK AND YE SHALL FIND E-0105	YR	*	55.00
84	SUMMER'S JOY MUSICAL 408743	LE	200.00	170.00
84	VOICE OF SPRING MUSICAL, THE- 408735	LE	200.00	165.00
84	WINTER'S SONG MUSICAL 408778	LE	200.00	165.00
84	WISHING YOU A MERRY CHRISTMAS E-5383	YR	17.00	35.00
85	ANGEL OF MERCY 102482	OP	20.00	35.00
85	BABY'S FIRST CHRISTMAS 15539	YR	13.00	30.00
85	BABY'S FIRST CHRISTMAS 15547	YR	13.00	35.00
85	BABY'S FIRST TRIP 16012	SU	33.00	225.00
85	BIRDS OF A FEATHER COLLECT E-0106	YR	*	47.00
85	BROTHERLY LOVE 100544	SU	37.00	80.00
85	BUNNY, TURTLE & LAMB- 3 PC 102296	SU	5.50	25.00
85	FRIENDS NEVER DRIFT APART 100250	OP	35.00	60.00
85	GOD BLESS AMERICA 102938	LE	30.00	80.00
85	GOD BLESS THE DAY WE FOUND YOU 100145	SU	40.00	65.00
85	GOD BLESS THE DAY WE FOUND YOU 100153	SU	40.00	65.00
85	GOD SENT HIS LOVE 15881	YR	17.00	32.00
85	GOD SENT YOU JUST IN TIME 15504	RT	45.00	100.00
85	HALO, AND MERRY CHRISTMAS 12351	SU	40.00	150.00
85	HE CLEANSED MY SOUL 100277	OP	24.00	45.00
85	HELP, LORD, I'M IN A SPOT 100269	RT	19.00	65.00
85	HONK IF YOU LOVE JESUS 15490	OP	13.00	27.00
85	I BELIEVE IN THE OLD RUGGED CROSS 103632	OP	25.00	45.00
85	I'M A POSSIBILITY 100188	RT	22.00	60.00
85	IT'S THE BIRTHDAY OF A KING 102962	SU	19.00	35.00
85	JESUS IS COMING SOON 12343	SU	23.00	40.00
85	JOY OF THE LORD...MY STRENGTH, THE-100137	OP	35.00	75.00
85	LET'S KEEP IN TOUCH 102520	OP	65.00	115.00
85	LORD I'M COMING HOME 100110	OP	23.00	45.00
85	LORD KEEP ME ON MY TOES 100129	RT	23.00	100.00
85	LOVE COVERS ALL 12009	SU	28.00	65.00
85	LOVE RESCUED ME 102393	OP	23.00	45.00
85	MAY YOUR BIRTHDAY BE GIGANTIC 15970	OP	12.50	35.00
85	MAY YOUR CHRISTMAS BE DELIGHTFUL 15482	OP	25.00	45.00
85	O WORSHIP THE LORD 100064	OP	24.00	45.00
85	O WORSHIP THE LORD 102229	OP	24.00	40.00
85	SENDING MY LOVE 100056	SU	23.00	55.00
85	SERVING THE LORD 100161	SU	19.00	65.00
85	SERVING THE LORD 100293	SU	19.00	45.00
85	SHEPHERD OF LOVE 102261	OP	10.00	21.00
85	SILENT NIGHT 15814	SU	38.00	75.00
85	TO MY FAVORITE PAW 100021	SU	23.00	85.00
85	TO MY FOREVER FRIEND 100072	OP	33.00	90.00
85	WISHING YOU A COZY CHRISTMAS 102342	YR	18.00	35.00
85	WISHING YOU GRR-EATNESS 109479	OP	19.00	28.00
85	YOU CAN FLY 12335	SU	25.00	65.00
86	A TUB FULL OF LOVE 104587	OP	23.00	35.00
86	BEAR THE GOOD NEWS OF CHRISTMAS 104515	YR	12.50	19.00
86	CHEERS TO THE LEADER 104035	RT	23.00	38.00
86	COME LET US ADORE HIM 104000 (SET OF 9)	OP	95.00	135.00
86	COME LET US ADORE HIME 104523	OP	400.00	465.00
86	CONGRATULATIONS, PRINCESS 106208	OP	20.00	35.00
86	GOD BLESS YOU GRADUATE 106194	OP	20.00	35.00
86	GREATEST GIFT IS A FRIEND, THE- 109231	OP	30.00	45.00
86	HALLELUJAH COUNTRY 105821	OP	35.00	150.00
86	HAPPY DAYS ARE HERE AGAIN 104396	SU	25.00	60.00
86	HAVE I GOT NEWS FOR YOU 105635	SU	23.00	50.00
86	HE WALKS WITH ME 107999	LE	25.00	33.00
86	HE'S THE HEALER OF BROKEN HEARTS 100080	OP	33.00	55.00
86	HEAVEN BLESS YOUR TOGETHERNESS 106755	OP	65.00	100.00
86	I PICKED A VERY SPECIAL MOM 100536	LE	38.00	70.00
86	I WOULD BE SUNK WITHOUT YOU 102970	OP	15.00	24.00
86	LORD GIVETH...TAKETH AWAY, THE- 100226	RT	34.00	40.00
86	LORD, HELP US KEEP...ACT TOGETHER 101850	RT	35.00	135.00
86	LOVE IS THE BEST GIFT OF ALL 110930	YR	23.00	40.00
86	LOVE IS THE GLUE THAT MENDS 104027	SU	34.00	60.00
86	MAKE ME A BLESSING 100102	RT	35.00	90.00
86	MY LOVE WILL NEVER LET YOU GO 103497	OP	25.00	45.00
86	NO TEARS PAST THE GATE 101826	OP	40.00	80.00
86	PRECIOUS MEMORIES 106763	OP	38.00	65.00
86	SHARING OUR CHRISTMAS TOGETHER 102490	SU	40.00	75.00

YR	NAME	LIMIT	ISSUE	TREND
86	SITTING PRETTY 104825	SU	23.00	53.00
86	SMILE ALONG THE WAY 101842	RT	30.00	155.00
86	SPIRIT IS WILLING...IS WEAK , THE-100196	RT	19.00	75.00
86	THEY FOLLOWED THE STAR 108243	OP	75.00	125.00
86	THIS IS THE DAY THE LORD HATH MADE 12157	SU	23.00	45.00
86	TO MY DEER FRIEND 100048	OP	33.00	75.00
86	TO TELL THE TOOTH YOU'RE SPECIAL 105813	SU	39.00	100.00
86	WE ARE ALL PRECIOUS IN HIS SIGHT 102903	OP	30.00	80.00
86	WE BELONG TO THE LORD 103004	SP	50.00	180.00
86	WE GATHER TO ASK/LORD'S BLESSING 109762	RT	130.00	150.00
86	WE'RE PULLING FOR YOU 106151	SU	40.00	70.00
86	WISHING YOU A MERRY CHRISTMAS 109754	OP	35.00	55.00
86	WITH THIS RING... 104019	OP	40.00	65.00
87	A GROWING LOVE E-0108	YR	*	46.00
87	A TUB FULL OF LOVE 112313	OP	23.00	35.00
87	BLESSED ARE THEY THAT OVERCOME 115479	YR	28.00	35.00
87	FAITH TAKES THE PLUNGE 111155	OP	28.00	45.00
87	GOOD LORD HAS BLESSED US TENFOLD, THE	LE	90.00	150.00
87	HAPPINESS DIVINE 109584	RT	25.00	60.00
87	HAPPY BIRTHDAY POPPY 106836	SU	28.00	60.00
87	HIS EYE IS ON THE SPARROW E-0530	RT	29.00	125.00
87	HOLY SMOKES E-2351	RT	30.00	125.00
87	I BELIEVE IN MIRACLES E-7156R	RT	23.00	70.00
87	LET LOVE REIGN E-9273	RT	28.00	75.00
87	LORD HELP ME MAKE THE GRADE 106216	SU	25.00	55.00
87	LORD/KEEP OUR ACT TOGETHER 101850	RT	35.00	155.00
87	LOVE IS KIND E-5377	RT	28.00	85.00
87	MOMMY, I LOVE YOU 109975	OP	23.00	35.00
87	MOMMY, I LOVE YOU 112143	OP	23.00	35.00
87	O COME LET US ADORE HIM 111333	SU	200.00	240.00
87	OH WHAT FUN IT IS TO RIDE 109819	OP	85.00	140.00
87	PUPPY LOVE IS FROM ABOVE 106798	RT	45.00	55.00
87	SCENT FROM ABOVE 100528	RT	19.00	60.00
87	SENDING YOU MY LOVE 109967	OP	35.00	55.00
87	SEW IN LOVE 106844	OP	45.00	65.00
87	SHARING IS UNIVERSAL E-0107	YR	*	45.00
87	SPIRIT IS WILLING, THE- 100196	RT	19.00	65.00
87	THIS IS THE DAY...LORD HATH MADE E2838	SU	20.00	60.00
87	THIS TOO SHALL PASS 114014	OP	23.00	35.00
87	WISHING YOU A BASKET/BLESSINGS 109924	OP	23.00	40.00
88	A FRIEND IS SOMEONE WHO CARES 520632	RT	30.00	35.00
88	BELIEVE THE IMPOSSIBLE 109487	SU	35.00	75.00
88	BON VOYAGE! 522201	SU	75.00	90.00
88	DON'T LET THE HOLIDAYS...DOWN 522112	RT	43.00	90.00
88	EGGSPECIALLY FOR YOU 520667	OP	45.00	60.00
88	FRIENDSHIP HITS THE SPOT 520748	OP	55.00	70.00
88	GREATEST OF THESE IS LOVE, THE- 521868	SU	28.00	45.00
88	HAVE A BERRY MERRY CHRISTMAS 522856	SU	15.00	27.00
88	HE IS THE STAR OF THE MORNING 522252	SU	55.00	75.00
88	HIS LOVE WILL SHINE ON YOU 522376	YR	30.00	55.00
88	I BELONG TO THE LORD 520853	SU	25.00	45.00
88	ISN'T HE PRECIOUS 522988	SU	15.00	20.00
88	JESUS IS THE ONLY WAY 520756	SU	40.00	60.00
88	JESUS LOVES ME 104531	1000	500.00	1550.00
88	JESUS THE SAVIOR IS BORN 520357	OP	25.00	50.00
88	JUST A LINE TO WISH...A HAPPY DAY 520721	SU	65.00	75.00
88	LIGHT OF THE WORLD IS JESUS, THE- 521507	OP	60.00	80.00
88	LORD HAS BLESSED US TENFOLD, THE- 114022	YR	90.00	175.00
88	LORD IS YOUR LIGHT..HAPPINESS, THE- 520837	OP	50.00	70.00
88	LORD, TURN MY LIFE AROUND 520551	SU	35.00	38.00
88	MAKE A JOYFUL NOISE 520322	1500	500.00	900.00
88	MANY MOONS...CANOE, BLESSUM YOU 520772	RT	50.00	365.00
88	MAY YOUR LIFE BE...W/TOUCHDOWNS 522023	OP	45.00	60.00
88	MEOWIE CHRISTMAS 109800	OP	30.00	45.00
88	MERRY CHRISTMAS DEER 522317	RT	50.00	65.00
88	MY DAYS ARE BLUE WITHOUT YOU 520802	SU	65.00	100.00
88	MY HEART IS EXPOSED WITH LOVE 520624	OP	45.00	55.00
88	OH HOLY NIGHT 522546	YR	25.00	40.00
88	OUR FIRST CHRISTMAS TOGETHER 115290	SU	50.00	75.00
88	PEACE ON EARTH 109749	SU	100.00	145.00
88	PUPPY LOVE 520764	OP	12.50	20.00
88	REJOICE O EARTH 520268	OP	13.00	22.00
88	SENDING YOU SHOWERS OF BLESSINGS 520683	RT	33.00	75.00
88	SOME BUNNY'S SLEEPING 115274	SU	13.50	19.00
88	SOMEDAY MY LOVE 520799	RT	40.00	75.00
88	SOMETHING'S MISSING...NOT AROUND 105643	SU	33.00	70.00
88	TELL IT TO JESUS 521477	OP	35.00	42.00
88	THANK YOU LORD FOR EVERYTHING 522031	SU	55.00	75.00
88	TIME TO WISH YOU/MERRY CHRISTMAS 115339	YR	24.00	32.00
88	TIS THE SEASON 111163	SU	28.00	35.00
88	TO BE WITH YOU IS UPLIFTING 522260	OP	20.00	35.00
88	WE NEED A GOOD FRIEND..RUFF TIMES 520810	SU	35.00	45.00
88	WISHING YOU A COZY CHRISTMAS 521949	SU	43.00	60.00
88	WISHING YOU A HAPPY EASTER 109886	OP	23.00	35.00
88	WISHING YOU A PERFECT CHOICE 520845	OP	55.00	70.00

YR	NAME	LIMIT	ISSUE	TREND
88	WISHING YOU A...SUCCESSFUL SEASON 522120	OP	60.00	75.00
88	WISHING YOU ROADS OF HAPPINESS 520780	OP	60.00	80.00
88	YOU ARE MY NUMBER ONE 520829	OP	25.00	35.00
88	YOUR LOVE IS SO UPLIFTING 520675	OP	60.00	80.00
89	ALWAYS IN HIS CARE 225290	YR	8.00	15.00
89	ALWAYS IN HIS CARE 524522	YR	30.00	45.00
89	ALWAYS ROOM FOR ONE MORE C-0109	YR	*	40.00
89	BLESSINGS FROM ABOVE 523747	OP	45.00	90.00
89	EASTER'S ON ITS WAY 521892	OP	60.00	70.00
89	FAITH IS A VICTORY 521396	RT	25.00	145.00
89	GOD IS LOVE DEAR VALENTINE 523518	OP	28.00	35.00
89	GOOD FRIENDS ARE FOREVER 521817	OP	50.00	55.00
89	GOOD FRIENDS ARE FOREVER 525049	*	*	N/A
89	GOOD LORD ALWAYS DELIVERS, THE- 523453	OP	28.00	35.00
89	HAPPY BIRTHDAY DEAR JESUS 524875	SU	13.50	25.00
89	HAPPY TRIP 521280	OP	35.00	65.00
89	HEAVEN BLESS YOU 520934	OP	35.00	45.00
89	HIGH HOPES 521957	SU	30.00	47.00
89	HOPE YOU'RE UP...THE TRAIL AGAIN 521205	SU	35.00	47.00
89	I'LL NEVER STOP LOVING YOU 521418	RT	38.00	42.00
89	I'M SO GLAD YOU FLUTTERED...LIFE 520640	RT	40.00	390.00
89	JESUS IS THE SWEETEST NAME I KNOW 523097	SU	23.00	35.00
89	LORD, HELP ME STICK TO MY JOB 521450	RT	30.00	45.00
89	LOVE IS FROM ABOVE 521841	SU	45.00	50.00
89	MY HAPPINESS C-0110	YR	*	40.00
89	ONCE UPON A HOLY NIGHT 523836	YR	25.00	40.00
89	REJOICE O EARTH 617334	OP	125.00	125.00
89	SOME BUNNIES SLEEPING 522996	SU	12.00	30.00
89	SWEEP ALL YOUR WORRIES AWAY 521779	RT	40.00	90.00
89	THAT'S WHAT FRIENDS ARE FOR 521183	OP	45.00	55.00
89	THERE SHALL BE SHOWERS..BLESSINGS 522090	OP	60.00	80.00
89	THINKING OF YOU IS...LIKE TO DO 522287	SU	30.00	33.00
89	THIS DAY HAS BEEN MADE IN HEAVEN 523496	OP	30.00	35.00
89	TIME HEALS 523739	OP	38.00	42.00
89	WE'RE GOING TO MISS YOU 524913	OP	50.00	55.00
89	YIELD NOT TO TEMPTATION 521310	SU	28.00	46.00
90	A REFLECTION OF HIS LOVE 522279	OP	50.00	55.00
90	A SPECIAL DELIVERY 521493	OP	30.00	35.00
90	ANGELS WE HAVE HEARD ON HIGH 524921	RT	60.00	70.00
90	BEING 9 IS JUST DIVINE 521833	OP	25.00	30.00
90	BLESS THOSE WHO SERVE... (A.F.) 526584	SU	33.00	45.00
90	BLESS THOSE WHO SERVE... (ARMY) 526576	SU	33.00	45.00
90	BLESS THOSE WHO SERVE... (BLACK) 527297	SU	33.00	42.00
90	BLESS THOSE WHO SERVE... (GIRL) 527289	SU	33.00	45.00
90	BLESS THOSE WHO SERVE... (MARINE) 527521	SU	33.00	42.00
90	BLESS THOSE WHO SERVE... (NAVY) 526568	SU	33.00	50.00
90	BRING THE LITTLE ONES TO JESUS 527556	OP	90.00	100.00
90	CLUB IS OUT OF THIS WORLD, THE C0112	YR	*	45.00
90	FRIENDSHIP GROWS WHEN YOU PLANT 524271	OP	40.00	100.00
90	GOD BLESS THE U.S.A. 527564	LE	33.00	40.00
90	GOOD FRIENDS ARE FOR ALWAYS 524123	OP	28.00	35.00
90	GOOD NEWS IS SO UPLIFTING 523615	OP	60.00	70.00
90	HE IS MY INSPIRATION 523038	OP	60.00	65.00
90	HOPPY EASTER, FRIEND 521906	OP	40.00	45.00
90	HUG ONE ANOTHER 521299	RT	45.00	50.00
90	I CAN'T SPELL SUCCESS W/O YOU 523763	OP	40.00	50.00
90	I WILL CHERISH ..OLD RUGGED CROSS 523534	YR	28.00	40.00
90	I WOULD BE LOST W/O YOU 526142	OP	28.00	32.00
90	IN THE SPOTLIGHT OF HIS GRACE 520543	SU	35.00	38.00
90	IT'S A PERFECT BOY 525286	OP	16.50	20.00
90	IT'S NO YOLK/I SAY I LOVE YOU 522104	OP	60.00	70.00
90	JOY ON ARRIVAL 523178	OP	50.00	55.00
90	MAY ONLY GOOD THINGS...YOUR WAY 524425	OP	30.00	40.00
90	MAY YOU HAVE AN OLD.....CHRISTMAS 417777	LE	200.00	165.00
90	MAY YOUR BIRTHDAY BE A BLESSING 524301	OP	30.00	35.00
90	MAY YOUR CHRISTMAS BE MERRY 524166	YR	28.00	35.00
90	MAY YOUR WORLD BE TRIMMED W/JOY 522082	SU	55.00	55.00
90	MY WARMEST THOUGHTS ARE YOU 524085	RT	55.00	64.00
90	SHARING A GIFT OF LOVE 527114	YR	30.00	50.00
90	SHARING THE GOOD NEWS TOGETHER-C0111	YR	*	40.00
90	TAKE HEED WHEN YOU STAND 521272	OP	55.00	60.00
90	THERE'S A LIGHT....TUNNEL 521485	SU	55.00	60.00
90	THUMB-BODY LOVES YOU 521698	SU	55.00	60.00
90	TO A SPECIAL MUM 521965	OP	30.00	40.00
90	TO A VERY SPECIAL MOM & DAD 521434	SU	35.00	45.00
90	WE ARE GOD'S WORKMANSHIP 525960	YR	28.00	40.00
90	WE HAVE COME FROM A FAR 526959	OP	17.50	25.00
90	WHAT THE WORLD NEEDS NOW 524352	RT	50.00	60.00
90	YOU ARE MY HAPPINESS 526185	YR	38.00	47.00
90	YOU ARE SUCH A PURR-FECT FRIEND 526010	2000	500.00	625.00
90	YOU ARE THE TYPE I LOVE 523542	OP	40.00	45.00
90	YOU DESERVE AN OVATION 520578	OP	35.00	40.00
90	YOU HAVE TOUCHED SO MANY HEARTS 523283	2000	600.00	610.00
90	YOU HAVE TOUCHED.....HEARTS 422282	LE	175.00	175.00
91	BLESSED ARE THE MEEK.. .EARTH 523313	LE	55.00	60.00

YR	NAME	LIMIT	ISSUE	TREND
91	BLESSED ARE THE PEACEMAKERS..523348	LE	55.00	55.00
91	BLESSED ARE THE POOR IN SPIRIT...523437	LE	55.00	70.00
91	BLESSED ARE THE PURE IN HEART...523399	LE	55.00	55.00
91	BLESSED ARE THEY THAT MOURN..523380	LE	55.00	60.00
91	BLESSED ARE THEY...BE FILLED 523321	LE	55.00	60.00
91	BLESSED ARE....SHALL OBTAIN MERCY 523291	LE	55.00	55.00
91	GOING HOME 525979	OP	60.00	65.00
91	HE LOVES ME 524263	YR	35.00	45.00
92	A SPECIAL CHIME FOR JESUS 524468	RT	33.00	33.00
92	A UNIVERSAL LOVE 527173	YR	33.00	50.00
92	AMERICA, YOU'RE BEAUTIFUL 528862	OP	35.00	40.00
92	AN EVENT FOR ALL SEASONS 530158	OP	30.00	45.00
92	BABY'S FIRST BIRTHDAY 524069	OP	25.00	30.00
92	BLESS-UM YOU 527335	OP	35.00	35.00
92	BRINGING YOU A MERRY CHRISTMAS 527599	RT	45.00	45.00
92	BUT THE GREATEST OF THESE IS LOVE 527688	YR	28.00	32.00
92	FRUIT..SPIRIT IS LOVE, THE- 521213	OP	30.00	32.00
92	GATHER YOUR DREAMS 529680	2000	550.00	550.00
92	HAPPINESS IS AT OUR FINGERTIPS 529931	LE	35.00	60.00
92	HAPPY BIRTHDAY JESUS 530492	OP	20.00	22.00
92	HIS LITTLE TREASURE PM931	OP	30.00	35.00
92	HOPE YOU'RE OVER THE HUMP 521671	SU	17.50	19.00
92	I ONLY HAVE ARMS FOR YOU 527769	OP	15.00	17.00
92	I'M LOST WITHOUT YOU 526142	YR	28.00	32.00
92	I'M SO GLAD GOD...FRIEND LIKE YOU 523623	RT	50.00	55.00
92	IT'S SO UPLIFTING/FRIEND LIKE YOU 524905	OP	40.00	45.00
92	JESUS IS THE ANSWER E-1381R	RT	55.00	60.00
92	LORD TURNED MY LIFE AROUND, THE- 520535	SU	35.00	38.00
92	LOVING PM932	OP	30.00	32.00
92	MAGIC STARTS W/YOU, THE- 529648	LE	16.00	24.00
92	MAKE A JOYFUL NOISE 528617	YR	28.00	30.00
92	MAY YOUR EVERY WISH COME TRUE 524298	OP	50.00	55.00
92	MAY YOUR FUTURE BE BLESSED	OP	35.00	35.00
92	OUR FRIENDSHIP IS SODA-LICIOUS 524336	OP	65.00	70.00
92	RING OUT THE GOOD NEWS 529966	RT	17.50	20.00
92	RING THOSE CHRISTMAS BELLS 525898	RT	95.00	100.00
92	SAFE IN THE ARMS OF JESUS 521922	OP	30.00	35.00
92	SEALED W/A KISS 524441	RT	50.00	55.00
92	THERE IS NO GREATER...A FRIEND...521000	OP	30.00	32.00
92	THIS LAND IS OUR LAND 527777	YR	35.00	40.00
92	TIED UP FOR THE HOLIDAYS 527580	SU	40.00	45.00
92	TO THE APPLE OF GOD'S EYE 522015	OP	33.00	35.00
92	TUBBY'S FIRST CHRISTMAS 525278	OP	10.00	15.00
92	WISHING YOU A COMFY CHRISTMAS 527750	OP	28.00	30.00
92	WISHING YOU A HO HO HO 527629	OP	40.00	45.00
92	WISHING YOU WERE HERE 526916	OP	100.00	115.00
92	WISHING YOU/SWEETEST CHRISTMAS 530166	YR	28.00	40.00
92	YOU ARE MY FAVORITE STAR 527378	RT	60.00	63.00
92	YOU'RE MY NUMBER ONE FRIEND 530026	LE	30.00	30.00
92	YOU'RE THE END OF MY RAINBOW C0014	OP	25.00	30.00
93	A REFLECTION OF HIS LOVE 529095	YR	28.00	28.00
93	BRING THE LITTLE ONES TO JESUS 531359	LE	50.00	50.00
93	FRIENDS TO THE VERY END 526150	RT	40.00	40.00
93	HE IS NOT HERE FOR HE IS RISEN..527106	OP	60.00	60.00
93	I WILL ALWAYS BE THINKING OF YOU 523631	RT	45.00	45.00
93	I'M SO GLAD I PICKED YOU...FRIEND 524379	OP	40.00	40.00
93	IT IS NO SECRET WHAT GOD CAN DO 531111	LE	30.00	30.00
93	LORD BLESS...KEEP YOU, THE- 532134	OP	30.00	30.00
93	LORD BLESS..KEEP YOU, THE- 532118	OP	40.00	40.00
93	LORD BLESS..KEEP YOU, THE- 532126	OP	30.00	30.00
93	LORD IS COUNTING ON YOU, THE- 531707	OP	33.00	33.00
93	LORD TEACH US TO PRAY 524158	OP	35.00	35.00
93	LORD WILL PROVIDE, THE- 523593	LE	40.00	45.00
93	NOTHING CAN DAMPEN..CARING 603864	OP	35.00	35.00
93	SERENITY PRAYER GIRL 530697	OP	35.00	35.00
93	SHARING SWEET MEMORIES TOGETHER 526487	OP	45.00	45.00
93	SURROUNDED W/JOY 531677	OP	30.00	30.00
93	SURROUNDED W/JOY 531685	OP	17.50	18.00
93	TO A VERY SPECIAL SISTER 528633	OP	60.00	60.00
93	YOU ARE/ROSE OF HIS CREATION 531243	2000	*	500.00
93	YOU SUIT ME TO A TEE 526193	OP	35.00	35.00
94	CARING	OP	35.00	35.00
94	PRECIOUS MOMENTS LAST FOREVER E6901	SU	10.00	100.00
94	SERENITY PRAYER BOY 530700	OP	35.00	35.00
94	SHARING	OP	35.00	35.00
94	SO GLAD I PICKED YOU AS A FRIEND	OP	40.00	40.00
94	YOU'RE AS PRETTY AS A CHRISTMAS TREE	OP	28.00	28.00
95	A POPPY FOR YOU 604208	OP	35.00	35.00
95	ALWAYS TAKE TIME TO PRAY	OP	35.00	35.00
95	ANOTHER YEAR AND MORE GREY HARES 128686	OP	17.50	18.00
95	BLESS YOUR SOLE 531162	OP	25.00	25.00
95	COME LET US ADORE HIM/MINI NAT. STARTER SET 142743	OP	35.00	35.00
95	COME LET US ADORE HIM/NATIVITY STARTER SET 142735	OP	50.00	50.00
95	DREAMS REALLY DO COME TRUE 128309	OP	38.00	38.00
95	GOD BLESS THE DAY WE FOUND YOU 100145R	OP	60.00	60.00

YR	NAME	LIMIT	ISSUE	TREND
95	GOD BLESS THE DAY WE FOUND YOU 100153R	OP	60.00	60.00
95	GOD CARED ENOUGH TO SEND HIS BEST 524476	RT	50.00	90.00
95	HALLELUJAH FOR THE CROSS 532002	OP	35.00	35.00
95	HAPPY HULA DAYS 128694	OP	30.00	30.00
95	HE COVERS THE EARTH WITH..BEAUTY 142654	YR	30.00	30.00
95	HE'S GOT THE WHOLE WORLD IN HIS HANDS	2000	*	N/A
95	I CAN'T BEAR TO LET YOU GO 532037	OP	50.00	50.00
95	I GIVE YOU MY LOVE FOREVER TRUE 129100	OP	70.00	70.00
95	I ONLY HAVE ICE FOR YOU 530956	OP	55.00	55.00
95	I'LL GIVE HIM MY HEART 150088	OP	40.00	40.00
95	JUST A LINE TO SAY YOU'RE SPECIAL 522864	OP	50.00	50.00
95	LORD HELP ME TO STAY ON COURSE 532096	OP	35.00	35.00
95	LOVE BLOOMS ETERNAL 127019	OP	35.00	35.00
95	MAKING A TRAIL TO BETHLEHEM 142751	OP	30.00	30.00
95	MAKING SPIRITS BRIGHT 150118	OP	38.00	38.00
95	MONEY'S NOT THE ONLY GREEN THING..SAVING 531073	RT	50.00	50.00
95	SENDING MY LOVE YOUR WAY 528609	OP	40.00	40.00
95	SENDING YOU OCEANS OF LOVE 532010	RT	35.00	35.00
95	TAKE TIME TO SMELL THE FLOWERS 524387	OP	30.00	30.00
95	VAYA CON DIOS (GO WITH GOD) 531146	OP	33.00	33.00
95	WALK IN THE SUNSHINE 524212	OP	35.00	35.00
95	WHAT THE WORLD NEEDS IS LOVE 531065	OP	45.00	45.00
95	YOU FILL THE PAGES OF MY LIFE	OP	68.00	68.00
95	YOU WILL ALWAYS BE OUR HERO 136271	YR	40.00	40.00
95	YOU'RE ONE IN A MILLION TO ME	OP	35.00	35.00
96	ALL SING HIS PRAISES 184012	OP	33.00	33.00
96	ANGELS ON EARTH 183776	OP	40.00	40.00
96	COLOR YOUR WORLD WITH THANKSGIVING 183857	OP	50.00	50.00
96	ENTER HIS COURT WITH THANKSGIVING 521221	OP	35.00	35.00
96	IT MAY BE GREENER, BUT....HARD TO CUT 163899	OP	38.00	38.00
96	LORD IS WITH YOU, THE 526835	OP	28.00	28.00
96	LOVE NEVER LEAVES A MOTHER'S ARMS 523941	OP	40.00	40.00
96	MAKING A TRAIL TO BETHLEHEM 184004	OP	19.00	19.00
96	MATCHING TO THE BEAT OF FREEDOM'S DRUM 521981	OP	35.00	35.00
96	MINI SET ADDITION/WEE THREE KINGS 213624 3 PC	OP	55.00	55.00
96	MY TRUE LOVE GAVE TO ME 529273	OP	40.00	40.00
96	NATIVITY SET ADDITION/SHEPHERD W/LAMBS 183954 3 PC	OP	40.00	40.00
96	PEACH ON EARTH...ANYWAY 183342	YR	33.00	33.00
96	SING IN EXCELSIS DEO 183830	OP	125.00	125.00
96	SNOWBUNNY LOVES YOU LIKE I DO 183792	OP	19.00	20.00
96	STANDING IN THE PRESENCE OF THE LORD 163732	YR	38.00	38.00
96	SUN IS ALWAYS SHINING SOMEWHERE, THE 163775	OP	38.00	38.00
96	SWEETER AS THE YEARS GO BY 522333	OP	60.00	60.00
96	TAKE IT TO THE LORD IN PRAYER 163767	OP	30.00	30.00
96	WHAT A DIFFERENCE...MADE IN MY LIFE 531138	OP	50.00	50.00
96	YOU DESERVE A HALO-THANK YOU 531693	OP	55.00	55.00
97	AND A CHILD SHALL LEAD THEM	OP	50.00	50.00
97	CANE YOU JOIN US FOR A MERRY CHRISTMAS 272698	YR	30.00	30.00
97	FRIENDS FROM THE VERY BEGINNING	OP	50.00	50.00
97	HAPPY BIRTHDAY JESUS	OP	35.00	35.00
97	HAVE YOU ANY ROOM FOR JESUS	OP	35.00	35.00
97	I THINK YOU'RE JUST DIVINE	OP	40.00	40.00
97	I'M DREAMING OF A WHITE CHRISTMAS	OP	25.00	25.00
97	LEAD ME TO CALVARY 260916	YR	38.00	38.00
97	LET US PRAY	OP	17.50	18.00
97	LORD IS THE HOPE OF OUR FUTURE, THE	OP	40.00	40.00
97	LORD, SPARE ME	OP	38.00	38.00
97	LOVE LETTERS IN THE SAND	OP	35.00	35.00
97	MAY YOUR CHRISTMAS BE DELIGHTFUL	OP	40.00	40.00
97	MOST PRECIOUS GIFT OF ALL	OP	38.00	38.00
97	MY LOVE WILL KEEP YOU WARM	OP	38.00	38.00
97	ON MY WAY TO A PERFECT DAY	OP	45.00	45.00
97	PIZZA ON EARTH	OP	55.00	55.00
97	POTTY TIME	OP	25.00	25.00
97	SAY I DO	OP	55.00	55.00
97	SHARING OUR CHRISTMAS TOGETHER	OP	35.00	35.00
97	SHARING THE LIGHT OF LOVE	OP	35.00	35.00
97	SOMETHING PRECIOUS FROM ABOVE	OP	50.00	50.00
97	SOMETIMES YOU'RE NEXT TO IMPOSSIBLE	OP	50.00	50.00
97	WE ALL HAVE OUR BAD HAIR DAYS	OP	35.00	35.00
97	WHO'S GONNA FILL YOUR SHOES- 531634	OP	38.00	38.00
97	YOU ARE ALWAYS THERE FOR ME- I	OP	50.00	50.00
97	YOU ARE ALWAYS THERE FOR ME- II	OP	50.00	50.00
97	YOU HAVE TOUCHED SO MANY HEARTS- I	OP	38.00	38.00
97	YOU'RE A LIFE SAVER TO ME	OP	35.00	35.00
97	YOU'RE JUST TO SWEET TO BE SCARY	OP	55.00	55.00

S. BUTCHER   **PRECIOUS MOMENTS ANNIVERSARY FIGURINES**

YR	NAME	LIMIT	ISSUE	TREND
83	GOD BLESSED OUR YEARS TOGETHER E-2853	OP	35.00	55.00
84	GOD BLESSED/LOVE & HAPPINESS E-2854	OP	35.00	55.00
84	GOD BLESSED/LOVE & HAPPINESS E-2855	OP	35.00	55.00
84	GOD BLESSED/LOVE & HAPPINESS E-2856	OP	35.00	55.00
84	GOD BLESSED/LOVE & HAPPINESS E-2857	OP	35.00	55.00
84	GOD BLESSED/LOVE & HAPPINESS E-2859	OP	35.00	55.00
84	GOD BLESSED/LOVE & HAPPINESS E-2860	OP	35.00	55.00

YR	NAME	LIMIT	ISSUE	TREND
93	I STILL DO 530999	OP	30.00	30.00
93	I STILL DO 531006	OP	30.00	30.00
S. BUTCHER		**PRECIOUS MOMENTS BABY CLASSICS**		
97	GOD LOVETH A CHEERFUL GIVER	OP	25.00	25.00
97	GOOD FRIENDS ARE FOREVER	OP	30.00	30.00
97	I BELIEVE IN MIRACLES	OP	25.00	25.00
97	LOVE IS SHARING	OP	25.00	25.00
97	LOVE ONE ANOTHER	OP	30.00	30.00
97	MAKE A JOYFUL NOISE	OP	30.00	30.00
97	WE ARE GOD'S WORKMANSHIP	OP	25.00	25.00
97	YOU HAVE TOUCHED SO MANY HEARTS- II	OP	25.00	25.00
S. BUTCHER		**PRECIOUS MOMENTS BABY'S FIRST**		
84	BABY'S FIRST HAIRCUT 12211	SU	33.00	138.00
84	BABY'S FIRST PICTURE E-2841	RT	45.00	155.00
84	BABY'S FIRST STEP E-2840	SU	35.00	80.00
88	BABY'S FIRST PET 520705	SU	45.00	70.00
90	BABY'S FIRST MEAL 524077	OP	35.00	42.00
92	BABY'S FIRST WORD 527238	OP	25.00	30.00
S. BUTCHER		**PRECIOUS MOMENTS BIRTHDAY CLUB**		
82	LET US CALL THE CLUB TO ORDER E-0103	YR	25.00	55.00
86	FISHING FOR FRIENDS BC-861	YR	10.00	150.00
86	OUR CLUB CAN'T BE BEAT B-0001	YR	*	75.00
87	A SMILE'S THE CYMBAL OF JOY B-0002	YR	*	60.00
87	A SMILE'S THE CYMBAL OF JOY B-0102	YR	*	70.00
87	HI SUGAR BC-871	YR	11.00	100.00
88	SOMEBUNNY CARES BC-881	YR	13.50	60.00
88	SWEETEST CLUB AROUND, THE- B-0003	YR	*	45.00
88	SWEETEST CLUB AROUND, THE- B-0103	YR	*	60.00
89	CAN'T BEEHIVE MYSELF WITHOUT YOU BC-891	YR	13.50	50.00
89	HAVE A BEARY SPECIAL BIRTHDAY B 0104	YR	*	45.00
89	HAVE A BEARY SPECIAL BIRTHDAY B0004	YR	*	N/A
90	COLLECTING MAKES GOOD SCENTS BC-901	YR	15.00	40.00
90	I'M NUTS OVER MY COLLECTION BC-902	YR	15.00	40.00
90	OUR CLUB IS A TOUGH ACT TO FOLLOW B-0005	YR	*	30.00
90	OUR CLUB IS A TOUGH ACT TO FOLLOW B-0105	YR	*	40.00
90	TRUE BLUE FRIENDS BC912	YR	15.00	35.00
91	EVERY MAN'S HOUSE IS HIS CASTLE BC921	YR	16.50	40.00
91	JEST TO LET YOU KNOW YOU'RE TOPS B-0106	YR	*	55.00
91	JEST TO LET YOU KNOW YOU'RE TOPS B0006	YR	*	45.00
91	LOVE PACIFIES BC911	YR	15.00	35.00
92	ALL ABOARD FOR BIRTHDAY CLUB FUN B0007	OP	16.00	35.00
92	ALL ABOARD FOR BIRTHDAY CLUB FUN B0107	YR	16.00	40.00
93	I'VE GOT YOU UNDER MY SKIN BC911	YR	16.50	33.00
94	CAN'T GET ENOUGH OF OUR CLUB B 0109	YR	*	28.00
94	CAN'T GET ENOUGH OF OUR CLUB B0009	YR	*	27.00
94	GOD BLESS OUR HOME BC941	YR	16.00	30.00
94	HAPPINESS IS BELONGING B0008	YR	*	25.00
94	HAPPINESS IS BELONGING B0108	YR	16.00	25.00
94	OWL ALWAYS BE YOUR FRIEND B932	OP	16.00	16.00
94	PUT A LITTLE PUNCH INTO YOUR BIRTHDAY BC931	OP	15.00	15.00
95	HOPPY BIRTHDAY B0010	YR	*	N/A
95	HOPPY BIRTHDAY B0110	YR	*	N/A
95	YER A PEL I CAN COUNT ON	YR	16.00	20.00
96	SCOOTIN' BY JUST TO SAY HI! B0011	YR	*	N/A
96	SCOOTIN' BY JUST TO SAY HI! B0111	YR	*	N/A
96	THERE'S A SPOT IN MY HEART FOR YOU BC961	YR	15.00	15.00
S. BUTCHER		**PRECIOUS MOMENTS BIRTHDAY SERIES**		
86	BRIGHTEN SOMEONE'S DAY 105953	SU	12.50	35.00
86	SHOWERS OF BLESSINGS 105945	RT	16.00	50.00
88	FRIENDS TO THE END 104418	SU	15.00	40.00
88	HELLO WORLD! 521175	OP	13.50	24.00
89	NOT A CREATURE WAS STIRRING 524484	SU	17.00	30.00
89	TO MY FAVORITE FAN 521043	SU	16.00	40.00
90	CAN'T BE WITHOUT YOU 524492	OP	16.00	20.00
90	HOW CAN I EVER FORGET YOU 526924	OP	15.00	18.00
90	LET'S BE FRIENDS 527270	RT	15.00	18.00
92	HAPPY BIRDIE 527343	SU	16.00	18.00
93	HAPPY BIRTHDAY JESUS 530492	OP	20.00	20.00
93	HOPE YOU'RE OVER THE HUMP 521671	SU	16.00	16.00
94	OINKY BIRTHDAY 524506	OP	13.50	14.00
95	WISHING YOU A HAPPY BEAR HUG 520659	SU	28.00	28.00
96	I HAVEN'T SEEN MUCH OF YOU LATELY 531057	OP	13.50	14.00
96	I HAVEN'T SEEN MUCH OF YOU LATELY 531057	OP	13.50	14.00
97	FROM THE FIRST TIME I SPOTTED YOU I KNEW ...	OP	20.00	20.00
S. BUTCHER		**PRECIOUS MOMENTS BIRTHDAY TRAIN**		
85	BLESS THE DAYS OF OUR YOUTH 16004	OP	15.00	35.00
85	GOD BLESS YOU ON YOUR BIRTHDAY 15962	OP	11.00	30.00
85	HAPPY BIRTHDAY LITTLE LAMB 15946	OP	10.00	30.00
85	HEAVEN BLESS YOUR SPECIAL DAY 15954	OP	11.00	30.00
85	KEEP LOOKING UP 15997	OP	13.50	30.00
85	MAY YOUR BIRTHDAY BE WARM 15938	OP	10.00	30.00
85	THIS DAY IS SOMETHING...ROAR ABOUT 15989	OP	13.50	30.00
88	ISN'T EIGHT JUST GREAT 109460	OP	19.00	27.00
88	WISHING YOU GRR-EATNESS 109479	OP	19.00	27.00

YR	NAME	LIMIT	ISSUE	TREND
90	MAY YOUR BIRTHDAY BE MAMMOTH 521825	OP	25.00	30.00
92	BEING NINE IS JUST DIVINE 521833	OP	25.00	30.00

S. BUTCHER — PRECIOUS MOMENTS BOYS & GIRLS CLUBS OF AMERICA

YR	NAME	LIMIT	ISSUE	TREND
97	HE IS OUR SHELTER FROM THE STORM	OP	75.00	75.00
97	SHOOT FOR THE STARS..STRIKE OUT 521701	LE	60.00	60.00

S. BUTCHER — PRECIOUS MOMENTS BRIDAL PARTY

YR	NAME	LIMIT	ISSUE	TREND
83	BRIDE E-2846	OP	18.00	30.00
83	GROOMSMAN WITH FROG E-2836	OP	13.00	35.00
83	JUNIOR BRIDESMAID E-2845	OP	12.00	25.00
83	NO FLOWER IS AS SWEET AS YOU E-2831	OP	13.00	24.00
84	FLOWER GIRL E-2835	OP	11.00	24.00
84	RINGBEARER E-2833	OP	11.00	22.00
86	GOD BLESS..FAMILY (PARENTS/BRIDE) 100501	OP	35.00	60.00
86	GOD BLESS..FAMILY (PARENTS/GROOM) 100498	OP	35.00	55.00
86	GROOM E-2837	OP	13.50	38.00
87	WEDDING ARCH 102369	SU	23.00	45.00

S. BUTCHER — PRECIOUS MOMENTS CALENDAR GIRL

YR	NAME	LIMIT	ISSUE	TREND
87	APRIL 110027	OP	28.00	75.00
87	FEBRUARY 109991	OP	28.00	45.00
87	JANUARY 109983	OP	38.00	55.00
87	JUNE 110043	OP	40.00	80.00
87	MARCH 110019	OP	28.00	45.00
87	MAY 110035	OP	28.00	95.00
88	AUGUST 110078	OP	40.00	55.00
88	DECEMBER 110116	OP	28.00	45.00
88	JULY 110051	OP	35.00	50.00
88	NOVEMBER 110108	OP	33.00	42.00
88	OCTOBER 110094	OP	35.00	50.00
88	SEPTEMBER 110086	OP	28.00	45.00

S. BUTCHER — PRECIOUS MOMENTS CENTURY CIRCLE EVENT

YR	NAME	LIMIT	ISSUE	TREND
97	PEARL OF GREAT PRICE, THE	YR	50.00	50.00

S. BUTCHER — PRECIOUS MOMENTS CENTURY CIRCLE EXCLUSIVE

YR	NAME	LIMIT	ISSUE	TREND
97	IN GOD'S BEAUTIFUL GARDEN OF LOVE	15000	150.00	150.00

S. BUTCHER — PRECIOUS MOMENTS CLOWN

YR	NAME	LIMIT	ISSUE	TREND
85	I GET A BANG OUT OF YOU 12262	RT	35.00	60.00
85	LORD KEEP ME ON THE BALL 12270	OP	35.00	60.00
85	LORD WILL CARRY YOU THROUGH, THE- 12467	RT	30.00	80.00
85	WADDLE I DO WITHOUT YOU 12459	RT	30.00	85.00

S. BUTCHER — PRECIOUS MOMENTS COLLECTORS CLUB

YR	NAME	LIMIT	ISSUE	TREND
81	HELLO, LORD, IT'S ME AGAIN PM-811	CL	25.00	495.00
81	PUT ON A HAPPY FACE PM-822	CL	25.00	200.00
82	BUT LOVE GOES ON FOREVER-PLAQUE E-0202	YR	*	65.00
82	LET US CALL THE CLUB TO ORDER E-0303	YR	*	60.00
82	SMILE, GOD LOVES YOU PM-821	CL	25.00	225.00
83	DAWN'S EARLY LIGHT PM-831	CL	28.00	90.00
83	GOD'S RAY OF MERCY PM-841	CL	25.00	60.00
84	I LOVE TO TELL THE STORY PM-852	CL	28.00	55.00
84	JOIN IN ON THE BLESSINGS E-0404	YR	*	40.00
84	LORD IS MY SHEPHERD, THE- PM-851	SU	25.00	80.00
84	SEEK AND YE SHALL FIND E-0005	YR	*	50.00
84	TRUST IN THE LORD TO THE FINISH PM-842	CL	25.00	55.00
86	BIRDS OF A FEATHER...TOGETHER E-0006	YR	*	50.00
86	FEED MY SHEEP PM-871	CL	25.00	50.00
86	GRANDMA'S PRAYER PM-861	CL	25.00	80.00
86	I'M FOLLOWING JESUS PM-862	CL	25.00	85.00
86	LOVING YOU DEAR VALENTINE PM873	OP	25.00	35.00
86	LOVING YOU DEAR VALENTINE PM874	OP	25.00	40.00
87	A GROWING LOVE E-0008	YR	*	35.00
87	IN HIS TIME PM-872	CL	25.00	48.00
87	SHARING IS UNIVERSAL E-0007	YR	*	45.00
88	ALWAYS ROOM FOR ONE MORE C-0009	YR	*	35.00
88	GOD BLESS YOU/TOUCHING MY LIFE PM-881	CL	28.00	55.00
88	YOU JUST CAN'T CHUCK...FRIENDSHIP PM-882	CL	28.00	46.00
89	MOW POWER TO YOU PM-892	CL	28.00	40.00
89	MY HAPPINESS C-0010	YR	*	40.00
89	YOU WILL ALWAYS BE MY CHOICE PM-891	CL	28.00	40.00
90	LORD, KEEP ME/TEE PEE TOP SHAPE PM-912	YR	28.00	40.00
90	ONE STEP AT A TIME PM-911	YR	33.00	40.00
90	SHARING THE GOOD NEWS TOGETHER C0011	YR	*	35.00
90	TEN YEARS AND STILL GOING STRONG PM-901	CL	30.00	50.00
90	YOU ARE A BLESSING TO ME PM-902	CL	28.00	50.00
91	THIS LAND IS OUR LAND 527386	LE	350.00	385.00
92	ONLY LOVE CAN MAKE A HOME PM-921	YR	30.00	45.00
92	SOWING THE SEEDS OF LOVE PM922	OP	30.00	35.00
93	LOVING, CARING..ALONG THE WAY C0113	OP	25.00	30.00
93	MEMORIES ARE MADE OF THIS 529982	LE	30.00	30.00
97	BLESSED ARE THE MERCIFUL	YR	40.00	40.00
97	YOU WILL ALWAYS BE A TREASURE TO ME	YR	50.00	50.00

S. BUTCHER — PRECIOUS MOMENTS EASTER SEALS

YR	NAME	LIMIT	ISSUE	TREND
91	WE ARE GOD'S WORKMANSHIP 523879	2000	*	650.00
96	YOU CAN ALWAYS COUNT ON ME 526827	OP	30.00	30.00
97	GIVE ABILITY A CHANCE	LE	30.00	30.00
97	LOVE GROWS HERE	2000	*	N/A

YR	NAME	LIMIT	ISSUE	TREND
S. BUTCHER		**PRECIOUS MOMENTS EVENTS**		
87	YOU ARE MY MAIN EVENT 115231	YR	30.00	75.00
88	SHARING BEGINS IN THE HEART 520861	YR	25.00	60.00
90	I'M A PRECIOUS MOMENTS FAN 523526	YR	25.00	45.00
90	YOU CAN ALWAYS BRING A FRIEND 527122	YR	28.00	50.00
92	AN EVENT WORTH WADING FOR 527319	YR	33.00	45.00
S. BUTCHER		**PRECIOUS MOMENTS FAMILY CHRISTMAS SCENE**		
85	GOD GAVE HIS BEST 15806	SU	13.00	35.00
85	MAY YOU HAVE...SWEETEST CHRISTMAS 15776	SU	17.00	45.00
85	STORY OF GOD'S LOVE, THE- 15784	SU	23.00	55.00
85	TELL ME A STORY 15792	SU	10.00	32.00
86	SHARING OUR CHRISTMAS TOGETHER 102490	SU	37.00	70.00
89	HAVE A BEARY MERRY CHRISTMAS 522856	SU	15.00	20.00
90	CHRISTMAS FIREPLACE 524883	SU	38.00	55.00
S. BUTCHER		**PRECIOUS MOMENTS GROWING IN GOD'S GARDEN OF LOVE**		
97	BOUQUET FROM GOD'S GARDEN OF LOVE, A	OP	38.00	38.00
S. BUTCHER		**PRECIOUS MOMENTS GROWING IN GRACE**		
97	AGE 11	OP	38.00	38.00
97	AGE 12	OP	38.00	38.00
97	AGE 13	OP	40.00	40.00
97	AGE 14	OP	35.00	35.00
97	AGE 15	OP	40.00	40.00
S. BUTCHER		**PRECIOUS MOMENTS HOLIDAY PREVIEW**		
97	PACK YOUR TRUNK FOR THE HOLIDAYS	YR	20.00	20.00
S. BUTCHER		**PRECIOUS MOMENTS LITTLE MOMENTS**		
97	APRIL	OP	20.00	20.00
97	AUGUST	OP	20.00	20.00
97	BLESS YOUR LITTLE TUTU	OP	20.00	20.00
97	DECEMBER	OP	20.00	20.00
97	FEBRUARY	OP	20.00	20.00
97	IT'S RUFF TO ALWAYS BE CHEERY	OP	20.00	20.00
97	JANUARY	OP	20.00	20.00
97	JULY	OP	20.00	20.00
97	JUNE	OP	20.00	20.00
97	MARCH	OP	20.00	20.00
97	MAY	OP	20.00	20.00
97	NOVEMBER	OP	20.00	20.00
97	OCTOBER	OP	20.00	20.00
97	SEPTEMBER	OP	20.00	20.00
97	YOU'LL ALWAYS BE A WINNER TO ME- 272612	OP	20.00	20.00
97	YOU'LL ALWAYS BE A WINNER TO ME- 283460	OP	20.00	20.00
S. BUTCHER		**PRECIOUS MOMENTS MINI NATIVITY**		
97	CAMEL, COW, DONKEY	OP	30.00	30.00
97	FOR AN ANGEL YOU'RE SO DOWN TO EARTH	OP	17.50	18.00
97	NATIVITY WALL	OP	40.00	40.00
97	SHEPHERD W/ LAMBS- SET OF 2	OP	23.00	23.00
S. BUTCHER		**PRECIOUS MOMENTS MUSICAL**		
79	COME LET US ADORE HIM E-2810	SU	60.00	150.00
79	LORD BLESS YOU AND KEEP YOU, THE- E-7180	OP	55.00	110.00
79	MOTHER SEW DEAR E-7182	OP	35.00	80.00
79	PURR-FECT GRANDMA, THE- E-7184	SU	35.00	80.00
80	CHRISTMAS IS A TIME TO SHARE E-2806	RT	45.00	165.00
80	CROWN HIM LORD OF ALL E-2807	SU	45.00	115.00
80	JESUS IS BORN E-2809	SU	45.00	145.00
80	MY GUARDIAN ANGEL E-5205	SU	28.00	90.00
80	MY GUARDIAN ANGEL E-5206	SU	28.00	100.00
80	PEACE ON EARTH E-4726	SU	29.00	145.00
80	REJOICE O EARTH E-5645	RT	40.00	110.00
80	SILENT NIGHT E-5642	SU	55.00	220.00
80	UNTO US A CHILD IS BORN E-2808	SU	45.00	110.00
81	HAND THAT ROCKS THE FUTURE, THE-E-5204	OP	38.00	85.00
81	LET THE WHOLE WORLD KNOW E-7165	SU	60.00	100.00
81	LET THE WHOLE WORLD KNOW E-7186	SU	60.00	160.00
81	LOVE IS SHARING E-7185	RT	40.00	165.00
82	I'LL PLAY MY DRUM FOR HIM E-2355	SU	45.00	165.00
83	LET HEAVEN AND NATURE SING E2345	SU	30.00	165.00
83	SHARING OUR SEASON TOGETHER E-0519	RT	70.00	150.00
83	WEE THREE KINGS E-0520	SU	60.00	135.00
84	HEAVEN BLESS YOU 100285	SU	45.00	95.00
84	WE SAW A STAR 12408	SU	50.00	100.00
84	WISHING YOU A MERRY CHRISTMAS E-5394	SU	55.00	115.00
85	OUR 1ST CHRISTMAS TOGETHER 101702	RT	50.00	128.00
87	I'M SENDING YOU A WHITE CHRISTMAS 112402	RT	55.00	145.00
88	YOU HAVE TOUCHED SO MANY HEARTS 112577	SU	40.00	65.00
90	LORD HELP KEEP ME IN BALANCE 520691	SU	60.00	75.00
91	SLEEPING BABY BOY 429570	OP	65.00	70.00
91	SLEEPING BABY GIRL 429589	OP	65.00	70.00
92	DO NOT OPEN TILL CHRISTMAS 522244	OP	75.00	90.00
S. BUTCHER		**PRECIOUS MOMENTS NATIVITY**		
97	AND YOU SHALL SEE A STAR	OP	33.00	33.00
97	LIGHTED INN	OP	100.00	100.00
97	NATIVITY WELL	OP	30.00	30.00
97	PALM TREES, HAY BAIL, BABY FOOD	OP	60.00	60.00
97	SHEPHERD W/ LAMBS- SET OF 3	OP	40.00	40.00

YR	NAME	LIMIT	ISSUE	TREND
S. BUTCHER				
	PRECIOUS MOMENTS NOAH'S ARK			
92	BUNNIES 530123	OP	9.00	9.00
92	ELEPHANTS 530131	OP	18.00	18.00
92	GIRAFFES 530115	OP	16.00	16.00
92	NOAH'S ARK 8/PC COLL. SET 530948	OP	190.00	190.00
92	PIGS 530085	OP	12.00	12.00
92	SHEEP 530077	OP	10.00	10.00
93	LLAMAS 531375	OP	15.00	15.00
S. BUTCHER				
	PRECIOUS MOMENTS REGIONAL CONFERENCE			
97	FESTIVAL OF PRECIOUS MOMENTS, A	YR	*	N/A
S. BUTCHER				
	PRECIOUS MOMENTS REJOICE IN THE LORD			
84	HAPPINESS IS THE LORD 12378	SU	15.00	40.00
84	HE IS MY SONG 12394	SU	17.50	45.00
84	LORD GIVE ME A SONG 12386	SU	15.00	40.00
84	THERE'S A SONG IN MY HEART 12173	SU	11.00	38.00
86	LORD KEEP MY LIFE IN TUNE 12580	SU	38.00	110.00
S. BUTCHER				
	PRECIOUS MOMENTS SPRING CATALOG			
97	HAPPINESS TO THE CORE	YR	38.00	38.00
S. BUTCHER				
	PRECIOUS MOMENTS SPRING CELEBRATION			
97	WE'RE SO HOPPY YOU'RE HERE	YR	33.00	33.00
S. BUTCHER				
	PRECIOUS MOMENTS SUGAR TOWN			
92	AUNT RUTH AND AUNT DOROTHY 529486	RT	20.00	21.00
92	CAR 529443	OP	23.00	24.00
92	CHAPEL 529621	RT	85.00	85.00
92	DUSTY 529435	RT	15.00	18.00
92	EVERGREEN TREE 528684	OP	15.00	17.00
92	FENCE 529796	RT	10.00	11.00
92	GRANDFATHER 529516	OP	15.00	17.00
92	KATYLYNNE 529524	RT	20.00	21.00
92	NATIVITY 529508	RT	20.00	21.00
92	PHILIP 529494	RT	17.00	18.00
92	SAM BUTCHER 529567	YR	23.00	32.00
92	SAMMY 528668	RT	17.00	150.00
93	SAM BUTCHER 529842	YR	23.00	24.00
95	BIRD BATH 150223	RT	8.50	9.00
95	BUS STOP 150207	RT	8.50	9.00
95	CONDUCTOR 150169	OP	20.00	20.00
95	DOG AND KITTEN ON PARK BENCH 529540	OP	13.00	13.00
95	FIRE HYDRANT 150215	RT	5.00	5.00
95	FUEL BOY 531871	OP	23.00	23.00
95	GIRLS WITH GIFTS 531812	OP	23.00	23.00
95	LUGGAGE CART WITH KITTEN 150185	RT	13.00	13.00
95	RAILROAD CROSSING SIGN 150177	OP	12.00	12.00
95	STREET SIGN 532185	RT	10.00	10.00
95	SUGAR TOWN ENHANCEMENT SET 152269	OP	45.00	45.00
95	SUGAR TOWN TRAIN STATION/COLLECTORS SET 150193	OP	190.00	190.00
95	TRAIN STATION NIGHT LIGHT 150150	OP	100.00	100.00
95	WE HAVE COME FROM AFAR 530913	OP	12.00	12.00
96	A PRINCE OF A GUY 526037	OP	35.00	35.00
96	BONFIRE WITH BUNNIES 184152	RT	10.00	10.00
96	COCOA 184063	RT	7.50	8.00
96	FLAG POLE WITH KITTEN 184136	RT	15.00	15.00
96	HANK AND SHARON 184098	RT	25.00	25.00
96	LEROY 184071	RT	19.00	18.00
96	LIGHTED TREE 184039	RT	45.00	45.00
96	LIGHTED WARMING HUT 192341	OP	60.00	60.00
96	MAZIE 184055	RT	19.00	19.00
96	MY LOVE BLOOMS FOR YOU 521728	OP	50.00	50.00
96	PRETTY AS A PRINCESS 526053	OP	35.00	35.00
96	SKATING POND 184047	RT	40.00	40.00
96	SKATING SIGN 184020	LE	15.00	15.00
96	SUGAR TOWN ENCHANCEMENT SET 184160	OP	40.00	40.00
96	SUGAR TOWN SKATING POND SET 184128 7 PC	OP	185.00	185.00
96	WOODEN BARREL HOT COCOA STAND 184144	OP	15.00	15.00
97	AUNT BULAH & UNCLE SAM	RT	23.00	23.00
97	AUNT CLEO	RT	19.00	19.00
97	BIKE RACK	RT	15.00	15.00
97	BUNNIES	RT	10.00	10.00
97	CHUCK	YR	23.00	23.00
97	ENHANCEMENTS- SET	OP	25.00	25.00
97	GARBAGE CAN	RT	20.00	20.00
97	HEATHER	RT	20.00	20.00
97	LIGHTED SCHOOL HOUSE	OP	80.00	80.00
97	MERRY GO ROUND	RT	20.00	20.00
97	SCHOOL HOUSE- COLL SET	RT	184.00	184.00
97	SKATING POND COLL SET	RT	170.00	170.00
S. BUTCHER				
	PRECIOUS MOMENTS THE FOUR SEASONS			
85	SUMMER'S JOY 12076	YR	30.00	100.00
85	VOICE OF SPRING, THE- 12068	YR	30.00	300.00
86	AUTUMN'S PRAISE 12084	YR	30.00	70.00
86	WINTER'S SONG 12092	YR	30.00	135.00
S. BUTCHER				
	SAMMY'S CIRCUS			
93	COLLIN 529214	SU	20.00	20.00
93	DUSTY 529176	SU	23.00	12.00

YR	NAME	LIMIT	ISSUE	TREND
93	KATIE 529184	SU	17.50	17.00
93	MARKIE 528099	SU	19.00	19.00
93	SAMMY 529222	OP	20.00	20.00
93	TIPPY 529192	SU	12.00	12.00
95	JORDAN 529168	SU	20.00	20.00
96	JENNIFER 163708	SU	20.00	20.00
S. BUTCHER			**SHARING SEASON GIFTS**	
92	CLUB'S THAT'S OUT...THIS WORLD, THE PM038	OP	*	70.00
*			**SMALL WORLD OF MUSIC**	
94	1963 CHEVROLET CORVETTE STING RAY	7500	300.00	300.00
95	'53 CORVETTE- MUSICAL	*	30.00	30.00
95	'55 FORD THUNDERBIRD- MUSICAL	*	30.00	30.00
95	'57 CHEVROLET BEL AIR- MUSICAL	*	30.00	30.00
95	'64 1/2 FORD MUSTANG- MUSICAL	*	30.00	30.00
95	'65 CORVETTE STING RAY- MUSICAL	*	30.00	30.00
95	A CHEESE RING CIRCUS/MUSICAL 869023	*	30.00	30.00
95	A REFRESHING PAUSE/MUSICAL 153168	*	30.00	30.00
95	A THRIST FOR FUN/MUSCIAL 128775	*	250.00	250.00
95	A-B-C- SAW/MUSICAL 868965	*	50.00	50.00
95	CALLING TO COLLECT/MUSICAL	*	250.00	250.00
95	CLARA'S DREAM/MUSICAL	*	30.00	30.00
95	FLEET SWEETS/MUSICAL	*	30.00	30.00
95	IT'S THE REAL THING/MUSICAL 128910	*	50.00	50.00
95	LITTLE LOVE BOAT/MUSICAL 551104	*	30.00	30.00
95	MAESTRO OF MISCHIEF/MUSICAL 138126	*	70.00	70.00
95	MINI MOUSEICIANS/MUSICAL 868981	*	30.00	30.00
95	MONTMARTRE/MUSICAL 869007	*	30.00	30.00
95	POP HOP SOAD SHOPPE/MUSICAL 138282	*	30.00	30.00
95	PRACTICE MAKES PERFECT/MUSICAL	*	50.00	50.00
95	PRESENTING..PINOCCHIO/MUSICAL 596302	*	350.00	350.00
95	ROCK-A-BEAR BABY/MUSICAL 868973	*	50.00	50.00
95	ROCKIN' & ROLLIN'/MUSICAL 598003	*	150.00	150.00
95	SANTA'S SECRET HELPER/MUSICAL	*	30.00	30.00
95	SIR MICKEY TO THE RESCUE/MUSICAL 123633	*	400.00	400.00
95	SPINING TAILS/MUSICAL 114944	*	200.00	200.00
95	SPINNING A YARN/MUSICAL 137006	*	30.00	30.00
95	THAT'S ALL FOLKS/MUSICAL	*	100.00	100.00
95	TO BOLDLY GO.../MUSICAL 323608	*	300.00	300.00
95	TO THE RESCUE/MUSICAL 551163	*	30.00	30.00
95	WISHES A-WEIGH/MUSICAL	*	70.00	70.00
96	'56 CORVETTE- MUSICAL	*	30.00	30.00
96	'59 CADILLAC- MUSICAL	*	30.00	30.00
96	BAKING SWEET MEMORIES/MUSICAL 184861	*	30.00	30.00
96	CHEVY BLAZER/MUSICAL 175021	*	30.00	30.00
96	COLOSSAL, THE/MUSICAL	*	600.00	600.00
96	COWARDLY LION, THE/MUSICAL 175110	*	30.00	30.00
96	DODGE RAM TRUCK/MUSICAL 174106	*	30.00	30.00
96	DOROTHY/MUSICAL 175099	*	30.00	30.00
96	F100 FORD PICK-UP/MUSICAL	*	30.00	30.00
96	FORD EXPLORER/MUSICAL 174092	*	30.00	30.00
96	HOLIDAY HORSEPLAY/MUSICAL	*	30.00	30.00
96	I'D LIKE TO BUY THE WORLD A COKE/MUSICAL	*	250.00	250.00
96	IT SEAMS LIKE CHRISTMAS/MUSICAL	*	30.00	30.00
96	JEEP GRAND CHEROKEE/MUSICAL 175013	*	30.00	30.00
96	LAST MINUTE SHOP WORK/MUSICAL	*	30.00	30.00
96	LULLABY LAND/MUSICAL	*	30.00	30.00
96	MERRY-GO-ROUND MAGIC/MUSICAL 167150	*	30.00	30.00
96	MICEST DECORATIONS, THE/MUSICAL	*	30.00	30.00
96	PERFECT HARMONY/MUSICAL 920339	*	30.00	30.00
96	SCARECROW. THE/MUSICAL 175129	*	30.00	30.00
96	SERVING UP FUN/MUSICAL 168025	*	30.00	30.00
96	SEW PETTY/MUSICAL 165360	*	30.00	30.00
96	SPOTTIN' ADVENTURE/MUSICAL 165387	*	30.00	30.00
96	TASTEFULLY TRIMMED/MUSICAL 184888	*	30.00	30.00
96	TEA FOR TWO/MUSICAL 902675	*	30.00	30.00
96	TIN MAN, THE/MUSICAL 175099	*	30.00	30.00
96	TINY TOONLAND/MUSICAL	*	30.00	30.00
96	TOGETHER W/COCA-COLA/MUSICAL 165409	*	150.00	150.00
96	WHAT CHILD IS THIS?/MUSICAL 184365	*	30.00	30.00
K. HAHN			**SMALL WORLD OF MUSIC**	
95	BAKING YOU HAPPY/MUSICAL 136999	*	30.00	30.00
95	SUPPLIES IN DEMAND/MUSICAL 136980	*	30.00	30.00
S. BUTCHER			**TO HAVE AND TO HOLD**	
96	A SILVER CELEBRATION TO SHARE 163813	OP	70.00	70.00
96	A YEAR OF BLESSINGS 163783	OP	70.00	70.00
96	EACH HOUR IS PRECIOUS WITH YOU 163791	OP	70.00	70.00
96	FIFTY YEARS AS PRECIOUS AS GOLD 163848	OP	70.00	70.00
96	FORTY YEARS OF PRECIOUS MEMORIES 163821	OP	70.00	70.00
96	LOVE VOWS TO ALWAYS BLOOM 129097	OP	70.00	70.00
96	TEN YEARS HEART TO HEART 163805	OP	70.00	70.00
S. BUTCHER			**YOU ARE ALWAYS THERE FOR ME**	
96	FATHER HELPING SON BAT 163627	OP	50.00	50.00
96	MOTHER KISSING DAUGHTER'S OWIE 163600	OP	50.00	50.00
96	SISTER CONSOLING SISTER 163635	OP	50.00	50.00

YR NAME	LIMIT	ISSUE	TREND

ERTL COLLECTIBLES
EPSTEIN/GAGE

		CAT HALL OF FAME	
98 ALBERT FELINESTEIN	OP	20.00	20.00
98 BETTY CROCKAT	OP	20.00	20.00
98 CATS DOMINO'	5000	60.00	60.00
98 CATS FIFTH AVENUE	OP	20.00	20.00
98 CATSABLANCA	5000	57.00	57.00
98 GEORGE S. CATTON	OP	20.00	20.00
98 LIZA MEWNELLI	OP	20.00	20.00
98 LUCY & RICKY RICATTO	5000	57.00	57.00
98 MARIE CATOINETTE	OP	20.00	20.00
98 MISS AMERICAT	OP	20.00	20.00
98 SITTING CAT	OP	20.00	20.00
98 WILLIAM SHAKESPURR	OP	20.00	20.00

L. DAVIS

		LOWELL DAVIS AMERICA	
97 A FRIEND IN NEED	4500	70.00	70.00
97 CAN'T WAIT	3500	150.00	150.00
97 COUNTRY DOCTOR	3500	290.00	290.00
97 DOG DAYS	3500	60.00	60.00
97 GET ONE FOR ME	4500	75.00	75.00
97 LAST OF THE LITTER	5500	60.00	60.00
97 NEXT!	4500	70.00	70.00
97 NINE LIVES	3500	120.00	120.00
97 OH! SHE'LL BE...	3500	180.00	180.00
97 RED OAK II 1923 CHEVY PANEL TRUCK	OP	16.00	16.00
97 SOOIE	3500	160.00	160.00
97 WASH DAY BLUES	3500	75.00	75.00

FENTON ART GLASS
*

* BASKET 5838CC	*	*	55.00
* BEAR BIRTHSTONE C5151W10	*	*	20.00
* BOWL 8065 OVAL 6-1/2"	*	*	65.00
* CANDY 8088 COVERED	*	*	32.00
* CANDY Q7580UD DOLPHIN HANDLED	*	*	70.00
* DECANTER 8068 SQUARE	*	*	75.00
* JAR 8075 APOTHECARY 36 OZ.	*	*	28.00
* JAR 8076A8 APOTHECARY 32 OZ.	*	*	40.00
* JAR 8077 APOTHECARY 48 OZ.	*	*	40.00
* LAMP 7503P5 MARIETTA BICENT 23-1/2"	*	*	500.00
* LAMP 7507N6 PARKERSBURG 25-1/2"	*	*	600.00
* MINIATURE AMETHYST LEMONADE SET	*	*	135.00
* MINIATURE BURMESE LEMONADE SET	*	*	400.00
* MINIATURE CUSTARD LEMONADE SET HP	*	*	125.00
* MINIATURE CUSTARD LEMONADE SET PLAIN	*	*	65.00
* MINIATURE CUSTARD TUMBLE UP HP VIOLETS	*	*	95.00
* MINIATURE CUSTARD TUMBLE UP PLAIN	*	*	55.00
* MINIATURE RUBY TUMBLE UP SET	*	*	135.00
* MINIATURE XMAS LEMONADE SET	*	*	115.00
* VASE R9451MI RIBBED FABERGE BUD 7"	*	*	14.00
* WATER SET HOBNAIL 5 PC.	*	*	375.00
79 COMPORT 8431BO 5" WATER LILY	*	*	32.00
79 VASA MURRHINA COBALT FOR FAGCA	*	*	55.00
80 BASKET 7237CD 7"	*	*	55.00
80 BASKET 7536VR 8-1/2"	*	*	80.00
80 BASKET 7537JA 7"	*	*	65.00
80 BASKET 9334BD BASKETWEAVE 7"	*	*	45.00
80 BASKET 9435IO RIBBON EDGE 8-1/2"	*	*	125.00
80 BASKET 9436IO ROSE BOWL 8-1/2"	*	*	120.00
80 BIRD 5011 OFFHAND VASA MURRHINA	*	*	65.00
80 BIRD 5163BD	*	*	30.00
80 BIRD 5163JA SMALL	*	*	32.00
80 BIRD 5197CD HAPPINESS	*	*	35.00
80 BOTTLE 7363BD HANDLED	*	*	70.00
80 BOWL 7523JA ROLLED RIM	*	*	30.00
80 BOWL 7526VR 6-1/2"	*	*	48.00
80 BOWL 8454IO ROSE 5"	*	*	65.00
80 BOWL 9425IO RIBBON EDGE 8"	*	*	75.00
80 BOY & GIRL 5100JA PAIR	*	*	53.00
80 BUNNY 5162BD	*	*	35.00
80 BUNNY 5162JA	*	*	48.00
80 BUTTERFLY 5171VR ON STAND	*	*	45.00
80 CANDLEHOLDERS 7572JA	*	*	32.00
80 CANDLEHOLDERS 7572VR	*	*	35.00
80 CAT 5165JA	*	*	43.00
80 COMPORT 7527VR FOOTED	*	*	40.00
80 COMPORT 7528JA	*	*	30.00
80 COMPORT 9422VR PERSIAN	*	*	43.00
80 ELEPHANT 5012 OFFHAND VASA MURRHINA	*	*	65.00
80 FAIRY LIGHT 7500JA 2 PC.	*	*	48.00
80 FAIRY LIGHT 8408VR PERSIAN	*	*	85.00
80 FROG 5166CD	*	*	35.00
80 HATPIN HOLDER	*	*	65.00
80 LAMP 2805IO STUDENT 20"	*	*	295.00
80 LAMP 7215CD HAMMERED 20-1/2"	*	*	180.00

YR	NAME	LIMIT	ISSUE	TREND
80	NUT DISH 7229BD	*	*	24.00
80	NUT DISH 7529JA	*	*	25.00
80	NUT DISH 7529VR FOOTED	*	*	32.00
80	OWL 5168JA	*	*	32.00
80	SALVER 7516VR 9"	*	*	35.00
80	SHADE LC	*	*	165.00
80	TEMPLE JAR 7488BD SMALL	*	*	40.00
80	TEMPLE JAR 7488CD SMALL	*	*	40.00
80	TEMPLE JAR 7488JA SMALL	*	*	40.00
80	TEMPLE JAR 7588JA LARGE	*	*	65.00
80	TOWN PUMP MINIATURE	*	*	38.00
80	VASE 7252BD 7"	*	*	38.00
80	VASE 7252CD 7"	*	*	38.00
80	VASE 7550JA 7"	*	*	45.00
80	VASE 7551VR FAN DOLPHIN	*	*	60.00
80	VASE 7557JA 10"	*	*	45.00
80	VASE 8251JA MANDARIN	*	*	105.00
80	VASE 8252JA EMPRESS	*	*	105.00
80	VASE 9054JA BUD TALL	*	*	15.00
80	VASE 9056BD BUD 8"	*	*	15.00
80	VASE 9056CD BUD	*	*	15.00
80	VASE 9056VR BUD FOOTED	*	*	26.00
80	VASE 9456IO SWUNG 12"	*	*	80.00
80	VASE MELON OVERLAY FAGCA	*	*	45.00
80	WATER SET 3407IO 7 PC.	*	*	350.00
81	BASKET 7235PC 5"	*	*	65.00
81	BASKET 7437SS 7-1/4"	*	*	95.00
81	BASKET 7535PD 7-1/2"	*	*	125.00
81	BASKET 8435VY 9"	*	*	95.00
81	BASKET 8437BO LILY OF VALLEY	*	*	48.00
81	BASKET 9334SF 7"	*	*	55.00
81	BASKET 9431VE MINIATURE	*	*	25.00
81	BASKET 9432VR 11"	*	*	95.00
81	BASKET 9536BQ	*	*	45.00
81	BASKET MINIATURE	*	*	32.00
81	BIRD 5163SF SMALL	*	*	25.00
81	BON BON 9128VB 7-1/2"	*	*	28.00
81	BOOT 9590PY	*	*	18.00
81	BOWL 5150PI HI ATLANTIS	*	*	240.00
81	BOWL 8250VR ROSE MINIATURE	*	*	20.00
81	BOX 9589BQ JEWEL OVAL	*	*	20.00
81	CANDY JAR 9488VB	*	*	75.00
81	CAT 5165SF	*	*	35.00
81	COMPORT 7429SF	*	*	35.00
81	COMPORT 7429SF 6"	*	*	28.00
81	COMPORT 8431VR WATER LILY	*	*	40.00
81	COMPOTE 9422VB	*	*	32.00
81	CUP 7581VY LOVING DOLPHIN HANDLE	*	*	65.00
81	DUCKLING 5169SF	*	*	30.00
81	EPERGNE 7505VY 5 PC.	*	*	325.00
81	FAIRY LIGHT 7300AC XMAS 2 PC.	*	*	45.00
81	FAIRY LIGHT 7501PD 3 PC.	*	*	75.00
81	FAIRY LIGHT 8405VR BEADED	*	*	125.00
81	FAIRY LIGHT 9102CY FINE CUT & BLOCK	*	*	25.00
81	FAIRY LIGHT 9304DR BASKETWEAVE	*	*	50.00
81	FAIRY LIGHT 9304SF 2 PC.	*	*	45.00
81	FAIRY LIGHT 9401FL NATIVITY	*	*	50.00
81	FAIRY LIGHT 9401FT NATIVITY	*	*	55.00
81	FAIRY LIGHT 9401TB NATIVITY	*	*	55.00
81	FAIRY LIGHT 9401TG NATIVITY	*	*	40.00
81	FAIRY LIGHT 9401VE NATIVITY	*	*	40.00
81	FENTON LOGO	*	*	25.00
81	IVY BALL 7522PE	*	*	50.00
81	LAMP 7204OW HAM. COLONIAL 16"	*	*	325.00
81	LAMP 7508OW FRENCH PROV. 22"	*	*	575.00
81	LAMP 7510OW 20"	*	*	425.00
81	LAMP 9305SF STUDENT 20"	*	*	295.00
82	PITCHER, 70 OZ. 8560AY	*	30.00	55.00
84	BEAR 5151FA	*	*	65.00
84	FAWN 5160FA	*	*	65.00
84	PENGUIN 5014 (OFF-HAND BY DELMER STOWASSER)	*	*	65.00
85	BASKET 3132OP 7 1/2"	*	*	85.00
85	VASE 3161OP 11"	*	*	65.00
86	BEAR 5151IK	*	*	55.00
86	BIRD 5163IK	*	*	45.00
86	CAT 5165IK	*	*	55.00
86	KITTEN	*	*	55.00
86	MALLARD 5147IK	*	*	45.00
86	MOUSE 5148IK	*	*	55.00
86	PIG 5220IK	*	*	50.00
88	ELEPHANT HEISEY COLLECTORS FO-SMALL	*	*	45.00
90	COLT BALKING RE FOR HCA	*	*	65.00
90	COLT KICKING RE FOR HCA	*	*	65.00
90	COLT STANDING RE FOR HCA	*	*	60.00
90	CYGNET RE FOR HCA	*	*	35.00

Proceeds from Dean Griff's charity piece You Are Not Alone *were given to benefit The Gift for Life. A part of the Charming Tails Collection, the figurine has more than doubled in value since its 1995 release.*

On the Move, *which retailed for $340 when it was released by Lladró in 1991, has increased in value.*

The Classic Motorcycle *from Crystal World was limited to 950 in 1995 and retailed for $420.*

YR	NAME	LIMIT	ISSUE	TREND
90	DIAMOND H SIGN RE FOR HCA	*	*	40.00
90	DUCKLING RE FOR HCA	*	*	35.00
90	FILLY HEAD FORWARD RE FOR HCA	*	*	125.00
90	FISH BOOKEND RE FOR HCA	*	*	85.00
90	GAZELLE RE FOR HCA	*	*	85.00
90	GIRAFFE RE FOR HCA	*	*	95.00
90	HEN RE FOR HCA	*	*	55.00
90	RABBIT PAPERWEIGHT RE FOR HCA	*	*	50.00
90	SOW RE FOR HCA	*	*	110.00
90	TIGER PAPERWEIGHT RE FOR HCA	*	*	225.00
95	WATER SET 9001KA	*	135.00	160.00
*				
81	MUG MINIATURE TOPAZ OPAL CARNIVAL	*	*	40.00
81	NUT DISH 7229SF	*	*	25.00
81	NUT DISH 9229SF	*	*	24.00
81	PITCHER MINIATURE GOD & HOME	*	*	35.00
81	SPITTOON 5150PI C. ATLANTIS	*	*	240.00
81	TOOTHPICK 7590VY	*	*	18.00
81	TOOTHPICK HOLDER 9592BQ	*	*	20.00
81	TRAY 1976CY LEAF DAISY & BUTTON	*	*	15.00
81	TUMBLER MINIATURE GOD & HOME	*	*	20.00
81	VASE 5150PI B. ATLANTIS	*	*	165.00
81	VASE 5153VY MINIATURE HAND	*	*	30.00
81	VASE 6056SF 6"	*	*	28.00
81	VASE 7255PD TULIP 10-1/2"	*	*	110.00
81	VASE 7255SS TULIP 10-3/4"	*	*	110.00
81	VASE 7442PD 5"	*	*	60.00
81	VASE 7546PD 4-1/2"	*	*	65.00
81	VASE 7547PD 5-1/2"	*	*	68.00
81	VASE 7551VY DOLPHIN HANDLED	*	*	65.00
81	VASE 7552PD TULIP 6-3/4"	*	*	90.00
81	VASE 7554BQ 5"	*	*	24.00
81	VASE 7558PD BUD 6"	*	*	65.00
81	VASE 7559PD 7-1/2"	*	*	75.00
81	VASE 7560PD 6-1/2"	*	*	75.00
81	VASE 7561PE 10-3/4"	*	*	95.00
81	VASE 8450CO HANDKERCHIEF	*	*	20.00
81	VASE 8455VY DIAMOND & THREAD	*	*	60.00
81	VASE 8458BO BUD 11"	*	*	25.00
81	VASE 9054RD BUD	*	*	28.00
81	VASE 9056SF BUD	*	*	24.00
81	VASE 9320SF BASKETWEAVE 4-1/2"	*	*	24.00
81	VASE 9356DR BUD BASKETWEAVE	*	*	28.00
81	VASE 9356SF BUD	*	*	28.00
81	VASE 9423VR 6"	*	*	30.00
81	VASE 9451VE BUD 7"	*	*	20.00
81	VASE 9455VR HANDKERCHIEF 9"	*	*	25.00
81	VASE 9556PY BUD 8-1/2"	*	*	26.00
81	VASE HANGING HEART FAGCA	*	*	100.00
81	WATER SET 7509VY 7 PC.	*	*	350.00
81	WATER SET MINIATURE	*	*	80.00
82	ASHTRAY 6371KL FLOWER BAND	*	*	10.00
82	BASKET 2534CC DAISY 7"	*	*	72.00
82	BASKET 3431RN CRACKER	*	*	125.00
82	BASKET 3432RN BANANA	*	*	120.00
82	BASKET 3433RN DOUBLE CRIMPED 10"	*	*	125.00
82	BASKET 3436RN LOOPED HANDLE 7-1/2"	*	*	85.00
82	BASKET 7235WQ 5"	*	*	65.00
82	BASKET 7434VI 7"	*	*	40.00
82	BASKET 7435CC 11"	*	*	110.00
82	BASKET 7435KB 11"	*	*	65.00
82	BASKET 7437MV	*	*	90.00
82	BASKET 7533KB 7"	*	*	45.00
82	BASKET 7539IN IRIS 7-1/2"	*	*	50.00
82	BOOT 3992MI HOBNAIL 4"	*	*	18.00
82	BOWL 6320KL FLOWER BAND 9"	*	*	24.00
82	BOWL 7521IN IRIS 6"	*	*	40.00
82	BOWL 7521PE 6"	*	*	42.00
82	BOWL 8520BB 12"	*	*	50.00
82	BOWL 9558WQ ROSE BURMESE MINIATURE	*	*	75.00
82	BOWL R8430GS FOOTED WATER LILY	*	*	24.00
82	BOWL R9426GS RIBBED FABERGE 4-1/2"	*	*	20.00
82	BOWL R9426MI RIBBED 4-1/2"	*	*	15.00
82	BOWL R9426RU RIBBED FABERGE 4-1/2"	*	*	18.00
82	BOWL R9430GS WATER LILY 6"	*	*	24.00
82	BOWL R9430RU RIBBED FABERGE 6"	*	*	24.00
82	BUNNY 5162DR	*	*	35.00
82	BUTTER 9580CK BUTTON & ARCH	*	*	125.00
82	CANDLEHOLDERS 6370KL FLOWER BAND	*	*	24.00
82	CANDY BOX 7484DR	*	*	40.00
82	COMPORT 3429RN FOOTED	*	*	50.00
82	COMPORT 6380KL LARGE	*	*	28.00
82	COMPORT 7431BA FOOTED	*	*	35.00
82	COMPORT 7431VI FOOTED	*	*	38.00
82	COMPORT 7582AY DOLPHIN	*	*	45.00

YR	NAME	LIMIT	ISSUE	TREND
82	COMPORT 8487CK OVAL PINWHEEL	*	*	40.00
82	CRACKER JACK 3480RN COVERED	*	*	90.00
82	CREAMER & COVERED SUGAR 3408RN	*	*	60.00
82	CRUET 3463RN	*	*	110.00
82	CUSPIDOR	*	*	55.00
82	CUSPIDOR 3426RN LADIES	*	*	50.00
82	CUSPIDOR 3427RN MANS	*	*	60.00
82	EGG 5140DR ON STAND	*	*	38.00
82	FAIRY LAMP 7501PD 3 PC.	*	*	125.00
82	FENTON LOGO CHOCOLATE FAGCA	*	*	60.00
82	HAT WHIMSY FAGCA	*	*	65.00
82	JAR 3480CK CRACKER CACTUS	*	*	85.00
82	JAR 7580AY DOLPHIN	*	*	65.00
82	LAMP 7503CQ STUDENT 23-1/2"	*	*	495.00
82	LAMP 7504CQ PRINCESS 19"	*	*	325.00
82	LAMP 7504YB PRINCESS 19"	*	*	325.00
82	LAMP 7506MV SWAG	*	*	475.00
82	LAMP 7506PD HANGING	*	*	450.00
82	LAMP 7507YB FRENCH PROV. 25-1/2"	*	*	525.00
82	LAMP 9301PD COLUMN 20"	*	*	325.00
82	MAYO SET 3803MI HOBNAIL 3 PC.	*	*	32.00
82	MUG 9640CK CRAFTSMAN	*	*	50.00
82	NAPPY GRAPE 8225BO	*	*	25.00
82	NUT DISH 6321KL FLOWER BAND	*	*	12.00
82	NUT DISH 8248RT SCROLL & EYE	*	*	15.00
82	PITCHER 1432CC COIN DOT 32 OZ.	*	*	65.00
82	PITCHER 1432KB COIN DOT 32 OZ.	*	*	50.00
82	PITCHER 1866CC FERN 16 OZ.	*	*	50.00
82	PITCHER 2060CC FEATHER 70 OZ.	*	*	100.00
82	PITCHER 8560AY 70 OZ.	*	*	50.00
82	SLIPPER 3985CK KITTEN	*	*	39.00
82	SUGAR & CREAMER 8402CK CHERRY	*	*	65.00
82	TEMPLE JAR 7488BA	*	*	35.00
82	TEMPLE JAR 7488KY SMALL	*	*	45.00
82	TEMPLE JAR 7488PE SMALL	*	*	45.00
82	TEMPLE JAR 7488VI SMALL	*	*	45.00
82	TEMPLE JAR 7588PE LARGE	*	*	75.00
82	TOOTHPICK 3495RN	*	*	28.00
82	TOOTHPICK 8295CK STRAWBERRY	*	*	28.00
82	VASE 1433CC COIN 9-1/2"	*	*	75.00
82	VASE 1824CC FERN 4-1/2"	*	*	40.00
82	VASE 2050CC FEATHER 6-1/2"	*	*	55.00
82	VASE 3434RN BASKET 10"	*	*	85.00
82	VASE 3441RN JACK IN THE PULPIT	*	*	75.00
82	VASE 3483RN SWUNG 9"	*	*	40.00
82	VASE 5858CC WHEAT 8"	*	*	60.00
82	VASE 5858KB WHEAT 8"	*	*	55.00
82	VASE 6056CR WAVE CREST	*	*	45.00
82	VASE 7241BA 4-1/2"	*	*	20.00
82	VASE 7241VI 4-1/2"	*	*	22.00
82	VASE 7255PD LARGE TULIP	*	*	95.00
82	VASE 7257MV MTN. REFLECT 10"	*	*	95.00
82	VASE 7530BA 6-1/2"	*	*	40.00
82	VASE 7530VI 6-1/2"	*	*	35.00
82	VASE 7550IN IRIS 6-1/2"	*	*	45.00
82	VASE 7550KP 6-1/2"	*	*	40.00
82	VASE 7550PE 6-1/2"	*	*	45.00
82	VASE 7552PD SMALL TULIP	*	*	60.00
82	VASE 7557IN IRIS 9"	*	*	50.00
82	VASE 7557PE 9-1/2"	*	*	65.00
82	VASE 7558PE BUD	*	*	28.00
82	VASE 7559IN IRIS 7-1/2"	*	*	60.00
82	VASE 7559IY SAND CARVED 7-1/2"	*	*	95.00
82	VASE 7559PD 7-1/2"	*	*	75.00
82	VASE 7560PD 6-1/2"	*	*	75.00
82	VASE 7561KY SAND CARVED 10-3/4"	*	*	95.00
82	VASE 7561PE 10-3/4"	*	*	85.00
82	VASE 7561SX SAND CARVED 10-3/4"	*	*	110.00
82	VASE 7582RT DOLPHIN HANDLE	*	*	35.00
82	VASE 7651SX SAND CARVED	*	*	110.00
82	VASE 7655SX SPHERE 10"	*	*	195.00
82	VASE 8251HU MANDARIN 9"	*	*	135.00
82	VASE 8252HU EMPRESS 7-1/2"	*	*	105.00
82	VASE 8528CC SPHERE 8"	*	*	65.00
82	VASE 8550AY 10"	*	*	45.00
82	VASE 8551AY CYLINDER 10-1/2"	*	25.00	48.00
82	VASE 8551BB CYLINDER 10-1/2"	*	*	42.00
82	VASE 8551CC CYLINDER 10-1/2"	*	*	60.00
82	VASE 8552AY 9-1/2"	*	*	45.00
82	VASE 8553AY 6-1/2"	*	18.00	32.00
82	VASE 9454RT BUD 10"	*	*	15.00
82	VASE CORN/GOOD LUCK	*	*	50.00
82	VASE R9451GS BUD RIBBED FABERGE 6"	*	*	35.00
82	VASE R9457GS RIBBED FABERGE 7"	*	*	25.00
82	WATER SET 3407RN 7 PC.	*	*	320.00

YR	NAME	LIMIT	ISSUE	TREND
82	WATER SET 9003CK LINCOLN INN	*	*	298.00
83	BASKET 8636CN SUNBURST	*	*	45.00
83	BASKET 9134HG BUTTERFLY & BERRY 7"	*	*	48.00
83	BASKET G1636AY	*	*	30.00
83	BOWL G1625AY OVAL 11"	*	*	45.00
83	BOWL G1625FB OVAL 11"	*	*	42.00
83	BOWL K7722KN MEDIUM	*	*	65.00
83	BOWL K7724KO 9-3/4"	*	*	75.00
83	CAKE PLATE 8613CY REGENCY	*	*	30.00
83	CANDLEHOLDERS G9071YL	*	*	30.00
83	CLOCK 8600LC	*	*	80.00
83	CREAM & SUGAR 6300CY FLOWER BANK	*	*	25.00
83	CREAMER & SUGAR 8602CY REGENCY	*	*	28.00
83	CRUET G1674AY AMERICAN LEGACY	*	*	60.00
83	CRUET G1674YL	*	*	45.00
83	DECANTER G1678AY	*	*	65.00
83	FAIRY LIGHT FAGCA 1 PC. CRANBERRY OPALESCENT (CO)	*	*	125.00
83	GOBLET G1645AY 10 OZ.	*	*	24.00
83	GOBLET G1645HG	*	*	18.00
83	GOBLET G1645YL	*	*	20.00
83	LAMP 3106OF PANCAKE	*	*	165.00
83	LAMP 3107OY OVERLAY 19"	*	*	150.00
83	LAMP 7514B8 KNIGHTS OF THE SEA	*	*	475.00
83	LAMP MARIETTA COLLEGE	*	*	450.00
83	PAPERWEIGHT TOWN PUMP MARIGOLD IR.	*	*	40.00
83	PITCHER 8664CY REGENCY 64 OZ.	*	*	45.00
83	PITCHER G1660AY 70 OZ.	*	*	85.00
83	PITCHER G1660HG 70 OZ.	*	*	40.00
83	PITCHER G1660YL	*	*	75.00
83	RELISH G1618AY OVAL 8"	*	*	75.00
83	SALT & PEPPER 8606CY REGENCY	*	*	16.00
83	SALT & PEPPER SHAKERS G1606AY	*	*	20.00
83	SUGAR & CREAMER G1603YL	*	*	55.00
83	SUGAR SHAKER G1692AY	*	*	38.00
83	SUGAR SHAKER G1692YL	*	*	32.00
83	TEMPLE JAR 7488TT SMALL	*	*	49.00
83	TUMBLER 8644CY REGENCY	*	*	40.00
83	VASE 1850OH OVERLAY 7-1/2"	*	*	38.00
83	VASE 7530DN 6-1/2"	*	*	30.00
83	VASE 7530TT 6-1/2"	*	*	50.00
83	VASE 9056DN BUD 7-1/2"	*	*	20.00
83	VASE G1652FB 10"	*	*	40.00
83	VASE G1652YL 10"	*	*	45.00
83	VASE G1659AY AMERICAN LEGACY 7"	*	*	40.00
83	VASE G1659YL	*	*	35.00
83	VASE K7751KE SMALL BLOWN	*	*	45.00
83	VASE K7753KC LARGE BLOWN	*	*	85.00
83	VASE K7754KE SMALL BLOWN	*	*	45.00
83	VASE K7755KN MEDIUM	*	*	55.00
83	WATER SET VICTORIAN	*	*	475.00
83	WINE G1644AY 5 OZ.	*	*	20.00
83	WINE G1644YL	*	*	18.00
84	APPLE 5019OD	*	*	55.00
84	APPLE 5019OF	*	*	50.00
84	BANANA STAND 3720PO HIGH FOOTED PIE CRUST CRIMP	*	*	150.00
84	BASKET 3734PO 12"	*	*	350.00
84	BASKET 3735PO 5-1/2"	*	*	105.00
84	BASKET 3838PO 8-1/2"	*	*	145.00
84	BASKET 7534DN	*	*	42.00
84	BASKET 7635RK	*	*	42.00
84	BASKET 9635DK 7"	*	*	26.00
84	BEAR CUB 5151RK	*	*	35.00
84	BOOT 3992MI	*	*	15.00
84	BOWL 3-TOED LIONS/FENTON FLOWERS	*	*	45.00
84	BOWL 3938PO 12"	*	*	175.00
84	BOWL 7549PF MELON 9"	*	*	35.00
84	BOWL 7622RK 9"	*	*	32.00
84	BOWL 9425IP RIBBON EDGE 8"	*	*	65.00
84	BOWL BUTTERFLY & BERRY/GOOD LUCK	*	*	65.00
84	BUTTERFLY BON BON	*	*	45.00
84	CANDLEHOLDERS 7475RK	*	*	36.00
84	CANDLEHOLDERS 7573PF MELON	*	*	35.00
84	CANDLELIGHT 9504FA BASKETWEAVE	*	*	80.00
84	CANDY BOX 3786MI OVAL	*	*	20.00
84	CANDY BOX 3886MI	*	*	24.00
84	CANDY/BUTTER 3802MI COVERED	*	*	30.00
84	CAT 5165RK	*	*	38.00
84	COMPORT 1628RK	*	*	32.00
84	ELEPHANT 5158FA	*	*	35.00
84	ELEPHANT 5158RK	*	*	30.00
84	EPERGNE 3701PO 4 PART	*	*	375.00
84	FAIRY LIGHT 3804PO 3 PC.	*	*	195.00
84	JAM 3600MI COVERED	*	*	30.00
84	LAMP 7514TL SMOKE & CINDERS 23" VERY RARE	250	*	513.00
84	LIGHT 9605VP GIRL	*	*	48.00

YR	NAME	LIMIT	ISSUE	TREND
84	MUG 9648VK BOY	*	*	20.00
84	MUG 9649VE PRAYER CHILDREN	*	*	20.00
84	PENGUIN 5014 OFFHAND BY DELMER STOWASSER	*	*	65.00
84	PICTURE FRAME 7596PY	*	*	25.00
84	PITCHER & BOWL SET 3303PO	*	*	300.00
84	PITCHER 3664PO ICE LIP 70 OZ.	*	*	165.00
84	PITCHER FISHERMAN'S	*	*	35.00
84	RELISH 3733PO HEART	*	*	65.00
84	SLIPPER 3700MI	*	*	15.00
84	SLIPPER 3995MI CAT	*	*	12.00
84	TEMPLE JAR 7488DN SMALL	*	*	40.00
84	VASE 3323PO CRIMPED 4-1/2"	*	*	65.00
84	VASE 3952MI FOOTED 4"	*	*	9.00
84	VASE 7544PF PETITE FLEUR 5"	*	*	35.00
84	VASE 8654NK 7-1/2"	*	*	35.00
84	VASE 9659DK 7-1/2"	*	*	20.00
84	VASE AZURE BLUE SATIN AVON	*	*	110.00
84	VASE MELON BLUE BURMESE FAGCA PELOTON	*	*	80.00
84	VOTIVE 7275RK FOOTED	*	*	24.00
84	VOTIVE 9671DK	*	*	15.00
84	WATER SET 3306PO 7 PC.	*	*	450.00
84	WHALE 5152FA	*	*	43.00
84	WHALE 5152RK	*	*	35.00
85	ANGEL 5114AB PRAYING	*	*	28.00
85	BASKET 2632BI LARGE 9-1/2"	*	*	125.00
85	BASKET 7437F7 8-1/4"	*	*	85.00
85	BASKET 8637XT OVAL	*	*	45.00
85	BASKET 9637NK LEAF W/BUTTERFLY	*	*	42.00
85	BOWL 2624BI LARGE 9"	*	*	80.00
85	BOWL 8810EP SHALLOW ARTISAN 9"	*	*	110.00
85	BOWL 8810ER SHALLOW ARTISAN 9"	*	*	110.00
85	BOWL 8811EP "V" ARTISAN 8"	*	*	120.00
85	BOWL 8811ER "V" ARTISAN 8"	*	*	120.00
85	CANDLE 8809EP ARTISAN 6-1/4"	*	*	125.00
85	CANDLEHOLDERS 3674	*	*	54.00
85	CAT 5165NG GRAY	*	*	35.00
85	CLOCK 8600F8 THE FARM	*	*	95.00
85	CLOWN 5111NE	*	*	35.00
85	CLOWN 5111NL	*	*	35.00
85	COASTER AUSTRALIAN	*	*	20.00
85	COMPORT 9626PH BASKETWEAVE 5-1/4"	*	*	28.00
85	CUSPIDOR	*	*	40.00
85	CUSPIDOR BASKETWEAVE	*	*	40.00
85	DOLL 5228 ALMOST HEAVEN 80TH ANNIV.	*	*	45.00
85	DRAKE MALLARD 5147NM	*	*	30.00
85	EPERGNE 4809GO DIAMOND 4PC.	*	*	375.00
85	FAIRY LIGHT 2604BI 3 PC.	*	*	120.00
85	FAIRY LIGHT 7300WP XMAS 2 PC.	*	*	50.00
85	FAWN 5160LB AUTUMN LEAVES	*	*	32.00
85	FAWN 5160NF	*	*	40.00
85	FAWN 5160PZ PEACH MEADOW	*	*	32.00
85	FAWN 5160VE	*	*	22.00
85	HOBBY HORSE 5135 SPOTTED	*	*	32.00
85	HOBBY HORSE 5135HY	*	*	32.00
85	JAR 9188 TOBACCO GRAPE & CABLE	*	*	75.00
85	KISSING KIDS 5101VE	*	*	30.00
85	KITTEN 5119NX	*	*	32.00
85	LAMP 2603BI STUDENT 20"	*	*	225.00
85	LAMP 7204DW 16"	250	*	325.00
85	LAMP 7204F5 HAMMERED COLONIAL 16"	*	*	275.00
85	LAMP 7602EB BUTTERFLY & BRANCH 22"	*	*	525.00
85	LUV BUG 5149CY	*	*	18.00
85	MALLARD 5147ND CANVASBACK	*	*	32.00
85	MALLARD 5147NQ BLUE WING TEAL	*	*	32.00
85	MELON VASE OVERLAY FAGCA COBALT BLUE W.MICA	*	*	65.00
85	MOUSE 5148NG GRAY	*	*	30.00
85	MOUSE 5148NJ BROWN	*	*	30.00
85	MUG BURMESE FAGCA	*	*	55.00
85	OIL LAMP 7609XT	*	*	30.00
85	PANDA BEAR 5151PJ	*	*	38.00
85	PIG 5220QP	*	*	40.00
85	PITCHER 2664BI 60 OZ. 9"	*	*	135.00
85	PITCHER 8667NK SUNBURST	*	*	75.00
85	PUNCH CUP 3847GO CC	*	*	24.00
85	SNAIL 5134NK	*	*	35.00
85	SPANIEL 5159SP	*	*	45.00
85	SPANIEL 5159VE	*	*	30.00
85	TEMPLE JAR 7488EF BOB EVANS	*	*	60.00
85	TUMBLER 2640FO	*	*	20.00
85	VASE 3140OP SPIRAL OPTIC 7-1/2"	*	*	65.00
85	VASE 5858OP WHEAT 8"	*	*	50.00
85	VASE 7530F7 6-1/2"	*	*	55.00
85	VASE 8801ER OVAL ARTISAN 12"	*	*	175.00
85	VASE 8801NV OVAL 12"	*	*	225.00
85	VASE 8802EG OVAL ARTISAN 12"	*	*	135.00

YR	NAME	LIMIT	ISSUE	TREND
85	VASE 8802ER OVAL ARTISAN 12"	*	*	150.00
85	VASE 8803KM TRIANGLE 15"	*	*	235.00
85	VASE 8803UV TRIANGLE 15"	*	*	235.00
85	VASE 8804KM SPHERE	*	*	225.00
85	VASE 8805ER ARTISAN 6"	*	*	85.00
85	VASE 8806ER ARTISAN 7-1/2"	*	*	120.00
85	VASE 8807EP ARTISAN 9"	*	*	110.00
85	VASE 9650OP DOGWOOD 11"	*	*	60.00
85	VASE 9658OP DOGWOOD 8"	*	*	50.00
85	VASE MELON OVERLAY FAGCA	*	*	95.00
85	VOTIVE 9673XN SANTA	*	*	45.00
86	BASE 9451DK BUD FABERGE	*	*	18.00
86	BASKET 6634UO 7"	*	*	36.00
86	BASKET 7635EW 7"	*	*	48.00
86	BASKET 8333PW BARRED OVAL 6"	*	*	30.00
86	BASKET 9230WQ 5"	*	*	45.00
86	BASKET 9234NK BUTTERFLY & BERRY	*	*	38.00
86	BASKET 9433DK STRAWBERRY	*	*	30.00
86	BASKET 9535FO MINIATURE	*	*	28.00
86	BASKET 9537DK STRAWBERRY	*	*	30.00
86	BASKET 9639JU 7-1/2"	*	*	40.00
86	BASKET V8637FX OVAL 7-1/2"	*	*	39.00
86	BEAR CUB 5151EW	*	*	32.00
86	BEAR CUB 5151FO	*	*	30.00
86	BEAR CUB V5151CY	*	*	15.00
86	BOOT 9590WQ	*	*	35.00
86	BOWL 6624UO REFLECTIONS 11"	*	*	40.00
86	BOWL 6626UO 5-1/2"	*	*	20.00
86	BOWL 8289BR ORANGE TR & CHERRY	*	*	65.00
86	BOWL 8289NK ORANGE TR & CHERRY	*	*	40.00
86	BOWL 8321PW BARRED OWL 6-1/2"	*	*	18.00
86	BOWL 9588WQ ROSE 3-1/4"	*	*	45.00
86	BOWL 9627PW BEAUTY	*	*	24.00
86	BOWL 9653NK ROSE FABERGE 4-1/2"	*	*	28.00
86	BOX V9589FX JEWEL 4-1/2"	*	*	24.00
86	BUTTERFLY 5171DK ON STAND	*	*	28.00
86	BUTTERFLY 5171PW ON STAND	*	*	28.00
86	CANDLEHOLDERS 6672UO	*	*	30.00
86	CANDY 6688UO COVERED	*	*	38.00
86	CANDY 9185 BR DAISY 8-3/4"	*	*	85.00
86	CANDY 9280DK COVERED BUTTERFLY	*	*	36.00
86	CANDY BOX 9551EO COVERED	*	*	32.00
86	CANDY BOX 9551UO COVERED	*	*	32.00
86	CAT V5165CY	*	*	15.00
86	COMPORT 1628EW FOOTED	*	*	38.00
86	COMPORT 8234BR PERSIAN	*	*	65.00
86	COMPORT 9120KD FINE CUT & BLOCK	*	*	20.00
86	COMPORT 9276NK INNOVATION 4-1/2"	*	*	35.00
86	COMPORT 9279NK MARQUETTE 7"	*	*	35.00
86	COMPORT 9626DK BASKETWEAVE 5-1/4"	*	*	18.00
86	COMPORT 9626PW BASKETWEAVE 5-1/4"	*	*	20.00
86	DESK PLAQUE 7698TP JUPITER	*	*	85.00
86	DISH 9125BR OVAL	*	*	75.00
86	ELEPHANT 5158CY	*	*	18.00
86	FAIRY LIGHT 8408BR 3 PC.	*	*	100.00
86	FAWN 5160BR W/WOOD BASE	*	*	55.00
86	FAWN 5160EW	*	*	35.00
86	FAWN 5160IK TRUE BLUE FRIENDS	*	*	53.00
86	FAWN V5160CY	*	*	15.00
86	FENTON LOGO 9799FO	*	*	25.00
86	HEN ON NEST 5186DK	*	*	20.00
86	KITTEN 5119NK	*	*	35.00
86	KITTEN V5119CY	*	*	18.00
86	LAMP 7514TP JUPITER 23"	*	*	450.00
86	MOUSE 5148FO	*	*	32.00
86	MOUSE 5148NK	*	*	40.00
86	MUG BUTTERFLY FAGCA	*	*	45.00
86	NUT DISH 9531DK STRAWBERRY	*	*	16.00
86	NUT DISH 9571FO FOOTED	*	*	20.00
86	RINGHOLDER 9144KD FINE CUT & BLOCK	*	*	5.00
86	RINGHOLDER 9144PW FINE CUT & BLOCK	*	*	5.00
86	SCOTTIE 5214CY	*	*	30.00
86	SLIPPER 1995BR DAISY & BUTTON	*	*	45.00
86	SLIPPER 1995DK DAISY & BUTTON	*	*	12.00
86	SLIPPER 1995PW DAISY & BUTTON	*	*	12.00
86	SLIPPER 9591WQ	*	*	30.00
86	SNAIL V5134CY	*	*	32.00
86	SPANIEL 5159SP	*	*	40.00
86	SQUIRREL 5215JU	*	*	30.00
86	SQUIRREL 5215VE	*	*	24.00
86	TOOTHPICK 9592WQ	*	*	29.00
86	TOOTHPICK/VOTIVE 8294BR	*	*	34.00
86	TOOTHPICK/VOTIVE 9292NK	*	*	18.00
86	TOOTHPICK/VOTIVE 9592WQ	*	*	40.00
86	URN 3194ZS HANDLED CC 13"	*	*	425.00

YR	NAME	LIMIT	ISSUE	TREND
86	VASE 1752WQ 5-1/2"	*	*	60.00
86	VASE 1752WQ FOOTED 5-1/2"	*	*	60.00
86	VASE 3190KF HANDLED CC 7"	*	*	225.00
86	VASE 6650UO BUD 6"	*	*	20.00
86	VASE 6654EO REFLECTIONS 11"	*	*	30.00
86	VASE 6654UO 11"	*	*	32.00
86	VASE 8257BR PEACOCK 8"	*	*	103.00
86	VASE 8351PW BUD BARRED OWL 8-1/2"	*	*	22.00
86	VASE 8812EK SILHOUETTES 10-1/2"	*	*	95.00
86	VASE 9056EW FOOTED BUD 7-1/2"	*	*	28.00
86	VASE 9157DK FINE CUT & BLOCK	*	*	18.00
86	VASE 9454DK BUD STRAWBERRY 11-1/2"	*	*	24.00
86	VASE 9652PW BEAUTY	*	*	24.00
86	VASE 9658NK DOGWOOD 8"	*	*	55.00
86	VASE 9659DK	*	*	18.00
86	VASE RUBY IRRIDIZED FAGCA	*	*	80.00
86	VASE V1759FX FOOTED 6-1/2"	*	*	24.00
86	VOTIVE 6655UO	*	*	18.00
86	VOTIVE 7275DK FOOTED	*	*	10.00
86	VOTIVE 7275EW FOOTED	*	*	24.00
86	VOTIVE 7275PW	*	*	12.00
86	VOTIVE 7675KR FOOTED	*	*	20.00
86	VOTIVE 8371PW BARRED OVAL	*	*	10.00
86	VOTIVE 9555EO	*	*	10.00
86	VOTIVE 9557RU 6"	*	*	15.00
87	BASKET 3032MI WAVE HOBNAIL	*	*	29.00
87	BASKET 3634MI OVAL HOBNAIL	*	*	18.00
87	BASKET 7635FS SQUARE	*	*	42.00
87	BASKET 7638CA AURORA	*	*	20.00
87	BASKET 8335OO OPEN EDGED	*	*	34.00
87	BASKET 9639BQ PANELED	*	*	40.00
87	BASKET 9639VJ PANELED	*	*	40.00
87	BEAR CUB 5151FS	*	*	35.00
87	BIRD 5197CA HAPPINESS	*	*	28.00
87	BON BON 3937MI 2 HANDLE HOBNAIL	*	*	12.00
87	BOWL 3022MI ROSE, HOBNAIL	*	*	18.00
87	BOWL 8323OO OPEN EDGED	*	*	18.00
87	BOWL 9728NK ACANTHUS	*	*	32.00
87	CANDLE 8376OO HURRICANE VALENCIA	*	*	30.00
87	CANDY 3033MI HEART HOBNAIL	*	*	20.00
87	CANDY 9284OO COVERED ROSE	*	*	32.00
87	CANDY 9519OO HEART	*	*	18.00
87	CANDY BOX 9280CA BUTTERFLY	*	*	35.00
87	COMPORT 1628FS	*	*	37.00
87	COMPORT 9223 FOOTED ROSE	*	*	20.00
87	COMPORT 9223OO ROSE FOOTED	*	*	22.00
87	COMPORT 9782VE DAISY	*	*	22.00
87	COMPOTE 3920MI FOOTED HOBNAIL	*	*	18.00
87	COOKIE JAR 3680MI HOBNAIL	*	*	95.00
87	FAWN 5160BQ	*	*	30.00
87	FAWN 5160FS PROVINCIAL BOUQUET	*	*	30.00
87	FOX 5226NK	*	*	30.00
87	HAT 3991MI HOBNAIL	*	*	12.00
87	KITTEN 5119FS	*	*	28.00
87	KITTEN 5119VC	*	*	30.00
87	LAMP 1400CC COIN DOT 20"	*	*	275.00
87	LAMP 2001CC FEATHER 17"	*	*	265.00
87	LAMP 3108CC SPIRAL PILLAR 30"	*	*	425.00
87	LAMP WILD TURKEY FEDERATION OF AMERICA	*	*	325.00
87	MOUSE 5148VC	*	*	24.00
87	NUT DISH 8327CA VALENCIA	*	*	10.00
87	NUT DISH 9531OO STRAWBERRY	*	*	15.00
87	PITCHER 3664MI HOBNAIL	*	*	55.00
87	PITCHER 9461NK PLYTEC 32 OZ.	*	*	45.00
87	PITCHER 9486QY CC	*	*	120.00
87	PITCHER HOLIDAY GREEN CARNIVAL	*	*	55.00
87	PUPPY 5225VC	*	*	30.00
87	ROCKING HORSE 5135VJ (COLOR CODE)	*	*	28.00
87	SLIPPER 1995CA DAISY & BUTTON	*	*	12.00
87	SWAN 5127OO OPEN	*	*	18.00
87	TRINKET BOX 8304OO VALENCIA	*	*	20.00
87	VASE 2057OO CURTAIN 7"	*	*	28.00
87	VASE 3161 OVERLAY 11"	*	*	75.00
87	VASE 3952CA HOBNAIL	*	*	9.00
87	VASE 7620CA AURORA	*	*	12.00
87	VASE 8252VE EMPRESS	*	*	85.00
87	VASE 8356CA BUD VALENCIA	*	*	12.00
87	VASE 9056BQ BUD FOOTED	*	*	28.00
87	VASE 9259VE SPRING 8-3/4"	*	*	75.00
87	VASE TULIP OVERLY FAGCA DUSTY ROSE/COBALT CREST	*	*	75.00
87	VOTIVE 8294CA	*	*	9.00
87	VOTIVE 8294OO PANELED DAISY	*	*	10.00
88	BASKET 7635VC SQUARE 7"	*	*	45.00
88	BASKET 9237OC ROSE 8-1/2"	*	*	36.00
88	BASKET 9238HL PANELED 7"	*	*	45.00

YR	NAME	LIMIT	ISSUE	TREND
88	BASKET 9537OC 6-1/2"	*	*	24.00
88	BASKET C3538TC SPANISH LACE	*	*	45.00
88	BASKET C9134OM BUTTERFLY & BERRY	*	*	45.00
88	BEAR 5233HL RECLINING	*	*	30.00
88	BEAR CUB 5151VC	*	*	24.00
88	BIRD 5115HL	*	*	28.00
88	BOWL C3524TX SPANISH LACE CRESTED	*	*	50.00
88	BOX 5780PT HEART PEARLY SENT.	*	*	30.00
88	BOX COVERED FAGCA	*	*	95.00
88	CANDLE 8376HL HURRICANE	*	*	38.00
88	CANDLE 8376OC HURRICANE	*	*	24.00
88	CANDLEHOLDER 9596OC 2-WAY	*	*	28.00
88	CANDLEHOLDER C3570TX SPANISH LACE	*	*	45.00
88	CAT 5165HL	*	*	45.00
88	CAT C5165EQ	*	*	30.00
88	CLOCK 8691VE DESK	*	*	75.00
88	CLOCK C8691EQ	*	*	65.00
88	COMPORT 1628VC 6"	*	*	35.00
88	COMPORT 9229HL EMPRESS	*	*	33.00
88	COMPORT C3522TC SPANISH LACE	*	*	35.00
88	ELEPHANT HEISEY COLLECTORS (LARGE)	*	*	55.00
88	FAIRY LIGHT 5106HL SANTA	*	*	55.00
88	FISHERMAN'S MUG PACIFIC NORTHWEST CARNIVAL	*	*	42.00
88	GOBLET 9245OC EMPRESS	*	*	18.00
88	HOBBY HORSE 5135BQ	*	*	28.00
88	ICEBERG 8740II 5" X 6"	*	*	32.00
88	ICEBERG 8741IH 3" X 4"	*	*	26.00
88	ICEBERG 8741II 3" X 4"	*	*	26.00
88	ICEBERG 8741MM 3" X 4"	*	*	28.00
88	LAMP 8376CA HURRICANE	*	*	26.00
88	LAMP 8376DK HURRICANE	*	*	30.00
88	LAMP 8376OO HURRICANE	*	*	30.00
88	LAMP 9308VC STUDENT 23"	*	*	225.00
88	NUT DISH 9531OC STRAWBERRY	*	*	18.00
88	SANTA 5235DS	*	*	59.00
88	SWAN 5127OC OPEN	*	*	18.00
88	VASE 1552CC URN 10-1/2"	*	*	95.00
88	VASE 3195FS PROVINCIAL BOUQUET 7"	*	*	95.00
88	VASE 3196FS PROVINCIAL BOUQUET 13"	*	*	150.00
88	VASE 7254HL 4-1/2"	*	*	32.00
88	VASE 7254VC 4-1/2"	*	*	28.00
88	VASE 7660VC RIBBED 7-1/2"	*	*	48.00
88	VASE 9056VC BUD 9-1/4"	*	*	28.00
88	VOTIVE 6655EO	*	*	18.00
88	VOTIVE 8294CA	*	*	9.00
88	VOTIVE 8294DK	*	*	10.00
88	VOTIVE 8294OO	*	*	10.00
88	VOTIVE 9555EO	*	*	18.00
88	VOTIVE 9555UO	*	*	18.00
88	VOTIVE 9576EO	*	*	15.00
88	VOTIVE 9576UO	*	*	15.00
89	BASKET 7630AF ANTIQUE ROSE 7"	*	*	45.00
89	BASKET 9127OI FINE CUT & BLOCK	*	*	35.00
89	BASKET 9139MG JACQUELINE 10-1/2"	*	*	150.00
89	BASKET 9239MP PANELED	*	*	45.00
89	BASKET 9434CC JACQUELINE 8-1/4"	*	*	85.00
89	BASKET 9539PT PEARLY	*	*	28.00
89	BASKET C5838LU CORNSHOCK	*	*	60.00
89	BASKET C9234DN BUTTERFLY & BERRY	*	*	45.00
89	BASKET Q9238	*	*	48.00
89	BEAR CUB Q5151RP	*	*	32.00
89	BOOT 1990OI DAISY & BUTTON	*	*	22.00
89	BOWL 8283OI ORANGE TR & CHERRY 10"	*	*	48.00
89	BOWL 9442MG JACQUELINE 9-1/2"	*	*	75.00
89	BOWL C3938DO	*	*	50.00
89	BOWL C8428XB BUTTERFLY & BERRY	*	*	60.00
89	BOX 9384MP TRINKET FLORAL	*	*	30.00
89	BUTTERFLY FAGCA	*	*	60.00
89	CANDLE 8376MP HURRICANE	*	*	30.00
89	CANDY 9185PE COVERED	*	*	32.00
89	CAT 5165OI	*	*	32.00
89	CLOCK 8600PG DEER SCENE	*	*	75.00
89	COMPORT 7980RU HEART	*	*	24.00
89	COMPORT 8227OI PINWHEEL	*	*	28.00
89	COMPORT 8324MP OPEN EDGED	*	*	25.00
89	COMPORT Q8625CY	*	*	32.00
89	EPERGNE 4801OI 4 PC.	*	*	150.00
89	FAIRY LIGHT 8406OI HEART	*	*	45.00
89	PITCHER 8464OI 36 OZ.	*	*	55.00
89	PITCHER C3360DO HOBNAIL	*	*	75.00
89	SWAN 5127OI OPEN	*	*	18.00
89	VASE 7691MP AURORA 7"	*	*	35.00
89	VASE 9056MP BUD 9-1/4"	*	*	24.00
89	VASE 9357MP BASKETWEAVE 4-1/2"	*	*	28.00
89	VASE C1353BX TULIP FINE DOT 10"	*	*	75.00

YR	NAME	LIMIT	ISSUE	TREND
89	VASE Q4453KK FOOTED	*	*	36.00
90	AIREDALE TERRIER RE FOR HCA	*	*	85.00
90	ASHTRAY 4469LK 5-1/2"	*	*	15.00
90	ATOMIZER 7948KP COPPER ROSE	*	*	60.00
90	ATOMIZER V7947E1 40TH	*	*	30.00
90	ATOMIZER V7947F1 50TH	*	*	30.00
90	ATOMIZER V7947H1 HAPPY	*	*	30.00
90	BASKET 1739CR DIAMOND OPTIC 7"	*	*	85.00
90	BASKET 3133CR SPIRAL OPTIC 6"	*	*	65.00
90	BASKET 7237LT COUNTRY SCENE	*	*	85.00
90	BASKET 7630AF AURORA 7"	*	*	48.00
90	BASKET 7630KP AURORA 7"	*	*	45.00
90	BASKET 7630TL AURORA	*	*	42.00
90	BASKET 8342SR VALENCIA	*	*	28.00
90	BASKET 9036DK PRISCILLA 12"	*	*	60.00
90	BASKET 9036SR PRISCILLA 12"	*	*	55.00
90	BASKET 9074RN GRAPE & CABLE	*	*	85.00
90	BASKET 9237LX ROSE 7-1/4"	*	*	36.00
90	BASKET 9240RN ROSE	*	*	40.00
90	BASKET 9335FH BASKETWEAVE	*	*	45.00
90	BASKET 9537DK FOOTED STRAWBERRY	*	*	24.00
90	BASKET 9544SR VULCAN	*	*	32.00
90	BASKET C1868XN MELON	*	*	55.00
90	BASKET C8355XB BASKETWEAVE	*	*	55.00
90	BASKET MELON GREEN CREST FAGCA JADE OPALESCENT	*	*	75.00
90	BEAR 5151NS SITTING HAPPY SANTA	*	*	48.00
90	BEAR 5233NS RECLINING HAPPY SANTA	*	*	50.00
90	BEAR C5151XT	*	*	32.00
90	BEAR CUB 5151ES	*	*	32.00
90	BEAR CUB 5151FH	*	*	32.00
90	BEAR CUB 5151KP	*	*	32.00
90	BEAR CUB 5151SR	*	*	20.00
90	BEAR CUB 5233FH RECLINING	*	*	32.00
90	BEAR DAYDREAMING 5239NS HAPPY SANTA	*	*	48.00
90	BIRD 5163TL	*	*	28.00
90	BIRD 5197DK HAPPINESS	*	*	24.00
90	BIRD 5197FH HAPPINESS	*	*	35.00
90	BIRD 5197LX HAPPINESS	*	*	39.00
90	BIRD 5197SR HAPPINESS	*	*	30.00
90	BOWL 1726CR DIAMOND OPTIC 10"	*	*	85.00
90	BOWL 7523KP ROLLED RIM 9-1/2"	*	*	45.00
90	BOWL 7727AG 14"	*	*	80.00
90	BOWL 7727KH 14"	*	*	89.00
90	BOWL 9059RN GRAPE & CABLE 10-1/2"	*	*	55.00
90	BOX 5780AF HEART ROSE	*	*	22.00
90	BOX 5780TL HEART	*	*	32.00
90	BOX 9384RN TRINKET FLORAL	*	*	35.00
90	BOX 9589FH OVAL TRINKET	*	*	30.00
90	BUNNY 5162TL	*	*	28.00
90	CANDLEHOLDER 9372KP 4-1/2"	*	*	45.00
90	CANDLEHOLDERS 9071EM 8-1/2"	*	*	60.00
90	CANDY 6780EM COVERED	*	*	60.00
90	CANDY BOX 6780ES COVERED PAISLEY	*	*	40.00
90	CANDY BOX 6780LX COVERED PAISLEY	*	*	36.00
90	CANDY BOX 6780SR COVERED PAISLEY	*	*	32.00
90	CANDY BOX 9480PE CHESSIE	*	*	75.00
90	CANDY DISH C7580EQ DOLPHIN HANDLES	*	*	65.00
90	CANDY DISH COVERED VALENCIA	*	*	45.00
90	CAT 5165AF	*	*	30.00
90	CAT 5165ES	*	*	32.00
90	CAT 5165FH	*	*	30.00
90	CAT 5165KP	*	*	30.00
90	CAT 5165TL	*	*	30.00
90	CAT 5243LX	*	*	40.00
90	CAT 5243SR	*	*	25.00
90	CAT C5165XT	*	*	35.00
90	CLOCK 8600BL DOWNY WOODPECKER	1500	*	95.00
90	CLOCK 8600LT ALARM COUNTRY SCENE	*	*	75.00
90	CLOCK 8600NB BLUEBIRD/SNOWFALL	1500	*	95.00
90	CLOCK 8691LX ALARM	*	*	75.00
90	CLOCK 8691RN ALARM	*	*	80.00
90	CLOCK 8691SR ALARM	*	*	50.00
90	CLOCK 8691TL ALARM	*	*	68.00
90	COMPORT 6322FH FLOWER BAND 5-1/2"	*	*	32.00
90	COMPORT 6322KP FLOWER BAND	*	*	30.00
90	COMPORT 6322TL FLOWER BAND	*	*	32.00
90	COMPORT 8625SR PURITAN 6-1/2"	*	*	24.00
90	COMPORT 9223DK FOOTED ROSE	*	*	22.00
90	COMPORT 9229ES EMPRESS	*	*	38.00
90	COMPORT C8625XB PURITAN 6-1/2"	*	*	40.00
90	CRUET 2095CR DRAPERY OPTIC	*	*	95.00
90	DUCKLING 5169TL	*	*	24.00
90	EGG 5140TL	*	*	35.00
90	FAIRY LIGHT 7300BL 2 PC.	4500	*	55.00
90	FAIRY LIGHT 7300NB 2 PC.	4500	*	45.00

YR	NAME	LIMIT	ISSUE	TREND
90	JAR 9188DK TOBACCO COVERED	*	*	100.00
90	JAR 9188RE TOBACCO COVERED	*	*	150.00
90	LAMP 7204BL HAMMERED COLONIAL 16"	500	*	275.00
90	LAMP 7204LT COUNTRY SCENE 16"	*	*	275.00
90	LAMP 7209BN STUDENT 21"	500	*	375.00
90	LAMP 7209LT STUDENT 21"	*	*	375.00
90	LION 5241KK	*	*	35.00
90	LION 5241RN	*	*	33.00
90	MOUSE 5148FH	*	*	24.00
90	MOUSE 5148NS HAPPY SANTA	*	*	48.00
90	NUT DISH 9531DK STRAWBERRY	*	*	18.00
90	PIG 5220NS HAPPY SANTA	*	*	48.00
90	PITCHER 3163CR SPIRAL OPTIC	*	*	60.00
90	PITCHER 7692ES BEADED MELON	*	*	50.00
90	PITCHER 9666LX SANDWICH	*	*	45.00
90	PITCHER 9666RN SANDWICH	*	*	50.00
90	PITCHER C1866XN FERN	*	*	50.00
90	PITCHER HOBNAIL	*	*	75.00
90	PLUG HOSE HEISEY COLLECTORS	*	*	40.00
90	RINGHOLDER 9144DK FINE CUT & BLOCK	*	*	6.00
90	SLIPPER 9295DK ROSE	*	*	12.00
90	SLIPPER 9295ES ROSE	*	*	18.00
90	SLIPPER 9295KP	*	*	22.00
90	SLIPPER 9295LX ROSE	*	*	18.00
90	SLIPPER 9295RN ROSE	*	*	18.00
90	SWAN 5127DK OPEN	*	*	15.00
90	TUMBLER 3008XB HOBNAIL SET	*	*	18.00
90	TUMBLER 7700QH 85TH ANNIVERSARY	*	*	40.00
90	VASE 1353CR TULIP FINE DOT 10"	*	*	85.00
90	VASE 1354CR DOT OPTIC 7"	*	*	65.00
90	VASE 1799CR DIAMOND OPTIC 6"	*	*	55.00
90	VASE 2557DK BEADED MELON	*	*	28.00
90	VASE 3161CR SPIRAL OPTIC 11"	*	*	95.00
90	VASE 5750DK ROSE 9"	*	*	28.00
90	VASE 7254LT COUNTRY SCENE 4-1/2"	*	*	48.00
90	VASE 7348KP	*	*	38.00
90	VASE 7371AG 7"	*	*	65.00
90	VASE 7371KH 7"	*	*	85.00
90	VASE 7372AG 13"	*	*	135.00
90	VASE 7372KH 13"	*	*	125.00
90	VASE 7373AG BUD TULIP 6"	*	*	39.00
90	VASE 7373KH BUD TULIP	*	*	39.00
90	VASE 7620AF AURORA 5"	*	*	32.00
90	VASE 7620SR AURORA 4"	*	*	16.00
90	VASE 7693ES BEADED MELON 6"	*	*	45.00
90	VASE 7694 AURORA 7"	*	*	45.00
90	VASE 7696KP 7-1/2"	*	*	55.00
90	VASE 8354AG BASKETWEAVE 9"	*	*	45.00
90	VASE 8354KH BASKETWEAVE 9"	*	*	55.00
90	VASE 8817KP 8-1/2"	*	*	80.00
90	VASE 9252AF ROSE 6-1/2"	*	*	45.00
90	VASE 9252ES ROSE 6-1/2"	*	*	45.00
90	VASE 9252FH ROSE 6-1/2"	*	*	38.00
90	VASE 9357ES BASKETWEAVE 4-1/2"	*	*	30.00
90	VASE 9357FH BASKETWEAVE 4-1/2"	*	*	30.00
90	VASE 9357TL BASKETWEAVE 4-1/2"	*	*	29.00
90	VASE 9752RN DAFFODIL	*	*	50.00
90	VASE 9754LX W/BOW 6-1/4"	*	*	38.00
90	VASE 9758PN STYLIZED 8"	*	*	40.00
90	VASE C1844CR FERN OPTIC SIGNED	*	*	95.00
90	VASE C5858NZ WHEAT 8"	*	*	55.00
90	VASE C8654GZ PINWHEEL 7-1/2"	*	*	30.00
90	VASE C9452MG JACQUELINE	*	*	75.00
90	VOTIVE 9578AF LEAF 2-WAY	*	*	18.00
90	WOOD DUCKLING STANDING RE FOR HCA	*	*	40.00
91	BASKET C7244QX 8-1/2"	*	*	85.00
91	BEAR 5151 NC, SCHWARZ	*	*	60.00
91	CANDY BOX C9388RN COVERED	*	*	55.00
91	CAT C5165KP	*	*	32.00
91	PITCHER C4661RB 5-1/2"	*	*	65.00
91	VASE 5150 ATLANTIS	*	*	80.00
92	GINGER JAR CB007CR COIN DOT	*	*	120.00
92	VASE CV0218T SPIRAL SIGNED 11"	*	*	95.00
*			**80TH ANNIVERSARY**	
85	BASKET 2635BI SQUARE 8"	*	*	85.00
85	PITCHER 8964BI BLUE RIDGE	*	*	135.00
*			**90TH ANNIVERSARY**	
95	BASKET 1135JE CORALENE FLORAL	OP	75.00	85.00
95	CANDLESTICKS 2911KA 3"	OP	50.00	50.00
95	CANDY BOX 9488KA W/COVER 10-1/2"	OP	50.00	50.00
95	CENTERPIECE 2990KA 4 PC.	OP	95.00	135.00
95	COMPORT 1134KA 5-1/4"	OP	33.00	33.00
95	EPERGNE 7601KA 5 PC. 13"	OP	185.00	235.00
95	LOGO 9499KA, OVAL 5"	OP	25.00	35.00

YR NAME	LIMIT	ISSUE	TREND
D. JOHNSON		**BIRDS OF WINTER ED. I**	
87 CLOCK 8600BC 6"	1500	50.00	75.00
87 FAIRY LIGHT 7300BC 4-1/2"	4500	30.00	55.00
87 LAMP 9702BC 18-1/2"	500	250.00	325.00
D. JOHNSON		**BIRDS OF WINTER ED. II**	
88 CLOCK 8600BD 6"	1500	55.00	75.00
88 FAIRY LIGHT 7300BD 4-1/2"	4500	30.00	55.00
88 LAMP 7209BD STUDENT 21"	500	274.00	225.00
D. JOHNSON		**BIRDS OF WINTER ED. III**	
90 CLOCK 8600BL 6"	1500	60.00	75.00
90 FAIRY LIGHT 7300BL 4-1/2"	4500	30.00	55.00
90 LAMP 7204BL 16"	500	250.00	275.00
D. JOHNSON		**BIRDS OF WINTER ED. IV**	
90 CLOCK 8600NB 6"	1500	60.00	75.00
90 FAIRY LIGHT 7300NB 4-1/2"	4500	30.00	65.00
90 LAMP 7209NB STUDENT 21"	500	275.00	375.00
F. BURTON		**CHRISTMAS AT HOME ED. I**	
90 CLOCK 8600HD 6" SLEIGH RIDE	1500	75.00	85.00
90 FAIRY LIGHT 7300HD 4-1/2" SLEIGH RIDE	3500	39.00	55.00
90 LAMP 7204HD 16" SLEIGH RIDE	1000	250.00	295.00
F. BURTON		**CHRISTMAS AT HOME ED. II**	
90 CLOCK 8600HJ 6" CHRISTMAS EVE	1500	75.00	85.00
90 FAIRY LIGHT 7300HJ 4-1/2" CHRISTMAS EVE	3500	39.00	55.00
90 LAMP 7204HJ 16"	1000	250.00	250.00
F. BURTON		**CHRISTMAS AT HOME ED. III**	
92 CLOCK 8600HQ 6" FAMILY TRADITIONS	1500	75.00	75.00
92 FAIRY LIGHT 7300HQ 4-1/2" FAMILY TRADITIONS	3500	39.00	50.00
92 LAMP 9830HQ 20"	1000	250.00	275.00
F. BURTON		**CHRISTMAS AT HOME ED. IV**	
93 CLOCK 8600HT	1500	79.00	85.00
93 FAIRY LIGHT 7300HT	3500	39.00	45.00
93 LAMP 7204HT 16"	1000	265.00	265.00
M. DICKINSON		**CHRISTMAS CLASSICS ED. I**	
78 FAIRY LIGHT 7300CV CHRISTMAS MORNING	*	25.00	55.00
78 LAMP 7204CV COLONIAL 16" CHRISTMAS MORN.	YR	125.00	225.00
K. CUNNINGHAM		**CHRISTMAS CLASSICS ED. II**	
79 FAIRY LIGHT 7300NC NATURE'S CHRISTMAS	*	30.00	55.00
79 LAMP 7204NC COLONIAL 16" NATURE'S CHRISTMAS	YR	150.00	225.00
D. JOHNSON		**CHRISTMAS CLASSICS ED. III**	
80 FAIRY LIGHT 7300GH GOING HOME	*	33.00	55.00
80 LAMP 7204GH COLONIAL 16" GOING HOME	YR	165.00	295.00
D. JOHNSON		**CHRISTMAS CLASSICS ED. IV**	
81 FAIRY LIGHT 7300AC ALL IS CALM	*	35.00	58.00
81 LAMP 7204AC COLONIAL 16" ALL IS CALM	YR	175.00	275.00
81 LAMP 7510AC STUDENT 20" ALL IS CALM	*	225.00	275.00
R. SPINDLER		**CHRISTMAS CLASSICS ED. V**	
82 FAIRY LIGHT 7300OC COUNTRY CHRISTMAS	*	35.00	55.00
82 LAMP 7204OC COLONIAL 16" COUNTRY CHRISTMAS	YR	175.00	295.00
82 LAMP 7510OC STUDENT 21" COUNTRY CHRISTMAS	*	225.00	225.00
D. JOHNSON		**CHRISTMAS FANTASY ED. I**	
83 FAIRY LIGHT 7300AI	7500	35.00	58.00
D. JOHNSON		**CHRISTMAS FANTASY ED. II**	
84 FAIRY LIGHT 7300GE	7500	38.00	55.00
84 LAMP 7512GE HURRICANE 10-1/2"	7500	75.00	135.00
D. JOHNSON		**CHRISTMAS FANTASY ED. III**	
85 FAIRY LIGHT 7300WP	7500	38.00	55.00
L. EVERSON		**CHRISTMAS FANTASY ED. IV**	
87 FAIRY LIGHT 7300CV	CL	38.00	55.00
*		**CHRISTMAS LIMITED EDITIONS**	
95 ANGEL 5144TW HEAVENLY BELL 5-3/4"	1900	35.00	38.00
M. DICKINSON		**CHRISTMAS LIMITED EDITIONS**	
86 BASKET 7439JW 9"	5000	100.00	125.00
86 LAMP 9702JW	2500	250.00	295.00
86 VASE 7661JW 9"	5000	95.00	125.00
L. PIPER		**CHRISTMAS LIMITED EDITIONS**	
86 CLOCK 8600XS 6"	5000	59.00	95.00
86 FAIRY LIGHT 7300XS 2 PC.	5000	35.00	75.00
86 LAMP 7204XS 16"	2500	195.00	225.00
M. REYNOLDS		**CHRISTMAS LIMITED EDITIONS**	
92 EGG 5140SD MANGER SCENE ON RUBY 3-1/2"	2500	30.00	45.00
92 EGG 5140SU POINSETTIA ON CRYSTAL IRID. 3-1/2"	2500	30.00	35.00
93 EGG 5140SV WOODS ON WHITE 3-1/2"	2500	35.00	37.00
93 EGG 5140SW ANGEL ON GREEN 3-1/2"	2500	35.00	37.00
94 EGG 5145VG MAGNOLIA ON GOLD 3-1/2"	1500	35.00	40.00
94 EGG 5145VK PARTRIDGE ON RUBY 3-1/2"	1500	35.00	45.00
95 ANGEL 5542TA RADIANT-MUSICAL BASE	900	85.00	85.00
95 EGG 5145TH BOW & HOLLY ON IVORY 3-1/2"	900	35.00	35.00
95 EGG 5145TP CHICKADEE ON GOLD 3-1/2"	900	35.00	38.00
95 PITCHER 2996V2 GOLDEN HOLIDAY PINE CONES	900	79.00	85.00
96 ANGEL 5542QB 7-1/2"	1000	60.00	60.00
96 EGG 5145AC 3-1/2"	1500	38.00	37.00
96 EGG 5145CH HOLLY BERRIES ON GOLD IND. 3-1/2"	1500	38.00	37.00

YR	NAME	LIMIT	ISSUE	TREND
96	EGG 5145QP PARTRIDGE ON SPRUCE 3-1/2"	1500	35.00	37.00
96	FAIRY LIGHT 7300AC 4-1/2"	2000	40.00	45.00
R. SPINDLER		**CHRISTMAS LIMITED EDITIONS**		
96	EGG 5145QV MOONLIT MEADOW ON RUBY 3-1/2"	1500	40.00	40.00
96	FAIRY LIGHT 9401N7 NATIVITY SCENE	1500	49.00	49.00
F. BURTON		**CHRISTMAS STAR "OUR HOME IS BLESSED"**		
95	EGG 5145VT 3-1/2"	1500	45.00	55.00
95	FAIRY LIGHT 7300VT 4-1/2"	1500	45.00	65.00
95	LAMP 2940VT 21" STUDENT	500	275.00	325.00
F. BURTON		**CHRISTMAS STAR "SILENT NIGHT"**		
94	EGG 5145VS ON STAND	1500	45.00	50.00
94	FAIRY LIGHT 7300VS 4-1/2"	1500	45.00	55.00
94	LAMP 7204VS 16"	500	275.00	275.00
F. BURTON		**CHRISTMAS STAR ED. III**		
96	EGG 5145SN 3-1/2"	1750	45.00	45.00
96	FAIRY LIGHT 7300SN 4-1/2"	1750	48.00	48.00
96	LAMP 7204SN 16"	750	275.00	260.00
*			**CLYDESDALE**	
83	BASKET 7237XA 7"	*	14.25	110.00
83	FAIRY LIGHT 7300XA	*	9.75	125.00
83	GINGER JAR 7488XA	*	12.50	75.00
83	LAMP HAMMERED BRASS7204XA 16"	*	70.00	250.00
83	LAMP HURRICANE ELECTRIFIED 7311XA 11"	*	43.00	195.00
83	PLATE 7418XA 8" W/STAND	*	12.50	80.00
83	VASE 7254XA 4 1/2"	*	9.75	45.00
83	VASE 7254XA 7"	*	13.75	58.00
*			**COLLECTIBLE EGGS EDITIONS**	
98	COLLECTIBLE EGGS	3000	50.00	50.00
F. BURTON		**COLLECTIBLE EGGS EDITIONS**		
94	EGG 5140A7 ENAMELED FLOWERS/BLUE	2500	38.00	55.00
S. JACKSON		**COLLECTIBLE EGGS EDITIONS**		
94	EGG 5140A2 TULIPS/SEA MIST	2500	33.00	35.00
94	EGG 5140A3 VIOLETS/MILK PEARL	2500	33.00	35.00
94	EGG 5140A5 SPRING LANDSCAPE/OPAL	2500	33.00	35.00
K. PLAUCHE		**COLLECTIBLE EGGS EDITIONS**		
93	EGG 5140D2 SCROLLING FLORAL/GRN	2500	30.00	32.00
93	EGG 5140D8 W/GOLD ON PLUM	2500	35.00	42.00
94	EGG 5140A6 METALLIC FLORAL/PLUM	2500	33.00	50.00
97	EGG DOLPHIN/FAVRENE HANDPAINTED & SANDCARVED	2500	65.00	70.00
97	EGG LIGHTHOUSE/FRENCH OPALESCENT IRIDIZED	2500	45.00	45.00
97	EGG VIOLAS/DUSTY ROSE	2500	39.00	39.00
M. REYNOLDS		**COLLECTIBLE EGGS EDITIONS**		
91	EGG 5140C9 PARTRIDGE	1500	30.00	35.00
91	EGG 5140E7 SKATER	1500	30.00	35.00
91	EGG 5140H7 WHITE SCENE	1500	30.00	35.00
91	EGG 5140N9 POINSETTIAS	1500	30.00	35.00
91	EGG 5140Q9 GOLD DESIGN	1500	30.00	35.00
91	EGG 5140X9 SHELL	1500	35.00	65.00
91	EGG 5140Z7 SNOW SCENE	1500	30.00	30.00
92	EGG 51407U CROQUET	2500	30.00	45.00
92	EGG 51407V FLORAL & BRONZE	2500	30.00	32.00
92	EGG 51407W BUTTERFLIES	2500	30.00	32.00
92	EGG 51407Y IRIS	2500	30.00	32.00
92	EGG 51407Y PINK FLORAL	2500	30.00	32.00
92	EGG 51407Z UNICORN	2500	30.00	40.00
93	EGG 5140D1 FUCHSIA FLORAL/WHITE	2500	30.00	32.00
93	EGG 5140D3 W/GOLD ON RUBY	2500	30.00	37.00
93	EGG 5140D4 SEA GULLS/OCEAN BLUE	2500	30.00	35.00
93	EGG 5140D5 COTTAGE/WHITE OPAL	2500	30.00	35.00
93	EGG 5140D6 PAISLEY/DUSTY ROSE	2500	30.00	35.00
93	EGG 5140ZN SANDCARVED/BL	1500	35.00	50.00
94	EGG 5140A1 GOLD	2500	33.00	37.00
95	EGG 5145S2 SCROLLS/BLACK	2500	33.00	38.00
95	EGG 5145S3 SCENE/WHITE	2500	33.00	45.00
95	EGG 5145S4 FLORAL/WHITE	2500	33.00	35.00
95	EGG 5145S5 FLORAL/GREEN	2500	33.00	38.00
95	EGG 5145S6 FLORAL/BLUE	2500	33.00	40.00
95	EGG 5145S7 FLORAL/GOLD	2500	33.00	38.00
95	EGG 5145S8 HUMMINGBIRD/DUSTY ROSE	2500	35.00	45.00
96	EGG 5145F2 HUMMINGBIRD/FRENCH OPAL	2500	38.00	45.00
96	EGG 5145F5 LAKE SCENE	2500	38.00	37.00
96	EGG 5145F6 JEWELED	2500	38.00	40.00
97	EGG DAISY/MISTY BLUE	2500	45.00	45.00
97	EGG ROSES/IVORY SANDBLASTED	2500	39.00	39.00
97	EGG, IRIS/SEAMIST GREEN	2500	45.00	45.00
R. SPINDLER		**COLLECTIBLE EGGS EDITIONS**		
96	EGG 5145F1 HONEYSUCKLE/DUSTY ROSE	2500	38.00	37.00
96	EGG 5145F3 BUTTERFLIES	2500	38.00	40.00
96	EGG 5145F4 MORNING GLORIES	2500	38.00	37.00
96	EGG 5145F7 FISH/SPRUCE	2500	38.00	45.00
97	EGG ROOSTER/SPRUCE	2500	39.00	39.00
*			**CONNOISSEUR COLLECTION**	
83	BASKET 6432IM 9"	1000	75.00	125.00
83	CRUET/STOPPER 6462IM	1000	75.00	150.00

YR	NAME	LIMIT	ISSUE	TREND
83	EPERGNE 7605BR 5 PC. SET BURMESE	500	200.00	500.00
83	VASE 7659GJ 7"	1500	50.00	135.00
84	BASKET 3134PV 10"	1250	85.00	175.00
84	CANDY BOX 9394UE 3 PC. W/COVER	1250	75.00	125.00
84	CANE 5090PV 18"	YR	35.00	125.00
84	HAT 3193PV SPIRAL CC 8"	1500	*	175.00
84	VASE 9458AV SWAN 8"	1500	65.00	150.00
85	EPERGNE 809GO 4 PC. SET 4809GO	1000	95.00	225.00
85	PUNCH SET 3712GO 14 PC.	500	250.00	475.00
85	VASE 8802LY 12"	800	150.00	295.00
86	BASKET 7438JD	1500	49.00	125.00
86	BOUDOIR LAMP 7802CZ	750	145.00	225.00
86	CRUET/STOPPER 7863CZ	1000	75.00	120.00
86	HANDLED URN 3194ZS 13"	1000	185.00	375.00
86	HANDLED VASE 3190KF 7"	1000	100.00	200.00
86	TOP HAT BASKET, 7438JD, TEAL/MILK OVERLAY 9	1500	49.00	175.00
86	VANITY SET 3104BI 4 PC.	1000	125.00	350.00
86	VASE, 10 1/2" DANIELLE 8812JY	1000	95.00	200.00
88	BASKET 3132OT	2500	65.00	95.00
88	PITCHER 2065ZC	3500	60.00	85.00
88	VASE 2556ZI TULIP 6"	3500	50.00	95.00
89	EPERGNE 7605RE 5 PC. SET	2000	250.00	475.00
89	PITCHER 7060RE	2500	55.00	75.00
89	VASE 6453RG VASA MURRHINA 8"	2000	65.00	130.00
89	VASE 8354RE	2500	45.00	90.00
90	BASKET 7732QD 5-1/2"	YR	58.00	125.00
90	LAMP 9308RB 20"	YR	250.00	350.00
90	VASE 7790RB 6"	YR	50.00	95.00
90	VASE 7791RB 6-1/2"	YR	45.00	100.00
90	VASE 7792QD 9"	YR	75.00	130.00
91	CANDY BOX 9394FN 3 PC.	1000	90.00	150.00
91	FISH PAPERWEIGHT 5193RE	2000	30.00	55.00
91	LAMP 6701RB 20"	500	275.00	425.00
93	OWL 5258FN 6"	1500	95.00	115.00

D. BARBOUR   **CONNOISSEUR COLLECTION**

YR	NAME	LIMIT	ISSUE	TREND
85	VASE 8808SB 7-1/2"	950	135.00	250.00
86	LAMP 7400SB 20"	500	350.00	595.00
87	VASE 1796BY 7-1/4"	950	95.00	125.00

F. BURTON   **CONNOISSEUR COLLECTION**

YR	NAME	LIMIT	ISSUE	TREND
91	VASE 8812G1	850	125.00	170.00
92	COVERED BOX 6080RH	1250	95.00	130.00
92	VASE 8817QZ 8"	750	150.00	200.00
93	LAMP 2780CX SPRING WOODS REVERSE	500	590.00	650.00
93	PERFUME/STOPPER 1710R5	1250	95.00	95.00
94	CLOCK 8691JV 4-1/2"	850	150.00	125.00
94	LAMP 5582JB HUMMINGBIRD REVERSE	300	590.00	850.00
94	PITCHER 2729JI LATTICE 10"	750	165.00	200.00
95	LAMP 5486VU BUTTEFLY 21"	300	595.00	625.00
96	LAMP 6805EA	400	750.00	800.00
96	PITCHER 2960WQ DRAGON FLY 8"	1250	165.00	165.00

R. DELANEY   **CONNOISSEUR COLLECTION**

YR	NAME	LIMIT	ISSUE	TREND
83	VASE 7542FJ OVAL 4-1/2"	2000	33.00	125.00
86	VASE 8812JY DANIELLE 10-1/2"	1000	95.00	210.00

L. EVERSON   **CONNOISSEUR COLLECTION**

YR	NAME	LIMIT	ISSUE	TREND
84	VASE 9651HD 9"	750	75.00	150.00
85	BASKET 7634EB 8-1/2"	1250	95.00	150.00
85	LAMP 7602EB 22"	350	300.00	525.00
85	VASE 8806GC 7-1/2"	1000	125.00	125.00
86	VASE 8812ET MISTY MORNING 10-1/2"	1000	95.00	185.00
87	PITCHER 9468QY 8"	950	85.00	100.00
88	CANDY 6080ZX	2000	95.00	125.00
89	BASKET 1330TE 7"	2500	85.00	95.00
89	CANDY BOX 2085TM W/COVER	2500	85.00	85.00
89	LAMP 9308TT 21"	1000	250.00	350.00
90	BASKET 7731QH 7"	YR	75.00	150.00
90	CRUET/STOPPER 7701QJ	YR	85.00	175.00
90	EPERGNE 7202QJ 2 PC. SET	YR	125.00	200.00
90	LAMP 7412QH 21"	YR	295.00	450.00
90	WATER SET 7700QH 7 PC.	YR	275.00	450.00
91	VASE 7252QH 7-1/2"	1500	65.00	150.00
92	VASE 5541QH 6-1/2"	1500	45.00	75.00

K. PLAUCHE   **CONNOISSEUR COLLECTION**

YR	NAME	LIMIT	ISSUE	TREND
96	BOX 6584CD W/LID-MELON	1250	150.00	150.00

M. REYNOLDS   **CONNOISSEUR COLLECTION**

YR	NAME	LIMIT	ISSUE	TREND
91	BASKET 4647MD	1500	64.00	70.00
91	VASE 8812FQ	850	125.00	160.00
92	PITCHER 1211RW 9"	950	110.00	125.00
92	PITCHER 5531QP 4-1/2"	1500	65.00	75.00
92	VASE 1684RP	950	110.00	155.00
93	AMPHORA W/STAND 2748FW	850	285.00	325.00
93	BOWL 2747RX RUBY STRETCH W/GOLD SCROLLS	1250	95.00	95.00
93	VASE 7661P4 GOLD LEAVES 9"	950	175.00	210.00
93	VASE 8805X3	950	125.00	125.00
94	VASE 2743JP 7"	850	185.00	200.00
94	VASE 2744JK PLUM OPAL. 8"	750	165.00	195.00

YR NAME	LIMIT	ISSUE	TREND
94 VASE 3161JQ GOLD 11"	750	175.00	125.00
95 AMPHORA W/STAND 2947US 10-1/4"	890	195.00	245.00
95 GINGER JAR 2950VN 3 PC. 8-1/2"	790	275.00	350.00
95 PITCHER 2796ZM 9-1/2"	490	250.00	250.00
95 VASE 7691WF 7"	890	125.00	150.00
96 VASE 2782DD 11"	1250	195.00	195.00
96 VASE 3254QJ QUEEN'S BIRD 11"	1150	250.00	275.00
96 VASE 9855EV	1150	195.00	195.00
REYNOLDS/DELANEY		**CONNOISSEUR COLLECTION**	
92 BOWL, 14" CRANBERRY CAMEO SANDCARVED 7727JC	500	390.00	400.00
94 BOWL 7727JC 14" BRANBERRY CAMEO	500	390.00	350.00
R. SPINDLER		**CONNOISSEUR COLLECTION**	
96 VASE 9866TR TROUT 8"	1350	135.00	165.00
M. YATES		**CONNOISSEUR COLLECTION**	
83 VASE 7661LJ 9"	850	75.00	200.00
84 VASE 7661MD 9"	750	125.00	200.00
*		**CRANBERRY OPALESCENT**	
98 HEART OPTIC BOX, 4 1/2"	TL	125.00	125.00
98 HEART OPTIC FAIRY LIGHT, 5"	TL	65.00	65.00
98 HEART OPTIC VASE, 5"	TL	40.00	40.00
F. BURTON		**DESIGNER SERIES**	
97 BELL 7" FOREST COTTAGE	2500	59.00	59.00
K. PLAUCHE		**DESIGNER SERIES**	
97 BELL 6 1/2" ROSES ON RIBBONS	2500	59.00	59.00
M. REYNOLDS		**DESIGNER SERIES**	
97 BELL 6" BUTTERFLIES	2500	59.00	59.00
R. SPINDLER		**DESIGNER SERIES**	
97 BELL 6 3/4" FEATHERS	2500	59.00	59.00
FINN		**DOWN HOME**	
83 LAMP 7209FV	300	*	475.00
M. REYNOLDS		**EASTER LIMITED EDITIONS**	
95 FAIRY LIGHT 8405YZ	CL	49.00	45.00
R. SPINDLER		**EASTER LIMITED EDITIONS**	
97 COVERED HEN & EGG PLATE	950	115.00	135.00
*		**FAMILY SIGNATURE SERIES**	
93 VASE 2752RN ALPINE THISTLE/RUBY CARNIVAL 9"	CL	105.00	125.00
94 BASKET 1217AO AUTUMN GOLD OPALESCENT 11"	CL	70.00	75.00
94 BASKET 2779RN RUBY CARNIVAL 8-1/2"	CL	65.00	70.00
94 VASE 1216EH FUCHSIA 10"	CL	95.00	90.00
95 CANDY 2970RN RED CARNIVAL W/COVER 9"	CL	65.00	75.00
95 SHOWCASE DEALER ITEM 3558CR	CL	75.00	95.00
96 SHOWCASE DEALER ITEM 9550DC FAN VASE 8"	CL	75.00	80.00
96 VASE 5357TE 8-1/2"	*	75.00	75.00
F. BURTON		**FAMILY SIGNATURE SERIES**	
93 VASE 1786PV VINTAGE ON PLUM 10"	CL	80.00	93.00
94 PITCHER 1568CW CRANBERRY 6-1/2"	CL	85.00	95.00
94 VASE 1559CW PANSIES ON CRANBERRY 9-1/2"	CL	95.00	95.00
95 PITCHER 1566FS THISTLE 9-1/2"	CL	125.00	125.00
95 VASE 1567CW 7"	CL	75.00	70.00
95 VASE 1649KG GOLDEN FLAX ON COBALT 9-1/2"	CL	95.00	110.00
96 BASKET 3076KT 8"	CL	85.00	95.00
97 BASKET 9" SWEETBRIAR ON PLUM ONERLAY	*	85.00	85.00
K. PLAUCHE		**FAMILY SIGNATURE SERIES**	
96 VASE 4759SE MAGNOLIA & BERRY ON SPRUCE 10"	OP	80.00	80.00
M. REYNOLDS		**FAMILY SIGNATURE SERIES**	
93 BASKET 6730PJ LILACS 8-1/2"	YR	65.00	70.00
93 VASE 1640C1 CRANBERRY 11"	CL	110.00	115.00
93 VASE 7661Z8 COTTAGE SCENE 9"	CL	90.00	118.00
94 BASKET 2738PJ LILACS 7-1/2"	CL	65.00	65.00
94 BASKET 2787ST STIEGEL GREEN 8"	CL	60.00	65.00
94 CANDY 7380AW W/COVER AUTUMN LEAVES 9-1/2"	CL	60.00	60.00
95 BASKET 1131DX TRELLIS 8-1/2"	CL	85.00	85.00
95 BASKET 1135JE CORALENE FLORAL 9-1/2"	CL	75.00	85.00
96 PITCHER 3065DP 6-1/2"	CL	70.00	70.00
97 FAIRY LIGHT 7 1/2" HYDRANGEAS ON TOPAZ	*	125.00	125.00
97 PITCHER 7 1/2" IRISES ON MISTY BLUE	*	85.00	85.00
97 VASE 6" FIELD FLOWERS ON CHAMP. SATIN	*	55.00	55.00
98 LYNN FENTON IRISES ON MISTY BLUE CLOCK, 4 1/2"	TL	95.00	95.00
98 NANCY & GEORGE FENTON FLORAL INTERLUDE VASE	TL	99.00	99.00
98 TOM FENTON TRELLIS BASKET, 9 1/2"	TL	95.00	95.00
R. SPINDLER		**FAMILY SIGNATURE SERIES**	
95 VASE 1554S9 SUMMER GARDEN ON SPRUCE 9"	CL	85.00	85.00
96 BASKET 3127NG 7"	OP	75.00	85.00
96 VASE 1563PD FEATHER 11"	CL	95.00	95.00
97 PITCHER 8 1/2" MEADOW BEAUTY FLORAL	*	95.00	95.00
97 VASE 8" MEDALLION COLLECT. FLORAL ON BLACK	*	75.00	70.00
98 SHELLY FENTON TOPAZ BASKET, 10 1/2"	TL	125.00	125.00
F. BURTON		**GLASS MESSENGER**	
98 MORNING GLORY ON BURMESE, GLASS MESSENGER	TL	99.00	99.00
*		**HEART OPTIC COLLECTION**	
97 HAT BASKET 7"	*	79.00	79.00
97 PITCHER 6 1/2" CRANBERRY OPALESCENT	*	89.00	89.00
97 PUFF BOX 4"	*	79.00	79.00

YR	NAME	LIMIT	ISSUE	TREND
*			**HISTORIC COLLECTION**	
88	BANANA BOWL A3720UP 12"	*	33.00	70.00
88	BASKET 9134TO BUTTERFLY & BERRY	*	25.00	65.00
88	BASKET 9435TO	*	30.00	65.00
88	BASKET 9436TO	*	33.00	70.00
88	BASKET A3335UO W/LOOPED HANDLE	*	23.00	75.00
88	BASKET A3830UO 10"	*	30.00	75.00
88	BASKET A3834UP 6-1/2"	*	16.50	45.00
88	BONBON A3937UO W/HANDLES	*	*	25.00
88	BOWL 8428TO FANTAIL FOOTED	*	28.00	40.00
88	BOWL 9425TO	*	23.00	35.00
88	BUTTERFLY 5171TO ON STAND	*	15.00	35.00
88	CRUET W/STOPPER A3863UP 6-1/2"	*	35.00	100.00
88	EPERGNE 4801TO 4 PC.	*	75.00	125.00
88	EPERGNE A3701UP 4 PC. 10"	*	55.00	195.00
88	EPERGNE A3801UO 4 PC. MINI	*	48.00	75.00
88	HAT BUTTERFLY & BERRY 9495TO	*	12.50	35.00
88	KITCHEN SET 8603TO 4 PC.	*	90.00	90.00
88	LAMP 9101TO 24"	*	200.00	300.00
88	LAMP A3308UO GONE W/THE WIND 25"	*	200.00	225.00
88	NUT DISH 8442TO 3 TOED	*	17.50	30.00
88	PITCHER 52 OZ. & 12" BOWL A3000UO	*	78.00	95.00
88	PUNCH SET A3712UP 14 PC.	*	275.00	400.00
88	ROSE BOWL 8454TO DRAPERY FOOTED	*	24.00	45.00
88	ROSE BOWL A3854UO 4-1/2"	*	12.50	30.00
88	ROSE BOWL A3861UP 4-1/4"	*	12.50	32.00
88	TOOTHPICK HOLDER A3795UP 2-3/4"	*	6.50	18.00
88	VASE A3362UO JACK IN THE PULPIT 6-1/2"	*	23.00	40.00
88	WATER SET 3407TO 7 PC. CACTUS	*	140.00	200.00
88	WATER SET A3908UP 7 PC.	*	99.00	250.00
89	BASKET 1435XC 5"	*	37.00	75.00
89	BASKET 1830XC 5-1/2"	*	37.00	69.00
89	BASKET 3138XC 7"	*	40.00	70.00
89	BASKET 3334XC 7"	*	25.00	50.00
89	BASKET 3834XC 4-1/2"	*	17.50	30.00
89	BASKET 8330XC 7"	*	25.00	45.00
89	BASKET 9638XC	*	23.00	45.00
89	BOWL 2323XC 10"	*	50.00	50.00
89	BOWL 9027XC	*	30.00	30.00
89	BUTTER 9580XC W/COVER	*	29.00	55.00
89	COMPORT 8234XC	*	20.00	40.00
89	CREAMER 1461XC	*	30.00	40.00
89	CRUET W/STOPPER 1865XC	*	49.00	95.00
89	CRUET W/STOPPER 3863XC 6-1/2"	*	35.00	65.00
89	EPERGNE 4801XC 4 PC.	*	75.00	125.00
89	FAIRY LIGHT 1803XC 3 PC.	*	85.00	150.00
89	FAIRY LIGHT 3608XC	*	16.50	45.00
89	LAMP 1413XC 22"	*	250.00	300.00
89	LAMP 3313XC STUDENT 21"	*	200.00	225.00
89	PUNCH SET 3712XC 14 PC	*	275.00	325.00
89	TOP HAT 1492XC	*	25.00	35.00
89	VASE 1353XC 10"	*	38.00	95.00
89	WATER SET 1404XC 7 PC.	*	200.00	290.00
89	WATER SET 3908XC 7 PC.	*	100.00	150.00
90	BASKET 1830BX 5-1/2"	*	37.00	60.00
90	BASKET 1832BX 7"	*	40.00	65.00
90	BASKET 8437BX	*	27.00	40.00
90	BOWL 1825BX W/BRIDE'S BASKET 10"	*	125.00	170.00
90	BOWL 1826BX 10"	*	55.00	40.00
90	BOWL 8229BX 10"	*	33.00	37.00
90	CANDY 8489BX W/COVER 7"	*	29.00	40.00
90	CRUET W/STOPPER 1860BX 7-1/2"	*	49.00	90.00
90	EPERGNE 4801BX 4 PC.	*	75.00	125.00
90	FENTON LOGO 9799BX 3" X 5"	*	15.00	25.00
90	LAMP 1800BX 22"	*	250.00	300.00
90	LAMP 1801BX 22"	*	250.00	325.00
90	ROSE BOWL 8453BX	*	16.50	25.00
90	TABLE SET 9700BX 4 PC. MINI	*	53.00	75.00
90	VASE 1853BX 10"	*	40.00	70.00
90	VASE 8458BX 10"	*	17.00	20.00
90	VASE 9651BX 3-1/2"	*	13.50	20.00
90	WATER SET 1802BX 7 PC.	*	200.00	275.00
91	BASKET 4617DT 7"	*	30.00	40.00
91	BASKET 4618DT 10"	*	33.00	45.00
91	BASKET 4632BO 7" WILDFLOWER	*	29.00	35.00
91	BASKET 4633BO 6"	*	25.00	30.00
91	BASKET 4646DT	*	29.00	40.00
91	BOWL 4619DT 10"	*	34.00	40.00
91	BOWL 4627BO 10-1/4"	*	35.00	35.00
91	BOX 4679DT	*	34.00	50.00
91	BUTTER 8680DT W/COVER	*	35.00	45.00
91	CANDLESTICKS 4672BO 3-1/2"	*	33.00	40.00
91	COMPORT 4693BO 6-1/2"	*	23.00	30.00
91	CUSPIDOR 4643DT	*	23.00	30.00
91	FENTON LOGO 9799DT 2-3/4" X 5"	*	20.00	25.00

YR	NAME	LIMIT	ISSUE	TREND
91	LAMP 4603BO 15"	*	195.00	225.00
91	LAMP 4603DT 15"	*	195.00	200.00
91	LAMP 4605BO/JU 20"	*	215.00	225.00
91	OWL 5254DT	*	30.00	35.00
91	PUNCH BOWL SET 4601BO 14 PC.	*	285.00	425.00
91	PUNCH SET 4601DT 14 PC.	*	300.00	300.00
91	TOOTHPICK HOLDER 4644DT	*	10.00	12.00
91	URN W/COVER 4602BO/JU	*	65.00	90.00
91	VASE 4651JO 10"	*	25.00	30.00
91	VASE 4653BO 9"	*	25.00	30.00
91	WATER SET 4609DT 5 PC.	*	88.00	95.00
92	BASKET 2725XV 7"	*	28.00	28.00
92	BASKET 2728XV 4"	*	20.00	20.00
92	BASKET 3077XV 11"	*	50.00	70.00
92	BASKET 3335GP	*	35.00	47.00
92	BASKET 5481GF 10-1/2"	*	49.00	60.00
92	BASKET 5483GF 10-1/2"	*	89.00	89.00
92	BOWL 3983XV 12"	*	35.00	38.00
92	BOWL 5482GF 9-1/2"	*	65.00	65.00
92	BOX 4600GP W/COVER	*	85.00	125.00
92	CANDLESTICK 5526GF 4"	*	59.00	59.00
92	CANDLESTICKS 3674XV 6"	*	33.00	33.00
92	CANDY BOX 3784XV	*	38.00	38.00
92	CREAMER 2726XV 4"	*	23.00	23.00
92	CRUET W/STOPPER 3863GP	*	45.00	75.00
92	EPERGNE 3701XV 4 PC.	*	99.00	125.00
92	EPERGNE 4801GP 4PC.	*	99.00	125.00
92	FENTON LOGO 9799XV	*	20.00	25.00
92	LAMP 1801XV 21"	*	295.00	320.00
92	LAMP 3313GP 21"	*	235.00	270.00
92	OWL 5252GP 7"	*	45.00	45.00
92	PITCHER 1875XV 8-1/2"	*	75.00	90.00
92	PUNCH CUP 4642XV	*	13.00	13.00
92	PUNCH SET 4601XV 14 PC.	*	315.00	315.00
92	TUMBLER 1876XV	*	25.00	25.00
92	TUMBLER 2727XV MINI 2"	*	9.50	10.00
92	TUMBLER 3949GP	*	12.50	13.00
92	VASE 2056XV 5"	*	40.00	40.00
92	VASE 3183XV 6-1/2"	*	25.00	50.00
92	VASE 3355GP 6"	*	27.00	45.00
92	VASE 5479GF 6"	*	35.00	38.00
92	VASE 5480GF 12"	*	45.00	35.00
92	WATER SET 1870XV 5 PC.	*	175.00	190.00
92	WATER SET 2730XV 5 PC.	*	60.00	65.00
92	WATER SET 3908GP 5 PC.	*	99.00	110.00
93	BASKET 3337RV 7"	OP	30.00	37.00
93	BASKET 3834RV 4-1/2"	OP	25.00	30.00
93	BASKET 9435XV DRAPERY	OP	45.00	47.00
93	BOWL 2754XV SWAN	OP	45.00	50.00
93	CANDLESTICKS 5172XV SWAN	OP	45.00	45.00
93	CANDY 3784RV W/COVER FOOTED	OP	38.00	38.00
93	CRUET W/STOPPER 3863RV 6-1/2"	OP	48.00	65.00
93	EPERGNE 3701RV 10" 4 PC.	CL	99.00	123.00
93	EPERGNE 3801XV MINI HOBNAIL	CL	50.00	60.00
93	FENTON LOGO 9799RV 2-3/4" X 5"	OP	20.00	25.00
93	LAMP 3313RV STUDENT W/PRISMS 21"	OP	250.00	325.00
93	LAMP 9101XV POPPY GONE W/THE WIND	OP	225.00	325.00
93	PITCHER 3764RV 54 OZ.	OP	59.00	65.00
93	PUNCH SET 3712RV 14 PC.	OP	275.00	300.00
93	ROSE BOWL 8454XV DRAPERY	OP	25.00	35.00
93	SWAN 5127XV	OP	15.00	18.00
93	TUMBLER 3949RV 9 OZ.	OP	12.50	15.00
93	VASE 3356RV JACK IN THE PULPIT 7-1/2"	OP	28.00	48.00
93	VASE 3854RV 4-1/2"	OP	17.50	22.00
93	WATER SET 3908RV 5 PC.	OP	109.00	130.00
94	BASKET 5551SS FOOTED 9"	OP	40.00	40.00
94	BASKET 5555SS FOOTED 7"	OP	30.00	35.00
94	BOWL 2773SS 8"	OP	38.00	38.00
94	BOWL 2799SS W/COVER-LION	OP	35.00	50.00
94	CANDLESTICKS 5526SS 4"	OP	45.00	45.00
94	CANDY COVER 4381ST 5-1/2"	OP	55.00	55.00
94	COMPORT 5554SS 5-1/4"	OP	30.00	30.00
94	EPERGNE 4802SS 2 PC.	OP	65.00	95.00
94	EPERGNE 7601SS 5 PC. SET	OP	175.00	275.00
94	FENTON LOGO 9799SS 5"	OP	25.00	28.00
94	GOBLET 5561SS 6-1/2"	OP	23.00	23.00
94	JUG 5562SS 8"	OP	60.00	60.00
94	ROSE BOWL 2759SS 3-1/2"	OP	25.00	25.00
94	ROSE BOWL 2759ST 3-1/2"	OP	30.00	35.00
94	SPARROW 5259ST 5"	OP	30.00	35.00
94	URN W/COVER 4602SS	OP	65.00	75.00
94	VASE 5553SS JACK IN THE PULPIT 7"	OP	30.00	40.00
94	VASE 5559SS HANDKERCHIEF 8"	OP	30.00	30.00
94	VASE 5559ST 8"	*	40.00	40.00
94	VASE 5559ST HANKERCHIEF 8"	OP	30.00	30.00

YR	NAME	LIMIT	ISSUE	TREND
94	WATER SET 5560SS 5 PC.	OP	150.00	150.00
95	BASKET 1142JE FOOTED 7"	OP	38.00	38.00
95	FENTON LOGO 9499KA OVAL 5"	OP	25.00	29.00
95	LAMP 7502UQ 33" DAYBREAK PILLAR	*	495.00	795.00
95	PITCHER 2968UN 10"	*	175.00	185.00
95	TOP HAT 1137JE 4-1/2"	OP	50.00	49.50
95	TUMBLER 9049KA 4-1/2"	OP	20.00	20.00
95	VASE 1136JE FAN 6"	OP	50.00	49.50
95	VASE 1140JE W/COLBALT BASE	OP	60.00	60.00
95	VASE 2767JE 4-1/2"	OP	33.00	33.00
95	VASE 2955UU 9"	*	150.00	180.00
95	WATER SET 9001KA 5 PC.	OP	135.00	175.00
96	BASKET 4833TG 6"	*	25.00	28.00
96	BASKET 4835TG 9-1/2"	*	50.00	65.00
96	COMPORT 4854TG 6-1/2"	*	35.00	35.00
96	COMPORT 8231XC	*	20.00	20.00
96	CRUET W/STOPPER 7701TE 7"	*	85.00	90.00
96	EPERGNE 4806TG MINI 4-1/2"	*	35.00	35.00
96	EPERGNE 4808TG 10"	*	115.00	125.00
96	LAMP 1705TE 24"	*	395.00	395.00
96	LOGO 9499TG 2 1/2"	*	25.00	25.00
96	PITCHER 5367TE 6-1/2"	*	75.00	75.00
96	VASE 1146TE 7"	*	50.00	50.00
96	VASE 1795TE 11"	*	85.00	85.00
97	BASKET 8 1/2" HOBNAIL	*	45.00	45.00
97	BELL 6 1/2" BEAUTY	*	25.00	25.00
97	EPERGNE 11 1/2" 5 PC.	*	250.00	250.00
97	LOGO 3 1/2" OVAL	*	28.00	28.00
97	NUT DISH 5" SCROLL	*	29.00	29.00
97	PUNCH CUPS	*	20.00	20.00
97	PUNCH SET W/8 CUPS HEART & HOBSTAR	*	350.00	350.00
97	SLIPPER 6" ROSE	*	15.00	15.00
97	VASE 6 1/2" ATLANTIS	*	50.00	50.00
97	VASE 8 1/2" WILDROSE	*	45.00	45.00
98	SEA GREEN SATIN	TL	*	N/A

F. BURTON — HISTORIC COLLECTION

YR	NAME	LIMIT	ISSUE	TREND
98	ROYAL PURPLE BASKET, 8"	2950	115.00	115.00
98	ROYAL PURPLE FAIRY LIGHT, 7 1/2"	2950	175.00	175.00
98	ROYAL PURPLE LAMP, 20"	1450	350.00	350.00
98	ROYAL PURPLE PERFUME, 6 1/2"	2950	125.00	125.00
98	ROYAL PURPLE VASE, 9 1/2"	2950	125.00	125.00

M. REYNOLDS — HISTORIC COLLECTION

YR	NAME	LIMIT	ISSUE	TREND
95	BASKET 2932UL 8"	750	135.00	165.00
95	BOWL 2909UK 10-1/4"	790	150.00	150.00
96	BASKET 1531MS 8"	1250	95.00	95.00
96	VASE 1689MS HUMMINGBIRD 9-1/2"	1250	95.00	95.00
96	VASE 2750MS 8"	1250	85.00	85.00
97	BASKET 8"	*	80.00	80.00
97	FAIRY LIGHT 3 PC.	*	125.00	125.00
97	LAMP W/ PRISMS	*	275.00	275.00
97	PITCHER 6 1/2"	*	55.00	55.00
97	VASE 9 1/2"	*	85.00	85.00
98	FLORAL INTERLUDE ON SEA GREEN SATIN	TL	*	N/A

R. SPINDLER — HISTORIC COLLECTION

YR	NAME	LIMIT	ISSUE	TREND
96	LAMP 5581MD 21"	500	495.00	495.00
96	PITCHER 1671MD 7-1/2"	1250	95.00	95.00
96	SHOWCASE DEALER 7603MD	1250	125.00	125.00

* — KATJA

YR	NAME	LIMIT	ISSUE	TREND
83	BOTTLE K7751KN SMALL	*	*	45.00
83	BOTTLE K7753KN LARGE	*	*	85.00
83	BOTTLE K7754KE SMALL BLOWN	*	*	45.00
83	BOTTLE K7761KN SMALL BLOWN	*	*	45.00
83	BOTTLE K7761KO SMALL BLOWN	*	*	45.00
83	BOTTLE K7762KN MEDIUM	*	*	65.00
83	BOTTLE K7762KO MEDIUM BLOWN	*	*	65.00
83	BOTTLE K7763KN LARGE	*	*	85.00
83	BOTTLE K7763KO LARGE BLOWN	*	*	85.00
83	BOTTLE K7765KN MEDIUM	*	*	65.00
83	CUP LOVING GOOD LUCK	*	*	50.00
83	CYLINDER K7743KN BLOWN	*	*	50.00
83	CYLINDER K7743KN SMALL	*	*	50.00
83	CYLINDER K7744KN MEDIUM	*	*	55.00

M. DICKINSON — LIGHTHOUSE POINT

YR	NAME	LIMIT	ISSUE	TREND
83	LAMP 7503LT STUDENT 23 1/2"	300	350.00	650.00
83	LAMP 7507LT LIGHTHOUSE POINT 25 1/2"	300	450.00	750.00

* — LOVES ME, LOVES ME NOT

YR	NAME	LIMIT	ISSUE	TREND
94	BASKET, OVAL, 7 1/2" 8637RY	TL	59.00	65.00

M. REYNOLDS — MARY GREGORY SERIES

YR	NAME	LIMIT	ISSUE	TREND
94	BASKET 8637RY OVAL 7-1/2"	CL	59.00	65.00
95	BASKET 8637RG OVAL 7-1/2"	CL	65.00	85.00
95	EGG 5145RG 4" RUBY ON STAND	CL	38.00	50.00
96	HAT BASKET 1532RK CRANBERRY 6-1/2"	2000	95.00	95.00
96	VASE 1554VP 9"	1500	135.00	135.00
97	BASKET 8"	1500	115.00	125.00
97	FAIRY LIGHT 5"	1500	79.00	85.00

YR	NAME	LIMIT	ISSUE	TREND
97	GUEST SET 7" CRANBERRY	1500	189.00	200.00
98	MARY GREGORY BASKET, 11 1/2"	1950	150.00	150.00
98	MARY GREGORY PERFUME, 5 1/2"	1950	115.00	115.00
98	MARY GREGORY PITCHER, 6 1/2"	1950	125.00	125.00
*				MINIATURES
96	EPERGNE 4806TG 4-1/2"	CL	35.00	35.00
96	PUNCH BOWL & CUPS 6800DZ 3-3/4" MINI	CL	59.00	59.00
97	PUNCH BOWL & CUPS 3 3/4" SEAMIST GREEN	*	59.00	59.00
98	MINIATURE EPERGNE, 4 1/2"	TL	65.00	65.00
98	MINIATURE PUNCH SET, 5 PC.	TL	75.00	75.00
98	MINIATURE WATER SET, 5 PC.	TL	85.00	85.00
*				MOUTHBLOWN EGGS
94	EGG 5031FU	YR	75.00	75.00
94	EGG 5031FV	YR	75.00	75.00
95	EGG 5031YW	YR	75.00	75.00
95	EGG 5031YX	YR	75.00	75.00
F. BURTON				MOUTHBLOWN EGGS
92	EGG 5031Q2 PETAL PINK IRID. 5"	CL	65.00	70.00
92	EGG 5031Q3 SEAMIST GREEN IRID. 5"	CL	65.00	70.00
94	EGG 5031FV BLUE 5"	CL	75.00	85.00
96	EGG 1642JM CRANBERRY-BLUE BIRD 5"	CL	95.00	95.00
M. REYNOLDS				MOUTHBLOWN EGGS
91	EGG 5030QB MOTHER OF PEARL 3-1/2"	CL	49.00	55.00
91	EGG 5031WD MOTHER OF PEARL 4-1/2"	CL	59.00	65.00
93	EGG 5031WE PLUM 5"	CL	69.00	85.00
93	EGG 5031WJ OCEAN BLUE 5"	CL	69.00	85.00
94	EGG 5031FU ROSE 5"	CL	75.00	85.00
95	EGG 5031YW SPRUCE 5"	CL	75.00	75.00
95	EGG 5031YX GOLD 5"	CL	75.00	75.00
96	EGG 1642JO FRENCH OPAL-BUTTERFLY 5"	CL	75.00	75.00
*				NATURAL ANIMALS
85	BIRD 5163NO	*	*	38.00
85	BIRD 5163NY SMALL	*	*	35.00
R. SPINDLER				ROSEBUDS ON ROSALENE
98	NATALIE BALLERINA 6 1/2"	TL	85.00	85.00
98	ROSALENE PERFUME 6 1/2"	TL	85.00	85.00
98	ROSALENE PUFF BOX, 4 1/4"	TL	100.00	100.00
98	ROSALENE VASE, 6"	TL	70.00	70.00
M. DICKINSON				SMOKE 'N CINDERS
84	LAMP, 23" STUDENT, 7514TL	250	*	550.00
M. DICKINSON				SMOKE'N CINDERS
84	LAMP 7204TL HAMMERED COLONIAL 16"	250	*	550.00
*				VALENTINE'S DAY
92	BASKET 6567CR CRANBERRY 6"	CL	50.00	65.00
92	PERFUME 6580CR W/OVAL STOPPER	CL	60.00	70.00
92	VASE 6568CR 4"	CL	35.00	40.00
93	BASKET 2732CR CAPRICE 7"	CL	59.00	65.00
93	SOUTHERN GIRL 5141NX ROSE PEARL IRID. 8"	CL	45.00	70.00
93	TRINKET BOX 2740CR 5"	CL	79.00	90.00
93	VASE 2749CR MELON 5-1/2"	CL	45.00	75.00
94	BASKET 2736CR CRANBERRY OPALESCENT 7"	CL	65.00	70.00
94	PERFUME 2760CR W/STOPPER 5"	CL	75.00	85.00
94	VASE 2755CR RIBBED 5-1/2"	CL	48.00	50.00
95	BASKET 2745CR MELON, CRANBERRY OPAL. 8"	CL	69.00	70.00
95	PITCHER 2774CR MELON 5-1/2"	CL	69.00	70.00
96	BASKET 7122CR MELON 8"	CL	75.00	75.00
96	FAIRY LIGHT 2903CR CRANBERRY	CL	135.00	135.00
96	PERFUME 7100CR MELON 5"	CL	95.00	95.00
M. REYNOLDS				VALENTINE'S DAY
93	SOUTHERN GIRL 5141NI 8"	CL	49.00	75.00
95	PERFUME 2785YB W/HEART STOPPER	2500	49.00	60.00
*		VALENTINE'S DAY LIMITED EDITIONS		
97	PENDANT & TRINKET BOX CHAMPAGNE SATIN	2500	65.00	95.00
R. SPINDLER		VALENTINE'S DAY LIMITED EDITIONS		
97	GIRL FIGURINE 8" FLORAL HANDPAINTED	2000	775.00	75.00
97	VANITY SET FLORAL & BUTTERFLY HANDPAINTED BURMESE	2000	225.00	225.00

FIGI COLLECTIONS INC.

*				SANTA'S CRYSTAL VALLEY
*	BEHOLD THE MAGIC HAMMER CV-204	OP	40.00	40.00
*	HEAVENLY CREATION CV-603	5000	190.00	190.00
*	MINING FOR MAGIC CV-202	OP	40.00	40.00
*	SHARING THE LEGEND CV-203	OP	40.00	40.00
*	THANKS SANTA!	OP	40.00	40.00
S. KEHRLI				SANTA'S CRYSTAL VALLEY
95	A GIFT FOR SANTA CV-701	1500	400.00	400.00
95	CAPTURE THE SPIRIT CV-106	RT	80.00	70.00
95	FINISHING TOUCH, THE CV-501	3500	225.00	225.00
95	POLAR BEAR ANGEL CV-101	OP	70.00	70.00
95	ROCKING HORSE DREAMS CV-104	OP	70.00	70.00
95	SANTA EXPRESS, THE CV-502	3500	225.00	225.00
95	SANTA'S DILEMMA CV-303	OP	100.00	100.00
95	SANTA'S REFLECTION CV-102	OP	70.00	70.00
95	SLEDDING WITH SANTA CV-302	OP	100.00	100.00

YR	NAME	LIMIT	ISSUE	TREND
95	SMILE MR. SNOWMAN CV-301	OP	100.00	100.00
95	STAR BRIGHT CV-103	RT	80.00	100.00
96	A VERY SPECIAL REQUEST CV-601	5000	190.00	190.00
96	AUDITION, THE CV-602	5000	190.00	190.00
96	DREAMS CAN COME TRUE CV-401	15000	100.00	100.00
96	FROLICKING FRIENDS CV-110	OP	70.00	70.00
96	JOURNEY TO CRYSTAL VALLEY CV-1001	SO	500.00	700.00
96	MAGIC IN THE MAKING CV-801	2500	500.00	500.00
96	ROOM FOR ONE MORE? CV-402	15000	100.00	100.00
96	SECRET RECIPE CV-109	OP	70.00	70.00
97	A CUDDLY MASTERPIECE CV-56	OP	25.00	25.00
97	ALL ABOARD! CV-53	OP	25.00	25.00
97	BEARLY FISNISHED CV-21	OP	10.00	10.00
97	BEARY BEST FRIEND CV-25	OP	10.00	10.00
97	BOOK OF LEGENDS,THE CV-802	3000	450.00	450.00
97	CHRISTMAS BLESSING CV-23	OP	10.00	10.00
97	DASHING THROUGH THE SNOW CV-107	OP	70.00	70.00
97	HOLIDAY ANTICIPATION CV-52	OP	25.00	25.00
97	IN THE SPIRIT CV-26	OP	10.00	10.00
97	MAGIC TOUCH CV-54	OP	25.00	25.00
97	PALACE PLAYGROUND CV-403	15000	100.00	100.00
97	SANTA'S CRYSTAL VALLEY CV-24	OP	10.00	10.00
97	SANTA'S DARING RESCUE CV-604	5000	190.00	190.00
97	SANTA'S JUNIOR EXPRESS CV-55	OP	25.00	25.00
97	WELCOME HOME CV-51	OP	25.00	25.00
97	WINGS OF LOVE CV-22	OP	10.00	10.00

FJ DESIGNS/CAT'S MEOW

F. JONES		**19TH CENTURY MASTER BUILDERS**		
93	ALEXANDER JACKSON DAVIS	RT	10.25	11.00
93	ANDREW JACKSON DOWNING	RT	10.30	11.00
93	HENRY HOBSON RICHARDSON	RT	10.30	11.00
93	SAMUEL SLOAN	RT	10.30	11.00
93	SET	RT	41.00	100.00
F. JONES			**ACCESSORIES**	
83	FALL TREE	RT	4.00	7.00
83	PINE TREE	RT	4.00	7.00
83	SUMMER TREE	RT	4.00	7.00
83	XMAS PINE TREE	RT	4.00	7.00
83	XMAS PINE TREE W/RED BOWS	RT	3.00	100.00
84	5 IN. HEDGE	RT	3.00	25.00
84	5 IN. PICKET FENCE	RT	3.00	3.00
84	8 IN. HEDGE	RT	3.25	25.00
84	8 IN. PICKET FENCE	RT	3.25	25.00
84	BANDSTAND	RT	6.50	7.00
84	DAIRY WAGON	RT	4.00	10.00
84	GAS LIGHT	RT	3.25	4.00
84	HORSE & CARRIAGE	RT	4.00	10.00
84	HORSE & SLEIGH	RT	4.00	4.00
84	LILAC BUSHES	RT	3.00	25.00
85	CHICKENS	RT	3.25	6.00
85	COWS	RT	4.00	10.00
85	DUCKS	RT	3.25	6.00
85	F.J. REAL ESTATE SIGN	RT	3.00	6.00
85	FLOWER POTS	RT	3.00	3.00
85	MAIN ST. SIGN	RT	3.25	4.00
85	TELEPHONE BOOTH	RT	3.00	3.00
85	U.S. FLAG	RT	3.25	4.00
86	5 IN. IRON FENCE	RT	3.00	45.00
86	8 IN. IRON FENCE	RT	3.25	25.00
86	CAROLERS	RT	4.00	10.00
86	CHERRY TREE	RT	4.00	5.00
86	ICE WAGON	RT	4.00	10.00
86	IRON GATE	RT	3.00	35.00
86	MAIL WAGON	RT	4.00	4.00
86	POPLAR TREE	RT	4.00	5.00
86	SKIPJACKS	RT	6.50	7.00
86	STREET CLOCK	OP	3.25	4.00
86	WISHING WELL	RT	3.25	6.00
86	WOODEN GATE	RT	3.00	3.00
87	CABLE CAR	RT	4.00	10.00
87	F.J. EXPRESS	RT	4.00	4.00
87	LIBERTY ST. SIGN	RT	3.25	6.00
87	RAILROAD SIGN	RT	3.00	3.00
87	WINDMILL	RT	3.25	4.00
88	ADA BELLE	RT	4.00	4.00
88	BUTCH & T.J.	RT	4.00	4.00
88	CHARLIE & CO	RT	4.00	4.00
88	COLONIAL BREAD WAGON	RT	4.00	4.00
89	CLOTHESLINE	RT	4.00	4.00
89	HARRY'S HOTDOGS	RT	4.00	4.00
89	MARKET ST. SIGN	RT	3.25	5.00
89	NANNY	RT	4.00	4.00
89	PASSENGER TRAIN CAR	RT	4.00	4.00
89	PONY EXPRESS RIDER	RT	4.00	4.00

YR	NAME	LIMIT	ISSUE	TREND
89	PUMPKIN WAGON	RT	3.25	4.00
89	QUAKER OATS TRAIN CAR	RT	4.00	4.00
89	ROSE TRELLIS	RT	3.25	4.00
89	RUDY & ALDINE	RT	4.00	4.00
89	SNOWMEN	RT	4.00	4.00
89	TAD & TONY	RT	4.00	4.00
89	TOURING CAR	RT	4.00	5.00
89	WELLS FARGO WAGON	RT	4.00	10.00
90	1909 FRANKLIN LIMOUSINE	RT	4.00	4.00
90	1913 PEERLESS TOURING CAR	RT	4.00	4.00
90	1914 FIRE PUMPER	RT	4.00	4.00
90	5 IN. WROUGHT IRON FENCE	RT	3.00	3.00
90	AMISH BUGGY	RT	4.00	4.00
90	BLUE SPRUCE	RT	4.00	4.00
90	BUS STOP	RT	4.00	4.00
90	CHRISTMAS TREE LOT	RT	4.00	4.00
90	EUGENE	RT	4.00	4.00
90	GERSTENSLAGER BUGGY	RT	4.00	4.00
90	LITTLE RED CABOOSE	RT	4.00	4.00
90	RED MAPLE TREE	RT	4.00	4.00
90	SANTA & REINDEER	RT	4.00	4.00
90	SCHOOL BUS	CL	4.00	4.00
90	TULIP TREE	RT	4.00	4.00
90	VETERINARY WAGON	RT	4.00	4.00
90	VICTORIAN OUTHOUSE	RT	4.00	4.00
90	WATKINS WAGON	RT	4.00	4.00
90	XMAS SPRUCE	RT	4.00	4.00
91	AMISH GARDEN	RT	4.00	4.00
91	BARNYARD	RT	4.00	4.00
91	CHESSIE HOPPER CAR	RT	4.00	4.00
91	CONCERT IN THE PARK	RT	4.00	4.00
91	JACK THE POSTMAN	RT	3.25	4.00
91	MARBLE GAME	RT	4.00	4.00
91	MARTIN HOUSE	RT	3.25	4.00
91	ON VACATION	RT	4.00	4.00
91	POPCORN WAGON	TL	4.00	4.00
91	SCAREY HARRY (SCARECROW)	OP	4.00	4.00
91	SKI PARTY	OP	4.00	4.00
91	USMC WAR MEMORIAL	OP	6.50	7.00
91	VILLAGE ENTRANCE SIGN	OP	6.50	7.00
92	DELIVERY TRUCK	OP	3.98	4.00
92	FORSYTHIA BUSH	OP	3.98	4.00
92	GASOLINE TRUCK	OP	3.98	4.00
92	MR. SOFTEE TRUCK	OP	3.98	4.00
92	NUTCRACKER BILLBOARD	OP	3.98	4.00
92	POLICE CAR	OP	3.98	4.00
92	SCHOOL CROSSING	OP	3.98	4.00
92	SILO	OP	3.98	4.00
92	SPRINGHOUSE	OP	3.25	4.00
93	CANNONBALL EXPRESS	OP	7.95	8.00
93	CHIPPEWA LAKE BILLBOARD	OP	7.95	8.00
93	GARDEN HOUSE	OP	6.50	7.00
93	GETTING DIRECTIONS	OP	7.95	8.00
93	GRAPE ARBOR	OP	7.95	8.00
93	JENNIE & GEORGE'S WEDDING	OP	7.95	8.00
93	JOHNNY APPLESEED STATUE	OP	7.95	8.00
93	LITTLE MARINE	OP	7.95	8.00
93	MARKET WAGON	OP	7.95	8.00
93	RUSTIC FENCE	OP	7.95	8.00

FLAMBRO

*		ANNUAL EMMETT KELLY JR. NUTCRACKER		
90	1990 NUTCRACKER	YR	50.00	50.00
*		CIRCUS WORLD MUSEUM CLOWNS		
85	FELIX ADLER (GROTESQUE)	9500	80.00	95.00
85	PAUL JEROME (HOBO)	9500	80.00	125.00
85	PAUL JUNG (NEAT)	9500	80.00	120.00
87	ABE GOLDSTEIN, KEYSTONE KOP	7500	90.00	90.00
87	FELIX ADLER WITH BALLOON	7500	90.00	90.00
87	PAUL JEROME WITH DOG	7500	90.00	90.00
87	PAUL JUNG, SITTING	7500	90.00	90.00
	C. PRACHT		DADDY LOVES YOU	
91	C'MON DADDY!	2500	100.00	100.00
91	MAKE YOU...GIGGLE!	2500	100.00	100.00
91	SOO...YOU LIKE IT?	2500	100.00	100.00
91	YOU'RE SOOO...SWEET	2500	100.00	100.00
*		EMMETT KELLY JR. A DAY AT THE FAIR		
90	75 CENTS PLEASE	RT	65.00	150.00
90	LOOK AT YOU	RT	65.00	150.00
90	RIDE THE WILD MOUSE	RT	65.00	150.00
90	STEP RIGHT UP	RT	65.00	150.00
90	STILT MAN, THE	RT	65.00	150.00
90	THANKS EMMETT	RT	65.00	150.00
90	THREE FOR A DIME	RT	65.00	150.00
90	YOU CAN DO IT, EMMETT	RT	65.00	150.00

Joining Goebel's M.I. Hummel Century Collection in 1994, Rock-A-Bye was produced for one year only and retailed for $1,150.

Sarah's Attic added the Buffalo Soldier to their Black Heritage Collection in 1992.

1987's Nap Time from Lladro´ was issued at $130 and has doubled in price.

Limited to 1995 production, You're at the Top of My List is part of Enesco Corp.'s Cherished Teddies "Santa's Workshop" series.

YR	NAME	LIMIT	ISSUE	TREND
90	YOU GO FIRST, EMMETT	RT	65.00	150.00
91	COIN TOSS	RT	65.00	150.00
91	POPCORN!	RT	65.00	150.00
91	TROUBLE WITH HOT DOGS, THE	RT	65.00	150.00
*		**EMMETT KELLY JR. FIGURINES**		
81	LOOKING OUT TO SEE	12000	75.00	2450.00
81	SWEEPING UP	12000	75.00	1600.00
82	THINKER, THE	15000	60.00	1200.00
82	WET PAINT	15000	80.00	825.00
82	WHY ME?	15000	65.00	500.00
83	BALANCING ACT, THE	10000	75.00	800.00
83	BALLOONS FOR SALE	10000	75.00	700.00
83	HOLE IN THE SOLE	10000	75.00	500.00
83	SPIRIT OF CHRISTMAS I	3500	125.00	1775.00
83	WISHFUL THNKING	10000	65.00	725.00
84	BIG BUSINESS	9500	110.00	850.00
84	EATING CABBAGE	12000	75.00	480.00
84	PIANO PLAYER	9500	160.00	750.00
84	SPIRIT OF CHRISTMAS II	3500	270.00	500.00
85	EMMETT'S FAN	12000	80.00	585.00
85	IN THE SPOTLIGHT	12000	103.00	400.00
85	MAN'S BEST FRIEND?	9500	98.00	600.00
85	NO STRINGS ATTACHED	9500	98.00	325.00
85	SPIRIT OF CHRISTMAS III	3500	220.00	600.00
86	BEDTIME	12000	98.00	300.00
86	COTTON CANDY	12000	98.00	400.00
86	ENTERTAINERS, THE	12000	120.00	200.00
86	FAIR GAME	2500	450.00	1900.00
86	MAKING NEW FRIENDS	9500	140.00	340.00
86	SPIRIT OF CHRISTMAS IV	3500	150.00	500.00
87	MY FAVORITE THINGS	9500	109.00	650.00
87	ON THE ROAD AGAIN	9500	109.00	425.00
87	OVER A BARREL	9500	130.00	350.00
87	SATURDAY NIGHT	7500	153.00	600.00
87	SPIRIT OF CHRISTMAS V	2400	170.00	640.00
87	TOOTHACHE	12000	98.00	250.00
88	AMEN	12000	120.00	450.00
88	DINING OUT	CL	120.00	350.00
88	SPIRIT OF CHRISTMAS VI	2400	194.00	700.00
88	WHEELER DEALER	7500	160.00	325.00
89	65TH BIRTHDAY COMMEMORATIVE	1989	275.00	2340.00
89	HURDY-GURDY MAN	9500	150.00	325.00
89	MAKING UP	7500	200.00	350.00
89	NO LOITERING	7500	200.00	475.00
90	BALLOONS FOR SALE II	7500	250.00	250.00
90	CONVENTION BOUND	7500	225.00	230.00
90	MISFORTUNE?	3500	400.00	650.00
90	SPIRIT OF CHRISTMAS VII	3500	275.00	400.00
90	WATCH THE BIRDIE	9500	200.00	210.00
91	ARTIST AT WORK	7500	295.00	295.00
91	FINISHING TOUCH	7500	245.00	245.00
91	FOLLOW THE LEADER	7500	200.00	200.00
91	SPIRIT OF CHRISTMAS VIII	3500	250.00	350.00
92	NO USE CRYING	7500	200.00	200.00
92	PEANUT BUTTER?	7500	200.00	200.00
92	READY-SET-GO	7500	200.00	200.00
93	SPIRIT OF CHRISTMAS IX	3500	200.00	200.00
93	SPIRIT OF CHRISTMAS X	3500	200.00	200.00
94	SPIRIT OF CHRISTMAS XI	3500	200.00	200.00
95	35 YEARS OF CLOWNING	5000	240.00	240.00
95	ALL-STAR CIRCUS 20TH ANNIVERSARY	5000	240.00	300.00
95	BEDTIME	OP	35.00	35.00
95	SPIRIT OF CHRISTMAS XII	3500	200.00	250.00
96	AM. CIRCUS EXTRAVAGANZAS 125TH ANNIVERSARY	5000	240.00	240.00
96	AMEN	OP	35.00	35.00
96	DAREDEVIL MOTOR SHOW 35TH ANNIVERSARY	5000	240.00	240.00
96	MISFORTUNE?	OP	60.00	60.00
96	SPIRIT OF CHRISTMAS XIII	3500	200.00	200.00
97	25TH ANNIVERSARY OF WHITE HOUSE APP.	5000	240.00	240.00
97	CATCH OF THE DAY	5000	240.00	240.00
97	SPIRIT OF CHRISTMAS XIV	5000	240.00	240.00
*		**EMMETT KELLY JR. JAPANESE FIGURINE**		
93	VIGILANTE, THE	OP	75.00	75.00
M. WU		**EMMETT KELLY JR. LITTLE EMMETTS**		
94	AGE 1	OP	9.00	9.00
94	AGE 10	OP	25.00	25.00
94	AGE 2	OP	9.50	10.00
94	AGE 3	OP	12.00	12.00
94	AGE 4	OP	12.00	12.00
94	AGE 5	OP	15.00	16.00
94	AGE 6	OP	15.00	16.00
94	AGE 7	OP	17.00	15.00
94	AGE 8	OP	21.00	21.00
94	AGE 9	OP	22.00	22.00
94	LITTLE ARTIST PICTURE FRAME	OP	22.00	22.00

YR	NAME	LIMIT	ISSUE	TREND
94	LITTLE EMMETT COUNTING LESSON-MUSICAL	OP	30.00	30.00
94	LITTLE EMMETT COUNTRY ROAD	OP	35.00	35.00
94	LITTLE EMMETT FISHING	OP	35.00	35.00
94	LITTLE EMMETT RAINDROPS	OP	35.00	35.00
94	LITTLE EMMETT SHADOW SHOW	OP	40.00	40.00
94	LITTLE EMMETT SOMEDAY	OP	50.00	50.00
94	LITTLE EMMETT WITH BLACKBOARD	OP	30.00	30.00
94	LITTLE EMMETT YOU'VE GOT A FRIEND	OP	33.00	33.00
94	PLAYFUL BOOKENDS	OP	40.00	40.00
95	BIRTHDAY HAUL	OP	30.00	30.00
95	DANCE LESSONS-MUSICAL	OP	50.00	50.00
95	LITTLE EMMETT NOEL, NOEL	OP	40.00	40.00
*	**EMMETT KELLY JR. MEMBERS ONLY FIGURINES**			
90	MERRY-GO-ROUND	CL	125.00	475.00
91	10 YEARS OF COLLECTING	CL	100.00	225.00
92	ALL ABOARD	CL	75.00	280.00
93	RINGMASTER	CL	125.00	150.00
94	BIRTHDAY MAIL	CL	100.00	250.00
95	SALUTE TO OUR VETS	CL	75.00	160.00
96	I LOVE YOU	CL	95.00	225.00
97	FILET OF SOLE	YR	130.00	130.00
*	**EMMETT KELLY JR. METAL SCULPTURES**			
91	BALANCING ACT, TOO	5000	125.00	125.00
91	CAROUSEL RIDER	5000	125.00	125.00
91	EMMETT'S POOCHES	5000	125.00	125.00
91	MAGICIAN, THE	5000	125.00	125.00
*	**EMMETT KELLY JR. MINIATURES**			
86	BALANCING ACT	RT	25.00	45.00
86	BALLOONS FOR SALE	RT	25.00	40.00
86	HOLE IN THE SOLE	RT	25.00	48.00
86	LOOKING OUT TO SEE	RT	25.00	100.00
86	SWEEPING UP	RT	25.00	100.00
86	THINKER, THE	RT	25.00	42.00
86	WET PAINT	RT	25.00	40.00
86	WHY ME?	RT	25.00	48.00
86	WISHFUL THINKING	RT	25.00	60.00
87	EATING CABBAGE	RT	30.00	42.00
87	EMMETT'S FAN	RT	30.00	45.00
87	SPIRIT OF CHRISTMAS I	RT	40.00	90.00
88	BIG BUSINESS	RT	35.00	39.00
89	COTTON CANDY	RT	30.00	30.00
89	MAN'S BEST FRIEND?	RT	35.00	35.00
90	MY FAVORITE THINGS	RT	45.00	45.00
90	SATURDAY NIGHT	RT	50.00	50.00
90	SPIRIT OF CHRISTMAS III	RT	50.00	50.00
91	IN THE SPOTLIGHT	RT	35.00	35.00
91	NO STRINGS ATTACHED	RT	35.00	35.00
94	SPIRIT OF CHRISTMAS V	OP	50.00	50.00
95	BEDTIME	OP	35.00	35.00
95	DINING OUT	OP	35.00	35.00
95	ENTERTAINERS, THE	OP	45.00	45.00
95	HURDY GURDY MAN	OP	40.00	40.00
95	NO LOITERING	OP	50.00	50.00
96	MAKING UP	OP	55.00	55.00
96	SPIRIT OF CHRISTMAS VI	OP	55.00	55.00
96	TOOTHACHE	OP	35.00	35.00
96	WHEELER DEALER	OP	65.00	65.00
97	BALLOONS FOR SALE II	OP	55.00	55.00
97	BIG BOSS	OP	55.00	55.00
97	CONVENTION BOUND	OP	55.00	55.00
97	MERRY GO ROUND	OP	65.00	65.00
97	SPIRIT OF CHRISTMAS VII	OP	50.00	50.00
97	WATCH THE BIRDIE	OP	55.00	55.00
*	**EMMETT KELLY JR. PROFESSIONALS**			
88	POLICEMAN	RT	50.00	85.00
93	AFTER THE PARADE	75000	190.00	190.00
93	KITTENS FOR SALE	75000	190.00	190.00
93	ON MANEUVERS	OP	50.00	50.00
93	PILOT	OP	50.00	50.00
93	REALTOR	OP	50.00	50.00
93	VETERINARIAN	OP	50.00	50.00
93	WORLD TRAVELER	75000	190.00	190.00
94	FOREST FRIENDS	75000	190.00	190.00
94	LET HIM EAT CAKE	RT	300.00	400.00
94	LION TAMER	75000	190.00	190.00
95	COACH	OP	55.00	55.00
95	DOCTOR	OP	55.00	55.00
95	FIREMAN	OP	55.00	55.00
95	GOLFER	OP	55.00	55.00
95	LAWYER	OP	55.00	55.00
95	POLICEMAN	OP	55.00	55.00
96	BOWLER	OP	55.00	55.00
96	DENTIST	OP	55.00	55.00
96	FARMER	OP	55.00	55.00
96	MAILMAN	OP	55.00	55.00

YR	NAME	LIMIT	ISSUE	TREND
96	SKIER	OP	55.00	55.00
96	TEACHER	OP	55.00	55.00
97	COMPUTER WIZ (WITH GARBAGE CAN)	OP	55.00	55.00
97	EXECUTIVE (TALKING ON PHONE)	OP	55.00	55.00
97	FISHERMAN (WITH FISH & DOG)	OP	55.00	55.00
97	FITNESS (RUNAWAY WEIGHTLESS)	OP	55.00	55.00
97	GARDENER (WITH RAKE)	OP	55.00	55.00
97	HUNTER (WITH ORANGE CAMOUFLAGE)	OP	55.00	55.00
*		**EMMETT KELLY JR. REAL RAGS COLLECTION**		
93	BIG BUSINESS II	RT	140.00	200.00
93	CHECKING HIS LIST	CL	100.00	250.00
93	LOOKING OUT TO SEE II	3000	100.00	100.00
93	SWEEPING UP II	3000	100.00	100.00
93	THINKER II	3000	120.00	150.00
94	A GOOD LIKENESS	3000	120.00	120.00
94	EATING CABBAGE II	3000	100.00	100.00
94	ON IN TWO	3000	100.00	150.00
94	RUDOLPH HAS A RED NOSE	3000	135.00	175.00
95	BALLOONS FOR SALE 2	3000	120.00	120.00
95	I'VE GOT RHYTHM	3000	140.00	140.00
95	NO STRINGS ATTACHED 2	3000	120.00	120.00
95	WATCH OUT BELOW	3000	120.00	120.00
*		**EMMETT KELLY JR. SPECIAL EVENT**		
97	SEND IN THE CLOWNS	YR	70.00	70.00
M. WU		**LITTLE EMMETT WATERGLOBE**		
95	LOOKING BACKWARD	OP	75.00	75.00
95	LOOKING FORWARD	OP	75.00	75.00
J. BERG VICTOR		**PLEASANTVILLE 1893**		
90	1ST CHURCH OF PLEASANTVILLE	OP	35.00	35.00
90	BAND STAND, THE	OP	12.00	12.00
90	DEPARTMENT STORE	OP	25.00	25.00
90	GERBER HOUSE, THE	OP	30.00	30.00
90	MASON'S HOTEL AND SALOON	OP	35.00	35.00
90	PLEASANTVILLE LIBRARY	OP	32.00	32.00
90	REVEREND LITTLEFIELD'S HOUSE	OP	34.00	34.00
90	SWEET SHOPPE & BAKERY	OP	40.00	40.00
90	TOY STORE	OP	30.00	30.00
91	COURT HOUSE	OP	36.00	36.00
91	FIRE HOUSE	OP	40.00	40.00
91	METHODIST CHURCH	OP	40.00	40.00
91	SCHOOL HOUSE	OP	36.00	36.00
92	APOTHECARY/ICE CREAM SHOP	OP	36.00	36.00
92	BANK/REAL ESTATE OFFICE	RT	36.00	36.00
92	BLACKSMITH/LIVERY	OP	40.00	40.00
92	COVERED BRIDGE	RT	36.00	36.00
92	MISS FOUNTAINS	OP	48.00	48.00
92	RAILROAD STATION	OP	40.00	40.00
92	TUBBS, JR. HOUSE	OP	40.00	40.00
93	BALCOMB'S FARM	OP	40.00	40.00
93	LIVERY STABLE AND RESIDENCE	OP	40.00	40.00
94	GAZEBO/BANDSTAND	OP	25.00	25.00
94	SACRED HEART CATHOLIC CHURCH	OP	40.00	40.00
94	SACRED HEART RECTORY	OP	40.00	40.00
R. MUSGRAVE		**POCKET DRAGONS**		
*	DENNIS THE DRAGON	*	*	117.00
89	WIZARDRY FOR FUN AND PROFIT	RT	375.00	650.00
93	BATH TIME	RT	90.00	100.00
93	BOOK END, THE	RT	90.00	90.00
93	FUZZY EARS	CL	16.50	17.00
93	I ATE THE WHOLE THING	RT	33.00	33.00
93	LET'S MAKE COOKIES	RT	90.00	90.00
93	LITTLE BIT	RT	16.50	17.00
93	LITTLE JEWEL-BROOCH	RT	20.00	30.00
93	OH GOODY!	CL	16.50	17.00
93	POCKET RIDER-BROOCH	RT	20.00	28.00
93	READING THE GOOD PARTS	CL	70.00	70.00
93	TREASURE	CL	90.00	90.00
93	WE'RE VERY BRAVE	RT	38.00	50.00
93	YOU CAN'T MAKE ME	OP	15.00	15.00
94	A BOOK MY SIZE	OP	30.00	30.00
94	A LITTLE SECURITY	OP	20.00	20.00
94	BUTTERFLY KISSES	OP	30.00	30.00
94	CANDY CANE	OP	55.00	55.00
94	COFFEE PLEASE	OP	24.00	24.00
94	DANCE PARTNER	OP	23.00	23.00
94	GARGOYLES JUST WANT TO HAVE FUN	CL	30.00	30.00
94	IN TROUBLE AGAIN	OP	35.00	35.00
94	IT'S DARK OUT THERE	OP	45.00	45.00
94	IT'S MAGIC	OP	31.00	31.50
94	PLAYING DRESS UP	CL	30.00	30.00
94	RAIDING THE COOKIE JAR	3500	200.00	275.00
94	SNUGGLES	OP	35.00	35.00
95	BUT I'M TOO LITTLE	OP	15.00	15.00
95	BYE...	OP	15.00	15.00
95	CLASSICAL DRAGON	OP	80.00	80.00

YR	NAME	LIMIT	ISSUE	TREND
95	ELEMENTARY MY DEAR	OP	35.00	35.00
95	HEDGEHOG'S JOKE, THE	OP	27.00	27.00
95	HI!	OP	15.00	15.00
95	I'LL BE THE BRIDE	OP	37.00	37.00
95	I'LL BE THE GROOM	OP	37.00	37.00
95	IT'S A PRESENT	OP	21.00	21.00
95	JINGLES	OP	23.00	23.00
95	PURPLE	OP	27.00	27.00
95	SEES ALL, KNOWS ALL	OP	35.00	35.00
95	TELLING SECRETS	OP	48.00	48.00
95	TUMBLY	OP	21.00	21.00
95	WATSON	OP	23.00	23.00
96	D-PRESSING	OP	28.00	28.00
96	I'M SO PRETTY	OP	23.00	23.00
96	PILLOW FIGHT	3500	157.00	200.00
96	POCKET PIPER	OP	37.00	37.00
96	QUARTET	OP	80.00	80.00
96	RED RIBBON	OP	17.00	17.00
96	SWEETIE PIE	OP	28.00	28.00
96	WHATCHA DOING	OP	23.00	23.00
97	DAISY	OP	17.00	17.00
97	DRIVER,THE	OP	28.00	28.00
97	NAVIGATOR,THE	OP	30.00	30.00
97	PRETTY PLEASE	OP	17.00	17.00

D. RUST   POCKET DRAGONS

| 93 | SANTA'S STOWAWAY | 10000 | 30.00 | 30.00 |
| 94 | 70 TH BIRTHDAY COMMEMORATIVE | 5000 | 30.00 | 30.00 |

R. MUSGRAVE   POCKET DRAGONS APPEARANCE FIGURINES

| 93 | A BIG HUG | RT | 35.00 | 80.00 |
| 94 | PACKED AND READY | RT | 47.00 | 47.00 |

R. MUSGRAVE   POCKET DRAGONS CHRISTMAS EDITIONS

89	PUTTING ME ON THE TREE	RT	53.00	78.00
92	A POCKET-SIZED TREE	RT	19.00	65.00
93	CHRISTMAS ANGEL	RT	45.00	65.00
94	DEAR SANTA	RT	50.00	75.00
95	CHASING SNOWFLAKES	RT	35.00	50.00
96	CHRISTMAS SKATES	RT	36.00	40.00
97	DECK THE HALLS	YR	39.00	39.00

R. MUSGRAVE   POCKET DRAGONS COLLECTORS CLUB GIFT

93	BITSY	RT	*	15.00
93	WANT A BITE?	RT	*	85.00
94	BLUE RIBBON DRAGON	RT	*	75.00
94	FRIENDSHIP PIN	RT	*	85.00
95	MAKING TIME FOR YOU	RT	30.00	30.00

R. MUSGRAVE   POCKET DRAGONS MEMBERS ONLY

93	PEN PALS	RT	90.00	135.00
94	BEST SEAT IN THE HOUSE, THE	RT	75.00	150.00
95	PARTY TIME	RT	75.00	85.00

C. BEYLON   RAGGEDY ANN & ANDY

88	70 YEARS YOUNG	2500	95.00	120.00
88	GIDDY UP	3500	95.00	120.00
88	OOPS!	3500	80.00	103.00
88	WET PAINT	3500	70.00	92.00

FRANKLIN MINT

N. ROCKWELL   JOYS OF CHILDHOOD

76	COASTING ALONG	3700	120.00	175.00
76	DRESSING UP	3700	120.00	175.00
76	FISHING HOLE, THE	3700	120.00	175.00
76	HOPSCOTCH	3700	120.00	175.00
76	MARBLE CHAMP, THE	3700	120.00	175.00
76	NURSE, THE	3700	120.00	175.00
76	RIDE 'EM COWBOY	3700	120.00	175.00
76	STILT WALKER, THE	3700	120.00	175.00
76	TIME OUT	3700	120.00	175.00
76	TRICK OR TREAT	3700	120.00	175.00

GANZ

C. THAMMAVONGSA   CHEESERVILLE PICNIC COLLECTION MINI

91	BASKET OF APPLES	OP	2.25	3.00
91	BASKET OF PEACHES	OP	2.00	2.00
91	BLUEBERRY CAKE	RT	2.50	3.00
91	BREAD BASKET	OP	2.50	3.00
91	CANDY	OP	2.00	2.00
91	CHERRY PIE	RT	2.00	2.00
91	CHOCOLATE CAKE	OP	2.50	3.00
91	CHOCOLATE CHEESECAKE	OP	2.00	2.00
91	DOUGHNUT BASKET	OP	2.50	3.00
91	EGG TART	OP	1.00	1.00
91	FOOD BKT. W/BLUE CLOTH	RT	6.50	7.00
91	FOOD BKT. W/GREEN CLOTH	OP	7.50	8.00
91	FOOD BKT. W/PINK CLOTH	RT	6.00	6.00
91	FOOD BKT. W/PURPLE CLOTH	OP	6.00	6.00
91	FOOD TROLLEY	RT	12.00	12.00
91	HAZELNUT ROLL	RT	2.00	2.00

YR	NAME	LIMIT	ISSUE	TREND
91	HONEY JAR	RT	2.00	2.00
91	HOT DOG	OP	2.25	3.00
91	ICE CREAM GROUP	OP	2.00	2.00
91	LEMON CAKE	RT	2.00	2.00
91	NAPKIN IN CAN	RT	2.00	2.00
91	SET OF FOUR BOTTLES	RT	10.00	10.00
91	STRAWBERRY CAKE	OP	2.00	2.00
91	SUNDAE	OP	2.00	2.00
91	WINE GLASS	OP	1.25	2.00
94	MAYFLOWER MEADOW BASE	OP	50.00	50.00

C. THAMMAVONGSA — CHEESERVILLE PICNIC COLLECTION MUSICALS

YR	NAME	LIMIT	ISSUE	TREND
91	BLOSSOM & HICKORY JEWELRY BX	RT	65.00	65.00
91	FLORAL TRINKET BOX	OP	32.00	32.00
91	MAMA & SWEET CICELY WATERGLOBE	RT	55.00	55.00
91	MEDLEY MEADOWMOUSE COOKIE JAR	RT	75.00	75.00
91	MEDLEY MEADOWMOUSE WATERGLOBE	OP	47.00	47.00
91	PICNIC BASE	OP	60.00	60.00
91	SUNFLOWER BASE	RT	65.00	65.00
91	SWEET CICELY DOLL BASKET	OP	85.00	85.00
91	TRINKET BOX	OP	30.00	30.00
91	VIOLET WOODSWORTH COOKIE JAR	RT	75.00	75.00
92	APRIL SHOWERS BRING MAY FLOWERS	OP	7.50	8.00
92	DECORATED W/LOVE	OP	7.50	8.00
92	FOR SOMEBUNNY SPECIAL	OP	7.50	8.00
93	SECRET TREASURES- TRINKET BX	OP	35.00	35.00
93	WISHING WELL	OP	50.00	50.00
94	BANDSTAND BASE, THE	OP	49.00	49.00

C. THAMMAVONGSA — CHRISTMAS COLLECTION

YR	NAME	LIMIT	ISSUE	TREND
94	CHRISTMAS TRIMMINGS	10000	24.00	24.00
94	JOY TO THE WORLD	OP	10.00	10.00
94	LET IT SNOW	OP	12.00	12.00
94	MISTLETOE MAGIC	OP	14.00	15.00
94	SANTA PIG	OP	11.00	11.00
94	YULETIDE CAROLS	OP	19.00	19.00

C. THAMMAVONGSA — COWTOWN COLLECTION

YR	NAME	LIMIT	ISSUE	TREND
93	BUFFALO BULL CODY	OP	15.00	16.00
93	BULL MASTERSON	OP	15.00	16.00
93	BULL ROGERS	OP	17.00	17.00
93	BULL RUTH	RT	13.00	13.00
93	BUTTERMILK & BUTTERCUP	OP	16.00	16.00
93	COWLAMITY JANE	OP	15.00	16.00
93	DAISY MOO	OP	11.00	11.00
93	GLORIA BOVINE & RUDOLPH BULLENTINO	OP	20.00	20.00
93	JETHRO BOVINE	RT	15.00	15.00
93	LI'L ORPHAN ANGUS	OP	11.00	11.00
93	MOO WEST	OP	15.00	16.00
93	OLD MOODONALD	OP	13.50	14.00
94	AMOOLIA STEERHEART	OP	25.00	25.00
94	COWSEY JONES & THE CANNONBULL EXPRESS	OP	27.00	27.00
94	GERONIMOO	OP	17.00	17.00
94	HEIFERELLA	OP	16.50	17.00
94	KING COWMOOAMOOA	OP	16.50	17.00
94	MA & PA CATTLE	OP	24.00	24.00
94	POCOWHANTIS	OP	16.50	17.00
94	SET OF THREE CACTI	OP	17.00	17.00
94	TCHAICOWSKY	OP	19.00	19.00
94	TEXAS LONESTEER	10000	50.00	50.00

C. THAMMAVONGSA — LITTLE CHEESERS/CHRISTMAS COLLECTION

YR	NAME	LIMIT	ISSUE	TREND
91	ABNER APPLETON RINGING BELL	RT	14.00	15.00
91	AUNTIE BLOSSOM W/ORNAMENTS	OP	14.00	15.00
91	CHEESER SNOWMAN	OP	7.50	8.00
91	CHRISTMAS TREE	OP	9.00	9.00
91	COUSIN WOODY PLAYING FLUTE	OP	14.00	15.00
91	FROWZY ROQUEFORT III SKATING	RT	14.00	15.00
91	GRANDMAMA & LITTLE TRUFFLE	RT	19.00	19.00
91	GRANDPAPA & SWEET CICELY	OP	19.00	19.00
91	GRANDPAPA BLOWING HORN	OP	14.00	15.00
91	GREAT AUNT ROSE W/TRAY	OP	14.00	15.00
91	HARLEY & HARRIET DANCING	RT	19.00	19.00
91	HICKORY PLAYING CELLO	OP	14.00	15.00
91	JENNY ON SLEIGH	OP	16.00	16.00
91	JEREMY W/TEDDY BEAR	OP	12.00	12.00
91	LAMP POST	OP	8.50	9.00
91	LITTLE TRUFFLE W/STOCKING	OP	8.00	8.00
91	MAMA POURING TEA	RT	14.00	15.00
91	MARIGOLD & OSCAR STEALING A CHRISTMAS KISS	OP	19.00	19.00
91	MEDLEY PLAYING DRUM	OP	8.00	8.00
91	MYRTLE MEADOWMOUSE W/BK	RT	14.00	15.00
91	OUTDOOR SCENE BASE	RT	35.00	35.00
91	PARLOR SCENE BASE	OP	38.00	38.00
91	SANTA CHEESER	OP	13.00	13.00
91	VIOLET W/SNOWBALL	OP	8.00	8.00
93	ALL I WANT FOR CHRISTMAS	OP	18.00	18.00
93	CANDLEHOLDER-SANTA CHEESER	OP	19.00	19.00
93	CANDY CANE	OP	2.00	2.00

YR	NAME	LIMIT	ISSUE	TREND
93	CHRISTMAS GIFT	OP	3.00	3.00
93	CHRISTMAS GREETINGS	OP	16.50	17.00
93	CHRISTMAS STOCKING	OP	3.00	3.00
93	GINGERBREAD HOUSE	OP	3.00	3.00
93	ICE POND BASE	OP	5.50	5.50
93	SLEIGH RIDE	OP	11.00	11.00
93	TOY SOLDIER	OP	3.00	3.00
93	TOY TRAIN	OP	3.00	3.00
94	CHRISTMAS COLLECTION BASE	OP	50.00	50.00
94	SANTA'S SLEIGH	10000	22.00	22.00
C. THAMMAVONGSA		**LITTLE CHEESERS/MUSICALS**		
92	J. BUTTERFIELD CHRISTMAS WATERGLOBE	RT	55.00	55.00
92	LITTLE TRUFFLE CHRISTMAS WATERGLOBE	OP	45.00	45.00
92	SANTA CHEESER ROLY-POLY	RT	55.00	55.00
93	I'LL BE HOME FOR X'MAS	OP	30.00	30.00
93	WE WISH YOU A MERRY CHRISTMAS	OP	25.00	25.00
C. THAMMAVONGSA		**LITTLE HOPPERS COLLECTION**		
94	BUBBLE BATH	OP	7.50	8.00
94	LET'S PLAY BALL	OP	7.00	7.00
94	SOMEBUNNY LOVES YOU	OP	7.50	8.00
94	SWEET NOTHINGS	OP	15.00	15.00
94	TENDER LOVING CARE	OP	10.00	10.00
94	TRICYCLE BUILT FOR TWO	OP	16.00	16.00
C. THAMMAVONGSA		**PIGSVILLE COLLECTION**		
93	BAKIN' AT THE BEACH	OP	11.00	11.00
93	ICE CREAM ANYONE?	RT	9.00	9.00
93	ME & MY ICE CREAM	RT	17.00	17.00
93	MOTHER LOVE	OP	13.00	13.00
93	NAP TIME	OP	11.00	11.00
93	P.O.P DISPLAY SIGN	OP	8.00	8.00
93	PIG AT THE BEACH	OP	9.00	9.00
93	PRIMA BALLERINA	RT	11.00	11.00
93	SOAP SUDS	OP	12.00	12.00
93	SQUEAKY CLEAN	OP	11.00	11.00
93	TIPSY	OP	9.00	9.00
93	TRUE LOVE	OP	12.00	12.00
93	WEE LITTLE PIGGY	OP	8.00	8.00
94	BEDTIME	OP	9.50	10.00
94	BIRTHDAY SURPRISE	OP	9.50	10.00
94	OLE FISHING HOLD	OP	16.00	16.00
94	PLAY BALL	OP	11.50	12.00
94	PRETTY PIGLET	OP	8.00	8.00
94	SANDCASTLE	OP	12.00	12.00
94	SNACKTIME	OP	11.50	12.00
94	SPECIAL TEST	OP	11.50	12.00
94	STORYTIME	OP	13.00	13.00
94	WEDDED BLISS	OP	16.00	16.00
C. THAMMAVONGSA		**PIGSVILLE COLLECTION ACCESSORIES**		
94	BARN	OP	35.00	35.00
94	SILO	OP	15.00	16.00
C. THAMMAVONGSA		**SPRINGTIME/CHEESERVILLE COLLECTION**		
92	A BASKET FULL OF JOY	OP	16.00	16.00
92	A WHEELBARROW OF SUNSHINE	OP	17.00	17.00
92	HIPPITY-HOP, IT'S EASTERTIME!	OP	16.00	16.00
92	SPRINGTIME DELIGHTS	OP	12.00	12.00
92	TULIPS & RIBBONS TRINKET BX MUSICAL	RT	28.00	28.00
93	BALLERINA SWEETHEART	OP	10.00	10.00
93	BLOSSOM HAS A LITTLE LAMB	OP	16.50	17.00
93	FIRST KISS	OP	24.00	24.00
93	FOR MY SWEETHEART	OP	22.00	22.00
93	FRIENDS FOREVER	OP	22.00	22.00
93	GENTLY DOWN THE STREAM	10000	27.00	27.00
93	GIFT FROM HEAVEN	OP	10.00	10.00
93	HIGS & KISSES	OP	11.00	11.00
93	I LOVE YOU	OP	22.00	22.00
93	PLAYING CUPID	OP	10.00	10.00
93	SUGAR & SPICE	OP	24.00	24.00
93	SUNDAY STROLL	OP	22.00	22.00
94	BIRTHDAY PARTY	OP	22.00	22.00
94	GET WELL	OP	22.00	22.00
94	HIP HIP HOORAY	OP	22.00	22.00
C. THAMMAVONGSA		**VALENTINE COLLECTION**		
94	CHAMPAGNE & ROSES	OP	14.00	15.00
94	I LOVE YOU	OP	9.50	10.00
94	I'M ALL YOURS	OP	11.50	12.00
94	LOVESTRUCK	OP	10.00	10.00
94	SWEETHEART PIG	OP	8.00	8.00
94	TOGETHER FOREVER	OP	15.00	16.00
C. THAMMAVONGSA		**WEDDING COLLECTION**		
92	BLOSSOM THISTLEDOWN BRIDE	OP	16.00	16.00
92	COUSIN WOODY & LI'L TRUFFLE	OP	20.00	20.00
92	FROWZY ROQUEFORT III W/GRAMOPHONE	OP	20.00	20.00
92	GRANDMAMA & GRANDPAPA THISTLEDOWN	RT	20.00	20.00
92	GREAT AUNT ROSE BESIDE TABLE	OP	20.00	20.00
92	HARLEY & HARRIET HARVESTMOUSE	OP	20.00	20.00

YR NAME	LIMIT	ISSUE	TREND
92 HICKORY HARVESTMOUSE GROOM	OP	16.00	16.00
92 J. BUTTERFIELD/SWEET CICELY BRIDESMAID	OP	20.00	20.00
92 LITTLE TRUFFLE RINGBEARER	OP	10.00	10.00
92 MAMA & PAPA WOODSWORTH DANCING	OP	20.00	20.00
92 MARIGOLD THISTLEDOWN & OSCAR ROBBINS	OP	20.00	20.00
92 MYRTLE MEADOWMOUSE W/MEDLEY	RT	20.00	20.00
92 PASTOR SMALLWOOD	OP	16.00	16.00
92 WEDDING PROCESSION	OP	40.00	40.00
93 BIG DAY, THE	OP	20.00	20.00
C. THAMMAVONGSA	**WEDDING COLLECTION ACCESSORIES**		
93 BANQUET TABLE	OP	14.00	15.00
93 GAZEBO BASE	OP	42.00	42.00
C. THAMMAVONGSA	**WEDDING COLLECTION MINI**		
92 BIBLE TRINKET BOX	OP	16.50	17.00
92 BIG CHOCOLATE CAKE	RT	4.50	5.00
92 BRIDE CANDLEHOLDER	OP	20.00	20.00
92 CAKE TRINKET BOX	OP	14.00	15.00
92 CANDLES	OP	3.00	3.00
92 CHERRY JELLO	OP	3.00	3.00
92 CHOCOLATE PASTRY	RT	2.00	2.00
92 CHOCOLATE PUDDING	OP	2.50	3.00
92 FLOUR BAG	RT	2.00	2.00
92 FLOWER VASE	RT	3.00	3.00
92 FRUIT SALAD	OP	3.00	3.00
92 GRASS BASE	RT	3.50	4.00
92 GROOM CANDLEHOLDER	OP	20.00	20.00
92 HONEY POT	OP	2.00	2.00
92 RING CAKE	OP	3.00	3.00
92 SALT CAN	RT	2.00	2.00
92 SOUFFLE	RT	2.50	3.00
92 SOUP POT	OP	3.00	3.00
92 TEA POT SET	RT	3.00	3.00
92 TEDDY MOUSE	RT	2.00	2.00
93 GOOSEBERRY CHAMPAGNE	OP	3.00	3.50
93 WEDDING CAKE	OP	4.50	5.00
C. THAMMAVONGSA	**WEDDING COLLECTION MUSICALS**		
92 BLOSSOM & HICKORY WEDDING WATERGLOBE	OP	55.00	55.00
92 WEDDING BASE	OP	32.00	32.00
92 WOODEN BASE FOR WEDDING PROCESSIONAL	OP	25.00	25.00
93 BLOSSOM & HICKORY MUSICAL	RT	50.00	50.00
93 WHITE MUSICAL WD. BASE/GAZEBO EVERGREEN	OP	25.00	25.00

GARTLAN USA

YR NAME	LIMIT	ISSUE	TREND
F. BARNUM	**ALL-STAR GEMS MINIATURE FIGURINES**		
90 GEORGE BRETT	10000	75.00	75.00
90 PETE ROSE	10000	75.00	75.00
90 WHITEY FORD	10000	75.00	75.00
90 YOGI BERRA	10000	75.00	75.00
91 JOE MONTANA	10000	79.00	79.00
92 HANK AARON	10000	79.00	79.00
V. BOVA	**ALL-STAR GEMS MINIATURE FIGURINES**		
91 MONTE IRVIN	10000	79.00	79.00
L. HEYDA	**ALL-STAR GEMS MINIATURE FIGURINES**		
89 CARL YASTRZEMSKI	10000	75.00	75.00
89 JOHNNY BENCH	10000	75.00	75.00
89 STEVE CARLTON	10000	75.00	75.00
89 TED WILLIAMS	10000	75.00	75.00
90 DARRYL STRAWBERRY	10000	75.00	75.00
90 JOHN WOODEN	10000	75.00	75.00
90 WAYNE GRETZKY	10000	75.00	75.00
91 BOBBY HULL	10000	75.00	75.00
91 BRETT HULL	10000	75.00	75.00
J. SLOCKBOWER	**ALL-STAR GEMS MINIATURE FIGURINES**		
90 LUIS APARICIO	10000	75.00	75.00
91 KEN GRIFFEY, JR.	10000	75.00	75.00
91 ROD CAREW	10000	75.00	75.00
91 WARREN SPAHN	10000	75.00	75.00
92 CARLTON FISK	10000	79.00	79.00
92 ISIAH THOMAS	10000	79.00	79.00
R. SUN	**ALL-STAR GEMS MINIATURE FIGURINES**		
90 MIKE SCHMIDT	10000	75.00	75.00
J. MARTIN	**BASEBALL/FOOTBALL/HOCKEY SERIES**		
86 GEORGE BRETT BASEBALL ROUNDER	OP	9.95	16.00
86 GEORGE BRETT BASEBALL ROUNDER, SIGNED	2000	30.00	30.00
86 GEORGE BRETT CERAMIC BASEBALL	OP	20.00	20.00
86 GEORGE BRETT CERAMIC BASEBALL, SIGNED	2000	50.00	50.00
T. SIZEMORE	**BASEBALL/FOOTBALL/HOCKEY SERIES**		
85 PETE ROSE CERAMIC BASEBALL	OP	9.95	16.00
85 PETE ROSE CERAMIC BASEBALL, SIGNED	4192	39.00	75.00
C. SOILEAU	**BASEBALL/FOOTBALL/HOCKEY SERIES**		
87 ROGER STAUBACH CERAMIC FOOTBALL	OP	9.95	16.00
87 ROGER STAUBACH CERAMIC FOOTBALL, SIGNED	1979	39.00	39.00
M. TAYLOR	**BASEBALL/FOOTBALL/HOCKEY SERIES**		
90 WAYNE GRETZKY CERAMIC HOCKEY	OP	18.00	18.00

YR	NAME	LIMIT	ISSUE	TREND
91	JOE MONTANA CERAMIC FOOTBALL	OP	18.00	18.00
92	CARLTON FISH CERAMIC BASEBALL	OP	18.00	18.00
L. HEYDA		**BOB COUSY COLLECTION**		
94	BOB COUSY	RT	225.00	300.00
94	BOB COUSY MINI	5000	40.00	40.00
R. SUN		**EDDIE MATHEWS COLLECTION**		
94	EDDIE MATHEWS	50	150.00	300.00
94	EDDIE MATHEWS MINI	RT	40.00	100.00
J. SLOCKBOWER			**FRANK THOMAS**	
95	FRANK THOMAS (AUTOGRAPHED)	SO	200.00	650.00
95	FRANK THOMAS MINI	RT	40.00	75.00
L. HEYDA		**KAREEM ABDUL-JABBAR SKY HOOK COLLECTION**		
89	KAREEM ABDUL-JABBAR A/P	100	200.00	450.00
89	KAREEM ABDUL-JABBAR H/S	1989	175.00	495.00
89	KAREEM ABDUL-JABBAR PURPLE UNIFORM H/S	33	275.00	5500.00
NOBLE STUDIO		**LEAVE IT TO BEAVER/JERRY MATHERS**		
95	LEAVE IT TO BEAVER 7 1/2" AP	234	250.00	250.00
95	LEAVE IT TO BEAVER AUTOGRAPHED	1963	195.00	195.00
95	LEAVE IT TO BEAVER MINI AUTOGRAPHED	5000	50.00	50.00
R. SUN		**MAGIC JOHNSON GOLD RIM COLLECTION**		
88	MAGIC JOHNSON COMMEMORATIVE	32	275.00	2800.00
88	MAGIC JOHNSON-MAGIC IN MOTION	1737	125.00	650.00
88	MAGIC JOHNSON-MAGIC IN MOTION, PROOF	250	175.00	3700.00
F. BARNUM		**MASTER'S MUSEUM COLLECTION**		
91	JOE MONTANA (SET)	500	*	N/A
L. HEYDA		**MASTER'S MUSEUM COLLECTION**		
91	KAREEM ABDUL-JABBAR	500	3,000.00	3000.00
91	TED WILLIAMS (SET)	500	*	N/A
91	WAYNE GRETZKY (SET)	500	*	N/A
F. BARNUM		**MEMBERS ONLY FIGURINE**		
91	JOE MONTANA-ROAD UNIFORM	CL	75.00	125.00
L. CELLA		**MEMBERS ONLY FIGURINE**		
94	SHAQUILLE O'NEAL	CL	40.00	80.00
L. HEYDA		**MEMBERS ONLY FIGURINE**		
90	WAYNE GRETZKY-HOME UNIFORM	CL	75.00	200.00
91	KAREEM ABDUL-JABBAR (MINI)	CL	75.00	79.00
R. SUN		**MIKE SCHMIDT 500TH HOME RUN COLLECTION**		
87	MIKE SCHMIDT H/S	1987	150.00	975.00
87	MIKE SCHMIDT H/S A/P	20	275.00	1500.00
V. BOVA			**NEGRO LEAGUE SERIES**	
91	BUCK LEONARD	1972	195.00	195.00
91	JAMES (COOL PAPA) BELL	1499	195.00	195.00
91	MATCHED-NUMBER SET #1-950	950	500.00	500.00
91	RAY DANDRIDGE	1987	195.00	195.00
B. FORBES		**PETE ROSE DIAMOND COLLECTION**		
88	FAREWELL CERAMIC BASEBALL CARD	OP	9.95	16.00
88	FAREWELL CERAMIC BASEBALL CARD, SIGNED	4258	39.00	65.00
H. REED		**PETE ROSE PLATINUM EDITION**		
85	PETE ROSE-FOR THE RECORD, SIGNED	4192	125.00	1375.00
PALUSO				**PLAQUES**
87	PLAQUE-ONLY PERFECT, SIGNED	500	150.00	340.00
J. MARTIN				**PLAQUES**
86	GEORGE BRETT-ROYALTY IN MOTION, SIGNED	2000	85.00	195.00
86	REGGIE JACKSON-THE ROUNDTRIPPER, PROOF	SO	200.00	300.00
86	REGGIE JACKSON-THE ROUNDTRIPPER, SIGNED	500	150.00	240.00
87	ROGER STAUBACH, SIGNED	1979	85.00	195.00
T. SIZEMORE				**PLAQUES**
85	PETE ROSE-DESIRE TO WIN, SIGNED	4192	75.00	75.00
J. MARTIN		**REGGIE JACKSON 500TH HOME RUN EDITION**		
86	CERAMIC BASEBALL CARD	OP	9.95	16.00
86	CERAMIC BASEBALL CARD, SIGNED	500	39.00	65.00
J. HOFFMAN				**RINGO STARR**
96	BEATLES, RINGO STARR 9 1/2"	1000	350.00	350.00
96	BEATLES, RINGO STARR MINI	10000	50.00	50.00
96	RINGO STARR 9 1/2" AP	250	600.00	600.00
96	RINGO STARR/DRUMMING	5000	150.00	150.00
L. CELLA		**SAM SNEAD COLLECTION**		
94	SAM SNEAD	RT	150.00	150.00
94	SAM SNEAD MINI	RT	40.00	40.00
R. SUH			**SHAQUILLE O'NEAL**	
95	SHAQUILLE O'NEAL (AUTOGRAPHED)	SO	225.00	800.00
95	SHAQUILLE O'NEAL MINI	RT	40.00	50.00
F. BARNUM			**SIGNED FIGURINES**	
89	YOGI BERRA	2000	225.00	250.00
89	YOGI BERRA H/S A/P	250	350.00	375.00
90	GEORGE BRETT	2500	225.00	225.00
90	WHITEY FORD	2360	225.00	225.00
91	JOE MONTANA A/P H/S	250	500.00	750.00
91	JOE MONTANA H/S	2250	325.00	425.00
92	HANK AARON	1982	225.00	225.00
V. BOVA			**SIGNED FIGURINES**	
91	AL BARLICK	1989	175.00	175.00
91	MONTE IRVIN	1973	225.00	225.00

YR	NAME	LIMIT	ISSUE	TREND
	L. HEYDA		**SIGNED FIGURINES**	
89	CARL YASTREZEMSKI H/S A/P	250	150.00	495.00
89	CARL YASTRZEMSKI-YAZ	1989	150.00	350.00
89	JOE DIMAGGIO H/S	2214	275.00	1375.00
89	JOHN WOODEN-COACHING CLASSICS	1975	175.00	175.00
89	JOHNNY BENCH H/S	1989	150.00	375.00
89	JOHNNY BENCH H/S A/P	250	150.00	550.00
89	STEVE CARLTON H/S	3290	175.00	235.00
89	TED WILLIAMS H/S	2654	295.00	575.00
89	WAYNE GRETZKY H/S	1851	225.00	1000.00
89	WAYNE GRETZKY, ARTIST PROOF H/S	300	695.00	1800.00
90	DARRYL STRAWBERRY	2500	225.00	225.00
90	JOE DIMAGGIO AP H/S	325	695.00	2400.00
91	BOBBY HULL-THE GOLDEN JET	1983	225.00	225.00
91	BRETT HULL-THE GOLDEN BRETT	1986	225.00	225.00
91	HULL MATCHED FIGURINES	950	500.00	500.00
	J. SLOCKBOWER		**SIGNED FIGURINES**	
90	LUIS APARICIO	1974	225.00	225.00
91	KEN GRIFFEY, JR.	1989	225.00	225.00
91	ROD CAREW-HITTING SPLENDOR	1991	225.00	225.00
91	WARREN SPAHN	1973	225.00	225.00
92	CARLTON FISK	1972	225.00	225.00
92	ISIAH THOMAS	1990	225.00	225.00
	K.L. SUN		**SIGNED FIGURINES**	
93	KRISTI YAMAGUCHI	RT	195.00	300.00
93	KRISTI YAMAGUCHI MINI	RT	79.00	79.00
	V. DAVIS		**TROY AIKMAN**	
95	TROY AIKMAN (AUTOGRAPHED)	SO	200.00	800.00
95	TROY AIKMAN MINI	RT	40.00	90.00

GENESIS DESIGNS

	NAME	LIMIT	ISSUE	TREND
	M. MORRIS		**BIBLICAL**	
00	THOMAS: RECEIVING THE KING	2000	*	N/A
98	MOSES: RECEIVING THE LAW	1998	150.00	150.00
99	MARY: RECEIVING THE WORD	1999	*	N/A
	M. MORRIS		**WILDLIFE**	
95	REX NANOOK	2500	160.00	160.00
95	REX NANOOK ARTIST PROOF	250	210.00	210.00

GEO. ZOLTAN LEFTON CO.

	NAME	LIMIT	ISSUE	TREND
	T. FRALEY		**AMERICAN CAROUSEL COLLECTION**	
87	CHARLES CARMEL 5968	CL	70.00	130.00
87	CHARLES CARMEL 5986	CL	35.00	75.00
87	CHARLES LOOFF	CL	70.00	100.00
87	CHARLES LOOFF	CL	70.00	160.00
87	CHARLES LOOFF 5967	CL	70.00	100.00
87	CHARLES LOOFF 5978	CL	100.00	195.00
87	CHARLES LOOFF 5979	CL	100.00	650.00
87	CHARLES LOOFF 5980	CL	100.00	750.00
87	CHARLES LOOFF 5984	CL	35.00	75.00
87	CHARLES LOOFF 5985	CL	35.00	75.00
87	CHARLES LOOFF 7125	CL	500.00	680.00
87	CHARLES LOOFF 7126	CL	500.00	800.00
87	CHARLES LOOFF 7127	CL	500.00	900.00
87	CHARLES LOOFF 7130	CL	125.00	260.00
87	CHARLES LOOFF 7131	CL	125.00	700.00
87	CHARLES LOOFF 7132	CL	125.00	125.00
87	DANIEL MULLER ROCKER 5982	CL	70.00	140.00
87	LOOFF 5972	CL	400.00	800.00
87	M.C. ILLIONS 5970	CL	70.00	100.00
87	M.C. ILLIONS 5971	CL	70.00	130.00
87	M.C. ILLIONS 5973	CL	500.00	900.00
87	M.C. ILLIONS 5988	CL	35.00	75.00
87	M.C. ILLIONS 5989	CL	35.00	75.00
87	M.C. ILLIONS 6390	CL	500.00	500.00
87	M.C. ILLIONS 7128	CL	100.00	225.00
87	M.C. ILLIONS 7129	CL	125.00	225.00
87	PTC 5969	CL	70.00	120.00
87	PTC 5987	CL	35.00	105.00
87	PTC. ROCKER 5981	CL	70.00	150.00
	T. FRALEY		**AMERICAN CAROUSEL COLLECTION II**	
88	C.W. PARKER 8322	CL	250.00	250.00
88	C.W. PARKER 8323	CL	135.00	300.00
88	C.W. PARKER 8468	CL	165.00	290.00
88	CHARLES LOOFF 8213	CL	65.00	190.00
88	CHARLES LOOFF 8214	CL	95.00	190.00
88	CHARLES LOOFF 8320	CL	250.00	250.00
88	CHARLES LOOFF 8321	CL	135.00	190.00
88	CHARLES LOOFF 8467	CL	165.00	240.00
88	CHARLES LOOFF SNOWGLOBE 8216	CL	80.00	80.00
88	DANIEL MULLER 8317	CL	55.00	100.00
88	DANIEL MULLER 8318	CL	85.00	130.00
88	DENTZEL 8329	CL	150.00	625.00
88	DENTZEL 8474	CL	235.00	235.00
88	DENTZEL 8475	CL	135.00	475.00

YR	NAME	LIMIT	ISSUE	TREND
88	HERSHELL-SPILLMAN CO. 8330	CL	150.00	450.00
88	HERSHELL-SPILLMAN CO. 8331	CL	150.00	475.00
88	HERSHELL-SPILLMAN CO. 8470	CL	235.00	235.00
88	HERSHELL-SPILLMAN CO. 8471	CL	135.00	475.00
88	HERSHELL-SPILLMAN CO. 8472	CL	235.00	235.00
88	HERSHELL-SPILLMAN CO. 8473	CL	135.00	475.00
88	M.C. ILLIONS 8319	CL	500.00	675.00
88	M.C. ILLIONS 8324	CL	235.00	235.00
88	M.C. ILLIONS 8325	CL	235.00	350.00
88	M.C. ILLIONS 8340	CL	550.00	650.00
88	M.C. ILLIONS 8469	CL	150.00	280.00
88	PTC 8218	CL	65.00	150.00
88	PTC 8219	CL	95.00	150.00
88	PTC 8221 SNOWGLOBE	CL	80.00	80.00
88	PTC 8222	CL	65.00	100.00
88	PTC 8223	CL	95.00	125.00
88	PTC 8224	CL	65.00	125.00
88	PTC 8225	CL	95.00	125.00
88	PTC 8315	CL	55.00	110.00
88	PTC 8316	CL	85.00	105.00

T. FRALEY

TOBIN FRALEY COLLECTION

YR	NAME	LIMIT	ISSUE	TREND
86	C.W. PARKER	CL	70.00	225.00
86	CHARLES CARMEL 5039	CL	75.00	165.00
86	CHARLES CARMEL 5043	CL	35.00	75.00
86	CHARLES LOOFF 5038	CL	75.00	165.00
86	CHARLES LOOFF 5040	CL	75.00	165.00
86	CHARLES LOOFF 5044	CL	35.00	75.00
86	CHARLES LOOFF/RAM	CL	35.00	75.00
86	D.C. MULLER & BROTHER 5049	CL	35.00	75.00
86	D.C. MULLER & BROTHER 5233	CL	25.00	55.00
86	FOUR HORSE MUSICAL CAROUSEL	CL	400.00	900.00
86	GUSTAV DENTZEL CO. 5036	CL	75.00	240.00
86	GUSTAV DENZEL CO. 5235	CL	35.00	140.00
86	HERSHELL-SPILLMAN 5230	CL	25.00	55.00
86	HERSHELL-SPILLMAN CO. 5046	CL	35.00	75.00
86	PTC 5047	CL	35.00	75.00
86	PTC. 5231	CL	25.00	55.00
86	SPILLMAN ENGINEERING 5041	CL	75.00	225.00
86	SPILLMAN ENGINEERING 5042	CL	35.00	75.00
86	STEIN & GOLDSTEIN 5037	CL	75.00	165.00
86	STEIN & GOLDSTEIN 5045	CL	35.00	75.00
86	WILLIAM DENTZEL CO. 5048	CL	35.00	75.00
86	WILLIAM DENTZEL CO. 5051	CL	70.00	300.00
86	WILLIAM DENTZEL CO. 5232	CL	25.00	45.00

T. FRALEY

TOBIN FRALEY COLLECTORS SOCIETY

YR	NAME	LIMIT	ISSUE	TREND
92	TOBIN FRALEY COLLECTOR SOCIETY	CL	35.00	90.00

GLASS EYE
*

YR	NAME	LIMIT	ISSUE	TREND
93	AQUARIUM	1000	17.50	20.00
93	CHERRY BLOSSOM	1000	17.50	20.00
94	CORAL REEF	1500	23.00	25.00
94	HEART AND VINES	1500	23.00	25.00
95	AURORA BOREALIS	150	165.00	175.00
95	GENESIS	500	50.00	55.00

GOEBEL INC.
Price ranges may reflect various demands in the market from one geographic region to another; condition of piece; specific markings found on piece; and/or changes in production of piece.

M.I. HUMMEL

YR	NAME	LIMIT	ISSUE	TREND
95	ANGLER, THE HUM 566	*	320.00	350.00
95	COME BACK SOON HUM 545	*	135.00	160.00
95	JUST DOZING HUM 451	*	220.00	240.00
95	PIXIE HUM 768	*	105.00	120.00
95	RING AROUND THE ROSIE MUSICAL HUM348	10000	675.00	2860.00
95	TO KEEP YOU WARM HUM 759		195.00	230.00
96	GOOSE GIRL HUM47	*	200.00	260.00

M.I. HUMMEL

BAVARIAN VILLAGE COLLECTION

YR	NAME	LIMIT	ISSUE	TREND
96	HAPPY PASTIME HUM 69	RT	175.00	175.00

G. BOCHMANN

BETSEY CLARK

YR	NAME	LIMIT	ISSUE	TREND
72	BLESS YOU	CL	18.00	275.00
72	FRIENDS	CL	21.00	400.00
72	LITTLE MIRACLE	CL	25.00	350.00
72	SO MUCH BEAUTY	CL	25.00	350.00

LORE

BLUMENKINDER

YR	NAME	LIMIT	ISSUE	TREND
66	A BUTTERFLY'S KISS	CL	28.00	N/A
66	APRONFUL OF FLOWERS	CL	25.00	N/A
66	BAREFOOT LAD	CL	28.00	N/A
66	BEARER OF GIFTS	CL	28.00	N/A
66	DISPLAY PLAQUE	CL	4.00	N/A
66	FLOWER FARMER, THE	CL	30.00	N/A
66	FLUTE RECITAL	CL	25.00	N/A
66	GARDEN ROMANCE	CL	50.00	N/A
66	HER FIRST BOUQUET	CL	30.00	N/A
66	HER KITTEN	CL	28.00	N/A

YR	NAME	LIMIT	ISSUE	TREND
66	NATURE'S TREASURES	CL	25.00	N/A
66	ST. VALENTINE'S MESSENGER	CL	30.00	N/A
66	TENDER LOVING CARE	CL	30.00	N/A
69	FIRST JOURNEY	CL	25.00	N/A
69	FIRST LOVE	CL	25.00	N/A
69	GARDEN PRINCES	CL	50.00	N/A
69	SUMMER MAGIC	CL	50.00	N/A
71	BIRD SONG	CL	65.00	N/A
71	BOYFRIEND, THE	CL	65.00	N/A
71	CELLO RECITAL	CL	80.00	N/A
71	COUNTRY LAD	CL	35.00	N/A
71	COUNTRY MAIDEN	CL	35.00	N/A
71	COURTING COUNTRY STYLE	CL	80.00	N/A
72	FIRST DATE	CL	95.00	N/A
72	PARTY GUEST	CL	95.00	N/A
73	ACCOMPANIST, THE	CL	95.00	115.00
73	BY A GARDEN POND	CL	75.00	N/A
73	EASTER TIME	CL	80.00	275.00
73	HITCHHIKER, THE	CL	80.00	N/A
73	KITTENS	CL	75.00	N/A
73	PATIENT, THE	CL	95.00	N/A
75	BOTH IN HARMONY	CL	95.00	N/A
75	COMPANIONS	CL	85.00	N/A
75	FOR YOU-WITH LOVE	CL	95.00	N/A
75	HAPPY MINSTREL	CL	95.00	N/A
75	LOYAL FRIEND	CL	85.00	N/A
75	LUCKY ONE, THE	CL	150.00	N/A
75	SPRINGTIME	CL	95.00	N/A
75	WITH LOVE	CL	150.00	N/A
79	BIRTHDAY MORNING	CL	201.00	N/A
79	FARMHOUSE COMPANIONS	CL	175.00	N/A
79	GARDEN FRIENDS	CL	175.00	N/A
79	HARVEST TREAT	CL	175.00	N/A
79	LOVING TOUCH	CL	201.00	N/A
79	SWEET TREAT	CL	149.00	N/A
80	DANCING SONG	CL	175.00	N/A
80	DRUMMER BOY	CL	180.00	N/A
80	FLUTIST	CL	175.00	N/A
80	ROMANCE	CL	175.00	N/A
80	SPRING SONG	CL	180.00	N/A
80	VIOLINIST	CL	180.00	N/A
82	AUTUMN DELIGHT	CL	165.00	N/A
82	HAPPY SAILING	CL	150.00	N/A
82	LITTLE MOMMY	CL	165.00	N/A
82	MAIL CALL	CL	165.00	N/A
82	PLAY BELL	CL	165.00	N/A
82	SPINNING TOP, THE	CL	150.00	N/A

B. TIMBERLAKE — **BOB TIMBERLAKE SIGNATURE**

YR	NAME	LIMIT	ISSUE	TREND
96	AUTUMN AFTERNOONS	500	490.00	490.00
96	FEBRUARY AT RIVERWOOD	OP	135.00	135.00
96	GATE LATCH	OP	60.00	60.00
96	LATE SNOW AT RIVERWOOD	500	500.00	500.00
96	RITUAL, THE	OP	135.00	135.00

M.I. HUMMEL — **CENTURY COLLECTION**

YR	NAME	LIMIT	ISSUE	TREND
87	PLEASANT JOURNEY HUM-406	CL	500.00	4375.00
95	STRIKE UP THE BAND HUM 668	CL	1,200.00	1450.00
96	LOVE'S BOUNTY HUM 751	*	1,200.00	1550.00

M.I. HUMMEL — **CLUB EXCLUSIVE**

YR	NAME	LIMIT	ISSUE	TREND
95	COUNTRY SUITOR HUM 760	*	195.00	210.00
95	STRUM ALONG HUM 557	*	135.00	143.00
96	AT GRANDPA'S HUM 621	CL	1,300.00	1550.00

G. SKROBEK — **CO-BOY**

YR	NAME	LIMIT	ISSUE	TREND
*	BERT THE SOCCER STAR	CL	*	50.00
*	CANDY THE BAKER'S DELIGHT	CL	*	50.00
*	CONNY THE NIGHT WATCHMAN	CL	*	50.00
*	ED THE WINE CELLAR STEWARD	CL	*	50.00
*	JACK THE PHARMACIST	CL	*	50.00
*	JIM THE BOWLER	CL	*	50.00
*	JOHN THE HAWKEYE HUNTER	CL	*	50.00
*	MARK-SAFETY FIRST	CL	*	50.00
*	MAX THE BOXING CHAMP	CL	*	50.00
*	PETRL THE VILLAGE ANGLER	CL	*	50.00
*	TONI THE SKIER	CL	*	50.00
71	BIT THE BACHELOR	CL	16.00	45.00
71	FIPS THE FOXY FISHERMAN	CL	16.00	60.00
71	FRITZ THE HAPPY BOOZER	CL	16.00	50.00
71	MIKE THE JAM MAKER	CL	16.00	60.00
71	PLUM THE PASTRY CHEF	CL	16.00	60.00
71	ROBBY THE VEGETARIAN	CL	16.00	90.00
71	SAM THE GOURMET	CL	16.00	60.00
71	TOM THE HONEY LOVER	CL	16.00	75.00
71	WIM THE COURT SUPPLIER	CL	16.00	60.00
72	BOB THE BOOKWORM	CL	20.00	50.00
72	BRUM THE LAWYER	CL	20.00	50.00
72	CO-BOY PLAQUE	CL	20.00	50.00

YR	NAME	LIMIT	ISSUE	TREND
72	KUNI THE BIG DIPPER	CL	20.00	60.00
72	PORZ THE MUSHROOM MUNCHER	CL	20.00	60.00
72	SEPP THE BEER BUDDY	CL	20.00	60.00
72	UTZ THE BANKER	CL	20.00	50.00
78	GIL THE GOALIE	CL	34.00	50.00
78	PAT THE PITCHER	CL	34.00	50.00
78	TOMMY TOUCHDOWN	CL	34.00	50.00
80	CARL THE CHEF	CL	49.00	50.00
80	DOC THE DOCTOR	CL	49.00	50.00
80	GERD THE DIVER	CL	49.00	50.00
80	HERB THE HORSEMAN	CL	49.00	50.00
80	MONTY THE MOUNTAIN CLIMBER	CL	49.00	50.00
80	TED THE TENNIS PLAYER	CL	49.00	50.00
81	AL THE TRUMPET PLAYER	CL	45.00	50.00
81	BEN THE BLACKSMITH	CL	45.00	50.00
81	GEORGE THE GOURMAND	CL	45.00	50.00
81	GREG THE GOURMET	CL	45.00	50.00
81	GRETA THE HAPPY HOUSEWIFE	CL	45.00	50.00
81	NICK THE NIGHTCLUB SINGER	CL	45.00	50.00
81	NIELS THE STRUMMER	CL	45.00	50.00
81	PETER THE ACCORDIONIST	CL	45.00	50.00
81	WALTER THE JOGGER	CL	45.00	50.00
84	BRAD THE CLOCKMASTER	CL	75.00	95.00
84	CHRIS THE SHOEMAKER	CL	45.00	50.00
84	CHUCK THE CHIMNEY SWEEP	CL	45.00	50.00
84	FELIX THE BAKER	CL	45.00	50.00
84	HERMAN THE BUTCHER	CL	45.00	50.00
84	HOMER THE DRIVER	CL	45.00	50.00
84	MARTHE THE NURSE	CL	45.00	50.00
84	PAUL THE DENTIST	CL	45.00	50.00
84	RICK THE FIREMAN	CL	45.00	50.00
84	RUDY THE WORLD TRAVELER	CL	45.00	50.00
84	SID THE VINTNER	CL	45.00	50.00
87	BANK-PETE THE PIRATE	CL	80.00	80.00
87	BANK-UTZ THE MONEY BAGS	CL	80.00	80.00
87	CHUCK ON HIS PIG	CL	75.00	75.00
87	CLOCK-CONY THE WATCHMAN	CL	125.00	125.00
87	CLOCK-SEPP AND THE BEER KEG	CL	125.00	125.00

T. DEGRAZIA | | | | **DEGRAZIA**

YR	NAME	LIMIT	ISSUE	TREND
84	DISPLAY PLAQUE	CL	45.00	95.00
84	FLOWER BOY	OP	65.00	110.00
84	FLOWER GIRL	OP	65.00	110.00
84	MY FIRST HORSE	OP	65.00	110.00
84	SUNFLOWER BOY	CL	65.00	300.00
84	WHITE DOVE	OP	45.00	80.00
84	WONDERING	OP	85.00	135.00
85	CHILD	OP	25.00	40.00
85	JOSEPH	OP	55.00	70.00
85	LITTLE MADONNA	OP	80.00	125.00
85	MARY	OP	55.00	65.00
85	NATIVITY SET (3 PIECES)	OP	135.00	195.00
85	PIMA DRUMMER BOY	OP	65.00	110.00
86	BLUE BOY, THE	OP	70.00	95.00
86	FESTIVAL LIGHTS	OP	75.00	95.00
86	MERRY LITTLE INDIAN	12500	175.00	245.00
87	LOVE ME	OP	95.00	110.00
87	WEE THREE	OP	180.00	195.00
88	ANGEL CHRISTMAS PRAYER	OP	70.00	80.00
88	BEAUTIFUL BURDEN	OP	175.00	185.00
88	FLOWER BOY PLAQUE	OP	80.00	80.00
88	LOS NINOS	5000	595.00	645.00
88	MERRILY, MERRILY, MERRILY	OP	95.00	110.00
89	MY BEAUTIFUL ROCKING HORSE	OP	225.00	245.00
89	MY FIRST ARROW	OP	95.00	110.00
89	TWO LITTLE LAMBS	OP	70.00	80.00
90	ALONE	OP	395.00	395.00
90	BIGGEST DRUM	YR	135.00	135.00
90	CRUCIFIXION	YR	295.00	295.00
90	DESERT HARVEST	5000	155.00	155.00
90	EL BURRITO	OP	60.00	60.00
90	LITTLE PRAYER	YR	85.00	85.00
90	NAVAJO BOY	YR	135.00	135.00
90	SUNFLOWER GIRL	OP	95.00	95.00
91	NAVAJO MOTHER	YR	*	N/A
91	SHEPHERD BOY	OP	95.00	95.00
91	WANDERER	YR	75.00	75.00
92	NAVAJO MADONNA	OP	135.00	135.00
92	SUN SHOWERS	5000	195.00	195.00

G. BOCHMANN | | | | **FASHIONS ON PARADE**

YR	NAME	LIMIT	ISSUE	TREND
82	AT THE TEA DANCE	OP	30.00	50.00
82	COSMOPOLITAN, THE	OP	30.00	50.00
82	EDWARDIAN GRACE	OP	30.00	50.00
82	GARDEN FANCIER, THE	OP	30.00	50.00
82	STROLLING ON THE AVENUE	OP	30.00	50.00
82	VISITOR, THE	OP	30.00	50.00

YR	NAME	LIMIT	ISSUE	TREND
83	BRIDE AND GROOM	OP	65.00	100.00
83	DEMURE ELEGANCE	OP	33.00	50.00
83	GENTLE THOUGHTS	OP	33.00	50.00
83	HER TREASURED DAY (BRIDE)	OP	33.00	50.00
83	IMPATIENCE	CL	33.00	50.00
83	REFLECTIONS	OP	33.00	50.00
83	WAITING FOR HIS LOVE (GROOM)	OP	33.00	50.00
84	CENTER COURT	CL	33.00	45.00
84	ON THE FAIRWAY	CL	33.00	45.00
84	SKIMMING GENTLY	CL	33.00	45.00
85	A GENTLE MOMENT	CL	23.00	35.00
85	A LAZY DAY	CL	23.00	35.00
85	AFTERNOON TEA	OP	33.00	50.00
85	GENTLE BREEZES	OP	33.00	50.00
85	RIVER OUTING	OP	33.00	50.00
85	TO THE HUNT	OP	33.00	50.00
86	EQUESTRIAN	OP	36.00	50.00
86	FASHIONS ON PARADE PLAQUE	OP	10.00	13.00
86	SOUTHERN BELLE	OP	36.00	50.00
87	PARIS IN FALL	OP	55.00	55.00
87	PROMENADE IN NICE	OP	55.00	55.00
87	SAY PLEASE	OP	55.00	55.00
87	SHEPHERDESS, THE	OP	55.00	55.00
87	SILVER LACE AND RHINESTONES	OP	55.00	55.00
87	VISCOUNTESS DIANA, THE	OP	55.00	55.00
88	BRIDE AND GROOM (2ND SET)	OP	110.00	110.00
88	FOREVER AND ALWAYS (BRIDE)	OP	55.00	55.00
88	PROMISE, THE- (GROOM)	OP	55.00	55.00

N. ROCKWELL   **GOEBEL**

YR	NAME	LIMIT	ISSUE	TREND
63	ADVERTISING PLAQUE	CL	*	600.00
63	BOYHOOD DREAMS	CL	12.00	400.00
63	BUTTERCUP TEST (BEGUILING BUTTERCUP)	CL	10.00	400.00
63	FIRST LOVE (A SCHOLARLY PACE)	CL	30.00	400.00
63	HOME CURE	CL	16.00	400.00
63	LITTLE VETERINARIAN (MYSTERIOUS MALADY)	CL	15.00	40.00
63	MOTHER'S HELPER (PRIDE OF PARENTHOOD)	CL	15.00	400.00
63	MY FIRST SMOKE	CL	9.00	400.00
63	MY NEW PAL (A BOY MEETS HIS DOG)	CL	12.00	400.00
63	PATIENT ANGLERS (FISHERMAN'S PARADISE)	CL	18.00	400.00
63	SHE LOVES ME (DAY DREAMER)	CL	8.00	400.00
63	TIMELY ASSISTANCE (LOVE AID)	CL	16.00	400.00

*   **LOONEY TUNES SPOTLIGHT COLLECTION**

YR	NAME	LIMIT	ISSUE	TREND
97	AND TO ALL A GOOD BITE	15098	75.00	75.00
97	BAD OL' PUDDY TAT	5098	400.00	400.00
97	BARBER SHOP BAD HARE DAY	10098	110.00	110.00
97	BARBER SHOP HARE-DO	10098	80.00	80.00
97	BARBER SHOP SCAPE	10098	85.00	85.00
97	CHRISTMAS MORNING KISS THE LITTLE BIRDIE	10098	100.00	100.00
97	CHRISTMAS MORNING SCAPE	10098	80.00	80.00
97	CHRISTMAS MORNING WHAT A PRESENT!	10098	70.00	70.00
97	CHRISTMAS TREE DISPLAY	15098	25.00	25.00
97	ISN'T SHE WOVEWE?	10098	185.00	185.00
97	MINE, MINE, MINE	7598	245.00	245.00
97	PLANET X IN THE NAME OF EARTH	10098	110.00	110.00
97	PLANET X IN THE NAME OF MARS	10098	110.00	110.00
97	PLANET X SCAPE	10098	80.00	80.00
97	ZIE BROKEN HEART OF LOVE	10098	150.00	150.00

M.I. HUMMEL   **M.I. HUMMEL**

YR	NAME	LIMIT	ISSUE	TREND
*	ADORATION HUM-23	CL	*	380.00
*	ADORATION HUM-23/I	OP	300.00	400.00-1300.00
*	ADORATION HUM-23/III	OP	470.00	595.00-2000.00
*	ANGEL DUET, CANDLEHOLDER HUM-193	OP	180.00	245.00
*	ANGEL LIGHTS, CANDLEHOLDER HUM-241	SU	*	250.00-350.00
*	ANGEL SERENADE HUM-83	OP	180.00	245.00-750.00
*	ANGEL/ACCORDION, CANDLEHLDER HUM111/39/0	SU	*	165.00-550.00
*	ANGEL/ACCORDION, CANDLEHLDER HUM111/39/1	CL	*	150.00-300.00
*	ANGEL/ACCORDION, CANDLEHOLDER HUM	OP	*	50.00-175.00
*	ANGEL/LUTE, CANDLEHOLDER HUM 1/38/0	OP	*	60.00
*	ANGEL/LUTE, CANDLEHOLDER HUM 111/38/0	SU	*	50.00-175.00
*	ANGEL/LUTE, CANDLEHOLDER HUM 111/38/1	CL	*	150.00-300.00
*	ANGEL/TRUMPET, CANDLEHOLDER HUM 1/40/0	SU	*	60.00
*	ANGEL/TRUMPET, CANDLEHOLDER HUM 111/40/0	SU	*	50.00-175.00
*	ANGEL/TRUMPET, CANDLEHOLDER HUM 111/40/1	CL	*	150.00-300.00
*	ANGEL/TWO CHILDREN AT FEET HUM-108	CL	*	3000.00-15000.00
*	ANGELIC SLEEP, CANDLEHOLDER HUM-25	SU	*	200.00-2000.00
*	ANGELIC SONG HUM-144	OP	125.00	165.00
*	APPLE TREE BOY HUM-142	CL	*	550.00-850.00
*	APPLE TREE BOY HUM-142/3/O	OP	120.00	160.00
*	APPLE TREE BOY HUM-142/I	OP	225.00	310.00
*	APPLE TREE BOY HUM-142/V	OP	1,000.00	1350.00
*	APPLE TREE BOY HUM-142/X	CL	*	28000.00
*	APPLE TREE BOY, CANDLEHOLDER HUM-677	OP	143.00	225.00
*	APPLE TREE BOY, TABLE LAMP HUM-230	TW	*	375.00-1000.00
*	APPLE TREE BOY/GIRL-BOOKENDS HUM-252 A&B	TW	*	300.00-425.00
*	APPLE TREE GIRL HUM-141	CL	*	600.00-900.00

YR	NAME	LIMIT	ISSUE	TREND
*	APPLE TREE GIRL HUM-141/3/O	OP	120.00	160.00
*	APPLE TREE GIRL HUM-141/I	OP	225.00	310.00
*	APPLE TREE GIRL HUM-141/V	OP	1,000.00	1350.00
*	APPLE TREE GIRL HUM-141/X	SU	*	24000.00
*	APPLE TREE GIRL, CANDLEHOLDER HUM-676	OP	143.00	225.00
*	APPLE TREE GIRL, TABLE LAMP HUM-229	TW	*	375.00-1000.00
*	ARTIST HUM-304	OP	200.00	275.00
*	AUF WIEDERSEHEN HUM-153	CL	*	650.00-1200.00
*	AUF WIEDERSEHEN HUM-153/I	OP	250.00	330.00
*	AUF WIEDERSEHEN HUM-153/O	OP	200.00	270.00
*	AUTHORIZED RETAILER PLAQUE HUM-460	CL	*	200.00-1500.00
*	AUTUMN HARVEST HUM-355	OP	180.00	200.00-3000.00
*	BA-BEE-RING 30/0 A&B RED	CL	*	6500.00
*	BA-BEE-RING 30/I A&B RED	CL	*	8500.00
*	BA-BEE-RING HUM-30/0 A&B	OP	160.00	220.00-700.00
*	BAKER HUM-128	OP	160.00	225.00
*	BAND LEADER HUM-129	OP	170.00	225.00
*	BAND LEADER HUM-129/4/O	OP	80.00	115.00
*	BARNYARD HERO HUM-195	CL	*	650.00-1200.00
*	BARNYARD HERO HUM-195/2/O	OP	140.00	185.00
*	BARNYARD HERO HUM-195/I	OP	265.00	350.00
*	BASHFUL HUM-377	OP	170.00	225.00
*	BE PATIENT HUM-197	CL	*	500.00-1000.00
*	BE PATIENT HUM-197/2/O	OP	160.00	225.00
*	BE PATIENT HUM-197/I	OP	230.00	335.00
*	BEGGING HIS SHARE HUM-9	OP	200.00	280.00
*	BIG HOUSECLEANING HUM-363	OP	230.00	315.00
*	BIRD DUET HUM-169	OP	120.00	160.00
*	BIRTHDAY SERENADE HUM-218	CL	*	950.00
*	BIRTHDAY SERENADE HUM-218/1	CL	*	1000.00-1500.00
*	BIRTHDAY SERENADE HUM-218/2/O	OP	150.00	190.00
*	BIRTHDAY SERENADE HUM-218/O	OP	250.00	330.00
*	BIRTHDAY SERENADE, TABLE LAMP HUM-231	TW	*	2500.00
*	BIRTHDAY SERENADE, TABLE LAMP HUM-234	TW	*	1600.00-2100.00
*	BLESSED CHILD (KRUMBAD) HUM-78/I	TW	*	30.00-50.00
*	BLESSED CHILD (KRUMBAD) HUM-78/II	TW	*	35.00-60.00
*	BLESSED CHILD (KRUMBAD) HUM-78/II 1/2	OP	35.00	75.00-150.00
*	BLESSED CHILD (KRUMBAD) HUM-78/III	TW	*	45.00-400.00
*	BLESSED CHILD (KRUMBAD) HUM-78/O	CL	*	150.00-300.00
*	BLESSED CHILD (KRUMBAD) HUM-78/V	TW	*	80.00-150.00
*	BLESSED CHILD (KRUMBAD) HUM-78/VI	TW	*	150.00-850.00
*	BLESSED CHILD (KRUMBAD) HUM-78/VIII	TW	*	300.00-1000.00
*	BLESSED EVENT HUM-333	OP	280.00	350.00
*	BOOK WORM BOOKENDS, BOY & GIRL HUM-14	CL	*	220.00-250.00
*	BOOK WORM HUM-3/I	OP	250.00	335.00
*	BOOK WORM HUM-3/II	TW	*	1200.00-3500.00
*	BOOK WORM HUM-3/III	TW	*	1250.00-4000.00
*	BOOK WORM HUM-8	OP	180.00	245.00
*	BOOK WORM, BOOKENDS, HUM-14 A&B	SU	*	1200.00-1600.00
*	BOOTS HUM-143	CL	*	650.00-1050.00
*	BOOTS HUM-143/I	OP	270.00	360.00
*	BOOTS HUM-143/O	OP	160.00	225.00
*	BOY W/HORSE, CANDLESTICK HUM-117	OP	50.00	60.00
*	BOY WITH ACCORDION HUM-390	OP	70.00	100.00
*	BOY WITH BIRD, ASHTRAY HUM-166	TW	*	140.00-650.00
*	BOY WITH HORSE HUM-239 C	OP	45.00	60.00
*	BOY WITH TOOTHACHE HUM-217	OP	185.00	230.00
*	BROTHER HUM-95	OP	165.00	230.00
*	BUILDER HUM-305	OP	200.00	275.00
*	BUSY STUDENT HUM-367	OP	140.00	180.00
*	CANDLELIGHT, CANDLEHOLDER HUM-192	OP	190.00	265.00
*	CARNIVAL HUM-328	OP	190.00	240.00
*	CELESTIAL MUSICIAN (MINI) HUM-188/4/0	OP	*	115.00
*	CELESTIAL MUSICIAN HUM-188	CL	*	320.00-2000.00
*	CELESTIAL MUSICIAN HUM-188/I	TW	230.00	295.00
*	CELESTIAL MUSICIAN HUM-188/O	OP	180.00	245.00
*	CHICK GIRL HUM-57	CL	*	500.00-1050.00
*	CHICK GIRL HUM-57/2/O	OP	125.00	165.00
*	CHICK GIRL HUM-57/I	OP	220.00	310.00
*	CHICK GIRL HUM-57/O	OP	145.00	185.00
*	CHICK GIRL, BOX (NEW STYLE) HUM III-57	TW	*	300.00-350.00
*	CHICK GIRL, BOX (OLD STYLE) HUM-III-57	CL	*	475.00-550.00
*	CHICKEN-LICKEN HUM-385	OP	240.00	310.00
*	CHICKEN-LICKEN HUM-385/4/O	OP	29.00	140.00
*	CHILD IN BED, LOOKING LEFT HUM-137 A	CL	*	5000.00-7000.00
*	CHILD IN BED, LOOKING RIGHT HUM-137 B	CL	*	350.00-550.00
*	CHILD IN BED, PLAQUE HUM-137	OP	55.00	70.00
*	CHIMNEY SWEEP HUM-12	CL	*	450.00-900.00
*	CHIMNEY SWEEP HUM-12/2/O	OP	110.00	130.00
*	CHIMNEY SWEEP HUM-12/I	OP	180.00	245.00
*	CHRIST CHILD HUM-18	TW	*	160.00
*	CHRISTMAS SONG HUM-343	OP	180.00	245.00
*	CINDERELLA HUM-337	OP	240.00	315.00
*	CLOSE HARMONY HUM-336	OP	240.00	330.00
*	CONFIDENTIALLY HUM-314	OP	230.00	325.00

YR NAME	LIMIT	ISSUE	TREND
* CONGRATULATIONS HUM-17/2	CL	*	4500.00-6500.00
* CONGRATULATIONS HUM-17/O	OP	160.00	225.00-700.00
* CROSSROADS HUM-331	CL	350.00	450.00
* CULPRITS HUM-56	CL	*	850.00-1100.00
* CULPRITS HUM-56 A	OP	245.00	325.00
* CULPRITS, TABLE LAMP HUM-44	CL	*	650.00-750.00
* CULPRITS, TABLE LAMP HUM-44 A	TW	*	325.00-650.00
* DOCTOR HUM-127	OP	135.00	170.00
* DOLL BATH HUM-319	OP	230.00	315.00
* DOLL MOTHER HUM-67	OP	190.00	230.00
* DOLL MOTHER/PRAYER..BKENDS HUM-76 A&B	CL	*	12500.00
* DUET (WITH "LIPS" BASE) HUM-130	CL	*	1250.00
* DUET (WITHOUT TIES), HUM-130	CL	*	2750.00
* DUET HUM-130	OP	225.00	300.00-1000.00
* EASTER GREETINGS! HUM-378	OP	185.00	225.00
* EVENTIDE (RARE) HUM-99	CL	*	3250.00
* EVENTIDE HUM-99	OP	290.00	360.00
* EVENTIDE, TABLE LAMP HUM-104	CL	*	9000.00
* FAREWELL HUM-65	CL	220.00	275.00-350.00
* FAREWELL HUM-65/I	CL	*	325.00-350.00
* FAREWELL HUM-65/O	CL	*	5000.00-8000.00
* FAREWELL, TABLE LAMP HUM-103	CL	*	9000.00
* FARM BOY HUM-66	OP	190.00	260.00
* FARM BOY/GOOSE GIRL BOOKENDS HUM-60 A&B	SU	*	400.00-1250.00
* FAVORITE PET HUM-361	OP	230.00	315.00
* FEATHERED FRIENDS HUM-344	OP	220.00	310.00
* FEEDING TIME HUM-199	CL	*	525.00-1000.00
* FEEDING TIME HUM-199/I	OP	220.00	315.00
* FEEDING TIME HUM-199/O	OP	160.00	225.00
* FESTIVAL HARMONY (FLUTE) HUM-173	CL	95.00	1000.OO-3500.00
* FESTIVAL HARMONY (FLUTE) HUM-173/4/O	OP	95.00	115.00
* FESTIVAL HARMONY (FLUTE) HUM-173/II	TW	*	450.00-800.00
* FESTIVAL HARMONY (FLUTE) HUM-173/O	OP	260.00	350.00
* FESTIVAL HARMONY (MANDOLIN) HUM-172	CL	*	1000.00-3500.00
* FESTIVAL HARMONY (MANDOLIN) HUM-172/4/O	OP	95.00	115.00
* FESTIVAL HARMONY (MANDOLIN) HUM-172/II	CL	95.00	450.00-800.00
* FESTIVAL HARMONY (MANDOLIN) HUM-172/O	OP	260.00	350.00
* FLITTING BUTTERFLY, PLAQUE HUM-139	OP	55.00	70.00
* FLOWER VENDOR HUM-381	OP	200.00	275.00
* FLYING ANGEL HUM-366	CL	105.00	145.00-275.00
* FOLLOW THE LEADER HUM-369	OP	1,000.00	1320.00
* FOR FATHER HUM-87	OP	180.00	240.00
* FOR MOTHER HUM-257	CL	*	225.00
* FOR MOTHER HUM-257/2/O	OP	105.00	130.00
* FOR MOTHER HUM-257/O	OP	170.00	225.00
* FOREST SHRINE HUM-183	OP	460.00	595.00
* FRIENDS HUM-136	CL	*	2000.00-4000.00
* FRIENDS HUM-136/I	OP	180.00	230.00
* FRIENDS HUM-136/V	OP	1,000.00	1350.00
* GAY ADVENTURE HUM-356	OP	160.00	220.00
* GIRL PLAYING A MANDOLIN HUM-254	CL	*	N/A
* GIRL W/BASKET HUM-253	CL	*	N/A
* GIRL W/FIR TREE, CANDLESTICK HUM-116	OP	50.00	60.00
* GIRL W/NOSEGAY, CANDLESTICK HUM-115	OP	50.00	60.00
* GIRL WITH DOLL HUM-239 B	OP	45.00	60.00
* GIRL WITH NOSEGAY HUM-239 A	OP	45.00	60.00
* GIRL WITH SHEET OF MUSIC HUM-389	OP	70.00	100.00
* GIRL WITH TRUMPET HUM-391	OP	70.00	100.00
* GLOBE TROTTER HUM-79	CL	170.00	200.00-750.00
* GOING TO GRANDMA'S HUM-52	CL	*	850.00-1600.00
* GOING TO GRANDMA'S HUM-52/I	TW	*	400.00-1500.00
* GOING TO GRANDMA'S HUM-52/O	OP	230.00	275.00
* GOOD FRIENDS HUM-182	OP	160.00	225.00
* GOOD FRIENDS, BOOKENDS HUM-251 A&B	TW	*	300.00-750.00
* GOOD FRIENDS, TABLE LAMP HUM-228	TW	*	375.00-850.00
* GOOD HUNTING HUM-307	OP	200.00	270.00
* GOOD SHEPHERD HUM-42/I	CL	*	5000.00-8000.00
* GOOD SHEPHERD HUM-42/O	OP	200.00	280.00-900.00
* GOOSE GIRL HUM-47	CL	*	850.00
* GOOSE GIRL HUM-47/3/O	OP	145.00	185.00
* GOOSE GIRL HUM-47/II	OP	380.00	400.00-1300.00
* GOOSE GIRL HUM-47/O	OP	185.00	260.00
* GUIDING ANGEL HUM-357	OP	70.00	100.00
* HAPPINESS HUM-86	OP	110.00	150.00
* HAPPY BIRTHDAY HUM-176	CL	*	600.00-1150.00
* HAPPY BIRTHDAY HUM-176/I	OP	250.00	330.00
* HAPPY BIRTHDAY HUM-176/O	OP	180.00	240.00
* HAPPY DAYS HUM-150	CL	*	900.00-1600.00
* HAPPY DAYS HUM-150/2/O	OP	150.00	190.00
* HAPPY DAYS HUM-150/I	OP	400.00	500.00
* HAPPY DAYS HUM-150/O	OP	250.00	330.00
* HAPPY DAYS, TABLE LAMP HUM-232	TW	*	500.00-1700.00
* HAPPY DAYS, TABLE LAMP HUM-235	TW	*	450.00-1100.00
* HAPPY PASTIME HUM-69	OP	135.00	190.00-650.00
* HAPPY PASTIME, ASHTRAY HUM-62	TW	*	150.00-650.00

YR	NAME	LIMIT	ISSUE	TREND
*	HAPPY PASTIME, BOX (NEW STYLE) HUM III/69	TW	*	150.00-200.00
*	HAPPY PASTIME, BOX (OLD STYLE) HUM III/69	CL	*	425.00-750.00
*	HAPPY TRAVELLER HUM-109	CL	*	1350.00
*	HAPPY TRAVELLER HUM-109	CL	*	180.00-250.00
*	HAPPY TRAVELLER HUM-109/II	CL	*	375.00-900.00
*	HAPPY TRAVELLER HUM-109/O	OP	120.00	165.00
*	HEAR YE, HEAR YE HUM-15	CL	*	1400.00-1700.00
*	HEAR YE, HEAR YE HUM-15/2/O	OP	125.00	190.00
*	HEAR YE, HEAR YE HUM-15/I	OP	200.00	280.00-900.00
*	HEAR YE, HEAR YE HUM-15/II	TW	400.00	450.00-1500.00
*	HEAR YE, HEAR YE HUM-15/O	OP	*	225.00-750.00
*	HEAVENLY ANGEL HUM-21/I	OP	210.00	295.00
*	HEAVENLY ANGEL HUM-21/II	TW	390.00	425.00-1600.00
*	HEAVENLY ANGEL HUM-21/O	OP	100.00	140.00
*	HEAVENLY ANGEL HUM-21/O 1/2	OP	170.00	245.00
*	HEAVENLY LULLABY HUM-262	OP	155.00	210.00
*	HEAVENLY PROTECTION HUM-88	CL	*	1100.00-2400.00
*	HEAVENLY PROTECTION HUM-88/I	OP	370.00	495.00
*	HEAVENLY PROTECTION HUM-88/II	TW	590.00	800.00
*	HEAVENLY SONG, CANDLEHOLDER, HUM-113	CL	*	3000.00-10000.00
*	HELLO HUM-124	CL	*	400.00-1000.00
*	HELLO HUM-124/I	TW	*	275.00-1000.00
*	HELLO HUM-124/O	OP	180.00	245.00
*	HERALD ANGELS, CANDLEHOLDER HUM-37	TW	*	180.00-800.00
*	HOLY CHILD HUM-70	TW	*	280.00
*	HOLY WATER FONT, ANGEL CLOUD HUM-206	OP	45.00	55.00
*	HOLY WATER FONT, ANGEL DUET HUM-146	OP	45.00	55.00
*	HOLY WATER FONT, ANGEL SHRINE HUM-147	OP	45.00	55.00
*	HOLY WATER FONT, ANGEL SITTING HUM-167	OP	45.00	55.00
*	HOLY WATER FONT, ANGEL W/BIRD HUM-22	CL	*	250.00-275.00
*	HOLY WATER FONT, ANGEL W/BIRD HUM-22/I	CL	*	300.00-600.00
*	HOLY WATER FONT, ANGEL W/BIRD HUM-22/O	OP	35.00	45.00
*	HOLY WATER FONT, ANGEL W/BIRD HUM-354C	CL	*	55.00
*	HOLY WATER FONT, ANGEL W/LANTERN HUM-354A	CL	*	N/A
*	HOLY WATER FONT, ANGEL W/TRUMPET	CL	*	N/A
*	HOLY WATER FONT, ANGEL/PRAYER HUM-91 A&B	OP	70.00	90.00-500.00
*	HOLY WATER FONT, CHILD JESUS HUM-26	CL	*	350.00-550.00
*	HOLY WATER FONT, CHILD JESUS HUM-26/I	CL	200.00	200.00-500.00
*	HOLY WATER FONT, CHILD JESUS HUM-26/O	OP	35.00	45.00
*	HOLY WATER FONT, CHILD W/FLOWERS HUM-36	CL	*	400.00-450.00
*	HOLY WATER FONT, CHILD/FLOWERS HUM-36/I	CL	*	175.00-425.00
*	HOLY WATER FONT, CHILD/FLOWERS HUM-36/O	OP	35.00	45.00
*	HOLY WATER FONT, CROSS WITH DOVES HUM-77	CL	*	5000.00-10000.00
*	HOLY WATER FONT, GOOD SHEPHERD HUM-35	CL	*	400.00-450.00
*	HOLY WATER FONT, GOOD SHEPHERD HUM-35/I	CL	*	175.00-425.00
*	HOLY WATER FONT, GOOD SHEPHERD HUM-35/O	OP	35.00	45.00
*	HOLY WATER FONT, GUARD. ANGEL HUM-248/I	CL	*	1300.00-1500.00
*	HOLY WATER FONT, GUARD. ANGEL HUM-248/O	OP	45.00	55.00
*	HOLY WATER FONT, GUARDIAN ANGEL HUM 29/0	CL	*	950.00-1500.00
*	HOLY WATER FONT, GUARDIAN ANGEL HUM 29/I	CL	*	1500.00-2000.00
*	HOLY WATER FONT, GUARDIAN ANGEL HUM-29	CL	*	1300.00-1500.00
*	HOLY WATER FONT, HEAVENLY ANGEL HUM-207	OP	45.00	55.00
*	HOLY WATER FONT, HOLY FAMILY HUM-246	OP	45.00	55.00
*	HOLY WATER FONT, MADONNA W/CHILD HUM-243	OP	45.00	55.00
*	HOLY WATER FONT, WHITE ANGEL HUM-75	OP	35.00	45.00
*	HOLY WATER FONT, WORSHIP HUM-164	OP	45.00	55.00
*	HOME FROM MARKET HUM-198	CL	*	425.00-750.00
*	HOME FROM MARKET HUM-198/2/O	OP	120.00	170.00
*	HOME FROM MARKET HUM-198/I	OP	180.00	240.00
*	HOMEWARD BOUND HUM-334	OP	295.00	360.00
*	JOYFUL & LET'S SING WD BOOKENDS, HUM-120	CL	*	15000.00
*	JOYFUL HUM-53	OP	100.00	140.00
*	JOYFUL, BOX (NEW STYLE)HUM III/53	CL	*	300.00-350.00
*	JOYFUL, BOX (OLD STYLE) HUM III/53	CL	*	475.00-550.00
*	JOYOUS NEWS HUM-27/3	CL	*	260.00-2000.00
*	JOYOUS NEWS HUM-27/I	CL	*	250.00-500.00
*	JOYOUS NEWS HUM-27/III	OP	180.00	245.00
*	JUST RESTING HUM-112	CL	*	700.00-850.00
*	JUST RESTING HUM-112/3/O	OP	125.00	165.00
*	JUST RESTING HUM-112/I	OP	225.00	310.00
*	JUST RESTING, TABLE LAMP HUM II/112	CL	*	375.00-800.00
*	JUST RESTING, TABLE LAMP HUM-225	CL	*	500.00-800.00
*	JUST RESTING, TABLE LAMP HUM-225/I	TW	*	350.00-600.00
*	JUST RESTING, TABLE LAMP HUM-225/II	TW	*	400.00-800.00
*	KISS ME HUM-311	OP	230.00	315.00
*	KNITTING LESSON HUM-256	OP	440.00	525.00
*	LATEST NEWS HUM-184	OP	240.00	320.00
*	LET'S SING HUM-110	CL	*	325.00-600.00
*	LET'S SING HUM-110/I	OP	140.00	185.00
*	LET'S SING HUM-110/O	OP	105.00	140.00
*	LET'S SING, ASHTRAY HUM-114	TW	*	150.00-1000.00
*	LET'S SING, BOX (NEW STYLE) III/110	TW	*	300.00-350.00
*	LET'S SING, BOX (OLD STYLE) III/110	CL	*	475.00-550.00
*	LETTER TO SANTA HUM-340	OP	285.00	360.00
*	LITTLE BAND (ON BASE) HUM-392	TW	*	275.00-450.00

YR NAME	LIMIT	ISSUE	TREND
* LITTLE BAND ON MUSIC BOX	TW	*	400.00-500.00
* LITTLE BAND, CANDLEHOLDER/BOX HUM-388	TW	*	275.00-500.00
* LITTLE BOOKKEEPER HUM-306	OP	240.00	315.00
* LITTLE CELLIST HUM-89	CL	*	1425.00
* LITTLE CELLIST HUM-89/I	OP	180.00	240.00
* LITTLE CELLIST HUM-89/II	TW	380.00	450.00-1500.00
* LITTLE DRUMMER HUM-240	OP	125.00	165.00
* LITTLE FIDDLER HUM-2/4/O	OP	80.00	115.00-140.00
* LITTLE FIDDLER HUM-2/I	TW	370.00	400.00-1500.00
* LITTLE FIDDLER HUM-2/II	TW	*	1100.00-3500.00
* LITTLE FIDDLER HUM-2/III	TW	*	1300.00-4000.00
* LITTLE FIDDLER HUM-2/O	OP	190.00	245.00
* LITTLE FIDDLER HUM-4	OP	170.00	225.00
* LITTLE FIDDLER, PLAQUE (RARE) HUM-93	CL	*	3000.00-5000.00
* LITTLE FIDDLER, PLAQUE HUM-93	TW	*	150.00-575.00
* LITTLE FIDDLER, PLAQUE WD FRAME, HUM-107	CL	*	5000.00-6000.00
* LITTLE GABRIEL HUM-32/I	CL	*	1200.00-2500.00
* LITTLE GABRIEL HUM-32/O	CL	*	180.00-550.00
* LITTLE GABRIEL, 5 IN. HUM-32	OP	115.00	165.00
* LITTLE GABRIEL, HUM-32	CL	*	1500.00-2500.00
* LITTLE GARDENER HUM-74	OP	100.00	130.00
* LITTLE GOAT HERDER HUM-200	CL	*	500.00-850.00
* LITTLE GOAT HERDER HUM-200/I	OP	200.00	260.00
* LITTLE GOAT HERDER HUM-200/O	OP	160.00	225.00
* LITTLE GOAT HERDER, BOOKENDS HUM-250 A&B	TW	*	300.00-750.00
* LITTLE GUARDIAN HUM-145	OP	125.00	165.00
* LITTLE HELPER HUM-73	OP	100.00	130.00
* LITTLE HIKER HUM-16	CL	*	450.00-750.00
* LITTLE HIKER HUM-16/2/O	OP	100.00	130.00
* LITTLE HIKER HUM-16/I	OP	180.00	245.00
* LITTLE PHARMACIST HUM-322	CL	*	2000.00-3000.00
* LITTLE PHARMACIST HUM-322/E	OP	200.00	270.00
* LITTLE SCHOLAR HUM-80	OP	180.00	240.00
* LITTLE SHOPPER HUM-96	OP	120.00	160.00
* LITTLE SWEEPER HUM-171	CL	*	170.00-500.00
* LITTLE SWEEPER HUM-171/4/O	OP	80.00	140.00
* LITTLE SWEEPER HUM-171/O	OP	110.00	160.00
* LITTLE TAILOR HUM-308	OP	200.00	275.00
* LITTLE THRIFTY, BANK HUM-118	OP	130.00	170.00
* LOST SHEEP HUM-68	CL	*	350.00-750.00
* LOST SHEEP HUM-68/2/O	CL	125.00	160.00-350.00
* LOST SHEEP HUM-68/O	CL	180.00	200.00-450.00
* LOST STOCKING HUM-374	OP	120.00	165.00
* LULLABY, CANDLEHOLDER HUM-24/I	TW	*	210.00
* LULLABY, CANDLEHOLDER HUM-24/III	TW	*	475.00-1900.00
* M.I. HUMMEL (ENGLISH), PLAQUE HUM-187 A	OP	75.00	110.00-225.00
* MAIL IS HERE, THE-PLAQUE HUM-140	TW	*	250.00-900.00
* MAIL IS HERE, THE-HUM-226	OP	470.00	595.00
* MAIL IS HERE, THE-PLAQ. OVERGLAZE HUM140	CL	*	1250.00
* MARCH WINDS HUM-43	OP	135.00	170.00
* MAX AND MORITZ HUM-123	OP	190.00	245.00-800.00
* MEDITATION HUM-13/2/O	OP	120.00	160.00
* MEDITATION HUM-13/II	TW	*	350.00-5000.00
* MEDITATION HUM-13/O	OP	190.00	245.00
* MEDITATION HUM-13/V	TW	*	1200.00-5000.00
* MEDITATION, HUM-13	CL	*	4000.00-5000.00
* MERRY WANDERER HUM-11	CL	*	600.00-750.00
* MERRY WANDERER HUM-11/2/O	OP	115.00	160.00
* MERRY WANDERER HUM-11/O	OP	160.00	225.00
* MERRY WANDERER HUM-7/I	TW	360.00	425.00-1750.00
* MERRY WANDERER HUM-7/II	TW	1,100.00	1200.00-3500.00
* MERRY WANDERER HUM-7/III	TW	*	1250.00-4000.00
* MERRY WANDERER HUM-7/O	OP	220.00	310.00
* MERRY WANDERER HUM-7/X	TW	*	24000.00
* MERRY WANDERER, PLAQUE HUM-92	TW	*	150.00-575.00
* MERRY WANDERER/PLAQ. WD FRAME, HUM-106	CL	*	5000.00-6000.00
* MISCHIEF MAKER HUM-342	OP	220.00	310.00
* MOTHER'S DARLING HUM-175	OP	180.00	245.00
* MOTHER'S HELPER HUM-133	OP	160.00	225.00
* MOUNTAINEER HUM-315	OP	180.00	240.00
* NOT FOR YOU! HUM-317	OP	200.00	270.00
* ON SECRET PATH HUM-386	OP	210.00	275.00
* OUT OF DANGER HUM-56 B	OP	245.00	325.00
* OUT OF DANGER, TABLE LAMP, HUM-44 B	TW	*	325.00-650.00
* PHOTOGRAPHER HUM-178	OP	230.00	315.00
* PLAYMATES HUM-58	CL	*	500.00-1050.00
* PLAYMATES HUM-58/2/O	OP	125.00	165.00-180.00
* PLAYMATES HUM-58/I	OP	220.00	310.00
* PLAYMATES HUM-58/O	OP	145.00	185.00
* PLAYMATES, BOX (NEW STYLE) HUM III/58	TW	*	300.00-350.00
* PLAYMATES, BOX (OLD STYLE) HUM III/58	CL	*	425.00-550.00
* PLAYMATES/CHICK GIRL BOOKENDS HUM-61 A&B	SU	*	400.00-1250.00
* POSTMAN HUM-119/2/O	OP	115.00	175.00
* POSTMAN HUM-119/O	OP	170.00	225.00
* PRAYER BEFORE BATTLE HUM-20	OP	145.00	185.00

YR	NAME	LIMIT	ISSUE	TREND
*	PRAYER BEFORE BATTLE, ASHTRAY HUM-19	CL	*	5000.00-10000.00
*	PUPPY LOVE & SERENADE/DOG BKENDS HUM-122	CL	*	15000.00
*	PUPPY LOVE HUM-1	RT	125.00	275.00-950.00
*	QUARTET, PLAQUE HUM-134	TW	*	250.00-1000.00
*	RETREAT TO SAFETY HUM-201	CL	*	650.00-1200.00
*	RETREAT TO SAFETY HUM-201/2/O	OP	140.00	180.00
*	RETREAT TO SAFETY HUM-201/I	OP	250.00	350.00
*	RETREAT TO SAFETY, PLAQUE HUM-126	TW	*	185.00-700.00
*	RIDE INTO CHRISTMAS HUM-396	CL	*	525.00-2500.00
*	RIDE INTO CHRISTMAS HUM-396/2/O	OP	200.00	260.00
*	RIDE INTO CHRISTMAS HUM-396/I	OP	360.00	485.00
*	RING AROUND THE ROSIE HUM-348	OP	2,300.00	2860.00
*	RUN-A-WAY HUM-327	OP	210.00	280.00
*	SAINT GEORGE HUM-55	OP	280.00	350.00
*	SCHOOL BOY HUM-82	CL	*	625.00-775.00
*	SCHOOL BOY HUM-82/2/O	OP	120.00	160.00
*	SCHOOL BOY HUM-82/II	OP	380.00	500.00-1600.00
*	SCHOOL BOY HUM-82/O	OP	160.00	225.00
*	SCHOOL BOYS HUM-170	CL	*	2150.00-5000.00
*	SCHOOL BOYS HUM-170/I	OP	1,000.00	1320.00
*	SCHOOL BOYS HUM-170/III	CL	*	1850.00-2250.00
*	SCHOOL GIRL HUM-81	CL	*	350.00-750.00
*	SCHOOL GIRL HUM-81/2/O	OP	120.00	160.00
*	SCHOOL GIRL HUM-81/O	OP	160.00	225.00
*	SCHOOL GIRLS HUM-177	CL	*	2150.00-5000.00
*	SCHOOL GIRLS HUM-177/I	OP	1,000.00	1320.00
*	SCHOOL GIRLS HUM-177/III	CL	*	1850.00-2250.00
*	SENSITIVE HUNTER HUM-6	CL	*	850.00-1000.00
*	SENSITIVE HUNTER HUM-6/2/O	OP	125.00	165.00
*	SENSITIVE HUNTER HUM-6/I	OP	210.00	280.00
*	SENSITIVE HUNTER HUM-6/II	TW	*	350.00-2000.00
*	SENSITIVE HUNTER HUM-6/O	OP	160.00	225.00
*	SERENADE HUM-85	CL	*	750.00-1500.00
*	SERENADE HUM-85/4/O	OP	80.00	120.00
*	SERENADE HUM-85/II	OP	380.00	500.00
*	SERENADE HUM-85/O	OP	110.00	150.00
*	SHE LOVES ME, SHE LOVES ME NOT! HUM-174	OP	150.00	220.00
*	SHE LOVES ME..NOT, TABLE LAMP HUM-227	TW	*	375.00-850.00
*	SHEPHERD'S BOY HUM-64	OP	185.00	260.00
*	SHINING LIGHT HUM-358	OP	70.00	100.00
*	SHRINE, TABLE LAMP HUM-100	CL	*	8000.00-10000.00
*	SIGNS OF SPRING HUM-203	CL	*	550.00-1000.00
*	SIGNS OF SPRING HUM-203/2/O	CL	*	225.00-1500.00
*	SIGNS OF SPRING HUM-203/I	CL	*	275.00-600.00
*	SIGNS OF SPRING W/TWO SHOES HUM 203/2/O	CL	120.00	1500.00
*	SILENT NIGHT CANDLEHLDR/BLK CHILD HUM-54	CL	*	7500.00-12000.00
*	SILENT NIGHT, CANDLEHOLDER HUM-54	TW	*	360.00
*	SILENT NIGHT/BLK CHILD/ADVENT GRP HUM-31	CL	*	22500.00
*	SILENT NIGHT/WHT CHILD/ADVENT GRP HUM-31	CL	*	12500.00
*	SINGING LESSON (WITHOUT BASE) HUM-41	CL	*	5000.00-10000.00
*	SINGING LESSON HUM-63	OP	100.00	135.00-500.00
*	SINGING LESSON, ASHTRAY HUM-34	TW	*	175.00-650.00
*	SINGING LESSON, BOX (NEW STYLE) HUM III/63	TW	*	300.00-350.00
*	SINGING LESSON, BOX (OLD STYLE) HUM III/63	CL	*	475.00-550.00
*	SISTER HUM-98	CL	*	325.00-700.00
*	SISTER HUM-98/2/O	OP	120.00	160.00
*	SISTER HUM-98/O	OP	165.00	230.00
*	SKIER HUM-59	OP	185.00	850.00
*	SMART LITTLE SISTER HUM-346	OP	210.00	275.00
*	SOLIDIER BOY HUM-332	OP	180.00	240.00
*	SOLOIST HUM-135	CL	*	160.00-500.00
*	SOLOIST HUM-135/4/O	OP	80.00	140.00
*	SOLOIST HUM-135/O	OP	110.00	150.00
*	SPRING CHEER HUM-72	TW	*	200.00-650.00
*	SPRING DANCE HUM-353/I	TW	*	550.00-2000.00
*	SPRING DANCE HUM-353/O	OP	*	350.00
*	STANDING BOY, PLAQUE HUM-168	TW	*	200.00-1100.00
*	STAR GAZER HUM-132	OP	180.00	230.00-800.00
*	STITCH IN TIME HUM-255	CL	*	340.00-800.00
*	STITCH IN TIME HUM-255/4/O	OP	80.00	115.00-140.00
*	STORMY WEATHER HUM-71	CL	*	525.00-1350.00
*	STORMY WEATHER HUM-71/2/O	OP	250.00	330.00-360.00
*	STORMY WEATHER HUM-71/I	OP	380.00	525.00
*	STREET SINGER HUM-131	OP	155.00	220.00
*	STROLLING ALONG HUM-5	CL	120.00	275.00-950.00
*	SUPREME PROTECTION HUM-364	CL	*	350.00-4000.00
*	SUPREME PROTECTION HUM-364 (ALTERED J)	CL	*	600.00-850.00
*	SURPRISE HUM-94	CL	*	550.00-1000.00
*	SURPRISE HUM-94/3/O	OP	130.00	170.00-550.00
*	SURPRISE HUM-94/I	OP	235.00	325.00-950.00
*	SWAYING LULLABY, PLAQUE HUM-165	TW	*	220.00-1100.00
*	SWEET MUSIC HUM-186	OP	160.00	225.00
*	SWEET MUSIC W/STRIPPED SLIPPERS HUM-186	CL	*	1200.00-1600.00
*	TELLING HER SECRET HUM-196	CL	*	800.00-1500.00
*	TELLING HER SECRET HUM-196/I	TW	*	400.00-950.00

YR	NAME	LIMIT	ISSUE	TREND
*	TELLING HER SECRET HUM-196/O	OP	250.00	330.00
*	TINY BABY IN CRIB, WALL PLAQ., HUM-138	CL	*	2000.00-4500.00
*	TO MARKET HUM-49	CL	*	600.00-1700.00
*	TO MARKET HUM-49/3/O	OP	140.00	175.00
*	TO MARKET HUM-49/I	TW	*	425.00-1700.00
*	TO MARKET HUM-49/O	OP	225.00	325.00
*	TO MARKET, TABLE LAMP HUM-101	CL	*	500.00-1000.00
*	TO MARKET, TABLE LAMP HUM-223	TW	*	495.00-850.00
*	TO MARKET,TABLE LAMP(PL. POST) HUM-101	CL	*	6000.00-10000.00
*	TO MARKET,TBL LAMP TREE TRK POST HUM-101	CL	*	1500.00-2000.00
*	TRUMPET BOY HUM-97	OP	110.00	525.00
*	TUNEFUL ANGEL HUM-359	OP	70.00	100.00
*	TUNEFUL GOOD NIGHT, PLAQUE HUM-180	TW	*	200.00-800.00
*	UMBRELLA BOY HUM-152	CL	*	2400.00-7000.00
*	UMBRELLA BOY HUM-152 A	CL	*	1500.00-2500.00
*	UMBRELLA BOY HUM-152/II A	OP	1,200.00	1600.00
*	UMBRELLA BOY HUM-152/O A	OP	490.00	650.00
*	UMBRELLA GIRL HUM-152 B	CL	*	1700.00-7000.00
*	UMBRELLA GIRL HUM-152/II B	OP	1,200.00	1600.00
*	UMBRELLA GIRL HUM-152/O B	OP	490.00	650.00
*	VACATION TIME, PLAQUE HUM-125	TW	*	185.00-750.00
*	VILLAGE BOY HUM-51	CL	*	900.00-1150.00
*	VILLAGE BOY HUM-51/2/O	OP	115.00	165.00
*	VILLAGE BOY HUM-51/3/O	OP	100.00	130.00
*	VILLAGE BOY HUM-51/I	TW	*	300.00-1100.00
*	VILLAGE BOY HUM-51/O	OP	195.00	280.00
*	VISITING AN INVALID HUM-382	OP	185.00	225.00
*	VOLUNTEER TABLE LAMP, HUM-102	CL	*	8000.00-10000.00
*	VOLUNTEERS HUM-50	CL	*	1250.00-1550.00
*	VOLUNTEERS HUM-50/2/O	OP	190.00	245.00
*	VOLUNTEERS HUM-50/I	TW	*	450.00-1500.00
*	VOLUNTEERS HUM-50/O	OP	250.00	330.00
*	WAITER HUM-154	CL	*	550.00-1150.00
*	WAITER HUM-154/I	OP	240.00	325.00
*	WAITER HUM-154/O	OP	180.00	240.00
*	WAITER W/WHISKY HUM 154/0	CL	*	1600.00-2100.00
*	WASH DAY HUM-321	OP	230.00	340.00-5000.00
*	WASH DAY HUM-321/4/O	OP	80.00	115.00-140.00
*	WATCHFUL ANGEL HUM-194	OP	270.00	340.00
*	WAYSIDE DEVOTION HUM-28	CL	*	1700.00-1900.00
*	WAYSIDE DEVOTION HUM-28/II	OP	370.00	450.00
*	WAYSIDE DEVOTION HUM-28/III	OP	480.00	600.00
*	WAYSIDE HARMONY HUM-111	CL	*	650.00-800.00
*	WAYSIDE HARMONY HUM-111/3/O	OP	125.00	165.00
*	WAYSIDE HARMONY HUM-111/I	OP	220.00	310.00
*	WAYSIDE HARMONY, TABLE LAMP HUM II/111	CL	*	375.00-800.00
*	WAYSIDE HARMONY, TABLE LAMP HUM-224	CL	*	500.00-800.00
*	WAYSIDE HARMONY, TABLE LAMP HUM-224/I	TW	*	350.00-600.00
*	WAYSIDE HARMONY, TABLE LAMP HUM-224/II	TW	*	400.00-800.00
*	WEARY WANDERER HUM-204	OP	200.00	290.00
*	WHICH HAND? HUM-258	OP	165.00	225.00
*	WHITSUNTIDE HUM-163	OP	270.00	330.00
*	WORSHIP HUM-84	CL	*	475.00-1500.00
*	WORSHIP HUM-84/O	OP	135.00	180.00
*	WORSHIP HUM-84/V	TW	*	1125.00-3000.00
38	ADORATION WITH BIRD, HUM-105	CL	*	7500.00
41	HUM 148	CL	*	N/A
41	HUM 149	CL	*	N/A
43	HUM-155	CL	*	N/A
43	HUM-156	CL	*	N/A
43	HUM-158 GIRL STANDING WITH DOG IN ARMS	CL	*	N/A
43	HUM-159 GIRL STANDING W/FLOWERS IN ARMS	CL	*	N/A
43	HUM-160 GIRL STANDING TIERED DRESS/FLWRS	CL	*	N/A
43	HUM-161 GIRL STANDING HANDS IN POCKETS	CL	*	N/A
46	HUM-162 GIRL STANDING WITH HANDBAG	CL	*	N/A
47	ACCORDION BOY HUM-185	RT	160.00	200.00-750.00
48	COQUETTES HUM-179	OP	230.00	325.00
48	OLD MAN READING NEWSPAPER HUM-181	CL	*	15000.00-20000.00
48	OLD MAN READING NEWSPAPER/TBL LAMPHUM202	CL	*	15000.00-20000.00
48	OLD MAN WALKING TO MARKET HUM-191	CL	*	15000.00-20000.00
48	OLD WOMAN KNITTING HUM-189	CL	*	15000.00-20000.00
48	OLD WOMAN WALKING TO MARKET HUM-190	CL	*	15000.00-20000.00
51	HUM-215 JESUS STANDING W/LAMB IN ARMS	CL	*	N/A
51	ORCHESTRA HUM-212	CL	*	N/A
52	HAPPY PASTIME/CANDY JAR HUM-221	CL	*	5000.00-10000.00
52	LITTLE VELMA HUM-219	CL	*	4000.00-6000.00
52	WE CONGRATULATE (WITH BASE) HUM-220	OP	135.00	170.00
52	WE CONGRATULATE W/BASE HUM-220/2/O	CL	*	475.00-575.00
54	HUM 236A & B	CL	*	10000.00-15000.00
54	HUM-233 BOY FEEDING BIRDS	CL	*	N/A
55	HOLY WATER FONT, ANGEL JOYOUS NEWS H-241	CL	*	1500.00-2000.00
55	HOLY WATER FONT, ANGEL JOYOUS NEWS H-242	CL	*	1250.00
55	HONEY LOVER HUM-312	RT	190.00	4000.00-5000.00
55	MADONNA HOLDING CHILD HUM-151	CL	44.00	9000.00-12000.00
55	PROFESSOR, THE HUM-320	CL	180.00	4000.00-5000.00

Mickey Mouse as the Brave Little Tailor was the first-ever "Animator's Choice" sculpture and was available exclusively to members of the Walt Disney Collectors Society in 1993.

Part of the Disney Woodcarvings collection from ANRI, Mickey Sorcerer's Apprentice is enhanced by a genuine Swarovski crystal.

Spring Bouquets, the 1987 members-only figurine for the Lladró Collectors Society, was issued at $125 and has appreciated greatly.

An M.I. Hummel collector's club piece, Honey Lover is now a closed edition. Produced by Goebel, it has increased in value since its 1991 release.

YR	NAME	LIMIT	ISSUE	TREND
55	STANDING MADONNA W/CHILD HUM-247	CL	*	10000.00-15000.00
56	BIRTHDAY PRESENT HUM-341	CL	140.00	4000.00-5000.00
56	LETTER TO SANTA CLAUS PROTOTYPE HUM-340	CL	30.00	15000.00-20000.00
57	RING AROUND THE ROSIE HUM-348	CL	70.00	12500.00
62	GIRL W/ACCORDION HUM-259	CL	*	5000.00-10000.00
64	MORNING STROLL HUM-375	CL	170.00	3000.00-4000.00
67	ANGEL WITH ACCORDION HUM-238 B	OP	45.00	60.00-125.00
67	ANGEL WITH LUTE HUM-238 A	OP	*	60.00-125.00
67	ANGEL WITH TRUMPET HUM-238 C	OP	45.00	60.00-125.00
68	ANGEL DUET HUM-261	OP	180.00	245.00
71	ADVENTURE BOUND HUM-347	OP	3,300.00	3980.00
72	A FAIR MEASURE HUM-345	OP	230.00	325.00
72	EASTER TIME HUM-384	OP	28.00	275.00
74	POET, THE HUM-397	CL	220.00	3000.00-4000.00
78	LITTLE ARCHITECT, THE HUM-410	CL	290.00	3000.00-4000.00
79	BIRD WATCHER HUM-300	OP	80.00	240.00
79	BOY AND GIRL, WALL VASE HUM-360 A	TW	*	160.00-675.00
79	BOY, WALL VASE HUM-360 B	TW	*	140.00-650.00
79	GIRL, WALL VASE HUM-360 C	TW	*	140.00-650.00
79	MERRY CHRISTMAS, PLAQUE HUM-323	OP	55.00	135.00
79	SEARCHING ANGEL, PLAQUE HUM-310	OP	55.00	130.00
81	IN TUNE HUM-414	OP	115.00	310.00
81	ON HOLIDAY "HOLIDAY SHOPPER" HUM-350	CL	85.00	4000.00-5000.00
81	ON HOLIDAY HUM-350	OP	85.00	170.00
81	SWEET GREETINGS HUM-352	OP	85.00	200.00
81	THOUGHTFUL HUM-415	OP	105.00	245.00
81	TIMID LITTLE SISTER HUM-394	OP	190.00	485.00
82	BOTANIST HUM-351	OP	84.00	200.00
82	LITTLE NURSE HUM-376	OP	95.00	270.00
83	KNIT ONE, PURL ONE HUM-432	OP	52.00	135.00
83	WITH LOVING GREETINGS HUM-309	OP	80.00	220.00
84	FLYING HIGH HUM-452	CL	75.00	175.00-300.00
84	JUST DOZING HUM-451	OP	220.00	240.00
85	BAKING DAY HUM-330	OP	95.00	310.00
85	GOING HOME HUM-383	OP	125.00	350.00
85	JUBILEE HUM-416	CL	200.00	500.00-600.00
85	JUST FISHING HUM-373	OP	85.00	250.00
85	SING WITH ME HUM-405	OP	125.00	350.00
87	GENTLE GLOW, CANDLEHOLDER HUM-439	OP	110.00	230.00
87	IN THE MEADOW HUM-459	OP	110.00	225.00
87	KINDERGARTNER HUM-467	OP	100.00	225.00
87	SING ALONG HUM-433	OP	145.00	310.00.
88	A BUDDING MAESTRO HUM-477	OP	45.00	120.00
88	ACCOMPANIST, THE HUM-453	OP	39.00	115.00
88	SONG OF PRAISE HUM-454	OP	39.00	115.00
88	SOUND THE TRUMPET HUM-457	OP	45.00	120.00
88	SOUNDS OF THE MANDOLIN HUM-438	OP	65.00	140.00
88	WINTER SONG HUM-476	OP	45.00	125.00
89	AN APPLE A DAY HUM-403	OP	195.00	310.00
89	BIRTHDAY CAKE, CANDLEHOLDER HUM-338	OP	95.00	160.00-5000.00
89	BIRTHDAY PRESENT HUM-341/3/O	OP	140.00	160.00
89	CHRISTMAS ANGEL HUM-301	OP	160.00	280.00
89	DADDY'S GIRLS HUM-371	OP	130.00	250.00
89	HOSANNA HUM-480	OP	68.00	120.00
89	I'LL PROTECT HIM HUM-483	OP	55.00	100.00
89	I'M HERE HUM-478	OP	50.00	120.00
89	IN D MAJOR HUM-430	OP	135.00	225.00
89	IS IT RAINING? HUM-420	OP	175.00	300.00
89	LOVE FROM ABOVE HUM-481	CL	75.00	125.00-150.00
89	MAKE A WISH HUM-475	OP	135.00	225.00
89	ONE FOR YOU, ONE FOR ME HUM-482	OP	50.00	120.00
89	POSTMAN HUM-119	CL	*	240.00-750.00
89	TUBA PLAYER HUM-437	OP	160.00	300.00
89	WASH DAY HUM-321	CL	*	325.00-350.00
90	BATH TIME HUM-412	OP	300.00	485.00
90	GOOD FRIENDS, CANDLEHOLDER HUM-679	OP	143.00	200.00-250.00
90	GRANDMA'S GIRL HUM-561	OP	100.00	160.00
90	GRANDPA'S BOY HUM-562	OP	100.00	160.00
90	HORSE TRAINER HUM-423	OP	155.00	245.00
90	SHE LOVES ME, CANDLEHOLDER HUM-678	OP	143.00	200.00-250.00
90	SLEEP TIGHT HUM-424	OP	155.00	245.00
90	WHAT'S NEW? HUM-418	OP	200.00	310.00
91	A NAP HUM-534	OP	95.00	130.00
91	ART CRITIC HUM-318	OP	230.00	315.00
91	EVENING PRAYER HUM-495	OP	95.00	120.00
91	FRIEND OR FOE HUM-434	OP	190.00	245.00
91	GUARDIAN, THE- HUM-455	OP	140.00	180.00
91	LAND IN SIGHT HUM-530	CL	1,600.00	1800.00-2250.00
91	SCAMP HUM-553	OP	95.00	120.00
91	STORYBOOK TIME HUM-458	OP	330.00	440.00
91	WE WISH YOU THE BEST HUM-600	CL	1,300.00	1400.00-1800.00
91	WHISTLER'S DUET HUM-413	OP	235.00	310.00
92	A SWEET OFFERING HUM-549	OP	75.00	100.00
92	LUCKY FELLOW HUM-560	CL	75.00	75.00-100.00
92	MY WISH IS SMALL HUM-463/O	CL	170.00	250.00-300.00

YR	NAME	LIMIT	ISSUE	TREND
93	A FREE FLIGHT HUM-569	OP	185.00	200.00
93	LITTLE ARCHITECT HUM-410/I	OP	*	330.00
93	ONE PLUS ONE HUM-556	CL	115.00	145.00
93	PARADE OF LIGHTS HUM-616	OP	235.00	275.00
94	CALL TO GLORY HUM-739	OP	250.00	275.00
94	HEAVENLY ANGEL TREE TOPPER HUM-755	OP	450.00	495.00
94	I'M CAREFREE HUM-633	OP	365.00	400.00
94	LITTLE VISITOR HUM-563	RT	180.00	200.00-225.00
94	MORNING STROLL HUM-375/3/O	OP	170.00	195.00
94	POET, THE HUM-397/I	OP	220.00	250.00
95	ANGLER, THE HUM-566	OP	320.00	350.00
95	COME BACK SOON HUM-545	OP	135.00	160.00
95	GOOSE GIRL ANN. CLOCK HUM-750	OP	200.00	220.00
95	LUCKY BOY HUM 335	15000	190.00	190.00
95	OOH, MY TOOTH HUM-533	OP	110.00	125.00
95	PIXIE HUM-768	OP	105.00	120.00
95	TO KEEP YOU WARM HUM-759	OP	195.00	230.00
96	A TUNEFUL TRIO HUM 757	20000	450.00	475.00
96	BLOSSOM TIME HUM 608	OP	155.00	155.00
96	CHRISTMAS SONG HUM 343 4/0	OP	115.00	115.00
96	DELICIOUS HUM 435	OP	155.00	155.00
96	NIMBLE FINGERS HUM 758	OP	225.00	230.00
96	PEN PALS	OP	55.00	55.00
96	SHEPHERD BOY HUM 395	OP	295.00	295.00
M.I. HUMMEL		**M.I. HUMMEL CENTURY COLLECTION**		
86	CHAPEL TIME, CLOCK HUM-442	CL	500.00	1500.00-3000.00
88	CALL TO WORSHIP, CLOCK HUM-441	CL	600.00	1250.00-1500.00
89	HARMONY IN FOUR PARTS HUM-471	CL	850.00	2000.00-2500.00
90	LET'S TELL THE WORLD HUM-487	CL	875.00	1500.00-1800.00
92	ON OUR WAY HUM-472	CL	950.00	1200.00-3000.00
93	WELCOME SPRING HUM-635	CL	1,085.00	1500.00-1800.00
94	ROCK-A-BYE HUM 574	CL	1,150.00	1500.00
95	STRIKE UP THE BAND HUM-668	OP	1,200.00	1400.00-1500.00
98	ECHOES OF JOY HUM 642/0	*	*	180.00
98	ECHOES OF JOY MINIATURE HUM 642/4/0	*	*	120.00
98	HEART'S DELIGHT HUM 698	*	*	220.00
98	HERE'S MY HEART HUM 766	*	*	1375.00
98	LOVE IN BLOOM HUM 699	*	*	220.00
98	ROSES ARE RED HUM 762	*	*	120.00
98	SUMMERTIME ENTERPRISE HUM 428/3/0	*	*	140.00
M.I. HUMMEL		**M.I. HUMMEL COLLECTORS CLUB ANNIVERSARY**		
90	FLOWER GIRL HUM-548	OP	105.00	140.00
90	LITTLE PAIR, THE- HUM-449	OP	170.00	220.00
91	HONEY LOVER HUM-312/I	CL	190.00	230.00
M.I. HUMMEL		**M.I. HUMMEL COLLECTORS CLUB EXCLUSIVES**		
77	VALENTINE GIFT HUM-387	CL	45.00	600.00-3000.00
78	SMILING THROUGH, PLAQUE HUM-690	CL	50.00	150.00-200.00
80	VALENTINE JOY HUM-399	CL	95.00	300.00-400.00
81	DAISIES DON'T TELL HUM-380	CL	80.00	350.00-400.00
82	IT'S COLD HUM-421	CL	80.00	350.00-400.00
83	WHAT NOW? HUM-422	CL	80.00	350.00-400.00
84	COFFEE BREAK HUM-409	CL	90.00	350.00-4000.00
85	SMILING THROUGH HUM-408	CL	125.00	350.00-375.00
86	BIRTHDAY CANDLE, CANDLEHOLDER HUM-440	CL	95.00	350.00-400.00
87	MORNING CONCERT HUM-447	CL	98.00	250.00-300.00
88	SURPRISE, THE- HUM-431	CL	125.00	300.00-350.00
89	HELLO WORLD HUM-429	CL	130.00	300.00-400.00
89	I BROUGHT YOU A GIFT HUM-479	RT	*	175.00
90	I WONDER HUM-486	CL	140.00	250.00-350.00
91	GIFT FROM A FRIEND HUM-485	CL	160.00	250.00-350.00
91	TWO HANDS, ONE TREAT HUM-493	CL	*	150.00
92	CHEEKY FELLOW HUM-554	CL	120.00	150.00
92	MY WISH IS SMALL HUM-463	CL	170.00	2000.00-2500.00
93	I DIDN'T DO IT HUM-626	CL	175.00	200.00-225.00
93	SWEET AS CAN BE HUM-541	OP	125.00	160.00
94	AT GRANDPA'S HUM-621	10000	1,300.00	1500.00-1600.00
94	FOR KEEPS HUM-630	OP	*	100.00-125.00
94	LITTLE TROUBADOUR HUM-558	RT	130.00	135.00-150.00
95	A STORY FROM GRANDMA HUM 620	10000	1,300.00	1550.00
G. SKROBEK		**M.I. HUMMEL COLLECTORS CLUB EXCLUSIVES**		
79	BUST OF SISTER M.I. HUMMEL HU-3	CL	75.00	300.00-7500.00
M.I. HUMMEL		**M.I. HUMMEL MADONNA**		
*	FLOWER MADONNA, COLOR HUM-10/I	CL	350.00	300.00-600.00
*	FLOWER MADONNA, COLOR HUM-10/III	CL	*	300.00-500.00
*	FLOWER MADONNA, WHITE HUM-10/I	OP	165.00	175.00-300.00
*	FLOWER MADONNA, WHITE HUM-10/III	TW	*	450.00-750.00
*	MADONNA PLAQUE HUM-48	CL	*	650.00-850.00
*	MADONNA PLAQUE HUM-48/II	TW	*	130.00-800.00
*	MADONNA PLAQUE HUM-48/O	TW	*	85.00-375.00
*	MADONNA PLAQUE HUM-48/V	CL	*	1000.00-2000.00
*	MADONNA W/HALO WHITE HUM-45/III	TW	150.00	105.00-350.00
*	MADONNA W/HALO, COLOR HUM-45/I	OP	105.00	145.00-400.00
*	MADONNA W/HALO, COLOR HUM-45/III	SU	*	150.00-600.00
*	MADONNA W/HALO, COLOR HUM-45/O	SU	*	60.00-275.00
*	MADONNA W/HALO, WHITE HUM-45/I	OP	70.00	75.00-200.00

YR	NAME	LIMIT	ISSUE	TREND
*	MADONNA W/HALO, WHITE HUM-45/O	OP	*	40.00-175.00
*	MADONNA W/O HALO, COLOR HUM-46/I	TW	*	140.00-400.00
*	MADONNA W/O HALO, COLOR HUM-46/III	TW	*	105.00-350.00
*	MADONNA W/O HALO, COLOR HUM-46/O	TW	*	60.00-275.00
*	MADONNA W/O HALO, WHITE HUM-46/I	SU	*	140.00-400.00
*	MADONNA W/O HALO, WHITE HUM-46/III	SU	*	105.00-350.00
*	MADONNA W/O HALO, WHITE HUM-46/O	SU	*	40.00-175.00
77	MADONNA HOLDING CHILD, BLUE HUM-151	TW	*	900.00-3000.00
77	MADONNA HOLDING CHILD, WHITE HUM-151	TW	*	400.00-2500.00

M.I. HUMMEL   **M.I. HUMMEL NATIVITY**

YR	NAME	LIMIT	ISSUE	TREND
*	ANGEL KNEELING/SERENADE HUM-214D (COLOR)	OP	70.00	100.00-200.00
*	ANGEL KNEELING/SERENADE HUM-214D (WHITE)	CL	*	165.00-290.00
*	ANGEL SERENADE (LARGE) HUM-260E	SU	*	155.00-170.00
*	ANGEL, GOOD NIGHT HUM-214C (WHITE)	CL	*	265.00-415.00
*	ANGEL/GOOD NIGHT HUM-214C (COLOR)	OP	70.00	100.00-200.00
*	COW, LYING (LARGE) HUM-260M	SU	*	170.00-190.00
*	DONKEY HUM-214J (COLOR)	OP	60.00	75.00-160.00
*	DONKEY HUM-214J (WHITE)	CL	*	130.00-255.00
*	DONKEY, STANDING (LARGE) HUM-260L	SU	*	135.00-150.00
*	GOOD NIGHT (LARGE) HUM-260D	SU	*	140.00-160.00
*	INFANT JESUS (LARGE) HUM-260C	SU	*	130.00
*	INFANT JESUS HUM-214A/K (COLOR)	OP	50.00	70.00-75.00
*	INFANT JESUS HUM-214A/K (WHITE)	CL	*	60.00-70.00
*	INFANT JESUS HUM-214A/K/1	OP	*	70.00
*	JOSEPH HUM-214B (COLOR)	OP	150.00	195.00-400.00
*	JOSEPH HUM-214B (WHITE)	CL	*	145.00-420.00
*	KING ON ONE KNEE HUM-214 M/O	OP	*	150.00-155.00
*	KING ON ONE KNEE HUM-214M (COLOR)	OP	150.00	195.00-415.00
*	KING ON ONE KNEE HUM-214M (WHITE)	CL	*	225.00-475.00
*	KING ON TWO KNEES HUM-214 N/O	OP	*	165.00-170.00
*	KING, KNEE W/CASH BOX HUM-214N (COLOR)	OP	140.00	175.00-385.00
*	KING, KNEE W/CASH BOX HUM-214N (WHITE)	CL	*	225.00-475.00
*	KING, KNEELING (LARGE) HUM-260P	SU	*	540.00-570.00
*	KING, STANDING (LARGE) HUM-260O	SU	*	565.00-615.00
*	LAMB HUM-214O	OP	*	55.00-130.00
*	LAMB HUM-214O (COLOR)	OP	18.00	22.00-52.00
*	LITTLE TOOTER (LARGE) HUM-260K	SU	*	195.00-220.00
*	MADONNA (LARGE) HUM-260A	SU	*	575.00-650.00
*	MOORISH KING, STANDING (LARGE) HUM-260N	SU	*	565.00-615.00
*	MOORISH KING, STANDING HUM-214L (COLOR)	OP	155.00	215.00-415.00
*	MOORISH KING, STANDING HUM-214L (WHITE)	CL	*	225.00-475.00
*	NATIVITY SET (LARGE) 16 PIECES HUM-260	TW	*	5745.00-6305.00
*	ONE SHEEP, LYING (LARGE) HUM-260R	SU	*	65.00-80.00
*	OX (COW) HUM-214K (COLOR)	OP	60.00	75.00-160.00
*	OX (COW) HUM-214K (WHITE)	CL	*	130.00-255.00
*	SAINT JOSEPH (LARGE) HUM-260B	SU	*	575.00-650.00
*	SHEEP, STANDING W/LAMB (LARGE) HUM-260H	SU	*	110.00-125.00
*	SHEPHERD BOY W/FLUTE HUM-214H (COLOR)	OP	100.00	135.00-280.00
*	SHEPHERD BOY W/FLUTE HUM-214H (WHITE)	CL	*	170.00-320.00
*	SHEPHERD BOY, KNEELING (LARGE) HUM-260J	SU	*	340.00-370.00
*	SHEPHERD KNEELING HUM-214G (COLOR)	OP	110.00	145.00-310.00
*	SHEPHERD KNEELING HUM-214G (WHITE)	CL	*	170.00-320.00
*	SHEPHERD W/SHEEP HUM-214F (COLOR)	OP	155.00	195.00-415.00
*	SHEPHERD W/SHEEP HUM-214F (WHITE)	CL	*	220.00-470.00
*	SHEPHERD, STANDING (LARGE) HUM-260G	SU	*	590.00-650.00
*	STABLE HUM-260S	OP	400.00	440.00
*	VIRGIN MARY HUM-214A (COLOR)	OP	150.00	195.00-2500.00
*	VIRGIN MARY HUM-214A (WHITE)	CL	*	195.00-3000.00
*	WE CONGRATULATE (LARGE) HUM-260F	SU	*	415.00-460.00
*	WE CONGRATULATE HUM-214E (COLOR)	OP	140.00	180.00-390.00
*	WE CONGRATULATE HUM-214E (WHITE)	CL	*	270.00-470.00
88	INFANT JESUS HUM-214A/K/O	OP	*	45.00
88	JOSEPH HUM-214B/O	OP	*	145.00
88	MARY HUM-214/A/M/O	OP	*	145.00
89	DONKEY HUM-214J/O	OP	*	55.00
89	LAMB HUM-214O/O	OP	*	22.00
89	OX HUM-214K/O	OP	*	55.00
90	KING STANDING HUM-214L/O	OP	*	165.00
91	LITTLE TOOTER HUM-214H/O	OP	*	110.00
91	SHEPHERD KNEELING HUM-214G/O	OP	*	130.00
91	SHEPHERD STANDING HUM-214F/O	OP	*	165.00

M.I. HUMMEL   **PEN PAL SERIES**

YR	NAME	LIMIT	ISSUE	TREND
96	FOR MOTHER HUM 257 5/O	*	55.00	55.00
96	MARCH WINDS HUM 43 5/O	*	55.00	55.00
96	ONE OF YOU, ONE OF ME HUM 482 5/O	*	55.00	55.00
96	SISTER HUM 98 5/O	*	55.00	55.00
96	SOLOIST HUM 135 5/O	*	55.00	55.00
96	VILLAGE BOY HUM 51 5/O	*	55.00	55.00

*   **PRECIOUS MOMENTS MINIATURES**

YR	NAME	LIMIT	ISSUE	TREND
95	LOVE IS KIND	OP	70.00	70.00
96	FRIENDS OF FRIENDSHIP	OP	135.00	135.00
96	GOD LOVETH A CHEERFUL GIVER	SO	70.00	70.00
96	HIS BURDEN IS LIGHT	SO	70.00	70.00
96	I'M SENDING YOU A WHITE CHRISTMAS	SO	100.00	100.00
96	LOVE ONE ANOTHER	OP	70.00	70.00

YR	NAME	LIMIT	ISSUE	TREND
96	MAKE A JOYFUL NOISE	SO	70.00	70.00
96	PRAISE THE LORD ANYHOW	OP	70.00	70.00
96	PRAYER CHANGES THINGS	OP	70.00	70.00
P. LARSEN			**PRECIOUS PLACES**	
95	FIELDS OF FRIENDSHIP	OP	625.00	625.00
M.I. HUMMEL			**TRIO COLLECTION**	
98	TRAVELING TRIO HUM 787	20000	490.00	490.00
M.I. HUMMEL		**UNICEF COMMEMORATIVE SERIES**		
94	FRIENDS TOGETHER 662/O	OP	260.00	300.00
95	GENTLE FELLOWSHIP HUM 628	25000	550.00	550.00
96	WE CAME IN PEACE HUM 754	*	350.00	385.00

GOEBEL MINIATURES

YR	NAME	LIMIT	ISSUE	TREND
R. OLSZEWSKI			**AMERICANA SERIES**	
81	PLAINSMAN, THE- 660-B	RT	45.00	245.00
82	AMERICAN BALD EAGLE 661-B	RT	45.00	305.00
83	SHE SOUNDS THE DEEP 662-B	RT	45.00	70.00
84	EYES ON THE HORIZON 663-B	RT	45.00	250.00
85	CENTRAL PARK SUNDAY 664-B	RT	45.00	70.00
86	AMERICANA DISPLAY 951-D	SU	80.00	105.00
86	CAROUSEL RIDE 665-B	RT	45.00	125.00
87	TO THE BANDSTAND 666-B	RT	45.00	70.00
89	BLACKSMITH 667-P	RT	55.00	165.00
R. OLSZEWSKI			**CHILDREN'S SERIES**	
80	BLUMENKINDER-COURTING 630-P	RT	55.00	275.00
81	SUMMER DAYS 631-P	RT	65.00	345.00
82	OUT AND ABOUT 632-P	RT	85.00	415.00
83	BACKYARD FROLIC 633-P	RT	65.00	100.00
84	GRANDPA 634-P	CL	75.00	110.00
85	SNOW HOLIDAY 635-P	CL	75.00	100.00
86	CLOWNING AROUND (OLD STYLE) 636-P	CL	85.00	210.00
87	CAROUSEL DAYS (PLAIN BASE) 637-P	CL	85.00	775.00
87	CAROUSEL DAYS 637-P	CL	85.00	200.00
88	CHILDREN'S DISPLAY (SMALL)	CL	45.00	60.00
88	LITTLE BALLERINA 638-P	CL	85.00	110.00
89	CLOWNING AROUND (NEW STYLE) 636-P	CL	85.00	100.00
90	BUILDING BLOCKS CASTLE (LARGE) 968-D	CL	75.00	100.00
LARSEN			**CLASSIC CLOCKS**	
95	ALEXIS	2500	200.00	200.00
95	BLINKING ADMIRAL	2500	200.00	200.00
95	PLAY	2500	250.00	250.00
R. OLSZEWSKI		**DEGRAZIA: GOEBEL MINIATURES**		
89	MERRY LITTLE INDIAN (NEW STYLE) 508-P	SU	110.00	175.00
R. OLSZEWSKI			**DISNEY-CINDERELLA**	
91	ANASTASIA 172-P	SU	85.00	100.00
91	CINDERELLA 176-P	SU	85.00	125.00
91	CINDERELLA'S COACH DISPLAY 978-D	SU	95.00	120.00
91	CINDERELLA'S DREAM CASTLE 976-D	SU	95.00	115.00
91	DRIZELLA 174-P	SU	85.00	100.00
91	FAIRY GODMOTHER 180-P	SU	85.00	105.00
91	FOOTMAN 181-P	SU	85.00	100.00
91	GUS 177-P	SU	75.00	80.00
91	JAQ 173-P	SU	75.00	80.00
91	LUCIFER 175-P	SU	75.00	95.00
91	PRINCE CHARMING 179-P	SU	85.00	135.00
91	STEPMOTHER 178-P	SU	85.00	100.00
R. OLSZEWSKI			**DISNEY-PETER PAN**	
92	JOHN 186-P	SU	90.00	130.00
92	MICHAEL 187-P	SU	90.00	110.00
92	NANA 189-P	SU	95.00	110.00
92	PETER PAN 184-P	SU	90.00	160.00
92	PETER PAN'S LONDON 986-D	SU	125.00	135.00
92	WENDY 185-P	SU	90.00	130.00
94	CAPTAIN HOOK 188-P	SU	160.00	175.00
94	LOST BOY-FOX 191-P	SU	130.00	130.00
94	LOST BOY-RABBIT 192-P	SU	130.00	130.00
94	NEVERLAND DISPLAY 997-D	SU	150.00	160.00
94	SMEE 190-P	SU	140.00	150.00
R. OLSZEWSKI			**DISNEY-PINOCCHIO**	
90	GEPPETTO'S TOY SHOP DISPLAY 965-D	SU	95.00	130.00
90	GEPPETTO/FIGARO 682-P	SU	90.00	110.00
90	GIDEON 683-P	SU	75.00	100.00
90	J. WORTHINGTON FOULFELLOW 684-P	SU	95.00	115.00
90	JIMINY CRICKET 685-P	SU	75.00	115.00
90	PINOCCHIO 686-P	SU	75.00	140.00
91	BLUE FAIRY 693-P	SU	95.00	120.00
91	LITTLE STREET LAMP DISPLAY 964-D	SU	65.00	100.00
91	STROMBOLI 694-P	SU	95.00	120.00
91	STROMBOLI'S STREET WAGON 979-D	SU	105.00	135.00
92	MONSTRO THE WHALE 985-D	SU	120.00	200.00
R. OLSZEWSKI			**DISNEY-SNOW WHITE**	
87	BASHFUL 165-P	SU	60.00	100.00
87	COZY COTTAGE DISPLAY 941-D	SU	35.00	260.00
87	DOC 162-P	SU	60.00	100.00

YR NAME	LIMIT	ISSUE	TREND
87 DOPEY 167-P	SU	60.00	160.00
87 GRUMPY 166-P	SU	60.00	100.00
87 HAPPY 164-P	SU	60.00	100.00
87 SLEEPY 163-P	SU	60.00	100.00
87 SNEEZY 161-P	SU	60.00	100.00
87 SNOW WHITE 168-P	SU	60.00	160.00
88 HOUSE IN THE WOODS DISPLAY 944-D	SU	60.00	120.00
90 SNOW WHITE'S PRINCE 170-P	SU	80.00	125.00
90 WISHING WELL DISPLAY, THE- 969-D	SU	65.00	115.00
91 CASTLE COURTYARD DISPLAY 981-D	SU	105.00	120.00
92 PATH IN THE WOODS 996-D	SU	140.00	170.00
92 SNOW WHITE'S QUEEN 182-P	SU	100.00	140.00
92 SNOW WHITE'S WITCH 183-P	SU	100.00	140.00
R. OLSZEWSKI		**DISNEYANA CONVENTION**	
94 MICKEY'S SELF-PORTRAIT	500	295.00	850.00
R. OLSZEWSKI		**FIRST EDITION M.I. HUMMEL**	
88 DOLL BATH HUM-252P	10000	95.00	105.00
88 LITTLE FIDDLER HUM-250P	10000	90.00	115.00
88 LITTLE SWEEPER HUM-253P	10000	90.00	105.00
88 MERRY WANDERER HUM-254P	10000	95.00	170.00
88 STORMY WEATHER HUM-251P	10000	115.00	130.00
89 APPLE TREE BOY HUM-257P	10000	115.00	130.00
89 POSTMAN HUM-255P	10000	95.00	105.00
89 VISITING AN INVALID HUM-256P	10000	105.00	115.00
90 BAKER HUM-262P	10000	100.00	105.00
90 CINDERELLA HUM-264P	10000	115.00	115.00
90 WAITER HUM-263P	10000	100.00	115.00
91 ACCORDION BOY HUM-266P	10000	105.00	115.00
91 BUSY STUDENT HUM-268P	10000	105.00	115.00
91 MERRY WANDERER DEALER PLAQUE HUM-280P	10000	130.00	435.00
91 MORNING CONCERT HUM-269P	TL	175.00	175.00
91 RIDE INTO CHRISTMAS HUM-279P	OP	195.00	195.00
91 SERENADE HUM-265P	10000	105.00	115.00
91 WE CONGRATULATE HUM-267P	10000	130.00	130.00-140.00
92 GOOSE GIRL HUM-283P	OP	130.00	130.00
92 SCHOOL BOY HUM-281P	OP	120.00	120.00
92 WAYSIDE HARMONY HUM-282P	OP	140.00	180.00
R. OLSZEWSKI		**HISTORICAL SERIES**	
80 CAPODIMONTE (OLD STYLE) 600-P	CL	90.00	495.00
81 MASQUERADE-ST. PETERSBURG 601-P	CL	65.00	220.00
83 CHERRY PICKERS, THE 602-P	SU	85.00	270.00
84 MOOR WITH SPANISH HORSE 603-P	OP	85.00	110.00
85 CAPODIMONTE (NEW STYLE) 600-P	SU	90.00	170.00
85 FLORAL BOUQUET POMPADOUR 604-P	OP	85.00	115.00
87 MEISSEN PARROT 605-P	OP	85.00	110.00
88 HISTORICAL DISPLAY 943-D	SU	45.00	60.00
88 MINTON ROOSTER 606-P	7500	85.00	110.00
89 FARMER W/DOVES 607-P	OP	85.00	110.00
90 ENGLISH COUNTRY GARDEN 970-D	OP	85.00	105.00
90 GENTLEMAN FOX HUNT 616-P	SU	145.00	180.00
92 POULTRY SELLER 608-G	1500	200.00	230.00
R. OLSZEWSKI		**JACK AND THE BEANSTALK**	
94 BEANSELLER 742-P	5000	210.00	210.00
94 JACK AND THE BEANSTALK DISPLAY 999-D	5000	225.00	250.00
94 JACK AND THE COW 743-P	5000	180.00	185.00
94 JACK'S MOM 741-P	5000	145.00	160.00
R. OLSZEWSKI		**MICKEY MOUSE**	
90 FANTASIA LIVING BROOMS 972-D	SU	85.00	215.00
90 MICKEY MOUSE SELLER	SU	165.00	430.00
90 SORCERER'S APPRENTICE , THE-171-P	SU	80.00	180.00
R. OLSZEWSKI		**NATIVITY COLLECTION**	
91 HOLY FAMILY DISPLAY 982-D	OP	85.00	90.00
91 JOSEPH 401-P	SU	95.00	125.00
91 JOYFUL CHERUBS 403-P	SU	130.00	175.00
91 MOTHER/CHILD 400-P	SU	120.00	150.00
91 STABLE DONKEY, THE- 402-P	SU	95.00	125.00
92 3 KINGS DISPLAY 987-D	OP	85.00	100.00
92 BALTHAZAR 405-P	SU	135.00	195.00
92 CASPAR 406-P	SU	135.00	195.00
92 MELCHIOR 404-P	SU	135.00	195.00
94 CAMEL & TENDER 819292	OP	380.00	390.00
94 FINAL NATIVITY DISPLAY 991-D	OP	260.00	270.00
94 GUARDIAN ANGEL 407-P	OP	200.00	220.00
94 SHEEP & SHEPHERD 819290	OP	230.00	235.00
YENAWINE		**NATURE'S MOMENTS**	
95 BATHING BEAUTIES	OP	95.00	95.00
95 FISH PARADISE	OP	110.00	110.00
95 GATHERING GOODIES	OP	95.00	95.00
95 HIDE AND SEEK	OP	110.00	110.00
95 PENGUINS PLUNGE	OP	95.00	95.00
95 POLAR PLAYGROUND	OP	110.00	110.00
95 PREPARING FOR FLIGHT	OP	80.00	80.00
95 ROBYN REFRESHER	OP	95.00	95.00
95 SUMMER SURPRISE	OP	95.00	95.00
95 TOUCH AND GO	OP	95.00	95.00

YR	NAME	LIMIT	ISSUE	TREND
R. OLSZEWSKI		**NIGHT BEFORE CHRISTMAS (1ST EDITION)**		
90	EIGHT TINY REINDEER 691-P	SU	110.00	120.00
90	MAMA & PAPA 692-P	SU	110.00	125.00
90	ST. NICHOLAS 690-P	SU	95.00	115.00
90	SUGAR PLUM BOY 687-P	SU	70.00	90.00
90	SUGAR PLUM GIRL 689-P	SU	70.00	90.00
90	YULE TREE 688-P	SU	90.00	100.00
91	UP TO THE HOUSETOP 966-D	5000	95.00	105.00
R. OLSZEWSKI		**ORIENTAL SERIES**		
80	KUAN YIN (OLD STYLE) 640-W	CL	40.00	255.00
82	GEISHA, THE- 641-P	SU	65.00	195.00
84	KUAN YIN (NEW STYLE) 640-W	SU	45.00	165.00
85	TANG HORSE 642-P	OP	65.00	95.00
86	BLIND MAN AND THE ELEPHANT, THE 643-P	SU	70.00	160.00
87	CHINESE WATER DRAGON 644-P	SU	70.00	155.00
87	ORIENTAL DISPLAY (SMALL) 945-D	SU	45.00	65.00
89	TIGER HUNT 645-P	OP	85.00	100.00
90	CHINESE TEMPLE LION 646-P	OP	90.00	110.00
90	EMPRESS GARDEN 967-D	OP	95.00	125.00
R. OLSZEWSKI		**PENDANTS**		
85	FLOWER GIRL PENDANT 561-P	OP	125.00	150.00
86	CAMPER BIALOSKY 151-P	CL	95.00	275.00
87	FESTIVAL OF LIGHTS 562-P	OP	90.00	195.00
88	MICKEY MOUSE 169-P	5000	92.00	255.00
90	HUMMINGBIRD 697-P	OP	125.00	145.00
91	CHRYSANTHEMUM PENDANT 222-P	OP	135.00	145.00
91	DAFFODIL PENDANT 221-P	OP	135.00	145.00
91	POINSETTIA PENDANT	OP	135.00	145.00
91	ROSE PENDANT	OP	135.00	145.00
N. ROCKWELL		**PORTRAIT OF AMERICA**		
88	BOTTOM OF THE SIXTH 365-P	SU	85.00	115.00
88	CHECK UP 363-P	SU	85.00	95.00
88	DOCTOR AND THE DOLL, THE 361-P	SU	85.00	135.00
88	MARBLES CHAMPION 362-P	CL	85.00	85.00
88	NO SWIMMING 360-P	CL	85.00	85.00
88	ROCKWELL DISPLAY 952-D	CL	80.00	93.00
88	TRIPLE SELF-PORTRAIT 364-P	SU	85.00	175.00
89	BOTTOM DRAWER 366-P	7500	85.00	85.00
HUGHES		**SATURDAY EVENING POST**		
92	BOY WITH WAGON	OP	*	N/A
92	CHILDREN CROSSING	OP	*	N/A
92	CROSSING GUARD	OP	*	N/A
92	MARKET VIGNETTE	OP	*	N/A
92	STORE OWNER	OP	*	N/A
R. OLSZEWSKI		**SATURDAY EVENING POST**		
92	CROSSING GUARD VIGNETTE	OP	*	N/A
N. ROCKWELL		**SATURDAY EVENING POST**		
91	CITY CLERK	OP	*	N/A
91	HOME COMING VIGNETTE 990-D	2000	190.00	250.00
91	MARRIAGE LICENSE VIGNETTE	OP	*	N/A
91	MOTHER 369-P	OP	*	N/A
91	SOLDIER 368-P	OP	*	N/A
91	WEDDING COUPLE	OP	*	N/A
92	TRIPLE SELF PORTRAIT	OP	*	N/A
92	TRIPLE SELF PORTRAIT VIGNETTE	OP	*	N/A
R. OLSZEWSKI		**SPECIAL RELEASE-ALICE IN WONDERLAND**		
82	ALICE IN THE GARDEN 670-P	CL	60.00	675.00
83	DOWN THE RABBIT HOLE 671-P	CL	75.00	425.00
84	CHESHIRE CAT, THE 672-P	CL	75.00	480.00
R. OLSZEWSKI		**SPECIAL RELEASE-WIZARD OF OZ**		
84	SCARECROW 673-P	CL	75.00	400.00
85	TINMAN 674-P	CL	80.00	240.00
86	COWARDLY LION, THE 675-P	CL	85.00	260.00
87	OZ DISPLAY 942-D	CL	45.00	565.00
87	WICKED WITCH, THE- 676-P	CL	85.00	105.00
88	MUNCHKINS, THE- 677-P	CL	85.00	100.00
92	DOROTHY/GLINDA 695-P	CL	120.00	142.00
92	GOOD-BYE.TO OZ DISPLAY 980-D	OP	110.00	160.00
R. OLSZEWSKI		**SPECIAL RELEASES**		
91	PORTRAIT OF THE ARTIST (CONVENTION) 658-P	CL	195.00	450.00
91	PORTRAIT OF THE ARTIST (PROMO) 658-P	OP	195.00	205.00
92	SUMMER DAYS COLLECTOR PLAQUE 659-P	OP	130.00	145.00
94	DRESDEN TIME PIECE 450-P	750	1,250.00	1300.00
REMINGTON		**THE AMERICAN FRONTIER COLLECTION**		
87	BRONCO BUSTER, THE 350-B	SU	80.00	175.00
87	EIGHT COUNT 310-B	SU	75.00	90.00
87	END OF THE TRAIL, THE340-B	SU	80.00	125.00
87	FIRST RIDE , THE-330-B	SU	85.00	100.00
87	GRIZZLY'S LAST STAND 320-B	SU	65.00	80.00
87	INDIAN SCOUT AND BUFFALO 300-B	SU	95.00	135.00
R. OLSZEWSKI		**THE AMERICAN FRONTIER COLLECTION**		
87	AMERICAN FRONTIER DISPLAY 947-D	SU	80.00	110.00
R. OLSZEWSKI		**THREE LITTLE PIGS**		
89	LITTLE STICKS PIG 678-P	7500	75.00	105.00

YR	NAME	LIMIT	ISSUE	TREND
89	THREE LITTLE PIGS HOUSE 956-D	7500	50.00	115.00
90	LITTLE STRAW PIG 679-P	7500	75.00	105.00
91	HUNGRY WOLF, THE- 681-P	7500	80.00	105.00
91	LITTLE BRICKS PIG 680-P	7500	75.00	105.00
*				**TRIO COLLECTION**
*	A TUNEFUL TRIO	SO	*	N/A
96	TRIO OF WISHES	20,000	475.00	475.00
R. OLSZEWSKI				**WILDLIFE SERIES**
80	CHIPPING SPARROW 620-P	OP	55.00	85.00
81	OWL-DAYLIGHT ENCOUNTER 621-P	CL	65.00	390.00
82	WESTERN BLUEBIRD 622-P	CL	65.00	150.00
83	RED-WINGED BLACKBIRD 623-P	CL	65.00	190.00
84	WINTER CARDINAL 624-P	CL	65.00	250.00
85	AMERICAN GOLDFINCH 625-P	OP	65.00	90.00
86	AUTUMN BLUE JAY 626-P	SU	65.00	175.00
87	COUNTRY DISPLAY (SMALL) 940-D	OP	45.00	65.00
87	MALLARD DUCK 627-P	OP	75.00	105.00
88	SPRING ROBIN 628-P	CL	75.00	165.00
89	HOODED ORIOLE 629-P	OP	80.00	100.00
90	COUNTRY LANDSCAPE (LG.) 957-D	OP	85.00	110.00
90	HUMMINGBIRD 696-P	CL	85.00	175.00
90	WILDLIFE DISPLAY (LARGE) 957-D	OP	85.00	95.00
92	AUTUMN BLUE JAY (ARCHIVE RELEASE) 626-P	OP	125.00	135.00
NORRGARD				**WINTER LIGHTS**
95	ONCE UPON A WINTER DAY	OP	275.00	275.00
R. OLSZEWSKI				**WOMEN'S SERIES**
80	DRESDEN DANCER 610-P	CL	55.00	350.00
81	HUNT WITH HOUNDS, THE (OLD STYLE) 611-P	CL	75.00	400.00
82	PRECIOUS YEARS 612-P	CL	65.00	230.00
83	ON THE AVENUE 613-P	CL	65.00	115.00
84	ROSES 614-P	CL	65.00	115.00
85	HUNT WITH HOUNDS, THE (NEW STYLE) 611-P	CL	75.00	110.00
86	I DO 615-P	CL	85.00	235.00
89	WOMEN'S DISPLAY (SMALL) 950-D	CL	40.00	65.00

GORHAM

N. ROCKWELL			**A BOY AND HIS DOG (FOUR SEASONS)**	
72	A BOY MEETS HIS DOG	RT	200.00	1450.00
72	ADVENTURERS BETWEEN ADVENTURES (SET)	RT	*	N/A
72	MYSTERIOUS MALADY, THE- (SET)	RT	*	N/A
72	PRIDE OF PARENTHOOD (SET)	RT	*	N/A
N. ROCKWELL			**A HELPING HAND (FOUR SEASONS)**	
80	CLOSED FOR BUSINESS (SET)	RT	*	N/A
80	COAL SEASONS COMING (SET)	RT	*	N/A
80	SWATTER'S RIGHT (SET)	RT	*	N/A
80	YEAR END COURT	RT	650.00	675.00
N. ROCKWELL			**DAD'S BOY (FOUR SEASONS)**	
81	CAREFUL AIM (SET)	RT	*	N/A
81	IN HIS SPIRITS (SET)	RT	*	N/A
81	SKI SKILLS	RT	750.00	775.00
81	TROUT DINNER (SET)	RT	*	N/A
N. ROCKWELL			**FOUR AGES OF LOVE (FOUR SEASONS)**	
74	FLOWERS IN TENDER BLOOM (SET)	RT	*	N/A
74	FONDLY DO WE REMEMBER (SET)	RT	*	N/A
74	GAILY SHARING VINTAGE TIMES	RT	300.00	950.00
74	SWEET SONG SO YOUNG (SET)	RT	*	N/A
N. ROCKWELL			**GOING ON SIXTEEN (FOUR SEASONS)**	
78	CHILLING CHORE	RT	400.00	660.00
78	PILGRIMAGE (SET)	RT	*	N/A
78	SHEAR AGONY (SET)	RT	*	N/A
78	SWEET SERENADE (SET)	RT	*	N/A
N. ROCKWELL			**GRAND PALS (FOUR SEASONS)**	
77	FISH FINDERS (SET)	RT	*	N/A
77	GHOSTLY GOURDS (SET)	RT	*	N/A
77	SNOW SCULPTURING	RT	350.00	660.00
77	SOARING SPIRITS (SET)	RT	*	N/A
N. ROCKWELL			**GRANDPA AND ME**	
75	DAY DREAMERS (SET)	RT	*	N/A
75	GAY BLADES	2500	300.00	900.00
75	GOIN' FISHING (SET)	RT	*	N/A
75	PENSIVE PALS (SET)	RT	*	N/A
J.C. LEYENDECKER		**LEYENDECKER ANNUAL CHRISTMAS FIGURINES**		
88	CHRISTMAS HUG	7500	95.00	95.00
N. ROCKWELL			**LIFE WITH FATHER (FOUR SEASONS)**	
83	A TOUGH ONE (SET)	RT	*	N/A
83	BIG DECISION	RT	250.00	250.00
83	BLASTING OUT (SET)	RT	*	N/A
83	CHEERING THE CHAMPS (SET)	RT	*	N/A
N. ROCKWELL			**ME AND MY PAL (FOUR SEASONS)**	
76	A LICKING GOOD BATH	RT	300.00	1050.00
76	DISASTROUS DARING (SET)	RT	*	N/A
76	FISHERMAN'S PARADISE (SET)	RT	*	N/A
76	YOUNG MAN'S FANCY (SET)	RT	*	N/A

YR	NAME	LIMIT	ISSUE	TREND
T. NAST		**MINIATURE CHRISTMAS FIGURINES**		
85	CHRISTMAS SANTA	RT	20.00	20.00
86	CHRISTMAS SANTA	RT	25.00	25.00
87	ANNUAL THOMAS NAST SANTA	RT	25.00	25.00
N. ROCKWELL		**MINIATURE CHRISTMAS FIGURINES**		
79	TINY TIM	RT	15.00	20.00
80	SANTA PLANS HIS TRIP	RT	15.00	16.00
81	YULETIDE RECKONING	RT	20.00	20.00
82	CHECKING GOOD DEEDS	RT	20.00	20.00
83	SANTA'S FRIEND	RT	20.00	20.00
84	DOWNHILL DARING	RT	20.00	20.00
N. ROCKWELL				**MINIATURES**
81	AT THE VETS	CL	28.00	35.00
81	BEGUILING BUTTERCUP	CL	45.00	45.00
81	BOY MEETS HIS DOG	CL	38.00	38.00
81	DOWNHILL DARING	CL	45.00	70.00
81	FLOWERS IN TENDER BLOOM	CL	60.00	60.00
81	GAY BLADES	CL	45.00	70.00
81	SNOW SCULPTURE	CL	45.00	60.00
81	SWEET SERENADE	CL	45.00	45.00
81	SWEET SONG SO YOUNG	CL	55.00	55.00
81	YOUNG MAN'S FANCY	CL	55.00	55.00
82	ANNUAL VISIT, THE	CL	50.00	70.00
82	MARRIAGE LICENSE	CL	60.00	70.00
82	RUNAWAY, THE	CL	50.00	50.00
82	TRIPLE SELF PORTRAIT	CL	60.00	135.00
82	VINTAGE TIMES	CL	50.00	50.00
83	TROUT DINNER	RT	60.00	60.00
84	CAREFUL AIMS	CL	55.00	55.00
84	GHOSTLY GOURDS	CL	60.00	60.00
84	GOIN' FISHING	CL	60.00	60.00
84	IN HIS SPIRITS	CL	60.00	60.00
84	PRIDE OF PARENTHOOD	CL	50.00	50.00
84	SHEAR AGONY	CL	60.00	60.00
84	YEARS END COURT	CL	60.00	60.00
85	BEST FRIENDS	CL	28.00	28.00
85	ENGINEER	CL	55.00	55.00
85	LITTLE RED TRUCK	CL	25.00	25.00
85	MUSCLE BOUND	CL	30.00	30.00
85	NEW ARRIVAL	CL	33.00	35.00
85	SPRING CHECKUP	CL	60.00	60.00
85	TO LOVE AND CHERISH	CL	33.00	35.00
86	FOOTBALL SEASON	CL	60.00	60.00
86	GRADUATE, THE	CL	30.00	40.00
86	LEMONADE STAND	CL	60.00	60.00
86	LITTLE ANGEL	CL	50.00	60.00
86	MORNING WALK	CL	60.00	60.00
86	OLD SIGN PAINTER, THE	CL	70.00	75.00
86	SHOULDER RIDE	CL	50.00	60.00
86	WELCOME MAT	CL	70.00	70.00
87	BABYSITTER	RT	75.00	75.00
87	BETWEEN THE ACTS	RT	60.00	60.00
87	CINDERELLA	RT	70.00	75.00
87	MILKMAID, THE	RT	80.00	80.00
87	PROM DRESS, THE	RT	75.00	75.00
87	SPRINGTIME	RT	65.00	70.00
87	STARSTRUCK	RT	75.00	75.00
N. ROCKWELL		**OLD BUDDIES (FOUR SEASONS)**		
84	ENDLESS DEBATES (SET)	RT	*	N/A
84	FINAL SPEECH (SET)	RT	*	N/A
84	HASTY RETREAT (SET)	RT	*	N/A
84	SHARED SUCCESS	RT	250.00	250.00
N. ROCKWELL		**OLD TIMERS (FOUR SEASONS MINIATURES)**		
82	CANINE SOLO	RT	250.00	250.00
82	FANCY FOOTWORK (SET)	RT	*	N/A
82	LAZY DAYS (SET)	RT	*	N/A
82	SWEET SURPRISE (SET)	RT	*	N/A
*			**PARASOL LADY**	
91	ON THE BOARDWALK	OP	95.00	95.00
94	AT THE FAIR	OP	95.00	95.00
94	SUNDAY PROMENADE	OP	95.00	95.00
N. ROCKWELL				**ROCKWELL**
74	AT THE VETS	CL	25.00	65.00
74	BATTER UP	CL	40.00	160.00
74	CAPTAIN	CL	45.00	95.00
74	FISHING	CL	50.00	100.00
74	MISSING TOOTH	CL	30.00	85.00
74	SKATING	CL	38.00	85.00
74	TINY TIM	CL	30.00	95.00
74	WEIGHING IN	RT	40.00	120.00
75	BOY AND HIS DOG	CL	38.00	90.00
75	NO SWIMMING	CL	35.00	150.00
75	OLD MILL POND	CL	45.00	95.00
76	GOD REST YE MERRY GENTLEMEN	CL	50.00	1200.00
76	INDEPENDENCE	CL	40.00	150.00

YR	NAME	LIMIT	ISSUE	TREND
76	MARRIAGE LICENSE	CL	50.00	165.00
76	OCCULTIST, THE	CL	50.00	175.00
76	SAYING GRACE RW42	CL	75.00	120.00
76	TACKLED (AD STAND)	CL	35.00	95.00
80	JOLLY COACHMAN	7500	75.00	140.00
81	A DAY IN THE LIFE BOY II	CL	75.00	85.00
81	CHRISTMAS DANCERS	RT	130.00	180.00
81	WET SPORT	CL	85.00	100.00
82	A DAY IN THE LIFE BOY III	CL	85.00	90.00
82	A DAY IN THE LIFE GIRL III	CL	85.00	115.00
82	APRIL FOOL'S (AT THE CURIOSITY SHOP)	CL	55.00	110.00
82	MARRIAGE LICENSE	RT	110.00	500.00
82	MERRIE CHRISTMAS	RT	75.00	150.00
82	SAYING GRACE RW12	RT	110.00	550.00
82	TACKLED (ROCKWELL NAME SIGNED)	CL	45.00	100.00
82	TRIPLE SELF PORTRAIT	5000	300.00	500.00
83	ANTIQUE DEALER	RT	130.00	175.00
83	CHRISTMAS GOOSE	7500	75.00	75.00
83	FACTS OF LIFE	RT	110.00	110.00
84	CARD TRICKS	RT	110.00	175.00
84	SANTA'S FRIEND	RT	75.00	150.00
84	SERENADE	RT	95.00	160.00
85	OLD SIGN PAINTER, THE	RT	130.00	200.00
85	PUPPET MAKER	RT	130.00	170.00
86	DRUM FOR TOMMY	RT	90.00	90.00
87	SANTA PLANNING HIS ANNUAL VISIT	RT	95.00	95.00
88	CONFRONTATION	RT	75.00	75.00
88	CRAMMING	RT	80.00	80.00
88	DELORES & EDDIE	RT	75.00	75.00
88	DIARY, THE	RT	75.00	80.00
88	GARY COOPER IN HOLLYWOOD	RT	90.00	90.00
88	HOME FOR THE HOLIDAYS	RT	100.00	100.00
N. ROCKWELL	**TENDER YEARS (FOUR SEASONS)**			
79	CHILLY RECEPTION (SET)	RT	*	N/A
79	COOL AID (SET)	RT	*	N/A
79	NEW YEAR LOOK	RT	500.00	600.00
79	SPRING TONIC (SET)	RT	*	N/A
N. ROCKWELL	**TRAVELING SALESMAN (FOUR SEASONS)**			
85	COUNTRY PEDDLER (SET)	RT	*	N/A
85	EXPERT SALESMAN (SET)	RT	*	N/A
85	HORSE TRADER	RT	275.00	275.00
85	TRAVELING SALESMAN (SET)	RT	*	N/A
VASARI	**VASARI FIGURINES**			
71	MERCENARY WARRIOR	250	250.00	500.00
71	MING WARRIOR	250	200.00	400.00
71	SWISS WARRIOR	250	250.00	1000.00
73	AUSTRIAN HUSSAR	250	400.00	800.00
73	CELLINI	250	400.00	800.00
73	CHRIST	250	250.00	500.00
73	COSSACK, THE	250	250.00	500.00
73	CRECHE	250	500.00	1000.00
73	D'ARTAGNAN	250	250.00	800.00
73	ENGLISH CRUSADER	250	250.00	500.00
73	FRENCH CRUSADER	250	250.00	500.00
73	GERMAN HUSSAR	250	250.00	500.00
73	GERMAN MERCENARY	250	250.00	500.00
73	ITALIAN CRUSADER	250	250.00	500.00
73	LEONARDO DA VINCI	200	250.00	500.00
73	MICHELANGELO	200	250.00	500.00
73	PIRATE	250	250.00	400.00
73	PORTHOS	250	250.00	500.00
73	ROMAN CENTURION	250	250.00	400.00
73	SPANISH GRANDEE	250	250.00	400.00
73	THREE KINGS (SET OF 3)	200	750.00	1500.00
73	THREE MUSKETEERS (SET OF 3)	200	750.00	1500.00
73	VENETIAN NOBLEMAN	250	200.00	400.00
73	VIKING	250	200.00	400.00
N. ROCKWELL	**YOUNG LOVE (FOUR SEASONS)**			
73	A SCHOLARLY PACE (SET)	2500	*	N/A
73	BEGUILING BUTTERCUP (SET)	2500	*	N/A
73	DOWNHILL DARING (SET)	2500	250.00	1100.00
73	FLYING HIGH (SET)	2500	*	N/A

GRANGET

G. GRANGET				GRANGET PORCELAINS
*	BOBWHITE QUAIL, OFF SEASON	350	*	3000.00
*	CALIFORNIA SEA LIONS, SEA FROLIC	500	1,375.00	4200.00
*	CANADIAN GEESE, HEADING SOUTH	150	4,650.00	14200.00
*	CEDAR WAXWINGS, ANXIOUS MOMENTS	175	2,675.00	2675.00
*	CROWNED CRANES, THE DANCE	25	20,000.00	20000.00
*	DOLPHIN GROUP	350	*	5000.00
*	DOLPHINS, PLAY TIME, DECORATED	100	9,000.00	N/A
*	DOLPHINS, PLAY TIME, UNDECORATED	500	3,500.00	3500.00
*	GREAT BLUE HERONS, THE CHALLENGE	150	5,000.00	14200.00
*	HALLA	350	*	4100.00

YR	NAME	LIMIT	ISSUE	TREND
*	MEADOWLARK, SPRING IS HERE	175	2,450.00	2450.00
*	MOURNING DOVES, ENGAGES	250	*	1475.00
*	OPEN JUMPER, THE CHAMPION	500	1,350.00	1350.00
*	PEREGRINE FALCON, WOOD, 10 IN.	2500	500.00	500.00
*	PEREGRINE FALCON, WOOD, 12.5 IN.	1500	700.00	700.00
*	PEREGRINE FALCON, WOOD, 20 IN.	250	2,000.00	2000.00
*	PINTAIL DUCKS, SAFE AT HOME	350	*	9700.00
*	RED DEER STAG, THE ROYAL STAG	150	4,850.00	4850.00
*	RING-NECKED PHEASANTS, TAKE COVER	125	*	5000.00
*	RUFFED GROUSE	150	2,000.00	2000.00
*	SCREECH OWL WITH CHICKADEES, DISTAIN	175	2,250.00	5650.00
*	SPRINGBOK, THE SENTINEL	150	2,000.00	2000.00
*	STAG	350	*	4400.00
*	WOODCOCKS, A FAMILY AFFAIR	200	*	1500.00
74	BLUE TITMOUSE, LIVELY FELLOW	750	1,295.00	1295.00
74	CATFINCH, SPRING MELODY	750	1,675.00	1675.00
74	GOLDEN-CRESTED WRENS, TINY ACROBATS	700	2,060.00	2060.00
74	GOLDFINCH, MORNING HOUR	750	1,250.00	1250.00
74	GREAT TITMOUSE ADULTS, BUSY ACTIVITY	750	2,175.00	2175.00
74	KINGFISHER, DEFECTED PREY	600	1,975.00	1975.00
74	ROBIN, A DAY BEGINS	750	1,795.00	1795.00
76	AMERICAN BALD EAGLE, FREEDOM IN FLIGHT	200	3,400.00	9500.00
76	AMERICAN ROBIN, IT'S SPRING AGAIN	150	1,950.00	1950.00
76	BLUEBIRDS, RELUCTANT FLEDGLING	350	1,750.00	4600.00
76	DOUBLE EAGLE, 24 KT GOLD VERMEIL/PEWTER	1200	250.00	250.00
76	SECRETARY BIRD, THE CONTEST	100	6,000.00	11000.00
77	RELUCTANT FLEDGLING	350	1,750.00	1750.00

GREENWICH WORKSHOP
W. BULLAS

98	ARTIST, THE	OP	95.00	95.00
98	BACK QUACKERS	OP	125.00	125.00
98	CALIFORNIA STYLIN'	OP	125.00	125.00
98	FOOL MOON	1750	125.00	125.00
98	FOWL BALL	OP	95.00	95.00
98	NURSE, THE	OP	95.00	95.00
98	SAND TRAP PRO	OP	95.00	95.00
98	SNOW BUDDIES	1250	125.00	125.00
98	SOCK HOP	OP	95.00	95.00
98	SPACE CADET	OP	95.00	95.00
98	SUPERMOM	OP	95.00	95.00

J. CHRISTENSEN

98	...HIS WIFE COULD EAT NO LEAN	1500	185.00	185.00
98	ANCIENT ANGEL, THE	1750	195.00	195.00
98	JACK SPRAT COULD EAT NO FAT	1500	175.00	175.00
98	LUTE PLAYER, THE	1500	450.00	450.00
98	MINIATURE ARTIST, THE	1500	95.00	95.00
98	MRS. CLAUS	2500	295.00	295.00
98	RESPONSIBLE MAN, THE	1950	495.00	495.00
98	WETLAND BIRD HUNTER	1950	250.00	250.00

S. GUSTAFSON

98	BABY BEAR	1950	60.00	60.00
98	BROTHER AVERY	2500	95.00	95.00
98	FROGGY GOES A-WOOING	2500	125.00	125.00
98	GOLDILOCKS	1950	150.00	150.00
98	HARE, THE	1950	95.00	95.00
98	MAMA BEAR	1950	165.00	165.00
98	OTTIST	1500	95.00	95.00
98	OWL AND THE PUSSYCAT, THE	2500	250.00	250.00
98	PAPA BEAR	1950	175.00	175.00
98	PUSS IN BOOTS	2500	165.00	165.00
98	TORTOISE, THE	1950	125.00	125.00

J. CHRISTENSEN

				BRONZE
*	CANDLEMAN, THE	*	*	3100.00
*	SIX BIRD HUNTERS	*	*	4500.00

F. MCCARTHY

				WESTERN
*	THUNDER OF HOOVES	*	*	10500.00

GUND INC.
R. SWEDLIN-RAIFFE

			SIGNATURE COLLECTION	
96	BEARMANI	575	150.00	150.00

HALLMARK
D. PALMITER

			KIDDIE CAR CLASSICS	
96	1935 STEELCRAFT AIRPLANE-MURRAY 9032	RT	50.00	50.00
96	1937 STEELCRAFT AUBURN LUX. ED. QHG9021	RT	65.00	170.00
96	1961 MURRAY SUPER DELUXE TRACTOR WITH TRAILER 9027	YR	55.00	55.00
97	1937 GARTON FORD 9035	RT	65.00	65.00
97	1939 GARTON FORD STATION WAGON 9034	YR	55.00	55.00
97	1941 STEELCRAFT OLDSMOBILE 9036	YR	55.00	55.00
97	1956 MURRAY GOLDEN EAGLE 9033	RT	50.00	50.00
98	1929 STEELCRAFT ROADSTER 9040	39500	70.00	70.00
98	1938 GARTON LINCOLN ZEPHYR 9038	RT	65.00	65.00
98	1940 GEDRON RED HOT ROADSTER 9037	YR	55.00	55.00
98	1941 STEELCRAFT FIRETRUCK 9042	YR	60.00	60.00

YR	NAME	LIMIT	ISSUE	TREND
98	1958 MURRAY CHAMPION 9041	YR	55.00	55.00
98	1960 EIGHT BALL RACER 9039	YR	55.00	55.00
E. WEIRICK			**KIDDIE CAR CLASSICS**	
92	1941 MURRAY AIRPLANE 9003	RT	50.00	400.00
92	1941 STEELCRAFT SPITFIRE AIRPLANE-MURRAY 9009	RT	50.00	75.00
92	1953 MURRAY DUMP TRUCK 9012	RT	48.00	265.00
92	1955 FIRE TRUCK- MURRAY 9001	RT	50.00	200.00
92	1955 CHAMPION BLUE- MURRAY 9008	RT	45.00	325.00
92	1955 TRACTOR & TRAILER- MURRAY 9004	RT	55.00	300.00
93	1955 FIRE CHIEF- MURRAY 9006	RT	50.00	200.00
93	1968 MURRAY BOAT JOLLY ROGER 9005	RT	50.00	100.00
94	1939 STEELCRAFT LINCOLN ZEPHYR- MURRAY 9015	RT	50.00	150.00
94	1955 RED CHAMPION- MURRAY 9002	RT	45.00	100.00
94	1955 DUMP TRUCK- MURRAY 9011	RT	48.00	125.00
94	1955 FIRE TRUCK- MURRAY 9010	RT	50.00	375.00
94	1955 RANCH WAGON- MURRAY 9007	RT	48.00	125.00
94	1956 GARTON DRAGNET POLICE CAR 9016	RT	50.00	60.00
94	1956 GARTON KIDILLAC 9094	RT	50.00	75.00
94	1956 GARTON MARK V 9022	RT	45.00	45.00
94	1958 MURRAY ATOMIC MISSILE 9018	RT	55.00	90.00
94	1961 MURRAY CIRCUS CAR 9014	RT	48.00	60.00
94	1961 MURRAY SPEEDWAY PACE CAR 9013	RT	45.00	60.00
95	1937 STEELCRAFT AIRFLOW- MURRAY LX. ED. 9024	RT	65.00	125.00
95	1948 PONTIAC- MURRAY 9026	RT	50.00	50.00
95	1950 TORPEDO- MURRAY 9020	RT	50.00	125.00
95	1955 ROYAL DELUXE- MURRAY LM. ED. 9025	29500	55.00	60.00
95	1959 GARTOM DELUXE KIDILLAC 9017	RT	55.00	100.00
95	1961 GARTON CASEY JONES LOCOMOTIVE 9019	RT	55.00	100.00
95	1962 MURRAY SUPER DELUXE FIRE TRUCK 9095	RT	55.00	70.00
95	1964 GARTON TIN LIZZIE 9023	RT	50.00	50.00
96	1935 STEELCRAFT- MURRAY LX. ED. 9029	RT	65.00	150.00
96	1956 GARTON HOT ROD RACER 9028	YR	55.00	75.00
96	1964-1/2 FORD MUSTANG 9030	*	55.00	50.00
D. PALMITER			**KIDDIE CAR CORNER**	
97	1941 JUNIOR SERVICE TRUCK 9031	YR	55.00	55.00
97	KC'S GARAGE 3601	RT	70.00	70.00
97	PEDAL POWER PREMIUM GAS PUMP 3603	YR	30.00	30.00
97	SIDEWALK SALES SIGNS 3605	YR	15.00	15.00
97	SIDEWALK SERVICE SIGNS 3604	YR	15.00	15.00
97	WELCOME SIGN 3606	YR	30.00	30.00
98	KC'S OIL CART 3609	YR	15.00	15.00
98	MECHANIC'S LIFT 3608	YR	25.00	25.00
98	PEDAL PETROLEUM GAS PUMP 3602	YR	25.00	25.00
*			**SIDEWALK CRUISER**	
95	1937 STEELCRAFT STREAMLINE SCOOTER/MURRAY QHG6301	RT	35.00	35.00
95	1939 MOBO HORSE QHG6304	*	45.00	45.00
95	1940 GARTON AERO FLITE WAGON LTD. ED. QHG6305	*	48.00	48.00
95	1958 MURRAY POLICE CYCLE LTD. ED. QHG6307	29500	55.00	55.00
95	1963 GARTON SPEEDSTER QHG6303	*	38.00	38.00
95	1966 GARTON SUPER-SONDA QHG6302	RT	45.00	45.00
96	1935 AMERICAN AIRFLOW COASTER LTD. ED. QHG6310	*	48.00	48.00
96	1935 SKY KING VELOCIPED QHG6311	*	45.00	45.00
96	1941 KEYSTONE LOCOMOTIVE QHG6312	*	38.00	38.00
96	1950 GARTON DELIVERY CYCLE QHG6309	*	38.00	38.00
96	LATE 1940S MOBO SULKY QHG6308	*	48.00	48.00
D. PALMITER			**SIDEWALK CRUISER**	
95	1935 STEELCRAFT STREAMLINE VELOPCIPEDE-MURRAY 6306	*	45.00	45.00
97	1937 SCAMP WAGON 6318	29,500	48.00	48.00
97	1939 AMERICAN-NATIONAL PEDAL BIKE 6314	YR	38.00	38.00
97	1939 GARTON BATWING SCOOTER 6317	YR	38.00	38.00
97	1960 MURRAY BLAZE-O-JET 6313	YR	45.00	45.00
98	1937 DE LUXE VELOCIPEDE 6319	YR	45.00	45.00
98	1960S SEALTEST MILK TRUCK 6315	YR	40.00	40.00

HAMILTON COLLECTION

*			**A CELEBRATION OF ROSES**	
89	BRANDY	OP	55.00	55.00
89	COLOR MAGIC	OP	55.00	55.00
89	HONOR	OP	55.00	55.00
89	MISS ALL-AMERICAN BEAUTY	OP	55.00	55.00
89	TIFFANY	OP	55.00	55.00
90	OREGOLD	OP	55.00	55.00
91	OLE'	OP	55.00	55.00
91	PARADISE	OP	55.00	55.00
D. FRYER			**AMERICAN GARDEN FLOWERS**	
87	AZALEA	15000	75.00	75.00
87	CAMELIA	9800	55.00	75.00
87	GARDENIA	15000	75.00	75.00
87	ROSE	15000	75.00	75.00
88	CALLA LILY	15000	75.00	75.00
88	DAY LILY	15000	75.00	75.00
88	PETUNIA	15000	75.00	75.00
89	PANSY	15000	75.00	75.00
H. DEATON			**AMERICAN WILDLIFE BRONZE COLLECTION**	
79	BOBCAT	7500	60.00	75.00

YR	NAME	LIMIT	ISSUE	TREND
79	COUGAR	7500	60.00	125.00
79	WHITE-TAILED DEER	7500	60.00	105.00
80	BEAVER	7500	60.00	65.00
80	POLAR BEAR	7500	60.00	65.00
80	SEA OTTER	7500	60.00	65.00

J. VILLENA — CELEBRATION OF OPERA

YR	NAME	LIMIT	ISSUE	TREND
86	CARMEN	7500	95.00	95.00
86	CIO-CIO-SAN	7500	95.00	95.00
87	FIGARO	7500	95.00	95.00
88	AIDA	7500	95.00	95.00
88	CANIO	7500	95.00	95.00
88	MIMI	7500	95.00	95.00
*				

CORAL KINGDOM

YR	NAME	LIMIT	ISSUE	TREND
95	ATHENA	OP	35.00	35.00

FRANCESCO — EXOTIC BIRDS OF THE WORLD

YR	NAME	LIMIT	ISSUE	TREND
84	BUDGERIGAR	7500	75.00	105.00
84	COCKATOO, THE	7500	75.00	115.00
84	DIAMOND DOVE, THE	7500	75.00	95.00
84	FISHER'S WHYDAH, THE	7500	75.00	95.00
84	PEACH-FACED LOVEBIRD, THE	7500	75.00	95.00
84	QUETZAL, THE	7500	75.00	95.00
84	RED LOG, THE	7500	75.00	95.00
84	RUBENIO PARAKEET, THE	7500	75.00	95.00

M. WALD — FRESHWATER CHALLENGE

YR	NAME	LIMIT	ISSUE	TREND
91	RAINBOW LURE	OP	75.00	75.00
91	STRIKE, THE	OP	75.00	75.00
91	SUN CATCHER	OP	75.00	75.00
92	PRIZED CATCH	OP	75.00	75.00
*				

GIBSON GIRLS

YR	NAME	LIMIT	ISSUE	TREND
86	ACTRESS, THE	OP	75.00	75.00
87	BRIDE, THE	OP	75.00	75.00
87	CAREER GIRL, THE	OP	75.00	75.00
87	COLLEGE GIRL, THE	OP	75.00	75.00
87	SPORTSWOMAN, THE	OP	75.00	75.00
88	ARTIST, THE	OP	75.00	75.00
88	DEBUTANTE, THE	OP	75.00	75.00
88	SOCIETY GIRL, THE	OP	75.00	75.00

H. DEATON — GREAT ANIMALS OF THE AMERICAN WILDERNESS

YR	NAME	LIMIT	ISSUE	TREND
83	BIGHORN	7500	75.00	75.00
83	ELK	7500	75.00	75.00
83	GRIZZLY BEAR	7500	75.00	75.00
83	MOUNTAIN LION	7500	75.00	75.00
83	MUSTANG	7500	75.00	75.00
83	PLAINS BISON	7500	75.00	75.00
83	PRONGHORN ANTELOPE	7500	75.00	75.00
83	TIMBER WOLF	7500	75.00	75.00
*				

HEROES OF BASEBALL-PORCELAIN BASEBALL CARDS

YR	NAME	LIMIT	ISSUE	TREND
90	BROOKS ROBINSON	OP	20.00	20.00
90	DUKE SNIDER	OP	20.00	20.00
90	GIL HODGES	OP	20.00	20.00
90	ROBERTO CLEMENTE	OP	20.00	20.00
90	WHITEY FORD	OP	20.00	20.00
90	WILLIE MAYS	OP	20.00	20.00
91	CASEY STENGEL	OP	20.00	20.00
91	ERNIE BANKS	OP	20.00	20.00
91	JACKIE ROBINSON	OP	20.00	20.00
91	MICKEY MANTLE	OP	20.00	20.00
91	SATCHEL PAGE	OP	20.00	20.00
91	YOGI BERRA	OP	20.00	20.00
*				

INTERNATIONAL SANTA

YR	NAME	LIMIT	ISSUE	TREND
92	FATHER CHRISTMAS	OP	55.00	55.00
92	GRANDFATHER FROST	OP	55.00	55.00
92	SANTA CLAUS	OP	55.00	55.00
93	BELSNICKEL	OP	55.00	55.00
93	JOLLY OLD ST. NICK	OP	55.00	55.00
93	KRIS KRINGLE	OP	55.00	55.00
94	PERE NOEL	OP	55.00	55.00
94	YULETIDE SANTA	OP	55.00	55.00
95	ALPINE SANTA	OP	55.00	55.00
95	DEDUSHKA MOROZ	OP	55.00	55.00

ITO — LEGENDARY FLOWERS OF THE ORIENT

YR	NAME	LIMIT	ISSUE	TREND
85	CHERRY BLOSSOM	15000	55.00	55.00
85	CHINESE PEONY	15000	55.00	55.00
85	CHRYSANTHEMUM	15000	55.00	55.00
85	GOLD BAND LILY	15000	55.00	55.00
85	IRIS	15000	55.00	55.00
85	JAPANESE ORCHID	15000	55.00	55.00
85	LOTUS	15000	55.00	55.00
85	WISTERIA	15000	55.00	55.00
*				

LITTLE FRIENDS OF THE ARCTIC

YR	NAME	LIMIT	ISSUE	TREND
95	YOUNG PRINCE, THE	OP	38.00	38.00

D.T. LYTTLETON — LITTLE NIGHT OWLS

YR	NAME	LIMIT	ISSUE	TREND
90	BARN OWL	OP	45.00	45.00
90	SNOWY OWL	OP	45.00	45.00

YR	NAME	LIMIT	ISSUE	TREND
90	TAWNY OWL	OP	45.00	45.00
91	BARRED OWL	OP	45.00	45.00
91	GREAT GREY OWL	OP	45.00	45.00
91	GREAT HORNED OWL	OP	45.00	45.00
91	SHORT-EARED OWL	OP	45.00	45.00
91	WHITE-FACED OWL	OP	45.00	45.00
FRANCESCO		**MAGNIFICENT BIRDS OF PARADISE**		
85	BLACK SICKLE-BILLED BIRD OF PARADISE	12500	75.00	95.00
85	BLUE BIRD OF PARADISE	12500	75.00	95.00
85	EMPEROR OF GERMANY	12500	75.00	95.00
85	GOLDIE'S BIRD OF PARADISE	12500	75.00	95.00
85	GREATER BIRD OF PARADISE	12500	75.00	95.00
85	MAGNIFICENT BIRD OF PARADISE	12500	75.00	95.00
85	PRINCESS STEPHANIE BIRD OF PARADISE	12500	75.00	95.00
85	RAGGIANA BIRD OF PARADISE	12500	75.00	95.00
H. DEATON		**MAJESTIC WILDLIFE OF NORTH AMERICA**		
85	ALASKAN MOOSE	7500	75.00	75.00
85	BARREN GROUND CARIBOU	7500	75.00	75.00
85	BLACK BEAR	7500	75.00	75.00
85	COYOTE	7500	75.00	75.00
85	HARBOUR SEAL	7500	75.00	75.00
85	MOUNTAIN GOAT	7500	75.00	75.00
85	OCELOT	7500	75.00	75.00
85	WHITE-TAILED DEER	7500	75.00	75.00
*		**MASTERS OF THE EVENING WILDERNESS**		
94	GREAT SNOWY OWL, THE	OP	38.00	38.00
95	AUTUMN BARN OWLS	OP	38.00	38.00
95	GREAT GREY OWL	OP	38.00	38.00
95	GREAT HORNED OWL	OP	38.00	38.00
S. DOUGLAS			**MYSTIC SPIRITS**	
95	SPIRIT OF THE WOLF	OP	55.00	55.00
D. GEENTZ		**NATURE'S MAJESTIC CATS**		
95	TIGRESS AND CUBS	OP	55.00	55.00
*		**NOBLE AMERICAN INDIAN WOMEN**		
93	SACAJAWEA	OP	55.00	55.00
93	WHITE ROSE	OP	55.00	55.00
94	FALLING STAR	OP	55.00	55.00
94	MINNEHAHA	OP	55.00	55.00
94	PINE LEAF	OP	55.00	55.00
95	LILY OF THE MOHAWKS	OP	55.00	55.00
95	LOZEN	OP	55.00	55.00
95	POCAHONTAS	OP	55.00	55.00
G. GRANGET			**NOBLE SWAN**	
85	NOBLE SWAN, THE	5000	295.00	295.00
*			**NOBLE WARRIORS**	
93	DELIVERANCE	OP	135.00	135.00
94	SPIRIT OF THE PLAINS	OP	135.00	135.00
95	TOP GUN	OP	135.00	135.00
95	WINDRIDER	OP	135.00	135.00
*		**NOLAN RYAN COLLECTORS ED./PORCELAIN BASEBALL**		
93	ANGELS 1972-C #595	OP	20.00	20.00
93	ASTROS 1985-C #7	OP	20.00	20.00
93	METS 1968-C #177	OP	20.00	20.00
93	METS 1969-C #533	OP	20.00	20.00
93	RANGERS 1990-C #1	OP	20.00	20.00
93	RANGERS 1992-C #1	OP	20.00	20.00
W. YOUNGSTROM			**OCEAN ODYSSEY**	
95	BREACHING THE WATERS	OP	55.00	55.00
95	RIDING THE WAVES	OP	55.00	55.00
*		**PRINCESS OF THE PLAINS**		
94	NOBLE GUARDIAN	OP	55.00	55.00
94	SNOW PRINCESS	OP	55.00	55.00
94	WILD FLOWER	OP	55.00	55.00
95	NATURE'S GUARDIAN	OP	55.00	55.00
95	WINTER'S ROSE	OP	55.00	55.00
R. MANNING		**PROTECT NATURE'S INNOCENTS**		
95	AFRICAN ELEPHANT	OP	14.95	15.00
J. LAMB		**PUPPY PLAYTIME SCULPTURE COLLECTION**		
90	DOUBLE TAKE	OP	30.00	30.00
91	A NEW LEASH ON LIFE	OP	30.00	30.00
91	CABIN FEVER	OP	30.00	30.00
91	CATCH OF THE DAY	OP	30.00	30.00
91	FUN AND GAMES	OP	30.00	30.00
91	GETTING ACQUAINTED	OP	30.00	30.00
91	HANGING OUT	OP	30.00	30.00
91	WEEKEND GARDENER	OP	30.00	30.00
P. COOPER			**PUSS IN BOOTS**	
92	CAUGHT NAPPING	OP	35.00	35.00
92	SWEET DREAMS	OP	35.00	35.00
93	ALL DRESSED UP	OP	35.00	35.00
93	HIDE'N GO SEEK	OP	35.00	35.00
93	SITTING PRETTY	OP	35.00	35.00
93	TENNIS ANYONE?	OP	35.00	35.00

YR NAME	LIMIT	ISSUE	TREND
94 DAYDREAMER	OP	35.00	35.00
94 TEE TIME	OP	35.00	35.00
P. COZZOLINO	**RINGLING BROS. CIRCUS ANIMALS**		
83 ACROBATIC SEAL	9800	50.00	50.00
83 BABY ELEPHANT	9800	50.00	55.00
83 MINIATURE SHOW HORSE	9800	50.00	70.00
83 MR. CHIMPANZEE	9800	50.00	50.00
83 PERFORMING POODLES	9800	50.00	50.00
83 SKATING BEAR	9800	50.00	50.00
84 PARADE CAMEL	9800	50.00	50.00
84 ROARING LION	9800	50.00	50.00
N. ROCKWELL	**ROCKWELL HOME OF THE BRAVE**		
82 BACK TO HIS OLD JOB	7500	75.00	75.00
82 HERO'S WELCOME	7500	75.00	75.00
82 REMINISCING	7500	75.00	85.00
82 TAKING MOTHER OVER THE TOP	7500	75.00	75.00
82 UNCLE SAM TAKES WINGS	7500	75.00	75.00
82 WILLIE GILLIS IN CHURCH	7500	75.00	75.00
*	**ROMANCE OF FLOWERS**		
87 SPRINGTIME BOUQUET	15000	95.00	95.00
87 SUMMER BOUQUET	15000	95.00	95.00
88 AUTUMN BOUQUET	15000	95.00	95.00
88 WINTER BOUQUET	15000	95.00	95.00
JACQUELINE B.	**SNUGGLE BABIES**		
88 BABY BEARS	OP	35.00	35.00
88 BABY BUNNIES	OP	35.00	35.00
88 BABY FOXES	OP	35.00	35.00
88 BABY SKUNKS	OP	35.00	35.00
89 BABY CHIPMUNKS	OP	35.00	35.00
89 BABY FAWNS	OP	35.00	35.00
89 BABY RACCOONS	OP	35.00	35.00
89 BABY SQUIRRELS	OP	35.00	35.00
T. SULLIVAN	**SPIRIT OF THE EAGLE**		
94 SPIRIT OF INDEPENDENCE	OP	55.00	55.00
95 BLAZING MAJESTIC SKIES	OP	55.00	55.00
95 NOBLE AND FREE	OP	55.00	55.00
95 PROUD SYMBOL OF FREEDOM	OP	55.00	55.00
E. DAUB	**SPLENDOR OF BALLET**		
87 GISELLE	15000	95.00	95.00
87 JULIET	15000	95.00	95.00
87 KITRI	15000	95.00	95.00
87 ODETTE	15000	95.00	95.00
88 AURORA	15000	95.00	95.00
89 CLARA	15000	95.00	95.00
89 FIREBIRD	15000	95.00	95.00
89 SWANILDA	15000	95.00	95.00
M. WALD	**TROPICAL TREASURES**		
89 FLAG-TAIL SURGEONFISH	OP	38.00	38.00
89 PENNANT BUTTERFLY FISH	OP	38.00	38.00
89 SAIL-FINNED SURGEONFISH	OP	38.00	38.00
89 SEA HORSE	OP	38.00	38.00
90 BEAKED CORAL BUTTERFLY FISH	OP	38.00	38.00
90 BLUE GIRDLED ANGEL FISH	OP	38.00	38.00
90 SPOTTED ANGEL FISH	OP	38.00	38.00
90 ZEBRA TURKEY FISH	OP	38.00	38.00
C. DEHAAN	**UNBRIDLED SPIRITS**		
94 WILD FURY	OP	135.00	135.00
M. GRIFFIN	**VISIONS OF CHRISTMAS**		
93 SANTA'S DELIVERY	OP	135.00	135.00
93 TOYS IN PROGRESS	OP	135.00	135.00
94 MRS. CLAUS' KITCHEN	OP	135.00	135.00
95 GIFTS FROM ST. NICK	OP	135.00	135.00
C. BURGESS	**WILD DUCKS OF NORTH AMERICA**		
87 COMMON MALLARD	15000	95.00	95.00
87 GREEN WINGED TAIL	15000	95.00	95.00
87 HOODED MERGANSER	15000	95.00	95.00
87 WOOD DUCK	15000	95.00	95.00
88 AMERICAN WIDGEON	15000	95.00	95.00
88 BUFFLEHEAD	15000	95.00	95.00
88 NORTHERN PINFALL	15000	95.00	95.00
88 RUDDY DUCK DRAKE	15000	95.00	95.00
D. GEENTY	**WOLVES OF THE WILDERNESS**		
95 A WOLF'S PRIDE	OP	55.00	55.00
95 MOTHER'S WATCH	OP	55.00	55.00

HAMILTON GIFTS

M. HUMPHREY BOGART	**MAUD HUMPHREY BOGART COLLECTOR'S CLUB FIGURINES**		
90 A FLOWER FOR YOU H5596	OP	65.00	65.00
91 FRIENDS FOR LIFE MH911	OP	60.00	140.00
M. HUMPHREY BOGART	**MAUD HUMPHREY BOGART FIGURINES**		
88 A PLEASURE TO MEET YOU H1310	RT	65.00	80.00
88 BRIDE, THE H1313	19500	90.00	90.00
88 CLEANING HOUSE H1303	RT	60.00	70.00
88 LITTLE CHICKADEES H1306	RT	65.00	70.00

YR	NAME	LIMIT	ISSUE	TREND
88	MAGIC KITTEN, THE- H1308	RT	66.00	85.00
88	MY FIRST DANCE H1311	RT	60.00	200.00
88	SARAH H1312	RT	60.00	275.00
88	SEAMSTRESS H1309	RT	66.00	250.00
88	SUSANNA H1305	RT	60.00	250.00
88	TEA AND GOSSIP H1301	RT	65.00	110.00
89	A SUNDAY OUTING H1386	15000	135.00	140.00
89	BRIDE, THE-PORCELAIN H1388	15000	125.00	128.00
89	GIFT OF LOVE H1319	RT	65.00	65.00
89	IN THE ORCHARD H1373	24500	33.00	36.00
89	KITTY'S LUNCH H1355	19500	60.00	66.00
89	LITTLE BO PEEP H1382	24000	45.00	49.00
89	LITTLE CAPTIVE, THE- H1374	19500	55.00	58.00
89	LITTLE CHICKADEES-PORCELAIN H1389	15000	*	110.00
89	LITTLE RED RIDING HOOD H1381	24500	43.00	46.00
89	MAGIC KITTEN, THE-PORCELAIN H5543	19500	125.00	125.00
89	MY FIRST BIRTHDAY H1320	RT	47.00	50.00
89	NO MORE TEARS H1351	24500	44.00	49.00
89	PLAYING BRIDESMAID H5500	19000	125.00	100.00
89	SCHOOL DAYS H1318	RT	43.00	60.00
89	SCHOOL LESSON H1356	19500	77.00	100.00
89	SEALED WITH A KISS H1316	RT	45.00	70.00
89	SPECIAL FRIENDS H1317	RT	66.00	115.00
89	SPECIAL FRIENDS-PORCELAIN H1390	15000	125.00	120.00
89	SPRING BEAUTIES H1387	15000	135.00	131.00
89	SPRINGTIME GATHERING H1385	7500	295.00	200.00
89	WINTER FUN H1354	15000	46.00	60.00
90	A CHANCE ACQUAINTANCE H5589	19500	70.00	135.00
90	A LITTLE ROBIN H1347	19500	55.00	58.00
90	A SPECIAL GIFT H5550	19500	70.00	99.00
90	AUTUMN DAYS H1348	24500	45.00	49.00
90	HOLIDAY SURPRISE H5551	24500	50.00	55.00
90	KITTY'S BATH H1384	19500	103.00	109.00
90	LITTLE PLAYMATES H1349	19500	48.00	53.00
90	MY WINTER HAT H5554	24500	40.00	46.00
90	PLAYTIME H1383	19500	60.00	66.00
90	SARAH (WATERBALL) H5594	19500	75.00	79.00
90	SUSANNA (WATERBALL) H5595	19500	75.00	79.00
90	WINTER DAYS H5553	24500	50.00	55.00
90	WINTER FRIENDS H5552	19500	64.00	69.00
91	ALL BUNDLED UP 910015	19500	85.00	85.00
91	CLEANING HOUSE (WATERBALL) H5654	19500	75.00	75.00
91	DOUBLES 910023	19500	70.00	70.00
91	GRADUATE, THE- H5559	19500	75.00	75.00
91	HUSH A BYE BABY H5695	19500	62.00	62.00
91	LITTLE BOY BLUE H5612	19500	55.00	55.00
91	LITTLE MISS MUFFET H5621	24500	75.00	75.00
91	MELISSA (WATERBALL) 910074	19500	40.00	40.00
91	MELISSA 910031	24500	55.00	55.00
91	MY FIRST DANCE (WATERBALL) H5655	19000	75.00	75.00
91	MY FIRST DANCE-PORCELAIN H5650	15000	110.00	110.00
91	MY SNOW SHOVEL 910058	19500	70.00	70.00
91	MY WINTER HAT 921017	15000	80.00	80.00
91	PINWHEEL, THE- H5600	24500	45.00	45.00
91	SARAH-PORCELAIN H5651	15000	110.00	110.00
91	SPRING BOUQUET H5598	24500	44.00	44.00
91	SPRING FROLIC H5590	15000	170.00	170.00
91	SUSANNA-PORCELAIN H5652	15000	110.00	110.00
91	TEA AND GOSSIP-PORCELAIN H5653	15000	132.00	132.00
91	WINTER DAYS (WATERBALL) 915130	19500	75.00	75.00
91	WINTER FRIENDS (WATERBALL) 915149	19500	75.00	75.00
91	WINTER FUN 921025	15000	90.00	90.00
91	WINTER RIDE 910066	19500	60.00	60.00

M. HUMPHREY BOGART   MAUD HUMPHREY BOGART GALLERY FIGURINES

YR	NAME	LIMIT	ISSUE	TREND
91	MOTHERS TREASURES H5619	15000	118.00	118.00
91	SHARING SECRETS 910007	15000	120.00	120.00

M. HUMPHREY BOGART   MAUD HUMPHREY BOGART PETITE FIGURINES

YR	NAME	LIMIT	ISSUE	TREND
91	CLEANING HOUSE H5611	OP	24.00	24.00
91	GIFT OF LOVE H5620	OP	24.00	24.00
91	MAGIC KITTEN, THE- H5623	OP	24.00	24.00
91	MY FIRST DANCE H-5623	OP	24.00	24.00
91	SARAH H5613	OP	24.00	24.00
91	SEAMSTRESS, THE- H5627	OP	24.00	24.00
91	SPECIAL FRIENDS H5625	OP	24.00	24.00
91	SUSANNA H5626	OP	24.00	24.00

HAMILTON/BOEHM
*

FAVORITE GARDEN FLOWERS

YR	NAME	LIMIT	ISSUE	TREND
85	CALIFORNIA POPPY	9800	195.00	225.00
85	CARNATION	9800	195.00	225.00
85	DAFFODIL	9800	195.00	225.00
85	HIBISCUS	9800	195.00	225.00
85	MORNING GLORY	9800	195.00	225.00
85	ROSE	9800	195.00	225.00

YR	NAME	LIMIT	ISSUE	TREND
85	SWEET PEA	9800	195.00	225.00
85	TULIP	9800	195.00	225.00
*				**ROSES OF DISTINCTION**
83	ANGEL FACE ROSE	9800	135.00	175.00
83	ELEGANCE ROSE	9800	135.00	175.00
83	MR. LINCOLN ROSE	9800	135.00	175.00
83	PEACE ROSE	9800	135.00	195.00
83	QUEEN ELIZABETH ROSE	9800	135.00	175.00
83	ROYAL HIGHNESS ROSE	9800	135.00	175.00
83	TROPICANA ROSE	9800	135.00	175.00
83	WHITE MASTERPIECE ROSE	9800	135.00	195.00

HANFORD'S
M. CRUNKLETON

				LINCOLN COUNTY GARDEN CLUB II
89	AUNT LENA	RT	40.00	95.00
89	BIG BEULAH	RT	40.00	40.00
89	CHARLOTTE DEAR	RT	40.00	95.00
89	GERTRUDE	RT	40.00	40.00
89	GRANDMA MATTIE	RT	40.00	125.00
89	JACKUELINE ADEL	RT	40.00	40.00
89	LADY MARGARET II	RT	40.00	40.00
89	LARRY LAVINSKI	RT	40.00	40.00
89	MISTER BOB	RT	40.00	40.00
89	MOLLY BLUME	RT	40.00	95.00
89	MOZELL	RT	40.00	95.00
89	SISTER ALMA	RT	40.00	95.00
89	TRUMAN WILLARD	RT	40.00	40.00

M. CRUNKLETON

				LINCOLN COUNTY GARDEN CLUB III
90	AGNES	RT	40.00	40.00
90	ANNIE LEA	RT	40.00	175.00
90	BIG GUY	RT	40.00	40.00
90	DINAH JANE	RT	40.00	40.00
90	DONNA JEAN	RT	40.00	40.00
90	FLORABEL'S MOM	RT	40.00	95.00
90	LADY MARGARET III	RT	40.00	125.00
90	LEONA MILLER	RT	40.00	95.00
90	MAUDE	RT	40.00	275.00
90	MISS TILLY	RT	40.00	95.00
90	MS LILA	RT	40.00	255.00
90	REBECCA MARIE	RT	40.00	95.00

HARMONY KINGDOM
M. PERRY

				HARMONY GARDEN
97	CHRYSANTHEMUM	OP	39.00	39.00
97	CRANBERRY	OP	39.00	39.00
97	DAISY	OP	39.00	39.00
97	HYACINTH	OP	39.00	39.00
97	HYDRANGEA	OP	39.00	39.00
97	MARSH MARIGOLD	OP	39.00	39.00
97	MORNING GLORY	OP	39.00	39.00
97	PEACE LILY	OP	39.00	39.00
97	RED ROSE	3600	39.00	225.00
97	RHODODENDRON	OP	39.00	39.00
97	ROSE BASKET	3600	65.00	150.00
97	SNOW DROP	OP	39.00	39.00
98	BEGONIA	*	45.00	45.00
98	CACTUS	*	45.00	45.00
98	DOUBLE ROSE	5000	55.00	55.00
98	FORGET-ME-NOT	*	45.00	45.00
98	GARDENIA	*	45.00	45.00
98	IRIS	*	45.00	45.00
98	PEONY	*	45.00	45.00
98	RAINBOW ROSE PARTY	5000	*	N/A
98	ROSE BUD	*	45.00	45.00
98	SNAP DRAGON	*	45.00	45.00
98	SUN FLOWER II	*	45.00	45.00

P. CALVESBERT

				HOLIDAY EDITIONS
96	NICK OF TIME	RT	35.00	125.00
97	SOMETHING'S GOTTA GIVE	TL	35.00	35.00

D. LAWRENCE

				HOLIDAY EDITIONS
95	CHATELAINE	RT	35.00	250.00
96	BON ENFANT	RT	35.00	125.00
97	CELESTE	TL	45.00	95.00

P. CALVESBERT

				LARGE TREASURE JESTS
90	PONDERING	RT	55.00	145.00
91	HORN O' PLENTY	RT	55.00	55.00
93	STANDING GUARD	RT	55.00	55.00

P. CALVESBERT

				LIMITED EDITIONS
95	NOAH'S LARK	5000	400.00	625.00
95	UNBEARABLES	2500	400.00	400.00
97	ORIGINAL KIN	2500	250.00	425.00

D. LAWRENCE

				LIMITED EDITIONS
97	KILLING TIME	3600	100.00	100.00

YR	NAME	LIMIT	ISSUE	TREND
P. CALVESBERT			**PARADOXICAL SERIES**	
95	PARADISE FOUND	RT	35.00	35.00
95	PARADISE LOST	OP	35.00	35.00
P. CALVESBERT		**ROYAL WATCH COLLECTOR'S CLUB**		
96	BIG BLUE	RT	75.00	175.00
96	BIG DAY, THE	RT	*	125.00
D. LAWRENCE		**ROYAL WATCH COLLECTOR'S CLUB**		
96	PURRFECT FIT	RT	*	85.00
P. CALVESBERT			**SMALL TREASURE JESTS**	
92	FORTY WINKS	RT	35.00	150.00
92	PRINCELY THOUGHTS	RT	35.00	150.00
93	ALL EARS	RT	35.00	60.00
93	ALL TIED UP	RT	35.00	70.00
93	AT ARM'S LENGTH	RT	35.00	185.00
93	BABY ON BOARD	RT	35.00	35.00
93	BACK SCRATCH	RT	35.00	950.00
93	DAY DREAMER	RT	35.00	200.00
93	HAMMING IT UP	RT	35.00	50.00
93	IT'S A FINE DAY	RT	35.00	199.00
93	JONAH'S HIDEAWAY	RT	35.00	185.00
93	REMINISCE	RT	35.00	165.00
93	SIDE STEPPING	RT	35.00	125.00
93	SWAMP SONG	RT	35.00	35.00
93	TOP BANANA	RT	35.00	180.00
93	TRUNK SHOW	RT	35.00	100.00
93	WHO'D A THOUGHT?	RT	35.00	950.00
94	GROUP THERAPY	RT	35.00	55.00
94	LET'S DO LUNCH	RT	35.00	260.00
94	LOVE SEAT	RT	35.00	35.00
94	NEIGHBORHOOD WATCH	RT	35.00	50.00
94	TEACHER'S PET	RT	35.00	40.00
94	UNTOUCHABLE	RT	35.00	250.00
95	BEAK TO BEAK	RT	35.00	35.00
95	DEN MOTHERS	RT	35.00	50.00
95	HORSE PLAY	RT	35.00	185.00
95	MAJOR'S MOUSERS	RT	45.00	55.00
95	MUD BATH	RT	35.00	45.00
P. CALVESBERT				**TREASURE JESTS**
97	FRIENDS IN HIGH PLACES	OP	45.00	45.00
97	IN FINE FEATHER	OP	45.00	45.00
97	PHOTO FINISH	OP	45.00	45.00
97	SLEEPY HOLLOW	OP	35.00	35.00
97	WHALE OF A TIME	OP	35.00	35.00
98	ALGERNON	OP	45.00	45.00
98	ANTIPASTO	OP	45.00	45.00
98	ARIA AMOROSA	OP	45.00	45.00
98	BABY BOOMERS	OP	45.00	45.00
98	CROC POT	OP	45.00	45.00
98	ROCKY'S RAIDERS	OP	45.00	45.00
98	WISHFUL THINKING	OP	45.00	45.00

HAWTHORNE
*

YR	NAME	LIMIT	ISSUE	TREND
			CLASSIC BALLPARKS	
95	WRIGLEY FIELD-ERNIE BANKS 78461	*	99.95	100.00
97	COMISKEY PARK 078470	*	50.00	50.00
*			**KINKADE ACCESSORIES**	
97	GARDEN OF PROMISE	*	20.00	20.00
97	GLORY OF MORNING	*	20.00	20.00
97	LAMPLIGHT BRIDGE	*	20.00	20.00
*		**MAYBERRY VILLAGE ACCESSORIES**		
97	SCHOOL BUS AND FLAG SET	*	24.00	24.00
97	VILLAGE STREETLIGHTS (SET OF 6)	*	24.00	24.00
S. SMITH			**THE FAIRY TALE FOREST**	
94	GOLDILOCKS & THE THREE BEARS 78651	*	25.00	25.00
94	GOLDILOCKS & THE THREE BEARS 78653	*	25.00	25.00
94	LITTLE RED RIDING HOOD 78654	CL	50.00	50.00
C. WYSOCKI			**WYSOCKI ACCESSORIES**	
97	SPECIAL DELIVERY	*	25.00	25.00

HELEN SABATTE DESIGNS INC.

YR	NAME	LIMIT	ISSUE	TREND
H. SABATTE		**AMERICAN CHRISTMAS CAROLLERS**		
93	FATHER	5000	48.00	48.00
93	GRADE SCHOOL BOY	5000	48.00	48.00
93	GRADE SCHOOL GIRL	5000	48.00	48.00
93	MOTHER	5000	48.00	48.00
93	PRE SCHOOL BOY	5000	48.00	48.00
93	PRE SCHOOL GIRL	5000	48.00	48.00
93	TEENAGE BOY	5000	48.00	48.00
93	TEENAGE GIRL	5000	48.00	48.00
93	TRADITIONAL GRANDFATHER	5000	48.00	48.00
93	TRADITIONAL GRANDMOTHER	5000	48.00	48.00
94	TEENAGE BOY HOLDING WATER SNOWGLOBE	200	45.00	50.00
94	TEENAGER GIRL HOLDING WATER SNOWGLOBE	200	45.00	50.00

YR	NAME	LIMIT	ISSUE	TREND
H. SABATTE			**CHILDHOOD MEMORIES**	
95	MAN WITH SNOWMAN	*	48.00	48.00
95	PRE-SCHOOL BOY WITH SNOWFLAKES	CL	45.00	45.00
95	PRE-SCHOOL BOY WITH SNOWMAN	*	45.00	45.00
95	PRE-SCHOOL GIRL WITH SNOWFLAKES	CL	45.00	45.00
95	PRE-SCHOOL GIRL WITH SNOWMAN	*	45.00	45.00
95	WOMAN WITH SNOWMAN	*	48.00	48.00
96	MOTHER WITH GINGERBREAD BOARD	*	65.00	65.00
96	PRE-SCHOOL BOY W/GINGERBREAD COOKIES	*	45.00	45.00
96	PRE-SCHOOL GIRL W/GINGERBREAD COOKIES	*	45.00	45.00
H. SABATTE			**COLLEGE**	
95	TEEN BOY WITH PENNANT	*	48.00	48.00
95	TEEN GIRL WITH PENNANT	*	48.00	48.00
H. SABATTE			**GARDEN**	
96	MAN W/GARDEN SUPPLIES	*	60.00	60.00
96	WOMAN W/GARDEN SUPPLIES	*	65.00	65.00
H. SABATTE			**NIGHT BEFORE CHRISTMAS**	
94	GRADE SCHOOL GIRL W/DEAR SANTA LETTER	CL	52.00	52.00
95	PRE-SCHOOL BOY WITH BEAR & BOOKS	*	50.00	50.00
96	MOTHER WITH CHRISTMAS WRAP	*	50.00	50.00
H. SABATTE			**OLDE ENGLISH**	
96	MAN/BROWN	*	80.00	80.00
96	MAN/GREEN	*	80.00	80.00
96	WOMAN/RED	*	80.00	80.00
H. SABATTE			**SPECIAL ACCESSORIES**	
95	FATHER WITH SKATES	*	45.00	45.00
95	FATHER WITH SKIS	*	48.00	48.00
95	MOTHER WITH SKATES	*	45.00	45.00
95	MOTHER WITH SKIS	*	48.00	48.00
95	PRE-SCHOOL BOY WITH CAT	*	45.00	45.00
95	PRE-SCHOOL BOY WITH DOG	*	45.00	45.00
95	PRE-SCHOOL BOY WITH PHOTO ALBUM	CL	48.00	48.00
95	PRE-SCHOOL GIRL WITH CAT	*	45.00	45.00
95	PRE-SCHOOL GIRL WITH DOG	*	45.00	45.00
95	PRE-SCHOOL GIRL WITH PHOTO ALBUM	CL	48.00	48.00
95	TEENAGE BOY WITH AIRPLANES	*	45.00	45.00
95	TEENAGE BOY WITH SKATES	*	45.00	45.00
95	TEENAGE BOY WITH SKIS	*	48.00	48.00
95	TEENAGE GIRL WITH SKATES	*	45.00	45.00
95	TEENAGE GIRL WITH SKIS	*	48.00	48.00
95	WOMAN WITH APPLES	*	48.00	48.00
96	GRADE SCHOOL GIRL W/RAGGEDY ANN	*	48.00	48.00
96	PRE-SCHOOL BOY WITH ADVENT CALENDAR	*	48.00	48.00
96	PRE-SCHOOL GIRL WITH ADVENT CALENDAR	*	48.00	48.00
H. SABATTE			**THE COLLECTOR**	
94	BEAR COLLECTOR-MAN	5000	60.00	65.00
94	BEAR COLLECTOR-WOMAN	5000	65.00	70.00
95	GRADE SCHOOL BOY WITH TEAPOT	CL	50.00	50.00
95	PRE-SCHOOL GIRL WITH 3 BEARS & BOOKS	*	50.00	50.00
95	TEENAGE BOY WITH BEARS & BOOKS	*	50.00	50.00
95	WOMAN WITH TEAPOTS	CL	65.00	65.00
96	GRADE SCHOOL BOY W/RAGGEDY ANDY	*	48.00	48.00
96	MOTHER WITH DOLLS & BOOKS	*	68.00	68.00
96	PRE-SCHOOL GIRL W/DOLL CASE, ETC.	*	50.00	50.00
H. SABATTE			**THE COLONIAL**	
95	PILGRIM MAN	*	48.00	48.00
95	PILGRIM WOMAN	*	48.00	48.00
96	PILGRIM BOY	*	48.00	48.00
96	PILGRIM GIRL	*	48.00	48.00
H. SABATTE			**THE FATHER CHRISTMAS SERIES**	
94	FATHER CHRISTMAS W/CHRISTMAS GREENERY	500	75.00	75.00
94	FATHER CHRISTMAS W/TRADITIONAL TREE	500	80.00	80.00
H. SABATTE			**THE NEW ENGLANDER**	
95	FISHERMAN-CHILD	*	48.00	48.00
95	FISHERMAN-OLD	*	48.00	48.00
95	FISHERMAN-YOUNG	*	48.00	48.00
95	LOBSTER BOY	*	48.00	48.00
95	LOBSTERMAN	*	49.00	49.00
95	MAN W/STARFISH SNOWMAN	*	47.00	47.00
95	MAN WITH BLUEBERRY SCOPE	*	48.00	48.00
95	MAN WITH CRANBERRY SCOPE	*	48.00	48.00
95	PRE-SCHOOL BOY W/STARFISH SNOWMAN	*	45.00	45.00
95	PRE-SCHOOL GIRL W/STARFISH SNOWMAN	*	45.00	45.00
95	SAILOR BOY WITH SAILBOAT	*	45.00	45.00
95	SAILOR BOY WITH XMAS SAILBOAT	*	46.00	46.00
95	SAILOR GIRL WITH SAILBOAT	*	45.00	45.00
95	SAILOR GIRL WITH XMAS SAILBOAT	*	46.00	46.00
95	WOMAN W/STARFISH SNOWMAN	*	47.00	47.00
95	WOMAN WITH BLUEBERRIES	*	48.00	48.00
95	WOMAN WITH CRANBERRIES	*	48.00	48.00
H. SABATTE			**THE PUPPETEER**	
95	MAN WITH SANTA PUPPET	*	54.00	54.00

YR	NAME	LIMIT	ISSUE	TREND
H. SABATTE				**WEDDING**
95	BRIDE	*	65.00	65.00
95	GROOM	*	60.00	60.00

HUTSCHENREUTHER

	GRANGET	**AMERICAN LIMITED EDITION COLLECTION**		
*	A FAMILY AFFAIR	200	*	3700.00
*	ANXIOUS MOMENT	175	*	5225.00
*	ARABIAN STALLION	300	*	8525.00
*	BLUE DOLPHINS	100	*	10000.00
*	CHALLENGE, THE	150	*	14000.00
*	CHRISTMAS ROSE	375	*	3050.00
*	CONTEST, THE	100	*	14000.00
*	DANCE-CROWNCRESTED CRANE, THE	25	*	30000.00
*	DECORATED SEA LIONS	100	*	6000.00
*	DISDAIN-OWL	175	*	5200.00
*	DOLPHIN GROUP	500	*	4000.00
*	ENGAGED	250	*	1750.00
*	FIRST LESSON	175	*	3550.00
*	FISH HAWK, THE	500	*	12000.00
*	FREEDOM IN FLIGHT	200	*	9000.00
*	FRIENDLY ENEMIES-WOODPECKER	175	*	5200.00
*	HEADING SOUTH	150	*	14000.00
*	IT'S SPRING AGAIN	250	*	3475.00
*	JOE-STAG	150	*	12000.00
*	LINNET ON EAR OF RYE	250	*	1175.00
*	OFF SEASON	125	*	4125.00
*	OLYMPIC CHAMPION	500	*	3650.00
*	PROUD PARENT	250	*	13750.00
*	PYGMY OWLS	650	*	6225.00
*	QUINCE	375	*	2850.00
*	REDSTART ON QUINCE BRANCH	250	*	1300.00
*	RELUCTANT FLEDGLING	350	*	3475.00
*	SAFE AT HOME	350	*	9000.00
*	SAW WHET OWL	750	*	3575.00
*	SEA FROLIC-SEA LION	500	*	3500.00
*	SENTINEL-SPRINGBOOK, THE	150	*	5200.00
*	SILVER HERON	500	*	5000.00
*	SPARROWHAWK W/KINGBIRD	500	*	8250.00
*	SPRING IS HERE	175	*	4500.00
*	TAKE COVER	125	*	14000.00
*	TO RIDE THE WIND	500	*	8650.00
*	WATER LILY	375	*	4150.00
*	WHOOPING CRANES	300	*	8000.00
*	WREN ON WILD ROSE	250	*	1675.00
D. VALENZA				**PORTRAIT FIGURINES**
77	CATHERINE THE GREAT	500	500.00	1100.00
77	HELEN OF TROY	500	500.00	1050.00
77	ISOLDE	500	500.00	2650.00
77	JENNIE CHURCHHILL	500	500.00	925.00
77	JUDITH	500	500.00	1575.00
77	LILLIAN RUSSELL	500	500.00	1825.00
77	QUEEN ISABELLE	500	500.00	925.00

IRIS ARC

	M. GENOA		**CRYSTAL KINGDOM**	
93	BASKET OF VIOLETS	RT	190.00	225.00
93	BIRDBATH	RT	190.00	225.00
93	COUNTRY CHURCH	OP	590.00	590.00
94	BLUEBIRD BASKET	OP	190.00	190.00
94	HUMMINGBIRDS	OP	290.00	290.00
94	MYSTIC STAR CASTLE	OP	390.00	390.00
C. HUGHES			**CRYSTAL KINGDOM**	
93	NOB HILL VICTORIAN	OP	1,000.00	1000.00
94	GARDEN COTTAGE	OP	390.00	390.00

ISPANKY

	L. ISPANKY		**ISPANKY PORCELAINS**	
*	EXODUS, BRONZE	100	1,500.00	1500.00
*	OWL	300	750.00	825.00
*	PRINCESS OF THE NILE	500	275.00	450.00
*	ROSH HASHANA, GRAY BEARD	2	275.00	10000.00
*	ROSH HASHANA, WHITE BEARD	400	275.00	1300.00
66	ORCHIDS	250	1,000.00	1500.00
67	ARTIST GIRL	500	200.00	1800.00
67	BALLERINA	500	350.00	1000.00
67	BALLET DANCERS	500	350.00	1000.00
67	BIRD OF PARADISE	250	1,500.00	1500.00
67	CAVALRY SCOUT, DECORATED	200	1,000.00	1200.00
67	CAVALRY SCOUT, WHITE	150	675.00	900.00
67	DRUMMER BOY, DECORATED	200	250.00	285.00
67	DRUMMER BOY, WHITE	600	150.00	185.00
67	DUTCH IRIS	250	1,400.00	1500.00
67	FORTY-NINER, DECORATED	200	450.00	650.00
67	FORTY-NINER, WHITE	350	250.00	250.00

From the Best Friends—First Friends Begin at Childhood
collection, Fishing Friends—produced by Band
Creations—is the work of artists Jeanette Richards and
Sandra Penfield.

Summer Stroll is a 1991
Lladró collectors club issue.

Just One More begs this little fellow of his
storytelling father. The piece is produced by
Lladró.

1992's Large Black Forest Santa by Jocelyn
Mostrom, limited to an edition of 3,000, is
part of the Christmas in Chelsea collection
from Kurt S. Adler Inc.

YR	NAME	LIMIT	ISSUE	TREND
67	GREAT SPIRIT, WHITE	150	750.00	750.00
67	HORSE	300	300.00	600.00
67	HUNT, DECORATED	200	2,000.00	3850.00
67	HUNT, WHITE	150	1,200.00	1485.00
67	KING ARTHUR	500	300.00	750.00
67	LOVE	300	375.00	950.00
67	MEDITATION	300	350.00	1000.00
67	MORNING	500	300.00	1500.00
67	MOSES	400	400.00	1800.00
67	ON THE TRAIL, WHITE	150	750.00	1125.00
67	PACK HORSE, DECORATED	200	700.00	1250.00
67	PACK HORSE, WHITE	150	500.00	350.00
67	PILGRIM FAMILY, DECORATED	200	500.00	750.00
67	PILGRIM FAMILY, WHITE	350	350.00	350.00
67	PIONEER SCOUT, DECORATED	200	1,000.00	1000.00
67	PIONEER SCOUT, WHITE	200	675.00	405.00
67	PIONEER WOMAN, DECORATED	200	350.00	550.00
67	PIONEER WOMEN, WHITE	150	225.00	350.00
67	PROMISES	100	225.00	2500.00
67	TULIPS, RED	50	1,800.00	4500.00
67	TULIPS, YELLOW	50	1,800.00	4500.00
68	PEGASUS, DECORATED	300	375.00	800.00
68	PEGASUS, WHITE	300	300.00	800.00
68	QUEEN OF SPRING	200	750.00	1200.00
69	AUTUMN WIND	500	300.00	1500.00
69	DAFFODILS	250	950.00	950.00
69	GREAT SPIRIT, DECORATED	200	1,500.00	1850.00
69	ISAIAH	300	475.00	1100.00
69	MARIA	350	750.00	1000.00
69	MERMAID GROUP, DECORATED	200	1,000.00	1800.00
69	MERMAID GROUP, WHITE	200	950.00	950.00
69	STORM	500	400.00	950.00
70	CELESTE	200	475.00	500.00
70	DAWN	300	500.00	1000.00
70	EVENING	300	375.00	650.00
70	HORSEPOWER	100	1,650.00	3250.00
70	ICARUS	350	350.00	650.00
70	KING AND QUEEN, PAIR	250	750.00	1200.00
70	ON THE TRAIL, DECORATED	200	1,700.00	1700.00
70	PEACE, DECORATED	100	375.00	750.00
70	PEACE, WHITE	100	300.00	450.00
70	REVERIE	200	200.00	850.00
70	THRASHER	300	1,000.00	1000.00
71	BEAUTY AND THE BEAST	15	4,500.00	4500.00
71	BETSY ROSS	350	750.00	1325.00
71	CHRISTINE	300	350.00	800.00
71	DAVID	400	450.00	600.00
71	DEBUTANTE	500	350.00	625.00
71	ETERNAL LOVE	300	400.00	650.00
71	EXCALIBUR	15	3,500.00	3500.00
71	FELICIA	15	2,500.00	2500.00
71	FREEDOM	250	300.00	500.00
71	JESSAMY 1	400	450.00	600.00
71	MR. AND MRS. OTTER	500	250.00	600.00
71	PEACE RIDERS	1	35,000.00	35000.00
71	QUEST	15	1,500.00	1500.00
71	ROMEO AND JULIET, DECORATED	500	375.00	950.00
71	SWAN LAKE	300	1,000.00	2500.00
71	TEKIEH	15	1,800.00	1800.00
72	ANNABEL LEE	500	750.00	750.00
72	CINDERELLA	400	375.00	375.00
72	MADAME BUTTERFLY	300	1,500.00	1500.00
72	PRINCESS AND THE FROG	500	675.00	675.00
72	SPIRIT OF THE SEA	450	500.00	500.00
72	SPRING BALLET	400	450.00	600.00
72	SPRING BOUQUET	50	3,000.00	15000.00
73	AARON	350	1,200.00	2400.00
73	ABRAHAM	500	600.00	1400.00
73	EMERALD DRAGON	100	2,500.00	3250.00
73	LORELEI	500	550.00	650.00
73	LOVE LETTERS	450	750.00	850.00
73	MAID OF THE MIST	350	450.00	850.00
73	MESSIAH	750	450.00	500.00
73	REBEKAH	300	400.00	775.00
73	TEXAS RANGERS	400	1,650.00	1650.00
74	BANBURY CROSS	350	550.00	1025.00
74	BELLE OF THE BALL	500	550.00	950.00
74	DIANNE	500	500.00	900.00
74	HAMLET AND OPHELIA	350	1,250.00	1350.00
74	HOLY FAMILY, DECORATED	450	900.00	1595.00
74	HOLY FAMILY, WHITE	450	750.00	700.00
74	KING LEAR AND CORDELIA	250	1,250.00	1250.00
74	SECOND BASE	500	650.00	1100.00
75	APOTHEOSIS OF THE SCULPTOR	250	495.00	1000.00
75	HEALING HAND, DECORATED	600	750.00	1250.00

YR	NAME	LIMIT	ISSUE	TREND
75	HEALING HAND, WHITE	600	650.00	800.00
75	JOSHUA	350	750.00	1200.00
75	MADONNA WITH HALO, DECORATED	500	350.00	495.00
75	MADONNA WITH HALO, WHITE	500	250.00	250.00
75	MADONNA, THE BLESSED SAINT, DECORATED	500	295.00	350.00
75	MADONNA, THE BLESSED SAINT, WHITE	500	195.00	250.00
75	MEMORIES	500	600.00	900.00
75	SPRING FEVER	600	650.00	1050.00
76	LYDIA	400	450.00	835.00
76	PIANO GIRL	800	300.00	725.00
76	SOPHISTICATION	800	350.00	575.00
76	SWANILDA	1000	285.00	800.00
77	DAISY	1000	325.00	575.00
77	DAY DREAMS	1000	300.00	600.00
77	MORNING GLORY	1000	325.00	620.00
77	POPPY	1000	325.00	575.00
77	SERENE HIGHNESS	100	2,500.00	4250.00
77	SNOW DROP	1000	325.00	430.00
77	THUNDER	500	500.00	795.00
78	LITTLE MERMAID	800	350.00	520.00
78	MY NAME IS IRIS	700	500.00	900.00
78	NARCISSUS	700	500.00	620.00
78	ROMANCE	500	800.00	1200.00
78	TEN COMMANDMENTS, DECORATED	500	950.00	1525.00
78	TEN COMMANDMENTS, WHITE	700	600.00	850.00
78	WATER LILY	1000	325.00	620.00

J.H. BOONE

N.J. ROSE / **BEAR CUB SOCIETY**

YR	NAME	LIMIT	ISSUE	TREND
95	HUCKLEBERRY BINGE	3000	80.00	80.00
96	SURPRISE	3000	80.00	80.00

N.J. ROSE / **CLASSIC**

YR	NAME	LIMIT	ISSUE	TREND
96	BUFFALO BILL	OP	125.00	125.00
96	FIRE WOLF	OP	100.00	100.00
96	FLY WITH EAGLES	OP	85.00	85.00
96	MEDICINE ROCK	OP	110.00	110.00

T. SNYDER / **EARTH MATES COLLECTION**

YR	NAME	LIMIT	ISSUE	TREND
95	WISDOM KEEPER	2500	155.00	155.00

T. SNYDER / **EARTH SONG COLLECTION**

YR	NAME	LIMIT	ISSUE	TREND
95	AMAZON	2500	135.00	135.00
95	CONGO	2500	140.00	140.00
95	EARTH MATES	2500	275.00	275.00
95	EARTH SONG	1950	275.00	275.00
95	IMPALA/MASAI	2500	160.00	160.00
95	KINGS IN THE CRADLE	2500	155.00	155.00
95	LAST FRONTIER	2500	140.00	140.00
95	MOUNTAIN FORTRESS	2500	155.00	155.00
95	NORTHERN WILDERNESS	2500	135.00	135.00
95	OUTBACK	2500	135.00	135.00
95	PRIDE OF AFRICA	1500	250.00	250.00
95	RHYTHM OF LIFE	2500	135.00	135.00
95	SACRED PATHS	2500	135.00	135.00
95	SAVAGE KINSHIP	2500	140.00	140.00
95	SAVANNA TITANS	2500	155.00	155.00
95	SPRINGBOK	2500	95.00	95.00
95	THIN ICE	2500	95.00	95.00
96	EMBRACE	2500	85.00	85.00
96	SAMBURU ELDER	1500	85.00	85.00
96	SEBRINA	1500	85.00	85.00
96	ZULU WARRIOR	2500	85.00	85.00

G. ROSE / **KINDRED SPIRIT COLLECTION**

YR	NAME	LIMIT	ISSUE	TREND
95	BUFFALO SPIRIT	1500	250.00	250.00
96	WOLF PAWS	3000	95.00	95.00

N.J. ROSE / **NEIL J. ROSE COLLECTION**

YR	NAME	LIMIT	ISSUE	TREND
95	ARCTIC PHANTOMS	2500	92.00	92.00
95	BUFFALO HEART	2500	85.00	85.00
95	COUGAR ROCK	1950	275.00	275.00
95	DENIZEN OF THE NORTH	2500	92.00	92.00
95	FLAME, THE	2500	105.00	105.00
95	FREE SPIRIT	2500	180.00	180.00
95	GIFT OF THE WOLF	2500	60.00	60.00
95	LEGEND OF SPIRIT LAKE	2500	95.00	95.00
95	MISTRAL	2500	75.00	75.00
95	PIPE HOLDER	1950	260.00	260.00
95	RISING SUN	3500	135.00	135.00
95	SILENT STALKER	2500	105.00	105.00
95	TOWERING ANTLERS	2500	115.00	115.00
95	WILDERNESS MARAUDER	1500	180.00	180.00
96	BETRAYAL	2500	275.00	275.00
96	ROCK MOUNTAIN RECLUSE	2500	100.00	100.00
96	SNOW FLOWER	2500	95.00	95.00

P. CARRICO / **TRACES**

YR	NAME	LIMIT	ISSUE	TREND
95	MATERNAL INSTINCT	2500	240.00	240.00
95	MONARCH MOUNTAIN	1950	280.00	280.00
95	REFUGE	1950	100.00	100.00

YR	NAME	LIMIT	ISSUE	TREND
95	SILENT LANDING	2500	105.00	105.00
96	SACRED SPIRITS	1950	250.00	250.00

JAN HAGARA COLLECTABLES

J. HAGARA

YR	NAME	LIMIT	ISSUE	TREND
95	DANA	7500	60.00	60.00
95	JENNIFER & BASKET	7500	73.00	72.50
95	TAMMY	7500	60.00	60.00

J. HAGARA — COUNTRY MUSIC GREATS

YR	NAME	LIMIT	ISSUE	TREND
*				
98	BUCK OWENS 5"	5000	39.00	39.00
98	BUCK OWENS 8"	10000	59.00	59.00
98	EDDY ARNOLD	5000	39.00	39.00
98	EDDY ARNOLD 8 "	10000	59.00	59.00
98	MARTY ROBBINS	5000	39.00	39.00
98	MARTY ROBBINS 8"	10000	59.00	59.00
98	PATSY CLINE 8"	10000	59.00	59.00
98	PORTER WAGONER	10000	59.00	59.00
98	TAMMY WYNETTE 5"	5000	39.00	39.00
98	TAMMY WYNETTE 8"	10000	59.00	59.00

J. HAGARA — GEORGETOWN

YR	NAME	LIMIT	ISSUE	TREND
98	ENYA & RYAN	3600	65.00	65.00
98	JUDIANNA	3600	55.00	55.00
98	LITTLE MEGAN	3600	69.00	69.00

J. HAGARA — MAKE BELIEVE

YR	NAME	LIMIT	ISSUE	TREND
98	BRIANNA ROSE	3000	45.00	45.00
98	BUTCHIE & OREO	3000	45.00	45.00
98	EMILY	3000	49.00	49.00
98	JASMINE	3000	49.00	49.00
98	JIMMY CHUCK	3000	49.00	49.00
98	KAYLA	3000	49.00	49.00
98	MARY LOU	3000	49.00	49.00
98	PEPPERMINT & CARMEL	3000	49.00	49.00

J. HAGARA — MINIATURES

YR	NAME	LIMIT	ISSUE	TREND
89	HEATHER	RT	18.00	18.00
89	MANDY	RT	18.00	25.00
89	RACHAEL	RT	18.00	18.00
89	TIPPI	RT	18.00	18.00

J. HAGARA — SHELFSITTER

YR	NAME	LIMIT	ISSUE	TREND
95	ADRIANNE	7500	47.00	47.00
95	MATTHEW HAS TURNED THE PAGE	7500	39.00	39.00
96	LITTLE SHARICE & ROCKER	7500	72.00	71.50

J. HAGARA — SIGNATURE

YR	NAME	LIMIT	ISSUE	TREND
85	ALICE AND ANDREA	RT	75.00	250.00
85	BECKY	RT	55.00	375.00
85	JESSICA	RT	55.00	100.00
85	MEMORIES	RT	75.00	250.00
85	STORYTIME	RT	135.00	300.00
85	THERESA	RT	55.00	260.00
87	NIKKI & SANTA	RT	135.00	260.00

J. HAGARA — VICTORIAN CHILDREN

YR	NAME	LIMIT	ISSUE	TREND
*	JAN AT AGE FOUR	*	*	75.00
*	MISSY	*	*	50.00
83	ANNE	RT	25.00	90.00
83	JENNY	RT	25.00	175.00
83	JODY	RT	25.00	60.00
83	LISA	RT	25.00	60.00
83	LYDIA	RT	25.00	100.00
83	VICTORIA	RT	25.00	65.00
84	AMANDA	RT	30.00	100.00
84	BRIAN	RT	30.00	40.00
84	CAROL	RT	30.00	200.00
84	CRISTINA	RT	30.00	75.00
85	ANGIE	RT	30.00	125.00
85	BRIAN & CINNAMON BEAR	RT	30.00	200.00
85	DAPHNE & UNICORN	RT	45.00	85.00
85	STACY	RT	30.00	125.00
85	STEPHEN	RT	30.00	125.00
86	ASHLEY	RT	25.00	60.00
86	CHRIS	RT	30.00	100.00
86	DAISIES FROM JIMMY	RT	45.00	125.00
86	LARRY	RT	30.00	75.00
86	MEG	RT	30.00	75.00
86	MELANIE	RT	30.00	100.00

JAN'S ORIGINALS

J. BENSON — GEORGIA SERIES

YR	NAME	LIMIT	ISSUE	TREND
92	BARNSLEY GARDENS RUINS	200	48.00	60.00
92	CARTERSVILLE DEPOT	200	48.00	48.00
92	FOX THEATRE	200	48.00	55.00
92	GEORGIA TECH	200	52.00	60.00
92	O'HARA HOMEPLACE	RT	50.00	200.00
92	UNIVERSITY OF GEORGIA	200	48.00	60.00
92	VARSITY, THE	200	50.00	50.00
93	4-WAY LUNCH	200	46.00	46.00
93	ROSELAWN	200	52.00	52.00

YR	NAME	LIMIT	ISSUE	TREND
94	1902 STOCK EXCHANGE	200	48.00	48.00
94	ADAIRSVILLE DEPOT	200	48.00	48.00
94	FIRST COCA COLA BOTTLING	200	48.00	48.00
94	GEORGIA STATE CAPITOL	200	76.00	76.00
94	GRAND THEATRE	200	46.00	46.00
94	LOEW'S GRAND THEATRE	200	52.00	52.00
94	WHITE COLUMNS WSB-TV	200	52.00	52.00

J. BENSON — **SIGNATURE SERIES**

YR	NAME	LIMIT	ISSUE	TREND
90	OLD DALLAS HIGH SCHOOL	200	48.00	48.00
90	PAULDING COURTHOUSE	200	52.00	52.00
91	LOST MOUNTAIN STORE	200	48.00	65.00
92	BIG CHICKEN	200	46.00	46.00
92	CLOCK TOWER	200	46.00	55.00
92	FIRST PRESBYTERIAN CHURCH, ST. MARY'S	200	48.00	60.00
92	OLD ST. MARY'S METHODIST CHURCH	200	48.00	60.00
92	ORANGE HALL	500	46.00	55.00
92	RIVERVIEW HOTEL	500	50.00	60.00
92	SHRIMP BOAT	200	48.00	63.00
92	TROLLEY, THE	200	46.00	55.00
92	WATERWHEEL OF BERRY COLLEGE	200	46.00	55.00
93	COBB CTY. YOUTH MUSEUM	200	48.00	48.00
93	FIRST BAPTIST CHURCH ST. MARY'S, GA.	200	48.00	48.00
93	MILLER'S DOCK	200	50.00	50.00
93	OLD COBB COUNTY COURTHOUSE	200	50.00	50.00
93	SPENCER HOUSE INN	500	48.00	48.00
94	BLUE GOOSE	500	48.00	48.00
94	CAMDEN CTY. HIGH SCHOOL	200	52.00	52.00
94	EPISCOPAL CHURCH OF THE ASCENIOUS	200	48.00	48.00
94	FIRST BAPTIST CHURCH-CARTERSVILLE	200	50.00	50.00
94	FIRST PRESBYTERIAN CHURCH-CARTERSVILLE	200	50.00	50.00
94	FLOYD CTY. COURTHOUSE	200	50.00	50.00
94	GOODBREAD HOUSE	200	48.00	48.00
94	JACKSON HOUSE, THE	200	52.00	52.00
94	MARIETTA DEPOT	200	50.00	50.00
94	PAVILION, THE	200	48.00	48.00
94	SAM JONES MEMORIAL METHODIST	200	50.00	50.00
94	YOUNG BROTHERS PHARMACY	200	48.00	48.00
95	GREYFIELD PLANTATION	1000	52.00	52.00
95	OLD CAMDEN CTY. COURTHOUSE	500	52.00	52.00
95	SKYLINE OF ATLANTA, GA. 1996	200	54.00	54.00

JEFFREY SCOTT CO.

M. GORETTI — **THE BIRD SANCTUARY**

YR	NAME	LIMIT	ISSUE	TREND
93	HERITAGE EAGLE	5000	50.00	60.00
94	HARMONY IN THE WILD	2500	65.00	75.00

JOHN HINE STUDIOS LTD.

* — **BUGABOOS**

YR	NAME	LIMIT	ISSUE	TREND
89	ARNOLD	CL	45.00	45.00
89	BERYL	CL	45.00	45.00
89	EDNA	CL	45.00	45.00
89	ENID	CL	45.00	45.00
89	GERALD	CL	45.00	45.00
89	LIZZIE	CL	45.00	45.00
89	OSCAR	CL	45.00	45.00
89	WESLEY	CL	45.00	45.00
89	WILBUR	CL	45.00	45.00

D. WINTER — **DAVID WINTER SCENES**

YR	NAME	LIMIT	ISSUE	TREND
92	AT ROSE COTTAGE/VIGNETTE	5000	39.00	39.00
92	AT THE BAKEHOUSE/VIGNETTE	5000	35.00	35.00
92	AT THE BOTHY/VIGNETTE BASE	5000	39.00	39.00
92	DAUGHTER	5000	30.00	30.00
92	FARM HAND AND SPADE	5000	40.00	40.00
92	FARMER AND PLOUGH	5000	60.00	60.00
92	FARMER'S WIFE	5000	45.00	45.00
92	FATHER	5000	45.00	45.00
92	GIRL SELLING EGGS	5000	30.00	30.00
92	GOOSE GIRL	5000	45.00	45.00
92	HOT CROSS BUN SELLER	5000	60.00	60.00
92	LADY CUSTOMER	5000	45.00	45.00
92	MOTHER	5000	50.00	50.00
92	SMALL BOY & DOG	5000	45.00	45.00
92	SON	5000	30.00	30.00
92	WOMAN AT PUMP	5000	45.00	45.00
93	BOB CRATCHIT & TINY TIM	5000	50.00	50.00
93	CHRISTMAS SNOW/VIGNETTE	5000	50.00	50.00
93	EBENEZER SCROOGE	5000	45.00	45.00
93	FRED	5000	35.00	35.00
93	MISS BELLE	5000	35.00	35.00
93	MRS. FEZZIWIG	5000	35.00	35.00
93	TOM THE STREET SHOVELER	5000	60.00	60.00
95	WINTERVILLE DIORAMA	RT	80.00	113.00

J. KING — **FATHER CHRISTMAS**

YR	NAME	LIMIT	ISSUE	TREND
88	FALLING	OP	70.00	70.00

YR NAME	LIMIT	ISSUE	TREND
88 FEET	OP	70.00	70.00
88 STANDING	OP	70.00	70.00
S. KUCK			**HEART STRINGS**
92 DAY DREAMING	15000	93.00	93.00
92 HUSH, IT'S SLEEPYTIME	15000	98.00	98.00
92 TAKING TEA	15000	93.00	93.00
92 WATCH ME WALTZ	15000	98.00	98.00

JUNE MCKENNA COLLECTIBLES INC.

YR NAME	LIMIT	ISSUE	TREND
J. MCKENNA			**12" LIMITED EDITION**
95 PEACEFUL JOURNEY	4000	250.00	250.00
96 MAGIC OF CHRISTMAS	4000	250.00	250.00
J. MCKENNA			**3-D BLACK FOLK ART**
96 ALL I WANT FOR CHRISTMAS	YR	70.00	70.00
96 I'VE GOT THE TREE	YR	70.00	70.00
96 JASMINE	YR	70.00	70.00
96 JEREMIAH	YR	70.00	70.00
96 SPLISH SPLASH	YR	70.00	70.00
96 UNCLE TOM'S CHRISTMAS	YR	160.00	160.00
J. MCKENNA			**3-D FIGURINES**
96 BRIDE & GROOM	YR	70.00	70.00
96 HELPFUL FRIENDS	YR	90.00	90.00
96 MR. SANTA W/ RAG DOLL	YR	70.00	70.00
96 MRS. SANTA W/ RAG DOLL	YR	70.00	70.00
96 SET OF THREE TREES	YR	60.00	60.00
97 A GIFT FOR CLARA	*	70.00	70.00
97 SNOWMAN AND ANGEL	*	70.00	70.00
98 BEARLY CHRISTMAS	TL	90.00	90.00
98 DRESSED FOR THE OCCASION	TL	80.00	80.00
98 YULETIDE CHRISTMAS	TL	80.00	80.00
J. MCKENNA			**6" CHRISTMAS FIGURINE**
95 FINISHING TOUCH	YR	70.00	70.00
95 JOEY'S CHRISTMAS	YR	70.00	70.00
J. MCKENNA			**7" LIMITED EDITION**
95 CHRISTMAS LULLABY/RED	RT	120.00	120.00
96 CHRISTMAS LULLABY/BLUE	7500	120.00	120.00
96 POLAR BEAR EXPRESS	2500	120.00	120.00
J. MCKENNA			**AMISH FLATBACK**
96 AMISH BROTHER	YR	30.00	30.00
96 AMISH FATHER	YR	30.00	30.00
96 AMISH GRANDPA	YR	32.00	32.00
96 AMISH MOTHER	YR	30.00	30.00
96 AMISH SISTER	YR	30.00	30.00
96 SUNDAY OUTING	YR	50.00	50.00
J. MCKENNA			**ANNIVERSARY SERIES**
97 APRIL EASTER	YR	30.00	30.00
97 AUGUST BEACH	YR	30.00	30.00
97 DECEMBER CHRISTMAS	YR	30.00	30.00
97 FEBRUARY VALENTINES DAY	YR	30.00	30.00
97 JANUARY PARTY	YR	30.00	30.00
97 JULY HAPPY FOURTH	YR	30.00	30.00
97 JUNE GRADUATION	YR	30.00	30.00
97 MARCH ST. PATRICKS DAY	YR	30.00	30.00
97 MAY FLOWERS	YR	30.00	30.00
97 NOVEMBER THANKSGIVING	YR	30.00	30.00
97 OCTOBER HALLOWEN	YR	30.00	30.00
97 SEPTEMBER BACK TO SCHOOL	YR	30.00	30.00
J. MCKENNA			**BLACK FOLK ART**
83 BLACK BOY WITH WATERMELON	CL	12.00	40.00
83 BLACK GIRL WITH WATERMELON	CL	12.00	40.00
84 BLACK MAN WITH PIG	CL	13.00	40.00
84 BLACK WOMAN WITH BROOM	CL	13.00	40.00
85 KIDS IN A TUB 3D	CL	30.00	60.00
85 KISSING COUSINS-SILL SITTER	CL	36.00	60.00
85 WATERMELON PATCH KIDS	CL	24.00	63.00
86 BLACK BUTLER	CL	13.00	40.00
87 AUNT BERTHA 3D	CL	36.00	72.00
87 LIL' WILLIE 3D	CL	36.00	72.00
87 SWEET PRISSY 3D	CL	36.00	72.00
87 UNCLE JACOB 3D	CL	36.00	72.00
88 NETTY	CL	16.00	50.00
88 RENTY	CL	16.00	40.00
89 DELIA	CL	16.00	40.00
89 JAKE	CL	16.00	40.00
90 TASHA	CL	17.00	40.00
90 TYREE	CL	17.00	40.00
J. MCKENNA			**CAROLERS**
85 BOY CAROLER	CL	36.00	75.00
85 GIRL CAROLER	CL	36.00	75.00
85 MAN CAROLER	CL	36.00	75.00
85 WOMAN CAROLER	CL	36.00	75.00
J. MCKENNA			**FLATBACK FIGURINES**
95 SANTA CAROLING	YR	60.00	60.00
95 TRAVEL PLANS	YR	70.00	70.00

YR	NAME	LIMIT	ISSUE	TREND
96	GREETINGS/DOORWAY	YR	50.00	50.00
96	SANTA/TREE TOPPER	YR	70.00	70.00
97	CHILDREN CAROLERS	*	70.00	70.00
97	CHRISTMAS WINDOW	*	70.00	70.00
97	MAN & WOMAN CAROLERS	*	70.00	70.00
J. MCKENNA				**ICICLE**
96	SANTA W/PIPE	YR	17.00	17.00
J. MCKENNA				**INTERNATIONAL**
97	SAMICHLAUS	YR	100.00	100.00
98	AUSTRALIAN SANTA	YR	110.00	110.00
J. MCKENNA			**JUNE MCKENNA FIGURINES**	
84	TREE TROPPER	CL	70.00	225.00
85	SOLDIER	CL	40.00	175.00
86	LITTLE ST. NICK	CL	50.00	100.00
86	MALE ANGEL	CL	44.00	1450.00
87	PATRIOTIC SANTA	CL	50.00	125.00
88	MRS. SANTA	CL	50.00	125.00
92	TAKING A BREAK	RT	60.00	70.00
93	A GOOD NIGHT'S SLEEP	RT	70.00	70.00
93	ANGEL NAME PLAQUE	OP	70.00	70.00
93	BAKING COOKIES	RT	450.00	450.00
93	BELLS OF CHRISTMAS	RT	40.00	40.00
93	CHILDREN ICE SKATERS	OP	70.00	70.00
93	CHRISTMAS CHEER	RT	120.00	120.00
93	CHRISTMAS EVE	4 YR	35.00	35.00
93	MR. SNOWMAN	OP	40.00	40.00
93	NATIVITY COW	OP	30.00	30.00
93	NATIVITY DONKEY	OP	30.00	30.00
93	NATIVITY RAM WITH EWE	OP	30.00	30.00
93	PATRIOT, THE	4000	250.00	250.00
93	SANTA AND FRIENDS	OP	70.00	70.00
93	SANTA NAME PLAQUE	RT	70.00	70.00
93	SANTA'S LOVE	RT	40.00	40.00
93	SNOW FAMILY, THE	OP	40.00	40.00
93	TOMORROW'S CHRISTMAS	RT	250.00	250.00
94	ALL ABOARD NORTH POLE EXPRESS	*	500.00	500.00
94	BRINGING HOME CHRISTMAS	4 YR	35.00	35.00
94	CHILDREN CAROLERS	OP	90.00	90.00
94	CONDUCTOR	OP	70.00	70.00
94	DECORATING FOR CHRISTMAS	OP	70.00	70.00
94	MRS. CLAUS, DANCING	7500	120.00	120.00
94	NOT ONCE BUT TWICE	10000	40.00	40.00
94	POSTMARKED NORTH POLE	10000	40.00	40.00
94	SANTA'S ONE MAN BAND	7500	120.00	120.00
94	SAY CHEESE, PLEASE	OP	250.00	250.00
94	SNOWMAN AND CHILD	OP	70.00	70.00
94	ST. NICHOLAS	4000	250.00	250.00
94	STAR OF BETHLEHEM	OP	40.00	40.00
94	WELCOME TO THE WORLD	RT	400.00	400.00
98	CHRISTMAS TOYS	2500	130.00	130.00
98	LENDING A HAND	OP	280.00	280.00
98	MEMORIES OF CHRISTMAS	4000	270.00	270.00
J. MCKENNA			**LIMITED EDITION**	
83	FATHER CHRISTMAS	RT	90.00	3500.00
84	OLD SAINT NICK	CL	100.00	1500.00
85	WOODLAND	CL	140.00	1900.00
86	VICTORIAN	CL	150.00	600.00
87	CHRISTMAS EVE	CL	170.00	575.00
87	KRIS KRINGLE	CL	350.00	500.00
88	BRINGING HOME CHRISTMAS	CL	170.00	325.00
88	REMEMBRANCE OF CHRISTMAS PAST	4000	400.00	550.00
89	SANTA'S WARDROBE	1500	750.00	750.00
89	SEASONS GREETINGS	CL	200.00	325.00
90	NIGHT BEFORE CHRISTMAS	1000	750.00	750.00
90	WILDERNESS	4000	200.00	200.00
91	COMING TO TOWN	RT	220.00	310.00
92	BEDTIME STORIES	2000	500.00	500.00
92	CHRISTMAS GATHERING	4000	220.00	220.00
92	HOT AIR BALLOON	1500	800.00	800.00
97	ALL I WANT FOR CHRISTMAS	2500	120.00	120.00
97	CHRISTMAS JOY	3000	40.00	40.00
97	LIGHTING THE WAY	4000	260.00	260.00
97	MERRY CHRISTMAS	3000	40.00	40.00
J. MCKENNA			**LIMITED FLATBACK**	
95	CHRISTMAS DELIVERY	10000	40.00	40.00
95	LIGHT OF CHRISTMAS	10000	40.00	40.00
96	HAPPY HOLIDAYS	3000	40.00	40.00
96	YULETIDE JOY	3000	40.00	40.00
J. MCKENNA			**NATIVITY SET**	
96	NATIVITY SET	OP	150.00	150.00
J. MCKENNA			**REGISTERED EDITION**	
86	COLONIAL	CL	150.00	425.00
87	WHITE CHRISTMAS	CL	170.00	1500.00
88	JOLLY OLE ST. NICK	CL	170.00	250.00
89	TRADITIONAL	OP	180.00	180.00

YR	NAME	LIMIT	ISSUE	TREND
90	TOY MAKER	OP	200.00	200.00
91	CHECKING HIS LIST	OP	230.00	230.00
92	FORTY WINKS	OP	250.00	250.00
95	A CHRISTMAS TREAT FOR ALL	YR	260.00	260.00
95	CHRISTMAS DOWN ON THE FARM	YR	260.00	260.00
96	CHRISTMAS OVER LOAD	YR	260.00	260.00
97	FOREST FRIENDS	*	260.00	260.00

J. MCKENNA — SPECIAL LIMITED EDITION

YR	NAME	LIMIT	ISSUE	TREND
89	LAST GENTLE NUDGE	RT	280.00	280.00
89	SANTA & HIS MAGIC SLEIGH	RT	280.00	280.00
90	CHRISTMAS DREAMS	4000	280.00	280.00
90	SANTA'S REINDEER	1500	400.00	400.00
90	UP ON THE ROOFTOP	RT	280.00	280.00
95	ALL ABOARD - TOY CAR	RT	250.00	250.00
96	INTERNATIONAL SANTA	YR	160.00	160.00
96	LOGGING CAR	YR	250.00	250.00
96	SHOW ME THE WAY	YR	500.00	500.00

J. MCKENNA — TRAIN SERIES

YR	NAME	LIMIT	ISSUE	TREND
97	NPE REINDEER CAR	YR	300.00	300.00
98	NORTH POLE EXPRESS CABOOSE	YR	310.00	310.00

J. MCKENNA — VICTORIAN LIMITED EDITION

YR	NAME	LIMIT	ISSUE	TREND
90	EDWARD 3D	CL	180.00	450.00
90	ELIZABETH 3D	CL	180.00	450.00

KAISER

W. GAWANTKA — ANIMALS

YR	NAME	LIMIT	ISSUE	TREND
69	PORPOISE GROUP (3), WHITE BISQUE	CL	85.00	400.00
75	DOLPHIN GROUP (5), 520/5, WHITE BISQUE	800	850.00	3000.00
75	GERMAN SHEPHERD 528, COLOR BISQUE	CL	250.00	675.00
75	GERMAN SHEPHERD 528, WHITE BISQUE	CL	185.00	450.00
76	IRISH SETTER 535, COLOR BISQUE	1000	290.00	675.00
76	IRISH SETTER 535, WHITE/BASE	1500	*	450.00
78	DOLPHIN GROUP (4), 596/4, WHITE BISQUE	4500	75.00	1000.00
78	KILLER WHALE 579, COLOR/BISQUE	2000	420.00	800.00
78	KILLER WHALE 579, WHITE/BISQUE	2000	85.00	425.00
78	KILLER WHALES (2), 594, COLOR	2000	925.00	2025.00
78	KILLER WHALES (2), 594, WHITE	2000	425.00	1050.00
79	BEAR & CUB 521, COLOR BISQUE	900	400.00	1100.00
79	BEAR & CUB 521, WHITE BISQUE	CL	125.00	400.00
85	BROOK TROUT 739, COLOR BISQUE	OP	250.00	500.00
85	PIKE 737, COLOR BISQUE	OP	350.00	700.00
85	RAINBOW TROUT 739, COLOR BISQUE	OP	250.00	500.00
85	TROUT 739, COLOR BISQUE	OP	95.00	500.00
91	LION 701201, WHITE BISQUE	1500	650.00	650.00
91	LION 701203, COLOR BISQUE	1500	1,300.00	1300.00

H. LIEDERLY — ANIMALS

YR	NAME	LIMIT	ISSUE	TREND
82	TWO WILD BOARS 664, COLOR BISQUE	1000	650.00	890.00

G. TAGLIARIOL — ANIMALS

YR	NAME	LIMIT	ISSUE	TREND
80	BISON 630, COLOR BISQUE	2000	620.00	1100.00
80	BISON 690, WHITE BISQUE	2000	350.00	500.00

* — BIRDS OF AMERICA COLLECTION

YR	NAME	LIMIT	ISSUE	TREND
*	BALD EAGLE II 497, COLORED	CL	*	1300.00
*	ROADRUNNER 492, COLOR/BASE	CL	350.00	900.00
*	ROBIN & WORM, COLOR/BASE	CL	60.00	90.00
*	ROBIN II 537, COLOR/BASE	1000	260.00	900.00
*	SCREECH OWL 532, WHITE/BASE	CL	175.00	200.00
*	SNOWY OWL 776, COLOR/BASE	1500	*	1200.00
*	SNOWY OWL 776, WHITE/BASE	1500	*	700.00
*	SPARROW HAWK 749, COLOR/BASE	3000	575.00	950.00
70	SCARLET TANAGER, COLOR/BASE	CL	60.00	90.00
85	PINTAILS 747, COLOR/BASE	1500	*	850.00
85	PINTAILS 747, WHITE/BASE	1500	*	375.00

W. GAWANTKA — BIRDS OF AMERICA COLLECTION

YR	NAME	LIMIT	ISSUE	TREND
*	BABY TITMICE 501, COLOR/BASE	CL	400.00	525.00
*	BABY TITMICE 501, WHITE/BASE	1200	200.00	800.00
72	BLUE BIRD 496, COLOR, BASE	2500	120.00	500.00
72	GOSHAWK 491, COLOR/BASE	1500	2,400.00	4400.00
72	GOSHAWK 491, WHITE/BASE	1500	850.00	2000.00
72	SEAGULL 498, COLOR/BASE	CL	850.00	1150.00
72	SEAGULL 498, WHITE/BASE	700	550.00	1600.00
73	BLUEJAY 503, COLOR/BASE	1500	475.00	1200.00
73	CARDINAL 504, COLOR/BASE	1500	60.00	600.00
73	ROBIN 502, COLOR/BASE	1500	340.00	725.00
74	FALCON 507, COLOR/BASE	1500	820.00	2000.00
76	BALD EAGLE IV 552, COLOR/BASE	1500	450.00	1000.00
76	BALD EAGLE IV 552, WHITE/BASE	1500	210.00	575.00
80	BALD EAGLE VI 634, WHITE/BASE	3000	*	700.00
84	BALD EAGLE IX 714, COLOR/BASE	3500	500.00	850.00
84	BALD EAGLE IX 714, WHITE/BASE	4000	190.00	400.00
85	BALD EAGLE X 746, COLOR/BASE	1500	*	1200.00
85	BALD EAGLE X 746, WHITE/BASE	1500	375.00	700.00
85	BALD EAGLE XI 751, COLOR/BASE	1000	880.00	1500.00
85	BALD EAGLE XI 751, WHITE/BASE	1000	*	925.00

U. NETZSCH — BIRDS OF AMERICA COLLECTION

YR	NAME	LIMIT	ISSUE	TREND
68	PAIR OF MALLARDS 456, COLOR/BASE	CL	150.00	500.00

YR	NAME	LIMIT	ISSUE	TREND
68	PAIR OF MALLARDS 456, WHITE/BASE	2000	75.00	525.00
68	PIGEON GROUP 475, COLOR/BASE	1500	150.00	825.00
68	PIGEON GROUP 475, WHITE/BASE	2000	60.00	425.00
G. TAGLIARIOL		**BIRDS OF AMERICA COLLECTION**		
*	BALD EAGLE VII 637, COLOR/BASE	200	*	20800.00
*	HORNED OWL II 524, COLOR/BASE	1000	650.00	2200.00
*	HORNED OWL II 524, WHITE/BASE	1000	*	1000.00
75	SPARROW 516, COLOR/BASE	1500	300.00	600.00
75	WOOD DUCKS 514, COLOR/BASE	800	*	2850.00
75	WOODPECKERS 515, COLOR/BASE	800	900.00	1800.00
76	BALTIMORE ORIOLE 536, COLOR/BASE	1000	280.00	750.00
76	CANADIAN GEESE 550, WHITE/BASE	1500	1,500.00	3500.00
76	PELICAN 534, COLOR/BASE	1200	925.00	1800.00
76	PELICAN 534, WHITE/BASE	CL	*	625.00
76	PHEASANT 556, COLOR/BASE	1500	3,200.00	6100.00
77	OWL IV 559, COLOR/BASE	1000	*	1300.00
78	BABY TITMICE 601, COLOR/BASE	2000	*	1000.00
78	BABY TITMICE 601, WHITE/BASE	2000	*	600.00
78	BALD EAGLE V 600, COLOR/BASE	1500	*	3900.00
78	PAIR OF MALLARDS II 572, COLOR/BASE	1500	*	1200.00
78	PAIR OF MALLARDS II 572, WHITE/BASE	1500	*	2400.00
79	SWAN 602, COLOR/BASE	2000	*	1400.00
81	KINGFISHER 639, COLOR/BASE	CL	45.00	60.00
81	QUAILS 640, COLOR/BASE	1500	*	2400.00
81	ROOSTER 642, COLOR/BASE	1500	860.00	1350.00
81	ROOSTER 642, WHITE/BASE	1500	380.00	700.00
82	BALD EAGLE VIII 656, COLOR/BASE	CL	800.00	900.00
82	BALD EAGLE VIII 656, WHITE/BASE	1000	400.00	925.00
82	HUMMINGBIRD GROUP 660, COLOR/BASE	3000	650.00	1300.00
84	PHEASANT 715, COLOR/BASE	1500	1,000.00	2000.00
M. TANDY		**BIRDS OF AMERICA COLLECTION**		
84	PEREGRINE FALCON 723, COLOR/BASE	1500	850.00	5000.00
86	SPARROW HAWK 777, COLORED BISQUE	10000	950.00	1400.00
86	SPARROW HAWK 777, WHITE BISQUE	1000	440.00	725.00
W. GAWANTKA		**HORSE SCULPTURE**		
71	PONY GROUP 488, COLOR/BASE	CL	150.00	350.00
71	PONY GROUP 488, WHITE/BASE	2500	50.00	425.00
74	MARE & FOAL II 510, COLOR/BASE	CL	650.00	800.00
75	LIPIZZANER/MAESTOSO 517, COLOR/BASE	CL	*	1150.00
75	LIPIZZANER/MAESTOSO 517, WHITE/BASE	CL	*	750.00
76	HASSAN/ARABIAN 553, COLOR/BASE	1500	600.00	1250.00
76	HASSAN/ARABIAN 553, WHITE/BASE	CL	250.00	600.00
78	CAPITANO/LIPIZZANER 597, COLOR	1500	625.00	1500.00
78	CAPITANO/LIPIZZANER 597, WHITE	CL	275.00	600.00
80	MARE & FOAL III 636, COLOR/BASE	1500	950.00	1650.00
80	MARE & FOAL III 636, WHITE/BASE	1500	300.00	675.00
80	ORION/ARABIAN 629, COLOR/BASE	2000	600.00	1050.00
80	ORION/ARABIAN 629, WHITE/BASE	2000	250.00	450.00
87	PACER 792, COLOR/BASE	1500	1,217.00	1350.00
87	PACER 792, WHITE/BASE	1500	574.00	675.00
87	TROTTER 780, COLOR/BASE	1500	1,217.00	1350.00
87	TROTTER 780, WHITE/BASE	1500	574.00	675.00
90	ARGOS 633101, WHITE BISQUE/BASE	1000	578.00	700.00
90	ARGOS 633103, LIGHT COLOR/BASE	1000	1,194.00	1400.00
90	ARGOS 633143, COLOR/BASE	1000	1,194.00	1400.00
*				**HUMAN FIGURES**
*	FATHER & DAUGHTER 752, COLOR	2500	390.00	725.00
*	FATHER & DAUGHTER 752, WHITE	2500	175.00	375.00
*	MOTHER & CHILD 757, COLOR	3500	600.00	900.00
*	MOTHER & CHILD 757, WHITE	4000	300.00	425.00
*	MOTHER & CHILD 775, COLOR	3500	600.00	900.00
*	MOTHER & CHILD 775, WHITE	4000	300.00	425.00
G. BOCHMANN				**HUMAN FIGURES**
60	MOTHER & CHILD 398, WHITE BISQUE	OP	*	325.00
W. GAWANTKA				**HUMAN FIGURES**
82	FATHER & SON 659, COLOR/BASE	2500	400.00	725.00
82	FATHER & SON 659, WHITE/BASE	2500	100.00	400.00
82	ICE PRINCESS 667, COLOR	5000	375.00	750.00
82	ICE PRINCESS 667, WHITE	5000	200.00	425.00
82	SWAN LAKE BALLET 641, COLOR	2500	650.00	1300.00
82	SWAN LAKE BALLET 641, WHITE	2500	200.00	1000.00
83	MOTHER & CHILD/BUST 696, COLOR	3500	500.00	1075.00
83	MOTHER & CHILD/BUST 696, WHITE	4000	225.00	450.00

KURT S. ADLER INC.

ANTONOV

97	FOR THE MRS.	OP	42.00	42.00

GIORDANO

97	UP ON THE ROOF	OP	67.00	67.00

KSA DESIGN

97	CHRISTMAS WISH LIST	OP	40.00	40.00
97	FROSTY FRIENDS	OP	40.00	40.00
97	GIFTS A PLENTY	OP	45.00	45.00
97	HOUSE CALLS	OP	40.00	40.00
97	LABOR OF LOVE	OP	45.00	45.00

YR	NAME	LIMIT	ISSUE	TREND
97	MAKING WAVES	OP	55.00	55.00
97	ONE MORE STORY	OP	55.00	55.00
97	PAPERWORK	OP	56.00	56.00
97	PUPPY LOVE	OP	50.00	50.00
97	SANTA ON LINE	OP	50.00	50.00
97	TEST DRIVE	OP	45.00	45.00
97	WHAT A CATCH	OP	45.00	45.00
KSA/STEINBACH				
97	MINI KING ARTHUR	15000	50.00	50.00
97	MINI NOAH	10000	50.00	50.00
97	MINI ST. NICHOLAS	15000	50.00	50.00
M. ROTHENBERG				
97	FAN MAIL	OP	50.00	50.00
97	HOLIDAY ON ICE	OP	135.00	135.00
97	MY HAVE YOU GROWN	OP	75.00	75.00
KSA/STEINBACH		AMERICAN PRESIDENTS STEINBACH NUTCRACKER		
93	BEN FRANKLIN ES922	RT	225.00	225.00
93	TEDDY ROOSEVELT ES644	10000	225.00	225.00
96	THOMAS JEFFERSON ES866	7500	260.00	260.00
C. STEINBACH		AMERICAN PRESIDENTS STEINBACH NUTCRACKER		
92	ABRAHAM LINCOLN ES622	RT	195.00	210.00
92	GEORGE WASHINGTON ES623	12000	195.00	210.00
N. BAILEY		ANGEL DARLINGS		
96	BOTTOMS UP	OP	15.00	15.00
96	BUDDIES H4765/3	OP	15.00	15.00
96	CUDDLES H4765/4	OP	15.00	15.00
96	DREAM BUILDERS H4765/4	OP	15.00	15.00
96	PEEK-A-BOO H4765/2	OP	15.00	15.00
97	FOR YOU	OP	20.00	20.00
97	SECRET, THE	OP	20.00	20.00
97	SHARING	OP	20.00	20.00
KSA/STEINBACH		BIBLICAL		
96	NOAH ES893	1000	260.00	260.00
97	MOSES	10000	250.00	250.00
KSA/STEINBACH		CAMELOT STEINBACH NUTCRACKER		
93	SIR LANCELOT ES638	12000	225.00	225.00
94	SIR GALAHAD ES862	12000	225.00	225.00
94	SIR LANCELOT SMOKER ES833	7500	150.00	150.00
95	QUEEN GUENEVERE ES869	10000	245.00	245.00
C. STEINBACH		CAMELOT STEINBACH NUTCRACKER		
91	MERLIN THE MAGICIAN ES610	RT	185.00	1650.00
92	KING ARTHUR ES621	RT	195.00	285.00
KSA/STEINBACH		CAMELOT STEINBACH SMOKING FIGURINE		
93	KING ARTHUR ES832	7500	175.00	175.00
C. STEINBACH		CAMELOT STEINBACH SMOKING FIGURINE		
92	MERLIN THE MAGICIAN ES830	7500	150.00	150.00
KSA/STEINBACH		CHRISTMAS CAROL		
97	EBENEZER SCROOGE	7500	250.00	250.00
KSA/STEINBACH		CHRISTMAS LEGENDS		
97	GRANDFATHER FROST	7500	250.00	250.00
KSA/STEINBACH		CLUB GIFT		
97	CHIMNEY SWEEP	YR	*	N/A
*		CURRIER & IVES WATERGLOBE COLLECTION		
92	OUR FIRST CHRISTMAS J1037	OP	40.00	40.00
92	WE WISH YOU A MERRY CHRISTMAS J1048	OP	40.00	40.00
K. ADLER		FABRICHE ANGEL SERIES		
92	HEAVENLY MESSENGER W1584	RT	41.00	41.00
K. ADLER		FABRICHE BEAR & FRIENDS		
92	LAUGHING ALL THE WAY J1567	RT	83.00	83.00
92	NOT A CREATURE WAS STIRRING W1534	RT	67.00	67.00
93	TEDDY BEAR PARADE W1601	RT	73.00	73.00
P. MAUK		FABRICHE CAMELOT FIGURE		
93	MERLIN THE MAGICIAN J7966	RT	120.00	120.00
93	YOUNG ARTHUR J7967	RT	120.00	120.00
94	KING ARTHUR J3372	RT	110.00	110.00
*		FABRICHE COLLECTION		
92	JOLLY OLD NICK W1557	OP	56.00	56.00
92	MASTER TOYMAKER W1566	OP	61.00	61.00
92	OLD FATHER FROST W1559	OP	56.00	56.00
92	SPECIAL DELIVERY W1558	OP	56.00	56.00
T. RUBEL		FABRICHE COLLECTION		
92	HE DID IT AGAIN J7944	OP	160.00	160.00
K. ADLER		FABRICHE HOLIDAY FIGURINES		
92	BUNDLES OF JOY W1578	RT	78.00	78.00
92	CHRISTMAS IS IN THE AIR W1590	OP	110.00	110.00
92	HOMEWARD BOUND W1566	OP	61.00	61.00
92	HUGS AND KISSES W1531	RT	67.00	67.00
92	ST. NICHOLAS THE BISHOP W1532	OP	78.00	78.00
93	ALL THAT JAZZ W1620	RT	67.00	67.00
93	BRINGING THE GIFTS W1605	OP	60.00	60.00
93	CHECKING IT TWICE W1604	OP	56.00	56.00
93	FOREVER GREEN W1607	RT	56.00	56.00
93	PAR FOR THE CLAUS W1603	OP	60.00	60.00

YR	NAME	LIMIT	ISSUE	TREND
93	PLAYTIME FOR SANTA W1619	RT	67.00	67.00
93	STOCKING STUFFER W1622	OP	56.00	56.00
93	TOP BRASS W1630	OP	67.00	67.00
93	WITH ALL THE TRIMMINGS W1616	OP	76.00	76.00
94	ALL STAR SANTA W1652	OP	56.00	56.00
94	BASKET OF GOODIES W1650	OP	60.00	60.00
94	CHECKING HIS LIST W1643	OP	60.00	60.00
94	FIREFIGHTING FRIENDS W1654	OP	72.00	72.00
94	FRIENDSHIP W1642	OP	65.00	65.00
94	HO, HO, HO SANTA W1632	OP	56.00	56.00
94	HOLIDAY EXPRESS W1636	OP	100.00	100.00
94	OFFICER CLAUS W1677	OP	56.00	56.00
94	PEACE SANTA W1631	OP	60.00	60.00
94	SANTA'S FISHTALES W1640	OP	60.00	60.00
94	SCHUSSING CLAUS W1651	OP	78.00	78.00
95	ALL ABOARD FOR CHRISTMAS W1679	OP	56.00	56.00
95	ARMCHAIR QUARTERBACK W1693	OP	90.00	90.00
95	CAPTAIN CLAUS W1680	OP	56.00	56.00
95	DIET STARTS TOMORROW W1691	OP	60.00	60.00
95	FATHER CHRISTMAS W1687	OP	56.00	56.00
95	GIFT FROM HEAVEN W1694	OP	60.00	60.00
95	KRIS KINGLE W1685	OP	55.00	55.00
95	MERRY MEMORIES W1735	OP	56.00	56.00
95	PERE NOEL W1686	OP	55.00	55.00
95	STRIKE UP THE BAND W1681	OP	55.00	55.00
95	TEE TIME W1734	OP	60.00	60.00
GIORDANO			**FABRICHE HOLIDAY FIGURINES**	
94	MERRY ST. NICK W1641	OP	100.00	100.00
W. JOYCE			**FABRICHE HOLIDAY FIGURINES**	
94	SANTA CALLS W1678	OP	55.00	55.00
KSA/WRG			**FABRICHE HOLIDAY FIGURINES**	
94	MAIL MUST GO THROUGH W1667	OP	110.00	110.00
M. ROTHENBERG			**FABRICHE HOLIDAY FIGURINES**	
91	SANTA FIDDLER W1549	RT	100.00	100.00
92	AN APRON FULL OF LOVE W1582	OP	75.00	75.00
92	BRINGING IN THE YULE LOG W1589	RT	200.00	200.00
92	MERRY KISSMAS W1548	RT	140.00	140.00
92	SANTA STEALS A KISS & A COOKIE W1581	RT	150.00	150.00
92	SANTA'S CAT NAP W1504	RT	98.00	98.00
92	SANTA'S ICE CAPADES W1588	OP	110.00	110.00
93	HERE KITTY W1616	RT	90.00	90.00
94	STAR GAZING SANTA W1656	OP	120.00	120.00
95	MRS. SANTA CAROLLER W1690	OP	70.00	70.00
95	SANTA CAROLER W1689	OP	70.00	70.00
T. RUBEL			**FABRICHE HOLIDAY FIGURINES**	
92	I'M LATE, I'M LATE J7947	OP	100.00	100.00
92	IT'S TIME TO GO J7943	RT	150.00	150.00
R. VOLPI			**FABRICHE HOLIDAY FIGURINES**	
95	WOODLAND SANTA W1731	RT	67.00	67.00
WD. RIVER GALL.			**FABRICHE HOLIDAY FIGURINES**	
95	NIGHT BEFORE CHRISTMAS W1692	OP	60.00	60.00
M. ROTHENBERG			**FABRICHE SANTA AT HOME**	
93	GRANDPA SANTA'S PIGGYBACK RIDE W1621	7500	84.00	84.00
94	CHRISTMAS WALTZ, THE W1635	RT	135.00	135.00
94	SANTA'S NEW FRIEND W1655	OP	110.00	110.00
95	BABY BURPING SANTA W1732	OP	80.00	80.00
95	FAMILY PORTRAIT W1727	OP	140.00	140.00
95	SANTA'S HORSEY RIDE W1728	OP	80.00	80.00
M. ROTHENBERG			**FABRICHE SANTA'S HELPERS**	
92	A STITCH IN TIME W1591	5000	135.00	135.00
93	LITTLE OLDE CLOCKMAKER W1629	RT	134.00	134.00
KSA/SMITHSONIAN			**FABRICHE SMITHSONIAN MUSEUM**	
91	SANTA ON A BICYCLE W1527	RT	150.00	150.00
92	HOLIDAY DRIVE W1556	OP	156.00	156.00
92	PEACE ON EARTH ANGEL TREETOP W1585	OP	52.00	52.00
92	PEACE ON EARTH FLYING ANGEL W1585	OP	49.00	49.00
93	HOLIDAY FLIGHT W1617	OP	144.00	144.00
95	TOYS FOR GOOD BOYS AND GIRLS W1696	OP	75.00	75.00
K. ADLER			**FABRICHE THOMAS NAST FIGURINES**	
91	HELLO! LITTLE ONE! W1552	12000	90.00	90.00
92	CAUGHT IN THE ACT W1577	RT	133.00	133.00
92	CHRISTMAS SING-A-LONG W1576	12000	110.00	110.00
93	DEAR SANTA W1602	RT	110.00	110.00
K. ADLER			**GALLERY OF ANGELS**	
94	GUARDIAN ANGEL M1099	2000	150.00	150.00
94	UNSPOKEN WORD M1100	2000	150.00	150.00
P.F. BOLINGER			**HALLOWEEN**	
96	DR PUMPKIN HW535	OP	50.00	50.00
96	EAT AT DRAC'S HW493	OP	22.00	22.00
96	PUMPKIN GRUMPKIN HW494	OP	18.00	18.00
96	PUMPKIN PLUMPKIN HW494	OP	18.00	18.00
96	PUMPKINS ARE US HW534	OP	17.00	17.00
P.F. BOLINGER			**HELPING HAND SANTAS**	
94	ALDWYN OF THE GREENWOOD J8196	OP	145.00	145.00

YR	NAME	LIMIT	ISSUE	TREND
94	BERWYN THE GRAND J8198	OP	175.00	190.00
94	CARADOC THE KIND J8199	OP	70.00	80.00
94	FLORIAN OF THE BERRY BUSH J8199	OP	70.00	80.00
94	GUSTAVE THE GUTSY J8199	OP	70.00	80.00
94	SILVANUS THE CHEERFUL J8197	OP	165.00	165.00
95	BOUNTIFUL J8234	OP	164.00	164.00
95	LUMINATUS J8241	OP	136.00	136.00
96	HARMONIOUS 56509	OP	115.00	115.00
96	NOAH J6487	OP	56.00	56.00
96	UNCLE SAM J6488	OP	56.00	56.00

P.F. BOLINGER — HO HO HO GANG

YR	NAME	LIMIT	ISSUE	TREND
94	CHRISTMAS GOOSE J8201	OP	25.00	25.00
94	HOLY MACKEREL J8202	OP	25.00	25.00
94	SANTA COB J8203	RT	28.00	28.00
94	SURPRISE J8201	OP	25.00	25.00
94	WILL HE MAKE IT? J8203	RT	28.00	28.00
95	COOKIE CLAUS J8286	OP	40.00	40.00
95	DO NOT DISTURB J8233	OP	56.00	56.00
95	LARGE NORTH POLE J8237	OP	56.00	56.00
95	NO HAIR DAY J8287	OP	50.00	50.00
95	SMALL NORTH POLE J8238	OP	45.00	45.00
95	WILL WORK FOR COOKIES J8235	OP	40.00	40.00
95	WISHFUL THINKING J8239	OP	39.00	39.00
96	BOX OF CHOCOLATE J6510	OP	33.00	33.00
96	CHRISTMAS SHOPPING SANTA J6497	OP	22.00	22.00
96	CLAUS A LOUNGER J6478	OP	33.00	33.00
96	FIRE DEPARTMENT NORTH POLE J6508	OP	50.00	50.00
96	FIREMAN SANTA J6476	OP	28.00	28.00
96	JOY OF COOKING J6496	OP	28.00	28.00
96	LOVE SANTA J6493	OP	18.00	18.00
96	NOAH	OP	56.00	56.00
96	NOEL ROLY POLY J6489	OP	20.00	20.00
96	NORTH POLE PRO-AM J6479	OP	28.00	28.00
96	ON STRIKE FOR MORE COOKIES J6506	OP	33.00	33.00
96	POLICE DEPARTMENT NORTH POLE J6507	OP	50.00	50.00
96	POLICEMAN SANTA J6475	OP	28.00	28.00
96	SAVE THE REINDEER J6498	OP	28.00	28.00
96	SOME ASSEMBLY REQUIRED J6477	OP	53.00	53.00
97	ANGEL WITH HEART	OP	20.00	20.00
97	BEHAVOMETER	OP	25.00	25.00
97	BOXERS OR BRIEFS	OP	25.00	25.00
97	CAPTAIN NOAH	OP	18.00	18.00
97	GOLF HEAVEN	OP	25.00	25.00
97	JAVA JUMPSTART	OP	15.00	15.00
97	NEVER SAY DIET	OP	15.00	15.00
97	NORTH POLE COUNTRY CLUB	OP	45.00	45.00
97	PEACE SANTA	2500	80.00	80.00
97	SAINT FRANCIS	OP	56.00	56.00
97	SANTA WITH BEAR	OP	8.00	8.00
97	SANTA'S DAY OFF	OP	25.00	25.00
97	SNOWMEN ARE COOL	OP	20.00	20.00
97	SPRING SALE SNOWMAN	OP	20.00	20.00
97	WINTER FUN	OP	25.00	25.00

H. ADLER — HOLLY BEARIES

YR	NAME	LIMIT	ISSUE	TREND
96	ANGEL BEAR J7342	OP	14.00	14.00
96	TEDDY TOWER J7221	OP	23.00	23.00
97	ANGEL STARCATCHER II	YR	20.00	20.00
97	BEARIES MAILING PACKAGES	OP	28.00	28.00
97	CHARLIE THE FISHERMAN	YR	34.00	34.00
97	SLEDDING BEARIES	OP	25.00	25.00

H. ADLER — HOLLY BEARIES CALENDAR BEARS

YR	NAME	LIMIT	ISSUE	TREND
96	CLAIRMONT, DEMPSEY & PETE J7215/JUL	OP	16.00	16.00
96	CLARA & CARNATION THE KITTY J7215/OCT	OP	16.00	16.00
96	FERGUS & FRITZI'S FROSTY FROLIC J7215/JAN	OP	16.00	16.00
96	GRANDMA GLADYS J7215/DEC	OP	16.00	16.00
96	MOTHERS DAY DEAR J7318	OP	15.00	15.00
96	NICOLE & NICOLAS SUN BATHING J7215/AUG	OP	16.00	16.00
96	PETUNIA & NATHAN PLANT ROSES J7215/MAY	OP	16.00	16.00
96	PHILO'S POT OF GOLD J7215/MAR	OP	16.00	16.00
96	PINKY & VICTORIA ARE SWEETIES J7215/FEB	OP	16.00	16.00
96	SKEETER & SIGOURNEY START SCHOOL J7215/SEP	OP	16.00	16.00
96	SUNSHINE CATCHING RAINDROPS J7215/APR	OP	16.00	16.00
96	THORNDIKE & FILBERT CATCH FISH J7215/JUN	OP	16.00	16.00
96	THORNDIKE ALL DRESSED UP J7215/NOV	OP	16.00	16.00

KSA/JHP — JIM HENSON'S MUPPET NUTCRACKERS

YR	NAME	LIMIT	ISSUE	TREND
93	KERMIT THE FROG H1223	RT	90.00	90.00

KSA/STEINBACH — MEMBERS ONLY

YR	NAME	LIMIT	ISSUE	TREND
97	MAREK, THE ROYAL GUARDSMAN	YR	225.00	225.00

KSA/DISNEY — MICKEY UNLIMITED

YR	NAME	LIMIT	ISSUE	TREND
92	GOOFY H1216	OP	78.00	78.00
92	MICKEY MOUSE SOLDIER H1194	OP	72.00	72.00
92	MICKEY MOUSE SORCERER H1221	OP	100.00	100.00
93	DONALD DUCK H1235	OP	90.00	90.00
93	MICKEY MOUSE W/GIFT BOXES W1608	RT	78.00	78.00
93	PINOCCHIO H1222	OP	110.00	110.00

YR	NAME	LIMIT	ISSUE	TREND
94	DONALD DUCK DRUMMER W1681	RT	45.00	45.00
94	MICKEY BANDLEADER W1669	RT	45.00	45.00
94	MICKEY SANTA NUTCRACKER H1237	OP	90.00	90.00
94	MINNIE MOUSE SOLDIER NUTCRACKER H1236	OP	90.00	90.00
94	MINNIE W/CYMBALS W1670	RT	45.00	45.00
	KSA/STEINBACH			**MINI SERIES**
96	MERLIN MINI NUTCRACKER ES335	15000	50.00	50.00
96	ROBIN HOOD MINI NUTCRACKER ES338	10000	50.00	50.00
	J. MOSTROM		**OLD WORLD SANTA SERIES**	
92	CHELSEA GARDEN SANTA W2721	RT	34.00	34.00
92	LARGE BLACK FOREST SANTA W2717	3000	110.00	110.00
92	LARGE FATHER CHRISTMAS W2719	3000	106.00	106.00
92	MRS. CLAUS W2714	5000	37.00	37.00
92	PATRIOTIC SANTA W2720	3000	128.00	128.00
92	PERE NOEL W2723	5000	34.00	34.00
92	SMALL BLACK FOREST SANTA W2712	5000	40.00	40.00
92	SMALL FATHER CHRISTMAS W2712	5000	34.00	34.00
92	SMALL FATHER FROST W2716	RT	43.00	43.00
92	SMALL GRANDFATHER FROST W2716	RT	106.00	106.00
92	ST. NICHOLAS W2713	5000	30.00	30.00
92	WORKSHOP SANTA W2715	5000	43.00	43.00
93	GOOD KING WENCESLAS W2928	3000	134.00	134.00
93	MEDIEVAL KING OF CHRISTMAS W2881	3000	390.00	390.00
	*		**OSCAR & BERTIE WATERGLOBE COLLECTION**	
92	BEARS ON ROCKING HORSE J1034	OP	56.00	56.00
92	SANTA BEAR WITH PACKAGES J1033	OP	41.00	41.00
	*	**SATURDAY EVENING POST WATERGLOBE COLLECTION**		
92	CHRISTMAS TRIO NORMAN ROCKWELL J1035	OP	40.00	40.00
92	SANTA'S SURPRISE J.C. LEYENDECKER J1036	OP	40.00	40.00
	KSA/JHP		**SESAME STREET SERIES**	
93	BIG BIRD FABRICHE J7928	OP	60.00	60.00
93	BIG BIRD NUTCRACKER H1199	RT	60.00	60.00
	P.F. BOLINGER			**SNOW PEOPLE**
96	COOLA HULA J6430	OP	20.00	20.00
96	SNOWPOKE J6431	OP	28.00	28.00
96	SNOWY J6429	OP	28.00	28.00
	C. STEINBACH		**STEINBACH MUSICAL COLLECTION**	
92	SKI LIFT MUSICAL ES27	2000	150.00	150.00
	KSA/STEINBACH	**STEINBACH NUTCRACKER CHRISTMAS LEGENDS**		
93	FATHER CHRISTMAS ES645	SO	225.00	225.00
94	ST. NICHOLAS, THE BISHOP ES865	7500	225.00	225.00
95	1930S SANTA CLAUS ES891	7500	245.00	245.00
	KSA/STEINBACH		**STEINBACH NUTCRACKER COLLECTION**	
84	OIL SHEIK	RT	100.00	300.00
91	COLUMBUS ES697	RT	194.00	210.00
92	HAPPY SANTA ES601	RT	190.00	205.00
	KSA/STEINBACH	**STEINBACH NUTCRACKER FAMOUS CHIEFTAINS**		
93	CHIEF SITTING BULL ES637	8500	225.00	225.00
94	CHIEF SITTING BULL SMOKER ES834	RT	150.00	150.00
94	RED CLOUD ES864	8500	225.00	225.00
95	BLACK HAWK ES889	7500	245.00	245.00
	KSA/STEINBACH		**TALES OF SHERWOOD FOREST**	
92	ROBIN HOOD ES863	SO	225.00	225.00
95	FRIAR TUCK ES890	7500	245.00	245.00
96	SHERIFF OF NOTTINGHAM ES892	7500	260.00	260.00
97	KING RICHARD THE LION HEARTED	7500	250.00	250.00
	KSA/STEINBACH			**THREE MUSKETEERS**
96	ARAMIS ES722	7500	130.00	130.00
	H. ADLER		**VATICAN LIBRARY COLLECTION**	
97	HOLY FAMILY SET	OP	*	N/A
97	THREE WISE MEN	OP	*	N/A
	K. ADLER		**VISIONS OF SANTA SERIES**	
92	SANTA COMING OUT OF FIREPLACE J1023	RT	29.00	29.00
92	SANTA HOLDING CHILD J826	RT	25.00	25.00
92	SANTA SPILLING BAG OF TOYS J1022	RT	26.00	26.00
92	SANTA W/LITTLE GIRLS ON LAP J1024	7500	25.00	25.00
92	SANTA W/SACK HOLDING TOY J827	RT	25.00	25.00
92	WORKSHOP SANTA J825	RT	27.00	27.00
	*		**WATERGLOBE COLLECTION**	
92	SANTA WITH TWO GIRLS J1038	OP	40.00	40.00
	KSA/ZUBER		**ZUBER NUTCRACKER SERIES**	
92	ANNAPOLIS MIDSHIPMAN, THE EK7	RT	125.00	125.00
92	BAVARIAN, THE EK16	RT	130.00	130.00
92	BRONCO BILLY THE COWBOY EK1	RT	125.00	125.00
92	CHIMNEY SWEEP, THE EK6	RT	125.00	125.00
92	COUNTRY SINGER, THE EK19	RT	125.00	125.00
92	FISHERMAN, THE EK17	5000	125.00	125.00
92	GEPETTO, THE TOYMAKER EK9	RT	125.00	125.00
92	GOLD PROSPECTOR, THE EK18	RT	125.00	125.00
92	GOLFER, THE EK5	RT	125.00	125.00
92	INDIAN, THE EK15	RT	135.00	135.00
92	NOR'EASTER SEA CAPTAIN, THE EK3	5000	125.00	125.00
92	PAUL BUNYAN THE LUMBERJACK EK2	RT	125.00	125.00
92	PILGRIM, THE EK14	RT	125.00	125.00

YR	NAME	LIMIT	ISSUE	TREND
92	TYROLEAN, THE EK4	RT	125.00	125.00
92	WEST POINT CADET W/CANON, THE EK6	RT	130.00	130.00
93	HERR DROSSELMEIR NUTCRACKER EK21	RT	150.00	150.00
93	ICE CREAM VENDOR, THE EK24	RT	150.00	150.00
93	NAPOLEON BONAPARTE EK23	RT	150.00	150.00
93	PIZZAMAKER, THE EK22	5000	150.00	150.00
94	GARDENER, THE EK26	RT	150.00	150.00
94	JAZZ PLAYER EK25	2500	145.00	145.00
94	KURT THE TRAVELING SALESMAN EK28	RT	155.00	155.00
94	MOUSE KING EK31	2500	150.00	150.00
94	PETER PAN EK28	2500	145.00	145.00
94	SCUBA DIVER EK27	2500	150.00	150.00
94	SOCCER PLAYER EK30	2500	145.00	145.00

LADIE & FRIENDS
B./P. WISBER

				SERIES I
96	AMANDA HIGH	TL	28.00	28.00
96	CASSIE YOCUM	TL	30.00	30.00
96	EDWARD BOWMAN	TL	28.00	28.00
96	GRACE VALENTINE	TL	25.00	25.00
96	KATIE BOWMAN	TL	28.00	28.00
96	LIZZIE HIGH	TL	27.00	27.00
96	MARISA VALENTINE	TL	25.00	25.00
96	MEGAN VALENTINE	TL	25.00	25.00
96	MINNIE VALENTINE	TL	35.00	35.00
96	NANCY BOWMAN	TL	30.00	30.00
96	NATALIE VALENTINE	TL	24.00	24.00
96	REBECCA BOWMAN	TL	28.00	28.00
96	SIGN	TL	37.00	37.00
		TL	37.00	37.00

LANCE CORP.
F. BARNUM

				CHILMARK
87	SURPRISE ENCOUNTER	RT	250.00	730.00
88	JOHNNY SHILOH	RT	100.00	225.00
92	KENNESAW MOUNTAIN	*	650.00	1000.00

M. BOYETT

				CHILMARK
81	PLIGHT OF THE HUNTSMAN	RT	495.00	825.00
82	BLOOD BROTHERS	RT	250.00	610.00
82	WINGS OF LIBERTY	SO	625.00	1250.00
84	FLAT OUT FOR RED RIVER STATION	RT	3,000.00	6000.00
86	EAGLE CATCHER	RT	300.00	1100.00
95	RAINMAKER, THE	YR	350.00	360.00

G. DELODZIA

				CHILMARK
81	FREEDOM EAGLE	SO	195.00	950.00

P. JACKSON

				CHILMARK
86	CAMELOT CHESS SET	RT	2,250.00	2250.00

KEIM/HAZEN

				CHILMARK
81	BUDWEISER WAGON	RT	2,000.00	3025.00

D. LAROCCA

				CHILMARK
79	CAVALRY OFFICER	RT	125.00	525.00
79	COWBOY	RT	125.00	650.00
88	DRAGON SLAYER	RT	385.00	500.00

A. MCGRORY

				CHILMARK
88	END OF THE TRAIL (MINI)	RT	225.00	300.00

D. POLLAND

				CHILMARK
74	CHEYENNE	RT	200.00	2850.00
76	RESCUE	RT	275.00	1200.00
77	FALL-MUSTANGS	3500	120.00	120.00
77	SPRING-MUSTANGS	3500	120.00	120.00
77	WINTER-MUSTANGS	3500	120.00	120.00
78	BUFFALO HUNT	RT	360.00	2220.00
78	COLD SADDLES, MEAN HORSES	RT	200.00	875.00
78	COUNTING COUP	RT	225.00	1800.00
78	CROW SCOUT	RT	250.00	1500.00
78	MAVERICK CALF	RT	250.00	1500.00
78	MONDAY MORNING WASH	RT	200.00	1100.00
78	OUTLAWS, THE	RT	450.00	1000.00
78	PAINTING THE TOWN	RT	300.00	1550.00
79	GETTING ACQUAINTED	RT	215.00	950.00
80	AFRICAN ELEPHANT	RT	275.00	400.00
80	BORDER RUSTLERS	RT	1,295.00	1500.00
80	MANDAN HUNTER	RT	65.00	825.00
81	AMBUSHED	RT	2,375.00	2725.00
81	BUFFALO ROBE	RT	200.00	315.00
81	DOG SOLDIER	2500	200.00	300.00
81	ENEMY TRACKS	RT	225.00	720.00
81	U.S. MARSHAL	RT	95.00	485.00
81	WAR PARTY	RT	550.00	1025.00
81	WHEN WAR CHIEFS MEET	RT	300.00	865.00
82	APACHE GAN DANCER	2500	95.00	110.00
82	APACHE HOSTILE	2500	95.00	110.00
82	ARAPAHO DRUMMER	2500	95.00	110.00
82	BUFFALO PRAYER	RT	95.00	300.00
82	COMANCHE PLAINES DRUMMER	2500	95.00	110.00
82	CROW MEDICINE DANCER	2500	95.00	110.00

YR	NAME	LIMIT	ISSUE	TREND
82	FLATHEAD WAR DANCER	2500	95.00	110.00
82	HOPI KACHINA DANCER	2500	95.00	110.00
82	JEMEZ EAGLE DANCER	RT	95.00	350.00
82	LAST ARROW	RT	95.00	350.00
82	NAVAJO KACHINA DANCER	2500	95.00	110.00
82	SIOUX WAR CHIEF	RT	95.00	350.00
82	YAKIMA SALMON FISHERMAN	RT	200.00	750.00
83	BOUNTY HUNTER	RT	250.00	450.00
83	CHIEF, THE	RT	275.00	1700.00
83	LINE RIDER	RT	195.00	1000.00
83	MUSTANGER	2500	425.00	550.00
83	TOO MANY ACES	RT	400.00	500.00
83	WILD BUNCH, THE	RT	200.00	325.00
84	EYE TO EYE	2500	375.00	475.00
84	GUIDON, THE	*	*	N/A
84	NOW OR NEVER	RT	265.00	800.00
84	UNIT COLORS	RT	250.00	1450.00
85	BAREBACK RIDER	2500	225.00	300.00
85	BARREL RACER	2500	275.00	325.00
85	BULL RIDER	2500	265.00	335.00
85	CALF ROPER	2500	300.00	375.00
85	OH GREAT SPIRIT	RT	300.00	1270.00
85	SADDLE BRONC RIDER	2500	250.00	300.00
85	STEER WRESTLING	2500	500.00	600.00
85	TEAM ROPING	2500	500.00	625.00
86	FIGHTING STALLIONS	2500	250.00	300.00
88	I WILL FIGHT NO MORE FOREVER	RT	350.00	825.00
89	GERONIMO	RT	375.00	700.00
90	BUFFALO SPIRIT	RT	110.00	195.00
90	COCHISE	RT	400.00	550.00
90	PEQUOT WARS	RT	395.00	675.00
90	RED RIVER WARS	RT	425.00	750.00
90	TECUMSEH'S REBELLION	RT	350.00	675.00
91	CRAZY HORSE	750	295.00	650.00
91	KIOWA PRINCESS	RT	300.00	300.00
92	STRONG HEARTS TO THE FRONT	RT	425.00	615.00
93	SACRED GROUND RECLAIMED	RT	495.00	600.00
94	HORSE BREAKING	RT	395.00	400.00
B. RODDEN				**CHILMARK**
79	MOSES	RT	100.00	250.00
80	CHARGE OF THE 7TH CALVARY	RT	600.00	975.00
C. ROUSELL				**CHILMARK**
84	CHEYENNE (REMINGTON)	RT	400.00	600.00
85	BRONCO BUSTER (LARGE)	RT	400.00	400.00
J. ROYCE				**CHILMARK**
84	GARDEN UNICORN	RT	160.00	200.00
J. SLOCKBOWER				**CHILMARK**
92	CHIEF JOSEPH METART	RT	975.00	1700.00
92	GERONIMO	RT	975.00	1000.00
93	CRAZY HORSE	750	975.00	1000.00
93	SITTING BULL	750	1,075.00	1100.00
R. SYLVAN				**CHILMARK**
79	CAROUSEL	RT	115.00	115.00
79	PEGASUS	RT	95.00	200.00
79	UNICORN	RT	115.00	600.00
D. POLLAND		**CHILMARK AMERICAN WEST CHRISTMAS**		
91	MERRY CHRISTMAS NEIGHBOR	RT	395.00	625.00
92	MERRY CHRISTMAS MY LOVE	RT	350.00	400.00
93	ALMOST HOME	RT	375.00	385.00
94	COWBOY CHRISTMAS	RT	250.00	260.00
M. BOYETT		**CHILMARK LEGACY OF COURAGE**		
81	APACHE SIGNALS	RT	175.00	550.00
81	BLACKFOOT SNOW HUNTER	RT	175.00	650.00
81	BUFFALO STALKER	RT	175.00	550.00
81	COMANCHE	RT	175.00	600.00
81	IROQUOIS WARFARE	RT	175.00	575.00
81	UNCONQUERED SEMINOLE	RT	175.00	550.00
81	VICTOR CHEYENNE	RT	175.00	500.00
82	ARAPAHO SENTINEL	RT	195.00	480.00
82	DANCE OF THE EAGLES	RT	150.00	225.00
82	KIOWA SCOUT	RT	195.00	525.00
82	LISTENING FOR HOOVES	RT	150.00	460.00
82	MANDAN BUFFALO DANCER	RT	195.00	575.00
82	PLAINS TALK, PAWNEE	RT	195.00	600.00
82	SHOSHONE EAGLE CATCHER	RT	225.00	1800.00
82	TRACKER NEZ PERCE, THE	RT	150.00	575.00
83	A WARRIOR'S TRIBUTE	RT	335.00	640.00
83	ALONG THE CHEROKEE TRACE	RT	295.00	700.00
83	CIRCLING THE ENEMY	RT	295.00	400.00
83	FOREST WATCHER	RT	215.00	550.00
83	MOMENT OF TRUTH	RT	295.00	575.00
83	RITE OF THE WHITETAIL	RT	295.00	400.00
83	WINTER HUNT	RT	295.00	375.00

YR	NAME	LIMIT	ISSUE	TREND

J. SLOCKBOWER — CHILMARK MICKEY & CO.

YR	NAME	LIMIT	ISSUE	TREND
92	CRUISING	RT	275.00	2000.00
93	SUNDAY DRIVE	RT	325.00	1200.00
94	BEACH BOUND	RT	350.00	875.00

A.T. MCGRORY — CHILMARK OFF CANVAS

90	SMOKE SIGNAL	RT	345.00	675.00
90	VIGIL	RT	345.00	600.00
90	WARRIOR	RT	300.00	450.00

* — CHILMARK PEWTER CIVIL WAR

87	SAVING THE COLORS	RT	350.00	650.00
92	KENNESAW MTN.	RT	650.00	1550.00
92	PARSON'S BATTERY	RT	495.00	525.00

F. BARNUM — CHILMARK PEWTER CIVIL WAR

88	A FATHER'S FAREWELL	RT	150.00	300.00
89	LEE TO THE REAR	RT	300.00	850.00
90	LEE AND JACKSON	RT	375.00	500.00
93	ABE LINCOLN BUST	RT	2,000.00	2275.00

D. POLLAND — CHILMARK PEWTER CIVIL WAR

77	SUMMER-MUSTANGS	3500	120.00	525.00

F. BARNUM — CHILMARK PEWTER CIVIL WAR CHRISTMAS SPECIALS

92	MERRY CHRISTMAS YANK	RT	350.00	525.00
93	SILENT NIGHT	RT	350.00	500.00
94	CHRISTMAS TRUCE	RT	295.00	300.00
95	PEACE ON EARTH	YR	350.00	360.00

F. BARNUM — CHILMARK PEWTER CIVIL WAR EVENT SPECIALS

93	JOHNNY REB	RT	95.00	135.00
94	BILLY YANK	RT	95.00	100.00
95	SEAMAN, CSS ALABAMA	RT	95.00	100.00

F. BARNUM — CHILMARK PEWTER CIVIL WAR REDEMPTION SPECIALS

92	ZOUAVES 1ST MANASSAS	RT	375.00	525.00
93	LETTER TO SARAH	RT	3,959.00	400.00
94	ANGEL OF FREDERICKSBURG	RT	275.00	300.00
95	REBEL YELL	YR	*	N/A

M. JOVINE — CHILMARK PEWTER HORSES

80	AFFIRMED	RT	850.00	1300.00

C. KEIM — CHILMARK PEWTER HORSES

81	CLYDESDALE WHEEL HORSE	RT	120.00	450.00

A. PETITTO — CHILMARK PEWTER HORSES

78	PADDOCK WALK	RT	85.00	225.00

D. POLLAND — CHILMARK PEWTER HORSES

86	WILD STALLION	RT	145.00	360.00

B. RODDEN — CHILMARK PEWTER HORSES

76	RUNNING FREE	RT	75.00	320.00
76	STALLION	RT	75.00	275.00
77	CHALLENGE, THE	RT	175.00	275.00
77	RISE AND SHINE	RT	135.00	200.00
80	BORN FREE	RT	250.00	700.00

* — CHILMARK PEWTER MICKEY & CO.

86	LIGHTS, CAMERA, ACTION/BRONZE	50	3,300.00	3300.00
89	GOLD EDITION HOLLYWOOD MICKEY	RT	200.00	780.00
89	HOLLYWOOD MICKEY	SU	165.00	250.00
91	MICKEY'S CAROUSEL RIDE	2500	150.00	150.00
94	LIGHTS, CAMERA, ACTION/PEWTER	500	1,525.00	1525.00
94	MICKEY ON PARADE/BRONZE	RT	975.00	975.00
94	MICKEY ON PARADE/METALART	RT	525.00	525.00
94	MICKEY ON PARADE/PEWTER	750	400.00	400.00
94	MOUSE IN A MILLION/BRONZE	RT	1,275.00	1275.00
94	MOUSE IN A MILLION/METALART	RT	675.00	675.00
94	MOUSE IN A MILLION/PEWTER	RT	525.00	525.00
94	PUTTIN' ON THE RITZ/BRONZE	RT	2,025.00	2025.00
94	PUTTIN' ON THE RITZ/METALART	250	1,025.00	1025.00
94	PUTTIN' ON THE RITZ/PEWTER	350	775.00	775.00

* — CHILMARK PEWTER MICKEY & CO. /THE SORCERER'S APPRENTICE

90	DREAM, THE	TL	225.00	235.00
90	INCANTATION, THE	TL	150.00	180.00
90	REPENTANT APPRENTICE, THE	RT	19,598.00	225.00
90	SORCERER'S APPRENTICE, THE	TL	225.00	235.00
90	WHIRLPOOL, THE	TL	225.00	250.00

P.W. BASTON — CHILMARK PEWTER MICKEY & CO. TWO WHEELING

94	GET YOUR MOTOR RUNNIN'/BRONZE	RT	1,200.00	1650.00
94	GET YOUR MOTOR RUNNIN'/METALART	RT	475.00	625.00
94	HEAD OUT ON THE HIGHWAY/METALART	950	475.00	500.00
95	LOOKING FOR ADVENTURE/BRONZE	50	1,200.00	1225.00
95	LOOKING FOR ADVENTURE/METALART	950	475.00	500.00

BASTON/ SLOCKBOWER — CHILMARK PEWTER MICKEY & CO. TWO WHEELING

94	HEAD OUT ON THE HIGHWAY/BRONZE	50	1,200.00	1225.00

A.T. MCGRORY — CHILMARK PEWTER OFF CANVAS

91	BLANKET SIGNAL	RT	750.00	875.00

F. BARNUM — CHILMARK PEWTER THE CAVALRY GENERALS

92	J.E.B. STUART	RT	375.00	525.00
93	GEORGE ARMSTRONG CUSTER	950	375.00	400.00
93	NATHAN BEDFORD FORREST	950	375.00	400.00
94	PHILIP SHERIDAN	950	375.00	400.00

YR	NAME	LIMIT	ISSUE	TREND
M. BOYETT		CHILMARK PEWTER WILDLIFE		
80	DUEL OF THE BIGHORNS	RT	725.00	1225.00
80	LEAD CAN'T CATCH HIM	RT	645.00	850.00
80	PRAIRIE SOVEREIGN	RT	645.00	800.00
80	VOICE OF EXPERIENCE	RT	645.00	875.00
V. HAYTON		CHILMARK PEWTER WILDLIFE		
80	RUBY-THROATED HUMMINGBIRD	RT	275.00	385.00
D. POLLAND		CHILMARK PEWTER WILDLIFE		
79	ELEPHANT	RT	315.00	500.00
79	RHINO	RT	135.00	400.00
80	GIRAFFE	RT	125.00	145.00
80	KUDU	RT	140.00	160.00
B. RODDEN		CHILMARK PEWTER WILDLIFE		
78	BUFFALO	RT	170.00	400.00
F. BARNUM		CHILMARK THE ADVERSARIES		
91	ROBERT E. LEE	RT	350.00	1750.00
92	STONEWALL JACKSON	RT	375.00	525.00
92	ULYSSES S. GRANT	RT	350.00	650.00
93	WM. TECUMSEH SHERMAN	RT	375.00	600.00
D. POLLAND		CHILMARK THE MEDICINE MEN		
92	FALSE FACE/METALART	1000	550.00	550.00
92	FALSE FACE/PEWTER	RT	375.00	375.00
A. MCGRORY		CHILMARK THE SEEKERS		
92	BUFFALO VISION	RT	1,075.00	1075.00
93	BEAR VISION	500	1,375.00	1375.00
93	EAGLE VISION	500	1,250.00	1250.00
D. POLLAND		CHILMARK THE WARRIORS		
92	SPIRIT OF THE WOLF/METALART	1000	500.00	510.00
92	SPIRIT OF THE WOLF/PEWTER	RT	350.00	875.00
93	SON OF THE MORNING STAR/METALART	1000	495.00	500.00
93	SON OF THE MORNING STAR/PEWTER	RT	375.00	475.00
T. SULLIVAN		CHILMARK TO THE GREAT SPIRIT		
92	SHOOTING STAR	RT	775.00	775.00
93	GRAY ELK	950	775.00	775.00
93	TWO EAGLES	950	775.00	775.00
94	THUNDER CLOUD	950	775.00	775.00
D. LIBERTY		CRYSTALS OF ZORN		
89	BATTLE ON THE PLAINS OF XENON	950	265.00	265.00
89	CHARGING THE STONE	950	395.00	395.00
89	GUARDING THE CRYSTAL	950	460.00	460.00
89	RESPONSE OF ORNIC FORCE	950	285.00	285.00
89	RESTORATION	950	435.00	435.00
89	U.S.S. STRIKES BACK	500	675.00	675.00
90	ASMUND'S WORKSHOP	950	275.00	275.00
90	STRUGGLING FOR SUPREMACY	950	400.00	400.00
90	VESTING THE GRAIL	950	200.00	200.00
*		GENERATIONS OF MICKEY		
87	ANTIQUE MICKEY	RT	95.00	600.00
89	MICKEY'S GALA PREMIERE	2500	150.00	150.00
89	SORCERER'S APPRENTICE	RT	150.00	400.00
89	STEAM BOAT WILLIE	RT	165.00	450.00
90	BAND CONCERT, THE	2000	185.00	200.00
90	BAND CONCERT, THE (PAINTED)	RT	215.00	390.00
90	DISNEYLAND MICKEY	2500	150.00	150.00
91	MOUSE, THE-1935	1200	185.00	185.00
91	PLANE CRAZY-1928	2500	175.00	175.00
P.W. BASTON		HUDSON PEWTER FIGURES		
69	BETSY ROSS	CL	30.00	110.00
69	COLONIAL BLACKSMITH	CL	30.00	110.00
69	GEORGE WASHINGTON (CANNON)	CL	35.00	90.00
69	JOHN HANCOCK	CL	15.00	110.00
72	BENJAMIN FRANKLIN	CL	15.00	90.00
72	GEORGE WASHINGTON	CL	15.00	90.00
72	JAMES MADISON	CL	15.00	65.00
72	JOHN ADAMS	CL	15.00	90.00
72	THOMAS JEFFERSON	CL	15.00	90.00
75	DECLARATION WALL PLAQUE	RT	*	400.00
75	FAVORED SCHOLAR, THE	RT	*	800.00
75	LEE'S NINTH GENERAL ORDER	CL	*	350.00
75	LINCOLN'S GETTYSBURG ADDRESS	CL	*	350.00
75	NEIGHBORING PEWS	RT	*	800.00
75	SPIRIT OF '76	RT	*	1100.00
75	WASHINGTON'S LETTER OF ACCEPTANCE	CL	*	350.00
75	WEIGHING THE BABY	RT	*	800.00
H. WILSON		HUDSON PEWTER FIGURES		
76	BALD EAGLE	CL	100.00	113.00
76	GREAT HORNED OWL	CL	*	42.00
D. LAROCCA		MILITARY COMMEMORATIVES		
91	DESERT LIBERATOR (PAINTED PORCELAIN)	5000	125.00	125.00
91	DESERT LIBERATOR (PEWTER)	950	295.00	295.00
D. POLLAND		MINIATURE SCULPTURE SOCIETY		
92	BLACK HAWK	*	25.00	250.00

YR	NAME	LIMIT	ISSUE	TREND
P.W. BASTON			**SEBASTIAN EXCHANGE**	
83	NEWSPAPER BOY	RT	29.00	80.00
84	FIRST THINGS FIRST	RT	30.00	40.00
P.W. BASTON, JR.			**SEBASTIAN EXCHANGE**	
85	NEWSSTAND	RT	30.00	40.00
86	NEWS WAGON	RT	35.00	50.00
87	IT'S ABOUT TIME	RT	25.00	40.00
P.W. BASTON			**SEBASTIAN MINIATURES**	
92	FIREFIGHTER	RT	28.00	55.00
92	I KNOW I LEFT IT HERE SOMEWHERE	1000	29.00	30.00
93	LAMPLIGHTER, THE	1000	28.00	30.00
93	PUMPKIN ISLAND LIGHT	3500	55.00	60.00
93	SOAP BOX DERBY	500	45.00	50.00
94	A JOB WELL DONE	1000	28.00	30.00
94	BOSTON LIGHT	3500	45.00	50.00
94	EGG ROCK LIGHT	3500	55.00	60.00
94	NUBBLE LIGHT	3500	45.00	50.00
P.W. BASTON, JR.			**SEBASTIAN MINIATURES**	
83	HARRY HOOD	RT	*	225.00
85	IT'S HOODS (WAGON)	RT	*	90.00
91	AMERICA SALUTES DESERT STORM-BRONZE	RT	27.00	100.00
91	AMERICA SALUTES DESERT STORM-PAINTED	RT	50.00	225.00
91	HAPPY HOOD HOLIDAYS	RT	33.00	75.00
P.W. BASTON			**SEBASTIAN MINIATURES AMERICA REMEMBERS**	
79	FAMILY SING	RT	30.00	90.00
80	FAMILY PICNIC	RT	30.00	80.00
81	FAMILY READS ALOUD	RT	35.00	60.00
82	FAMILY FISHING	RT	35.00	75.00
83	FAMILY FEAST	RT	38.00	75.00
P.W. BASTON			**SEBASTIAN MINIATURES CHILDREN AT PLAY**	
78	SIDEWALK DAYS BOY	RT	20.00	50.00
78	SIDEWALK DAYS GIRL	RT	20.00	50.00
79	BUILDING DAYS BOY	RT	20.00	40.00
79	BUILDING DAYS GIRL	RT	20.00	40.00
80	SNOW DAYS BOY	RT	20.00	50.00
80	SNOW DAYS GIRL	RT	20.00	50.00
81	SAILING DAYS BOY	RT	20.00	40.00
81	SAILING DAYS GIRL	RT	20.00	40.00
82	SCHOOL DAYS BOY	RT	20.00	50.00
82	SCHOOL DAYS GIRL	RT	20.00	50.00
P.W. BASTON			**SEBASTIAN MINIATURES COLLECTORS SOCIETY**	
80	S.M.C SOCIETY PLAQUE ('80 CHARTER)	RT	*	25.00
P.W. BASTON, JR.			**SEBASTIAN MINIATURES COLLECTORS SOCIETY**	
86	STATUE OF LIBERTY (AT&T)	RT	*	190.00
87	WHITE HOUSE (GOLD, OVAL BASE)	RT	17.00	50.00
P.W. BASTON, JR.			**SEBASTIAN MINIATURES HOLIDAY MEMORIES-MEMBER ONLY**	
90	LEPRECHAUN	YR	28.00	28.00
90	THANKSGIVING HELPER	YR	40.00	40.00
91	TRICK OR TREAT	YR	26.00	65.00
P.W. BASTON			**SEBASTIAN MINIATURES JIMMY FUND**	
83	SCHOOLBOY	RT	25.00	30.00
84	CATCHER	RT	25.00	60.00
P.W. BASTON, JR.			**SEBASTIAN MINIATURES JIMMY FUND**	
85	HOCKEY PLAYER	RT	25.00	40.00
86	SOCCER PLAYER	RT	25.00	25.00
87	FOOTBALL PLAYER	RT	27.00	27.00
88	SANTA	RT	33.00	33.00
P.W. BASTON, JR.			**SEBASTIAN MINIATURES MEMBER ONLY**	
89	COLLECTORS, THE	YR	40.00	40.00
P.W. BASTON			**SEBASTIAN MINIATURES SHAKESPEAREAN-MEMBER ONLY**	
84	ANNE BOYELIN	RT	17.50	30.00
84	HENRY VIII	RT	20.00	30.00
85	FALSTAFF	RT	20.00	30.00
85	MISTRESS FORD	RT	17.50	30.00
86	JULIET	RT	17.50	30.00
86	ROMEO	RT	20.00	30.00
87	COUNTESS OLIVIA	RT	20.00	30.00
87	MALVOLIO	RT	22.00	30.00
88	AUDREY	RT	23.00	30.00
88	TOUCHSTONE	RT	23.00	30.00
89	CLEOPATRA	RT	27.00	30.00
89	MARK ANTHONY	RT	27.00	30.00
P.W. BASTON, JR.			**SEBASTIAN MINIATURES SHAKESPEAREAN-MEMBER ONLY**	
88	SHAKESPEARE	RT	24.00	30.00
P.W. BASTON			**WASHINGTON IRVING-MEMBER ONLY**	
80	RIP VAN WINKLE	CL	20.00	20.00
81	DAME VAN WINKLE	CL	20.00	20.00
81	ICHABOD CRANE	CL	20.00	20.00
82	BROM BONES (HEADLESS HORSEMAN)	CL	23.00	23.00
82	KATRINA VAN TASSEL	CL	20.00	20.00
83	DIEDRICH KNICKERBOCKER	CL	23.00	23.00

LAND OF LEGEND

YR	NAME	LIMIT	ISSUE	TREND
	T. RAINE — CASTLE COLLECTION			
78	DENNIS THE DRAGON/COUNTERSIGN	CL	55.00	225.00
86	CASTLE OF THE EXILED PRINCE	CL	225.00	200.00
86	CASTLE OF THE GOLDEN CHALICE	CL	60.00	60.00
86	CASTLE OF THE RANSOMED KING	CL	250.00	200.00
86	CASTLE OF THE RED KNIGHT	CL	65.00	65.00
86	CASTLE OF THE SLEEPING PRINCESS	CL	235.00	235.00
86	SORCERER'S RETREAT	CL	50.00	55.00
87	WIZARD'S TOWER	CL	215.00	208.00
	H. HENRIKSEN — DRAGONS			
89	COUNTERSIGN FOR SERIES	*	75.00	90.00
90	DRAGON OF THE GOLDEN HOARD	*	270.00	350.00
90	GUARDIAN OF THE KEEP	*	295.00	375.00
90	HATCHED	*	295.00	395.00
90	LET SLEEPING DRAGONS LIE	3000	450.00	595.00
90	LEVIATHAN	*	325.00	424.00
90	WYVERN	*	295.00	375.00
	T. RAINE — DREAM CASTLES			
88	CAMELOT	CL	33.00	33.00
88	FAIRYTALE	CL	33.00	33.00
88	GRAND VIZIERS	CL	33.00	33.00
88	VALKYRIES TOWER	CL	33.00	33.00
	T. RAINE — DREAM DRAGONS			
88	BATHTIME	RT	32.00	32.00
88	BREAKOUT	RT	32.00	32.00
88	DOUBLE TROUBLE	RT	35.00	35.00
88	DREAM BABY	RT	32.00	32.00
88	HAZY DAZE	RT	32.00	32.00
88	HELP	RT	32.00	32.00
88	HI THERE	RT	32.00	32.00
88	LITTLE SISTER	RT	32.00	32.00
88	STRIKE ONE	RT	35.00	35.00
88	WILD WHEELS	RT	35.00	35.00
89	ESPECIALLY FOR YOU	RT	35.00	35.00
89	KISS, THE	RT	45.00	45.00
89	LIPSTICK AND LASHES	RT	35.00	35.00
89	LOVE LETTER	RT	35.00	35.00
89	OFF TO SCHOOL	RT	35.00	35.00
89	PARTY TIME	RT	45.00	45.00
89	SHE LOVES ME	RT	35.00	35.00
89	STAY COOL	RT	35.00	35.00
	T. RAINE — ETHELRED FLAMETAIL			
89	BLACK KNIGHT, THE	CL	80.00	80.00
89	EARLY DAYS	CL	38.00	38.00
89	EUREKA	CL	50.00	50.00
89	FLYING LESSON, THE	CL	65.00	65.00
89	HELLO WORLD	CL	38.00	38.00
89	JEREMY THE DANDY	CL	90.00	90.00
89	LIFT OFF	CL	105.00	105.00
89	MAGIC WATER, THE	CL	65.00	65.00
89	MERCHANT, THE	CL	68.00	68.00
89	MR. BONZER	CL	63.00	63.00
89	ON THE RUNWAY	CL	50.00	50.00
89	PRINCESS NYNEVE	CL	60.00	60.00
89	RANOL	CL	30.00	30.00
89	SCHOOL DAYS	CL	90.00	90.00
89	SWAMP BIRD	CL	40.00	40.00
89	TENDER LOVING CARE	CL	115.00	115.00
89	THREE CHEERS	CL	115.00	115.00
89	TREE POPPER	CL	45.00	45.00
89	TROLL, THE	CL	68.00	68.00
89	WILY WIZARD, THE	CL	80.00	80.00
89	YOUNG INVENTOR, THE	CL	45.00	45.00
	T. RAINE — FANTASY FIGURINES			
88	BEHEMOTH ON WOODEN BASE	2500	220.00	220.00
88	ELFIN KING ON WOODEN BASE	2500	275.00	275.00
88	ETERNAL HERO ON WOODEN BASE	CL	220.00	220.00
88	UNION OF OPPOSITES ON WOODEN BASE	CL	300.00	300.00
	T. RAINE — GENIES BY TOM RAINE			
89	FLIGHT TO BAGDAD	OP	170.00	170.00
89	FREE AT LAST	OP	150.00	150.00
89	KEY OF KNOWLEDGE	OP	170.00	170.00
89	YES MASTER	OP	150.00	150.00
	H. HENRIKSEN — JESTERS			
89	COUNTERSIGN FOR SERIES	OP	75.00	90.00
89	HIS MAJESTRY BALDWICK/INCREDIBLY SIMPLE	3000	295.00	375.00
89	JOCKOMO, THE DOG	RT	59.00	59.00
89	JOLLIES PITCHBELLY	OP	175.00	200.00
89	LA DI DA TOOGOODE	RT	185.00	185.00
89	MERRY ANDREW	RT	130.00	130.00
89	PUCK, BABY BEAR	RT	59.00	59.00
89	SMACK THICKWIT	OP	185.00	230.00

YR	NAME	LIMIT	ISSUE	TREND
89	TWIT COXCOMBE	RT	140.00	140.00
89	URSULA, MOTHER BEAR	RT	95.00	95.00
H. HENRIKSEN		**LAND OF LEGEND FELLOWSHIP**		
90	SELF TAUGHT	TL	100.00	100.00
R. MUSGRAVE		**LAND OF LEGEND FELLOWSHIP**		
90	TAKE A CHANCE	TL	*	N/A
T. RAINE		**LAND OF LEGEND FELLOWSHIP**		
89	HUBBLE BUBBLE	RT	95.00	130.00
89	SWORD IN THE STONE, THE	RT	*	75.00
T. RAINE		**LIMITED EDITION CASTLES**		
88	SCHLOSS NEUSCHWANSTEIN	CL	750.00	910.00
D. TATE		**LIMITED EDITION CASTLES**		
86	SCHLOSS RHEINIUNGFRAU	1500	335.00	335.00
R. MUSGRAVE		**POCKET DRAGONS**		
89	A GOOD EGG	RT	37.00	43.00
89	ATTACK	OP	45.00	55.00
89	BABY BROTHER	OP	20.00	24.00
89	DO I HAVE TO?	OP	53.00	63.00
89	DROWSY DRAGON	OP	35.00	35.00
89	FLOWERS FOR YOU	OP	43.00	48.00
89	GALLANT DEFENDER, THE	OP	37.00	43.00
89	GARGOYLE HOPING FOR RASPBERRY TEACAKE	RT	140.00	140.00
89	LOOK AT ME	RT	43.00	43.00
89	NEW BUNNY SHOES	OP	29.00	35.00
89	NO UGLY MONSTERS ALLOWED	OP	48.00	58.00
89	OPERA GARGOYLE	RT	85.00	105.00
89	PINK 'N PRETTY	OP	24.00	30.00
89	POCKET DRAGON COUNTERSIGN	RT	50.00	63.00
89	POCKET MINSTREL, THE	RT	37.00	43.00
89	SCRIBBLES	OP	38.00	45.00
89	SEA DRAGON	RT	45.00	55.00
89	SIR NIGEL SMYTHEBE-SMOKE	OP	148.00	175.00
89	STALKING THE COOKIE JAR	OP	31.00	39.00
89	STORYTIME AT WIZARD'S HOUSE	3000	375.00	450.00
89	TEDDY MAGIC	RT	85.00	105.00
89	TOADY GOLDTRAYLER	OP	53.00	63.00
89	WALKIES	OP	65.00	79.00
89	WHAT COOKIE?	OP	43.00	50.00
89	WIZARDRY FOR FUN AND PROFIT	3000	375.00	450.00
89	YOUR PAINT IS STIRRED	RT	43.00	53.00
90	APPRENTICE, THE	OP	25.00	30.00
90	TAG-A-LONG	OP	20.00	24.00
91	A JOYFUL NOISE	OP	28.00	28.00
91	FRIENDS	OP	85.00	85.00
91	I'M A KITTY	OP	50.00	50.00
91	PICK ME UP	OP	28.00	28.00
91	PLAYING FOOTSIE	OP	28.00	28.00
91	PRACTICE MAKES PERFECT	OP	43.00	43.00
91	SLEEPY HEAD	OP	53.00	53.00
91	TICKLE	OP	35.00	35.00
91	TWINKLE TOES	OP	28.00	28.00
T. RAINE		**SECRET OF THE SWAN PRINCESS**		
89	ALARCH SILVERBEARD	CL	80.00	80.00
89	ASPARD	CL	65.00	65.00
89	CASTLE OF THE SWAN PRINCESS	CL	100.00	100.00
89	DRAGON'S LAIR	CL	75.00	75.00
89	JUDGE'S RETREAT	CL	85.00	85.00
89	KIBOLD WALTER	CL	65.00	65.00
89	MASTERS OF THE FOREST	CL	75.00	75.00
89	PALACE OF THE EMPEROR CHILD	CL	75.00	75.00
89	RONTUNDO THE TUSCAN	CL	65.00	65.00
89	SALIX THE BOLD	CL	65.00	65.00
MUSGRAVE/ HENRIKSEN		**UNDER THE HEDGE**		
89	A WINTER'S FRIEND	RT	25.00	25.00
89	BASKETS OF LOVE	OP	40.00	48.00
89	CAREFULLY WRAPPED	RT	30.00	30.00
89	COUNTERSIGN	OP	40.00	48.00
89	COUSIN BERTHA'S REVENGE	OP	43.00	50.00
89	DECK THE HALLS	3000	100.00	120.00
89	FASHION PLATE, THE	RT	48.00	48.00
89	FATHER CHRISTMAS	OP	45.00	55.00
89	FAVORITE UNCLE	OP	43.00	58.00
89	KEEP YOUR TAIL WARM	OP	60.00	70.00
89	OUT OF TOWN GUEST	OP	43.00	58.00
89	SNOWBALLS AND TOP HATS	RT	40.00	40.00
89	TRAPPED ON THE SUMMIT	RT	38.00	38.00
90	ARTFUL BOWLER, THE	OP	48.00	60.00
90	ARTIST, THE	OP	63.00	75.00
90	AUNT VIOLET & PUDGY	OP	50.00	60.00
90	COUSIN REGGIE	OP	60.00	70.00
90	JELLY SANWICHES	OP	82.50	98.00
90	JUNIUS BUG	OP	43.00	50.00
90	JUST GUARDING THE HAMPER	OP	48.00	58.00
90	MIGHTY PERCY AT THE BAT	OP	50.00	60.00

From the Disneyana collection by Armani, Snow White originally retailed for $750 and is now retired.

A member of Kristin Haynes' Dreamsicles line, produced by Cast Art Industries, Forever Friends has tripled in value since its 1993 release.

Pluto Helps Decorate, from the "Holiday Series" by Walt Disney Classics Collection, features Mickey's best friend in a most compromising position.

There's A Light At the End of the Tunnel is from Enesco Corp.'s Precious Moments collection by Sam Butcher.

A favorite of young and old alike, Winnie the Pooh was the 1996 gift sculpture for members of Walt Disney Classics Collection's Collectors Society.

YR	NAME	LIMIT	ISSUE	TREND
90	MISS AMELIA'S TURN	OP	45.00	55.00
90	SLOW AND STEADY	OP	60.00	70.00
90	SPARKLING CLEAN	OP	95.50	115.00
90	SPOTTING STRAYS	OP	50.00	60.00
90	STEMS AND BOWLES LTD.	OP	159.00	190.00
90	SUNDAE AFTERNOON	OP	199.00	235.00
90	TEA TABLE, THE	OP	40.00	48.00
90	WAITING FOR A LIGHT	OP	82.50	98.00
90	WATCHING THE HERD	OP	45.00	55.00
90	WICKET KEEPER, THE	OP	55.00	70.00
H. HENRIKSEN				**WIZARDS**
89	COUNTERSIGN FOR WIZARDS' SERIES	OP	75.00	90.00
89	FORESHADOW THE SEER	OP	135.00	160.00
89	LACKEY	RT	95.00	95.00
89	MERLYN THE WIZARD WATCHER	RT	50.00	50.00
89	MERRYWEATHER SUNLIGHTER	3000	295.00	350.00
89	MORIAH	OP	159.00	190.00
89	MYDWYNTER	RT	135.00	135.00
89	REPOSITORY OF MAGIC	RT	130.00	130.00
89	RIMBAUGH	OP	159.00	190.00
89	THORBAULD	RT	175.00	175.00
91	BALANCE OF TRUTH	2500	270.00	270.00
91	DRAGON MASTER, THE	1500	675.00	675.00
91	FORESHADOW THE SEER (WITH CRYSTALS)	OP	190.00	190.00
91	HOWLAND THE WISE	2500	300.00	300.00
91	MORIAH (WITH CRYSTALS)	OP	225.00	225.00
91	PONDERING THE QUEST	2500	270.00	270.00
91	RIMBAUGH (WITH CRYSTALS)	OP	225.00	225.00

LEGENDS

	C. PARDELL			
90	LAKOTA LOVE SONG	RT	380.00	965.00
	C. PARDELL		**AMERICAN WEST PREMIER EDITION**	
91	FIRST COUP	SO	1,150.00	1200.00
91	UNEXPECTED RESCUER	SO	990.00	2000.00
92	AMERICAN HORSE TAKES HIS NAME	950	1,300.00	1300.00
	C. PARDELL		**ANNUAL COLLECTORS EDITION**	
*	MEDICINE GIFT OF MANHOOD	*	990.00	1900.00
90	NIGHT BEFORE, THE	SO	990.00	1900.00
91	MEDICINE GIFT OF MANHOOD	SO	990.00	1900.00
92	SPIRIT OF THE WOLF	500	950.00	1225.00
93	TOMORROW'S WARRIOR	*	590.00	1400.00
	K. CANTRELL		**ENDANGERED WILDLIFE COLLECTION**	
90	FOREST SPIRIT	SO	290.00	1195.00
92	SPIRIT SONG	*	350.00	695.00
	K. CANTRELL		**ENDANGERED WILDLIFE COLLECTION-EAGLE SERIES**	
89	SENTINEL	*	280.00	585.00
	C. PARDELL		**GALLERY EDITIONS**	
92	RESOLUTE	*	7,950.00	13,000.00
	C. PARDELL		**INDIAN ARTS COLLECTION**	
89	CHIEF'S BLANKET	SO	350.00	600.00
90	KACHINA CARVER	*	270.00	450.00
90	STORY TELLER	*	290.00	325.00
	C. PARDELL		**LEGACIES OF THE WEST PREMIER EDITION**	
90	MYSTIC VISION	SO	990.00	2895.00
90	VICTORIOUS	SO	1,275.00	3875.00
91	DEFIANT COMANCHE	SO	1,300.00	2550.00
91	NO MORE, FOREVER	SO	1,500.00	2900.00
92	ESTEEMED WARRIOR	SO	1,750.00	2250.00
	C. PARDELL		**LEGENDARY WEST COLLECTION**	
87	JOHNSON'S LAST FLIGHT	SO	590.00	1200.00
87	PONY EXPRESS	RT	320.00	450.00
87	WHITE FEATHER'S VISION	SO	390.00	2000.00
89	CRAZY HORSE	*	390.00	900.00
	C. PARDELL		**LEGENDARY WEST PREMIER EDITION**	
88	RED CLOUD'S COUP	SO	480.00	6000.00
89	PURSUED	SO	750.00	6000.00
89	SONGS OF GLORY	SO	850.00	4300.00
90	CROW WARRIOR	SO	1,225.00	4500.00
91	TRIUMPHANT	SO	1,150.00	2000.00
92	FINAL CHARGE, THE	750	1,250.00	1600.00

LENOX CHINA/CRYSTAL COLLECTION

	*		**AMERICAN FASHION**	
83	SPRINGTIME PROMENADE	OP	95.00	95.00
84	FIRST WALTZ	OP	95.00	95.00
84	TEA AT THE RITZ	OP	95.00	95.00
85	GOVERNOR'S GARDEN PARTY	OP	95.00	95.00
86	BELLE OF THE BALL	OP	95.00	95.00
86	GRAND TOUR	OP	95.00	95.00
87	CENTENNIAL BRIDE	OP	95.00	95.00
87	GALA AT THE WHITE HOUSE	OP	95.00	95.00
	*		**BABY BEARS**	
91	POLAR BEAR	OP	45.00	45.00

YR	NAME	LIMIT	ISSUE	TREND
*			**BABY BIRD PAIRS**	
91	ROBINS	OP	64.00	64.00
*			**BIBLICAL CHARACTERS**	
92	MOSES, THE LAWGIVER	OP	95.00	95.00
*			**CAROUSEL ANIMALS**	
87	CAROUSEL HORSE	9500	136.00	152.00
88	CAROUSEL UNICORN	9500	136.00	152.00
89	CAROUSEL CIRCUS HORSE	9500	136.00	152.00
89	CAROUSEL REINDEER	9500	136.00	152.00
90	CAROUSEL CHARGER	9500	136.00	152.00
90	CAROUSEL ELEPHANT	9500	136.00	152.00
90	CAROUSEL LION	9500	136.00	152.00
91	CAROUSEL POLAR BEAR	9500	152.00	152.00
91	PRIDE OF AMERICA	TL	152.00	152.00
91	WESTERN HORSE	OP	152.00	152.00
92	CAMELOT HORSE	OP	152.00	152.00
*			**COUNTRY KIDS**	
91	GOOSE GIRL	OP	75.00	75.00
*			**DOVES & ROSES**	
91	DOVES OF PEACE	OP	95.00	95.00
91	LOVE'S PROMISE	OP	95.00	95.00
92	DOVES OF HONOR	OP	119.00	119.00
*			**ENDANGERED BABY ANIMALS**	
90	PANDA	OP	39.00	39.00
91	BABY FLORIDA PANTHER	OP	57.00	57.00
91	BABY GREY WOLF	OP	57.00	57.00
91	ELEPHANT	OP	57.00	57.00
*			**EXOTIC BIRDS**	
91	COCKATOO	OP	50.00	50.00
*			**FLORAL SCULPTURES**	
86	RUBRUM LILY	OP	119.00	136.00
87	IRIS	OP	119.00	136.00
88	MAGNOLIA	OP	119.00	136.00
88	PEACE ROSE	OP	119.00	136.00
*			**GARDEN BIRDS**	
85	CHICKADEE	OP	39.00	45.00
86	BLUE JAY	OP	39.00	45.00
86	EASTERN BLUEBIRD	OP	39.00	45.00
86	TUFTED TITMOUSE	OP	39.00	45.00
87	AMERICAN GOLDFINCH	OP	39.00	45.00
87	CARDINAL	OP	39.00	45.00
87	RED-BREASTED NUTHATCH	OP	39.00	45.00
87	TURTLEDOVE	OP	39.00	45.00
88	CEDAR WAXWING	OP	39.00	45.00
88	HUMMINGBIRD	OP	39.00	45.00
89	DOWNY WOODPECKER	OP	39.00	45.00
89	ROBIN	OP	39.00	45.00
89	SAW WHET OWL	OP	45.00	45.00
90	BALTIMORE ORIOLE	OP	45.00	45.00
90	CHIPPING SPARROW	OP	45.00	45.00
90	WOOD DUCK	OP	45.00	45.00
90	WREN	OP	45.00	45.00
91	BROADBILLED HUMMINGBIRD	OP	45.00	45.00
91	DARK-EYED JUNCO	OP	45.00	45.00
91	GOLDEN CROWNED KINGLET	OP	45.00	45.00
91	PURPLE FINCH	OP	45.00	45.00
91	ROSE GROSBEAK	OP	45.00	45.00
92	SCARLET TANGER	OP	45.00	45.00
*			**GARDEN FLOWERS**	
88	CATTLEYA ORCHID	OP	39.00	45.00
88	PARROT TULIP	OP	39.00	39.00
88	TEA ROSE	OP	39.00	45.00
89	IRIS	OP	45.00	45.00
90	CARNATION	OP	45.00	45.00
90	DAFFODIL	OP	45.00	45.00
90	DAY LILY	OP	45.00	45.00
91	CALLA LILY	OP	45.00	45.00
91	CAMELIA	OP	45.00	45.00
91	MAGNOLIA	OP	45.00	45.00
91	MORNING GLORY	OP	45.00	45.00
91	POINSETTIA	OP	39.00	39.00
*			**GENTLE MAJESTY**	
90	BEAR HUG POLAR BEAR	OP	76.00	76.00
90	PENGUINS	OP	76.00	76.00
91	KEEPING WARM (FOXES)	OP	76.00	76.00
*			**INTERNATIONAL BRIDES**	
90	RUSSIAN BRIDE	OP	136.00	136.00
*			**INTERNATIONAL HORSE SCULPTURES**	
88	ARABIAN KNIGHT	OP	136.00	136.00
89	THOROUGHBRED	OP	136.00	136.00
90	APPALOOSA	OP	136.00	136.00
90	LIPPIZAN	OP	136.00	136.00

YR	NAME	LIMIT	ISSUE	TREND

J.W. SMITH

YR	NAME	LIMIT	ISSUE	TREND
91	FEEDING KITTY	OP	60.00	60.00
91	ROSEBUDS	OP	60.00	60.00

JESSIE WILCOX SMITH

KINGS OF THE SKY

YR	NAME	LIMIT	ISSUE	TREND
89	AMERICAN BALD EAGLE	OP	195.00	195.00
91	DEFENDER OF FREEDOM	TL	234.00	234.00
91	GOLDEN EAGLE	OP	234.00	234.00

LEGENDARY PRINCESSES

YR	NAME	LIMIT	ISSUE	TREND
85	RAPUNZEL	OP	119.00	136.00
86	SLEEPING BEAUTY	OP	119.00	136.00
87	SNOW QUEEN	OP	119.00	136.00
88	CINDERELLA	OP	136.00	136.00
89	SNOW WHITE	OP	136.00	136.00
89	SWAN PRINCESS	OP	136.00	136.00
90	CLEOPATRA	OP	136.00	136.00
90	GUINEVERE	OP	136.00	136.00
90	JULIET	OP	136.00	136.00
91	PEACOCK MAIDEN	OP	136.00	136.00
91	POCAHONTAS	9500	136.00	136.00
92	FIREBIRD	OP	156.00	156.00

LENOX BABY BOOK

YR	NAME	LIMIT	ISSUE	TREND
90	BABY'S FIRST SHOES	OP	57.00	57.00
91	BABY'S FIRST CHRISTMAS	OP	57.00	57.00
91	BABY'S FIRST STEPS	OP	57.00	57.00
92	BABY'S FIRST PORTRAIT	OP	57.00	57.00

LENOX PUPPY COLLECTION

YR	NAME	LIMIT	ISSUE	TREND
90	BEAGLE	OP	76.00	76.00
91	COCKER SPANIEL	OP	76.00	76.00
92	POODLE	OP	76.00	76.00

LENOX SEA ANIMALS

YR	NAME	LIMIT	ISSUE	TREND
91	DANCE OF THE DOLPHINS	OP	119.00	119.00

LIFE OF CHRIST

YR	NAME	LIMIT	ISSUE	TREND
90	CHILDREN'S BLESSING, THE	OP	95.00	95.00
90	GOOD SHEPHERD, THE	OP	95.00	95.00
90	MADONNA AND CHILD	OP	95.00	95.00
91	JESUS, THE TEACHER	9500	95.00	95.00
91	SAVIOR, THE	OP	95.00	95.00
92	A CHILD'S PRAYER	OP	95.00	95.00
92	CHILDREN'S DEVOTION PAINTED	OP	195.00	195.00

MOTHER & CHILD

YR	NAME	LIMIT	ISSUE	TREND
86	CHERISHED MOMENT	OP	119.00	119.00
86	SUNDAY IN THE PARK	OP	119.00	119.00
87	STORYTIME	OP	119.00	119.00
88	PRESENT, THE	OP	119.00	119.00
89	CHRISTENING	OP	119.00	119.00
90	BEDTIME PRAYERS	OP	119.00	119.00
91	AFTERNOON STROLL	7500	136.00	136.00
91	EVENING LULLABY	7500	136.00	136.00
92	MORNING PLAYTIME	OP	136.00	136.00

NATIVITY

YR	NAME	LIMIT	ISSUE	TREND
86	HOLY FAMILY	OP	119.00	136.00
87	THREE ANGELS	OP	119.00	152.00
88	ANIMALS OF THE NATIVITY	OP	119.00	152.00
88	SHEPHERDS	OP	119.00	152.00
89	ANGELS OF ADORATION	OP	136.00	152.00
90	CHILDREN OF BETHLEHEM	OP	136.00	152.00
91	STANDING CAMEL & DRIVER	9500	152.00	152.00
91	TOWNSPEOPLE OF BETHLEHEM	OP	136.00	152.00

NATURE'S BEAUTIFUL BUTTERFLIES

YR	NAME	LIMIT	ISSUE	TREND
89	BLUE TEMORA	OP	39.00	45.00
90	MONARCH	OP	39.00	45.00
90	PURPLE EMPEROR	OP	45.00	45.00
90	YELLOW SWALLOWTAIL	OP	39.00	45.00
91	ADONIS	OP	45.00	45.00
91	MALACHITE	OP	45.00	45.00

NORTH AMERICAN BIRD PAIRS

YR	NAME	LIMIT	ISSUE	TREND
90	HUMMINGBIRDS	OP	119.00	119.00
91	BLUE JAY PAIRS	9500	119.00	119.00
91	CHICKADEES	9500	119.00	119.00
92	CARDINAL	OP	119.00	119.00

NORTH AMERICAN WILDLIFE

YR	NAME	LIMIT	ISSUE	TREND
91	WHITE-TAILED DEER	OP	195.00	195.00

OWLS OF AMERICA

YR	NAME	LIMIT	ISSUE	TREND
88	SNOWY OWL	OP	136.00	136.00
89	BARN OWL	OP	136.00	136.00
90	SCREECH OWL	OP	136.00	136.00
91	GREAT HORNED OWL	9500	136.00	136.00

PARENT & CHILD BIRD PAIRS

YR	NAME	LIMIT	ISSUE	TREND
92	BLUE JAY PAIRS	OP	119.00	119.00

PORCELAIN DUCK COLLECTION

YR	NAME	LIMIT	ISSUE	TREND
91	MALLARD DUCK	OP	45.00	45.00
91	WOOD DUCK	OP	45.00	45.00
92	BLUE WINGED TEAL DUCK	OP	45.00	45.00

YR	NAME	LIMIT	ISSUE	TREND
*			**SANTA CLAUS COLLECTIONS**	
90	FATHER CHRISTMAS	OP	136.00	136.00
91	AMERICANA SANTA	OP	136.00	136.00
91	KRIS KRINGLE	OP	136.00	136.00
*			**STREET CRIER COLLECTION**	
90	FRENCH FLOWER MAIDEN	OP	136.00	136.00
91	BELGIAN LACE MAKER	OP	136.00	136.00
*		**WILDLIFE OF THE SEVEN CONTINENTS**		
84	NORTH AMERICAN BIGHORN SHEEP	OP	120.00	120.00
85	ASIAN ELEPHANT	OP	120.00	120.00
85	AUSTRALIAN KOALA	OP	120.00	120.00
86	SOUTH AMERICAN PUMA	OP	120.00	120.00
87	ANTARCTIC SEALS	OP	136.00	136.00
87	EUROPEAN RED DEER	OP	136.00	136.00
88	AFRICAN LION	OP	136.00	136.00
*			**WOODLAND ANIMALS**	
90	RACCOON	OP	39.00	39.00
90	RED SQUIRREL	OP	39.00	39.00
91	CHIPMUNK	OP	39.00	39.00

LLADRO

YR	NAME	LIMIT	ISSUE	TREND
*				**ANGELS**
69	ANGEL WITH BABY L4635G/M	OP	15.00	120.00
69	ANGEL WITH HORN L4540G/M	OP	13.00	92.00
69	ANGEL'S GROUP L4542G/M	OP	31.00	200.00
69	ANGEL, BLACK L4537G/M	OP	13.00	92.00
69	ANGEL, CHINESE L4536G/M	OP	13.00	92.00
69	ANGEL, PRAYING L4538G/M	OP	13.00	92.00
69	ANGEL, RECLINING L4541G/M	OP	13.00	92.00
69	ANGEL, THINKING L4539G/M	OP	13.00	92.00
72	ANGEL WITH CLARINET L1232G	RT	60.00	425.00
72	ANGEL WITH FLUTE L1233G	RT	60.00	425.00
72	ANGEL WITH LUTE L1231G	RT	60.00	425.00
77	ANGEL, DREAMING L4961G	OP	40.00	125.00
77	ANGEL, WONDERING L4962G	OP	40.00	125.00
77	CURIOUS ANGEL L4960G	OP	40.00	125.00
77	MIME ANGEL L4959G	OP	40.00	125.00
85	CAREFREE ANGEL WITH FLUTE L1463G	RT	220.00	650.00
85	CAREFREE ANGEL WITH LYRE L1464G	RT	220.00	650.00
90	ANGEL CARE L5727G	OP	190.00	210.00
90	ANGELIC VOICE L5724G	OP	125.00	145.00
90	HEAVENLY CHIMES L5723G	OP	100.00	120.00
90	HEAVENLY DREAMER L5728G	OP	100.00	120.00
90	MAKING A WISH L5725G	OP	125.00	145.00
90	SWEEP AWAY THE CLOUDS L5726G	OP	125.00	145.00
91	HEAVENLY SWING L1739G	1000	1,900.00	2050.00
93	ANGELIC MELODY L5963G	YR	145.00	165.00
*			**ANIMAL MINIATURES**	
85	MINIATURE BISON ATTACKING L5313G	RT	58.00	190.00
85	MINIATURE BISON RESTING L5312G	RT	50.00	140.00
85	MINIATURE CAT L5308G	RT	35.00	120.00
85	MINIATURE COCKER SPANIEL L5309G	RT	35.00	125.00
85	MINIATURE COCKER SPANIEL L5310G	RT	35.00	125.00
85	MINIATURE DEER L5314G	RT	40.00	170.00
85	MINIATURE DROMEDARY L5315G	RT	45.00	150.00
85	MINIATURE GIRAFFE L5316G	RT	50.00	200.00
85	MINIATURE KITTEN L5307G	RT	35.00	100.00
85	MINIATURE LAMB L5317G	RT	30.00	170.00
85	MINIATURE PUPPIES (3) L5311G	RT	65.00	175.00
85	MINIATURE SEAL FAMILY L5318G	RT	78.00	120.00
86	BALANCING ACT (SEAL) L5392G	RT	35.00	170.00
86	CURIOSITY (DOG) L5393G	RT	25.00	140.00
86	ON GUARD L5350G	RT	50.00	260.00
86	POOR PUPPY L5394G	RT	25.00	190.00
86	WOE IS ME (DOG) L5351G	RT	45.00	190.00
86	WOLF HOUND L5356G	RT	45.00	190.00
87	COUGAR L5435G	RT	65.00	240.00
87	ELEPHANT L5438G	RT	50.00	250.00
87	KANGAROO L5433G	RT	65.00	260.00
87	LION L5436G	RT	50.00	200.00
87	MONKEY L5432G	RT	60.00	190.00
87	POLAR BEAR L5434G	OP	65.00	110.00
87	RHINO L5437G	RT	50.00	175.00
*			**ANIMALS**	
69	AFGHAN L1069G	RT	36.00	600.00
69	BEAGLE PUPPY (LYING) L1072G	RT	16.50	250.00
69	BEAGLE PUPPY (POUNCING) L1070G	RT	17.00	350.00
69	BEAGLE PUPPY (SITTING) L1071G	RT	16.50	275.00
69	DEER L1064G	RT	28.00	375.00
69	FOX AND CUB L1065G	RT	17.50	400.00
69	GREAT DANE L1068G	RT	55.00	475.00
69	HORSE GROUP (2) L4655G	OP	110.00	760.00
69	HORSES GROUP (3) L1021G	OP	950.00	2380.00
69	HORSES GROUP/WHITE (3) L1022M	OP	465.00	2100.00
69	OLD DOG L1067G	RT	40.00	600.00

YR	NAME	LIMIT	ISSUE	TREND
69	RAM L1046	RT	*	600.00
69	TWO HORSES L4597	RT	240.00	1200.00
71	ELEPHANTS WALKING L1150G	OP	100.00	795.00
71	ORIENTAL HORSE L2030M	RT	1,100.00	4500.00
71	TWO ELEPHANTS L1151G	OP	45.00	420.00
72	ATTENTIVE POLAR BEAR L1207G	OP	16.00	75.00
72	POLAR BEAR L1208G	OP	16.00	75.00
72	SEATED POLAR BEAR L1209G	OP	16.00	75.00
73	HUNTING SCENE L1238	RT	800.00	2850.00
78	FLIGHT OF THE GAZELLES L1352	RT	1,450.00	3100.00
78	HORSE HEADS L3511M	RT	260.00	625.00
82	BORN FREE L1420G	OP	1,520.00	3250.00
82	ELK L3501M	RT	950.00	1500.00
83	KITTY CONFRONTATION L1442G	OP	155.00	285.00
83	PURR-FECT L1444G	OP	350.00	615.00
85	ANTELOPE DRINKING L5302G	RT	215.00	640.00
85	GAZELLE L5271G	RT	205.00	550.00
85	PACK OF HUNTING DOGS L5342	RT	925.00	2000.00
85	THOROUGHBRED HORSE L5340	RT	625.00	1100.00
90	BEAUTIFUL BURRO L5683G	RT	280.00	365.00
90	FAWN AND A FRIEND, A L5674G	RT	450.00	525.00
90	HI THERE! L5672G	RT	450.00	525.00
90	QUIET MOMENT, A L5673G	RT	450.00	525.00
92	ATTENTIVE BUNNY L5905G	OP	75.00	75.00
92	EASTER BUNNIES L5902G	RT	240.00	250.00
92	HIPPITY HOP L5886G	RT	95.00	120.00
92	PREENING BUNNY L5906G	RT	75.00	85.00
92	SITTING BUNNY L5907G	OP	75.00	85.00
92	SLEEPING BUNNY L5904G	RT	75.00	80.00
92	SNACK TIME L5889G	RT	95.00	120.00
92	THAT TICKLES L5888G	RT	95.00	120.00
92	WASHING UP L5887G	RT	95.00	115.00
*				**ASSORTED FIGURINES**
69	DON JUAN L4609G	RT	*	715.00
69	GIRL WITH CALLA LILIES L4650G	OP	18.00	155.00
72	PEACE/ALLEGORY TO PEACE L1202G	RT	550.00	7000.00
73	COUNTRY WOMAN L2049	RT	200.00	1300.00
74	EMBROIDERER L4865G	RT	115.00	700.00
74	EXQUISITE SCENT/SCHOOLGIRL L1313G	RT	201.00	620.00
74	ON THE FARM L1306G	RT	130.00	285.00
74	SEA BREEZE/WINDBLOWN GIRL L4922G	OP	150.00	375.00
74	SPRING BREEZE L4936G	OP	145.00	410.00
76	COUNTRY LADY L1330	RT	900.00	1570.00
77	GIRL WITH LILIES SITTING L4972G	RT	65.00	180.00
78	GIRL WATERING/GROWING ROSES L1354G	RT	485.00	620.00
79	DANCER L5050G	OP	85.00	205.00
80	FLOWERS IN POT L-5028G	RT	325.00	600.00
80	PLANNING THE DAY L-5026G	RT	90.00	260.00
82	CAT GIRL/KITTY L-5164G	RT	125.00	460.00
82	WINTER WONDERLAND L1429G	OP	1,025.00	2125.00
84	BOY GRADUATE L5198G	OP	160.00	290.00
84	CHARLIE THE TRAMP L5233G	RT	150.00	775.00
84	GIRL GRADUATE L5199G	OP	160.00	285.00
84	ON THE LAKE L5216G	RT	660.00	975.00
84	PREDICTING THE FUTURE L-5191G	RT	135.00	430.00
85	CLASSIC FALL L1466G	RT	620.00	1000.00
85	CLASSIC SPRING L1465G	RT	620.00	1000.00
85	LA GIACONDA (BUST) L5337G	RT	110.00	500.00
85	LOVE BOAT L5343	RT	825.00	1350.00
85	NATURE GIRL L5346G	RT	450.00	850.00
86	AT THE BALL L5398G	RT	375.00	700.00
86	CONSIDERATION (BUST) L5355M	RT	100.00	225.00
86	LOVERS SERENADE L5382G	RT	350.00	700.00
87	CARNIVAL TIME L5423	RT	2,400.00	3300.00
87	COURTING TIME L5409	RT	425.00	525.00
87	POETRY OF LOVE L5442G	RT	500.00	875.00
89	CIRCUS PARADE L1609G	750	5,200.00	6550.00
90	BARNYARD REFLECTIONS L5684G	RT	460.00	600.00
90	BARNYARD SCENE L5659G	OP	200.00	245.00
90	BREEZY AFTERNOON L5682G/M	OP	180.00	195.00
90	KING'S GUARD, THE- L5642G	RT	950.00	1100.00
90	MAY DANCE L5662G	OP	170.00	210.00
90	SPRING DANCE L5663G	OP	170.00	210.00
90	STREET HARMONIES L5692G	RT	3,200.00	3500.00
90	SUNNING IN IPANEMA L5660G	RT	370.00	500.00
90	TRINO AT THE BEACH L5666G	RT	390.00	500.00
90	TWILIGHT YEARS L5677G	RT	370.00	425.00
91	ALLEGORY OF LIBERTY L5819G	OP	1,950.00	2100.00
91	CHARM (BUST) L5801	RT	650.00	750.00
91	DANCE OF LOVE (BUST) L5820G	RT	575.00	650.00
91	ELEGANT PROMENADE L5802G	OP	775.00	825.00
91	LOVER'S PARADISE L5779G	RT	2,250.00	2450.00
91	ONWARD! L1742G	RT	2,500.00	2900.00
91	SHALL WE DANCE? L5799G	RT	600.00	710.00
92	AFTERNOON JAUNT L5855G	RT	420.00	525.00

YR	NAME	LIMIT	ISSUE	TREND
92	AT THE BALL L5859G	OP	295.00	330.00
92	EASTER BONNETS L5852G	RT	265.00	380.00
92	FEATHERED FANTASY L5851G	RT	1,200.00	1300.00
92	GRAND ENTRANCE L5857G	RT	265.00	315.00
92	LOVING FAMILY, THE- L5848G	RT	950.00	1060.00
92	QUIET AFTERNOON, A L5843G	RT	1,050.00	1180.00
92	READER, THE (BUST) L3560	200	2,650.00	2815.00
92	SPRING SPLENDOR L5898G	OP	440.00	450.00
92	WAITING TO DANCE L5858G	RT	295.00	350.00
93	AUTUMN GLOW (BUST, GRES) L2250M	RT	750.00	825.00
93	HOLIDAY GLOW (BUST, GRES) L2249	RT	750.00	825.00
94	AT PEACE (BUST) L3565M	1000	1,750.00	1750.00
94	CIRCUS FANFARE L1783G	RT	14,240.00	14300.00
*		**BALLET AND HARLEQUIN FIGURINES**		
69	BALLERINA/WAITING BACKSTAGE L4559G	RT	110.00	475.00
69	IDYLL L1017G/M	RT	115.00	700.00
69	SAD HARLEQUIN L4558G	RT	110.00	570.00
69	SEATED BALLERINA L4504G	RT	*	990.00
69	SEATED HARLEQUIN L4503G/M	RT	*	990.00
72	YOUNG HARLEQUIN L1229G	OP	70.00	520.00
73	DEATH OF THE SWAN L4855G	OP	45.00	330.00
73	PASSIONATE DANCE L2051M	RT	375.00	4275.00
74	CLOSING SCENE L4935G	RT	180.00	495.00
74	LADY WITH YOUNG HARLEQUIN L4883G	RT	100.00	2000.00
77	INFANTILE CANDOR L4963G	RT	285.00	1200.00
78	BETH L1358G	RT	75.00	210.00
78	HEATHER L1359G	RT	75.00	210.00
78	JULIA L1361G	RT	75.00	210.00
78	LAURA L1360G	RT	75.00	210.00
78	PHYLLIS L1356G	RT	75.00	210.00
78	SHELLEY L1357G	RT	75.00	210.00
79	ACT II L5035G	OP	700.00	1425.00
80	AFTER THE DANCE L-5092G	RT	165.00	380.00
80	BALLET FIRST STEP L5094G	RT	165.00	380.00
80	DANCING PARTNER, A L5903G	RT	165.00	380.00
80	HARLEQUIN "A" L5075G	RT	218.00	440.00
80	HARLEQUIN "B" L5076G	RT	185.00	360.00
80	HARLEQUIN "C" L5077G	RT	185.00	475.00
80	TAKING A BOW L5095G	RT	165.00	300.00
82	LOST LOVE L5128G	RT	400.00	665.00
83	CLOSING SCENE/WHITE L4935.30M	RT	213.00	455.00
83	DEATH OF THE SWAN, WHITE L4855.30M	RT	110.00	250.00
84	BALLET TRIO L5235G	OP	785.00	1675.00
85	WEARY BALLERINA L5275G/M	RT	175.00	325.00
90	FIRST BALLET L5714G	OP	370.00	420.00
91	BACKSTAGE PREPARATION L5817G/M	RT	490.00	570.00
91	CURTAIN CALL L5814G/M	RT	490.00	570.00
91	IN FULL RELEVE L5815G/M	RT	490.00	570.00
91	ON HER TOES L5818G/M	RT	490.00	570.00
91	PRECOCIOUS BALLERINA L5793G	RT	575.00	655.00
91	PRIMA BALLERINA L5816G/M	RT	490.00	570.00
92	DRESSING FOR THE BALLET L5865G	RT	395.00	470.00
92	FINAL TOUCHES L5866G	RT	395.00	470.00
92	SWAN BALLET L5920G	OP	210.00	215.00
93	GRACEFUL MOMENT L6033G	3000	1,475.00	1475.00
93	NUTCRACKER SUITE L5935G	OP	620.00	620.00
*				**BIRDS**
69	BIRD L1054G	RT	14.00	140.00
69	DOVE L1015G	RT	21.00	150.00
69	DOVE L1016G	RT	36.00	200.00
69	HEN L1041G	RT	13.00	100.00
71	KISSING DOVES L1169G	OP	32.00	155.00
71	KISSING DOVES L1169M	RT	32.00	200.00
72	EAGLES L1189	RT	900.00	3000.00
72	GROUP OF EAGLE OWLS L-1223M	RT	225.00	1000.00
72	SEA BIRDS WITH NEST L1194	RT	600.00	2500.00
72	TURKEY GROUP L1196M	RT	650.00	2500.00
73	FOREST, THE- L1243G	RT	625.00	4000.00
73	TURTLEDOVES L1240M	RT	500.00	2300.00
74	DUCK JUMPING L1265G	OP	20.00	90.00
74	DUCK RUNNING L1263G	OP	20.00	90.00
74	DUCKLINGS L1307G	OP	48.00	150.00
74	DUCKS AT THE POND L1317G	RT	4,250.00	5800.00
74	FLYING DUCK L1264G	OP	20.00	90.00
76	HERONS L1319G	OP	1,550.00	2625.00
77	DOVE GROUP L1335G	RT	950.00	1700.00
77	FLYING PARTRIDGES L2064	RT	3,500.00	4300.00
78	SPRING BIRDS L1368G	RT	1,600.00	2500.00
80	TURTLEDOVE NEST L3519	RT	3,600.00	5500.00
81	EAGLES NEST L3523	RT	6,900.00	12000.00
83	CRANES L1456G	OP	1,000.00	1950.00
83	HOW DO YOU DO? L1439G	OP	185.00	295.00
84	GRACEFUL SWAN L-5230G	OP	35.00	95.00
84	PENGUIN L-5247G	RT	70.00	225.00
84	PENGUIN L-5248G	RT	70.00	225.00

YR	NAME	LIMIT	ISSUE	TREND
84	PENGUIN L-5249G	RT	70.00	225.00
84	SWAN WITH WINGS SPREAD L-5231G	OP	50.00	135.00
85	FLOCK OF BIRDS L1462G	1500	1,125.00	1750.00
87	BARN OWL L5421G	RT	120.00	200.00
87	GREAT GRAY OWL L5419G	RT	190.00	250.00
87	HAWK OWL L5422G	RT	120.00	200.00
87	HORNED OWL L5420G	RT	150.00	225.00
87	SHORT EARED OWL L5418G	RT	200.00	300.00
89	BOWING CRANE L1613G	OP	385.00	485.00
89	COURTING CRANES L1611G	OP	565.00	695.00
89	DANCING CRANE L1614G	OP	385.00	485.00
89	FLUTTERING CRANE L1598G	RT	115.00	150.00
89	FREEDOM L5602G	RT	875.00	1015.00
89	LANDING CRANE L1600G	RT	115.00	150.00
89	NESTING CRANE L1599G	RT	95.00	120.00
89	PREENING CRANES L1612G	OP	385.00	485.00
90	FOLLOW ME L5722G	OP	140.00	160.00
90	MARSHLAND MATES L5691G	OP	950.00	1200.00
91	LIBERTY EAGLE L1738G	1500	1,000.00	1100.00
92	JUSTICE EAGLE L5863G	1500	1,700.00	1840.00
92	SWANS TAKE FLIGHT L5912G	OP	2,850.00	2950.00
*				**BRIDAL FIGURINES**
72	WEDDING L4808G/M	OP	50.00	190.00
82	WEDDING/MATRIMONY L1404G	RT	320.00	500.00
83	HERE COMES THE BRIDE L1446G	RT	518.00	900.00
85	OVER THE THRESHOLD L5282G	OP	150.00	290.00
85	WEDDING DAY L5274G	OP	240.00	435.00
86	MY WEDDING DAY L1494G	RT	800.00	1500.00
87	BRIDE, THE L5439G	RT	250.00	440.00
87	I LOVE YOU TRULY L1528G	OP	375.00	595.00
89	BRIDESMAID L5598G	OP	150.00	180.00
89	WEDDING CAKE L5587G	RT	595.00	750.00
91	BRIDAL PORTRAIT L5742G	RT	480.00	590.00
91	I DO L5835G	OP	165.00	190.00
91	VENICE VOWS L1732G	1500	3,755.00	4100.00
92	DOWN THE AISLE L5903G	RT	295.00	350.00
92	FROM THIS DAY FORWARD L5885G	OP	265.00	285.00
95	LOVE AND MARRIAGE L1802G	1500	2,650.00	2650.00
*				**CAPRICHO SERIES**
87	SM. BROWN FLOWER BASKET L1554.10M	RT	*	300.00
87	SM. BROWN FLOWER BASKET-BLUE LACE L1554M	RT	*	350.00
87	SM. BROWN FLOWER BASKET-PINK LACE L1553M	RT	*	350.00
87	SM. GREEN FLOWER BASKET L1554.30M	RT	*	325.00
87	SMALL VASE WITH IRIS L1551M	RT	199.00	475.00
87	VIOLET FAN W/BASE L1546M	YR	675.00	1000.00
87	WHITE FAN W/BASE L1546.03M	YR	675.00	1000.00
88	BASKET OF MARGARITAS L1543M	RT	550.00	1000.00
88	BASKET OF ROSES L1544M	RT	*	700.00
88	IRIS ARRANGEMENT L1542M	RT	*	1100.00
88	ORCHID ARRANGEMENT L1541M	RT	*	1300.00
88	PINK BALLET SLIPPERS L1540M	RT	275.00	450.00
88	WHITE BALLET SLIPPERS L1540.3M	RT	275.00	450.00
*			**CHILDREN WITH ANIMALS OR BIRDS**	
69	GIRL WITH FLOWERS L1088G	RT	45.00	700.00
69	GIRL WITH UMBRELLA L4510G	RT	40.00	350.00
71	BOYS PLAYING WITH GOAT L1129G	RT	*	2000.00
71	DOG IN THE BASKET L1128G	RT	18.00	450.00
71	PLATERO AND MARCELINO L1181G	RT	50.00	350.00
72	CARESS AND REST L1246G	RT	50.00	300.00
72	FRIENDSHIP L1230G/M	RT	68.00	400.00
73	FEEDING THE DUCKS L4849G/M	RT	60.00	350.00
74	AGGRESSIVE DUCK L1288G	RT	170.00	475.00
74	DEVOTION L1278G	RT	140.00	450.00
74	FEEDING TIME L1277G/M	RT	120.00	400.00
74	FOLLOWING HER CATS L1309G	OP	120.00	310.00
74	GIRL WITH PUPPIES L1311G	RT	120.00	350.00
74	SEESAW L4867G	RT	55.00	375.00
74	SWEETY/HONEY LICKERS L1248G	RT	100.00	500.00
78	NAUGHTY DOG L4982G	RT	130.00	300.00
79	AVOIDING THE GOOSE L5033G	RT	160.00	360.00
79	DOG AND CAT/LITTLE FRISKIES L5032G	RT	108.00	300.00
80	MY HUNGRY BROOD L5074G	RT	295.00	425.00
82	STUBBORN DONKEY L5178G	RT	250.00	500.00
84	ARACELY WITH HER PET DUCK L5202G	RT	125.00	300.00
84	JOSEFA FEEDING HER DUCK L5201G	RT	125.00	300.00
85	PLAYING WITH DUCKS AT THE POND L5303G	RT	425.00	700.00
86	LITTER OF FUN L5364G	OP	275.00	465.00
86	THIS ONE'S MINE L5376G	RT	300.00	575.00
87	BEDTIME/SLEEPY TRIO L5443G	RT	190.00	320.00
87	I HOPE SHE DOES L5450G	RT	190.00	340.00
89	JOY IN A BASKET L5595G	RT	215.00	315.00
89	MY NEW PET L5549G	OP	150.00	185.00
89	PLAYFUL ROMP L5594G	RT	215.00	300.00
90	BEHAVE! L5703G	RT	230.00	285.00
90	CAN I HELP? L5689G	RT	250.00	325.00

YR	NAME	LIMIT	ISSUE	TREND
90	CAT NAP L5640G	OP	125.00	145.00
90	CRADLE OF KITTENS, A L5784G	RT	360.00	400.00
90	DOG'S BEST FRIEND L5688G	OP	250.00	295.00
90	SLEEPY KITTEN L5712G	OP	110.00	130.00
90	WE CAN'T PLAY L5706G	OP	200.00	235.00
91	BEST FOOT FORWARD L5738G	RT	280.00	325.00
91	BIG SISTER L5735G	OP	650.00	685.00
91	COME OUT AND PLAY L5797G	RT	275.00	325.00
91	DON'T FORGET ME L5743G	OP	150.00	160.00
91	HOLD HER STILL L5753G	RT	650.00	725.00
91	INTERRUPTED NAP L5760G	RT	325.00	425.00
91	LAP FULL OF LOVE L5739G	RT	275.00	320.00
91	MY PUPPIES L5807G	RT	325.00	400.00
91	NOT TOO CLOSE L5781G	RT	365.00	450.00
91	OUT FOR A ROMP L5761G	RT	375.00	450.00
91	PRECIOUS CARGO L5794G	RT	460.00	575.00
91	PRESTO! L5759G	RT	275.00	325.00
91	PUPPET SHOW L5736G	RT	280.00	335.00
91	SHARING SWEETS L5836G	RT	220.00	260.00
91	SING WITH ME L5837G	RT	240.00	265.00
92	JUST A LITTLE MORE L5908G	RT	370.00	400.00
92	LOVING MOUSE L5883G	RT	285.00	325.00
92	MAKING A WISH L5910G	OP	790.00	825.00
92	MISCHIEVOUS MOUSE L5881G	OP	285.00	295.00
92	RESTFUL MOUSE L5882G	RT	285.00	325.00
92	TAKE YOUR MEDICINE L5921G	OP	360.00	370.00
*			**CHILDREN'S THEMES**	
69	GIRL MANICURING L1082G/M	RT	14.50	260.00
69	GIRL WITH BRUSH L1081G/M	RT	14.50	285.00
69	GIRL WITH DOLL L1083G/M	RT	14.50	285.00
69	GIRL WITH MOTHER'S SHOE L1084G/M	RT	14.50	260.00
71	GIRL WITH BONNET L1147G/M	RT	20.00	285.00
71	PUPPY LOVE L1127G	RT	50.00	350.00
72	BOY MEETS GIRL L1188G	RT	310.00	400.00
72	GIRL WITH DOLL L1211G/M	RT	72.00	450.00
74	SEESAW L1255G/M	RT	110.00	600.00
77	GIRL WITH WATERING CAN/BLOOMING ROSES L1339G	RT	325.00	500.00
77	LITTLE RED RIDING HOOD L-4965G	RT	210.00	550.00
80	LITTLE FLOWER SELLER L-5082G	RT	750.00	2700.00
80	NOSTALGIA L5071G	RT	185.00	360.00
80	PRECOCIOUS COURTSHIP L5072G	RT	327.00	700.00
80	ROSES FOR MY MOM/CUTTING THE FLOWERS L5088G	RT	645.00	1200.00
80	SLEIGH RIDE L5037G	RT	585.00	1250.00
82	"A" IS FOR AMY L-5145G	RT	110.00	1500.00
82	"E" IS FOR ELLEN L5146G	RT	110.00	1200.00
82	"I" IS FOR IVY L5147G	RT	100.00	600.00
82	"O" IS FOR OLIVIA L5148G	RT	100.00	450.00
82	"U" IS FOR URSULA L5149G	RT	100.00	450.00
82	BABY WITH PACIFIER (TEETHING) L-5102G	RT	58.00	275.00
82	BALLOON SELLER/BALLOONS FOR SALE L5141G	RT	90.00	275.00
82	BARROW OF BLOSSOMS, A L1419G	OP	390.00	675.00
82	BUDDING BLOSSOMS/FROM MY GARDEN L1416G	RT	140.00	300.00
82	FLOWER HARMONY L1418G	RT	130.00	285.00
82	GAYLE/LITTLE BALLET GIRL L-5109G	RT	85.00	350.00
82	KARENA/LITTLE BALLET GIRL L-5107G	RT	85.00	325.00
82	NATURE'S BOUNTY L1417G	RT	160.00	400.00
82	PONDERING L5173G	RT	160.00	600.00
82	REVERENT MATADOR/LITTLE BOY BULLFIGHTER L-5115G	RT	123.00	425.00
82	SALLIE/LITTLE BALLET GIRL L-5104G	RT	85.00	300.00
84	AUTUMN L5218G/M	OP	90.00	200.00
84	DANCING THE POLKA L5252G	RT	205.00	500.00
84	FISHING WITH GRAMPS L5215G	OP	410.00	895.00
84	FOLK DANCING L5256G	RT	205.00	500.00
84	PRETTY PICKINGS L5222G/M	OP	80.00	165.00
84	SPRING IS HERE L5223G/M	OP	80.00	165.00
84	SPRING L5217G/M	OP	90.00	200.00
84	STORYTIME L5229G	RT	245.00	950.00
84	SUMMER L5219G/M	OP	90.00	195.00
84	SWEET SCENT L5221G/M	OP	80.00	165.00
84	WINTER L5220G/M	OP	90.00	195.00
85	BOY ON CAROUSEL HORSE L1470G	OP	470.00	945.00
85	CHILDREN AT PLAY L5304	RT	220.00	525.00
85	FALL CLEAN-UP L5286G	OP	295.00	565.00
85	GIRL ON CAROUSEL HORSE L1469G	OP	470.00	945.00
85	GLORIOUS SPRING L5284G	OP	355.00	720.00
85	ICE CREAM VENDOR L5325G	RT	380.00	700.00
85	LOVE IN BLOOM L5292G	OP	225.00	435.00
85	SUMMER ON THE FARM L5285G	OP	235.00	455.00
85	VISIT WITH GRANNY, A L5305G	RT	275.00	575.00
85	WINTER FROST L5287G	OP	270.00	520.00
86	BEDTIME L5347G	OP	300.00	545.00
86	BOY & HIS BUNNY L1507G/M	RT	90.00	275.00
86	CHILDREN'S GAMES L5379G	RT	325.00	650.00
86	FORGOTTEN L1502G/M	RT	125.00	300.00
86	IN THE MEADOW L1508G/M	RT	100.00	275.00

YR	NAME	LIMIT	ISSUE	TREND
86	LITTLE SCULPTOR L5358G	RT	160.00	350.00
86	NATURE BOY L1505G/M	RT	100.00	275.00
86	NEGLECTED L1503G/M	RT	125.00	300.00
86	NEW FRIEND, A L1506G/M	RT	110.00	275.00
86	PUPPET PAINTER, THE- L5396G	OP	500.00	850.00
86	RAG DOLL L1501G/M	RT	125.00	300.00
86	RAGAMUFFIN L1500G/M	RT	125.00	300.00
86	SPRING FLOWERS L1509G/M	RT	100.00	275.00
86	STILL LIFE L5363G	RT	180.00	250.00
86	STITCH IN TIME, A L5344G	RT	425.00	800.00
86	SWEET HARVEST L5380G	RT	450.00	800.00
86	TRY THIS ONE L5361G	RT	225.00	400.00
87	AT ATTENTION L5407G	RT	175.00	310.00
87	BUGLER, THE L5406G	RT	175.00	350.00
87	CADET CAPTAIN L5404G	RT	175.00	360.00
87	CIRCUS TRAIN L1517G	RT	2,900.00	4500.00
87	DRUMMER BOY, THE L5403G	RT	225.00	400.00
87	FLAG BEARER, THE - L5405G	RT	200.00	400.00
87	HAPPY BIRTHDAY L5429G	OP	100.00	155.00
87	MUSIC TIME L5430G	RT	500.00	700.00
87	MY BEST FRIEND L5401G	OP	150.00	240.00
87	NAPTIME L5448G/M	OP	135.00	260.00
87	ONE, TWO, THREE L5426G	RT	240.00	420.00
87	TIME TO REST L5399G	RT	175.00	315.00
87	WANDERER, THE- L5400G	OP	150.00	245.00
89	BABY DOLL L5608G	OP	150.00	180.00
89	HELLO FLOWERS L5543G	RT	385.00	550.00
89	LET'S MAKE UP L5555G	OP	215.00	265.00
89	PRETTY POSIES L5548G	RT	425.00	575.00
89	PUPPY DOG TAILS L5539G	OP	1,200.00	1675.00
90	ACADEMY DAYS L5768G	RT	280.00	350.00
90	AFTER SCHOOL L5707G	RT	280.00	350.00
90	BACK TO SCHOOL L5702G	RT	350.00	425.00
90	BETWEEN CLASSES L5709G	RT	280.00	350.00
90	CATHY L5643G	OP	200.00	235.00
90	CHRISTMAS WISH, A L5711G	RT	350.00	410.00
90	CINDY L5646G	OP	190.00	215.00
90	COURTNEY L5648G	OP	200.00	230.00
90	DON'T LOOK DOWN L5698G	OP	330.00	405.00
90	ELIZABETH L5645G	OP	190.00	215.00
90	FANTASY FRIEND L5710G	RT	420.00	525.00
90	GIDDY UP L5664G	RT	190.00	250.00
90	HANG ON! L5665G	RT	225.00	300.00
90	I FEEL PRETTY L5678G	RT	190.00	245.00
90	IN NO HURRY L5679G	RT	550.00	650.00
90	JUST A LITTLE KISS L5701G	RT	320.00	375.00
90	LAND OF THE GIANTS L5716G	RT	275.00	400.00
90	MY FIRST CLASS L5708G	RT	280.00	350.00
90	NOTHING TO DO L5649G	RT	190.00	230.00
90	OVER THE CLOUDS L5697G	OP	275.00	310.00
90	ROCK A BYE BABY L5717G	OP	300.00	365.00
90	SARA L5647G	OP	200.00	230.00
90	SHARING SECRETS L5720G	RT	290.00	340.00
90	SITTING PRETTY L5699G	OP	300.00	340.00
90	SNOW MAN, THE- L5713G	OP	300.00	350.00
90	SUSAN L5644G	OP	190.00	215.00
90	TRAVELING IN STYLE L5680G	RT	425.00	525.00
91	CAREFREE L5790G	OP	300.00	325.00
91	CAROUSEL CANTER L5732G	RT	1,700.00	2000.00
91	CAROUSEL CHARM L5731G	RT	1,700.00	2000.00
91	DANCE CLASS L5741G	RT	340.00	400.00
91	FAITHFUL STEED L5769G	RT	300.00	400.00
91	LITTLE DREAMERS L5772G/M	OP	230.00	240.00
91	LITTLE PRINCE L5737G	RT	295.00	330.00
91	LITTLE VIRGIN L5752G	RT	295.00	330.00
91	MY CHORES L5782G	RT	325.00	395.00
91	OUT FOR A SPIN L5770G	RT	390.00	475.00
91	PLAYING TAG L5804G	RT	170.00	200.00
91	TICKLING L5806G/M	RT	130.00	175.00
91	TUMBLING L5805G/M	RT	130.00	175.00
91	WALK WITH FATHER L5751G	RT	375.00	475.00
92	ALL DRESSED UP L5909G	RT	440.00	475.00
92	BOUQUET OF BLOSSOMS L5895G	RT	295.00	295.00
92	FLIRTATIOUS JESTER L5844G	RT	890.00	925.00
92	FRAGRANT BOUQUET L5862G	OP	350.00	370.00
92	FRIENDSHIP IN BLOOM L5893G	RT	650.00	715.00
92	GUEST OF HONOR L5877G	RT	195.00	225.00
92	JUST ONE MORE L5899G	RT	450.00	500.00
92	SISTER'S PRIDE L5878G	RT	595.00	650.00
92	TRIMMING THE TREE L5897G	OP	900.00	925.00
92	VOYAGE OF COLUMBUS, THE- L5847G	RT	1,450.00	1650.00
*				**CLOWNS**
69	CLOWN WITH CONCERTINA L1027G	RT	95.00	750.00
71	CLOWN L4618G	OP	70.00	415.00
71	CLOWN WITH VIOLIN L1126G	RT	71.00	2000.00

YR	NAME	LIMIT	ISSUE	TREND
71	PELUSA CLOWN L1125G	RT	70.00	2000.00
76	LANGUID CLOWN L4924G	RT	200.00	1200.00
80	CLOWN WITH CLOCK L5056G	RT	290.00	800.00
80	CLOWN WITH CONCERTINA L5058G	RT	290.00	600.00
80	CLOWN WITH SAXOPHONE L5059G	RT	290.00	600.00
80	CLOWN WITH VIOLIN L5057G	RT	270.00	800.00
80	GIRL CLOWN WITH TRUMPET L5060G	RT	290.00	550.00
82	CLOWN'S HEAD (BUST) L5129G	OP	220.00	455.00
82	PENSIVE CLOWN (BUST) L5130G	OP	250.00	680.00
85	PIERROT WITH CONCERTINA L5279G	OP	95.00	160.00
85	PIERROT WITH PUPPY & BALL L5278G	OP	95.00	160.00
85	PIERROT WITH PUPPY L5277G	OP	95.00	160.00
89	BLUES, THE (BUST) L5600G	RT	265.00	400.00
89	FINE MELODY (BUST) L5585G	RT	225.00	325.00
89	MELANCHOLY (BUST) L5542G	OP	375.00	455.00
89	REFLECTING (BUST) L5612G	RT	335.00	420.00
89	SAD CLOWN (BUST) L5611G	RT	335.00	420.00
89	SAD NOTE (BUST) L5586G	RT	185.00	350.00
89	STAR STRUCK (BUST) L5610G	RT	335.00	420.00
91	CHECKING THE TIME L5762G	RT	170.00	600.00
91	HATS OFF TO FUN L5765G	RT	475.00	575.00
91	HAVING A BALL L5813G	OP	225.00	240.00
91	LITTLEST CLOWN L5811G	OP	225.00	240.00
91	MAGIC OF LAUGHTER, THE- L5771G	RT	950.00	1075.00
91	ON THE MOVE L5838G	RT	340.00	400.00
91	SEEDS OF LAUGHTER L5764G	RT	525.00	610.00
91	TIRED FRIEND L5812G	OP	225.00	245.00
91	YOUTH L5800	RT	650.00	725.00
92	ALL TUCKERED OUT L5846G/M	OP	220.00	255.00
92	CIRCUS MAGIC L5892G	RT	470.00	500.00
92	SURPRISE L5901G	OP	325.00	335.00
94	MOMENT'S PAUSE, A (BUST) L3569M	3500	1,635.00	1635.00
*	**DON QUIXOTE FIGURINES**			
69	DON QUIXOTE L1030G	OP	225.00	1450.00
69	DON QUIXOTE L1030M	RT	225.00	1450.00
69	SANCHO PANZA L1031G/M	RT	65.00	600.00
73	QUIXOTE STANDING UP L4854G	OP	40.00	205.00
74	MAN OF LA MANCHA L1269G	RT	700.00	3800.00
76	QUIXOTE & SANCHO PANZA/IMPOSSIBLE DREAM L1318G	RT	2,400.00	4350.00
77	WRATH OF DON QUIXOTE L1343G	RT	250.00	900.00
78	DON QUIXOTE & SANCHO PANZA L4998G	RT	875.00	2500.00
78	LETTERS TO DULCINEA (NUMBERED SERIES) L3509M	RT	260.00	2200.00
78	QUIXOTE ON GUARD/BRAVE KNIGHT L1385G	RT	350.00	800.00
82	TOAST BY SANCHO, A L5165G	RT	100.00	450.00
84	QUEST, THE- L5224G	OP	125.00	310.00
85	I HAVE FOUND THEE, DULCINEA L5341G	RT	1,850.00	2900.00
86	DON QUIXOTE & THE WINDMILL L1497G	RT	1,100.00	2000.00
86	ORATION L5357G	OP	170.00	300.00
87	LISTEN TO DON QUIXOTE (BUST) L1520G	RT	1,800.00	3000.00
*	**ELITE**			
76	PLAYING CARDS L1327M, NUMBERED	OP	3,800.00	6600.00
78	FEARFUL FLIGHT L1377G	750	7,000.00	18000.00
80	TURTLEDOVES GROUP L3520M	750	1,000.00	11900.00
85	18TH CENTURY COACH L1485G	500	14,000.00	28000.00
86	FANTASIA L1487G	5000	1,500.00	2700.00
86	FLORAL OFFERING L1490G	3000	2,500.00	2445.00
86	ORIENTAL MUSIC L1491G	5000	1,350.00	1445.00
86	THREE SISTERS L1492G	3000	1,850.00	3250.00
87	I AM DON QUIXOTE! L1522G	OP	2,600.00	3950.00
87	SUNDAY DRIVE, A L1510G	1000	3,400.00	5250.00
88	RETURN TO LA MANCHA L1580G	500	6,400.00	8350.00
89	MOUNTED WARRIORS L1608G	500	2,850.00	3450.00
90	LEPRECHAUN L1721G	OP	1,200.00	1400.00
90	SPRITE L1720G	OP	1,200.00	1400.00
91	OUTING IN SEVILLE L1756G	500	23,000.00	24500.00
92	CIRCUS TIME L1758G	2500	9,200.00	9650.00
92	HAWAIIAN CEREMONY L1757G	1000	9,800.00	10250.00
92	TEA IN THE GARDEN L1759G	2000	9,500.00	9750.00
93	ORIENTAL GARDEN L1775G	750	22,500.00	22500.00
93	PAELLA VALENCIANO L1762G	1000	10,000.00	10000.00
94	CINDERELLA'S ARRIVAL L1785G	1500	25,950.00	25950.00
*	**FANTASY FIGURINES**			
69	CENTAUR BOY L1013G/M	RT	45.00	425.00
69	CENTAUR GIRL L1012G/M	RT	45.00	425.00
69	FAIRY L4595G/M	RT	28.00	200.00
69	PAN WITH CYMBALS L1006G	RT	45.00	500.00
72	CINDERELLA L4828G	OP	47.00	245.00
82	BUTTERFLY GIRL/DAYDREAMING NYMPH L1402G/M	RT	210.00	550.00
82	BUTTERFLY GIRL/PONDERING NYMPH L1403G/M	RT	210.00	550.00
82	BUTTERFLY GIRL/SLEEPING NYMPH L1401G/M	RT	210.00	550.00
82	FANTASY L1414G	OP	115.00	260.00
82	ILLUSION L1413G	OP	115.00	260.00
82	MIRAGE L1415G	OP	115.00	260.00
85	DEMURE CENTAUR GIRL L5320G	RT	157.00	400.00
85	WISTFUL CENTAUR GIRL L5319G	RT	157.00	400.00

YR	NAME	LIMIT	ISSUE	TREND
86	AT THE STROKE OF TWELVE L1493	RT	4,250.00	7500.00
86	REY DE BASTOS L5369G	RT	325.00	650.00
86	REY DE COPAS L5366G	RT	325.00	650.00
86	REY DE ESPADAS L5368G	RT	325.00	650.00
86	REY DE OROS L5367G	RT	325.00	650.00
90	SWAN AND THE PRINCESS, THE- L5705G	RT	350.00	450.00
90	SWAN SONG L5704G	RT	350.00	450.00
91	ALICE IN WONDERLAND L5740G	OP	440.00	485.00
91	FAIRY GODMOTHER L5791G	RT	375.00	425.00
91	LITTLE UNICORN L5826G/M	RT	275.00	325.00
91	OCEAN BEAUTY L5785G	OP	625.00	665.00
91	PRINCESS AND THE UNICORN, THE- L1755G	RT	1,750.00	1900.00
92	FAIRY FLOWERS L5861G	RT	630.00	700.00
92	FAIRY GARLAND L5860G	RT	630.00	750.00
92	FLORAL ADMIRATION/EASTER BONNETS L5852G	RT	265.00	325.00
92	PLAYFUL UNICORN L5880G/M	OP	295.00	320.00
92	TINKERBELL L-7518G	RT	350.00	2400.00
93	PETER PAN L7529G	RT	400.00	2000.00
94	CINDERELLA AND HER FAIRY GODMOTHER L7553	RT	875.00	1200.00
*				**FLOWERS**
71	ANEMONES BUNCH L1184	RT	400.00	3225.00
71	FLORAL L1185	RT	475.00	1625.00
71	ROSES BUNCH L1186	RT	575.00	2000.00
84	CALIFORNIA POPPY L5190M	RT	98.00	250.00
84	CHRYSANTHEMUM L5189M	RT	100.00	250.00
84	DAHLIA WITH BASE L5180M	RT	65.00	150.00
84	JAPANESE CAMELLIA L5181M	RT	60.00	150.00
84	LACTIFLORA PEONY L5185M	RT	65.00	150.00
84	MINIATURE BEGONIA L5188M	RT	80.00	150.00
84	RHODODENDRON L5187M	RT	68.00	200.00
84	THREE PINK ROSES L5179M	RT	70.00	150.00
84	TWO YELLOW ROSES L5183M	RT	58.00	150.00
84	WHITE CARNATION L5184M	RT	65.00	150.00
84	WHITE PEONY WITH BASE L5182M	RT	85.00	150.00
84	YELLOW BEGONIA L5186M	RT	68.00	150.00
*				**GRES SERIES**
74	SHORT ORIENTAL L2057	OP	35.00	105.00
74	TALL CHINESE L2056	OP	35.00	105.00
74	THAI COUPLE/THAILANDIA L2058	OP	650.00	1885.00
74	WIND, THE- L1279	OP	250.00	830.00
77	GRACEFUL DUO L2073	RT	775.00	1700.00
77	MONK L2060	OP	60.00	155.00
77	NEW HAIRDO, A L2070	RT	1,060.00	1525.00
77	NUNS L2075	OP	90.00	250.00
77	THAI DANCER L2069	OP	300.00	760.00
78	NUDE WITH ROSE L3517	OP	225.00	780.00
78	PENSIVE L3514	OP	500.00	1050.00
78	RAIN IN SPAIN, THE/UNDER THE RAIN L2077	RT	190.00	525.00
78	WINTRY DAY, A L3513	RT	525.00	700.00
80	MOTHER'S LOVE/YOUNG MOTHER (BUST) L3521	RT	1,000.00	1200.00
81	CLASS WATER CARRIER/WEARY L3525	OP	360.00	750.00
81	LOST IN THOUGHT L2125	RT	210.00	350.00
82	STORMY SEA L3554	OP	675.00	1600.00
82	WATCHING THE DOVE/CONTEMPLATION L3526	OP	265.00	650.00
83	INDIAN CHIEF (BUST) L2127	RT	525.00	700.00
83	VENUS (BUST) L2128	OP	650.00	1330.00
84	FAIRY BALLERINA L2137	RT	500.00	1300.00
84	KING, THE- L2136	RT	570.00	1100.00
84	MYSTICAL JOSEPH L2135	RT	428.00	700.00
84	SEA HARVEST L2142	RT	535.00	700.00
85	HAWAIIAN FLOWER VENDOR L2154	OP	245.00	510.00
85	PEACE OFFERING L3559	OP	397.00	775.00
85	TRIBUTE TO PEACE, A (BUST) L2150	OP	470.00	1000.00
85	YOUNG MADONNA (BUST) L2149	RT	400.00	900.00
92	AFTERNOON VERSE L2231	OP	580.00	595.00
92	ARCTIC ALLIES L2227	OP	585.00	615.00
92	BOY'S BEST FRIEND L2226	OP	390.00	410.00
92	CHERISH (BUST) L2224	OP	1,750.00	1850.00
92	FRIENDLY SPARROW L2225	OP	295.00	325.00
92	GUESS WHAT I HAVE? L2233	OP	340.00	375.00
92	MARY'S CHILD L2230	RT	525.00	570.00
92	NEW LAMB L2223	OP	385.00	385.00
92	PLAYFUL PUSH L2234	OP	850.00	875.00
92	POOR LITTLE BEAR L2232	OP	250.00	265.00
92	SEASONAL GIFTS L2229	OP	450.00	475.00
92	SNOWY SUNDAY L2228	OP	550.00	625.00
92	TENDER MOMENT L2222	OP	400.00	425.00
92	UNDERFOOT L2219	OP	360.00	425.00
93	DAYS OF YORE L2248	1000	1,950.00	2050.00
*				**HISTORICAL FIGURINES**
74	QUEEN ELIZABETH II L1275G	RT	3,650.00	5000.00
78	HENRY VIII L1384G	RT	650.00	1050.00
82	COLUMBUS L1432G	RT	575.00	1350.00
85	NAPOLEON BONAPARTE L5338G	RT	275.00	625.00
85	NAPOLEON PLANNING THE BATTLE L1459G	RT	875.00	1375.00

YR	NAME	LIMIT	ISSUE	TREND
86	EL GRECO L5359G	RT	300.00	650.00
86	NEW WORLD, THE L1486G	RT	700.00	1400.00
87	CHRISTOPHER COLUMBUS (BUST) L2176G	RT	1,000.00	1350.00
91	COLUMBUS REFLECTING L1741G	RT	1,850.00	2000.00
91	COLUMBUS, TWO ROUTES L1740G	RT	1,500.00	1700.00
94	APOLLO LANDING, THE L6168G	RT	450.00	525.00
94	DR. MARTIN LUTHER KING L7528G	OP	345.00	375.00
95	ABRAHAM LINCOLN L7554G	RT	2,190.00	2190.00
*	**IN THE GARDEN FIGURINES**			
71	GIRL GATHERING FLOWERS L1172G/M	RT	27.00	350.00
74	FLOWER HARVEST L1286G	OP	200.00	495.00
74	LITTLE GARDENER L1283G	OP	250.00	785.00
74	MY FLOWERS L1284G	OP	200.00	550.00
74	MY GOODNESS L1285G	RT	190.00	435.00
74	PICKING FLOWERS L1287G	OP	170.00	440.00
74	SWINGING/VICTORIAN GIRL ON SWING L1297G	RT	520.00	1750.00
78	DAUGHTERS/SISTERS L5013G	RT	425.00	850.00
78	WATERING THE FLOWERS L1376G	RT	400.00	950.00
79	FLOWER CURTSY L5027G	OP	230.00	500.00
79	WILDFLOWER L5030G	OP	360.00	730.00
85	GIRL SITTING UNDER TRELLIS L5298G	RT	*	720.00
86	SCARECROW & THE LADY L5385G	RT	350.00	700.00
86	SUNDAY IN THE PARK L5365G	RT	375.00	625.00
86	TIME FOR REFLECTION L5378G	OP	425.00	745.00
87	FEEDING THE PIGEONS L5428G/M	RT	490.00	675.00
87	IN THE GARDEN L5416G/M	RT	200.00	400.00
87	INSPIRATION L5413	RT	1,200.00	2100.00
87	STUDYING IN THE PARK L5425G/M	RT	675.00	900.00
87	WILL YOU MARRY ME? L5447G	RT	750.00	1300.00
91	GARDEN CLASSIC L7617G	YR	295.00	500.00
92	GARDEN SONG L7618G	YR	295.00	450.00
*	**INTERNATIONAL & ETHNIC FIGURINES**			
69	ANDALUSIANS GROUP L4647G	RT	412.00	1100.00
69	BOLIVIAN MOTHER L4658	RT	75.00	400.00
69	FLAMENCO DANCERS L4519G	RT	150.00	1275.00
69	PERUVIAN GROUP L4610G	RT	190.00	1500.00
72	ESKIMO PLAYING WITH BEAR L1195G	OP	30.00	135.00
80	GRETEL/DUTCH GIRL, HANDS AKIMBO L5064G	RT	255.00	400.00
80	ILSA L5066G	RT	275.00	500.00
80	INGRID L5065G	RT	370.00	700.00
80	KRISTINA L5062G	RT	225.00	400.00
80	MARGARETTA/DUTCH GIRL WITH BRAIDS L5063G	RT	265.00	425.00
81	PHILIPPINE FOLKLORE L3522M	RT	1,450.00	2280.00
81	WATUSI QUEEN L3524M	RT	1,875.00	2900.00
82	BLUE GOD L3552	RT	553.00	1600.00
82	DESERT PEOPLE L3555	RT	1,680.00	3000.00
82	DUTCH GIRL L1399G/M	RT	*	700.00
82	FIRE BIRD L3553	RT	900.00	1375.00
82	GOYA LADY/AMPARO L5125G	RT	130.00	330.00
82	ROAD TO MANDALAY L3556M	RT	1,390.00	3000.00
83	VENETIAN SERENADE L1433	RT	2,600.00	3800.00
84	AZTEC DANCER L2143M	RT	463.00	600.00
84	AZTEC INDIAN L2139M	RT	553.00	1000.00
84	HEAD OF CONGOLESE WOMAN (BUST) L2148M	RT	*	600.00
84	LADY FROM MAJORCA L5240G	RT	120.00	385.00
85	AROMA OF THE ISLANDS L1480G	OP	260.00	480.00
85	HAWAIIAN DANCER/ALOHA L1478G	OP	230.00	440.00
85	IN A TROPICAL GARDEN L1479G	OP	230.00	440.00
85	LADY FROM ELCHE (BUST) L5269M	RT	432.00	750.00
86	DEEP IN THOUGHT L5389G	RT	170.00	375.00
86	ESKIMO RIDERS L5353G/M	OP	150.00	270.00
86	HAWAIIAN FESTIVAL L1496G	RT	1,850.00	3200.00
86	HINDU CHILDREN L5352G	OP	250.00	445.00
86	RIDE IN THE COUNTRY L5354G	RT	225.00	470.00
86	SPANISH DANCER L5390G	RT	170.00	430.00
86	TAHITIAN DANCING GIRLS L1498G	RT	750.00	1400.00
86	TIME TO REST, A L5391G	RT	170.00	300.00
87	DESERT TOUR L5402G	RT	950.00	1150.00
87	HAWAIIAN BEAUTY L1512G	RT	575.00	1250.00
87	LEHUA L1532G	RT	275.00	525.00
87	LEILANI L1530G	RT	275.00	525.00
87	MALIA L1531G	RT	275.00	525.00
87	MEXICAN DANCERS L5415G	OP	800.00	1195.00
87	MOMI L1529G	RT	275.00	525.00
90	LITTLE DUTCH GARDENER L5671G	RT	400.00	500.00
90	VENETIAN CARNIVAL L5658G	RT	500.00	625.00
92	FALLAS QUEEN L5869G	RT	420.00	465.00
94	INDIAN BRAVE L3562M	1500	2,250.00	2250.00
*	**LIMITED EDITION EGGS**			
93	LIMITED EDITION EGG L6083M	YR	145.00	240.00
94	LIMITED EDITION EGG L7532M	YR	150.00	175.00
95	LIMITED EDITION EGG L7548M	YR	150.00	160.00
96	LIMITED EDITION EGG L7550M	YR	155.00	155.00
97	LIMITED EDITION EGG L7552M	YR	155.00	155.00

YR	NAME	LIMIT	ISSUE	TREND
*			**LITERARY FIGURINES**	
71	HAMLET L1144G	RT	250.00	2800.00
71	OTHELLO AND DESDEMONA L1145G	RT	275.00	3000.00
71	ROMEO AND JULIET L4750G	OP	150.00	1250.00
74	HAMLET AND YORICK L1254G	RT	325.00	1200.00
77	SHAKESPEARE L1338G	RT	*	1450.00
78	OTHELLO L3510M	RT	575.00	1050.00
82	DANTE L5177G	RT	263.00	675.00
82	MIGUEL DE CERVANTES L5132G	RT	925.00	1400.00
83	REFLECTIONS OF HAMLET L1455G	RT	1,000.00	1550.00
85	CAMELOT L1458G	RT	1,000.00	1750.00
86	POET, THE L5397G	RT	425.00	800.00
92	INSPIRING MUSE L5850G	RT	1,200.00	1300.00
*			**LLADRO COLLECTORS SOCIETY**	
85	LITTLE PALS S7600G	RT	95.00	2400.00
86	LITTLE TRAVELER S7602G	RT	95.00	1400.00
87	SPRING BOUQUET S7603G	RT	125.00	800.00
88	FLOWER SONG S7607G	RT	175.00	650.00
88	SCHOOL DAYS S7604G	RT	125.00	550.00
89	MY BUDDY S7609G	RT	145.00	450.00
90	CAN I PLAY? S7610G	RT	150.00	450.00
91	PICTURE PERFECT/5TH ANNIVERSARY SPECIAL S7612G	YR	350.00	600.00
91	SUMMER STROLL S7611G	RT	195.00	450.00
92	ALL ABOARD S7619G	RT	165.00	400.00
93	BEST FRIEND S7620G	RT	195.00	300.00
94	BASKET OF LOVE S7622G	RT	225.00	340.00
95	AFTERNOON PROMENADE S7636G	RT	240.00	275.00
95	NOW AND FOREVER (10TH ANNIV. SPL.) S7642G	YR	395.00	425.00
96	INNOCENCE IN BLOOM S7644G	RT	250.00	275.00
97	POCKET FULL OF WISHES S7650G	RT	360.00	360.00
*			**LLADRO SCULPTURES**	
71	LYRIC MUSE L2031	RT	750.00	2500.00
81	ADORATION L3545	YR	1,050.00	1600.00
81	AFRICAN WOMAN L3546	YR	1,300.00	2400.00
82	TOGETHERNESS L3527	RT	375.00	900.00
83	ANXIETY L3530	RT	1,075.00	1800.00
83	BOXER L3550	RT	850.00	1500.00
83	COMPANIONSHIP L3529	65	1,000.00	1790.00
83	DAWN L3000	RT	325.00	990.00
83	DREAMING L3537	YR	475.00	1200.00
83	MONKS L3001	RT	1,675.00	2500.00
83	OBSERVER L3533	RT	900.00	1700.00
83	PLENTITUDE L3532	YR	1,000.00	1900.00
83	RELAXATION L3536	YR	525.00	1000.00
83	REPOSING L3549	RT	425.00	810.00
83	SERENITY L3548	RT	925.00	1600.00
83	SLAVE L3535	YR	950.00	1400.00
83	TRANQUILITY L3541	YR	1,000.00	1400.00
83	VICTORY L3531	YR	1,500.00	2200.00
83	WRESTLING L3528	YR	950.00	1700.00
87	CLASSIC BEAUTY L3012	500	1,300.00	1900.00
87	DIGNITY L3015	150	1,400.00	1900.00
87	YOUTHFUL INNOCENCE L3013	500	1,300.00	2300.00
88	CELLIST L3018	RT	650.00	900.00
88	MUSE L3017	RT	650.00	900.00
88	PASSION L3016	RT	865.00	1250.00
90	AFTER THE BATH L3023	RT	350.00	1400.00
90	DAYDREAMING L3022	500	550.00	775.00
90	DISCOVERIES L3024	RT	1,500.00	1800.00
93	AWAKENING, THE L2244	300	1,200.00	1200.00
93	FLIGHT OF FANCY L2243	RT	1,400.00	1500.00
94	DANAE L3029	300	2,880.00	3100.00
94	EBONY (BUST) L3027	300	1,295.00	1295.00
94	MODESTY (BUST) L3028	300	1,295.00	1295.00
*			**MOTHER & CHILD**	
69	MOTHER AND CHILD L4575G	RT	35.00	300.00
70	MOTHER AND CHILD L4701G	RT	45.00	300.00
76	BABY'S OUTING L4938G	OP	250.00	775.00
76	COMFORTING BABY/MOTHER KISSING CHILD(BUST) L1329M	RT	350.00	1100.00
76	MY BABY L1331	RT	275.00	1300.00
83	MOTHER & SON (BUST, GRES, NUMBERED SERIES) L2131M	RT	850.00	1600.00
85	MOTHER AND CHILD WITH LAMB L5299G/M	RT	225.00	500.00
86	FAMILY ROOTS L5371G	OP	575.00	935.00
87	GOODNIGHT L5449G	OP	225.00	375.00
87	TENDERNESS L1527G	OP	260.00	430.00
89	LATEST ADDITION L1606G	OP	385.00	495.00
89	MOTHER'S DAY/A GIFT OF LOVE L5596G	OP	400.00	495.00
90	ANTICIPATION L5650G	RT	300.00	400.00
90	MOMMY, IT'S COLD L5715G	RT	360.00	450.00
90	ONCE UPON A TIME L5721G	RT	550.00	650.00
91	BEAUTIFUL TRESSES L5757G	RT	725.00	850.00
91	FIRST SAMPLER L5767G	RT	625.00	715.00
91	STORY HOUR L5786G	RT	550.00	650.00
91	SUNDAY BEST L5758G	RT	725.00	825.00
92	DRESSING THE BABY L5845G	OP	295.00	295.00

YR	NAME	LIMIT	ISSUE	TREND
92	MATERNAL JOY L5864G	RT	1,600.00	1700.00
92	MODERN MOTHER L5873G	RT	325.00	375.00
92	OFF WE GO L5874G	RT	365.00	425.00
92	SLEEP TIGHT L5900G	RT	450.00	500.00
93	MOTHER'S TOUCH, A L5989G	RT	470.00	500.00
*				**MUSICIANS**
69	VIOLINIST AND GIRL L1039G/M	RT	120.00	1000.00
70	GIRL WITH GUITAR L2016M	RT	650.00	2250.00
71	BOY WITH CORNET (BUST) L1105G	RT	*	400.00
73	STUDENT FLUTE PLAYER L4837G	RT	*	400.00
77	VIOLIN PLAYER/CONCERTO (BUST) L2063M	RT	500.00	1300.00
85	BEETHOVEN L5339G	RT	800.00	1300.00
85	CONCERT VIOLINIST L5330G	RT	220.00	475.00
85	YOUNG STREET MUSICIANS L5306G	RT	300.00	1000.00
86	SERENADE L5381G	RT	450.00	625.00
86	SIDEWALK SERENADE L5388G	RT	750.00	1300.00
90	CIRCUS SERENADE L5694G	RT	300.00	425.00
90	CONCERTINA L5695G	RT	300.00	400.00
90	MANDOLIN SERENADE L5696G	RT	300.00	400.00
90	MUSICAL MUSE L5651G	RT	375.00	450.00
90	MUSICALLY INCLINED L5810G	RT	235.00	300.00
90	WANDERING MINSTREL L5676G	RT	270.00	325.00
91	JAZZ BASS L5834G	OP	395.00	425.00
91	JAZZ HORN L5832G	OP	295.00	310.00
91	JAZZ SAX L5833G	OP	295.00	315.00
91	MINSTREL'S LOVE L5821G	RT	525.00	600.00
91	MUSICAL PARTNERS L5763G	RT	625.00	675.00
92	JAZZ CLARINET L5928G	OP	295.00	295.00
92	JAZZ COMBO L5930G	OP	795.00	900.00
92	JAZZ DRUMS L5929G	OP	595.00	610.00
92	YOUNG MOZART L5915G	RT	500.00	1300.00
95	YOUNG BACH L1801G	2500	850.00	850.00
*				**NAO BY LLADRO**
69	CAT, HEAD DOWN N0008G	RT	7.00	70.00
69	CAT, HEAD UP N0010G	RT	7.00	70.00
69	GOOSE N0052G	OP	*	60.00
69	GOOSE N0052M	RT	*	100.00
69	GOOSE N0053G	OP	*	60.00
69	GOOSE N0053M	RT	*	100.00
70	GIRL WITH BIRD NOO92G	RT	*	250.00
70	GIRL WITH SLATE N0117G	RT	*	90.00
74	LITTER OF KITTENS N0104M	RT	*	150.00
75	GATHERING BUTTERFLIES N0181G	RT	*	140.00
84	LITTLE DUCK/DUCKLING N0370G	OP	*	30.00
84	LITTLE DUCK/DUCKLING NO369G	OP	*	30.00
84	LITTLE GIRL FEEDING DOVES N0382G	OP	*	395.00
84	LITTLE GIRL FEEDING DOVES N0382M	OP	*	540.00
84	TWERP AND MIKIE/TIRELESS PUPPIES N0386G	OP	*	110.00
85	TAHITIAN GIRLS (GRES) N0473	OP	*	1975.00
87	BEAR N0718G	OP	*	90.00
91	TRADITIONAL DANCE N1174G	RT	*	535.00
91	WHEN I GROW UP N1166G	RT	*	110.00
92	PLAYING WITH MY DOG N1190G	RT	*	200.00
92	SHOWER TIME! N1186G	RT	*	245.00
92	YOUNG SKATEBOARDER N1191G	RT	*	125.00
*				**NATIVITY FIGURINES**
69	BABY JESUS L4670G	OP	18.00	55.00
69	BABY JESUS L4670M	RT	18.00	75.00
69	COW L4680G	OP	37.00	90.00
69	COW L4680M	RT	37.00	125.00
69	KING BALTHASAR L4675G	OP	35.00	95.00
69	KING BALTHASAR L4675M	RT	35.00	130.00
69	KING GASPAR L4674G	OP	35.00	95.00
69	KING GASPAR L4674M	RT	35.00	130.00
69	KING MELCHIOR L4673G	OP	35.00	95.00
69	KING MELCHIOR L4673M	RT	35.00	130.00
69	MARY L4671G	OP	18.00	75.00
69	MARY L4671M	RT	18.00	110.00
69	SHEPHERD WITH LAMB L4676G	OP	14.00	110.00
69	SHEPHERD WITH LAMB L4676M	RT	14.00	175.00
69	SHEPHERDESS WITH BASKET L4678G	OP	13.00	90.00
69	SHEPHERDESS WITH BASKET L4678M	RT	13.00	125.00
69	SHEPHERDESS WITH ROOSTER L4677G	OP	14.00	90.00
69	SHEPHERDESS WITH ROOSTER L4677M	RT	14.00	150.00
69	ST. JOSEPH L4672G	OP	33.00	90.00
69	ST. JOSEPH L4672M	RT	33.00	125.00
81	BABY JESUS L1388G	OP	85.00	140.00
81	COW L1390G	OP	95.00	215.00
81	DONKEY L1389G	OP	95.00	215.00
81	ST. JOSEPH L1386G	OP	250.00	385.00
81	VIRGIN MARY L1387G	OP	240.00	385.00
82	KING BALTHASAR L1425G	OP	315.00	585.00
82	KING GASPAR L1424G	OP	265.00	475.00
82	KING MELCHIOR L1423G	OP	225.00	440.00
85	NATIVITY SCENE, HAUTE RELIEF L5281M	RT	210.00	410.00

YR	NAME	LIMIT	ISSUE	TREND
86	BLESSED FAMILY L1499G	OP	200.00	395.00
91	BABY JESUS L5745G	RT	170.00	195.00
91	BULL & DONKEY L5744G	RT	250.00	275.00
91	HOLY NIGHT L5796G	RT	330.00	375.00
91	LITTLE LAMB L5750G	RT	40.00	55.00
91	MARY L5747G	RT	275.00	325.00
91	SHEPHERD BOY L5749G	RT	225.00	275.00
91	SHEPHERD GIRL L5748G	RT	150.00	175.00
91	ST. JOSEPH L5746G	RT	350.00	385.00
93	HUMBLE GRACE L2255M	2000	2,150.00	2150.00
94	BABY JESUS (GRES) L2277	OP	85.00	85.00
94	DONKEY (GRES) L2282	OP	185.00	185.00
94	KING BALTHASAR (GRES) L2280	OP	290.00	290.00
94	KING GASPAR (GRES) L2279	OP	290.00	290.00
94	KING MELCHIOR (GRES) L2278	OP	290.00	290.00
94	LOST LAMB (GRES) L2283	OP	140.00	140.00
94	MARY (GRES) L2276	OP	175.00	175.00
94	OX (GRES) L2281	OP	185.00	185.00
94	SHEPHERD BOY (GRES) L2284	OP	285.00	285.00
94	ST. JOSEPH (GRES) L2275	OP	270.00	270.00
*				

NAUTICAL FIGURINES

YR	NAME	LIMIT	ISSUE	TREND
69	SEA CAPTAIN L4621G/M	RT	45.00	325.00
72	BOY WITH YACHT/YOUNG SAILOR L4810G	OP	33.00	175.00
76	SEAMAN/HELMSMAN, THE- L1325M	RT	600.00	1100.00
78	RESCUE, THE (GRES) L3504	RT	2,900.00	4500.00
80	HARPOONER/WHALER, THE (GRES) L2121	RT	820.00	1100.00
82	SEA FEVER L5166G/M	RT	130.00	325.00
84	NAUTICAL WATCH (BUST, GRES) L2134	RT	450.00	725.00
84	TALL YARN, A L5207G	OP	260.00	545.00
84	YACHTSMAN L5206G	RT	110.00	235.00
85	SAILOR'S SERENADE, A L5276G	RT	315.00	850.00
93	INSPIRED VOYAGE L2245M	1000	4,800.00	4800.00
*				

NORMAN ROCKWELL

YR	NAME	LIMIT	ISSUE	TREND
82	COURT JESTER L1405/RL405G/#328	RT	600.00	1250.00
82	DAY DREAMER L1411/RL404G/	RT	450.00	1300.00
82	LOVE LETTERS L1408/RL400G/#902	RT	650.00	1000.00
82	PRACTICE MAKES PERFECT L1408/RL402G/#1234	RT	725.00	1100.00
82	SPRINGTIME '27 L1410/RL406G/#860	RT	450.00	1500.00
82	SUMMER STOCK L1407/RL401G/#861	RT	750.00	900.00
82	YOUNG LOVE L1409/RL403G/#522	RT	450.00	1500.00
*				

NUDES

YR	NAME	LIMIT	ISSUE	TREND
71	THREE GRACES, THE L2028M	RT	950.00	4500.00
78	NATIVE L3502M	OP	700.00	2450.00
78	NUDE WITH DOVE L3503M	RT	250.00	1100.00
81	VENUS AND CUPID L1392M	RT	1,100.00	1800.00
83	BATHER (BUST) L3551M	YR	975.00	1350.00
83	DAINTINESS L3539M	YR	1,000.00	1400.00
83	DEMURE L3543M	YR	1,250.00	1700.00
83	IN THE DISTANCE L3534M	RT	525.00	1300.00
83	INDOLENCE L3003M	YR	1,465.00	2000.00
83	POSE L3540M	YR	1,250.00	1500.00
83	RECLINING NUDE L3547M	YR	650.00	900.00
83	REFLECTIONS L3544M	75	650.00	1100.00
83	VENUS IN THE BATH L3005M	YR	1,175.00	1500.00
83	WAITING L3002M	YR	1,550.00	1900.00
83	YOGA L3542M	YR	650.00	900.00
83	YOUTH L3538M	YR	525.00	1100.00
84	INNOCENCE W/BASE, GREEN L3558M	RT	960.00	2500.00
84	INNOCENCE WBASE,RED L3558.30M	RT	960.00	2000.00
85	YOUTHFUL BEAUTY L1461M	RT	750.00	1200.00
87	ARTIST'S MODEL L5417G/M	RT	425.00	520.00
87	NYMPH, THE- L3014M	250	1,000.00	1450.00
89	DEMURENESS L3020M	RT	400.00	650.00
91	RESTING NUDE L3025M	RT	650.00	1000.00
91	UNADORNED BEAUTY L3026M	200	1,700.00	1800.00
*				

ORIENTAL FIGURINES

YR	NAME	LIMIT	ISSUE	TREND
71	ORIENTAL WOMAN L2026M	RT	*	400.00
71	YOUNG ORIENTAL MAN L2021M	RT	500.00	1900.00
72	GEISHA L4807G	RT	190.00	475.00
73	ORIENTAL GIRL/ORIENTAL FLOWER ARRANGER L4840G/M	RT	90.00	525.00
74	CHINESE NOBLEMAN L4921G	RT	325.00	2500.00
74	CHINESE NOBLEWOMAN L4916G	RT	300.00	2500.00
77	CHINESE FARMER L2068M	RT	*	1000.00
78	CHRYSANTHEMUM L4990G	OP	125.00	310.00
78	MADAME BUTTERFLY L4991G	OP	125.00	295.00
78	ORIENTAL SPRING L4988G	RT	125.00	350.00
78	RICKSHAW RIDE, A L1383G	OP	1,500.00	2150.00
78	SAYONARA L4989G	RT	125.00	325.00
82	AUGUST MOON L5122G	RT	185.00	350.00
82	CHINESE BOY L2153M	RT	90.00	225.00
82	CHINESE GIRL L2152M	RT	90.00	225.00
82	FISH A'PLENTY L5172G	RT	190.00	400.00
82	MARIKO W/BASE L1421G	RT	860.00	1500.00
82	MY PRECIOUS BUNDLE L5123G	OP	150.00	245.00
83	KIYOKO L1450G	OP	235.00	550.00

YR	NAME	LIMIT	ISSUE	TREND
83	MAYUMI L1449G	RT	235.00	500.00
83	MICHIKO L1447G	OP	235.00	460.00
83	SPRINGTIME IN JAPAN L1445G	RT	965.00	1800.00
83	TERUKO L1451G	OP	235.00	550.00
83	YUKI L1448G	RT	285.00	550.00
85	NIPPON LADY L5327G	OP	325.00	595.00
86	LADY OF THE EAST L1488G	RT	625.00	1200.00
89	KITAKAMI CRUISE W/BASE L1605	RT	5,800.00	7500.00
89	SIAMESE DANCER L5593G	RT	345.00	475.00
91	GIFT OF BEAUTY L5775G	RT	850.00	1000.00
91	GRACEFUL OFFERING L5773G	RT	850.00	1000.00
91	NATURE'S GIFTS L5774G	RT	900.00	1100.00
91	SINGAPORE DANCERS L5754G	RT	950.00	1100.00
*	**PASTORAL FIGURINES**			
69	BOY WITH GOAT/BOY WITH KID L4506M	RT	23.00	350.00
69	BOY WITH LAMBS L4509G	RT	38.00	325.00
69	GIRL W/ COCKEREL/SHEPHERDESS W/BASKET L4591G/M	RT	20.00	275.00
69	GIRL WITH BASKET/SHEPHERDESS WITH DOG L1034G	RT	30.00	225.00
69	GIRL WITH DUCK L1052G/M	OP	30.00	205.00
69	GIRL WITH GEESE L1035G/M	RT	38.00	225.00
69	GIRL WITH LAMB L1010G/M	RT	26.00	250.00
69	GIRL WITH LAMB L4505G	OP	20.00	130.00
69	GIRL WITH LAMB L4505M	RT	20.00	150.00
69	GIRL WITH LAMB L4584G/M	RT	27.00	200.00
69	GIRL WITH PIG L1011G	OP	13.00	95.00
69	GIRL WITH PIG L1011M	RT	13.00	150.00
69	SHEPHERD L4659G	RT	*	325.00
69	SHEPHERD RESTING L4571G	RT	60.00	450.00
69	SHEPHERDESS W/DUCKS/GIRL W/GEESE L4568G/M	RT	45.00	325.00
69	SHEPHERDESS WITH DOVE L4660G/M	RT	21.00	325.00
69	SHEPHERDESS WITH GOATS L1001G/M	RT	80.00	700.00
70	GIRL WITH MILKPAIL L4682G/M	RT	28.00	300.00
70	SHEPHERDESS SLEEPING/SHEPHERDESS W/LAMB-BUSTL2005M	RT	100.00	700.00
71	SHEPHERD SLEEPING L1104G	RT	*	2200.00
72	GIRL WITH GOOSE L4815G/M	RT	72.00	325.00
72	GIRL WITH LAMB/SHEPHERDESS L4835G/M	RT	42.00	250.00
72	LITTLE GIRL W/GOAT/GETTING HER GOAT L4812G	RT	55.00	425.00
72	LITTLE SHEPHERD WITH GOAT L4817M	RT	50.00	450.00
72	RABBIT'S FOOD/GIRL FEEDING RABBIT L4826G	RT	40.00	300.00
74	GIRL WITH GOOSE AND DOG L4866G/M	RT	26.00	300.00
74	GIRL WITH PIGEONS L4915G	RT	110.00	400.00
74	SHEPHERD'S REST L1252G	RT	100.00	600.00
74	WATCHING THE PIGS L4892G	RT	350.00	1000.00
86	PASTORAL SCENE W/BASE L5386G	RT	1,100.00	2500.00
88	SHEPHERD BOY L5485G	OP	140.00	205.00
91	MILKMAID L5798G	RT	450.00	515.00
91	WALKING THE FIELDS L5780G	RT	725.00	825.00
*	**PERIOD FIGURINES**			
69	OLD FOLKS L1033G/M	RT	140.00	1400.00
70	DRESSMAKER L4700G/M	RT	45.00	450.00
71	WOMAN/LADY WITH DOG L4761G	RT	60.00	400.00
74	ARANJUEZ LITTLE LADY/LADY WITH PARASOL L4879G	RT	48.00	325.00
74	LADY WITH SHAWL L4914G	OP	220.00	730.00
74	LOVERS FROM VERONA L1250G	RT	330.00	1300.00
74	LOVERS IN THE PARK L1274G	RT	450.00	1375.00
74	MEDIEVAL LADY L4928G	RT	275.00	1150.00
74	REMINISCING L1270G	RT	975.00	1285.00
74	THOUGHTS L1272G	OP	88.00	3490.00
74	WALK WITH THE DOG/MY DOG L4893G	OP	85.00	235.00
78	ANNIVERSARY WALTZ L1372G	OP	260.00	570.00
78	GIRLS IN THE SWING/SWINGING L1366G	RT	825.00	1500.00
78	MISS TERESA L-4999G	RT	*	375.00
78	READING L5000G	OP	150.00	275.00
78	SUNNY DAY, A L5003G/M	RT	193.00	400.00
78	UNDER THE WILLOW L1346G	RT	1,600.00	2000.00
78	WAITING IN THE PARK L1374G	RT	235.00	515.00
78	WALK IN VERSAILLES L5004	RT	*	900.00
82	AFTERNOON TEA L1428G/M	OP	115.00	300.00
82	DEBUTANTE, THE L1431G/M	OP	115.00	300.00
82	FLAPPER/LADY GRAND CASINO L5175G	RT	185.00	425.00
82	HIGH SOCIETY L1430G/M	RT	305.00	700.00
82	ROARING TWENTIES L5174G	RT	172.50	390.00
82	SEWING A TROUSSEAU/MED. LADY EMBROIDERER L5126G	RT	185.00	450.00
83	ON THE TOWN L1452G	RT	220.00	475.00
83	PLEASANTRIES L1440G	RT	960.00	1800.00
83	VOWS L1434G	RT	600.00	860.00
84	SCHOOL MARM L5209G	RT	205.00	850.00
85	ENGLISH LADY L5324G	RT	225.00	475.00
85	MEDIEVAL COURTSHIP L5300G	RT	735.00	850.00
85	MILANESE LADY L5323G	RT	180.00	375.00
85	PARISIAN LADY L5321G	RT	193.00	375.00
85	SOCIALITE OF THE TWENTIES L5283G	OP	175.00	345.00
85	VIENNESE LADY L5322G	RT	160.00	325.00
86	CAN CAN L5370G	RT	700.00	1200.00
86	LADY OF TASTE, A L1495G	OP	575.00	1020.00

YR	NAME	LIMIT	ISSUE	TREND
86	NEW HAT, A L5345G	RT	200.00	385.00
86	PETITE MAIDEN L5383G	RT	110.00	300.00
86	PETITE PAIR L5384G	RT	225.00	300.00
86	RECEPTION, THE- L1504G	RT	625.00	1050.00
86	TOUCH OF CLASS, A L5377G	OP	475.00	795.00
87	CAFE DE PARIS L1511G	RT	1,900.00	3000.00
87	FLOWER FOR MY LADY, A L1513G	RT	1,150.00	1600.00
87	INTERMEZZO L5424G/M	RT	325.00	550.00
87	ISABEL L5412G	RT	225.00	400.00
87	PILAR L5410G	RT	200.00	375.00
87	STROLL IN THE PARK L1519G	RT	1,600.00	2700.00
87	SUNDAY STROLL L5408G	RT	250.00	550.00
87	TERESA L5411G	RT	225.00	400.00
88	GARDEN PARTY L1578	RT	5,500.00	7200.00
89	SOUTHERN TEA L1597G	RT	1,775.00	2500.00
90	AFTERNOON STROLL L5687G	RT	275.00	360.00
90	INVINCIBLE L2188M	300	1,100.00	1250.00
90	ON THE AVENUE L5686G	RT	275.00	350.00
90	PROMENADE L5685G	RT	275.00	350.00
90	SOUTHERN CHARM L5700G	RT	675.00	1100.00
91	ASHLEY L5756G	RT	265.00	315.00
91	CHARMING DUET L5766G	RT	575.00	650.00
91	CLAUDETTE L5755G	RT	265.00	375.00
91	FLIRT, THE - L5789G	OP	185.00	195.00
91	PILGRIM COUPLE L5734G	RT	490.00	530.00
91	SOPHISTICATE L5787G	OP	185.00	195.00
91	TALK OF THE TOWN L5788G	OP	185.00	195.00
*				

PROFESSIONAL FIGURINES

YR	NAME	LIMIT	ISSUE	TREND
69	DOCTOR L4602G	OP	33.00	220.00
69	HARVESTER, THE L4581G	RT	*	650.00
69	HARVESTER, WOMAN L4582 G	RT	*	650.00
69	ORCHESTRA CONDUCTOR L4653G	RT	95.00	800.00
69	PAINTER L4663G	RT	*	900.00
69	WOODCUTTER L4656G	RT	*	900.00
71	DENTIST L4762G	RT	36.00	600.00
71	LAWYER L1089G	RT	*	900.00
71	LAWYER L1090G	RT	*	900.00
71	NURSE L4603G	OP	35.00	220.00
71	OBSTETRICIAN L4763G/M	RT	40.00	450.00
72	TEACHER, THE (MALE) L4801G	RT	45.00	475.00
72	VETERINARIAN L4825G/M	RT	48.00	450.00
73	PHARMACIST L4844G	RT	70.00	1500.00
74	BARRISTER, THE L4908G	RT	100.00	550.00
74	JUDGE L1281G	RT	325.00	1500.00
77	SHERIFF PUPPET L4969G	RT	85.00	650.00
79	FLOWER PEDDLER L-5029G	RT	675.00	1350.00
80	BOY POTTERY SELLER L5080	RT	320.00	550.00
80	GIRL POTTERY SELLER L5081G	RT	300.00	550.00
80	TEACHER WOMAN L5048G	RT	115.00	625.00
83	FLOWERS OF THE SEASON L1454G	OP	1,460.00	2550.00
84	ARCHITECT L5214G	RT	140.00	475.00
84	ARTISTIC ENDEAVOR L5234G	RT	225.00	550.00
84	FEMALE PHYSICIAN L5197G	OP	120.00	275.00
84	LAMPLIGHTER L5205G	OP	170.00	425.00
84	MAESTRO, MUSIC PLEASE! L5196G	RT	135.00	465.00
84	PROFESSOR L5208G	RT	205.00	550.00
84	ROVING PHOTOGRAPHER L5194G	RT	145.00	1500.00
84	SAY CHEESE L5195G	RT	170.00	500.00
84	SHARPENING THE CUTLERY L5204G	RT	210.00	950.00
84	SPANISH SOLDIER L5255G	RT	185.00	500.00
84	WINE TASTER L5239G	OP	190.00	425.00
85	TAILOR, THE- L5326G	RT	335.00	900.00
87	MIDWIFE L5431G/M	RT	175.00	550.00
90	ON THE ROAD L5681G	RT	320.00	450.00
90	TRAVELING ARTIST L5661G	RT	250.00	300.00
91	HORTICULTURIST L5733G	RT	450.00	525.00
91	SPECIAL DELIVERY L5783G	RT	525.00	600.00
92	AVIATOR, THE L5891G	RT	375.00	425.00
93	FIREMAN, THE L5976G	RT	395.00	475.00
93	HAND OF JUSTICE, THE L6035G	RT	1,250.00	1300.00
93	ON PATROL L5960G	RT	395.00	475.00
94	AMERICAN COWBOY L3568M	3000	950.00	950.00
94	TRAIL BOSS L3561M	1500	2,595.00	2595.00
*				

RELIGIOUS FIGURINES

YR	NAME	LIMIT	ISSUE	TREND
69	KING BALTHASAR L1020M	OP	345.00	1850.00
69	KING GASPAR L1018M	OP	345.00	1895.00
69	KING MELCHIOR L1019M	OP	345.00	1850.00
69	NUNS L4611G/M	OP	38.00	155.00
70	MADONNA WITH CHILD L2018M	RT	450.00	1800.00
71	EVE AT THE TREE L2029M	RT	450.00	3500.00
71	MADONNA SEATED L2043M	RT	400.00	1700.00
72	BUDDHA L1235G	RT	*	600.00
77	SINGING LESSON/CHOIR LESSON L4973G	RT	350.00	1600.00
77	ST. THERESA L2061	RT	388.00	1400.00
78	ST. FRANCIS L2090M	RT	565.00	1700.00

YR	NAME	LIMIT	ISSUE	TREND
78	ST. MICHAEL L3515M	1500	2,200.00	4900.00
80	SAMSON AND DELILAH L5051G	RT	350.00	1675.00
82	ABRAHAM L5169G	RT	155.00	725.00
82	HOLY MARY, NUMBERED SERIES L1394G	OP	1,000.00	1475.00
82	JESUS L5167G	OP	130.00	265.00
82	KING SOLOMON L5168G	RT	205.00	900.00
82	MONKS AT PRAYER L5155M	OP	130.00	300.00
82	MOSES L5170G	OP	175.00	410.00
82	OUR LADY WITH FLOWERS L5171G	OP	172.50	310.00
84	FRIAR JUNIPER L2138M	RT	160.00	350.00
84	JESUS IN TIBERIUS L3557M	1200	2,600.00	5250.00
84	ST. CRISTOBAL/ST. CHRISTOPHER L5246G	RT	265.00	550.00
86	SEWING CIRCLE L5360G	RT	600.00	1250.00
86	ST. VINCENT L5387G	RT	190.00	400.00
87	BALTHASAR'S PAGE L1516G	RT	275.00	850.00
87	GASPAR'S PAGE L1514G	RT	275.00	650.00
87	KING MELCHIOR'S PAGE L1515G	RT	290.00	650.00
87	SAINT NICHOLAS L5427G	RT	425.00	700.00
88	BLESSED LADY L1579G	RT	1,150.00	2500.00
89	JESUS THE ROCK L1615G	RT	1,175.00	2600.00
89	PIETA L5541G	RT	1,075.00	1500.00
91	REVERENT MOMENT L5792G	RT	295.00	360.00
92	LOAVES & FISHES, THE- L5896G	RT	695.00	795.00
92	SORROWFUL MOTHER L5849G	1500	1,750.00	1850.00
92	WAY OF THE CROSS, THE- L5890G	2000	975.00	1050.00
93	BLESSING, THE L5942G	2000	1,345.00	1345.00
93	OUR LADY OF ROCIO L5951G	2000	3,500.00	3500.00
95	RABBI, THE L6209G	RT	250.00	275.00
95	READING THE TORAH L6208G	OP	535.00	535.00
*				**SPORTS FIGURINES**
69	FEMALE EQUESTRIAN L4516G	OP	170.00	745.00
69	HUNTERS L1048G/M	RT	115.00	1400.00
72	FISHER BOY/GOING FISHING L4809G	OP	33.00	160.00
72	GOLFER L4824G	OP	66.00	295.00
73	WOMAN GOLFER/LADY GOLFER L4851G	OP	70.00	280.00
74	HUNT, THE- L1308G	RT	4,750.00	7000.00
74	RACE, THE- L1249G	RT	450.00	2000.00
74	SOCCER PLAYERS L1266G	RT	1,000.00	7500.00
77	DERBY L1344G	RT	1,125.00	2500.00
77	JOCKEY L1341G	RT	120.00	500.00
77	OLYMPIC PUPPET L4968G	RT	65.00	1000.00
77	SKIER PUPPET L4970G	RT	85.00	500.00
77	TENNIS PLAYER PUPPET L-4966G	RT	60.00	500.00
79	JOCKEY AND LADY L5036G	RT	950.00	2300.00
80	JOCKEY, THE L5089G	RT	*	1200.00
80	SUCCESSFUL HUNT L5098G	RT	*	8500.00
82	BILLY SOCCER PLAYER L-5135G	RT	140.00	600.00
82	BILLY THE BASEBALL PLAYER L5137G	RT	140.00	700.00
82	BILLY THE GOLFER L5138G	RT	140.00	950.00
82	BILLY THE SKIER L5136G	RT	140.00	850.00
82	FEMALE TENNIS PLAYER L1427M	RT	200.00	350.00
82	LILY SOCCER PLAYER/GIRL SOCCER PLAYER L-5134G	RT	140.00	600.00
82	MALE TENNIS PLAYER L1426M	RT	200.00	350.00
83	GOLFING COUPLE L1453G	OP	248.00	530.00
84	SOCCER PLAYER L5200G	RT	155.00	450.00
84	SPECIAL MALE SOCCER PLAYER L5200.30G	RT	150.00	600.00
84	TORCH BEARER L5251G	RT	100.00	400.00
85	AEROBICS FLOOR EXERCISE L-5335G	RT	110.00	300.00
85	AEROBICS PULL-UPS L-5334G	RT	110.00	300.00
85	AEROBICS SCISSOR FIGURE L-5336G	RT	110.00	300.00
85	BIKING IN THE COUNTRY L5272G	RT	295.00	825.00
85	GENTLEMAN EQUESTRIAN L5329G	RT	160.00	500.00
85	GYMNAST BALANCING BALL L-5332G	RT	95.00	350.00
85	GYMNAST EXERCISING WITH BALL L5333G	RT	95.00	350.00
85	GYMNAST WITH RING L5331G	RT	95.00	350.00
85	HIKER L5280G	RT	195.00	400.00
85	LADY EQUESTRIAN L5328G	RT	160.00	500.00
85	LITTLE LEAGUER EXERCISING L-5289G	RT	150.00	450.00
85	LITTLE LEAGUER ON BENCH L-5291G	RT	150.00	450.00
85	LITTLE LEAGUER, CATCHER L-5290G	RT	150.00	450.00
85	RACING MOTORCYCLIST L5270G	RT	360.00	775.00
85	WAITING TO TEE OFF L5301G	OP	145.00	295.00
86	FOX HUNT L5362G	1000	5,200.00	8750.00
90	TEE TIME L5675G	RT	280.00	350.00
91	NEXT AT BAT L5828G	OP	170.00	180.00
92	SHOT ON GOAL L5879G	RT	1,100.00	1200.00
93	COURAGE/SPECIAL OLYMPICS L7522G	RT	195.00	235.00
94	HOCKEY PLAYER L6108G	OP	295.00	310.00
95	REGATTA L6248G	RT	695.00	725.00
95	TO THE RIM L1800G	1500	2,475.00	2475.00
*				**VALENCIAN FIGURINES**
69	VALENCIAN COUPLE ON HORSEBACK L4648G	RT	900.00	1000.00
73	VALENCIAN GIRL L4841G	OP	35.00	235.00
74	VALENCIAN GIRL WITH FLOWERS L1304G	OP	200.00	625.00
82	APPRECIATION L1396G	RT	420.00	1000.00

YR	NAME	LIMIT	ISSUE	TREND
82	FULL OF MISCHIEF L1395G	RT	420.00	1000.00
82	MISS VALENCIA L1422G	RT	175.00	415.00
82	REVERIE L1398G	RT	490.00	1100.00
82	SECOND THOUGHTS L1397G	RT	420.00	1000.00
82	VALENCIAN BOY L1400G	RT	298.00	475.00
84	MAKING PAELLA L5254G	RT	215.00	500.00
85	FESTIVAL IN VALENCIA L1457G	RT	1,400.00	2400.00
85	VALENCIAN COUPLE L1472G	3000	885.00	1225.00
86	CARMENCITA L5373G	RT	120.00	250.00
86	LOLITA L5372G	RT	120.00	250.00
86	PEPITA L5374G	RT	120.00	250.00
86	TERESITA L5375G	RT	120.00	250.00
86	VALENCIAN BOY L5395G	RT	200.00	400.00
86	VALENCIAN CHILDREN L1489G	OP	700.00	1225.00
87	VALENCIAN BOUQUET L1524G	RT	250.00	400.00
87	VALENCIAN DREAMS L1525G	RT	240.00	400.00
87	VALENCIAN FLOWERS L1526G	RT	375.00	550.00
87	VALENCIAN GARDEN L1518G	RT	1,100.00	1800.00
90	VALENCIAN BEAUTY (BUST) L5670G	RT	175.00	275.00
90	VALENCIAN FLOWERS (BUST) L5669G	RT	370.00	500.00
90	VALENCIAN HARVEST (BUST) L5668G	RT	175.00	275.00
91	VALENCIAN CRUISE L1731G	1000	2,700.00	2950.00
92	LOVING VALENCIA L5868G	RT	365.00	410.00
92	SERENE VALENCIA L5867G	RT	365.00	410.00
*			**VEHICULAR FIGURINES**	
71	ANTIQUE AUTO L1146G	RT	1,000.00	8000.00
72	HANSOM CARRIAGE L1225G	RT	1,450.00	9000.00
78	CAR IN TROUBLE L1375G	RT	3,000.00	6500.00
78	IN THE GONDOLA (NUMBERED SERIES) L1350G	OP	1,350.00	3250.00
80	SEDAN CHAIR GROUP/HER LADYSHIP L5097G	RT	5,900.00	6000.00
82	FIRST DATE L1393G	1500	3,800.00	5900.00
82	SCOOTING L5143G	RT	575.00	900.00
87	HAPPY ENCOUNTER, A L1523G	1500	2,900.00	4900.00
87	LANDAU CARRIAGE, THE L1521G	RT	2,500.00	4000.00
90	RIDE IN THE PARK, A L5718	RT	3,200.00	4200.00
91	FLORAL GETAWAY L5795G	RT	625.00	810.00
92	MOTORING IN STYLE L5884G	RT	3,700.00	3900.00
92	PRESENTING CREDENTIALS L5911G	1500	19,500.00	20500.00
93	HONEYMOON RIDE WITH BASE L5968G	RT	2,750.00	3000.00
93	WHERE TO SIR? L5952G	1500	5,250.00	5250.00

LONGTON CROWN
*

YR	NAME	LIMIT	ISSUE	TREND
			GREAT MOMENTS IN BASEBALL	
97	BABE RUTH/WILLY MAYS	*	40.00	40.00
97	CY YOUNG/STAN MUSIAL	*	40.00	40.00
97	DON LARSON/BOBBY THOMPSON	*	40.00	40.00
97	LOU GEHRIG/JACKIE ROBINSON	*	40.00	40.00
97	ROBERTO CLEMENTE/LOU BROCK	*	40.00	40.00
97	TED WILLIAMS/TY COBB	*	40.00	40.00
*			**GRIDIRON HEROES OF THE NFL**	
97	BOB LILLY/KELLEN WINSLOW	*	40.00	40.00
97	GALE SAYERS/DEACON JONES	*	40.00	40.00
97	JOE MONTANA/JERRY RICE	*	40.00	40.00
97	JOHNNY UNITAS/"MEAN" JOE GREENE	*	40.00	40.00
97	RAY NITCHKE/RONNIE LOTT	*	40.00	40.00
97	REGGIE WHITE/TBD	*	40.00	40.00

MAFEKING COLLECTION
M. GREEN

YR	NAME	LIMIT	ISSUE	TREND
			MAN'S BEST FRIEND	
95	MICKEY'S EYES	75	295.00	300.00

MARGARET FURLONG DESIGNS
M. FURLONG

YR	NAME	LIMIT	ISSUE	TREND
			2" ANGEL SERIES	
97	VIOLA ANGEL	OP	12.00	12.00
	M. FURLONG		**3" ANGEL SERIES**	
97	DOGWOOD ANGEL	OP	14.00	14.00
	M. FURLONG		**4" ANGEL SERIES**	
97	IRIS ANGEL	YR	23.00	23.00
	M. FURLONG		**MADONNA SERIES**	
97	MADONNA OF THE CROSS	20,000	80.00	80.00

MARK HOPKINS SCULPTURE
M. HOPKINS

YR	NAME	LIMIT	ISSUE	TREND
			ARTS GALLERY	
93	JAZZ BASS	750	550.00	550.00
93	JAZZ DRUMS	750	850.00	850.00
	M. HOPKINS		**EAGLES COLLECTION**	
95	MOUNTAIN MAJESTY	450	975.00	975.00
	M. HOPKINS		**EARTH COLLECTION**	
95	BEAR	750	400.00	400.00
95	COUGAR	750	400.00	400.00
95	WOLF	750	400.00	400.00
	M. HOPKINS		**FISHING COLLECTION**	
95	GOTCHA!	950	375.00	375.00
	M. HOPKINS		**GOLF COLLECTION**	
95	WOODS	950	395.00	395.00

The first release in Lance Corp.'s "The Adversaries" series as part of the Chilmark collection, Robert E. Lee is worth approximately five times its 1991 issue price of $350.

A member of "The Adversaries" series from Lance Corp.'s Chilmark collection, Ulysses S. Grant has nearly doubled in value since its 1992 release.

A musical that plays "Summertime" and has moving parts, Willie the Fisherman is a member of the Melody in Motion line by WACO Products.

YR	NAME	LIMIT	ISSUE	TREND
96	DOWN THE MIDDLE	950	300.00	950.00
96	GREEN, THE	OP	160.00	160.00
96	LINING IT UP	950	300.00	300.00
M. HOPKINS		**GREAT CATS OF AMERICA COLLECTION**		
95	SACRED GROUND	750	1,495.00	1495.00
M. HOPKINS		**GREAT MYSTERY COLLECTION**		
95	WAKAN TONKA	450	1,495.00	1495.00
M. HOPKINS		**KIDS ON THE MOVE**		
95	RACE YA! (BOY)	950	435.00	435.00
95	RACE YA! (GIRL)	950	435.00	435.00
M. HOPKINS		**KIDS PLAY GALLERY**		
93	FASTBREAK	950	315.00	315.00
93	TIRE SWING, THE	550	650.00	650.00
T. RUSH		**LIVING REEF COLLECTION**		
95	LORD OF THE REEF	950	775.00	775.00
M. HOPKINS		**MARK HOPKINS PREMIERE EDITIONS**		
96	SURVIVAL - LARGE	250	3,500.00	3500.00
M. HOPKINS		**MARK HOPKINS STUDIO**		
94	BORN TO FLY	450	925.00	925.00
T. RUSH		**MARK HOPKINS STUDIO**		
93	CHASE, THE	950	695.00	695.00
93	SPOOKED	950	975.00	975.00
93	TURNING POINT	950	695.00	695.00
94	ALPHA WOLF	950	225.00	225.00
94	FACES IN THE DEEP	950	600.00	600.00
94	FIRST STRIKE	950	775.00	775.00
94	HONEY	950	225.00	225.00
94	LURED AWAY	950	750.00	750.00
94	OCEAN MONARCHS	950	575.00	575.00
94	PROTECTING THE INNOCENT	950	550.00	550.00
94	RACE TO THE FLY	950	675.00	675.00
94	RETURN TO THE SKIES	950	225.00	225.00
94	RISE TO THE CHALLENGE	950	225.00	225.00
M. HOPKINS		**NATURE'S CHILDREN COLLECTION**		
95	BEAR HUG	750	825.00	825.00
M. HOPKINS		**NAUTICAL & SEA LIFE GALLERY**		
93	FAIR WIND	RT	550.00	600.00
93	HEAVY WEATHER AHEAD	SU	500.00	500.00
93	TAKING A SIGHT	SU	450.00	450.00
M. HOPKINS		**NOBLESSENCE GALLERY**		
93	AMONG THE ASPEN	550	1,125.00	1125.00
93	BREAK OUT	250	1,250.00	1250.00
93	EAGLE DANCE	750	700.00	700.00
93	GOLDEN EAGLE	RT	975.00	1050.00
93	PHANTOMS OF THE FOREST	SU	685.00	685.00
93	SONS & BROTHERS	250	1,250.00	1250.00
94	ANCIENT OF DAYS	750	1,250.00	1250.00
94	BATTLE WORN	250	975.00	975.00
94	CRY OF FREEDOM	450	1,100.00	1100.00
94	EARTH MOTHER	750	1,250.00	1250.00
94	GATHERING WISDOM	450	875.00	875.00
94	GENERATIONS OF TIME	750	1,250.00	1250.00
94	GUARDIAN OF THE PLAINS	750	975.00	975.00
94	I HAVE SEEN TOMORROW	450	1,000.00	1000.00
94	LICK AND A PROMISE, A	750	850.00	850.00
94	MATERNAL PRIDE	750	975.00	975.00
94	NIGHT HUNTER	750	875.00	875.00
94	PEACE NO MORE	450	950.00	950.00
94	POUNCING LYNX	750	650.00	650.00
94	VISION QUEST	250	1,500.00	1500.00
M. HOPKINS		**NOBLESSENCE GALLERY MHS ANNUAL**		
94	MOTHER'S NATURE	YR	685.00	800.00
95	SURVIVAL	YR	795.00	1400.00
M. HOPKINS		**NOBLESSENCE GALLERY NATIVE AMERICAN**		
91	FIRST BUFFALO	250	1,498.00	2000.00
93	BROKEN TREATY	450	1,100.00	1800.00
M. HOPKINS		**NOBLESSENCE GALLERY NATURE**		
92	CRY OF THE WOLVES	950	850.00	1950.00
92	FISHING GRIZZLY	450	875.00	1890.00
92	STALKING COUGAR	450	750.00	1725.00
93	SOARING	450	975.00	1250.00
97	SHADOW IN THE GRASS	250	1,625.00	1625.00
M. HOPKINS		**NOBLESSENCE GALLERY WILD DOMAIN**		
93	MOUNTAIN OVERLOOK	550	975.00	1400.00
94	CATCH OF THE DAY	550	1,150.00	4000.00
97	EAGLE'S LEDGE	250	875.00	875.00
97	GRIZZLY CANYON	250	925.00	925.00
M. HOPKINS		**ON THE RIDGE COLLECTION**		
95	FISHING ROCK	550	750.00	750.00
95	SPIRIT OF THE MOUNTAIN	550	750.00	750.00
M. HOPKINS		**PORTRAITS OF THE WILD COLLECTION**		
95	LONE SCOUT	650	600.00	600.00

YR	NAME	LIMIT	ISSUE	TREND
95	NO LIMIT	650	600.00	600.00
95	SILENT APPROACH	650	600.00	600.00
M. HOPKINS		**SKY COLLECTION**		
96	RED-TAILED HAWK	450	450.00	450.00
M. HOPKINS		**SPORTS & WILDLIFE GALLERY**		
93	DOWNRIVER RUN	450	950.00	1450.00
93	FISHING HOLE	450	650.00	650.00
93	I CAN'T LOOK	950	325.00	325.00
93	NOT AGAIN	950	325.00	325.00
93	TEACHING THE WAY	450	750.00	750.00
94	FOREVER FREE	950	625.00	625.00
97	BALD EAGLE	950	225.00	225.00
97	PATRIOT'S DREAM	950	325.00	325.00
M. HOPKINS		**VOICE OF JAZZ COLLECTION**		
95	BODY AND SOUL	750	625.00	625.00
95	TRIO	750	675.00	675.00
M. HOPKINS		**WAY OF THE PEOPLE COLLECTION I**		
95	LEGEND KEEPER	450	925.00	925.00
M. HOPKINS		**WAY OF THE PEOPLE COLLECTION II**		
95	SEASON OF INNOCENCE	450	925.00	925.00
M. HOPKINS		**WAY OF THE WARRIOR COLLECTION**		
96	HOKA HAY	450	1,350.00	1350.00
M. HOPKINS		**WILD WATERS COLLECTION**		
95	RELEASE, THE	450	1,095.00	1095.00
T. RUSH		**WILDLIFE STUDIES COLLECTION II**		
95	CLAP OF THUNDER	950	250.00	250.00
95	CURIOSITY	950	250.00	250.00
95	SCENT OF DANGER	950	285.00	285.00
95	TERRITORIAL RIGHT	950	250.00	250.00
T. RUSH		**WILDLIFE STUDIES COLLECTION III**		
95	ELK COUNTRY	950	335.00	335.00
95	GREAT PLAINS BUFFALO	950	310.00	310.00
95	HAWK EYE	950	275.00	275.00

MARTY SCULPTURE

YR	NAME	LIMIT	ISSUE	TREND
M. CAREY		**THE HERD**		
95	PRIDE & JOY PORTRAIT HEAD	5000	130.00	130.00
95	RUMBLE BASE	*	45.00	45.00
95	RUMBLE SIGHS	*	29.00	29.00
95	RUMBLE TRIES	*	29.00	29.00
95	THUNDER PORTRAIT HEAD	5000	150.00	150.00

MARURI USA

YR	NAME	LIMIT	ISSUE	TREND
W. GAITHER		**AFRICAN SAFARI ANIMALS**		
81	MYALA	300	1,450.00	1450.00
83	AFRICAN ELEPHANT	CL	3,500.00	3500.00
83	BLACK MANED LION	CL	1,450.00	1450.00
83	CAPE BUFFALO	CL	2,200.00	2200.00
83	GRANT'S ZEBRAS, PAIR	500	1,200.00	1200.00
83	SABLE	CL	1,200.00	1200.00
83	SOUTHERN GREATER KUDU	CL	1,800.00	1800.00
83	SOUTHERN IMPALA	CL	1,200.00	1200.00
83	SOUTHERN LEOPARD	CL	1,450.00	1450.00
83	SOUTHERN WHITE RHINO	150	3,200.00	3200.00
*		**AMERICAN EAGLE GALLERY**		
85	E-8501	CL	45.00	70.00
85	E-8502	OP	55.00	65.00
85	E-8503	OP	60.00	67.00
85	E-8504	OP	65.00	75.00
85	E-8505	CL	65.00	140.00
85	E-8506	OP	75.00	90.00
85	E-8507	OP	75.00	90.00
85	E-8508	CL	75.00	80.00
85	E-8509	CL	85.00	130.00
85	E-8510	OP	85.00	85.00
85	E-8511	CL	85.00	130.00
85	E-8512	OP	295.00	300.00
87	E-8521	CL	40.00	50.00
87	E-8522	OP	45.00	50.00
87	E-8523	CL	55.00	55.00
87	E-8524	OP	175.00	195.00
89	E-8931	OP	55.00	60.00
89	E-8932	OP	75.00	80.00
89	E-8933	OP	95.00	95.00
89	E-8934	OP	135.00	135.00
89	E-8935	OP	175.00	185.00
89	E-8936	OP	185.00	195.00
91	E-9141 EAGLE LANDING	OP	60.00	60.00
91	E-9142 EAGLE W/TOTEM POLE	OP	75.00	75.00
91	E-9143 PAIR IN FLIGHT	OP	95.00	95.00
91	E-9144 EAGLE W/SALMON	OP	110.00	110.00
91	E-9145 EAGLE W/SNOW	OP	135.00	135.00
91	E-9146 EAGLE W/BABIES	OP	145.00	145.00
95	EAGLE E-9551	OP	60.00	60.00

YR	NAME	LIMIT	ISSUE	TREND
95	EAGLE E-9552	OP	65.00	65.00
95	EAGLE E-9553	OP	75.00	75.00
95	EAGLE E-9554	OP	80.00	80.00
95	EAGLE E-9555	OP	90.00	90.00
95	EAGLE E-9556	OP	110.00	110.00
W. GAITHER				**AMERICANA**
81	GRIZZLY BEAR AND INDIAN	CL	650.00	650.00
82	SIOUX BRAVE AND BISON	CL	985.00	985.00
W. GAITHER				**BABY ANIMALS**
81	AFRICAN LION CUBS	RT	195.00	195.00
81	BLACK BEAR CUBS	CL	195.00	195.00
81	WOLF CUBS	CL	195.00	195.00
W. GAITHER				**BIRDS OF PREY**
81	AMERICAN BALD EAGLE I	CL	165.00	1700.00
81	SCREECH OWL	300	960.00	960.00
82	AMERICAN BALD EAGLE II	CL	245.00	2700.00
83	AMERICAN BALD EAGLE III	CL	445.00	1700.00
84	AMERICAN BALD EAGLE IV	CL	360.00	1700.00
86	AMERICAN BALD EAGLE V	CL	325.00	1200.00
*				**EYES OF THE NIGHT**
90	DOUBLE BARN OWL O-8807	CL	125.00	125.00
90	DOUBLE SNOWY OWL O-8809	CL	245.00	245.00
90	SINGLE GREAT HORNED OWL O-8803	CL	60.00	60.00
90	SINGLE GREAT HORNED OWL O-8808	CL	145.00	145.00
90	SINGLE SCREECH OWL O-8801	CL	50.00	50.00
90	SINGLE SCREECH OWL O-8806	CL	90.00	90.00
90	SINGLE SNOWY OWL O-8802	CL	50.00	50.00
90	SINGLE SNOWY OWL O-8805	CL	80.00	80.00
90	SINGLE TAWNY OWL O-8804	CL	60.00	60.00
*				**GRACEFUL REFLECTIONS**
91	MUTE SWAN WITH BABY SW-9152	CL	95.00	95.00
91	PAIR-MUTE SWAN SW-9153	CL	145.00	145.00
91	PAIR-MUTE SWAN SW-9154	CL	195.00	195.00
91	SINGLE MUTE SWAN SW-9151	CL	85.00	85.00
*				**HUMMINGBIRDS**
91	ALLEW'S WITH HIBISCUS H-8906	OP	195.00	195.00
91	ANNA'S W/LILY H-8905	OP	160.00	160.00
91	RUBY-THROATED W/AZALEA H-8911	OP	75.00	75.00
91	RUBY-THROATED W/ORCHID H-8901	OP	150.00	150.00
91	RUFOUS WITH TRUMPET CREEPER H-8901	OP	70.00	70.00
91	VIOLET-CROWNED W/GENTIAN H-8913	OP	75.00	75.00
91	WHITE-EARED W/MORNING GLORY H-8912	OP	75.00	75.00
95	ALLEN'S & BABIES W/ROSE	OP	120.00	120.00
95	ALLEN'S W/EASTER LILY	OP	95.00	95.00
95	ANNA'S W/TRUMPET CREEPER	OP	130.00	130.00
95	BROAD-BILLED W/AMARYLLIS	OP	150.00	150.00
95	VIOLET-CROWNED W/IRIS	OP	95.00	95.00
95	WHITE-EARED W/TULIP	OP	145.00	145.00
ITO				**LEGENDARY FLOWERS OF THE ORIENT**
85	CHERRY BLOSSOM	15000	45.00	55.00
85	CHINESE PEONY	15000	45.00	55.00
85	CHRYSANTHEMUM	15000	45.00	55.00
85	IRIS	15000	45.00	55.00
85	LILY	15000	45.00	55.00
85	LOTUS	15000	45.00	55.00
85	ORCHID	15000	45.00	45.00
85	WISTERIA	15000	45.00	55.00
*				**MAJESTIC OWLS OF THE NIGHT**
87	BURROWING OWL	15000	55.00	55.00
88	BARRED OWL	15000	55.00	55.00
88	ELF OWL	15000	55.00	55.00
W. GAITHER				**NORTH AMERICAN GAME ANIMALS**
84	WHITE TAIL DEER	950	285.00	285.00
W. GAITHER				**NORTH AMERICAN GAME BIRDS**
81	CANADIAN GEESE, PAIR	CL	2,000.00	2000.00
81	EASTERN WILD TURKEY	CL	300.00	300.00
82	RUFFED GROUSE	CL	1,745.00	1745.00
83	BOBTAIL QUAIL, FEMALE	CL	375.00	375.00
83	BOBTAIL QUAIL, MALE	CL	375.00	375.00
83	WILD TURKEY HEN WITH CHICKS	CL	300.00	300.00
W. GAITHER				**NORTH AMERICAN SONGBIRDS**
82	BLUEBIRD	CL	95.00	95.00
82	CARDINAL, MALE	CL	95.00	95.00
82	CAROLINA WREN	CL	95.00	95.00
82	CHICKADEE	CL	95.00	95.00
82	MOCKINGBIRD	CL	95.00	95.00
83	CARDINAL, FEMALE	CL	95.00	95.00
83	ROBIN	CL	95.00	95.00
W. GAITHER				**NORTH AMERICAN WATERFOWL I**
81	BLUE WINGED TEAL	200	980.00	980.00
81	CANVASBACK DUCKS	CL	780.00	780.00
81	FLYING WOOD DUCKS	CL	880.00	880.00
81	MALLARD DUCKS	CL	2,380.00	2380.00
81	WOOD DUCK, DECOY	950	480.00	480.00

YR NAME	LIMIT	ISSUE	TREND
W. GAITHER	**NORTH AMERICAN WATERFOWL II**		
81 MALLARD DUCKS, PAIR	1500	225.00	225.00
82 BUFFLEHEAD DUCKS, PAIR	1500	225.00	225.00
82 GOLDENEYE DUCKS, PAIR	CL	225.00	225.00
82 PINTAIL DUCKS, PAIR	CL	225.00	225.00
82 WIDGEON, FEMALE	CL	225.00	225.00
82 WIDGEON, MALE	CL	225.00	225.00
83 LOON	CL	245.00	245.00
*	**POLAR EXPEDITION**		
90 BABY ARCTIC FOX P-9002	OP	50.00	50.00
90 BABY EMPEROR PENGUIN P-9001	OP	45.00	45.00
90 BABY HARP SEALS P-9005	OP	65.00	65.00
90 MOTHER & BABY EMPEROR PENGUINS P-9006	OP	80.00	80.00
90 MOTHER & BABY HARP SEALS P-9007	OP	90.00	90.00
90 MOTHER & BABY POLAR SEALS P-9008	OP	125.00	125.00
90 POLAR BEAR CUB P-9003	OP	50.00	50.00
90 POLAR BEAR CUBS P-9004	OP	60.00	60.00
90 POLAR EXPEDITION SIGN P-9009	OP	18.00	18.00
92 ARCTIC FOX CUBS PLAYING P-9223	OP	65.00	65.00
92 BABY HARP SEAL P-221	OP	55.00	55.00
92 EMPEROR PENGUINS P-9222	OP	60.00	60.00
92 POLAR BEAR FAMILY P-9224	OP	90.00	90.00
*	**PRECIOUS PANDA**		
92 LAZY LUNCH PP-9202	OP	60.00	60.00
92 MOTHER'S CUDDLE PP-9204	OP	120.00	120.00
92 SNACK TIME PP-9201	OP	60.00	60.00
92 TUG OF WAR PP-9203	OP	70.00	70.00
*	**SANTA'S WORLD TRAVELS**		
96 SANTA'S SAFARI	5000	225.00	225.00
W. GAITHER	**SIGNATURE COLLECTION**		
85 AMERICAN BALD EAGLE	CL	60.00	60.00
85 CANADA GOOSE	CL	60.00	60.00
85 HAWK	CL	60.00	60.00
85 PINTAIL DUCK	CL	60.00	60.00
85 SNOW GOOSE	CL	60.00	60.00
85 SWALLOW	CL	60.00	60.00
*	**SONGBIRD SERENADE**		
97 BLUEBIRD FAMILY W/APPLE BLOSSOM	OP	95.00	95.00
97 BLUEJAY W/OAK	OP	70.00	70.00
97 CARDINAL FAMILY W/ROSE	OP	90.00	90.00
97 CEDAR WAXWING PAIR W/BERRIES	OP	80.00	80.00
97 CHICKADEE PAIR W/HOLLY & BERRY	OP	85.00	85.00
97 GOLDFINCH W/VIOLETS	OP	65.00	65.00
97 ROBIN W/BLACKBERRY	OP	70.00	70.00
97 ROBIN W/LILY	OP	70.00	70.00
97 WREN PAIR W/CACTUS	OP	80.00	80.00
*	**SONGBIRDS OF BEAUTY**		
91 BLUEBIRD WITH APPLE BLOSSOM SB-9105	CL	85.00	85.00
91 CARDINAL WITH CHERRY BLOSSOM SB-9103	CL	85.00	85.00
91 CHICKADEE WITH ROSES SB-9101	CL	85.00	85.00
91 DOUBLE BLUEBIRD W/PEACH BLOSSOM SB-9107	CL	145.00	145.00
91 DOUBLE CARDINAL WITH DOGWOOD SB-9108	CL	145.00	145.00
91 GOLDFINCH WITH HAWTHORNE SB-9102	CL	85.00	85.00
91 ROBIN & BABY WITH AZALEA SB-9106	CL	115.00	115.00
91 ROBIN WITH LILIES SB-9104	CL	85.00	85.00
W. GAITHER	**SPECIAL COMMISSIONS**		
81 WHITE BENGAL TIGER	240	340.00	340.00
82 CHEETAH	CL	995.00	995.00
83 ORANGE BENGAL TIGER	240	340.00	340.00
*	**STUDIO COLLECTION**		
90 MAJESTIC EAGLES MS-100	SO	350.00	780.00
91 DELICATE MOTION MS-200	SO	325.00	325.00
92 IMPERIAL PANDA MS-300	SO	350.00	350.00
93 WILD WINGS	SO	395.00	450.00
94 WALTZ OF THE DOLPHINS	3500	300.00	300.00
98 FANTASY IN FLIGHT	3500	295.00	295.00
W. GAITHER	**STUMP ANIMALS**		
82 RED FOX	CL	175.00	175.00
83 OWL	CL	175.00	175.00
83 RACCOON	CL	175.00	175.00
84 BOBCAT	CL	175.00	175.00
84 CHIPMUNK	CL	175.00	175.00
84 GRAY SQUIRREL	1200	175.00	175.00
84 PELICAN	CL	260.00	260.00
84 SAND PIPER	CL	260.00	260.00
W. GAITHER	**UPLAND BIRDS**		
81 MOURNING DOVES	CL	780.00	780.00
*	**WINGS OF LOVE DOVES**		
87 D-8701 SINGLE DOVE	OP	45.00	58.00
87 D-8702 DOUBLE DOVE	OP	55.00	65.00
87 D-8703 SINGLE DOVE	CL	65.00	65.00
87 D-8704 DOUBLE DOVE	OP	75.00	85.00
87 D-8705 SINGLE DOVE	CL	95.00	95.00
87 D-8706 DOUBLE DOVE	OP	175.00	175.00

YR	NAME	LIMIT	ISSUE	TREND
90	D-9021 DOUBLE DOVE	OP	50.00	55.00
90	D-9022 DOUBLE DOVE	OP	75.00	75.00
90	D-9023 DOUBLE DOVE	OP	115.00	115.00
90	D-9024 DOUBLE DOVE	OP	150.00	150.00

MAZE CREEK STUDIO
A. THOMAS

93	STRIDE THE TENTS- BRONZE	50	2,300.00	2300.00
96	CAVALRY DUEL	250	329.00	329.00
97	PURITY	25	229.00	229.00

MCMEMORIES
*

97	MCDUTIES	*	22.00	22.00
97	THUMBS UP	*	25.00	25.00
98	RONALD AND ME	*	40.00	40.00
*			**MCDONALD'S GOLDEN CLASSIC**	
98	DOMED SCULPTURE	*	*	N/A

MICHAEL GARMAN PRODUCTIONS
M. GARMAN — CITYSCAPES

95	MINI POLL HALL BLUES	OP	250.00	275.00
95	MINI WEST SIDE NEWS	OP	250.00	275.00

M. GARMAN — FIREFIGHTER

95	ADVANCING THE LINE	OP	72.00	72.00

M. GARMAN — PROFESSIONAL

95	HEALING TOUCH	OP	70.00	70.00

M. GARMAN — SPORT

96	LONG BALL	OP	60.00	60.00
96	TEE TIME	OP	60.00	60.00

MIDWEST OF CANNON FALLS
C. ULBRICHT — A CHRISTMAS CAROL

93	BOB CRATCHIT AND TINY TIM NUTCRACKER 09577-5	CL	240.00	240.00
93	EBENEZER SCROOGE NUTCRACKER	6000	210.00	210.00
94	GHOST OF CHRISTMAS PRESENT NUTCRACKER 12041-5	CL	190.00	190.00
95	SCROOGE NUTCRACKER 09584-3	CL	210.00	210.00

C. ULBRICHT — AMERICAN FOLK HERO

94	DAVY CROCKETT NUTCRACKER 12960-9	CL	190.00	190.00
94	JOHNNY APPLESEED NUTCRACKER 12959-3	CL	196.00	196.00
95	PAUL BUNYAN NUTCRACKER 12800-8	CL	220.00	220.00

J.P. LLOBERA — BELENES PUIG NATIVITY COLLECTION

85	NATIVITY, SET OF 6 00205-6	OP	250.00	250.00
85	SHEPHERD, SET OF 2 00458-6	OP	110.00	110.00
85	WISE MEN, SET OF 3 00459-3	OP	185.00	185.00
86	SHEEP, SET OF 3 00475-3	OP	28.00	28.00
87	SHEPHERD & ANGEL SCENE, SET OF 7 06084-1	OP	305.00	305.00
88	STANDING CAMEL 08792-3	OP	115.00	115.00
89	ANGEL 02087-6	OP	50.00	50.00
89	BABY JESUS 02085-2	OP	62.00	62.00
89	DONKEY 02082-1	OP	26.00	26.00
89	JOSEPH 02086-9	OP	62.00	62.00
89	MOTHER MARY 02084-5	OP	62.00	62.00
89	OX 02083-8	OP	26.00	26.00
89	SHEPHERD CARRYING LAMB 02092-0	OP	56.00	56.00
89	SHEPHERD W/STAFF 02091-3	OP	56.00	56.00
89	WISE MAN W/FRANKINCENSE 02088-3	OP	66.00	66.00
89	WISE MAN W/FRANKINCENSE ON CAMEL 02077-7	OP	155.00	155.00
89	WISE MAN W/GOLD 02089-0	OP	66.00	66.00
89	WISE MAN W/GOLD ON CAMEL 02075-3	OP	155.00	155.00
89	WISE MAN W/MYRRH 02090-6	OP	66.00	66.00
89	WISE MAN W/MYRRH ON CAMEL 02076-0	OP	155.00	155.00
90	RESTING CAMEL 04025-6	OP	115.00	115.00
*			**CANNON VALLEY COLLECTION**	
94	APPLE TREE, 2 ASSTD. 11484-1	OP	10.00	10.00
94	CANNON VALLEY SIGN 11297-7	OP	5.50	5.50
94	CHICKEN, 3 ASSTD. 11299-1	OP	2.00	2.00
94	CHILDREN, 2 ASSTD. 11461-2	OP	5.50	5.50
94	COW, 3 ASSTD. 11309-7	OP	5.50	5.50
94	FAMILY FARMHOUSE/LIGHTED 11292-2	OP	43.00	43.00
94	FARM COUPLE, 2 ASSTD. 11458-2	OP	7.50	8.00
94	FARM TOWN WINDMILL 11306-6	OP	9.50	10.00
94	FARM TRACTOR 11305-9	OP	9.50	10.00
94	FLAGPOLE 11300-4	OP	5.30	5.30
94	GENERAL STORE/LIGHTED 11295-3	OP	43.00	43.00
94	HAY WAGON & HORSE SET 11303-5	OP	19.00	19.00
94	HEN HOUSE/LIGHTED 11294-6	RT	33.00	33.00
94	HORSE, 2 ASSTD. 11485-8	OP	10.00	10.00
94	LITTLE RED SCHOOLHOUSE/LIGHTED 11293-9	OP	43.00	43.00
94	MAILBOX & WATER PUMP, 2 ASSTD. 11301-1	RT	4.00	4.00
94	PICK UP TRUCK 11304-2	OP	12.00	12.00
94	RED BARN/LIGHTED 11296-0	OP	43.00	43.00
94	SPLIT RAIL FENCE 12676-9	OP	2.00	2.00
94	SUNDAY BEST COUPLE W/CHILDREN, 2 ASSTD. 12670-7	OP	7.50	8.00
95	ACE'S GARAGE/LIGHTED 12665-3	OP	45.00	45.00

YR	NAME	LIMIT	ISSUE	TREND
95	APPLE TREE, SET OF 3 12677-6	OP	7.00	7.00
95	CHICKEN, 2 ASSTD. 12657-8	OP	3.00	3.00
95	CHURCH/LIGHTED 12664-6	OP	45.00	45.00
95	COW W/CALF, 2 ASSTD. 12673-8	OP	6.50	6.50
95	DAIRY BARN/LIGHTED 12666-0	CL	49.00	49.00
95	DOG BU BOGHOUSE 12658-5	OP	5.00	5.00
95	FARM CAT 12808-4	OP	5.00	5.00
95	FARM CHILDREN, 4 ASSTD. 12671-4	OP	7.50	8.00
95	FARMER W/FEED BAG 12672-1	OP	7.50	8.00
95	FARMYARD LIGHT 12683-7	OP	5.00	5.00
95	FIRE HYDRANT 12685-1	OP	3.00	3.00
95	FOUR SQUARE FARMHOUSE/LIGHTED 12662-2	OP	49.00	49.00
95	GRAIN ELEVATOR/LIGHTED 12663-9	OP	45.00	45.00
95	GRANDPARENTS, 2 ASSTD. 12661-5	OP	6.00	6.00
95	GRAVEL ROAD 12682-0	OP	9.00	9.00
95	MECHANIC 12660-8	OP	6.00	6.00
95	MINISTER 12674-5	OP	6.00	6.00
95	OUTHOUSE 12668-4	OP	11.00	11.00
95	PARKING METER 12686-8	OP	3.00	3.00
95	PICKET FENCE 13260-9	OP	6.00	6.00
95	PIG & PIGLETS 11302-8	OP	5.30	5.30
95	PINE TREE, SET OF 2 12680-6	OP	7.50	8.00
95	SILO 12667-7	OP	16.00	16.00
95	STOREKEEPER 11459-9	OP	5.50	5.50
95	TEACHER & CHILDREN, 3 ASSTD. 11460-5	OP	5.50	5.50
95	TELEPHONE POLE 12684-4	OP	5.00	5.00
95	TURKEY, 2 ASSTD. 12659-2	OP	5.00	5.00
95	WATER TOWER 13116-9	OP	13.00	13.00
95	WOODU CAR 12669-1	OP	12.00	12.00
96	BATTERY OPERATED MINI LIGHT, SET OF 10 16937-7	OP	9.00	9.00
96	BORDER COLLIE & SHEEP, SET OF 3 16677-2	OP	10.00	10.00
96	CHRISTMAS DECORATION, SET OF 12 16964-3	OP	10.00	10.00
96	CORNSTALK 16679-6	OP	5.50	5.50
96	FIRE FIGHTERS, 2 ASSTD. 16674-1	OP	8.00	8.00
96	FIRE TRUCK 16676-5	OP	13.00	13.00
96	GARDENERS, SET OF 2 16675-8	OP	13.00	13.00
96	HAY RAKE 16759-5	OP	8.00	8.00
96	HOMETOWN CAFE/LIGHTED 16669-7	3600	45.00	45.00
96	HORSE, 2 ASSTD. 16930-8	OP	6.00	6.00
96	OLD OAK TREE 16681-9	OP	11.00	11.00
96	PLAYING CHECKERS 16680-2	OP	13.00	13.00
96	PLOW 16761-8	OP	6.50	6.50
96	PRAIRIE STYLE BARN/LIGHTED 16667-3	OP	49.00	49.00
96	SPREADER 16760-1	OP	9.00	9.00
96	TRACTOR 16678-9	OP	9.50	10.00
96	VICTORIAN FARM HOUSE/LIGHTED 16666-6	OP	45.00	45.00
96	VOLUNTEER FIRE DEPT./LIGHTED 16668-0	OP	49.00	49.00
*			**COTTONTAIL LANE COLLECTION**	
93	ARBOR W/FENCE SET 02188-0	OP	14.00	15.00
93	BIRDBATH, BENCH & MAILBOX 02184-2	RT	4.00	4.00
93	BRIDGE & GAZEBO, 2 ASSTD. 02182-9	OP	11.50	12.00
93	BUNNY COUPLE ON BICYCLE 02978-7	RT	5.30	6.00
93	LAMPPOST, BIRDHOUSE & MAILBOX, 3 ASSTD. 02187-3	RT	4.50	5.00
93	STROLLING BUNNY, 2 ASSTD. 02976-3	RT	4.20	5.00
93	TREES, 3 ASSTD. 02194-1	RT	6.20	7.00
94	BIRDHOUSE, SUNDIAL & FOUNTAIN, 3 ASSTD. 00371-8	OP	4.50	5.00
94	BUNNY MARCHING BAND, 6 ASSTD. 00355-8	OP	4.20	5.00
94	BUNNY PREPARING FOR EASTER, 3 ASSTD. 02971-8	OP	4.20	5.00
94	BUNNY SHOPPING COUPLE, 2 ASSTD. 10362-3	OP	4.20	5.00
94	COBBLESTONE ROAD 10072-1	OP	9.00	9.00
94	CONE-SHAPED TREE SET 10369-2	OP	7.50	8.00
94	COTTONTAIL LANE SIGN 10063-9	OP	5.00	5.00
94	EASTER BUNNY, 2 ASSTD. 00356-5	OP	4.20	5.00
94	EGG STAND & FLOWER CART, 2 ASSTD. 10354-8	OP	6.00	6.00
94	POLICEMAN, CONDUCTOR BUNNY, 2 ASSTD. 00367-1	OP	4.20	5.00
94	SWEEPER & FLOWER PEDDLER BUNNY COUPLE 00359-6	OP	4.20	5.00
94	TOPIARY TREES, 3 ASSTD. 00346-6	RT	2.50	3.00
94	TRAIN STATION COUPLE, 2 ASSTD. 00357-2	OP	4.20	5.00
94	TREE & SHRUB, 2 ASSTD. 00382-4	OP	5.00	5.00
94	WEDDING BUNNY COUPLE, 2 ASSTD. 00347-3	OP	4.20	5.00
95	BUNNY CHEF, 2 ASSTD. 12433-8	OP	5.00	5.00
95	BUNNY CHILD COLLECTING EGG, 2 ASSTD. 02880-3	RT	4.20	5.00
95	BUNNY COUPLE AT CAFE 12444-4	OP	7.00	7.00
95	BUNNY KIDS AT CARROT JUICE STAND 12437-6	OP	5.30	5.30
95	BUNNY MINISTER, SOLOIST, 2 ASSTD. 12434-8	OP	5.00	5.00
95	BUNNY PLAYING PIANO 12439-0	OP	5.30	5.30
95	BUNNY PLAYING, 2 ASSTD. 12442-0	OP	6.50	6.50
95	BUNNY POPCORN, BALLOON VENDOR, 2 ASSTD. 12443-7	OP	6.70	7.00
95	ELECTRIC STREET LAMPPOST, SET OF 4 12461-1	OP	25.00	25.00
95	MAYOR BUNNY & BUNNY W/FLAG POLE, 2 ASSTD. 12441-3	OP	5.50	5.50
95	OUTDOOR BUNNY, 3 ASSTD. 12435-2	OP	5.00	5.00
95	PROFESSIONAL BUNNY, 3 ASSTD. 12438-3	OP	5.00	5.00
95	STREET SIGN, 3 ASSTD. 12433-8	OP	4.50	5.00
95	STROLLING BUNNY, 2 ASSTD. 12440-6	OP	5.50	5.50
96	BUNNIES SITTING IN GAZEBO 15801-2	OP	10.00	10.00

YR	NAME	LIMIT	ISSUE	TREND
96	BUNNY BAND QUARTET, SET OF 4 15799-2	OP	16.00	16.00
96	BUNNY CHILDREN WORKING IN GARDEN 15796-1	OP	3.50	4.00
96	BUNNY PICNICKING, SET OF 4 15798-5	OP	15.00	15.00
96	GARDEN SHOPKEEPER, SET OF 2 15800-5	OP	10.00	10.00
96	GARDEN TABLE W/POTTED PLANTS & FLOWERS 15802-9	OP	9.00	9.00
96	GARDEN W/WATERFALL & POND 15797-8	OP	15.00	15.00
96	TREE W/PAINTED FLOWERS, SET OF 3 15924-8	OP	20.00	20.00
*			**CREEPY HOLLOW COLLECTION**	
92	HALLOWEEN SIGN, 2 ASSTD. 06709-3	RT	6.00	6.00
92	WITCH 06706-2	OP	6.00	6.00
93	HAUNTED TREE, 2 ASSTD. 05892-3	OP	7.00	7.00
93	HINGED DRACULA'S COFFIN 08545-5	RT	11.00	11.00
93	PUMPKIN HEAD GHOST 06661-4	RT	5.50	5.50
93	PUMPKIN PATCH SIGN, 2 ASSTD. 05898-5	RT	6.50	6.50
93	SKELETON 06651-5	RT	5.50	5.50
93	TRICK OR TREATER, 3 ASSTD. 08591-2	RT	5.50	5.50
94	BLACK PICKET FENCE 10685-3	OP	13.50	14.00
94	CREEPY HOLLOW SIGN 10647-1	OP	5.50	5.50
94	GHOST, 3 ASSTD. 10652-5	OP	6.00	6.00
94	MAD SCIENTIST 10646-4	OP	6.00	6.00
94	OUTHOUSE 10648-8	OP	7.00	7.00
94	PHANTOM OF THE OPERA 10645-7	OP	6.00	6.00
94	STREET SIGN, 2 ASSTD. 10644-0	OP	5.70	6.00
94	TOMBSTONE SIGN, 3 ASSTD. 10642-6	OP	3.50	4.00
94	WEREWOLF 10643-4	OP	6.00	6.00
95	CEMETERY GATE 13366-8	OP	16.00	16.00
95	FLYING WITCH, GHOST, 2 ASSTD. 13362-0	OP	11.00	11.00
95	GHOUL USHER 13515-0	OP	6.50	6.50
95	GHOULISH ORGANIST PLAYING ORGAN 13363-7	OP	13.00	13.00
95	GRAVE DIGGER, 2 ASSTD. 13360-6	OP	10.00	10.00
95	HEARSE W/MONSTERS 13364-4	OP	15.00	15.00
95	HINGED TOMB 13516-7	RT	15.00	15.00
95	HUNCHBACK 13359-0	OP	9.00	9.00
95	PUMPKIN STREET LAMP, SET OF 4 13365-1	OP	25.00	25.00
95	ROAD OF BONES 13371-2	OP	9.00	9.00
95	STREET SIGN, 3 ASSTD. 13357-6	OP	5.50	5.50
95	THEATER GOER, SET OF 2 13358-3	OP	9.00	9.00
95	TICKET SELLER 13361-3	OP	10.00	10.00
96	BONE FENCE 16961-2	OP	9.50	10.00
96	COVERED BRIDGE 16664-2	OP	22.00	22.00
96	DRAGON 16936-0	OP	8.50	9.00
96	GHOSTLY KING 16659-8	OP	8.00	8.00
96	GYPSY 16656-7	OP	8.00	8.00
96	GYPSY WITCH 16655-0	OP	8.00	8.00
96	HEADLESS HORSEMAN 16658-1	OP	11.00	11.00
96	INN KEEPER 16660-4	OP	7.00	7.00
96	SCHOOL TEACHER 16657-4	OP	8.00	8.00
96	SKELETON BUTLER 16661-1	OP	7.00	7.00
E. WALKER			**EDDIE WALKER CHRISTMAS**	
98	1998 SANTA IN HOLIDAY PLANE	YR	55.00	55.00
98	SANTA AT NORTH POLE TREE FARM (SET OF 5)	7500	200.00	200.00
E. WALKER		**EDDIE WALKER GREAT PUMPKIN PATCH**		
98	1998 SIGNATURE WITCH ON PUMPKIN	YR	40.00	40.00
L.R. SMITH III			**LEO R. SMITH III COLLECTION**	
91	COSSACK SANTA 01092-1	RT	103.00	103.00
91	FISHERMAN SANTA 03311-1	RT	270.00	270.00
91	MILKMAKER 03541-2	RT	170.00	170.00
91	PILGRIM MAN 03313-5	RT	84.00	84.00
91	PILGRIM RIDING TURKEY 03312-8	RT	230.00	230.00
91	PILGRIM WOMAN 03315-9	RT	84.00	84.00
91	STARS & STRIPES SANTA 01743-2	RT	190.00	190.00
91	TIS A WITCHING TIME 03544-3	RT	140.00	140.00
91	TOYMAKER 03540-5	RT	120.00	120.00
91	WOODSMAN SANTA 03310-4	RT	230.00	230.00
92	DREAMS OF NIGHT BUFFALO 07999-7	CL	250.00	250.00
92	GREAT PLAINS SANTA 08049-8	RT	270.00	270.00
92	MS. LIBERTY 07866-2	RT	190.00	190.00
92	SANTA OF PEACE 07328-5	RT	250.00	250.00
92	WOODLAND BRAVE 07867-9	RT	87.00	87.00
93	DANCING SANTA 09042-8	RT	170.00	170.00
93	FOLK ANGEL 05444-4	RT	145.00	145.00
93	GNOME SANTA ON DEER 05206-8	CL	270.00	270.00
93	SANTA FISHERMAN 08979-8	CL	250.00	250.00
93	VOYAGEUR 09043-5	CL	170.00	170.00
94	GIFT GIVER SANTA 12056-9	CL	180.00	180.00
94	OLD WORLD SANTA 12053-8	RT	75.00	75.00
94	SANTA SKIER 12054-5	RT	190.00	190.00
94	STAR OF THE ROUNDUP COWBOY 11966-1	CL	100.00	100.00
94	WEATHERWISE ANGEL 12055-2	CL	150.00	150.00
95	ANGEL W/LION & LAMB 13990-5	RT	125.00	125.00
95	CIRCLE OF NATURE WREATH 16120-3	CL	200.00	200.00
95	GARDENING ANGEL 16118-0	CL	130.00	130.00
95	HARE LEAPING OVER THE GARDEN 16121-0	CL	100.00	100.00
95	MAIZE MAIDEN ANGEL 13992-9	CL	45.00	45.00
95	ORCHARD SANTA 13989-9	CL	125.00	125.00

YR	NAME	LIMIT	ISSUE	TREND
95	OTTER WALL HANGING 16122-7	CL	150.00	150.00
95	OWL LADY 13988-2	RT	100.00	100.00
95	SANTA IN SLEIGH 13987-5	CL	125.00	125.00
95	SUNBRINGER SANTA 13991-2	CL	125.00	125.00
95	WEE WILLIE SANTA 13993-6	RT	50.00	50.00
98	NORTHWOODS SANTA IN CANOE	1000	140.00	140.00
98	SANTA FISHERMAN	1000	90.00	90.00
98	SANTA ON MOOSE	750	150.00	150.00
98	SNOWSHOE SANTA	750	120.00	120.00

C. ULBRICHT   **NUTCRACKER COLLECTION**

YR	NAME	LIMIT	ISSUE	TREND
86	PILGRIM 00393-0	CL	145.00	145.00
93	MR. CLAUS 09588-1	CL	180.00	180.00
93	MRS. CLAUS 09587-4	CL	180.00	180.00
94	PRINCE ON ROCKING HORSE 12964-7	CL	160.00	160.00
95	FATHER TIME 12794-0	OP	220.00	220.00
95	FEMALE HEALTH CARE PROFESSIONAL 13189-3	OP	200.00	200.00
95	FEMALE VOLLEYBALL PLAYER 13986-8	OP	200.00	200.00
95	HUCK FINN 12788-9	CL	220.00	220.00
95	KING NUTCRACKER 13190-9	OP	200.00	200.00
95	LEPRECHAUN 09110-4	CL	170.00	170.00
95	MOSES 13186-2	CL	220.00	220.00
95	MOTHER GOOSE 13182-4	OP	220.00	220.00
95	NATURE SANTA W/BIRDHOUSE 12790-2	CL	220.00	220.00
95	PINOCCHIO 13184-8	CL	200.00	200.00
95	SANTA COOKIE BAKER 13191-6	CL	220.00	220.00
95	SANTA RIDING ROCKING REINDEER 12786-5	RT	200.00	200.00
95	SANTA W/TREE 12791-9	CL	200.00	200.00
95	WITCH 13183-1	OP	220.00	220.00
96	CANDYLAND SANTA 17016-8	OP	200.00	200.00
96	CINDERELLA 17014-4	OP	200.00	200.00
96	FIREFIGHTER 17017-5	OP	200.00	200.00
96	FLY FISHERMAN 17022-9	OP	190.00	190.00
96	GARDENING SANTA 17025-0	OP	190.00	190.00
96	GHOST OF CHRISTMAS PAST 18299-4	CL	200.00	200.00
96	GHOST OF CHRISTMAS YET TO COME 17021-2	CL	190.00	190.00
96	PIED PIPER 17026-7	OP	190.00	190.00
96	ROCK & ROLL SINGER 17020-5	OP	200.00	200.00
96	SACAJAWEA 17018-2	CL	200.00	200.00
96	SCARECROW 17023-6	OP	190.00	190.00
96	WYATT EARP 17019-9	1000	200.00	200.00

C. ULBRICHT   **NUTCRACKER FANTASY**

YR	NAME	LIMIT	ISSUE	TREND
91	CLARA 03657-0	OP	125.00	125.00
91	HERR DROSSELMEYER 03656-3	OP	170.00	170.00
91	MOUSE KING NUTCRACKER 04510-7	OP	170.00	170.00
91	PRINCE 03665-5	OP	160.00	160.00
91	TOY SOLDIER 03666-2	OP	160.00	160.00
95	BIKER NUTCRACKER 13187-9	OP	220.00	220.00
95	CLOWN NUTCRACKER 13188-6	OP	200.00	200.00
95	DRUMMER NUTCRACKER 12792-6	CL	220.00	220.00
95	KING OF CHRISTMAS NUTCRACKER 13665-2	OP	250.00	250.00

*   **ORE MOUNTAIN A CHRISTMAS CAROL**

YR	NAME	LIMIT	ISSUE	TREND
93	BOB CRATCHIT 09421-1	RT	120.00	120.00
93	GHOST OF CHRISTMAS PRESENT 12041-5	CL	116.00	116.00
93	SCROOGE 05522-9	RT	104.00	104.00
94	GHOST OF CHRISTMAS FUTURE 10449-1	RT	116.00	116.00
94	GHOST OF CHRISTMAS PAST10447-7	RT	116.00	116.00
94	MARLEY'S GHOST NUTCRACKER	4000	116.00	116.00

*   **ORE MOUNTAIN EASTER NUTCRACKER COLLECTION**

YR	NAME	LIMIT	ISSUE	TREND
84	MARCH HARE 00312-1	RT	77.00	77.00

*   **ORE MOUNTAIN NUTCRACKER COLLECTION**

YR	NAME	LIMIT	ISSUE	TREND
84	PINOCCHIO 00160-8	OP	60.00	60.00
88	NORDIC SANTA 08872-2	RT	84.00	84.00
88	SANTA W/TREE & TOYS 07666-8	RT	117.00	117.00
89	COUNTRY SANTA 09326-9	OP	95.00	95.00
89	FISHERMAN 09327-6	RT	90.00	90.00
89	GOLFER 09325-2	RT	85.00	85.00
90	ELF 04154-3	RT	70.00	70.00
90	MERLIN THE MAGICIAN 04207-6	RT	67.00	67.00
90	SEA CAPTAIN 04157-4	RT	108.00	108.00
90	SORCERER 10471-2	RT	100.00	100.00
90	UNCLE SAM 04206-9	RT	50.00	50.00
90	WINDSOR CLUB 04160-4	RT	85.00	85.00
90	WITCH 04159-8	RT	75.00	75.00
90	WOODLAND SANTA 04191-8	RT	105.00	105.00
91	CLOWN 03561-0	RT	115.00	115.00
91	NUTCRACKER-MAKER 03601-3	RT	62.00	62.00
92	CHRISTOPHER COLUMBUS 00152-3	RT	80.00	80.00
92	COWBOY 00298-8	RT	97.00	97.00
92	FARMER 01109-6	RT	65.00	65.00
92	INDIAN 00195-0	RT	96.00	96.00
92	PILGRIM 00188-2	RT	96.00	96.00
92	RINGMASTER 00196-7	RT	135.00	135.00
92	SANTA W/SKIS 01305-2	RT	86.00	86.00
92	VICTORIAN SANTA 00187-5	RT	130.00	130.00
93	CAT WITCH 09426-6	OP	93.00	93.00

YR	NAME	LIMIT	ISSUE	TREND
93	FIREMAN W/DOG 06592-1	OP	134.00	134.00
93	GEPETTO SANTA 09417-4	RT	115.00	115.00
93	SANTA W/ANIMALS 09424-2	RT	80.00	80.00
93	WHITE SANTA 09533-1	RT	100.00	100.00
94	ANNIE OAKLEY 10464-4	RT	128.00	128.00
94	BASEBALL PLAYER 10459-0	RT	111.00	111.00
94	BLACK SANTA 10460-6	OP	74.00	74.00
94	CAVALIER 12952-4	OP	80.00	80.00
94	CAVALIER 12953-1	OP	65.00	65.00
94	CAVALIER 12958-6	OP	57.00	57.00
94	CONFEDERATE SOLDIER 12837-4	OP	93.00	93.00
94	ENGINEER 10454-5	RT	108.00	108.00
94	GARDENING LADY 10450-7	OP	104.00	104.00
94	MINER 10493-4	RT	110.00	110.00
94	NATURE LOVER 10446-0	RT	112.00	112.00
94	PINECONE SANTA 10461-3	RT	92.00	92.00
94	PRINCE CHARMING 10457-6	RT	125.00	125.00
94	PUMPKIN HEAD SCARECROW 10451-1	OP	127.00	127.00
94	REGAL PRINCE 10452-1	OP	140.00	140.00
94	SANTA IN NIGHTSHIRT 10462-0	RT	76.00	76.00
94	SANTA W/BASKET 10472-9	OP	100.00	100.00
94	SNOW KING 10470-5	RT	97.00	97.00
94	SOCCER PLAYER 10494-1	OP	100.00	100.00
94	SULTAN KING 104552-2	RT	130.00	130.00
94	TOY VENDOR 11987-7	OP	124.00	124.00
94	UNION SOLDIER 12836-7	OP	93.00	93.00
95	AMERICAN COUNTRY SANTA 13195-4	OP	165.00	165.00
95	AUGUST THE STRONG 13185-5	OP	190.00	190.00
95	BARBEQUE DAD 13193-0	OP	176.00	176.00
95	BASKETBALL PLAYER 12784-1	OP	135.00	135.00
95	BEEFEATER 12797-1	OP	175.00	175.00
95	CHIMNEY SWEEP 00326-8	OP	70.00	70.00
95	DOWNHILL SANTA SKIER 13197-8	OP	145.00	145.00
95	HANDYMAN 12806-0	OP	135.00	136.00
95	HOCKEY PLAYER 12783-4	OP	155.00	155.00
95	HUNTER 12785-8	OP	136.00	136.00
95	JACK FROST 12803-9	OP	150.00	150.00
95	JOLLY ST. NICK W/TOYS 13709-3	OP	135.00	135.00
95	KING RICHARD THE LIONHEARTED 12798-8	OP	165.00	165.00
95	LAW SCHOLAR 12789-6	OP	127.00	127.00
95	PEDDLER 12805-3	OP	140.00	140.00
95	PIERRE LE CHEF 12802-2	OP	147.00	147.00
95	PIZZA BAKER 13194-7	OP	170.00	170.00
95	RIVERBOAT GAMBLER 12787-2	OP	137.00	137.00
95	ROYAL LION 13985-1	OP	130.00	130.00
95	SANTA AT WORKBENCH 13335-4	OP	108.00	108.00
95	TEACHER 13196-1	OP	165.00	165.00
96	ANGEL WCANDLE 17010-6	OP	220.00	220.00
96	ATTORNEY 17012-0	OP	120.00	120.00
96	CHIMNEY SWEEP 17043-4	OP	120.00	120.00
96	COUNT DRACULA 17050-2	OP	150.00	150.00
96	COW FARMER 17054-0	OP	120.00	120.00
96	DRUMMER 17044-1	OP	120.00	120.00
96	EAST COAST SANTA 17047-2	OP	200.00	200.00
96	EMERGENCY MEDICAL TECHNICIAN 17013-7	OP	140.00	140.00
96	FEMALE FARMER 17011-3	OP	145.00	145.00
96	FRANKENSTEIN 17009-0	OP	170.00	170.00
96	GUARD 17046-5	OP	120.00	120.00
96	HARLEQUIN SANTA 17174-5	OP	180.00	180.00
96	KING W/SCEPTER 17045-8	OP	120.00	120.00
96	MALE FARMER 17015-1	OP	145.00	145.00
96	NORTHWOODS SANTA 17048-9	OP	200.00	200.00
96	PRINCE 17038-0	OP	120.00	120.00
96	SANTA ONE-MAN BAND MUSICAL 17051-9	OP	170.00	170.00
96	SPORTS FAN 17173-8	OP	120.00	120.00
96	VICTORIAN SANTA 17172-1	OP	180.00	180.00
96	WESTERN 17049-6	OP	250.00	250.00

ORE MOUNTAIN NUTCRACKER FANTASY COLLECTION

YR	NAME	LIMIT	ISSUE	TREND
*				
88	HERR DROSSELMEYER 14 1/2" 07506-7	OP	75.00	75.00
88	MOUSE KING, THE 10" 07509-8	OP	60.00	60.00
88	PRINCE, THE 12 3/4", 2 ASSTD. 07507-4	OP	75.00	75.00
88	TOY SOLDIER, THE 11" 07508-1	OP	70.00	70.00
91	BUNNY W/EGG 00145--5	RT	77.00	77.00
91	CLARA 8" 01254-3	RT	77.00	77.00
92	BUNNY PAINTER 06480-1	RT	77.00	77.00
93	MOUSE KING, THE 05350-8	CL	100.00	100.00
94	HERR DROSSELMEYER 10456-9	CL	110.00	110.00
94	MARLEY'S GHOST 10448-4	RT	116.00	116.00
94	NUTCRACKER PRINCE 11001-0	CL	104.00	104.00
95	CLARA 12801-5	CL	125.00	125.00
95	TOY SOLDIER 12804-6	CL	125.00	125.00

C. ULBRICHT   **SANTA SERIES**

YR	NAME	LIMIT	ISSUE	TREND
93	MR. SANTA CLAUS NUTCRACKER	5000	180.00	180.00
93	MRS. CLAUS NUTCRACKER	5000	180.00	180.00

YR	NAME	LIMIT	ISSUE	TREND
C. ULBRICHT			**TRADITIONAL SANTA SERIES**	
92	FATHER CHRISTMAS NUTCRACKER 07094-9	RT	190.00	190.00
93	TOYMAKER NUTCRACKER 09531-7	CL	220.00	220.00
94	VICTORIAN SANTA NUTCRACKER 12961-1	CL	220.00	220.00
WENDT & KUHN				**WENDT & KUHN**
76	ANGEL W/SLED 02940-4	RT	37.00	37.00
76	SANTA W/ANGEL 00473-9	OP	50.00	50.00
78	MADONNA W/CHILD 01207-9	OP	120.00	120.00
79	ANGEL PLAYING VIOLIN 00403-6	RT	34.00	34.00
79	ANGEL TRIO 00471-5	OP	140.00	140.00
79	BAVARIAN MOVING VAN 02854-4	OP	134.00	134.00
79	GIRL W/CRADLE, SET OF 2 01203-1	RT	38.00	38.00
79	GIRL W/PORRIDGE BOWL 01198-0	OP	29.00	29.00
79	GIRL W/SCISSORS 01197-3	OP	29.00	29.00
79	MARGARITA ANGELS, SET OF 6 02938-1	OP	94.00	94.00
79	PIED PIPER & CHILDREN, SET OF 7 02843-8	RT	120.00	120.00
80	ANGEL PULLING WAGON 00553-8	RT	43.00	43.00
80	LITTLE PEOPLE NAPKIN RINGS, 6 ASSTD. 03504-7	OP	22.00	22.00
81	ANGEL W/TREE & BASKET 01190-8	RT	24.00	24.00
81	ANGELS AT CRADLE 01193-5	OP	73.00	73.00
81	SANT W/ANGEL IN SLEIGH 01192-8	RT	52.00	52.00
83	ANGEL BRASS MUSICIANS, SET OF 6 00470-8	OP	92.00	92.00
83	ANGEL CONDUCTOR ON STAND 00469-2	OP	21.00	21.00
83	ANGEL PERCUSSION MUSICIANS, SET OF 6 00443-2	OP	110.00	110.00
83	ANGEL STRING & WOODLAND MUSICIANS SET OF 6-00465-4	OP	108.00	108.00
83	ANGEL STRING MUSICIANS, SET OF 6 00455-5	RT	105.00	105.00
83	GIRL W/WAGON 01196-6	RT	27.00	27.00
83	MARGARITA BIRTHDAY ANGELS, SET OF 3 00480-7	RT	44.00	44.00
84	ANGELS BEARING TOYS, SET OF 6 00451-7	RT	97.00	97.00
87	CHILD ON SKIS, 2 ASSTD. 06083-4	RT	28.00	28.00
87	CHILD ON SLED 06085-8	RT	26.00	26.00
88	CHILDREN CARRYING LANTERNS PROCESSION, 6 01213-0	OP	117.00	117.00
88	LUCIA PARADE, SET OF 3 07667-5	RT	75.00	75.00
89	ANGEL AT PIANO 09403-7	OP	31.00	31.00
90	ANGEL DUET IN CELESTIAL STARS 04158-1	RT	60.00	60.00
91	BIRDHOUSE 01209-3	RT	23.00	23.00
91	BOY ON ROCKING HORSE, 2 ASSTD/ 01202-4	RT	35.00	35.00
91	DISPLAY BASE FOR WENDT & KUHN FIGURINES 01214-7	OP	32.00	32.00
91	FLOWER CHILDREN, SET OF 6 01213-0	OP	130.00	130.00
91	GIRL W/DOLL 01200-0	OP	32.00	32.00
91	WHITE ANGELS W/VIOLIN 01205-5	RT	26.00	26.00
92	WENDT & KUHN DISPLAY SIGN W/SITTING ANGEL 07535-7	OP	20.00	20.00
94	BUSY ELF, 3 ASSTD. 12856-5	OP	22.00	22.00
94	CHILD W/FLOWERS SET 12947-0	OP	45.00	45.00
94	SANTA W/TREE 12942-5	OP	29.00	29.00
94	SUN, MOON, STAR SET 12943-2	OP	69.00	69.00
96	ANGELS BEARING GIFTS 17039-0	OP	120.00	120.00
96	BLUEBERRY CHILDREN 17040-3	OP	110.00	110.00

MILL POND PRESS

YR	NAME	LIMIT	ISSUE	TREND
R. BATEMAN			**BATEMAN SCULPTURES**	
82	RED-TAILED HAWK STUDY	250	950.00	1750.00
83	MERGANSER DUCKLING	250	695.00	695.00
84	PEREGRINE IN FLIGHT	90	850.00	1500.00

MISS MARTHA ORIGINALS

YR	NAME	LIMIT	ISSUE	TREND
M. ROOT				
*	ANIKA 2600	*	*	350.00
*	ERIC & LIGHTNING 1570	RT	*	90.00
*	ERIKA 1578	RT	*	80.00
*	IDA B. WELLS 1906	RT	*	170.00
*	NAKIA 3500 (MAT)	RT	*	115.00
*	NAKIA 3500 (MATT)	RT	*	120.00
*	SANTA & SCOOTY 1571	RT	*	90.00
*	SHANI (BLACK EYES/WHITE DOTS) 1583	*	*	58.00
*	WILLIE W/BASE 1406W	RT	*	70.00
*	ZAMIKA 1581	RT	*	100.00
*	ZIZI	RT	*	45.00
M. ROOT			**ALL GOD'S CHILDREN**	
*	JANE 2001	RT	*	150.00
*	PATTI (DARK BLUE) 2002B	RT	*	100.00
*	PATTI (ROSE) 2002	RT	*	100.00
85	ABE 1357	RT	25.00	1520.00
85	BOOKER T 1320	RT	19.00	1490.00
85	CALLIE, 2 1/4 IN. 1362	RT	12.00	316.00
85	CALLIE, 4 1/2 IN. 1361	RT	19.00	536.00
85	EMMA 1322	RT	27.00	2040.00
85	TOM 1353	RT	16.00	475.00
86	AMY 1405W	RT	22.00	75.00
86	ANGEL 1401W	RT	20.00	79.00
86	ANNIE MAE, 6 IN. 1311	RT	19.00	187.00
86	ANNIE MAE, 8 1/2 IN. 1310	RT	27.00	275.00
86	BECKY 1402W	RT	22.00	82.00
86	GRANDMA 1323	RT	30.00	3750.00
86	JACOB 1407W	RT	26.00	84.00

YR	NAME	LIMIT	ISSUE	TREND
86	LI'L EMMIE, 3 1/2 IN. 1345	RT	13.00	188.00
86	LI'L EMMIE, 4 1/4 IN. 1344	RT	16.00	215.00
86	PRISSY (BEAR) 1358	RT	18.00	52.00
86	PRISSY (MOON PIE) 1557	OP	20.00	32.00
86	RACHEL 1404W	OP	20.00	28.00
86	SELINA JANE (6 STRANDS) 1338	RT	22.00	320.00
86	SELINA JANE (9 STRANDS) 1338	RT	22.00	638.00
86	ST. NICHOLAS BLACK 1316	RT	30.00	175.00
86	ST. NICHOLAS WHITE 1315	RT	30.00	175.00
86	TOBY, 3 1/2 IN. 1332	RT	13.00	190.00
86	TOBY, 4 1/2 IN. 1331	RT	16.00	220.00
86	UNCLE BUD, 6 IN. 1304	RT	19.00	220.00
86	UNCLE BUD, 8 1/2 IN. 1303	RT	27.00	420.00
87	AUNT SARAH IN BLUE 1440	RT	45.00	310.00
87	AUNT SARAH IN RED 1440	RT	45.00	425.00
87	BECKY WITH PATCH 1402	RT	19.00	254.00
87	BEN 1504	RT	22.00	447.00
87	BLOSSOM IN BLUE 1500	RT	60.00	440.00
87	BLOSSOM IN RED 1500	RT	750.00	830.00
87	BONNIE & BUTTONS 1502	RT	24.00	175.00
87	CASSIE 1503	RT	22.00	215.00
87	CHARITY 1408	RT	28.00	130.00
87	GINNIE 1508	RT	22.00	454.00
87	JESSIE-NO BASE 1501	RT	19.00	460.00
87	MOSES 1506	RT	30.00	190.00
87	PADDY PAW & LUCY 1553	SU	24.00	104.00
87	PADDY PAW & LUKE 1551	SU	24.00	104.00
87	PRIMAS JONES 1377	RT	40.00	862.00
87	PRIMAS JONES W/BASE 1377	RT	40.00	862.00
87	PRISSY W/BASKET 1346	RT	16.00	183.00
87	PRISSY W/YARN HAIR (6 STRANDS) 1343	RT	19.00	325.00
87	PRISSY W/YARN HAIR (9 STRANDS) 1343	RT	19.00	560.00
87	PUD 1550	RT	10.00	1385.00
87	TAT 1801	RT	30.00	79.00
87	TIFFANY1511	OP	32.00	32.00
87	WILLIE-NO BASE 1406W	RT	22.00	468.00
88	BEAN (CLEAR WATER) 1521	RT	36.00	334.00
88	BETSY (CLEAR WATER) 1513	RT	36.00	340.00
88	BOONE 1510	RT	125.00	190.00
88	CALVIN 777	RT	200.00	2180.00
88	HANNAH 1515	OP	36.00	37.00
88	JOHN 1514	RT	30.00	260.00
88	KEZIA 1518	RT	36.00	76.00
88	LISA 1512	RT	30.00	275.00
88	MAYA 1520	RT	36.00	163.00
88	MEG (LONG HAIR) 1505	RT	21.00	500.00
88	MEG (SHORT HAIR) 1505	RT	21.00	990.00
88	MEG IN BEIGE DRESS 1505	RT	21.00	1240.00
88	MICHAEL & KIM 1517	OP	36.00	38.00
88	MOE & POKEY 1552	RT	16.00	110.00
88	PEANUT 1509	RT	16.00	195.00
88	SALLY 1507	RT	19.00	225.00
88	TANSY & TEDI 1516	OP	30.00	38.00
88	TANSY & TEDI W/GREEN SOCKS 1516	RT	30.00	338.00
89	ADAM 1525	RT	25.00	1300.00
89	BEVERLY 1525	RT	50.00	660.00
89	BO 1530	RT	22.00	98.00
89	BOOTSIE 1529	RT	60.00	98.00
89	DAVID 1528	OP	28.00	30.00
89	JESSICA & JEREMY 1522-23	RT	195.00	1998.00
89	JESSIE 1501	OP	30.00	32.00
89	SASHA 1531	OP	30.00	32.00
89	TARA 1527	OP	36.00	37.00
90	JEROME 1532	OP	30.00	32.00
90	JOSEPH 1537	OP	30.00	30.00
90	KACIE 1533	OP	38.00	38.00
90	MARY 1536	OP	30.00	30.00
90	PRESHUS 1538	OP	24.00	24.00
90	SUNSHINE 1535	RT	38.00	78.00
90	TESS 1534	OP	30.00	32.00
90	THALIYAH 778	RT	150.00	1900.00
91	BESSIE & CORKIE 1547	OP	70.00	70.00
91	BILLY 1545	RT	36.00	165.00
91	DORI IN GREEN DRESS 1544	RT	30.00	419.00
91	DORI/PEACH DRESS 1544	OP	28.00	30.00
91	FATHER CHRISTMAS BLACK 1772	RT	195.00	695.00
91	NELLIE 1546	RT	36.00	175.00
91	SAMANTHA 1542	RT	38.00	145.00
91	SAMUEL 1541	RT	30.00	139.00
92	BARNEY 1557	RT	32.00	100.00
92	BEAN (PAINTED WATER) 1521	RT	36.00	150.00
92	BETH 1558	RT	32.00	100.00
92	BETSY (PAINTED WATER) 1513	RT	36.00	150.00
92	CAITLIN 1554	RT	36.00	135.00
92	FAITH 1555	RT	32.00	134.00

YR	NAME	LIMIT	ISSUE	TREND
92	JOY 1548	OP	30.00	30.00
92	MELISSA 1556	RT	32.00	110.00
92	MERCI 1559	OP	36.00	37.00
92	RAKIYA 1561	OP	36.00	36.00
92	STEPHEN (NATIVITY SHEPHERD) 1563	OP	36.00	36.00
92	THOMAS 1549	OP	30.00	30.00
92	VALERIE 1560	OP	36.00	37.00
93	NATHANIEL	OP	36.00	36.00
93	SIMON & ANDREW 1565	OP	45.00	45.00
93	SYLVIA 1564	OP	36.00	37.00
93	ZACK 1566	OP	34.00	34.00
94	CHANTEL 1573	OP	39.00	39.00
94	CHERI 1574	OP	38.00	38.00
94	JUSTIN 1576	OP	37.00	37.00
94	NIAMBI 1577	OP	34.00	34.00
94	TISH 1572	OP	38.00	38.00
94	URIEL 2000	RT	45.00	185.00
98	DENISE	OP	39.00	39.00
98	KRISHNA	OP	40.00	40.00
98	LEROY	OP	40.00	40.00
98	SISSY	OP	38.00	38.00

M. ROOT — **ANGELIC MESSENGERS**

YR	NAME	LIMIT	ISSUE	TREND
94	CIEARA 2500	OP	38.00	38.00
94	MARIAH 2501	*	38.00	100.00

M. ROOT — **CHRISTMAS**

YR	NAME	LIMIT	ISSUE	TREND
86	SAINT NICHOLAS BLACK 1316	RT	30.00	110.00
86	SAINT NICHOLAS WHITE 1315	RT	30.00	85.00
87	FATHER CHRISTMAS BLACK 1751	RT	145.00	745.00
87	FATHER CHRISTMAS WHITE 1750	RT	145.00	745.00
88	FATHER CHRISTMAS BLACK 1758	RT	195.00	640.00
88	FATHER CHRISTMAS WHITE 1757	RT	195.00	640.00
88	SANTA CLAUS BLACK 1768	RT	185.00	665.00
88	SANTA CLAUS WHITE 1767	RT	185.00	665.00
89	FATHER CHRISTMAS BLACK 1770	RT	195.00	720.00
89	FATHER CHRISTMAS WHITE 1769	RT	195.00	720.00
91	FATHER CHRISTMAS WHITE 1771	RT	195.00	695.00
92	FATHER CHRISTMAS BLACK 1774	RT	195.00	500.00
92	FATHER CHRISTMAS BLACK BUST 1776	RT	145.00	380.00
92	FATHER CHRISTMAS WHITE 1773	RT	195.00	500.00
92	FATHER CHRISTMAS WHITE BUST 1775	RT	145.00	380.00

M. ROOT — **COLLECTOR'S CLUB**

YR	NAME	LIMIT	ISSUE	TREND
89	MOLLY 1524	RT	38.00	650.00
90	JOEY 1539	RT	32.00	525.00
91	MANDY 1540	RT	36.00	330.00
92	OLIVIA 1562	RT	36.00	272.00
93	GARRETT 1567	RT	36.00	250.00
93	PEEK-A-BOO	RT	*	95.00
94	ALEXANDRIA 1575	RT	36.00	140.00
94	LINDY	RT	*	83.00

M. ROOT — **ENDEARING MEMORIES**

YR	NAME	LIMIT	ISSUE	TREND
*	KALIA 8010	*	*	110.00
*	MARCUS/NICOLE 8014	*	*	120.00
*	SAVANNAH 8017	RT	*	135.00
*	WIL 8012	*	*	112.00

M. ROOT — **FAMILY REUNION**

YR	NAME	LIMIT	ISSUE	TREND
94	BEAR	*	*	125.00
95	TILLIE	*	*	120.00
96	DILLIE	*	*	80.00

M. ROOT — **HISTORICAL**

YR	NAME	LIMIT	ISSUE	TREND
89	HARRIET TUBMAN 1900	RT	65.00	285.00
90	SOJOURNER TRUTH 1901	OP	65.00	65.00
91	FREDERICK DOUGLASS 1902	OP	70.00	70.00
92	DR. DANIEL WILLIAMS 1903	RT	70.00	185.00
92	FRANCES HARPER 1905	OP	70.00	70.00
92	GEORGE WASHINGTON CARVER 1907	OP	70.00	70.00
92	MARY BETHUNE 1904 (MISSPELLED)	CL	70.00	290.00
94	AUGUSTUS WALLEY (BUFFALO SOLDIER) 1908	RT	95.00	260.00
94	BESSIE SMITH 1909	OP	70.00	70.00
98	BESSIE COLEMAN	OP	71.50	72.00

M. ROOT — **INTERNATIONAL**

YR	NAME	LIMIT	ISSUE	TREND
87	KAMEOK 1802	OP	26.00	28.00
87	KARL 1808	RT	26.00	68.00
87	KELLI 1805	OP	30.00	30.00
87	LITTLE CHIEF 1804	OP	32.00	32.00
87	PIKE 1806	OP	30.00	32.00
88	KATRINA 1803	RT	26.00	167.00
93	MINNIE 1568	OP	36.00	36.00

M. ROOT — **SUGAR AND SPICE**

YR	NAME	LIMIT	ISSUE	TREND
87	BLESSED ARE THE PEACEMAKERS (ELI) 1403	RT	22.00	500.00
87	FRIENDS SHOW LOVE (BECKY) 1402	RT	22.00	500.00
87	FRIENDSHIP WARMS...HEART (JACOB) 1407	RT	22.00	500.00
87	GOD IS LOVE (ANGEL) 1401	RT	22.00	500.00
87	JESUS LOVES ME (AMY) 1405	RT	22.00	500.00
87	OLD FRIENDS ARE BEST (RACHEL) 1404	RT	22.00	500.00

YR	NAME	LIMIT	ISSUE	TREND
87	SHARING WITH FRIENDS (WILLIE) 1406	RT	22.00	500.00
88	JUAN 1807	RT	22.00	162.00

MUSEUM COLLECTIONS INC.

	N. ROCKWELL		AMERICAN FAMILY I	
79	BABY'S FIRST STEP	22500	90.00	220.00
80	BIRTHDAY PARTY	22500	110.00	150.00
80	FIRST HAIRCUT	22500	90.00	140.00
80	HAPPY BIRTHDAY, DEAR MOTHER	22500	90.00	150.00
80	LITTLE MOTHER	22500	110.00	110.00
80	SWEET SIXTEEN	22500	90.00	90.00
80	WASHING OUR DOG	22500	110.00	110.00
81	BRIDE AND GROOM	22500	110.00	180.00
81	MOTHER'S LITTLE HELPERS	22500	110.00	110.00
	N. ROCKWELL		**CHRISTMAS**	
80	CHECKING HIS LIST	YR	65.00	85.00
81	RINGING IN GOOD CHEER	YR	95.00	95.00
82	WAITING FOR SANTA	YR	95.00	95.00
83	HIGH HOPES	YR	95.00	95.00
84	SPACE-AGE SANTA	YR	65.00	65.00
	N. ROCKWELL		**CLASSIC**	
80	BEDTIME	OP	65.00	95.00
80	COBBLER, THE	OP	65.00	85.00
80	FOR A GOOD BOY	OP	65.00	75.00
80	LIGHTHOUSE KEEPER'S DAUGHTER	OP	65.00	65.00
80	MEMORIES	OP	65.00	65.00
80	TOYMAKER, THE	OP	65.00	85.00
81	A DOLLHOUSE FOR SIS	OP	65.00	65.00
81	MUSIC LESSON, THE	OP	65.00	65.00
81	MUSIC MASTER	OP	65.00	65.00
81	OFF TO SCHOOL	OP	65.00	65.00
81	PUPPY LOVE	OP	65.00	65.00
81	WHILE THE AUDIENCE WAITS	OP	65.00	65.00
82	COUNTRY DOCTOR, THE	OP	65.00	65.00
82	DREAMS IN THE ANTIQUE SHOP	OP	65.00	65.00
82	KITE MAKER, THE	OP	65.00	65.00
82	SPRING FEVER	OP	65.00	65.00
82	WORDS OF WISDOM	OP	65.00	65.00
83	A FINAL TOUCH	OP	65.00	65.00
83	A SPECIAL TREAT	OP	65.00	65.00
83	BORED OF EDUCATION	OP	65.00	65.00
83	BRAVING THE STORM	OP	65.00	65.00
83	HIGH STEPPING	OP	65.00	65.00
83	WINTER FUN	OP	65.00	65.00
84	ALL WRAPPED UP	OP	65.00	65.00
84	BIG RACE, THE	OP	65.00	65.00
84	GOIN' FISHIN'	OP	65.00	65.00
84	SATURDAY'S HERO	OP	65.00	65.00
	N. ROCKWELL		**COMMEMORATIVE**	
81	NORMAN ROCKWELL DISPLAY	5000	125.00	150.00
82	SPIRIT OF AMERICA	5000	125.00	125.00
83	NORMAN ROCKWELL, AMERICA'S ARTIST	5000	125.00	125.00
84	OUTWARD BOUND	5000	125.00	125.00
85	ANOTHER MASTERPIECE BY NORMAN ROCKWELL	5000	125.00	150.00
86	PAINTER AND THE PUPS, THE	5000	125.00	150.00

N. ROCKWELL GALLERY

	N. ROCKWELL			
97	IS HE COMING? STOCKING HOLDER	*	40.00	40.00
97	ROCKWELL'S STUDIO MUSIC BOX	*	35.00	35.00
97	SANTA'S WORKSHOP MUSIC BOX	*	35.00	35.00
	N. ROCKWELL		**HOME FOR CHRISTMAS**	
97	THE LIBRARY (BOX)	*	35.00	35.00

OLD WORLD CHRISTMAS

	E.M. MERCK		NUTCRACKERS	
87	AUSTRIAN MUSKETEER NUTCRACKER 72048	RT	32.00	75.00
87	BRITISH GUARD NUTCRACKER 72041	RT	35.00	65.00
87	PRUSSIAN SERGEANT NUTCRACKER 72045	RT	36.00	75.00
92	LG. BAVARIAN DUKE NUTCRACKER 72242	RT	99.00	150.00

OLSZEWSKI STUDIOS

	R. OLSZEWSKI		CORE 1ST QUARTER	
97	AMERICAN BEAUTY	750	225.00	225.00
	R. OLSZEWSKI		**CORE 2ND QUARTER**	
97	SUMMER	750	240.00	240.00
	R. OLSZEWSKI		**CORE 3RD QUARTER**	
97	WINTER	750	230.00	230.00
	R. OLSZEWSKI		**CORE 4TH QUARTER**	
97	DOLLHOUSE DREAMS	750	235.00	235.00
	R. OLSZEWSKI		**LANDSCAPE**	
97	FOX HUNT, THE	500	480.00	480.00
	R. OLSZEWSKI		**MINIATURES**	
94	GRAND ENTRANCE, THE	1500	225.00	300.00
94	LITTLE TINKER, THE	750	235.00	400.00

YR	NAME	LIMIT	ISSUE	TREND
94	TINKER'S TREASURE CHEST & TO BE..., THE	CL	235.00	350.00
97	NOT TO BE TOWER	OP	165.00	165.00
R. OLSZEWSKI			**PRECIOUS METALS**	
97	DASHING THROUGH THE SNOW GIFT BOX	OP	850.00	850.00
97	GARDEN BRACELET	OP	225.00	225.00

PACIFIC RIM

	*			**BUNNY TOES**
94	HANNAH WITH MAXIMILIAN	RT	13.00	13.00
94	MAZIE AT PLAY	OP	13.00	13.00
94	SWEETHEARTS	OP	50.00	50.00
94	TILLIE MAKING A WREATH	OP	13.00	13.00
94	TIMOTHY WITH FLOWER CART	OP	17.00	17.00
94	TIMOTHY WITH TULIPS	OP	13.00	13.00
94	WENDELL AT THE MAILBOX	OP	17.00	17.00
94	WENDELL WITH EGGS IN HAT	OP	13.00	13.00
94	WENDELL WITH FLOWERS	RT	13.00	13.00
94	WILLIS & SKEETER	OP	17.00	17.00
94	WINIFRED WITH BLOOMS	OP	13.00	13.00
95	BUNNY GAZEBO	OP	50.00	50.00
95	GARDEN TRELLIS	OP	30.00	30.00
95	TILLIE WITH HER BIKE	OP	15.00	15.00
95	TIMOTHY WITH EGGS	OP	13.00	13.00
95	WILLIS & SKEETER GARDENING	OP	15.00	15.00
95	WINIFRED PAINTS EGGS	OP	15.00	15.00
96	BETSY & JUSTIN	1440	15.00	15.00
97	ANNIE ON THE SWING	OP	30.00	30.00
97	BIRTHDAY PARTY	1200	60.00	60.00
97	HANNAH'S PRIDE & JOY	OP	20.00	20.00
97	MAZIE FROLICS	OP	15.00	15.00
97	MISS AMANDA'S CLASS	OP	20.00	20.00
97	OH CHRISTMAS TREE	OP	20.00	20.00
97	SOPHIE TRIMS THE TREE	OP	20.00	20.00
97	TIMOTHY & TILLIE GIVE THANKS	OP	20.00	20.00
97	WINIFRED & WENDELL CAROLING	OP	20.00	20.00
P. SEBERN			**BUNNY TOES**	
95	BUNNY TOES LOGO SIGN	OP	20.00	20.00
96	BETSY-CELEBRATE	1440	7.50	8.00
96	JUSTINE-STARS & STRIPES	1440	7.50	8.00
P. SEBERN		**BUNNY TOES BIRTHDAY BUNNIES**		
95	ANABELL GLIDING ALONG	OP	20.00	20.00
95	BETH BACK TO SCHOOL	OP	20.00	20.00
95	CALLIE BUNDLE UP	OP	20.00	20.00
95	CARLY STRIKING A POSE	OP	20.00	20.00
95	CHARLOTTE BEST OF THE BUNCH	OP	20.00	20.00
95	CHESTER SHARING WITH FRIENDS	OP	20.00	20.00
95	CHRISTOPHER & CORY THE BEST SHOT	OP	20.00	20.00
95	DINAH IRRESISTIBLE	OP	20.00	20.00
95	DOUGLAS FROSTY FRIENDS	OP	20.00	20.00
95	GOLDIE TAKING TURNS	OP	20.00	20.00
95	HARVEY GIDDY-UP AND GO	OP	20.00	20.00
95	JEREMY CLEAR SAILING	OP	20.00	20.00
95	JOEY AUTUMN CHORES	OP	20.00	20.00
95	MAGGIE JOY OF LIVING	OP	20.00	20.00
95	MOLLY SWEET WISHES	OP	20.00	20.00
95	NICHOLAS BETWEEN TIDES	OP	20.00	20.00
95	PENELOPE WISHFUL THINKING	OP	20.00	20.00
95	PHOEBE FIRST OUTING	OP	20.00	20.00
95	PIETER HIGHER EDUCATION	OP	20.00	20.00
95	RUSSEL & ROBBY SHARING THE HARVEST	OP	20.00	20.00
95	VIOLET THANK YOU NOTES	OP	20.00	20.00
95	WILBUR LAZY DAZE	OP	20.00	20.00
95	WILEY WINTER GAMES	OP	20.00	20.00
95	ZACHARY WAITIN' ON THE WIND	OP	20.00	20.00
	*			**PATRIOTIC SERIES**
97	BETSY SEWS THE FLAG	1200	15.00	15.00
97	JUSTIN ON PARADE	1200	15.00	15.00

PAPEL GIFTWARE

C. JOHNSON			**LIFE'S ENDEARMENTS**	
94	COACHING	OP	30.00	32.00
94	LEARNING TO SHARE	OP	25.00	27.00
94	MY FIRST FRIEND	OP	23.00	25.00
94	MY TEDDY TALKS	OP	25.00	27.00
94	PUPPY LOVE	OP	23.00	25.00
94	SISTERS	OP	30.00	32.00
	*	**WINDSOR BEARS OF CRANBURY COMMONS**		
98	AMBER-THINKING OF YOU	OP	16.50	17.00
98	CONNOR-FOLLOW YOUR DREAMS	OP	22.50	23.00
98	REBECCA-THANK YOU	OP	16.50	17.00
	*	**WINDSOR HARES OF CRANBURY COMMONS**		
98	A TIME TO REMEMBER	*	*	N/A
98	AMBER & BRANDON-DASHING THROUGH THE SNOW	OP	30.00	30.00
98	COURTNEY & RYAN-BOO!	OP	20.00	20.00
98	DANIEL-SHOW DAY!	OP	15.00	15.00

YR	NAME	LIMIT	ISSUE	TREND
98	DOROTHY & SCOTT-PERFECT PAIR	OP	17.50	18.00
98	EMILY-BUILDING A FRIENDSHIP	OP	20.00	20.00
98	FRED-TE-RIFIC GOLFER	OP	10.00	10.00
98	LAURA-PAR-FECT PUTT	OP	10.00	10.00
98	LAUREN-SWEET & DELICIOUS	OP	25.00	25.00
98	MOMMY & BECKY-HOMEMADE WITH LOVE	OP	20.00	20.00
98	MORGAN & TAYLOR-FRIENDSHIP WARMS THE HEART	OP	20.00	20.00
98	SANTA & COREY-ALL I WANT FOR CHRISTMAS	OP	17.50	18.00

PAVILION OF T'SANG YING-HSUAN

S. FU   **THE FORBIDDEN CITY MUSIC BOX COLLECTION**

91	EMPEROR'S WEDDING, THE	84-DAY	40.00	45.00

PEMBERTON & OAKES

D. ZOLAN   **MUSIC BOXES**

89	DOZENS OF DAISIES	*	48.00	110.00
91	BROTHERLY LOVE	*	54.00	140.00
91	FOR YOU	*	35.00	46.00
91	TINY TREASURES	*	27.00	48.00

D. ZOLAN   **ZOLAN'S CHILDREN**

81	ERIK AND THE DANDELION	17000	48.00	71.00
82	SABINA IN THE GRASS	6800	48.00	97.00
84	WINTER WONDER	8000	28.00	59.00
85	TENDER MOMENT	10000	29.00	48.00

PENDELFIN

J. HEAP   **40TH ANNIVERSARY**

94	AUNT RUBY	10000	275.00	275.00

J. HEAP   **FAMILY CIRCLE**

93	BOSUN	RT	50.00	90.00
94	PUFFER	RT	85.00	85.00
95	GEORGIE & THE DRAGON	RT	125.00	125.00
96	DELIA	RT	125.00	125.00
97	WOODY	YR	125.00	125.00

J. HEAP   **FAMILY CIRCLE EVENT**

94	WALMSLEY	RT	75.00	75.00
95	RUNAWAY	RT	90.00	90.00

J. HEAP   **GALLERY SERIES**

71	WAKEY, PIEFACE, POPPET, ROBERT, DODGER	RT	300.00	300.00

J. HEAP   **RETIRED FIGURINES/COTTAGES**

53	PENDLE WITCH	RT	4.00	1000.00
55	MARGO	RT	2.00	450.00
55	OLD FATHER (REMODELED)	RT	50.00	850.00
55	ORIGINAL FATHER	RT	50.00	1250.00
56	MIDGE	RT	2.00	450.00
56	ORIGINAL ROBERT	RT	2.50	300.00
56	TIMBER STAND	RT	35.00	175.00
57	OLD MOTHER	RT	6.25	675.00
58	RABBIT BOOK ENDS	RT	10.00	1750.00
59	CHA CHA	RT	*	1000.00
59	ROCKY	RT	32.00	40.00
59	UNCLE SOAMES	RT	105.00	350.00
60	GUSSIE	RT	*	375.00
60	LUCY POCKET	RT	4.20	350.00
60	MODEL STAND	RT	4.00	575.00
60	SHINER WITH BLACK EYE	RT	2.50	400.00
60	SQUEEZY	RT	2.50	425.00
61	FATHER MOUSE (GRAY)	RT	*	625.00
61	GRAND STAND MOLD 1	RT	35.00	590.00
61	LOLLIPOP (GRAY MOUSE)	RT	*	600.00
61	MEGAN	RT	3.00	450.00
61	MOTHER GOOSE (GRAY)	RT	*	625.00
62	CORNISH PRAYER (CORNY)	RT	*	700.00
63	AUNT AGATHA	RT	*	1750.00
63	CYRIL SQUIRREL	RT	*	1025.00
64	BANDSTAND	RT	70.00	80.00
64	DODGER	RT	24.00	24.00
65	MOTHER GOOSE (BRONZE)	RT	*	350.00
65	MOTHER HOUSE (STONEWARE)	RT	*	600.00
65	PICNIC STAND	RT	63.00	160.00
66	CAKESTAND	RT	2.00	350.00
66	MILK JUG STAND	RT	2.00	375.00
66	PICNIC BASKET	RT	2.00	475.00
67	BATH TUB	RT	4.50	85.00
67	MAUD	RT	*	425.00
67	PHUMF	RT	24.00	80.00
67	PICNIC TABLE	RT	*	425.00
71	TOTTY	RT	21.00	200.00
85	APPLE BARREL	RT	*	20.00
88	HUMPHREY GO KART	RT	70.00	110.00
92	GRAND STAND MOLD 2	RT	150.00	150.00

D. ROBERTS   **RETIRED FIGURINES/COTTAGES**

57	TAMMY	RT	25.00	70.00
62	POOCH	RT	25.00	65.00
64	BONGO	RT	31.00	115.00

YR	NAME	LIMIT	ISSUE	TREND
65	MUNCHER	RT	26.00	80.00
66	PIEFACE	RT	31.00	68.00
67	ROBERT WITH LOLLIPOP	RT	12.00	175.00
80	CROCKER	RT	20.00	70.00
81	NIPPER	RT	21.00	80.00
81	SHRIMP STAND	RT	70.00	75.00
84	BLOSSOM	RT	35.00	65.00
84	OLIVER	RT	25.00	33.00
85	CHRISTMAS SET	RT	*	500.00
85	JINGLE	RT	11.25	35.00
85	SOLO	RT	40.00	65.00
86	JIM LAD	RT	23.00	60.00
86	LITTLE MO	RT	35.00	45.00
87	TENNYSON	RT	35.00	40.00
89	CHIRPY	RT	32.00	80.00
89	HONEY	RT	40.00	65.00
90	CHARLOTTE	RT	25.00	80.00
91	WORDSWORTH	RT	60.00	70.00
93	FORTY WINKS	RT	57.00	57.00

PHILIP L. MARCACCI STUDIO
P. MARCACCI

YR	NAME	LIMIT	ISSUE	TREND
93	HOTEL ARIZONA	33	2,800.00	3000.00
93	KEEPER OF THE WIND	33	2,800.00	3000.00
93	NOSEY NEIGHBOR	33	865.00	925.00
93	ONE LOST MITTEN	33	1,200.00	1400.00
93	SEBASTIAN	33	1,050.00	1200.00
93	WOULD YA LOOK AT THAT	33	925.00	1000.00
94	ALMOST	33	900.00	1000.00
94	CROWN PRINCESS	33	575.00	650.00
94	HEIRS TO THE THRONE	33	885.00	950.00
94	NOWHERE TO HIDE	33	750.00	800.00
94	SAVANNAH SOVEREIGN	33	4,800.00	5000.00

PIPPSYWOGGINS
M. CARLSON — FRIAR FOLK

YR	NAME	LIMIT	ISSUE	TREND
98	KNEELING PRAYING	*	10.00	10.00
98	STANDING BASEBALL PLAYER	*	10.00	10.00
98	STANDING EATING COOKIE	*	10.00	10.00
98	STANDING HOLDING BOOKS	*	10.00	10.00
98	STANDING HOLDING CUT FLOWERS	*	10.00	10.00
98	STANDING HOLDING FISH	*	10.00	10.00

M. CARLSON — PIPPSYWOGGINS

YR	NAME	LIMIT	ISSUE	TREND
94	DESSIE ROSALIA	RT	38.00	38.00
94	PETERJON THOMAS	RT	38.00	38.00
97	FRANNIE JANE	OP	42.00	42.00
97	MILLIE ROSEANNA	OP	42.00	42.00
97	OPAL VERONICA	OP	42.00	42.00

M. CARLSON — WISHING YOU...

YR	NAME	LIMIT	ISSUE	TREND
98	COMFORT	*	20.00	20.00
98	HAPPINESS	*	20.00	20.00
98	HOPE	*	20.00	20.00
98	JOY	*	20.00	20.00
98	LOVE	*	20.00	20.00
98	PEACE	*	20.00	20.00

POLLAND STUDIOS
D. POLLAND — AMERICAN SPIRIT COLLECTION

YR	NAME	LIMIT	ISSUE	TREND
98	DAMNED KNOTHEAD	900	195.00	195.00
98	FIGHTING MUSTANGS	1200	188.00	188.00
98	ON THE PROD	900	195.00	195.00
98	SACKING OUT	900	195.00	195.00
98	SEARS CATALOG	900	195.00	195.00
98	STOLEN PONY	1200	195.00	195.00
98	TEXAS SAGE	1200	195.00	195.00
98	WARRING TRIBES #1	600	250.00	250.00
98	WARRING TRIBES #2	600	250.00	250.00
98	WARRING TRIBES #3	600	250.00	250.00

D. POLLAND — COLLECTIBLE BRONZES

YR	NAME	LIMIT	ISSUE	TREND
67	BULL SESSION	11	200.00	1200.00
69	BLOWIN' COLD	30	375.00	1250.00
69	BREED, THE	30	350.00	975.00
69	BUFFALO HUNT	30	450.00	1250.00
69	COMANCHERO	30	350.00	750.00
69	DANCING INDIAN WITH LANCE	50	250.00	775.00
69	DANCING INDIAN WITH TOMAHAWK	50	250.00	775.00
69	DANCING MEDICINE MAN	50	250.00	775.00
69	DRAWN SABERS	50	2,000.00	5650.00
69	LOOKOUTS	30	375.00	1300.00
69	TOP MONEY	30	275.00	800.00
69	TRAIL HAZZARD	30	700.00	1750.00
69	WAR CRY	30	350.00	975.00
69	WHEN ENEMIES MEET	30	700.00	2350.00
70	COFFEE TIME	50	1,200.00	2900.00
70	LOST DISPATCH, THE	50	1,200.00	2950.00

YR	NAME	LIMIT	ISSUE	TREND
70	WANTED	50	500.00	1150.00
71	AMBUSH AT ROCK CANYON	5	20,000.00	45000.00
71	OH SUGAR!	40	700.00	1525.00
71	SHAKIN' OUT A LOOP	40	500.00	1075.00
72	BUFFALO ROBE	50	1,000.00	2350.00
73	BUNCH QUITTER	60	750.00	1975.00
73	CHALLENGE	60	750.00	1800.00
73	TRACKING	60	500.00	1500.00
73	WAR PARTY	60	1,500.00	5500.00
75	CHEYENNE	6	1,300.00	1800.00
75	COUNTING COUP	6	1,450.00	1950.00
75	CROW SCOUT	6	1,300.00	1800.00
76	BUFFALO HUNT	6	2,200.00	3500.00
76	MANDAN HUNTER	12	775.00	775.00
76	MONDAY MORNING WASH	6	2,800.00	2800.00
76	PAINTING THE TOWN	6	3,000.00	4200.00
76	RESCUE	6	2,400.00	3000.00
80	BUFFALO PRAYER	25	375.00	675.00
D. POLLAND			**COLLECTOR SOCIETY**	
87	I COME IN PEACE	CL	35.00	230.00
87	I COME IN PEACE, SILENT TRAIL (SET)	CL	335.00	1000.00
87	SILENT TRAIL	CL	300.00	750.00
88	DISPUTED TRAIL	CL	300.00	500.00
88	HUNTER, THE	CL	35.00	250.00
88	HUNTER, THE- DISPUTED TRAIL (SET)	CL	335.00	825.00
89	APACHE BIRDMAN	CL	300.00	450.00
89	CRAZY HORSE	CL	35.00	150.00
89	CRAZY HORSE, APACHE BIRDMAN (SET)	CL	335.00	700.00
90	BUFFALO PONY	CL	300.00	350.00
90	CHIEF PONTIAC	CL	35.00	125.00
90	CHIEF PONTIAC, BUFFALO PONY (SET)	CL	335.00	625.00
91	SIGNAL, THE	YR	350.00	350.00
91	WAR DANCER	YR	35.00	35.00
91	WAR DANCER & THE SIGNAL (SET)	YR	385.00	385.00
D. POLLAND			**PEWTER COLLECTION**	
84	FEDERAL STALLION	1500	145.00	185.00
85	HUNTING COUGAR	1500	145.00	180.00
85	RUNNING FREE	1500	250.00	300.00

POSITIVE IMAGE

N. HUGHES			**BLACK LEGENDS**	
94	BILL PICKETT	4000	164.00	164.00
94	GEORGE W. CARVER	4000	164.00	164.00
94	I.B. WELLS	4000	190.00	190.00
94	MAHALIA JACKSON	4000	164.00	164.00
94	SATCHEL PAGE	4000	164.00	164.00
N. HUGHES			**POSITIVE IMAGE**	
91	BALLERINA	RT	56.00	56.00
91	BANJO PLAYER	RT	90.00	90.00
91	BOY IN CHOIR	RT	54.00	54.00
91	BOY WITH DOG	RT	42.00	42.00
91	EASTER EGG HUNT	RT	42.00	42.00
91	FATHER AND SON	RT	62.00	62.00
91	GIRL IN CHAIR	RT	54.00	54.00
91	GIRL WITH BIRD	RT	56.00	56.00
91	GIRL WITH CAT	RT	42.00	42.00
91	GIRLS ON CAROUSEL	RT	210.00	210.00
91	MOTHER AND CHILD	RT	62.00	62.00
91	SURPRISE	RT	62.00	62.00
92	BUFFALO SOLDIER	*	102.00	102.00
92	CIVIL WAR SOLDIER	*	102.00	102.00
92	DISPLAY PIECE	*	22.00	22.00
92	GIRL WITH GOOSE	*	62.00	62.00
92	LIL WILLIE	RT	82.00	82.00
92	NEWSPAPER BOY	*	42.00	42.00
92	SERENA	RT	78.00	78.00
92	TUSKEGEE AIRMAN	*	102.00	102.00
93	GIRL AND DOG DISPLAY	*	38.00	38.00
93	PRAYING ANGEL LEROY	*	42.00	42.00
93	REACH FOR A STAR ANGEL	*	42.00	42.00
93	SAILOR	*	102.00	102.00
94	BOY ON A CAROUSEL RABBIT	*	104.00	104.00
94	PRAYING SLAVE	RT	120.00	120.00
94	WHY ME LORD ANGEL	*	42.00	42.00
95	DRESS-UP ANGEL	*	46.00	46.00
95	FEMALE GRADUATE	*	48.00	48.00
95	HIP HOP ANGEL	*	46.00	46.00
95	MALE GRADUATE	*	48.00	48.00
95	TKO ANGEL	*	46.00	46.00
95	VIETNAM FIELD NURSE	*	102.00	102.00
95	VIETNAM SOLDIER	*	102.00	102.00
96	CUPID	2500	116.00	116.00
96	DANCER	2500	116.00	116.00
96	HIGH YELLOW (HERMINE)	2500	144.00	144.00
96	MILLION MAN MARCH	2500	148.00	148.00

YR	NAME	LIMIT	ISSUE	TREND
96	PRAYING SLAVE	2500	92.00	92.00
96	ROLLIN ROUND HEAVEN DISPLAY PIECE	*	24.00	24.00

POSSIBLE DREAMS
*

YR	NAME	LIMIT	ISSUE	TREND
*	CRINKLE BASEBALL PLAYER 4 1/2"	*	20.00	20.00
*	CRINKLE DOCTOR 3 1/2"	*	20.00	20.00
*	CRINKLE FIREMAN 4 1/2"	*	20.00	20.00
*	CRINKLE FISHERMAN 4 1/2"	*	20.00	20.00
*	CRINKLE FOOTBALL PLAYER 4 1/4"	*	20.00	20.00
*	CRINKLE GOLFER 4 1/4"	*	20.00	20.00
*	CRINKLE HOCKEY PLAYER 4 1/4"	*	20.00	20.00
*	CRINKLE POLICEMAN 4 1/2"	*	20.00	20.00
*	CRINKLE POSTMAN 4 1/2"	*	20.00	20.00
*	CRINKLE SOCCER PLAYER 4"	*	20.00	20.00
*	SANTA W/CANDY CANE 6 1/2"	*	17.50	18.00

J.C. LEYENDECKER

YR	NAME	LIMIT	ISSUE	TREND
*	TRADITIONAL SANTA 7 1/2"	OP	66.00	66.00
91	HUGGING SANTA 8"	OP	53.00	53.00
91	TRADITIONAL SANTA 10"	RT	100.00	130.00
92	SANTA ON LADDER 8 1/2"	RT	59.00	59.00

W. STILL — AFRICAN SPIRIT

YR	NAME	LIMIT	ISSUE	TREND
98	BUSHMAN AND SON	*	140.00	140.00
98	RENDILLE WOMAN & CHILD	*	136.00	136.00

CLOTHTIQUE AMERICAN ARTIST COLLECTION
*

YR	NAME	LIMIT	ISSUE	TREND
*	AND FEATHERED FRIEND 10"	OP	80.00	80.00
*	CHRISTMAS LIGHT 10"	OP	54.00	54.00
*	CHRISTMAS STORIES 8"	OP	64.00	64.00
*	DRESSED FOR THE HOLIDAY 10 1/4"	OP	47.00	47.00
*	FRESH FROM THE OVEN 11"	OP	49.00	49.00
*	MUSICAL READY FOR CHRISTMAS 10"	OP	99.00	99.00
*	NEW SUIT FOR SANTA 9 1/2" SET OF TWO	OP	90.00	90.00
*	NOT A CREATURE STIRRING 8 3/4"	OP	44.00	44.00
*	REFUGE FROM THE STORM 10 1/2"	OP	49.00	49.00
*	TWELVE DAYS OF CHRISTMAS 10 3/4"	OP	48.00	48.00
*	VISIONS OF SUGARPLUMS 10"	OP	50.00	50.00
91	ALPINE CHRISTMAS 11 1/4"	RT	129.00	133.00
91	FATHER CHRISTMAS 10 1/4"	RT	60.00	61.00
91	FRIENDLY VISIT 11 1/2"	RT	100.00	103.00
91	MAGIC OF CHRISTMAS 11 1/4"	RT	132.00	140.00
91	PEACEFUL EVE 10"	RT	100.00	103.00
91	SANTA'S CUISINE 10 1/2"	RT	138.00	150.00
91	TRADITIONS 10 "	RT	50.00	60.00
92	AN ANGEL'S KISS 10 1/2"	RT	85.00	90.00
92	CHRISTMAS COMPANY 9"	RT	73.00	120.00
92	HERALDING THE WAY 10 1//4"	RT	72.00	76.00
92	LIGHTING THE WAY 11"	RT	85.00	85.00
92	MUSIC MAKERS 9"	RT	135.00	170.00
92	OUT OF THE FOREST 10 1/4"	RT	60.00	70.00
92	PEACE ON EARTH 10 1/4"	RT	88.00	95.00
92	SANTA IN R. CHAIR 9 1/4"	RT	85.00	103.00
93	BEACON OF LIGHT 11"	OP	60.00	64.00
93	BRIGHTER DAY 9 1/2"	OP	68.00	68.00
93	EASY PUTT 9"	OP	110.00	110.00
93	FATHER EARTH 10"	OP	77.00	77.00
93	ICE CAPERS 7 3/4"	OP	100.00	100.00
93	JUST SCOOTING ALONG 10"	OP	80.00	80.00
93	NATURE'S LOVE 10"	OP	75.00	80.00
93	STRUMMING THE LUTE 9"	OP	79.00	79.00
93	TREE PLANTER, THE 10"	OP	80.00	80.00
93	WORKSHOP, THE 9 3/4" MUSIC	RT	140.00	160.00
94	CAPTAIN CLAUS 10"	OP	74.00	74.00
94	CHRISTMAS SURPRISE 10"	OP	84.00	84.00
94	GENTLE CRAFTSMAN, THE 8 1/2"	OP	77.00	77.00
94	GIFTS FROM GARDEN 10"	RT	74.00	74.00
94	SPIRIT OF SANTA 11"	OP	65.00	65.00
94	SPIRIT/CHRISTMAS PAST 10"	OP	76.00	76.00
94	TEA TIME 10"	OP	86.00	86.00
94	TEDDY LOVE 10"	OP	85.00	85.00
94	TOUCH OF MAGIC 10"	OP	90.00	90.00
95	CHRISTMAS CALLER 10 1/2"	OP	58.00	58.00
95	COUNTRY SOUNDS 8 1/2"	OP	74.00	74.00
95	GIVING THANKS 7 1/4"	OP	46.00	46.00
95	GOOD ROUND 11"	OP	73.00	73.00
95	PATCHWORK SANTA 10"	OP	68.00	68.00
95	RIDING HIGH 10 1/2"	OP	115.00	115.00
95	SANTA AND THE ARK 10 1/2"	OP	72.00	72.00
95	SOUTHWEST SANTA 10"	OP	65.00	65.00
95	STORY TELLER, THE 8 1/4"	OP	76.00	76.00
95	SUN FLOWER SANTA 10"	OP	75.00	75.00

G. BENVENUTI — CLOTHTIQUE AMERICAN ARTIST COLLECTION

YR	NAME	LIMIT	ISSUE	TREND
98	BONE APPETIT!	*	54.00	54.00
98	FELICE NATALE!	*	46.00	46.00

YR	NAME	LIMIT	ISSUE	TREND
	T. BROWNING	CLOTHTIQUE AMERICAN ARTIST COLLECTION		
98	DREAMS COME TRUE	*	69.00	69.00
98	PLAYING THROUGH	*	50.00	50.00
	L. FLETCHER	CLOTHTIQUE AMERICAN ARTIST COLLECTION		
98	DRESS REHEARSAL	*	50.00	50.00
98	TRAILSIDE PRAYER	*	60.00	60.00
98	WOMAN BEHIND CHRISTMAS, THE	*	58.00	58.00
	M. HUMPHRIES	CLOTHTIQUE AMERICAN ARTIST COLLECTION		
98	CLEAN SWEEP	*	47.00	47.00
	S. RUSINKO	CLOTHTIQUE AMERICAN ARTIST COLLECTION		
98	NEW ARRIVAL	*	48.00	48.00
	J. SORENSON	CLOTHTIQUE AMERICAN ARTIST COLLECTION		
98	YULETIDE ROUNDUP	*	43.00	43.00
	W. STILL	CLOTHTIQUE AMERICAN ARTIST COLLECTION		
98	SANTA'S ON A ROLL	*	42.00	42.00
	J. VAILLANCOURT	CLOTHTIQUE AMERICAN ARTIST COLLECTION		
98	SCANDINAVIAN FATHER CHRISTMAS	*	40.00	40.00
*		CLOTHTIQUE COCA-COLA COLLECTION		
98	BUSY MAN'S PAUSE	*	49.00	49.00
98	SANTA'S GREETINGS	*	*	N/A
98	STEP UP TO REFRESHMENT	*	47.00	47.00
98	THANKS FOR THE PAUSE THAT REFRESHES	*	47.00	47.00
*			CLOTHTIQUE ELVES	
*	WORKING ELVES 6" SET OF THREE	OP	66.00	66.00
*			CLOTHTIQUE GIRL	
*	GIRL AT MANGER 7" SET OF THREE	OP	74.00	74.00
*		CLOTHTIQUE LI'L DRUMMER BOY		
*	LI'L DRUMMER BOY 7" SET OF TWO	OP	60.00	60.00
*			CLOTHTIQUE LONDONSHIRE	
*	ALBERT 10"	RT	65.00	70.00
*	EARL OF HAMLETT 12"	RT	65.00	70.00
*	MAGGIE 10 1/2"	RT	57.00	57.00
*	WALTER 8"	RT	33.00	33.00
*	WENDY 8"	RT	33.00	33.00
93	NIGEL AS SANTA 10"	OP	54.00	54.00
95	ADMIRAL WALDO 11"	OP	65.00	65.00
95	BETH 7 1/4"	OP	35.00	35.00
95	CHRISTOPHER 7 1/2"	OP	35.00	35.00
95	COUNTESS OF HAMLETT 10 3/4"	OP	65.00	65.00
95	DAVID 7 1/2"	OP	38.00	38.00
95	DEBBIE 7 1/2"	OP	38.00	38.00
95	DIANNE 8"	OP	33.00	33.00
95	DR. ISAAC 11"	RT	65.00	70.00
95	EARL'S FREE TIME 11"	OP	57.00	57.00
95	JEAN CLAUDE 7 1/2"	OP	35.00	35.00
95	LORD WINSTON 12"	RT	65.00	70.00
95	MARGARET OF FOXCROFT 11"	OP	65.00	65.00
95	NICOLE 7 1/2"	OP	35.00	35.00
95	OFFICER KEVIN 11"	RT	65.00	70.00
95	PHILLIP 8"	OP	33.00	33.00
95	REBECCA 7 1/2"	OP	35.00	35.00
95	RICHARD 7 1/2"	OP	35.00	35.00
95	RODNEY 10 1/2"	OP	65.00	65.00
95	SIR RED 11"	RT	72.00	72.00
95	TIFFANY SORBET 8"	OP	65.00	65.00
96	SIR ROBERT 12"	OP	65.00	65.00
*			CLOTHTIQUE NATIVITIES	
*	HOLY FAMILY 9" - 11 3/4" SET OF TWO	OP	150.00	150.00
*	HOLY FAMILY SET 10 1/2" 3 PC	OP	90.00	90.00
*	HOLY FAMILY SET 12" 2 PC	OP	166.00	166.00
*	WISE MEN 7 1/2-11 3/4" SET OF THREE	OP	174.00	174.00
*		CLOTHTIQUE PEPSI SANTA COLLECTION		
*	PEPSI SANTA W/LIST 6"	OP	9.90	10.00
90	PEPSI COLA SANTA 10"	OP	68.00	68.00
92	PEPSI COLA SANTA SITTING 8"	*	84.00	84.00
94	HOLIDAY HOST 10"	OP	59.00	59.00
95	JOLLY TRAVELER 7 1/2"	OP	90.00	90.00
*			CLOTHTIQUE PROFESSIONALS	
*	DOCTOR 9 1/2"	OP	38.00	38.00
*	FIREMAN 9 1/2"	OP	38.00	38.00
*	GOLFER 9 1/2"	OP	38.00	38.00
*	LIFESTYLES-FISHERMAN 10"	OP	38.00	38.00
*	LIFESTYLES-WOMAN GOLFER 9 3/4"	OP	30.00	30.00
*	NURSE 9 1/2"	OP	38.00	38.00
*	POLICEMAN 9 1/2"	OP	38.00	38.00
*	POSTMAN 9 1/2"	OP	38.00	38.00
*			CLOTHTIQUE ROCKWELLS	
89	DEAR SANTA 7 3/4"	RT	71.00	71.00
89	SANTA W/GLOBE 8"	RT	73.00	73.00
90	HOBO 11 1/2"	OP	159.00	159.00
90	LOVE LETTERS 11"	OP	172.00	172.00
91	GIFT, THE 12 1/2"	OP	160.00	160.00
91	GRAMPS W/REINS 12 1/2"	OP	290.00	290.00
91	MAN W/GEESE 12 1/4"	OP	120.00	120.00

A members-only figurine for members of the Enesco Corp. Precious Moments Birthday Club in 1994, God Bless Our Home *has nearly doubled in value since its release.*

One of Kristin Hayne's early creations for Cast Art Industries, Best Pals *has doubled in value since its 1992 release.*

Three children play a game of Ring Around the Rosie *in this figurine from the A Child's World 6th Edition collection by Frances Hook. Produced by Roman Inc.*

Christmas Prayer Angel *by Ted DeGrazia, produced by Artists of the World, is a closed edition that has increased in value since its 1988 release.*

The 1985 members-only figurine and the first issue for the Lladró Collectors Society, Little Pals—*originally released in 1985 at $95—sold at a 1997 auction for $3,750.*

YR	NAME	LIMIT	ISSUE	TREND
91	SANTA PLOTTING 12"	OP	160.00	160.00
91	SPRINGTIME 11 1/2"	OP	130.00	130.00
92	BALANCING BUDGET 11"	OP	120.00	120.00
92	MARRIAGE LICENSE 11 3/4"	OP	195.00	195.00
*				

CLOTHTIQUE SANTAS COLLECTION

YR	NAME	LIMIT	ISSUE	TREND
*	FIRST NOEL MUSICAL, THE 8 1/4"	OP	62.00	62.00
*	FOR SOMEONE SPECIAL 9 1/2"	OP	39.00	39.00
*	GINGERBREAD BAKER, THE 10"	OP	35.00	35.00
*	HEAVEN SENT	OP	50.00	50.00
*	HO HO HOLE IN ONE	OP	43.00	43.00
*	JUMPIN' JACK SANTA 9 1/2"	OP	46.00	46.00
*	MASTER TOYMAKER 9 1/2"	OP	45.00	45.00
*	MODERN SKIER SANTA 10"	OP	67.00	67.00
*	SANTA W/DOLL 10 1/2"	OP	40.00	40.00
*	SANTA'S PET PROJECT 7"	OP	37.00	37.00
*	SHAMROCK SANTA 9 1/2"	OP	41.50	42.00
*	THREE ALARM SANTA 11 1/2"	OP	43.00	43.00
*	WISHES COME TRUE 9"	OP	59.00	59.00
86	CHRISTMAS MAN 10"	RT	60.00	60.00
86	SANTA W/PACK 10"	RT	60.00	60.00
86	TRADITIONAL SANTA 10"	RT	60.00	60.00
87	COLONIAL SANTA 10"	RT	32.00	32.00
87	TRADITIONAL DELUXE SANTA 10"	RT	32.00	32.00
87	UKKO 10"	RT	32.00	32.00
88	CARPENTER, SANTA 10"	RT	40.00	40.00
88	FRONTIER SANTA 10"	RT	38.00	40.00
88	RUSSIAN ST. NICHOLAS 10"	OP	38.00	38.00
88	ST. NICHOLAS 10"	RT	38.00	40.00
88	WEIHNACHTSMAN 10"	RT	38.00	40.00
89	BABY'S FIRST CHRISTMAS 10"	CL	42.00	42.00
89	EXHAUSTED SANTA 7 3/4"	RT	60.00	60.00
89	MRS. CLAUS W/DOLL 10"	RT	42.00	42.00
89	PELZE NICHOL 10"	RT	40.00	45.00
89	SANTA W/EMBLEM ROBE 10"	*	40.00	40.00
89	TRADITIONAL SANTA 10"	RT	40.00	40.00
90	HARLEM SANTA 10"	RT	46.00	50.00
90	SANTA PLEASE STOP HERE 10"	RT	63.00	63.00
90	SANTA W/BLUE ROBE 10"	RT	46.00	51.00
90	SKIING SANTA 10"	RT	62.00	162.00
90	WORKBENCH SANTA 8"	RT	72.00	75.00
91	FATHER CHRISTMAS 10"	RT	43.00	49.00
91	KRIS KRINGLE 10"	RT	43.00	43.00
91	MRS. CLAUS IN COAT 10"	RT	47.00	60.00
91	SANTA DECORATING TREE 7 1/4"	RT	60.00	60.00
91	SANTA SHELF SITTER 7 1/4"	RT	56.00	60.00
91	SIBERIAN SANTA 10"	RT	49.00	50.00
91	TRUE SPIRIT OF XMAS 8"	RT	97.00	97.00
92	1940 TRADITIONAL SANTA 10 1/2"	RT	44.00	68.00
92	AFRICAN/AMERICAN SANTA 8"	RT	65.00	65.00
92	ENGINEER SANTA MUSIC 9 3/4"	RT	130.00	130.00
92	FIREMAN SANTA 11 1/4"	OP	60.00	60.00
92	NICHOLAS 10"	RT	58.00	61.00
92	SANTA ON BED 6 3/4" H X 8 1/2" L	RT	76.00	76.00
92	SANTA ON SLED 8"	RT	75.00	75.00
92	SANTA-SLEIGH MUSIC 9 1/4"	RT	79.00	80.00
92	SANTA/MOTORBIKE 11 1/4"	RT	115.00	125.00
92	SANTA/REINDEER 12 1/2"	RT	79.00	81.00
93	EUROPEAN SANTA 10"	OP	53.00	53.00
93	FIREMAN & CHILD 10"	OP	55.00	55.00
93	HIS FAVORITE COLOR 10"	OP	48.00	48.00
93	MODERN SHOPPER, THE 10"	OP	40.00	40.00
93	SANTA W/GROCERIES 10 1/2"	OP	48.00	48.00
93	VICTORIAN SANTA 9 1/2"	OP	56.00	60.00
94	CHRISTMAS CHEER 10"	OP	55.00	55.00
94	CHRISTMAS IS FOR CHILDREN 10"	OP	59.00	59.00
94	GOOD TIDINGS 10"	OP	49.00	49.00
94	HOLIDAY FRIEND 8"	OP	99.00	99.00
94	MRS. CLAUS 10"	OP	55.00	55.00
94	MRS. CLAWS 10"	OP	69.00	69.00
94	MUSICAL CHRISTMAS GUEST 10"	OP	75.00	75.00
94	OUR HERO 11"	OP	60.00	60.00
94	PLAYMATES 6 1/2"	OP	99.00	99.00
94	PUPPY LOVE 9"	OP	59.00	59.00
94	WELCOME VISIT 10"	OP	60.00	60.00
94	YULETIDE JOURNEY 10"	OP	56.00	56.00
95	FINISHING TOUCH 9 3/4"	OP	55.00	55.00
95	FRISKY FRIEND 10"	OP	46.00	46.00
95	HOME SPUN HOLIDAY 8 3/4"	OP	50.00	49.50
95	HOOK, LINE & SANTA 9 1/2"	OP	50.00	50.00
95	LONG TRIP 10 1/2"	OP	95.00	95.00
95	SOUNDS OF CHRISTMAS 9 1/2"	OP	58.00	58.00
95	SPECIAL TREAT 9 3/4"	OP	51.00	50.50
95	STOCKINGS WERE HUNG 8 1/2"	OP	65.00	65.00
95	VICTORIAN EVERGREEN SANTA 10 1/2"	OP	49.00	49.00
95	VICTORIAN PUPPETEER 10"	OP	51.00	52.00

YR	NAME	LIMIT	ISSUE	TREND
96	AUTOGRAPH FOR A FAN 10"	OP	39.00	39.00
98	CHRISTMAS IN THE ALPS	*	48.00	48.00
98	FOR A SPECIAL LITTLE GIRL	*	44.00	44.00
98	HIGHLAND SANTA	*	42.50	43.00
98	LANDING BEACON	*	43.40	44.00
98	MEXICAN MARIACHI SANTA	*	48.80	49.00
98	NORTH POLE PARTY LINE	*	44.90	45.00
98	OFFICER CLAUS	*	37.80	38.00
98	PURRY FRIEND, A	*	42.50	43.00
98	SANTA WITH TREE	*	38.50	39.00
98	SANTA'S CHECKUP	*	37.00	37.00
98	SANTA'S FLYING MACHINES	*	39.60	40.00
98	SANTA'S NEW LIST	*	44.90	45.00
98	SANTA'S TREE	*	36.40	37.00
98	SNACK FOR SANTA, A	*	37.00	37.00
98	TOP O' THE MORNING	*	41.50	42.00
98	VISITOR FROM THE NORTH	*	39.50	40.00
*	**CLOTHTIQUE SIGNATURE SERIES**			
*	2 PC SET- 721001 & 721002	OP	198.00	198.00
*	2 PC SET- 721004 & 721005	OP	198.00	198.00
*	KRIS KRINGLE USA 12"	OP	99.00	99.00
*	ST. NICHOLAS 12" CIRCA 1300	OP	99.00	99.00
95	DEPT STORE SANTA USA 1940	OP	108.00	108.00
95	FATHER XMAS ENGLAND 12"	OP	90.00	90.00
*	**CRINKLE ANGEL**			
*	CRINKLE ANGEL W/CANDLE 4 3/4"	*	20.00	20.00
*	CRINKLE ANGEL W/DOVE 4 1/2"	*	20.00	20.00
*	CRINKLE ANGEL W/HARP 4 1/2"	*	20.00	20.00
*	CRINKLE ANGEL W/LAMB 4 3/4"	*	20.00	20.00
*	CRINKLE ANGEL W/LANTERN 4 1/2"	*	20.00	20.00
*	CRINKLE ANGEL W/MANDOLIN 4 3/4"	*	20.00	20.00
*	**CRINKLE CAROUSEL**			
98	CHECKMATE CRINKLE	*	9.00	9.00
98	CRINKLE ANTLERS	*	16.00	16.00
98	CRINKLE DOODLE-DOO	*	15.00	15.00
98	CRINKLE FILLY	*	16.00	16.00
98	CRINKLE PONY WITH DOME	*	40.00	40.00
98	CRINKLE STALLION WITH DOME	*	40.00	40.00
98	FRISKY CRINKLE	*	12.00	12.00
98	GALLOPING CRINKLE	*	16.00	16.00
98	HAPPY HOG CRINKLE	*	15.00	15.00
98	HIPPITY HOP CRINKLE	*	15.00	15.00
98	HONEY BEAR CRINKLE	*	15.00	15.00
98	LAUGHING LION CRINKLE	*	15.40	16.00
98	MERRY-GO-CRINKLE	*	34.00	34.00
98	PACHYDERM CRINKLE	*	16.00	16.00
98	PARASOL CRINKLE	*	13.30	14.00
98	PRANCING CRINKLE MUSIC BOX	*	30.00	30.00
98	SURF RIDER CRINKLE	*	16.00	16.00
*	**CRINKLE CLAUS**			
*	AMERICAN SANTA 4"	*	15.50	16.00
*	ARCTIC SANTA 3 1/2"	*	15.70	16.00
*	AUSTRIAN SANTA 3 3/4"	*	15.80	16.00
*	AUTUMN PEPPERGRASS 4 1/2"	OP	31.00	31.00
*	BELL SHAPE SANTA 5/12"	*	24.00	24.00
*	BISHOP OF MAYA 4 3/4"	*	20.00	20.00
*	BLACK FOREST GIFT GIVER 4 3/4"	*	20.00	20.00
*	BLACK FOREST SANTA 3 1/4"	*	7.80	8.00
*	BUCKETS OF FRUIT FOR....5"	*	45.00	45.00
*	C/C ROLY POLY SANTA 3 1/2"	RT	12.50	13.00
*	CANDLE STICK SANTA 5"	*	15.80	16.00
*	CELTIC SANTA 4 1/2"	*	20.00	20.00
*	CHOO-CHOOS FOR CHILDREN 5"	*	25.00	25.00
*	CHRISTMAS TREE SANTA 5 3/4"	*	20.00	20.00
*	CRESCENT MOON SANTA 4 3/4"	*	19.00	19.00
*	CRINKLE CLAUS W/DOME GERMAN SANTA 120mm	*	45.00	45.00
*	CRINKLE CLAUS W/DOME SANTA/CHIMNEY 6"	*	45.00	45.00
*	CRINKLE CLAUS W/DOME ST. NICHOLAS 120mm	*	45.00	45.00
*	DAINTY WHISKERS 4 1/2"	OP	30.00	30.00
*	DASHING THROUGH THE SNOW 5 3/4"	*	45.00	45.00
*	DISPLAY FIGURINE 4"	*	11.00	11.00
*	ENGLISH SANTA 3 3/4"	*	15.80	16.00
*	FEEDIN' FOREST FRIENDS 5"	*	28.00	28.00
*	FOREST SANTA 4 1/4"	*	15.50	16.00
*	FRENCH SANTA 3 1/2"	*	15.70	16.00
*	GERMAN SANTA 3 3/4"	*	15.80	16.00
*	GOODY PRINGLE 4 3/4"	OP	31.00	31.00
*	HARD BOILED SANTA 3 1/4"	*	13.70	14.00
*	HIGH HAT SANTA 6 1/4"	*	13.40	14.00
*	HOUR GLASS SANTA 5 1/2"	*	15.00	15.00
*	ICELAND VISITOR 4 1/2"	*	20.00	20.00
*	ITALIAN SANTA 3 1/2"	*	15.70	16.00
*	JOLLY ST. NICK 3 1/2"	*	15.00	15.00
*	MERRY HEART 4 1/2"	OP	30.00	30.00
*	MERRY OL'ENGLAND 4 1/4"	*	20.00	20.00

YR	NAME	LIMIT	ISSUE	TREND
*	NETHERLANDS SANTA 4"	*	15.70	16.00
*	NORTHLAND SANTA 4 1/2"	*	20.00	20.00
*	PATIENCE FINNEY 4 1/4"	OP	31.00	31.00
*	PINE CONE SANTA 4"	*	15.50	16.00
*	RAG DOLL DELIVERY 6"	*	35.00	35.00
*	ROLY POLY SANTA 5 1/2"	*	23.00	23.00
*	RUNNING DOWN THE LIST 5 3/4"	*	33.00	33.00
*	RUSSIAN SANTA 3 1/2"	*	15.70	16.00
*	RUSSIAN SANTA 4"	RT	15.50	16.00
*	SANTA IN SLED 4 1/2"	RT	17.00	17.00
*	SANTA ON BAG 4"	RT	15.00	15.00
*	SANTA ON ROOF 5"	*	29.00	29.00
*	SANTA SITTING PRETTY 3 1/4"	*	13.90	14.00
*	SANTA W/ANIMALS 4"	RT	15.00	15.00
*	SANTA W/BOOK 4"	*	13.80	14.00
*	SANTA W/CANDY CANE 4 1/2"	RT	13.00	13.00
*	SANTA W/CANDY CANE 5"	*	27.00	27.00
*	SANTA W/CANE & BAG 3 1/4"	RT	12.00	12.00
*	SANTA W/GIFTS 5"	RT	27.00	27.00
*	SANTA W/LANTERN & BAG 4 1/2"	RT	15.50	16.00
*	SANTA W/LANTERN 5"	RT	27.00	27.00
*	SANTA W/LIST 4 1/2"	RT	15.00	15.00
*	SANTA W/NOAH'S ARK 4 1/2"	*	15.50	16.00
*	SANTA W/PATCHWORK BAG 6 1/2"	*	19.00	19.00
*	SANTA W/STAR 4 3/4"	*	14.00	15.00
*	SANTA W/TEDDY BEAR 4 1/4"	*	16.00	16.00
*	SANTA W/TREE 3 3/4"	*	14.20	15.00
*	SANTA W/WREATH 4"	RT	16.30	17.00
*	SCANDINAVIAN SANTA 3 3/4"	*	15.80	16.00
*	SLIM LINE SANTA 6 1/4"	RT	12.00	12.00
*	TICK TOCK SANTA 4 3/4"	*	15.00	15.00
*	TIP TOP SANTA 5 1/2"	*	24.00	24.00
*	VELVET WINTERBERRY 5"	OP	30.00	30.00
98	BAVARIAN OM-PAH CRINKLE MUSICAL	*	38.80	39.00
98	BOTTLE CRINKLE	*	15.90	16.00
98	CHRISTMAS EXPEDITION	*	26.90	27.00
98	CLICKETY-CLACK CRINKLE	*	17.20	18.00
98	CRINKLE CELLO	*	14.80	15.00
98	CRINKLE CHRISTMAS EVE	*	28.50	29.00
98	CRINKLE CLAUS CRUISE	*	17.20	18.00
98	CRINKLE CROSS	*	15.00	15.00
98	CRINKLE ELF CARPENTER	*	8.50	9.00
98	CRINKLE ELF CHEF	*	8.50	9.00
98	CRINKLE ELF FIREMAN	*	8.50	9.00
98	CRINKLE ELF POSTMAN	*	8.50	9.00
98	CRINKLE ELF TOYMAKER	*	8.50	9.00
98	CRINKLE ELF WITH JESTER	*	8.50	9.00
98	CRINKLE ELF WITH SNOWMAN	*	8.50	9.00
98	CRINKLE ELF WITH TEDDY	*	8.50	9.00
98	CRINKLE FLAG BEARER	*	12.40	13.00
98	CRINKLE LYRE	*	16.70	17.00
98	CRINKLE MAIL CAR	*	18.80	19.00
98	CRINKLE SPIRIT OF GIVING	*	23.50	24.00
98	CRINKLE UNCLE SAM	*	13.50	14.00
98	DEPARTMENT STORE CRINKLE	*	23.50	24.00
98	DING-DONG CRINKLE	*	16.60	17.00
98	DUTCH TREAT CRINKLE MUSICAL	*	38.80	39.00
98	EMERALD ISLE CRINKLE	*	13.40	14.00
98	ENGLISH CRINKLE AT WESTMINSTER ABBEY	*	28.50	29.00
98	FINE FEATHERED FRIENDS	*	25.40	26.00
98	FIRECRACKER CRINKLE	*	14.60	15.00
98	GERMAN CRINKLE AT ROTHENBURG	*	28.50	29.00
98	GRIZZLY BEAR HELPER	*	25.90	26.00
98	HIGH FLYING CRINKLE	*	32.50	33.00
98	IRISH CRINKLE AT ST. PATRICK'S CATHEDRAL	*	28.50	29.00
98	KREMLIN CRINKLE MUSICAL	*	38.80	39.00
98	LIBERTY CRINKLE	*	12.40	13.00
98	NUTTY NOEL, A	*	25.90	26.00
98	OLD GLORY CRINKLE	*	12.40	13.00
98	ROYAL CRINKLE MUSICAL	*	38.80	39.00
98	RUSSIAN CRINKLE AT ST. BASIL'S	*	28.50	29.00
98	SCOTTISH CRINKLE AT GLAMIS CASTLE	*	28.50	29.00
98	SHAMROCK CRINKLE	*	13.40	14.00
98	TEDDY BEEFEATER CRINKLE	*	20.00	20.00
98	TEDDY CRINKLE ITALIANO	*	20.00	20.00
98	TEDDY DUTCH CRINKLE	*	20.00	20.00
98	TEDDY MCCRINKLE	*	24.80	25.00
98	TEDDY O'CRINKLE	*	24.80	25.00
98	TEDDY RUSSIAN CRINKLE	*	20.00	20.00
98	TEDDY VON CRINKLE	*	20.00	20.00
98	US CRINKLE AT THE CAPITOL	*	28.50	29.00
*				**CRINKLE COUSIN**
*	CRINKLE COUSIN W/CLOCK 3"	*	15.50	16.00
*	CRINKLE COUSIN W/CLOWN 2 3/4"	*	15.50	16.00
*	CRINKLE COUSIN W/DOLLS 2 1/2"	*	15.50	16.00

YR	NAME	LIMIT	ISSUE	TREND
*	CRINKLE COUSIN W/LANTERN 3 1/2"	*	15.50	16.00
*	CRINKLE COUSIN W/TEDDY 3"	*	15.50	16.00
*			**CRINKLE CRACKERS**	
95	CRINKLE CRACKER ADMIRAL 5 3/4"	*	19.00	19.00
95	CRINKLE CRACKER CAPTAIN 6"	*	13.00	13.00
95	CRINKLE CRACKER CORPORAL 5 3/4"	*	14.60	15.00
95	CRINKLE CRACKER FRENCH 4"	*	13.50	14.00
95	CRINKLE CRACKER FRENCH ROLY POLY 3 3/4"	*	13.90	14.00
95	CRINKLE CRACKER GENERAL 4 3/4"	*	15.50	16.00
95	CRINKLE CRACKER LIEUTENANT 8"	*	27.00	27.00
95	CRINKLE CRACKER MAJOR 5"	*	14.50	15.00
95	CRINKLE CRACKER PRIVATE 6"	*	15.00	15.00
95	CRINKLE CRACKER ROLY POLY SERGEANT 4"	*	13.50	14.00
95	CRINKLE CRACKER RUSSIAN 4"	*	13.50	14.00
95	CRINKLE CRACKER RUSSIAN ROLY POLY 3 3/4"	*	13.50	14.00
95	CRINKLE CRACKER U.S. 3 3/4"	*	13.50	14.00
95	CRINKLE CRACKER U.S. ROLY POLY 3 3/4"	*	13.90	14.00
95	FRENCH CRINKLE CRACKER 5 1/2"	*	22.00	22.00
95	RUSSIAN CRINKLE CRACKER 7 3/4"	*	30.00	30.00
95	U.S. CRINKLE CRACKER 7 1/2"	*	29.00	29.00
*			**LIMITED EDITION SANTAS**	
88	FATHER CHRISTMAS 17"	RT	240.00	240.00
88	KRIS KRINGLE 17"	RT	240.00	240.00
88	PATRIOTIC SANTA 17"	RT	240.00	240.00
89	TRADITIONAL SANTA 17"	RT	240.00	240.00
*		**SANTA CLAUS NETWORK COLLECTORS CLUB**		
*	FROSTY FRIENDS 10"	OP	47.00	47.00
92	GIFT GIVER, THE	OP	30.00	30.00
93	SANTA'S SPECIAL FRIENDS 7 1/2"	RT	59.00	59.00
93	SPECIAL DELIVERY	RT	30.00	30.00
94	JOLLY ST. NICK PREMIUM	OP	30.00	30.00
94	ON A WINTER'S EVE 10"	RT	65.00	65.00
95	CHECKING HIS LIST	OP	30.00	30.00
95	MARIONETTE SANTA 8"	YR	50.00	50.00
96	COOKIE FROM SANTA PREMIUM	OP	30.00	30.00
*			**SANTA GO ROUNDS**	
*	ROLY POLY CHRISTMAS TREE 4 1/4"	RT	15.80	16.00
*	SANTA ON SLED 4 1/4"	RT	15.80	16.00
	J.C. LEYENDECKER		**SATURDAY EVENING POST**	
91	HUGGING SANTA 10 3/4"	RT	129.00	145.00
92	SANTA ON LADDER 11"	RT	135.00	145.00
	N. ROCKWELL		**SATURDAY EVENING POST**	
*	DEAR SANTA 11 1/2"	RT	180.00	180.00
89	SANTA W/GLOBE 11 1/2"	RT	175.00	175.00
91	DOCTOR & DOLL 12 1/2"	RT	196.00	210.00
91	GONE FISHING 11 3/4"	RT	250.00	275.00
92	SANTA'S HELPERS 11"	RT	170.00	180.00
92	SELF PORTRAIT 14"	RT	230.00	255.00
	R. SPANGLER		**SPANGLER'S REALM**	
98	CHRISTMAS COOKIE EXPRESS	*	28.00	28.00
98	DRAGLING ON THE SCALE	*	36.00	36.00
98	NO SMOKING SIGN	*	*	N/A
98	SLEEPY TIME	*	18.50	19.00
*			**THICKETS AT SWEETBRIAR**	
93	CLOVIS BUTTONS 3 1/2"	OP	23.00	23.00
93	JEWEL BLOSSOM 4 3/4"	OP	35.00	35.00
93	LILY BLOSSOM 4 3/4"	RT	35.00	35.00
93	MAUDE TWEEDY 3 1/2"	RT	25.00	26.00
93	MORNING GLORY 4"	OP	29.00	29.00
93	MR. CLAWS 5"	RT	32.00	32.00
93	MRS. CLAWS 4 3/4"	OP	32.00	32.00
93	MUSICAL - LILY BLOSSOM 6 3/4"	OP	60.00	60.00
93	OLIVER DOONE, THE GROOM 4 1/2"	RT	30.00	30.00
93	ORCHID BEASLEY 3 3/4"	RT	25.00	25.00
93	PEABLOSSOM THORNDIKE 3 1/2"	RT	25.00	25.00
93	RAINDROP 5 3/4"	OP	45.00	45.00
93	ROSE BLOSSOM 4 3/4"	OP	35.00	35.00
94	LADY SLIPPER 3 1/2"	OP	20.00	20.00
94	MORNING DEW 5"	OP	29.00	29.00
94	PRECIOUS PETALS 5"	OP	32.00	32.00
94	SUNSHINE 4 3/4"	OP	32.00	32.00
94	SWEETIE FLOWERS	OP	32.00	32.00
95	ANGEL DEAR 4"	OP	32.00	32.00
95	BUTTERCUP 4 3/4"	OP	32.00	32.00
95	CECILY PICKWICK 4 1/2"	OP	37.00	37.00
95	CLEM JINGLES 5 1/4"	OP	30.00	30.00
95	EMILY FEATHERS THE BRIDE 4 1/2"	OP	35.00	35.00
95	KATY HOLLYBERRY 5"	OP	11.50	12.00
95	MERRY TAILS 2 1/2"	OP	46.00	46.00
95	P. BLOSSOM THORNDIKE 5" MUSICAL	OP	37.00	37.00
95	PARSLEY DIVINE 5 1/4"	OP	32.00	32.00
95	PENNY PRINGLE 4 1/2"	OP	32.00	32.00
95	PITTYPAT 4 3/4"	OP	56.00	56.00
95	RAINDROP 8" MUSICAL	OP		

YR	NAME	LIMIT	ISSUE	TREND
95	RILEY PICKENS 4 1/2"	OP	32.00	32.00
95	TILLIE LILY 4 3/4"	OP	32.00	32.00
95	TIMMY EVERGREEN 4 1/4"	OP	29.00	29.00
95	VIOLET WIGGLES 4 1/2"	OP	32.00	32.00
	B. ROSS		**THICKETS AT SWEETBRIAR**	
98	CELESTE	*	27.00	27.00
98	CHIP WEEZLEY	*	10.50	11.00
98	DOTTIE CRISPIN	*	27.00	27.00
98	ERIN PENNY	*	26.00	26.00
98	MARIE PERIWINKLE	*	26.00	26.00
98	MAYBELLE PUDDING	*	26.00	26.00
98	SAMUEL GOOLEY	*	21.00	21.00

PRECIOUS ART/PANTON/KRYSTONIA

YR	NAME	LIMIT	ISSUE	TREND
*	SMALL TOKKEL	*		**KRYSTONIA**
			*	50.00
87	GRUMBLYPEG GRUNCH-1081	RT	52.00	100.00
87	LARGE GRAFFYN ON GRUMBLYPEG GRUNCH-1011	RT	52.00	100.00
87	LARGE HAAPF-1901	RT	38.00	85.00
87	LARGE KRAK N'BORG-3001	RT	240.00	650.00
87	LARGE MOPLOS-1021	RT	90.00	350.00
87	LARGE MYZER-1201	RT	50.00	180.00
87	LARGE RUEGGAN-1701	RT	55.00	115.00
87	LARGE TURFEN-1601	RT	50.00	100.00
87	LARGE WODEMA-1301	RT	50.00	125.00
87	MEDIUM STOOPE-1101	RT	52.00	85.00
87	OWHEY-1071	RT	32.00	115.00
87	SMALL GRAFFYN/GRUNCH-1012	RT	45.00	200.00
87	SMALL GROC-1042B	RT	34.00	3700.00
87	SMALL N'BORG-1091	RT	50.00	225.00
87	SMALL SHEPF-1152	RT	40.00	100.00
88	LARGE N'GRALL-2201	RT	108.00	220.00
88	SMALL TULAN CAPTAIN-2502	RT	44.00	100.00
88	TARNHOLD - 3203	RT	60.00	280.00
88	TARNHOLD MED.-3202	RT	120.00	160.00
89	CAUGHT AT LAST!-1107	RT	150.00	215.00
91	DRAGONS PLAY	RT	65.00	245.00
91	N'BORG 6" 609	RT	29.00	30.00
91	PULTZR - 501	RT	55.00	325.00
93	ALL MINE	OP	40.00	45.00
93	ESCUBLAR	7500	170.00	185.00
93	GILBRAN OF WENLOCK	15000	65.00	75.00
93	HAGGA-BEAST	7500	125.00	150.00
93	HIS SECRET	15000	60.00	70.00
93	HULBERT	OP	38.00	45.00
93	MUFFLER	OP	24.00	28.00
93	OOPS	OP	38.00	43.00
93	POMPON	OP	24.00	28.00
93	SHEPF	OP	23.00	28.00
93	STOOPE	RT	23.00	28.00
93	TAG THE TROLL	OP	48.00	53.00
94	BOLL	RT	52.00	57.00
94	CHECKIN IT OUT	15000	36.00	40.00
94	ELDER PHYL	OP	20.00	22.00
94	IKSHAR	OP	46.00	50.00
94	LEARNING IS GWEAT	OP	48.00	52.00
94	OH SWEET DREAMS	OP	35.00	40.00
94	OKINAWATHE	7500	99.00	120.00
94	ONE UNHAAPFY RIDE	4500	125.00	140.00
94	PHYLONEOUS POOK	OP	20.00	22.00
94	POOKBALL	OP	20.00	22.00
94	SCHNOOGLES	OP	48.00	53.00
94	SPYKE	OP	20.00	25.00
94	WELCOME TO KRYSTONIA	15000	60.00	65.00
94	WODEMA	OP	23.00	28.00
95	A DEFINITE MAYBE	15000	60.00	70.00
95	AH HAH!	OP	48.00	53.00
95	DELTA	OP	70.00	75.00
95	ENOUGH IS ENOUGH	2999	250.00	280.00
95	POPOTOMPOTAN	OP	32.00	35.00
95	ROOT	15000	85.00	95.00
95	STOOPE THE STUPENDOUS	15000	65.00	70.00
95	TINCHACHUIK	7500	104.00	120.00
95	WHEY	OP	20.00	73.00
97	ALMOST THERE	OP	75.00	75.00
97	FLAW GRINTAWD	3500	125.00	125.00
97	GLOWING MASHAL	OP	30.00	30.00
97	GRUNCHIE	OP	35.00	35.00
97	PLOOT	7500	67.00	67.00
97	PULTZ	OP	35.00	35.00
97	SPYKESTER	OP	35.00	35.00
97	STORYTELLER	3500	145.00	145.00
98	DOWSER	3000	50.00	50.00
98	FOREVER FRIENDS	1000	300.00	300.00
98	GRUNCHESTA	3000	50.00	50.00

YR	NAME	LIMIT	ISSUE	TREND
98	GULBAR-GUL	3000	50.00	50.00
98	READY OR NOT	OP	27.00	27.00
98	SEER, THE	3000	70.00	70.00
98	SHOOF	3000	50.00	50.00
*			**KRYSTONIA COLLECTOR'S CLUB**	
		RT	*	100.00
89	KEY	RT	55.00	150.00
89	PULTZR	RT	55.00	150.00
89	PULTZR W/KEY			

PRINCETON GALLERY

*				**PEGASUS**
92	WINGS OF MAGIC	OP	95.00	95.00

PRIZM
P. ULVILDEN

			PIPKA 'EARTH ANGELS'	
96	ANGEL OF HEARTS	5400	85.00	85.00
96	COTTAGE ANGEL	5400	85.00	85.00
96	GARDENING ANGEL	5400	85.00	85.00
96	MESSENGER ANGEL	5400	85.00	85.00
97	ANGEL OF ROSES	5400	85.00	85.00
97	GUARDIAN ANGEL	5400	85.00	85.00

P. ULVILDEN

			PIPKA MEMORIES OF CHRISTMAS	
95	CZECH SANTA	SO	85.00	85.00
95	GINGERBREAD SANTA	SO	85.00	85.00
95	MIDNIGHT VISITOR	SO	85.00	85.00
95	SANTA'S ARK	SO	85.00	85.00
95	STAR CATCHER SANTA	SO	85.00	85.00
95	STAR COAT SANTA	SO	85.00	85.00
96	AUSSIE SANTA W/BOOMER	SO	85.00	85.00
96	GOOD NEWS SANTA	3600	85.00	85.00
96	STORYTIME SANTA	3600	85.00	85.00
96	UKRAINIAN SANTA	3600	85.00	85.00
97	NORWEGIAN SANTA	3600	90.00	90.00
97	POLISH SANTA	3600	90.00	90.00
97	RUSSIAN SANTA	3600	90.00	90.00
97	SANTA'S SPOTTED GREY	3600	90.00	90.00
97	ST. NICHOLAS	3600	90.00	90.00
97	WHERE'S RUDOLF	3600	90.00	90.00

P. ULVILDEN

			PIPKA REFLECTIONS OF CHRISTMAS	
97	AMISH COUNTRY SANTA	9700	40.00	40.00
97	BETTER WATCH OUT SANTA	9700	40.00	40.00
97	CZECH SANTA	9700	40.00	40.00
97	MIDNIGHT VISITOR	9700	40.00	40.00
97	STAR CATCHER SANTA	9700	40.00	40.00
97	STAR COAT SANTA	9700	40.00	40.00

P. ULVILDEN

			PIPKA'S EARTH ANGELS	
98	CELESTE-ANGEL OF STARS	5400	90.00	90.00
98	CHRISTINE-THE CHRISTMAS ANGEL	5400	90.00	90.00
98	ELIZABETH-FORGET-ME-NOT ANGEL	5400	90.00	90.00
98	MIKAELA-ANGEL OF INNOCENCE	5400	40.00	40.00
98	SAMANTHA-PLAYFUL ANGEL	5400	40.00	40.00
98	SARAH-LITTLEST ANGEL	5400	40.00	40.00

P. ULVILDEN

			PIPKA'S MEMORIES OF CHRISTMAS	
98	FATHER CHRISTMAS	3600	95.00	95.00
98	PEACE MAKER	3600	95.00	95.00
98	SAN NICOLAS	3600	95.00	95.00
98	TEDDY BEAR SANTA	3600	95.00	95.00

P. ULVILDEN

			PIPKA'S REFLECTIONS OF CHRISTMAS	
98	AUSSIE SANTA	9700	40.00	40.00
98	DEAR SANTA	9700	40.00	40.00
98	GINGERBREAD SANTA	9700	40.00	40.00
98	GOOD NEWS SANTA	9700	40.00	40.00
98	NORWEGIAN JULENISSE	9700	40.00	40.00
98	POLISH FATHER CHRISTMAS	9700	40.00	40.00
98	STORYTIME SANTA	9700	40.00	40.00
98	TEDDY BEAR SANTA	9700	40.00	40.00
98	UKRAINIAN SANTA	9700	40.00	40.00
98	WHERE'S RUDOLPH?	9700	40.00	40.00

R.J. ERNST ENTERPRISES
A. MURRAY

			LITTLE MISSES YOUNG AND FAIR	
82	HEART OF A CHILD	5000	65.00	65.00
83	WHERE WILD FLOWERS GROW	2000	65.00	65.00
85	FINAL TOUCH	2000	75.00	75.00
85	WHISPERED MOMENTS	2000	75.00	75.00

R. MONEY

			MY FAIR LADIES	
82	LADY SABRINA	5000	85.00	85.00

R. MONEY

			SEEMS LIKE YESTERDAY	
81	STOP AND SMELL THE ROSES	5000	25.00	25.00
82	HOME BY LUNCH	5000	25.00	25.00
82	IT'S GOT MY NAME ON IT	5000	25.00	25.00
82	LISA'S CREEK	5000	25.00	25.00
82	MY MAGIC HAT	5000	25.00	25.00

GLENICE

			YESTERDAYS	
82	AMBER	5000	25.00	25.00

YR	NAME	LIMIT	ISSUE	TREND
84	ELMER	5000	25.00	25.00
85	KATIE	600	25.00	25.00

RAWCLIFFE CORP.

J. DESTEFANO — ANGEL FAIRIES OF THE SEASONS

YR	NAME	LIMIT	ISSUE	TREND
94	ANGEL FAIRY OF FALL	4500	95.00	95.00
94	ANGEL FAIRY OF SPRING	4500	95.00	95.00
94	ANGEL FAIRY OF SUMMER	4500	95.00	95.00
94	ANGEL FAIRY OF WINTER	4500	95.00	95.00

J. DESTEFANO — BABY BUBBLE FAIRIES

YR	NAME	LIMIT	ISSUE	TREND
93	AMBER, OCTOBER FAIRY	6700	70.00	70.00
93	AZURE, AUGUST FAIRY	6700	70.00	70.00
93	BABY BUBBLE FAIRIES	OP	*	20.00
93	BLUSH, MARCH FAIRY	6700	70.00	70.00
93	CHARTREUSE, APRIL FAIRY	6700	70.00	70.00
93	CORAL, JUNE FAIRY	6700	70.00	70.00
93	EMERALD, DECEMBER FAIRY	6700	70.00	70.00
93	LAVENDER, SEPTEMBER, FAIRY	6700	70.00	70.00
93	MAGENTA, FEBRUARY FAIRY	6700	70.00	70.00
93	SAFFRON, JULY FAIRY	6700	70.00	70.00
93	TURQUOISE, JANUARY FAIRY	6700	70.00	70.00
93	VERMILLION, NOVEMBER FAIRY	6700	70.00	70.00
93	VIOLET, MAY FAIRY	6700	70.00	70.00

J. DESTEFANO — FOUR SEASONS FAIRIES

YR	NAME	LIMIT	ISSUE	TREND
93	ARIA, SUMMER FAIRY	9500	95.00	95.00
93	HARVEST, FALL FAIRY	9500	95.00	95.00
93	PETAL, SPRING FAIRY	9500	95.00	95.00
93	SNOW, WINTER FAIRY	9500	95.00	95.00

J. DESTEFANO — GARDEN FAIRIES

YR	NAME	LIMIT	ISSUE	TREND
93	DEW FAIRY, THE	4500	115.00	115.00
93	DREAM FAIRY, THE	4500	115.00	115.00
93	FAIRY SLIPPER, THE	4500	115.00	115.00
93	ILLUSIVE FAIRY, THE	4500	115.00	115.00

J. DESTEFANO — STAR TREK

YR	NAME	LIMIT	ISSUE	TREND
93	LUKE SKYWALKER X-WING FIGHTER	15000	95.00	95.00
93	USS ENTERPRISE NCC-1701-D	4500	100.00	100.00
94	DARTH VADER TIE FIGHTER	15000	135.00	135.00
94	DEEP SPACE NINE SPACE STATION	4500	300.00	300.00
94	HAN SOLO MILLENNIUM FALCON	15000	115.00	115.00

RECO INTERNATIONAL

J. MCCLELLAND — CLOWN FIGURINES BY JOHN MCCLELLAND

YR	NAME	LIMIT	ISSUE	TREND
87	MR. CURE-ALL	9500	35.00	35.00
87	MR. LOVABLE	9500	35.00	35.00
87	MR. ONE-NOTE	9500	35.00	35.00
87	MR. TIP	9500	35.00	35.00
88	MR. COOL	9500	35.00	35.00
88	MR. HEART-THROB	9500	35.00	35.00
88	MR. MAGIC	9500	35.00	35.00

J. MCCLELLAND — FACES OF LOVE

YR	NAME	LIMIT	ISSUE	TREND
88	CUDDLES	OP	30.00	33.00
88	SUNSHINE	OP	30.00	33.00

G. GRANGET — GRANGET CRYSTAL SCULPTURE

YR	NAME	LIMIT	ISSUE	TREND
*	RUFFED GROUSE	350	1,000.00	1000.00
73	LONG EARED OWL, ASIO OTUS	350	2,250.00	2250.00

J. BERGSMA — LAUGHABLES

YR	NAME	LIMIT	ISSUE	TREND
95	ANNIE, GEORGE & HARRY	OP	17.50	18.00
95	CODY & SPOT	OP	15.00	16.00
95	DAFFODIL & PRINCE	OP	13.50	14.00
95	DAISY & JEREMIAH	OP	15.00	16.00
95	JOEY & JUMPER	OP	15.00	16.00
95	MERLIN & GEMINI	OP	15.00	16.00
95	MILLIE & MITTENS	OP	15.00	16.00
95	PATCHES AND POKEY	OP	15.00	16.00
95	PATTY & PETUNIA	OP	16.50	17.00
95	SUNNY	OP	13.50	14.00
95	WHISKERS & WILLIE	OP	13.50	14.00
96	NICHOLAS & CHELSEA 43511	SO	*	N/A

J. MCCLELLAND — RECO ANGEL COLLECTION

YR	NAME	LIMIT	ISSUE	TREND
86	ADORATION	OP	22.00	24.00
86	DEVOTION	OP	14.50	15.00
86	FAITH	OP	22.00	24.00
86	GLORIA	OP	12.00	12.00
86	HARMONY	OP	12.00	12.00
86	HOPE	OP	22.00	24.00
86	INNOCENCE	OP	12.00	12.00
86	JOY	OP	14.50	15.00
86	LOVE	OP	12.00	12.00
86	PEACE	OP	18.00	24.00
86	PRAISE	OP	18.00	20.00
86	SERENITY	OP	22.00	24.00
88	MINSTRAL	OP	12.00	12.00
88	REVERENCE	OP	12.00	12.00

J. MCCLELLAND — RECO CLOWN COLLECTION

YR	NAME	LIMIT	ISSUE	TREND
85	ARABESQUE	OP	12.00	13.00

YR	NAME	LIMIT	ISSUE	TREND
85	BOW JANGLES	OP	12.00	12.00
85	CURLY	OP	12.00	13.00
85	HOBO	OP	12.00	13.00
85	PROFESSOR, THE	OP	12.00	13.00
85	RUFFLES	OP	12.00	13.00
85	SAD EYES	OP	12.00	13.00
85	SCAMP	OP	12.00	13.00
85	SPARKLES	OP	12.00	13.00
85	TOP HAT	OP	12.00	13.00
85	WHOOPIE	OP	12.00	13.00
85	WINKIE	OP	12.00	13.00
87	DISCO DAN	OP	12.00	13.00
87	DOMINO	OP	12.00	13.00
87	HAPPY GEORGE	OP	12.00	13.00
87	JOKER, THE	OP	12.00	13.00
87	JOLLY JOE	OP	12.00	13.00
87	LOVE	OP	12.00	13.00
87	MR. BIG	OP	12.00	13.00
87	SMILEY	OP	12.00	13.00
87	TRAMP	OP	12.00	13.00
87	TWINKLE	OP	12.00	13.00
87	WISTFUL	OP	12.00	13.00
87	ZANY JACK	OP	12.00	13.00

J. MCCLELLAND
RECO COLLECTION CLOWN BUSTS

YR	NAME	LIMIT	ISSUE	TREND
88	DOMINO	5000	40.00	40.00
88	HOBO	5000	40.00	40.00
88	LOVE	5000	40.00	40.00
88	SPARKLES	5000	40.00	40.00

A. FAZIO
SOPHISTICATED LADIES FIGURINES

YR	NAME	LIMIT	ISSUE	TREND
87	BIANKA	9500	30.00	33.00
87	CERISSA	9500	30.00	33.00
87	CHELSEA	9500	30.00	33.00
87	CLEO	9500	30.00	33.00
87	FELICIA	9500	30.00	33.00
87	NATASHA	9500	30.00	33.00
87	PHOEBE	9500	30.00	33.00
87	SAMANTHA	9500	30.00	33.00

RED MILL MFG.

C. BUCHER

YR	NAME	LIMIT	ISSUE	TREND
96	HARMONY ANGEL	2500	35.00	35.00

T. FITZGERALD

95	NICOLE ANGEL	2500	35.00	35.00

R. WETHERBEE

96	SANTA	2500	35.00	35.00

ANGEL II COLLECTION

L. JOHNSON

94	CHRISTINA	2500	35.00	35.00

FLIGHTS OF FANCY

R. BENJAMIN

93	LIBERTY	5000	38.00	38.00

FLIGHTS OF FANCY

R.C. SOMMERS

93	INTEGRITY	3000	78.00	78.00
93	VALOR	2500	49.00	49.00

FLIGHTS OF FANCY

J. TEASDALE

93	SENTINEL	2500	55.00	55.00

FLIGHTS OF FANCY

R. WETHERBEE

93	COURAGEOUS	2500	65.95	66.00
93	MAJESTIC	3000	75.00	75.00

RHODES STUDIO

ROCKWELL INSPIRED
ROCKWELL'S AGE OF WONDER

YR	NAME	LIMIT	ISSUE	TREND
91	HUSH-A-BYE	TL	35.00	35.00
91	SPLISH SPLASH	TL	35.00	35.00
91	STAND BY ME	TL	37.00	37.00

ROCKWELL INSPIRED
ROCKWELL'S BEAUTIFUL DREAMERS

91	DEAR DIARY	TL	38.00	38.00
91	SECRET SONNETS	TL	40.00	40.00
91	SITTING PRETTY	TL	38.00	38.00

ROCKWELL INSPIRED
ROCKWELL'S GEMS OF WISDOM

91	LOVE CURES ALL	TL	40.00	40.00
91	PRACTICE MAKES PERFECT	TL	40.00	40.00

ROCKWELL INSPIRED
ROCKWELL'S HEIRLOOM SANTA COLLECTION

90	SANTA'S WORKSHOP	150-DAY	50.00	50.00
91	CHRISTMAS DREAM	150-DAY	50.00	50.00

ROCKWELL INSPIRED
ROCKWELL'S HOMETOWN

91	BELL TOWER	TL	37.00	37.00
91	FIREHOUSE	TL	37.00	37.00
91	GREYSTONE CHURCH	TL	35.00	35.00
91	ROCKWELL'S RESIDENCE	TL	35.00	35.00

ROCKWELL INSPIRED
ROCKWELL'S MAIN STREET

90	ANTIQUE SHOP, THE	150-DAY	28.00	28.00
90	COUNTRY STORE, THE	150-DAY	32.00	32.00
90	ROCKWELL'S STUDIO	150-DAY	28.00	28.00
90	TOWN OFFICES, THE	150-DAY	32.00	32.00
91	BANK, THE	150-DAY	36.00	36.00

YR NAME	LIMIT	ISSUE	TREND
91 LIBRARY, THE	150-DAY	36.00	36.00
91 RED LION INN	150-DAY	39.00	39.00

RIVER SHORE
R. BROWN

		BABIES OF ENDANGERED SPECIES	
84 BAXTER (BEAR)	15000	45.00	45.00
84 CAROLINE (ANTELOPE)	15000	45.00	45.00
84 CHESTER (PRAIRIE DOG)	15000	45.00	45.00
84 DAISY (WOOD BISON)	15000	45.00	45.00
84 SIDNEY (COUGAR)	15000	45.00	45.00
84 TREVOR (FOX)	15000	45.00	45.00
84 VIOLET (OTTER)	15000	45.00	45.00
84 WEBSTER (TIMBERWOLF)	15000	45.00	45.00

M. HAGUE

		LOVABLE TEDDY MUSICAL FIGURINE COLLECTION	
87 APRIL	OP	30.00	30.00
87 AUSTIN	OP	30.00	30.00
87 GILBERT	OP	30.00	30.00
87 WILLIAM	OP	30.00	30.00
88 ADAM	OP	30.00	30.00
88 HARVEY	OP	30.00	30.00
88 HENRY	OP	30.00	30.00
88 KATIE	OP	30.00	30.00

R. BROWN

		LOVEABLE BABY ANIMALS	
78 AKIKU-SEAL	15000	38.00	150.00
78 ALFRED-RACCOON	15000	43.00	45.00
79 MATILDA-KOALA	15000	45.00	45.00
79 SCOOTER-CHIPMUNK	15000	45.00	55.00

N. ROCKWELL

		ROCKWELL SINGLE ISSUES	
82 GRANDPA'S GUARDIAN	9500	125.00	125.00

R. BROWN

		WILDERNESS BABIES	
85 ABERCROMBIE (POLAR BEAR)	15000	45.00	45.00
85 ANNABEL (MOUNTAIN GOAT)	15000	45.00	45.00
85 ARIANNE (RABBIT)	15000	45.00	45.00
85 CARMEN (BURRO)	15000	45.00	45.00
85 ELROD (FOX)	15000	45.00	45.00
85 PENELOPE (DEER)	15000	45.00	45.00
85 REGGIE (RACCOON)	15000	45.00	45.00
85 ROCKY (BOBCAT)	15000	45.00	45.00

R. BROWN

		WILDLIFE BABY ANIMALS	
78 FANNY-FAWN	15000	45.00	90.00
79 ROOSEVELT-BEAR	15000	50.00	65.00
79 ROSCOE-RED FOX	15000	50.00	50.00
80 PRISCILLA-SKUNK	15000	50.00	50.00

RJB DESIGNS
R. BRENNAN

		CINDER CLAUS	
93 SANTA (3 FT.)	75	950.00	1000.00
93 SANTA (4 FT.)	40	1,300.00	1500.00
93 SANTA-SPECIAL EDITION	850	200.00	225.00
94 AMBERT	250	200.00	225.00
94 CUTHBERT	250	200.00	225.00
94 DRUSILLA	100	20.00	23.00
94 GARRICK	250	200.00	225.00
94 MONTGOMERY	250	200.00	225.00
94 SANTA (3 FT.)	60	950.00	975.00
94 SANTA (4 FT.)	20	1,300.00	1400.00
94 SANTA (5 FT.)	3	3,500.00	3750.00
95 CORNELIUS	250	200.00	200.00
95 CULVER	250	200.00	200.00
95 ROSCOE	250	200.00	200.00
95 STODDARD	250	200.00	200.00
95 WILHELMINA	100	200.00	200.00

R. BRENNAN

		OH FOR HEAVEN'S SAKE SERIES I	
95 BETTY	5600	30.00	30.00
95 BUD	5600	30.00	30.00
95 CHARLIE	5600	30.00	30.00
95 CLAUDE	5600	30.00	30.00
95 EDNA	5600	30.00	30.00
95 EVELYN	5600	30.00	30.00
95 LESTER	5600	30.00	30.00
95 VERA	5600	30.00	30.00

R. BRENNAN

		OH FOR HEAVEN'S SAKE SERIES II	
96 BOB	5600	30.00	30.00
96 ELIZABETH	5600	30.00	30.00
96 IVA	5600	30.00	30.00
96 LOIS	5600	30.00	30.00
96 LOUISE	5600	30.00	30.00
96 O'BRIAN	5600	30.00	30.00
96 REX	5600	30.00	30.00
96 ROY	5600	30.00	30.00

ROHN
E. ROHN

		AROUND THE WORLD	
71 COOLIE	100	700.00	1300.00
72 GYPSY	125	1,450.00	1850.00

YR	NAME	LIMIT	ISSUE	TREND
73	MATADOR	90	2,400.00	3100.00
73	SHERIFF	100	1,500.00	2250.00
74	AUSSIE-HUNTER	90	1,000.00	1300.00
E. ROHN	*CLOWNS-BIG TOP SERIES*			
79	WHITE FACE	100	1,000.00	3500.00
80	TRAMP	100	1,200.00	2500.00
81	AUGUSTE	100	1,400.00	1700.00
83	SWEETHEART	200	925.00	1500.00
E. ROHN	*CLOWNS-HEY RUBE*			
79	AUGUSTE	300	190.00	350.00
79	TRAMP	300	190.00	350.00
79	WHITEFACE	300	190.00	350.00
E. ROHN	*FAMOUS PEOPLE*			
75	HARRY S. TRUMAN	75	2,400.00	4000.00
79	NORMAN ROCKWELL	200	1,950.00	2300.00
81	RONALD REAGAN	200	3,000.00	3000.00
85	SHERLOCK HOLMES	2210	155.00	190.00
86	DR. JOHN WATSON	2210	155.00	155.00
93	SHERLOCK HOLMES & DR. WATSON	OP	185.00	200.00
E. ROHN	*FAMOUS PEOPLE-BISQUE*			
79	LINCOLN	500	100.00	500.00
79	NORMAN ROCKWELL	YR	100.00	200.00
81	REAGAN	2500	140.00	200.00
83	J.F. KENNEDY	500	140.00	400.00
E. ROHN	*KINARA SERIES*			
92	KENTE WOMAN	OP	40.00	45.00
E. ROHN	*PORTRAIT SERIES*			
92	MARTIN LUTHER KING	OP	60.00	75.00
E. ROHN	*RELIGIOUS & BIBLICAL*			
77	ZAIDE	70	1,950.00	5000.00
78	SABBATH	70	1,825.00	5000.00
85	MENTOR, THE	15	9,500.00	9500.00
E. ROHN	*REMEMBER WHEN*			
71	AMERICAN GI	100	600.00	1750.00
71	RIVERBOAT CAPTAIN	100	1,000.00	2400.00
73	APPRENTICE	175	500.00	850.00
73	JAZZ MAN	150	750.00	3500.00
74	MISSY	250	250.00	500.00
74	RECRUIT (SET W/FN-5)	250	250.00	500.00
77	CASEY	300	275.00	500.00
77	FLAPPER	500	325.00	500.00
77	SOU' WESTER	450	300.00	500.00
77	WALLY	250	250.00	500.00
80	SHOWMAN (W.C. FIELDS)	300	220.00	500.00
81	CLOWN PRINCE	25	2,000.00	2400.00
E. ROHN	*ROHN'S CLOWNS*			
84	AUGUSTE	7500	95.00	100.00
84	HOBO	7500	95.00	100.00
84	WHITE FACE	7500	95.00	100.00
E. ROHN	*SMALL WORLD SERIES*			
*	JOHNNIE'S	1500	90.00	90.00
74	BIG BROTHER	250	90.00	90.00
74	BURGLERS	250	120.00	120.00
74	KNEE DEEP	500	60.00	60.00
74	QUACKERS	250	75.00	75.00
75	FIELD MUSHROOMS	250	90.00	90.00
75	OYSTER MUSHROOM	250	140.00	140.00
E. ROHN	*WESTERN*			
71	APACHE INDIAN	125	800.00	2000.00
71	CHOSEN ONE (INDIAN MAID)	125	850.00	2000.00
71	CROW INDIAN	100	800.00	1500.00
71	TRAIL-HAND	100	1,200.00	1600.00
E. ROHN	*WILD WEST*			
82	RODEO CLOWN	100	2,600.00	3500.00

ROMAN INC.

YR	NAME	LIMIT	ISSUE	TREND
F. HOOK	*A CHILD'S WORLD 1ST EDITION*			
80	BEACH BUDDIES, SIGNED	15000	29.00	600.00
80	BEACH BUDDIES, UNSIGNED	15000	29.00	500.00
80	HELPING HANDS	15000	45.00	75.00
80	KISS ME GOOD NIGHT	15000	29.00	50.00
80	MY BIG BROTHER	15000	39.00	200.00
80	NIGHTTIME THOUGHTS	15000	25.00	75.00
80	SOUNDS OF THE SEA	15000	45.00	150.00
F. HOOK	*A CHILD'S WORLD 2ND EDITION*			
81	ALL DRESSED UP	15000	36.00	75.00
81	CAT NAP	15000	42.00	100.00
81	I'LL BE GOOD	15000	36.00	75.00
81	MAKING FRIENDS	15000	42.00	46.00
81	SEA AND ME, THE	15000	39.00	50.00
81	SUNDAY SHCOOL	15000	39.00	75.00
F. HOOK	*A CHILD'S WORLD 3RD EDITION*			
81	BEAR HUG	15000	42.00	55.00
81	PATHWAY TO DREAMS	15000	47.00	80.00

YR	NAME	LIMIT	ISSUE	TREND
81	ROAD TO ADVENTURE	15000	47.00	50.00
81	SISTERS	15000	64.00	110.00
81	SPRING BREEZE	15000	38.00	50.00
81	YOUTH	15000	38.00	50.00
F. HOOK		**A CHILD'S WORLD 4TH EDITION**		
82	ALL BUNDLED UP	15000	38.00	50.00
82	BEDTIME	15000	35.00	38.00
82	BIRDIE	15000	38.00	50.00
82	FLOWER GIRL	15000	42.00	50.00
82	MY DOLLY!	15000	39.00	50.00
82	RING BEARER	15000	39.00	50.00
F. HOOK		**A CHILD'S WORLD 5TH EDITION**		
83	BROTHERS	15000	64.00	75.00
83	FINISH LINE	15000	39.00	42.00
83	HANDFUL OF HAPPINESS	15000	36.00	50.00
83	HE LOVES ME...	15000	49.00	60.00
83	PUPPY'S PAL	15000	39.00	42.00
83	RING AROUND THE ROSIE	15000	99.00	105.00
F. HOOK		**A CHILD'S WORLD 6TH EDITION**		
84	CAN I HELP?	15000	38.00	50.00
84	FUTURE ARTIST	15000	42.00	50.00
84	GOOD DOGGIE	15000	47.00	50.00
84	LET'S PLAY CATCH	15000	33.00	40.00
84	NATURE'S WONDERS	15000	29.00	40.00
84	SAND CASTLES	15000	38.00	50.00
F. HOOK		**A CHILD'S WORLD 7TH EDITION**		
85	ART CLASS	15000	99.00	105.00
85	DON'T TELL ANYONE	15000	49.00	50.00
85	LOOK AT ME!	15000	42.00	50.00
85	MOTHER'S HELPER	15000	45.00	50.00
85	PLEASE HEAR ME	15000	29.00	30.00
85	YUMMM!	15000	36.00	40.00
F. HOOK		**A CHILD'S WORLD 8TH EDITION**		
85	CHANCE OF SHOWERS	15000	33.00	40.00
85	DRESS REHEARSAL	15000	33.00	40.00
85	ENGINE	15000	36.00	50.00
85	JUST STOPPED BY	15000	36.00	50.00
85	PRIVATE OCEAN	15000	29.00	40.00
85	PUZZLING	15000	36.00	50.00
F. HOOK		**A CHILD'S WORLD 9TH EDITION**		
87	HOPSCOTCH	15000	68.00	75.00
87	LI'L BROTHER	15000	60.00	75.00
I. SPENCER		**CATNIPPERS**		
85	A BAFFLING YARN	15000	45.00	50.00
85	A CHRISTMAS MOURNING	15000	45.00	50.00
85	A TAIL OF TWO KITTIES	15000	45.00	50.00
85	CAN'T WE BE FRIENDS	15000	45.00	50.00
85	FLORA AND FELINA	15000	45.00	50.00
85	FLYING TIGER-RETIRED	15000	45.00	50.00
85	PAW THAT REFRESHES, THE	15000	45.00	50.00
85	SANDY CLAWS	15000	45.00	50.00
*		**CERAMICA EXCELSIS**		
77	CHRIST KNOCKING AT THE DOOR	5000	60.00	60.00
77	MADONNA AND CHILD WITH ANGELS	5000	60.00	60.00
77	MADONNA WITH CHILD	5000	65.00	75.00
77	ST. FRANCIS	5000	60.00	60.00
77	WHAT HAPPENED TO YOUR HAND?	5000	60.00	60.00
78	ASSUMPTION MADONNA	5000	56.00	56.00
78	CHRIST ENTERING JERUSALEM	5000	96.00	96.00
78	CHRIST IN THE GARDEN OF GETHSEMANE	5000	40.00	60.00
78	FLIGHT INTO EGYPT	5000	59.00	90.00
78	GUARDIAN ANGEL WITH BOY	5000	69.00	69.00
78	GUARDIAN ANGEL WITH GIRL	5000	69.00	69.00
78	HOLY FAMILY AT WORK	5000	96.00	96.00
78	INFANT OF PRAGUE	5000	38.00	60.00
79	JESUS SPEAKS IN PARABLES	5000	90.00	90.00
79	MOSES	5000	77.00	77.00
79	NOAH	5000	77.00	77.00
80	DANIEL IN THE LION'S DEN	5000	80.00	80.00
80	DAVID	5000	77.00	77.00
80	WAY TO EMMAUS	5000	155.00	155.00
81	INNOCENCE	5000	95.00	100.00
81	JOURNEY TO BETHLEHEM	5000	89.00	89.00
81	SERMON ON THE MOUNT	5000	56.00	56.00
81	WAY OF THE CROSS	5000	59.00	59.00
83	GOOD SHEPHERD	5000	49.00	49.00
83	HOLY FAMILY	5000	72.00	72.00
83	JESUS WITH CHILDREN	5000	74.00	74.00
83	KNEELING SANTA	5000	95.00	100.00
83	ST. ANNE	5000	49.00	49.00
83	ST. FRANCIS	5000	60.00	60.00
E. WILLIAMS		**CLASSIC BRIDES OF THE CENTURY**		
89	1900-FLORA	5000	175.00	175.00
89	1910-ELIZABETH GRACE	5000	175.00	175.00

YR	NAME	LIMIT	ISSUE	TREND
89	1920-MARY CLAIRE	5000	175.00	175.00
89	1930-KATHLEEN	5000	175.00	175.00
89	1940-MARGARET	5000	175.00	175.00
89	1950-BARBARA ANN	5000	175.00	175.00
89	1960-DIANNE	5000	175.00	175.00
89	1970-HEATHER	5000	175.00	175.00
89	1980-JENNIFER	5000	175.00	175.00
89	1990-STEPHANIE HELEN	5000	175.00	175.00
D. FEARON			**DECLAN'S FINNIANS**	
95	AILERAN, THE CURIOUS	RT	35.00	35.00
95	CAELON, THE LOVER	RT	30.00	30.00
95	CUCHULAINN, THE TRAVELER	2000	75.00	75.00
95	ENID, THE SWIFT	RT	30.00	30.00
95	JACK, THE CLIMBER	RT	30.00	30.00
95	LAIDECH, THE SONGFUL	RT	30.00	30.00
95	SENAN, THE STEADFAST	2000	75.00	75.00
L. MARTIN			**DOLFI ORIGINAL-10 IN. STONEART**	
89	A SHOULDER TO LEAN ON	OP	400.00	400.00
89	BAREFOOT IN SPRING	OP	400.00	400.00
89	BIG CHIEF SITTING DOG	OP	325.00	325.00
89	BIRDLAND CAFE	OP	300.00	300.00
89	DRESS REHEARSAL	OP	495.00	495.00
89	FLOWER CHILD	OP	300.00	300.00
89	FRIENDS & FLOWERS	OP	400.00	400.00
89	GARDEN SECRETS	OP	300.00	300.00
89	HAVE I BEEN THAT GOOD	OP	495.00	495.00
89	HOLIDAY HERALD	OP	300.00	300.00
89	LITTLE SANTA	OP	325.00	325.00
89	MARY & JOEY	OP	495.00	495.00
89	MERRY LITTLE LIGHT	OP	325.00	325.00
89	MOTHER HEN	OP	300.00	300.00
89	MUD PUDDLES	OP	300.00	300.00
89	MY FAVORITE THINGS	OP	400.00	400.00
89	MY FIRST CAKE	OP	300.00	300.00
89	MY FIRST KITTEN	OP	300.00	300.00
89	PAMPERED PUPPIES	OP	300.00	300.00
89	PUPPY EXPRESS	OP	300.00	300.00
89	SING A SONG OF JOY	OP	400.00	400.00
89	SLEEPYHEAD	OP	300.00	300.00
89	STUDY BREAK	OP	325.00	325.00
89	WRAPPED IN LOVE	OP	300.00	300.00
L. MARTIN			**DOLFI ORIGINAL-10 IN. WOOD**	
89	A SHOULDER TO LEAN ON	2000	1,000.00	1000.00
89	BAREFOOT IN SPRING	2000	1,000.00	1000.00
89	BIG CHIEF SITTING DOG	2000	825.00	825.00
89	BIRDLAND CAFE	2000	750.00	750.00
89	DRESS REHEARSAL	2000	1,250.00	1250.00
89	FLOWER CHILD	2000	750.00	750.00
89	FRIENDS & FLOWERS	2000	1,000.00	1000.00
89	GARDEN SECRETS	2000	750.00	750.00
89	HAVE I BEEN THAT GOOD	2000	1,250.00	1250.00
89	HOLIDAY HERALD	2000	750.00	750.00
89	LITTLE SANTA	2000	825.00	825.00
89	MARY & JOEY	2000	1,250.00	1250.00
89	MERRY LITTLE LIGHT	2000	825.00	825.00
89	MOTHER HEN	2000	750.00	750.00
89	MUD PUDDLES	2000	750.00	750.00
89	MY FAVORITE THINGS	2000	1,000.00	1000.00
89	MY FIRST CAKE	2000	750.00	750.00
89	MY FIRST KITTEN	2000	750.00	750.00
89	PAMPERED PUPPIES	2000	750.00	750.00
89	PUPPY EXPRESS	2000	1,000.00	1000.00
89	SING A SONG OF JOY	2000	750.00	750.00
89	SLEEPYHEAD	2000	825.00	825.00
89	STUDY BREAK	2000	750.00	750.00
89	WRAPPED IN LOVE			
L. MARTIN			**DOLFI ORIGINAL-5 IN. WOOD**	
89	A SHOULDER TO LEAN ON	5000	300.00	300.00
89	BAREFOOT IN SPRING	5000	300.00	300.00
89	BIG CHIEF SITTING DOG	5000	250.00	250.00
89	BIRDLAND CAFE	5000	230.00	230.00
89	DRESS REHEARSAL	5000	375.00	375.00
89	FLOWER CHILD	5000	230.00	230.00
89	FRIENDS & FLOWERS	5000	300.00	300.00
89	GARDEN SECRETS	5000	230.00	230.00
89	HAVE I BEEN THAT GOOD	5000	375.00	375.00
89	HOLIDAY HERALD	5000	230.00	230.00
89	LITTLE SANTA	5000	250.00	250.00
89	MARY & JOEY	5000	375.00	375.00
89	MERRY LITTLE LIGHT	5000	250.00	250.00
89	MOTHER HEN	5000	230.00	230.00
89	MUD PUDDLES	5000	230.00	230.00
89	MY FAVORITE THINGS	5000	300.00	300.00
89	MY FIRST CAKE	5000	230.00	230.00
89	MY FIRST KITTEN	5000	230.00	230.00

YR	NAME	LIMIT	ISSUE	TREND
89	PAMPERED PUPPIES	5000	230.00	230.00
89	PUPPY EXPRESS	5000	230.00	230.00
89	SING A SONG OF JOY	5000	300.00	300.00
89	SLEEPYHEAD	5000	230.00	230.00
89	STUDY BREAK	5000	250.00	250.00
89	WRAPPED IN LOVE	5000	230.00	230.00

L. MARTIN — DOLFI ORIGINAL-7 IN. STONEART

YR	NAME	LIMIT	ISSUE	TREND
89	A SHOULDER TO LEAN ON	OP	150.00	150.00
89	BAREFOOT IN SPRING	OP	150.00	150.00
89	BIG CHIEF SITTING DOG	OP	120.00	120.00
89	BIRDLAND CAFE	OP	110.00	110.00
89	DRESS REHEARSAL	OP	185.00	185.00
89	FLOWER CHILD	OP	110.00	110.00
89	FRIENDS & FLOWERS	OP	150.00	150.00
89	GARDEN SECRETS	OP	110.00	110.00
89	HAVE I BEEN THAT GOOD	OP	185.00	185.00
89	HOLIDAY HERALD	OP	110.00	110.00
89	LITTLE SANTA	OP	120.00	120.00
89	MARY & JOEY	OP	185.00	185.00
89	MERRY LITTLE LIGHT	OP	120.00	120.00
89	MOTHER HEN	OP	110.00	110.00
89	MUD PUDDLES	OP	110.00	110.00
89	MY FAVORITE THINGS	OP	150.00	150.00
89	MY FIRST CAKE	OP	110.00	110.00
89	MY FIRST KITTEN	OP	110.00	110.00
89	PAMPERED PUPPIES	OP	110.00	110.00
89	PUPPY EXPRESS	OP	110.00	110.00
89	SING A SONG OF JOY	OP	150.00	150.00
89	SLEEPYHEAD	OP	110.00	110.00
89	STUDY BREAK	OP	120.00	120.00
89	WRAPPED IN LOVE	OP	110.00	110.00

E. SIMONETTI — FONTANINI CLUB SYMBOL OF MEMBERSHIP

YR	NAME	LIMIT	ISSUE	TREND
90	I FOUND HIM	CL	*	N/A
96	ROSANNAH, ANGEL OF THE ROSES	YR	*	N/A
97	LEAH, ANGEL OF LIGHT	YR	*	N/A
98	CANDACE, THE CAREGIVER	YR	*	N/A

E. SIMONETTI — FONTANINI HEIRLOOM NATIVITIES 5-IN. FIGURINES

YR	NAME	LIMIT	ISSUE	TREND
66	ANGELS, GLORIA ANGEL	RT	5.50	6.00
66	BABY JESUS	RT	5.50	12.00
66	BALTHAZAR	RT	5.50	12.00
66	GASPAR	RT	5.50	12.00
66	JOSEPH	RT	5.50	12.00
66	MARY	RT	5.50	12.00
66	WISE MEN, MELCHIOR	RT	5.50	12.00
67	AARON	RT	5.50	6.00
67	GABRIEL	RT	12.50	13.00
67	JOSIAH	RT	5.50	12.00
67	KNEELING ANGEL	RT	5.50	12.00
67	LEVI	RT	5.50	13.00
67	MIRIAM	RT	5.50	12.00
67	MORDECAI	RT	5.50	12.00
67	STANDING ANGEL	RT	5.50	13.00
83	MICAH	RT	5.50	12.00

E. SIMONETTI — FONTANINI HEIRLOOM NATIVITIES 5-IN. LIMITED ED. FIGURINES

YR	NAME	LIMIT	ISSUE	TREND
92	ARIEL	YR	30.00	30.00
93	JOSHUA & ADIN	YR	30.00	30.00
94	14-PC. GOLDEN EDITION NATIVITY SET	2500	375.00	375.00
94	ABIGAIL & PETER	YR	30.00	30.00
95	GABRIELA	YR	18.00	18.00
96	RAPHAEL	YR	18.00	18.00
97	JUDAH	YR	19.50	20.00
98	CELESTE, ANGEL WITH DOVE	YR	19.50	20.00

E. SIMONETTI — FONTANINI HEIRLOOM NATIVITIES 7.5-IN. FIGURINES

YR	NAME	LIMIT	ISSUE	TREND
79	BABY JESUS	RT	13.00	25.00
79	GABRIEL	RT	13.00	25.00
79	JOSEPH	RT	13.00	25.00
79	MARY	RT	13.00	25.00
82	KNEELING ANGEL	RT	13.00	25.00
82	STANDING ANGEL	RT	13.00	25.00

E. SIMONETTI — FONTANINI HEIRLOOM NATIVITIES 90TH ANNIVERSARY

YR	NAME	LIMIT	ISSUE	TREND
98	10-PC. FIGURE SET WITH STABLE	YR	300.00	300.00
98	CHARIS, 90TH ANNIVERSARY ANGEL	YR	30.00	30.00

E. SIMONETTI — FONTANINI HEIRLOOM NATIVITIES CLUB MEMBERS ONLY

YR	NAME	LIMIT	ISSUE	TREND
91	PILGRIMAGE, THE	YR	25.00	25.00
92	SHE RESCUED ME	YR	24.00	24.00
93	CHRISTMAS SYMPHONY	YR	13.50	14.00
94	SWEET HARMONY	YR	13.50	14.00
95	FAITH, THE FIFTH ANGEL	YR	22.50	23.00
96	MARA	YR	12.50	13.00
97	BENJAMIN	YR	15.00	15.00

E. SIMONETTI — FONTANINI HEIRLOOM NATIVITIES CLUB RENEWAL GIFT

YR	NAME	LIMIT	ISSUE	TREND
93	HE COMFORTS ME	YR	13.00	13.00
94	I'M HEAVEN BOUND	YR	13.00	13.00

YR	NAME	LIMIT	ISSUE	TREND
95	GIFT OF JOY	YR	13.00	13.00
98	HANNAH	YR	15.00	15.00
E. SIMONETTI	**FONTANINI HEIRLOOM NATIVITIES CRECHE**			
73	10 CM 15 PC. SET	RT	64.00	90.00
73	12 CM. 15 PC. SET	RT	77.00	100.00
73	19 CM. 15 PC. SET	RT	176.00	275.00
79	16 CM. 15 PC. SET	RT	179.00	300.00
80	30 CM. 15 PC. SET	RT	670.00	750.00
82	17 CM. 15 PC. SET	RT	189.00	189.00
E. SIMONETTI	**FONTANINI HEIRLOOM NATIVITIES SPECIAL EVENT**			
94	SUSANNA	YR	12.00	12.00
95	DOMINICA	YR	15.00	15.00
96	SARAH	YR	15.00	15.00
97	MARTHA	YR	15.00	15.00
E. SIMONETTI	**FONTANINI HEIRLOOM NATIVITIES TOUR EXCLUSIVE**			
90	GIDEON	CL	15.00	15.00
95	LUKE	CL	15.00	15.00
F. HOOK	**FRANCES HOOK'S FOUR SEASONS**			
84	WINTER	12500	95.00	100.00
85	FALL	12500	95.00	100.00
85	SPRING	12500	95.00	100.00
85	SUMMER	12500	95.00	100.00
I. SPENCER	**HEARTBEATS**			
86	MIRACLE	5000	145.00	150.00
87	STORYTIME	5000	145.00	150.00
F. HOOK	**HOOK**			
82	SAILOR MATES	2000	290.00	325.00
82	SUN SHY	2000	290.00	325.00
86	CARPENTER BUST	YR	95.00	100.00
86	CARPENTER BUST-HEIRLOOM EDITION	YR	95.00	100.00
87	LITTLE CHILDREN, COME TO ME	15000	45.00	50.00
87	MADONNA AND CHILD	15000	40.00	50.00
E. ROHN	**JAM SESSION**			
85	BANJO PLAYER	7500	145.00	150.00
85	BASS PLAYER	7500	145.00	150.00
85	CLARINET PLAYER	7500	145.00	150.00
85	CORONET PLAYER	7500	145.00	150.00
85	DRUMMER	7500	145.00	150.00
85	TROMBONE PLAYER	7500	145.00	150.00
G. DELLE NOTTI	**MASTERPIECE COLLECTION**			
81	HOLY FAMILY, THE	5000	98.00	100.00
R. FERRUZZI	**MASTERPIECE COLLECTION**			
82	MADONNA OF THE STREETS	5000	65.00	75.00
F. LIPPE	**MASTERPIECE COLLECTION**			
79	ADORATION	5000	73.00	80.00
P. MIGNARD	**MASTERPIECE COLLECTION**			
80	MADONNA WITH GRAPES	5000	85.00	90.00
M.J. DORCY	**MILLENIUM COLLECTION**			
96	PRINCE OF PEACE	RT	30.00	30.00
A. TRIPI	**MUSEUM COLLECTION BY ANGELA TRIPI**			
90	MENTOR, THE	1000	290.00	300.00
91	A GENTLEMAN'S GAME	1000	175.00	175.00
91	CADDIE, THE	1000	135.00	150.00
91	CHRISTOPHER COLUMBUS	1000	250.00	250.00
91	FIDDLER, THE	1000	175.00	175.00
91	ST. FRANCIS OF ASSISI	1000	175.00	175.00
91	TEE TIME AT ST. ANDREW'S	1000	175.00	175.00
SERAPHIM STUDIOS	**SERAPHIM CLASSICS 12-IN. LIMITED EDITIONS**			
95	ALYSSA-NATURE'S ANGEL	CL	145.00	145.00
96	ROSALIE-NATURE'S DELIGHT	OP	55.00	55.00
96	VANESSA-HEAVENLY MAIDEN	CL	150.00	150.00
97	ARIEL-HEAVEN'S SHINING STAR	CL	159.00	159.00
97	CHLOE-NATURE'S GIFT	CL	159.00	159.00
98	AVALON-FREE SPIRIT	YR	175.00	175.00
98	HOPE-LIGHT IN THE DISTANCE	TL	175.00	175.00
SERAPHIM STUDIOS	**SERAPHIM CLASSICS 4-IN.**			
95	CYMBELINE-PEACEMAKER	OP	19.50	20.00
95	EVANGELINE-ANGEL OF MERCY	OP	19.50	20.00
95	FELICIA-ADORING MAIDEN	OP	19.50	20.00
95	IRISH-RAINBOW'S END	OP	19.50	20.00
95	ISABEL-GENTLE SPIRIT	OP	19.50	20.00
95	LAURICE-WISDOM'S CHILD	OP	19.50	20.00
95	LYDIA-WINGED POET	OP	19.50	20.00
95	OPHELIA-HEART SEEKER	OP	19.50	20.00
95	PRISCILLA-BENEVOLENT GUIDE	OP	19.50	20.00
95	SERAPHINA-HEAVEN'S HELPER	OP	19.50	20.00
SERAPHIM STUDIOS	**SERAPHIM CLASSICS 7-IN.**			
94	CYMBELINE-PEACEMAKER	RT	50.00	50.00
94	EVANGELINE-ANGEL OF MERCY	OP	50.00	50.00
94	IRIS-RAINBOW'S END	OP	50.00	50.00
94	ISABEL-GENTLE SPIRIT	OP	50.00	50.00
94	LYDIA-WINGED POET	RT	50.00	50.00
94	OPHELIA-HEART SEEKER	RT	50.00	50.00
95	FELICIA-ADORING MAIDEN	OP	50.00	50.00

YR	NAME	LIMIT	ISSUE	TREND
95	PRISCILLA-BENEVOLENT GUIDE	OP	50.00	50.00
95	SERAPHINA-HEAVEN'S HELPER	RT	50.00	50.00
96	CELINE-THE MORNING STAR	OP	55.00	55.00
96	FAITH-THE EASTER ANGEL	OP	55.00	55.00
96	FRANCESCA-LOVING GUARDIAN	OP	65.00	65.00
96	GABRIEL-CELESTIAL MESSENGER	OP	60.00	60.00
96	MARIAH-HEAVENLY JOY	OP	60.00	60.00
96	SERENA-ANGEL OF PEACE	OP	65.00	65.00
97	CHELSEA-SUMMER'S DELIGHT	OP	55.00	55.00
97	GRACE-BORN ANEW	OP	55.00	55.00
97	HANNAH-ALWAYS NEAR	OP	55.00	55.00
97	HARMONY-LOVE'S GUARDIAN	OP	55.00	55.00
97	HEATHER-AUTUMN BEAUTY	OP	55.00	55.00
97	LAURICE-WISDOM'S CHILD	RT	50.00	50.00
97	MELODY-HEAVEN'S SONG	OP	55.00	55.00
97	RACHEL-CHILDREN'S JOY	OP	55.00	55.00
97	SABRINA-ETERNAL GUIDE	RT	55.00	55.00
97	TAMARA-BLESSED GUARDIAN	OP	65.00	65.00
98	AMELIA-ETERNAL BLOOM	YR	65.00	65.00
98	ANGEL'S TOUCH-DEDICATION ANGEL	OP	60.00	60.00
98	ANNABELLA-ANNOUNCEMENT F JOY	YR	60.00	60.00
98	DIANA-HEAVEN'S ROSE	OP	60.00	60.00
98	NOELLE-GIVING SPIRIT	OP	60.00	60.00
98	SAMANTHA-BLESSED AT BIRTH	OP	60.00	60.00
98	SIMONE-NATURE'S OWN	OP	100.00	100.00

SERAPHIM STUDIOS   **SERAPHIM CLASSICS ANGELS TO WATCH OVER ME**

YR	NAME	LIMIT	ISSUE	TREND
96	FIFTH YEAR GIRL	OP	40.00	40.00
96	FIRST YEAR GIRL	OP	40.00	40.00
96	FOURTH YEAR GIRL	OP	40.00	40.00
96	NEWBORN GIRL	OP	40.00	40.00
96	SECOND YEAR GIRL	OP	40.00	40.00
96	THIRD YEAR GIRL	OP	40.00	40.00
97	FIFTH YEAR BOY	OP	40.00	40.00
97	FIRST YEAR BOY	OP	40.00	40.00
97	FOURTH YEAR BOY	OP	40.00	40.00
97	NEWBORN BOY	OP	40.00	40.00
97	SECOND YEAR BOY	OP	40.00	40.00
97	SEVENTH YEAR GIRL	OP	40.00	40.00
97	SIXTH YEAR BOY	OP	40.00	40.00
97	SIXTH YEAR GIRL	OP	40.00	40.00
97	THIRD YEAR BOY	OP	40.00	40.00

SERAPHIM STUDIOS   **SERAPHIM CLASSICS COLLECTORS CLUB**

YR	NAME	LIMIT	ISSUE	TREND
97	TESS-TENDER ONE	YR	55.00	55.00
98	LILLIAN-NUTURING LIFE	YR	65.00	65.00

SERAPHIM STUDIOS   **SERAPHIM CLASSICS GLITTERDOMES**

YR	NAME	LIMIT	ISSUE	TREND
95	FRANCESCA-LOVING GUARDIAN	OP	50.00	50.00
97	IRIS-RAINBOW'S END	OP	50.00	50.00

SERAPHIM STUDIOS   **SERAPHIM CLASSICS HEAVEN SENT COLLECTION**

YR	NAME	LIMIT	ISSUE	TREND
97	HOPE ETERNAL	OP	30.00	30.00
97	LOVING SPIRIT	OP	30.00	30.00
97	PURE AT HEART	OP	30.00	30.00

SERAPHIM STUDIOS   **SERAPHIM CLASSICS HEAVEN SENT COLLECTION MUSICALS**

YR	NAME	LIMIT	ISSUE	TREND
97	HOPE ETERNAL	OP	38.00	38.00
97	LOVING SPIRIT	OP	38.00	38.00
97	PURE AT HEART	OP	38.00	38.00
98	PEACEFUL EMBRACE	OP	85.00	85.00

SERAPHIM STUDIOS   **SERAPHIM CLASSICS MUSICALS**

YR	NAME	LIMIT	ISSUE	TREND
94	FRANCESCA-LOVING GUARDIAN	OP	75.00	75.00
96	IRIS-RAINBOW'S END	OP	65.00	65.00
98	EVANGELINE-ANGEL OF MERCY	OP	75.00	75.00

SERAPHIM STUDIOS   **SERAPHIM CLASSICS NATIVITY**

YR	NAME	LIMIT	ISSUE	TREND
96	NATIVITY SET 5 PCS.	OP	125.00	125.00
97	THREE KINGS	OP	125.00	125.00
98	GLORIA ANGEL	OP	60.00	60.00
98	SHEPHERDS 2-PC. SET	OP	65.00	65.00

SERAPHIM STUDIOS   **SERAPHIM CLASSICS SPECIAL EVENT**

YR	NAME	LIMIT	ISSUE	TREND
96	DAWN-SUNSHINE'S GUARDIAN ANGEL	CL	55.00	55.00
97	MONICA-UNDER LOVE'S WING	YR	55.00	55.00

I. SPENCER   **SPENCER**

YR	NAME	LIMIT	ISSUE	TREND
85	FLOWER PRINCESS	5000	195.00	200.00
85	MOON GODDESS	5000	195.00	200.00

RON LEE'S WORLD OF CLOWNS

R. LEE   **ORIGINAL RON LEE COLLECTION**

YR	NAME	LIMIT	ISSUE	TREND
76	ALLIGATOR BOWLING 504	CL	15.00	50.00
76	BEAR FISHING 512	CL	15.00	50.00
76	CLOWN AND DOG ACT 101	CL	48.00	125.00
76	CLOWN AND ELEPHANT ACT 107	CL	56.00	110.00
76	CLOWN TIGHTROPE WALKER 104	CL	50.00	125.00
76	DOG FISHING 512	CL	15.00	50.00
76	FROG SURFING 502	CL	15.00	50.00
76	HIPPO ON SCOOTER 505	CL	15.00	50.00
76	HOBO JOE HITCHHIKING 116	CL	55.00	65.00
76	HOBO JOE WITH BALLOONS 120	CL	66.00	90.00

YR	NAME	LIMIT	ISSUE	TREND
76	HOBO JOE WITH PAL 115	CL	66.00	150.00
76	HOBO JOE WITH UMBRELLA 117	CL	58.00	110.00
76	KANGAROOS BOXING 508	CL	15.00	50.00
76	OWL WITH GUITAR 500	CL	15.00	50.00
76	PENGUIN ON SNOWSKIS 503	CL	15.00	50.00
76	PIG PLAYING VIOLIN 510	CL	15.00	50.00
76	PINKY LYING DOWN 112	CL	25.00	— 40.00
76	PINKY SITTING 119	CL	25.00	40.00
76	PINKY STANDING 118	CL	25.00	75.00
76	PINKY UPSIDE DOWN 111	CL	25.00	◄ 40.00
76	RABBIT PLAYING TENNIS 507	CL	15.00	50.00
76	TURTLE ON SKATEBOARD 501	CL	15.00	50.00
77	BEAR ON ROCK 523	CL	18.00	55.00
77	KOALA BEAR IN TREE 514	CL	15.00	50.00
77	KOALA BEAR ON LOG 516	CL	15.00	50.00
77	KOALA BEAR WITH BABY 515	CL	15.00	50.00
77	MONKEY WITH BANANA 521	CL	18.00	55.00
77	MOUSE AND CHEESE 520	CL	18.00	55.00
77	MR. PENGUIN 518	CL	18.00	60.00
77	OWL GRADUATE 519	CL	22.00	60.00
77	PELICAN AND PYTHON 522	CL	18.00	55.00
78	BOBBI ON UNICYCLE 204	CL	45.00	80.00
78	BOW TIE 222	CL	68.00	150.00
78	BUTTERFLY AND FLOWER 529	CL	22.00	60.00
78	CLANCY, THE COP 210	CL	55.00	100.00
78	CLARA-BOW 205	CL	52.00	90.00
78	COCO-HANDS ON HIPS 218	CL	70.00	125.00
78	CORKY THE DRUMMER BOY 202	CL	53.00	110.00
78	CUDDLES 208	CL	37.00	75.00
78	DOLPHINS 525	CL	22.00	60.00
78	DRIVER THE GOLFER 211	CL	55.00	75.00
78	ELEPHANT ON BALL 214	CL	26.00	60.00
78	ELEPHANT ON STAND 213	CL	26.00	60.00
78	ELEPHANT SITTING 215	CL	26.00	60.00
78	FANCY PANTS 224	CL	55.00	110.00
78	FIREMAN WITH HOSE 216	CL	62.00	110.00
78	HEY RUBE 220	CL	35.00	75.00
78	HUMMINGBIRD 528	CL	22.00	60.00
78	JERI IN A BARREL 219	CL	75.00	145.00
78	JOCKO WITH LOLLIPOP 221	CL	68.00	150.00
78	OSCAR ON STILTS 223	CL	55.00	110.00
78	PIERROT PAINTING 207	CL	50.00	130.00
78	POLLY THE PARROT & CRACKERS 201	CL	63.00	135.00
78	POPPY WITH PUPPET 209	CL	60.00	100.00
78	PRINCE FROG 526	CL	22.00	60.00
78	SAD SACK 212	CL	48.00	150.00
78	SAILFISH 524	CL	18.00	75.00
78	SEA OTTER ON BACK 531	CL	22.00	60.00
78	SEA OTTER ON ROCK 532	CL	22.00	60.00
78	SEAGULL 527	CL	22.00	60.00
78	SKIPPY SWINGING 239	CL	52.00	◄— 75.00
78	SPARKY SKATING 206	CL	55.00	175.00
78	TINKER BOWING 203	CL	37.00	75.00
78	TOBI-HANDS OUTSTRETCHED 217	CL	70.00	225.00
78	TURTLE ON ROCK 530	CL	22.00	60.00
79	BUTTONS BICYCLING 229	CL	75.00	150.00
79	CAROUSEL HORSE 232	CL	119.00	165.00
79	DARBY TIPPING HAT 238	CL	35.00	100.00
79	DARBY WITH FLOWER 235	CL	35.00	100.00
79	DARBY WITH UMBRELLA 236	CL	35.00	100.00
79	DARBY WITH VIOLIN 237	CL	35.00	100.00
79	DOCTOR SAWBONES 228	CL	75.00	150.00
79	FEARLESS FRED IN CANNON 234	CL	80.00	200.00
79	HARRY AND THE HARE 233	CL	69.00	175.00
79	KELLY AT THE PIANO 241	CL	185.00	400.00
79	KELLY IN KAR 230	CL	164.00	300.00
79	KELLY'S KAR 231	CL	75.00	150.00
79	LILI 227	CL	75.00	145.00
79	TIMMY TOOTING 225	CL	35.00	65.00
79	TUBBY TUBA 226	CL	35.00	60.00
80	BANJO WILLIE 258	CL	68.00	150.00
80	CAROUSEL HORSE 248	CL	88.00	200.00
80	CAROUSEL HORSE 249	CL	88.00	200.00
80	CHUCKLES JUGGLING 244	CL	98.00	◄— 150.00
80	CUBBY HOLDING BALLOON 240	CL	50.00	70.00
80	DENNIS PLAYING TENNIS 252	CL	74.00	140.00
80	DOCTOR JAWBONES 260	CL	85.00	200.00
80	DONKEY WHAT? 243	CL	60.00	175.00
80	EMILE 257	CL	43.00	140.00
80	HAPPY WAVING 255	CL	43.00	140.00
80	HOBO JOE IN TUB 259	CL	96.00	125.00
80	JAQUE DOWNHILL RACER 253	CL	74.00	150.00
80	JINGLES TELLING TIME 242	CL	75.00	140.00
80	JO-JO AT MAKE-UP MIRROR 250	CL	86.00	◄— 150.00
80	MONKEY 251	CL	60.00	150.00

YR	NAME	LIMIT	ISSUE	TREND
80	P.T. DINGHY 245	CL	65.00	135.00
80	PEANUTS PLAYING CONCERTINA 247	CL	65.00	225.00
80	RONI RIDING HORSE 246	CL	115.00	230.00
80	RUFORD 254	CL	43.00	140.00
80	ZACH 256	CL	43.00	140.00
81	AL AT THE BASS 284	CL	48.00	75.00
81	BOSOM BUDDIES 299	CL	135.00	150.00
81	BOZO ON UNICYCLE 279	CL	28.00	110.00
81	BOZO PLAYING CYMBALS 277	CL	28.00	110.00
81	BOZO RIDING CAR 278	CL	28.00	110.00
81	CARNEY AND SEAL ACT 300	CL	63.00	100.00
81	CAROUSEL HORSE 280	CL	88.00	180.00
81	CAROUSEL HORSE 281	CL	88.00	175.00
81	EXECUTIVE HITCHHIKING 267	CL	23.00	80.00
81	EXECUTIVE READING 264	CL	23.00	80.00
81	EXECUTIVE RESTING 266	CL	23.00	80.00
81	EXECUTIVE WITH UMBRELLA 265	CL	23.00	80.00
81	HARPO 296	CL	120.00	270.00
81	HOBO JOE PRAYING 298	CL	57.00	75.00
81	KEVIN AT THE DRUMS 283	CL	50.00	125.00
81	LARRY AND HIS HOTDOGS 274	CL	76.00	150.00
81	LOUIE HITCHING A RIDE 269	CL	47.00	90.00
81	LOUIE ON PARK BENCH 268	CL	56.00	75.00
81	LOUIE ON RAILROAD CAR 270	CL	77.00	140.00
81	MICKEY TIGHTROPE WALKER 292	CL	50.00	100.00
81	MICKEY UPSIDE DOWN 293	CL	50.00	100.00
81	MICKEY WITH UMBRELLA 291	CL	50.00	100.00
81	MY SON DARREN 295	CL	57.00	100.00
81	NICKY SITTING ON BALL 289	CL	39.00	65.00
81	NICKY STANDING ON BALL 290	CL	39.00	65.00
81	PERRY SITTING WITH BALLOON 287	CL	37.00	70.00
81	PERRY STANDING WITH BALLOON 288	CL	37.00	70.00
81	PICKLES AND POOCH 297	CL	90.00	190.00
81	PISTOL PETE 272	CL	76.00	150.00
81	ROCKETMAN 294	CL	77.00	140.00
81	RON AT THE PIANO 285	CL	46.00	75.00
81	RON LEE TRIO 282	CL	144.00	375.00
81	TIMOTHY IN BIG SHOE 286	CL	37.00	70.00
82	ALI ON HIS MAGIC CARPET 335	CL	105.00	180.00
82	BARNUM FEEDING BACON 315	CL	120.00	210.00
82	BEAVER PLAYING ACCORDIAN 807	CL	23.00	60.00
82	BENNY PULLING CAR 310	CL	190.00	300.00
82	BURRITO BANDITO 334	CL	150.00	225.00
82	BUSTER IN BARREL 308	CL	85.00	110.00
82	CAMEL 818	CL	57.00	125.00
82	CAPTAIN CRANBERRY 320	CL	115.00	165.00
82	CAPTAIN MIS-ADVENTURE 703	CL	250.00	400.00
82	CARNEY AND DOG ACT 301	CL	63.00	125.00
82	CHARLIE CHAPLAIN 701	CL	230.00	450.00
82	CHARLIE IN THE RAIN 321	CL	80.00	140.00
82	CHICO PLAYING GUITAR 336	CL	70.00	140.00
82	CLANCY, THE COP AND DOG 333	CL	115.00	190.00
82	CLARENCE, THE LAWYER 331	CL	100.00	170.00
82	DENNY EATING ICE CREAM 305	CL	39.00	110.00
82	DENNY HOLDING GIFT BOX 306	CL	39.00	110.00
82	DENNY JUGGLING BALL 307	CL	39.00	110.00
82	DOG PLAYING GUITAR 805	CL	23.00	60.00
82	DR. PAINLESS AND PATIENT 311	CL	195.00	310.00
82	FIREMAN WATERING HOUSE 303	CL	99.00	140.00
82	FISH WITH SHOE 803	CL	23.00	60.00
82	FOX IN AN AIRPLANE 806	CL	23.00	60.00
82	GEORGIE GOING ANYWHERE 302	CL	95.00	125.00
82	GIRAFFE 816	CL	57.00	125.00
82	HERBIE BALANCING HAT 327	CL	26.00	75.00
82	HERBIE DANCING 325	CL	26.00	75.00
82	HERBIE HANDS OUTSTRETCHED 326	CL	26.00	75.00
82	HERBIE LEGS IN AIR 329	CL	26.00	75.00
82	HERBIE LYING DOWN 328	CL	26.00	75.00
82	HERBIE TOUCHING GROUND 330	CL	26.00	75.00
82	HOBO JOE ON CYCLE 322	CL	125.00	225.00
82	HORSE 819	CL	57.00	125.00
82	KUKLA AND FRIEND 316	CL	100.00	175.00
82	LAUREL & HARDY 700	CL	225.00	400.00
82	LIMOUSINE SERVICE 705	CL	330.00	575.00
82	LION 817	CL	57.00	125.00
82	LITTLE HORSE-HEAD UP 341	CL	29.00	72.00
82	MARION WITH MARRIONETTE 317	CL	105.00	180.00
82	MURPHY ON UNICYCLE 337	CL	115.00	225.00
82	NAPPY SNOOZING 346	CL	110.00	170.00
82	NORMAN PAINTING DUMBO 314	CL	126.00	180.00
82	OSTRICH 813	CL	57.00	125.00
82	PARROT ROLLERSKATING 809	CL	23.00	60.00
82	PIG BRICK LAYER 800	CL	23.00	60.00
82	PINBALL PAL 332	CL	150.00	250.00
82	QUINCY LYING DOWN 304	CL	80.00	150.00

YR	NAME	LIMIT	ISSUE	TREND
82	RABBIT WITH EGG 801	CL	23.00	60.00
82	REINDEER 812	CL	57.00	125.00
82	ROBIN RESTING 338	CL	110.00	170.00
82	RON LEE CAROUSEL	CL	10,000.00	12500.00
82	ROOSTER 815	CL	57.00	125.00
82	ROOSTER WITH BARBELL 808	CL	23.00	60.00
82	SAMMY RIDING ELEPHANT 309	CL	90.00	140.00
82	SEAL BLOWING HIS HORNS 804	CL	23.00	60.00
82	SELF PORTRAIT 702	CL	1,000.00	2450.00
82	SLIM CHARGING BULL 313	CL	195.00	350.00
82	SMOKEY, THE BEAR 802	CL	23.00	60.00
82	STEPPIN' OUT 704	CL	325.00	550.00
82	THREE MAN VALENTINOS 319	CL	55.00	90.00
82	TIGER 814	CL	57.00	125.00
82	TOO LOOSE-L'ARTISTE 312	CL	150.00	230.00
82	TOU TOU 323	CL	70.00	140.00
82	TOY SOLDIER 324	CL	95.00	200.00
82	TURTLE WITH GUN 811	CL	57.00	125.00
82	TWO MAN VALENTINOS 318	CL	45.00	90.00
82	WALRUS WITH UMBRELLA 810	CL	23.00	60.00
83	BANDWAGON, THE 707	CL	900.00	1800.00
83	BEETHOVEN'S FOURTH PAWS 358	CL	59.00	80.00
83	BLACK CAROUSEL HORSE 1001	CL	450.00	640.00
83	BUMBLES SELLING BALLOONS 353	CL	80.00	140.00
83	BUSTER AND HIS BALLOONS 363	CL	47.00	60.00
83	CAPTAIN FREDDY 375	CL	85.00	310.00
83	CASEY CRUISING 351	CL	57.00	80.00
83	CATCH THE BRASS RING 708	CL	510.00	1250.00
83	CECIL AND SAUSAGE 354	CL	90.00	150.00
83	CHEF'S CUISINE 361	CL	57.00	80.00
83	CHESTNUT CAROUSEL HORSE 1002	CL	450.00	640.00
83	CIMBA THE ELEPHANT 706	CL	225.00	375.00
83	CLYDE JUGGLING 339	CL	39.00	45.00
83	CLYDE UPSIDE DOWN 340	CL	39.00	45.00
83	COCO AND HIS COMPACT 369	CL	55.00	100.00
83	COTTON CANDY 377	CL	150.00	245.00
83	DARING DUDLEY 367	CL	65.00	125.00
83	DOOR TO DOOR DABNEY 373	CL	100.00	175.00
83	ENGINEER BILLIE 356	CL	190.00	350.00
83	FLIPPER DIVING 345	CL	115.00	175.00
83	GAZEBO 1004	CL	450.00	640.00
83	GILBERT TEE'D OFF 376	CL	60.00	95.00
83	HOBI IN HIS HAMMOCK 344	CL	85.00	140.00
83	I LOVE YOU FROM MY HEART 360	CL	35.00	50.00
83	JOGGER, THE- 372	CL	75.00	95.00
83	JOSEPHINE 370	CL	55.00	100.00
83	KNICKERS BALANCING FEATHER 366	CL	47.00	75.00
83	LAST SCOOP, THE 900	CL	325.00	325.00
83	LAST SCOOP, THE- 379	CL	175.00	275.00
83	LITTLE HORSE-HEAD DOWN 342	CL	29.00	72.00
83	LITTLE SATURDAY NIGHT 348	CL	53.00	80.00
83	LOU PROPOSING 365	CL	57.00	70.00
83	MATINEE JITTERS 378	CL	175.00	200.00
83	MATINEE JITTERS 901	CL	325.00	400.00
83	MY DAUGHTER DEBORAH 357	CL	63.00	90.00
83	NO CAMPING OR FISHING 902	CL	325.00	375.00
83	ON THE ROAD AGAIN 355	CL	220.00	400.00
83	RICHES TO RAGS 374	CL	55.00	175.00
83	RIDE 'EM RONI 347	CL	125.00	175.00
83	RUFUS AND HIS REFUSE 343	CL	65.00	160.00
83	SAY IT WITH FLOWERS 359	CL	35.00	70.00
83	SINGIN' IN THE RAIN 362	CL	105.00	180.00
83	TATTERS AND BALLOONS 352	CL	65.00	75.00
83	TEETER TOTTIE SCOTTIE 350	CL	55.00	85.00
83	TOTTIE SCOTTIE 349	CL	39.00	60.00
83	UP, UP AND AWAY 364	CL	50.00	80.00
83	WHITE CAROUSEL HORSE 1003	CL	450.00	640.00
83	WILT THE STILT 368	CL	49.00	75.00
84	A BOZO LUNCH 390	CL	148.00	225.00
84	BAGGY PANTS 387	CL	98.00	180.00
84	BLACK CIRCUS HORSE 711A	CL	305.00	440.00
84	CHESTNUT CIRCUS HORSE 710A	CL	305.00	440.00
84	GIVE A DOG A BONE 383	CL	95.00	140.00
84	JUST FOR YOU 386	CL	110.00	225.00
84	LOOK AT THE BIRDY 388	CL	138.00	200.00
84	MY FELLOW AMERICAN 391	CL	138.00	275.00
84	NO CAMPING OR FISHING 380	CL	175.00	318.00
84	NO LOITERING 392	CL	113.00	160.00
84	PEPPERMINTS, THE- 384	CL	150.00	210.00
84	RUDY HOLDING BALLOONS 713	CL	230.00	350.00
84	SATURDAY NIGHT 714	CL	250.00	500.00
84	T.K. AND OH!! 385	CL	85.00	150.00
84	TISKET AND TASKET 393	CL	93.00	190.00
84	WHEELER SHEILA 381	CL	75.00	140.00
84	WHITE CIRCUS HORSE 709	CL	305.00	440.00

YR	NAME	LIMIT	ISSUE	TREND
85	CLOWNS OF THE CARIBBEAN PS101	CL	1,250.00	2000.00
85	GIRAFFE GETTING A BATH 428	CL	160.00	340.00
85	WHISKERS BATHING 749	CL	305.00	305.00
85	WHISKERS HITCHHIKING 745	CL	240.00	750.00
85	WHISKERS HOLDING BALLOON 746	CL	265.00	600.00
85	WHISKERS HOLDING UMBRELLA 747	CL	265.00	600.00
85	WHISKERS ON THE BEACH 750	CL	230.00	650.00
85	WHISKERS SWEEPING 744	CL	240.00	875.00
86	BATHING BUDDIES 450	CL	145.00	200.00
86	CAPTAIN CRANBERRY 469	CL	140.00	165.00
86	GETTING EVEN 485	CL	85.00	110.00
86	HARI AND HARE 454	CL	57.00	75.00
86	RIDE 'EM PEANUTS 463	CL	55.00	68.00
86	WET PAINT 436	CL	80.00	125.00
87	FIRST & MAIN L110	CL	368.00	525.00
87	HEARTBROKEN HARRY L101	CL	63.00	125.00
87	LOVABLE LUKE L102	8500	70.00	70.00
87	PUPPY LOVE L103	8500	71.00	145.00
87	SUGARLAND EXPRESS L109	CL	342.00	375.00
87	WOULD YOU LIKE TO RIDE? L104	CL	246.00	— 325.00
88	FIFTH WHEEL, THE L117	CL	250.00	295.00
88	NEW RON LEE CAROUSEL	CL	7,000.00	9500.00
88	TO THE RESCUE L127	CL	130.00	350.00
88	TUNNEL OF LOVE L123	CL	490.00	550.00
88	WHEN YOU'RE HOT, YOU'RE HOT! L128	CL	221.00	525.00
89	BE IT EVER SO HUMBLE L111	CL	900.00	1100.00
89	CATCH A FALLING STAR L148	CL	57.00	57.00
89	CIRCUS LITTLE L143	CL	990.00	1265.00
89	FIREMAN, THE L169	CL	68.00	85.00
89	FISHERMAN, THE - L194	7500	72.00	72.00
89	GOLFER, THE- L188	CL	72.00	90.00
89	GREATEST LITTLE SHOE ON EARTH, THE- L210	CL	165.00	210.00
89	HUGHIE MUNGUS L144	CL	250.00	325.00
89	I PLEDGE ALLEGIANCE L134	3750	131.00	131.00
89	IF I WERE A RICH MAN L133	CL	315.00	425.00
89	IN OVER MY HEAD L135	CL	95.00	125.00
89	LAWYER, THE- L171	CL	68.00	75.00
89	O' SOLO MIA L139	CL	85.00	150.00
89	POLICEMAN, THE- L165	CL	68.00	80.00
89	SH-H-H-H! L146	CL	210.00	700.00
89	SNOWDRIFTER L163	CL	230.00	350.00
89	TEE FOR TWO L141	CL	125.00	150.00
89	TODAY'S CATCH L147	CL	230.00	300.00
89	WISHFUL THINKING L114	CL	230.00	375.00
90	BIG WHEEL, THE L236	2750	240.00	240.00
90	CANDY MAN L217	2750	350.00	350.00
90	FILL'ER UP L248	2250	280.00	280.00
90	HEARTBROKEN HOBO L233	CL	116.00	145.00
90	HENRY 8-3/4 L260	2750	37.00	37.00
90	HORSIN' AROUND L262	2750	37.00	37.00
90	KISS! KISS! L251	2750	37.00	37.00
90	ME TOO! L231	3500	70.00	70.00
90	N/A! N/A! L252	2750	33.00	33.00
90	NEW SELF PORTRAIT, THE- L218	CL	800.00	950.00
90	PUSH AND PULL L249	2250	260.00	260.00
90	SCOOTER L234	2750	240.00	240.00
90	SNOWDRIFTER II L250	1250	340.00	340.00
90	TANDEM MANIA L235	2750	360.00	360.00
90	UNI-CYCLE L237	2750	240.00	240.00
91	ANYWHERE? L269	1500	125.00	125.00
91	BUSINESS IS BUSINESS L266	1500	110.00	110.00
91	CRUISING L265	1500	170.00	170.00
91	FALL L282	1500	120.00	120.00
91	GILBERT'S DILEMMA L270	1750	90.00	90.00
91	GIVE ME LIBERTY L313	1776	155.00	155.00
91	HAPPY BIRTHDAY PUPPY LOVE L278	1750	73.00	73.00
91	I'M SINGIN' IN THE RAIN L268	1500	135.00	135.00
91	LIT'L SNOWDRIFTER L298	1750	70.00	70.00
91	OUR NATION'S PRIDE L312	1776	150.00	150.00
91	PUPPY LOVE SCOOTIN' L275	1750	73.00	73.00
91	PUPPY LOVE'S FREE RIDE L276	1750	73.00	73.00
91	PUPPY LOVE'S TREAT L277	1750	73.00	73.00
91	SPRING L280	1500	95.00	95.00
91	SUMMER L281	1500	95.00	95.00
91	TA DA! L294	1500	120.00	120.00
91	UNITED WE STAND L314	1776	150.00	150.00
91	WINTER L279	1500	115.00	115.00

R. LEE   RON LEE COLLECTOR'S CLUB RENEWAL SCULPTURES

YR	NAME	LIMIT	ISSUE	TREND
87	DOGGIN' ALONG CC1	YR	75.00	120.00
88	MIDSUMMER'S DREAM CC2	YR	97.00	145.00
89	PEEK-A-BOO CHARLIE CC3	YR	65.00	95.00

R. LEE   RON LEE LOONEY TUNE COLLECTION

YR	NAME	LIMIT	ISSUE	TREND
91	1940 BUGS BUNNY LT165	2750	85.00	85.00
91	BUGS BUNNY LT150	2750	123.00	123.00
91	DAFFY DUCK LT140	2750	80.00	85.00

American Bald Eagle I is *from the "Birds of Prey" collection by W.D. Gaither. The porcelain sculpture is produced by Maruri.*

Artist W.D. Gaither captures the movements and majesty of the American Bald Eagle III *in his third sculpture for Maruri's "Birds of Prey" series.*

American Bald Eagle II is *crafted in porcelain by W.D. Gaither and produced by Maruri as part of the "Bird of Prey" collection.*

American Bald Eagle IV *by W.D. Gaither portrays the creature searching for food. The figure is from the "Birds of Prey" series produced by Maruri.*

YR	NAME	LIMIT	ISSUE	TREND
91	ELMER FUDD LT125	2750	87.00	90.00
91	FOGHORN LEGHORN & HENRY HAWK LT160	2750	115.00	115.00
91	MARVIN THE MARTIAN LT170	2750	75.00	75.00
91	MICHIGAN J. FROG LT110	2750	115.00	115.00
91	MT. YOSEMITE LT180	850	160.00	225.00
91	PEPE LEPEW & PENELOPE LT145	2750	115.00	115.00
91	PORKY PIG LT115	2750	97.00	100.00
91	SYLVESTER & TWEETY LT135	2750	110.00	115.00
91	TASMANIAN DEVIL LT120	2750	105.00	105.00
91	TWEETY LT155	2750	110.00	115.00
91	WESTERN DAFFY DUCK LT105	2750	87.00	90.00
91	WILE E. COYOTE & ROADRUNNER LT175	2750	165.00	175.00
91	YOSEMITE SAM LT130	2750	110.00	110.00

ROYAL DOULTON

N. PEDLEY — AGE OF INNOCENCE

YR	NAME	LIMIT	ISSUE	TREND
91	FEEDING TIME	9500	245.00	245.00
91	MAKING FRIENDS	9500	270.00	270.00
91	PUPPY LOVE	9500	270.00	270.00

M. ABBERLEY — ANTAGONISTS CHARACTER JUGS

86	GEORGE III & GEORGE WASHINGTON	9500	195.00	195.00

M. ALCOCK — BEATRIX POTTER

93	BENJAMIN BUNNY	OP	65.00	65.00
93	JEMIMA PUDDLEDUCK	OP	65.00	65.00
93	JEREMY FISHER	OP	65.00	65.00
93	MRS. RABBIT	OP	65.00	65.00
93	PETER RABBIT	OP	65.00	65.00
93	TOM KITTEN	OP	65.00	65.00
95	PETER IN BED	OP	40.00	40.00

A. HUGHES — BEATRIX POTTER

95	FOXY WHISKERED GENTLEMAN	OP	65.00	65.00

W. PLATT — BEATRIX POTTER

95	TAILOR OF GLOUCESTER	OP	65.00	65.00

W. PLATT — BRAMBLY HEDGE FIGURES

93	MR. SALTAPPLE	OP	40.00	40.00
93	MRS. SALTAPPLE	OP	40.00	40.00

V. ANNAND — BRITISH SPORTING HERITAGE

93	HENLEY	5000	475.00	475.00
94	ASCOT	5000	450.00	450.00
95	WIMBLEDON	5000	475.00	475.00

M. ALCOCK — CHARACTER JUG OF THE YEAR

94	CAPTAIN HOOK	OP	235.00	235.00

S. TAYLOR — CHARACTER JUG OF THE YEAR

93	VICE-ADMIRAL LORD NELSON	OP	225.00	225.00
95	CAPTAIN BLIGH	OP	200.00	200.00

* — CHARACTER JUGS

91	FORTUNE TELLER	YR	130.00	130.00
91	SANTA CLAUS MINIATURE	5000	50.00	50.00
92	WINSTON CHURCHILL	YR	195.00	195.00

W. HARPER — CHARACTER JUGS

91	HENRY VIII	1991	395.00	395.00

D. BIGGS — CHARACTER SCULPTURES

95	GULLIVER	OP	285.00	285.00

A. MASLANKOWSKI — CHARACTER SCULPTURES

93	LONG JOHN SILVER	OP	250.00	250.00
93	ROBIN HOOD	OP	250.00	250.00
94	PIED PIPER	OP	260.00	260.00
94	WIZARD	OP	340.00	340.00

R. TABBENOR — CHARACTER SCULPTURES

93	CAPTAIN HOOK	OP	250.00	250.00
93	DICK TURPIN	OP	250.00	250.00
94	D'ARTAGNAN	OP	260.00	260.00

P. GEE — CHARACTER STUDIES

94	PIPER, THE	OP	295.00	295.00

P. PARSONS — CHARACTER STUDIES

94	GRANDPA'S STORY	OP	275.00	275.00
94	WHEN I WAS YOUNG	OP	275.00	275.00
95	RICHARD THE LIONHEART	OP	500.00	500.00

R. TABBENOR — CHARACTER STUDIES

93	FATHER CHRISTMAS	OP	195.00	195.00

A. MASLANKOWSKI — CHILD FIGURES

93	BALLET SHOES	OP	74.00	74.00
93	DADDY'S GIRL	OP	75.00	75.00

P. PARSONS — CHILD FIGURES

94	FLOWERS FOR MOTHER	OP	98.00	98.00

N. PEDLEY — CHILD FIGURES

93	ALMOST GROWN	OP	65.00	65.00
93	BEST WISHES	OP	165.00	165.00
93	BIRTHDAY GIRL	OP	130.00	130.00
93	FLOWERGIRL	OP	99.00	99.00
93	MY FIRST FIGURINE	OP	110.00	110.00
94	A POSY FOR YOU	OP	98.00	98.00
94	FIRST RECITAL	OP	98.00	98.00

YR	NAME	LIMIT	ISSUE	TREND
94	HELLO DADDY	OP	125.00	125.00
94	MOTHER'S HELPER	OP	98.00	98.00
94	SPECIAL FRIEND	OP	98.00	98.00
94	YOUNG MELODY	OP	98.00	98.00
95	HOMETIME	OP	135.00	135.00
95	SPECIAL TREAT	OP	135.00	135.00
95	WHAT'S THAT MATTER	OP	135.00	135.00
M. ALCOCK			**CHRISTMAS MINI JUGS**	
94	SNOWMAN MINI	2500	62.00	62.00
W. HARPER			**CHRISTMAS MINI JUGS**	
93	ELE MINI	2500	55.00	55.00
M. DAVIES			**DANCERS OF THE WORLD**	
77	DANCERS, FLAMENCO	750	400.00	1300.00
77	DANCERS, INDIAN TEMPLE	750	400.00	1300.00
78	DANCERS, PHILIPPINE	750	450.00	675.00
78	DANCERS, SCOTTISH	750	450.00	1050.00
79	DANCERS, KURDISH	750	550.00	550.00
79	DANCERS, MEXICAN	750	550.00	550.00
80	DANCERS, CHINESE	750	750.00	625.00
80	DANCERS, NORTH AMERICAN INDIAN	750	950.00	575.00
80	DANCERS, POLISH	750	750.00	675.00
81	DANCERS, BRETON	750	850.00	575.00
81	DANCERS, WEST INDIAN	750	850.00	625.00
82	DANCERS, BALINESE	750	950.00	575.00
M. DAVIES			**FEMMES FATALES**	
79	CLEOPATRA	750	750.00	1300.00
81	HELEN OF TROY	750	1,250.00	1100.00
82	QUEEN OF SHEBA	750	1,250.00	1100.00
83	TZ'U-HSI	750	1,250.00	1100.00
84	EVE	750	1,250.00	1100.00
85	LUCREZIA BORGIA	750	1,250.00	1300.00
V. ANNAND			**FIGURE OF THE YEAR**	
93	PATRICIA	RT	250.00	275.00
P. GEE			**FIGURE OF THE YEAR**	
91	AMY	YR	245.00	245.00
92	MARY	YR	225.00	225.00
94	JENNIFER	OP	250.00	260.00
N. PEDLEY			**FIGURE OF THE YEAR**	
95	DEBORAH	OP	225.00	225.00
V. ANNAND			**FLOWERS OF LOVE**	
95	CAMELLIAS	OP	325.00	325.00
95	FORGET ME NOTS	OP	325.00	325.00
V. ANNAND			**FOUR SEASONS**	
93	SPRINGTIME	OP	325.00	325.00
94	AUTUMNTIME	OP	325.00	325.00
94	SUMMERTIME	OP	325.00	325.00
95	WINTERTIME	OP	325.00	325.00
P. GEE			**GAINSBOROUGH LADIES**	
*	MARY, COUNTESS HOWE	5000	650.00	650.00
91	COUNTESS OF SEFTON	5000	650.00	650.00
91	HON FRANCES DUNCOMBE	5000	650.00	650.00
91	LADY SHEFFIELD	5000	650.00	650.00
*			**GENTLE ARTS**	
*	ADORNMENT	750	1,350.00	1350.00
*	FLOWER ARRANGING	750	1,350.00	1350.00
M. DAVIES			**GENTLE ARTS**	
84	SPINNING	750	1,250.00	1400.00
P. PARSONS			**GENTLE ARTS**	
85	TAPESTRY WEAVING	750	1,250.00	1250.00
86	WRITING	750	1,350.00	1350.00
87	PAINTING	750	1,350.00	1350.00
R. JEFFERSON			**GREAT LOVERS**	
93	ROMEO & JULIET	150	5,250.00	5250.00
94	ROBIN HOOD & MAID MARIAN	150	5,250.00	5250.00
V. ANNAND			**HN FIGURES**	
94	ANNIVERSARY	OP	575.00	575.00
P. GEE			**IMAGES**	
93	GIFT OF FREEDOM	OP	85.00	85.00
A. HUGHES			**IMAGES**	
93	BROTHER & SISTER	OP	50.00	50.00
P. PARSONS			**IMAGES**	
93	OUR FIRST CHRISTMAS	OP	475.00	175.00
A. HUGHES			**IMAGES OF NATURE**	
93	ALWAYS AND FOREVER	OP	55.00	55.00
A. MASLANKOWSKI			**IMAGES OF NATURE**	
94	NEW ARRIVAL	OP	50.00	50.00
M. DAVIES			**LADY MUSICIANS**	
70	CELLO	750	250.00	1100.00
71	VIRGINALS	750	250.00	1250.00
72	LUTE	750	250.00	800.00
72	VIOLIN	750	250.00	1000.00
73	FLUTE	750	250.00	900.00
73	HARP	750	275.00	1300.00

YR	NAME	LIMIT	ISSUE	TREND
74	CHITARRONE	750	250.00	625.00
74	CYMBALS	750	325.00	600.00
75	DULCIMER	750	375.00	575.00
75	HURDY GURDY	750	375.00	550.00
76	FRENCH HORN	750	400.00	500.00
76	VIOLA D'AMORE	750	400.00	500.00
D. BIGGS			**LARGE SIZE JUGS**	
95	ALFRED HITCHCOCK	OP	200.00	200.00
W. HARPER			**LARGE SIZE JUGS**	
94	GLENN MILLER	OP	270.00	270.00
R. JEFFERSON			**LES SAISONS**	
*	L'ETE	300	850.00	895.00
*	L'HIVER	300	850.00	795.00
86	AUTOMNE	300	850.00	940.00
87	PRINTEMPS	300	825.00	825.00
A. MASLANKOWSKI			**LIMITED EDITION FIGURES**	
93	WINSTON S. CHURCHILL	5000	595.00	595.00
R. TABBENOR			**LIMITED EDITION FIGURES**	
93	ROBERT E. LEE	5000	1,175.00	1175.00
93	ULYSSES S. GRANT	5000	1,175.00	1175.00
94	FIELD MARSHAL MONTGOMERY	1994	1,100.00	1100.00
D. BIGGS			**LIMITED EDITION TOBY JUGS**	
94	ALADDIN'S GENIE	1500	335.00	335.00
W. HARPER			**LIMITED EDITION TOBY JUGS**	
93	FATHER CHRISTMAS TOBY	3500	125.00	125.00
93	WILLIAM SHAKESPEARE	2500	625.00	625.00
94	OLIVER CROMWELL	2500	475.00	475.00
95	CHARLES DICKENS	2500	500.00	500.00
NOKE/FENTON			**LIMITED EDITION TOBY JUGS**	
94	DIAMOND ANNIVERSARY TINIES	2500	325.00	325.00
S. TAYLOR			**LIMITED EDITION TOBY JUGS**	
93	CLOWN TOBY	3000	175.00	175.00
93	NAPOLEON	2000	225.00	225.00
94	KING & QUEEN OF DIAMONDS TOBY	2500	260.00	260.00
94	LEPRECHAUN TOBY	2500	150.00	150.00
95	JUDGE AND THIEF TOBY	OP	185.00	185.00
P. GEE			**MINIATURES**	
93	TOP O' THE HILL	OP	120.00	120.00
N. PEDLEY			**MINIATURES**	
94	HANNAH	OP	142.00	142.00
R. JEFFERSON			**MYTHS & MAIDENS**	
82	LADY & UNICORN	300	2,500.00	3000.00
83	LEDA & SWAN	300	2,500.00	2950.00
84	JUNO & PEACOCK	300	2,500.00	2950.00
85	EUROPA & BULL	300	2,500.00	2950.00
86	DIANA THE HUNTRESS	300	2,500.00	2950.00
A MASLANKOWSKI			**NATIVITY**	
93	HOLY FAMILY (JESUS, MARY & JOSEPH)	RT	250.00	275.00
S. TAYLOR			**PRESIDENTIAL SERIES**	
93	ABRAHAM LINCOLN	25000	190.00	190.00
94	THOMAS JEFFERSON	2500	200.00	200.00
95	GEORGE WASHINGTON	2500	200.00	200.00
*			**PRESTIGE FIGURES**	
91	COLUMBINE	*	1,250.00	1250.00
91	FIGHTER ELEPHANT	*	2,500.00	2500.00
91	FOX	*	1,550.00	1550.00
91	HARLEQUIN	*	1,250.00	1250.00
91	JACK POINT	*	2,900.00	2900.00
91	KING CHARLES	*	2,500.00	2500.00
91	LEOPARD ON ROCK	*	3,000.00	3000.00
91	LION ON ROCK	*	3,000.00	3000.00
91	MATADOR AND BULL	*	21,500.00	21500.00
91	MOOR, THE	*	2,500.00	2500.00
91	PRINCESS BADOURA	*	28,000.00	28000.00
91	ST. GEORGE AND DRAGON	*	13,600.00	13600.00
91	TIGER	*	1,950.00	1950.00
91	TIGER ON ROCK	*	3,000.00	3000.00
A. MASLANKOWSKI			**PRESTIGE FIGURES**	
93	DUKE OF WELLINGTON	1500	1,750.00	1750.00
93	VICE-ADMIRAL LORD NELSON	950	1,750.00	1750.00
95	CHARGE OF THE LIGHT BRIGADE	SP	16,000.00	16000.00
P. GEE			**PRETTY LADIES**	
93	AMY'S SITER	OP	225.00	225.00
N. PEDLEY			**PRETTY LADIES**	
93	HELEN	OP	225.00	225.00
93	JOANNE	OP	185.00	185.00
93	NICOLE	OP	155.00	155.00
94	HOLLY	OP	195.00	195.00
95	GEMMA	OP	195.00	195.00
95	HANNAH	OP	250.00	250.00
95	HAPPY BIRTHDAY	OP	250.00	250.00
D. TOTTLE			**PRETTY LADIES**	
94	ALEXANDRA	OP	250.00	250.00

YR	NAME	LIMIT	ISSUE	TREND
*				
		QUEENS OF REALM		
*	MARY, QUEEN OF SCOTS	SO	550.00	750.00
*	QUEEN ANNE	5000	525.00	550.00
	P. PARSONS	**QUEENS OF REALM**		
*	QUEEN ELIZABETH I	SO	495.00	550.00
*	QUEEN VICTORIA	SO	495.00	950.00
	P. GEE	**REYNOLDS COLLECTION**		
91	LADY WORSLEY HN3318	5000	550.00	575.00
	P. GEE	**REYNOLDS LADIES**		
93	COUNTESS SPENCER	5000	595.00	595.00
*		**ROYAL DOULTON COLLECTORS' CLUB**		
80	JOHN DOULTON JUG (8 O'CLOCK)	YR	70.00	125.00
81	SLEEPY DARLING FIGURE	YR	100.00	195.00
82	DOG OF FO	YR	50.00	150.00
82	PRIZED POSSESSIONS FIGURE	YR	125.00	475.00
83	LOVING CUP	YR	75.00	275.00
83	SPRINGTIME	YR	125.00	350.00
84	PRIDE & JOY FIGURE	YR	125.00	225.00
84	SIR HENRY DOULTON JUG	YR	50.00	125.00
85	TOP OF THE HILL PLATE	YR	35.00	75.00
85	WINTERTIME FIGURE	YR	125.00	195.00
86	ALBERT SAGGER TOBY JUG	YR	35.00	70.00
86	AUCTIONEER FIGURE	YR	150.00	195.00
87	COLLECTOR BUNNYKINS	YR	40.00	295.00
87	SUMMERTIME FIGURE	YR	140.00	150.00
88	BEEFEATER TINY JUG	YR	25.00	125.00
88	OLD SALT TEA POT	YR	135.00	250.00
88	TOP OF THE HILL MINIATURE FIGURINE	YR	95.00	125.00
	M. DAVIES	**ROYAL DOULTON FIGURINES**		
67	INDIAN BRAVE	500	2,500.00	7000.00
71	PALIO, THE	500	2,500.00	6550.00
	R. GARBE	**ROYAL DOULTON FIGURINES**		
33	BEETHOVEN	25	*	6250.00
	M. DAVIES	**ROYALTY**		
73	QUEEN ELIZABETH II	750	200.00	1900.00
80	QUEEN MOTHER	1500	650.00	1300.00
81	DUKE OF EDINBURGH	750	395.00	400.00
	E. GRIFFITHS	**ROYALTY**		
82	LADY DIANA SPENCER HN2885	1500	395.00	800.00
82	PRINCE OF WALES HN2883	1500	395.00	525.00
82	PRINCE OF WALES HN2884	1500	750.00	800.00
82	PRINCESS OF WALES HN2887	1500	750.00	1000.00
86	DUCHESS OF YORK	1500	495.00	500.00
*		**SEASONAL FIGURES**		
94	CHRISTMAS SURPRISE BUNNYKINS	OP	50.00	50.00
	M. ALCOCK	**SEASONAL FIGURES**		
93	HALLOWEEN BUNNYKINS	OP	50.00	50.00
	W. PLATT	**SEASONAL FIGURES**		
95	EASTER GREETINGS BUNNYKINS	OP	50.00	50.00
	A. MASLANKOWSKI	**SENTIMENTS**		
93	CHRISTMAS DAY	OP	65.00	65.00
94	CHRISTMAS PARCELS	OP	60.00	60.00
	S. KEENAN	**SHIP FIGUREHEADS**		
*	AJAX	950	*	550.00
*	BENMORE	950	*	550.00
*	CHIEFTAIN	950	*	650.00
*	HIBERNIA	950	*	850.00
*	LALLA ROOKH	950	*	750.00
*	LORD NELSON	950	*	750.00
*	MARY, QUEEN OF SCOTS	950	*	1200.00
*	POCAHONTAS	950	*	950.00
	W. HARPER	**SMALL SIZE JUGS**		
93	SHAKESPEARE	OP	95.00	95.00
	S. TAYLOR	**SMALL SIZE JUGS**		
93	WINSTON CHURCHILL	OP	99.00	99.00
	E. GRIFFITHS	**SOLDIERS OF THE REVOLUTION**		
75	SOLDIERS, CONNECTICUT	350	750.00	800.00
75	SOLDIERS, DELAWARE	350	750.00	800.00
75	SOLDIERS, GEORGIA	350	750.00	875.00
75	SOLDIERS, MARYLAND	350	750.00	800.00
75	SOLDIERS, MASSACHUSETTS	350	750.00	800.00
75	SOLDIERS, NEW HAMPSHIRE	350	750.00	825.00
75	SOLDIERS, NEW JERSEY	350	750.00	1500.00
75	SOLDIERS, NEW YORK	350	750.00	800.00
75	SOLDIERS, NORTH CAROLINA	350	750.00	800.00
75	SOLDIERS, PENNSYLVANIA	350	750.00	800.00
75	SOLDIERS, RHODE ISLAND	350	750.00	800.00
75	SOLDIERS, SOUTH CAROLINA	350	750.00	800.00
75	SOLDIERS, VIRGINIA	350	1,500.00	2800.00
	L. ISPANKY	**SOLDIERS OF THE REVOLUTION**		
77	SOLDIERS, WASHINGTON	750	*	2250.00

YR	NAME	LIMIT	ISSUE	TREND
M. ABBERLEY		**STAR CROSSED LOVERS CHARACTER JUGS**		
*	ANTHONY & CLEOPATRA	SO	195.00	195.00
86	NAPOLEON & JOSEPHINE	9500	195.00	195.00
S. TAYLOR		**STAR CROSSED LOVERS CHARACTER JUGS**		
88	SAMSON & DELILAH	9500	195.00	195.00
89	KING ARTHUR & GUINEVERE	9500	195.00	195.00
N. PEDLEY				**VANITY FAIR**
93	DAWN	OP	125.00	125.00
93	GIFT OF LOVE	OP	125.00	125.00
94	GOOD COMPANION	OP	185.00	185.00
94	LINDSAY	OP	142.00	142.00
95	TAKE ME HOME	OP	195.00	195.00
T. POTTS				**VANITY FAIR**
93	MARIA	OP	125.00	125.00

ROYAL WORCESTER
*

YR	NAME	LIMIT	ISSUE	TREND
		200TH ANNIVERSARY COLLECTION		
89	AUGUSTA VASE	200	4,500.00	4500.00
89	CHAMBERLAIN CROCUS POT	200	4,000.00	4000.00
89	CLARENCE VASE	200	1,500.00	1500.00
89	ELIZABETH VASE	200	1,500.00	1500.00
89	FLIGHT BOWL	200	1,200.00	1200.00
89	GLOUCESTER ICE PAIL	200	4,000.00	4000.00
89	HANCOCK VASE	200	2,500.00	2500.00
89	KING GEORGE III VASE	200	4,000.00	4000.00
89	QUEEN CHARLOTTE VASE	200	4,000.00	4000.00
89	REGENT POT POURRI	200	3,500.00	3500.00
P.W. BASTON		**BICENTENNIAL LIMITED EDITION COMMEMORATIVES**		
74	BLACKSMITH	500	200.00	400.00
74	CABINETMAKER	500	200.00	400.00
74	CLOCKMAKER	500	200.00	500.00
74	POTTER	500	200.00	400.00
D. FRIAR		**BIRDS AND FLOWERS OF AMERICA SCULPTURES**		
84	BLUEBIRD AND FIR, THE	9800	135.00	135.00
84	CARDINAL AND DOWNY HAWTHORNE, THE	9800	135.00	135.00
84	CHICKADEE AND DAISY, THE	9800	135.00	135.00
84	GOLDFINCH AND DOGWOOD, THE	9800	135.00	135.00
84	KINGFISHER AND WATER LILY, THE	9800	135.00	135.00
84	ROBIN AND NARCISSUS, THE	9800	135.00	135.00
84	SWALLOW AND WILD ROSE, THE	9800	135.00	135.00
84	WREN AND BLACKBERRY, THE	9800	135.00	135.00
D. LINDER			**DORIS LINDER PORCELAINS**	
47	QUEEN ELIZABETH ON TOMMY	100	275.00	13200.00
59	HEREFORD BULL	1000	350.00	710.00
60	FOX HUNTER	500	500.00	N/A
61	ANGUS BULL	500	350.00	N/A
61	JERSEY COW	500	300.00	575.00
61	OFFICER OF ROYAL HORSE GUARDS	150	500.00	N/A
61	OFFICER OF THE LIFE GUARDS	150	500.00	N/A
61	SANTA GERTRUDIS BULL	500	350.00	700.00
62	QUARTER HORSE	500	400.00	N/A
63	ARAB STALLION	500	450.00	N/A
63	MERANO	500	500.00	1375.00
64	BRITISH FRIESIAN BULL	500	400.00	850.00
64	JERSEY BULL	500	400.00	940.00
64	SHIRE STALLION	500	700.00	1350.00
65	HYPERION	500	525.00	850.00
66	DAIRY SHORTHORN BULL	500	475.00	890.00
66	PERCHERON STALLION	500	725.00	N/A
66	ROYAL CANADIAN MOUNTY	500	875.00	1500.00
66	WELSH MOUNTAIN PONY	500	3,000.00	2750.00
67	ARKLE	500	525.00	825.00
68	BRAHMA BULL	500	400.00	N/A
68	BULLDOG	500	*	N/A
68	CHAROLAIS BULL	500	400.00	840.00
68	DUKE OF EDINBURGH	750	100.00	N/A
69	APPALOOSA	750	550.00	1350.00
69	SULFOLK PUNCH	500	650.00	975.00
70	MARION COAKES-MOULD	750	750.00	1500.00
71	PALOMINO	750	975.00	N/A
71	PRINCESS GRACE & FOAL, COLOR	750	1,500.00	1600.00
71	PRINCESS GRACE & FOAL, WHITE	250	1,400.00	1500.00
72	NIJINSKY	500	2,000.00	2000.00
73	AMERICAN SADDLE HORSE	750	1,450.00	N/A
73	PRINCESS ANNE ON DOUBLET	750	4,250.00	4250.00
75	GALLOPING PONIES, COLORED	500	3,300.00	N/A
75	GALLOPING, CLASSIC	250	2,500.00	N/A
76	DUKE OF MARLBOROUGH	350	5,200.00	5200.00
76	GALLOPING IN WINTER	250	3,500.00	N/A
76	HACKNEY	500	1,500.00	1500.00
76	MILL REEF	500	2,000.00	2000.00
76	NEW BORN, COLOR	500	1,800.00	1800.00
76	NEW BORN, WHITE	150	1,250.00	1250.00
76	RED RUM	250	2,000.00	2000.00
76	RICHARD MEADE	500	2,450.00	2450.00

YR	NAME	LIMIT	ISSUE	TREND
77	CLYDESDALE	500	1,250.00	1250.00
77	GRUNDY	500	1,800.00	1800.00
77	HIGHLAND BULL	500	900.00	900.00
D. DOUGHTY		**DOROTHY DOUGHTY PORCELAINS**		
35	AMERICAN REDSTARTS AND HEMLOCK	66	*	5500.00
36	BLUEBIRDS	350	500.00	8550.00
36	GOLDFINCHES & THISTLE	250	350.00	4500.00
37	CARDINALS	500	500.00	6000.00
38	BALTIMORE ORIOLES	250	350.00	N/A
38	CHICKADEES & LARCH	300	350.00	8700.00
40	BOBWHITE QUAIL	22	275.00	11000.00
40	CRABAPPLES	250	400.00	4000.00
40	MOCKINGBIRDS	500	450.00	7500.00
41	APPLE BLOSSOMS	250	400.00	2500.00
42	CRABAPPLE BLOSSOM SPRAYS AND A BUTTERFLY	250	*	800.00
42	INDIGO BUNTING AND PLUM TWIG	5000	*	N/A
42	INDIGO BUNTINGS, BLACKBERRY SPRAYS	500	375.00	2700.00
42	MOCKINGBIRDS AND PEACH BLOSSOM	500	*	N/A
47	ORANGE BLOSSOMS & BUTTERFLY	250	500.00	4400.00
50	HUMMINGBIRDS AND FUCHSIA	500	*	2800.00
50	MAGNOLIA WARBLER	150	1,100.00	2700.00
50	MEXICAN FEIJOA	250	600.00	3500.00
52	KINGLETS & NOBLE PINE	500	450.00	2500.00
52	RED-EYED VIREOS	500	450.00	2000.00
52	YELLOW-HEADED BLACKBIRDS	350	650.00	2200.00
55	GNATCATCHERS	500	600.00	3750.00
55	MYRTLE WARBLERS	500	550.00	2500.00
56	BEWICK'S WRENS & YELLOW JASMINE	500	600.00	3000.00
56	SCARLET TANAGERS	500	675.00	3600.00
57	OVENBIRDS	250	650.00	4500.00
57	PARULA WARBLERS	500	600.00	2700.00
58	PHOEBES ON FLAME VINE	500	750.00	4000.00
58	YELLOWTHROATS ON WATER HYACINTH	350	750.00	3000.00
59	CACTUS WRENS	500	1,250.00	3500.00
59	ELF OWL	500	875.00	N/A
60	CANYON WRENS	500	750.00	3000.00
61	HOODED WARBLERS	500	950.00	4300.00
62	LAZULI BUNTING & CHOKECHERRIES, COLOR	500	1,350.00	3700.00
62	LAZULI BUNTING & CHOKECHERRIES, WHITE	100	1,350.00	2800.00
62	SCISSOR-TAILED FLYCATCHER, COLOR	250	950.00	N/A
62	SCISSOR-TAILED FLYCATCHER, WHITE	75	950.00	1450.00
63	AUDUBON WARBLERS	500	1,350.00	3100.00
63	VERMILLION FLYCATCHERS	500	250.00	1700.00
64	BLUE TITS & PUSSY WILLOW	500	250.00	3000.00
64	LESSER WHITETHROATS	500	350.00	2600.00
64	MOORHEN CHICK	500	1,000.00	N/A
64	MOUNTAIN BLUEBIRDS	500	950.00	2000.00
64	ROBIN	500	750.00	N/A
64	WRENS & BURNET ROSE	500	650.00	1000.00
65	CERULEAN WARBLERS & RED MAPLE	500	1,350.00	2400.00
65	CHUFFCHAFF	500	1,500.00	2400.00
65	KINGFISHER COCK & AUTUMN BEECH	500	1,250.00	2100.00
66	LARK SPARROW	500	750.00	N/A
67	DOWNY WOODPECKER & PECAN, COLOR	400	1,500.00	1700.00
67	DOWNY WOODPECKER & PECAN, WHITE	75	1,000.00	1900.00
68	CAROLINA PAROQUET, COLOR	350	1,200.00	2000.00
68	CAROLINA PAROQUET, WHITE	75	600.00	N/A
68	GRAY WAGTAIL	500	600.00	N/A
68	REDSTARTS & GORSE	500	1,900.00	2300.00
71	NIGHTINGALE & HONEYSUCKLE	500	2,500.00	2000.00
72	GOLDCRESTS, PAIR	500	4,200.00	N/A
77	MEADOW PIPIT	500	1,800.00	1800.00
N. ROESSLER		**NORBERT E.J. ROESSLER BRONZES**		
76	HUMMER, WITH FUCHSIA	500	225.00	225.00
76	MARLIN	500	250.00	250.00
R. VAN RUYCKEVELT		**RONALD VAN RUYCKEVELT PORCELAINS**		
*	ALICE	500	1,875.00	1875.00
*	CECILIA	500	1,875.00	1875.00
56	HOGFISH & SERGEANT MAJOR	500	375.00	650.00
58	RED HIND	500	375.00	900.00
61	PASSIONFLOWER	500	300.00	400.00
61	SQUIRRELFISH	500	400.00	9000.00
62	FLYING FISH	300	400.00	450.00
62	HIBISCUS	500	300.00	350.00
62	SAILFISH	500	400.00	550.00
64	ROCK BEAUTY	500	425.00	850.00
64	TARPON	500	500.00	975.00
65	BLUE MARLIN	500	500.00	1000.00
66	SWORDFISH	500	575.00	650.00
67	BLUEFIN TUNA	500	500.00	N/A
67	BUTTERFLY FISH	500	375.00	1600.00
68	BLUE ANGEL FISH	500	375.00	900.00
68	DOLPHIN	500	500.00	900.00
68	HONFLEUR A-105	290	*	600.00
68	HONFLEUR A-106	290	*	600.00

YR	NAME	LIMIT	ISSUE	TREND
68	MALLARDS	500	*	2000.00
68	MENNECY A-101	338	*	725.00
68	MENNECY A-102	334	*	725.00
68	RAINBOW PARROT FISH	500	1,500.00	1500.00
68	RING-NECKED PHEASANTS	500	*	3300.00
69	ARGENTEUIL A-108	338	*	N/A
69	BOBWHITE QUAIL, PAIR	500	*	2000.00
69	CASTELNEAU PINK	429	*	850.00
69	CASTELNEAU YELLOW	163	*	850.00
69	SAINT DENIS A-109	500	*	950.00
70	AMERICAN PINTAIL, PAIR	500	*	3000.00
71	ELAINE	750	600.00	625.00
71	GREEN-WINGED TEAL	500	1,450.00	1450.00
71	LANGUEDOC	216	*	1150.00
72	WHITE DOVES	25	3,600.00	28000.00
76	PICNIC	250	2,850.00	2850.00
76	QUEEN ELIZABETH I	250	3,850.00	3850.00
76	QUEEN MARY I	250	4,850.00	4850.00
77	QUEEN ELIZABETH II	250	*	N/A

D. FRIAR — ROYAL WORCESTER GREAT AMERICAN BIRDS OF PREY

YR	NAME	LIMIT	ISSUE	TREND
85	AMERICAN KESTREL	9800	195.00	195.00
85	BALD EAGLE	9800	195.00	195.00
85	COOPERS HAWK	9800	195.00	195.00
85	GREAT HORNED OWL	9800	195.00	195.00
85	GYRFALCON	9800	195.00	195.00
85	PEREGRINE FALCON	9800	195.00	195.00
85	RED TAIL HAWK	9800	195.00	195.00
85	SCREECH OWL	9800	195.00	195.00

R. VAN RUYCKEVELT — RUTH VAN RUYCKEVELT PORCELAINS

YR	NAME	LIMIT	ISSUE	TREND
59	LISETTE	500	100.00	N/A
59	PENELOPE	500	100.00	N/A
60	BEATRICE	500	125.00	N/A
60	CAROLINE	500	125.00	N/A
62	LOUISA	500	400.00	975.00
63	SISTER OF LONDON HOSPITAL	500	*	500.00
63	SISTER OF ST. THOMAS HOSPITAL	500	*	500.00
64	MELANIE	500	150.00	N/A
64	ROSALIND	500	150.00	N/A
64	TEA PARTY	250	400.00	7000.00
66	SISTER OF UNIVERSITY COLLEGE HOSPITAL	500	*	500.00
67	ELIZABETH	750	300.00	800.00
68	CHARLOTTE AND JANE	500	1,000.00	1600.00
68	MADELINE	500	300.00	800.00
68	MARION	500	275.00	600.00
69	BRIDGET	500	300.00	650.00
69	EMILY	500	300.00	600.00
70	SISTER OF THE RED CROSS	750	*	500.00
71	FELICITY	750	600.00	600.00
78	ESTHER	500	*	N/A

K. POTTS — SPECIAL ISSUE

YR	NAME	LIMIT	ISSUE	TREND
88	QUEEN ELIZABETH I	100	15,000.00	15000.00

SAMSONS STUDIOS

S. BUTCHER — MCCOONS COUNTY

NAME	LIMIT	ISSUE	TREND
* BOX SOCIAL	RT	80.00	100.00
* CHECKERBOARD SQUARE	RT	85.00	125.00
* GOOD-BYE MARY LOU - ARMY	RT	60.00	70.00
* GOOD-BYE MARY LOU - NAVY	RT	60.00	80.00
* MAMA SANG TENOR	RT	70.00	90.00
* MCCOON COUNTY FAIR	RT	80.00	100.00
* WISHING YOU A TWO TON CHRISTMAS	RT	70.00	100.00

S. BUTCHER — MCCOONS STUDIOS

NAME	LIMIT	ISSUE	TREND
* SATURDAY NIGHT HO-DOWN	RT	150.00	175.00

S. BUTCHER — SNUGGLE BUGS

NAME	LIMIT	ISSUE	TREND
* BON VOYAGE	RT	15.00	75.00
* HAPPY BIRTHDAY TO YOU	RT	15.00	45.00
* I'M SENDING YOU MY BERRY VEST	RT	15.00	80.00
* LET LOVE BLOOM	RT	15.00	70.00
* LET'S POOL OUR RESOURCES	RT	15.00	75.00
* YOU ARE MY FAVORITE PAIL	RT	15.00	80.00
* YOU ARE MY NO. 1	RT	15.00	45.00
* YOU ARE OUT OF THIS WORLD	RT	15.00	45.00
* YOU ARE THE END OF MY RAINBOW	RT	15.00	300.00
* YOU TAKE THE CAKE	RT	15.00	45.00

T. CLARK — TOM CLARK CREATIONS

NAME	LIMIT	ISSUE	TREND
* DAISY AND ERIC	*	*	750.00

SANDICAST

S. BRUE — BARKITECTURE

YR	NAME	LIMIT	ISSUE	TREND
93	BEACON HILL TOWNHOUSE & BOSTON TERRIER	RT	25.00	25.00
93	EIFFEL TOWER & POODLE	RT	25.00	25.00
93	ENGLISH THATCHED COTTAGE & LABRADOR	RT	25.00	25.00
93	GERMAN CASTLE & ROTTWEILER	RT	25.00	25.00
93	IGLOO & HUSKY	RT	25.00	25.00
93	IRISH COTTAGE & SETTER	RT	25.00	25.00

Issued in the late 1980s, The Competition by Jim Deneen was part of the "Classic American Trains" series produced by Artaffects.

A touching moment between mother and child is captured in Motherhood from the "Times of Our Lives Collection" by Rob Sauber for Artaffects.

he First Kiss, ased on artwork by J. Bouguereau, was sued in 1994 as art of the "Cherubs of nnocence" series by he Bradford xchange.

The Wizard Troll was the second issue in the "Enchanted Norfin Trolls" plate series by Reco International. The series was based on the Norfin Trolls developed in Denmark by Danish artist Thomas Dam.

This three-dimensional plate titled The Wolf, rom the "Faces of the Wild" series by D. Parker, vas issued by The Bradford Exchange in 1994.

The blown-glass creations of Christopher Radko rank highly among ornament collectors. Esquire Santa is currently bringing approximately $400 on the secondary market.

This popular Barbie ornament was issued by Hallmark in 1994 to commemorate the 35th anniversary of the doll's debut in 1959.

One of the most valuable Hallmark ornaments, Starship Enterprise has a current secondary market value of around $350.

Hansel & Gretel by Christopher Radko is a must-have for collectors of fairy tale art.

Daisy, *the Cherished Teddies figurine by Priscilla Hillman, is currently worth around $800 on the secondary market.*

Lead Me—
The Dolphins *by artist Michael Stamey was issued by Swarovski America Ltd. in 1990 as a Swarovski Collectors Society Edition. Issued at $225, the piece is currently worth approximately $1,500.*

Sister M.I. Hummel's artwork will be forever remembered through the line of figurines by Goebel that bears her name. Crossroads *was first introduced in the U.S. market in 1972. Several variations exist.*

One of today's most popular figurine lines is the Precious Moments Collection based on the artwork of Sam Butcher and produced by Enesco Corp. God Loveth a Cheerful Giver *currently commands around $1,000 on the secondary market.*

Issued by Enesco Corp. in 1989, We Need a Good Friend Through the Ruff Times—*from the Precious Moments Collection by Sam Butcher—was eventually suspended.*

Glynda Turley excels at painting flowers. A Southern Tradition V is the fifth in her popular series featuring magnolias.

A fearsome black wolf blends into the shadows in Dark Encounter by John Seerey-Lester, Mill Pond Press

Fresh tire tracks in a snow-covered driveway indicate a special Homecoming, painted by Tim Schultz and produced by Northwoods Craftsman.

or years Robert Bateman has been known as the *quintessential wildlife artist.* Arctic Evening—White Wolf, *which was published in 1982, now fetches around $1,500 on the secondary market.*

The evocative artwork of "Painter of Light" Thomas Kinkade—including Petals of Hope *released in 1995 by Lightpost Publishing— touches the hearts of thousands.*

Folk artist Charles Wysocki touches the heart of every feline enthusiast in Maggie the Messmaker, *produced by AMCAL Fine Art.*

Flossie *and* Freddie, *the younger set of Bobb* *Twins, were created by Wendy Lawton and* *produced by the Lawton Doll Co. in 1991. T* *have risen significantly in value since then.*

James & Olivia—*groom and bride—were issued as a set for $250 in 1992. Now the couple, created by Karen Germany and produced by Daddy's Long Legs, averages $640 on the secondary market.*

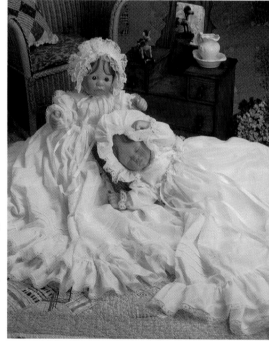

One of life's most precious events was commemorated with First Moments Cristening Awake *and* First Moments Christening Asleep *from the "First Moments Series,"* Lee Middleton Original Dolls Inc.

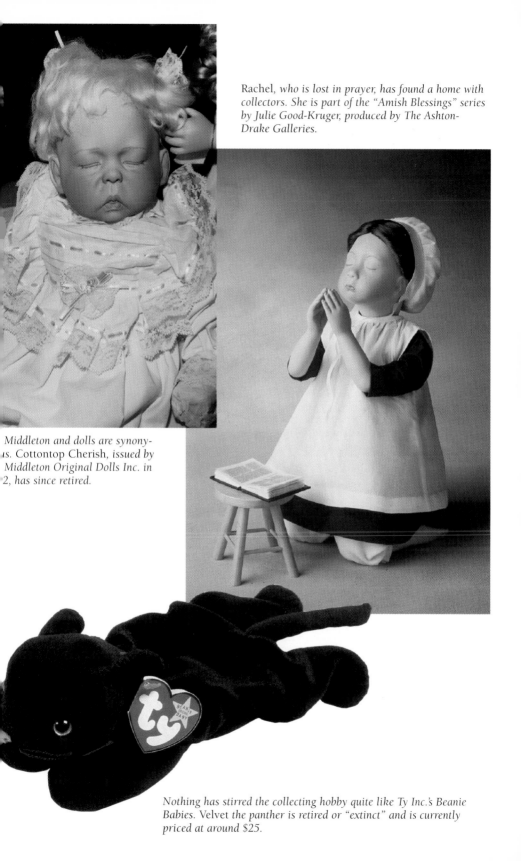

Rachel, *who is lost in prayer, has found a home with collectors. She is part of the "Amish Blessings" series by Julie Good-Kruger, produced by The Ashton-Drake Galleries.*

Middleton and dolls are synony- *us.* Cottontop Cherish, *issued by* *Middleton Original Dolls Inc. in* *2, has since retired.*

Nothing has stirred the collecting hobby quite like Ty Inc.'s Beanie Babies. Velvet *the panther is retired or "extinct" and is currently priced at around $25.*

In 1994 Lilliput Lane issued Waterside Mill *as part of the "English Cottages" series of collectible architectural structures.*

The art of Cheryl Spencer Collin is recognized by its incredible detail, as evidenced in Diamond Head Lighthouse *from the "Admiral's Lights— Flag Quarter Series."*

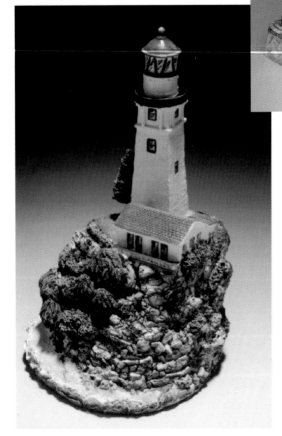

Collectors purchasing David Winter's Birthstone Wishing Well *were given a choice of gemstones signify the month in which they were born.*

The Red Schoolhouse *was issued with the original set of seven pieces that comprised Department 56's New England Village.*

YR	NAME	LIMIT	ISSUE	TREND
93	JAPANESE PAGODA & AKITA	RT	25.00	25.00
93	LOG CABIN & BLOODHOUND	RT	25.00	25.00
93	MAYAN TEMPLE & CHIHUAHUA	RT	25.00	25.00
93	SCOTTISH CASTLE & WESTIE	RT	25.00	25.00
93	SWISS CHALET & ST. BERNARD	RT	25.00	25.00
93	TIBETAN TEMPLE & LHASA	RT	25.00	25.00
S. BRUE			**COLLECTOR'S GUILD**	
94	COLLECTOR'S GUILD MEMBERSHIP KIT	YR	40.00	40.00
S. BRUE			**FOREVER FRIENDS**	
93	BASSET & PUP	*	70.00	70.00
93	BEAGEL & PUP	*	70.00	70.00
93	BOXER PUP, BRINDLE	RT	70.00	70.00
93	BOXER PUP, FAWN	*	70.00	70.00
93	CAT & KITTEN, BLACK	*	70.00	70.00
93	CAT & KITTEN, BLACK AND WHITE	*	70.00	70.00
93	CAT & KITTEN, CALICO	*	70.00	70.00
93	CAT & KITTEN, ORANGE AND WHITE	*	70.00	70.00
93	CAT, GRAY AND WHITE	*	70.00	70.00
93	CAT, WHITE	*	70.00	70.00
93	COCKER & PUP, BLACK	RT	70.00	70.00
93	COCKER & PUP, BUFF	RT	70.00	70.00
93	COCKER & PUP, PARTI BLACK	RT	70.00	70.00
93	COCKER & PUP, PARTI BUFF	RT	70.00	70.00
93	GOLDEN RETRIEVER & PUP	*	70.00	70.00
93	HARP SEAL & PUP	*	70.00	70.00
93	LION & CUB	*	70.00	70.00
93	PENGUIN & CHICK	*	70.00	70.00
93	SCHNAUZER & PUP	*	70.00	70.00
94	LAB & PUP, BLACK	*	70.00	11.00
94	LAB & PUP, CHOCOLATE	*	70.00	70.00
94	LAB & PUP, YELLOW	*	70.00	70.00
94	POLAR BEAR & CUB	*	62.00	62.00
S. BRUE			**LIFE SIZE**	
93	CAT, BLACK AND WHITE	*	108.00	108.00
93	CAVALIER KING CHARLES SPANIEL	*	108.00	108.00
93	PANDA CUB	*	69.00	80.00
94	COLLIE PUP, SABLE	*	108.00	108.00
94	JACK RUSSELL TERRIER	*	108.00	108.00
94	JACK RUSSELL TERRIER, BLACK AND WHITE	*	108.00	108.00
94	ST. BERNARD PUP	*	108.00	108.00
S. BRUE			**LIL' SNOOZERS**	
94	KITTEN, MIDNIGHT	*	9.00	9.00
94	NODDER, MIDNIGHT	*	9.00	9.00
94	YAWNER, BLACK	*	9.00	9.00
S. BRUE			**LION KING**	
94	ADULT SIMBA	RT	68.00	68.00
94	MUFASA & SIMBA	RT	68.00	68.00
94	PRIDE ROCK DISPLAY	RT	60.00	60.00
94	SIMBA & NALA	RT	68.00	68.00
94	YOUNG NALA	RT	18.00	18.00
94	YOUNG SIMBA	RT	18.00	18.00
S. BRUE			**NATURE'S HABITAT**	
94	BISON	5000	80.00	80.00
94	GRIZZLY BEAR	5000	80.00	80.00
94	HABITAT	5000	100.00	100.00
94	MOOSE	5000	80.00	80.00
94	TIMBER WOLF	RT	40.00	40.00
S. BRUE			**ORIGINALS**	
93	DOBIE, RED (II), UNCROPPED	*	40.00	40.00
94	AUSTRALIAN SHEPHERD	*	40.00	40.00
94	GREYHOUND	*	40.00	40.00
94	GREYHOUND, FAWN	*	40.00	40.00
94	GREYHOUND, WHITE & BRINDLE	*	40.00	40.00
S. BRUE			**PESKY PEEPERS**	
94	CHOW, BLACK	*	11.00	11.00
94	CHOW, RED	*	11.00	11.00
94	COCKER, BLACK	*	11.00	11.00
94	JACK RUSSELL TERRIER	*	11.00	11.00
94	KITTY, BLACK	*	11.00	11.00
94	ROTTWEILER	*	11.00	11.00
94	SHIH TZU, BLACK/WHITE	*	11.00	11.00
94	SHIH TZU, GOLD/WHITE	*	11.00	11.00
94	ST. BERNARD	*	11.00	11.00
S. BRUE			**WILD CREATURES**	
94	FERRET	*	48.00	48.00
94	WOLF	*	48.00	48.00

SANDY DOLLS INC.

YR	NAME	LIMIT	ISSUE	TREND
A. LEE			**SASS 'N CLASS**	
98	5TH GRADE SUBSTITUTE	OP	40.00	40.00
98	BLUE MONDAY	OP	40.00	40.00
98	BURN YOU BABY?	OP	55.00	55.00
98	GIMME DAT GUM	5000	70.00	70.00
98	HOLY GHOST	5000	40.00	40.00

YR	NAME	LIMIT	ISSUE	TREND
98	LOVING ARMS	OP	35.00	35.00
98	METAMORPHOSIS	OP	60.00	60.00
98	MOTHER BOARD	5000	85.00	85.00
98	SPRINKLIN' & PRESSIN'	OP	55.00	55.00
G. DY		**SEASONAL ACCENTS ANGELIC COLLECTION**		
98	DIANNA MUSICAL	OP	80.00	80.00
98	JOELLE MUSICAL	OP	80.00	80.00
98	ZAHRA MUSICAL	OP	80.00	80.00
S. BEDARD		**SOUL MATES OCCASIONS**		
98	FOR A SPECIAL FRIEND	OP	15.00	15.00
98	GET WELL (CLOWN)	OP	15.00	15.00
98	GET WELL (SOAP)	OP	15.00	15.00
98	HAPPY BIRTHDAY (CAT)	OP	15.00	15.00
98	HAPPY BIRTHDAY (DOG)	OP	15.00	15.00
98	MISSING YOU	OP	15.00	15.00

SARAH'S ATTIC
S. SCHULTZ

YR	NAME	LIMIT	ISSUE	TREND
*	BEVERLY JANE SUNDAY BEST	500	160.00	300.00
88	SUNSHINE DOLL	RT	118.00	700.00
89	BEVERLY JANE AMERICAN (RED DRESS)	500	160.00	300.00
89	LONG JOURNEY	RT	19.00	35.00
90	SLEEPY RABBIT	RT	15.50	25.00
90	THELMA RABBIT	RT	33.00	40.00
91	SILENT NIGHT	RT	33.00	44.00
97	APRIL WH. ANGEL	2000	36.00	36.00
97	BASKET OF MEMORIES	RT	35.00	35.00
97	BASKET OF TREASURES	*	35.00	35.00
97	BENJAMIN BANNEKER	2000	65.00	65.00
97	BLACK SEMINOLE SCOUT	2000	48.00	48.00
97	BLANCHE KELSO BRUCE	2000	55.00	55.00
97	BLESSED IS HE IV	2000	65.00	65.00
97	BONDING BUDDIES RABBITS	RT	25.00	25.00
97	BUN-NARD RABBIT- BLUE	RT	80.00	80.00
97	BUN-NARD RABBIT- RUST	RT	80.00	80.00
97	BUN-NETTE RABBIT- BLUE	RT	80.00	80.00
97	BUN-NETTE RABBIT- RUST	RT	80.00	80.00
97	BURLEY BEAR- ABC'S	5000	24.00	24.00
97	BURLEY BEAR- BLUE	RT	20.00	20.00
97	BURLEY BEAR- GREEN	RT	20.00	20.00
97	BURLEY BEAR- PASTEL	RT	20.00	20.00
97	BURLEY BEAR- RED	RT	20.00	20.00
97	CORETTA- NOBEL PRIZE	10000	65.00	65.00
97	CUPCAKE- HOUSEWORK	5000	40.00	40.00
97	DO LORD!- PURPLE	3000	45.00	45.00
97	DO LORD!- RED	3000	45.00	45.00
97	FAITH BL. ANGEL- PASTEL	RT	70.00	70.00
97	FAITH WH. ANGEL- PASTEL	RT	70.00	70.00
97	FLOPPER W/ VEG. RABBIT	RT	25.00	25.00
97	FOREVER PEACE	1000	110.00	110.00
97	GENERATIONS OF QUILTING	2000	300.00	300.00
97	GIGGLES BL. ANGEL	2500	14.50	15.00
97	HEATHER RABBIT	RT	30.00	30.00
97	HEAVENLY REFLECTIONS	1000	30.00	30.00
97	HERBIE RABBIT	RT	30.00	30.00
97	JALEESA- PRAYING	2500	28.00	28.00
97	JEB- PRAYING	2500	28.00	28.00
97	JESSICA- PRAYING	2500	28.00	28.00
97	JESSIE	RT	25.00	25.00
97	JODI	RT	25.00	25.00
97	JUSTIN- PRAYING	2500	28.00	28.00
97	KATIE- SHOPPING	5000	38.00	38.00
97	KWANZAA	2000	200.00	200.00
97	LET THE SUNSHINE	4040	30.00	30.00
97	LEWIS H. DOUGLASS	2500	50.00	50.00
97	MAGGIE SCHOOL- GREEN	RT	35.00	35.00
97	MAGGIE SCHOOL- PASTEL	RT	35.00	35.00
97	MAGGIE- LGE	RT	75.00	75.00
97	MATT SCHOOL- GREEN	RT	27.00	27.00
97	MATT SCHOOL- PASTEL	RT	27.00	27.00
97	MATT- LGE	RT	754.00	75.00
97	MAY BL. ANGEL	2000	36.00	36.00
97	MIKEY II BEAR- BLUE	RT	60.00	60.00
97	MIKEY II BEAR- GREEN	RT	60.00	60.00
97	MIKEY II BEAR- PASTEL	RT	60.00	60.00
97	MISSY II BEAR- BLUE	RT	60.00	60.00
97	MISSY II BEAR- GREEN	RT	60.00	60.00
97	MISSY II BEAR- PASTEL	RT	60.00	60.00
97	MLK- NOBEL PRIZE	10000	65.00	65.00
97	NAT SCHOOL- BLUE	RT	27.00	27.00
97	NAT SCHOOL- YELLOW	RT	27.00	27.00
97	NAT- LGE	RT	75.00	75.00
97	NETTIE SCHOOL- BLUE	RT	35.00	35.00
97	NETTIE SCHOOL- YELLOW	RT	35.00	35.00
97	NETTIE- LGE	RT	75.00	75.00

YR	NAME	LIMIT	ISSUE	TREND
97	OSCEOLA INDIAN CHIEF	RT	55.00	55.00
97	PATTER GIRL ANGEL	5000	24.00	24.00
97	PEEK-A-BOO RABBIT	RT	19.00	19.00
97	PITTER BOY ANGEL	5000	24.00	24.00
97	RACHEL- PRINCESS	5000	34.00	34.00
97	SERENITY CROSS	500	44.00	44.00
97	SHARING MEMORIES	RT	85.00	85.00
97	SIMON HOUSE PIN	OP	8.00	8.00
97	SMILES, WH. ANGEL	2500	14.50	15.00
97	SPIRITUAL GUIDANCE	500	65.00	65.00
97	SUNDAY TILLIE- BLUE	RT	75.00	75.00
97	SUNDAY TILLIE- PASTEL	500	75.00	75.00
97	SUNDAY WILLIE- BLUE	RT	75.00	75.00
97	SUNDAY WILLIE- PASTEL	500	75.00	75.00
97	TABBY BEAR- BLUE	RT	25.00	25.00
97	TABBY BEAR- GREEN	RT	25.00	25.00
97	TABBY BEAR- PASTEL	RT	25.00	25.00
97	TILLIE- PREACHER'S WIFE	5000	30.00	30.00
97	TOMMY BEAR- BLUE	RT	27.00	27.00
97	TOMMY BEAR- GREEN	RT	27.00	27.00
97	TOMMY BEAR- PASTEL	RT	27.00	27.00
97	TOOTSIE BEAR- BLUE	RT	20.00	20.00
97	TOOTSIE BEAR- PASTEL	RT	20.00	20.00
97	TOOTSIE BEAR- RED	RT	20.00	20.00
97	TRANQUILITY W/ LION	1000	130.00	130.00
97	TREASURED MOMENTS	*	85.00	85.00
97	TUSKEGEE AIRMAN II	4000	60.00	60.00
97	TWINKIE- REMOTE	5000	34.00	34.00
97	WHIMPY- EXECUTIVE	5000	36.00	36.00
97	WILLIE- PREACHER	5000	30.00	30.00

S. SCHULTZ — AMERICANA COLLECTION

YR	NAME	LIMIT	ISSUE	TREND
88	AMERICANA BEAR	CL	17.50	18.00
88	AMERICANA BEAR	CL	70.00	70.00
88	AMERICANA BUNNY	CL	70.00	70.00
88	AMERICANA CLOWN	OP	80.00	80.00
88	BETSY BEAR W/FLAG	CL	23.00	23.00
88	BETSY ROSS	OP	34.00	40.00
88	COLONIAL BEAR W/HAT	CL	23.00	23.00
88	INDIAN BRAVE	OP	10.00	10.00
88	INDIAN GIRL	OP	10.00	10.00
88	PILGRIM BOY	OP	12.50	13.00
88	PILGRIM GIRL	OP	12.50	13.00
88	TURKEY	OP	10.00	12.00
90	BRIGHT SKY	TL	70.00	70.00
90	IRON HAWK	TL	70.00	70.00
90	LITTLE DOVE	TL	40.00	40.00
90	SPOTTED EAGLE	TL	30.00	30.00

S. SCHULTZ — ANGELS IN THE ATTIC

YR	NAME	LIMIT	ISSUE	TREND
89	ANGEL ABBEE	CL	9.50	18.00
89	ANGEL ALEX	CL	10.00	15.00
89	ANGEL AMELIA	CL	10.00	15.00
89	ANGEL ASHBEE	CL	9.50	18.00
89	ANGEL ASHLEE	CL	14.00	25.00
89	ANGEL BEVIE	CL	10.00	10.00
89	ANGEL BONNIE	CL	17.00	21.00
89	ANGEL CLYDE	CL	17.00	20.00
89	ANGEL DAISY	CL	14.00	15.00
89	ANGEL DUSTY	CL	12.00	85.00
89	ANGEL EDDIE	CL	10.00	10.00
89	ANGEL EMMY LOU	CL	12.00	12.00
89	ANGEL FLOPPY	CL	10.00	10.00
89	ANGEL GRAMPS	CL	17.00	90.00
89	ANGEL GRAMS	CL	17.00	90.00
89	ANGEL JEFFREY	CL	14.00	15.00
89	ANGEL JESSICA	CL	14.00	15.00
89	ANGEL PATSY	CL	13.00	15.00
89	ANGEL RAYBURN	CL	12.00	20.00
89	ANGEL REBA	CL	12.00	15.00
89	ANGEL REGGIE	CL	12.00	14.00
89	ANGEL RUTHIE	CL	12.00	13.00
89	ANGEL SHOOTER	CL	12.50	18.00
89	ANGEL WENDALL	CL	10.00	15.00
89	ANGEL WENDY	CL	10.00	15.00
89	ANGEL WILBUR	CL	9.50	14.00
89	ANGEL WINNIE	CL	10.00	14.00
89	SAINT WILLIE BILL	CL	30.00	40.00
89	ST. ANNE	CL	29.00	32.00
89	ST. GABBE	CL	30.00	33.00
89	ST. GEORGE	CL	60.00	65.00
90	ANGEL BEAR IN BASKET	CL	23.00	23.00
90	ANGEL BILLI	CL	18.00	21.00
90	ANGEL BUSTER	CL	15.00	16.00
90	ANGEL CINDI	CL	18.00	20.00
90	ANGEL FLOSSY	CL	15.00	25.00
90	ANGEL LENA	CL	36.00	38.00

YR	NAME	LIMIT	ISSUE	TREND
90	ANGEL LOUISE	CL	17.00	21.00
90	ANGEL RABBIT IN BASKET	CL	25.00	25.00
90	ANGEL TRAPPER	CL	17.00	21.00
90	ANGEL TRUDY	CL	36.00	36.00
91	ANGEL BERT GOLFING	1000	60.00	60.00
91	ANGEL DONALD WITH DOG	1000	50.00	50.00
91	CONTENTMENT	RT	100.00	180.00
92	LOVE	RT	80.00	180.00
95	DIGNITY ANGEL/4330	OP	55.00	55.00
95	LOUISE ANGEL/4472	2500	34.00	34.00
95	LOVE ANGEL/4328	OP	40.00	40.00
95	PRAYER OF LOVE/4437	SO	85.00	170.00
95	RESPECT ANGEL/4329	OP	32.00	32.00
95	WILLIE BILL ANGEL/4471	2500	34.00	34.00
96	APRIL ANGEL/4514	4000	40.00	40.00
96	MAY ANGEL/4515	4000	40.00	40.00

S. SCHULTZ — BEARY ADORABLES COLLECTION

YR	NAME	LIMIT	ISSUE	TREND
87	ABBEE BEAR	CL	10.00	10.00
87	ALEX BEAR	CL	11.50	12.00
87	AMELIA BEAR	CL	11.50	12.00
87	ASHBEE BEAR	CL	10.00	10.00
87	BEAR ON TRUNK	CL	20.00	20.00
87	COLLECTIBLE BEAR	CL	16.00	16.00
88	ARCTIC PICNIC BEAR	CL	7.00	7.00
88	BEAR IN BASKET	CL	48.00	48.00
88	BENNI BEAR	CL	7.00	7.00
88	EINSTEIN BEAR	CL	8.50	9.00
88	GHOST BEAR	CL	12.00	12.00
88	HONEY PICNIC BEAR	CL	16.50	17.00
88	JESTER CLOWN BEAR	CL	12.50	13.00
88	LEFTY BEAR	CL	80.00	80.00
88	MARTI PICNIC BEAR	CL	12.50	13.00
88	RUFUS PICNIC BEAR	CL	15.00	16.00
89	ANGEL BEAR	CL	25.00	25.00
89	DAISY BEAR	CL	48.00	55.00
89	GRISWALD BEAR	CL	48.00	55.00
89	MIKEY BEAR	CL	26.00	26.00
89	MINI TEDDY BEAR	CL	5.00	5.00
89	MISSY BEAR	CL	26.00	26.00
89	SAMMY BEAR	CL	12.00	15.00
89	SID BEAR	CL	18.00	25.00
89	SOPHIE BEAR	CL	18.00	25.00
89	SPICE BEAR	RT	12.00	15.00
89	SUGAR BEAR	CL	12.00	12.00
90	BAILEY 50'S BEAR	RT	30.00	30.00
90	BELINDA 50'S BEAR	RT	25.00	25.00
90	BEULAH 50'S BEAR	RT	30.00	30.00
90	BIRKEY 50'S BEAR	RT	25.00	25.00
90	DUDLEY BROWN BEAR	RT	32.00	32.00
90	FRANNY BROWN BEAR	RT	32.00	32.00
90	JOEY BROWN BEAR	RT	32.00	32.00
90	MARGIE BROWN BEAR	RT	32.00	32.00
90	MISS LOVE BROWN BEAR	RT	42.00	42.00
90	OLIVER BLACK BEAR	RT	32.00	32.00
91	DUDLEY BEAR	CL	32.00	32.00
91	FRANNY BEAR	RT	32.00	32.00
91	JOEY BEAR	RT	32.00	32.00
91	MISS LOVE BEAR	RT	42.00	42.00
91	NARGI BEAR	RT	32.00	32.00
91	OLIVER BEAR	RT	32.00	32.00
92	ANDY-FATHER BEAR	RT	20.00	21.00
92	AUNT EUNICE BEAR	OP	24.00	24.00
92	BELLHOP & SECOND HAND ROSE	OP	40.00	40.00
92	BELLHOP BEAR	OP	24.00	24.00
92	BRANDY BABY BEAR	CL	14.00	15.00
92	DOWAGER TWINS BEAR	OP	24.00	24.00
92	EDDIE BEAR WITH TRUNK	OP	40.00	40.00
92	IRISH BEAR	OP	24.00	24.00
92	IRISH BEAR AT PUB	OP	40.00	40.00
92	JUST TED BEAR	OP	24.00	24.00
92	JUST TED WITH MIRROR	OP	40.00	40.00
92	LIBRARIAN WITH DESK	OP	40.00	40.00
92	MANDY MOTHER BEAR	RT	20.00	20.00
92	ME AND MY SHADOW	OP	26.00	26.00
92	MICHAUD BEAR	OP	35.00	35.00
92	PROFESSOR WITH BOARD	OP	40.00	40.00
92	SECOND HAND ROSE BEAR	OP	24.00	24.00
92	TOMMY WITH DOG	OP	40.00	40.00
92	TOMMY'S BEAR	OP	24.00	24.00
93	ANGEL FAITH BLACK	1994	40.00	40.00
93	ANGEL GRACE WHITE	1994	40.00	40.00
93	BEARY HAPPY HALLOWEEN	CL	18.00	18.00
93	BEARY HUGGABLE BEAR	CL	18.00	18.00
93	BEARY MERRY CHRISTMAS	CL	20.00	20.00
93	BEARY SPECIAL BROTHER BEAR	CL	18.00	18.00

YR	NAME	LIMIT	ISSUE	TREND
93	BEARY SPECIAL FATHER BEAR	CL	22.00	22.00
93	BEARY SPECIAL MOTHER BEAR	CL	18.00	18.00
93	BEARY SPECIAL SISTER BEAR	CL	18.00	18.00
93	BLESSED IS HE	CL	48.00	150.00
93	DOWAGER TWINS ON COUCH	CL	60.00	60.00
93	EDDIE BEAR	CL	24.00	24.00
93	HEAVENLY PEACE	RT	47.00	47.00
93	HEAVENLY UNITING	RT	45.00	45.00
93	I LOVE YOU BEARS	CL	22.00	22.00
93	I'M BEARY SORRY BEAR	CL	18.00	18.00
93	LIBRARIAN BEAR	CL	24.00	24.00
93	ME AND MY SHADOW WITH CHAIR	CL	45.00	45.00
93	MISS YOU BEARY MUCH BEAR	CL	18.00	18.00
93	MR. WARD	RT	40.00	40.00
93	PROFESSOR BEAR	OP	24.00	24.00
93	RISEN CHRIST	1994	48.00	48.00
93	WITCHIE BEAR	CL	24.00	24.00
93	WITCHIE WITH POT	CL	40.00	40.00
93	YOU'RE BEARY SPECIAL BEAR	CL	18.00	18.00
94	ADORA WITH HARP	SO	26.00	26.00
94	ANGEL BEAR WITH HORSE	2050	26.00	26.00
94	ANGEL BUNNY WITH CAGE	2050	20.00	20.00
94	ANGEL CASEY	2050	32.00	32.00
94	ANGEL JONATHON	2050	32.00	32.00
94	ANGEL LACY	2050	32.00	32.00
94	ANGEL PUP WITH VICTROLA	2050	20.00	20.00
94	BEARY SPECIAL BIRTHDAY BEAR	CL	20.00	20.00
94	BEARY SPECIAL FRIEND BEAR	CL	20.00	20.00
94	BLESSED IS HE II	2500	66.00	66.00
94	ENOS WITH HORN	4000	26.00	26.00
94	GET WELL SOON BEAR	CL	20.00	20.00
94	WINGS OF LOVE BLACK BOY	RT	36.00	36.00
94	WINGS OF LOVE BLACK GIRL	RT	36.00	36.00
95	BAY CITY BEAUTY	CL	26.00	27.00
95	BAY CITY BEAUTY W/TRUNK	OP	40.00	40.00
S. SCHULTZ		**BLACK HERITAGE COLLECTION**		
87	GRAMPS	RT	16.00	16.00
87	GRAMS	CL	16.00	16.00
89	PAPPY JAKE	CL	40.00	95.00
89	QUILTING LADIES	CL	90.00	285.00
90	BROTHERLY LOVE	RT	80.00	160.00
90	CALEB	CL	23.00	30.00
90	HARPSTER W/BANJO	RT	60.00	250.00
90	HATTIE	RT	40.00	85.00
90	LIBBY W/BIBS	RT	36.00	145.00
90	LUCAS W/BIBS	CL	36.00	145.00
90	PEARL, TAP DANCER	RT	45.00	65.00
90	PERCY, TAP DANCER	RT	45.00	65.00
90	PORTIA	CL	30.00	30.00
90	PREACHER I	RT	55.00	150.00
90	SUSIE MAE	CL	22.00	22.00
90	WHOOPIE & WOOSTER	RT	50.00	250.00
91	BLACK BABY TANSY	CL	40.00	45.00
91	BRAIDED RUG	*	35.00	35.00
91	CALEB W/VEGETABLES	RT	50.00	50.00
91	CALEB WITH FOOTBALL	6000	40.00	40.00
91	CHIPS, BLACK BOY GRADUATE	6000	46.00	46.00
91	CORPORAL PERVIS	RT	60.00	110.00
91	CRICKET, BLACK GIRL GRADUATE	6000	46.00	46.00
91	GENERAL OF LOVE, COOKSTOVE	*	100.00	100.00
91	HARPSTER W/HARMONICA	RT	60.00	110.00
91	HATTIE QUILTING	RT	60.00	115.00
91	KETTLES	*	13.00	13.00
91	LIBBY W/PUPPY	RT	50.00	75.00
91	LUCAS W/DOG	RT	50.00	75.00
91	NIGHTTIME PEARL	CL	50.00	60.00
91	NIGHTTIME PERCY	CL	50.00	60.00
91	PAPPY JAKE & SUSIE MAE	RT	60.00	60.00
91	PIE	*	7.00	7.00
91	PORTIA QUILTING	RT	40.00	40.00
91	PRAISE THE LORD II	RT	100.00	100.00
91	SADIE & OSIE MAE	RT	70.00	70.00
91	UNCLE REUBEN	RT	70.00	120.00
91	VICTORIAN PORTIA	RT	35.00	35.00
91	VICTORIAN WEBSTER	RT	35.00	35.00
91	WHOOPIE & WOOSTER II	RT	70.00	70.00
92	BLACK TEACHER MISS LETTIE	RT	50.00	50.00
92	BUFFALO SOLDIER	RT	80.00	115.00
92	CLARENCE, PORTER	RT	80.00	120.00
92	ESTHER WITH BUTTER CHURN	CL	70.00	70.00
92	GRANNY WYNNE & OLIVIA	RT	85.00	85.00
92	MUSIC MASTERS	CL	300.00	350.00
95	AHMAD/4453	7500	23.00	23.00
95	ALICIA/YVETTE/4410	5000	50.00	50.00
95	ANGELIKA/4456	7500	25.00	25.00

YR	NAME	LIMIT	ISSUE	TREND
95	BESSIE COLEMAN/4313	2500	50.00	50.00
95	BILL PICKET/4281	2500	56.00	56.00
95	BLESSED FAMILY NATIVITY/4364	5000	70.00	70.00
95	BLESSED IS HE III/4387	YR	60.00	60.00
95	BLESSED IS SHE/4312	RT	50.00	50.00
95	BOOK OF WISDOM/4315	4000	52.00	52.00
95	BUFFALO BILL/4311	RT	60.00	60.00
95	BUFFALO SOLDIER/4285	5000	165.00	165.00
95	CALF & CHICKS/4459	OP	25.00	25.00
95	CALVIN/4319	RT	28.00	28.00
95	CHARITY/4318	4000	28.00	28.00
95	CHIEF JOSEPH/4282	RT	56.00	56.00
95	ELROY/4411	5000	25.00	25.00
95	F. DOUGLASS/4402	2500	55.00	55.00
95	H.O. FLIPPER/4403	2500	55.00	55.00
95	HUGS/4185	OP	36.00	36.00
95	IDA B. WELLS/4400	2500	65.00	65.00
95	ISHAMAEL/4454	7500	23.00	23.00
95	JABARI/4455	7500	23.00	23.00
95	JARRELL/4452	7500	23.00	23.00
95	JOAH/4451	7500	*	23.00
95	KISSES/4186	RT	30.00	30.00
95	LAKEISHA/4450	7500	25.00	25.00
95	LAMB & DUCKS/4458	OP	25.00	25.00
95	LEAN ON ME/4369	5000	55.00	55.00
95	LIBBY W/CANDLE/4396	RT	26.00	26.00
95	LIFT YOUR HEARTS/4413	5000	50.00	50.00
95	LOVE/4187	OP	50.00	50.00
95	LOVING TOUCH/4314	4000	66.00	66.00
95	LUCAS W/BEAR/4397	RT	26.00	26.00
95	O.A.D. WASH./4404	2500	51.00	51.00
95	OLD TIME TUNE/4317	4000	54.00	54.00
95	PIGLET/4457	OP	11.00	11.00
95	ROSA PARKS/4401	RT	65.00	65.00
95	STITCH OR LOVE/4316	4000	60.00	60.00
95	TUSKEGEE AIRMAN WWII /4405	SO	60.00	60.00
95	WAGS/4412	RT	9.00	9.00
96	BELIEVE IN YOUR/4522	3000	70.00	70.00
96	BLESSED IS HE IV/4520	2000	70.00	70.00
96	BREEZE/4537	RT	24.00	24.00
96	CARTER/4536	2500	30.00	30.00
96	CAYLA/4535	2500	36.00	36.00
96	CLOWN HICKORY/4485	10000	29.00	29.00
96	CLOWN SASSAFRAS/4484	10000	29.00	29.00
96	JAZZ MAN/4499	2000	150.00	150.00
96	LOVE OF MY LIFE II/4534	2500	75.00	75.00
96	MA RAINEY/4500	2000	50.00	50.00
96	MARY ELIZA MAHONEY/4501	SO	50.00	50.00
96	MISTY/4539	RT	50.00	24.00
96	NOAH'S ARK/4529	SO	130.00	130.00
96	SPECIAL BEAR/4476	5000	23.00	23.00
96	SPECIAL BLACK GIRL/4477	5000	29.00	29.00
96	SPECIAL WHITE GIRL/4478	5000	29.00	29.00
96	SUMMER-4538	RT	24.00	24.00
96	SUNDAY TILLIE/BW/4530	2500	75.00	75.00
96	SUNDAY TILLIE/YG/4532	RT	75.00	75.00
96	SUNDAY WILLIE/BW/4531	2500	75.00	75.00
96	SUNDAY WILLIE/YG/4533	RT	75.00	75.00
96	TRUST IN EACH OTHER/4523	RT	70.00	70.00
98	PRAISE THE LORD V	4000	65.00	65.00
98	SPREAD WORD	4000	65.00	65.00

S. SCHULTZ   **CHERISHED MEMORIES**

YR	NAME	LIMIT	ISSUE	TREND
91	BLACK BABY BOY (1-2 YRS.)	*	50.00	50.00
91	BLACK BABY BOY (BIRTH-1 YR.)	*	50.00	50.00
91	BLACK BABY GIRL (1-2 YRS.)	*	50.00	50.00
91	BLACK BABY GIRL (BIRTH-1 YR.)	*	50.00	50.00
91	WHITE BABY BOY (1-2 YRS.)	*	60.00	60.00
91	WHITE BABY BOY (BIRTH-1 YR.)	*	60.00	60.00
91	WHITE BABY GIRL (1-2 YRS.)	*	60.00	60.00
91	WHITE BABY GIRL (BIRTH-1 YR.)	*	60.00	60.00

S. SCHULTZ   **CHILDREN OF LOVE**

YR	NAME	LIMIT	ISSUE	TREND
91	BENJAMIN WITH DRUMS	10000	46.00	46.00
91	CHARITY SEWING FLAGS	10000	46.00	46.00
91	SKIP BUILDING HOUSE	10000	50.00	50.00
91	SUSIE PAINTING TRAIN	10000	46.00	46.00

S. SCHULTZ   **CLASSROOM MEMORIES**

YR	NAME	LIMIT	ISSUE	TREND
88	MISS PRITCHETT	CL	28.00	38.00
91	ACHIEVING OUR GOALS	RT	80.00	83.00
91	CLASSROOM MEMORIES	6000	80.00	80.00

S. SCHULTZ   **COLLECTOR'S CLUB**

YR	NAME	LIMIT	ISSUE	TREND
95	FRIENDS FOREVER/4444	YR	65.00	65.00
95	HORSIN' AROUND/4445	YR	65.00	65.00
95	PLAYTIME PALS/4446	YR	65.00	65.00

N. HUGHES   **COLORS OF LIFE**

YR	NAME	LIMIT	ISSUE	TREND
97	ANCESTORS	5797	195.00	195.00

YR	NAME	LIMIT	ISSUE	TREND
97	EMBRACE	5797	115.00	115.00
97	FRIENDS	5797	125.00	125.00
97	PEACE	5797	95.00	95.00
97	RITES	5797	99.00	99.00
97	SHELTER	5797	99.00	99.00

S. SCHULTZ — COOKIE KIDS & FRIENDS

YR	NAME	LIMIT	ISSUE	TREND
95	CHIP/C004	OP	30.00	30.00
95	COOKIE KIDS SIGN/C001	OP	39.00	39.00
95	HONEY/C007	OP	30.00	30.00
95	OATIE/C002	OP	30.00	30.00
95	PEANUT/C005	OP	30.00	30.00
95	SPRINKLES/C006	OP	30.00	30.00
95	SUGAR/C003	RT	30.00	30.00

S. SCHULTZ — COTTON TALE COLLECTION

YR	NAME	LIMIT	ISSUE	TREND
86	WINNIE MOM RABBIT	CL	14.00	17.00
87	BONNIE	CL	30.00	100.00
87	CLYDE	CL	30.00	100.00
87	FLOPPY	CL	19.00	21.00
87	WENDALL BOY RABBIT	CL	14.00	27.00
87	WENDALL PA RABBIT	CL	17.00	25.00
87	WENDY GIRL RABBIT	CL	15.00	27.00
88	AMOS HARE	CL	11.00	12.00
88	BILLI RABBIT	CL	27.00	36.00
88	BOY RABBIT RES. CANDLE	CL	9.00	10.00
88	CINDI RABBIT	CL	27.00	36.00
88	GIRL RABBIT RES. CANDLE	CL	9.00	10.00
88	IZZY HARE	CL	8.00	10.00
88	LIZZY HARE	CL	8.00	10.00
88	MADDY HARE	CL	11.00	11.00
88	RABBIT IN BASKET	CL	48.00	48.00
88	WENDALL MINI BOY RABBIT	CL	7.50	10.00
88	WENDY MINI GIRL RABBIT	CL	7.50	10.00
88	WILBUR MINI PAPA RABBIT	CL	8.50	10.00
88	WINNIE MINI MAMA RABBIT	CL	8.50	10.00
89	COOKIE RABBIT	CL	29.00	110.00
89	CRUMB RABBIT	CL	29.00	40.00
89	NANA RABBIT	RT	50.00	65.00
89	PAPA RABBIT	RT	50.00	65.00
89	SLEEPING BABY BUNNY	CL	15.50	16.00
89	THELMA RABBIT	CL	33.00	41.00
89	TOBY RABBIT	CL	17.00	21.00
90	CHUCKLES FARM RABBIT	TL	53.00	54.00
90	COOKIE FARM RABBIT	TL	47.00	48.00
90	CRUMB FARM RABBIT	TL	53.00	54.00
90	HANNAH RABBIT QUILTING	CL	32.00	32.00
90	HEATHER RABBIT W/DOLL	OP	20.00	22.00
90	HENRY RABBIT W/PIPE	CL	32.00	32.00
90	HERBIE RABBIT W/BOOK	CL	22.00	22.00
90	MOLLY RABBIT W/VEST	CL	75.00	75.00
90	NANA FARM RABBIT	CL	100.00	100.00
90	OLLY RABBIT W/VEST	CL	65.00	100.00
90	PAPA FARM RABBIT	CL	80.00	80.00
90	SLEEPY FARM RABBIT	CL	35.00	35.00
90	THOMAS RABBIT	RT	33.00	40.00
90	ZEB SAILOR DAD	CL	26.00	28.00
90	ZEB W/CARROTS	RT	18.00	35.00
90	ZEKE SAILOR BOY	CL	26.00	26.00
90	ZEKE W/CARROTS	CL	17.00	35.00
90	ZELDA SAILOR MOM	CL	28.00	28.00
90	ZELDA W/CARROTS	RT	18.00	35.00
90	ZOE SAILOR GIRL	CL	26.00	26.00
90	ZOE W/CARROTS	RT	17.00	35.00
91	TESSY RABBIT	RT	20.00	37.00
91	VICTORIAN TABITHA	CL	30.00	48.00
91	VICTORIAN TESSY	CL	20.00	38.00
91	VICTORIAN THELMA	CL	60.00	60.00
91	VICTORIAN THOMAS	CL	60.00	60.00
91	VICTORIAN TOBY	TL	40.00	60.00
91	VICTORIAN TUCKER	CL	37.00	37.00
93	X-MAS TOBY	RT	20.00	20.00
95	GLIMMER/4362	RT	50.00	50.00
95	GLITZ/4363	RT	50.00	50.00
98	CLARA NIBBLES	1998	50.00	50.00
98	CLEM NIBBLES	1998	50.00	50.00

S. SCHULTZ — CUDDLY CRITTERS COLLECTION

YR	NAME	LIMIT	ISSUE	TREND
87	SPARKY	OP	9.00	10.00
88	BUSTER BOY CAT	CL	14.00	15.00
88	CAROUSEL HORSE	CL	31.00	31.00
88	COW W/BELL	CL	35.00	35.00
88	FLOSSY GIRL CAT	CL	9.50	10.00
88	KITTY CAT W/BONNET	CL	12.00	12.00
88	LAZY-CAT ON BACK	CL	13.00	13.00
88	LILA MRS. MOUSE	CL	17.50	18.00
88	LOUISE MAMA CAT	CL	20.00	20.00
88	LUCKY BOY MOUSE	CL	13.00	13.00

YR	NAME	LIMIT	ISSUE	TREND
88	LUCKY GIRL MOUSE	CL	12.00	12.00
88	MYRTLE THE PIG	CL	38.00	45.00
88	PAPA MOUSE	CL	17.50	18.00
88	ROCKING HORSE	CL	56.00	56.00
88	SLEEPING CAT	CL	6.00	6.00
88	TRAPPER PAPA CAT	CL	20.00	20.00
89	MADAM DONNA	CL	36.00	45.00
89	MESSIEUR PIERRE	CL	36.00	45.00
89	OTIS PAPA CAT	CL	13.00	13.00
89	PUDDIN GIRL CAT	CL	10.00	10.00
89	WHISKERS BOY CAT	CL	10.00	10.00
89	WIGGLY PIG	CL	17.00	25.00
90	BOY SQUIRREL SONNY	CL	18.00	18.00
90	GIRL SQUIRREL SIS	CL	18.00	18.00
90	HORACE & SISSY DOGS	OP	50.00	50.00
90	JASPER DAD CAT	OP	36.00	36.00
90	LULU GIRL CAT	OP	26.00	26.00
90	MA SQUIRREL SASHA	CL	19.00	19.00
90	PA SQUIRREL SHERMAN	CL	19.00	19.00
90	PENNY GIRL DOG	OP	35.00	35.00
90	REBECCA MOM DOG	OP	40.00	40.00
90	SCOOTER BOY DOG	OP	30.00	30.00
90	SCUFFY BOY CAT	OP	26.00	26.00
90	WINNIE MOM CAT	OP	36.00	36.00
91	JIGGS, SLEEPING CAT	*	10.00	10.00
95	GIDDY-UP/4180	RT	38.00	38.00
S. SCHULTZ			**DAISY COLLECTION**	
89	SALLY BOOBA	CL	40.00	65.00
90	BOMBER	CL	52.00	60.00
90	JACK BOY BALL & GLOVE	CL	40.00	45.00
90	JEWEL	CL	62.00	70.00
90	SPARKY	CL	55.00	60.00
90	SPIKE	RT	46.00	50.00
90	STRETCH	CL	52.00	60.00
S. SCHULTZ			**DREAMS OF TOMORROW**	
96	NURSE TILLIE II/4502	5000	29.00	29.00
S. SCHULTZ			**FACES OF COURAGE**	
98	BUFFALO SOLDIER BUST	9898	48.00	48.00
98	HARRIET TUBMAN BUST	9898	48.00	48.00
98	ROSA PARKS BUST	9898	48.00	48.00
98	TUSKEGEE AIRMAN BUST	9898	48.00	48.00
S. SCHULTZ			**FOREVER ICE SCULPTURES**	
98	CLARA NIBBLES	1998	45.00	45.00
98	CLEM NIBBLES	1998	45.00	45.00
S. SCHULTZ			**GINGER BABIES COLLECTION**	
89	GINGER	RT	17.00	17.00
89	MOLASSES	RT	17.00	17.00
90	GINGER BOY NUTMEG	RT	15.50	20.00
90	GINGER GIRL CINNAMON	RT	15.50	20.00
S. SCHULTZ			**HAPPY COLLECTION**	
87	HAPPY W/BALLOONS	CL	22.00	22.00
87	LARGE HAPPY CLOWN	CL	22.00	22.00
87	SITTING HAPPY	CL	26.00	26.00
88	LADY CLOWN	CL	20.00	20.00
90	ENCORE CLOWN W/DOG	2000	100.00	100.00
S. SCHULTZ			**HEAVENLY WINGS COLLECTION**	
89	ANGELICA ANGEL	6000	21.00	25.00
89	HEAVENLY GUARDIAN	CL	40.00	40.00
89	REGINA	CL	24.00	30.00
90	ADORA W/BUNNY	10000	50.00	50.00
90	ADORA W/PINK GOWN	CL	35.00	75.00
90	BOY ANGEL INST. ADAIR	CL	29.00	29.00
90	ENOS W/BLUE GOWN	CL	33.00	75.00
90	ENOS W/FROG	10000	50.00	50.00
S. SCHULTZ			**HISTORICALS**	
98	BASEBALL LEGEND	2500	60.00	60.00
98	SCOTT JOPLIN	2500	60.00	60.00
S. SCHULTZ			**LABOR OF LOVE**	
95	BABY/4288	OP	25.00	25.00
95	BEACH/4302	RT	29.00	29.00
95	BIRTHDAY/4290	OP	29.00	29.00
95	BIRTHDAY/4299	OP	29.00	29.00
95	BIRTHDAY/4301	OP	29.00	29.00
95	BIRTHDAY/4303	OP	29.00	29.00
95	BOTTLE/4306	RT	29.00	29.00
95	BOY STOCKING/4436	OP	18.00	18.00
95	BOY TRUMPET/4432	OP	18.00	18.00
95	BOY WREATH/4434	OP	18.00	18.00
95	CAMPFIRE/4293	RT	29.00	29.00
95	CANNING/4297	RT	29.00	29.00
95	COMPUTER/4304	OP	29.00	29.00
95	FISHING/4300	OP	29.00	29.00
95	GIRL PRAYING/4431	OP	18.00	18.00
95	GIRL WREATH/4435	OP	18.00	18.00

YR	NAME	LIMIT	ISSUE	TREND
95	GOLFING/4308	OP	29.00	29.00
95	GROWING/4305	OP	29.00	29.00
95	HAPPINESS/4291	OP	29.00	29.00
95	HEALING/4292	OP	29.00	29.00
95	IRONING/4289	OP	29.00	29.00
95	MECHANIC/4298	RT	29.00	29.00
95	MOWING/4296	RT	29.00	29.00
95	PLANTING/4287	OP	29.00	29.00
95	PROTECT. BLUE/4383	OP	12.00	12.00
95	PROTECT. BLUE/4385	OP	12.00	12.00
95	PROTECT. GOLD/4378	OP	12.00	12.00
95	PROTECT. GOLD/4380	OP	12.00	12.00
95	PROTECT. GOLD/4382	OP	12.00	12.00
95	PROTECT. GOLD/4384	OP	12.00	12.00
95	PROTECT. PINK/4379	OP	12.00	12.00
95	PROTECT. PINK/4381	OP	12.00	12.00
95	ROLLER BLADING/4309	OP	29.00	29.00
95	SENDING SMILES/4307	OP	29.00	29.00
95	SEWING/4296	RT	29.00	29.00
95	STUDYING/4294	OP	25.00	25.00
95	TOOLS/4310	RT	29.00	29.00
96	COMPTR. BOY/4487	RT	29.00	29.00
96	COMPTR. GIRL/4486	RT	29.00	29.00
96	COMPTR. GIRL/4488	RT	29.00	29.00
96	COMPTR. SEWING/4489	OP	29.00	29.00
96	GOLFER/4490	RT	29.00	29.00

S. SCHULTZ — LITTLE CHARMERS COLLECTION

YR	NAME	LIMIT	ISSUE	TREND
87	AMBER-SMALL GIRL STANDING	CL	15.00	18.00
87	ARCHIE-SMALL BOY STANDING	CL	15.00	16.00
87	ASHLEE	CL	60.00	65.00
87	BARE BOTTOM BABY	CL	9.50	15.00
87	BASEBALL PLAYER	CL	24.00	30.00
87	BEAU-CUPIE BOY	CL	20.00	22.00
87	BEVIE	CL	18.00	20.00
87	BLONDIE-GIRL DOLL SITTING	CL	16.00	18.00
87	BUTCH-BOY BOOK SITTING	CL	16.00	18.00
87	BUTTONS-CUPIE GIRL	CL	20.00	22.00
87	CHEERLEADER	CL	16.00	18.00
87	CLEMENTINE-GIRL SAILOR SUIT	CL	14.50	17.00
87	CORKY-BOY SAILOR SUIT	CL	14.50	17.00
87	CUPCAKE W/ROPE	CL	19.00	21.00
87	DAISY	CL	36.00	40.00
87	DUSTY	CL	19.00	21.00
87	EDDIE	CL	18.00	20.00
87	EMMY LOU	CL	14.00	16.00
87	FOOTBALL PLAYER	CL	24.00	26.00
87	MAN GOLFER	CL	24.00	26.00
87	SHOOTER	CL	19.00	21.00
87	TWINKLE W/POLE	CL	19.00	21.00
87	WILLIE BILL	CL	20.00	22.00
87	WOMAN GOLFER	CL	24.00	26.00
88	BASKETBALL PLAYER	CL	24.00	26.00
88	BOWLER	CL	24.00	26.00
88	BOY W/CLOWN DOLL	CL	40.00	45.00
88	GIRL W/DOG	CL	43.00	47.00
88	GIRL W/TEACUP	CL	37.00	40.00
88	JESSICA	CL	44.00	45.00
89	JENNIFER & DOG	CL	57.00	60.00
89	MOOSE BOY SITTING	OP	18.00	20.00
90	WHITE BABY TANSY	10000	40.00	40.00

S. SCHULTZ — MARTIN LUTHER KING, JR.

YR	NAME	LIMIT	ISSUE	TREND
95	BIRMINGHAM JAIL/4407	YR	65.00	65.00
95	WEDDING DAY/4406	YR	85.00	85.00
96	I HAVE A DREAM/4540	10000	50.00	65.00
96	RACIAL HARMONY/4541	5000	114.00	114.00

S. SCHULTZ — MATT & MAGGIE

YR	NAME	LIMIT	ISSUE	TREND
86	MAGGIE	RT	14.00	25.00
86	MAGGIE CANDLEHOLDER	CL	12.00	12.00
86	MATT	CL	14.00	25.00
86	MATT CANDLEHOLDER	CL	12.00	12.00
87	MAGGIE ON HEART	CL	9.00	13.00
87	MATT & MAGGIE W/BEAR	RT	100.00	155.00
87	MATT ON HEART	CL	9.00	13.00
87	STANDING MAGGIE	CL	11.00	13.00
87	STANDING MATT	CL	11.00	13.00
88	LARGE MAGGIE	RT	48.00	60.00
88	LARGE MATT	RT	48.00	60.00
88	SMALL SITTING MAGGIE	CL	11.50	37.00
88	SMALL SITTING MATT	CL	11.50	37.00
89	MAGGIE BENCH SITTER	CL	32.00	40.00
89	MATT BENCH SITTER	CL	32.00	40.00
89	MINI MAGGIE	CL	6.00	10.00
89	MINI MATT	CL	6.00	10.00

S. SCHULTZ — MEMORY LANE COLLECTION

YR	NAME	LIMIT	ISSUE	TREND
87	BARBER SHOP	CL	13.00	15.00

YR	NAME	LIMIT	ISSUE	TREND
87	BARN	CL	16.50	18.00
87	CHURCH	CL	19.00	20.00
87	COTTAGE	CL	13.00	15.00
87	DRUG STORE	CL	13.00	15.00
87	GENERAL STORE	CL	13.00	15.00
87	GRANDMA'S HOUSE	CL	13.00	15.00
87	HOUSE W/DORMERS	CL	15.00	16.00
87	MILL	CL	16.50	18.00
87	SCHOOL	CL	14.00	15.00
88	BANK	CL	13.00	15.00
88	MINI BARBER SHOP	CL	6.50	10.00
88	MINI BARN	CL	6.00	8.00
88	MINI CHURCH	CL	6.50	10.00
88	MINI DRUG STORE	CL	6.00	8.00
88	MINI GENERAL STORE	CL	6.00	8.00
88	MINI GRANDMA'S HOUSE	CL	7.00	8.00
88	MINI MILL	CL	6.50	7.00
88	MINI SALT BOX	CL	6.00	6.00
88	MINI SCHOOL	CL	6.50	7.00
88	TRAIN DEPOT	CL	13.50	14.00
89	BRITON CHURCH	CL	25.00	25.00
89	FIRE STATION	CL	20.00	20.00
89	MINI BANK	CL	6.00	6.00
89	MINI DEPOT	CL	7.00	7.00
89	POST OFFICE	CL	25.00	25.00

S. SCHULTZ — MICHAUD BEARS

YR	NAME	LIMIT	ISSUE	TREND
95	BAY CITY BEAUTY/4334	RT	26.00	26.00
95	BEAU W/TRUNK/4335	RT	40.00	40.00
95	LOVE HEALS ALL/4438	RT	28.00	28.00
95	PROXY BEAR/4332	RT	20.00	20.00
95	PROXY W/JEWELRY/4333	RT	33.00	33.00

S. SCHULTZ — PREMIER EDITION FOR CLUB CONTEST WINNERS

YR	NAME	LIMIT	ISSUE	TREND
96	ANGELS ON ASSIGN/4544	YR	65.00	65.00

S. SCHULTZ — PROMOTION FIGURINES

YR	NAME	LIMIT	ISSUE	TREND
95	FLAGS IN HEAV./4386	YR	45.00	45.00
96	ABIGAIL/4543	YR	36.00	36.00
96	ARETHA/4542	YR	36.00	36.00

S. SCHULTZ — ROSE COLLECTION

YR	NAME	LIMIT	ISSUE	TREND
89	SWEET ROSE	CL	50.00	50.00
90	TIFFANY VICTORIAN GIRL	TL	40.00	40.00
90	TYLER VICTORIAN BOY	TL	40.00	40.00
90	VICTORIAN BOY CODY	CL	46.00	46.00

S. SCHULTZ — SANTAS OF THE MONTH

YR	NAME	LIMIT	ISSUE	TREND
88	APRIL SANTA BLACK	CL	50.00	250.00
88	APRIL SANTA WHITE	CL	50.00	125.00
88	AUGUST SANTA WHITE	CL	50.00	125.00
88	DECEMBER SANTA BLACK	TL	50.00	250.00
88	DECEMBER SANTA WHITE	CL	50.00	125.00
88	FEBRUARY SANTA BLACK	TL	50.00	250.00
88	FEBRUARY SANTA WHITE	CL	50.00	125.00
88	JANUARY SANTA BLACK	TL	50.00	250.00
88	JANUARY SANTA WHITE	CL	50.00	125.00
88	JULY SANTA BLACK	TL	50.00	250.00
88	JULY SANTA WHITE	CL	50.00	125.00
88	JUNE SANTA BLACK	TL	50.00	250.00
88	JUNE SANTA WHITE	CL	50.00	125.00
88	MARCH SANTA BLACK	TL	50.00	250.00
88	MARCH SANTA WHITE	CL	50.00	125.00
88	MAY SANTA BLACK	CL	50.00	250.00
88	MAY SANTA WHITE	CL	50.00	125.00
88	MINI APRIL SANTA	CL	14.00	30.00
88	MINI AUGUST SANTA	CL	14.00	30.00
88	MINI DECEMBER SANTA	CL	14.00	30.00
88	MINI FEBRUARY SANTA	CL	14.00	30.00
88	MINI JANUARY SANTA	CL	14.00	30.00
88	MINI JULY SANTA	CL	14.00	30.00
88	MINI JUNE SANTA	CL	14.00	30.00
88	MINI MARCH SANTA	CL	14.00	30.00
88	MINI MAY SANTA	CL	14.00	30.00
88	MINI NOVEMBER SANTA	CL	14.00	30.00
88	MINI OCTOBER SANTA	CL	14.00	30.00
88	MINI SEPTEMBER SANTA	CL	14.00	30.00
88	NOVEMBER SANTA BLACK	TL	50.00	250.00
88	NOVEMBER SANTA WHITE	CL	50.00	125.00
88	OCTOBER SANTA BLACK	TL	50.00	250.00
88	OCTOBER SANTA WHITE	CL	50.00	125.00
88	SEPTEMBER SANTA BLACK	TL	50.00	250.00
88	SEPTEMBER SANTA WHITE	CL	50.00	125.00
90	APR. SANTA SPRING/JOY	CL	150.00	150.00
90	APR. SPRING TIME	CL	90.00	100.00
90	APRIL, MRS.	CL	110.00	110.00
90	AUG. FUN IN THE SUN	CL	90.00	100.00
90	AUGUST SANTA BLACK	CL	50.00	250.00
90	AUGUST SANTA SUMMERS TRN.	CL	110.00	125.00
90	AUGUST, MRS.	CL	90.00	100.00

YR	NAME	LIMIT	ISSUE	TREND
90	DEC. A GIFT OF PEACE	CL	90.00	90.00
90	DEC. SANTA PEACE	CL	120.00	125.00
90	DECEMBER, MRS.	CL	110.00	130.00
90	FEB. FROM THE HEART	CL	90.00	90.00
90	FEB. SANTA CUPIDS HELP	CL	120.00	120.00
90	FEBRUARY, MRS.	CL	110.00	110.00
90	JAN. FRUITS OF LOVE	CL	90.00	90.00
90	JAN. SANTA WINTER FUN	CL	80.00	85.00
90	JANUARY, MRS.	CL	80.00	105.00
90	JULY CELEBRATE AMERICA	CL	90.00	95.00
90	JULY SANTA GOD BLESS	CL	100.00	110.00
90	JULY, MRS.	CL	100.00	120.00
90	JUNE HOMERUN	CL	90.00	95.00
90	JUNE SANTA GRADUATION	CL	70.00	70.00
90	JUNE, MRS.	CL	70.00	95.00
90	MAR. IRISH LOVE	CL	100.00	100.00
90	MAR. SANTA IRISH DELIGHT	CL	120.00	145.00
90	MARCH, MRS.	CL	80.00	95.00
90	MASQUERADE TILLIE	TL	45.00	45.00
90	MAY CADDY CHATTER	CL	100.00	100.00
90	MAY SANTA PAR FOR COURSE	CL	100.00	100.00
90	MAY, MRS.	CL	80.00	110.00
90	NOV. HARVEST OF LOVE	TL	120.00	120.00
90	NOV. SANTA GIVE THANKS	CL	100.00	120.00
90	NOVEMBER, MRS.	CL	90.00	110.00
90	OCT. MASQUERADE	CL	120.00	120.00
90	OCT. SANTA SEASONS PLENTY	CL	120.00	120.00
90	OCTOBER, MRS.	CL	90.00	110.00
90	SEP. SANTA TOUCHDOWN	CL	90.00	90.00
90	SEPT. LESSONS IN LOVE	TL	90.00	90.00
90	SEPTEMBER, MRS.	CL	90.00	95.00

S. SCHULTZ **SARAH'S GANG**

YR	NAME	LIMIT	ISSUE	TREND
86	ORIGINAL KATIE	CL	14.00	20.00
86	ORIGINAL TILLIE	CL	14.00	25.00
86	ORIGINAL TWINKIE	CL	14.00	20.00
86	ORIGINAL WHIMPY	CL	14.00	20.00
86	ORIGINAL WILLIE	CL	14.00	28.00
86	TILLIE CANDLE HOLDER	CL	12.00	13.00
87	CUPCAKE ON HEART	CL	12.00	21.00
87	KATIE ON HEART	CL	12.00	21.00
87	ORIGINAL CUPCAKE	CL	16.00	20.00
87	SITTING KATIE	CL	14.00	21.00
87	SITTING WHIMPY	CL	14.00	21.00
87	TILLIE ON HEART	CL	9.00	21.00
87	TWINKIE ON HEART	CL	9.00	21.00
87	WHIMPY ON HEART	CL	9.00	19.00
87	WILLIE CANDLE HOLDER	CL	12.00	13.00
87	WILLIE ON HEART	CL	9.00	21.00
88	CUPCAKE	CL	20.00	21.00
88	KATIE	CL	20.00	21.00
88	TILLIE	CL	20.00	21.00
88	TWINKIE	CL	20.00	21.00
88	WHIMPY	CL	20.00	21.00
88	WILLIE	CL	20.00	21.00
89	AMERICANA CUPCAKE	CL	21.00	24.00
89	AMERICANA KATIE	CL	21.00	24.00
89	AMERICANA TILLIE	CL	21.00	24.00
89	AMERICANA TWINKIE	CL	21.00	24.00
89	AMERICANA WHIMPY	CL	21.00	24.00
89	AMERICANA WILLIE	CL	21.00	24.00
89	BABY RACHEL	CL	20.00	20.00
89	SMALL COUNTRY TILLIE	CL	16.00	25.00
89	SMALL COUNTRY WILLIE	CL	18.00	25.00
89	SMALL SAILOR KATIE	CL	14.00	18.00
89	SMALL SAILOR WHIMPY	CL	14.00	18.00
89	SMALL SCHOOL CUPCAKE	CL	11.00	18.00
89	SMALL SCHOOL TWINKIE	CL	11.00	18.00
90	AMERICANA RACHEL	CL	30.00	30.00
90	BEACHTIME BABY RACHEL	CL	35.00	50.00
90	BEACHTIME CUPCAKE	CL	35.00	50.00
90	BEACHTIME KATIE & WHIMPY	CL	60.00	70.00
90	BEACHTIME TILLIE	CL	35.00	50.00
90	BEACHTIME TWINKIE	CL	35.00	50.00
90	BEACHTIME WILLIE	CL	35.00	50.00
90	CLOWN TILLIE	CL	40.00	45.00
90	CLOWN WILLIE	CL	40.00	45.00
90	DEVIL CUPCAKE	CL	40.00	40.00
90	DEVIL TWINKIE	CL	40.00	45.00
90	PUMPKIN RACHEL	CL	40.00	45.00
90	SCARECROW WHIMPY	CL	40.00	40.00
90	WITCH KATIE	CL	40.00	45.00
91	CRACKER, COCKER SPANIEL	TL	9.00	9.00
91	DOCTOR TWINKIE	6000	50.00	50.00
91	EXECUTIVE WHIMP	6000	46.00	46.00
91	KATIE, WHITE BRIDE	TL	47.00	47.00

YR	NAME	LIMIT	ISSUE	TREND
91	NURSE CUPCAKE	6000	46.00	46.00
91	PEACHES, BLACK FLOWER GIRL	CL	40.00	40.00
91	PERCY, BLACK MINISTER	CL	50.00	50.00
91	PUG, BLACK RING BEARER	CL	40.00	40.00
91	RACHEL, WHITE FLOWER GIRL	CL	40.00	40.00
91	TEACHER TILLIE	6000	50.00	50.00
91	THANKSGIVING KATIE	RT	32.00	32.00
91	THANKSGIVING RACHEL	RT	32.00	32.00
91	THANKSGIVING TILLIE	RT	32.00	32.00
91	THANKSGIVING WHIMPY	RT	32.00	32.00
91	THANKSGIVING WILLIE	10000	32.00	32.00
91	TILLIE, BLACK BRIDE	CL	47.00	50.00
91	TWINKIE, WHITE MINISTER	CL	50.00	52.00
91	TYLER, WHITE RING BEARER	CL	40.00	40.00
91	WHIMPY, WHITE GROOM	CL	47.00	50.00
91	WILLIE, BLACK GROOM	CL	47.00	47.00
95	CUPCAKE/4346	OP	28.00	28.00
95	KATIE/4344	OP	28.00	28.00
95	LARGE FLOWER POT84355	OP	6.00	6.00
95	PORCE SET 5 PC./4353	OP	250.00	250.00
95	RACHEL/4348	OP	28.00	28.00
95	ROLLER BLADES/4356	OP	8.00	8.00
95	SMALL FLOWER POT/4354	OP	5.00	5.00
95	SPARKY/4357	OP	10.00	10.00
95	TILLIE/4342	OP	28.00	28.00
95	TRAP/4360	OP	6.50	7.00
95	TWINKIE/4347	OP	28.00	28.00
95	WAGON OF FUN/4361	OP	25.00	25.00
95	WHIMPY/4345	OP	28.00	28.00
95	WICKER CHAIR/4358	OP	20.00	20.00
95	WICKER SETTEE/4359	OP	25.00	25.00
95	WILLIE/4343	OP	28.00	28.00

S. SCHULTZ

SARAH'S NEIGHBORHOOD FRIENDS

YR	NAME	LIMIT	ISSUE	TREND
90	ANNIE W/FLOWER BASKET	CL	56.00	56.00
90	ANNIE W/VIOLIN	CL	40.00	40.00
90	BUBBA W/LANTERN	CL	40.00	40.00
90	BUBBA W/LEMONADE	CL	54.00	100.00
90	BUD W/BOOK	CL	40.00	40.00
90	BUD W/NEWSPAPER	CL	40.00	40.00
90	HEWETT W/APPLES	CL	40.00	40.00
90	HEWETT W/DRUM	CL	40.00	40.00
90	PANSY W/BUGGY	CL	40.00	40.00
90	PANSY W/SLED	CL	50.00	50.00
90	WALDO DOG	CL	35.00	35.00
90	WALDO W/FLOWERS	CL	10.00	10.00
90	WEASEL W/CAP	CL	14.00	15.00
90	WEASEL W/PAPER	CL	40.00	40.00
91	ANNIE, WHITE MARY	CL	40.00	40.00
91	BABES, BLACK BABY JESUS	CL	30.00	30.00
91	BUBBA, BLACK KING	CL	20.00	20.00
91	BUD, WHITE JOSEPH	CL	40.00	40.00
91	CRATE OF LOVE, BLACK	CL	34.00	34.00
91	CRATE OF LOVE, WHITE	CL	40.00	40.00
91	DOLLY, WHITE BABY JESUS	CL	40.00	40.00
91	EXECUTIVE NOAH	CL	20.00	20.00
91	HEWITT, WHITE KING W/DRUM	CL	46.00	46.00
91	KITTEN IN BASKET	CL	40.00	40.00
91	NOAH, BLACK JOSEPH	TL	15.00	16.00
91	NURSE PANSY	TL	36.00	36.00
91	PANSY, BLACK ANGEL	6000	46.00	46.00
91	SHELBY, BLACK MARY	TL	30.00	30.00
91	TEACHER ANNIE	CL	30.00	30.00
91	WALDO, DOG W/SHOE	6000	55.00	55.00
91	WEASEL, WHITE KING W/KITTEN	TL	15.00	16.00
		CL	40.00	40.00

S. SCHULTZ

SNOWFLAKE COLLECTION

YR	NAME	LIMIT	ISSUE	TREND
89	BOO MINI SNOWMAN	CL	6.00	10.00
89	FLURRY	CL	12.00	18.00
89	WINTER FROLIC	CL	60.00	72.00
90	AMERICAN SNOW OLD GLORY	RT	24.00	25.00
95	CHILLY/4418	1000	44.00	44.00
95	CHILLY/JINGLES/4417	SO	80.00	80.00
95	FLURRY & BOO/4414	1000	30.00	30.00
95	SNOWY/4416	1000	30.00	30.00
96	CHILLY/SNOWFLAKE/4482	5000	32.00	32.00
96	FILLY/SNOWCRYSTAL/4483	5000	36.00	36.00
96	TOPPER/TABBY/4481	5000	32.00	32.00

S. SCHULTZ

SPARKLING WONDERLAND

YR	NAME	LIMIT	ISSUE	TREND
98	BURLEY B & W	1998	50.00	50.00
98	BURLEY PASTEL	1998	50.00	50.00
98	CLARA NIBBLES	1998	45.00	45.00
98	CLEM NIBBLES	1998	45.00	45.00

S. SCHULTZ

SPIRIT OF AMERICA

YR	NAME	LIMIT	ISSUE	TREND
96	BETSY/4491	2500	40.00	40.00
96	GOD BLESS AMERICA/4497	RT	30.00	30.00
96	GOD BLESS AMERICA/4498	RT	30.00	30.00

To A Special Mum, *with an issue price of $30 in 1990, has increased in value since that time. It is a member of Sam Butcher's Precious Moments collection, produced by Enesco Corp.*

Produced by Creart, Jim Robison's Vigilant Eagle *is part of the Birds of Prey collection.*

Cub E. Bear, *the club piece for Enesco's Cherished Teddies Club's charter year, has increased in value since its 1995 release.*

Produced by ANRI, Sarah Kay's woodcarving I Know, I Know *is from the School Days collection.*

YR	NAME	LIMIT	ISSUE	TREND
96	I'M PROUD BEAR/4495	2500	10.00	10.00
96	PEACHES/4493	RT	26.00	26.00
96	PUG/4494	2500	26.00	26.00
96	ROSS/4492	RT	36.00	36.00
96	USA SANTA/4496	RT	100.00	100.00
S. SCHULTZ		**SPIRIT OF CHRISTMAS COLLECTION**		
87	COLONEL SANTA	CL	30.00	30.00
87	FATHER SNOW	CL	42.00	46.00
87	JINGLE BELLS	CL	20.00	28.00
87	KRIS KRINGLE	CL	100.00	120.00
87	LARGE SANTA W/CANE	CL	27.00	33.00
87	LONG JOURNEY	CL	19.00	36.00
87	MINI SANTA W/CANE	CL	8.00	10.00
87	MRS. CLAUS	CL	26.00	28.00
87	NAUGHTY OR NICE SANTA AT D	CL	100.00	100.00
87	SANTA SITTING	CL	18.00	20.00
87	SANTA W/POCKETS	CL	34.00	34.00
87	SANTA'S WORKSHOP	CL	50.00	90.00
87	SMALL SANTA W/TREE	CL	14.00	17.00
88	BLESSED CHRISTMAS	RT	100.00	100.00
88	CHRISTMAS CLOWN	CL	88.00	88.00
88	CHRISTMAS W/CHILDREN	4000	80.00	80.00
88	COW/OX	CL	16.50	17.00
88	ELF GRABBING HAT	CL	8.00	10.00
88	ELF W/GIFT	CL	8.00	9.00
88	JESUS-NATURAL	CL	11.00	11.00
88	JOSEPH-NATURAL	CL	11.00	11.00
88	LARGE MRS. CLAUS RES. CANDLE	CL	11.00	12.00
88	LARGE SANTA RES. CANDLE	CL	11.00	12.00
88	MARY-NATURAL	CL	12.00	12.00
88	MINI JESUS	CL	4.00	5.00
88	MINI JESUS-NATURAL	CL	4.00	5.00
88	MINI JOSEPH	CL	6.00	6.00
88	MINI JOSEPH-NATURAL	CL	5.00	5.00
88	MINI LONG JOURNEY	CL	11.00	11.00
88	MINI MARY	CL	8.00	8.00
88	MINI MARY-NATURAL	CL	5.00	5.00
88	MINI SANTA RES. CANDLE	CL	7.00	7.00
88	SANTA IN CHIMNEY	CL	110.00	140.00
88	SANTA KNEELING	CL	22.00	22.00
88	SANTA W/ELF	CL	90.00	90.00
88	SHEEP	CL	8.00	8.00
88	SITTING ELF	CL	7.00	15.00
88	SMALL ANGEL RES. CANDLE	CL	9.50	10.00
88	SMALL MRS. CLAUS	CL	8.50	9.00
88	SMALL MRS. CLAUS RES. CANDLE	CL	10.00	10.00
88	SMALL SANTA RES. CANDLE	CL	10.00	10.00
88	SMALL SITTING SANTA	CL	11.00	11.00
89	BLINKEY ELF BALL	CL	16.00	20.00
89	CHRISTMAS JOY	RT	32.00	33.00
89	COLONEL SANTA 2	CL	35.00	36.00
89	FATHER SNOW 2	RT	32.00	40.00
89	JINGLE BELLS 2	RT	25.00	25.00
89	JOLLY 2	RT	17.00	18.00
89	LONG JOURNEY 2	RT	35.00	45.00
89	MAMA SANTA SITTING	CL	30.00	42.00
89	MAMA SANTA STOCKING	CL	50.00	51.00
89	MINI COLONEL SANTA	CL	14.00	20.00
89	MINI FATHER SNOW	CL	16.00	17.00
89	MINI JINGLE BELLS	CL	16.00	17.00
89	MINI JOLLY	CL	10.00	11.00
89	MINI NAUGHTY OR NICE	CL	20.00	21.00
89	MINI ST. NICK	CL	14.00	15.00
89	PAPA SANTA SITTING	CL	30.00	41.00
89	PAPA SANTA STOCKING	CL	50.00	62.00
89	SILENT NIGHT	RT	33.00	45.00
89	ST. NICK 2	CL	43.00	45.00
89	STINKY ELF SITTING	CL	16.00	18.00
89	WINKY ELF LETTER	CL	16.00	21.00
89	WOODLAND SANTA	RT	100.00	140.00
89	YULE TIDINGS 2	RT	23.00	31.00
90	BELLS OF CHRISTMAS	RT	35.00	38.00
90	CHRISTMAS MUSIC	RT	60.00	65.00
90	CHRISTMAS WISHES	RT	50.00	51.00
90	CHRISTMAS WONDER SANTA	RT	50.00	55.00
90	LOVE THE CHILDREN	RT	75.00	78.00
90	SANTA CLAUS EXPRESS	RT	150.00	155.00
91	SHARING LOVE SANTA	RT	120.00	130.00
91	TREASURES OF LOVE SANTA	RT	140.00	145.00
95	AMERICAN SANTA/4467	RT	100.00	100.00
95	CARE BASKET/4424	5000	26.00	26.00
95	CARING/4423	5000	29.00	29.00
95	CHERISH THE CHILDREN/4466	7500	70.00	70.00
95	CHRISTINE/4420	5000	26.00	26.00
95	CHRISTMAS DREAMS/4463	RT	64.00	64.00

YR	NAME	LIMIT	ISSUE	TREND
95	CHRISTMAS JOY/4331	2000	60.00	60.00
95	CHRISTMAS WARM./4421	OP	90.00	90.00
95	COFFEE POT/4422	OP	5.00	5.00
95	COUNTRY TREE/4419	OP	33.00	33.00
95	HAPPINESS/4426	5000	34.00	34.00
95	HELPFULNESS/4425	5000	37.00	37.00
95	JOY TO THE WORLD/4462	1000	64.00	64.00
95	JOYFULNESS/4428	5000	28.00	28.00
95	KINDNESS/4427	5000	30.00	30.00
95	MRS. SANTA/4430	5000	42.00	42.00
95	PEACE ON EARTH/4464	7500	80.00	80.00
95	SANTA'S LOVE/4465	7500	98.00	98.00
95	SANTA/4429	5000	45.00	45.00
95	TILLIE CAROLING/4461	5000	26.00	26.00
95	WILLIE CAROLING/4460	5000	26.00	26.00

S. SCHULTZ SPRINGTIME TREASURES

YR	NAME	LIMIT	ISSUE	TREND
96	AMEN BIBLE/4524	RT	20.00	20.00
96	BUNNY BUN/4510	RT	18.00	18.00
96	BUNNY LOVE/4513	1500	18.00	18.00
96	HERBIE RABBIT/4509	1500	33.00	33.00
96	HETHER RABBIT/4508	1500	33.00	33.00
96	JANGLES RABBIT/4511	RT	24.00	24.00
96	JINGLES RABBIT/4512	RT	24.00	24.00
96	SANTA & FRIENDS/4517	1000	100.00	100.00
96	SPIRITUAL GUID-B 4518	RT	65.00	65.00
96	SPIRITUAL GUID-G 4519	RT	65.00	65.00
96	SPRING TREASURES/4516	1000	100.00	100.00

S. SCHULTZ TATTERED N' TORN COLLECTION

YR	NAME	LIMIT	ISSUE	TREND
90	BLACK MUFFIN & PUFFIN	10000	55.00	55.00
90	BLACK PRISSY & PEANUT	2000	120.00	120.00
90	BOY RAG DOLL OPIE	4000	50.00	50.00
90	GIRL RAG DOLL POLLY	4000	50.00	50.00
90	MUFFIN BLACK RAG DOLL	500	90.00	200.00
90	PUFFIN BLACK RAG DOLL	OP	90.00	200.00
90	WHITE MUFFIN & PUFFIN	10000	55.00	55.00
90	WHITE PRISSY & PEANUT	2000	120.00	120.00

S. SCHULTZ TENDER MOMENTS

YR	NAME	LIMIT	ISSUE	TREND
95	ALL DONE/4395	RT	29.00	29.00
95	BUNDLE OF JOY/4392	3000	20.00	20.00
95	BUNDLE OF LOVE/4393	3000	29.00	29.00
95	FAMILY IS LOVE/4320	RT	60.00	60.00
95	HAVING FUN/4322	RT	44.00	44.00
95	LITTLE ENGINEER/4389	RT	25.00	25.00
95	LULLABY/4390	RT	29.00	29.00
95	ME BIG GIRL/4394	RT	29.00	29.00
95	PRECIOUS DREAMS/4391	RT	28.00	28.00
95	REFRESHMENTS/4326	RT	16.00	16.00
95	REMEMBRANCE/4470	RT	100.00	100.00
95	SQUEAKS/4327	RT	5.00	5.00
95	STUDY TIME/4325	RT	32.00	32.00
95	SWEET DREAMS/4388	3000	29.00	29.00
95	TIME. KNOWL./4323	RT	47.00	47.00
95	TREASURE MOMENTS/4321	RT	70.00	70.00
95	WOW/4324	RT	36.00	36.00
96	BUBBLES/4503	3000	35.00	35.00
96	DINNER TIME/4507	RT	32.00	32.00
96	MIKEY BEAR II/BW/4528	2500	60.00	60.00
96	MIKEY BEARII-VG/4526	2500	60.00	60.00
96	MISSY BEAR II-VG/4525	2500	60.00	60.00
96	MISSY BEAR II/BW/4527	2500	60.00	60.00
96	TA DA/4506	3000	32.00	32.00
96	YACKY JACKIE/4504	RT	32.00	32.00
98	CHERISHED DREAMS	9898	85.00	85.00
98	CHERISHED MOMENTS	9898	85.00	85.00

S. SCHULTZ UNITED HEARTS COLLECTION

YR	NAME	LIMIT	ISSUE	TREND
91	BARNEY THE GREAT BEAR	CL	40.00	50.00
91	BEACH ANNIE & WALDO	CL	40.00	41.00
91	BEACH BUBBA W/INNERTUBE	CL	34.00	40.00
91	BEACH PANSY WITH KITTEN	CL	34.00	40.00
91	BIBI-MISS LIBERTY BEAR	CL	30.00	35.00
91	CHILLY SNOWMAN	CL	33.00	41.00
91	CHRISTMAS ADORA	CL	36.00	42.00
91	CHRISTMAS ENOS	CL	36.00	37.00
91	CHRISTMAS TREE WITH HEARTS	CL	40.00	40.00
91	CLOWN BIBI & BIFF BEARS	CL	35.00	40.00
91	EMILY W/BUGGY	CL	53.00	58.00
91	GIDEON WITH BEAR & ROSE	CL	40.00	42.00
91	HEWITT W/LEPRECHAUN	CL	56.00	65.00
91	JACK BOY GRADUATION	CL	40.00	41.00
91	LIBERTY PAPA BARNEY & BIFF	CL	64.00	75.00
91	NOAH W/POT OF GOLD	CL	36.00	45.00
91	SALLY BOOBA GRADUATION	RT	45.00	48.00
91	SCHOOL CHUCKLES RABBIT	CL	26.00	27.00
91	SCHOOL COOKIE RABBIT W/KIT	CL	28.00	29.00
91	SCHOOL CRUMB RABBIT-DUNCE	CL	32.00	40.00

YR	NAME	LIMIT	ISSUE	TREND
91	SCHOOL DESK WITH BOOK	TL	15.00	16.00
91	SHELBY W/SHAMROCK	CL	36.00	40.00
91	THANKSGIVING CORNSTALK	TL	30.00	30.00
91	THANKSGIVING CUPCAKE	CL	36.00	37.00
91	THANKSGIVING TWINKIE	CL	32.00	33.00
91	TILLIE WITH SKATES	CL	32.00	38.00
91	TOBY & TESSIE W/WHEELBARROW	CL	44.00	45.00
91	VALENTINE PEANUT W/CANDY	CL	32.00	33.00
91	VALENTINE PRISSY WITH DOG	CL	36.00	37.00
91	WILLIE ON SLED	CL	32.00	41.00
91	WOOLY LAMB	CL	16.00	16.00
92	SPARKY DOG GRADUATION	TL	16.00	16.00
92	TABITHA RABBIT W/BUNNY	TL	32.00	33.00

SCHMID
L. DAVIS

				CAT TALES
82	COMPANY'S COMING	RT	60.00	250.00
82	FLEW THE COOP	RT	60.00	350.00
82	ON THE MOVE	RT	70.00	600.00
82	RIGHT CHURCH, WRONG PEW	RT	70.00	350.00

L. DAVIS

				CHRISTMAS FIGURINES
83	HOOKER AT MAILBOX W/PRESENTS	CL	80.00	750.00
84	COUNTRY CHRISTMAS	CL	80.00	450.00
84	KITTENS WITH PRESENTS	2500	80.00	465.00
85	CHRISTMAS AT FOXFIRE FARM	CL	80.00	260.00
86	CHRISTMAS AT RED OAK	CL	80.00	200.00
87	BLOSSOM'S GIFT	CL	150.00	300.00
88	CUTTING THE FAMILY CHRISTMAS TREE	CL	80.00	325.00
89	PETER AND THE WREN	2250	165.00	375.00
90	WINTERING DEER	CL	165.00	275.00
91	CHRISTMAS AT RED OAK II	CL	250.00	250.00
92	BORN ON A STARRY NIGHT	2500	225.00	225.00
94	VISIONS OF SUGAR PLUMS	2500	250.00	250.00
95	BAH HUMBUG	2500	200.00	200.00

L. DAVIS

				COUNTRY PRIDE
81	BUSTIN' WITH PRIDE	RT	100.00	240.00
81	DUKE'S MIXTURE	RT	100.00	225.00
81	PLUM TUCKERED OUT	RT	100.00	950.00
81	SURPRISE IN THE CELLAR	RT	100.00	965.00

L. DAVIS

				DEALER COUNTER SIGNS
80	RFD AMERICA	CL	40.00	225.00
81	UNCLE REMUS	CL	30.00	300.00
85	FOX FIRE FARM	CL	30.00	250.00
90	MR. LOWELL'S FARM	OP	50.00	60.00
92	LITTLE CRITTERS	OP	50.00	50.00

D. POLLAND

				DON POLLAND FIGURINES I
83	A SECOND CHANCE	RT	350.00	650.00
83	CHALLENGE	RT	275.00	600.00
83	DANGEROUS MOMENT	RT	250.00	350.00
83	DOWNED	RT	250.00	600.00
83	ESCAPE	RT	175.00	650.00
83	FIGHTING BULLS	RT	200.00	600.00
83	GREAT HUNT, THE	RT	3,750.00	3775.00
83	HOT PURSUIT	RT	225.00	550.00
83	HUNTER, THE	RT	225.00	500.00
83	YOUNG BULL	RT	125.00	250.00
86	DOWN FROM THE HIGH COUNTRY	RT	225.00	300.00
86	EAGLE DANCER	RT	170.00	300.00
86	PLAINS WARRIOR	RT	350.00	550.00
86	RUNNING WOLF-WAR CHIEF	RT	170.00	300.00
86	SECOND CHANCE	RT	125.00	650.00
86	SHOOTING THE RAPIDS	RT	195.00	500.00
86	WAR TROPHY	RT	225.00	500.00

L. DAVIS

				FARM CLUB
85	BRIDE, THE	RT	45.00	450.00
86	THIRSTY?	YR	*	85.00
87	CACKLE BERRIES	RT		N/A
87	PARTY'S OVER, THE	RT	50.00	145.00
88	CHOW TIME	RT	55.00	95.00
88	ICE CREAM CHURN	RT	*	50.00
89	CAN'T WAIT	RT	75.00	125.00
90	NOT A SHARING SOUL	RT	*	40.00
90	PIT STOP	RT	75.00	140.00
91	ARRIVAL OF STANLEY	RT	100.00	90.00
91	DON'T PICK THE FLOWERS	RT	100.00	145.00
91	NEW ARRIVAL	RT	*	40.00
92	CHECK'S IN THE MAIL	RT	100.00	100.00
92	GARDEN TOAD	RT	*	N/A
92	HOG WILD	RT	100.00	100.00
93	LUKE 12:6	RT	*	N/A
93	SUMMER DAYS	YR	100.00	100.00
93	SURVIVOR, THE	RT	70.00	75.00
94	DUTCH TREAT	YR	100.00	100.00
95	FREE KITTENS	YR	40.00	40.00

YR	NAME	LIMIT	ISSUE	TREND
L. DAVIS				**FARM SET**
85	BARN	RT	48.00	400.00
85	CHICKEN HOUSE	RT	19.00	50.00
85	CORN CRIB AND SHEEP PEN	RT	25.00	75.00
85	GARDEN AND WOOD SHED	RT	25.00	60.00
85	GOAT YARD AND STUDIO	RT	33.00	80.00
85	HEN HOUSE	RT	33.00	80.00
85	HOG HOUSE	RT	28.00	80.00
85	MAIN HOUSE	RT	43.00	105.00
85	PRIVY	OP	12.50	40.00
85	REMUS' CABIN	RT	43.00	100.00
85	SMOKE HOUSE	RT	12.50	70.00
85	WINDMILL	RT	25.00	45.00
L. DAVIS				**FRIENDS OF MINE**
89	SUN WORSHIPPERS	RT	120.00	140.00
89	SUN WORSHIPPERS MINI	RT	33.00	40.00
90	SUNDAY AFTERNOON TREAT MINI	CL	33.00	40.00
91	WARM MILK	RT	120.00	200.00
91	WARM MILK MINI	RT	33.00	40.00
92	CAT AND JENNY WREN	5000	170.00	200.00
92	CAT AND JENNY WREN MINI	CL	35.00	35.00
92	SUNDAY AFTERNOON TREAT	5000	120.00	185.00
L. DAVIS				**LITTLE CRITTERS**
89	GITTIN' A NIBBLE	CL	50.00	60.00
90	GREAT AMERICAN CHICKEN RACE	2500	225.00	270.00
90	HOME SQUEEZINS	CL	90.00	90.00
90	OUTING WITH GRANDPA	RT	200.00	250.00
90	PRIVATE TIME	CL	18.00	45.00
90	PUNKIN' PIG	RT	250.00	325.00
91	HITTIN THE SACK	CL	70.00	70.00
91	ITISKIT, ITASKET	CL	45.00	45.00
91	MILK MOUSE	2500	175.00	230.00
91	PUNKIN' WINE	CL	100.00	145.00
91	TOAD STRANGLER	CL	57.00	60.00
91	WHEN COFFEE NEVER TASTED SO GOOD	1250	800.00	800.00
92	CHARIVARI	950	250.00	250.00
92	CHRISTOPHER CRITTER	RT	150.00	150.00
92	DOUBLE YOLKER	YR	70.00	70.00
92	MISS PRIVATE TIME	YR	35.00	35.00
92	WOLF IN SHEEP'S CLOTHING, A	YR	110.00	110.00
L. DAVIS				**PROMOTIONAL FIGURINE**
91	LEAVING THE RAT RACE	RT	80.00	225.00
92	HEN SCRATCH	RT	90.00	100.00
93	LEAPIN' LIZARD	RT	80.00	80.00
94	DON'T FORGET ME	RT	70.00	70.00
95	NASTY STUFF	OP	40.00	40.00
L. DAVIS				**QUILTIN' BEE**
92	BIG LIKE DADDY	OP	80.00	80.00
92	BIRDS OF A FEATHER	OP	80.00	80.00
92	CORN FLABIN	OP	80.00	80.00
92	LUNCH BREAK	OP	80.00	80.00
92	WHAT'S FOR DESSERT	OP	80.00	80.00
L. DAVIS				**RFD AMERICA**
79	BLOSSOM	RT	180.00	1700.00
79	BROKEN DREAMS	RT	165.00	1200.00
79	COUNTRY ROAD	RT	100.00	875.00
79	FOWL PLAY	RT	100.00	300.00
79	IGNORANCE IS BLISS	RT	165.00	1250.00
79	SLIM PICKINS	RT	165.00	650.00
80	CREEK BANK BANDIT	RT	38.00	385.00
80	FORBIDDEN FRUIT	RT	25.00	160.00
80	GOOD, CLEAN FUN	RT	40.00	105.00
80	ITCHING POST	RT	30.00	100.00
80	MILKING TIME	RT	20.00	250.00
80	NEW DAY	RT	20.00	175.00
80	STRAWBERRY PATCH	RT	25.00	100.00
80	SUNDAY AFTERNOON	RT	23.00	235.00
80	WILBUR	RT	110.00	600.00
81	COUNTRY BOY	RT	38.00	325.00
81	DOUBLE TROUBLE	RT	35.00	500.00
81	DRY AS A BONE	RT	45.00	300.00
81	HIGHTAILING IT	RT	50.00	425.00
81	PUNKIN' SEEDS	RT	225.00	1600.00
81	ROOTED OUT	RT	45.00	100.00
81	SCALLAWAGS	RT	65.00	165.00
81	SPLIT DECISION	RT	45.00	255.00
81	STUDIO MOUSE	RT	60.00	325.00
81	UNDER THE WEATHER	RT	25.00	90.00
81	UP TO NO GOOD	RT	200.00	890.00
82	BABY BLOSSOM	RT	40.00	300.00
82	BABY BOBS	RT	48.00	225.00
82	BLOSSOM & CALF	RT	250.00	900.00
82	BRAND NEW DAY	RT	24.00	160.00
82	COUNTRY CROOK	RT	38.00	375.00
82	IDLE HOURS	RT	38.00	275.00

YR	NAME	LIMIT	ISSUE	TREND
82	MOON RAIDERS	RT	190.00	300.00
82	MOVING DAY	RT	44.00	300.00
82	SHOE TO FILL, A	RT	38.00	175.00
82	STRAY DOG	RT	35.00	70.00
82	THINKING BIG	RT	35.00	90.00
82	TREED	RT	155.00	300.00
82	TWO'S COMPANY	RT	44.00	225.00
82	WAITING FOR HIS MASTER	RT	50.00	225.00
82	WHEN MAMA GETS MAD	RT	38.00	340.00
83	CITY SLICKER	RT	150.00	275.00
83	COUNTING THE DAYS	RT	40.00	65.00
83	FAIR WEATHER FRIEND	RT	25.00	80.00
83	FALSE ALARM	RT	65.00	170.00
83	HAPPY HUNTING GROUND	RT	160.00	240.00
83	HI GIRLS, THE NAME'S BIG JACK	RT	200.00	380.00
83	HIS EYES ARE BIGGER THAN HIS STOMACH	RT	235.00	350.00
83	LICKIN' GOOD	RT	35.00	250.00
83	MAKIN' TRACKS	RT	70.00	115.00
83	MAMA'S PRIZE LEGHORN	RT	55.00	120.00
83	STIRRING UP TROUBLE	RT	160.00	245.00
83	WOMEN'S WORK	RT	35.00	85.00
84	ANYBODY HOME	RT	35.00	125.00
84	CATNAPPING TOO	RT	70.00	140.00
84	COUNTRY KITTY	RT	52.00	120.00
84	COURTIN'	RT	45.00	125.00
84	GONNA PAY FOR HIS SINS	RT	28.00	50.00
84	GOSSIPS	RT	110.00	225.00
84	HEADED HOME	RT	25.00	53.00
84	HIS MASTER'S DOG	RT	45.00	150.00
84	HUH?	RT	40.00	125.00
84	MAD AS A WET HEN	RT	185.00	750.00
84	ONE FOR THE ROAD	RT	38.00	65.00
84	PASTURE PALS	RT	52.00	125.00
84	PRAIRIE CHORUS	RT	135.00	1200.00
85	BARN CATS	RT	40.00	75.00
85	COUNTRY COUSINS	RT	43.00	75.00
85	COUNTRY CROONER	OP	25.00	50.00
85	DON'T PLAY WITH YOUR FOOD	RT	29.00	105.00
85	FURS GONNA FLY	1500	145.00	250.00
85	HOG HEAVEN	RT	165.00	350.00
85	LOVE AT FIRST SIGHT	RT	70.00	120.00
85	OUT-OF-STEP	RT	45.00	95.00
85	OZARK BELLE	RT	35.00	75.00
85	RENOIR	RT	45.00	75.00
85	TOO GOOD TO WASTE ON KIDS	RT	70.00	125.00
85	WILL YOU STILL RESPECT ME IN THE MORNING	RT	35.00	80.00
86	BIT OFF MORE THAN HE COULD CHEW	RT	40.00	60.00
86	COMFY?	OP	40.00	75.00
86	FEELIN' HIS OATS	1500	150.00	250.00
86	MAMA?	RT	15.00	48.00
87	BOTTOMS UP	RT	80.00	100.00
87	CHICKEN THIEF	RT	200.00	360.00
87	EASY PICKINS	RT	45.00	85.00
87	GLUTTON FOR PUNISHMENT	RT	95.00	155.00
87	MAIL ORDER BRIDE	RT	150.00	225.00
87	ORPHANS, THE	RT	50.00	90.00
87	TWO IN THE BUSH	RT	150.00	325.00
87	WHEN THE CAT'S AWAY	RT	40.00	60.00
88	BROTHERS	RT	55.00	85.00
88	FLEAS	OP	20.00	25.00
88	GOLDIE AND HER PEEPS	RT	25.00	35.00
88	HAPPY HOUR	RT	58.00	90.00
88	IN A PICKLE	RT	40.00	50.00
88	MAKING A BEE LINE	RT	75.00	130.00
88	MISSOURI SPRING	RT	115.00	185.00
88	NO PRIVATE TIME	RT	200.00	350.00
88	PERFECT TEN	RT	95.00	175.00
88	SAWIN' LOGS	RT	85.00	100.00
88	WHEN THREE FOOT'S A MILE	RT	230.00	270.00
88	WINTER LAMB	RT	200.00	260.00
88	WISHFUL THINKING	RT	55.00	75.00
89	BOY'S NIGHT OUT, THE	1500	190.00	225.00
89	COON CAPERS	RT	68.00	85.00
89	FAMILY OUTING	RT	45.00	65.00
89	LEFTOVERS	RT	90.00	95.00
89	MEETING OF SHELDON	RT	120.00	150.00
89	MOTHER HEN	RT	38.00	55.00
89	NEW FRIEND	RT	45.00	65.00
89	SUN WORSHIPPERS MINI FIGURINE	OP	33.00	43.00
89	TRIBUTE TO HOOKER, A	RT	180.00	250.00
89	WOODSCOLT	RT	300.00	375.00
90	CORN CRIB MOUSE	RT	35.00	40.00
90	DEALER COUNTER SIGN	OP	50.00	70.00
90	FINDERS KEEPERS	OP	40.00	50.00
90	FOREPLAY	RT	60.00	75.00

YR	NAME	LIMIT	ISSUE	TREND
90	HANKY PANKY	RT	65.00	100.00
90	LAST STRAW, THE	RT	125.00	175.00
90	LITTLE BLACK LAMB (BABA)	RT	30.00	40.00
90	LONG DAYS, COLD NIGHTS	RT	175.00	200.00
90	PIGGIN' OUT	RT	190.00	245.00
90	PRIVATE TIME	OP	18.00	18.00
90	SEEIN' RED	RT	35.00	50.00
90	TRICKS OF THE TRADE	RT	300.00	330.00
91	COCK OF THE WALK	2500	300.00	300.00
91	FIRST OFFENSE	RT	70.00	75.00
91	GUN SHY	RT	70.00	70.00
91	HEADING FOR THE PERSIMMON GROVE	RT	80.00	80.00
91	KISSIN COUSINS	RT	80.00	80.00
91	LONG HOT SUMMER	1950	250.00	250.00
91	SOOIEEE	1500	350.00	350.00
91	WASHED ASHORE	RT	70.00	70.00
92	DON'T PLAY WITH FIRE	RT	120.00	120.00
92	FREE LUNCH	RT	85.00	85.00
92	GRASS IS ALWAYS GREENER, THE	RT	195.00	195.00
92	HEADED SOUTH	RT	45.00	45.00
92	HONEYMOON'S OVER, THE	1950	300.00	300.00
92	LOWELL DAVIS PROFILE	OP	65.00	65.00
92	MY FAVORITE CHORES	1500	750.00	750.00
92	OH SHEEEIT...	RT	120.00	120.00
92	OZARK'S VITTLES	RT	60.00	60.00
92	SAFE HAVEN	RT	95.00	95.00
92	SCHOOL YARD DOGS	RT	100.00	100.00
92	SHE LAY LOW	RT	120.00	120.00
92	SNAKE DOCTOR	RT	70.00	70.00
93	BE MY VALENTINE	RT	35.00	35.00
93	DON'T OPEN TILL CHRISTMAS	RT	35.00	35.00
93	DRY HOLE	RT	30.00	30.00
93	FREELOADERS, THE	1250	230.00	230.00
93	HAPPY BIRTHDAY MY SWEET	RT	35.00	35.00
93	I'M THANKFUL FOR YOU	RT	35.00	35.00
93	IF YOU CAN'T BEAT 'EM JOIN 'EM	1750	250.00	250.00
93	KING OF THE MOUNTAIN	750	500.00	500.00
93	NO HUNTING	1000	95.00	95.00
93	OH WHERE IS HE NOW?	1250	250.00	250.00
93	PEEP SHOW	RT	35.00	35.00
93	POLLYWOGS	750	650.00	650.00
93	SHEEP SHEARIN' TIME	1200	500.00	500.00
93	SWEET TOOTH	RT	60.00	60.00
93	TRICK OR TREAT	RT	35.00	35.00
93	WAITING FOR MR. LOWELL	2500	250.00	250.00
93	YOU'RE A BASKET OF FUN	OP	35.00	165.00
94	AND DOWN THE HATCH- COMP PC	6 MO	135.00	135.00
94	ATTIC ANTICS	RT	100.00	100.00
94	FIRST OUTING	OP	65.00	65.00
94	HELPIN' HIMSELF	RT	65.00	65.00
94	HITTIN' THE TRAIL	1250	250.00	250.00
94	MAMA CAN WILLIE STAY FOR SUPPER?	1250	200.00	200.00
94	NOT A HAPPY CAMPER	RT	75.00	75.00
94	OH MOTHER WHAT IS IT?	1000	250.00	250.00
94	OPEN THE LID	6 MO	135.00	135.00
94	PECKING ORDER	RT	200.00	200.00
94	QU'EST-CEQUE C'EST?	RT	200.00	200.00
94	TWO TIMER	RT	95.00	95.00
94	WARMIN' THEIR BUNS	1250	270.00	270.00
95	BLOSSOM'S BEST	750	300.00	300.00
95	CUSSIN' UP A STORM	RT	45.00	45.00
95	STICKS & STONES	RT	30.00	30.00
95	UNINVITED CALLER	RT	35.00	35.00

L. DAVIS — ROUTE 66

YR	NAME	LIMIT	ISSUE	TREND
91	JUST CHECK THE AIR	RT	700.00	1450.00
91	JUST CHECK THE AIR	2500	550.00	550.00
91	LITTLE BIT OF SHADE	RT	100.00	100.00
91	NEL'S DINER	RT	700.00	1550.00
91	NEL'S DINER	2500	550.00	550.00
92	FRESH SQUEEZED	2500	450.00	425.00
92	FRESH SQUEEZED- W/ WOOD BASE	350	600.00	700.00
92	GOING TO GRANDMA	RT	80.00	80.00
92	QUIET DAY AT MAPLE GROVE	RT	130.00	130.00
92	RELIEF	RT	80.00	80.00
92	WELCOME MAT- W/ WOOD BASE	1500	400.00	400.00
92	WHAT ARE PALS FOR?	RT	100.00	100.00
93	HOME FOR CHRISTMAS	RT	80.00	150.00
93	KICKIN' HIMSELF	RT	80.00	125.00
93	SUMMER DAYS	YR	100.00	100.00

L. DAVIS — SPECIAL EDITION FIGURINES

YR	NAME	LIMIT	ISSUE	TREND
83	CRITICS, THE	RT	400.00	1100.00
85	HOME FROM MARKET	RT	400.00	1400.00
89	FROM A FRIEND TO A FRIEND	1200	750.00	1650.00
90	WHAT RAT RACE?	1200	800.00	1000.00
92	LAST LAFF	1200	900.00	975.00

YR	NAME	LIMIT	ISSUE	TREND
L. DAVIS				**UNCLE REMUS**
81	BRER BEAR	RT	80.00	1050.00
81	BRER COYOTE	RT	80.00	500.00
81	BRER FOX	RT	70.00	900.00
81	BRER RABBIT	RT	85.00	1900.00
81	BRER WEASEL	RT	80.00	675.00
81	BRER WOLF	RT	85.00	595.00

SCULPTURE BY SHALAH

YR	NAME	LIMIT	ISSUE	TREND
S. PERKINS				**BRONZE**
93	FARMER, THE	20	*	1800.00
93	MISS DOLLIE	20	*	1500.00
94	CALL OF THE LAND	20	*	1800.00
94	CELEBRATION OF A COWGIRL	10	*	9000.00
94	NEIGHBOR	20	*	1050.00
94	REMEMBERING	20	*	950.00
S. PERKINS				**BRONZE FOUNTAIN**
94	JOY IN THE MORNING	13	*	5500.00
95	WISHFUL THINKING	20	*	7500.00

SEBASTIAN STUDIOS

YR	NAME	LIMIT	ISSUE	TREND
P.W. BASTON				**LARGE CERAMASTONE FIGURES**
*	SANTA FE...ALL THE WAY	CL	*	800.00
*	ST. FRANCIS PLAQUE	CL	*	800.00
39	PAUL REVERE PLAQUE	CL	*	425.00
40	BASKET	CL	*	350.00
40	BRETON MAN	CL	*	800.00
40	BRETON WOMAN	CL	*	800.00
40	CANDLE HOLDER	CL	*	350.00
40	CAROLER	CL	*	350.00
40	HORN OF PLENTY	CL	*	350.00
40	JESUS	CL	*	350.00
40	LAMB	CL	*	350.00
40	MARY	CL	*	350.00
47	LARGE VICTORIAN COUPLE	CL	*	800.00
48	WOODY AT THREE	CL	*	800.00
56	JELL-O COW MILK PITCHER	CL	*	800.00
58	SWIFT INSTRUMENT GIRL	CL	*	200.00
59	WASP PLAQUE	CL	*	600.00
63	ABRAHAM LINCOLN TOBY JUG	CL	*	600.00
63	ANNE BOLEYN	CL	*	800.00
63	DAVID COPPERFIELD	CL	*	800.00
63	DORA	CL	*	800.00
63	GEORGE WASHINGTON TOBY JUG	CL	*	800.00
63	HENRY VIII	CL	*	800.00
63	JOHN F. KENNEDY TOBY JUG	CL	*	800.00
63	MENDING TIME	CL	*	800.00
63	TOM SAWYER	CL	*	800.00
64	COLONIAL BOY	CL	*	800.00
64	COLONIAL GIRL	CL	*	800.00
64	COLONIAL MAN	CL	*	800.00
64	COLONIAL WOMAN	CL	*	800.00
64	IBM FATHER	CL	*	800.00
64	IBM MOTHER	CL	*	800.00
64	IBM PHOTOGRAPHER	CL	*	800.00
64	IBM SON	CL	*	800.00
64	IBM WOMAN	CL	*	800.00
65	DENTIST, THE	CL	*	800.00
65	N.E. HOME FOR LITTLE WANDERERS	CL	*	800.00
65	STANLEY MUSIC BOX	CL	*	400.00
66	GUITARIST	CL	*	800.00
67	INFANT OF PRAGUE	CL	*	800.00
73	BLACKSMITH	CL	*	350.00
73	CABINETMAKER	CL	*	350.00
73	CLOCKMAKER	CL	*	800.00
73	POTTER	CL	*	350.00
75	MINUTEMAN	CL	*	800.00
78	MT. RUSHMORE	CL	*	425.00
P.W. BASTON				**SEBASTIAN MINIATURES**
*	BABE RUTH	CL	*	800.00
*	BOB HOPE	CL	*	800.00
*	CORONATION CROWN	CL	*	800.00
*	EAGLE PLAQUE	CL	*	1500.00
*	KING, THE	CL	*	800.00
*	ORTHO GYNECIC	CL	*	800.00
*	SYLVANIA ELECTRIC-BULB DISPLAY	CL	*	800.00
38	SHAKER LADY	CL	*	100.00
38	SHAKER MAN	CL	*	100.00
39	BENJAMIN FRANKLIN	CL	*	100.00
39	CORONADO	CL	*	100.00
39	CORONADO'S SENORA	CL	*	100.00
39	DEBORAH FRANKLIN	CL	*	100.00
39	EVANGELINE	CL	*	125.00
39	GABRIEL	CL	*	125.00
39	GEORGE WASHINGTON	CL	*	55.00

YR	NAME	LIMIT	ISSUE	TREND
39	INDIAN MAIDEN	CL	*	125.00
39	INDIAN WARRIOR	CL	*	125.00
39	JOHN ALDEN	CL	*	45.00
39	MARGARET HOUSTON	CL	*	100.00
39	MARTHA WASHINGTON	CL	*	55.00
39	PRISCILLA	CL	*	45.00
39	SAM HOUSTON	CL	*	100.00
39	WILLIAMSBURG GOVERNOR	CL	*	100.00
39	WILLIAMSBURG LADY	CL	*	100.00
40	ANN STVYVESANT	CL	*	100.00
40	ANNIE OAKLEY	CL	*	100.00
40	BUFFALO BILL	CL	*	100.00
40	CATHERINE LAFITTE	CL	*	100.00
40	DAN'L BOONE	CL	*	100.00
40	ELIZABETH MONROE	CL	*	165.00
40	HANNAH PENN	CL	*	125.00
40	JAMES MONROE	CL	*	165.00
40	JEAN LAFITTE	CL	*	100.00
40	JOHN HARVARD	CL	*	135.00
40	JOHN SMITH	CL	*	135.00
40	MRS. DAN'L BOONE	CL	*	100.00
40	MRS. HARVARD	CL	*	135.00
40	PETER STVYVESANT	CL	*	100.00
40	POCAHONTAS	CL	*	135.00
40	WILLIAM PENN	CL	*	125.00
41	DOVES	CL	*	800.00
41	DUCKLINGS	CL	*	800.00
41	KITTEN (SITTING)	CL	*	800.00
41	KITTEN (SLEEPING)	CL	*	800.00
41	PEACOCK	CL	*	800.00
41	PHEASANT	CL	*	800.00
41	ROOSTER	CL	*	800.00
41	SECRETS	CL	*	800.00
41	SWAN	CL	*	800.00
42	ACCORDION	CL	*	350.00
42	CYMBALS	CL	*	350.00
42	DRUM	CL	*	350.00
42	HORN	CL	*	350.00
42	MAJORETTE	CL	*	350.00
42	TUBA	CL	*	350.00
46	PURITAN SPINNER	CL	*	800.00
46	SATCHEL-EYE DYER	CL	*	135.00
47	DAHL'S FISHERMAN	CL	*	165.00
47	DILEMMA	CL	*	300.00
47	DOWN EAST	CL	*	135.00
47	FIRST COOKBOOK AUTHOR	CL	*	135.00
47	FISHER PAIR PS	CL	*	800.00
47	HOWARD JOHNSON PIEMAN	CL	*	425.00
47	MR. BEACON HILL	CL	*	125.00
47	MRS. BEACON HILL	CL	*	125.00
47	PRINCE PHILIP	CL	*	250.00
47	PRINCESS ELIZABETH	CL	*	250.00
47	TOLLHOUSE TOWN CRIER	CL	*	150.00
48	A HARVEY GIRL	CL	*	275.00
48	DEMOCRATIC VICTORY	CL	*	425.00
48	JORDAN MARSH OBSERVER	CL	*	165.00
48	MARY LYON	CL	*	275.00
48	MR. RITTENHOUSE SQUARE	CL	*	165.00
48	MR. SHERATON	CL	*	375.00
48	MRS. RITTENHOUSE SQUARE	CL	*	165.00
48	NATHANIEL HAWTHORNE	CL	*	185.00
48	REPUBLICAN VICTORY	CL	*	800.00
48	SITZMARK	CL	*	185.00
48	SLALOM	CL	*	185.00
48	SWEDISH BOY	CL	*	400.00
48	SWEDISH GIRL	CL	*	400.00
49	BOY SCOUT PLAQUE	CL	*	325.00
49	DUTCHMAN'S PIPE	CL	*	200.00
49	EMMETT KELLY	CL	*	275.00
49	EUSTACE TILLY	CL	*	1250.00
49	GATHERING TULIPS	CL	*	250.00
49	GIANT ROYAL BENGAL TIGER	CL	*	1500.00
49	MARK TWAIN HOME IN HANNIBAL, MO, THE	CL	*	800.00
49	MENOTOMY INDIAN	CL	*	220.00
49	PATRICK HENRY	CL	*	125.00
49	PAUL BUNYAN	CL	*	250.00
49	SARAH HENRY	CL	*	125.00
49	THINKER, THE	CL	*	220.00
49	UNCLE MISTLETOE	CL	*	250.00
50	MR. OBOCELL	CL	*	100.00
50	NATIONAL DIAPER SERVICE	CL	*	275.00
50	PHOEBE, HOUSE OF 7 GABLES	CL	*	165.00
51	CARL MOORE (WEEI)	CL	*	250.00
51	CAROLINE CABOT (WEEI)	CL	*	275.00
51	CHARLES ASHLEY (WEEI)	CL	*	275.00

YR	NAME	LIMIT	ISSUE	TREND
51	CHIEF PONTIAC	CL	*	550.00
51	CHIQUITA BANANA	CL	*	375.00
51	CHRISTOPHER COLUMBUS	CL	*	275.00
51	E.B. RIDEOUT (WEEI)	CL	*	275.00
51	GREAT STONE FACE	CL	*	800.00
51	IRON MASTER'S HOUSE, THE	CL	*	425.00
51	JESSE BUFFMAN (WEEI)	CL	*	275.00
51	JORDON MARSH/RIDES THE A.W. HORSE	CL	*	325.00
51	JUDGE PYNCHEON	CL	*	200.00
51	MIT SEAL	CL	*	400.00
51	MOTHER PARKER (WEEI)	CL	*	275.00
51	OBSERVER & DAME NEW ENGLAND, THE	CL	*	350.00
51	PRISCILLA FORTESUE (WEEI)	CL	*	275.00
51	SEB. DEALER PLAQUE (MARBLEHEAD)	CL	*	325.00
51	SIR FRANCES DRAKE	CL	*	275.00
52	AERIAL TRAMWAY	CL	*	450.00
52	BABY (JELL-O)	CL	*	575.00
52	FAT MAN, THE (JELL-O)	CL	*	575.00
52	FAVORED SCHOLAR	CL	*	250.00
52	FIRST HOUSE, THE - PLYMOUTH PLANTATION	CL	*	175.00
52	LOST IN THE KITCHEN (JELL-O)	CL	*	475.00
52	MARBLEHEAD HIGH SCHOOL PLAQUE	CL	*	250.00
52	NEIGHBORING PEWS	CL	*	250.00
52	OLD POWDER HOUSE	CL	*	275.00
52	OUR LADY OF GOOD VOYAGE	CL	*	225.00
52	SCOTTISH GIRL (JELL-O)	CL	*	375.00
52	ST. JOAN D'ARC	CL	*	325.00
52	ST. SEBASTIAN	CL	*	325.00
52	STORK (JELL-O)	CL	*	475.00
52	TABASCO SAUCE	CL	*	425.00
52	WEIGHING THE BABY	CL	*	250.00
53	BLESSED JULIE BILLART	CL	*	425.00
53	BOY JESUS IN THE TEMPLE	CL	*	375.00
53	DARNED WELL HE CAN	CL	*	325.00
53	HOLGRAVE THE DAGUERROTYPIST	CL	*	225.00
53	LION (JELL-O)	CL	*	375.00
53	OLD PUT ENJOYS A LICKING	CL	*	325.00
53	R.H. STEARNS CHESTNUT HILL MALL	CL	*	250.00
53	SCHOOLBOY OF 1850, THE	CL	*	375.00
53	ST. TERESA OF LISIEUX	CL	*	250.00
54	BLUEBIRD GIRL	CL	*	425.00
54	CAMPFIRE GIRL	CL	*	425.00
54	DACHSHUND (AUDIOVOX)	CL	*	325.00
54	HORIZON GIRL	CL	*	425.00
54	KERNEL-FRESH ASHTRAY	CL	*	425.00
54	MOOSE (JELL-O)	CL	*	375.00
54	OUR LADY OF LALECHE	CL	*	325.00
54	RABBIT (JELL-O)	CL	*	375.00
54	RESOLUTE INS. CO. CLIPPER PS	CL	*	325.00
54	SCUBA DIVER	CL	*	425.00
54	ST. PIUS X	CL	*	440.00
54	STIMALOSE (MEN)	CL	*	800.00
54	STIMALOSE (WOMAN)	CL	*	185.00
54	SWAN BOAT BROOCH-EMPTY SEATS	CL	*	800.00
54	SWAN BOAT BROOCH-FULL SEATS	CL	*	800.00
54	WHALE (JELL-O)	CL	*	375.00
54	WILLIAM PENN	CL	*	200.00
55	CAPTAIN DOLIBER	CL	*	325.00
55	DAVY CROCKETT	CL	*	250.00
55	GIRAFFE (JELL-O)	CL	*	375.00
55	HORSE HEAD PS	CL	*	375.00
55	OLD WOMAN IN THE SHOE (JELL-O)	CL	*	550.00
55	SANTA (JELL-O)	CL	*	550.00
55	SECOND BANK-STATE ST. TRUST PS	CL	*	325.00
56	77TH BENGAL LANCER (JELL-O)	CL	*	800.00
56	ALIKE, BUT OH SO DIFFERENT	CL	*	325.00
56	ARTHRITIC HANDS (J&J)	CL	*	800.00
56	EASTERN PAPER PLAQUE	CL	*	375.00
56	ELSIE THE COW BILLBOARD	CL	*	800.00
56	GIRL ON DIVING BOARD	CL	*	425.00
56	GREEN GIANT, THE	CL	*	425.00
56	MICHIGAN MILLERS PS	CL	*	240.00
56	MRS. OBOCELL	CL	*	425.00
56	NYU GRAD SCHOOL OF BUS. ADMIN. BLDG.	CL	*	325.00
56	PERMACEL TOWER OF TAPE ASHTRAY	CL	*	800.00
56	PRAYING HANDS	CL	*	275.00
56	RARICAL BLACKSMITH	CL	*	400.00
56	ROBIN HOOD & FRIAR TUCK	CL	*	425.00
56	ROBIN HOOD & LITTLE JOHN	CL	*	425.00
56	TEXCEL TAPE BOY	CL	*	400.00
56	THREE LITTLE KITTENS (JELL-O)	CL	*	400.00
57	ALONG THE ALBANY ROAD PS	CL	*	800.00
57	BORDEN'S CENTENNIAL (ELSIE THE COW)	CL	*	800.00
57	COLONIAL FUND DOORWAY PS	CL	*	800.00
57	IBM 305 RAMAC	CL	*	425.00

YR	NAME	LIMIT	ISSUE	TREND
57	JAMESTOWN CHURCH	CL	*	425.00
57	JAMESTOWN SHIPS	CL	*	400.00
57	MAYFLOWER PS	CL	*	325.00
57	NABISCO BUFFALO BEE	CL	*	800.00
57	NABISCO SPOONMAN	CL	*	800.00
57	OLDE JAMES FORT	CL	*	275.00
57	SPEEDY ALKA SELTZER	CL	*	800.00
58	CBS MISS COLUMBIA PS	CL	*	800.00
58	CLIQUOT CLUB ESKIMO PS	CL	*	1600.00
58	COMMODORE STEPHEN DECATUR	CL	*	150.00
58	CONNECTICUT BANK & TRUST	CL	*	250.00
58	HANNAH DUSTON PS	CL	*	285.00
58	HARVARD TRUST COLONIAL MAN	CL	*	300.00
58	JACKIE GLEASON	CL	*	800.00
58	JORDAN MARSH OBSERVER	CL	*	225.00
58	MT. VERNON	CL	*	425.00
58	ROMEO & JULIET	CL	*	425.00
58	SALEM SAVINGS BANK	CL	*	275.00
59	ALCOA WRAP PS	CL	*	375.00
59	ALEXANDER SMITH WEAVER	CL	*	400.00
59	FIORELLO LAGUARDIA	CL	*	150.00
59	FLEISCHMAN'S MARGARINE PS	CL	*	275.00
59	GIOVANNI VERRAZZANO	CL	*	150.00
59	H.P. HOOD CO. CIGAR STORE INDIAN	CL	*	800.00
59	HARVARD TRUST CO. TOWN CRIER	CL	*	375.00
59	HENRY HUDSON	CL	*	150.00
59	MRS. S.O.S.	CL	*	325.00
59	SIESTA COFFEE PS	CL	*	800.00
60	INFANTRYMAN, THE	CL	*	800.00
60	MARINE MEMORIAL	CL	*	350.00
60	MASONIC BIBLE	CL	*	350.00
60	METROPOLITAN LIFE TOWER PS	CL	*	375.00
60	PETER STVYVESANT	CL	*	150.00
60	SON OF THE DESERT	CL	*	240.00
60	SUPP-HOSE LADY	CL	*	325.00
60	TONY PIET	CL	*	800.00
61	BUNKY KNUDSEN	CL	*	800.00
61	MERCHANT'S WARREN SEA CAPTAIN	CL	*	225.00
61	POPE JOHN 23RD	CL	*	425.00
61	ST. JUDE THADDEUS	CL	*	425.00
62	BIG BROTHER BOB EMERY	CL	*	800.00
62	BLUE BELLE HIGHLANDER	CL	*	225.00
62	SEAMAN'S BANK FOR SAVINGS	CL	*	350.00
62	YANKEE CLIPPER SULFIDE	CL	*	800.00
63	DIA-MEL FAT MAN	CL	*	400.00
63	JACKIE KENNEDY TOBY JUG	CL	*	800.00
63	JOHN F. KENNEDY TOBY JUG	CL	*	800.00
63	NAUMKEAG INDIAN	CL	*	250.00
65	HENRY WADSWORTH LONGFELLOW	CL	*	300.00
65	PANTI-LEGS GIRL PS	CL	*	275.00
65	POPE PAUL VI	CL	*	425.00
65	STATE STREET BANK GLOBE	CL	*	275.00
66	GARDENER MAN	CL	*	275.00
66	GARDENER WOMEN	CL	*	275.00
66	GARDENERS (THERMOMETER)	CL	*	350.00
66	LITTLE GEORGE	CL	*	400.00
66	MASSACHUSETTS SPCA	CL	*	300.00
66	PAUL REVERE PLAQUE (W.T. GRANT)	CL	*	325.00
66	TOWN LYNE INDIAN	CL	*	800.00
67	DOC BERRY OF BERWICK (YELLOW SHIRT)	CL	*	325.00
67	ORTHO-NOVUM	CL	*	800.00
68	CAPTAIN JOHN PARKER	CL	*	325.00
68	WATERMILL CANDY PLAQUE	CL	*	800.00
70	UNCLE SAM IN ORBIT	CL	*	375.00
71	BOSTON GAS TANK	CL	*	400.00
71	TOWN MEETING PLAQUE	CL	*	375.00
72	GEORGE & HATCHET	CL	*	425.00
72	MARTHA & THE CHERRY PIE	CL	*	375.00

SEYMOUR MANN
KENJI

			BUNNY MUSICAL	
91	BUNNY IN TEACUP MH-781	OP	25.00	25.00
91	BUNNY IN TEAPOT MH-780	OP	25.00	25.00

KENJI

			CAT MUSICAL FIGURINES	
85	CATS BALL SHAPE	CL	25.00	25.00
86	CATS W/RIBBON MH-481 A/C	RT	30.00	30.00
87	BROWN CAT IN BAG	CL	30.00	30.00
87	BROWN CAT IN TEACUP	RT	30.00	30.00
87	CAT IN BAG MH-614	RT	30.00	30.00
87	CAT IN BAG MH-617	RT	30.00	30.00
87	CAT IN GARBAGE CAN MH-190	RT	35.00	35.00
87	CAT IN ROSE TEACUP MH-600VG	RT	30.00	30.00
87	CAT IN TEACUP MH-600VGG	RT	30.00	30.00
87	CAT ON TIPPED GARBAGE CAN MH-498	RT	35.00	35.00
87	KITTENS W/BALLS OF YARN MH-612	RT	30.00	30.00

YR	NAME	LIMIT	ISSUE	TREND
87	MUSICAL BEAR MH-602	RT	28.00	28.00
87	TEAPOT CAT MH-631	RT	30.00	30.00
87	VALENTINE CAT IN BAG MUSICAL MH-600	RT	34.00	34.00
87	VALENTINE CAT IN TEACUP MH-600VLT	RT	34.00	34.00
88	BROWN CAT IN HAT MH-634B/6	RT	35.00	35.00
88	CAT IN HAT BOX MH-634	RT	35.00	35.00
88	CAT IN HAT MH-634B	RT	35.00	35.00
89	CAT IN BASINET MH-714	RT	35.00	35.00
89	CAT IN BASKET MH-713B	RT	35.00	35.00
89	CAT IN FLOWER MH-709	RT	35.00	35.00
89	CAT IN GIFT BOX MUSICAL MH-732	RT	40.00	40.00
89	CAT IN SHOE MH-718	RT	30.00	30.00
89	CAT IN WATER CAN MUSICAL MH-712	RT	35.00	35.00
89	CAT ON BASKET MH-713	RT	35.00	35.00
89	CAT W/COFFEE CUP MUSICAL MH-706	RT	35.00	35.00
89	CAT W/SWING MUSICAL MH-710	RT	35.00	35.00
90	BRIDE/GROOM CAT MH-738	RT	38.00	38.00
90	CAT ASLEEP MH-735	RT	17.50	18.00
90	CAT CALICO IN EASY CHAIR MH-743VG	RT	28.00	28.00
90	CAT IN BOOTIE MH-728	RT	35.00	35.00
90	CAT IN DRESS MH-751VG	RT	38.00	38.00
90	CAT ON GIFT BOX MUSIC MH-740	RT	40.00	40.00
90	CAT ON PILLOW MH-731	RT	17.50	18.00
90	CAT SAILOR IN ROCKING BOAT MH-734	RT	45.00	45.00
90	CAT W/BOW ON PINK PILLOW MH-741P	RT	34.00	36.00
90	CAT W/PARROT MH-730	RT	38.00	38.00
90	CATS GRADUATION MH-745	RT	28.00	28.00
90	GREY CAT IN BOOTIE MH-728G/6	CL	35.00	35.00
90	KITTEN TRIO IN CARRIAGE MH-742	CL	38.00	38.00
91	BROWN CAT IN BAG	RT	30.00	30.00
91	BROWN CAT IN HAT	RT	35.00	35.00
91	BROWN CAT IN TEACUP	CL	30.00	30.00
91	CAT IN BAG	CL	30.00	30.00
91	CAT IN BASKET MH-768	RT	35.00	35.00
91	CAT IN BOOTIE	CL	35.00	35.00
91	CAT IN GARBAGE CAN	RT	35.00	35.00
91	CAT IN HAT	CL	35.00	35.00
91	CAT IN HAT BOX	CL	35.00	35.00
91	CAT IN ROSE TEACUP	RT	30.00	30.00
91	CAT IN TEACUP	CL	30.00	30.00
91	CAT MOMMA MH-758	RT	35.00	35.00
91	CAT ON TIPPED GARBAGE CAN	CL	35.00	35.00
91	CAT WATCHING BUTTERFLY MH-784	RT	17.50	18.00
91	CAT WATCHING CANARY MH-783	RT	25.00	25.00
91	CATS BALL SHAPE	CL	25.00	25.00
91	CATS W/RIBBON	CL	30.00	30.00
91	FAMILY CAT MH-770	RT	35.00	35.00
91	GREY CAT IN BOOTIE	CL	35.00	35.00
91	KITTEN PICKING TULIPS MH-756	RT	40.00	40.00
91	KITTENS W/BALLS OF YARN	CL	30.00	30.00
91	MUSICAL BEAR	CL	28.00	28.00
91	REVOLVING CAT W/BUTTERFLY MH-759	RT	40.00	40.00
91	TEAPOT CAT	CL	30.00	30.00

JAIMY

			CHRISTMAS COLLECTION	
89	SANTA IN SLED W/REINDEER CJ-3	RT	25.00	25.00
89	SANTA MUSICALS CJ-1/4	RT	28.00	28.00
89	SANTA ON HORSE CJ-33A	RT	34.00	34.00
89	SANTA W/LIST CJ-23	RT	28.00	28.00
90	MR. & MRS. SANTA MUSICAL	CL	38.00	38.00
90	ROLY POLY SANTA 3 ASST. CJ-263/4/7	RT	17.50	18.00
90	SANTA ON CHIMNEY MUSICAL	CL	34.00	34.00
90	SANTA PACKING BAG CJ-210	CL	34.00	34.00
90	SANTA W/LIST CJ-23	RT	28.00	28.00
91	APOTHECARY LITE UP CJ-128	RT	34.00	34.00
91	BEIGE CHURCH LITE UP HOUSE MER-360A	RT	35.00	35.00
91	BOY & GIRL ON BELL CJ-132	RT	13.50	14.00
91	BOY ON HORSE CJ-457	RT	6.00	6.00
91	CAROLERS UNDER LAMPPOST CJ-114A	RT	7.50	8.00
91	CHURCH LITE UP MER-410	RT	17.50	18.00
91	COVERED BRIDGE CJ-101	RT	28.00	28.00
91	EMILY'S TOYS CJ-127	RT	35.00	35.00
91	FATHER & MOTHER W/DAUGHTER CJ-133	RT	13.50	14.00
91	FATHER CHRISTMAS CJ-233	RT	34.00	34.00
91	FATHER CHRISTMAS W/HOLLY CJ-239	RT	35.00	35.00
91	FIRE STATION CJ-129	RT	50.00	50.00
91	FOUR MEN TALKING CJ-138	RT	28.00	28.00
91	GIFT SHOP LITE UP CJ-125	RT	34.00	34.00
91	GIRLS W/INSTRUMENTS CJ-131	RT	13.50	14.00
91	HORSE & COACH CJ-207	RT	25.00	25.00
91	KIDS BUILDING IGLOO CJ-137	RT	13.50	14.00
91	LADY W/DOGS CJ-208	RT	13.50	14.00
91	MAN W/WHEELBARROW CJ-134	RT	13.50	14.00
91	NEWSBOY UNDER LAMPPOST CJ-144B	RT	15.00	15.00
91	OLD CURIOSITY LITE UP CJ-201	RT	38.00	38.00
91	PLAYHOUSE LITE UP CJ-122	RT	50.00	50.00

YR	NAME	LIMIT	ISSUE	TREND
91	REINDEER BARN LITE UP HOUSE	CL	55.00	55.00
91	SANTA CAT ROLY POLY CJ-252	RT	17.50	18.00
91	SANTA FIXING SLED CJ-237	RT	35.00	35.00
91	SANTA IN BARREL WATERBALL CJ-243	RT	34.00	34.00
91	SANTA IN TOY SHOP CJ-441	RT	34.00	34.00
91	SANTA ON TRAIN CJ-458	RT	6.00	6.00
91	SANTA PACKING BAG CJ-210	RT	34.00	34.00
91	SANTA PACKING BAG CJ-236	RT	35.00	35.00
91	SANTA SLEEPING MUSICAL CJ-214	RT	30.00	30.00
91	SANTA W/BAG & LIST CJ-431	RT	34.00	34.00
91	SANTA W/DEER MUSICAL	RT	34.00	34.00
91	SANTA W/GIRL WATERBALL	RT	34.00	34.00
91	SANTA W/LANTERN MUSICAL CJ-211	RT	34.00	34.00
91	SANTA W/LIST CJ-23R	RT	28.00	28.00
91	SKATER, THE CJ-205	RT	25.00	25.00
91	SNOWBALL FIGHT CJ-124B	RT	25.00	25.00
91	SOUP SELLER WATERBALL CJ-209	RT	25.00	25.00
91	STONE COTTAGE LITE UP CJ-100	RT	38.00	38.00
91	STONE HOUSE LITE UP CJ-102	RT	45.00	45.00
91	THREE LADDIES W/FOOD CJ-136	RT	13.50	14.00
91	TOY SELLER, THE CJ-206	RT	13.50	14.00
91	TRADER SANTA MUSICAL CJ-442	RT	30.00	30.00
91	TWO OLD MEN TALKING CJ-107	RT	13.50	14.00
91	VILLAGE MILL LITE UP CJ-104	RT	30.00	30.00
91	VILLAGE PEOPLE CJ-116A	RT	60.00	60.00
91	WOMAN W/COW CJ-135	RT	15.00	15.00
91	YE OLDE TOWN TAVERN CJ-130	RT	45.00	45.00
E. MANN			**CHRISTMAS COLLECTION**	
89	CATS IN BASKET XMAS-664	RT	7.50	8.00
90	FIRE STATION LITE UP HOUSE	CL	25.00	25.00
90	SANTA ON SEE SAW TR-14	RT	30.00	30.00
91	ELF W/DOLL HOUSE CB-14	RT	30.00	30.00
91	ELF W/HAMMER CB-11	RT	30.00	30.00
91	ELF W/ROCKING HORSE CB-10	RT	30.00	30.00
91	ELF W/TEDDY BEAR CB-12	RT	30.00	30.00
91	SANTA ON WHITE HORSE CJ-338	RT	34.00	34.00
91	TEDDY BEAR ON WHEELS CB-42	RT	25.00	25.00
J. WHITE			**CHRISTMAS COLLECTION**	
85	TRUMPETING ANGEL W/JESUS XMAS-627	RT	40.00	40.00
85	VIRGIN W/CHRIST MUSICAL XMAS-528	RT	34.00	34.00
86	ANTIQUE SANTA MUSICAL XMAS-364	RT	20.00	20.00
86	JUMBO SANTA/TOYS XMAS-38	RT	45.00	45.00
89	CAT IN TEACUP MUSICAL XMAS-600	RT	30.00	30.00
90	ANTIQUE SHOP LITE UP HOUSE MER-373	RT	28.00	28.00
90	BAKERY LITE UP HOUSE MER-376	RT	28.00	28.00
90	BETHLEHEM LITE UP SET 3 CP-59893	RT	120.00	120.00
90	BRICK CHURCH LITE UP HOUSE MER-360C	RT	35.00	35.00
90	CATHEDRAL LITE UP HOUSE MER-362	RT	38.00	38.00
90	CHURCH LITE UP HOUSE MER-310	RT	28.00	28.00
90	DEEP GOLD CHURCH LITE UP HOUSE MER-360D	RT	35.00	35.00
90	DOUBLE STORE LITE UP HOUSE MER-311	RT	28.00	28.00
90	GRIST MILL LITE UP HOUSE MER-372	CL	28.00	28.00
90	INN LITE UP HOUSE MER-316	CL	28.00	28.00
90	LEATHERWORKS LITE UP HOUSE	CL	28.00	28.00
90	LIBRARY LITE UP HOUSES	CL	28.00	28.00
90	LIGHT HOUSE LITE UP HOUSE	CL	28.00	28.00
90	MANSION LITE UP HOUSE	CL	28.00	28.00
90	N. ENG. CHURCH LITE UP HOUSE MER-375	CL	28.00	28.00
90	N. ENG. GEN. STORE LITE UP HSE MER-377	CL	28.00	28.00
90	RAILROAD STATION LITE UP HOUSE	CL	28.00	28.00
90	SCHOOL LITE UP HOUSE	CL	28.00	28.00
90	TOWN HALL LITE UP HOUSE	CL	28.00	28.00
91	CHURCH W/BLU ROOF LITE UP HSE MER-360E	RT	35.00	35.00
91	FLORAL PLAQUE XMAS-911	OP	10.00	10.00
91	FLOWER BASKET XMAS-912	OP	10.00	10.00
91	RESTAURANT LITE UP HOUSE	CL	28.00	28.00
91	TOY STORE LITE UP HOUSE	CL	28.00	28.00
91	TRAIN SET MER-378	RT	25.00	25.00
91	TWO-TONE STONE CHURCH MER-360B	RT	35.00	35.00
E. MANN			**CHRISTMAS IN AMERICA**	
88	CAPITOL, WHITE HOUSE, MT. VERNON	RT	75.00	150.00
88	DOCTOR'S OFFICE LITE UP	RT	28.00	28.00
89	SANTA IN SLEIGH	CL	25.00	45.00
90	CART WITH PEOPLE	RT	25.00	35.00
J. WHITE			**CHRISTMAS IN AMERICA**	
91	NEW ENGLAND CHURCH LITE UP MER-375	RT	28.00	28.00
91	NEW ENGLAND GEN'L STORE LITE UP MER-377	RT	28.00	28.00
L. SCIOLA			**CHRISTMAS VILLAGE**	
91	AWAY, AWAY	CL	30.00	30.00
91	COUNSEL HOUSE	CL	60.00	60.00
91	CURIOSITY SHOP	CL	45.00	45.00
91	EMILY'S TOYS	CL	45.00	45.00
91	FIRE STATION, THE	CL	60.00	60.00
91	ON THIN ICE	CL	30.00	30.00
91	PLAYHOUSE, THE	CL	60.00	60.00

YR	NAME	LIMIT	ISSUE	TREND
91	PUBLIC LIBRARY	CL	50.00	50.00
91	SCROOGE/MARLEY'S COUNTING HOUSE	CL	45.00	45.00
91	STORY TELLER, THE CJ-204	CL	20.00	20.00
91	YE OLD GIFT SHOPPE	CL	50.00	50.00
JAIMY			**DICKENS COLLECTION**	
91	CRATCHIT'S LITE UP HOUSE CJ-200	RT	38.00	38.00
91	CRATCHIT/TINY TIM MUSICAL CJ-117	RT	34.00	34.00
91	SCROOGE MUSICAL	RT	30.00	30.00
91	SCROOGE/MARLEY COUNTING HOUSE CJ-202	RT	38.00	38.00
J. WHITE			**DICKENS COLLECTION**	
89	CRATCHIT'S LITE UP XMS-7000A	RT	30.00	30.00
89	FEZZIWIG'S LITE UP XMS-7000C	RT	30.00	30.00
89	GIFT SHOPPE LITE UP XMS-7000H	RT	30.00	30.00
89	SCROOGE/MARLEY LITE UP XMS-7000B	RT	30.00	30.00
90	BLACK SWAN INN LITE UP XMS-7000E	RT	30.00	30.00
90	CRATCHIT FAMILY MER-121	RT	38.00	38.00
90	CRATCHIT/TINY TIM MUSICAL MER-105	RT	34.00	34.00
90	HEN POULTRY LITE UP	CL	30.00	30.00
90	TEA AND SPICE LITE UP	CL	30.00	30.00
90	WAITE FISH STORE LITE UP	CL	30.00	30.00
J. SAUERBREY			**GINGERBREAD CHRISTMAS COLLECTION**	
91	GINGERBREAD CHURCH LITE UP HSE CJ-403	CL	65.00	65.00
91	GINGERBREAD HOUSE LITE UP CJ-404	CL	65.00	65.00
91	GINGERBREAD MANSION LITE UP	CL	70.00	70.00
91	GINGERBREAD ROCKING HORSE MUSIC	CL	34.00	34.00
91	GINGERBREAD SWAN MUSICAL	CL	34.00	34.00
91	GINGERBREAD SWEET SHOP LITE UP HOUSE	CL	60.00	60.00
91	GINGERBREAD TEDDY BEAR MUSIC	CL	34.00	34.00
91	GINGERBREAD TOY SHOP LITE UP HOUSE	CL	60.00	60.00
91	GINGERBREAD VILLAGE LITE UP HOUSE	CL	60.00	60.00
JAIMY			**VICTORIAN CHRISTMAS COLLECTION**	
90	TWO BOYS WITH SNOWMAN	CL	12.00	12.00
91	LITTLE MATCH GIRL	CL	9.00	9.00
J. WHITE			**VICTORIAN CHRISTMAS COLLECTION**	
90	TOY/DOLL HOUSE LITE UP	CL	28.00	28.00
90	VICTORIAN HOUSE LITE UP HOUSE	CL	28.00	28.00
90	YARN SHOP LITE UP HOUSE	CL	28.00	28.00
91	ANTIQUE SHOP LITE UP HOUSE	CL	28.00	28.00
91	BEIGE CHURCH LITE UP HOUSE MER351	CL	35.00	35.00
91	BOOK STORE LITE UP HOUSE	CL	28.00	28.00
91	CHURCH LITE UP HOUSE	CL	38.00	38.00
91	COUNTRY STORE LITE UP HOUSE	CL	28.00	28.00
91	INN LITE UP HOUSE MER-352	CL	28.00	28.00
E. MANN			**WIZARD OF OZ-40TH ANNIVERSARY**	
79	DOROTHY, SCARECROW, LION, TINMAN	RT	7.50	45.00
79	DOROTHY, SCARECROW, LION, TINMAN-MUSICAL	RT	12.50	75.00

SHADE TREE CREATIONS INC.

B. VERNON				**COWBOYS**
80	BEER DRINKER	RT	20.00	240.00
80	CARD SHARK	RT	20.00	165.00
80	EARLY RISER	RT	20.00	190.00
81	GUNFIGHTER (1ST RELEASE)	RT	20.00	165.00
81	REDNECK (1ST RELEASE)	RT	20.00	150.00
81	URBAN COWBOY (PAINTED)	RT	20.00	1275.00
83	URBAN COWBOY (BROWN)	RT	15.00	550.00
86	BATHER	OP	*	N/A
86	SNOOZER	RT	*	45.00
87	FISHERMAN	OP	*	N/A
87	GOLFER	RT	30.00	125.00
87	GOODBYE CRUEL WORLD	RT	*	N/A
88	COMPUTER WIZARD	RT	25.00	125.00
88	HUNTER	RT	*	60.00
89	BIKER	OP	*	N/A
89	BOSS, THE	OP	*	N/A
89	EXECUTIVE	RT	30.00	115.00
89	HAPPY HOUR	RT	30.00	65.00
89	HENPECKED & HOGTIED	RT	30.00	110.00
89	PROMISE, THE	OP	*	N/A
89	YEE HAW	RT	25.00	125.00
90	CAMERA CRAZY	RT	30.00	60.00
90	HELLO FROM... CUSTOM EDITION	RT	*	N/A
90	MAN'S BEST FRIEND	RT	*	55.00
90	SMOKIN'-STURGIS RALLY	RT	35.00	550.00
90	THIS JOB	RT	30.00	65.00
90	TOURIST	RT	30.00	40.00
90	TRUCKER	RT	*	80.00
91	BOWLER	RT	30.00	45.00
91	COUCH POTATO	RT	*	60.00
91	GUNFIGHTER (2ND RELEASE)	RT	30.00	65.00
91	MECHANIC	RT	30.00	150.00
91	POOL SHARK	RT	*	50.00
91	REDNECK (2ND RELEASE)	RT	30.00	165.00
91	SKIER	RT	30.00	45.00
92	FIRST CUP, THE	OP	*	N/A

YR	NAME	LIMIT	ISSUE	TREND
92	GOLF MY WAY	OP	*	N/A
92	RODEO CLOWN	RT	*	75.00
92	SADDLE SORES	OP	*	N/A
92	SMOKIN' BIKER	OP	*	N/A
93	BUT...I DIDN'T INHALE!	*	*	N/A
93	COOKIES FOR SANTA	5000	*	N/A
93	EXECUTIVE LIBRARY	OP	*	N/A
93	PARTY ANIMAL	OP	*	N/A
93	YARD WARRIOR	OP	*	N/A
94	DEFENDERS OF THE FLAG	*	*	N/A
94	DR. FEELGOOD	OP	*	N/A
94	FIRE FIGHTIN'	OP	*	N/A
94	HOUSEWORK STINKS!	*	*	N/A
94	TESTIN' THE TOYS	5000	*	N/A
95	DRAGGIN BUTT	OP	35.00	35.00
95	KEEPER OF THE PEACE	OP	*	N/A
95	LOUNGIN' WITH THE LADIES	OP	*	N/A
95	MEAN AND ORNERY!	*	*	N/A
95	PLUMB'IN TROUBLE	OP	*	N/A
95	SEX MACHINE	OP	40.00	40.00
95	WOAH DERNIT	RT	40.00	40.00
97	DANCIN' FOOL!	*	*	N/A
97	GOIN' POSTAL	OP	*	N/A
97	REDNECK & FED UP!	*	*	N/A
98	BAR-B-Q-IN'	*	*	N/A
98	REAL MEN DON'T NEED...	*	*	N/A
98	ROAD RAGE	*	*	N/A

SHENANDOAH DESIGNS
N. LINDBLADE   ARCADIAN PEWTER

YR	NAME	LIMIT	ISSUE	TREND
95	AEROPLANE MONOCOUPE	10000	46.00	46.00
95	BUS-SAFETY COACH	10000	46.00	46.00
95	COFFEE MILL	10000	46.00	46.00
95	COUPE A RUMBLE SEAT	10000	46.00	46.00
95	COUPE MODEL T	10000	46.00	46.00
95	EXPRESS FLYER WAGON	10000	46.00	46.00
95	FIRE ENGINE AUTO	10000	56.00	56.00
95	FIREWAGON (HORSE-DRAWN)	10000	70.00	70.00
95	MAIL BOX SPECIAL EDITION	10000	40.00	40.00
95	SEDAN A TUDOR	10000	46.00	46.00
95	STATE BANK	10000	*	N/A
95	STEAMBOAT	10000	46.00	46.00
95	TRACTOR	10000	46.00	46.00
95	TRUCK A-STAKES SIDES	10000	46.00	46.00
95	TRUCK T STAKE SIDES	10000	56.00	56.00
96	A-EXPRESS TRUCK	10000	46.00	46.00
96	AMBULANCE	10000	46.00	46.00
96	COTTAGE BANK	10000	30.00	30.00
96	FARM MOWER	10000	40.00	40.00
96	FIRE LADDER TRUCK	10000	46.00	46.00
96	MOTORCYCLE COP	10000	46.00	46.00
96	NO. 1501 SEDAN	10000	30.00	30.00
96	NO. 1810 FIRE ENGINE	10000	46.00	46.00
96	PLYMOUTH SEDAN	10000	40.00	40.00
96	PRACING HORSE BANK	10000	40.00	40.00
96	ROCKING CHAIR	10000	30.00	30.00
96	TOW CROP TRACTOR	10000	46.00	46.00
96	TOY POLICE BANK	10000	40.00	40.00
96	TWO-MAN RACER	10000	46.00	46.00
96	WHEELBARROW WITH TOOLS	10000	46.00	46.00

SHENANDOAH DESIGN TEAM   D. MORGANS

YR	NAME	LIMIT	ISSUE	TREND
96	ACCESSORY GROUP	2000	70.00	70.00
96	FATHER CHRISTMAS	6000	100.00	100.00
96	MAGIC NEVER ENDS	6000	100.00	100.00
96	ST. NICHOLAS	6000	100.00	100.00

C.M. BARKER   FLOWER FAIRIES SERIES I

YR	NAME	LIMIT	ISSUE	TREND
95	GREATER CELANDINE FAIRY	OP	20.00	20.00
95	LAVENDER FAIRY	OP	20.00	20.00
95	MOUNTAIN ASH FAIRY	OP	20.00	20.00
95	ROSEHIP FAIRY	OP	20.00	20.00
95	WAYFARING TREE FAIRY	OP	20.00	20.00
95	WILD CHERRY BLOSSOM FAIRY	OP	20.00	20.00

C.M. BARKER   FLOWER FAIRIES SERIES II

YR	NAME	LIMIT	ISSUE	TREND
96	BLACKTHORN FAIRY	OP	20.00	20.00
96	CANTERBURY FAIRY	OP	20.00	20.00
96	FUMITORY FAIRY	OP	20.00	20.00
96	NASTURTIUM FAIRY	OP	20.00	20.00
96	POPPY FAIRY	OP	20.00	20.00
96	STRAWBERRY FAIRY	OP	20.00	20.00

C.M. BARKER   FLOWER FAIRIES SERIES III

YR	NAME	LIMIT	ISSUE	TREND
96	CANDYTUFT FAIRY	OP	20.00	20.00
96	CHRISTMAS TREE FAIRY	OP	20.00	20.00
96	COLUMBINE FAIRY	OP	20.00	20.00
96	DANDELION FAIRY	OP	20.00	20.00

YR	NAME	LIMIT	ISSUE	TREND
96	MAY FAIRY	OP	20.00	20.00
96	WHITE BINDWEED FAIRY	OP	20.00	20.00
C.M. BARKER			**FLOWER FAIRIES SERIES IV**	
97	BLACK MEDICH BOY FAIRY	OP	20.00	20.00
97	BLACK MEDICH GIRL FAIRY	OP	20.00	20.00
97	BOX TREE FAIRY	OP	20.00	20.00
97	ELM TREE FAIRY	OP	20.00	20.00
97	HAZELNUT FAIRY	OP	20.00	20.00
97	PEAR BLOSSOM FAIRY	OP	20.00	20.00
SHENANDOAH DESIGN TEAM			**KEEPER KLUB**	
96	KEEPER OF COLLECTORS	YR	35.00	35.00
96	KEEPER SHELF	YR	*	N/A
SHENANDOAH DESIGN TEAM			**KEEPER OF CHRISTMAS SCENES**	
95	CHRISTMAS 1995	RT	40.00	225.00
96	CHRISTMAS 1996	RT	40.00	125.00
97	CHRISTMAS 1997	6000	40.00	40.00
SHENANDOAH DESIGN TEAM			**KEEPER SERIES I**	
93	BATH	OP	35.00	35.00
93	BEDCHAMBER	OP	35.00	35.00
93	ENTRY	OP	35.00	35.00
93	HEARTH	OP	35.00	35.00
93	KITCHEN	RT	35.00	75.00
93	LAUNDRY	OP	35.00	35.00
93	LIBRARY	RT	35.00	100.00
93	NURSERY	OP	35.00	35.00
SHENANDOAH DESIGN TEAM			**KEEPER SERIES II**	
94	COWBOY SPIRIT	OP	35.00	35.00
94	HOME OFFICE	OP	35.00	35.00
94	HOME WORKSHOP	OP	35.00	35.00
94	LOVE	OP	35.00	35.00
94	MOTHERS	OP	35.00	35.00
94	NATIVE AMERICAN	RT	35.00	100.00
94	SUNROOM	OP	35.00	35.00
94	TIME	OP	35.00	35.00
SHENANDOAH DESIGN TEAM			**KEEPER SERIES III**	
95	BEARS	OP	35.00	35.00
95	FATHERS	OP	35.00	35.00
95	FLIGHT	OP	35.00	35.00
95	RAILS	OP	35.00	35.00
95	THANKSGIVING	OP	35.00	35.00
95	THE CATCH	OP	35.00	35.00
SHENANDOAH DESIGN TEAM			**KEEPER SERIES IV**	
95	BIRTHDAYS	OP	35.00	35.00
95	FAITH	OP	35.00	35.00
95	FIREFIGHTERS	OP	35.00	35.00
95	GARDEN	OP	35.00	35.00
95	GOLFING	OP	35.00	35.00
95	MUSIC	OP	35.00	35.00
95	SEA	OP	35.00	35.00
95	TRAILS	OP	35.00	35.00
95	WOODLAND ANIMALS	OP	35.00	35.00
SHENANDOAH DESIGN TEAM			**KEEPER SERIES V**	
96	CHECKERED FLAG	OP	35.00	35.00
96	FRIENDSHIP	OP	35.00	35.00
96	PEACE	OP	35.00	35.00
96	PHOTOGRAPHY	OP	35.00	35.00
96	SECRETS	OP	35.00	35.00
SHENANDOAH DESIGN TEAM			**KEEPER SERIES VI**	
97	CATS	OP	35.00	35.00
97	CROWN JEWELS	6000	40.00	40.00
97	GALAXY	OP	35.00	35.00
97	HALLOWEEN	3500	45.00	45.00
97	PUBS	OP	35.00	35.00
SHENANDOAH DESIGN TEAM			**LEAPERS**	
97	KISS A LEAPER	6000	50.00	50.00
97	LEAP OF FAITH	6000	50.00	50.00
97	LEAPER WENT A COURTIN'	6000	50.00	50.00
97	LEARN & LEAP	6000	50.00	50.00
97	TO LEAP OR NOT TO LEAP	6000	50.00	50.00
97	TO LEAP...TO DREAM	6000	50.00	50.00
SHENANDOAH DESIGN TEAM			**LIMBIES**	
97	BRUNO	6000	40.00	40.00
97	FIRST BEAR	6000	40.00	40.00
97	GRACE	6000	40.00	40.00
97	GUITARIST	6000	40.00	40.00
97	QUEEN	6000	40.00	40.00
97	ZEUS	6000	50.00	50.00

SILVER DEER LTD.
G. TRUEX

*	CRYSTAL STARSHIP	*	*	410.00
G. TRUEX			**CRYSTAL COLLECTIBLES**	
84	PINOCCHIO, 120MM	CL	195.00	250.00
90	JOE COOL CRUISIN	CL	165.00	165.00

YR	NAME	LIMIT	ISSUE	TREND

SO! STUDIO ORIGINALS

K. GRAVES				**ANIMAL LOVE**
95	BROWN BEAR LOVE	1000	85.00	85.00
95	FERRET LOVE	1000	85.00	85.00
95	HAMADRYAD BABOON	1000	85.00	85.00
95	LEOPARD LOVE	1000	85.00	85.00
95	MANDRILL BABOON LOVE	1000	85.00	85.00
95	PANDA LOVE	1000	85.00	85.00
K. GRAVES				**CHESS SET**
93	KATALIN'S ADV. IN ALICE'S WONDERLAND	500	1,100.00	1100.00
93	TOURNAMENT OF THE TREE FROGS	500	750.00	750.00
94	A WEE MAC CHESS TOURNAMENT	500	850.00	850.00
94	IMAGES OF THE SOUTHWEST	500	2,500.00	2500.00
K. GRAVES				**IMAGINALS**
93	BILLY THE KITTY (KITTEN)	5000	50.00	50.00
93	BLACK BARK (STAFFORDSHIRE TERRIER)	5000	50.00	50.00
93	CHIEF SITTING BULLDOG	5000	50.00	50.00
93	CHOW MEIN	5000	50.00	50.00
93	DACHS HOLIDAY (DACHSHUND)	5000	50.00	50.00
93	DOLLY POODLE	5000	50.00	50.00
93	FLUIGATOR, THE (SKUNK)	5000	50.00	50.00
93	KAT FLOOSIE (CAT)	5000	50.00	50.00
93	MA BARKER (BEAGLE)	5000	50.00	50.00
93	MISS KITTY (CAT)	5000	50.00	50.00
93	ONE NOTE E. COYOTE	5000	50.00	50.00
93	PANCHO GATO (CAT)	5000	50.00	50.00
93	WILD NANOOK/NORTH (ALASKAN MALAMUTE)	5000	50.00	50.00
93	WYATT MOUSETRAP (CAT)	5000	50.00	50.00
94	BIG NOST KAT (WILD CAT)	5000	50.00	50.00
94	BLACK FOOTED FERRET, THE	5000	50.00	50.00
94	BOSTON BEENE (BOSTON TERRIER)	5000	50.00	50.00
94	CALAMITY CAIRN (CAIRN TERRIER)	5000	50.00	50.00
94	DANIEL SPANIEL (ENG. SPRINGER SPANIEL)	5000	50.00	50.00
94	DAVY COCKER (COCKER SPANIEL PUPPY)	5000	50.00	50.00
94	GERONIMEOW (CAT)	5000	50.00	50.00
94	GOLD N. TREEVER	5000	50.00	50.00
94	HERR MAX VON SCHAFERHUND (GERMAN SHPRD.)	5000	50.00	50.00
94	JUDGE ROY MEAN (BULL TERRIER)	5000	50.00	50.00
94	MALTESE FALCONIER, THE	5000	50.00	50.00
94	MELANIE COLLIE ROSE	5000	50.00	50.00
94	PUGLIACCI (PUG)	5000	50.00	50.00
94	RED EYED AL (ALBINO FERRET)	5000	50.00	50.00
94	REV. LUTHER ST. BERNARD	5000	50.00	50.00
94	RITA RAT	5000	50.00	50.00
94	ROUGH RIDER ROTTIE (ROTTWEILER)	5000	50.00	50.00
94	RUDOLPHO RAT	5000	50.00	50.00
94	SIAM SAM (SIAMESE CAT)	5000	50.00	50.00
94	SIAM SUE (SIAMESE CAT)	5000	50.00	50.00
94	TY-PHOON SHAR-PEI	5000	50.00	50.00
94	WILD SPOTS DOOLIN (DALMATIAN)	5000	50.00	50.00
94	WILD, WILD WESTIE (W. HIGHLAND TERRIER)	5000	50.00	50.00
94	YORKIE YORKIER PUDDIN' (YORKSHIRE TERR.)	5000	50.00	50.00
95	CATS DOMINO	5000	50.00	50.00
95	CHEF BRIARD DEE	5000	50.00	50.00
95	COUNT BORZOI	5000	45.00	45.00
95	LABRACADABRA	5000	50.00	50.00
95	MADAMA PAPILLION	5000	45.00	45.00
95	PUGLIACCI	5000	45.00	45.00
96	DOGGIE SCHNAUZER MD	5000	50.00	50.00
96	SHAGGY BOB TALE	5000	55.00	55.00
96	ZANE GREYHOUND	5000	50.00	50.00

SPORTS IMPRESSIONS

*				
	DON MATTINGLY ERROR	500	125.00	850.00
*				**500 HOME RUN CLUB**
90	EDDIE MATTHEWS	5512	100.00	125.00
90	FRANK ROBINSON	5586	150.00	150.00
90	HARMON KILLEBREW	5573	150.00	150.00
90	JIMMY FOX	5534	150.00	150.00
90	MEL OTT	5511	150.00	150.00
90	TED WILLIAMS	5251	150.00	150.00
90	WILLIE MCCOVEY	5521	150.00	150.00
*				**BASEBALL SUPERSTAR FIGURINE SERIES**
87	DON MATTINGLY	CL	125.00	400.00
87	KEITH HERNANDEZ	2500	125.00	185.00
87	MICKEY MANTLE	CL	125.00	300.00
87	TED WILLIAMS F/S	CL	125.00	150.00
87	WADE BOGGS F/S	CL	125.00	150.00
88	ABBOTT & COSTELLO	5000	145.00	145.00
88	AL KALINE G/E	2500	125.00	150.00
88	ANDRE DAWSON G/E	2500	125.00	150.00
88	BABE RUTH	5000	125.00	125.00
88	BOB FELLER	2500	125.00	185.00
88	JOSE CANSECO	CL	125.00	250.00

YR	NAME	LIMIT	ISSUE	TREND
88	LOU GEHRIG	5000	125.00	125.00
88	PAUL MOLITOR	2500	125.00	125.00
88	REGGIE JACKSON (YANKEES)	CL	125.00	275.00
88	ROBERTO CLEMENTE	5000	125.00	125.00
88	TY COBB	5000	125.00	125.00
89	ALAN TRAMMELL	2500	125.00	125.00
89	CY YOUNG	5000	125.00	125.00
89	DUKE SNIDER	2500	125.00	125.00
89	FRANK VIOLA	2500	125.00	125.00
89	HONUS WAGNER	5000	125.00	125.00
89	KIRK GIBSON	CL	125.00	185.00
89	REGGIE JACKSON (ANGELS)	CL	125.00	165.00
89	THURMAN MUNSON	5000	125.00	125.00
89	WILL CLARK F/S	CL	125.00	225.00
*			**BASEBALL'S 3000 HIT CLUB**	
89	ROD CAREW	3053	150.00	150.00
*		**BASEBALL'S 3000 HIT WINNERS PITCHERS SERIES**		
89	TOM SEAVER	CL	150.00	150.00
*			**BASEBALL'S 500 HOME RUN HITTERS**	
89	ERNIE BANKS	5512	150.00	150.00
89	HANK AARON	5755	150.00	150.00
89	WILLIE MAYS	5660	150.00	150.00
*		**BASEBALL'S CY YOUNG AWARD WINNERS**		
89	OREL HERSHISER	5055	125.00	165.00
*			**COLLECTORS' CLUB FIGURINE**	
89	MICK-MICKEY MANTLE, THE- H/S	TL	125.00	375.00
*				**KINGS OF K**
90	NOLAN RYAN	500	195.00	195.00
90	STEVE CARLTON	500	195.00	195.00
90	TOM SEAVER	500	195.00	195.00
*		**NEW YORK METS SUPERSTAR FIGURINES**		
89	DARRYL STRAWBERRY	5018	125.00	125.00
89	DWIGHT GOODEN	5016	125.00	125.00
89	GARY CARTER	5008	125.00	125.00
89	GREGG JEFFERIES	5009	125.00	125.00
89	HOWARD JOHNSON	5020	125.00	125.00
89	KEVIN MCREYNOLDS	5022	125.00	125.00
*			**NFL LIMITED EDITION FIGURINES**	
90	BOOMER ESIASON-AWAY	995	195.00	195.00
90	BOOMER ESIASON-HOME	995	195.00	195.00
90	DAN MARINO-AWAY	995	195.00	195.00
90	DAN MARINO-HOME	995	195.00	195.00
90	JOE MONTANA-AWAY	995	195.00	195.00
90	JOE MONTANA-HOME	995	195.00	195.00
90	JOHN ELWAY-AWAY	995	195.00	195.00
90	JOHN ELWAY-HOME	995	195.00	195.00
90	LAWRENCE TAYLOR-AWAY	995	195.00	195.00
90	LAWRENCE TAYLOR-HOME	995	195.00	195.00
90	RANDALL CUNNINGHAM-AWAY	995	195.00	195.00
90	RANDALL CUNNINGHAM-HOME	995	195.00	195.00
*			**RENAISSANCE 13 IN. SCULPTURES**	
90	DON MATTINGLY	2950	395.00	395.00
*			**SPECIAL INDIVIDUAL RELEASES**	
89	MANTLE-SWITCH HITTER	CL	295.00	345.00
90	JOE MORGAN-NEWEST HALL OF FAMER	1990	195.00	195.00
91	RICKEY HENDERSON	939	150.00	150.00
91	ROCKWELL-YER OUT	2500	195.00	195.00
*			**SUPER SIZE FIGURINES**	
89	JOSE CANSECO	CL	250.00	275.00
89	TED WILLIAMS	CL	250.00	275.00
90	MICKEY MANTLE	CL	250.00	275.00
90	REGGIE JACKSON	CL	250.00	250.00
90	THURMAN MUNSON	995	250.00	250.00
90	TOM SEAVER	CL	250.00	250.00
*				**TEAM OF DREAMS**
90	CAL RIPKEN, JR.	1990	150.00	150.00
90	DON MATTINGLY	1990	150.00	150.00
90	ERIC DAVIS	1990	150.00	150.00
90	KEN GRIFFEY, JR.	1990	150.00	150.00
90	KEVIN MITCHELL	1990	150.00	150.00
90	KIRBEY PUCKETT	1990	150.00	150.00
90	LENNY DYKSTRA	1990	150.00	150.00
90	MARK LANGSTON	1990	150.00	150.00
*			**TODAY'S STAR SERIES**	
90	DON MATTINGLY	2950	65.00	65.00
90	DWIGHT GOODEN	2950	65.00	65.00
90	KEN GRIFFEY, JR.	2950	65.00	65.00
90	LENNY DYKSTRA	2950	65.00	65.00
90	NOLAN RYAN	2950	65.00	65.00

STUDIO COLLECTION
D. WOOD

				HAPPY HABITS
98	SISTER MARY ELLIOTT	*	35.00	35.00
98	SISTER MARY GLEE	*	35.00	35.00

YR	NAME	LIMIT	ISSUE	TREND
98	SISTER MARY GUIDANCE	*	35.00	35.00
98	SISTER MARY PRAISES	*	35.00	35.00

T. RUBEL   HEAVENLY ANGELS

YR	NAME	LIMIT	ISSUE	TREND
98	AND IF I COULD I'D HEAL ALL	*	20.00	20.00
98	FOOTPRINTS IN THE SAND	*	18.00	18.00
98	HUG ME!	*	18.00	18.00
98	IF I CAN TEACH THE WORLD ONE THING--KINDNESS	*	22.50	23.00
98	MY MON'S #1	*	22.50	23.00
98	THERE'S ENOUGH TO GO AROUND	*	25.00	25.00
98	WHAT WOULD JESUS DO?	*	18.00	18.00

T. RUBEL   RETIRED PEARL ANGELS

YR	NAME	LIMIT	ISSUE	TREND
98	MR. SO LATE & MS. TRULY	*	80.00	80.00
98	MS. DEARING	*	35.00	35.00
98	MS. FLORA SWEET	*	35.00	35.00
98	MS. NELLIE, MS. STELLA & MS. SOPHIE	*	100.00	100.00
98	MS. PENNY SAVER	*	35.00	35.00
98	MS. WANDERER	*	36.00	36.00
98	MS. WEATHERBEE	*	35.00	35.00

T. RUBEL   SANTA'S ANIMAL KINGDOM

YR	NAME	LIMIT	ISSUE	TREND
94	SANTA'S ANIMAL KINGDOM-STIFFENED	2500	125.00	135.00

STUDIOS OF HARRY SMITH
H. SMITH

YR	NAME	LIMIT	ISSUE	TREND
91	CAT ON PILLOW	150	145.00	300.00
91	MYSTICAL DRAGON	SO	175.00	350.00

SUMMERHILL CRYSTAL
*   SUMMERHILL CRYSTAL

YR	NAME	LIMIT	ISSUE	TREND
92	BICYCLE	500	64.00	64.00
92	L'ARC DU TRIOMPHE	5000	220.00	220.00
92	LARGE DRAGON	1500	320.00	320.00
92	PRINCESS COACH	1500	700.00	700.00
92	SACRE COEUR	5000	190.00	190.00
92	VENUS	500	96.00	96.00

SWAROVSKI AMERICA
E. MAIR   A PET'S CORNER

YR	NAME	LIMIT	ISSUE	TREND
96	ST. BERNARD	OP	*	N/A

M. STAMEY   A PET'S CORNER

YR	NAME	LIMIT	ISSUE	TREND
91	KITTEN 7634NR028000	RT	48.00	100.00
91	SITTING CAT	OP	75.00	85.00

A. STOCKER   A PET'S CORNER

YR	NAME	LIMIT	ISSUE	TREND
90	BEAGLE, PUPPY	OP	40.00	50.00
90	TERRIER 7619NR000002	RT	60.00	120.00
92	POODLE	RT	125.00	140.00

A. STOCKER   AFRICAN WILDLIFE

YR	NAME	LIMIT	ISSUE	TREND
88	ELEPHANT, LARGE 7640NR60	RT	70.00	175.00
88	HIPPOPOTAMUS 7626NR65	RT	70.00	160.00
89	ELEPHANT, SMALL	OP	50.00	65.00
89	HIPPOPOTAMUS, SMALL 7626NR055000	RT	70.00	120.00

M. ZENDRON   AFRICAN WILDLIFE

YR	NAME	LIMIT	ISSUE	TREND
95	BABY ELEPHANT	OP	155.00	155.00

C. SCHNEIDERBAUER   AMONG FLOWERS AND FOLIAGE

YR	NAME	LIMIT	ISSUE	TREND
92	BUMBLEBEE	RT	85.00	85.00
92	HUMMINGBIRD	RT	195.00	210.00
94	BUTTERFLY ON LEAF	OP	75.00	75.00
95	DRAGONFLY	OP	85.00	85.00

*   ANIMALS

YR	NAME	LIMIT	ISSUE	TREND
*	TURTLE, KING SIZE 7632NR75	RT	58.00	500.00
84	BLOWFISH, LARGE 7644NR41	RT	40.00	150.00
85	BEE-GOLD 7553NR100	RT	200.00	2000.00
85	BEE-RHODUIM 7553NR200	RT	200.00	2500.00
85	BUTTERFLY-GOLD 7551NR100	RT	*	2000.00
85	BUTTERFLY-RHODIUM 7551NR200	RT	*	2500.00
88	DUMBO NO TUSKS 7640NR35-3	RT	*	4500.00
88	DUMBO W/SM. TUSKS 7640NR35-2	RT	*	5500.00
88	ORLANDO DUMBO W/LG. TUSKS 7640NB35-1	RT	*	5500.00
89	DUMBO W/LG. EARS & TUSKS 7640NR35-4	RT	*	5000.00
89	DUMBO W/LG. EARS, NO TUSKS	RT	*	4500.00
90	DUMBO W/FLYING EARS	RT	*	1500.00
93	DUMBO '93 7640NR100001	RT	*	500.00

M. SCHRECK   ANIMALS

YR	NAME	LIMIT	ISSUE	TREND
*	BEAR, GIANT 7637NR112	RT	125.00	2600.00
*	BEAR, KING SIZE 7637NR92	RT	95.00	2750.00
*	CAT, MEDIUM 7634NR52	RT	38.00	500.00
*	CHICKEN, MINI 7651NR20	RT	16.00	100.00
*	DUCK, LARGE 7653NR75	RT	44.00	325.00
*	DUCK, MINI 7653NR45	RT	16.00	120.00
*	HEDGEHOG, KING SIZE 7630NR60	RT	98.00	700.00
*	MOUSE, KING SIZE 7631NR60	RT	95.00	900.00
*	MOUSE, LARGE 7631NR50	RT	69.00	600.00
*	MOUSE, MINI 7655NR23	RT	16.00	125.00
*	MOUSE, SMALL 2 TAIL STYLES	RT	*	90.00
*	MOUSE, SMALL 7631NR30	RT	35.00	60.00
*	PIG, LARGE 7638NR65	RT	50.00	450.00

YR	NAME	LIMIT	ISSUE	TREND
*	RABBIT, MINI 7652NR20	RT	16.00	125.00
77	CAT, LARGE 7634NR70	RT	44.00	150.00
82	CAT, MINI 7659NR31	RT	16.00	85.00
84	DACHSHUND 7641NR75	RT	48.00	150.00
84	FALCON HEAD, LARGE 7645NR100	RT	600.00	1200.00
84	FROG 7642NR48	RT	30.00	190.00
86	FALCON HEAD, SMALL 7645NR45	RT	60.00	200.00
M. STAMEY				**ANIMALS**
88	WHALE 7628NR80	RT	70.00	240.00
89	TOUCAN 7621NR000002	RT	70.00	200.00
A. STOCKER				**ANIMALS**
87	PARTRIDGE 7625NR50	RT	85.00	200.00
M. SCHRECK				**BARNYARD FRIENDS**
*	PIG, MEDIUM (CRYSTAL TAIL) 7638NR50 STYLE CHANGE	RT	42.00	300.00
82	PIG, MINI	OP	16.00	30.00
84	PIG, MEDIUM	OP	35.00	47.50
G. STAMEY				**BARNYARD FRIENDS**
87	HEN, MINI	OP	35.00	45.00
87	ROOSTER, MINI	OP	35.00	55.00
88	CHICKS (SET OF 3) MINI	RT	35.00	45.00
A. STOCKER				**BARNYARD FRIENDS**
93	DICK GOSLING	OP	38.00	38.00
93	HARRY GOSLING	OP	38.00	38.00
93	MOTHER GOOSE	OP	75.00	75.00
93	TOM GOSLING	OP	38.00	38.00
A. HIRZINGER				**BEAUTIES OF THE LAKE**
95	SWAN, MAXI	OP	4,500.00	4500.00
M. SCHRECK				**BEAUTIES OF THE LAKE**
77	SWAN, LARGE	OP	55.00	95.00
77	SWAN, MEDIUM	OP	44.00	85.00
83	DRAKE, MINI	OP	20.00	45.00
86	MALLARD 7647NR80	RT	80.00	200.00
89	SWAN, SMALL	OP	35.00	50.00
M. STAMEY				**BEAUTIES OF THE LAKE**
89	MALLARD, GIANT	OP	2,000.00	4500.00
94	FROG	OP	50.00	50.00
96	GOLDFISH, MINI	OP	*	N/A
A. STOCKER				**BEAUTIES OF THE LAKE**
86	DUCK - STANDING, MINI	OP	22.00	38.00
86	DUCK - SWIMMING, MINI	OP	16.00	38.00
A. HIRZINGER				**CENTENARY EDITION**
95	CENTENARY SWAN	YR	150.00	225.00
G. STAMEY		**COLLECTORS SOCIETY ANNUAL EDITIONS**		
92	BIRTHDAY CAKE, THE 003-0169678	RT	85.00	275.00
M. SCHRECK		**COLLECTORS SOCIETY ANNUAL EDITIONS/CARING AND SHARING**		
87	LOVE BIRDS, THE DO1X861/TOGETHERNESS	RT	150.00	4800.00
A. STOCKER		**COLLECTORS SOCIETY ANNUAL EDITIONS/CARING AND SHARING**		
88	WOODPECKERS, THE DO1X881/SHARING	RT	165.00	2200.00
89	TURTLEDOVES, THE DO1X891/AMOUR	RT	195.00	1200.00
M. ZENDRON		**COLLECTORS SOCIETY ANNUAL EDITIONS/FABULOUS CREATURES**		
96	UNICORN, THE	OP	325.00	600.00
M. STAMEY		**COLLECTORS SOCIETY ANNUAL EDITIONS/INSPIRATION AFRICA**		
94	KUDU, THE DO1X941/INSPIRATION AFRICA	RT	*	600.00
A. STOCKER		**COLLECTORS SOCIETY ANNUAL EDITIONS/INSPIRATION AFRICA**		
95	LION, THE DO1X951/INSPIRATION AFRICA	RT	*	600.00
M. ZENDRON		**COLLECTORS SOCIETY ANNUAL EDITIONS/INSPIRATION AFRICA**		
93	ELEPHANT, THE DO1X931/INSPIRATION AFRICA	RT	325.00	1750.00
M. STAMEY		**COLLECTORS SOCIETY ANNUAL EDITIONS/MOTHER AND CHILD**		
90	DOLPHINS, THE DO1X901/LEAD ME	RT	225.00	1500.00
91	SEALS, THE DO1X911/SAVE ME	RT	225.00	600.00
92	WHALES, THE DO1X921/CARE FOR ME	RT	265.00	650.00
DESIGN TEAM		**COLLECTORS SOCIETY MEMBER EDITIONS**		
91	DOLPHINS BROOCH 003-8901707	RT	*	175.00
93	ELEPHANT BROOCH 003-8902448	RT	*	150.00
95	CENTENARY SWAN BROOCH	YR	125.00	175.00
DESIGN TEAM		**COMMEMORATIVE SINGLE ISSUE**		
90	ELEPHANT-COMMEMORATIVE ITEM/WALT DISNEY	CL	125.00	1250.00
93	ELEPHANT	OP	150.00	150.00
M. STAMEY				**CRYSTAL MELODIES**
96	VIOLIN	OP	*	N/A
M. ZENDRON				**CRYSTAL MELODIES**
92	HARP	OP	175.00	210.00
92	LUTE	RT	125.00	140.00
*				**ENDANGERED SPECIES**
77	TORTOISE, SMALL 7632NR030000	RT	*	N/A
M. SCHRECK				**ENDANGERED SPECIES**
77	TURTLE, LARGE	RT	48.00	75.00
77	TURTLE, SMALL	OP	35.00	70.00
81	TURTLE, GIANT	OP	2,500.00	4500.00
M. STAMEY				**ENDANGERED SPECIES**
91	KIWI 7617NR043000	RT	38.00	75.00
93	MOTHER KANGAROO WITH BABY	OP	95.00	95.00

YR	NAME	LIMIT	ISSUE	TREND
A. STOCKER			**ENDANGERED SPECIES**	
87	KOALA	OP	50.00	65.00
89	KOALA, MINI	OP	35.00	45.00
92	BEAVER, LYING BABY	RT	48.00	75.00
92	BEAVER, MOTHER 7616NR000001	RT	110.00	195.00
92	BEAVER, SITTING BABY	OP	48.00	50.00
93	PANDA, BABY	OP	25.00	25.00
93	PANDA, MOTHER	OP	120.00	120.00
DESIGN TEAM			**EXQUISITE ACCENTS**	
87	BIRD'S NEST 7470NR050000	RT	90.00	175.00
M. SCHRECK			**EXQUISITE ACCENTS**	
80	BIRDBATH	OP	150.00	210.00
87	DINNER BELL, MEDIUM	OP	80.00	95.00
87	DINNER BELL, SMALL	OP	60.00	65.00
M. STAMEY			**EXQUISITE ACCENTS**	
92	ROSE, THE	OP	150.00	150.00
95	ORCHID, THE/PINK	OP	140.00	140.00
95	ORCHID, THE/YELLOW	OP	140.00	140.00
A. STOCKER			**EXQUISITE ACCENTS**	
95	ANGEL	OP	210.00	210.00
A. HIRZINGER			**FEATHERED FRIENDS**	
93	PELICAN	OP	38.00	38.00
E. MAIR			**FEATHERED FRIENDS**	
95	DOVE	OP	55.00	55.00
*				**FRUIT**
*	GRAPES, LARGE 7550NR30015	RT	250.00	1500.00
M. SCHRECK				**FRUIT**
*	APPLE PHOTO STAND, LARGE/RHODIUM	RT	80.00	350.00
*	APPLE PHOTO STAND, SMALL/RHODIUM	RT	40.00	275.00
*	GIANT PINEAPPLE-RHODIUM 7507NR260002	RT	1,750.00	3750.00
M. SCHRECK			**GAME OF KINGS**	
84	CHESS SET	OP	950.00	3000.00
*			**IN A SUMMER MEADOW**	
82	BUTTERFLY	OP	44.00	85.00
85	HEDGEHOG 7630NR070000	RT	*	N/A
E. MAIR			**IN A SUMMER MEADOW**	
95	LADYBUG	OP	30.00	30.00
C. SCHNEIDERBAUER			**IN A SUMMER MEADOW**	
92	SPARROW	RT	30.00	30.00
M. SCHRECK			**IN A SUMMER MEADOW**	
76	MOUSE, MEDIUM 7631NR40	RT	48.00	140.00
85	HEDGEHOG, LARGE 7630NR50	RT	65.00	300.00
85	HEDGEHOG, MEDIUM 7630NR40	RT	70.00	250.00
87	HEDGEHOG, SMALL 7630NR30	RT	50.00	450.00
A. STOCKER			**IN A SUMMER MEADOW**	
88	MOTHER RABBIT	OP	60.00	75.00
88	RABBIT - SITTING, MINI	OP	35.00	45.00
91	FIELD MOUSE	OP	48.00	50.00
94	FIELD MICE	OP	43.00	43.00
*			**JULIA'S WORLD**	
90	JULIA W/MANDOLIN	OP	30.00	30.00
90	LENA & PEPI/BENCH	OP	55.00	55.00
90	LENA W/LUTE	OP	30.00	30.00
90	MARIAN	OP	30.00	30.00
90	PEPI & MOPSY	OP	55.00	55.00
90	PEPI W/DRUM	OP	30.00	30.00
90	SALI	OP	30.00	30.00
90	SALI W/ACCORDION	OP	30.00	30.00
M. SCHRECK			**KINGDOM OF ICE AND SNOW**	
84	PENGUIN, LARGE 7643NR85	RT	44.00	125.00
84	PENGUIN, MINI	OP	16.00	38.00
A. STOCKER			**KINGDOM OF ICE AND SNOW**	
86	BABY SEAL, MINI	OP	30.00	45.00
86	POLAR BEAR, LARGE	RT	140.00	210.00
*				**NATIVITY**
91	HOLY FAMILY WITH ARCH 7475NR001	RT	250.00	375.00
92	ANGEL 7475NR000009	RT	65.00	175.00
92	SHEPHERD 7475NR000007	RT	65.00	175.00
92	WISE MEN (SET OF 3)	RT	175.00	300.00
*			**OUR CANDLEHOLDERS**	
87	STAR, LARGE 7600NR143000	RT	250.00	450.00
89	STAR, MEDIUM	OP	200.00	260.00
M. SCHRECK			**OUR CANDLEHOLDERS**	
83	WATER LILY, MEDIUM	OP	150.00	260.00
85	WATER LILY, LARGE	OP	200.00	375.00
85	WATER LILY, SMALL	OP	100.00	175.00
A. STOCKER			**OUR CANDLEHOLDERS**	
90	NEO-CLASSIC, LARGE	RT	220.00	400.00
90	NEO-CLASSIC, MEDIUM	RT	190.00	300.00
90	NEO-CLASSIC, SMALL	RT	170.00	250.00
A. HIRZINGER			**OUR WOODLAND FRIENDS**	
95	OUTLET	OP	45.00	45.00

YR	NAME	LIMIT	ISSUE	TREND
E. MAIR			**OUR WOODLAND FRIENDS**	
94	ROE DEER FAWN	RT	75.00	75.00
M. SCHRECK			**OUR WOODLAND FRIENDS**	
79	OWL, LARGE	OP	90.00	125.00
79	OWL, MINI	OP	16.00	30.00
81	BEAR, LARGE	OP	75.00	95.00
83	OWL, GIANT	OP	1,200.00	2000.00
85	BEAR, MINI	OP	16.00	55.00
85	SQUIRREL	OP	35.00	65.00
A. STOCKER			**OUR WOODLAND FRIENDS**	
87	FOX	RT	50.00	150.00
88	FOX - SITTING, MINI	OP	35.00	45.00
89	MUSHROOMS	RT	35.00	45.00
M. SCHRECK			**PAPERWEIGHTS**	
82	CONE	RT	80.00	225.00
87	CHATON, LARGE	RT	190.00	260.00
87	CHATON, SMALL	RT	50.00	65.00
87	PYRAMID, LARGE	OP	90.00	250.00
87	PYRAMID, SMALL	RT	100.00	125.00
90	CHATON, GIANT	OP	3,900.00	4500.00
*			**RETIRED**	
*	SPARROW, LARGE 7650NR32	RT	38.00	175.00
85	BUTTERFLY	RT	200.00	1100.00
85	HUMMINGBIRD RHODIUM 7552NR200	RT	200.00	3750.00
85	HUMMINGBIRD-GOLD 7552NR100	RT	200.00	2000.00
86	BUTTERFLY, MINI 7671NR30	RT	16.00	200.00
M. SCHRECK			**RETIRED**	
*	APPLE PHOTO STAND, KING SIZE/RHODIUM	RT	120.00	750.00
*	DACHSHUND, MINI 7672NR42	RT	35.00	225.00
*	DOG 7635NR70	RT	44.00	150.00
*	DUCK, MEDIUM 7653NR55	RT	38.00	150.00
*	ELEPHANT, LARGE 7640NR55	RT	90.00	300.00
*	PINEAPPLE, LARGE/RHODIUM 7507NR105002	RT	150.00	450.00
*	RABBIT, LARGE 7652NR45	RT	38.00	350.00
*	SEAL, BLACK NOSE 7646NR85	RT	85.00	275.00
*	SEAL, SILVER WHISKERS 7646NR85	RT	85.00	165.00
79	OWL, SMALL 7636NR46	RT	59.00	120.00
79	SPARROW, MINI 7650NR20	RT	16.00	90.00
81	DINNER BELL, LARGE	RT	80.00	150.00
81	EGG	RT	60.00	150.00
82	BEAR, SMALL 7637NR54	RT	44.00	150.00
84	BEAR, MINI 7670NR32	RT	16.00	250.00
84	FROG W/CLEAR EYES 7642NR48	RT	30.00	400.00
85	SEAL, LARGE 7645NR85	RT	44.00	140.00
87	PINEAPPLE, SMALL/RHODIUM 7507NR060002	RT	55.00	200.00
88	SWAN, MINI 7658NR27	RT	16.00	175.00
M. STAMEY			**RETIRED**	
86	SNAIL 7648NR30	RT	35.00	95.00
89	OWL 7621NR000003	RT	85.00	220.00
89	WALRUS 7620NR100000	RT	120.00	200.00
91	SOUTH SEA SHELL 7624NR072000	RT	110.00	140.00
A. STOCKER			**RETIRED**	
87	DACHSHUND, MINI 7672NR042	RT	20.00	125.00
88	FOX - RUNNING, MINI	RT	35.00	60.00
88	RABBIT, LYING MINI 7678NR030	RT	35.00	125.00
88	RHINOCEROS 7622NR70	RT	70.00	180.00
90	RHINOCEROS, SMALL 7622NR60	RT	70.00	130.00
G. STAMEY			**SILVER CRYSTAL CITY**	
*	TOWN HALL 7474NR000027	RT	135.00	250.00
90	CATHEDRAL	RT	95.00	250.00
90	HOUSES I & II	RT	75.00	150.00
90	HOUSES III & IV	RT	75.00	150.00
90	POPLARS	RT	40.00	125.00
91	CITY GATES 7474NR000023	RT	95.00	175.00
91	CITY TOWER 7474NR000022	RT	38.00	125.00
A. STOCKER			**SILVER CRYSTAL WORLDWIDE LIMITED EDITION**	
95	EAGLE	RT	1,750.00	5000.00
*			**SOUTH SEA**	
86	BLOWFISH, SMALL	OP	35.00	55.00
87	BLOWFISH, MINI	OP	22.00	30.00
M. STAMEY			**SOUTH SEA**	
88	OPEN SHELL WITH PEARL	OP	120.00	200.00
91	BUTTERFLY FISH	RT	150.00	175.00
93	SEA HORSE	OP	85.00	85.00
95	CONCH	OP	30.00	30.00
95	DOLPHIN	OP	210.00	210.00
95	MARITIME TRIO	OP	104.00	104.00
95	SHELL	OP	30.00	30.00
95	STARFISH	OP	30.00	30.00
DESIGN TEAM			**SPARKLING FRUIT**	
85	GRAPES, MEDIUM 7550NR20029	RT	300.00	450.00
85	GRAPES, SMALL 7550NR20015	RT	200.00	300.00
M. SCHRECK			**SPARKLING FRUIT**	
*	APPLE PHOTO STAND, KING SIZE/GOLD	RT	150.00	600.00

YR	NAME	LIMIT	ISSUE	TREND
*	APPLE PHOTO STAND, LARGE/GOLD	RT	80.00	300.00
*	APPLE PHOTO STAND, SMALL/GOLD	RT	60.00	225.00
81	PINEAPPLE, GIANT	OP	1,750.00	3250.00
81	PINEAPPLE, LARGE	RT	150.00	450.00
86	PINEAPPLE, SMALL	RT	55.00	85.00
M. STAMEY			**SPARKLING FRUIT**	
91	APPLE 7476NR000001	RT	175.00	225.00
91	PEAR	RT	175.00	185.00
M. STAMEY			**UP IN THE TREES**	
89	PARROT 7621NR000004	RT	70.00	200.00
90	KINGFISHER 7621NR000001	RT	75.00	200.00
*			**WHEN WE WERE YOUNG**	
94	REPLICA HEDGEHOG	OP	38.00	38.00
94	REPLICA CAT	OP	38.00	38.00
94	REPLICA MOUSE	OP	38.00	38.00
94	STARTER SET	OP	113.00	113.00
G. STAMEY			**WHEN WE WERE YOUNG**	
88	LOCOMOTIVE	OP	150.00	155.00
88	TENDER	OP	55.00	55.00
88	WAGON	OP	85.00	95.00
89	OLD TIMER AUTOMOBILE	RT	130.00	175.00
90	PETROL WAGON	OP	75.00	95.00
91	SANTA MARIA	OP	375.00	375.00
93	TIPPING WAGON	OP	95.00	95.00
94	SAILBOAT	OP	195.00	195.00
95	TRAIN, MINI	OP	125.00	125.00
A. STOCKER			**WHEN WE WERE YOUNG**	
90	AIRPLANE	OP	135.00	155.00
M. ZENDRON			**WHEN WE WERE YOUNG**	
93	KRIS BEAR	OP	75.00	75.00
95	KRIS BEAR ON SKATES	OP	75.00	75.00

THOMAS F. CLARK CO.

T. CLARK			**TOM CLARK CREATIONS**	
*	ABEDNEGO	*	*	75.00
*	ABRAHAM	*	*	180.00
*	ADAM	*	*	125.00
*	AHAB	*	*	350.00
*	ALPHA	*	*	150.00
*	BELLE KRINGLE	*	*	200.00
*	BLACKSMITH	*	*	280.00
*	CALEB	*	*	200.00
*	COWBOY	*	*	150.00
*	DAFFY	*	*	225.00
*	ERNEST	*	*	270.00
*	GERBER	*	*	400.00

TUDOR MINT

J. WATSON				
91	POWER OF THE CRYSTAL, THE	3500	478.00	525.00
S. RILEY			**EXHIBITION ONLY STUDIES**	
93	DACTRIUS	*	64.00	70.00
J. WATSON			**EXHIBITION ONLY STUDIES**	
94	VEXIUS	*	67.00	70.00
S. RILEY			**EXTRAVAGANZA STUDIES**	
92	SAURIA	403	32.00	40.00
94	LITHIA	*	32.00	33.00
J. WATSON			**EXTRAVAGANZA STUDIES**	
93	DEINOS	463	32.00	35.00
S. RILEY			**MYTH & MAGIC CLUB**	
90	QUEST FOR THE TRUTH, THE	1282	80.00	83.00
92	FRIENDS	*	30.00	32.00
92	PLAYMATES	3778	27.00	30.00
93	MYSTICAL ENCOUNTER, THE	*	32.00	35.00
94	CRYSTAL SHIELD, THE	OP	44.00	48.00
94	KEEPER OF THE DRAGONS, THE	*	80.00	85.00
95	BATTLE FOR THE CRYSTAL, THE	OP	108.00	108.00
J. WATSON			**MYTH & MAGIC CLUB**	
91	GAME OF STRAX, THE	2533	24.00	25.00
91	WELL OF ASPIRATIONS, THE	2973	80.00	85.00
92	ENCHANTED POOL, THE	*	80.00	85.00
S. RILEY			**MYTH & MAGIC-LARGE STUDIES**	
90	DANCE OF THE DOLPHINS, THE	1537	280.00	300.00
90	DRAGON MASTER, THE	1500	280.00	300.00
90	VII SEEKERS OF KNOWLEDGE, THE	7500	280.00	300.00
J. WATSON			**MYTH & MAGIC-LARGE STUDIES**	
92	GATHERING OF THE UNICORNS, THE	5000	296.00	325.00
S. RILEY			**ONE YEAR ONLY STUDIES**	
94	DRAGON OF THE UNDERWORLD, THE	YR	67.00	70.00
95	GUARDIAN OF THE CRYSTAL, THE	YR	108.00	108.00
J. WATSON			**ONE YEAR ONLY STUDIES**	
93	FLYING DRAGON, THE	YR	64.00	70.00

YR	NAME	LIMIT	ISSUE	TREND

UNITED DESIGN CORP.

S. BRADFORD

ANGELS COLLECTION

YR	NAME	LIMIT	ISSUE	TREND
91	CHRISTMAS ANGEL AA-003	10000	125.00	125.00
91	CLASSICAL ANGEL AA-005	10000	79.00	79.00
91	GIFT, THE- AA-009	3500	140.00	500.00
91	HEAVENLY SHEPHERDESS AA-008	10000	99.00	99.00
91	MESSENGER OF PEACE AA-006	RT	75.00	75.00
91	TRUMPETER ANGEL AA-004	RT	99.00	99.00
91	WINTER ROSE ANGEL AA-007	10000	65.00	65.00
93	GIFT, THE- '93	RT	120.00	140.00
94	EARTH ANGEL	RT	84.00	84.00
94	HARVEST ANGEL	RT	84.00	84.00

P. JONAS

ANGELS COLLECTION

YR	NAME	LIMIT	ISSUE	TREND
91	ANGEL WAIF AA-012	OP	15.00	16.00
91	PEACE DESCENDING ANGEL AA-013	OP	20.00	20.00
91	ROSETTI ANGEL AA-011	OP	20.00	20.00
91	VICTORIAN CUPID ANGEL AA-010	OP	15.00	16.00

K. MEMOLI

ANGELS COLLECTION

YR	NAME	LIMIT	ISSUE	TREND
93	ANGEL OF FLIGHT	10000	100.00	100.00
93	MADONNA	10000	100.00	100.00
94	ANGEL WITH CHRIST CHILD	10000	84.00	84.00
94	DREAMING OF ANGELS	10000	120.00	120.00

D. NEWBURN

ANGELS COLLECTION

YR	NAME	LIMIT	ISSUE	TREND
93	ANGEL WITH BIRDS	10000	75.00	75.00
93	ANGEL WITH LEAVES	10000	70.00	70.00
93	ANGEL WITH LEAVES, EMERALD	RT	70.00	90.00
93	ANGEL WITH LILIES	10000	80.00	80.00
93	ANGELS WITH LILIES, CRIMSON	RT	80.00	100.00
94	ANGEL WITH BOOK	10000	84.00	84.00
94	ANGEL, ROSES & BLUEBIRDS	10000	65.00	65.00
94	GIFT, THE- '94	RT	140.00	150.00

S. BRADFORD

BACKYARD BIRDS

YR	NAME	LIMIT	ISSUE	TREND
88	BABY ROBIN, SMALL BB-006	OP	10.00	10.00
88	BABY ROBINS BB-008	OP	15.00	18.00
88	BLUEBIRD BB-009	OP	15.00	20.00
88	BLUEBIRD, SMALL BB-001	OP	10.00	10.00
88	CARDINAL, SMALL BB-002	OP	10.00	10.00
88	CHICKADEE BB-010	OP	15.00	17.00
88	CHICKADEE, SMALL BB-003	OP	10.00	10.00
88	FEMALE CARDINAL BB-011	OP	15.00	17.00
88	FEMALE HUMMINGBIRD, SMALL BB-005	RT	10.00	10.00
88	FLYING HUMMINGBIRD, SMALL BB-004	OP	10.00	10.00
88	HANGING BLUEBIRD BB-017	RT	11.00	17.00
88	HANGING CARDINAL BB-018	RT	11.00	11.00
88	HANGING CHICKADEE BB-019	RT	11.00	11.00
88	HANGING HUMMINGBIRD, LARGE BB-023	RT	15.00	16.00
88	HANGING HUMMINGBIRD, SMALL BB-022	RT	11.00	11.00
88	HANGING ROBIN BB-020	RT	11.00	11.00
88	HANGING SPARROW BB-021	RT	11.00	11.00
88	HUMMINGBIRD BB-012	OP	15.00	17.00
88	MALE CARDIDNAL BB-013	OP	15.00	17.00
88	RED-WINGED BLACKBIRD BB-014	RT	15.00	17.00
88	ROBIN BB-015	OP	15.00	20.00
88	SPARROW BB-016	OP	15.00	17.00
88	SPARROW, SMALL BB-007	OP	10.00	10.00
89	BABY BLUE JAY BB-027	OP	15.00	16.00
89	BALTIMORE ORIOLE BB-024	OP	20.00	22.00
89	BLUE JAY BB-026	OP	20.00	22.00
89	GOLDFINCH BB-028	OP	16.50	20.00
89	HOOT OWL BB-025	OP	15.00	20.00
89	SAW-WHET OWL BB-029	OP	15.00	20.00
89	WOODPECKER BB-030	OP	16.50	20.00
90	BABY CEDAR WAXWINGS BB-033	OP	22.00	22.00
90	BLUEBIRD (UPRIGHT) BB-031	OP	20.00	20.00
90	CEDAR WAXWING BB-032	OP	20.00	20.00
90	EVENING GROSBEAK BB-034	OP	22.00	22.00
90	FEMALE INDIGO BUNTING BB-039	OP	20.00	20.00
90	INDIGO BUNTING BB-036	OP	20.00	20.00
90	NUTHATCH, WHITE-THROATED BB-037	OP	20.00	20.00
90	PAINTED BUNTING BB-040	OP	20.00	20.00
90	PAINTED BUNTING, FEMALE BB-041	OP	20.00	20.00
90	PURPLE FINCH BB-038	OP	20.00	20.00
90	ROSE BREASTED GROSBEAK BB-042	OP	20.00	20.00

D. KENNICUTT

EASTER BUNNY FAMILY

YR	NAME	LIMIT	ISSUE	TREND
88	BUNNIES, BASKET OF SEC-001	RT	13.00	18.00
88	BUNNY BOY W/DUCK SEC-002	RT	13.00	18.00
88	BUNNY GIRL W/HEN SEC-004	RT	13.00	18.00
88	BUNNY, EASTER SEC-003	RT	13.00	18.00
88	RABBIT, GRANDMA SEC-005	RT	15.00	18.00
88	RABBIT, GRANDPA SEC-006	RT	15.00	18.00
88	RABBIT, MOMMA W/BONNET SEC-007	RT	15.00	18.00
89	AUNTIE BUNNY SEC-008	RT	20.00	23.00
89	BUNNY W/PRIZE EGG SEC-010	OP	20.00	20.00
89	DUCKY W/BONNET, BLUE SEC-015	OP	10.00	12.00

YR	NAME	LIMIT	ISSUE	TREND
89	DUCKY W/BONNET, PINK SEC-014	OP	10.00	12.00
89	EASTER EGG HUNT SEC-012	OP	16.50	20.00
89	LITTLE SIS W/LOLLY SEC-009	OP	14.50	18.00
89	ROCK-A-BYE BUNNY SEC-013	OP	20.00	23.00
89	SIS & BUBBA SHARING SEC-011	OP	23.00	23.00
90	BUBBA W/WAGON SEC-016	OP	16.50	18.00
90	EASTER BUNNY W/CRYSTAL SEC-017	OP	23.00	23.00
90	HEN W/CHICK SEC-018	OP	23.00	23.00
90	MOMMA MAKING BASKET SEC-019	OP	23.00	23.00
90	MOTHER GOOSE SEC-020	OP	16.50	20.00
91	BABY IN BUGGY, BOY SEC-027	RT	20.00	20.00
91	BABY IN BUGGY, GIRL SEC-029	RT	20.00	20.00
91	BUBBA IN WHEELBARROW SEC-021	OP	20.00	20.00
91	BUNNY BOY W/ BASKET SEC-025	OP	20.00	20.00
91	FANCY FIND SEC-028	OP	20.00	20.00
91	LOP-EAR W/CRYSTAL SEC-022	OP	23.00	23.00
91	NEST OF BUNNY EGGS SEC-023	OP	17.50	18.00
91	VICTORIAN AUNTIE BUNNY SEC-026	OP	20.00	20.00
91	VICTORIAN MOMMA SEC-024	OP	20.00	20.00

K. MEMOLI | | | | **FAERIE TALES**

YR	NAME	LIMIT	ISSUE	TREND
90	FAERIE FLIGHT	7500	39.00	39.00
90	SLEEPING FAERIE	7500	39.00	39.00
90	WATER SPRITE	7500	39.00	39.00
90	WIND SPRITE	7500	39.00	39.00
90	WINTER FAERIE	7500	39.00	39.00
90	WOOD SPRITE	7500	39.00	39.00

MEMOLI/JONAS | | | | **LEGEND OF SANTA CLAUS**

YR	NAME	LIMIT	ISSUE	TREND
90	SAFE ARRIVAL CF-027	7500	150.00	150.00

S. BRADFORD | | | | **LEGEND OF SANTA CLAUS**

YR	NAME	LIMIT	ISSUE	TREND
86	ROOFTOP SANTA CF-004	RT	65.00	79.00
86	SANTA WITH PUPS CF-003	RT	65.00	250.00
87	DREAMING OF SANTA CF-008	RT	65.00	250.00
87	MRS. SANTA CF-006	RT	60.00	75.00
87	ON SANTA'S KNEE CF-007	15000	65.00	79.00
87	SANTA ON HORSEBACK CF-011	RT	75.00	250.00
88	FATHER CHRISTMAS CF-018	7500	75.00	85.00
88	LOAD 'EM UP CF-016	RT	79.00	250.00
89	A PURRR-FECT CHRISTMAS CF-019	7500	95.00	95.00
89	CHRISTMAS HARMONY CF-020	7500	85.00	85.00
90	VICTORIAN SANTA CF-028	7500	125.00	125.00
90	WAITING FOR SANTA CF-026	7500	100.00	100.00
91	VICTORIAN SANTA W/TEDDY CF-033	7500	150.00	150.00
93	NORTHWOODS SANTA	7500	100.00	110.00
93	VICT., LION AND LAMB SANTA	7500	100.00	110.00
94	STAR SANTA WITH POLAR BEAR	7500	130.00	130.00

K. MEMOLI | | | | **LEGEND OF SANTA CLAUS**

YR	NAME	LIMIT	ISSUE	TREND
91	BLESSED FLIGHT CF-032	7500	159.00	159.00
91	REINDEER WALK CF-031	7500	150.00	150.00
93	DEAR SANTA	7500	170.00	185.00
93	JOLLY ST. NICK	7500	130.00	140.00
93	JOLLY ST. NICK, VICT.	7500	120.00	130.00
94	LONGSTOCKING DILEMMA	7500	170.00	170.00
94	LONGSTOCKING DILEMMA, VICT.	7500	170.00	170.00
94	STORY OF CHRISTMAS, THE	10000	180.00	180.00

L. MILLER | | | | **LEGEND OF SANTA CLAUS**

YR	NAME	LIMIT	ISSUE	TREND
86	ELF PAIR CF-005	10000	60.00	75.00
86	KRIS KRINGLE CF-002	RT	60.00	75.00
86	SANTA AT REST CF-001	RT	70.00	250.00
87	CHECKING HIS LIST CF-009	15000	75.00	85.00
87	LOADING SANTA'S SLEIGH CF-010	15000	100.00	100.00
88	ASSEMBLY REQUIRED CF-017	7500	79.00	95.00
88	ST. NICHOLAS CF-015	7500	75.00	85.00
89	HITCHING UP CF-021	7500	90.00	90.00
90	FOREST FRIENDS CF-025	7500	90.00	90.00
90	PUPPY LOVE CF-024	7500	100.00	100.00
91	FOR SANTA CF-029	7500	99.00	99.00
91	SANTA AT WORK CF-030	7500	99.00	99.00
93	NIGHT BEFORE CHRISTMAS	7500	100.00	110.00
93	SANTA'S FRIENDS	7500	100.00	110.00
94	SANTA RIDING DOVE	7500	120.00	120.00

L. MILLER | | | | **LEGEND OF THE LITTLE PEOPLE**

YR	NAME	LIMIT	ISSUE	TREND
89	A FRIENDLY TOAST LL-003	RT	35.00	45.00
89	ADVENTURE BOUND LL-002	RT	35.00	45.00
89	CADDY'S HELPER LL-007	RT	35.00	45.00
89	MAGICAL DISCOVERY LL-005	RT	45.00	45.00
89	SPRING WATER SCRUB LL-006	RT	35.00	45.00
89	TREASURE HUNT LL-004	RT	45.00	45.00
89	WOODLAND CACHE LL-001	RT	35.00	45.00
90	A LITTLE JIG LL-018	RT	45.00	45.00
90	A LOOK THROUGH THE SPYGLASS LL-015	RT	40.00	45.00
90	A PROCLAMATION LL-013	RT	45.00	50.00
90	FISHIN' HOLE LL-012	RT	35.00	45.00
90	GATHERING ACORNS LL-014	RT	100.00	100.00
90	HEDGEHOG IN HARNESS LL-010	RT	45.00	45.00
90	HUSKING ACORNS LL-008	RT	60.00	60.00

YR	NAME	LIMIT	ISSUE	TREND
90	MINSTRAL MAGIC LL-017	RT	45.00	45.00
90	TRAVELING FAST LL-009	RT	45.00	45.00
90	WOODLAND SCOUT LL-011	RT	40.00	45.00
90	WRITING THE LEGEND LL-016	RT	65.00	65.00
91	EASTER BUNNY'S CART, THE LL-020	RT	45.00	45.00
91	FIRE IT UP LL-023	RT	50.00	50.00
91	GOT IT LL-021	RT	45.00	45.00
91	IT'S ABOUT TIME LL-022	RT	55.00	55.00
91	VIKING LL-019	RT	45.00	45.00
P. JONAS				**LIL' DOLLS**
91	ANGELA BEAR LD-010	10000	35.00	35.00
91	ARCHIBALD BEAR LD-009	10000	35.00	35.00
91	BETTY BUTTON'S SURPRISE LD-008	10000	35.00	35.00
91	GEORGIE BEAR LD-001	10000	35.00	35.00
91	JENNY BEAR LD-002	10000	35.00	35.00
91	NUTCRACKER LD-006	RT	35.00	35.00
D. NEWBURN				**LIL' DOLLS**
91	ADDIE LD-013	10000	35.00	35.00
91	AMY LD-003	10000	35.00	35.00
91	BECKY BUNNY LD-005	10000	35.00	35.00
91	KRISTA LD-014	10000	35.00	35.00
91	MARCHING IN TIME LD-007	10000	35.00	35.00
91	SAM LD-004	10000	35.00	35.00
91	SARA LD-011	10000	35.00	35.00
91	TESS LD-015	10000	35.00	35.00
91	TOM LD-012	10000	35.00	35.00
S. BRADFORD				**MUSICMAKERS**
89	HERALD ANGEL MM-011	12000	79.00	79.00
89	TEDDY BEAR BAND MM-012	12000	99.00	99.00
D. KENNICUTT				**MUSICMAKERS**
89	CHRISTMAS TREE MM-008	OP	69.00	69.00
89	EVENING CAROLERS MM-005	OP	69.00	69.00
89	SNOWSHOE SLED RIDE MM-007	OP	69.00	69.00
89	TEDDIES AND FROSTY MM-010	OP	69.00	69.00
89	TEDDY DRUMMERS MM-009	OP	69.00	69.00
89	WINTER FUN MM-006	OP	69.00	69.00
91	A CHRISTMAS GIFT MM-015	OP	59.00	59.00
91	CRYSTAL ANGEL MM-017	OP	59.00	59.00
91	DASHING THROUGH THE SNOW MM-013	OP	59.00	59.00
91	TEDDY SOLDIERS MM-018	OP	69.00	69.00
91	TWO FAERIES MM-014	OP	59.00	59.00
L. MILLER				**MUSICMAKERS**
89	COMING TO TOWN MM-001	OP	69.00	69.00
89	MERRY LITTLE CHRISTMAS MM-002	OP	69.00	69.00
89	MERRY MAKING MM-003	RT	69.00	90.00
89	SANTA'S SLEIGH MM-004	OP	69.00	69.00
D. KENNICUTT				**PARTY ANIMALS**
84	DEMOCRATIC DONKEY ('84)	RT	14.50	16.00
90	DEMOCRATIC DONKEY ('90)	RT	16.00	16.00
90	GOP ELEPHANT ('90)	RT	16.00	16.00
L. MILLER				**PARTY ANIMALS**
84	GOP ELEPHANT ('84)	RT	14.50	16.00
86	DEMOCRATIC DONKEY ('86)	RT	14.50	15.00
86	GOP ELEPHANT ('86)	RT	14.50	15.00
88	DEMOCRATIC DONKEY ('88)	RT	14.50	16.00
88	GOP ELEPHANT ('88)	RT	14.50	16.00
P. JONAS				**PENNIBEARS**
90	ATTIC FUN PB-019	RT	20.00	22.00
90	BABY HUGS PB-007	RT	20.00	22.00
90	BATHTIME BUDDIES PB-023	RT	20.00	22.00
90	BEAUTIFUL BRIDE PB-004	RT	20.00	24.00
90	BIRTHDAY BEAR PB-018	RT	20.00	24.00
90	BOOOO BEAR PB-025	RT	20.00	22.00
90	BOUQUET BOY PB-003	RT	20.00	20.00
90	BOUQUET GIRL PB-001	RT	20.00	22.00
90	BUTTERFLY BEAR PB-005	RT	20.00	22.00
90	BUTTONS & BOWS PB-012	RT	20.00	22.00
90	COOKIE BANDIT PB-006	RT	20.00	22.00
90	COUNT BEARACULA PB-027	RT	22.00	24.00
90	COUNTRY QUILTER PB-030	RT	22.00	26.00
90	COUNTRY SPRING PB-013	RT	20.00	22.00
90	DOCTOR BEAR PB-008	RT	20.00	22.00
90	DRESS UP FUN PB-028	RT	22.00	24.00
90	GARDEN PATH PB-014	RT	20.00	22.00
90	GIDDIAP TEDDY PB-011	RT	20.00	24.00
90	HANDSOME GROOM PB-015	RT	20.00	22.00
90	HONEY BEAR PB-002	RT	20.00	20.00
90	LAZY DAYS PB-009	RT	20.00	22.00
90	NAP TIME PB-016	RT	20.00	22.00
90	NURSE BEAR PB-017	RT	20.00	22.00
90	PETITE MADEMOISELLE PB-010	RT	20.00	22.00
90	PUPPY BATH PB-020	RT	20.00	22.00
90	PUPPY LOVE PB-021	RT	20.00	22.00
90	SANTA BEAR-ING GIFTS PB-031	RT	24.00	26.00

YR	NAME	LIMIT	ISSUE	TREND
90	SCARECROW TEDDY PB-029	RT	24.00	24.00
90	SNEAKY SNOWBALL PB-026	RT	20.00	22.00
90	SOUTHERN BELLE PB-024	RT	20.00	22.00
90	STOCKING SURPRISE PB-032	RT	22.00	26.00
90	TUBBY TEDDY PB-022	RT	20.00	22.00
91	A WILD RIDE PB-052	RT	26.00	26.00
91	BAKING GOODIES PB-043	RT	26.00	26.00
91	BEAR FOOTIN' IT PB-037	RT	24.00	24.00
91	BEARLY AWAKE PB-033	RT	22.00	22.00
91	BOO HOO BEAR PB-050	RT	22.00	22.00
91	BOUNTIFUL HARVEST PB-045	RT	24.00	24.00
91	BUMP-BEAR CROP PB-035	RT	26.00	26.00
91	BUNNY BUDDIES PB-042	RT	22.00	22.00
91	CHRISTMAS REINBEAR PB-046	RT	28.00	28.00
91	COUNTRY LULLABYE PB-036	RT	24.00	24.00
91	CURTAIN CALL PB-049	RT	24.00	24.00
91	GOODNIGHT LITTLE PRINCE PB-041	RT	26.00	26.00
91	GOODNIGHT SWEET PRINCESS PB-040	RT	26.00	26.00
91	HAPPY HOBO PB-051	RT	26.00	26.00
91	LIL' MER-TEDDY PB-034	RT	24.00	24.00
91	PILGRIM PROVIDER PB-047	RT	32.00	32.00
91	SUMMER SAILING PB-039	RT	26.00	26.00
91	SWEET LIL 'SIS PB-048	RT	22.00	22.00
91	SWEETHEART BEARS PB-044	RT	28.00	28.00
91	WINDY DAY PB-038	RT	24.00	24.00

P. JONAS   PENNIBEARS COLLECTOR'S CLUB MEMBERS ONLY EDITIONS

YR	NAME	LIMIT	ISSUE	TREND
90	FIRST COLLECTION PB-C90	RT	26.00	26.00
91	COLLECTING MAKES CENTS PB-C91	RT	26.00	26.00

H. HENRIKSEN   STORYTIME RHYMES & TALES

YR	NAME	LIMIT	ISSUE	TREND
91	HUMPTY DUMPTY 008	RT	64.00	64.00
91	LITTLE JACK HORNER 007	RT	50.00	50.00
91	LITTLE MISS MUFFET 006	RT	64.00	64.00
91	MISTRESS MARY 002	RT	64.00	64.00
91	MOTHER GOOSE 001	RT	64.00	64.00
91	OWL & PUSSY CAT 004	RT	100.00	100.00
91	SIMPLE SIMON 003	RT	90.00	90.00
91	THREE LITTLE PIGS 005	RT	100.00	100.00

S. BRADFORD   SUZY'S ZOO

YR	NAME	LIMIT	ISSUE	TREND
90	BABY QUACKER	OP	20.00	20.00
90	BUNNY BABY	OP	20.00	20.00
90	BUNNY BRIDE & GROOM	OP	25.00	25.00
90	CORKY PILGRIM	OP	25.00	25.00
90	CORKY TURTLE & HAT	OP	23.00	23.00
90	CORKY, HEART FELT	OP	23.00	23.00
90	JACK & FLOWERS	OP	23.00	23.00
90	MARMOT BABY, RAINY DAY	OP	20.00	20.00
90	MARMOT CAROLERS	OP	25.00	25.00
90	MARMOT SISTERS/PALS	OP	25.00	25.00
90	MARMOTS DANCING	OP	25.00	25.00
90	MARTHA MARMOT	OP	23.00	23.00
90	OLLIE MARMOT	OP	23.00	23.00
90	POLLY QUACKER	OP	23.00	23.00
90	RITZ, SIGNING-I LOVE YOU	OP	23.00	23.00
90	RITZ-HAY THERE	OP	20.00	20.00
90	SUZY & FAVORITE PILLOW	OP	23.00	23.00
90	SUZY & TEDDY	OP	23.00	23.00
90	SUZY, ARTIST	OP	23.00	23.00
90	SUZY, BEAUTY QUEEN	OP	25.00	25.00
90	TEDDY	OP	20.00	20.00
90	TILLIAMOOK & FLOWERS	OP	23.00	23.00
90	TILLIAMOOK, BALLERINA	OP	23.00	23.00

VAILLANCOURT FOLK ART

N. BAILEY   ANGEL DARLINGS

YR	NAME	LIMIT	ISSUE	TREND
96	ALMOST FITS H4765/1	OP	15.00	15.00

J. VAILLANCOURT   COLLECTIBLE RABBIT

YR	NAME	LIMIT	ISSUE	TREND
95	CHALKWARE PEDDLAR, 9513	OP	130.00	130.00
95	LTD. LADY RABBIT, 9502	250	190.00	190.00
95	RABBIT AND CHICKS, 9505	OP	90.00	90.00
95	RABBIT AND LAMB, 9504	OP	150.00	150.00
95	RABBIT LEANING ON EGG, 9508	OP	130.00	130.00
95	RABBIT ON DUCK, 9506	OP	60.00	60.00
95	RABBIT ON MALLARD, 9507	OP	80.00	80.00
95	RABBIT W/APRON, 9511	OP	65.00	65.00
95	RABBIT/BARREL, 9512	OP	110.00	110.00
95	RABBIT/UMBRELLA, 9514	OP	140.00	140.00
95	ROCKER RABBIT, 9503	OP	130.00	130.00
95	SMALL BUNNY, 9509	OP	50.00	50.00
95	SMALL RABBIT, 9510	OP	40.00	40.00
95	TWO RABBITS, 9501	OP	190.00	190.00
96	CAT, 9602	OP	150.00	150.00
96	LARGE RABBIT, 9601	OP	180.00	180.00
96	LTD BOY/CHICK, 9603	OP	190.00	190.00
96	RABBIT, 9604	OP	100.00	100.00
96	RABBIT, 9605	OP	90.00	90.00

YR	NAME	LIMIT	ISSUE	TREND
96	RUNNING RABBIT, 9606	OP	150.00	150.00
96	TINY RABBIT, 9607	OP	40.00	40.00

J. VAILLANCOURT

COLLECTIBLE SANTA

YR	NAME	LIMIT	ISSUE	TREND
95	ANGEL, 9539	OP	40.00	40.00
95	BELSNICKLE, 9529	OP	70.00	70.00
95	BELSNICKLE, 9533	OP	90.00	90.00
95	BELSNICKLE, 9534	OP	80.00	80.00
95	BELSNICKLE, 9538	OP	50.00	50.00
95	BLUE FATHER CHRISTMAS, 9537	OP	110.00	110.00
95	F.C. ON DONKEY, 9541	250	300.00	300.00
95	F.C. PULLING SLED, 9543	250	300.00	300.00
95	LARGE F.C. ON DONKEY, 9542	OP	250.00	250.00
95	LARGE WALKING, 9531	OP	1,900.00	1900.00
95	SANTA HOLDING LARGE BAG, 9532	OP	250.00	250.00
95	SANTA, 9535	OP	130.00	130.00
95	SNOW ANGEL, 9540	OP	70.00	70.00
95	STOCKING, 9536	OP	190.00	190.00
96	ANGEL	OP	90.00	90.00
96	BELSNICKLE, 9637	OP	70.00	70.00
96	BELSNICKLE, 9643	OP	140.00	140.00
96	CHILDREN ON SLED, 9636	OP	350.00	350.00
96	F.C. ON MOTORCYCLE	OP	130.00	130.00
96	F.C., 9644	OP	130.00	130.00
96	FATHER CHRISTMAS, 9633	OP	90.00	90.00
96	FATHER CHRISTMAS, 9635	OP	350.00	350.00
96	GERMAN TREE, 9638	OP	30.00	30.00
96	LTD. F.C., 9641	250	300.00	300.00
96	SANTA, 9631	OP	150.00	150.00
96	SANTA, 9632	OP	90.00	90.00
96	SNOWMAN ARTIST, 9640	OP	120.00	120.00
96	SNOWMAN, 9639	OP	50.00	50.00
96	STARLIGHT SANTA, 9630	RT	100.00	100.00

VICKILANE

V. ANDERSON

YR	NAME	LIMIT	ISSUE	TREND
94	BUNNY ANGEL #1610	OP	13.00	13.00
94	BUNNY ANGEL #1611	OP	13.00	13.00
94	BUNNY ANGEL #1612	OP	13.00	13.00
94	BUNNY ANGEL #1613	OP	13.00	13.00
94	BUNNY ANGEL #1614	OP	13.00	13.00
94	BUNNY ANGEL #1615	OP	13.00	13.00
94	CHILD ANGEL #6011	OP	20.00	20.00

V. ANDERSON

ACCESSORIES

YR	NAME	LIMIT	ISSUE	TREND
93	FIREPLACE	OP	20.00	20.00

V. ANDERSON

AMISH/COUNTRY KIDS

YR	NAME	LIMIT	ISSUE	TREND
94	BROTHERLY LOVE	OP	*	N/A
94	PATIENCE	OP	20.00	20.00

V. ANDERSON

BLESSINGS FROM ABOVE

YR	NAME	LIMIT	ISSUE	TREND
94	CHILD ANGEL #6009	OP	18.00	18.00
94	CHILD ANGEL #6010	OP	25.00	25.00

V. ANDERSON

CHARACTER CAPERS

YR	NAME	LIMIT	ISSUE	TREND
94	DILIGENCE	OP	20.00	20.00
94	FAITH	OP	*	N/A

V. ANDERSON

CHRISTMAS

YR	NAME	LIMIT	ISSUE	TREND
93	FUZZY	OP	23.00	23.00
93	GRANDMA & GRANDPA	OP	25.00	25.00
93	ROSEBERRY	OP	22.00	22.00
93	SPARKY	OP	18.00	18.00
93	SUGAR PLUM	OP	22.00	22.00

V. ANDERSON

CLUB PIECE

YR	NAME	LIMIT	ISSUE	TREND
94	MISS APRIL	OP	28.00	28.00
94	SWEET SECRETS	RT	*	N/A

V. ANDERSON

COW-LLECTOR

YR	NAME	LIMIT	ISSUE	TREND
94	COW WITH BAG OF OATS	OP	*	N/A
94	COW WITH SUNGLASSES	OP	*	N/A

V. ANDERSON

LIL BLESSINGS

YR	NAME	LIMIT	ISSUE	TREND
94	BUNNY ANGEL CLOUD	OP	12.00	12.00

V. ANDERSON

NITE BEAR-FORE

YR	NAME	LIMIT	ISSUE	TREND
93	PAPA BEARS	OP	22.00	22.00

V. ANDERSON

PURRFECTLY PRECIOUS KITTY

YR	NAME	LIMIT	ISSUE	TREND
94	KITTIES BEHIND FENCE	OP	*	N/A

V. ANDERSON

SCHOOL HOUSE BUNNIES

YR	NAME	LIMIT	ISSUE	TREND
94	BOY WITH BASKETBALL	OP	18.00	18.00
94	BOYS WITH BOOKS	OP	20.00	20.00
94	GIRL READING	OP	20.00	20.00
94	SCHOOL TEACHER	OP	20.00	20.00

V. ANDERSON

SKIN TONE

YR	NAME	LIMIT	ISSUE	TREND
94	CHILD ANGEL #6013	OP	20.00	20.00
94	CHILD ANGEL #6014	OP	22.00	22.00

V. ANDERSON

SWEET THUMPINS

YR	NAME	LIMIT	ISSUE	TREND
94	BUNNY THROWING SNOW	RT	31.00	31.00
94	HAPPY EARS	OP	31.00	31.00
94	INJURED BUNNY	OP	31.00	31.00
94	NEW BORN EXCITEMENT	OP	31.00	31.00

YR	NAME	LIMIT	ISSUE	TREND
94	NURSE BUNNY	OP	31.00	31.00
94	SWEETHEART BUNNIES	OP	31.00	31.00
V. ANDERSON		**THE LORD IS MY SHEPHERD**		
94	LAMB ANGEL	OP	*	N/A
94	LAMB AT DOOR	OP	*	N/A
94	LAMB BUILD ALTAR	OP	*	N/A
94	LAMB READING	OP	*	N/A
94	LAMB WORSHIPPING	OP	*	N/A
V. ANDERSON		**THIS LITTLE PIGGY**		
94	PIG EATING APPLES	OP	22.00	22.00
V. ANDERSON		**TIME FOR TEDDY**		
93	NEWLYWED BEAR	OP	20.00	20.00
93	SNOWMEN BEARS	OP	*	N/A
93	TEDDY BEAR	OP	10.00	10.00
V. ANDERSON		**WHITE OR BLACK**		
94	CHILD ANGEL #6012	OP	20.00	20.00

WACO PRODUCTS CORP.

YR	NAME	LIMIT	ISSUE	TREND
J. UNGER		**HERMAN COLLECTION**		
90	BIRTHDAY/CAKE	OP	36.00	36.00
90	BOWLING/WIFE	OP	32.00	32.00
90	DOCTOR/FAT MAN	OP	36.00	36.00
90	DOCTOR/HIGH COST	OP	32.00	32.00
90	FRY PAN	OP	40.00	40.00
90	GOLF/CAMEL	OP	44.00	44.00
90	HUSBAND/CHECK	OP	36.00	36.00
90	HUSBAND/NEWSPAPER	OP	41.00	41.00
90	LAWYER/CABINET	OP	44.00	44.00
90	STOP SMOKING	OP	40.00	40.00
90	TENNIS/WIFE	OP	32.00	32.00
90	WEDDING RING	OP	41.00	41.00
*		**MELODY IN MOTION**		
89	SANTA CLAUS-1989	RT	130.00	600.00
90	LULL'A BYE WILLIE II (EUROPEAN)	RT	*	400.00
92	SANTA CLAUS-1992	RT	160.00	180.00
93	MADAME CELLO, GLAZE	RT	170.00	310.00
93	MADAME FLUTE, GLAZE	RT	170.00	310.00
93	MADAME HARP, GLAZE	RT	190.00	320.00
93	SANTA CLAUSE-1993 (EUROPEAN)	RT	*	413.00
93	WALL STREET (JAPANESE)	RT	*	N/A
96	SANTA CLAUS-1996	RT	220.00	220.00
96	WILLIE THE ARTIST/SIGNING PIECE	RT	240.00	240.00
97	GLAZED TRUMPETER/SIGNING PIECE	RT	220.00	220.00
97	SANTA CLAUS-1997	RT	220.00	220.00
C. JOHNSON		**MELODY IN MOTION**		
90	LITTLE JOHN	RT	180.00	300.00
90	ROBIN HOOD	RT	180.00	325.00
K. MAEDA		**MELODY IN MOTION**		
98	CAROLER BOY II	*	190.00	190.00
98	COCA-COLA SANTA CLAUS CLOCK	3000	250.00	250.00
98	NEW FIDDLER	*	200.00	200.00
98	SANTA CLAUS	4000	220.00	220.00
98	WEDDING COUPLE	*	196.00	196.00
98	WILLIE THE WANDERER	*	170.00	170.00
S. NAKANE		**MELODY IN MOTION**		
85	SALTY N' PEPPER	RT	90.00	550.00
85	WILLIE THE HOBO	RT	90.00	225.00
85	WILLIE THE TRUMPETER	OP	96.00	130.00
85	WILLIE THE WHISTLER	RT	90.00	185.00
86	CELLIST, THE	RT	100.00	240.00
86	FIDDLER, THE	RT	100.00	250.00
86	GUITARIST, THE	RT	100.00	300.00
86	SANTA CLAUS-1986	RT	100.00	2750.00
87	ACCORDION CLOWN	RT	85.00	300.00
87	BALLOON CLOWN	OP	110.00	110.00
87	CAROUSEL, THE	RT	190.00	300.00
87	CLARINET CLOWN	RT	85.00	325.00
87	LAMPPOST WILLIE	OP	84.00	110.00
87	MADAME CELLO PLAYER	RT	130.00	240.00
87	MADAME FLUTE PLAYER	RT	130.00	265.00
87	MADAME HARPSICHORD PLAYER	RT	130.00	265.00
87	MADAME LYRE PLAYER	RT	130.00	210.00
87	MADAME MANDOLIN PLAYER	RT	130.00	240.00
87	MADAME VIOLIN PLAYER	RT	130.00	240.00
87	ORGAN GRINDER	RT	100.00	275.00
87	SANTA CLAUS-1987	RT	110.00	1500.00
87	SAXOPHONE CLOWN	RT	85.00	275.00
87	VIOLIN CLOWN	RT	85.00	275.00
88	ICE CREAM VENDOR	RT	140.00	250.00
88	MADAME HARP PLAYER	OP	130.00	130.00
88	PEANUT VENDOR	RT	140.00	325.00
88	SANTA CLAUS-1988	RT	130.00	1000.00
88	SPOTLIGHT CLOWN BANJO	RT	85.00	275.00
88	SPOTLIGHT CLOWN CORNET	RT	85.00	250.00
88	SPOTLIGHT CLOWN TROMBONE	RT	85.00	275.00

YR NAME	LIMIT	ISSUE	TREND
88 SPOTLIGHT CLOWN TUBA	RT	85.00	250.00
88 SPOTLIGHT CLOWN WITH BINGO THE DOG	RT	85.00	180.00
89 GRAND CAROUSEL, THE	RT	3,000.00	4500.00
89 GRANDFATHER'S CLOCK	RT	200.00	300.00
89 LULL'ABY WILLIE	RT	170.00	285.00
89 SPOTLIGHT CLOWN WITH UPRIGHT BASS	RT	130.00	130.00
89 WILLIE THE SANTA	RT	130.00	150.00
90 ACCORDION BOY	RT	120.00	200.00
90 BLACKSMITH	RT	110.00	200.00
90 CLOCKPOST WILLIE	RT	150.00	400.00
90 HUNTER	RT	110.00	225.00
90 ROBIN HOOD TIMEPIECE	RT	180.00	350.00
90 SANTA CLAUS-1990	RT	150.00	300.00
90 SHOEMAKER	RT	110.00	175.00
90 WOODCHOPPER	RT	110.00	175.00
91 CAROUSEL, THE, 2ND ED.	RT	240.00	350.00
91 HUNTER TIMEPIECE	RT	250.00	300.00
91 SANTA CLAUS-1991	RT	150.00	325.00
91 VICTORIA PARK CAROUSEL	OP	300.00	300.00
91 WILLIE THE FISHERMAN	OP	150.00	150.00
92 AMAZING WILLIE/ONE MAN BAND	RT	130.00	250.00
92 KING OF CLOWNS CAROUSEL	RT	740.00	850.00
93 1993 COCA-COLA SANTA	RT	180.00	240.00
93 ARTIST, THE	RT	240.00	240.00
93 HEARTBREAK WILLIE	OP	180.00	190.00
93 LAMPLIGHT WILLIE	RT	220.00	220.00
93 MADAME HARPSICHORD, GLAZE	RT	170.00	310.00
93 SOUTH OF THE BORDER	RT	180.00	203.00
93 WHEN I GROW UP	RT	200.00	250.00
93 WILLIE THE GOLFER	RT	240.00	240.00
94 1994 COCA-COLA SANTA	RT	190.00	250.00
94 CAROLER BOY, THE	10000	172.00	180.00
94 CAROLER GIRL, THE	10000	172.00	180.00
94 CHATTANOOGA CHOO-CHOO	OP	180.00	190.00
94 CHRISTMAS CAROLER BOY	10000	172.00	180.00
94 CHRISTMAS CAROLER GIRL	10000	172.00	180.00
94 DAY'S END	RT	240.00	240.00
94 JACKPOT WILLIE	OP	180.00	190.00
94 LONGEST DRIVE	OP	150.00	160.00
94 LOW PRESSURE JOB	RT	240.00	240.00
94 SMOOTH SAILING	RT	200.00	200.00
94 WILLIE THE GOLFER CLOCK	RT	240.00	240.00
95 BLUE DANUBE CAROUSEL	OP	280.00	280.00
95 CAMPFIRE COWBOY	RT	180.00	275.00
95 COCA-COLA NORMAN ROCKWELL GONE FISHIN'	YR	194.00	200.00
95 COCA-COLA POLAR BEAR	6000	180.00	180.00
95 LOW PRESSURE JOB CLOCK	RT	240.00	240.00
95 SANTA CLAUS-1995	RT	190.00	190.00
95 WILLIE THE CONDUCTOR	10000	220.00	220.00
95 WILLIE THE FIREMAN	RT	200.00	200.00
96 WILLIE THE ORGAN GRINDER	3000	200.00	200.00

K. MAEDA   MELODY IN MOTION MEMBERS-ONLY FIGURINE

YR NAME	LIMIT	ISSUE	TREND
98 WILLIE & JUMBO	YR	180.00	180.00

WALT DISNEY CLASSICS COLLECTION
*

101 DALMATIANS

YR NAME	LIMIT	ISSUE	TREND
96 LUCKY WITH TV 41131	OP	150.00	150.00
96 OPENING TITLE 41169	OP	29.00	29.00
96 PERDITA 41133	OP	175.00	175.00
96 PONGO (DISNEYANA BACKSTAMP)	OP	375.00	375.00
96 PROUD PONGO 41132	OP	175.00	175.00
96 ROLLY THE PUPPY 41130	OP	65.00	65.00
96 TWO PUPS ON NEWSPAPER 41129	OP	120.00	120.00

*

BAMBI

YR NAME	LIMIT	ISSUE	TREND
92 BAMBI & FLOWER-WHEEL 41010	10000	298.00	475.00
92 BAMBI OPENING TITLE-WHEEL 41015	CL	29.00	35.00
92 BAMBI-WHEEL 41033	CL	195.00	225.00
92 FIELD MOUSE-HANDS NOT TOUCHING 41012	RT	195.00	1400.00
92 FIELD MOUSE-HANDS TOUCHING 41012	RT	195.00	1200.00
92 FLOWER-WHEEL 41034	CL	78.00	160.00
92 FRIEND OWL-WHEEL 41011	CL	195.00	175.00
92 THUMPER'S SISTERS-WHEEL 41014	CL	69.00	70.00
92 THUMPER-WHEEL 41013	CL	55.00	55.00

*

BEAUTY AND THE BEAST

YR NAME	LIMIT	ISSUE	TREND
97 BELLE & BEAST 41156	OP	295.00	295.00
97 COGSWORTH 41182	OP	120.00	120.00
97 LUMIERO 41181	OP	115.00	115.00
97 MRS. POTTS/CHIP 41183	OP	125.00	125.00
97 OPENING TITLE 41189	OP	29.00	29.00

*

CINDERELLA

YR NAME	LIMIT	ISSUE	TREND
92 BIRDS WITH SASH-WHEEL 41005	RT	149.00	170.00
92 BRUNO	RT	69.00	120.00
92 CHALK MOUSE-WHEEL 41006	RT	65.00	96.00
92 CINDERELLA OPENING TITLE TECHNICOLOR 41009	RT	29.00	35.00
92 CINDERELLA'S DRESS 41030	RT	800.00	2289.00

YR	NAME	LIMIT	ISSUE	TREND
92	CINDERELLA-CLEF 41000	RT	195.00	400.00
92	CINDERELLA-WHEEL 41000	RT	195.00	420.00
92	GUS-WHEEL 41007	RT	65.00	115.00
92	JAQ-WHEEL 41008	RT	65.00	110.00
92	LUCIFER-WHEEL 41001	RT	69.00	120.00
92	NEEDLE MOUSE-WHEEL 41004	RT	69.00	110.00
92	SEWING BOOK (NO MARK) 41003	RT	69.00	80.00
95	CINDERELLA AND THE PRINCE 41079	OP	275.00	275.00

COLLECTORS SOCIETY

YR	NAME	LIMIT	ISSUE	TREND
92	JIMINY CRICKET-KIT C	RT	*	220.00
92	JIMINY CRICKET-KIT W	RT	*	240.00
93	BRAVE LITTLE TAILOR-CLEF	RT	160.00	250.00
93	BRAVE LITTLE TAILOR-TROWEL	RT	160.00	325.00
94	ADMIRAL DUCK	RT	165.00	195.00
94	CHESHIRE CAT "TWAS BRILLIG"-CLEF	RT	*	120.00
94	CHESHIRE CAT KIT-FLOWER	RT	*	85.00
94	PECOS BILL & WIDOWMAKER	RT	650.00	350.00
95	CRUELLA DE VIL "101 DALMATIANS"	RT	250.00	350.00
95	DUMBO	RT	*	80.00
95	SLUE FOOT SUE 41075	RT	695.00	575.00
96	CASEY AT THE BAT 41107	YR	395.00	360.00
96	PRINCESS MINNIE	RT	165.00	165.00
96	WINNIE THE POOH	RT	*	80.00
97	GOOFY-MOVING DAY 41138	RT	185.00	185.00
97	MAGICIAN MICKEY 41134	RT	25.00	25.00
97	MALEFICENT	RT	450.00	450.00
97	STEAMBOAT WILLIE-CHARTER	RT	175.00	375.00

DELIVERY BOY

YR	NAME	LIMIT	ISSUE	TREND
92	DELIVERY BOY MICKEY-WHEEL 41020	RT	125.00	170.00
92	DELIVERY BOY MINNIE-WHEEL 41021	RT	125.00	160.00
92	PLUTO (FLAT) 41022	RT	125.00	175.00
92	PLUTO (INCISED)-WHEEL	CL	125.00	230.00
92	THE DELIVERY BOY OPENING TITLE-NO MARK	RT	29.00	100.00

EVENT PIECES

YR	NAME	LIMIT	ISSUE	TREND
93	FLIGHT OF FANCY	RT	35.00	45.00
94	MR. SMEE-TEAL	RT	90.00	90.00
94	MR. SMEE-WHITE	RT	90.00	90.00
95	LUCKY 41080	RT	40.00	55.00
95	WICKED WITCH	RT	130.00	205.00
96	FAIRY GODMOTHER	RT	125.00	125.00
97	BLUE FAIRY	RT	150.00	150.00
97	EVIL QUEEN	RT	150.00	150.00

FANTASIA

YR	NAME	LIMIT	ISSUE	TREND
92	BROOM NO SPOTS	RT	*	100.00
92	BROOM-WHEEL (WITH WATER SPOTS)	RT	75.00	186.00
92	SORCERER MICKEY	RT	195.00	285.00
93	BLUE CENTAURETTE-CLEF	RT	195.00	165.00
93	FANTASIA OPENING TITLE-RECALL	RT	29.00	55.00
93	FANTASIA OPENING TITLE-TECHNICOLOR-WHEEL	RT	29.00	40.00
93	PINK CENTAURETTE-CLEF	RT	175.00	155.00
94	CUPIDS ON PILLAR	RT	290.00	290.00
94	LG. MUSHROOM-TEAL LOGO	CL	60.00	60.00
94	MED. MUSHROOM-TEAL LOGO	CL	50.00	50.00
94	SM. MUSHROOM HOP LOW	OP	35.00	35.00

HOLIDAY SERIES

YR	NAME	LIMIT	ISSUE	TREND
95	PRESENTS FOR MY PALS	RT	150.00	150.00
96	PLUTO HELPS DECORATE	RT	150.00	150.00
97	CHIP 'N DALE	RT	150.00	150.00

JUNGLE BOOK

YR	NAME	LIMIT	ISSUE	TREND
97	BAGHEERE	OP	135.00	135.00
97	BALOO	OP	185.00	185.00
97	FLUNKY MONKEY	OP	135.00	135.00
97	KING LOUIE	OP	175.00	175.00
97	MOWGLI	OP	115.00	115.00
97	OPENING TITLE	OP	29.00	29.00

LADY AND THE TRAMP

YR	NAME	LIMIT	ISSUE	TREND
96	LADY & THE TRAMP OPENING TITLE	OP	29.00	29.00
96	LADY-TROWEL	RT	120.00	150.00
96	TRAMP-TROWEL	RT	100.00	120.00

LITTLE MERMAID

YR	NAME	LIMIT	ISSUE	TREND
97	ARIEL	OP	275.00	275.00
97	BLACKFISH	OP	95.00	95.00
97	FLOUNDER	OP	150.00	150.00
97	OPENING TITLE	OP	29.00	29.00
97	TURTLE	OP	85.00	85.00

MR. DUCK STEPS OUT

YR	NAME	LIMIT	ISSUE	TREND
93	DEWEY	RT	65.00	65.00
93	DONALD & DAISY "OH BOY,WHAT A JITTERBUG"-WHEEL	RT	298.00	600.00
93	DONALD AND DAISY-CLEF	RT	298.00	500.00
93	HUEY-CLEF	RT	65.00	55.00
93	LOUIE-CLEF	RT	65.00	55.00
93	MR. DUCK STEPS OUT OPENING TITLE	RT	29.00	30.00
94	DONALD "WITH LOVE FROM DAISY"-TEAL LOGO	RT	180.00	180.00

YR	NAME	LIMIT	ISSUE	TREND
*				**PETER PAN**
93	CAPT. HOOK-CLEF	CL	275.00	550.00
93	CROCODILE-FLOWER	CL	315.00	315.00
93	PETER PAN OPENING TITLE-CLEF	CL	29.00	35.00
93	PETER PAN-CLEF	CL	165.00	225.00
93	TINKERBELL-CLEF	12500	215.00	525.00
93	TINKERBELL-FLOWER	*	*	340.00
*				**PINOCCHIO**
96	FIGARO	OP	55.00	55.00
96	GEPPETTO	OP	145.00	145.00
96	JIMINY CRICKET	OP	85.00	85.00
96	PINOCCHIO	OP	125.00	125.00
96	PINOCCHIO OPENING TITLE	OP	29.00	29.00
*				**POCAHONTAS**
96	POCAHONTAS	RT	225.00	240.00
96	POCAHONTAS DEALER PROTOTYPE	RT	225.00	500.00
*				**RELUCTANT DRAGON**
96	RELUCTANT DRAGON-HAT	7500	695.00	725.00
96	RELUCTANT DRAGON-TROWEL	7500	695.00	800.00
*				**SNOW WHITE**
94	SNOW WHITE-FLOWER	RT	165.00	200.00
95	BASHFUL	OP	95.00	95.00
95	DOC	OP	95.00	95.00
95	DOPEY	OP	95.00	95.00
95	GRUMPY	OP	180.00	180.00
95	HAPPY	OP	125.00	125.00
95	SLEEPY	OP	95.00	95.00
95	SNEEZY	OP	90.00	90.00
95	SNOW WHITE OPENING TITLE	OP	29.00	29.00
*				**SONG OF THE SOUTH**
96	BRER BEAR	RT	175.00	185.00
96	BRER FOX	RT	120.00	185.00
96	BRER RABBIT	RT	150.00	185.00
96	SONG OF THE SOUTH OPENING TITLE	OP	29.00	50.00
*				**SYMPHONY HOUR**
93	CLARABELLE-WHEEL	CL	198.00	244.00
93	GOOFY-CLEF	CL	198.00	240.00
93	GOOFY-WHEEL	CL	198.00	2700.00
93	HORACE-WHEEL	CL	198.00	244.00
93	MAESTRO MICKEY	RT	185.00	244.00
93	SYMPHONY HOUR OPENING TITLE	CL	29.00	35.00
94	CLARA CLUCK	OP	185.00	185.00
96	SYLVESTER MACARONI	12500	395.00	395.00
*				**THREE CABALLEROS**
95	AMIGO DONALD	RT	180.00	180.00
95	AMIGO JOSE	RT	180.00	180.00
95	AMIGO PANCHITO	RT	180.00	180.00
*				**THREE LITTLE PIGS**
93	BIG BAD WOLF (1ST, SHORT STRAIGHT TEETH)	7500	295.00	1400.00
93	BIG BAD WOLF (2ND, SHORT STRAIGHT TEETH)	7500	295.00	1200.00
93	BIG BAD WOLF (3RD, LONG CURVED TEETH)	7500	295.00	675.00
93	FIDDLER PIG-CLEF	CL	75.00	90.00
93	FIFER PIG-CLEF	CL	75.00	90.00
93	PRACTICAL PIG-CLEF	CL	75.00	90.00
93	THREE LITTLE PIGS OPENING TITLE-CLEF	CL	29.00	33.00
96	WOLF IN SHEEP'S CLOTHING	OP	225.00	225.00
*				**TRIBUTE SERIES**
95	PALS FOREVER	RT	175.00	175.00

WEE FOREST FOLK
A. PETERSEN

YR	NAME	LIMIT	ISSUE	TREND
72	MISS MOUSEY W/BOW HAT M-2B	CL	4.25	300.00
72	MISS MOUSEY W/STRAW HAT M-2A	CL	4.25	300.00
76	MRS. MOUSEY W/HAT M-15A	CL	4.25	300.00
82	OFFICE MOUSEY M-68	CL	23.00	550.00
83	RUNNING DOE/LITTLE DEER B-107B	OP	35.00	42.00
92	GRETA M-169A	CL	35.00	90.00
92	HANS M-169A	CL	35.00	90.00
92	TUCKERED OUT! M-136A	CL	46.00	160.00
93	CHRISTMAS EVE M-191	OP	145.00	155.00
93	FIRST KISS! M-192	OP	65.00	65.00
93	LITTLE MICE WHO LIVED IN A SHOE M-189	OP	395.00	420.00
93	LORD & LADY MOUSEBATTEN M-195	OP	85.00	140.00
93	MUMMY, THE M-194	OP	34.00	37.00
93	ONE-MOUSE BAND M-196	OP	95.00	100.00
93	PETER PUMPKIN EATER M-190	CL	98.00	140.00
93	WELCOME CHICK! M-193	OP	64.00	68.00
94	CHIEF MOUSE-ASOIT M-197	OP	90.00	90.00
94	MIDNIGHT SNACK M-201	OP	230.00	230.00
94	PILGRIM'S WELCOME M-198	OP	55.00	55.00
94	WE GATHER TOGETHER M-199	OP	90.00	90.00
94	WEDDING PAIR, THE M-200	OP	98.00	98.00
94	YARD SALE, THE M-202	OP	325.00	325.00
95	BROOM SERVICE M-205	OP	62.00	60.00

YR	NAME	LIMIT	ISSUE	TREND
95	CAUGHT IN THE ACT M-209	OP	49.00	49.00
95	CHRISTMAS WISH M-203	OP	156.00	156.00
95	CLEMENTINE M-204	OP	86.00	86.00
95	HEAVENLY SLUMBER M-210	OP	49.00	45.00
95	HIGH FLYER M-207	OP	88.00	85.00
95	JACK IN THE SANDBOX M-206	OP	108.00	100.00
95	STRUGGLING ARTIST M-208	OP	49.00	49.00
95	WANDERLUST M-211	OP	68.00	68.00
A. PETERSEN				**ANIMALS**
73	MISS DUCKY	CL	6.00	N/A
74	BABY HIPPO	CL	7.00	N/A
74	MISS AND BABY HIPPO	CL	15.00	900.00
74	MISS HIPPO	CL	8.00	N/A
75	"DOC" RAT	CL	12.00	250.00
75	SPEEDY RAT	CL	11.50	250.00
77	NUTSY SQUIRREL	CL	3.00	450.00
78	BEAVER WOOD CUTTER	CL	8.00	350.00
78	MOLE SCOUT	CL	9.00	175.00
79	TURTLE JOGGER	CL	4.00	350.00
A. PETERSEN				**BEARS**
77	BLUEBERRY BEARS	CL	8.75	525.00
77	BOY BLUEBERRY BEAR	CL	4.50	475.00
77	GIRL BLUEBERRY BEAR	CL	4.25	450.00
78	BIG LADY BEAR	CL	7.50	N/A
78	TRAVELING BEAR	CL	8.00	320.00
95	DON'T BE SHY BB-1	OP	76.00	75.00
95	FATHER'S NIGHT BB-5	OP	159.00	155.00
95	GOOD PICKIN'S BB-4	OP	64.00	60.00
95	JUST A PEEK BB-6	OP	159.00	155.00
95	LUNCH ON A LOG BB-3	OP	89.00	85.00
95	WELCOME HOME BB-2	OP	108.00	100.00
W. PETERSEN				**BOOK/FIGURINE**
88	TOM & EON BK-1	SU	45.00	22.00
A. PETERSEN				**BUNNIES**
72	DOUBLE BUNNIES	CL	4.25	350.00
72	HOUSEKEEPING BUNNY	CL	4.50	350.00
73	BROOM BUNNY	CL	9.50	N/A
73	MARKET BUNNY	CL	9.00	N/A
73	MUFF BUNNY	CL	9.00	N/A
73	PROFESSOR, THE	CL	4.75	360.00
73	SIR RABBIT	CL	4.50	350.00
73	SUNDAY BUNNY	CL	4.75	N/A
77	BATTER BUNNY	CL	4.50	480.00
77	TENNIS BUNNY	CL	3.75	300.00
78	WEDDING BUNNIES	CL	12.50	450.00
80	PROFESSOR RABBIT	CL	14.00	450.00
85	TINY EASTER BUNNY	CL	25.00	85.00
92	WINDY DAY! B-13	OP	37.00	40.00
A. PETERSEN				**CHRISTMAS CAROL**
87	BOB CRATCHIT AND TINY TIM CC-2	OP	36.00	43.00
87	GHOST OF CHRISTMAS PAST CC-4	OP	24.00	30.00
87	GHOST OF CHRISTMAS PRESENT CC-5	OP	54.00	57.00
87	GHOST OF CHRISTMAS YET TO COME CC-6	OP	24.00	28.00
87	MARLEY'S GHOST CC-3	OP	24.00	28.00
87	SCROOGE CC-1	OP	23.00	28.00
88	FEZZIWIGS, THE CC-7	OP	65.00	80.00
A. PETERSEN				**CINDERELLA**
88	CINDERELLA'S SLIPPER W/PRINCE C-1	CL	62.00	170.00
88	CINDERELLA'S WEDDING C-5	CL	62.00	150.00
88	FLOWER GIRL C-6	CL	22.00	80.00
88	FLOWER GIRLS, THE C-4	CL	42.00	105.00
88	MEAN STEPMOTHER, THE C-3	CL	32.00	125.00
88	UGLY STEPSISTERS, THE C-2	CL	62.00	145.00
89	CINDERELLA'S SLIPPER C-1A	CL	32.00	110.00
89	FAIRY GODMOTHER, THE C-7	CL	69.00	200.00
A. PETERSEN				**FAIRY TALE SERIES**
80	RED RIDING HOOD	CL	13.00	500.00
80	RED RIDING HOOD & WOLF	CL	29.00	1150.00
W. PETERSEN				**FOREST SCENE**
88	WOODLAND SERENADE	RT	125.00	285.00
89	HEARTS AND FLOWERS	OP	110.00	112.00
90	MOUSIE COMES A-CALLING	OP	128.00	145.00
91	MOUNTAIN STREAM	OP	128.00	140.00
92	LOVE LETTER	OP	98.00	108.00
93	PICNIC ON THE RIVERBANK FS-6	OP	150.00	175.00
94	WAYSIDE CHAT FS-7	OP	170.00	165.00
A. PETERSEN				**FOXES**
77	DANDY FOX	CL	6.00	475.00
77	FANCY FOX	CL	4.75	475.00
78	BARRISTER FOX	CL	7.50	675.00
A. PETERSEN				**FROGS**
74	FROG ON ROCK	CL	6.00	N/A
74	PRINCE CHARMING	CL	7.50	450.00
77	FROG FRIENDS	CL	5.95	400.00

YR	NAME	LIMIT	ISSUE	TREND
77	GRAMPA FROG	CL	6.00	450.00
77	SPRING PEEPERS	CL	3.50	N/A
78	SINGING FROG	CL	5.50	275.00
W. PETERSEN				**LIMITED EDITION**
81	BEAUTY AND THE BEAST	CL	89.00	1750.00
84	POSTMOUSTER	CL	46.00	725.00
85	HELPING HAND	RT	62.00	700.00
87	STATUE IN THE PARK	CL	93.00	915.00
88	UNCLE SAMMY	CL	85.00	275.00
A. PETERSEN				**MICE**
72	MARKET MOUSE	CL	4.25	250.00
72	MISS MOUSE	CL	4.25	325.00
72	MISS MOUSEY	CL	4.00	300.00
73	MISS NURSEY MOUSE	CL	4.00	550.00
74	FARMER MOUSE	CL	3.75	400.00
74	GOOD KNIGHT MOUSE	CL	7.50	425.00
74	WOOD SPRITE	CL	4.00	425.00
75	BRIDE MOUSE	CL	4.00	500.00
75	TWO MICE WITH CANDLE	CL	4.50	400.00
75	TWO TINY MICE	CL	4.50	425.00
76	FAN MOUSE	CL	5.75	470.00
76	JUNE BELLE	CL	4.25	375.00
76	MAMA MOUSE WITH BABY	CL	6.00	400.00
76	MAY BELLE	CL	4.25	300.00
76	MOUSE WITH MUFF	CL	9.00	N/A
76	MRS. MOUSEY	CL	4.00	N/A
76	NIGHTIE MOUSE	CL	4.75	425.00
76	SHAWL MOUSE	CL	9.00	N/A
76	TEA MOUSE	CL	5.75	475.00
77	BABY SITTER	CL	5.75	375.00
77	KING "TUT" MOUSE	CL	4.50	N/A
77	QUEEN "TUT" MOUSE	CL	4.50	N/A
78	BRIDGE CLUB MOUSE	CL	6.00	275.00
78	BRIDGE CLUB MOUSE PARTNER	CL	6.00	275.00
78	CHIEF NIP-A-WAY MOUSE	CL	7.00	450.00
78	COWBOY MOUSE	CL	6.00	450.00
78	PICNIC MICE	CL	14.50	425.00
78	PIRATE MOUSE	CL	6.50	375.00
78	SECRETARY, MISS SPELL/MISS PELL	CL	4.50	425.00
78	TOWN CRIER MOUSE	CL	10.50	475.00
78	WEDDING MICE	CL	7.50	550.00
79	CHRIS-MISS	CL	9.00	375.00
79	CHRIS-MOUSE	CL	9.00	175.00
79	GARDENER MOUSE	CL	12.00	400.00
79	MOUSE ARTISTE	CL	12.50	500.00
79	MOUSE BABY, HEART BOOK	CL	9.50	350.00
79	MOUSE BALLERINA	CL	12.50	425.00
79	MOUSE DUET	CL	25.00	625.00
79	MOUSE PIANIST	CL	17.00	550.00
79	MOUSE VIOLINIST	CL	9.00	305.00
79	RAGGEDY AND MOUSE	CL	12.00	375.00
79	ROCK-A-BYE BABY MOUSE	CL	17.00	400.00
80	CARPENTER MOUSE	CL	15.00	375.00
80	COMMO-DOORMOUSE	CL	14.00	700.00
80	FISHERMOUSE	CL	16.00	600.00
80	MISS BOBBIN	OP	22.00	60.00
80	MISS POLLY MOUSE	CL	23.00	420.00
80	MISS TEACH	CL	18.00	450.00
80	MRS. TIDY AND HELPER	CL	24.00	525.00
80	PHOTOGRAPHER MOUSE	CL	23.00	550.00
80	PIRATE MOUSE	CL	16.00	600.00
80	SANTA MOUSE	CL	12.00	315.00
80	WITCH MOUSE	CL	12.00	225.00
81	BARRISTER MOUSE	CL	16.00	475.00
81	BLUE DEVIL	CL	12.50	100.00
81	CAROLERS, THE	CL	29.00	500.00
81	DOC MOUSE & PATIENT	CL	14.00	425.00
81	FLOWER GIRL	CL	15.00	300.00
81	GRADUATE MOUSE	CL	15.00	110.00
81	LITTLE DEVIL	CL	12.50	30.00
81	LITTLE GHOST	CL	8.50	20.00
81	LONE CAROLER	CL	15.50	475.00
81	MOM AND SQUEAKY CLEAN	CL	27.00	55.00
81	MOTHER'S HELPER	CL	11.00	490.00
81	MOUSEY EXPRESS	CL	22.00	125.00
81	NURSE MOUSEY	CL	14.00	400.00
81	PEARL KNIT MOUSE	CL	20.00	235.00
81	SCHOOL MARM MOUSE	CL	20.00	475.00
82	ARTY MOUSE	CL	19.00	110.00
82	BABY SITTER	CL	24.00	85.00
82	BEACH MOUSEY	CL	19.00	100.00
82	BEDDY-BYE MOUSEY	CL	29.00	50.00
82	BOY SWEETHEART	CL	13.50	450.00
82	EASTER BUNNY MOUSE	CL	18.00	35.00
82	GIRL SWEETHEART	CL	13.50	25.00

YR	NAME	LIMIT	ISSUE	TREND
82	HAPPY BIRTHDAY!	CL	17.50	30.00
82	HOLLY MOUSE	CL	13.50	30.00
82	LAMPLIGHT CAROLERS	CL	35.00	350.00
82	LITTLE FIRE CHIEF	CL	29.00	550.00
82	LITTLE SLEDDERS	CL	24.00	325.00
82	LITTLEST ANGEL	CL	15.00	80.00
82	ME AND RAGGEDY ANN	CL	19.00	35.00
82	MISS TEACH & PUPIL	CL	30.00	425.00
82	MOON MOUSE	CL	15.50	625.00
82	MOUSEY'S TEDDY	CL	29.00	465.00
82	POOREST ANGEL	CL	15.00	125.00
82	SAY "CHEESE"	CL	15.50	525.00
82	SNOWMOUSE & FRIEND	CL	24.00	425.00
82	SWEETHEARTS	CL	26.00	425.00
82	TEA FOR TWO	CL	26.00	350.00
82	WEDDING MICE	CL	30.00	135.00
83	BIRTHDAY GIRL	CL	19.00	30.00
83	CHIEF GERONIMOUSE	CL	21.00	90.00
83	CHRISTMAS MORNING	CL	35.00	300.00
83	CLOWN MOUSE	CL	22.00	400.00
83	CUPID MOUSE	CL	22.00	40.00
83	FIRST CHRISTMAS	CL	16.00	325.00
83	GET WELL SOON!	CL	15.00	375.00
83	HARVEST MOUSE	CL	23.00	425.00
83	MERRY CHRIS-MISS	CL	17.00	370.00
83	MERRY CHRIS-MOUSE	CL	16.00	370.00
83	MOUSE CALL	CL	24.00	750.00
83	MOUSEY NURSE	CL	15.00	30.00
83	MOUSEY'S CONE	*	22.00	70.00
83	MOUSEY'S DOLLHOUSE	CL	30.00	450.00
83	MOUSEY'S TRICYCLE	OP	24.00	45.00
83	PACK MOUSE	CL	19.00	325.00
83	ROCKING TOT	CL	19.00	75.00
83	ROPE 'EM MOUSEY	CL	19.00	375.00
83	WASH DAY	CL	23.00	500.00
84	CAMPFIRE MOUSE	CL	26.00	375.00
84	CHRIS-MOUSE PAGEANT	OP	38.00	55.00
84	FIRST DAY OF SCHOOL	CL	27.00	175.00
84	MOM & GINGER BAKER	*	38.00	65.00
84	PEN PAL MOUSEY	CL	26.00	350.00
84	PETER'S PUMPKIN	CL	19.00	105.00
84	PRUDENCE PIE MAKER	CL	19.00	115.00
84	SANTA'S TRAINEE	CL	37.00	500.00
84	SPRING GARDENER	CL	26.00	40.00
84	TIDY MOUSE	CL	38.00	500.00
84	TRAVELING MOUSE	CL	28.00	275.00
84	WITCHY BOO!	RT	21.00	35.00
85	ATTIC TREASURE	RT	42.00	140.00
85	CHRIS-MOUSE TREE	OP	28.00	45.00
85	COME PLAY!	CL	18.00	85.00
85	FAMILY PORTRAIT	CL	54.00	280.00
85	FIELD MOUSE	OP	46.00	90.00
85	MOUSE TALK	CL	44.00	165.00
85	PAGEANT SHEPHERDS	CL	35.00	215.00
85	PAGEANT WISEMAN	CL	58.00	250.00
85	PIGGY-BACK MOUSEY	CL	28.00	425.00
85	QUILTING BEE	OP	30.00	40.00
85	SHEPHERD KNEELING	OP	20.00	25.00
85	SHEPHERD STANDING	OP	20.00	25.00
85	STROLLING WITH BABY	OP	42.00	60.00
85	SUNDAY DRIVERS	CL	58.00	275.00
85	UNDER THE CHRIS-MOUSE TREE	OP	48.00	80.00
85	WISEMAN IN ROBE	OP	26.00	35.00
85	WISEMAN KNEELING	OP	29.00	35.00
85	WISEMAN WITH TURBAN	OP	28.00	35.00
86	CHRIST-MOUSE STOCKING	OP	34.00	40.00
86	COME & GET IT!	CL	34.00	120.00
86	DOWN THE CHIMNEY	CL	48.00	300.00
86	FIRST DATE	OP	60.00	65.00
86	FIRST HAIRCUT	CL	58.00	185.00
86	FUN FLOAT	OP	34.00	40.00
86	JUST CHECKING	OP	34.00	40.00
86	MOUSE ON CAMPUS	CL	25.00	115.00
86	SWEET DREAMS	CL	58.00	175.00
86	WALTZING MATILDA	CL	48.00	160.00
87	BAT MOUSE	CL	25.00	75.00
87	CHOIR MOUSE	CL	23.00	110.00
87	DON'T CRY!	CL	33.00	110.00
87	DRUMMER MOUSE	CL	29.00	60.00
87	LITTLEST WITCH	CL	24.00	85.00
87	LITTLEST WITCH AND SKELETON	OP	49.00	60.00
87	MARKET MOUSE	CL	49.00	135.00
87	MISS NOEL	OP	32.00	40.00
87	PAGEANT ANGEL	OP	19.00	25.00
87	PAGEANT STABLE	OP	56.00	70.00

YR	NAME	LIMIT	ISSUE	TREND
87	RED WAGON, THE	CL	54.00	200.00
87	SCOOTER MOUSE	OP	34.00	40.00
87	SKELETON MOUSEY	CL	27.00	90.00
87	TOOTH FAIRY	OP	32.00	40.00
87	TRUMPETER	CL	29.00	65.00
87	TUBA PLAYER	CL	29.00	65.00
88	ALOHA!	CL	32.00	80.00
88	FORTY WINKS	OP	36.00	45.00
88	MOUSEY'S EASTER BASKET	CL	32.00	120.00
89	COMMENCEMENT DAY	OP	28.00	35.00
89	ELF TALES	RT	48.00	85.00
89	FATHER CHRIS-MOUSE	OP	34.00	40.00
89	HAUNTED MOUSE HOUSE	OP	125.00	180.00
89	PRIMA BALLERINA	OP	35.00	40.00
90	CHRIS-MOUSE SLIPPER	OP	35.00	40.00
90	COLLEEN O'GREEN	OP	40.00	45.00
90	HANS & GRETA	CL	64.00	175.00
90	POLLY'S PARASOL	CL	39.00	115.00
90	STARS & STRIPES	OP	34.00	40.00
90	ZELDA	OP	37.00	45.00
91	APRIL SHOWERS	OP	27.00	35.00
91	GRAMMY-PHONE	OP	75.00	85.00
91	LITTLE SQUIRT	OP	49.00	55.00
91	MOUSIE'S EGG FACTORY	OP	73.00	90.00
91	NIGHT PRAYER	OP	52.00	60.00
91	NUTCRACKER, THE	OP	49.00	60.00
91	RED RIDING HOOD/GRANDMOTHER'S HOUSE	OP	295.00	295.00
91	SEA SOUNDS	OP	34.00	40.00
91	SILENT NIGHT	OP	64.00	75.00
91	TEA FOR THREE	OP	135.00	160.00
92	ADAM'S APPLES	OP	148.00	148.00
92	HIGH ON THE HOG	CL	52.00	130.00
92	MISS DAISY	OP	42.00	48.00
92	MRS. MOUSEY'S STUDIO	OP	150.00	160.00
92	OLD BLACK STOVE, THE	OP	130.00	140.00
92	PEEKABOO!	OP	52.00	55.00
92	SNOW BUDDIES	OP	58.00	65.00

A. PETERSEN — MINUTEMICE

YR	NAME	LIMIT	ISSUE	TREND
74	CONCORDIAN ON DRUM W/GLASSES MM-4	CL	9.00	N/A
74	CONCORDIAN WOOD BASE W/HAT MM-4B	CL	8.00	N/A
74	CONCORDIAN WOOD BASE W/TAN COAT MM-4A	CL	8.00	N/A
74	LITTLE FIFER ON DRUM MM-5B	CL	8.00	N/A
74	LITTLE FIFER ON DRUM W/FOFE MM-5	CL	8.00	N/A
74	LITTLE FIFER ON WOOD BASE MM-5A	CL	8.00	N/A
74	MOUSE CARRYING LARGE DRUM BB-3	CL	8.00	N/A
74	MOUSE ON DRUM W/BLACK HAT MM-2	CL	9.00	N/A
74	MOUSE ON DRUM W/FIFE MM-1	CL	9.00	N/A
74	MOUSE ON DRUM W/FIFE WOOD BASE MM-1A	CL	9.00	N/A
79	CONCORD MINUTE MOUSE MM-10	OP	14.00	15.00
79	MINUTE MOUSE AND RED COAT MM-9	OP	28.00	28.00
79	RED COAT MOUSE MM-11	OP	14.00	15.00

A. PETERSEN — MOLES

YR	NAME	LIMIT	ISSUE	TREND
78	MOLE SCOUT MO-1	CL	4.25	325.00
94	BELL FINGER MOLE MO-2	OP	44.00	44.00
95	MOLE'S BED SLED MO-3	OP	59.00	59.00

A. PETERSEN — MOUSE SPORTS

YR	NAME	LIMIT	ISSUE	TREND
75	BOBSLED THREE	CL	12.00	450.00
75	SKATER MOUSE	CL	4.50	350.00
76	MOUSE SKIER	CL	4.25	350.00
76	TENNIS STAR	CL	3.75	225.00
77	GOLFER MOUSE	CL	5.25	275.00
77	SKATING STAR MOUSE	CL	3.75	325.00
80	SKATER MOUSE	CL	16.50	375.00
80	SKIER MOUSE MS-9	CL	13.00	325.00
81	GOLFER MOUSE	CL	15.50	510.00
82	TWO IN A CANOE	OP	29.00	60.00
84	LAND HO!	CL	37.00	240.00
84	TENNIS ANYONE?	CL	18.00	130.00
85	FISHIN' CHIP	CL	46.00	310.00
89	JOE DI'MOUSIO	OP	39.00	45.00
94	CAMPING OUT MS-16	OP	75.00	75.00

A. PETERSEN — OWLS

YR	NAME	LIMIT	ISSUE	TREND
74	MR. AND MRS. OWL	CL	6.00	475.00
74	MR. OWL	CL	3.25	225.00
74	MRS. OWL	CL	3.00	225.00
75	COLONIAL OWLS	CL	11.50	425.00
79	"GRAD" OWL	CL	4.25	450.00
80	GRADUATE OWL	CL	12.00	425.00

A. PETERSEN — PIGGIES

YR	NAME	LIMIT	ISSUE	TREND
78	BOY PIGLET/PICNIC PIGGY	CL	4.00	675.00
78	GIRL PIGLET/PICNIC PIGGY	CL	4.00	675.00
78	JOLLY TAR PIGGY	CL	4.50	225.00
78	MISS PIGGY SCHOOL MARM	CL	4.50	275.00
78	PICNIC PIGGIES	CL	7.75	250.00
78	PIGGY BAKER	CL	4.50	325.00

YR	NAME	LIMIT	ISSUE	TREND
78	PIGGY JOGGER	CL	4.50	160.00
80	NURSE PIGGY	CL	15.50	21.00
80	PIG O' MY HEART	CL	12.00	235.00
80	PIGGY BALLERINA	CL	15.50	235.00
80	PIGGY POLICEMAN	CL	17.50	275.00
81	HOLLY HOG	CL	25.00	390.00
A. PETERSEN				**RACCOONS**
77	HIKER RACCOON	CL	4.50	650.00
77	MOTHER RACCOON	CL	4.50	335.00
78	BIRD WATCHER RACCOON	CL	6.50	550.00
78	RACCOON SKATER	CL	4.75	325.00
78	RACCOON SKIER	CL	6.00	400.00
A. PETERSEN				**ROBIN HOOD SERIES**
90	FRIAR TUCK	CL	32.00	85.00
90	MAID MARION	CL	32.00	85.00
90	ROBIN HOOD	CL	37.00	85.00
D. PETERSEN				**TINY TEDDIES**
83	TINY TEDDY	CL	16.00	165.00
84	BOO BEAR	SU	20.00	75.00
84	DRUMMER BEAR	SU	22.00	70.00
84	HUGGY BEAR	SU	26.00	80.00
84	LITTLE TEDDY	CL	20.00	120.00
84	RIDE 'EM TEDDY!	SU	32.00	90.00
84	SAILOR TEDDY	SU	20.00	75.00
84	SANTA BEAR	SU	27.00	110.00
84	SEASIDE TEDDY	SU	28.00	90.00
87	CHRISTMAS TEDDY	SU	26.00	75.00
87	WEDDING BEARS	SU	54.00	130.00
88	HANSEL & GRETEL/WITCH'S HOUSE	SU	175.00	240.00
89	MOMMA BEAR	SU	27.00	135.00
A. PETERSEN				**WIND IN THE WILLOWS**
82	BADGER	CL	18.00	480.00
82	MOLE	CL	18.00	575.00
82	RATTY	CL	18.00	475.00
82	TOAD	CL	18.00	575.00

WHITLEY BAY

L. HEYDA				**SANTA SERIES**
87	GLOBE	10000	225.00	225.00
87	SANTA	10000	150.00	150.00
89	ELF	10000	225.00	225.00
89	ENTRY	10000	275.00	275.00
89	HUG	10000	225.00	225.00
89	LETTERS	10000	375.00	375.00
89	LISTS	10000	275.00	275.00
89	SLEIGH	10000	375.00	375.00

WILLITTS DESIGNS

A. DEZENDORF				**AMISH HERITAGE COLLECTION**
*	CAROLINE	RT	*	N/A
*	SARAH AND MAGGIE	RT	*	N/A
*	TAKING DOWN THE CLOTHES	RT	*	N/A
*	WINTER FUN	RT	*	N/A
96	CAROLING	3500	300.00	300.00
96	DOLL QUILT, THE	RT	60.00	60.00
96	FIRST KISS	RT	110.00	110.00
96	SPECIAL PLAYMATES	RT	95.00	95.00
96	TUCKERED OUT	RT	60.00	60.00
A. DEZENDORF				**CAROUSEL CLASSICS**
98	LION WITH CHERUB	9500	75.00	75.00
98	MIDDLE ROW JUMPER WITH DOG	9500	70.00	70.00
98	OUTSIDE ROW STANDER WITH SCALLOPED MANE	9500	70.00	70.00
98	OUTSIDE ROW ZEBRA STANDER	9500	75.00	75.00
98	STANDER WITH ROACHED MANE	9500	70.00	70.00
T. BLACKSHEAR				**EBONY VISIONS COLLECTION**
95	WINTER HOLIDAY, A	RT	120.00	120.00
95	AUTUMN LEAVE	RT	120.00	120.00
95	CAROLINE'S BEDTIME PRAYER	RT	75.00	75.00
95	KATIE AND BETH	RT	95.00	95.00
95	MADONNA, THE	RT	160.00	160.00
95	MIRACLE OF SPRING, THE	RT	120.00	120.00
95	NURTURER, THE	RT	160.00	160.00
95	PREMIER COMMUNION SERVICE	1500	300.00	300.00
95	PROTECTOR, THE	RT	195.00	300.00
95	SADIE MAE'S HUNGRY GEESE	RT	85.00	85.00
95	SIBLINGS, THE	RT	120.00	150.00
95	STORY TELLER PREMIER, THE	SO	410.00	1100.00
95	SUMMERTIME FUN	RT	120.00	120.00
95	TENDER TOUCH, THE	RT	185.00	185.00
96	BATH TIME	RT	110.00	110.00
96	CHANCE TO DREAM, A	RT	135.00	135.00
96	DREAMER, THE	RT	135.00	150.00
96	GUARDIAN, THE	RT	300.00	300.00
96	MUSIC MAKER, THE	RT	300.00	250.00
98	CATCHING THE EYE	RT	235.00	235.00

YR	NAME	LIMIT	ISSUE	TREND
98	COMFORTER, THE	RT	250.00	250.00
98	FRUITS OF FRIENDSHIP	RT	115.00	115.00
C. PYLE	**HISTORY OF ANGELS COLLECTION BY BILL DALE**			
95	ANGEL GABRIEL, THE	9500	120.00	120.00
95	MUSICAL ANGELS	9500	160.00	160.00
96	ANGELIC DOUBLE/STRUGGLE OF THE SOUL, THE	9500	200.00	200.00
T. BLACKSHEAR	**MASTER PEACE COLLECTION**			
98	FORGIVEN	RT	200.00	200.00
C. M. DUDASH	**MASTER PEACE COLLECTION**			
98	VICTORIOUS LION OF JUDAH	RT	175.00	175.00
M. WEISTLING	**MASTER PEACE COLLECTION**			
98	INVITATION, THE	RT	250.00	250.00
A. BLACKSHEAR	**RAINBOW BABIES**			
98	BELOVED	*	*	N/A
98	LIL' BLOSSOM	*	33.00	33.00
98	PEEK-A-BOO PALS	*	*	N/A

Ornaments

Clara Johnson Scroggins

Who would have guessed that one day ornament manufacturers would sponsor collector's clubs, offer special "member's only issues" and host gatherings at which "event-only" ornaments could be purchased on a limited basis?

Who could have predicted that one day collectors would be insuring their collections, carefully ascertaining reliable secondary market values for the appraisal of their ornaments? Or cataloging their collections with the aid of sourcebooks and storing their collections, carefully logged and labeled, in climate controlled quarters?

Who could have known that "first in a series" would be a phrase that sent shivers down the spines of ornament collectors and drove them into buying frenzies or that one day ornaments would sell on the secondary market for up to 10 times their original retail value?

That's the point to which ornament collecting has evolved today. And did you notice that these once holiday-only items are rarely referred to as Christmas ornaments in today's marketplace? Ornament makers have broadened their scope to include more than just Yuletide treasures, thus making ornaments a year-round collectible. Easter, Independence Day and Thanksgiving are just some of the holidays that are often commemorated in the form of ornaments. Producers are also personalizing ornaments, making them wonderful gifts for friends and loved ones.

But more importantly, and perhaps more than any other collectible, ornaments reflect the changes in our lives and times. From the early beginnings of elegant European blown glass, to the lively and often humorous artplas ornaments of today, this is a collectible that represents all passions and interests. Ornaments offer something for everyone. The themes are so varied and the media so diverse that this is a collectible with an affinity for the unique. Children are thrilled to own an ornament depicting their favorite sports figure and delight in the ornaments featuring licensed characters from their favorite movies or products. Hallmark, Enesco and Carlton Cards are just a few of the makers leading the way in this ever-changing industry rapidly aligning itself with the era of pop culture.

Timeless themes also abound in this diverse class of collecting. Generations-old themes, mediums and traditions are even more prevalent, and perhaps just as popular, as the "here today, gone tomorrow" themes of the '90s. Nostalgic collectors entranced by the magical look of blown glass can revel in the designs brought back by today's importers and makers such as Old World Christmas, Christopher Radko and Kurt S. Adler. Crystal, sterling silver and porcelain offered by Reed and Barton, Anna-Perenna, Swarovski and many, many more offer a variety of appealing themes in media just as alluring.

What drives the secondary market of this somewhat new arena? Perhaps diversity is its greatest thrust. In an industry producing for the masses, it's only logical that the laws of supply and demand would dictate the growth of the secondary market. Sports collectors, car enthusiasts, train aficionados, bear lovers, angel adorers and animation zealots frequently "cross over" to the realm of ornament collecting when the subject matter lends itself to their particular area of interest—which it often does. The competition to attain an ornament aligned with that area of interest often makes buying at the retail level somewhat difficult. That's where the secondary market begins. And so too does our chapter on the prices and trends of perhaps the world's most popular collectible.

CLARA JOHNSON SCROGGINS, who has authored six books on Hallmark ornaments, is a consultant and speaker who appears at collectibles events around the country. Her ornament collection is recognized as the largest in the country.

ORNAMENTS

YR NAME	LIMIT	ISSUE	TREND
ADRIAN TARON & SONS			
S. ROSAS			
97 BUSTER & BELLE	3000	32.00	32.00
S. ROSAS		**NURSERY RHYME**	
97 HUMPTY DUMPTY	5000	17.00	17.00

AMERICAN GREETINGS

YR NAME	LIMIT	ISSUE	TREND
*	**AMERICAN GREETINGS CHRISTMAS ORNAMENTS**		
80 ACRYLIC DISC-HOLLY HOBBIE C-23	YR	1.75	5.00
80 ACRYLIC DISC-MOTHER C-22	YR	1.75	4.00
80 STRAWBERRY SHORTCAKE/XMAS SUGARPLUM C-27	CL	3.50	4.00
81 ACRYLIC DISC-FIRST XMAS TOGETHER WXX-240	YR	4.00	4.00
81 ACRYLIC DISC-HOLLY HOBBIE WXX-239	YR	4.00	5.00
81 ACRYLIC DISC-MOTHER WXX-237	YR	4.00	5.00
81 ACRYLIC DISC-ZIGGY & FRIENDS WXX-236	YR	4.00	5.00
81 PORCELAIN HOLLY HOBBIE WXX-56	CL	3.00	4.00
82 ACRYLIC DISC-FRIENDSHIP/DESIGN WXO-32	YR	5.00	6.00
82 HOLLY HOB. PLUM PUDD PORCLN BELL WXO-45	CL	5.25	6.00
82 HOLLY HOBBIE FIG. PORCLN BELL WXO-48	YR	12.00	14.00
83 ACRYLIC DISC-FIRST XMAS TOGETHER CO-1901	YR	5.75	7.00
83 ACRYLIC DISC-FRIENDSHIP CO-1902	YR	5.75	7.00
83 ACRYLIC DISC-LOVE CO-1903	YR	5.75	7.00
83 HIMSELF THE ELF/PORC. BELL CO-1403	CL	12.00	12.00
83 RELIGIOUS ACRYLIC DISC CO-1904	YR	5.75	7.00
83 STRAWBERRY SHORTCAKE/PORC. BELL CO-1401	CL	12.00	12.00
83 STRWBRRY SHORTCAKE..SPECIAL GIFT CO-1225	CL	9.00	12.00
83 ZIGGY PORCELAIN FIGURINE BELL CO-1402	CL	12.00	12.00
84 CAREBEARS DECORATING THE TREE AO-1102	CL	15.00	20.00
84 HIMSELF THE ELF SCULPTED ORN. AO-407	CL	7.50	8.00
84 HOLLY HOBBIE CERAMIC FIGURE BELL AO-701	CL	10.00	10.00
84 HOLLY HOBBIE SCULPTED ORNAMENT AO-403	CL	7.50	15.00
84 MUSICAL-BABY'S FIRST CHRISTMAS AO-1001	YR	17.50	22.00
84 STRAWBERRY SHORTCAKE & FRIENDS AO-1101	CL	15.00	30.00
84 STRWBRRY SHORTCAKE SCULPTED ORN. AO-402	CL	9.00	12.00
84 TENDERHEART BEAR SCULPTED ORN. AO-406	CL	6.50	10.00
85 BABY'S FIRST CHRISTMAS BX-302	YR	7.00	10.00
85 HOLLY HOBBIE PORCELAIN/BELL BX-901	YR	10.00	10.00
85 MOUSE ON WATCH BX-303	CL	7.00	7.00
85 ZIGGY & FRIENDS ADMIRING TREE BX-1102	CL	13.00	13.00
86 ACRYLIC DISC A WREATH OF LOVE DX-503	CL	3.75	5.00
86 ACRYLIC DISC BABY'S FIRST XMAS DX-504	YR	3.75	5.00
86 ACRYLIC DISC FIRST XMAS TOGETHER DX-502	YR	3.75	5.00
86 ACRYLIC DISC SPECIAL FRIEND DX-501	YR	3.75	5.00
86 BABY'S FIRST CHRISTMAS DX-1609	CL	7.50	10.00
86 CERAMIC BELL BABY'S FIRST XMAS DX-1002	YR	6.50	8.00
86 CERAMIC BELL CHRISTMAS IS LOVE DX-1003	CL	6.50	7.00
86 CERAMIC BELL FIRST XMAS TOGETHER DX-1001	YR	6.50	13.00
86 GONE FISHIN' DX-1605	CL	8.00	8.00
86 OUT W/OLD IN W/NEW - ZIGGY DX-1501	YR	6.50	7.00
87 BRASS SAILBOAT CX-702	YR	6.50	7.00
87 CERAMIC OLD-FASHIONED TEDDY CX-402	CL	5.00	5.00
87 IRIDESCENT UNICORN CX-203	CL	4.00	4.00
87 PORCELAIN BELLS 1ST XMAS TOGETHER CX-302	YR	6.50	7.00
87 PORCELAIN BELLS BABY'S FIRST XMAS CX-301	YR	6.50	7.00
87 SCULPTED DIMEN. 1ST XMAS TOGETHER CX-104	YR	7.00	9.00
87 SCULPTED DIMEN./BOY FIRST XMAS CX-403	YR	7.50	9.00
87 SCULPTED DIMEN./CAROUSEL HORSE CX-801	CL	8.50	9.00
87 SCULPTED DIMEN./GIRL FIRST XMAS CX-404	YR	7.50	9.00
87 SCULPTED DIMEN./SANTA REF CX-112	YR	7.00	7.00
87 WOODEN ORNAMENT ROCKING HORSE CX-1104	YR	3.25	5.00
87 WOODEN ORNAMENT ZIGGY & FUZZ CX-1003	CL	4.50	5.00
88 ACRYLIC DISC FIRST XMAS TOGETHER AX-1007	YR	4.00	5.00
88 ACRYLIC DISC MADONNA & CHILD AX-1039	UD	4.25	5.00
88 BABY BOY'S FIRST XMAS AX-1004	YR	7.50	8.00
88 BABY GIRL'S FIRST XMAS AX-1005	YR	7.50	8.00
88 BABY'S FIRST XMAS PHOTO FRAME AX-1001	YR	5.00	5.00
88 BOWLING MOUSE AX-1017	UD	7.00	7.00
88 BRASS OUR HOME TO YOUR HOME AX-1010	YR	5.50	6.00
88 CAROUSEL HORSE AX-1040	UD	8.50	9.00
88 CERAMIC COW BELL AX-1034	UD	6.50	7.00
88 COPPER REINDEER WEATHERVANE	YR	4.50	5.00
88 LOVEBIRDS FIRST XMAS TOGETHER AX-1006	YR	7.00	7.00
88 MUSICAL ZIGGY & FUZZ FRIENDSHIP AX-1013	YR	7.00	7.00
88 NEW YEAR ZIGGY AX-1049	YR	6.50	7.00
88 ROCKING HORSE BABY'S FIRST XMAS AX-1003	YR	3.50	4.00
89 ACRYLIC DISC REWORK DX-1012	YR	4.24	5.00
89 BEAR ON ROCKING HORSE DX-1001	YR	7.95	8.00
89 BEAR ON ROCKING HORSE DX-1002	YR	7.95	8.00
89 BEAR ON ROCKING HORSE DX-1030	YR	7.50	8.00
89 BRASS SAILBOAT DX-1022	YR	6.50	7.00
89 BUNNIES IN SWING DX-1005	YR	8.50	9.00

YR	NAME	LIMIT	ISSUE	TREND
89	CAMEO-LOOK DOVE DISK DX-1016	YR	5.95	6.00
89	COOKING BEAR DX-1029	YR	7.50	8.00
89	DEER LEAPING OVER LANDSCAPE DX-1004	YR	4.95	5.00
89	DINOSAUR DRIVING TRAIN DX-1010	YR	7.95	8.00
89	HEART PHOTO FRAME-CANDY CANE DX-1023	YR	5.95	6.00
89	HEART SHAPE W/HOLLY DX-1007	YR	5.95	6.00
89	KITTEN IN STOCKING DX-1011	YR	4.50	5.00
89	LACE-LOOK BEAR EMBROID HOOP DX-1003	YR	5.50	6.00
89	NAUTICAL-LIFE RING W/HOLLY DX-1028	YR	5.95	6.00
89	PAPER DOLL CHAIN ON CERAMIC BELL DX-1009	YR	6.95	7.00
89	POLAR BEARS HOLDING HANDS DX-1035	YR	6.95	7.00
89	VICTORIAN EMBROIDERY HOOP DX-1008	YR	6.50	7.00
89	VICTORIAN HOUSE DX-1013	YR	4.50	5.00
89	WOOD DISC W/TREE DX-1033	YR	4.50	5.00
89	WOOD HEART W/SILK MISTLETOE DX-1015	YR	4.50	5.00
89	ZIGGY ELF W/JINGLE BELLS DX-1014	YR	6.95	7.00
90	2 BEARS W/GIFT ON SLED DX-1010	YR	4.50	5.00
90	ANGEL HOLDING HEART DX-1012	YR	4.50	5.00
90	BEAR ON BLOCK DX-1001	YR	7.95	8.00
90	BEAR ON BLOCK DX-1002	YR	7.95	8.00
90	BEAR ON ROCKING HORSE DX-1003	YR	4.50	5.00
90	BEARS PUTTING STAR ON XMAS TREE DX-1007	YR	5.95	6.00
90	BI-PLANE WITH SANTA DX-1015	YR	7.95	8.00
90	BIRDS IN MAILBOX DX-1008	YR	6.95	7.00
90	CAROUSEL REINDEER DX-1033	YR	7.95	8.00
90	CONV. HEART SHAPED DISC W/LTG. DX-1006	YR	5.50	6.00
90	FATHER CHRISTMAS DX-1035	YR	7.50	8.00
90	NATIVITY...CHRIST CHILD DX-1019	YR	5.50	6.00
90	SLEIGH & HOUSE DX-1009	YR	5.95	6.00
90	TOY SOLDIER W/DRUM DX-1034	YR	5.95	6.00
90	VICKY BELL DX-1014	YR	7.50	8.00

ANHEUSER-BUSCH INC.
*

			A & EAGLE COLLECTOR ORNAMENT SERIES	
91	BUDWEISER GIRL N3178	RT	15.00	15.00
92	1893 COLUMBIAN EXPOSITION N3649	RT	15.00	15.00
93	GREATEST TRIUMPH N4089	RT	15.00	15.00

S. SAMPSON

			CHRISTMAS ORNAMENT SERIES	
92	CLYDESDALES MINI PLATE ORNAMENTS N3650	RT	23.00	23.00

M. URDAHL

			CHRISTMAS ORNAMENT SERIES	
93	BUDWEISER 6-PK MINI PLATE ORN. N4220	RT	10.00	10.00

ANNA-PERENNA
P. BUCKLEY MOSS

93	SECOND ANGEL	YR	28.00	50.00
94	CHRISTMAS SKATERS	YR	28.00	28.00
94	THIRD ANGEL	YR	28.00	50.00
95	CHRISTMAS NIGHT	OP	28.00	28.00

P. BUCKLEY MOSS

			ANNUAL CHRISTMAS ORNAMENTS	
91	NOEL	*	25.00	120.00
92	SLEIGHRIDE	*	28.00	60.00

P. BUCKLEY MOSS

			HOLLY SERIES	
93	SNOWMAN, THE	YR	28.00	70.00

P. BUCKLEY MOSS

			TWELVE DAYS OF CHRISTMAS	
*	FIVE GOLDEN RINGS	*		N/A
*	FOUR CALLING BIRDS	*		N/A
*	PARTRIDGE IN A PEAR TREE	*		N/A
*	THREE FRENCH HENS	*		N/A
*	TWO TURTLEDOVES	*		N/A
98	SEVEN SWANS A SWIMMING	*	27.50	28.00
98	SIX GEESE A LAYING	*	27.50	28.00

ANNALEE MOBILITEE
A. THORNDIKE

82	ELF HEAD	1908	2.95	25.00
83	GINGERBREAD BOY	11835	11.00	35.00
84	SNOWMAN HEAD	13677	7.95	30.00
84	STAR	3275	5.95	25.00
85	3 IN. ANGEL ON CLOUD	*	6.50	30.00
85	SUN	1692	6.50	25.00
86	ANGEL HEAD	*	7.95	30.00
86	BABY ANGEL	YR	11.95	35.00
86	CLOWN HEAD	5701	7.95	150.00
93	3 IN. BEAR ORNAMENT W/ STAND	OP	13.00	13.00
93	5 IN. GINGERBREAD BOY ORNAMENT	OP	16.95	17.00
93	DEER HEAD ORNAMENT	OP	35.00	18.00
93	SANTA HEAD ORNAMENT	OP	8.95	9.00
93	SNOWMAN HEAD ORNAMENT	OP	11.45	12.00
94	3 IN. SUN W/SANTA HAT ORNAMENT	12881	7.95	8.00
94	5 IN. GINGERBREAD BOY ORNAMENT	RT	17.50	18.00
94	5 IN. OLD WORLD SANTA ORN.	7540	24.00	24.00
94	7 IN. SANTA HEAD ORNAMENT	12616	9.50	10.00
94	7 IN. SNOWMAN HEAD ORNAMENT	10062	11.95	12.00
94	DEER HEAD ORNAMENT	RT	10.50	11.00
94	PEPI HERRMAN CRYSTAL ORNAMENT	OP	29.95	30.00

YR	NAME	LIMIT	ISSUE	TREND
95	3 IN. ANGEL W/INSTRUMENT	SU	14.50	15.00
95	3 IN. BABY IN BLUE PJ'S	OP	11.95	12.00
95	3 IN. BABY IN PINK PJ'S	OP	11.95	12.00
95	3 IN. HONEY BEAR	OP	13.00	13.00
95	3 IN. STARBRIGHT ELF ORNAMENT-GREEN #7821	SU	12.00	12.00
95	3 IN. STARBRIGHT ELF ORNAMENT-RED #7822	SU	12.00	12.00
95	3 IN. SUN W/SANTA HAT	OP	8.50	9.00
95	3 IN. WINTER ELF	OP	11.95	12.00
95	5 IN. GINGERBREAD BOY	OP	17.95	18.00
95	5 IN. OLD WORLD SANTA	OP	24.00	24.00
95	DEER HEAD	OP	11.00	11.00
95	SANTA HEAD	OP	9.95	10.00
95	SNOWMAN HEAD	OP	11.95	12.00
96	18 IN. SANTA HANGING GINGERGREAD	OP	77.00	77.00
96	3 IN. ANGEL W/INSTRUMENT	OP	16.00	16.00
96	3 IN. GINGERBREAD BOY	OP	15.00	15.00
96	3 IN. HOLLY BERRY ANGEL	OP	17.00	17.00
96	3 IN. HONEY BEAR	OP	14.00	14.00
96	3 IN. JUST-A-JESTER	OP	21.00	20.50
96	3 IN. MIDNIGHT SNACK MOUSE	OP	18.00	18.00
96	3 IN. MOUSE IN SANTA'S HAT	SU	18.00	18.00
96	3 IN. MRS. SANTA	SU	16.50	16.50
96	3 IN. RED ELF W/STAR	OP	13.00	13.00
96	3 IN. SANTA	SU	16.50	16.50
96	3 IN. SKI BUNNY	RT	20.00	20.00
96	3 IN. SNOWMAN	OP	16.50	16.50
96	3 IN. WINTER ELF	OP	14.00	14.00
96	5 IN. OLD WORLD SANTA	OP	24.00	23.50
96	ELF HEAD/GREEN	SU	10.00	10.00
96	ELF HEAD/RED	SU	10.00	10.00
96	SANTA HEAD	OP	10.00	10.00
96	SNOWMAN HEAD	OP	12.50	13.00
96	TRIM-A-TREE PUPPY	RT	18.00	18.00

ANRI

	L. GAITHER		CHRISTMAS EVE SERIES	
95	HITCHING PRANCER	500	140.00	140.00
96	GETTING READY	500	140.00	140.00
98	FIRST GIFT OF CHRISTMAS	500	165.00	165.00
	DISNEY		DISNEY FOUR STAR COLLECTION	
89	MAESTRO MICKEY	YR	25.00	80.00
90	MINNIE MOUSE	YR	25.00	45.00
	J. FERRANDIZ		FERRANDIZ MESSAGE COLLECTION	
89	LET THE HEAVENS RING	1000	215.00	215.00
90	HEAR THE ANGELS SING	1000	225.00	225.00
	J. FERRANDIZ		FERRANDIZ WOODCARVINGS	
88	HEAVENLY DRUMMER	1000	175.00	225.00
89	HEAVENLY STRINGS	1000	190.00	190.00
	S. KAY		SARAH KAY'S FIRST CHRISTMAS	
95	FIRST XMAS STOCKING	500	99.00	99.00
96	ALL I WANT FOR CHRISTMAS	500	198.00	195.00
97	CHRISTMAS PUPPY	500	295.00	295.00

ARMANI

	G. ARMANI			ANNUAL
98	CHRISTMAS EVE 123F	YR	35.00	35.00
	G. ARMANI			COMMEMORATIVE
91	1991 CHRISTMAS ORNAMENT 799A	RT	11.50	12.00
92	1992 CHRISTMAS ORNAMENT 788F	RT	24.00	100.00
93	1993 CHRISTMAS ORNAMENT 982P	RT	25.00	75.00
94	1994 CHRISTMAS ORNAMENT 801P	RT	25.00	25.00
95	1995 CHRISTMAS ORNAMENT 640P	RT	30.00	30.00
96	1996 CHRISTMAS ORNAMENT 355P	RT	30.00	30.00
97	1997 CHRISTMAS ORNAMENT	YR	38.00	38.00

ARTAFFECTS

	G. PERILLO		ANNUAL BELL ORNAMENT	
85	HOME SWEET WIGWAM	OP	14.00	14.00
86	PEEK-A-BOO	OP	15.00	33.00
87	ANNUAL BELL ORNAMENT	YR	15.00	33.00
88	ANNUAL BELL ORNAMENT	YR	17.50	18.00
89	ANNUAL BELL ORNAMENT	YR	17.50	18.00
90	ANNUAL BELL ORNAMENT	YR	17.50	18.00
91	ANNUAL BELL ORNAMENT	YR	20.00	20.00
	G. PERILLO		ANNUAL CHRISTMAS ORNAMENTS	
85	PAPOOSE ORNAMENT	YR	14.00	40.00
86	CHRISTMAS CACTUS	YR	15.00	50.00
87	ANNUAL ORNAMENT	YR	15.00	35.00
88	ANNUAL ORNAMENT	YR	17.50	25.00
89	ANNUAL ORNAMENT	YR	17.50	25.00
90	ANNUAL ORNAMENT	YR	17.50	18.00
91	ANNUAL ORNAMENT	YR	20.00	19.50
	G. PERILLO		KACHINA ORNAMENTS	
91	DAWN KACHINA	OP	17.50	18.00
91	KACHINA MOTHER	OP	17.50	18.00

YR NAME	LIMIT	ISSUE	TREND
91 OLD KACHINA	OP	17.50	18.00
91 SNOW KACHINA	OP	17.50	18.00
91 SUN KACHINA	OP	17.50	18.00
91 TOTEM KACHINA	OP	17.50	18.00
G. PERILLO		**SAGEBRUSH KIDS BELL ORNAMENTS**	
87 CAROLERS, THE	OP	9.00	9.00
87 CHRISTMAS CANDLE	OP	9.00	9.00
87 CHRISTMAS HORN	OP	9.00	9.00
87 FIDDLER, THE	OP	9.00	9.00
87 GIFT, THE	OP	9.00	9.00
87 HARPIST, THE	OP	9.00	9.00
G. PERILLO		**SAGEBRUSH KIDS COLLECTION**	
91 MOCCASIN ORNAMENT	OP	15.00	16.00
91 SHIELD ORNAMENT	OP	15.00	16.00
91 TEE-PEE ORNAMENT	OP	15.00	16.00
C. ROEDA		**SIMPLE WONDERS**	
91 ASHLEY	OP	23.00	23.00
91 BRITTANY	OP	23.00	23.00
91 KIM	OP	23.00	23.00
91 LITTLE FEATHER	OP	23.00	23.00
91 MEGAN	OP	23.00	23.00
91 NICOLE	OP	23.00	23.00
92 SWEET SURPRISE	YR	15.00	16.00

ARTHUR COURT DESIGNS

A. COURT		CHRISTMAS ORNAMENT SERIES	
94 BUNNIES ON A SLEIGH	8200	22.00	24.00

ARTISTS OF THE WORLD

T. DEGRAZIA		DEGRAZIA ANNUAL ORNAMENTS	
86 PIMA, INDIAN DRUMMER BOY	YR	28.00	375.00
87 WHITE DOVE	YR	30.00	75.00
88 FLOWER GIRL	YR	33.00	50.00
89 FLOWER BOY	YR	35.00	50.00
90 MERRY LITTLE INDIAN	10000	88.00	100.00
90 PINK PAPOOSE	YR	35.00	50.00
91 CHRISTMAS PRAYER	YR	50.00	50.00
92 BEARING GIFT	YR	55.00	55.00
93 LIGHTING THE WAY	YR	58.00	58.00
93 WARM WISHES	YR	65.00	75.00
94 LITTLE PRAYER	YR	50.00	52.00
94 WARM WISHES	YR	65.00	85.00
95 HEAVENLY FLOWERS	YR	65.00	65.00
95 LITTLE PRAYER	YR	50.00	70.00
95 MY BEAUTIFUL ROCKING HORSE	YR	125.00	125.00
96 OH HOLY NIGHT	YR	68.00	68.00
97 CHRISTMAS SPIRIT	YR	65.00	65.00
98 LITTLE COLOPAH INDIAN GIRL	OP	67.50	68.00

ASHTON-DRAKE GALLERIES

J. MEYERAAN		AND HIS NAME SHALL BE CALLED	
97 LIGHT OF THE WORLD	*	*	N/A
97 PRINCE OF PEACE	*	*	N/A
B.P. GUTMANN		**BESSIE P. GUTMANN ORNAMENTS COLLECTION**	
97 FRIENDLY ENEMIES/HELPING HANDS	*	35.00	35.00
97 JUST A TASTE/MINE	*	35.00	35.00
97 LOVE IS BLIND/SLEEPYHEADS	*	35.00	35.00
97 ON HIS WAY/THE LULLABY	*	35.00	35.00
97 REWARD, THE/DRESSING MYSELF	*	35.00	35.00
97 TAPS/BEST OF FRIENDS	*	35.00	35.00

BAND CREATIONS

RICHARDS/PENFIELD AMERICA'S FARMLAND COLLECTION - AMERICA'S COUNTRY BARN			
96 DOUBLE-CRIB BARN	OP	29.95	30.00
96 DUTCH BARN	OP	29.95	30.00
96 ENGLISH BARN	OP	29.95	30.00
96 GAMBREL ROOF BARN	OP	29.95	30.00
96 LOG BARN	OP	29.95	30.00
96 POLYGONAL BARN	OP	29.95	30.00
96 ROUND BARN	OP	29.95	30.00
RICHARDS/PENFIELD		**BEST FRIENDS**	
94 ANGEL ORNAMENTS-4 ASSORTED	OP	5.00	5.00
95 DOUBLE ANGELS	OP	8.00	8.00
RICHARDS/PENFIELD		**BEST FRIENDS - ANGELS OF THE MONTH**	
93 APRIL ANGEL	OP	10.00	10.00
93 AUGUST ANGEL	OP	10.00	10.00
93 DECEMBER ANGEL	OP	10.00	10.00
93 FEBRUARY ANGEL	OP	10.00	10.00
93 JANUARY ANGEL	OP	10.00	10.00
93 JULY ANGEL	OP	10.00	10.00
93 JUNE ANGEL	OP	10.00	10.00
93 MARCH ANGEL	OP	10.00	10.00
93 MAY ANGEL	OP	10.00	10.00
93 NOVEMBER ANGEL	OP	10.00	10.00
93 OCTOBER ANGEL	OP	10.00	10.00

YR	NAME	LIMIT	ISSUE	TREND
93	SEPTEMBER ANGEL	OP	10.00	10.00
96	APRIL ANGEL	OP	10.00	10.00
96	AUGUST ANGEL	OP	10.00	10.00
96	DECEMBER ANGEL	OP	10.00	10.00
96	FEBRUARY ANGEL	OP	10.00	10.00
96	JANUARY ANGEL	OP	10.00	10.00
96	JULY ANGEL	OP	10.00	10.00
96	JUNE ANGEL	OP	10.00	10.00
96	MARCH ANGEL	OP	10.00	10.00
96	MAY ANGEL	OP	10.00	10.00
96	NOVEMBER ANGEL	OP	10.00	10.00
96	OCTOBER ANGEL	OP	10.00	10.00
96	SEPTEMBER ANGEL	OP	10.00	10.00

RICHARDS/PENFIELD — BEST FRIENDS - KRINGLE TOPPERS

YR	NAME	LIMIT	ISSUE	TREND
96	AMERICA, SANTA CLAUS	OP	10.00	10.00
96	AUSTRIA, CHRISTKIND	OP	10.00	10.00
96	ENGLAND, FATHER CHRISTMAS	OP	10.00	10.00
96	GERMANY, PELSNICKEL	OP	10.00	10.00
96	NETHERLANDS, ST. NICKOLAS	OP	10.00	10.00
96	PERE NOEL, FRANCE	OP	10.00	10.00
96	RUSSIAN, FATHER FROST	OP	10.00	10.00
96	SCANDINAVIA, JULNISSE	OP	10.00	10.00

BIEDERMANN & SONS
*

YR	NAME	LIMIT	ISSUE	TREND
93	BABY'S FIRST CHRISTMAS	400	12.00	14.00
93	FOUR CALLING BIRDS (BRASS)	RT	12.50	19.00
93	FOUR CALLING BIRDS (SILVER)	500	18.00	55.00
94	BABY'S FIRST CHRISTMAS	400	12.00	13.00
94	DRUMMER BOY (BRASS)	14500	12.50	18.00
94	DRUMMER BOY (SILVER)	500	18.00	140.00

* — COMMEMORATIVE ORNAMENTS

YR	NAME	LIMIT	ISSUE	TREND
71	THREE KINGS	10000	7.00	580.00
72	SLEIGH RIDE	10000	8.00	910.00
76	ANGEL PLAYING LUTE	10000	10.00	126.00
87	PARTRIDGE IN A PEAR TREE	10000	12.00	264.00
90	HERALD ANGEL	10000	14.00	236.00
94	DRUMMER BOY (BRASS)	10000	15.00	130.00

G. NEUMEIER — COMMEMORATIVE ORNAMENTS

YR	NAME	LIMIT	ISSUE	TREND
98	TOY ROCKING HORSE RIDE	10000	15.50	16.00

* — SILVER COMMEMORATIVES

YR	NAME	LIMIT	ISSUE	TREND
88	SANTA'S SLEIGH RIDE	288	15.00	135.00
89	TWO TURTLEDOVES	288	16.00	142.00
92	CHRISTMAS MORNING	288	17.00	102.00

R. RIECHERT — SILVER COMMEMORATIVES

YR	NAME	LIMIT	ISSUE	TREND
95	FIVE GOLDEN RINGS (SILVER)	288	20.00	170.00

K. VON KLUGE — SILVER COMMEMORATIVES

YR	NAME	LIMIT	ISSUE	TREND
94	DRUMMER BOY (SILVER)	288	18.00	400.00

BING & GRONDAHL
H. HANSEN

YR	NAME	LIMIT	ISSUE	TREND
98	CHRISTMAS AROUND THE WORLD	YR	25.00	25.00

S. VESTERGAARD

YR	NAME	LIMIT	ISSUE	TREND
98	CHRISTMAS	YR	38.00	38.00

C. MAGADINE — CHRISTMAS

YR	NAME	LIMIT	ISSUE	TREND
96	CHRISTMAS EVE AT THE STATUE OF LIBERTY	YR	25.00	25.00

J. WOODSON — CHRISTMAS IN AMERICA

YR	NAME	LIMIT	ISSUE	TREND
86	CHRISTMAS EVE IN WILLIAMSBURG	CL	12.50	50.00
87	CHRISTMAS EVE AT THE WHITE HOUSE	CL	15.00	25.00
88	CHRISTMAS EVE AT ROCKEFELLER CENTER	CL	19.00	19.00
89	CHRISTMAS IN NEW ENGLAND	CL	20.00	20.00
90	CHRISTMAS EVE AT THE CAPITOL	CL	20.00	30.00
91	INDEPENDENCE HALL	CL	24.00	24.00
92	CHRISTMAS IN SAN FRANCISCO	CL	25.00	35.00
93	COMING HOME FOR CHRISTMAS	CL	25.00	25.00

H. HANSEN — SANTA CLAUS

YR	NAME	LIMIT	ISSUE	TREND
89	SANTA'S WORKSHOP	YR	20.00	55.00
90	SANTA'S SLEIGH	YR	20.00	50.00
91	JOURNEY, THE	YR	24.00	50.00
92	SANTA'S ARRIVAL	YR	25.00	40.00
93	SANTA'S GIFTS	YR	25.00	30.00

BOYDS COLLECTION LTD.
G. LOWENTHAL — BEARSTONE COLLECTION

YR	NAME	LIMIT	ISSUE	TREND
94	CHARITY 2502	RT	10.00	30.00
94	FAITH 2500	RT	10.00	30.00
94	HOPE 2501	RT	10.00	30.00
95	EDMUND	CL	10.00	10.00
95	ELLIOT WITH TREE 2507	CL	10.00	10.00
95	MANHEIM THE MOOSE	CL	10.00	10.00
96	BAILEY & MATTHEW	*	70.00	70.00
96	CLAIR WITH GINGERBREAD MAN 25701	*	11.00	25.00
96	EDMUND 25700	*	11.00	25.00
96	WILSON WITH SHOOTING STAR 25702	*	11.00	25.00

YR	NAME	LIMIT	ISSUE	TREND

BRADFORD EDITIONS

YR	NAME	LIMIT	ISSUE	TREND
*			**ALMOST ANGELS**	
97	COOKIE/FRECKLES	*	20.00	20.00
L. LIU			**BEAUTIFUL HUMMINGBIRDS**	
97	GARDEN WHISPERS/WINGS OF GRACE	*	30.00	30.00
97	RUBY THROATED HUMMINGBIRD/ANNA'S HUMMINGBIRD	*	30.00	30.00
*			**CAT'S MEOW**	
97	CAT NAP/HOUSE SITTING	*	25.00	25.00
97	OUT ON A LIMB/HAPPY AS A LARK	*	25.00	25.00
D. BROOKS		**HEAVEN'S LITTLE SWEETHEARTS**		
97	AN ANGEL'S CARING/AN ANGEL'S SHARING	*	20.00	20.00
97	AN ANGEL'S KINDNESS/AN ANGEL'S LOVE	*	20.00	20.00
T. CATHEY	**HEAVENLY HEARTS PORCELAIN ORNAMENTS COLLECTION**			
97	HUMILITY/INNOCENCE SET	95 DAYS	20.00	20.00
97	JOY/PRUDENCE SET	95 DAYS	20.00	20.00
97	LIBERTY/FAITH SET	95 DAYS	20.00	20.00
97	PATIENCE/INSPIRATION SET	95 DAYS	20.00	20.00
97	PURITY/LOVING SET	95 DAYS	20.00	20.00
97	SERENITY/HONESTY SET	95 DAYS	20.00	20.00
97	SWEETNESS/GRACE SET	95 DAYS	20.00	20.00
97	TRUTH/MODESTY SET	95 DAYS	20.00	20.00
*			**KINDRED MOMENTS**	
97	FOREVER FRIENDS/LIFE'S GREATEST TREASURE	95 DAYS	20.00	20.00
97	SISTERS ARE BLOSSOMS/CLOSE AT HEART	95 DAYS	20.00	20.00
J. SCHOLZ			**KITTEN EXPEDITION**	
97	BY THE LILY POND/AT THE GARDEN FENCE	*	30.00	30.00
97	IN THE MEADOW/IN THE ROCK GARDEN	*	30.00	30.00
LEPAGE/DANIEL			**SPIRIT OF THE WILDERNESS**	
97	GRAY GUARDIAN/GOLDEN GENERATIONS	*	20.00	20.00
97	SILVER SCOUT/BLACK KNIGHT (SET OF 2)	*	20.00	20.00

BRANDYWINE WOODCRAFTS

YR	NAME	LIMIT	ISSUE	TREND
M. WHITING			**WILLIAMSBURG ORNAMENTS**	
94	GUNSMITH	350	9.50	10.00

BRIERCROFT

YR	NAME	LIMIT	ISSUE	TREND
B. FARLOW				
94	BELL ANGEL	5000	6.00	10.00

BUCCELLATI

YR	NAME	LIMIT	ISSUE	TREND
G. BUCCELLATI			**CHRISTMAS ORNAMENTS**	
86	SNOWY VILLAGE SCENE-2464	500	195.00	400.00
87	SHOOTING STAR-2469	500	240.00	350.00
88	SANTA CLAUS-2470	500	225.00	300.00
89	CHRISTMAS TREE-2471	750	230.00	230.00
90	ZENITH-2479	750	250.00	250.00
91	WREATH-3561	750	300.00	300.00
92	CHERUBS 3562	500	300.00	300.00
93	CHRISTMAS CANDLE	500	300.00	320.00
94	CHRISTMAS FIREPLACE	500	300.00	320.00

CARRIAGE HOUSE STUDIO INC.

YR	NAME	LIMIT	ISSUE	TREND
M. FURLONG			**GIFTS FROM GOD**	
85	CHARIS ANGEL, THE	3000	45.00	100.00
86	ANGEL OF LIGHT, THE	3000	45.00	100.00
86	HALLELUJAH ANGEL, THE	3000	45.00	125.00
88	CELESTIAL ANGEL, THE	3000	45.00	100.00
89	CORONATION ANGEL	3000	45.00	60.00
M. FURLONG			**JOYEUX NOEL**	
90	CELEBRATION ANGEL	10000	45.00	45.00
91	THANKSGIVING ANGEL	10000	45.00	45.00
92	JOYEUX NOEL ANGEL	10000	45.00	45.00
M. FURLONG			**MUSICAL SERIES**	
80	CAROLER, THE	3000	50.00	100.00
81	LYRIST, THE	3000	45.00	60.00
82	LUTIST, THE	3000	45.00	75.00
83	CONCERTINIST, THE	3000	45.00	75.00
84	HERALD ANGEL, THE	3000	45.00	75.00

CAVANAGH GROUP

YR	NAME	LIMIT	ISSUE	TREND
H. SUNDBLOM	**COCA-COLA BRAND HERITAGE COLLECTION**			
95	CHRISTMAS IS LOVE	OP	10.00	10.00
95	SANTA AT THE MANTLE	OP	10.00	10.00
95	SSSHHH!	OP	10.00	10.00
96	HOSPITALITY IN YOUR REFRIGERATOR	10000	25.00	25.00
96	IT WILL REFRESH YOU TOO (PORCELAIN)	10000	25.00	25.00
96	PLEASE PAUSE HERE	10000	25.00	25.00
97	IT WILL REFRESH YOU TOO	OP	10.00	10.00
97	SSSHHH!	OP	10.00	10.00
*	THAT EXTRA SOMETHING	OP	10.00	10.00
*		**COCA-COLA BRAND HERITAGE COLLECTION POLAR BEARS**		
96	BABY'S FIRST CHRISTMAS	OP	12.00	12.00
96	OUR FIRST CHRISTMAS	OP	12.00	12.00
96	STOCKING STUFFERS	OP	12.00	12.00

White Dove *by Ted DeGrazia, produced by Artists of the World, has more than doubled in value since its 1987 release.*

Hallmark helps newlyweds commemorate Our First Christmas Together *with this Keepsake Ornament from 1995.*

Sculpted by Hallmark artist Don Palmiter for the Olympic Spirit Collection, IZZY— the Mascot ornament has increased in value since its 1996 release.

The Surprised Cherub *Christmas ornament debuted in Lladró's ornament line for $120 in 1995.*

YR	NAME	LIMIT	ISSUE	TREND
97	ALWAYS FAMILY	OP	10.00	10.00
97	TRIMMING THE TREE	OP	10.00	10.00
H. SUNDBLOM	**COCA-COLA BRAND HERITAGE COLLECTION POLAR BEARS**			
97	REFRESHING BREAK	OP	10.00	10.00
*	**COCA-COLA BRAND HISTORICAL BUILDING**			
91	1930S SERVICE STATION	CL	10.00	20.00
91	EARLY COCA-COLA BOTTLING COMPANY	CL	10.00	20.00
91	JACOB'S PHARMACY	CL	10.00	20.00
91	PEMBERTON HOUSE, THE	CL	10.00	20.00
*	**COCA-COLA BRAND NORTH POLE BOTTLING WORKS**			
93	BLAST OFF	CL	9.00	9.00
93	DELIVERY FOR SANTA	CL	9.00	9.00
93	FILL'ER UP	CL	9.00	20.00
93	ICE SCULPTING	CL	9.00	9.00
93	LONG WINTER'S NAP	CL	9.00	13.00
93	NORTH POLE EXPRESS	CL	9.00	20.00
93	THIRSTING FOR ADVENTURE	CL	9.00	15.00
93	TOPS ON REFRESHMENT	CL	9.00	13.00
94	POWER DRIVE	CL	9.00	9.00
94	SANTA'S REFRESHMENT	CL	9.00	13.00
94	SELTZER SURPRISE	CL	9.00	13.00
94	TOPS OFF REFRESHMENT	CL	9.00	9.00
95	BARREL OF BEARS	CL	9.00	9.00
95	FOUNTAIN GLASS FOLLIES	OP	9.00	9.00
95	NORTH POLE FLYING SCHOOL	CL	9.00	9.00
96	REFRESHING SURPRISE	OP	9.00	9.00
96	RUSH DELIVERY	OP	9.00	9.00
96	TO: MRS. CLAUS	OP	9.00	9.00
*	**COCA-COLA BRAND POLAR BEAR COLLECTION**			
94	DOWNHILL SLEDDER	CL	9.00	9.00
94	NORTH POLE DELIVERY	CL	9.00	13.00
94	SKATING COCA-COLA POLAR BEAR	CL	9.00	12.00
94	VENDING MACHINE MISCHIEF	CL	9.00	9.00
95	POLAR BEAR ON BOTTLE OPENER	OP	9.00	9.00
95	SNOWBOARDIN' BEAR	OP	9.00	9.00
96	CHRISTMAS STAR, THE	OP	9.00	9.00
96	HOLLYWOOD	OP	9.00	9.00
97	DOUBLE THE FUN	OP	9.00	9.00
97	DOWNHILL RACERS	OP	9.00	9.00
H. SUNDBLOM	**COCA-COLA BRAND TRIM A TREE COLLECTION**			
90	AWAY WITH A TIRED & THIRSTY FACE	CL	10.00	25.00
90	HOSPITALITY	CL	10.00	13.00
90	MERRY CHRISTMAS AND A HAPPY NEW YEAR	CL	10.00	40.00
90	SEASON'S GREETINGS	CL	10.00	13.00
91	CHRISTMAS IS LOVE	CL	10.00	25.00
91	TIME TO SHARE	CL	10.00	25.00
92	HAPPY HOLIDAYS	CL	10.00	25.00
92	SSSHHH!	CL	10.00	27.00
93	DECORATING THE TREE	CL	10.00	20.00
93	EXTRA BRIGHT REFRESHMENT	CL	10.00	17.00
93	TRAVEL REFRESHED	CL	10.00	13.00
94	BUSY MAN'S PAUSE	CL	10.00	10.00
94	FOR SPARKLING HOLIDAYS	CL	10.00	10.00
94	THINGS GO BETTER WITH COKE	CL	10.00	10.00
95	IT WILL REFRESH YOU TOO	CL	10.00	10.00
95	PLEASE PAUSE HERE	OP	10.00	10.00
96	PAUSE THAT REFRESHES	OP	10.00	10.00
96	THEY REMEMBERED ME	OP	10.00	10.00
97	GOOD BOYS AND GIRLS	OP	9.00	9.00
*	**COCA-COLA CHRISTMAS COLLECTORS SOCIETY**			
93	HO HO HO - SANTA	CL		30.00
94	FISHING BEAR	CL		28.00
95	HOSPITALITY - SANTA	CL		25.00
96	SPRITE	CL		N/A
97	CAROUSEL CAPERS	CL		N/A
*	**COCA-COLA POLAR BEAR CUBS**			
97	BABY'S FIRST CHRISTMAS	OP	8.00	8.00
97	COOKIES FOR SANTA	OP	8.00	8.00
97	DREAMING OF A MAGICAL CHRISTMAS	YR	8.00	8.00
97	REFRESHING ICE COLD TREAT	OP	8.00	8.00
97	STOCKING STUFFER SURPRISE	YR	8.00	8.00
97	TWAS THE NIGHT BEFORE CHRISTMAS	OP	8.00	8.00

CAZENOVIA ABROAD

*			**CHRISTMAS ORNAMENTS**	
68	BUNNY P104B	*	9.00	40.00
68	CAT P105C	*	9.00	40.00
68	DUCK P103D	*	9.00	40.00
68	ELEPHANT P102E	*	9.00	40.00
68	ROOSTER P106R	*	10.00	40.00
68	STANDING ANGEL P107SA	*	9.00	45.00
68	TEDDY BEAR P101TB	*	9.00	40.00
68	TIPTOE ANGEL P108TTA	*	10.00	40.00
69	FAWN P109F	*	12.00	45.00
70	PEACE P111P	*	12.00	45.00

YR	NAME	LIMIT	ISSUE	TREND
70	PORKY P112PK	*	15.00	45.00
70	SNOW MAN P110SM	*	12.00	45.00
71	KNEELING ANGEL P113KA	*	15.00	55.00
72	ROCKING HORSE P114RH	*	15.00	55.00
73	TREETOP ANGEL P115TOP	*	10.00	42.00
74	OWL P116O	*	15.00	45.00
75	STAR P117ST	*	15.00	45.00
76	HATCHING CHICK P118CH	*	15.00	45.00
77	RAGGEDY ANN P119RA	*	17.50	45.00
78	SHELL P120SH	*	20.00	40.00
79	TOY SOLDIER P121TS	*	20.00	40.00
80	BURRO P122BU	*	20.00	40.00
81	CLOWN P123CL	*	25.00	40.00
82	REBECCA P124RE	*	25.00	40.00
83	MOUSE P126MO	*	28.00	45.00
83	RAGGEDY ANDY P125AND	*	28.00	45.00
84	CHERUB P127CB	*	30.00	45.00
84	REINDEER & SLEIGH H100	*	1,250.00	1500.00
85	SHAGGY DOG P132SD	*	45.00	50.00
86	BIG SISTER P134BS	*	60.00	60.00
86	LITTLE BROTHER P135LB	*	55.00	55.00
86	PETER RABBIT P133PR	*	50.00	50.00
87	LAMB P136LA	*	60.00	60.00
87	SEA HORSE P137SE	*	35.00	30.00
88	PARTRIDGE P138PA	*	70.00	70.00
88	SQUIRREL P139SQ	*	70.00	70.00
89	SWAN P140SW	OP	45.00	45.00
90	MORAVIAN STAR P141PS	OP	65.00	65.00
91	ANGEL P144A	OP	63.00	63.00
91	BUNNY RABBIT P143BR	OP	65.00	65.00
91	HEDGEHOG P142HH	OP	65.00	65.00
92	HUMPTY DUMPTY P145HD	OP	70.00	70.00

CHARMING TAILS
D. GRIFF

YR	NAME	LIMIT	ISSUE	TREND
92	CATCHIN' ZZZS	RT	12.00	38.00
92	CHICKADEES ON BALL	RT	14.00	14.00
92	DRIFTERS-MOUSE HOLDS STEM	RT	12.00	38.00
92	DRIFTERS-MOUSE WITH LEAF PARACHUTE	RT	12.00	38.00
92	FRESH FRUIT-BIRD AND APPLE	RT	12.00	34.00
92	FRESH FRUIT-MOUSE AND PEAR	RT	12.00	34.00
92	FRESH FRUIT-RABBIT AND APPLE	RT	12.00	36.00
92	MICE IN LEAF SLEIGH	RT	26.00	200.00
92	MICE/RABBIT BALL	RT	12.00	75.00
92	MICE/RABBIT BALL-RABBIT	RT	12.00	70.00
93	BUNNY/MOUSE BELL-BUNNY	RT	11.00	11.00
93	BUNNY/MOUSE BELL-MOUSE	RT	11.00	11.00
93	HANG IN THERE-CURLED TAIL	RT	10.00	28.00
93	HANG IN THERE-MOUSE WITH BERRIES	RT	10.00	28.00
93	HANG IN THERE-TAIL WRAPPED ON LEG	RT	10.00	28.00
93	HOLIDAY WREATH-MOUSE	RT	12.00	47.00
93	HOLIDAY WREATH-RABBIT	RT	12.00	47.00
93	MACKENZIE NAPPING	RT	12.00	38.00
93	MAXINE LIGHTS A CANDLE	RT	11.00	37.00
93	MOUSE ON DRAGONFLY	RT	17.00	245.00
93	MOUSE ON SNOWFLAKE	RT	11.00	38.00
93	PORCELAIN MOUSE BELL	RT	5.00	5.00
94	APPLE HOUSE	RT	13.00	60.00
94	BABY'S FIRST CHRISTMAS	SO	12.00	45.00
94	BINKEY & REGINALD ON ICE-RABBIT	RT	10.00	10.00
94	BINKEY & REGINALD ON ICE-RACCOON	RT	10.00	10.00
94	BINKEY IN THE BERRY PATCH	RT	12.00	50.00
94	EASTER PARADE	RT	10.00	32.00
94	FRIENDS IN FLIGHT	RT	18.00	100.00
94	GRAPE ESCAPE-GREEN	RT	18.00	80.00
94	GRAPE ESCAPE-PURPLE	RT	18.00	60.00
94	HIGH FLYING MACKENZIE	RT	20.00	36.00
94	HOLIDAY LIGHTS	RT	10.00	47.00
94	HORSING AROUND	RT	18.00	35.00
94	MACKENZIE BLOWING BUBBLE	RT	12.00	67.00
94	MACKENZIE ON ICE	RT	10.00	38.00
94	MACKENZIE'S BUBBLE RIDE	RT	13.00	52.00
94	MAXINE AND MACKENZIE	RT	12.00	37.00
94	MAXINE AND MACKENZIE-MACKENZIE ON LEAF	RT	12.00	37.00
94	MOUSE ON YELLOW BULB	CL	10.00	65.00
94	PEAR HOUSE	RT	12.00	80.00
94	PEEK-A-BOO	RT	12.00	35.00
94	REGINALD'S BUBBLE RIDE	RT	12.00	70.00
94	STICKY SITUATIONS-CANDY CANE	RT	16.00	38.00
94	STICKY SITUATIONS-RIBBON CANDY	RT	16.00	38.00
95	BINKEY & REGINALD IN STOCKING	SO	16.00	30.00
95	BINKEY'S POINTSETTIA	RT	12.00	30.00
95	HELLO, SWEET PEA	RT	12.00	24.00
95	HOLIDAY BALLOON RIDE	RT	16.00	34.00
95	MACKENZIE'S WHIRLYGIG	RT	20.00	37.00
95	MOUSE IN STRAWBERRY	RT	12.00	50.00

YR	NAME	LIMIT	ISSUE	TREND
95	PICKING PEPPERS	RT	12.00	25.00
95	REGINALD IN LEAVES-RIDING LEAF	RT	10.00	19.00
95	STEWART AT PLAY	RT	12.00	47.00
95	STEWART'S WINTER FUN/ICICLE	RT	10.00	36.00
95	STEWART'S WINTER FUN/SNOWFLAKE	RT	10.00	38.00
96	ALL WRAPPED UP	SO	12.00	43.00
96	BABY'S FIRST CHRISTMAS	SO	12.00	25.00
96	I'M BERRY HAPPY!	RT	15.00	32.00
96	OUR FIRST CHRISTMAS	SO	18.00	37.00
97	MACKENZIE'S JACK IN THE BOX	YR	10.00	10.00
D. GRIFF			**EASTER BASKET**	
94	EASTER PARADE	RT	10.00	28.00
D. GRIFF			**EVERYDAY SERIES**	
93	MOUSE ON A BEE	CL	17.00	240.00
94	BINKEY IN A BERRY PATCH	RT	12.00	50.00
94	SPRINGTIME SHOWERS	RT	10.00	35.00
95	I'M FULL	CL	15.00	28.00
95	THIS IS HOT	RT	15.00	25.00

CHRISTINA'S WORLD
*

YR	NAME	LIMIT	ISSUE	TREND
97	AH SO PORCELAIN CHINAMAN 3.5"- ART125	OP	3.00	3.00
97	ANGEL IN THE SNOW W/ BLUE WINGS 100MM- ART137	OP	9.00	9.00
97	ANGEL IN THE SNOW W/ PINK WINGS 100MM- ART136	OP	9.00	9.00
97	ANGEL OF PEACE 100MM- ART138	OP	15.00	15.00
97	CHAMPAGNE GARDEN OF EDEN W/ COCKATOO	300	30.00	30.00
97	CHINESE FARMER PORCELAIN 100MM- ART126	OP	6.50	7.00
97	DELICATE IRIS PORCELAIN100MM- ART129	OP	6.50	7.00
97	DOVE & CHERUB CLEAR AMETHYST100MM- ART130-C	OP	4.00	4.00
97	GARDEN OF EDEN FROSTED 100MM- ART132	OP	15.00	15.00
97	GARDEN OF EDEN GOLD ANTIQUE 100MM- ART133	OP	15.00	15.00
97	LITTLE SNOW BOY 100MM- ART135	OP	9.00	9.00
97	LITTLE SNOW GIRL 100MM- ART134	OP	9.00	9.00
97	PAGODA PORCELAIN 100MM- ART128	OP	6.50	7.00
97	SAMURAI PORCELAIN 100MM- ART127	OP	6.50	7.00
97	THREE GRACES 100MM- ART131	OP	6.50	7.00
C. MALLOUK				
97	BUTTON SANTA	500	30.00	30.00
97	HANS W/ TREE	300	30.00	30.00
97	MIDNIGHT MASQUERADE	500	30.00	30.00
IWANA				
97	WILD PONIES ON A BURGUNDY SKY	500	40.00	40.00
O. NOVITOVA				
97	EDO COURTESANS	300	80.00	80.00
SEGUSO				
97	MURANO VARIATION- 11 PC	50	85.00	85.00
C. MALLOUK			**ABSTRACTS**	
94	OP ART 80 MM - ART970	48	9.00	9.00
*			**BIRDS**	
97	MARCASITE HUMMINGBIRD BALL BLACK 100MM- BIR163-B	OP	5.00	5.00
97	MARCASITE HUMMINGBIRD BALL FROSTE 100MM- BIR163-F	OP	5.00	5.00
97	PHOENIX RISING WHITE ON BLUE 112MM- BIR604	OP	15.00	15.00
97	SNOW SWAN W/ CROWN CLIP ON BIRD IRIDESCENT- BIR164	OP	5.00	5.00
*			**BY THE SEA**	
97	BARREL BEAD GARLAND COPPER 6'- SUN125	OP	20.00	20.00
97	GOLDEN CONCH- SEA342	OP	2.25	2.00
*			**CIRQUE DE NOEL**	
97	HARLEQUIN MASQUE BALL 112MM- CIR456	OP	15.00	15.00
97	JESTER, THE, PETITE TETE W/ RUFFLE COLLAR- CIR452	OP	15.00	15.00
97	JESTER, THE, PETITE TETE- CIR453	OP	15.00	15.00
97	NIGHT & DAY, PETITE TETE W/ RUFFLE COLLAR- CIR454	OP	15.00	15.00
97	NIGHT & DAY, PETITE TETE- CIR455	OP	15.00	15.00
97	PIERRETTE, PETITE TETE- CIR451	OP	15.00	15.00
97	PIERROT, PETITE TETE W/ RUFFLE COLLAR- CIR450	OP	15.00	15.00
*			**FINIALS & TREE TOPS**	
97	TREE TOP BURGUNDY GOLD 10"- CAS702	OP	10.00	10.00
97	TREE TOP GREEN GOLD 10"- CAS703	OP	10.00	10.00
97	TREE TOP MARDI GRAS MULTI COLOR 20"- FIN916	OP	18.00	18.00
97	TREE TOP OLD WORLD FLORAL 20"- FIN917	OP	18.00	18.00
97	TREE TOP OLD WORLD GOLD RED 24"- FIN915	OP	25.00	25.00
97	TREE TOP OLD WORLD SILVER RED 24"- FIN914	OP	25.00	25.00
*			**GARDEN FLOWERS**	
97	PEONY GIANT CLEAR GOLD 5"- FLO562	OP	6.50	7.00
97	PEONY GIANT PINK 5"- FLO561	OP	6.50	7.00
97	SPIDER MUM BALL 100MM- FLO560	OP	6.50	7.00
97	SUNFLOWER GIANT 5"- FLO563	OP	6.50	7.00
*			**GARDEN OF EDEN 1997**	
97	AFRICAN DAISY PINK 100MM- GAR950	YR	12.00	12.00
97	ANTHURIUM ORCHID BOUQUET 112MM- GAR958	YR	15.00	15.00
97	CALADIUM LAVENDER GREEN 112MM- GAR955	YR	13.00	13.00
97	CLEARLY IRIS 112MM- GAR957	YR	12.00	12.00
97	CLEMATIS VINE LIME GREEN 112MM- GAR953	YR	13.00	13.00
97	CLEMATIS VINE PINK 112MM- GAR952	YR	13.00	13.00
97	CLEMATIS VINE TURQUOISE 112MM- GAR954	YR	13.00	13.00

YR	NAME	LIMIT	ISSUE	TREND
97	DELICATE PUSSY WILLOW CLEAR 112MM- GAR956	YR	12.00	12.00
97	DRAGONFLY BALL 112MM- GAR951	YR	12.00	12.00
97	FLORAL EMBROIDERY ON CLEAR 112MM- GAR961	YR	12.00	12.00
97	GLITTERED PEONY ON FROSTED 112MM- GAR965	YR	12.00	12.00
97	GLITTERFLEURS 90MM 6 PC- GAR964	YR	42.00	42.00
97	HIBISCUS RUBY 112MM- GAR962	YR	12.00	12.00
97	RED POPPY IN THE SNOW 112MM- GAR963	YR	15.00	15.00
97	ROSES ARE PINK 112MM- GAR959	YR	12.00	12.00
97	TULIPS ON A CLEAR DAY 112MM- GAR960	YR	12.00	12.00
*			**GIFT WRAP/RED GOLD PLAID**	
97	BUTTON SANTA COPPER LTD 112MM- GIF339	OP	15.00	15.00
97	CAROUSEL HORSE ON SHINY BLACK 100MM- GIF342	OP	7.00	7.00
97	CAROUSEL ROYAL BLUE 6"- GIF340	OP	7.50	8.00
97	CHRISTINA'S WORLD LOGO GLOBE 80MM- GIF346	OP	5.00	5.00
97	DUTCH WINDMILL 6"- GIF345	OP	7.00	7.00
97	JOLLY ST. NICK 5"- GIF347	OP	6.00	6.00
97	SKATING BOY 5"- GIF348	OP	4.50	5.00
97	SNOWMAN W/GLITTER BOWTIE 7"- GIF343	OP	7.00	7.00
97	STOCKING SANTA W/TEDDY 6.5"- GIF341	OP	7.00	7.00
*			**HERBAL GARDEN**	
97	CATMINT BALL MINT/WHITE 112MM- HRB653	OP	9.00	9.00
97	CORIANDER BALL MINT/WHITE 112MM- HRB651	OP	9.00	9.00
97	DILL BALL MINT/WHITE 112MM- HRB652	OP	9.00	9.00
97	HERBAL GARDEN AST. BALLS 80MM- HRB700	OP	7.00	7.00
97	MYRRH BALL MINT/WHITE 112MM- HRB654	OP	9.00	9.00
97	TANSY BALL MINT/WHITE 112MM- HRB650	OP	9.00	9.00
97	TREESCAPE TURQUOISE 100MM- HRB700	OP	6.50	6.50
C. MALLOUK			**HUNDERTWASSER**	
94	BLUE SEA & GOLDEN SHIPS- HUN853	48	13.00	13.00
94	GOLDEN ONION DOMES- HUN852	48	13.00	13.00
94	RED ONION DOMES- HUN854	48	13.00	13.00
*			**IMPERIAL GARDEN BUTTERFLIES**	
97	BEVY OF BUTTERFLIES BLUE BLACK 5"- BUT623B	OP	8.00	8.00
97	BEVY OF BUTTERFLIES RED MULTI 5"- BUT623R	OP	8.00	8.00
97	BUTTERFLY BALL BRONZE 100MM- BUT620	OP	6.50	7.00
97	MARCASITE BUMBLEBEE FROSTED BALL 80MM- BUT621	OP	5.00	5.00
97	MARCASITE BUTTERFLY FROSTED 80MM- BUT622	OP	5.00	5.00
C. MALLOUK			**KIMONO PRINTS**	
94	MANDARIN GLITTER FANS- ART995	48	13.00	13.00
94	SILVER GREY GLITTER MOUNTAINS- ART95	48	13.00	13.00
*			**KING ARTHUR'S COURT**	
97	BEAD GARLAND BURGUNDY GLITTER LARGE 6'- CAS704-B	OP	15.00	15.00
97	BEAD GARLAND GREEN GLITTER LARGE 6'- CAS704-G	OP	15.00	15.00
97	BEAD GARLAND REGAL BURGUNDY 6'- CAS700	OP	18.00	18.00
97	BEAD GARLAND REGAL GREEN 6'- CAS701	OP	18.00	18.00
97	BURGUNDY BALL W/ GOLD TASSLE 80MM- CAS705	OP	3.50	4.00
97	GOLD CATHEDRAL BURGUNDY SKY 100MM- CAS708	OP	9.00	9.00
97	GOLD STARS ON BURGUNDY 100MM- CAS711	OP	5.00	5.00
97	SNOW CHURCH FUCHSIA SKY 100MM- CAS709	OP	9.00	9.00
97	SNOW CHURCH RED SKY 100MM- CAS710	OP	9.00	9.00
97	TREE TOP BURGUNDY GOLD 10"- CAS702	OP	10.00	10.00
97	TREE TOP GREEN GOLD 10"- CAS703	OP	10.00	10.00
*			**LACE LEGACY**	
97	FLOCKED SNOWFLAKE BALL 100MM- LAC386	OP	4.50	5.00
*			**LIMITED EDITION 1997**	
97	GARDEN OF EDEN CHAMPAGNE 100MM- LTD851	YR	15.00	15.00
97	HANS W/TREE 100MM- LTD850	YR	15.00	15.00
*		**LIMITED EDITION CONNOISSEURS' CIRCLE SELECTION**		
97	EDO COURTESANS RUSSIAN 100MM- LTD853	YR	40.00	40.00
97	WILD PONIES ON A BURGUNDY SKY 112MM- LTD852	YR	20.00	20.00
*			**MARDI GRAS**	
97	AND HER SISTER! W/BLACK HAT & PEARLS- MAR672	OP	15.00	15.00
97	FLAPPER PRINCESS W/SEQUINED CLOCH 112MM- MAR671	OP	15.00	15.00
97	MIDNIGHT MASQUERADE LTD 112MM- MAR671	YR	15.00	15.00
C. MALLOUK			**MARDI GRAS**	
94	RED GLACIER 115MM- MAR662	48	18.00	18.00
C. MALLOUK			**MATISSE REMEMBERED**	
94	MATISSE UMBRELLA	200	18.00	18.00
*		**MILLE FIORI OF MURANO/EXCLUSIVE**		
97	MILLE FIORE W/OUT GOLD LEAF 80MM- MUR904	OP	40.00	40.00
97	MILLE FIORI W/GOLD LEAF 70MM- MUR901	OP	42.00	42.00
97	MILLE FIORI W/GOLD LEAF 80MM- MUR900	OP	45.00	45.00
97	MURANO VAR 5C: GOLD TURQ YELLOW CINNABAR RED WHITE	OP	32.00	32.00
97	PEACOCK FEATHERS BLUE 80MM- MUR903	OP	40.00	40.00
97	PEACOCK FEATHERS WHITE 80MM- MUR902	OP	40.00	40.00
*			**OH BABY!**	
97	OH BABY W/ POODLE & BUNTINGS 2 PC- BAB901	OP	3.00	3.00
*			**OJIBWA VARIATIONS**	
97	GLASS BEAD GARLAND GOLD & COPPER 6'- OJB835-C	OP	15.00	15.00
*			**PEACE ON EARTH 1997**	
97	CHERUBS & ROSES PINK/TEAL 100MM- PEC818	YR	6.50	7.00
97	NATIVITY IN THE ROUND 6" GIANT- PEC815	YR	12.00	12.00
97	OUR LADY OF CZESTOCHOWA 100MM- PEC817	YR	7.00	7.00
97	THREE WISEMEN ICICLE DROP TRICOLOR- PEC812	YR	7.00	7.00

YR	NAME	LIMIT	ISSUE	TREND
C. MARROUK			**SECRET GARDEN**	
95	90 MM ETCHED FEATHER- GAR916	96	9.00	9.00
*			**SIBERIAN WINTER**	
97	CAROUSEL ICE CRYSTALS 6"- ICE650	OP	9.00	9.00
97	CASTLE OF THE OWL PRINCE- ICE106	OP	7.00	7.00
97	CATHEDRAL FROSTED ICE CRYSTALS 6"- ICE651	OP	4.00	4.00
97	CLEARING IN THE WOODS, A 100MM- ICE104	OP	5.00	5.00
97	GARLAND ICE CRYSTALS PEARL DROP 6'- ICE660	OP	18.00	18.00
97	GARLAND WHITE SILVER ICE CRYSTALS 6'- ICE656	OP	15.00	15.00
97	GREY SNOW OWL FROSTED BLUE 5"- ICE658	OP	2.50	3.00
97	MEDALLION TASSEL FROSTED ICE CRYSTALS- ICE659	OP	5.00	5.00
97	METEORITE ICE CRYSTALS 70MM- ICE663	OP	4.00	4.00
97	MOONSPOTS SILVER ICE CRYSTALS 80MM- ICE655	OP	3.00	3.00
97	OWL FROSTED WHITE ICE CRYSTALS 5"- ICE657	OP	2.50	3.00
97	OWL PRINCE 5"- ICE105	OP	6.00	6.00
97	PINE TREE FROSTED ICE CRYSTALS 5"- ICE109	OP	5.00	5.00
97	SANTA W/MAGIC BLUE COAT 5.5"- ICE107	OP	6.00	6.00
97	SIBERIAN EXPRESS TRAIN GARLAND 18"- ICE102	OP	13.00	13.00
97	SIBERIAN ICE CRYSTALS SANTA 10" LTD- ICE100	*	15.00	15.00
97	SIBERIAN WEDDING BALL 80MM- ICE103	OP	6.00	6.00
97	SNOBALLS FROSTED ICE CRYSTALS AST. 100MM- ICE654	OP	3.50	4.00
97	SNOBALLS FROSTED ICE CRYSTALS AST. 80MM- ICE653	OP	3.00	3.00
97	SNOWBIRDS BALL FROSTED 70MM- INE664	OP	2.25	2.00
97	THREE WISEMEN IN BETHLEHEM 100MM- ICE108	OP	6.50	7.00
97	TINY BLUE SANTA 2"- ICE666	OP	2.50	3.00
97	TINY RED SANTA 2"- ICE667	OP	2.50	3.00
97	TREE TOP FROSTED SILVER ICE CRYSTALS 18"- ICE662	OP	18.00	18.00
97	TRIPLE ICICLE FROSTED CRYSTALS 6"- ICE652	OP	3.00	3.00
*			**TUTTI FRUTTI**	
97	GOLDEN FRUIT BOWL 100MM- TUT150-G	OP	3.00	3.00
*			**WINTER WONDERLAND**	
97	BEAD GARLAND CANDY STRIPE 6' TINY-WIN541	OP	18.00	18.00
97	BLACK BELT SANTA 6"- WIN536	OP	5.00	5.00
97	ENCHANTED FOREST BALL 112MM- WIN591	OP	15.00	15.00
97	GLASS BEAD GARLAND FLOWER 6' MINI- WIN540	OP	18.00	18.00
97	GOLD STARRY NIGHT VILLAGE ON BURGUNDY 70MM- WIN545	OP	2.50	3.00
97	MOON BALLS GOLD BURGUNDY 100MM- WIN538	OP	4.00	4.00
97	MOON BALLS GOLD RED 80MM- WIN539	OP	3.50	4.00
97	NORTHWIND SANTA PETITE TETE 6"- WIN590	OP	12.00	12.00
97	QUIZICAL SANTA BURGUNDY CAP 6"- WIN535	OP	4.00	4.00
97	SANTA BALL FROSTY 70MM- WIN542	OP	2.00	2.00
97	SANTA W/TOYS 5"- WIN537	OP	3.50	4.00
97	SNOWBALL MAN 9"- WIN566	OP	9.00	9.00
97	TREE BALL GREEN GLITTER 100MM- WIN544	OP	3.50	4.00
97	TREES FOR ALL SEASONS 100MM- WIN534	OP	6.50	7.00
97	WHITE COUNTRY CHURCH 3"- WIN543	OP	3.00	3.00

CHRISTOPHER RADKO

YR	NAME	LIMIT	ISSUE	TREND
C. RADKO				
*	RUSSIAN SANTA JOLLY HOLIDAYS	*	34.00	50.00
86	ALPINE FLOWERS	RT	12.00	130.00
86	BIG TOP	RT	15.00	175.00
86	DEEP SEA	RT	*	65.00
86	EMERALD CITY	RT	5.00	78.00
86	GOLDEN ALPINE	RT	*	50.00
86	LONG ICICLES	RT	7.00	90.00
86	MIDAS TOUCH	RT	15.00	150.00
86	ROSES	RT	16.00	120.00
86	SANTA'S CANE-PINK	RT	*	100.00
86	SIBERIAN SLEIGHRIDE	RT	15.00	100.00
86	SILENT BELLS	RT	5.00	300.00
86	THREE RIBBON OVAL	RT	12.00	150.00
87	AMERICAN SOUTHWEST	RT	15.00	250.00
87	BABY BALLOONS	RT	6.00	100.00
87	DECO FLORAL	RT	14.00	120.00
87	FABERGE BALL	RT	*	50.00
87	GRECIAN COLUMN	RT	*	100.00
87	KAT KONCERT	RT	16.00	125.00
87	MEMPHIS	RT	15.00	100.00
87	NEOPOLITAN ANGELS 87-014-0	RT	13.00	65.00
87	SAMOVAR	RT	6.00	300.00
87	SANTA'S CANE	*	7.00	90.00
87	TWIN FINIAL	RT	20.00	125.00
87	VICTORIAN LAMP	RT	7.00	120.00
88	ALPINE FLOWERS	RT	16.00	100.00
88	BABY BALLOON	RT	8.00	115.00
88	BIRDHOUSE	RT	10.00	100.00
88	BLUE RAINBOW	RT	16.00	145.00
88	BUDS IN BLOOM	RT	16.00	115.00
88	CELESTIAL	RT	15.00	65.00
88	CELESTIAL-BLUE	RT	16.00	60.00
88	CHRISTMAS FANFARE	RT	15.00	140.00
88	CIRCLE OF SANTAS	RT	15.00	200.00
88	CORNUCOPIA	RT	15.00	300.00
88	CRESCENT MOON SANTA	RT	15.00	150.00

YR	NAME	LIMIT	ISSUE	TREND
88	CROWN JEWELS	RT	15.00	150.00
88	DOUBLE ROYAL STAR	RT	23.00	150.00
88	EXCLAMATION FLASK	RT	8.00	85.00
88	FABERGE OVAL	RT	15.00	100.00
88	GILDED LEAVES	RT	16.00	130.00
88	GRECIAN COLUMN	RT	10.00	100.00
88	HOT AIR BALLOON	RT	15.00	130.00
88	LILAC SPARKLE	RT	15.00	150.00
88	MUSHROOM IN WINTER	RT	12.00	100.00
88	NEOPOLITAN ANGEL	RT	16.00	140.00
88	OZ BALLOON	RT	18.00	150.00
88	PEAR	*	15.00	300.00
88	RIPPLES ON OVAL	RT	6.00	80.00
88	ROYAL DIADEM	RT	25.00	125.00
88	ROYAL PORCELAIN	RT	16.00	150.00
88	RUSSIAN ST. NICK	RT	15.00	120.00
88	SATIN SCEPTER	RT	9.00	100.00
88	SHINY BRITE	RT	5.00	30.00
88	SIMPLY CARTIERE	RT	17.00	125.00
88	SPIN TOP	RT	8.00	60.00
88	SQUIGGLIES	RT	15.00	125.00
88	STAINED GLASS	RT	16.00	150.00
88	STRIPED BALLOON	RT	15.00	108.00
88	TIGER	RT	15.00	425.00
88	TREE ON BALL	RT	9.00	100.00
88	TWIN FINIAL	RT	24.00	125.00
88	ZEBRA	RT	15.00	150.00
89	ALPINE FLOWERS	RT	17.00	35.00
89	BAROUQUE ANGEL	RT	17.00	130.00
89	CHARLIE CHAPLIN	RT	9.00	75.00
89	CIRCLE OF SANTAS	RT	17.00	75.00
89	DOUBLE TOP	RT	7.00	45.00
89	DROP REFLECTOR	RT	23.00	90.00
89	ELF ON BALL	RT	10.00	108.00
89	FISHER FROG	RT	7.00	70.00
89	FLUERS DE PROVENCE	RT	17.00	120.00
89	GILDED BIRDS	RT	18.00	150.00
89	GRECIAN URN	RT	9.00	30.00
89	H.M. SCEPTER	RT	25.00	144.00
89	HIS BOY ELROY	RT	8.00	120.00
89	HURRICANE LAMP	RT	7.00	50.00
89	IVY, THE	RT	17.00	125.00
89	JESTER	RT	17.00	120.00
89	JOEY CLOWN 89-058-0	RT	9.00	225.00
89	KIM ONO	RT	7.00	50.00
89	KING ARTHUR 89-103-0	RT	12.00	85.00
89	KITE FACE	RT	9.00	50.00
89	LILAC SPARKLE	RT	17.00	100.00
89	LUCKY FISH	RT	8.00	50.00
89	PARACHUTE	RT	7.00	85.00
89	PATCHWORK	RT	17.00	125.00
89	PEPPERMINT STRIPES	RT	29.00	275.00
89	ROYAL ROOSTER	RT	17.00	100.00
89	ROYAL STAR TREE FINIAL	RT	42.00	100.00
89	SEAHORSE	RT	10.00	135.00
89	SERPENT	RT	7.00	35.00
89	SHY KITTEN	RT	7.00	60.00
89	SILENT MOVIE 89-055-0	*	9.00	65.00
89	SMALL REFLECTOR	RT	8.00	30.00
89	SMILING SUN	RT	7.00	45.00
89	SONG BIRDS	RT	18.00	230.00
89	TIFFANY	RT	17.00	600.00
89	VINEYARD	RT	17.00	125.00
89	WALRUS	RT	8.00	125.00
89	WINTER LANDSCAPE	RT	17.00	220.00
89	ZEBRA	RT	18.00	100.00
90	ANGEL ON HARP	RT	9.00	75.00
90	BALLOONING SANTA	RT	20.00	225.00
90	BATHING BABY	RT	11.00	50.00
90	BOY CLOWN ON REFLECTOR	RT	18.00	130.00
90	CALLA LILY	RT	7.00	65.00
90	CANDY TRUMPET MAN	RT	28.00	100.00
90	CANDY TRUMPET MAN-BLUE	RT	28.00	40.00
90	CARMEN MIRANDA	RT	19.00	135.00
90	CHEERFUL SUN	*	9.00	50.00
90	CHIMNEY SWEEP BELL	RT	27.00	100.00
90	CHRISTMAS CARDINALS	RT	18.00	130.00
90	CONCH SHELL	RT	9.00	90.00
90	CROWNED PRINCE	RT	14.00	115.00
90	DECO FLORAL	RT	19.00	125.00
90	DUBLIN PIPE	RT	14.00	45.00
90	EAGLE MEDALLION	RT	9.00	60.00
90	EARLY WINTER	RT	10.00	45.00
90	ELEPHANT ON BALL 90-086-0	*	20.00	150.00
90	EMERALD CITY	RT	8.00	55.00

YR	NAME	LIMIT	ISSUE	TREND
90	FAT LADY	RT	7.00	30.00
90	FATHER CHRISTMAS	RT	8.00	50.00
90	FROG UNDER BALLOON	RT	14.00	75.00
90	FROSTY	RT	14.00	75.00
90	GOGGLE EYES	*	9.00	100.00
90	GOLDEN PUPPY	RT	8.00	100.00
90	GYPSY QUEEN	RT	12.00	35.00
90	HAPPY GNOME	RT	8.00	65.00
90	HEARTS & FLOWERS	*	19.00	75.00
90	HOLLY BALL	RT	19.00	135.00
90	JESTER	RT	17.00	125.00
90	JOEY CLOWN 89-058-1	RT	15.00	100.00
90	KIM ONO	RT	6.00	50.00
90	KING ARTHUR-RED	RT	16.00	100.00
90	LULLABYE	RT	9.00	48.00
90	MARACCA	RT	9.00	130.00
90	MEDITERRANEAN SUNSHINE	RT	27.00	30.00
90	MISSION BALL	RT	18.00	50.00
90	MOTHER GOOSE 90-052-0	RT	10.00	60.00
90	MUNCHKIN 90-035-0	RT	7.00	40.00
90	NATIVITY	RT	6.00	45.00
90	PEACOCK	RT	18.00	80.00
90	PIERRE LE BERRY	RT	10.00	100.00
90	POINSETTIA	RT	18.00	110.00
90	POLISH FOLK DANCE	RT	18.00	135.00
90	PRAYING ANGEL	RT	5.00	80.00
90	PROUD PEACOCK	RT	18.00	130.00
90	PUDGY CLOWN	RT	7.00	60.00
90	RAINBOW UMBRELLA	RT	14.00	60.00
90	ROLY POLY SANTA	RT	13.00	72.00
90	ROSE LAMP	RT	14.00	120.00
90	SANTA ON BALL	RT	16.00	110.00
90	SILENT MOVIE 89-055-1	RT	9.00	65.00
90	SMALL NAUTILUS SHELL	RT	7.00	25.00
90	SMILING KITE	RT	14.00	90.00
90	SNOW BALL TREE	RT	17.00	65.00
90	SNOWMAN ON BALL	RT	14.00	80.00
90	SOUTHWEST INDIAN BALL	RT	19.00	250.00
90	SPIN TOP	RT	11.00	100.00
90	SUNBURST FISH	RT	13.00	45.00
90	TROPICAL FISH	RT	24.00	70.00
90	TRUMPET PLAYER	RT	18.00	100.00
90	TUXEDO PENGUIN	RT	8.00	700.00
90	WALRUS	RT	9.00	125.00
90	YARN FIGHT	RT	17.00	130.00
91	ALADDIN	RT	14.00	50.00
91	ALL WEATHER SANTA	RT	32.00	200.00
91	ALTAR BOY	RT	16.00	40.00
91	ANCHOR OF AMERICA	RT	22.00	60.00
91	APACHE	RT	9.00	40.00
91	ASPEN	RT	21.00	75.00
91	AZTEC	RT	22.00	90.00
91	AZTEC BIRD	RT	20.00	80.00
91	BALLOONING SANTA	RT	23.00	175.00
91	BARNUM CLOWN	RT	15.00	85.00
91	BISHOP	RT	15.00	45.00
91	BLACK FOREST CONE	RT	8.00	36.00
91	BLUE RAINBOW	RT	22.00	100.00
91	BOWERY KID	RT	15.00	50.00
91	BY THE NILE	RT	22.00	55.00
91	CARDINAL RICHELIEU	RT	16.00	96.00
91	CHANCE ENCOUNTER	RT	14.00	35.00
91	CHIEF SITTING BULL	RT	16.00	80.00
91	CHIMNEY SANTA	RT	15.00	40.00
91	CLOWN DRUM	RT	14.00	95.00
91	COMET	RT	9.00	75.00
91	COSETTE	RT	16.00	75.00
91	COWBOY SANTA	*	16.00	75.00
91	CROWN JEWELS	RT	22.00	100.00
91	DAPPER SHOE	RT	10.00	70.00
91	DAWN & DUSK	RT	14.00	75.00
91	DECO FLORAL	RT	22.00	100.00
91	DECO SPARKLE	RT	21.00	95.00
91	DUTCH BOY	RT	11.00	45.00
91	DUTCH GIRL	RT	11.00	65.00
91	EDWARDIAN LACE	RT	22.00	130.00
91	EINSTEIN KITE 91-098-0	RT	20.00	100.00
91	ELEPHANT ON BALL 90-086-1	RT	23.00	500.00
91	ELF REFLECTOR	RT	23.00	45.00
91	EVENING SANTA	RT	15.00	150.00
91	FANFARE	RT	22.00	100.00
91	FISHER FROG	RT	11.00	80.00
91	FLORENTINE	RT	22.00	75.00
91	FLOWER CHILD	RT	13.00	60.00
91	FROG UNDER BALLOON	RT	16.00	50.00

YR	NAME	LIMIT	ISSUE	TREND
91	FROGGY CHILD	RT	9.00	50.00
91	FRUIT IN BALLOON	RT	22.00	120.00
91	FU MANCHU	RT	15.00	75.00
91	GALAXY	RT	22.00	100.00
91	GRAPEFRUIT TREE	RT	23.00	175.00
91	HAPPY ELF	*	10.00	90.00
91	HARVEST	RT	14.00	25.00
91	HATCHING DUCK	RT	14.00	55.00
91	HEARTS & FLOWERS	RT	53.00	250.00
91	HER MAJESTY	RT	21.00	110.00
91	HER PURSE	RT	10.00	60.00
91	HOLLY BALL	RT	22.00	70.00
91	IRISH LADDIE	RT	12.00	80.00
91	JEMIMA'S CHILD	RT	16.00	70.00
91	KING ARTHUR 89-103-1	RT	19.00	75.00
91	LION'S HEAD	RT	16.00	70.00
91	MADELEINE'S PUPPY 91-025-0	RT	11.00	100.00
91	MADONNA AND CHILD	RT	15.00	130.00
91	MELON SLICE	RT	18.00	35.00
91	MOTHER GOOSE 90-052-1	RT	11.00	35.00
91	MS. MAUS	RT	14.00	180.00
91	MUNCHKIN 90-035-1	RT	8.00	16.00
91	OLYMPIAD	RT	22.00	140.00
91	PATRICK'S BUNNY 91-024-0	RT	11.00	45.00
91	PEAR FACE	RT	15.00	75.00
91	PERUVIAN	RT	22.00	240.00
91	PIERRE LE BERRY	RT	14.00	150.00
91	PINK CLOWN ON BALL	RT	14.00	60.00
91	PINK ELEPHANTS	RT	22.00	150.00
91	PIPE MAN	RT	20.00	70.00
91	PIPE SMOKING MONEY	RT	11.00	80.00
91	PRINCE ON BALL	RT	15.00	125.00
91	PRINCE UMBRELLA	RT	15.00	125.00
91	PROUD PEACOCK	RT	23.00	40.00
91	PUSS IN BOOTS 91-023-0	*	11.00	35.00
91	RAINBOW BIRD	RT	16.00	40.00
91	RAINBOW CONE	RT	10.00	44.00
91	RASPBERRY & LIME	RT	12.00	45.00
91	RED STAR	RT	22.00	60.00
91	ROLY POLY CLOWN 91-032-0	*	14.00	45.00
91	RUSSIAN SANTA	RT	22.00	90.00
91	SALLY ANN	RT	8.00	48.00
91	SANTA BOOTIE 91-055-0	RT	10.00	70.00
91	SHIRLEY	RT	16.00	100.00
91	SHY ELF	RT	10.00	45.00
91	SLEEPYTIME SANTA 91-052-2	RT	15.00	100.00
91	SMITTY	RT	15.00	100.00
91	STAR QUILT	RT	22.00	60.00
91	SUNBURST FISH	RT	15.00	30.00
91	SUNSHINE	RT	22.00	40.00
91	TABBY	RT	8.00	40.00
91	TIFFANY	RT	22.00	55.00
91	TIGER	RT	15.00	80.00
91	TRIGGER	RT	15.00	150.00
91	TRUMPET MAN	RT	21.00	100.00
91	TULIP FAIRY 91-063-0	RT	16.00	75.00
91	VIENNA	RT	22.00	195.00
91	VILLANDRY	RT	21.00	175.00
91	WINKING ST. NICK	RT	16.00	80.00
91	WOODLAND SANTA	RT	14.00	75.00
91	ZEBRA	RT	22.00	450.00
92	ALADDIN 91-029-1	*	20.00	36.00
92	ALPINE FLOWERS	RT	28.00	60.00
92	ALPINE VILLAGE	RT	24.00	100.00
92	ASPEN	RT	26.00	60.00
92	BARBIE'S MOM	RT	18.00	60.00
92	BENJAMIN'S NUTCRACKERS	RT	58.00	350.00
92	BINKIE THE CLOWN	RT	12.00	25.00
92	BLUE SANTA	RT	18.00	60.00
92	BUTTERFLY BOUQUET	RT	27.00	140.00
92	BY THE NILE	RT	27.00	80.00
92	CABARET	RT	28.00	70.00
92	CANDY TRUMPET MAN	RT	27.00	75.00
92	CELESTIAL	RT	26.00	110.00
92	CHEERFUL SUN	RT	18.00	45.00
92	CHEVRON	RT	28.00	100.00
92	CHEVRON TIFFANY	RT	28.00	100.00
92	CHIMNEY SWEEP BELL	RT	27.00	140.00
92	CHOIR BOY	RT	24.00	60.00
92	CHRISTMAS CARDINALS	RT	26.00	130.00
92	CHRISTMAS ROSE	RT	26.00	45.00
92	CHRISTMAS TRIM	RT	16.00	50.00
92	CIRCLE OF SANTAS 89-032-1	*	27.00	50.00
92	CIRCUS GARLAND	RT	30.00	65.00
92	CIRCUS LADY	RT	12.00	30.00

YR	NAME	LIMIT	ISSUE	TREND
92	CLOWN SNAKE	RT	22.00	85.00
92	COUNTRY SCENE	RT	12.00	85.00
92	COUNTRY STAR QUILT	RT	12.00	100.00
92	COWBOY SANTA	RT	24.00	105.00
92	DELFT DESIGN	RT	27.00	150.00
92	DIAMOND BALLOON 92-157-0	*	27.00	50.00
92	DIVA	RT	17.00	50.00
92	DOLLY MADISON	RT	17.00	90.00
92	DOWNHILL RACER	RT	34.00	125.00
92	ELEPHANT ON PARADE	RT	26.00	90.00
92	ELEPHANT REFLECTOR	RT	17.00	85.00
92	ELF REFLECTORS	RT	28.00	40.00
92	EVENINGSTAR SANTA	RT	60.00	175.00
92	FABERGE 87-034-1	RT	27.00	65.00
92	FAITH, HOPE & LOVE	RT	12.00	40.00
92	FANTASY CONE	RT	18.00	30.00
92	FESTIVE SMITTY	RT	29.00	100.00
92	FLORAL CASCADE FINIAL	RT	68.00	85.00
92	FLORAL CASCADE TIER DROP	RT	32.00	300.00
92	FLORENTINE	RT	27.00	60.00
92	FLUTTER BYS	RT	11.00	60.00
92	FOLK ART SET	RT	10.00	10.00
92	FOREST FRIENDS	RT	14.00	20.00
92	FRENCH COUNTRY	RT	26.00	55.00
92	FRUIT IN BALLOON	RT	28.00	260.00
92	GABRIEL'S TRUMPETS	RT	20.00	20.00
92	GLASS SLEIGH	RT	14.00	15.00
92	GOLD LINK CHAIN	RT	16.00	50.00
92	HARLEQUIN TIER DROP	RT	36.00	100.00
92	HAROLD LLOYD REFLECTOR	RT	70.00	350.00
92	HER SLIPPER	RT	17.00	20.00
92	HOLLY FINIAL	RT	70.00	75.00
92	HONEY BEAR	*	14.00	45.00
92	ICE BERRIES	RT	36.00	75.00
92	ICE PEAR	RT	20.00	60.00
92	ICE POPPIES	RT	26.00	65.00
92	JUMBO	RT	31.00	50.00
92	KEWPIE	RT	18.00	60.00
92	KING OF PRUSSIA	RT	27.00	110.00
92	KITTY RATTLE	RT	18.00	75.00
92	LITTLE ESKIMO 92-038-0	RT	14.00	30.00
92	LITTLE LEAGUER	RT	20.00	90.00
92	LITTLEST SNOWMAN	RT	14.00	50.00
92	LOCOMOTIVE GARLAND	RT	60.00	120.00
92	MADELEINE'S PUPPY 91-025-1	*	18.00	35.00
92	MEDITERRANEAN SUNSHINE	RT	27.00	35.00
92	MERLIN SANTA	RT	32.00	75.00
92	MERRY CHRISTMAS MAIDEN	RT	26.00	50.00
92	MOTHER GOOSE	RT	15.00	20.00
92	MR. & MRS. CLAUS	RT	18.00	225.00
92	MUSHROOM ELF 92-087-0	RT	18.00	55.00
92	NEOPOLITAN ANGEL 87-014-2	RT	27.00	350.00
92	NORTHSTARS	RT	12.00	15.00
92	NORWEGIAN PRINCESS	RT	15.00	100.00
92	OLD SALEM QUILT SERIES 92-194-A	RT	28.00	60.00
92	OLD SALEM QUILT SERIES 92-194-B	RT	28.00	60.00
92	OLYMPIAD	RT	26.00	90.00
92	PIERRE WINTERBURY	RT	17.00	125.00
92	PINE CONE	RT	50.00	60.00
92	PINK LACE TIFFANY	RT	28.00	150.00
92	PINK PASSION	RT	18.00	45.00
92	POLAR BEAR	RT	16.00	45.00
92	PRIMARY COLORS	RT	30.00	150.00
92	QUILTED HEARTS	RT	28.00	50.00
92	RAINBOW PARASOL	RT	30.00	125.00
92	ROLY POLY CLOWN 91-032-1	*	18.00	45.00
92	ROYAL SEPTER	RT	36.00	100.00
92	RUBY BEADS	RT	15.00	40.00
92	RUSSIAN IMPERIAL	RT	25.00	85.00
92	RUSSIAN JEWEL HEARTS	RT	27.00	100.00
92	RUSSIAN STAR	RT	26.00	45.00
92	SAIL AWAY	RT	22.00	50.00
92	SANKE PRINCE	RT	19.00	40.00
92	SANTA BOOTIE 91-055-1	RT	16.00	65.00
92	SANTA BOOTIE 91-055-2	RT	10.00	75.00
92	SANTA CLAUS GARLAND	RT	66.00	100.00
92	SANTA IN WINTER WHITE 91-112-1	RT	28.00	150.00
92	SANTA'S HELPER	RT	17.00	35.00
92	SEAHORSE-PINK	RT	20.00	85.00
92	SERPENTS OF PARADISE	RT	13.00	40.00
92	SIBERIAN SLEIGHRIDE	RT	27.00	125.00
92	SITTING BULL	RT	26.00	70.00
92	SLEEPYTIME SANTA 91-052-1	RT	18.00	100.00
92	SLOOPY SNOWMAN	RT	20.00	80.00
92	SNOW FLAKES	RT	10.00	35.00

YR	NAME	LIMIT	ISSUE	TREND
92	SORBET	RT	22.00	50.00
92	SPUTNIKS	RT	26.00	100.00
92	ST. NICKCICLE	RT	26.00	75.00
92	STAR OF WONDER	RT	27.00	30.00
92	STARBURST TREE TOPPER	RT	20.00	25.00
92	STARBURSTS	RT	12.00	80.00
92	STARDUST JOEY	RT	16.00	125.00
92	STARLIGHT SANTA	RT	18.00	60.00
92	STERLING SILVER	RT	12.00	50.00
92	TALKING PIPE 91-093-1	RT	26.00	100.00
92	THUNDERBOLT	RT	60.00	60.00
92	TIFFANY ALPINE FLOWERS	RT	28.00	35.00
92	TIFFANY BRIGHT HARLEQUIN	RT	28.00	70.00
92	TIFFANY CHEVRON	RT	28.00	180.00
92	TIFFANY PASTEL HARLEQUIN	RT	28.00	110.00
92	TO GRANDMOTHER'S HOUSE WE GO	RT	20.00	40.00
92	TOPIARY	RT	30.00	350.00
92	TROPICAL FISH	RT	17.00	70.00
92	TRUMPET ANGEL GARLAND	RT	66.00	100.00
92	TULIP FAIRY	RT	18.00	50.00
92	TUXEDO SANTA	RT	22.00	150.00
92	TWO SIDED SANTA REFLECTOR	RT	28.00	80.00
92	UMBRELLA SANTA	RT	60.00	165.00
92	VICTORIAN SANTA & ANGEL BALLOON	RT	68.00	550.00
92	VIENNA	RT	27.00	160.00
92	VILLAGE CAROLERS	RT	17.00	35.00
92	VIRGIN MARY	RT	10.00	50.00
92	WACKO'S BROTHER DOOFUS	RT	20.00	75.00
92	WATER LILIES	RT	26.00	225.00
92	WEDDING BELLS	RT	40.00	240.00
92	WINTER KISS	RT	18.00	40.00
92	WINTER WONDERLAND	RT	26.00	125.00
92	WOODLAND SANTA	RT	20.00	80.00
92	ZIEGFELD FOLLIES	RT	27.00	125.00
93	1939 WORLD'S FAIR	RT	27.00	95.00
93	A SHY RABBIT'S HEART	RT	15.00	85.00
93	ACCORDION ELF 93-189-0	RT	21.00	45.00
93	ALADDIN'S LAMP	RT	20.00	35.00
93	ALLEGRO	RT	27.00	72.00
93	ALPINE VILLAGE	RT	24.00	140.00
93	ALPINE WINGS	RT	58.00	110.00
93	ANASSAZI	RT	27.00	125.00
93	ANCHOR SANTA	RT	32.00	72.00
93	ANGEL OF PEACE	RT	17.00	100.00
93	ANGELS WE HAVE HEARD ON HIGH	RT	50.00	500.00
93	APACHE	RT	14.00	80.00
93	AULD LANG SYNE	RT	15.00	60.00
93	BAVARIAN SANTA	RT	23.00	32.00
93	BEDTIME BUDDY	RT	29.00	125.00
93	BELL HOUSE BOY	RT	21.00	35.00
93	BELLS ARE RINGING	RT	18.00	60.00
93	BEYOND THE STARS	RT	19.00	80.00
93	BISHOP OF MYRA	RT	20.00	60.00
93	BISHOP'S CROSS	RT	49.00	60.00
93	BLUE TOP	RT	16.00	80.00
93	BOWZER	RT	23.00	160.00
93	BY JIMINY	RT	17.00	50.00
93	CALLA LILY	RT	13.00	30.00
93	CANDIED CITRUS 93-278-0	*	9.00	13.00
93	CANDIED CITRUS 93-278-0A	*	9.00	13.00
93	CARNIVAL RIDES	RT	18.00	100.00
93	CELESTE	RT	26.00	150.00
93	CELESTIAL PEACOCK FINIAL	RT	69.00	300.00
93	CENTER RING	RT	31.00	40.00
93	CENTURIAN	RT	26.00	175.00
93	CHIMNEY SWEEP BELL	RT	26.00	200.00
93	CHRISTMAS EXPRESS 93-394-0	RT	58.00	200.00
93	CHRISTMAS STARS	RT	14.00	40.00
93	CHURCH BELL	RT	24.00	50.00
93	CINDERELLA'S BLUEBIRDS	RT	26.00	100.00
93	CIRCLE OF SANTAS FINIAL	RT	69.00	100.00
93	CIRCUS SEAL	RT	28.00	100.00
93	CIRCUS STAR BALLOON	RT	28.00	60.00
93	CLASS CLOWN	RT	21.00	75.00
93	CLOWNING AROUND	RT	43.00	70.00
93	CONFUCIUS	RT	19.00	60.00
93	COOL CAT	RT	21.00	125.00
93	COPENHAGEN	RT	27.00	80.00
93	COUNTRY FLOWERS	RT	16.00	35.00
93	CROWNED PASSION	RT	23.00	50.00
93	CRYSTAL FOUNTAIN	*	34.00	75.00
93	CRYSTAL RAINBOW	RT	30.00	275.00
93	DANCING HARLEQUIN 93-232-0	RT	36.00	60.00
93	DECO SNOW FALL	RT	27.00	48.00
93	DEER DROP	RT	34.00	215.00

YR	NAME	LIMIT	ISSUE	TREND
93	DON'T HOLD YOUR BREATH	RT	11.00	55.00
93	DOWNHILL RACER	RT	30.00	80.00
93	EGGMAN	RT	23.00	45.00
93	EMERALD WIZARD	RT	18.00	50.00
93	EMPEROR'S PET	RT	22.00	150.00
93	ENCHANTED GARDENS	RT	6.00	15.00
93	ENGLISH KITCHEN	RT	26.00	60.00
93	EPIPHANY	RT	29.00	100.00
93	ESKIMO KITTY	RT	15.00	40.00
93	EVENING STAR SANTA	RT	59.00	100.00
93	FABERGE EGG	RT	18.00	35.00
93	FANTASIA	RT	24.00	145.00
93	FAR OUT SANTA	RT	39.00	64.00
93	FIESTA BALL	RT	27.00	80.00
93	FIRST SNOW 93-365-0	*	10.00	17.00
93	FLORA DORA	RT	25.00	100.00
93	FLY BOY 93-235-0	RT	33.00	60.00
93	FOREST FRIENDS	RT	28.00	75.00
93	FRENCH ROSE	RT	27.00	45.00
93	FRUIT IN BALLOON	RT	28.00	85.00
93	GEISHA GIRLS	RT	12.00	65.00
93	GEORGIAN SANTA 93-292-0	*	30.00	34.00
93	GERARD	RT	26.00	36.00
93	GILDED CAGE	*	44.00	75.00
93	GLORY ON HIGH	RT	17.00	135.00
93	GOLD FISH	RT	26.00	80.00
93	GOLDEN ALPINE	*	27.00	48.00
93	GOOFY FRUITS	RT	14.00	75.00
93	GOOFY GARDEN	RT	15.00	200.00
93	GRANDPA BEAR	RT	13.00	25.00
93	GRECIAN URN	RT	23.00	55.00
93	GUARDIAN ANGEL	RT	36.00	125.00
93	GYPSY GIRL	RT	16.00	25.00
93	HEAVENLY CHORDS	RT	64.00	100.00
93	HOLIDAY SPICE	RT	24.00	45.00
93	ICE BEAR	RT	18.00	50.00
93	ICE STAR SANTA	RT	38.00	350.00
93	INJUN JOE	RT	25.00	70.00
93	JACK FROST	RT	23.00	85.00
93	JACK N JILL	RT	41.00	150.00
93	JACQUES LE BERRY	RT	17.00	150.00
93	JOEY B. CLOWN	RT	26.00	125.00
93	JUMBO SPINTOPS	RT	27.00	50.00
93	JUST LIKE GRANDMA'S	RT	8.00	45.00
93	KISSING COUSINS	RT	30.00	150.00
93	KITTY RATTLE	RT	18.00	100.00
93	LETTER TO SANTA	RT	22.00	60.00
93	LIGHT IN THE WINDOWS	RT	25.00	25.00
93	LITTLE BOY BLUE	RT	26.00	35.00
93	LITTLE DOGGIE	RT	7.00	50.00
93	LITTLE ESKIMO 92-038-1	RT	14.00	30.00
93	LITTLE SLUGGER	RT	22.00	30.00
93	MAJESTIC REFLECTOR	RT	70.00	125.00
93	MAXINE	*	20.00	72.00
93	MEDITERRANEAN SUNSHINE	RT	27.00	80.00
93	MIDAS TOUCH	RT	28.00	75.00
93	MONKEY MAN	RT	16.00	80.00
93	MONTEREY	RT	15.00	100.00
93	MOON DUST	RT	15.00	45.00
93	MOON JUMP	RT	29.00	50.00
93	MOONING OVER YOU	RT	17.00	60.00
93	MR. & MRS. CLAUS	RT	18.00	100.00
93	MUSHROOM ELF 92-087-1	RT	18.00	50.00
93	MUSHROOM SANTA	RT	28.00	80.00
93	NELLIE	RT	28.00	150.00
93	NORTH WOODS	RT	27.00	70.00
93	NORTHWIND	*	17.00	60.00
93	PARTRIDGE IN A PEAR TREE	RT	33.00	900.00
93	PENNSYLVANIA DUTCH	RT	27.00	60.00
93	PIGGLY WIGGLY	RT	11.00	70.00
93	PINEAPPLE QUILT	RT	27.00	60.00
93	PINOCCHIO	RT	30.00	90.00
93	PIXIE SANTA	RT	16.00	70.00
93	POINSETTIA SANTA	RT	20.00	55.00
93	POLAR BEARS	RT	16.00	16.00
93	POMPADOUR	RT	9.00	30.00
93	PRINCE ALBERT	RT	23.00	75.00
93	PURSE	RT	16.00	16.00
93	QUARTET	RT	4.00	15.00
93	RAINBOW REFLECTOR	RT	27.00	50.00
93	RAINBOW SHARK	RT	18.00	60.00
93	RAINBOW SNOW 93-366-0	*	10.00	16.00
93	RAINY DAY FRIEND	RT	22.00	60.00
93	RAMBLING ROSE	RT	27.00	50.00
93	REGAL ROOSTER	RT	26.00	80.00

YR	NAME	LIMIT	ISSUE	TREND
93	REMEMBRANCE	RT	27.00	50.00
93	RISING STARS	*	9.50	13.00
93	RISING STARS 93-182-0A	*	9.50	13.00
93	ROLY POLY CLOWN 91-032-2	RT	18.00	70.00
93	ROSE POINTE FINIAL	RT	34.00	45.00
93	RUSSIAN JEWEL HEARTS FINIAL	RT	27.00	90.00
93	SAIL BY STARLIGHT	RT	12.00	17.00
93	SAILOR MAN	RT	22.00	120.00
93	SANTA BABY	RT	18.00	50.00
93	SANTA IN SPACE	RT	39.00	210.00
93	SANTA IN WINTER WHITE 91-112-2	RT	28.00	60.00
93	SANTA STAR	*	58.00	68.00
93	SANTA TREE	RT	66.00	250.00
93	SANTA'S HELPER	RT	17.00	45.00
93	SARABAND	RT	28.00	175.00
93	SCOTCH PINE	RT	27.00	100.00
93	SERENADE PINK	RT	27.00	60.00
93	SHY RABBIT	RT	14.00	80.00
93	SIEGFRED 93-227-0	RT	25.00	60.00
93	SILENT NIGHT	RT	18.00	80.00
93	SKATING BETTINAS, THE	RT	29.00	140.00
93	SKI BABY	RT	21.00	170.00
93	SLOOPY SNOWMAN	RT	20.00	60.00
93	SMITTY	RT	18.00	85.00
93	SNOW DANCE	RT	29.00	100.00
93	SNOWDAY SANTA	RT	20.00	75.00
93	SNOWMAN BY CANDLELIGHT	RT	27.00	70.00
93	SOUTH SEA SPARKLE	RT	48.00	60.00
93	SOUTHERN COLONIAL	RT	27.00	105.00
93	SPIDER & THE FLY	RT	7.00	35.00
93	SPORTY	RT	20.00	60.00
93	ST. NICK'S PIPE	RT	5.00	80.00
93	ST. NICKCICLE	RT	26.00	40.00
93	STAR CHILDREN	RT	18.00	65.00
93	STAR FIRE	RT	27.00	60.00
93	STARLIGHT SANTA	RT	12.00	20.00
93	STOCKING STUFFERS	RT	16.00	25.00
93	SUGAR SHACK	*	22.00	24.00
93	SUNNY SIDE UP	RT	22.00	50.00
93	SWEETHEART	RT	16.00	60.00
93	TALKING PIPE	RT	26.00	60.00
93	TANNENBAUM	RT	24.00	34.00
93	TEA & SYMPATHY	*	20.00	34.00
93	TEXAS STAR	RT	8.00	8.00
93	THOMAS NAST SANTA	RT	23.00	36.00
93	TUXEDO SANTA	RT	22.00	160.00
93	TWEETER	RT	4.00	20.00
93	TWINKLE TOES 93-233-0	RT	28.00	52.00
93	TWINKLE TREE	RT	16.00	40.00
93	TWISTER	RT	17.00	60.00
93	U-BOAT	RT	16.00	52.00
93	V.I.P.	RT	23.00	150.00
93	VICTORIAN SANTA REFLECTOR	RT	28.00	75.00
93	WADDLES	RT	4.00	70.00
93	WALLY	*	26.00	34.00
93	WINTER BIRDS 93-164-0	RT	27.00	90.00
93	WINTER BIRDS 93-164-0A	RT	27.00	90.00
94	ACCORDION ELF	RT	23.00	70.00
94	AIRPLANE	*	56.00	76.00
94	ALL WRAPPED UP	RT	26.00	28.00
94	ANDY GUMP	RT	18.00	40.00
94	ANGEL SONG	RT	46.00	150.00
94	BABY BOOTIES	RT	17.00	30.00
94	BAG OF GOODIES	*	26.00	50.00
94	BATTER UP	RT	13.00	20.00
94	BERRY STRIPE	RT	48.00	100.00
94	BIRD BRAIN	RT	33.00	80.00
94	BLUE SATIN	RT	29.00	32.00
94	BRAZILIA	*	38.00	48.00
94	BRIGHT HEAVENS ABOVE	RT	56.00	110.00
94	BUBBLES	*	42.00	54.00
94	BUBBLY	*	43.00	48.00
94	CAMILLE	*	29.00	32.00
94	CANDELABRA	RT	33.00	90.00
94	CAPTAIN	*	48.00	145.00
94	CASTANETTA	RT	37.00	100.00
94	CHIC OF ARABY	RT	17.00	60.00
94	CHIQUITA	*	15.00	16.00
94	CHRISTMAS EXPRESS 93-394-1	*	72.00	80.00
94	CHRISTMAS HARLEQUIN	*	29.00	32.00
94	CHRISTMAS IN CAMELOT	RT	27.00	50.00
94	CHUBBS & SLIM	RT	29.00	45.00
94	CIRCUS BAND	RT	34.00	100.00
94	CONCHITA	RT	37.00	55.00
94	CONCORD	*	16.00	20.00

YR	NAME	LIMIT	ISSUE	TREND
94	COOL CAT	RT	26.00	75.00
94	CORN HUSK	RT	13.00	25.00
94	COW POKE	*	42.00	56.00
94	CRESCENT MOONS	RT	29.00	55.00
94	CROCK O' DILE	RT	33.00	80.00
94	CROWN OF THORNS	*	26.00	30.00
94	CROWNED PEACOCK	*	15.00	18.00
94	DANCING HARLEQUIN 93-232-1	*	44.00	60.00
94	DEEP SEA	*	29.00	48.00
94	DEERCICLE 94-291-0	*	29.00	48.00
94	DOLLY	*	42.00	60.00
94	EGG HEAD	*	19.00	22.00
94	EINSTEIN'S KITE	RT	30.00	50.00
94	ELEPHANT PRINCE	RT	15.00	30.00
94	EPIPHANY BALL 94-211-0	*	29.00	34.00
94	FIRST SNOW 93-365-1	*	15.00	17.00
94	FLEET'S IN	RT	38.00	50.00
94	FLORENTINE	RT	29.00	50.00
94	FOREST HOLIDAY	RT	64.00	90.00
94	FORGET YOUR TROUBLES	RT	17.00	35.00
94	FRENCH COUNTRY	RT	29.00	80.00
94	FRENCH REGENCY BALLOON	RT	33.00	50.00
94	FRENCH REGENCY FINIAL	*	78.00	90.00
94	FROSTY CARES	RT	25.00	72.00
94	GEORGIAN SANTA 93-292-1	*	46.00	34.00
94	GIFTED SANTA	RT	25.00	50.00
94	GLOW WORM	RT	32.00	90.00
94	GOLDEN CRESCENDO FINIAL	RT	42.00	130.00
94	HANSEL & GRETEL	RT	35.00	75.00
94	HARVEST HOME	RT	29.00	55.00
94	HIEROGLYPH	RT	29.00	50.00
94	HOLIDAY SPARKLE FINIAL	*	84.00	90.00
94	HOLLY HEART	RT	24.00	35.00
94	HOLLY RIBBONS FINIAL	RT	78.00	100.00
94	HONEY BELLE	RT	74.00	130.00
94	HORSE OF A DIFFERENT COLOR	RT	28.00	140.00
94	HOUSE SITTING SANTA	RT	26.00	35.00
94	ICE MAN COMETH	RT	22.00	75.00
94	JACK CLOWN	RT	22.00	55.00
94	JOCKEY PIPE	RT	36.00	145.00
94	JOLLY STRIPES	RT	28.00	40.00
94	JUMBO HARLEQUIN	*	48.00	60.00
94	JUST LIKE US	RT	30.00	130.00
94	KAYO	RT	14.00	35.00
94	KEWPIE	RT	22.00	45.00
94	KING OF KINGS	RT	22.00	80.00
94	KING'S GUARD	*	44.00	60.00
94	KISSING COUSINS	RT	28.00	210.00
94	KITTY TAMER	RT	65.00	375.00
94	LEADER OF THE BAND-SIGNED	RT	22.00	350.00
94	LEMON TWIST	*	15.00	35.00
94	LETTER TO SANTA	RT	31.00	60.00
94	LIBERTY BALL 94-172-0	*	26.00	50.00
94	LITTLE ORPHAN	RT	18.00	70.00
94	LOS ANGELES, THE	RT	26.00	50.00
94	MAMA'S LITTLE ANGEL	*	23.00	24.00
94	MARTIAN HOLIDAY	RT	42.00	100.00
94	MASQUERADE	RT	16.00	60.00
94	MEDIUM NAUTILUS	RT	16.00	60.00
94	MESSIAH	*	22.00	24.00
94	METAMORPHOSIS	RT	16.00	25.00
94	MISSION BALL FINIAL	*	78.00	90.00
94	MITTENS FOR KITTENS	RT	22.00	100.00
94	MOON MARTIAN	RT	26.00	160.00
94	MOON MULLINS	RT	18.00	50.00
94	MOON RIDE	RT	28.00	70.00
94	MOTHER AND CHILD	RT	29.00	70.00
94	MR. MOTO	RT	36.00	160.00
94	MR. SMEDLEY DRYSDALE	RT	44.00	225.00
94	MY DARLING	RT	22.00	50.00
94	MY WHAT BIG TEETH 94-248-0	*	29.00	75.00
94	MY WHAT BIG TEETH 94-248-0A	*	29.00	75.00
94	NEW YEAR'S BABE	*	21.00	22.00
94	NIGHTY NIGHT	RT	36.00	90.00
94	OLD SOUR PUSS	RT	34.00	85.00
94	OLLIE	*	50.00	74.00
94	ON THE RUN	RT	45.00	100.00
94	ONE SMALL STEP	*	58.00	72.00
94	OVER THE WAVES	RT	38.00	100.00
94	OWL REFLECTOR	RT	54.00	80.00
94	PAPA'S JAMBOREE	RT	29.00	50.00
94	PARTY HOPPER	RT	37.00	190.00
94	PEAS ON EARTH	*	16.00	22.00
94	PEKING SANTA	RT	18.00	25.00
94	PICKLED	RT	26.00	65.00

A dated ornament by Linda Sickman for Hallmark as part of its Anniversary Ornaments, Pewter Rocking Horse *has increased in value since its 1995 release.*

Freedom 7, *the first piece in Hallmark's "Journeys Into Space" series, celebrates the 35th anniversary of the first American manned space flight.*

Captain Jean-Luc Picard, Captain James T. Kirk *and the* Romulan Warbird *were produced by Hallmark in 1995, marking the fifth year Hallmark offered Keepsake Ornaments based on Star Trek images.*

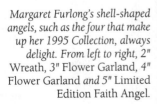

Margaret Furlong's shell-shaped angels, such as the four that make up her 1995 Collection, always delight. From left to right, 2" Wreath, 3" Flower Garland, 4" Flower Garland and 5" Limited Edition Faith Angel.

YR	NAME	LIMIT	ISSUE	TREND
94	PIGLET	RT	13.00	50.00
94	PINECONE SANTA 93-142-1	RT	30.00	85.00
94	PINOCCHIO GETS HITCHED 94-250-0	RT	30.00	125.00
94	PINOCCHIO GETS HITCHED 94-250-0A	RT	30.00	125.00
94	PIXIE SANTA	RT	20.00	45.00
94	POLAR BEAR	*	18.00	19.00
94	PRESIDENT TAFT	RT	18.00	45.00
94	PRINCE PHILIP	RT	20.00	160.00
94	PRIVATE EYE	RT	18.00	40.00
94	QUICK DRAW	RT	65.00	310
94	RAIN DANCE	RT	34.00	80.00
94	RAINBOW SNOW 93-366-1	*	15.00	16.00
94	RAINY DAY SMILE	*	22.00	36.00
94	RAZZLE DAZZLE	*	38.00	50.00
94	RED CAP	RT	22.00	30.00
94	RING MASTER	RT	22.00	55.00
94	RINGING RED BOOTS	RT	46.00	90.00
94	ROLY POLY CLOWN	RT	20.00	80.00
94	ROLY POLY PINOCCHIO	RT	54.00	66.00
94	ROYALE FINIAL	RT	64.00	100.00
94	RUBY REFLECTOR	RT	26.00	50.00
94	SANTA BY STARLIGHT	*	60.00	68.00
94	SANTA COPTER	RT	47.00	70.00
94	SANTA REFLECTOR FINIAL	RT	92.00	125.00
94	SANTA'S HELPER	RT	20.00	30.00
94	SCOTCH PINE FINIAL	*	78.00	90.00
94	SEX APPEAL	*	22.00	24.00
94	SHIP'S AHOY	RT	38.00	65.00
94	SHIVERS	RT	25.00	225.00
94	SIBERIAN TIGER	*	24.00	26.00
94	SIEGRED 93-227-1	*	26.00	34.00
94	SILENT NIGHT	RT	27.00	60.00
94	SMILEY	RT	16.00	55.00
94	SNOW BELL	RT	13.00	55.00
94	SNOWY	*	32.00	44.00
94	SOLDIER BOY	RT	19.00	110.00
94	SPECIAL DELIVERY	*	18.00	32.00
94	SQUASH MAN	*	28.00	38.00
94	SQUIGGLES	RT	30.00	50.00
94	STAFFORD FLORAL	RT	29.00	112.00
94	STAR FIRE FINIAL	*	84.00	90.00
94	STARBUCK SANTA	RT	75.00	340.00
94	STOCKING FULL	*	24.00	32.00
94	STOCKING SAM	*	23.00	72.00
94	STRAWBERRY	*	12.00	16.00
94	SUGAR CONE	*	47.00	86.00
94	SUGAR PEAR	*	13.00	18.00
94	SURF'S UP	RT	36.00	70.00
94	SWAMI	RT	18.00	30.00
94	SWAN FOUNTAIN	*	44.00	85.00
94	SWEET GHERKIN	*	12.00	14.00
94	SWEET PEAR	RT	24.00	70.00
94	TANGERINE	*	12.00	13.00
94	TEDDY ROOSEVELT	RT	22.00	70.00
94	TEE TIME	*	16.00	18.00
94	TEENAGE MERMAID	RT	28.00	60.00
94	TERRANCE	RT	16.00	50.00
94	TINY NAUTILUS	RT	12.00	55.00
94	TOMBA	*	34.00	55.00
94	TOPO	*	33.00	42.00
94	TUXEDO CAROUSEL	RT	52.00	72.00
94	TWINKLE TOES 93-233-1	RT	38.00	52.00
94	TWO TURTLEDOVES	RT	28.00	175.00
94	UNCLE MAX	RT	26.00	65.00
94	VALCOURT	RT	29.00	95
94	VAUDEVILLE SAM	RT	18.00	30.00
94	WALNUT	*	11.00	12.00
94	WEDDED BLISS	RT	88.00	200.00
94	WEDNESDAY	RT	42.00	80.00
94	WHAT A DONKEY	RT	34.00	36.00
94	WHITE NIGHTS	RT	26.00	70.00
94	WILBUR	*	33.00	48.00
94	WINDSWEPT	*	29.00	32.00
94	WINGS AND A SNAIL	RT	32.00	130.00
94	WINTER FROLIC	RT	18.00	60.00
94	XENON	RT	38.00	210
95	ALOISIUS BEER	RT	75.00	130.00
95	ALPINE	RT	24.00	35.00
95	ANDREW JACKSONS, THE (PAIR)	RT	68.00	210.00
95	ANGEL FLIGHT	*	44.00	46.00
95	AUTUMN PINE 95-067-0	*	16.00	17.00
95	BAILEY	RT	46.00	95
95	BEAR MAIL	RT	28.00	40.00
95	BISHOP, THE	*	74.00	90.00
95	BRINGING HOME THE BACON	RT	26.00	60.00

YR	NAME	LIMIT	ISSUE	TREND
95	BUFORD T	RT	14.00	35.00
95	CARIBBEAN CONSTABLE	RT	24.00	48.00
95	CATCH O' DAY	RT	14.00	25.00
95	CHEEKY ST. NICK	RT	32.00	80.00
95	CHUBBY DECKER	RT	36.00	45.00
95	CLAUDETTE	RT	22.00	90.00
95	CLIMBING HIGHER	RT	26.00	35.00
95	CLOWN RAFFLE	RT	16.00	36.00
95	COWBOY SANTA	RT	32.00	60.00
95	DASH AWAY ALL	RT	34.00	100.00
95	DAVID	RT	28.00	35.00
95	DEERCICLE 94-291-1	*	46.00	48.00
95	DIAMOND BALLOON 92-157-1	RT	32.00	55.00
95	DUTCH DOLLS	RT	22.00	90.00
95	DUTCH DOLLS	RT	22.00	35.00
95	EAGLE EYE	RT	26.00	40.00
95	EPIPHANY BALL 94-211-1	RT	32.00	34.00
95	EVENING OWL	RT	36.00	50.00
95	FARMER BOY	RT	28.00	72.00
95	FLYING HIGH	RT	22.00	55.00
95	FOREST CABIN	RT	15.00	18.00
95	FOREVER LUCY	RT	32.00	75.00
95	FRENCH LACE	RT	24.00	50.00
95	FROG LADY	RT	24.00	50.00
95	FROSTED SANTA	*	25.00	30.00
95	FRUIT KAN CHU	RT	50.00	65.00
95	FRUIT NUTS	RT	14.00	25.00
95	GARDEN GIRLS	RT	18.00	72.00
95	GAY BLADES	RT	46.00	60.00
95	GLORIANNA	RT	56.00	70.00
95	GOBBLES	RT	52.00	90.00
95	GRANDPA JONES	RT	22.00	75.00
95	GUARDIAN ANGEL	RT	84.00	120.00
95	GUNTHER	RT	32.00	150.00
95	HELMUT'S BELLS	RT	18.00	40.00
95	HERE BOY	RT	12.00	48.00
95	HIGH FLYING	RT	22.00	60.00
95	HOOTY HOOT	RT	26.00	35.00
95	HUBBARD'S THE NAME	RT	26.00	108.00
95	IMPERIAL HELMUT	RT	22.00	60.00
95	JAZZ SANTA	RT	28.00	50.00
95	JOY TO THE WORLD 95-042-0	*	68.00	90.00
95	JUMBO WALNUT	RT	18.00	48.00
95	KALEIDOSCOPE CONE	RT	44.00	70.00
95	KITTY VITTLES	RT	18.00	55.00
95	LAUGH TILL YOU CRY	RT	24.00	50.00
95	LAVENDER LIGHT	RT	28.00	80.00
95	LITTLE DRUMMER BEAR	RT	22.00	35.00
95	LITTLE PRINCE	RT	39.00	130.00
95	LITTLE RED	RT	22.00	90.00
95	LITTLE TOY MAKER	RT	26.00	78.00
95	MICKEY'S TREE	RT	45.00	300.00
95	MISS MAMIE	RT	34.00	50.00
95	MUGSY	RT	22.00	60.00
95	MY BONNIE LASS	RT	24.00	40.00
95	MY FAVORITE CHIMP	*	26.00	28.00
95	OFF TO MARKET	RT	24.00	75.00
95	OFFICER JOE	RT	22.00	75.00
95	ON TOP OF THE WORLD	YR	32.00	80.00
95	ON WINGS OF HOPE	RT	30.00	50.00
95	PAPA BEAR REFLECTOR	RT	52.00	90.00
95	PENELOPE	RT	26.00	60.00
95	PERCUSSION	RT	50.00	130.00
95	PERSONAL DELIVERY	RT	36.00	96.00
95	POLAR EXPRESS-SOUTH BEND	*	27.00	60.00
95	POOH'S FAVORITE GIFT	RT	45.00	360.00
95	PRINCE OF THIEVES	RT	28.00	45.00
95	PURRFECT PRESENT	RT	*	65.00
95	QUAKERS	RT	24.00	36.00
95	RAKISH CHARM	RT	22.00	50.00
95	REFLECTO	RT	46.00	60.00
95	ROCKETEER	RT	44.00	70.00
95	ROUND ABOUT SANTA	RT	42.00	50.00
95	SANTA BUGS	*	45.00	96.00
95	SANTA FANTASY	RT	44.00	100.00
95	SANTA MARIA	RT	64.00	150.00
95	SHY ELEPHANT	RT	32.00	90.00
95	SIAMESE SLIPPERS	RT	16.00	60.00
95	SISTER ACT	RT	18.00	120.00
95	SKATER'S WALTZ	RT	28.00	50.00
95	SPRING ARRIVAL	RT	44.00	70.00
95	SPRINGTIME SPARROW	RT	14.00	30.00
95	ST. PETER'S KEYS	RT	8.00	20.00
95	STORK LANTERN	RT	18.00	25.00
95	SWAN LAKE	RT	36.00	70.00

YR	NAME	LIMIT	ISSUE	TREND
95	SWEET MADAME	RT	48.00	110.00
95	SWINGING ON A STAR	RT	44.00	55.00
95	TAZ ANGEL	RT	40.00	96.00
95	TEDDY'S TREE	RT	22.00	50.00
95	THREE FRENCH HENS	RT	34.00	175.00
95	TIME FLIES	RT	28.00	40.00
95	TOPOLIMA	RT	42.00	65.00
95	TRICK OR TREAT	RT	23.00	35.00
95	TURTLE BIRD	RT	22.00	48.00
95	TWEETY SPRITE	RT	45.00	120.00
95	TWINKLE TOES 93-233-2	RT	48.00	52.00
95	WESTMINSTER SANTA	RT	24.00	40.00
95	WINTER SUN	RT	31.00	50.00
96	ASTRO PUP	RT	32.00	50.00
96	BABY ELEPHANTS	RT	18.00	35.00
96	ESKIMO CHEER	RT	22.00	35.00
96	ESQUIRE SANTA	RT	150.00	800.00
96	FOUR CALLING BIRDS	RT	44.00	175.00
96	FROSTY WEATHER	RT		25.00
96	LILAC WINTER	RT	44.00	50.00
96	MIDNIGHT RIDE	RT	51.00	65.00
96	MINUET	RT	54.00	70.00
96	MONTE CARLO	RT	52.00	70.00
96	MS. PEANUT	RT	30.00	95.00
96	ROUND MIDNIGHT	RT	30.00	45.00
96	SNOW CASTLE	RT	12.00	20.00

CYBIS

			CHRISTMAS	COLLECTION
*				
83	1983 HOLIDAY BELL	YR	145.00	1000.00
84	1984 HOLIDAY BELL	YR	145.00	695.00
85	1985 HOLIDAY ANGEL	YR	75.00	490.00
86	1986 HOLIDAY CHERUB ORNAMENT	YR	75.00	490.00
87	1987 HEAVENLY ANGELS	YR	95.00	400.00
88	1988 HOLIDAY ORNAMENT	YR	95.00	400.00

DAVE GROSSMAN CREATIONS

N. ROCKWELL — **ANNUAL ROCKWELL BALL ORNAMENTS**

75	SANTA WITH FEATHER QUILL	RT	3.50	25.00
76	SANTA AT GLOBE	RT	4.00	20.00
77	GRANDPA ON ROCKING HORSE	RT	4.00	15.00
78	SANTA WITH MAP	RT	4.50	15.00
79	SANTA AT DESK WITH MAIL BAG	RT	5.00	15.00
80	SANTA ASLEEP WITH TOYS	RT	5.00	12.00
81	SANTA WITH BOY ON FINGER	RT	5.00	10.00
82	SANTA FACE ON WINTER SCENE	RT	5.00	10.00
83	COACHMAN WITH WHIP	RT	5.00	10.00
84	CHRISTMAS BOUNTY MAN	RT	5.00	10.00
85	OLD ENGLISH TRIO	RT	5.00	10.00
86	TINY TIM ON SHOULDER	RT	5.00	5.00
87	SKATING LESSON	RT	5.00	5.00
88	BIG MOMENT	RT	5.50	5.50
89	DISCOVERY	RT	6.00	6.00
90	BRINGING HOME THE TREE	RT	6.00	6.00
91	DOWNHILL DARING	RT	6.00	6.00
92	ON THE ICE	YR	6.00	6.00
93	GRAMPS	YR	6.00	10.00
94	COMMEMORATIVE	YR	6.00	8.00
94	TRIPLE SELF PORTRAIT	RT	6.00	10.00

N. ROCKWELL — **ANNUAL ROCKWELL FIGURINE ORNAMENTS**

78	CAROLER	RT	15.00	75.00
79	DRUM FOR TOMMY	RT	20.00	50.00
80	SANTA'S GOOD BOYS	RT	20.00	40.00
81	LETTERS TO SANTA	RT	20.00	40.00
82	CORNETTIST	RT	20.00	30.00
83	FIDDLER	RT	20.00	30.00
84	CHRISTMAS BOUNTY	RT	20.00	30.00
85	JOLLY COACHMAN	RT	20.00	30.00
86	GRANDPA AND ROCKING HORSE	RT	20.00	35.00
87	SKATING LESSON	RT	20.00	30.00
88	BIG MOMENT	RT	20.00	30.00
89	DISCOVERY	RT	20.00	25.00
90	BRINGING HOME THE TREE	RT	20.00	25.00
91	DOWNHILL DARING	RT	20.00	25.00
92	ON THE ICE	RT	20.00	25.00
93	GRAMPS	RT	24.00	30.00
94	MERRY CHRISTMAS	RT	24.00	28.00

ROCKWELL INSPIRED — **CHARACTER DOLL ORNAMENTS**

83	DOCTOR AND DOLL	RT	20.00	30.00
83	LOVERS	RT	20.00	30.00
83	SAMPLERS	RT	20.00	30.00
*				EMMETT KELLY
92	CHRISTMAS TUNES	YR	15.00	16.00
95	MERRY CHRISTMAS MR. SCROOGE	RT	20.00	20.00
96	CHRISTMAS TREE	RT	20.00	20.00

YR	NAME	LIMIT	ISSUE	TREND
97	EMMETT THE SANTA	*	20.00	20.00
98	100TH BIRTHDAY	*	20.00	20.00

B. LEIGHTON-JONES — **EMMETT KELLY**

YR	NAME	LIMIT	ISSUE	TREND
86	A CHRISTMAS CAROL	CL	12.00	12.00
87	CHRISTMAS WREATH	CL	14.00	14.00
88	CHRISTMAS DINNER	CL	15.00	16.00
89	CHRISTMAS FEAST	YR	15.00	16.00
90	JUST WHAT I NEEDED	YR	15.00	16.00
91	EMMETT THE SNOWMAN	YR	15.00	16.00
93	DOWNHILL ORNAMENT	YR	20.00	24.00

B. LEIGHTON-JONES — **EMMETT KELLY ORIGINAL CIRCUS COLLECTION**

YR	NAME	LIMIT	ISSUE	TREND
94	HOLIDAY SKATER	RT	20.00	24.00

GONE WITH THE WIND

YR	NAME	LIMIT	ISSUE	TREND
92	SCARLETT-GREEN DRESS	CL	20.00	20.00
93	RHETT WHITE SUIT	CL	20.00	24.00
94	GOLD PLATED DISC ORNAMENT	OP	13.00	13.00
94	LIMITED EDITION ORNAMENT	*	25.00	28.00
94	SCARLETT BBQ DRESS	RT	20.00	20.00
96	SCARLETT & RHETT SET OF 5	*	100.00	100.00
96	SCARLETT BLUE DRESS	*	24.00	24.00
96	SCARLETT WITH SUITORS	*	24.00	24.00
97	BONNIE	*	24.00	24.00

R. BROWN — **GONE WITH THE WIND**

YR	NAME	LIMIT	ISSUE	TREND
91	PRISSY	CL	20.00	20.00

D. GEENTY — **GONE WITH THE WIND**

YR	NAME	LIMIT	ISSUE	TREND
87	ASHLEY	CL	15.00	45.00
87	RHETT	CL	15.00	45.00
87	SCARLETT	CL	15.00	45.00
87	TARA	CL	15.00	45.00
88	RHETT AND SCARLETT	CL	20.00	40.00
89	MAMMY	CL	20.00	20.00
90	SCARLETT-RED DRESS	CL	20.00	20.00

MOUSEHOLE COLLECTION

YR	NAME	LIMIT	ISSUE	TREND
93	MOUSEHOLE	RT	15.00	15.00
94	MOUSEHOLE	RT	15.00	15.00

DEPARTMENT 56

YR	NAME	LIMIT	ISSUE	TREND
97	GAD'S HILL PLACE 98732	RT	*	N/A

CCP ORNAMENTS

YR	NAME	LIMIT	ISSUE	TREND
86	APOTHECARY SHOP	CL	3.50	20.00
86	CHRISTMAS CAROL VILLAGE (SET OF 3)	CL	13.00	35.00
86	GENERAL STORE	CL	3.50	20.00
86	LIVERY STABLE & BOOT SHOP	CL	3.50	20.00
86	NATHANIEL BINGHAM FABRICS	CL	3.50	20.00
86	NEW ENGLAND VILLAGE (SET OF 7)	CL	25.00	290.00
86	RED SCHOOLHOUSE	CL	3.50	20.00
86	SCROOGE	CL	4.35	16.00
86	STEEPLE CHURCH	CL	3.50	20.00

CHRISTMAS CAROL CHARACTER ORNAMENTS

YR	NAME	LIMIT	ISSUE	TREND
86	BOB CRATCHIT & TINY TIM	CL	4.35	16.00
86	CHRISTMAS CAROL CHARACTERS (SET OF 3)	CL	13.00	35.00
86	POULTERER	CL	4.35	16.00

CLASSIC ORNAMENT SERIES

YR	NAME	LIMIT	ISSUE	TREND
98	CITY HALL	*	15.00	15.00
98	CRAGGY COVE LIGHTHOUSE	*	15.00	15.00
98	DICKENS' VILLAGE CHURCH	*	15.00	15.00
98	DOROTHY'S DRESS SHOP	*	15.00	15.00
98	J. YOUNG'S GRANARY	*	15.00	15.00
98	NANTUCKET	*	15.00	15.00
98	OLD CURIOSITY SHOP, THE	*	15.00	15.00
98	SANTA'S LOOKOUT TOWER	*	15.00	15.00
98	STEEPLED CHURCH	*	15.00	15.00

DICKENS' VILLAGE

YR	NAME	LIMIT	ISSUE	TREND
94	DEDLOCK ARMS INN 9872-8	RT	12.50	10.00
95	SIR JOHN FALSTAFF INN 9870-1	RT	15.00	10.00

HERITAGE VILLAGE

YR	NAME	LIMIT	ISSUE	TREND
96	CROWN & CRICKET INN #98730	RT	15.00	15.00
96	GRAPES INN, THE #98729	RT	15.00	15.00
96	PIED BULL INN, THE #98731	RT	15.00	15.00

MISCELLANEOUS ORNAMENTS

YR	NAME	LIMIT	ISSUE	TREND
84	DICKENS TIN ORNAMENTS (SET OF 6)	CL	12.00	165.00
88	BALSAM BELL BRASS DICKENS' CANDLESTICK	CL	3.00	10.00
88	BOB & MRS. CRATCHIT	CL	18.00	35.00
88	SCROOGE'S HEAD	CL	13.00	24.00
88	TINY TIM'S HEAD	CL	10.00	24.00

PIERRO/KIRCHNER — **SNOWBABIES**

YR	NAME	LIMIT	ISSUE	TREND
86	CRAWLING, LITE-UP, CLIP-ON 7953-7	CL	7.00	20.00
86	ORNAMENT ON BRASS RIBBON 7961-8	RT	8.00	50.00
86	SITTING, LITE-UP, CLIP-ON 7952-9	RT	7.00	32.00
86	WINGED, LITE-UP, CLIP-ON 7954-5	RT	7.00	35.00
87	ADRIFT, LITE-UP, CLIP-ON	RT	8.50	100.00
87	MINI, LITE-UP, CLIP-ON 7976-6	OP	9.00	12.00
87	MOON BEAMS 7951-0	OP	7.50	9.00

YR	NAME	LIMIT	ISSUE	TREND
88	TWINKLE LITTLE STAR 7980-4	RT	7.00	25.00
89	NOEL 7988-0	OP	7.50	8.00
89	STAR BRIGHT 7990-1	OP	7.50	8.00
89	SURPRISE 7989-8	CL	12.00	20.00
90	PENGUIN, LITE-UP, CLIP ON 7940-5	CL	5.00	25.00
90	POLAR BEAR, LITE-UP, CLIP-ON 7941-3	CL	5.00	25.00
90	ROCK-A-BYE BABY 7939-1	RT	7.00	7.00
91	MY FIRST STAR 6811-0	OP	7.00	7.00
91	SWINGING ON A STAR 6810-1	OP	9.50	10.00
93	SPRINKLING STARS IN THE SKY 6848-9	RT	13.50	14.00
93	WEE... THIS IS FUN! 6847-9	RT	13.50	14.00
93	YOU DIDN'T FORGET ME! 68500	RT	*	N/A
94	CATCH A FALLING STAR 68713	RT	*	N/A
94	FIRST STAR JINGLEBABY 68586	RT	10.00	10.00
94	GATHERING STARS IN THE SKY 68551	RT	12.50	13.00
94	LITTLE DRUMMER JINGLEBABY 68594	RT	10.00	10.00
95	ARE YOU ON MY LIST? 68797	RT	*	N/A
96	BABY'S 1ST RATTLE	OP	15.00	15.00
96	JINGLEBELL JINGLEBABY	OP	11.00	11.00
96	JOY TO THE WORLD- SET OF 2	OP	17.50	17.00
96	NIGHT BEFORE CHRISTMAS, THE - WREATH	OP	18.00	18.00
96	NIGHT BEFORE CHRISTMAS, THE- BELL	OP	18.00	18.00
96	NIGHT BEFORE CHRISTMAS, THE- DRUMMER	OP	18.00	18.00
96	NIGHT BEFORE CHRISTMAS, THE- MOON	OP	18.00	18.00
96	NIGHT BEFORE CHRISTMAS, THE- PACKAGE	OP	18.00	18.00
96	NIGHT BEFORE CHRISTMAS, THE- SISAL TREE	OP	18.00	18.00
96	NIGHT BEFORE CHRISTMAS, THE- SNOWBALL	OP	18.00	18.00
96	NIGHT BEFORE CHRISTMAS, THE- SOLDIER	OP	18.00	18.00
96	NIGHT BEFORE CHRISTMAS, THE- STAR	OP	18.00	18.00
96	SNOWBABY IN MY STOCKING	OP	10.00	10.00
96	STARRY PINE JINGLEBABY	OP	11.00	11.00
98	CANDLE LIGHT...SEASON BRIGHT	*	14.00	14.00
98	FIVE, SIX, A DRUM WITH STICKS		14.00	14.00

*
VILLAGE LIGHT-UP ORNAMENTS

YR	NAME	LIMIT	ISSUE	TREND
85	ABEL BEASLEY BUTCHER	CL	6.00	20.00
85	BEAN AND SON SMITHY SHOP	CL	6.00	20.00
85	CANDLE SHOP	CL	6.00	25.00
85	CROWNTREE INN	CL	6.00	40.00
85	DICKENS' VILLAGE (SET OF 8)	CL	48.00	210.00
85	DICKENS' VILLAGE CHURCH	CL	6.00	50.00
85	GOLDEN SWAN BAKER	CL	6.00	20.00
85	GREEN GROCER	CL	6.00	30.00
85	JONES & CO. BRUSH & BASKET SHOP	CL	6.00	35.00
86	APOTHECARY SHOP	CL	6.00	16.00
86	BRICK TOWN HALL	CL	6.00	35.00
86	GENERAL STORE	CL	6.00	35.00
86	LIVERY STABLE & BOOT SHOP	CL	6.00	25.00
86	NATHANIEL BINGHAM FABRICS	CL	6.00	25.00
86	NEW ENGLAND VILLAGE (SET OF 7)	CL	42.00	300.00
86	RED SCHOOLHOUSE	CL	6.00	78.00
86	STEEPLE CHURCH	CL	6.00	150.00
87	BARLEY BREE FARMHOUSE	CL	6.00	20.00
87	BLYTHE POND MILL HOUSE	CL	6.00	35.00
87	BRICK ABBEY	CL	6.00	80.00
87	CHESTERTON MANOR HOUSE	CL	6.00	40.00
87	CHRISTMAS CAROL COTTAGES (SET OF 3)	CL	16.95	70.00
87	COTTAGE OF BOB CRATCHIT & TINY TIM, THE	CL	6.00	35.00
87	CRAGGY COVE LIGHTHOUSE	CL	6.00	175.00
87	DICKENS' VILLAGE (SET OF 6)	CL	36.00	130.00
87	FEZZIWIG'S WAREHOUSE	CL	6.00	25.00
87	JACOB ADAMS BARN	CL	6.00	55.00
87	JACOB ADAMS FARMHOUSE	CL	6.00	40.00
87	KENILWORTH CASTLE	CL	6.00	50.00
87	NEW ENGLAND VILLAGE (SET OF 6)	CL	36.00	250.00
87	OLD CURIOSITY SHOP, THE	CL	6.00	50.00
87	SCROOGE & MARLEY COUNTINGHOUSE	CL	6.00	30.00
87	SMYTHE WOOLEN MILL	CL	6.00	100.00
87	TIMBER KNOLL LOG CABIN	CL	6.00	125.00
87	WESTON TRAIN STATION	CL	6.00	40.00

ENESCO CORP.
*
ANGEL SERIES-DATED

YR	NAME	LIMIT	ISSUE	TREND
89	WARM WISHES AND HAPPINESS-117706	YR	12.00	12.00
90	CHRISTMAS IS A TIME OF LOVE-119970	YR	17.00	17.00
90	XMAS BRING JOY OF BEAUT. SEASON-120413	YR	35.00	35.00

*
BABY'S FIRST CHRISTMAS-DATED SERIES

YR	NAME	LIMIT	ISSUE	TREND
89	SOMEWHERE IN THE EVENING SKY-117587	YR	12.00	15.00
90	MAY BABY'S FIRST XMAS BE FILLED-119741	YR	17.00	17.00

P. HILLMAN
CALICO KITTENS FOR YOU WITH MESSAGES

YR	NAME	LIMIT	ISSUE	TREND
96	TITLE N/A 178497	*	12.50	13.00

P. HILLMAN
CALICO KITTENS I LOVE MY KITTY

YR	NAME	LIMIT	ISSUE	TREND
95	BIRD SEED FROM KITTY 144355	*	13.50	14.00
95	I LOVE MY CAT 144320	*	11.00	11.00
95	MERRY CHRISTMAS KITTY 144266	*	11.00	11.00
95	TITLE N/A	*	11.00	11.00

YR	NAME	LIMIT	ISSUE	TREND
95	TO MY CAT 144398	*	11.00	11.00
95	TO MY KITTY 144274	*	11.00	11.00
P. HILLMAN	**CALICO KITTENS ITTY BITTY KITTY CHRISTMAS KITTY**			
96	TITLE N/A 178462	*	7.00	7.00
96	TITLE N/A 178489	*	12.50	13.00
96	TITLE N/A 178500	*	12.50	13.00
96	TITLE N/A 178519	*	12.50	13.00
96	TITLE N/A 178551	*	10.00	10.00
P. HILLMAN	**CALICO KITTENS/ 1993 CHRISTMAS INTRODUCTION**			
93	BABY'S FIRST ORNAMENT- BOY	RT	16.00	16.00
93	BABY'S FIRST ORNAMENT- GIRL	RT	16.00	16.00
93	CAT WITH BLUE HAT- 3 PC	RT	11.00	11.00
93	CAT WITH GREEN HAT- 3 PC	RT	11.00	11.00
93	CAT WITH RED HAT- 3 PC	RT	11.00	11.00
P. HILLMAN	**CALICO KITTENS/ 1994 CHRISTMAS INTRODUCTION**			
94	JOY TO THE WORLD- 2 PC	RT	13.50	14.00
94	OUR FIRST CHRISTMAS TOGETHER	RT	15.00	15.00
94	PEACE ON EARTH- 2 PC	RT	13.50	14.00
P. HILLMAN	**CHERISHED TEDDIES**			
95	BABY ANGEL ON CLOUD 141240	OP	13.50	14.00
95	BOY AND GIRL WITH BANNER 141259	OP	13.50	20.00
95	YOU'RE SKATED INTO MY HEART 141232	YR	12.50	13.00
96	BEAR W/DANGLING MITTENS 177768	OP	12.50	13.00
97	1997 DATED	YR	12.50	13.00
98	GINGERBREAD	YR	12.50	13.00
P. HILLMAN	**CHERISHED TEDDIES CHRISTMAS**			
92	ANGEL BEAR	SU	12.50	55.00
92	BEAR IN STOCKING	YR	16.00	50.00
92	BEAR ON ROCKING REINDEER	SU	20.00	45.00
92	SISTER WITH BLUE HAT	SU	12.50	21.00
92	SISTER WITH RED HAT	SU	12.50	21.00
92	SISTER WITH SANTA'S CAP	SU	12.50	21.00
93	ANGEL WITH BELLS	OP	12.50	13.00
93	ANGEL WITH HARP	OP	12.50	13.00
93	ANGEL WITH HORN	OP	12.50	13.00
93	BABY BOY'S FIRST CHRISTMAS	YR	12.50	32.00
93	BABY GIRL'S FIRST CHRISTMAS	YR	12.50	36.00
93	BEAR IN SANTA CAP	*	12.50	20.00
93	GIRL WITH MUFF	YR	13.50	50.00
94	BEARS IN SLED	*	15.00	37.00
94	BEARY CHRISTMAS-BABY IN BASKET	YR	15.00	40.00
94	DRUMMER BOY	YR	10.00	25.00
95	BEAR WITH ICE SKATES	YR	12.50	20.00
P. HILLMAN	**CHERISHED TEDDIES HOLIDAY DANGLING**			
96	JOY AND HO HO	*	12.50	12.00
P. HILLMAN	**CHERISHED TEDDIES MESSENGERS OF THE HEART**			
95	BOY BEAR FLYING CUPID	SU	13.00	20.00
95	GIRL BEAR FLYING CUPID	SU	13.00	20.00
P. HILLMAN	**CHERISHED TEDDIES SANTA'S WORKSHOP**			
95	ELF BEAR WITH CANDY CANE 651389	SU	12.50	15.00
95	ELF BEAR WITH DOLL 625434	SU	12.50	15.00
95	ELF BEAR WITH REINDEER TOY 625442	SU	12.50	15.00
95	MRS. CLAUS HOLDING TRAY OF COOKIES 625426	SU	12.50	21.00
95	SANTA BEAR 651370	OP	12.50	15.00
*****	**FROM BARBIE WITH LOVE**			
96	BARBIE AS S. O'HARA IN GRN VELVET 182028	YR	12.50	13.00
96	DECOUPAGE HEART 189103	*	9.00	9.00
96	DECOUPAGE ROUND 189030	*	7.50	8.00
96	HAPPY HOLIDAY BARBIE, 1989 188867	YR	12.50	13.00
96	HAPPY HOLIDAY BARBIE, 1996 188824	YR	12.50	13.00
96	HOLIDAY DANCE 1965 188808	*	12.50	13.00
96	QUEEN OF HEARTS BARBIE 157724	*	9.00	9.00
S. BUTCHER	**JOY TO THE WORLD**			
95	JOY TO THE WORLD 1ST ISSUE 150320	OP	20.00	20.00
96	JOY TO THE WORLD 2ND ISSUE 153338	OP	20.00	20.00
KINKA	**KINKA**			
89	BABIES ARE CHRISTMAS DREAMS-117722	OP	15.00	16.00
89	MAY THE CHRISTMAS STAR TOUCH-117595	OP	13.50	14.00
89	MAY THIS SEASON BE FILLED WITH-117714	OP	13.50	14.00
89	MAY YOU SHARE A NEW YEAR FILLED-119733	OP	23.00	23.00
89	SOMEWHERE IN THE EVENING SKY-117587	YR	12.00	15.00
89	WARM WISHES AND EVERY HAPPINESS-117706	YR	12.00	12.00
90	LOVE TO YOU-119954	YR	13.50	14.00
90	MAY CHRISTMAS BRING YOU-120413	YR	35.00	35.00
91	CHRISTMAS IS A TIME WHEN GOD-122742	YR	23.00	23.00
91	MAY THE TRUE SPIRIT-122750 (DATED)	YR	40.00	40.00
91	MAY THIS SPECIAL SEASON-122696	OP	23.00	23.00
91	MEMORIES ARE MADE OF-122661	OP	23.00	23.00
91	WISHING YOU SPECIAL BLESSINGS-122785	YR	17.50	18.00
92	CHRISTMAS IS LOVE-125369	OP	10.00	10.00
92	HEAVEN'S BUNDLE OF JOY-122734	OP	10.00	10.00
92	LIFE IS ONE JOYOUS STEP-125350	OP	10.00	10.00
92	LOVE TO YOU/THIS WONDROUS TIME-119954	OP	7.50	8.00
92	MAY THE CHRISTMAS STAR TOUCH-117595	OP	7.50	8.00

YR	NAME	LIMIT	ISSUE	TREND
92	MAY THIS SEASON BE FILLED W/JOY-117714	OP	7.50	8.00
92	MAY THIS SPECIAL SEASON-122688	OP	11.25	12.00
92	MEMORIES ARE MADE OF SIMPLE JOYS-122661	OP	11.25	12.00
92	SOUND OF LOVE IS FELT, THE-120693	OP	10.00	10.00
92	SWEET MUSIC & BEAUTIFUL MEMORIES-120707	OP	10.00	10.00

M. RHYNER-NADIG — **MARY'S MOO MOOS COWABUNGAS**

YR	NAME	LIMIT	ISSUE	TREND
96	I LOVE MOO	OP	7.50	8.00
96	SHUCK'S YOU'RE SWEET	OP	7.50	8.00
96	UDDERLY WONDERFUL	OP	7.50	8.00

M. RHYNER-NADIG — **MARY'S MOO MOOS MOO-SENGERS OF LOVE**

YR	NAME	LIMIT	ISSUE	TREND
96	CUPID H/O W/STAND	OP	6.75	7.00
96	GIRL/HEART H/O	OP	6.75	7.00

M. RHYNER-NADIG — **MARY'S MOO MOOS MOOEY CHRISTMAS**

YR	NAME	LIMIT	ISSUE	TREND
96	BABY'S 1ST CHRISTMAS	OP	12.50	13.00
96	BOY/GIRL ON SLED	OP	12.50	13.00
96	COWBOY	OP	12.50	13.00
96	GIRL SKATER	OP	12.50	13.00
96	SANTA/DATED	OP	6.25	7.00
96	WHEEE ARE MOOVIN!	YR	25.00	25.00

M. RHYNER-NADIG — **MARY'S MOO MOOS-DATED 1997**

YR	NAME	LIMIT	ISSUE	TREND
97	IT'S BUTTER TO GIVE THAN TO RECIEVE	YR	12.50	13.00

M. ATTWELL — **MEMORIES OF YESTERDAY**

YR	NAME	LIMIT	ISSUE	TREND
88	BABY'S FIRST CHRISTMAS-520373	YR	13.50	30.00
88	SPECIAL DELIVERY!-520381	YR	13.50	35.00
89	A SURPRISE FOR SANTA-522473	YR	13.50	22.00
89	BABY'S FIRST CHRISTMAS-522465	OP	15.00	20.00
89	CHRISTMAS TOGETHER-522562	CL	15.00	34.00
90	MOONSTRUCK-524794	RT	15.00	20.00
90	NEW MOON-524646	CL	15.00	25.00
90	TIME FOR BED-524638	YR	15.00	16.00
91	JUST WATCHIN' OVER YOU-525421	RT	17.50	25.00
91	LUCKY ME-525448	RT	16.00	20.00
91	LUCKY YOU-525847	RT	16.00	16.00
91	S'NO USE LOOKIN' BACK NOW!-527181	YR	17.50	18.00
91	STAR FISHIN'-525820	OP	16.00	16.00
92	I'LL FLY ALONG TO SEE YOU SOON-525804	YR	16.00	16.00
92	MERRY CHRISTMAS, LITTLE BOO-BOO-528803	OP	38.00	38.00
92	MOMMY, I TEARED IT-527041	YR	15.00	16.00
92	SAILIN' WITH MY FRIENDS-587575	OP	25.00	25.00
92	STAR LIGHT, STAR BRIGHT-528838	OP	16.00	16.00
92	SWINGING TOGETHER-580481	YR	17.50	18.00
93	HOW 'BOUT A LITTLE KISS?	CL	16.50	45.00
93	WISH I COULD FLY TO YOU?	YR	16.00	16.00
94	GIVE YOURSELF A HUG FROM ME	YR	17.50	18.00
95	HAPPY LANDINGS	YR	16.00	16.00
95	I PRAY THE LORD MY SOUL TO KEEP	OP	15.00	15.00
95	NOW I LAY ME DOWN TO SLEEP	OP	15.00	15.00
96	CAN I KEEP HER, MOMMY?	OP	13.50	14.00
97	SHARING GINGERBREAD BLESSINGS	YR	17.50	18.00

M. ATTWELL — **MEMORIES OF YESTERDAY 97 EVENT ONLY**

YR	NAME	LIMIT	ISSUE	TREND
97	YOU WARM MY HEART WITH FRIENDSHIP	YR	15.00	15.00

M. ATTWELL — **MEMORIES OF YESTERDAY 97 NATIVITY PAGEANT**

YR	NAME	LIMIT	ISSUE	TREND
97	ANGEL WITH HOLDER	OP	17.50	18.00

M. ATTWELL — **MEMORIES OF YESTERDAY FRIENDSHIP**

YR	NAME	LIMIT	ISSUE	TREND
96	I LOVE YOU THIS MUCH!	OP	13.50	14.00

M. ATTWELL — **MEMORIES OF YESTERDAY SOCIETY MEMBERS ONLY**

YR	NAME	LIMIT	ISSUE	TREND
92	WITH LUCK/I'S IN HEAVEN-MY922	YR	16.00	20.00
93	I'M BRINGING GOOD LUCK-WHEREVER YOU ARE	YR	16.00	20.00

M. ATTWELL — **MEMORIES OF YESTERDAY-WINTER MEMORIES SERIES**

YR	NAME	LIMIT	ISSUE	TREND
89	I'SE SWINGIN'-564923 (DATED)	YR	15.00	30.00
90	MAY EVERYTHING GO WITH A SWING-569550	YR	16.00	16.00
91	SWING WITH ME-580473 (DATED)	YR	16.00	16.00

S. BUTCHER — **PRECIOUS MOMENTS**

YR	NAME	LIMIT	ISSUE	TREND
80	BABY'S FIRST CHRISTMAS E-5631	SU	6.00	60.00
80	BABY'S FIRST CHRISTMAS E-5632	SU	6.00	60.00
80	WE HAVE SEEN HIS STAR E-6120	RT	9.00	60.00
80	WEE THREE KINGS (3PC SET) E-5634	SU	25.00	150.00
81	BUT LOVE GOES ON FOREVER E-5627	SU	6.00	115.00
81	BUT LOVE GOES ON FOREVER E-5628	SU	6.00	110.00
81	COME LET US ADORE HIM (4PC SET) E-5633	SU	20.00	135.00
81	LET THE HEAVENS REJOICE E-5629	YR	6.00	260.00
81	UNTO US A CHILD IS BORN E-5630	SU	6.00	65.00
82	BABY'S FIRST CHRISTMAS E-2362	SU	9.00	40.00
82	BABY'S FIRST CHRISTMAS E-2372	SU	9.00	45.00
82	CAMEL, DONKEY & COW (3 PC SET) E-2386	SU	25.00	100.00
82	DROPPING IN FOR CHRISTMAS E-2369	RT	9.00	58.00
82	DROPPING OVER FOR CHRISTMAS E-2376	RT	9.00	65.00
82	FIRST NOEL , THE-E-2367	SU	9.00	55.00
82	FIRST NOEL, THE- E-2368	RT	9.00	55.00
82	I'LL PLAY MY DRUM FOR HIM E-2359	YR	9.00	85.00
82	JOY TO THE WORLD E-2343	SU	9.00	45.00
82	MOUSE WITH CHEESE E-2381	SU	9.00	135.00
82	OUR FIRST CHRISTMAS TOGETHER E-2385	SU	9.00	45.00
82	SET OF 3-CAMEL, DONKEY & COW E2386	SU	25.00	100.00

YR	NAME	LIMIT	ISSUE	TREND
82	UNICORN E-2371	RT	9.00	60.00
83	BLESSED ARE THE PURE IN HEART E-0518	YR	9.00	45.00
83	JESUS IS THE LIGHT THAT SHINES E-0537	SU	9.00	65.00
83	LET HEAVEN AND NATURE SING E-0532	RT	9.00	45.00
83	LOVE IS PATIENT E-0535	SU	9.00	55.00
83	LOVE IS PATIENT E-0536	SU	9.00	60.00
83	MOTHER SEW DEAR E-0514	OP	9.00	24.00
83	O COME ALL YE FAITHFUL E-0531	SU	10.00	55.00
83	PERFECT GRANDPA, THE- E-0517	SU	9.00	40.00
83	PURR-FECT GRANDMA, THE- E-0516	OP	9.00	27.00
83	SURROUND US WITH JOY E-0513	YR	9.00	55.00
83	TELL ME THE STORY OF JESUS E-0533	SU	9.00	50.00
83	TO A SPECIAL DAD E-0515	SU	9.00	45.00
83	TO THEE WITH LOVE E-0534	RT	9.00	45.00
84	BLESSED ARE THE PURE IN HEART E-5392	YR	10.00	32.00
84	HAVE A HEAVENLY CHRISTMAS 12416	OP	12.00	30.00
84	JOY TO THE WORLD E-5388	RT	10.00	45.00
84	LOVE IS KIND E-5391	SU	10.00	35.00
84	MAY GOD BLESS YOU/PERFECT SEASON E-5390	SU	10.00	35.00
84	PEACE ON EARTH E-5389	SU	10.00	35.00
84	WISHING YOU A MERRY CHRISTMAS E-5387	YR	10.00	30.00
85	ANGEL OF MERCY 102407	OP	10.00	20.00
85	BABY'S FIRST CHRISTMAS 102504	YR	10.00	32.00
85	BABY'S FIRST CHRISTMAS 102512	YR	10.00	30.00
85	BABY'S FIRST CHRISTMAS 15903	YR	10.00	45.00
85	BABY'S FIRST CHRISTMAS 15911	YR	10.00	35.00
85	GOD SENT HIS LOVE 15768	YR	10.00	30.00
85	HAPPINESS IS THE LORD 15830	SU	10.00	32.00
85	HONK IF YOU LOVE JESUS 15857	SU	10.00	25.00
85	IT'S A PERFECT BOY 102415	SU	10.00	25.00
85	LORD KEEP ME ON MY TOES 102423	RT	10.00	45.00
85	LOVE RESCUE ME 102385	OP	10.00	22.00
85	MAY YOUR CHRISTMAS BE DELIGHTFUL 15849	SU	10.00	25.00
85	MAY YOUR CHRISTMAS BE HAPPY 15822	SU	10.00	35.00
85	OUR FIRST CHRISTMAS TOGETHER 102350	YR	10.00	30.00
85	ROCKING HORSE 102474	SU	10.00	25.00
85	SERVE WITH A SMILE 102431	SU	10.00	30.00
85	SERVE WITH A SMILE 102458	SU	10.00	30.00
85	SHEPHERD OF LOVE 102288	SU	10.00	25.00
85	TRUST AND OBEY 102377	OP	10.00	22.00
85	WISHING YOU A COZY CHRISTMAS 102326	YR	10.00	32.00
86	BABY'S FIRST CHRISTMAS 109401	YR	12.00	45.00
86	BABY'S FIRST CHRISTMAS 109428	YR	12.00	45.00
86	HE CLEANSED MY SOUL 112380	OP	12.00	24.00
86	I'M A POSSIBILITY 111120	SU	10.00	27.00
86	I'M SENDING YOU A WHITE CHRISTMAS 112372	SU	11.00	27.00
86	LOVE IS THE BEST GIFT OF ALL 109770	YR	11.00	30.00
86	OUR FIRST CHRISTMAS TOGETHER 112399	YR	11.00	30.00
86	REINDEER 102466	YR	11.00	175.00
86	WADDLE I DO WITHOUT YOU 112364	OP	10.00	20.00
86	YOU HAVE TOUCHED SO MANY HEARTS 112356	RT	10.00	20.00
87	BABY'S FIRST CHRISTMAS 109401	YR	12.00	45.00
87	BABY'S FIRST CHRISTMAS 109428	YR	12.00	45.00
87	BEAR THE GOOD NEWS IF CHRISTMAS 104515	YR	11.00	30.00
87	DASHING THROUGH THE SNOW 521574	OP	15.00	20.00
87	I'M A POSSIBILITY 111120	OP	10.00	25.00
88	A GROWING LOVE 520349	*		85.00
88	ALWAYS ROOM FOR ONE MORE 522961	OP		100.00
88	BABY'S FIRST CHRISTMAS 115282	YR	15.00	30.00
88	BABY'S FIRST CHRISTMAS 520241	YR	13.00	30.00
88	BABY'S FIRST CHRISTMAS 523194	YR	15.00	25.00
88	BABY'S FIRST CHRISTMAS 523208	YR	15.00	25.00
88	CHEERS TO THE LEADER 113999	SU	13.50	35.00
88	CHRISTMAS IS RUFF WITHOUT YOU 520462	YR	13.00	32.00
88	DON'T LET THE HOLIDAYS..DOWN 521590	OP	15.00	20.00
88	GLIDE THROUGH THE HOLIDAYS 521566	RT	13.50	35.00
88	GOD SENT YOU JUST IN TIME 113972	SU	13.50	35.00
88	HANG ON FOR THE HOLLY DAYS 520292	YR	13.00	25.00
88	I BELIEVE IN THE OLD RUGGED CROSS 522953	OP	15.00	20.00
88	MAKE A JOYFUL NOISE 522910	SU	15.00	19.00
88	MAY ALL YOUR CHRISTMASES..521302	OP	13.50	20.00
88	MY LOVE WILL NEVER LET YOU GO 114006	SU	13.50	33.00
88	OH HOLY NIGHT 522848	YR	13.50	32.00
88	OUR FIRST CHRISTMAS TOGETHER 520233	YR	13.00	21.00
88	OUR FIRST CHRISTMAS TOGETHER 521558	YR	17.50	35.00
88	PEACE ON EARTH 523062	YR	25.00	75.00
88	REJOICE O EARTH 113980	RT	13.50	40.00
88	SMILE ALONG THE WAY 113964	SU	15.00	26.00
88	TIME TO WISH YOU/MERRY CHRISTMAS 115320	YR	13.00	45.00
88	TO MY FOREVER FRIEND 113956	OP	16.00	25.00
88	YOU ARE MY GIFT COME TRUE 520276	YR	12.50	19.00
89	BABY'S FIRST CHRISTMAS 523771	YR	15.00	22.00
89	BABY'S FIRST CHRISTMAS 523798	YR	15.00	22.00
89	BUNDLES OF JOY 525057	LE	17.50	32.00
89	CELEBRATING...SHARING & CARING 227986	YR	7.00	10.00

YR	NAME	LIMIT	ISSUE	TREND
89	FRIENDS NEVER DRIFT APART 522937	RT	17.50	19.00
89	HAPPY TRAILS IS TRUSTING JESUS 523224	OP	15.00	20.00
89	LOVE ONE ANOTHER 522929	OP	17.50	20.00
89	MAY YOUR CHRISTMAS BE/HAPPY HOME 523704	YR	28.00	50.00
89	OH HOLY NIGHT 522848	YR	13.50	40.00
89	ONCE UPON A HOLY NIGHT 523852	YR	15.00	30.00
89	OUR FIRST CHRISTMAS TOGETHER 522945	YR	17.50	27.00
89	OUR FIRST CHRISTMAS TOGETHER 525324	YR	17.50	30.00
89	WISHING YOU A PURR-FECT HOLIDAY 520497	YR	15.00	30.00
90	A UNIVERSAL LOVE 238899	YR	8.00	12.00
90	BABY'S FIRST CHIRSTMAS (GIRL) 527092	YR	15.00	25.00
90	BABY'S FIRST CHRISTMAS (BOY) 527084	YR	15.00	20.00
90	GOOD LORD ALWAYS DELIVERS, THE- 527165	SU	15.00	20.00
90	MAY YOUR CHRISTMAS BE MERRY 524174	YR	15.00	30.00
90	MAY YOUR CHRISTMAS BE MERRY 526940	YR	30.00	35.00
90	SHARING A GIFT OF LOVE 233196	YR	8.00	8.00
90	SNO-BUNNY FALLS FOR YOU LIKE I DO 520438	YR	15.00	28.00
91	MAY YOUR CHRISTMAS BE MERRY 526940	YR	30.00	40.00
92	15 YEARS-TWEET MUSIC TOGETHER 530840	LE	15.00	20.00
92	BABY'S FIRST CHRISTMAS 527475	YR	15.00	19.00
92	BABY'S FIRST CHRISTMAS 527483	YR	15.00	19.00
92	BABY'S FIRST CHRISTMAS 530859	YR	15.00	19.00
92	BABY'S FIRST CHRISTMAS 530867	YR	15.00	19.00
92	BUT THE GREATEST OF THESE IS LOVE 527696	YR	15.00	24.00
92	BUT THE GREATEST OF THESE IS LOVE 527734	YR	30.00	32.00
92	GOOD FRIENDS ARE FOR ALWAYS 524131	RT	15.00	18.00
92	I'M NUTS ABOUT YOU 520411	YR	16.00	27.00
92	IT'S SO UPLIFTING...FRIEND...YOU 528846	OP	16.00	17.00
92	LORD KEEP ME ON MY TOES 525332	OP	15.00	17.00
92	OUR FIRST CHRISTMAS TOGETHER 528870	YR	17.50	21.00
92	OUR FIRST CHRISTMAS TOGETHER 530506	OP	17.50	19.00
92	SHARE IN THE WARMTH OF CHRISTMAS	OP	15.00	18.00
92	SLOW DOWN & ENJOY THE HOLIDAYS 520489	YR	16.00	19.00
92	THERE'S A CHRISTIAN WELCOME HERE 528021	YR	23.00	30.00
92	WISHING YOU/SWEETEST CHRISTMAS 530190	YR	30.00	35.00
92	WISHING YOU/SWEETEST CHRISTMAS 530212	OP	15.00	30.00
93	AN EVENT FOR ALL SEASONS 529974	LE	15.00	15.00
93	AN EVENT FOR ALL SEASONS 530158	OP	30.00	30.00
93	WISHING YOU/SWEETEST CHRISTMAS 530182	OP	8.00	8.00
94	BABY'S FIRST CHRISTMAS 530255	YR	16.00	16.00
94	BABY'S FIRST CHRISTMAS 530263	YR	16.00	16.00
94	MEMORIES ARE MADE OF THIS 529982	OP	30.00	30.00
94	OUR FIRST CHRISTMAS TOGETHER 529206	OP	19.00	19.00
94	TAKE A BOW CUZ YOU'RE MY CHRISTMAS STAR	OP	16.00	16.00
94	YER A PEL-I-CAN COUNT ON	OP	16.00	16.00
94	YOU ARE ALWAYS IN MY HEART 530972	OP	16.00	16.00
94	YOU'RE AS PRETTY AS A CHRISTMAS TREE 530387	YR	28.00	28.00
94	YOU'RE AS PRETTY AS A CHRISTMAS TREE 530395	YR	30.00	30.00
95	BABY'S FIRST CHRISTMAS 142719	OP	17.50	18.00
95	BABY'S FIRST CHRISTMAS 142727	OP	17.50	18.00
95	FOLLOW YOUR HEART 528080	OP	30.00	30.00
95	HE COVERS THE EARTH W/HIS BEAUTY 142662	OP	17.00	17.00
95	HE COVERS THE EARTH W/HIS BEAUTY 142689	OP	30.00	30.00
95	HIPPO HOLIDAYS	OP	17.00	17.00
95	JOY FROM HEAD TO MISTLETOE 150126	OP	17.00	17.00
95	MERRY CHRISMOOSE 150134	OP	17.00	17.00
95	OUR FIRST CHRISTMAS TOGETHER 142700	OP	19.00	19.00
95	YOU'RE "A" NUMBER ONE IN MY BOOK, TEACHER 150142	OP	17.00	17.00
96	BABY'S FIRST CHRISTMAS-BOY 183946	YR	17.50	18.00
96	BABY'S FIRST CHRISTMAS-GIRL 183938	YR	17.50	18.00
96	GOD'S PRECIOUS GIFT 183881	OP	20.00	20.00
96	OUR FIRST CHRISTMAS TOGETHER 183911	YR	23.00	23.00
96	PEACH ON EARTH...ANYWAY 183350	YR	30.00	30.00
96	PEACH ON EARTH...ANYWAY 183369	YR	19.00	19.00
96	WHEN THE SKATING'S RUFF, TRY PRAYER 183903	OP	19.00	19.00
97	PUPPY PUSHING SLED	OP	19.00	19.00

S. BUTCHER   **PRECIOUS MOMENTS BIRTHDAY**

YR	NAME	LIMIT	ISSUE	TREND
95	HIPPO HOLIDAYS 520403	OP	17.00	17.00
96	OWL BE HOME FOR CHRISTMAS 128708	YR	19.00	19.00
97	SLOW DOWN FOR THE HOLIDAYS	YR	19.00	19.00

S. BUTCHER   **PRECIOUS MOMENTS COLLECTORS' CLUB PIECES**

YR	NAME	LIMIT	ISSUE	TREND
84	CELEBRATING A DECADE..SHARING 227986	YR	7.00	10.00
90	7 CHAPEL WINDOWS ORNAMENT SET PM890	OP	105.00	105.00
90	BLESSED ARE THE MEEK...PM390	OP	15.00	15.00
90	BLESSED ARE THE MERCIFUL..PM590	OP	15.00	15.00
90	BLESSED ARE THE PEACEMAKERS...PM790	OP	15.00	15.00
90	BLESSED ARE THE POOR...PM190	OP	15.00	15.00
90	BLESSED ARE THE PURE... PM690	OP	15.00	15.00
90	BLESSED ARE THEY THAT HUNGER...PM490	OP	15.00	15.00
90	BLESSED ARE THEY THAT MOURN..PM290	OP	15.00	15.00
92	LOVING...SHARING ALONG THE WAY PM040	OP	12.50	30.00

S. BUTCHER   **PRECIOUS MOMENTS COMMEMORATIVE EASTER SEALS ORNAMENTS**

YR	NAME	LIMIT	ISSUE	TREND
93	YOU'RE MY NUMBER ONE FRIEND 250112	OP	8.00	8.00
94	IT IS NO SECRET WHAT GOD CAN DO	YR	6.50	7.00
95	TAKE TIME TO SMELL THE FLOWERS	YR	7.50	8.00

YR	NAME	LIMIT	ISSUE	TREND
96	YOU CAN ALWAYS COUNT ON ME	YR	6.50	7.00
97	SOMEBODY CARES	YR	40.00	40.00
S. BUTCHER		**PRECIOUS MOMENTS DATED**		
97	BABY'S FIRST CHRISTMAS	YR	19.00	19.00
97	BABY'S FIRST ORNAMENT	YR	19.00	19.00
97	CANE YOU JOIN US FOR A MERRY CHRISTMAS	YR	19.00	19.00
97	CANE YOU JOIN US FOR A MERRY CHRISTMAS- BALL	YR	30.00	30.00
97	OUR FIRST CHRISTMAS TOGETHER	YR	20.00	20.00
S. BUTCHER		**PRECIOUS MOMENTS JOY TO THE WORLD**		
97	JOY TO THE WORLD	OP	20.00	20.00
S. BUTCHER	**PRECIOUS MOMENTS SPECIAL EDITION MEMBERS ONLY**			
93	LOVING,CARING & SHARING ALONG THE WAY	OP	15.00	15.00
94	YOU ARE THE END OF MY RAINBOW	OP	15.00	15.00
S. BUTCHER		**PRECIOUS MOMENTS SUGAR TOWN**		
92	BOY STANDING BY CHAPEL 530484	LE	17.50	20.00
95	SUGAR TOWN DOCTOR'S OFFICE 530441	RT	17.50	18.00
96	TRAIN STATION 184101	RT	19.00	19.00
*			**SHARING SEASON GIFTS**	
86	BIRDS OF A FEATHER COLLECT... PM864	OP	*	160.00
87	BRASS FILIGREE BELL SHAPED PM009	OP	*	45.00
88	A GROWING LOVE 520349	OP	*	85.00
89	ALWAYS ROOM FOR ONE MORE 522961	OP	*	100.00
90	MY HAPPINESS PM904	OP	*	95.00
91	SHARING THE GOOD NEWS TOGETHER PM037	OP	*	80.00
*		**TREASURY MASTERPIECE EDITIONS**		
97	100 YEARS OF SOUP-ERB GOOD TASTE	YR	20.00	20.00
97	50 YEARS OF MIRACLES	YR	20.00	20.00
97	ALWAYS COOL WITH COKE	YR	23.00	23.00
97	BEEP ME UP!	YR	20.00	20.00
97	BEST BET'S A 'VETTE	YR	23.00	23.00
97	COCA-COLA CABOOSE	YR	25.00	25.00
97	CRACKER JACK...THE HOME RUN SNACK	YR	25.00	25.00
97	DEERE SANTA	YR	25.00	25.00
97	EVERYONE KNOWS IT'S SLINKY	YR	23.00	23.00
97	FOR ALL YOU DO, MERRY CHRISTMAS TO YOU	YR	25.00	25.00
97	FORECAST ALWAYS CALLS FOR COKE, THE	YR	20.00	20.00
97	G.I. JOE LOVES CHRISTMAS	YR	20.00	20.00
97	HAVE YOUR CAKE AND BAKE IT, TOO	YR	20.00	20.00
97	HEADING 4-WHEEL MERRY CHRISTMAS	YR	23.00	23.00
97	HO HO HO, A GRILLING WE WILL GO!	YR	20.00	20.00
97	HOME SWEET HOME	YR	25.00	25.00
97	HULA HOOP HOLIDAYS	YR	20.00	20.00
97	ICE CREAM OF THE CROP	YR	20.00	20.00
97	MOVIN' AND GROOVIN'	YR	23.00	23.00
97	ON TRACK WITH SANTA	YR	20.00	20.00
97	ORDERING UP A MERRY CHRISTMAS	YR	25.00	25.00
97	PLAY IT AGAIN, SANTA	YR	20.00	20.00
97	PREPARE FOR BATTLE	YR	25.00	25.00
97	STOCKIN' UP FOR THE HOLIDAYS	YR	23.00	23.00
97	TWIST & SHOUT "HAVE A COKE"	YR	25.00	25.00
97	WORKIN' ROUND THE CLOCK	YR	23.00	23.00
97	WWW. HAPPY HOLIDAYS!.COM	YR	25.00	25.00
T. FRALEY		**TREASURY MASTERPIECE EDITIONS**		
97	TOBIN'S GRACEFUL STEED	YR	20.00	20.00
K. HAHN		**TREASURY MASTERPIECE EDITIONS**		
97	ADVENT-URES IN ORNAMENT COLLECTING- CHARTER MEMBER	YR	20.00	20.00
97	ADVENT-URES IN ORNAMENT COLLECTING- SILVER STAR	YR	20.00	20.00
97	BUBBLING WITH CHEER	YR	20.00	20.00
97	FIRED UP FOR CHRISTMAS	YR	23.00	23.00
97	HOWL-A-DAY PET SHOPPE	YR	25.00	25.00
97	I'M SO GLAD I FONDUE AS A FRIEND	YR	20.00	20.00
97	ON COURSE WITH SANTA	YR	20.00	20.00
97	PRIMPING IRON	YR	20.00	20.00
97	SPARE TIME FOR CHRISTMAS FUN	YR	25.00	25.00
97	SWEETEST NATIVITY, THE	YR	20.00	20.00
P. HILLMAN		**TREASURY MASTERPIECE EDITIONS**		
97	CHERISH THE JOY	YR	25.00	25.00
*			**TREASURY OF CHRISTMAS**	
81	BABY'S FIRST CHRISTMAS 1981-E-6145	YR	6.00	22.00
81	FLYIN' SANTA CHRISTMAS SPECIAL-E6136	YR	9.00	110.00
81	LOOK OUT BELOW-E-6135	TL	6.00	60.00
81	NOT A CREATURE WAS STIRRING-E-6149	TL	4.00	45.00
81	OUR HERO-E-6146	TL	4.00	55.00
81	SAWIN' ELF HELPER-E-6138	TL	6.00	45.00
81	SNOW SHOE-IN SANTA-E-6139	TL	6.00	50.00
81	WHOOPS, IT'S 1981-E-6148	YR	7.50	75.00
81	WHOOPS-E-6147	TL	3.50	95.00
82	A SAVIOR IS BORN THIS DAY-E-6949	TL	4.00	18.00
82	BABY'S FIRST CHRISTMAS 1982-E-6952	YR	4.00	10.00
82	BABY'S FIRST CHRISTMAS 1982-E-6979	YR	10.00	35.00
82	BUNNY WINTER PLAYGROUND 1982-E-6978	YR	10.00	55.00
82	CAROUSEL HORSES-E-6958	TL	8.00	65.00
82	FLYIN' SANTA CHRISTMAS SPECIAL-E6136	YR	9.00	105.00
82	GRANDCHILD'S FIRST CHRISTMAS 1982-E-6983	YR	5.00	15.00

YR	NAME	LIMIT	ISSUE	TREND
82	MERRY CHRISTMAS GRANDMA-E-6975	TL	5.00	5.00
82	MERRY CHRISTMAS TEACHER-E-6984	TL	7.00	7.00
82	PENGUIN POWER-E-6977	TL	6.00	18.00
82	POLAR BEAR FUN WHOOPS IT'S 1982-E-6953	YR	10.00	85.00
82	TOY SOLDIER 1982-E-6957	YR	6.50	65.00
82	VICTORIAN SLEIGH-E-6946	TL	9.00	9.00
83	ARCTIC CHARMER-E-6945	TL	7.00	35.00
83	BABY'S FIRST CHRISTMAS-E-0271	YR	6.00	6.00
83	BABY'S FIRST CHRISTMAS-E-0273	TL	9.00	9.00
83	CAROUSEL HORSE-E-0278	TL	9.00	50.00
83	CAROUSEL HORSES-E-6980	TL	8.00	65.00
83	GRANDCHILD'S FIRST CHRISTMAS-E0272	YR	5.00	5.00
83	TO A SPECIAL TEACHER-E-0276	TL	5.00	15.00
83	TOY DRUM TEDDY-E-0274	TL	9.00	9.00
83	TOY SHOP-E-0277	TL	8.00	32.00
83	WATCHING AT THE WINDOW-E-0275	TL	13.00	40.00
83	WIDE OPEN THROTTLE-E-0242	TL	12.00	35.00
83	WING-A-DING ANGEL-E-6948	TL	7.00	40.00
84	BABY'S FIRST CHRISTMAS 1984-E-6215	YR	6.00	6.00
84	BUNNY'S CHRISTMAS STOCKING-E-6251	YR	2.00	28.00
84	CAROUSEL HORSE-E-6913	TL	1.50	20.00
84	CHRISTMAS NEST-E-6249	TL	3.00	3.00
84	CUCKOO CLOCK-E-6217	TL	8.00	40.00
84	FERRIS WHEEL MICE-E-6216	TL	9.00	9.00
84	GODCHILD'S FIRST CHRISTMAS-E-6287	TL	7.00	7.00
84	GRANDCHILD'S FIRST CHRISTMAS 1984-E-6286	YR	5.00	5.00
84	HAPPY HOLIDAYS-E-6248	TL	2.00	2.00
84	HOLIDAY PENGUIN-E-6240	TL	1.50	20.00
84	JOY TO THE WORLD-E-6209	TL	9.00	48.00
84	LETTER TO SANTA-E-6210	TL	5.00	35.00
84	LITTLE DRUMMER-E-6241	TL	2.00	2.00
84	MERRY CHRISTMAS MOTHER-E-6213	TL	10.00	35.00
84	OWL BE HOME FOR CHRISTMAS-E-6230	TL	10.00	10.00
84	PEEK-A-BEAR BABY'S/CHRISTMAS-E-6228	TL	10.00	10.00
84	PEEK-A-BEAR BABY'S/CHRISTMAS-E-6229	TL	9.00	9.00
84	PENGUINS ON ICE-E-6280	TL	7.50	30.00
84	SANTA IN THE BOX-E-6292	TL	6.00	35.00
84	SANTA ON ICE-E-6252	TL	2.50	25.00
84	SANTA'S TROLLEY-E-6231	TL	11.00	55.00
84	TREASURED MEMORIES THE NEW SLED-E-6256	TL	7.00	70.00
84	UP ON THE HOUSE TOP-E-6280	TL	9.00	30.00
85	A STOCKING FULL FOR 1985-56464	YR	6.00	6.00
85	ANGEL IN FLIGHT-55816	TL	8.00	25.00
85	BABY BLOCKS-55883	TL	12.00	12.00
85	BABY RATTLE PHOTO FRAME-56006	TL	5.00	5.00
85	BABY'S FIRST CHRISTMAS-55840	TL	15.00	16.00
85	CAROUSEL REINDEER-55808	TL	12.00	50.00
85	CHILD'S SECOND CHRISTMAS-55867	TL	11.00	20.00
85	CHRISTMAS LIGHTS-56200	TL	8.00	40.00
85	CHRISTMAS PENGUIN-55824	TL	7.50	40.00
85	CHRISTMAS TOY CHEST-55891	TL	10.00	25.00
85	CHRISTMAS TREE PHOTOFRAME-56871	TL	10.00	10.00
85	FISHING FOR STARS-55875	TL	9.00	15.00
85	FLYING SANTA CHRISTMAS SPECIAL-56383	TL	8.00	45.00
85	GRANDCHILD'S FIRST ORNAMENT-55921	TL	7.00	12.00
85	LOOK OUT BELOW-56375	TL	6.00	50.00
85	MERRY CHRISTMAS GRANDMA-56197	YR	7.00	7.00
85	MERRY CHRISTMAS TEACHER-56448	YR	9.00	9.00
85	NIGHT BEFORE CHRISTMAS, THE-55972	TL	5.00	5.00
85	NORTH POLE EXPRESS-56073	TL	9.00	50.00
85	NOT A CREATURE WAS STIRRING-56421	YR	5.50	45.00
85	OLD FASHIONED ROCKING HORSE-55859	TL	10.00	10.00
85	OUR HERO-56413	YR	5.50	55.00
85	SANTA CLAUS BALLOON-55794	YR	8.50	40.00
85	SAWIN ELF HELPER-56391	YR	8.00	45.00
85	SCOTTIE CELEBRATING CHRISTMAS-56065	TL	10.00	15.00
85	SKATING WALRUS-56081	TL	9.00	45.00
85	SNOW SHOE-IN SANTA-56405	YR	8.00	50.00
85	ST. NICHOLAS CIRCA 1910-56359	TL	6.00	15.00
85	TOBOGGAN RIDE-56286	TL	6.00	12.00
85	VICTORIAN DOLL HOUSE-56251	YR	13.00	30.00
85	WE THREE KINGS-55964	YR	4.50	15.00
86	1ST CHRISTMAS TOGETHER 1986-551171	YR	9.00	22.00
86	ANTIQUE TOY-551317	TL	9.00	25.00
86	BABY BEAR SLEIGH, THE-551651	TL	9.00	25.00
86	BABY'S FIRST CHRISTMAS 1986-551724	YR	6.50	7.00
86	BABY'S FIRST CHRISTMAS-551716	TL	5.50	10.00
86	BAH, HUMBUG!-553387	TL	9.00	20.00
86	CHRISTMAS ANGEL, THE-551244	10000	23.00	55.00
86	CHRISTMAS CALENDAR-551333	TL	7.00	20.00
86	CHRISTMAS RATTLE-553379	TL	8.00	25.00
86	CHRISTMAS SCOTTIE-551201	TL	7.00	15.00
86	CHRISTMAS WISHES FROM PANDA-552623	TL	6.00	10.00
86	COUNTRY COUSINS MERRY XMAS, DAD-552704	TL	7.00	10.00
86	COUNTRY COUSINS MERRY XMAS, DAD-552712	TL	7.00	15.00

YR	NAME	LIMIT	ISSUE	TREND
86	COUNTRY COUSINS MERRY XMAS, MOM-552704	TL	7.00	10.00
86	COUNTRY COUSINS MERRY XMAS, MOM-552712	TL	7.00	15.00
86	ELF STRINGING POPCORN-551198	TL	10.00	18.00
86	FIRST CHRISTMAS TOGETHER-551708	TL	6.00	23.00
86	FROM OUR HOUSE TO YOUR HOUSE-553360	TL	15.00	20.00
86	GOD BLESS US EVERYONE-553395	TL	10.00	22.00
86	GRANDMOTHER'S LITTLE ANGEL-552747	TL	8.00	15.00
86	HAVE A HEAVENLY HOLIDAY-551260	TL	9.00	1.00
86	HOLIDAY FISHERMAN-551309	TL	8.00	35.00
86	HOLIDAY TRAIN-553417	TL	10.00	24.00
86	I LOVE MY GRANDPARENTS-553263	YR	6.00	6.00
86	M.V.B. (MOST VALUABLE BEAR)-554219	TL	3.00	3.00
86	MERRY CHRISTMAS MOM & DAD-553271	YR	6.00	6.00
86	MERRY CHRISTMAS TEACHER-552666	TL	6.50	12.00
86	MERRY CHRISTMAS-553646	TL	8.00	14.00
86	MY SPECIAL FRIEND-552615	TL	2.50	18.00
86	OLD FASHIONED DOLL HOUSE-551287	TL	15.00	25.00
86	PEEK-A-BEAR GRANDCHILD'S/XMAS-552070	YR	6.00	6.00
86	PEEK-A-BEAR PRESENT-552089	TL	2.50	3.00
86	S. CLAUS HOLLYCOPTER-553344	TL	13.50	30.00
86	SANTA AND CHILD-551236	TL	13.50	25.00
86	SANTA'S HELPERS-552607	TL	2.50	3.00
86	SIAMESE KITTEN-551279	TL	9.00	20.00
87	1ST CHRISTMAS TOGETHER 1987-556335	YR	9.00	25.00
87	BABY'S FIRST CHRISTMAS 1987-556254	YR	7.00	25.00
87	BABY'S FIRST CHRISTMAS 1987-556297	YR	2.00	5.00
87	BABY'S FIRST CHRISTMAS-555061	TL	12.00	15.00
87	BABY'S FIRST CHRISTMAS-555088	TL	7.50	12.00
87	BABY'S FIRST CHRISTMAS-555118	TL	6.00	10.00
87	BABY'S FIRST CHRISTMAS-556041	TL	10.00	10.00
87	BEARY CHRISTMAS FAMILY-556300	TL	2.00	5.00
87	BOY ON A ROCKING HORSE-555983	TL	12.00	20.00
87	BUCKET O'LOVE-556491	TL	2.50	3.00
87	CAROUSEL GOOSE-556076	TL	17.00	40.00
87	CAROUSEL MOBILE-553409	TL	15.00	60.00
87	CHRISTMAS TRAIN-557196	TL	10.00	18.00
87	COUNTRY COUSINS KATIE/ICE SKATING-556378	TL	8.00	30.00
87	COUNTRY COUSINS SCOOTER SNOWMAN-556386	TL	8.00	35.00
87	GRANDCHILD'S FIRST CHRISTMAS-556416	TL	10.00	25.00
87	I'M DREAMING OF/BRIGHT CHRISTMAS-556602	TL	2.50	3.00
87	KITTY'S 1ST CHRISTMAS-552917	TL	4.00	5.00
87	KITTY'S BED-556408	TL	12.00	50.00
87	KITTY'S JACK-IN-THE-BOX-555959	TL	11.00	15.00
87	LITTLE SAILOR ELF-556068	TL	10.00	20.00
87	MERRY CHRISTMAS KITTY-552933	TL	3.50	5.00
87	MERRY CHRISTMAS PUPPY-552925	TL	3.50	5.00
87	MERRY CHRISTMAS TEACHER-555967	TL	7.50	10.00
87	MERRY CHRISTMAS TEACHER-556319	TL	2.00	5.00
87	MOUSE IN A MITTEN-555975	TL	7.50	30.00
87	NIGHT CAPS-556084	TL	5.50	8.00
87	OUR FIRST CHRISTMAS TOGETHER-556548	TL	13.00	18.00
87	PEAK-A-BEAR MY SPECIAL FRIEND-556513	TL	6.00	20.00
87	PEAK-A-BEAR LETTER TO SANTA-555991	TL	8.00	15.00
87	PUPPY LOVE-556505	TL	6.00	15.00
87	PUPPY'S 1ST CHRISTMAS-552909	TL	4.00	5.00
87	ROCKING HORSE PAST JOYS-556157	TL	10.00	10.00
87	SANTA'S LIST-556394	TL	7.00	25.00
87	SKATING SANTA 1987-556211	YR	13.50	80.00
87	SLEIGH AWAY-555401	TL	12.00	20.00
87	SUGAR PLUM BEARIES-555193	TL	4.50	5.00
87	TEDDY TAKES A SPIN-556467	TL	13.00	18.00
87	TEDDY'S SUSPENDERS-556262	TL	8.50	16.00
87	THREE LITTLE BEARS-556556	TL	7.50	12.00
87	TINY TOY THIMBLE MOBILE-556475	TL	12.00	15.00
88	1ST CHRISTMAS TOGETHER 1988-554596	YR	17.50	18.00
88	BABY'S FIRST CHRISTMAS 1988-554928	YR	7.50	10.00
88	CHRISTMAS IS COMING-554901	TL	12.00	18.00
88	CHRISTMAS PIN-UP 489409	TL	11.00	25.00
88	CHRISTMAS THIM-BELL-558389	YR	4.00	6.00
88	CHRISTMAS TRAIN, THE-554944	TL	15.00	20.00
88	GRAMOPHONE KEEPSAKE-558818	TL	13.00	22.00
88	HAPPY HOWLADAYS-558605	YR	7.00	12.00
88	MERRY CHRISTMAS ENGINE-554561	TL	23.00	35.00
88	MERRY CHRISTMAS GRANDPA-560065	TL	8.00	10.00
88	NORTH POLE DEADLINE-489387	TL	13.50	18.00
88	SANTA TURTLE-558559	TL	10.00	20.00
88	SANTA'S SURVEY-554642	TL	35.00	70.00
88	TEDDY BEAR BALL, THE-558567	TL	10.00	12.00
88	TURTLE GREETINGS-558583	TL	8.50	22.00
89	BABY'S FIRST CHRISTMAS 1989-562807	YR	8.00	12.00
89	BOTTOM'S UP 1989-830003	TL	11.00	20.00
89	CAUGHT IN THE ACT-830046	TL	12.50	13.00
89	CLARA-568406	YR	12.50	22.00
89	COWARDLY LION, THE-567787	YR	12.00	22.00
89	DOROTHY-567760	YR	12.00	25.00

YR	NAME	LIMIT	ISSUE	TREND
89	FIRST CHRISTMAS TOGETHER 1989-562823	TL	11.00	12.00
89	GONE WITH THE WIND-567698	YR	13.50	25.00
89	HOE! HOE! HOE!-564761	YR	20.00	31.00
89	PAUSE THAT REFRESHES, THE-563226	TL	15.00	20.00
89	PURR-FECT FIT!, THE-566462	TL	15.00	16.00
89	SANTA'S LITTLE REINDEAR-568430	TL	15.00	16.00
89	SCARECROW, THE-567795	YR	12.00	20.00
89	STATIC IN THE ATTIC-562947	TL	13.00	15.00
89	TIN MAN, THE-567779	YR	12.00	20.00
89	VICTORIAN SLEIGH RIDE-562890	TL	23.00	23.00
89	YE OLDE PUPPET SHOW-562939	TL	17.50	20.00
90	A CALLING HOME AT CHRISTMAS-568457	TL	15.00	16.00
90	BREWING WARM WISHES-564974	TL	10.00	12.00
90	CLARA'S PRINCE-568422	YR	12.50	18.00
90	FESTIVE FLIGHT-566101	TL	11.00	14.00
90	HANG IN THERE-566055	TL	13.50	14.00
90	HAPPY HOLIDAY READINGS-568104	TL	8.00	10.00
90	HAVE A COKE AND A SMILE-571512	TL	15.00	16.00
90	HEADING FOR HAPPY HOLIDAYS-577537	TL	17.50	18.00
90	MCHAPPY HOLIDAYS-577529	TL	17.50	18.00
90	MERRY CHRISTMAS TEACHER-566098	TL	11.00	11.00
90	MOUSE HOUSE-575186	TL	16.00	16.00
90	NUTCRACKER, THE-568422	YR	12.50	18.00
90	OVER ONE MILLION HOLIDAY WISHES!-577553	YR	17.50	20.00
90	PURR-FECT PALS-563218	TL	8.00	12.00
90	SANTA'S SUITCASE-566462	TL	25.00	25.00
90	SEAMAN'S GREETINGS-566047	TL	11.00	11.00
90	TEN LORDS A-LEAPING-573949	TL	15.00	16.00
90	TONS OF TOYS-577510	TL	13.00	18.00
90	TWAS THE NIGHT BEFORE CHRISTMAS-577545	TL	17.50	18.00
90	YOU MALT MY HEART-577596	TL	25.00	25.00
91	A REAL CLASSIC-831603	YR	10.00	10.00
91	ALL CAUGHT UP IN CHRISTMAS-583537	TL	10.00	10.00
91	ALL I WANT FOR CHRISTMAS-577596	TL	25.00	25.00
91	BABY'S FIRST CHRISTMAS 1991-586935	YR	12.50	13.00
91	CHECKING IT TWICE-583936	TL	25.00	25.00
91	CHRISTMAS CHEER-585769	TL	13.50	14.00
91	CHRISTMAS COUNTDOWN-568376	TL	20.00	20.00
91	CHRISTMAS CUTIE-576182	TL	13.50	14.00
91	CHRISTMAS IS IN THE AIR-581453	YR	15.00	16.00
91	CHRISTMAS IS MY GOAL-581550	TL	17.50	18.00
91	CHRISTMAS KAYAK-583723	TL	13.50	15.00
91	DREAM A LITTLE DREAM-575593	TL	17.50	18.00
91	FROSTY THE SNOWMAN-576425	TL	15.00	16.00
91	GLOW OF CHRISTMAS, THE-581801	TL	20.00	20.00
91	HAPPY MEAL ON WHEELS-583715	TL	23.00	23.00
91	HERE'S THE SCOOP-583693	TL	13.50	14.00
91	HOLIDAY AHOY-568368	TL	12.50	13.00
91	HOLIDAY TREATS-581542	YR	17.50	18.00
91	HOLIDAY WING DING-574333	TL	23.00	23.00
91	IT'S TEA-LIGHTFUL-694789	TL	13.50	15.00
91	JUGGLIN' THE HOLIDAYS-587028	TL	13.00	13.00
91	LIGHTING THE WAY-588776	TL	20.00	20.00
91	MARILYN MONROE-583774	YR	20.00	20.00
91	MEOW MATES-576220	TL	12.00	12.00
91	NORTH POLE HERE I COME-574333	TL	23.00	23.00
91	OUR MOST PRECIOUS GIFT-585726	YR	17.50	18.00
91	PEDAL PUSHIN' SANTA-566098	TL	20.00	20.00
91	RUDOLPH-588784	TL	17.50	18.00
91	SANTA'S STEED-587044	YR	15.00	18.00
91	STARRY EYED SANTA-587176	TL	15.00	16.00
91	THINGS GO BETTER WITH COKE-580597	TL	17.00	18.00
91	TUBA TOTIN' TEDDY-568449	TL	15.00	16.00
91	WARMEST WISHES-573825	YR	17.50	25.00
92	A CHILD'S CHRISTMAS-586358	TL	25.00	25.00
92	A CHRISTMAS TOAST-588261	TL	20.00	20.00
92	A POUND OF GOOD CHEERS-582034	TL	17.50	18.00
92	A SURE SIGN OF CHRISTMAS-588857	TL	23.00	23.00
92	A WATCHFUL EYE-595713	YR	15.00	16.00
92	A-B-C-SON'S GREETINGS-588806	TL	16.50	17.00
92	BABY'S FIRST CHRISTMAS-586943	YR	12.50	13.00
92	BEGINNING TO LOOK/CHRISTMAS-588253	TL	15.00	16.00
92	BLESS OUR HOME-595772	YR	12.00	12.00
92	CARTIN' HOME HOLIDAY TREATS-832790	TL	13.50	14.00
92	CHECKIN' HIS LIST-595756	YR	12.50	13.00
92	CHRISTMAS BIZ-593168	TL	23.00	23.00
92	CHRISTMAS CAT NAPPIN'-595764	YR	12.00	12.00
92	CHRISTMAS CURE-ALLS-588938	TL	20.00	20.00
92	CHRISTMAS EVE-MERGENCY-588849	TL	27.00	27.00
92	CHRISTMAS IS IN THE AIR-831174	TL	25.00	25.00
92	CHRISTMAS LIFTS THE SPIRITS-582018	TL	25.00	25.00
92	CHRISTMAS TRIMMIN'-590932	TL	17.00	17.00
92	COLD, CRISP TASTE OF COKE, THE-583766	TL	17.00	17.00
92	DIAL 'S' FOR SANTA-589373	TL	25.00	25.00
92	FESTIVE FIDDLERS-586501	YR	20.00	20.00

YR	NAME	LIMIT	ISSUE	TREND
92	FESTIVE NEWSFLASH-588792	TL	17.50	18.00
92	FIRED UP FOR CHRISTMAS-595799	YR	12.00	12.00
92	FIRESIDE FRIENDS-588830	TL	20.00	20.00
92	GOOD CATCH-595721	YR	12.50	13.00
92	GUTEN CHEERS-587192	YR	23.00	23.00
92	HAVE A SOUP-ER CHRISTMAS-588911	TL	17.50	18.00
92	HOLIDAY TAKE-OUT-593508	YR	17.50	18.00
92	HOLIDAYS ARE A HIT, THE-581577	TL	17.50	18.00
92	HOLIDAYS GIVE ME A LIFT-588865	TL	30.00	30.00
92	HOPPY HOLIDAYS-588814	YR	13.50	14.00
92	LIGHTS...CAMERA...CHRISTMAS!-594369	TL	20.00	20.00
92	MC HO HO HO-585181	TL	23.00	23.00
92	MERRY KISSES-831166	TL	17.50	18.00
92	MERRY MISTLE TOAD-588288	TL	15.00	16.00
92	MOON WATCH-587184	TL	20.00	20.00
92	MUSIC MICE-TRO!-575143	TL	12.00	12.00
92	ON TARGET TWO-GETHER-575623	YR	17.00	17.00
92	PUT ON A HAPPY FACE-588237	TL	15.00	16.00
92	SMALL FRY'S FIRST CHRISTMAS-586749	TL	17.00	17.00
92	SPECIAL DELIVERY-832812	TL	12.00	12.00
92	SPECIAL DELIVERY-840440	YR	23.00	23.00
92	SPIRITED STALLION-594407	YR	15.00	16.00
92	SPREADING SWEET JOY-580465	YR	13.50	14.00
92	SUNDAE RIDE-583707	TL	20.00	20.00
92	SWINGIN' CHRISTMAS-584096	TL	15.00	16.00
92	TAKE A CHANCE ON THE HOLIDAYS-594075	TL	20.00	20.00
92	TEE-RIFIC HOLIDAYS-590827	TL	25.00	25.00
92	TIC-TAC-MISTLE-TOE-588296	YR	23.00	23.00
92	TIP TOP TIDINGS-581828	TL	13.00	13.00
92	TO A DEAR BABY-587168	YR	19.00	19.00
92	TOYFUL' RUDOLPH-593982	TL	23.00	23.00
92	TRUNK OF TREASURES-588636	YR	20.00	20.00
92	WARMTH OF THE SEASON, THE-586994	TL	20.00	20.00
92	WATCHING FOR SANTA-840432	TL	25.00	25.00
92	WEAR THE SEASON WITH A SMILE-595829	YR	10.00	10.00
92	WRAPPIN' UP WARM WISHES-593141	YR	17.50	18.00
92	YULE TIDE TOGETHER-588903	TL	20.00	20.00
93	25 POINTS FOR CHRISTMAS	OP	25.00	25.00
93	A BRIGHT IDEA	OP	23.00	23.00
93	A KICK OUT OF CHRISTMAS	OP	10.00	10.00
93	A MISTLE-TOW	OP	15.00	15.00
93	A PAUSE FOR CLAUS	OP	23.00	23.00
93	ALL YOU ADD IS LOVE	OP	19.00	19.00
93	ARIEL'S UNDER-THE-SEA TREE	OP	23.00	23.00
93	BABY'S FIRST CHRISTMAS	OP	17.50	18.00
93	BABY'S FIRST CHRISTMAS DINNER	OP	12.00	12.00
93	BEARLY BALANCED	OP	15.00	15.00
93	BORN TO SHOP	OP	27.00	27.00
93	CARVING CHRISTMAS WISHES	OP	25.00	25.00
93	CELEBRATING W/A SPLASH	OP	17.00	17.00
93	CHRISTMAS DANCER	OP	15.00	15.00
93	CHRISTMAS IN THE MAKING	OP	20.00	20.00
93	CHRISTMAS IS IN THE AIR	OP	25.00	25.00
93	CHRISTMAS KICKS	OP	17.50	18.00
93	CHRISTMAS MAIL CALL	OP	20.00	20.00
93	CHRISTMAS-TO-GO	OP	26.00	26.00
93	CLOWNIN' AROUND	OP	10.00	10.00
93	COOL YULE	OP	12.00	12.00
93	COUNTIN' ON A MERRY CHRISTMAS	OP	23.00	23.00
93	DELIVERED TO THE NICK IN TIME	OP	13.50	14.00
93	DESIGNED W/YOU IN MIND	OP	16.00	16.00
93	DREAM WHEELS	OP	30.00	30.00
93	DUCKING THE SEASON'S RUSH	OP	17.50	18.00
93	DUNK THE HALLS	OP	19.00	19.00
93	FAIREST ONE OF ALL, THE	OP	20.00	20.00
93	FESTIVE FIREMAN	OP	17.00	17.00
93	FOCUSING ON CHRISTMAS	OP	28.00	28.00
93	FOR A SHARP UNCLE	OP	10.00	10.00
93	FOR A STAR AUNT	OP	12.00	12.00
93	FRIENDS THROUGH THICK & THIN	OP	10.00	10.00
93	GOOFY ABOUT SKIING	OP	23.00	23.00
93	GRANDMA'S LIDDLE GRIDDLE	OP	10.00	10.00
93	HANGING OUT FOR THE HOLIDAYS	OP	15.00	15.00
93	HAPPILY EVER AFTER	OP	25.00	25.00
93	HAPPY HAUL-IDAYS	OP	30.00	30.00
93	HAVE A CHERRY CHRISTMAS, SISTER	OP	13.50	14.00
93	HAVE A COOL CHRISTMAS	OP	10.00	10.00
93	HAVE A DARN GOOD CHRISTMAS	OP	21.00	21.00
93	HAVE A HOLLY JELL-O CHRISTMAS	OP	20.00	20.00
93	HEART FILLED DREAMS	OP	10.00	10.00
93	HEARTS AGLOW	OP	19.00	19.00
93	HERE COMES RUDOLPH	OP	17.50	18.00
93	HERE COMES SANTA CLAWS	OP	23.00	23.00
93	HOLIDAY MEW-SIC	OP	20.00	20.00
93	HOLIDAY ORDERS	OP	20.00	20.00

YR	NAME	LIMIT	ISSUE	TREND
93	HOLIDAY TREASURES	OP	19.00	19.00
93	HOLIDAY WISHES	OP	17.50	18.00
93	HOME TWEET HOME	OP	10.00	10.00
93	HOT OFF THE PRESS	OP	28.00	28.00
93	I'M DREAMING OF A WHITE-OUT CHRISTMAS	OP	23.00	23.00
93	IT'S BEGINNING TO LOOK A LOT LIKE...	OP	23.00	23.00
93	JOYEUX NOEL	OP	25.00	25.00
93	LIGHT UP YOUR HOLIDAYS W/COKE	OP	28.00	28.00
93	LIGHTS..CAMERA..CHRISTMAS	OP	20.00	20.00
93	LOVE'S SWEET DANCE	OP	30.00	30.00
93	MAGIC CARPET RIDE	OP	25.00	25.00
93	MERRY CHRISTMAS, BABY	OP	10.00	10.00
93	MERRY CHRISTMAS, DAUGHTER	OP	20.00	20.00
93	MERRY MC-CHOO-CHOO	OP	30.00	30.00
93	MICKEY'S HOLIDAY TREASURE	OP	12.00	12.00
93	MY SPECIAL CHRISTMAS	OP	17.50	18.00
93	NOT A CREATURE WAS STIRRING...	OP	28.00	28.00
93	ON YOUR MARK, GET SET, IS THAT TO GO?	OP	13.50	14.00
93	PITTER-PATTER POST OFFICE	OP	20.00	20.00
93	PLANE O' HOLIDAY FUN	OP	28.00	28.00
93	POOL HALL-IDAYS	OP	19.00	19.00
93	ROCKIN' W/SANTA	OP	13.50	14.00
93	ROUNDIN' UP CHRISTMAS TOGETHER	OP	25.00	25.00
93	SANTA'S MAGIC RIDE	OP	24.00	24.00
93	SAY CHEESE	OP	13.50	14.00
93	SEE-SAW SWEETHEARTS	OP	10.00	10.00
93	SEEING IS BELIEVING	OP	20.00	20.00
93	SLEDDIN' MR. SNOWMAN	OP	13.00	13.00
93	SLIMMIN' SANTA	OP	19.00	19.00
93	SMOOTH MOVE, MOM	OP	20.00	20.00
93	SNEAKING A PEEK	OP	10.00	10.00
93	SPECIAL DELIVERY FOR SANTA	OP	10.00	10.00
93	SPOT OF LOVE	OP	20.00	20.00
93	SPREADING JOY	OP	28.00	28.00
93	SUGAR CHEF SHOPPE	OP	24.00	24.00
93	SWEET SEASONS EATINGS	OP	23.00	23.00
93	SWEET WHISKERED WISHES	OP	17.00	17.00
93	SWEETEST RIDE, THE	OP	19.00	19.00
93	TANGLED UP FOR CHRISTMAS	OP	14.50	15.00
93	TERRIFIC TOYS	OP	20.00	20.00
93	TIME FOR SANTA	OP	17.50	18.00
93	TO A GRADE A TEACHER	OP	10.00	10.00
93	TO MY GEM	OP	28.00	28.00
93	TOASTY TIDINGS	OP	20.00	20.00
93	TOOL TIME, YULE TIME	OP	19.00	19.00
93	TOP MARKS FOR TEACHER	OP	10.00	10.00
93	TOY TO THE WORLD	OP	25.00	25.00
93	TREASURE THE HOLIDAYS, MAN	OP	25.00	25.00
93	TREE FOR TWO	OP	17.50	18.00
93	TWAS THE NIGHT BEFORE CHRISTMAS	OP	23.00	23.00
93	WARM & HEARTY WISHES	OP	17.50	18.00
93	WATCHING FOR SANTA	OP	25.00	25.00
94	'A' FOR SANTA	OP	17.50	18.00
94	A BOUGH FOR BELLE!	OP	19.00	19.00
94	A CHRISTMAS TAIL	OP	20.00	20.00
94	A HOLIDAY OPPORTUNITY	OP	20.00	20.00
94	A REAL BOY FOR CHRISTMAS	OP	15.00	15.00
94	A SIGN OF PEACE	OP	19.00	19.00
94	AHOY JOY!	OP	20.00	20.00
94	ALMOST TIME FOR SANTA	OP	25.00	25.00
94	ANSWERING CHRISTMAS WISHES	OP	17.50	18.00
94	ARIEL'S CHRISTMAS SURPRISE!	OP	20.00	20.00
94	BUBBLIN' W/JOY	OP	12.50	13.00
94	BUILDING A SEW-MAN	OP	19.00	19.00
94	BUNDLE OF JOY	OP	10.00	10.00
94	BUTTONS 'N' BOW BOUTIQUE	OP	23.00	23.00
94	CHIMINY CHEER	OP	23.00	23.00
94	CHRISTMAS CROSSROADS	OP	20.00	20.00
94	CHRISTMAS CRUISIN'	OP	23.00	23.00
94	CHRISTMAS CUSTOMS	10000	17.50	18.00
94	CHRISTMAS FISHES FROM SANTA PAWS	OP	19.00	19.00
94	CHRISTMAS FLY-BY	OP	15.00	15.00
94	CHRISTMAS SWISHES	OP	17.50	18.00
94	CHRISTMAS TEE TIME	OP	25.00	25.00
94	CHRISTMAS TWO-GETHER	OP	12.50	13.00
94	COCOA 'N' KISSES FOR SANTA	OP	23.00	23.00
94	COOL CRUISE	19640	20.00	20.00
94	COZY CANDLELIGHT DINNER	OP	25.00	25.00
94	ESPECIALLY FOR YOU	OP	28.00	28.00
94	EXERCISING GOOD TASTE	OP	17.50	18.00
94	FEATURED PRESENTATION	OP	20.00	20.00
94	FINE FEATHERED FESTIVITIES	OP	23.00	23.00
94	FINISHING FIRST	OP	20.00	20.00
94	FROM OUR HOUSE TO YOURS	OP	25.00	25.00
94	GALIANT GREETING	OP	20.00	20.00

YR	NAME	LIMIT	ISSUE	TREND
94	GOOD FORTUNE TO YOU	OP	25.00	25.00
94	GOOD FRIENDS ARE FOREVER	OP	13.50	14.00
94	GOOD THINGS CROP UP AT CHRISTMAS	OP	25.00	25.00
94	GOOD TIDINGS, TIDINGS, TIDINGS...	OP	20.00	20.00
94	GOOFY DELIVERY	OP	23.00	23.00
94	GRANDMAS ARE SEW SPECIAL	OP	12.50	13.00
94	HAND-TOSSED TIDINGS	OP	17.50	18.00
94	HANDLE W/CARE	OP	20.00	20.00
94	HAPPY HOWL-IDAYS	OP	23.00	23.00
94	HAVE A BALL AT CHRISTMAS	OP	15.00	15.00
94	HAVE A MERRY DAIRY CHRISTMAS	OP	23.00	23.00
94	HAVE A TOTEM-LY TERRIFIC CHRISTMAS	OP	30.00	30.00
94	HOLIDAY CHEW-CHEW	OP	23.00	23.00
94	HOLIDAY FREEZER TEASER	OP	25.00	25.00
94	HOLIDAY HONEYS	OP	20.00	20.00
94	HOLIDAY SHOW-STOPPER	OP	15.00	15.00
94	HOLIDAY STARS	OP	20.00	20.00
94	I CAN BEAR-LY WAIT FOR A COKE	OP	19.00	19.00
94	JOY FROM HEAR TO HOSE	OP	15.00	15.00
94	L'IL STOCKING STUFFER	OP	17.50	18.00
94	LATEST MEWS FROM HOME, THE	OP	16.00	16.00
94	LATEST SCOOP FROM SANTA, THE	OP	19.00	19.00
94	MELTED MY HEART	OP	15.00	15.00
94	MERRY CHRISTMAS TOOL YOU, DAD	OP	23.00	23.00
94	MERRY LITTLE TWO-STEP	OP	12.50	13.00
94	MERRY MEMO-RIES	OP	23.00	23.00
94	MERRY MENAGE	OP	20.00	20.00
94	MERRY MISCHIEF	OP	15.00	15.00
94	MERRY REINDEER RIDE	OP	20.00	20.00
94	MINNIE'S HOLIDAY TREASURE	OP	12.00	12.00
94	NUTCRACKER SWEETHEART	OP	15.00	15.00
94	ON THE ROAD W/COKE	OP	25.00	25.00
94	ONCE UPON A TIME	OP	15.00	15.00
94	PEACE ON EARTH 132942	OP	12.50	13.00
94	PEACE ON EARTHWORM	OP	20.00	20.00
94	PICTURE PERFECT CHRISTMAS	OP	15.00	15.00
94	PURDY PACKAGES, PARDNER!	OP	20.00	20.00
94	PURE CHRISTMAS PLEASURE	OP	20.00	20.00
94	ROCKIN' RANGER	OP	25.00	25.00
94	SANTA CLAUS IS COMIN'	OP	20.00	20.00
94	SANTA DELIVERS	OP	12.00	12.00
94	SANTA' S SING-A-LONG	OP	20.00	20.00
94	SANTA' SECRET TEST DRIVE	OP	20.00	20.00
94	SANTA'S GINGER-BRED DOE	OP	15.00	1500
94	SANTA'S L'IL HELPER	OP	12.50	13.00
94	SANTA...PHONE HOME	OP	25.00	25.00
94	SANTA..YOU'RE THE POPS!	OP	23.00	23.00
94	SEASONED W/LOVE	OP	23.00	23.00
94	SKI-SON'S GREETINGS	OP	20.00	20.00
94	SPECIAL DELIVERY	OP	20.00	20.00
94	SUGAR 'N SPICE FOR SOMEONE NICE	OP	30.00	30.00
94	SWEET DREAMS	OP	12.50	13.00
94	SWEET GREETINGS	OP	12.50	13.00
94	SWEETS FOR MY SWEETIE	OP	15.00	15.00
94	TEED-OFF DONALD	OP	15.00	15.00
94	TO COIN A PHRASE, MERRY CHRISTMAS	OP	20.00	20.00
94	TO MY FAVORITE V.I.P.	OP	20.00	20.00
94	TO THE SWEETEST BABY	OP	19.00	19.00
94	TOY TINKER TOPPER	OP	20.00	20.00
94	TWAS THE NITE BEFORE CHRISTMAS	OP	19.00	19.00
94	WAY TO A MOUSE'S HEART, THE	OP	15.00	15.00
94	WHAT'S SHAKIN' FOR CHRISTMAS	OP	19.00	19.00
94	WISHING UPON A STAR	OP	19.00	19.00
94	WISHING YOU WELL AT CHRISTMAS	OP	25.00	25.00
94	YOU'RE A WHEEL COOL BROTHER	OP	23.00	23.00
94	YOU'RE A WINNER SON!	OP	19.00	19.00
94	YULE FUEL	OP	20.00	20.00
94	YULETIDE YUMMIES	OP	20.00	20.00
95	1955 BLACK FORD THUNDERBIRD 146838	OP	20.00	20.00
95	1955 RED FORD THUNDERBIRD 128821	19550	20.00	20.00
95	1956 FORD F-100 TRUCK 128813	YR	25.00	25.00
95	1957 CHEVY BEL AIR 128848	YR	20.00	20.00
95	1959 CADILLAC ELDORADO 132705	YR	20.00	20.00
95	1965 CHEVROLET CORVETTE STINGRAY 128856	YR	20.00	20.00
95	A CAROUSEL FOR ARIEL 142212	YR	17.50	18.00
95	A LITTLE SOMETHING EXTRA..EXTRA 137251	10000	25.00	25.00
95	A SIP OF GOOD MEASURE 139610	YR	17.50	18.00
95	A WELL BALANCED MEAL FOR SANTA 4TH & FINAL 592633	OP	17.50	18.00
95	ABOVE THE CROWD-R.MCDONALD HOUSE 129089	YR	20.00	20.00
95	ALL TUCKED IN 139734	YR	15.00	15.00
95	BUBBLIN' W/JOY 136581	YR	15.00	15.00
95	CHOC FULL OF WISHES 128945	YR	20.00	20.00
95	CHRISTMAS BELLE 142182	YR	20.00	20.00
95	CHRISTMAS EVE MISCHIEF 139726	YR	18.00	18.00
95	CHRISTMAS IN THE BAG 139645	YR	18.00	18.00

YR	NAME	LIMIT	ISSUE	TREND
95	CHRISTMAS VACATION 142158	YR	20.00	20.00
95	CRACKIN' A SMILE 129046	YR	17.50	18.00
95	DASHING THROUGH THE SNOW 128996	YR	20.00	20.00
95	DREAMIN OF THE ONE I LOVE 139696	YR	25.00	25.00
95	FRIENDS FUR-EVER	OP	20.00	20.00
95	FUN IN HAND 139661	YR	17.50	18.00
95	GOOFED-UP! 136697	YR	20.00	20.00
95	GOTTA HAVE A CLUE 139653	YR	20.00	20.00
95	HAPPY YULEGLIDE 129003	YR	17.50	18.00
95	HAVE A COKE & A SMILE 128953	YR	23.00	23.00
95	HO, HO, HOLE IN ONE! 111953	YR	20.00	20.00
95	HOLIDAY BIKE HIKE 111937	YR	20.00	20.00
95	HOLIDAY BOUND 136689	YR	20.00	20.00
95	HOLIDAY RIDE 14224	YR	17.50	18.00
95	HOME FOR THE HOWL-I-DAYS 111732	YR	20.00	20.00
95	HOW DO I LOVE THEE 7TH ISSUE 104949	YR	23.00	23.00
95	HUSTLING UP SOME CHEER 112038	YR	20.00	20.00
95	JUST FORE CHRISTMAS 142174	YR	15.00	15.00
95	LOOKING OUR HOLIDAY BEST 139750	YR	25.00	25.00
95	MAKE MINE A COKE 7TH ISSUE 128988	YR	25.00	25.00
95	MAKIN' TRACKS W/MICKEY 136662	YR	20.00	20.00
95	MAZE OF OUR LIVES, THE 139599	YR	17.50	18.00
95	MERRY CHRISTMAS TO ME 139742	YR	20.00	20.00
95	MERRY MCMEAL 6TH & FINAL 129070	YR	17.50	18.00
95	MERRY MONOPOLY 132969	YR	23.00	23.00
95	MICKEY AT THE HELM 132063	YR	17.50	18.00
95	MICKEY'S AIRMAIL 136670	YR	20.00	20.00
95	MINNIE'S MERRY CHRISTMAS 136611	YR	20.00	20.00
95	MOM'S TAXI/DODGE CARAVAN 128872	YR	25.00	25.00
95	NO TIME TO SPARE AT CHRISTMAS 111961	YR	20.00	20.00
95	NUTTY ABOUT CHRISTMAS 137030	YR	23.00	23.00
95	ON THE BALL AT CHRISTMAS	YR	15.00	15.00
95	ON THE BALL AT CHRISTMAS 136700	YR	15.00	15.00
95	PLANELY DELICIOUS 109665	YR	20.00	20.00
95	PUPPY LOVE	YR	17.50	18.00
95	RX:MAS GREETINGS 129054	YR	17.50	18.00
95	SALUTE' 3RD & FINAL 593133	YR	23.00	23.00
95	SANTA'S SPEEDWAY 129011	YR	20.00	20.00
95	SCORING BIG AT CHRISTMAS 112046	YR	20.00	20.00
95	SERVING UP THE BEST 3RD & FINAL 112054	YR	17.50	18.00
95	SNACK THAT HITS THE SPOT	YR	15.00	15.00
95	SNEAKING A PEEK 139718	YR	23.00	23.00
95	STARRING ROLL AT CHRISTMAS 137057	YR	17.50	18.00
95	SWEET ON YOU 136719	YR	23.00	23.00
95	SWISHING YOU SWEET GREETINGS 105201	YR	20.00	20.00
95	TAIL WAGGIN' WISHES 142190	YR	17.50	18.00
95	TIME FOR REFRESHMENTS 111872	YR	20.00	20.00
95	TINKERTOY JOY 137049	YR	20.00	20.00
95	TOYS TO TREASURE 6TH ISSUE 112119	YR	20.00	20.00
95	TRUCKIN'	YR	25.00	25.00
95	TRUNK FULL OF TREASURES 128961	20000	25.00	25.00
95	WISHING YOU A PERFECT HOLIDAY	OP	5.00	5.00
95	YOU'RE MY CUP OF TEA 129038	YR	20.00	20.00
95	YULE LOG ON FOR CHRISTMAS CHEER 122513	YR	20.00	20.00
95	YULE TIDE PRANCER 6TH & FINAL 588660	YR	15.00	15.00
96	#1 COACH 168440	YR	9.00	9.00
96	'TIS THE SEASON TO BE NUTTY 175234	YR	18.00	18.00
96	100 YEARS..AND STILL ON A ROLL 173770	19960	18.00	18.00
96	1956 CHEVROLET CORVETTE 175269	19560	23.00	23.00
96	1965 FORD MUSTANG 173800	YR	23.00	23.00
96	A BOOT FULL OF CHEER 166952	YR	20.00	20.00
96	A CENTURY OF GOOD TASTE 8TH & FINAL 166774	YR	20.00	20.00
96	A MAGIC MOMENT 172197	YR	18.00	18.00
96	A PICTURE PERFECT PAIR 8TH ISSUE 167002	YR	25.00	25.00
96	A SPLASH OF COOL YULE 213713	YR	20.00	20.00
96	A WORLD OF GOOD TASTE 175420	20000	20.00	20.00
96	A-JOY MATIE, THROW ME A LIFESAVERS 166677	YR	20.00	20.00
96	ALL FIRED UP FOR CHRISTMAS 168475	YR	25.00	25.00
96	AN APPOINTMENT WITH SANTA 166979	YR	20.00	20.00
96	BABY'S FIRST CHRISTMAS 166944	YR	9.00	9.00
96	CAMPAIGN FOR CHRISTMAS 176818	19960	18.00	18.00
96	CHEVY BLAZER 167223	YR	23.00	23.00
96	DELIVERING HOLIDAY CHEERS 177318	YR	25.00	25.00
96	DODGE RAM TRUCK 167258	YR	23.00	23.00
96	DOWNHILL DELIVERY 167053	YR	25.00	25.00
96	FORD EXPLORER 167231	YR	23.00	23.00
96	GIFTS FROM MICKEY 168467	YR	20.00	20.00
96	GOIN' FISHIN' 168459	YR	23.00	23.00
96	HAPPY'S HOLIDAY 172200	YR	18.00	18.00
96	HAVE A CRACKER JACK CHRISTMAS 172979	YR	25.00	25.00
96	HOLD ON, SANTA! 1ST ISSUE 167088	YR	25.00	25.00
96	HOLIDAY IN BLOOM 172669	YR	25.00	25.00
96	HOLIDAY TINKERTOY TREE 166995	YR	17.50	18.00
96	I LOVE DAD 166901	YR	9.00	9.00
96	I LOVE GRANDMA 166898	YR	9.00	9.00

YR	NAME	LIMIT	ISSUE	TREND
96	I LOVE MOM 166928	YR	9.00	9.00
96	I LOVE MY DAUGHTER 166863	YR	9.00	9.00
96	I LOVE MY GODCHILD 166944	YR	9.00	9.00
96	I LOVE MY SON 168432	YR	9.00	9.00
96	IN STORE FOR MORE 167134	YR	25.00	25.00
96	IN-LINE TO HELP SANTA 166855	YR	20.00	20.00
96	IT'S PLANE TO SEE..COKE IS IT 166723	YR	25.00	25.00
96	IT'S TIME FOR CHRISTMAS 1ST ISSUE 175455	YR	25.00	25.00
96	JEEP GRAND CHEROKEE 167215	YR	23.00	23.00
96	LIFE'S SWEET CHOICES 172634	YR	25.00	25.00
96	MINNIE'S MALL HAUL 168491	YR	25.00	25.00
96	MOTORCYCLE MICKEY 136654	YR	25.00	25.00
96	ON A ROLL WITH DIET COKE 167061	YR	20.00	20.00
96	PLANE CRAZY 168386	YR	23.00	23.00
96	PLAY IT AGAIN, NICK 166987	YR	17.50	18.00
96	SANTA'S ON THE LINE 167037	YR	25.00	25.00
96	SERVIN' UP JOY 166847	YR	20.00	20.00
96	SITTING PRETTY 172219	YR	18.00	18.00
96	SPECIAL BEAR-LIVERY 129062	YR	15.00	15.00
96	SPICE UP THE SEASON 1ST ISSUE 111724	YR	20.00	20.00
96	STEPPIN' WITH MINNIE 136603	YR	13.50	14.00
96	SUMMONS FOR A MERRY CHRISTMAS 166960	YR	23.00	23.00
96	SWINGING ON A STAR 166642	YR	20.00	20.00
96	TAILS A'WAGON 167126	YR	20.00	20.00
96	THOU ART MY LAMP, O LORD 173894	YR	25.00	25.00
96	TOYLAND, TOYLAND 7TH ISSUE 173878	YR	20.00	20.00
96	TREES TO PLEASE 168386	YR	25.00	25.00

G. ARMGARDT — TREASURY OF CHRISTMAS

YR	NAME	LIMIT	ISSUE	TREND
90	JINGLE BELL ROCK 1990-563390	YR	13.50	18.00

C. BAKER — TREASURY OF CHRISTMAS

YR	NAME	LIMIT	ISSUE	TREND
89	HOLLY-FAIRY-565199	YR	15.00	35.00
90	CHRISTMAS TREE FAIRY, THE-565202	YR	15.00	25.00

S. BUTCHER — TREASURY OF CHRISTMAS

YR	NAME	LIMIT	ISSUE	TREND
94	A CHILD IS BORN	OP	25.00	25.00
94	BABY'S FIRST CHRISTMAS	OP	20.00	20.00
94	DROPPING IN FOR THE HOLIDAYS	OP	20.00	20.00
94	DRUMMING UP A SEASON OF JOY	OP	19.00	19.00
94	FRIENDSHIPS WARM THE HOLIDAYS	OP	20.00	20.00
94	MAY ALL YOUR WISHES COME TRUE	OP	20.00	20.00
94	MAY YOUR HOLIDAY BE BRIGHTENED W/LOVE	OP	15.00	15.00
94	OUR FIRST CHRISTMAS TOGETHER	OP	25.00	25.00
94	RINGING UP HOLIDAY WISHES	OP	19.00	19.00
94	SENDING YOU A SEASON'S GREETING	OP	25.00	25.00
94	SWEET HOLIDAYS	OP	11.00	11.00
94	TIS THE SEASON TO GO SHOPPING	OP	23.00	23.00
95	BABY'S FIRST CHRISTMAS 125946	OP	15.00	15.00
95	BABY'S FIRST CHRISTMAS125954	OP	15.00	15.00
95	BRINGING HOLIDAY WISHES TO YOU 125911	OP	23.00	23.00
95	FRIENDS ARE THE GREATEST TREASURE 125962	20000	25.00	25.00
95	HAPPY BIRTHDAY JESUS 125857	OP	15.00	15.00
95	I'M IN A SPIN OVER YOU 125873	OP	15.00	15.00
95	LET'S SNUGGLE TOGETHER FOR CHRISTMAS 125865	OP	15.00	15.00
95	OUR FIRST CHRISTMAS TOGETHER 125881	OP	23.00	23.00
95	PRETTY UP FOR THE HOLIDAYS 125830	OP	20.00	20.00
95	TWINKLE, TWINKLE CHRISTMAS STAR 125903	OP	17.50	18.00
95	YOU BRING THE LOVE TO CHRISTMAS 125849	OP	15.00	15.00
95	YOU PULL THE STRINGS TO MY HEART 125938	OP	20.00	20.00

M. COOK — TREASURY OF CHRISTMAS

YR	NAME	LIMIT	ISSUE	TREND
88	DAIRY CHRISTMAS-557501	TL	10.00	15.00
89	CHRISTMAS COOK-OUT-561045	TL	9.00	12.00
89	DECK THE HOGS-565490	TL	12.00	16.00
89	FELIZ NAVIDAD! 1989-564842	YR	11.00	20.00
89	PINATA RIDIN'-565504	TL	11.00	18.00
89	SCRUB-A-DUB CHIPMUNK-561037	TL	8.00	10.00
89	SPREADING CHRISTMAS JOY-564850	TL	10.00	10.00
89	TOP OF THE CLASS-565237	TL	11.00	11.00
90	CHRISTMAS IS MAGIC-564826	TL	10.00	10.00
90	FLEECE NAVIDAD-571903	TL	13.50	14.00
90	HAVE A NAVAHO-HO-HO 1990-571970	YR	15.00	18.00
90	LIGHTING UP CHRISTMAS-564834	TL	10.00	14.00
90	MERRY MOUSTRONAUTS-573558	TL	20.00	20.00
90	REELING IN THE HOLIDAYS-560405	TL	8.00	10.00
91	CHRISTMAS TO GO-580600	YR	23.00	23.00
91	DOUBLE SCOOP SNOWMOUSE-564796	TL	13.50	14.00
91	HAVE A MARIACHI CHRISTMAS-580619	TL	13.50	14.00
91	WALKIN' WITH MY BABY-561029	TL	10.00	10.00
92	LA LUMINARIA-586579	TL	13.50	14.00

J. DAVIS — TREASURY OF CHRISTMAS

YR	NAME	LIMIT	ISSUE	TREND
82	HOLIDAY SKIER-E-6954	TL	7.00	30.00
83	GARFIELD CUTS THE ICE-E-8771	TL	6.00	45.00
83	STOCKING FULL FOR 1983-E-8773	YR	8.00	45.00
84	DEER! ODIE-E6226	TL	6.00	40.00
84	FUN IN SANTA'S SLEIGH-E-6225	TL	12.00	35.00
84	GARFIELD HARK! THE HERALD ANGEL-E-6224	TL	7.50	45.00
84	GARFIELD THE SNOW CAT-E-6227	TL	12.00	12.00

YR	NAME	LIMIT	ISSUE	TREND
84	STOCKING FULL FOR 1984-E-8773	YR	6.00	35.00
85	GARFIELD-IN-THE-BOX-56189	YR	6.50	7.00
85	HOPPY CHRISTMAS-56154	YR	8.50	30.00
85	MERRY CHRISTMAS MOTHER-56146	YR	8.50	9.00
85	MERRY CHRISTMAS TEACHER-56170	YR	6.00	6.00
85	NORTH POLE EXPRESS-56138	YR	12.00	35.00
85	SKI TIME-56111	YR	13.00	40.00
86	GIFT WRAP OLDIE-553611	YR	7.00	7.00
86	LIGHTEN UP!-553603	TL	10.00	22.00
87	GARFIELD MERRY KISSMAS-555215	TL	8.50	20.00
87	GARFIELD SUGAR PLUM FAIRY-556009	TL	8.50	25.00
87	GARFIELD THE NUTCRACKER-556017	TL	8.50	15.00
88	DEER GARFIELD-558702	TL	12.00	18.00
88	GARFIELD BAGS O'FUN-558761	YR	3.30	5.00
88	NIGHT-WATCH CAT-558362	TL	13.00	20.00
88	SPECIAL DELIVERY-558699	TL	9.00	16.00
89	A CHAINS OF PACE FOR ODIE-563269	TL	12.00	12.00
89	GOD BLESS US EVERYONE-563242	TL	13.50	14.00
89	HO-HO HOLIDAY SCROOGE-563234	TL	13.50	14.00
89	JOY RIDIN'-563463	TL	15.00	18.00
89	MINE, ALL MINE!-564079	YR	15.00	25.00
89	SCROOGE WITH THE SPIRIT-563250	TL	13.50	15.00
90	AN APPLE A DAY-572594	TL	12.00	15.00
90	DEAR SANTA-572608	TL	17.00	17.00
90	FROSTY GARFIELD 1990-572551	YR	13.50	20.00
90	GARFIELD NFL ATLANTA FALCONS-573159	TL	12.50	13.00
90	GARFIELD NFL BUFFALO BILLS-573108	TL	12.50	13.00
90	GARFIELD NFL CHICAGO BEARS-573248	TL	12.50	13.00
90	GARFIELD NFL CINCINNATI BENGALS-573000	TL	15.50	13.00
90	GARFIELD NFL CLEVELAND BROWNS-573019	TL	12.50	13.00
90	GARFIELD NFL DALLAS COWBOYS-573183	TL	12.50	13.00
90	GARFIELD NFL DENVER BRONCOS-573043	TL	12.50	13.00
90	GARFIELD NFL DETROIT LIONS-573256	TL	12.50	13.00
90	GARFIELD NFL GREEN BAY PACKERS-573264	TL	12.50	13.00
90	GARFIELD NFL HOUSTON OILERS-573027	TL	12.50	13.00
90	GARFIELD NFL INDIANAPOLIS COLTS-573116	TL	12.50	13.00
90	GARFIELD NFL KANSAS CITY CHIEFS-573051	TL	12.50	13.00
90	GARFIELD NFL LOS ANGELES RAIDERS-573078	TL	12.50	13.00
90	GARFIELD NFL LOS ANGELES RAMS-572764	TL	12.50	13.00
90	GARFIELD NFL MIAMI DOLPHINS-573124	TL	12.50	13.00
90	GARFIELD NFL MINNESOTA VIKINGS-573272	TL	12.50	13.00
90	GARFIELD NFL NEW ENGLAND PATRIOTS-573132	TL	12.50	13.00
90	GARFIELD NFL NEW ORLEANS SAINTS-573167	TL	12.50	13.00
90	GARFIELD NFL NEW YORK GIANTS-573191	TL	12.50	13.00
90	GARFIELD NFL NEW YORK JETS-573140	TL	12.50	13.00
90	GARFIELD NFL PHILADELPHIA EAGLES-573205	TL	12.50	13.00
90	GARFIELD NFL PHOENIX CARDINALS-573213	TL	12.50	13.00
90	GARFIELD NFL PITTSBURGH STEELERS-573035	TL	12.50	13.00
90	GARFIELD NFL SAN DIEGO CHARGERS-573086	TL	12.50	13.00
90	GARFIELD NFL SAN FRANCISCO 49ERS-573175	TL	12.50	13.00
90	GARFIELD NFL SEATTLE SEAHAWKS-573094	TL	12.50	13.00
90	GARFIELD NFL TAMPA BAY BUCCANEERS-573280	TL	12.50	13.00
90	GARFIELD NFL WASHINGTON REDSKINS-573221	TL	12.50	13.00
90	LITTLE RED RIDING CAT-572632	YR	13.50	18.00
90	OH SHOOSH!-572624	TL	17.00	17.00
90	OVER THE ROOFTOPS-572721	TL	17.50	18.00
90	POP GOES THE ODIE-572578	TL	15.00	16.00
90	TROUBLE ON WHEELS-564052	TL	20.00	20.00
91	ALL DECKED OUT-572659	TL	13.50	14.00
91	HAVE A BALL THIS CHRISTMAS-572616	YR	15.00	20.00
91	HERE COMES SANTA PAWS-572535	TL	20.00	20.00
91	HOLIDAY HIDEOUT-585270	TL	15.00	16.00
91	HOT STUFF SANTA-573523	TL	25.00	30.00
91	MERRY CHRISTMAS GO-ROUND-585203	TL	20.00	20.00
91	PINOCCHIO-577391	TL	15.00	16.00
91	STRAIGHT TO SANTA-830534	TL	13.50	14.00
91	SWEET BEAMS-572586	TL	13.50	14.00
92	4 X 4 HOLIDAY FUN-580783	TL	20.00	20.00
92	A ROCKIN' GARFIELD CHRISTMAS-572527	TL	17.50	18.00
92	FAST TRACK CAT-585289	TL	17.50	18.00
92	HOLIDAY CAT NAPPING-585319	TL	20.00	20.00
92	HOLIDAY ON ICE-585254	TL	17.50	17.00
92	RING MY BELL-580740	YR	13.50	14.00
93	BAH HUMBUG	OP	15.00	15.00
93	GRADE A WISHES FROM GARFIELD	OP	20.00	20.00
94	MINE, MINE, MINE	OP	20.00	20.00

T. FRALEY   **TREASURY OF CHRISTMAS**

YR	NAME	LIMIT	ISSUE	TREND
96	TOBIN'S DEBUT DANCER 1ST ISSUE 173886	20000	20.00	20.00

M. GILMORE   **TREASURY OF CHRISTMAS**

YR	NAME	LIMIT	ISSUE	TREND
82	CRESCENT SANTA-E-6950	TL	10.00	65.00
82	DEAR SANTA-E-6959	TL	10.00	15.00
84	BABY'S FIRST CHRISTMAS 1984-E-6212	YR	10.00	10.00
85	BABY'S FIRST CHRISTMAS 1985-56014	YR	6.00	6.00
85	MERRY CHRISTMAS GODCHILD-55832	TL	8.00	30.00
86	BABY BEAR SLEIGH-551651	TL	9.00	30.00

YR	NAME	LIMIT	ISSUE	TREND
86	BABY'S FIRST CHRISTMAS 1986-551678	YR	10.00	15.00
86	CAROUSEL UNICORN-551252	TL	12.00	75.00
86	MERRY CHRISTMAS-551341	TL	8.00	75.00
86	TIME FOR CHRISTMAS-551325	TL	13.00	25.00
87	BABY'S FIRST CHRISTMAS 1987-556238	YR	10.00	25.00
87	CAROUSEL LION-556025	TL	12.00	25.00
87	HOME SWEET HOME-556033	TL	15.00	55.00
87	PARTRIDGE IN A PEAR TREE-556173	TL	9.00	33.00
87	TEDDY'S STOCKING-555940	TL	10.00	20.00
87	THREE FRENCH HENS-556440	TL	9.00	25.00
87	TWINKLE BEAR-556572	TL	8.00	15.00
87	TWO TURTLEDOVES-556432	TL	9.00	33.00
88	1ST CHRISTMAS TOGETHER-554537	TL	15.00	16.00
88	A CHIPMUNK HOLIDAY-554898	TL	11.00	18.00
88	A MOUSE CHECK-554553	TL	13.50	18.00
88	AIRMAIL FOR TEACHER-489425	TL	13.50	25.00
88	AN EYE ON CHRISTMAS-554545	TL	23.00	35.00
88	BABY'S FIRST CHRISTMAS 1988-554936	YR	10.00	16.00
88	CHRISTMAS TRADITION-558400	TL	10.00	18.00
88	FIVE GOLDEN RINGS-559121	TL	11.00	30.00
88	FOREVER FRIENDS-554626	TL	12.00	27.00
88	FOUR CALLING BIRDS-556459	TL	11.00	30.00
88	LI'L DRUMMER BEAR-554952	TL	12.00	20.00
88	NORTH POLE LINEMAN-558834	TL	10.00	20.00
88	SIX GEESE A-LAYING-559148	TL	11.00	30.00
88	TWO FOR TEA-559776	TL	20.00	30.00
89	ALL SET FOR SANTA-563080	TL	17.50	18.00
89	BABY'S FIRST CHRISTMAS 1989-562815	YR	10.00	13.00
89	BY THE LIGHT OF THE MOON-563005	TL	12.00	15.00
89	CAUGHT IN THE ACT-830046	TL	12.50	13.00
89	CHESTNUTS ROASTIN'-562912	TL	13.00	28.00
89	CHRISTMAS COOKIN'-563048	TL	23.00	25.00
89	EIGHT MAIDS A-MILKING-562750	TL	12.00	18.00
89	MERRY CHRISTMAS POPS-562971	TL	12.00	24.00
89	MISTLE-TOAST-1989-562963	YR	15.00	21.00
89	NINE DANCERS DANCING-562769	TL	15.00	18.00
89	OLD TOWN'S CHURCH-554871	TL	17.50	18.00
89	READIN' & RIDIN'-830054	TL	13.50	14.00
89	SARDINE EXPRESS-554588	TL	17.50	20.00
89	SEVEN SWANS A-SWIMMING-562742	TL	12.00	12.00
89	STICKIN' TO IT-563013	TL	10.00	16.00
89	TRAVELIN' TRIKE-562882	TL	15.00	16.00
90	A CAROLING WEE GO-573671	TL	12.00	12.00
90	ALL ABOARD-567671	TL	17.50	18.00
90	ALL EYE WANT FOR CHRISTMAS-573647	TL	28.00	28.00
90	BABY'S FIRST CHRISTMAS 1990-573973	YR	10.00	10.00
90	BABY'S FIRST CHRISTMAS 1990-573981	YR	12.00	14.00
90	DECK THE HALLS-573701	TL	23.00	23.00
90	ELEVEN DRUMMERS DRUMMING-573957	TL	15.00	16.00
90	FIRST CLASS CHRISTMAS-830038	TL	10.00	10.00
90	HAVE A COOL YULE-830496	TL	12.00	12.00
90	HERE'S LOOKING AT YOU-830259	TL	17.50	18.00
90	LITTLE JACK HORNER-574058	TL	17.50	18.00
90	MERRY MAILMAN-573698	TL	15.00	16.00
90	NORTH POLE OR BUST-562998	TL	25.00	25.00
90	OLD KING COLE-575682	TL	20.00	20.00
90	OLD MOTHER MOUSE-573922	TL	17.50	18.00
90	PROF. MICHAEL BEAR/ONE BEAR BAND-573663	TL	23.00	23.00
90	RAILROAD REPAIRS-573930	TL	12.50	13.00
90	SANTA'S SWEETS-563196	TL	20.00	20.00
90	STUCK ON YOU-573655	TL	12.50	13.00
90	SWEETEST GREETINGS 1990-830011	YR	10.00	15.00
90	TH-INK-IN' OF YOU-562920	TL	20.00	20.00
90	TWELVE PIPERS PIPING-573965	TL	15.00	16.00
90	WARMEST WISHES-573825	YR	17.50	25.00
90	YOU'RE WHEEL SPECIAL-573728	TL	15.00	16.00
90	YULETIDE RIDE 1990-577502	YR	13.50	22.00
91	A CHRISTMAS CAROL-583928	TL	23.00	23.00
91	A DECADE OF TREASURES-587052	YR	38.00	38.00
91	A QUARTER POUNDER WITH CHEER-581569	TL	20.00	20.00
91	A SONG FOR SANTA-573779	TL	25.00	25.00
91	AIMING FOR THE HOLIDAYS-830941	TL	12.00	12.00
91	CHRISTMAS CABOOSE-574856	TL	25.00	25.00
91	CHRISTMAS FILLS THE AIR-831921	TL	12.00	12.00
91	CHRISTMAS TRIMMINGS-575631	TL	17.00	17.00
91	COME LET US ADORE HIM-573736	TL	9.00	9.00
91	CRYSTAL BALL CHRISTMAS-575666	TL	23.00	23.00
91	DREAMIN' OF A WHITE CHRISTMAS-583669	TL	15.00	16.00
91	FINISHING TOUCH, THE-831530	YR	10.00	12.00
91	FIRED UP FOR CHRISTMAS-586587	TL	33.00	33.00
91	FITTIN' MITTENS-830976	TL	12.00	12.00
91	FOR A DOG-GONE GREAT UNCLE-586706	YR	12.00	12.00
91	FOR A PURR-FECT AUNT-586692	YR	12.00	12.00
91	FOR A PURR-FECT MOM-586641	YR	12.00	12.00
91	FOR A SPECIAL DAD-586668	YR	17.50	18.00

YR	NAME	LIMIT	ISSUE	TREND
91	FROM THE SAME MOLD-581798	TL	17.00	17.00
91	GUMBALL WIZARD-575658	TL	13.00	13.00
91	KURIOUS KITTY-573868	TL	17.50	19.00
91	LETTERS TO SANTA-830925	TL	15.00	16.00
91	LIGHTS..CAMERA..KISSMAS!-583626	YR	15.00	18.00
91	MARY, MARY QUITE CONTRARY-574066	TL	23.00	23.00
91	MERRY MILLIMETERS-583677	TL	17.00	17.00
91	MOON BEAM DREAMS-573760	TL	12.00	12.00
91	MR. MAILMOUSE-587109	TL	17.00	17.00
91	ODE TO JOY-830968	TL	10.00	10.00
91	ONE FOGGY CHRISTMAS EVE-586625	TL	30.00	30.00
91	PEDDLING FUN-586714	YR	16.00	16.00
91	PETER, PETER PUMPKIN EATER-574015	TL	20.00	20.00
91	SANTA DELIVERS LOVE-562904	TL	17.50	18.00
91	SANTA'S KEY MAN-830461	TL	11.00	11.00
91	SNEAKING SANTA'S SNACK-830933	TL	13.00	13.00
91	SPECIAL KEEPSAKES-586722	YR	13.50	14.00
91	SWEET STEED-583634	TL	15.00	16.00
91	THROUGH THE YEARS-574252	YR	17.50	18.00
91	TIE-DINGS OF JOY-830488	YR	12.00	12.00
91	TOM, TOM THE PIPER'S SON-575690	TL	15.00	16.00
91	WITH LOVE-586676	YR	13.00	13.00
92	A BOOT-IFUL CHRISTMAS-840165	YR	20.00	20.00
92	A CHRISTMAS YARN-593516	YR	20.00	20.00
92	A GOLD STAR FOR TEACHER-831948	TL	15.00	16.00
92	A MUG FULL OF LOVE-832928	YR	13.50	14.00
92	A TALL ORDER-832758	TL	12.00	12.00
92	BEARLY SLEEPY-578029	YR	17.50	18.00
92	BUBBLE BUDDY-586978	TL	13.50	14.00
92	CANDLELIGHT SERENADE-832766	TL	12.00	12.00
92	CATCH A FALLING STAR-583944	TL	15.00	16.00
92	CHRISTMAS NITE CAP-834424	TL	13.50	14.00
92	CHRISTOPHER COLUMOUSE-832782	YR	12.00	12.00
92	COZY CHRISTMAS CARRIAGE-586730	TL	23.00	23.00
92	FIREHOUSE FRIENDS-586951	YR	23.00	23.00
92	FUR-EVER FRIENDS-590797	TL	13.50	14.00
92	GINGER-BRED GREETING-831581	YR	12.00	12.00
92	HAVE A COOL CHRISTMAS-832944	YR	13.50	14.00
92	HOLIDAY GLOW PUPPET SHOW-832774	TL	15.00	16.00
92	HOLIDAY HAPPENINGS-588555	TL	30.00	30.00
92	HOLIDAY HONORS-833029	YR	15.00	16.00
92	HUMPTY DUMPTY-574244	TL	25.00	25.00
92	IT'S A GO FOR CHRISTMAS-587095	TL	15.00	16.00
92	KNITTEN' KITTENS-832952	YR	17.50	18.00
92	MAKING TRACKS TO SANTA-832804	TL	15.00	16.00
92	NORTH POLE PEPPERMINT PATROL-840157	TL	25.00	25.00
92	NUTCRACKER, THE-574023	TL	25.00	25.00
92	POPPIN' HOPPIN' HOLIDAYS-831263	YR	25.00	25.00
92	POST-MOUSTER GENERAL-587117	TL	20.00	20.00
92	QUEEN OF HEARTS-575712	TL	17.50	18.00
92	ROCK-A-BYE BABY-575704	TL	13.50	14.00
92	SANTA'S MIDNIGHT SNACK-588598	TL	20.00	20.00
92	SEED-SON'S GREETINGS-588571	TL	27.00	27.00
92	SEW CHRISTMASY-583820	TL	25.00	25.00
92	SWEET AS CANEBE-583642	TL	15.00	16.00
92	TANKFUL TIDINGS-831271	TL	30.00	30.00
92	THROUGH THE YEARS-586862	YR	17.50	18.00
92	TO THE POINT-831182	TL	13.50	14.00
92	WINDOW WISH LIST-586854	TL	30.00	30.00
95	4-ALARM CHRISTMAS 6TH & FINAL ISSUE 128767	OP	17.50	18.00
95	A THIMBLE OF THE SEASON 2ND ISSUE 137243	OP	23.00	23.00
95	BABY'S SWEET FEAST 3RD & FINAL 588733	OP	17.50	18.00
95	FILLED TO THE BRIM 3RD & FINAL 595039	OP	25.00	25.00
95	FIRST CLASS CHRISTMAS TR954	YR	22.50	23.00
95	SEA-SON'S GREETINGS, TEACHER 112070	OP	17.50	18.00
95	SIESTA SANTA 5TH & FINAL 112089	OP	25.00	25.00
95	SWEET HARMONY 3RD & FINAL 586773	OP	17.50	18.00
95	TO SANTA, POST HASTE 112151	OP	15.00	15.00
95	WE'VE SHARED SEW MUCH 9TH ISSUE 112097	OP	25.00	25.00
96	A CUP OF CHEER 10TH & FINAL 135070	YR	25.00	25.00

J. GROSSMAN — **TREASURY OF CHRISTMAS**

YR	NAME	LIMIT	ISSUE	TREND
86	SANTA CLAUS SHOPPE, THE- CIRCA 1905-551562	TL	8.00	18.00

K. HAHN — **TREASURY OF CHRISTMAS**

YR	NAME	LIMIT	ISSUE	TREND
89	FULL HOUSE MOUSE-565016	TL	13.50	22.00
89	I FEEL PRETTY-565024	TL	20.00	25.00
90	BABY'S CHRISTMAS FEAST-565040	TL	13.50	22.00
90	BUBBLE TROUBLE-575038	TL	20.00	20.00
90	CATCH OF THE DAY-575070	TL	25.00	25.00
90	COFFEE BREAK-564990	TL	15.00	16.00
90	DON'T OPEN 'TIL CHRISTMAS-575089	TL	16.50	17.00
90	I CAN'T WEIGHT TIL CHRISTMAS-575119	TL	17.50	18.00
90	SLOTS O LUCK-830518	TL	13.50	22.00
90	WARMEST WISHES-565032	TL	15.00	16.00
90	YIPPIE-I-YULETIDE-564982	TL	15.00	24.00
90	YOU'RE SEW SPECIAL-565008	YR	20.00	25.00

Angel Starcatcher *from Holly Adler's Holly Bearies Collection for Kurt S. Adler Inc., is an open edition piece that debuted in 1996.*

Betty Boop *wears a billowing scarlet dress and has side-glancing green eyes in this blown glass ornament from Kurt S. Adler Inc.'s Polonaise Collection.*

Beary Christmas, *a 1994 dated ornament from Enesco's Cherished Teddies Collection, has more than doubled in value.*

The first in the edition of Barbie ornaments for Hallmark, Barbie—Debut 1959 *honors the staying power of this all-glamour icon*

YR	NAME	LIMIT	ISSUE	TREND
91	A HOLIDAY SCENT STATION-575054	TL	15.00	16.00
91	BATHING BEAUTY-860581	TL	13.50	14.00
91	DECK THE HALLS-575127	TL	15.00	15.00
91	HATS OFF TO CHRISTMAS-586757	YR	23.00	23.00
91	MERRY MOTHER-TO-BE-575046	TL	13.50	14.00
91	TEA FOR TWO-573299	TL	30.00	30.00
92	CAMPIN' COMPANIONS-590282	TL	20.00	20.00
92	FRIENDSHIPS PRESERVED-586749	YR	23.00	23.00
92	JESUS LOVES ME-595837	YR	10.00	10.00
92	JOY TO THE WHIRLED-589551	TL	20.00	20.00
92	MERRY CHRISTMAS MOTHER EARTH-595810	YR	11.00	11.00
92	MERRY MAKE-OVER-589586	TL	20.00	20.00
92	SALUTE THE SEASON-595780	YR	12.00	12.00
92	SPINNING CHRISTMAS DREAMS-590908	TL	23.00	23.00
92	SQUIRRELIN' IT WAY-595748	YR	12.00	12.00
92	TREASURE THE EARTH-593826	TL	25.00	25.00
93	A TOAST LADLED W/LOVE	OP	15.00	15.00
93	DECEMBER 25..DEAR DIARY	OP	10.00	10.00
93	DO NOT OPEN 'TIL CHRISTMAS	OP	15.00	15.00
93	GOOD GROUNDS FOR FRIENDSHIP	OP	25.00	25.00
93	GREETINGS IN STEREO	OP	20.00	20.00
93	JEWEL BOX BALLET	OP	20.00	20.00
93	MICE CAPADES	OP	27.00	27.00
93	PAINT YOUR HOLIDAYS BRIGHT	OP	10.00	10.00
93	WHEEL MERRY WISHES	OP	15.00	15.00
93	YOU'RE A HIT W/ME, BROTHER	OP	10.00	10.00
94	BUILDING MEMORIES	OP	25.00	25.00
94	EXPECTING JOY	OP	12.50	13.00
94	FRIENDS ARE THE SPICE OF LIFE	OP	20.00	20.00
94	HAPPY HOLI-DATE	OP	23.00	23.00
94	HAVE A DINO-MITE CHRISTMAS	OP	19.00	19.00
94	HOLIDAY CATCH	OP	12.50	13.00
94	MERRY MISS MERRY	OP	12.00	12.00
94	O' COME ALL YE FAITHFUL	OP	15.00	15.00
94	ONE SMALL STEP...	19690	30.00	30.00
94	OPEN FOR BUSINESS	OP	17.50	18.00
94	RING IN THE HOLIDAYS	OP	12.50	13.00
95	CHRISTMAS FISHES, DAD 139629	OP	17.50	18.00
95	FRIENDSHIPS BLOOM THROUGH ALL SEASONS 6TH 132950	OP	23.00	23.00
95	GET IN THE SPIRIT...RECYCLE 7TH & FINAL 132918	YR	17.50	18.00
95	GOOD WILL TOWARD MEN 132942	19450	25.00	25.00
95	JACKPOT JOY! 7TH ISSUE 132896	OP	17.50	18.00
95	MISS MERRY'S SECRET 7TH ISSUE 132934	OP	20.00	20.00
95	NIGHT B 4 CHRISTMAS, THE 134848	OP	20.00	20.00
95	ON THE MOVE AT CHRISTMAS 142220	OP	17.50	18.00
96	15 YEARS OF HITS 175463	10000	25.00	25.00
96	CATCH OF THE HOLIDAY 132888	YR	20.00	20.00
96	DECKED OUT FOR CHRISTMAS 176796	YR	25.00	25.00
96	HAIR'S THE PLACE 173029	YR	25.00	25.00
96	HOLIDAY DREAMS OF GREEN 173797	YR	15.00	15.00
96	MERRY MANICURE 8TH ISSUE 173339	YR	25.00	25.00
96	SANTA'S SACKS 111945	YR	15.00	15.00
96	SEW DARN CUTE 3RD ISSUE 176761	YR	25.00	25.00
96	THERE'S A FRIENDSHIP BREWING 7TH ISSUE 167096	YR	25.00	25.00
96	TRACKING REINDEER PAUSE 173789	YR	25.00	25.00
J. HENSON			**TREASURY OF CHRISTMAS**	
84	MUPPET BABIES BABY'S/CHRISTMAS-E-6222	YR	10.00	60.00
84	MUPPET BABIES BABY'S/CHRISTMAS-E-6223	YR	10.00	60.00
J. JONIK			**TREASURY OF CHRISTMAS**	
89	STAR OF STARS-564389	TL	9.00	10.00
89	YULETIDE TREE HOUSE-564915	TL	20.00	22.00
90	HANG ONTO YOUR HAT-564397	TL	8.00	9.00
91	SANTA WINGS IT-573612	TL	13.00	13.00
92	JOLLY OL' GENT-585645	TL	13.50	14.00
R. MOREHEAD			**TREASURY OF CHRISTMAS**	
88	OLD FASHIONED ANGEL-559164	TL	12.50	15.00
88	PRETTY BABY-559156	TL	12.50	13.00
D. OLSEN			**TREASURY OF CHRISTMAS**	
94	FORMULA FOR LOVE	OP	10.00	10.00
D. PARKER			**TREASURY OF CHRISTMAS**	
88	BABY'S FIRST CHRISTMAS-558397	TL	16.00	25.00
J. PENCHOFF			**TREASURY OF CHRISTMAS**	
92	HEAVEN SENT-588423	TL	12.50	13.00
M. PETERS			**TREASURY OF CHRISTMAS**	
89	JUST WHAT I WANTED-563668	TL	13.50	14.00
90	FLEAS NAVIDAD-563978	TL	13.50	14.00
90	PUCKER UP!-563676	TL	11.00	11.00
90	TWEET GREETINGS-564044	TL	15.00	16.00
90	WHAT'S THE BRIGHT IDEA-563684	TL	13.50	14.00
91	DECK THE HALLS-860573	TL	12.00	12.00
M. RHYNER			**TREASURY OF CHRISTMAS**	
92	SPEEDIN' MR. SNOWMAN-595802	YR	12.00	12.00
L. RIGG			**TREASURY OF CHRISTMAS**	
85	CHRISTMAS PLANE RIDE-56049	TL	10.00	20.00

YR	NAME	LIMIT	ISSUE	TREND
86	LUCY & ME CHRISTMAS TREE-552542	TL	7.00	25.00
86	LUCY & ME SKI TIME-552658	TL	6.50	7.00
86	MERRY CHRISTMAS 1986-552186	YR	8.00	8.00
86	MERRY CHRISTMAS 1986-552534	YR	8.00	20.00
87	LUCY & ME ANGEL ON A CLOUD-555452	TL	12.00	20.00
87	LUCY & ME MAILBOX BEAR-556564	TL	3.00	5.00
87	LUCY & ME STORYBOOK BEAR-555444	TL	6.50	14.00
87	MERRY CHRISTMAS 1987-555428	TL	8.00	8.00
87	MERRY CHRISTMAS 1987-555436	YR	8.00	8.00
87	TIME FOR CHRISTMAS-555452	TL	12.00	20.00
88	JESTER BEAR-558222	TL	8.00	20.00
88	MERRY CHRISTMAS 1988-557595	YR	10.00	12.00
88	MERRY CHRISTMAS 1988-557609	YR	10.00	12.00
88	TEDDY BEAR GREETINGS-558214	TL	8.00	12.00
88	TOY CHEST KEEPSAKE-558206	TL	12.50	15.00
89	CHRISTMAS 1989-565210	YR	12.00	12.00
89	CHRISTMAS 1989-568325	YR	12.00	12.00
90	A SPOONFUL OF LOVE-568570	TL	10.00	10.00
90	BABY BEAR CHRISTMAS 1990-575860	YR	12.00	13.00
90	BEARING HOLIDAY WISHES-568619	TL	23.00	23.00
90	BEARY CHRISTMAS 576158	YR	12.00	15.00
90	CHRISTMAS SWINGTIME 1990-568597	TL	13.00	13.00
90	CHRISTMAS SWINGTIME 1990-568600	YR	13.00	13.00
91	BEARY MERRY MAILMAN-830151	TL	13.50	14.00
91	CHRISTMAS SWINGTIME 1991-576166	YR	13.00	15.00
91	CHRISTMAS SWINGTIME 1991-5761714	YR	13.00	15.00
91	CHRISTMAS TWO-GETHER-575615	TL	23.00	23.00
91	CRANK UP THE CAROLS-575887	TL	17.50	18.00
91	LOVE IS THE SECRET INGREDIENT-568562	TL	15.00	16.00
91	TIRE-D LITTLE BEAR-575852	YR	12.50	13.00
92	MOONLIGHT SWING-568627	TL	15.00	16.00
92	TASTY TIDINGS-575836	YR	13.50	14.00
G.G. SANTIAGO		**TREASURY OF CHRISTMAS**		
88	CHRISTMAS VACATION-558451	TL	8.00	15.00
88	CHRISTMAS WATCH-558443	TL	11.00	15.00
88	ICE FAIRY, THE-558516	TL	23.00	30.00
88	MOUSE UPON A PIPE-489220	TL	10.00	24.00
88	PARTY MOUSE-558435	TL	12.00	15.00
88	SANTA CLAUS BALLOON-489212	TL	10.00	16.00
88	STOCKING STORY-558419	TL	10.00	16.00
88	SWEET CHERUB-558478	TL	7.00	9.00
88	TIME OUT-558486	TL	11.00	27.00
88	WINTER TALE-558427	TL	6.00	19.00
89	HO! HO! YO-YO!-565105	YR	12.00	12.00
89	SPECIAL DELIVERY-565091	YR	12.00	20.00
89	WEIGHTIN' FOR SANTA-565148	TL	7.50	8.00
90	BUMPER CAR SANTA-565083	YR	20.00	25.00
N. TEIBER		**TREASURY OF CHRISTMAS**		
89	TEA FOR TWO-693758	TL	12.50	14.00
89	TEA TIME-694797	TL	12.50	14.00
90	FIREPLACE FROLIC-564435	TL	25.00	25.00
90	HOLIDAY TEA TOAST-694770	TL	13.50	14.00
T. WILSON		**TREASURY OF CHRISTMAS**		
90	A NIGHT BEFORE CHRISTMAS-572438	TL	17.50	18.00
90	CHEERS 1990-572411	YR	13.50	15.00
90	MERRY KISSMAS-572446	TL	10.00	10.00
91	RIS-SKI BUSINESS-576719	TL	10.00	10.00
92	FINISHING TOUCHES, THE-585610	TL	17.50	18.00
K. WISE		**TREASURY OF CHRISTMAS**		
89	HANGIN' IN THERE 1989-565598	YR	10.00	15.00
90	MEOW-Y CHRISTMAS 1990-565601	YR	10.00	12.00
S. ZIMNICKI		**TREASURY OF CHRISTMAS**		
89	BUNKIE-561835	TL	23.00	25.00
89	POPPER-561878	TL	12.00	15.00
89	SPARKLES-561843	TL	17.50	20.00
90	BLINKIE-570214	TL	15.00	16.00
90	SMITCH-570184	TL	23.00	23.00
90	TUMBLES 1990-566519	YR	16.00	22.00
90	TWIDDLES-566551	TL	15.00	16.00
90	TWINKLE & SPRINKLE-570206	TL	23.00	23.00
91	SNUFFY-566578	TL	17.50	19.00
91	STAMPER-830267	YR	13.50	15.00
92	CARVER-570192	YR	17.50	18.00
92	SPARKY & BUFFER-561851	TL	25.00	25.00
93	CHIMIER	OP	25.00	25.00
93	SPEEDY	OP	25.00	25.00
94	TOODLES	OP	25.00	25.00
*		**TREASURY OF CHRISTMAS COLLECTORS CLUB**		
93	CAN'T WEIGHT FOR THE HOLIDAYS-MOO	OP	19.00	19.00
93	TREASURE CARD, THE - SOM	OP	20.00	20.00
94	SPRY FRY - MOO	OP	15.00	15.00
95	BUTTONING UP OUR HOLIDAY BEST-MOO	YR	23.00	23.00
95	FIRST CLASS CHRISTMAS - MOO	YR	23.00	23.00
95	HOLIDAY HIGH-LIGHT- MOO	YR	15.00	15.00
95	THINGS GO BETTER WITH COKE TR951	YR	15.00	15.00

YR	NAME	LIMIT	ISSUE	TREND
96	COCA-COLA CHOO CHOO 1ST ISSUE TR961	YR	35.00	35.00
96	FRIENDS ARE TEA-RIFFIC TR962	YR	25.00	25.00
96	ON TRACK WITH COKE 2ND ISSUE TR963	YR	25.00	25.00
96	YO HO HOLIDAYS T0003	YR	*	20.00
96	YO HO HOLIDAYS T0103	YR	*	20.00

K. HAHN · TREASURY OF CHRISTMAS COLLECTORS CLUB

YR	NAME	LIMIT	ISSUE	TREND
93	TOGETHER WE CAN SHOOT FOR THE STARS-MOO	OP	17.50	19.00
94	SEEDLINGS GREETINGS-MOO	OP	23.00	23.00
95	YOU'RE THE PERFECT FIT T0002	YR	*	N/A
96	RIDING HIGH 1ST ISSUE TR964	YR	20.00	20.00

ERTL COLLECTIBLES
EPSTEIN/GAGE · CAT HALL OF FAME

YR	NAME	LIMIT	ISSUE	TREND
98	NUTCATTER BALLET-HERR DROSSELMEOWER	OP	15.00	15.00
98	NUTCATTER BALLET-MEWRIA	OP	15.00	15.00
98	NUTCATTER BALLET-MOTHER GINGER	OP	15.00	15.00
98	NUTCATTER BALLET-NUTCATTER PURRINCE	OP	15.00	15.00
98	NUTCATTER BALLET-RAT KING	OP	15.00	15.00
98	NUTCATTER BALLET-SUGAR PLUM FURRY	OP	15.00	15.00

L. DAVIS · SPARROWSVILLE

YR	NAME	LIMIT	ISSUE	TREND
97	BACHELOR PAD	OP	17.00	17.00
97	COZY CABIN	OP	17.00	17.00
97	HAYLOFT, THE	OP	17.00	17.00
97	HEARTHSIDE MANOR	OP	17.00	17.00
97	HOME SWEET HOME	OP	17.00	17.00
97	LEATHER NEST	OP	17.00	17.00
97	LOVE NEST	OP	17.00	17.00
97	SMITH'S, THE	OP	17.00	17.00
97	SNOWBIRDS	OP	17.00	17.00
97	STONE HAVEN	OP	17.00	17.00
97	WINTER RETREAT	OP	17.00	17.00
97	WINTER SQUASH	OP	17.00	17.00

FENTON ART GLASS
*

YR	NAME	LIMIT	ISSUE	TREND
82	ORNAMENT 1714CY	*	*	14.00
82	ORNAMENT 1714DH	*	*	18.00
82	ORNAMENT 1714KG	*	*	15.00
82	ORNAMENT 1714RU	*	*	15.00
82	ORNAMENT 9414FL NATIVITY	*	*	25.00
82	ORNAMENT 9414TD NATIVITY	*	*	20.00

M. REYNOLDS · CHRISTMAS LIMITED EDITIONS

YR	NAME	LIMIT	ISSUE	TREND
96	ORNAMENT 1714AC	2000	28.00	28.00

FIGI COLLECTIONS INC.
* · SANTA'S CRYSTAL VALLEY

YR	NAME	LIMIT	ISSUE	TREND
*	BEARY CHRISTMAS ORNAMENT	OP	13.00	13.00
*	PEACE ON EARTH ORNAMENT	OP	13.00	13.00
97	1997 SANTA ORNAMENT CVO-101	OP	13.00	13.00

FJ DESIGNS/CAT'S MEOW
F. JONES

YR	NAME	LIMIT	ISSUE	TREND
98	CHRIST'S BIRTH	OP	9.00	9.00
98	SANTA CASPER ORNAMENT	OP	9.00	9.00
98	SNOW GLOBE ORNAMENT	OP	9.00	9.00
98	WRAPPED HOUSE ORNAMENT	OP	9.00	9.00

F. JONES · CHRISTMAS ORNAMENTS

YR	NAME	LIMIT	ISSUE	TREND
85	1986, 1987 CHRISTMAS ORNAMENT SET	RT	*	750.00
85	BANCROFT HOUSE	RT	4.00	40.00
85	CHAPEL	RT	4.00	40.00
85	GRAYLING HOUSE	RT	4.00	40.00
85	MORTON HOUSE	RT	4.00	40.00
85	RUTLEDGE HOUSE	RT	4.00	75.00
85	SCHOOL	RT	4.00	40.00
87	1988 CHRISTMAS ORNAMENT SET	RT	20.00	185.00
87	BLACKSMITH SHOP	RT	5.00	60.00
87	DISTRICT #17 SCHOOL	RT	5.00	60.00
87	GLOBE CORNER BOOKSTORE	RT	5.00	60.00
87	KENNEDY BIRTHPLACE	RT	5.00	50.00
95	CARNEGIE LIBRARY	RT	9.00	9.00
95	HOLLY HILL FARMOUSE	RT	9.00	9.00
95	NORTH CENTRAL SCHOOL	RT	9.00	9.00
95	ST. JAMES GENERAL STORE	RT	9.00	9.00
95	UNITARIAN CHURCH	RT	9.00	9.00
95	YAQUINA BAY LIGHT	RT	9.00	9.00
96	CHRIST CHURCH	YR	9.00	9.00
96	DEERFIELD POST OFFICE	YR	9.00	9.00
96	GIMBEL & SONS COUNTRY STORE	YR	9.00	9.00
96	HOOK WINDMILL	YR	9.00	9.00
96	MAPLE MANOR	YR	9.00	9.00
96	PARSONAGE	YR	9.00	9.00

F. JONES · NANTUCKET CHRISTMAS ORNAMENTS

YR	NAME	LIMIT	ISSUE	TREND
98	CHRISTMAS CHOP ORNAMENT	OP	9.00	9.00
98	POWELL HOUSE ORNAMENT	OP	9.00	9.00

YR	NAME	LIMIT	ISSUE	TREND
98	SHAW HOUSE ORNAMENT	OP	9.00	9.00
98	WINTHROP HOUSE ORNAMENT	OP	9.00	9.00

FLAMBRO
*

			EMMETT KELLY JR.	
89	65TH BIRTHDAY CHRISTMAS ORNAMENT	CL	24.00	47.00
90	30 YEARS OF CLOWNING	YR	30.00	53.00
91	EKJ WITH STOCKING AND TOYS	YR	30.00	30.00
92	HOME FOR CHRISTMAS	YR	24.00	24.00
93	CHRISTMAS MAIL	YR	25.00	50.00
94	70TH BIRTHDAY COMMEMORATIVE	YR	24.00	24.00
95	ALL-STAR CIRCUS 20TH ANNIVERSARY	YR	25.00	25.00
97	1997 DATED ORNAMENT	YR	30.00	30.00

M. WU
			LITTLE EMMETT	
95	CHRISTMAS WRAP	OP	11.50	12.00
95	DECK THE NECK	OP	11.50	12.00

R. MUSGRAVE
			POCKET DRAGONS	
90	ONE SIZE FITS ALL	OP	20.00	20.00
90	PUTTING ME ON THE TREE	5000	48.00	48.00

*
			RAGGEDY ANN & ANDY	
89	RAGGEDY ANDY W/CANDY CANE	YR	13.50	18.00
89	RAGGEDY ANN W/GIFT STOCKING	YR	13.50	18.00

GANZ
C. THAMMAVONGSA
			CHEESERVILLE PICNIC COLLECTION	
91	AUNTIE MARIGOLD EATING COOKIE	OP	13.00	13.00
91	BABY CICELY	OP	8.00	8.00
91	BABY TRUFFLE	OP	8.00	8.00
91	BLOSSOM & HICKORY IN LOVE	OP	19.00	19.00
91	COUSIN WOODY WITH BEAD & FRUIT	OP	14.00	15.00
91	FELLOW W/PICNIC HAMPER	RT	13.00	13.00
91	FELLOW W/PLATE OF COOKIES	RT	13.00	13.00
91	GRANDMAMA THISTLEDOWN HOLDING BREAD	OP	14.00	15.00
91	GRANDPAPA THISTLEDOWN CARRYING BKT	OP	13.00	13.00
91	HARLEY HARVESTMOUSE WAVING	OP	13.00	13.00
91	HARRIET HARVESTMOUSE	RT	13.00	13.00
91	JENNY BUTTERFIELD KNEELING	OP	13.00	13.00
91	JEREMY BUTTERFIELD	OP	13.00	13.00
91	LADY W/GRAPES	RT	14.00	15.00
91	LI'L TRUFFLE EATING GRAPES	OP	8.00	8.00
91	LI'L TRUFFLE SMELLING FLOWERS	OP	16.50	17.00
91	MAMA FIXING SWEET CICELY'S HAIR	RT	16.50	17.00
91	MAMA WITH ROLLING PIN	OP	13.00	13.00
91	MAMA WOODSWORTH W/CAFE	RT	14.00	15.00
91	MARIGOLD THISTLEDOWN PICKING UP JAR	OP	14.00	15.00
91	MEDLEY MEADOWMOUSE/BOUQUET	OP	13.00	13.00
91	PAPA WOODSWORTH	OP	13.00	13.00
91	PICNIC BUDDIES	OP	19.00	19.00
91	VIOLET WITH PEACHES	OP	13.00	13.00
92	SWEET CICELY MUSICAL DOLL IN BKT	OP	85.00	85.00
93	CHUCKLES THE CLOWN	OP	16.00	16.00
93	CLOWNIN' AROUND	OP	10.50	11.00
93	FOR SOMEONE SPECIAL	OP	13.50	14.00
93	LI'L CHEESERS DISPLAY PLAQUE	OP	25.00	25.00
93	STORYTELLER, THE	10000	25.00	25.00
93	STRUMMIN' AWAY	OP	13.00	13.00
93	SUNDAY DRIVE	OP	40.00	40.00
93	SWEET DREAMS	OP	28.00	28.00
93	WILLY'S TOE-TAPPIN' TUNES	OP	15.00	15.00
93	WORDS OF WISDOM	OP	14.00	15.00
94	FIDDLE-DEE-DEE	OP	13.00	13.00
94	MELODY MAKER	OP	17.00	17.00
94	OOM-PAH-PAH	OP	13.00	13.00
94	SWINGIN' SAX	OP	13.00	13.00
94	WASHBOARD BLUES	OP	13.00	13.00
94	WHAT A HOOT!	OP	13.00	13.00

C. THAMMAVONGSA
			COWTOWN/CHRISTMAS COLLECTION	
94	BILLY THE CALF	OP	14.00	15.00
94	BRONCO BULLY	OP	13.00	13.00
94	CALF-IN-THE-BOX	OP	12.50	13.00
94	CHRISTMAS CACTUS	OP	13.50	14.00
94	CHRISTMOOS EVE	OP	12.00	12.00
94	DOWNHILL DAR DEBULL	OP	12.00	12.00
94	HALLEMOOAH	OP	12.00	12.00
94	JINGLE BELL	OP	15.50	16.00
94	LI'L RED GLIDING HOOF	OP	12.00	12.00
94	LITTLE DRUMMER CALF	OP	12.00	12.00
94	SAINT NICOWLAS	OP	16.00	16.00
94	SANTA COWS	OP	18.00	18.00
94	SANTA'S LITTLE HEIFER	OP	12.50	13.00

C. THAMMAVONGSA
			COWTOWN/VALENTINE COLLECTION	
94	I LOVE MOO	OP	15.00	16.00
94	ROBIN HOOF & MAID MOOIAN	OP	23.00	23.00
94	ROMECOW & MOOLIET	OP	22.00	22.00
94	WANTED: A SWEETHEART	OP	16.00	16.00

YR	NAME	LIMIT	ISSUE	TREND
C. THAMMAVONGSA		**LITTLE CHEESERS/CHRISTMAS COLLECTION**		
92	ABNER APPLETON	OP	15.00	15.00
92	JENNY BUTTERFIELD	OP	17.00	17.00
92	JEREMY/ TEDDY BEAR	OP	13.00	13.00
92	LITTLE TRUFFLE	OP	9.50	10.00
92	MYRTLE MEADOWMOUSE	OP	15.00	15.00
92	SANTA CHEESER	OP	14.00	15.00
93	BABY'S FIRST XMAS	OP	12.50	13.00
93	DASHING THROUGH THE SNOW	OP	11.00	11.00
93	LITTLE STOCKING STUFFER	OP	10.50	11.00
93	MEADLEY MEADOWMOUSE XMAS BELL	OP	17.00	17.00
93	OUR 1ST CHRISTMAS TOGETHER	OP	19.00	19.00
93	SANTA'S LITTLE HELPER	OP	11.00	11.00
93	SKATING INTO YOUR HEART	OP	10.00	10.00
94	ALL I WANT FOR CHRISTMAS	RT	13.50	14.00
94	ANGEL	OP	8.00	8.00
94	CANDY CANE CAPER	OP	9.00	9.00
94	CHEESER SHOWMAN	RT	5.00	5.00
94	CHELSEA'S STOCKING BELL	OP	15.50	16.00
94	COUSIN WOODY PLAYING FLUTE	RT	10.00	10.00
94	GRANDPA BLOWING HORN	RT	10.00	10.00
94	HICKORY PLAYING CELLO	RT	10.00	10.00
94	MEDLEY PLAYING DRUM	RT	5.50	6.00
94	MRS. CLAUS	OP	9.00	9.00
94	PEACE ON EARTH	OP	8.00	8.00
94	SANTA SILVERWOOD	OP	9.00	9.00
94	SANTA'S WORKSHOP	OP	10.00	10.00
94	SLEIGH RIDE	RT	9.00	9.00
94	SWINGING INTO THE SEASON	OP	11.00	11.00
94	VIOLET WITH SNOWBALL	RT	5.50	6.00
C. THAMMAVONGSA		**LITTLE CHEESERS/THE SILVERWOODS**		
94	CHRISTMAS SURPRISE	OP	8.50	9.00
94	COMFORT AND JOY	OP	6.00	6.00
94	DECK THE HALLS	OP	9.50	10.00
94	GIDDY UP!	OP	8.50	9.00
94	HICKORY DICKORY DOCK	OP	9.50	10.00
94	XMAS EXPRESS	OP	8.50	9.00
C. THAMMAVONGSA		**PIGSVILLE/CHRISTMAS COLLECTION**		
94	CAROLER	OP	10.00	10.00
94	CHRISTMAS TREATS	OP	9.00	9.00
94	DRUMMER PIG	OP	10.00	10.00
94	JOY TO THE WORLD	OP	10.00	10.00
94	SANTA PIG	OP	11.00	11.00
94	WHEEEEEE! PIGGY	OP	9.00	9.00
C. THAMMAVONGSA		**PIGSVILLE/THE VALENTINE COLLECTION**		
94	LOVESTRUCK	OP	10.50	11.00

GLASS EYE
*

YR	NAME	LIMIT	ISSUE	TREND
93	COBALT WAVE	2000	19.00	22.00
94	CRANBERRY OPALESCENT LACE	2000	19.00	22.00

GOEBEL INC.
*

YR	NAME	LIMIT	ISSUE	TREND
		ANGEL BELLS ANNUAL ORNAMENT		
76	ANGEL WITH FLUTE-BLUE	YR	9.00	100.00
76	ANGEL WITH FLUTE-PINK	YR	9.00	100.00
76	ANGEL WITH FLUTE-RED	YR	9.00	100.00
76	ANGEL WITH FLUTE-WHITE	YR	7.00	70.00
77	ANGEL WITH BANJO-GREEN	YR	9.00	35.00
77	ANGEL WITH BANJO-PURPLE	YR	9.00	35.00
77	ANGEL WITH BANJO-WHITE	YR	7.00	30.00
77	ANGEL WITH BANJO-YELLOW	YR	9.00	35.00
78	ANGEL WITH HARP-BLUE	YR	11.00	35.00
78	ANGEL WITH HARP-PINK	YR	11.00	35.00
78	ANGEL WITH HARP-RUST	YR	11.00	35.00
78	ANGEL WITH HARP-WHITE	YR	9.00	30.00
79	ANGEL WITH ACCORDION-GREEN	YR	11.00	35.00
79	ANGEL WITH ACCORDION-PURPLE	YR	11.00	35.00
79	ANGEL WITH ACCORDION-WHITE	YR	9.00	30.00
79	ANGEL WITH ACCORDION-YELLOW	YR	11.00	35.00
80	ANGEL WITH SAXAPHONE-BLUE	YR	13.50	35.00
80	ANGEL WITH SAXAPHONE-PINK	YR	13.50	35.00
80	ANGEL WITH SAXAPHONE-RUST	YR	13.50	35.00
80	ANGEL WITH SAXAPHONE-WHITE	YR	11.50	30.00
81	ANGEL WITH SONG SHEET-GREEN	YR	14.00	35.00
81	ANGEL WITH SONG SHEET-PURPLE	YR	14.00	35.00
81	ANGEL WITH SONG SHEET-WHITE	YR	12.00	30.00
81	ANGEL WITH SONG SHEET-YELLOW	YR	14.00	35.00
82	ANGEL WITH FRENCH HORN-GREEN	YR	14.00	35.00
82	ANGEL WITH FRENCH HORN-RED	YR	14.00	35.00
82	ANGEL WITH FRENCH HORN-RUST	YR	14.00	35.00
82	ANGEL WITH FRENCH HORN-WHITE	YR	12.00	30.00
83	ANGEL WITH REED PIPE-BROWN	YR	14.00	35.00
83	ANGEL WITH REED PIPE-ORANGE	YR	14.00	35.00
83	ANGEL WITH REED PIPE-PURPLE	YR	14.00	35.00

YR	NAME	LIMIT	ISSUE	TREND
83	ANGEL WITH REED PIPE-WHITE	YR	12.00	30.00
84	ANGEL WITH DRUM-GREEN	YR	14.00	35.00
84	ANGEL WITH DRUM-RED	YR	14.00	35.00
84	ANGEL WITH DRUM-WHITE	YR	12.00	30.00
85	ANGEL WITH TRUMPET-BLUE	YR	14.00	35.00
85	ANGEL WITH TRUMPET-GREEN	YR	14.00	35.00
85	ANGEL WITH TRUMPET-RED	YR	14.00	35.00
85	ANGEL WITH TRUMPET-WHITE	YR	12.00	30.00
86	ANGEL WITH BELLS-GREEN	YR	15.00	35.00
86	ANGEL WITH BELLS-RED	YR	15.00	35.00
86	ANGEL WITH BELLS-WHITE	YR	12.50	30.00
86	ANGEL WITH BELLS-YELLOW	YR	15.00	35.00
87	ANGEL CONDUCTOR-BLUE	YR	17.25	35.00
87	ANGEL CONDUCTOR-GREEN	YR	17.25	35.00
87	ANGEL CONDUCTOR-RED	YR	17.25	35.00
87	ANGEL CONDUCTOR-WHITE	YR	15.00	30.00
88	ANGEL WITH STAR-GREEN	YR	20.00	20.00
88	ANGEL WITH STAR-RED	YR	20.00	20.00
88	ANGEL WITH STAR-WHITE	YR	17.00	17.00
88	ANGEL WITH STAR-YELLOW	YR	20.00	20.00
*		**ANNUAL CHRISTMAS BELL ORNAMENT**		
84	CHRISTMAS TREE	YR	14.00	25.00
85	SANTA	YR	14.00	15.00
86	WREATH	YR	15.00	16.00
87	TEDDY BEAR	YR	17.25	18.00
88	CRYSTAL BELL	YR	7.50	15.00
*		**ANNUAL ORNAMENT**		
78	SANTA-COLOR	YR	15.00	17.00
78	SANTA-WHITE	YR	7.50	12.00
79	ANGEL/TREE-COLOR	YR	16.00	18.00
79	ANGEL/TREE-WHITE	YR	8.00	13.00
80	MRS. SANTA-COLOR	YR	17.00	17.00
80	MRS. SANTA-WHITE	YR	9.00	14.00
81	NUTCRACKER, THE-COLOR	YR	18.00	18.00
81	NUTCRACKER, THE-WHITE	YR	10.00	10.00
82	SANTA IN CHIMNEY-COLOR	YR	18.00	18.00
82	SANTA IN CHIMNEY-WHITE	YR	10.00	10.00
83	CLOWN-COLOR	YR	18.00	18.00
83	CLOWN-WHITE	YR	10.00	10.00
84	SNOWMAN-COLOR	YR	18.00	18.00
84	SNOWMAN-WHITE	YR	10.00	10.00
85	ANGEL-COLOR	YR	18.00	18.00
85	ANGEL-WHITE	YR	9.00	9.00
86	DRUMMER BOY-COLOR	YR	18.00	18.00
86	DRUMMER BOY-WHITE	YR	9.00	9.00
87	ROCKING HORSE-COLOR	YR	20.00	20.00
87	ROCKING HORSE-WHITE	YR	10.00	10.00
88	DOLL-COLOR	YR	23.00	23.00
88	DOLL-WHITE	YR	12.50	13.00
89	DOVE-COLOR	YR	20.00	20.00
89	DOVE-WHITE	YR	12.50	13.00
90	GIRL IN SLEIGH	YR	30.00	30.00
91	BABY ON MOON	YR	35.00	35.00
*		**ANNUAL ORNAMENT-GLASS**		
79	SANTA	15000	12.00	12.00
80	ANGEL WITH TREE	15000	12.00	12.00
81	MRS. SANTA	15000	12.00	12.00
82	NUTCRACKER, THE	15000	4.00	4.00
B. TIMBERLAKE		**BOB TIMBERLAKE SIGNATURE**		
96	CHRISTMAS CARDINAL	YR	35.00	35.00
C. BYJ		**CHARLOT BYJ ANNUAL ORNAMENT**		
86	SANTA LUCIA ANGEL	CL	18.00	25.00
87	CHRISTMAS PAGEANT	CL	20.00	20.00
88	ANGEL WITH SHEET MUSIC	CL	22.00	22.00
C. BYJ		**CHARLOT BYJ BABY ORNAMENT**		
86	BABY ORNAMENT	CL	18.00	18.00
87	BABY SNOW	CL	20.00	20.00
88	BABY'S 1ST STOCKING	CL	28.00	28.00
*		**CHRISTMAS ORNAMENTS**		
86	ANGEL WITH HORN-COLOR	OP	8.00	8.00
86	ANGEL WITH HORN-WHITE	OP	6.00	6.00
86	ANGEL WITH LANTERN-COLOR	OP	8.00	8.00
86	ANGEL WITH LANTERN-WHITE	OP	6.00	6.00
86	ANGEL WITH LUTE-COLOR	OP	8.00	8.00
86	ANGEL WITH LUTE-WHITE	OP	6.00	6.00
86	ANGEL-RED WITH BELL	OP	6.00	6.00
86	ANGEL-RED WITH BOOK	OP	6.00	6.00
86	ANGEL-RED WITH SONG	OP	6.00	6.00
86	TEDDY BEAR-RED BOOTS	OP	5.00	5.00
86	TEDDY BEAR-RED HAT	OP	5.00	5.00
86	TEDDY BEAR-RED SCARF	OP	5.00	5.00
87	THREE ANGELS WITH INSTRUMENTS (SET)	OP	30.00	30.00
87	THREE ANGELS WITH TOYS (SET)	OP	30.00	30.00
88	ANGEL WITH ACCORDION	OP	10.00	10.00
88	ANGEL WITH BANJO	OP	10.00	10.00

YR	NAME	LIMIT	ISSUE	TREND
88	ANGEL WITH MUSIC (SET)	OP	30.00	30.00
88	ANGEL WITH TOY ROCKING HORSE	OP	10.00	10.00
88	ANGEL WITH TOY TEDDY BEAR	OP	10.00	10.00
88	ANGEL WITH TOY TRAIN	OP	10.00	10.00
88	ANGEL WITH TOYS (SET OF 3)	OP	30.00	30.00
88	ANGEL WITH VIOLIN	OP	10.00	10.00
88	NUTCRACKER	OP	15.00	16.00
88	SAINT NICK	OP	15.00	16.00
88	SANTA'S BOOT	OP	7.50	8.00
88	SNOWMAN	OP	10.00	10.00

G. SKROBEK — CO-BOY ANNUAL ORNAMENT

YR	NAME	LIMIT	ISSUE	TREND
86	COBOY WITH WREATH	CL	18.00	25.00
87	COBOY WITH CANDY CANE	CL	25.00	25.00
88	COBOY WITH TREE	CL	30.00	30.00

M.I. HUMMEL — M.I. HUMMEL ANNUAL FIGURINE ORNAMENTS

YR	NAME	LIMIT	ISSUE	TREND
88	FLYING HIGH HUM-452	CL	75.00	165.00
89	LOVE FROM ABOVE HUM-481	CL	75.00	125.00
90	PEACE ON EARTH HUM-484	CL	80.00	125.00
91	ANGELIC GUIDE HUM-571	CL	95.00	125.00
92	LIGHT UP THE NIGHT HUM-622	CL	95.00	135.00
93	HERALD ON HIGH HUM-623	CL	155.00	185.00

M.I. HUMMEL — M.I. HUMMEL CENTURY COLLECTION

YR	NAME	LIMIT	ISSUE	TREND
98	ECHOES OF JOY HUM 597	*	*	N/A

M.I. HUMMEL — M.I. HUMMEL CHRISTMAS BELL ORNAMENTS

YR	NAME	LIMIT	ISSUE	TREND
89	RIDE INTO CHRISTMAS HUM-775	CL	35.00	55.00
90	LETTER TO SANTA CLAUS HUM-776	CL	38.00	55.00
91	HEAR YE, HEAR YE HUM-777	CL	40.00	55.00
92	HARMONY IN FOUR PARTS HUM-778	CL	45.00	50.00
93	CELESTIAL MUSICIAN HUM-779	CL	50.00	50.00
95	FESTIVAL HARMONY W/FLUTE HUM 781	CL	55.00	55.00
96	CHRISTMAS SONG HUM 782	CL	55.00	55.00

M.I. HUMMEL — M.I. HUMMEL MINIATURE ORNAMENTS

YR	NAME	LIMIT	ISSUE	TREND
93	CELESTIAL MUSICIAN HUM-646	CL	90.00	110.00
94	FESTIVAL HARMONY W/MANDOLIN HUM-647	CL	95.00	110.00
95	FESTIVAL HARMONY W/FLUTE HUM-648	CL	100.00	100.00

M.I. HUMMEL — UNICEF

YR	NAME	LIMIT	ISSUE	TREND
93	FRIENDS FOREVER HUM-662	25000	260.00	390.00

GORHAM

*

ANNUAL CRYSTAL ORNAMENTS

YR	NAME	LIMIT	ISSUE	TREND
85	CRYSTAL ORNAMENT	CL	22.00	22.00
86	CRYSTAL ORNAMENT	CL	25.00	25.00
87	CRYSTAL ORNAMENT	CL	25.00	25.00
88	CRYSTAL ORNAMENT	CL	28.00	28.00
89	CRYSTAL ORNAMENT	CL	28.00	28.00
90	CRYSTAL ORNAMENT	CL	30.00	30.00
91	CRYSTAL ORNAMENT	CL	35.00	35.00
92	CRYSTAL ORNAMENT	CL	33.00	33.00

*

ANNUAL SNOWFLAKE ORNAMENTS

YR	NAME	LIMIT	ISSUE	TREND
70	STERLING SNOWFLAKE	CL	10.00	290.00
71	STERLING SNOWFLAKE	CL	10.00	110.00
72	STERLING SNOWFLAKE	CL	10.00	100.00
73	STERLING SNOWFLAKE	CL	11.00	90.00
74	STERLING SNOWFLAKE	CL	17.50	60.00
75	STERLING SNOWFLAKE	CL	17.50	60.00
76	STERLING SNOWFLAKE	CL	20.00	60.00
77	STERLING SNOWFLAKE	CL	23.00	60.00
78	STERLING SNOWFLAKE	CL	23.00	60.00
79	STERLING SNOWFLAKE	CL	33.00	70.00
80	SILVERPLATED SNOWFLAKE	CL	15.00	75.00
81	STERLING SNOWFLAKE	CL	50.00	65.00
82	STERLING SNOWFLAKE	CL	38.00	75.00
83	STERLING SNOWFLAKE	CL	45.00	60.00
84	STERLING SNOWFLAKE	CL	45.00	60.00
85	STERLING SNOWFLAKE	CL	45.00	60.00
86	STERLING SNOWFLAKE	CL	45.00	55.00
87	STERLING SNOWFLAKE	CL	50.00	60.00
88	STERLING SNOWFLAKE	CL	50.00	50.00
89	STERLING SNOWFLAKE	CL	50.00	50.00
90	STERLING SNOWFLAKE	CL	50.00	50.00
91	STERLING SNOWFLAKE	CL	55.00	55.00
92	STERLING SNOWFLAKE	CL	50.00	50.00

*

ARCHIVE COLLECTIBLE

YR	NAME	LIMIT	ISSUE	TREND
88	VICTORIAN HEART	CL	50.00	50.00
89	VICTORIAN WREATH	CL	50.00	50.00
90	ELIZABETHAN CUPID	CL	60.00	60.00
91	STERLING BAROQUE ANGELS	CL	55.00	55.00
92	MADONNA AND CHILD	YR	50.00	50.00

*

BABY'S FIRST CHRISTMAS CRYSTAL

YR	NAME	LIMIT	ISSUE	TREND
91	BABY'S FIRST ROCKING HORSE	CL	35.00	35.00

HADLEY COMPANIES

A. AGNEW — HADLEY COLLECTION

YR	NAME	LIMIT	ISSUE	TREND
95	ARCTIC WOLVES	45 DAYS	20.00	30.00

YR NAME	LIMIT	ISSUE	TREND
D. BARNHOUSE		**HADLEY COLLECTION**	
95 REPAIRS	45 DAYS	20.00	30.00
D. BRESH		**HADLEY COLLECTION**	
95 WARMTH OF WINTER II	45 DAYS	20.00	30.00
T. REDLIN		**HADLEY COLLECTION**	
95 SHARING THE EVENING	45 DAYS	20.00	30.00

HALLMARK
*

76 BABY'S FIRST CHRISTMAS 250QX211-1	YR	2.50	145.00
76 HAPPY HOLIDAYS KISSING BALLS QX225-1	YR	5.00	225.00
77 HOLLY & POINSETTIA TABLE DECOR. OHD320-2	YR	8.00	132.00
77 MR. & MRS. SNOWMAN KISSING BALL QX 225-2	YR	5.00	100.00
77 OLD FASHION CUSTOMS KISSING BALL QX225-5	YR	5.00	147.00
78 CHRISTMAS STAR TREE TOPPERS QX 702-3	YR	7.50	40.00
78 HEAVENLY MINSTREL TABLETOP QHD 921-9	YR	35.00	375.00
78 HOLIDAY MEMORIES KISSING BALL QHD 900-3	YR	5.00	120.00
78 LITTLE TRIMMER COLLECTION QX 132-3	YR	9.00	320.00
79 LITTLE TRIMMER SET QX 159-9	YR	9.00	300.00
80 BELLRINGER-2ND EDITION 1500QX157-4	YR	15.00	66.00
80 BRASS STAR TREE TOPPERS QX 705-4	YR	25.00	52.00
80 CHRISTMAS KITTEN TEST ORNAMENT QX353-4	YR	4.00	260.00
81 YARN & FABRIC ORNAMENT ANGEL QX 162-1	YR	3.00	11.00
81 YARN & FABRIC ORNAMENT SANTA QX 161-4	YR	3.00	11.00
81 YARN & FABRIC ORNAMENT SNOWMAN QX 163-4	YR	3.00	11.00
81 YARN & FABRIC ORNAMENT SOLDIER QX 164-1	YR	3.00	11.00
82 BRASS PROMOTIONAL ORNAMENT NO NUMBER	YR	3.50	42.00
83 SILVER BELL QX 110-9	YR	12.00	31.00
84 BABY'S FIRST CHRISTMAS-GIRL QX 240-1	YR	4.50	20.00
84 CHRISTMAS MEMORIES PHOTOHOLDER QX 300-4	YR	6.50	21.00
85 DISNEY CHRISTMAS QX 271-2	YR	4.75	24.00
85 HEAVENLY TRUMPETER 2750QX405-2	YR	28.00	82.00
86 SNOOPY AND WOODSTOCK 434-6	YR	8.00	58.00
87 ELVES-EMIL PAINTER ELF-FIGURINE QSP930-9	YR	10.00	30.00
87 ELVES-HANS CARPENTER ELF-FIGURE QSP930-7	YR	10.00	30.00
87 ELVES-KURT BLUE PRINT ELF FIGUREQSP931-7	YR	10.00	30.00
87 HALLIS STAR-TREE TOPPER EPCA	YR	*	32.00
89 CANDY CANE 450QXM560-2	YR	4.50	19.00
90 FESTIVE ANGEL TREE TOPPER 975QXM578-3	YR	9.75	29.00
90 PENGUIN PAL 450QXM574-6	YR	4.50	19.00
90 PORCELAIN BEAR 8TH ED. QX 442-6	YR	8.75	21.00
90 SNOOPY AND WOODSTOCK 427-3	YR	6.75	30.00
93 HOLIDAY EXPRESS QXM 545-2	YR	50.00	50.00
94 BETSEY'S COUNTRY CHRISTMAS 3RD ED. 500QX240-3	YR	5.00	10.00
94 FEELIN' GROOVY 795QX595-3	YR	8.00	20.00
94 GODPARENT 500QX242-3	YR	5.00	15.00
94 GRANDPARENTS 500QX242-6	YR	5.00	10.00
94 MARY ENGELBREIT 500QX241-6	YR	5.00	13.00
95 BABY'S FIRST CHRISTMAS-BABY BOY QX 231-9	YR	5.00	8.00
95 BABY'S FIRST CHRISTMAS-BABY GIRL QX231-7	YR	5.00	8.00
95 MAGIC SCHOOL BUS, THE QX584-9	YR	11.00	20.00
95 MARY ENGELBRIET QX240-9	YR	5.00	13.00
95 NUMBER ONE TEACHER QX594-9	YR	8.00	12.00
95 SPACE SHUTTLE COLUMBIA 739-6	YR	24.50	32.00
96 PEZ SNOWMAN QX653-4	YR	8.00	20.00
97 CORVETTE 16455	YR	14.00	14.00
97 CORVETTE MINIATURE 1433-2	YR	7.00	7.00
97 INCREDIBLE HULK 547-1	YR	13.00	13.00
97 LONE RANGER LUNCH BOX 626-5	YR	13.00	35.00
98 GARDEN OF PIGLET AND POOH 1295QEO8403	YR	13.00	13.00
98 PRACTICE SWING-DONALD DUCK 1095QEO8396	YR	11.00	11.00
98 TIGGER IN THE GARDEN 995QEO8436	YR	10.00	10.00
P. ANDREWS			
94 CANDY CAPER 895QX577-6	YR	9.00	15.00
94 DAUGHTER 695QX562-3	YR	7.00	11.00
94 GRANDMOTHER 695QX567-3	YR	8.00	13.00
94 HEARTS IN HARMONY 1095QX440-6	YR	11.00	16.00
94 ICE SHOW 795QX594-6	YR	8.00	15.00
94 IN THE PINK 995QX576-3	YR	10.00	18.00
94 JOYOUS SONG 895QX447-3	YR	9.00	15.00
94 NEW HOME 895QX566-3	YR	9.00	20.00
94 OUR FIRST CHRISTMAS TOGETHER 1895QX570-6	YR	19.00	22.00
94 SON 695QX562-6	YR	7.00	13.00
94 TIME OF PEACE 795QX581-3	YR	8.00	12.00
95 BABY'S FIRST CHRISTMAS QX 554-7	YR	19.00	25.00
95 BABY'S FIRST CHRISTMAS QX 555-7	YR	10.00	16.00
95 CELEBRATION OF ANGELS FIRST SERIES QX507-7	YR	13.00	35.00
95 CHRISTMAS PATROL QX595-9	YR	8.00	16.00
95 COWS OF BALI QX599-9	YR	9.00	13.00
95 GRANDMOTHER QX576-7	YR	8.00	11.00
95 HEAVEN'S GIFT QX605-7	YR	20.00	26.00
95 IN A HEARTBEAT QX581-7	YR	9.00	16.00
95 JOY TO THE WORLD QX586-7	YR	9.00	16.00
95 MERRY OLDE SANTA 6TH SERIES QX513-9	YR	15.00	25.00
95 NEW HOME QX583-9	YR	9.00	16.00

YR	NAME	LIMIT	ISSUE	TREND
95	THREE WISHES QX597-9	YR	8.00	16.00
96	A CHILD'S GIFTS QXM423-4	YR	6.75	7.00
96	JOYOUS ANGEL QXM423-1	YR	4.75	5.00
96	LONG WINTER'S NAP QXM424-4	YR	5.75	6.00
98	MIDGE 35TH ANNIVERSARY 1495QEO8413	YR	15.00	15.00
N. AUBE				
95	CHRISTMAS FEVER QX596-7	YR	8.00	18.00
95	TENNIS, ANYONE? QX590-7	YR	8.00	16.00
96	HILLSIDE EXPRESS QX613-4	YR	13.00	13.00
98	BASHFUL GIFT-SET OF TWO 1195QEO8446	YR	12.00	12.00
M. BASTIN				
95	VERA THE MOUSE QX553-7	YR	9.00	10.00
R. BISHOP				
94	LOU RANKIN SEAL 995QX545-6	YR	10.00	18.00
94	OUR FIRST CHRISTMAS TOGETHER 995QX564-3	YR	10.00	15.00
T. BLACKSHEAR				
80	CHECKING IT TWICE 2000QX158-4	YR	20.00	200.00
A. BROWNSWORD				
95	FOREVER FRIENDS BEAR QX525-8	YR	9.00	18.00
R. CHAD				
94	HELPFUL SHEPHERD 895QX553-6	YR	9.00	16.00
94	MERRY OLDE SANTA 5TH ED. 1495QX525-6	YR	15.00	25.00
95	MULETIDE GREETINGS QX600-9	YR	8.00	15.00
95	OUR FAMILY QX570-9	YR	8.00	11.00
95	SPECIAL CAT QX571-7	YR	8.00	11.00
95	SPECIAL DOG QX571-9	YR	8.00	11.00
95	SUPERMAN QLX730-9	YR	28.00	45.00
96	HIGH STYLE QX606-4	YR	9.00	9.00
K. CROW				
87	NORTH POLE POWER & LIGHT 627XPR933-3	YR	3.00	20.00
88	CHRISTMAS MORNING 2450QLX701-3	YR	25.00	34.00
88	MISTLETOAD 700QLX468-7	YR	7.00	24.00
88	NIGHT BEFORE CHRISTMAS QX 451-7	YR	6.50	25.00
91	WOODLAND BABIES 600QXM566-7	YR	6.00	24.00
93	PEEK-A-BOO TREE QX524-4	YR	10.75	18.00
94	CHEERS TO YOU! 1095QX579-6	YR	11.00	20.00
94	CHEERY CYCLISTS 1295QX578-6	YR	13.00	26.00
94	DEAR SANTA MOUSE 1495QX580-6	YR	15.00	21.00
94	EXTRA-SPECIAL DELIVERY 795QX583-3	YR	8.00	15.00
94	FOLLOW THE SUN 895QX584-6	YR	9.00	15.00
94	JINGLE BELL BAND 1095QX578-3	YR	11.00	22.00
94	SANTA'S LEGO SLEIGH 1095QX545-3	YR	11.00	20.00
95	BOBBIN' ALONG QX587-9	YR	9.00	30.00
95	GRANDPA QX576-9	YR	9.00	14.00
95	HAPPY WRAPPERS QX603-7	YR	11.00	15.00
95	HOCKEY PUP QX591-7	YR	10.00	11.00
95	IN TIME WITH CHRISTMAS QX604-9	YR	13.00	20.00
95	LEGO FIREPLACE WITH SANTA QX476-9	YR	11.00	20.00
95	MY FIRST HOT WHEELS QLX727-9	YR	28.00	44.00
95	ON THE ICE QX604-7	YR	8.00	15.00
95	OUR LITTLE BLESSINGS QX520-9	YR	13.00	16.00
95	POLAR COASTER QX611-7	YR	9.00	15.00
95	SANTA'S SERENADE QX601-7	YR	9.00	15.00
95	SPACE SHUTTLE QLX739-	YR	25.00	31.00
95	SURFIN' SANTA QX601-9	YR	10.00	20.00
95	WEE LITTLE CHRISTMAS QLX732-9	YR	22.00	30.00
96	A LITTLE SONG AND DANCE QX621-1	YR	10.00	10.00
96	JETSONS, THE QLX741-1	YR	28.00	35.00
96	JOLLY WOLLY ARK QX622-1	YR	13.00	13.00
96	PINBALL WONDER QLX745-1	YR	28.00	28.00
P. DUTKIN				
87	FAVORITE SANTA 2250QX445-7	YR	23.00	50.00
88	ST. LOUIE NICK QX 453-9	YR	7.75	21.00
J. FRANCIS				
93	A CHILD'S CHRISTMAS QX588-2	YR	9.75	15.00
94	JUMP-ALONG JACKALOPE 895QX575-6	YR	9.00	15.00
94	NEPHEW 795QX554-6	YR	8.00	11.00
94	NIECE 795QX554-3	YR	8.00	15.00
94	RELAXING MOMENT 1495QX535-6	YR	15.00	25.00
95	ACROSS THE MILES QX 584-7	YR	9.00	15.00
95	BARREL-BACK RIDER QX518-9	YR	10.00	20.00
95	CHRISTMAS MORNING QX599-7	YR	11.00	13.00
95	DREAM ON QX600-7	YR	11.00	20.00
95	GRANDCHILD'S FIRST CHRISTMAS QX577-7	YR	8.00	11.00
95	JUMPING FOR JOY QLX734-7	YR	28.00	45.00
95	PEZ SANTA QX526-7	YR	8.00	20.00
95	TAKIN' A HIKE QX602-9	YR	8.00	15.00
96	REGAL CARDINAL QX620-4	YR	10.00	10.00
T. KINKADE				
97	VICTORIAN CHRISTMAS 1613-5	YR	11.00	11.00
97	WARMTH OF HOME 1754-5	YR	19.00	19.00
K. KLINE				
98	WHAT'S YOUR NAME? 795QEO8443	YR	8.00	8.00

YR	NAME	LIMIT	ISSUE	TREND
D. LEE				
80	HEAVENLY MINSTREL 15QX156-7	YR	15.00	300.00
81	ANGEL QX 139-6	YR	5.50	82.00
83	DIANA DOLL QX 423-7	YR	9.00	23.00
84	CLASSICAL ANGEL 2750QX459-1	YR	28.00	75.00
90	GOLF'S MY BAG 775QX496-3	YR	7.75	17.00
94	FOR MY GRANDMA,PHOTOHOLDER 695QX561-3	YR	7.00	13.00
95	HEADIN' HOME QLX732-7	YR	22.00	32.00
95	TWO FOR TEA QX582-9	YR	10.00	25.00
J. LYLE				
89	BROTHER 725QX445-2	YR	7.25	15.00
93	OUR FIRST CHRISTMAS TOGETHER 975QX564-2	YR	9.75	13.00
94	GENTLE NURSE 695QX597-3	YR	7.00	16.00
94	HAPPY BIRTHDAY, JESUS 1295QX542-3	YR	13.00	20.00
94	NORMAN ROCKWELL ART 500QX241-3	YR	5.00	12.00
95	BROTHER QX567-9	YR	7.00	10.00
95	GRANDPARENTS QX241-9	YR	5.00	6.00
95	OUR CHRISTMAS TOGETHER QX579-9	YR	10.00	18.00
95	OUR FIRST CHRISTMAS TOGETHER QX317-7	YR	7.00	15.00
95	OUR FIRST CHRISTMAS TOGETHER QX579-7	YR	17.00	25.00
95	REJOICE! QX598-7	YR	11.00	20.00
95	SISTER QX568-7	YR	7.00	9.00
D. PALMITER				
94	MERRY FISHMAS 895QX591-3	YR	9.00	15.00
94	OUR FIRST CHRISTMAS..PHOTOHOLDER QX565-3	YR	9.00	15.00
94	PRACTICE MAKES PERFECT 895QX586-3	YR	9.00	12.00
94	SWEET GREETING 1095QX580-3	YR	11.00	19.00
95	COMING TO SEE SANTA QLX736-9	YR	32.00	48.00
95	DAUGHTER QX567-7	YR	7.00	8.00
95	FOR MY GRANDMA: PHOTOHOLDER QX572-9	YR	9.00	9.00
95	FRIENDLY BOOST QX582-7	YR	9.00	11.00
95	GODCHILD QX570-7	YR	8.00	10.00
95	MERRY RV QX602-7	YR	13.00	25.00
95	PEANUTS FIFTH AND FINAL QLX727-7	YR	25.00	40.00
95	SON QX566-9	YR	7.00	14.00
95	WAITING UP FOR SANTA QX610-6	YR	9.00	12.00
96	JUKEBOX PARTY QLX733-9	YR	25.00	45.00
S. PIKE				
88	OWLIDAY WISH	YR	6.50	16.00
90	SPENCER SPARROW, ESQ. 675QX431-2	YR	6.75	17.00
90	STOCKING KITTEN 675QX456-5	YR	6.75	13.00
94	BROTHER 695QX551-6	YR	7.00	11.00
94	DAD-TO-BE 795QX547-3	YR	8.00	14.00
94	GRANDDAUGHTER 695QX552-3	YR	7.00	16.00
94	GRANDSON 695QX552-6	YR	7.00	14.00
94	MOM-TO-BE 795QX550-6	YR	8.00	16.00
94	SISTER 695QX551-3	YR	7.00	15.00
95	DUDLEY THE DRAGON QX620-9	YR	11.00	20.00
95	FOREST FROLICS 7TH & FINAL QLX729-9	YR	28.00	45.00
96	MAXINE 10TH ANN. OF SHOEBOX GREETINGS QX622-4	YR	10.00	10.00
96	PEPPERMINT SURPRISE QX623-4	YR	8.00	8.00
98	FOREVER FRIENDS/ANDREW BROWNSWORD COLLECTION 8423	YR	10.00	10.00
M. PYDA-SEVCIK				
90	FIRST CHRISTMAS TOGETHER QX 488-3	YR	9.75	17.00
D. RHODUS				
94	HOLIDAY PATROL 895QX582-6	YR	9.00	11.00
94	MAKING IT BRIGHT 895QX540-3	YR	9.00	15.00
94	REINDEER PRO 795QX592-6	YR	8.00	16.00
94	SISTER TO SISTER 995QX553-3	YR	10.00	15.00
94	SPECIAL CAT, PHOTOHOLDER 795QX560-6	YR	8.00	9.00
94	SPECIAL DOG, PHOTOHOLDER 795QX560-3	YR	8.00	12.00
95	DAD-TO-BE QX566-7	YR	8.00	9.00
95	FELIZ NAVIDAD QX586-9	YR	8.00	16.00
95	MOM-TO-BE QX565-9	YR	8.00	15.00
95	SKI HOUND QX590-9	YR	9.00	11.00
95	THOMAS THE TANK ENGINE NO. 1 QX585-7	YR	10.00	25.00
96	HATTIE CHAPEAU QXM425-1	YR	4.75	5.00
N. ROCKWELL				
95	SANTA'S VISITOR: NORMAN ROCKWELL QX240-7	YR	5.00	11.00
A. ROGERS				
90	NUTSHELL HOLIDAY 575QX465-2	YR	5.75	21.00
92	KRINGLES, THE- 600QXM538-1	YR	6.00	22.00
93	MERRY OLDE SANTA 4TH ED. 1475QX484-2	YR	14.75	27.00
94	BEATLES GIFT SET QX 537-3	YR	48.00	92.00
94	CARING DOCTOR 895QX582-3	YR	9.00	15.00
94	DAD 795QX546-3	YR	8.00	11.00
94	FELIZ NAVIDAD 895QX579-3	YR	9.00	16.00
94	GODCHILD 895QX445-3	YR	9.00	9.00
94	MOM 795QX546-6	YR	8.00	12.00
94	OUR CHRISTMAS TOGETHER 995QX481-6	YR	10.00	14.00
94	RED HOT HOLIDAY 795QX584-3	YR	8.00	12.00
94	THICK 'N THIN 1095QX569-3	YR	11.00	14.00
94	TOU CAN LOVE 895QX564-6	YR	9.00	14.00
95	FRIENDS SHARE FUN QLX734-9	YR	16.50	25.00

YR	NAME	LIMIT	ISSUE	TREND
95	GRANDDAUGHTER QX577-9	YR	7.00	11.00
95	GRANDSON QX578-7	YR	7.00	9.00
95	HOLIDAY SWIM QLX731-9	YR	19.00	21.00
95	MOM AND DAD QX565-7	YR	10.00	13.00
E. SEALE				
87	CHRISTMAS IS GENTLE 1750QX444-9	YR	17.50	75.00
88	TREETOP DREAMS QX 459-7	YR	6.75	22.00
88	WONDERFUL SANTACYCLE, THE- 225QX411-4	YR	23.00	45.00
93	YOU'RE ALWAYS WELCOME QXC569-2	YR	9.75	50.00
94	COLORS OF JOY 795QX589-3	YR	8.00	20.00
94	KITTY'S CATAMARAN 1095QX541-6	YR	11.00	13.00
94	KRINGLE'S KAYAK 795QX588-6	YR	8.00	18.00
94	MAGIC CARPET RIDE 795QX588-3	YR	8.00	17.00
94	MISTLETOE SURPRISE 1295QX599-6	YR	13.00	25.00
95	AIR EXPRESS	YR	8.00	10.00
95	NORTH POLE 911 QX595-7	YR	11.00	17.00
95	OUR FIRST CHRISTMAS TOGETHER:PHOTOHOLDER QX580-7	YR	9.00	11.00
95	PACKED WITH MEMORIES:PHOTOHOLDER QX563-9	YR	8.00	11.00
95	ROLLER WHIZ QX593-7	YR	8.00	16.00
95	SANTA IN PARIS QX587-7	YR	9.00	20.00
96	CHRISTMAS BEAR QXM424-1	YR	4.75	5.00
96	MESSAGE FOR SANTA QXM425-4	YR	6.75	7.00
96	TINY CHRISTMAS HELPERS SET OF 6 QXM426-1	YR	29.00	29.00
L. SICKMAN				
85	TUFTED TITMOUSE QX 479-5	YR	6.50	26.00
86	OPEN HOUSE ORNAMENT QX0440-3	YR	12.75	47.00
89	ORNAMENT EXPRESS, THE- 2200QX580-5	YR	22.00	39.00
90	DOVE OF PEACE 2475QXC447-6	25400	25.00	65.00
94	FRIENDSHIP SUNDAE 1095QX476-6	YR	11.00	18.00
94	STAMP OF APPROVAL 795QX570-3	YR	8.00	11.00
95	DELIVERING KISSES QX410-7	YR	11.00	16.00
95	IMPORTANT MEMO QX584-7	YR	9.00	11.00
96	HOLIDAY HAUL QX620-1	YR	15.00	15.00
96	WOODLAND SANTA QX613-1	YR	13.00	13.00
B. SIEDLER				
88	HAPPY HOLIDATA QX 471-4	YR	6.50	24.00
88	REINDOGGY QX 452-7	YR	5.75	26.00
93	MESSAGES OF CHRISTMAS QLX747-2	YR	35.00	35.00
94	BIG SHOT 795QX587-3	YR	8.00	13.00
94	BUSY BATTER 795QX587-6	YR	8.00	12.00
94	CHAMPION TEACHER 695QX583-6	YR	7.00	11.00
94	FRIENDLY PUSH 895QX568-6	YR	9.00	13.00
94	IT'S A STRIKE 895QX585-6	YR	9.00	15.00
94	KEEP ON MOWIN' 895QX541-3	YR	9.00	11.00
94	KICKIN' ROO 795QX591-6	YR	8.00	10.00
94	MOM AND DAD 995QX566-6	YR	10.00	13.00
94	OPEN-AND-SHUT HOLIDAY 995QX569-6	YR	10.00	15.00
94	THRILL A MINUTE 895QX586-6	YR	9.00	12.00
94	WINNIE THE POOH AND TIGGER 1295QX574-6	YR	13.00	30.00
95	ACORN 500 QX 592-9	YR	11.00	11.00
95	CATCH THE SPIRIT QX589-9	YR	8.00	12.00
95	DAD QX564-9	YR	8.00	11.00
95	FAITHFUL FAN QX589-7	YR	9.00	10.00
95	GOODY GUMBALLS! QLX736-7	YR	12.50	21.00
95	GOPHER FUN QX588-7	YR	10.00	13.00
95	LOU RANKIN BEAR QX406-9	YR	10.00	13.00
95	MOM QX564-7	YR	8.00	11.00
95	OUR FIRST CHRISTMAS TOGETHER QX579-9	YR	9.00	11.00
95	PEANUTS GANG 3RD SERIES QX505-9	YR	10.00	25.00
95	PERFECT BALANCE QX592-7	YR	8.00	9.00
95	WATER SPORTS QX603-9	YR	15.00	19.00
95	WINNIE THE POOH -TOO MUCH HUNNY QLX729-7	YR	25.00	35.00
95	WINNIE THE POOH AND TIGGER QX500-9	YR	13.00	30.00
95	WINNING PLAY, THE QX588-9	YR	8.00	13.00
96	VIDEO PARTY QLX743-1	YR	28.00	28.00
S. TAGUE				
98	BOUQUET OF MEMORIES 795QEO8456	YR	8.00	8.00
D. UNRUH				
86	JOLLY ST. NICK 2250QX429-6	YR	23.00	60.00
86	MAGICAL UNICORN 2750QX429-3	YR	28.00	100.00
87	CHRISTMAS TIME MIME 2750QX442-9	YR	28.00	40.00
88	IN A NUTSHELL 550QX469-7	YR	5.50	19.00
93	GLOWING PEWTER WREATH 1875QX530-2	YR	19.00	39.00
94	COACH 795QX593-3	YR	8.00	11.00
94	GRANDCHILD'S FIRST CHRISTMAS 795QX567-6	YR	8.00	10.00
94	GRANDPA 795QX561-6	YR	8.00	11.00
94	LUCINDA AND TEDDY 2175QX481-3	SPEC. ED	22.00	35.00
94	OUT OF THIS WORLD TEACHER 795QX576-6	YR	8.00	16.00
94	SECRET SANTA 795QX573-6	YR	8.00	9.00
95	ANNIVERSARY YEAR: PHOTOHOLDER QX 581-9	YR	9.00	11.00
95	REFRESHING GIFT QX406-7	YR	15.00	19.00
96	PEACEFUL CHRISTMAS QXM421-4	YR	4.75	5.00
98	VICTORIAN CROSS 895QEO8453	YR	9.00	9.00
L. VOTRUBA				
90	FIRST CHRISTMAS TOGETHER QX 213-6	YR	4.75	15.00

YR	NAME	LIMIT	ISSUE	TREND
90	FIRST CHRISTMAS TOGETHER QX 314-6	YR	6.75	16.00
90	FIRST XMAS TOGETHER PHOTOHOLDER QX488-6	YR	7.75	15.00
93	BABY'S FIRST CHRISTMAS-GIRL 475QX209-2	YR	4.75	8.00
94	CHILD CARE GIVER 795QX590-6	YR	8.00	13.00
94	COCK-A-DOODLE CHRISTMAS QX 539-6	YR	9.00	12.00
94	OUR FIRST CHRISTMAS TOGETHER 695QX318-6	YR	7.00	16.00
95	BABY'S FIRST CHRISTMAS: PHOTOHOLDER QX554-9	YR	8.00	11.00
95	BINGO BEAR QX591-9	YR	8.00	16.00
95	GODPARENT QX241-7	YR	5.00	6.00
95	HAPPY HOLIDAYS: PHOTOHOLDER QX630-7	YR	3.00	9.00
95	SANTA'S DINER QLX733-7	YR	25.00	35.00
95	SISTER TO SISTER QX568-9	YR	8.00	12.00
D. LEE			**20TH ANNIVERSARY**	
93	TANNENBAUM'S DEPT. STORE 2600QX561-2	YR	26.00	50.00
D. UNRUH			**20TH ANNIVERSARY**	
93	GLOWING PEWTER WREATH QX530-2	YR	19.00	30.00
P. ANDREWS		**A CELEBRATION OF ANGELS**		
96	A CELEBRATION OF ANGELS 2ND ED. QX563-4	YR	13.00	25.00
97	A CELEBRATION OF ANGELS 3RD ED.	YR	14.00	14.00
D. UNRUH		**A CHRISTMAS CAROL COLLECTION**		
91	BOB CRATCHIT 1375QX499-7	YR	13.75	23.00
91	EBENEZER SCROOGE 1375QX498-9	YR	13.75	35.00
91	MERRY CAROLERS 2975QX479-9	YR	30.00	75.00
91	MRS. CRATCHIT 1375QX499-7	YR	13.75	30.00
91	TINY TIM 1075QX503-7	YR	10.75	30.00
J. LEE		**ACCESSORIES FOR COLLECTOR'S SERIES**		
95	NOSTALGIC HOUSES AND SHOPS QX508-9	YR	9.00	11.00
P. ANDREWS			**ALICE IN WONDERLAND**	
96	MAD HATTER 2ND ED. QXM407-4	YR	6.75	15.00
M. ROOT			**ALL GOD'S CHILDREN**	
96	CHRISTY 1ST ED. QX556-4	YR	13.00	13.00
97	NIKKI	YR	13.00	13.00
P. ANDREWS			**ALL IS BRIGHT**	
95	ANGEL OF LIGHT QK115-9	YR	12.00	14.00
95	GENTLE LULLABY QK115-7	YR	12.00	14.00
D. PALMITER			**ALL-AMERICAN TRUCKS**	
95	1956 FORD TRUCK FIRST SERIES QX 552-7	YR	14.00	35.00
96	1955 CHEVROLET CAMEO 2ND ED. QX524-1	YR	14.00	20.00
97	1953 GMC QX610-5	YR	14.00	14.00
*		**AMERICAN COUNTRY COLLECTION**		
86	MARY EMMERLING 795QX275-2	YR	8.00	19.00
*			**ANGEL BELLS**	
95	CAROLE QX114-7	YR	13.00	25.00
L. VOTRUBA			**ANGEL BELLS**	
95	JOY QK113-7	YR	13.00	25.00
95	NOELLE QK113-9	YR	13.00	25.00
*		**ANNIVERSARY ORNAMENTS**		
92	25 YEARS TOGETHER 1000AGA711-3	YR	10.00	22.00
92	25 YEARS TOGETHER ANN. BELL 800AGA713-4	YR	10.00	16.00
92	40 YEARS TOGETHER 1000AGA731-6	YR	10.00	27.00
92	50 YEARS TOGETHER 1000AGA721-4	YR	10.00	27.00
92	50 YEARS TOGETHER ANN. BELL 800AGA723-5	YR	10.00	17.00
92	OUR FIFTH ANNIVERSARY 1000AGA731-9	YR	10.00	20.00
92	OUR FIRST ANNIVERSARY 1000AGA731-8	YR	10.00	22.00
92	OUR TENTH ANNIVERSARY 1000AGA731-7	YR	10.00	20.00
93	25 YEARS TOGETHER 1000AGA768-6	YR	10.00	24.00
93	25 YEARS TOGETHER ANN. BELL 800AGA768-7	YR	10.00	24.00
93	40 YEARS TOGETHER 1000AGA786-8	YR	10.00	24.00
93	50 YEARS TOGETHER 1000AGA778-7	YR	10.00	22.00
93	50 YEARS TOGETHER ANN. BELL 800AGA778-8	YR	10.00	22.00
93	OUR FIFTH ANNIVERSARY 1000AGA786-6	YR	10.00	22.00
93	OUR FIRST ANNIVERSARY 1000AGA786-5	YR	10.00	22.00
93	OUR TENTH ANNIVERSARY 1000AGA786-7	YR	10.00	22.00
L. SICKMAN			**ANNIVERSARY ORNAMENTS**	
95	PEWTER ROCKING HORSE QX616-7	YR	20.00	50.00
B. SIEDLER		**ANNIVERSARY ORNAMENTS**		
95	WHEEL OF FORTUNE QX588-9	YR	13.00	25.00
D. MCGEHEE			**ART MASTERPIECE**	
86	MADONNA & CHILD 3RD & FINAL QX 350-6	YR	6.75	21.00
R. CHAD			**ARTISTS' FAVORITES**	
88	BABY REDBIRD 500QX410-1	YR	5.00	12.00
92	ELFIN MARIONETTE 1175QX593-1	YR	11.75	21.00
K. CROW			**ARTISTS' FAVORITES**	
90	WELCOME, SANTA 1175QX477-3	YR	11.75	24.00
91	NOAH'S ARK 1375QX486-7	YR	13.75	32.00
92	MOTHER GOOSE 1375QX498-4	YR	13.75	35.00
P. DUTKIN			**ARTISTS' FAVORITES**	
88	VERY STRAWBERRY 475QX409-1	YR	4.75	13.00
J. FRANCIS			**ARTISTS' FAVORITES**	
89	BABY PARTRIDGE 675QX452-5	YR	6.75	13.00
90	GENTLE DREAMERS 875QX475-6	YR	8.75	20.00
91	TRAMP AND LADDIE 775QX439-7	YR	7.75	21.00

YR	NAME	LIMIT	ISSUE	TREND
D. LEE			**ARTISTS' FAVORITES**	
87	DECEMBER SHOWERS 550QX448-7	YR	5.50	19.00
87	THREE MEN IN A TUB 800QX454-7	YR	8.00	20.00
88	CYMBALS OF CHRISTMAS 550QX411-1	YR	5.50	22.00
89	PLAYFUL ANGEL 675QX453-5	YR	6.75	21.00
90	DONDER'S DINER 1375QX482-3	YR	13.75	25.00
90	HAPPY WOODCUTTER 975QX476-3	YR	9.75	20.00
91	HOOKED ON SANTA 775QX410-9	YR	7.75	18.00
92	TURTLE DREAMS 875QX499-1	YR	8.75	20.00
M. PYDA-SEVCIK			**ARTISTS' FAVORITES**	
90	ANGEL KITTY 875QX474-6	YR	8.75	21.00
A. ROGERS			**ARTISTS' FAVORITES**	
88	MERRY MINT UNICORN 850QX423-4	YR	8.50	17.00
89	MERRY-GO-ROUND UNICORN 1075QX447-2	YR	10.75	16.00
E. SEALE			**ARTISTS' FAVORITES**	
87	WEE CHIMNEY SWEEP 625QX451-9	YR	6.25	18.00
89	MAIL CALL 875QX452-2	YR	8.75	15.00
90	MOUSEBOAT 775QX475-3	YR	7.75	12.00
91	SANTA SAILOR 975QX438-9	YR	9.75	18.00
92	POLAR POST 875QX491-4	YR	8.75	15.00
L. SICKMAN			**ARTISTS' FAVORITES**	
89	CAROUSEL ZEBRA 925QX451-5	YR	9.25	18.00
89	CHERRY JUBILEE 500QX453-2	YR	5.00	20.00
91	POLAR CIRCUS WAGON 1375QX439-9	YR	13.75	17.00
92	STOCKED WITH JOY 775QX593-4	YR	7.75	16.00
B. SIEDLER			**ARTISTS' FAVORITES**	
87	BEARY SPECIAL 475QX455-7	YR	4.75	15.00
88	LITTLE JACK HORNER 800QX408-1	YR	8.00	18.00
88	MIDNIGHT SNACK 600QX410-4	YR	6.00	18.00
89	BEAR-I-TONE 475QX454-2	YR	4.75	15.00
92	UNCLE ART'S ICE CREAM 875QX500-1	YR	8.75	20.00
L. VOTRUBA			**ARTISTS' FAVORITES**	
91	FIDDLIN' AROUND 775QX438-7	YR	7.75	16.00
D. RHODUS			**AT THE BALLPARK**	
96	NOLAN RYAN 1ST ED. QXI571-1	YR	15.00	15.00
97	HANK AARON 2ND. ED. 16152	YR	15.00	15.00
*			**BABY CELEBRATIONS**	
89	BABY'S CHRISTENING KEEPSAKE 700BBY132-5	YR	7.00	30.00
89	BABY'S FIRST BIRTHDAY 5500BBY172-9	YR	5.50	31.00
89	BABY'S FIRST CHRISTMAS-BOY 475BB145-3	YR	4.75	13.00
89	BABY'S FIRST CHRISTMAS-GIRL 475BBY155-3	YR	4.75	11.00
90	BABY'S CHRISTENING 1000BBY132-6	YR	10.00	22.00
90	BABY'S FIRST CHRISTMAS-BOY PONY BBY145-4	YR	10.00	22.00
90	BABY'S FIRST CHRISTMAS-GIRL BUNNY BBY155	YR	10.00	35.00
91	BABY'S CHRISTENING LAMB 1000BBY131-7	YR	10.00	14.00
91	BABY'S FIRST CHRISTMAS-BOY PONY BBY141-6	YR	10.00	14.00
91	BABY'S FIRST CHRISTMAS-GIRL BUNNY BBY151	YR	10.00	25.00
92	BABY'S CHRISTENING-WHITE HEART BBY133-1	YR	8.50	11.00
92	BABY'S FIRST CHRISTMAS-BLUE PONY BBY145-6	YR	8.50	11.00
92	BABY'S FIRST CHRISTMAS-BUNNY 850BBY155-7	YR	8.50	10.00
93	BABY'S 1ST CHRISTMAS PHOTOHOLDER BBY147-0	YR	10.00	29.00
93	BABY'S CHRISTENING 1200BBY291-7	YR	12.00	15.00
93	BABY'S CHRISTENING PHOTOHOLDER BBY 133-5	YR	10.00	13.00
93	BABY'S FIRST CHRISTMAS MOON 1400BBY291-9	YR	14.00	17.00
93	BABY'S FIRST CHRISTMAS RABBIT BBY291-8	YR	12.00	29.00
93	GRANDDAUGHTER FIRST CHRISTMAS BBY 280-2	YR	14.00	28.00
93	GRANDSON'S FIRST CHRISTMAS BBY 280-1	YR	14.00	28.00
*			**BABY'S FIRST CHRISTMAS**	
94	BABY'S FIRST CHRISTMAS-BOY 500QX243-6	YR	5.00	6.00
94	BABY'S FIRST CHRISTMAS-GIRL 500QX243-3	YR	5.00	6.00
K. CROW			**BABY'S FIRST CHRISTMAS**	
94	BABY'S FIRST CHRISTMAS 795QX571-3	YR	8.00	13.00
95	BABY'S FIRST CHRISTMAS MUSICAL QLX 731-7	YR	22.00	25.00
P. ANDREWS				**BARBIE**
94	BARBIE 1ST IN ED. QX 500-6	YR	15.00	30.00
95	BARBIE: SOLO IN SPOTLIGHT 2ND IN ED. QX1504-9	YR	15.00	31.00
96	BARBIE: ENCHANTED EVENING 3RD IN ED. QXI654-1	YR	15.00	25.00
97	WEDDING DAY 4TH ED. 1959-1962	YR	16.00	16.00
D. RHODUS			**BASEBALL HEROES**	
94	BABE RUTH 1ST ED. 1295QX532-3	YR	13.00	50.00
95	LOU GEHRIG QX502-9	YR	13.00	25.00
96	SATCHEL PAIGE 3RD ED. QX530-4	YR	13.00	15.00
97	JACKIE ROBINSON 620-2	YR	13.00	13.00
R. CHAD				**BATMAN**
94	BATMAN 1295QX585-3	YR	13.00	40.00
D. PALMITER				**BATMAN**
95	BATMOBILE QX573-9	YR	15.00	35.00
*			**BEARINGERS OF VICTORIA CIRCLE**	
93	ABEARNATHY/SON 495XPR974-7	YR	5.00	7.00
93	BEARNADETTE/DAUGHTER 495XPR974-8	YR	5.00	7.00
93	FIREPLACE HEARTH XPR974-9	YR	5.00	8.00
93	MAMA BEARINGER 495XPR974-5	YR	5.00	8.00
93	PAPA BEARINGER 495XPR974-6	YR	5.00	7.00

YR	NAME	LIMIT	ISSUE	TREND
L. VOTRUBA				
				BEATRIX POTTER
96	PETER RABBIT	YR	9.00	60.00
97	JEMIMA PUDDLE-DUCK	YR	9.00	18.00
98	BENJAMIN BUNNY 895QE8383	YR	9.00	9.00
*				**BEAUTY OF AMERICA COLLECTION**
77	DESERT 250QX159-5	YR	2.50	30.00
77	MOUNTAINS 250QX158-2	YR	2.50	27.00
77	SEASHORE 250QX160-2	YR	2.50	50.00
77	WHARF 250QX161-5	YR	2.50	36.00
*				**BELLRINGER SERIES**
81	SWINGIN' BELLRINGER QX 441-5	YR	15.00	92.00
84	ELFIN ARTIST QX 438-4	YR	15.00	35.00
D. LEE				**BELLRINGER SERIES**
82	ANGEL QX 455-6	YR	15.00	90.00
*				**BETSEY CLARK**
73	BETSEY CLARK-FIRST EDITION 250XHD110-2	YR	2.50	120.00
74	BETSEY CLARK-SECOND EDITION 250QX108-1	YR	2.50	70.00
75	BETSEY CLARK-THIRD EDITION 300QX133-1	YR	3.00	30.00
76	BETSEY CLARK-FOURTH ED 300QX195-1	YR	3.00	80.00
77	BETSEY CLARK-FIFTH ED 350QX264-2	YR	3.50	440.00
78	BETSEY CLARK-SIXTH ED 350QX201-6	YR	3.50	50.00
79	BETSEY CLARK-SEVENTH EDITION 350QX201-9	YR	3.50	31.00
80	BETSEY CLARK-EIGHTH ED 400QX215-4	YR	4.00	28.00
81	BETSEY CLARK-NINTH ED 450QX802-2	YR	4.50	26.00
82	BETSEY CLARK-TENTH ED QX 215-6	YR	4.50	26.00
83	BETSEY CLARK-ELEVENTH EDITION 450QX211-9	YR	4.50	26.00
84	BETSEY CLARK-TWELFTH EDITION 500QX249-4	YR	5.00	25.00
S. PIKE				**BETSEY CLARK**
85	BETSEY CLARK THIRTEENTH & FINAL 500QX263-2	YR	5.00	25.00
*				**BICENTENNIAL COMMEMORATIVES**
76	BICENTENNIAL '76 COMMEMORATIVE QX 203-1	YR	2.50	60.00
76	BICENTENNIAL CHARMERS 300QX198-1	YR	3.00	43.00
76	COLONIAL CHILDREN (2) 400QX208-1	YR	4.00	42.00
D. LEE				**BRASS ORNAMENTS**
82	BRASS BELL 1200QX460-6	YR	12.00	17.00
E. SEALE				**BRASS ORNAMENTS**
82	SANTA'S SLEIGH 900QX478-6	YR	9.00	26.00
L. SICKMAN				**BRASS ORNAMENTS**
82	SANTA AND REINDEER 900QX467-6	YR	9.00	43.00
*				**CAROUSEL SERIES**
78	CAROUSEL SERIES-1ST EDITION 600QX146-3	YR	6.00	400.00
79	CAROUSEL-2ND EDITION 650QX146-7	YR	6.50	155.00
80	MERRY CAROUSEL 750QX141-4	YR	7.50	150.00
81	CAROUSEL-4TH EDITION 900QX427-5	YR	9.00	75.00
E. SEALE				**CAROUSEL SERIES**
82	SNOWMAN CAROUSEL-5TH EDITION 1000QX478-3	YR	10.00	85.00
L. SICKMAN				**CAROUSEL SERIES**
83	SANTA & FRIENDS 1100QX401-9	YR	11.00	40.00
K. BRICKER				**CAT NAPS**
97	CAT IN BRIEFCASE 4TH ED. 620-5	YR	9.00	9.00
D. RHODUS				**CAT NAPS**
94	CAT NAPS 1ST ED. 795QX531-3	YR	7.75	38.00
95	CAT NAPS 2ND SERIES QX509-7	YR	8.00	25.00
96	CAT NAP 3RD ED. QX564-1	YR	8.00	15.00
L. SICKMAN				**CENTURIES OF SANTA**
96	CENTURIES OF SANTA 3RD ED. QXM409-1	YR	5.75	6.00
*				**CHARLIE BROWN CHRISTMAS**
95	CHARLIE BROWN 420-7	YR	4.00	38.00
95	LINUS 421-7	YR	4.00	25.00
95	LUCY 420-9	YR	4.00	25.00
95	SNOOPY 421-9	YR	4.00	29.00
A.M. ROGERS				**CHILDREN'S COLLECTOR BARBIE**
98	BARBIE AS LITTLE BO PEEP 1495QEO8373	YR	15.00	15.00
*				**CHRIS MOUSE**
97	CHRIS MOUSE LUMINARIA 13TH EDITION QLX752-5	YR	*	15.00
P. DUTKIN				**CHRIS MOUSE**
86	CHRIS MOUSE DREAMS 2ND EDITION 1300QLX705-6	YR	13.00	80.00
A. ROGERS				**CHRIS MOUSE**
89	CHRIS MOUSE COOKOUT 5TH EDITION 950QLX722-5	YR	9.50	50.00
90	CHRIS MOUSE WREATH 6TH EDITION 1000QLX729-6	YR	10.00	33.00
92	CHRIS MOUSE SHOE 8TH EDITION 1200QLX707-4	YR	12.00	27.00
93	CHRIS MOUSE FLIGHT 9TH EDITION 1200QLX715-2	YR	12.00	23.00
94	CHRIS MOUSE JELLY 10TH EDITION 1200QLX739-3	YR	12.00	22.00
95	CHRIS MOUSE TREE 11TH EDITION QLX730-7	YR	12.50	20.00
B. SIEDLER				**CHRIS MOUSE**
85	CHRIS MOUSE 1ST EDITION 1250QLX703-2	YR	12.50	70.00
87	CHRIS MOUSE 3RD EDITION 100QLX705-7	YR	11.00	52.00
88	CHRIS MOUSE STAR 4TH EDITION QLX 715-4	YR	8.75	50.00
91	CHRIS MOUSE MAIL 7TH EDITION 1000QLX720-7	YR	10.00	30.00
96	CHRIS MOUSE INN 12TH EDITION QLX737-1	YR	14.50	20.00
E. SEALE				**CHRISTMAS BELLS**
96	CHRISTMAS BELLS 2ND ED. QXM407-1	YR	4.75	5.00

YR	NAME	LIMIT	ISSUE	TREND
	*	CHRISTMAS CAROUSEL HORSE COLLECTION		
89	CAROUSEL DISPLAY STAND 629XPR972-3	YR	1.00	11.00
	J. LEE	CHRISTMAS CAROUSEL HORSE COLLECTION		
89	GINGER 629XPR972-1	YR	4.00	18.00
89	HOLLY 629XPR972-2	YR	4.00	18.00
89	SNOW 929XPR971-9	YR	4.00	28.00
89	STAR 629XPR972-0	YR	4.00	18.00
	*	CHRISTMAS CLASSICS		
86	NUTCRACKER BALLET 1750QLX704-3	YR	17.50	80.00
87	A CHRISTMAS CAROL 1600QLX702-9	YR	16.00	45.00
	J. FRANCIS	CHRISTMAS CLASSICS		
90	LITTLEST ANGEL , THE-1400QLX730-3	YR	14.00	36.00
	D. LEE	CHRISTMAS CLASSICS		
88	NIGHT BEFORE CHRISTMAS-3RD ED. 1500QLX716-1	YR	15.00	27.00
89	LITTLE DRUMMER BOY 1350QLX724-2	YR	13.50	35.00
	*	CHRISTMAS EXPRESSIONS COLLECTION		
77	BELL 350QX154-2	YR	3.50	40.00
77	MANDOLIN 350QX157-5	YR	3.50	40.00
77	ORNAMENTS 350QX155-5	YR	3.50	40.00
77	WREATH 350QX156-2	YR	3.50	37.00
	L. SICKMAN	CHRISTMAS MEDLEY COLLECTION		
86	FAVORITE TIN DRUM 850QX514-3	YR	8.50	21.00
86	JOYFUL CAROLERS 975QX513-6	YR	9.75	29.00
	B. SIEDLER	CHRISTMAS MEDLEY COLLECTION		
86	FESTIVE TREBLE CLEF 875QX513-3	YR	8.75	20.00
	D. UNRUH	CHRISTMAS MEDLEY COLLECTION		
86	CHRISTMAS GUITAR 700QX512-6	YR	7.00	18.00
86	HOLIDAY HORN 800QX514-6	YR	8.00	26.00
	K. CROW	CHRISTMAS PIZZAZZ COLLECTION		
87	JOLLY FOLLIES 850QX466-9	YR	8.50	23.00
87	MISTLETOAD 700QX468-7	YR	7.00	24.00
	P. DUTKIN	CHRISTMAS PIZZAZZ COLLECTION		
87	ST. LOUIE NICK 775QX453-9	YR	7.75	21.00
	D. LEE	CHRISTMAS PIZZAZZ COLLECTION		
87	CHRISTMAS FUN PUZZLE 800QX467-9	YR	8.00	18.00
	E. SEALE	CHRISTMAS PIZZAZZ COLLECTION		
87	DOC HOLIDAY 800QX467-7	YR	8.00	31.00
	B. SIEDLER	CHRISTMAS PIZZAZZ COLLECTION		
87	HAPPY HOLIDATA 650QX471-7	YR	6.50	24.00
	D. UNRUH	CHRISTMAS PIZZAZZ COLLECTION		
87	HOLIDAY HOURGLASS 800QX470-7	YR	8.00	17.00
	L. SICKMAN	CHRISTMAS SKY LINE COLLECTION		
92	CABOOSE 975QX532-1	YR	9.75	23.00
92	COAL CAR 975QX540-1	YR	9.75	18.00
92	LOCOMOTIVE 975QX531-1	YR	9.75	48.00
92	STOCK CAR 975QX531-4	YR	9.75	18.00
	*	CHRISTMAS VISITORS		
96	CHRISTKINDL 563-1	YR	15.00	25.00
97	KOLYADA 617-2	YR	15.00	15.00
	A. ROGERS	CHRISTMAS VISITORS		
95	ST. NICHOLAS 1ST ED. QX508-7	YR	15.00	35.00
	L. VOTRUBA	CHRISTMAS VISITORS		
96	CHRISTKINDL 2ND ED. QX563-1	YR	15.00	25.00
	D. PALMITER	CLASSIC AMERICAN CARS		
91	1957 CORVETTE-1ST EDITION 1275QX431-9	YR	12.75	185.00
92	1966 MUSTANG 1275QX428-4	YR	12.75	45.00
93	1956 FORD THUNDERBIRD 1275QX527-5	YR	12.75	30.00
94	1957 CHEVROLET BEL AIR 4TH ED. 1275QX542-2	YR	13.00	25.00
95	1969 CHEVROLET CAMARO QX523-9	YR	13.00	19.00
96	1959 CADILLAC DE VILLE 6TH ED. QX538-4	YR	13.00	20.00
97	1969 HURST OLDSMOBILE 442	YR	14.00	14.00
	D. PALMITER	CLAUS & CO. R.R. ORNAMENTS		
91	CABOOSE 395XPR973-3	YR	4.00	11.00
91	GIFT CAR 395XPR973-1	YR	4.00	11.00
91	PASSENGER CAR 395XPR973-2	YR	4.00	11.00
91	TRESTLE TRACK FOR TRAIN 295XPR973-4	YR	3.00	8.00
	*	CLOTH DOLL ORNAMENTS		
77	ANGEL 175QX220-2	YR	1.75	52.00
77	SANTA 175QX221-5	YR	1.75	60.00
	L. SICKMAN	CLOTHESPIN SOLDIER		
84	CANADIAN MOUNTIE QX447-1	YR	5.00	22.00
85	SCOTTISH-4TH EDITION 550QX471-5	YR	5.50	22.00
86	CLOTHESPIN SOLDIER-5TH ED. 550QX406-3	YR	5.50	22.00
87	SAILOR 550QX480-7	YR	5.50	20.00
	D. UNRUH	COCA-COLA SANTA		
96	WELCOME GUEST QX539-4	YR	15.00	15.00
	*	COLLECTIBLE SERIES		
79	BELLRINGER-1ST EDITION 10QX147-9	YR	10.00	250.00
79	SNOOPY AND FRIENDS 800QX141-9	YR	8.00	120.00
80	BELLRINGERS, THE-2ND EDITION 15QX157-4	YR	15.00	75.00
81	NORMAN ROCKWELL-2ND EDITION 850QX511-5	YR	8.50	37.00
83	BELLRINGER, THE-5TH EDITION 1500QX403-9	YR	15.00	119.00

YR	NAME	LIMIT	ISSUE	TREND
84	CINNAMON BEAR-2ND EDITION 700QX454-1	YR	7.00	33.00
84	WOOD CHILDHOOD ORNAMENTS 650QX439-4	YR	6.50	36.00
86	CINNAMON BEAR-4TH EDITION 775QX405-6	YR	7.75	44.00
87	CINNAMON BEAR-5TH EDITION 775QX442-7	YR	7.75	25.00
89	BETSEY CLARK-HOME FOR XMAS, 4TH ED. 500QX230-2	YR	5.00	22.00
89	WINTER SURPRISE-1ST EDITION 1075QX427-2	YR	10.75	20.00
90	BETSEY CLARK: HOME FOR XMAS 5TH ED. 500QX203-3	YR	5.00	16.00
90	CINNAMON BEAR-8TH EDITION 875QX442-6	YR	8.75	20.00
91	BETSEY CLARK: HOME FOR XMAS 6TH ED. 500QX210-9	YR	5.00	16.00
92	BETSEY'S COUNTRY CHRISTMAS 1ST ED. 500QX210-4	YR	5.00	20.00
93	BETSEY'S COUNTRY CHRISTMAS 2ND ED. 500QX206-2	YR	5.00	10.00
K. CROW			**COLLECTIBLE SERIES**	
89	HARK! IT'S HERALD-1ST EDITION 675QX455-5	YR	6.75	21.00
90	HARK! IT'S HERALD-2ND EDITION 675QX446-3	YR	6.75	19.00
P. DUTKIN			**COLLECTIBLE SERIES**	
83	CINNAMON BEAR-1ST EDITION 700QX428-9	YR	7.00	75.00
85	CINNAMON BEAR-3RD EDITION 750QX479-2	YR	7.50	50.00
J. FRANCIS			**COLLECTIBLE SERIES**	
80	SNOOPY & FRIENDS-2ND EDITION 900QX154-1	YR	9.00	97.00
81	SNOOPY & FRIENDS-3RD EDITION 1200QX436-2	YR	12.00	82.00
90	WINTER SURPRISE-2ND EDITION 1075QX444-3	YR	10.75	18.00
92	WINTER SURPRISE 4TH ED. 1175QX427-1	YR	11.75	17.00
J. LEE			**COLLECTIBLE SERIES**	
91	MERRY OLDE SANTA-2ND EDITION 1475QX435-9	YR	14.75	80.00
92	HARK! IT'S HERALD 4TH ED. 775QX446-4	YR	7.75	18.00
J. LYLE			**COLLECTIBLE SERIES**	
91	HEAVENLY ANGELS-1ST EDITION 775QX436-7	YR	7.75	30.00
91	WINTER SURPRISE-3RD EDITION 1075QX427-7	YR	10.75	20.00
92	HEAVENLY ANGELS 2ND ED. 775QX445-4	YR	7.75	24.00
93	HEAVENLY ANGELS 3RD ED. 775QX494-5	YR	7.75	15.00
D. MCGEHEE			**COLLECTIBLE SERIES**	
84	ART MASTERPIECE-1ST EDITION 650QX349-4	YR	6.50	13.00
85	ART MASTERPIECE-2ND EDITION 675QX377-2	YR	6.75	14.00
J. PATTEE			**COLLECTIBLE SERIES**	
87	CONSTITUTION, THE 600QZ377-7	YR	6.50	14.00
S. PIKE			**COLLECTIBLE SERIES**	
86	BETSEY CLARK: HOME FOR XMAS 500QX277-6	YR	5.00	21.00
87	BETSEY CLARK-HOME FOR CHRISTMAS 500QX272-7	YR	5.00	20.00
88	BETSEY CLARK: HOME FOR XMAS 500QX271-4	YR	5.00	18.00
88	CINNAMON BEAR 800QX404-4	YR	8.00	30.00
88	FIVE GOLDEN RINGS-5TH EDITION 650QX371-4	YR	6.50	20.00
89	CINNAMON TEDDY-7TH EDITION 875QX461-5	YR	8.75	20.00
93	FABULOUS DECADE 775QX447-5	YR	7.75	14.00
A. ROGERS			**COLLECTIBLE SERIES**	
89	CHRISTMAS KITTY-1ST EDITION 1475QX544-5	YR	14.75	23.00
89	MINIATURE CRECHE-5TH EDITION 925QX459-2	YR	9.25	18.00
90	CHRISTMAS KITTY-2ND EDITION 1475QX450-6	YR	14.75	26.00
91	CHRISTMAS KITTY-3RD EDITION 1475QX437-7	YR	14.75	21.00
91	HARK! IT'S HERALD-3RD ED. 675QX437-9	YR	6.75	17.00
E. SEALE			**COLLECTIBLE SERIES**	
82	SNOOPY & FRIENDS-4TH EDITION 1300QX480-3	YR	13.00	105.00
85	MINIATURE CRECHE-1ST EDITION 875QX482-5	YR	8.75	29.00
86	MINIATURE CRECHE-2ND EDITION 900QX407-6	YR	9.00	55.00
87	MINIATURE CRECHE-3RD EDITION 900QX481-9	YR	9.00	23.00
90	CLAUS CONSTRUCTION 775QX488-5	YR	7.75	23.00
90	FABULOUS DECADE-1ST EDITION 775QX446-6	YR	7.75	35.00
90	HEART OF CHRISTMAS-1ST ED. 1375QX472-6	YR	13.75	50.00
90	MERRY OLDE SANTA-1ST EDITION 1475QX473-6	YR	14.75	70.00
91	FABULOUS DECADE-2ND EDITION 775QX411-9	YR	7.75	31.00
91	HEART OF CHRISTMAS-2ND ED. 1375QX435-7	YR	13.75	30.00
92	FABULOUS DECADE 3RD ED. 775QX424-4	YR	7.75	30.00
92	HEART OF CHRISTMAS 3RD ED. 1375QX441-1	YR	13.75	30.00
93	HEART OF CHRISTMAS 4TH ED. 1475QX448-2	YR	14.75	23.00
94	FABULOUS DECADE 5TH ED. 795QX526-3	YR	8.00	18.00
94	HEART OF CHRISTMAS 5TH ED. 1495QX526-6	YR	15.00	20.00
95	FABULOUS DECADE 6TH SERIES QX514-7	YR	8.00	12.00
96	FABULOUS DECADE 7TH ED. QX566-1	YR	8.00	20.00
97	FABULOUS DECADE 8TH ED. 623-2	YR	8.00	8.00
L. SICKMAN			**COLLECTIBLE SERIES**	
82	CLOTHESPIN SOLDIER-1ST ED. 500QX458-3	YR	5.00	115.00
83	CLOTHESPIN SOLDIER-2ND ED. 500QX402-9	YR	5.00	52.00
83	SNOOPY & FRIENDS-5TH EDITION 1300QX416-9	YR	13.00	75.00
D. UNRUH			**COLLECTIBLE SERIES**	
87	HOLIDAY HEIRLOOM QX 485-7	34600	25.00	29.00
88	MINIATURE CRECHE-4TH EDITION 850QX403-4	YR	8.50	17.00
92	MERRY OLDE SANTA 3RD ED. 1475QX441-4	YR	14.75	30.00
L. VOTRUBA			**COLLECTIBLE SERIES**	
90	GIFT BRINGERS-ST. LUCIA 500QX280-3	YR	5.00	24.00
90	GREATEST STORY-1ST EDITION 1275QX465-6	YR	12.75	22.00
91	GREATEST STORY-2ND EDITION 1275QX412-9	YR	12.75	24.00
92	GIFT BRINGERS, THE/KOLYADA 4TH ED. 500QX212-4	YR	5.00	14.00
92	GREATEST STORY 3RD ED. 1275QX425-1	YR	12.75	20.00
K. CROW			**COLLECTOR'S CHOICE**	
96	COME ALL YE FAITHFUL QX624-4	YR	13.00	13.00

YR NAME	LIMIT	ISSUE	TREND
J. LYLE		**COLLECTOR'S CHOICE**	
96 GLAD TIDINGS QX623-1	YR	15.00	15.00
96 PRAYER FOR PEACE QX626-1	YR	8.00	8.00
S. TAGUE		**COLLECTOR'S CHOICE**	
96 WELCOME HIM QX626-4	YR	9.00	9.00
D. UNRUH		**COLLECTOR'S CHOICE**	
96 CHRISTMAS JOY QX624-1	YR	15.00	15.00
L. VOTRUBA		**COLLECTOR'S CHOICE**	
96 PRECIOUS CHILD QX624-1	YR	9.00	9.00
P. ANDREWS		**COLLECTOR'S CLASSIC**	
96 GONE WITH THE WIND 3 PC. SET QXM421-1	YR	20.00	50.00
S. PIKE		**COLLECTOR'S CLASSIC**	
96 COOL DELIVERY COCA-COLA QXM402-1	YR	5.75	6.00
E. SEALE		**COLLECTOR'S CLASSIC**	
96 STATUE OF LIBERTY, THE QLX742-1	YR	25.00	25.00
B. SIEDLER		**COLLECTOR'S CLASSIC**	
96 A TREE FOR WOODSTOCK QXM476-7	YR	5.75	10.00
96 WINNIE THE POOH & TIGGER QXM404-4	YR	9.75	25.00
K. CROW		**COLORFUL WORLD**	
95 CRAYOLA QX551-9	YR	11.00	18.00
*		**COLORS OF CHRISTMAS**	
77 CANDLE 350QX203-5	YR	3.50	59.00
77 JOY 350QX201-5	YR	3.50	45.00
77 WREATH 350QX202-2	YR	3.50	59.00
78 ANGEL 350QX354-3	YR	3.50	50.00
78 CANDLE 350QX357-6	YR	3.50	85.00
78 LOCOMOTIVE 350QX356-3	YR	3.50	45.00
79 HOLIDAY WREATH 350QX353-9	YR	3.50	40.00
79 PARTRIDGE IN A PEAR TREE 350QX351-9	YR	3.50	40.00
79 WORDS OF CHRISTMAS 350QX350-7	YR	3.50	75.00
80 JOY 400QX350-1	YR	4.00	20.00
82 NATIVITY 450QX308-3	YR	4.50	45.00
82 SANTA'S FLIGHT 450QX308-6	YR	4.50	45.00
D. PALMITER		**COLORS OF CHRISTMAS**	
78 MERRY CHRISTMAS 350QX355-6	YR	3.50	47.00
L. SICKMAN		**COLORS OF CHRISTMAS**	
77 BELL 350QX200-2	YR	3.50	52.00
79 STAR OVER BETHLEHEM 350QX352-7	YR	3.50	62.00
*		**COMMEMORATIVES**	
77 BABY'S FIRST CHRISTMAS 350QX131-5	YR	3.50	70.00
77 FIRST CHRISTMAS TOGETHER 350QX132-2	YR	3.50	64.00
77 FOR YOUR NEW HOME 350QX263-5	YR	3.50	37.00
77 GRANDDAUGHTER 350QX208-2	YR	3.50	27.00
77 GRANDMOTHER 350QX260-2	YR	3.50	42.00
77 GRANDSON 350QX209-5	YR	3.50	27.00
77 LOVE 350QX262-2	YR	3.50	27.00
77 MOTHER 350QX261-5	YR	3.50	22.00
78 25TH CHRISTMAS TOGETHER 350QX269-3	YR	3.50	20.00
78 BABY'S FIRST CHRISTMAS 350QX200-3	YR	3.50	70.00
78 FIRST CHRISTMAS TOGETHER 350QX218-3	YR	3.50	38.00
78 FOR YOUR NEW HOME 350QX217-6	YR	3.50	27.00
78 GRANDDAUGHTER 350QX216-3	YR	3.50	35.00
78 GRANDMOTHER 350QX267-6	YR	3.50	39.00
78 GRANDSON 350QX215-6	YR	3.50	37.00
78 LOVE 350QX268-3	YR	3.50	35.00
78 MOTHER 350QX266-3	YR	3.50	35.00
79 BABY'S FIRST CHRISTMAS 350QX208-7	YR	3.50	25.00
79 BABY'S FIRST CHRISTMAS 800QX154-7	YR	8.00	165.00
79 FRIENDSHIP 350QX203-9	YR	3.50	25.00
79 GRANDDAUGHTER 350QX211-9	YR	3.50	27.00
79 GRANDMOTHER 350QX252-7	YR	3.50	24.00
79 GRANDSON 350QX210-7	YR	3.50	27.00
79 LOVE 350QX258-7	YR	3.50	26.00
79 MOTHER 350QX251-9	YR	3.50	20.00
79 NEW HOME 350QX212-7	YR	3.50	27.00
79 OUR FIRST CHRISTMAS TOGETHER 350QX209-9	YR	3.50	47.00
79 OUR TWENTY-FIFTH ANNIVERSARY 350QX250-7	YR	3.50	22.00
79 TEACHER 350QX213-9	YR	3.50	13.00
80 25TH CHRISTMAS TOGETHER 400QX206-1	YR	4.00	15.00
80 BABY'S FIRST CHRISTMAS 400QX200-1	YR	4.00	23.00
80 BEAUTY OF FRIENDSHIP 400QX303-4	YR	4.00	47.00
80 BLACK BABY'S FIRST CHRISTMAS 400QX229-4	YR	4.00	20.00
80 CHRISTMAS AT HOME 400QX210-1	YR	4.00	14.00
80 CHRISTMAS LOVE 400QX207-4	YR	4.00	29.00
80 DAD 400QX214-1	YR	4.00	15.00
80 DAUGHTER 400QX212-1	YR	4.00	27.00
80 FIRST CHRISTMAS TOGETHER 400QX205-4	YR	4.00	24.00
80 FIRST CHRISTMAS TOGETHER 400QX305-4	YR	4.00	50.00
80 FRIENDSHIP 400QX208-1	YR	4.00	15.00
80 GRANDDAUGHTER 400QX202-1	YR	4.00	25.00
80 GRANDFATHER 400QX231-4	YR	4.00	17.00
80 GRANDMOTHER 400QX204-1	YR	4.00	14.00
80 GRANDPARENTS 400QX213-4	YR	4.00	22.00
80 GRANDSON 400QX201-4	YR	4.00	22.00

YR	NAME	LIMIT	ISSUE	TREND
80	LOVE 400QX302-1	YR	4.00	60.00
80	MOTHER 400QX203-4	YR	4.00	15.00
80	MOTHER 400QX304-1	YR	4.00	31.00
80	MOTHER AND DAD 400QX230-1	YR	4.00	16.00
80	SON 400QX211-4	YR	4.00	29.00
80	TEACHER 400QX209-4	YR	4.00	14.00
81	25TH CHRISTMAS TOGETHER 450QX707-5	YR	4.50	16.00
81	25TH CHRISTMAS TOGETHER 550QX504-2	YR	5.50	21.00
81	50TH CHRISTMAS TOGETHER QX 708-2	YR	4.50	15.00
81	BABY'S FIRST CHRISTMAS 1300QX440-2	YR	13.00	47.00
81	BABY'S FIRST CHRISTMAS 550QX516-2	YR	5.50	26.00
81	BABY'S FIRST CHRISTMAS 850QX513-5	YR	8.50	19.00
81	BABY'S FIRST CHRISTMAS-BLACK 450QX602-2	YR	4.50	25.00
81	BABY'S FIRST CHRISTMAS-BOY 450QX601-5	YR	4.50	25.00
81	BABY'S FIRST CHRISTMAS-GIRL 450QX600-2	YR	4.50	25.00
81	DAUGHTER 450QX607-5	YR	4.50	35.00
81	FATHER 450QX609-5	YR	4.50	13.00
81	FIRST CHRISTMAS TOGETHER 450QX706-2	YR	4.50	20.00
81	FIRST CHRISTMAS TOGETHER 550QX505-5	YR	5.50	15.00
81	FRIENDSHIP 450QX704-2	YR	4.50	14.00
81	FRIENDSHIP 550QX503-5	YR	5.50	26.00
81	GIFT OF LOVE, THE- 450QX705-5	YR	4.50	17.00
81	GODCHILD 450QX603-5	YR	4.50	13.00
81	GRANDDAUGHTER 450QX605-5	YR	4.50	21.00
81	GRANDFATHER 450QX701-5	YR	4.50	14.00
81	GRANDMOTHER 450QX702-2	YR	4.50	15.00
81	GRANDPARENTS 450QX703-5	YR	4.50	14.00
81	GRANDSON 450QX604-2	YR	4.50	20.00
81	HOME 450QX709-5	YR	4.50	17.00
81	LOVE 550QX502-2	YR	5.50	45.00
81	MOTHER 450QX608-2	YR	4.50	15.00
81	MOTHER AND DAD 450QX700-2	YR	4.50	11.00
81	SON 450QX606-2	YR	4.50	22.00
81	TEACHER 450QX800-2	YR	4.50	12.00
82	25TH CHRISTMAS TOGETHER 450QX211-6	YR	4.50	13.00
82	50TH CHRISTMAS TOGETHER 450QX212-3	YR	4.50	16.00
82	BABY'S FIRST CHRISTMAS (BOY) 450QX216-3	YR	4.50	20.00
82	BABY'S FIRST CHRISTMAS (GIRL) 450QX207-3	YR	4.50	21.00
82	BABY'S FIRST XMAS-PHOTOHOLDER 650QX312-6	YR	6.50	25.00
82	DAUGHTER 450QX204-6	YR	4.50	25.00
82	FIRST CHRISTMAS TOGETHER 450QX211-3	YR	4.50	25.00
82	FIRST CHRISTMAS TOGETHER 550QX302-6	YR	5.50	14.00
82	FIRST CHRISTMAS TOGETHER 850QX306-6	YR	8.50	22.00
82	FRIENDSHIP 450QX208-6	YR	4.50	17.00
82	FRIENDSHIP 550QX304-6	YR	5.50	24.00
82	GODCHILD 450QX222-6	YR	4.50	15.00
82	GRANDDAUGHTER 450QX224-3	YR	4.50	15.00
82	GRANDFATHER 450QX207-6	YR	4.50	11.00
82	GRANDMOTHER 450QX200-3	YR	4.50	14.00
82	GRANDPARENTS 450QX214-6	YR	4.50	13.00
82	GRANDSON 450QX224-6	YR	4.50	21.00
82	LOVE 450QX209-6	YR	4.50	16.00
82	LOVE 550QX304-3	YR	5.50	25.00
82	MOMENTS OF LOVE 450QX209-3	YR	4.50	15.00
82	MOTHER 450QX205-3	YR	4.50	14.00
82	MOTHER AND DAD 450QX222-3	YR	4.50	13.00
82	NEW HOME 450QX212-6	YR	4.50	16.00
82	SISTER 450QX208-3	YR	4.50	22.00
82	SON 450QX204-3	YR	4.50	21.00
82	TEACHER 450QX214-3	YR	4.50	9.00
83	10TH CHRISTMAS TOGETHER 650QX430-7	YR	6.50	17.00
83	25TH CHRISTMAS TOGETHER 450QX224-7	YR	4.50	18.00
83	BABY'S 1ST XMAS PHOTOHOLDER QX 302-9	YR	7.00	20.00
83	BABY'S FIRST CHRISTMAS 450QX200-7	YR	4.50	21.00
83	BABY'S FIRST CHRISTMAS 450QX200-9	YR	4.50	21.00
83	BABY'S SECOND CHRISTMAS 450QX226-7	YR	4.50	24.00
83	CHILD'S THIRD CHRISTMAS 450QX226-9	YR	4.50	19.00
83	DAUGHTER 450QX203-7	YR	4.50	27.00
83	FIRST CHRISTMAS TOGETHER 600QX306-9	YR	6.00	19.00
83	FIRST CHRISTMAS TOGETHER 600QX310-9	YR	6.00	29.00
83	FIRST CHRISTMAS TOGETHER 750QX301-7	YR	7.50	17.00
83	FRIENDSHIP 450QX207-7	YR	4.50	16.00
83	FRIENDSHIP 600QX305-9	YR	6.00	16.00
83	GODCHILD 450QX201-7	YR	4.50	13.00
83	GRANDCHILD'S FIRST CHRISTMAS 400Q430-9	YR	14.00	32.00
83	GRANDCHILD'S FIRST CHRISTMAS 600QX312-9	YR	6.00	22.00
83	GRANDDAUGHTER 450QX202-7	YR	4.50	29.00
83	GRANDMOTHER 450QX205-7	YR	4.50	19.00
83	GRANDPARENTS 650QX429-9	YR	6.50	19.00
83	GRANDSON 450QX201-9	YR	4.50	29.00
83	LOVE 450QX207-9	YR	4.50	18.00
83	LOVE 600QX305-7	YR	6.00	17.00
83	LOVE 600QX310-9	YR	6.00	30.00
83	LOVE IS A SONG 450QX223-9	YR	4.50	24.00
83	MOTHER 600QX306-7	YR	6.00	16.00

YR	NAME	LIMIT	ISSUE	TREND
83	NEW HOME 450QX210-7	YR	4.50	20.00
83	SISTER 450QX206-9	YR	4.50	17.00
83	SON 450QX202-9	YR	4.50	24.00
83	TEACHER 450QX224-9	YR	4.50	16.00
83	TEACHER 600QX304-9	YR	6.00	11.00
84	A GIFT OF FRIENDSHIP 450QX260-4	YR	4.50	18.00
84	BABY BOY FIRST CHRISTMAS 450QX240-4	YR	4.50	19.00
84	BABY GIRL FIRST CHRISTMAS 450QX340-1	YR	4.50	35.00
84	BABY'S 1ST XMAS PHOTOHOLDER QX 300-1	YR	7.00	18.00
84	BABY'S FIRST CHRISTMAS 1400QX438-1	YR	14.00	41.00
84	BABY'S FIRST CHRISTMAS 600QX340-1	YR	6.00	35.00
84	BABY'S SECOND CHRISTMAS 450QX241-1	YR	4.50	11.00
84	BABYSITTER 450QX253-1	YR	4.50	12.00
84	CHILD'S THIRD CHRISTMAS 450QX261-1	YR	4.50	17.00
84	DAUGHTER 450QX244-4	YR	4.50	24.00
84	FATHER 600QX257-1	YR	6.00	16.00
84	FIRST CHRISTMAS TOGETHER 450QX245-1	YR	4.50	18.00
84	FIRST CHRISTMAS TOGETHER 600QX342-1	YR	6.00	16.00
84	FRIENDSHIP 450QX248-1	YR	4.50	13.00
84	FROM OUR HOME TO YOURS 450QX248-4	YR	4.50	21.00
84	FUN OF FRIENDSHIP, THE- 600QX343-1	YR	6.00	30.00
84	GODCHILD 450QX242-1	YR	4.50	16.00
84	GRANDCHILD'S FIRST CHRISTMAS 110QX460-1	YR	11.00	21.00
84	GRANDCHILD'S FIRST CHRISTMAS 450QX257-4	YR	4.50	13.00
84	GRANDDAUGHTER 450QX243-1	YR	4.50	20.00
84	GRANDMOTHER 450QX244-1	YR	4.50	15.00
84	GRANDPARENTS 450QX256-1	YR	4.50	13.00
84	GRANDSON 450QX242-4	YR	4.50	20.00
84	GRATITUDE 600QX344-4	YR	6.00	10.00
84	HEARTFUL OF LOVE 1000QX443-4	YR	10.00	40.00
84	LOVE 450QX255-4	YR	4.50	19.00
84	LOVE-THE SPIRIT OF CHRISTMAS 450QX247-4	YR	4.50	22.00
84	MIRACLE OF LOVE, THE- 600QX342-4	YR	6.00	26.00
84	MOTHER 600QX343-4	YR	6.00	13.00
84	MOTHER AND DAD 650QX258-1	YR	6.50	20.00
84	NEW HOME 450QX245-4	YR	4.50	50.00
84	SISTER 650QX259-4	YR	6.50	20.00
84	SON 450QX243-4	YR	4.50	21.00
84	TEACHER 450QX249-1	YR	4.50	11.00
84	TEN YEARS TOGETHER 650QX258-4	YR	6.50	16.00
84	TWENTY-FIVE YEARS TOGETHER 650QX259-1	YR	6.50	18.00
85	BABY'S FIRST CHRISTMAS 1500QX499-2	YR	15.00	50.00
85	BABY'S FIRST CHRISTMAS 1600QX499-5	YR	16.00	40.00
85	BABY'S FIRST CHRISTMAS 500QX260-2	YR	5.00	18.00
85	BABY'S SECOND CHRISTMAS 600QX478-5	YR	6.00	27.00
85	DAUGHTER 550QX503-2	YR	5.50	11.00
85	FIRST CHRISTMAS TOGETHER 475QX261-2	YR	4.75	15.00
85	FIRST CHRISTMAS TOGETHER 675QX370-5	YR	6.75	11.00
85	FIRST CHRISTMAS TOGETHER 800QX507-2	YR	8.00	9.00
85	GOOD FRIENDS 475QX265-2	YR	4.75	17.00
85	GRANDCHILD'S FIRST CHRISTMAS 500QX260-5	YR	5.00	11.00
85	GRANDDAUGHTER 475QX263-5	YR	4.75	18.00
85	HEART FULL OF LOVE 675QX378-2	YR	6.75	11.00
85	HOLIDAY HEART 800QX498-2	YR	8.00	15.00
85	NIECE 575QX520-5	YR	5.75	8.00
85	TEACHER,OWL 600QX505-2	YR	6.00	12.00
85	TWENTY-FIVE YEARS TOGETHER 800QX500-5	YR	8.00	15.00
85	WITH APPRECIATION 675QX375-2	YR	6.75	7.00
86	BABY'S FIRST CHRISTMAS 550QX271-3	YR	5.50	20.00
86	BABY-SITTER 475QX275-6	YR	4.75	7.00
86	FIFTY YEARS TOGETHER 1000QX400-6	YR	10.00	18.00
86	FIRST CHRISTMAS TOGETHER 1600QX400-3	YR	16.00	17.00
86	FIRST CHRISTMAS TOGETHER 475QX270-3	YR	4.75	16.00
86	FIRST CHRISTMAS TOGETHER 7000QX379-3	YR	7.00	14.00
86	FRIENDSHIP GREETING 800QX427-3	YR	8.00	10.00
86	FRIENDSHIP'S GIFT 600QX381-6	YR	6.00	9.00
86	FROM OUR HOME TO YOURS 600QX383-3	YR	6.00	12.00
86	GODCHILD 475QX271-6	YR	4.75	12.00
86	GRANDCHILD'S FIRST CHRISTMAS 1000QX411-6	YR	10.00	13.00
86	GRANDPARENTS 750QX432-3	YR	7.50	16.00
86	MOTHER 700QX382-6	YR	7.00	17.00
86	NEPHEW 675QX381-3	YR	6.25	10.00
86	NIECE 600QX426-6	YR	6.00	8.00
86	SEASON OF THE HEART 475QX270-6	YR	4.75	11.00
86	TEACHER 475QX275-3	YR	4.75	11.00
86	TEN YEARS TOGETHER 750QX401-3	YR	7.50	17.00
87	BABY LOCKET 1500QX461-7	YR	15.00	21.00
87	BABY'S 1ST XMAS PHOTOHOLDER 750QX461-9	YR	7.50	25.00
87	BABY'S FIRST CHRISTMAS 600QX372-9	YR	6.00	15.00
87	FIRST CHRISTMAS TOGETHER 1500QX446-9	YR	15.00	22.00
87	FIRST CHRISTMAS TOGETHER 650QX371-9	YR	6.50	14.00
87	FIRST CHRISTMAS TOGETHER 800QX445-9	YR	8.00	25.00
87	GRANDMOTHER 475QX277-9	YR	4.75	11.00
87	HOLIDAY GREETINGS 600QX375-7	YR	6.00	11.00
87	NIECE 475QX275-9	YR	4.75	10.00

YR	NAME	LIMIT	ISSUE	TREND
87	TWENTY-FIVE YEARS TOGETHER 750QX443-9	YR	7.50	23.00
87	WARMTH OF FRIENDSHIP 600QX375-9	YR	6.00	11.00
87	WORD OF LOVE 800QX447-7	YR	8.00	15.00
88	BABY BOY'S FIRST CHRISTMAS 475QX272-1	YR	4.75	15.00
88	BABY GIRL'S FIRST CHRISTMAS 475QX272-4	YR	4.75	25.00
88	BABY'S FIRST CHRISTMAS PHOTOHOLDER 750QX470-4	YR	7.50	21.00
88	FIFTY YEARS TOGETHER 675QX374-1	YR	6.75	16.00
88	FIRST CHRISTMAS TOGETHER 475QX274-1	YR	4.75	17.00
88	GODCHILD 475QX278-4	YR	4.75	16.00
88	GRANDMOTHER 475QX276-4	YR	4.75	14.00
88	LOVE GROWS 475QX275-4	YR	4.75	19.00
88	MOTHER 650QX375-1	YR	6.50	15.00
88	TEN YEARS TOGETHER 475QX275-1	YR	4.75	14.00
88	YEAR TO REMEMBER 700QX416-4	YR	7.00	16.00
89	FIRST CHRISTMAS TOGETHER 475QX273-2	YR	4.75	17.00
89	FIVE YEARS TOGETHER 475QX273-5	YR	4.75	17.00
89	FROM OUR HOME TO YOURS 625QX384-5	YR	6.25	12.00
89	GRANDDAUGHTER 475QX278-2	YR	4.75	14.00
89	GRANDSON 475QX278-5	YR	4.75	13.00
89	LANGUAGE OF LOVE 625QX383-5	YR	6.25	16.00
89	MOTHER 975QX440-5	YR	9.75	21.00
89	SISTER 475QX279-2	YR	4.75	13.00
89	TEACHER 575QX412-5	YR	5.75	21.00
89	WORLD OF LOVE 475QX274-5	YR	4.75	21.00
90	BABY'S FIRST CHRISTMAS: BABY BOY QX 206-3	YR	4.75	17.00
90	BABY'S FIRST CHRISTMAS: BABY GIRL QX 206-6	YR	4.75	17.00
90	BABY'S FIRST XMAS PHOTOHOLDER 775QX484-3	YR	7.75	22.00
90	CHILD CARE GIVER 675QX316-6	YR	6.75	11.00
90	FROM OUR HOME TO YOURS 475QX216-6	YR	4.75	10.00
90	GRANDPARENTS 475QX225-3	YR	4.75	10.00
90	OUR FIRST CHRISTMAS TOGETHER 475QX213-6	YR	4.75	16.00
90	OUR FIRST CHRISTMAS TOGETHER 675QX314-6	YR	6.75	17.00
90	OUR FIRST CHRISTMAS TOGETHER 975QX488-3	YR	9.75	19.00
90	OUR FIRST XMAS/PHOTOHOLDER 775QX488-6	YR	7.75	17.00
90	PEACEFUL KINGDOM 475QX210-6	YR	4.75	16.00
90	SISTER 475QX227-3	YR	4.75	11.00
91	EXTRA-SPECIAL FRIENDS 475QX227--9	YR	4.75	11.00
91	FIRST CHRISTMAS TOGETHER QX 222-9	YR	4.75	12.00
91	FIVE YEARS TOGETHER 775QX492-7	YR	7.75	14.00
91	FORTY YEARS TOGETHER 775QX493-9	YR	7.75	12.00
91	GRANDMOTHER 475QX230-7	YR	4.75	11.00
91	MOM AND DAD 975QX546-7	YR	9.75	17.00
91	MOTHER 975QX545-7	YR	9.75	20.00
91	SWEETHEART 975QX495-7	YR	9.75	19.00
91	TEN YEARS TOGETHER 775QX492-9	YR	7.75	15.00
92	FOR MY GRANDMA PHOTOHOLDER QX 518-4	YR	7.75	12.00
92	GRANDMOTHER 475QX201-1	YR	4.75	10.00
92	GRANDPARENTS 475QX200-4	YR	4.75	10.00
92	TEACHER 475QX226-4	YR	4.75	11.00

P. ANDREWS COMMEMORATIVES

92	BABY'S FIRST CHRISTMAS 1875QX458-1	YR	19.00	31.00

R. BISHOP COMMEMORATIVES

91	GODCHILD 675QX548-9	YR	6.75	13.00
91	NEW HOME 675QX544-9	YR	6.75	19.00

R. CHAD COMMEMORATIVES

88	CHILD'S THIRD CHRISTMAS 600QX471-4	YR	6.00	21.00
89	BABY'S FIRST CHRISTMAS 725QX449-2	YR	7.25	90.00
90	MOM AND DAD 875QX459-3	YR	8.75	18.00
91	GRANDDAUGHTER'S 1ST CHRISTMAS 675QX511-9	YR	6.75	11.00
91	GRANDSON'S FIRST CHRISTMAS 675QX511-7	YR	6.75	15.00
92	FRIENDLY GREETINGS 775QX504-1	YR	7.75	13.00
92	SPECIAL CAT PHOTOHOLDER QX 541-4	YR	7.75	13.00
92	SPECIAL DOG PHOTOHOLDER QX 542-1	YR	7.75	21.00

K. CROW COMMEMORATIVES

86	FRIENDS ARE FUN 475QX272-3	YR	4.75	26.00
86	NEW HOME 475QX274-6	YR	4.75	25.00
87	CHILD'S THIRD CHRISTMAS 575QX459-9	YR	5.75	22.00
88	BABY'S FIRST CHRISTMAS 975QX470-1	YR	9.75	35.00
91	FRIENDS ARE FUN 975QX528-9	YR	9.75	17.00
92	BROTHER 675QX468-4	YR	6.75	12.00
92	SISTER 675QX468-1	YR	6.75	12.00

J. FRANCIS COMMEMORATIVES

89	BABY'S FIRST CHRISTMAS 675QX381-5	YR	6.75	13.00
89	BABY'S SECOND CHRISTMAS 675QX449-5	YR	6.75	30.00
89	CHILD'S FOURTH CHRISTMAS 675QX543-2	YR	6.75	16.00
89	CHILD'S THIRD CHRISTMAS 675QX469-5	YR	6.75	19.00
89	GODCHILD 625QX311-2	YR	6.25	9.00
89	GRANDDAUGHTER'S FIRST XMAS 675QX382-2	YR	6.75	15.00
89	GRANDSON'S FIRST CHRISTMAS 675QX382-5	YR	6.75	15.00
90	BABY'S FIRST CHRISTMAS 775QX485-6	YR	7.75	35.00
90	BABY'S FIRST CHRISTMAS 975QX485-3	YR	9.75	18.00
90	BABY'S SECOND CHRISTMAS 675QX486-3	YR	6.75	25.00
90	CHILD'S FOURTH CHRISTMAS 675QX487-3	YR	6.75	16.00
90	CHILD'S THIRD CHRISTMAS 675QX486-6	YR	6.75	19.00
90	GODCHILD 675QX317-6	YR	6.75	11.00

YR	NAME	LIMIT	ISSUE	TREND
90	GRANDDAUGHTER'S FIRST XMAS 675QX310-6	YR	6.75	13.00
90	GRANDSON'S FIRST CHRISTMAS 675QX306-3	YR	6.75	12.00
91	A CHILD'S CHRISTMAS 975QX488-7	YR	9.75	13.00
91	BABY'S FIRST CHRISTMAS 1775QX510-7	YR	17.75	30.00
91	BABY'S FIRST CHRISTMAS 775QX488-9	YR	7.75	27.00
91	BABY'S SECOND CHRISTMAS 675QX489-7	YR	6.75	25.00
91	CHILD'S FOURTH CHRISTMAS 675QX490-7	YR	6.75	16.00
91	CHILD'S THIRD CHRISTMAS 675QX489-9	YR	6.75	19.00
92	A CHILD'S CHRISTMAS 975QX457-4	YR	9.75	17.00
92	BABY'S FIRST CHRISTMAS 775QX464-4	YR	7.75	24.00
92	BABY'S SECOND CHRISTMAS 675QX465-1	YR	6.75	12.00
92	CHILD'S FOURTH CHRISTMAS 675QX466-1	YR	6.75	16.00
92	CHILD'S THIRD CHRISTMAS 675QX465-4	YR	6.75	15.00
92	DAUGHTER 675QX503-1	YR	6.75	17.00
92	SON 675QX502-4	YR	6.75	15.00

M. HAMILTON COMMEMORATIVES

YR	NAME	LIMIT	ISSUE	TREND
91	BABY'S FIRST CHRISTMAS-BOY 475QX221-7	YR	4.75	17.00
91	BABY'S FIRST CHRISTMAS-GIRL 475QX222-7	YR	4.75	14.00

D. LEE COMMEMORATIVES

YR	NAME	LIMIT	ISSUE	TREND
83	BABY'S FIRST CHRISTMAS 1400QX402-7		14.00	35.00
84	BABY'S FIRST CHRISTMAS 1600QX904-1		16.00	32.00
85	BABY'S FIRST CHRISTMAS 575QX370-2	YR	5.75	16.00
87	BABY'S FIRST CHRISTMAS 975QX411-3	YR	9.75	27.00
87	BABY'S SECOND CHRISTMAS 575QX460-7	YR	5.75	24.00
87	FIRST CHRISTMAS TOGETHER 950QX446-7	YR	9.50	22.00
89	DAD 725QX441-2	YR	7.25	12.00
89	FRIENDSHIP TIME 975QX413-2	YR	9.75	26.00
90	DAD 675QX453-3	YR	6.75	13.00
91	DAD 775QX512-7	YR	7.75	15.00
91	DAD-TO-BE 575QX487-9	YR	5.75	13.00
91	FLAG OF LIBERTY 675QX524-9	YR	6.75	7.00
91	MOM-TO-BE 575QX487-7	YR	5.75	15.00
92	DAD-TO-BE 675QX461-1	YR	6.75	16.00
92	MOM-TO-BE 675QX461-4	YR	6.75	16.00
92	OUR FIRST CHRISTMAS TOGETHER 975QX506-1	YR	9.75	16.00

J. LYLE COMMEMORATIVES

YR	NAME	LIMIT	ISSUE	TREND
86	GRANDDAUGHTER 475QX273-6	YR	4.75	17.00
87	FIRST CHRISTMAS TOGETHER 450QX272-9	YR	4.75	18.00
87	LOVE IS EVERYWHERE 475QX278-7	YR	4.75	26.00
88	MOTHER AND DAD 800QX414-4	YR	8.00	17.00
88	SPIRIT OF CHRISTMAS 475QX276-1	YR	4.75	15.00
89	GRANDMOTHER 475QX277-5	YR	4.75	12.00
89	GRANDPARENTS 475QX277-2	YR	4.75	11.00
89	TEN YEARS TOGETHER 475QX274-2	YR	4.75	16.00
90	GRANDDAUGHTER 475QX228-6	YR	4.75	11.00
90	TEN YEARS TOGETHER 475QX215-3	YR	4.75	10.00
91	ACROSS THE MILES 675QX315-7	YR	6.75	11.00
91	SISTER 675QX548-7	YR	6.75	17.00
92	FOR THE ONE I LOVE 975QX484-4	YR	9.75	17.00

D. MCGEHEE COMMEMORATIVES

YR	NAME	LIMIT	ISSUE	TREND
84	FIRST CHRISTMAS TOGETHER 1600QX904-4	YR	16.00	26.00
84	FIRST CHRISTMAS TOGETHER 750QX340-4	YR	7.50	17.00
85	BABY LOCKET 1600QX401-2	YR	16.00	19.00
85	GODCHILD 675QX380-2	YR	6.75	8.00
85	LOVE AT CHRISTMAS 575QX371-5	YR	5.75	32.00
86	BABY LOCKET 1600QX412-3	YR	16.00	20.00
88	FIVE YEARS TOGETHER 475QX274-4	YR	4.75	16.00
91	GIFT OF JOY 875QX531-9	YR	8.75	18.00

D. PALMITER COMMEMORATIVES

YR	NAME	LIMIT	ISSUE	TREND
85	SPECIAL FRIENDS 575QX372-5	YR	5.75	7.00
86	BABY'S FIRST CHRISTMAS 600QX380-3	YR	6.00	20.00

J. PATTEE COMMEMORATIVES

YR	NAME	LIMIT	ISSUE	TREND
85	FRIENDSHIP 775QX506-2	YR	7.75	9.00
85	FROM OUR HOUSE TO YOURS 775QX520-2	YR	7.75	6.00
85	GRANDMOTHER 475QX262-5	YR	4.75	10.00
85	SISTER 725QX506-5	YR	7.25	14.00
86	BABY'S FIRST XMAS PHOTOHOLDER 800QX379-2	YR	8.00	24.00
86	CHILD'S THIRD CHRISTMAS 650QX413-6	YR	6.50	17.00
86	GRANDMOTHER 475QX274-3	YR	4.75	12.00
86	JOY OF FRIENDS 675QX382-3	YR	6.75	14.00
86	SWEETHEART 1100QX408-6	YR	11.00	37.00
87	BABY'S FIRST CHRISTMAS-BOY 475QX274-9	YR	4.75	20.00
87	BABY'S FIRST CHRISTMAS-GIRL 475QX274-7	YR	4.75	14.00
87	NEW HOME 600QX376-7	YR	6.00	22.00
88	DAUGHTER 575QX415-1	YR	5.75	47.00
88	FROM OUR HOME TO YOURS 475QX279-4	YR	4.75	14.00
88	GRANDPARENTS 475QX277-1	YR	4.75	13.00
88	GRATITUDE 600QX375-4	YR	6.00	10.00
88	SON 575QX415-4	YR	5.75	36.00
88	TWENTY-FIVE YEARS TOGETHER 675QX373-4	YR	6.75	16.00
90	FIFTY YEARS TOGETHER 975QX490-6	YR	9.75	16.00
90	FORTY YEARS TOGETHER 975QX490-3	YR	9.75	12.00
90	JESUS LOVES ME 675QX315-6	YR	6.75	13.00
90	TWENTY-FIVE YEARS TOGETHER 975QX489-6	YR	9.75	13.00

YR	NAME	LIMIT	ISSUE	TREND
S. PIKE			**COMMEMORATIVES**	
83	MOM AND DAD 650QX429-7	YR	6.50	20.00
85	GRANDPARENTS 700QX380-5	YR	7.00	7.00
85	MOTHER 675QX372-2	YR	6.75	12.00
86	GRATITUDE 600QX432-6	YR	6.00	10.00
86	HUSBAND 800QX383-6	YR	8.00	12.00
87	BABYSITTER 475QX279-7	YR	4.75	11.00
87	GRANDPARENTS 475QX277-7	YR	4.75	13.00
87	MOTHER 650QX373-7	YR	6.50	13.00
87	MOTHER AND DAD 700QX462-7	YR	7.00	18.00
88	BABY'S FIRST CHRISTMAS 600QX372-1	YR	6.00	17.00
88	BABY'S SECOND CHRISTMAS 600QX471-1	YR	6.00	27.00
88	FIRST CHRISTMAS TOGETHER 900QX489-4	YR	9.00	19.00
88	TEACHER 625QX417-1	YR	6.25	15.00
89	MOM AND DAD 975QX442-5	YR	9.75	18.00
91	FIRST CHRISTMAS TOGETHER QX 313-9	YR	6.75	17.00
91	UNDER THE MISTLETOE 875QX494-9	YR	8.75	18.00
92	NEW HOME 875QX519-1	YR	8.75	16.00
M. PYDA-SEVCIK			**COMMEMORATIVES**	
85	BABY-SITTER 475QX264-2	YR	4.75	13.00
85	FRIENDSHIP 675QX378-5	YR	6.75	13.00
85	NEW HOME 475QX269-5	YR	4.75	19.00
86	MOTHER AND DAD 750QX431-6	YR	7.50	17.00
87	FROM OUR HOME TO YOURS 475QX279-9	YR	4.75	15.00
87	GODCHILD 475QX276-7	YR	4.75	16.00
90	NEW HOME 675QX434-3	YR	6.75	18.00
91	GRANDDAUGHTER 475QX229-9	YR	4.75	16.00
91	GRANDPARENTS 475QX230-9	YR	4.75	9.00
91	GRANDSON 475QX229-7	YR	4.75	11.00
D. RHODUS			**COMMEMORATIVES**	
89	CHILD'S FIFTH CHRISTMAS 675QX543-5	YR	6.75	16.00
89	FIRST CHRISTMAS TOGETHER 675QX383-2	YR	6.75	20.00
90	CHILD'S FIFTH CHRISTMAS 675QX487-6	YR	6.75	16.00
90	FRIENDSHIP KITTEN 675QX414-3	YR	6.75	14.00
90	SWEETHEART 1175QX489-3	YR	11.75	22.00
91	CHILD'S FIFTH CHRISTMAS 675QX490-9	YR	6.75	16.00
91	JESUS LOVES ME 775QX314-7	YR	7.75	12.00
92	ACROSS THE MILES 675QX304-4	YR	6.75	11.00
92	CHILD'S FIFTH CHRISTMAS 675QX466-4	YR	6.75	16.00
A. ROGERS			**COMMEMORATIVES**	
89	25 YEARS TOGETHER PHOTOHOLDER 875QX485-5	YR	8.75	12.00
89	40 YEARS TOGETHER PHOTOHOLDER 875QX545-2	YR	8.75	15.00
89	50 YEARS TOGETHER PHOTOHOLDER 875QX486-2	YR	8.75	15.00
89	FIRST CHRISTMAS TOGETHER 675QX485-2	YR	9.75	21.00
90	BABY'S FIRST CHRISTMAS 675QX303-6	YR	6.75	18.00
91	TEACHER 475QX228-9	YR	4.75	9.00
92	HOLIDAY MEMO 775QX504-4	YR	7.75	14.00
92	LOVE TO SKATE 875QX484-1	YR	8.75	17.00
92	MOM 775QX516-4	YR	7.75	15.00
92	SECRET PAL 775QX542-4	YR	7.75	12.00
E. SEALE			**COMMEMORATIVES**	
82	BABY'S FIRST CHRISTMAS 1300QX455-3	YR	13.00	45.00
82	BABY'S FIRST CHRISTMAS 550QX302-3	YR	5.50	35.00
82	FIRST XMAS TOGETHER-LOCKET 1500QX456-3	YR	15.00	28.00
82	TEACHER-APPLE 550QX301-6	YR	5.50	11.00
83	FIRST XMAS TOGETHER-LOCKET 1500QX432-9	YR	15.00	31.00
84	FIRST CHRISTMAS TOGETHER 1500QX436-4	YR	15.00	20.00
85	CHILD'S THIRD CHRISTMAS 600QX475-5	YR	6.00	23.00
85	FIRST CHRISTMAS TOGETHER 1675QX400-5	YR	16.75	19.00
86	DAUGHTER 575QX430-6	YR	5.75	27.00
86	LOVING MEMORIES 900QX409-3	YR	9.00	25.00
86	SON 575QX430-3	YR	5.75	30.00
87	FIFTY YEARS TOGETHER 800QX443-7	YR	8.00	17.00
87	GRANDCHILD'S FIRST CHRISTMAS 900QX460-9	YR	9.00	18.00
90	TEACHER 775QX448-3	YR	7.75	10.00
92	1ST CHRISTMAS TOGETHER PHOTO. QX 469-4	YR	8.75	18.00
92	FRIENDSHIP LINE 975QX503-4	YR	9.75	21.00
92	GRANDDAUGHTER 675QX560-4	YR	6.75	15.00
92	GRANDSON 675QX561-1	YR	6.75	17.00
L. SICKMAN			**COMMEMORATIVES**	
80	BABY'S FIRST CHRISTMAS 1200QX156-1	YR	12.00	45.00
82	CHRISTMAS MEMORIES 650QX311-6	YR	6.50	16.00
82	FATHER 450QX205-6	YR	4.50	13.00
82	TEACHER 650QX312-3	YR	6.50	13.00
83	BABY'S FIRST CHRISTMAS 750QX301-9	YR	7.50	14.00
83	FIRST CHRISTMAS TOGETHER 450QX208-9	YR	4.50	23.00
83	LOVE 1300QX422-7	YR	13.00	27.00
85	FIRST CHRISTMAS TOGETHER 1300QX493-5	YR	13.00	21.00
86	BABY'S FIRST CHRISTMAS 900QX412-6	YR	9.00	35.00
86	FIRST CHRISTMAS TOGETHER 1200QX409-6	YR	12.00	19.00
87	DAUGHTER 575QX463-7	YR	5.75	20.00
87	SISTER 600QX474-7	YR	6.00	10.00
87	SON 575QX463-9	YR	5.75	30.00
87	SWEETHEART 1100QX447-9	YR	11.00	22.00
88	BABYSITTER 475QX279-1	YR	4.75	9.00

YR	NAME	LIMIT	ISSUE	TREND
89	DAUGHTER 625QX443-2	YR	6.25	15.00
89	SON 625QX444-5	YR	6.25	15.00
89	SWEETHEART 975QX486-5	YR	9.75	28.00
91	FIRST CHRISTMAS TOGETHER QX 491-9	YR	8.75	20.00
91	TERRIFIC TEACHER 675QX530-9	YR	6.75	12.00
B. SIEDLER			**COMMEMORATIVES**	
85	SON 550QX502-5	YR	5.50	28.00
86	BABY'S SECOND CHRISTMAS 650QX413-3	YR	6.50	22.00
87	DAD 600QX462-9	YR	6.00	31.00
87	TEACHER 575QX466-7	YR	5.75	16.00
88	DAD 700QX414-1	YR	7.00	18.00
90	BROTHER 575QX449-3	YR	5.75	14.00
90	COPY OF CHEER 775QX448-6	YR	7.75	14.00
90	DAD-TO-BE 575QX491-3	YR	5.75	18.00
90	DAUGHTER 575QX449-6	YR	5.75	15.00
90	MOM-TO-BE 575QX491-6	YR	5.75	27.00
90	SON 575QX451-6	YR	5.75	13.00
91	BIG CHEESE, THE 675QX532-7	YR	6.75	15.00
91	BROTHER 675QX547-9	YR	6.75	13.00
91	DAUGHTER 575QX547-7	YR	5.75	20.00
91	SON 575QX546-9	YR	5.75	14.00
92	DAD 775QX467-4	YR	7.75	17.00
92	GRANDDAUGHTER'S 1ST CHRISTMAS 675QX463-4	YR	6.75	14.00
92	GRANDSON'S 1ST CHRISTMAS 675QX462-1	YR	6.75	16.00
92	MOM AND DAD 975QX467-1	YR	9.75	32.00
92	V.P. OF IMPORTANT STUFF 675QX505-1	YR	6.75	12.00
92	WORLD-CLASS TEACHER 775QX505-4	YR	7.75	15.00
D. UNRUH			**COMMEMORATIVES**	
88	SWEETHEART 975QX490-1	YR	9.75	14.00
92	ANNIVERSARY YEAR, PHOTOHOLDER 975QX485-1	YR	9.75	20.00
92	GODCHILD 675QX594-1	YR	6.75	15.00
L. VOTRUBA			**COMMEMORATIVES**	
85	BABY'S FIRST CHRISTMAS 700QX478-2	YR	7.00	14.00
85	FATHER 650QX376-2	YR	6.50	7.00
85	GRANDCHILD'S FIRST CHRISTMAS 1100QX495-5	YR	11.00	16.00
85	GRANDSON 475QX262-2	YR	4.75	25.00
85	MOTHER AND DAD 775QX509-2	YR	7.75	18.00
86	FATHER 650QX431-3	YR	6.50	13.00
86	GRANDSON 475QX273-3	YR	4.75	17.00
86	SISTER 675QX380-6	YR	6.75	14.00
86	TIMELESS LOVE 600QX379-6	YR	6.00	16.00
86	TWENTY-FIVE YEARS TOGETHER 800QX410-3	YR	8.00	19.00
87	GRANDDAUGHTER 600QX374-7	YR	6.00	12.00
87	GRANDSON 475QX276-9	YR	4.75	16.00
87	HEART IN BLOSSOM 600QX372-7	YR	6.00	18.00
87	HUSBAND 700QX373-9	YR	7.00	9.00
87	TEN YEARS TOGETHER 700QX444-7	YR	7.00	20.00
87	TIME FOR FRIENDS 475QX280-7	YR	4.75	15.00
88	FIRST CHRISTMAS TOGETHER 675QX373-1	YR	6.75	24.00
88	GRANDDAUGHTER 475QX277-4	YR	4.75	20.00
88	GRANDSON 475QX278-1	YR	4.75	20.00
88	LOVE FILLS THE HEART 600QX374-4	YR	6.00	17.00
88	NEW HOME 600QX376-1	YR	6.00	17.00
88	SISTER 800QX499-4	YR	8.00	25.00
89	BABY'S 1ST XMAS PHOTOHOLDER 625QX468-2	YR	6.25	40.00
89	BABY'S FIRST CHRISTMAS-BOY 475QX272-5	YR	4.75	15.00
89	BABY'S FIRST CHRISTMAS-GIRL 475QX272-2	YR	4.75	15.00
89	FESTIVE YEAR 775QX384-2	YR	7.75	15.00
89	GRATITUDE 675QX385-2	YR	6.75	11.00
89	NEW HOME 475QX275-5	YR	4.75	16.00
90	ACROSS THE MILES 675QX317-3	YR	6.75	13.00
90	FIVE YEARS TOGETHER 475QX210-3	YR	4.75	15.00
90	GRANDMOTHER 475QX223-6	YR	4.75	11.00
90	GRANDSON 475QX229-3	YR	4.75	10.00
90	MOTHER 875QX453-6	YR	8.75	17.00
91	25 YEARS TOGETHER PHOTOHOLDER QX493-7	YR	8.75	16.00
91	BABY'S FIRST XMAS-PHOTOHOLDER 775QX486-9	YR	7.75	20.00
91	FIFTY YEARS TOGETHER-PHOTOHOLDER 875QX494-7	YR	8.75	15.00
91	FIRST CHRISTMAS TOGETHER QX 491-7	YR	8.75	15.00
91	FROM OUR HOME TO YOURS 475QX228-7	YR	4.75	14.00
92	BABY'S 1ST CHRISTMAS PHOTOHOLDER QX464-1	YR	7.75	17.00
92	BABY'S FIRST CHRISTMAS-BOY 475QX219-1	YR	4.75	10.00
92	BABY'S FIRST CHRISTMAS-GIRL 475QX220-4	YR	4.75	10.00
92	FROM OUR HOME TO YOURS 475QX213-1	YR	4.75	10.00
92	OUR FIRST CHRISTMAS TOGETHER 675QX301-1	YR	6.75	14.00
N. AUBE			**COOKIE JAR FRIENDS**	
96	CLYDE QK116-1	YR	16.00	16.00
A. ROGERS			**COOKIE JAR FRIENDS**	
96	CARMEN QK116-4	YR	16.00	16.00
K. CROW			**COTTONTAIL EXPRESS**	
98	PASSENGER CAR 995QEO8376	YR	10.00	10.00
*			**COUNTRY CHRISTMAS COLLECTION**	
85	OLD-FASHIONED DOLL 1450QX519-5	YR	14.50	30.00
85	WHIRLIGIG SANTA 1250QX519-2	YR	12.50	19.00

YR	NAME	LIMIT	ISSUE	TREND
M. PYDA-SEVCIK		**COUNTRY CHRISTMAS COLLECTION**		
85	COUNTRY GOOSE 775QX518-5	YR	7.75	11.00
L. SICKMAN		**COUNTRY CHRISTMAS COLLECTION**		
85	SHEEP AT CHRISTMAS 825QX517-5	YR	8.25	20.00
L. VOTRUBA		**COUNTRY CHRISTMAS COLLECTION**		
85	ROCKING HORSE MEMORIES 1000QX518-2	YR	10.00	11.00
*		**COUNTRY TREASURES COLLECTION**		
86	REMEMBERING CHRISTMAS 865QX510-6	YR	8.75	20.00
K. CROW		**COUNTRY TREASURES COLLECTION**		
86	LITTLE DRUMMERS 1250QX511-6	YR	12.50	22.00
86	WELCOME CHRISTMAS 825QX510-3	YR	8.25	21.00
L. SICKMAN		**COUNTRY TREASURES COLLECTION**		
86	COUNTRY SLEIGH 1000QX511-3	YR	10.00	18.00
D. UNRUH		**COUNTRY TREASURES COLLECTION**		
86	NUTCRACKER SANTA 1000QX512-3	YR	10.00	45.00
K. CROW		**CRAYOLA CRAYON**		
90	BRIGHT MOVING COLORS 875QX458-6	YR	8.75	50.00
91	BRIGHT VIBRANT CAROLS 975QX421-9	YR	9.75	30.00
92	BRIGHT BLAZING COLORS 975QX426-4	YR	9.75	28.00
93	BRIGHT SHINING CASTLE 1075QX442-2	YR	10.75	22.00
94	BRIGHT PLAYFUL COLORS 1095QX527-3	YR	11.00	19.00
95	BRIGHT N'SUNNY TEEPEE QX524-7	YR	11.00	17.00
96	BRIGHT FLYING COLORS QX539-1	YR	11.00	11.00
L. SICKMAN		**CRAYOLA CRAYON**		
89	BRIGHT JOURNEY 875QX-435-2	YR	8.75	50.00
S. TAGUE		**CRAYOLA CRAYON**		
97	BRIGHT ROCKING COLORS	YR	13.00	13.00
*		**CROWN CLASSICS COLLECTION**		
81	ANGEL 450QX507-5	YR	4.50	24.00
81	TREE PHOTOHOLDER 550QX515-5	YR	5.50	20.00
81	UNICORN 850QX516-5	YR	8.50	20.00
83	ENAMELED CHRISTMAS WREATH 900QX311-9	YR	9.00	11.00
83	MEMORIES TO TREASURE 700QX303-7	YR	7.00	18.00
83	MOTHER AND CHILD 750QX302-7	YR	7.50	31.00
*		**CURRIER & IVES**		
74	CURRIER & IVES (2) 350QX112-1	YR	3.50	40.00
76	CURRIER & IVES 250QX209-1	YR	2.50	40.00
76	CURRIER & IVES 300QX197-1	YR	3.00	40.00
77	CURRIER & IVES 350QX130-2	YR	3.50	50.00
82	CURRIER & IVES 450QX201-3	YR	4.50	16.00
83	CURRIER & IVES 450QX215-9	YR	4.50	15.00
84	CURRIER & IVES 450QX250-1	YR	4.50	20.00
J. LYLE		**CURRIER & IVES**		
87	CURRIER & IVES: AMERICAN FARM 475QX282-9	YR	4.75	20.00
L. SICKMAN		**CURRIER & IVES**		
75	CURRIER & IVES (2) 250QX164-1	YR	2.50	40.00
75	CURRIER & IVES (2) 400QX137-1	YR	4.00	35.00
*		**DECORATIVE BALL ORNAMENTS**		
76	CARDINALS 225QX205-1	YR	2.25	45.00
76	CHICKADEES 225QX204-1	YR	2.25	55.00
77	CHRISTMAS MOUSE 350QX134-2	YR	3.50	60.00
77	RABBIT 250QX139-5	YR	2.50	99.00
77	SQUIRREL 250QX138-2	YR	2.50	95.00
77	STAINED GLASS 350QX152-2	YR	3.50	42.00
78	DRUMMER BOY 350QX252-3	YR	3.50	25.00
78	HALLMARK'S ANTIQUE CARD COLL. 350QX220-3	YR	3.50	40.00
78	JOY 350QX254-3	YR	3.50	45.00
78	MERRY CHRISTMAS (SANTA) 350QX202-3	YR	3.50	55.00
78	NATIVITY 350QX253-6	YR	3.50	55.00
78	QUAIL, THE- 350QX251-6	YR	3.50	40.00
78	YESTERDAY'S TOYS 350QX250-3	YR	3.50	25.00
79	BEHOLD THE STAR 350QX255-9	YR	3.50	30.00
79	BLACK ANGEL 350QX207-9	YR	3.50	19.00
79	CHRISTMAS CHICKADEES 350QX204-7	YR	3.50	30.00
79	CHRISTMAS COLLAGE 350QX257-9	YR	3.50	21.00
79	LIGHT OF CHRISTMAS, THE- 350QX256-7	YR	3.50	21.00
79	NIGHT BEFORE CHRISTMAS 350QX214-7	YR	3.50	40.00
80	CHRISTMAS CARDINALS 400QX224-1	YR	4.00	23.00
80	CHRISTMAS CHOIR 400QX228-1	YR	4.00	70.00
80	CHRISTMAS TIME 400QX226-1	YR	4.00	23.00
80	HAPPY CHRISTMAS 400QX222-1	YR	4.00	25.00
80	JOLLY SANTA 400QX227-4	YR	4.00	22.00
80	NATIVITY 400QX225-4	YR	4.00	26.00
80	SANTA'S WORKSHOP 400QX223-4	YR	4.00	20.00
81	CHRISTMAS 1981-SCHNEEBERG 450QX809-5	YR	4.50	17.00
81	CHRISTMAS IN THE FOREST 450QX813-5	YR	4.50	120.00
81	CHRISTMAS MAGIC 450QX810-2	YR	4.50	18.00
81	LET US ADORE HIM 450QX811-5	YR	4.50	50.00
81	MERRY CHRISTMAS 450QX814-2	YR	4.50	15.00
81	SANTA'S COMING 450QX812-2	YR	4.50	22.00
81	SANTA'S SURPRISE 450QX815-5	YR	4.50	19.00
81	TRADITIONAL (BLACK SANTA) 450QX801-5	YR	4.50	76.00
82	CHRISTMAS ANGEL 450QX220-6	YR	4.50	17.00
82	SEASON FOR CARING 450QX221-3	YR	4.50	18.00

YR	NAME	LIMIT	ISSUE	TREND
83	1983 450QX220-9	YR	4.50	22.00
83	AN OLD FASHIONED CHRISTMAS 450QX217-9	YR	4.50	20.00
83	ANGELS 500QX219-7	YR	5.00	19.00
83	ANNUNCIATION, THE 450QX216-7	YR	4.50	21.00
83	CHRISTMAS JOY 450QX216-9	YR	4.50	24.00
83	CHRISTMAS WONDERLAND 450QX221-9	YR	4.50	90.00
83	HERE COMES SANTA 450QX217-7	YR	4.50	34.00
83	ORIENTAL BUTTERFLIES 450QX218-7	YR	4.50	23.00
83	SEASON'S GREETING 450QX219-9	YR	4.50	18.00
83	WISE MEN, THE- 450QX220-7	YR	4.50	37.00
T. BLACKSHEAR		**DECORATIVE BALL ORNAMENTS**		
82	SANTA 450QX221-6	YR	4.50	15.00
L. SICKMAN		**DECORATIVE BALL ORNAMENTS**		
79	CHRISTMAS TRADITIONS 350QX253-9	YR	3.50	30.00
*		**DESIGNER KEEPSAKES**		
82	MERRY CHRISTMAS 450QX225-6	YR	4.50	16.00
82	OLD FASHIONED CHRISTMAS 450QX227-6	YR	4.50	33.00
82	OLD WORLD ANGELS 450QX226-3	YR	4.50	20.00
82	PATTERNS OF CHRISTMAS 450QX226-6	YR	4.50	19.00
82	STAINED GLASS 450QX228-3	YR	4.50	17.00
82	TWELVE DAYS OF CHRISTMAS 450QX203-6	YR	4.50	22.00
P. ANDREWS		**DOLLS OF THE WORLD**		
96	NATIVE AMERICAN BARBIE QX556-1	YR	15.00	15.00
A. MARRA ROGERS		**DOLLS OF THE WORLD**		
97	CHINESE BARBIE	YR	15.00	15.00
*		**EASTER ORNAMENTS**		
91	BABY'S FIRST EASTER 875QEO518-9	YR	8.75	27.00
91	DAUGHTER 575QEO517-9	YR	5.75	29.00
91	EASTER MEMORIES PHOTOHOLDER QEO 513-7	YR	7.75	19.00
91	FULL OF LOVE 775QEO514-9	YR	7.75	39.00
91	GENTLE LAMB 675QEO515-9	YR	6.75	19.00
91	GRANDCHILD 675QEO517-7	YR	6.75	22.00
91	LI'L DIPPER 675QEO514-7	YR	6.75	22.00
91	LILY EGG 975QEO513-9	YR	9.75	24.00
91	SON 575QEO518-7	YR	5.75	24.00
91	SPIRIT OF EASTER 775QEO516-9	YR	7.75	34.00
91	SPRINGTIME STROLL 675QEO516-7	YR	6.75	20.00
94	SPRINGTIME BONNETS 775QEO809-6	YR	7.75	23.00
94	SWEET EASTER WISHES 875QEO819-6	YR	8.75	24.00
95	APRIL SHOWERS QEO 826-3	YR	7.00	12.00
95	BABY'S FIRST EASTER QEO 823-7	YR	8.00	13.00
95	BUGS BUNNY QEO 827-9	YR	9.00	12.00
95	BUNNY WITH CRAYONS QEO 824-9	YR	8.00	14.00
95	BUNNY WITH SEED PACKETS QEO 825-9	YR	9.00	16.00
95	DAUGHTER QEO 823-9	YR	6.00	10.00
95	EASTER BEAGLE QEO 825-7	YR	8.00	17.00
95	EASTER EGG COTTAGES QEO 820-7	YR	9.00	15.00
95	GARDEN CLUB QEO 820-9	YR	8.00	15.00
95	HAM 'N EGGS QEO 827-7	YR	8.00	11.00
95	HERE COMES EASTER QEO 821-7	YR	8.00	20.00
95	LILY QEO 826-7	YR	7.00	8.00
95	MINIATURE TRAIN QEO 826-9	YR	5.00	10.00
95	SON QEO 824-7	YR	6.00	12.00
95	SPRINGTIME BARBIE, FIRST SERIES QEO 806-9	YR	13.00	32.00
95	SPRINGTIME BONNETS, THIRD SERIES QEO 822-7	YR	8.00	13.00
95	THREE FLOWERPOT FRIENDS QEO 822-9	YR	15.00	20.00
P. ANDREWS		**EASTER ORNAMENTS**		
93	BARROW OF GIGGLES 875QEO840-2	YR	8.75	24.00
93	DAUGHTER 575QEO834-2	YR	5.75	22.00
93	SON 575QEO833-5	YR	5.75	22.00
94	DAUGHTER 575QEO815-6	YR	5.75	15.00
94	SON 575QEO816-3	YR	5.75	12.00
R. CHAD		**EASTER ORNAMENTS**		
93	TIME FOR EASTER 875QEO838-5	YR	8.75	24.00
96	PORK N' BEANS QEO817-4	YR	8.00	10.00
K. CROW		**EASTER ORNAMENTS**		
92	EASTER PARADE 675QEO930-1	YR	6.75	20.00
92	GRANDCHILD 675QEO927-4	YR	6.75	16.00
94	COLORFUL SPRING 775QEO816-6	YR	7.75	27.00
94	HERE COMES EASTER 775QEO809-3	YR	7.75	24.00
96	HIPPITY HOP DELIVERY QEO814-4	YR	8.00	8.00
96	LOCOMOTIVE QEO807-4	YR	8.00	40.00
J. FRANCIS		**EASTER ORNAMENTS**		
92	BABY'S FIRST EASTER 675QEO927-1	YR	6.75	22.00
92	BLESS YOU 675QEO929-1	YR	6.75	15.00
92	SOMEBUNNY LOVES YOU 675QEO929-4	YR	6.75	27.00
93	MAYPOLE STROLL 2800QEO839-5 SET OF THREE	YR	28.00	38.00
94	BABY'S FIRST EASTER 675QEO815-3	YR	6.75	19.00
96	APPLE BLOSSOM LANE QEO808-4	YR	9.00	9.00
96	LOOK WHAT I FOUND! QEO818-1	YR	8.00	10.00
J. LEE		**EASTER ORNAMENTS**		
92	SPRINGTIME EGG 875QEO932-1	YR	8.75	23.00
93	BEST-DRESSED TURTLE 575QEO839-2	YR	5.75	12.00
93	EASTER PARADE 675QEO832-5	YR	6.75	18.00

YR	NAME	LIMIT	ISSUE	TREND
93	LI'L PEPPER 775QEO831-2	YR	7.75	20.00
93	NUTTY EGGS 675QEO838-2	YR	6.75	12.00
93	SPRINGTIME BONNETS 775QEO832-2	YR	7.75	25.00
J. LYLE			**EASTER ORNAMENTS**	
92	PROMISE OF EASTER 875QEO931-4	YR	8.75	22.00
93	CHICKS-ON-A-TWIRL 775QEO837-5	YR	7.75	12.00
96	JOYFUL ANGELS FIRST SERIES QEO818-4	YR	10.00	40.00
97	JOYFUL ANGELS 2ND. SERIES 865-5	YR	*	11.00
D. PALMITER			**EASTER ORNAMENTS**	
92	JOY BEARER 875QEO933-4	YR	8.75	32.00
93	BABY'S FIRST EASTER 675QEO834-5	YR	6.75	12.00
94	RIDING A BREEZE 575QEO821-3	YR	5.75	15.00
96	GARDEN CLUB QEO809-1	YR	8.00	10.00
96	HERE COMES EASTER QEO809-4	YR	8.00	10.00
S. PIKE			**EASTER ORNAMENTS**	
92	EVERYTHING'S DUCKY! 675QEO933-1	YR	6.75	22.00
92	SUNNY WISHER 575QEO934-4	YR	5.75	22.00
D. RHODUS			**EASTER ORNAMENTS**	
94	EASTER PARADE 675QEO813-6	YR	6.75	19.00
96	PARADE PALS QEO815-1	YR	8.00	8.00
A. ROGERS			**EASTER ORNAMENTS**	
92	CRAYOLA BUNNY 775QEO930-4	YR	7.75	34.00
92	DAUGHTER 575QEO928-4	YR	5.75	22.00
92	SON 575QEO928-1	YR	5.75	22.00
94	SWEET AS SUGAR 875QEO808-6	YR	8.75	17.00
94	YUMMY RECIPE 775QEO814-3	YR	7.75	20.00
96	DAFFY DUCK QEO815-4	YR	9.00	10.00
E. SEALE			**EASTER ORNAMENTS**	
94	SUNNY BUNNY GARDEN 1500QEO814-6 SET OF 3	YR	15.00	30.00
96	EGGSTRA SPECIAL SURPRISE QEO816-1	YR	9.00	9.00
96	STRAWBERRY PATCH QEO817-1	YR	7.00	10.00
L. SICKMAN			**EASTER ORNAMENTS**	
93	BACKYARD BUNNY 675QEO840-5	YR	6.75	22.00
93	LOP-EARED BUNNY 575QEO831-5	YR	5.75	19.00
94	TREETOP COTTAGE 975QEO818-6	YR	9.75	20.00
B. SIEDLER			**EASTER ORNAMENTS**	
92	COSMIC RABBIT 775QEO936-4	YR	7.75	23.00
92	CULTIVATED GARDENER 575QEO935-1	YR	5.75	19.00
92	EGGS IN SPORTS 675QEO934-1	YR	6.75	37.00
92	EGGSPERT PAINTER 675QEO936-1	YR	6.75	24.00
93	EGGS IN SPORTS 675QEO833-2	YR	6.75	30.00
93	GRANDCHILD 675QEO835-2	YR	6.75	22.00
94	EGGS IN SPORTS 675QEO813-3	YR	6.75	19.00
D. UNRUH			**EASTER ORNAMENTS**	
93	BEAUTIFUL MEMORIES,PHOTOHLDR 675QEO836-2	YR	6.75	18.00
93	RADIANT WINDOW 775QEO836-5	YR	7.75	24.00
94	JOYFUL LAMB 575QEO820-6	YR	5.75	15.00
94	PEANUTS 775QEO817-6	YR	7.75	27.00
94	PEEPING OUT 675QEO820-3	YR	6.75	15.00
96	EASTER MORNING QEO816-4	YR	8.00	8.00
96	STRIKE UP THE BAND! QEO814-1	YR	15.00	16.00
L. VOTRUBA			**EASTER ORNAMENTS**	
92	BELLE BUNNY 975QEO935-4	YR	9.75	24.00
92	ROCKING BUNNY 975QEO932-4	YR	9.75	24.00
92	WARM MEMORIES 775QEO931-1	YR	7.75	19.00
93	LOVELY LAMB 975QEO837-2	YR	9.75	22.00
94	COLLECTOR'S PLATE 775QEO823-3	YR	7.75	25.00
94	DIVINE DUET 675QEO818-3	YR	6.75	16.00
94	EASTER ART SHOW 775QEO819-3	YR	7.75	17.00
96	PETER RABBIT FIRST SERIES QEO807-1	YR	9.00	75.00
*			**FABRIC ORNAMENTS**	
81	CALICO KITTY 300QX403-5	YR	3.00	20.00
81	CARDINAL CUTIE 300QX400-2	YR	3.00	23.00
81	GINGHAM DOG 300QX402-2	YR	3.00	19.00
81	PEPPERMINT MOUSE 300QX401-5	YR	3.00	25.00
P. ANDREWS			**FAMILY AND FRIENDS**	
96	BABY'S FIRST CHRISTMAS QX575-4	YR	10.00	10.00
K. BRICKER			**FAMILY AND FRIENDS**	
96	CLOSE-KNIT FRIENDS QX587-4	YR	10.00	10.00
96	THANK YOU, SANTA PHOTO HOLDER QX585-4	YR	8.00	8.00
K. CROW			**FAMILY AND FRIENDS**	
96	BABY'S FIRST CHRISTMAS QX576-4	YR	8.00	8.00
96	BABY'S SECOND CHRISTMAS QX577-1	YR	8.00	8.00
96	CHILD'S FOURTH CHRISTMAS QX578-1	YR	8.00	8.00
96	CHILD'S THIRD CHRISTMAS QX577-4	YR	8.00	8.00
96	OUR CHRISTMAS TOGETHER PHOTO HOLDER QX580-4	YR	9.00	9.00
J. FRANCIS			**FAMILY AND FRIENDS**	
96	BABY'S FIRST CHRISTMAS QLX740-4	YR	22.00	22.00
J. LYLE			**FAMILY AND FRIENDS**	
96	MOM QX582-4	YR	8.00	8.00
96	SISTER TO SISTER QX583-4	YR	10.00	10.00
D. PALMITER			**FAMILY AND FRIENDS**	
96	DAUGHTER QX607-7	YR	9.00	9.00

YR	NAME	LIMIT	ISSUE	TREND
96	OUR CHRISTMAS TOGETHER QX579-4	YR	19.00	19.00
96	SON QX607-9	YR	9.00	9.00
D. RHODUS			**FAMILY AND FRIENDS**	
96	CHILD'S FIFTH CHRISTMAS QX578-4	YR	7.00	7.00
96	HEARTS FULL OF LOVE QX581-4	YR	10.00	10.00
96	MOM AND DAD QX582-1	YR	10.00	10.00
A. ROGERS			**FAMILY AND FRIENDS**	
96	GODCHILD QX584-1	YR	9.00	9.00
96	GRANDDAUGHTER QX569-7	YR	8.00	8.00
96	GRANDSON QX569-9	YR	8.00	8.00
E. SEALE			**FAMILY AND FRIENDS**	
96	BABY'S FIRST CHRISTMAS QX576-1 PHOTO HOLDER	YR	8.00	8.00
96	NEW HOME QX588-1	YR	9.00	9.00
B. SIEDLER			**FAMILY AND FRIENDS**	
96	DAD QX573-1	YR	8.00	8.00
S. TAGUE			**FAMILY AND FRIENDS**	
96	ON MY WAY, PHOTO HOLDER QX586-1	YR	8.00	8.00
96	SPECIAL DOG PHOTO HOLDER QX586-4	YR	8.00	8.00
D. UNRUH			**FAMILY AND FRIENDS**	
96	MOM-TO-BE QX579-1	YR	8.00	8.00
L. VOTRUBA			**FAMILY AND FRIENDS**	
96	BABY'S FIRST CHRISTMAS QX574-4	YR	19.00	19.00
96	GRANDMA QX584-4	YR	9.00	9.00
96	GRANDPA QX585-1	YR	9.00	9.00
96	OUR FIRST CHRISTMAS TOGETHER QX305-1	YR	7.00	7.00
D. RHODUS			**FLINTSTONES**	
94	FRED & BARNEY 1495QX500-3	YR	15.00	30.00
95	BETTY AND WILMA QX541-7	YR	15.00	25.00
95	FRED AND DINO QLX728-9	YR	28.00	40.00
*			**FOLK ART AMERICANA**	
95	FETCHING THE FIREWOOD QKL105-7	YR	17.00	30.00
95	FISHING PARTY QK103-9	YR	16.00	30.00
95	GUIDING SANTA QK103-7	YR	19.00	35.00
95	LEARNING TO SKATE QK104-7	YR	15.00	25.00
L. SICKMAN			**FOLK ART AMERICANA**	
93	ANGEL IN FLIGHT 1575QK105-2	YR	15.75	30.00
93	POLAR BEAR ADV. 1500QK105-5	YR	15.00	42.00
93	RIDING IN THE WOODS 1575QK106-5	YR	15.75	55.00
93	RIDING THE WIND 1575QK104-5	YR	15.75	40.00
93	SANTA CLAUS 1675QK107-2	YR	16.75	130.00
94	CATCHING 40 WINKS 1675QK118-3	YR	16.75	35.00
94	GOING TO TOWN 1575QK116-6	YR	15.75	30.00
94	RACING THROUGH THE SNOW 1575QK117-3	YR	15.75	30.00
94	RARIN' TO GO 1575QK119-3	YR	15.75	35.00
94	ROUNDUP TIME 1675QK117-6	YR	16.75	40.00
96	CAROLING ANGEL QK113-4	YR	17.00	35.00
96	MRS. CLAUS QK120-4	YR	19.00	40.00
96	SANTA'S GIFTS QK112--4	YR	19.00	60.00
*			**FOOTBALL HELMET COLLECTION**	
96	CAROLINA PANTHERS FOOTBALL HELMET	YR	10.00	28.00
96	CHICAGO BEARS FOOTBALL HELMET	YR	10.00	40.00
96	DALLAS COWBOYS FOOTBALL HELMET	YR	10.00	55.00
96	KANSAS CITY CHIEFS FOOTBALL HELMET	YR	10.00	40.00
96	MINNESOTA VIKINGS FOOTBALL HELMET	YR	10.00	25.00
96	NEW ENGLAND PATRIOTS FOOTBALL HELMET	YR	10.00	25.00
96	OAKLAND RAIDERS FOOTBALL HELMET	YR	10.00	85.00
96	PHILADELPHIA EAGLES FOOTBALL HELMET	YR	10.00	25.00
96	SAN FRANCISCO 49ERS FOOTBALL HELMET	YR	10.00	39.00
96	WASHINGTON REDSKINS FOOTBALL HELMET	YR	10.00	25.00
D. RHODUS			**FOOTBALL LEGENDS**	
95	JOE MONTANA/KANSAS CITY QXI620-7	YR	15.00	80.00
95	JOE MONTANA/SAN FRANCISCO QX1575-9	YR	15.00	35.00
96	TROY AIKMAN QXI502-1	YR	15.00	20.00
97	JOE NAMATH QX16182	YR	15.00	15.00
*			**FROSTED IMAGES**	
80	DOVE 400QX308-1	YR	4.00	35.00
80	DRUMMER BOY 400QX309-4	YR	4.00	21.00
80	SANTA 400QX310-1	YR	4.00	20.00
81	ANGEL 400QX509-5	YR	4.00	47.00
81	MOUSE 400QX508-2	YR	4.00	19.00
81	SNOWMAN 400QX510-2	YR	4.00	20.00
*			**FROSTY FRIENDS**	
80	A COOL YULE-1ST EDITION 650QX137-4	YR	6.50	630.00
81	ESKIMO & HUSKY IN IGLOO-2ND EDITION QX 433-5	YR	8.00	400.00
J. LEE			**FROSTY FRIENDS**	
90	LITTLE SEAL 620XPR972-1	YR	3.00	10.00
90	MEMORY WREATH 620XPR972-4	YR	3.00	10.00
92	WHALE-13TH EDITION 975QX429-1	YR	9.75	30.00
93	IGLOO DOGHOUSE 14TH ED. 975QX414-2	YR	9.75	30.00
S. PIKE			**FROSTY FRIENDS**	
91	ICE HOCKEY-12TH EDITION 975QX432-7	YR	9.75	30.00
E. SEALE			**FROSTY FRIENDS**	
82	ICICLE-3RD EDITION 800QX452-3	YR	8.00	275.00

YR NAME	LIMIT	ISSUE	TREND
83 ESKIMO & SEAL ON ICE-4TH EDITION 800QX400-7	YR	8.00	255.00
84 ICE FISHING-5TH EDITION 800QX437-1	YR	8.00	70.00
85 ARCTIC PALS/KAYAK-6TH EDITION 850QX482-2	YR	8.50	60.00
87 ESKIMO & SEAL -8TH EDITION 850QX440-9	YR	8.50	50.00
88 ESKIMO & POLAR BEAR-9TH EDITION 875QX403-1	YR	8.75	52.00
89 SLED-10TH EDITION 925QX457-2	YR	9.25	38.00
90 ICE BERG-11TH EDITION 975QX439-6	YR	9.75	30.00
90 LITTLE HUSKY 620XPR972-2	YR	3.00	15.00
93 20TH ANNIVERSARY 2000QX568-2	YR	20.00	45.00
94 BEAR AND WREATH-15TH EDITION 995QX529-3	YR	10.00	25.00
95 ESKIMO WITH POLAR BEAR-16TH SERIES QX516-9	YR	11.00	20.00
96 FROSTY FRIENDS 17TH ED. QX568-1	YR	11.00	20.00
97 WIND SURF SKIING 18TH EDITION 625-5	YR	11.00	11.00
B. SIEDLER		**FROSTY FRIENDS**	
86 ESKIMO & REINDEER-7TH EDITION 850QX405-3	YR	8.50	57.00
90 LITTLE BEAR 620XPR972-3	YR	3.00	10.00
90 LITTLE FROSTY 620XPR972-0	YR	3.00	12.00
S. PIKE		**GARDEN CLUB**	
98 GARDEN CLUB 795QEO8426	YR	8.00	
R. CHAD		**GARDEN ELVES COLLECTION**	
94 DAISY DAYS 995QX598-6	YR	10.00	10.00
94 HARVEST JOY 995QX599-3	YR	10.00	10.00
94 TULIP TIME 995QX598-3	YR	10.00	10.00
94 YULETIDE CHEER 995QX597-6	YR	10.00	10.00
L. VOTRUBA		**GIFT BRINGERS**	
89 ST. NICHOLAS 1ST EDITION 550QX279-5	YR	5.00	13.00
91 CHRISTKINDL 3RD ED. 500QX211-7	YR	5.00	16.00
93 MAGI, THE 5TH ED. 500QX206-5	YR	5.00	12.00
*		**GOLD CROWN ORNAMENTS**	
91 SANTA'S PREMIERE 1075QX523-7	YR	10.75	33.00
P. DUTKIN		**GOLD CROWN ORNAMENTS**	
86 ON THE RIGHT TRACK QSP 420-1	YR	15.00	37.00
E. SEALE		**GOLD CROWN ORNAMENTS**	
94 EAGER FOR...TENDER TOUCHES 1500QX533-6	YR	15.00	23.00
L. VOTRUBA		**GOLD CROWN ORNAMENTS**	
92 O CHRISTMAS TREE 1075QX541-1	YR	10.75	21.00
*		**HALLMARK EXPO ORNAMENTS**	
93 GOLD DOVE OF PEACE	SO	10.00	10.00
93 GOLD SANTA	SO	10.00	10.00
93 GOLD SLEIGH	SO	10.00	10.00
93 GOLD STAR AND HOLLY	SO	10.00	10.00
94 GOLD BOWS	SO	10.00	10.00
94 GOLD POINSETTIA	SO	10.00	10.00
94 MRS. CLAUS' CUPBOARD QXC484-3	YR	55.00	225.00
*		**HALLMARK KEEPSAKE ORNAMENTS**	
73 BETSEY CLARK 250XHD100-2	YR	2.50	80.00
73 CHRISTMAS IS LOVE 250XHD106-2	YR	2.50	65.00
73 ELVES 250XHD103-5	YR	2.50	67.00
73 MANGER SCENE 250XHD102-2	YR	2.50	95.00
73 SANTA WITH ELVES 250XHD101-5	YR	2.50	75.00
74 ANGEL 250QX110-1	YR	2.50	70.00
74 BUTTONS & BO (2) 350QX113-1	YR	3.50	47.00
74 CHARMERS 250QX109-1	YR	2.50	37.00
74 LITTLE MIRACLES (4) 450QX115-1	YR	4.50	55.00
74 NORMAN ROCKWELL 250QX106-1	YR	2.50	80.00
74 NORMAN ROCKWELL 250QX111-1	YR	2.50	75.00
74 RAGGEDY ANN & RAGGEDY ANDY(4) 450QX114-1	YR	4.50	80.00
74 SNOWGOOSE 250QX107-1	YR	2.50	75.00
89 FESTIVE ANGEL 975QXM578-3	YR	9.75	12.00
93 MARY ENGELBREIT 500QX207-5	YR	5.00	11.00
94 BARNEY 995QX596-6	YR	10.00	24.00
P. ANDREWS		**HALLMARK KEEPSAKE ORNAMENTS**	
93 BABY'S FIRST CHRISTMAS 1075QX551-5	YR	10.75	17.00
93 GRANDMOTHER 675QX566-5	YR	6.75	10.00
93 ON HER TOES 875QX526-5	YR	8.75	16.00
93 OUR FIRST CHRISTMAS TOGETHER 675QX301-5	YR	6.75	12.00
93 STAR TEACHER PHOTOHOLDER QX564-5	YR	5.75	12.00
93 SWAT TEAM, THE 1275QX539-5	YR	12.75	21.00
94 A FELINE OF CHRISTMAS 895QX581-6	YR	9.00	23.00
R. BISHOP		**HALLMARK KEEPSAKE ORNAMENTS**	
94 ANNIVERSARY YR. PHOTOHOLDER 1095QX568-3	YR	11.00	15.00
R. CHAD		**HALLMARK KEEPSAKE ORNAMENTS**	
93 GODCHILD 875QX587-5	YR	8.75	12.00
93 GRANDDAUGHTER 675QX563-5	YR	6.75	10.00
93 GRANDSON 675QX563-2	YR	6.75	10.00
93 ONE-ELF MARCHING BAND 1275QX534-2	YR	12.75	22.00
93 POPPING GOOD TIMES 1475QX539-2	YR	14.75	24.00
93 SUPERMAN 1275QX575-2	YR	12.75	40.00
K. CROW		**HALLMARK KEEPSAKE ORNAMENTS**	
93 BABY'S FIRST CHRISTMAS 775QX552-5	YR	7.75	17.00
93 BEARY GIFTED 775QX576-2	YR	7.75	13.00
93 CURLY 'N' KINGLY 1075QX528-5	YR	10.75	18.00
93 QUICK AS A FOX 875QX579-2	YR	8.75	13.00

YR NAME	LIMIT	ISSUE	TREND
93 ROOM FOR ONE MORE 875QX538-2	YR	8.75	37.00
94 A SHARP FLAT 1095QX577-3	YR	9.00	15.00
J. FRANCIS	**HALLMARK KEEPSAKE ORNAMENTS**		
93 ACROSS THE MILES 875QX591-2	YR	8.75	13.00
93 BABY'S SECOND CHRISTMAS 675QX599-2	YR	6.75	19.00
93 BOWLING FOR ZZZS 775QX556-5	YR	7.75	13.00
93 CARING NURSE 675QX578-5	YR	6.75	15.00
93 CHILD'S FOURTH CHRISTMAS 675QX521-5	YR	6.75	13.00
93 CHILD'S THIRD CHRISTMAS 675QX599-5	YR	6.75	14.00
93 GRANDCHILD'S FIRST CHRISTMAS QX 555-2	YR	6.75	11.00
93 SNOWY HIDEWAWAY 975QX531-2	YR	9.75	16.00
J. LEE	**HALLMARK KEEPSAKE ORNAMENTS**		
93 BIRD WATCHER 975QX525-2	YR	9.75	18.00
93 DAD 775QX585-5	YR	7.75	14.00
93 DAD-TO-BE 675QX553-2	YR	6.75	13.00
93 FELIZ NAVIDAD 875QX536-5	YR	8.75	14.00
93 ICICLE BICYCLE 975QX583-5	YR	9.75	15.00
93 LOOK FOR THE WONDER 1275QX568-5	YR	12.75	23.00
93 MOM 775QX585-2	YR	7.75	15.00
93 MOM-TO-BE 675QX553-5	YR	6.75	11.00
93 OUR CHRISTMAS TOGETHER 1075QX594-2	YR	10.75	17.00
93 PEEP INSIDE 1375QX532-2	YR	13.75	20.00
93 PUTT-PUTT PENGUIN 975QX579-5	YR	9.75	15.00
93 SNOW BEAR ANGEL 775QX535-5	YR	7.75	14.00
93 SNOWBIRD 775QX576-5	YR	7.75	13.00
93 TO MY GRANDMA 775QX555-5	YR	7.75	11.00
93 WATER BED SNOOZE 975QX537-5	YR	9.75	17.00
J. LYLE	**HALLMARK KEEPSAKE ORNAMENTS**		
93 ANNIVERSARY YEAR PHOTOHOLDER QX597-2	YR	9.75	14.00
93 HE IS BORN 975QX536-2	YR	9.75	30.00
93 READY FOR FUN 775QX512-4	YR	7.75	13.00
93 SILVERY NOEL 1275QX530-5	YR	12.75	19.00
93 STAR OF WONDER 675QX598-2	YR	6.75	20.00
D. PALMITER	**HALLMARK KEEPSAKE ORNAMENTS**		
93 BABY'S FIRST CHRISTMAS 1875QX551-2	YR	19.00	23.00
93 COACH 675QX593-5	YR	6.75	12.00
93 LITTLE DRUMMER BOY 875QX537-2	YR	8.75	15.00
93 MAKING WAVES 975QX577-5	YR	9.75	21.00
93 MOM AND DAD 975QX584-5	YR	9.75	14.00
93 NEW HOME 775QX590-5	YR	7.75	35.00
93 PINK PANTHER, THE 1275QX575-5	YR	12.75	19.00
D. RHODUS	**HALLMARK KEEPSAKE ORNAMENTS**		
93 CHILD'S FIFTH CHRISTMAS 675QX522-2	YR	6.75	13.00
93 LOU RANKIN POLAR BEAR 975QX574-5	YR	9.75	22.00
94 ALL PUMPED UP 895QX592-3	YR	9.00	17.00
A. ROGERS	**HALLMARK KEEPSAKE ORNAMENTS**		
93 BABY'S FIRST CHRISTMAS PHOTOHOLDER QX 552-2	YR	7.75	19.00
93 BROTHER 675QX554-2	YR	6.75	10.00
93 GREAT CONNECTIONS 1075QX540-2	YR	10.75	21.00
93 HOWLING GOOD TIME 975QX525-5	YR	9.75	15.00
93 NEPHEW 675QX573-5	YR	6.75	10.00
93 NIECE 675QX573-2	YR	6.75	10.00
93 OUR FIRST CHRISTMAS TOGETHER 1875QX595-5	YR	19.00	29.00
93 SISTER 675QX554-5	YR	6.75	13.00
93 TOP BANANA 775QX592-5	YR	7.75	15.00
E. SEALE	**HALLMARK KEEPSAKE ORNAMENTS**		
93 APPLE FOR TEACHER 775QX590-2	YR	7.75	12.00
93 CHRISTMAS BREAK 775QX582-5	YR	7.75	20.00
93 HIGH TOP-PURR 875QX533-2	YR	8.75	20.00
93 MAKIN' MUSIC 975QX532-5	YR	9.75	16.00
93 PEOPLE FRIENDLY 875QX593-2	YR	8.75	12.00
93 SISTER TO SISTER 975QX588-5	YR	9.75	40.00
93 SMILE! IT'S CHRISTMAS PHOTOHOLDERQX533-5	YR	9.75	17.00
94 BABY'S FIRST CHRISTMAS 1295QX574-3	YR	13.00	18.00
L. SICKMAN	**HALLMARK KEEPSAKE ORNAMENTS**		
87 VILLAGE EXPRESS 2450QLX707-2	YR	25.00	90.00
93 CLEVER COOKIE 775QX566-2	YR	7.75	16.00
93 MAXINE 875QX538-5	YR	8.75	18.00
93 STRANGE AND WONDERFUL LOVE QX596-5	YR	8.75	14.00
93 WARM AND SPECIAL FRIENDS QX589-5	YR	10.75	18.00
94 ANGEL HARE 895QX589-6	YR	9.00	19.00
B. SIEDLER	**HALLMARK KEEPSAKE ORNAMENTS**		
93 BIG ROLLER 875QX535-2	YR	8.75	13.00
93 DUNKIN' ROO 775QX557-5	YR	7.75	14.00
93 FILLS THE BILL 875QX557-2	YR	8.75	13.00
93 HOME FOR CHRISTMAS 775QX556-2	YR	7.75	13.00
93 PERFECT MATCH 875QX577-2	YR	8.75	15.00
93 THAT'S ENTERTAINMENT 875QX534-5	YR	8.75	12.00
D. UNRUH	**HALLMARK KEEPSAKE ORNAMENTS**		
93 JULIANNE AND TEDDY 2175QX529-5	YR	22.00	44.00
93 OUR 1ST CHRISTMAS TOGETHER PHOTO.QX595-2	YR	8.75	12.00
93 OUR FAMILY PHOTOHOLDER 775QX589-2	YR	7.75	12.00
93 WAKE-UP CALL 875QX526-2	YR	8.75	16.00
94 BABY'S FIRST CHRISTMAS 1895QX563-3	YR	19.00	27.00

YR	NAME	LIMIT	ISSUE	TREND
L. VOTRUBA		HALLMARK KEEPSAKE ORNAMENTS		
93	BABY'S FIRST CHRISTMAS-BOY QX 210-5	YR	4.75	10.00
93	BIG ON GARDENING 975QX584-2	YR	9.75	14.00
93	DAUGHTER 675QX587-2	YR	6.75	10.00
93	FAITHFUL FIRE FIGHTER 775QX578-2	YR	8.00	15.00
93	GRANDPARENTS 475QX208-5	YR	4.75	12.00
93	SON 675QX586-5	YR	6.75	10.00
93	SPECIAL CAT PHOTOHOLDER QX523-5	YR	7.75	12.00
93	SPECIAL DOG PHOTOHOLDER QX596-2	YR	7.75	11.00
*		HALLMARK KEEPSAKE ORNAMENTS COLLECTOR'S CLUB		
91	FIVE YEARS TOGETHER QXC315-9	YR	*	40.00
94	SWEET BOUQUET QXC480-6	YR	*	15.00
P. ANDREWS		HALLMARK KEEPSAKE ORNAMENTS COLLECTOR'S CLUB		
90	SUGAR PLUM FAIRY 2775QXC447-3	25400	28.00	50.00
93	GENTLE TIDINGS 2500QXC544-2	YR	25.00	40.00
95	BARBIE: BRUNETTE DEBUT 1959 QXC539-7	YR	15.00	35.00
96	1988 HAPPY HOLIDAY BARBIE DOLL 1ST EDITION	YR	*	N/A
R. CHAD		HALLMARK KEEPSAKE ORNAMENTS COLLECTOR'S CLUB		
92	CHRISTMAS TREASURES 2200QXC546-4	YR	22.00	125.00
K. CROW		HALLMARK KEEPSAKE ORNAMENTS COLLECTOR'S CLUB		
89	VISIT FROM SANTA QXC580-2	YR	*	30.00
90	CLUB HOLLOW QXC445-6	YR	*	30.00
91	HIDDEN TREASURE/LI'L KEEPER 1500QXC476-9	YR	*	35.00
P. DUTKIN		HALLMARK KEEPSAKE ORNAMENTS COLLECTOR'S CLUB		
89	SITTING PURRTY QXC581-2	YR	*	45.00
J. FRANCIS		HALLMARK KEEPSAKE ORNAMENTS COLLECTOR'S CLUB		
90	ARMFUL OF JOY 975QXC445-3	YR	9.75	35.00
93	FORTY WINKS QXC 529-4	YR	*	18.00
94	HOLIDAY PURSUIT QXC 482-3	YR	*	19.00
D. LEE		HALLMARK KEEPSAKE ORNAMENTS COLLECTOR'S CLUB		
88	ANGELIC MINSTREL 2950QX408-4	YR	30.00	30.00
92	RODNEY TAKES FLIGHT QXC508-1	YR	*	21.00
94	ON CLOUD NINE 1200QXC485-3	YR	12.00	15.00
J. LYLE		HALLMARK KEEPSAKE ORNAMENTS COLLECTOR'S CLUB		
93	SHARING CHRISTMAS 2000QXC543-5	YR	20.00	40.00
94	JOLLY HOLLY SANTA QXC 483-3	YR	22.00	37.00
D. PALMITER		HALLMARK KEEPSAKE ORNAMENTS COLLECTOR'S CLUB		
95	1958 FORD EDSEL CITATION CONVERTIBLE QXC 416-7	YR	13.00	50.00
S. PIKE		HALLMARK KEEPSAKE ORNAMENTS COLLECTOR'S CLUB		
89	COLLECT A DREAM 900QXC428-5	YR	9.00	32.00
A. ROGERS		HALLMARK KEEPSAKE ORNAMENTS COLLECTOR'S CLUB		
90	CROWN PRINCE QXC560-3	YR	*	40.00
91	SECRETS FOR SANTA 2375QXC479-7	28700	24.00	58.00
96	AIRMAIL FOR SANTA	YR	9.00	9.00
96	WIZARD OF OZ, THE	YR	13.00	50.00
E. SEALE		HALLMARK KEEPSAKE ORNAMENTS COLLECTOR'S CLUB		
88	CHRISTMAS IS SHARING 1750QX407-1	YR	17.50	31.00
89	CHRISTMAS IS PEACEFUL 1850QXC451-2	YR	19.00	30.00
92	CHIPMUNK PARCEL SERVICE QXC519-4	YR	7.00	22.00
92	SANTA'S CLUB LIST 1500QXC729-1	YR	15.00	29.00
93	IT'S IN THE MAIL QXC527-2	YR	10.00	20.00
95	FISHING FOR FUN QXC520-7	YR	11.00	20.00
L. SICKMAN		HALLMARK KEEPSAKE ORNAMENTS COLLECTOR'S CLUB		
87	CAROUSEL REINDEER QXC 581-7	YR	8.00	60.00
88	SLEIGHFUL OF DREAMS 800QXC580-1	YR	8.00	53.00
90	CHRISTMAS LIMITED 1975QXC476-6	38700	20.00	92.00
91	GALLOPING INTO CHRISTMAS 1975QXC477-9	28400	20.00	57.00
93	TRIMMED W/MEMORIES 1200QXC543-2	YR	12.00	19.00
95	HOME FROM THE WOODS QXC105-9	YR	16.00	25.00
B. SIEDLER		HALLMARK KEEPSAKE ORNAMENTS COLLECTOR'S CLUB		
88	HOLD ON TIGHT QXC570-4	YR	*	75.00
88	OUR CLUBHOUSE QXC580-4	YR	*	39.00
91	BEARY ARTISTIC 1000QXC725-9	YR	10.00	35.00
95	COLLECTING MEMORIES QXC411-7	YR	20.00	19.00
96	RUDLOPH THE RED-NOSED REINDEER	YR	*	25.00
96	RUDOLPH'S HELPER	YR	*	15.00
D. UNRUH		HALLMARK KEEPSAKE ORNAMENTS COLLECTOR'S CLUB		
87	WREATH OF MEMORIES QXC580-9	YR	*	50.00
88	HOLIDAY HEIRLOOM-2ND EDITION 2500QX406-4	34600	25.00	25.00
89	HOLIDAY HEIRLOOM-3RD ED. 2500QXC460-5	YR	25.00	26.00
89	NOELLE 1975QXC448-3	YR	20.00	29.00
92	VICTORIAN SKATER 2500QXC406-7	14700	25.00	120.00
94	MAJESTIC DEER 2500QXC483-6	YR	25.00	29.00
*		HANDCRAFTED ORNAMENTS		
78	ANGELS 800QX150-3	YR	8.00	347.00
78	CALICO MOUSE 450QX137-6	YR	4.50	174.00
78	JOY 450QX138-3	YR	4.50	75.00
78	PANORAMA BALL 600QX145-6	YR	6.00	130.00
78	RED CARDINAL 450QX144-3	YR	4.50	157.00
78	SCHNEEBERG BELL 800QX152-3	YR	8.00	182.00
78	SKATING RACCOON 600QX142-3	YR	6.00	85.00
79	A CHRISTMAS TREAT 500QX134-7	YR	5.00	65.00
79	CHRISTMAS EVE SURPRISE 650QX157-9	YR	6.50	55.00

YR	NAME	LIMIT	ISSUE	TREND
79	CHRISTMAS HEART 650QX140-7	YR	6.50	90.00
79	CHRISTMAS IS FOR CHILDREN 500QX135-9	YR	5.00	80.00
79	DRUMMER BOY, THE 800QX143-9	YR	8.00	112.00
79	HOLIDAY SCRIMSHAW 400QX152-7	YR	4.00	200.00
79	SANTA'S HERE 500QX138-7	YR	5.00	62.00
79	SKATING SNOWMAN, THE- 500QX139-9	YR	5.00	72.00
80	A CHRISTMAS TREAT 550QX134-7	YR	5.50	65.00
80	CHRISTMAS IS FOR CHILDREN 550QX135-9	YR	5.50	80.00
80	ELFIN ANTICS 900QX142-1	YR	9.00	190.00
80	HEAVENLY SOUNDS 750QX152-1	YR	7.50	80.00
80	SANTA 1980 550QX146-1	YR	5.50	87.00
80	SKATING SNOWMAN 550QX139-9	YR	5.50	72.00
80	SNOWFLAKE SWING, THE- 400QX133-4	YR	4.00	42.00
81	A HEAVENLY NAP 650QX139-4	YR	6.50	48.00
81	A WELL-STOCKED STOCKING 900QX154-7	YR	9.00	75.00
81	CANDYVILLE EXPRESS 750QX418-2	YR	7.50	100.00
81	CHRISTMAS FANTASY 1300QX155-4	YR	13.00	74.00
81	DOUGH ANGEL 550QX139-6	YR	5.50	90.00
81	DRUMMER BOY 250QX148-1	YR	2.50	40.00
81	LOVE AND JOY 900QX425-2	YR	9.00	87.00
81	MR. & MRS. CLAUS SET 1200QX448-5	YR	12.00	120.00
81	SAILING SANTA 1300QX439-5	YR	13.00	250.00
81	SPACE SANTA 650QX430-2	YR	6.50	97.00
82	CHRISTMAS FANTASY 1300QX155-4	YR	13.00	74.00
82	CLOISONNE ANGEL 1200QX145-4	YR	12.00	90.00
82	COWBOY SNOWMAN 800QX480-6	YR	8.00	45.00
82	CYCLING SANTA 2000QX435-5	YR	20.00	120.00
82	EMBROIDERED TREE 650QX494-6	YR	6.50	33.00
82	JOGGING SANTA 800QX457-6	YR	8.00	45.00
82	JOLLY CHRISTMAS TREE 650QX465-3	YR	6.50	78.00
82	PEEKING ELF 650QX419-5	YR	6.50	20.00
82	SANTA BELL 1500QX148-7	YR	15.00	50.00
82	TIN SOLDIER 650QX483-6	YR	6.50	45.00
83	CHRISTMAS KITTEN 400QX454-3	YR	4.00	31.00
83	CYCLING SANTA 2000QX435-6	YR	20.00	120.00
83	EMBROIDERED HEART 650QX421-7	YR	6.50	19.00
83	HOLIDAY PUPPY 350QX412-7	YR	3.50	29.00
83	JACK FROST 900QX407-9	YR	9.00	50.00
83	JOLLY SANTA 350QX425-9	YR	3.50	27.00
83	MADONNA AND CHILD 1200QX428-7	YR	12.00	35.00
83	MAILBOX KITTEN 650QX415-7	YR	6.50	51.00
83	MOUSE IN BELL 1000QX419-7	YR	10.00	59.00
83	PEPPERMINT PENGUIN 650QX408-9	YR	6.50	37.00
83	PORCELAIN DOLL-DIANA 900QX423-7	YR	9.00	32.00
83	SANTA'S MANY FACES 600QX311-7	YR	6.00	27.00
83	SANTA'S ON HIS WAY 1000QX426-9	YR	10.00	27.00
83	SKATING RABBIT 800QX409-7	YR	8.00	45.00
83	SKI LIFT SANTA 800QX418-7	YR	8.00	60.00
83	UNICORN 1000QX426-7	YR	10.00	60.00
88	JINGLE BELL CLOWN 1500QX477-4	YR	15.00	19.00
88	KRINGLE PORTRAIT 750QX421-4	YR	7.50	23.00
88	KRINGLE TREE 650QX495-4	YR	6.50	36.00
88	PEANUTS 475QX280-1	YR	4.75	24.00

T. BLACKSHEAR   **HANDCRAFTED ORNAMENTS**

YR	NAME	LIMIT	ISSUE	TREND
81	CHECKING IT TWICE 2250QX158-4	YR	23.00	182.00
82	THREE KINGS 850QX307-3	YR	8.50	18.00

R. CHAD   **HANDCRAFTED ORNAMENTS**

YR	NAME	LIMIT	ISSUE	TREND
88	SOFT LANDING 700QX475-1	YR	7.00	18.00
88	WINTER FUN 850QX478-1	YR	8.50	20.00

K. CROW   **HANDCRAFTED ORNAMENTS**

YR	NAME	LIMIT	ISSUE	TREND
88	CHRISTMAS CUCKOO 800QX480-1	YR	8.00	22.00
88	COOL JUGGLER 650QX487-4	YR	6.50	17.00
88	PEEK-A-BOO KITTENS 750QX487-1	YR	7.50	19.00
88	SLIPPER SPANIEL 450QX472-4	YR	4.50	12.00

D. LEE   **HANDCRAFTED ORNAMENTS**

YR	NAME	LIMIT	ISSUE	TREND
78	ANGEL 400QX139-6	YR	4.50	80.00
78	ANIMAL HOME 600QX149-6	YR	6.00	150.00
79	DOWNHILL RUN, THE 650QX145-9	YR	6.50	150.00
79	READY FOR CHRISTMAS 650QX133-9	YR	6.50	130.00
79	SKATING RACCOON 650QX142-3	YR	6.50	85.00
80	A CHRISTMAS VIGIL 900QX144-1	YR	9.00	100.00
80	A HEAVENLY NAP 650QX139-4	YR	6.50	50.00
80	A SPOT OF CHRISTMAS CHEER 800QX153-4	YR	8.00	132.00
80	ANIMAL'S CHRISTMAS, THE 800QX150-1	YR	8.00	55.00
80	CAROLING BEAR 750QX140-1	YR	7.50	125.00
80	DRUMMER BOY 550QX147-4	YR	5.50	87.00
81	CHRISTMAS DREAMS 1200QX437-5	YR	12.00	210.00
81	FRIENDLY FIDDLER, THE- 800QX434-2	YR	8.00	67.00
81	ICE FAIRY 650QX431-5	YR	6.50	70.00
81	ICE SCULPTOR, THE- 800QX432-2	YR	8.00	75.00
81	TOPSY-TURVY TUNES 750QX429-5	YR	7.50	72.00
82	BAROQUE ANGEL 1500QX456-6	YR	15.00	150.00
82	PINECONE HOME 800QX461-3	YR	8.00	160.00
82	RACCOON SURPRISES 900QX479-3	YR	9.00	142.00
82	SANTA'S WORKSHOP 1000QX450-3	YR	10.00	65.00

YR	NAME	LIMIT	ISSUE	TREND
83	BAROQUE ANGELS 1300QX422-9	YR	13.00	115.00
83	RAINBOW ANGEL 550QX416-7	YR	5.50	97.00
83	SANTA'S WORKSHOP 1000QX450-3	YR	10.00	80.00
83	SKIING FOX 800QX420-7	YR	8.00	37.00
88	TRAVELS WITH SANTA 1000QX477-1	YR	10.00	28.00
88	UNCLE SAM NUTCRACKER 700QX488-4	YR	7.00	23.00

J. LYLE   HANDCRAFTED ORNAMENTS

YR	NAME	LIMIT	ISSUE	TREND
88	CHRISTMAS SCENES 475QX273-1	YR	4.75	18.00

J. PATTEE   HANDCRAFTED ORNAMENTS

YR	NAME	LIMIT	ISSUE	TREND
88	CHRISTMAS MEMORIES PHOTOHOLDER QX 372-4	YR	6.50	20.00
88	GLOWING WREATH 600QX492-1	YR	6.00	13.00
88	SHINY SLEIGH 575QX492-4	YR	5.75	16.00
88	SPARKLING TREE 600QX483-1	YR	6.00	16.00

S. PIKE   HANDCRAFTED ORNAMENTS

YR	NAME	LIMIT	ISSUE	TREND
88	PARTY LINE 875QX476-1	YR	8.75	24.00
88	SQUEAKY CLEAN 675QX475-4	YR	6.75	19.00

M. PYDA-SEVCIK   HANDCRAFTED ORNAMENTS

YR	NAME	LIMIT	ISSUE	TREND
88	SANTA FLAMINGO 475QX483-4	YR	4.75	25.00

A. ROGERS   HANDCRAFTED ORNAMENTS

YR	NAME	LIMIT	ISSUE	TREND
88	CHRISTMAS CARDINAL 475QX494-1	YR	4.75	13.00
88	JOLLY WALRUS 450QX473-1	YR	4.50	16.00
88	KRINGLE MOON 550QX495-1	YR	5.50	28.00
88	LOVING BEAR 475QX493-4	YR	4.75	12.00
88	PURRFECT SNUGGLE 625QX474-4	YR	6.25	21.00
88	STARRY ANGEL 475QX494-4	YR	4.75	17.00

E. SEALE   HANDCRAFTED ORNAMENTS

YR	NAME	LIMIT	ISSUE	TREND
83	ANGEL MESSENGER 650QX408-7	YR	6.50	90.00
83	BRASS SANTA 900QX423-9	YR	9.00	19.00
83	CAROLING OWL 450QX411-7	YR	4.50	37.00
83	CHRISTMAS KOALA 400QX419-9	YR	4.00	27.00
83	HITCHHIKING SANTA 800QX424-7	YR	8.00	39.00
83	MOUNTAIN CLIMBING SANTA 650QX407-7	YR	6.50	30.00
83	SCRIMSHAW REINDEER 800QX424-9	YR	8.00	30.00
83	SNEAKER MOUSE 450QX400-9	YR	4.50	32.00
88	FILLED WITH FUDGE 475QX419-1	YR	4.75	25.00
88	SWEET STAR 500QX418-4	YR	5.00	25.00
88	TEENY TASTER 475QX418-1	YR	4.75	19.00
88	TOWN CRIER, THE- 550QX473-4	YR	5.50	16.00

L. SICKMAN   HANDCRAFTED ORNAMENTS

YR	NAME	LIMIT	ISSUE	TREND
78	DOVE 450QX190-3	YR	4.50	80.00
78	HOLLY & POINSETTIA BALL 600QX147-6	YR	6.00	80.00
79	OUTDOOR FUN 800QX150-7	YR	8.00	115.00
80	SANTA'S FLIGHT 550QX138-1	YR	5.50	110.00
81	ST. NICHOLAS 550QX446-2	YR	5.50	45.00
81	STAR SWING 550QX421-5	YR	5.50	28.00
82	ELFIN ARTIST 900QX457-3	YR	9.00	47.00
82	SPIRIT OF CHRISTMAS, THE- 1000QX452-6	YR	10.00	120.00
83	BELL WREATH 650QX420-9	YR	6.50	27.00
83	EMBROIDERED STOCKING 650QX479-6	YR	6.50	16.00
83	MOUSE ON CHEESE 650QX413-7	YR	6.50	45.00
83	OLD-FASHIONED SANTA 1100QX409-9	YR	11.00	62.00
83	TIN ROCKING HORSE 650QX414-9	YR	6.50	45.00
88	AMERICANA DRUM 775QX488-1	YR	7.75	22.00
88	GOIN' CROSS COUNTRY 850QX476-4	YR	8.50	22.00
88	NOAH'S ARK 850QX490-4	YR	8.50	31.00
88	OLD-FASHIONED CHURCH 400QX498-1	YR	4.00	15.00
88	OLD-FASHIONED SCHOOL HOUSE 400QX497-1	YR	4.00	18.00
88	SAILING! SAILING! 850QX491-1	YR	8.50	22.00

B. SIEDLER   HANDCRAFTED ORNAMENTS

YR	NAME	LIMIT	ISSUE	TREND
88	ARCTIC TENOR 400QX472-1	YR	4.00	14.00
88	GO FOR THE GOLD 800QX417-4	YR	8.00	21.00
88	GONE FISHING 500QX479-4	YR	5.00	20.00
88	HOE-HOE-HOE 500QX422-1	YR	5.00	14.00
88	HOLIDAY HERO 500QX423-1	YR	5.00	14.00
88	LOVE SANTA 500QX486-4	YR	5.00	15.00
88	NICK THE KICK 500QX422-4	YR	5.00	16.00
88	PAR FOR SANTA 500QX479-1	YR	5.00	15.00
88	POLAR BOWLER 500QX478-1	YR	5.00	14.00

D. UNRUH   HANDCRAFTED ORNAMENTS

YR	NAME	LIMIT	ISSUE	TREND
88	A KISS FROM SANTA 450QX482-1	YR	4.50	21.00
88	FELIZ NAVIDAD 675QX416-1	YR	6.75	23.00
88	KISS THE CLAUS 500QX486-1	YR	5.00	12.00
88	OREO 400QX481-4	YR	4.00	35.00
88	SNOOPY & WOODSTOCK 600QX474-1	YR	6.00	40.00

D. LEE   HANDCRAFTED ORNAMENTS: ADORABLE ADORNMENTS

YR	NAME	LIMIT	ISSUE	TREND
75	BETSEY CLARK 250QX157-1	YR	2.50	230.00
75	DRUMMER BOY 250QX161-1	YR	2.50	200.00
75	MRS. SANTA 250QX156-1	YR	2.50	130.00
75	RAGGEDY ANDY 250QX160-1	YR	2.50	330.00
75	RAGGEDY ANN 250QX159-1	YR	2.50	290.00
75	SANTA 250QX155-1	YR	2.50	130.00

*   HANDCRAFTED ORNAMENTS: NOSTALGIA

YR	NAME	LIMIT	ISSUE	TREND
77	NATIVITY 500QX181-5	YR	5.00	130.00

YR	NAME	LIMIT	ISSUE	TREND
D. LEE		**HANDCRAFTED ORNAMENTS: NOSTALGIA**		
77	ANGEL 500QX182-2	YR	5.00	95.00
L. SICKMAN		**HANDCRAFTED ORNAMENTS: NOSTALGIA**		
75	DRUMMER BOY 350QX130-1	YR	3.50	135.00
75	JOY 350QX132-1	YR	3.50	115.00
75	LOCOMOTIVE (DATED) 350QX127-1	YR	3.50	145.00
75	PEACE ON EARTH (DATED) 350QX131-1	YR	3.50	145.00
75	SANTA & SLEIGH 350QX129-1	YR	3.50	225.00
76	DRUMMER BOY 400QX130-1	YR	4.00	135.00
76	LOCOMOTIVE 400QX222-1	YR	4.00	140.00
76	PEACE ON EARTH 400QX223-1	YR	4.00	110.00
77	ANTIQUE CAR 500QX180-2	YR	5.00	42.00
77	TOYS 500QX183-5	YR	5.00	120.00
*		**HANDCRAFTED ORNAMENTS: TREE TREATS**		
76	ANGEL 300QX176-1	YR	3.00	160.00
76	REINDEER 300QX178-1	YR	3.00	100.00
76	SANTA 300QX177-1	YR	3.00	197.00
76	SHEPHERD 300QX175-1	YR	3.00	95.00
*		**HANDCRAFTED ORNAMENTS: TWIRL-ABOUTS**		
77	BELLRINGER 600QX192-2	YR	6.00	62.00
77	WEATHER HOUSE 600QX191-5	YR	6.00	101.00
D. LEE		**HANDCRAFTED ORNAMENTS: TWIRL-ABOUTS**		
77	DELLA ROBIA WREATH 450QX193-5	YR	4.50	117.00
L. SICKMAN		**HANDCRAFTED ORNAMENTS: TWIRL-ABOUTS**		
76	ANGEL 450QX171-1	YR	4.50	140.00
76	PARTRIDGE 450QX174-1	YR	4.50	160.00
76	SANTA 450QX172-1	YR	4.50	100.00
76	SOLDIER 450QX173-1	YR	4.50	70.00
77	SNOWMAN 450QX190-2	YR	4.50	50.00
*		**HANDCRAFTED ORNAMENTS: YESTERYEARS**		
76	DRUMMER BOY 500QX184-1	YR	5.00	120.00
76	PARTRIDGE 500QX183-1	YR	5.00	100.00
76	SANTA 500QX182-1	YR	5.00	125.00
76	TRAIN 500QX181-1	YR	5.00	100.00
*		**HEIRLOOM CHRISTMAS COLLECTION**		
85	LACY HEART 875QX511-2	YR	8.75	16.00
85	VICTORIAN LADY 950QX513-2	YR	9.50	21.00
J. PATTEE		**HEIRLOOM CHRISTMAS COLLECTION**		
85	SNOWFLAKE 650QX510-5	YR	6.50	12.00
S. PIKE		**HEIRLOOM CHRISTMAS COLLECTION**		
85	KEEPSAKE BASKET 1500QX514-5	YR	15.00	16.00
M. PYDA-SEVCIK		**HEIRLOOM CHRISTMAS COLLECTION**		
85	CHARMING ANGEL 975QX512-5	YR	9.75	19.00
*		**HERE COMES SANTA**		
79	SANTA'S MOTORCAR 1ST SERIES 900QX155-9	YR	9.00	625.00
80	SANTA'S EXPRESS 1200QX143-4	YR	12.00	170.00
81	ROOFTOP DELIVERIES 1300QX438-2	YR	13.00	235.00
K. CROW		**HERE COMES SANTA**		
87	SANTA'S WOODY 1400QX484-7	YR	14.00	45.00
88	KRINGLE KOACH 1400QX400-1	YR	14.00	38.00
89	CHRISTMAS CABOOSE 11TH ED. 1475QX458-5	YR	14.75	37.00
E. SEALE		**HERE COMES SANTA**		
96	SANTA'S 4x4 18TH ED. QX568-4	YR	15.00	15.00
L. SICKMAN		**HERE COMES SANTA**		
82	JOLLY TROLLEY QX 464-3	YR	15.00	107.00
83	SANTA'S EXPRESS 1300QX403-7	YR	13.00	275.00
84	SANTA'S DELIVERIES 1300QX432-4	YR	13.00	82.00
85	SANTA'S FIRE ENGINE 1400QX496-5	YR	14.00	75.00
90	FESTIVE SURREY 12TH ED. 1475QX492-3	YR	14.75	36.00
91	SANTA'S ANTIQUE CAR-13TH ED. 1475QX434-9	YR	14.75	40.00
92	KRINGLE TOURS 14TH ED. 1475QX434-1	YR	14.75	31.00
93	HAPPY HAULI-DAYS 15TH ED. 1475QX410-2	YR	14.75	28.00
93	SHOPPING WITH SANTA QX567-5	YR	24.00	36.00
94	MAKIN' TRACTOR TRACKS 16TH ED. 1495QX529-6	YR	15.00	50.00
95	SANTA'S ROADSTER 17TH SERIES QX517-9	YR	15.00	20.00
B. SIEDLER		**HERE COMES SANTA**		
86	KRINGLES KOOL TREATS 1400QX404-3	YR	14.00	60.00
S. TAGUE		**HERE COMES SANTA**		
97	CLAUS MOBILE	YR	15.00	15.00
L. SICKMAN		**HERSHEY'S**		
96	TIME FOR A TREAT QX546-4	YR	12.00	12.00
N. AUBE		**HOBBIES**		
96	SEW SWEET QX592-1	YR	9.00	10.00
96	STAR OF THE SNOW QX600-4	YR	9.00	9.00
R. CHAD		**HOBBIES**		
96	ANTLERS AWEIGH! QX590-1	YR	10.00	10.00
96	FAN-TASTIC SEASON QX592-4	YR	10.00	10.00
K. CROW		**HOBBIES**		
96	MATCHLESS MEMORIES QX606-1	YR	10.00	10.00
96	MERRY CARPOOLERS QX558-4	YR	15.00	15.00
D. PALMITER		**HOBBIES**		
96	PUP-TENTING QX601-1	YR	8.00	8.00

YR	NAME	LIMIT	ISSUE	TREND
D. RHODUS				**HOBBIES**
96	HAPPY HOLI-DOZE QX590-4	YR	10.00	10.00
96	I DIG GOLF QX589-1	YR	11.00	11.00
N. ROCKWELL				**HOBBIES**
96	GROWTH OF A LEADER BOYS SCOUTS OF AMERICA QX554-1	YR	10.00	10.00
E. SEALE				**HOBBIES**
96	GOAL LINE GLORY QX600-1	YR	13.00	13.00
96	THIS BIG! QX591-4	YR	10.00	10.00
B. SIEDLER				**HOBBIES**
96	BOUNCE PASS QX603-1	YR	8.00	8.00
96	BOWL'EM OVER QX601-4	YR	8.00	8.00
96	JACKPOT JINGLE QX591-1	YR	10.00	10.00
D. UNRUH				**HOBBIES**
96	POLAR CYCLE QX603-4	YR	13.00	13.00
L. VOTRUBA				**HOBBIES**
96	YULETIDE CHEER QX605-4	YR	8.00	8.00
*				**HOCKEY GREATS**
97	WAYNE GRETZKY 1627-5	YR	16.00	16.00
P. ANDREWS				**HOLIDAY BARBIE COLLECTION**
93	HOLIDAY BARBIE 1ST IN ED. 1495QX572-5	YR	15.00	125.00
94	HOLIDAY BARBIE 2ND IN ED. 1495QX521-6	YR	15.00	45.00
95	HOLIDAY BARBIE 3RD IN ED. QXI505-7	YR	15.00	35.00
96	HOLIDAY BARBIE 4TH IN ED. QXI537-1	YR	15.00	30.00
97	HOLIDAY BARBIE 5TH IN ED. QX16212	YR	15.00	15.00
*				**HOLIDAY CHIMES**
80	SANTA MOBILE 550QX136-1	YR	5.50	41.00
81	SANTA MOBILE 550QX136-1	YR	5.50	41.00
81	SNOWMAN CHIMES 550QX445-5	YR	5.50	26.00
82	ANGEL CHIMES 550QX502-6	YR	5.50	25.00
E. SEALE				**HOLIDAY CHIMES**
82	TREE CHIMES 550QX484-6	YR	5.50	51.00
L. SICKMAN				**HOLIDAY CHIMES**
78	REINDEER CHIMES 450QX320-3	YR	4.50	30.00
79	REINDEER CHIMES 450QX320-3	YR	4.50	36.00
79	STAR CHIMES 450QX137-9	YR	4.50	60.00
80	REINDEER CHIMES 550QX320-3	YR	5.50	39.00
80	SNOWFLAKE CHIMES 550QX165-4	YR	5.50	24.00
81	SNOWFLAKE CHIMES 550QX165-4	YR	5.50	24.00
82	BELL CHIMES 550QX494-3	YR	5.50	21.00
*				**HOLIDAY ENCHANTMENT**
93	JOURNEY TO THE FOREST 1375QK101-2	YR	13.75	25.00
93	MAGI, THE 1375QK102-5	YR	13.75	30.00
R. CHAD				**HOLIDAY ENCHANTMENT**
93	BRINGING HOME THE TREE 1375QK104-2	YR	13.75	27.00
L. VOTRUBA				**HOLIDAY ENCHANTMENT**
93	ANGELIC MESSENGER 1375QK103-2	YR	13.75	29.00
93	VISION OF SUGARPLUMS 1375QK100-5	YR	13.75	27.00
95	AWAY IN A MANGER QK109-7	YR	14.00	16.00
95	FOLLOWING THE STAR QK109-9	YR	14.00	16.00
L. VOTRUBA				**HOLIDAY FAVORITES**
94	DAPPER SNOWMAN 1375QK105-3	YR	13.75	16.00
94	GRACEFUL FAWN 1175QK103-3	YR	11.75	14.00
94	JOLLY SANTA 1375QK104-6	YR	13.75	19.00
94	JOYFUL LAMB 1175QK103-6	YR	11.75	16.00
94	PEACEFUL DOVE 1175QK104-3	YR	11.75	17.00
L. SICKMAN				**HOLIDAY FLIERS**
93	TIN AIRPLANE 775QX562-2	YR	7.75	25.00
93	TIN BLIMP 775QX562-5	YR	7.75	25.00
93	TIN HOT AIR BALLOON 775QX561-5	YR	7.75	19.00
*				**HOLIDAY HIGHLIGHTS**
77	DRUMMER BOY 350QX312-2	YR	3.50	50.00
77	JOY 350QX310-2	YR	3.50	30.00
77	PEACE ON EARTH 350QX311-5	YR	3.50	48.00
77	STAR 350QX313-5	YR	3.50	48.00
78	DOVE 350QX310-3	YR	3.50	100.00
78	SANTA 350QX307-6	YR	3.50	72.00
78	SNOWFLAKE 350QX308-3	YR	3.50	52.00
79	CHRISTMAS ANGEL 350QX300-7	YR	3.50	80.00
79	CHRISTMAS CHEER 350QX303-9	YR	3.50	60.00
79	CHRISTMAS TREE 350QX302-7	YR	3.50	60.00
79	LOVE 350QX304-7	YR	3.50	90.00
79	SNOWFLAKE 350QX301-9	YR	3.50	37.00
80	THREE WISE MEN 400QX300-1	YR	4.00	24.00
80	WREATH 400QX301-4	YR	4.00	60.00
81	CHRISTMAS STAR 550QX501-5	YR	5.50	16.00
81	SHEPHERD SCENE 550QX500-2	YR	5.50	21.00
82	ANGEL 550QX309-6	YR	5.50	27.00
82	CHRISTMAS MAGIC 550QX311-3	YR	5.50	26.00
82	CHRISTMAS SLEIGH 550QX309-3	YR	5.50	70.00
83	CHRISTMAS STOCKING 600QX303-9	YR	6.00	34.00
83	TIME FOR SHARING 600QX307-7	YR	6.00	32.00
D. PALMITER				**HOLIDAY HIGHLIGHTS**
78	NATIVITY 350QX309-6	YR	3.50	72.00

YR	NAME	LIMIT	ISSUE	TREND
E. SEALE			**HOLIDAY HIGHLIGHTS**	
83	STAR OF PEACE 600QX304-7	YR	6.00	17.00
*			**HOLIDAY HUMOR**	
84	A CHRISTMAS PRAYER 450QX246-1	YR	4.50	20.00
84	FLIGHTS OF FANTASY 450QX256-4	YR	4.50	13.00
84	FRISBEE PUPPY 500QX444-4	YR	5.00	45.00
84	NAPPING MOUSE 550QX435-1	YR	5.50	42.00
84	REINDEER RACETRACK 450QX254-4	YR	4.50	18.00
84	SANTA STAR 550QX450-4	YR	5.50	32.00
84	SNOWMOBILE SANTA 650QX431-4	YR	6.50	26.00
85	DOGGY IN A STOCKING 550QX474-2	YR	5.50	29.00
85	LAMB IN LEGWARMERS 700QX480-2	YR	7.00	18.00
85	MOUSE WAGON 575QX476-2	YR	5.75	55.00
85	NATIVITY SCENE 475QX264-5	YR	4.75	21.00
86	OPEN ME FIRST 725QX422-6	YR	7.25	24.00
87	CHRISTMAS CUDDLE 575QX453-7	YR	5.75	24.00
87	DR SEUSS: GRINCH'S CHRISTMAS 475QX278-3	YR	4.75	40.00
87	JAMMIE PIES 475QX283-9	YR	4.75	10.00
87	JOY RIDE 1150QX440-7	YR	11.50	75.00
87	LET IT SNOW 650QX458-9	YR	6.50	15.00
87	PEANUTS 475QX281-9	YR	4.75	25.00
87	SANTA AT THE BAT 775QX457-9	YR	7.75	17.00
87	SPOTS 'N STRIPES 550QX452-9	YR	5.50	16.00
K. CROW			**HOLIDAY HUMOR**	
86	CHATTY PENGUIN 575QX417-6	YR	5.75	17.00
86	PLAYFUL POSSUM 1100QX425-3	YR	11.00	20.00
86	RAH RAH RABBIT 700QX421-6	YR	7.00	25.00
87	HAPPY SANTA 475QX456-9	YR	4.75	22.00
87	NIGHT BEFORE CHRISTMAS 650QX451-7	YR	6.50	25.00
87	PRETTY KITTEN 1100QX448-9	YR	11.00	18.00
87	SLEEPY SANTA 625QX450-7	YR	6.25	30.00
P. DUTKIN			**HOLIDAY HUMOR**	
85	KITTY MISCHIEF 500QX474-5	YR	5.00	19.00
85	MERRY MOUSE 450QX403-2	YR	4.50	22.00
85	SKATEBOARD RACCOON 650QX473-2	YR	6.50	25.00
85	SOCCER BEAVER 650QX477-5	YR	6.50	16.00
86	KITTY MISCHIEF 500QX474-5	YR	5.00	19.00
86	MERRY MOUSE 450QX403-2	YR	4.50	22.00
86	SKATEBOARD RACCOON 650QX473-2	YR	6.50	25.00
86	SNOW BUDDIES 800QX423-6	YR	8.00	29.00
86	SOCCER BEAVER 650QX477-5	YR	6.50	16.00
86	TIPPING THE SCALES 675QX418-6	YR	6.75	21.00
86	TOUCHDOWN SANTA 800QX423-3	YR	8.00	29.00
87	FUDGE FOREVER 500QX449-7	YR	5.00	29.00
87	JOGGING THROUGH THE SNOW 725QX457-7	YR	7.25	16.00
D. LEE			**HOLIDAY HUMOR**	
84	MUSICAL ANGEL 550QX434-4	YR	5.50	57.00
84	PEPPERMINT 1984 450QX456-1	YR	4.50	47.00
84	THREE KITTENS IN A MITTEN 800QX431-1	YR	8.00	37.00
85	SNOW-PITCHING SNOWMAN 450QX470-2	YR	4.50	19.00
85	STARDUST ANGEL 575QX475-2	YR	5.75	30.00
85	THREE KITTENS IN A MITTEN 800QX431-1	YR	8.00	37.00
86	HEAVENLY DREAMER 575QX 417-3	YR	5.75	25.00
86	SNOW-PITCHING SNOWMAN 450QX470-2	YR	4.50	19.00
86	TREETOP TRIO 975QX424-6	YR	11.00	25.00
86	WYNKEN, BLYNKEN AND NOD 975QX424-6	YR	9.75	40.00
87	TREETOP TRIO 1100QX425-6	YR	11.00	25.00
D. MCGEHEE			**HOLIDAY HUMOR**	
86	COOKIES FOR SANTA 450QX414-6	YR	4.50	20.00
S. PIKE			**HOLIDAY HUMOR**	
87	OWLIDAY WISH 650QX455-9	YR	6.50	16.00
87	PADDINGTON BEAR 550QX472-7	YR	5.50	21.00
E. SEALE			**HOLIDAY HUMOR**	
84	BELL RINGER SQUIRREL 1000QX443-1	YR	10.00	30.00
84	CHRISTMAS OWL 600QX444-1	YR	6.00	26.00
84	MARATHON SANTA 800QX456-4	YR	8.00	32.00
84	MOUNTAIN CLIMBING SANTA 650QX407-7	YR	6.50	30.00
84	POLAR BEAR DRUMMER 450QX430-1	YR	4.50	20.00
84	RACCOON'S CHRISTMAS 900QX-447-4	YR	9.00	43.00
84	ROLLER SKATING RABBIT 500QX457-1	YR	5.00	26.00
84	SNOWY SEAL 400QX450-1	YR	4.00	17.00
85	BAKER ELF 575QX491-2	YR	5.75	26.00
85	CHILDREN IN THE SHOE 950QX490-5	YR	9.50	34.00
85	DAPPER PENGUIN 500QX477-2	YR	5.00	22.00
85	DO NOT DISTURB BEAR 775QX481-2	YR	7.75	23.00
85	NIGHT BEFORE CHRISTMAS 1300QX449-4	YR	13.00	33.00
85	ROLLER SKATING RABBIT 500QX457-1	YR	5.00	26.00
85	SANTA'S SKI TRIP 1200QX496-2	YR	12.00	56.00
85	SNOWY SEAL 400QX450-1	YR	4.00	17.00
85	TRUMPET PANDA 450QX471-2	YR	4.50	14.00
86	DO NOT DISTURB BEAR 775QX481-2	YR	7.75	24.00
86	LI'L JINGLER 675QX419-3	YR	6.75	35.00
86	MOUSE IN THE MOON 550QX416-6	YR	5.50	18.00
86	SANTA'S HOT TUB 1200QX426-3	YR	12.00	43.00

YR	NAME	LIMIT	ISSUE	TREND
86	WALNUT SHELL RIDER 600QX419-6	YR	6.00	18.00
87	CHOCOLATE CHIPMUNK 600QX456-7	YR	6.00	40.00
87	JACK FROSTING 700QX449-9	YR	7.00	53.00
87	LI'L JINGLER 675QX419-3	YR	6.75	45.00
87	MOUSE IN THE MOON 550QX416-6	YR	5.50	18.00
87	SEASONED GREETINGS 625QX454-9	YR	6.25	16.00
87	TREETOP DREAMS 675QX459-7	YR	6.75	22.00
87	WALNUT SHELL RIDER 600QX419-6	YR	6.00	18.00
L. SICKMAN			**HOLIDAY HUMOR**	
84	FORTUNE COOKIE ELF 450QX452-4	YR	4.50	35.00
84	SNOWSHOE PENGUIN 650QX453-1	YR	6.50	42.00
85	BEARY SMOOTH RIDE 650QX480-5	YR	6.50	17.00
85	CANDY APPLE MOUSE 750QX470-5	YR	6.50	55.00
86	BEARY SMOOTH RIDE 650QX480-5	YR	6.50	17.00
86	MERRY KOALA 500QX415-3	YR	5.00	16.00
86	POPCORN MOUSE 675QX421-3	YR	6.75	33.00
87	MERRY KOALA 500QX415-3	YR	5.00	16.00
B. SIEDLER			**HOLIDAY HUMOR**	
84	SANTA MOUSE 450QX433-4	YR	4.50	40.00
85	BOTTLECAP FUN BUNNIES 775QX481-5	YR	7.75	29.00
85	ENGINEERING MOUSE 550QX473-5	YR	5.50	18.00
85	ICE-SKATING OWL 500QX476-5	YR	5.00	16.00
85	SUN AND FUN SANTA 775QX492-2	YR	7.75	32.00
85	SWINGING ANGEL BELL 1100QX492-5	YR	11.00	27.00
86	JOLLY HIKER 500QX483-2	YR	5.00	17.00
86	SKI TRIPPER 675QX420-6	YR	6.75	14.00
86	SPECIAL DELIVERY 500QX415-6	YR	5.00	18.00
87	BRIGHT CHRISTMAS DREAMS QX 473-7	YR	7.25	80.00
87	ICY TREAT 450QX450-9	YR	4.50	16.00
87	JOLLY HIKER 500QX483-2	YR	5.00	17.00
87	RACCOON BIKER 700QX458-7	YR	7.00	16.00
87	REINDOGGY 575QX452-7	YR	5.75	26.00
87	SNOOPY AND WOODSTOCK 725QX472-9	YR	7.25	50.00
D. UNRUH			**HOLIDAY HUMOR**	
86	ACORN INN 850QX424-3	YR	8.50	26.00
86	HAPPY CHRISTMAS TO OWL 600QX418-3	YR	6.00	15.00
86	PUPPY'S BEST FRIEND 650QX420-3	YR	6.50	20.00
87	HOT DOGGER 650QX471-9	YR	6.50	20.00
L. VOTRUBA			**HOLIDAY HUMOR**	
87	NATURE'S DECORATIONS 475QX273-9	YR	4.75	19.00
*			**HOLIDAY SCULPTURE**	
83	SANTA 400QX308-7	YR	4.00	26.00
L. SICKMAN			**HOLIDAY SCULPTURE**	
83	HEART 400QX307-9	YR	4.00	39.00
*			**HOLIDAY TRADITIONS**	
89	FIRST CHRISTMAS, THE- 775QX547-5	YR	7.75	12.00
89	GENTLE FAWN 775QX548-5	YR	7.75	14.00
89	GEORGE WASHINGTON BICENTEN. 625QX386-2	YR	6.25	12.00
89	OLD-WORLD GNOME 775QX434-5	YR	7.75	23.00
89	SWEET MEMORIES PHOTOHOLDER 675QX438-5	YR	6.75	16.00
P. ANDREWS			**HOLIDAY TRADITIONS**	
96	KINDLY SHEPHERD QX627-4	YR	13.00	13.00
JOHNSON/ BRICKER			**HOLIDAY TRADITIONS**	
96	TAMIKA QX630-1	YR	8.00	8.00
R. CHAD			**HOLIDAY TRADITIONS**	
96	LIGHTING THE WAY QX612-4	YR	13.00	13.00
K. CROW			**HOLIDAY TRADITIONS**	
89	HANG IN THERE 525QX430-5	YR	5.25	30.00
89	PEEK-A-BOO KITTIES 750QX487-1	YR	7.50	19.00
J. FRANCIS			**HOLIDAY TRADITIONS**	
89	JOYFUL TRIO 975QX437-2	YR	9.75	14.00
89	PADDINGTON BEAR 575QX429-2	YR	5.75	17.00
96	MAKING HIS ROUNDS QX627-1	YR	15.00	15.00
J. LYLE			**HOLIDAY TRADITIONS**	
89	NORMAN ROCKWELL 475QX276-2	YR	4.75	15.00
S. PIKE			**HOLIDAY TRADITIONS**	
89	OWLIDAY GREETINGS 400QX436-5	YR	4.00	14.00
89	PARTY LINE 875QX476-1	YR	8.75	24.00
89	SPENCER SPARROW, ESQ. 675QX431-2	YR	6.75	17.00
89	STOCKING KITTEN 675QX456-5	YR	6.75	13.00
M. PYDA-SEVCIK			**HOLIDAY TRADITIONS**	
89	FELIZ NAVIDAD 675QX439-2	YR	6.75	23.00
D. RHODUS			**HOLIDAY TRADITIONS**	
89	SNOOPY & WOODSTOCK 675QX433-2	YR	6.75	35.00
A. ROGERS			**HOLIDAY TRADITIONS**	
89	CRANBERRY BUNNY 575QX426-2	YR	5.75	14.00
89	SPECIAL DELIVERY 525QX432-5	YR	5.75	16.00
E. SEALE			**HOLIDAY TRADITIONS**	
89	TEENY TASTER 475QX418-1	YR	4.75	18.00
L. SICKMAN			**HOLIDAY TRADITIONS**	
96	FELIZ NAVIDAD QX630-4	YR	10.00	10.00
96	MADONNA AND CHILD QX632-4	YR	13.00	13.00

YR NAME	LIMIT	ISSUE	TREND
B. SIEDLER		**HOLIDAY TRADITIONS**	
89 CAMERA CLAUS 575QX546-5	YR	5.75	13.00
89 DEER DISGUISE 575QX426-5	YR	5.75	18.00
89 GONE FISHING 575QX479-4	YR	5.75	16.00
89 GYM DANDY 575QX418-5	YR	5.75	14.00
89 HERE'S THE PITCH 575QX545-5	YR	5.75	14.00
89 HOPPY HOLIDAYS 775QX469-2	YR	7.75	17.00
89 KRISTY CLAUS 575QX424-5	YR	5.75	12.00
89 NORTH POLE JOGGER 575QX546-2	YR	5.75	13.00
89 ON THE LINKS 575QX419-2	YR	5.75	17.00
89 POLAR BOWLER 575QX478-4	YR	5.75	14.00
89 SEA SANTA 575QX415-2	YR	5.75	19.00
89 SNOWPLOW SANTA 575QX420-5	YR	5.75	16.00
D. UNRUH		**HOLIDAY TRADITIONS**	
89 A KISS FROM SANTA 450QX482-1	YR	4.50	22.00
89 OREO COOKIE 400QX481-4	YR	4.00	10.00
*		**HOLIDAY WILDLIFE**	
82 CARDINALS QX 313-3	YR	7.00	350.00
83 CHICKADEE 700QX309-9	YR	7.00	67.00
84 PHEASANTS 725QX347-4	YR	7.25	25.00
85 PARTRIDGE 750QX376-5	YR	7.50	22.00
86 CEDAR WAXWING 750QX321-6	YR	7.50	23.00
88 PURPLE FINCH 775QX371-1	YR	7.75	16.00
L. VOTRUBA		**HOLIDAY WILDLIFE**	
87 SNOW GOOSE 750QX371-7	YR	7.50	15.00
*		**HOOP STARS**	
95 SHAQUILLE O'NEAL 1ST ED. QX1551-7	YR	15.00	25.00
96 LARRY BIRD 2ND ED. QXI501-4	YR	15.00	15.00
97 MAGIC JOHNSON	YR	15.00	15.00
K. CROW		**HUNCHBACK OF NOTRE DAME**	
96 ESMERALDA AND DJALO QXI635-1	YR	15.00	20.00
96 LAVERNE, VICTOR AND HUGO QXI635-4	YR	13.00	15.00
96 QUASIMODO QXI634-1	YR	10.00	15.00
*		**ICE SCULPTURES**	
82 ARCTIC PENGUIN 400QX300-3	YR	4.00	15.00
82 SNOWY SEAL 400QX300-6	YR	4.00	18.00
P. ANDREWS		**INVITATION TO TEA**	
95 COZY COTTAGE TEAPOT QK112-7	YR	16.00	19.00
95 EUROPEAN CASTLE QK112-9	YR	16.00	19.00
95 VICTORIAN HOME TEAPOT QX111-9	YR	16.00	19.00
*		**IT'S A WONDERFUL LIFE**	
91 IT'S A WONDERFUL LIFE 719-9	YR	20.00	60.00
K. CROW		**IT'S A WONDERFUL LIFE**	
96 IT'S A WONDERFUL LIFE QXI653-1	YR	15.00	45.00
E. SEALE		**JOURNEYS INTO SPACE**	
96 FREEDOM 7 1ST ED. QLX752-4	YR	24.00	60.00
97 FRIENDSHIP 7 2ND ED.	YR	24.00	24.00
J. LYLE		**JOYFUN ANGELS**	
98 JOYFUL ANGELS 1095QEO8386	YR	11.00	11.00
*		**KEEPSAKE MAGIC COLLECTION**	
89 HOLIDAY BELL 1750QLX722-2	YR	17.50	28.00
R. CHAD		**KEEPSAKE MAGIC COLLECTION**	
89 MOONLIT NAP 875QLX713-4	YR	8.75	22.00
89 RUDOLPH RED-NOSED REINDEER 1950QLX725-2	YR	20.00	47.00
K. CROW		**KEEPSAKE MAGIC COLLECTION**	
89 TINY TINKER 1950QLX717-4	YR	20.00	42.00
J. FRANCIS		**KEEPSAKE MAGIC COLLECTION**	
89 ANIMALS SPEAK , THE1350QLX723-2	YR	13.50	100.00
D. LEE		**KEEPSAKE MAGIC COLLECTION**	
89 BUSY BEAVER 1750QLX724-5	YR	17.50	47.00
89 FIRST CHRISTMAS TOGETHER 1750QLX734-2	YR	17.50	33.00
S. PIKE		**KEEPSAKE MAGIC COLLECTION**	
89 FOREST FROLICS-1ST EDITION 2450QLX728-2	YR	25.00	80.00
D. RHODUS		**KEEPSAKE MAGIC COLLECTION**	
89 UNICORN FANTASY 950QLX723-5	YR	9.50	20.00
E. SEALE		**KEEPSAKE MAGIC COLLECTION**	
89 BABY'S FIRST CHRISTMAS 3000QLX727-2	YR	30.00	57.00
89 KRINGLE'S TOY SHOP 2450QLX701-7	YR	25.00	52.00
89 SPIRIT OF ST. NICK 2450QLX728-5	YR	25.00	57.00
L. SICKMAN		**KEEPSAKE MAGIC COLLECTION**	
89 METRO EXPRESS 2800QLX727-5	YR	28.00	67.00
B. SIEDLER		**KEEPSAKE MAGIC COLLECTION**	
89 BACKSTAGE BEAR 1350QLX721-5	YR	13.50	25.00
89 LOVING SPOONFUL 1950QLX726-2	YR	20.00	32.00
D. UNRUH		**KEEPSAKE MAGIC COLLECTION**	
89 JOYOUS CAROLERS 3000QLX729-5	YR	30.00	57.00
L. VOTRUBA		**KEEPSAKE MAGIC COLLECTION**	
89 ANGEL MELODY 950QLX720-2	YR	9.50	19.00
N. AUBE		**KEEPSAKE ORNAMENT PREMIERE**	
96 BASHFUL MISTLETOE MERRY MINIATURES	YR	13.00	13.00
E. SEALE		**KEEPSAKE ORNAMENT PREMIERE**	
96 WELCOME SIGN TENDER TOUCHES	YR	15.00	15.00

Released for Lladró's 1995 Christmas season, the Doll Christmas ornament, with a delicate blue bow tied at her neck, retailed for $69.

This Flying Woodman Santa *ornament from Midwest of Cannon Falls was limited to 2,500 pieces in 1994. The three-inch Leo R. Smith III ornament retailed for $35 and has been retired.*

Enesco Corp. offered Give Yourself a Hug From Me *in their Memories of Yesterday line in 1994.*

This sterling ornament speaks for itself. I Love Santa *is produced by Hand & Hammer.*

YR	NAME	LIMIT	ISSUE	TREND
*		KEEPSAKE ORNAMENT SIGNATURE COLLECTION		
96	SANTA'S TOY SHOP QXC420-1	YR	60.00	60.00
D. PALMITER		KIDDIE CAR CLASSICS		
94	MURRAY CHAMPION 1ST ED. 1395QX542-6	RT	14.00	40.00
95	MURRAY FIRE TRUCK 2ND SERIES QX502-7	YR	14.00	31.00
D. RHODUS		KIDDIE CAR CLASSICS		
96	MURRAY AIRPLANE 3RD ED. QX536-4	OP	14.00	14.00
K. CROW		KITTENS IN TOYLAND		
88	KITTENS IN TOYLAND/TRAIN 500QXM562-1	YR	5.00	29.00
89	SCOOTER 450QXM561-2	YR	4.50	19.00
90	SAILBOAT 450QXM573-6	YR	4.50	22.00
91	AIRPLANE 450QXM563-0	YR	4.50	19.00
92	POGO STICK 450QXM5391	YR	4.50	17.00
A. ROGERS		KRINGLES		
93	WREATH QXM 513-5	YR	5.75	12.00
S. TAGUE		LANGUAGE OF FLOWERS		
96	PANSY 1ST ED. QK117-1	YR	16.00	55.00
97	SNOWDROP ANGEL 2ND ED.	YR	16.00	16.00
N. AUBE		LIFESTYLES		
96	APPLE FOR TEACHER QX612-1	YR	8.00	8.00
J. FRANCIS		LIFESTYLES		
96	HURRYING DOWNSTAIRS QX607-4	YR	9.00	9.00
E. SEALE		LIFESTYLES		
96	TENDER LOVIN' CARE QX611-4	YR	8.00	8.00
B. SIEDLER		LIFESTYLES		
96	CHILD CARE GIVER QX607-1	YR	9.00	9.00
*		LIGHTED ORNAMENTS COLLECTION		
86	MR. & MRS. SANTA 1450QLX705-2	YR	14.50	60.00
86	SANTA AND SPARKY-1ST ED. 2200QLX703-3	YR	22.00	75.00
86	SUGARPLUM COTTAGE 1100QLX701-1	YR	11.00	36.00
K. CROW		LIGHTED ORNAMENTS COLLECTION		
86	BABY'S FIRST CHRISTMAS 1950QLX710-3	YR	20.00	41.00
86	KEEP ON GLOWIN' 1000QLX707-6	YR	10.00	37.00
86	SANTA'S SNACK 1000QLX706-6	YR	10.00	52.00
D. LEE		LIGHTED ORNAMENTS COLLECTION		
86	GENERAL STORE 1575QLX705-3	YR	15.75	42.00
E. SEALE		LIGHTED ORNAMENTS COLLECTION		
86	CHRISTMAS SLEIGH RIDE 2450QLX701-2	YR	25.00	125.00
86	FIRST CHRISTMAS TOGETHER 2200QLX707-3	YR	14.00	30.00
L. SICKMAN		LIGHTED ORNAMENTS COLLECTION		
86	GENTLE BLESSINGS 1500QLX708-3	YR	15.00	137.00
86	VILLAGE EXPRESS 2450QLX707-2	YR	25.00	90.00
D. UNRUH		LIGHTED ORNAMENTS COLLECTION		
86	SANTA'S ON HIS WAY 1500QLX711-5	YR	15.00	62.00
L. VOTRUBA		LIGHTED ORNAMENTS COLLECTION		
86	MERRY CHRISTMAS BELL 850QLX709-3	YR	8.50	20.00
86	SHARING FRIENDSHIP 850QLX706-3	YR	8.50	16.00
*		LION KING		
94	MUFASA AND SIMBA 1495QX540-6	YR	15.00	25.00
94	SIMBA AND NALA 1295QX530-3	YR	13.00	30.00
94	SIMBA, SARABI, MUFASA 751-3	YR	20.00	50.00
94	TIMON & PUMBAA 895QX536-6	YR	9.00	30.00
97	TIMON, PUMBAA 406-5	YR	13.00	13.00
K. CROW		LION KING		
94	SIMBA, SARABI AND MUFASA QLX 751-3	YR	32.00	70.00
95	SIMBA, PUMBAA & TIMON QX615-9	YR	13.00	30.00
*		LIONEL TRAIN		
96	700E HUDSON STEAM LOCOMOTIVE 1ST ED. QX553-1	YR	19.00	60.00
97	1950 SANTA FE F3 DIESEL LOCOMOTIVE 2ND ED.	YR	19.00	25.00
*		LITTLE TRIMMERS		
78	DRUMMER BOY 250QX136-3	YR	2.50	57.00
78	SANTA 250QX135-6	YR	2.50	45.00
79	A MATCHLESS CHRISTMAS 400QX132-7	YR	4.00	65.00
79	ANGEL DELIGHT 300QX130-7	YR	3.00	75.00
79	SANTA 300QX135-6	YR	3.00	45.00
79	THIMBLE SERIES-MOUSE 300QX133-6	YR	3.00	265.00
80	CHRISTMAS OWL 400QX131-4	YR	4.00	35.00
80	CHRISTMAS TEDDY 250QX135-4	YR	2.50	90.00
80	CLOTHESPIN SOLDIER 350QX134-4	YR	3.50	35.00
80	MERRY REDBIRD 350QX160-1	YR	3.50	50.00
80	SWINGIN' ON A STAR 400QX130-1	YR	4.00	65.00
81	CLOTHESPIN DRUMMER BOY 450QX408-2	YR	4.50	35.00
81	JOLLY SNOWMAN 350QX407-5	YR	3.50	35.00
81	PERKY PENGUIN 350QX409-5	YR	3.50	45.00
81	PUPPY LOVE 350QX406-2	YR	3.50	34.00
81	STOCKING MOUSE, THE- 450QX412-2	YR	4.50	75.00
82	CHRISTMAS KITTEN 400QX454-3	YR	4.00	27.00
82	CHRISTMAS OWL 450QX131-4	YR	4.50	35.00
82	MERRY MOOSE 550QX415-5	YR	5.50	47.00
82	PERKY PENGUIN 400QX409-5	YR	4.00	45.00
D. LEE		LITTLE TRIMMERS		
78	PRAYING ANGEL 250QX134-3	YR	2.50	75.00
82	MUSICAL ANGEL 550QX459-6	YR	5.50	120.00

YR	NAME	LIMIT	ISSUE	TREND
E. SEALE			**LITTLE TRIMMERS**	
82	JINGLING TEDDY 400QX477-6	YR	4.00	33.00
L. SICKMAN			**LITTLE TRIMMERS**	
82	COOKIE MOUSE 450QX454-6	YR	4.50	52.00
82	DOVE LOVE 450QX462-3	YR	4.50	51.00
P. ANDREWS			**LOONEY TUNES COLLECTION**	
93	PORKY PIG 875QX565-2	YR	8.75	16.00
R. CHAD			**LOONEY TUNES COLLECTION**	
94	ROAD RUNNER AND WILE E. COYOTE QX 560-2	YR	13.00	25.00
95	BUGS BUNNY QX501-9	YR	9.00	15.00
95	POPEYE QX525-7	YR	11.00	24.00
95	SYLVESTER AND TWEETY QX501-7	YR	14.00	19.00
96	FOGHORN LEGHORN & HENERY HAWK QX544-4	YR	14.00	14.00
96	MARVIN THE MARTIAN QX545-1	YR	11.00	20.00
96	OLIVE OYL AND SWEE' PEA QX548-1	YR	11.00	20.00
96	SPIDERMAN QX575-7	YR	13.00	20.00
96	ZIGGY QX652--4	YR	10.00	10.00
J. LYLE			**LOONEY TUNES COLLECTION**	
93	ELMER FUDD 875QX549-5	YR	8.75	20.00
D. PALMITER			**LOONEY TUNES COLLECTION**	
93	SYLVESTER & TWEETY 975QX540-5	YR	9.75	30.00
94	DAFFY DUCK 895QX541-6	YR	9.00	20.00
94	SPEEDY GONZALES 895QX534-3	YR	9.00	16.00
94	TASMANIAN DEVIL 895QX560-5	YR	9.00	50.00
94	YOSEMITE SAM 895QX534-6	YR	9.00	20.00
A. ROGERS			**LOONEY TUNES COLLECTION**	
96	WONDER WOMAN QX594-1	YR	13.00	20.00
96	YOGI BEAR AND BOO BOO QX552-1	YR	13.00	15.00
L. SICKMAN			**LOONEY TUNES COLLECTION**	
93	BUGS BUNNY 875QX541-2	YR	9.75	25.00
D. PALMITER			**LOONEY TUNES LOVABLES**	
96	BABY SYLVESTER QXM415-4	YR	5.75	15.00
96	BABY TWEETY QXM401-4	YR	5.75	25.00
J. COLLINS			**MADAME ALEXANDER**	
96	CINDERELLA-1995 1ST ED. QX631-1	YR	15.00	40.00
J. FRANCIS			**MADAME ALEXANDER**	
97	LITTLE RED RIDING HOOD-1991 2ND ED.	YR	15.00	15.00
L. VOTRUBA			**MAGI BELLS**	
96	BALTHAZAR (FRANKINCENSE) QK1174	YR	14.00	14.00
96	CASPAR (MYRRH) QK118-4	YR	14.00	14.00
96	MELCHIOR (GOLD) QK118-1	YR	14.00	14.00
*			**MAGIC ORNAMENTS**	
84	ALL ARE PRECIOUS 800QLX704-1	YR	8.00	22.00
84	BRASS CAROUSEL 900QLX707-1	YR	9.00	82.00
84	CHRISTMAS IN THE FOREST 800QLX703-4	YR	8.00	17.00
84	SANTA'S WORKSHOP 1300QLX700-4	YR	13.00	50.00
84	STAINED GLASS 800QLX703-1	YR	8.00	17.00
84	SUGARPLUM COTTAGE 1100QLX701-1	YR	11.00	36.00
85	ALL ARE PRECIOUS 800QLX704-4	YR	8.00	22.00
85	CHRISTMAS EVE VISIT 1200QLX710-5	YR	12.00	24.00
85	KATYBETH 1075QLX710-2	YR	10.75	36.00
85	MR. AND MRS. SANTA 1450QLX705-2	YR	14.50	60.00
85	SANTA'S WORKSHOP 1300QLX700-4	YR	13.00	50.00
85	SUGARPLUM COTTAGE 1100QLX701-1	YR	11.00	36.00
85	SWISS CHEESE LANE 1300QLX706-5	YR	13.00	43.00
87	BABY'S FIRST CHRISTMAS 1350QLX704-9	YR	13.50	31.00
87	FIRST CHRISTMAS TOGETHER 1150QLX708-7	YR	11.50	40.00
87	LACY BRASS SNOWFLAKE 1150QLX709-7	YR	11.50	18.00
87	SEASON FOR FRIENDSHIP 850QLX706-9	YR	8.50	16.00
88	FIRST CHRISTMAS TOGETHER 1200QLX702-7	YR	12.00	31.00
88	SONG OF CHRISTMAS 850QLX711-1	YR	8.50	20.00
88	TREE OF FRIENDSHIP 850QLX710-4	YR	8.50	18.00
90	BLESSINGS OF LOVE 1400QLX736-3	YR	14.00	37.00
91	ANGEL OF LIGHT 3000QLT723-9	YR	30.00	60.00
92	ANGEL OF LIGHT 3000QLX723-9	YR	30.00	37.00
94	BARNEY 2400QLX750-6	YR	24.00	40.00
P. ANDREWS			**MAGIC ORNAMENTS**	
90	ELF OF THE YEAR 1000QLX735-6	YR	10.00	17.00
91	KITTY IN A MITTY 450QXM587-9	YR	4.50	12.00
92	LIGHTING THE WAY 1800QLX723-1	YR	18.00	37.00
93	SONG OF THE CHIMES 2500QLX740-5	YR	25.00	38.00
R. CHAD			**MAGIC ORNAMENTS**	
88	MOONLIT NAP 875QLX713-4	YR	8.75	22.00
90	HOLIDAY FLASH 1800QLX733-3	YR	18.00	32.00
91	ELFIN ENGINEER 1000QLX720-9	YR	10.00	20.00
91	SPARKLING ANGEL 1800QLX715-7	YR	18.00	28.00
92	OUR FIRST CHRISTMAS TOGETHER2000QLX722-1	YR	20.00	33.00
93	OUR FIRST CHRISTMAS TOGETHER QLX735-5	YR	20.00	31.00
93	ROAD RUNNER AND WILE E. COYOTE QLX741-5	YR	30.00	57.00
K. CROW			**MAGIC ORNAMENTS**	
87	CHRISTMAS MORNING 2450QLX701-3	YR	25.00	34.00
87	KEEP ON GLOWIN! 1000QLX707-6	YR	10.00	42.00
87	KEEPING COZY 1175QLX704-7	YR	11.75	27.00
88	CHRISTMAS IS MAGIC 1200QLX717-1	YR	12.00	45.00

YR	NAME	LIMIT	ISSUE	TREND
88	CIRCLING THE GLOBE 1050QLX712-4	YR	10.50	30.00
90	ELFIN WHITTLER 2000QLX726-5	YR	20.00	45.00
90	SANTA'S HO-HO-HOEDOWN 2500QLX725-6	YR	25.00	80.00
91	ARCTIC DOME 2500QLX711-7	YR	25.00	46.00
91	SANTA'S HOT LINE 1800QLX715-9	YR	18.00	35.00
91	TOYLAND TOWER 2000QLX712-9	YR	20.00	34.00
92	BABY'S FIRST CHRISTMAS 2200QLX728-1	YR	22.00	72.00
92	ENCHANTED CLOCK 3000QLX727-4	YR	30.00	48.00
92	NUT SWEET NUT 1000QLX708-1	YR	10.00	20.00
92	SANTA SUB 1800QLX732-1	YR	18.00	36.00
93	BELLS ARE RINGING 2800QLX740-2	YR	28.00	46.00
93	DOLLHOUSE DREAMS 2200QLX737-2	YR	22.00	35.00
93	SANTA'S SNOW-GETTER 1800QLX735-2	YR	18.00	32.00
94	FELIZ NAVIDAD 2800QLX743-3	YR	28.00	31.00
94	KRINGLE TROLLEY 2000QLX741-3	YR	20.00	32.00
94	SANTA'S SING-ALONG 2400QLX747-3	YR	24.00	40.00
94	WINNIE THE POOH PARADE 3200QLX749-3	YR	32.00	60.00

P. DUTKIN   **MAGIC ORNAMENTS**

YR	NAME	LIMIT	ISSUE	TREND
91	FRIENDSHIP TREE 1000QLX716-9	YR	10.00	20.00

J. FRANCIS   **MAGIC ORNAMENTS**

YR	NAME	LIMIT	ISSUE	TREND
92	WATCH OWLS 1200QLX708-4	YR	12.00	19.00
93	BABY'S FIRST CHRISTMAS 2200QLX736-5	YR	22.00	36.00
94	BABY'S FIRST CHRISTMAS 2000QLX746-6	YR	20.00	31.00
94	CANDY CANE LOOKOUT 1800QLX737-6	YR	18.00	35.00

D. LEE   **MAGIC ORNAMENTS**

YR	NAME	LIMIT	ISSUE	TREND
84	SANTA'S ARRIVAL 1300QLX702-4	YR	13.00	60.00
84	VILLAGE CHURCH 1500QLX702-1	YR	15.00	40.00
85	LITTLE RED SCHOOLHOUSE 1575QLX711-2	YR	15.75	80.00
85	VILLAGE CHURCH 1500QLX702-1	YR	15.00	40.00
87	TRAIN STATION 1275QLX703-9	YR	12.75	36.00
90	FIRST CHRISTMAS TOGETHER QLX 725-5	YR	18.00	36.00
91	IT'S A WONDERFUL LIFE 2000QLX723-7	YR	20.00	60.00
91	JINGLE BEARS 2500QLX732-3	YR	25.00	45.00
91	MOLE FAMILY HOME 2000QLX714-9	YR	20.00	32.00
92	LOOK! IT'S SANTA 1400QLX709-4	YR	14.00	32.00
92	SANTA'S ANSWERING MACHINE 2200QLX724-1	YR	22.00	18.00
93	DOG'S BEST FRIEND 1200QLX717-2	YR	12.00	21.00
93	RADIO NEWS FLASH 2200QLX736-2	YR	22.00	35.00
94	WHITE CHRISTMAS 2800QLX746-3	YR	28.00	40.00

J. LYLE   **MAGIC ORNAMENTS**

YR	NAME	LIMIT	ISSUE	TREND
85	SEASON OF BEAUTY 800QLX712-2	YR	8.00	20.00
88	RADIANT TREE 1175QLX712-1	YR	11.75	15.00
90	PARTRIDGES IN A PEAR 1400QLX721-2	YR	14.00	26.00
94	AWAY IN A MANGER 1600QLX738-3	YR	16.00	26.00

D. MCGEHEE   **MAGIC ORNAMENTS**

YR	NAME	LIMIT	ISSUE	TREND
91	FESTIVE BRASS CHURCH 1400QLX717-9	YR	14.00	22.00

L. NORTON   **MAGIC ORNAMENTS**

YR	NAME	LIMIT	ISSUE	TREND
93	U.S.S ENTERPRISE QLX741-2	YR	24.00	60.00

D. PALMITER   **MAGIC ORNAMENTS**

YR	NAME	LIMIT	ISSUE	TREND
90	BABY'S FIRST CHRISTMAS 2800QLX724-6	YR	28.00	51.00
92	GOOD SLEDDING AHEAD 2800QLX724-4	YR	28.00	45.00
92	UNDER CONSTRUCTION 1800QLX732-4	YR	18.00	31.00
93	LAMPLIGHTER, THE 1800QLX719-2	YR	18.00	30.00
94	GINGERBREAD FANTASY 4400QLX738-2	YR	44.00	65.00

S. PIKE   **MAGIC ORNAMENTS**

YR	NAME	LIMIT	ISSUE	TREND
87	MEOWY CHRISTMAS 1000QLX708-9	YR	10.00	51.00
88	KITTY CAPERS 1300QLX716-4	YR	13.00	33.00
90	FOREST FROLICS 2500QLX723-6	YR	25.00	55.00
91	FOREST FROLICS 2500QLX721-9	YR	25.00	55.00
91	HOLIDAY GLOW 1400QLX717-7	YR	14.00	20.00
92	FOREST FROLICS 2800QLX725-4	YR	28.00	49.00
93	FOREST FROLICS 2500QLX716-5	YR	25.00	42.00
94	FOREST FROLICS 2800QLX743-6	YR	28.00	30.00

M. PYDA-SEVCIK   **MAGIC ORNAMENTS**

YR	NAME	LIMIT	ISSUE	TREND
88	HEAVENLY GLOW 1175QLX711-4	YR	11.75	20.00

D. RHODUS   **MAGIC ORNAMENTS**

YR	NAME	LIMIT	ISSUE	TREND
90	MRS. SANTA'S KITCHEN 2500QLX726-3	YR	25.00	67.00
91	PEANUTS 1800QLX722-9	YR	18.00	52.00
92	PEANUTS 1800QLX721-4	YR	18.00	42.00
92	SHUTTLECRAFT "GALILEO" 2400QLX133-1	YR	21.00	50.00
93	PEANUTS 1800QLX715-5	YR	18.00	32.00
94	PEANUTS 2000QLX740-6	YR	20.00	30.00

A. ROGERS   **MAGIC ORNAMENTS**

YR	NAME	LIMIT	ISSUE	TREND
90	LETTER TO SANTA 1400QLX722-6	YR	14.00	23.00
90	SONG AND DANCE 2000QLX725-3	YR	20.00	77.00
90	STARLIGHT ANGEL 1400QLX730-6	YR	14.00	29.00
93	BEARYMORES, THE 575QXM512-5	YR	5.75	18.00
93	RAIDING THE FRIDGE 1600QLX718-5	YR	16.00	28.00
94	PEEKABOO PUP 2000QLX742-3	YR	20.00	26.00

E. SEALE   **MAGIC ORNAMENTS**

YR	NAME	LIMIT	ISSUE	TREND
84	NATIVITY 1200QLX700-1	YR	12.00	27.00
85	BABY'S FIRST CHRISTMAS 1650QLX700-5	YR	16.50	37.00
85	NATIVITY 1200QLX700-1	YR	12.00	27.00
87	LOVING HOLIDAY 2200QLX701-6	YR	22.00	37.00

YR	NAME	LIMIT	ISSUE	TREND
87	MEMORIES ARE FOREVER-PHOTO 850QLX706-7	YR	8.50	23.00
88	BABY'S FIRST CHRISTMAS 2400QLX718-4	YR	24.00	38.00
88	KRINGLE'S TOY SHOP 2450QLX701-7	YR	25.00	52.00
91	BABY'S FIRST CHRISTMAS 3000QLX724-7	YR	30.00	75.00
91	SANTA SPECIAL 4000QLX716-7	YR	40.00	70.00
91	SKI TRIP 2800QLX726-6	YR	28.00	54.00
92	SANTA SPECIAL 4000QLX716-7	YR	40.00	70.00
92	YULETIDE RIDER 2800QLX731-4	YR	28.00	42.00
93	NORTH POLE MERRYTHON QLX739-2	YR	25.00	45.00
94	CONVERSATION W/SANTA 2800QLX742-6	YR	28.00	40.00
94	EAGLE HAS LANDED, THE 2400QLX768-6	YR	24.00	50.00
L. SICKMAN			**MAGIC ORNAMENTS**	
87	GOOD CHEER BLIMP 1600QLX704-6	YR	16.00	45.00
88	BEARLY REACHING 950QLX715-1	YR	9.50	27.00
88	COUNTRY EXPRESS 2450QLX721-1	YR	25.00	60.00
88	FESTIVE FEEDER 1150QLX720-4	YR	11.50	41.00
88	PARADE OF THE TOYS 2200QLX719-4	YR	25.00	30.00
90	CHILDREN'S EXPRESS 2800QLX724-3	YR	28.00	55.00
91	FIRST CHRISTMAS TOGETHER QX 713-7	YR	25.00	47.00
91	KRINGLES'S BUMPER CARS 2500QLX711-9	YR	25.00	50.00
92	CHRISTMAS PARADE 3000QLX727-1	YR	30.00	56.00
92	CONTINENTAL EXPRESS 3200QLX726-4	YR	32.00	62.00
92	FEATHERED FRIENDS 1400QLX709-1	YR	14.00	27.00
93	HOME ON THE RANGE 3200QLX739-5	YR	32.00	45.00
94	COUNTRY SHOWTIME 2200QLX741-6	YR	22.00	34.00
94	MAXINE 2000QLX750-3	YR	20.00	32.00
B. SIEDLER			**MAGIC ORNAMENTS**	
84	CITY LIGHTS 1000QLX701-4	YR	10.00	42.00
90	BEARY SHORT NAP 1000QLX732-6	YR	10.00	24.00
90	DEER CROSSING 1800QLX721-3	YR	18.00	35.00
90	HOP 'N POP POPPER 2000QLX735-3	YR	20.00	77.00
90	STARSHIP CHRISTMAS 1800QLX733-6	YR	18.00	40.00
93	SANTA'S WORKSHOP 2800QLX737-5	YR	28.00	44.00
93	WINNIE THE POOH 2400QLX742-2	YR	24.00	50.00
94	ROCK CANDY MINER 2000QLX740-3	YR	20.00	28.00
D. UNRUH			**MAGIC ORNAMENTS**	
87	ANGELIC MESSENGERS 1875QLX711-3	YR	19.00	55.00
88	LAST-MINUTE HUG 1950QLX718-1	YR	22.00	40.00
88	SKATER'S WALTZ 2450QLX720-1	YR	25.00	49.00
90	CHRISTMAS MEMORIES 2500QLX727-6	YR	25.00	47.00
91	BRINGING HOME THE TREE 2800QLX724-9	YR	28.00	47.00
91	FATHER CHRISTMAS 1400QLX714-7	YR	14.00	35.00
91	SALVATION ARMY BAND 3000QLX727-3	YR	30.00	67.00
L. VOTRUBA			**MAGIC ORNAMENTS**	
85	LOVE WREATH 850QLX702-5	YR	8.50	26.00
87	BRIGHT NOEL 700QLX705-9	YR	7.00	27.00
92	DANCING NUTCRACKER, THE 3000QLX726-1	YR	30.00	45.00
93	LAST MINUTE SHOPPING 2800QLX738-5	YR	28.00	45.00
94	VERY MERRY MINUTES 2400QLX744-3	YR	24.00	40.00
D. UNRUH			**MARCH OF THE TEDDY BEARS**	
96	MARCH OF THE TEDDY BEARS 4TH & FINAL QXM409-4	YR	4.75	5.00
*			**MARILYN MONROE**	
97	PINK GOWN 570-4	YR	15.00	15.00
D. UNRUH			**MARJOLEIN BASTIN**	
96	CHRISTMAS SNOWMAN QX621-4	YR	10.00	10.00
R. CHAD			**MARY'S ANGELS**	
88	BUTTERCUP 500QX407-4	YR	5.00	95.00
89	BLUEBELL 2ND ED. 575QX454-5	YR	5.75	110.00
90	ROSEBUD 575QX442-3	YR	5.75	50.00
91	IRIS 675QX427-9	YR	6.75	35.00
92	LILY 5TH ED. 675QX427-4	YR	6.75	55.00
93	IVY 6TH ED. 675QX428-2	YR	6.75	20.00
94	JASMINE 7TH ED. 695QX527-6	YR	7.00	15.00
95	CAMELLIA 8TH ED. QX514-9	YR	7.00	20.00
96	VIOLET 9TH ED. QX566-4	YR	7.00	7.00
97	DAISY 10TH ED.	YR	8.00	8.00
E. SEALE			**MATCHBOX MEMORIES**	
91	EVERGREEN INN 875QX538-9	YR	8.75	17.00
91	HOLIDAY CAFE 875QX539-9	YR	8.75	14.00
91	SANTA'S STUDIO 875QX539-7	YR	8.75	15.00
K. CROW			**MERRY OLDE SANTA**	
96	MERRY OLDE SANTA 7TH ED. QX565-4	YR	15.00	15.00
J. LYLE			**MERRY OLDE SANTA**	
97	SANTA WITH CARDINALS 8TH ED.	YR	15.00	15.00
L. SICKMAN			**METAL ORNAMENTS**	
77	SNOWFLAKE COLLECTION (4) 500QX210-2	YR	5.00	92.00
*			**MINIATURE ORNAMENTS**	
88	SNEAKER MOUSE 400QXM571-1	YR	4.00	12.00
88	SWEET DREAMS 700QXM560-4	YR	7.00	15.00
89	HEAVENLY GLOW TREE TOPPER QXM 566-1	YR	9.75	14.00
89	KITTENS IN TOYLAND-2ND ED. 450QXM561-2	YR	4.50	19.00
89	KRINGLES, THE-1ST EDITION 600QXM562-2	YR	6.00	25.00
89	MOTHER 600QXM564-5	YR	6.00	9.00
89	ROLY-POLY RAM 300QXM570-5	YR	3.00	10.00

YR	NAME	LIMIT	ISSUE	TREND
89	SPECIAL FRIEND 450QXM565-2	YR	4.50	11.00
90	AIR SANTA 450QXM565-6	YR	4.50	12.00
90	BRASS HORN 300QXM579-3	YR	3.00	5.00
90	BRASS PEACE 300QXM579-6	YR	3.00	5.00
90	BRASS YEAR 300QXM583-3	YR	3.00	6.00
90	LOVING HEARTS 300QXM552-3	YR	3.00	7.00
91	BRASS CHURCH 300QXM597-9	YR	3.00	6.00
91	BRASS SOLDIER 300QXM598-7	YR	3.00	6.00
91	INN-4TH EDITION 850QXM562-7	YR	8.50	19.00
91	OUR 1ST CHRISTMAS TOGETHER 600QXM581-9	YR	6.00	17.00
92	DANCING ANGELS TREE TOPPER QXM 589-1	YR	9.75	12.00
92	HOLIDAY HOLLY 975QXM536-4	YR	9.75	13.00
93	DANCING ANGELS TREE-TOPPER QXM 589-1	YR	9.75	13.00
94	DANCING ANGELS TREE-TOPPER QXM 589-1	YR	9.75	13.00
94	GRACEFUL CAROUSEL HORSE 775QXM405-6	YR	7.75	17.00
95	NIGHT BEFORE CHRISTMAS 4TH ED. 480-7	YR	4.75	15.00

P. ANDREWS — MINIATURE ORNAMENTS

YR	NAME	LIMIT	ISSUE	TREND
90	FIRST CHRISTMAS TOGETHER 600QXM553-6	YR	6.00	11.00
91	BRASS BELLS 300QXM597-7	YR	3.00	7.00
92	GOING PLACES 375QXM587-1	YR	3.75	6.00
92	MOM 450QXM550-4	YR	4.50	14.00
92	SKI FOR TWO 450QXM582-1	YR	4.50	10.00
92	VISIONS OF ACORNS 450QXM585-1	YR	4.50	9.00
93	EARS TO PALS 375QXM407-5	YR	3.75	9.00
93	MOM 450QXM515-5	YR	4.50	13.00
93	NATURE'S ANGELS 450QXM512-2	YR	4.50	14.00
93	SNUGGLE BIRDS 575QXM518-2	YR	5.75	14.00

R. BISHOP — MINIATURE ORNAMENTS

YR	NAME	LIMIT	ISSUE	TREND
91	WEE TOYMAKER 850QXM596-7	YR	8.50	15.00
94	BEARY PERFECT TREE 475QXM407-6	YR	4.75	10.00
94	HEARTS A-SAIL 575QXM540-6	YR	5.75	12.00
94	JUST MY SIZE 375QXM408-6	YR	3.75	9.00

R. CHAD — MINIATURE ORNAMENTS

YR	NAME	LIMIT	ISSUE	TREND
90	PERFECT FIT 450QXM551-6	YR	4.50	10.00
90	TYPE OF JOY 450QXM564-6	YR	4.50	9.00
91	ALL ABOARD 450QXM586-9	YR	4.50	10.00
91	RING-A-DING ELF 850QXM566-9	YR	8.50	14.00
91	TREELAND TRIO 850QXM589-9	YR	8.50	14.00
91	VISION OF SANTA 450QXM593-7	YR	4.50	11.00
92	HICKORY, DICKORY, DOCK 375QXM586-1	YR	3.75	10.00
92	SPUNKY MONKEY 300QXM592-1	YR	3.00	14.00
93	LEARNING TO SKATE 300QXM412-2	YR	3.00	9.00
93	LIGHTING A PATH 300QXM411-5	YR	3.00	9.00
93	REFRESHING FLIGHT 575QXM411-2	YR	5.75	14.00
94	POUR SOME MORE 575QXM515-6	YR	5.75	12.00
96	FATHER TIME QLX739-1	YR	25.00	25.00

K. CROW — MINIATURE ORNAMENTS

YR	NAME	LIMIT	ISSUE	TREND
89	SANTA'S ROADSTER 600QXM566-5	YR	6.00	14.00
90	ACORN WREATH 600QXM568-6	YR	6.00	10.00
90	BUSY CARVER 450QXM567-3	YR	4.50	7.00
90	STAMP COLLECTOR 450QXM562-3	YR	4.50	7.00
91	FLY BY 450QXM585-9	YR	4.50	17.00
91	KEY TO LOVE 450QXM568-9	YR	4.50	16.00
92	BUCK-A-ROO 450QXM581-4	YR	4.50	10.00
92	FEEDING TIME 575QXM548-1	YR	5.75	12.00
92	FRIENDS ARE TOPS 450QXM552-1	YR	4.50	8.00
92	HOOP IT UP 450QXM583-1	YR	4.50	9.00
93	'ROUND THE MOUNTAIN QXM 402-5	YR	7.25	14.00
94	A MERRY FLIGHT 575QX407-3	YR	5.75	12.00
94	CUTE AS A BUTTON 375QXM410-3	YR	3.75	9.00
94	SWEET DREAMS 300QXM409-6	YR	3.00	11.00
96	CHICKEN COOP CHORUS QLX749-1	YR	25.00	25.00
96	SHARING A SODA QLX742-4	YR	25.00	25.00

P. DUTKIN — MINIATURE ORNAMENTS

YR	NAME	LIMIT	ISSUE	TREND
89	SHARING A RIDE 850QXM576-5	YR	8.50	15.00

J. FRANCIS — MINIATURE ORNAMENTS

YR	NAME	LIMIT	ISSUE	TREND
89	MERRY SEAL 600QXM575-5	YR	6.00	12.00
90	BABY'S FIRST CHRISTMAS 850QXM570-3	YR	8.50	17.00
90	HOLIDAY CARDINAL 300QXM552-6	YR	3.00	12.00
90	PANDA'S SURPRISE 450QXM561-6	YR	4.50	13.00
91	BABY'S FIRST CHRISTMAS 600QXM579-9	YR	6.00	16.00
91	UPBEAT BEAR 600QXM590-7	YR	6.00	13.00
92	BLACK-CAPPED CHICKADEE 300QXM548-4	YR	3.00	12.00
92	CHRISTMAS COPTER 575QXM584-4	YR	5.75	10.00
92	GRANDCHILD'S FIRST CHRISTMAS 575QXM550-1	YR	5.75	8.00
92	HOLIDAY SPLASH 575QXM583-4	YR	5.75	10.00
93	COUNTRY FIDDLING 375QXM406-2	YR	3.75	10.00
93	PULL OUT A PLUM 575QXM409-5	YR	5.75	12.00
93	SPECIAL FRIENDS 450QXM516-5	YR	4.50	10.00
93	WOODLAND BABIES 575QXM510-2	YR	5.75	11.00
94	SCOOTING ALONG 675QXM517-3	YR	6.75	12.00

D. LEE — MINIATURE ORNAMENTS

YR	NAME	LIMIT	ISSUE	TREND
88	BABY'S FIRST CHRISTMAS 600QXM574-4	YR	5.00	12.00
89	STOCKING PAL 450QXM567-2	YR	4.50	7.00
90	GOING SLEDDING 450QXM568-3	YR	4.50	9.00

YR	NAME	LIMIT	ISSUE	TREND
90	SANTA'S STREETCAR 850QXM576-6	YR	8.50	12.00
90	SNOW ANGEL 600QXM577-3	YR	6.00	10.00
90	STOCKING PAL 450QXM567-2	YR	4.50	12.00
91	FRIENDLY FAWN 600QXM594-7	YR	6.00	12.00
91	HEAVENLY MINSTREL 975QXM568-7	YR	9.75	17.00
91	OLD ENGLISH VILLAGE 850QXM562-7	YR	8.50	21.00
91	SILVERY SANTA 975QXM567-9	YR	9.75	21.00
91	SPECIAL FRIENDS 850QXM579-7	YR	8.50	15.00
92	COOL UNCLE SAM 300QXM556-1	YR	3.00	10.00
92	COZY KAYAK 375QXM555-1	YR	3.75	10.00
94	HAVE A COOKIE 575QXM516-6	YR	5.75	14.00
J. LYLE			**MINIATURE ORNAMENTS**	
88	BRASS ANGEL 150QXM567-1	YR	1.50	17.00
88	BRASS STAR 150QXM566-4	YR	1.50	17.00
88	BRASS TREE 150QXM567-4	YR	1.50	17.00
89	BRASS PARTRIDGE 300QXM572-5	YR	3.00	9.00
89	BRASS SNOWFLAKE 450QXM570-2	YR	4.50	9.00
89	COZY SKATER 450QXM573-5	YR	4.50	10.00
89	LITTLE STAR BRINGER 600QXM562-2	YR	6.00	13.00
90	BRASS BOUQUET 600QMX577-6	YR	6.00	6.00
90	COZY SKATER 450QXM573-5	YR	4.50	9.00
90	MOTHER 450QXM571-6	YR	4.50	11.00
91	CARDINAL CAMEO 600QXM595-7	YR	6.00	12.00
91	CARING SHEPHERD 600QXM594-9	YR	6.00	12.00
91	FANCY WREATH 450QXM591-7	YR	4.50	10.00
92	ANGELIC HARPIST 450QXM552-4	YR	4.50	13.00
92	BABY'S FIRST CHRISTMAS 450QXM5494	YR	4.50	12.00
92	THIMBLE BELLS 600QXM546-1	YR	6.00	15.00
93	PEAR-SHAPED TONES 375QXM405-2	YR	3.75	8.00
94	BABY'S FIRST CHRISTMAS 575QXM400-3	YR	5.75	10.00
94	FRIENDS NEED HUGS 450QXM401-6	YR	4.50	12.00
94	JOURNEY TO BETHLEHEM 575QXM403-6	YR	5.75	12.00
96	LET US ADORE HIM QLX738-1	YR	16.50	17.00
D. MCGEHEE			**MINIATURE ORNAMENTS**	
88	FIRST CHRISTMAS TOGETHER 400QXM574-1	YR	4.00	9.00
88	JOYOUS HEART 350QXM569-1	YR	3.50	22.00
D. PALMITER			**MINIATURE ORNAMENTS**	
90	BEAR HUG 600QXM563-3	YR	6.00	13.00
90	PUPPY LOVE 600QXM566-6	YR	6.00	10.00
91	N. POLE BUDDY 450QXM592-7	YR	4.50	11.00
92	CHRISTMAS BONUS 300QXM581-1	YR	3.00	6.00
92	WEE THREE KINGS 575QXM553-1	YR	5.75	17.00
92	WOODLAND BABIES 600QXM544-4	YR	6.00	10.00
93	CRYSTAL ANGEL 975QXM401-5	YR	9.75	68.00
93	NORTH POLE FIRE TRUCK 475QXM410-5	YR	4.75	13.00
93	VISIONS OF SUGARPLUMS 725QXM402-2	YR	7.25	16.00
96	MURRAY FIRE TRUCK 2ND ED. QXM403-1	OP	6.75	7.00
J. PATTEE			**MINIATURE ORNAMENTS**	
88	FOLK ART LAMB 250QXM568-1	YR	2.75	17.00
88	FOLK ART REINDEER 250QXM568-4	YR	3.00	15.00
88	FRIENDS SHARE JOY 200QXM576-4	YR	2.00	12.00
88	HAPPY SANTA 450QXM561-4	YR	4.50	14.00
88	LOVE IS FOREVER 200QXM577-4	YR	2.00	12.00
89	FOLK ART BUNNY 450QXM569-2	YR	4.50	7.00
89	KITTY CART 300QXM572-2	YR	3.00	6.00
90	BRASS SANTA 300QXM578-6	YR	3.00	7.00
90	RUBY REINDEER 600QXM581-6	YR	6.00	10.00
S. PIKE			**MINIATURE ORNAMENTS**	
88	MOTHER 300QXM572-4	YR	3.00	9.00
88	THREE LITTLE KITTENS 600QXM569-4	YR	6.00	14.00
89	ACORN SQUIRREL 450QXM568-2	YR	4.50	8.00
89	BABY'S FIRST CHRISTMAS 600QXM573-2	YR	6.00	11.00
89	LOVEBIRDS 600QXM563-5	YR	6.00	11.00
89	ROLY-POLY PIG 300QXM571-2	YR	3.00	12.00
89	THREE LITTLE KITTENS 600QXM569-4	YR	6.00	14.00
90	ACORN SQUIRREL 450QXM568-2	YR	4.50	9.00
90	ROLY-POLY PIG 300QXM571-2	YR	3.00	12.00
90	SPECIAL FRIENDS 600QXM572-6	YR	6.00	10.00
90	TEACHER 450QXM565-3	YR	4.50	6.00
91	COOL 'N' SWEET 450QXM586-7	YR	4.50	15.00
91	COURIER TURTLE 450QXM585-7	YR	4.50	11.00
92	NATURE'S ANGELS 450QXM545-1	YR	4.50	14.00
92	SNUG KITTY 375QXM555-4	YR	3.75	12.00
M. PYDA-SEVCIK			**MINIATURE ORNAMENTS**	
90	THIMBLE BELLS 600QXM554-3	YR	6.00	27.00
91	THIMBLE BELLS-2ND EDITION 600QXM565-9	YR	6.00	22.00
D. RHODUS			**MINIATURE ORNAMENTS**	
89	LOAD OF CHEER 600QXM574-5	YR	6.00	13.00
89	PINECONE BASKET 450QXM573-4	YR	4.50	6.00
89	STARLIT MOUSE 450QXM565-5	YR	4.50	13.00
91	BRIGHT BOXERS 450QXM587-7	YR	4.50	14.00
91	BUSY BEAR 450QXM593-9	YR	4.50	12.00
91	HOLIDAY SNOWFLAKE 300QXM599-7	YR	3.00	9.00
92	FAST FINISH 375QXM530-1	YR	3.75	9.00
94	CORNY ELF 450QXM406-3	YR	4.50	7.00

YR	NAME	LIMIT	ISSUE	TREND
A. ROGERS			**MINIATURE ORNAMENTS**	
88	COUNTRY WREATH 400QXM573-1	YR	4.00	9.00
89	COUNTRY WREATH 450QXM573-1	YR	4.50	9.00
89	HAPPY BLUEBIRD 450QXM566-2	YR	4.50	10.00
89	KRINGLES, THE QXM 562-5	YR	6.00	30.00
89	SANTA'S MAGIC RIDE 850QXM563-2	YR	8.50	10.00
90	BASKET BUDDY 600QXM569-6	YR	6.00	12.00
90	COUNTRY HEART 450QXM569-3	YR	4.50	9.00
90	KRINGLES, THE- 600QXM575-3	YR	6.00	24.00
90	MADONNA AND CHILD 600QXM564-3	YR	6.00	9.00
91	FELIZ NAVIDAD 600QXM588-7	YR	6.00	11.00
91	GRANDCHILD'S 1ST CHRISTMAS 450QXM569-7	YR	4.50	14.00
91	KRINGLES, THE-3RD EDITION 6000QXM564-7	YR	6.00	20.00
91	LULU & FAMILY 600QXM567-7	YR	6.00	10.00
92	BEARYMORES, THE 575QXM554-4	YR	5.75	15.00
92	PERFECT BALANCE 300QXM557-1	YR	3.00	12.00
93	SECRET PAL 375QXM517-2	YR	3.75	8.00
94	BEARYMORES, THE 575QXM513-3	YR	5.75	14.00
94	MELODIC CHERUB 375QXM406-6	YR	3.75	10.00
94	MOM 450QXM401-3	YR	4.50	10.00
94	TEA W/TEDDY 725QXM404-6	YR	7.25	12.00
E. SEALE			**MINIATURE ORNAMENTS**	
90	STRINGING ALONG 850QXM560-6	YR	8.50	12.00
90	WARM MEMORIES 450QXM571-3	YR	4.50	9.00
91	TINY TEA PARTY 2900QXM582-7	YR	29.00	150.00
91	TOP HATTER 600QXM588-9	YR	6.00	17.00
92	BRIGHT STRINGERS 375QXM584-1	YR	3.75	14.00
92	INSIDE STORY 725QXM588-1	YR	7.25	19.00
92	POLAR POLKA 450QXM553-4	YR	4.50	14.00
92	SEW, SEW TINY 2900QXM579-4	YR	29.00	40.00
93	CHRISTMAS CASTLE 575QXM408-5	YR	5.75	11.00
93	GRANDMA 450QXM516-2	YR	4.50	12.00
93	INTO THE WOODS 375QXM404-5	YR	3.75	8.00
93	TINY GREEN THUMBS QXM 403-2 SET OF SIX	YR	29.00	45.00
94	BAKING TINY TREATS QXM 403-3 SET OF SIX	YR	29.00	52.00
96	OVER THE ROOFTOPS QLX737-4	YR	14.50	15.00
L. SICKMAN			**MINIATURE ORNAMENTS**	
89	LITTLE SOLDIER 450QXM567-5	YR	4.50	8.00
89	PUPPY CART 300QXM571-5	YR	3.00	6.00
90	LION AND LAMB 450QXM567-6	YR	4.50	10.00
90	LITTLE SOLDIER 450QXM567-5	YR	4.50	10.00
90	SANTA'S JOURNEY 850QXM582-6	YR	8.50	13.00
91	LI'L POPPER 450QXM589-7	YR	4.50	13.00
91	NOEL 300QXM598-9	YR	3.00	10.00
92	FRIENDLY TIN SOLDIER 450QXM587-4	YR	4.50	15.00
92	LITTLE TOWN OF BETHLEHEM 300QXM586-4	YR	3.00	15.00
93	I DREAM OF SANTA 375QXM405-5	YR	3.75	15.00
93	MONKEY MELODY 575QXM409-2	YR	5.75	14.00
94	CENTURIES OF SANTA 600QXM515-3	YR	6.00	18.00
94	JOLLY VISITOR 575QXM405-3	YR	5.75	14.00
94	LOVE WAS BORN 450QXM404-3	YR	4.50	12.00
94	NOAH'S ARK 2450QXM410-6 SET OF THREE	YR	25.00	70.00
94	NUTCRACKER GUILD 575QXM514-6	YR	5.75	15.00
96	MINIATURE CLOTHESPIN SOLDIER 2ND ED. QXM414-4	YR	4.75	7.00
96	TREASURED MEMORIES QLX738-4	YR	19.00	19.00
B. SIEDLER			**MINIATURE ORNAMENTS**	
88	CANDY CANE ELF 300QXM570-1	YR	3.00	19.00
88	LITTLE DRUMMER BOY 450QXM578-4	YR	4.50	20.00
88	PENGUIN PAL-1ST EDITION 375QXM563-1	YR	3.75	20.00
88	SNUGGLY SKATER 450QXM571-4	YR	4.50	20.00
89	OLD-WORLD SANTA 300QXM569-5	YR	3.00	8.00
89	SLOW MOTION 600QXM575-2	YR	6.00	7.00
89	STROLLIN' SNOWMAN 450QXM574-2	YR	4.50	13.00
90	CHRISTMAS DOVE 450QXM563-6	YR	4.50	13.00
90	GRANDCHILD'S FIRST XMAS 600QXM572-3	YR	6.00	13.00
90	OLD-WORLD SANTA 300QXM569-5	YR	3.00	9.00
90	SWEET SLUMBER 450QXM566-3	YR	4.50	12.00
90	WEE NUTCRACKER 850QXM584-3	YR	8.50	17.00
91	MOM 600QXM569-9	YR	6.00	17.00
91	PENGUIN PAL-4TH EDITION 450QXM562-9	YR	4.50	17.00
91	SEASIDE OTTER 450QXM590-9	YR	4.50	12.00
92	GERBIL INC. 375QXM592-4	YR	3.75	8.00
92	PUPPET SHOW 300QXM557-4	YR	3.00	12.00
93	CHEESE PLEASE 375QXM407-2	YR	3.75	8.00
93	MERRY MASCOT 375QXM404-2	YR	3.75	10.00
D. UNRUH			**MINIATURE ORNAMENTS**	
88	HOLY FAMILY 850QXM561-1	YR	8.50	10.00
88	JOLLY ST. NICK 800QXM572-1	YR	8.00	30.00
88	SKATER'S WALTZ 700QXM560-1	YR	7.00	18.00
89	HOLY FAMILY 850QXM561-1	YR	8.50	10.00
90	NATIVITY 450QXM570-6	YR	4.50	14.00
91	FIRST CHRISTMAS TOGETHER QXM 581-9	YR	6.00	19.00
92	A+ TEACHER 375QXM551-1	YR	3.75	6.00
92	COCA-COLA SANTA 575QXM588-4	YR	5.75	25.00
92	GRANDMA 450QXM551-4	YR	4.50	14.00

YR	NAME	LIMIT	ISSUE	TREND
92	MINTED FOR SANTA 375QXM585-4	YR	3.75	10.00
93	MARCH OF THE TEDDY BEARS 450QXM400-5	YR	4.50	17.00
94	MARCH OF THE TEDDY BEARS 450QXM510-6	YR	4.50	12.00
94	NIGHT BEFORE CHRISTMAS 450QXM512-3	YR	4.50	12.00
96	NIGHT BEFORE CHRISTMAS QXM410-4	YR	5.75	12.00
L. VOTRUBA		**MINIATURE ORNAMENTS**		
88	GENTLE ANGEL 200QXM577-1	YR	2.00	16.00
89	BUNNY HUG 300QXM577-5	YR	3.00	8.00
89	FIRST CHRISTMAS TOGETHER 850QXM564-2	YR	8.50	10.00
89	HOLIDAY DEER 300QXM577-2	YR	3.00	8.00
89	REJOICE 300QXM578-2	YR	3.00	8.00
89	SCRIMSHAW REINDEER 450QXM568-5	YR	4.50	9.00
90	CLOISONNE POINSETTIA 1050QMX553-3	YR	10.50	24.00
91	COUNTRY SLEIGH 450QXM599-9	YR	4.50	11.00
91	LOVE IS BORN 600QXM595-9	YR	6.00	15.00
92	HARMONY TRIO 1175QXM547-1	YR	11.75	15.00
92	NIGHT BEFORE CHRISTMAS 1375QXM5541	YR	13.75	35.00
92	SNOWSHOE BUNNY 375QXM556-4	YR	3.75	8.00
93	BABY'S FIRST CHRISTMAS 575QXM514-5	YR	5.75	12.00
93	CLOISONNE SNOWFLAKE 975QXM401-2	YR	9.75	18.00
93	NIGHT BEFORE CHRISTMAS 450QXM511-5	YR	4.50	18.00
93	THIMBLE BELLS 575QXM514-2	YR	5.75	15.00
94	DAZZLING REINDEER 975QXM402-6	YR	9.75	20.00
94	JOLLY WOLLY SNOWMAN 375QXM409-3	YR	3.75	10.00
94	NATURE'S ANGELS 450QXM512-6	YR	4.50	12.00
*		**MINIATURE ORNAMENTS-OLD ENGLISH VILLAGE**		
95	TUDOR HOUSE 481-9	YR	6.75	14.00
97	VILLAGE DEPOT 418-2	YR	7.00	7.00
P. ANDREWS		**MINIATURE ORNAMENTS-OLD ENGLISH VILLAGE**		
94	HAT SHOP 700QXM514-3	YR	7.00	16.00
D. LEE		**MINIATURE ORNAMENTS-OLD ENGLISH VILLAGE**		
88	FAMILY HOME 850QXM563-4	YR	8.50	45.00
89	SWEET SHOP 850QXM561-5	YR	8.50	30.00
90	SCHOOL 850QXM576-3	YR	8.50	20.00
91	COUNTRY INN QXM 562-7	YR	8.50	25.00
92	CHURCH 700QXM5384	YR	7.00	25.00
93	TOY SHOP 700QXM513-2	YR	7.00	17.00
D. RHODUS		**MINIATURE ORNAMENTS-OLD ENGLISH VILLAGE**		
96	VILLAGE MILL QXM412-4	YR	6.75	10.00
L. SICKMAN		**MINIATURE ORNAMENTS-ON THE ROAD**		
93	ON THE ROAD 575QXM400-2	YR	5.75	17.00
94	ON THE ROAD 575QXM510-3	YR	5.75	12.00
95	ON THE ROAD 479-7	YR	5.75	10.00
96	ON THE ROAD QXM410-1	YR	5.75	6.00
97	ON THE ROAD 417-2	YR	6.00	6.00
L. SICKMAN		**MINIATURE ORNAMENTS-NOEL RAILROAD**		
89	LOCOMOTIVE 850QXM576-2	YR	8.50	44.00
90	COAL CAR 850QXM575-6	YR	8.50	29.00
91	PASSENGER CAR-3RD EDITION 850QXM564-9	YR	8.50	30.00
92	BOX CAR 700QXM5441	YR	7.00	22.00
93	FLATBED CAR 700QXM510-5	YR	7.00	19.00
94	STOCK CAR 700QXM511-3	YR	7.00	16.00
95	MILK TANK CAR 481-7	YR	6.75	12.00
96	COOKIE CAR 8TH ED. QXM411-4	YR	6.75	7.00
97	CANDY CAR 417-5	YR	7.00	7.00
*		**MOTHER GOOSE**		
97	LITTLE BOY BLUE 621-5	YR	14.00	14.00
E. SEALE		**MOTHER GOOSE**		
93	HUMPTY DUMPTY 1ST ED. 1375QX528-2	YR	13.75	35.00
94	HEY DIDDLE, DIDDLE 2ND ED. 1395QX521-3	YR	14.00	40.00
SEALE/VOTRUBA		**MOTHER GOOSE**		
95	JACK AND JILL 3RD SERIES QX509-9	YR	14.00	25.00
96	MARY HAD A LITTLE LAMB QX564-4	YR	14.00	20.00
J. FRANCIS		**MR. AND MRS. CLAUS**		
93	A FITTING MOMENT 8TH ED. 1475QX420-2	YR	14.75	26.00
D. UNRUH		**MR. AND MRS. CLAUS**		
86	MERRY MISTLETOE TIME 1300QX402-6	YR	13.00	200.00
87	HOME COOKING 1325QX483-7	YR	13.25	70.00
88	SHALL WE DANCE? 1300QX401-1	YR	13.00	42.00
89	HOLIDAY DUET 1325QX457-5	YR	13.25	42.00
90	POPCORN PARTY 5TH ED. 1375QX439-3	YR	13.75	45.00
91	CHECKING HIS LIST 6TH ED. 1375QX433-9	YR	13.75	30.00
92	GIFT EXCHANGE 7TH ED. 1475QX429-4	YR	14.75	27.00
94	A HANDWARMING PRESENT 9TH ED. 1495QX528-3	YR	15.00	25.00
95	CHRISTMAS EVE KISS 10TH & FINAL SERIES QX515-7	YR	15.00	25.00
*		**MUSICAL**		
82	BABY'S FIRST CHRISTMAS 1600QMB900-7	YR	16.00	67.00
82	FIRST CHRISTMAS TOGETHER 1600QMB901-9	YR	16.00	75.00
82	LOVE 1600QMB900-9	YR	16.00	70.00
83	BABY'S FIRST CHRISTMAS 1600QMB903-9	YR	16.00	70.00
83	FRIENDSHIP 1600QMB904-7	YR	16.00	102.00
83	MOTHER'S DAY-A MOTHER'S LOVE MDQ 340-7	YR	14.00	75.00
83	NATIVITY 1600QMB904-9	YR	16.00	150.00

YR	NAME	LIMIT	ISSUE	TREND
E. SEALE				**MUSICAL**
83	TWELVE DAYS OF CHRISTMAS 1500QMB415-9	YR	15.00	77.00
S. PIKE				**NATURE'S ANGELS**
91	PUPPY 450QXM565-7	YR	4.50	22.00
96	NATURE'S ANGELS 7TH ED. QXM411-1	YR	4.75	5.00
E. SEALE				**NATURE'S ANGELS**
90	BUNNY 450QXM573-3	YR	4.50	24.00
BASTIN/FRANCIS				**NATURE'S SKETCHBOOK**
95	BACKYARD ORCHARD QK106-9	YR	19.00	22.00
95	CHRISTMAS CARDINAL QK107-7	YR	19.00	22.00
96	CHRISTMAS BUNNY QK110-4	YR	19.00	19.00
BASTIN/LYLE				**NATURE'S SKETCHBOOK**
95	RAISING A FAMILY QK106-7	YR	19.00	22.00
95	VIOLETS AND BUTTERFLIES QK107-9	YR	17.00	22.00
96	HOLLY BASKET, THE QK109-4	YR	19.00	19.00
BASTIN/UNRUH				**NATURE'S SKETCHBOOK**
96	BIRDS' CHRISTMAS TREE, THE QK111-4	YR	19.00	19.00
*				**NEW ATTRACTIONS**
89	FESTIVE ANGEL 675QX463-5	YR	6.75	18.00
89	GRACEFUL SWAN 675QX464-2	YR	6.75	17.00
89	ROOSTER WEATHERVANE 575QX467-5	YR	5.75	11.00
90	COUNTRY ANGEL 675QX504-6	YR	6.75	85.00
90	FELIZ NAVIDAD 675QX517-3	YR	6.75	20.00
90	GARFIELD 475QX230-3	YR	4.75	25.00
90	GINGERBREAD ELF 575QX503-3	YR	5.75	13.00
90	GOOSE CART 775QX523-6	YR	7.75	11.00
90	HOME FOR THE OWLIDAYS 675QX518-3	YR	6.75	11.00
90	MOOY CHRISTMAS 675QX493-3	YR	6.75	17.00
90	NUTSHELL CHAT 675QX519-3	YR	6.75	19.00
90	PEANUTS 475QX223-3	YR	4.75	18.00
91	MARY ENGELBREIT 475QX223-7	YR	4.75	18.00
91	PEANUTS 500QX225-7	YR	5.00	17.00
92	EGG NOG NEST 775QX512-1	YR	7.75	14.00
92	PEANUTS 500QX224-4	YR	5.00	20.00
92	SANTA JOLLY WOLLY 775QX537-4	YR	7.75	7.00
94	GARFIELD 1295QX575-3	YR	13.00	25.00
95	GARFIELD QX500-7	YR	11.00	25.00
P. ANDREWS				**NEW ATTRACTIONS**
90	SPOON RIDER 975QX549-6	YR	9.75	16.00
90	TWO PEAS IN A POD 475QX492-6	YR	4.75	27.00
92	FELIZ NAVIDAD 675QX518-1	YR	6.75	15.00
92	JESUS LOVES ME 775QX302-4	YR	7.75	11.00
92	LOVING SHEPHERD 775QX515-1	YR	7.75	14.00
92	MEMORIES TO CHERISH 1075QX516-1	YR	10.75	16.00
92	TOBOGGAN TAIL 775QX545-9	YR	7.75	16.00
R. CHAD				**NEW ATTRACTIONS**
89	BALANCING ELF 675QX489-5	YR	6.75	20.00
89	NUTSHELL DREAMS 575QX465-5	YR	5.75	16.00
89	NUTSHELL WORKSHOP 575QX487-2	YR	5.75	16.00
91	DINOCLAUS 775QX527-7	YR	7.75	17.00
92	SPIRIT OF CHRISTMAS STRESS 875QX523-1	YR	8.75	19.00
K. CROW				**NEW ATTRACTIONS**
89	COOL SWING 625QX487-5	YR	6.25	25.00
89	GOIN' SOUTH 425QX410-5	YR	4.25	20.00
89	LET'S PLAY 725QX488-2	YR	7.25	20.00
90	BEARBACK RIDER 975QX548-3	YR	9.75	20.00
90	HOT DOGGER 775QX497-6	YR	7.75	13.00
90	JOY IS IN THE AIR 775QX550-3	YR	7.75	20.00
90	SANTA SCHNOZ 675QX498-3	YR	6.75	18.00
90	THREE LITTLE PIGGIES 775QX499-6	YR	7.75	15.00
91	ON A ROLL 675QX534-7	YR	6.75	16.00
91	UP 'N' DOWN JOURNEY 975QX504-7	YR	9.75	24.00
92	DOWN-UNDER HOLIDAY 775QX514-4	YR	7.75	18.00
92	FUN ON A BIG SCALE 1075QX513-4	YR	10.75	18.00
92	GENIUS AT WORK 1075QX537-1	YR	10.75	18.00
92	HELLO-HO-HO 975QX514-1	YR	9.75	18.00
92	SANTA MARIA 1275QX507-4	YR	12.75	25.00
P. DUTKIN				**NEW ATTRACTIONS**
89	CACTUS COWBOY 675QX411-2	YR	6.75	37.00
89	PEPPERMINT CLOWN 2475QX450-5	YR	25.00	25.00
90	S. CLAUS TAXI 1175QX468-6	YR	11.75	23.00
J. FRANCIS				**NEW ATTRACTIONS**
90	KITTY'S BEST PAL 675QX471-6	YR	6.75	16.00
92	DECK THE HOGS 875QX520-4	YR	8.75	16.00
D. LEE				**NEW ATTRACTIONS**
89	TV BREAK 625QX409-2	YR	6.25	16.00
90	BILLBOARD BUNNY 775QX519-6	YR	7.75	13.00
90	COYOTE CAROLS 875QX499-3	YR	8.75	19.00
90	POOLSIDE WALRUS 775QX498-6	YR	7.75	15.00
90	STITCHES OF JOY 775QX518-6	YR	7.75	20.00
91	CHILLY CHAP 675QX533-9	YR	6.75	15.00
91	FELIZ NAVIDAD 675QX527-9	YR	6.75	20.00
91	SKI LIFT BUNNY 675QX544-7	YR	6.75	16.00
92	A SANTA-FULL 975QX599-1	YR	9.75	31.00

YR	NAME	LIMIT	ISSUE	TREND
92	COOL FLIERS 1075QX547-4	YR	10.75	17.00
92	GONE WISHIN' 875QX517-1	YR	8.75	13.00
92	HONEST GEORGE 775QX506-4	YR	7.75	15.00
92	PLEASE PAUSE HERE 1475QX529-1	YR	14.75	32.00
92	SANTA'S ROUNDUP 875QX508-4	YR	8.75	19.00
92	SKIING 'ROUND 875QX521-4	YR	8.75	17.00
92	TASTY CHRISTMAS 975QX599-4	YR	9.75	17.00
J. LYLE			**NEW ATTRACTIONS**	
89	SPARKLING SNOWFLAKE 775QX547-2	YR	7.75	17.00
90	HOLIDAY CARDINALS 775QX524-3	YR	7.75	16.00
90	NORMAN ROCKWELL ART 475QX229-6	YR	4.75	14.00
91	NORMAN ROCKWELL ART 500QX225-9	YR	5.00	16.00
92	NORMAN ROCKWELL ART 500QX222-4	YR	5.00	13.00
D. PALMITER			**NEW ATTRACTIONS**	
92	GARFIELD 775QX537-4	YR	7.75	20.00
92	GREEN THUMB SANTA 775QX510-1	YR	7.75	14.00
92	RAPID DELIVERY 875QX509-4	YR	8.75	17.00
S. PIKE			**NEW ATTRACTIONS**	
90	BORN TO DANCE 775QX504-3	YR	7.75	17.00
90	CHIMING IN 975QX436-6	YR	9.75	18.00
90	COZY GOOSE 575QX496-6	YR	5.75	10.00
90	MEOW MART 775QX444-6	YR	7.75	18.00
91	NUTTY SQUIRREL 575QX483-3	YR	5.75	13.00
92	HOLIDAY WISHES 775QX513-1	YR	7.75	14.00
M. PYDA-SEVCIK			**NEW ATTRACTIONS**	
89	COUNTRY CAT 625QX467-2	YR	6.25	16.00
89	NOSTALGIC LAMB 675QX466-5	YR	6.75	13.00
90	CHRISTMAS CROC 775QX437-3	YR	7.75	16.00
D. RHODUS			**NEW ATTRACTIONS**	
89	WIGGLY SNOWMAN 675QX489-2	YR	6.75	20.00
90	SNOOPY & WOODSTOCK 675QX472-3	YR	6.75	28.00
91	GARFIELD 775QX517-7	YR	7.75	25.00
91	SNOOPY AND WOODSTOCK 675QX519-7	YR	6.75	40.00
A. ROGERS			**NEW ATTRACTIONS**	
89	NUTSHELL HOLIDAY 575QX465-2	YR	5.75	21.00
90	BABY UNICORN 975QX548-6	YR	9.75	17.00
90	JOLLY DOLPHIN 675QX468-3	YR	6.75	19.00
90	LONG WINTER'S NAP 675QX470-3	YR	6.75	15.00
91	CUDDLY LAMB 675QX519-9	YR	6.75	13.00
91	NUTSHELL NATIVITY 675QX517-6	YR	6.75	21.00
92	HOLIDAY TEATIME 1475QX543-1	YR	14.75	25.00
92	SNOOPY & WOODSTOCK 875QX595-4	YR	8.75	27.00
L. SCHULER			**NEW ATTRACTIONS**	
92	GOLF'S A BALL 675QX598-4	YR	6.75	16.00
E. SEALE			**NEW ATTRACTIONS**	
89	CLAUS CONSTRUCTION 775QX488-5	YR	7.75	23.00
90	HANG IN THERE 675QX471-3	YR	6.75	17.00
90	KING KLAUS 775QX410-6	YR	7.75	20.00
90	STOCKING PALS 1075QX549-3	YR	10.75	18.00
91	BASKET BELL PLAYERS 775QX537-7	YR	7.75	18.00
91	YULE LOGGER 875QX496-7	YR	8.75	23.00
92	BEAR BELL CHAMP 775QX507-1	YR	7.75	17.00
92	MERRY "SWISS" MOUSE 775QX511-4	YR	7.75	13.00
92	NORTH POLE FIRE FIGHTER 975QX510-4	YR	9.75	18.00
92	SANTA'S HOOK SHOT 1275QX543-4	YR	12.75	25.00
92	TREAD BEAR 875QX509-1	YR	8.75	16.00
L. SICKMAN			**NEW ATTRACTIONS**	
89	HORSE WEATHERVANE 575QX463-2	YR	5.75	14.00
90	CHRISTMAS PARTRIDGE 775QX524-6	YR	7.75	15.00
91	CHRISTMAS WELCOME 975QX529-9	YR	9.75	16.00
91	JOLLY WOLLY SANTA 775QX541-9	YR	7.75	19.00
91	JOLLY WOLLY SNOWMAN 775QX542-7	YR	7.75	16.00
91	JOLLY WOLLY SOLDIER 775QX542-9	YR	7.75	15.00
91	NIGHT BEFORE CHRISTMAS 975QX530-7	YR	9.75	19.00
91	OLD-FASHIONED SLED 875QX431-7	YR	8.75	13.00
91	PARTRIDGE IN A PEAR TREE 975QX529-7	YR	9.75	17.00
91	SNOWY OWL 775QX526-9	YR	7.75	16.00
92	SILVER STAR 2800QX532-4	YR	28.00	50.00
B. SIEDLER			**NEW ATTRACTIONS**	
89	RODNEY REINDEER 675QX407-2	YR	6.75	11.00
90	BEARY GOOD DEAL 675QX473-3	YR	6.75	13.00
90	PEPPERONI MOUSE 675QX497-3	YR	6.75	14.00
90	PERFECT CATCH 775QX469-3	YR	7.75	15.00
90	POLAR JOGGER 575QX466-6	YR	5.75	11.00
90	POLAR PAIR 575QX462-6	YR	5.75	13.00
90	POLAR SPORT 775QX515-6	YR	7.75	15.00
90	POLAR TV 775QX516-6	YR	7.75	10.00
90	POLAR V.I.P. 575QX466-3	YR	5.75	10.00
90	POLAR VIDEO 575QX463-3	YR	5.75	10.00
91	ALL STAR 675QX532-9	YR	6.75	16.00
91	NOTES OF CHEER 575QX535-7	YR	5.75	13.00
91	POLAR CLASSIC 675QX528-7	YR	6.75	16.00
92	PARTRIDGE IN PEAR TREE 875QX523-4	YR	8.75	13.00

YR NAME	LIMIT	ISSUE	TREND
D. UNRUH		**NEW ATTRACTIONS**	
90 LITTLE DRUMMER BOY 775QX523-3	YR	7.75	14.00
90 LOVABLE DEARS 875QX547-6	YR	8.75	14.00
91 SWEET TALK 875QX536-7	YR	8.75	15.00
92 CHEERFUL SANTA 975QX515-4	YR	9.75	50.00
L. VOTRUBA		**NEW ATTRACTIONS**	
90 HAPPY VOICES 675QX464-5	YR	6.75	11.00
91 FOLK ART REINDEER 875QX535-9	YR	8.75	13.00
91 JOYOUS MEMORIES-PHOTOHOLDER 675QX536-9	YR	6.75	18.00
*		**NFL COLLECTION**	
96 NFL BALL ORNAMENTS	YR	6.00	6.00
D. UNRUH		**NFL COLLECTION**	
96 ARIZONA CARDINALS NFL TEAM QSR648-4	YR	10.00	10.00
96 ATLANTA FALCONS NFL TEAM QSR636-4	YR	10.00	10.00
96 BROWNS NFL TEAM QSR639-1	YR	10.00	10.00
96 BUFFALO BILLS NFL TEAM QSR637-1	YR	10.00	10.00
96 CAROLINA PANTHERS NFL TEAM QSR637-4	YR	10.00	10.00
96 CHICAGO BEARS NFL TEAM QSR638-1	YR	10.00	10.00
96 CINCINNATI BENGALS NFL TEAM QSR638-4	YR	10.00	10.00
96 DALLAS COWBOYS NFL TEAM QSR639-4	YR	10.00	10.00
96 DENVER BRONCOS NFL TEAM QSR641-1	YR	10.00	10.00
96 DETROIT LIONS NFL TEAM QSR641-1	YR	10.00	10.00
96 GREEN BAY PACKERS NFL TEAM QSR642-1	YR	10.00	10.00
96 INDIANAPOLIS COLTS NFL TEAM QSR643-1	YR	10.00	10.00
96 JACKSONVILLE JAGUARS NFL TEAM QSR643-4	YR	10.00	10.00
96 KANSAS CITY CHIEFS NFL TEAM QSR636-1	YR	10.00	10.00
96 MIAMI DOLPHINS NFL TEAM QSR645-1	YR	10.00	10.00
96 MINNESOTA VIKINGS NFL TEAM QSR645-4	YR	10.00	10.00
96 NEW ENGLAND PATRIOTS NFL TEAM QSR646-1	YR	10.00	10.00
96 NEW ORLEANS SAINTS NFL TEAM QSR646-4	YR	10.00	10.00
96 NEW YORK GIANTS NFL TEAM QSR647-1	YR	10.00	10.00
96 OAKLAND RAIDERS NFL TEAM QSR644-1	YR	10.00	10.00
96 OILERS NFL TEAM QSR642-4	YR	10.00	10.00
96 PHILADELPHIA EAGLES NFL TEAM QSR648-1	YR	10.00	10.00
96 PITTSBURGH STEELERS NFL TEAM QSR649-1	YR	10.00	10.00
96 SAN DIEGO CHARGERS NFL TEAM QSR649-4	YR	10.00	10.00
96 SAN FRANCISCO 49ERS NFL TEAM QSR650-1	YR	10.00	30.00
96 SEATTLE SEAHAWKS NFL TEAM QSR650-4	YR	10.00	10.00
96 ST. LOUIS RAMS NFL TEAM QSR644-4	YR	10.00	10.00
96 TAMPA BAY BUCCANEERS NFL TEAM QSR651-1	YR	10.00	10.00
96 WASHINGTON REDSKINS NFL TEAM QSR651-4	YR	10.00	10.00
*		**NORMAN ROCKWELL**	
80 SANTA'S VISITORS 650QX306-1	YR	6.50	195.00
83 DRESS REHEARSAL-4TH EDITION 750QX300-7	YR	7.50	28.00
88 AND TO ALL A GOOD NIGHT 775QX340-4	YR	7.75	16.00
P. DUTKIN		**NORMAN ROCKWELL**	
93 FILLING THE STOCKINGS 1575QK115-5	YR	15.75	35.00
93 JOLLY POSTMAN 1575QK116-2	YR	15.75	35.00
J. LYLE		**NORMAN ROCKWELL**	
88 CHRISTMAS SCENES 475QX273-1	YR	4.75	16.00
D. MCGEHEE		**NORMAN ROCKWELL**	
84 CAUGHT NAPPING 750QX341-1	YR	7.50	27.00
85 POSTMAN & KIDS-6TH EDITION 750QX374-5	YR	7.50	21.00
D. PALMITER		**NORMAN ROCKWELL**	
87 CHRISTMAS DANCE-8TH EDITION 775QX370-7	YR	7.75	15.00
S. PIKE		**NORMAN ROCKWELL**	
86 CHECKING UP 775QX321-3	YR	7.75	18.00
D. UNRUH		**NORMAN ROCKWELL**	
96 LITTLE SPOONERS QX550-4	YR	13.00	13.00
L. SICKMAN		**NORTH POLE NUTCRACKERS**	
92 ERIC THE BAKER 875QX524-4	YR	8.75	15.00
92 FRANZ THE ARTIST 875QX526-1	YR	8.75	20.00
92 FRIEDA THE ANIMALS' FRIEND 875QX526-4	YR	8.75	19.00
92 LUDWIG THE MUSICIAN 875QX528-1	YR	8.75	17.00
92 MAX THE TAILOR 875QX525-1	YR	8.75	17.00
92 OTTO THE CARPENTER 875QX525-4	YR	8.75	17.00
D. LEE		**NOSTALGIC HOUSES & SHOPS**	
84 VICTORIAN DOLLHOUSE 1300QX448-1	YR	13.00	250.00
85 TOY SHOP 1375QX497-5	YR	13.75	97.00
86 CHRISTMAS CANDY SHOPPE 1375QX403-3	YR	13.75	275.00
87 HOUSE ON MAIN ST. 1400QX483-9	YR	14.00	67.00
88 HALL BROS CARD SHOP 1450QX401-4	YR	14.50	75.00
89 U.S. POST OFFICE 1425QX458-2	YR	14.25	50.00
90 HOLIDAY HOME 7TH ED 1475QX469-6	YR	14.75	60.00
91 FIRE STATION-8TH ED 1475QX413-9	YR	14.75	51.00
92 FIVE-AND-TEN-CENT STORE 9TH ED 1475QX425-4	YR	14.75	32.00
93 COZY HOME 10TH ED 1475QX417-5	YR	14.75	32.00
94 NEIGHBORHOOD DRUGSTORE 11TH ED 1495QX528-6	YR	15.00	32.00
D. PALMITER		**NOSTALGIC HOUSES & SHOPS**	
95 TOWN CHURCH 12TH ED QX515-9	YR	15.00	22.00
96 VICTORIAN PAINTED LADY 13TH ED. QX567-1	YR	15.00	15.00
97 CAFE 14TH ED.	YR	17.00	17.00
L. VOTRUBA		**NUTCRACKER BALLET**	
96 NUTCRACKER BALLET, THE 1ST ED. QXM406-4	YR	14.75	15.00

YR	NAME	LIMIT	ISSUE	TREND
L. SICKMAN			**NUTCRACKER GUILD**	
96	NUTCRACKER GUILD 3RD ED QXM408-4	YR	5.75	6.00
D. PALMITER			**OLD WORLD SILVER**	
93	SILVER DOVE OF PEACE 2475QK107-5	YR	25.00	34.00
93	SILVER SLEIGH 2475QK108-2	YR	25.00	34.00
93	SILVER STAR AND HOLLY 2475QK108-5	YR	25.00	34.00
94	SILVER BOWS 2475QK102-3	YR	25.00	26.00
D. UNRUH			**OLD WORLD SILVER**	
93	SILVER SANTA 2475QK109-2	YR	25.00	60.00
94	SILVER BELLS 2475QK102-6	YR	25.00	26.00
94	SILVER POINSETTIA 2475QK100-6	YR	25.00	30.00
94	SILVER SNOWFLAKES 2475QK101-6	YR	25.00	26.00
P. DUTKIN			**OLD-FASHIONED CHRISTMAS COLLECTION**	
87	LITTLE WHITTLER 600QX469-9	YR	6.00	25.00
M. PYDA-SEVCIK			**OLD-FASHIONED CHRISTMAS COLLECTION**	
87	COUNTRY WREATH 575QX470-9	YR	5.75	18.00
L. SICKMAN			**OLD-FASHIONED CHRISTMAS COLLECTION**	
87	FOLK ART SANTA 525QX474-9	YR	5.25	27.00
87	NOSTALGIC ROCKER 650QX468-9	YR	6.50	20.00
D. UNRUH			**OLD-FASHIONED CHRISTMAS COLLECTION**	
87	IN A NUTSHELL 550QX469-7	YR	5.50	15.00
*			**OLYMPIC SPIRIT COLLECTION**	
95	CENTENNIAL GAMES ATLANTA 1996 QX316-9	YR	8.00	16.00
96	PARADE OF NATIONS QXE574-1	YR	11.00	18.00
D. MCGEHEE			**OLYMPIC SPIRIT COLLECTION**	
96	CLOISONNE MEDALLION QXE404-1	YR	9.75	19.00
96	INVITATION TO THE GAMES QXE551-1	YR	15.00	18.00
D. PALMITER			**OLYMPIC SPIRIT COLLECTION**	
96	IZZY - THE MASCOT QXE572-4	YR	10.00	13.00
E. SEALE			**OLYMPIC SPIRIT COLLECTION**	
96	OLYMPIC TRIUMPH QXE573-1	YR	11.00	15.00
D. UNRUH			**OLYMPIC SPIRIT COLLECTION**	
96	LIGHTING THE FLAME QXE744-4	YR	28.00	30.00
*			**OPEN HOUSE ORNAMENTS**	
86	SANTA & HIS REINDEER 975QX0440-6	YR	9.75	28.00
86	SANTA'S PANDA PAL 550QX0441-3	YR	5.00	17.00
E. SEALE			**ORNAMENT PREMIERE**	
95	WISH LIST QX585-9	YR	15.00	18.00
B. SIEDLER			**OWLIVER**	
92	OWLIVER 1ST ED. 775QX454-4	YR	7.75	20.00
93	OWLIVER 2ND ED. 775QX542-5	YR	7.75	15.00
94	OWLIVER 795QX522-6	YR	8.00	15.00
L. SICKMAN			**PEACE ON EARTH**	
91	ITALY FIRST ED 1175QX512-9	YR	11.75	27.00
92	SPAIN 2ND ED 1175QX517-4	YR	11.75	21.00
93	POLAND 3RD ED 1175QX524-2	YR	11.75	19.00
R. CHAD			**PEANUTS**	
96	SCHROEDER AND LUCY QLX739-4	YR	19.00	30.00
S. PIKE			**PEANUTS**	
98	GOING UP? CHARLIE BROWN 995QEO8433	YR	10.00	10.00
B. SIEDLER			**PEANUTS**	
96	A TREE FOR SNOOPY QX550-7	YR	9.00	15.00
*			**PEANUTS COLLECTION**	
77	PEANUTS (2) 400QX163-5	YR	4.00	72.00
77	PEANUTS 250QX162-2	YR	2.50	47.00
77	PEANUTS 350QX135-5	YR	3.50	61.00
78	PEANUTS 250QX203-6	YR	2.50	52.00
78	PEANUTS 250QX204-3	YR	2.50	60.00
78	PEANUTS 350QX205-6	YR	3.50	58.00
78	PEANUTS 350QX206-3	YR	3.50	50.00
89	A CHARLIE BROWN CHRISTMAS 475QX276-5	YR	4.75	35.00
R. BISHOP			**PEANUTS COLLECTION**	
94	LUCY QX 520-3	YR	10.00	30.00
J. FRANCIS			**PEANUTS COLLECTION**	
96	PEANUTS GANG,THE- FINAL ED. QX538-1	YR	10.00	15.00
D. RHODUS			**PEANUTS COLLECTION**	
93	PEANUTS GANG 1ST ED 975QX531-5	YR	9.75	50.00
*			**PERSONALIZED ORNAMENTS**	
93	COOL SNOWMAN 875QP605-2	YR	8.75	9.00
93	PEANUTS 900QP604-5	YR	9.00	9.00
93	REINDEER IN THE SKY 875QP605-5	YR	8.75	6.00
P. ANDREWS			**PERSONALIZED ORNAMENTS**	
95	BABY BEAR QP615-7	YR	13.00	14.00
K. CROW			**PERSONALIZED ORNAMENTS**	
93	MAILBOX DELIVERY 1475QP601-5	YR	14.75	11.00
93	ON THE BILLBOARD 1275QP602-2	YR	12.75	11.00
94	ETCH-A-SKETCH 1295QP600-6	YR	13.00	10.00
94	MAILBOX DELIVERY 1495QP601-5	YR	15.00	11.00
94	ON THE BILLBOARD 1295QP602-2	YR	13.00	11.00
94	REINDEER ROOTERS 1295QP605-6	YR	13.00	13.00
95	ETCH-A-SKETCH QP601-5	YR	13.00	14.00
95	MAILBOX DELIVERY QP601-5	YR	15.00	15.00

YR NAME	LIMIT	ISSUE	TREND
95 ON THE BILLBOARD QP602-2	YR	13.00	14.00
95 REINDEER ROOTERS QP605-6	YR	13.00	14.00
J. FRANCIS	**PERSONALIZED ORNAMENTS**		
93 BABY BLOCK PHOTOHOLDER QP603-5	YR	14.75	16.00
93 PLAYING BALL 1275QP603-2	YR	12.75	11.00
94 BABY BLOCK PHOTOHOLDER 1495QP603-5	YR	15.00	16.00
94 PLAYING BALL 1295QP603-2	YR	13.00	11.00
95 PLAYING BALL 603-2	YR	13.00	14.00
D. PALMITER	**PERSONALIZED ORNAMENTS**		
93 GOING GOLFIN' 1275QP601-2	YR	12.75	11.00
94 GOIN' FISHIN' 1495QP602-3	YR	15.00	15.00
94 GOIN' GOLFIN' 1295QP601-2	YR	12.75	11.00
D. RHODUS	**PERSONALIZED ORNAMENTS**		
94 FROM THE HEART 1495QP603-6	YR	25.00	25.00
95 FROM THE HEART QP603-6	YR	15.00	15.00
A. ROGERS	**PERSONALIZED ORNAMENTS**		
93 FILLED W/COOKIES 1275QP604-2	YR	12.75	11.00
E. SEALE	**PERSONALIZED ORNAMENTS**		
93 HERE'S YOUR FORTUNE 1075QP600-2	YR	10.75	9.00
93 SANTA SAYS 1475QP600-5	YR	12.75	13.00
94 COMPUTER CAT 'N' MOUSE 1295QP604-6	YR	13.00	10.00
94 SANTA SAYS 1495QP600-5	YR	15.00	13.00
95 CHAMP, THE QP604-6	YR	13.00	14.00
95 KEY NOTE QP614-9	YR	13.00	15.00
B. SIEDLER	**PERSONALIZED ORNAMENTS**		
94 HOLIDAY HELLO 2495QXR611-6	YR	25.00	25.00
L. VOTRUBA	**PERSONALIZED ORNAMENTS**		
93 FESTIVE ALBUM PHOTOHOLDER QP602-5	YR	12.75	13.00
94 COOKIE TIME 1295QP607-3	YR	13.00	10.00
94 FESTIVE ALBUM PHOTOHOLDER 1295QP602-5	YR	13.00	13.00
94 NOVEL IDEA 1295QP606-6	YR	13.00	13.00
95 COOKIE TIME QP607-3	YR	13.00	14.00
95 NOVEL IDEA QP606-6	YR	13.00	14.00
A. ROGERS	**PLAYFUL PALS**		
93 COCA-COLA SANTA 1475QX574-2	YR	14.75	24.00
*	**PLUSH ANIMALS**		
81 CHRISTMAS TEDDY 500QX404-2	YR	5.50	17.00
81 RACCOON TUNES 550QX405-5	YR	5.50	18.00
K. CROW	**POCAHONTAS**		
95 CAPTAIN JOHN SMITH AND MEEKO QX1617-9	YR	13.00	20.00
95 PERCY, FLIT AND MEEKO QX1617-9	YR	10.00	17.00
95 POCAHONTAS AND CAPT. JOHN SMITH QX1619-7	YR	15.00	18.00
95 POCAHONTAS QX1617-7	YR	13.00	20.00
*	**PORTRAITS IN BISQUE**		
93 JOY OF SHARING 1575QK114-2	YR	15.75	30.00
S. PIKE	**PORTRAITS IN BISQUE**		
93 CHRISTMAS FEAST 1575QK115-2	YR	15.75	35.00
93 MISTLETOE KISS 1575QK114-5	YR	15.75	30.00
L. VOTRUBA	**PRECIOUS EDITION**		
96 SPARKLING CRYSTAL ANGEL QXM426-4	YR	9.75	10.00
*	**PROPERTY ORNAMENTS**		
75 BETSEY CLARK (2) 350QX167-1	YR	3.50	35.00
75 BETSEY CLARK (4) 450QX168-1	YR	4.50	50.00
75 BUTTONS & BO (4) 500QX139-1	YR	5.00	45.00
75 CHARMERS 300QX135-1	YR	3.00	40.00
75 LITTLE MIRACLES (4) 500QX140-1	YR	5.00	40.00
75 MARTY LINKS 300QX136-1	YR	3.00	40.00
75 NORMAN ROCKWELL 250QX166-1	YR	2.50	35.00
75 NORMAN ROCKWELL 300QX134-1	YR	3.00	35.00
76 BETSEY CLARK (3) 450QX218-1	YR	4.50	52.00
76 BETSEY CLARK 250QX210-1	YR	2.50	35.00
76 CHARMERS (2) 350QX215-1	YR	3.50	45.00
76 HAPPY THE SNOWMAN (2) QX216-1	YR	3.50	38.00
76 MARTY LINKS (2) 400QX207-1	YR	4.00	37.00
76 NORMAN ROCKWELL 300QX196-1	YR	3.00	60.00
76 RAGGEDY ANN 250QX212-1	YR	2.50	52.00
76 RUDOLPH AND SANTA 250QX213-1	YR	2.50	72.00
77 CHARMERS 350QX153-5	YR	3.50	48.00
77 DISNEY (2) 400QX137-5	YR	4.00	42.00
77 DISNEY 350QX133-5	YR	3.50	47.00
77 GRANDMA MOSES 350QX150-2	YR	3.50	50.00
77 NORMAN ROCKWELL 350QX151-5	YR	3.50	57.00
78 DISNEY 350QX207-6	YR	3.50	70.00
78 JOAN WALSH ANGLUND 350QX221-6	YR	3.50	70.00
78 SPENCER SPARROW 350QX219-6	YR	3.50	50.00
79 JOAN WALSH ANGLUND 350QX205-9	YR	3.50	32.00
79 MARY HAMILTON 350QX254-7	YR	3.50	21.00
79 PEANUTS-TIME TO TRIM 350QX202-7	YR	3.50	33.00
79 SPENCER SPARROW 350QX200-7	YR	3.50	24.00
79 WINNIE-THE-POOH 350QX206-7	YR	3.50	39.00
80 BETSEY CLARK 650QX307-4	YR	6.50	51.00
80 BETSEY CLARK'S CHRISTMAS 750QX149-4	YR	7.50	26.00
80 DISNEY 400QX218-1	YR	4.00	26.00
80 JOAN WALSH ANGLUND 400QX217-4	YR	4.00	20.00

YR	NAME	LIMIT	ISSUE	TREND
80	MARTY LINKS 400QX221-4	YR	4.00	14.00
80	MARY HAMILTON 400QX219-4	YR	4.00	17.00
80	MUPPETS 400QX220-1	YR	4.00	31.00
80	PEANUTS 400QX216-1	YR	4.00	25.00
81	BETSEY CLARK 900QX423-5	YR	9.00	61.00
81	BETSEY CLARK BLUE CAMEO QX 512-2	YR	8.50	25.00
81	DISNEY 450QX805-5	YR	4.50	22.00
81	JOAN WALSH ANGLUND 450QX804-2	YR	4.50	25.00
81	MARTY LINKS 450QX808-2	YR	4.50	16.00
81	MARY HAMILTON 450QX806-2	YR	4.50	17.00
81	MUPPETS 450QX807-5	YR	4.50	25.00
81	PEANUTS 450QX803-5	YR	4.50	28.00
82	BETSEY CLARK 850QX305-6	YR	8.50	24.00
82	DISNEY 450QX217-3	YR	4.50	30.00
82	JOAN WALSH ANGLUND 450QX219-3	YR	4.50	17.00
82	MARY HAMILTON 450QX217-6	YR	4.50	18.00
82	MISS PIGGY & KERMIT 450QX218-3	YR	4.50	40.00
82	MUPPETS PARTY 450QX218-6	YR	4.50	37.00
82	NORMAN ROCKWELL 450QX202-3	YR	4.50	21.00
82	NORMAN ROCKWELL-3RD EDITION 850QX305-3	YR	8.50	20.00
82	PEANUTS 450QX200-6	YR	4.50	30.00
83	BETSEY CLARK 900QX440-1	YR	9.00	28.00
83	DISNEY 450QX212-9	YR	4.50	42.00
83	MARY HAMILTON 450QX213-7	YR	4.50	26.00
83	MISS PIGGY 1300QX405-7	YR	13.00	155.00
83	MUPPETS, THE- 450QX214-7	YR	4.50	47.00
83	NORMAN ROCKWELL 450QX215-7	YR	4.50	42.00
83	PEANUTS 450QX212-7	YR	4.50	30.00
83	SHIRT TALES 450QX214-9	YR	4.50	19.00
84	BETSEY CLARK ANGEL 900QX462-4	YR	9.00	30.00
84	DISNEY 450QX250-4	YR	4.50	34.00
84	KATYBETH 900QX463-1	YR	9.00	22.00
84	KIT 550QX453-4	YR	5.50	22.00
84	MUPPETS, THE- 450QX251-4	YR	4.50	30.00
84	PEANUTS 450QX252-1	YR	4.50	32.00
84	SHIRT TALES 450QX252-4	YR	4.50	20.00
85	BETSEY CLARK 850QX508-5	YR	8.50	25.00
85	DISNEY CHRISTMAS 475QX271-2	YR	4.75	20.00
85	FRAGGLE ROCK HOLIDAY 475QX265-5	YR	4.75	16.00
85	HUGGA BUNCH 500QX271-5	YR	5.00	20.00
85	MERRY SHIRT TALES 475QX267-2	YR	4.75	17.00
85	PEANUTS 475QX266-5	YR	4.75	29.00
85	RAINBOW BRITE AND FRIENDS 475QX268-2	YR	4.75	18.00
86	KATYBETH W/STAR 700QX435-3	YR	7.00	18.00
86	NORMAN ROCKWELL 475QX276-3	YR	4.75	21.00
86	PEANUTS 475QX276-6	YR	4.75	27.00
86	SHIRT TALES PARADE 475QX277-3	YR	4.75	13.00
J. FRANCIS			**PROPERTY ORNAMENTS**	
81	KERMIT THE FROG 900QX424-2	YR	9.00	80.00
82	DIVINE MISS PIGGY, THE 1200QX425-5	YR	12.00	85.00
D. LEE			**PROPERTY ORNAMENTS**	
82	KERMIT THE FROG 1100QX495-6	YR	11.00	90.00
83	KERMIT THE FROG 1100QX495-6	YR	11.00	90.00
84	MUFFIN 550QX442-1	YR	5.50	23.00
D. MCGEHEE			**PROPERTY ORNAMENTS**	
84	NORMAN ROCKWELL QX 251-1	YR	4.50	25.00
85	NORMAN ROCKWELL 475QX266-2	YR	4.75	25.00
M. PYDA-SEVCIK			**PROPERTY ORNAMENTS**	
86	STATUE OF LIBERTY, THE 600QX384-3	YR	6.00	19.00
E. SEALE			**PROPERTY ORNAMENTS**	
83	BETSEY CLARK 650QX404-7	YR	6.50	20.00
84	SNOOPY & WOODSTOCK 750QX439-1	YR	7.50	100.00
86	HEATHCLIFF 750QX436-3	YR	7.50	18.00
L. SICKMAN			**PROPERTY ORNAMENTS**	
75	BETSEY CLARK 250QX163-1	YR	2.50	38.00
75	RAGGEDY ANN & RAGGEDY ANDY 400QX138-1	YR	4.00	65.00
75	RAGGEDY ANN 250QX165-1	YR	2.50	45.00
B. SIEDLER			**PROPERTY ORNAMENTS**	
85	KIT THE SHEPHERD 575QX484-5	YR	5.75	20.00
85	MUFFIN THE ANGEL 575QX483-5	YR	5.75	23.00
85	SNOOPY AND WOODSTOCK 750QX491-5	YR	7.50	75.00
86	PADDINGTON BEAR 600QX435-6	YR	6.00	33.00
86	SNOOPY AND WOODSTOCK 800QX438-3	YR	8.00	38.00
A. ROGERS			**PUPPY LOVE**	
91	PUPPY LOVE 1ST ED. 775QX537-9	YR	7.75	50.00
92	PUPPY LOVE 2ND ED. 775QX448-4	YR	7.75	40.00
93	PUPPY LOVE 3RD ED. 775QX504-5	YR	7.75	20.00
94	PUPPY LOVE 4TH ED. 795QX525-3	YR	8.00	20.00
95	PUPPY LOVE 5TH ED. QX513-7	YR	8.00	20.00
96	PUPPY LOVE 6TH ED. QX565-1	YR	8.00	14.00
97	PUPPY LOVE 7TH ED. QX622-2	YR	8.00	8.00
B. SIEDLER			**REINDEER CHAMPS**	
86	DASHER 1ST ED 750QX422-3	YR	7.50	122.00
87	DANCER 750QX480-9	YR	7.50	45.00

YR	NAME	LIMIT	ISSUE	TREND
88	PRANCER 750QX405-1	YR	7.50	30.00
89	VIXEN 4TH ED 775QX456-2	YR	7.75	20.00
90	COMET 5TH ED 775QX443-3	YR	7.75	25.00
91	CUPID 6TH ED 775QX434-7	YR	7.75	20.00
92	DONNER 7TH ED 875QX528-4	YR	8.75	28.00
93	BLITZEN 8TH ED 875QX433-1	YR	8.75	25.00
*				**ROCKING HORSE**
78	ROCKING HORSE 600QX148-3	YR	6.00	87.00
80	ROCKING HORSE QX 340-7	YR	2.00	23.00
84	ROCKING HORSE 1000QX435-4	YR	10.00	80.00
L. SICKMAN				**ROCKING HORSE**
75	ROCKING HORSE 350QX128-1	YR	3.50	140.00
76	ROCKING HORSE 400QX128-1	YR	4.00	140.00
81	ROCKING HORSE 900QX422-2	YR	9.00	580.00
82	ROCKING HORSE 1000QX502-3	YR	10.00	400.00
83	ROCKING HORSE 1000QX417-7	YR	10.00	290.00
85	ROCKING HORSE 1075QX493-2	YR	10.75	65.00
86	ROCKING HORSE 1075QX401-6	YR	10.75	55.00
87	ROCKING HORSE 1075QX482-9	YR	10.75	50.00
88	DAPPLED 450QXM562-4	YR	4.50	42.00
88	ROCKING HORSE 1075QX402-4	YR	10.75	50.00
89	PALOMINO 450QXM560-5	YR	4.50	27.00
89	ROCKING HORSE 1075QX462-2	YR	10.75	35.00
90	PINTO 450QXM574-3	YR	4.50	22.00
90	ROCKING HORSE 1075QX464-6	YR	10.75	75.00
91	GREY ARABIAN 450QXM563-7	YR	4.50	22.00
91	ROCKING HORSE 1075QX414-7	YR	10.75	30.00
92	BROWN HORSE 450QXM5454	YR	4.50	17.00
92	ROCKING HORSE 1075QX426-1	YR	10.75	35.00
93	APPALOOSA 450QXM511-2	YR	4.50	12.00
93	ROCKING HORSE 1075QX416-2	YR	10.75	30.00
94	ROCKING HORSE 1095QX501-6	YR	11.00	30.00
94	WHITE 450QXM511-6	YR	4.50	14.00
95	ROCKING HORSE QX516-7	YR	11.00	30.00
96	ROCKING HORSE QX567-4	YR	11.00	20.00
96	ROCKING HORSE QXM412-1	YR	4.75	5.00
L. SICKMAN				**SACRED MASTERWORKS**
96	MADONNA AND CHILD QK114-4	YR	16.00	16.00
96	PRAYING MADONNA QK115-4	YR	16.00	16.00
K. CROW			**SANTA & HIS REINDEER COLLECTION**	
92	COMET & CUPID 495XPR973-7	YR	5.00	11.00
92	DASHER & DANCER 495XPR973-5	YR	5.00	16.00
92	DONDER & BLITZEN 495XPR973-8	YR	5.00	16.00
92	PRANCER & VIXEN 495XPR973-6	YR	5.00	11.00
92	SANTA & SLEIGH 495XPR973-9	YR	5.00	17.00
*				**SANTA & SPARKY**
87	PERFECT PORTRAIT 1950QLX701-9	YR	20.00	45.00
88	ON WITH THE SNOW 1950QLX719-1	YR	20.00	30.00
*			**SANTA CLAUS-THE MOVIE**	
85	SANTA CLAUS 675QX300-5	YR	6.75	5.00
85	SANTA'S VILLLAGE 675QX300-2	YR	6.75	5.00
K. CROW			**SANTA'S LITTLE BIG TOP**	
96	SANTA'S LITTLE BIG TOP 2ND ED QXM408-1	YR	6.75	10.00
*			**SARAH, PLAIN AND TALL COLLECTION**	
94	COUNTRY CHURCH, THE 795XPR945-0	YR	8.00	19.00
94	HAYS TRAIN STATION, THE-795XPR945-2	YR	8.00	17.00
94	MRS. PARKLEY'S GENERAL STORE 795XPR945-1	YR	8.00	16.00
94	SARAH'S MAINE HOME 795XPR945-4	YR	8.00	22.00
94	SARAH'S PRAIRIE HOME 795XPR945-3	YR	8.00	20.00
*				**SEWN TRIMMERS**
79	ANGEL MUSIC 200QX343-9	YR	2.00	19.00
79	MERRY SANTA 200QX342-7	YR	2.00	21.00
79	ROCKING HORSE, THE 200QX340-7	YR	2.00	23.00
79	STUFFED FULL STOCKING 200QX341-9	YR	2.00	24.00
P. ANDREWS		**SHOWCASE ORNAMENTS/CHRISTMAS LIGHTS**		
94	MOONBEAMS 1575QK111-6	YR	15.75	21.00
R. CHAD		**SHOWCASE ORNAMENTS/CHRISTMAS LIGHTS**		
94	PEACEFUL VILLAGE 1575QK110-6	YR	15.75	23.00
D. PALMITER		**SHOWCASE ORNAMENTS/CHRISTMAS LIGHTS**		
94	HOME FOR THE HOLIDAYS 1575QK112-3	YR	15.75	21.00
A. ROGERS		**SHOWCASE ORNAMENTS/CHRISTMAS LIGHTS**		
94	MOTHER AND CHILD 1575QK112-6	YR	15.75	27.00
*				**SIDEWALK CRUISERS**
98	1939 MOBO HORSE 1295QEO8393	YR	13.00	13.00
J. LYLE				**SPECIAL EDITION**
95	VICTORIAN TOY BOX QLX735-7	YR	42.00	47.00
96	EVERGREEN SANTA QX571-4	YR	22.00	40.00
D. RHODUS				**SPECIAL EDITION**
96	O HOLY NIGHT- 4 PC QXM420-4	YR	25.00	25.00
E. SEALE				**SPECIAL EDITION**
96	NORTH POLE VOLUNTEERS QLX747-1	YR	42.00	70.00
L. SICKMAN				**SPECIAL EDITION**
96	AFRICAN ELEPHANTS QXM422-4	YR	5.75	6.00

YR	NAME	LIMIT	ISSUE	TREND
D. UNRUH				**SPECIAL EDITION**
95	BEVERLY AND TEDDY QX525-9	YR	22.00	24.00
*				**STAR TREK**
*	ROMULAN WAR BIRD	YR	*	35.00
96	COMMANDER WILLIAM T. RIKER 1555-1	YR	15.00	25.00
96	MR. SPOCK	YR	15.00	25.00
97	COMMANDER DATA 1634-5	YR	15.00	15.00
97	DR. LEONARD H. MCCOY 1635-2	YR	15.00	15.00
97	U.S.S. DEFIANT	YR	24.00	25.00
L. NORTON				**STAR TREK**
91	STARSHIP ENTERPRISE 2000QLX719-9	YR	20.00	375.00
94	KLINGON BIRD OF PREY 2400QLX738-6	YR	24.00	31.00
95	ROMULAN WARBIRD QX1726-7	YR	24.00	35.00
96	STAR TREK 30 YEARS QXI753-4	YR	45.00	45.00
96	U.S.S. VOYAGER QXI754-4	YR	24.00	35.00
D. RHODUS				**STAR TREK**
96	U.S.S. ENTERPRISE QXI753-4	YR	45.00	45.00
A. ROGERS				**STAR TREK**
95	CAPTAIN JAMES T. KIRK QX1553-9	YR	14.00	31.00
95	CAPTAIN JEAN-LUC PICARD QX1573-7	YR	14.00	27.00
A. ROGERS				**STAR TREK COLLECTION**
96	MR. SPOCK QXI554-4	OP	14.95	15.00
*				**STAR WARS**
97	C-3PO & R2-D2 1426-5	YR	13.00	13.00
97	DARTH VADER 1753-1	YR	24.00	25.00
97	LUKE SKYWALKER 1548-4	YR	14.00	20.00
98	STAR WARS LUNCHBOX 1259QEO8406	YR	13.00	13.00
K. CROW				**STAR WARS**
96	MILLENNIUM FALCON QLX747-4	YR	24.00	55.00
D. RHODUS				**STAR WARS**
96	VEHICLES OF STAR WARS, THE SET OF 3 QXM402-4	YR	20.00	40.00
E. SEALE				**STOCK CAR CHAMPIONS**
97	JEFF GORDON 1616-5	YR	16.00	30.00
*				**SYMBOLS OF CHRISTMAS**
95	JOLLY SANTA QX108-7	YR	16.00	20.00
95	SWEET SONG QX108-9	YR	16.00	20.00
*				**TALE OF PETER RABBIT**
94	BEATRIX POTTER 500QX244-3	YR	5.00	11.00
K. CROW				**TEDDY BEAR YEARS COLLECTION**
94	BABY'S SECOND CHRISTMAS 795QX571-6	YR	8.00	12.00
95	BABY'S FIRST CHRISTMAS QX 555-9	YR	8.00	18.00
95	BABY'S SECOND CHRISTMAS QX556-7	YR	8.00	13.00
95	CHILD'S THIRD CHRISTMAS QX562-7	YR	8.00	15.00
J. FRANCIS				**TEDDY BEAR YEARS COLLECTION**
94	CHILD'S FOURTH CHRISTMAS 695QX572-6	YR	7.00	12.00
94	CHILD'S THIRD CHRISTMAS 695QX572-3	YR	7.00	11.00
95	CHILD'S FOURTH CHRISTMAS QX562-9	YR	7.00	15.00
D. RHODUS				**TEDDY BEAR YEARS COLLECTION**
94	CHILD'S FIFTH CHRISTMAS 695QX573-3	YR	7.00	11.00
95	CHILD'S FIFTH CHRISTMAS QX563-7	YR	7.00	13.00
E. SEALE				**TENDER TOUCHES**
91	FANFARE BEAR 875QX533-7	YR	8.75	17.00
91	GLEE CLUB BEARS 875QX496-9	YR	8.75	18.00
91	LOOK OUT BELOW 875QX495-9	YR	8.75	18.00
91	LOVING STITCHES 875QX498-7	YR	8.75	28.00
91	PLUM DELIGHTFUL 875QX497-7	YR	8.75	16.00
91	SNOW TWINS 875QX497-9	YR	8.75	16.00
93	DOWNHILL DASH	YR	23.00	23.00
93	GARDEN CAPERS	YR	20.00	20.00
93	HANDLING BIG THIRST	YR	21.00	21.00
93	LIBERTY MOUSE	YR	21.00	21.00
93	MR. REPAIR BEAR	YR	18.00	18.00
93	PATRIOT GEORGE	YR	25.00	25.00
93	SCULPTING SANTA	YR	20.00	20.00
93	STITCHING STARS	YR	21.00	21.00
93	TEETER FOR TWO	YR	23.00	23.00
94	"TENTS" SITUATIONS	YR	25.00	25.00
94	CHIPMUNK KETTLEDRUM	RT	18.00	21.00
94	CHRISTMAS PLAYERS	YR	25.00	25.00
94	EASTER STROLL	YR	21.00	21.00
94	LOVE AT FIRST SIGHT	YR	23.00	23.00
94	MAKING A SPLASH	YR	20.00	20.00
94	OLD SWIMMING HOLE, THE	9500	60.00	60.00
94	PLAYGROUND GO ROUND	YR	23.00	23.00
94	SOMETHING'S BREWING	YR	23.00	23.00
94	TEE FOR TWO	YR	23.00	23.00
94	WHERE'S THE FIRE	YR	25.00	25.00
A. ROGERS				**THE NEXT GENERATION**
96	COMMANDER WILLIAM T. RIKER QXI555-1	OP	14.95	15.00
*				**THIMBLE SERIES**
78	THIMBLE W/MOUSE 300QX133-6	YR	3.00	250.00
79	THIMBLE CHRISTMAS SALUTE, A 400QX131-9	YR	4.00	120.00
80	THIMBLE ELF 400QX132-1	YR	4.00	135.00

YR	NAME	LIMIT	ISSUE	TREND
81	THIMBLE ANGEL 450QX413-5	YR	4.50	120.00
82	THIMBLE 500QX451-3	YR	5.00	62.00
83	THIMBLE ELF 500QX401-7	YR	5.00	35.00
86	THIMBLE PARTRIDGE 575QX406-6	YR	5.75	25.00
A. ROGERS				**THIMBLE SERIES**
89	THIMBLE PUPPY 575QX455-2	YR	5.75	20.00
B. SIEDLER				**THIMBLE SERIES**
84	THIMBLE ANGEL 500QX430-4	YR	5.00	46.00
85	THIMBLE SANTA QX 472-5	YR	5.50	27.00
87	THIMBLE DRUMMER 575QX441-9	YR	5.75	24.00
88	THIMBLE SNOWMAN 575QX405-4	YR	5.75	20.00
D. RHODUS			**THOMAS THE TANK ENGINE & FRIENDS**	
96	PERCY THE SMALL ENGINE-NO. 6 QX631-4	YR	10.00	25.00
J. LYLE				**TIME FOR LOVE**
90	CARDINALS 475QX213-3	YR	4.75	14.00
L. SICKMAN				**TIN LOCOMOTIVE**
82	TIN LOCOMOTIVE-1ST EDITION 1300QX460-3	YR	13.00	600.00
83	TIN LOCOMOTIVE-2ND EDITION 1300QX404-9	YR	13.00	260.00
84	TIN LOCOMOTIVE-3RD EDITION 1400QX440-4	YR	14.00	75.00
85	TIN LOCOMOTIVE-4TH EDITION 1475QX497-2	YR	14.75	71.00
86	TIN LOCOMOTIVE-5TH EDITION 1475QX403-6	YR	14.75	50.00
87	TIN LOCOMOTIVE-6TH EDITION 1475QX484-9	YR	14.75	57.00
88	TIN LOCOMOTIVE-7TH EDITION 1475QX400-4	YR	14.75	41.00
89	TIN LOCOMOTIVE-8TH EDITION 1475QX460-2	YR	14.75	35.00
D. PALMITER				**TINY TOON ADVENTURE**
94	BABS BUNNY 575QXM411-6	YR	5.75	12.00
94	BUSTER BUNNY 575QXM516-3	YR	5.75	12.00
94	DIZZY DEVIL 575QXM413-3	YR	5.75	14.00
94	HAMTON 575QXM412-6	YR	5.75	12.00
94	PLUCKY DUCK 575QXM412-3	YR	5.75	12.00
T. FRALEY				**TOBIN FRALEY CAROUSEL**
92	TOBIN FRALEY CAROUSEL 2800QX489-1	YR	28.00	50.00
93	TOBIN FRALEY CAROUSEL 2ND ED. 2800QX550-2	YR	28.00	30.00
94	TOBIN FRALEY CAROUSEL 3RD ED. 2800QX522-3	YR	28.00	50.00
95	TOBIN FRALEY CAROUSEL 4TH AND FINAL QX506-9	YR	28.00	29.00
95	TOBIN FRALEY HOLIDAY CAROUSEL 2ND ED. QLX726-9	YR	32.00	40.00
J. FRANCIS				**TOBIN FRALEY CAROUSEL**
96	TOBIN FRALEY HOLIDAY CAROUSEL 3RD/ FINAL QLC746-1	YR	32.00	32.00
D. UNRUH				**TOBIN FRALEY CAROUSEL**
94	TOBIN FRALEY HOLIDAY CAROUSEL 1ST ED. 3200QLX749-6	YR	32.00	50.00
*				**TONKA**
96	TONKA MIGHTY DUMP TRUCK QX632-1	YR	14.00	25.00
97	MIGHTY FRONT LOADER 636-2	YR	14.00	14.00
*				**TRADITIONAL ORNAMENTS**
84	AMANDA DOLL 900QX432-1	YR	9.00	30.00
84	EMBROIDERED HEART 650QX421-7	YR	6.50	19.00
84	HOLIDAY FRIENDSHIP 1300QX445-1	YR	13.00	26.00
84	HOLIDAY STARBURST 500QX253-4	YR	5.00	16.00
84	OLD FASHIONED ROCKING HORSE 750QX346-4	YR	7.50	16.00
84	PEACE ON EARTH 750QX341-4	YR	7.50	20.00
84	SANTA 750QX458-4	YR	7.50	15.00
84	SANTA SULKY DRIVER 900QX436-1	YR	9.00	22.00
84	SAVIOR IS BORN, A 450QX254-1	YR	4.50	25.00
84	WHITE CHRISTMAS 1600QX905-1	YR	16.00	75.00
84	XMAS MEMORIES PHOTOHOLDER 650QX300-4	YR	6.50	24.00
85	CHRISTMAS TREATS 550QX507-5	YR	5.50	15.00
85	OLD-FASHIONED WREATH 750QX373-5	YR	7.50	19.00
86	HOLIDAY JINGLE BELL 1600QX404-6	YR	16.00	37.00
86	MEMORIES TO CHERISH PHOTO. QX 427-6	YR	7.50	21.00
87	SPECIAL MEMORIES PHOTOHOLDER 675QX464-7	YR	6.75	17.00
K. CROW				**TRADITIONAL ORNAMENTS**
87	HEAVENLY HARMONY 1500QX465-9	YR	15.00	31.00
87	PROMISE OF PEACE 650QX374-9	YR	11.00	16.00
P. DUTKIN				**TRADITIONAL ORNAMENTS**
85	SANTA PIPE 950QX494-2	YR	9.50	19.00
D. LEE				**TRADITIONAL ORNAMENTS**
84	CUCKOO CLOCK 1000QX455-1	YR	10.00	43.00
85	SPIRIT OF SANTA CLAUS, THE- 2250QX498-5	YR	23.00	80.00
J. LYLE				**TRADITIONAL ORNAMENTS**
87	I REMEMBER SANTA 475QX278-9	YR	4.75	22.00
87	NORMAN ROCKWELL: XMAS SCENES 475QX282-7	YR	4.75	18.00
D. PALMITER				**TRADITIONAL ORNAMENTS**
84	MADONNA AND CHILD 600QX344-1	YR	6.00	27.00
J. PATTEE				**TRADITIONAL ORNAMENTS**
86	CHRISTMAS BEAUTY 600QX322-3	YR	6.00	7.00
86	GLOWING CHRISTMAS TREE 700QX428-6	YR	7.00	12.00
86	HEIRLOOM SNOWFLAKE 675QX515-3	YR	6.75	14.00
S. PIKE				**TRADITIONAL ORNAMENTS**
84	NEEDLEPOINT WREATH 650QX459-4	YR	6.50	12.00
85	CANDLE CAMEO 675QX374-2	YR	6.75	14.00
85	PEACEFUL KINGDOM 575QX373-2	YR	5.75	16.00
85	SEWN PHOTOHOLDER 700QX379-5	YR	7.00	25.00
86	MAGI, THE- 475QX272-6	YR	4.75	17.00

YR NAME	LIMIT	ISSUE	TREND
E. SEALE		**TRADITIONAL ORNAMENTS**	
84 ALPINE ELF 600QX452-1	YR	6.00	29.00
84 GIFT OF MUSIC 1500QX451-1	YR	15.00	87.00
84 TWELVE DAYS OF CHRISTMAS 1500QX415-9	YR	15.00	77.00
87 JOYOUS ANGEL 775QX465-7	YR	7.75	17.00
L. SICKMAN		**TRADITIONAL ORNAMENTS**	
84 CHICKADEE 600QX451-4	YR	6.00	33.00
84 EMBROIDERED STOCKING 650QX479-6	YR	6.50	16.00
84 HOLIDAY JESTER 1100QX437-4	YR	11.00	26.00
84 NOSTALGIC SLED 600QX442-4	YR	6.00	15.00
84 UNCLE SAM 600QX449-1	YR	6.00	37.00
85 NOSTALGIC SLED 600QX442-4	YR	6.00	20.00
86 BLUEBIRD 725QX428-3	YR	7.25	42.00
87 GOLDFINCH 700QX464-9	YR	7.00	49.00
D. UNRUH		**TRADITIONAL ORNAMENTS**	
87 CHRISTMAS KEYS 575QX473-9	YR	5.75	22.00
L. VOTRUBA		**TRADITIONAL ORNAMENTS**	
86 STAR BRIGHTENERS 600QX322-6	YR	6.00	10.00
*		**TREE TOPPER**	
77 ANGEL TREE TOPPER 900HD230-2	YR	9.00	425.00
79 TIFFANY ANGEL TREE TOPPER 1000QX703-7	YR	10.00	31.00
84 ANGEL TREE TOPPER 2450QTT710-1	YR	25.00	36.00
86 SANTA TREE TOPPER 1800QTO700-6	SAN	18.00	35.00
86 SHINING STAR 1750QLT709-6	YR	17.50	20.00
K. CROW		**TURN OF THE CENTURY PARADE**	
95 FIREMAN, THE FIRST ED QK102-7	YR	17.00	45.00
96 UNCLE SAM 2ND ED QK108-4	YR	17.00	25.00
*		**TWELVE DAYS OF CHRISTMAS**	
84 PARTRIDGE IN A PEAR TREE 600QX348-4	YR	6.00	300.00
89 SIX GEESE A-LAYING 675QX381-2	YR	6.75	25.00
90 SEVEN SWANS-A-SWIMMING 675QX303-3	YR	6.75	18.00
91 EIGHT MAIDS-A-MILKING 675QX308-9	YR	6.75	18.00
93 TEN LORDS A LEAPING 301-2	YR	*	20.00
94 ELEVEN PIPERS PIPING 695QX318-3	YR	7.00	14.00
95 TWELVE DRUMMERS DRUMMING QX300-9	YR	7.00	15.00
S. PIKE		**TWELVE DAYS OF CHRISTMAS**	
85 TWO TURTLEDOVES 650QX371-2	YR	6.50	70.00
87 FOUR COLLY BIRDS 650QX370-9	YR	6.50	34.00
88 FIVE GOLDEN RINGS 650QX371-4	YR	6.50	30.00
M. PYDA-SEVCIK		**TWELVE DAYS OF CHRISTMAS**	
92 NINE LADIES DANCING 675QX303-1	YR	6.75	18.00
L. VOTRUBA		**TWELVE DAYS OF CHRISTMAS**	
86 THREE FRENCH HENS 650QX378-6	YR	6.50	46.00
*		**U.S. CHRISTMAS STAMPS**	
94 U.S. CHRISTMAS STAMPS 1095QX520-6	YR	11.00	20.00
95 U.S. CHRISTMAS STAMPS QX506-7	YR	11.00	20.00
L. SICKMAN		**U.S. CHRISTMAS STAMPS**	
93 U.S. CHRISTMAS STAMPS 1075QX529-2	YR	10.75	40.00
D. PALMITER		**VINTAGE ROADSTER**	
98 1931 FORD MODEL A ROADSTER 1495QEO8416	YR	15.00	15.00
D. LEE		**WINDOWS OF THE WORLD**	
85 MEXICAN QX 490-2	YR	9.75	70.00
87 HAWAIIAN 1000QX482-7	YR	10.00	18.00
88 FRENCH 1000QX402-1	YR	10.00	22.00
89 GERMAN 5TH ED. 1075QX462-5	YR	10.75	20.00
90 IRISH 1075QX463-6	YR	10.75	16.00
B. SIEDLER		**WINDOWS OF THE WORLD**	
86 DUTCH 1000QX408-3	YR	10.00	45.00
B. SIEDLER		**WINNIE THE POOH COLLECTION**	
91 CHRISTOPHER ROBIN 975QX557-9	YR	9.75	40.00
91 KANGA AND ROO 975QX561-7	YR	9.75	35.00
91 PIGLET AND EEYORE 975QX557-7	YR	9.75	50.00
91 RABBIT 975QX560-7	YR	9.75	30.00
91 TIGGER 975QX560-9	YR	9.75	97.00
91 WINNIE-THE POOH 975QX556-9	YR	9.75	52.00
92 OWL 975QX561-4	YR	9.75	24.00
93 EEYORE 975-QX571-2	YR	9.75	20.00
93 KANGA AND ROO 975QX567-2	YR	9.75	20.00
93 OWL 975QX569-5	YR	9.75	20.00
93 RABBIT 975QX570-2	YR	9.75	20.00
93 TIGGER AND PIGLET 975QX570-5	YR	9.75	40.00
93 WINNIE THE POOH 975QX571-5	YR	9.75	30.00
96 SLIPPERY DAY QLX741-4	YR	25.00	40.00
P. ANDREWS		**WIZARD OF OZ COLLECTION**	
94 COWARDLY LION, THE 995QX544-6	YR	10.00	40.00
K. CROW		**WIZARD OF OZ COLLECTION**	
96 EMERALD CITY QLX745-4	YR	32.00	60.00
J. LYLE		**WIZARD OF OZ COLLECTION**	
94 DOROTHY AND TOTO 1095QX543-3	YR	11.00	60.00
95 GLINDA, WITCH OF THE NORTH QX574-9	YR	14.00	30.00
96 WITCH OF THE WEST QX555-4	YR	14.00	25.00
97 MISS GULCH 637-2	YR	14.00	16.00

YR	NAME	LIMIT	ISSUE	TREND
D. UNRUH		**WIZARD OF OZ COLLECTION**		
94	SCARECROW 995QX543-6	YR	10.00	45.00
94	TIN MAN 995QX544-3	YR	10.00	45.00
*		**WOOD CHILDHOOD**		
89	TRUCK 6TH ED. 775QX459-5	YR	7.75	18.00
K. CROW		**WOOD CHILDHOOD**		
86	REINDEER 750QX407-3	YR	7.50	22.00
P. DUTKIN		**WOOD CHILDHOOD**		
85	TRAIN-2ND IN SERIES 700QX472-2	YR	7.00	36.00
88	AIRPLANE, 5TH ED. 750QX404-1	YR	7.50	16.00
B. SIEDLER		**WOOD CHILDHOOD**		
87	HORSE 750QX441-7	YR	7.50	17.00
T. HADDIX		**WORLD OF WISHES**		
98	HAPPY DIPLOMA DAY! 795QEO8476	YR	8.00	8.00
K. KLINE		**WORLD OF WISHES**		
98	SWEET BIRTHDAY 795QEO8473	YR	8.00	8.00
S. TAGUE		**WORLD OF WISHES**		
98	PRECIOUS BABY 995QEO8463	YR	10.00	10.00
L. VOTRUBA		**WORLD OF WISHES**		
98	WEDDING MEMORIES 995QEO8466	YR	10.00	10.00
L. VOTRUBA		**WORLD OF WISHES-SPOONFUL OF STARS**		
98	SPECIAL FRIENDS 1295QEO8523	YR	13.00	13.00
*		**YARN ORNAMENTS**		
73	ANGEL 125XHD78-5	YR	1.25	29.00
73	BLUE GIRL 125XHD85-2	YR	1.25	25.00
73	BOY CAROLER 125XHD83-2	YR	1.25	26.00
73	CHOIR BOY 125XHD80-5	YR	1.25	27.00
73	ELF 125XHD79-2	YR	1.25	26.00
73	GREEN GIRL 125XHD84-5	YR	1.25	26.00
73	LITTLE GIRL 125XHD82-5	YR	1.25	23.00
73	MR. SANTA 125XHD74-5	YR	1.25	27.00
73	MR. SNOWMAN 125XHD76-5	YR	1.25	23.00
73	MRS. SANTA 125XHD75-2	YR	1.25	25.00
73	MRS. SNOWMAN 125XHD77-2	YR	1.25	23.00
73	SOLDIER 100XHD81-2	YR	1.00	23.00
74	ANGEL 150QX103-1	YR	1.50	30.00
74	ELF 150QX101-1	YR	1.50	26.00
74	MRS. SANTA 150QX100-1	YR	1.50	27.00
74	SANTA 150QX105-1	YR	1.50	27.00
74	SNOWMAN 150QX104-1	YR	1.50	23.00
74	SOLDIER 150QX102-1	YR	1.50	23.00
75	DRUMMER BOY 175QX123-1	YR	1.75	26.00
75	LITTLE GIRL 175QX126-1	YR	1.75	22.00
75	MRS. SANTA 175QX125-1	YR	1.75	24.00
75	RAGGEDY ANDY 175QX122-1	YR	1.75	35.00
75	RAGGEDY ANN 175QX121-1	YR	1.75	37.00
75	SANTA 175QX124-1	YR	1.75	23.00
76	CAROLER 175QX126-1	YR	1.75	22.00
76	DRUMMER BOY 175QX123-1	YR	1.75	27.00
76	MRS. SANTA 175QX125-1	YR	1.75	24.00
76	RAGGEDY ANDY 175QX122-1	YR	1.75	35.00
76	RAGGEDY ANN 175QX121-1	YR	1.75	35.00
76	SANTA 175QX124-1	YR	1.75	23.00
78	GREEN BOY 200QX123-1	YR	2.00	23.00
78	GREEN GIRL 200QX126-1	YR	2.00	19.00
78	MR. CLAUS 200QX340-3	YR	2.00	23.00
78	MRS. CLAUS 200QX125-1	YR	2.00	24.00
80	ANGEL 300QX162-1	YR	3.00	11.00
80	SANTA 300QX161-4	YR	3.00	11.00
80	SNOWMAN 300QX163-4	YR	3.00	11.00
80	SOLDIER 300QX164-1	YR	3.00	11.00
*		**YESTERYEARS COLLECTION**		
77	ANGEL 600QX172-2	YR	6.00	90.00
77	HOUSE 600QX170-2	YR	6.00	100.00
77	JACK-IN-THE-BOX 600QX171-5	YR	6.00	80.00
77	REINDEER 600QX173-5	YR	6.00	100.00
L. SICKMAN		**YULETIDE CENTRAL**		
94	LOCOMOTIVE 1ST ED. 1895QX531-6	YR	19.00	50.00
95	RAILROAD COAL CAR 2ND SERIES QX507-9	YR	19.00	35.00
96	MAIL CAR 3RD ED. QX501-1	YR	19.00	19.00
97	TOY FREIGHT CAR 4TH ED. 5812	YR	19.00	19.00

HAMILTON GIFTS

	M. HUMPHREY BOGART	MAUD HUMPHREY BOGART ORNAMENTS		
89	SARAH H1367	19500	35.00	38.00
90	CATHERINE H1366	19500	35.00	38.00
90	GRETCHEN H1369	19500	35.00	38.00
90	MICHELLE H1370	19500	35.00	38.00
90	REBECCA H5513	19500	35.00	38.00
90	VICTORIA H1365	19500	35.00	38.00
91	CLEANING HOUSE 915084	OP	24.00	24.00
91	GIFT OF LOVE 915092	OP	24.00	24.00
91	MY FIRST DANCE 915106	OP	24.00	24.00
91	SARAH 915165	OP	24.00	24.00

Snuffy, *one of the many elves Sandi Zimnicki has designed for Enesco Corp.'s Treasury of Christmas collection, stands just 3-3/4" tall.*

Produced by Enesco Corp., Bundles of Joy *from the Precious Moments collection was named the 1991 Ornament of the Year by NALED, the Worldwide Association of Gift and Collectible Retailers.*

Oh Holy Night, *produced by Enesco Corp. as part of Sam Butcher's Precious Moments collection, had an issue price of $13.50 in 1989. It is now worth almost three times as much.*

Gorham produced these two sterling silver ornaments for 1988. The Victorian Heart *and* Sterling Snowflake *were both issued at $50.*

YR	NAME	LIMIT	ISSUE	TREND
91	SPECIAL FRIENDS 915114	OP	24.00	24.00
91	SUSANNA 915122	OP	24.00	24.00
92	HOLLIES FOR YOU 915726	YR	24.00	24.00

HAND & HAMMER
C. DEMATTEO

YR	NAME	LIMIT	ISSUE	TREND
		HAND & HAMMER ANNUAL ORNAMENTS		
87	SILVER BELLS-737	CL	38.00	50.00
88	SILVER BELLS-792	CL	40.00	40.00
89	SILVER BELLS-843	CL	40.00	40.00
90	SILVER BELLS REV.-964	CL	39.00	39.00
90	SILVER BELLS-1080	CL	40.00	40.00
90	SILVER BELLS-865	CL	39.00	39.00
91	SILVER BELLS-1080	CL	40.00	40.00
92	SILVER BELLS-1148	CL	40.00	40.00

C. DEMATTEO

YR	NAME	LIMIT	ISSUE	TREND
		HAND & HAMMER ORNAMENTS		
80	ICICLE-009	490	25.00	30.00
81	GABRIEL WITH LIBERTY CAP-301	275	25.00	50.00
81	GABRIEL-320	SU	25.00	32.00
81	ROUNDEL-109	220	25.00	45.00
82	CARVED HEART-425	SU	29.00	48.00
82	FLEUR DE LYS ANGEL-343	320	28.00	75.00
82	MADONNA & CHILD-388	175	28.00	50.00
82	STRAW STAR-448	590	25.00	40.00
83	CALLIGRAPHIC DEER-511	SU	25.00	29.00
83	CHERUB-528	295	29.00	50.00
83	DOVE-522	*	13.00	13.00
83	EGYPTIAN CAT-521	*	13.00	13.00
83	FIRE ANGEL-473	315	25.00	30.00
83	INDIAN-494	190	29.00	50.00
83	JAPANESE SNOWFLAKE-534	350	29.00	35.00
83	POLLOCK ANGEL-502	SU	35.00	50.00
83	SARGENT ANGEL-523	690	29.00	34.00
83	SUNBURST-543	*	13.00	50.00
83	WISE MAN-549	RT	29.00	55.00
84	BEARDSLEY ANGEL-398	OP	28.00	48.00
84	BIRD & CHERUB-588	*	13.00	30.00
84	BUNNY-582	*	13.00	30.00
84	CRESCENT ANGEL-559	SU	30.00	32.00
84	FREER STAR-553	*	13.00	30.00
84	IBEX-584	400	29.00	70.00
84	MANGER-601	RT	29.00	50.00
84	MORAVIAN STAR-595	OP	38.00	50.00
84	MT. VERNON WEATHERVANE-602	SU	32.00	39.00
84	NINE HEARTS-572	275	34.00	50.00
84	PINEAPPLE-558	SU	30.00	38.00
84	PRAYING ANGEL-576	SU	29.00	30.00
84	ROCKING HORSE-581	*	13.00	13.00
84	ROSETTE-571	220	32.00	50.00
84	USHS 1984 ANGEL-574	SU	35.00	50.00
84	WILD SWAN-592	SU	35.00	50.00
84	WREATH-575	*	13.00	30.00
85	ABIGAIL-613	500	32.00	50.00
85	ANGEL-607	225	36.00	50.00
85	ANGEL-612	217	32.00	50.00
85	ART DECO DEER-620	SU	34.00	38.00
85	AUDUBON BLUEBIRD-615	SU	48.00	60.00
85	AUDUBON SWALLOW-614	SU	48.00	60.00
85	BICYCLE-669	*	13.00	30.00
85	BUTTERFLY-646	RT	39.00	39.00
85	CAMEL-655	*	13.00	30.00
85	CAROUSEL PONY-618	*	13.00	13.00
85	CHERUB-642	815	37.00	37.00
85	CRANE-606	150	39.00	50.00
85	EAGLE-652	375	30.00	120.00
85	FAMILY-659	915	32.00	40.00
85	FRENCH QUARTER HEART-647	OP	37.00	37.00
85	GEORGE WASHINGTON-629	SU	35.00	39.00
85	GRASSHOPPER-634	OP	32.00	39.00
85	GUARDIAN ANGEL-616	1340	35.00	39.00
85	HALLEY'S COMET-621	432	35.00	50.00
85	HERALD ANGEL-641	RT	36.00	40.00
85	HOSANNA-635	715	32.00	50.00
85	LAFARGE ANGEL-658	SU	32.00	50.00
85	LIBERTY BELL-611	SU	32.00	40.00
85	MADONNA-666	227	35.00	50.00
85	MERMAID-622	RT	35.00	75.00
85	MILITIAMAN-608	460	25.00	30.00
85	MODEL A FORD-604	*	13.00	30.00
85	NUTCRACKER-609	510	30.00	50.00
85	OLD NORTH CHURCH-661	OP	35.00	39.00
85	PEACOCK-603	470	34.00	37.00
85	PIAZZA-653	SU	32.00	50.00
85	REINDEER-656	*	13.00	30.00
85	SAMANTHA-648	SU	35.00	36.00
85	SHEPHERD-617	1770	35.00	39.00

YR	NAME	LIMIT	ISSUE	TREND
85	ST. NICHOLAS-670	*	13.00	30.00
85	TEDDY-637	SU	37.00	40.00
85	UNICORN-660	RT	37.00	50.00
85	USHS BLUEBIRD-631	SU	29.00	50.00
85	USHS MADONNA-630	SU	35.00	50.00
85	USHS SWALLOW-632	SU	29.00	50.00
86	ARCHANGEL-684	RT	29.00	65.00
86	BEAR CLAUS-692	*	13.00	13.00
86	CHRISTMAS TREE-708	*	13.00	13.00
86	HALLELUJAH-686	*	38.00	38.00
86	KRINGLE BEAR-723	*	13.00	30.00
86	LAFARGE ANGEL-710	SU	31.00	50.00
86	MOTHER GOOSE-719	OP	34.00	40.00
86	NATIVITY-679	RT	36.00	50.00
86	NIGHTINGALE-716	RT	35.00	70.00
86	NUTCRACKER-681	1356	37.00	37.00
86	PHAETON-683	*	13.00	13.00
86	PRANCER-698	OP	38.00	38.00
86	SALEM LAMB-712	RT	32.00	70.00
86	SANTA SKATES-715	SU	36.00	36.00
86	SNOWFLAKE-713	RT	36.00	50.00
86	TEDDY BEAR-685	RT	38.00	60.00
86	TEDDY-707	*	13.00	30.00
86	USHS ANGEL-703	SU	35.00	50.00
86	VICTORIAN SANTA-724	250	32.00	35.00
86	WINGED DOVE-680	RT	35.00	55.00
86	WREATH-714	SU	36.00	38.00
87	ANGEL WITH LYRE-750	SU	32.00	40.00
87	ART DECO ANGEL-765	RT	38.00	40.00
87	BUFFALO-777	SU	36.00	36.00
87	CAT-754	SU	37.00	37.00
87	CLIPPER SHIP-756	SU	35.00	35.00
87	DOVE-747	*	13.00	13.00
87	FIRST CHRISTMAS-771	*	13.00	13.00
87	HUNTING HORN-738	SU	37.00	37.00
87	MINUTEMAN-776	SU	35.00	105.00
87	NOEL-731	SU	38.00	38.00
87	OLD IRONSIDES-767	OP	35.00	39.00
87	PEGASUS-745	*	13.00	13.00
87	REINDEER-752	RT	38.00	45.00
87	RIDE A COCK HORSE-757	RT	34.00	40.00
87	SANTA AND SLEIGH-751	RT	32.00	95.00
87	SANTA-741	*	13.00	13.00
87	SNOW QUEEN-746	RT	35.00	70.00
87	SNOWMAN-753	825	38.00	38.00
87	STOCKING-772	*	13.00	13.00
87	SWEETHEART STAR-740	RT	40.00	60.00
87	USHS GLORIA ANGEL-748	SU	39.00	50.00
88	ANGEL-797	*	13.00	13.00
88	ANGEL-818	SU	32.00	40.00
88	BANK-812	400	40.00	115.00
88	BOSTON STATE HOUSE	OP	34.00	40.00
88	BUGGY-817	*	13.00	13.00
88	CABLE CAR-848	OP	38.00	38.00
88	CAROUSEL HORSE-811	2150	34.00	34.00
88	CHRISTMAS TREE-798	*	13.00	13.00
88	CONN. STATE HOUSE-833	OP	38.00	38.00
88	CORONADO-864	SU	38.00	70.00
88	DOVE-786	112	36.00	50.00
88	DRUMMER BEAR-773	*	13.00	13.00
88	EIFFEL TOWER-861	225	38.00	100.00
88	FIRST CHRISTMAS-842	*	13.00	13.00
88	JACK IN THE BOX-789	RT	40.00	40.00
88	LOCKET BEAR-844	*	25.00	25.00
88	MADONNA-787	600	35.00	35.00
88	MADONNA-809	15	39.00	50.00
88	MADONNA-815	SU	39.00	50.00
88	MAGI-788	SU	40.00	40.00
88	NATIVITY-821	SU	32.00	39.00
88	NIGHT BEFORE CHRISTMAS COL.-841	10000	160.00	160.00
88	OLD KING COLE-824	RT	34.00	40.00
88	RABBIT-816	*	13.00	13.00
88	SANTA WITH SCROLL-814	250	34.00	37.00
88	SKATERS-790	RT	40.00	45.00
88	SLEIGH-834	OP	34.00	38.00
88	STAR OF THE EAST-785	RT	35.00	50.00
88	STAR-806	311	13.00	150.00
88	STAR-854	275	32.00	35.00
88	STOCKING BEAR-835	*	13.00	13.00
88	STOCKING-774	*	13.00	13.00
88	STOCKING-827	*	13.00	13.00
88	THUMBELINA-803	RT	35.00	70.00
88	US CAPITOL-820	OP	38.00	40.00
89	1989 BARNESVILLE BUGGY-950	*	13.00	13.00
89	1989 NUTCRACKER-872	1790	38.00	38.00

YR	NAME	LIMIT	ISSUE	TREND
89	1989 SANTA-856	1715	35.00	35.00
89	1989 USHS ANGEL-901	SU	38.00	38.00
89	BUGLE BEAR-935	*	12.00	12.00
89	GOOSE-857	650	37.00	37.00
89	INDEPENDENCE HALL-908	OP	38.00	38.00
89	JACK IN THE BOX BEAR-936	*	12.00	12.00
89	L&T UGLY DUCKLING-917	RT	38.00	70.00
89	MFA ANGEL WITH TREE-906	SU	36.00	42.00
89	MFA DURER SNOWFLAKE-907	2000	36.00	42.00
89	MFA LAFARGE ANGEL SET-937	SU	98.00	98.00
89	MFA NOEL-905	SU	36.00	42.00
89	PRESIDENTIAL SEAL-858	500	39.00	39.00
89	STOCKING BEAR-95	*	12.00	12.00
89	STOCKING WITH TOYS-956	*	12.00	12.00
89	SWAN BOAT-904	OP	38.00	38.00
89	VICTORIAN HEART-954	*	13.00	13.00
90	1990 PETER RABBIT-1018	4315	40.00	40.00
90	1990 SANTA-869	2250	38.00	38.00
90	1990 SNOWFLAKE-1033	1415	36.00	38.00
90	1990 USHS ANGEL-1061	SU	39.00	39.00
90	ANGEL WITH HORN-939	*	*	N/A
90	ANGEL WITH STAR-871	SU	38.00	38.00
90	ANGEL WITH VIOLIN-1024	SU	39.00	39.00
90	ANGELS-1039	RT	36.00	36.00
90	BEARDSLEY ANGEL-1040	RT	34.00	34.00
90	BLAKE ANGEL-961	*	36.00	36.00
90	BOSTON LIGHT, THE-1032	OP	40.00	40.00
90	CARDINALS-870	RT	39.00	39.00
90	CAROUSEL HORSE-866	1915	38.00	38.00
90	CARRIAGE-960	*	13.00	13.00
90	CAT ON PILLOW-915	*	13.00	13.00
90	CHRISTMAS SEAL-931	*	25.00	25.00
90	CHURCH-921	RT	37.00	37.00
90	CLOWN WITH DOG-958	*	13.00	13.00
90	COCKATOO-969	*	13.00	13.00
90	COLONIAL CAPITOL-965	OP	39.00	39.00
90	CONESTOGA WAGON-1027	OP	38.00	38.00
90	COVERED BRIDGE-920	RT	37.00	37.00
90	CURRIER & IVES VICTORIAN VILLAGE-923	2000	140.00	140.00
90	DUCKLINGS-1114	OP	38.00	38.00
90	ELK-1023	*	13.00	13.00
90	FARMHOUSE-919	RT	37.00	37.00
90	FATHER CHRISTMAS-970	SU	36.00	36.00
90	FERREL'S ANGEL 1990-1084	*	15.00	16.00
90	FIRST BAPTIST ANGEL-997	200	35.00	35.00
90	FIRST CHRISTMAS BEAR-940	SU	35.00	35.00
90	FLOPSY BUNNIES-995	SU	40.00	40.00
90	FLORIDA STATE CAPITOL-1044	2000	40.00	40.00
90	GEORGIA STATE CAPITOL-1042	2000	40.00	40.00
90	GOOSE & WREATH-868	RT	37.00	37.00
90	GOVERNOR'S PALACE-966	OP	39.00	39.00
90	HEART ANGEL-959	SU	39.00	39.00
90	JEMIMA PUDDLEDUCK-1020	*	30.00	30.00
90	JEREMY FISHER-992	OP	40.00	40.00
90	JOY-1047	RT	39.00	39.00
90	JOY-867	1140	36.00	36.00
90	KOALA SAN DIEGO ZOO-1095	SU	36.00	36.00
90	LANDING DUCK-1021	*	13.00	13.00
90	LIBERTY BELL-1028	OP	38.00	38.00
90	LOCOMOTIVE-1100	SU	39.00	39.00
90	MERRY CHRISTMAS LOCKET-948	*	25.00	25.00
90	MILL-922	RT	37.00	37.00
90	MOLE & RAT WIND IN WILLOWS-944	SU	36.00	36.00
90	MONTPELIER-1113	OP	36.00	36.00
90	MOUSE WITH CANDY CANE-916	*	13.00	13.00
90	MRS. RABBIT-991	OP	40.00	40.00
90	NORTH CAROLINA STATE CAPITOL-1043	2000	40.00	40.00
90	OLD FASHIONED SANTA-971	SU	36.00	36.00
90	PATRIOTIC SANTA-972	SU	36.00	36.00
90	PEGASUS-1037	SU	35.00	35.00
90	PETER RABBIT LOCKET ORNAMENT-1019	*	30.00	30.00
90	PETER RABBIT-993	OP	40.00	40.00
90	PETER'S FIRST CHRISTMAS-994	SU	40.00	40.00
90	PRESIDENTIAL HOMES-990	SU	350.00	390.00
90	SAN FRANCISCO ROW HOUSE-1071	OP	40.00	40.00
90	SANTA & REINDEER-929	395	39.00	43.00
90	SANTA IN BALLOON-973	SU	36.00	36.00
90	SANTA IN THE MOON-941	SU	38.00	38.00
90	SANTA ON REINDEER-974	SU	36.00	36.00
90	SANTA UP TO DATE-975	SU	36.00	36.00
90	SOUTH CAROLINA STATE CAPITOL-1045	2000	40.00	40.00
90	STEADFAST TIN SOLDIER-1050	RT	36.00	70.00
90	TEDDY BEAR LOCKET-949	*	25.00	25.00
90	TEDDY BEAR WITH HEART-957	*	13.00	13.00
90	TOAD WIND IN WILLOWS-945	SU	38.00	38.00

YR	NAME	LIMIT	ISSUE	TREND
90	WHITE TAIL DEER-1022	*	13.00	13.00
91	1991 SANTA-1056	3750	38.00	38.00
91	ALICE IN WONDERLAND-1159	OP	140.00	140.00
91	ALICE-1119	OP	39.00	39.00
91	ANGEL WITH HORN-1026	OP	32.00	32.00
91	APPLY DAPPLY-1091	OP	40.00	40.00
91	CAROUSEL HORSE-1025	RT	38.00	38.00
91	COLUMBUS-1140	1500	39.00	39.00
91	COW JUMPED OVER THE MOON-1055	SU	38.00	38.00
91	FIR TREE-1145	RT	39.00	39.00
91	I LOVE SANTA-998	OP	36.00	36.00
91	LARGE JEMIMA PUDDLEDUCK-1083	OP	50.00	50.00
91	LARGE PETER RABBIT-1116	OP	50.00	50.00
91	LARGE TAILOR OF GLOUCESTER-1117	OP	50.00	50.00
91	MAD TEA PARTY-1120	OP	39.00	39.00
91	MFA SNOWFLAKE 1991-1143	RT	36.00	45.00
91	MOMMY & BABY KANGAROO-1078	OP	36.00	36.00
91	MOMMY & BABY KOALA BEAR-1077	OP	36.00	36.00
91	MOMMY & BABY PANDA BEAR-1079	RT	36.00	40.00
91	MOMMY & BABY SEAL-1075	OP	36.00	36.00
91	MOMMY & BABY WOLVES-1076	OP	36.00	36.00
91	MRS. RABBIT 1991-1086	RT	40.00	40.00
91	NATIVITY-1118	OP	38.00	38.00
91	NUTCRACKER-1151	OP	50.00	50.00
91	OLIVERS ROCKING HORSE-1085	RT	37.00	37.00
91	PAUL REVERE-1158	OP	39.00	39.00
91	PETER RABBIT WITH BOOK-1093	OP	40.00	40.00
91	PIG ROBINSON-1090	OP	40.00	40.00
91	PRECIOUS PLANET-1142	2000	120.00	120.00
91	QUEEN OF HEARTS-1122	OP	39.00	39.00
91	TAILOR OF GLOUCESTER-1087	OP	40.00	40.00
91	USHS ANGEL 1991-1139	SU	38.00	50.00
91	VOYAGES OF COLUMBUS, THE-1141	1500	39.00	50.00
91	WAITING FOR SANTA-1123	OP	38.00	38.00
91	WHITE RABBIT-1121	OP	39.00	39.00
92	AMERICA AT PEACE-1245	2000	85.00	85.00
92	ANDREA-1163	RT	36.00	36.00
92	ANGEL W/DOUBLE HORN-1212	2000	50.00	50.00
92	ANGEL-1213	2000	39.00	39.00
92	BOB & TINY TIM-1242	OP	36.00	36.00
92	CHOCOLATE POT-1209	RT	50.00	70.00
92	CHRISTMAS TREE & HEART-1162	RT	36.00	36.00
92	COWARDLY LION-1287	RT	36.00	50.00
92	DELLA ROBBIA ORNAMENT-1219	RT	39.00	45.00
92	DOROTHY-1284	RT	36.00	50.00
92	FAIRY TALE ANGEL-1222	OP	36.00	36.00
92	JEMIMA PUDDLEDUCK 1992-1167	RT	40.00	40.00
92	JOY-1164	OP	40.00	40.00
92	MARLEY'S GHOST-1243	OP	36.00	36.00
92	MFA SNOWFLAKE-1246	RT	39.00	45.00
92	MRS. CRATCHIT-1244	OP	36.00	36.00
92	MRS. RABBIT-1181	OP	40.00	40.00
92	NOAH'S ARK-1166	OP	36.00	36.00
92	PARROT-1233	OP	37.00	37.00
92	PRINCESS & THE PEA-1247	RT	39.00	50.00
92	REVERE TEAPOT-1207	RT	50.00	75.00
92	ROUND TEAPOT-1206	RT	50.00	50.00
92	SCARECROW-1286	RT	36.00	45.00
92	SCROOGE-1241	OP	36.00	36.00
92	ST. JOHN ANGEL-1236	10000	39.00	39.00
92	ST. JOHN LION-1235	10000	39.00	39.00
92	TIN MAN-1285	RT	36.00	50.00
92	UNICORN-1165	RT	36.00	36.00

J. WALPOLE
HAND & HAMMER ORNAMENTS

YR	NAME	LIMIT	ISSUE	TREND
87	NAPTIME-732	RT	32.00	50.00
87	SANTA STAR-739	RT	32.00	50.00

HARBOUR LIGHTS
*

CHRISTMAS ORNAMENTS

YR	NAME	LIMIT	ISSUE	TREND
96	30 MILE POINT, NY 7044	CL	15.00	15.00
96	BIG BAY POINT, MI 7040	CL	15.00	15.00
96	BURROWS ISLAND, WA 7043	CL	15.00	15.00
96	CAPE NEDDICK, ME 7047	OP	15.00	15.00
96	HOLLAND, MI 7041	OP	15.00	15.00
96	NEW LONDON LEDGE, CT 7046	OP	15.00	15.00
96	SAND ISLAND, WI 7042	CL	15.00	15.00
96	SE BLOCK ISLAND, RI 7045	OP	15.00	15.00
96	SET OF FOUR 702	OP	60.00	60.00
96	SET OF FOUR 703	OP	60.00	60.00

HAWTHORNE
*

GONE WITH THE WIND ORNAMENTS

YR	NAME	LIMIT	ISSUE	TREND
95	RED HORSE SALOON/BUTLER MANSION 79043	*	30.00	30.00
95	TARA/ATLANTA CHURCH 79041	*	30.00	30.00
95	TWELVE OAKS/KENNEDY STORE 79042	*	30.00	30.00

YR	NAME	LIMIT	ISSUE	TREND
	ROCKWELL- INSPIRED	**ROCKWELL'S MAIN STREET/ILLUMINATED**		
94	ANTIQUE SHOP & TOWN OFFICES 79902	*	30.00	30.00
94	BANK & LIBRARY 79903	*	30.00	30.00
94	RED LION INN & ROCKWELL RESIDENCE 79904	*	30.00	30.00
94	STUDIO & COUNTRY STORE 79901	*	30.00	30.00
	KINKADE- INSPIRED	**THOMAS KINKADE'S CANDLELIGHT COTTAGES**		
95	CEDAR NOOKE/CANDLELIT 79964	*	30.00	30.00
95	OLD PORTERFIELD TEA ROOM/MERRITT'S 79962	*	30.00	30.00
95	SEASIDE/SWEETHEART 79963	*	30.00	30.00
95	SWANBROOKE/CHANDLER'S 79961	CL	30.00	30.00

JAN HAGARA COLLECTABLES

	J. HAGARA		**VICTORIAN CHILDREN**	
84	ANNE	RT	10.00	125.00
84	BETSY	RT	10.00	50.00
84	JENNY	RT	10.00	125.00
84	JIMMY	RT	10.00	150.00
84	JODY	RT	10.00	45.00
84	LISA	RT	10.00	50.00
84	LYDIA	RT	10.00	45.00
84	VICTORIA	RT	10.00	125.00
85	CHRIS	RT	7.00	50.00
86	JILL	RT	15.00	30.00
86	NOEL	RT	10.00	50.00
87	AMANDA	RT	14.00	45.00
87	BRIAN	RT	14.00	45.00
87	CRISTINA	RT	14.00	30.00
87	HOLLY	RT	15.00	18.00
87	LAURIE	RT	14.00	30.00
87	MARC	RT	14.00	35.00
87	NIKKI	RT	10.00	50.00
87	STACY	RT	14.00	45.00
87	STEPHEN	RT	14.00	45.00

JOHN HINE STUDIOS LTD.

	D. WINTER		**CHRISTMAS ORNAMENTS**	
91	A CHRISTMAS CAROL	RT	15.00	19.00
91	HOGMANAY	RT	15.00	19.00
91	MR. FEZZIWIG'S EMPORIUM	RT	15.00	21.00
91	SCROOGE'S COUNTING HOUSE	RT	15.00	21.00
92	FAIRYTALE CASTLE	RT	15.00	19.00
92	FRED'S HOME	RT	15.00	19.00
92	SET	YR	60.00	100.00
92	SUFFOLK HOUSE	RT	15.00	19.00
92	TUDOR MANOR HOUSE	RT	15.00	19.00
93	GRANGE, THE	RT	15.00	17.00
93	SCROOGE'S SCHOOL	RT	15.00	15.00
93	TOMFOOL'S COTTAGE	RT	15.00	17.00
93	WILL-'O-THE-WISP	RT	15.00	17.00
94	OLD JOE'S BEETLING SHOP	OP	17.50	17.00
94	SCROOGES' FAMILY HOME	OP	17.50	17.00
94	WHAT COTTAGE?	OP	17.50	17.00
95	BUTTERCUP COTTAGE	OP	17.50	22.00
95	FLOWER SHOP, THE	OP	17.50	22.00
95	LOOKING FOR SANTA	OP	17.50	18.00
95	MISS BELLES COTTAGE	OP	17.50	18.00
95	ROBIN HOOD MOUSE	OP	17.50	18.00
95	SEASON'S GREETINGS	OP	17.50	18.00
96	JOLLY ROGER MOUSE	RT	17.50	18.00
96	PLOUGH FARMSTEAD	RT	17.50	18.00
96	PUNCH STABLES	RT	17.50	18.00
96	STABLE MOUSE	RT	17.50	18.00
96	STOCKING MOUSE	RT	17.50	18.00
96	TINY TIM	RT	17.50	18.00

JUNE MCKENNA COLLECTIBLES INC.

	J. MCKENNA			
93	ANGEL OF PEACE-PINK	OP	30.00	30.00
93	ANGEL OF PEACE-WHITE	OP	30.00	30.00
93	CHRISTMAS TREAT	OP	30.00	30.00
93	ELF BERNIE	OP	30.00	30.00
93	FINAL NOTES	OP	30.00	30.00
93	OLD LAMPLIGHTER	OP	30.00	30.00
94	ELF RICKEY	OP	30.00	30.00
94	ELF TAMMY	OP	30.00	30.00
94	GUIDING LIGHT ANGEL-GREEN	OP	30.00	30.00
94	GUIDING LIGHT ANGEL-PINK	OP	30.00	30.00
94	GUIDING LIGHT ANGEL-WHITE	OP	30.00	30.00
94	NUTCRACKER	OP	30.00	30.00
94	PRIMITIVE	OP	16.00	17.00
94	QUICK AS A WINK	OP	16.00	17.00
94	RINGING IN CHRISTMAS	OP	30.00	30.00
94	SANTA WITH PIPE	OP	30.00	30.00
94	SANTA WITH SKIS	OP	30.00	30.00
94	SNOW SHOWERS	OP	30.00	30.00
94	WHISPERING	OP	16.00	17.00

YR	NAME	LIMIT	ISSUE	TREND
	J. MCKENNA		**3-D BLACK FOLK ART**	
96	FUN AT THE BEACH/SANTA	YR	70.00	70.00
	J. MCKENNA		**FLATBACK ORNAMENTS**	
82	ANGEL WITH TOYS	CL	14.00	85.00
82	BABY BEAR, TEESHIRT	CL	11.00	60.00
82	CANDY CANE	CL	10.00	45.00
82	COLONIAL MAN	CL	12.00	150.00
82	COLONIAL WOMAN	CL	12.00	150.00
82	KATE GREENAWAY BOY	CL	12.00	275.00
82	KATE GREENAWAY GIRL	CL	12.00	300.00
82	MAMA BEAR, BLUE CAPE	CL	12.00	90.00
82	PAPA BEAR, RED CAPE	CL	12.00	90.00
82	SANTA WITH TOYS	CL	14.00	80.00
83	BABY	CL	11.00	60.00
83	BABY BEAR IN VEST	CL	11.00	50.00
83	FATHER BEAR IN SUIT	CL	12.00	75.00
83	GLORIA ANGEL	CL	14.00	475.00
83	GRANDMA	CL	12.00	65.00
83	GRANDPA	CL	12.00	65.00
83	MOTHER BEAR IN DRESS	CL	12.00	75.00
83	RAGGEDY ANDY	CL	12.00	75.00
83	RAGGEDY ANN	CL	12.00	75.00
83	ST. NICK WITH LANTERN	CL	14.00	75.00
84	ANGEL WITH HORN	CL	14.00	75.00
84	COUNTRY BOY	CL	12.00	70.00
84	COUNTRY GIRL	CL	12.00	70.00
84	MR. CLAUS	CL	14.00	65.00
84	MRS. CLAUS	CL	14.00	60.00
84	OLD WORLD SANTA	CL	14.00	65.00
85	AMISH MAN	CL	13.00	50.00
85	AMISH WOMAN	CL	13.00	50.00
85	BABY PIG	CL	11.00	60.00
85	BRIDE	CL	25.00	125.00
85	FATHER PIG	CL	12.00	75.00
85	GROOM	CL	25.00	125.00
85	MOTHER PIG	CL	12.00	75.00
85	PRIMITIVE SANTA	CL	17.00	85.00
86	AMISH BOY	CL	13.00	65.00
86	SANTA WITH BAG	CL	16.00	65.00
86	SANTA WITH BEAR	CL	14.00	40.00
86	SANTA WITH BELLS (BLUE)	CL	14.00	65.00
86	SANTA WITH BELLS (GREEN)	CL	14.00	375.00
88	1776 SANTA	CL	17.00	40.00
88	ELIZABETH, SILL SITTER	CL	20.00	150.00
88	GUARDIAN ANGEL	CL	16.00	40.00
88	SANTA WITH BOOK (BLUE & RED)	CL	17.00	75.00
88	SANTA WITH TOYS	CL	17.00	40.00
88	SANTA WITH WREATH	CL	17.00	40.00
89	GLORIOUS ANGEL	OP	17.00	17.00
89	SANTA WITH TREE	CL	17.00	40.00
89	WINKING SANTA	CL	17.00	40.00
90	ELF JEFFREY	CL	17.00	40.00
90	HARVEST SANTA	CL	17.00	40.00
90	HO HO HO	CL	17.00	40.00
91	BOY ANGEL	CL	20.00	20.00
91	ELF JOEY	OP	20.00	20.00
91	GIRL ANGEL	OP	20.00	20.00
91	SANTA WITH BANNER	OP	20.00	20.00
91	SANTA WITH LIGHTS, BLACK	OP	20.00	20.00
92	ELF SCOTTY	OP	25.00	25.00
92	NORTH POLE NEWS	OP	25.00	25.00
92	PRAYING ANGEL	OP	25.00	25.00
92	SANTA WITH BASKET	OP	25.00	25.00
92	SANTA WITH SACK	OP	25.00	25.00
95	ANGEL W/TEDDY	YR	30.00	30.00
95	ANGEL W/WREATH	YR	30.00	30.00
95	COUNTRY SANTA	YR	30.00	30.00
95	ELF/DANNY	YR	30.00	30.00
95	SANTA & HELPER/BROWN	YR	30.00	30.00
95	SANTA NUTCRACKER	YR	30.00	30.00
95	SANTA TEACHER	YR	30.00	30.00
95	WHO'S THIS FROSTY	YR	30.00	30.00
96	ANGEL W/HARPE - ELIZABETH	YR	30.00	30.00
96	ANGEL W/HORN - MARY	YR	30.00	30.00
96	ANGEL W/LYRE - KATHLEEN	YR	30.00	30.00
96	CHRISTMAS TREAT/RED	YR	30.00	30.00
96	ELF CADDIE	YR	30.00	30.00
96	FIREMAN SANTA	YR	30.00	30.00
96	FISHING SANTA	YR	30.00	30.00
96	GOLFING SANTA	YR	30.00	30.00
96	MR. GOODBY KISS	YR	30.00	30.00
96	MRS. GOODBY KISS	YR	30.00	30.00
96	NUTCRACKER	YR	30.00	30.00
96	SANTA & HELPER/WHITE	YR	30.00	30.00
96	SANTA W/TEDDY	YR	30.00	30.00

YR	NAME	LIMIT	ISSUE	TREND
96	SNOWMAN	YR	30.00	30.00
97	NUTCRACKER W/ HORN	*	30.00	30.00
97	OLD WORLD SANTA	*	30.00	30.00
97	SABRINA'S ANGEL	*	30.00	30.00
97	SANTA DOCTOR	*	30.00	30.00
97	TENNIS SANTA	*	30.00	30.00

J. MCKENNA — **HEAD ORNAMENTS**

YR	NAME	LIMIT	ISSUE	TREND
95	CHRISTMAS KISS	RT	17.00	17.00
95	HELPING HAND	YR	17.00	17.00
95	I LOVE YOU SANTA	RT	17.00	17.00
95	MOON SHAPE SANTA	YR	17.00	17.00
95	PRIMITIVE SANTA	YR	17.00	17.00
95	QUICK AS A WINK	YR	17.00	17.00
95	SANTA W/HOLLY	YR	17.00	17.00
95	SANTA W/PIPE	YR	17.00	17.00
95	WHISPERING SANTA	YR	17.00	17.00
96	PATRIOTIC SANTA	YR	17.00	17.00
96	SANTA W/TASSEL	YR	17.00	17.00
96	SNOWMAN	YR	17.00	17.00

J. MCKENNA — **ICICLE**

YR	NAME	LIMIT	ISSUE	TREND
96	ANGEL/LONG RED HAIR	YR	17.00	17.00
96	ANGEL/SHORT BLONDE HAIR	YR	17.00	17.00
96	ANGEL/SHORT BROWN HAIR	YR	17.00	17.00
96	BLACK ANGEL	YR	17.00	17.00
96	SANTA W/HAT	YR	17.00	17.00
96	SNOWMAN	YR	17.00	17.00

KIRK STIEFF

D. BACORN — **COLONIAL WILLIAMSBURG**

YR	NAME	LIMIT	ISSUE	TREND
83	SILVERPLATE TREETOP STAR	YR	30.00	30.00
87	SILVERPLATE ROCKING HORSE	CL	20.00	30.00
87	SILVERPLATE TIN DRUM	CL	20.00	30.00
88	SILVERPLATE LAMB	CL	20.00	22.00
88	SILVERPLATE UNICORN	CL	22.00	30.00
89	SILVERPLATE DOLL ORNAMENT	CL	22.00	30.00

D. BACORN — **KIRK STIEFF ORNAMENTS**

YR	NAME	LIMIT	ISSUE	TREND
83	CHARLESTON LOCOMOTIVE	CL	17.50	20.00
84	UNICORN	CL	17.50	20.00
86	STERLING SILVER ICICLE	CL	35.00	50.00

K. STIEFF — **KIRK STIEFF ORNAMENTS**

YR	NAME	LIMIT	ISSUE	TREND
89	SMITHSONIAN CAROUSEL HORSE	CL	50.00	50.00
89	SMITHSONIAN CAROUSEL SEAHORSE	CL	50.00	50.00
90	TOY SHIP	CL	23.00	35.00

K. STIEFF — **THE NUTCRACKER STAINED GLASS ORNAMENT**

YR	NAME	LIMIT	ISSUE	TREND
86	BATTLE, THE	CL	17.50	18.00
86	CLARA'S GIFT	CL	17.50	18.00
86	NUTCRACKER PRINCE, THE	CL	17.50	18.00
86	SET OF FOUR	CL	69.95	40.00
86	SUGAR PLUM FAIRY, THE	CL	17.50	18.00

J. BARATA — **TWELVE DAYS OF CHRISTMAS**

YR	NAME	LIMIT	ISSUE	TREND
85	PARTRIDGE IN A PEAR TREE	YR	9.95	11.00
85	TWO TURTLEDOVES	YR	9.95	11.00
86	FOUR CALLING BIRDS	YR	9.95	11.00
86	THREE FRENCH HENS	YR	9.95	11.00
87	FIVE GOLDEN RINGS	YR	9.95	11.00
87	SIX GEESE A-LAYING	YR	9.95	11.00
88	EIGHT MAIDS A-MILKING	YR	9.95	11.00
88	SEVEN SWANS A-SWIMMING	YR	9.95	11.00
89	NINE LADIES DANCING	YR	11.00	11.00
89	TEN LORDS A-LEAPING	YR	11.00	11.00

KURT S. ADLER INC.

* — **CAROUSEL ORNAMENTS**

YR	NAME	LIMIT	ISSUE	TREND
97	GRACEFUL HORSE	*	20.00	20.00
97	SEA MONSTER	*	20.00	20.00

J. MOSTROM — **CHILDREN'S HOUR**

YR	NAME	LIMIT	ISSUE	TREND
95	ALICE IN WONDERLAND J5751	RT	23.00	23.00
95	BOW PEEP J5753	OP	27.00	27.00
95	CINDERELLA J5762	RT	28.00	28.00
95	LITTLE BOY BLUE J5755	RT	18.00	18.00
95	MISS MUFFET J5753	OP	27.00	27.00
95	MOTHER GOOSE J5754	RT	27.00	27.00
95	RED RIDING HOOD J5751	RT	23.00	23.00

J. MOSTROM — **CHRISTMAS IN CHELSEA**

YR	NAME	LIMIT	ISSUE	TREND
92	ALLISON SITTING IN CHAIR W2812	RT	26.00	26.00
92	ALLISON W2729	RT	21.00	21.00
92	AMANDA W2709	RT	21.00	21.00
92	AMY W2729	RT	21.00	21.00
92	CHRISTINA W2812	RT	26.00	26.00
92	CHRISTOPHER W2709	RT	21.00	21.00
92	DELPHINIUM W2728	OP	20.00	20.00
92	HOLLY HOCK W2728	OP	20.00	20.00
92	HOLLY W2709	RT	21.00	21.00
92	PEONY W2728	OP	20.00	20.00
92	ROSE W2728	OP	20.00	20.00

YR	NAME	LIMIT	ISSUE	TREND
94	ALICE, MARGUERITE W2973	RT	28.00	28.00
94	GUARDIAN ANGEL W/BABY W2974	RT	31.00	31.00
95	JOSE W/VIOLIN W3078	RT	32.00	32.00

M. ROTHENBERG — **CORNHUSK MICE**

93	BALLERINA CORNHUSK MICE W2700	RT	13.50	14.00
93	NUTCRACKER STE. FANTASY CORNHUSK MOUSE	RT	15.50	16.00
94	CLARA, PRINCE W2948	OP	16.00	16.00
94	COWBOY W2951	RT	18.00	18.00
94	DROSSELMEIR FAIRY, MOUSE KING W2949	OP	16.00	16.00
94	FATHER CHRISTMAS W2979	RT	18.00	18.00
94	FATHER CHRISTMAS W2982	OP	25.00	25.00
94	LITTLE POCAHONTAS, INDIAN BRAVE W2950	OP	18.00	18.00
95	ANGEL MICE W3088	OP	10.00	10.00
95	BABY'S FIRST MOUSE W3087	OP	10.00	10.00
95	MISS TAMMIE MOUSE W3086	RT	17.00	17.00
95	MR. JAMIE MOUSE W3086	RT	17.00	17.00
95	MRS. MOLLY MOUSE W3086	RT	17.00	17.00

* — **FABRICHE COLLECTION**

92	HELLO LITTLE ONE! W1561	RT	22.00	22.00
92	HUGS AND KISSES W1560	RT	22.00	22.00
92	MERRY CHRISMOUSE W1565	RT	10.00	10.00
92	NOT A CREATURE WAS STIRRING W1563	RT	22.00	22.00

K. ADLER — **FABRICHE COLLECTION**

92	CHRISTMAS IN THE AIR W1593	RT	36.00	36.00
93	HOMEWARD BOUND W1596	RT	27.00	27.00
93	MASTER TOYMAKER W1595	RT	27.00	27.00
93	PAR FOR THE CLAUS W1625	RT	27.00	27.00
93	SANTA W/LIST W1510	RT	20.00	20.00
94	ALL STAR SANTA W1665	RT	27.00	27.00
94	CHECKING HIS LIST W1634	RT	24.00	24.00
94	COOKIES FOR SANTA W1639	RT	28.00	28.00
94	FIREFIGHTING FRIENDS W1668	RT	28.00	28.00
94	SANTA'S FISHTALES W1666	RT	29.00	29.00
95	CAPTAIN CLAUS W1711	RT	25.00	25.00
95	STRIKE UP THE BAND W1710	RT	25.00	25.00

M. ROTHENBERG — **FABRICHE COLLECTION**

92	AN APRON FULL OF LOVE W1594	RT	27.00	27.00

H. ADLER — **HOLLY BEARIES**

96	ANGEL STARCATCHER 57222	OP	20.00	20.00

J. MOSTROM — **INTERNATIONAL CHRISTMAS**

94	CATHY, JOHNNY W2945	RT	24.00	24.00
94	ESKIMO-ATOM UKPIK W2967	RT	28.00	28.00
94	GERMANY-KATERINA,HANS W2969	RT	27.00	27.00
94	NATIVE AMERICAN-WHITE DOVE,LITTLE WOLF	RT	28.00	28.00
94	POLAND-MARISSA, HEDWIG W2965	RT	27.00	27.00
94	SCOTLAND-BONNIE, DOUGLAS W2966	RT	27.00	27.00
94	SPAIN-MARIA. MIGUEL W2968	RT	27.00	27.00

J. MOSTROM — **LITTLE DICKENS**

94	LITTLE BOB CRACHIT W2961	RT	30.00	30.00
94	LITTLE MARLEY'S GHOST W2964	RT	34.00	34.00
94	LITTLE MRS. CRACHIT W2962	RT	27.00	27.00
94	LITTLE SCROOGE IN BATHROBE W2959	RT	30.00	30.00
94	LITTLE SCROOGE IN OVERCOAT W2960	RT	30.00	30.00
94	LITTLE TINY TIM W2963	RT	23.00	23.00

* — **POLONAISE COLLECTION**

94	GOLDEN ANGEL HEAD GP372	RT	18.00	150.00
94	GOLDEN ROCKING HORSE GP355	RT	23.00	125.00
95	WIZARD OF OZ 4 PC. BOXED SET GP508	5000	170.00	250.00
96	COCA COLA BEAR GP630	OP	37.00	37.00
96	COCA COLA BOTTLE GP631	OP	33.00	33.00
96	COCA COLA BOTTLE TOP GP633	OP	27.00	27.00
96	COCA COLA DISK GP632	OP	26.00	26.00
96	COCA COLA VENDING MACHINE GP634	OP	37.00	37.00
96	POLONAISE MEDIEVAL HORSE GP640	OP	35.00	35.00
97	ALICE COLLECTION- 4 PC GP548	OP	150.00	150.00
97	ALICE COLLECTION- 5 PC LIMITED EDITIONGP547	7500	175.00	175.00
97	ALICE IN WONDERLAND GP692	OP	30.00	30.00
97	BABAR ELEPHANT GP817	OP	*	N/A
97	BIG BIRD- GLASS GP699	OP	35.00	35.00
97	CAVALRY, GUNNER, DRUMMER GP645	OP	30.00	30.00
97	CHARLIE BROWN PEANUTS GP824	OP	*	N/A
97	CIRCUS COLLECTION- 5 PC GP545	OP	180.00	180.00
97	CIRCUS RINGMASTER GP691	OP	35.00	35.00
97	CIRCUS SEAL- GLASS GP688	OP	30.00	30.00
97	CIRCUS STRONGMAN GP690	OP	35.00	35.00
97	CLOWNS- 3 PC GLASS GP682	OP	35.00	35.00
97	COCA COLA 6 PACK GP803	OP	35.00	35.00
97	COCA COLA TRUCK GP804	OP	38.00	38.00
97	COLA BEAR SKIING GP801	OP	35.00	35.00
97	COLA BEAR SNOWMOBILE GP802	OP	35.00	35.00
97	DR. WATSON- GLASS	OP	30.00	30.00
97	EGYPTIAN COLLECTION- 4 PC GP515	OP	150.00	150.00
97	ENGLISH BOBBIE GP814	OP	30.00	30.00
97	FOUR CALLING BIRDS GP828	OP	*	N/A

YR	NAME	LIMIT	ISSUE	TREND
97	GINGERBREAD HOUSE GP664	OP	30.00	30.00
97	GOLDEN COCA COLA BOTTLE GP800	OP	35.00	35.00
97	GONE WITH THE WIND RHETT BUTLER GP815	OP	*	N/A
97	GONE WITH THE WIND SCARLETT O'HARA GP805	OP	*	N/A
97	GONE WITH THE WIND TARA GP816	OP	*	N/A
97	GONE WITH THE WIND- 3 PC BOX GP557	OP	*	N/A
97	GRANDFATHER FROST GP801COL	YR	*	50.00
97	HANDBLOWN WITCH GP661	OP	35.00	35.00
97	HANSEL & GRETEL GP662	OP	30.00	30.00
97	HANSEL/GRETEL- 4 PC GP538	OP	150.00	150.00
97	HAT BOXES- GLASS GP620	OP	28.00	30.00
97	HERALD RABBIT GP693	OP	35.00	35.00
97	HOLLY BEAR- GLASS GP827	OP	*	N/A
97	HUNTER- GLASS GP667	OP	30.00	30.00
97	JEWELRY BOXES- 3 PC GP637	OP	15.95	16.00
97	JUST MARRIED GP829	OP	23.00	23.00
97	KRAKOW CASTLE GP670	OP	35.00	35.00
97	KRAKOW MAN- GLASS GP674	OP	30.00	30.00
97	LITTLE RED RIDING HOOD GP665	OP	30.00	30.00
97	LITTLE RED RIDING HOOD- 3 PC GP544	OP	110.00	110.00
97	LUCY PEANUTS GP825	OP	*	N/A
97	MAD HATTER- GLASS GP696	OP	35.00	35.00
97	MADONNA VATICAN EGG GP830	OP	38.00	38.00
97	MAGICIANS HAT GP689	OP	35.00	35.00
97	MARILYN MONROE GP818	OP	*	N/A
97	MGM COWARDLY LION GP821	OP	*	N/A
97	MGM DOROTHY GP819	OP	*	N/A
97	MGM SCARECROW GP822	OP	*	N/A
97	MGM TIN MAN GP820	OP	*	N/A
97	MGM WIZ OF OZ- 4 PC BOX GP555	OP	*	N/A
97	NAPOLEONIC SOLDIER GP543	OP	150.00	150.00
97	NEW COCA COLA- 3PC GP553	OP	130.00	130.00
97	NY BALL- 5 PC GP677	OP	25.00	25.00
97	PEANUTS- 3 PC BOX GP 556	OP	*	N/A
97	POLISH MOUNTAIN MAN GP675	OP	30.00	30.00
97	QUEEN OF HEARTS GP695	OP	35.00	35.00
97	RAG ANN/ANDY GP550	OP	75.00	75.00
97	RAGGEDY ANN- GLASS GP322	OP	24.95	25.00
97	RED RIDING HOOD- 4 PC LIMITED EDITION GP539		*	N/A
97	ROYAL SUITE- 4 PC GP552	OP	140.00	140.00
97	ROYAL SUITE- 4 PC GP806	OP	30.00	30.00
97	SANTA HEAD- GLASS GP811	OP	23.00	23.00
97	SEVEN DWARFS- 7 PC GP611	OP	30.00	30.00
97	SHERLOCK HOLMES GP812	OP	30.00	30.00
97	SHERLOCK HOLMES-3 PC BOX GP551	OP	125.00	125.00
97	SMITHSONIAN ASTRONAUT GP826	OP	*	N/A
97	SNOOPY PEANUTS GP823	OP	*	N/A
97	SNOW WHITE & 7 DWARFS- BOX GP558	OP	*	N/A
97	SNOW WHITE- GLASS GP660	OP	30.00	30.00
97	STAR BOY- GLASS GP676	OP	35.00	35.00
97	STAR- 3 PC GLASS GP671	OP	20.00	20.00
97	TATAR PRINCE- GLASS GP672	OP	35.00	35.00
97	TROPICAL FISH- 4 PC GP554	OP	110.00	110.00
97	WOLF, THE- GLASS GP666	OP	35.00	35.00
97	X-MAS IN POLAND- 4 PC GP534	OP	150.00	150.00

KING FEATURES
POLONAISE COLLECTION

96	BETTY BOOP GP624	OP	32.00	32.00

KSA/KOMOZJA
POLONAISE COLLECTION

94	ANGEL HEAD GP372	RT	18.00	18.00
94	ANGEL W/BEAR GP396	RT	20.00	35.00
94	BEER GLASS GP366	OP	18.00	18.00
94	CARDINAL GP420	RT	18.00	30.00
94	CAT W/BALL GP390	RT	18.00	50.00
94	DINOSAURS GP397	RT	23.00	23.00
94	EGYPTIANS 12 PC. GP500	RT	200.00	400.00
94	GLASS ACORN GP342	RT	11.00	150.00
94	GLASS ANGEL GP309	RT	18.00	18.00
94	GLASS APPLE GP339	RT	11.00	20.00
94	GLASS CHURCH GP369	OP	18.00	18.00
94	GLASS CLOWN GP301	RT	13.50	50.00
94	GLASS CLOWN GP302	RT	23.00	30.00
94	GLASS CLOWN GP303	RT	23.00	38.00
94	GLASS DICE GP363	RT	18.00	75.00
94	GLASS DOLL GP377	RT	13.50	30.00
94	GLASS GNOME GP347	RT	18.00	30.00
94	GLASS KNIGHT GP304	RT	18.00	20.00
94	GLASS OWL GP328	OP	20.00	20.00
94	GLASS TOP GP359	OP	9.00	9.00
94	GLASS TURKEY GP326	RT	20.00	20.00
94	GUARDMAN GP407	OP	15.50	16.00
94	HOLY FAMILY GP371	OP	28.00	28.00
94	LOCOMOTIVE GP353	OP	23.00	23.00
94	MADONNA W/CHILD GP370	OP	23.00	23.00
94	MERLIN GP373	RT	20.00	28.00
94	MOOSE KING GP406	OP	20.00	20.00

YR	NAME	LIMIT	ISSUE	TREND
94	NEFERTITI GP349	OP	25.00	25.00
94	NIGHT & DAY GP307	OP	23.00	23.00
94	NUTCRACKER GP404	OP	20.00	20.00
94	OLD FASHIONED CAR GP380	RT	13.50	14.00
94	PARROT GP332	RT	15.50	45.00
94	PEACOCK GP323	RT	28.00	28.00
94	PEACOCK GP324	RT	18.00	20.00
94	PIERROT THE CLOWN GP405	RT	18.00	30.00
94	PUPPY GP333	RT	15.50	30.00
94	PYRAMID GP352	OP	23.00	23.00
94	ROCKING HORSE GP355	OP	23.00	23.00
94	ROCKING HORSE GP356	OP	23.00	23.00
94	SAINT NICK GP316	OP	28.00	28.00
94	SANTA BOOT GP375	OP	20.00	20.00
94	SANTA GP317	OP	23.00	23.00
94	SANTA HEAD GP315	RT	13.50	20.00
94	SANTA HEAD GP374	OP	18.00	18.00
94	SNOWMAN W/PARCEL GP313	OP	23.00	23.00
94	SNOWMAN W/SPECS GP312	RT	20.00	30.00
94	SPARROW GP329	RT	15.50	55.00
94	SPHINX GP350	RT	23.00	60.00
94	SWAN GP325	OP	20.00	20.00
94	TEDDY BEAR GP338	RT	15.50	38.00
94	TRAIN COACHES GP354	OP	15.50	16.00
94	TRAIN SET GP501	OP	90.00	90.00
94	TROPICAL FISH GP409	OP	23.00	23.00
94	TUTANKHAMEN GP348	RT	25.00	30.00
94	ZODIAC SUN GP381	RT	23.00	50.00
95	ALARM CLOCK GP452	RT	25.00	25.00
95	BLESSED MOTHER GP413	OP	23.00	23.00
95	CAESAR GP422	OP	25.00	25.00
95	CAT IN BOOT GP478	OP	28.00	28.00
95	CAT W/BOW GP446	OP	23.00	23.00
95	CHRIST CHILD GP414	OP	20.00	20.00
95	CHRISTMAS TREE GP461	OP	23.00	23.00
95	CLARA GP408	OP	20.00	20.00
95	CLOWN HEAD GP460	OP	25.00	25.00
95	COWBOY HEAD GP462	OP	30.00	30.00
95	CROCODILE GP468	RT	28.00	28.00
95	EAGLE GP453	OP	28.00	28.00
95	EGYPTIAN SET 4 PC. GP500/4	OP	110.00	110.00
95	ELEPHANT GP	OP	28.00	28.00
95	FISH 4 PC. GP506	OP	110.00	110.00
95	HERR DROSSELMEIR GP465	OP	30.00	30.00
95	HOLY FAMILY 3 PC. GP504	OP	84.00	84.00
95	INDIAN GP463	OP	30.00	30.00
95	LOCOMOTIVE GP447	OP	28.00	28.00
95	NOAH'S ARK GP469	OP	25.00	25.00
95	NUTCRACKER SUITE 4 PC. GP507	OP	110.00	110.00
95	PETER PAN GP419	OP	23.00	23.00
95	PETER PAN SET 4 PC. GP503	OP	124.00	124.00
95	POLONAISE AFRO-AM. SANTA GP389/1	OP	25.00	25.00
95	POLONAISE CARDINAL GP473	OP	25.00	25.00
95	POLONAISE HOUSE GP455	RT	25.00	30.00
95	POLONAISE SANTA GP389	OP	25.00	25.00
95	ROMAN CENTURIAN GP427	OP	23.00	23.00
95	ROMAN SET 7 PC. GP502	RT	164.00	200.00
95	SAILING SHIP GP415	OP	30.00	30.00
95	SANTA GP442	OP	25.00	25.00
95	SANTA ON GOOSE ON SLED GP479	OP	30.00	30.00
95	SHARK GP417	RT	18.00	24.00
95	ST. JOSEPH GP412	OP	23.00	23.00
95	TELEPHONE GP448	RT	25.00	25.00
95	TREASURE CHEST GP416	RT	20.00	20.00
95	WIZARD OF OZ 6 PC. GP508	RT	170.00	200.00
95	WIZARD OF OZ DOROTHY GP434	OP	25.00	25.00
95	WIZARD OF OZ LION GP433	OP	23.00	23.00
95	WIZARD OF OZ SCARECROW GP435	OP	25.00	25.00
95	WIZARD OF OZ TINMAN GP436	OP	25.00	25.00
96	ANTIQUE CARS BOXED SET GP522	OP	124.00	124.00
96	BOXED SET OF DICE GP509	OP	60.00	60.00
96	CANDLEHOLDER GP450	OP	20.00	20.00
96	CINDERELLA 4 BOXED SET GP512	OP	134.00	134.00
96	CINDERELLA BOXED SET GP511	7500	190.00	190.00
96	CINDERELLA COACH GP487	OP	33.00	33.00
96	CINDERELLA GP488	OP	28.00	28.00
96	COCA COLA 4 PC BOXED SET GP517	OP	135.00	135.00
96	COSSACK GP604	OP	35.00	35.00
96	EGYPTIAN CAT GP351	OP	30.00	30.00
96	EGYPTIAN II BOXED SET GP510	OP	170.00	170.00
96	EGYPTIAN PRINCESS GP482	OP	33.00	33.00
96	ELVES GP611/23	OP	30.00	30.00
96	EMERALD CITY GP623	OP	32.00	32.00
96	FIRE ENGINE GP605	OP	30.00	30.00
96	GIFT BOXES GP614	OP	25.00	25.00

YR	NAME	LIMIT	ISSUE	TREND
96	GLASS SLIPPER GP490	OP	20.00	20.00
96	GLINDA THE GOOD WITCH GP621	OP	32.00	32.00
96	GRAMOPHONE GP446	RT	23.00	23.00
96	HORUS GP484	OP	33.00	33.00
96	KING BALTHAZAR GP607	OP	30.00	30.00
96	KING NEPTUNE GP496	OP	35.00	35.00
96	LIGHT BULB GP449	RT	20.00	20.00
96	LITTLE MERMAID GP492	OP	28.00	28.00
96	MEDIEVAL BOXED SET GP519	OP	160.00	160.00
96	MEDIEVAL DRAGON GP642	OP	35.00	35.00
96	MEDIEVAL KNIGHT GP641	OP	35.00	35.00
96	MEDIEVAL LADY GP643	OP	35.00	35.00
96	MUMMY GP483	OP	33.00	33.00
96	NEFERTITI 96 GP485	OP	33.00	33.00
96	PHARAOH GP481	OP	35.00	35.00
96	PRINCE CHARMING GP489	OP	28.00	28.00
96	RAGGEDY ANN GP321	OP	28.00	28.00
96	RUSSIAN 5 BOXED SET GP514	OP	190.00	190.00
96	RUSSIAN BISHOP GP603	OP	35.00	35.00
96	RUSSIAN WOMEN GP602	OP	35.00	35.00
96	SANTA CAR GP367	OP		N/A
96	SANTA PILOT GP365	OP	33.00	33.00
96	SEA HORSE GP494	OP	25.00	25.00
96	SPHINX GP480	OP	33.00	33.00
96	ST. BASILS CATHEDRAL GP600	OP	35.00	35.00
96	STING RAY GP495	RT	28.00	28.00
96	THREE KINGS BOXED SET GP516	OP	144.00	144.00
96	TSAR IVAN GP601	OP	35.00	35.00
96	TUTANKHAMEN #2 GP476	OP	35.00	35.00
96	WICKED WITCH GP606	OP	32.00	32.00
96	WINTER BOY GP615	OP	23.00	23.00
96	WINTER GIRL GP615	OP	23.00	23.00
96	WIZARD IN BALLOON GP622	OP	32.00	32.00
96	WIZARD OF OZ II BOXED SET GP518	RT	164.00	164.00
STEFAN		**POLONAISE COLLECTION**		
95	CRECHE GP358	OP	28.00	28.00
95	DOVE ON BALL GP472	RT	32.00	32.00
95	GOOSE W/WREATH GP475	OP	25.00	25.00
95	HUMPTY DUMPTY GP477	OP	25.00	25.00
95	ICICLE SANTA GP474	RT	25.00	40.00
95	PARTRIDGE GP467	OP	34.00	34.00
95	SANTA MOON GP454	OP	28.00	28.00
95	STAR SANTA GP470	OP	25.00	25.00
95	TURTLEDOVES GP471	OP	25.00	25.00
96	FRENCH HEN GP626	OP	33.00	33.00
96	STAR SNOWMAN GP625	OP	32.00	32.00
J. MOSTROM		**ROYAL HERITAGE**		
93	ANASTASIA W2922	RT	28.00	28.00
93	CAROLINE W2924	RT	26.00	26.00
93	CHARLES W2924	RT	26.00	26.00
93	ELIZABETH W2924	RT	26.00	26.00
93	JOELLA W2979	RT	27.00	27.00
93	KELLY W2979	RT	27.00	27.00
93	NICHOLAS W2923	RT	26.00	26.00
93	PATINA W2923	RT	26.00	26.00
93	SASHA W2923	RT	26.00	26.00
95	BENJAMIN J5756	RT	25.00	25.00
95	BLYTHE J5756	RT	25.00	25.00
95	EDMOND W/VIOLIN W3078	RT	32.00	32.00
95	PAULINE W/VIOLIN W3078	RT	32.00	32.00
96	ANGELIQUE ANGEL BABY W3278	RT	25.00	25.00
96	BRIANNA IVORY W7663	OP	25.00	25.00
96	BRIANNA PINK W7663	OP	25.00	25.00
96	ETOILE ANGEL BABY W3278	RT	25.00	25.00
96	FRANCIS WINTER BOY W 3279	OP	28.00	28.00
96	GABRIELLE IN PINK COAT W3276	OP	28.00	28.00
96	GISELLE W/BOW W3277	RT	28.00	28.00
96	GISELLE WINTER GIRL W/PACKAGE W3279	OP	28.00	28.00
96	LADY COLETTE IN SLED W3301	OP	32.00	32.00
96	LAURIELLE LADY SKATER W3281	OP	36.00	36.00
96	MINIOTTE W/MUFF W3279	OP	28.00	28.00
96	MONIQUE W/HAT BOX W3217	OP	28.00	28.00
96	NICOLE W/BALLOON W3277	OP	28.00	28.00
96	RENE VICTORIAN LADY W3280	OP	36.00	36.00
KSA/SMITHSONIAN		**SMITHSONIAN MUSEUM CAROUSEL**		
87	ANTIQUE CAROUSEL BUNNY, THE S3027/12	RT	14.50	15.00
87	ANTIQUE CAROUSEL GOAT, THE S3027/1	RT	14.50	15.00
88	ANTIQUE CAROUSEL GIRAFFE, THE S3027/4	RT	14.50	15.00
88	ANTIQUE CAROUSEL HORSE, THE S3027/3	RT	14.50	15.00
89	ANTIQUE CAROUSEL CAT, THE S3027/6	RT	14.50	15.00
89	ANTIQUE CAROUSEL LION, THE S3027/5	RT	14.50	15.00
90	ANTIQUE CAROUSEL SEAHORSE, THE S3027/8	RT	14.50	15.00
90	ANTIQUE CAROUSEL ZEBRA, THE S3027/17	RT	14.50	15.00
91	ANTIQUE CAROUSEL HORSE, THE S3027/10	RT	14.50	15.00
91	ANTIQUE CAROUSEL ROOSTER, THE S3027/9	RT	14.50	15.00

YR	NAME	LIMIT	ISSUE	TREND
92	ANTIQUE CAROUSEL ELEPHANT, THE S3027/11	RT	14.50	15.00
93	ANTIQUE CAROUSEL HORSE, THE S3027/14	OP	15.00	15.00
93	ANTIQUE CAROUSEL TIGER, THE S3027/13	OP	15.00	15.00
94	ANTIQUE CAROUSEL PIG, THE S3027/16	OP	15.50	16.00
94	ANTIQUE CAROUSEL REINDEER, THE S3027/15	OP	15.50	16.00
95	ANTIQUE CAROUSEL CAMEL, THE S3027/14	OP	15.00	15.00
95	ANTIQUE FROG S32027/18	OP	15.50	16.00
95	ARMORED HORSE S3027/17	OP	15.50	16.00

KSA/SMITHSONIAN — **SMITHSONIAN MUSEUM FABRICHE**

YR	NAME	LIMIT	ISSUE	TREND
92	HOLIDAY DRIVE W1580	RT	38.00	38.00
92	SANTA ON A BICYCLE W1547	RT	31.00	31.00
94	HOLIDAY FLIGHT W1637	RT	40.00	40.00

J. MOSTROM — **SNOW CHILDREN COLLECTION**

YR	NAME	LIMIT	ISSUE	TREND
94	ICE FAIRY	RT	26.00	26.00
94	SNOW PRINCESS W2971	RT	28.00	28.00
94	WINTER FAIRY	RT	25.00	25.00

K. ADLER — **STEINBACH ORNAMENT SERIES**

YR	NAME	LIMIT	ISSUE	TREND
92	KING'S GUARD, THE ES300	OP	27.00	27.00

* — **VATICAN LIBRARY**

YR	NAME	LIMIT	ISSUE	TREND
96	CHERUBUM BOXED SET GP521	OP	150.00	150.00
96	DANCING CHERUBS ON BALL GP652	OP	40.00	40.00
96	FULL BODY CHERUB GP650	OP	35.00	35.00
96	GARDEN OF MAY BOXED SET GP520	OP	135.00	145.00
96	LILY GLASS GP655	OP	35.00	35.00
96	MADONNA & CHILD GP653	OP	35.00	35.00
96	ROSE GLASS GP654	OP	35.00	35.00

LANCE CORP.

P.W. BASTON — **SEBASTIAN CHRISTMAS ORNAMENTS**

YR	NAME	LIMIT	ISSUE	TREND
43	MADONNA OF THE CHAIR	CL	2.00	175.00
81	SANTA CLAUS	CL	29.00	30.00
82	MADONNA OF THE CHAIR (REISSUE)	CL	15.00	35.00

P.W. BASTON, JR. — **SEBASTIAN CHRISTMAS ORNAMENTS**

YR	NAME	LIMIT	ISSUE	TREND
85	HOME FOR THE HOLIDAYS	CL	10.00	17.00
86	HOLIDAY SLEIGH RIDE	CL	10.00	14.00
87	SANTA	CL	10.00	13.00
88	DECORATING THE TREE	CL	12.50	14.00
89	FINAL PREPARATIONS FOR CHRISTMAS	CL	13.90	14.00
90	STUFFING THE STOCKINGS	CL	14.00	15.00
91	MERRY CHRISTMAS	OP	14.50	15.00
92	FINAL CHECK	OP	14.50	15.00

LENOX CHINA/CRYSTAL COLLECTION

* — **ANNUAL BELL SERIES**

YR	NAME	LIMIT	ISSUE	TREND
87	PARTRIDGE BELL	YR	45.00	45.00
88	ANGEL BELL	OP	45.00	45.00
89	ST. NICHOLAS BELL	OP	45.00	45.00
90	CHRISTMAS TREE BELL	OP	49.00	49.00
91	TEDDY BEAR BELL	YR	49.00	49.00
92	SNOWMAN BELL	YR	49.00	49.00

* — **ANNUAL ORNAMENT**

YR	NAME	LIMIT	ISSUE	TREND
82	1982 ORNAMENT	YR	30.00	70.00
83	1983 ORNAMENT	YR	35.00	75.00
84	1984 ORNAMENT	YR	38.00	65.00
85	1985 ORNAMENT	YR	38.00	60.00
86	1986 ORNAMENT	YR	39.00	50.00
87	1987 ORNAMENT	YR	39.00	45.00
88	1988 ORNAMENT	YR	39.00	45.00
89	1989 ORNAMENT	YR	39.00	39.00
90	1990 ORNAMENT	YR	42.00	42.00
91	1991 ORNAMENT	YR	39.00	39.00
92	1992 ORNAMENT	YR	39.00	39.00

BOTTICELLI — **CATHEDRAL PORTRAITS**

YR	NAME	LIMIT	ISSUE	TREND
91	15TH CENTURY MADONNA & CHILD	OP	29.00	29.00
91	16TH CENTURY MADONNA & CHILD	OP	29.00	29.00

* — **CHRISTMAS CAROUSEL**

YR	NAME	LIMIT	ISSUE	TREND
89	BLACK HORSE	OP	20.00	20.00
89	CAT	OP	20.00	20.00
89	CHRISTMAS CAROUSEL SET	OP	470.00	470.00
89	ELEPHANT	OP	20.00	20.00
89	GOAT	OP	20.00	20.00
89	HARE	OP	20.00	20.00
89	LION	OP	20.00	20.00
89	PALOMINO	OP	20.00	20.00
89	PINTO	OP	20.00	20.00
89	POLAR BEAR	OP	20.00	20.00
89	REINDEER	OP	20.00	20.00
89	SEA HORSE	OP	20.00	20.00
89	SWAN	OP	20.00	20.00
89	TIGER	OP	20.00	20.00
89	UNICORN	OP	20.00	20.00
89	WHITE HORSE	OP	20.00	20.00
89	ZEBRA	OP	20.00	20.00
90	CAMEL	OP	20.00	20.00
90	FROG	OP	20.00	20.00

YR	NAME	LIMIT	ISSUE	TREND
90	GIRAFFE	OP	20.00	20.00
90	MEDIEVAL HORSE	OP	20.00	20.00
90	PANDA	OP	20.00	20.00
90	PIG	OP	20.00	20.00
90	ROOSTER	OP	20.00	20.00
90	SET OF 24	OP	468.00	468.00
90	ST. BERNARD	OP	20.00	20.00
*				**COMMEMORATIVES**
89	BABY'S FIRST CHRISTMAS (DATED)	YR	23.00	25.00
89	FIRST CHRISTMAS TOGETHER (DATED)	YR	23.00	25.00
*				**DAYS OF CHRISTMAS**
87	PARTRIDGE	OP	23.00	23.00
88	TWO TURTLEDOVES	OP	23.00	23.00
89	THREE FRENCH HENS	OP	23.00	23.00
90	FOUR CALLING BIRDS	OP	25.00	25.00
91	FIVE GOLDEN RINGS	OP	25.00	25.00
92	SIX GEESE A-LAYING	OP	25.00	25.00
*			**GOLDEN RENAISSANCE ANGELS**	
91	ANGEL WITH MANDOLIN	OP	25.00	25.00
91	ANGEL WITH TRUMPET	OP	25.00	25.00
91	ANGEL WITH VIOLIN	OP	25.00	25.00
*				**HOLIDAY HOMECOMING**
88	HEARTH	CL	23.00	23.00
89	DOOR-DATED	OP	23.00	23.00
90	HUTCH-DATED	YR	25.00	25.00
91	WINDOW (DATED)	YR	25.00	25.00
92	STOVE (DATED)	YR	25.00	25.00
*			**LENOX CARVED ORNAMENTS**	
87	PORTRAIT WREATH	CL	21.00	21.00
89	GEORGIAN FRAME	OP	21.00	25.00
*			**LENOX CHRISTMAS KEEPSAKES**	
90	ROCKING HORSE	OP	42.00	42.00
90	SWAN	OP	42.00	42.00
91	SLEIGH	OP	42.00	42.00
92	FIRE ENGINE	OP	42.00	42.00
*			**LENOX CHRISTMAS VILLAGE**	
89	VILLAGE CHURCH-DATED	OP	39.00	39.00
90	VILLAGE INN-DATED	YR	39.00	39.00
91	VILLAGE TOWN HALL (DATED)	YR	39.00	39.00
92	SWEET SHOP (DATED)	YR	39.00	39.00
*		**LENOX CRYSTAL BALL ORNAMENTS**		
84	DEEP CUT BALL	YR	35.00	50.00
85	CUT BALL	YR	35.00	50.00
86	CUT BALL	YR	35.00	45.00
87	CUT BALL	YR	29.00	29.00
88	CHRISTMAS LIGHTS BALL	YR	30.00	30.00
89	CRYSTAL LIGHTS ORNAMENT	OP	30.00	30.00
89	STARLIGHT ORNAMENT	OP	34.00	34.00
91	CRYSTAL ABBEY BALL	OP	45.00	45.00
91	CRYSTAL STARLIGHT BALL-BLUE	OP	45.00	45.00
91	CRYSTAL STARLIGHT BALL-GREEN	OP	45.00	45.00
91	CRYSTAL STARLIGHT BALL-RED	OP	45.00	45.00
92	CRYSTAL OPTIKA	OP	37.00	37.00
*			**LENOX CRYSTAL ORNAMENTS**	
89	ANNUAL CHRISTMAS TREE	YR	26.00	26.00
89	BABY'S FIRST CHRISTMAS	YR	26.00	26.00
89	CANDLELIGHT BELL	OP	38.00	38.00
89	CHRISTMAS LIGHTS TREE TOP ORNAMENT	OP	55.00	55.00
89	CRYSTAL ICICLE	OP	30.00	30.00
89	NATIVITY	OP	26.00	26.00
89	OUR FIRST CHRISTMAS	YR	26.00	26.00
89	SNOWFLAKE	OP	26.00	32.00
90	1990 CHRISTMAS TREE	YR	30.00	30.00
90	BABY'S FIRST CHRISTMAS-1990	YR	30.00	30.00
90	CANDY CANE	OP	30.00	30.00
90	CHRISTMAS GOOSE	OP	30.00	29.00
90	OUR FIRST CHRISTMAS-1990	YR	32.00	32.00
91	ABBEY TREETOPPER	OP	54.00	54.00
91	ANGEL PENDANT	OP	29.00	29.00
91	BABY'S FIRST CHRISTMAS-1991	YR	29.00	29.00
91	BIRD-BLUE	OP	29.00	29.00
91	BIRD-CLEAR	OP	29.00	29.00
91	BIRD-GREEN	OP	29.00	29.00
91	BIRD-RED	OP	29.00	29.00
91	CHRISTMAS STOCKING	OP	29.00	29.00
91	CHRISTMAS TREE-1991	YR	29.00	29.00
91	DOVE	OP	32.00	32.00
91	HERALD ANGEL-BLUE	OP	29.00	29.00
91	HERALD ANGEL-CLEAR	OP	29.00	29.00
91	HERALD ANGEL-GREEN	OP	29.00	29.00
91	HERALD ANGEL-RED	OP	29.00	29.00
91	OUR FIRST CHRISTMAS-1991	YR	29.00	29.00
91	SNOWMAN	OP	32.00	32.00

YR	NAME	LIMIT	ISSUE	TREND
*				**NATIVITY**
89	JOSEPH	OP	21.00	21.00
89	MARY & CHILD	OP	21.00	21.00
90	BALTHAZAR	OP	22.00	22.00
90	CASPAR	OP	22.00	22.00
90	MELCHIOR	OP	22.00	22.00
*				**RENAISSANCE ANGELS**
87	ANGEL WITH MANDOLIN	CL	21.00	21.00
87	ANGEL WITH TRUMPET	OP	21.00	21.00
87	ANGEL WITH VIOLIN	CL	21.00	21.00
89	ANGEL TREETOPPER	OP	100.00	100.00
*				**SANTA'S PORTRAITS**
89	SANTA'S VISIT	OP	27.00	27.00
90	SANTA WITH GARLAND	OP	29.00	29.00
90	SANTA'S RIDE	OP	29.00	29.00
91	SANTA AND CHILD	OP	29.00	29.00
92	SANTA IN CHIMNEY	OP	29.00	29.00
*				**VICTORIAN HOMES**
90	SHEFFIELD MANOR	OP	25.00	25.00
91	CAMBRIDGE MANOR	OP	25.00	25.00
*				**VICTORIAN LACE**
91	CHRISTMAS TREE	OP	25.00	25.00
91	FAN	OP	25.00	25.00
*				**YULETIDE**
85	CHRISTMAS TREE	OP	18.00	18.00
85	TEDDY BEAR	CL	18.00	18.00
89	ANGEL WITH HORN	OP	18.00	18.00
89	SANTA WITH TREE	OP	18.00	18.00
90	DOVE	OP	20.00	20.00
91	SNOWMAN	OP	20.00	20.00
92	GOOSE	OP	20.00	20.00
*				**YULETIDE EXPRESS**
88	LOCOMOTIVE	OP	39.00	39.00
89	CABOOSE-DATED	OP	39.00	90.00
90	PASSENGER-DATED	OP	39.00	39.00
91	DINING CAR (DATED)	YR	39.00	39.00
92	TENDER CAR (DATED)	YR	39.00	39.00

LILLIPUT LANE LTD.

YR	NAME	LIMIT	ISSUE	TREND
*				**CHRISTMAS ORNAMENT SERIES**
92	MISTLETOE COTTAGE	RT	28.00	50.00
93	ROBIN COTTAGE	RT	35.00	50.00
94	IVY HOUSE	RT	38.00	50.00
95	PLUM COTTAGE	RT	40.00	40.00
96	FIR TREE COTTAGE	RT	30.00	30.00
98	GREAT EXPECTATIONS	YR	35.00	35.00

R. DAY

YR	NAME	LIMIT	ISSUE	TREND
96	SANTA'S CORNER	RT	38.00	38.00

LLADRO

YR	NAME	LIMIT	ISSUE	TREND
*				**ANGEL ORCHESTRA**
91	HEAVENLY HARPIST	YR	135.00	135.00
92	ANGELIC CYMBALIST	YR	140.00	140.00
94	ANGELIC VIOLINIST	RT	150.00	175.00
*				**ANNUAL CHRISTMAS BALLS**
88	CHRISTMAS BALL L1603M	YR	60.00	85.00
89	CHRISTMAS BALL L5656M	YR	65.00	80.00
90	CHRISTMAS BALL L5730M	YR	70.00	70.00
91	CHRISTMAS BALL L5829M	YR	52.00	65.00
92	CHRISTMAS BALL L5914M	YR	52.00	60.00
93	CHRISTMAS BALL L6009M	RT	54.00	60.00
94	CHRISTMAS BALL L6105M	RT	55.00	60.00
95	CHRISTMAS BALL L6207M	YR	55.00	60.00
96	CHRISTMAS BALL L6298M	YR	55.00	60.00
97	CHRISTMAS BALL L6442M	YR	55.00	55.00
*				**MINIATURE ORNAMENTS**
88	ANGEL ORNAMENTS L-1604G SET OF 3	YR	75.00	140.00
89	HOLY FAMILY L5657G (SET OF 3)	YR	80.00	100.00
90	THREE KINGS L5729G (SET OF 3)	YR	88.00	110.00
91	HOLY SHEPHERDS L-5809 SET OF 3	YR	98.00	110.00
93	NATIVITY TRIO SET OF 3 L6095G	YR	115.00	200.00
*				**ORNAMENTS**
91	BABY'S FIRST CHRISTMAS L5839G	YR	55.00	55.00
91	OUR FIRST CHRISTMAS L5840G	YR	50.00	55.00
91	SANTA L5842G	YR	55.00	60.00
91	SNOWMAN L5841G	YR	50.00	60.00
92	BABY'S FIRST L5922G	YR	55.00	55.00
92	CHRISTMAS MORNING L5940G SET OF 3	YR	98.00	105.00
92	ELF L5938G	YR	50.00	60.00
92	MRS. CLAUS L5939G	YR	55.00	65.00
92	OUR FIRST CHRISTMAS L5923G	YR	50.00	55.00
93	BABY'S FIRST CHRISTMAS L6037G	YR	57.00	57.00
93	OUR FIRST CHRISTMAS L6038G	YR	52.00	55.00
94	JOYFUL OFFERING	RT	245.00	275.00

COCA COLA COUNTRY

YR	NAME	LIMIT	ISSUE	TREND
95	DOLL	CL	69.00	69.00
95	SURPRISED CHERUB	CL	120.00	120.00
*				TREE TOPPERS
90	ANGEL TREE TOPPER L-5719 BLUE	YR	115.00	200.00
91	ANGEL TREE TOPPER L5831G PINK	YR	115.00	200.00
92	ANGEL TREE TOPPER L5875G GREEN	YR	120.00	150.00
93	1993 ANGEL TREE TOPPER LAVENDER	RT	125.00	150.00

MARGARET FURLONG DESIGNS
M. FURLONG

				ANNUAL ORNAMENTS
96	SUNFLOWER ANGEL	CL	21.00	30.00
97	FROM THE HEART	OP	8.00	8.00

M. FURLONG

				FLORA ANGELICA
95	FAITH ANGEL	RT	45.00	115.00
96	HOPE ANGEL	CL	45.00	100.00
97	CHARITY ANGEL	10000	50.00	50.00

M. FURLONG

				VICTORIA
94	VICTORIA HEART ANGEL	RT	24.95	75.00
95	VICTORIA LILY OF THE VALLEY ANGEL	30000	24.95	75.00

MCMEMORIES

*		CHRISTMAS TREASURES GLASS ORNAMENTS		
97	RONALD AND FRENCH FRIEDS	*	40.00	40.00
*				MERRY MCNUGGETS
97	MERRY MCNUGGETS SET OF 24 ORNAMENTS	*	20.00	20.00

MIDWEST OF CANNON FALLS
I. STEELHAMMER

98	1998 DATED SANTA ON REINDEER	YR	10.00	10.00

E. WALKER

				EDDIE WALKER CHRISTMAS
98	1998 DATED SANTA HOLDING ROCKING HORSE	YR	15.00	15.00

L.R. SMITH III

			LEO R. SMITH III COLLECTION	
94	FLYING WOODSMAN SANTA 11921-1	RT	35.00	175.00
95	ANGEL OF LOVE 16123-4	CL	32.00	40.00
95	ANGEL OF PEACE 16199-9	CL	32.00	40.00
95	ANGEL OF YOUR DREAMS 16130-2	CL	32.00	32.00
95	PARTRIDGE ANGEL 13994-3	CL	30.00	30.00
95	SANTA ON REINDEER 13780-2	CL	35.00	85.00
96	ANGEL OF HEAVEN & EARTH 18396-0	CL	33.00	33.00
96	ANGEL OF LIGHT 18076-1	CL	33.00	33.00
96	ANGEL OF MUSIC 18073-4	CL	33.00	33.00
96	BELSNICKLE SANTA 18074-7	CL	39.00	39.00
98	SANTA WITH FITS 1998 DATED ORNAMENT	YR	40.00	40.00
*				MOUSEKINS
94	HEATHCLIFF GREY "TIME TO CELEBRATE"	YR	10.00	10.00

WENDT & KUHN

			WENDT & KUHN ORNAMENTS	
78	ANGEL CLIP-ON 00729-7	RT	20.00	20.00
89	TRUMPETING ANGEL, 2 ASSTD. 09402-0	RT	14.00	15.00
91	ANGEL IN RING 01208-6	RT	12.00	12.00
94	ANGEL ON MOON, STAR, 12 AASTED 12945-6	OP	20.00	20.00

MISS MARTHA ORIGINALS
M. ROOT

			ALL GOD'S CHILDREN	
87	CAMEO D-1912	ST	24.00	185.00
87	DOLL D-1924	ST	28.00	156.00

OLD WORLD CHRISTMAS
E.M. MERCK

			ANGELS AND FEMALE FIGURES	
85	RED GIRL WITH TREE 1010309	RT	4.25	10.00
85	SMALL GIRL WITH TREE 101029	RT	3.00	6.00
92	ANGEL ON FORM 1044	RT	9.00	11.00
92	GUARDIAN ANGEL 1043	RT	8.00	10.00
92	HONEY CHILD 1042	RT	7.50	8.00

E.M. MERCK

				ANIMALS
88	JUMBO ELEPHANT 1213	RT	7.00	10.00
93	PASTEL BUTTERFLY 1268	RT	8.45	10.00
94	WOODLAND SQUIRREL 1291	RT	20.00	21.00

E.M. MERCK

			BIRDS FOR HANGING	
84	COCK ROBIN 161012	RT	3.50	8.00
88	SWANS ON LAKE 1612	RT	5.50	10.00
90	DUCK 1613	RT	5.00	7.00
91	LARGE PARROT ON BALL 1617	RT	10.00	12.00
93	ROOSTER AT HEN HOUSE 1629	RT	6.50	12.00

E.M. MERCK

				BIRDS WITH CLIP
85	BLUE BIRD 181078	RT	3.30	8.00
85	MED. PEACOCK WITH TINSEL TAIL 187215	RT	4.80	10.00
85	NUTHATCH 181076	RT	3.60	8.00
86	BIRD IN NEST 1801	RT	6.75	12.00
87	FAT BURGUNDY BIRD 1813	RT	5.00	10.00
87	LILAC BIRD 1811	RT	5.70	10.00
87	RED-BREASTED SONGBIRD 1812	RT	6.25	7.00
87	SHINY GOLD BIRD 1807	RT	3.50	6.00
90	SMALL RED-HEADED SONGBIRD 1823	RT	6.25	7.00
91	FESTIVE BIRD 1832	RT	6.25	8.00

Picture Perfect Christmas *offers a triple dose of Mickey Mouse, introduced as part of Enesco Corp.'s 1994 offerings.*

The ornament for charter members of Hallmark's Keepsake Ornament Collectors' Club, Carousel Reindeer *was available originally for $8 in 1987. It is now worth over seven times as much.*

Have A Cracker Jack Christmas, *part of Enesco Corp.'s Treasury of Christmas collection, brings America's favorite snack to our Christmas trees.*

Cherished Teddies by Priscilla Hillman is one of Enesco's most popular lines. I'll Play My Drum For You *was issued in 1994 for $10.*

YR	NAME	LIMIT	ISSUE	TREND
B. MUELLER-BLECH		**BIRGIT'S CHRISTMAS COLLECTION**		
96	O'TANNENBAUM #131	RT	35.00	50.00
96	OLD CHRISTMAS BARN, THE #133	RT	50.00	100.00
E.M. MERCK		**CHURCHES AND HOUSES**		
85	SQUARE HOUSE 201040	RT	4.00	10.00
90	CHRISTMAS CHALET 2014	RT	6.75	10.00
91	THATCHED COTTAGE 2019	RT	6.30	8.00
E.M. MERCK		**CLOWNS AND MALE FIGURES**		
86	CLOWN WITH ACCORDION 2409	RT	5.60	12.00
86	CLOWN WITH BANJO 2407	RT	3.75	8.00
86	CLOWN WITH DRUM 2408	RT	5.60	12.00
86	JESTER 2419	RT	4.00	8.00
E.M. MERCK		**COLLECTOR'S EDITIONS**		
92	FLYING PEACOCK WITH WINGS 1550	RT	23.00	24.00
92	FLYING SONGBIRD WITH WINGS 1551	RT	22.00	24.00
E.M. MERCK		**FRUITS AND VEGETABLES**		
85	LARGE BASKET OF GRAPES 281053	RT	6.00	12.00
86	PEAR WITH FACE 2805	RT	3.75	8.00
90	STRAWBERRY CLUSTER 2836	RT	4.20	7.00
E.M. MERCK		**HEARTS**		
87	BURGUNDY HEART W/GLITTER 3004	RT	4.30	8.00
88	VALENTINE 3005	RT	4.20	7.00
E.M. MERCK		**MISCELLANEOUS FORMS**		
88	CLIP-ON TULIP 3605	RT	6.30	7.00
89	MORNING GLORIES 3608	RT	8.90	10.00
90	ASSORTED CHRISTMAS STARS 3620	RT	5.70	8.00
90	LARGE SNOWFLAKE 3622	RT	11.25	14.00
92	ASSORTED NORTHERN STARS 3640	RT	6.20	7.00
92	ASSORTED SPIRALS 3636	RT	8.25	9.00
94	VICTORIAN FLORAL DROP 3659	RT	21.00	25.00
E.M. MERCK		**MUSICAL INSTRUMENTS**		
86	CELLO 3801	RT	3.60	8.00
88	LARGE BELL WITH ACORNS 3804	RT	7.00	8.00
E.M. MERCK		**REFLECTORS**		
86	PINK REFLECTOR 4202	RT	5.98	10.00
90	ASSORTED 6 CM. REFLECTORS 4207	RT	5.80	8.00
90	ASSORTED REFLECTORS W/DIAMONDS 4206	RT	8.00	11.00
E.M. MERCK		**SANTAS**		
84	LARGE SANTA IN BASKET 401001	RT	7.00	15.00
85	BLUE FATHER CHRISTMAS 4010498	RT	4.20	10.00
85	JOLLY FATHER CHRISTMAS 401043	RT	3.50	8.00
85	PINK FATHER CHRISTMAS 4010499	RT	4.20	10.00
85	SANTA WITH TREE ON FORM 401026	RT	4.80	10.00
85	SMALL SANTA IN BASKET 401105	RT	4.95	10.00
85	SMALL SANTA WITH PACK 401065	RT	2.90	6.00
86	SANTA IN CHIMNEY 4005	RT	5.25	65.00
86	SANTA WITH GLUED ON TREE 4009	RT	4.80	10.00
86	SMALL BLUE SANTA 4010	RT	3.00	6.00
86	ST. NICHOLAS HEAD 4008	RT	3.55	8.00
89	ST. NICHOLAS 4020	RT	10.00	10.00
90	FESTIVE SANTA HEAD 4039	RT	9.75	12.00
90	WHITE CLIP-ON SANTA 4026	RT	6.00	11.00
93	LG. FATHER CHRISTMAS HEAD 4066	RT	23.00	25.00
E.M. MERCK		**STORYBOOK SANTAS**		
94	POLAR EXPRESS 9701	RT	9.00	12.00
E.M. MERCK		**TRANSPORTATION**		
90	LARGE ZEPPELIN 4605	RT	6.75	10.00
92	RACE CAR 4609	RT	5.50	8.00
E.M. MERCK		**TREE TOPS**		
89	ANGEL IN INDENT TREE TOP 5009	RT	27.00	27.00

ORREFORS

YR	NAME	LIMIT	ISSUE	TREND
O. ALBERIUS		**CHRISTMAS ORNAMENTS**		
84	DOVE	YR	30.00	45.00
85	ANGEL	YR	30.00	40.00
86	REINDEER	YR	30.00	35.00
87	SNOWMAN	YR	30.00	35.00
88	SLEIGH	YR	30.00	35.00
89	CHRISTMAS TREE 1989	YR	35.00	35.00
90	HOLLY LEAVES AND BERRIES	YR	35.00	35.00
91	STOCKING	YR	40.00	40.00
92	STAR	YR	35.00	35.00
93	BELL	OP	35.00	35.00

PACIFIC RIM

YR	NAME	LIMIT	ISSUE	TREND
P. SEBERN		**BRISTOL WATERFRONT**		
95	PORTSHEAD LIGHTHOUSE LIGHT COVER ORN.	OP	10.00	10.00

PFALTZGRAFF

YR	NAME	LIMIT	ISSUE	TREND
B.B. RICHARDS				
93	LITTLEST ANGEL	5000	12.50	15.00

POSSIBLE DREAMS

YR	NAME	LIMIT	ISSUE	TREND
	B. STEBELTON		**BOB STEBLETON'S FOLKART**	
98	SANTA	*	19.50	20.00
	B. STEBLETON		**BOB STEBLETON'S FOLKART**	
98	EGG SHAPE SANTA	*	5.20	5.20
98	SANTA BALL SHAPE BODY W/CONE SHAPE HEAD	*	6.80	7.00
98	SANTA BALL SHAPE WITH CONE HAT	*	6.30	7.00
98	SANTA BELL SHAPE	*	6.30	7.00
98	SANTA CANDLE STICK SHAPE	*	5.90	6.00
98	SANTA CONE SHAPE	*	7.00	7.00
98	SANTA LONG CONE HEAD HAT	*	6.90	7.00
98	SANTA ON HOLDER	*	5.90	6.00
98	SANTA PEAR BODY WITH HANDLE HEAD	*	5.90	6.00
98	SANTA PEAR SHAPE WITH HANDLE HEAD	*	6.30	7.00
98	SANTA SPINNING TOP SHAPE	*	4.80	5.00
*			**CLOTHTIQUE ANGEL TREE TOPPER**	
*	ANGEL 12 IN.	OP	54.00	54.00
*	ANGEL 14 1/2 IN.	OP	59.00	59.00
*	ANGEL 14 1/4 IN.	OP	59.00	59.00
*	ANGEL 7 IN.	OP	25.00	26.00
*	ANGEL 7 IN. SET OF THREE	OP	73.00	73.00
*	ANGEL 8 IN. SET OF THREE	OP	70.00	70.00
*	ANGEL 9 1/2 IN.	OP	35.00	35.00
*	ANGEL 9 1/2 IN. SET OF THREE	OP	96.00	96.00
*	ANGEL 9 IN.	OP	33.00	33.00
*	ANGEL GOLD 10 IN.	OP	33.00	33.00
*	ANGEL GOLD 14 IN.	OP	58.00	58.00
*	ANGEL GOLD/BEIGE 13 IN.	OP	65.00	65.00
*	ANGEL GREEN/WHITE 13 IN.	OP	65.00	65.00
*	ANGEL MAUVE/LILAC 7 IN.	OP	24.00	24.00
*	ANGEL MAUVE/LILAC 9 IN.	OP	32.00	32.00
*	ANGEL PEACH/TEAL 12 IN.	OP	53.00	53.00
*	ANGEL PEACH/TEAL 7 IN.	OP	24.00	24.00
*	ANGEL PEACH/TEAL 9 IN.	OP	32.00	32.00
*	ANGEL PURPLE/TEAL 7 IN.	OP	24.00	24.00
*	ANGEL PURPLE/TEAL 9 IN.	OP	32.00	32.00
*	ANGEL RED/CREAM 7 IN.	OP	24.00	24.00
*	ANGEL RED/CREAM 9 IN.	OP	32.00	32.00
*	ANGEL W/SCROLL 10 IN.	OP	40.00	40.00
*	ANGELS 10 IN. SET OF THREE	OP	78.00	78.00
*	CLOTHTIQUE & LACE ANGEL 10 1/2 IN.	OP	37.00	37.00
*			**CLOTHTIQUE ELVES**	
*	ELVES 7 IN. SET OF THREE	OP	57.00	57.00
*			**CLOTHTIQUE ORNAMENTS**	
*	1040s SANTA 5 1/2 IN.	OP	20.00	20.00
*	1940s SANTA 7 IN.	OP	24.00	24.00
*	ANGEL 10 IN.	OP	44.00	44.00
*	ANGEL 9 1/2 IN.	OP	37.00	37.00
*	ANGEL 9 1/2 IN.	OP	37.00	37.00
*	ANGEL 9 1/2 IN. SET OF THREE	OP	108.00	108.00
*	ANGEL GOLD 7 IN.	OP	26.00	26.00
*	ANGEL GOLD 9 IN.	OP	34.00	34.00
*	ANGEL MAUVE/LILAC 7 IN.	OP	24.00	24.00
*	ANGEL MAUVE/LILAC 9 IN.	OP	32.00	32.00
*	ANGEL PEACH/TEAL 7 IN.	OP	24.00	24.00
*	ANGEL PEACH/TEAL 9 IN.	OP	32.00	32.00
*	ANGEL PURPLE/TEAL 7 IN.	OP	24.00	24.00
*	ANGEL PURPLE/TEAL 9 IN.	OP	32.00	32.00
*	ANGEL RED/CREAM 7 IN.	OP	24.00	24.00
*	ANGEL RED/CREAM 9 IN.	OP	32.00	32.00
*	ANGEL/BLUE 9 IN.	OP	44.00	44.00
*	ANGEL/GOLD 9 IN.	OP	44.00	44.00
*	ANGEL/RED 9 IN.	OP	44.00	44.00
*	ANGELS 6 IN. SET OF THREE	OP	57.00	57.00
*	ANGELS 7 1/4 IN. SET OF THREE	OP	79.00	79.00
*	ANGELS 7 IN. SET OF THREE	OP	79.00	79.00
*	BEIGE SANTA 7 IN.	OP	23.00	23.00
*	CHERUB 5 1/3 IN. SET OF THREE	OP	43.00	43.00
*	CHERUBS 5 1/2 IN. SET OF THREE	OP	45.00	45.00
*	CHERUBS 5 IN. SET OF THREE	OP	45.00	45.00
*	CHERUBS GOLD 5 1/2 IN. SET OF THREE	OP	40.00	40.00
*	COLONIAL SANTA 7 IN.	OP	23.00	23.00
*	FATHER CHRISTMAS 7 1/4 IN.	OP	20.00	20.00
*	FIREMAN SANTA 6 IN.	OP	17.50	18.00
*	FIREMAN SANTA 7 3/4 IN.	OP	24.00	24.00
*	FIRST CHRISTMAS 7 IN.	OP	23.00	23.00
*	KRIS KRINGLE 7 IN.	OP	20.00	20.00
*	MRS. CLAUS 5 1/2 IN.	OP	16.00	16.00
*	MRS. CLAUS 6 1/2 IN.	OP	22.00	22.00
*	NICHOLAS 5 1/2 IN.	OP	20.00	20.00
*	NICHOLAS 7 IN.	OP	24.00	24.00
*	PATRIOTIC SANTA 7 1/4 IN.	OP	20.00	20.00
*	SANTA 5 1/2 IN.	OP	16.00	16.00
*	SANTA GREEN COAT 5 1/2 IN.	OP	13.50	14.00

YR	NAME	LIMIT	ISSUE	TREND
*	SANTA GREEN COAT 7 IN.	OP	15.00	15.00
*	SANTA IN BED 6 3/4 IN.	OP	36.00	36.00
*	SANTA IN RED 7 IN.	OP	23.00	23.00
*	SANTA RED COAT 5 1/2 IN.	OP	13.50	14.00
*	SANTA RED COAT 7 IN.	OP	15.00	15.00
*	SANTA W/BLUE CAPE 7 IN.	OP	22.00	22.00
*	SANTA W/LIST 7 IN.	OP	22.00	22.00
*	SANTA W/STAFF 7 IN.	OP	22.00	22.00
*	SANTA WHITE COAT 5 1/2 IN.	OP	13.50	14.00
*	SANTA WHITE COAT 7 IN.	OP	15.00	15.00
*	SKIING SANTA 7 1/2 IN.	OP	26.00	26.00
*	STOP HERE PLEASE 6 1/4 IN.	OP	30.00	30.00
*	TRADITIONAL SANTA 5 1/2 IN.	OP	16.00	16.00
*	TRADITIONAL SANTA 7 IN.	OP	22.00	22.00
*	WORKING SANTA 7 IN.	OP	22.00	22.00
*				**CLOTHTIQUE SANTAS**
*	SANTA CLAWS 9 3/4 IN.	OP	69.00	69.00
*				**CRINKLE CLAUS**
*	BISHOP OF MAYA	*	7.80	8.00
*	FATHER CHRISTMAS 3 IN.	*	7.80	8.00
*	GERMAN SANTA 3 IN.	*	7.80	8.00
*	NIBBLY DO 2 3/4 IN.	OP	10.50	11.00
*	PERE NOEL SANTA 3 1/4 IN.	*	7.80	8.00
*	SNUGGLES 3 1/4 IN.	OP	11.70	12.00
*	ST. NICHOLAS 3 IN.	*	7.80	8.00
*				**PEPSI**
*	PEPSI BOTTLE CAP 2 1/2 IN.	OP	2.90	3.00
*	PEPSI BOTTLE IN WREATH 4 IN.	OP	7.90	8.00
*	PEPSI SANTA 7 IN.	OP	27.00	27.00
*	PEPSI SANTA IN WREATH 3 1/2 IN.	OP	7.40	8.00
*	PEPSI SANTA ON BOTTLE 3 1/2 IN.	OP	13.50	14.00
*	PEPSI SANTA W/BARREL 4 IN.	OP	12.20	12.20
*	PEPSI SANTA/BALLOON 4 1/2 IN.	OP	14.00	15.00
*	PEPSI SANTA/PEPSI CAN 2 1/2 IN.	OP	13.00	13.00
*	PEPSI SANTA/XMAS BALL 3 1/2 IN.	OP	13.50	14.00
*	PEPSI SIGN/WREATH 3 1/2 IN.	OP	7.40	8.00
*				**THICKETS**
*	BEAU PEEK 3 IN.	OP	14.00	15.00
*	CANDY TAILS 2 1/4 IN.	RT	11.50	12.00
*	CHRISTMAS WHISKERS 3 IN.	RT	11.50	12.00
*	FICKLE TAILS 2 3/4 IN.	OP	11.50	12.00
*	HARMONY HOLIDAY 2 1/4 IN.	OP	12.00	12.00
*	JINGLE BELLS 3 1/4 IN.	RT	12.00	12.00
*	KRIS KRINKLE 3 IN.	OP	12.50	13.00
*	MELODY TWINKLE PAWS 2 3/4 IN.	OP	13.00	13.00
*	RASCAL DOODLE 3 IN.	OP	20.00	20.00
*	TINSEL TUNE 2 1/2 IN.	OP	11.50	12.00
*	TRICKY TAILS 2 3/4 IN.	OP	11.50	12.00
*	TWINKLE TAILS 2 3/4 IN.	OP	11.50	12.00
95	HOLLY TAILS 2 1/4 IN.	OP	11.50	12.00

PRECIOUS ART/PANTON/KRYSTONIA

	*			**WORLD OF KRYSTONIA**
94	GRAFYNSSORPRISE	RT	19.00	23.00
94	WHAT KRYSTAL	RT	19.00	23.00

PRIZM
P. ULVILDEN

				PIPKA'S STORIES OF CHRISTMAS
98	FATHER CHRISTMAS	OP	15.00	15.00
98	NORWEGIAN JULENISSE	OP	15.00	15.00
98	PEACE MAKER	OP	15.00	15.00
98	POLISH FATHER CHRISTMAS	OP	15.00	15.00
98	SAN NICOLAS	OP	15.00	15.00
98	SANTA'S SPOTTED GREY	OP	15.00	15.00
98	ST. NICHOLAS	OP	15.00	15.00
98	STORYTIME SANTA	OP	15.00	15.00
98	TEDDY BEAR SANTA	OP	15.00	15.00
98	WHERE'S RUDOLPH?	OP	15.00	15.00

RAYMON TROUP STUDIO
W.R. TROUP

				ANGELS
98	SNOW BUBBLES	OP	28.00	28.00
98	STAR LIGHT, STAR BRIGHT	OP	28.00	28.00

RECO INTERNATIONAL
J. MCCLELLAND

				RECO ANGEL COLLECTION HANG-UPS
87	ADORATION	OP	10.00	10.00
87	DEVOTION	OP	7.50	8.00
87	GLORIA	OP	7.50	8.00
87	HARMONY	OP	7.50	8.00
87	HOPE	OP	10.00	10.00
87	INNOCENCE	OP	7.50	8.00
87	JOY	OP	7.50	8.00
87	LOVE	OP	7.50	8.00

YR	NAME	LIMIT	ISSUE	TREND
87	PEACE	OP	10.00	10.00
87	SERENITY	OP	10.00	10.00

J. MCCLELLAND

RECO CLOWN COLLECTION HANG-UPS

YR	NAME	LIMIT	ISSUE	TREND
87	ARABESQUE	OP	8.00	8.00
87	BOW JANGLES	OP	8.00	8.00
87	CURLY	OP	8.00	8.00
87	HOBO	OP	8.00	8.00
87	PROFESSOR, THE	OP	8.00	8.00
87	RUFFLES	OP	8.00	8.00
87	SAD EYES	OP	8.00	8.00
87	SCAMP	OP	8.00	8.00
87	SPARKLES	OP	8.00	8.00
87	TOP HAT	OP	8.00	8.00
87	WHOOPIE	OP	8.00	8.00
87	WINKIE	OP	8.00	8.00

S. KUCK

RECO ORNAMENT COLLECTION

YR	NAME	LIMIT	ISSUE	TREND
88	BILLY	YR	15.00	16.00
88	LISA	YR	15.00	16.00
89	HEATHER	YR	15.00	16.00
89	TIMOTHY	YR	15.00	16.00
90	AMY	YR	15.00	16.00
90	JOHNNY	YR	15.00	16.00
90	PEACE ON EARTH	17500	17.50	18.00

REED & BARTON

12 DAYS OF CHRISTMAS

YR	NAME	LIMIT	ISSUE	TREND
83	PARTRIDGE IN A PEAR TREE	YR	16.50	20.00
83	TURTLEDOVES	YR	16.50	20.00
84	CALLING BIRDS	YR	19.00	20.00
84	FRENCH HENS	YR	19.00	20.00
85	GEESE A'LAYING	YR	20.00	20.00
85	GOLD RINGS	YR	20.00	20.00
86	MAIDS A'MILKING	YR	20.00	20.00
86	SWANS A'SWIMMING	YR	20.00	20.00
87	LADIES DANCING	YR	20.00	20.00
87	LORDS A'LEAPING	YR	20.00	20.00
88	DRUMMERS DRUMMING	YR	20.00	20.00
88	PIPERS PIPING	YR	20.00	20.00

12 DAYS OF CHRISTMAS STERLING & LEAD CRYSTAL

YR	NAME	LIMIT	ISSUE	TREND
88	PARTRIDGE IN A PEAR TREE	YR	25.00	28.00
89	TWO TURTLEDOVES	YR	25.00	28.00
90	FRENCH HENS	YR	28.00	28.00
91	CALLING BIRDS	YR	28.00	28.00
92	FIVE GOLDEN RINGS	YR	28.00	28.00

CAROUSEL HORSE

YR	NAME	LIMIT	ISSUE	TREND
88	GOLD COVERED-1988	YR	15.00	16.00
88	SILVERPLATE-1988	YR	13.50	14.00
89	GOLD COVERED-1989	YR	15.00	16.00
89	SILVERPLATE-1989	YR	13.50	14.00
90	GOLD COVERED-1990	YR	14.50	15.00
90	SILVERPLATE-1990	YR	13.50	14.00
91	GOLD COVERED-1991	YR	15.00	16.00
91	SILVERPLATE-1991	YR	13.50	14.00
92	GOLD COVERED-1992	YR	15.00	16.00
92	SILVERPLATE-1992	YR	13.50	14.00

CATHEDRALS

YR	NAME	LIMIT	ISSUE	TREND
90	GOTHIC	YR	12.50	13.00
90	MOORISH	YR	12.50	13.00

CHRISTMAS CROSS

YR	NAME	LIMIT	ISSUE	TREND
71	24KT. GOLD OVER STERLING-V1971	YR	17.50	225.00
71	STERLING SILVER-1971	YR	10.00	300.00
72	24KT. GOLD OVER STERLING-V1972	YR	17.50	80.00
72	STERLING SILVER-1972	YR	10.00	125.00
73	24KT. GOLD OVER STERLING-V1973	YR	17.50	60.00
73	STERLING SILVER-1973	YR	10.00	70.00
74	24KT. GOLD OVER STERLING-V1974	YR	20.00	55.00
74	STERLING SILVER-1974	YR	13.00	45.00
75	24KT. GOLD OVER STERLING-V1975	YR	20.00	50.00
75	STERLING SILVER-1975	YR	13.00	45.00
76	24KT. GOLD OVER STERLING-V1976	YR	20.00	50.00
76	STERLING SILVER-1976	YR	14.00	55.00
77	24KT. GOLD OVER STERLING-V1977	YR	19.00	50.00
77	STERLING SILVER-1977	YR	15.00	45.00
78	24KT. GOLD OVER STERLING-V1978	YR	20.00	50.00
78	STERLING SILVER-1978	YR	16.00	60.00
79	24KT. GOLD OVER STERLING-V1979	YR	24.00	45.00
79	STERLING SILVER-1979	YR	20.00	60.00
80	24KT. GOLD OVER STERLING-V1980	YR	40.00	50.00
80	STERLING SILVER-1980	YR	35.00	60.00
81	24KT. GOLD OVER STERLING-V1981	YR	40.00	45.00
81	STERLING SILVER-1981	YR	35.00	45.00
82	24KT. GOLD OVER STERLING-V1982	YR	40.00	45.00
82	STERLING SILVER-1982	YR	35.00	53.00
83	24KT. GOLD OVER STERLING-V1983	YR	40.00	45.00
83	STERLING SILVER-1983	YR	35.00	50.00

YR	NAME	LIMIT	ISSUE	TREND
84	24KT. GOLD OVER STERLING-V1984	YR	45.00	45.00
84	STERLING SILVER-1984	YR	35.00	45.00
85	24KT. GOLD OVER STERLING-V1985	YR	40.00	40.00
85	STERLING SILVER-1985	YR	35.00	40.00
86	24KT. GOLD OVER STERLING-V1986	YR	40.00	40.00
86	STERLING SILVER-1986	YR	39.00	39.00
87	24KT. GOLD OVER STERLING-V1987	YR	40.00	40.00
87	STERLING SILVER-1987	YR	35.00	35.00
88	24KT. GOLD OVER STERLING-V1988	YR	40.00	40.00
88	STERLING SILVER-1988	YR	35.00	35.00
89	24KT. GOLD OVER STERLING-V1989	YR	40.00	40.00
89	STERLING SILVER-1989	YR	35.00	35.00
90	24KT. GOLD OVER STERLING-V1990	YR	45.00	45.00
90	STERLING SILVER-1990	YR	40.00	40.00
91	24KT. GOLD OVER STERLING-V1991	YR	45.00	45.00
91	STERLING SILVER-1991	YR	40.00	40.00
92	24KT GOLD OVER STERLING-1992	YR	45.00	45.00
92	STERLING SILVER-1992	YR	40.00	40.00
*				
			COLORS OF CHRISTMAS	
90	VICTORIAN HOUSE	YR	12.50	13.00
90	WREATH	YR	12.50	13.00
*				
			DISNEY CHRISTMAS ORNAMENTS	
87	MICKEY	YR	25.00	40.00
88	MINNIE	YR	25.00	25.00
*				
			FLORA OF CHRISTMAS	
90	POINSETTIA/SNOWDROP (PAIR)	YR	25.00	25.00
91	MISTLETOE & CHRISTMAS IVY	YR	25.00	25.00
*				
			HOLLY BALL	
76	1976 SILVER PLATED	YR	14.00	50.00
77	1977 SILVER PLATED	YR	15.00	35.00
78	1978 SILVER PLATED	YR	15.00	35.00
79	1979 SILVER PLATED	YR	15.00	35.00
*				
			HOLLY BELL	
80	1980 BELL	YR	23.00	40.00
80	GOLD PLATE BELL-V1980	YR	25.00	45.00
81	1981 BELL	YR	23.00	35.00
81	GOLD PLATE BELL-V1981	YR	28.00	35.00
82	1982 BELL	YR	23.00	35.00
82	GOLD PLATE BELL-V1982	YR	28.00	35.00
83	1983 BELL	YR	24.00	40.00
83	GOLD PLATE BELL-V1983	YR	30.00	35.00
84	1984 BELL	YR	25.00	30.00
84	GOLD PLATE BELL-V1984	YR	29.00	35.00
85	1985 BELL	YR	25.00	35.00
85	GOLD PLATE BELL-V1985	YR	29.00	29.00
86	1986 BELL	YR	25.00	35.00
86	GOLD PLATE BELL-V1986	YR	29.00	33.00
87	1987 BELL	YR	28.00	30.00
87	GOLD PLATE BELL-V1987	YR	30.00	30.00
88	1988 BELL	YR	28.00	30.00
88	GOLD PLATE BELL-V1988	YR	30.00	30.00
89	1989 BELL	YR	28.00	28.00
89	GOLD PLATE BELL-V1989	YR	30.00	30.00
90	1990 BELL	YR	28.00	28.00
90	GOLD PLATE BELL-V1990	YR	30.00	30.00
91	1991 BELL	YR	28.00	28.00
91	GOLD PLATE BELL-V1991	YR	30.00	30.00
92	GOLD PLATE BELL-V1992	YR	30.00	30.00
92	SILVER PLATE BELL-1992	YR	28.00	28.00

RJB DESIGNS
R. BRENNAN

				CINDER CLAUS
93	'93 CINDER CLAUS	1000	42.00	45.00
94	'94 CINDER CLAUS	1000	42.00	45.00
96	CINDER CLAUS	1000	38.00	38.00

ROMAN INC.
I. SPENCER

				CATNIPPERS
88	CHRISTMAS MOURNING	OP	15.00	15.00
88	PUSS IN BERRIES	OP	15.00	15.00
88	RING A DING-DING	OP	15.00	15.00
89	BOW BRUMMEL	OP	15.00	15.00
89	HAPPY HOLIDAZE	OP	15.00	15.00
89	SANDY CLAWS	OP	15.00	15.00
90	FELIX NAVIDAD	OP	15.00	15.00
90	SOCK IT TO ME SANTA	OP	15.00	15.00
90	STUCK ON CHRISTMAS	OP	15.00	15.00
91	CHRISTMAS KNIGHT	OP	15.00	15.00
91	FAUX PAW	OP	15.00	15.00
91	MEOWY CHRISTMAS	OP	15.00	15.00
92	HOLLY DAYS ARE HAPPY DAYS	OP	15.00	15.00
92	PAWTRIDGE IN A PURR TREE	OP	15.00	15.00
92	SNOW BIZ	OP	15.00	15.00

YR NAME	LIMIT	ISSUE	TREND
I. SPENCER		**DISCOVERY OF AMERICA**	
91 KITSTOPHER KOLUMBUS	1992	15.00	16.00
91 QUEEN KITSABELLA	1992	15.00	16.00
E. SIMONETTI		**FONTANINI ANNUAL CHRISTMAS ORNAMENT**	
91 1991 ANNUAL (BOY)	YR	8.50	9.00
91 1991 ANNUAL (GIRL)	YR	8.50	9.00
92 1992 ANNUAL (BOY)	YR	8.50	9.00
92 1992 ANNUAL (GIRL)	YR	8.50	9.00
E. SIMONETTI		**FONTANINI HEIRLOOM NATIVITIES BAS RELIEF ORNAMENTS**	
95 ANNUNCIATION, THE	20000	20.00	20.00
96 JOURNEY TO BETHLEHEM	20000	20.00	20.00
97 GLORIA ANGEL	YR	20.00	20.00
M.J. DORCY		**MILLENIUM COLLECTION**	
92 SILENT NIGHT	20000	20.00	20.00
93 ANNUNCIATION	20000	20.00	20.00
94 PEACE ON EARTH	20000	20.00	20.00
95 CAUSE OF OUR JOY	20000	20.00	20.00
96 PRINCE OF EACE	30000	20.00	20.00
97 GENTLE LOVE	YR	20.00	20.00
SERAPHIM STUDIOS		**SERAPHIM CLASSICS DIMENSIONAL ORNAMENT**	
98 NOELLE-GIVING SPIRIT	OP	19.50	20.00
FARO STUDIOS		**SERAPHIM CLASSICS FARO COLLECTION ORNAMENTS**	
94 ROSALYN-RAREST OF HEAVEN	CL	25.00	25.00
95 HELENA-HEAVEN'S HERALD	20000	25.00	25.00
96 FLORA-FLOWER OF HEAVEN	20000	25.00	25.00
97 EMILY-HEAVEN'S TREASURE	YR	25.00	25.00
98 ELISE-HEAVEN'S GLORY	YR	25.00	25.00
SERAPHIM STUDIOS		**SERAPHIM CLASSICS WAFER ORNAMENT**	
95 CYMBELINE-PEACEMAKER	RT	15.00	15.00
95 EVANGELINE-ANGEL OF MERCY	RT	15.00	15.00
95 IRIS-RAINBOW'S END	OP	15.00	15.00
95 ISABEL-GENTLE SPIRIT	OP	15.00	15.00
95 LYDIA-WINGED POET	RT	15.00	15.00
95 OPHELIA-HEART SEEKER	RT	15.00	15.00
96 FELICIA-ADORING MAIDEN	RT	15.00	15.00
96 LAURICE-WISDOM'S CHILD	RT	15.00	15.00
96 PRISCILLA-BENEVOLENT GUIDE	RT	15.00	15.00
96 SERAPHINA-HEAVEN'S HELPER	RT	15.00	15.00
97 CELINE-THE MORNING STAR	OP	15.00	15.00
97 FRANCESCA-LOVING GUARDIAN	OP	15.00	15.00
97 GABRIEL-CELESTIAL MESSENGER	OP	15.00	15.00
97 MARIAH-HEAVENLY JOY	OP	15.00	15.00
97 ROSALIE-NATURE'S DELIGHT	OP	15.00	15.00
97 SERENA-ANGEL OF PEACE	OP	15.00	15.00
98 CHELSEA-SUMMER'S DELIGHT	OP	15.00	15.00
98 HARMONY-LOVE'S GUARDIAN	OP	15.00	15.00
98 HOPE-LIGHT IN THE DISTANCE	OP	15.00	15.00
98 MELODY- HEAVEN'S SONG	OP	15.00	15.00
98 RACHEL-CHILDREN'S JOY	OP	15.00	15.00
98 TAMARA-BLESSED GUARDIAN	OP	15.00	15.00

ROYAL COPENHAGEN

YR NAME	LIMIT	ISSUE	TREND
F. NAESS-SCHMIDT		**CHRISTMAS**	
98 CHRISTMAS SHEAF 1998	YR	65.00	65.00
S. VESTERGAARD		**CHRISTMAS**	
98 CHRISTMAS	YR	38.00	38.00

SAMSONS STUDIOS

YR NAME	LIMIT	ISSUE	TREND
S. BUTCHER		**MCCOONS COUNTY**	
87 HERE COMES SANTA CLAUS	CL	15.00	40.00

SARAH'S ATTIC

YR NAME	LIMIT	ISSUE	TREND
S. SCHULTZ		**GOLD PLATED ORNAMENTS**	
95 ADORA/X001	1000	20.00	20.00
95 BLESSED FAMILY/X003	1000	24.00	24.00
95 BLESSED IS HE III/X002	1000	24.00	24.00
95 CLAUDIA/BREWSTER/X006	1000	23.00	23.00
95 OH MY!/X005	RT	23.00	23.00
95 TILLIE/X004	1000	23.00	23.00
S. SCHULTZ		**SANTAS OF THE MONTH ORNAMENTS**	
88 APRIL MINI SANTA	CL	14.00	17.00
88 AUG. MINI SANTA	CL	14.00	17.00
88 DEC. MINI SANTA	CL	14.00	17.00
88 FEB. MINI SANTA	CL	14.00	17.00
88 JAN. MINI SANTA	CL	14.00	17.00
88 JULY MINI SANTA	CL	14.00	17.00
88 JUNE MINI SANTA	CL	14.00	17.00
88 MARCH MINI SANTA	CL	14.00	17.00
88 MAY MINI SANTA	CL	14.00	17.00
88 NOV. MINI SANTA	CL	14.00	17.00
88 OCT. MINI SANTA	CL	14.00	17.00
88 SEPT. MINI SANTA	CL	14.00	17.00

YR	NAME	LIMIT	ISSUE	TREND

SCHMID

*

			DISNEY ANNUAL	
85	SNOW BIZ	YR	8.50	20.00
86	TREE FOR TWO	YR	8.50	15.00
87	MERRY MOUSE MEDLEY	YR	8.50	10.00
88	WARM WINTER RIDE	YR	11.00	45.00
89	MERRY MICKEY CLAUS	YR	11.00	11.00
90	HOLLY JOLLY CHRISTMAS	YR	13.50	30.00
91	MICKEY & MINNIE'S ROCKIN' CHRISTMAS	YR	13.50	14.00

L. DAVIS

			FRIENDS OF MINE	
89	SUN WORSHIPPERS	YR	33.00	35.00
90	SUNDAY AFTERNOON TREAT	YR	38.00	35.00
91	WARM MILK	YR	38.00	38.00
92	CAT AND JENNY WREN	YR	35.00	35.00

M. LILLEMOE

			KITTY CUCUMBER ANNUAL	
89	RING AROUND THE ROSIE	YR	25.00	25.00
90	SWAN LAKE	YR	12.00	12.00
91	TEA PARTY	YR	12.00	24.00

L. DAVIS

			LOWELL DAVIS COUNTRY CHRISTMAS	
83	MAILBOX & GIFTS	YR	17.50	70.00
84	CAT IN BOOT	YR	17.50	75.00
85	WILBUR IN TROUGH	YR	17.50	70.00
86	CHURCH	YR	17.50	48.00
87	BLOSSOM IN WREATH	YR	20.00	53.00
88	WISTERIA IN WREATH	YR	20.00	33.00
89	WREN	YR	20.00	44.00
90	BARN	YR	20.00	20.00
91	CHURCH AT RED OAK II	YR	25.00	27.00
92	BORN ON A STARRY NIGHT	YR	25.00	25.00

L. DAVIS

			LOWELL DAVIS GLASS ORNAMENTS	
86	CHRISTMAS AT RED OAK	YR	5.00	20.00
87	BLOSSOM'S GIFT	YR	5.50	15.00
88	HOPE MOM LIKES IT	YR	6.00	18.00
89	PETER AND THE WREN	YR	6.50	15.00
90	WINTERING DEER	YR	6.50	15.00
91	CHURCH AT RED OAK II	YR	7.50	28.00
92	BORN ON A STARRY NIGHT BALL	YR	7.50	15.00

SCULPTURE WORKSHOP DESIGNS

F. KREITCHET

				ANNUAL
85	RETURN OF THE CHRISTMAS COMET, THE	7500	39.00	100.00
86	LIBERTY/PEACE	7500	49.00	150.00
87	CHRISTMAS AT HOME	2500	57.00	90.00
88	CHRISTMAS DOVES	2500	57.00	80.00
89	SANTA'S REINDEER	2500	60.00	75.00
90	JOYFUL ANGELS	2500	75.00	75.00
91	ANGEL & SHEPHERDS	2500	75.00	75.00

F. KREITCHET

			ANNUAL-SPECIAL COMMEMORATIVE	
87	BICENTENNIAL OF/U.S. CONSTITUTION, THE	200	95.00	250.00
89	PRESIDENTIAL SIGNATURES, THE	200	95.00	125.00
91	U.S. BILL OF RIGHTS, THE	200	150.00	150.00

F. KREITCHET

				SANTA SERIES
92	FOREVER SANTA	2500	68.00	68.00

SEYMOUR MANN

JAIMY

			CHRISTMAS COLLECTION	
89	FLAT RED SANTA ORNAMENT CJ-115R	OP	2.88	3.00
89	FLAT SANTA ORNAMENT CJ-115	OP	7.50	8.00
91	ELF WITH REINDEER CJ-422	CL	9.00	9.00

J. WHITE

			CHRISTMAS COLLECTION	
85	ANGEL WALL ORNAMENT CHRISTMAS-523	CL	12.00	12.00
86	CUPID HEAD ORNAMENT CHRISTMAS-53	OP	25.00	25.00
86	SANTA ORNAMENT CHRISTMAS-384	CL	7.50	8.00
89	CHRISTMAS CAT IN TEACUP CHRISTMAS-660	OP	13.50	14.00

J. SAUERBREY

			GINGERBREAD CHRISTMAS COLLECTION	
91	GINGERBREAD ANGEL CJ-411	CL	7.50	8.00
91	GINGERBREAD HOUSE CJ-416	CL	7.50	8.00
91	GINGERBREAD MAN CJ-415	CL	7.50	8.00
91	GINGERBREAD MOUSE/BOOT CJ-409	CL	7.50	8.00
91	GINGERBREAD MRS. CLAUS CJ-414	CL	7.50	8.00
91	GINGERBREAD REINDEER CJ-410	CL	7.50	8.00
91	GINGERBREAD SANTA CJ-408	CL	7.50	8.00
91	GINGERBREAD SLEIGH CJ-406	CL	7.50	8.00
91	GINGERBREAD SNOWMAN CJ-412	CL	7.50	8.00
91	GINGERBREAD TREE CJ-407	CL	7.50	8.00

JAIMY

			VICTORIAN CHRISTMAS COLLECTION	
93	COUPLE AGAINST WIND CJ-420	CL	15.00	16.00

SHELIA'S COLLECTIBLES

S. THOMPSON

				MIDAS TOUCH
95	BLUE COTTAGES (FIRST ED.)	RT	15.00	35.00
95	CAPE HATTERAS LIGHT (FIRST ED.)	RT	15.00	35.00
95	CHESTNUTT HOUSE (FIRST ED.)	RT	19.00	30.00
95	DRAYTON HOUSE (FIRST ED.)	RT	19.00	35.00

YR	NAME	LIMIT	ISSUE	TREND
95	EAST BROTHER LIGHTHOUSE (FIRST ED.)	RT	15.00	35.00
95	ECLECTIC BLUE (FIRST ED.)	RT	15.00	35.00
95	GOELLER HOUSE (FIRST ED.)	RT	19.00	35.00
95	POINT FERMIN LIGHT (FIRST ED.)	RT	19.00	35.00
95	STOCKTON PLACE ROW (FIRST ED.)	RT	19.00	35.00
96	ARTIST HOUSE	OP	19.00	19.00
96	BLUE COTTAGE (SECOND ED.)	RT	15.00	25.00
96	CAPE HATTERAS LIGHT (SECOND ED.)	RT	15.00	25.00
96	CAPITOL	OP	19.00	19.00
96	CHESTNUTT HOUSE (SECOND ED.)	RT	15.00	25.00
96	DRAYTON HOUSE (FIRST ED.)	RT	19.00	35.00
96	DRAYTON HOUSE (SECOND ED.)	RT	15.00	25.00
96	E.B. HALL	OP	19.00	19.00
96	EAST BROTHER LIGHTHOUSE (SECOND ED.)	RT	15.00	25.00
96	ECLECTIC BLUE (SECOND ED.)	RT	15.00	25.00
96	GOELLER HOUSE (SECOND ED.)	RT	15.00	25.00
96	MAIL POUCH BARN	RT	19.00	35.00
96	MARKET	OP	19.00	19.00
96	PINK HOUSE	OP	19.00	19.00
96	POINT FERMIN LIGHT (SECOND ED.)	RT	15.00	25.00
96	RUTLEDGE	OP	19.00	19.00
96	ST. PHILIPS CHURCH	OP	19.00	19.00
96	STOCKTON PLACE ROW (SECOND ED.)	RT	15.00	25.00
96	THOMAS POINT LIGHT	RT	19.00	35.00
96	TITMAN HOUSE	OP	19.00	19.00
96	VICTORIA	OP	19.00	19.00
96	WHITE COTTAGE	OP	19.00	19.00

S. THOMPSON

OUR STARS

YR	NAME	LIMIT	ISSUE	TREND
96	BANTA HOUSE	RT	23.00	23.00
96	GREENMAN HOUSE	RT	21.00	23.00
96	RILEY-CUTLER HOUSE	RT	23.00	23.00
96	WELLER HOUSE	RT	23.00	23.00

STUDIOS OF HARRY SMITH

H. SMITH

CHRISTMAS TREE ORNAMENTS

YR	NAME	LIMIT	ISSUE	TREND
95	ANGEL	150	350.00	350.00
95	HUMMINGBIRD	150	250.00	250.00

SWAROVSKI AMERICA

*

HOLIDAY ORNAMENTS

YR	NAME	LIMIT	ISSUE	TREND
86	ANGEL/NOEL, LARGE	YR	35.00	75.00
86	DOVE/PEACE, SMALL	YR	18.00	60.00
86	HOLLY/MERRY CHRISTMAS, SMALL	YR	18.00	60.00
86	LARGE PARTRIDGE/MERRY CHRISTMAS	YR	35.00	75.00
86	MEDIUM ANGEL/JOYEUX NOEL	YR	23.00	75.00
86	MEDIUM BELL/MERRY CHRISTMAS	YR	23.00	75.00
86	SMALL ANGEL/NOEL	YR	18.00	60.00
86	SMALL BELL/MERRY CHRISTMAS	YR	18.00	60.00
86	SNOWFLAKE, MEDIUM	YR	23.00	75.00
86	SNOWFLAKE, SMALL	YR	18.00	70.00
87	1987 HOLIDAY ETCHING-CANDLE	YR	20.00	280.00
88	1988 HOLIDAY ETCHING-WREATH	YR	25.00	110.00
89	1989 HOLIDAY ETCHING-DOVE	YR	35.00	250.00
90	1990 HOLIDAY ETCHING-MERRY CHRISTMAS	YR	25.00	175.00
91	1991 HOLIDAY ORNAMENT	YR	35.00	175.00

M. ZENDRON

HOLIDAY ORNAMENTS

YR	NAME	LIMIT	ISSUE	TREND
95	SWAROVSKI '95 HOLIDAY ORNAMENT	YR	40.00	75.00
96	SWAROVSKI '96 HOLIDAY ORNAMENT	YR	45.00	65.00

TOWLE SILVERSMITHS

*

CHRISTMAS ANGEL

YR	NAME	LIMIT	ISSUE	TREND
91	1991 ANGEL	CL	45.00	70.00

*

GRANDE BAROQUE 12 DAYS SERIES

YR	NAME	LIMIT	ISSUE	TREND
91	FOUR COLLY BIRDS	CL	40.00	95.00
92	FIVE GOLDEN RINGS	CL	40.00	50.00
93	SIX GEESE A LAYING	CL	40.00	43.00
94	SEVEN SWANS A SWIMMING	OP	40.00	40.00
95	EIGHT MAIDS A MILKING	OP	40.00	40.00

*

REMEMBRANCE COLLECTION

YR	NAME	LIMIT	ISSUE	TREND
90	OLD MASTER SNOWFLAKE-1990	CL	45.00	85.00
91	OLD MASTER SNOWFLAKE-1991	CL	45.00	80.00
92	OLD MASTER SNOWFLAKE-1992	CL	45.00	75.00

*

SONGS OF CHRISTMAS MEDALLIONS

YR	NAME	LIMIT	ISSUE	TREND
78	SILENT NIGHT MEDALLION	CL	35.00	75.00
79	DECK THE HALLS	CL	35.00	75.00
80	JINGLE BELLS	CL	53.00	75.00
81	HARK THE HEARLD ANGELS SING	CL	53.00	140.00
82	O CHRISTMAS TREE	CL	35.00	75.00
83	SILVER BELLS	CL	40.00	60.00
84	LET IT SNOW	CL	30.00	50.00
85	CHESTNUTS ROASTING ON OPEN FIRE	CL	35.00	75.00
86	IT CAME UPON A MIDNIGHT CLEAR	CL	35.00	75.00
87	WHITE CHRISTMAS	CL	35.00	75.00

*

STERLING CHRISTMAS ORNAMENTS

YR	NAME	LIMIT	ISSUE	TREND
89	FACETED BALL	OP	38.00	38.00

YR	NAME	LIMIT	ISSUE	TREND
89	FLUTED BALL	OP	38.00	38.00
89	PLAIN BALL	OP	38.00	38.00
89	POMANDER BALL	OP	33.00	33.00
*			STERLING FLORAL MEDALLIONS	
83	CHRISTMAS ROSE	CL	40.00	50.00
84	HAWTHORNE/GLASTONBURY THORN	CL	40.00	50.00
85	POINSETTIA	CL	35.00	60.00
86	LAUREL BAY	CL	35.00	70.00
87	MISTLETOE	CL	35.00	75.00
88	HOLLY	CL	40.00	60.00
89	IVY	CL	35.00	50.00
90	CHRISTMAS CACTUS	CL	40.00	50.00
91	CHRYSANTHEMUM	CL	40.00	50.00
92	STAR OF BETHLEHEM	CL	40.00	45.00
*			STERLING NATIVITY MEDALLION	
88	ANGEL GABRIEL	CL	40.00	100.00
89	JOURNEY, THE	CL	40.00	70.00
90	NO ROOM AT THE INN	CL	40.00	60.00
91	TIDINGS OF JOY	CL	40.00	60.00
92	STAR OF BETHLEHEM	CL	40.00	60.00
*		STERLING TWELVE DAYS OF CHRISTMAS MEDALLIONS		
71	PARTRIDGE IN PEAR TREE	CL	20.00	700.00
72	TWO TURTLEDOVES	CL	20.00	250.00
73	THREE FRENCH HENS	CL	20.00	150.00
74	FOUR MOCKINGBIRDS	CL	20.00	100.00
75	FIVE GOLDEN RINGS	CL	30.00	100.00
76	SIX GEESE-A-LAYING	CL	30.00	125.00
77	SEVEN SWANS-A-SWIMMING	CL	35.00	75.00
78	EIGHT MAIDS-A-MILKING	CL	37.00	90.00
79	NINE LADIES DANCING	CL	37.00	75.00
80	TEN LORDS-A-LEAPING	CL	76.00	80.00
81	ELEVEN PIPERS PIPING	CL	50.00	80.00
82	TWELVE DRUMMERS DRUMMING	CL	35.00	80.00

UNITED DESIGN CORP.
S. BRADFORD

YR	NAME	LIMIT	ISSUE	TREND
			ANGELS COLLECTION	
91	FRA ANGELICO DRUMMER, BLUE IBO-414	RT	20.00	20.00
91	FRA ANGELICO DRUMMER, IVORY IBO-420	RT	20.00	20.00
91	GIRL CUPID W/ROSE, IVORY IBO-413	RT	15.00	16.00
91	VICTORIAN CUPID IBO-415	OP	15.00	16.00
92	ANGEL AND TAMBOURINE IBO-422	RT	20.00	20.00
92	ANGEL AND TAMBOURINE, IVORY IBO-425	RT	20.00	20.00
92	MARY AND DOVE IBO-424	RT	20.00	20.00
92	ST. FRANCIS AND CRITTERS IBO-423	RT	20.00	20.00

P. JONAS

YR	NAME	LIMIT	ISSUE	TREND
			ANGELS COLLECTION	
90	CRYSTAL ANGEL IBO-401	RT	20.00	20.00
90	CRYSTAL ANGEL, IVORY IBO-405	RT	20.00	20.00
90	ROSE OF SHARON IBO-402	RT	20.00	20.00
90	ROSE OF SHARON, IVORY IBO-406	OP	20.00	20.00
90	STAR GLORY IBO-403	RT	15.00	16.00
90	STAR GLORY, IVORY IBO-407	RT	15.00	16.00
90	VICTORIAN ANGEL IBO-404	RT	15.00	16.00
90	VICTORIAN ANGEL, IVORY IBO-408	RT	15.00	16.00
91	ANGEL WAIF, IVORY IBO-411	OP	15.00	16.00
91	PEACE DESCENDING IBO-418	RT	20.00	20.00
91	PEACE DESCENDING, IVORY IBO-412	RT	20.00	20.00
91	ROSETTI ANGEL IBO-416	RT	20.00	20.00
91	ROSETTI ANGEL, IVORY IBO-410	RT	20.00	20.00
91	VICTORIAN CUPID, IVORY IBO-409	OP	15.00	16.00

VICKILANE
V. ANDERSON

YR	NAME	LIMIT	ISSUE	TREND
			LIL BLESSINGS	
94	BUNNY ANGEL #1610	OP	13.00	13.00
94	BUNNY ANGEL #1611	OP	13.00	13.00
94	BUNNY ANGEL #1612	OP	13.00	13.00
94	BUNNY ANGEL #1613	OP	13.00	13.00
94	BUNNY ANGEL #1614	OP	13.00	13.00
94	BUNNY ANGEL #1615	OP	13.00	13.00

WALLACE SILVERSMITHS

YR	NAME	LIMIT	ISSUE	TREND
*			24K GOLDPLATE SCULPTURES	
88	ANGEL	CL	16.00	16.00
88	CANDY CANE	CL	16.00	16.00
88	CHRISTMAS TREE	CL	16.00	16.00
88	DOVE	CL	16.00	16.00
88	NATIVITY SCENE	CL	16.00	16.00
88	SNOWFLAKE	CL	16.00	16.00
*			ANNUAL SILVERPLATED BELLS	
71	1ST EDITION SLEIGH BELL	CL	13.00	1150.00
72	2ND EDITION SLEIGH BELL	CL	13.00	600.00
73	3RD EDITION SLEIGH BELL	CL	13.00	550.00
74	4TH EDITION SLEIGH BELL	CL	14.00	350.00
75	5TH EDITION SLEIGH BELL	CL	14.00	250.00
76	6TH EDITION SLEIGH BELL	CL	14.00	350.00
77	7TH EDITION SLEIGH BELL	CL	15.00	225.00

YR	NAME	LIMIT	ISSUE	TREND
78	8TH EDITION SLEIGH BELL	CL	15.00	100.00
79	9TH EDITION SLEIGH BELL	CL	16.00	175.00
80	10TH EDITION SLEIGH BELL	CL	19.00	50.00
81	11TH EDITION SLEIGH BELL	CL	19.00	100.00
82	12TH EDITION SLEIGH BELL	CL	20.00	130.00
83	13TH EDITION SLEIGH BELL	CL	20.00	130.00
84	14TH EDITION SLEIGH BELL	CL	22.00	100.00
85	15TH EDITION SLEIGH BELL	CL	22.00	110.00
86	16TH EDITION SLEIGH BELL	CL	22.00	55.00
87	17TH EDITION SLEIGH BELL	CL	22.00	45.00
88	18TH EDITION SLEIGH BELL	CL	22.00	45.00
89	19TH EDITION SLEIGH BELL	CL	25.00	50.00
90	20TH EDITION SLEIGH BELL	CL	25.00	40.00
90	SPECIAL EDITION SLEIGH BELL, GOLD	CL	35.00	75.00
91	21ST EDITION SLEIGH BELL	CL	25.00	25.00
92	22ND EDITION SLEIGH BELL	CL	25.00	40.00
93	23RD EDITION SLEIGH BELL	CL	25.00	40.00
94	24TH EDITION SLEIGH BELL	CL	25.00	25.00
95	25TH EDITION SLEIGH BELL	CL	30.00	30.00
*			**ANTIQUE PEWTER BELLS**	
89	REINDEER	CL	16.00	16.00
89	TEDDY BEAR	CL	16.00	16.00
89	TOY SOLDIER	CL	16.00	16.00
90	CAROUSEL HORSE	CL	16.00	16.00
90	SANTA CLAUS	CL	16.00	16.00
*			**ANTIQUE PEWTER ORNAMENTS**	
*	CANDY CANE	CL	10.00	10.00
*	DOVE	CL	10.00	10.00
*	GINGERBREAD HOUSE	CL	10.00	10.00
*	ROCKING HORSE	CL	10.00	10.00
*	TEDDY BEAR	CL	10.00	10.00
*	TOY SOLDIER	CL	10.00	10.00
89	ANGEL WITH CANDLES	CL	10.00	10.00
89	CHERUB WITH HORN	CL	10.00	10.00
89	SANTA	CL	10.00	10.00
89	TEDDY BEAR	CL	10.00	10.00
89	WREATH	CL	10.00	10.00
*			**CAMEO FRAME ORNAMENTS**	
89	ANGEL	OP	15.00	15.00
89	CHRISTMAS BALL	OP	15.00	15.00
89	DINO	OP	15.00	15.00
89	ELEPHANT	OP	15.00	15.00
89	KITTEN	OP	15.00	15.00
89	SANTA	OP	15.00	15.00
89	SNOWMAN	OP	15.00	15.00
89	SOLDIER	OP	15.00	15.00
89	WREATH	OP	15.00	15.00
*			**CANDY CANES**	
81	PEPPERMINT	CL	9.00	225.00
82	WINTERGREEN	CL	10.00	60.00
83	CINNAMON	CL	11.00	50.00
84	CLOVE	CL	11.00	50.00
85	DOVE MOTIF	CL	11.95	50.00
86	BELL MOTIF	CL	11.95	125.00
87	TEDDY BEAR	CL	13.00	75.00
88	CHRISTMAS ROSE	CL	13.99	40.00
89	CHRISTMAS CANDLE	CL	15.00	35.00
90	REINDEER	CL	16.00	30.00
*			**CATHEDRAL ORNAMENT**	
88	1988-1ST EDITION	CL	25.00	40.00
89	1989-2ND EDITION	CL	25.00	35.00
90	1990-3RD EDITION	CL	25.00	30.00
*			**CHRISTMAS COOKIE ORNAMENT**	
80	ANGEL	CL	6.00	20.00
80	SANTA	CL	6.00	10.00
80	SNOWMAN	CL	6.00	15.00
80	TREE	CL	6.00	15.00
81	BELL	CL	6.00	15.00
81	DRUM	CL	6.00	15.00
81	REINDEER	CL	6.00	15.00
82	DOVE	CL	6.00	20.00
82	MOUSE	CL	6.00	15.00
82	TRAIN	CL	6.00	15.00
83	BOY CAROLER	CL	6.00	15.00
83	GINGERBREAD HOUSE	CL	6.00	10.00
83	HUSKY	CL	6.00	20.00
83	JACK-IN-THE-BOX	CL	6.00	10.00
83	MRS. CLAUS	CL	6.00	10.00
83	ROCKING HORSE	CL	6.00	10.00
83	TOY SOLDIER	CL	6.00	10.00
84	CAROL SINGER	CL	7.00	15.00
84	HORN	CL	7.00	10.00
84	MOTHER AND CHILD	CL	7.00	15.00
84	PUPPY IN BOOT	CL	7.00	10.00
85	BOY SKATER	CL	11.00	10.00

YR	NAME	LIMIT	ISSUE	TREND
85	CLOWN	CL	7.00	10.00
85	HOT-AIR BALLOON	CL	11.00	10.00
85	TEDDY BEAR	OP	7.00	10.00
85	UNICORN	CL	7.00	10.00
86	CAROUSEL HORSE	CL	7.00	20.00
86	DOG ON SLED	CL	7.00	20.00
86	DRESSED KITTEN	CL	7.00	15.00
86	GIRL HONEY BEAR	CL	7.00	10.00
86	GOOSE	CL	7.00	15.00
86	NEW DESIGN SNOWMAN	CL	7.00	20.00
86	PANDA	CL	6.00	10.00
86	PENGUIN	CL	7.00	10.00
86	SANTA HEAD	CL	7.00	10.00
86	TUGBOAT	CL	7.00	10.00
87	ANGEL WITH HEART	OP	8.00	10.00
87	GIRAFFE	CL	8.00	10.00
87	POLAR BEAR	OP	8.00	10.00
87	SKI CABIN	CL	8.00	10.00
87	SNOWBIRD	CL	8.00	10.00
88	ANGEL	OP	9.00	10.00
88	BABY BEAR	OP	9.00	10.00
88	CHRISTMAS VILLAGE	OP	9.00	10.00
88	DRAGON	OP	9.00	10.00
88	ELEPHANT	OP	9.00	10.00
88	GOOSE	OP	9.00	10.00
88	NIGHT BEFORE, THE	OP	9.00	10.00
88	POLAR BEAR	OP	9.00	10.00
88	TEDDY BEAR	OP	9.00	10.00
89	ROCKING HORSE	OP	10.00	10.00
89	SANTA	OP	10.00	10.00
89	SNOWBIRD	OP	10.00	10.00
*	**GRANDE BAROQUE 12 DAY SERIES**			
88	PARTRIDGE	CL	40.00	80.00
89	TWO TURTLEDOVES	CL	40.00	100.00
90	THREE FRENCH HENS	CL	40.00	75.00
*	**STERLING MEMORIES**			
89	BEAR WITH BLOCKS	OP	35.00	35.00
89	CAROLERS	OP	35.00	35.00
89	CHURCH	OP	35.00	35.00
89	DOVE	OP	35.00	35.00
89	DRUMMER BOY	OP	35.00	35.00
89	MOTHER & CHILD	OP	35.00	35.00
89	NATIVITY ANGEL	OP	35.00	35.00
89	REINDEER	OP	35.00	35.00
89	ROCKING HORSE	OP	35.00	35.00
89	SLEIGH	OP	35.00	35.00
89	SNOWFLAKE	OP	35.00	35.00
89	SNOWMAN	OP	35.00	35.00
*	**STERLING MEMORIES-HAND ENAMELED WITH COLOR**			
89	CANDY CANE	OP	35.00	35.00
89	CHURCH	OP	35.00	35.00
89	ELF WITH GIFT	OP	35.00	35.00
89	FIREPLACE	OP	35.00	35.00
89	KNEELING ANGEL	OP	35.00	35.00
89	SANTA	OP	35.00	35.00
89	SINGLE CANDLE	OP	35.00	35.00
89	TOY SOLDIER	OP	35.00	35.00
89	TRAIN	OP	35.00	35.00

WALT DISNEY CLASSICS COLLECTION

		LIMIT	ISSUE	TREND
*	**COLLECTORS SOCIETY**			
93	FLIGHT OF FANCY	*	35.00	50.00
94	DUMBO "SIMPLY ADORABLE"	RT	20.00	35.00
96	WINNIE THE POOH 41096	RT	25.00	35.00
97	MAGICIAN MICKEY 41135	RT		50.00
*	**EVENT PIECES**			
96	TINKERBELL	RT	50.00	77.00
97	HERCULES	RT	55.00	55.00
97	WINNIE THE POOH	RT	59.00	59.00

WATERFORD WEDGWOOD USA

		LIMIT	ISSUE	TREND
*	**WATERFORD CRYSTAL CHRISTMAS ORNAMENTS**			
78	1978 ORNAMENT	YR	25.00	100.00
79	1979 ORNAMENT	YR	28.00	75.00
80	1980 ORNAMENT	YR	28.00	65.00
81	1981 ORNAMENT	YR	28.00	45.00
82	1982 ORNAMENT	YR	28.00	45.00
83	1983 ORNAMENT	YR	28.00	50.00
84	1984 ORNAMENT	YR	28.00	50.00
85	1985 ORNAMENT	YR	28.00	75.00
86	1986 ORNAMENT	YR	28.00	50.00
87	1987 ORNAMENT	YR	29.00	40.00
88	1988 ORNAMENT	YR	30.00	35.00
89	1989 ORNAMENT	YR	32.00	35.00

YR	NAME	LIMIT	ISSUE	TREND
*			**WEDGWOOD CHRISTMAS ORNAMENTS**	
88	JASPER CHRISTMAS TREE ORNAMENT	OP	20.00	28.00
89	JASPER ANGEL ORNAMENT	OP	25.00	28.00
90	JASPER SANTA CLAUS ORNAMENT	OP	28.00	28.00
91	JASPER WREATH ORNAMENT	OP	28.00	28.00
92	JASPER STOCKING ORNAMENT	OP	25.00	25.00

WILLITTS DESIGNS

YR	NAME	LIMIT	ISSUE	TREND
	A. DEZENDORF		**AMISH HERITAGE COLLECTION**	
96	POCKET QUILT 3RD OF 4	YR	20.00	20.00
	C. SCHULZ		**CERAMIC PEANUTS ORNAMENTS**	
88	CHARLIE BROWN	SO	7.50	8.00
88	FLYING ACE	SO	7.50	8.00
88	JOE COOL	SO	7.50	8.00
88	LUCY	SO	7.50	8.00
88	SKATING SNOOPY	SO	7.50	8.00
88	SLEDDING SNOOPY	SO	7.50	8.00
88	WOODSTOCK (BELL)	SO	7.50	8.00
*			**COCA-COLA SANTA**	
90	COCA-COLA SIX PACK ORNAMENT	OP	20.00	20.00
90	HAPPY HOLIDAYS COKE BOTTLE	OP	10.00	10.00
	T. BLACKSHEAR		**EBONY VISIONS COLLECTION**	
95	POCKET QUILT 2ND OF 4	YR	20.00	20.00
97	LITTLE BLUE WINGS	SO	*	N/A
98	ON WINGS OF PRAISE	YR	30.00	30.00
	C. PYLE	**HISTORY OF ANGELS COLLECTION BY BILL DALE**		
95	ASCENSION OF THE SOUL	RT	25.00	25.00
95	CHERUB ORNAMENT W/FLUTE	RT	17.50	17.50
95	CHERUB ORNAMENT W/HARP	RT	17.50	17.50
	C. SCHULZ		**PEANUTS**	
90	CHARLIE BROWN SHEPHERD ORNAMENT	SO	10.00	10.00
90	SNOOPY SHEPHERD ORNAMENT	SO	10.00	10.00
	C. SCHULZ		**PEANUTS BASEBALL ORNAMENTS**	
88	CHARLIE BROWN	SO	10.00	10.00
88	LINUS	SO	10.00	10.00
88	LUCY	SO	10.00	10.00
88	PEPPERMINT PATTY	SO	10.00	10.00
88	SCHROEDER	SO	10.00	10.00
88	SNOOPY	SO	10.00	10.00
	A. BLACKSHEAR		**RAINBOW BABIES**	
98	FLUTTERBY	*	29.00	29.00
	C. SCHULZ		**WOODEN SNOOPY ORNAMENTS**	
88	SNOOPY-8438	SO	5.50	5.50
88	SNOOPY-8439	OP	5.50	5.50
88	SNOOPY-8440	SO	5.50	5.50

Plates

Susan K. Elliott

If the circle can be considered a form of perfection, then plate collectors enjoy a perfect form of art.

Since the first dated annual Christmas plates appeared in 1895 in Denmark, collectors have been happily anticipating the "next" edition to be released. Bing & Grondahl issued that first blue and white collector's plate, *Behind the Frozen Window,* at approximately 50 cents. Today, as the series enjoys over 100 years of continuous production, that rare first edition sells for about $5,000.

Of course, these days not all plates are round, made of porcelain, or colored blue and white. New shapes include ovals, rounded squares, and even hearts. Today's plates may be sculpted in bas relief, incised, lighted or able to play a tune. They're made of wood, molded resin, pewter, crystal or porcelain. Subjects range from cute to elegant, with every possibility in between, and in a full range of colors and accent borders.

Until the 1960s, collector's plates continued to be made in Europe and produced only for Christmas. Royal Copenhagen introduced a second "Danish Christmas" series in 1908, and Rosenthal began a dated "Christmas" series in Germany in 1907.

Other key events in plate collecting history include:

- 1965: Lalique introduces a crystal plate, *Deux Oiseeaux (Two Birds)*

- 1969: Bing & Grondahl releases the first Mother's Day plate, *Dog and Puppies,* in blue and white

- 1969: Wedgwood issues *Windsor Castle* as first in a new "Christmas" series, produced in its famous blue and white jasperware

- 1970: Franklin Mint introduces original art by Norman Rockwell on a sterling silver plate, *Bringing Home the Tree*

- 1971: two Christmas series featuring art by Sister Maria Innocentia Hummel begin, with the Goebel Hummel issue, *Heavenly Angel,* later becoming one of the most valuable plates in the market.

The 1970s saw a boom in collecting of all types, spurred by the celebration of the U.S. Bicentennial in 1976. Historical subject plates abounded, and more and more makers, both American and European, focused on plates as a collectible. New artists entered the field, elevating the art and focusing more attention on the artists themselves.

The development of the First International Plate Collectors Convention in 1975 provided a platform for the limited edition hobby to grow, and grow it has, expanding into many related art forms such as figurines, cottages, ornaments, dolls and graphics. The number of platemakers peaked in the 1980s, with production shifting by the 1990s to fewer, major producers such as The Bradford Exchange.

Plate collectors of the '90s are likely to collect other media besides plates, searching for graphics by favorite artists such as Thomas Kinkade, Sandra Kuck, Terry Redlin and Lena Liu to round out their collections.

As plate collecting enters its second hundred years, the art form remains an ever-changing and always growing collectible.

SUSAN K. ELLIOTT began enjoying plates just before attending the first International Plate Collectors Convention in 1975. She writes extensively about collectibles and is the executive director of the Worldwide Association of Gift and Collectible Retailers (NALED).

PLATES

YR NAME	LIMIT	ISSUE	TREND
AMERICAN ARTISTS			
F. STONE			
* CIGAR/SIGNED	*	95.00	95.00
* CIGAR/UNSIGNED	*	75.00	75.00
D. ZOLAN		**FAMILY TREASURES**	
81 CORA'S RECITAL	18500	40.00	72.00
82 CORA'S TEA PARTY	18500	40.00	72.00
83 CORA'S GARDEN PARTY	18500	40.00	65.00
F. STONE		**FAMOUS FILLIES**	
87 LADY'S SECRET	9500	65.00	97.00
88 GENUINE RISK	9500	65.00	97.00
88 RUFFIAN	9500	65.00	97.00
92 GO FOR THE WAND	9500	65.00	97.00
F. STONE		**FRED STONE CLASSIC SERIES**	
86 ETERNAL LEGACY, THE	950	75.00	110.00
86 SHOE-8,000 WINS, THE	9500	75.00	110.00
88 FOREVER FRIENDS	9500	75.00	120.00
89 ALYSHEBA	9500	75.00	110.00
F. STONE		**GOLD SIGNATURE SERIES**	
90 SECRETARIAT FINAL TRIBUTE, SIGNED	4500	150.00	295.00
90 SECRETARIAT FINAL TRIBUTE, UNSIGNED	7500	75.00	75.00
91 OLD WARRIORS, SIGNED	4500	150.00	310.00
91 OLD WARRIORS, UNSIGNED	7500	75.00	75.00
F. STONE		**GOLD SIGNATURE SERIES II**	
91 KELSO, DBL. SIGNATURES	1500	175.00	175.00
91 KELSO, SGL. SIGNATURE	3000	150.00	200.00
91 KELSO, UNSIGNED	7500	75.00	75.00
91 NORTHERN DANCER, DBL. SIGNATURES	1500	175.00	225.00
91 NORTHERN DANCER, SGL. SIGNATURE	3000	150.00	150.00
91 NORTHERN DANCER, UNSIGNED	7500	75.00	75.00
F. STONE		**GOLD SIGNATURE SERIES III**	
92 DANCE SMARTLY-P. DAY, DBL. SIGNATURES	1500	175.00	175.00
92 DANCE SMARTLY-P. DAY, SGL. SIGNATURE	3000	150.00	200.00
92 DANCE SMARTLY-P. DAY, UNSIGNED	7500	75.00	75.00
93 AMERICAN TRIPLE CROWN, SIGNED 1937-46	2500	195.00	195.00
93 AMERICAN TRIPLE CROWN, SIGNED 1948-78	2500	195.00	200.00
93 AMERICAN TRIPLE CROWN, UNSIGNED 1937-46	7500	75.00	75.00
93 AMERICAN TRIPLE CROWN, UNSIGNED 1948-78	7500	75.00	75.00
94 AMERICAN TRIPLE CROWN, SIGNED 1919-35	2500	95.00	200.00
94 AMERICAN TRIPLE CROWN, UNSIGNED 1919-35	7500	75.00	75.00
F. STONE		**GOLD SIGNATURE SERIES IV**	
95 JULIE KRONA/DBL. SIGNATURE	2500	150.00	150.00
95 JULIE KRONA/UNSIGNED	7500	75.00	75.00
F. STONE		**HORSES OF FRED STONE**	
82 ARABIAN MARE AND FOAL	9500	55.00	130.00
82 PATIENCE	9500	55.00	150.00
82 SAFE AND SOUND	9500	55.00	100.00
83 CONTENTMENT	9500	55.00	95.00
F. STONE		**MARES & FOALS 6 1/2 IN. SERIES**	
86 TRANQUILITY	12500	25.00	25.00
91 PATIENCE	19500	25.00	25.00
92 KIDNAPPED MARE	19500	25.00	25.00
92 PASTURE PEST	19500	25.00	25.00
92 WATER TROUGH	19500	25.00	25.00
93 ARABIAN MARE & FOAL	19500	25.00	25.00
93 CONTENTMENT	19500	25.00	25.00
F. STONE		**MARES & FOALS SERIES**	
86 PASTURE PEST	12500	50.00	78.00
86 TRANQUILITY	12500	50.00	95.00
86 WATER TROUGH	12500	50.00	160.00
87 ARABIANS, THE	12500	50.00	50.00
F. STONE		**MARES & FOALS SERIES II**	
89 DIAMOND IN THE ROUGH	RT	35.00	50.00
89 FIRST DAY, THE	CL	35.00	50.00
F. STONE		**RACING LEGENDS**	
89 PHAR LAP	9500	75.00	110.00
89 SUNDAY SILENCE	9500	75.00	110.00
90 JOHN HENRY-SHOEMAKER	9500	75.00	110.00
F. STONE		**SPORT OF KINGS SERIES**	
84 MAN O'WAR	9500	65.00	250.00
84 SECRETARIAT	9500	65.00	225.00
85 JOHN HENRY-MCCARRON	9500	65.00	120.00
86 SEATTLE SLEW	9500	65.00	110.00
F. STONE		**STALLION SERIES**	
83 ANDALUSIAN	12500	50.00	140.00
83 BLACK STALLION	12500	50.00	140.00
AMERICAN RAILS & HIGHWAYS			
*			**CORVETTE**
95 VIPER GTS-R	*	40.00	40.00
96 GRAND SPORT CORVETTE	*	40.00	40.00

YR	NAME	LIMIT	ISSUE	TREND
P. ADAMS				**CORVETTE**
94	1964/94 MUSTANG	*	40.00	40.00
95	1978 CORVETTE	*	40.00	40.00
95	1982 CORVETTE	*	40.00	40.00
95	35TH CORVETTE	*	40.00	40.00
95	40TH ANNIV. THUNDERBIRD	*	40.00	40.00
95	40TH CORVETTE	*	40.00	40.00
95	VIPER GTS-RT/10	*	40.00	40.00
B. HUBBOCK				**CORVETTE**
96	VIPER 1996 PACE CAR/INDY	*	40.00	40.00
R. PEDERSEN				**CORVETTE**
95	1995 75TH INDY PACE CAR	*	40.00	40.00
*				**TRAIN**
95	B&O CHESSIE	*	33.00	33.00
95	CHIEF, THE	*	33.00	33.00
95	SANTA FE SUPER CHIEF	*	33.00	33.00
95	UNION PAC, E-9	*	33.00	33.00
P. ADAMS				**TRAIN**
93	G6-1	*	33.00	33.00
94	HIAWATHA	*	33.00	33.00
94	N.Y. CENTRAL	*	33.00	33.00
95	BLACK JACK	*	33.00	33.00
95	K-4	*	33.00	33.00
95	MAPLE LEAF	*	33.00	33.00
R. PEDERSEN				**TRAIN**
96	ERIE F-8	*	33.00	33.00
96	NEW HAVEN	*	33.00	33.00

AMERICAN ROSE SOCIETY

YR	NAME	LIMIT	ISSUE	TREND
*				**ALL-AMERICAN ROSE**
75	ARIZONA	9800	39.00	142.00
75	OREGOLD	9800	39.00	142.00
75	ROSE PARADE	9800	39.00	137.00
76	AMERICA	9800	39.00	140.00
76	CATHEDRAL	9800	39.00	115.00
76	SEASHELL	9800	39.00	110.00
76	YANKEE DOODLE	9800	39.00	115.00
77	DOUBLE DELIGHT	9800	39.00	100.00
77	FIRST EDITION	9800	39.00	100.00
77	PROMINENT	9800	39.00	100.00
78	CHARISMA	9800	39.00	89.00
78	COLOR MAGIC	9800	39.00	90.00
79	FRIENDSHIP	9800	39.00	79.00
79	PARADISE	9800	39.00	75.00
79	SUNDOWNER	9800	39.00	75.00
80	CHERISH	9800	49.00	80.00
80	HONOR	9800	49.00	75.00
80	LOVE	9800	49.00	80.00
81	BING CROSBY	9800	49.00	80.00
81	MARINA	9800	49.00	75.00
81	WHITE LIGHTNIN'	9800	49.00	80.00
82	BRANDY	9800	49.00	80.00
82	FRENCH LACE	9800	49.00	80.00
82	MON CHERI	9800	49.00	80.00
82	SHREVEPORT	9800	49.00	80.00
83	SUN FLARE	9800	49.00	80.00
83	SWEET SURRENDER	9800	49.00	80.00
84	IMPATIENT	9800	49.00	80.00
84	INTRIGUE	9800	49.00	78.00
84	OLYMPIAD	9800	49.00	78.00
85	PEACE	9800	50.00	80.00
85	QUEEN ELIZABETH	9800	50.00	81.00
85	SHOW BIZ	9800	50.00	78.00

ANHEUSER-BUSCH INC.

YR	NAME	LIMIT	ISSUE	TREND
D. LANGENECKERT				**ARCHIVES PLATE SERIES**
92	1893 COLUMBIAN EXPOSITION N3477	CL	28.00	28.00
92	GANYMEDE N4004	CL	28.00	28.00
D. LANGENECKERT				**CIVIL WAR SERIES**
92	GENERAL GRANT N3478	CL	45.00	45.00
93	GENERAL ROBERT E. LEE N3590	CL	45.00	45.00
93	PRESIDENT ABRAHAM LINCOLN N3591	CL	45.00	45.00
B. KEMPER				**HOLIDAY PLATE SERIES**
89	WINTER'S DAY N2295	RT	30.00	80.00
89	WINTER'S EVENING N2295	RT	30.00	75.00
94	HOMETOWN HOLIDAY N4572	CL	28.00	28.00
N. KOERBER				**HOLIDAY PLATE SERIES**
93	SPECIAL DELIVERY N4002	RT	28.00	28.00
S. SAMPSON				**HOLIDAY PLATE SERIES**
90	AN AMERICAN TRADITION N2767	RT	30.00	50.00
91	SEASON'S BEST, THE- N3034	CL	30.00	30.00
92	A PERFECT CHRISTMAS N3440	CL	28.00	28.00
M. URDAHL				**MAN'S BEST FRIEND SERIES**
90	BUDDIES N2615	RT	30.00	75.00
90	SIX PACK N3005	RT	30.00	40.00
92	SOMETHING'S BREWING N3147	CL	30.00	30.00

YR	NAME	LIMIT	ISSUE	TREND
93	OUTSTANDING IN THEIR FIELD N4003	CL	28.00	28.00
95	THIS BUD'S FOR YOU N4945	25 DAYS	28.00	28.00
*			**OLYMPIC TEAM SERIES**	
91	'92 OLYMPIC TEAM- WINTER	CL	35.00	35.00
92	'92 OLYMPIC TEAM- SUMMER	CL	35.00	35.00

ANNA-PERENNA

P. BUCKLEY MOSS				
89	HELLO GRANDMA	CL	75.00	110.00
93	STORYTELLER, THE	5000	100.00	100.00
94	SCHOOL DAYS	5000	85.00	85.00
94	VISITING NURSE	5000	85.00	85.00
95	FRIENDS FOREVER	5000	85.00	85.00
P. BUCKLEY MOSS		**AMERICAN SILHOUETTES FAMILY SERIES**		
81	FAMILY OUTING	5000	75.00	100.00
82	JOHN AND MARY	5000	75.00	100.00
83	LEISURE TIME	5000	75.00	90.00
84	HOMEMAKERS QUILTING	5000	75.00	140.00
P. BUCKLEY MOSS		**AMERICAN SILHOUETTES VALLEY SERIES**		
81	FROSTY FROLIC	5000	75.00	90.00
82	HAY RIDE	5000	75.00	90.00
83	SUNDAY RIDE	5000	75.00	90.00
84	MARKET DAY	5000	75.00	120.00
P. BUCKLEY MOSS		**AMERICAN SILHOUETTES-CHILDREN'S SERIES**		
81	FIDDLERS TWO	5000	75.00	100.00
82	MARY WITH THE LAMBS	5000	75.00	90.00
83	RING-AROUND-THE-ROSIE	5000	75.00	100.00
84	WAITING FOR TOM	5000	75.00	100.00
P. BUCKLEY MOSS		**ANNUAL CHRISTMAS PLATE**		
84	NOEL, NOEL	5000	68.00	210.00
85	HELPING HANDS	5000	68.00	100.00
86	NIGHT BEFORE CHRISTMAS	5000	68.00	100.00
87	CHRISTMAS SLEIGH	5000	75.00	100.00
88	CHRISTMAS JOY	7500	75.00	100.00
89	CHRISTMAS CAROL	7500	80.00	130.00
90	CHRISTMAS EVE	7500	80.00	140.00
91	SNOWMAN, THE	7500	80.00	140.00
92	CHRISTMAS WARMTH	7500	85.00	125.00
93	JOY TO THE WORLD	7500	85.00	125.00
94	CHRISTMAS NIGHT	7500	85.00	125.00
95	CHRISTMAS AT HOME	5000	85.00	125.00
96	UNDER THE MISTLETOE	7500	85.00	85.00
P. BUCKLEY MOSS		**CELEBRATION SERIES**		
86	WEDDING JOY	5000	100.00	150.00
87	CHRISTENING, THE	5000	100.00	135.00
88	ANNIVERSARY, THE	5000	100.00	200.00
89	FAMILY REUNION	5000	100.00	175.00
P. BUCKLEY MOSS		**FESTIVAL SERIES**		
98	LOVE ETERNAL VALENTINE	*	75.00	75.00
P. BUCKLEY MOSS		**HEARTLAND SERIES**		
89	BLACKSMITH, THE	OP	90.00	155.00
91	SUNDAY OUTING	OP	90.00	155.00
92	PRAIRIE WINTER	OP	90.00	155.00
93	SCHOOLHOUSE, THE	5000	90.00	155.00
P. BUCKLEY MOSS		**JOYFUL CHILDREN COLLECTION**		
93	DANCE OF THE BUTTERFLIES	5000	70.00	70.00
93	PURPLE UMBRELLA	5000	70.00	70.00
94	DOLL'S HOUSE, THE	5000	70.00	70.00
94	MEDICS, THE	5000	70.00	70.00
P. BUCKLEY MOSS		**MOTHER'S LOVE SERIES**		
91	TENDER HANDS	CL	85.00	135.00
92	MOTHER'S LOVE	OP	85.00	125.00
93	MOTHER'S WORLD	5000	80.00	125.00
94	MOTHER'S JOY	5000	80.00	125.00
95	NEWBORN, THE	5000	80.00	125.00
96	TREASURED BABE	5000	80.00	80.00
98	PRECIOUS MOMENT, A	*	80.00	80.00
P. BUCKLEY MOSS		**SINGLE ISSUE ART PLATE**		
93	SUMMER WEDDING	5000	100.00	100.00
95	MUSEUM PLATE, THE	5000	80.00	80.00
95	SKATING JOY	5000	80.00	80.00
96	WEDDING DAY	5000	90.00	90.00
P. BUCKLEY MOSS		**TREASURED FRIENDS COLLECTION**		
95	LEARNED PAIR	5000	85.00	125.00
95	LORDS OF THE REALM	5000	85.00	125.00
96	NOBLE FILLY	5000	85.00	125.00
T. KRUMEICH		**UNCLE TAD'S CATS**		
79	OLIVER'S BIRTHDAY	5000	75.00	175.00
80	PEACHES & CREAM	5000	75.00	130.00
81	PRINCESS AURORA	5000	80.00	100.00
81	WALTER'S WINDOW	5000	80.00	115.00

ANRI

*			**ANRI FATHER'S DAY**	
72	ALPINE FATHER & CHILDREN	CL	35.00	130.00
73	ALPINE FATHER & CHILDREN	CL	40.00	130.00

YR	NAME	LIMIT	ISSUE	TREND
74	CLIFF GAZING	CL	50.00	140.00
76	SAILING	CL	60.00	160.00
*			ANRI MOTHER'S DAY	
72	ALPINE MOTHER & CHILDREN	CL	35.00	75.00
73	ALPINE MOTHER & CHILDREN	CL	40.00	90.00
74	ALPINE MOTHER & CHILDREN	CL	50.00	90.00
75	ALPINE STROLL	CL	60.00	100.00
76	KNITTING	CL	60.00	95.00
*			CHRISTMAS	
79	MOSS GATHERERS	RT	135.00	180.00
80	WINTRY CHURCHGOING	RT	165.00	250.00
81	SANTA CLAUS IN TYROL	RT	165.00	250.00
82	STAR SINGERS, THE	RT	165.00	225.00
83	UNTO US A CHILD IS BORN	RT	165.00	250.00
84	YULETIDE IN THE VALLEY	RT	165.00	350.00
J. MALFERTHEINER			CHRISTMAS	
71	ST. JAKOB IN GARDEN	RT	38.00	135.00
72	PIPERS AT ALBEROBELLO	RT	45.00	160.00
73	ALPINE HORN	RT	45.00	700.00
74	YOUNG MAN AND GIRL	RT	50.00	130.00
75	CHRISTMAS IN IRELAND	RT	60.00	140.00
76	ALPINE CHRISTMAS	RT	65.00	300.00
77	LEGEND OF HELIGENBLUT	RT	65.00	240.00
78	KLOCKLER SINGERS	RT	80.00	175.00
85	GOOD MORNING, GOOD CHEER	RT	165.00	165.00
87	DOWN FROM THE ALPS	RT	195.00	250.00
88	FLIGHT INTO EGYPT	RT	275.00	280.00
TORIART			CHRISTMAS	
86	A GRODEN CHRISTMAS	RT	165.00	325.00
88	CHRISTKINDL MARKET	RT	220.00	340.00
90	HOLY NIGHT	RT	300.00	355.00
*			DISNEY FOUR STAR COLLECTION	
89	MICKEY MINI PLATE	RT	40.00	50.00
90	MINNIE MINI PLATE	RT	40.00	50.00
91	DONALD MINI PLATE	RT	50.00	50.00
J. FERRANDIZ			FERRANDIZ CHRISTMAS	
72	CHRIST IN THE MANGER	RT	35.00	250.00
73	CHRISTMAS	RT	40.00	225.00
74	HOLY NIGHT	RT	50.00	350.00
75	FLIGHT INTO EGYPT	RT	60.00	250.00
76	GIRL WITH FLOWERS	RT	65.00	200.00
76	TREE OF LIFE	RT	60.00	100.00
78	LEADING THE WAY	RT	78.00	180.00
79	DRUMMER, THE	RT	120.00	200.00
80	REJOICE	RT	150.00	200.00
81	SPREADING THE WORD	RT	150.00	200.00
82	SHEPHERD FAMILY, THE	RT	150.00	250.00
83	PEACE ATTEND THEE	RT	150.00	200.00
J. FERRANDIZ			FERRANDIZ MOTHER'S DAY SERIES	
72	MOTHER SEWING	RT	35.00	200.00
73	ALPINE MOTHER & CHILD	RT	40.00	150.00
74	MOTHER HOLDING CHILD	RT	50.00	200.00
75	DOVE GIRL	RT	60.00	170.00
76	MOTHER KNITTING	RT	60.00	200.00
78	BEGINNING, THE	RT	75.00	150.00
79	ALL HEARTS	RT	120.00	175.00
80	SPRING ARRIVALS	RT	150.00	230.00
81	HARMONY	RT	150.00	200.00
82	WITH LOVE	RT	150.00	200.00
J. FERRANDIZ			FERRANDIZ WOODEN WEDDING PLATES	
72	BOY AND GIRL EMBRACING	CL	40.00	275.00
73	WEDDING SCENE	CL	40.00	150.00
74	WEDDING	CL	48.00	100.00
75	WEDDING	CL	60.00	100.00
76	WEDDING	CL	60.00	100.00
L. GAITHER			RELIGIOUS	
98	HOLY FAMILY	OP	995.00	995.00

ARABIA ANNUAL

R. UOSIKKINEN			KALEVALA	
76	VAINAMOINEN'S SOWING	*	30.00	400.00
77	AINO'S FATE	*	30.00	110.00
78	LEMMINKAINEN'S CHASE	2500	39.00	100.00
79	KULLERVO'S REVENGE	YR	40.00	80.00
80	VAINAMOINEN'S RESCUE	YR	45.00	200.00
81	VAINAMOINEN'S MAGIC	YR	50.00	80.00
82	JOUKAHAINEN SHOOTS THE HORSE	YR	56.00	80.00
83	LEMMINKAINEN'S ESCAPE	YR	60.00	100.00
84	LEMMINKAINEN'S MAGIC FEATHERS	YR	50.00	110.00
85	LEMMINKAINEN'S GRIEF	YR	60.00	100.00
86	OSMATAR CREATING ALE	YR	60.00	80.00
87	VAINAMOINEN TRICKS ILMARINEN	YR	65.00	85.00
88	HEAR VAINAMOINEN WEEP	YR	69.00	115.00
89	FOUR MAIDENS	YR	75.00	95.00
90	ANNIKKA	YR	85.00	105.00
91	LEMMINKAIN'S MOTHER SAYS DON'T/WAR	YR	85.00	100.00

YR	NAME	LIMIT	ISSUE	TREND

ARMSTRONG'S
R. SKELTON — COMMEMORATIVE ISSUES

YR	NAME	LIMIT	ISSUE	TREND
83	70 YEARS YOUNG	15000	85.00	90.00
84	FREDDIE THE TORCHBEARER	15000	63.00	90.00

A. D'ESTREHAN — CONSTITUTION SERIES

87	GREAT CHASE, THE	10000	40.00	75.00
87	U.S. CONSTITUTION VS. GUERRIERE	10000	40.00	75.00
87	U.S. CONSTITUTION VS. JAVA	10000	40.00	75.00
87	U.S. CONSTITUTION VS. TRIPOLI	10000	40.00	75.00

L. DEWINNE — FACES OF THE WORLD

88	CLARA (BELGIUM)	14 DAYS	25.00	43.00
88	COLLETTE (FRANCE)	14 DAYS	25.00	43.00
88	ERIN (IRELAND)	14 DAYS	25.00	43.00
88	GRETA (AUSTRIA)	14 DAYS	25.00	43.00
88	HEATHER (ENGLAND)	14 DAYS	25.00	43.00
88	LUISA (SPAIN)	14 DAYS	25.00	43.00
88	MARIA (ITALY)	14 DAYS	25.00	43.00
88	TAMIKO (JAPAN)	14 DAYS	25.00	43.00

R. SKELTON — FREDDIE'S ADVENTURES

82	CAPTAIN FREDDIE	15000	60.00	100.00
84	GERTRUDE AND HEATHCLIFFE	15000	63.00	95.00

R. SKELTON — FREEDOM COLLECTION

90	ALL-AMERICAN, THE	9000	63.00	90.00
90	ALL-AMERICAN, THE-SIGNED	1000	195.00	300.00
91	INDEPENDENCE DAY	9000	63.00	90.00
91	INDEPENDENCE DAY-SIGNED	1000	195.00	300.00
92	LET FREEDOM RING	9000	63.00	100.00
92	LET FREEDOM RING-SIGNED	1000	195.00	280.00
93	FREDDIE'S GIFT OF LIFE	9000	63.00	100.00
93	FREDDIE'S GIFT OF LIFE-SIGNED	1000	195.00	280.00

W. LANTZ — HAPPY ART SERIES

81	WOODY'S TRIPLE SELF-PORTRAIT	9000	40.00	40.00
81	WOODY'S TRIPLE SELF-PORTRAIT-SIGNED	1000	100.00	100.00
83	GOTHIC WOODY	9000	40.00	40.00
83	GOTHIC WOODY-SIGNED	1000	100.00	100.00
84	BLUE BOY WOODY	9000	40.00	40.00
84	BLUE BOY WOODY-SIGNED	1000	100.00	100.00

S. ETEM — INFINITE LOVE

87	A PAIR OF DREAMS	CL	25.00	40.00
87	EYES SAY I LOVE YOU, THE	14 DAYS	25.00	40.00
87	KISS A LITTLE GIGGLE	14 DAYS	25.00	43.00
87	ONCE UPON A SMILE	14 DAYS	25.00	43.00
88	BUNDLE OF JOY	14 DAYS	25.00	40.00
88	GRINS FOR GRANDMA	14 DAYS	25.00	43.00
88	LOVE GOES FORTH IN LITTLE FEET	14 DAYS	25.00	43.00
89	A MOMENT TO CHERISH	CL	25.00	40.00

S. ETEM — MISCHIEF MAKERS

86	BUCKLES	10000	40.00	60.00
86	PUDDLES	10000	40.00	75.00
87	TRIX	10000	40.00	60.00
88	NAP	10000	40.00	60.00

R. SKELTON — SIGNATURE COLLECTION

86	ANYONE FOR TENNIS?	9000	63.00	90.00
86	ANYONE FOR TENNIS?-SIGNED	1000	125.00	300.00
87	IRONING THE WAVES	9000	63.00	80.00
87	IRONING THE WAVES-SIGNED	1000	125.00	270.00
88	CLIFFHANGER, THE	9000	63.00	85.00
88	CLIFFHANGER, THE-SIGNED	1000	150.00	280.00
88	HOOKED ON FREDDIE	9000	63.00	85.00
88	HOOKED ON FREDDIE-SIGNED	1000	175.00	250.00

SCHENKEN — SPORTS

*	PETE ROSE- UNSIGNED	10000	45.00	60.00
*	PETE ROSE-HANDSIGNED	1000	100.00	600.00

A. D'ESTREHAN — STATUE OF LIBERTY

86	DEDICATION	10000	40.00	60.00
86	IMMIGRANTS, THE	10000	40.00	60.00
86	INDEPENDENCE	10000	40.00	60.00
86	RE-DEDICATION	10000	40.00	60.00

ART WORLD OF BOURGEAULT
R. BOURGEAULT — ENGLISH COUNTRYSIDE

80	COUNTRY SQUIRE, THE	1500	70.00	280.00
81	WILLOWS, THE	1500	85.00	280.00
82	ROSE COTTAGE	1500	90.00	310.00
83	THATCHED BEAUTY	1500	95.00	280.00

R. BOURGEAULT — ENGLISH COUNTRYSIDE SINGLE ISSUES

84	ANNE HATHAWAY COTTAGE, THE	500	150.00	640.00
85	LILAC COTTAGE	500	125.00	350.00
87	SUFFOLK PINK	50	220.00	427.00
88	STUART HOUSE	50	325.00	571.00
89	LARK RISE	50	450.00	603.00

R. BOURGEAULT — ROYAL GAINSBOROUGH SERIES

90	LISA-CAROLINE, THE	*	65.00	100.00
91	A GAINSBOROUGH LADY	*	*	N/A

R. BOURGEAULT — ROYAL LITERARY SERIES

85	JOHN BUNYAN COTTAGE, THE	4500	60.00	100.00

YR	NAME	LIMIT	ISSUE	TREND
87	THOMAS HARTY COTTAGE, THE	4500	65.00	100.00
88	JOHN MILTON COTTAGE, THE	4500	65.00	100.00
89	ANNE HATHAWAY COTTAGE, THE	4500	65.00	100.00

R. BOURGEAULT

WHERE IS ENGLAND

YR	NAME	LIMIT	ISSUE	TREND
90	FORGET-ME-NOT	50	525.00	500.00
91	FLEECE INN, THE	50	525.00	705.00
92	MILLBROOK HOUSE	50	525.00	525.00
93	COTSWOLD BEAUTY	50	525.00	525.00

ARTAFFECTS
T. NEWSOM

ADVENTURES OF PETER PAN

YR	NAME	LIMIT	ISSUE	TREND
90	ENCOUNTER, THE	CL	30.00	40.00
90	FLYING OVER LONDON	CL	30.00	40.00
90	LOOK AT ME	CL	30.00	40.00
90	NEVER LAND	CL	30.00	40.00

G. PERILLO

AMERICA'S INDIAN HERITAGE

YR	NAME	LIMIT	ISSUE	TREND
87	CHEYENNE NATION	CL	25.00	65.00
88	ARAPAHO NATION	CL	25.00	50.00
88	BLACKFOOT NATION	CL	25.00	50.00
88	CHIPPEWA NATION	CL	25.00	50.00
88	CROW NATION	CL	25.00	50.00
88	KIOWA NATION	CL	25.00	40.00
88	NEZ PERCE NATION	CL	25.00	40.00
88	SIOUX NATION	CL	25.00	50.00

R. SAUBER

AMERICAN BLUES SPECIAL OCCASION

YR	NAME	LIMIT	ISSUE	TREND
92	HAPPILY EVER AFTER - WEDDING	*	35.00	50.00
92	MY SUNSHINE - MOTHERHOOD	*	35.00	50.00
92	PERFECT TREE, THE - CHRISTMAS	*	35.00	50.00

K. SOLDWEDEL

AMERICAN MARITIME HERITAGE

YR	NAME	LIMIT	ISSUE	TREND
87	U.S.S. CONSTITUTION	CL	35.00	40.00

R. SAUBER

AN OLD FASHIONED CHRISTMAS

YR	NAME	LIMIT	ISSUE	TREND
93	UP ON THE ROOF TOP	*	30.00	45.00
94	CHRISTMAS DELIGHT	*	30.00	45.00
94	CHRISTMAS EVE	*	30.00	45.00
94	TOY SHOPPE, THE	*	30.00	45.00

J. EGGERT

ANGLER'S DREAM

YR	NAME	LIMIT	ISSUE	TREND
83	BROOK TROUT	9800	55.00	75.00
83	CHINOOK SALMON	9800	55.00	75.00
83	LARGEMOUTH BASS	9800	55.00	75.00
83	STRIPED BASS	9800	55.00	75.00

G. PERILLO

ARABIANS

YR	NAME	LIMIT	ISSUE	TREND
86	SILVER STREAK	3500	95.00	155.00

R. SAUBER

BABY'S FIRSTS

YR	NAME	LIMIT	ISSUE	TREND
89	BABY'S FIRST STEP	CL	22.00	30.00
89	CHRISTMAS MORN	CL	22.00	30.00
89	FIRST BIRTHDAY	CL	22.00	30.00
89	PICTURE PERFECT	CL	22.00	30.00
89	VISITING THE DOCTOR	CL	22.00	30.00

B. LEIGHTON-JONES

BACKSTAGE

YR	NAME	LIMIT	ISSUE	TREND
90	BUBBLING OVER	CL	30.00	30.00
90	LETTER, THE	CL	30.00	30.00
90	RUNAWAY, THE	CL	30.00	30.00

M. HOOKS

BAKER STREET

YR	NAME	LIMIT	ISSUE	TREND
83	SHERLOCK HOLMES	CL	55.00	90.00
83	WATSON	9800	55.00	90.00

C. BECKER

BECKER BABIES

YR	NAME	LIMIT	ISSUE	TREND
83	SNOW PUFF	CL	30.00	60.00
84	PALS	CL	30.00	60.00
84	SMILING THROUGH	CL	30.00	60.00

B.P. GUTMANN

BESSIE'S BEST

YR	NAME	LIMIT	ISSUE	TREND
84	LOOKING FOR TROUBLE	CL	30.00	45.00
84	MY BABY	CL	30.00	50.00
84	NEW LOVE, THE	CL	30.00	40.00
84	OH! OH! A BUNNY	CL	30.00	50.00
84	TAPS	CL	30.00	40.00

MAGO

BRING UNTO ME THE CHILDREN

YR	NAME	LIMIT	ISSUE	TREND
94	A LITTLE LOVE SONG	CL	30.00	46.00
94	BAPTISM, THE	CL	30.00	46.00
94	COMMUNION	CL	30.00	46.00
94	HEAVENLY EMBRACE	CL	30.00	46.00
94	LORD'S PRAYER, THE	CL	30.00	46.00
94	LOVE'S BLESSING	CL	30.00	46.00
94	SWEET DREAMS	CL	30.00	46.00
94	SWEET SERENITY	CL	30.00	46.00

T. NEWSOM

CARNIVAL SERIES

YR	NAME	LIMIT	ISSUE	TREND
82	CAROUSEL	19500	35.00	50.00
82	KNOCK EM' DOWN	19500	35.00	50.00

R. SAUBER

CHILDHOOD DELIGHTS

YR	NAME	LIMIT	ISSUE	TREND
83	AMANDA	7500	45.00	75.00

G. PERILLO

CHILDREN OF THE PRAIRIE

YR	NAME	LIMIT	ISSUE	TREND
93	BEACH COMBER	*	30.00	46.00
93	DAYDREAMERS	*	30.00	46.00
93	PATIENCE	*	30.00	46.00
93	PLAY TIME	*	30.00	46.00
93	SENTINAL, THE	*	30.00	46.00
93	SISTERS	*	30.00	46.00

YR	NAME	LIMIT	ISSUE	TREND
93	TENDER LOVING CARE	*	30.00	46.00
93	WATCHFUL WAITING	*	30.00	46.00
A. TOBEY			**CHRISTIAN COLLECTION**	
87	BRING TO ME THE CHILDREN	*	35.00	60.00
87	HEALER, THE	*	35.00	40.00
87	WEDDING FEAST AT CANA	*	35.00	40.00
M. LEONE		**CHRISTMAS CELEBRATIONS OF YESTERDAY**		
93	CHRISTMAS BLESSINGS	*	27.00	42.00
93	CHRISTMAS EVE	*	27.00	42.00
93	CHRISTMAS ON MAIN STREET	*	27.00	42.00
93	CHRISTMAS ON THE FARM	*	27.00	42.00
93	CHRISTMAS PARTY	*	27.00	42.00
93	HOME FOR CHRISTMAS	*	27.00	42.00
93	TRIMMING THE TREE	*	27.00	42.00
93	WREATH MAKER	*	27.00	42.00
J. DENEEN			**CLASSIC AMERICAN CARS**	
89	CADILLAC	CL	35.00	50.00
89	CORD	CL	35.00	50.00
89	DUESENBERG	CL	35.00	50.00
89	RUXTON	CL	35.00	50.00
90	HUDSON	CL	35.00	50.00
90	LINCOLN	CL	35.00	50.00
90	PACKARD	CL	35.00	50.00
90	PIERCE-ARROW	CL	35.00	50.00
J. DENEEN			**CLASSIC AMERICAN TRAINS**	
88	COMPETITION	CL	35.00	50.00
88	HOMEWARD BOUND	CL	35.00	50.00
88	MIDDAY STOP	CL	35.00	60.00
88	RACE AGAINST TIME, A	CL	35.00	60.00
88	ROUND THE BEND	CL	35.00	60.00
88	SILVER BULLET, THE	CL	35.00	70.00
88	TAKING THE HIGH ROAD	CL	35.00	50.00
88	TRAVELING IN STYLE	CL	35.00	60.00
G. PERILLO			**CLUB MEMBER LIMITED EDITION**	
92	PENCIL, THE	YR	35.00	80.00
92	STUDIES IN B/W SET OF FOUR	YR	75.00	80.00
93	WATCHER OF THE WILDERNESS	YR	60.00	65.00
G. PERILLO				**COLTS**
85	APPALOOSA	5000	40.00	105.00
85	ARABIAN	5000	40.00	105.00
85	PINTO	5000	40.00	115.00
85	THOROUGHBRED	5000	40.00	105.00
G. PERILLO			**COUNCIL OF NATIONS**	
92	BOLDNESS OF THE SENECA	CL	30.00	40.00
92	COURAGE OF THE ARAPAHO	CL	30.00	40.00
92	DIGNITY OF THE NEZ PERCE	CL	30.00	40.00
92	NOBILITY OF THE ALGONQUIN	CL	30.00	40.00
92	POWER OF THE BLACKFOOT	CL	30.00	40.00
92	PRIDE OF THE CHEYENNE	CL	30.00	40.00
92	STRENGTH OF THE SIOUX	CL	30.00	40.00
92	WISDOM OF THE CHEROKEE	CL	30.00	40.00
S. MILLER-MAXWELL				**GOOD SPORTS**
89	ALLEY CATS	CL	23.00	35.00
89	PURRFECT GAME	CL	23.00	35.00
89	QUARTERBACK SNEAK	CL	23.00	35.00
89	TEE TIME	CL	23.00	35.00
89	TWO/LOVE	CL	23.00	35.00
89	WHAT'S THE CATCH?	CL	23.00	35.00
J. DENEEN			**GREAT AMERICAN TRAINS**	
92	ALTON LIMITED, THE	CL	27.00	46.00
92	BLACKHAWK LIMITED, THE	CL	27.00	46.00
92	BROADWAY LIMITED, THE	CL	27.00	46.00
92	CAPITOL LIMITED, THE	CL	27.00	46.00
92	MERCHANTS LIMITED, THE	CL	27.00	46.00
92	PANAMA SPECIAL LIMITED, THE	CL	27.00	46.00
92	SOUTHWESTERN LIMITED, THE	CL	27.00	46.00
92	SUNSHINE SPECIAL LIMITED, THE	CL	27.00	46.00
J. DENEEN				**GREAT TRAINS**
85	SANTA FE	7500	35.00	60.00
85	TWENTIETH CENTURY LTD.	7500	35.00	60.00
86	EMPIRE BUILDER	7500	35.00	60.00
MAGO				**HEAVENLY ANGELS**
92	ANGEL CAKE	CL	27.00	50.00
92	ANGEL'S KISS, THE	CL	27.00	50.00
92	CAUGHT IN THE ACT	CL	27.00	50.00
92	HEAVENLY HELPER	CL	27.00	50.00
92	HEAVENLY LIGHT	CL	27.00	50.00
92	HUSH-A-BYE	CL	27.00	70.00
92	MY ANGEL	CL	27.00	50.00
92	SLEEPY SENTINEL	CL	27.00	50.00
R. SAUBER			**HOW DO I LOVE THEE?**	
82	ALAINA	19500	40.00	60.00
82	TAYLOR	19500	40.00	60.00
83	EMBRACE	19500	40.00	60.00
83	RENDEZVOUS	19500	40.00	60.00
G. PERILLO				**INDIAN BRIDAL**
90	AUTUMN BLOSSOM	CL	25.00	30.00

YR	NAME	LIMIT	ISSUE	TREND
90	MISTY WATERS	CL	25.00	30.00
90	SUNNY SKIES	CL	25.00	30.00
90	YELLOW BIRD	CL	25.00	30.00
A. CHESTERMAN			**LANDS BEFORE TIME**	
94	IMPERIAL DYNASTY	CL	30.00	43.00
94	KNIGHTS IN SHINING ARMOUR	CL	30.00	43.00
94	PHARAOH'S RETURN	CL	30.00	43.00
94	ROMAN HOLIDAY	CL	30.00	43.00
L. MARCHETTI			**LIFE OF JESUS**	
92	AGONY IN THE GARDEN, THE	CL	27.00	46.00
92	BLESSING OF THE CHILDREN, THE	CL	27.00	46.00
92	DESCENT FROM THE CROSS, THE	CL	27.00	46.00
92	ENTRY INTO JERUSALEM, THE	CL	27.00	46.00
92	HEALING OF THE SICK, THE	CL	27.00	46.00
92	LAST SUPPER, THE	CL	27.00	46.00
92	RESURRECTION, THE	CL	27.00	46.00
92	SERMON ON THE MOUNT, THE	CL	27.00	46.00
G. PERILLO			**LIVING IN HARMONY**	
91	PEACEABLE KINGDOM	CL	30.00	45.00
B.P. GUTMANN			**MAGICAL MOMENT**	
81	HAPPY DREAMS	CL	30.00	65.00
81	HARMONY	CL	30.00	70.00
82	HIS MAJESTY	CL	30.00	60.00
82	THANK YOU GOD	CL	30.00	50.00
82	WAITING FOR DADDY	CL	30.00	50.00
83	LULLABY, THE	CL	30.00	75.00
MAGO			**MAGO'S MOTHERHOOD**	
90	SERENITY	CL	50.00	80.00
MONET/ CASSAT		**MASTERPIECES OF IMPRESSIONISM**		
80	WOMAN WITH PARASOL	17500	35.00	75.00
81	YOUNG MOTHER SEWING	17500	35.00	60.00
82	SARA IN GREEN BONNET	17500	35.00	60.00
83	MARGOT IN BLUE	17500	35.00	50.00
N. ROCKWELL			**MASTERPIECES OF ROCKWELL**	
80	AFTER THE PROM	17500	43.00	90.00
80	CHALLENGER, THE	17500	50.00	75.00
82	GIRL AT THE MIRROR	17500	50.00	75.00
82	MISSING TOOTH	17500	50.00	75.00
B. JOHNSON			**MASTERPIECES OF THE WEST**	
80	TEXAS NIGHT HERDER	17500	35.00	75.00
LEIGH			**MASTERPIECES OF THE WEST**	
82	COWBOY STYLE	17500	35.00	75.00
G. PERILLO			**MASTERPIECES OF THE WEST**	
82	INDIAN STYLE	17500	35.00	150.00
REMINGTON			**MASTERPIECES OF THE WEST**	
80	INDIAN TRAPPER	17500	35.00	100.00
H. GARRIDO			**MELODIES OF CHILDHOOD**	
83	MARY HAD A LITTLE LAMB	19500	35.00	50.00
83	ROW, ROW, ROW YOUR BOAT	19500	35.00	50.00
83	TWINKLE, TWINKLE, LITTLE STAR	19500	35.00	50.00
B.P. GUTMANN			**MOTHER'S LOVE**	
84	DADDY'S HERE	CL	30.00	50.00
G. PERILLO			**MOTHER'S LOVE**	
88	FEELINGS	YR	35.00	60.00
89	MOONLIGHT	YR	35.00	60.00
90	PRIDE & JOY	YR	40.00	50.00
91	LITTLE SHADOW	YR	40.00	50.00
G. PERILLO			**NATIVE AMERICAN CHRISTMAS**	
93	LITTLE SHEPHERD, THE	YR	35.00	75.00
94	JOY TO THE WORLD	YR	45.00	75.00
G. PERILLO			**NORTH AMERICAN WILDLIFE**	
89	MOUNTAIN LION	CL	30.00	50.00
89	MUSTANG	CL	30.00	50.00
89	WHITE-TAILED DEER	CL	30.00	50.00
90	AMERICAN BALD EAGLE	CL	30.00	50.00
90	BIGHORN SHEEP	CL	30.00	40.00
90	BUFFALO	CL	30.00	40.00
90	POLAR BEAR	CL	30.00	40.00
90	TIMBER WOLF	CL	30.00	40.00
C. BECKER			**NURSERY PAIR**	
83	AWAKENING, THE	CL	25.00	60.00
83	IN SLUMBERLAND	CL	25.00	50.00
N. ROCKWELL			**ON THE ROAD SERIES**	
84	CITY PRIDE	CL	35.00	65.00
84	COUNTRY PRIDE	CL	35.00	65.00
84	PRIDE OF STOCKBRIDGE	CL	35.00	65.00
G. PERILLO			**PERILLO CHRISTMAS**	
87	SHINING STAR	YR	30.00	60.00
88	SILENT LIGHT	YR	35.00	75.00
89	SNOW FLAKE	YR	35.00	55.00
90	BUNDLE UP	YR	40.00	55.00
91	CHRISTMAS JOURNEY	YR	40.00	55.00
G. PERILLO			**PERILLO SANTAS**	
80	SANTA'S JOY	CL	30.00	55.00
81	SANTA'S BUNDLE	CL	30.00	50.00

YR	NAME	LIMIT	ISSUE	TREND
G. PERILLO			**PERILLO'S FAVORITES**	
94	BUFFALO AND THE BRAVE	CL	45.00	68.00
94	HOME OF THE BRAVE AND FREE	CL	35.00	40.00
G. PERILLO			**PERILLO'S FOUR SEASONS**	
91	AUTUMN	CL	25.00	35.00
91	SPRING	CL	25.00	35.00
91	SUMMER	CL	25.00	35.00
91	WINTER	CL	25.00	35.00
G. PERILLO			**PLAINSMEN**	
78	BUFFALO HUNT (BRONZE)	2500	300.00	390.00
79	PROUD ONE, THE (BRONZE)	2500	300.00	390.00
J.H. DOLPH			**PLAYFUL PETS**	
82	CURIOSITY	7500	45.00	75.00
82	MASTER'S HAT	7500	45.00	75.00
J. EGGERT			**PORTRAIT SERIES**	
86	CHANTILLY	CL	25.00	43.00
86	DYNASTY	CL	25.00	43.00
86	JAMBALAYA	CL	25.00	43.00
86	VELVET	CL	25.00	43.00
G. PERILLO			**PORTRAITS BY PERILLO-MINI PLATES**	
89	BRIGHT SKY	9500	20.00	30.00
89	LITTLE FEATHER	9500	20.00	43.00
89	RUNNING BEAR	9500	20.00	20.00
89	SMILING EYES	9500	20.00	30.00
90	BLUE BIRD	9500	20.00	43.00
90	PROUD EAGLE	9500	20.00	20.00
90	SPRING BREEZE	9500	20.00	43.00
90	WILDFLOWER	9500	20.00	43.00
R. SAUBER			**PORTRAITS OF AMERICAN BRIDES**	
86	CAROLINE	CL	30.00	70.00
86	JACQUELINE	CL	30.00	50.00
87	ELIZABETH	CL	30.00	50.00
87	EMILY	CL	30.00	50.00
87	LAURA	CL	30.00	50.00
87	MEREDITH	CL	30.00	50.00
87	REBECCA	CL	30.00	50.00
87	SARAH	CL	30.00	60.00
G. PERILLO			**PRIDE OF AMERICA'S INDIANS**	
86	BRAVE AND FREE	CL	25.00	60.00
86	DARK-EYED FRIENDS	CL	25.00	60.00
86	NOBLE COMPANIONS	CL	25.00	60.00
87	KINDRED SPIRITS	CL	25.00	50.00
87	LOYAL ALLIANCE	CL	25.00	75.00
87	PEACEFUL COMRADES	CL	25.00	55.00
87	SMALL AND WISE	CL	25.00	55.00
87	WINTER SCOUTS	CL	25.00	50.00
G. PERILLO			**PROUD YOUNG SPIRITS**	
90	BIRDS OF A FEATHER	CL	30.00	40.00
90	FAST FRIENDS	CL	30.00	40.00
90	FREEDOM'S WATCH	CL	30.00	40.00
90	LOYAL GUARDIAN	CL	30.00	40.00
90	PRAIRIE PALS	CL	30.00	40.00
90	PROTECTOR OF THE PLAINS	CL	30.00	55.00
90	WATCHFUL EYES	CL	30.00	60.00
90	WOODLAND SCOUTS	CL	30.00	40.00
MAGO			**REFLECTIONS OF YOUTH**	
88	AMY	CL	30.00	45.00
88	ANDREW	CL	30.00	70.00
88	BETH	CL	30.00	50.00
88	JESSICA	CL	30.00	50.00
88	JULIA	CL	30.00	50.00
88	LAUREN	CL	30.00	50.00
88	MICHELLE	CL	30.00	50.00
88	SEBASTIAN	CL	30.00	50.00
N. ROCKWELL			**ROCKWELL AMERICANA**	
81	SHUFFLETON'S BARBERSHOP	17500	75.00	125.00
82	BREAKING HOME TIES	17500	75.00	125.00
83	WALKING TO CHURCH	17500	75.00	125.00
N. ROCKWELL			**ROCKWELL TRILOGY**	
81	STOCKBRIDGE IN WINTER 1	CL	35.00	60.00
82	STOCKBRIDGE IN WINTER 2	CL	35.00	60.00
82	STOCKBRIDGE IN WINTER 3	CL	35.00	65.00
L. MARCHETTI			**ROMANTIC CITIES OF EUROPE**	
89	PARIS	CL	35.00	55.00
89	VENICE	CL	35.00	55.00
90	LONDON	CL	35.00	55.00
90	MOSCOW	CL	35.00	50.00
KNOX/ROBERTSON			**ROSE WREATHS**	
93	GENTLE PERSUASION	*	27.00	46.00
93	SUMMER'S BOUNTY	*	27.00	46.00
93	SUNSET SPLENDOR	*	27.00	46.00
93	VICTORIAN FANTASY	*	27.00	46.00
94	FLORAL FASCINATION	*	27.00	46.00
94	LOVE'S EMBRACE	*	27.00	46.00
94	SWEET SUNSHINE	*	27.00	46.00
94	SWEETHEART'S DELIGHT	*	27.00	46.00

YR	NAME	LIMIT	ISSUE	TREND
K. SOLDWEDEL		SAILING THROUGH HISTORY		
86	FLYING CLOUD	CL	30.00	55.00
86	MAYFLOWER	CL	30.00	55.00
86	SANTA MARIA	CL	30.00	55.00
N. ROCKWELL		SIMPLER TIMES SERIES		
84	LAZY DAZE	7500	35.00	50.00
84	ONE FOR THE ROAD	7500	35.00	50.00
R. SAUBER		SONGS OF STEPHEN FOSTER		
84	BEAUTIFUL DREAMER	3500	60.00	100.00
84	JEANIE WITH THE LIGHT BROWN HAIR	3500	60.00	100.00
84	OH! SUSANNAH	3500	60.00	100.00
MAGO		SPECIAL ISSUE		
94	DIVINE INTERVENTION	CL	35.00	40.00
H.C. CHRISTY		SPECIAL ISSUE		
87	WE THE PEOPLE	OP	35.00	40.00
F. TIPTON HUNTER		SPECIAL OCCASIONS		
82	BUBBLES	OP	30.00	50.00
82	BUTTERFLIES	OP	30.00	50.00
G. PERILLO		SPIRITS OF NATURE		
93	DEFENDER OF THE MOUNTAIN	3500	60.00	82.00
93	GUARDIAN OF SAFE PASSAGE	3500	60.00	82.00
93	KEEPER OF THE FOREST	3500	60.00	82.00
93	PROTECTOR OF THE NATIONS	3500	60.00	82.00
93	SPIRIT OF THE PLAINS	3500	60.00	82.00
G. PERILLO		STUDIES IN BLACK & WHITE COLLECTOR'S CLUB ONLY		
92	DETERMINATION	YR	*	N/A
92	DEVOTION	YR	*	N/A
92	DIGNITY	YR	75.00	80.00
92	DILIGENCE	YR	*	N/A
MAGO		STUDIES OF EARLY CHILDHOOD		
90	ANYBODY HOME?	CL	35.00	45.00
90	CHRISTOPHER & KATE	CL	35.00	46.00
90	PEEK-A-BOO	CL	35.00	45.00
90	THREE-PART HARMONY	OP	35.00	75.00
R. SAUBER		TIMELESS LOVE		
89	PROPOSAL, THE	CL	35.00	65.00
89	SWEET EMBRACE	CL	35.00	50.00
90	AFTERNOON LIGHT	CL	35.00	50.00
90	QUIET MOMENTS	CL	35.00	50.00
R. SAUBER		TIMES OF OUR LIVES COLLECTION		
82	WEDDING, THE 10 1/4 IN.	CL	38.00	40.00
84	HAPPY BIRTHDAY 10 1/4 IN.	CL	38.00	40.00
85	ALL ADORE HIM 10 1/4 IN.	CL	38.00	40.00
85	HOME SWEET HOME 10 1/4 IN.	CL	38.00	40.00
86	ANNIVERSARY, THE 10 1/4 IN.	CL	38.00	40.00
86	CHRISTENING, THE 10 1/4 IN.	CL	38.00	40.00
86	SWEETHEARTS 10 1/4 IN.	CL	38.00	50.00
87	FATHERHOOD 10 1/4 IN.	CL	38.00	40.00
87	MOTHERHOOD 10 1/4 IN.	CL	38.00	40.00
87	SWEET SIXTEEN	CL	38.00	40.00
88	ALL ADORE HIM 6 1/2 IN.	CL	20.00	23.00
88	ANNIVERSARY, THE 6 1/2 IN.	CL	20.00	23.00
88	CHRISTENING, THE 6 1/2 IN.	CL	20.00	23.00
88	FATHERHOOD 6 1/2 IN.	CL	20.00	23.00
88	HAPPY BIRTHDAY 6 1/2 IN.	CL	20.00	23.00
88	HOME SWEET HOME 6 1/2 IN.	CL	20.00	23.00
88	MOTHERHOOD 6 1/2 IN.	CL	20.00	23.00
88	SWEETHEARTS 6 1/2 IN.	CL	20.00	23.00
88	WEDDING, THE 6 1/2 IN..	CL	20.00	23.00
89	GOD BLESS AMERICA 10 1/4 IN.	CL	40.00	40.00
89	GOD BLESS AMERICA 6 1/4 IN.	CL	22.00	23.00
89	VISITING THE DOCTOR	CL	40.00	40.00
90	MOTHER'S JOY 10 1/4 IN.	CL	40.00	40.00
90	MOTHER'S JOY 6 1/2 IN.	CL	23.00	40.00
G. PERILLO		TRIBAL IMAGES		
94	BLACKFOOT CHIEFTAINS	CL	35.00	45.00
94	CHEYENNE CHIEFTAINS	CL	35.00	45.00
94	CROW CHIEFTAINS	CL	35.00	45.00
94	SIOUX CHIEFTAINS	CL	35.00	45.00
H.C. CHRISTY		TRIBUTE SERIES		
82	GEE, I WISH	CL	30.00	50.00
J.M. FLAGG		TRIBUTE SERIES		
82	I WANT YOU	CL	30.00	50.00
N. ROCKWELL		TRIBUTE SERIES		
83	SOLDIER'S FAREWELL	CL	30.00	50.00
J. TERRESON		UNICORN MAGIC		
83	AFTERNOON OFFERING	7500	50.00	75.00
83	MORNING ENCOUNTER	7500	50.00	75.00
G. PERILLO		WAR PONIES OF THE PLAINS		
92	FREE SPIRIT	CL	27.00	47.00
92	GENTLE WARRIOR	CL	27.00	47.00
92	NIGHTSHADOW	CL	27.00	47.00
92	PRAIRIE PRANCER	CL	27.00	47.00
92	PROUD COMPANION	CL	27.00	47.00
92	SUN DANCER	CL	27.00	47.00

YR	NAME	LIMIT	ISSUE	TREND
92	THUNDERFOOT	CL	27.00	47.00
92	WINDCATCHER	CL	27.00	47.00
R. SAUBER				**WINTER MINDSCAPE**
89	PEACEFUL VILLAGE	CL	30.00	40.00
89	SNOWBOUND	CL	30.00	40.00
90	COUNTRY MORNING	CL	30.00	40.00
90	FIRST FREEZE	CL	30.00	40.00
90	JANUARY THAW	CL	30.00	40.00
90	PAPA'S SURPRISE	CL	30.00	40.00
90	SLEIGH RIDE	CL	30.00	40.00
90	WELL TRAVELED ROAD	CL	30.00	40.00
G. PERILLO				**YOUNG EMOTIONS**
86	SMILES	5000	*	N/A
86	TEARS	5000	75.00	255.00

ARTISTS OF THE WORLD

YR	NAME	LIMIT	ISSUE	TREND
T. DEGRAZIA				**CELEBRATION**
93	CAROLING	5000	40.00	100.00
93	HOLIDAY LULLABY	5000	40.00	100.00
93	LORD'S CANDLE, THE	5000	40.00	100.00
93	PINATA PARTY	5000	40.00	100.00
T. DEGRAZIA				**CHILDREN**
76	LOS NINOS	5000	35.00	785.00
77	WHITE DOVE	5000	40.00	90.00
78	FLOWER GIRL	9500	45.00	70.00
78	FLOWER GIRL-SIGNED	500	100.00	455.00
78	LOS NINOS-SIGNED	500	100.00	905.00
78	WHITE DOVE-SIGNED	500	100.00	455.00
79	FLOWER BOY	9500	45.00	55.00
79	FLOWER BOY-SIGNED	500	100.00	455.00
80	LITTLE COCOPAH	9500	50.00	70.00
80	LITTLE COCOPAH GIRL-SIGNED	500	100.00	325.00
81	BEAUTIFUL BURDEN	9500	50.00	55.00
81	BEAUTIFUL BURDEN-SIGNED	500	100.00	325.00
81	MERRY LITTLE INDIAN-SIGNED	500	100.00	455.00
82	MERRY LITTLE INDIAN	9500	55.00	55.00
83	WONDERING	10000	60.00	50.00
84	PINK PAPOOSE	10000	65.00	45.00
85	SUNFLOWER BOY	10000	65.00	65.00
T. DEGRAZIA				**CHILDREN AT PLAY**
85	MY FIRST HORSE	15000	65.00	100.00
86	GIRL WITH SEWING MACHINE	15000	65.00	100.00
87	LOVES ME	15000	65.00	100.00
88	MERRILY, MERRILY, MERRILY	15000	65.00	100.00
89	MY FIRST ARROW	15000	65.00	100.00
90	AWAY WITH MY KITE	15000	65.00	100.00
T. DEGRAZIA				**CHILDREN MINI-PLATES**
80	LOS NINOS	5000	15.00	305.00
81	WHITE DOVE	5000	15.00	40.00
82	FLOWER BOY	5000	15.00	40.00
82	FLOWER GIRL	5000	15.00	40.00
83	BEAUTIFUL BURDEN	5000	20.00	55.00
83	LITTLE COCOPAH INDIAN GIRL	5000	15.00	30.00
84	MERRY LITTLE INDIAN	5000	20.00	30.00
84	WONDERING	5000	20.00	30.00
85	PINK PAPOOSE	5000	20.00	30.00
85	SUNFLOWER BOY	5000	20.00	30.00
K. FUNG NG				**CHILDREN OF ABERDEEN**
79	GIRL WITH LITTLE BROTHER	*	50.00	100.00
80	SAMPAN GIRL	*	50.00	60.00
81	GIRL WITH LITTLE SISTER	*	55.00	75.00
82	GIRL WITH SEASHELLS	*	60.00	110.00
83	GIRL WITH SEABIRDS	*	60.00	105.00
84	BROTHER AND SISTER	*	60.00	85.00
T. DEGRAZIA				**CHILDREN OF THE SUN**
87	BRIGHT FLOWERS OF THE DESERT	150 DAYS	38.00	50.00
87	MY LITTLE PINK BIRD	150 DAYS	35.00	50.00
87	SPRING BLOSSOMS	150 DAYS	35.00	50.00
88	GENTLE WHITE DOVE, THE	150 DAYS	38.00	50.00
88	GIFTS FROM THE SUN	150 DAYS	38.00	50.00
88	GROWING GLORY	150 DAYS	38.00	50.00
88	SUNFLOWER MAIDEN	150 DAYS	40.00	55.00
89	SUN SHOWERS	150 DAYS	40.00	55.00
T. DEGRAZIA				**FIESTA OF THE CHILDREN**
90	CASTANETS IN BLOOM	150 DAYS	35.00	50.00
90	WELCOME TO THE FIESTA	150 DAYS	35.00	40.00
91	FIESTA FLOWERS	150 DAYS	35.00	50.00
92	FIESTA ANGELS	150 DAYS	35.00	45.00
T. DEGRAZIA				**FLORAL FIESTA**
94	FLOWERS FOR MOTHER	5000	40.00	42.00
94	LITTLE FLOWER VENDOR	5000	40.00	42.00
T. DEGRAZIA				**HOLIDAY**
76	FESTIVAL OF LIGHTS	9500	45.00	90.00
76	FESTIVAL OF LIGHTS-SIGNED	500	100.00	325.00
77	BELL OF HOPE	9500	45.00	60.00
77	BELL OF HOPE-SIGNED	500	100.00	190.00
78	LITTLE MADONNA	9500	45.00	55.00

YR	NAME	LIMIT	ISSUE	TREND
78	LITTLE MADONNA-SIGNED	500	100.00	340.00
79	NATIVITY, THE	9500	50.00	80.00
79	NATIVITY, THE-SIGNED	500	100.00	185.00
80	LITTLE PIMA DRUMMER	9500	50.00	60.00
80	LITTLE PIMA DRUMMER-SIGNED	500	100.00	190.00
81	A LITTLE PRAYER	9500	55.00	50.00
81	A LITTLE PRAYER-SIGNED	500	100.00	195.00
82	BLUE BOY	10000	60.00	50.00
82	BLUE BOY-SIGNED	96	100.00	200.00
83	HEAVENLY BLESSINGS	10000	65.00	30.00
84	NAVAJO MADONNA	10000	65.00	50.00
85	SAGUARO DANCE	10000	65.00	50.00

T. DEGRAZIA — HOLIDAY-MINI PLATES

80	FESTIVAL OF LIGHTS	5000	15.00	255.00
81	BELL OF HOPE	5000	15.00	55.00
82	LITTLE MADONNA	5000	15.00	100.00
82	NATIVITY, THE	5000	15.00	100.00
83	LITTLE PIMA DRUMMER	5000	15.00	30.00
83	LITTLE PRAYER	5000	20.00	30.00
84	BLUE BOY	5000	20.00	30.00
84	HEAVENLY BLESSINGS	5000	20.00	30.00
85	NAVAJO MADONNA	5000	20.00	30.00
85	SAGUARO DANCE	5000	20.00	30.00

T. DEGRAZIA — WESTERN

86	MORNING RIDE	5000	65.00	105.00
87	BRONCO	5000	65.00	105.00
88	APACHE SCOUT	5000	65.00	105.00
89	ALONE	5000	65.00	105.00

BAREUTHER
H. MUELLER — CHRISTMAS

67	STIFTSKIRCHE	10000	12.00	200.00
68	KAPPLKIRCHE	10000	12.00	75.00
69	CHRISTKINDLESMARKT	10000	12.00	40.00
70	CHAPEL IN OBERNDORF	10000	12.50	75.00
72	CHRISTMAS IN MUNICH	10000	14.50	30.00
73	SLEIGH RIDE	10000	15.00	40.00
74	BLACK FOREST CHURCH	10000	19.00	40.00
75	SNOWMAN	10000	22.00	50.00
76	CHAPEL IN THE HILLS	10000	24.00	30.00
77	STORY TIME	10000	25.00	45.00
78	MITTENWALD	10000	28.00	75.00
79	WINTER DAY	10000	35.00	63.00
80	MITTENBERG	10000	38.00	65.00
81	WALK IN THE FOREST	10000	40.00	60.00
82	BAD WIMPFEN	10000	40.00	50.00
83	NIGHT BEFORE CHRISTMAS, THE	10000	40.00	50.00
84	ZEIL ON THE RIVER MAIN	10000	43.00	70.00
85	WINTER WONDERLAND	10000	43.00	60.00
86	CHRISTMAS IN FORCHHEIM	10000	43.00	35.00
87	DECORATING THE TREE	10000	43.00	90.00
88	ST. COLOMAN CHURCH	10000	53.00	85.00
89	SLEIGH RIDE	10000	53.00	30.00
90	OLD FORGE IN ROTHENBURG, THE	10000	53.00	55.00
91	CHRISTMAS JOY	10000	56.00	60.00
92	MARKET PLACE IN HEPPENHEIM	10000	60.00	60.00
93	WINTER FUN	10000	60.00	60.00
94	COMING HOME FOR CHRISTMAS	10000	60.00	75.00

L. RICHTER — CHRISTMAS

71	TOYS FOR SALE	10000	12.75	30.00

BELLEEK
* — CHRISTMAS

70	CASTLE CALDWELL	7500	25.00	200.00
71	CELTIC CROSS	7500	25.00	85.00
72	FLIGHT OF THE EARLS	7500	30.00	70.00
73	TRIBUTE TO YEATS	7500	39.00	100.00
74	DEVENISH ISLAND	7500	45.00	90.00
75	CELTIC CROSS, THE	7500	48.00	90.00
76	DOVE OF PEACE	7500	55.00	120.00
77	WREN	7500	55.00	80.00

BERLIN DESIGN
* — CHRISTMAS

70	CHRISTMAS IN BERNKASTEL	4000	14.50	130.00
71	CHRISTMAS IN ROTHENBURG	20000	14.50	50.00
72	CHRISTMAS IN MICHELSTADT	20000	15.00	60.00
73	CHRISTMAS IN WENDLESTEIN	20000	20.00	60.00
74	CHRISTMAS IN BREMEN	20000	25.00	55.00
75	CHRISTMAS IN DORTLAND	20000	30.00	40.00
76	CHRISTMAS IN AUGSBURG	20000	32.00	80.00
77	CHRISTMAS IN HAMBURG	20000	32.00	35.00
78	CHRISTMAS IN BERLIN	20000	36.00	90.00
79	CHRISTMAS IN GREETSIEL	20000	48.00	65.00
80	CHRISTMAS IN MITTENBERG	20000	50.00	60.00
81	CHRISTMAS EVE IN HAHNENKLEE	20000	55.00	60.00
82	CHRISTMAS EVE IN WASSERBERG	20000	55.00	55.00
83	CHRISTMAS IN OBERNDORF	20000	55.00	70.00

YR	NAME	LIMIT	ISSUE	TREND
84	CHRISTMAS IN RAMSAU	20000	55.00	60.00
85	CHRISTMAS IN BAD WIMPFEN	20000	55.00	60.00
86	CHRISTMAS EVE IN GELNHAUS	20000	65.00	70.00
87	CHRISTMAS EVE IN GOSLAR	20000	65.00	70.00
88	CHRISTMAS EVE IN RUHPOLDING	20000	65.00	95.00
89	CHRISTMAS EVE IN FRIEDECHSDADT	20000	80.00	85.00
90	CHRISTMAS EVE IN PARTENKIRCHEN	20000	80.00	85.00
91	CHRISTMAS EE IN ALLENDORF	20000	80.00	85.00
*				HISTORICAL
75	WASHINGTON CROSSING THE DELAWARE	YR	30.00	40.00
76	TOM THUMB	YR	32.00	35.00
77	ZEPPELIN	YR	32.00	35.00
78	BENZ MOTOR CAR MUNICH	10000	36.00	36.00
79	JOHANNES GUTENBERG	10000	48.00	48.00
*		HOLIDAY WEEK OF THE FAMILY KAPPELMANN		
84	MONDAY	*	33.00	33.00
84	TUESDAY	*	33.00	37.00
85	FRIDAY	*	35.00	40.00
85	THURSDAY	*	35.00	38.00
85	WEDNESDAY	*	33.00	37.00
86	SATURDAY	*	35.00	40.00
86	SUNDAY	*	35.00	40.00

BIEDERMANN & SONS
*

YR	NAME	LIMIT	ISSUE	TREND
93	FOUR CALLING BIRDS	250	17.50	20.00
94	DRUMMER BOY	250	20.00	50.00

BING & GRONDAHL
C. MAGADINI
98	AMERICAN CHRISTMAS HERITAGE COLLECTION	YR	35.00	35.00

J. NIELSEN
98	PLACES OF ENCHANTMENT 1998	7500	70.00	70.00

A. HALLIN
			CENTENNIAL COLLECTION	
95	BEHIND THE FROZEN WINDOW	YR	60.00	85.00

D. JENSEN
			CENTENNIAL COLLECTION	
92	CROWS ENJOYING CHRISTMAS	YR	60.00	75.00

H. THELANDER
			CENTENNIAL COLLECTION	
93	CHRISTMAS ELF	YR	60.00	80.00
94	CHRISTMAS IN CHURCH	YR	60.00	80.00

H. VLUGENRING
			CENTENNIAL COLLECTION	
92	COPENHAGEN CHRISTMAS	YR	60.00	60.00

C. ROLLER
			CHILDREN'S DAY PLATE	
85	MAGICAL TEA PARTY, THE	YR	25.00	30.00
86	A JOYFUL FLIGHT	YR	27.00	35.00
86	LITTLE GARDENERS, THE	YR	30.00	45.00
88	WASH DAY	YR	35.00	45.00
89	BEDTIME	YR	37.00	30.00

S. VESTERGAARD
			CHILDREN'S DAY PLATE	
90	MY FAVORITE DRESS	YR	37.00	45.00
91	FUN ON THE BEACH	YR	45.00	60.00
92	A SUMMER DAY IN THE MEADOW	YR	45.00	69.00
93	CAROUSEL, THE	YR	45.00	60.00
94	LITTLE FISHERMAN, THE	YR	45.00	60.00
98	CHILDREN'S DAY 1998	YR	35.00	35.00

AARESTRUP
			CHRISTMAS	
30	YULE TREE	YR	1.50	99.00

K. BONFILS
			CHRISTMAS	
54	ROYAL BOAT	YR	7.00	89.00
55	KAULUNDORG CHURCH	YR	8.00	123.00
56	CHRISTMAS IN COPENHAGEN	YR	8.50	123.00
57	CHRISTMAS CANDLES	YR	9.00	139.00
58	SANTA CLAUS	YR	9.50	115.00
59	CHRISTMAS EVE	YR	10.00	129.00
60	VILLAGE CHURCH	YR	10.00	170.00
61	WINTER HARMONY	YR	10.50	80.00
62	WINTER NIGHT	YR	11.00	79.00

C. ERSGAARD
			CHRISTMAS	
10	OLD ORGANIST. THE	YR	1.50	110.00

H. FLUGENRING
			CHRISTMAS	
31	TOWN HALL SQUARE	YR	2.50	90.00
32	LIFE BOAT	YR	2.50	95.00
33	KORSOR-NYBORG FERRY	YR	3.00	77.00
34	CHURCH BELL IN TOWER	YR	3.00	77.00

A. FRIIS
			CHRISTMAS	
17	CHRISTMAS BOAT	YR	1.50	90.00
18	FISHING BOAT	YR	1.50	90.00
19	OUTSIDE LIGHTED WINDOW	YR	2.00	89.00
20	HARE IN THE SNOW	YR	2.00	82.00
21	PIGEONS	YR	2.00	82.00
22	STAR OF BETHLEHEM	YR	2.00	55.00
23	ERMITAGE, THE	YR	2.00	79.00
24	LIGHTHOUSE	YR	2.50	79.00
25	CHILD'S CHRISTMAS	YR	2.50	79.00
26	CHURCHGOERS	YR	2.50	79.00
27	SKATING COUPLE	YR	2.50	95.00
28	ESKIMOS	YR	2.50	69.00

The Snowman *by K. Lange was Royal Copenhagen's 1985 addition to the "Christmas" series.*

The fourth release in The Bradford Exchange's Visions of the Sacred collection, Buffalo Caller *has increased in value from its 1995 issue price of $32.90.*

As part of the "Kinkade's Illuminated Cottages" series, The Flagstone Path *is based on the art of Thomas Kinkade and was released in 1994 by The Bradford Exchange.*

Ladies Secret *from the "Famous Fillies" series by Fred Stone illustrates why Stone is considered a master in the genre. This 1987 print from American Artists was limited to 9,500 and sold for $65.*

YR	NAME	LIMIT	ISSUE	TREND
29	FOX OUTSIDE FARM	YR	2.50	89.00
31	CHRISTMAS TRAIN	YR	2.50	87.00
F. GARDE				**CHRISTMAS**
00	CHURCH BELLS	YR	0.75	1600.00
98	ROSES AND STAR	YR	0.75	978.00
99	CROWS	YR	0.75	2000.00
F. HALLIN				**CHRISTMAS**
95	BEHIND THE FROZEN WINDOW	YR	0.50	7000.00
96	NEW MOON	YR	0.50	2400.00
97	SPARROWS	YR	0.75	1400.00
E. HANSEN				**CHRISTMAS**
02	GOING TO CHURCH	YR	1.50	99.00
98	CHRISTMAS AROUND THE WORLD 1998	7500	70.00	70.00
M. HYLDAHL				**CHRISTMAS**
00	EXPECTANT CHILDREN	YR	1.00	290.00
46	COMMEMORATION CROSS	YR	5.00	79.00
47	DYBBOL MILL	YR	5.00	99.00
48	WATCHMAN	YR	5.50	65.00
49	LANDSOLDATEN	YR	5.50	73.00
50	KRONBORG CASTLE	YR	5.50	109.00
51	JENS BANG	YR	6.00	95.00
D. JENSEN				**CHRISTMAS**
02	GOTHIC CHURCH INTERIOR	YR	1.00	437.00
05	CHRISTMAS NIGHT	YR	1.00	179.00
06	SLEIGHING TO CHURCH	YR	1.00	110.00
15	DOG OUTSIDE WINDOW	YR	1.50	139.00
84	CHRISTMAS LETTER, THE	YR	55.00	75.00
85	CHRISTMAS EVE AT THE FARMHOUSE	YR	55.00	77.00
86	SILENT NIGHT, HOLY NIGHT	YR	55.00	75.00
87	SNOWMAN'S CHRISTMAS EVE, THE	YR	60.00	77.00
88	IN THE KINGS GARDEN	YR	65.00	77.00
89	CHRISTMAS ANCHORAGE	YR	60.00	71.00
90	CHANGING OF THE GUARDS	YR	65.00	71.00
91	COPENHAGEN STOCK EXCHANGE	YR	70.00	55.00
P. JORGENSEN				**CHRISTMAS**
00	ST. PETRI CHURCH	YR	1.00	80.00
16	SPARROWS AT CHRISTMAS	YR	1.50	65.00
T. LARSEN				**CHRISTMAS**
13	BRINGING HOME THE TREE	YR	1.50	49.00
14	AMALIENBORG CASTLE	YR	1.50	25.00
O. LARSON				**CHRISTMAS**
35	LILLEBELT BRIDGE	YR	3.00	77.00
36	ROYAL GUARD	YR	3.00	77.00
37	ARRIVAL OF CHRISTMAS GUESTS	YR	3.00	80.00
40	CHRISTMAS LETTERS	YR	4.00	149.00
41	HORSES ENJOYING MEAL	YR	4.00	243.00
42	DANISH FARM	YR	4.00	174.00
43	RIBE CATHEDRAL	YR	5.00	174.00
44	SORGENFRI CASTLE	YR	5.00	99.00
45	OLD WATER MILL, THE	YR	5.00	119.00
H. MOLTKE				**CHRISTMAS**
00	ANGELS AND SHEPHERDS	YR	1.50	79.00
J. NIELSEN				**CHRISTMAS**
98	CHRISTMAS 1998	YR	70.00	70.00
C. OLSEN				**CHRISTMAS**
04	FREDERICKSBERG HILL	YR	1.00	179.00
F. PLOCKROSS				**CHRISTMAS**
07	LITTLE MATCH GIRL	YR	1.00	133.00
B. PRAMVIG				**CHRISTMAS**
52	THORSVALDSEN MUSEUM	YR	6.00	70.00
53	SNOWMAN	YR	7.50	79.00
S. SABRA				**CHRISTMAS**
00	THREE WISE MEN	YR	1.00	450.00
J. STEENSEN				**CHRISTMAS**
92	CHRISTMAS AT THE RECTORY	YR	70.00	79.00
93	FATHER CHRISTMAS IN COPENHAGEN	YR	70.00	72.00
H. THELANDER				**CHRISTMAS**
63	CHRISTMAS ELF	YR	11.00	127.00
64	FIR TREE AND HARE, THE	YR	11.50	47.00
65	BRINGING HOME THE TREE	YR	12.00	49.00
66	HOME FOR CHRISTMAS	YR	12.00	47.00
67	SHARING THE JOY	YR	13.00	65.00
68	CHRISTMAS IN CHURCH	YR	14.00	39.00
69	ARRIVAL OF GUESTS	YR	14.00	30.00
70	PHEASANTS IN SNOW	YR	14.50	25.00
71	CHRISTMAS AT HOME	YR	15.00	25.00
72	CHRISTMAS IN GREENLAND	YR	16.50	25.00
73	COUNTRY CHRISTMAS	YR	20.00	25.00
74	CHRISTMAS IN THE VILLAGE	YR	22.00	25.00
75	OLD WATER MILL	YR	28.00	39.00
76	CHRISTMAS WELCOME	YR	28.00	39.00
77	COPENHAGEN CHRISTMAS	YR	30.00	39.00
78	CHRISTMAS TALE	YR	32.00	49.00
79	WHITE CHRISTMAS	YR	37.00	20.00
80	CHRISTMAS IN WOODS	YR	43.00	49.00
81	CHRISTMAS PEACE	YR	50.00	49.00

YR NAME	LIMIT	ISSUE	TREND
82 CHRISTMAS TREE	YR	55.00	83.00
83 CHRISTMAS IN OLD TOWN	YR	55.00	75.00
I. TJERNE			**CHRISTMAS**
38 LIGHTING THE CANDLES	YR	3.00	109.00
39 OLD LOCK-EYE, THE SANDMAN	YR	3.00	149.00
S. VESTERGAARD			**CHRISTMAS**
98 CHRISTMAS 1998	YR	70.00	70.00
J. WOODSON			**CHRISTMAS IN AMERICA**
86 CHRISTMAS EVE IN WILLIAMSBURG	YR	30.00	45.00
87 CHRISTMAS EVE AT THE WHITE HOUSE	YR	35.00	40.00
88 CHRISTMAS EVE AT ROCKEFELLER CENTER	YR	35.00	50.00
89 CHRISTMAS IN NEW ENGLAND	YR	37.00	50.00
90 CHRISTMAS EVE AT THE CAPITOL	YR	40.00	50.00
91 CHRISTMAS EVE AT INDEPENDENCE HALL	YR	45.00	50.00
91 CHRISTMAS EVE IN WILLIAMSBURG	YR	70.00	74.00
92 CHRISTMAS IN SAN FRANCISCO	YR	48.00	50.00
93 COMING HOME FOR CHRISTMAS	YR	48.00	65.00
94 CHRISTMAS EVE IN ALASKA	YR	48.00	65.00
AARESTRUP			**JUBILEE-5 YEAR CYCLE**
80 YULE TREE	YR	60.00	75.00
J. BONFILS			**JUBILEE-5 YEAR CYCLE**
90 ROYAL YACHT DANNEBROG, THE	YR	95.00	79.00
C. ERSGAARD			**JUBILEE-5 YEAR CYCLE**
30 OLD ORGANIST, THE	YR	*	199.00
H. FLUGENRING			**JUBILEE-5 YEAR CYCLE**
85 LIFEBOAT AT WORK	YR	65.00	90.00
A. FRIIS			**JUBILEE-5 YEAR CYCLE**
50 ESKIMOS	YR	*	239.00
65 CHURCHGOERS	YR	25.00	105.00
F. GARDE			**JUBILEE-5 YEAR CYCLE**
20 CHURCH BELLS	YR	*	75.00
F. HALLIN			**JUBILEE-5 YEAR CYCLE**
15 FROZEN WINDOW	YR	*	189.00
M. HYLDAHL			**JUBILEE-5 YEAR CYCLE**
55 DYBBOL MILL	YR	*	239.00
60 KRONBORG CASTLE	YR	25.00	159.00
D. JENSEN			**JUBILEE-5 YEAR CYCLE**
25 DOG OUTSIDE WINDOW	YR	*	159.00
T. LARSEN			**JUBILEE-5 YEAR CYCLE**
45 AMALIENBORG CASTLE	YR	*	219.00
70 AMALIENBORG CASTLE	YR	30.00	25.00
O. LARSON			**JUBILEE-5 YEAR CYCLE**
75 HORSES ENJOYING MEAL	YR	40.00	59.00
E. PLOCKROSS			**JUBILEE-5 YEAR CYCLE**
35 LITTLE MATCH GIRL	YR	*	759.00
S. SABRA			**JUBILEE-5 YEAR CYCLE**
40 THREE WISE MEN	YR	*	1839.00
L. JENSEN			**MOTHER'S DAY**
90 HEN WITH CHICKS	YR	53.00	60.00
91 NANNY GOAT AND HER TWO FRISKY KIDS, THE	YR	55.00	75.00
92 PANDA WITH CUBS	YR	60.00	75.00
J. NIELSEN			**MOTHER'S DAY**
98 MOTHER'S DAY 1998	YR	50.00	50.00
H. THELANDER			**MOTHER'S DAY**
69 DOGS AND PUPPIES	YR	9.75	65.00
70 BIRD AND CHICKS	YR	10.00	30.00
71 CAT AND KITTEN	YR	11.00	14.00
72 MARE AND FOAL	YR	12.00	13.00
73 DUCK AND DUCKLINGS	YR	13.00	14.00
74 BEAR AND CUBS	YR	16.50	17.00
75 DOE AND FAWNS	YR	20.00	20.00
76 SWAN FAMILY	YR	23.00	20.00
77 SQUIRREL AND YOUNG	YR	24.00	20.00
78 HERON	YR	25.00	20.00
79 FOX AND CUBS	YR	28.00	30.00
80 WOODPECKER AND YOUNG	YR	30.00	29.00
81 HARE AND YOUNG	YR	37.00	30.00
82 LIONESS AND CUBS	YR	40.00	50.00
83 RACCOON AND YOUNG	YR	40.00	50.00
84 STORK AND NESTLINGS	YR	40.00	50.00
85 BEAR AND CUBS	YR	40.00	39.00
86 ELEPHANT WITH CALF	YR	40.00	39.00
87 SHEEP WITH LAMBS	YR	43.00	89.00
88 CRESTED PLOYER & YOUNG	YR	48.00	70.00
88 LAPWING MOTHER WITH CHICKS	YR	50.00	60.00
89 COW WITH CALF	YR	50.00	70.00
A. THERKELSEN			**MOTHER'S DAY**
93 ST. BERNARD DOG AND PUPPIES	YR	60.00	75.00
*			**OLYMPIC**
72 MUNICH, GERMANY	CL	20.00	35.00
76 MONTREAL, CANADA	CL	30.00	45.00
80 MOSCOW, RUSSIA	CL	43.00	50.00
84 LOS ANGELES, USA	CL	45.00	75.00
88 SEOUL, KOREA	CL	60.00	85.00
92 BARCELONA, SPAIN	CL	75.00	90.00

YR	NAME	LIMIT	ISSUE	TREND
H. HANSEN			SANTA CLAUS COLLECTION	
89	SANTA'S WORKSHOP	YR	60.00	70.00
90	SANTA'S SLEIGH	YR	60.00	85.00
91	SANTA'S JOURNEY	YR	70.00	95.00
92	SANTA'S ARRIVAL	YR	75.00	95.00
93	SANTA'S GIFTS	YR	75.00	95.00
94	CHRISTMAS STORIES	YR	75.00	100.00
*			STATUE OF LIBERTY	
85	STATUE OF LIBERTY	10000	60.00	90.00
S. VESTERGAARD			YOUNG ADVENTURER	
90	LITTLE VIKING, THE	YR	53.00	70.00

BOEHM STUDIOS

YR	NAME	LIMIT	ISSUE	TREND
*			EGYPTIAN COMMEMORATIVE	
78	TUTANKHAMUN	5000	125.00	170.00
78	TUTANKHAMUN, HANDPAINTED	225	975.00	975.00
*			PANDA	
82	PANDA, HARMONY	5000	65.00	70.00
82	PANDA, PEACE	5000	65.00	70.00

BRADFORD EXCHANGE

YR	NAME	LIMIT	ISSUE	TREND
*			100 ACRE WOOD HOLIDAY	
98	DECORATING THE TREE	*	30.00	30.00
*			101 DALMATIANS	
97	BED TIME	95 DAYS	35.00	35.00
97	CRUELLA IS SPOTTED	95 DAYS	40.00	40.00
97	MANSION AWAITS, THE	95 DAYS	40.00	40.00
97	OVER THE WALL	95 DAYS	40.00	40.00
97	PUPPIES ON THE LOOSE	95 DAYS	40.00	40.00
97	SERGEANT TIBS SAVES THE DAY	95 DAYS	33.00	33.00
97	TRUE LOVE	95 DAYS	35.00	35.00
A. WHITE			101 DALMATIANS	
93	WATCH DOGS	CL	30.00	40.00
94	A HAPPY REUNION	CL	30.00	40.00
94	HALFWAY HOME	CL	33.00	45.00
94	HELLO DARLINGS	CL	33.00	45.00
95	A MESSY GOOD TIME	95 DAYS	30.00	50.00
B. BENGER			500 HOME RUN CLUB	
97	TED WILLIAMS	*	30.00	30.00
98	WILLIE MAYS	*	30.00	30.00
L. GARRISON			A CHRISTMAS CAROL	
93	GHOST OF CHRISTMAS PRESENT	CL	30.00	40.00
93	GOD BLESS US EVERYONE	CL	30.00	40.00
94	A MERRY CHRISTMAS TO ALL	CL	30.00	40.00
94	A SPIRIT'S WARNING	CL	30.00	40.00
94	A VISIT FROM MARLEY'S GHOST	CL	30.00	40.00
94	REMEMBERING CHRISTMAS PAST	CL	30.00	40.00
94	TRUE SPIRIT OF CHRISTMAS, THE	CL	30.00	40.00
L. MARTIN			A GARDEN OF LITTLE JEWELS	
97	A SPLENDID MOMENT	*	35.00	35.00
97	A WHISPER OF WINGS	*	35.00	35.00
97	DELICATE BEAUTY	*	35.00	35.00
97	GARDEN GRACE	*	35.00	35.00
97	PERFECT ENCHANTMENT	*	35.00	35.00
97	PRECIOUS TREASURES	*	35.00	35.00
R. DOCKEN			A GATHERING OF NATIONS	
97	DEFENDER OF HONOR	*	35.00	35.00
97	DEFENDER OF TRUTH	*	35.00	35.00
98	DEFENDER OF PRIDE	*	35.00	35.00
98	DEFENDER OF SPIRITS	*	35.00	35.00
J. ANDERSON			A MOTHER'S LOVE	
95	KINDNESS	*	*	40.00
95	PATIENCE	*	*	40.00
95	REMEMBRANCE	95 DAYS	30.00	40.00
95	THOUGHTFULNESS	*	*	40.00
N. ROCKWELL			A MOTHER'S LOVE	
97	A SONG IN YOUR HEART	*	35.00	35.00
97	CONSTANT COMFORT	*	35.00	35.00
98	SHARING GENTLE MOMENTS	*	35.00	35.00
N. STRELKINA			A SYMPHONY OF ANGELS	
97	SERENITY'S SONG	*	30.00	30.00
97	TRANQUILITY'S SERENADE	*	30.00	30.00
98	DIVINE MELODY	*	33.00	33.00
98	HARMONY'S HYMN	*	33.00	33.00
98	PEACEFUL PRELUDE	*	33.00	33.00
*			ALADDIN	
93	A FRIEND LIKE ME	CL	30.00	40.00
93	MAGIC CARPET RIDE	CL	30.00	40.00
94	ALADDIN IN LOVE	CL	30.00	40.00
94	ALLADIN'S WISH	95 DAYS	30.00	40.00
94	MAKE WAY FOR PRINCE ALIABAWA	95 DAYS	30.00	40.00
94	TRAVELING COMPANIONS	CL	30.00	40.00
95	BEE YOURSELF	95 DAYS	30.00	40.00
95	GROUP HUG	95 DAYS	30.00	40.00
D. O'LEARY		ALAN JACKSON: AS COUNTRY AS COUNTRY GETS		
98	EVERYTHING I LOVE	*	30.00	30.00

YR	NAME	LIMIT	ISSUE	TREND
S. GUSTAFSON			**ALICE IN WONDERLAND**	
93	ADVICE FROM A CATERPILLAR	CL	30.00	40.00
93	CHESHIRE CAT, THE	CL	30.00	40.00
93	MAD TEA PARTY, THE	CL	30.00	40.00
94	CROQUET WITH THE QUEEN	CL	30.00	40.00
E. JERINS			**ALWAYS BY MY SIDE**	
97	PEACEFUL HARMONY	*	30.00	30.00
98	DIVINE INSPIRATION		30.00	30.00
E. JERRINS			**ALWAYS BY MY SIDE**	
97	GIFTS OF LOVE	*	30.00	30.00
97	SWEET EMBRACE	*	30.00	30.00
D. EVERHART		**AMERICA'S FAVORITE CLASSIC CARS**		
93	CORVETTE 1957	*	54.00	65.00
93	THUNDERBIRD 1956	*	54.00	60.00
94	BEL AIR 1957	*	54.00	65.00
94	MUSTANG 1965	*	54.00	60.00
R. SCHAAR			**AMERICA'S TRIUMPH IN SPACE**	
93	BEYOND THE BOUNDS OF EARTH	CL	33.00	45.00
93	EAGLE HAS LANDED, THE	CL	30.00	40.00
93	FLIGHT OF GLORY	CL	33.00	45.00
93	MARCH TOWARDS DESTINY, THE	CL	30.00	40.00
94	CONQUERING THE NEW FRONTIER	CL	33.00	45.00
94	NEW EXPLORERS, THE	CL	35.00	50.00
94	RENDEZVOUS W/VICTORY	CL	35.00	45.00
94	TRIUMPHANT FINALE, THE	CL	35.00	50.00
C. WYSOCKI			**AMERICAN FRONTIER**	
93	TIMBERLINE JACK'S TRADING POST	CL	30.00	40.00
94	BUSTLING BOOMTOWN	CL	30.00	40.00
94	DR. LIVINGWELL'S MEDICINE SHOW	CL	30.00	40.00
94	HEARTY HOMESTEADERS	CL	30.00	40.00
94	KIRBYVILLE	CL	30.00	40.00
94	OKLAHOMA OR BUST	CL	30.00	40.00
M. SILVERSMITH			**ANCIENT SEASONS**	
95	EDGE OF NIGHT	95 DAYS	30.00	40.00
95	JOURNEY THROUGH MIDNIGHT	*	*	40.00
95	MID-WINTER PASSAGE	*	*	40.00
95	WINTER SOJOURN	*	*	40.00
95	WINTER STORM	*	*	40.00
E. TADIELLO			**ANGELS OF GRACE**	
97	TRANQUILITY'S RELEASE	*	35.00	35.00
98	LOVE'S REFLECTION	*	35.00	35.00
*			**ANTIQUE LANE**	
98	GRANDMA'S ATTIC ANTIQUES	*	40.00	40.00
98	SWEET ADELINE'S CLOSET	*	40.00	40.00
P. HEFFERNAN			**BABE RUTH CENTENNIAL**	
95	60TH HOMER, THE	CL	35.00	50.00
95	BARNSTORMING DAYS	CL	35.00	65.00
95	FINAL HOME RUN	CL	30.00	75.00
95	RUTH'S PITCHING DEBUT	CL	30.00	75.00
A. ISAKOV			**BASKETS OF LOVE**	
93	ANDREW AND ABBEY	CL	30.00	45.00
93	CODY AND COURTNEY	CL	30.00	40.00
93	EMILY AND ELLIOTT	CL	33.00	45.00
93	HEATHER AND HANNAH	CL	33.00	45.00
93	JUSTIN AND JESSICA	CL	33.00	45.00
93	KATIE AND KELLY	CL	35.00	45.00
93	LOUIE & LIBBY	CL	35.00	45.00
94	SAMMY AND SARAH	CL	35.00	45.00
J. GRIFFIN		**BATTLES OF THE AMERICAN CIVIL WAR**		
95	CHANCELLORSVILLE	*	*	40.00
95	FREDERICKSBURG	*	*	40.00
95	GETTYSBURG	95 DAYS	30.00	40.00
95	MONITOR & THE MERRIMAC	*	*	40.00
95	VICKSBURG	95 DAYS	30.00	40.00
96	ANTIETAM	*	*	40.00
96	ATLANTA	*	*	40.00
96	SHILOH	*	*	40.00
S. SHERWOOD			**BEARY MERRY CHRISTMAS**	
96	A MOMENT TO TREASURE	*	30.00	40.00
96	A ROMANTIC RIDE	*	30.00	40.00
*			**BEATITUDES**	
96	BLESSED/THE PURE IN HEART	*	*	40.00
L. LIU			**BEAUTIFUL GARDENS**	
94	IRIS GARDEN	CL	34.00	45.00
94	ORCHID GARDEN	CL	44.00	50.00
94	PEONY GARDEN	CL	34.00	45.00
94	POPPY GARDEN	CL	44.00	55.00
94	ROSE GARDEN	CL	39.00	50.00
94	TULIP GARDEN	CL	39.00	50.00
95	CLEMATIS GARDEN	95 DAYS	47.00	60.00
95	LILY GARDEN	95 DAYS	44.00	50.00
96	HIBISCUS GARDEN	95 DAYS	47.00	60.00
96	MORNING GLORY GARDEN	CL	44.00	60.00
*			**BEAUTY AND THE BEAST**	
94	A SPOT OF TEA	CL	35.00	40.00
97	A BLOSSOMING ROMANCE	150 DAYS	30.00	30.00

YR	NAME	LIMIT	ISSUE	TREND
97	A GIFT FOR BELLE	150 DAYS	37.00	37.00
97	A MISMATCH	150 DAYS	35.00	35.00
97	BE OUR GUEST	150 DAYS	35.00	35.00
97	BELLE'S FAVORITE STORY	150 DAYS	35.00	35.00
97	ENCHANTE' CHERIE	150 DAYS	37.00	37.00
97	LEARNING TO LOVE	150 DAYS	33.00	33.00
97	LOVE'S FIRST DANCE	150 DAYS	30.00	30.00
97	PAPA'S WORKSHOP	150 DAYS	33.00	33.00
97	SPELL IS BROKEN, THE	150 DAYS	37.00	37.00
97	WARMING UP	150 DAYS	33.00	33.00
G. OLSEN				**BEST OF TIMES**
97	DENIM TO LACE	*	30.00	30.00
97	MELODIES REMEMBERED	*	30.00	30.00
R. BROWN			**BRETT FAVRE COLLECTION**	
97	3 DEGREES TO VICTORY	*	30.00	30.00
97	BACK TO TITLETOWN	*	30.00	30.00
97	LEADER OF THE PACK	*	30.00	30.00
98	PACK IS BACK, THE	*	30.00	30.00
98	PACKER TOUCHDOWN HIGH	*	30.00	30.00
V. CRANDALL				**BUNNY TALES**
97	APPLE DUMPLIN'	*	30.00	30.00
97	FOOTLOOSE	*	30.00	30.00
97	FUZZBALL	*	30.00	30.00
97	I'M ALL EARS	*	30.00	30.00
97	MUNCHKIN	*	30.00	30.00
98	BASKET CASE	*	30.00	30.00
98	CARROT TOP	*	30.00	30.00
98	QUITE AN EARFUL	*	30.00	30.00
98	SNOW BUNNY	*	30.00	30.00
J. MADAY			**BUNNY WORKSHOP**	
95	MAKE TODAY EGGSTRA SPECIAL	95 DAYS	20.00	40.00
95	SMILE MAKES THE DAY SO SWEET	*	*	40.00
L. DUBIN			**BYGONE DAYS**	
94	SODA FOUNTIAN	CL	*	40.00
95	BARBER SHOP,THE	95 DAYS	30.00	40.00
95	CORNER NEWSSTAND,THE	CL	30.00	40.00
95	MAIN STREET SPLENDOR	95 DAYS	30.00	40.00
95	SAM'S GROCERY STORE	CL	30.00	40.00
95	SATURDAY MATINEE	CL	30.00	40.00
F. BUCHWITZ		**CABINS OF COMFORT RIVER**		
95	COMFORT BY CAMPLIGHTS FIRE	95 DAYS	30.00	30.00
C. JAGODITS			**CANINE CAPERS**	
97	FISHING FOR TROUBLE	*	30.00	30.00
TSENG			**CAROUSEL DAYDREAMS**	
95	ALL ABOARD	CL	45.00	55.00
95	BIG HOPES, BRIGHT DREAMS	95 DAYS	50.00	60.00
95	FLIGHT OF FANCY	CL	45.00	55.00
95	HOLD ONTO YOUR DREAMS	CL	45.00	55.00
95	MY FAVORITE MEMORY	95 DAYS	50.00	60.00
95	SWEPT AWAY	CL	40.00	50.00
95	VICTORIAN REVERIE	95 DAYS	50.00	60.00
95	WHEN I GROW UP	CL	40.00	50.00
96	DREAMS OF DESTINY	95 DAYS	50.00	60.00
96	WISHFUL THINKING	95 DAYS	50.00	60.00
J. KRAMER COLE			**CELESTIAL SPIRITS**	
97	HOMEWARD JOURNEY	*	35.00	35.00
97	LIGHTING THE WAY	*	35.00	35.00
C. WYSOCKI		**CHARLES WYSOCKI'S COUNTRY HEARTLAND**		
97	BUDZEN'S ROADSIDE FOOD STAND	*	*	N/A
97	PEPPERCRICKET FARMS	*	*	N/A
97	PUMPKIN HOLLOW	*	*	N/A
97	VIRGINIA'S NEST	*	*	N/A
M.A. LASHER			**CHERISHED TRADITIONS**	
95	DRESDEN	*	*	40.00
95	LOG CABIN	*	*	40.00
95	OCEAN WAVE	*	*	40.00
95	STAR, THE	*	*	40.00
95	WEDDING RING, THE	95 DAYS	30.00	40.00
96	GOOSE IN THE POND	OP	30.00	40.00
96	GRANDMOTHER'S FLOWER GARDEN	*	*	40.00
96	STARBURST	*	*	40.00
W. BOUGUEREAU			**CHERUBS OF INNOCENCE**	
94	FIRST KISS, THE	CL	30.00	40.00
95	LOVE AT REST	95 DAYS	30.00	40.00
95	THOUGHTS OF LOVE	95 DAYS	30.00	40.00
ZATZKA			**CHERUBS OF INNOCENCE**	
95	LOVING GAZE	*	*	45.00
P.L. TOOLE			**CHOIR OF ANGELS**	
95	SONG OF JOY	*	*	40.00
96	SONG OF HARMONY	*	*	40.00
96	SONG OF HOPE	*	*	40.00
96	SONG OF PEACE	*	35.00	40.00
G. RUNNING WOLF			**CHOSEN MESSENGERS**	
94	OVERSEERS, THE	CL	30.00	45.00
94	PATHFINDERS, THE	CL	30.00	45.00

YR	NAME	LIMIT	ISSUE	TREND
94	PROVIDERS, THE	CL	33.00	45.00
94	SURVEYORS, THE	CL	33.00	45.00
R. MCGINNIS			**CHRISTMAS IN THE VILLAGE**	
95	LITTLE CHURCH IN THE VALE	CL	30.00	40.00
95	VILLAGE TOY SHOP, THE	CL	30.00	40.00
96	GOODNIGHT DEAR FRIENDS	CL	30.00	40.00
96	VILLAGE CONFECTIONARY	CL	30.00	40.00
96	VILLAGE INN	CL	30.00	40.00
N. ROCKWELL			**CHRISTMAS MEMORIES**	
97	SANTA'S WORKSHOP	*	40.00	40.00
98	CHRISTMAS DREAM	*	40.00	40.00
J. TANTON			**CHRISTMAS MEMORIES**	
93	A WINTER'S TALE	CL	30.00	40.00
93	CHRISTMAS CELEBRATION	CL	30.00	40.00
93	FINISHING TOUCHES	CL	30.00	40.00
93	WELCOME TO OUR HOME	CL	30.00	40.00
P. FRYER			**CLASSIC ELEGANCE**	
97	FAIREST OF THEM ALL, THE	*	35.00	35.00
97	PRETTY AS A PICTURE	*	30.00	30.00
98	ALL SWEETNESS AND LIGHT	*	30.00	30.00
98	SUGAR AND SPICE	*	30.00	30.00
M. HAMPSHIRE		**CLASSIC MELODIES FROM "THE SOUND OF MUSIC"**		
95	ALPINE REFUGE	CL	30.00	43.00
95	DROP OF GOLDEN SUN	CL	30.00	43.00
95	SING ALONG WITH MARIA	CL	30.00	40.00
95	VON TRAPP FAMILY SINGERS	CL	30.00	43.00
L. MOSER			**CLASSIC ROSES**	
96	BEAUTY IN BLOOM	OP	35.00	40.00
96	MAGIC IN MAUVE	*	*	45.00
96	PRECIOUS IN PURPLE	*	*	45.00
96	PRETTY IN PINK	*	35.00	40.00
K. BURNETT			**CLIFF DWELLERS**	
97	AN EAGLE RULES THE HEIGHTS	*	40.00	40.00
97	BIGHORNS LINGER ON THE EDGE	*	40.00	40.00
97	THE WOLVES ASCEND THE ROCKY SLOPE	*	40.00	40.00
97	WITHIN THE COUGAR'S SIGHTS	*	40.00	40.00
D. KLAUBA		**COSTUMING OF A LEGEND: GONE WITH THE WIND**		
93	BLACK & WHITE BENGALINE DRESS	95 DAYS	*	45.00
93	GREEN DRAPERY DRESS	95 DAYS	*	45.00
93	GREEN SPRIGGED DRESS	95 DAYS	*	53.00
93	MOURNING GOWN	95 DAYS	*	45.00
93	ORCHID PERCALE DRESS	95 DAYS	*	45.00
93	RED DRESS, THE	CL	30.00	45.00
93	WIDOW'S WEEDS	95 DAYS	*	45.00
94	COUNTRY WALKING DRESS	95 DAYS	*	45.00
94	GREEN MUSLIN DRESS	95 DAYS	*	45.00
94	PLAID BUSINESS ATTIRE	95 DAYS	*	45.00
W. GOEBEL			**COUNTRY WONDERLAND**	
95	QUIET HOUR, THE	95 DAYS	30.00	40.00
D. CASEY			**COW-HIDE**	
95	INCOWGNITO	*	*	40.00
95	INCOWSPICUOUS	*	*	40.00
96	COWMOOFLAGE	*	35.00	40.00
96	COWPANSIONS	OP	35.00	40.00
*			**CROWN JEWELS OF DISNEY**	
97	ARIEL'S DREAM COMES TRUE	95 DAYS	40.00	40.00
97	BEAUTY AND THE BEAST	95 DAYS	40.00	40.00
97	SLEEPING BEAUTY	95 DAYS	40.00	40.00
97	THAT SPECIAL SPARKLE	95 DAYS	40.00	40.00
*			**CURRIER & IVES CHRISTMAS**	
96	WINTER MOON-FEEDING CHICKENS	*	35.00	40.00
CURRIER & IVES			**CURRIER & IVES CHRISTMAS**	
95	AMERICAN HOMESTEAD WINTER	*	*	40.00
95	AMERICAN WINTER SCENES	*	*	40.00
95	EARLY WINTER	*	*	40.00
D. SIVAVEC			**DAN MARINO: RECORD BREAKER**	
98	51,636 AND COUNTING	*	35.00	35.00
*			**DANCE OF THE UNICORNS**	
98	MIDNIGHT DREAMER	*	50.00	50.00
98	MOONLIGHT CANTER	*	50.00	50.00
98	TWILIGHT DANCER	*	50.00	50.00
E. KUCERA			**DAUGHTERS OF THE WIND**	
97	UNBRIDLED BEAUTY	*	35.00	35.00
98	NOURISHING THE SPIRIT	*	35.00	35.00
98	PATH TO SERENITY	*	35.00	35.00
98	PEACEFUL REFLECTION	*	35.00	35.00
J. THORNBRUGH			**DEER FRIENDS AT CHRISTMAS**	
94	A GLISTENING SEASON	CL	30.00	40.00
94	ALL A GLOW	CL	30.00	40.00
94	RADIANT COUNTRYSIDE	CL	30.00	40.00
94	STARRY NIGHT	CL	30.00	40.00
95	WOODLAND SPLENDOR	CL	30.00	40.00
B. CHAMBERS			**DIANA: QUEEN OF OUR HEARTS**	
98	OUR ROYAL PRINCESS	*	30.00	30.00
98	TRUE PRINCESS, A	*	30.00	30.00
98	VERY SPECIAL PRINCESS, A	*	30.00	30.00

YR	NAME	LIMIT	ISSUE	TREND
J. MONTI				
	DIANA: QUEEN OF OUR HEARTS			
97	THE PEOPLE'S PRINCESS	95 DAYS	30.00	30.00
*				
	DISNEY TREASURED MOMENTS COLLECTION			
97	ALICE IN WONDERLAND	150 DAYS	33.00	33.00
97	BEAUTY AND THE BEAST	150 DAYS	35.00	35.00
97	JUNGLE BOOK, THE	150 DAYS	35.00	35.00
97	PETER PAN	150 DAYS	33.00	33.00
97	PINOCCHIO	150 DAYS	35.00	35.00
97	SLEEPING BEAUTY	150 DAYS	33.00	33.00
97	SNOW WHITE AND THE SEVEN DWARFS	150 DAYS	30.00	30.00
*				
	DISNEY WORLD'S 25TH ANNIVERSARY			
97	ADVENTURELAND	*	30.00	30.00
97	FANTASYLAND	95 DAYS	30.00	30.00
97	FRONTIERLAND	*	30.00	30.00
97	MAIN STREET, USA	95 DAYS	30.00	30.00
97	TOMORROWLAND	*	30.00	30.00
98	BIRTHDAY CELEBRATION, A	*	30.00	30.00
98	LIBERTY SQUARE	*	30.00	30.00
98	MICKEY'S TOON TOWN FAIR	*	30.00	30.00
*				
	DISNEY'S MUSICAL MEMORIES			
95	FAIREST ONE OF ALL	95 DAYS	30.00	40.00
96	ALADDIN'S MAGICAL NEW WORLD	95 DAYS	33.00	40.00
97	A TALE AS OLD AS TIME	95 DAYS	33.00	33.00
97	CINDERELLA'S WISH COME TRUE	95 DAYS	30.00	30.00
97	FLIGHT TO NEVERLAND	95 DAYS	33.00	33.00
97	FUTURE KING OF PRIDE ROCK	95 DAYS	35.00	35.00
97	ONCE UPON A DREAM	95 DAYS	35.00	35.00
97	THE JUNGLE BOOK	95 DAYS	35.00	35.00
97	UNDER THE SEA	95 DAYS	35.00	35.00
97	WELCOME TO WONDERLAND	95 DAYS	35.00	35.00
98	COLORS OF THE WIND	*	35.00	35.00
98	MOONLIGHT ROMANCE	*	35.00	35.00
*				
	DISNEYLAND'S 40TH ANNIVERSARY			
95	CINDERELLA'S WISH COME TRUE	*	*	40.00
95	DISNEYLAND RAILROAD	*	30.00	43.00
95	FAIREST ONE OF ALL	*	*	40.00
95	SLEEPING BEAUTY'S CASTLE	*	30.00	43.00
95	TALE AS OLD AS TIME	*	*	45.00
96	FLIGHT TO NEVERLAND	*	*	45.00
96	HAUNTED MANSION	*	35.00	53.00
96	IT'S A SMALL WORLD	OP	33.00	50.00
96	MATTERHORN	*	35.00	53.00
96	MICKEY'S TOONTOWN	*	33.00	48.00
96	PIRATES OF THE CARIBBEAN	*	33.00	48.00
96	WELCOME TO WONDERLAND	*	*	50.00
97	BIG THUNDER MOUNTAIN RAILROAD	95 DAYS	35.00	35.00
97	JUNGLE CRUISE	*	35.00	35.00
97	MAIN STREET ELECTRICAL PARADE	95 DAYS	35.00	35.00
97	MARK TWAIN'S RIVERBOAT	95 DAYS	35.00	35.00
97	SUBMARINE VOYAGE	95 DAYS	35.00	35.00
R. MCCAUSLAND				
	DIVINE LIGHT			
95	SAVIOUR IS BORN	*	*	45.00
96	BIRTH OF A KING	*	*	45.00
96	BLESSED IS THE CHILD	OP	35.00	45.00
96	WE SHALL PRAISE HIM	*	*	45.00
J. GADAMUS				
	DOG DAYS			
93	FIRST FLUSH	CL	33.00	45.00
93	LITTLE RASCALS	CL	33.00	45.00
93	PIER GROUP	CL	30.00	45.00
93	SWEET DREAMS	CL	30.00	45.00
93	WAGON TRAIN	CL	33.00	45.00
93	WHERE'D HE GO	CL	33.00	45.00
A. CASAY				
	DOLPHIN KISSES			
98	KISSING COUSINS	*	30.00	30.00
98	ROMANCING THE MOON	*	30.00	30.00
98	SEAL OF APPROVAL	*	30.00	30.00
98	SEALED WITH A KISS	*	30.00	30.00
*				
	DOLPHIN SPLENDOR			
98	AT ONE WITH THE SEA	*	40.00	40.00
*				
	ELVIS IN THE SPOTLIGHT			
98	LAS VEGAS	*	60.00	60.00
J. BOWSER				
	EMBRACED BY THE SPIRITS			
97	MYSTIC PASSAGE	*	30.00	30.00
98	PHANTOM OF THE FALLS	*	30.00	30.00
98	SHADOW RAPIDS	*	30.00	30.00
D. DAY				
	EMMITT SMITH: RUNNING TO DAYLIGHT			
98	SUPERBOWL XXX	*	30.00	30.00
M. DUDASH				
	ENCHANTED CHARMS OF OZ			
96	CAN'T EVEN SCARE A CROW	*	*	40.00
96	FRESH FROM BRUSH UP SHOP	*	*	40.00
96	THERE'S NO PLACE LIKE HOME	OP	*	N/A
96	WONDERFUL WIZARD OF OZ	*	*	40.00
S. KUCK				
	ENCHANTED GARDENS			
98	SWEETEST DELIGHTS	*	33.00	33.00
98	TEA FOR THREE	*	33.00	33.00

YR	NAME	LIMIT	ISSUE	TREND
J. PATTI			**ENCHANTED JOURNEY**	
97	MOONLIT DREAMS	*	30.00	30.00
97	MOONLIT TRAIL	*	30.00	30.00
97	REFLECTIONS OF A DREAM	*	30.00	30.00
97	WINGS OF BEAUTY	*	30.00	30.00
98	JOURNEY'S END	*	30.00	30.00
98	REFLECTIVE INTERLUDE	*	30.00	30.00
T. KINKADE			**END OF A PERFECT DAY**	
97	AUTUMN SERENITY	95 DAYS	40.00	40.00
97	PEACEFUL REFLECTIONS	95 DAYS	40.00	40.00
97	TWILIGHT TRANQUILITY	95 DAYS	40.00	40.00
D. HENDERSON			**ESCAPE TO THE COUNTRY**	
96	COUNTRY CORNUCOPIA	*	*	40.00
96	COUNTRY WELCOME	*	*	40.00
96	COUNTY LINE FARMER'S MARKET	*	30.00	40.00
G. TURLEY			**ETERNAL BEAUTY**	
97	ETERNAL BEAUTY (SET OF 5)	*	175.00	175.00
S. KUCK			**EVERLASTING FRIENDS**	
97	SHARING BEAUTY	*	30.00	30.00
97	SHARING DREAMS	*	30.00	30.00
97	SHARING LOVE	*	30.00	30.00
*			**EVERLASTING LOVE**	
97	BASKETS OF LOVE	*	45.00	45.00
97	HEARTSTRINGS OF LOVE	*	40.00	40.00
97	RINGS OF LOVE	*	45.00	45.00
98	BOOK OF LOVE	*	45.00	45.00
98	HEART OF LOVE	*	45.00	45.00
D. PARKER			**FACES OF THE WILD**	
95	BEAR	95 DAYS	45.00	55.00
95	BOBCAT	95 DAYS	45.00	55.00
95	COUGAR	95 DAYS	45.00	55.00
95	DEAR	95 DAYS	45.00	55.00
95	FOX	95 DAYS	45.00	60.00
95	WHITE WOLF	CL	40.00	50.00
95	WOLF, THE	CL	40.00	50.00
96	LYNX	95 DAYS	45.00	60.00
M. JOBE			**FAIRYLAND**	
94	FOREST ENCHANTMENT	95 DAYS	33.00	46.00
94	SILVERY SPLASHES	95 DAYS	33.00	46.00
94	TRAILS OF STARLIGHT	95 DAYS	30.00	40.00
94	TWILIGHT TRIO	95 DAYS	30.00	40.00
95	FAREWELL TO THE NIGHT	95 DAYS	35.00	45.00
95	MAGICAL MISCHIEF	95 DAYS	33.00	45.00
96	DAZZLING BEGINNINGS	95 DAYS	35.00	50.00
C. BRENDERS			**FAMILY AFFAIR**	
94	CLOSE TO MOM	*	*	41.00
95	DEN MOTHER	95 DAYS	30.00	40.00
95	FULL HOUSE	*	*	41.00
95	SHADOWS IN THE GRASS	*	*	41.00
95	UNDER MOTHER'S WATCHFUL EYE	*	*	41.00
R. RUST			**FAMILY AFFAIR**	
95	ROCKY CAMP	*	*	40.00
R. RUST			**FAMILY CIRCLES**	
93	GREAT GRAY OWL FAMILY	CL	30.00	40.00
94	BARRED OWL FAMILY	CL	30.00	40.00
94	GREAT HORNED OWL FAMILY	CL	30.00	40.00
94	SPOTTED OWL FAMILY	CL	30.00	40.00
J. SCHOLZ			**FAMILY OUTING**	
97	A BEAUTIFUL RESTING PLACE	*	40.00	40.00
97	CLIMBING IS NOT SO EASY	*	40.00	40.00
97	HOW PRETTY IT SMELLS	*	40.00	40.00
97	WHAT'S THAT FLUTTERING IN THE AIR?	*	40.00	40.00
S. WHEELER			**FAMILY'S LOVE**	
96	GIVING THANKS	*	30.00	40.00
L. KAATZ			**FIELD PUP FOLLIES**	
94	FOWL PLAY	CL	30.00	35.00
94	HAT CHECK	CL	30.00	35.00
94	SLEEPING ON THE JOB	CL	30.00	30.00
G. BEECHAM			**FIERCE & FREE: THE BIG CATS**	
95	BLACK LEOPARD	*	*	55.00
95	COUGAR	*	*	55.00
95	JAGUAR	*	*	55.00
95	SNOW LEOPARD	*	*	50.00
96	AFRICAN LION	*	*	55.00
96	TIGER, THE	*	40.00	55.00
M. BUDDEN			**FLEETING ENCOUNTERS**	
95	AUTUMN RETREAT	95 DAYS	30.00	40.00
J. MEGER			**FLIGHT OF THE PHEASANTS**	
98	ROYAL FLUSH	*	30.00	30.00
G. KURZ			**FLORAL FROLICS**	
94	BEE CAREFUL	CL	30.00	40.00
94	SPRING SURPRISES	CL	30.00	45.00
95	FUZZY FUN	CL	33.00	45.00
95	SUNNY HIDEOUT	CL	33.00	45.00
L. LIU			**FLORAL GREETINGS**	
94	CIRCLE OF ELEGANCE	95 DAYS	30.00	44.00

YR	NAME	LIMIT	ISSUE	TREND
94	CIRCLE OF HARMONY	95 DAYS	33.00	44.00
94	CIRCLE OF JOY	95 DAYS	33.00	45.00
94	CIRCLE OF LOVE	95 DAYS	30.00	39.00
94	CIRCLE OF ROMANCE	95 DAYS	35.00	44.00
95	CIRCLE OF BEAUTY	95 DAYS		45.00
95	CIRCLE OF DELIGHT	95 DAYS	*	50.00
95	CIRCLE OF INSPIRATION	95 DAYS	35.00	50.00
S. RICKERT			**FOOTPRINTS IN THE SAND**	
97	ALONG THE PATH	*	40.00	40.00
97	I CARRIED YOU	*	40.00	40.00
97	WALK WITH ME	*	40.00	40.00
97	WALKING WITH THE LORD	*	40.00	40.00
H. SCHAARE			**FOOTSTEPS OF THE BRAVE**	
93	AT JOURNEY'S END	CL	30.00	50.00
93	AT STORM'S PASSAGE	CL	25.00	40.00
93	HORIZONS OF DESTINY	CL	28.00	45.00
93	NOBLE QUEST	CL	25.00	40.00
93	PATH OF HIS FOREFATHERS	CL	28.00	45.00
93	REVERENT TRAIL, THE	CL	30.00	50.00
93	SOULFUL REFLECTION	CL	30.00	50.00
93	WITH BOUNDLESS VISION	CL	28.00	45.00
C. FALBERG			**FOREVER GLAMOROUS BARBIE**	
95	ENCHANTED EVENING	CL	50.00	50.00
96	MIDNIGHT BLUE	CL	50.00	50.00
M.A. LASHER			**FOREVER MY DAUGHTER**	
97	ALWAYS MY DAUGHTER	*	30.00	30.00
98	DAUGHTER KNOWS, A	*	30.00	30.00
98	FOREVER MY DAUGHTER	*	30.00	30.00
*			**FRAGILE BEAUTY**	
98	HEAVENLY HIBISCUS	*	40.00	40.00
J. LARSON			**FREE SPIRITS**	
97	CROW PONIES	*	35.00	35.00
E. TOTTEN		**FRESHWATER GAME FISH OF NORTH AMERICA**		
94	BLUE GILLS	95 DAYS	30.00	46.00
94	LARGEMOUTH BASS	95 DAYS	30.00	40.00
94	RAINBOW TROUT	95 DAYS	30.00	40.00
94	SMALL MOUTH BASS	*	*	50.00
95	BROOK TROUT	*	*	50.00
95	BROWN TROUT	*		50.00
95	NORTHERN PIKE	95 DAYS	30.00	45.00
95	WALLEYE	95 DAYS	30.00	45.00
		*	*	50.00
L. CHANG			**FRIENDSHIP IN BLOOM**	
94	PAWS IN THE POSIES	CL	35.00	40.00
95	COZY PETUNIA PATCH	95 DAYS	35.00	40.00
95	PATIENCE & IMPATIENCE	95 DAYS	35.00	40.00
95	PRIMROSE PLAYMATES	*	*	38.00
*			**FUN IN 100 ACRE WOODS**	
97	A CELEBRATION FOR EEYORE	*	30.00	30.00
97	A STICKY SITUATION	95 DAYS	30.00	30.00
97	AN APPLE FOR YOU WINNIE THE POOH	*	30.00	30.00
97	GOING FISHING	95 DAYS	30.00	30.00
97	HARVEST TIME	95 DAYS	30.00	30.00
97	HELLO POOH!	95 DAYS	30.00	30.00
97	POOH'S PICNIC	*	30.00	30.00
97	TREE TOP TRIO	95 DAYS	30.00	30.00
97	TROUBLES WITH BUBBLES	95 DAYS	30.00	30.00
98	BLUSTERY DAYS ARE BEST WITH FRIENDS	*	30.00	30.00
98	PARADE	*	30.00	30.00
J. STRAIN			**GALLANT MEN OF THE CIVIL WAR**	
94	STONEWALL JACKSON	95 DAYS	30.00	40.00
95	BEN HARDIN HELM	*	*	40.00
95	JOHN C. BRECKINRIDGE	*	*	40.00
95	JOHN HUNT MORGAN	95 DAYS	30.00	40.00
95	JOSHUA CHANBERLAIN	95 DAYS	30.00	40.00
95	NATHAN BEDFORD FORREST	95 DAYS	30.00	40.00
95	ROBERT E. LEE	95 DAYS	30.00	40.00
95	TURNER ASHBY	*	*	40.00
R. DEFELICE			**GAME'S GREATEST, THE**	
97	DETROIT LIONS' BARRY SANDERS	*	30.00	30.00
C. HOPKINS			**GAME'S GREATEST, THE**	
98	GREEN BAY'S BRETT FAVRE	*	30.00	30.00
98	MIAMI'S DAN MARINO	*	30.00	30.00
D. GELSINGER			**GARDEN BLESSINGS**	
96	AN ANGEL'S CARE	95 DAYS	30.00	30.00
96	AN ANGEL'S GIFT	95 DAYS	30.00	30.00
96	AN ANGEL'S GUIDANCE	95 DAYS	30.00	30.00
96	AN ANGEL'S TOUCH	95 DAYS	30.00	30.00
96	AN ANGEL'S WARMTH	95 DAYS	30.00	30.00
97	AN ANGEL'S GRACE	*	30.00	30.00
97	AN ANGEL'S SPIRIT	95 DAYS	30.00	30.00
97	AN ANGELS TENDERNESS	*	30.00	30.00
98	AN ANGEL'S GENTLENESS	*	30.00	30.00
L. CHANG			**GARDEN GIFTS**	
98	BASKET OF LOVE	*	30.00	30.00
98	BUNDLE OF JOY	*	30.00	30.00

YR	NAME	LIMIT	ISSUE	TREND

Z. KENYON — GARDEN SONGS OF INNOCENCE

YR	NAME	LIMIT	ISSUE	TREND
97	AFTERNOON RECITAL	*	40.00	40.00
97	MY MORNING FRIEND	*	40.00	40.00
97	WARM WELCOME	*	40.00	40.00
98	SUNSHINE SERENADE	*	40.00	40.00

D. RICHARDSON — GARDENS OF INNOCENCE

YR	NAME	LIMIT	ISSUE	TREND
93	CHARITY	95 DAYS	30.00	40.00
93	FAITH	95 DAYS	33.00	45.00
94	GRACE	95 DAYS	33.00	46.00
94	HOPE	CL	30.00	40.00
94	JOY	95 DAYS	33.00	45.00
95	COMPASSION	*	*	55.00
95	HARMONY, (BRADFORD)	*	*	56.00
95	KINDNESS	*	*	56.00
95	PATIENCE	95 DAYS	35.00	50.00
95	PEACE	95 DAYS	35.00	50.00
95	SERENITY	95 DAYS	35.00	50.00
96	LOVE	OP	37.00	55.00

T. KINKADE — GATHER AT OUR HOME

YR	NAME	LIMIT	ISSUE	TREND
97	A CHRISTMAS WELCOME	95 DAYS	30.00	30.00
97	DEER CREEK COTTAGE	95 DAYS	30.00	30.00
97	SUNDAY EVENING SLEIGHRIDE	*	30.00	30.00
98	MOONLIT VILLAGE	*	30.00	30.00

D. RUST — GETTING AWAY FROM IT ALL

YR	NAME	LIMIT	ISSUE	TREND
95	MOUNTAIN HIDEAWAY	95 DAYS	30.00	30.00

L. TUCCI — GIFTS FROM THE GARDEN

YR	NAME	LIMIT	ISSUE	TREND
97	A BUTTERFLY'S RETERAT	*	*	N/A
98	BEAUTY IN BLOOM	*	30.00	30.00
98	BLUSHING BEAUTIES	*	30.00	30.00
98	SUNNY BLOSSOM	*	30.00	30.00

L. BOGLE — GIFTS OF LOVE

YR	NAME	LIMIT	ISSUE	TREND
97	BUDDING DESIRE	*	35.00	35.00
97	PASSION'S FIRST BLOOM	*	35.00	35.00

B. BARRETT — GLORY OF CHRIST

YR	NAME	LIMIT	ISSUE	TREND
95	CHRIST FEEDS THE MULTITUDES	*	*	38.00
95	CHRIST WALKS ON WATER	*	*	41.00
96	CHRIST BEFORE THE APOSTLES	*	*	40.00
96	RAISING OF LAZARUS	*	*	42.00
96	WEDDING AT CANA	OP	30.00	40.00

M. PHALEN — GONE WITH THE WIND

YR	NAME	LIMIT	ISSUE	TREND
95	RHETT'S BRIGHT PROMISE	CL	40.00	40.00
95	SCARLETT RADIANCE	CL	40.00	40.00

A. JENKS — GONE WITH THE WIND MUSICAL TREASURES

YR	NAME	LIMIT	ISSUE	TREND
95	CHARITY BAZAAR	95 DAYS	33.00	33.00
95	PROPOSAL,THE	95 DAYS	33.00	33.00

C. NOTARILE — GONE WITH THE WIND: CAMEO MEMORIES

YR	NAME	LIMIT	ISSUE	TREND
97	EMERALD ELEGANCE	*	35.00	35.00
98	SUNLIGHT RADIANCE	*	35.00	35.00

* — GONE WITH THE WIND: MOVIE OF THE CENTURY

YR	NAME	LIMIT	ISSUE	TREND
97	PASSION, THE	*	30.00	30.00
97	ROMANCE, THE	*	30.00	30.00
98	COURAGE, THE	*	30.00	30.00
98	DEVOTION, THE	*	30.00	30.00

S. GARDNER — GREAT MOMENTS IN BASEBALL

YR	NAME	LIMIT	ISSUE	TREND
93	BILL MAZEROSKI: WINNING HOME RUN	95 DAYS	33.00	39.00
93	BOBBY THOMSON: SHOT HEARD	95 DAYS	33.00	40.00
93	JOE DIMAGGIO: THE STREAK	CL	30.00	35.00
93	STAN MUSIAL: 5-HOMER DBL. HEAD	95 DAYS	30.00	34.00
94	BILLY MARTIN: RESCUE CATCH	95 DAYS	35.00	47.00
94	DIZZY DEAN	95 DAYS	35.00	45.00
94	DON LARSEN: PERFECT SERIES	95 DAYS	35.00	40.00
94	JACKIE ROBINSON: SAVED PENNANT	95 DAYS	35.00	46.00
94	SATCHEL PAIGE	CL	35.00	40.00
95	CARL HUBBELL: THE 1934 ALL STATE	95 DAYS	37.00	45.00
95	ENOS SLAUGHTER: THE MAD DASH	*	*	50.00
95	RALPH KINER: HOME RUN STREAK	*	*	50.00

R. JOHNSON — GREAT MOMENTS IN NFL FOOTBALL

YR	NAME	LIMIT	ISSUE	TREND
97	HISTORY MAKER, THE (JERRY RICE)	*	35.00	35.00
98	FIRST SUDDEN DEATH	*	35.00	35.00

R. BROWN — GREAT SUPERBOWL QUARTERBACKS

YR	NAME	LIMIT	ISSUE	TREND
95	BART STARR, WINNING THE FIRST SUPERBOWL	*	*	46.00
95	JOE MONTANA: KING OF THE COMEBACKS	95 DAYS	30.00	40.00
95	JOE NAMATH, THE GUARANTEE	*	*	41.00
95	JOHNNY UNITAS, CHAMPION COL.	*	*	45.00
95	LEN DAWSON, MOST VALUABLE CHI.	*	*	50.00
96	BOB GRIESE	*	33.00	45.00
96	KEN STABLER, THE SNAKE STRIKES	*	*	51.00

B. JAXON — GUIDANCE FROM ABOVE

YR	NAME	LIMIT	ISSUE	TREND
94	PRAYER TO THE STORM	CL	30.00	41.00
95	APPEAL TO THUNDER	CL	30.00	40.00
95	BLESSING THE FUTURE	CL	33.00	40.00

J. DALY — HAPPY HEARTS

YR	NAME	LIMIT	ISSUE	TREND
95	CHILDHOOD FRIENDS	95 DAYS	30.00	45.00
95	CONTENTMENT	95 DAYS	30.00	40.00
95	FAVORITE GIFT	95 DAYS	30.00	45.00
95	GOOD COMPANY	*	*	46.00

YR	NAME	LIMIT	ISSUE	TREND
95	HER SECRET PLACE	*	*	51.00
95	PLAYMATES	95 DAYS	30.00	40.00
	R. NANINI		**HEART OF CAT COUNTRY**	
96	ALL ABOARD	*	30.00	30.00
	J. GIBSON		**HEART STRINGS**	
96	FAMILY TIES	*	30.00	40.00
96	GIFT OF FRIENDSHIP	*	*	45.00
	FIORENTINO INSPIRED		**HEART TO HEART**	
95	TALES OF FANCY	*	*	45.00
	MARATTA INSPIRED		**HEART TO HEART**	
95	ECHOES OF AFFECTION	*	*	45.00
95	WHISPERS IN ROMANCE	*	*	45.00
	RAPHAEL INSPIRED		**HEART TO HEART**	
95	SPEAKING OF LOVE	*	*	40.00
95	THINKING OF YOU	TL	30.00	40.00
	E. STEINBRUCK		**HEART TO HEART**	
96	FEELINGS OF ENDEARMENT	OP	30.00	45.00
	T. KINKADE		**HEAVEN ON EARTH**	
94	I AM THE LIGHT OF THE WORLD	95 DAYS	30.00	41.00
95	BUT THE PATH OF THE JUST	95 DAYS	30.00	40.00
95	FOR THOU ART MY LAMP	95 DAYS	30.00	40.00
95	FOR WITH THEE	*	*	41.00
95	I AM THE WAY	95 DAYS	30.00	40.00
95	IN HIM WAS LIFE	95 DAYS	30.00	40.00
95	LET YOUR LIGHT SO SHINE	*	*	40.00
95	THY WORD IS A LAMP	95 DAYS	30.00	40.00
	L. BOGLE		**HEAVEN SENT**	
94	PUPPY DOG TAILS	95 DAYS	30.00	40.00
94	SWEET DREAMS	CL	30.00	40.00
94	TIMELESS TREASURE	95 DAYS	30.00	45.00
95	PRECIOUS GIFT	95 DAYS	33.00	45.00
	D. BROOKS		**HEAVEN'S LITTLE ANGELS**	
97	ANGEL'S HOPE	*	30.00	30.00
97	ANGEL'S JOY	*	30.00	30.00
97	ANGEL'S LOVE	*	30.00	30.00
98	ANGEL'S BLESSING	*	30.00	30.00
98	ANGEL'S DELIGHT	*	30.00	30.00
	R. AKERS		**HEAVEN'S LITTLE SWEETHEARTS**	
95	FIRST NOEL	*	*	55.00
	D. BROOKS		**HEAVEN'S LITTLE SWEETHEARTS**	
96	AN ANGEL'S CARING	*	*	41.00
96	AN ANGEL'S DEVOTION	*	*	39.00
96	AN ANGEL'S KINDNESS	*	30.00	40.00
96	AN ANGEL'S LOVE	*	*	40.00
	J. MONTI		**HEAVEN'S PRECIOUS BLESSINGS**	
97	TENDER MOMENT	*	30.00	30.00
97	WARM EMBRACE	*	30.00	30.00
97	WINGS OF LOVE	*	30.00	30.00
	R. AKERS		**HEAVENLY CHORUS**	
95	ANGELS WE HAVE HEARD ON HIGH	*	*	51.00
95	HARK THE HERALD ANGELS SING	CL	40.00	50.00
96	O COME ALL YE FAITHFUL	*	40.00	40.00
	A. PECH		**HEIRLOOM MEMORIES**	
94	PINK LEMONADE ROSES	CL	30.00	40.00
94	PORCELAIN TREASURE	CL	30.00	40.00
94	RHYTHMS IN LACE	CL	30.00	40.00
94	TEATIME TULIPS	CL	30.00	40.00
94	VICTORIAN ROMANCE	CL	30.00	40.00
	A. PECH		**HEIRLOOMS AND LACE**	
94	TOUCH OF THE IRISH	*	*	40.00
	R. DEFELICE		**HEROES ON ICE**	
97	LE MAGNIFIQUE (MARIO LEMIEUX)	*	30.00	30.00
98	HEART AND SOUL	*	30.00	30.00
98	SWIFT 77	*	30.00	30.00
	S. TARABAY		**HEROES ON ICE**	
98	SUPER 16	*	30.00	30.00
	R. RUST		**HIDDEN WORLD**	
93	HUNTER GROWLS, SPIRITS PROWL	CL	33.00	33.00
93	IN MOONGLOW ONE DRINKS	CL	33.00	33.00
93	SINGS AT THE MOON, SPIRITS SING IN TUNE	CL	35.00	35.00
93	TWO BY NIGHT, TWO BY LIGHT	CL	30.00	30.00
93	TWO BY STEAM, TWO IN DREAM	CL	33.00	33.00
93	TWO ON SLY, TWO WATCH NEARBY	CL	33.00	36.00
94	TWO CUBS PLAY, SPIRITS SHOW THE WAY	CL	35.00	39.00
94	YOUNG ONES HOLD ON TIGHT	CL	35.00	40.00
	R. RUST		**HIDEAWAY LAKE**	
93	ECHOES OF MORNING	CL	35.00	40.00
93	FISHING FOR DREAMS	CL	35.00	40.00
93	RUSTY'S RETREAT	CL	35.00	40.00
93	SUNSET CABIN	CL	35.00	40.00
	L. LIU		**HOLIDAY ANGELS**	
97	CELEBRATION	95 DAYS	33.00	33.00
97	GLAD TIDINGS	95 DAYS	30.00	30.00
97	JUBILEE	95 DAYS	33.00	33.00
97	NOEL	95 DAYS	33.00	33.00

YR	NAME	LIMIT	ISSUE	TREND
97	REJOICE	95 DAYS	30.00	30.00
97	YULETIDE	95 DAYS	33.00	33.00
T. KINKADE				
HOLIDAY MEMORIES: THOMAS KINKADE				
97	HOME FOR THE HOLIDAYS	95 DAYS	40.00	40.00
97	VICTORIAN CHRISTMAS CELEBRATION	95 DAYS	40.00	40.00
97	VICTORIAN CHRISTMAS MEMORIES	95 DAYS	40.00	40.00
M. LEONE				
HOME IN THE HEARTLAND				
95	BARN RAISING	*	*	44.00
96	APPLE BLOSSOM FESTIVAL, THE	OP	35.00	45.00
96	COUNTRY FAIR	*	*	44.00
C. WYSOCKI				
HOMETOWN MEMORIES				
95	A FAREWELL KISS	95 DAYS	30.00	40.00
95	CAPTURING THE MOMENT	95 DAYS	30.00	40.00
95	JASON SPARKLING THE LIGHTHOUSE	95 DAYS	30.00	40.00
95	SMALL TALK AT BIRDIE'S PERCH	95 DAYS	*	40.00
95	SUMMER DELIGHTS	95 DAYS	30.00	40.00
95	TRANQUIL DAYS/RAVENSWHIP COVER	95 DAYS	30.00	40.00
*				
HUNCHBACK OF NOTRE DAME				
97	A FEATHERED FRIEND	*	35.00	35.00
97	A GOOD DAY TO FLY	95 DAYS	35.00	35.00
97	DANCE OF ENCHANTMENT	95 DAYS	35.00	35.00
97	TOPSY TURVY PARADE	95 DAYS	35.00	35.00
97	TOUCHED BY LOVE	95 DAYS	35.00	35.00
R. DOCKEN				
HUNTERS OF THE SPIRIT				
95	DEFENDER	*	*	41.00
95	GATHERER	*	*	39.00
95	PROVIDER	95 DAYS	30.00	40.00
95	SEEKER	*	*	40.00
96	HUNTER, THE	OP	30.00	40.00
M. BIERLINSKI				
ILLUSIONS OF NATURE				
95	A TRIO OF WOLVES	95 DAYS	30.00	40.00
95	RUNNING DEER	*	*	40.00
J. GRENDE				
ILLUSIONS OF NATURE				
95	AUTUMN ILLUSION	*	*	41.00
J. GRENDE				
ILLUSIVE WINGS				
95	AUTUMN MIRAGE	*	*	39.00
96	AMETHYST APPARITION	*	*	42.00
96	GLIMPSE OF GOLD	*	*	40.00
96	NUTMEG IMPRESSIONS	*	30.00	40.00
C. JACKSON				
IMMORTALS OF THE DIAMOND				
94	SULTAN OF SWAT	CL	40.00	50.00
95	GEORGIA PEACH	CL	40.00	51.00
95	PRIDE OF THE YANKEES	CL	40.00	50.00
95	WINNINGIST PITCHER	CL	40.00	50.00
T. CLAUSNITZER				
IN A HIDDEN GARDEN				
93	CURIOUS KTTENS	CL	30.00	40.00
94	AMBER GAZE	CL	30.00	40.00
94	FASCINATING FIND	CL	30.00	40.00
94	THROUGH EYES OF BLUE	CL	30.00	40.00
D. SIVAVEC				
IT'S A WONDERFUL LIFE				
95	AN ANGEL GETS HIS WINGS	*	*	40.00
95	WELCOME HOME	*	*	41.00
96	BY THE LIGHT OF THE MOON	OP	35.00	40.00
96	I'M THE ANSWER TO YOUR PRAYER	*	35.00	40.00
S. MICHAELS				
JAMES DEAN COLLECTION				
97	HOLLYWOOD COOL	*	35.00	35.00
97	HOLLYWOOD GIANT	*	35.00	35.00
J. WOOSTER SCOTT				
JANE WOOSTER SCOTT'S SEASIDE MEMORIES				
97	BEACHFRONT FUN	*	35.00	35.00
97	PEACEFUL HARBOR	*	35.00	35.00
98	SHIPS AHOY!	*	35.00	35.00
98	SUMMER AT THE SEASHORE	*	35.00	35.00
D. SMITH				
JOE MONTANA: TICKET TO GLORY				
97	SUPERBOWL XVI	*	35.00	35.00
98	SUPER BOWL XIX	*	35.00	35.00
R. BROWN				
JOHN ELWAY: KING OF THE MOUNTAIN				
98	SUPER BOWL CHAMPIONS	*	30.00	30.00
*				
KEEPERS OF THE SHORE				
98	SUMMER BY THE SEA	*	40.00	40.00
C. LAYTON				
KEEPSAKES OF THE HEART				
93	AFTERNOON TEA	CL	30.00	40.00
93	FOREVER FRIENDS	CL	30.00	40.00
93	RIDING COMPANIONS	CL	30.00	40.00
93	SENTIMENTAL SWEETHEARTS	CL	30.00	45.00
C. POULIN				
KINDRED MOMENTS				
95	SISTERS ARE BLOSSOMS	95 DAYS	20.00	30.00
96	FOREVER FRIENDS	*	23.00	40.00
97	SISTERS SHARE TRIUMPHS AND TEARS	*	27.00	27.00
97	SISTERS WISH ON THE SAME STAR	*	27.00	27.00
D. CASEY				
KINDRED SPIRITS				
96	SPIRIT OF THE WOLF	OP	30.00	40.00
C. PUOLIN				
KINDRED THOUGHTS				
95	SISTERS	95 DAYS	30.00	30.00
M. JOBE				
KINGDOM OF ENCHANTMENT				
96	MOONBEAM TRAILS	*	30.00	40.00
96	MOONLIGHT WONDER	*	*	40.00

YR	NAME	LIMIT	ISSUE	TREND
C. FRACE			**KINGDOM OF GREAT CATS**	
94	AMERICAN MONARCH	*	*	43.00
94	EMPEROR OF SIBERIA	*	*	45.00
94	HIS DOMAIN	*	*	44.00
94	MYSTIC REALM	CL	40.00	45.00
94	RADIANT MOMENT	*	*	43.00
94	SNOW LEOPARD	*	*	45.00
M. FERRARO			**KINGDOM OF THE UNICORN**	
93	CHASING A DREAM	CL	30.00	40.00
93	FOUNTAIN OF YOUTH, THE	CL	30.00	40.00
93	IN CRYSTAL WATERS	CL	30.00	40.00
93	MAGIC BEGINS, THE	CL	30.00	40.00
T. KINKADE			**KINKADE'S ILLUMINATED COTTAGES**	
94	FLAGSTONE PATH, THE	CL	35.00	50.00
95	CHERRY BLOSSOM HIDEAWAY	CL	35.00	50.00
95	GARDEN WALK,THE	CL	35.00	50.00
95	LIGHTED GATE	CL	38.00	51.00
J. SCHOLZ			**KITTEN EXPEDITIONS**	
97	AT THE LITTLE WATERFALL	*	37.00	37.00
97	ON THE GARDEN BENCH		37.00	37.00
97	ON THE WOODPILE		37.00	37.00
T. KINKADE			**LAMPLIGHT VILLAGE**	
95	LAMPLIGHT BRIDGE	*	*	40.00
95	LAMPLIGHT BROOKE	95 DAYS	30.00	40.00
95	LAMPLIGHT COUNTY	95 DAYS	*	40.00
95	LAMPLIGHT GLEN		*	40.00
95	LAMPLIGHT INN	95 DAYS	30.00	40.00
95	LAMPLIGHT LANE	95 DAYS	30.00	40.00
96	LAMPLIGHT FARM	*	*	40.00
96	LAMPLIGHT MILL		*	40.00
D. CHERRY			**LAND OF OZ: NEW DIMENSION**	
95	STEP INTO THE EMERALD CITY	95 DAYS	35.00	40.00
95	WIZ LENTICULAR		*	40.00
D. STANLEY			**LEGEND OF THE WHITE BUFFALO**	
95	CALL OF THE CLOUDS	*	*	40.00
95	MYSTIC SPIRIT	95 DAYS	30.00	40.00
95	VALLEY OF THE SACRED	*	*	40.00
96	BUFFALO SPIRIT OF THE VILLAGE	*	*	40.00
96	SPIRIT OF THE BUFFALO SHAMAN	*	30.00	40.00
96	WHITE BUFFALO CALF WOMAN	*	*	40.00
E. JERINS			**LEGENDARY HOME RUNS**	
97	FINAL HOME RUN, THE	*	30.00	30.00
J. WALKER			**LEGENDARY HOME RUNS**	
97	TWELFTH INNING ROCKET	*	35.00	35.00
98	GIBSON'S WORLD SERIES HOME RUNS	*	35.00	35.00
B. BENGER			**LEGENDARY JACKIE ROBINSON**	
97	BREAKING BARRIERS	*	50.00	50.00
W. TERRY			**LEGENDS OF THE MOON**	
96	MOON OF RUNNING WOLVES	*	35.00	35.00
L. LIU			**LENA LIU'S COUNTRY ACCENTS**	
97	GARDEN DELIGHTS	95 DAYS	30.00	30.00
97	GARDEN ELEGANCE	95 DAYS	33.00	33.00
97	GARDEN GRACE	95 DAYS	33.00	33.00
97	GARDEN PLEASURES	95 DAYS	30.00	30.00
L. LIU			**LENA LIU'S FLIGHTS OF FANCY**	
97	GARDEN JEWELS	95 DAYS	35.00	35.00
97	ON GOSSAMER WINGS	*	35.00	35.00
98	FLEETING BEAUTY	*	35.00	35.00
98	WHISPERING WINGS	*	35.00	35.00
L. LIU			**LENA LIU'S FLORAL CAMEOS**	
97	CHERISHED	95 DAYS	33.00	33.00
97	ENCHANTMENT	95 DAYS	30.00	30.00
97	EVERLASTING	95 DAYS	33.00	33.00
97	EXQUISITE	*	35.00	35.00
97	GLORY	95 DAYS	35.00	35.00
97	MAGICAL	*	35.00	35.00
97	PRECIOUS	95 DAYS	33.00	33.00
97	REMEMBRANCE	95 DAYS	30.00	30.00
97	TREASURED	95 DAYS	35.00	35.00
98	HONORED	*	35.00	35.00
98	RADIANCE	*	35.00	35.00
L. LIU			**LENA LIU'S WINGS OF LOVE**	
97	PRECIOUS IS THE GIFT OF LOVE	95 DAYS	30.00	30.00
97	SACRED IS THE PROMISE OF LOVE	95 DAYS	30.00	30.00
97	SWEET ARE THE DREAMS OF LOVE	*	30.00	30.00
97	TENDER ARE THE HEARTS OF LOVE	95 DAYS	30.00	30.00
98	BRIGHT IS LIGHT OF LOVE	*	30.00	30.00
R. BARRETT			**LIFE OF CHRIST**	
94	ASCENSION	CL	35.00	50.00
94	JESUS CALMS THE WATERS	CL	33.00	45.00
94	JESUS ENTERS JERUSALEM	CL	30.00	40.00
94	PASSION IN THE GARDEN, THE	CL	30.00	40.00
94	RESURRECTION	CL	35.00	50.00
94	SERMON ON THE MOUNT	CL	33.00	46.00
95	CRUCIFIXION,THE	CL	35.00	50.00

YR	NAME	LIMIT	ISSUE	TREND
	C. NICK			**LIGHT OF THE WORLD**
95	BETRAYAL IN THE GARDEN	*	*	40.00
95	FACING HIS ACCUSERS	*	*	40.00
95	LAST SUPPER	95 DAYS	30.00	40.00
96	JESUS GOES BEFORE PILATE	*	*	40.00
96	PRAYER IN THE GARDEN	*	30.00	40.00
96	WAY OF THE CROSS	*	*	40.00
*				**LION KING**
97	CIRCLE CONTINUES, THE	95 DAYS	35.00	35.00
97	RISE AND SHINE	95 DAYS	35.00	35.00
97	STARGAZING	95 DAYS	35.00	35.00
*				**LION KING**
95	A CRUNCHY FEAST	95 DAYS	33.00	45.00
95	CIRCLE OF LIFE, THE	95 DAYS	30.00	40.00
95	COURTING THE FUTURE KING	95 DAYS	*	50.00
95	HAKUNA MATATA	95 DAYS	*	50.00
95	I'M GONNA BE KING	95 DAYS	*	45.00
95	KING WITHIN	95 DAYS	*	50.00
95	LIKE FATHER, LIKE SON	95 DAYS	30.00	40.00
95	WE'LL ALWAYS BE FRIENDS	95 DAYS	*	45.00
96	BEST FRIENDS	*	*	50.00
	DISNEY			**LION KING: THE CIRCLE OF LIFE**
98	LIFE LONG FRIENDS	*	30.00	30.00
98	REMEMBER WHO YOU ARE	*	30.00	30.00
98	SIMBA AND NALA	*	30.00	30.00
	C. JAGODITS			**LITTER RASCALS**
96	SNEAKING SECONDS	*	30.00	30.00
	J. SCHOLZ			**LITTER RASCALS**
97	FRISKY BUSINESS	*	30.00	30.00
98	KITCHEN CAPERS	*	30.00	30.00
	C. JAGODITS			**LITTLE BANDITS**
93	ALL TIED UP	CL	30.00	40.00
93	EVERYTHING'S COMING UP DAISIES	CL	33.00	35.00
93	HANDLE WITH CARE	CL	30.00	50.00
93	OUT OF HAND	CL	33.00	35.00
93	PUPSICLES	CL	33.00	33.00
93	UNEXPECTED GUESTS	CL	33.00	33.00
	G. BEECHAM			**LORD OF FOREST & CANYON**
94	MOUNTAIN MAJESTY	95 DAYS	30.00	40.00
95	FOREST EMPEROR	95 DAYS	30.00	45.00
95	GOLDEN MONARCH	95 DAYS	30.00	45.00
95	GRAND DOMAIN	*	*	46.00
95	PROUD LEGACY	95 DAYS	30.00	40.00
*				**LOVE'S HEAVENLY MESSENGERS**
97	WATCHING OVER ME	*	40.00	40.00
	B.P. GUTMANN			**LOVE'S HEAVENLY MESSENGERS**
97	ENCHANTING DREAMS	*	30.00	30.00
97	GENTLE FRIEND	*	30.00	30.00
97	SILENT BEAUTY	*	30.00	30.00
98	BUBBLING JOY	*	30.00	30.00
98	ENCHANTING MELODY	*	30.00	30.00
98	LOVELY THOUGHTS	*	30.00	30.00
	R. MCGINNIS			**LOVING HEARTS**
95	UNSELFISH AND GIVING	*	*	40.00
96	BEAUTY & SPLENDOR	*	30.00	40.00
96	PATIENT & KIND	*	30.00	40.00
	W. BOUGUERAEU			**MADONNA AND CHILD: THE MASTERS SERIES**
97	VIRGIN WITH ANGELS, THE	*	35.00	35.00
98	DIVINE MOTHER	*	35.00	35.00
98	MADONNA OF GLORY	*	35.00	35.00
	W. RAFFAEL			**MADONNA AND CHILD: THE MASTERS SERIES**
97	SISTER MADONNA	*	35.00	35.00
	G. DIECKHONER			**MAJESTIC PATRIOTS**
95	MY COUNTRY TIS OF THEE	95 DAYS	30.00	40.00
	C. NOTARILE			**MARILYN: THE GOLD COLLECTION**
97	FOREVER RADIANT	*	35.00	35.00
97	RADIANT IN RED	*	35.00	35.00
	M. GREENE			**MARILYN: UP CLOSE AND PERSONAL**
98	BODY AND SOUL	*	35.00	35.00
98	LADY IN RED	*	35.00	35.00
*				**MASTERS OF LAND & SKY**
96	SUPREME SUMMONS	*	30.00	40.00
	GIANNINI			**MASTERS OF LAND & SKY**
95	MAJESTIC HARMONY	*	*	40.00
95	SOUL MATES	*	*	40.00
95	UNITED IN SPIRIT	*	*	40.00
	STRONGIN			**MASTERS OF LAND & SKY**
95	NOBLE BOND	*	*	40.00
96	ENDURING PRESENCE	*	*	40.00
96	SOVEREIGN UNITY	*	*	40.00
*				**MESSAGES FROM HEAVEN**
97	ANGEL OF HARMONY	*	40.00	40.00
97	ANGEL OF JOY	*	40.00	40.00
98	ANGEL OF KINDNESS	*	40.00	40.00
98	ANGEL OF LOVE	*	40.00	40.00

YR	NAME	LIMIT	ISSUE	TREND
L. BOGLE				
	MESSENGERS OF THE SPIRIT			
97	BLESSING, THE	*	30.00	30.00
97	DREAM, THE	*	30.00	30.00
97	GIFT, THE	*	30.00	30.00
97	HOPE, THE	*	30.00	30.00
97	SHARING, THE	*	30.00	30.00
97	SIGN, THE	*	30.00	30.00
97	THE GUIDE	*	30.00	30.00
97	VISION, THE	*	30.00	30.00
R. SPANGLER				
	MEWSIC FOR THE HOLIDAYS			
97	SANTA CLAWS IS COMING TO TOWN	*	35.00	35.00
C. GILLIES				
	MICHAEL JORDAN COLLECTION			
97	1991 EASTERN FINALS	*	35.00	35.00
98	CAREER HIGH 69 IN OVERTIME	*	35.00	35.00
98	RECORD 23 IN A ROW	*	35.00	35.00
	MICHAEL JORDAN: FLYING HIGH			
98	BREAKING THE RECORDS	*	60.00	60.00
	MICHAEL JORDAN: LEGEND FOR ALL TIME			
98	SLAM JAMMER	*	80.00	80.00
S. GREENWELL				
	MICHAEL JORDAN: LEGEND FOR ALL TIME			
97	RIM ROCKER	*	80.00	80.00
G. GREEN				
	MICHAEL JORDAN: TICKET TO GREATNESS			
97	HEART OF A CHAMPION	*	35.00	35.00
97	TAKING IT PERSONALLY	*	38.00	38.00
98	IN THE ZONE	*	38.00	38.00
98	LEADER OF THE LEAGUE	*	38.00	38.00
	MICKEY & MINNIE			
94	BRAVE LITTLE TAILOR	TL	30.00	40.00
95	MICKEY MOUSE CLUB	*	33.00	46.00
95	MICKEY'S 65TH BIRTHDAY	*	35.00	45.00
95	MICKEY'S GALA PREMIERE	*	33.00	46.00
95	STEAMBOAT WILLIE	*	33.00	45.00
	MICKEY & MINNIE THROUGH THE YEARS			
97	MICKEY'S BIRTHDAY PARTY, 1942	95 DAYS	30.00	30.00
S. GARDNER				
	MICKEY MANTLE COLLECTION			
96	500TH HOME RUN CLUB	*	*	41.00
96	BRONX BOMBER	*	40.00	40.00
96	TRIPLE CROWN SEASON	*	*	40.00
	MICKEY MANTLE: ALL AMERICAN LEGEND			
97	TRIPLE CROWN KING	*	80.00	80.00
	MICKEY'S CHRISTMAS MAGIC			
97	NAUGHTY OR NICE?	95 DAYS	35.00	35.00
97	SANTA'S FAVORITE HELPERS	95 DAYS	35.00	35.00
97	SPECIAL DELIVERY	95 DAYS	35.00	35.00
97	THANKS PLUTO	95 DAYS	35.00	35.00
	MICKEY'S HOLIDAY MAGIC			
97	SPECIAL DELIVERY	*	35.00	35.00
J. WELTY				
	MIRACLE OF CHRISTMAS			
96	ONCE UPON A HOLY NIGHT	OP	35.00	45.00
S. KUCK				
	MOMENTS AT HOME			
95	MOMENTS OF SHARING	95 DAYS	30.00	40.00
C. FISHER				
	MOMENTS IN THE GARDEN			
95	RUBY TREASURES	*	*	41.00
96	LUMINOUS JEWELS	*	30.00	40.00
96	LUSTROUS SAPPHIRE	*	*	42.00
96	RADIANT GEMS	OP	30.00	40.00
96	SHIMMERING SPLENDOR	OP	30.00	40.00
L. LIU				
	MORNING JEWELS			
97	AMETHYST GLORY	*	40.00	40.00
97	CRIMSON BLUSH	*	45.00	45.00
97	CRYSTAL DAYBREAK	*	45.00	45.00
97	FUCHSIA MAJESTY	*	45.00	45.00
97	GARNET GRANDEUR	*	45.00	45.00
97	LILY SPLENDOUR	*	45.00	45.00
97	REGAL MORNING	*	45.00	45.00
97	ROSE-COLORED DAWN	*	40.00	40.00
97	RUBY REFLECTIONS	*	45.00	45.00
98	PEARL TREASURE	*	45.00	45.00
R. AKERS				
	MUSICAL CAROUSEL TREASURES			
93	SWEET STANDER	CL	49.00	60.00
B. EMMETT				
	MUSICAL TRIBUTE TO ELVIS THE KING			
94	HOUND DOG BOP	95 DAYS	30.00	40.00
94	RED, WHITE, AND G.I. BLUES	95 DAYS	33.00	40.00
94	ROCKIN' BLUE SUEDE SHOES	CL	30.00	40.00
95	AMERICAN DREAM	95 DAYS	33.00	45.00
95	FALLING IN LOVE WITH/KING	*	*	45.00
95	GOSPEL IN HIS SOUL	*	*	50.00
95	YOUR FUN LOVIN' TEDDY BEAR	*	*	50.00
96	LOVE: THE GREATEST GIFT	OP	35.00	50.00
	MY GUARDIAN ANGEL			
97	GUIDING MY WAY	*	40.00	40.00
B. BURKE				
	MY LITTLE GUARDIAN			
97	BLESSING MY DREAMS	*	30.00	30.00
97	WATCHING OVER ME	*	30.00	30.00
98	HEARING MY PRAYERS	*	30.00	30.00

The Dance of Snow White & the Seven Dwarfs *was the first issue in the "Snow White & the Seven Dwarfs" series by the Edwin M. Knowles China Co. Issued in 1991 for $29.90, the secondary market on this plate has almost doubled.*

The first of four editions in Fenton Art Glass' "Christmas Fantasy Series" by Diane Johnson, the design was also produced as a bell and a fairy light.

Royal Copenhagen's 1987 addition to the "Christmas" series was Winter Birds *by Sven Vestergaard.*

Limited to 150 firing days, Spring Blossoms *from Ted DeGrazia's Children of the Sun collection was produced by Artists of the World.*

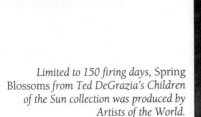

YR	NAME	LIMIT	ISSUE	TREND
B.H. BOND		MYSTERIOUS CASE OF FOWL PLAY		
94	GLAMOURPUSS	CL	30.00	40.00
94	INSPECTOR CLAWSEAU	CL	30.00	40.00
94	KOOL CAT	CL	30.00	40.00
94	SNEAKERS AND HIGH-TOP	CL	30.00	40.00
94	SOPHISICAT	CL	30.00	40.00
95	TUXEDO	CL	30.00	40.00
S. HILL		MYSTIC GUARDIANS		
93	COMPANION SPIRITS	CL	33.00	45.00
93	FAITHFUL FELLOWSHIP	CL	33.00	45.00
93	MAJESTIC MESSENGER	CL	30.00	40.00
93	ROYAL UNITY	CL	35.00	45.00
93	SOUL MATES	CL	30.00	40.00
93	SPIRITUAL HARMONY	CL	33.00	45.00
V. CRANDALL		MYSTIC SPIRITS		
94	MIDNIGHT SNOW	95 DAYS	30.00	41.00
95	ARCTIC NIGHTS	95 DAYS	33.00	45.00
95	ENTRANCING GLANCE	*	*	51.00
95	KEEPER OF THE NIGHT	*	*	45.00
95	MOON SHADOWS	95 DAYS	30.00	40.00
95	SILENT ENCOUNTER	*	*	46.00
96	SILENT NIGHT	*	*	52.00
C. JACKSON		NATIVE AMERICAN LEGENDS: CHIEFS OF DESTINY		
95	RED CLOUD	CL	45.00	45.00
95	SITTING BULL	CL	40.00	40.00
96	TECUMSEH	95 DAYS	45.00	45.00
L. BOGLE		NATIVE BEAUTY		
94	AFTERGLOW	95 DAYS	30.00	41.00
94	PROMISE, THE	CL	30.00	40.00
94	WHITE FEATHER	95 DAYS	30.00	39.00
95	FIRST GLANCE	95 DAYS	30.00	40.00
95	MORNING STAR	95 DAYS	30.00	40.00
95	QUIET TIME	95 DAYS	30.00	40.00
95	STIRRING OF THE HEART	*	30.00	41.00
95	WARM THOUGHTS	95 DAYS	30.00	40.00
97	LOVERS, THE	*	30.00	30.00
J. KRAMER COLE		NATIVE VISIONS		
94	BROTHER TO THE MOON	*	*	42.00
95	BRINGERS OF THE STORM	95 DAYS	30.00	40.00
95	RED SHIELD	*	*	40.00
95	SON OF SUN	*	*	43.00
95	WATER VISION	95 DAYS	30.00	40.00
96	LISTENING	OP	30.00	40.00
96	MAN WHO SEES FAR	OP	30.00	40.00
96	TOPONAS	*	*	39.00
G. TURLEY		NATURE'S ELEGANCE		
97	ABUNDANT DELIGHTS	*	30.00	30.00
97	SWEET SPLENDOR	*	30.00	30.00
98	FRUITFUL PLEASURES	*	30.00	30.00
98	RIPENED RICHES	*	30.00	30.00
D. GELSINGER		NATURE'S HEAVENLY GUARDIANS		
97	GENTLE GUIDANCE	95 DAYS	30.00	30.00
97	MAKING NEW FRIENDS	95 DAYS	30.00	30.00
97	WONDROUS DISCOVERY, A	95 DAYS	30.00	30.00
98	GIFT OF LOVE, A	*	30.00	30.00
L. MARTIN		NATURE'S LITTLE TREASURES		
93	GARDEN WHISPERS	CL	30.00	40.00
94	DELICATE SPLENDOR	CL	33.00	45.00
94	MINIATURE GLORY	CL	33.00	45.00
94	MINUTE ENCHANTMENT	CL	35.00	50.00
94	PERFECT JEWELS	CL	33.00	45.00
94	PRECIOUS BEAUTIES	95 DAYS	35.00	52.00
94	RARE PERFECTION	95 DAYS	35.00	50.00
94	WINGS OF GRACE	CL	33.00	40.00
95	MISTY MORNING	95 DAYS	37.00	55.00
95	WHISPER IN THE WIND	95 DAYS	*	55.00
D. PARKER		NATURE'S NOBILITY		
96	BUCK, THE	OP	40.00	50.00
96	DALL SHEEP	*	*	52.00
L. CABLE		NATURE'S TENDERNESS		
98	SOUL MATES	*	35.00	35.00
*		NESTING NEIGHBORS		
97	OUR COZY HAVEN	*	45.00	45.00
97	OUR PRECIOUS RETREAT	*	45.00	45.00
97	OUR SWEET HIDEAWAY	*	40.00	40.00
98	OUR HEARTFELT HOME	*	45.00	45.00
98	OUR LOVELY LODGING	*	45.00	45.00
R. COPPLE		NEW HORIZONS		
93	BUILDING FOR A NEW GENERATION	CL	30.00	40.00
93	POWER OF GOD, THE	CL	30.00	40.00
93	WINGS OF SNOWY GRANDEUR	CL	33.00	45.00
94	MASTER OF THE CHASE	CL	33.00	45.00
95	COASTAL DOMAIN	95 DAYS	33.00	45.00
M. CORNING		NFL 75TH ANNIV. ALL-TIME TEAM		
95	FOREST GREGG/JOE GREEN	*	*	39.00
95	MIKE WEBSTER/RAY NITSCHKE	*	*	40.00

YR	NAME	LIMIT	ISSUE	TREND
96	GALE SAYERS/JACK LAMBERT	*	35.00	40.00
96	JOHNNY UNITAS/BOB LILY	*	35.00	40.00
R. BROWN			**NFL QUARTERBACK CLUB**	
97	BRETT FAVRE	*	30.00	30.00
97	JOHN ELWAY	*	30.00	30.00
97	TROY AIKMAN	*	30.00	30.00
98	DREW BLEDSOE	*	30.00	30.00
98	STEVE YOUNG	*	30.00	30.00
C. GILLIES		**NIGHT BEFORE CHRISTMAS 175TH ANNIVERSARY**		
97	HAPPY CHRISTMAS TO ALL	*	35.00	35.00
J. HANSEL			**NIGHTSONG: THE LOON**	
94	EVENING MIST	CL	30.00	40.00
94	MOONLIGHT ECHOES	CL	30.00	40.00
94	NIGHT LIGHT	CL	35.00	50.00
94	NOCTURNAL GLOW	CL	33.00	45.00
94	TRANQUIL REFLECTIONS	CL	33.00	45.00
95	LOONS BY THE LILY PAD	95 DAYS	35.00	35.00
95	PEACEFUL HOMESTEAD	CL	35.00	50.00
95	SERENE SANCTUARY	95 DAYS	37.00	55.00
95	SILENT PASSAGE	CL	35.00	54.00
95	TRANQUIL REFUGE	CL	37.00	52.00
D. NINGEWANCE			**NIGHTWATCH: THE WOLF**	
94	MIDNIGHT GUARD	CL	30.00	40.00
94	MOONLIGHT SERENADE	CL	30.00	40.00
94	SILENT SENTRIES	CL	30.00	38.00
94	SNOWY LOOKOUT	CL	30.00	40.00
94	SONG TO THE NIGHT	CL	30.00	40.00
94	WINTER PASSAGE	CL	30.00	41.00
K. WEISBERG			**NORTHERN COMPANIONS**	
95	MIDNIGHT HARMONY	95 DAYS	30.00	40.00
D. WENZEL			**NORTHWOODS SPIRIT**	
94	TIMELESS WATCH	CL	30.00	35.00
95	EVENING RESPITE	95 DAYS	30.00	30.00
95	FOREST ECHO	95 DAYS	30.00	30.00
95	TIMBERLAND GAZE	95 DAYS	30.00	30.00
P. WEIRS			**NOSY NEIGHBORS**	
94	CAT NAP	95 DAYS	30.00	40.00
94	SPECIAL DELIVERY	95 DAYS	30.00	42.00
95	HOUSE SITTING	95 DAYS	30.00	40.00
95	OBSERVATION DECK	95 DAYS	33.00	45.00
95	SURPRISE VISIT	95 DAYS	33.00	45.00
96	FULL HOUSE	*	*	51.00
96	LIFEGUARD ON DUTY	*	35.00	50.00
*		**NOTORIOUS DISNEY VILLAINS**		
93	WICKED QUEEN, THE	CL	30.00	40.00
94	CRUELLA DE VIL	CL	30.00	40.00
94	MALEFICENT	CL	30.00	40.00
94	URSELLA	CL	30.00	40.00
C. POULIN			**NOW AND FOREVER**	
97	SIDE BY SIDE	*		N/A
T. KINKADE			**OLD FASHIONED CHRISTMAS**	
93	A HOLIDAY GATHERING	CL	33.00	45.00
93	ALL FRIENDS ARE WELCOME	CL	30.00	40.00
93	CHRISTMAS TREE COTTAGE	CL	33.00	45.00
93	WINTER'S MEMORIES	CL	30.00	40.00
95	BEST TRADITION, THE	95 DAYS	33.00	45.00
95	STONEHEARTH HUTCH	95 DAYS	*	52.00
S. GUSTAFSON			**ONCE UPON A TIME**	
98	GOLDILOCKS AND THE THREE BEARS	*	35.00	35.00
98	LITTLE RED RIDING HOOD	*	35.00	35.00
98	THREE LITTLE PIGS, THE	*	35.00	35.00
H. GARRIDO			**OUR HEAVENLY MOTHER**	
95	ADORATION	*	*	45.00
95	FAITHFULNESS	*	*	45.00
95	HEAVENLY DEVOTION	*	*	45.00
96	CONSTANCY	*	35.00	45.00
W. NELSON			**PANDA BEAR HUGS**	
93	ROCK-A-BYE	CL	39.00	50.00
94	A PLAYFUL INTERLUDE	CL	39.00	62.00
94	A TASTE OF LIFE	CL	39.00	62.00
94	LOVING ADVICE	CL	39.00	54.00
J. BARNES			**PATHWAYS OF THE HEART**	
93	DAYBREAK	CL	30.00	40.00
93	OCTOBER RADIANCE	CL	30.00	40.00
94	A NIGHT TO REMEMBER	CL	30.00	40.00
94	DISTANT LIGHTS	CL	30.00	40.00
94	HARMONY WITH NATURE	CL	30.00	40.00
94	PEACEFUL EVENING	CL	30.00	40.00
M. RIEN			**PAWS IN ACTION**	
95	PLAYFUL DREAMS	*	*	45.00
95	SWEET SLUMBER	*	*	45.00
96	NESTLED WRESTLE	*	*	45.00
M. RIEN			**PAWS IN PLAY**	
95	BEDTIME TAILS	*	*	45.00
95	CUDDLE BUDDIES	*	*	45.00

YR	NAME	LIMIT	ISSUE	TREND
96	BREAK TIME	*	35.00	45.00
96	WAKE-UP CALL	*	*	45.00
D. GEISNESS			**PEACE ON EARTH**	
93	WINTER LULLABY	CL	30.00	30.00
94	HEAVENLY SLUMBER	CL	30.00	30.00
94	SNOWY SILENCE	CL	33.00	37.00
94	SWEET EMBRACE	CL	33.00	33.00
M. HARVEY			**PEACEABLE KINGDOM**	
94	NOAH'S ARK	CL	30.00	35.00
C. WYSOCKI			**PEPPERCRICKET GROVE**	
93	BLACK CROW ANTIQUE SHOPPE	95 DAYS	25.00	40.00
93	BUDZEN'S FRUIT & VEGETABLES	95 DAYS	25.00	40.00
93	GINGERNUT VALLEY INN	CL	25.00	40.00
93	LIBERTY STAR FARMS	95 DAYS	25.00	40.00
93	OVERFLOW ANTIQUE MARKET	95 DAYS	25.00	40.00
93	PEPPERCRICKET FARMS	CL	25.00	40.00
93	PUMPKIN HOLLOW EMPORIUM	95 DAYS	25.00	40.00
93	VIRGINIA'S MARKET	95 DAYS	25.00	40.00
W. VON SCHWARZBEK		**PICKED FROM AN ENGLISH GARDEN**		
95	LASTING TREASURES	CL	30.00	30.00
95	NATURE'S WONDERS	CL	30.00	30.00
*			**POCAHONTAS**	
97	BEST FRIENDS	95 DAYS	35.00	35.00
97	FATHER'S LOVE	95 DAYS	33.00	33.00
97	JUST AROUND THE RIVERBEND	95 DAYS	30.00	30.00
97	LISTEN TO YOUR HEART	95 DAYS	33.00	33.00
97	LOVE'S EMBRACE	95 DAYS	30.00	30.00
97	MOMENT THEY TOUCH, THE	95 DAYS	33.00	33.00
A. HARTZELL			**POLAR PALS**	
98	BEAR HUG	*	35.00	35.00
98	BUBBLE TROUBLE	*	35.00	35.00
C. JACKSON		**POOH'S HONEYPOT ADVENTURES**		
98	A WISH FOR FRIENDS	*	45.00	45.00
*		**POOH'S HUNNYPOT ADVENTURES**		
97	A POOH-ISH SORT OF PICNIC	*	45.00	45.00
97	HIP HIP POOHRAY	*	40.00	40.00
97	JUST A SMALL PIECE OF WEATHER	*	40.00	40.00
C. JACKSON		**POOH'S HUNNYPOT ADVENTURES**		
97	FISHIN' FOR FUN	*	45.00	45.00
97	HAPPY WINDSDAY	*	45.00	45.00
97	TIGGER'S TANGLE	*	45.00	45.00
98	FRIENDSHIP MAKES A STAR SHINE BRIGHTER	*	45.00	45.00
98	SHARING A RIDE	*	45.00	45.00
*			**PORTRAITS OF DIANA**	
98	ALWAYS, DIANA	*	30.00	30.00
D. BRAUD			**PORTRAITS OF MAJESTY**	
95	EMPEROR OF HIS REALM	95 DAYS	30.00	30.00
95	REFLECTIONS OF KINGS	95 DAYS	30.00	30.00
95	SOLEMN SOVEREIGN	95 DAYS	30.00	30.00
*			**PORTRAITS OF VALOR**	
93	EMANCIPATION PROCLAMATION	CL	30.00	30.00
93	GETTYSBURG ADDRESS, THE	CL	30.00	30.00
93	LINCOLN-DOUGLAS DEBATE, THE	CL	30.00	30.00
T. KINKADE		**POSTCARDS FROM THOMAS KINKADE**		
95	NEW YORK CITY	95 DAYS	35.00	35.00
95	PARIS	95 DAYS	35.00	35.00
95	SAN FRANCISCO	95 DAYS	35.00	35.00
97	BOSTON	95 DAYS	35.00	35.00
97	CARMEL	95 DAYS	35.00	35.00
97	MARKET STREET--SAN FRANCISCO	95 DAYS	35.00	35.00
L. KAATZ			**PRACTICE MAKES PERFECT**	
94	ONES THAT GOT AWAY, THE	CL	30.00	30.00
94	WHAT'S A MOTHER TO DO?	CL	30.00	30.00
95	MORE THAN A MOUTHFUL	CL	35.00	35.00
95	ON THE RIGHT TRACK	CL	35.00	35.00
B. BURKE		**PRECIOUS GIFTS DAY BY DAY**		
97	MONDAY'S CHILD	*	30.00	30.00
98	TUESDAY'S CHILD	*	30.00	30.00
98	WEDNESDAY'S CHILD	*	30.00	30.00
*			**PRECIOUS ROSES**	
97	DAWN'S PROMISE	*	40.00	40.00
98	DAYLIGHT SPLENDOR	*	40.00	40.00
J. GRANDE			**PRECIOUS VISIONS**	
95	BRIEF INTERLUDE	95 DAYS	30.00	30.00
95	BRILLIANT MOMENT	95 DAYS	30.00	30.00
95	ENDURING ELEGANCE	95 DAYS	33.00	33.00
95	TIMELESS RADIANCE	95 DAYS	30.00	30.00
J. SPURLOCK			**PRIDE OF AMERICA**	
95	WINGS OF GLORY	95 DAYS	30.00	30.00
P. KULL			**PROFILES OF NIGHT**	
97	MIDNIGHT MAGIC	*	35.00	35.00
98	EVENING TWILIGHT	*	35.00	35.00
98	NIGHT RADIANCE	*	35.00	35.00
98	WATCHFUL NIGHT	*	35.00	35.00
*			**PROMISE OF A SAVIOR**	
93	A CHILD IS BORN	CL	30.00	30.00

YR	NAME	LIMIT	ISSUE	TREND
93	AN ANGEL'S MESSAGE	CL	30.00	40.00
93	ANGELS WERE WATCHING	CL	30.00	30.00
93	GIFTS TO JESUS	CL	30.00	40.00
93	HEAVENLY KING, THE	CL	30.00	40.00
93	HOLY MOTHER AND CHILD	CL	30.00	40.00
M. AMERMAN			**PROUD HERITAGE**	
95	PEACEFUL DEFENDER	CL	35.00	35.00
M. RODERICK			**PURRFECTLY AT HOME**	
96	HOME SWEET HOME	*	40.00	40.00
96	KITTY CORNER	*	40.00	40.00
K. DANIEL			**QUIET MOMENTS**	
95	A LOVING HAND	95 DAYS	30.00	30.00
95	KEPT WITH CARE	95 DAYS	30.00	30.00
95	PUPPY LOVE	95 DAYS	30.00	30.00
L. MARTIN			**RADIANT MESSENGERS**	
94	BEAUTY	CL	30.00	35.00
94	PEACE	CL	30.00	30.00
95	INSPIRATION	95 DAYS	30.00	30.00
K. DANIEL			**REALM OF THE WOLF**	
97	MOONGLOW	*	30.00	30.00
97	MOONLIT PHANTOM	*	30.00	30.00
97	SHADOW SPIRITS	*	30.00	30.00
C. NOTARILE			**REFLECTIONS OF MARILYN**	
94	ALL THAT GLITTERS	CL	30.00	30.00
94	SHIMMERING HEAT	CL	30.00	35.00
95	A TWINKLE IN HER EYE	95 DAYS	30.00	30.00
E. CSELKO			**REFLECTIONS OF THE SOUL**	
97	INSPIRATION	*	35.00	35.00
C. POULIN			**REFLECTIONS ON SISTERHOOD**	
97	A SISTER IS A SPECIAL GIFT FILLING LIFE	*	33.00	33.00
97	A SISTER IS A SPECIAL GIFT FULL OF LOVE	*	30.00	30.00
N. GIORGIO			**REMEMBERING ELVIS**	
95	LEGEND,THE	95 DAYS	30.00	30.00
96	DREAM, THE	*	30.00	30.00
97	VISION, THE	*	30.00	30.00
C. BOGLE			**REMEMBERING ENGLAND'S ROSE**	
98	DIANA, A ROSE EVERLASTING	*	*	N/A
98	DIANA, ROSE OF OUR HEARTS	*	35.00	35.00
G. GREEN			**RETURN TO GREATNESS**	
97	A MIRACLE FINISH	*	40.00	40.00
97	DOUBLE NICKEL GAME	*	40.00	40.00
97	NBA SEASON HIGH	*	40.00	40.00
98	1996 FINALS MVP	*	40.00	40.00
98	MICHAEL VS. LAKERS	*	40.00	40.00
98	NBA 101	*	40.00	40.00
A. JENKINS			**ROAD TO OZ**	
97	GREETINGS DOROTHY	*	35.00	35.00
97	IT'S PLEASANT DOWN THAT WAY	*	35.00	35.00
98	I'M A LITTLE RUSTY YET	*	35.00	35.00
98	NOBODY'S EVER SEEN THE GREAT OZ	*	35.00	35.00
N. ROCKWELL			**ROCKWELL COMMEMORATIVE STAMPS**	
94	FREEDOM FROM FEAR	CL	30.00	35.00
94	FREEDOM FROM WANT	CL	30.00	35.00
95	FREEDOM OF SPEECH	95 DAYS	30.00	30.00
95	FREEDOM OF WORSHIP	95 DAYS	30.00	30.00
ROCKWELL INSPIRED			**ROCKWELL SOCIETY CHRISTMAS ANNUAL**	
97	FOR GOOD BOYS AND GIRLS	*	35.00	35.00
N. ROCKWELL			**ROCKWELL SOCIETY HERITAGE**	
94	APPRENTICE, THE	*	30.00	35.00
97	FAMILY GRACE	*	33.00	33.00
J. PENCHOFF			**ROYAL ENCHANTMENTS**	
95	COURTSHIP, THE	CL	40.00	40.00
95	GIFT, THE	CL	40.00	40.00
L. BOGLE			**SACRED BOND**	
97	CHERISHED UNION	*	30.00	30.00
97	GENTLE EMBRACE	*	30.00	30.00
97	PRECIOUS LOVE	*	30.00	30.00
97	SHELTERING HEART	*	30.00	30.00
97	SOFTEST CARESS	*	30.00	30.00
97	TENDER MOMENT	*	30.00	30.00
K. RANDLE			**SACRED CIRCLE**	
93	BEFORE THE HUNT	CL	30.00	30.00
93	GHOST DANCE	CL	33.00	33.00
93	SPIRITUAL GUARDIAN	CL	30.00	30.00
94	DEER DANCE	CL	33.00	33.00
94	PAINTED HORSE, THE	CL	35.00	35.00
94	WOLF DANCE, THE	CL	33.00	33.00
S. KUCK			**SANDRA KUCK'S GARDENS OF INNOCENCE**	
97	SWEETLY SWINGING	*	33.00	33.00
98	GENTLY GIVING	*	33.00	33.00
98	PRECIOUS PARTY	*	33.00	33.00
S. KUCK			**SANDRA KUCK'S MOTHER'S DAY COLLECTION**	
95	HOME IS WHERE THE HEART IS	95 DAYS	35.00	35.00
98	WINGS OF LOVE	*	35.00	35.00
B.H. BOND			**SANTA'S LITTLE HELPERS**	
94	STOCKING STUFFERS	CL	30.00	35.00

YR	NAME	LIMIT	ISSUE	TREND
94	WRAPPING UP THE HOLIDAYS	CL	25.00	30.00
95	COZY KITTENS	CL	25.00	25.00
95	HOLIDAY MISCHIEF	CL	25.00	25.00
S. GUSTAFSON			**SANTA'S ON HIS WAY**	
94	CHECKING IT TWICE	CL	30.00	35.00
95	GIFTS FOR ONE AND ALL	CL	30.00	30.00
95	SANTA'S FIRST STOP	CL	30.00	30.00
*			**SAVIOR IS BORN, THE**	
97	A BLESSING BEYOND MEASURE	*	40.00	40.00
98	FAITH'S INFINITE SPLENDOR	*	40.00	40.00
L. GARRISON			**SCENES OF CHRISTMAS PAST**	
94	A GATHERING OF FAITH	CL	33.00	37.00
M. SARNAT			**SEASON OF LOVE**	
96	A CHERISHED MOMENT	*	30.00	30.00
E. JERINS			**SEASONS OF JOY**	
97	SPRING'S BLOSSOM	*	30.00	30.00
98	AUTUMN'S HARVEST	*	30.00	30.00
98	SPRING BLESSING, A	*	30.00	30.00
98	WINTER'S MAJESTY	*	30.00	30.00
E. JERRINS			**SEASONS OF JOY**	
97	SUMMER'S RADIANCE	*	30.00	30.00
C. POULIN			**SEASONS OF SHARING: SISTERS FOR LIFE**	
97	SISTERS SHARE A BOUQUET OF LOVE	*	30.00	30.00
97	SISTERS SHARE A SPECIAL WARMTH	*	30.00	30.00
98	SISTERS SHARE SWEET MEMORIES	*	30.00	30.00
98	SISTERS SHARE TENDER TIMES	*	30.00	30.00
C. BRENDERS			**SEASONS OF THE TIGER: A MASTER'S COLLECTION**	
98	ON THE PROWL	*	35.00	35.00
98	SILENT PURSUIT	*	35.00	35.00
98	SNOWY QUEST	*	35.00	35.00
T. ISAAC			**SEASONS OF THE TIGER: A MASTER'S COLLECTION**	
98	WITH GUARDED EYE	*	35.00	35.00
L. ZABEL			**SEASONS ON THE OPEN RANGE**	
96	SEASON OF GOLD	OP	30.00	30.00
*			**SERAPHIM CLASSICS: ANGELS OF INSPIRATION**	
96	ISABEL-GENTLE SPIRIT	*	50.00	50.00
T. ISAAC			**SHADES OF THE SEASONS**	
98	APRIL SONG	*	40.00	40.00
98	SPRINGTIME BLUES	*	40.00	40.00
D. PIERCE			**SHADOW GUARDIANS**	
97	EVENING PATROL	*	30.00	30.00
97	MYSTIC GUARDIANS	*	30.00	30.00
97	NIGHT WATCH	*	30.00	30.00
98	FOREST SENTINELS	*	30.00	30.00
98	LOOKOUTS, THE	*	30.00	30.00
B.P. GUTMANN			**SHARING WITH MY BEST FRIEND**	
97	TIME OUT	*	35.00	35.00
98	FRIENDLY ENEMIES	*	35.00	35.00
98	OFF TO BED	*	35.00	35.00
98	REWARD, THE	*	35.00	35.00
J. THORNBRUGH			**SIGNS OF SPRING**	
94	A FAMILY FEAST	CL	*	N/A
95	AWAITING NEW ARRIVALS	95 DAYS	30.00	30.00
95	HOW FAST THEY GROWN	95 DAYS	30.00	30.00
95	OUR FIRST HOME	95 DAYS	30.00	30.00
D. CASEY			**SILENT JOURNEY**	
95	JOURNEY OF THE WILD	95 DAYS	30.00	30.00
95	UNBRIDLED MAJESTY	95 DAYS	30.00	30.00
95	WHERE PATHS CROSS	95 DAYS	30.00	30.00
95	WHERE THE BUFFALO ROAM	95 DAYS	30.00	30.00
95	WISDOM SEEKER	95 DAYS	30.00	30.00
V. GADINO			**SILVER SCREEN MARILYN**	
97	EVERYTHING ABOUT IT IS APPEALING	*	30.00	30.00
98	LOOKING LIKE A MILLION	*	30.00	30.00
*			**SNOW WHITE**	
97	FOLLOW ME HERE	95 DAYS	40.00	40.00
97	HERE'S A LITTLE KISS	95 DAYS	40.00	40.00
97	HUMPH	95 DAYS	40.00	40.00
R. IVERSON			**SOFT ELEGANCE**	
94	PRISCILLA IN PEARLS	*	*	40.00
95	ALEXANDRA IN AMETHYSTS	95 DAYS	30.00	40.00
95	EMILY IN EMERALDS	95 DAYS	30.00	40.00
95	TABITHA ON TAFFETA	95 DAYS	30.00	40.00
N. GIORGIO			**SOLID GOLD ELVIS**	
97	HEARTBREAK HOTEL	*	33.00	33.00
98	HOUND DOG	*	33.00	33.00
J. TANTON			**SOME BEARY NICE PLACES**	
94	WELCOME TO THE LIBEARY	CL	30.00	40.00
95	BEARENIAL GARDEN	CL	33.00	40.00
95	WELCOME TO OUR MUSIC	CL	33.00	40.00
L. LEWIS			**SOMEONE IS WATCHING OVER ME**	
97	PROTECTED ALONG THE PATH	*	33.00	33.00
*			**SOMEONE TO WATCH OVER ME**	
93	GUIDING THE WAY	*	*	41.00
94	WELCOME TO OUR CONSERBEARTOR	*	*	41.00

YR	NAME	LIMIT	ISSUE	TREND
95	GUIDED JOURNEY	*	*	41.00
95	HELPING HAND ON HIGH	*	*	41.00
95	NURTURING INNOCENCE	*	*	41.00
95	PROTECTED SLEEP	*	*	41.00
95	SAFE AT PLAY	*	*	41.00
96	BY MY SIDE	*	30.00	40.00
96	FAITHFUL CARE	*		41.00
WEISMANN		**SOMEONE TO WATCH OVER ME**		
96	DIVINE COMFORT	*	*	41.00
96	PERPETUAL LOVE	*	*	41.00
L. BOGLE		**SOUL MATES**		
95	AWAKENING, THE	95 DAYS	30.00	40.00
95	EMBRACE	*	*	40.00
95	HEART'S DESIRE	*	*	41.00
95	LOVERS, THE	95 DAYS	30.00	40.00
95	WAKING DREAM	*	*	43.00
96	PERFECT HARMONY	OP	30.00	40.00
96	STIRRING, THE	OP	30.00	40.00
96	WARM INTERLUDE	OP	30.00	40.00
B. PARRISH		**SOUL OF THE WILDERNESS**		
95	CHANCE OF FLURRIES	*	*	45.00
95	ONE LAST LOOK	*	*	45.00
95	SILENT WATCH	*	*	45.00
96	WINTER SOLSTICE	*	35.00	45.00
96	WINTER WHITES	*	*	45.00
G. DIECKHONER		**SOVEREIGNS OF THE SKY**		
94	SPIRIT OF FREEDOM	CL	39.00	55.00
94	SPIRIT OF MAJESTY	CL	44.00	55.00
94	SPIRIT OF PRIDE	CL	39.00	55.00
94	SPIRIT OF VALOR	CL	44.00	55.00
95	SPIRIT OF BRAVERY	95 DAYS	49.00	68.00
95	SPIRIT OF COURAGE	95 DAYS	49.00	55.00
95	SPIRIT OF GLORY	95 DAYS	44.00	55.00
95	SPIRIT OF HONOR	95 DAYS	49.00	68.00
D. GRANT		**SOVEREIGNS OF THE WILD**		
93	FIRST OUTING	CL	30.00	41.00
93	SNOW QUEEN, THE	CL	30.00	40.00
94	AFRICAN EVENING	CL	30.00	40.00
94	COOL CATS	CL	30.00	40.00
94	LET US SURVIVE	CL	30.00	40.00
94	SIBERIAN SNOW TIGERS	CL	30.00	40.00
J. KRAMER COLE		**SPIRIT JOURNEYS**		
97	BRINGING THE SHIELD	*	30.00	30.00
97	JOURNEY OF RENEWAL	*	30.00	30.00
97	REVERENCE	*	30.00	30.00
J. KRAMER-COLE		**SPIRIT JOURNEYS**		
97	SPIRIT BROTHERS	*	30.00	30.00
98	REVERENCE	*	30.00	30.00
E. LEPAGE		**SPIRITS OF THE WILDERNESS**		
96	EBONY CHIEF	OP	35.00	35.00
D. GELSINGER		**STAR LIGHT, STAR BRIGHT**		
97	WISH UPON A STAR	*	30.00	30.00
*		**STAR TREK 30TH ANNIVERSARY**		
97	CHIEF SCIENCE OFFICER SPOCK	*	40.00	40.00
98	CHIEF ENGINEER SCOTT	*	40.00	40.00
98	DOCTOR LEONARD MCCOY	*	40.00	40.00
B. LANGTON		**STUDY OF A CHAMPION**		
95	DEVOTED PARTNER	*	*	43.00
95	LOYAL COMPANION	*	*	43.00
95	TRUSTED FRIEND	*	*	43.00
96	FAITHFUL BUDDY	OP	30.00	40.00
*		**SUGAR N SPICE**		
97	ALLSPICE	*	40.00	40.00
97	CINNAMON	*		N/A
D. HENDERSON		**SUMMER'S SWEET PURSUITS**		
97	EVENING'S TRANQUILITY	*	30.00	30.00
97	GARDEN HIDEAWAY	*	30.00	30.00
97	GARDEN LOFT	*	30.00	30.00
97	SUMMER'S REFLECTIONS	*	30.00	30.00
98	COZY COURTYARD	*	30.00	30.00
98	FRIENDLY VISITORS	*	30.00	30.00
T. SIZEMORE		**SUPERSTARS OF BASEBALL**		
94	WILLIE 'SAY HEY' MAYS	CL	30.00	40.00
95	BOB GIBSON	CL	30.00	40.00
95	CARL "YAZ" YASTRZEMSKI	CL	30.00	40.00
95	DON DRYSDALE	CL	35.00	46.00
95	FRANK "ROBBY" ROBINSON	CL	30.00	45.00
95	HARMON KILLEBREW	CL	33.00	46.00
N. GIORGIO		**SUPERSTARS OF COUNTRY MUSIC**		
93	BARBARA MANDRELL	CL	33.00	45.00
93	DOLLY PARTON: I WILL ALWAYS LOVE YOU	CL	30.00	45.00
93	GLEN CAMPBELL: RHINESTONE COWBOY	CL	33.00	45.00
93	KENNY ROGERS: SWEET MUSIC MAN	CL	30.00	40.00
R. AKERS		**TALE OF PETER RABBIT & BENJAMIN BUNNY**		
94	A POCKET FULL OF ONIONS	CL	39.00	50.00
94	BESIDE HIS COUSIN	CL	39.00	53.00

YR	NAME	LIMIT	ISSUE	TREND
94	ROUND THAT CORNER	CL	39.00	55.00
95	AMONGST THE FLOWERPOTS	95 DAYS	44.00	62.00
95	MR. MCGREGOR'S GARDEN	CL	44.00	55.00
95	ROSEMARY TEA AND LAVENDER	CL	44.00	63.00
95	SAFELY HOME	CL	44.00	60.00
96	UPON THE SCARECROW	95 DAYS	44.00	55.00
J. MONTI				**TEA FOR TWO**
96	SPRING ROSE TEAPOT	*	35.00	35.00
T. DUBOIS				**TEDDY BEAR FAIR**
94	BEAR HUGS AND HONEY PIES	*	*	32.00
A. ISAKOV				**THAT'S WHAT FRIENDS ARE FOR**
94	FRIENDS ARE COMFORT	CL	30.00	40.00
94	FRIENDS ARE FOREVER	CL	30.00	40.00
94	FRIENDS ARE LOVING	CL	30.00	40.00
95	FRIENDS ARE FUN	CL	30.00	40.00
T. KINKADE				**THOMAS KINKADE'S ENCHANTED COTTAGES**
97	ROSE GARDEN COTTAGE	95 DAYS	30.00	30.00
97	WEATHERVANE COTTAGE	95 DAYS	30.00	30.00
T. KINKADE				**THOMAS KINKADE'S GUIDING LIGHTS**
97	A LIGHT IN THE STORM	95 DAYS	30.00	30.00
97	BEACON OF HOPE	95 DAYS	30.00	30.00
97	THE LIGHT OF PEACE	*	30.00	30.00
98	CLEARING STORMS	*	30.00	30.00
T. KINKADE				**THOMAS KINKADE'S INSPIRATIONS**
98	IRISH BLESSING	*	30.00	30.00
98	ROAD NOT TAKEN, THE	*	30.00	30.00
T. KINKADE				**THOMAS KINKADE'S INSPIRATIONS OF HOPE**
97	SERENITY PRAYER	95 DAYS	30.00	30.00
T. KINKADE				**THOMAS KINKADE'S PEACEFUL RETREATS**
98	TWILIGHT COTTAGE	*	*	N/A
T. KINKADE				**THOMAS KINKADE'S ROMANTIC HIDEAWAYS**
97	BROOKSIDE HIDEAWAY	95 DAYS	35.00	35.00
97	LOCHAVEN COTTAGE	95 DAYS	35.00	35.00
97	MEADOWOOD COTTAGE	95 DAYS	35.00	35.00
97	STEPPING STONE COTTAGE	95 DAYS	35.00	35.00
T. KINKADE				**THOMAS KINKADE'S SCENES OF SERENITY**
97	ASHLEY'S COTTAGE	95 DAYS	30.00	30.00
97	COLLECTOR'S COTTAGE	95 DAYS	30.00	30.00
97	EMERALD ISLE COTTAGE	95 DAYS	30.00	30.00
97	HEATHER'S HUTCH	95 DAYS	30.00	30.00
97	HOPE'S COTTAGE	95 DAYS	30.00	30.00
97	LIGHTHOUSE COTTAGE	95 DAYS	30.00	30.00
97	MORNING GLORY COTTAGE	95 DAYS	30.00	30.00
97	RAINBOW'S END COTTAGE	95 DAYS	30.00	30.00
H. GARRIDO				**THOSE WHO GUIDE US**
95	ST. FRANCIS OF ASSISI	*	*	43.00
95	ST. JOSEPH	*	*	43.00
96	ST. ANTHONY	*	30.00	40.00
96	ST. JUDE	OP	30.00	40.00
K. NOLES				**THROUGH A CHILD'S EYES**
94	LITTLE BUTTERFLY	CL	30.00	40.00
94	TREETOP SCOUT	CL	30.00	42.00
95	LITTLE RED SQUIRREL	CL	33.00	46.00
95	PRAIRIE SONG	CL	33.00	50.00
95	TREETOP WONDER	CL	30.00	30.00
95	WATER LILY	CL	33.00	45.00
95	WOODLAND ROSE	CL	30.00	40.00
R. TAYLOR				**THUNDER IN THE SKY**
96	D-DAY, THE AIRBORN ASSAULT	*	*	43.00
96	MIGHTY 8TH, THE- COMING HOME	*	30.00	40.00
F. MILLER				**THUNDERING WATERS**
94	BRIDAL VEIL FALLS	CL	35.00	42.00
94	NIAGARA FALLS	CL	35.00	40.00
95	HAVASU FALLS	CL	30.00	40.00
95	LOWER FALLS, YELLOWSTONE	CL	35.00	40.00
J. TSCHELTER				**TIMBERLAND CHORUS**
97	HEAR THE ANCIENT VOICES	*	40.00	40.00
97	HUNTERS PROUD AND FREE	*	40.00	40.00
97	JOIN THE HOWLING CHORUS	*	40.00	40.00
97	MASTERS OF THE MOONLIGHT	*	40.00	40.00
L. DANIELS				**TIMBERLAND SECRETS**
95	GENTLE AWAKENING	*	*	43.00
95	GOOD DAY TO PLAY	*	*	43.00
95	SWEET DREAMS	*	*	43.00
96	A MOMENT'S PAUSE	OP	30.00	40.00
96	TRANQUIL RETREAT	*	*	43.00
96	WINTRY WATCH	OP	30.00	40.00
KOLLER				**TO MOM WITH LOVE**
95	CASCADING INSPIRATION	*	*	43.00
KOLLER				**TO SOAR WITH EAGLES**
95	THROUGH THE CRYSTAL MIST	*	*	43.00
P.C. WEIRS				**TO SOAR WITH EAGLES**
96	ABOVE THE TURBULENT TIDE	*	33.00	40.00
96	SOARING TO GREATER HEIGHTS	*	*	45.00
J.K. COLE				**TOUCHING THE SPIRIT**
93	RUNNING WITH THE WIND	CL	30.00	35.00

YR	NAME	LIMIT	ISSUE	TREND
*				
			TOY STORY	
96	FRIENDS AT LAST	*	35.00	45.00
97	FEELIN' SHEEPISH	95 DAYS	35.00	35.00
97	TO INFINITY AND BEYOND	95 DAYS	35.00	35.00
97	WOODY BREAKS THE NEWS	95 DAYS	35.00	35.00
SIEVE				
			TRAIL OF THE WHITETAIL	
95	HOMEWARD BOUND	*	*	45.00
96	AFTER THE STORM	*	*	45.00
96	FAST BREAK	*	*	45.00
96	MAPLE RUSH	*	*	45.00
96	SECOND SEASON	*	*	45.00
K. RANDLE				
			TRAINS OF THE GREAT WEST	
93	EARLY MORNING ARRIVAL	CL	30.00	30.00
93	MOONLIT JOURNEY	CL	30.00	40.00
93	MOUNTAIN HIDEAWAY	CL	30.00	40.00
93	SNOWY PASS, THE	CL	30.00	40.00
J. GIBSON				
			TRANQUIL RETREATS	
96	DAY'S END	*	*	45.00
96	DAYBREAK	*	*	45.00
97	DUSK'S SERENITY	*	30.00	30.00
FERRIS				
			TREASURED DUCKS OF CANADA	
93	DAWN LIGHT: PINTAIL	*	*	43.00
93	EARLY SPRING: HOODED MERGANZER	*	*	45.00
93	GENTLE REFLECTIONS: GREENTEAL	*	*	43.00
93	QUIET WATERS: MALLARD	*	*	43.00
*				
			TREASURES FROM VATICAN	
96	BIRTH OF CHRIST	*	*	41.00
E. LEPAGE				
			TREASURES OF OUR NATION	
96	WEST COAST TREASURES	*	*	40.00
I. MAKAROVA				
		TREASURES OF RUSSIAN TRADITION		
96	COLBALT MAJESTY	*	*	45.00
96	GOLDEN PEARLESCENCE	*	*	40.00
96	LAPIS RADIANCE	*	*	42.00
96	SAPPHIRE SPLENDOUR	*	*	42.00
*				
			TRIBUTE TO DIANA	
98	DIANA-ENGLAND'S ROSE	*	40.00	40.00
B. EMMETT				
			TRIBUTE TO SELENA	
96	SELENA FOREVER	*	*	40.00
DODGE				
			TRIBUTE TO THE ARMED FORCES	
95	PROUD TO SERVE	*	*	40.00
J. WALKER				
			TRIPLE CROWN CHAMPIONS	
97	LOU GEHRIG: 1934	*	35.00	35.00
J. WALKER				
			TRIPLE CROWN WINNERS	
97	MICKEY MANTLE: 1956	*	35.00	35.00
H. KREBS				
			TRIUMPH IN THE AIR	
94	CHECKMATE	95 DAYS	35.00	40.00
94	HUNTING FEVER	95 DAYS	35.00	40.00
94	ONE HECK OF A DEFLECTION SHOT	95 DAYS	35.00	40.00
95	STRUCK BY A THUNDERBOLT	95 DAYS	35.00	40.00
J. BARNES				
			TWILIGHT MEMORIES	
95	HOLIDAY HOMECOMING	*	*	43.00
95	WINTER'S TWILIGHT	95 DAYS	30.00	40.00
S. EIDE				
			TWO'S COMPANY	
95	BROTHERLY LOVE	95 DAYS	30.00	30.00
95	GOLDEN HARVEST	CL	30.00	30.00
95	SEEING DOUBLE	95 DAYS	30.00	30.00
95	SPRING SPANIELS	95 DAYS	30.00	30.00
K. MCELROY				
			UNBRIDLED MYSTERY	
95	MIDNIGHT MAJESTY	*	*	40.00
95	SHADOW DANCER	*	*	40.00
96	DARK SPLENDOR	OP	30.00	40.00
C. SAMS				
			UNDER A SNOWY VEIL	
95	FIRST SNOW	95 DAYS	30.00	40.00
95	SNOW MATES	95 DAYS	30.00	40.00
95	WINTER'S DAWN	95 DAYS	30.00	40.00
95	WINTER'S WARMTH	95 DAYS	30.00	40.00
D. MCCAFFREY				
			UNDER MOTHER'S WING	
95	ECHOES ALONG THE RIVER	*	*	40.00
95	MONARCH'S LIGHT	*	*	40.00
95	RUNNING WITH THE LIGHT	*	*	40.00
D. MCCAFFREY				
			UNDER THE NORTHERN LIGHTS	
96	CATCHING THE ELUSIVE LIGHT	*	30.00	40.00
P. WEIRS				
			UNEXPECTED GUESTS	
98	DO NOT DISTURB	*	40.00	40.00
P. WEIRS				
			UNTAMED SPIRITS	
93	WILD HEARTS	CL	30.00	33.00
94	BREAKAWAY	CL	30.00	30.00
94	DISTANT THUNDER	CL	30.00	30.00
94	FOREVER FREE	CL	30.00	30.00
P. WEIRS				
			UNTAMED WILDERNESS	
95	LONESOME BULL	*	*	43.00
95	PAUSE FROM THE JOURNEY	*	*	43.00
95	UNEXPECTED ENCOUNTER	95 DAYS	30.00	40.00
95	WHITETAIL CROSSING	*	*	43.00

YR	NAME	LIMIT	ISSUE	TREND
96	FLEETING SPLENDOR	OP	30.00	40.00
96	SILENT BEAUTY	*	*	43.00
G. DIECKHONER			**VANISHING PARADISES**	
93	AN AFRICAN SAFARI	CL	30.00	40.00
93	PANDA'S WORLD, THE	CL	30.00	40.00
93	RAINFOREST, THE	CL	30.00	40.00
93	SPLENDORS OF INDIA	CL	30.00	40.00
HUNT			**VICTORIAN GARDEN JEWELS**	
95	PRIMROSE PATCH/ROSE ARBOUR	*	*	40.00
C. LASSEN			**VISIONS BENEATH THE SEA**	
96	DIAMOND HEAD DAWN	*	*	42.00
96	MAUI WHALE SONG	*	*	42.00
96	MIRACLE IN LIFE	*	*	45.00
96	MOTHER'S LOVE	*	*	45.00
D. CASEY			**VISIONS FROM EAGLE RIDGE**	
95	ASSEMBLY OF PRIDE	95 DAYS	30.00	40.00
96	LEGACY OF LIBERTY	*	30.00	40.00
G. OLSEN			**VISIONS OF FAITH**	
98	BE NOT AFRAID	*	35.00	35.00
98	GOOD SHEPHERD, THE	*	35.00	35.00
98	LIGHT OF THE WORLD	*	35.00	35.00
98	LOST NO MORE	*	35.00	35.00
D. COOK			**VISIONS OF GLORY**	
95	FREEING OF PARIS	CL	30.00	42.00
95	IWO JIMA	CL	30.00	40.00
*			**VISIONS OF OUR BLESSED MOTHER**	
97	OUR LADY OF CHARITY	*	45.00	45.00
97	OUR LADY OF DEVOTION	*	45.00	45.00
97	OUR LADY OF GRACE	*	45.00	45.00
98	OUR LADY OF MIRACLES	*	45.00	45.00
98	OUR LADY OF SALVATION	*	45.00	45.00
H. GARRIDO			**VISIONS OF OUR LADY**	
94	OUR LADY OF FATIMA	95 DAYS	30.00	42.00
94	OUR LADY OF GRACE	CL	30.00	40.00
94	OUR LADY OF GUADALUPE	95 DAYS	30.00	42.00
94	OUR LADY OF LA SALETTE	*	*	42.00
94	OUR LADY OF LOURDES	CL	30.00	40.00
94	OUR LADY OF MEDJUGORJE	CL	30.00	40.00
94	OUR LADY OF MT. CARMEL	95 DAYS	30.00	42.00
94	OUR LADY OF SILENCE	*	*	42.00
95	OUR LADY OF HOPE	*	*	42.00
95	OUR LADY OF SNOW	*	*	42.00
95	VIRGIN OF THE POOR	*	*	42.00
95	VIRGIN WITH THE GOLDEN HEART	*	*	42.00
C. NICK			**VISIONS OF OUR LORD**	
98	LIGHT OF LIFE		30.00	30.00
L. MEDARIS			**VISIONS OF THE SACRED**	
94	SNOW RIDER	CL	30.00	40.00
D. STANLEY			**VISIONS OF THE SACRED**	
94	CHEYENNE PROPHET	95 DAYS	33.00	46.00
94	SPRING'S MESSENGER	95 DAYS	30.00	42.00
95	BUFFALO CALLER	95 DAYS	33.00	45.00
95	CELEBRATION OF SPIRIT	*	*	51.00
95	COUNCIL OF ANIMALS	*	*	51.00
95	JOURNEY OF HARMONY	95 DAYS	33.00	45.00
95	THUNDERBIRD	*	*	51.00
96	APACHE WAR WOMAN	*	*	55.00
96	GATHERER, THE	OP	37.00	55.00
D. STANLEY			**VISIONS OF THE WEST**	
95	HEALER	*	*	55.00
C. JACKSON			**VISIT FROM ST. NICK**	
95	BUNDLE OF TOYS	CL	54.00	62.00
95	HAPPY CHRISTMAS TO ALL	95 DAYS	59.00	66.00
95	STOCKINGS WERE FILLED	CL	54.00	62.00
95	TWAS THE NIGHT BEFORE CHRISTMAS	CL	49.00	55.00
95	UP TO THE HOUSETOP	CL	49.00	55.00
95	VISIONS OF SUGARPLUMS	95 DAYS	54.00	62.00
95	WINK IN HIS EYE	95 DAYS	59.00	66.00
96	TO MY WONDERING EYES	95 DAYS	59.00	65.00
J. BARKLEM			**VISIT TO BRAMBLEY HEDGE**	
94	AUTUMN STORY	CL	40.00	46.00
94	SPRING STORY	CL	40.00	47.00
94	SUMMER STORY	CL	40.00	45.00
94	WINTER STORY	CL	40.00	46.00
M.A. LASHER			**WARM COUNTRY MOMENTS**	
94	ANNEBELL'S SIMPLE PLEASURE	95 DAYS	30.00	40.00
94	CHARLOTTE'S SUMMER HARVEST	*	*	53.00
94	EMILY AND ALICE IN A JAM	95 DAYS	30.00	46.00
94	HARRIET'S LOVING TOUCH	95 DAYS	30.00	46.00
94	MABEL'S SUNNY RETREAT	CL	30.00	40.00
95	HANNA'S SECRET GARDEN	95 DAYS	30.00	45.00
95	HENRIETTA'S FLORAL FANTASY	*	*	53.00
95	SOPHIE & PEARL'S GARDEN	*	*	53.00
LOQUE			**WARMTH OF HOME AT CRISTMAS**	
95	WARM WINTER'S EVE	*	*	43.00

YR	NAME	LIMIT	ISSUE	TREND
	G. KURZ		**WELCOME HOME**	
98	CHERISH YOUR FAMILY	*	30.00	30.00
	B. MOCK		**WELCOME TO THE NEIGHBORHOOD**	
94	DAFFODIL DRIVE	CL	30.00	43.00
94	IVY LANE	CL	30.00	43.00
95	LILAC LANE	CL	35.00	40.00
95	TULIP TERRACE	CL	35.00	40.00
	J. BARNES		**WHEN ALL HEARTS COME HOME**	
93	CHRISTMAS WISH	CL	30.00	45.00
93	COMFORT AND JOY	CL	30.00	40.00
93	GRANDPA'S FARM	CL	30.00	40.00
93	NIGHT BEFORE CHRISTMAS	CL	30.00	40.00
93	NIGHT DEPARTURE	CL	30.00	40.00
93	OH CHRISTMAS TREE	CL	30.00	40.00
93	PEACE ON EARTH	CL	30.00	40.00
93	SUPPER AND SMALL TALK	CL	30.00	40.00
	R. MCGINNIS		**WHEN DREAMS BLOSSOM**	
94	DREAMS OF POETRY	95 DAYS	33.00	46.00
94	DREAMS TO GATHER	CL	30.00	42.00
94	SWEETEST OF DREAMS	95 DAYS	33.00	46.00
94	WHERE FRIENDS DREAM	95 DAYS	33.00	43.00
95	A PLACE TO DREAM	95 DAYS	33.00	45.00
95	DREAMING OF YOU	95 DAYS	33.00	45.00
	C. NICK		**WHEN I GROW UP**	
94	ON THE COUNT OF THREE	*	*	45.00
	TIRITILLI		**WHEN STORIES COME ALIVE**	
94	AT THE ROUND-UP	*	*	44.00
	F. MITTELSTADT		**WHERE EAGLES SOAR**	
94	ALLEGIANCE WITH THE WIND	CL	30.00	44.00
94	ON FREEDOM'S WING	CL	30.00	44.00
95	LAKESIDE EAGLES	95 DAYS	30.00	30.00
95	LIGHTHOUSE EAGLES	95 DAYS	30.00	30.00
95	NOBLE LEGACY	CL	30.00	40.00
95	PRIDE OF THE SKY	CL	30.00	44.00
95	PRISTINE DOMAIN	CL	30.00	44.00
95	ROYAL ASCENT	95 DAYS	30.00	44.00
95	SPLENDOR IN FLIGHT	95 DAYS	30.00	44.00
95	WINDWARD MAJESTY	CL	30.00	44.00
	D. CASEY		**WHERE PATHS JOIN**	
97	SHARED WORLDS	*	30.00	30.00
98	MESSENGERS, THE	*	30.00	30.00
98	PROTECTORS, THE	*	30.00	30.00
98	WATCHFUL EYES	*	30.00	30.00
	D. CASEY		**WHERE PATHS MEET**	
96	NATIVE HARMONY	*	*	46.00
97	AMONGST FRIENDS	*	30.00	30.00
	J. GRENDE		**WHISPERING WINGS**	
96	MORNING GLORY	*	*	46.00
96	PERFECT HARMONY	*	*	46.00
	K. O'MALLEY		**WHISPERS ON THE WIND**	
95	ANNA'S HUMMINGBIRD	*	*	53.00
95	RUBY THROATED HUMMINGBIRD	*	*	53.00
96	ALLEN'S HUMMINGBIRD	*	45.00	50.00
96	RUFOUS WITH FOXGLOVES	*	*	53.00
	L. CABLE		**WILD BUNCH**	
97	WAKE-UP CALL	*	30.00	30.00
98	KING OF THE HILL	*	30.00	30.00
98	ROUGH HOUSE	*	30.00	30.00
98	STICKING TOGETHER	*	30.00	30.00
	K. KAYOMI		**WILD HEARTS**	
97	EYES FOR YOU	*	35.00	35.00
97	TENDER PAUSE	*	35.00	35.00
98	LAP OF LUXURY	*	35.00	35.00
98	WALKING ON AIR	*	35.00	35.00
	F. MITTLESTADT		**WILD PAGEANTRY**	
95	FLIGHT OF PHEASANT	*	*	53.00
95	THUNDERING WINGS: RUFF GROUSE	*	*	53.00
	R. MCGINNIS		**WILDFLOWER LEGACY**	
95	NATURE'S SPLENDOUR	*	*	43.00
	K. DANIEL		**WINDOWS ON A WORLD OF SONG**	
93	BEDROOM, THE: BLUEBIRDS	CL	35.00	42.00
93	DEN, THE: BLACK-CAPPED CHICKADEES	CL	35.00	42.00
93	LIBRARY, THE: CARDINALS	CL	35.00	40.00
94	KITCHEN, THE: GOLDFINCHES	CL	35.00	40.00
	D. CASEY		**WINDOWS TO THE SOUL**	
97	EYES OF THE FOREST	*	30.00	30.00
97	MOONLIT PHANTOM	*	30.00	30.00
97	TOGETHER IN SPIRIT	*	30.00	30.00
	F. MITTLESTADT		**WINGS OF GLORY**	
95	PORTRAIT OF LIBERTY	CL	33.00	43.00
96	PARAGON OF COURAGE	CL	33.00	43.00
	J. SPURLOCK		**WINGS OF GLORY**	
94	PRIDE OF AMERICA	CL	33.00	43.00
95	SPIRIT OF FREEDOM	CL	33.00	43.00
	G. BEECHAM		**WINGS OF THE TOTEM**	
94	EAGLE: SYMBOL OF POWER	*	*	43.00

YR	NAME	LIMIT	ISSUE	TREND
	C. JACKSON		**WINNIE THE POOH & FRIENDS**	
94	TIME FOR A LITTLE SOMETHING	CL	40.00	60.00
95	BOUNCING'S WHAT TIGGERS DO BEST	CL	40.00	65.00
95	YOU'RE A REAL FRIEND	95 DAYS	45.00	60.00
96	RUMBLY IN MY TUMBLY	95 DAYS	45.00	45.00
97	A FINE DAY TO BUZZ WITH THE BEES	95 DAYS	50.00	50.00
97	DO YOU THINK IT'S A WOOZLE?	95 DAYS	50.00	50.00
97	MANY HAPPY RETURNS OF THE DAY	95 DAYS	50.00	50.00
97	NOBODY CAN BE UNCHEERED WITH A BALLOON	95 DAYS	50.00	50.00
97	PLAYING POOHSTICKS	95 DAYS	50.00	50.00
97	T IS FOR TIGGER	95 DAYS	50.00	50.00
97	THREE CHEERS FOR POOH	95 DAYS	50.00	50.00
*			**WINNIE THE POOH STORYBOOK COLLECTION**	
98	BOUNCY FUN-FUN-FUN	*	40.00	40.00
98	TOO MUCH HONEY	*	40.00	40.00
	C. JACKSON		**WINNIE THE POOH: 3D**	
95	BOUNCING IS WHAT TIGGERS DO BEST	CL	40.00	40.00
*			**WINNIE THE POOH: A HONEY OF A FRIEND**	
97	FRIENDSHIP IS AS SWEET AS HONEY			N/A
98	LITTLE FIXING IS REQUIRED, A	*	30.00	30.00
98	WELCOME LITTLE FRIENDS	*	30.00	30.00
	S. KOZAR		**WINTER EVENING REFLECTIONS**	
96	AS TWILIGHT FALLS	*	40.00	45.00
96	DAY FADES TO MEMORY	*	*	45.00
96	DOWN BY THE STREAM	*	*	45.00
96	SHADOWS GROW LONGER	*	*	45.00
	S. TIMM		**WINTER GARLANDS**	
96	CRISP MORNING CALL	*	*	40.00
96	FROSTY SEASON	*	*	40.00
96	JEWELS IN THE SNOW	OP	35.00	40.00
	T. ISAAC		**WINTER GUARDIANS: A MASTER COLLECTION**	
97	TRACKING THE EDGE	*	30.00	30.00
	D. SMITH		**WINTER GUARDIANS: A MASTER COLLECTION**	
97	EVENING QUEST	*	30.00	30.00
	P. WEIRS		**WINTER RETREAT**	
96	WHITETAILS PAUSE	*	*	40.00
	N. GLAZIER		**WINTER SHADOWS**	
95	CANYON MOON	95 DAYS	30.00	40.00
95	SHADES OF GRAY	95 DAYS	30.00	40.00
	P. WEIRS		**WINTER SHADOWS**	
95	BROKEN WATCH	*	*	40.00
95	DECEMBER WATCH	*	*	40.00
95	MOONLIGHT SHADOWS	*	*	40.00
95	TRACKERS	*	*	40.00
95	VIGILANT COMPANIONS	*	*	40.00
96	ICY SHADOWS	OP	30.00	40.00
	T. KINKADE		**WISH YOU WERE HERE**	
93	END OF A PERFECT DAY	95 DAYS	30.00	43.00
94	AFTERNOON ON FOREST LAKE	95 DAYS	*	45.00
94	QUIET EVENING/RIVERLODGE	95 DAYS	30.00	40.00
94	SOFT MORNING LIGHT	95 DAYS	30.00	45.00
95	SIMPLER TIMES	95 DAYS	*	50.00
97	EVENING IN THE FOREST	95 DAYS	33.00	33.00
	SOLBERG		**WITH WATCHFUL EYES**	
94	WINTER WHITE	*	*	40.00
	L. DANIELS		**WOLF PUPS: YOUNG FACES OF THE WILDERNESS**	
95	MORNING INNOCENTS	*	*	42.00
95	NEW ADVENTURE	*	*	42.00
95	TOMORROW'S PRIDE	*	*	42.00
96	CALL TO THE FUTURE	OP	30.00	40.00
96	EARLY ASPIRATIONS	*	*	42.00
96	ONE TO ONE	*	*	42.00
96	ROSY BEGINNINGS	*	*	42.00
	G. ALEXANDER		**WOODLAND TRANQUILITY**	
94	WINTER'S CALM	CL	30.00	40.00
95	BROKEN SILENCE	*	*	40.00
95	CROSSING BOUNDARIES	95 DAYS	30.00	40.00
95	FROSTY MORN	95 DAYS	30.00	40.00
95	SNOWY VEIL	*	*	46.00
96	RIVER REFLECTIONS	*	*	52.00
96	SUNSET AT CORNUCOPIA	OP	35.00	50.00
96	TWILIGHT APPROACH	*	*	52.00
	J. HANSEL		**WOODLAND WINGS**	
94	GLIDING ON GILDED SKIES	CL	35.00	43.00
94	SUNSET VOYAGE	CL	35.00	46.00
94	TWILIGHT FLIGHT	CL	35.00	40.00
95	PEACEFUL JOURNEY	CL	35.00	40.00
	D. TERBUSH		**WORLD BENEATH THE WAVES**	
94	ALL GOD'S CHILDREN	95 DAYS	30.00	38.00
94	CIRCLE OF LIGHT	*	*	38.00
94	SEA OF LIGHT	95 DAYS	30.00	38.00
95	FOLLOW YOUR HEART	*	*	38.00
95	HUMPBACK WHALES	95 DAYS	30.00	30.00
95	LONG BEFORE MAN	*	*	38.00
95	REACH FOR YOUR DREAMS	*	*	38.00

YR	NAME	LIMIT	ISSUE	TREND
95	SHARE THE LOVE	*	*	38.00
96	ALL THE MIRACLES TO SEA	OP	30.00	40.00
J. HANSEL			**WORLD OF THE EAGLE**	
93	SILENT GUARD	CL	30.00	39.00
94	NIGHT FLYER	CL	33.00	44.00
94	SENTINEL OF THE NIGHT	CL	30.00	40.00
95	MIDNIGHT DUTY	CL	33.00	40.00
T. CLAUSNITZER			**WORLD OF WILDLIFE**	
95	A DELICATE BALANCE	95 DAYS	30.00	30.00
95	AFRICA: EXQUISITE TRANQUILITY	*	*	40.00
95	EUROPE: IN NATURAL HARMONY	*	*	40.00
95	NORTH AMERICA: A DELICATE BALANCE	*	*	40.00
96	SOUTH AMERICA: EXOTIC KINGDOM	*	*	40.00
KOLLER			**WORLD RECORD HOLDERS**	
95	JORDAN BUCK	*	*	38.00
*			**WORLD WAR II: 50TH ANNIVERSARY**	
94	1941: A WORLD AT WAR	*	*	38.00
94	1941: TAKING A STAND	*	*	38.00
J. GRIFFIN			**WORLD WAR II: A REMEMBRANCE**	
94	BATTLE OF MIDWAY	95 DAYS	30.00	40.00
94	BATTLE OF THE BULGE	95 DAYS	33.00	43.00
94	D-DAY	CL	30.00	40.00
95	BATTLE OF THE PHILIPPINES	95 DAYS	33.00	45.00
95	DOOLITTLE'S RAID OVER TOKYO	95 DAYS	33.00	45.00
95	LIBERATION OF FRANCE	95 DAYS	*	43.00
C. WYSOCKI			**WYSOCKI CHRISTMAS MEMORIES**	
98	SMALL TOWN CHRISTMAS	*	45.00	45.00
C. WYSOCKI			**WYSOCKI COUNTRY CORNERS**	
98	GRAIN, FEED & SEED	*	35.00	35.00
98	IGGIE'S EXTRACTS	*	35.00	35.00
98	OLD TIMES ANTIQUE SHOP	*	35.00	35.00
98	PETER'S GROCERY	*	35.00	35.00
98	SHAVERS & HAIRCUTS	*	35.00	35.00
98	TICK-TOCK CLOCK SHOP	*	35.00	35.00
C. WYSOCKI			**WYSOCKI'S FOLKTOWN**	
96	BIRDIE'S PERCH COFFEE SHOP	*	*	53.00
96	CHIPS AND FELTS	*	*	53.00
96	QUILT LADIES SOCIAL CLUB	*	*	53.00
96	STOOL PIGEON GOSSIP SHOP	*	*	53.00
96	SWEET SHOP	*	*	53.00
96	TOWN FLORIST	*	*	53.00

BRIERCROFT

D. WINDBERG			**AMERICAN SNOWSCAPE**	
95	JOYOUS EVENSONG	1500	65.00	65.00

BYLINY'S PORCELAIN

ROGATOV			**FLIGHTS OF FANCY**	
91	ENCHANTMENT	*	*	42.00
91	FANTASIE (ROGATOV)	*	*	45.00
91	RHAPSODY	*	*	41.00
91	SPLENDOUR	*	*	45.00
92	REVERIE	*	*	45.00
U.L. DUBOVIKOV			**JEWELS OF THE GOLDEN RING**	
91	BORIS AND GLEB MONASTERY	*	*	45.00
91	NIKITSKY MONASTERY	*	*	45.00
91	ROSTOV THE GREAT	*	*	45.00
91	ST. BASIL'S, MOSCOW	195 DAYS	30.00	46.00
91	TRINITY MONASTERY, ZAGORSK	*	*	41.00
91	YAROSLAVI KREMLIN	*	*	50.00
92	GOLDEN GATES OF VLADIMIR	*	*	50.00
92	SUZOAL, PEARL OF GOLDEN RING	*	*	50.00
NAZARUK			**LEGEND OF SCARLET FLOWER**	
91	ENCHANTED GARDEN	*	*	46.00
92	MAGIC RING	*	*	45.00
92	MERCHANT'S FARWELL	*	*	49.00
92	SCARLET FLOWER	*	*	49.00
92	SPIRIT OF LOVE	*	*	61.00
92	VOICE OF KINDNESS	*	*	52.00
ZHIRYAKOVA			**LEGEND OF THE TSAR SALTAN**	
91	ARRIVAL OF TSAR SALTAN	*	*	49.00
91	MAGIC LAND OF PRINCE GUIDON	*	*	49.00
91	MAGIC SQUIRREL	*	*	48.00
91	SWAN PRINCESS	*	*	48.00
DEVYATKIN			**RUSSIAN FAIRY PRINCESSES**	
92	LUDMILLA	*	*	50.00
92	SLEEPING BEAUTY	*	*	50.00
92	SNOWMAIDEN	*	*	50.00
92	VASILISA THE BEAUTIFUL	*	*	51.00
DEVYATKIN			**RUSSIAN SEASONS**	
92	AUTUMN FANTASIE	*	*	50.00
92	SPRINGTIME REJOICE	*	*	50.00
92	SPRINGTIME SPLENDOR	*	*	46.00
92	SUMMERTIME SERENADE	*	*	47.00
92	WINTER IDYLL	*	*	47.00
92	WINTER MAJESTY	*	*	43.00

YR	NAME	LIMIT	ISSUE	TREND
93	AUTUMN MEDLEY	*	*	50.00
93	SUMMERTIME BOUNTY	*	*	50.00
AN			**TALE OF FATHER FROST**	
92	CIRCLE DANCE	*	*	51.00
92	FOR ALL BOYS AND GIRLS	*	*	50.00
92	ON THIS COLD WINTERY NIGHT	*	*	53.00
92	SNOWY PLAYLAND	*	*	52.00
92	TREE TRIMMING TIME	*	*	50.00
LEONOVA			**VILLAGE LIFE OF RUSSIA**	
90	BRINGING HOME THE HARVEST	*	*	51.00
90	CELEBRATION OF FRIENDSHIP	*	*	51.00
90	WINTER SLEIGH RIDE	*	*	51.00
91	COUNTRY PEDDLAR	*	*	51.00
91	MERRY MUSICIANS	*	*	51.00
91	TO THE SPRING FESTIVAL	*	*	51.00
91	VILLAGE COBBLER	*	*	51.00
91	VILLAGE WEDDING	*	*	51.00

C.U.I./CAROLINA COLLECTION

YR	NAME	LIMIT	ISSUE	TREND
*			**CHRISTMAS**	
91	CHECKIN' IT TWICE FIRST ED.	RT	40.00	40.00
G. GEIVETTE			**CLASSIC CAR**	
92	CHEVY 1957	RT	40.00	45.00
*			**COORS FACTORY**	
92	COORS FACTORY FIRST ED.	CL	30.00	30.00
93	COORS FACTORY SECOND ED.	CL	30.00	30.00
T. STORTZ			**COORS WINTERFEST**	
92	SKATING PARTY	RT	30.00	30.00
G. GEIVETTE			**CORVETTE**	
92	CORVETTE 1953	CL	40.00	45.00
C.L. BRAGG			**ENVIRONMENTAL**	
91	REINFOREST MAGIC FIRST ED.	RT	40.00	40.00
M. HOFFMAN			**ENVIRONMENTAL**	
92	FIRST BREATH	RT	40.00	40.00
R. CRUWYS			**FIRST ENCOUNTER**	
93	STAND OFF	CL	30.00	30.00
94	CLASS CLOWN	CL	30.00	30.00
*			**GIRL IN THE MOON**	
91	MILLER GIRL IN THE MOON FIRST ED.	9950	40.00	40.00
J. KILLEN			**GREAT AMERICAN SPORTING DOGS**	
92	BLACK LAB FIRST ED.	20000	40.00	45.00
93	BRITTANY SPANIEL SIXTH ED.	CL	40.00	45.00
93	ENGLISH SETTER FIFTH ED.	CL	40.00	45.00
93	GOLDEN RETRIEVER SECOND ED.	CL	40.00	45.00
93	SPRINGER SPANIEL THIRD ED.	CL	40.00	45.00
93	YELLOW LABRADOR FOURTH ED.	CL	40.00	45.00
P. KETHLEY			**NATIVE AMERICAN**	
91	HUNT FOR THE BUFFALO FIRST ED.	RT	40.00	40.00

CAVANAGH GROUP

YR	NAME	LIMIT	ISSUE	TREND
*			**COCA-COLA BRAND HERITAGE COLLECTION**	
94	SANTA AT HIS DESK	5000	60.00	65.00
95	HILDA CLARK WITH ROSES	5000	60.00	65.00
N. ROCKWELL			**COCA-COLA BRAND HERITAGE COLLECTION**	
95	BOY FISHING	5000	60.00	60.00
H. SUNDBLOM			**COCA-COLA BRAND HERITAGE COLLECTION**	
96	TRAVEL REFRESHED	OP	60.00	60.00
H. SUNDBLOM			**COCA-COLA SANTA**	
95	GOOD BOYS AND GIRLS	CL	60.00	60.00

CLARISSA'S CREATIONS

YR	NAME	LIMIT	ISSUE	TREND
C. JOHNSON				
90	LITTLE BALLERINA	14 DAYS	48.00	55.00
94	MEMORIES	25000	48.00	50.00

CRESTLEY COLLECTION

YR	NAME	LIMIT	ISSUE	TREND
GUISEWITE			**A TRIBUTE TO ROY ROGERS**	
94	HOME ON THE RANGE	*	*	30.00
S. WOODS			**BACKYARD BUDDIES**	
94	APRIL OUTING	*	*	30.00
94	DECEMBER CUDDLE	*	*	30.00
94	JULY JUBILEE	*	*	30.00
94	JUNE DELIGHT	*	*	30.00
94	MAY DAY	*	*	30.00
94	OCTOBER HARVEST	*	20.00	30.00
95	JANUARY JINGLE	*	*	30.00
S. WHEELER			**CHRISTMAS/PRIMROSE HILL**	
94	BE IT EVER SO HUMBLE	*	20.00	30.00
A. CASAY			**CORAL KINGDOMS**	
94	AFTERNOON FROLIC	*	*	30.00
94	DAYBREAK DELIGHT	*	*	30.00
94	MOONLIGHT DISCOVERY	*	*	30.00
94	MORNING ENCHANTMENT	*	*	30.00
94	SUNSET SERENADE	*	*	30.00
94	TWILIGHT WONDER	*	*	30.00

YR	NAME	LIMIT	ISSUE	TREND
WHITTEN			**FRIENDS FOREVER**	
94	BUDDING FRIENDSHIP	*	*	30.00
94	CUDDLE UP	*	*	30.00
94	DRINKIN BUDDIES	*	*	30.00
94	PUPPY LOVE	*	*	30.00
94	SHARING THE WONDER	*	*	30.00
94	TIGHT-KNIT FRIENDS	*	*	30.00
T. CATHEY			**HEAVENLY HEARTS**	
94	FAITH AND CHARITY	*	*	29.00
94	GOODNESS AND HOPE	*	*	31.00
94	JOY	*	*	30.00
94	LIBERTY AND PEACE	*	*	30.00
94	PATIENCE	*	*	29.00
94	PRUDENCE	*	20.00	30.00
94	SWEETNESS AND GRACE	*	*	30.00
95	INSPIRATION	*	*	31.00
LAKOFKA			**NATIVE BEAUTY**	
94	DANCE IN THE SUN	*	*	32.00
LAKOFKA			**NATIVE SKY**	
94	ONE WITH THE SKY	*	*	31.00
94	SPIRIT OF THE FULL MOON	*	*	31.00
94	WHEN LIGHTNING CASTS SHADOWS	*	*	30.00
*			**PICTURE PURRFECT CATS**	
94	EVERYONE NEEDS A TEDDY	*	20.00	30.00
94	FLUFF AND FLOWERS	*	*	33.00
94	PEEK-A-BOO KITTY	*	*	33.00
94	PERFECTLY POISED	*	*	33.00
94	TEATIME TABBY	*	*	33.00
95	IN THE PINK	*	*	33.00
95	KITTEN ON THE KEYS	OP	20.00	20.00
JAXON			**PRAYERS TO THE GREAT SPIRIT**	
94	PRAYER TO THE DAWN	*	20.00	30.00
94	PRAYER TO THE FOREFATHERS	*	20.00	30.00
S. WHEELER			**PRIMROSE HILL**	
93	LOVE'S A GIFT FROM THE HEART	*	20.00	34.00
94	GOD BLESS OUR HOME	*	20.00	33.00
94	HOME IS WHERE THE HEART IS	*	20.00	33.00
94	LET HEAVEN AND NATURE SING	*	20.00	33.00
94	SENDING SMILES ACROSS MILES	*	20.00	33.00
S. EVANS			**PROFILES OF BRAVERY**	
93	BOLD AND THE FREE	*	*	32.00
93	NOBLE AND THE PROUD	*	*	33.00
94	FIERCE & THE MIGHTY, THE	*	20.00	22.00
94	STRONG AND THE BRAVE	*	*	33.00
94	WILD AND THE WISE	*	*	32.00
T. DUBOIS			**TEDDY BEAR FAIR**	
94	AND AWAY WE GO	*	*	32.00
94	HERE WE GO 'ROUND	*	*	32.00
94	JUST THE TWO OF US	*	*	32.00
94	POWER OF LOVE, THE	*	20.00	30.00
94	SITTING ON TOP OF THE WORLD	*	*	32.00
94	SWEETEST OF ALL	*	*	32.00
94	YOUR HEART'S DESIRE	*	*	32.00
*			**TRIBUTE TO ROY ROGERS**	
94	HAPPY TRAILS TO YOU	*	20.00	30.00
T. DUBOIS			**TROLLS**	
93	MONDAY'S TROLL	*	*	32.00
93	TUESDAY'S TROLL	*	*	32.00
93	WEDNESDAY'S TROLL	*	*	32.00
94	FRIDAY'S TROLL	*	*	32.00
94	SATURDAY'S TROLL	*	*	32.00
94	SUNDAY'S TROLL	*	20.00	22.00
94	THURSDAY'S TROLL	*	*	32.00
L. KENDRICK			**VISION QUEST**	
93	EAGLE DANCE	*	*	32.00
93	SHARING THE SPIRIT	*	*	32.00
94	CALLING THE STORM	*	*	32.00
94	HIGHER POWER, A	*	*	32.00
94	SEEKING THE DAWN	*	*	32.00
94	SOARING SPIRIT	*	*	32.00
94	VALLEY OF THE SPIRIT	*	20.00	30.00
GRAY			**YOUNG AND THE RESTLESS**	
93	NIKKI'S WORLD	*	*	32.00
94	CRICKET'S TRAILS	*	*	32.00
94	JILL'S ESCAPADES	*	*	32.00
94	KATHERINE'S LEGACY	*	*	32.00
94	VICTOR'S EMPIRE	*	*	32.00

CROWN PARIAN

YR	NAME	LIMIT	ISSUE	TREND
T. BOYER			**AMERICAN FOLK HEROES**	
83	JOHNNY APPLESEED	*	*	83.00
84	DAVY CROCKETT	*	*	61.00
85	BETSY ROSS	*	*	61.00
86	BUFFALO BILL	*	*	61.00
87	CASEY JONES	*	*	61.00
87	SACAJAWEA (BOYER)	*	*	61.00

YR NAME	LIMIT	ISSUE	TREND
CALDER			**CALDER**
78 AFFECTION	*	*	91.00
R. SKELTON			**FREDDIE THE FREELOADER**
79 FREDDIE IN THE BATHTUB	OP	55.00	� 350.00
80 FREDDIE'S SHACK	OP	55.00	—145.00
81 FREDDIE ON THE GREEN	10000	60.00	—115.00
82 LOVE THAT FREDDIE	OP	60.00	➤100.00
R. SKELTON			**FREDDIE'S ADVENTURES**
82 CAPTAIN FREDDIE	OP	60.00	—100.00
83 BRONCO FREDDIE	OP	60.00	➤100.00
83 SIR FREDDIE	OP	63.00	➤ 85.00
G. ERIKSON			**GLORIA ERIKSON**
82 APRIL SPRING	*	*	48.00
RUTHVEN			**MOMENTS OF NATURE**
79 CALIFORNIA QUAIL	*	*	70.00
JONES			**OLD WEST**
79 TURNING THE LEAD	*	*	48.00
RUTHVEN			**OWL FAMILY**
83 BARRED OWL	*	*	100.00
83 SAW-WHET OWL	*	*	100.00
83 SNOWY OWL FAMILY	*	*	100.00
84 GREAT HORNED OWL	*	*	100.00
MCGREW			**THANKSGIVING DAY**
83 DINNER	*	*	112.00

D'ARCEAU LIMOGES

YR NAME	LIMIT	ISSUE	TREND
CAMBIER			
80 LA JEUNE FILLE DU PRINTEMP	*	*	151.00
CAMBIER			**CAMBIER MOTHER'S DAY**
83 MICHELE ET SYLVIE	*	*	61.00
84 MARIE ET JACQUELINE	*	*	57.00
86 MARIANNE AND THERESE	*	*	54.00
A. RESTIEAU			**CHRISTMAS**
75 LA FRUITE EN EGYPTE	*	24.00	150.00
76 DANS LA CRECHE	*	24.00	60.00
77 REFUS D'HEBERGEMENT	*	24.00	45.00
78 LA PURIFICATION	YR	27.00	50.00
79 L'ADORATION DES ROIS	YR	27.00	60.00
80 JOYEUSE NOUVELLE	YR	29.00	45.00
81 GUIDES PAR L'ETOILE	YR	29.00	45.00
82 L'ANNUCIATION	YR	31.00	60.00
JULIEN			**FRENCH COUNTRY LANDSCAPES**
87 ALONG THE RIVERSIDE	*	*	50.00
87 HARVEST IN CHAMPAGNE	*	*	55.00
87 SUNDAY IN A VILLAGE	*	*	50.00
88 FLOCK OF SHEEP IN AUVERGNE	*	*	55.00
88 HARBOUR SCENE IN PROVENCE	*	*	55.00
88 OLD WATER MILL IN ALSACE	*	*	60.00
88 PICNIC ON THE GRASS	*	*	55.00
89 PROMENADE IN THE ALOS	*	*	60.00
GUIDOU			**GIGI**
85 GIGI	*	*	40.00
85 NIGHT THEY INVENTED CHAMPAGNE	*	*	40.00
86 GIGI IN LOVE	*	*	41.00
86 I REMEMBER IT WELL	*	*	42.00
CAMBIER			**JEUNES FILLES**
78 LA JEUNE FILLE D'ETE	*	*	186.00
79 LA JEUNE FILLE D'HIVER	*	*	153.00
81 LA JEUNE FILLE D'AUTOMNE	*	*	162.00
BOULME			**JOSEPHINE AND NAPOLEON**
84 BONAPARTE TRAVERSANT ALPS	*	*	49.00
84 L'IMPERATRICE JOSEPHINE	*	*	68.00
84 LA RECONTRE	*	*	109.00
85 LE DIVORCE	*	*	51.00
85 SACRE DE NAPOLEON	*	*	57.00
86 LE SOUVENIR	*	*	50.00
BRENOT			**LA BELLE EPOQUE**
86 LIANE DE POUGY	*	*	38.00
86 SARAH BERNHARDT	*	*	36.00
87 ANNA PAVLOVA	*	*	39.00
A. RESTIEAU			**LAFAYETTE**
73 NORTH ISLAND LANDING	*	20.00	80.00
73 SECRET CONTRACT, THE	*	14.82	75.00
74 BATTLE OF BRANDYWINE	*	20.00	45.00
74 CITY TAVERN MEETING	*	20.00	75.00
75 MESSAGES TO FRANKLIN	*	20.00	95.00
75 SIEGE AT YORKTOWN	*	20.00	80.00
DALI			**LES DUOZE SITES**
80 L' ARC DE TRIUMPHE	*	*	40.00
81 LA CATHEDRAL NOTRE DAME	*	*	38.00
81 LA PLACE DE LA CONCORD	*	*	39.00
82 L'EGLISE SAINT PIERRE	*	*	42.00
82 LA POINTE DU VERT GALANT	*	*	49.00
82 LE MARCHE AUX FLEURS	*	*	42.00
83 L'HOTEL DE VILLE	*	*	44.00
83 L'OPERA	*	*	49.00

Limited to one year of production, The Jolly Coachmen *from the "Rockwell Christmas" series was issued in 1982 by Gorham Corp. for $29.50.*

Imagine how The Immigrants *felt when experiencing this scene from the "Statue of Liberty" series by A. D'Estrehan of Armstrong's.*

Jacqueline and Renée, *the third plate in Edna Hibel's "Mother's Day" series, closed on May 8, 1994.*

Now an extremely valuable plate, Deux Oiseaux (Two Birds) *from Lalique, an edition limit of 2,000, was released in 1965 for $25.*

YR	NAME	LIMIT	ISSUE	TREND
83	LA TOUR EIFFEL	*	*	50.00
83	LE JARDIN DES TUILERIES	*	*	47.00
83	LE MOULIN ROUGE	*	*	49.00
83	LE PONT ALEXANDRE	*	*	55.00
GUIDOU			**LES NOELS DE FRANCE**	
86	MAGICAL WINDOW	*	*	41.00
87	STARLIT CRECHE	*	*	41.00
88	CHRISTMAS IN ALSACE	*	*	45.00
DUTHEIL			**LES TRES HEURES**	
82	JUIN	*	*	180.00
83	MAI	*	*	130.00
83	OCTOBRE	*	*	117.00
87	FEVRIER	*	*	114.00
87	MARS	*	*	116.00
87	NOVEMBER	*	*	122.00
DUTHEIL			**LES TRES RICHES**	
79	JANVIER	*	*	128.00
80	AVRIL	*	*	120.00
81	AOUT	*	*	130.00
DUTHEIL			**LES TRES RICHES HEURES**	
88	DECEMBRE	*	*	121.00
88	JUILLET	*	*	122.00
88	SEPTEMBRE	*	*	121.00
GANEAU			**WOMEN OF THE CENTURY**	
76	COLETTE LA FEMME	*	*	45.00
76	EDITH	*	*	45.00
76	FRANCOISE	*	*	45.00
76	LEA LA FEMME FLEUR	*	*	45.00
76	MARLENE LA VAMP	*	*	45.00
76	SARAH EN TOURNURE	*	*	45.00
76	SCARLET EN CRINOLINE	*	*	62.00
76	SOPHIE	*	*	45.00
77	ALBERTINE LA FEMME	*	*	45.00
77	DAISY	*	*	45.00
78	HELENE L'INTREPIDE	*	*	45.00
79	BRIDGETTE	*	*	45.00

DANBURY MINT

*			**BICENTENNIAL**	
73	BOSTON TEA PARTY	*	*	195.00
74	FIRST CONTINENTAL CONGRESS	*	*	195.00
75	PAUL REVERE'S RIDE	*	*	195.00
76	DECLARATION OF INDEPENDENCE	*	*	195.00
76	WASHINGTON AT VALLEY FORGE	*	*	195.00
78	MOLLY PITCHER	*	*	195.00
79	BON HOMME RICHARD	*	*	195.00
DALY			**BOYS WILL BE BOYS**	
93	CLEAN AS A WHISTLE	*	*	46.00
93	FAVORITE READER	*	*	46.00
93	HER HERO	*	*	46.00
93	KEPT IN	*	*	46.00
93	SHOESHINE BOY	*	*	46.00
93	SLINGSHOT PAL	*	*	46.00
93	THIEF, THE	*	*	46.00
93	TRANQUIL MOMENT	*	*	46.00
CAMBIER			**CAMBIER MOTHER'S DAY**	
85	MONIQUE ET FRANCOIS	*	*	54.00
*			**CHRISTMAS**	
75	SILENT NIGHT (DANBURY MINT)	*	*	40.00
76	JOY TO THE WORLD	*	*	42.00
77	AWAY IN THE MANGER	*	*	42.00
78	FIRST NOEL	*	*	51.00
REICHARDT			**COUNTRY MEMORIES**	
92	BY THE OLD MILL	*	*	38.00
92	SO GOOD TO BE HOME	*	*	38.00
95	EARLY SNOWFALL	*	*	38.00
95	NATURE'S SWEET SYRUP	*	*	38.00
95	PEACEFUL RETREAT	*	*	38.00
95	RUSTIC BEAUTY	*	*	38.00
95	SNUG HARBOUR	*	*	38.00
95	SUMMERTIME	*	*	38.00
REICHARDT			**EAGLES ACROSS AMERICA**	
95	CATCH OF THE DAY	*	*	40.00
95	EVERGLADE SUNRISE	*	*	40.00
95	GUARDIANS, THE	*	*	40.00
95	KING OF THE CANYON	*	*	40.00
95	PERFECT HARMONY	*	*	40.00
95	PRIDE OF AMERICA	*	*	40.00
95	SPIRIT OF ALASKA	*	*	40.00
95	TRYING THEIR WINGS	*	*	40.00
ST. CLAIR			**ENCHANTED GARDEN**	
95	FLOWER GIRL	*	*	40.00
95	GOLDEN BUTTERFLY	*	*	40.00
KAYE			**FARMING THE HEARTLAND**	
92	BEATING THE STORM	*	*	29.00
92	BOUNTIFUL HARVEST	*	*	64.00
92	HARVESTING AT LAST	*	*	31.00

YR	NAME	LIMIT	ISSUE	TREND
93	BAILING THE HAY	*	*	28.00
93	TAKING A BREAK	*	*	31.00
93	WELL DESERVED BREAK	*	*	31.00

REICHARDT — GOD BLESS AMERICA

YR	NAME	LIMIT	ISSUE	TREND
93	AFTER THE STORM	*	*	39.00
93	CASCADING THUNDER	*	*	39.00
93	FLYING FREE	*	*	39.00
93	FROSTY MORNING	*	*	39.00
93	ICE-CAPPED MAJESTY	*	*	39.00
93	PEACEFUL SOLITUDE	*	*	39.00
93	PROUD GUARDIAN	*	*	39.00
93	SUNLIT RETREAT	*	*	39.00
93	TRANQUIL BEAUTY	*	*	39.00
93	UNTAMED GLORY	*	*	39.00
93	VIGILANT BEACON	*	*	39.00
93	WHERE EAGLES SOAR	*	*	39.00

* — GREAT ART MASTERPIECES

YR	NAME	LIMIT	ISSUE	TREND
75	LAST SUPPER	*	*	211.00
76	SUNFLOWER	*	*	210.00

MANNING — KITTEN COUSINS

YR	NAME	LIMIT	ISSUE	TREND
92	PLAYFUL COMPANIONS	*	*	36.00

M.I. HUMMEL — LITTLE COMPANIONS

YR	NAME	LIMIT	ISSUE	TREND
91	APPLE TREE BOY AND GIRL	*	*	51.00
91	BUDDING SCHOLARS	*	*	51.00
91	COME BACK SOON	*	*	51.00
91	COUNTRY CROSSROAD	*	*	51.00
91	HELLO DOWN THERE	*	*	51.00
91	LITTLE EXPLORERS	*	*	51.00
91	LITTLE MUSICIANS	*	*	51.00
91	PRIVATE PARADE	*	*	51.00
91	SQUEAKY CLEAN	*	*	51.00
91	STORMY WEATHER	*	*	51.00
91	SURPRISE	*	*	51.00
91	TENDER LOVING CARE	*	*	51.00

D. ZOLAN — LITTLE FARMHANDS

YR	NAME	LIMIT	ISSUE	TREND
98	PIGLET ROUNDUP	75 DAYS	30.00	30.00
98	TOO BUSY TO PLAY	75 DAYS	30.00	30.00

* — MICHAELANGELO

YR	NAME	LIMIT	ISSUE	TREND
72	CREATION OF ADAM	*	*	118.00
73	MOSES	*	*	117.00
73	PEITA	*	*	117.00
74	HOLY FAMILY	*	*	115.00

* — PORCELAIN PLATES

YR	NAME	LIMIT	ISSUE	TREND
77	OFFICIAL AMERICA'S CUP	*	*	30.00
77	QUEENS SILVER JUBILEE	*	*	140.00
77	TALL SHIPS	*	*	30.00

TRAVERS — PRIDE OF THE WILDERNESS

YR	NAME	LIMIT	ISSUE	TREND
93	FALL RETREAT	*	*	43.00
93	FULL ALERT	*	*	43.00
93	SNOWBOUND	*	*	43.00
93	WINTER STAG	*	*	43.00

NELSON — UNDERWATER PARADISE

YR	NAME	LIMIT	ISSUE	TREND
93	DISCOVERY OFF ANAHOLA	*	*	37.00
94	CALIFORNIA SPIRITS	*	*	37.00
94	CHEZ PAUL	*	*	37.00
94	HAWAIIAN MUSES	*	*	37.00
94	HONOLUA: BAY OF PIILANI	*	*	37.00
94	LA LE'S SACRED PRINCESS	*	*	37.00
94	LAHAINA SEA FLIGHT	*	*	37.00
94	MOONLIT MOMENT	*	*	37.00
94	NEW MOON OVER WINGWORD OHU	*	*	37.00
94	SEARCH FOR HARMONY	*	*	37.00
94	SERENITY OF WAIPIO	*	*	37.00
94	SUNLIT GOLD	*	*	37.00

D. GELSINGER — WINTER WONDERLAND

YR	NAME	LIMIT	ISSUE	TREND
93	DEAR SANTA	75 DAYS	30.00	30.00
93	MY FIRST SNOWMAN	75 DAYS	30.00	30.00
93	NOELLE	75 DAYS	30.00	30.00
94	CHORUS OF CAROLERS	75 DAYS	30.00	30.00
94	CHRISTMAS PRARYER, A	75 DAYS	30.00	30.00
94	JUST MY SIZE	75 DAYS	30.00	30.00
94	SEASON OF SHARING, A	75 DAYS	30.00	30.00
94	SKATER'S DREAM	75 DAYS	30.00	30.00

LAWRENCE — YOUNG INNOCENCE

YR	NAME	LIMIT	ISSUE	TREND
92	BEDTIME PRAYERS	*	*	43.00

DAVE GROSSMAN CREATIONS

N. ROCKWELL — BOY SCOUT

YR	NAME	LIMIT	ISSUE	TREND
81	CAN'T WAIT	RT	30.00	50.00
82	GUIDING HAND	RT	30.00	40.00
83	TOMORROW'S LEADER	RT	30.00	45.00

* BARNARD — CHILDREN OF THE WEEK

YR	NAME	LIMIT	ISSUE	TREND
78	MONDAY'S CHILD	*	*	46.00
79	TUESDAY'S CHILD	*	*	46.00
79	WEDNESDAY'S CHILD	*	*	46.00
80	FRIDAY'S CHILD	*	*	46.00
80	THURSDAY'S CHILD	*	*	62.00

YR	NAME	LIMIT	ISSUE	TREND
81	SATURDAY'S CHILD	*	*	46.00
81	SUNDAY'S CHILD	*	*	46.00
* BARNARD				**CHRISTMAS**
78	PEACE	*	*	63.00
79	SANTA	*	*	63.00
N. ROCKWELL				**CHRISTMAS**
*	FACES OF CHRISTMAS (82)	RT	75.00	75.00
			EMMETT KELLY CHRISTMAS	
93	DOWNHILL	RT	30.00	30.00
94	HOLIDAY SKATER	RT	30.00	30.00
B. LEIGHTON-JONES			**EMMETT KELLY CHRISTMAS**	
86	CHRISTMAS CAROL	CL	20.00	25.00
86	CHRISTMAS CAROL (GROSSMAN)	YR	20.00	49.00
86	CHRISTMAS CAROL (KELLY)	YR	20.00	46.00
87	CHRISTMAS WREATH	YR	20.00	46.00
88	CHRISTMAS DINNER	YR	20.00	31.00
89	CHRISTMAS FEAST	YR	20.00	40.00
89	CHRISTMAS FEAST	YR	20.00	34.00
90	JUST WHAT I NEEDED	YR	24.00	39.00
91	EMMETT AND THE SNOWMAN	YR	25.00	39.00
92	CHRISTMAS TUNES	YR	25.00	30.00
93	DOWNHILL PLATE	YR	30.00	47.00
94	HOLIDAY SKATERS (EMMETT KELLY)	YR	30.00	44.00
95	MERRY CHRISTMAS MR. SCROOGE	YR	30.00	44.00
B. LEIGHTON-JONES		**EMMETT KELLY ORIGINAL CIRCUS COLLECTION**		
94	HOLIDAY SKATER	YR	30.00	35.00
N. ROCKWELL				**HUCK FINN**
79	SECRET	RT	40.00	45.00
80	LISTENING	RT	40.00	45.00
80	NO KINGS	RT	40.00	45.00
81	SNAKE ESCAPES	RT	40.00	45.00
* LUPETTI				**MAGIC PEOPLE**
82	FANTASY FESTIVAL	*	*	114.00
82	MUSIC FOR A QUEEN	*	*	112.00
M. KEANE				**MARGARET KEANE**
76	BALLOON GIRL	*	*	55.00
77	MY KITTY	*	*	48.00
78	BEDTIME (GROSSMAN)	*	*	40.00
*			**MOUSEHOLE COLLECTION**	
94	CHRISTMAS TRIO	RT	18.00	18.00
E. ROBERTS			**NATIVE AMERICAN SERIES**	
91	LONE WOLF	10000	45.00	65.00
92	TORTOISE LADY	10000	45.00	65.00
94	BUFFALO CHIEF	*	*	68.00
94	CORN PRINCESS	*	*	72.00
D. GROSSMAN		**NORMAN ROCKWELL COLLECTION**		
81	DREAMS OF LONG AGO	RT	60.00	90.00
82	DOCTOR	RT	*	90.00
N. ROCKWELL		**NORMAN ROCKWELL COLLECTION**		
78	YOUNG DOCTOR	RT	50.00	70.00
79	BUTTERBOY	RT	40.00	45.00
79	LEAPFROG	RT	50.00	50.00
80	BACK TO SCHOOL	RT	24.00	40.00
80	CHRISTMAS TRIO	RT	75.00	116.00
80	LOVERS	RT	60.00	65.00
81	NO SWIMMING	RT	25.00	40.00
81	SANTA'S GOOD BOYS	RT	75.00	51.00
82	AMERICAN MOTHER	RT	45.00	50.00
82	LOVE LETTER	RT	27.00	40.00
83	CHRISTMAS CHORES	RT	75.00	76.00
83	CIRCUS	RT	65.00	70.00
83	DOCTOR AND DOLL	RT	27.00	40.00
83	DREAMBOATS	RT	24.00	25.00
84	BIG MOMENT	RT	27.00	30.00
84	TINY TIM	RT	75.00	99.00
84	VISIT WITH ROCKWELL	RT	65.00	70.00
N. ROCKWELL			**SATURDAY EVENING POST**	
91	DOWNHILL DARING	YR	25.00	30.00
91	MISSED	YR	25.00	30.00
92	CHOOSIN UP	YR	25.00	30.00
N. ROCKWELL				**TOM SAWYER**
75	WHITEWASHING THE FENCE	RT	26.00	40.00
76	FIRST SMOKE	RT	26.00	40.00
77	TAKE YOUR MEDICINE	RT	26.00	45.00
78	LOST IN CAVE	RT	26.00	45.00

DELPHI

N. GIORGIO			**BEATLES COLLECTION**	
91	A HARD DAY'S NIGHT	CL	28.00	50.00
91	BEATLES, LIVE IN CONCERT	CL	25.00	71.00
91	HELLO AMERICA	CL	25.00	41.00
92	BEATLES '65	CL	28.00	48.00
92	BEATLES AT SHEA STADIUM	CL	30.00	58.00
92	HARD DAYS NIGHT	CL	28.00	45.00
92	HELP!	CL	28.00	49.00
92	RUBBER SOUL	CL	30.00	54.00
92	YESTERDAY AND TODAY	CL	30.00	50.00

YR	NAME	LIMIT	ISSUE	TREND
	D. SIVAVEC		**BEATLES COLLECTION**	
92	ALL YOU NEED IS LOVE	CL	28.00	45.00
92	SGT. PEPPER, THE 25TH ANNIVERSARY	CL	28.00	40.00
93	ABBEY ROAD	CL	31.00	58.00
93	HEY JUDE	CL	31.00	45.00
93	LET IT BE	CL	31.00	53.00
93	MAGICAL MYSTERY TOUR	CL	31.00	45.00
	HERRING		**CLASSIC DINERS**	
93	TWILIGHT AT THE GALAXY	*	*	40.00
	M. STUTZMAN		**COMMEMORATING THE KING**	
93	BLUES AND BLACK LEATHER	CL	30.00	35.00
93	GOLDEN BOY	CL	30.00	30.00
93	LAS VEGAS, LIVE	CL	30.00	41.00
93	OUTSTANDING YOUNG MAN	95 DAYS	30.00	35.00
93	PRIVATE PRESLEY	CL	30.00	35.00
93	ROCK AND ROLL LEGEND ELVIS	CL	30.00	41.00
93	SCREEN IDOL	CL	30.00	35.00
93	TIGER: FAITH, SPIRIT & DISCIPLINE, THE	OP	30.00	30.00
	P. PALMA		**DREAM MACHINES**	
88	'56 T-BIRD	CL	25.00	45.00
88	'57 'VETTE	CL	25.00	45.00
89	'56 CONTINENTAL- MURRAY	CL	28.00	50.00
89	'57 BEL AIR	CL	28.00	55.00
89	'57 CHRYSLER 300C	CL	28.00	43.00
89	'58 BIARRITZ	CL	28.00	30.00
	B. EMMETT		**ELVIS ON THE BIG SCREEN**	
92	G.I. BLUES	CL	30.00	40.00
92	LOVING YOU	CL	30.00	45.00
92	VIVA LAS VEGAS	CL	33.00	45.00
93	BLUE HAWAII	CL	33.00	45.00
93	HARUM SCARUM	CL	35.00	50.00
93	JAILHOUSE ROCK	CL	33.00	45.00
93	SPEEDWAY	CL	35.00	50.00
93	SPINOUT	CL	35.00	50.00
	N. GIORGIO		**ELVIS PRESLEY HIT PARADE**	
92	BLUE CHRISTMAS	CL	33.00	45.00
92	BLUE SUEDE SHOES	CL	30.00	40.00
92	HEARTBREAK HOTEL	CL	30.00	45.00
92	HOUND DOG	CL	33.00	45.00
92	RETURN TO SENDER	CL	33.00	45.00
93	ALWAYS ON MY MIND	CL	35.00	50.00
93	BLUE MOON OF KENTUCKY	CL	35.00	55.00
93	MYSTERY TRAIN	CL	35.00	55.00
93	PEACE IN THE VALLEY	CL	37.00	55.00
93	SUSPICIOUS MINDS	CL	37.00	55.00
93	TEDDY BEAR	CL	35.00	50.00
93	WEAR MY RING ROUND YOUR NECK	CL	37.00	55.00
	B. EMMETT		**ELVIS PRESLEY: IN PERFORMANCE**	
90	'68 COMEBACK SPECIAL	CL	25.00	79.00
91	ALOHA FROM HAWAII	CL	28.00	50.00
91	BACK IN TUPELO, 1956	CL	28.00	45.00
91	BENEFIT FOR THE USS ARIZONA	CL	30.00	45.00
91	CONCERT IN BATON ROUGE, 1974	CL	30.00	50.00
91	IF I CAN DREAM	CL	28.00	50.00
91	KING OF LAS VEGAS	CL	25.00	50.00
91	MADISON SQUARE GARDEN, 1972	CL	30.00	50.00
91	TAMPA, 1955	CL	30.00	45.00
92	IN THE SPOTLIGHT: HAWAII '72	CL	32.00	50.00
92	ON STAGE IN WICHITA, 1974	CL	32.00	50.00
92	TOUR FINALE: INDIANAPOLIS '77	CL	32.00	55.00
	B. EMMETT		**ELVIS PRESLEY: LOOKING AT A LEGEND**	
88	ELVIS AT THE GATES OF GRACELAND	RT	25.00	100.00
89	HOMECOMING	CL	28.00	65.00
89	JAILHOUSE ROCK	CL	25.00	70.00
89	MEMPHIS FLASH, THE	CL	28.00	70.00
90	A STUDIO SESSION	CL	28.00	55.00
90	ELVIS AND GLADYS	CL	28.00	60.00
90	ELVIS IN HOLLYWOOD	CL	30.00	60.00
90	ELVIS ON HIS HARLEY	CL	30.00	70.00
90	STAGE DOOR AUTOGRAPHS	CL	30.00	55.00
91	CHRISTMAS AT GRACELAND	CL	33.00	65.00
91	CLOSING THE DEAL	CL	35.00	70.00
91	ENTERING SUN STUDIO	CL	33.00	50.00
91	GOING FOR THE BLACK BELT	CL	33.00	62.00
91	HIS HAND IN MINE	CL	33.00	55.00
91	LETTERS FROM FANS	CL	33.00	55.00
92	ELVIS RETURNS TO THE STAGE	CL	35.00	70.00
	G. ANGELINI		**FABULOUS CARS OF THE FIFTIES**	
93	'57 BLUE BELAIR	CL	28.00	30.00
93	'57 RED CORVETTE	CL	25.00	30.00
93	'57 WHITE T-BIRD	CL	25.00	30.00
93	'59 PINK CADILLAC	CL	28.00	30.00
94	'56 LINCOLN PREMIER	CL	28.00	30.00
94	'59 RED FORD FAIRLANE	CL	28.00	32.00
	D. SIVAVEC		**IN THE FOOTSTEPS OF THE KING**	
93	ELVIS' BIRTHPLACE: TUPELO	CL	30.00	41.00
93	FLYING CIRCLE G RANCH: WALLS, MS	CL	33.00	45.00

YR	NAME	LIMIT	ISSUE	TREND
93	GRACELAND: MEMPHIS, TN	CL	28.00	47.00
94	DAY JOB: MEMPHIS TN	CL	33.00	45.00
94	LAUDERDALE COURTS: MEMPHIS	CL	33.00	45.00
94	PATRIOTIC SOLDIER	95 DAYS	35.00	50.00
V. GADINO				**INDIANA JONES**
89	INDIANA JONES	CL	25.00	50.00
89	INDIANA JONES AND HIS DAD	CL	25.00	50.00
90	A FAMILY DISCUSSION	CL	28.00	50.00
90	INDIANA JONES/DR. SCHNEIDER	CL	28.00	45.00
90	YOUNG INDIANA JONES	CL	28.00	60.00
91	INDIANA JONES/THE HOLY GRAIL	CL	28.00	60.00
J. BARSON				**LEGENDS OF BASEBALL**
92	LOU GEHRIG: THE LUCKIEST MAN	CL	25.00	35.00
93	CHRISTY MATHEWSON	*	*	50.00
93	CY YOUNG: THE PERFECT GAME	CL	28.00	40.00
93	HONUS WAGNER: FLYING DUTCHMAN	CL	30.00	45.00
93	JIMMIE FOX: THE BEAST	CL	30.00	45.00
93	MEL OTT: MASTER MELVIN	*	*	50.00
93	ROGER HORNSBY: 424 SEASON	CL	28.00	40.00
93	TRIS SPEAKER: THE GRAY EAGLE	CL	30.00	50.00
93	TY COBB: THE GEORGIA PEACH	CL	28.00	40.00
93	WALTER JOHNSON: THE SHUTOUT	CL	30.00	45.00
94	LEFTY GROVE	CL	32.00	36.00
94	LEFTY GROVE: HIS GREATEST	*	*	50.00
94	MICKEY COCKRANE: BLACK MIKE	*	*	50.00
94	PIE TRAYNOR: PITTSBURG CHAMPION	*	*	50.00
94	SHOELESS JOE JACKSON: TRIPLES	*	*	50.00
95	GROVER ALEXANDER	*	*	50.00
B. BENGER				**LEGENDS OF BASEBALL**
92	BABE RUTH: THE CALLED SHOT	CL	25.00	35.00
C. NOTARILE				**MAGIC OF MARILYN**
92	FOR OUR BOYS IN KOREA	*	*	43.00
92	FOR OUR BOYS IN KOREA, 1954	CL	25.00	40.00
92	OPENING NIGHT	*	*	41.00
92	RISING STAR	*	*	46.00
92	STRASBERG'S CLASS	CL	30.00	30.00
93	CURTAIN CALL	CL	30.00	46.00
93	PHOTO OPPORTUNITY	*	*	46.00
93	SHINING STAR	*	*	46.00
93	STOPPING TRAFFIC	*	*	46.00
93	STRASBERG'S STUDENT	*	*	46.00
C. NOTARILE				**MARILYN MONROE**
89	MARILYN MONROE/7 YEAR ITCH	CL	25.00	90.00
90	DIAMONDS/GIRL'S BEST FRIEND	CL	25.00	68.00
91	MARILYN MONROE/RIVER OF NO RETURN	CL	28.00	50.00
92	ALL ABOUT EVE	CL	30.00	49.00
92	DON'T BOTHER TO KNOCK	CL	32.00	50.00
92	HOW TO MARRY A MILLIONAIRE	CL	28.00	60.00
92	MARILYN MONROE AS CHERIE IN BUS STOP	CL	30.00	50.00
92	MARILYN MONROE IN NIAGARA	CL	30.00	60.00
92	MONKEY BUSINESS	CL	32.00	55.00
92	MY HEART BELONGS TO DADDY	CL	30.00	55.00
92	THERE'S NO BUSINESS/SHOW BUSINESS	CL	28.00	50.00
92	WE'RE NOT MARRIED	CL	32.00	50.00
N. GIORGIO				**MICHAEL JACKSON**
90	BILLIE JEAN	*	*	38.00
D. ZWIERZ				**PORTRAITS OF THE KING**
91	ARE YOU LONESOME TONIGHT?	CL	28.00	50.00
91	I'M YOURS	CL	31.00	50.00
91	LOVE ME TENDER	CL	28.00	45.00
91	TREAT ME NICE	CL	31.00	35.00
92	FOLLOW THAT DREAM	CL	33.00	35.00
92	JUST BECAUSE	CL	33.00	35.00
92	WONDER OF YOU, THE	CL	31.00	32.00
92	YOU'RE A HEARTBREAKER	CL	33.00	35.00
D. HENDERSON				**TAKE ME OUT TO THE BALLGAME**
93	BRIGGS STADIUM: HOME OF TIGERS	*	*	53.00
93	COMISKEY PARK: HOME OF WHITE SOCKS	*	*	53.00
93	FENWAY PARK: HOME OF THE GREEN MONSTER	CL	33.00	50.00
93	MEMORIAL STADIUM: HOME OF THE ORIOLES	CL	35.00	50.00
93	WRIGLEY FIELD: FRIENDLY CONFINES	CL	30.00	53.00
93	YANKEE STADIUM: HOUSE BABE RUTH	CL	30.00	53.00
94	CLEVELAND STADIUM: INDIANS	*	*	53.00
94	COUNTY STADIUM: MILWAUKEE BREWERS	CL	35.00	50.00
94	EBBETS FIELD: HOME OF THE DODGERS	CL	35.00	53.00
94	SHIBE PARK: PHILADELPHIA HOME	*	*	53.00
95	FORBES FIELD: PITTSBURG PIRATES	*	*	53.00
95	POLO GROUNDS: N.Y. GIANTS	*	*	53.00

DEPARTMENT 56

R. INNOCENTI

YR	NAME	LIMIT	ISSUE	TREND
				A CHRISTMAS CAROL
91	CRATCHIT'S CHRISTMAS PUDDING, THE	18000	60.00	75.00
92	MARLEY'S GHOST APPEARS TO SCROOGE	18000	60.00	65.00
92	SPIRIT OF CHRISTMAS PRESENT, THE	18000	60.00	65.00
94	VISIONS OF CHRISTMAS PAST	18000	60.00	65.00
*				**DICKENS' VILLAGE**
87	DICKENS' VILLAGE 5917-0 (SET OF 4)	CL	140.00	225.00

YR	NAME	LIMIT	ISSUE	TREND

DIANA ART
D. CALISTI

YR	NAME	LIMIT	ISSUE	TREND
96	DOWN THE CHIMNEY HE GOES	25 DAYS	30.00	30.00

S. WILLIAMS

| 95 | KITTY'S QUILT | 15 DAYS | 30.00 | 30.00 |

R. HOLYFIELD — BACKYARD BIRDS

96	MOUNTIAN LAUREL CARDINAL	5000	30.00	30.00
97	APPLE BLOSSOM TIME	5000	30.00	30.00
97	GOLD IN THE DOGWOOD	5000	30.00	30.00
97	JEWELS IN THE ORCHARD	5000	30.00	30.00

R. ROGERS — DUCKS FOR ALL SEASONS

97	AUTUMN'S JEWELS	5000	30.00	30.00
97	SPRING SPLENDOR	5000	30.00	30.00
97	SUMMER SWIM	5000	30.00	30.00
97	WINTER VISITORS	5000	30.00	30.00

L. THOMPSON — ENDANGERED SPECIES

97	FROLICKING DOLPHINS	5000	30.00	30.00
97	LAST REFUGE MANATEES	5000	30.00	30.00
97	WHALE OF A TIME	5000	30.00	30.00
97	WOLF DEN	5000	30.00	30.00

G. HACKING — EXOTIC ANIMALS

96	ELEPHANT COUNTRY	25 DAYS	30.00	30.00
96	GIRAFFES	25 DAYS	30.00	30.00
96	TIGER REFLECTION	25 DAYS	30.00	30.00
96	YOUNG SILVERBACK	25 DAYS	30.00	30.00

D. CALISTE — FARM ANIMALS

| 96 | GOOD MOOOOD! | 15 DAYS | 30.00 | 30.00 |

DUNCAN ROYALE
S. MORTON — HISTORY OF SANTA CLAUS I

YR	NAME	LIMIT	ISSUE	TREND
*	COLLECTION OF 12 PLATES	RT	480.00	485.00
85	KRIS KRINGLE	RT	40.00	70.00
85	MEDIEVAL	RT	40.00	55.00
85	PIONEER	10000	40.00	45.00
86	CIVIL WAR	10000	40.00	45.00
86	NAST	RT	40.00	80.00
86	RUSSIAN	RT	40.00	45.00
86	SODA POP	RT	40.00	70.00
87	BLACK PETER	10000	40.00	45.00
87	DEDT MOROZ	10000	40.00	45.00
87	ST. NICHOLAS	RT	40.00	80.00
87	VICTORIAN	RT	40.00	45.00
87	WASSAIL	RT	40.00	45.00

EDNA HIBEL STUDIOS
E. HIBEL — ALLEGRO

YR	NAME	LIMIT	ISSUE	TREND
78	PLATE & BOOK	7500	120.00	140.00

E. HIBEL — ARTE OVALE

80	TAKARA, BLANCO	700	450.00	665.00
80	TAKARA, COBALT BLUE	1000	595.00	890.00
80	TAKARA, GOLD	300	1,000.00	1450.00
84	TARO-KUN, BLANCO	700	450.00	830.00
84	TARO-KUN, COBALT BLUE	1000	995.00	1100.00
84	TARO-KUN, GOLD	300	1,000.00	2650.00

E. HIBEL — CHRISTMAS ANNUAL

85	ANGELS' MESSAGE, THE	YR	45.00	230.00
86	GIFT OF THE MAGI	YR	45.00	280.00
88	ADORATION OF THE SHEPHERDS	YR	49.00	180.00
90	NATIVITY, THE	YR	49.00	155.00

E. HIBEL — DAVID SERIES

79	WEDDING OF DAVID & BATHSHEBA	5000	250.00	450.00
80	DAVID, BATHSHEBA & SOLOMON	5000	275.00	425.00
82	DAVID THE KING	5000	275.00	415.00
82	DAVID THE KING, COBALT A/P	25	275.00	1150.00
84	BATHSHEBA	5000	275.00	400.00
84	BATHSHEBA, COBALT A/P	100	275.00	1150.00

E. HIBEL — EROICA

| 90 | COMPASSION | 10000 | 50.00 | 80.00 |
| 92 | DARYA | 10000 | 50.00 | 80.00 |

E. HIBEL — FAMOUS WOMEN & CHILDREN

80	PHARAOH'S DAUGHTER & MOSES, COBALT BLUE	500	350.00	1400.00
80	PHARAOH'S DAUGHTER & MOSES, GOLD	2500	350.00	515.00
82	ANNA & THE CHILDREN OF THE KING OF SIAM - GOLD	2500	350.00	515.00
82	ANNA & THE CHILDREN OF THE KING OF SIAM-COBALT BLU	500	350.00	1400.00
82	CORNELIA & HER JEWELS, COBALT BLUE	500	350.00	1400.00
82	CORNELIA & HER JEWELS, GOLD	2500	350.00	515.00
84	MOZART & THE EMPRESS MARIE THERESA-GOLD	2500	350.00	515.00

E. HIBEL — FLOWER GIRL ANNUAL

85	LILY	15000	79.00	130.00
86	IRIS	15000	79.00	130.00
87	ROSE	15000	79.00	130.00
88	CAMELLIA	15000	79.00	130.00
89	PEONY	15000	79.00	145.00
92	WISTERIA	15000	79.00	130.00

E. HIBEL — HIBEL HOLIDAYS

| 91 | FIRST HOLIDAY | YR | 49.00 | 73.00 |

YR	NAME	LIMIT	ISSUE	TREND
91	FIRST HOLIDAY, THE - GOLD	1000	99.00	145.00
92	CHRISTMAS ROSE	YR	49.00	73.00
92	CHRISTMAS ROSE, THE - GOLD	1000	99.00	100.00
93	HOLIDAY JOY	*	*	79.00

E. HIBEL   **HIBEL MOTHER'S DAY**

YR	NAME	LIMIT	ISSUE	TREND
84	ABBY & LISA	YR	30.00	350.00
85	ERICA AND JAMIE	YR	30.00	350.00
86	EMILY AND JENNIFER	YR	30.00	350.00
87	CATHERINE AND HEATHER	YR	35.00	350.00
88	SARAH AND TESS	YR	35.00	350.00
89	JESSICA AND KATE	YR	35.00	350.00
90	ELIZABETH, JORDAN & JANIE	YR	37.00	350.00
91	MICHELE AND ANNA	YR	37.00	350.00
92	MOLLY AND ANNIE	YR	39.00	75.00
93	OLIVIA AND HILDY	YR	40.00	350.00
94	JACQUELINE AND RENEE	YR	*	66.00
95	TAMMY AND KAILE JO	YR	*	63.00

E. HIBEL   **INTERNATIONAL MOTHER LOVE FRENCH**

YR	NAME	LIMIT	ISSUE	TREND
85	YVETTE AVEC SES ENFANTS	5000	125.00	230.00
91	LIBERTE, EGALITE, FRATERNITE	5000	95.00	100.00

E. HIBEL   **INTERNATIONAL MOTHER LOVE GERMAN**

YR	NAME	LIMIT	ISSUE	TREND
82	GESA UND KINDER	5000	195.00	200.00
83	ALEXANDER UND KINDER	5000	195.00	200.00

E. HIBEL   **MOTHER AND CHILD**

YR	NAME	LIMIT	ISSUE	TREND
73	COLETTE & CHILD	15000	40.00	340.00
74	SAYURI & CHILD	15000	40.00	245.00
75	KRISTINA & CHILD	15000	50.00	175.00
76	MARILYN & CHILD	15000	55.00	165.00
77	LUCIA & CHILD	15000	60.00	90.00
81	KATHLEEN & CHILD	15000	85.00	95.00

E. HIBEL   **MUSEUM COMMEMORATIVE**

YR	NAME	LIMIT	ISSUE	TREND
77	FLOWER GIRL OF PROVENCE	12750	175.00	430.00
80	DIANA	3000	350.00	400.00

E. HIBEL   **NOBILITY OF CHILDREN**

YR	NAME	LIMIT	ISSUE	TREND
77	LE MARQUIS MAURICE PIERRE	12750	120.00	230.00
79	CHIEF RED FEATHER	12750	140.00	195.00

E. HIBEL   **NORDIC FAMILIES**

YR	NAME	LIMIT	ISSUE	TREND
87	A TENDER MOMENT	7500	79.00	100.00

E. HIBEL   **ORIENTAL THEME**

YR	NAME	LIMIT	ISSUE	TREND
80	ARTE OVALE	*	*	2355.00
80	TAKARA-BLUE	*	*	110.00
80	TAKARA-WHITE	*	*	110.00

E. HIBEL   **SCANDINAVIAN MOTHER & CHILD**

YR	NAME	LIMIT	ISSUE	TREND
87	PEARLS & FLOWERS	7500	55.00	230.00
89	ANEMONE & VIOLET	7500	75.00	95.00
90	HOLLY & TALIA	7500	75.00	90.00

E. HIBEL   **TO LIFE ANNUAL**

YR	NAME	LIMIT	ISSUE	TREND
86	GOLDEN'S CHILD	5000	99.00	280.00
87	TRIUMPH! EVERYONE A WINNER	19500	55.00	65.00
88	WHOLE EARTH BLOOMED AS A SACRED PLACE	15000	85.00	95.00
89	LOVERS OF THE SUMMER PALACE	5000	65.00	80.00
92	PEOPLE OF THE FIELDS	5000	49.00	50.00

E. HIBEL   **TRIBUTE TO ALL CHILDREN**

YR	NAME	LIMIT	ISSUE	TREND
84	GERARD	19500	55.00	100.00
84	GISELLE	19500	55.00	100.00
85	WENDY	19500	55.00	130.00
86	TODD	19500	55.00	130.00

E. HIBEL   **WORLD I LOVE**

YR	NAME	LIMIT	ISSUE	TREND
81	LEAH'S FAMILY	17500	85.00	230.00
82	KAYLIN	17500	85.00	380.00
83	EDNA'S MUSIC	17500	85.00	200.00
83	O'HANA	17500	85.00	200.00

EDWIN M. KNOWLES

L. ROBERTS   **A SWAN IS BORN**

YR	NAME	LIMIT	ISSUE	TREND
87	AT THE BARRE	CL	25.00	40.00
87	HOPES AND DREAMS	CL	25.00	40.00
87	IN POSITION	CL	25.00	40.00
88	JUST FOR SIZE	CL	25.00	45.00

M. HAMPSHIRE   **AESOP'S FABLES**

YR	NAME	LIMIT	ISSUE	TREND
88	GOOSE THAT LAID THE GOLDEN EGG, THE	CL	28.00	40.00
88	HARE & THE TORTOISE, THE	CL	28.00	40.00
89	FOX & THE GRAPES, THE	CL	31.00	40.00
89	JAY AND THE PEACOCK, THE	CL	31.00	40.00
89	LION & THE MOUSE, THE	CL	31.00	40.00
89	MILK MAID AND HER PAIL, THE	CL	31.00	40.00

MARSTEN/ MANDRAJJI   **AMERICAN INNOCENTS**

YR	NAME	LIMIT	ISSUE	TREND
86	ABIGAIL IN THE ROSE GARDEN	CL	20.00	30.00
86	ANN BY THE TERRACE	CL	20.00	30.00
86	ELLEN AND JOHN IN THE PARLOR	CL	20.00	30.00
86	WILLIAM ON THE ROCKING HORSE	CL	20.00	45.00

M. KUNSTLER   **AMERICAN JOURNEY**

YR	NAME	LIMIT	ISSUE	TREND
87	WESTWARD HO	CL	30.00	35.00
88	CHRISTMAS AT THE NEW CABIN	CL	30.00	40.00
88	CROSSING THE RIVER	CL	30.00	40.00
88	KITCHEN WITH A VIEW	CL	30.00	35.00

YR NAME	LIMIT	ISSUE	TREND
D. SPAULDING		**AMERICANA HOLIDAYS**	
78 FOURTH OF JULY	YR	26.00	55.00
79 THANKSGIVING	YR	26.00	65.00
80 EASTER	YR	26.00	80.00
81 VALENTINE'S DAY	YR	26.00	45.00
82 FATHER'S DAY	YR	26.00	40.00
83 CHRISTMAS	YR	26.00	40.00
84 MOTHER'S DAY	YR	26.00	40.00
A. BRACKENBURY		**AMY BRACKENBURY'S CAT TALES**	
87 A CHANCE MEETING: WHITE AM. SHORTHAIRS	CL	22.00	45.00
87 GONE FISHING: MAINE COONS	CL	22.00	60.00
88 ALL WRAPPED UP: HIMALAYANS	CL	25.00	70.00
88 FLOWER BED: BRITISH SHORTHAIRS	CL	25.00	45.00
88 KITTENS AND MITTENS: SILVER TABBIES	CL	25.00	45.00
88 STRAWBERRIES AND CREAM: CREAM PERSIANS	CL	25.00	65.00
W. CHAMBERS		**ANNIE**	
83 ANNIE AND GRACE	CL	19.00	40.00
83 ANNIE AND SANDY	CL	19.00	40.00
83 DADDY WARBUCKS	CL	19.00	50.00
84 ANNIE AND THE ORPHANS	CL	21.00	40.00
85 TOMORROW	CL	21.00	35.00
86 ANNIE AND MISS HANNIGAN	CL	21.00	50.00
86 ANNIE, LILY AND ROOSTER	CL	24.00	50.00
86 GRAND FINALE	CL	24.00	35.00
J. THORNBRUGH		**BABY OWLS OF NORTH AMERICA**	
91 BEGINNING TO EXPLORE: BOREAL OWLS	CL	33.00	45.00
91 FORTY WINKS: SAW-WHET OWLS	CL	28.00	45.00
91 OUT ON A LIMB: GREAT GRAY OWL	CL	31.00	50.00
91 PEEK-A-WHOO: SCREECH OWLS	CL	28.00	40.00
91 THREE OF A KIND: GREAT HORNED OWLS	CL	31.00	45.00
91 TREE HOUSE, THE: NORTHERN PYGMY OWLS	CL	31.00	45.00
92 THREE'S COMPANY: LONG EARED OWLS	CL	33.00	50.00
92 WHOO'S THERE: BARRED OWLS	CL	33.00	45.00
J. THORNBRUGH		**BACKYARD HARMONY**	
91 ANNOUNCING SPRING	CL	31.00	53.00
91 SINGING LESSON, THE	CL	28.00	39.00
91 WELCOMING A NEW DAY	CL	28.00	48.00
92 AT THE PEEP OF DAY	CL	33.00	40.00
92 MORNING HARVEST, THE	CL	31.00	48.00
92 SPRING TIME PRIDE	CL	31.00	50.00
92 TODAY'S DISCOVERIES	CL	33.00	50.00
92 TREETOP SERENADE	CL	33.00	50.00
DISNEY		**BAMBI**	
91 BASHFUL BAMBI	CL	35.00	50.00
92 BAMBI'S MORNING GREETINGS	CL	38.00	50.00
92 BAMBI'S NEW FRIENDS	CL	35.00	50.00
92 BAMBI'S SKATING LESSON	CL	38.00	50.00
92 HELLO LITTLE PRINCE	CL	38.00	50.00
93 WHAT'S UP POSSUMS?	CL	38.00	55.00
DISNEY		**BEAUTY AND THE BEAST**	
93 A BLOSSOMING ROMANCE	CL	30.00	40.00
93 A MISMATCH	CL	35.00	45.00
93 BE OUR GUEST	CL	35.00	50.00
93 BELLE'S FAVORITE STORY	CL	35.00	50.00
93 LEARNING TO LOVE	CL	33.00	45.00
93 LOVE'S FIRST DANCE	CL	30.00	40.00
93 PAPA'S WORKSHOP	CL	33.00	45.00
93 WARMING UP	CL	33.00	45.00
94 A GIFT FOR BELLE	CL	37.00	55.00
94 A SPOT OF TEA	CL	35.00	55.00
94 ENCHANTE'S CHERIE	CL	37.00	55.00
94 SPELL IS BROKEN	*	*	55.00
E. LICEA		**BIBLICAL MOTHERS**	
83 BATHSHEBA AND SOLOMON	YR	40.00	110.00
84 JUDGMENT OF SOLOMON	YR	40.00	110.00
84 PHARAOH'S DAUGHTER AND MOSES	YR	40.00	90.00
85 MARY AND JESUS	YR	40.00	55.00
85 SARAH AND ISAAC	YR	45.00	75.00
86 REBEKAH, JACOB AND ESAU	YR	45.00	75.00
S. TIMM		**BIRDS OF THE SEASONS**	
90 BLUEBIRDS IN SPRING	CL	25.00	42.00
90 CARDINALS IN WINTER	CL	25.00	45.00
91 BALTIMORE ORIOLES IN SUMMER	CL	28.00	40.00
91 BLACK-CAPPED CHICKADEES/WINTER	CL	30.00	54.00
91 BLUE JAYS IN EARLY FALL	CL	28.00	45.00
91 CEDAR WAXWINGS IN FALL	CL	30.00	50.00
91 CHICKADEES IN WINTER	CL	30.00	43.00
91 NUTHATCHES IN FALL	CL	28.00	40.00
91 ROBINS IN EARLY SPRING	CL	28.00	45.00
K. DANIEL		**BRITANNICA'S BIRDS OF YOUR GARDEN**	
85 BALTIMORE ORIOLE, THE	CL	23.00	40.00
85 BLUE JAY, THE	CL	20.00	75.00
85 CARDINAL, THE	CL	20.00	70.00
86 BLUEBIRD, THE	CL	23.00	35.00
86 CHICKADEES, THE	CL	23.00	40.00
86 HUMMINGBIRD, THE	CL	25.00	55.00
86 ROBIN, THE	CL	23.00	35.00

YR	NAME	LIMIT	ISSUE	TREND
87	CEDAR WAXWING, THE	CL	25.00	50.00
87	DOWNY WOODPECKER, THE	CL	25.00	40.00
87	GOLDFINCH, THE	CL	25.00	45.00

K. DANIEL — CALL OF THE WILDERNESS

YR	NAME	LIMIT	ISSUE	TREND
91	FIRST OUTING	CL	30.00	61.00
91	HOWLING LESSON	CL	30.00	85.00
91	SILENT WATCH	CL	33.00	70.00
91	WINTER TRAVELERS	CL	33.00	75.00
92	A NEW FUTURE	CL	35.00	50.00
92	AHEAD OF THE PACK	CL	33.00	55.00
92	MORNING MIST	CL	37.00	50.00
92	NORTHERN SPIRITS	CL	35.00	50.00
92	SILENT ONE, THE	CL	37.00	50.00
92	TWILIGHT FRIENDS	CL	35.00	50.00

D. BROWN — CAROUSEL

YR	NAME	LIMIT	ISSUE	TREND
87	IF I LOVED YOU	CL	25.00	30.00
88	CAROUSEL WALTZ, THE	CL	25.00	40.00
88	MR. SNOW	CL	25.00	35.00
88	YOU'LL NEVER WALK ALONE	CL	25.00	35.00

J. GRIFFIN — CASABLANCA

YR	NAME	LIMIT	ISSUE	TREND
90	HERE'S LOOKING AT YOU, KID	CL	35.00	50.00
90	WE'LL ALWAYS HAVE PARIS	CL	35.00	41.00
91	A FRANC FOR YOUR THOUGHTS	CL	38.00	50.00
91	PLAY IT AGAIN SAM	CL	38.00	55.00
91	RICK'S CAFE AMERICCAIN	CL	38.00	45.00
91	WE LOVED EACH OTHER ONCE	CL	38.00	50.00

J.W. SMITH — CHILDHOOD HOLIDAYS

YR	NAME	LIMIT	ISSUE	TREND
86	CHRISTMAS	CL	20.00	20.00
86	CHRISTMAS (SMITH)	*	*	32.00
86	EASTER	CL	20.00	25.00
86	EASTER (SMITH)	*	*	36.00
86	THANKSGIVING	CL	20.00	30.00
86	VALENTINE'S DAY	CL	23.00	35.00
87	FOURTH OF JULY	*	*	36.00
87	MOTHER'S DAY	CL	23.00	23.00
87	MOTHER'S DAY (SMITH)	*	*	34.00

T.C. CHIU — CHINA'S NATURAL TREASURES

YR	NAME	LIMIT	ISSUE	TREND
91	GIANT PANDA, THE	CL	33.00	50.00
91	SIBERIAN TIGER, THE	CL	30.00	44.00
91	SNOW LEOPARD, THE	CL	30.00	45.00
92	ASIAN ELEPHANT, THE	CL	33.00	60.00
92	GOLDEN MONKEY, THE	CL	35.00	50.00
92	TIBETAN BROWN BEAR, THE	CL	33.00	50.00

A. LEIMANIS — CHRISTMAS IN THE CITY

YR	NAME	LIMIT	ISSUE	TREND
92	A CHRISTMAS SNOWFALL	CL	35.00	44.00
92	YULETIDE CELEBRATION	CL	35.00	45.00
93	HOLIDAY CHEER	CL	35.00	45.00
93	MAGIC OF CHRISTMAS, THE	CL	35.00	45.00

DISNEY — CINDERELLA

YR	NAME	LIMIT	ISSUE	TREND
88	A DREAM IS A WISH YOUR HEART MAKES	CL	30.00	70.00
88	BIBBIDI-BOBBIDI-BOO	CL	30.00	75.00
89	A DRESS FOR CINDERELLY	CL	33.00	80.00
89	OH SING SWEET NIGHTINGALE	CL	33.00	60.00
89	SO THIS IS LOVE	CL	33.00	85.00
90	AT THE STROKE OF MIDNIGHT	CL	33.00	65.00
90	HAPPILY EVER AFTER	CL	35.00	80.00
90	IF THE SHOE FITS	CL	35.00	70.00

S. GUSTAFSON — CLASSIC FAIRY TALES

YR	NAME	LIMIT	ISSUE	TREND
91	FROG PRINCE, THE	CL	33.00	60.00
91	GOLDILOCKS AND THE 3 BEARS	CL	30.00	65.00
91	LITTLE RED RIDING HOOD	CL	30.00	54.00
91	THREE LITTLE PIGS, THE	CL	33.00	75.00
92	HANSEL AND GRETEL	CL	35.00	66.00
92	JACK AND THE BEANSTALK	CL	33.00	56.00
92	PUSS IN BOOTS	CL	35.00	50.00
92	TOM THUMB	CL	35.00	50.00

S. GUSTAFSON — CLASSIC MOTHER GOOSE

YR	NAME	LIMIT	ISSUE	TREND
92	LITTLE BO PEEP	CL	30.00	40.00
92	LITTLE MISS MUFFET	CL	30.00	45.00
92	MARY HAD A LITTLE LAMB	CL	30.00	40.00
92	MARY, MARY, QUITE CONTRARY	CL	30.00	40.00

H.H. INGMIRE — COMFORTS OF HOME

YR	NAME	LIMIT	ISSUE	TREND
92	CURIOUS PAIR	CL	25.00	45.00
92	SLEEPYHEADS	CL	25.00	45.00
93	A COZY FIRESIDE	CL	30.00	50.00
93	FELINE FROLIC	CL	30.00	50.00
93	MOTHER'S RETREAT	CL	28.00	50.00
93	PLAYTIME	CL	28.00	50.00
93	WASHDAY HELPERS	CL	30.00	50.00
93	WELCOME FRIENDS	CL	28.00	50.00

H.H. INGMIRE — COZY COUNTRY CORNERS

YR	NAME	LIMIT	ISSUE	TREND
90	LAZY MORNING	CL	25.00	50.00
90	WARM RETREAT	CL	25.00	40.00
91	A SUNNY SPOT	CL	28.00	40.00
91	APPLE ANTICS	CL	30.00	55.00
91	ATTIC AFTERNOON	CL	28.00	58.00
91	HIDE AND SEEK	CL	30.00	45.00

YR	NAME	LIMIT	ISSUE	TREND
91	MIRROR MISCHIEF	CL	28.00	58.00
91	TABLE TROUBLE	CL	30.00	70.00
J. CSATARI			**CSATARI GRANDPARENT**	
80	BEDTIME STORY	CL	18.00	40.00
81	SKATING LESSON, THE	CL	20.00	30.00
82	COOKIE TASTING, THE	CL	20.00	60.00
83	SWINGER, THE	CL	20.00	32.00
84	SKATING QUEEN, THE	CL	22.00	32.00
85	PATRIOT'S PARADE, THE	CL	22.00	35.00
86	HOME RUN, THE	CL	22.00	35.00
87	SNEAK PREVIEW, THE	CL	22.00	35.00
DISNEY			**DISNEY TREASURED MOMENTS COLLECTION**	
92	CINDERELLA	CL	30.00	50.00
92	SNOW WHITE & THE SEVEN DWARFS	CL	30.00	50.00
93	ALICE IN WONDERLAND	CL	33.00	50.00
93	BEAUTY AND THE BEAST	CL	35.00	50.00
93	JUNGLE BOOK, THE	CL	35.00	50.00
93	PETER PAN	CL	33.00	50.00
93	PINOCCHIO	CL	35.00	50.00
93	SLEEPING BEAUTY	CL	33.00	50.00
T. KINKADE			**ENCHANTED COTTAGES**	
93	FALLBROOKE COTTAGE	CL	30.00	40.00
93	JULIANNE'S COTTAGE	CL	30.00	40.00
93	ROSE GARDEN COTTAGE	CL	30.00	40.00
93	SEASIDE COTTAGE	CL	30.00	40.00
93	SWEETHEART COTTAGE	CL	30.00	40.00
93	WEATHERVANE COTTAGE	CL	30.00	40.00
DISNEY		**FANTASIA: (THE SORCERER'S APPRENTICE) GOLDEN ANNIVERSARY**		
90	APPRENTICE'S DREAM, THE	CL	30.00	65.00
90	MISCHIEVOUS APPRENTICE	CL	30.00	40.00
91	DREAMS OF POWER	CL	33.00	65.00
91	MICKEY MAKES MAGIC	CL	35.00	50.00
91	MICKEY'S MAGICAL WHIRLPOOL	CL	33.00	50.00
91	PENITENT APPRENTICE, THE	CL	35.00	50.00
91	WIZARDRY GONE WILD	CL	33.00	45.00
92	AN APPRENTICE AGAIN	CL	35.00	50.00
B. BRADLEY			**FATHER'S LOVE**	
84	BATTER UP	CL	20.00	30.00
84	OPEN WIDE	CL	20.00	30.00
85	LITTLE SHAVER	CL	20.00	30.00
85	SWING TIME	CL	23.00	50.00
L. KAATZ			**FIELD PUPPIES**	
87	CAUGHT IN THE ACT-THE GOLDEN RETRIEVER	CL	25.00	55.00
87	DOG TIRED-THE SPRINGER SPANIEL	CL	25.00	70.00
88	A PERFECT SET-LABRADOR	CL	28.00	50.00
88	FRITZ'S FOLLY-GERMAN SHORTHAIRED POINTER	CL	28.00	50.00
88	MISSING/POINT/IRISH SETTER	CL	28.00	50.00
88	SHIRT TALES-COCKER SPANIEL	CL	28.00	60.00
89	COMMAND PERFORMANCE-WIEMARANER	CL	30.00	65.00
89	FINE FEATHERED FRIENDS-ENGLISH SETTER	CL	30.00	50.00
L. KAATZ			**FIELD TRIPS**	
90	GONE FISHING	CL	25.00	50.00
91	BOXED IN	CL	28.00	40.00
91	CHESAPEAKE BAY RETRIEVERS	CL	30.00	45.00
91	DUCKING DUTY	CL	25.00	45.00
91	HAT TRICK	CL	30.00	45.00
91	PAIL PALS	CL	30.00	45.00
91	PUPPY TALES	CL	28.00	40.00
91	PUPS 'N BOOTS	CL	28.00	40.00
J. GIORDANO			**FIRST IMPRESSIONS**	
91	ALL EARS	CL	33.00	45.00
91	FINE FEATHERED FRIEND	CL	33.00	44.00
91	TAKING A GANDER	CL	30.00	40.00
91	TWO'S COMPANY	CL	30.00	40.00
91	WHAT'S UP?	CL	33.00	45.00
92	BETWEEN FRIENDS	CL	33.00	50.00
G. LAMBERT			**FOUR ANCIENT ELEMENTS**	
84	EARTH	CL	28.00	100.00
84	WATER	CL	28.00	85.00
85	AIR	CL	30.00	65.00
85	FIRE	CL	30.00	50.00
F. HOOK			**FRANCES HOOK LEGACY**	
85	DAY DREAMING	CL	20.00	35.00
85	FASCINATION	CL	20.00	59.00
86	DISAPPOINTMENT	CL	23.00	34.00
86	DISCOVERY	CL	23.00	34.00
87	EXPECTATION	CL	23.00	37.00
M. BUDDEN			**FREE AS THE WIND**	
92	AIRBORNE	CL	33.00	45.00
92	ALOFT	CL	30.00	40.00
92	SKYWARD	CL	30.00	40.00
93	ASCENT	CL	33.00	45.00
93	FLIGHT	CL	33.00	45.00
93	HEAVENWARD	CL	33.00	45.00
J. DOWN			**FRIENDS I REMEMBER**	
83	FISH STORY	CL	17.50	50.00
84	OFFICE HOURS	CL	17.50	30.00

YR	NAME	LIMIT	ISSUE	TREND
85	A COAT OF PAINT	CL	17.50	28.00
85	FRINGE BENEFITS	CL	20.00	30.00
85	HERE COMES THE BRIDE	CL	20.00	30.00
86	FLOWER ARRANGEMENT	CL	22.00	30.00
86	HIGH SOCIETY	CL	20.00	30.00
86	TASTE TEST	CL	22.00	30.00

K. DANIEL — FRIENDS OF THE FOREST

YR	NAME	LIMIT	ISSUE	TREND
87	RABBIT, THE	CL	25.00	40.00
87	RACCOON, THE	CL	25.00	50.00
87	SQUIRREL, THE	CL	28.00	50.00
88	CHIPMUNK, THE	CL	28.00	50.00
88	FOX, THE	CL	28.00	50.00
88	OTTER, THE	CL	28.00	50.00

T. KINKADE — GARDEN COTTAGES OF ENGLAND

YR	NAME	LIMIT	ISSUE	TREND
91	CANDLELIT COTTAGE	CL	31.00	50.00
91	CEDAR NOOK COTTAGE	CL	28.00	50.00
91	CHANDLER'S COTTAGE	CL	28.00	75.00
91	MCKENNA'S COTTAGE	CL	31.00	57.00
91	OPEN GATE COTTAGE	CL	31.00	50.00
91	WOODSMAN'S THATCH COTTAGE	CL	33.00	58.00
92	MERRITT'S COTTAGE	CL	33.00	55.00
92	STONEGATE COTTAGE	CL	33.00	60.00

B. HIGGINS BOND — GARDEN SECRETS

YR	NAME	LIMIT	ISSUE	TREND
93	BLOOMIN' KITTIES	CL	25.00	35.00
93	FLORAL PURR-FUME	CL	25.00	35.00
93	FLOWER FANCIERS	CL	25.00	35.00
93	FRISKY BUSINESS	CL	25.00	35.00
93	KITTY CORNER	CL	25.00	35.00
93	MEADOW MISCHIEF	CL	25.00	35.00
93	NINE LIVES	CL	25.00	35.00
93	PUSSYCAT POTPOURRI	CL	25.00	35.00

R. KURSAR — GONE WITH THE WIND

YR	NAME	LIMIT	ISSUE	TREND
78	SCARLETT	CL	22.00	390.00
79	ASHLEY	CL	22.00	140.00
80	MELANIE	CL	22.00	70.00
81	RHETT	CL	24.00	50.00
82	MAMMY LACING SCARLETT	CL	24.00	50.00
83	MELANIE GIVES BIRTH	CL	24.00	55.00
84	SCARLET'S GREEN DRESS	CL	26.00	70.00
85	RHETT AND BONNIE	CL	26.00	70.00
85	SCARLETT AND RHETT: THE FINALE	CL	30.00	62.00

L. CABLE — GREAT CATS OF THE AMERICAS

YR	NAME	LIMIT	ISSUE	TREND
89	COUGAR, THE	CL	30.00	45.00
89	JAGUAR, THE	CL	30.00	60.00
89	LYNX, THE	CL	33.00	35.00
90	BOBCAT, THE	CL	33.00	35.00
90	JAGUARUNDI, THE	CL	33.00	35.00
90	MARGAY, THE	CL	35.00	40.00
90	OCELOT, THE	CL	33.00	35.00
91	PAMPAS CAT, THE	CL	35.00	35.00

C. LAYTON — HEIRLOOMS AND LACE

YR	NAME	LIMIT	ISSUE	TREND
89	ANNA	CL	35.00	75.00
89	VICTORIA	CL	35.00	90.00
90	OLIVIA	CL	38.00	115.00
90	TESS	CL	38.00	90.00
91	BRIDGET	CL	38.00	100.00
91	REBECCA	CL	38.00	125.00

E. HIBEL — HIBEL CHRISTMAS

YR	NAME	LIMIT	ISSUE	TREND
85	ANGEL'S MESSAGE, THE	YR	45.00	60.00
86	GIFTS OF THE MAGI, THE	YR	45.00	60.00
87	FLIGHT INTO EGYPT, THE	YR	49.00	60.00
88	ADORATION OF THE SHEPHERD	YR	49.00	60.00
89	PEACEFUL KINGDOM	YR	49.00	67.00
90	NATIVITY	YR	49.00	75.00

T. KINKADE — HOME FOR THE HOLIDAYS

YR	NAME	LIMIT	ISSUE	TREND
91	HOME BEFORE CHRISTMAS	CL	33.00	50.00
91	HOME TO GRANDMA'S	CL	30.00	40.00
91	SLEIGH RIDE HOME	CL	30.00	49.00
92	HOME AWAY FROM HOME	CL	35.00	52.00
92	HOMESPUN HOLIDAY	CL	33.00	45.00
92	HOMETIME YULETIDE	CL	35.00	50.00
92	JOURNEY HOME, THE	CL	35.00	50.00
92	WARMTH OF HOME, THE	CL	33.00	45.00

T. KINKADE — HOME IS WHERE THE HEART IS

YR	NAME	LIMIT	ISSUE	TREND
92	A CARRIAGE RIDE HOME	CL	33.00	45.00
92	A WARM WELCOME HOME	CL	30.00	45.00
92	HOME SWEET HOME	CL	30.00	65.00
93	AMBER AFTERNOON	CL	33.00	45.00
93	COUNTRY MEMORIES	CL	33.00	49.00
93	HOMETOWN HOSPITALITY	CL	35.00	55.00
93	OUR SUMMER HOME	CL	35.00	52.00
93	TWILIGHT CAFE, THE	CL	35.00	52.00

R. MCGINNIS — HOME SWEET HOME

YR	NAME	LIMIT	ISSUE	TREND
89	GEORGIAN, THE	CL	40.00	45.00
89	GREEK REVIVAL, THE	CL	40.00	35.00
89	VICTORIAN, THE	CL	40.00	45.00
90	MISSION, THE	CL	40.00	40.00

YR	NAME	LIMIT	ISSUE	TREND
F. HOOK			HOOK'S WORDS OF LOVE	
86	I LOVE YOU	*	*	38.00
87	THAT'S MY BOY	*	*	38.00
91	DON'T BE SCARED	*	*	39.00
91	HAPPILY EVER AFTER	*	*	37.00
91	LET'S SEE YOU SMILE	*	*	38.00
91	YOU'RE DOING FINE	*	*	38.00
L. KAATZ			IT'S A DOG'S LIFE	
92	LITERARY LABS	CL	30.00	40.00
92	WE'VE BEEN SPOTTED	CL	30.00	40.00
93	BARRELING ALONG	CL	33.00	40.00
93	DOGS AND SUDS	CL	35.00	50.00
93	LODGING A COMPLAINT	CL	33.00	45.00
93	PAWS FOR A PICNIC	CL	35.00	50.00
93	PLAY BALL	CL	35.00	50.00
93	RETRIEVING OUR DIGNITY	CL	33.00	45.00
B. JERNER			JERNER'S DUCKS	
86	MALLARD	*	*	54.00
86	PINTAIL	*	*	54.00
87	AMERICAN WIGEON	CL	23.00	42.00
87	GREEN WINGED TEAL	CL	23.00	44.00
87	NORTHERN SHOVELER	CL	23.00	39.00
87	WOOD DUCK	CL	23.00	53.00
88	BLUE-WINGED TEAL	*	*	42.00
88	GADWALL			41.00
T.C. CHIU			JEWELS OF THE FLOWERS	
91	AMETHYST FLIGHT	CL	33.00	45.00
91	EMERALD PAIR	CL	33.00	60.00
91	OPAL SPLENDOR	CL	35.00	50.00
91	RUBY ELEGANCE	CL	33.00	55.00
91	SAPPHIRE WINGS	CL	30.00	60.00
91	TOPAZ BEAUTIES	CL	30.00	35.00
92	AQUAMARINE GLIMMER	CL	35.00	35.00
92	PEARL LUSTER	CL	35.00	55.00
S. GUSTAFSON			KEEPSAKE RHYMES	
92	HUMPTY DUMPTY	CL	30.00	43.00
93	OLD KING COLE	CL	30.00	40.00
93	PAT-A-CAKE	CL	30.00	40.00
93	PETER PUMPKIN EATER	CL	30.00	40.00
W. CHAMBERS			KING AND I	
84	A PUZZLEMENT	CL	20.00	50.00
85	GETTING TO KNOW YOU	CL	20.00	40.00
85	SHALL WE DANCE?	CL	20.00	60.00
85	WE KISS IN A SHADOW	CL	20.00	35.00
DISNEY			LADY AND THE TRAMP	
92	DOG POUND BLUES	CL	38.00	45.00
92	FIRST DATE	CL	35.00	45.00
92	MERRY CHRISTMAS TO ALL	CL	38.00	45.00
92	PUPPY LOVE	CL	35.00	40.00
93	DOUBLE SIAMESE TROUBLE	CL	38.00	45.00
93	MOONLIGHT ROMANCE	CL	40.00	50.00
93	RUFF HOUSE	CL	40.00	50.00
93	TELLING TAILS	CL	40.00	50.00
B. JERNER			LESS TRAVELED ROAD	
88	COVERED BRIDGE, THE	CL	33.00	40.00
88	MURMURING STREAM, THE	CL	30.00	40.00
88	WEATHERED BARN, THE	CL	30.00	40.00
89	FLOWERING MEADOW, THE	CL	33.00	40.00
89	HIDDEN WATERFALL, THE	CL	33.00	40.00
89	WINTER'S PEACE	CL	33.00	40.00
M. KUNSTLER			LINCOLN, MAN OF AMERICA	
86	GETTYSBURG ADDRESS, THE	CL	25.00	30.00
87	BEGINNINGS IN NEW SALEM	CL	28.00	35.00
87	INAUGURATION, THE	CL	25.00	35.00
87	LINCOLN-DOUGLAS DEBATES, THE	CL	28.00	35.00
88	EMANCIPATION PROCLAMATION	CL	28.00	35.00
88	FAMILY MAN, THE	CL	28.00	35.00
DISNEY			LITTLE MERMAID	
93	A SONG FROM THE SEA	CL	30.00	40.00
93	A VISIT TO THE SURFACE	CL	30.00	40.00
93	ARIEL'S TREASURED COLLECTION	CL	33.00	45.00
93	DADDY'S GIRL	CL	33.00	45.00
93	FOREVER LOVE	CL	35.00	51.00
93	KISS THE GIRL	CL	33.00	50.00
93	UNDERWATER BUDDIES	CL	33.00	45.00
94	FIREWORKS AT FIRST SIGHT	CL	35.00	51.00
D. SMITH			MAJESTIC BIRDS OF NORTH AMERICA	
88	BALD EAGLE, THE	CL	30.00	50.00
88	GREAT HORNED OWL, THE	CL	33.00	40.00
88	PEREGRINE FALCON, THE	CL	30.00	40.00
89	AMERICAN KESTRAL, THE	CL	33.00	40.00
89	RED-TAILED HAWK, THE	CL	33.00	40.00
89	WHITE GYRFALCON, THE	CL	33.00	40.00
90	GOLDEN EAGLE, THE	CL	35.00	45.00
90	OSPREY, THE	CL	35.00	45.00
E. HIBEL			MARCH OF DIMES: OUR CHILDREN, OUR FUTURE	
90	TIME TO EMBRACE	150 DAYS	29.00	49.00

YR	NAME	LIMIT	ISSUE	TREND
S. KUCK		MARCH OF DIMES: OUR CHILDREN, OUR FUTURE		
89	TIME TO LOVE	*	*	63.00
J. MCCLELLAND		MARCH OF DIMES: OUR CHILDREN, OUR FUTURE		
89	TIME TO PLANT	*	*	45.00
G. PERILLO		MARCH OF DIMES: OUR CHILDREN, OUR FUTURE		
89	A TIME TO BE BORN	CL	29.00	40.00
A. WILLIAMS		MARCH OF DIMES: OUR CHILDREN, OUR FUTURE		
90	A TIME TO LAUGH	CL	29.00	35.00
D. ZOLAN		MARCH OF DIMES: OUR CHILDREN, OUR FUTURE		
89	TIME FOR PEACE	*	*	50.00
M. HAMPSHIRE				MARY POPPINS
89	A SPOONFUL OF SUGAR	CL	30.00	40.00
89	MARY POPPINS	CL	30.00	43.00
90	A JOLLY HOLIDAY WITH MARY	CL	33.00	45.00
90	WE LOVE TO LAUGH	CL	33.00	50.00
91	CHIM CHIM CHER-EE	CL	33.00	45.00
91	TUPPENCE A BAG	CL	33.00	44.00
DISNEY				MICKEY'S CHRISTMAS CAROL
92	BAH HUMBUG!	CL	30.00	45.00
92	WHAT'S SO MERRY ABOUT CHRISTMAS?	CL	30.00	45.00
93	A CHRISTMAS FEAST	CL	35.00	55.00
93	A CHRISTMAS SURPRISE	CL	33.00	50.00
93	A COZY CHRISTMAS	CL	35.00	55.00
93	GOD BLESS US EVERY ONE	CL	33.00	50.00
93	MARLEY'S WARNING	CL	35.00	55.00
93	YULETIDE GREETINGS	CL	33.00	50.00
K. MILNAZIK		MUSICAL MOMENTS FROM THE WIZARD OF OZ		
93	IF I ONLY HAD A BRAIN	CL	30.00	65.00
93	IF I WERE KING OF THE FOREST	CL	30.00	55.00
93	LULLABYE LEAGUE	CL	30.00	50.00
93	MUNCHKINLAND	CL	30.00	48.00
93	OVER THE RAINBOW	CL	30.00	42.00
93	WE'RE OFF TO SEE THE WIZARD	CL	30.00	46.00
94	DING, DONG, THE WITCH IS DEAD	CL	30.00	49.00
94	MERRY OLD LAND OF OZ	CL	30.00	50.00
W. CHAMBERS				MY FAIR LADY
89	I COULD HAVE DANCED ALL NIGHT	CL	25.00	40.00
89	OPENING DAY AT ASCOT	CL	25.00	40.00
89	RAIN IN SPAIN, THE	CL	28.00	45.00
89	SHOW ME	CL	28.00	45.00
90	GET ME TO THE CHURCH ON TIME	CL	28.00	45.00
90	I'VE GROWN ACCUSTOMED TO YOUR FACE	CL	28.00	45.00
M. JOBE				NATURE'S CHILD
90	FAITHFUL FRIENDS	CL	33.00	50.00
90	LOST LAMB, THE	CL	30.00	45.00
90	SEEMS LIKE YESTERDAY	CL	33.00	50.00
90	SHARING	CL	30.00	45.00
90	TRUSTED COMPANION	CL	33.00	50.00
91	HAND IN HAND	CL	33.00	50.00
C. DECKER				NATURE'S GARDEN
93	A MORNING SPLASH	CL	30.00	40.00
93	FLURRY OF ACTIVITY	CL	33.00	45.00
93	HANGING AROUND	CL	33.00	45.00
93	SPRINGTIME FRIENDS	CL	30.00	45.00
93	TINY TWIRLING TREASURES	CL	33.00	45.00
J. THORNBRUGH				NATURE'S NURSERY
92	TESTING THE WATERS	CL	30.00	40.00
93	HIDE AND SEEK	CL	30.00	40.00
93	PIGGYBACK RIDE	CL	30.00	40.00
93	RACE YA MOM	CL	30.00	40.00
93	TAKING THE PLUNGE	CL	30.00	40.00
93	TIME TO WAKE UP	CL	30.00	40.00
WEIR				NORTH WOODS HERITAGE
92	BRINGING HOME THE TREE	*	*	50.00
92	CROSSING THE BRIDGE	*	*	52.00
92	MAPLE SUGAR SEASON	*	*	50.00
92	WINTER'S WORK	*	*	50.00
93	END OF DAY	*	*	52.00
93	NORTHERN HAYRIDE	*	*	82.00
J.W. SMITH				NOT SO LONG AGO
88	MOTHER'S LITTLE HELPER	CL	25.00	42.00
88	STORY TIME	CL	25.00	42.00
88	SUPPERTIME FOR KITTY	CL	25.00	42.00
88	WASH DAY FOR DOLLY	CL	25.00	42.00
M. KUNSTLER				OKLAHOMA!
85	OH, WHAT A BEAUTIFUL MORNIN'	CL	20.00	30.00
86	I CAIN'T SAY NO	CL	20.00	30.00
86	OKLAHOMA!	CL	20.00	33.00
86	SURREY W/THE FRINGE ON TOP	CL	20.00	30.00
M. WEBER				OLD FASHIONED FAVORITES
91	APPLE CRISP	CL	30.00	73.00
91	BLUEBERRY MUFFINS	CL	30.00	50.00
91	CHOCOLATE CHIP OATMEAL COOKIES	CL	30.00	95.00
91	PEACH COBBLER	CL	30.00	75.00
C. TENNANT				OLD MILL STREAM
90	NEW LONDON GRIST MILL	CL	40.00	45.00

YR NAME	LIMIT	ISSUE	TREND
91 GLADE CREEK GRIST MILL	CL	40.00	45.00
91 OLD RED MILL	CL	40.00	45.00
91 WAYSIDE INN GRIST MILL	CL	40.00	45.00
K. PRITCHETT			**ONCE UPON A TIME**
88 LITTLE RED RIDING HOOD	CL	25.00	45.00
88 RAPUNZEL	CL	25.00	45.00
88 THREE LITTLE PIGS	CL	28.00	50.00
89 BEAUTY AND THE BEAST	CL	28.00	50.00
89 GOLDILOCKS AND THE THREE BEARS	CL	28.00	50.00
89 PRINCESS AND THE PEA, THE	CL	28.00	50.00
*			**PINOCCHIO**
89 GEPETTO CREATES PINOCCHIO	CL	30.00	65.00
90 I'VE GOT NO STRINGS ON ME	CL	33.00	50.00
90 IT'S AN ACTOR' S LIFE FOR ME	CL	33.00	50.00
90 PINOCCHIO AND THE BLUE FAIRY	CL	30.00	67.00
91 A REAL BOY	CL	33.00	70.00
91 PLEASURE ISLAND	CL	33.00	50.00
W. CHAMBERS			**PORTRAITS OF MOTHERHOOD**
87 MOTHER'S HERE	CL	30.00	45.00
88 FIRST TOUCH	CL	30.00	45.00
M.T. FANGEL			**PRECIOUS LITTLE ONES**
88 LITTLE FLEDGLINGS	CL	30.00	35.00
88 LITTLE RED ROBINS	CL	30.00	35.00
88 PEEK-A-BOO	CL	30.00	40.00
88 SATURDAY NIGHT BATH	CL	30.00	35.00
N. GLAZIER		**PROUD SENTINELS OF THE AMERICAN WEST**	
93 CAT NAP	CL	30.00	30.00
93 CROWN PRINCE	CL	33.00	33.00
93 DESERT BIGHORN-MORMON RIDGE	CL	33.00	33.00
93 YOUNGBLOOD	CL	30.00	45.00
J. GIORDANO			**PURRFECT POINT OF VIEW**
91 UNEXPECTED VISITORS	CL	30.00	38.00
91 WISTFUL MORNING	CL	30.00	40.00
92 AFTERNOON CATNAP	CL	30.00	45.00
92 COZY COMPANY	CL	30.00	40.00
C. WILSON			**PUSSYFOOTING AROUND**
91 FISH TALES	CL	25.00	40.00
91 TEATIME TABBIES	CL	25.00	35.00
91 TWO MAESTROS	CL	25.00	35.00
91 YARN SPINNERS	CL	25.00	35.00
R.B. PIERCE			**ROMANTIC AGE OF STEAM**
92 BROADWAY LIMITED, THE	CL	30.00	45.00
92 CHIEF, THE	CL	33.00	45.00
92 CRESCENT LIMITED, THE	CL	33.00	45.00
92 EMPIRE BUILDER, THE	CL	30.00	40.00
92 TWENTIETH CENTURY LIMITED	CL	33.00	50.00
93 DAYLIGHT, THE	CL	35.00	50.00
93 JUPITER, THE	CL	35.00	50.00
93 OVERLAND LIMITED, THE	CL	35.00	50.00
T. BROWNING			**SANTA'S CHRISTMAS**
91 SANTA'S CHEER	CL	30.00	44.00
91 SANTA'S GIFT	CL	33.00	50.00
91 SANTA'S LOVE	CL	30.00	40.00
91 SANTA'S PROMISE	CL	33.00	65.00
92 SANTA'S MAGIC	CL	33.00	69.00
92 SANTA'S SURPRISE	CL	33.00	60.00
M. JOBE			**SEASON FOR SONG**
91 FROSTY CHORUS	CL	35.00	45.00
91 SILVER SERENADE	CL	35.00	50.00
91 SNOWY SYMPHONY	CL	35.00	60.00
91 WINTER CONCERT	CL	35.00	50.00
K. RANDLE			**SEASON OF SPLENDOR**
92 A COUNTRY WEEKEND	CL	33.00	45.00
92 AUTUMN GRANDEUR	CL	30.00	43.00
92 HARVEST MEMORIES	CL	33.00	54.00
92 SCHOOL DAYS	CL	30.00	38.00
92 WOODLAND MILL STREAM	CL	33.00	64.00
93 INDIAN SUMMER	CL	33.00	59.00
N. GLAZIER		**SHADOWS & LIGHT: WINTER'S WILDLIFE**	
92 WINTER'S CHILDREN	CL	30.00	50.00
93 CUB SCOUTS	CL	30.00	59.00
93 LITTLE SNOWMAN	CL	30.00	47.00
93 SNOW CAVE, THE	CL	30.00	40.00
M. SKOLSKY			**SINGIN' IN THE RAIN**
90 GOOD MORNING	CL	33.00	50.00
90 SINGIN' IN THE RAIN	CL	33.00	50.00
91 BROADWAY MELODY	CL	33.00	50.00
91 WE'RE HAPPY AGAIN	CL	33.00	50.00
DISNEY			**SLEEPING BEAUTY**
91 AWAKENED BY A KISS	CL	40.00	50.00
91 HAPPY BIRTHDAY BRIAR ROSE	CL	43.00	58.00
91 ONCE UPON A DREAM	CL	40.00	43.00
92 TOGETHER AT LAST	CL	43.00	60.00
C. LAYTON			**SMALL BLESSINGS**
92 BLESS US O LORD FOR THESE, THY GIFTS	CL	30.00	62.00
92 BLESSED ARE THE PURE IN HEART	CL	33.00	50.00

YR	NAME	LIMIT	ISSUE	TREND
92	JESUS LOVES ME, THIS I KNOW	CL	33.00	65.00
92	NOW I LAY ME DOWN TO SLEEP	CL	30.00	59.00
92	THIS LITTLE LIGHT OF MINE	CL	33.00	50.00
93	BLESS OUR HOME	CL	33.00	50.00
DISNEY		**SNOW WHITE AND THE SEVEN DWARFS**		
91	A SPECIAL TREAT	CL	33.00	49.00
91	DANCE OF SNOW WHITE/SEVEN DWARFS, THE	CL	30.00	55.00
91	WITH A SMILE AND A SONG	CL	30.00	45.00
92	A KISS FOR DOPEY	CL	33.00	45.00
92	A WISH COME TRUE	CL	35.00	50.00
92	FIRESIDE LOVE STORY	CL	35.00	68.00
92	POISON APPLE, THE	CL	33.00	66.00
92	STUBBORN GRUMPY	CL	35.00	45.00
92	TIME TO TIDY UP	CL	35.00	55.00
93	A SURPRISE IN THE CLEARING	CL	37.00	55.00
93	HAPPY ENDING	CL	37.00	60.00
93	MAY I HAVE THIS DANCE?	CL	37.00	55.00
H. BOND		**SONGS OF THE AMERICAN SPIRIT**		
91	AMERICA THE BEAUTIFUL	CL	30.00	45.00
91	BATTLE HYMN OF THE REPUBLIC	CL	30.00	49.00
91	MY COUNTRY TIS OF THEE	CL	30.00	44.00
91	STAR SPANGLED BANNER, THE	CL	30.00	30.00
T. CRNKOVICH		**SOUND OF MUSIC**		
86	DO-RE-MI	CL	20.00	35.00
86	MY FAVORITE THINGS	CL	23.00	40.00
86	SOUND OF MUSIC	CL	20.00	35.00
87	CLIMB EV'RY MOUNTAIN	CL	25.00	50.00
87	EDELWEISS	CL	23.00	35.00
87	I HAVE CONFIDENCE	CL	23.00	35.00
87	LAENDLER WALTZ	CL	23.00	35.00
87	MARIA-WEDDING SCENE	CL	25.00	50.00
E. GIGNILLIAT		**SOUTH PACIFIC**		
87	DITES MOI	CL	25.00	35.00
87	HAPPY TALK	CL	25.00	35.00
87	SOME ENCHANTED EVENING	CL	25.00	35.00
88	HONEY BUN	CL	25.00	35.00
J. BEAUDOIN		**STATELY OWLS**		
89	GREAT HORNED OWL, THE	CL	30.00	40.00
89	SNOWY OWL, THE	CL	30.00	55.00
90	BARN OWL, THE	CL	33.00	40.00
90	BARRED OWL, THE	CL	33.00	50.00
90	GREAT GREY OWL, THE	CL	35.00	50.00
90	SCREECH OWL, THE	CL	33.00	33.00
90	SHORT-EARED OWL, THE	CL	33.00	45.00
91	SAW-WHET OWL, THE	CL	35.00	60.00
E. LICEA		**STORY OF CHRISTMAS BY EVE LICEA**		
87	ANNUNCIATION, THE	YR	45.00	60.00
88	NATIVITY, THE	YR	45.00	60.00
89	ADORATION OF THE SHEPHERDS	YR	50.00	60.00
90	JOURNEY OF THE MAGI	YR	50.00	70.00
91	GIFTS OF THE MAGI	YR	50.00	70.00
92	REST ON THE FLIGHT INTO EGYPT	YR	50.00	70.00
LAWSON		**STORYBOOK TREASURY**		
92	GOLDILOCKS AND THE THREE BEARS	*	*	42.00
92	LITTLE RED RIDING HOOD	*	*	42.00
H. SUNDBLOM		**SUNDBLOM SANTAS**		
89	SANTA BY THE FIRE	CL	28.00	50.00
90	CHRISTMAS VIGIL	CL	28.00	45.00
91	TO ALL A GOOD NIGHT	CL	33.00	50.00
92	SANTA'S ON HIS WAY	CL	33.00	65.00
J. WELTY		**SWEETNESS AND GRACE**		
92	FAVORITE BUDDY	CL	35.00	40.00
92	GOD BLESS TEDDY	CL	35.00	45.00
92	SUNSHINE AND SMILES	CL	35.00	40.00
92	SWEET DREAMS	CL	35.00	40.00
T. KINKADE		**THOMASHIRE**		
92	OLD THOMASHIRE MILL	CL	30.00	50.00
92	OLDE PORTERFIELD TEA ROOM	CL	30.00	50.00
92	PYE CORNER COTTAGE	CL	33.00	50.00
92	SWANBROOK COTTAGE	CL	33.00	50.00
93	BLOSSOM HILL CHURCH	CL	33.00	60.00
93	OLDE GARDEN COTTAGE	CL	33.00	45.00
W. CHAMBERS		**TOM SAWYER**		
87	TOM AND BECKY	CL	28.00	33.00
87	TOM SAWYER THE PIRATE	CL	28.00	33.00
87	WHITEWASHING THE FENCE	CL	28.00	33.00
88	FIRST PIPES	CL	28.00	33.00
J. BEAUDOIN		**UNDER MOTHER'S WING**		
92	ARCTIC SPRING: SNOWY OWLS	CL	30.00	44.00
92	FOREST EDGE: GREAT GRAY OWLS	CL	30.00	40.00
92	LOFTY-LIMB: GREAT HORNED OWLS	CL	35.00	50.00
92	TREETOP TRIO: LONG EARED OWLS	CL	33.00	45.00
92	VAST VIEW: SAW WHET OWLS	CL	33.00	45.00
92	WOODLAND WATCH: SPOTTED OWLS	CL	33.00	45.00
93	HAPPY HOME: SHORT EARED OWL	CL	35.00	50.00
93	PERFECT PERCH: BARRED OWL	CL	35.00	50.00

Andalusian *by Fred Stone from "The Stallion Series" by American Artists was issued in 1983. Limited to 12,500, it is currently valued at $125.*

Issued in 1986, Lesley *was the third release in the "Country Series" by Jan Hagara, an artist known for her elegantly dressed Victorian-era children.*

Schmid introduced Young Reader *as its 17th annual Mother's Day plate inspired by the work of Berta Hummel.*

Released in 1994 for the The Bradford Exchange's Gardens of Innocence collection, Hope *is a closed edition.*

The 1982 issue in Incolay Studios' Romantic Poets Collection, My Heart Leaps Up When I Behold *has increased in value from its issue price of $70.*

YR	NAME	LIMIT	ISSUE	TREND
W. ANDERSON		**UPLAND BIRDS OF NORTH AMERICA**		
86	GROUSE, THE	CL	25.00	35.00
86	PHEASANT, THE	CL	25.00	35.00
87	GRAY PARTRIDGE, THE	CL	28.00	40.00
87	QUAIL, THE	CL	28.00	40.00
87	WILD TURKEY, THE	CL	28.00	40.00
87	WOODCOCK, THE	CL	28.00	40.00
J. WELTY		**WINDOWS OF GLORY**		
93	EVERLASTING FATHER, THE	CL	33.00	33.00
93	GOOD SHEPHERD, THE	CL	33.00	33.00
93	KING OF KINGS	CL	30.00	30.00
93	LIGHT OF THE WORLD, THE	CL	33.00	33.00
93	MESSIAH, THE	CL	33.00	33.00
93	PRINCE OF PEACE	CL	30.00	30.00
J. AUCKLAND		**WIZARD OF OZ**		
77	OVER THE RAINBOW	CL	19.00	145.00
78	IF I ONLY HAD A BRAIN	CL	19.00	85.00
78	IF I ONLY HAD A HEART	CL	19.00	60.00
78	IF I WERE KING OF THE FOREST	CL	19.00	55.00
79	FOLLOW THE YELLOW BRICK ROAD	CL	19.00	45.00
79	WICKED WITCH OF THE WEST	CL	19.00	45.00
79	WONDERFUL WIZARD OF OZ	CL	19.00	45.00
80	GRAND FINALE, THE	CL	24.00	70.00
R. LASLO		**WIZARD OF OZ, A NATIONAL TREASURE**		
91	FOLLOW THE YELLOW BRICK ROAD	CL	30.00	54.00
92	I EVEN SCARE MYSELF	CL	33.00	51.00
92	I HAVEN'T GOT A BRAIN	CL	30.00	51.00
92	I'LL NEVER GET HOME	CL	35.00	51.00
92	I'M A LITTLE RUSTY YET	CL	33.00	49.00
92	I'M MELTING	CL	35.00	53.00
92	THERE'S NO PLACE LIKE HOME	CL	35.00	51.00
92	WE'RE OFF TO SEE THE WIZARD	CL	33.00	51.00
J. WILCOX SMITH		**YESTERDAY'S INNOCENTS**		
92	MY FIRST BOOK	CL	30.00	40.00
92	TIME TO SMELL THE ROSES	CL	30.00	53.00
93	HUSH, BABY'S SLEEPING	CL	33.00	45.00
93	READY AND WAITING	CL	33.00	49.00
T. KINKADE		**YULETIDE MEMORIES**		
92	A BEACON OF FAITH	CL	30.00	40.00
92	MAGIC OF CHRISTMAS, THE	CL	30.00	45.00
93	A WINTER'S WALK	CL	30.00	40.00
93	MOONLIT SLEIGHRIDE	CL	30.00	40.00
93	OLDE PORTERFIELD GIFT SHOPPE	CL	30.00	45.00
93	SILENT NIGHT	CL	30.00	40.00
93	SKATER'S DELIGHT	CL	30.00	40.00
93	WONDER OF THE SEASON, THE	CL	30.00	40.00

ENCHANTICA

YR	NAME	LIMIT	ISSUE	TREND
J. WOODWARD		**DRAGON COLLECTION**		
92	SPRING DRAGON-GORGOYLE	RT	50.00	65.00
92	WINTER DRAGON-GRAWLFANG	RT	50.00	65.00
93	AUTUMN DRAGON-SNARLGARD	RT	50.00	65.00
93	SUMMER DRAGON-ARANGAST	RT	50.00	65.00

ENESCO CORP.

YR	NAME	LIMIT	ISSUE	TREND
*				**BARBIE**
94	35TH ANNIVERSARY	5000	30.00	45.00
94	HOLIDAY 1994	5000	30.00	45.00
P. HILLMAN		**CALICO KITTENS/ 1997 CHRISTMAS INTRODUCTION**		
97	FRIENDSHIP IS HEAVENLY- DATED	5000	35.00	35.00
P. HILLMAN		**CHERISHED TEDDIES**		
95	SANTA COOKIE 141585	*	25.00	25.00
95	SEASON OF JOY, THE 141550	YR	35.00	35.00
96	BEAR IN BUNNY OUTFIT DATED 1996 156590	YR	35.00	35.00
96	MOTHER'S DAY 156493	YR	35.00	35.00
96	SEASON OF PEACE, THE DATED 1996 176060	*	35.00	35.00
97	OUR LOVE IS EVER-BLOOMING	YR	35.00	35.00
97	SEASON TO BELIEVE, THE- DATED	YR	35.00	35.00
97	SPRINGTIME HAPPINESS	YR	35.00	35.00
97	WE BEAR THANKS	OP	35.00	35.00
98	SEASON OF MAGIC	YR	35.00	35.00
M. JANNINCK		**CHERISHED TEDDIES**		
97	EASTER- DATED	YR	35.00	35.00
97	MOTHER'S DAY- DATED	YR	35.00	35.00
P. HILLMAN		**CHERISHED TEDDIES NURSERY RHYME PLATES**		
95	JACK AND JILL 114901	OP	35.00	35.00
95	LITTLE BO PEEP 164658	*	35.00	35.00
95	MARY HAD A LITTLE LAMB 128902	OP	35.00	35.00
95	MOTHER GOOSE/FRIENDS 170968	*	35.00	35.00
95	OLD KING COLE 135437	OP	35.00	35.00
95	WEE WILLIE WINKIE 170941	*	35.00	35.00
96	LITTLE JACK HORNER 151998	OP	35.00	35.00
96	LITTLE MISS MUFFET 145033	OP	35.00	35.00
P. HILLMAN		**CHERISHED TEDDIES ONCE UPON A TEDDY**		
95	GIRL IN GREEN DRESS	OP	35.00	35.00
96	EASTER	OP	35.00	35.00

YR	NAME	LIMIT	ISSUE	TREND
P. HILLMAN		**CHERISHED TEDDIES VILLAGE**		
96	A PICNIC FOR TWO	*	45.00	45.00
P. HILLMAN		**CHERISHED TEDDIES/CHERISHED SEASONS**		
97	AUTUMN BRINGS A SEASON OF THANKSGIVING	OP	35.00	35.00
97	SPRING BRINGS A SEASON OF BEAUTY	OP	35.00	35.00
97	SUMMER BRINGS A SEASON OF WARMTH	OP	35.00	35.00
97	WINTER BRINGS A SEASON OF JOY	OP	35.00	35.00
*		**FROM BARBIE WITH LOVE**		
95	HAPPY HOLIDAYS BARBIE 1988 154180	YR	30.00	30.00
95	HAPPY HOLIDAYS BARBIE 1995 143154	YR	30.00	30.00
95	SOLO IN SPOTLIGHT 1960 114383	5000	30.00	30.00
96	1920'S FLAPPER BARBIE 174777	YR	30.00	30.00
96	A ROYAL SURPRISE, 1964 MINI 171050	*	12.50	13.00
96	ARABIAN NIGHTS, 1964 MINI 171069	*	12.50	13.00
96	BARBIE AS SCARLETT O'HARA IN GREEN VELVET 171085	10000	35.00	35.00
96	CINDERELLA, 1964 MINI 171042	*	12.50	13.00
96	ENCHANTED EVENING, 1960 185787	10000	100.00	100.00
96	GIBSON GIRL BARBIE 174769	10000	30.00	30.00
96	HAPPY HOLIDAYS BARBIE 1996 188816	YR	30.00	30.00
96	HAPPY HOLIDAYS BARBIE, 1989 188859	YR	30.00	30.00
96	HERE COMES THE BRIDE 170984	*	30.00	30.00
96	HOLIDAY DANCE 1965 188786	10000	100.00	100.00
96	QUEENS OF HEARTS BARBIE 157678	OP	25.00	25.00
96	RED RIDING HOOD, 1964 MINI 171077	*	12.50	12.50
KINKA		**KINKA COLLECTOR PLAQUE**		
89	KINKA 119601	OP	10.00	10.00
L. RIGG		**LUCY & ME**		
97	CHRISTMAS PAGEANT- DATED W/EASEL	YR	20.00	20.00
M. RHYNER-NADIG		**MARY'S MOO MOOS DATED 1997**		
97	IT'S BUTTER TO GIVE THAN TO RECEIVE	YR	35.00	35.00
M. RHYNER-NADIG		**MARY'S MOO MOOS MOOEY CHRISTMAS**		
96	WHEEE ARE MOVIN!	YR	17.50	18.00
M. ATTWELL		**MEMORIES OF YESTERDAY**		
93	LOOK OUT-SOMETHING GOOD..YOUR WAY!	YR	50.00	55.00
94	PLEASANT DREAMS & SWEET REPOSE	CL	50.00	75.00
95	JOIN ME FOR A LITTLE SONG	OP	50.00	50.00
S. BUTCHER		**PRECIOUS MOMENTS BEAUTY OF CHRISTMAS COLLECTION**		
92	WISHING YOU/SWEETEST CHRISTMAS 530204	YR	50.00	60.00
94	YOU'RE AS PRETTY AS A CHRISTMAS TREE	OP	50.00	50.00
95	HE COVERS THE EARTH W/HIS BEAUTY 142670	OP	50.00	50.00
96	PEACE ON EARTH...ANYWAY 183377	YR	50.00	50.00
97	CANE YOU JOIN US FOR A MERRY CHRISTMAS	YR	50.00	50.00
S. BUTCHER		**PRECIOUS MOMENTS CHRISTMAS BLESSINGS**		
90	WISHING YOU A YUMMY CHRISTMAS 523801	YR	50.00	75.00
91	BLESSING FROM ME TO THEE 523860	YR	50.00	65.00
92	BUT THE GREATEST/LOVE 527742	YR	50.00	55.00
S. BUTCHER		**PRECIOUS MOMENTS CHRISTMAS COLLECTION**		
81	COME LET US ADORE HIM E-5646	15000	40.00	55.00
82	LET HEAVEN AND NATURE SING E-2347	15000	40.00	60.00
83	WEE THREE KINGS E-0538	15000	40.00	60.00
84	UNTO US A CHILD IS BORN E-5395	15000	40.00	60.00
S. BUTCHER		**PRECIOUS MOMENTS CHRISTMAS LOVE**		
86	I'M SENDING YOU A WHITE CHRISTMAS 101834	YR	45.00	60.00
87	MY PEACE I GIVE TO THEE 102954	YR	45.00	95.00
88	MERRY CHRISTMAS DEER 520284	YR	50.00	85.00
89	MAY YOUR CHRISTMAS BE/HAPPY HOME 523003	YR	50.00	60.00
S. BUTCHER		**PRECIOUS MOMENTS INSPIRED THOUGHTS**		
82	MAKE A JOYFUL NOISE E-7174	15000	40.00	50.00
83	I BELIEVE IN MIRACLES E-9257	15000	40.00	50.00
84	LOVE IS KIND E-2847	15000	40.00	50.00
85	LOVE ONE ANOTHER E-5215	15000	40.00	70.00
S. BUTCHER		**PRECIOUS MOMENTS JOY OF CHRISTMAS**		
82	I'LL PLAY MY DRUM FOR HIM E2357	YR	40.00	75.00
83	CHRISTMASTIME IS FOR SHARING E-0505	YR	40.00	100.00
84	TELL ME THE STORY OF JESUS 15237	YR	40.00	100.00
84	WONDER OF CHRISTMAS, THE E-5396	YR	40.00	85.00
S. BUTCHER		**PRECIOUS MOMENTS MOTHER'S DAY**		
80	MOTHER SEW DEAR E-5217	15000	40.00	55.00
82	PURR-FECT GRANDMA, THE E-7173	15000	40.00	50.00
83	HAND THAT ROCKS THE FUTURE, THE E-9256	15000	40.00	50.00
84	LOVING THY NEIGHBOR E-2848	15000	40.00	50.00
93	THINKING OF YOU...REALLY..TO DO 531766	YR	50.00	55.00
95	HE HATH MADE EVERYTHING...TIME 2ND ED. 129151	YR	50.00	50.00
96	OF ALL THE MOTHERS....AS PRECIOUS AS MY OWN 163716	YR	50.00	50.00
S. BUTCHER		**PRECIOUS MOMENTS OPEN EDITIONS**		
81	LORD BLESS YOU AND KEEP YOU, THE E-5216	SU	30.00	40.00
82	JESUS LOVES ME E-9275	SU	30.00	45.00
82	JESUS LOVES ME E-9276	SU	30.00	45.00
82	OUR FIRST CHRISTMAS TOGETHER E-2378	SU	30.00	50.00
82	REJOICING WITH YOU E-7172	SU	30.00	45.00
94	BRING THE LITTLE ONES TO JESUS 531359	YR	50.00	50.00
S. BUTCHER		**PRECIOUS MOMENTS THE FOUR SEASONS SERIES**		
85	SUMMER'S JOY 12114	YR	40.00	60.00
85	VOICE OF SPRING, THE 12106	YR	40.00	75.00
86	AUTUMN'S PRAISE 12122	YR	40.00	50.00
86	WINTER'S SONG 12130	YR	40.00	60.00

YR	NAME	LIMIT	ISSUE	TREND

FAIRMONT

T. DEGRAZIA — ARTISTS OF THE WORLD/CHILDREN

YR	NAME	LIMIT	ISSUE	TREND
78	FLOWER GIRL	9500	45.00	50.00
79	FLOWER BOY	9500	45.00	59.00
80	LITTLE COCOPAH INDIAN GIRL	9500	50.00	65.00
81	BEAUTIFUL BURDEN	9500	50.00	59.00
82	MERRY LITTLE INDIAN	9500	55.00	85.00
83	WONDERING	10000	60.00	27.00
84	PINK PAPOOSE	10000	65.00	24.00
84	SUNFLOWER BOY	10000	65.00	32.00

T. DEGRAZIA — ARTISTS OF THE WORLD/CHILDREN AT PLAY

YR	NAME	LIMIT	ISSUE	TREND
85	MY FIRST HORSE	15000	65.00	65.00
86	GIRL AT SEWING MACHINE	15000	65.00	65.00
87	LOVE ME	15000	65.00	60.00
88	MERRILY, MERRILY, MERRILY	15000	65.00	65.00
89	MY FIRST ARROW	15000	65.00	83.00

T. DEGRAZIA — ARTISTS OF THE WORLD/HOLIDAY

YR	NAME	LIMIT	ISSUE	TREND
76	FESTIVAL OF LIGHTS	9500	45.00	120.00
77	BELL OF HOPE	9500	45.00	43.00
78	LITTLE MADONNA	9500	45.00	50.00
79	NATIVITY, THE	9500	50.00	63.00
80	PRIME INDIAN DRUMMER	9500	50.00	61.00
81	LITTLE PRAYER ANGEL	9500	55.00	33.00
82	BLUE BOY	10000	60.00	34.00
83	HEAVENLY BLESSINGS	10000	65.00	24.00
84	NAVAJO MADONNA	10000	65.00	27.00
85	SAGUARO DANCE	10000	65.00	40.00

R. SKELTON — FAMOUS CLOWNS

YR	NAME	LIMIT	ISSUE	TREND
76	FREDDIE THE FREELOADER	10000	55.00	— 550.00
77	W.C. FIELDS	10000	55.00	— 150.00
78	HAPPY	10000	55.00	— 80.00
79	PLEDGE, THE	10000	55.00	— 70.00

I. SPENCER — SPENCER SPECIAL

YR	NAME	LIMIT	ISSUE	TREND
78	HUG ME	10000	55.00	155.00
78	SLEEP LITTLE BABY	10000	65.00	130.00

FENTON ART GLASS

YR	NAME	LIMIT	ISSUE	TREND
*	PLATE 8011 9"	*	*	15.00
81	PLATE 7418FN MOTHER'S DAY 8"	*	*	45.00
81	PLATE 8281FL XMAS IN AMERICA 8"	*	*	50.00
81	PLATE 8417TN HARVEST C&I	*	*	35.00
81	PLATE 8418TB CURRIER & IVES 8"	*	*	25.00
81	PLATE 9412FL NATIVITY	*	*	25.00
81	PLATE 9412FT NATIVITY	*	*	25.00
81	PLATE 9412TB NATIVITY	*	*	25.00
81	PLATE 9412TG NATIVITY	*	*	25.00
81	PLATE 9412VE	*	*	30.00
82	PLATE 7418OC XMAS 8"	*	*	45.00
82	PLATE 7615TC CUP ARTIST SERIES	*	*	20.00
82	PLATE 8415TB OLD HOME C&I	*	*	35.00
83	PLATE 7418AO XMAS FANTASY 8"	*	*	40.00
83	PLATE 7418CU MINERVA OH SESQ 8"	*	*	50.00
83	PLATE 7418FV DESIGNER SERIES 8"	*	*	95.00
83	PLATE 7418LT DESIGNER SERIES 8"	*	*	85.00
83	PLATE 7418RQ MOTHER'S DAY 8"	*	*	50.00
83	PLATE 7615WC CUP ARTIST SERIES	*	*	20.00
83	PLATE CUP 7615WC	*	*	20.00
84	PLATE 7618EE DESIGNER SERIES 8"	1250	*	50.00
84	PLATE 8418CN CURRIER & IVES	*	*	35.00
85	PLATE 7418 GARDEN OF EDEN 8"	*	*	40.00
85	PLATE 7418WP XMAS FANTASY 8"	*	*	45.00
85	PLATE 7615CL CUP CLOWN	*	*	20.00
85	PLATE 7615FG CUP ARTIST SERIES	*	*	20.00
85	PLATE 7615HQ CUP HOBBY HORSE	*	*	20.00
85	PLATE 7618 IN SEASON 8"	*	*	120.00
85	PLATE 8011LE DESIGNER 9"	*	*	50.00
85	PLATE 9614NK 8"	19500	*	35.00
86	7418SU STUDEBAKER 8"	*	*	135.00
86	PLAQUE 7698SU STUDEBAKER	5000	*	85.00
86	PLATE 7418TP JUPITER 8"	5000	*	100.00
86	PLATE 7618LE DESIGNER 9"	*	*	65.00
87	PLATE 7615PN CUP CHILDHOOD	*	*	18.00
87	PLATE 7615PN CUP FRISKY PUP	*	*	20.00
87	PLATE 7615SF CUP ARTIST SERIES	*	*	20.00
88	PLATE 7418 BOB EVANS 8"	*	*	50.00
88	PLATE 7418 EVANS XMAS 8"	*	*	50.00
88	PLATE 7418 LEVEE 8"	*	*	50.00
88	PLATE 7418 MARIETTA 8"	*	*	95.00
89	PLATE 7615AC ARTIST SERIES	*	*	20.00
89	PLATE 7615CX CUP CHILDHOOD	*	*	18.00
90	PLATE 7418BL 8"	*	*	75.00
90	PLATE 7418LT COUNTRY SCENE 8"	*	*	75.00
90	PLATE 7418NB 8"	*	*	75.00
90	PLATE 7418SN MOTHER'S DAY 8"	*	*	75.00
94	PLATE 7418PM PRECIOUS PANDA 8"	*	*	50.00

YR	NAME	LIMIT	ISSUE	TREND
*			**AMERICAN CRAFTSMAN CARNIVAL**	
70	GLASSMAKER	CL	10.00	55.00
71	PRINTER	CL	10.00	55.00
72	BLACKSMITH	CL	10.00	55.00
73	SHOEMAKER	CL	12.50	55.00
74	COOPER	CL	12.50	55.00
75	SILVERSMITH REVERE	CL	12.50	55.00
76	GUNSMITH	CL	15.00	55.00
77	POTTER	CL	15.00	55.00
78	WHEELWRIGHT	CL	15.00	55.00
79	CABINETMAKER	CL	15.00	55.00
80	TANNER	CL	16.50	55.00
81	HOUSEWRIGHT 9681	CL	17.50	55.00
	D. JOHNSON		**BIRDS OF WINTER ED. I**	
87	PLATE 7418BC W/STAND 8"	4500	40.00	35.00
	D. JOHNSON		**BIRDS OF WINTER ED. II**	
88	PLATE 7418BD W/STAND 8"	4500	40.00	50.00
	D. JOHNSON		**BIRDS OF WINTER ED. III**	
90	PLATE 7418BL W/STAND 8"	4500	40.00	75.00
	D. JOHNSON		**BIRDS OF WINTER ED. IV**	
80	PLATE 7418NB W/STAND 8"	4500	40.00	40.00
	F. BURTON		**CHRISTMAS AT HOME ED. I**	
90	PLATE 7418HD W/STAND 8"	3500	45.00	45.00
	F. BURTON		**CHRISTMAS AT HOME ED. II**	
90	PLATE 7418HJ W/ STAND 8"	3500	45.00	45.00
	F. BURTON		**CHRISTMAS AT HOME ED. III**	
92	PLATE 7418HQ W/STAND 8"	3500	49.00	50.00
	F. BURTON		**CHRISTMAS AT HOME ED. IV**	
93	PLATE 7418HT W/STAND	3500	49.00	49.00
	K. CUNNINGHAM		**CHRISTMAS CLASSICS ED. II**	
79	PLATE 7418NC 8" NATURE'S CHRISTMAS	YR	35.00	30.00
	D. JOHNSON		**CHRISTMAS CLASSICS ED. III**	
80	PLATE 7418GH 8" GOING HOME	YR	39.00	45.00
	D. JOHNSON		**CHRISTMAS CLASSICS ED. IV**	
81	PLATE 7418AC 8" ALL IS CALM	YR	43.00	30.00
	R. SPINDLER		**CHRISTMAS CLASSICS ED. V**	
82	PLATE 7418NA 8" COUNTRY CHRISTMAS	YR	43.00	50.00
	D. JOHNSON		**CHRISTMAS FANTASY ED. I**	
83	PLATE 7418AO 8" ANTICIPATION	7500	45.00	40.00
	D. JOHNSON		**CHRISTMAS FANTASY ED. II**	
84	PLATE 7418GE 8" EXPECTATION	7500	50.00	50.00
	D. JOHNSON		**CHRISTMAS FANTASY ED. III**	
85	PLATE 7418WP 8" HEART'S DESIRE	7500	50.00	45.00
	L. EVERSON		**CHRISTMAS FANTASY ED. IV**	
87	PLATE 7418CV 8" SHARING THE SPIRIT	YR	50.00	50.00
	F. BURTON		**CHRISTMAS STAR**	
94	SILENT NIGHT	1500	65.00	65.00
95	OUR HOME IS BLESSED 7418VT W/STAND 8"	1500	65.00	65.00
	F. BURTON		**CHRISTMAS STAR ED. III**	
96	PLATE 7418SN 8" STAR OF WONDER	1750	65.00	65.00
	M. REYNOLDS		**EASTER LIMITED EDITIONS**	
95	COVERED HEN & EGG 5188YZ	950	95.00	110.00
	M. REYNOLDS		**HANDPAINTED MOTHER'S DAY**	
80	NEW BORN	CL	29.00	25.00
81	GENTLE FAWN	CL	33.00	30.00
82	NATURES AWAKENING	CL	35.00	35.00
84	PRECIOUS PANDA	CL	35.00	25.00
85	MOTHER'S LITTLE LAMB	CL	35.00	35.00
90	WHITE SWAN	CL	45.00	50.00
91	MOTHER'S WATCHFUL EYE	CL	45.00	45.00
92	LET'S PLAY WITH MOM 7418X5 8" W/STAND	CL	50.00	35.00
93	MOTHER DEER	CL	50.00	35.00
94	LOVING PUPPY	CL	50.00	50.00
*			**HISTORICAL COLLECTION**	
91	CAKEPLATE 4671BO 11-1/4"	*	40.00	40.00
91	PLATE 4611DT 12"	*	35.00	35.00
*			**LOVES ME, LOVES ME NOT**	
94	PLATE WITH STAND, 9" 8319RY	TL	65.00	65.00
	M. REYNOLDS		**MARY GREGORY**	
94	PLATE 8319RY W/STAND	CL	65.00	70.00
95	PLATE 8319RG W/STAND 9"	CL	65.00	65.00
	M. DICKINSON		**SMOKE 'N CINDERS**	
84	PLATE WITH STAND, 8" 7618TL	1250	*	110.00
*			**STATUE OF LIBERTY**	
85	PLATE 7618LO DESIGNER 9"	1250	*	105.00

FITZ & FLOYD

YR	NAME	LIMIT	ISSUE	TREND
	R. HAVINS		**ANNUAL CHRISTMAS PLATE**	
92	MAGIC OF THE NUTCRACKER, THE	CL	65.00	70.00
	T. KERR		**ANNUAL CHRISTMAS PLATE**	
93	A DICKENS CHRISTMAS	5000	75.00	80.00
94	NIGHT BEFORE CHRISTMAS	7500	75.00	80.00

YR	NAME	LIMIT	ISSUE	TREND
	R. HAVINS		**MYTH OF SANTA CLAUS**	
93	FATHER FROST	5000	70.00	75.00
94	CANDYLAND SANTA	5000	75.00	80.00
	R. HAVINS		**TWELVE DAYS OF CHRISTMAS**	
93	TWELVE DAYS OF CHRISTMAS	5000	75.00	80.00
	R. HAVINS		**WONDERLAND**	
93	A MAD TEA PARTY	5000	70.00	75.00

FLAMBRO

YR	NAME	LIMIT	ISSUE	TREND
	D. RUST		**EMMETT KELLY JR.**	
83	WHY ME?-PLATE I	10000	40.00	455.00
84	BALLOONS FOR SALE-PLATE II	10000	40.00	355.00
85	BIG BUSINESS-PLATE III	10000	40.00	355.00
86	AND GOD BLESS AMERICA-PLATE IV	10000	40.00	— 330.00
88	TIS THE SEASON	10000	50.00	80.00
89	LOOKING BACK-65TH BIRTHDAY	6500	50.00	130.00
91	WINTER	10000	60.00	60.00
92	AUTUMN	10000	60.00	60.00
92	SPRING	10000	60.00	60.00
92	SUMMER	10000	60.00	60.00
93	SANTA'S STOWAWAY	10000	30.00	35.00
94	70TH BIRTHDAY COMMEMORATIVE	5000	30.00	35.00
95	ALL WRAPPED UP IN CHRISTMAS	5000	30.00	30.00
	C. BEYLON		**RAGGEDY ANN & ANDY**	
88	70 YEARS YOUNG	10000	35.00	35.00

FOUNTAINHEAD

YR	NAME	LIMIT	ISSUE	TREND
	M. FERNANDEZ		**AS FREE AS THE WIND**	
89	AS FREE AS THE WIND	*	295.00	450.00
	M. FERNANDEZ		**SEASONS**	
86	FALL CARDINALS	5000	85.00	150.00
87	SPRING ROBINS	5000	85.00	150.00
87	SUMMER GOLDFINCHES	5000	85.00	150.00
87	WINTER CHICKADEES	5000	85.00	150.00
	M. FERNANDEZ		**TWELVE DAYS OF CHRISTMAS**	
88	A PARTRIDGE IN A PEAR TREE	7500	155.00	155.00
88	TWO TURTLEDOVES	7500	*	155.00
89	FOUR CALLING BIRDS	7500	*	155.00
89	THREE FRENCH HENS	7500	155.00	155.00
	M. FERNANDEZ		**WINGS OF FREEDOM**	
85	COURTSHIP FLIGHT	2500	250.00	1650.00
86	WINGS OF FREEDOM	2500	250.00	1100.00

FRANKLIN MINT

YR	NAME	LIMIT	ISSUE	TREND
	N. MATTHEWS			
95	KITTEN COMPANIONS	45 DAYS	55.00	55.00
	T. POLITOWICZ			
95	IMPERIAL HUMMINGBIRD, THE	45 DAYS	30.00	30.00
	BROOKS		**TEDDY BEAR MUSEUM**	
94	JUST MARRIED	*	*	43.00

GARTLAN USA

YR	NAME	LIMIT	ISSUE	TREND
	M./J. TAYLOR			
91	AL BARLICK PLATE	15	*	20.00
	M./J. TAYLOR		**BOB COUSY COLLECTION**	
94	BOB COUSY 10 1/4"	RT	175.00	200.00
94	BOB COUSY 3 1/4"	OP	15.00	15.00
94	BOB COUSY 8 1/4"	5000	30.00	30.00
	M. TAYLOR		**BRETT & BOBBY HULL**	
91	HOCKEY'S GOLDEN BOYS 3 1/4"	OP	15.00	25.00
91	HOCKEY'S GOLDEN BOYS 8 1/2"	10000	30.00	40.00
91	HOCKEY'S GOLDEN BOYS SIGNED 10 1/4"	950	250.00	500.00
92	PLATE A/P	300	350.00	355.00
	M. TAYLOR		**CARL YASTRZEMSKI-THE IMPOSSIBLE DREAM**	
93	PLATE 3 1/4"	OP	15.00	20.00
93	PLATE 8 1/2"	10000	30.00	40.00
93	SIGNED PLATE 10 1/4"	950	150.00	165.00
	M. TAYLOR		**CARLTON FISK**	
92	PLATE 3 1/4"	OP	15.00	20.00
92	PLATE 8 1/2"	10000	30.00	35.00
92	SIGNED PLATE 10 1/4"	950	70.00	110.00
92	SIGNED PLATE, A/P 10 1/4"	300	175.00	230.00
	M. TAYLOR		**COACHING CLASSICS-JOHN WOODEN**	
89	COLLECTOR PLATE 3 1/4"	OP	15.00	20.00
89	COLLECTOR PLATE 8 1/2"	10000	30.00	35.00
89	COLLECTOR PLATE, SIGNED 10 1/4"	1975	100.00	105.00
	M. TAYLOR		**DALE EARNHARDT**	
95	PLATE 3 1/4"	OP	14.95	15.00
95	PLATE 8 1/2"	10000	30.00	30.00
95	SIGNED PLATE 10 1/4"	1994	150.00	155.00
	M. TAYLOR		**DARRYL STRAWBERRY**	
90	PLATE 3 1/4"	OP	15.00	20.00
90	PLATE 8 1/2"	10000	30.00	50.00
90	SIGNED PLATE 10 1/4"	2500	70.00	130.00
	M. TAYLOR		**FRANK THOMAS**	
94	PLATE 3 1/4"	OP	14.95	15.00

YR	NAME	LIMIT	ISSUE	TREND
94	PLATE 8 1/2"	10000	30.00	30.00
94	SIGNED PLATE 10 1/4"	1994	150.00	155.00
J. MARTIN	**GEORGE BRETT GOLD CROWN COLLECTION**			
86	GEORGE BRETT, BASEBALL ALL STAR 3 1/4"	OP	12.95	25.00
86	GEORGE BRETT, SIGNED 10 1/4"	2000	100.00	500.00
M. TAYLOR	**GORDIE HOWE**			
92	SIGNED PLATE 10 1/4"	2358	90.00	120.00
92	SIGNED PLATE 3 1/4"	OP	15.00	20.00
92	SIGNED PLATE 8 1/2"	10000	30.00	55.00
92	SIGNED PLATE, A/P 10 1/4"	250	150.00	175.00
M. TAYLOR	**JOE MONTANA**			
91	PLATE 3 1/4"	OP	15.00	20.00
91	PLATE 8 1/2"	10000	30.00	40.00
91	SIGNED PLATE 10 1/4"	2250	125.00	130.00
91	SIGNED PLATE, A/P 10 1/4"	250	195.00	200.00
94	PLATE, K.C. CHIEFS 3 1/4"	OP	14.95	15.00
94	PLATE, K.C. CHIEFS 8 1/2"	10000	30.00	30.00
M. TAYLOR	**JOHNNY BENCH**			
89	COLLECTOR PLATE 3 1/4"	OP	15.00	20.00
89	COLLECTOR PLATE, SIGNED 10 1/4"	1989	100.00	205.00
M. TAYLOR	**KAREEM ABDUL-JABBAR SKY-HOOK COLLECTION**			
89	COLLECTOR PLATE 3 1/4"	CL	16.00	35.00
89	KAREEM ABDUL-JABBAR, SIGNED 10 1/4"	1989	100.00	210.00
M. TAYLOR	**KEN GRIFFEY JR.**			
92	PLATE 3 1/4"	OP	15.00	20.00
92	PLATE 8 1/2"	10000	30.00	40.00
92	SIGNED PLATE 10 1/4"	1989	100.00	115.00
92	SIGNED PLATE, A/P 10 1/2"	300	195.00	200.00
M. TAYLOR	**KRISTI YAMAGUCHI COLLECTION**			
93	KRISTI YAMAGUCHI 8 1/4"	5000	30.00	30.00
93	KRISTI YAMAGUCHI 10 1/4"	50	150.00	200.00
93	KRISTI YAMAGUCHI 3 1/4"	OP	15.00	15.00
93	PLATE 3 1/4"	OP	15.00	20.00
93	PLATE 8 1/2"	5000	30.00	40.00
93	SIGNED PLATE 10 1/4"	950	100.00	130.00
M. TAYLOR	**LEAVE IT TO BEAVER/JERRY MATHERS**			
95	LEAVE IT TO BEAVER 10 1/4"	1963	125.00	170.00
95	LEAVE IT TO BEAVER 10 1/4" AP	234	175.00	175.00
95	LEAVE IT TO BEAVER 3 1/4"	OP	15.00	15.00
95	LEAVE IT TO BEAVER 8 1/4"	10000	40.00	55.00
M. TAYLOR	**LUIS APARICIO**			
90	PLATE 3 1/4"	OP	15.00	25.00
90	PLATE 8 1/2"	10000	30.00	50.00
90	SIGNED PLATE 10 1/4"	1984	70.00	130.00
90	SIGNED PLATE, A/P 10 1/4"	250	150.00	155.00
R. WINSLOW	**MAGIC JOHNSON GOLD RIM COLLECTION**			
87	MAGIC JOHNSON-THE MAGIC SHOW	CL	14.50	30.00
87	MAGIC JOHNSON-THE MAGIC SHOW SIGNED	1987	100.00	450.00
C. PALUSO	**MIKE SCHMIDT 500TH HOME RUN EDITION**			
87	MIKE SCHMIDT (A/P)	56	150.00	155.00
87	MIKE SCHMIDT H/S DATED	50	100.00	600.00
87	MIKE SCHMIDT-POWER AT THE PLATE	OP	14.50	20.00
87	MIKE SCHMIDT-POWER AT THE PLATE SIGNED	1987	100.00	400.00
M. TAYLOR	**PATRICK EWING**			
95	PLATE 3 1/4"	OP	14.95	15.00
95	PLATE 8 1/2"	10000	30.00	30.00
95	SIGNED PLATE 10 1/4"	950	150.00	155.00
B. FORBES	**PETE ROSE DIAMOND COLLECTION**			
88	PETE ROSE SIGNED A/P 10 1/4"	50	300.00	400.00
88	PETE ROSE-THE REIGNING LEGEND 3 1/4"	OP	14.50	20.00
88	PETE ROSE-THE REIGNING LEGEND SIGNED	950	195.00	285.00
T. SIZEMORE	**PETE ROSE PLATINUM EDITION**			
85	PETE ROSE "THE BEST OF BASEBALL"	4192	100.00	400.00
85	PETE ROSE H/S DATED	50	100.00	680.00
85	PETE ROSE-THE BEST OF BASEBALL 3 1/4"	OP	12.95	25.00
M. TAYLOR	**PHIL ESPOSITO**			
92	PLATE 3 1/4"	OP	15.00	20.00
92	PLATE 8 1/2"	10000	30.00	40.00
92	SIGNED PLATE 10 1/4"	1984	150.00	155.00
92	SIGNED PLATE, A/P 10 1/2"	300	195.00	200.00
M. TAYLOR	**RINGO STARR**			
96	RINGO STARR 10 1/4" AP	250	400.00	400.00
96	RINGO STARR 10"	1000	225.00	225.00
96	RINGO STARR 3 3/4" MINI	OP	15.00	15.00
96	RINGO STARR 8 1/4"	10000	30.00	30.00
M. TAYLOR	**ROD CAREW**			
91	HITTING FOR THE HALL 3 1/4"	OP	15.00	25.00
91	HITTING FOR THE HALL 8 1/2"	10000	30.00	50.00
91	HITTING FOR THE HALL, SIGNED	950	70.00	155.00
C. SOILEAU	**ROGER STAUBACH STERLING COLLECTION**			
87	ROGER STAUBACH 3 1/4"	OP	12.95	25.00
87	ROGER STAUBACH, SIGNED 10 1/4"	1979	100.00	160.00
J. MARTIN	**ROUND TRIPPER**			
86	REGGIE JACKSON 3 1/4"	OP	12.95	25.00
M. TAYLOR	**SAM SNEAD COLLECTION**			
94	SAM SNEAD 10 1/4"	50	100.00	200.00

YR	NAME	LIMIT	ISSUE	TREND
94	SAM SNEAD 3 1/4"	OP	15.00	15.00
94	SAM SNEAD 8 1/4"	5000	30.00	30.00
M. TAYLOR			**SHAQUILLE O'NEAL**	
94	PLATE 3 1/4"	OP	14.95	15.00
94	PLATE 8 1/2"	10000	30.00	40.00
94	SIGNED PLATE 10 1/4"	1993	195.00	200.00
M. TAYLOR		**SHAQUILLE O'NEAL CLUB PLATE**		
94	SHAQUILLE O'NEAL	*	30.00	50.00
M. TAYLOR			**TOM SEAVER**	
92	SIGNED PLATE 10 1/4"	1992	90.00	120.00
92	SIGNED PLATE 3 1/4"	OP	15.00	20.00
92	SIGNED PLATE 8 1/2"	10000	30.00	40.00
92	SIGNED PLATE, A/P 10 1/4"	250	195.00	200.00
M. TAYLOR			**TROY AIKMAN**	
94	PLATE 3 1/2"	OP	14.95	15.00
94	PLATE 8 1/2"	10000	30.00	40.00
94	SIGNED PLATE 10 1/4"	1993	150.00	155.00
95	TROY AIKMAN 10 1/4" AUTOGRAPHED	SO	125.00	200.00
95	TROY AIKMAN 8 1/4"	10000	30.00	30.00
95	TROY AIKMAN MINI 3 1/4"	OP	15.00	15.00
M. TAYLOR			**WAYNE GRETZKY**	
89	COLLECTOR PLATE	300	300.00	430.00
89	COLLECTOR PLATE 3 1/4"	OP	15.00	25.00
89	COLLECTOR PLATE 8 1/2"	10000	45.00	55.00
89	COLLECTOR PLATE, H/S BY GRETZKY & HOWE	1851	225.00	290.00
M. TAYLOR			**WHITEY FORD**	
90	PLATE 3 1/4"	OP	15.00	20.00
90	PLATE 8 1/2"	10000	30.00	40.00
90	SIGNED PLATE 10 1/4"	2360	70.00	110.00
90	SIGNED PLATE, A/P 10 1/4"	250	175.00	180.00
M. TAYLOR			**YOGI BERRA**	
89	COLLECTOR PLATE 3 1/4"	OP	15.00	25.00
89	COLLECTOR PLATE 8 1/2"	10000	30.00	40.00
89	COLLECTOR PLATE, SIGNED 10 1/4"	2150	100.00	125.00
89	COLLECTOR PLATE, SIGNED A/P 10 1/4"	250	175.00	180.00

GEORGETOWN COLLECTION INC.

C. THEROUX		**CHILDREN OF THE GREAT SPIRIT**		
93	BUFFALO CHILD	CL	30.00	35.00
93	WINTER BABY	CL	30.00	35.00

GHENT COLLECTION

E. BIERLY		**AMERICAN BICENTENNIAL WILDLIFE**		
76	AMERICAN WHITETAIL DEER	2500	95.00	500.00
C. FRACE		**AMERICAN BICENTENNIAL WILDLIFE**		
76	AMERICAN BISON	2500	95.00	500.00
A. GILBERT		**AMERICAN BICENTENNIAL WILDLIFE**		
76	AMERICAN WILD TURKEY	2500	95.00	500.00
H. MOELLER		**AMERICAN BICENTENNIAL WILDLIFE**		
76	AMERICAN BALD EAGLE	2500	95.00	500.00
N. ROCKWELL			**APRIL FOOL ANNUAL**	
78	APRIL FOOL	10000	35.00	75.00
79	APRIL FOOL	10000	35.00	60.00
80	APRIL FOOL	10000	38.00	60.00

GOEBEL INC.

Price ranges may reflect various demands in the market from one geographic region to another; condition of piece; specific markings found on piece; and/or changes in production of piece.

M.I. HUMMEL		**FIGURAL CHRISTMAS PLATES**		
95	FESTIVAL HARMONY W/FLUTE HUM 693	CL	125.00	115.00
96	CHRISTMAS SONG HUM 692	CL	130.00	115.00
97	THANKSGIVING PRAYER HUM 694	YR	140.00	140.00
M.I. HUMMEL			**FOUR SEASONS**	
96	WINTER MELODY HUM 296	YR	195.00	200.00
98	SUMMERTIME STROLL HUM 298	YR	*	195.00
M.I. HUMMEL			**FRIENDS FOREVER**	
92	MEDITATION HUM-292	CL	180.00	200.00
93	FOR FATHER HUM-293	CL	195.00	200.00
94	SWEET GREETINGS PLATE HUM-294	CL	205.00	210.00
95	SURPRISE PLATE HUM-295	OP	210.00	215.00
M.I. HUMMEL		**KITCHEN MOULD COLLECTION**		
91	KITCHEN MOULD COLLECTION HUM-669	CL	99.00	163.00
91	KITCHEN MOULD COLLECTION HUM-670	CL	99.00	163.00
91	KITCHEN MOULD COLLECTION HUM-671	CL	99.00	163.00
91	KITCHEN MOULD COLLECTION HUM-672	CL	99.00	163.00
M.I. HUMMEL			**LITTLE HOMEMAKERS**	
88	LITTLE SWEEPER HUM-745	CL	45.00	88.00
89	WASH DAY HUM-746	CL	50.00	88.00
90	A STITCH IN TIME HUM-747	CL	50.00	88.00
91	CHICKEN LICKEN HUM-748	CL	70.00	88.00
M.I. HUMMEL			**LITTLE MUSIC MAKER**	
84	LITTLE FIDDLER HUM-744	CL	30.00	88.00
85	SERENADE HUM-741	CL	30.00	88.00
86	SOLOIST HUM-743	CL	35.00	88.00
87	BAND LEADER HUM-742	CL	40.00	88.00

YR	NAME	LIMIT	ISSUE	TREND
M.I. HUMMEL		**M.I. HUMMEL ANNIVERSARY PLATES**		
75	STORMY WEATHER HUM-280	CL	100.00	225.00
80	RING AROUND THE ROSIE HUM-281	CL	225.00	200.00
85	AUF WIEDERSEHEN HUM-282	CL	225.00	275.00
M.I. HUMMEL		**M.I. HUMMEL ANNUAL COLLECTIBLE PLATES**		
71	HEAVENLY ANGEL HUM-264	CL	25.00	875.00
72	HEAR YE, HEAR YE HUM-265	CL	30.00	104.00
73	GLOBE TROTTER HUM-266	CL	33.00	225.00
74	GOOSE GIRL HUM-267	CL	40.00	103.00
75	RIDE INTO CHRISTMAS HUM-268	CL	50.00	103.00
76	APPLE TREE GIRL HUM-269	CL	50.00	103.00
77	APPLE TREE BOY HUM-270	CL	53.00	103.00
78	HAPPY PASTIME HUM-271	CL	65.00	103.00
79	SINGING LESSON HUM-272	CL	90.00	88.00
80	SCHOOL GIRL HUM-273	CL	100.00	88.00
81	UMBRELLA BOY HUM-274	CL	100.00	103.00
82	UMBRELLA GIRL HUM-275	CL	100.00	88.00
83	POSTMAN HUM-276	CL	108.00	263.00
84	LITTLE HELPER HUM-277	CL	108.00	125.00
85	CHICK GIRL HUM-278	CL	110.00	125.00
86	PLAYMATES HUM-279	CL	125.00	200.00
87	FEEDING TIME HUM-283	CL	135.00	375.00
88	LITTLE GOAT HERDER HUM-284	CL	145.00	188.00
89	FARM BOY HUM-285	CL	160.00	213.00
90	SHEPHERD'S BOY HUM-286	CL	170.00	238.00
91	JUST RESTING HUM-287	CL	196.00	238.00
92	WAYSIDE HARMONY HUM-288	CL	210.00	238.00
93	DOLL BATH HUM-289	CL	210.00	238.00
94	DOCTOR HUM-290	CL	225.00	238.00
95	COME BACK SOON HUM 291	CL	250.00	263.00
M.I. HUMMEL		**M.I. HUMMEL CHRISTMAS PLATES**		
87	CELESTIAL MUSICIAN	20000	35.00	69.00
88	ANGEL DUET	20000	40.00	50.00
89	GUIDING LIGHT	20000	*	75.00
90	TENDER WATCH	20000	*	75.00
M.I. HUMMEL		**M.I. HUMMEL CLUB EXCLUSIVE-CELEBRATION**		
86	VALENTINE GIFT HUM-738	CL	90.00	125.00
87	VALENTINE JOY HUM-737	CL	98.00	125.00
88	DAISIES DON'T TELL HUM-736	CL	115.00	125.00
89	IT'S COLD HUM-735	CL	120.00	125.00
M.I. HUMMEL		**M.I. HUMMEL FIGURAL CHRISTMAS PLATES**		
98	ECHOES OF JOY HUM 695	*	*	N/A
M.I. HUMMEL		**M.I. HUMMEL PLAQUES**		
47	M.I. HUMMEL PLAQUES (IN ENGLISH) HUM-187	CL	*	175.00-1500.00
49	M.I. HUMMEL DEALER'S PLAQ FRENCH HUM-208	CL	*	3000.00-6000.00
54	STAR GLAZER, WALL PLAQUE HUM-237	CL	*	12500.00
68	MERRY WANDERER WALL PLAQUE HUM-263	CL	*	12500.00
93	ARTIST PLAQUE HUM-756	CL	260.00	350.00-500.00
95	PUPPY LOVE, DISPLAY PLAQUE HUM-767	OP	240.00	325.00
M.I. HUMMEL		**M.I. HUMMEL PLAQUES MADE IN GERMANY**		
49	M.I. HUMMEL DEALER'S PLAQ GERMAN HUM-205	CL	*	850.00-1700.00
M.I. HUMMEL		**M.I. HUMMEL PLAQUES MADE IN SWEDEN**		
49	M.I. HUMMEL DEALER'S PLAQ SWED. HUM-209	CL	*	4000.00-6000.00
M.I. HUMMEL		**M.I. HUMMEL PLAQUES SCHMID BROS.**		
35	M.I. HUMMEL DEALER'S PLAQ/SCHMID HUM-210	CL	*	20000.00-25000.00
M.I. HUMMEL		**M.I. HUMMEL PLAQUES- BRITISH VERSION**		
86	GOEBEL AUTHORIZED RETAILER PLAQ. HUM-460	OP	*	300.00-750.00
M.I. HUMMEL		**M.I. HUMMEL PLAQUES- DUTCH VERSION**		
86	GOEBEL AUTHORIZED RETAILER PLAQ. HUM-460	OP	*	300.00-1500.00
M.I. HUMMEL		**M.I. HUMMEL PLAQUES- FRENCH VERISON**		
86	GOEBEL AUTHORIZED RETAILER PLAQ. HUM-460	OP	*	300.00-1000.00
M.I. HUMMEL		**M.I. HUMMEL PLAQUES- GERMAN VERSION**		
86	GOEBEL AUTHORIZED RETAILER PLAQ. HUM-460	OP	*	300.00-1000.00
M.I. HUMMEL		**M.I. HUMMEL PLAQUES- ITALIAN VERSION**		
86	GOEBEL AUTHORIZED RETAILER PLAQ. HUM-460	OP	*	300.00-1500.00
M.I. HUMMEL		**M.I. HUMMEL PLAQUES- U.S. VERSION**		
86	GOEBEL AUTHORIZED RETAILER PLAQ. HUM-460	CL	*	225.00
M.I. HUMMEL		**M.I. HUMMEL PLAQUES-SPANISH VERSION**		
51	M.I. HUMMEL DEALER'S PLAQ SPAN. HUM-213	CL	*	9000.00
86	GOEBEL AUTHORIZED RETAILER PLAQ. HUM-460	OP	*	300.00-1500.00
M.I. HUMMEL		**M.I. HUMMEL PLAQUES-SWEDISH VERSION**		
86	GOEBEL AUTHORIZED RETAILER PLAQ. HUM-460	OP	*	300.00-1000.00

GORHAM

*		**AMERICAN ARTISTS COLLECTION**		
76	BLACK REGIMENT	*	*	86.00
R. DONNELLY		**AMERICAN ARTISTS COLLECTION**		
76	APACHE MOTHER & CHILD	9800	25.00	80.00
N. ROCKWELL		**AMERICAN ARTISTS COLLECTION**		
80	CHILLY RECEPTION	*	*	98.00
BARRYMORE		**BARRYMORE**		
71	QUIET WATERS	15000	25.00	30.00
72	LITTLE BOATYARD, STERLING	1000	100.00	150.00
72	NANTUCKET, STERLING	1000	100.00	105.00
72	SAN PEDRO HARBOR	15000	25.00	30.00

YR	NAME	LIMIT	ISSUE	TREND
N. ROCKWELL				**BAS RELIEF**
81	BEGUILING BUTTERCUP	UD	63.00	75.00
81	SWEET SONG SO YOUNG	UD	100.00	105.00
82	FLOWERS IN TENDER BLOOM	UD	100.00	105.00
82	FLYING HIGH	UD	63.00	70.00
N. ROCKWELL		**BOY AND HIS DOG FOUR SEASONS PLATES**		
71	ADVENTURERS BETWEEN ADVENTURES (SET)	YR	*	125.00
71	BOY MEETS HIS DOG	YR	50.00	145.00
71	MYSTERIOUS MALADY, THE (SET)	YR	*	125.00
71	PRIDE OF PARENTHOOD (SET)	YR	*	125.00
N. ROCKWELL				**BOY SCOUT PLATES**
75	OUR HERITAGE	18500	20.00	90.00
76	A SCOUT IS LOYAL	18500	20.00	90.00
77	A GOOD SIGN	18500	20.00	55.00
77	SCOUTMASTER, THE	18500	20.00	90.00
78	CAMPFIRE STORY	18500	20.00	45.00
78	POINTING THE WAY	18500	20.00	45.00
80	BEYOND THE EASEL	18500	45.00	60.00
C. RUSSELL				**CHARLES RUSSELL**
80	IN WITHOUT KNOCKING	9800	38.00	80.00
81	BRONC TO BREAKFAST	9800	38.00	95.00
82	WHEN IGNORANCE IS BLISS	9800	45.00	95.00
83	COWBOY LIFE	9800	45.00	105.00
GORHAM				**CHINA BICENTENNIAL**
72	1776 PLATE	18500	17.50	40.00
76	1776 BICENTENNIAL	8000	17.50	40.00
N. ROCKWELL				**CHRISTMAS**
74	TINY TIM	YR	12.50	40.00
75	GOOD DEEDS	YR	17.50	40.00
76	CHRISTMAS TRIO	YR	20.00	25.00
77	YULETIDE RECKONING	YR	20.00	35.00
78	PLANNING CHRISTMAS VISIT	YR	25.00	30.00
79	SANTA'S HELPERS	YR	25.00	30.00
80	LETTER TO SANTA	YR	28.00	35.00
81	SANTA PLANS HIS VISIT	YR	30.00	55.00
82	JOLLY COACHMAN	YR	30.00	35.00
83	CHRISTMAS DANCERS	YR	30.00	40.00
84	CHRISTMAS MEDLEY	17500	30.00	35.00
85	HOME FOR THE HOLIDAYS	17500	30.00	35.00
86	MERRY CHRISTMAS GRANDMA	17500	30.00	70.00
87	HOMECOMING, THE	17500	35.00	55.00
88	DISCOVERY	17500	38.00	40.00
*		**CHRISTMAS/CHILDREN'S TELEVISION WORKSHOP**		
81	SESAME STREET CHRISTMAS	YR	17.50	20.00
82	SESAME STREET CHRISTMAS	YR	17.50	20.00
83	SESAME STREET CHRISTMAS	YR	20.00	25.00
N. ROCKWELL		**DAD'S BOYS FOUR SEASONS PLATES**		
80	CAREFUL AIM (SET)	YR	*	N/A
80	SKI SKILLS	YR	135.00	105.00
80	TROUT DINNER (SET)	YR	*	N/A
J. CLYMER		**ENCOUNTERS, SURVIVAL AND CELEBRATIONS**		
82	A FINE WELCOME	7500	50.00	120.00
83	ALOUETTE	7500	63.00	120.00
83	TRADER, THE	7500	63.00	120.00
83	TRAPPER TAKES A WIFE, THE	7500	63.00	120.00
83	WINTER CAMP	7500	63.00	120.00
83	WINTER TRAIL	7500	50.00	120.00
J. RITTER				**FALL IN LOVE**
77	ENCHANTMENT	5000	100.00	105.00
77	FROLIC (SET)	5000	*	N/A
77	GUTSY GAL (SET)	5000	*	N/A
77	LONELY CHILL (SET)	5000	*	N/A
N. ROCKWELL				**FOUR AGES OF LOVE**
73	FONDLY WE DO REMEMBER (SET)	YR	*	N/A
73	GAILY SHARING VINTAGE TIME	YR	60.00	170.00
73	SWEET SONG SO YOUNG (SET)	YR	*	N/A
REMBRANDT INSPIRED				**GALLERY OF MASTERS**
71	MAN WITH A GILT HELMET	10000	50.00	55.00
72	SELF PORTRAIT WITH SASKIA	10000	50.00	55.00
73	HONORABLE MRS. GRAHAM, THE	7500	50.00	55.00
N. ROCKWELL		**GOING ON SIXTEEN FOUR SEASONS PLATES**		
77	CHILLING CHORE	YR	75.00	100.00
77	PILGRIMAGE (SET)	YR	*	N/A
77	SHEAR AGONY (SET)	YR	*	N/A
77	SWEET SERENADE (SET)	YR	*	N/A
GORHAM				**GORHAM MUSEUM DOLL PLATES**
84	BELTON BEBE	5000	29.00	60.00
84	CHRISTMAS LADY	7500	33.00	40.00
84	LYDIA	5000	29.00	130.00
85	JUMEAU	5000	29.00	40.00
85	LUCILLE	5000	29.00	40.00
N. ROCKWELL		**GRAND PALS FOUR SEASONS PLATES**		
76	FISH FINDERS	YR	*	N/A
76	GHOSTLY GOURDS	YR	*	N/A
76	SNOW SCULPTURING	YR	70.00	100.00
76	SOARING SPIRITS	YR	*	N/A

YR	NAME	LIMIT	ISSUE	TREND
N. ROCKWELL		**GRANDPA AND ME FOUR SEASONS PLATES**		
74	DAY DREAMERS	YR	*	N/A
74	GAY BLADES	YR	60.00	120.00
74	GOIN' FISHING	YR	*	N/A
74	PENSIVE PALS	YR	*	N/A
N. ROCKWELL		**HELPING HAND FOUR SEASONS PLATES**		
79	CLOSED FOR BUSINESS	YR	*	N/A
79	COAL SEASON'S COMING	YR	*	N/A
79	SWATTER'S RIGHTS	YR	*	N/A
79	YEAR END COURT	YR	100.00	100.00
J. RITTER		**JULIAN RITTER**		
77	CHRISTMAS VISIT	9800	25.00	35.00
78	VALENTINE, FLUTTERING HEART	7500	45.00	50.00
N. ROCKWELL		**LANDSCAPES**		
80	SUMMER RESPITE	YR	45.00	85.00
81	AUTUMN REFLECTION	YR	45.00	80.00
82	WINTER DELIGHT	YR	50.00	80.00
83	SPRING RECESS	YR	60.00	100.00
J.C. LEYENDECKER		**LEYENDECKER ANNUAL CHRISTMAS PLATES**		
88	CHRISTMAS HUG	10000	38.00	55.00
N. ROCKWELL		**LIFE WITH FATHER FOUR SEASONS PLATES**		
82	A TOUGH ONE	YR	*	N/A
82	BIG DECISION	YR	100.00	250.00
82	BLASTING OUT	YR	*	N/A
82	CHEERING THE CHAMPS	YR	*	N/A
N. ROCKWELL		**ME AND MY PALS FOUR SEASONS PLATES**		
75	A LICKIN' GOOD BATH	YR	70.00	70.00
75	DISASTROUS DARING	YR	*	N/A
75	FISHERMAN'S PARADISE	YR	*	N/A
75	YOUNG MAN'S FANCY	YR	*	N/A
*		**MOPPET PLATES-ANNIVERSARY**		
76	MOPPET PLATE ANNIVERSARY	20000	13.00	20.00
*		**MOPPET PLATES-CHRISTMAS**		
73	CHRISTMAS MARCH	YR	10.00	50.00
74	DECORATING THE TREE	YR	12.00	35.00
75	CARRYING THE TREE	YR	13.00	20.00
76	ASLEEP UNDER THE TREE	YR	13.00	20.00
77	STAR FOR THE TOP	YR	13.00	20.00
78	PRESENTS	YR	10.00	15.00
79	MOPPET PLATE CHRISTMAS	YR	12.00	15.00
80	MOPPET PLATE CHRISTMAS	YR	12.00	20.00
81	HAPPY MERRY CHRISTMAS TREE	YR	12.00	20.00
82	MOPPET PLATE CHRISTMAS	YR	12.00	15.00
83	MOPPET PLATE CHRISTMAS	YR	12.00	15.00
*		**MOPPET PLATES-MOTHER'S DAY**		
73	FLOWERS FOR MOTHER	YR	10.00	60.00
74	MOTHER'S HAT	YR	12.00	30.00
75	IN MOTHER'S CLOTHES	YR	13.00	20.00
76	FLOWERS	YR	13.00	25.00
77	GIFT FOR MOTHER	YR	13.00	20.00
78	ICING THE CAKE	YR	10.00	20.00
N. ROCKWELL		**OLD BUDDIES FOUR SEASONS PLATES**		
83	ENDLESS DEBATE	YR	*	N/A
83	FINAL SPEECH	YR	*	N/A
83	HASTY RETREAT	YR	*	N/A
83	SHARED SUCCESS	YR	115.00	120.00
N. ROCKWELL		**OLD TIMERS FOUR SEASONS PLATES**		
81	CANINE SOLO	YR	100.00	105.00
81	FANCY FOOTWORK (SET)	YR	*	N/A
81	LAZY DAYS (SET)	YR	*	N/A
81	SWEET SURPRISE (SET)	YR	*	N/A
B. FELDER		**PASTORAL SYMPHONY**		
*	HE LOVES ME	7500	43.00	75.00
82	GATHER THE CHILDREN	7500	43.00	75.00
82	WHEN I WAS A CHILD	7500	43.00	75.00
84	SUGAR AND SPICE	7500	43.00	75.00
R. PAILTHORPE		**PEWTER BICENTENNIAL**		
71	BURNING OF THE GASPEE	5000	35.00	40.00
72	BOSTON TEA PARTY	5000	35.00	40.00
N. ROCKWELL		**PRESIDENTIAL**		
76	DWIGHT D. EISENHOWER	9800	30.00	40.00
76	JOHN F. KENNEDY	9800	30.00	40.00
F. REMINGTON		**REMINGTON WESTERN**		
73	A NEW YEAR ON THE CIMARRON	YR	25.00	40.00
73	AIDING A COMRADE	YR	25.00	80.00
73	FIGHT FOR THE WATER HOLE, THE	YR	25.00	80.00
73	FLIGHT, THE	YR	25.00	70.00
75	A BREED	YR	20.00	50.00
75	OLD RAMOND	YR	20.00	50.00
76	A TRAPPER	5000	38.00	70.00
76	CAVALRY OFFICER	5000	38.00	70.00
GORHAM		**SILVER BICENTENNIAL**		
72	1776 PLATE	500	500.00	500.00
R. PAILTHORPE		**SILVER BICENTENNIAL**		
72	BURNING OF THE GASPEE	750	500.00	500.00
73	BOSTON TEA PARTY	750	550.00	580.00

YR	NAME	LIMIT	ISSUE	TREND
F. QUAGON			**SINGLE RELEASE**	
76	BLACK REGIMENT, THE 1778	7500	25.00	60.00
N. ROCKWELL			**SINGLE RELEASE**	
74	GOLDEN RULE, THE	YR	12.50	65.00
74	WEIGHING IN	YR	12.50	90.00
75	BEN FRANKLIN	YR	20.00	40.00
76	MARRIAGE LICENSE	*	38.00	60.00
78	TRIPLE SELF PORTRAIT MEMORIAL PLATE	YR	38.00	65.00
80	ANNUAL VISIT, THE	YR	33.00	75.00
81	DAY IN LIFE OF BOY	YR	50.00	85.00
81	DAY IN LIFE OF GIRL	YR	50.00	105.00
N. ROCKWELL		**TENDER YEARS FOUR SEASONS PLATES**		
78	CHILLY RECEPTION	YR	*	N/A
78	COOL AID	YR	*	N/A
78	NEW YEAR LOOK	YR	100.00	40.00
78	SPRING TONIC	YR	*	N/A
B. PORT		**TIME MACHINE TEDDIES PLATES**		
86	MISS EMILY, BEARING UP	5000	33.00	60.00
87	BIG BEAR, THE TOY COLLECTOR	5000	33.00	65.00
88	HUNNY MUNNY	5000	38.00	70.00
J. RITTER			**TO LOVE A CLOWN**	
78	AWAITED REUNION	5000	120.00	125.00
78	SHOWTIME BECKONS	5000	120.00	125.00
78	TOGETHER IN MEMORIES	5000	120.00	125.00
78	TWOSOME TIME	5000	120.00	125.00
GORHAM			**VERMEIL BICENTENNIAL**	
72	1776 PLATE	250	750.00	800.00
N. ROCKWELL		**YOUNG LOVE FOUR SEASONS PLATES**		
72	A SCHOLARLY PACE	YR	*	N/A
72	BEGUILING BUTTERCUP	YR	*	N/A
72	DOWNHILL DARING	YR	60.00	155.00
72	FLYING HIGH	YR	*	N/A

GRANDE COPENHAGEN

YR	NAME	LIMIT	ISSUE	TREND
*				**CHRISTMAS**
75	ALONE TOGETHER	UD	25.00	25.00
76	CHRISTMAS WREATH	UD	25.00	30.00
77	FISHWIVES AT GAMMELSTRAND	UD	27.00	30.00
78	HANS CHRISTIAN ANDERSON	UD	33.00	38.00
79	PHEASANTS	UD	35.00	53.00
80	SNOW QUEEN IN THE TIVOLI	UD	40.00	40.00
81	LITTLE MATCH GIRL IN NYHAVN	UD	43.00	43.00
82	SHEPHERDESS/CHIMNEY SWEEP	UD	45.00	55.00
83	LITTLE MERMAID NEAR KRONBORG	UD	45.00	115.00
84	SANDMAN AT AMALIENBORG	UD	45.00	60.00

H & G STUDIOS

YR	NAME	LIMIT	ISSUE	TREND
B. BURKE		**ANNUAL MOTHER'S DAY PLATE**		
96	A MOTHER'S JOY	7500	39.00	39.00
B. BURKE		**CHRISTMAS MEMORIES**		
95	CHRISTMAS PRESENTS	7500	39.00	39.00
D. PATRICK LEWAN			**CITY OF BEARS**	
95	BEARY PATCH PARK	7500	35.00	35.00
A. MURRAY			**GENTLE HEARTS**	
95	A PROMISE KEPT	5000	35.00	35.00
D. PATRICK LEWAN			**OVAL PLATE**	
95	VICTORIAN COUNTRY HOME	5000	39.00	39.00
D. PATRICK LEWAN		**VICTORIAN TREASURES**		
95	VICTORIAN DREAMS	7500	35.00	35.00
96	VICTORIAN ROMANCE	7500	35.00	35.00
S. CEPELLO		**WOLVES & WARRIORS**		
95	SPIRIT TRAIL	7500	35.00	35.00

HACKETT AMERICAN

YR	NAME	LIMIT	ISSUE	TREND
ALEXANDER				**SPORTS**
*	ARNOLD PALMER H/S	RT	125.00	230.00
*	GARY PLAYER H/S	RT	125.00	400.00
83	REGGIE JACKSON, PROOF	RT	250.00	1000.00
86	JOE MONTANA D/S	RT	125.00	800.00
PALUSO				**SPORTS**
81	REGGIE JACKSON H/S	RT	100.00	900.00
82	STEVE GARVEY H/S	RT	100.00	160.00
83	NOLAN RYAN H/S	RT	100.00	800.00
83	TOM SEAVER H/S	RT	100.00	330.00
84	STEVE CARLTON H/S	RT	100.00	270.00
85	E. MATHEWS D/S	RT	125.00	230.00
85	H. KILLEBREW D/S	RT	125.00	330.00
85	HANK AARON H/S	RT	125.00	300.00
85	SANDY KOUFAX H/S	RT	125.00	385.00
85	WHITEY FORD H/S	RT	125.00	300.00
85	WILLIE MAYS H/S	RT	125.00	335.00
86	DON SUTTON D/S	RT	125.00	330.00
86	REGGIE JACKSON D/S	RT	125.00	400.00
86	ROGER CLEMENS D/S	RT	125.00	600.00
86	TOM SEAVER 300 D/S	RT	125.00	255.00
86	WALLY JOYNER D/S	RT	125.00	300.00

YR	NAME	LIMIT	ISSUE	TREND
SIMON				**SPORTS**
*	DWIGHT GOODEN U/S	RT	55.00	105.00
*	GARY CARTON D/S	RT	125.00	180.00

HADLEY COMPANIES

YR	NAME	LIMIT	ISSUE	TREND
T. REDLIN				**AMERICAN MEMORIES**
87	COMING HOME	9500	85.00	135.00
88	LIGHTS OF HOME	9500	85.00	135.00
89	HOMEWARD BOUND	9500	85.00	135.00
91	FAMILY TRADITIONS	9500	85.00	135.00
T. REDLIN				**ANNUAL CHRISTMAS**
91	HEADING HOME	9500	65.00	100.00
92	PLEASURES OF WINTER	19500	65.00	100.00
93	WINTER WONDERLAND	19500	65.00	90.00
94	ALMOST HOME	19500	65.00	89.00
95	SHARING THE EVENING	45 DAYS	30.00	30.00
T. REDLIN				**COUNTRY DOCTOR COLLECTION**
95	HOUSE CALLS	45 DAYS	30.00	50.00
95	MORNING ROUNDS	45 DAYS	30.00	50.00
95	OFFICE HOURS	45 DAYS	30.00	50.00
95	WEDNESDAY AFTERNOON	45 DAYS	30.00	50.00
S. HANKS				**DAYS OF INNOCENCE**
94	WORLD FOR OUR CHILDREN	*	*	53.00
95	DUET	45 DAYS	30.00	50.00
95	STEPPING STONES	*	*	53.00
T. REDLIN				**GLOW SERIES**
85	EVENING GLOW	5000	55.00	475.00
85	MORNING GLOW	5000	55.00	225.00
85	TWILIGHT GLOW	5000	55.00	105.00
88	AFTERNOON GLOW	5000	55.00	60.00
D. BARNHOUSE				**HEARTLAND COLLECTION**
95	REPAIRS	45 DAYS	30.00	30.00
M. CAPSER				**HEARTLAND COLLECTION**
95	PICKETS AND VINES	45 DAYS	30.00	30.00
S. HAMRICK				**HEARTLAND COLLECTION**
95	BIRD'S EYE VIEW	45 DAYS	30.00	30.00
T. REDLIN				**LOVERS COLLECTION**
92	LOVERS	9500	50.00	55.00
T. REDLIN				**NAVAJO VISIONS SUITE**
93	NAVAJO FANTASY	5000	50.00	75.00
93	YOUNG WARRIOR	5000	50.00	75.00
T. REDLIN				**NAVAJO WOMAN**
90	FEATHERED HAIR TIES	5000	50.00	85.00
91	NAVAJO SUMMER	5000	50.00	75.00
92	TURQUOISE NECKLACE	5000	50.00	75.00
93	PINK NAVAJO	5000	50.00	75.00
T. REDLIN				**RETREAT**
87	EVENING RETREAT	9500	65.00	70.00
87	MORNING RETREAT	9500	65.00	105.00
88	GOLDEN RETREAT	9500	65.00	100.00
89	MOONLIGHT RETREAT	9500	65.00	70.00
T. REDLIN				**SEASONS**
94	AUTUMN EVENING	45 DAYS	30.00	55.00
95	SPRING FEVER	45 DAYS	30.00	50.00
95	SUMMERTIME	45 DAYS	30.00	50.00
95	WINTERTIME	45 DAYS	30.00	50.00
T. REDLIN				**THAT SPECIAL TIME**
90	THAT SPECIAL TIME	9500	65.00	112.00
91	EVENING SOLITUDE	9500	65.00	100.00
92	AROMA OF FALL	9500	65.00	100.00
93	WELCOME TO PARADISE	9500	65.00	100.00
O. FRANCA				**TRANQUILITY SUITE**
93	BLUE TRANQUILITY	9500	50.00	78.00
94	BLUE NAVAJO	9500	50.00	78.00
94	NAVAJO MEDITATING	9500	50.00	78.00
T. REDLIN				**WINDOWS TO THE WILD**
90	MASTER'S DOMAIN	9500	65.00	100.00
91	WINTER WINDBREAK	9500	65.00	100.00
92	EVENING COMPANY	9500	65.00	100.00
94	NIGHT MAPLING	9500	65.00	100.00

HALLMARK

YR	NAME	LIMIT	ISSUE	TREND
L. VOTRUBA				
87	LIGHT SHINES AT CHRISTMAS 800QX481-7	YR	8.00	63.00
88	WAITING FOR SANTA 800QX406-1	YR	8.00	43.00
89	MORNING OF WONDER 825QX461-2	YR	8.25	27.00
90	COOKIES FOR SANTA 875QX443-6	YR	8.75	25.00
91	LET IT SNOW!-5TH EDITION 875QX436-9	YR	8.75	23.00
92	SWEET HOLIDAY HARMONY 6TH ED. 875QX446-1	YR	8.75	24.00
*				**AUTHENTIC OLYMPIC GAMES COLLECTION**
96	PARADE OF NATIONS QHC819-4	OP	*	N/A
*				**EASTER COLLECTION**
95	COLLECTOR'S PLATE QEO 821-9	YR	7.95	15.00
L. VOTRUBA				**EASTER COLLECTION**
96	KEEPING A SECRET QEO822-1	YR	7.95	8.00

YR	NAME	LIMIT	ISSUE	TREND
*			**FAMILY AND FRIENDS**	
96	OUR FIRST CHRISTMAS TOGETHER COLL. PLATE QX580-1	OP	10.95	11.00

B.P. GUTMANN   FAMILY AND FRIENDS

| 96 | BABY'S FIRST CHRISTMAS QX575-1 | OP | 10.95 | 11.00 |

HAMILTON COLLECTION

*

| 98 | YOU'VE MISSED A SPOT | * | 30.00 | 30.00 |

S. BASS

| 98 | INTIMIDATOR, THE (DALE EARNHARDT) | * | 35.00 | 35.00 |

C. REN

| 98 | DELIVERANCE | * | 40.00 | 40.00 |

L. YENCHO

| 98 | KITTENS IN THE CUPBOARD | * | 40.00 | 40.00 |

J. LAMB   ALL IN A DAY'S WORK

94	BUDDING ARTISTS	28 DAYS	30.00	44.00
94	DECOY DELIVERY	CL	30.00	40.00
94	GARDEN GUARDS	28 DAYS	30.00	44.00
94	LUNCH BREAK	CL	30.00	40.00
94	PUPPY PATROL	CL	30.00	40.00
94	WHERE'S THE FIRE?	CL	30.00	40.00
95	SADDLING UP	28 DAYS	30.00	44.00
95	TAKING THE LEAD	28 DAYS	30.00	44.00

T. FREEMAN   AMERICA'S GREATEST SAILING SHIPS

88	AMERICA	CL	30.00	60.00
88	BONHOMME RICHARD	CL	30.00	60.00
88	CHARLES W. MORGAN	CL	30.00	60.00
88	EAGLE	CL	30.00	60.00
88	ENTERPRISE	CL	30.00	60.00
88	GERTRUDE L. THEBAUD	CL	30.00	60.00
88	GREAT REPUBLIC	CL	30.00	60.00
88	U.S.S. CONSTITUTION	CL	30.00	60.00

D. PRECHTEL   AMERICAN CIVIL WAR

90	ABRAHAM LINCOLN	CL	38.00	65.00
90	GENERAL ROBERT E. LEE	CL	38.00	80.00
90	GENERAL THOMAS "STONEWALL" JACKSON	CL	38.00	55.00
90	GENERALS GRANT AND LEE AT APPOMATTOX	CL	38.00	50.00
91	A LETTER FFOM HOME	CL	38.00	65.00
91	GENERAL J.E.B. STUART	CL	38.00	50.00
91	GENERAL PHILIP SHERIDAN	CL	38.00	65.00
91	GOING HOME	CL	38.00	50.00
92	ASSEMBLING THE TROOP	CL	38.00	80.00
92	STANDING WATCH	CL	38.00	80.00

P.J. SWEANY   AMERICAN ROSE GARDEN

88	AMERICAN SPIRIT	CL	30.00	50.00
88	PEACE ROSE	CL	30.00	50.00
89	AMERICAN HERITAGE	CL	30.00	50.00
89	BLUE MOON	CL	30.00	50.00
89	CORAL CLUSTER	CL	30.00	50.00
89	ECLIPSE	CL	30.00	50.00
89	PRESIDENT HERBERT HOOVER	CL	30.00	50.00
89	WHITE KNIGHT	CL	30.00	50.00

R. TANENBAUM   ANDY GRIFFITH

92	A STARTLING CONCLUSION	CL	30.00	40.00
92	SHERIFF ANDY TAYLOR	CL	30.00	40.00
93	AN EXPLOSIVE SITUATION	CL	30.00	40.00
93	AUNT BEE'S KITCHEN	CL	30.00	40.00
93	MAYBERRY SING-ALONG	CL	30.00	40.00
93	MEETING AUNT BEE	CL	30.00	40.00
93	OPIE'S BIG CATCH	CL	30.00	40.00
93	SURPRISE! SURPRISE!	CL	30.00	40.00

M. SUSINNO   ANGLER'S PRIZE

91	AUTUMN BEAUTY	CL	30.00	40.00
91	BLUE RIBBON TROUT	CL	30.00	30.00
91	BRONZEBACK FIGHTER	CL	30.00	40.00
91	FRESHWATER BARRACUDA	CL	30.00	40.00
91	SUN DANCERS	CL	30.00	40.00
91	TROPHY BASS	CL	30.00	40.00
92	OLD MOONEYES	CL	30.00	40.00
92	SILVER KING	CL	30.00	30.00

*   BEAUTY OF WINTER

| 92 | SILENT NIGHT | CL | 30.00 | 40.00 |
| 93 | MOONLIGHT SLEIGHRIDE | CL | 30.00 | 40.00 |

R. TANENBAUM   BEST OF BASEBALL

93	EXCEPTIONAL BROOKS ROBINSON, THE	CL	30.00	30.00
93	EXTRAORDINARY LOU GEHRIG, THE	CL	30.00	30.00
93	GREAT WILLIE MAYS, THE	CL	30.00	30.00
93	IMMORTAL BABE RUTH, THE	CL	30.00	30.00
93	INCREDIBLE NOLAN RYAN, THE	CL	30.00	30.00
93	LEGENDARY MICKLE MANTLE, THE	CL	30.00	30.00
93	PHENOMENAL ROBERTO CLEMENTE, THE	CL	30.00	30.00
93	REMARKABLE JOHNNY BENCH, THE	CL	30.00	30.00
93	UNBEATABLE DUKE SNIDER, THE	CL	30.00	30.00
93	UNFORGETTABLE PHIL RIZZUTO, THE	CL	30.00	30.00
94	ULTIMATE COMPETITOR: MIKE SCHMIDT, THE	CL	30.00	30.00

P./A. BIALOSKY   BIALOSKY & FRIENDS

| 92 | FAMILY ADDITION | CL | 30.00 | 40.00 |

YR	NAME	LIMIT	ISSUE	TREND
93	BREAKFAST IN BED	CL	30.00	40.00
93	HONEY FOR SALE	CL	30.00	40.00
93	LET'S GO FISHING	CL	30.00	40.00
93	MY FIRST TWO-WHEELER	CL	30.00	40.00
93	SLEIGH RIDE	CL	30.00	40.00
93	SWEETHEART	CL	30.00	40.00
93	U.S. MAIL	CL	30.00	40.00

D. MANNING   **BIG CATS OF THE WORLD**

YR	NAME	LIMIT	ISSUE	TREND
89	AFRICAN SHADE	CL	30.00	35.00
89	VIEW FROM ABOVE	CL	30.00	35.00
90	ABOVE THE TREETOPS	CL	30.00	35.00
90	DEEP IN THE JUNGLE	CL	30.00	35.00
90	MOUNTAIN DWELLER	CL	30.00	35.00
90	ON THE PROWL	CL	30.00	35.00
90	SPIRIT OF THE MOUNTAIN	CL	30.00	35.00
90	SPOTTED SENTINEL	CL	30.00	35.00

J. CHENG   **BIRDS OF THE TEMPLE GARDENS**

YR	NAME	LIMIT	ISSUE	TREND
89	CRANES OF ETERNAL LIFE	CL	30.00	35.00
89	DOVES OF FIDELITY	CL	30.00	50.00
89	GOLDFINCHES OF VIRTUE	CL	30.00	35.00
89	HONORABLE SWALLOWS	CL	30.00	35.00
89	IMPERIAL GOLDCREST	CL	30.00	35.00
89	MAGPIES: BIRDS OF GOOD OMEN	CL	30.00	35.00
89	ORIENTAL WHITE EYES OF BEAUTY	CL	30.00	35.00
89	PHEASANTS OF GOOD FORTUNE	CL	30.00	35.00

B.P. GUTMANN   **BUNDLES OF JOY**

YR	NAME	LIMIT	ISSUE	TREND
88	A LITTLE BIT OF HEAVEN	CL	25.00	80.00
88	AWAKENING	CL	25.00	90.00
88	BILLY	CL	25.00	45.00
88	HAPPY DREAMS	CL	25.00	80.00
88	SUN KISSED	CL	25.00	45.00
88	SWEET INNOCENCE	CL	25.00	45.00
88	TASTING	CL	25.00	50.00
88	TOMMY	CL	25.00	45.00

P.J. SWEANY   **BUTTERFLY GARDEN**

YR	NAME	LIMIT	ISSUE	TREND
87	COMMON BLUE	CL	30.00	40.00
87	CRIMSON PATCHED LONGWING	CL	30.00	40.00
87	MONARCH	CL	30.00	40.00
87	ORANGE SULPHUR	CL	30.00	35.00
87	SPICEBUSH SWALLOWTAIL	CL	30.00	50.00
87	TIGER SWALLOWTAIL	CL	30.00	35.00
88	MORNING CLOAK	CL	30.00	35.00
88	RED ADMIRAL	CL	30.00	40.00

J. TIFT   **CALL OF THE NORTH**

YR	NAME	LIMIT	ISSUE	TREND
93	WINTER'S DAWN	CL	30.00	40.00
94	ARCTIC SECLUSION	CL	30.00	40.00
94	EVENING SILENCE	CL	30.00	40.00
94	FOREST TWILIGHT	CL	30.00	40.00
94	MOONLIT WILDERNESS	CL	30.00	40.00
94	SENTINELS OF THE SUMMIT	CL	30.00	40.00
94	SILENT SNOWFALL	CL	30.00	40.00
94	SNOWY WATCH	CL	30.00	40.00

R. CROSS   **CALL TO ADVENTURE**

YR	NAME	LIMIT	ISSUE	TREND
93	BOUNTY, THE	CL	30.00	40.00
93	USS CONSTITUTION	CL	30.00	40.00
94	BONHOMME RICHARD	CL	30.00	40.00
94	BOSTON	CL	30.00	40.00
94	GOLDEN WEST	CL	30.00	40.00
94	HANNAH	CL	30.00	40.00
94	IMPROVEMENT	CL	30.00	40.00
94	OLD NANTUCKET	CL	30.00	40.00

Q. LEMONDS   **CAMEO KITTENS**

YR	NAME	LIMIT	ISSUE	TREND
93	BLOSSOM	CL	30.00	40.00
93	CAT TAILS	CL	30.00	40.00
93	GINGER SNAP	CL	30.00	40.00
93	LADY BLUE	CL	30.00	40.00
93	TINY HEART STEALER	CL	30.00	40.00
94	SCOUT	CL	30.00	40.00
94	TIGER'S TEMPTATION	CL	30.00	40.00
94	WHISKER ANTICS	CL	30.00	40.00

T. UTZ   **CAREFREE DAYS**

YR	NAME	LIMIT	ISSUE	TREND
82	AUTUMN WANDERER	CL	25.00	50.00
82	BATHTIME VISITOR	CL	25.00	50.00
82	BEST FRIENDS	CL	25.00	50.00
82	FEEDING TIME	CL	25.00	50.00
82	FIRST CATCH	CL	25.00	50.00
82	MONKEY BUSINESS	CL	25.00	50.00
82	NATURE HUNT	CL	25.00	60.00
82	TOUCHDOWN	CL	25.00	60.00

B.P. GUTMANN   **CHILD'S BEST FRIEND**

YR	NAME	LIMIT	ISSUE	TREND
85	GOING TO TOWN	CL	25.00	80.00
85	GOOD MORNING	CL	25.00	80.00
85	IN DISGRACE	CL	25.00	95.00
85	MINE	CL	25.00	95.00
85	ON THE UP AND UP	CL	25.00	90.00
85	REWARD, THE	CL	25.00	65.00

YR	NAME	LIMIT	ISSUE	TREND
85	SYMPATHY	CL	25.00	60.00
85	WHO'S SLEEPY	CL	25.00	95.00

B.P. GUTMANN — CHILDHOOD REFLECTIONS

YR	NAME	LIMIT	ISSUE	TREND
91	FRIENDLY ENEMIES	CL	30.00	40.00
91	HARMONY	CL	30.00	80.00
91	KITTY'S BREAKFAST	CL	30.00	40.00
91	LITTLE MOTHER	CL	30.00	30.00
91	LULLABY	CL	30.00	40.00
91	OH! OH! A BUNNY	CL	30.00	30.00
91	SMILE, SMILE, SMILE	CL	30.00	40.00
91	THANK YOU, GOD	CL	30.00	40.00

D. CROOK — CHILDREN OF THE AMERICAN FRONTIER

YR	NAME	LIMIT	ISSUE	TREND
86	A LADY NEEDS A LITTLE PRIVACY	CL	25.00	45.00
86	DESPERADOES, THE	CL	25.00	30.00
86	IN TROUBLE AGAIN	CL	25.00	40.00
86	RIDERS WANTED	CL	25.00	35.00
86	TUBS AND SUDS	CL	25.00	30.00
87	A COWBOY'S DOWNFALL	CL	25.00	30.00
87	A SPECIAL PATIENT	CL	25.00	45.00
87	RUNAWAY BLUES	CL	25.00	30.00

M. GNATEK — CIVIL WAR GENERALS

YR	NAME	LIMIT	ISSUE	TREND
94	CONFEDERATE HEROES	28 DAYS	30.00	44.00
94	GEORGE ARMSTRONG CUSTER	CL	30.00	40.00
94	J.E.B. STEWART	CL	30.00	40.00
94	JAMES LONGSTREET	CL	30.00	40.00
94	JOSHUA L. CHAMBERLAIN	CL	30.00	40.00
94	NATHAN BEDFORD FORREST	CL	30.00	40.00
94	ROBERT E. LEE	CL	30.00	40.00
94	STONEWALL JACKSON	28 DAYS	30.00	44.00

G. HINKE — CLASSIC AMERICAN SANTAS

YR	NAME	LIMIT	ISSUE	TREND
93	A CHRISTMAS EVE VISITOR	CL	30.00	40.00
94	A CHRISTMAS CHORUS	CL	30.00	40.00
94	AN EXCITING CHRISTMAS EVE	CL	30.00	40.00
94	PREPARING THE SLEIGH	CL	30.00	40.00
94	REINDEER'S STABLE, THE	CL	30.00	40.00
94	REST YE MERRY GENTLEMEN	CL	30.00	40.00
94	SANTA'S CANDY KITCHEN	CL	30.00	40.00
94	UP ON THE ROOFTOP	CL	30.00	40.00

M. LACOURCIERE — CLASSIC CORVETTES

YR	NAME	LIMIT	ISSUE	TREND
94	1957 CORVETTE	CL	30.00	30.00
94	1963 CORVETTE	CL	30.00	30.00
94	1968 CORVETTE	CL	30.00	30.00
94	1986 CORVETTE	CL	30.00	30.00

B. CHRISTIE — CLASSIC SPORTING DOGS

YR	NAME	LIMIT	ISSUE	TREND
89	BEAGLES	CL	25.00	40.00
89	GOLDEN RETRIEVERS	CL	25.00	60.00
89	LABRADOR RETRIEVERS	CL	25.00	65.00
89	POINTERS	CL	25.00	35.00
89	SPRINGER SPANIELS	CL	25.00	45.00
90	BRITTANY SPANIELS	CL	25.00	50.00
90	GERMAN SHORT-HAIRED POINTERS	CL	25.00	60.00
90	IRISH SETTERS	CL	25.00	40.00

K. MILNAZIK — CLASSIC TV WESTERNS

YR	NAME	LIMIT	ISSUE	TREND
90	BONANZA	CL	30.00	60.00
90	LONE RANGER AND TONTO, THE	CL	30.00	70.00
90	ROY ROGERS AND DALE EVANS	CL	30.00	65.00
91	HAVE GUN, WILL TRAVEL	CL	30.00	50.00
91	HOPALONG CASSIDY	CL	30.00	65.00
91	RAWHIDE	CL	30.00	50.00
91	VIRGINIAN, THE	CL	30.00	70.00
91	WILD WILD WEST	CL	30.00	65.00

H. BOND — CORAL PARADISE

YR	NAME	LIMIT	ISSUE	TREND
89	LIVING OASIS, THE	CL	30.00	30.00
90	CARIBBEAN SPECTACLE	CL	30.00	30.00
90	FOREST BENEATH THE SEA	CL	30.00	30.00
90	MYSTERIES OF THE GALAPAGOS	CL	30.00	30.00
90	RICHES OF THE CORAL SEA	CL	30.00	30.00
90	SHIMMERING REEF DWELLERS	CL	30.00	40.00
90	TROPICAL PAGEANTRY	CL	30.00	40.00
90	UNDERSEA VILLAGE	CL	30.00	40.00

K. GEORGE — COTTAGE PUPPIES

YR	NAME	LIMIT	ISSUE	TREND
93	ENDEARING INNOCENCE	CL	30.00	40.00
93	LITTLE GARDENERS	CL	30.00	40.00
93	SPRINGTIME FANCY	CL	30.00	40.00
94	A GARDENING TRIO	CL	30.00	40.00
94	LAZY AFTERNOON	CL	30.00	40.00
94	PICNIC PLAYTIME	CL	30.00	40.00
94	SUMMERTIME PALS	CL	30.00	40.00
94	TAKING A BREAK	CL	30.00	40.00

G. PERILLO — COUNCIL OF NATIONS

YR	NAME	LIMIT	ISSUE	TREND
92	BOLDNESS OF THE SENECA	CL	30.00	40.00

E. DERTNER — COUNTRY GARDEN COTTAGES

YR	NAME	LIMIT	ISSUE	TREND
92	RIVERBANK COTTAGE	CL	30.00	40.00
92	SHEPHERD'S COTTAGE	CL	30.00	40.00
92	SUNDAY OUTING	CL	30.00	40.00
93	APRIL COTTAGE	CL	30.00	40.00
93	DAYDREAM COTTAGE	CL	30.00	40.00

Evening Retreat *is from the "Retreat" series by Terry Redlin, produced by Hadley Companies.*

That Special Time, *released in 1990 as part of the "That Special Time" series by wildlife artist Terry Redlin, is produced by Hadley Companies.*

The Christening, *an open edition piece by Abbie Williams, is produced by Roman Inc.*

Thy Kingdom Come *by Abbie Williams is the second issue in "The Lord's Prayer" series produced by Roman. The piece was limited to just a 10-day firing period.*

YR	NAME	LIMIT	ISSUE	TREND
93	GARDEN GLORIOUS	CL	30.00	40.00
93	SUMMER SYMPHONY	CL	30.00	40.00
93	THIS SIDE OF HEAVEN	CL	30.00	40.00
G. GERARDI				**COUNTRY KITTIES**
89	ALL WASHED UP	CL	25.00	40.00
89	ATTIC ATTACK	CL	25.00	50.00
89	CAPTIVE AUDIENCE	CL	25.00	40.00
89	JUST FOR THE FERN OF IT	CL	25.00	35.00
89	MISCHIEF MAKERS	CL	25.00	50.00
89	ROCK AND ROLLERS	CL	25.00	35.00
89	STROLLER DERBY	CL	25.00	40.00
89	TABLE MANNERS	CL	25.00	40.00
J.M. VASS			**COUNTRY SEASON OF HORSES**	
90	A WINTER'S WALK	CL	30.00	30.00
90	AUTUMN GRANDEUR	CL	30.00	35.00
90	CLIFFSIDE BEAUTY	CL	30.00	30.00
90	CRISP COUNTRY MORNING	CL	30.00	30.00
90	FIRST DAY OF SPRING	CL	30.00	45.00
90	FROSTY MORNING	CL	30.00	30.00
90	RIVER RETREAT	CL	30.00	30.00
90	SUMMER SPLENDOR	CL	30.00	30.00
N. NOEL				**COUNTRY SUMMER**
85	BUTTERFLY BEAUTY	CL	30.00	40.00
85	GOLDEN PUPPY, THE	CL	30.00	40.00
86	MY BUNNY	CL	30.00	40.00
86	ROCKING CHAIR, THE	CL	30.00	40.00
88	PIGLET, THE	CL	30.00	40.00
88	TEAMMATES	CL	30.00	40.00
B. HARRISON				**CURIOUS KITTENS**
90	KEEPING IN STEP	CL	30.00	45.00
90	RAINY DAY FRIENDS	CL	30.00	45.00
91	A PAW'S IN THE ACTION	CL	30.00	45.00
91	ALL WOUND UP	CL	30.00	45.00
91	CHANCE MEETING	CL	30.00	45.00
91	DELIGHTFUL DISCOVERY	CL	30.00	45.00
91	MAKING TRACKS	CL	30.00	45.00
91	PLAYING CAT AND MOUSE	CL	30.00	45.00
92	CAT BURGLAR	CL	30.00	45.00
92	LITTLE SCHOLAR	CL	30.00	45.00
K. THAYER			**DAUGHTERS OF THE SUN**	
93	A SECRET GLANCE	CL	30.00	40.00
93	CHIPPEWA CHARMER	CL	30.00	40.00
93	DELIGHTED DANCER	CL	30.00	40.00
93	EVENING DANCER	CL	30.00	40.00
93	SHINING FEATHER	CL	30.00	40.00
93	SUN DANCER	CL	30.00	40.00
94	PRIDE OF YAKIMA	CL	30.00	40.00
94	RADIANT BEAUTY	CL	30.00	40.00
J. HAGARA				**DEAR TO MY HEART**
90	ADDIE	CL	30.00	50.00
90	CATHY	CL	30.00	50.00
90	DACY	CL	30.00	50.00
90	JIMMY	CL	30.00	50.00
90	PAUL	CL	30.00	50.00
91	JENNY	CL	30.00	50.00
91	JOY	CL	30.00	50.00
91	SHELLY	CL	30.00	50.00
J. LAMB			**DELIGHTS OF CHILDHOOD**	
89	CRAYON CREATIONS	CL	30.00	45.00
89	LITTLE MOTHER	CL	30.00	45.00
90	BATHING BEAUTY	CL	30.00	45.00
90	IS THAT YOU, GRANNY?	CL	30.00	45.00
90	NATURE'S LITTLE HELPER	CL	30.00	45.00
90	SHOWER TIME	CL	30.00	45.00
90	SO SORRY	CL	30.00	45.00
90	STORYTIME FRIENDS	CL	30.00	45.00
K. HAYNES			**DREAMSICLES CLASSICS**	
94	FLYING LESSON, THE	CL	20.00	30.00
95	BLOSSOMS & BUTTERFLIES	28 DAYS	20.00	32.00
95	BY THE LIGHT OF THE MOON	28 DAYS	20.00	32.00
95	HEAVENLY PIROUETTES	28 DAYS	20.00	32.00
95	LOVE'S SHY GLANCE	28 DAYS	20.00	32.00
95	RECITAL, THE	28 DAYS	20.00	32.00
95	WISHING UPON A STAR	28 DAYS	20.00	32.00
K. HAYNES			**DREAMSICLES HEAVEN SENT**	
96	QUIET BLESSINGS	28 DAYS	20.00	32.00
K. HAYNES			**DREAMSICLES LIFE'S BLESSING**	
95	HAPPINESS	28 DAYS	20.00	40.00
K. HAYNES			**DREAMSICLES SCULPTURAL**	
95	FLYING LESSON, SCULPTURAL	OP	38.00	54.00
96	BLOSSOMS & BUTTERFLIES, SCULPTURAL	OP	38.00	54.00
96	BY THE LIGHT/MOON SCULPTURAL	OP	38.00	54.00
96	HEAVENLY PIROUETTES, SCULPTURAL	OP	38.00	54.00
96	LOVE'S SHY GLANCE	OP	38.00	54.00
96	RECITAL, SCULPTURAL	OP	38.00	54.00
96	WISHING UPON A STAR, SCULPTURAL	OP	38.00	54.00

YR	NAME	LIMIT	ISSUE	TREND
K. HAYNES		**DREAMSICLES SPECIAL FRIEND**		
95	HEAVEN'S LITTLE HELPER	28 DAYS	30.00	32.00
95	HUG FROM THE HEART	28 DAYS	30.00	32.00
96	BLESS US ALL	28 DAYS	30.00	32.00
K. HAYNES		**DREAMSICLES SWEETHEARTS**		
96	STOLEN KISS	28 DAYS	35.00	35.00
R. TANENBAUM		**DRIVERS OF VICTORY LANE**		
94	BILL ELLIOTT	CL	30.00	30.00
94	JEFF GORDON	CL	30.00	30.00
J. ENRIGHT		**ENCHANTED SEASCAPES**		
93	BLUE PARADISE	CL	30.00	42.00
93	SANCTUARY OF THE DOLPHIN	CL	30.00	42.00
94	EDGE OF TIME	CL	30.00	42.00
94	LOST BENEATH THE BLUE	CL	30.00	42.00
94	OASIS OF THE GODS	CL	30.00	42.00
94	RHAPSODY OF HOPE	CL	30.00	42.00
94	SEA OF LIGHT	CL	30.00	42.00
94	SPHERE OF LIFE	CL	30.00	42.00
M. BELL		**ENGLISH COUNTRY COTTAGES**		
90	PERIWINKLE TEA ROOM	CL	30.00	50.00
91	CHAPLAIN'S GARDEN, THE	CL	30.00	40.00
91	GAMEKEEPER'S COTTAGE	CL	30.00	80.00
91	GINGER COTTAGE	CL	30.00	65.00
91	LARKSPUR COTTAGE	CL	30.00	50.00
91	LORNA DOONE COTTAGE	CL	30.00	50.00
91	LULLABYE COTTAGE	CL	30.00	40.00
91	MURRLE COTTAGE	CL	30.00	40.00
J. LAMB		**FARMYARD FRIENDS**		
92	LITTLE COWHANDS	CL	30.00	40.00
92	MISTAKEN IDENTITY	CL	30.00	40.00
93	AN APPLE A DAY	CL	30.00	40.00
93	FOLLOW THE LEADER	CL	30.00	40.00
93	FOWL PLAY	CL	30.00	40.00
93	PARTNERS IN CRIME	CL	30.00	40.00
93	PONY TALES	CL	30.00	40.00
93	SHREADING THE EVIDENCE	CL	30.00	40.00
D. O'DRISCOLL		**FAVORITE AMERICAN SONGBIRDS**		
89	BLUE JAYS OF SPRING	CL	30.00	40.00
89	GOLDFINCHES OF SUMMER	CL	30.00	40.00
89	RED CARDINALS OF WINTER	CL	30.00	40.00
89	ROBINS & APPLE BLOSSOMS	CL	30.00	40.00
90	AUTUMN CHICKADEES	CL	30.00	40.00
90	BLUEBIRDS AND MORNING GLORIES	CL	30.00	40.00
90	TUFTED TITMOUSE AND HOLLY	CL	30.00	30.00
91	CAROLINA WRENS OF SPRING	CL	30.00	30.00
F. MCCARTHY		**FIERCE AND THE FREE**		
92	BIG MEDICINE	CL	30.00	40.00
93	LAND OF THE WINTER HAWK	CL	30.00	40.00
93	WARRIOR OF SAVAGE SPLENDOR	CL	30.00	40.00
94	AMBUSH	28 DAYS	30.00	43.00
94	CHALLENGE, THE	CL	30.00	40.00
94	DANGEROUS CROSSING	28 DAYS	30.00	42.00
94	OUT OF RISING MIST	28 DAYS	30.00	44.00
94	WAR PARTY	CL	30.00	40.00
T. BLACKSHEAR		**FIFTY YEARS OF OZ**		
89	FIFTY YEARS OF OZ	CL	38.00	70.00
J. DENEEN		**FORGING NEW FRONTIERS**		
94	BIG BOY	CL	30.00	40.00
94	CRESTING THE SUMMIT	CL	30.00	40.00
94	HIGH COUNTRY LOGGING	CL	30.00	40.00
94	RACE IS ON, THE	CL	30.00	40.00
94	SPRING ROUNDUP	CL	30.00	40.00
94	WINTER IN THE ROCKIES	CL	30.00	40.00
S. HARDOCK		**FOUR SEASONS OF THE EAGLE**		
98	SPRING'S AWAKENING	*	40.00	40.00
98	WINTER SOLSTICE	*	40.00	40.00
M. HANSON		**GARDEN SONG**		
94	AUTUMN'S ELEGANCE	28 DAYS	30.00	45.00
94	GOLDEN GLORIES	CL	30.00	45.00
94	IN FULL BLOOM	CL	30.00	45.00
94	WINTER'S SPLENDOR	CL	30.00	45.00
95	FALL'S SERENADE	28 DAYS	30.00	46.00
95	FIRST SNOWFALL	28 DAYS	30.00	44.00
95	ROBINS IN SPRING	28 DAYS	30.00	46.00
95	SUMMER'S GLOW	28 DAYS	30.00	44.00
C. MICARELLI		**GLORY OF CHRIST**		
92	ASCENSION, THE	CL	30.00	40.00
T. FOGARTY		**GLORY OF THE GAME**		
94	B. THOMPSON'S SHOT HEARD ROUND THE WORLD	CL	30.00	30.00
94	HANK AARON'S RECORD-BREAKING HOME RUN	CL	30.00	30.00
T. XARAS		**GOLDEN AGE OF AMERICAN RAILROADS**		
91	ABOVE THE CANYON	CL	30.00	95.00
91	BIG BOY, THE	CL	30.00	65.00
91	BLUE COMET, THE	CL	30.00	50.00
91	EMPIRE BUILDER, THE	CL	30.00	65.00
91	MORNING LOCAL, THE	CL	30.00	65.00

YR	NAME	LIMIT	ISSUE	TREND
91	PENNSYLVANIA K-4, THE	CL	30.00	95.00
91	PORTRAIT IN STEAM	CL	30.00	80.00
91	SANTA FE SUPER CHIEF, THE	CL	30.00	110.00
92	AN AMERICAN CLASSIC	CL	30.00	35.00
92	FINAL DESTINATION	CL	30.00	40.00

C. LAWSON — GOLDEN CLASSICS

YR	NAME	LIMIT	ISSUE	TREND
87	HANSEL AND GRETEL	CL	38.00	40.00
87	JACK AND THE BEANSTALK	CL	38.00	40.00
87	RUMPELSTILTSKIN	CL	38.00	40.00
87	SLEEPING BEAUTY	CL	38.00	40.00
87	SNOW WHITE AND ROSE RED	CL	38.00	40.00
88	CINDERELLA	CL	38.00	40.00
88	GOLDEN GOOSE, THE	CL	38.00	40.00
88	SNOW QUEEN, THE	CL	38.00	40.00

J. LAMB — GOOD SPORTS

YR	NAME	LIMIT	ISSUE	TREND
90	BASS MASTERS, THE	CL	30.00	40.00
90	DOUBLE PLAY	CL	30.00	40.00
90	HOLE IN ONE	CL	30.00	65.00
90	SLAP SHOT	CL	30.00	50.00
90	SPOTTED ON THE SIDELINE	CL	30.00	40.00
90	WIDE RETRIEVER	CL	30.00	50.00
91	BASSETBALL	CL	30.00	40.00
91	NET PLAY	CL	30.00	50.00
92	BOXER REBELLION	CL	30.00	30.00
92	GREAT TRY	CL	30.00	40.00

R. WADDEY — GREAT FIGHTER PLANES OF WW II

YR	NAME	LIMIT	ISSUE	TREND
92	BIG HOG	CL	30.00	40.00
92	F4F WILDCAT	CL	30.00	40.00
92	OLD CROW	CL	30.00	40.00
92	P-38F LIGHTNING	CL	30.00	40.00
92	P-40 FLYING TIGER	CL	30.00	40.00
92	P-47 THUNDERBOLT	CL	30.00	40.00
93	F6F HELLCAT	CL	30.00	40.00
93	MEMPHIS BELLE	14 DAYS	*	45.00
93	P-39M AIRACOBRA	CL	30.00	40.00
95	DRAGON AND HIS TAIL	14 DAYS	*	44.00

WYLAND — GREAT MAMMALS OF THE SEA

YR	NAME	LIMIT	ISSUE	TREND
91	CHILDREN OF THE SEA	CL	35.00	65.00
91	DOLPHIN PARADISE	CL	35.00	50.00
91	HAWAII DOLPHINS	CL	35.00	40.00
91	ISLANDS	CL	35.00	65.00
91	KISSING DOLPHINS	CL	35.00	40.00
91	ORCA JOURNEY	CL	35.00	40.00
91	ORCA TRIO	CL	35.00	50.00
91	ORCAS	CL	35.00	50.00

F. MOODY — GREATEST SHOW ON EARTH

YR	NAME	LIMIT	ISSUE	TREND
81	AERIALISTS	CL	30.00	45.00
81	CLOWNS	CL	30.00	50.00
81	ELEPHANTS	CL	30.00	45.00
81	EQUESTRIANS	CL	30.00	45.00
81	GREAT PARADE	CL	30.00	45.00
81	MIDWAY	CL	30.00	45.00
82	GRANDE FINALE	CL	30.00	45.00
82	LION TAMER	CL	30.00	45.00

P. BROOKS — GROWING UP TOGETHER

YR	NAME	LIMIT	ISSUE	TREND
90	MY VERY BEST FRIENDS	CL	30.00	40.00
90	PICNIC PALS	CL	30.00	40.00
90	TEA FOR TWO	CL	30.00	40.00
90	TENDER LOVING CARE	CL	30.00	40.00
91	BEDTIME BLESSINGS	CL	30.00	40.00
91	FISHING BUDDIES	CL	30.00	40.00
91	KITTEN CABOODLE	CL	30.00	40.00
91	NEWFOUND FRIENDS	CL	30.00	40.00

D. BOBNICK — HONEYMOONERS

YR	NAME	LIMIT	ISSUE	TREND
93	OFFICAL HONEYMOONER'S COMM. PLATE, THE	CL	38.00	95.00

D. KILMER — HONEYMOONERS

YR	NAME	LIMIT	ISSUE	TREND
87	BABY, YOU'RE THE GREATEST	CL	25.00	145.00
87	HONEYMOONERS, THE	CL	25.00	135.00
87	HUCKLEBUCK, THE	CL	25.00	135.00
88	BANG! ZOOM!	CL	25.00	135.00
88	GOLFER, THE	CL	25.00	135.00
88	HONEYMOON EXPRESS, THE	CL	25.00	275.00
88	ONLY WAY TO TRAVEL, THE	CL	25.00	140.00
88	TV CHEFS, THE	CL	25.00	140.00

J. KRITZ — I LOVE LUCY PLATE COLLECTION

YR	NAME	LIMIT	ISSUE	TREND
89	CALIFORNIA, HERE WE COME	CL	30.00	120.00
89	IT'S JUST LIKE CANDY	CL	30.00	100.00
90	BIG SQUEEZE, THE	CL	30.00	105.00
90	EATING THE EVIDENCE	CL	30.00	110.00
90	TWO OF A KIND	CL	30.00	70.00
91	QUEEN OF THE GYPSIES	CL	30.00	70.00
92	A RISING PROBLEM	CL	30.00	110.00
92	NIGHT AT THE COPA	CL	30.00	90.00

KOSEKI/EBIHARA — JAPANESE BLOSSOMS OF AUTUMN

YR	NAME	LIMIT	ISSUE	TREND
85	ARROWROOT	CL	45.00	50.00
85	BELLFLOWER	CL	45.00	50.00
85	BUSH CLOVER	CL	45.00	50.00

YR	NAME	LIMIT	ISSUE	TREND
85	MAIDEN FLOWER	CL	45.00	50.00
85	PAMPAS GRASS	CL	45.00	50.00
85	PURPLE TROUSERS	CL	45.00	50.00
85	WILD CARNATION	CL	45.00	50.00
SHUHO/KAGE		JAPANESE FLORAL CALENDAR		
81	NEW YEAR'S DAY	CL	33.00	75.00
82	AUTUMN	CL	33.00	75.00
82	BOY'S DOLL DAY FESTIVAL	CL	33.00	75.00
82	BUDDHA'S BIRTHDAY	CL	33.00	75.00
82	EARLY SPRING	CL	33.00	75.00
82	EARLY SUMMER	CL	33.00	35.00
82	GIRL'S DOLL DAY FESTIVAL	CL	33.00	75.00
82	SPRING	CL	33.00	75.00
82	SUMMER	CL	33.00	75.00
83	FESTIVAL OF THE FULL MOON	CL	33.00	75.00
83	LATE AUTUMN	CL	33.00	75.00
83	WINTER	CL	33.00	75.00
S. BASS		JEFF GORDON COLLECTION		
98	ON THE WARPATH	*	35.00	35.00
J. LANDENBERGER		JEWELED HUMMINGBIRDS PLATE COLLECTION		
89	AMETHYST-THROATED HUMMINGBIRDS	CL	38.00	40.00
89	ANDEAN EMERALD HUMMINGBIRDS	CL	38.00	50.00
89	BLUE-HEADED SAPPHIRE HUMMINGBIRDS	CL	38.00	40.00
89	GARNET-THROATED HUMMINGBIRDS	CL	38.00	40.00
89	GREAT SAPPHIRE WING HUMMINGBIRDS	CL	38.00	40.00
89	PEARL CORONET HUMMINGBIRDS	CL	38.00	50.00
89	RUBY-THROATED HUMMINGBIRDS	CL	38.00	60.00
89	RUBY-TOPAZ HUMMINGBIRDS	CL	38.00	50.00
P. COOPER		KITTEN CLASSICS		
85	BIRDWATCHER	CL	30.00	60.00
85	CAT NAP	CL	30.00	60.00
85	COUNTRY KITTY	CL	30.00	60.00
85	FIRST PRIZE	CL	30.00	60.00
85	LITTLE RASCALS	CL	30.00	60.00
85	PURRFECT TREASURE	CL	30.00	60.00
85	TIGER'S FANCY	CL	30.00	60.00
85	WILD FLOWER	CL	30.00	60.00
M. WEISTLING		L.A. AT LAST		
98	LUCY MEETS THE STARS	*	35.00	35.00
C. REN		LAST WARRIORS		
93	LONE WINTER JOURNEY	CL	30.00	40.00
93	MORNING OF RECKONING	CL	30.00	40.00
93	TWILIGHTS LAST GLEAMING	CL	30.00	40.00
93	WINTER OF '41	CL	30.00	40.00
94	CONFRONTING DANGER	CL	30.00	40.00
94	SOLEMN REFLECTION	CL	30.00	40.00
94	SOLITARY HUNTER	CL	30.00	40.00
94	VICTORY'S REWARD	CL	30.00	40.00
V. DEZERIN		LEGEND OF FATHER CHRISTMAS		
94	FEAST OF THE HOLIDAY, THE	CL	30.00	40.00
94	GIFTS FROM FATHER CHRISTMAS	CL	30.00	40.00
94	RETURN OF FATHER CHRISTMAS, THE	CL	30.00	40.00
95	CHRISTMAS DAY VISITORS	28 DAYS	30.00	45.00
95	DECORATING THE TREE	28 DAYS	30.00	44.00
95	HOLY NIGHT	28 DAYS	30.00	45.00
95	SKATING ON THE POND	28 DAYS	30.00	44.00
95	SNOW SCULPTURE	28 DAYS	30.00	45.00
L. MARTIN		LISI MARTIN CHRISTMAS		
92	SANTA'S LITTLES REINDEER	CL	30.00	30.00
93	A TASTE OF THE HOLIDAYS	CL	30.00	30.00
93	CHRISTMAS DREAMS	CL	30.00	30.00
93	CHRISTMAS STORY, THE	CL	30.00	30.00
93	CHRISTMAS WATCH	CL	30.00	30.00
93	NIGHT BEFORE CHRISTMAS, THE	CL	30.00	30.00
93	NOT A CREATURE WAS STIRRING	CL	30.00	30.00
93	TRIMMING THE TREE	CL	30.00	30.00
M. HUMPHREY BOGART		LITTLE LADIES		
89	PLAYING BRIDESMAID	CL	30.00	90.00
90	A DAY IN THE COUNTRY	CL	30.00	50.00
90	KITTY'S BATH	CL	30.00	60.00
90	LITTLE CAPTIVE	CL	30.00	50.00
90	PLAYING MAMA	CL	30.00	65.00
90	SEAMSTRESS, THE	CL	30.00	65.00
90	SUSANNA	CL	30.00	50.00
91	FIRST PARTY	CL	30.00	30.00
91	MAGIC KITTEN, THE	CL	30.00	30.00
91	SARAH	CL	30.00	50.00
*		LITTLE RASCALS		
85	BUTCH'S CHALLENGE	CL	25.00	30.00
85	DARLA'S DEBUT	CL	25.00	30.00
85	MY GAL	CL	25.00	50.00
85	PETE'S PAL	CL	25.00	30.00
85	ROUGHIN' IT	CL	25.00	50.00
85	SKELETON CREW	CL	25.00	30.00
85	SPANKY'S PRANKS	CL	25.00	30.00
85	THREE FOR THE SHOW	CL	25.00	40.00

YR NAME	LIMIT	ISSUE	TREND
G. GERARDI		**LITTLE SHOPKEEPERS**	
90 SEW TIRED	CL	30.00	30.00
91 BREAK TIME	CL	30.00	30.00
91 CANDY CAPERS	CL	30.00	40.00
91 CHAIN REACTION	CL	30.00	50.00
91 INFERIOR DECORATORS	CL	30.00	40.00
91 PURRFECT FIT	CL	30.00	30.00
91 TOYING AROUND	CL	30.00	40.00
91 TULIP TAG	CL	30.00	40.00
L. DANIELLE		**LORE OF THE WEST**	
93 A CHIEF'S PRIDE	CL	30.00	45.00
93 A MILE IN HIS MOCASSINS	CL	30.00	45.00
93 PATH OF HONOR	CL	30.00	45.00
94 GREAT SPIRIT OF THE PLAINS	*	*	44.00
94 GROWING UP BRAVE	CL	30.00	45.00
94 IN HER STEPS	CL	30.00	45.00
94 LEGACY TO MY SON	*	*	44.00
94 NOMADS OF THE SOUTHWEST	CL	30.00	45.00
94 PATHWAYS OF THE PUEBLO	CL	30.00	45.00
94 SACRED SPIRIT OF THE PLAINS	CL	30.00	45.00
95 END OF THE TRAIL	*	*	45.00
95 WE'LL FIGHT NO MORE	*	*	44.00
M. WEISTLING		**LUCY COLLAGE**	
93 LUCY	CL	38.00	225.00
S. BOTTICELLI		**MADONNA AND CHILD**	
93 MADONNA COL BAMBINO	CL	38.00	50.00
93 MADONNA DEL MAGNIFICAT	CL	38.00	50.00
A. CORREGGIO		**MADONNA AND CHILD**	
93 VIRGIN ADORING CHRIST CHILD	CL	38.00	50.00
L. DAVINCI		**MADONNA AND CHILD**	
92 VIRGIN OF THE ROCKS	CL	38.00	50.00
P. MIGNARD		**MADONNA AND CHILD**	
93 VIRGIN OF THE GRAPE	CL	38.00	50.00
B.E. MURILLO		**MADONNA AND CHILD**	
93 MADONNA OF ROSARY	CL	38.00	50.00
R. SANZIO		**MADONNA AND CHILD**	
92 MADONNA DELLA SEDIA	CL	38.00	50.00
93 SISTINE MADONNA	CL	38.00	50.00
T. HIRATA		**MAJESTY OF FLIGHT**	
89 COASTAL JOURNEY	CL	38.00	70.00
89 COMMANDING THE MARSH	CL	38.00	70.00
89 EAGLE SOARS, THE	CL	38.00	70.00
89 REALM OF THE RED-TAIL	CL	38.00	70.00
89 SENTRY OF THE NORTH	CL	38.00	70.00
90 FIERCE AND FREE	CL	30.00	70.00
90 SILENT WATCH	CL	30.00	70.00
90 VANTAGE POINT, THE	CL	30.00	70.00
L. PICKEN		**MAN'S BEST FRIEND**	
92 GOOD CATCH	CL	30.00	45.00
92 MAKING WAVES	CL	30.00	45.00
92 SPECIAL DELIVERY	CL	30.00	45.00
93 BEDTIME STORY	CL	30.00	45.00
93 FAITHFUL FRIEND	CL	30.00	45.00
93 LET'S PLAY BALL	CL	30.00	45.00
93 SITTING PRETTY	CL	30.00	45.00
93 TIME FOR A WALK	CL	30.00	75.00
93 TRUSTED COMPANION	CL	30.00	45.00
P. COOPER		**MIXED COMPANY**	
90 A STICKY SITUATION	CL	30.00	40.00
90 ALL WRAPPED UP	CL	30.00	40.00
90 PICTURE PERFECT	CL	30.00	35.00
90 TWO AGAINST ONE	CL	30.00	40.00
90 WHAT'S UP	CL	30.00	35.00
91 A MOMENT TO UNWIND	CL	30.00	40.00
91 OLE	CL	30.00	40.00
91 PICNIC PROWLERS	CL	30.00	35.00
C. REN		**MYSTIC WARRIORS**	
92 DELIVERANCE	CL	30.00	45.00
92 MAN WHO WALKS ALONE	CL	30.00	45.00
92 MYSTIC WARRIOR	CL	30.00	45.00
92 SPIRIT OF THE PLAINS	CL	30.00	45.00
92 SUN SEEKER	CL	30.00	45.00
92 TOP GUN	CL	30.00	45.00
92 WINDRIDER	CL	30.00	45.00
93 BLUE THUNDER	CL	30.00	45.00
93 PEACE MAKER	CL	30.00	45.00
93 SUN GLOW	CL	30.00	45.00
M. RICHTER		**NATURE'S MAJESTIC CATS**	
93 AFRICAN LION	CL	30.00	45.00
93 HIMALAYAN SNOW LEOPARD	CL	30.00	45.00
93 SIBERIAN TIGER	CL	30.00	45.00
94 AFRICAN CHEETAH	CL	30.00	45.00
94 AMERICAN COUGAR	CL	30.00	45.00
94 ASIAN CLOUDED LEOPARD	CL	30.00	45.00
94 CANADIAN LYNX	CL	30.00	45.00
94 EAST AFRICAN LEOPARD	CL	30.00	45.00

YR	NAME	LIMIT	ISSUE	TREND
G. MURRAY			**NATURE'S NIGHTTIME REALM**	
92	BOBCAT	CL	30.00	45.00
92	COUGAR	CL	30.00	45.00
93	CHEETAH	CL	30.00	45.00
93	JAGUAR	CL	30.00	45.00
93	LION	CL	30.00	45.00
93	LYNX	CL	30.00	45.00
93	SNOW LEOPARD	CL	30.00	45.00
93	WHITE TIGER	CL	30.00	45.00
R. PARKER			**NATURE'S QUIET MOMENTS**	
88	A CURIOUS PAIR	CL	38.00	40.00
88	JUST RESTING	CL	38.00	40.00
88	NORTHERN MORNINGS	CL	38.00	40.00
89	AUTUMN FORAGING	CL	38.00	40.00
89	CREEKSIDE	CL	38.00	40.00
89	MOUNTAIN BLOOMS	CL	38.00	40.00
89	OLD MAN OF THE MOUNTAIN	CL	38.00	40.00
89	WAITING OUT THE STORM	CL	38.00	40.00
D. WRIGHT			**NOBLE AMERICAN INDIAN WOMEN**	
89	SACAJAWEA	CL	30.00	50.00
90	LILY OF THE MOHAWK	CL	30.00	40.00
90	MINNEHAHA	CL	30.00	40.00
90	PINE LEAF	CL	30.00	50.00
90	POCAHONTAS	CL	30.00	50.00
90	WHITE ROSE	CL	30.00	50.00
91	FALLING STAR	CL	30.00	50.00
91	LOZEN	CL	30.00	30.00
J. SEEREY-LESTER			**NOBLE OWLS OF AMERICA**	
86	MORNING MIST	15000	55.00	100.00
87	AUTUMN MIST	15000	55.00	100.00
87	DAWN IN THE WILLOWS	15000	55.00	100.00
87	PRAIRIE SUNDOWN	15000	55.00	100.00
87	SNOWY WATCH	15000	55.00	100.00
87	WINTER VIGIL	15000	55.00	100.00
88	HIDING PLACE	15000	55.00	100.00
88	WAITING FOR DUSK	15000	55.00	100.00
R. TANENBAUM			**NOLAN RYAN**	
94	27 SEASONS	CL	30.00	30.00
94	BIRTH OF A LEGEND	CL	30.00	30.00
94	FAREWELL	CL	30.00	30.00
94	MILLION-DOLLAR PLAYER	CL	30.00	30.00
94	MR. FASTBALL	CL	30.00	30.00
94	STRIKEOUT EXPRESS, THE	CL	30.00	30.00
R. LAWRENCE			**NORTH AMERICAN DUCKS**	
91	AUTUMN FLIGHT	CL	30.00	40.00
91	RESTING PLACE, THE	CL	30.00	40.00
91	TWIN FLIGHT	CL	30.00	40.00
92	MISTY MORNING	CL	30.00	40.00
92	OVERCAST	CL	30.00	40.00
92	PERFECT PINTAILS	CL	30.00	40.00
92	SPRINGTIME THAW	CL	30.00	40.00
92	SUMMER RETREAT	CL	30.00	40.00
J. KILLEN			**NORTH AMERICAN GAMEBIRDS**	
90	BOBWHITE QUAIL	CL	38.00	50.00
90	GAMBEL QUAIL	CL	38.00	40.00
90	MOURNING DOVE	CL	38.00	50.00
90	RING-NECKED PHEASANT	CL	38.00	40.00
90	RUFFED GROUSE	CL	38.00	40.00
90	WOODCOCK	CL	38.00	50.00
91	CHUKAR PARTRIDGE	CL	38.00	50.00
91	WILD TURKEY	CL	38.00	50.00
R. LAWRENCE			**NORTH AMERICAN WATERBIRDS**	
88	CANADA GEESE	CL	38.00	50.00
88	HOODED MERGANSERS	CL	38.00	60.00
88	PINTAILS	CL	38.00	50.00
88	WOOD DUCKS	CL	38.00	60.00
89	AMERICAN WIDGEONS	CL	38.00	60.00
89	CANVASBACKS	CL	38.00	60.00
89	MALLARD PAIR	CL	38.00	65.00
89	SNOW GEESE	CL	38.00	50.00
S. FISHER			**NUTCRACKER BALLET**	
78	CLARA	CL	20.00	40.00
79	GODFATHER	CL	20.00	20.00
79	SNOW QUEEN AND KING	CL	20.00	45.00
80	CLARA AND THE PRINCE	CL	20.00	50.00
80	WALTZ OF THE FLOWERS	CL	20.00	25.00
J. PITCHER			**ON WINGS OF EAGLES**	
95	CHANGING OF THE GUARD	28 DAYS	30.00	40.00
95	FREE FLIGHT	28 DAYS	30.00	40.00
95	MORNING MAJESTY	28 DAYS	30.00	40.00
95	OVER THE LAND OF THE FREE	28 DAYS	30.00	40.00
95	WINTER'S MAJESTIC FLIGHT	28 DAYS	30.00	40.00
R. MASSEY			**PASSAGE TO CHINA**	
83	ALLIANCE	15000	55.00	60.00
83	EMPRESS OF CHINA	15000	55.00	60.00
85	CHALLENGE	15000	55.00	60.00
85	FLYING CLOUD	15000	55.00	60.00

YR	NAME	LIMIT	ISSUE	TREND
85	GRAND TURK	15000	55.00	60.00
85	ROMANCE OF THE SEAS	15000	55.00	60.00
85	SEA SERPENT	15000	55.00	60.00
85	SEA WITCH	15000	55.00	60.00
B. HARRISON			**PETALS AND PURRS**	
88	BLUSHING BEAUTIES	CL	25.00	60.00
88	FORGET-ME-NOT	CL	25.00	50.00
88	MORNING GLORIES	CL	25.00	50.00
88	SPRING FEVER	CL	25.00	50.00
89	GOLDEN FANCY	CL	25.00	50.00
89	PINK LILIES	CL	25.00	50.00
89	SIAMESE SUMMER	CL	25.00	50.00
89	SUMMER SUNSHINE	CL	25.00	50.00
T. BLACKSHEAR			**PORTRAITS FROM OZ**	
89	DOROTHY	CL	30.00	160.00
89	SCARECROW	CL	30.00	120.00
89	TIN MAN	CL	30.00	130.00
90	COWARDLY LION	CL	30.00	135.00
90	GLINDA	CL	30.00	105.00
90	TOTO	CL	30.00	225.00
90	WICKED WITCH	CL	30.00	200.00
90	WIZARD	CL	30.00	110.00
T. UTZ			**PORTRAITS OF CHILDHOOD**	
81	BUTTERFLY MAGIC	CL	25.00	50.00
82	SWEET DREAMS	CL	25.00	50.00
83	TURTLE TALK	CL	25.00	50.00
84	FRIENDS FOREVER	CL	25.00	50.00
J. PITCHER			**PORTRAITS OF THE BALD EAGLE**	
93	IN BOLD DEFIANCE	CL	38.00	55.00
93	MASTER OF THE SUMMER SKIES	CL	38.00	55.00
93	RULER OF THE SKY	CL	38.00	55.00
93	SPRING'S SENTINEL	CL	38.00	55.00
J. MEGER			**PORTRAITS OF THE WILD**	
94	CALL OF AUTUMN	CL	30.00	40.00
94	DEVOTED PROTECTOR	CL	30.00	40.00
94	INTERLUDE	CL	30.00	40.00
94	WATCHFUL EYES	CL	30.00	40.00
94	WINTER SOLITUDE	CL	30.00	40.00
95	BABIES OF SPRING (BEAR CUBS)	28 DAYS	30.00	40.00
95	BIGHORN (SHEEP)	28 DAYS	30.00	40.00
95	MONARCH OF THE PLAINS	28 DAYS	30.00	45.00
95	MOONLIGHT VIGIL	28 DAYS	30.00	45.00
95	TENDER COURTSHIP	28 DAYS	30.00	40.00
95	UNBRIDLED POWER	28 DAYS	30.00	45.00
S. BUTCHER			**PRECIOUS MOMENTS BIBLE STORY**	
90	COME LET US ADORE HIM	CL	30.00	30.00
92	CARPENTER SHOP, THE	CL	30.00	30.00
92	CRUCIFIXION, THE	CL	30.00	30.00
92	FLIGHT INTO EGYPT, THE	CL	30.00	30.00
92	JESUS IN THE TEMPLE	CL	30.00	30.00
92	THEY FOLLOWED THE STAR	CL	30.00	30.00
93	HE IS NOT HERE	CL	30.00	30.00
S. BUTCHER			**PRECIOUS MOMENTS CLASSICS**	
93	GOD LOVETH A CHEERFUL GIVER	CL	35.00	40.00
93	MAKE A JOYFUL NOISE	CL	35.00	40.00
T. UTZ			**PRECIOUS MOMENTS PLATES**	
79	FRIEND IN THE SKY	CL	22.00	55.00
80	SAND IN HER SHOE	CL	22.00	30.00
80	SEASHELLS	CL	22.00	35.00
80	SNOW BUNNY	CL	22.00	25.00
81	DAWN	CL	22.00	30.00
82	MY KITTY	CL	22.00	50.00
B.P. GUTMANN			**PRECIOUS PORTRAITS**	
87	BUNNY	CL	25.00	50.00
87	FAIRY GOLD	CL	25.00	50.00
87	GOLDILOCKS	CL	25.00	50.00
87	MISCHIEF	CL	25.00	50.00
87	PEACH BLOSSOM	CL	25.00	50.00
87	SUNBEAM	CL	25.00	50.00
D. WRIGHT			**PRINCESSES OF THE PLAINS**	
93	GENTLE BEAUTY	CL	30.00	45.00
93	NOBLE BEAUTY	CL	30.00	45.00
93	PRAIRIE FLOWER	CL	30.00	45.00
93	SNOW PRINCESS	CL	30.00	45.00
93	WILD FLOWER	CL	30.00	45.00
93	WINTER'S ROSE	CL	30.00	45.00
94	MOUNTAIN PRINCESS	CL	30.00	45.00
94	NATURE'S GUARDIAN	CL	30.00	45.00
95	PROUD DREAMER	28 DAYS	30.00	45.00
95	SPRING MAIDEN	28 DAYS	30.00	45.00
A. AGNEW			**PROTECTOR OF THE WOLF**	
98	WINTER MAJESTY	*	40.00	40.00
K. FREEMAN			**PROUD INDIAN FAMILIES**	
91	NAMING CEREMONY, THE	CL	30.00	45.00
91	PLAYING WITH TRADITION	CL	30.00	45.00
91	POWER OF THE BASKET, THE	CL	30.00	45.00
91	STORYTELLER, THE	CL	30.00	45.00

YR	NAME	LIMIT	ISSUE	TREND
92	CEREMONIAL DRESS	CL	30.00	45.00
92	MARRIAGE CEREMONY, THE	CL	30.00	45.00
92	PREPARING THE BERRY HARVEST	CL	30.00	45.00
92	SOUNDS OF THE FOREST	CL	30.00	45.00
93	BEAUTIFUL CREATIONS	CL	30.00	45.00
93	JEWELRY MAKER, THE	CL	30.00	45.00
J. SCHMIDT				**PROUD INNOCENCE**
94	DESERT FLOWER	CL	30.00	40.00
95	LAUGHING HEART	28 DAYS	30.00	45.00
95	LITTLE DRUMMER	28 DAYS	30.00	44.00
95	MORNING CHILD	28 DAYS	30.00	44.00
95	SUN BLOSSOM	28 DAYS	30.00	44.00
95	WISE ONE	28 DAYS	30.00	45.00
95	YOUNG ARCHER	28 DAYS	30.00	45.00
R. SWANSON				**PROUD NATION**
89	AUTUMN TREAT	CL	25.00	50.00
89	DRESSED UP FOR THE POW WOW	CL	25.00	50.00
89	IN A BIG LAND	CL	25.00	50.00
89	JUST A FEW DAYS OLD	CL	25.00	50.00
89	NAVAJO LITTLE ONE	CL	25.00	50.00
89	NEWEST LITTLE SHEEPHERDER	CL	25.00	50.00
89	OUT WITH MAMA'S FLOCK	CL	25.00	50.00
89	UP THE RED ROCKS	CL	25.00	85.00
J. LAMB				**PUPPY PLAYTIME**
87	CABIN FEVER-BLACK LABRADORS	CL	25.00	50.00
87	CATCH OF THE DAY-GOLDEN RETRIEVERS	CL	25.00	50.00
87	DOUBLE TAKE-COCKER SPANIELS	CL	25.00	80.00
87	FUN AND GAMES-POODLE	CL	25.00	50.00
87	GETTING ACQUAINTED-BEAGLES	CL	25.00	55.00
87	HANGING OUT-GERMAN SHEPHERD	CL	25.00	50.00
87	NEW LEASH ON LIFE-MINI SCHNAUZER	CL	25.00	55.00
87	WEEKEND GARDENER-LHASA APSOS	CL	25.00	55.00
D. GREEN			**QUIET MOMENTS OF CHILDHOOD**	
91	CHRISTINA'S SECRET GARDEN	CL	30.00	40.00
91	ELIZABETH'S AFTERNOON TEA	CL	30.00	50.00
91	ERIC & ERIN'S STORYTIME	CL	30.00	40.00
92	CHILDREN'S DAY BY THE SEA	CL	30.00	40.00
92	DANIELS' MORNING PLAYTIME	CL	30.00	40.00
92	JESSICA'S TEA PARTY	CL	30.00	35.00
92	JORDAN'S PLAYFUL PUPS	CL	30.00	35.00
92	MEGAN & MONIQUE'S BAKERY	CL	30.00	40.00
M. STEELE				**QUILTED COUNTRYSIDE**
91	COUNTRY MERCHANT, THE	CL	30.00	40.00
91	OLD COUNTRY STORE, THE	CL	30.00	55.00
91	QUILTER'S CABIN, THE	CL	30.00	50.00
91	SPRING CLEANING	CL	30.00	40.00
91	SUMMER HARVEST	CL	30.00	40.00
91	WINTER'S END	CL	30.00	40.00
92	ANTIQUES STORE, THE	CL	30.00	40.00
92	WASH DAY	CL	30.00	40.00
L. BYWATERS				**RENAISSANCE ANGELS**
94	ANGELIC INNOCENCE	CL	30.00	45.00
94	DOVES OF PEACE	CL	30.00	45.00
94	JOY TO THE WORLD	28 DAYS	30.00	44.00
95	ANGEL OF FAITH	28 DAYS	30.00	45.00
95	ANGELS SING, THE	28 DAYS	30.00	44.00
95	CHRISTMAS STAR	28 DAYS	30.00	44.00
95	HARMONIOUS HEAVENS	28 DAYS	30.00	45.00
95	TRUMPETER'S CALL	28 DAYS	30.00	44.00
S. MORTON		**REPUBLIC PICTURES FILM LIBRARY COLLECTION**		
92	FIGHTING SEABEES, THE	CL	38.00	60.00
92	QUIET MAN, THE	CL	38.00	60.00
93	ANGEL & THE BADMAN	CL	38.00	60.00
N. ROCKWELL			**ROCKWELL HOME OF THE BRAVE**	
81	BACK TO HIS OLD JOB	18000	35.00	60.00
81	HERO'S WELCOME	18000	35.00	60.00
81	REMINISCING	18000	35.00	60.00
81	WAR HERO	18000	35.00	40.00
82	TAKING MOTHER OVER THE TOP	18000	35.00	40.00
82	UNCLE SAM TAKES WINGS	18000	35.00	80.00
82	WAR BOND	18000	35.00	40.00
82	WILLIE GILLIS IN CHURCH	18000	35.00	60.00
D. TUTWEILER				**ROMANCE OF THE RAILS**
94	BLUE BONNET	28 DAYS	30.00	45.00
94	CRESCENT LIMITED	CL	30.00	45.00
94	MORNING STAR	CL	30.00	45.00
94	ORANGE BLOSSOM SPECIAL	CL	30.00	45.00
94	PINE TREE LIMITED	28 DAYS	30.00	44.00
94	PORTLAND ROSE	CL	30.00	45.00
94	STARLIGHT LIMITED	CL	30.00	45.00
94	SUNRISE LIMITED	CL	30.00	45.00
94	SUNSET LIMITED	CL	30.00	45.00
94	WESTERN STAR	CL	30.00	45.00
Q. LEMONDS			**ROMANTIC FLIGHTS OF FANCY**	
94	EVENING SOLO	28 DAYS	30.00	44.00
94	MORNING MINUET	CL	30.00	45.00
94	SUNLIT WALTZ	CL	30.00	45.00

YR	NAME	LIMIT	ISSUE	TREND
95	EXOTIC INTERLUDE	28 DAYS	30.00	44.00
95	SUMMER SONATA	28 DAYS	30.00	44.00
95	SUNRISE SAMBA	28 DAYS	30.00	44.00
95	SUNSET BALLET	28 DAYS	30.00	44.00
95	TWILIGHT TANGO	28 DAYS	30.00	44.00
J. GROSSMAN	**ROMANTIC VICTORIAN KEEPSAKE**			
92	AS FAIR AS A ROSE	CL	35.00	50.00
92	BONNIE BLUE EYES	CL	35.00	50.00
92	DEAREST KISS	CL	35.00	50.00
92	FIRST LOVE	CL	35.00	50.00
92	PRECIOUS FRIENDS	CL	35.00	50.00
92	SPRINGTIME BEAUTY	CL	35.00	50.00
92	SUMMERTIME FANCY	CL	35.00	50.00
94	BONNETS AND BOUQUETS	CL	35.00	50.00
N. ROCKWELL	**SATURDAY EVENING POST BASEBALL COLLECTION**			
92	100TH YEAR OF BASEBALL	CL	20.00	25.00
93	BOTTOM OF THE SIXTH	CL	20.00	25.00
93	DUGOUT, THE	CL	20.00	25.00
93	ROOKIE, THE	CL	20.00	25.00
N. ROCKWELL	**SATURDAY EVENING POST PLATE COLLECTION**			
89	EASTER MORNING	CL	35.00	65.00
89	FACTS OF LIFE, THE	CL	35.00	40.00
89	WONDERS OF RADIO, THE	CL	35.00	40.00
90	FIRST FLIGHT	CL	35.00	55.00
90	FURLOUGH	CL	35.00	40.00
90	JURY ROOM	CL	35.00	40.00
90	TRAVELING COMPANION	CL	35.00	40.00
90	WINDOW WASHER, THE	CL	35.00	50.00
B. PERRY	**SCENES OF AN AMERICAN CHRISTMAS**			
94	CHRISTMAS EVE WORSHIP	CL	30.00	45.00
94	I'LL BE HOME FOR CHRISTMAS	CL	30.00	45.00
95	AFTERNOON OUTING	28 DAYS	30.00	45.00
95	DEAR SANTA	28 DAYS	30.00	45.00
95	HOLIDAY HAPPENING	28 DAYS	30.00	44.00
95	LONG WINTER'S NIGHT	28 DAYS	30.00	44.00
95	SOUNDS OF CHRISTMAS	28 DAYS	30.00	45.00
95	WINTER WORSHIP	28 DAYS	30.00	45.00
J. PITCHER	**SEASONS OF THE BALD EAGLE**			
91	AUTUMN IN THE MOUNTAINS	CL	38.00	40.00
91	SPRING ON THE RIVER	CL	38.00	40.00
91	SUMMER ON THE SEACOAST	CL	38.00	40.00
91	WINTER IN THE VALLEY	CL	38.00	40.00
T. UTZ	**SINGLE ISSUE**			
83	PRINCESS GRACE	CL	40.00	65.00
C. FRACE	**SMALL WONDERS OF THE WILD**			
89	HIDEAWAY	CL	30.00	50.00
90	EXPLORING A NEW WORLD	CL	30.00	45.00
90	EYES OF WONDER	CL	30.00	45.00
90	QUIET MORNING	CL	30.00	45.00
90	READY FOR ADVENTURE	CL	30.00	45.00
90	THREE OF A KIND	CL	30.00	45.00
90	UNO	CL	30.00	45.00
90	YOUNG EXPLORERS	CL	30.00	45.00
J. LAMB	**SPORTING GENERATION**			
91	GOLDEN MOMENTS	CL	30.00	45.00
91	LIKE FATHER, LIKE SON	CL	30.00	45.00
91	LOOKOUT, THE	CL	30.00	45.00
92	FIRST TIME OUT	CL	30.00	45.00
92	PICKING UP THE SCENT	CL	30.00	45.00
92	POINT OF INTEREST	CL	30.00	45.00
92	SPRINGING INTO ACTION	CL	30.00	45.00
92	WHO'S TRACKING WHO	CL	30.00	45.00
*	**STAINED GLASS GARDENS**			
89	COCKATOO'S GARDEN, THE	15000	55.00	60.00
89	GARDEN SUNSET	15000	55.00	60.00
89	PEACOCK AND WISTERIA	15000	55.00	60.00
89	WATERFALL AND IRIS	15000	55.00	60.00
90	A HOLLYHOCK SUNRISE	15000	55.00	60.00
90	PEACEFUL WATERS	15000	55.00	60.00
90	ROSES AND MAGNOLIAS	15000	55.00	60.00
90	SPRINGTIME IN THE VALLEY	15000	55.00	60.00
*	**STAR TREK**			
94	CAPTAIN JEAN-LUC PICARD (AUTOGRAPHED)	5000	195.00	200.00
94	FIRST OFFICER SPOCK (AUTOGRAPHED)	2500	195.00	200.00
T. BLACKSHEAR	**STAR TREK 25TH ANNIVERSARY COMMEMORATIVE COLLECTION**			
91	KIRK	CL	35.00	100.00
91	SPOCK	CL	35.00	115.00
91	STAR TREK 25TH ANNIVERSARY PLATE	CL	38.00	135.00
92	MCCOY	CL	35.00	40.00
92	SCOTTY	CL	35.00	40.00
92	UHURA	CL	35.00	40.00
93	CHEKOV	CL	35.00	40.00
93	SULU	CL	35.00	40.00
94	U.S.S. ENTERPRISE NCC-1701	CL	35.00	40.00
K. BIRDSONG	**STAR TREK GENERATIONS**			
95	ULTIMATE CONFRONTATION	28 DAYS	35.00	60.00

YR	NAME	LIMIT	ISSUE	TREND
T. BLACKSHEAR		**STAR TREK NEXT GENERATION**		
93	CAPTAIN JEAN-LUC PICARD	CL	35.00	135.00
93	COMMANDER WILLIAM T. RIKER	CL	35.00	50.00
94	LIEUTENANT COMMANDER DATA	CL	35.00	95.00
94	LIEUTENANT WORF	CL	35.00	50.00
K. BIRDSONG		**STAR TREK NEXT GENERATION THE EPISODES**		
94	ALL GOOD THINGS	28 DAYS	35.00	60.00
94	BEST OF BOTH WORLDS, THE	CL	35.00	50.00
94	ENCOUNTER AT FAR POINT	CL	35.00	50.00
94	UNIFICATION	28 DAYS	35.00	60.00
94	YESTERDAY'S ENTERPRISE	28 DAYS	35.00	60.00
95	BIG GOODBYE	28 DAYS	35.00	60.00
95	DESCENT	28 DAYS	35.00	60.00
95	INNER LIGHT	28 DAYS	35.00	60.00
95	REDEMPTION	28 DAYS	35.00	60.00
95	RELICS	28 DAYS	35.00	60.00
M. WEISTLING		**STAR TREK THE MOVIES**		
94	FINAL FRONTIER	28 DAYS	35.00	60.00
94	MOTION PICTURE, THE	28 DAYS	35.00	60.00
94	SEARCH FOR SPOCK	28 DAYS	35.00	60.00
94	STAR TREK II: THE WRATH OF KHAN	CL	35.00	50.00
94	STAR TREK IV: THE VOYAGE HOME	CL	35.00	50.00
94	UNDISCOVERED COUNTRY	28 DAYS	35.00	60.00
K. BIRDSONG		**STAR TREK THE VOYAGERS**		
94	KLINGON BATTLECRUISER	CL	35.00	50.00
94	ROMULAN WARBIRD	CL	35.00	50.00
94	U.S.S. ENTERPRISE NCC-1701	CL	35.00	50.00
94	U.S.S. ENTERPRISE NCC-1701-D	CL	35.00	50.00
95	CARDASSIAN GALOR WARSHIP	28 DAYS	35.00	60.00
95	FERENGI MARAUDER	28 DAYS	35.00	60.00
95	KLINGON BIRD OF PREY	28 DAYS	35.00	60.00
95	TRIPLE NACELLED ENTERPRISE	28 DAYS	35.00	60.00
95	U.S.S. ENTERPRISE, NCC 1701A VOYAGER	TL	35.00	60.00
95	U.S.S. EXCELSIOR	TL	35.00	60.00
T. BLACKSHEAR		**STAR WARS 10TH ANNIVERSARY COMMEMORATIVE PLATE**		
90	STAR WARS 10TH ANNIVERSARY PLATE	CL	40.00	90.00
*		**STAR WARS HEROES AND VILLAINS**		
98	LUKE SKYWALKER	*	35.00	35.00
T. BLACKSHEAR		**STAR WARS PLATE COLLECTION**		
87	HAN SOLO	CL	30.00	85.00
87	IMPERIAL WALKERS, THE	CL	30.00	105.00
87	LUKE AND YODA	CL	30.00	95.00
87	LUKE SKYWALKER AND DARTH VADER	CL	30.00	70.00
87	PRINCESS LEIA	CL	30.00	125.00
87	R2-D2 AND WICKET	CL	30.00	85.00
88	CREW IN THE COCKPIT	CL	30.00	175.00
88	SPACE BATTLE	CL	30.00	325.00
M. WEISTLING		**STAR WARS TRILOGY**		
93	EMPIRE STRIKES BACK, THE	CL	38.00	50.00
93	RETURN OF THE JEDI	CL	38.00	50.00
93	STAR WARS	CL	38.00	50.00
T. UTZ		**SUMMER DAYS OF CHILDHOOD**		
83	A JUMPING CONTEST	CL	30.00	50.00
83	A STOLEN KISS	CL	30.00	50.00
83	BALLOON CARNIVAL	CL	30.00	50.00
83	BIRTHDAY PARTY, THE	CL	30.00	50.00
83	BLOWING BUBBLES	CL	30.00	50.00
83	COOLING OFF	CL	30.00	50.00
83	FIRST CUSTOMER	CL	30.00	50.00
83	GARDEN MAGIC	CL	30.00	50.00
83	KITTY'S BATHTIME	CL	30.00	50.00
83	LITTLE BEACHCOMBER	CL	30.00	50.00
83	MOUNTAIN FRIENDS	CL	30.00	50.00
83	PLAYING DOCTOR	CL	30.00	50.00
T. UTZ		**THORNTON UTZ 10TH ANNIVERSARY PLATE COLLECTION**		
89	AMONG THE DAFFODILS	CL	30.00	45.00
89	BEST FRIENDS	CL	30.00	35.00
89	DAWN	CL	30.00	35.00
89	FRIENDS IN THE SKY	CL	30.00	35.00
89	JUST LIKE MOMMY	CL	30.00	35.00
89	LITTLE EMILY	CL	30.00	35.00
89	MY KITTY	CL	30.00	35.00
89	PLAYING DOCTOR	CL	30.00	35.00
89	TEDDY'S BATHTIME	CL	30.00	35.00
89	TURTLE TALK	CL	30.00	35.00
M. TSANG		**TIMELESS EXPRESSIONS OF THE ORIENT**		
90	FIDELITY	15000	75.00	100.00
91	BEAUTY	15000	55.00	60.00
91	FEMININITY	15000	75.00	80.00
91	LONGEVITY	15000	75.00	80.00
92	COURAGE	15000	55.00	60.00
H. BOND		**TREASURED DAYS**		
87	AMANDA	CL	25.00	50.00
87	ASHLEY	CL	30.00	65.00
87	CHRISTOPHER	CL	25.00	50.00
87	JEREMY	CL	25.00	50.00
87	SARA	CL	25.00	35.00

YR	NAME	LIMIT	ISSUE	TREND
88	JUSTIN	CL	25.00	50.00
88	LINDSAY	CL	25.00	50.00
88	NICHOLAS	CL	25.00	50.00
P. HILLMAN		**TREASURY OF CHERISHED TEDDIES**		
95	A NEW YEAR WITH OLD FRIENDS	CL	30.00	30.00
95	VALENTINES FOR YOU	CL	30.00	30.00
K. MCELROY		**UNBRIDLED MYSTERY**		
96	WILD SPIRIT	*	*	40.00
C. DEHAAN		**UNBRIDLED SPIRIT**		
92	DESERT SHADOWS	CL	30.00	40.00
92	SURF DANCER	CL	30.00	44.00
92	WINTER RENEGADE	CL	30.00	40.00
93	AUTUMN REVERIE	CL	30.00	40.00
93	BLIZZARD'S PERIL	CL	30.00	40.00
93	DESERT DUEL	CL	30.00	40.00
93	MIDNIGHT RUN	CL	30.00	40.00
93	MOONLIGHT MAJESTY	CL	30.00	40.00
93	PAINTED SUNRISE	CL	30.00	40.00
93	SUNRISE SURPRISE	CL	30.00	40.00
T. UTZ		**UTZ MOTHER'S DAY**		
83	A GIFT OF LOVE	TL	28.00	40.00
83	MOTHER'S ANGEL	TL	28.00	30.00
83	MOTHER'S HELPING HAND	TL	28.00	30.00
J. HARRISON		**VANISHING RURAL AMERICA**		
91	AMERICA'S HEARTLAND	CL	30.00	30.00
91	AUTUMN'S PASSAGE	CL	30.00	50.00
91	COUNTRY PATH	CL	30.00	40.00
91	COVERED IN FALL	CL	30.00	50.00
91	QUIET REFLECTIONS	CL	30.00	50.00
91	RURAL DELIVERY	CL	30.00	30.00
91	STOREFRONT MEMORIES	CL	30.00	50.00
91	WHEN THE CIRCUS CAME TO TOWN	CL	30.00	40.00
J. GROSSMAN		**VICTORIAN CHRISTMAS MEMORIES**		
92	A VISIT FROM ST. NICHOLAS	CL	30.00	40.00
92	WITH VISIONS OF SUGAR PLUMS	CL	30.00	40.00
93	CHRISTMAS ANGELS	CL	30.00	40.00
93	CHRISTMAS DELIVERY	CL	30.00	40.00
93	CHRISTMAS INNOCENCE	CL	30.00	40.00
93	GRANDFATHER FROST	CL	30.00	40.00
93	JOYOUS NOEL	CL	30.00	40.00
93	MERRY OLDE KRIS KRINGLE	CL	30.00	40.00
M. HUMPHREY BOGART		**VICTORIAN PLAYTIME**		
91	A BUSY DAY	CL	30.00	40.00
92	A LITTLE PERSUASION	CL	30.00	40.00
92	CLEANING HOUSE	CL	30.00	40.00
92	LITTLE MASTERPIECE	CL	30.00	40.00
92	PEEK-A-BOO	CL	30.00	40.00
92	PLAYING BRIDE	CL	30.00	40.00
92	TEA AND GOSSIP	CL	30.00	40.00
92	WAITING FOR A NIBBLE	CL	30.00	40.00
C. DEHAAN		**WARRIOR'S PRIDE**		
94	BATTLE COLORS	*	*	45.00
94	BLACKFOOT WAR PONY	CL	30.00	40.00
94	CALL OF THE DRUMS	*	*	45.00
94	CHAMPION'S REVELRY	*	*	45.00
94	CROW WAR PONY	CL	30.00	40.00
94	RUNNING FREE	CL	30.00	40.00
94	SHOSHONI WAR PONY	*	*	45.00
94	SOUTHERN CHEYENNE	CL	30.00	40.00
D. CROOK		**WE THE CHILDREN**		
87	FREEDOM OF SPEECH, THE	14 DAYS	25.00	40.00
88	CRUEL AND UNUSUAL PUNISHMENT	14 DAYS	25.00	40.00
88	QUARTERING OF SOLDIERS	14 DAYS	25.00	40.00
88	RIGHT TO BEAR ARMS	14 DAYS	25.00	40.00
88	RIGHT TO VOTE	14 DAYS	25.00	40.00
88	SELF INCRIMINATION	14 DAYS	25.00	40.00
88	TRIAL BY JURY	14 DAYS	25.00	40.00
88	UNREASONABLE SEARCH AND SEIZURE	14 DAYS	25.00	40.00
F. MCCARTHY		**WEST OF FRANK MCCARTHY**		
91	ATTACKING THE IRON HORSE	CL	38.00	65.00
91	ATTEMPT ON THE STAGE	CL	38.00	50.00
91	BRINGING OUT THE FURS	CL	38.00	50.00
91	HEADED NORTH	CL	38.00	40.00
91	HOSTILE THREAT, THE	CL	38.00	50.00
91	KIOWA RAIDER	CL	38.00	50.00
91	ON THE OLD NORTH TRAIL	CL	38.00	50.00
91	PRAYER, THE	CL	38.00	55.00
R. PARKER		**WINGED REFLECTIONS**		
89	ABOVE THE BREAKERS	CL	38.00	40.00
89	AMONG THE REEDS	CL	38.00	40.00
89	FOLLOWING MAMA	CL	38.00	40.00
89	FREEZE UP	CL	38.00	40.00
89	WINGS ABOVE THE WATER	CL	38.00	40.00
90	AT THE WATER'S EDGE	CL	30.00	30.00
90	EARLY SPRING	CL	30.00	30.00
90	SUMMER LOON	CL	30.00	30.00

YR	NAME	LIMIT	ISSUE	TREND

T. XARAS — WINTER RAILS

YR	NAME	LIMIT	ISSUE	TREND
92	WINTER CLOSING	CL	30.00	40.00
93	BY SEA OR RAIL	CL	30.00	40.00
93	COAL COUNTRY	CL	30.00	40.00
93	COUNTRY CROSSROADS	CL	30.00	40.00
93	DARBY CROSSING	CL	30.00	40.00
93	DAYLIGHT RUN	CL	30.00	40.00
93	LONG HAUL, THE	CL	30.00	40.00
93	TIMBER LINE	CL	30.00	40.00
95	EAST BROAD TOP	28 DAYS	30.00	45.00
95	LANSDOWN STATION	28 DAYS	30.00	45.00

J. SEEREY-LESTER — WINTER WILDLIFE

YR	NAME	LIMIT	ISSUE	TREND
89	AMONG THE CATTAILS	15000	55.00	60.00
89	CLOSE ENCOUNTERS	15000	55.00	60.00
89	EARLY SNOW	15000	55.00	60.00
89	FIRST SNOW	15000	55.00	60.00
89	LYING IN WAIT	15000	55.00	60.00
89	OUT OF THE BLIZZARD	15000	55.00	60.00
89	REFUGE, THE	15000	55.00	60.00
89	WINTER HIDING	15000	55.00	60.00

T. BLACKSHEAR — WIZARD OF OZ COMMEMORATIVE

YR	NAME	LIMIT	ISSUE	TREND
88	DOROTHY MEETS THE SCARECROW	CL	25.00	115.00
88	WE'RE OFF TO SEE THE WIZARD	CL	25.00	215.00
89	A GLIMPSE OF THE MUNCHKINS	CL	25.00	120.00
89	GREAT AND POWERFUL OZ, THE	CL	25.00	150.00
89	IF I WERE KING OF THE FOREST	CL	25.00	150.00
89	THERE'S NO PLACE LIKE HOME	CL	25.00	155.00
89	TIN MAN SPEAKS, THE	CL	25.00	130.00
89	WITCH CASTS A SPELL, THE	CL	25.00	145.00

R. ORR — WOODLAND CREATURES

YR	NAME	LIMIT	ISSUE	TREND
85	FIRST ADVENTURE	10 DAYS	38.00	40.00
85	FISHING TRIP	10 DAYS	38.00	40.00
85	HIDING PLACE, THE	10 DAYS	38.00	40.00
85	MEADOWLAND VIGIL	10 DAYS	38.00	40.00
85	MORNING LESSON	10 DAYS	38.00	40.00
85	RESTING IN THE GLEN	10 DAYS	38.00	40.00
85	SPRINGTIME FROLIC	10 DAYS	38.00	40.00
85	STARTLED SENTRY	10 DAYS	38.00	40.00

G. GIORDANO — WOODLAND ENCOUNTERS

YR	NAME	LIMIT	ISSUE	TREND
91	ANYONE FOR A SWIM?	CL	30.00	40.00
91	HI NEIGHBOR	CL	30.00	40.00
91	LUNCHTIME VISITOR	CL	30.00	40.00
91	MEADOW MEETING	CL	30.00	40.00
91	NATURE SCOUTS	CL	30.00	40.00
91	PEEK-A-BOO!	CL	30.00	40.00
91	WANT TO PLAY?	CL	30.00	40.00
92	FIELD DAY			

D. ZOLAN — WORLD OF ZOLAN

YR	NAME	LIMIT	ISSUE	TREND
92	FIRST KISS	CL	30.00	45.00
92	MORNING DISCOVERY	CL	30.00	45.00
93	FLOWERS FOR MOTHER	CL	30.00	45.00
93	LETTER TO GRANDMA	CL	30.00	45.00
93	LITTLE FISHERMAN, THE	CL	30.00	30.00
93	TWILIGHT PRAYER	CL	30.00	30.00

A. AGNEW — YEAR OF THE WOLF

YR	NAME	LIMIT	ISSUE	TREND
93	BROKEN SILENCE	CL	30.00	40.00
93	LEADER OF THE PACK	CL	30.00	40.00
93	SOLITUDE	CL	30.00	40.00
94	A SECOND GLANCE	CL	30.00	40.00
94	FREE AS THE WIND	CL	30.00	40.00
94	GUARDIANS OF THE HIGH COUNTRY	CL	30.00	40.00
94	SONG OF THE WOLF	CL	30.00	40.00
94	TUNDRA LIGHT	CL	30.00	40.00
95	LORDS OF THE TUNDRA	28 DAYS	30.00	45.00
95	WILDERNESS COMPANIONS	28 DAYS	30.00	45.00

HAMILTON/BOEHM

BOEHM — AWARD WINNING ROSES

YR	NAME	LIMIT	ISSUE	TREND
79	ANGEL FACE ROSE	15000	45.00	65.00
79	ELEGANCE ROSE	15000	45.00	65.00
79	MR. LINCOLN ROSE	15000	45.00	65.00
79	PEACE ROSE	15000	45.00	65.00
79	QUEEN ELIZABETH ROSE	15000	45.00	65.00
79	ROYAL HIGHNESS ROSE	15000	45.00	65.00
79	TROPICANA ROSE	15000	45.00	65.00
79	WHITE MASTERPIECE ROSE	15000	45.00	65.00

BOEHM — GAMEBIRDS OF NORTH AMERICA

YR	NAME	LIMIT	ISSUE	TREND
84	AMERICAN WOODCOCK	15000	63.00	65.00
84	BOB WHITE QUAIL	15000	63.00	65.00
84	CALIFORNIA QUAIL	15000	63.00	65.00
84	PRAIRIE GROUSE	15000	63.00	65.00
84	RING-NECKED PHEASANT	15000	63.00	65.00
84	RUFFED GROUSE	15000	63.00	65.00
84	WILD TURKEY	15000	63.00	65.00
84	WILLOW PARTRIDGE	15000	63.00	65.00

BOEHM — HUMMINGBIRD COLLECTION

YR	NAME	LIMIT	ISSUE	TREND
80	BLUE THROATED	15000	63.00	85.00

YR	NAME	LIMIT	ISSUE	TREND
80	BRAZILIAN RUBY	15000	63.00	85.00
80	BROADBILLED	15000	63.00	65.00
80	BROADTAIL	15000	63.00	65.00
80	CALLIOPE	15000	63.00	85.00
80	CRIMSON TOPAZ	15000	63.00	65.00
80	RUFOUS FLAME BEARER	15000	63.00	85.00
80	STREAMERTAIL	15000	63.00	85.00

BOEHM — OWL COLLECTION

YR	NAME	LIMIT	ISSUE	TREND
80	BARN OWL	15000	45.00	65.00
80	BARRED OWL	15000	45.00	65.00
80	BOREAL OWL	15000	45.00	80.00
80	GREAT HORNED OWL	15000	45.00	65.00
80	SAW WHET OWL	15000	45.00	65.00
80	SCREECH OWL	15000	45.00	65.00
80	SHORT EARED OWL	15000	45.00	65.00
80	SNOWY OWL	15000	45.00	65.00

BOEHM — WATER BIRDS

YR	NAME	LIMIT	ISSUE	TREND
81	AMERICAN PINTAIL	15000	63.00	65.00
81	CANADA GEESE	15000	63.00	80.00
81	CANVAS BACK	15000	63.00	65.00
81	COMMON MALLARD	15000	63.00	65.00
81	GREEN WINGED TEAL	15000	63.00	65.00
81	HOODED MERGANSER	15000	63.00	90.00
81	ROSS'S GEESE	15000	63.00	65.00
81	WOOD DUCKS	15000	63.00	65.00

HAVILAND
R. HETREAU — TWELVE DAYS OF CHRISTMAS

YR	NAME	LIMIT	ISSUE	TREND
70	PARTRIDGE	30000	25.00	300.00
71	TWO TURTLEDOVES	30000	25.00	80.00
72	THREE FRENCH HENS	30000	28.00	40.00
73	FOUR CALLING BIRDS	30000	29.00	60.00
74	FIVE GOLDEN RINGS	30000	30.00	40.00
75	SIX GEESE A'LAYING	30000	33.00	40.00
76	SEVEN SWANS	30000	38.00	60.00
77	EIGHT MAIDS	30000	40.00	80.00
78	NINE LADIES DANCING	30000	45.00	75.00
79	TEN LORDS A'LEAPING	30000	50.00	40.00
80	ELEVEN PIPERS PIPING	30000	55.00	40.00
81	TWELVE DRUMMERS	30000	60.00	65.00

HAVILAND & PARLON
*
CHRISTMAS MADONNAS

YR	NAME	LIMIT	ISSUE	TREND
72	BY RAPHAEL	5000	35.00	45.00
73	BY FERUZZI	5000	40.00	80.00
74	BY RAPHAEL	5000	43.00	45.00
75	BY MURILLO	7500	43.00	45.00
76	BY BOTTICELLI	7500	45.00	50.00
77	BY BELLINI	7500	48.00	50.00
78	BY LIPPI	7500	48.00	55.00
79	MADONNA OF THE EUCHARIST	7500	50.00	115.00

*
LADY AND THE UNICORN

YR	NAME	LIMIT	ISSUE	TREND
77	TO MY ONLY DESIRE	20000	45.00	130.00
78	SIGHT	20000	45.00	75.00
79	SOUND	20000	48.00	80.00
80	TOUCH	15000	53.00	150.00
81	SCENT	10000	59.00	125.00
82	TASTE	10000	59.00	125.00

*
TAPESTRY I

YR	NAME	LIMIT	ISSUE	TREND
71	UNICORN IN CAPTIVITY	10000	35.00	150.00
72	START OF THE HUNT	10000	35.00	75.00
73	CHASE OF THE UNICORN	10000	35.00	120.00
74	END OF THE HUNT	10000	38.00	120.00
75	UNICORN SURROUNDED	10000	40.00	80.00
76	BROUGHT TO THE CASTLE	10000	43.00	80.00

HUTSCHENREUTHER
W.C. HALLETT — GLORY OF CHRISTMAS

YR	NAME	LIMIT	ISSUE	TREND
82	NATIVITY, THE	25000	80.00	130.00
83	ANNUNCIATION, THE	25000	80.00	120.00
84	SHEPHERDS, THE	25000	80.00	105.00
85	WISEMAN, THE	25000	80.00	105.00

G. GRANGET — GUNTHER GRANGET

YR	NAME	LIMIT	ISSUE	TREND
72	AMERICAN SPARROWS	5000	50.00	155.00
72	EUROPEAN SPARROWS	5000	30.00	70.00
73	AMERICAN KILDEER	2250	75.00	95.00
73	AMERICAN SQUIRREL	2500	75.00	80.00
73	EUROPEAN SQUIRREL	2500	35.00	55.00
74	AMERICAN PARTRIDGE	2500	75.00	95.00
75	AMERICAN RABBITS	2500	90.00	95.00
76	FREEDOM IN FLIGHT	5000	100.00	105.00
76	FREEDOM IN FLIGHT, GOLD	200	200.00	195.00
76	WRENS	5000	100.00	105.00
77	BEARS	2500	100.00	105.00
78	FOXES' SPRING JOURNEY	1000	125.00	205.00

IMPERIAL CHING-TE CHEN

Z. HUIMIN

BEAUTIES OF THE RED MANSION

YR	NAME	LIMIT	ISSUE	TREND
86	PAO-CHAI	CL	28.00	75.00
86	YUAN-CHUN	CL	28.00	50.00
87	HSI-CHUN	CL	31.00	50.00
87	HSI-FENG	CL	31.00	60.00
88	HSIANG-YUN	CL	35.00	65.00
88	KO-CHING	CL	33.00	50.00
88	LI-WAN	CL	33.00	50.00
88	MIAO-YU	CL	31.00	50.00
88	TAI-YU	CL	33.00	50.00
88	YING-CHUN	CL	31.00	55.00
89	CHIAO-CHIEH	CL	35.00	70.00
89	TAN-CHUN	CL	35.00	75.00

Z. SONG MAO

BLESSINGS FROM A CHINESE GARDEN

YR	NAME	LIMIT	ISSUE	TREND
88	GIFT OF PURITY, THE	CL	40.00	45.00
89	GIFT OF BEAUTY, THE	CL	43.00	50.00
89	GIFT OF GRACE, THE	CL	40.00	45.00
89	GIFT OF HAPPINESS, THE	CL	43.00	45.00
90	GIFT OF JOY, THE	CL	43.00	50.00
90	GIFT OF TRUTH, THE	CL	43.00	50.00

Z. HUIMIN

FLOWER GODDESSES OF CHINA

YR	NAME	LIMIT	ISSUE	TREND
91	CAMELLIA GODDESS, THE	CL	38.00	55.00
91	CHRYSANTHEMUM GODDESS, THE	CL	35.00	40.00
91	LOTUS GODDESS, THE	CL	35.00	40.00
91	NARCISSUS GODDESS, THE	CL	38.00	65.00
91	PEONY GODDESS, THE	CL	38.00	45.00
91	PLUM BLOSSOM GODDESS, THE	CL	38.00	45.00

S. FU

FORBIDDEN CITY

YR	NAME	LIMIT	ISSUE	TREND
90	FLYING KITES/SPRING DAY	CL	40.00	45.00
90	PAVILION OF 10,000 SPRINGS	CL	40.00	45.00
90	PAVILION/FLOATING JADE GREEN	CL	43.00	45.00
91	DRESSING THE EMPRESS	CL	46.00	45.00
91	HALL OF THE CULTIVATING MIND, THE	CL	43.00	50.00
91	LANTERN FESTIVAL, THE	CL	43.00	50.00
91	NINE DRAGON SCREEN	CL	43.00	65.00
91	PAVILION OF FLOATING CUPS	CL	46.00	48.00

J. XUE-BING

GARDEN OF SATIN WINGS

YR	NAME	LIMIT	ISSUE	TREND
92	A MORNING DREAM	CL	30.00	45.00
93	A GARDEN WHISPER	CL	30.00	45.00
93	AN EVENING MIST	CL	30.00	45.00

J. XUE-BING

LEGENDS OF WEST LAKE

YR	NAME	LIMIT	ISSUE	TREND
89	LADY WHITE	CL	30.00	45.00
90	APRICOT FAIRY, THE	CL	33.00	40.00
90	BRIGHT PEARL	CL	33.00	45.00
90	LADY SILKWORM	CL	30.00	45.00
90	LAUREL PEAK	CL	30.00	40.00
90	RISING SUN TERRACE	CL	33.00	45.00
90	THREAD OF SKY	CL	35.00	50.00
91	ANCESTORS OF TEA	CL	35.00	60.00
91	CASE OF THE FOLDING FANS, THE	CL	37.00	55.00
91	FLY-IN PEAK	CL	37.00	55.00
91	PHOENIX MOUNTAIN	CL	35.00	45.00
91	THREE POOLS MIRRORING/MOON	CL	37.00	70.00

J. XUE-BING

MAIDENS OF THE FOLDING SKY

YR	NAME	LIMIT	ISSUE	TREND
92	BRIDE YEN CHUN	CL	33.00	50.00
92	LADY LU	CL	30.00	45.00
92	MISTRESS YANG	CL	30.00	45.00
93	PARROT MAIDEN	CL	33.00	50.00

Z. SONG MAO

SCENES FROM THE SUMMER PALACE

YR	NAME	LIMIT	ISSUE	TREND
88	JADE BELT BRIDGE	CL	30.00	45.00
88	MARBLE BOAT, THE	CL	30.00	65.00
89	BOATERS ON KUMMING LAKE	CL	35.00	55.00
89	GARDEN/HARMONIOUS PLEASURE	CL	33.00	45.00
89	GREAT STAGE, THE	CL	33.00	45.00
89	HALL THAT DISPELS THE CLOUDS	CL	33.00	50.00
89	LONG PROMENADE, THE	CL	33.00	50.00
89	SEVENTEEN ARCH BRIDGE	CL	35.00	55.00

INCOLAY

R. AKERS

CHRISTMAS CAMEO COLLECTION

YR	NAME	LIMIT	ISSUE	TREND
90	HOME WITH THE TREE	*	60.00	73.00
91	SKATERS AT TWILIGHT	YR	60.00	76.00
92	EVENING CAROLERS	OP	65.00	84.00
93	SLEDDING BY STARLIGHT	YR	65.00	99.00
94	PROPOSAL UNDER THE STARS	YR	65.00	65.00
*				

FALL OF TROY

YR	NAME	LIMIT	ISSUE	TREND
87	JUDGMENT OF PARIS, THE	CL	55.00	80.00
88	HECTOR AND ANDROMACHE	CL	55.00	80.00
88	HELEN AND PARIS	CL	55.00	80.00
88	TROJAN HORSE, THE	CL	55.00	80.00
*				

LOVE SONNETS OF SHAKESPEARE

YR	NAME	LIMIT	ISSUE	TREND
87	LOVE ALTERS NOT	CL	60.00	95.00
87	SHALL I COMPARE THEE	CL	55.00	95.00
87	SINCE I FIRST SAW YOU	CL	60.00	100.00
87	THOU ART TOO DEAR	CL	55.00	95.00

YR	NAME	LIMIT	ISSUE	TREND
88	YOU SHALL SHINE MORE BRIGHT	CL	60.00	100.00
88	YOUR FAIR EYES	CL	60.00	95.00

R. AKERS — LOVE THEMES FROM GRAND OPERA

YR	NAME	LIMIT	ISSUE	TREND
90	CARMEN	*	65.00	65.00
90	MADAME BUTTERFLY	CL	65.00	65.00
90	MARRIAGE OF FIGARO, THE	CL	70.00	89.00
91	AIDA	CL	70.00	100.00
91	LA TRAVIATA	CL	70.00	80.00
91	TRISTAN AND ISOIDE	CL	70.00	77.00

D. STAPLEFORD — MAJESTIC SAILING SHIPS

YR	NAME	LIMIT	ISSUE	TREND
92	FLYING CLOUD, THE	YR	65.00	65.00
92	SEA WITCH, THE	YR	65.00	65.00
93	CHARLES W. MORGAN	YR	65.00	90.00
94	DREADNOUGHT, THE	YR	65.00	65.00

R. AKERS — NIGHT BEFORE CHRISTMAS

YR	NAME	LIMIT	ISSUE	TREND
93	HAPPY CHRISTMAS	YR	69.00	69.00
94	VISIONS OF SUGAR PLUMS	YR	74.00	74.00

D. CLIFF — NORTH AMERICA'S WILDLIFE HERITAGE

YR	NAME	LIMIT	ISSUE	TREND
91	AT STREAM'S EDGE	OP	65.00	68.00
91	IN THE POND'S SHALLOWS	OP	65.00	65.00
92	BENEATH THE OPEN SKY	OP	70.00	70.00
92	BESIDE THE SHELTERING KNOLL	OP	75.00	75.00
92	ON THE RIVERBANK	OP	70.00	75.00
92	THROUGH THE GRASSY CLEARING	OP	75.00	75.00
92	UPON THE ROCKY LEDGE	OP	70.00	75.00
93	AT STREAMS EDGE (DEER)	YR	65.00	65.00
93	IN PONDS SHALLOW (MOOSE)	YR	65.00	65.00
93	NEAR THE RUNNING BROOK	YR	75.00	90.00
94	GRASSY CLEARING, THE (ELK)	YR	75.00	75.00

R. AKERS — ROMANTIC POET SERIES

YR	NAME	LIMIT	ISSUE	TREND
81	KISS, THE	YR	65.00	95.00
82	MY HEART LEAPS UP	YR	70.00	100.00
83	I STOOD TIPTOE	YR	70.00	110.00
84	DREAM, THE	YR	70.00	90.00
85	RECOLLECTION, THE	YR	70.00	90.00

G. APPLEBY — ROMANTIC POET SERIES

YR	NAME	LIMIT	ISSUE	TREND
77	SHE WALKS IN BEAUTY	YR	60.00	85.00
78	A THING OF BEAUTY	YR	60.00	70.00
79	ODE TO A SKYLARK	YR	65.00	85.00
80	PHANTOM OF DELIGHT	YR	65.00	80.00

R. AKERS — SHAKESPEARE LOVERS

YR	NAME	LIMIT	ISSUE	TREND
88	ROMEO AND JULIET	OP	65.00	110.00
89	HAMLET AND OPHELIA	OP	65.00	95.00
89	MACBETH AND LADY MACBETH	OP	70.00	100.00
89	PETRUCHIO AND KATHARINA	OP	70.00	120.00
90	BENEDICK AND BEATRICE	OP	70.00	100.00
90	FERDINAND AND MIRANDA	OP	75.00	100.00
90	LYSANDER AND HERMIA	OP	70.00	100.00
90	OTHELLO AND DESDEMONA	OP	75.00	100.00

R. AKERS — TWAS THE NIGHT BEFORE CHRISTMAS

YR	NAME	LIMIT	ISSUE	TREND
92	HAPPY CHRISTMAS TO ALL	OP	69.00	90.00
92	I SPRANG FROM MY BED	OP	74.00	88.00
92	IT MUST BE ST. NICK	YR	74.00	85.00
92	UP ON THE ROOFTOP	YR	69.00	80.00
92	WITH VISIONS OF SUGAR PLUMS	OP	74.00	125.00
93	UP THE CHIMNEY HE ROSE	YR	74.00	145.00

C. WORKMASTER — VICTORIAN DREAM HOMES

YR	NAME	LIMIT	ISSUE	TREND
92	125 MAIN STREET	OP	55.00	90.00
92	212 THIRD AVENUE	OP	55.00	79.00
92	367 RIVERSIDE DRIVE	OP	60.00	85.00
92	432 FAIRVIEW LANE	OP	60.00	78.00

INTERNATIONAL SILVER

M. DEOLIVEIRA — BICENTENNIAL

YR	NAME	LIMIT	ISSUE	TREND
72	SIGNING DECLARATION	7500	40.00	450.00
73	PAUL REVERE	7500	40.00	200.00
74	CONCORD BRIDGE	7500	40.00	175.00
75	CROSSING DELAWARE	7500	50.00	125.00
76	VALLEY FORGE	7500	50.00	80.00
77	SURRENDER AT YORKTOWN	7500	50.00	65.00

JAN HAGARA COLLECTABLES

J. HAGARA — FALL IN LOVE AGAIN

YR	NAME	LIMIT	ISSUE	TREND
95	TAMMY	7500	39.00	39.00

J. HAGARA — VICTORIAN CHILDREN

YR	NAME	LIMIT	ISSUE	TREND
79	DAISIES FROM MARYBETH	*	38.00	150.00
79	LISA	5000	60.00	90.00
80	ADRIANNE	5000	60.00	250.00
80	CARA	*	25.00	250.00
80	DAISIES FROM JIMMY	*	38.00	300.00
81	HEARTS & FLOWERS	*	25.00	250.00
81	LYDIA	5000	60.00	175.00
82	DAISIES FOR MOMMY	*	38.00	120.00
82	MELANEE	5000	60.00	125.00
83	CAROL	15000	45.00	210.00
84	CHRIS	15000	45.00	150.00
85	NOEL	15000	45.00	100.00

Sleigh Ride *by H. Mueller was issued in an edition of 10,000 by Bareuther for $52.50 in 1989.*

Gorham's first doll plate, Lydia, *from the Gorham Museum Doll Plates collection, debuted in 1984 with an edition of 5,000. The gold-banded 8 1/2-inch plate retailed for $29 and is currently valued at $125.*

Share the sweet melody of Morning Song *by Jody Bergsma. Issued in 1985 as part of the* Days Gone By *collection by Reco International, production was limited to 14 days.*

To All A Good Night, *produced by the Edwin M. Knowles China Co., portrays the artwork of famous Santa illustrator, Haddon Sundblom.*

YR	NAME	LIMIT	ISSUE	TREND
86	LESLEY	RT	43.00	120.00
86	NIKKI	15000	45.00	100.00
88	HANNAH	15000	50.00	125.00

JOHN HINE STUDIOS LTD.

D. WINTER — COLLECTORS GUILD EXCLUSIVE

89	STREET SCENE (BAS RELIEF PLAQUE)	RT	*	150.00

M. FISHER — DAVID WINTER PLATE COLLECTION

91	A CHRISTMAS CAROL	10000	30.00	65.00
91	COTSWOLD VILLAGE	10000	30.00	43.00
92	CHICHESTER CROSS	10000	30.00	30.00
92	LITTLE MILL	10000	30.00	30.00
92	OLD CURIOSTY SHOP, THE	10000	30.00	48.00
92	SCROOGE'S COUNTING HOUSE	10000	30.00	30.00

D. WINTER — DAVID WINTER PLATE COLLECTION

93	DOVE COTTAGE	10000	30.00	30.00
93	FORGE, THE	10000	30.00	30.00

D. WINTER — DICKENS CHRISTMAS CAROL COLLECTION

94	SCROOGE FAMILY HOME, THE-PLAQUE	3500	125.00	130.00
95	MISS BELLE'S COTTAGE-PLAQUE	4000	120.00	125.00
96	TINY TIM-PLAQUE	4000	110.00	110.00

* — SPECIAL EVENTS

90	CARTWRIGHT'S COTTAGE	RT	40.00	90.00

KAISER

G. NEUBACHER — AMERICA, THE BEAUTIFUL

88	CALIFORNIA QUAIL	9500	50.00	59.00
88	SNOWY EGRET	9500	50.00	50.00
90	BROWSING FOR DELICACIES	9500	50.00	59.00
90	SCANNING THE TERRITORY	9500	50.00	59.00

G. WILLIAMS — AMERICAN CATS

91	KITS IN A CRADLE, SIAMESE	7500	50.00	50.00
91	LAZY RIVER DAYS, SHORTHAIRS	7500	50.00	50.00
91	TAKING IT EASY, PERSIANS	7500	50.00	50.00
91	TREE VIEW, SHORTHAIRS	7500	50.00	50.00

K. BAUER — ANNIVERSARY

75	TENDER MOMENT	CL	25.00	40.00
82	BETROTHAL	CL	40.00	40.00

H. BLUM — ANNIVERSARY

79	ROMANTIC INTERLUDE	CL	32.00	32.00
80	LOVE AT PLAY	CL	40.00	40.00
81	RENDEZVOUS	CL	40.00	40.00

T. SCHOENER — ANNIVERSARY

72	LOVE BIRDS	CL	16.50	30.00
73	IN THE PARK	CL	16.50	25.00
74	CANOEING	CL	20.00	30.00
76	SERENADE	CL	25.00	25.00
77	SIMPLE GIFT	CL	25.00	25.00
78	VIKING TOAST	CL	30.00	30.00
83	SUNDAY AFTERNOON	CL	40.00	40.00

R. HERSEY — ARABIAN NIGHTS

89	SCHEHERAZADE	9500	75.00	75.00

J. TRUMBALL — BICENTENNIAL PLATE

76	SIGNING DECLARATION	CL	75.00	175.00

J. FRANCIS — BIRD DOG SERIES

*	BEAGLE	19500	40.00	50.00
*	BLACK LABRADOR	19500	40.00	50.00
*	COCKER SPANIEL	19500	40.00	50.00
*	ENGLISH POINTER	19500	40.00	50.00
*	ENGLISH SETTER	19500	40.00	50.00
*	GERMAN SHORT HAIR POINTER	19500	40.00	50.00
*	GOLDEN LABRADOR	19500	40.00	50.00
*	IRISH SETTER	19500	40.00	50.00

A. SCHLESINGER — CHILDHOOD MEMORIES

85	WAIT A LITTLE	CL	29.00	29.00

W. ZEUNER — CHILDREN'S PRAYER

82	NOW I LAY ME DOWN TO SLEEP	CL	30.00	30.00
82	SAYING GRACE	CL	30.00	30.00

K. BAUER — CHRISTMAS PLATES

71	SILENT NIGHT	CL	13.50	35.00
72	WELCOME HOME	CL	16.50	45.00
74	CHRISTMAS CAROLERS	CL	25.00	40.00
81	ADORATION BY THREE KINGS	CL	40.00	55.00
82	BRINGING HOME THE TREE	CL	40.00	50.00

H. BLUM — CHRISTMAS PLATES

79	CHRISTMAS EVE	CL	32.00	50.00
80	JOYS OF WINTER	CL	40.00	45.00

C. MARATTI — CHRISTMAS PLATES

76	CHRIST/SAVIOUR BORN	CL	25.00	40.00

J. NORTHCOTT — CHRISTMAS PLATES

75	BRINGING HOME THE TREE	CL	25.00	35.00

T. SCHOENER — CHRISTMAS PLATES

70	WAITING FOR SANTA CLAUS	CL	12.50	30.00
73	HOLY NIGHT	CL	18.00	45.00
77	THREE KINGS, THE	CL	25.00	30.00
78	SHEPHERDS IN THE FIELD	CL	30.00	35.00

YR	NAME	LIMIT	ISSUE	TREND
G. NEUBACHER		CLASSIC FAIRY TALES COLLECTION		
82	FROG KING	*	40.00	50.00
83	LITTLE RED RIDING HOOD	*	40.00	50.00
83	PUSS IN BOOTS	*	40.00	50.00
84	CINDERELLA	*	40.00	45.00
84	HANSEL AND GRETEL	*	40.00	45.00
84	SLEEPING BEAUTY	*	40.00	45.00
R. CLARKE		DANCE, BALLERINA, DANCE		
*	OPENING NIGHT	CL	48.00	48.00
*	PIROUETTE	CL	48.00	48.00
*	RECITAL, THE	CL	48.00	48.00
*	SWAN LAKE	CL	48.00	48.00
82	FIRST SLIPPERS	CL	48.00	48.00
83	AT THE BARRE	CL	48.00	48.00
*		EGYPTIAN		
80	NEFERTITI	10000	275.00	475.00
80	TUTANKHAMEN	10000	275.00	475.00
R.J. MAY		FAITHFUL COMPANIONS		
90	BEAGLE	9500	50.00	50.00
90	BOXER	*	*	54.00
90	COCKER SPANIEL	9500	50.00	50.00
90	DASHCHUND	9500	50.00	50.00
90	DOBERMAN	9500	50.00	50.00
90	ENGLISH SPRINGER SPANIEL	9500	50.00	50.00
90	GERMAN SHEPHERD	9500	50.00	50.00
90	GOLDEN RETRIEVER	9500	50.00	50.00
90	POODLE	*	*	54.00
90	ROTTWEILER	9500	50.00	50.00
90	ROUGH COLLIE (MAY)	*	*	54.00
91	LABRADOR RETRIEVER	*	*	53.00
91	YORKSHIRE TERRIERS	*	*	53.00
A. LOHMANN		FAMOUS HORSES		
83	SNOW KNIGHT	CL	95.00	95.00
84	NORTHERN DANCER	CL	95.00	95.00
G. NEUBACHER		FAMOUS LULLABIES		
85	SLEEP BABY SLEEP	*	40.00	40.00
86	A MOCKINGBIRD	*	40.00	46.00
86	AU CLAIR DE LUNE	*	40.00	44.00
86	ROCKABYE BABY	*	40.00	41.00
87	WELSH LULLABYE	*	40.00	57.00
88	BRAHMS' LULLABYE	*	40.00	45.00
G. LOATES		FEATHERED FRIENDS		
78	BLUE JAYS	CL	70.00	150.00
79	CARDINALS	CL	80.00	150.00
80	WAXWINGS	CL	80.00	150.00
81	GOLDFINCH	CL	80.00	150.00
G. NEUBACHER		FOREST SURPRISES		
89	DEERHEAD ORCHID	9500	50.00	59.00
89	MARSH MARIGOLD	9500	50.00	59.00
90	VIOLETS	9500	50.00	59.00
90	WILD IRIS	9500	50.00	59.00
I. CENKOVCAN		FOUR SEASONS		
81	AUTUMN	*	50.00	64.00
81	SPRING	*	50.00	64.00
81	SUMMER	*	50.00	64.00
81	WINTER	*	50.00	64.00
W. GAWANTKA		GARDEN AND SONG BIRDS		
73	CARDINALS	CL	200.00	250.00
73	TITMOUSE	CL	200.00	250.00
J. MCKERNAN		GRADUATE		
86	BOY	7500	40.00	40.00
86	GIRL	7500	40.00	40.00
K. BAUER		GREAT YACHTS		
72	CETONIA	CL	50.00	50.00
72	WESTWARD	CL	50.00	50.00
G. NEUBACHER		HAPPY DAYS		
79	AEROPLANE, THE	CL	75.00	75.00
80	JULIE	CL	75.00	75.00
81	WINTER FUN	CL	75.00	75.00
82	LOOKOUT, THE	CL	75.00	75.00
J. LITTLEJOHN		HARMONY AND NATURE		
85	SPRING ENCORE	CL	40.00	40.00
E. HIBEL		HIBEL HOLIDAYS		
94	AND UNTO US A CHILD IS BORN	*	*	78.00
95	WONDER OF LOVE	*	*	79.00
*		KING TUT		
78	KING TUT	CL	65.00	110.00
G. NEUBACHER		MEMORIES OF CHRISTMAS		
83	WONDER OF CHRISTMAS, THE	CL	43.00	43.00
84	A CHRISTMAS DREAM	CL	40.00	43.00
85	CHRISTMAS EVE	CL	40.00	40.00
86	A VISIT WITH SANTA	CL	40.00	40.00
K. BAUER		MOTHER'S DAY		
82	PHEASANT FAMILY	CL	40.00	45.00
83	TENDER CARE	CL	40.00	85.00

YR	NAME	LIMIT	ISSUE	TREND
H. BLUM				MOTHER'S DAY
81	SAFE NEAR MOTHER	CL	40.00	45.00
J. NORTHCOTT				MOTHER'S DAY
80	RACCOON FAMILY	CL	40.00	60.00
N. PETERNER				MOTHER'S DAY
79	A MOTHER'S DEVOTION	CL	32.00	45.00
T. SCHOENER				MOTHER'S DAY
71	MARE AND FOAL	CL	13.00	45.00
72	FLOWERS FOR MOTHER	CL	16.50	40.00
73	CATS	CL	17.00	50.00
74	FOX	CL	20.00	70.00
75	GERMAN SHEPHERD	CL	25.00	95.00
76	SWAN AND CYGNETS	CL	25.00	30.00
77	MOTHER RABBIT AND YOUNG	CL	25.00	35.00
78	HEN AND CHICKS	CL	30.00	55.00
L. TURNER				NOBLE HORSE COLLECTION
88	ARABIAN	OP	50.00	50.00
88	GELDERLANDER	OP	50.00	50.00
88	HOLSTEIN	OP	50.00	50.00
88	QUARTER HORSE	OP	50.00	50.00
88	THOROUGHBRED	OP	50.00	50.00
88	TRAKEHNER	OP	50.00	50.00
*				OBERAMMERGAU PASSION PLAY
91	OBERAMMERGAU, COBALT	400	64.00	64.00
91	OBERAMMERGAU, SEPIA	700	38.00	38.00
K. BAUER				OBERAMMERGAU PASSION PLAY
70	OBERAMMERGAU	CL	40.00	40.00
T. SCHOENER				OBERAMMERGAU PASSION PLAY
70	OBERAMMERGAU	CL	25.00	30.00
A. LOHMANN				ON THE FARM
*	DUCKS ON THE POND	*	50.00	108.00
*	GIRL FEEDING ANIMALS	*	50.00	108.00
*	GIRL WITH GOATS	*	50.00	108.00
*	WHITE HORSE	*	50.00	108.00
81	DUCK, THE	*	50.00	108.00
82	ROOSTER, THE	*	50.00	108.00
83	HORSES, THE	*	50.00	108.00
83	POND, THE	*	50.00	108.00
R. HORTON				RACING FOR PRIDE AND PROFIT
*	PROFIT OR PRISON	9500	*	60.00
84	AGING VICTOR, THE	9500	50.00	50.00
85	SECOND GOES HUNGRY	9500	50.00	50.00
86	NO TIME TO BOAST	9500	50.00	50.00
87	FIRST FISH TO MARKET	9500	50.00	60.00
88	GYPSY TRADERS	9500	60.00	60.00
G. NEUBACHER				ROMANTIC PORTRAITS
81	LILIE	CL	200.00	210.00
82	CAMELIA	CL	175.00	180.00
83	ROSE	CL	175.00	185.00
84	DAISY	CL	175.00	180.00
D. TWINNEY				STABLE DOOR COLLECTION
88	FIRST STEPS	OP	30.00	30.00
88	IMPUDENCE	OP	30.00	30.00
88	PRIDE	OP	30.00	30.00
88	VISITOR, THE	OP	30.00	30.00
D. KING				TRADITIONAL FAIRY TALES
83	CINDERELLA	*	40.00	40.00
83	JACK AND THE BEANSTALK	*	40.00	40.00
84	THREE LITTLE PIGS	*	40.00	40.00
84	TOM THUMB	*	40.00	40.00
85	DICK WITTINGTON	*	40.00	40.00
85	GOLDILOCKS	*	40.00	40.00
E. BIERLY				WATER FOWL COLLECTION
85	CANVASBACK DUCKS	19500	55.00	89.00
85	MALLARD DUCKS	19500	55.00	50.00
85	PINTAIL DUCKS	19500	55.00	50.00
85	WOOD DUCKS	19500	55.00	60.00
T. BOYER				WATER FOWL COLLECTION
89	CAROLINA WOODDUCKS	*	*	48.00
89	GREENWINGED TEALS	*	*	48.00
89	PAIR OF CANVASBACKS	15000	50.00	50.00
89	PAIR OF CAROLINA WOOD DUCKS	15000	50.00	50.00
89	PAIR OF GREENWINGED TEALS	15000	50.00	50.00
89	PAIR OF MALLARDS	15000	50.00	50.00
89	PAIR OF PINTAILS	15000	50.00	50.00
89	PAIR OF REDHEADS	15000	50.00	50.00
89	REDHEADS	*	*	48.00
G. NEUBACHER				WILDFLOWERS
86	TRILLIUM	9500	40.00	80.00
87	SPRING BEAUTY	9500	45.00	64.00
87	WILD ASTERS	9500	50.00	59.00
87	WILD ROSES	9500	50.00	59.00

KONIGSZELT BAYERN

YR	NAME	LIMIT	ISSUE	TREND
H. KELLER				HEDI KELLER CHRISTMAS
79	ADORATION, THE	*	30.00	33.00

YR	NAME	LIMIT	ISSUE	TREND
80	FLIGHT INTO EGYPT	*	30.00	33.00
81	RETURN INTO GALILEE	*	30.00	31.00
82	FOLLOWING THE STAR	*	30.00	32.00
83	REST ON THE FLIGHT	*	30.00	35.00
84	NATIVITY, THE	*	30.00	35.00
85	GIFT OF THE MAGI	*	35.00	40.00
86	ANNUNCIATION	*	35.00	40.00

KPM-ROYAL CORPORATION
*   CHRISTMAS

YR	NAME	LIMIT	ISSUE	TREND
69	CHRISTMAS STAR	5000	28.00	400.00
70	THREE KINGS	5000	28.00	300.00
71	CHRISTMAS TREE	5000	28.00	300.00
72	CHRISTMAS ANGEL	5000	31.00	320.00
73	CHRIST CHILD ON SLED	5000	33.00	300.00
74	ANGEL AND HORN	5000	35.00	200.00
75	SHEPHERDS	5000	40.00	175.00
76	STAR OF BETHLEHEM	5000	43.00	150.00
77	MARY AT CRIB	5000	46.00	100.00
78	THREE WISE MEN	5000	49.00	60.00
79	MANGER, THE	5000	55.00	60.00
80	SHEPHERDS IN FIELDS	5000	55.00	60.00

L.L. KNICKERBOCKER CO. INC.
R.T. GORDON

YR	NAME	LIMIT	ISSUE	TREND
94	VARSITY BEAR PHOTO C15001	2500	31.00	32.00

LALIQUE
M. LALIQUE   ANNUAL

YR	NAME	LIMIT	ISSUE	TREND
65	DEUX OISEAUX (TWO BIRDS)	2000	25.00	1200.00
66	ROSE DE SONGERIE (DREAM ROSE)	5000	25.00	125.00
67	BALLET DE POISSON (FISH BALLET)	5000	25.00	100.00
68	GAZELLE FANTAISIE (GAZELLE FANTASY)	5000	25.00	65.00
69	PAPILLON (BUTTERFLY)	5000	30.00	40.00
70	PAON (PEACOCK)	5000	30.00	60.00
71	HIBOU (OWL)	5000	35.00	70.00
72	COQUILLAGE (SHELL)	5000	40.00	65.00
73	PETIT GEAI (JAYLING)	5000	43.00	100.00
74	SOUS D'ARGENT (SILVER PENNIES)	5000	48.00	100.00
75	DUO DE POISSON (FISH DUET)	5000	50.00	140.00
76	AIGLE (EAGLE)	5000	60.00	75.00

LANCE CORP.
*   12 DAYS OF CHRISTMAS (CHILMARK PEWTER/STAINED GLASS)

YR	NAME	LIMIT	ISSUE	TREND
79	PARTRIDGE IN A PEAR TREE 8 IN.	RT	100.00	100.00
80	TWO TURTLEDOVES 8 IN.	RT	100.00	100.00

C. TERRIS   AMERICA'S FAVORITE BIRDS (HUDSON PEWTER/CRYSTAL)
| 78 | CRYSTAL WREN 8 IN. | RT | 80.00 | 80.00 |

R. LAMB   AMERICAN COMM. (HUDSON PEWTER)
75	HYDE PARK 6 IN.	RT	*	55.00
75	LOG CABIN 6 IN.	RT	*	55.00
75	MONTICELLO 6 IN.	RT	*	55.00
75	MT. VERNON 6 IN.	RT	*	55.00
75	SPIRIT OF '76 6 IN.	RT	*	55.00

P.W. BASTON   AMERICAN EXPANSION (HUDSON PEWTER)
75	AMERICAN EXPANSION	CL	*	60.00
75	AMERICAN INDEPENDENCE	CL	*	110.00
75	AMERICAN WAR BETWEEN THE STATES, THE	CL	*	175.00
75	SPIRIT OF '76 (6 IN. PLATE)	CL	28.00	110.00

A. PETITTO   CHILD'S CHRISTMAS (HUDSON PEWTER)
78	BEDTIME STORY	SU	35.00	60.00
79	LITTLEST ANGELS	SU	35.00	60.00
80	HEAVEN'S CHRISTMAS TREE	SU	43.00	60.00
81	FILLING THE SKY	SU	48.00	60.00

*   CHRISTMAS (CHILMARK PEWTER)
77	CURRIER & IVES CHRISTMAS 8 IN.	RT	60.00	75.00
78	TRIMMING THE TREE 8 IN.	RT	65.00	75.00
79	THREE WISEMEN 8 IN.	RT	65.00	75.00

A. MCGRORY   CHRISTMAS (HUDSON PEWTER)
| 93 | CRACK THE WHIP | 950 | 55.00 | 55.00 |
| 94 | HOME FOR CHRISTMAS | 950 | 50.00 | 50.00 |

A. PETITTO   CHRISTMAS (HUDSON PEWTER)
| 87 | CAROLING ANGELS, THE | SU | 48.00 | 60.00 |

J. WANAT   CHRISTMAS (HUDSON PEWTER)
| 86 | BRINGING HOME THE TREE | SU | 48.00 | 60.00 |

D. EVERHART   MICKEY'S CHRISTMAS (HUDSON PEWTER)
86	GOD BLESS US, EVERY ONE	SU	48.00	60.00
87	JOLLY OLD SAINT NICK	SU	55.00	60.00
88	HE'S CHECKING IT TWICE	SU	50.00	60.00

*   MOTHER'S DAY (CHILMARK PEWTER)
| 74 | FLOWERS OF THE FIELD 8 IN. | RT | 60.00 | 75.00 |
| 80 | 1980 MOTHER'S DAY | RT | 90.00 | 90.00 |

A. PETITTO   MOTHER'S DAY (HUDSON PEWTER)
| 79 | CHERISHED 6 IN. | RT | 43.00 | 55.00 |
| 80 | 1980 MOTHER'S DAY 6 IN. | RT | 43.00 | 55.00 |

A. PETITTO   SAILING SHIPS (HUDSON PEWTER)
| 78 | AMERICA 6 IN. | RT | 35.00 | 55.00 |

YR	NAME	LIMIT	ISSUE	TREND
78	CONSTITUTION 6 IN.	RT	35.00	55.00
78	FLYING CLOUD 6 IN.	RT	35.00	55.00
78	MORGAN 6 IN.	RT	35.00	55.00

P.W. BASTON   **SEBASTIAN PLATES**

YR	NAME	LIMIT	ISSUE	TREND
74	SPIRIT OF '76 (9 IN.)	RT	28.00	75.00
76	DECLARATION OF INDEPENDENCE (8 1/2 IN.)	RT	25.00	50.00
78	MOTIF NO. 1	CL	75.00	60.00
78	ZODIAC (8 IN.)	RT	60.00	75.00
79	GRAND CANYON	CL	75.00	60.00
80	IN THE CANDY STORE	CL	40.00	45.00
80	LONE CYPRESS	CL	75.00	160.00
81	DOCTOR, THE	CL	40.00	45.00
83	LITTLE MOTHER	CL	40.00	45.00
84	SWITCHING THE FREIGHT	CL	43.00	90.00

HOLLIS/YOURDON   **SONG BIRDS OF THE FOUR SEASONS (HUDSON PEWTER)**

YR	NAME	LIMIT	ISSUE	TREND
78	CARDINAL (WINTER 6 IN.)	RT	35.00	55.00
78	HUMMINGBIRD (SUMMER 6 IN.)	RT	35.00	55.00
78	SPARROW (AUTUMN 6 IN.)	RT	35.00	55.00
78	WOOD THRUSH (SPRING 6 IN.)	RT	35.00	55.00

A. MCGRORY   **SONGS OF CHRISTMAS (HUDSON PEWTER)**

YR	NAME	LIMIT	ISSUE	TREND
88	SILENT NIGHT	SU	55.00	60.00
89	HARK! THE HERALD ANGELS SING	SU	60.00	60.00
90	FIRST NOEL, THE	SU	60.00	60.00
91	WE THREE KINGS	SU	60.00	60.00

A. HOLLIS   **TWAS THE NIGHT BEFORE CHRISTMAS (HUDSON PEWTER)**

YR	NAME	LIMIT	ISSUE	TREND
82	NOT A CREATURE WAS STIRRING	SU	48.00	70.00
83	VISIONS OF SUGAR PLUMS	SU	48.00	60.00
84	HIS EYES HOW THEY TWINKLED	SU	48.00	60.00
85	HAPPY CHRISTMAS TO ALL	SU	48.00	60.00

LENOX CHINA/CRYSTAL COLLECTION

N. ADAMS   **AMERICAN WILDLIFE**

YR	NAME	LIMIT	ISSUE	TREND
82	BLACK BEARS	9500	65.00	70.00
82	BUFFALO	9500	65.00	70.00
82	DALL SHEEP	9500	65.00	80.00
82	JACK RABBITS	9500	65.00	70.00
82	MOUNTAIN LIONS	9500	65.00	70.00
82	OCELOTS	9500	65.00	80.00
82	OTTERS	9500	65.00	70.00
82	POLAR BEARS	9500	65.00	70.00
82	RACCOONS	9500	65.00	70.00
82	RED FOXES	9500	65.00	70.00
82	SEA LIONS	9500	65.00	80.00
82	WHITE TAILED DEER	9500	65.00	70.00

*   **ANNUAL CHRISTMAS PLATES**

YR	NAME	LIMIT	ISSUE	TREND
92	SLEIGH	YR	75.00	75.00

L. BYWATERS   **ANNUAL CHRISTMAS PLATES**

YR	NAME	LIMIT	ISSUE	TREND
93	MIDNIGHT SLEIGH RIDE	CL	119.00	125.00

J. VAN ZYLE   **ARCTIC WOLVES**

YR	NAME	LIMIT	ISSUE	TREND
93	CRY OF THE WILD	CL	30.00	30.00
93	FAR COUNTRY CROSSING	CL	30.00	30.00
93	MIDNIGHT RENEGADE	CL	30.00	30.00
93	NIGHTWATCH	CL	30.00	30.00
93	ON THE EDGE	CL	30.00	30.00
93	PICKING UP THE TRAIL	CL	30.00	30.00

Q. LEMONDS   **BIG CATS OF THE WORLD**

YR	NAME	LIMIT	ISSUE	TREND
93	BLACK PANTHER	OP	40.00	40.00
93	BOBCAT	OP	40.00	40.00
93	CHINESE LEOPARD	OP	40.00	40.00
93	COUGAR	OP	40.00	40.00
93	LION	OP	40.00	40.00
93	SNOW LEOPARD	OP	40.00	40.00
93	TIGER	OP	40.00	40.00
93	WHITE TIGER	OP	40.00	40.00

W. MUMM   **BIRDS OF THE GARDEN**

YR	NAME	LIMIT	ISSUE	TREND
92	SPRING GLORY, CARDINALS	OP	40.00	40.00
93	BLOSSOMING BOUGH, CHICKADEES	OP	40.00	40.00
93	BLUEBIRDS HAVEN, BLUEBIRDS	OP	40.00	40.00
93	INDIGO MEADOW, INDIGO BUNTINGS	OP	40.00	40.00
93	JEWELS OF THE GARDEN, HUMMINGBIRDS	OP	40.00	40.00
93	SCARLET TANAGERS	OP	40.00	40.00
93	SUNBRIGHT SONGBIRDS, GOLDFINCH	OP	40.00	40.00

E. BOEHM   **BOEHM BIRDS**

YR	NAME	LIMIT	ISSUE	TREND
70	WOOD THRUSH	YR	35.00	500.00
71	GOLDFINCH	YR	35.00	175.00
72	MOUNTAIN BLUEBIRD	YR	38.00	120.00
73	MEADOWLARK	YR	41.00	100.00
74	RUFOUS HUMMINGBIRD	YR	45.00	85.00
75	AMERICAN REDSTART	YR	50.00	80.00
76	CARDINALS	YR	53.00	100.00
77	ROBINS	YR	55.00	85.00
78	MOCKINGBIRDS	YR	58.00	100.00
79	GOLDEN-CROWNED KINGLETS	YR	65.00	100.00
80	BLACK-THROATED BLUE WARBLERS	YR	80.00	125.00
81	EASTERN PHOEBES	YR	90.00	140.00

E. BOEHM   **BOEHM WOODLAND WILDLIFE**

YR	NAME	LIMIT	ISSUE	TREND
73	RACCOONS	YR	50.00	125.00

YR	NAME	LIMIT	ISSUE	TREND
74	RED FOXES	YR	53.00	70.00
75	COTTONTAIL RABBITS	YR	59.00	100.00
76	EASTERN CHIPMUNKS	YR	63.00	100.00
77	BEAVER	YR	68.00	100.00
78	WHITETAIL DEER	YR	70.00	95.00
79	SQUIRRELS	YR	76.00	110.00
80	BOBCATS	YR	83.00	140.00
81	MARTENS	YR	100.00	150.00
82	RIVER OTTERS	YR	100.00	150.00
D. CROWLEY		**CHILDREN OF THE SUN & MOON**		
93	DESERT BLOSSOM	OP	40.00	40.00
93	FEATHERS & FURS	OP	40.00	40.00
93	SHY ONE	OP	40.00	40.00
94	DAUGHTER OF THE SUN	OP	40.00	40.00
94	INDIGO GIRL	OP	40.00	40.00
94	LITTLE FLOWER	OP	40.00	40.00
94	RED FEATHERS	OP	40.00	40.00
94	STARS IN HER EYES	OP	40.00	40.00
*		**CHRISTMAS TREES AROUND THE WORLD**		
91	GERMANY	YR	75.00	78.00
92	FRANCE	YR	75.00	80.00
*		**COLONIAL CHRISTMAS WREATH**		
81	COLONIAL VIRGINIA	YR	65.00	100.00
82	MASSACHUSETTS	YR	70.00	95.00
83	MARYLAND	YR	70.00	175.00
84	RHODE ISLAND	YR	70.00	100.00
85	CONNECTICUT	YR	70.00	100.00
86	NEW HAMPSHIRE	YR	70.00	115.00
87	PENNSYLVANIA	YR	70.00	100.00
88	DELAWARE	YR	70.00	150.00
89	NEW YORK	YR	75.00	150.00
90	NEW JERSEY	YR	75.00	100.00
91	SOUTH CAROLINA	YR	75.00	78.00
92	NORTH CAROLINA	YR	75.00	140.00
Q. LEMONDS		**CUBS OF THE BIG CATS**		
93	JAGUAR CUB	CL	30.00	30.00
L. PICKEN		**DARLING DALMATIANS**		
93	ALL FIRED UP	CL	30.00	30.00
93	CAUGHT IN THE ACT	CL	30.00	30.00
93	FIRE BRIGADE	CL	30.00	30.00
93	PLEASE DON'T PICK THE FLOWERS	CL	30.00	30.00
93	PUPS IN BOOTS	CL	30.00	30.00
93	THREE ALARM FIRE	CL	30.00	30.00
J. HOLDERBY		**DOLPHINS OF THE SEVEN SEAS**		
93	BOTTLENOSE DOLPHINS	OP	40.00	40.00
R. KELLY		**EAGLE CONSERVATION**		
93	DAYBREAK ON RIVER'S EDGE	OP	40.00	40.00
93	EAGLES ON MT. MCKINLEY	OP	40.00	40.00
93	LONE SENTINEL	OP	40.00	40.00
93	NORTHERN HERITAGE	OP	40.00	40.00
93	NORTHWOOD'S LEGEND	OP	40.00	40.00
93	RIVER SCOUT	OP	40.00	40.00
93	SOARING THE PEAKS	OP	40.00	40.00
93	SOLO FLIGHT	OP	40.00	40.00
*		**GARDEN BIRD PLATE COLLECTION**		
88	BLUEJAY	OP	48.00	53.00
88	CHICKADEE	OP	48.00	53.00
89	HUMMINGBIRD	OP	48.00	53.00
91	CARDINAL	OP	48.00	53.00
91	DOVE	OP	48.00	53.00
92	GOLDFINCH	OP	48.00	53.00
G. COHELEACH		**GREAT CATS OF THE WORLD**		
93	CHINESE LEOPARD	OP	40.00	40.00
93	COUGAR	OP	40.00	40.00
93	JAGUAR	OP	40.00	40.00
93	LION	OP	40.00	40.00
93	LIONESS	OP	40.00	40.00
93	SIBERIAN TIGER	OP	40.00	40.00
93	SNOW LEOPARD	OP	40.00	40.00
93	WHITE TIGER	OP	40.00	40.00
R. HOOVER		**INTERNATIONAL VICTORIAN SANTAS**		
92	KRIS KRINGLE	CL	40.00	40.00
93	FATHER CHRISTMAS	CL	40.00	40.00
94	GRANDFATHER FROST	CL	40.00	40.00
95	AMERICAN SANTA CLAUS	CL	40.00	40.00
S. COMBES		**KING OF THE PLAINS**		
94	AFRICAN ANCIENTS	OP	40.00	40.00
94	END OF THE LINE	OP	40.00	40.00
94	GUARDIAN	OP	40.00	40.00
94	LAST ELEPHANT, THE	OP	40.00	40.00
94	PROTECTING THE FLANKS	OP	40.00	40.00
94	RAINBOW TRAIL	OP	40.00	40.00
94	SPARRING BULLS	OP	40.00	40.00
94	TSAVA ELEPHANT	OP	40.00	40.00
L. BYWATERS		**MAGIC OF CHRISTMAS**		
93	GIFTS FOR ALL	OP	40.00	40.00
93	SANTA OF THE NORTHERN FOREST	OP	40.00	40.00

YR	NAME	LIMIT	ISSUE	TREND
93	SANTA'S GIFT OF PEACE	OP	40.00	40.00
94	A BERRY MERRY CHRISTMAS	OP	40.00	40.00
94	COMING HOME	OP	40.00	40.00
94	SANTA'S SENTINELS	OP	40.00	40.00
94	WONDER OF WONDERS	OP	40.00	40.00
C. MCCLUNG			**NATURE'S COLLAGE**	
92	CEDAR WAXWING, AMONG THE BERRIES	OP	35.00	35.00
92	GOLD FINCHES, GOLDEN SPLENDOR	OP	35.00	35.00
93	BLUEBIRDS, SUMMER INTERLUDE	CL	40.00	40.00
93	BLUEJAYS, WINTER SONG	CL	40.00	40.00
93	CARDINALS, SPRING COURTSHIP	CL	40.00	40.00
93	CHICKADEES, ROSE MORNING	CL	40.00	40.00
93	HUMMINGBIRDS, JEWELED GLORY	CL	40.00	40.00
93	INDIGO BUNTINGS, INDIGO EVENING	CL	40.00	40.00
L. LAFFIN			**OWLS OF NORTH AMERICA**	
93	SPIRIT OF THE ARCTIC, SNOWY OWL	OP	40.00	40.00
*			**PIERCED NATIVITY**	
93	HOLY FAMILY	OP	45.00	45.00
94	HERALDING ANGELS	OP	45.00	45.00
94	SHEPHERDS	OP	45.00	45.00
94	THREE KINGS	OP	45.00	45.00
G. COHELEACH		**ROYAL CATS OF GUY COHELEACH**		
94	AFTERNOON SHADE	OP	40.00	40.00
94	AMBUSH IN THE SNOW	OP	40.00	40.00
94	CAT NAP	OP	40.00	40.00
94	JUNGLE JAGUAR	OP	40.00	40.00
94	LION IN WAIT	OP	40.00	40.00
94	ROCKY MOUNTAIN PUMA	OP	40.00	40.00
94	ROCKY REFUGE	OP	40.00	40.00
94	SIESTA	OP	40.00	40.00
J. HOLDERBY			**WHALE CONSERVATION**	
93	ORCA	OP	40.00	40.00

LIGHTPOST PUBLISHING

YR	NAME	LIMIT	ISSUE	TREND
T. KINKADE		**T. KINKADE SIGNATURE COLLECTION**		
91	CEDAR NOOK	2500	50.00	65.00
91	CHANDLER'S COTTAGE	2500	50.00	60.00
91	HOME TO GRANDMA'S	2500	50.00	60.00
91	SLEIGH RIDE HOME	2500	50.00	65.00

LILLIPUT LANE LTD.

YR	NAME	LIMIT	ISSUE	TREND
R. DAY		**AMERICAN LANDMARKS COLLECTION**		
90	COUNTRY CHURCH	RT	35.00	35.00
90	MAIL BARN	5000	35.00	125.00
90	RIVERSIDE CHAPEL	RT	35.00	35.00
R. DAY			**COCA COLA COUNTRY**	
98	CATCH OF THE DAY	OP	40.00	40.00
98	ICE-COLD COKE	OP	40.00	40.00
98	SPRING HAS SPRUNG	OP	40.00	40.00
98	WHEN I WAS YOUR AGE	OP	40.00	40.00

LLADRO

YR	NAME	LIMIT	ISSUE	TREND
*			**CHRISTMAS PLATES**	
71	CHRISTMAS CAROLING L7006	YR	*	185.00
72	CHRISTMAS CAROLERS L7008	YR	*	165.00
73	BOY AND GIRL AT CHRISTMAS L7010	YR	*	150.00
74	CHRISTMAS CAROLERS L7012	YR	*	150.00
75	CHRISTMAS CHERUBS L7014	YR	*	150.00
76	CHRIST CHILD L7016	YR	*	150.00
77	NATIVITY L7022	YR	*	150.00
78	CHRISTMAS CAROLING CHILD L7106	YR	*	140.00
79	CHRISTMAS SNOW DANCE L7108	YR	*	130.00
80	CHRISTMAS PLATE L7024	YR	*	125.00
*			**LLADRO PLATE COLLECTION**	
93	DUCK PLATE L-6000G	OP	38.00	40.00
93	GREAT VOYAGE, THE L-5964G	CL	50.00	50.00
93	LOOKING OUT L-5998G	OP	38.00	40.00
93	SWINGING L-5999G	OP	38.00	40.00
94	APPLE PICKING L-6159M	OP	32.00	35.00
94	FLAMINGO L-6161M	OP	32.00	35.00
94	FRIENDS L-6158	OP	32.00	35.00
94	RESTING L-6162M	OP	32.00	35.00
94	TURTLEDOVE L-6160	OP	32.00	35.00
*			**MOTHER'S DAY PLATES**	
71	MOTHER'S DAY PLATE L7025	YR	*	150.00
72	BIRDS AND CHICKS L-7007	YR	*	150.00
73	MOTHER AND CHILDREN L7009	YR	*	140.00
74	NURSING MOTHER L7011	YR	*	130.00
75	MOTHER AND CHILD L7013	YR	*	120.00
76	TENDER VIGIL L7015	YR	*	115.00
77	MOTHER AND DAUGHTER L7021	YR	*	110.00
78	NEW ARRIVAL L7105	YR	*	100.00
79	OFF TO SCHOOL L7107	YR	*	90.00
80	MOTHER'S DAY PLATE L7023	YR	*	80.00

YR	NAME	LIMIT	ISSUE	TREND

MAFEKING COLLECTION

M. GREEN — **FOREVER FRIENDS**

YR	NAME	LIMIT	ISSUE	TREND
93	HIDE AWAY, THE	500	85.00	100.00
94	RUFOUS (THE HUMMINGBIRD)	500	35.00	85.00

M. GREEN — **LORD'S CHILDREN**

YR	NAME	LIMIT	ISSUE	TREND
93	A FRAGRANCE IN TIME	500	85.00	100.00
93	HEAR MY PRAYERS	500	75.00	85.00
94	TRADITIONS	500	40.00	85.00

M. GREEN — **MAN'S BEST FRIEND**

YR	NAME	LIMIT	ISSUE	TREND
93	DEREK (THE LABRADOR RETRIEVER)	500	65.00	85.00
93	DIVOT (THE GERMAN SHEPHERD)	500	85.00	100.00
94	MICKEY (SPANIEL CROSS)	500	40.00	45.00
94	PEPPER (THE AIREDALE)	500	40.00	85.00

M. GREEN — **MY LITTLE BEAR**

YR	NAME	LIMIT	ISSUE	TREND
93	BEAR WITH ME	500	85.00	100.00
93	SHIZAM (THE MAGICIAN)	500	85.00	100.00

MARIGOLD

CARRENO — **SPORT**

YR	NAME	LIMIT	ISSUE	TREND
89	JOE DIMAGGIO F/BLUE SIGNATURE	RT	60.00	110.00
89	JOE DIMAGGIO H/S	RT	100.00	1200.00
89	MICKEY MANTLE H/S	RT	100.00	645.00
89	MICKEY MANTLE U/S	RT	60.00	95.00
90	JOE DIMAGGIO AP H/S	RT	*	2200.00

MARURI USA

*

YR	NAME	LIMIT	ISSUE	TREND
98	HUMMINGBIRD PLATE ALLEN'S W/HIBISCUS	OP	40.00	40.00
98	HUMMINGBIRD PLATE ANNA'S W/LILY	OP	40.00	40.00
98	HUMMINGBIRD PLATE RUBY-THROATED W/TRUMPET CREEPER	OP	40.00	40.00

W. GAITHER — **EAGLE PLATE SERIES**

YR	NAME	LIMIT	ISSUE	TREND
84	FREE FLIGHT	CL	150.00	175.00

MORGANTOWN

C. YATES — **HEAVENS ABOVE**

YR	NAME	LIMIT	ISSUE	TREND
89	CASSIOPEIA	OP	65.00	75.00
90	ORION	OP	65.00	120.00
90	PEGASUS	OP	65.00	200.00
91	CYGNUS	OP	65.00	150.00

C. YATES — **STAR OF BETHLEHEM**

YR	NAME	LIMIT	ISSUE	TREND
88	HOLY FAMILY, THE	OP	35.00	50.00
89	SHEPHERDS IN THE FIELD	OP	35.00	54.00
90	LED BY THE STAR	OP	38.00	50.00
91	TIDINGS OF GREAT JOY	OP	38.00	50.00

C. YATES — **YATE'S COUNTRY LADIES**

YR	NAME	LIMIT	ISSUE	TREND
81	ANGELICA	OP	75.00	110.00
82	VIOLET	OP	75.00	110.00
83	HEATHER	OP	75.00	110.00
84	LAUREL	OP	75.00	110.00

MUSEUM COLLECTIONS INC.

N. ROCKWELL — **AMERICAN FAMILY I**

YR	NAME	LIMIT	ISSUE	TREND
79	BABY'S FIRST STEP	9900	29.00	85.00
79	BIRTHDAY PARTY	9900	29.00	38.00
79	BRIDE AND GROOM	9900	29.00	38.00
79	FIRST HAIRCUT	9900	29.00	40.00
79	FIRST PROM	9900	29.00	40.00
79	HAPPY BIRTHDAY DEAR MOTHER	9900	29.00	65.00
79	LITTLE MOTHER	9900	29.00	45.00
79	MOTHER'S LITTLE HELPERS	9900	29.00	38.00
79	STUDENT, THE	9900	29.00	40.00
79	SWEET SIXTEEN	9900	29.00	100.00
79	WASHING OUR DOG	9900	29.00	40.00
79	WRAPPING CHRISTMAS PRESENTS	9900	29.00	40.00

N. ROCKWELL — **AMERICAN FAMILY II**

YR	NAME	LIMIT	ISSUE	TREND
80	ALMOST GROWN UP	22500	35.00	50.00
80	COURAGEOUS HERO	22500	35.00	50.00
80	GIVING THANKS	22500	35.00	50.00
80	HOME RUN SLUGGER	22500	35.00	50.00
80	LITTLE SALESMAN	22500	35.00	50.00
80	LITTLE SHAVER	22500	35.00	50.00
80	NEW ARRIVAL	22500	35.00	50.00
80	SPACE PIONEERS	22500	35.00	50.00
80	SWEET DREAMS	22500	35.00	50.00
80	WE MISSED YOU DADDY	22500	35.00	50.00
81	AT THE CIRCUS	22500	35.00	50.00
81	GOOD FOOD, GOOD FRIENDS	22500	35.00	50.00

N. ROCKWELL — **CHRISTMAS**

YR	NAME	LIMIT	ISSUE	TREND
79	DAY AFTER CHRISTMAS	YR	75.00	100.00
80	CHECKING HIS LIST	YR	75.00	100.00
81	RINGING IN GOOD CHEER	YR	75.00	100.00
82	WAITING FOR SANTA	YR	75.00	100.00
83	HIGH HOPES	YR	75.00	100.00
84	SPACE AGE SANTA	YR	55.00	100.00

YR NAME	LIMIT	ISSUE	TREND
N. ROCKWELL GALLERY			
N. ROCKWELL	**N. ROCKWELL CENTENNIAL**		
93 COBBLER, THE	CL	40.00	60.00
93 TOYMAKER, THE	CL	40.00	60.00
N. ROCKWELL	**ROCKWELL'S CHRISTMAS LEGACY**		
92 SANTA'S WORKSHOP	CL	50.00	70.00
93 MAKING A LIST	CL	50.00	60.00
93 VISIONS OF SANTA	CL	55.00	65.00
93 WHILE SANTA SLUMBERS	CL	55.00	60.00
NEWELL			
S. STILWELL	**WEBER'S CALENDAR**		
84 JULY	OP	19.00	19.00
84 JUNE	OP	19.00	19.00
85 AUGUST	OP	19.00	19.00
85 NOVEMBER	OP	19.00	19.00
85 OCTOBER	OP	19.00	19.00
85 SEPTEMBER	OP	19.00	19.00
86 APRIL	OP	19.00	25.00
86 DECEMBER	OP	19.00	20.00
86 FEBRUARY	OP	19.00	19.00
86 JANUARY	OP	19.00	19.00
86 MARCH	OP	19.00	22.00
86 MAY	OP	19.00	55.00
NOSTALGIA			
L. CASIGA	**HISPANIC COLLECTORS**		
95 RINCONCITO CRIOLLO	12000	30.00	30.00
E. DIUZ	**HISPANIC COLLECTORS**		
95 LA GARITA	9000	30.00	30.00
J. FELLIN	**HISPANIC COLLECTORS**		
95 A LA LUZ DE MI BALCON	12000	30.00	30.00
OSIRIS PORCELAIN			
N.N. BICHAY	**LEGEND OF TUTANKHAMEN**		
91 TUTANKHAMEN AND HIS PRINCESS	195 DAYS	40.00	45.00
PEMBERTON & OAKES			
D. ZOLAN	**ADVENTURES OF CHILDHOOD**		
89 ALMOST HOME	RT	20.00	55.00
89 CRYSTAL'S CREEK	RT	20.00	40.00
89 SUMMER SUDS	RT	22.00	45.00
90 SNOWY ADVENTURE	RT	22.00	50.00
91 FORESTS & FAIRY TALES	RT	24.00	50.00
D. ZOLAN	**ANNIVERSARY (10TH)**		
88 RIBBONS AND ROSES	RT	24.00	45.00
D. ZOLAN	**BEST OF ZOLAN IN MINIATURE**		
85 SABINA IN THE GRASS	RT	12.50	119.00
86 ERIK AND DANDELION	RT	12.50	90.00
86 TENDER MOMENT	RT	12.50	87.00
86 TOUCHING THE SKY	RT	12.50	75.00
87 A GIFT FOR LAURIE	RT	12.50	67.00
87 SMALL WONDER	RT	12.50	64.00
D. ZOLAN	**CHILDHOOD DISCOVERIES (MINIATURE)**		
90 AUTUMN LEAVES	RT	14.40	35.00
90 COLORS OF SPRING	RT	14.40	40.00
90 FIRST KISS	RT	14.40	55.00
91 ENCHANTED FOREST	RT	16.60	35.00
91 JUST DUCKY	RT	16.60	30.00
91 RAINY DAY PALS	RT	16.60	35.00
92 DOUBLE TROUBLE	RT	16.60	35.00
93 PEPPERMINT KISS	RT	16.60	30.00
95 TENDER HEARTS	RT	16.60	17.00
D. ZOLAN	**CHILDHOOD FRIENDSHIP**		
86 BEACH BREAK	RT	19.00	50.00
87 LITTLE ENGINEERS	RT	19.00	60.00
88 DOZENS OF DAISIES	RT	19.00	35.00
88 SHARING SECRETS	RT	19.00	50.00
89 TINY TREASURES	RT	19.00	50.00
90 COUNTRY WALK	RT	19.00	35.00
D. ZOLAN	**CHILDREN AND PETS**		
84 GOLDEN MOMENT	RT	19.00	50.00
84 TENDER MOMENT	RT	19.00	60.00
85 MAKING FRIENDS	RT	19.00	40.00
85 TENDER BEGINNING	RT	19.00	40.00
86 BACKYARD DISCOVERY	RT	19.00	40.00
86 WAITING TO PLAY	RT	19.00	40.00
D. ZOLAN	**CHILDREN AT CHRISTMAS**		
81 A GIFT FOR LAURIE	RT	48.00	100.00
82 CHRISTMAS PRAYER	RT	48.00	70.00
83 ERIK'S DELIGHT	RT	48.00	80.00
84 CHRISTMAS SECRET	RT	48.00	80.00
85 CHRISTMAS KITTEN	RT	48.00	80.00
86 LAURIE AND THE CRECHE	RT	48.00	80.00
D. ZOLAN	**CHRISTMAS**		
91 CANDLELIGHT MAGIC	RT	25.00	55.00

YR	NAME	LIMIT	ISSUE	TREND
D. ZOLAN			**CHRISTMAS (MINIATURE)**	
93	SNOWY ADVENTURE	RT	16.60	25.00
94	CANDLELIGHT MAGIC	CL	16.60	17.00
D. ZOLAN			**EASTER (MINIATURE)**	
91	EASTER MORNING (EASTER)	RT	16.60	35.00
D. ZOLAN			**FATHER'S DAY**	
86	DADDY'S HOME	RT	19.00	100.00
D. ZOLAN			**FATHER'S DAY (MINIATURE)**	
94	TWO OF A KIND	RT	16.60	25.00
D. ZOLAN			**GRANDPARENT'S DAY**	
90	IT'S GRANDMA & GRANDPA	RT	24.00	50.00
93	GRANDPA'S FENCE	RT	24.00	35.00
D. ZOLAN			**HEIRLOOM OVALS**	
92	MY KITTY	RT	19.00	40.00
D. ZOLAN		**MEMBERS ONLY SINGLE ISSUE (MINIATURE)**		
90	BY MYSELF	RT	14.40	60.00
93	SUMMER'S CHILD	RT	16.60	30.00
94	LITTLE SLUGGER	CL	16.60	17.00
D. ZOLAN			**MEMBERSHIP (MINIATURE)**	
87	FOR YOU	RT	12.50	75.00
88	MAKING FRIENDS	RT	12.50	75.00
89	GRANDMA'S GARDEN	RT	12.50	65.00
90	A CHRISTMAS PRAYER	RT	14.40	45.00
91	GOLDEN MOMENT	RT	15.00	35.00
92	BROTHERLY LOVE	RT	15.00	50.00
93	NEW SHOES	RT	17.00	35.00
94	MY KITTY	CL	*	30.00
D. ZOLAN			**MOMENTS TO REMEMBER (MINIATURE)**	
92	ALMOST HOME	RT	16.60	25.00
92	JUST WE TWO	RT	16.60	35.00
93	FOREST FRIENDS	RT	16.60	25.00
93	TINY TREASURES	RT	16.60	25.00
D. ZOLAN			**MOTHER'S DAY**	
88	MOTHER'S ANGELS	RT	19.00	65.00
D. ZOLAN			**MOTHER'S DAY (MINIATURE)**	
90	FLOWERS FOR MOTHER (MOTHER'S DAY)	RT	14.40	45.00
92	TWILIGHT PRAYER (MOTHER'S DAY)	RT	16.60	35.00
93	JESSICA'S FIELD	RT	16.60	35.00
94	ONE SUMMER DAY	RT	16.60	25.00
R. ANDERSON			**NUTCRACKER II**	
88	ROYAL WELCOME, THE	RT	24.00	40.00
S. FISHER			**NUTCRACKER II**	
81	GRAND FINALE	RT	24.00	35.00
82	ARABIAN DANCERS	RT	24.00	65.00
83	DEW DROP FAIRY	RT	24.00	55.00
84	CLARA'S DELIGHT	RT	24.00	50.00
85	BEDTIME FOR NUTCRACKER	RT	24.00	45.00
86	CROWNING OF CLARA, THE	RT	24.00	40.00
M. VICKERS			**NUTCRACKER II**	
89	SPANISH DANCER, THE	RT	24.00	45.00
D. ZOLAN			**NUTCRACKER II**	
87	DANCE OF THE SNOWFLAKES	RT	24.00	45.00
D. ZOLAN			**PLAQUES**	
91	FLOWERS FOR MOTHER	RT	16.80	25.00
91	NEW SHOES	RT	19.00	30.00
92	EASTER MORNING	RT	19.00	25.00
92	GRANDMA'S GARDEN	RT	19.00	25.00
92	SMALL WONDER	RT	19.00	25.00
D. ZOLAN			**SINGLE ISSUE**	
93	WINTER FRIENDS	RT	19.00	35.00
D. ZOLAN			**SINGLE ISSUE (MINIATURE)**	
86	BACKYARD DISCOVERY	RT	12.50	110.00
86	DADDY'S HOME	RT	12.50	650.00
89	MY PUMPKIN	RT	14.40	60.00
89	SUNNY SURPRISE	RT	12.50	60.00
91	BACKYARD BUDDIES	RT	16.60	35.00
91	THINKER, THE	RT	16.60	35.00
93	QUIET TIME	RT	16.60	40.00
94	LITTLE FISHERMAN	RT	16.60	25.00
D. ZOLAN		**SINGLE ISSUE BONE CHINA (MINIATURE)**		
92	WINDOWS OF DREAMS	RT	19.00	25.00
D. ZOLAN		**SINGLE ISSUE DAY TO DAY SPODE**		
91	DAISY DAYS	RT	48.00	50.00
D. ZOLAN			**SPECIAL MOMENTS**	
88	BROTHERLY LOVE	RT	19.00	90.00
88	SUNNY SURPRISE	RT	19.00	40.00
89	SISTERLY LOVE	RT	22.00	35.00
89	SUMMER'S CHILD	RT	22.00	45.00
90	CONE FOR TWO	RT	25.00	50.00
90	MEADOW MAGIC	RT	22.00	40.00
90	RODEO GIRL	RT	25.00	40.00
D. ZOLAN			**THANKSGIVING**	
81	I'M THANKFUL TOO	RT	19.00	85.00
D. ZOLAN			**THANKSGIVING (MINIATURE)**	
93	I'M THANKFUL TOO	RT	16.60	25.00

YR	NAME	LIMIT	ISSUE	TREND
D. ZOLAN		TIMES TO TREASURE BONE CHINA (MINIATURE)		
93	GARDEN SWING	RT	16.60	30.00
93	LITTLE TRAVELER	RT	16.60	30.00
94	SEPTEMBER GIRL	CL	16.60	40.00
94	SUMMER GARDEN	CL	16.60	40.00
D. ZOLAN		WONDER OF CHILDHOOD		
82	TOUCHING THE SKY	RT	19.00	60.00
83	SPRING INNOCENCE	RT	19.00	100.00
84	WINTER ANGEL	RT	22.00	85.00
85	SMALL WONDER	RT	22.00	65.00
86	GRANDMA'S GARDEN	RT	22.00	45.00
87	DAY DREAMER	RT	22.00	45.00
D. ZOLAN		YESTERDAY'S CHILDREN (MINIATURE)		
94	LITTLE FRIENDS	CL	16.60	30.00
94	SEASIDE TREASURES	CL	16.60	30.00
D. ZOLAN		ZOLAN'S CHILDREN		
78	ERIK AND DANDELION	RT	19.00	120.00

PFALTZGRAFF
B.B. RICHARDS

YR	NAME	LIMIT	ISSUE	TREND
93	LITTLEST ANGEL	5000	19.00	23.00
94	CHRISTMAS TRADITION	10000	15.00	18.00
94	HARVEST MEMORIES	10000	15.00	18.00

PICKARD
RAPHAEL

YR	NAME	LIMIT	ISSUE	TREND
		ANNUAL CHRISTMAS		
76	ALBA MADONNA	7500	60.00	400.00
79	ADORATION OF THE MAGI	10000	70.00	100.00
80	MADONNA AND CHILD	10000	80.00	125.00
81	MADONNA AND CHILD WITH ANGELS	10000	90.00	125.00
G. DAVID		ANNUAL CHRISTMAS		
78	REST ON FLIGHT INTO EGYPT	10000	65.00	175.00
L. LOTTO		ANNUAL CHRISTMAS		
77	NATIVITY, THE	7500	65.00	200.00
J. SANCHEZ		CHILDREN OF MEXICO		
81	MARIA	5000	85.00	225.00
81	MIGUEL	5000	85.00	120.00
82	REGINA	5000	90.00	120.00
83	RAPHAEL	5000	90.00	120.00
*		GEMS OF NATURE: HUMMINGBIRDS		
89	RUBY-THROATED HUMMINGBIRD	CL	29.00	55.00
90	BLACK-CHINNED HUMMINGBIRD	CL	32.00	60.00
90	BROAD-BILLED HUMMINGBIRD	CL	32.00	40.00
90	CALLIOPE HUMMINGBIRD	CL	32.00	50.00
90	RUFOUS HUMMINGBIRD	CL	29.00	50.00
91	ANNA'S HUMMINGBIRD/PETUNIAS	CL	34.00	50.00
91	COSTA'S HUMMINGBIRD & HOLLYHOCKS	CL	34.00	50.00
91	WHITE-EARED HUMMINGBIRD	CL	32.00	44.00
*		HAWAIIAN SPLENDOR		
92	AN EVENING IN THE ISLANDS	CL	34.00	50.00
92	COASTAL HARMONY	CL	34.00	52.00
92	TROPICAL ENCHANTMENT	CL	34.00	37.00
92	TWILIGHT PARADISE	CL	34.00	55.00
*		HOLIDAY TRADITIONS		
92	CHRISTMAS HOMECOMING	CL	29.00	45.00
92	QUIET UNDER THE EAVES	CL	29.00	65.00
93	HEART OF CHRISTMAS, THE	CL	29.00	29.00
93	SNOWS OF YESTERYEAR	CL	29.00	30.00
*		INNOCENT ENCOUNTERS		
88	JUST PASSING BY	CL	34.00	50.00
88	MAKING FRIENDS	CL	34.00	55.00
89	EYE TO EYE	CL	34.00	60.00
89	LET'S PLAY	CL	34.00	60.00
J. LOCKHART		LOCKHART WILDLIFE		
70	WOODCOCK/RUFFED GROUSE, PAIR	2000	150.00	550.00
71	TEAL/MALLARD, PAIR	2000	150.00	325.00
72	MOCKINGBIRD/CARDINAL, PAIR	2000	163.00	300.00
73	TURKEY/PHEASANT, PAIR	2000	163.00	350.00
74	AMERICAN BALD EAGLE	2000	150.00	1000.00
75	WHITE TAILED DEER	2500	100.00	250.00
76	AMERICAN BUFFALO	2500	165.00	300.00
77	GREAT HORNED OWL	2500	100.00	200.00
78	AMERICAN PANTHER	2000	175.00	350.00
79	RED FOXES	2500	120.00	175.00
80	TRUMPETER SWAN	2000	200.00	300.00
I. SPENCER		MOTHER'S LOVE		
80	MIRACLE	7500	95.00	100.00
81	STORY TIME	7500	110.00	110.00
82	FIRST EDITION	7500	115.00	120.00
83	PRECIOUS MOMENT	7500	120.00	120.00
D. SWEET		ROMANTIC CASTLES OF EUROPE		
90	LUDWIG'S CASTLE	19500	55.00	80.00
91	DAVINCI'S CHAMBORD	19500	55.00	80.00
91	EILEAN DONAN	19500	55.00	80.00
91	LEGENDARY CASTLE OF LEEDS, THE	19500	55.00	80.00
91	PALACE OF THE MOORS	19500	55.00	80.00
91	SWISS ISLE FORTRESS	19500	55.00	80.00

YR	NAME	LIMIT	ISSUE	TREND
92	ELTZ CASTLE	19500	55.00	80.00
92	KYLEMORE ABBEY	19500	55.00	80.00

I. SPENCER — SYMPHONY OF ROSES

YR	NAME	LIMIT	ISSUE	TREND
82	WILD IRISH ROSE	10000	85.00	120.00
83	YELLOW ROSE OF TEXAS	10000	90.00	125.00
84	HONEYSUCKLE ROSE	10000	95.00	140.00
85	ROSE OF WASHINGTON SQUARE	10000	100.00	300.00

PORSGRUND
G. BRATILE — CHRISTMAS (ANNUAL)

YR	NAME	LIMIT	ISSUE	TREND
68	CHURCH SCENE	UD	12.00	300.00
69	THREE KINGS	UD	12.00	30.00
70	ROAD TO BETHLEHEM	UD	12.00	30.00
71	A CHILD IS BORN	UD	12.00	30.00
72	HARK THE HERALD ANGELS	UD	12.00	30.00
73	PROMISE OF THE SAVIOR	UD	12.00	30.00
74	SHEPHERDS, THE	UD	15.00	75.00
75	ROAD TO TEMPLE	UD	20.00	20.00
76	JESUS AND THE ELDERS	UD	22.00	26.00
77	DRAUGHT OF THE FISH	UD	24.00	40.00

PORTERFIELD'S
R. ANDERS — FATHER'S DAY

YR	NAME	LIMIT	ISSUE	TREND
97	COOKIES FOR DADDY	19 DAYS	16.60	38.00

R. ANDERS — HALLOWEEN

97	SPOOKY STORIES	10 DAYS	16.60	17.00

R. ANDERS — MOMENTS OF WONDER

96	DIGGING IN	19 DAYS	16.60	38.00
96	FIRST LOVE	CL	16.60	50.00
96	SAFE HARBOR	SO	16.60	34.00
96	TIME OUT	SO	16.60	38.00
97	SWEET DREAMS	19 DAYS	16.60	17.00
97	TWO BITES TO GO	SO	16.60	34.00

R. ANDERS — MOTHER'S DAY

98	TUCKED IN	10 DAYS	16.60	17.00

R. ANDERS — ROB ANDERS SOCIETY

97	SHORT STORIES	YR	19.00	45.00
98	CUDDLING UP	10 DAYS	19.00	19.00

R. ANDERS — TREASURES OF THE HEART

97	IN GOOD HANDS	10 DAYS	16.60	17.00
98	BUBBLES AWAY	10 DAYS	16.60	17.00

PRINCETON GALLERY
K. MCELROY

95	UNICORN BY THE SEA, THE	95 DAYS	30.00	30.00

J. VAN ZYLE — ARCTIC WOLVES

91	SONG OF THE WILDERNESS	CL	30.00	30.00
92	IN THE EYE OF THE MOON	CL	30.00	30.00

R. SANDERSON — CIRCUS FRIENDS COLLECTION

89	DON'T BE SHY	*	30.00	30.00
90	CHEER UP MR. CLOWN	*	30.00	30.00
90	LOOKS LIKE RAIN	*	30.00	30.00
90	MAKE ME A CLOWN	*	30.00	30.00

Q. LEMOND — CUBS OF THE BIG CATS

90	COUGAR CUB	*	30.00	40.00
91	CHEETAH	CL	30.00	40.00
91	LION CUB	CL	30.00	40.00
91	SNOW LEOPARD	CL	30.00	40.00
91	TIGER	CL	30.00	40.00
92	LYNX CUB	CL	30.00	40.00
92	WHITE TIGER CUB	CL	30.00	40.00

L. PICKEN — DARLING DALMATIANS

91	DALMATIAN	CL	30.00	30.00
92	FIREHOUSE FROLIC	CL	30.00	30.00

R. SANDERSON — ENCHANTED WORLD OF THE UNICORN

91	RAINBOW VALLEY	CL	30.00	40.00
92	ENCHANTED SHORES	CL	30.00	40.00
92	HIDDEN GLADE OF UNICORN	CL	30.00	40.00
92	JOYFUL MEADOW OF UNICORN	CL	30.00	40.00
92	MISTY HILLS OF UNICORN	CL	30.00	40.00
92	SECRET GARDEN OF UNICORN	CL	30.00	40.00
92	SPRINGTIME PASTURE OF UNICORN	CL	30.00	40.00
92	TROPICAL PARADISE OF UNICORN	CL	30.00	40.00

R.J. ERNST ENTERPRISES
S. MORTON — BEAUTIFUL WORLD

81	TAHITIAN DREAMER	RT	28.00	50.00
82	FLIRTATION	RT	28.00	50.00
84	ELKE OF OSLO	RT	28.00	50.00

S. KUHNLY — CLASSY CARS

82	26T, THE	RT	25.00	50.00
82	31A, THE	RT	25.00	45.00
83	PICKUP, THE	RT	25.00	45.00
84	PANEL VAN	RT	25.00	45.00

S. MORTON — COMMEMORATIVES

81	JOHN LENNON	RT	40.00	160.00
82	MARILYN MONROE	RT	40.00	80.00

YR	NAME	LIMIT	ISSUE	TREND
83	JUDY GARLAND	RT	40.00	100.00
84	JOHN WAYNE	RT	40.00	80.00

S. MORTON — ELVIRA

YR	NAME	LIMIT	ISSUE	TREND
88	MISTRESS OF THE DARK	RT	30.00	50.00
88	NIGHT ROSE	CL	30.00	50.00
88	RED VELVET	RT	30.00	50.00

S. MORTON — ELVIS PRESLEY

YR	NAME	LIMIT	ISSUE	TREND
88	ELVIS PRESLEY	RT	40.00	80.00
88	FOREVER YOURS	RT	40.00	90.00
88	MOODY BLUES	RT	40.00	80.00
89	ELVIS PRESLEY- SPECIAL REQUEST	RT	150.00	275.00

S. MORTON — ELVIS REMEMBERED

YR	NAME	LIMIT	ISSUE	TREND
89	EARLY YEARS	CL	38.00	90.00
89	KING, THE	CL	38.00	100.00
89	LOVING YOU	CL	38.00	90.00
89	ROCKIN' IN THE MOONLIGHT	CL	38.00	90.00
89	TENDERLY	RT	38.00	90.00

S. MORTON — HOLLYWOOD GREATS

YR	NAME	LIMIT	ISSUE	TREND
81	GARY COOPER	RT	30.00	50.00
81	JOHN WAYNE	RT	30.00	75.00
82	CLARK GABLE	RT	30.00	75.00
84	ALAN LADD	RT	30.00	50.00

S. MORTON — HOLLYWOOD, WALK OF FAME

YR	NAME	LIMIT	ISSUE	TREND
89	ELIZABETH TAYLOR	RT	40.00	70.00
89	JIMMY STEWART	RT	40.00	70.00
89	JOAN COLLINS	RT	40.00	70.00
89	TOM SELLECK	RT	40.00	70.00
90	BURT REYNOLDS	RT	40.00	70.00
90	SYLVESTER STALLONE	RT	40.00	70.00

S. MORTON — REPUBLIC PICTURES LIBRARY

YR	NAME	LIMIT	ISSUE	TREND
91	ATTACK AT TARAWA	RT	38.00	40.00
91	RIDE HOME, THE	RT	38.00	40.00
91	SHOWDOWN WITH LAREDO	RT	38.00	40.00
91	THOUGHTS OF ANGELIQUE	RT	38.00	60.00
92	ANGEL AND THE BADMAN	RT	38.00	40.00
92	FLIGHTING SEABEES, THE	RT	38.00	40.00
92	WAR OF THE WILDCATS	RT	38.00	60.00
93	FLYING TIGERS	RT	38.00	60.00
93	SANDS OF IWO JIMA	RT	38.00	60.00
93	TRIBUTE, THE 12 IN.	RT	98.00	100.00
94	TRIBUTE, THE 8 1/4 IN.	9500	30.00	30.00

R. MONEY — SEEMS LIKE YESTERDAY

YR	NAME	LIMIT	ISSUE	TREND
81	STOP & SMELL THE ROSES	RT	25.00	50.00
82	HOME BY LUNCH	RT	25.00	50.00
82	LISA'S CREEK	RT	25.00	50.00
83	IT'S GOT MY NAME ON IT	RT	25.00	50.00
83	MY MAGIC HAT	RT	25.00	50.00
84	LITTLE PRINCE	RT	25.00	50.00

S. MORTON — STAR TREK

YR	NAME	LIMIT	ISSUE	TREND
84	MR. SPOCK	RT	30.00	70.00
85	BEAM US DOWN SCOTTY	RT	30.00	50.00
85	CAPTAIN KIRK	RT	30.00	60.00
85	CHEKOV	RT	30.00	50.00
85	DR. MCCOY	RT	30.00	60.00
85	ENTERPRISE, THE	RT	40.00	105.00
85	SCOTTY	RT	30.00	50.00
85	SULU	RT	30.00	50.00
85	UHURA	RT	30.00	55.00

S. MORTON — STAR TREK: COMMEMORATIVE COLLECTION

YR	NAME	LIMIT	ISSUE	TREND
87	A PIECE OF THE ACTION	RT	30.00	110.00
87	AMOK TIME	RT	30.00	105.00
87	CITY ON THE EDGE OF FOREVER, THE	RT	30.00	210.00
87	DEVIL IN THE DARK, THE	RT	30.00	105.00
87	JOURNEY TO BABEL	RT	30.00	145.00
87	MENAGERIE, THE	RT	30.00	130.00
87	MIRROR, MIRROR	RT	30.00	180.00
87	TROUBLE WITH TRIBBLES, THE	RT	30.00	110.00

R. MONEY — TURN OF THE CENTURY

YR	NAME	LIMIT	ISSUE	TREND
81	RIVERBOAT HONEYMOON	RT	35.00	40.00
82	CHILDREN'S CAROUSEL	RT	35.00	40.00
84	FLOWER MARKET	RT	35.00	40.00
85	BALLOON RACE	RT	35.00	40.00

D. PUTNAM — WOMEN OF THE WEST

YR	NAME	LIMIT	ISSUE	TREND
79	EXPECTATIONS	RT	40.00	60.00
81	SILVER DOLLAR SAL	RT	40.00	60.00
82	SCHOOL MARM	RT	40.00	60.00
83	DOLLY	RT	40.00	60.00

RAYMON TROUP STUDIO

W. RAYMON — AMERICAN LANDMARKS COLLECTION

YR	NAME	LIMIT	ISSUE	TREND
95	IVY GREEN	1500	40.00	40.00
95	OLD MILL, THE	1500	40.00	40.00

W.R. TROUP — ANGELS

YR	NAME	LIMIT	ISSUE	TREND
98	SNOW BUBLES	OP	70.00	70.00
98	STAR LIGHT, STAR BRIGHT	OP	70.00	70.00

RECO INTERNATIONAL

YR	NAME	LIMIT	ISSUE	TREND
S. DEVLIN				**AMERICANA**
72	GASPEE INCIDENT	RT	200.00	350.00
B. FARNSWORTH				**AMISH TRADITIONS**
94	FAMILY OUTING	CL	30.00	30.00
94	GOLDEN HARVEST	CL	30.00	30.00
94	QUILTING BEE, THE	CL	30.00	30.00
95	LAST DAY OF SCHOOL	95 DAYS	30.00	30.00
S. KUCK				**BAREFOOT CHILDREN**
87	GOLDEN AFTERNOON	RT	30.00	40.00
87	NIGHT-TIME STORY	RT	30.00	40.00
88	CAROUSEL MAGIC	RT	30.00	50.00
88	GRANDMA'S TRUNK	RT	30.00	40.00
88	LITTLE SWEETHEARTS	RT	30.00	40.00
88	PRETTY AS A PICTURE	RT	30.00	40.00
88	REHEARSAL, THE	RT	30.00	40.00
88	UNDER THE APPLE TREE	RT	30.00	40.00
J. MCCLELLAND				**BECKY'S DAY**
85	AWAKENING	CL	25.00	30.00
85	GETTING DRESSED	RT	25.00	35.00
86	BREAKFAST	RT	28.00	35.00
86	EVENING PRAYER	RT	28.00	45.00
86	LEARNING IS FUN	RT	28.00	40.00
86	MUFFIN MAKING	RT	28.00	40.00
86	TUB TIME	CL	28.00	40.00
G. RATNAVIRA				**BIRDS OF THE HIDDEN FOREST**
94	MACAW WATERFALL	CL	30.00	30.00
94	PARADISE VALLEY	CL	30.00	30.00
95	TOUCAN TREASURE	96 DAYS	30.00	30.00
*				**BOHEMIAN ANNUALS**
74	1974	RT	130.00	160.00
75	1975	RT	140.00	160.00
76	1976	RT	150.00	160.00
J. BERGSMA				**CASTLES & DREAMS**
92	BIRTH OF A DREAM, THE	CL	30.00	30.00
92	DREMAS COME TRUE	CL	30.00	30.00
93	BELIEVE IN YOUR DREAMS	CL	30.00	30.00
94	FOLLOW YOUR DREAMS	CL	30.00	30.00
J. HALL				**CELEBRATION OF LOVE**
92	10TH ANNIVERSARY (6 1/2 IN.)	OP	25.00	30.00
92	10TH ANNIVERSARY (9 1/4 IN.)	OP	35.00	40.00
92	25TH ANNIVERSARY (6 1/2 IN.)	OP	25.00	30.00
92	25TH ANNIVERSARY (9 1/4 IN.)	OP	35.00	40.00
92	50TH ANNIVERSARY (6 1/2 IN.)	OP	25.00	30.00
92	50TH ANNIVERSARY (9 1/4 IN.)	OP	35.00	40.00
92	HAPPY ANNIVERSARY (6 1/2 IN.)	OP	25.00	30.00
92	HAPPY ANNIVERSARY (9 1/4 IN.)	OP	35.00	40.00
S. KUCK				**CHILDHOOD ALMANAC**
85	BE MINE-FEBRUARY	RT	30.00	40.00
85	CHRISTMAS MAGIC-DECEMBER	RT	35.00	50.00
85	EASTER MORNING-APRIL	RT	30.00	50.00
85	FIRESIDE DREAMS-JANUARY	RT	30.00	50.00
85	FOR MOM-MAY	RT	30.00	40.00
85	GIVING THANKS-NOVEMBER	RT	30.00	40.00
85	INDIAN SUMMER-OCTOBER	RT	30.00	40.00
85	JUST DREAMING-JUNE	RT	30.00	50.00
85	SCHOOL DAYS-SEPTEMBER	RT	30.00	50.00
85	STAR SPANGLED SKY-JULY	RT	30.00	40.00
85	SUMMER SECRETS-AUGUST	RT	30.00	50.00
85	WINDS OF MARCH-MARCH	RT	30.00	40.00
S. KUCK				**CHILDREN'S CHRISTMAS PAGEANT**
86	SILENT NIGHT	RT	33.00	60.00
87	HARK THE HERALD ANGELS SING	RT	33.00	60.00
88	WHILE SHEPHERDS WATCHED...	RT	33.00	60.00
89	WE THREE KINGS	YR	33.00	60.00
J. MCCLELLAND				**CHILDREN'S GARDEN**
93	GARDEN FRIENDS	RT	30.00	30.00
93	PUPPY LOVE	RT	30.00	30.00
93	TEA FOR THREE	RT	30.00	30.00
S. KUCK				**CHRISTENING GIFT**
95	GOD'S GIFT	OP	30.00	30.00
J. BERGSMA				**CHRISTMAS SERIES**
90	DOWN THE GLISTENING LANE	RT	35.00	30.00
91	A CHILD IS BORN	RT	35.00	30.00
92	CHRISTMAS DAY	RT	35.00	30.00
J. BERGSMA				**CHRISTMAS WISHES**
93	I WISH YOU AN ANGEL	75 DAYS	30.00	30.00
94	I WISH YOU LOVE	CL	30.00	30.00
95	I WISH YOU JOY	75 DAYS	30.00	30.00
S. KUCK				**DAYS GONE BY**
83	AMY'S MAGIC HORSE	RT	30.00	75.00
83	SUNDAY BEST	RT	30.00	100.00
84	AFTERNOON RECITAL	RT	30.00	80.00
84	EASTER AT GRANDMA'S	RT	30.00	60.00
84	LITTLE ANGLERS	RT	30.00	75.00
84	LITTLE TUTOR	RT	30.00	60.00

YR	NAME	LIMIT	ISSUE	TREND
85	MORNING SONG	RT	30.00	50.00
85	SURREY RIDE, THE	RT	30.00	55.00
*				
		DRESDEN CHRISTMAS		
71	SHEPHERD SCENE	RT	15.00	50.00
72	NIKLAS CHURCH	RT	15.00	30.00
73	SCHWANSTEIN CHURCH	RT	18.00	40.00
74	VILLAGE SCENE	RT	20.00	30.00
75	ROTHENBURG SCENE	RT	24.00	30.00
76	VILLAGE CHURCH	RT	26.00	40.00
77	OLD MILL (ISSUE CLOSED)	RT	28.00	30.00
*				
		DRESDEN MOTHER'S DAY		
72	DOE AND FAWN	RT	15.00	20.00
73	MARE AND COLT	RT	16.00	30.00
74	TIGER AND CUB	RT	20.00	25.00
75	DACHSHUNDS	RT	24.00	30.00
76	OWL AND OFFSPRING	RT	26.00	30.00
77	CHAMOIS (ISSUE CLOSED)	RT	28.00	30.00
	C. HOPKINS			
		ENCHANTED NORFIN TROLLS		
93	TROLL AND HIS DRAGON, THE	RT	20.00	20.00
93	TROLL MAIDEN	RT	20.00	20.00
93	WIZARD TROLL, THE	RT	20.00	20.00
94	CHEF LE TROLL	RT	20.00	20.00
94	IF TROLLS COULD FLY	RT	20.00	20.00
94	MINSTREL TROLL	RT	20.00	20.00
94	QUEEN OF THE TROLLS	RT	20.00	20.00
94	TROLL IN SHINNING ARMOR	RT	20.00	20.00
	C.M. BARKER			
		FLOWER FAIRIES YEAR COLLECTION		
90	PINE TREE FAIRY, THE	RT	30.00	30.00
90	RED CLOVER FAIRY, THE	RT	30.00	30.00
90	ROSE HIP FAIRY, THE	RT	30.00	30.00
90	WILD CHERRY BLOSSOM FAIRY, THE	RT	30.00	30.00
	J. POLUSZYNSKI			
		FOUR SEASONS		
73	FALL	RT	50.00	75.00
73	SPRING	RT	50.00	75.00
73	SUMMER	RT	50.00	75.00
73	WINTER	RT	50.00	75.00
*				
		FURSTENBERG CHRISTMAS		
71	RABBITS	RT	15.00	30.00
72	SNOWY VILLAGE	RT	15.00	20.00
73	CHRISTMAS EVE	RT	18.00	40.00
74	SPARROWS	RT	20.00	30.00
75	DEER FAMILY	RT	22.00	30.00
76	WINTER BIRDS	RT	25.00	30.00
	E. GROSSBERG			
		FURSTENBERG DELUXE CHRISTMAS		
71	WISE MEN	RT	45.00	50.00
72	HOLY FAMILY	RT	45.00	50.00
73	CHRISTMAS EVE	RT	60.00	85.00
*				
		FURSTENBERG EASTER		
71	SHEEP	RT	15.00	160.00
72	CHICKS	RT	15.00	65.00
73	BUNNIES	RT	16.00	85.00
74	PUSSYWILLOW	RT	20.00	40.00
75	EASTER WINDOW	RT	22.00	30.00
76	FLOWER COLLECTING	RT	25.00	30.00
*				
		FURSTENBERG MOTHER'S DAY		
72	HUMMINGBIRDS, FE	RT	15.00	50.00
73	HEDGEHOGS	RT	16.00	40.00
74	DOE AND FAWN	RT	20.00	30.00
75	SWANS	RT	22.00	30.00
76	KOALA BEARS	RT	25.00	40.00
	J. POLUSZYNSKI			
		FURSTENBERG OLYMPIC		
72	MUNICH	RT	20.00	75.00
76	MONTREAL	RT	38.00	40.00
	S. KUCK			
		GAMES CHILDREN PLAY		
79	ME FIRST	RT	45.00	80.00
80	FOREVER BUBBLES	RT	45.00	80.00
81	SKATING PALS	RT	45.00	80.00
82	JOIN ME	10000	45.00	75.00
	D. BARLOWE			
		GARDENS OF AMERICA		
92	COLONIAL SPLENDOR	CL	30.00	30.00
	D. BARLOWE			
		GARDENS OF BEAUTY		
88	DUTCH COUNTRY GARDEN	RT	30.00	45.00
88	ENGLISH COUNTRY GARDEN	RT	30.00	45.00
88	JAPANESE GARDEN	RT	30.00	45.00
88	NEW ENGLAND GARDEN	RT	30.00	45.00
89	GERMAN COUNTRY GARDEN	RT	30.00	45.00
89	HAWAIIAN GARDEN	RT	30.00	45.00
89	ITALIAN GARDEN	RT	30.00	45.00
89	MEXICAN GARDEN	RT	30.00	45.00
	S. KUCK			
		GIFT OF LOVE		
93	MORNING GLORY	RT	65.00	90.00
94	FIELD OF DREAMS	*	*	90.00
94	MEMORIES FROM THE HEART	RT	65.00	90.00
	C. MICARELLI			
		GLORY OF CHRIST		
92	ASCENSION, THE	CL	30.00	30.00
93	JESUS HEALS THE SICK	CL	30.00	30.00

"Bah Humbug" *says old Mr. Scrooge to Tiny Tim. The Disney plate is from the "Mickey's Christmas Carol" series distributed by The Bradford Exchange.*

Released by W.S. George in 1991, Fleeting Encounter *is the first issue in The World's Most Magnificent Cats collection. Limited to 150 days of production, it retailed for $24.50 and is currently valued at $70.*

Zhivago and Lara share a brisk outing in this first issue in the Dr. Zhivago collection. Issued by W.S. George in 1990, production was limited to 150 days.

Is the Santa Fe *picking up speed or rolling into the train station? The work was created by Jim Deneen for Artaffects.*

YR	NAME	LIMIT	ISSUE	TREND
93	JESUS TEACHING	CL	30.00	30.00
93	LAST SUPPER, THE	CL	30.00	30.00
94	BAPTISM OF CHRIST, THE	CL	30.00	30.00
94	DESCENT FROM THE CROSS	CL	30.00	30.00
94	JESUS WALKS ON WATER	CL	30.00	30.00
94	NATIVITY, THE	CL	30.00	30.00
I. DRECHSLER			**GOD'S OWN COUNTRY**	
90	COMING HOME	RT	30.00	45.00
90	DAYBREAK	RT	30.00	45.00
90	PEACEFUL GATHERING	RT	30.00	45.00
90	QUIET WATERS	RT	30.00	45.00
J. MCCLELLAND			**GOLF COLLECTION**	
92	PAR EXCELLENCE	CL	35.00	40.00
*			**GRAFBURG CHRISTMAS**	
75	BLACK-CAPPED CHICKADEE	RT	20.00	60.00
76	SQUIRRELS	RT	22.00	30.00
S. KUCK		**GRANDPARENT COLLECTOR'S PLATES**		
81	GRANDMA'S COOKIE JAR	YR	38.00	55.00
81	GRANDPA AND THE DOLLHOUSE	YR	38.00	55.00
G. KATZ		**GREAT STORIES FROM THE BIBLE**		
87	JOSEPH'S COAT OF MANY COLORS	RT	30.00	50.00
87	KING SAUL & DAVID	RT	30.00	50.00
87	MOSES AND THE TEN COMMANDMENTS	RT	30.00	50.00
87	MOSES IN THE BULRUSHES	RT	30.00	50.00
88	DANIEL READS THE WRITING ON THE WALL	RT	30.00	50.00
88	KING SOLOMON	RT	30.00	50.00
88	REBEKAH AT THE WELL	RT	30.00	50.00
88	STORY OF RUTH, THE	RT	30.00	50.00
J. BERGSMA		**GUARDIANS OF THE KINGDOM**		
90	GUARDIANS OF THE INNOCENT CHILDREN	17500	35.00	50.00
90	MIRACLE OF LOVE, THE	17500	35.00	50.00
90	RAINBOW TO RIDE ON	RT	35.00	50.00
90	SPECIAL FRIENDS ARE FEW	17500	35.00	50.00
91	IN FAITH I AM FREE	17500	35.00	50.00
91	MAGIC OF LOVE, THE	17500	35.00	50.00
91	ONLY WITH THE HEART	17500	35.00	50.00
91	TO FLY WITHOUT WINGS	17500	35.00	50.00
H. ROE			**HAVEN OF THE HUNTERS**	
94	EAGLE'S CASTLE	RT	30.00	45.00
94	SANCTUARY OF THE HAWK	RT	30.00	45.00
J. YORK			**HEART OF THE FAMILY**	
92	SHARING SECRETS	CL	30.00	45.00
93	SPINNING DREAMS	CL	30.00	45.00
S. KUCK			**HEARTS & FLOWERS**	
91	PATIENCE	120 DAYS	30.00	53.00
91	TEA PARTY	CL	30.00	43.00
92	CAROUSEL OF DREAMS	CL	33.00	45.00
92	CATS IN THE CRADLE	120 DAYS	33.00	44.00
92	DELIGHTFUL BUNDLE	120 DAYS	35.00	51.00
92	EASTER MORNING VISITOR	120 DAYS	35.00	50.00
92	STORYBOOK MEMORIES	120 DAYS	33.00	45.00
93	ME AND MY PONY	120 DAYS	35.00	50.00
W. LOWE			**IN THE EYE OF THE STORM**	
91	FIRST STRIKE	RT	30.00	30.00
92	NIGHT FORCE	RT	30.00	30.00
92	TRACKS ACROSS THE SAND	RT	30.00	30.00
MERLI			**KING'S CHRISTMAS**	
73	ADORATION	RT	100.00	275.00
74	MADONNA	RT	150.00	250.00
75	HEAVENLY CHOIR	RT	160.00	240.00
76	SIBLINGS	RT	200.00	230.00
A. FALCHI			**KING'S FLOWERS**	
73	CARNATION	RT	85.00	200.00
74	RED ROSE	RT	100.00	215.00
75	YELLOW DAHLIA	RT	110.00	250.00
76	BLUEBELLS	RT	130.00	250.00
77	ANEMONES	RT	130.00	250.00
MERLI			**KING'S MOTHER'S DAY**	
73	DANCING GIRL	RT	100.00	230.00
74	DANCING BOY	RT	115.00	250.00
75	MOTHERLY LOVE	RT	140.00	230.00
76	MAIDEN	RT	180.00	200.00
P. JEPSON		**KINGDOM OF THE GREAT CATS**		
94	SNOWY TIGER	*	*	40.00
94	SUMMIT SANCTUARY	CL	30.00	40.00
95	OUT OF THE MIST	36 DAYS	30.00	40.00
S. SOMERVILLE			**KITTENS 'N HATS**	
94	OPENING NIGHT	CL	30.00	45.00
94	SITTING PRETTY	CL	30.00	45.00
95	LITTLE LEAGUE	48 DAYS	30.00	45.00
J. BERGSMA			**LAND OF OUR DREAMS**	
89	LAND OF NOD	19000	35.00	40.00
89	SECRET DOOR, THE	19000	35.00	40.00
89	STARS, THE	19500	35.00	40.00
89	SWING, THE	19000	35.00	40.00

YR NAME	LIMIT	ISSUE	TREND
S. KUCK	**LITTLE ANGEL PLATE COLLECTION**		
94 ANGEL OF CHARITY	CL	30.00	30.00
94 ANGEL OF JOY	CL	30.00	30.00
S. KUCK	**LITTLE PROFESSIONALS**		
82 ALL IS WELL	RT	40.00	65.00
83 TENDER LOVING CARE	RT	40.00	65.00
84 LOST AND FOUND	RT	40.00	65.00
85 READING, WRITING AND...	RT	40.00	65.00
J. BERGSMA	**MAGIC COMPANIONS**		
94 BELIEVE IN LOVE	CL	30.00	40.00
94 IMAGINE PEACE	CL	30.00	40.00
96 LIVE IN HARMONY	48 DAYS	30.00	43.00
96 TRUST IN LOVE	48 DAYS	30.00	44.00
*	**MARMOT CHRISTMAS**		
70 POLAR BEAR, FE	RT	13.00	60.00
71 AMERICAN BUFFALO	RT	14.50	40.00
71 BUFFALO BILL	RT	16.00	60.00
72 BOY AND GRANDFATHER	RT	20.00	50.00
73 SNOWMAN	RT	22.00	50.00
74 DANCING	RT	24.00	30.00
75 QUAIL	RT	30.00	40.00
76 WINDMILL	RT	40.00	50.00
*	**MARMOT FATHER'S DAY**		
70 STAG	RT	12.00	100.00
71 HORSE	RT	12.50	40.00
*	**MARMOT MOTHER'S DAY**		
72 SEAL	RT	16.00	65.00
73 BEAR WITH CUB	RT	20.00	150.00
74 PENGUINS	RT	24.00	50.00
75 RACCOONS	RT	30.00	50.00
76 DUCKS	RT	40.00	50.00
J. MCCLELLAND	**MCCLELLAND CHILDREN'S CIRCUS COLLECTION**		
82 KATIE THE TIGHTROPE WALKER	RT	30.00	50.00
82 TOMMY THE CLOWN	RT	30.00	50.00
83 JOHNNY THE STRONGMAN	RT	30.00	40.00
84 MAGGIE THE ANIMAL TRAINER	RT	30.00	65.00
M. ATTWELL	**MEMORIES OF YESTERDAY**		
93 HUSH	RT	30.00	45.00
93 I'VE BEEN PAINTING	RT	30.00	45.00
93 JUST LOOKING PRETTY	RT	30.00	45.00
93 TIME FOR BED	RT	30.00	45.00
94 GIVE IT YOUR BEST SHOT	RT	30.00	45.00
94 I PRAY THE LORD MY SOUL TO KEEP	RT	30.00	45.00
94 JUST THINKING ABOUT YOU	RT	30.00	45.00
94 WHAT WILL I GROW UP TO BE	RT	30.00	45.00
*	**MOSER CHRISTMAS**		
70 HARDCANY CASTLE	RT	75.00	175.00
71 KARLSTEIN CASTLE	RT	75.00	85.00
72 OLD TOWN HALL	RT	85.00	95.00
73 KARLOVY VARY CASTLE	RT	90.00	100.00
*	**MOSER MOTHER'S DAY**		
71 PEACOCKS	RT	75.00	150.00
72 BUTTERFLIES	RT	85.00	350.00
73 SQUIRRELS	RT	90.00	100.00
J. MCCLELLAND	**MOTHER GOOSE**		
79 MARY, MARY	RT	23.00	200.00
80 LITTLE BOY BLUE	RT	23.00	100.00
81 LITTLE MISS MUFFET	YR	25.00	60.00
82 LITTLE JACK HORNER	RT	25.00	40.00
83 LITTLE BO PEEP	YR	25.00	45.00
84 DIDDLE, DIDDLE DUMPLING	YR	25.00	35.00
85 MARY HAD A LITTLE LAMB	YR	28.00	50.00
86 JACK AND JILL	RT	28.00	50.00
J. BERGSMA	**MOTHER'S DAY COLLECTION**		
91 BEAUTY OF LIFE	*	*	49.00
92 LIFE'S BLESSING	*	*	48.00
93 MY GREATEST TREASURES	CL	35.00	50.00
94 FOREVER IN MY HEART	*	*	49.00
S. KUCK	**MOTHER'S DAY COLLECTION**		
85 ONCE UPON A TIME	RT	30.00	65.00
86 TIMES REMEMBERED	YR	30.00	65.00
87 A CHERISHED TIME	YR	30.00	50.00
88 A TIME TOGETHER	YR	30.00	60.00
95 HOME IS WHERE THE HEART IS	48 DAYS	35.00	40.00
KELLY	**NOBLE AND FREE**		
94 GATHERING STORM	CL	30.00	40.00
94 MOONLIGHT RUN	CL	30.00	40.00
94 PROTECTED JOURNEY	CL	30.00	40.00
C. MICARELLI	**NUTCRACKER BALLET**		
89 CHRISTMAS EVE PARTY	RT	35.00	50.00
90 CLARA AND HER PRINCE	CL	35.00	50.00
90 DREAM BEGINS, THE	CL	35.00	50.00
91 DANCE OF THE SNOW FAIRIES	RT	35.00	50.00
92 LAND OF SWEETS, THE	CL	35.00	50.00
92 SUGAR PLUM FAIRY, THE	CL	35.00	50.00

YR	NAME	LIMIT	ISSUE	TREND
J. PITCHER				
			ON WINGS OF EAGLES	
94	BY DAWN'S EARLY LIGHT	CL	30.00	45.00
P.D. JACKSON				
		OSCAR & BERTIE'S EDWARDIAN HOLIDAY		
91	SNAPSHOT	RT	30.00	40.00
92	EARLY RISE	RT	30.00	40.00
93	ALL ABOARD	RT	30.00	42.00
93	LEARNING TO SWIM	RT	30.00	43.00
S. BARLOWE				
			OUR CHERISHED SEAS	
91	FLIGHT OF THE DOLPHINS	CL	38.00	50.00
91	LIONS OF THE SEA	CL	38.00	50.00
91	WHALE SONG	CL	38.00	50.00
92	PALACE OF THE SEALS	CL	38.00	50.00
93	EMPERORS OF THE ICE	CL	38.00	50.00
93	ORCA BALLET	48 DAYS	38.00	45.00
93	SEA TURTLES	CL	38.00	50.00
93	SPLENDOR OF THE SEA	48 DAYS	38.00	45.00
93	TURTLE TREASURE	48 DAYS	38.00	45.00
S. KUCK				
			PLATE OF THE MONTH COLLECTION	
90	APRIL	RT	25.00	30.00
90	AUGUST	RT	25.00	30.00
90	DECEMBER	RT	25.00	30.00
90	FEBRUARY	RT	25.00	30.00
90	JANUARY	RT	25.00	30.00
90	JULY	RT	25.00	30.00
90	JUNE	RT	25.00	30.00
90	MARCH	RT	25.00	30.00
90	MAY	RT	25.00	30.00
90	NOVEMBER	RT	25.00	30.00
90	OCTOBER	RT	25.00	30.00
90	SEPTEMBER	RT	25.00	30.00
S. KUCK				
			PRECIOUS ANGELS	
94	ANGEL OF SHARING	CL	30.00	40.00
95	ANGEL OF GRACE	95 DAYS	30.00	40.00
95	ANGEL OF HAPPINESS	95 DAYS	30.00	40.00
95	ANGEL OF HOPE	CL	30.00	30.00
95	ANGEL OF LAUGHTER	95 DAYS	30.00	40.00
95	ANGEL OF LOVE	95 DAYS	30.00	40.00
95	ANGEL OF PEACE	95 DAYS	30.00	40.00
95	ANGEL OF SUNSHINE	95 DAYS	30.00	40.00
S. KUCK				
			PREMIER COLLECTION	
91	KITTEN	RT	95.00	175.00
91	PUPPY	RT	95.00	140.00
J. MCCLELLAND				
			PREMIER COLLECTION	
91	LOVE	7500	75.00	75.00
*				
69	APOLLO MOON LANDING	RT	30.00	85.00
				ROYALE
*				
			ROYALE CHRISTMAS	
69	CHRISTMAS FAIR	RT	12.00	130.00
70	VIGIL MASS	RT	13.00	110.00
71	CHRISTMAS NIGHT	RT	16.00	50.00
72	ELKS	RT	16.00	50.00
73	CHRISTMAS DOWN	RT	20.00	40.00
74	VILLAGE CHRISTMAS	RT	22.00	65.00
75	FEEDING TIME	RT	26.00	40.00
76	SEAPORT CHRISTMAS	RT	28.00	30.00
77	SLEDDING	RT	30.00	40.00
*				
			ROYALE FATHER'S DAY	
70	FRIGATE CONSTITUTION	RT	13.00	85.00
71	MAN FISHING	RT	13.00	50.00
72	MOUNTAINEER	RT	16.00	80.00
73	CAMPING	RT	18.00	50.00
74	EAGLE	RT	22.00	50.00
75	REGATTA	RT	26.00	45.00
76	HUNTING	RT	28.00	45.00
77	FISHING	RT	30.00	45.00
J. POLUSZYNSKI				
			ROYALE GAME PLATES	
72	SETTERS	RT	180.00	300.00
73	FOX	RT	200.00	375.00
W. SCHIENER				
			ROYALE GAME PLATES	
74	OSPREY	RT	250.00	360.00
75	CALIFORNIA QUAIL	RT	265.00	360.00
*				
		ROYALE GERMANIA CHRISTMAS ANNUAL		
70	ORCHID	RT	200.00	675.00
71	CYCLAMEN	RT	200.00	330.00
72	SILVER THISTLE	RT	250.00	300.00
73	TULIPS	RT	275.00	325.00
74	SUNFLOWERS	RT	300.00	350.00
75	SNOWDROPS	RT	450.00	500.00
76	FLAMING HEART	RT	450.00	500.00
*				
		ROYALE GERMANIA CRYSTAL MOTHER'S DAY		
71	ROSES	RT	135.00	675.00
72	ELEPHANT AND YOUNGSTER	RT	180.00	250.00
73	KOALA BEAR AND CUB	RT	200.00	230.00
74	SQUIRRELS	RT	240.00	250.00
75	SWAN AND YOUNG	RT	350.00	375.00

YR	NAME	LIMIT	ISSUE	TREND
*			**ROYALE MOTHER'S DAY**	
70	SWAN AND YOUNG	RT	12.00	85.00
71	DOE AND FAWN	RT	13.00	60.00
72	RABBITS	RT	16.00	40.00
73	OWL FAMILY	RT	18.00	40.00
74	DUCK AND YOUNG	RT	22.00	40.00
75	LYNX AND CUBS	RT	26.00	40.00
76	WOODCOCK AND YOUNG	RT	28.00	35.00
77	KOALA BEAR	RT	30.00	40.00
A. FAZIO			**SOPHISTICATED LADIES COLLECTION**	
85	CLEO	CL	30.00	50.00
85	FELICIA	CL	30.00	50.00
85	PHOEBE	CL	30.00	50.00
85	SAMANTHA	CL	30.00	50.00
86	BIANKA	CL	30.00	50.00
86	CERISSA	CL	30.00	50.00
86	CHELSEA	CL	30.00	50.00
86	NATASHA	CL	30.00	50.00
S. KUCK			**SPECIAL OCCASIONS**	
88	WEDDING, THE	OP	35.00	50.00
89	WEDDING DAY (6 1/2 IN.)	RT	25.00	30.00
90	SPECIAL DAY, THE	RT	25.00	30.00
92	WEDDING (BRIDE & GROOM)	*	*	43.00
C. MICARELLI			**SPECIAL OCCASIONS-WEDDING**	
91	FROM THIS DAY FORWARD (6 1/2 IN.)	RT	25.00	30.00
91	FROM THIS DAY FORWARD (9 1/2 IN.)	OP	35.00	40.00
91	TO HAVE AND TO HOLD (6 1/2 IN.)	RT	25.00	30.00
91	TO HAVE AND TO HOLD (9 1/2 IN.)	OP	35.00	40.00
T. UTZ			**SPRINGTIME OF LIFE**	
85	TEDDY'S BATHTIME	CL	30.00	60.00
86	AMONG THE DAFFODILS	CL	30.00	60.00
86	AUNT TILLIE'S HATS	CL	30.00	60.00
86	GRANNY'S BOOTS	CL	30.00	60.00
86	JUST LIKE MOMMY	CL	30.00	60.00
86	LITTLE EMILY	CL	30.00	60.00
86	MY FAVORITE DOLLS	CL	30.00	60.00
86	MY MASTERPIECE	CL	30.00	60.00
S. KUCK			**SUGAR & SPICE**	
93	BEST FRIENDS	CL	30.00	45.00
93	SISTERS	CL	30.00	40.00
94	GARDEN OF SUNSHINE	CL	35.00	40.00
94	LITTLE ONE	CL	33.00	45.00
94	MORNING PRAYERS	CL	33.00	40.00
94	TEDDY BEAR TALES	CL	33.00	40.00
95	A SPECIAL DAY	95 DAYS	35.00	50.00
95	FIRST SNOW	95 DAYS	35.00	50.00
S. KUCK			**TIDINGS OF JOY**	
92	PEACE ON EARTH	RT	35.00	50.00
93	REJOICE	RT	35.00	50.00
94	NOEL	RT	35.00	40.00
J. BERGSMA			**TOTEMS OF THE WEST**	
94	PEACE AT LAST	CL	30.00	40.00
94	WATCHMEN, THE	CL	30.00	40.00
96	NEVER ALONE	96 DAYS	35.00	45.00
S. BARLOWE			**TOWN AND COUNTRY DOGS**	
90	FOX HUNT	CL	35.00	48.00
91	GOLDEN FIELDS (GOLDEN RETRIEVER)	CL	35.00	48.00
91	RETRIEVAL, THE	CL	35.00	48.00
93	FAITHFUL COMPANIONS	36 DAYS	35.00	53.00
R. JOHNSON			**TRAINS OF THE ORIENT**	
93	GOLDEN ARROW-ENGLAND, THE	RT	30.00	40.00
94	AUSTRIA	RT	30.00	40.00
94	BAVARIA	RT	30.00	40.00
94	FRANCE	RT	30.00	40.00
94	FRANKONIA	RT	30.00	40.00
94	GREECE	RT	30.00	40.00
94	RUMANIA	RT	30.00	40.00
94	TURKEY	RT	30.00	40.00
J. MCCLELLAND			**TREASURED SONGS OF CHILDHOOD**	
88	A TISKET, A TASKET	RT	30.00	40.00
88	BAA, BAA, BLACK SHEEP	RT	33.00	50.00
88	TWINKLE, TWINKLE, LITTLE STAR	RT	30.00	40.00
89	I'M A LITTLE TEAPOT	RT	33.00	40.00
89	PAT-A-CAKE	CL	35.00	50.00
89	RAIN, RAIN GO AWAY	RT	33.00	45.00
89	ROUND THE MULBERRY BUSH	CL	33.00	45.00
90	HUSH LITTLE BABY	CL	35.00	50.00
S. BARLOWE			**VANISHING ANIMAL KINGDOMS**	
86	OLEPI THE BUFFALO	21500	35.00	63.00
86	RAMA THE TIGER	21500	35.00	63.00
87	COOLIBAH THE KOALA	21500	35.00	63.00
87	ORTWIN THE DEER	21500	35.00	63.00
87	YEN-POH THE PANDA	21500	35.00	63.00
88	MAMAKUU THE ELEPHANT	21500	35.00	63.00
S. KUCK			**VICTORIAN CHRISTMAS**	
95	DEAR SANTA	72 DAYS	35.00	42.00
96	NIGHT BEFORE CHRISTMAS	72 DAYS	35.00	42.00

YR	NAME	LIMIT	ISSUE	TREND
S. KUCK			**VICTORIAN MOTHER'S DAY**	
89	MOTHER'S SUNSHINE	RT	35.00	65.00
90	REFLECTION OF LOVE	RT	35.00	65.00
91	A PRECIOUS TIME	RT	35.00	60.00
91	BOUQUETS OF LOVE	YR	35.00	40.00
92	LOVING TOUCH	RT	35.00	40.00
E. BERKE			**WESTERN**	
74	MOUNTAIN MAN	RT	165.00	250.00
C. CORCILIUS			**WOMEN OF THE PLAINS**	
94	NO BOUNDARIES	CL	30.00	50.00
94	PRIDE OF A MAIDEN	CL	30.00	50.00
95	SILENT COMPANIONS	36 DAYS	35.00	49.00
J. MCCLELLAND			**WONDER OF CHRISTMAS**	
91	MY FAVORITE ORNAMENT	RT	30.00	50.00
91	SANTA'S SECRET	RT	30.00	50.00
92	WAITING FOR SANTA	RT	30.00	50.00
93	CANDELIGHT CHRISTMAS	RT	30.00	50.00
93	CAROLER, THE	RT	30.00	50.00
J. MCCLELLAND			**WORLD OF CHILDREN**	
77	RAINY DAY FUN	10000	50.00	60.00
78	WHEN I GROW UP	15000	50.00	60.00
79	YOU'RE INVITED	15000	50.00	60.00
80	KITTENS FOR SALE	15000	50.00	60.00

REECE
*

YR	NAME	LIMIT	ISSUE	TREND
			WATERFOWL	
73	MALLARDS & WOOD DUCKS (PAIR)	900	250.00	375.00
74	CANVASBACK & CANADIAN GEESE (PAIR)	900	250.00	375.00
75	PINTAILS & TEAL (PAIR)	900	250.00	425.00

REED & BARTON
AUDUBON

YR	NAME	LIMIT	ISSUE	TREND
			AUDUBON	
70	PINE SISKIN	5000	60.00	175.00
71	RED-SHOULDERED HAWK	5000	60.00	100.00
72	STILT SANDPIPER	5000	60.00	100.00
73	RED CARDINAL	5000	60.00	100.00
74	BOREAL CHICKADEE	5000	65.00	100.00
75	YELLOW-BREASTED CHAT	5000	65.00	100.00
76	BAY-BREASTED WARBLER	5000	65.00	100.00
77	PURPLE FINCH	5000	65.00	100.00
J. DOWNING			**TWAS THE NIGHT BEFORE CHRISTMAS**	
89	'TWAS THE NIGHT BEFORE CHRISTMAS	4000	75.00	85.00
90	VISIONS OF SUGARPLUMS	3500	75.00	85.00
91	AWAY TO THE WINDOW	3500	74.00	79.00

RHODES STUDIO
*

YR	NAME	LIMIT	ISSUE	TREND
			BOUNTIFUL HARVEST	
92	BASKET FULL OF APPLES	CL	39.00	50.00
92	BUSHEL OF PEACHES	CL	39.00	50.00
93	FRESH OFF THE PLUM TREE	CL	39.00	50.00
93	PEARS FROM THE GROVE	CL	39.00	75.00
*			**LEGENDARY STEAM TRAINS**	
89	AMERICAN STANDARD 4-4-0	CL	65.00	89.00
90	BEST FRIEND/CHARLESTON 0-4-OT	CL	70.00	110.00
90	CHALLENGER CLASS, THE 4-6-6-4	CL	70.00	110.00
90	HUDSON J3 STREAMLINER 4-6-4	CL	65.00	92.00
91	K-28, THE- 2-8-2	CL	70.00	100.00
91	K4 CLASS, THE- 4-6-2	CL	70.00	125.00
*			**MIRACLES OF LIGHT**	
92	NATIVITY OF HOPE	CL	90.00	100.00
92	NATIVITY OF JOY	CL	90.00	100.00
92	NATIVITY OF LOVE	CL	85.00	100.00
92	NATIVITY OF PEACE	CL	85.00	100.00
93	NATIVITY OF FAITH	CL	90.00	100.00
93	NATIVITY OF PRAISE	CL	90.00	100.00
*			**TREASURES OF THE DORE BIBLE**	
86	MOSES/TEN COMMANDMENTS	CL	59.00	90.00
87	JACOB AND THE ANGEL	CL	59.00	90.00
87	REBEKAH AT THE WELL	CL	64.00	90.00
88	DANIEL IN THE LION'S DEN	CL	64.00	90.00
88	ELIJAH AND/CHARIOT OF FIRE	CL	64.00	100.00
88	JUDGMENT OF SOLOMON	CL	64.00	90.00
*			**VILLAGE LIGHTS**	
93	CHURCH AT THE BEND	CL	54.00	65.00
93	EVERGREEN BOOKS	CL	54.00	65.00
93	HOLLY STREET BAKERY	CL	49.00	60.00
93	KRINGLE'S GENERAL STORE	CL	54.00	65.00
93	MISTLETOE TOY SHOP	CL	49.00	60.00
93	MRS. SUGARPLUM'S CHOCOLATES	CL	54.00	65.00
*			**WATERFOWL LEGACY**	
91	MALLARD'S DESCENT	CL	69.00	80.00
92	IN FLIGHT	CL	69.00	75.00
92	TAKING OFF	CL	74.00	70.00
92	WIND RIDERS	CL	74.00	70.00
93	FLYING IN	CL	74.00	70.00
93	RISING UP	CL	74.00	70.00

YR NAME	LIMIT	ISSUE	TREND

RICHARD DI SILVIO STUDIO
R. DISILVIO

92 COLUMBUS DISCOVERY OF AMERICA	2000	30.00	30.00

R. DISILVIO — **PANTHEON OF COMPOSERS**

92 GIACOMO PUCCINI	YR	30.00	30.00
92 GIOACCHINO ROSSINI	YR	30.00	30.00
92 LUDWIG VAN BEETHOVEN	YR	30.00	30.00
92 WOLFGANG A. MOZART	YR	30.00	30.00
93 FRANZ LISZT	YR	30.00	30.00
93 GIUSEPPE VERDI	YR	30.00	30.00
93 PETER TEHACKOVSKY	YR	30.00	30.00
93 RICHARD WAGNER	YR	30.00	30.00

R. DISILVIO — **WEDDING COLLECTION**

93 KISS OF ETERNAL LOVE	10000	30.00	30.00

RIVER SHORE
R. BROWN — **BABY ANIMALS**

79 AKIKU	20000	50.00	75.00
80 ROOSEVELT	20000	50.00	90.00
81 CLOVER	20000	50.00	70.00
82 ZUELA	20000	50.00	70.00

ROCKWELL/ BROWN — **FAMOUS AMERICANS**

76 BROWN'S LINCOLN	9500	40.00	600.00
77 ROCKWELL'S TRIPLE SELF-PORTRAIT	9500	45.00	180.00
78 PEACE CORPS	9500	45.00	100.00
79 SPIRIT OF LINDBERGH	9500	50.00	85.00

N. ROCKWELL — **FOUR FREEDOMS**

81 FREEDOM OF SPEECH	17000	65.00	85.00
82 FREEDOM FROM FEAR	17000	65.00	65.00
82 FREEDOM FROM WANT	17000	65.00	65.00
82 FREEDOM OF WORSHIP	17000	65.00	75.00

E. CHRISTOPHERSON — **LITTLE HOUSE ON THE PRAIRIE**

85 A BELL FOR WALNUT GROVE	10 DAYS	30.00	60.00
85 CAROLINE'S EGGS	10 DAYS	30.00	60.00
85 FOUNDER'S DAY PICNIC	10 DAYS	30.00	60.00
85 INGALLS FAMILY	10 DAYS	30.00	60.00
85 MARY'S GIFT	10 DAYS	30.00	60.00
85 MEDICINE SHOW	10 DAYS	30.00	60.00
85 SWEETHEART TREE, THE	10 DAYS	30.00	60.00
85 WOMEN'S HARVEST	10 DAYS	30.00	60.00

M. HAGUE — **LOVABLE TEDDIES**

85 BEARLY FRIGHTFUL	10 DAYS	22.00	50.00
85 BEDTIME BLUES	10 DAYS	22.00	50.00
85 CAUGHT IN THE ACT	10 DAYS	22.00	50.00
85 FIRESIDE FRIENDS	10 DAYS	22.00	50.00
85 HARVEST TIME	10 DAYS	22.00	50.00
85 MISSED A BUTTON	10 DAYS	22.00	50.00
85 SUNDAY STROLL	10 DAYS	22.00	50.00
85 TENDER LOVING BEAR	10 DAYS	22.00	50.00

N. ROCKWELL — **NORMAN ROCKWELL SINGLE ISSUE**

79 SPRING FLOWERS	17000	75.00	150.00
80 LOOKING OUT TO SEA	17000	75.00	140.00
82 GRANDPA'S GUARDIAN	17000	80.00	75.00
82 GRANDPA'S TREASURES	17000	80.00	75.00

J. LAMB — **PUPPY PLAYTIME**

87 DOUBLE TAKE	14 DAYS	25.00	75.00
87 FUN AND GAMES	14 DAYS	25.00	50.00
88 A NEW LEASH ON LIFE	14 DAYS	25.00	50.00
88 CABIN FEVER	14 DAYS	25.00	50.00
88 CATCH OF THE DAY	14 DAYS	25.00	50.00
88 GETTING ACQUAINTED	14 DAYS	25.00	50.00
88 HANGING OUT	14 DAYS	25.00	50.00
88 WEEKEND GARDENER	14 DAYS	25.00	50.00

HICKS — **SIGNS OF LOVE**

81 A KISS FOR MOTHER	CL	19.00	30.00
81 A WATCHFUL EYE	CL	22.00	30.00
82 A GENTLE PERSUASION	CL	24.00	30.00
83 A PROTECTIVE EMBRACE	CL	24.00	40.00
83 A TENDER COAXING	CL	24.00	100.00
84 A REASSURING TOUCH	CL	24.00	30.00
85 A LOVING GUIDANCE	CL	27.00	40.00
85 A TRUSTING HUG	CL	27.00	40.00

ROCKWELL SOCIETY
N. ROCKWELL — **CHRISTMAS**

74 SCOTTY GETS HIS TREE	YR	25.00	90.00
75 ANGEL WITH BLACK EYE	YR	25.00	34.00
76 GOLDEN CHRISTMAS	YR	25.00	35.00
77 TOY SHOP WINDOW	YR	25.00	25.00
78 CHRISTMAS DREAM	YR	25.00	30.00
79 SOMEBODY'S UP THERE	YR	25.00	30.00
80 SCOTTY PLAYS SANTA	YR	25.00	28.00
81 WRAPPED UP IN CHRISTMAS	YR	26.00	26.00
82 CHRISTMAS COURTSHIP	YR	26.00	26.00
83 SANTA IN THE SUBWAY	YR	26.00	26.00
84 SANTA IN THE WORKSHOP	YR	28.00	28.00
85 GRANDPA PLAYS SANTA	YR	28.00	28.00

YR	NAME	LIMIT	ISSUE	TREND
86	DEAR SANTY CLAUS	YR	28.00	27.00
87	SANTA'S GOLDEN GIFT	YR	30.00	30.00
88	SANTA CLAUS	YR	30.00	30.00
89	JOLLY OLD ST. NICK	YR	30.00	30.00
90	A CHRISTMAS PRAYER	YR	30.00	30.00
91	SANTA'S HELPERS	YR	33.00	33.00
92	CHRISTMAS SURPRISE, THE	YR	33.00	44.00
93	TREE BRIGADE, THE	YR	33.00	39.00
94	CHRISTMAS MARVEL	YR	33.00	50.00

N. ROCKWELL — **COLONIALS-THE RAREST ROCKWELLS**

YR	NAME	LIMIT	ISSUE	TREND
85	UNEXPECTED PROPOSAL	CL	28.00	28.00
86	LIGHT FOR THE WINTER	CL	31.00	38.00
86	WORDS OF COMFORT	CL	28.00	28.00
87	CLINCHING THE DEAL	CL	31.00	31.00
87	JOURNEY HOME, THE	CL	31.00	31.00
87	PORTRAIT FOR A BRIDEGROOM	CL	31.00	31.00
88	SIGN OF THE TIMES	CL	33.00	33.00
88	YE GLUTTON	CL	33.00	33.00

N. ROCKWELL — **COMING OF AGE**

YR	NAME	LIMIT	ISSUE	TREND
90	A NEW LOOK	CL	33.00	35.00
90	BACK TO SCHOOL	CL	30.00	30.00
90	HER FIRST FORMAL	CL	33.00	40.00
90	HOME FROM CAMP	CL	30.00	30.00
90	MUSCLEMAN, THE	CL	33.00	33.00
91	A BALCONY SEAT	CL	33.00	33.00
91	DOORWAY TO THE PAST	CL	35.00	49.00
91	MEN ABOUT TOWN	CL	35.00	35.00
91	PATHS OF GLORY	CL	35.00	35.00
91	SCHOOL'S OUT!	CL	35.00	60.00

N. ROCKWELL — **GOLDEN MOMENTS**

YR	NAME	LIMIT	ISSUE	TREND
87	GRANDMA'S LOVE	CL	20.00	44.00
87	GRANDPA'S GIFT	CL	20.00	50.00
88	BEST FRIENDS	CL	23.00	40.00
88	END OF DAY	CL	23.00	40.00
89	EVENING'S REPOSE	CL	25.00	50.00
89	KEEPING COMPANY	CL	25.00	40.00
89	LOVE LETTERS	CL	23.00	40.00
89	NEWFOUND WORLDS	CL	23.00	50.00

N. ROCKWELL — **HERITAGE**

YR	NAME	LIMIT	ISSUE	TREND
77	TOY MAKER	YR	14.50	175.00
78	COBBLER	YR	20.00	75.00
79	LIGHTHOUSE KEEPER'S DAUGHTER	YR	20.00	75.00
80	SHIP BUILDER	YR	20.00	65.00
81	MUSIC MAKER	YR	20.00	45.00
82	TYCOON	YR	20.00	40.00
83	PAINTER	YR	20.00	40.00
84	STORYTELLER	YR	20.00	45.00
85	GOURMET	YR	20.00	35.00
86	PROFESSOR	YR	23.00	40.00
87	SHADOW ARTIST	YR	23.00	40.00
88	BANJO PLAYER, THE	YR	23.00	40.00
88	VETERAN, THE	YR	23.00	40.00
90	OLD SCOUT, THE	YR	25.00	40.00
91	FAMILY DOCTOR, THE	YR	28.00	50.00
91	YOUNG SCHOLAR, THE	YR	25.00	40.00
93	HALLOWEEN FROLIC	YR	28.00	64.00
93	JEWELER	YR	28.00	49.00
95	APPRENTICE	YR	30.00	50.00
97	DREAMER	YR	*	50.00

N. ROCKWELL — **INNOCENCE & EXPERIENCE**

YR	NAME	LIMIT	ISSUE	TREND
91	AMERICAN HEROES, THE	150 DAYS	33.00	40.00
91	MAGICIAN, THE	150 DAYS	33.00	40.00
91	RADIO OPERATOR, THE	150 DAYS	30.00	40.00
91	SEA CAPTAIN, THE	150 DAYS	30.00	40.00

N. ROCKWELL — **MIND OF HER OWN**

YR	NAME	LIMIT	ISSUE	TREND
86	SITTING PRETTY	CL	25.00	40.00
87	BREAKING THE RULES	CL	28.00	40.00
87	GOOD INTENTIONS	CL	28.00	40.00
87	SERIOUS BUSINESS	CL	25.00	40.00
88	KISS AND TELL	CL	30.00	40.00
88	ON MY HONOR	CL	30.00	40.00
88	SECOND THOUGHTS	CL	28.00	40.00
88	WORLD'S AWAY	CL	28.00	40.00

N. ROCKWELL — **MOTHER'S DAY**

YR	NAME	LIMIT	ISSUE	TREND
76	A MOTHER'S LOVE	YR	25.00	125.00
77	FAITH	YR	25.00	80.00
78	BEDTIME	YR	25.00	40.00
79	REFLECTIONS	YR	25.00	40.00
80	A MOTHER'S PRIDE	YR	25.00	35.00
81	AFTER THE PARTY	YR	25.00	35.00
82	COOKING LESSON, THE	YR	26.00	75.00
83	ADD TWO CUPS AND LOVE	YR	26.00	35.00
84	GRANDMA'S COURTING DRESS	YR	26.00	35.00
85	MENDING TIME	YR	28.00	35.00
86	PANTRY RAID	YR	28.00	40.00
87	GRANDMA'S SURPRISE	YR	30.00	40.00
88	MY MOTHER	YR	30.00	40.00
89	SUNDAY DINNER	YR	30.00	40.00

YR	NAME	LIMIT	ISSUE	TREND
90	EVENING PRAYERS	YR	30.00	40.00
91	BUILDING OUR FUTURE	YR	33.00	40.00
91	GENTLE REASSURANCE	YR	33.00	40.00
92	A SPECIAL DELIVERY	YR	33.00	40.00
N. ROCKWELL			**ROCKWELL ON TOUR**	
83	PROMENADE A PARIS	CL	16.00	20.00
83	WALKING THROUGH MERRIE ENGLANDE	CL	16.00	30.00
83	WHEN IN ROME	CL	16.00	20.00
84	WALK ON THE RHINE	CL	16.00	30.00
N. ROCKWELL			**ROCKWELL'S AMERICAN DREAM**	
85	A COUPLE'S COMMITMENT	CL	20.00	40.00
85	A FAMILY'S FULL MEASURE	CL	23.00	34.00
85	A YOUNG GIRL'S DREAM	CL	20.00	60.00
86	A MOTHER'S WELCOME	CL	23.00	30.00
86	MUSICIAN'S MAGIC, THE	CL	23.00	50.00
86	YOUNG MAN'S DREAM	CL	23.00	40.00
87	AN ORPHAN'S HOPE	CL	25.00	40.00
87	LOVE'S REWARD	CL	25.00	50.00
N. ROCKWELL			**ROCKWELL'S CHRISTMAS LEGACY**	
93	FILLING EVERY STOCKING (3D)	*	*	70.00
93	SANTA'S MAGICAL VIEW (3D)	*	*	70.00
N. ROCKWELL			**ROCKWELL'S LIGHT CAMPAIGN**	
83	THIS IS THE ROOM THAT LIGHT MADE	CL	20.00	80.00
84	BIRTHDAY WISH, THE	CL	22.00	35.00
84	CLOSE HARMONY	CL	22.00	30.00
84	EVENING'S EASE	CL	20.00	35.00
84	FATHER'S HELP	CL	20.00	20.00
84	GRANDPA'S TREASURE CHEST	CL	20.00	20.00
N. ROCKWELL			**ROCKWELL'S REDISCOVERED WOMEN**	
*	COMPLETE COLLECTION	100 DAYS	267.00	267.00
84	CONFIDING IN THE DEN	CL	23.00	23.00
84	DREAMING IN THE ATTIC	CL	20.00	20.00
84	FLIRTING IN THE PARLOR	CL	23.00	30.00
84	GOSSIPING IN THE ALCOVE	CL	23.00	23.00
84	MAKING BELIEVE AT THE MIRROR	CL	23.00	25.00
84	MEETING ON THE PATH	CL	23.00	23.00
84	PONDERING ON THE PORCH	CL	23.00	23.00
84	REMINISCING IN THE QUIET	CL	23.00	23.00
84	STANDING IN THE DOORWAY	CL	23.00	25.00
84	WAITING AT THE DANCE	CL	23.00	25.00
84	WAITING ON THE SHORE	CL	23.00	23.00
84	WORKING IN THE KITCHEN	CL	23.00	23.00
N. ROCKWELL			**ROCKWELL'S THE ONES WE LOVE**	
88	TENDER LOVING CARE	CL	20.00	35.00
89	A TIME TO KEEP	CL	20.00	27.00
89	GROWING STRONG	CL	23.00	23.00
89	INVENTOR AND THE JUDGE, THE	CL	23.00	30.00
89	READY FOR THE WORLD	CL	23.00	23.00
90	COUNTRY DOCTOR, THE	CL	25.00	25.00
90	HOMECOMING, THE	CL	25.00	22.00
90	OUR LOVE OF COUNTRY	CL	25.00	25.00
90	STORY HOUR, THE	CL	23.00	24.00
91	A HELPING HAND	CL	25.00	25.00
N. ROCKWELL			**ROCKWELL'S TREASURED MEMORIES**	
91	EVENING PASSAGE	CL	33.00	33.00
91	HEAVENLY DREAMS	OP	33.00	33.00
91	QUIET REFLECTIONS	CL	30.00	15.00
91	ROMANTIC REVERIE	CL	30.00	30.00
91	SENTIMENTAL SHORES	OP	33.00	35.00
91	TENDER ROMANCE	CL	33.00	33.00

ROMAN INC.

A. WILLIAMS			**ABBIE WILLIAMS COLLECTION**	
91	BLESS THE CHILD	OP	30.00	30.00
91	LEGACY OF LOVE	OP	30.00	30.00
I. SPENCER			**CATNIPPERS**	
86	CHRISTMAS MOURNING	9500	35.00	35.00
92	HAPPY HOLIDAZE	9500	35.00	35.00
F. HOOK			**CHILD'S PLAY**	
82	BREEZY DAY	CL	30.00	35.00
82	KITE FLYING	CL	30.00	35.00
84	BATHTUB SAILOR	CL	30.00	35.00
84	FIRST SNOW, THE	CL	30.00	35.00
F. HOOK			**CHILD'S WORLD**	
80	LITTLE CHILDREN, COME TO ME	15000	45.00	65.00
E. SIMONETTI			**FONTANINI ANNUAL CHRISTMAS PLATE**	
86	A KING IS BORN	YR	60.00	60.00
87	O COME, LET US ADORE HIM	YR	60.00	65.00
88	ADORATION OF THE MAGI	YR	70.00	75.00
89	FLIGHT INTO EGYPT	YR	75.00	85.00
F. HOOK			**FRANCES HOOK COLLECTION-SET I**	
82	BABY BLOSSOMS	15000	25.00	75.00
82	DAISY DREAMER	15000	25.00	75.00
82	I WISH, I WISH	15000	25.00	75.00
82	TREES SO TALL	15000	25.00	75.00
F. HOOK			**FRANCES HOOK COLLECTION-SET II**	
83	CAN I KEEP HIM	15000	25.00	50.00

YR	NAME	LIMIT	ISSUE	TREND
83	CAUGHT IT MYSELF	15000	25.00	50.00
83	SO CUDDLY	15000	25.00	50.00
83	WINTER WRAPPINGS	15000	25.00	50.00

F. HOOK   **FRANCES HOOK LEGACY**

YR	NAME	LIMIT	ISSUE	TREND
86	WONDERMENT	CL	23.00	33.00

A. WILLIAMS   **GOD BLESS YOU, LITTLE ONE**

YR	NAME	LIMIT	ISSUE	TREND
91	BABY'S FIRST BIRTHDAY (BOY)	OP	30.00	30.00
91	BABY'S FIRST BIRTHDAY (GIRL)	OP	30.00	30.00
91	BABY'S FIRST SMILE	OP	20.00	20.00
91	BABY'S FIRST STEP	OP	20.00	20.00
91	BABY'S FIRST TOOTH	OP	20.00	20.00
91	BABY'S FIRST WORD	OP	20.00	20.00

G. PETTY   **ICE CAPADES CLOWN**

YR	NAME	LIMIT	ISSUE	TREND
83	PRESENTING FREDDIE TRENKLER	CL	25.00	35.00

A. WILLIAMS   **LORD'S PRAYER**

YR	NAME	LIMIT	ISSUE	TREND
86	AS WE FORGIVE	CL	25.00	30.00
86	DELIVER US FROM EVIL	CL	25.00	30.00
86	FORGIVE OUR TRESPASSES	CL	25.00	30.00
86	GIVE US THIS DAY	CL	25.00	30.00
86	LEAD US NOT	CL	25.00	30.00
86	OUR FATHER	CL	25.00	30.00
86	THINE IS THE KINGDOM	CL	25.00	30.00
86	THY KINGDOM COME	CL	25.00	30.00

A. WILLIAMS   **LOVE'S PRAYER**

YR	NAME	LIMIT	ISSUE	TREND
88	LOVE BELIEVES ALL THINGS	CL	30.00	35.00
88	LOVE DOES NOT INSIST ON ITS OWN WAY	CL	30.00	35.00
88	LOVE IS NEVER ARROGANT OR RUDE	CL	30.00	35.00
88	LOVE IS NEVER IRRITABLE OR RESENTFUL	CL	30.00	35.00
88	LOVE IS NEVER JEALOUS OR BOASTFUL	CL	30.00	35.00
88	LOVE IS PATIENT AND KIND	CL	30.00	35.00
88	LOVE NEVER ENDS	CL	30.00	35.00
88	LOVE REJOICES IN THE RIGHT	CL	30.00	35.00

A. WILLIAMS   **MAGIC OF CHILDHOOD**

YR	NAME	LIMIT	ISSUE	TREND
85	BEST BUDDIES	CL	25.00	35.00
85	FEEDING TIME	CL	25.00	30.00
85	GETTING ACQUAINTED	CL	25.00	30.00
85	SPECIAL FRIENDS	CL	25.00	30.00
86	A HANDFUL OF LOVE	CL	25.00	30.00
86	LAST ONE IN	CL	25.00	30.00
86	LOOK ALIKES	CL	25.00	30.00
86	NO FAIR PEEKING	CL	25.00	30.00

G. DELLE NOTTI   **MASTERPIECE COLLECTION**

YR	NAME	LIMIT	ISSUE	TREND
81	HOLY FAMILY, THE	5000	95.00	115.00

R. FERRUZZI   **MASTERPIECE COLLECTION**

YR	NAME	LIMIT	ISSUE	TREND
82	MADONNA OF THE STREETS	5000	85.00	100.00

F. LIPPE   **MASTERPIECE COLLECTION**

YR	NAME	LIMIT	ISSUE	TREND
79	ADORATION	5000	65.00	75.00

P. MIGNARD   **MASTERPIECE COLLECTION**

YR	NAME	LIMIT	ISSUE	TREND
80	MADONNA WITH GRAPES	5000	88.00	100.00

M.J. DORCY   **MILLENIUM COLLECTION**

YR	NAME	LIMIT	ISSUE	TREND
92	SILENT NIGHT	2000	50.00	50.00
93	ANNUNCIATION	5000	50.00	50.00
94	PEACE ON EARTH	5000	50.00	50.00
95	CAUSE OF OUR JOY	7500	50.00	50.00
96	PRINCE OF PEACE	15000	50.00	50.00
97	GENTLE LOVE	YR	50.00	50.00

A. WILLIAMS   **PRECIOUS CHILDREN**

YR	NAME	LIMIT	ISSUE	TREND
93	BLESS BABY BROTHER	*	30.00	30.00
93	BLOWING BUBBLES	*	30.00	30.00
93	DON'T WORRY, MOTHER DUCK	*	30.00	30.00
93	LET'S SAY GRACE	*	30.00	30.00
93	MOTHER'S LITTLE ANGEL	*	30.00	30.00
93	PICKING DAISIES	*	30.00	30.00
93	TEA PARTY, THE	*	30.00	30.00
93	TREETOP DISCOVERY	*	30.00	30.00

G. PETTY   **PRETTY GIRLS OF THE ICE CAPADES**

YR	NAME	LIMIT	ISSUE	TREND
83	ICE PRINCESS	CL	25.00	35.00

*   **PROMISE OF A SAVIOR**

YR	NAME	LIMIT	ISSUE	TREND
93	A CHILD IS BORN	CL	30.00	30.00

R.J. ZOLAN   **RICHARD JUDSON ZOLAN COLLECTION**

YR	NAME	LIMIT	ISSUE	TREND
92	BUTTERFLY NET, THE	CL	30.00	30.00
94	RING, THE	CL	30.00	30.00
94	TERRACE DANCING	CL	30.00	30.00
95	CHILDHOOD DREAMS	OP	7.50	8.00
95	VISIT, THE	OP	7.50	8.00

*   **ROMAN CATS**

YR	NAME	LIMIT	ISSUE	TREND
84	GRIZABELLA	CL	30.00	35.00
84	MR. MISTOFFELEES	CL	30.00	35.00
84	RUM RUM TUGGER	CL	30.00	35.00

F. HOOK   **ROMAN MEMORIAL**

YR	NAME	LIMIT	ISSUE	TREND
84	CARPENTER, THE	YR	100.00	140.00

FARO STUDIOS   **SERAPHIM CLASSICS FARO COLLECTION PLATES**

YR	NAME	LIMIT	ISSUE	TREND
94	ROSALYN-RAREST OF HEAVEN	CL	65.00	65.00
95	HELENA-HEAVEN'S HERALD	CL	65.00	65.00
96	FLORA-FLOWER OF HEAVEN	CL	65.00	65.00

YR	NAME	LIMIT	ISSUE	TREND
97	EMILY-HEAVEN'S TREASURE	CL	65.00	65.00
98	ELISE-HEAVEN'S GLORY	YR	65.00	65.00
SERAPHIM STUDIO		**SERAPHIM CLASSICS OVAL PLATES**		
96	CYMBELINE-PEACEMAKER	TL	50.00	50.00
96	ISABEL-GENTLE SPIRIT	TL	50.00	50.00
96	LYDIA-WINGED POET	TL	50.00	50.00
96	PRISCILLA-BENEVOLENT GUIDE	TL	50.00	50.00
A. WILLIAMS			**SINGLE RELEASES**	
87	CHRISTENING, THE	OP	30.00	30.00
90	DEDICATION, THE	OP	30.00	30.00
I. SPENCER			**SWEETEST SONGS**	
86	A BABY'S PRAYER	CL	40.00	45.00
86	THIS LITTLE PIGGIE	CL	40.00	45.00
88	LONG, LONG AGO	CL	40.00	45.00
89	ROCKABYE	CL	40.00	45.00
B. SARGENT			**TENDER EXPRESSIONS**	
92	THOUGHTS OF YOU ARE IN MY HEART	CL	30.00	30.00

RORSTRAND

YR	NAME	LIMIT	ISSUE	TREND
G. NYLUND				**CHRISTMAS**
68	BRINGING HOME THE TREE	YR	12.00	510.00
69	FISHERMAN SAILING HOME	YR	13.50	50.00
70	NILS WITH HIS GEESE	YR	13.50	50.00
71	NILS IN LAPLAND	YR	15.00	20.00
72	DALECARLIAN FIDDLER	YR	15.00	20.00
73	FARM IN SMALAND	YR	16.00	60.00
74	VADSLENA	YR	19.00	40.00
75	NILS IN VASTMANLAND	YR	20.00	35.00
76	NILS IN UAPLAND	YR	20.00	40.00
77	NILS IN VARMLAND	YR	30.00	30.00
78	NILS IN FJALLBACKA	YR	33.00	50.00
79	NILS IN VAESTERGOETLAND	YR	39.00	39.00
80	NILS IN HALLAND	YR	55.00	65.00
81	NILS IN GOTLAND	YR	55.00	45.00
82	NILS AT SKANSEN	YR	48.00	40.00
83	NILS IN OLAND	YR	43.00	55.00
84	ANGERMAN LAND	YR	43.00	35.00
85	NILS IN JAMTLAND	YR	43.00	65.00
86	NILS IN KARLSKR	YR	43.00	50.00
87	DALSLAND, FORGET-ME-NOT	YR	48.00	150.00
88	NILS IN HALSINGLAND	YR	55.00	60.00
89	NILS VISITS GOTHENBORG	YR	60.00	60.00
A. WILLIAMS				**CHRISTMAS**
90	NILS IN KVIKKJOKK	YR	75.00	75.00
91	NILS IN MEDELPAD	YR	85.00	85.00
92	GASTRIKLAND, LILY OF THE VALLEY	YR	93.00	93.00
93	NARKE'S CASTLE	YR	93.00	93.00

ROSENTHAL

YR	NAME	LIMIT	ISSUE	TREND
*				**CHRISTMAS**
10	WINTER PEACE	YR	*	575.00
11	THREE WISE MEN	YR	*	350.00
12	STARDUST	YR	*	265.00
13	CHRISTMAS LIGHTS	YR	*	250.00
14	CHRISTMAS SONG	YR	*	350.00
15	WALKING TO CHURCH	YR	*	190.00
16	CHRISTMAS DURING WAR	YR	*	240.00
17	ANGEL OF PEACE	YR	*	210.00
18	PEACE ON EARTH	YR	*	210.00
19	ST. CHRISTOPHER WITH CHRIST CHILD	YR	*	225.00
20	MANGER IN BETHLEHEM	YR	*	350.00
21	CHRISTMAS IN MOUNTAINS	YR	*	210.00
22	ADVENT BRANCH	YR	*	210.00
23	CHILDREN IN WINTER WOODS	YR	*	210.00
24	DEER IN THE WOODS	YR	*	210.00
25	THREE WISE MEN	YR	*	210.00
26	CHRISTMAS IN MOUNTAINS	YR	*	200.00
27	STATION ON THE WAY	YR	*	210.00
28	CHALET CHRISTMAS	YR	*	200.00
29	CHRISTMAS IN ALPS	YR	*	225.00
30	GROUP OF DEER UNDER PINES	YR	*	225.00
31	PATH OF THE MAGI	YR	*	225.00
32	CHRIST CHILD	YR	*	200.00
33	THRU THE NIGHT TO LIGHT	YR	*	200.00
34	CHRISTMAS PEACE	YR	*	200.00
35	CHRISTMAS BY THE SEA	YR	*	200.00
36	NURNBERG ANGELS	YR	*	200.00
37	BERCHTESGADEN	YR	*	200.00
38	CHRISTMAS IN THE ALPS	YR	*	200.00
39	SCHNEEKOPPE MOUNTAIN	YR	*	200.00
40	MARIEN CHURCH IN DANZIG	YR	*	250.00
41	STRASSBURG CATHEDRAL	YR	*	250.00
42	MARIANBURG CASTLE	YR	*	300.00
43	WINTER IDYLL	YR	*	300.00
44	WOOD SCAPE	YR	*	300.00
45	CHRISTMAS PEACE	YR	*	400.00
46	CHRISTMAS IN AN ALPINE VALLEY	YR	*	240.00
47	DILLINGEN MADONNA	YR	*	985.00

YR	NAME	LIMIT	ISSUE	TREND
48	MESSAGE TO THE SHEPHERDS	YR	*	875.00
49	HOLY FAMILY, THE	YR	*	200.00
50	CHRISTMAS IN THE FOREST	YR	*	200.00
51	STAR OF BETHLEHEM	YR	*	450.00
52	CHRISTMAS IN THE ALPS	YR	*	200.00
53	HOLY LIGHT, THE	YR	*	200.00
54	CHRISTMAS EVE	YR	*	200.00
55	CHRISTMAS IN A VILLAGE	YR	*	200.00
56	CHRISTMAS IN THE ALPS	YR	*	200.00
57	CHRISTMAS BY THE SEA	YR	*	200.00
58	CHRISTMAS EVE	YR	*	200.00
59	MIDNIGHT MASS	YR	*	200.00
60	CHRISTMAS IN A SMALL VILLAGE	YR	*	200.00
61	SOLITARY CHRISTMAS	YR	*	225.00
62	CHRISTMAS EVE	YR	*	200.00
63	SILENT NIGHT	YR	*	200.00
64	CHRISTMAS MARKET IN NUREMBERG	YR	*	225.00
65	CHRISTMAS IN MUNICH	YR	*	200.00
66	CHRISTMAS IN ULM	YR	*	275.00
67	CHRISTMAS IN REGINBURG	YR	*	200.00
68	CHRISTMAS IN BREMEN	YR	*	200.00
69	CHRISTMAS IN ROTHENBURG	YR	*	220.00
70	CHRISTMAS IN COLOGNE	YR	*	175.00
71	CHRISTMAS IN GARMISCH	YR	42.00	100.00
72	CHRISTMAS IN FRANCONIA	YR	50.00	100.00
73	LUBECK-HOLSTEIN	YR	77.00	110.00
74	CHRISTMAS IN WURZBURG	YR	85.00	100.00

E. HIBEL **NOBILITY OF CHILDREN**

YR	NAME	LIMIT	ISSUE	TREND
76	LA CONTESSA ISABELLA	12750	120.00	300.00
77	LA MARQUIS MAURICE-PIERRE	12750	120.00	120.00
78	BARONESSE JOHANNA	12750	130.00	230.00
79	CHIEF RED FEATHER	12750	140.00	180.00

E. HIBEL **ORIENTAL GOLD**

YR	NAME	LIMIT	ISSUE	TREND
76	YASUKO	2000	275.00	1710.00
77	MR. OBATA	2000	275.00	1050.00
78	SAKURA	2000	295.00	740.00
79	MICHIO	2000	325.00	750.00

B. WIINBLAD **WIINBLAD CHRISTMAS**

YR	NAME	LIMIT	ISSUE	TREND
71	MARIA & CHILD	UD	100.00	700.00
72	CASPAR	UD	100.00	290.00
73	MELCHIOR	UD	125.00	335.00
74	BALTHAZAR	UD	125.00	300.00
75	ANNUNCIATION, THE	UD	195.00	200.00
76	ANGEL WITH TRUMPET	UD	195.00	200.00
77	ADORATION OF SHEPHERDS	UD	225.00	225.00
78	ANGEL WITH HARP	UD	275.00	295.00
79	EXODUS FROM EGYPT	UD	310.00	310.00
80	ANGEL WITH GLOCKENSPIEL	UD	360.00	360.00
81	CHRIST CHILD VISITS TEMPLE	UD	375.00	375.00
82	CHRISTENING OF CHRIST	UD	375.00	375.00

ROYAL BAYREUTH
*

CHRISTMAS

YR	NAME	LIMIT	ISSUE	TREND
72	CARRIAGE IN THE VILLAGE	4000	15.00	80.00
73	SNOW SCENE	4000	16.50	20.00
74	OLD MILL, THE	4000	24.00	24.00
75	FOREST CHALET 'SERENITY'	4000	28.00	28.00
76	CHRISTMAS IN THE COUNTRY	5000	40.00	40.00
77	PEACE ON EARTH	5000	40.00	40.00
78	PEACEFUL INTERLUDE	5000	45.00	45.00
79	HOMEWARD BOUND	5000	50.00	50.00

ROYAL COPENHAGEN
S. VESTERGAARD

YR	NAME	LIMIT	ISSUE	TREND
98	GRANDPARENTS	YR	35.00	35.00
98	YOUNG ANDVENTURERS	YR	35.00	35.00

S. VESTERGAARD **AMERICA'S MOTHER'S DAY**

YR	NAME	LIMIT	ISSUE	TREND
88	WESTERN TRAIL	YR	35.00	35.00
89	INDIAN LOVE CALL	YR	37.00	35.00
90	SOUTHERN BELLE	YR	40.00	39.00
91	MOTHER'S DAY AT THE MISSION	YR	43.00	39.00
92	TURN OF THE CENTURY BOSTON	YR	45.00	40.00

* **CHRISTMAS**

YR	NAME	LIMIT	ISSUE	TREND
62	LITTLE MERMAID, THE	YR	11.00	309.00

R. BOCHER **CHRISTMAS**

YR	NAME	LIMIT	ISSUE	TREND
16	SHEPHERD AT CHRISTMAS	YR	1.50	129.00
26	CHRISTIANSHAVN CANAL	YR	2.00	145.00
36	ROSKILDE CATHEDRAL	YR	2.50	243.00
45	A PEACEFUL MOTIF	YR	4.00	599.00
51	CHRISTMAS ANGEL	YR	5.00	439.00

A. BOESEN **CHRISTMAS**

YR	NAME	LIMIT	ISSUE	TREND
13	FREDERIK CHURCH SPIRE	YR	1.50	163.00
14	HOLY SPIRIT CHURCH	YR	1.50	210.00

H. HANSEN **CHRISTMAS**

YR	NAME	LIMIT	ISSUE	TREND
49	OUR LADY'S CATHEDRAL	YR	5.00	339.00
57	GOOD SHEPHERD, THE	YR	8.00	163.00
58	SUNSHINE OVER GREENLAND	YR	9.00	163.00

YR	NAME	LIMIT	ISSUE	TREND
59	CHRISTMAS NIGHT	YR	9.00	163.00
60	STAG, THE	YR	10.00	185.00
O. JENSEN				CHRISTMAS
11	DANISH LANDSCAPE	YR	1.00	210.00
17	OUR SAVIOR CHURCH	YR	2.00	129.00
18	SHEEP AND SHEPHERDS	YR	2.00	129.00
19	IN THE PARK	YR	2.00	115.00
21	AABENRAA MARKETPLACE	YR	2.00	115.00
23	DANISH LANDSCAPE	YR	2.00	97.00
25	CHRISTIANSHAVN	YR	2.00	115.00
29	GRUNDTVIG CHURCH	YR	2.00	113.00
32	FREDERIKSBERG GARDENS	YR	2.50	129.00
34	HERMITAGE CASTLE, THE	YR	2.50	210.00
98	CHILDREN'S CHRISTMAS	*	40.00	40.00
98	CHILDREN'S CHRISTMAS (REG. ED.)	YR	40.00	40.00
T. KJOLNER				CHRISTMAS
41	DANISH VILLAGE CHURCH	YR	3.00	499.00
48	NODEBO CHURCH	YR	4.50	309.00
53	FREDERIKSBERG CASTLE	YR	6.00	163.00
A. KROG				CHRISTMAS
15	DANISH LANDSCAPE	YR	1.50	210.00
K. LANGE				CHRISTMAS
40	GOOD SHEPHERD, THE	YR	3.00	597.00
47	GOOD SHEPHERD, THE	YR	4.50	339.00
52	CHRISTMAS IN THE FOREST	YR	5.00	163.00
54	AMALIENBORG PALACE	YR	6.00	195.00
55	FANO GIRL	YR	7.00	243.00
56	ROSENBORG CASTLE	YR	7.00	210.00
61	TRAINING SHIP	YR	10.00	195.00
63	HOJSAGER MILL	YR	11.00	109.00
64	FETCHING THE TREE	YR	11.00	69.00
65	LITTLE SKATERS	YR	12.00	74.00
66	BLACKBIRD	YR	12.00	38.00
67	ROYAL OAK, THE	YR	13.00	38.00
68	LAST UMIAK, THE	YR	13.00	38.00
69	OLD FARMYARD, THE	YR	14.00	38.00
70	CHRISTMAS ROSE AND CAT	YR	14.00	38.00
71	HARE IN WINTER	YR	15.00	25.00
72	IN THE DESERT	YR	16.00	27.00
73	TRAIN HOMEWARD BOUND	YR	22.00	27.00
74	WINTER TWILIGHT	YR	22.00	30.00
75	QUEEN'S PALACE	YR	28.00	25.00
77	IMMERVAD BRIDGE	YR	32.00	27.00
78	GREENLAND SCENERY	YR	35.00	27.00
79	CHOOSING CHRISTMAS TREE	YR	43.00	82.00
80	BRINGING HOME THE TREE	YR	50.00	35.00
81	ADMIRING CHRISTMAS TREE	YR	53.00	82.00
82	WAITING FOR CHRISTMAS	YR	55.00	82.00
83	MERRY CHRISTMAS	YR	55.00	82.00
84	JINGLE BELLS	YR	55.00	82.00
85	SNOWMAN	YR	55.00	95.00
86	CHRISTMAS VACATION	YR	55.00	83.00
H. NIELSEN				CHRISTMAS
38	ROUND CHURCH IN OSTERLARS	YR	3.00	439.00
39	GREENLAND PACK-ICE	YR	3.00	597.00
B. OLSEN				CHRISTMAS
24	SAILING SHIP	YR	2.00	129.00
27	SHIP'S BOY AT TILLER	YR	2.00	173.00
30	FISHING BOATS	YR	2.50	145.00
33	FERRY AND THE GREAT BELT	YR	2.50	195.00
35	KRONBORG CASTLE	YR	2.50	309.00
V. OLSON				CHRISTMAS
44	DANISH VILLAGE SCENE	YR	4.00	405.00
50	BOESLUNDE CHURCH	YR	5.00	399.00
G. RODE				CHRISTMAS
20	MARY AND CHILD JESUS	YR	2.00	115.00
28	VICAR'S FAMILY	YR	2.00	145.00
31	MOTHER AND CHILD	YR	2.50	145.00
E. SELSCHAU				CHRISTMAS
22	THREE SINGING ANGELS	YR	2.00	97.00
C. THOMSEN				CHRISTMAS
08	MADONNA AND CHILD	YR	1.00	4900.00
10	MAGI, THE	YR	1.00	179.00
12	CHRISTMAS TREE	YR	1.00	210.00
N. THORSSON				CHRISTMAS
37	MAIN STREET COPENHAGEN	YR	2.50	339.00
42	BELL TOWER	YR	4.00	565.00
43	FLIGHT INTO EGYPT	YR	4.00	759.00
46	ZEALAND VILLAGE CHURCH	YR	4.00	275.00
S. USSING				CHRISTMAS
09	DANISH LANDSCAPE	YR	1.00	243.00
S. VESTERGAARD				CHRISTMAS
76	DANISH WATERMILL	YR	28.00	27.00
87	WINTER BIRDS	YR	60.00	98.00
88	CHRISTMAS EVE IN COPENHAGEN	YR	60.00	98.00
89	OLD SKATING POND, THE	YR	60.00	113.00
90	CHRISTMAS AT TIVOLI	YR	70.00	210.00

YR NAME	LIMIT	ISSUE	TREND
91 FESTIVAL OF SANTA LUCIA, THE	YR	70.00	113.00
92 QUEEN'S CARRIAGE	YR	70.00	83.00
93 CHRISTMAS GUESTS	YR	70.00	113.00
94 CHRISTMAS SHOPPING	YR	73.00	83.00
95 CHRISTMAS AT THE MANOR HOUSE	YR	73.00	75.00
98 CHRISTMAS 1998	YR	70.00	70.00
H. HANSEN		**CHRISTMAS IN DENMARK**	
91 BRINGING HOME THE TREE	YR	73.00	113.00
92 CHRISTMAS SHOPPING	YR	73.00	83.00
93 SKATING PARTY, THE	YR	75.00	113.00
94 SLEIGH RIDE, THE	YR	75.00	83.00
C. MAGADINE		**FIRST/BING & GRONDAHL**	
96 CHRISTMAS EVE AT THE STATUE OF LIBERTY	YR	48.00	48.00
J. NIELSEN		**NATURE'S CHILDREN**	
93 ROBINS, THE	YR	40.00	40.00
94 FAWN, THE	YR	40.00	40.00
98 NATURE'S CHILDREN 1998	YR	40.00	40.00

ROYAL CORNWALL

Y. KOUTSIS			**CREATION**
77 IN HIS IMAGE	10000	45.00	130.00
77 IN THE BEGINNING	10000	38.00	90.00
77 NOAH AND THE ARK	10000	45.00	180.00
77 TOWER OF BABEL	19500	30.00	70.00
78 ADAM'S RIB	10000	45.00	125.00
78 BANISHED FROM EDEN	10000	45.00	125.00
78 JACOB'S LADDER	19500	30.00	70.00
78 JACOB'S WEDDING	19500	30.00	70.00
78 JOSEPH INTERPRETS PHARAOH'S DREAM	19500	30.00	70.00
78 JOSEPH'S COAT OF MANY COLORS	19500	30.00	70.00
78 REBEKAH AT THE WELL	19500	30.00	80.00
78 SODOM AND GOMORRAH	19500	30.00	70.00

ROYAL DEVON

N. ROCKWELL		**ROCKWELL CHRISTMAS**	
75 DOWNHILL DARING	YR	25.00	30.00
76 CHRISTMAS GIFT, THE	YR	25.00	35.00
77 BIG MOMENT, THE	YR	28.00	50.00
78 PUPPETS FOR CHRISTMAS	YR	28.00	30.00
79 ONE PRESENT TOO MANY	YR	32.00	30.00
80 GRAMPS MEETS GRAMPS	YR	33.00	35.00
N. ROCKWELL		**ROCKWELL MOTHER'S DAY**	
75 DOCTOR AND DOLL	YR	24.00	45.00
76 PUPPY LOVE	YR	25.00	100.00
77 FAMILY, THE	YR	25.00	80.00
78 MOTHER'S DAY OFF	YR	27.00	35.00
79 MOTHER'S EVENING OUT	YR	30.00	35.00
80 MOTHER'S TREAT	YR	33.00	35.00

ROYAL DOULTON

*		**CHRISTMAS PLATES**	
93 SLEIGH RIDE	YR	45.00	45.00
93 TOGETHER FOR CHRISTMAS	YR	45.00	50.00
*		**FAMILY CHRISTMAS PLATES**	
91 DAD PLAYS SANTA	CL	60.00	60.00

ROYAL GRAFTON/THE COLLECTOR'S TREASURY

M. JACKSON		**BEAUTY OF POLAR WILDLIFE**	
90 BABY SEALS	150 DAYS	*	43.00
90 POLAR BEAR CUBS	*	*	38.00
91 ARCTIC FOX CUBS	*	*	42.00
91 ARCTIC HARE FAMILY	*	*	44.00
91 ARCTIC WOLF FAMILY	*	*	49.00
91 DALL SHEEP	*	*	49.00
91 EMPEROR PENGUINS	*	*	42.00
92 REINDEER YOUNG	*	*	47.00

ROYAL WICKFORD PORCELAIN

G. TERP		**ALICE IN WONDERLAND**	
87 CATERPILLAR, THE	45 DAYS	30.00	48.00
87 DUCHESS AND COOK, THE	45 DAYS	30.00	48.00
87 TEA PARTY, THE	45 DAYS	30.00	43.00
87 TWEEDLEDEE-TWEEDLEDUM	45 DAYS	30.00	30.00
87 WHITE KNIGHT, THE	45 DAYS	30.00	48.00
88 HUMPTY DUMPTY	45 DAYS	30.00	30.00
88 LION AND THE UNICORN, THE	45 DAYS	30.00	30.00
88 OFF WITH THEIR HEADS	45 DAYS	30.00	30.00
88 RED AND WHITE QUEENS	45 DAYS	30.00	30.00
88 TALKING FLOWERS	45 DAYS	30.00	30.00
88 WALRUS AND CARPENTER	45 DAYS	30.00	30.00
88 WHITE RABBIT, THE	45 DAYS	30.00	30.00
L. DUBIN			**LIL' PEDDLERS**
87 APPLE A DAY	YR	30.00	48.00
87 BALLOONS N' THINGS	YR	30.00	30.00
87 CHIMNEY SWEEP	YR	30.00	30.00
87 COBBLESTONE DELI	YR	30.00	30.00
87 COOLIN' OFF	YR	30.00	50.00
87 EXTRA, EXTRA	YR	30.00	50.00

YR	NAME	LIMIT	ISSUE	TREND
87	FORGET ME NOTS	YR	30.00	50.00
87	JUST PICKED	YR	30.00	30.00
87	OVEN FRESH	YR	30.00	30.00
87	PENNY CANDY	YR	30.00	30.00
87	POPPIN' CORN	YR	30.00	30.00
87	TODAY'S CATCH	YR	30.00	30.00

ROYAL WORCESTER

P.W. BASTON — BIRTH OF A NATION

YR	NAME	LIMIT	ISSUE	TREND
72	BOSTON TEA PARTY	10000	45.00	210.00
73	PAUL REVERE	10000	45.00	195.00
74	CONCORD BRIDGE	10000	50.00	135.00
75	SIGNING DECLARATION	10000	65.00	135.00
76	CROSSING DELAWARE	10000	65.00	135.00
77	WASHINGTON'S INAUGURATION	1250	65.00	135.00

P.W. BASTON — CURRIER AND IVES PLATES

YR	NAME	LIMIT	ISSUE	TREND
74	ROAD IN WINTER	5570	60.00	100.00
75	OLD GRIST MILL	3200	60.00	100.00
76	WINTER PASTIME	1500	60.00	90.00
77	HOME TO THANKSGIVING	546	60.00	225.00

P. COOPER — KITTEN CLASSICS

YR	NAME	LIMIT	ISSUE	TREND
85	CAT NAP	CL	30.00	35.00
85	COUNTRY KITTY	CL	30.00	35.00

P. COOPER — KITTEN ENCOUNTERS

YR	NAME	LIMIT	ISSUE	TREND
87	BEDTIME BUDDIES	CL	30.00	30.00
87	BUNNY CHASE	CL	30.00	30.00
87	FISHFUL THINKING	CL	30.00	42.00
87	FLUTTER BY	CL	30.00	30.00
87	JUST DUCKY	CL	30.00	35.00
87	PUPPY PAL	CL	30.00	35.00
88	CAT AND MOUSE	CL	30.00	35.00
88	STABLEMATES	CL	30.00	50.00

* — SPODE MARITIME PLATES

YR	NAME	LIMIT	ISSUE	TREND
80	CONSTITUTION & GUERRIRE	2000	150.00	150.00
80	CONSTITUTION & JAVA	2000	150.00	150.00
80	PELICAN & ARGUS	2000	150.00	150.00
80	PRESIDENT & LITTLE BELT	2000	150.00	150.00
80	SHANNON & CHESAPEAKE	2000	150.00	150.00
80	UNITED STATES/MACEDONIAN	2000	150.00	150.00

J. COOKE — WATER BIRDS OF NORTH AMERICA

YR	NAME	LIMIT	ISSUE	TREND
85	AMERICAN PINTAILS	15000	55.00	55.00
85	CANADA GEESE	15000	55.00	55.00
85	CANVASBACKS	15000	55.00	55.00
85	GREEN WINGED TEALS	15000	55.00	55.00
85	HOODED MERGANSERS	15000	55.00	55.00
85	MALLARDS	15000	55.00	55.00
85	SNOW GEESE	15000	55.00	55.00
85	WOOD DUCKS	15000	55.00	55.00

SARAH'S ATTIC

S. SCHULTZ — CLASSROOM MEMORIES

YR	NAME	LIMIT	ISSUE	TREND
91	CLASSROOM MEMORIES	CL	80.00	80.00

SCHMID

L. DAVIS — CAT TALES

YR	NAME	LIMIT	ISSUE	TREND
82	COMPANY'S COMING	12500	38.00	100.00
82	FLEW THE COOP	12500	38.00	100.00
82	ON THE MOVE	12500	38.00	100.00
82	RIGHT CHURCH, WRONG PEW	12500	38.00	100.00

L. DAVIS — CHRISTMAS

YR	NAME	LIMIT	ISSUE	TREND
83	HOOKER AT MAILBOX W/ PRESENT	7500	45.00	120.00
84	COUNTRY CHRISTMAS	7500	45.00	85.00
85	CHRISTMAS AT FOXFIRE FARM	7500	45.00	130.00
86	CHRISTMAS AT RED OAK	7500	45.00	60.00
87	BLOSSOM'S GIFT	7500	48.00	100.00
88	CUTTING THE FAMILY CHRISTMAS TREE	7500	48.00	60.00
89	PETER AND THE WREN	7500	48.00	80.00
90	WINTER DEER	7500	48.00	50.00
91	CHRISTMAS AT RED OAK II	7500	55.00	75.00
92	BORN ON A STARRY NIGHT	7500	55.00	75.00
93	WAITING FOR MR. LOWELL	7500	55.00	55.00
94	VISIONS OF SUGARPLUMS	5000	55.00	55.00
95	BAH HUMBUG	5000	55.00	55.00

B. HUMMEL — CHRISTMAS

YR	NAME	LIMIT	ISSUE	TREND
71	ANGEL	YR	15.00	29.00
72	ANGEL WITH FLUTE	YR	15.00	20.00
73	NATIVITY, THE	YR	15.00	70.00
74	GUARDIAN ANGEL, THE	YR	19.00	20.00
75	CHRISTMAS CHILD	YR	25.00	30.00
76	SACRED JOURNEY	YR	28.00	30.00
77	HERALD ANGEL	YR	28.00	30.00
78	HEAVENLY TRIO	YR	33.00	33.00
79	STARLIGHT ANGEL	YR	38.00	40.00
80	PARADE INTO TOYLAND	YR	45.00	50.00
81	A TIME TO REMEMBER	YR	45.00	50.00
82	ANGELIC PROCESSION	YR	45.00	50.00
83	ANGELIC MESSENGER	YR	45.00	50.00
84	A GIFT FROM HEAVEN	YR	45.00	50.00

YR	NAME	LIMIT	ISSUE	TREND
85	HEAVENLY LIGHT	YR	45.00	47.00
86	TELL THE HEAVENS	YR	45.00	50.00
87	ANGELIC GIFTS	YR	48.00	50.00
88	CHEERFUL CHERUBS	YR	53.00	75.00
89	ANGELIC MUSICIAN	YR	53.00	75.00
90	ANGEL'S LIGHT	YR	53.00	75.00
91	MESSAGE FROM ABOVE	YR	60.00	75.00
92	SWEET BLESSINGS	YR	65.00	75.00

L. DAVIS — COUNTRY PRIDE

YR	NAME	LIMIT	ISSUE	TREND
81	DUKE'S MIXTURE	7500	35.00	185.00
81	PLUM TUCKERED OUT	7500	35.00	80.00
81	SURPRISE IN THE CELLAR	7500	35.00	200.00
82	BUSTIN' WITH PRIDE	7500	35.00	60.00
*				

DISNEY ANNUAL

83	SNEAK PREVIEW	20000	23.00	25.00
84	COMMAND PERFORMANCE	20000	23.00	25.00
85	SHOW BIZ	20000	23.00	25.00
86	TREE FOR TWO	20000	23.00	25.00
87	MERRY MOUSE MEDLEY	20000	25.00	25.00
88	WARM WINTER RIDE	20000	25.00	25.00
89	MERRY MICKEY CLAUS	20000	33.00	75.00
90	HOLLY JOLLY CHRISTMAS	20000	33.00	35.00
91	MICKEY AND MINNIE'S ROCKIN' CHRISTMAS	20000	37.00	40.00
*				

DISNEY CHRISTMAS

73	SLEIGH RIDE	YR	10.00	275.00
74	DECORATING THE TREE	YR	10.00	75.00
75	CAROLING	YR	12.50	15.00
76	BUILDING A SNOWMAN	YR	13.00	15.00
77	DOWN THE CHIMNEY	YR	13.00	15.00
78	NIGHT BEFORE CHRISTMAS	YR	15.00	30.00
79	SANTA'S SURPRISE	15000	17.50	30.00
80	SLEIGH RIDE	15000	17.50	35.00
81	HAPPY HOLIDAYS	15000	17.50	22.00
82	WINTER GAMES	15000	19.00	30.00
*				

DISNEY MOTHER'S DAY

74	FLOWERS FOR MOTHER	YR	10.00	50.00
75	SNOW WHITE & DWARFS	YR	12.50	50.00
76	MINNIE MOUSE	YR	13.00	25.00
77	PLUTO'S PALS	YR	13.00	25.00
78	FLOWERS FOR BAMBI	YR	15.00	35.00
79	HAPPY FEET	10000	17.50	20.00
80	MINNIE'S SURPRISE	10000	17.50	30.00
81	PLAYMATES	10000	17.50	35.00
82	A DREAM COME TRUE	10000	19.00	40.00

J. FERRANDIZ — FERRANDIZ BEAUTIFUL BOUNTY PORCELAIN PLATES

82	A MID-WINTER'S DREAM	10000	40.00	50.00
82	AUTUMN'S BLESSING	10000	40.00	50.00
82	SPRING BLOSSOMS	10000	40.00	40.00
82	SUMMER'S GOLDEN HARVEST	10000	40.00	40.00

J. FERRANDIZ — FERRANDIZ MUSIC MAKERS PORCELAIN PLATES

81	ENTERTAINER, THE	10000	25.00	30.00
81	FLUTIST, THE	10000	25.00	30.00
82	MAGICAL MEDLEY	10000	25.00	30.00
82	SWEET SERENADE	10000	25.00	30.00

J. FERRANDIZ — FERRANDIZ PORCELAIN CHRISTMAS PLATES

72	CHRIST IN THE MANAGER	*	30.00	175.00
73	CHRISTMAS	*	30.00	230.00

J. FERRANDIZ — FERRANDIZ WOODEN BIRTHDAY PLATES

72	BOY	*	15.00	150.00
72	GIRL	*	15.00	175.00
73	BOY	*	20.00	200.00
73	GIRL	*	20.00	150.00
74	BOY	*	22.00	175.00
74	GIRL	*	22.00	175.00

L. DAVIS — FRIENDS OF MINE

89	SUNDAY WORSHIPPERS	7500	53.00	75.00
90	SUNDAY AFTERNOON TREAT	7500	53.00	75.00
91	WARM MILK	7500	55.00	75.00
92	CAT AND JENNY WREN	7500	55.00	75.00

M. LILLEMOE — KITTY CUCUMBER ANNUAL

89	RING AROUND THE ROSIE	20000	25.00	25.00
90	SWAN LAKE	20000	25.00	25.00
91	TEA PARTY	2500	25.00	25.00
92	DANCE ROUND THE MAYPOLE	2500	25.00	50.00

B. HUMMEL — MOTHER'S DAY

72	PLAYING HOOKY	YR	15.00	16.00
73	LITTLE FISHERMAN	YR	15.00	35.00
74	BUMBLEBEE	YR	19.00	20.00
75	MESSAGE OF LOVE	YR	25.00	30.00
76	DEVOTION FOR MOTHER	YR	28.00	30.00
77	MOONLIGHT RETURN	YR	28.00	30.00
78	AFTERNOON STROLL	YR	33.00	33.00
79	CHERUB'S GIFT	YR	38.00	38.00
80	MOTHER'S LITTLE HELPERS	YR	45.00	50.00
81	PLAYTIME	YR	45.00	52.00
82	FLOWER BASKET, THE	YR	45.00	50.00
83	SPRING BOUQUET	YR	45.00	75.00

The first plate in Pickard Inc.'s Gems of Nature collection, Ruby-Throated Hummingbird with Lily was released in 1989 for $29 and has since increased in value.

Made of pristine white oxolyte, Silent Night, the first issue in Roman Inc.'s "Millenium" series, was limited to 2,000.

Sapphire Wings light gently on glorious flowers in this first issue in the "Jewels of the Flower" series from Edwin M. Knowles China Co. in 1991.

YR	NAME	LIMIT	ISSUE	TREND
84	A JOY TO SHARE	YR	45.00	50.00
85	A MOTHER'S JOURNEY	YR	45.00	50.00
86	HOME FROM SCHOOL	YR	45.00	75.00
88	YOUNG READER	YR	53.00	80.00
89	PRETTY AS A PICTURE	YR	53.00	80.00
90	MOTHER'S LITTLE ATHLETE	YR	53.00	75.00
91	SOFT & GENTLE	YR	55.00	75.00
*	**PADDINGTON BEAR/MUSICIAN'S DREAM PLATES**			
83	BEAT GOES ON, THE	10000	17.50	25.00
83	KNOWING THE SCORE	10000	17.50	20.00
83	PERFECT HARMONY	10000	17.50	25.00
83	TICKLING THE IVORY	10000	17.50	25.00
C. SCHULZ			**PEANUTS CHRISTMAS**	
72	SNOOPY GUIDES THE SLEIGH	YR	10.00	35.00
73	CHRISTMAS EVE AT DOGHOUSE	YR	10.00	90.00
74	CHRISTMAS AT FIREPLACE	YR	10.00	50.00
75	WOODSTOCK AND SANTA CLAUS	YR	12.50	20.00
76	WOODSTOCK'S CHRISTMAS	YR	13.00	20.00
77	DECK THE DOGHOUSE	YR	13.00	20.00
78	FILLING THE STOCKING	YR	15.00	40.00
79	CHRISTMAS AT HAND	15000	17.50	25.00
80	WAITING FOR SANTA	15000	17.50	25.00
81	A CHRISTMAS WISH	15000	17.50	30.00
82	PERFECT PERFORMANCE	15000	19.00	50.00
C. SCHULZ			**PEANUTS MOTHER'S DAY PLATES**	
72	LINUS	*	10.00	10.00
73	MOM?	*	10.00	10.00
74	SNOOPY/WOODSTOCK/PARADE	*	10.00	15.00
75	A KISS FOR LUCY	*	12.50	15.00
76	LINUS AND SNOOPY	*	13.00	35.00
77	DEAR MOM	*	13.00	30.00
78	THOUGHTS THAT COUNT	*	15.00	25.00
79	A SPECIAL LETTER	*	17.50	25.00
80	A TRIBUTE TO MOM	*	17.50	25.00
81	MISSION FOR MOM	*	17.50	20.00
82	WHICH WAY TO MOTHER	*	19.00	20.00
C. SCHULZ			**PEANUTS SPECIAL EDITION PLATE**	
76	BICENTENNIAL	*	13.00	30.00
C. SCHULZ			**PEANUTS VALENTINE'S DAY PLATES**	
77	HOME IS WHERE THE HEART IS	*	13.00	35.00
78	HEAVENLY BLISS	*	13.00	30.00
79	LOVE MATCH	*	17.50	30.00
80	FROM SNOOPY, WITH LOVE	*	17.50	25.00
81	HEARTS-A-FLUTTER	*	17.50	20.00
82	LOVE PATCH	*	17.50	25.00
C. SCHULZ			**PEANUTS WORLD'S GREATEST ATHLETE**	
82	CROWD WENT WILD, THE	10000	17.50	25.00
82	GO DEEP	10000	17.50	25.00
82	PUCK STOPS HERE, THE	10000	17.50	25.00
82	WAY YOU PLAY THE GAME, THE	10000	17.50	20.00
*	**RAGGEDY ANN ANNUAL PLATES**			
80	SUNSHINE WAGON, THE	10000	17.50	90.00
81	RAGGEDY SHUFFLE, THE	10000	17.50	50.00
82	FLYING HIGH	10000	19.00	20.00
83	WINNING STREAK	10000	23.00	25.00
84	ROCKING RODEO	10000	23.00	25.00
*	**RAGGEDY ANN BICENTENNIAL PLATE**			
76	BICENTENNIAL PLATE	*	13.00	50.00
*	**RAGGEDY ANN CHRISTMAS PLATES**			
75	GIFTS OF LOVE	*	12.50	50.00
76	MERRY BLADES	*	13.00	40.00
77	CHRISTMAS MORNING	*	13.00	25.00
78	CHECKING THE LIST	*	15.00	20.00
79	LITTLE HELPER	*	17.50	20.00
*	**RAGGEDY ANN VALENTINE'S DAY PLATES**			
78	AS TIME GOES BY	*	13.00	25.00
79	DAISIES DO TELL	*	17.50	20.00
L. DAVIS			**RED OAK SAMPLER**	
85	GENERAL STORE	5000	45.00	150.00
87	COUNTRY WEDDING	5000	45.00	120.00
89	COUNTRY SCHOOL	5000	45.00	75.00
90	BLACKSMITH SHOP	5000	53.00	75.00
L. DAVIS			**SPECIAL EDITION**	
84	CRITICS, THE	12500	45.00	100.00
84	GOOD OLE DAYS PRIVY- 2 PC	5000	60.00	110.00
85	HOME FROM MARKET	7500	55.00	150.00
*	**WALT DISNEY SPECIAL EDITION PLATES**			
78	MICKEY MOUSE AT FIFTY	15000	25.00	90.00
80	HAPPY BIRTHDAY PINOCCHIO	7500	17.50	50.00
81	ALICE IN WONDERLAND	7500	17.50	25.00
82	GOOFY'S GOLDEN JUBILEE	7500	19.00	30.00
82	HAPPY BIRTHDAY PLUTO	7500	17.50	40.00
87	SNOW WHITE GOLDEN ANNIVERSARY	5000	48.00	50.00
88	MICKEY MOUSE & MINNIE MOUSE-60TH ANNIV.	10000	50.00	110.00
89	SLEEPING BEAUTY-30TH ANNIVERSARY	5000	80.00	95.00
90	FANTASIA RELIEF PLATE	20000	25.00	40.00

YR	NAME	LIMIT	ISSUE	TREND
90	FANTASIA-SORCERER'S APPRENTICE	5000	59.00	80.00
90	PINOCCHIO'S FRIEND	YR	25.00	25.00
*				

YEAR WITH PADDINGTON BEAR PLATES

YR	NAME	LIMIT	ISSUE	TREND
79	PYRAMID OF PRESENTS	25000	12.50	28.00
80	SPRINGTIME	25000	12.50	25.00
81	SANDCASTLES	25000	12.50	25.00
82	SCHOOL DAYS	25000	12.50	13.00

SEELEY CERAMICS
M. SEELEY — OLD FRENCH DOLL COLLECTION

YR	NAME	LIMIT	ISSUE	TREND
79	A.T., THE	5000	39.00	55.00
79	BRU, THE	5000	39.00	200.00
79	E.J., THE	5000	39.00	75.00
80	ALEZANDRE	5000	39.00	45.00
81	MARQUE, THE	5000	39.00	43.00
81	SCHMITT, THE	5000	39.00	43.00

SEYMOUR MANN
BERNINI — CONNOISSEUR PLATE COLLECTION

YR	NAME	LIMIT	ISSUE	TREND
96	BUTTERFLY/LILY CLT 330	25000	45.00	45.00
96	HUMMINGBIRDS/MORNING GLORY CLT 320	25000	45.00	45.00
96	ROSES/FORGET ME NOT CLT 340	25000	45.00	45.00

SILVER DEER LTD.
E. ERIKSEN — CHRISTMAS

YR	NAME	LIMIT	ISSUE	TREND
72	MAID OF COPENHAGEN	YR	16.50	37.00

S. OTTO — CHRISTMAS

YR	NAME	LIMIT	ISSUE	TREND
73	FIR TREE, THE	YR	22.00	25.00
74	CHIMNEY SWEEP, THE	YR	25.00	25.00
75	UGLY DUCKLING, THE	YR	28.00	28.00
77	SNOWMAN	YR	30.00	30.00
78	LAST DREAM OF THE OLD OAK TREE	YR	32.00	32.00
79	OLD STREET LAMP, THE	YR	37.00	37.00
80	WILLIE WINKIE	YR	43.00	43.00
81	UTTERMOST PARTS OF THE SEA	YR	50.00	50.00
82	TWELVE BY THE MAILCOACH	YR	55.00	55.00
83	STORY OF THE YEAR, THE	YR	55.00	55.00
84	NIGHTINGALE, THE	YR	55.00	55.00
85	KRONBERG CASTLE	YR	60.00	60.00
86	BELL, THE	YR	60.00	75.00
87	THUMBELINA	YR	60.00	60.00
88	BELL DEEP, THE	YR	60.00	60.00
89	OLD HOUSE, THE	YR	60.00	60.00
90	GRANDFATHER'S PICTURE BOOK	YR	65.00	72.00
91	WINDMILL, THE	YR	65.00	75.00

G. SAUSMARK — CHRISTMAS

YR	NAME	LIMIT	ISSUE	TREND
70	H.C. ANDERSON HOUSE	YR	14.50	39.00

M. STAGE — CHRISTMAS

YR	NAME	LIMIT	ISSUE	TREND
71	LITTLE MATCH GIRL	YR	15.00	38.00
76	SNOW QUEEN, THE	YR	28.00	28.00
*				

MOTHER'S DAY

YR	NAME	LIMIT	ISSUE	TREND
70	BOUQUET FOR MOTHER	*	14.50	75.00
71	MOTHER'S LOVE	*	15.00	40.00
72	GOOD NIGHT	*	16.50	35.00
73	FLOWERS FOR MOTHER	*	20.00	35.00
74	DAISIES FOR MOTHER	*	25.00	35.00
75	SURPRISE FOR MOTHER	*	28.00	28.00
76	COMPLETE GARDENER, THE	*	28.00	28.00
77	LITTLE FRIENDS	*	30.00	30.00
78	DREAMS	*	32.00	32.00
79	PROMENADE	*	37.00	37.00
80	NURSERY SCENE	*	43.00	43.00
81	DAILY DUTIES	*	50.00	50.00
82	MY BEST FRIEND	*	55.00	55.00
83	AN UNEXPECTED MEETING	*	55.00	55.00

S. OTTO — MOTHER'S DAY

YR	NAME	LIMIT	ISSUE	TREND
87	COMPLETE ANGLER, THE	YR	60.00	60.00
88	LITTLE BAKERY, THE	YR	60.00	60.00
89	SPRINGTIME	YR	60.00	60.00
90	SPRING EXCURSION, THE	YR	65.00	65.00
91	WALKING AT THE BEACH	YR	65.00	65.00

M. STAGE — MOTHER'S DAY

YR	NAME	LIMIT	ISSUE	TREND
84	WHO ARE YOU?	YR	55.00	55.00
86	MEETING ON THE MEADOW	YR	60.00	60.00

SPODE
R. HARM — AMERICAN SONG BIRDS

YR	NAME	LIMIT	ISSUE	TREND
72	SET OF TWELVE	UD	350.00	765.00

G. WEST — CHRISTMAS

YR	NAME	LIMIT	ISSUE	TREND
70	PARTRIDGE	UD	35.00	35.00
71	ANGEL'S SINGING	UD	35.00	35.00
72	THREE SHIPS A'SAILING	UD	35.00	38.00
73	WE THREE KINGS OF ORIENT	UD	35.00	55.00
74	DECK THE HALLS	UD	35.00	55.00
75	CHRISTBAUM	UD	45.00	45.00
76	GOOD KING WENCESLAS	UD	45.00	55.00
77	HOLLY & IVY	UD	45.00	45.00
78	WHILE SHEPHERDS WATCHED	UD	45.00	45.00

YR	NAME	LIMIT	ISSUE	TREND
79	AWAY IN A MANGER	UD	50.00	50.00
80	BRINGING IN THE BOAR'S HEAD	UD	60.00	60.00
81	MAKE WE MERRY	UD	65.00	65.00

SPORTS IMPRESSIONS

*

C. HAYES

YR	NAME	LIMIT	ISSUE	TREND
95	CHARLES BARKLEY	2500	150.00	150.00

GLENICE

YR	NAME	LIMIT	ISSUE	TREND
95	DREAM TEAM II	1994	150.00	150.00

CELEBRITY IMPRESSIONS

YR	NAME	LIMIT	ISSUE	TREND
*	HULK HOGAN	5000	40.00	40.00
*	MIKE TYSON	5000	40.00	40.00

J. CATALANO — COLLECTOVAL PLATES

YR	NAME	LIMIT	ISSUE	TREND
90	KINGS OF K	*	195.00	195.00

T. FOGARTY — COLLECTOVAL PLATES

YR	NAME	LIMIT	ISSUE	TREND
90	LIFE OF A LEGEND	1968	195.00	195.00

B. JOHNSON — COLLECTOVAL PLATES

YR	NAME	LIMIT	ISSUE	TREND
90	FENWAY TRADITION	1000	195.00	195.00

M. PETRONELLA — COLLECTOVAL PLATES

YR	NAME	LIMIT	ISSUE	TREND
90	GOLDEN YEARS	1000	195.00	195.00

* — GOLD EDITION PLATES

YR	NAME	LIMIT	ISSUE	TREND
*	JACKIE ROBINSON	1956	150.00	150.00
89	KIRK GIBSON	2500	125.00	125.00

J. CATALANO — GOLD EDITION PLATES

YR	NAME	LIMIT	ISSUE	TREND
88	JOSE CANSECO	2500	125.00	125.00
88	YANKEE TRADITION	CL	150.00	155.00
89	MANTLE SWITCH HITTER	CL	150.00	300.00
89	OREL HERSHISER	2500	125.00	125.00
89	WILL CLARK	CL	125.00	150.00
91	MICHAEL JORDAN	CL	150.00	200.00

T. FOGARTY — GOLD EDITION PLATES

YR	NAME	LIMIT	ISSUE	TREND
88	PAUL MOLITOR	1000	125.00	125.00
89	DARRYL STRAWBERRY #2	CL	125.00	130.00
89	DWIGHT GOODEN	5000	125.00	125.00
89	FRANK VIOLA	2500	125.00	125.00

B. JOHNSON — GOLD EDITION PLATES

YR	NAME	LIMIT	ISSUE	TREND
86	DON MATTINGLY	CL	125.00	180.00
86	WADE BOGGS	CL	125.00	145.00
88	DUKE SNIDER	1500	125.00	125.00

E. LAPERE — GOLD EDITION PLATES

YR	NAME	LIMIT	ISSUE	TREND
87	AL KALINE	1000	125.00	125.00
88	BOB FELLER	2500	125.00	125.00
89	ALAN TRAMMELL	1000	125.00	125.00

R. LEWIS — GOLD EDITION PLATES

YR	NAME	LIMIT	ISSUE	TREND
89	GREATEST CENTERFIELDERS	5000	150.00	150.00
90	ANDRE DAWSON	CL	150.00	150.00
90	LIVING TRIPLE CROWN WINNERS	CL	150.00	190.00
90	TOM SEAVER	CL	150.00	150.00

C.W. MUNDY — GOLD EDITION PLATES

YR	NAME	LIMIT	ISSUE	TREND
91	MAGIC JOHNSON	CL	150.00	200.00

L. SALK — GOLD EDITION PLATES

YR	NAME	LIMIT	ISSUE	TREND
92	TEAM USA BASKETBALL	CL	150.00	250.00

R. SIMON — GOLD EDITION PLATES

YR	NAME	LIMIT	ISSUE	TREND
86	KEITH HERNANDEZ	CL	125.00	170.00
86	LARRY BIRD	CL	125.00	200.00
86	MICKEY MANTLE AT NIGHT	CL	95.00	275.00
87	CARL YASTRZEMSKI	CL	125.00	170.00
87	DARRYL STRAWBERRY #1	CL	125.00	130.00
87	GARY CARTER	CL	125.00	150.00
87	LENNY DYKSTRA	1000	125.00	125.00
87	MICKEY, WILLIE, & DUKE	CL	150.00	525.00
87	TED WILLIAMS U/S	CL	95.00	335.00
88	BROOKS ROBINSON	CL	125.00	200.00

M. PETRONELLA — GOLDEN YEARS

YR	NAME	LIMIT	ISSUE	TREND
90	DUKE SNIDER	5000	60.00	60.00
90	MICKEY MANTLE	5000	60.00	60.00
90	WILLIE MAYS	5000	60.00	60.00

J. CATALANO — NFL GOLD EDITION PLATES

YR	NAME	LIMIT	ISSUE	TREND
90	BOOMER ESIASON	1990	150.00	150.00
90	DAN MARINO	*	150.00	150.00
90	JOE MONTANA 49ERS	CL	150.00	150.00
90	JOHN ELWAY	*	150.00	150.00
90	LAWRENCE TAYLOR	*	150.00	150.00
90	RANDALL CUNNINGHAM	*	150.00	150.00

M. PETRONELLA — NFL PLATINUM EDITION PLATES

YR	NAME	LIMIT	ISSUE	TREND
90	BOOMER ESIASON	*	50.00	50.00
90	DAN MARINO	5000	50.00	50.00
90	JOE MONTANA	5000	50.00	50.00
90	JOHN ELWAY	5000	50.00	50.00
90	LAWRENCE TAYLOR	5000	50.00	50.00
90	RANDALL CUNNINGHAM	5000	50.00	50.00

J. CATALANO — REGULAR EDITION PLATES

YR	NAME	LIMIT	ISSUE	TREND
*	JOSE CANSECO	10000	50.00	65.00
*	WHO'S ON FIRST	10000	50.00	75.00
*	WILL CLARK	10000	50.00	65.00
*	YANKEE TRADITION	10000	50.00	65.00

YR	NAME	LIMIT	ISSUE	TREND
T. FOGARTY			**REGULAR EDITION PLATES**	
*	FRANK VIOLA	10000	50.00	65.00
*	KIRK GIBSON	10000	50.00	65.00
*	PAUL MOLITOR	10000	50.00	65.00
B. JOHNSON			**REGULAR EDITION PLATES**	
*	BABE RUTH	10000	50.00	75.00
*	DON MATTINGLY R/E	5000	50.00	75.00
*	DUKE SNIDER	5000	50.00	75.00
*	LOU GEHRIG	10000	50.00	75.00
*	WADE BOGGS	2000	50.00	65.00
E. LAPERE			**REGULAR EDITION PLATES**	
*	AL KALINE	10000	50.00	65.00
*	ALAN TRAMMEL	10000	50.00	65.00
*	BOB FELLER	10000	50.00	65.00
R. LEWIS			**REGULAR EDITION PLATES**	
*	ANDRE DAWSON	10000	50.00	65.00
*	CY YOUNG	10000	50.00	75.00
*	HONUS WAGNER	10000	50.00	75.00
*	LIVING TRIPLE CROWN	10000	50.00	75.00
*	NOLAN RYAN	5000	150.00	150.00
*	R. CLEMENTE	10000	50.00	75.00
*	TY COBB	10000	50.00	75.00
R. SIMON			**REGULAR EDITION PLATES**	
*	B. ROBINSON	2000	50.00	75.00
*	CARL YASTRZEMSKI	3000	50.00	65.00
*	CARY CARTER	2000	50.00	65.00
*	DARRYL STRAWBERRY R/E	2000	50.00	75.00
*	DEM BUMS	10000	50.00	75.00
*	K. HERNANDEZ	2000	50.00	65.00
*	LARRY BIRD	2000	50.00	65.00
*	LENNY DYKSTRA	2000	50.00	65.00
*	MICKEY MANTLE R/E	3500	50.00	75.00
*	MICKEY, WILLIE, DUKE F/S	3500	50.00	175.00
*	TED WILLIAMS	3000	50.00	65.00
*	THURMAN MUNSON	10000	50.00	75.00

STUDIO COLLECTION

T. RUBEL			**SANTA'S ANIMAL KINGDOM**	
94	SANTA'S ANIMAL KINGDOM COLLECTORS PLATE	5000	30.00	32.00

U.S. HISTORICAL SOCIETY

W. HOMER			**YOUNG AMERICA**	
73	YOUNG AMERICA OF WINSLOW HOMER-6 PLATES	2500	425.00	1100.00

V. PALEKH ART STUDIOS

A. KOVALEV			**RUSSIAN LEGENDS**	
88	PRINCESS/SEVEN BOGATYRS, THE	195 DAYS	30.00	60.00
G. LUBIMOV			**RUSSIAN LEGENDS**	
88	RUSSIAN AND LUDMILLA	195 DAYS	30.00	55.00
V. VLESHKO			**RUSSIAN LEGENDS**	
88	GOLDEN COCKEREL, THE	195 DAYS	33.00	33.00
88	LUKOMORYA	195 DAYS	33.00	33.00
89	FISHERMAN AND THE MAGIC FISH	195 DAYS	33.00	33.00
89	PRIEST AND HIS SERVANT, THE	195 DAYS	35.00	35.00
89	TSAR SALTAN	195 DAYS	33.00	33.00
90	MOROZKO	195 DAYS	37.00	37.00
90	SADKO	195 DAYS	35.00	35.00
90	SILVER HOOF	195 DAYS	37.00	37.00
90	STONE FLOWER	195 DAYS	35.00	35.00
90	TWELVE MONTHS, THE	195 DAYS	37.00	37.00

VAGUE SHADOWS

G. PERILLO			**ARCTIC FRIENDS**	
82	SIBERIAN LOVE	7500	100.00	150.00
82	SNOW PALS	7500	*	N/A
G. PERILLO			**CHIEFTAINS I**	
79	CHIEF JOSEPH	7500	65.00	115.00
79	CHIEF SITTING BULL	7500	65.00	405.00
80	CHIEF GERONIMO	7500	65.00	90.00
80	CHIEF RED CLOUD	7500	65.00	125.00
81	CHIEF CRAZY HORSE	7500	65.00	235.00
G. PERILLO			**CHIEFTAINS II**	
83	CHIEF PONTIAC	7500	70.00	100.00
83	CHIEF VICTORIO	7500	70.00	100.00
84	CHIEF BLACK KETTLE	7500	70.00	100.00
84	CHIEF COCHISE	7500	70.00	100.00
84	CHIEF TECUMSEH	7500	70.00	100.00
G. PERILLO			**CHILD LIFE**	
83	SIESTA	10000	45.00	60.00
84	SWEET DREAMS	10000	45.00	60.00
G. PERILLO			**INDIAN NATIONS**	
83	APACHE (SET)	7500	*	50.00
83	BLACKFOOT	7500	140.00	115.00
83	CHEYENNE (SET)	7500	*	50.00
83	SIOUX (SET)	7500	*	50.00
G. PERILLO			**LEGENDS OF THE WEST**	
82	DANIEL BOONE	10000	65.00	100.00

YR	NAME	LIMIT	ISSUE	TREND
83	BUFFALO BILL	10000	65.00	100.00
83	DAVY CROCKETT	10000	65.00	100.00
83	KIT CARSON	10000	65.00	100.00
G. PERILLO				**MAIDENS**
85	SHIMMERING WATERS	5000	60.00	155.00
85	SNOW BLANKET	5000	60.00	155.00
85	SONG BIRD	5000	60.00	155.00
G. PERILLO				**MOTHERHOOD SERIES**
83	MADRE	10000	50.00	80.00
84	MADONNA OF THE PLAINS	3500	50.00	90.00
85	ABUELA	3500	50.00	80.00
86	NAP TIME	3500	50.00	80.00
G. PERILLO				**NATURE'S HARMONY**
82	BENGAL TIGER	12500	50.00	75.00
82	PEACEABLE KINGDOM, THE	12500	100.00	160.00
82	ZEBRA	12500	50.00	75.00
83	BLACK PANTHER	12500	50.00	75.00
83	ELEPHANT	12500	50.00	75.00
G. PERILLO				**PRINCESSES**
82	LILY OF THE MOHAWKS	7500	50.00	90.00
82	MINNEHAHA	7500	50.00	70.00
82	POCAHONTAS	7500	50.00	60.00
82	SACAJAWEA	7500	50.00	90.00
G. PERILLO				**PROFESSIONALS**
79	BIG LEAGUER, THE	15000	30.00	100.00
80	BALLERINA'S DILEMMA	15000	33.00	50.00
81	QUARTERBACK	15000	33.00	50.00
81	RODEO JOE	15000	35.00	45.00
82	MAJOR LEAGUER	15000	35.00	50.00
83	HOCKEY PLAYER, THE	15000	35.00	50.00
G. PERILLO				**SPECIAL ISSUE**
81	APACHE BOY	5000	95.00	180.00
83	PAPOOSE	3000	100.00	130.00
84	LOVERS, THE	OP	50.00	105.00
84	NAVAJO GIRL	3500	95.00	355.00
86	NAVAJO BOY	3500	95.00	175.00
G. PERILLO				**STORYBOOK COLLECTION**
80	LITTLE RED RIDING HOOD	CL	30.00	45.00
81	CINDERELLA	CL	30.00	45.00
81	HANSEL & GRETEL	CL	30.00	45.00
82	GOLDILOCKS & THE 3 BEARS	CL	30.00	45.00
G. PERILLO				**TENDER MOMENTS**
85	SUNSET	2000	150.00	255.00
85	WINTER ROMANCE	2000	*	N/A
G. PERILLO				**THOROUGHBREDS**
84	MAN O' WAR	9500	50.00	80.00
84	SEABISCUIT	9500	50.00	85.00
84	SECRETARIAT	9500	50.00	85.00
84	WHIRLAWAY	9500	50.00	85.00
G. PERILLO				**TRIBAL PONIES**
84	ARAPAHO TRIBAL PONY	3500	65.00	100.00
84	COMANCHE TRIBAL PONY	3500	65.00	100.00
84	CROW TRIBAL PONY	3500	65.00	100.00
G. PERILLO				**WAR PONIES**
83	APACHE WAR PONY	7500	60.00	100.00
83	NEZ PERCE WAR PONY	7500	60.00	105.00
83	SIOUX WAR PONY	7500	60.00	100.00
G. PERILLO				**YOUNG CHIEFTAINS**
85	YOUNG JOSEPH	5000	50.00	85.00
85	YOUNG SITTING BULL	5000	50.00	85.00
86	YOUNG CRAZY HORSE	5000	50.00	85.00
86	YOUNG GERONIMO	5000	50.00	85.00
86	YOUNG RED CLOUD	5000	50.00	85.00

VENETO FLAIR

V. TIZIANO				**BELLINI**
71	MADONNA	500	45.00	400.00
*				**BIRDS**
72	FALCON	2000	38.00	38.00
72	OWL	2000	38.00	100.00
73	MALLARD	2000	45.00	45.00
V. TIZIANO				**CHRISTMAS**
71	THREE KINGS	1500	55.00	160.00
72	SHEPHERDS	2000	55.00	90.00
73	CHRIST CHILD	2000	55.00	55.00
74	ANGEL	*	55.00	55.00
V. TIZIANO				**DOGS**
72	GERMAN SHEPHERD	2000	38.00	75.00
73	COLLIE	2000	40.00	45.00
73	DACHSHUND	2000	45.00	43.00
73	DOBERMAN	2000	38.00	35.00
73	POODLE	2000	38.00	45.00
*				**EASTER**
73	RABBITS	2000	50.00	90.00
74	CHICKS	2000	50.00	55.00

YR	NAME	LIMIT	ISSUE	TREND
75	LAMB	2000	50.00	55.00
76	COMPOSITE	2000	55.00	55.00

*

ST. MARK'S OF VENICE

YR	NAME	LIMIT	ISSUE	TREND
84	NOAH AND THE DOVE	UD	60.00	65.00
85	MOSES AND THE BURNING BUSH	UD	60.00	65.00
86	ABRAHAM AND THE JOURNEY	UD	60.00	66.00
86	JOSEPH AND THE COAT	UD	63.00	65.00

V. TIZIANO

WILDLIFE

YR	NAME	LIMIT	ISSUE	TREND
71	DEER	500	38.00	450.00
72	ELEPHANT	1000	38.00	275.00
73	PUMA	2000	38.00	65.00
74	TIGER	2000	40.00	50.00

VILETTA

*

DISNEYLAND

YR	NAME	LIMIT	ISSUE	TREND
76	BETSY ROSS	3000	15.00	100.00
76	CROSSING THE DELAWARE	3000	15.00	100.00
76	SIGNING THE DECLARATION	3000	15.00	100.00
76	SPIRIT OF '76	3000	15.00	100.00
79	MICKEY'S 50TH ANNIVERSARY	5000	37.00	50.00

*

NUTCRACKER BALLET

YR	NAME	LIMIT	ISSUE	TREND
78	CLARA AND NUTCRACKER	OP	20.00	10.00
79	GIFT FROM GODFATHER	OP	20.00	9.00
79	SNOW KING AND QUEEN	OP	20.00	24.00
80	CARLA AND THE PRINCE	OP	20.00	15.00
80	WALTZ OF THE FLOWERS	OP	20.00	11.00

S. FISHER

NUTCRACKER BALLET

YR	NAME	LIMIT	ISSUE	TREND
79	SUGARPLUM FAIRY, THE	CL	20.00	25.00

D. ZOLAN

ZOLAN'S CHILDREN

YR	NAME	LIMIT	ISSUE	TREND
78	ERIK AND DANDELION	OP	19.00	240.00
79	SABINA IN THE GRASS	RT	22.00	300.00
80	BY MYSELF	OP	24.00	24.00
81	FOR YOU	OP	24.00	24.00

VILLEROY & BOCH

C. BARKER

FLOWER FAIRY

YR	NAME	LIMIT	ISSUE	TREND
79	LAVENDER	CL	35.00	130.00
80	CANDYTUFT	CL	35.00	90.00
80	SWEET PEA	CL	35.00	130.00
81	APPLEBLOSSOM	CL	35.00	100.00
81	BLACKTHORN	CL	35.00	80.00
81	HELIOTROPE	CL	35.00	80.00

B. ZVORYKIN

RUSSIAN FAIRY TALES MARIA MOREVNA

YR	NAME	LIMIT	ISSUE	TREND
82	KOSHCHEY CARRIES OFF MARIA MOREVNA	27500	70.00	75.00
82	MARIA MOREVNA AND TSAREVICH IVAN	27500	70.00	85.00
82	TSAREVICH IVAN AND THE BEAUTIFUL CASTLE	27500	70.00	105.00

B. ZVORYKIN

RUSSIAN FAIRY TALES SNOW MAIDEN

YR	NAME	LIMIT	ISSUE	TREND
80	SNOW MAIDEN, THE	27500	70.00	120.00
81	SNEGUROCHKA AND LEI, THE SHEPHERD BOY	27500	70.00	70.00
81	SNEGUROCHKA AT THE COURT/TSAR BERENDEI	27500	70.00	70.00

B. ZVORYKIN

RUSSIAN FAIRY TALES THE FIREBIRD

YR	NAME	LIMIT	ISSUE	TREND
81	IN SEARCH OF THE FIREBIRD	27500	70.00	105.00
81	IVAN AND TSAREVNA ON THE GREY WOLF	27500	70.00	75.00
81	WEDDING OF TSAREVNA ELENA THE FAIR, THE	27500	70.00	109.00

B. ZVORYKIN

RUSSIAN FAIRY TALES THE RED KNIGHT

YR	NAME	LIMIT	ISSUE	TREND
81	RED KNIGHT, THE	27500	70.00	55.00
81	VASSILISSA AND HER STEPSISTERS	27500	70.00	55.00
81	VASSILISSA IS PRESENTED TO THE TSAR	27500	70.00	65.00

W.S. GEORGE

H. LAMBSON

ALASKA: THE LAST FRONTIER

YR	NAME	LIMIT	ISSUE	TREND
91	AUTUMN GRANDEUR	CL	35.00	40.00
91	ICY MAJESTY	CL	35.00	40.00
92	ARCTIC JOURNEY	CL	40.00	45.00
92	DOWN THE TRAIL	CL	38.00	45.00
92	GRACEFUL PASSAGE	CL	40.00	45.00
92	MOONLIGHT LOOKOUT	CL	38.00	45.00
92	MOUNTAIN MONARCH	CL	38.00	40.00
92	SUMMIT DOMAIN	CL	40.00	45.00

M. HARVEY

ALONG AN ENGLISH LANE

YR	NAME	LIMIT	ISSUE	TREND
93	COTTAGE AROUND THE BEND	CL	30.00	35.00
93	FRIENDS AND FLOWERS	CL	30.00	35.00
93	GREETING THE DAY	CL	30.00	35.00
93	SUMMER'S BRIGHT WELCOME	CL	30.00	35.00

H. JOHNSON

AMERICA THE BEAUTIFUL

YR	NAME	LIMIT	ISSUE	TREND
88	GRAND CANYON, THE	CL	35.00	40.00
88	YOSEMITE FALLS	CL	35.00	40.00
89	GREAT SMOKEY MOUNTAINS, THE	CL	38.00	40.00
89	YELLOWSTONE RIVER	CL	38.00	40.00
90	ACADIA	CL	38.00	45.00
90	CRATER LAKE	CL	40.00	45.00
90	EVERGLADES, THE	CL	38.00	40.00
90	GRAND TETONS, THE	CL	40.00	45.00

R. RICHERT

AMERICA'S PRIDE

YR	NAME	LIMIT	ISSUE	TREND
92	MISTY FJORDS	CL	30.00	70.00
92	RUGGED SHORES	CL	30.00	55.00
93	CANYON CLIMB	CL	35.00	40.00

YR	NAME	LIMIT	ISSUE	TREND
93	GOLDEN VISTA	CL	35.00	40.00
93	LOFTY REFLECTIONS	CL	33.00	40.00
93	MIGHTY SUMMIT	CL	33.00	70.00
93	MOUNTAIN MAJESTY	CL	35.00	40.00
93	TRANQUIL WATERS	CL	33.00	40.00
M. MCDONALD				**ART DECO**
89	A FLAPPER WITH GREYHOUNDS	CL	40.00	55.00
90	ARRIVING IN STYLE	CL	40.00	80.00
90	ON THE TOWN	CL	40.00	80.00
90	TANGO DANCERS	CL	40.00	65.00
J. SEEREY-LESTER				**BEAR TRACKS**
92	DENALI FAMILY	CL	30.00	35.00
93	ALONG THE ICE FLOW	CL	30.00	35.00
93	BREAKING COVER	CL	30.00	35.00
93	HEAVY GOING	CL	30.00	35.00
93	HIGH COUNTRY CHAMPION	CL	30.00	35.00
93	THEIR FIRST SEASON	CL	30.00	35.00
C. BARKER				**BELOVED HYMNS OF CHILDHOOD**
88	AWAY IN A MANGER	CL	30.00	35.00
88	LORD'S MY SHEPHERD, THE	CL	30.00	50.00
89	ALL GLORY, LAUD AND HONOUR	CL	33.00	35.00
89	I LOVE TO HEAR THE STORY	CL	33.00	35.00
89	LOVE DIVINE	CL	33.00	35.00
89	NOW THANK WE ALL OUR GOD	CL	33.00	35.00
90	ALL PEOPLE ON EARTH DO DWELL	CL	35.00	40.00
90	LOVING SHEPHERD OF THY SHEEP	OP	35.00	40.00
C. JAGODITS				**BLACK TIE AFFAIR: THE PENGUIN**
92	BABY-SITTERS	CL	30.00	35.00
92	LITTLE EXPLORER	CL	30.00	35.00
92	PENGUIN PARADE	CL	30.00	35.00
93	BELLY FLOPPING	CL	30.00	35.00
W. RANE				**BLESSED ARE THE CHILDREN**
90	I AM THE GOOD SHEPHERD	CL	30.00	55.00
91	BLESSED ARE THE PEACEMAKERS	CL	35.00	50.00
91	HOSANNA IN THE HIGHEST	CL	33.00	45.00
91	I AM THE VINE, YOU ARE THE BRANCHES	CL	35.00	65.00
91	JESUS HAD COMPASSION ON THEM	CL	33.00	40.00
91	LET THE LITTLE CHILDREN COME TO ME	CL	30.00	40.00
91	SEEK AND YOU WILL FIND	CL	35.00	45.00
91	WHOEVER WELCOMES THIS LITTLE CHILD	CL	33.00	45.00
B. BURKE				**BONDS OF LOVE**
89	PRECIOUS EMBRACE	CL	30.00	40.00
90	CHERISHED MOMENT	CL	30.00	35.00
91	TENDER CARESS	CL	33.00	40.00
92	LOVING TOUCH	CL	33.00	45.00
92	TREASURED KISSES	CL	33.00	50.00
94	ENDEARING WHISPERS	CL	33.00	35.00
H. GARRIDO				**CHRISTMAS STORY**
92	GIFTS OF THE MAGI	CL	30.00	35.00
93	ADORATION OF THE SHEPHERDS	CL	30.00	35.00
93	ANNUNCIATION, THE	CL	30.00	35.00
93	JOURNEY OF THE MAGI	CL	30.00	35.00
93	NATIVITY, THE	CL	30.00	35.00
93	REST ON THE FLIGHT INTO EGYPT	CL	30.00	35.00
J. PENALVA		**COLUMBUS DISCOVERS AMERICA: THE 500TH ANNIVERSARY**		
92	ASHORE AT DAWN	CL	30.00	50.00
92	BRINGING TOGETHER TWO CULTURES	CL	33.00	65.00
92	COLUMBUS RAISES THE FLAG	CL	33.00	60.00
92	QUEEN'S APPROVAL, THE	CL	33.00	60.00
92	TREASURES FROM THE NEW WORLD	CL	33.00	55.00
92	UNDER FULL SAIL	CL	30.00	55.00
G. KURZ				**COUNTRY BOUQUETS**
91	GARDEN'S BOUNTY	CL	33.00	40.00
91	MORNING SUNSHINE	CL	30.00	45.00
91	SUMMER PERFUME	CL	30.00	55.00
91	WARM WELCOME	CL	33.00	55.00
M. HARVEY				**COUNTRY NOSTALGIA**
89	APPLE CIDER PRESS, THE	CL	30.00	45.00
89	OLD HAND PUMP, THE	CL	33.00	45.00
89	SPRING BUGGY, THE	CL	30.00	35.00
89	VINTAGE SEED PLANTER, THE	CL	30.00	45.00
90	ANTIQUE SPINNING WHEEL, THE	CL	35.00	40.00
90	DAIRY CANS, THE	CL	33.00	40.00
90	FORGOTTEN PLOW, THE	CL	35.00	40.00
90	WOODEN BUTTER CHURN, THE	CL	33.00	50.00
P. JENNIS		**CRITIC'S CHOICE: GONE WITH THE WIND**		
91	A DECLARATION OF LOVE	CL	31.00	60.00
91	MARRY ME, SCARLETT	CL	28.00	50.00
91	PARIS HAT, THE	CL	31.00	50.00
91	SCARLETT ASKS A FAVOR	CL	31.00	50.00
91	WAITING FOR RHETT	CL	28.00	50.00
92	BUGGY RIDE, THE	CL	33.00	35.00
92	SCARLETT GETS DOWN TO BUSINESS	CL	35.00	40.00
92	SCARLETT GETS HER WAY	CL	33.00	55.00
92	SCARLETT'S SHOPPING SPREE	CL	33.00	35.00
92	SMITTEN SUITOR, THE	CL	33.00	50.00

YR	NAME	LIMIT	ISSUE	TREND
93	AT CROSS PURPOSES	CL	35.00	35.00
93	SCARLETT'S HEART IS W/TARA	CL	35.00	35.00
G. BEECHAM		DELICATE BALANCE: VANISHING WILDLIFE		
92	TOMORROW'S HOPE	CL	30.00	35.00
93	EYES ON THE NEW DAY	CL	33.00	40.00
93	PRESENT DREAMS	CL	33.00	40.00
93	TODAY'S FUTURE	CL	30.00	35.00
G. BUSH				DR. ZHIVAGO
91	LARA'S LOVE	CL	40.00	50.00
91	LOVE POEMS FOR LARA	CL	40.00	45.00
91	ZHIVAGO AND LARA	CL	40.00	45.00
91	ZHIVAGO SAYS FAREWELL	CL	40.00	45.00
*				DUCKS UNLIMITED
88	CANADA GEESE/AUTUMN FIELDS	OP	37.00	37.00
90	PINTAILS IN INDIAN SUMMER	OP	40.00	40.00
L. KAATZ				DUCKS UNLIMITED
88	MALLARDS AT SUNRISE	*	*	55.00
89	CANVAS BACKS BREAKING AWAY	*	*	53.00
89	GREEN WINGS AT MORNING MARSH	*	*	51.00
90	BLUEBILLS COMING IN	*	*	53.00
90	SNOWGEESE AGAINST NOV. SKIES	*	*	53.00
90	WOOD DUCKS TAKING FLIGHT	*	*	49.00
J. FAULKNER				ELEGANT BIRDS
88	GREAT BLUE HERON	CL	33.00	35.00
88	SWAN, THE	CL	33.00	35.00
89	ANHINGA, THE	CL	36.00	40.00
89	FLAMINGO, THE	CL	36.00	40.00
89	SNOWY EGRET	CL	33.00	40.00
90	SANDHILL AND WHOOPING CRANE	CL	36.00	40.00
E. ANTONACCIO				ENCHANTED GARDEN
93	A PEACEFUL RETREAT	CL	25.00	30.00
93	A PLACE TO DREAM	CL	25.00	30.00
93	PLEASANT PATHWAYS	CL	25.00	30.00
93	TRANQUIL HIDEAWAY	CL	25.00	30.00
*				ENDANGERED SPECIES
89	RED WOLF, THE	OP	31.00	31.00
D. PIERCE				EYES OF THE WILD
93	EYES IN THE MIST	CL	30.00	35.00
93	EYES IN THE PINES	CL	30.00	35.00
93	EYES IN THE SNOW	CL	30.00	35.00
93	EYES OF GOLD	CL	30.00	35.00
93	EYES OF SILENCE	CL	30.00	35.00
93	EYES OF WONDER	CL	30.00	35.00
93	EYES ON THE SLY	CL	30.00	35.00
94	EYES OF STRENGTH	CL	30.00	35.00
J. KRAMER-COLE				FACES OF NATURE
92	CANYON OF THE CAT	RT	30.00	35.00
92	WOLF RIDGE	CL	30.00	35.00
93	TRAIL OF THE TALISMAN	CL	30.00	35.00
93	TWO BEARS CAMP	CL	30.00	35.00
93	WAMBLI OKIYE	CL	30.00	35.00
93	WINTERING WITH THE WAPITI	CL	30.00	35.00
93	WITHIN SUNRISE	CL	30.00	35.00
93	WOLFPACK OF THE ANCIENTS	CL	30.00	35.00
N. ANDERSON		FEDERAL DUCK STAMP PLATE COLLECTION		
90	CANVASBACKS	CL	31.00	40.00
90	LESSER SCAUP, THE	CL	28.00	45.00
90	MALLARD	CL	28.00	60.00
90	RUDDY DUCKS, THE	CL	31.00	30.00
91	CINNAMON TEAL	CL	33.00	35.00
91	FULVOUS WISTLING DUCK	CL	33.00	50.00
91	PINTAILS	CL	31.00	32.00
91	REDHEADS, THE	CL	33.00	50.00
91	SNOW GOOSE	CL	33.00	35.00
91	WIGEONS	CL	31.00	40.00
H. RONNER				FELINE FANCY
93	GEOGRAPHERS, THE	CL	35.00	40.00
93	GLOBETROTTERS	CL	35.00	40.00
93	LITTLE ATHLETES	CL	35.00	40.00
93	YOUNG ADVENTURERS	CL	35.00	40.00
D. BUSH		FIELD BIRDS OF NORTH AMERICA		
91	AUTUMN MOMENT: AMERICAN WOODCOCK	CL	43.00	75.00
91	IN DISPLAY: RUFFED GOOSE	CL	40.00	50.00
91	MISTY CLEARING: WILD TURKEY	CL	43.00	60.00
91	MORNING LIGHT: BOBWHITE QUAIL	CL	43.00	65.00
91	WINTER COLORS: RING-NECKED PHEASANT	CL	40.00	55.00
92	SEASON'S END: WILLOW PTARMIGAN	CL	43.00	50.00
C. CALLOG				FLORAL FANCIES
93	SITTING PINK	CL	35.00	40.00
93	SITTING PRETTY	CL	35.00	40.00
93	SITTING SUNNY	CL	35.00	40.00
L. LIU				FLOWER FAIRIES
93	ARMOROUS ANGELS	*	33.00	45.00
93	DELICATE DANCER	*	*	50.00
93	FANCIFUL FAIRIES	*	35.00	55.00
93	MAGIC MAKERS	CL	30.00	40.00
93	MISCHIEF MASTERS	*	33.00	45.00

YR	NAME	LIMIT	ISSUE	TREND
93	PETAL PLAYMATE	*	30.00	40.00
95	MINIATURE MERMAIDS	*	35.00	50.00
G. KURZ		**FLOWERS FROM GRANDMA'S GARDEN**		
90	COUNTRY CUTTINGS	CL	25.00	50.00
90	MORNING BOUQUET, THE	CL	25.00	45.00
91	A COUNTRY WELCOME	CL	30.00	60.00
91	GARDENER'S DELIGHT	CL	28.00	65.00
91	HARVEST IN THE MEADOW	CL	28.00	35.00
91	HOMESPUN BEAUTY	CL	28.00	40.00
91	NATURE'S BOUNTY	CL	28.00	55.00
91	SPRINGTIME ARRANGEMENT, THE	CL	30.00	55.00
V. MORLEY		**FLOWERS OF YOUR GARDEN**		
88	CHRYSANTHEMUMS	CL	28.00	30.00
88	DAISIES	CL	28.00	45.00
88	LILACS	CL	25.00	50.00
88	PEONIES	CL	28.00	30.00
88	ROSES	CL	25.00	70.00
89	DAFFODILS	CL	28.00	30.00
89	IRISES	CL	30.00	35.00
89	TULIPS	CL	30.00	35.00
C. GILLIES		**GARDEN OF THE LORD**		
92	ASK IN PRAYER	CL	35.00	40.00
92	LORD BLESS YOU, THE	CL	33.00	40.00
92	LORD'S LOVE, THE	CL	33.00	40.00
92	LOVE ONE ANOTHER	CL	30.00	35.00
92	PERFECT PEACE	CL	30.00	35.00
92	TRUST IN THE LORD	CL	33.00	40.00
93	GIVE THANKS TO THE LORD	CL	35.00	40.00
93	PEACE BE WITH YOU	CL	35.00	40.00
L. CHANG		**GARDENS OF PARADISE**		
92	SPLENDOR	CL	33.00	40.00
92	TRANQUILITY	CL	30.00	35.00
93	BEAUTY	CL	33.00	40.00
93	ELEGANCE	CL	33.00	40.00
93	GRANDEUR	CL	33.00	40.00
93	HARMONY	CL	33.00	40.00
93	MAJESTY	CL	33.00	40.00
93	SERENITY	CL	30.00	35.00
W. NELSON		**GENTLE BEGINNINGS**		
91	A TOUCH OF LOVE	CL	35.00	70.00
91	LAP OF LOVE	CL	38.00	45.00
91	TENDER LOVING CARE	CL	35.00	60.00
91	UNDER WATCHFUL EYES	CL	38.00	65.00
92	FIRST STEPS	CL	38.00	50.00
92	HAPPY TOGETHER	CL	38.00	50.00
R. COBANE		**GLORIOUS SONGBIRDS**		
91	BALTIMORE ORIOLES/AUTUMN LEAVES	CL	35.00	40.00
91	BLUEBIRDS IN A BLUEBERRY BUSH	CL	35.00	40.00
91	CARDINALS ON A SNOWY BRANCH	CL	30.00	40.00
91	CEDAR WAXWING/WINTER BERRIES	CL	33.00	35.00
91	CHICKADEES AMONG THE LILACS	CL	33.00	35.00
91	GOLDFINCHES IN THE THISTLE	CL	33.00	35.00
91	INDIGO BUNTINGS AND/BLOSSOMS	CL	30.00	35.00
91	ROBINS WITH DOGWOOD IN BLOOM	CL	35.00	40.00
C. VICKERY		**GOLDEN AGE OF THE CLIPPER SHIP**		
89	BLUE JACKET AT SUNSET, THE	CL	30.00	35.00
89	TWILIGHT UNDER FULL SAIL, THE	CL	30.00	35.00
89	YOUNG AMERICA, HOMEWARD	CL	33.00	35.00
90	DAVY CROCKETT AT DAYBREAK	CL	33.00	40.00
90	FLYING CLOUD	CL	33.00	50.00
90	GOLDEN EAGLE CONQUERS WIND	CL	33.00	40.00
90	LIGHTNING IN LIFTING FOG, THE	CL	35.00	40.00
90	SEA WITCH, MISTRESS/OCEANS	CL	35.00	50.00
H. ROGERS		**GONE WITH THE WIND: GOLDEN ANNIVERSARY**		
88	BURNING OF ATLANTA, THE	CL	25.00	70.00
88	PROPOSAL, THE	CL	28.00	110.00
88	SCARLETT AND ASHLEY AFTER THE WAR	CL	28.00	75.00
88	SCARLETT AND HER SUITORS	CL	25.00	75.00
89	A QUESTION OF HONOR	CL	30.00	45.00
89	FRANKLY MY DEAR	CL	30.00	65.00
89	HOME TO TARA	CL	28.00	50.00
89	MELANIE AND ASHLEY	CL	33.00	50.00
89	SCARLETT'S RESOLVE	CL	30.00	50.00
89	STROLLING IN ATLANTA	CL	28.00	55.00
90	A TOAST TO BONNIE BLUE	CL	33.00	55.00
90	SCARLETT & RHETT'S HONEYMOON	CL	33.00	60.00
C. FRACE		**GRAND SAFARI: IMAGES OF AFRICA**		
92	A MOMENT'S REST	CL	35.00	40.00
92	ELEPHANTS OF KILIMANJARO	CL	35.00	40.00
92	GREATER KUDO, THE	CL	38.00	45.00
92	LONE HUNTER	CL	38.00	45.00
92	QUIET TIME IN SAMBURU	CL	38.00	45.00
92	UNDIVIDED ATTENTION	CL	38.00	45.00
G. BEECHAM		**HEART OF THE WILD**		
91	A GENTLE TOUCH	CL	30.00	55.00
92	AN AFTERNOON TOGETHER	CL	33.00	50.00

Artist P. Buckley Moss captures the simplistic pleasures of Amish life in Family Outing, *the first issue in "The Family Collection" produced by Anna Perenna.*

Recalling a historic moment for baby boomers, 1991's The Beatles, Live in Concert *was the first issue in "The Beatles" series from Delphi.*

Valentine Joy *was produced as a M.I. Hummel Club exclusive available to members only.*

R. Cobane's Cardinals on a Snowy Branch *was the first issue in the "Glorious Songbirds" series from W.S. George.*

YR	NAME	LIMIT	ISSUE	TREND
92	MOTHER'S PRIDE	CL	30.00	105.00
92	QUIET TIME?	CL	33.00	35.00

E. DZENIS — **HOLLYWOOD'S GLAMOUR GIRLS**

YR	NAME	LIMIT	ISSUE	TREND
89	JEAN HARLOW-DINNER AT EIGHT	CL	25.00	45.00
90	CAROL LOMBAR/THE GAY BRIDE	CL	30.00	35.00
90	GRETA GARBO-IN GRAND HOTEL	CL	30.00	35.00
90	LANA TURNER-POSTMAN RINGS TWICE	CL	30.00	35.00

H.T. BECKER — **HOMETOWN MEMORIES**

YR	NAME	LIMIT	ISSUE	TREND
93	A WINTER RIDE	CL	30.00	30.00
93	HEADING HOME	CL	30.00	30.00
93	MOONLIGHT SKATERS	CL	30.00	30.00
93	MOUNTAIN SLEIGH RIDE	CL	30.00	30.00

W. NELSON — **LAST OF THEIR KIND: THE ENDANGERED SPECIES**

YR	NAME	LIMIT	ISSUE	TREND
88	PANDA, THE	CL	28.00	50.00
88	SNOW LEOPARD, THE	CL	28.00	50.00
89	ASIAN ELEPHANT, THE	CL	31.00	30.00
89	RED WOLF, THE	CL	31.00	30.00
90	BLACK-FOOTED FERRET, THE	CL	34.00	35.00
90	BRIDLED WALLABY, THE	CL	31.00	30.00
90	SIBERIAN TIGER, THE	CL	34.00	40.00
90	SLENDER-HORNED GAZELLE, THE	CL	31.00	30.00
91	PRZEWALSKI'S HORSE	CL	34.00	35.00
91	VICUNA, THE	CL	34.00	35.00

L. LIU — **LENA LIU'S BASKET BOUQUETS**

YR	NAME	LIMIT	ISSUE	TREND
92	IRISES	CL	33.00	55.00
92	LILIES	CL	33.00	65.00
92	PANSIES	CL	30.00	50.00
92	PARROT TULIPS	CL	33.00	50.00
92	PEONIES	CL	33.00	50.00
92	ROSES	CL	30.00	35.00
92	TULIPS AND LILACS	CL	33.00	40.00
93	BEGONIAS	CL	33.00	32.50
93	CALLA LILIES	CL	33.00	40.00
93	HYDRANGEAS	CL	33.00	40.00
93	MAGNOLIAS	CL	33.00	40.00
93	ORCHIDS	CL	33.00	40.00

L. LIU — **LENA LIU'S HUMMINGBIRD TREASURY**

YR	NAME	LIMIT	ISSUE	TREND
92	ANNA'S HUMMINGBIRD	CL	30.00	35.00
92	RUBY-THROATED HUMMINGBIRD, THE	CL	30.00	35.00
92	RUFOUS HIUMMINGBIRD, THE	CL	33.00	40.00
92	VIOLET-CROWNED HUMMINGBIRD	CL	33.00	40.00
93	ALLEN'S HUMMINGBIRD, THE	CL	35.00	40.00
93	BOARD-BILLED HUMMINGBIRD	CL	35.00	40.00
93	CALLIOPE HUMMINGBIRD	CL	35.00	40.00
93	WHITE-EARED HUMMINGBIRD	CL	33.00	40.00

B. BURKE — **LITTLE ANGELS**

YR	NAME	LIMIT	ISSUE	TREND
92	ANGELS WE HAVE HEARD ON HIGH	CL	30.00	48.00
92	O TANNENBAUM	CL	30.00	60.00
93	FIRST NOEL, THE	CL	33.00	58.00
93	HARK THE HERALD ANGELS SING	CL	33.00	33.00
93	IT CAME UPON A MIDNIGHT CLEAR	CL	33.00	33.00
93	JOY TO THE WORLD	CL	33.00	40.00

B. LANGTON — **LOVING LOOK: DUCK FAMILIES**

YR	NAME	LIMIT	ISSUE	TREND
90	FAMILY OUTING	CL	35.00	40.00
91	FAMILY TREE, THE	CL	38.00	55.00
91	QUIET MOMENT	CL	38.00	40.00
91	SAFE AND SOUND	CL	38.00	40.00
91	SLEEPY START	CL	35.00	40.00
91	SPRING ARRIVALS	CL	38.00	75.00

P. WILDERMUTH — **MAJESTIC HORSE**

YR	NAME	LIMIT	ISSUE	TREND
92	AMERICAN GOLD: THE QUARTERHORSE	CL	35.00	45.00
92	CLASSIC BEAUTY: THOROUGHBRED	CL	35.00	50.00
92	REGAL SPIRIT: THE ARABIAN	CL	35.00	55.00
92	WESTERN FAVORITE: AM. PAINT HORSE	CL	35.00	60.00

A. SAKHAVARZ — **MELODIES IN THE MIST**

YR	NAME	LIMIT	ISSUE	TREND
93	AMONG THE DEWDROPS	CL	35.00	40.00
93	EARLY MORNING RAIN	CL	35.00	40.00
93	FEEDING TIME	CL	38.00	45.00
93	GARDEN PARTY, THE	CL	38.00	45.00
93	SPRING RAIN	CL	38.00	45.00
93	UNPLEASANT SURPRISE	CL	38.00	45.00

* — **MEMORIES OF A VICTORIAN CHILDHOOD**

YR	NAME	LIMIT	ISSUE	TREND
92	AN ARMFUL OF TREASURES	CL	33.00	50.00
92	SWEET SLUMBER	CL	30.00	60.00
92	THROUGH THICK AND THIN	CL	33.00	55.00
92	YOU'D BETTER NOT POUT	CL	30.00	30.00
93	A TRIO OF BOOKWORMS	CL	33.00	65.00
93	PUGNACIOUS PLAYMATE	CL	33.00	65.00

J. SIAS — **NATURE'S LEGACY**

YR	NAME	LIMIT	ISSUE	TREND
90	BLUE SNOW AT HALF DOME	CL	25.00	35.00
91	AUTUMN SPLENDOR IN THE SMOKEY MTNS.	CL	28.00	30.00
91	GOLDEN MAJESTY/ROCKY MOUNTAINS	CL	30.00	35.00
91	HAVASU CANYON	CL	28.00	30.00
91	MISTY MORNING/MT. MCKINLEY	CL	25.00	40.00
91	MOUNT RANIER	CL	28.00	28.00
91	MT. RANIER/TWILIGHT REFLECTIONS	CL	28.00	40.00

YR	NAME	LIMIT	ISSUE	TREND
91	RADIANT SUNSET OVER THE EVERGLADES	CL	30.00	35.00
91	WINTER PEACE IN YELLOWSTONE PARK	CL	30.00	35.00

C. FRACE — NATURE'S LOVABLES

YR	NAME	LIMIT	ISSUE	TREND
90	KOALA, THE	CL	28.00	45.00
91	BABY HARP SEAL	CL	31.00	65.00
91	BANDIT	CL	33.00	45.00
91	BOBCAT: NATURE'S DAWN	CL	31.00	35.00
91	CHINESE TREASURE	CL	28.00	30.00
91	CLOUDED LEOPARD	CL	33.00	40.00
91	NEW ARRIVAL	CL	28.00	50.00
91	ZEBRA FOAL	CL	33.00	65.00

C. FRACE — NATURE'S PLAYMATES

YR	NAME	LIMIT	ISSUE	TREND
91	DOUBLE TROUBLE	CL	33.00	50.00
91	PALS	CL	33.00	50.00
91	PARTNERS	CL	30.00	50.00
91	RECESS	CL	33.00	50.00
91	SECRET HEIGHTS	CL	30.00	40.00
92	AMBASSADORS	CL	37.00	40.00
92	CURIOUS TRIO	CL	35.00	40.00
92	PEACE ON ICE	CL	37.00	40.00
92	PLAYMATES	CL	35.00	40.00
92	SURPRISE	CL	35.00	40.00

L. LIU — NATURE'S POETRY

YR	NAME	LIMIT	ISSUE	TREND
89	MORNING SERENADE	CL	25.00	40.00
89	SONG OF PROMISE	CL	25.00	45.00
90	GENTLE REFRAIN	CL	28.00	35.00
90	MELODY AT DAYBREAK	CL	30.00	35.00
90	MORNING CHORUS	CL	28.00	40.00
90	NATURE'S HARMONY	CL	28.00	55.00
90	TENDER LULLABY	CL	28.00	30.00
91	CHERUB CHORALE	CL	33.00	55.00
91	DELICATE ACCORD	CL	30.00	40.00
91	LYRICAL BEGINNINGS	CL	30.00	40.00
91	MOTHER'S MELODY	CL	33.00	45.00
91	SONG OF SPRING	CL	33.00	45.00

W. GOEBEL — ON GOLDEN WINGS

YR	NAME	LIMIT	ISSUE	TREND
93	AS DAY BREAKS	CL	33.00	40.00
93	DAYLIGHT FLIGHT	CL	33.00	40.00
93	EARLY RISERS	CL	30.00	35.00
93	MORNING LIGHT	CL	30.00	35.00
93	WINTER DAWN	CL	33.00	40.00
94	FIRST LIGHT	CL	35.00	40.00

L. LIU — ON GOSSAMER WINGS

YR	NAME	LIMIT	ISSUE	TREND
88	MALACHITES	CL	28.00	30.00
88	MONARCH BUTTERFLIES	CL	25.00	40.00
88	RED-SPOTTED PURPLE	CL	28.00	35.00
88	WESTERN TIGER SWALLOWTAILS	CL	25.00	40.00
88	WHITE PEACOCKS	CL	28.00	50.00
89	EASTERN TAILED BLUES	CL	28.00	30.00
89	RED ADMIRALS	CL	30.00	40.00
89	ZEBRA SWALLOWTAILS	CL	30.00	35.00

T. HUMPHREY — ON THE WING

YR	NAME	LIMIT	ISSUE	TREND
92	GLORIOUS ASCENT	CL	33.00	40.00
92	RISING MALLARD	CL	30.00	35.00
92	TAKING WING	CL	33.00	40.00
92	UPWARD BOUND	CL	33.00	40.00
92	WINGED SPLENDOR	CL	30.00	35.00
93	ON THE WING	CL	35.00	40.00
93	SPRINGING FORTH	CL	25.00	40.00
93	WONDROUS MOTION	CL	35.00	40.00

L. LIU — ON WINGS OF SNOW

YR	NAME	LIMIT	ISSUE	TREND
91	COCKATOOS, THE	CL	38.00	45.00
91	DOVES, THE	CL	35.00	40.00
91	EGRETS, THE	CL	38.00	40.00
91	PEACOCKS, THE	CL	38.00	40.00
91	SWANS, THE	CL	35.00	40.00
92	HERONS, THE	CL	38.00	40.00

C. BRENDERS — OUR WOODLAND FRIENDS

YR	NAME	LIMIT	ISSUE	TREND
89	FASCINATION	CL	30.00	30.00
90	BENEATH THE PINES	CL	30.00	30.00
90	HIGH ADVENTURE	CL	33.00	35.00
90	SHY EXPLORERS	CL	33.00	40.00
91	A JUMP INTO LIFE: SPRING FAWN	CL	35.00	45.00
91	FOREST SENTINEL: BOBCAT	CL	35.00	45.00
91	FULL HOUSE FOX FAMILY	CL	33.00	65.00
91	GOLDEN SEASON: GRAY SQUIRREL	CL	33.00	40.00

P. JENNIS — PASSIONS OF SCARLETT O'HARA

YR	NAME	LIMIT	ISSUE	TREND
92	AS GOD IS MY WITNESS	CL	35.00	55.00
92	DREAMS OF ASHLEY	CL	33.00	75.00
92	FIERY EMBRACE	CL	30.00	70.00
92	FOND FAREWELL, THE	CL	33.00	55.00
92	PRIDE AND PASSION	CL	30.00	70.00
92	WALTZ, THE	CL	33.00	80.00
93	BRAVE SCARLETT	CL	35.00	40.00
93	DANGEROUS ATTRACTION	CL	37.00	40.00
93	EVENING PRAYERS	CL	35.00	40.00
93	NAPTIME	CL	37.00	40.00

YR	NAME	LIMIT	ISSUE	TREND
93	NIGHTMARE	CL	35.00	40.00
94	END OF AN ERA, THE	CL	37.00	40.00
C. FRACE		**PAW PRINTS: BABY CATS OF THE WILD**		
92	MORNING MISCHIEF	CL	30.00	35.00
93	BUDDY SYSTEM, THE	CL	33.00	40.00
93	NAP TIME	CL	33.00	40.00
93	TOGETHERNESS	CL	30.00	35.00
L. CHANG			**PETAL PALS**	
92	FLOWERING FASCINATION	CL	25.00	30.00
92	GARDEN DISCOVERY	CL	25.00	30.00
93	ALLURING LILIES	CL	25.00	30.00
93	BLOSSOMING ADVENTURE	CL	25.00	30.00
93	DANCING DAFFODILS	CL	25.00	30.00
93	MORNING MELODY	CL	25.00	30.00
93	SPRINGTIME OASIS	CL	25.00	30.00
93	SUMMER SURPRISE	CL	25.00	30.00
C. VALENTE			**POETIC COTTAGES**	
92	BEDFORDSHIRE EVENING SKY	CL	33.00	40.00
92	GARDEN PATHS OF OXFORDSHIRE	CL	30.00	35.00
92	STONEWALL BROOK BLOSSOMS	CL	33.00	40.00
92	TWILIGHT AT WOODGREEN POND	CL	30.00	35.00
93	ALDERBURY GARDENS	CL	33.00	40.00
93	HAMPSHIRE SPRING SPLENDOR	CL	33.00	40.00
93	WILTSHIRE ROSE ARBOR	CL	33.00	40.00
93	WISTERIA SUMMER	CL	33.00	40.00
J. SALAMANCA			**PORTRAITS OF CHRIST**	
91	BECOME AS LITTLE CHILDREN	CL	33.00	65.00
91	FATHER, FORGIVE THEM	CL	30.00	95.00
91	LO, I AM WITH YOU	CL	33.00	65.00
91	PEACE I LEAVE WITH YOU	CL	35.00	70.00
91	THIS IS MY BELOVED SON	CL	33.00	55.00
91	THY WILL BE DONE	CL	30.00	55.00
92	FOLLOW ME	CL	35.00	40.00
92	FOR GOD SO LOVED THE WORLD	CL	35.00	70.00
92	I AM THE WAY, THE TRUTH & THE LIFE	CL	35.00	85.00
92	WEEP NOT FOR ME	CL	35.00	55.00
C. BRENDERS		**PORTRAITS OF EXQUISITE BIRDS**		
90	BACKYARD TREASURE-CHICKADEE	CL	30.00	40.00
90	BEAUTIFUL BLUEBIRD, THE	CL	30.00	40.00
91	IVORY-BILLED WOODPECKER	CL	33.00	35.00
91	MEADOWLARK'S SONG, THE	CL	33.00	35.00
91	RED-WINGED BLACKBIRD	CL	33.00	35.00
91	SUMMER GOLD: THE ROBIN	CL	33.00	40.00
D. SCHWARTZ		**PUREBRED HORSES OF THE AMERICAS**		
89	APPALOOSA, THE	CL	35.00	40.00
89	TENNESSEE WALKER, THE	CL	35.00	40.00
90	MORGAN, THE	CL	38.00	75.00
90	MUSTANG, THE	CL	38.00	40.00
90	QUARTERHORSE, THE	CL	38.00	40.00
90	SADDLEBRED, THE	CL	38.00	50.00
J. SEEREY-LESTER			**RARE ENCOUNTERS**	
93	BLACK MAGIC	CL	30.00	35.00
93	FUTURE SONG	CL	33.00	40.00
93	HIGH AND MIGHTY	CL	33.00	40.00
93	LAST SANCTUARY	CL	33.00	40.00
93	SOFTLY, SOFTLY	CL	30.00	35.00
93	SOMETHING STIRRED	CL	35.00	40.00
C. SMITH			**ROMANTIC GARDENS**	
89	PLANTATION GARDEN, THE	CL	30.00	35.00
89	WOODLAND GARDEN, THE	CL	30.00	35.00
90	COLONIAL GARDEN, THE	CL	33.00	35.00
90	COTTAGE GARDEN, THE	CL	33.00	45.00
C. VICKERY			**ROMANTIC HARBORS**	
93	ADVENT OF THE GOLDEN BOUGH	CL	35.00	40.00
93	CHRISTMAS TREE SCHOONER	CL	35.00	40.00
93	PRELUDE TO THE JOURNEY	CL	38.00	45.00
93	SHIMMERING LIGHT OF DUSK	CL	38.00	45.00
V. MORLEY			**ROMANTIC ROSES**	
93	COUNTRY CHARM	CL	33.00	40.00
93	OLD-FASHIONED GRACE	CL	30.00	35.00
93	PASTORAL DELIGHT	CL	33.00	40.00
93	SPRINGTIME ELEGANCE	CL	35.00	40.00
93	SUMMER ROMANCE	CL	33.00	40.00
93	VICTORIAN BEAUTY	CL	30.00	35.00
93	VINTAGE SPLENDOR	CL	35.00	40.00
94	HEAVENLY PERFECTION	CL	35.00	40.00
L. GARRISON		**SCENES OF CHRISTMAS PAST**		
87	HOLIDAY SKATERS	CL	28.00	55.00
88	CHRISTMAS EVE	CL	28.00	40.00
89	HOMECOMING, THE	CL	31.00	35.00
90	TOY STORE, THE	CL	31.00	35.00
91	CAROLLERS, THE	CL	31.00	31.00
92	FAMILY TRADITIONS	CL	33.00	45.00
93	HOLIDAY PAST	OP	33.00	45.00
94	A GATHERING OF FAITH	OP	33.00	33.00
J. BRIDGETT		**SECRET WORLD OF THE PANDA**		
90	A MOTHER'S CARE	CL	28.00	35.00

YR	NAME	LIMIT	ISSUE	TREND
91	A BAMBOO FEAST	CL	33.00	80.00
91	A DAY OF EXPLORING	CL	31.00	35.00
91	A FROLIC IN THE SNOW	CL	28.00	30.00
91	A GENTLE HUG	CL	33.00	35.00
91	LAZY AFTERNOON	CL	31.00	35.00
C. FRACE			**SOARING MAJESTY**	
91	FREEDOM	CL	30.00	50.00
91	GOLDEN EAGLE, THE	CL	35.00	65.00
91	GYRFALCON, THE	CL	35.00	50.00
91	NORTHERN GOSHAWK, THE	CL	30.00	45.00
91	OSPREY, THE	CL	33.00	40.00
91	PEREGRINE FALCON	CL	33.00	35.00
91	RED-TAILED HAWK	CL	33.00	35.00
92	RED-SHOULDERED HAWK	CL	35.00	40.00
G. KURZ			**SONNETS IN FLOWERS**	
92	SONNET OF BEAUTY	CL	35.00	45.00
92	SONNET OF HAPPINESS	CL	35.00	40.00
92	SONNET OF LOVE	CL	35.00	40.00
92	SONNET OF PEACE	CL	35.00	40.00
V. GADINO		**SOUND OF MUSIC: SILVER ANNIVERSARY**		
91	HILLS ARE ALIVE, THE	CL	30.00	35.00
92	LET'S START AT THE VERY BEGINNING	CL	30.00	35.00
92	MARIA'S WEDDING DAY	CL	33.00	40.00
92	SOMETHING GOOD	CL	33.00	40.00
J. SIAS			**SPIRIT OF CHIRSTMAS**	
90	SILENT NIGHT	CL	30.00	45.00
91	DECK THE HALLS	CL	33.00	50.00
91	I'LL BE HOME FOR CHRISTMAS	CL	33.00	55.00
91	JINGLE BELLS	CL	30.00	30.00
J. SIAS			**SPIRIT OF CHRISTMAS**	
91	O CHRISTMAS TREE	CL	33.00	40.00
91	WINTER WONDERLAND	CL	33.00	45.00
C. FISHER			**SPIRITS OF THE SKY**	
92	EVENING GLIMMER	CL	33.00	40.00
92	FIRST LIGHT	CL	30.00	35.00
92	GOLDEN DUSK	CL	33.00	40.00
92	TWILIGHT GLOW	CL	30.00	35.00
93	AMBER FLIGHT	CL	35.00	40.00
93	DAY'S END	CL	35.00	40.00
93	SUNSET SPLENDOR	CL	33.00	40.00
93	WINGED RADIANCE	CL	35.00	40.00
L. LIU		**SYMPHONY OF SHIMMERING BEAUTIES**		
91	HIBISCUS MEDLEY	CL	35.00	40.00
91	IRIS QUARTET	CL	30.00	55.00
91	LILY CONCERTO	CL	33.00	55.00
91	PEONY PRELUDE	CL	33.00	35.00
91	POPPY PASTORALE	CL	33.00	40.00
91	ROSE FANTASY	CL	35.00	40.00
91	TULIP ENSEMBLE	CL	30.00	40.00
92	CARNATION SERENADE	CL	37.00	40.00
92	DAHLIA MELODY	CL	35.00	40.00
92	GLADIOLUS ROMANCE	CL	37.00	40.00
92	HOLLYHOCK MARCH	CL	35.00	40.00
92	ZINNIA FINALE	CL	37.00	40.00
J. SIAS			**TIS THE SEASON**	
93	A TIME FOR TRADITION	CL	30.00	35.00
93	A WORLD DRESSED IN SNOW	CL	30.00	35.00
93	OUR FAMILY TREE	CL	30.00	42.00
93	WE SHALL COME REJOICING	CL	30.00	35.00
W. NELSON			**TOMORROW'S PROMISE**	
92	CURIOSITY: ASIAN ELEPHANTS	CL	30.00	55.00
92	FRISKINESS: KIT FOXES	CL	33.00	50.00
92	INNOCENCE: RHINOS	CL	33.00	65.00
92	PLAYTIME PANDAS	CL	30.00	35.00
J. KRAMER-COLE			**TOUCHING THE SPIRIT**	
93	CAMP OF THE SACRED DOGS	CL	30.00	35.00
93	HE WHO WATCHES	CL	30.00	35.00
93	KEEPER OF THE SECRET	CL	30.00	35.00
93	KINDRED SPIRITS	CL	30.00	35.00
93	MARKING TREE, THE	CL	30.00	35.00
93	RUNNING WITH THE WIND	CL	30.00	35.00
93	TWICE TRAVELED TRAIL	CL	30.00	35.00
93	WAKAN TANKA	CL	30.00	35.00
R. STINE			**TREASURY OF SONGBIRDS**	
92	AFTERNOON CALM	CL	33.00	50.00
92	ALLURING DAYLIGHT	CL	35.00	50.00
92	DAWN'S RADIANCE	CL	33.00	50.00
92	GOLDEN DAYBREAK	CL	33.00	48.00
92	MORNING GLORY	CL	30.00	35.00
92	SAPPHIRE DAWN	CL	35.00	50.00
92	SCARLET SUNRISE	CL	35.00	50.00
92	SPRINGTIME SPLENDOR	CL	30.00	49.00
A. CASAY			**VANISHING GENTLE GIANTS**	
91	JUMPING FOR JOY	CL	33.00	40.00
91	MONARCH OF THE DEEP	CL	36.00	50.00
91	SONG OF THE HUMPBACK	CL	33.00	40.00
91	TRAVELERS OF THE SEA	CL	36.00	55.00

YR	NAME	LIMIT	ISSUE	TREND
91	UNICORN OF THE SEA	CL	36.00	60.00
91	WHITE WHALE OF THE NORTH	CL	36.00	55.00
H. BONNER				**VICTORIAN CAT**
90	MISCHIEF WITH THE HATBOX	CL	25.00	50.00
91	DAYDREAMS	CL	28.00	50.00
91	FRISKY FELINES	CL	28.00	55.00
91	KITTENS AT PLAY	CL	28.00	50.00
91	PERFECTLY POISED	CL	30.00	50.00
91	PLAYING IN THE PARLOR	CL	30.00	60.00
91	STRING QUARTET	CL	25.00	60.00
92	MIDDAY REPOSE	CL	30.00	35.00
*				**VICTORIAN CAT CAPERS**
92	A CURIOUS KITTY	CL	28.00	55.00
92	FORBIDDEN FRUIT	CL	30.00	30.00
92	MY BOWL IS EMPTY	CL	28.00	36.00
92	PUSS IN BOOT	CL	25.00	62.00
92	VANITY FAIR	CL	28.00	28.00
92	WHO'S THE FAIREST OF THEM ALL?	CL	25.00	68.00
93	KITTEN EXPRESS, THE	CL	30.00	30.00
93	PURR-FECT PEN PAL, THE	CL	30.00	30.00
*				**WILD INNOCENTS**
93	LION CUB	CL	30.00	40.00
93	REFLECTIONS	CL	30.00	40.00
93	SPIRITUAL HEIR	CL	30.00	40.00
93	SUNNY SPOT	CL	30.00	40.00
T. HIRATA				**WILD SPIRITS**
92	MOUNTAIN MAGIC	CL	33.00	45.00
92	SOLITARY WATCH	CL	30.00	45.00
92	TIMBER GHOST	CL	30.00	43.00
93	LONE VANGUARD	CL	35.00	50.00
93	MIGHTY PRESENCE	CL	35.00	50.00
93	QUIET VIGIL	CL	35.00	50.00
93	SILENT GUARD	CL	33.00	45.00
93	SLY EYES	CL	33.00	45.00
D.L. RUST				**WINGS OF WINTER**
93	FULL MOON COMPANIONS	CL	30.00	30.00
93	MOONLIGHT RETREAT	CL	30.00	40.00
93	NIGHT LIGHTS	CL	30.00	30.00
93	SILENT SUNSET	CL	30.00	30.00
93	TWILIGHT SERENADE	CL	30.00	30.00
93	WHITE NIGHT	CL	30.00	30.00
93	WINTER HAVEN	CL	30.00	30.00
93	WINTER REFLECTIONS	150 DAYS	30.00	30.00
C. FRACE				**WINTER'S MAJESTY**
92	CHASE, THE	CL	35.00	40.00
92	QUEST, THE	CL	35.00	40.00
93	ALASKAN FRIEND	CL	35.00	40.00
93	AMERICAN COUGAR	CL	35.00	40.00
93	ON WATCH	CL	35.00	40.00
93	SOLITUDE	CL	35.00	40.00
R. HARM				**WONDERS OF THE SEA**
91	A FAMILY AFFAIR	CL	35.00	35.00
91	HEART TO HEART	CL	35.00	40.00
91	STAND BY ME	CL	35.00	40.00
91	WARM EMBRACE	CL	35.00	45.00
C. FRACE				**WORLD'S MOST MAGNIFICENT CATS**
91	AFRICAN LEOPARD, THE	CL	30.00	60.00
91	CLOUDED LEOPARD, THE	CL	30.00	110.00
91	COUGAR	CL	25.00	80.00
91	FLEETING ENCOUNTER	CL	25.00	70.00
91	JAGUAR	CL	28.00	80.00
91	MIGHTY WARRIOR	CL	30.00	75.00
91	POWERFUL PRESENCE	CL	28.00	65.00
91	ROYAL BENGAL	CL	28.00	45.00
92	CHEETAH, THE	CL	32.00	70.00
92	SIBERIAN TIGER	CL	32.00	70.00

WATERFORD WEDGWOOD USA

YR	NAME	LIMIT	ISSUE	TREND
*				**BICENTENNIAL**
72	BOSTON TEA PARTY	YR	40.00	45.00
73	PAUL REVERE'S RIDE	YR	40.00	120.00
74	BATTLE OF CONCORD	YR	40.00	60.00
75	ACROSS THE DELAWARE	YR	40.00	110.00
75	VICTORY AT YORKTOWN	YR	45.00	55.00
76	DECLARATION SIGNED	YR	45.00	50.00
*				**MOTHER'S DAY**
71	SPORTIVE LOVE	*	20.00	20.00
72	SEWING LESSON, THE	*	20.00	20.00
73	BAPTISM OF ACHILLES, THE	*	20.00	25.00
74	DOMESTIC EMPLOYMENT	*	30.00	33.00
75	MOTHER AND CHILD	*	35.00	37.00
76	SPINNER, THE	*	35.00	35.00
77	LEISURE TIME	*	35.00	35.00
78	SWAN AND CYGNETS	*	40.00	40.00
79	DEER AND FAWN	*	45.00	45.00
80	BIRDS	*	48.00	48.00
81	MARE AND FOAL	*	50.00	60.00

YR	NAME	LIMIT	ISSUE	TREND
82	CHERUBS WITH SWING	*	55.00	60.00
83	CUPID AND BUTTERFLY	*	55.00	55.00
84	MUSICAL CUPIDS	*	55.00	59.00
85	CUPIDS AND DOVES	YR	55.00	80.00
86	CUPIDS FISHING	YR	55.00	55.00
87	SPRING FLOWERS	YR	55.00	80.00
88	TIGER LILY	YR	55.00	59.00
89	IRISES	YR	65.00	65.00
91	PEONIES	YR	65.00	65.00
*			**WATERFORD WEDGWOOD**	
89	MOSS ROSE	*	*	*70.00
*			**WEDGWOOD CHRISTMAS**	
79	BUCKINGHAM PALACE	YR	65.00	70.00
80	ST. JAMES PALACE	YR	70.00	75.00
81	MARBLE ARCH	YR	75.00	80.00
82	LAMBETH PALACE	YR	80.00	85.00
83	ALL SOULS, LANGHAM PALACE	YR	80.00	85.00
84	CONSTITUTION HILL	YR	80.00	85.00
85	TATE GALLERY, THE	YR	80.00	85.00
86	ALBERT MEMORIAL, THE	YR	80.00	145.00
87	GUILDHALL	YR	80.00	90.00
88	OBSERVATORY/GREENWICH, THE	YR	80.00	95.00
89	WINCHESTER CATHEDRAL	YR	88.00	90.00
T. HARPER			**WEDGWOOD CHRISTMAS**	
69	WINDSOR CASTLE	YR	25.00	185.00
70	TRAFALGAR SQUARE	YR	30.00	55.00
71	PICADILLY CIRCUS	YR	30.00	40.00
72	ST. PAUL'S CATHEDRAL	YR	35.00	45.00
73	TOWER OF LONDON	YR	40.00	85.00
74	HOUSES OF PARLIAMENT	YR	40.00	45.00
75	TOWER BRIDGE	YR	45.00	50.00
76	HAMPTON COURT	YR	50.00	55.00
77	WESTMINISTER ABBEY	YR	55.00	60.00
78	HORSE GUARDS	YR	60.00	65.00

WENDELL AUGUST FORGE

L. YOUNGO		**COLLECTORS GUILD MEMBER'S ONLY**		
95	HOLIDAY EXPRESS	YR	*	N/A
96	FIRST LOVE	5000	39.00	39.00

WILD WINGS INC.

R. ABBETT

98	ENGLISH POINTER HEAD	14 DAYS	50.00	50.00

S. BOURDET

98	BACK TO NATURE-BLUEBIRDS	14 DAYS	50.00	50.00

R. MILLETTE

98	RUSTIC RETREAT-RED FOX	14 DAYS	50.00	50.00
98	RUSTIC RETREAT-WHITETAIL DEER	14 DAYS	50.00	50.00

M. SUSINNO

98	HOOKED-FLY FISHING	14 DAYS	50.00	50.00
98	MATCHING THE HATCH-BROOK TROUT	14 DAYS	50.00	50.00
98	MATCHING THE HATCH-BROWN TROUT	14 DAYS	50.00	50.00
98	MATCHING THE HATCH-CUTTHROAT TROUT	14 DAYS	50.00	50.00
98	MATCHING THE HATCH-RAINBOW TROUT	14 DAYS	50.00	50.00

WILDLIFE INTERNATIONALE

J. RUTHVEN			**SPORTING DOGS**	
85	DECOY (LABORADOR RETRIEVER)	5000	55.00	150.00
85	DUSTY (GOLDEN RETRIEVER)	5000	55.00	80.00
85	RUMMY (ENGLISH SETTER)	5000	55.00	55.00
85	SCARLETT (IRISH SETTER)	5000	55.00	150.00

WILLITTS DESIGNS

T. BLACKSHEAR		**EBONY VISIONS COLLECTION**		
95	KATIE'S FIRST QUILT	RT	30.00	30.00

WINDBERG ENTERPRISES

D. WINDBERG

75	AUTUMN'S WAY	*	650.00	650.00
75	MOUNTAIN'S MAJESTY, THE	*	*	650.00

ZOLAN FINE ARTS/WINSTON ROLAND

D. ZOLAN

96	HARP SONG	SO	30.00	79.00
97	RAINED OUT	CL	20.00	33.00

D. ZOLAN			**COUNTRY FRIENDS**	
98	HELPING OUT	15 DAYS	20.00	20.00
98	LITTLE GARDENER	15 DAYS	20.00	20.00
98	LITTLE TOMBOY	15 DAYS	20.00	20.00
98	PUPPY LOVE	15 DAYS	20.00	20.00

D. ZOLAN			**SINGLE ISSUE**	
98	DOWNHILL DELIGHT	15 DAYS	20.00	20.00
98	SUMMER THUNDER	*	20.00	20.00

Prints

Jay Brown

Selling a print can be as emotional as losing a favorite pet. But often with art, the financial reward can be the perfect compensation. Perhaps you need a few quick bucks or want to clear a little wall space for a new masterpiece. What do you do?

First, determine the value of the work you wish to sell. There are magazines such as *Collector's mart* on the market that can give you some idea of the current trend. The gallery where the print was purchased or the publisher of the print should also be able to give you an idea of the current market price.

Remember that a framed or unframed print in mint condition is easier to sell and will bring you more dollars than the same print in average condition. Hopefully, you will find that the current market price is in line with what is personally acceptable to you. If you are lucky, the gallery or publisher you're dealing with will make a good offer or direct you to a collector or gallery who is looking for the work you wish to sell.

If not, you have two main options: sell at retail to a private collector, perhaps someone you know; or sell (usually on consignment) at wholesale through a dealer. In either case, it often helps to show a would-be buyer evidence that the print was purchased from (and was framed by, if applicable) a gallery with a good reputation.

One way to locate a retail buyer is to place a classified advertisement in a local newspaper and/or check to see if your friends are interested in buying the print. If the artist is in high demand, your chances for making a sale will be increased tremendously.

If your ad doesn't result in a buyer, don't fret. Selling your print through a reputable gallery is often the preferred way to go. Look for a gallery with experience in dealing with the artist whose work you wish to sell. That gallery should have a marketing plan and a clientele interested in the print. The sales commission that the gallery receives will vary from 10-50 percent of the selling price. The most common commission is 33-40 percent.

Occasionally, a print will be difficult to sell due to the timing of the attempted resale. Perhaps the economy is in a decline or the artist is not in demand due to a change in collecting trends. Remember, as with any investment, there are peak times to sell. For example, you'll have better luck with an artist who is in his prime as opposed to one whose art is not as popular.

There are companies that specialize in matching buyers with sellers on the secondary market. These companies provide dealers and collectors with listings of clients interested in selling works of art. Such listings are based on information provided by the sellers. Using such a list, galleries are able to see what it costs to obtain a work of art.

Even though these listing companies make locating works on the secondary market easy for art dealers, many reputable galleries prefer to use their own client base whenever possible. By using their own collector base, galleries can normally avoid shipping costs and be assured that the condition of the work of art is as represented. But most important, by using their own client base, galleries are able to reward clients who exhibit loyalty to them.

Art is a fabulous investment, not because of the amount of potential profit that can be made upon its sale, but because of the amount of enjoyment it can give. Even though many prints turn out to be great monetary investments, it is highly recommended that buyers follow the golden rule of collecting: "Buy what you like, and all your purchases are guaranteed to be good investments."

JAY BROWN owns and operates Gallery One with locations in Mentor and Strongsville, Ohio, where he specializes in the retail sales of limited edition prints and original paintings and sculptures by the industry's most popular artists. He also deals extensively in the secondary market sale of these collectibles.

PRINTS

YR	NAME	LIMIT	ISSUE	TREND

3-DIMENSIONAL EDITIONS
F. MILLER
YR	NAME	LIMIT	ISSUE	TREND
*	ONE WINNER, OR TWO LOSERS	1500	155.00	155.00
*	WHEN TIMES WERE GOOD	1500	165.00	165.00
89	WINNER TAKES ALL, THE	1000	145.00	322.00
91	NATURE'S MONARCH	1000	145.00	595.00
92	TIME TO REMEMBER, A	SO	145.00	250.00
93	AUTUMN SONG	SO	145.00	220.00
93	NO MARGIN FOR ERROR	SO	145.00	220.00
94	HIGH MTN. PEACE	1000	145.00	220.00
94	ON THE WINGS OF EAGLES	1000	145.00	145.00
94	THUNDERING WATERS NIAGARA FALLS	1000	145.00	145.00
95	ELUSIVE PRIZE, THE	SO	95.00	146.00
95	KEEPER OF THE FALLS	1000	145.00	145.00
95	RETURN, THE	1000	165.00	200.00
95	YOSEMITE'S MESSENGER TO THE GODS	1000	145.00	145.00
96	THERE WAS A PLACE	1000	155.00	175.00
96	WILDERNESS RETREAT	1000	155.00	200.00

AMCAL FINE ARTS
C. WYSOCKI
YR	NAME	LIMIT	ISSUE	TREND
97	YOUNG HEARTS AT SEA	1500	185.00	325.00
97	YOUNG HEARTS AT SEA (FR. CANVAS TRANSFER)	300	850.00	1150.00

C. WYSOCKI
				FRAMED CANVAS
95	MABEL THE STOWAWAY	CL	750.00	900.00
96	BLACK BIRDS ROOST AT MILL CREEK	CL	795.00	1000.00
96	MAGGIE THE MESSMAKER	500	795.00	975.00

S. ROSS
				PRINT
95	FLORA AND FIONA	500	75.00	65.00

M. STACK
				PRINT
95	UNDER A SUMMER SKY	750	150.00	250.00

C. WYSOCKI
				PRINT
95	MABEL THE STOWAWAY	CL	175.00	225.00
95	OLDE CAPE COD	2500	195.00	225.00
95	ROOT BEER BREAK AT THE BUTTERFIELD'S	2500	165.00	200.00
96	MAGGIE THE MESSMAKER	6500	175.00	450.00
96	UNCLE JACK'S TOPIARY TENDENCIES	SO	185.00	210.00

C. WYSOCKI
				THE FOUR SEASONS-SET
97	PAPERBOYS,THE	2000	*	N/A
97	PROMISES, PROMISES	2000	*	N/A
97	SO PROULDY WE HAIL	2000	*	N/A
97	THERE'S A RIGHT WAY, A WRONG WAY AND THE AMISH WAY	2000	*	N/A

C. WYSOCKI
				UNFRAMED CANVAS
95	MABEL THE STOWAWAY	500	495.00	1100.00

AMERICAN ARTISTS
A. SEHRING
YR	NAME	LIMIT	ISSUE	TREND
88	AUTUMN FIELDS	445	300.00	300.00
88	FIELDS OF SUMMER	445	300.00	300.00
88	HIGH ON THE HILL	445	300.00	300.00
88	PICNIC BY THE POND	445	300.00	620.00
88	PINK BONNET	445	300.00	300.00
88	STRAWBERRY TIME	445	300.00	300.00
88	SUMMER WILDFLOWER	445	300.00	300.00
88	SUMMERS BY THE SEA	445	300.00	300.00
88	SUN & SHADE	445	300.00	300.00
88	VIOLETS	445	300.00	460.00
89	REFLECTIONS OF THE JUNGLE	445	300.00	775.00
89	THREATENING GESTURES	445	300.00	300.00
90	FACE OF THE JUNGLE	445	300.00	300.00
90	SOLITARY HUNTER	445	300.00	300.00
95	LOOK WHAT I CAUGHT	445	300.00	300.00
95	WILDFLOWERS	445	300.00	450.00
96	QUIET MOMENTS	68	1,600.00	1600.00
97	IRISES	150	1,000.00	1000.00
97	WHERE THE LILIES GROW II	68	1,600.00	1600.00

F. STONE
YR	NAME	LIMIT	ISSUE	TREND
*	CIGAR	*	150.00	250.00
*	SUNDAY SILENCE	950	195.00	725.00
78	AFFIRMED, STEVE CAUTHEN UP	750	100.00	625.00
78	MARE AND FOAL	500	90.00	600.00
78	MOMENT AFTER, THE	500	90.00	350.00
79	ONE, TWO, THREE	500	100.00	1000.00
79	PATIENCE	1000	90.00	1550.00
79	RIVALS, THE: AFFIRMED & ALYDAR	500	90.00	500.00
80	BELMONT, THE: BOLD FORBES	500	100.00	625.00
80	EXCELLER: BILL SHOEMAKER	500	90.00	800.00
80	GENUINE RISK	500	100.00	875.00
80	KENTUCKY DERBY, THE	750	100.00	1300.00
80	KIDNAPPED MARE: FRANFRELUCHE	750	115.00	775.00
80	PASTURE PEST, THE	500	100.00	1050.00
80	SPECTACULAR BID	500	65.00	350.00
81	ARABIANS, THE	750	115.00	500.00
81	CONTENTMENT	750	115.00	460.00

YR	NAME	LIMIT	ISSUE	TREND
81	SHOE, THE: 8,000 WINS	395	200.00	5300.00
81	THOROUGHBREDS, THE	750	115.00	425.00
82	JOHN HENRY: BILL SHOEMAKER UP	595	160.00	600.00
82	MAN O' WAR: FINAL THUNDER	750	175.00	3100.00
82	OFF AND RUNNING	750	125.00	500.00
82	POWER HORSES, THE	750	125.00	390.00
82	WATER TROUGH, THE	750	125.00	550.00
83	ANDALUSIAN, THE	750	150.00	350.00
83	DUEL, THE	750	150.00	405.00
83	FOR ONLY A MOMENT: RUFFIAN	750	175.00	950.00
83	TRANQUILITY	750	150.00	600.00
84	NORTHERN DANCER	950	175.00	620.00
84	SECRETARIAT	950	175.00	1325.00
84	TURNING FOR HOME	750	150.00	500.00
85	ETERNAL LEGACY	950	175.00	660.00
85	FRED STONE PAINTS THE SPORT OF KINGS	750	265.00	750.00
85	JOHN HENRY: MCCARRON UP	750	175.00	750.00
85	KELSO	950	175.00	775.00
85	LEGACY, THE	950	175.00	950.00
86	FOREVER FRIENDS	950	175.00	600.00
86	NIJINSKI II	950	175.00	200.00
86	RUFFIAN & FOOLISH PLEASURE	950	175.00	1270.00
87	FIRST DAY, THE	950	175.00	350.00
87	LADY'S SECRET	950	175.00	330.00
87	RIVALRY, THE: ALYSHEBA AND BET TWICE	950	195.00	330.00
88	ALYSHEBA	950	195.00	375.00
88	CAM-FELIA	950	175.00	175.00
88	SHOE & BALD EAGLE	950	195.00	450.00
89	BATTLE FOR THE TRIPLE CROWN	950	225.00	500.00
89	PHAR LAP	950	195.00	275.00
90	FINAL TRIBUTE: SECRETARIAT	1150	265.00	650.00
90	OLD WARRIORS SHOEMAKER: JOHN HENRY	1950	265.00	625.00
91	BLACK STALLION	1500	225.00	225.00
91	FOREGO	1150	225.00	225.00
91	GO FOR WAND: A CANDLE IN THE WIND	1150	225.00	225.00
92	AMERICAN TRIPLE CROWN I (1948-1978)	1500	325.00	450.00
92	DANCE SMARTLY	950	225.00	225.00
93	AMERICAN TRIPLE CROWN II (1937-1946)	1500	325.00	325.00
93	AMERICAN TRIPLE CROWN III (1919-1935)	1500	225.00	225.00
95	HOLY BULL	1150	225.00	175.00
95	HOLY BULL (CANVAS)	350	375.00	375.00
95	JULIE KRONE - COLONIAL AFFAIR	1150	225.00	200.00
95	SUMMER DAYS	1150	225.00	250.00

AMERICAN LEGACY
S. ETEM

	NAME	LIMIT	ISSUE	TREND
*	FOUNTAIN, THE	CL	150.00	150.00
*	INDIANA SUMMER	CL	150.00	150.00
*	LITTLE BANDIT	CL	150.00	150.00

AMERICAN MASTERS
P. CROWE

YR	NAME	LIMIT	ISSUE	TREND
85	FOGGY MORNING MALLARDS	950	90.00	90.00
86	OUTLAWS II, THE	1950	60.00	275.00
87	MASTERS OF DISASTER, THE	950	90.00	100.00
87	WILD BUNCH, THE	950	90.00	150.00
87	WINTER RETREAT	950	90.00	125.00

L. DYKE

YR	NAME	LIMIT	ISSUE	TREND
78	ISAIAH 40:3 S/N	1000	40.00	300.00
78	ISAIAH 40:3 S/O	1500	30.00	30.00
78	ISAIAH 58:8 S/N	1000	35.00	390.00
78	JOHN 3:8 S/N	1000	30.00	725.00
78	PSALMS 27:4 S/N	1000	40.00	675.00
79	COLLECTOR'S SUITE S/N	1000	48.00	48.00
79	JOHN 9:4 S/N	1000	45.00	50.00
79	JOHN 9:4 S/O	2000	30.00	90.00
79	PROVERBS 8:25 S/N	1000	45.00	45.00
79	PROVERBS 8:25 S/O	1800	30.00	80.00
79	PSALM 113:3 S/N	1000	40.00	40.00
79	PSALM 113:3 S/O	1500	30.00	100.00
79	PSALM 147:16 S/N	1000	45.00	50.00
79	PSALM 147:16 S/O	1200	30.00	100.00
79	SONG OF SOLOMON 2:17 S/N	1000	45.00	45.00
79	SONG OF SOLOMON 2:17 S/O	1800	30.00	95.00
80	COLLECTOR'S SUITE S/O	1800	35.00	90.00
80	DEUTERONOMY 28:8 S/N	1000	55.00	55.00
80	DEUTERONOMY 28:8 S/O	1800	37.50	200.00
80	EZEKIEL 34:15 S/N	1000	55.00	60.00
80	EZEKIEL 34:15 S/O	1800	37.50	80.00
80	PSALM 42:1 S/N	1000	55.00	55.00
80	PSALM 42:1 S/O	1200	37.50	175.00
80	PSALM 91:1 S/N	1000	45.00	45.00
80	PSALM 91:1 S/O	2200	30.00	50.00
80	QUIET ENCOUNTER (PSALM 104:13) S/N	1600	85.00	105.00
80	REVELATIONS 21:6 S/N	1000	55.00	1050.00
80	REVELATIONS 21:6 S/O	1800	35.00	1300.00
80	ROMANS 15:32 S/N	1000	57.50	60.00
80	ROMANS 15:32 S/O	2200	37.50	50.00
81	EZEKIEL 32:14 S/N	1500	65.00	65.00

YR	NAME	LIMIT	ISSUE	TREND
81	EZEKIEL 32:14 S/O	2500	40.00	40.00
81	JOHN 10:27 S/N	1000	60.00	60.00
81	JOHN 10:27 S/O	2700	37.50	100.00
81	LAMENTATIONS 3:28 S/N	1500	68.00	200.00
81	LAMENTATIONS 3:28 S/O	2500	45.00	200.00
81	MATTHEW 6:30 S/N	1000	40.00	40.00
81	MATTHEW 9:37 S/N	1000	65.00	65.00
81	MATTHEW 9:37 S/O	2200	38.00	40.00
81	PROVERBS 23:10 S/N	1000	60.00	60.00
81	PROVERBS 23:10 S/O	2200	37.50	130.00
81	PSALMS 90:2 S/N	1500	67.50	70.00
81	PSALMS 90:2 S/O	2500	45.00	90.00
82	DANIEL 2:21 S/N	1500	70.00	85.00
82	DANIEL 2:21 S/O	2500	45.00	45.00
82	ECCLESIASTES 3:1 S/N	1500	70.00	70.00
82	ISAIAH 45:3 S/N	1950	80.00	150.00
82	JOB 39:8 S/N	1500	70.00	80.00
82	JOB 39:8 S/O	2500	45.00	90.00
82	JOHN 8:32 S/N	1500	85.00	85.00
82	JOSHUA 2:22 S/N	1500	70.00	70.00
82	JOSHUA 2:22 S/O	2500	45.00	45.00
83	EARLY ARRIVAL (EPHESIANS 5:8) S/N	1600	75.00	250.00
83	ISAIAH 58:11 S/N	1600	85.00	350.00
83	MATTHEW 18:12 S/N	1500	75.00	215.00
83	ZACHARIAH 14:7 S/N	1600	85.00	85.00
84	MAJESTIC MORNING (AMOS 4:13) S/N	1600	85.00	135.00
84	MORGAN'S CLEARING S/N	1600	80.00	85.00
84	SHARING THE FAITH (PSALM 23) S/N	5000	85.00	95.00
84	TRANQUIL REFUGE (JEREMIAH 48:40) S/N	1600	80.00	90.00
85	A NEW PROMISE (GENESIS 9:16) S/N	1600	85.00	415.00
85	OFFERING, THE (MARK 12:41-44) S/N	3000	125.00	275.00
85	SHADY CREEK MILL (JOB 40:22) S/N	1600	85.00	175.00
87	MISSION, THE (ISAIAH 40:8) S/N	1503	85.00	460.00
88	AFTER THE STORM (LAMENTATIONS 3:26) S/N	1000	110.00	160.00

C. FRACE

YR	NAME	LIMIT	ISSUE	TREND
73	GIANT PANDA	5000	45.00	215.00
73	GOLDEN EAGLE	1000	75.00	170.00
73	PRONGHORN	5000	50.00	135.00
73	TIGER	3000	35.00	200.00
74	CHEETAH KITTEN	5000	40.00	325.00
74	HARP SEAL	2000	75.00	950.00
74	HERRING GULL	5000	45.00	300.00
74	LIONS, THE	5000	40.00	115.00
74	RACCOON	5000	50.00	180.00
74	ZEBRA	4000	60.00	400.00
75	BIGHORN COUNTRY	2500	75.00	200.00
75	LION CUB	3500	35.00	100.00
75	NORTHERN GOSHAWK	4000	50.00	1150.00
75	SAFE RETURN	3000	140.00	140.00
75	SIBERIAN TIGER	2000	80.00	115.00
75	TIGER CUB	3500	35.00	200.00
75	ZEBRA FOAL	4000	35.00	265.00
76	DOUBLE TROUBLE	2500	90.00	270.00
76	ELEPHANTS AT KILIMANJARO	1000	75.00	500.00
76	FLEETING ENCOUNTER	3000	150.00	650.00
76	FLORIDA BOBCAT	3000	40.00	280.00
76	GREATER KUDU	3000	50.00	85.00
76	MASAI GIRAFFES	3000	40.00	350.00
76	OCELOTS	5000	35.00	225.00
76	WHITE TIGER	1500	75.00	225.00
76	WHITE TIGER (REMARQUE)	1000	125.00	260.00
77	CANADA LYNX	3000	50.00	150.00
77	CAVALIER SPANIELS	1500	35.00	200.00
77	CHEETAH	3000	50.00	145.00
77	COUGAR	1000	90.00	925.00
77	GYRFALCON	3000	40.00	175.00
78	AFRICAN LEOPARD	1500	75.00	625.00
78	AFRICAN LEOPARD (REMARQUE)	1000	125.00	975.00
78	BISON	2000	50.00	190.00
78	CHINESE TREASURE	3000	140.00	240.00
78	CLOUDED LEOPARD	2000	65.00	85.00
78	CLOUDED LEOPARD CUB	2000	75.00	145.00
78	HIMALAYAN PRINCE	2000	75.00	300.00
78	RACCOONS (3)	5000	100.00	400.00
78	RED SHOULDERED HAWK	2000	60.00	100.00
79	KOALA	2000	65.00	400.00
79	SNOW LEOPARD	1500	75.00	250.00
79	SNOW LEOPARD (REMARQUE)	1000	125.00	1450.00
79	SNOW LEOPARD HEAD	15000	20.00	200.00
79	SNOWY OWLS	2000	65.00	120.00
80	IMPALA	2000	60.00	85.00
80	POLAR BEAR	2000	100.00	110.00
80	SCREECH OWLS	3500	20.00	85.00
80	SIBERIAN LYNX CUB	2000	75.00	80.00
80	WHITE TIGER HEAD	20000	25.00	30.00
81	AFRICAN LEOPARD CUB	2000	65.00	275.00
81	AFRICAN LEOPARD HEAD	12500	25.00	30.00
81	HIGH MOUNTAIN PATH	3000	140.00	140.00
81	LOFTY VIEW	2500	75.00	200.00

YR	NAME	LIMIT	ISSUE	TREND
81	ROYAL PRIDE	2500	100.00	125.00
82	HARLAN'S HAWK	1500	60.00	100.00
82	JAGUAR	2000	75.00	500.00
82	JAGUAR HEAD	12500	25.00	30.00
82	LONE HUNTER	2500	100.00	240.00
82	MAJESTY	2500	80.00	80.00
82	ON WATCH	2500	80.00	550.00
82	RACCOON (TENNESSEE CONSERVATION STAMP)	2000	50.00	400.00
82	UNO	2500	75.00	80.00
83	A MOMENT'S REST	2500	100.00	300.00
83	AFRICAN LION	3000	35.00	140.00
83	ALASKAN AUTUMN	2500	80.00	380.00
83	BLACK LEOPARD	3000	50.00	525.00
83	BOBCAT (MS WILDLIFE FED. STAMP)	5000	90.00	100.00
83	LABRADOR RETRIEVER (NTL. RETR. CLUB)	2192	125.00	175.00
83	LABRADOR RETRIEVER (NTL. RETR. CLUB/REM)	190	250.00	400.00
83	MY FRIEND	7500	35.00	65.00
83	RED RASCAL	2500	80.00	670.00
83	YOUNG EXPLORER	2500	80.00	80.00
84	AMERICAN EAGLE	2000	75.00	155.00
84	AMERICAN MONARCH	3750	120.00	275.00
84	BANDIT	2500	90.00	125.00
84	COUGAR CUB	3000	50.00	100.00
84	NEW ARRIVAL	7500	35.00	250.00
84	SOLITUDE	2500	100.00	160.00
85	A RADIANT MOMENT	3000	155.00	155.00
85	A SUNNY SPOT	2500	100.00	100.00
85	KING'S FAVORITE	2500	110.00	110.00
85	PALS	2500	70.00	70.00
85	QUIET TIME IN SAMBURU	2500	100.00	100.00
85	ROYAL BENGAL	3950	125.00	130.00
86	FIRST LIGHT	3950	125.00	125.00
86	FREEDOM	2500	120.00	440.00
86	HIDEAWAY	3950	85.00	260.00
86	THREE OF A KIND	3950	110.00	230.00
86	TREASURES OF THE SEA (FRIEND/SEA OTTER)	500	150.00	150.00
87	CHALLENGER, THE	3000	140.00	150.00
87	MIGHTY WARRIOR	3000	140.00	140.00
87	MORRIS THE CAT	5000	30.00	420.00
87	PLAYMATES	2500	120.00	250.00
87	READY FOR ADVENTURE	3950	115.00	125.00
87	TAKING A BREAK	3950	100.00	110.00
88	OUT ON A LIMB	3000	140.00	150.00
88	RECESS	2500	140.00	150.00
88	WANDERER, THE	3000	140.00	800.00
89	NATURE'S DAWN	3000	140.00	140.00
89	POWERFUL PRESENCE	5619	155.00	160.00
89	SURPRISE	3000	140.00	140.00
90	AMBASSADORS	3000	155.00	155.00
90	PARTNERS	3000	55.00	500.00
C. FRAZIER				
87	BURST OF SPRING	950	65.00	90.00
87	PARADISAL SETTING	950	65.00	90.00
87	PASSING THROUGH	950	65.00	200.00
87	ROSE GARDENS	950	65.00	200.00
L. GORDON				
88	EVENING RIDE	950	75.00	280.00
88	FLOWER MARKET, THE	950	70.00	175.00
88	PLEASANT PROMENADE	950	70.00	110.00
88	SUMMER CAROUSEL	950	70.00	185.00
R. SUMMERS				
78	BOSQUE TERRITORY	1500	35.00	200.00
78	FORBIDDEN WILDERNESS	1500	35.00	135.00
78	WHITE BUFFALO	1500	35.00	200.00
79	COLTER'S QUEST	1500	50.00	170.00
79	COMANCHE MOON	1500	36.00	220.00
79	FOOTPRINTS IN THE SNOW	1500	40.00	850.00
79	MIGHTY OAK ENDURETH, THE	1500	25.00	50.00
80	ANOTHER DAY	1500	52.00	260.00
80	NATURE'S CLASSROOM	1500	52.00	90.00
80	RECEDING STORM	1500	50.00	140.00
80	SLICKER TIME	1500	52.00	1350.00
81	CAMP COFFEE	1500	75.00	80.00
81	COMMUNE WITH GOD	1500	75.00	240.00
81	FIRST VISIT	1500	62.00	165.00
81	HEADIN' HOME	1500	57.00	60.00
81	LEADIN' LOOSE	1500	60.00	90.00
81	RENDEZVOUS	1500	55.00	75.00
82	BOOM TOWN	1950	75.00	200.00
82	COOLING OFF	1500	80.00	175.00
82	FAMILY TREE	1500	80.00	135.00
82	I'D LIKE TO BE THERE	1500	80.00	100.00
82	PEACEFUL VALLEY	1500	80.00	80.00
82	TEXAS GOLD	1950	90.00	200.00
83	AGAINST THE WIND	1500	90.00	90.00
83	ALL IS CALM	1500	90.00	90.00
83	PERFECT DAY, THE	1500	90.00	100.00
83	RANGE FARE	1500	95.00	125.00

YR	NAME	LIMIT	ISSUE	TREND
84	CHANGING TIMES	1500	85.00	225.00
84	COWTOWN	1500	90.00	110.00
86	LEGEND OF THE WEST	1500	85.00	85.00
87	BARON'S DAUGHTER	750	100.00	280.00
87	COUNTRY SLICKERS	750	100.00	325.00

ANNA-PERENNA
T. KRUMEICH — KRUMEICH HECTOR'S WINDOW

*	13-COLOR LITHO, FRAMED	995	95.00	95.00
*	GENUINE STONE LITHO	325	175.00	225.00

APPLEJACK LTD.
C. CORCILIUS — APPLEJACK LTD.

90	CLAN OF THE WOLF	SO	150.00	351.00

ARMSTRONG'S
A. D'ESTREHAN

87	SAN PEDRO	500	95.00	250.00
87	SAN PEDRO A/P	CL	95.00	250.00
87	U.S.S. CONSTITUTION	500	95.00	95.00
87	U.S.S. CONSTITUTION A/P	CL	95.00	95.00

L. DEWINNE

87	WINDSWEPT	500	95.00	95.00
87	WINDSWEPT A/P	CL	95.00	95.00

S. ETEM

87	BOYS, THE	500	70.00	70.00
87	BOYS, THE A/P	CL	70.00	70.00
87	SISSY AND MISSY	500	70.00	70.00
87	SISSY AND MISSY A/P	CL	70.00	70.00

G. LAMBERT

87	LADY CUNNINGHAM	500	95.00	95.00
87	LADY CUNNINGHAM A/P	CL	95.00	95.00

ART IMPRESSIONS WEST
R. VAN BEEK

87	COMPANIONS	450	48.00	900.00
87	DAYS OF AUTUMN	450	28.00	50.00
87	PALLET OF SPRING	450	28.00	575.00
87	SUMMER MEMORIES	450	28.00	575.00
88	END OF DAY	450	28.00	325.00
88	FOUR SEASONS SET	450	112.00	3250.00
90	MT. BAKER TWIN SISTER SET	250	74.00	2000.00
94	SPRING BREEZE	950	75.00	120.00

R. VAN BEEK — CANVAS

93	MORNING LIGHT ON SKAGIT FIELDS	750	195.00	475.00
94	CASCADE FAMILY TREE	450	195.00	575.00
94	SATURDAY IN OCTOBER	450	195.00	575.00
94	SPRING BREEZE	450	195.00	575.00
94	WINTER MEMORIES	450	195.00	575.00

R. VAN BEEK — FOUR SEASONS COLLECTIONS

95	DAYS OF AUTUMN	450	28.00	75.00
95	END OF DAY	450	28.00	325.00
95	PALLET OF SPRING	450	28.00	575.00
95	SUMMER MEMORIES	450	28.00	575.00

R. VAN BEEK — LIMITED EDITION

95	COMPANIONS	450	45.00	825.00
95	MT. BAKER TWIN SISTER SET	450	74.00	2000.00
95	SPRING BREEZE	450	75.00	430.00

R. VAN BEEK — LIMITED EDITION/CANVAS

95	CASCADE FAMILY TREE	450	195.00	430.00
95	MORNING LIGHT ON SKAGIT FIELDS	450	195.00	430.00
95	SATURDAY IN OCTOBER	450	195.00	430.00
95	SPRING BREEZE	450	195.00	430.00
95	WINTER MEMORIES	450	195.00	430.00

ART WORLD OF BOURGEAULT
R. BOURGEAULT — ROYAL LITERARY SERIES

89	ANNE HATHAWAY COTTAGE	OP	75.00	115.00
89	JOHN BUNYAN COTTAGE	OP	75.00	115.00
89	JOHN MILTON COTTAGE	OP	75.00	115.00
89	THOMAS HARDY COTTAGE	OP	75.00	115.00

R. BOURGEAULT — THE ENGLISH COUNTRYSIDE

89	COUNTRY SQUIRE, THE	550	130.00	500.00

ARTAFFECTS
MAGO

88	BETH	950	95.00	200.00
88	JESSICA AND SEBASTIAN (PR.)	550	225.00	325.00
88	SERENITY	950	95.00	200.00

J. DENEEN

88	EMPIRE BUILDER	950	75.00	75.00
88	SANTA FE	950	75.00	75.00
88	TWENTIETH CENTURY LIMITED	950	75.00	75.00

G. PERILLO

77	MADRE	500	125.00	410.00
78	MADONNA OF THE PLAINS	500	125.00	500.00
78	SNOW PALS	500	125.00	260.00

YR	NAME	LIMIT	ISSUE	TREND
79	SIOUX SCOUT/BUFFALO HUNT (PR.)	500	150.00	750.00
80	BABYSITTER	3000	60.00	120.00
80	PUPPIES	3000	45.00	260.00
81	PEACEABLE KINGDOM	950	100.00	104.00
82	CHIEF PONTIAC	950	75.00	100.00
82	HOOFBEATS	950	100.00	150.00
82	INDIAN STYLE	950	75.00	325.00
82	LONESOME COWBOY	950	75.00	390.00
82	MARIA	550	150.00	350.00
82	TENDER LOVE	950	75.00	104.00
82	TINKER	3000	45.00	100.00
83	MOMENT, THE (POSTER)	OP	20.00	60.00
84	NAVAJO LOVE	300	125.00	550.00
84	OUT OF THE FOREST	*	*	450.00
85	CHIEF CRAZY HORSE	950	125.00	450.00
85	CHIEF SITTING BULL	500	125.00	350.00
85	MARIGOLD	500	125.00	350.00
85	SECRETARIAT	950	125.00	125.00
85	WHIRLAWAY	950	125.00	125.00
86	LEARNING HIS WAYS	325	150.00	150.00
86	POUT	325	150.00	350.00
86	RESCUE, THE	325	150.00	450.00
86	WAR PONY	325	150.00	250.00
88	BY THE STREAM	950	100.00	100.00
88	MAGNIFICENT SEVEN	950	125.00	125.00
90	PACK, THE	950	150.00	150.00

R. SAUBER

YR	NAME	LIMIT	ISSUE	TREND
82	BUTTERFLY	3000	45.00	100.00

MAGO   GRAND GALLERY COLLECTION

YR	NAME	LIMIT	ISSUE	TREND
88	AMY	2500	75.00	90.00
88	LAUREN	2500	75.00	90.00
88	MISCHIEF	2500	75.00	90.00
88	TOMORROWS	2500	75.00	90.00

L. MARCHETTI   GRAND GALLERY COLLECTION

YR	NAME	LIMIT	ISSUE	TREND
88	PARIS	2500	75.00	90.00
88	VENICE	2500	75.00	90.00

G. PERILLO   GRAND GALLERY COLLECTION

YR	NAME	LIMIT	ISSUE	TREND
88	BLACKFOOT HUNTER	2500	75.00	90.00
88	BRAVE & FREE	2500	75.00	200.00
88	CHEYENNE NATION, THE	2500	75.00	90.00
88	CHIEF CRAZY HORSE	2500	75.00	90.00
88	CHIEF RED CLOUD	2500	75.00	98.00
88	LAST FRONTIER, THE	2500	75.00	90.00
88	LATE MAIL	2500	75.00	98.00
88	LILY OF THE MOHAWKS	2500	75.00	90.00
88	NATIVE AMERICAN	2500	75.00	220.00
88	NOBLE HERITAGE	2500	75.00	220.00
88	PEACEABLE KINGDOM, THE	2500	75.00	90.00
88	TENDER LOVE	2500	75.00	130.00

R. SAUBER   GRAND GALLERY COLLECTION

YR	NAME	LIMIT	ISSUE	TREND
88	GOD BLESS AMERICA	2500	75.00	90.00
88	HOME SWEET HOME	2500	75.00	90.00
88	MOTHERHOOD	2500	75.00	90.00
88	VISITING THE DOCTOR	2500	75.00	90.00
88	WEDDING, THE	2500	75.00	90.00

ARTISTS OF THE WORLD

T. DEGRAZIA

YR	NAME	LIMIT	ISSUE	TREND
94	ADORATION	950	79.50	83.00
94	BEAUTIFUL HARVEST	950	79.50	83.00
94	SPRING BLOSSOMS	950	79.50	83.00
94	YOUNG MADONNA	950	79.50	83.00

AVIATION ART MUSEUM

K. FOX

YR	NAME	LIMIT	ISSUE	TREND
80	P-40 WARHAWKS AVG FLYING TIGERS	1000	150.00	N/A
82	B-17F MEMPHIS BELLE 26TH MISSION	1000	150.00	150.00
82	MEMPHIS BELLE 26TH MISSION	1000	150.00	N/A

K. FOX   50TH ANNIVERSARY COMMEMORATIVE

YR	NAME	LIMIT	ISSUE	TREND
77	LINDBERGH	3000	150.00	1100.00
82	EARHART	2000	150.00	1100.00

K. FOX   90TH ANNIVERSARY COMMEMORATIVE

YR	NAME	LIMIT	ISSUE	TREND
93	WRIGHT BROS.	1903	150.00	N/A

K. FOX   ARTISTS PROOFS

YR	NAME	LIMIT	ISSUE	TREND
93	WRIGHT BROS.	90	200.00	N/A

B. BOURGEAU RICHARDS COLLECTION

B.B. RICHARDS

YR	NAME	LIMIT	ISSUE	TREND
93	ALWAYS	1000	25.00	30.00
93	BARNEY	1000	20.00	23.00
93	DAPHNEY DUBUNNY	1000	20.00	23.00
93	FOR THE CHILDREN	1000	45.00	55.00
93	GRANDMA'S TEAPOT	1000	20.00	23.00
93	MARY & PETE NEWEST ARRIVAL	1000	20.00	23.00
93	MEDORE'S PRIZE PIG	1000	40.00	45.00
93	RED ROSES FOR CONSTANCE	1000	30.00	35.00
93	SUNFLOWER FOR FLORENCE	1000	20.00	23.00
94	BIRD WATCHING	1000	15.00	18.00

YR	NAME	LIMIT	ISSUE	TREND
94	CYNTHIA'S TEAPOT	1000	15.00	18.00
94	FISHERMAN, THE	1000	15.00	18.00
94	FRIENDSHIP GARDEN, THE	1000	37.00	42.00
94	FROM THE HEART	1000	15.00	18.00
94	INDIAN SUMMER	1000	37.00	42.00
94	INNOCENCE	1000	40.00	45.00
94	JOSEPHINE WEDS CHARLES	1000	15.00	18.00
94	JUST THREE ANGELS	1000	15.00	18.00
94	MA	1000	35.00	40.00
94	PEARL LOVES HELEN	1000	15.00	18.00
94	SARAH ON WASH DAY	1000	15.00	18.00
94	WAITING FOR PAPA	1000	25.00	30.00

B.B. RICHARDS   AMANDA MOORE SERIES

YR	NAME	LIMIT	ISSUE	TREND
93	APPLE FOR MISS AMANDA	1000	40.00	45.00
93	HOUSE ON HOLLISTER	1000	30.00	35.00

B.B. RICHARDS   CHRISTMAS SERIES

YR	NAME	LIMIT	ISSUE	TREND
93	PEACE, LOVE AND JOY	1050	32.00	40.00
94	WHERE MY HEART FINDS CHRISTMAS	1452	32.00	40.00

B.B. RICHARDS   FLORAL SERIES

YR	NAME	LIMIT	ISSUE	TREND
93	WILD ROSES	1000	40.00	45.00
94	PURPLE IRIS	1000	40.00	45.00

B.B. RICHARDS   FOUR SEASONS WEDDING SERIES

YR	NAME	LIMIT	ISSUE	TREND
93	WINTER WEDDING BELLS	1000	34.00	40.00
94	WEDDING IN SPRING	1000	35.00	40.00

BARBER GALLERY

J.M. BARBER   STANDARD PRINT

YR	NAME	LIMIT	ISSUE	TREND
78	ATLANTIC SENTINEL	SO	40.00	650.00
78	BOAT SHED	SO	40.00	350.00
78	CHESAPEAKE BAY SKIPJACK	SO	40.00	600.00
78	NELLIE CROCKETT OYSTER BOAT	SO	40.00	1850.00
79	BUTLER'S BOAT YARD	SO	40.00	380.00
79	HAMPTON CREEK DERELICT	SO	40.00	405.00
79	PARRAMORE ISLAND GUARDIAN	SO	250.00	2500.00
79	SPRING PAINTING	SO	40.00	120.00
79	WILD DUCK ROUNDING HOOPER ST.	SO	40.00	1800.00
80	SKIPJACK ELSWORTH, THE	SO	40.00	1500.00
81	CAP'N WALTER'S WHARF	SO	40.00	450.00
81	SKIPJACK LADY KATIE, THE	SO	40.00	450.00
81	SKIPJACK MARTHA LEWIS, THE	SO	40.00	500.00
82	BUYBOAT WILLIAM B. TENNYSON	SO	55.00	351.00
82	GOOD DAY'S CATCH, A	SO	55.00	875.00
82	SIGSBEE- B&W	SO	25.00	120.00
82	SKIPJACK SIGSBEE, THE	SO	55.00	110.00
83	AT THE NETS- B&W	SO	25.00	50.00
83	CHESAPEAKE OYSTER TONGERS- B&W	SO	25.00	100.00
83	DISTANT THUNDER	SO	75.00	300.00
83	MORNING AT BELL BUOY- B&W	SO	25.00	212.00
83	SKIPJACK MAGGIE LEE, THE	SO	55.00	500.00
84	BUYING OYSTERS AT DRUM POINT	SO	100.00	422.00
84	COMING SQUALL	SO	50.00	515.00
84	GUARDIAN OF DIAMOND SHOALS	SO	65.00	225.00
84	MISTY MORNING	SO	65.00	250.00
84	MORNING AT COVE POINT	SO	75.00	790.00
84	TRADEWINDS	SO	65.00	460.00
85	BUYBOATS ON JACKSON CREEK	SO	65.00	380.00
85	CHESAPEAKE MORNING	SO	130.00	500.00
85	GLOUCESTER POINT WATERMEN	SO	75.00	765.00
85	NIGHT CROSSING	SO	95.00	2780.00
85	SPINNAKER REACH	SO	85.00	350.00
85	WINDWARD START	SO	85.00	300.00
86	AUGUST AFTERNOON	SO	95.00	270.00
86	DAWN ON THE CHOPTANK	SO	95.00	266.00
86	ON THE RAILWAY	SO	75.00	196.00
86	TWILIGHT HARBOR	SO	125.00	1160.00
86	VANISHING FLEET, THE	SO	145.00	1290.00
87	BAY COUNTRY MILL- B&W	OP	35.00	35.00
87	BAY COUNTRY MILL- COLOR	SO	135.00	270.00
87	MOONLIGHT HARBOR	SO	175.00	1076.00
87	RACING FOR THE OYSTERS- B&W	OP	35.00	35.00
87	RACING FOR THE OYSTERS- COLOR	SO	175.00	418.00
87	RETURNING HOME	SO	145.00	1400.00
88	BREEZING UP	SO	140.00	400.00
88	NIGHT PASSAGE	SO	225.00	650.00
88	UNCERTAIN WEATHER	SO	125.00	266.00
89	FOG OVER BLOODY POINT BAR	SO	165.00	330.00
89	MOONLIGHT OVER ST. MICHAELS	SO	285.00	935.00
89	TOWN DOCK	SO	95.00	190.00
89	UP FOR REPAIR	OP	95.00	95.00
90	AUTUMN MORNING	SO	85.00	170.00
90	DAWN'S EARLY LIGHT	SO	85.00	447.00
90	SKIPJACKS AT SANDY POINT	SO	165.00	220.00
90	SUNRISE OVER MOBJACK BAY	SO	185.00	370.00
91	ANNAPOLIS, CIRCA 1900	SO	195.00	423.00
91	MOONLIGHT RUN	SO	245.00	561.00
91	TILGHMAN ISLAND SUNSET	OP	120.00	120.00
92	CHESAPEAKE COUNTRY	OP	75.00	75.00
92	FAIR BREEZE & A FULL MOON, A	SO	145.00	383.00

YR	NAME	LIMIT	ISSUE	TREND
92	ROUNDING THE WINDWARD MARK	OP	115.00	115.00
92	SKIPJACKS AT POINT NO POINT	OP	125.00	125.00
93	DAY'S END ON DAVIS CREEK	OP	120.00	120.00
93	MORNING ARRIVAL AT BALTIMORE	OP	195.00	195.00
93	SUMMER MEMORIES	SO	165.00	330.00
94	FOGGY RUN	OP	130.00	130.00
94	SPRING BREEZES	OP	165.00	165.00
94	TANGIER AFTERNOON	OP	85.00	135.00
94	WINTER IN ANNAPOLIS	SO	95.00	190.00
95	DEAL ISLAND MORNING	OP	75.00	75.00
95	ENCOUNTER AT SMITH POINT LIGHT	OP	110.00	110.00
95	GOLDEN DAWN	OP	115.00	115.00
95	OLD NORFOLK EVENING	OP	195.00	195.00
95	OLD TOWN ALEXANDRIA	SO	195.00	390.00
95	WINTER ON THE EASTERN SHORE	OP	95.00	95.00
96	HARVESTERS	OP	100.00	100.00
96	MOONLIGHT FLIGHT	OP	65.00	65.00
96	SUMMER AFTERNOON AT ST. MICHAEL'S	OP	195.00	195.00
96	WINTER HARBOR	SO	95.00	95.00
97	MORNING ON THE POTOMAC	OP	100.00	100.00
97	OFF WINDMILL POINT	OP	120.00	120.00

BARTZ STUDIOS
D. CLAPP-BARTZ

YR	NAME	LIMIT	ISSUE	TREND
*	LITTLE NIGHT MUSIC, A	600	25.00	100.00
84	CASA DE VIDA	445	45.00	65.00
84	ENCHANTMENT	245	75.00	500.00
84	GOLDEN MEMORIES	445	45.00	65.00
84	GOLDEN TREASURES	245	75.00	200.00
84	GUARDIAN	445	45.00	200.00
84	INSPIRATION	245	75.00	275.00
84	MIDWINTER'S DREAM	245	75.00	500.00
84	NEW BEGINNINGS	445	45.00	65.00
85	DREAMMAKER	500	85.00	175.00
85	EMERALD MAGIC	950	30.00	30.00
85	GIFT, THE	500	85.00	375.00
85	SUMMER RETROSPECT	500	85.00	130.00
86	AUTUMN HIDEAWAY	500	135.00	125.00
86	FRIENDS	600	25.00	100.00
86	MAGIC MOMENTS	500	55.00	350.00
86	MOONGLO	600	40.00	350.00
86	QUIET SERENADE	500	135.00	500.00
86	REFUGE	500	60.00	350.00
87	AUTUMN COMES	500	110.00	200.00
87	MORNING MAGIC, THE	500	110.00	450.00
87	MORNING SONGS	500	165.00	1200.00
87	NATURE'S VEIL	500	95.00	1200.00
87	PATTERNS	500	150.00	165.00
88	ARABESQUE	500	115.00	125.00
88	ARCADIA	600	45.00	100.00
88	BLUE MOON	500	155.00	165.00
88	DISCOVERIES	500	155.00	165.00
88	DREAMIN'	500	155.00	155.00
88	IMAGES	600	45.00	100.00
88	WELCOME	500	45.00	75.00
89	AMBROSIA	500	185.00	415.00
89	FORUM I	285	500.00	950.00
89	SUNLIT PASSAGE	500	125.00	130.00
89	TIME PASSAGE	500	115.00	125.00
90	AUDIENCE, THE	600	45.00	45.00
90	NY POSTER	4000	25.00	25.00
90	PRELUDE	500	165.00	165.00
90	WHITE KNIGHTS	500	165.00	165.00
91	DEJA VU	500	125.00	125.00
91	INTERLUDE	500	165.00	240.00
91	MYSTIC HUES	500	190.00	190.00
91	SMOOTH JOURNEY	500	150.00	165.00
91	SUNDAY AFTERNOON	290	750.00	950.00
92	BLUE NOTES	20	700.00	1200.00
92	ESSENTIALS	20	800.00	1400.00
92	SERENDIPITY	20	500.00	1000.00
92	STRING OF PEARLS	20	500.00	1200.00
92	VERNAL FALLS	20	1,000.00	1400.00
92	YO MAXFIELD	20	800.00	1000.00
93	AH ROMANCE	600	95.00	95.00
93	PATRIOT, THE	600	50.00	50.00
93	PREREQUISITE	500	110.00	110.00
93	RHAPSODIES	500	195.00	195.00
93	SOLITUDES ILLUSION	600	65.00	65.00
95	MEMORIES	500	195.00	195.00
96	AU NATURAL	500	195.00	195.00

BENSON FINE ART PRINTS
G. BENSON

YR	NAME	LIMIT	ISSUE	TREND
92	AT THE LAKE	750	95.00	300.00
92	QUIET MOMENT	950	85.00	85.00
92	STORM RETREAT	750	85.00	150.00
93	AUTUMN TREASURES	175	95.00	95.00
93	TOGETHER AT DAWN	250	95.00	170.00

YR	NAME	LIMIT	ISSUE	TREND
G. BENSON			**REMEMBERING AMERICA**	
94	HOMELAND REFLECTIONS	950	125.00	185.00
94	TIME PASSAGES	950	125.00	175.00
95	OUT OF THE MIST	1500	65.00	110.00
95	TIMBER COUNTRY	950	125.00	180.00
96	CAMPFIRE POINT	950	125.00	125.00
96	RETURNING HOME	950	125.00	200.00

BISHOP FINE ART LTD.

J. MARIE				
93	DREAMING	1100	125.00	125.00
J. MARIE			**ANGELIC SERENITY**	
96	HEAVEN AND EARTH IN HARMONY	1100	125.00	125.00
96	TRANQUILITY	1100	125.00	125.00
97	MOMENTS OF BLISS	110	395.00	395.00
97	PARADISE FOUND	220	395.00	395.00

BRIERCROFT

D. WINDBERG		**WINDBERG COLLECTORS SOCIETY MEMBERS ONLY**		
95	PERFECT SERENITY	*	150.00	150.00

BRIGHTER IMAGE PUBLISHING

K. AUNCHMAN				
95	18TH HOLE HARBOURTOWN	1000	90.00	90.00

CANEY CREEK PUBLISHING

P. MURRAY				
95	AUNTY EMILY	CL	205.00	330.00
95	DENIM	680	35.00	35.00
95	LID'L FANNIE	680	30.00	30.00
95	MAUDE	680	35.00	35.00
95	MILT	680	30.00	30.00
P. MURRAY			**LAST OF THE LEGEND**	
93	DANIEL	CL	385.00	325.00
95	WASHBOARD COMPLAINT	680	285.00	285.00

CAT CORCILIUS

C. CORCILIUS			**CORCILIUS STUDIOS**	
89	BEAR TRACKS	SO	95.00	553.00
89	BUFFALO ROBE	SO	125.00	425.00
89	HAWK'S WOMAN	SO	95.00	180.00
91	NINTOTEM	SO	125.00	765.00
92	RAINDANCE	SO	100.00	225.00
93	DREAMWEAVER	SO	150.00	300.00
94	CHINA TRADE	SO	175.00	468.00
94	PRIDE OF A WARRIOR	SO	150.00	200.00
C. CORCILIUS			**SECOND EMERALD**	
92	LITTLE PRINCESS	SO	60.00	120.00
92	LITTLE WARRIOR	SO	60.00	120.00
C. CORCILIUS			**WIEGHORST MUSEUM**	
95	SHARED VISION	SO	150.00	270.00

CHRISTOPHER PALUSO ART WORKS

C. PALUSO				
*	AL KALINE	750	5.00	30.00
*	ALAN TRAMMELL	750	5.00	30.00
*	ANDY HAWKINS	750	5.00	30.00
*	BABE RUTH	500	85.00	125.00
*	BASEBALL'S IRON MAN	10000	15.00	35.00
*	CHUCK CONNORS	750	5.00	50.00
*	DARRYL STRAWBERRY	1000	10.00	30.00
*	DAVE DRAVECKY	750	5.00	30.00
*	DON MATTINGLY	1000	10.00	30.00
*	DUKE SNIDER	500	5.00	30.00
*	DWIGHT GOODEN	1000	10.00	30.00
*	K. MCREYNOLDS	500	5.00	30.00
*	NOLAN RYAN	1000	50.00	300.00
*	OREL HERSHISER	750	5.00	30.00
*	RICKY HENDERSON	1000	10.00	30.00
*	RON CEY	250	5.00	30.00
*	RUPPERT JONES	750	5.00	30.00
*	RYNE SANDBERG	500	5.00	30.00
*	SPARKY ANDERSON	250	5.00	30.00
*	STEVE GARVEY	1000	10.00	30.00
*	TED WILLIAMS	500	5.00	35.00
*	TERRY KENNEDY	750	5.00	30.00
*	TONY GWYNN	351	85.00	150.00
*	WILLIE MAYS	500	5.00	35.00
*	WILLIE MCCOVEY	500	5.00	30.00

CHUST COUNTRY

T. NEIFFER				
93	AND THE ANIMALS CAME	450	98.00	98.00
94	ADVENTURES OF COLE THE CAT, THE	850	98.00	98.00

CIRCLE FINE ART

L. NEIMAN			**NEIMAN**	
*	12 METER YACHT RACE	250	*	1800.00

Rockland Breakwater Light, *a print by Charles Wysocki for The Greenwich Workshop, has nearly tripled in value since its release in 1991.*

The canvas edition of Thomas Kinkade's award-winning image End of A Perfect Day II, A Quiet Evening at Riverlodge, *produced by Lightpost Publishing, has increased in value since its 1994 release.*

YR	NAME	LIMIT	ISSUE	TREND
*	AL CAPONE	300	*	2000.00
*	BACKHAND	300	*	1450.00
*	CASINO	300	*	4100.00
*	CHIPPING ON	275	*	1500.00
*	DEUCE	275	*	2000.00
*	DOUBLES	300	*	3150.00
*	DOWNHILL	600	*	1800.00
*	END AROUND	300	2,800.00	2800.00
*	FOUR ACES	300	*	1500.00
*	FOX HUNT	300	*	1500.00
*	GOAL	300	*	1500.00
*	HARLEQUIN	200	3,600.00	3600.00
*	HARLEQUIN W/SWORD	250	*	1150.00
*	HARLEQUIN W/TEXT	200	*	1150.00
*	HOCKEY PLAYER	300	*	2800.00
*	HOMMAGE TO BOUCHER	250	*	1700.00
*	IN THE STRETCH	250	*	1400.00
*	INNSBRUCK	300	*	2000.00
*	JOCKEY	300	3,200.00	2800.00
*	LEOPARD	300	*	5500.00
*	LION PRIDE	300	*	4000.00
*	MARATHON	300	*	1800.00
*	OCELOT	250	*	2500.00
*	PADDOCK	300	*	3900.00
*	PIERROT	250	*	1150.00
*	PIERROT THE JUGGLER	200	*	1150.00
*	POOL ROOM	350	*	6500.00
*	PUNCHINELLO	250	*	2200.00
*	PUNCHINELLO W/TEXT	200	*	1600.00
*	RACE, THE	300	*	700.00
*	ROULETTE	40	*	11000.00
*	SAILING	275	*	1700.00
*	SCRAMBLE	300	*	1800.00
*	SKIER	300	*	1500.00
*	SLALOM	300	*	2500.00
*	SLAPSHOT	300	*	2000.00
*	SLIDING HOME	300	*	2450.00
*	SMASH	300	*	1700.00
*	STOCK MARKET	300	*	7500.00
*	SUDDEN DEATH	250	*	2350.00
*	TEE SHOT	300	*	4000.00
*	TENNIS PLAYER	300	*	1500.00
*	TIGER	300	*	5100.00
*	TROTTERS	300	*	1850.00

N. ROCKWELL — **ROCKWELL**

YR	NAME	LIMIT	ISSUE	TREND
*	AMERICAN FAMILY FOLIO	200	*	17550.00
*	ARTIST AT WORK, THE	130	*	3550.00
*	AT THE BARBER	200	*	5000.00
*	AUTUMN	200	*	3550.00
*	AUTUMN/JAPON	25	*	3700.00
*	AVIARY	200	*	3850.00
*	BARBERSHOP QUARTET	200	*	2000.00
*	BASEBALL	200	*	3650.00
*	BEN FRANKLIN'S PHILADELPHIA	200	*	3675.00
*	BEN'S BELLES	200	*	3675.00
*	BIG DAY, THE	200	*	3500.00
*	BIG TOP, THE	148	*	3400.00
*	BLACKSMITH SHOP	200	*	5000.00
*	BOOKSELLER	200	*	2775.00
*	BOOKSELLER/JAPON	25	*	2800.00
*	BRIDGE, THE	200	*	3150.00
*	CAT	200	*	3500.00
*	CAT/COLLOTYPE	200	*	4050.00
*	CHEERING	200	*	3650.00
*	CHILDREN AT WINDOW	200	*	3650.00
*	CHURCH	200	*	3450.00
*	CHURCH/COLLOTYPE	200	*	4075.00
*	CIRCUS	200	*	2700.00
*	COUNTY AGRICULTURAL	200	*	2300.00
*	CRITIC, THE	200	*	4700.00
*	DAY IN THE LIFE OF A BOY	25	*	3850.00
*	DEBUT	200	*	3650.00
*	DISCOVERY	200	*	3000.00
*	DOCTOR AND BOY	200	*	9500.00
*	DOCTOR AND DOLL	200	*	8500.00
*	DRESSING UP/INK	60	*	4500.00
*	DRESSING UP/PENCIL	200	*	3775.00
*	DRUNKARD, THE	200	*	3675.00
*	EXPECTED AND UNEXPECTED, THE	200	*	3750.00
*	FAMILY TREE	200	*	6000.00
*	FIDO'S HOUSE	200	*	3600.00
*	FOOTBALL MASCOT	200	*	3700.00
*	FOUR SEASONS FOLIO	200	*	5500.00
*	FOUR SEASONS FOLIO/JAPON	25	*	14000.00
*	FREEDOM FROM FEAR	200	*	6500.00
*	FREEDOM FROM WANT	200	*	6500.00
*	FREEDOM OF RELIGION	200	*	6500.00
*	FREEDOM OF SPEECH	200	*	6500.00
*	GAIETY DANCE TEAM	200	*	3000.00

YR	NAME	LIMIT	ISSUE	TREND
*	GIRL AT MIRROR	200	*	8500.00
*	GOLDEN AGE, THE	200	*	3500.00
*	GOLDEN RULE	200	*	4500.00
*	GOLF	200	*	3700.00
*	GOSSIPS	200	*	5000.00
*	GOSSIPS/JAPON	25	*	5200.00
*	GROTTO	200	*	3500.00
*	GROTTO/COLLOTYPE	200	*	4000.00
*	HIGH DIVE	200	*	2500.00
*	HOMECOMING, THE	200	*	3700.00
*	HOUSE, THE	200	*	3700.00
*	HUCK FINN FOLIO	200	*	16000.00
*	ICHABOD CRANE	200	*	6800.00
*	INVENTOR, THE	200	*	3600.00
*	JERRY	200	*	4800.00
*	JIM GOT DOWN ON HIS KNEES	200	*	4500.00
*	LINCOLN	200	*	5000.00
*	LOBSTERMAN	200	*	5500.00
*	LOBSTERMAN/JAPON	25	*	5600.00
*	MARRIAGE LICENSE	200	*	1000.00
*	MEDICINE	200	*	3500.00
*	MEDICINE/COLOR LITHO	200	*	6000.00
*	MISS MARY JANE	200	*	4500.00
*	MOVING DAY	200	*	4000.00
*	MUSIC HATH CHARMS	200	*	4200.00
*	MY HAND SHOOK	200	*	4500.00
*	OUT THE WINDOW	200	*	3400.00
*	OUT THE WINDOW/COLLOTYPE	200	*	4000.00
*	OUTWARD BOUND	200	*	8000.00
*	POOR RICHARD'S ALMANAC	200	*	11500.00
*	PRESCRIPTION	200	*	5000.00
*	PRESCRIPTION/JAPON	25	*	5000.00
*	PROBLEM WE ALL LIVE WITH, THE	200	*	3150.00
*	PUPPIES	200	*	3700.00
*	RALEIGH THE DOG	200	*	4000.00
*	ROCKET SHIP	200	*	4000.00
*	ROYAL CROWN, THE	200	*	3500.00
*	RUNAWAY	200	*	4600.00
*	SAFE AND SOUND	200	*	3800.00
*	SATURDAY PEOPLE	200	*	3300.00
*	SAVE ME	200	*	3600.00
*	SAVING GRACE	200	*	7500.00
*	SCHOOL DAYS FOLIO	200	*	18000.00
*	SCHOOLHOUSE, THE	200	*	4500.00
*	SCHOOLHOUSE/JAPON	25	*	4700.00
*	SEE AMERICA FIRST	200	*	2600.00
*	SEE AMERICA FIRST/JAPON	25	*	5700.00
*	SETTLING IN	200	*	5000.00
*	SHUFFELTON'S BARBERS	200	*	7500.00
*	SMOKING	200	*	4000.00
*	SMOKING/COLLOTYPE	200	*	4000.00
*	SPANKING	200	*	3500.00
*	SPANKING/COLLOTYPE	200	*	3600.00
*	SPELLING BEE	200	*	5000.00
*	SPRING	200	*	2500.00
*	SPRING FLOWERS	200	*	5200.00
*	SPRING/JAPON	25	*	3650.00
*	STUDY FOR THE DOCTOR	200	*	6000.00
*	STUDYING	200	*	3600.00
*	SUMMER	200	*	3600.00
*	SUMMER STOCK	200	*	5000.00
*	SUMMER STOCK/JAPON	25	*	5000.00
*	SUMMER/JAPON	25	*	3600.00
*	TEACHER'S PET	200	*	3600.00
*	TEACHER, THE	200	*	3400.00
*	TEACHER, THE/JAPON	25	*	3500.00
*	TEXAN, THE	200	*	2000.00
*	THEN FOR THREE MINUTES	200	*	4500.00
*	THEN MISS WATSON	200	*	4500.00
*	THERE WARN'T NO HARM	200	*	4500.00
*	THREE FARMERS	200	*	3600.00
*	TICKETSELLER	200	*	2700.00
*	TOM SAWYER COLOR SUITE	200	*	30500.00
*	TOM SAWYER FOLIO	200	*	11000.00
*	TOP OF THE WORLD	200	*	4300.00
*	TRUMPETER	200	*	4000.00
*	TRUMPETER/JAPON	25	*	4100.00
*	TWO O'CLOCK FEEDING	200	*	3600.00
*	VILLAGE SMITHY, THE	200	*	3500.00
*	WELCOME	200	*	3500.00
*	WET PAINT	200	*	2000.00
*	WHEN I LIT MY CANDLE	200	*	4500.00
*	WHITEWASHING	200	*	3450.00
*	WHITEWASHING THE FENCE	200	*	4000.00
*	WINDOW WASHER	200	*	6500.00
*	WINTER	200	*	2300.00
*	WINTER/JAPON	25	*	3600.00
*	YE OLD PRINT SHOPPE	200	*	3500.00
*	YOUR EYES IS LOOKIN'	200	*	4600.00

YR	NAME	LIMIT	ISSUE	TREND

COLE FINE ART

J. KRAMER COLE

COLE CONCEPT

YR	NAME	LIMIT	ISSUE	TREND
93	HOMEWARD JOURNEY			
95	MAHTOLA	5000	95.00	134.00
		5000	125.00	155.00

J. KRAMER COLE

COLLECTORS SERIES

YR	NAME	LIMIT	ISSUE	TREND
86	MAN WHO SEES FAR	417	25.00	3000.00
92	HE WHO WATCHES	495	185.00	198.00
92	WHEN SILENCE WARNS	495	185.00	297.00
93	LISTENING	750	185.00	189.00
94	BRINGING THE SHIELD	950	185.00	234.00
95	RED SHIELD, THE	950	235.00	313.00
96	JOURNEY OF RENEWAL	950	235.00	276.00
97	WOLF CREEK	950	235.00	235.00

J. KRAMER COLE

EMERGING IMAGE

YR	NAME	LIMIT	ISSUE	TREND
88	CANYON OF THE CAT	950	50.00	350.00
88	WOLF RIDGE	950	50.00	525.00
89	MANY WINTERS I AM	950	75.00	339.00
89	TWO BEARS CAMP	950	100.00	1200.00
89	WAMBLI OKIYE	950	75.00	299.00
90	TRAIL OF THE TALISMAN	950	110.00	549.00
90	WITHIN SUNRISE	1150	95.00	166.00
91	TWICE TRAVELED TRAIL	950	135.00	333.00
91	WINTERING WITH THE WAPITI	950	135.00	275.00
91	WOLFPACK OF THE ANCIENTS	950	135.00	219.00
92	MARKING TREE, THE	950	145.00	328.00
92	SACRED DOGS	950	145.00	1077.00
93	KEEPERS OF THE SECRET	3500	185.00	185.00
93	WAKAN TANKA	2500	185.00	411.00
94	CIRCLE OF THE SACRED DOGS	6408	185.00	185.00
95	TOPONAS	3850	185.00	185.00
96	FEATHER, THE	2850	235.00	235.00
96	SUMMONED SPIRITS	2500	255.00	255.00
97	OFFERING, THE	1500	255.00	255.00
98	ANIMAL DREAMS	1500	195.00	195.00

J. KRAMER COLE

LIFESTYLES SERIES

YR	NAME	LIMIT	ISSUE	TREND
91	ISABEL	950	135.00	247.00
94	MEMORY, A	950	185.00	185.00

J. KRAMER COLE

MASTER EDITION SERIES

YR	NAME	LIMIT	ISSUE	TREND
94	BROTHER TO THE MOON, SUN OF THE SUN	185	295.00	314.00

COMPETITIVE IMAGES

RUSH

YR	NAME	LIMIT	ISSUE	TREND
76	GUARANTEED WINNER (SUPER BOWL III)	900	100.00	1150.00
78	SUGAR BOWL 1987: ALABAMA VS OHIO STATE	275	200.00	3000.00
79	TURN, THE (THOROUGHBRED)	275	300.00	900.00
79	YOU BETTER PASS (SUGAR BOWL)	130	300.00	4500.00
80	SPINNAKER RUN (12 M. YACHTS)	325	400.00	1000.00
80	SPIRIT OF VICTORY (USA OLYM. HOCKEY)	325	400.00	3500.00
81	CHAMPIONSHIP SEASON (U. OF GEORGIA)	325	400.00	500.00
81	HAPPY BIRTHDAY AMERICA (MCENROE)	325	400.00	1500.00
81	JACK NICKLAUS: THE GOLDEN BEAR	325	400.00	800.00
81	SLALOM	325	400.00	2500.00
81	SUPER BOWL GIANTS	410	500.00	550.00
82	COACH PAUL BEAR BRYANT	200	425.00	2500.00
82	HILTON HEAD: THE HERITAGE CLASSIC	325	425.00	2500.00
82	LAST CHUKKER, THE (POLO)	500	400.00	500.00
82	NATIONAL CHAMPION CLEMSON UNIV.	500	450.00	1000.00
82	NORTH CAROLINA NATIONAL CHAMPION	500	450.00	500.00
82	PEBBLE BEACH	500	500.00	1200.00
83	DINNER WHITE NIGHT (PENN STATE)	350	450.00	500.00
83	GREENTRACK (GREYHOUND RACING)	225	425.00	500.00
83	UCLA	500	450.00	500.00
84	A DREAM OF GOLD (XXIII OLYMPIAD)	500	500.00	600.00
84	FAIRBANKS, THE (XXXIII OLYM. EQUES.)	200	500.00	550.00
84	ONE AND ONLY, THE (NEBRASKA)	225	450.00	500.00
84	WIMBLEDON WOMEN (100TH ANNIVERSARY)	500	450.00	800.00
85	A CENTURY OF EXCELLENCE (GA TECH)	225	500.00	550.00
85	CHRIS EVERT LLOYD	275	500.00	500.00
85	MIAMI ON THE MOVE (DOLPHINS)	225	500.00	600.00
85	TWENTY SIX & GLORY (OK STATE)	100	450.00	450.00
86	GLORY YEARS, THE (ICE BOWL)	135	500.00	2000.00
86	INDY 500, THE	175	500.00	600.00
86	KENTUCKY DERBY, THE	500	450.00	550.00
86	MARTINA NAVRATILOVA	275	500.00	550.00
86	OKLAHOMA NATIONAL CHAMPION (B. SWITZER)	100	500.00	800.00
86	ROYAL FINISH (KANSAS CITY)	300	522.00	600.00
86	SHOW ME SERIES, THE (K.C. WORLD SERIES)	375	450.00	550.00
86	WON FOR PAPA (SUPER BOWL)	200	500.00	4000.00
87	AMAZIN AGAIN: N.Y. METS	320	525.00	550.00
87	AMERICA'S COWBOYS (DALLAS)	310	500.00	550.00
87	BURGUNDY IN GOLD (REDSKINS)	165	500.00	550.00
87	MILE HIGH DENVER BRONCOS	425	500.00	500.00
88	CUMMINGS AGAIN: BUCKS	175	500.00	550.00
88	LED BY THE SPIRIT (COTTON BOWL 88)	150	525.00	1500.00
88	NATIONAL CHAMPION HOOSIERS	250	525.00	525.00
88	NATIONAL CHAMPION JAYHAWKS	275	450.00	450.00
88	ON WISCONSIN	185	500.00	500.00
88	REACHING THE MARK (AMERICA'S CUP)	*	525.00	700.00

YR	NAME	LIMIT	ISSUE	TREND
89	A TRADITION OF GOLD (NOTRE DAME)	275	550.00	550.00
89	HIGH FLYING CARDINALS (BASEBALL)	190	525.00	525.00
89	HIT & RUN BREWERS 1987	190	525.00	550.00
89	SECOND AND GOLD: 1987 ROSE BOWL	150	525.00	525.00
90	ABOVE THE CROWD (M. JORDAN)	200	525.00	600.00

CROSS GALLERY
P. CROSS — HALF BREED SERIES

YR	NAME	LIMIT	ISSUE	TREND
89	ACH-HUA DLUBH: HALF BREED	475	190.00	700.00
90	ACH-HUA DLUBH: HALF BREED II	475	225.00	480.00
90	ACH-HUA DLUBH: HALF BREED III	475	225.00	600.00
95	HALF-BREED IV	865	225.00	225.00
96	BANDITS, THE	865	225.00	225.00
96	HEALER, THE	250	795.00	225.00
96	WOLVES	865	225.00	225.00

P. CROSS — LIMITED EDITION ORIGINAL GRAPHICS

YR	NAME	LIMIT	ISSUE	TREND
85	CAROLINE (STONE LITHO)	47	300.00	600.00
88	MAIDENHOOD HOPI (STONE LITHO)	74	950.00	1150.00
89	RED CAPOTE, THE (SERIGRAPH)	275	750.00	400.00
89	ROSAPINA (ETCHING)	74	1,200.00	1260.00
90	NIGHTEYES I (SERIGRAPH)	275	225.00	250.00

P. CROSS — LIMITED EDITION PRINTS

YR	NAME	LIMIT	ISSUE	TREND
83	AYLA-SA-XUH-XAH (PRETTY COLOURS)	475	150.00	150.00
83	ISBAALOO EETSCHIILEEHCHEE (SORTING BEAD)	475	150.00	1800.00
84	BLUE BEADED HAIR TIES	475	85.00	400.00
84	DII-TAH-SHTEH EE-WIHZA-AHOOK (COAT)	475	90.00	560.00
84	PROFILE OF CAROLINE	475	85.00	125.00
84	THICK LODGE CLAN BOY: CROW	475	85.00	180.00
84	WHISTLING WATER CLAN GIRL: CROW	475	85.00	330.00
85	CAROLINE	475	45.00	70.00
85	WATER VISION, THE	475	150.00	275.00
86	GRAND ENTRY	475	85.00	95.00
86	RED CAPOTE, THE	475	150.00	245.00
86	WINTER MORNING	475	185.00	1100.00
86	WINTER SHAWL, THE	475	150.00	2600.00
87	ELKSKIN ROBE, THE	475	190.00	325.00
87	RED NECKLACE, THE	475	90.00	150.00
87	TINA	475	45.00	115.00
88	DANCE APACHE	475	190.00	250.00
88	MA-A-LUPPIS-SHE-LA-DUS (SHE IS ABOVE)	475	190.00	450.00
89	B'ACHUA DLUBH-BIA BII NOSKIIYAHI, II	475	225.00	415.00
89	BIAACHEE-ITAH BAH-ACHBEH	475	225.00	225.00
89	CHEY-AYJEH: PREY	475	190.00	300.00
89	DREAMER, THE	475	190.00	190.00
89	TEESA WAITS TO DANCE	475	135.00	135.00
90	BAAPE OCHIA (NIGHT WIND, TURQUOISE)	475	185.00	225.00
90	ESHTE	475	185.00	185.00
90	ISHIA-KAHDA #1 (QUIET ONE)	475	185.00	190.00

P. CROSS — MINIATURE LINE

YR	NAME	LIMIT	ISSUE	TREND
91	BJ	447	80.00	85.00
91	FLORAL SHAWL, THE	447	80.00	125.00
91	KENDRA	447	80.00	100.00
91	WATERCOLOR STUDY #32 FOR HALF BREED	447	80.00	80.00

P. CROSS — PAINTED LADIES' SUITE

YR	NAME	LIMIT	ISSUE	TREND
92	ACORIA (CROW: SEAT OF HONOR)	447	185.00	140.00
92	AVISOLA	475	185.00	185.00
92	DAH-SAY (CROW HEART)	475	185.00	185.00
92	ITZA-CHU (APACHE: THE EAGLE)	475	185.00	165.00
92	KEL'HOYA (HOPI: LITTLE SPARROW HAWK)	475	185.00	185.00
92	PAINTED LADIES, THE	475	225.00	975.00
92	SUS(H)GAH-DAYDUS(H) (CROW: QUICK)	447	185.00	185.00
92	TZE-GO-JUNI (CHIRICAHUA APACHE)	447	80.00	80.00

P. CROSS — STAR QUILT

YR	NAME	LIMIT	ISSUE	TREND
85	WINTER WARMTH	475	150.00	1600.00
86	REFLECTIONS	475	185.00	975.00
88	QUILT MAKERS, THE	475	190.00	245.00

P. CROSS — WOLF SERIES

YR	NAME	LIMIT	ISSUE	TREND
85	DII-TAH-SHTEH BII-WIK; CHEDAH-BAH LIIDAH	475	185.00	2000.00
87	MORNING STAR GIVES LONG OTTER HIS HOOP	475	190.00	1300.00
89	BIAGOHT EECUEBEH HEHSHEESH-CHEDAH	475	225.00	225.00
90	AGNJNAUG AMAGUUT; INUPIAG (WOMEN/WOLVES)	1050	325.00	325.00

DAVE GROSSMAN CREATIONS
* — GONE WITH THE WIND

YR	NAME	LIMIT	ISSUE	TREND
94	ATLANTA BURNING CANVAS PRINT 18X24	RT	200.00	200.00
94	ATLANTA BURNING CANVAS PRINT 8X10	RT	100.00	100.00
94	MISS SCARLETT CANVAS PRINT 18X24	RT	200.00	200.00
94	MISS SCARLETT MONTAGE CANVAS PRINT 8X10	RT	100.00	100.00
94	OPENING SCENE CANVAS PRINT 18X24	RT	200.00	200.00
94	OPENING SCENE CANVAS PRINT 8X10	RT	100.00	100.00
94	SCARLETT & TARA CANVAS PRINT 8X10	RT	100.00	100.00
94	SCARLETT AND TARA CANVAS PRINT 18X24	RT	200.00	200.00

DEBORAH ROBINSON
D. ROBINSON

YR	NAME	LIMIT	ISSUE	TREND
84	JEWELS IN THE SUNSET	CL	*	N/A
84	TO GOD GIVE THE GLORY	CL	*	N/A
85	ME TOO	CL	*	N/A

YR	NAME	LIMIT	ISSUE	TREND
87	BEAR YOUR HEART	CL	*	N/A
87	EVERYTHING'S COMING UP ROSES	CL	*	N/A
89	HIBISCUS	500	125.00	125.00
89	TIDEPOOL	CL	*	N/A
90	GIVE IT A WHIRL	500	125.00	125.00
91	SECRETS	CL	*	N/A
92	FRIENDS	500	50.00	50.00
92	SAND CASTLE	500	85.00	85.00
92	SAND TIME	500	85.00	85.00
92	WHEN WE WERE YOUNG	500	225.00	225.00
92	YESTERDAY	500	85.00	85.00

DELGADO STUDIO
DELGADO

	NAME	LIMIT	ISSUE	TREND
*	CAMACHO VS MACINI S/N	500	25.00	100.00
*	CATCH, THE A/P	49	149.00	275.00
*	CATCH, THE S/N H/S	750	100.00	200.00
*	HEAD TO HEAD EASY GOER & SUNDAY SILENCE	500	100.00	250.00
*	JOHN HENRY	750	75.00	275.00
*	MICKEY AT NIGHT H/S	750	125.00	450.00
*	MONTANA TO RICE A/P	49	300.00	400.00
*	MONTANTA TO RICE H/S S/N	500	250.00	300.00
*	PAEZ VS LOPEZ S/N	500	25.00	100.00
*	RONNIE LOTT H/S S/N	1049	149.00	225.00
*	SHOES ROSES A/P, THE	25	150.00	300.00
*	SHOES ROSES S/N, THE	500	50.00	200.00
*	WITAKER, TAYLER, CAMACHO AT CAESARS S/N	500	25.00	125.00

DENNIS P. LEWAN FINE ART STUDIOS
D. PATRICK LEWAN — A/P CANVAS FRAMED

	NAME	LIMIT	ISSUE	TREND
*	BEAR COTTAGE	30	505.00	2000.00
*	BEAR HAUS INN, THE	45	230.00	300.00
*	BEARLY EVE	40	410.00	1675.00
*	FLOWER HARVEST	45	230.00	300.00
*	GATE TO THE COURTYARD	30	230.00	275.00
*	GRAND MANOR	40	850.00	950.00
*	KINGSBERRY COTTAGE	40	175.00	200.00
*	LITTLE BEAR COTTAGE	40	300.00	900.00
*	MANOR HOUSE, THE	40	500.00	1675.00
*	MEAGAN'S FRIENDS	30	230.00	400.00
*	MILL CREEK MANOR	40	525.00	1675.00
*	OLDE AMSTERDAM	30	495.00	1000.00
*	SEACLIFF COTTAGE	40	175.00	250.00
*	SPRING IN BAVARIA	30	155.00	285.00
*	VICTORIAN FANTASY	40	410.00	930.00
*	WENTWORTH COTTAGE	30	155.00	285.00

D. PATRICK LEWAN — A/P PAPER UNFRAMED

	NAME	LIMIT	ISSUE	TREND
*	BEAR COTTAGE	50	225.00	540.00
*	MANOR HOUSE, THE	55	175.00	245.00

D. PATRICK LEWAN — S/N CANVAS FRAMED

	NAME	LIMIT	ISSUE	TREND
*	BEAR COTTAGE	300	430.00	1300.00
*	BEAR HAUS INN, THE	450	190.00	250.00
*	BEARLY EVE	375	260.00	900.00
*	FLOWER HARVEST	450	190.00	230.00
*	GATE TO THE COURTYARD	300	200.00	250.00
*	GRAND MANOR	400	700.00	1100.00
*	KINGSBERRY COTTAGE	400	150.00	225.00
*	LITTLE BEAR COTTAGE	400	250.00	1000.00
*	MANOR HOUSE, THE	400	440.00	1250.00
*	MEAGAN'S FRIENDS	300	200.00	325.00
*	MILL CREEK MANOR	375	450.00	600.00
*	OLDE AMSTERDAM	300	390.00	390.00
*	SEACLIFF COTTAGE	400	150.00	225.00
*	SPRING IN BAVARIA	300	130.00	260.00
*	VICTORIAN FANTASY	375	360.00	975.00

D. PATRICK LEWAN — S/N CANVAS UNFRAMED

	NAME	LIMIT	ISSUE	TREND
*	SEACLIFF COTTAGE	400	120.00	170.00
*	WENTWORTH COTTAGE	300	100.00	230.00

D. PATRICK LEWAN — S/N PAPER UNFRAMED

	NAME	LIMIT	ISSUE	TREND
*	BEAR COTTAGE	500	150.00	300.00
*	MANOR HOUSE, THE	550	125.00	170.00
*	VICTORIAN FANTASY	500	150.00	200.00

DIANE PHALEN WATERCOLORS
D. PHALEN — AMERICANA QUILT

YR	NAME	LIMIT	ISSUE	TREND
94	COUNTRY STORE QUILTS	750	20.00	20.00
95	AMISH ROADSIDE MARKET	1500	30.00	30.00
95	AMISH SPRING	1500	30.00	30.00
95	CHRISTMAS QUILTS	1500	30.00	30.00
95	GRANDMA'S TREASURES	1500	30.00	30.00
95	LOG CABIN QUILTS	1500	40.00	40.00
95	QUILTS FOR SALE	1500	40.00	40.00
95	SUMMER BREEZE	1500	30.00	30.00
96	AMISH NEIGHBORS	1500	60.00	60.00
96	CHRISTMAS EVE QUILTS	1500	40.00	40.00
96	COTTAGE IRISES	1500	30.00	30.00
96	LLAMAS AND QUILTS	1500	40.00	40.00
96	SEPTEMBER GOLD	1500	40.00	40.00

YR	NAME	LIMIT	ISSUE	TREND
96	SPRING GARDEN	1500	60.00	60.00
96	THREE SISTERS' QUILTS	1500	40.00	40.00
97	A QUILTED VIEW	1500	60.00	60.00
97	HOLIDAY AIRING	1500	60.00	60.00
97	SHORELINE TREASURES	1500	60.00	60.00

DIMENSIONAL AESTHETICS
B. HAILS

YR	NAME	LIMIT	ISSUE	TREND
85	GAZEBO, THE	*	40.00	65.00
86	BRIGHT NEW DAY	*	40.00	60.00
86	RIVER VISTA (THE GAP)	*	40.00	60.00
86	SOLITUDE	*	40.00	60.00
86	TAVERN, THE	*	40.00	65.00
87	CITY BREEZES	*	80.00	90.00
87	INDIAN SUMMER	*	40.00	90.00
87	LOCK, THE	*	95.00	95.00
87	QUIET LIGHT	*	40.00	60.00
88	AZALEA BANK A/P	*	90.00	130.00
89	AZALEA GLOW	*	40.00	40.00
89	TRACERY	*	40.00	50.00

EAGLE EDITIONS LTD.
J. CRANDALL

YR	NAME	LIMIT	ISSUE	TREND
77	SMOKE UP AHEAD	450	60.00	400.00
79	I FOUND THE PASS	500	60.00	360.00
79	PURSUED	525	60.00	1000.00
80	ON TO TAOS	560	65.00	125.00
80	SHRINE TO THE BUFFALO	525	65.00	170.00
81	CAUTION	650	40.00	145.00
81	NOT ALONE	650	55.00	300.00
82	COUREURS DES BOIS	1000	85.00	250.00
83	AN EARLY SNOW	750	85.00	100.00

J. CRANDALL — WINGS OF VALOR

YR	NAME	LIMIT	ISSUE	TREND
85	MOUSE AND THE FLEA, THE: B-17	950	85.00	300.00
87	TOMCATS 2-FITTERS 0: F-14	950	85.00	95.00
89	BLOND KNIGHT, THE: ME 109	950	145.00	900.00

EDNA HIBEL STUDIOS
E. HIBEL — HIBEL LITHOGRAPHY ON PORCELAIN

YR	NAME	LIMIT	ISSUE	TREND
78	LENORE AND CHILD (ON PORCELAIN)	395	600.00	2100.00
80	CHERYLL AND WENDY (ON PORCELAIN)	100	3,900.00	11500.00

E. HIBEL — HIBEL STONE LITHOGRAPHY

YR	NAME	LIMIT	ISSUE	TREND
*	BEGGAR	70	250.00	4700.00
74	MOTHER AND FOUR CHILDREN	60	150.00	1675.00
75	SANDY (STONE LITHO)	140	75.00	1550.00
76	ELSA & BABY	300	150.00	4200.00
76	JAPANESE DOLL	28	160.00	2600.00
76	KIKUE (SILK)	145	195.00	2700.00
76	MOTHER & FOUR CHILDREN (HORIZONTAL)	300	250.00	2000.00
76	SOPHIA & CHILDREN	296	325.00	4300.00
76	SWITZERLAND	270	350.00	2000.00
77	COLETTE & CHILD	275	195.00	1100.00
77	MAYAN MAN	295	350.00	4300.00
77	MUSEUM SUITE	375	1,900.00	9700.00
78	FELICIA	148	900.00	2250.00
79	AKIKO & CHILDREN	335	450.00	2800.00
79	INTERNATIONAL YEAR OF THE CHILD SUITE	420	900.00	2250.00
79	JOSEPH	335	495.00	1325.00
79	NORA	394	175.00	750.00
79	PETRA MIT KINDER	320	345.00	2475.00
79	THAI PRINCESS	335	495.00	1450.00
80	CHERYLL & WENDY	100	3,900.00	11500.00
80	CHO CHO SAN	396	500.00	1050.00
80	HOPE	396	400.00	1100.00
80	SPIRIT OF MAINAU SUITE, THE	385	1,200.00	3150.00
80	TINA	200	750.00	1175.00
81	JACKLIN & CHILD	197	110.00	400.00
81	LITTLE EMPEROR, THE	275	1,000.00	2250.00
81	LITTLE EMPRESS	319	1,000.00	2100.00
82	BETTINA AND CHILDREN	300	310.00	1400.00
82	FAMILY OF THE MOUNTAIN LAKE	305	395.00	2250.00
82	JOELLE	348	295.00	1400.00
82	KELLY	347	320.00	1700.00
82	LYDIA	298	295.00	650.00
82	NARO-SAN	322	310.00	675.00
82	RENA & RACHEL	329	345.00	1025.00
83	VALERIE & CHILDREN	400	295.00	625.00
84	ARIELLE & AMY	275	295.00	675.00
84	BEVERLY & CHILD	216	160.00	425.00
84	CARESS, THE	430	325.00	700.00
84	CELESTE	256	175.00	400.00
84	CLAIRE	206	335.00	975.00
84	DES FLEURS ROUGES	298	245.00	750.00
84	DORENE & CHILD	331	250.00	525.00
84	DREAM SKETCHBOOK	298	175.00	475.00
84	GERARD	200	250.00	725.00
84	JENNIFER & CHILDREN	318	445.00	775.00
84	NATASHA & CHILDREN	308	195.00	500.00
84	NAVA & CHILDREN	385	385.00	750.00

YR	NAME	LIMIT	ISSUE	TREND
84	SANDY & CHILDREN	419	365.00	750.00
84	SARAH & JOSHUA	343	475.00	850.00
84	WENDY WITH HAT	308	395.00	725.00
85	LA TOSCA	355	595.00	725.00
86	BELINDA & NINA	320	295.00	625.00
86	DUCHESS	320	325.00	525.00
86	NANCY WITH MEGAN	367	450.00	900.00
87	FINNISH MOTHER & CHILD	343	185.00	325.00
87	FLOWERS OF KASHMIR	297	275.00	525.00
87	MONICA MATTEAO & VANESSA	300	350.00	650.00
87	ONCE UPON A TIME	287	365.00	550.00
88	AMELIA & CHILDREN	268	675.00	825.00
88	FLOWERS OF THE ADRIATIC	286	300.00	500.00
88	JOHN M	308	185.00	325.00
88	LINDA T	302	185.00	325.00
88	NEW HAT, THE	298	310.00	550.00
88	XIN-XIN OF THE HIGH MOUNTAINS	325	1,300.00	2000.00
89	HELENE & CHILDREN	280	365.00	495.00
90	TAMARA	254	360.00	500.00

EIGHTH AVENUE GRAPHICS
D. DAY

YR	NAME	LIMIT	ISSUE	TREND
94	DADDY'S GIRL	2500	225.00	350.00

T. DOUGLAS

YR	NAME	LIMIT	ISSUE	TREND
96	MENTOR, THE	565	380.00	700.00

FANTASTIC ART
R. SPANGLER

YR	NAME	LIMIT	ISSUE	TREND
78	MORNING ON THE BALCONY	*	20.00	40.00
83	DREAMER	*	45.00	150.00
83	GREAT, GREAT GRANDDRAGON	*	25.00	125.00
84	DRAGONSLAYER	*	35.00	125.00
84	STORYTELLER	*	25.00	450.00
84	WIZARD'S GIFT	*	24.00	36.00
85	GUARDIAN OF THE CANDLES	*	15.00	24.00
85	NEW ARRIVAL	*	25.00	45.00
85	PIPELIGHTER	*	20.00	45.00
85	STOCKING STUFFERS	*	24.00	34.00
85	TEA PARTY	*	20.00	34.00
85	WIZARD'S NEW PET	*	35.00	55.00
86	ASTRONOMER	*	45.00	400.00
86	DRAGON AWAY!	*	25.00	250.00
86	JUST A LITTLE BIT HIGHER	*	20.00	40.00
86	PERFECT AIM	*	24.00	37.00
86	SPRING CLEANING	*	24.00	37.00
86	YOU LIGHT UP MY LIFE	*	15.00	35.00
87	CANDLEHOLDER I	*	15.00	17.00
87	CANDLEHOLDER II	*	15.00	17.00
87	FASCINATION	*	48.00	125.00
87	FLOATING CITIES OF ELAN	*	35.00	49.00
87	MORNING COFFEE	*	20.00	50.00
87	OVERLOAD	*	24.00	30.00
87	SWEET DREAMS	*	25.00	350.00
87	TWILIGHT STORIES	*	45.00	450.00
87	WHAT COOKIES?	*	15.00	30.00
88	CHRISTMAS COOKIES	*	20.00	24.00
88	MIDNIGHT MUNCHIES	*	24.00	44.00
88	MISGUIDED MAGIC	*	20.00	40.00
88	MOONLIGHT MAGIC	*	45.00	450.00
88	MYSTIC CAT I	*	30.00	37.00
88	MYSTIC CAT II	*	25.00	45.00
88	MYSTIC CAT III	*	15.00	25.00
88	MYSTIC CAT IV	*	32.00	42.00
88	WAKING THE WIZARD	*	25.00	42.00
88	WANNA PLAY?	*	24.00	45.00
89	DRAGLING'S WORK IS NEVER DONE, A	*	28.00	38.00
89	GREY LADY	*	48.00	65.00
89	GUARD DUTY	*	24.00	34.00
89	GUARDIAN OF THE COOKIES	*	24.00	34.00
89	MIDNIGHT RAID	*	35.00	44.00
89	SATURDAY NIGHT BATH	*	28.00	55.00
90	BEST FRIENDS	*	34.00	55.00
90	BIRTHDAY COOKIE	*	15.00	24.00
90	BUBBLE BATH	*	34.00	55.00
90	CHOCOLATE LOVER'S DELIGHT	*	24.00	31.00
90	CHRISTMAS TREASURES	*	17.00	24.00
90	ENCHANTED	*	55.00	75.00
90	FETCHING FIREFLIES	*	24.00	75.00
90	FLOUR JUST FOR YOU, A	*	20.00	31.00
90	I BELIEVE IN DRAGONS	*	22.00	28.00
90	I LOVE TREES	*	24.00	34.00
90	PRINCE OF FISH	*	26.00	42.00
90	PRINCESS OF NATURE	*	30.00	47.00
90	RUPERT	*	26.00	32.00
90	SNACK TIME	*	24.00	28.00
90	STOP & SMELL THE COOKIES	*	28.00	46.00
90	WHO'S THERE?	*	25.00	40.00
91	ANXIOUS ANGLER	*	14.00	21.00
91	BLUE SUEDE GROUPER	*	14.00	21.00

The paper edition of Thomas Kinkade's Simpler Times I *was published by Lightpost Publishing in 1995 in a limited edition of 3,350.*

Jerry Gadamus' Spring Rose, *limited to an edition of 850, is produced by Northwoods Craftsman.*

The old fishing hole is the centerpiece of Terry Redlin's 1992 Summertime *from Hadley House.*

YR	NAME	LIMIT	ISSUE	TREND
91	CAT & MOUSE	*	85.00	85.00
91	FANTASY FLIGHT	*	38.00	48.00
91	GUARDIAN	*	38.00	48.00
91	NEPTUNE'S MOUNT	*	26.00	35.00
91	SEA RIDER	*	42.00	49.00
91	STORYTIME	*	35.00	200.00
91	WITH A LITTLE HELP...	*	28.00	38.00
91	WOULD BE APPRENTICE	*	30.00	50.00
92	ADMIRAL LADNAR'S MECHANICAL MACKEREL	*	85.00	85.00
92	AMBUSH	*	38.00	75.00
92	BIRD IN HAND	*	20.00	24.00
92	CAUGHT WITH THE COOKIE	*	24.00	29.00
92	COOKIE SNEAK	*	26.00	34.00
92	COSMIC CONTEMPLATION	*	20.00	24.00
92	DRAGGIN' IN THE MORNING	*	24.00	35.00
92	DRAGON DREAMS	*	24.00	45.00
92	EASTER DRAGON	*	26.00	34.00
92	FIRESIDE FAIRYTAILS	*	95.00	450.00
92	LET'S SHARE: 1 FOR YOU, 2 FOR ME	*	26.00	29.00
92	NEVER REFUSE HOMEMADE COOKIES	*	16.00	20.00
92	NO SMOKING I	*	18.00	45.00
92	ONLY WAY TO HAVE A FRIEND	*	25.00	34.00
92	WE THREE KINGS	*	40.00	49.00
92	WHAT CHOCOLATE?	*	24.00	45.00
92	WIZARD'S RAIN MACHINE	*	55.00	67.00
93	ALWAYS HAVE FRESH COOKIES FOR YOUR GUESTS	950	20.00	24.00
93	BERRY HEIST	*	38.00	49.00
93	BUBBLES	*	20.00	33.00
93	EMERALD EYES	*	58.00	65.00
93	FISHGAZING	*	55.00	67.00
93	FULL DRAGON/HAPPY DRAGON	*	22.00	28.00
93	MUSHROOM INN	*	34.00	39.00
93	NEON FISH	*	15.00	18.00
93	NO SMOKING II	*	25.00	45.00
93	OVERWEIGHT AGAIN!	*	35.00	38.00
93	STOWAWAY	*	22.00	28.00
94	CAT-THEDRAL	*	28.00	36.00
94	CHERISH THE SMALL WONDERS OF LIFE	1100	20.00	30.00
94	COOKIES BY CANDLELIGHT	*	20.00	20.00
94	DRAGONS' DREAM	1100	65.00	68.00
94	FAERIE I: THE GUIDE	*	24.00	28.00
94	FAERIE II: THE GIFT	*	24.00	28.00
94	FIREFLY FANTASY	1100	45.00	52.00
94	HIDDEN TREASURE	950	28.00	32.00
94	I'M DRAGGIN' EVERY MORNING	*	28.00	36.00
94	MONDAY MORNING	1100	42.00	48.00
94	MOUNTAIN DWARF	950	15.00	18.00
94	MYSTIC CAT V	*	68.00	75.00
94	NO SMOKING III	*	28.00	36.00
94	ONCE AROUND THE CASTLE	950	36.00	39.00
94	ROYAL GUARD	950	15.00	18.00
94	SAMANTHA'S SEARCH	*	26.00	34.00
94	SWORDSMAN, THE	950	15.00	18.00
94	TIMELY TASK, A	950	27.00	40.00
94	WINTER WARRIOR	950	15.00	18.00
95	HEAVENLY COMPANION	950	36.00	38.00
95	HOME IS WHERE THE MAGIC IS	950	125.00	125.00
95	HOW MUCH WOULD I WEIGH?	950	38.00	38.00
95	MAKING TIME FOR SOMEONE SPECIAL	950	24.00	28.00
95	MYSTERY SHELF, THE	950	36.00	40.00
95	NO ME!	950	36.00	38.00
95	SANTA'S SURPRISE	950	28.00	32.00
95	YOU SCRUB MY BACK & I'LL SCRUB YOURS	950	36.00	38.00
96	ALL IN A DAYS WORK	*	40.00	40.00
96	BREAKFAST OF CHAMPIONS	*	38.00	38.00
96	DELIGHT IN LIFE'S WONDERS	*	24.00	24.00
96	EVENING PLEASURES	*	78.00	78.00
96	FANTAIL	950	20.00	28.00
96	FLIGHT OF THE FIREFLIES	*	38.00	38.00
96	I'M FOREVER BLOWING BUBBLES	950	24.00	24.00
96	JADE EYES	*	17.00	17.00
96	JOURNEY OVER OHM	*	55.00	55.00
96	MILK MOUSTACHE	950	24.00	24.00
96	NO SMOKING IV	950	34.00	34.00
96	PURR-FECT HARMONY	*	40.00	40.00
96	SAPPHIRE EYES	*	17.00	17.00
96	SHARE THE MAGIC OF LOVE	*	24.00	24.00
96	WISHFUL THINKING	950	38.00	38.00

R. SPANGLER — **FAERIEL I**

95	GUIDE, THE	950	25.00	25.00

R. SPANGLER — **FAERIEL II**

95	GIFT, THE	950	25.00	25.00

FARAWAY
L. STONE

74	BLUE NOSE ON THE GRAND BANKS	2000	75.00	125.00
78	VIGIL	1300	75.00	125.00

YR	NAME	LIMIT	ISSUE	TREND

FLAMBRO
B. LEIGHTON-JONES

EMMETT KELLY JR. LITHOGRAPHS

YR	NAME	LIMIT	ISSUE	TREND
94	70TH BIRTHDAY COMMEMORATIVE	YR	150.00	150.00
94	A PICTURE IS WORTH 1,000 WORDS	YR	90.00	95.00
94	I LOVE YOU	YR	90.00	95.00
94	JOYFUL NOISE	YR	90.00	95.00
95	ALL STAR CIRCUS	2 YR	150.00	150.00

FOR ARTS SAKE
B. ABBOTT

YR	NAME	LIMIT	ISSUE	TREND
95	BLUE JAY/FALL COLOR	900	25.00	25.00
95	CARDINAL/WINTER BERRIES	900	25.00	25.00
95	GOLD FINCH/SPRING GOLD	900	25.00	25.00
95	HUMMINGBIRDS/TRUMPET NECTAR	900	25.00	25.00
97	BUOY'S CLUB, THE	50	90.00	90.00
97	EGRETS IN THE MIST	25	200.00	200.00
97	SWAN SERENITY	50	90.00	90.00
98	BUOY #9 OSPREY	250	40.00	40.00
98	FUTURE BEST BUDDIES-LABS	100	25.00	25.00
98	MALLARDS N MAPLES	250	30.00	30.00
98	SPORTSMEN, THE-GOLDENS	100	25.00	25.00
98	WOODUCKS WATER LILY	250	30.00	30.00

FOUNTAINHEAD
M. FERNANDEZ

YR	NAME	LIMIT	ISSUE	TREND
*	HEART OF SEVEN COLORS	*	*	950.00
*	MOST PRECIOUS GIFT	*	*	950.00
*	OH, SMALL CHILD	*	*	245.00
*	SPREADING THE WORD	*	*	100.00

FRAME HOUSE
C. HARPER

YR	NAME	LIMIT	ISSUE	TREND
*	ARCTIC CIRCLE-MUSKOX	*	*	175.00
*	BARK EYES-OWL	*	90.00	90.00
*	BIG RAC' ATTACK-RACCOON	*	*	125.00
*	BLACKBERRY JAM	*	90.00	135.00
*	CARDINAL COURTSHIP	*	175.00	240.00
*	CARDINAL CRADLE	*	175.00	185.00
*	CHRISTMAS CAPER	*	25.00	35.00
*	CLAIR DE LOON	*	175.00	185.00
*	CONFISKATION-ROBIN	*	90.00	160.00
*	CONVIVIAL PURSUIT	*	125.00	180.00
*	COTTONTAIL IN A COTTONFIELD-RABBIT	*	125.00	125.00
*	CRABITAT	*	125.00	125.00
*	DREAM TEAM	*	20.00	26.00
*	EVERGLADE KITE	*	*	250.00
*	FEARLESS FEATHERS	*	125.00	125.00
*	FLAMINGO A GO GO	*	150.00	150.00
*	FROG IN GRASS	*	*	250.00
*	GIFT RAPT-RACCOON	*	175.00	175.00
*	KOALA, KOALA-KOALA BEAR	*	*	20.00
*	LOVE ON A LIMB-MONKEY	*	125.00	135.00
*	LUCKY LADYBUG	*	8.00	25.00
*	MANATEE IN THE MANGROVE	*	195.00	195.00
*	MYSTERY OF THE MISSING MIGRANT-BIRD	*	*	30.00
*	OWLTERCATION	*	175.00	185.00
*	PACK PACT-MILL	*	175.00	175.00
*	PELICAN PANTRY	*	60.00	100.00
*	PISCINE QUEUES	*	125.00	125.00
*	QUAILSAFE	*	90.00	95.00
*	RACCROBAT	*	*	10.00
*	RACCSNACK-RACCOON	*	90.00	100.00
*	SQUIRREL IN A SQUALL	*	90.00	115.00
*	SUGAR FREE	*	125.00	135.00
*	TAILGATOR	*	125.00	170.00
*	UPSIDE DOWNY	*	125.00	145.00
*	WINGDING	*	90.00	90.00
68	HOUSE WRENS	500	20.00	175.00
68	LADYBUG	500	20.00	300.00
68	LADYBUG (LITHO)	10000	6.00	50.00
68	PORTFOLIO OF FOUR PRINTS	500	60.00	375.00
69	ANHINGA (LITHO ON CANVAS)	500	50.00	225.00
69	HUNGRY EYES	500	20.00	600.00
69	WATER STRIDER	500	40.00	475.00
70	BOBWHITE FAMILY	750	30.00	150.00
70	BURROWING OWL	500	30.00	100.00
70	CARDINAL (ON CORN)	500	30.00	400.00
70	CRAYFISH MOLTING	750	30.00	125.00
70	PILEATED WOODPECKER	750	30.00	150.00
71	BEETLE BATTLE	750	30.00	125.00
71	BLUE JAY BATHING	1500	30.00	145.00
71	LADYBUG LOVERS	1500	30.00	160.00
71	PUFFIN	750	30.00	140.00
71	RED-BELLIED WOODPECKER	1500	30.00	100.00
72	BEAR IN THE BIRCHES	1500	35.00	525.00
72	BOX TURTLE	1500	30.00	125.00
72	CHIPMUNK	1500	30.00	100.00
72	FAMILY OWLBUM	1500	30.00	125.00

YR	NAME	LIMIT	ISSUE	TREND
72	PELICAN IN A DOWNPOUR	1500	30.00	400.00
72	YELLOW BELLIED SAPSUCKER	1500	30.00	50.00
73	LAST SUNFLOWER SEED, THE	1500	30.00	300.00
73	ROUND ROBIN	1500	30.00	135.00
73	WATERMELON MOON	1500	30.00	375.00
73	WEDDING FEAST	1500	30.00	115.00
73	WOOD DUCK	1500	30.00	350.00
74	BIRDS OF A FEATHER	2000	50.00	100.00
74	COOL CARDINAL	2000	30.00	435.00
74	CROW IN THE SNOW	1500	35.00	300.00
74	FINE FEATHER	1500	30.00	150.00
74	PAINTED BUNTING	1500	30.00	125.00
74	TALL TAIL	2000	30.00	100.00
75	BIRDWATCHER	2000	40.00	775.00
75	BLUEBIRDS IN THE BLUEGRASS	2000	45.00	65.00
75	PFWHOOOO	*	*	145.00
75	RACCPACK	2000	35.00	160.00
75	WHITECOAT	2000	30.00	200.00
76	CLAWS	2000	40.00	190.00
76	CORNPONE	2500	40.00	150.00
76	DEVOTION IN THE OCEAN	2000	40.00	100.00
76	LOVE FROM ABOVE	2000	40.00	375.00
76	SKIMMERSCAPE	2000	40.00	140.00
77	BRRRTHDAY	2500	40.00	90.00
77	CATNIP	2500	50.00	125.00
77	DOLFUN	2500	50.00	90.00
77	DOWN UNDER, DOWN UNDER	2500	40.00	80.00
77	PHANCY PHEATHERS	2500	50.00	175.00
77	SEEING RED	2500	40.00	150.00
77	SKIPPING SCHOOL	2500	50.00	50.00
78	BITTERN SUITE	2500	50.00	50.00
78	CRAWLING TALL	3500	50.00	50.00
78	FROG EAT FROG	2500	50.00	60.00
78	HARE'S BREADTH	2500	50.00	50.00
78	LOVEY DOVEY	2500	50.00	160.00
79	BUZZ OFF YOU TURKEY	2500	55.00	75.00
79	COOL CARNIVORE	2500	50.00	50.00
79	FURRED FEEDER	2500	50.00	60.00
79	SERENGETI SPAGHETTI	2500	55.00	110.00
80	HEXIT	1500	60.00	90.00
80	JUMBRELLA	1500	60.00	100.00
80	POTLUCK	1500	60.00	120.00
80	REDBIRDS AND REDBUDS	1500	60.00	60.00
81	FOXSIMILES	1500	60.00	60.00
81	LAST APHID	1500	60.00	135.00
81	RACC & RUIN	1500	60.00	180.00
81	ROMANCE ON THE RICHTER SCALE-WHALE	1500	60.00	140.00
82	ARMADITTO	1500	60.00	90.00
82	PRICKLEY PAIR	1500	60.00	300.00
82	TERN, STONES, AND TURNSTONES	1500	60.00	110.00
84	GREEN CUISINE	1000	90.00	110.00
84	PIER GROUP	1000	90.00	380.00
84	RACCOONNAISSANCE	1000	90.00	120.00
85	HERONDIPITY	500	175.00	300.00
85	VOWLENTINE	1000	45.00	140.00
86	B-R-R-R-R-R-DBATH	1000	125.00	170.00
86	LOONRISE-LOON DUCK	500	175.00	200.00

J. HARRISON

YR	NAME	LIMIT	ISSUE	TREND
74	RURAL AMERICANA	1500	40.00	350.00
75	AMERICAN BYWAYS	1500	40.00	330.00
75	COUNTRY SEASONIN'	1500	40.00	300.00
75	DISAPPEARING AMERICA	1500	40.00	1400.00
76	RURAL DELIVERY	1500	40.00	400.00
76	YESTERYEAR	1500	50.00	210.00
77	BURMA SHAVE	1500	50.00	300.00
77	COMMUNITY CHURCH	1500	50.00	230.00
77	DR. PEPPER	1500	50.00	300.00
77	FALLOW AND FORGOTTON	1500	50.00	200.00
78	666 COLD TABLETS	1500	50.00	270.00
78	PHILIP MORRIS	1500	50.00	280.00
78	RC COLA	975	135.00	135.00
78	RED COVERED BRIDGE	1500	50.00	300.00
78	TOOLS	300	275.00	450.00
78	WOODPILE	1500	75.00	145.00
79	CLABBER GIRL	1500	75.00	350.00
79	GOLD DUST TWINS	1500	55.00	180.00
79	GOODY'S	1500	50.00	145.00
79	LUCKY STRIKE	1500	50.00	170.00
80	PEANUTS AND PEPSI	1500	60.00	270.00
80	TONIC AND LINIMENT	1500	85.00	225.00
80	TUBE ROSE SNUFF	1500	60.00	180.00
80	UNPAINTED COVERED BRIDGE	1500	60.00	200.00
81	7-UP AND BLACK EYED SUSANS	1500	75.00	200.00
81	BRUSH AND BUCKET	300	300.00	350.00
81	HOUSE AND BARN	1500	50.00	235.00
81	OLD DUTCH CLEANSER	1500	75.00	155.00
82	BULL OF THE WOODS	1500	75.00	115.00
82	RAILROAD CROSSING	1500	75.00	300.00
82	WINDMILL	1500	75.00	140.00

YR	NAME	LIMIT	ISSUE	TREND
83	FILLIN' STATION	1500	80.00	275.00
83	FRESH GRITS	1500	80.00	860.00
83	LEE OVERALLS	OP	7.50	20.00
83	LIGHTHOUSE	975	135.00	315.00
83	MOUNTAIN BRIDGE	1500	80.00	300.00
83	SHRINE CIRCUS	1500	80.00	80.00
84	MEMORIES	408	90.00	200.00
84	MORTON SALT AND ROCK CITY	1500	135.00	240.00
84	RED GOOSE SHOES	1500	90.00	90.00
85	MEMORIES II	431	90.00	200.00
85	OLD STONE BARN	1500	90.00	150.00
85	SPRING CLOUDS	1500	90.00	180.00
86	FISHING VILLAGE	975	135.00	165.00
87	COCA-COLA BRIDGE	975	135.00	468.00
87	JEFFERSON ISLAND SALT	975	135.00	135.00
87	UNCLE JOHN'S SYRUP	975	135.00	175.00
88	HERSHEY BAR	975	135.00	200.00
88	RED BOAT	975	135.00	275.00

A. HUNT

YR	NAME	LIMIT	ISSUE	TREND
84	LAZY AFTERNOON	1500	75.00	75.00
85	FOX IN REEDS	1500	75.00	75.00
86	SNOW LEOPARD	1000	150.00	475.00
88	DAWN ALERT	TL	160.00	165.00

GARTLAN USA

J. MARTIN   LITHOGRAPH

YR	NAME	LIMIT	ISSUE	TREND
86	GEORGE BRETT: THE SWING	2000	85.00	85.00

C. SOILEAU   LITHOGRAPH

YR	NAME	LIMIT	ISSUE	TREND
87	ROGER STAUBACH	1979	85.00	85.00

M. TAYLOR   LITHOGRAPH

YR	NAME	LIMIT	ISSUE	TREND
89	KAREEM ABDUL-JABBAR: THE RECORD SETTER	1989	85.00	300.00
90	DARRYL STRAWBERRY	500	295.00	295.00
91	JOE MONTANA, SIGNED, H/S	500	495.00	545.00

GREENWICH WORKSHOP

M. BASTIN

YR	NAME	LIMIT	ISSUE	TREND
97	DINNER GUESTS	SO	95.00	95.00
98	GARDEN PICNIC	1950	119.00	119.00

A. BEAN

YR	NAME	LIMIT	ISSUE	TREND
94	IN THE BEGINNING	SO	450.00	545.00

C. BLISH

YR	NAME	LIMIT	ISSUE	TREND
98	FATHER, THE HOUR HAS COME	OP	70.00	70.00

C. BLOSSOM

YR	NAME	LIMIT	ISSUE	TREND
98	GOLD RUSH TWILIGHT	550	195.00	195.00

W. BULLAS

YR	NAME	LIMIT	ISSUE	TREND
95	DOG BITE	SO	95.00	95.00
98	A FOOL AND HIS BUNNY	950	95.00	95.00

S. COMBES

YR	NAME	LIMIT	ISSUE	TREND
98	SENTINELS	550	125.00	125.00

E. DUBOWSKI

YR	NAME	LIMIT	ISSUE	TREND
98	ERRAND, THE	550	125.00	125.00

L. FRAZIER

YR	NAME	LIMIT	ISSUE	TREND
98	CONSTANT TRAVELER	750	150.00	150.00

S. GUSTAFSON

YR	NAME	LIMIT	ISSUE	TREND
*	ADVICE FROM CATERPILLAR	*	*	200.00
*	FAIRY TALE SET OF 5	*	*	120.00
*	MAD TEA PARTY	*	*	190.00
*	OWL & PUSSYCAT	*	*	160.00
93	GOLDILOCKS AND THE THREE BEARS	RT	125.00	450.00
93	HUMPTY DUMPTY	RT	125.00	150.00
93	LITTLE RED RIDING HOOD	RT	125.00	125.00
93	SNOW WHITE AND THE SEVEN DWARFS	RT	165.00	400.00
94	FROG PRINCE	RT	125.00	150.00
94	PAT-A-CAKE	RT	125.00	145.00
95	ALICE IN WONDERLAND SUITE	4000	195.00	195.00
95	HANSEL & GRETEL	3000	125.00	150.00
95	JACK AND THE BEANSTALK	3500	125.00	160.00
95	RUMPLESTILTSKIN	2750	125.00	150.00
95	TOUCHED BY MAGIC	4000	185.00	185.00
96	OLD KING COLE	2750	125.00	135.00
96	PUSS IN BOOTS	2750	145.00	160.00
97	TOM THUMB	SO	125.00	150.00
98	LITTLE BO PEEP	950	125.00	125.00
98	MOONBEAR LISTENS TO THE EARTH	1250	175.00	175.00

J. HOLM

YR	NAME	LIMIT	ISSUE	TREND
98	FIVE PERSIANS	550	130.00	130.00

S. KENNEDY

YR	NAME	LIMIT	ISSUE	TREND
94	QUIET TIME COMPANIONS-SAMOYED	SO	125.00	125.00
98	CROSSING OVER	750	145.00	145.00

P. LANDRY

YR	NAME	LIMIT	ISSUE	TREND
96	AFTERNOON TEA	SO	495.00	495.00

S. LYMAN

YR	NAME	LIMIT	ISSUE	TREND
97	WINTER SHADOWS	SO	225.00	225.00

B. MARRIS

YR	NAME	LIMIT	ISSUE	TREND
96	LITTLE PIG WITH A BIG HEART (BABE)	SO	95.00	95.00
98	UNDERCOVER	750	145.00	145.00

YR	NAME	LIMIT	ISSUE	TREND
F. MCCARTHY				
95	MEDICINE MAN	SO	165.00	165.00
98	PATROL AT BROKEN FINGER	750	165.00	165.00
W.S. PHILLIPS				
96	LIGHTKEEPER'S GIFT	SO	175.00	175.00
H. PRESSE				
98	DANCE OF THE SUN	550	125.00	125.00
J. REYNOLDS				
94	QUIET PLACE, THE	SO	185.00	185.00
98	SWING SHIFT (CANVAS)	450	495.00	495.00
H. TERPNING				
*	CROW PIPE CEREMONY	SO	*	N/A
98	HOLY MAN OF THE BLACKFOOT (CANVAS)	975	895.00	895.00
J. WEISS				
*	GOOD AS GOLD	SO	*	N/A
98	DOUBLE TROUBLE	1450	95.00	95.00
J. CHRISTENSEN				**CHRISTENSEN**
*	ANGEL WITH FISH	*	*	275.00
*	BIRDS HUNTERS FULL CAMO.	*	*	165.00
*	FISH WATER	*	*	3200.00
85	GIFT FOR MRS. CLAUS, THE	3500	80.00	700.00
86	JONAH	850	95.00	500.00
86	OLDE WORLD SANTA	3500	80.00	1100.00
86	YOUR PLACE, OR MINE?	850	125.00	270.00
87	OLD MAN WITH A LOT ON HIS MIND	850	85.00	925.00
87	VOYAGE OF THE BASSET	850	225.00	1475.00
88	MAN WHO MINDS THE MOON, THE	850	145.00	775.00
88	WIDOW'S MITE, THE	850	145.00	200.00
89	ANNUNCIATION, THE	850	175.00	175.00
90	BURDEN OF THE RESPONSIBLE MAN, THE	850	145.00	1600.00
90	RHYMES & REASONS	OP	150.00	175.00
90	TWO SISTERS	650	325.00	400.00
91	CANDLEMAN, THE	850	160.00	450.00
91	LAWRENCE AND A BEAR	850	145.00	400.00
91	ONCE UPON A TIME	1500	175.00	1975.00
91	ONCE UPON A TIME (REMARQUE)	500	375.00	2000.00
91	PELICAN KING	850	115.00	400.00
92	OLDEST ANGEL, THE	850	125.00	1150.00
92	RESPONSIBLE WOMAN, THE	2500	175.00	825.00
92	ROYAL PROCESSIONAL, THE	1500	185.00	600.00
92	ROYAL PROCESSIONAL, THE- REMARQUE	1500	185.00	700.00
93	COLLEGE OF MAGICAL KNOWLEDGE	*	185.00	400.00
93	GETTING IT RIGHT	4000	185.00	185.00
93	ROYAL MUSIC BARQUE, THE	2750	375.00	375.00
93	SCHOLAR, THE	3250	125.00	200.00
93	WAITING FOR THE TIDE	2250	150.00	175.00
94	SIX BIRD HUNTERS	*	165.00	185.00
98	SUPERSTITIONS	RT	195.00	195.00
B. DOOLITTLE				**DOOLITTLE**
*	GHOST OF THE GRIZZLY	*	*	3000.00
*	GRIZZLY TREE	*	*	3500.00
79	PINTOS	1000	65.00	8000.00
80	BUGGED BEAR	1000	85.00	3700.00
80	GOOD OMEN, THE	1000	85.00	2450.00
80	WHOO!?	1000	75.00	2000.00
81	SPIRIT OF THE GRIZZLY	1500	150.00	3700.00
81	UNKNOWN PRESENCE	1500	135.00	2700.00
81	WOODLAND ENCOUNTER	1500	145.00	7000.00
82	EAGLE'S FLIGHT	1500	185.00	3100.00
83	CHRISTMAS DAY, GIVE OR TAKE A WEEK	4800	80.00	1800.00
83	ESCAPE BY A HARE	1500	80.00	850.00
83	RUNS WITH THUNDER	1500	150.00	1400.00
83	RUSHING WAR EAGLE	1500	150.00	1475.00
84	LET MY SPIRIT SOAR	1500	195.00	4600.00
85	TWO INDIAN HORSES	12253	225.00	3400.00
85	WOLVES OF THE CROW	2650	225.00	1600.00
86	TWO BEARS OF THE BLACKFEET	2650	225.00	1100.00
86	WHERE SILENCE SPEAKS, ART OF DOOLITTLE	3500	650.00	2760.00
87	CALLING THE BUFFALO	8500	245.00	1300.00
87	GUARDIAN SPIRITS	13238	295.00	1000.00
87	SEASON OF THE EAGLE	36548	245.00	825.00
88	DOUBLED BACK	15000	285.00	1600.00
89	SACRED GROUND	70000	265.00	500.00
90	HIDE AND SEEK SUITE	25000	900.00	1980.00
90	HIDE AND SEEK-7 PC. COMP SET	RT	1,200.00	1200.00
90	HIDE AND SEEK-LG	RT	300.00	300.00
90	HIDE AND SEEK-MINI	*	*	250.00
91	SACRED CIRCLE	*	265.00	500.00
91	SACRED CIRCLE (PC)	40192	325.00	725.00
91	SENTINEL, THE	35000	275.00	775.00
92	EAGLE HEART	48000	285.00	375.00
93	PRAYER FOR THE WILD THINGS	*	325.00	425.00
93	WILDERNESS...WILDERNESS!	RT	65.00	80.00
94	WHEN THE WIND HAD WINGS	*	325.00	400.00
95	TWO MORE INDIAN HORSES	48000	385.00	825.00
J. CHRISTENSEN				**ETCHING**
*	ARTIST, THE	*	*	450.00

YR	NAME	LIMIT	ISSUE	TREND
*	GIFT, THE	*	*	350.00
*	OLD ANGEL	*	*	350.00
*	WIZARD	*	*	50.00
J. CHRISTENSEN				**FANTASY**
94	EVENING ANGELS	4000	195.00	200.00
94	SOMETIMES THE SPIRIT..W/BOOK	3600	195.00	260.00
94	TWO ANGELS DISCUSS BOTTICELLI	2950	145.00	160.00
95	PISCATORIAL PERCUSSIONIST	3000	125.00	130.00
95	SERENADE FOR AN ORANGE CAT	3000	125.00	135.00
95	SISTERS OF THE SEA	SO	195.00	210.00
J. CHRISTENSEN				**FANTASY/ETCHING**
*	FISHE	*	*	325.00
*	FISHWALKER	*	*	1000.00
*	MECHANICAL FISH	*	*	300.00
*	MIDNIGHT SCHOLAR	*	*	350.00
*	MUSICIAN	*	*	300.00
J. CHRISTENSEN				**FANTASY/LITHO**
*	ANGEL IN PURSUIT FISH KNOW.	*	*	300.00
*	CONVERSATION AROUND FISH	*	*	600.00
*	FISH ANGEL	*	*	400.00
B. DOOLITTLE				**HORSE**
*	HIDE AND SEEK-NUM MINI-1C	*	*	150.00
*	HIDE AND SEEK-NUM MINI-2A	*	*	150.00
*	HIDE AND SEEK-NUM MINI-2C	*	*	150.00
*	HIDE AND SEEK-NUM MINI-3B	*	*	150.00
*	HIDE AND SEEK-NUM MINI-3D	*	*	150.00
B. DOOLITTLE				**INDIAN**
84	FOREST HAS EYES, THE	RT	175.00	4000.00
F. MCCARTHY				**INDIAN**
92	NAVAJO PONIES FOR COMANCHE	1000	225.00	225.00
92	WHEN THE LAND WAS THEIRS	1000	225.00	225.00
92	WHERE OTHERS HAD PASSED	1000	245.00	245.00
93	IN THE LAND OF ANCIENT ONES	1250	245.00	350.00
93	SIGHTING THE INTRUDERS	1000	225.00	240.00
94	SHOW OF DEFIANCE	1000	195.00	195.00
94	WAY OF ANCIENT MIGRATION	1250	245.00	245.00
S. LYMAN				**LANDSCAPE**
93	LAKE OF THE SHINING ROCKS-LANDSCAPE	*	235.00	625.00
94	NORTH COUNTRY SHORES-LANDSCAPE	*	225.00	500.00
95	CATHEDRAL SNOW-LANDSCAPE	4000	245.00	380.00
J. CHRISTENSEN				**LITHO**
*	COPADEORA	*	*	140.00
S. LYMAN				**LYMAN**
*	BIG COUNTRY, THE-GRIZZLY	*	*	200.00
83	EARLY WINTER IN THE MOUNTAINS	850	95.00	1150.00
83	END OF THE RIDGE	850	95.00	850.00
83	PASS, THE	850	95.00	1150.00
84	FREE FLIGHT	850	70.00	200.00
84	NOISY NEIGHBORS (R)	25	95.00	1450.00
85	AUTUMN GATHERING-LANDSCAPE	850	115.00	950.00
85	BEAR & BLOSSOMS-BLACK BEAR	850	75.00	725.00
86	COLORS OF TWILIGHT	850	75.00	175.00
86	HIGH TRAIL AT SUNSET-MOUNTAIN GOAT	1000	125.00	1100.00
86	MORNING SOLITUDE-GREY BLUE HERON	850	115.00	775.00
86	SNOWY THRONE (C)	850	85.00	1125.00
87	AN ELEGANT COUPLE	1000	125.00	550.00
87	CANADIAN AUTUMN-MOOSE	1500	165.00	360.00
87	ELEGANT COUPLE-WOOD DUCK	1000	125.00	150.00
87	HIGH CREEK CROSSING-BISON	1000	165.00	1650.00
87	MOON SHADOWS-CANADA GOOSE	1500	135.00	210.00
87	NEW TERRITORY-GRIZZLY BEAR	1000	135.00	575.00
87	TWILIGHT SNOW-BLUE JAY	950	85.00	550.00
88	INTRUDER, THE	1500	150.00	275.00
88	RAPTOR'S WATCH, THE-EAGLE	1500	150.00	1000.00
88	RETURN OF THE FALCON	1500	150.00	450.00
88	SNOW HUNTER-BOBCAT	1500	135.00	200.00
88	UZUMATI: GREAT BEAR OF YOSEMITE	1750	150.00	250.00
89	COLOR IN THE SNOW-PHEASANT	1500	165.00	600.00
89	HIGH LIGHT	1250	165.00	525.00
89	LAST LIGHT OF WINTER-CANADA GOOSE	1500	175.00	1825.00
89	QUIET RAIN-CANADA GOOSE	1500	165.00	1100.00
90	A MOUNTAIN CAMPFIRE	1500	195.00	2650.00
90	AMONG THE WILD BRAMBLES-KESTREL	1750	185.00	1075.00
90	EVENING LIGHT	2500	225.00	3200.00
90	SILENT SNOWS-WOLF	1750	210.00	480.00
91	DANCE OF CLOUD AND CLIFF-LANDSCAPE	1500	225.00	640.00
91	DANCE OF WATER AND LIGHT	3000	225.00	275.00
91	EMBERS AT DAWN	3500	225.00	1900.00
91	RIVER OF LIGHT	2950	225.00	300.00
91	SECRET WATCH-LYNX	2250	150.00	175.00
92	WARMED BY THE VIEW-CAMPFIRE	8500	235.00	600.00
92	WILDERNESS WELCOME	8500	235.00	1225.00
92	WILDFLOWER SUITE	2250	175.00	360.00
92	WOODLAND HAVEN-ELK	2500	195.00	325.00
93	FIRE DANCE-CAMPFIRE	8500	235.00	750.00
93	RIPARIAN RICHES-G/B HERON	2500	235.00	350.00
93	SPIRIT OF CHRISTMAS-SANTA	RT	165.00	550.00

YR	NAME	LIMIT	ISSUE	TREND
94	MOONFIRE	7500	245.00	1400.00
94	MOONLIT FLIGHT, CHRISTMAS	2750	165.00	300.00
94	NEW KID ON THE ROCK-OTTER	2250	185.00	275.00
95	MIDNIGHT FIRE	8500	245.00	300.00
95	THUNDERBOLT	7000	235.00	975.00
F. MCCARTHY				**MCCARTHY**
74	HUNT, THE	1000	75.00	500.00
74	LONE SENTINEL	1000	55.00	1150.00
74	LONG COLUMN	1000	75.00	620.00
74	NIGHT THEY NEEDED A GOOD RIBBON MAN, THE	1000	65.00	300.00
75	RETURNING RAIDERS	1000	75.00	400.00
75	SMOKE WAS THEIR ALLY	1000	75.00	200.00
75	SURVIVOR, THE	1000	65.00	250.00
75	WAITING FOR THE ESCORT	1000	75.00	110.00
76	HOSTILES, THE	1000	55.00	525.00
76	PACKING IN	1000	65.00	825.00
76	SIOUX WARRIORS	650	55.00	230.00
76	WARRIOR, THE	650	55.00	200.00
77	AN OLD TIME MOUNTAIN MAN	1000	65.00	175.00
77	BEAVER MEN, THE	1000	75.00	375.00
77	COMANCHE MOON	1000	75.00	240.00
77	DISTANT THUNDER	1500	75.00	1000.00
77	DUST STAINED POSSE	1000	75.00	1075.00
77	ROBE SIGNAL	850	60.00	450.00
78	AMBUSH, THE	1000	125.00	300.00
78	BEFORE THE NORTHER	1000	90.00	500.00
78	FORDING, THE	1000	75.00	275.00
78	IN THE PASS	1500	90.00	250.00
78	NIGHT CROSSING	1000	75.00	225.00
78	SINGLE FILE	1000	75.00	900.00
78	TO BATTLE	1000	75.00	600.00
79	LONER, THE	1000	75.00	380.00
79	ON THE WARPATH	1000	75.00	175.00
79	PRAYER, THE	1500	90.00	550.00
79	RETREAT TO HIGHER GROUND	2000	90.00	260.00
80	A TIME OF DECISION	1150	125.00	275.00
80	BEFORE THE CHARGE	1000	115.00	170.00
80	BURNING THE WAY STATION	1000	125.00	250.00
80	FORBIDDEN LAND	1000	125.00	300.00
80	ROAR OF THE NORTHER	1000	90.00	200.00
80	SNOW MOON	1000	115.00	200.00
80	TROOPER, THE	1000	90.00	175.00
81	COUP, THE	1000	125.00	500.00
81	CROSSING THE DIVIDE/THE OLD WEST	1500	850.00	850.00
81	HEADED NORTH	1000	150.00	370.00
81	RACE WITH THE HOSTILES	1000	135.00	225.00
81	SURROUNDED	1000	150.00	560.00
81	UNDER HOSTILE FIRE	1000	150.00	175.00
82	ALERT	1000	135.00	175.00
82	APACHE SCOUT	1000	165.00	245.00
82	ATTACK ON THE WAGON TRAIN	1400	150.00	200.00
82	CHALLENGE, THE	1000	175.00	400.00
82	WARRIORS, THE	1000	150.00	200.00
83	BLACKFEET RAIDERS	1000	90.00	340.00
83	IN THE LAND OF THE SPARROW HAWK PEOPLE	1000	165.00	175.00
83	MOONLIT TRAIL	1000	90.00	300.00
83	OUT OF THE MIST THEY CAME	1000	165.00	200.00
83	UNDER ATTACK	5676	125.00	525.00
84	AFTER THE DUST STORM	1000	145.00	200.00
84	ALONG THE WEST FORK	1000	175.00	320.00
84	DECOYS, THE	450	325.00	510.00
84	SAVAGE TAUNT, THE	1000	225.00	260.00
84	WATCHING THE WAGONS	1400	175.00	900.00
84	WHIRLING HE RACED TO MEET THE CHALLENGE	1000	175.00	515.00
85	CHARGING THE CHALLENGER	1000	150.00	425.00
85	FIREBOAT, THE	1000	175.00	245.00
85	LAST CROSSING, THE	550	350.00	400.00
85	LONG KNIVES, THE	1000	175.00	500.00
85	SCOUTING THE LONG KNIVES	1400	195.00	325.00
85	TRADERS, THE	1000	195.00	195.00
86	CHILDREN OF THE RAVEN	1000	185.00	960.00
86	COMANCHE WAR TRAIL	1000	165.00	165.00
86	DRIVE, THE	1000	95.00	400.00
86	RED BULL'S WAR PARTY	1000	165.00	160.00
86	SPOOKED	1400	195.00	200.00
86	WHERE TRACKS WILL BE LOST	550	350.00	600.00
87	CHIRICAHUA RAIDERS	1000	165.00	200.00
87	FOLLOWING THE HERDS	1000	195.00	375.00
87	FROM THE RIM	1000	225.00	225.00
87	IN THE LAND OF THE WINTER HAWK	1000	225.00	400.00
87	WHEN OMENS TURN BAD	1000	165.00	500.00
88	APACHE TRACKERS	1000	95.00	100.00
88	BUFFALO RUNNERS, THE	1000	195.00	275.00
88	HOSTILE LAND, THE	1000	225.00	225.00
88	IN PURSUIT OF THE WHITE BUFFALO	1500	225.00	450.00
88	LAST STAND, THE: LITTLE BIG HORN	2250	225.00	225.00
88	SABER CHARGE	2250	225.00	225.00
88	TURNING THE LEADERS	1500	225.00	225.00
89	BIG MEDICINE	1000	225.00	475.00

YR	NAME	LIMIT	ISSUE	TREND
89	CANYON LANDS	1250	225.00	225.00
89	COMING OF THE IRON HORSE, THE	1500	225.00	225.00
89	COMING OF/IRON HORSE, THE (PRINT/PEWTER)	100	1,500.00	3600.00
89	DOWN FROM THE MOUNTAINS	1500	245.00	240.00
89	LOS DIABLOS	1250	225.00	225.00
90	BELOW THE BREAKING DAWN	1250	225.00	225.00
90	HOKA HEY: SIOUX WAR CRY	1250	225.00	225.00
90	ON THE OLD NORTH TRAIL	650	550.00	900.00
90	OUT OF THE WINDSWEPT RAMPARTS	1250	225.00	225.00
90	WINTER TRAIL	1500	235.00	235.00
91	PONY EXPRESS	1000	225.00	225.00
91	PURSUIT, THE	650	550.00	550.00
91	WILD ONES, THE	1000	225.00	225.00
93	SHADOWS OF THE WARRIORS	1000	225.00	225.00

F. MCCARTHY — WESTERN

YR	NAME	LIMIT	ISSUE	TREND
91	CHASE, THE	1000	225.00	225.00
92	BREAK'G THE MOONLIT SILENCE	650	375.00	375.00
92	HEADING BACK	1000	225.00	225.00
92	WHERE ANCIENT ONES HUNTED	1000	245.00	275.00
93	BY ANCIENT TRAILS THEY PASS	1000	245.00	245.00
93	WITH PISTOLS DRAWN	1000	195.00	200.00
94	BENEATH THE CLIFF OF SPIRIT	1500	295.00	295.00
94	FLASHES OF LIGHTNING	550	435.00	435.00
95	CHARGE OF BUFFALO SOLDIERS	1000	195.00	245.00
95	SPLITTING THE HERD	550	465.00	560.00

C. WYSOCKI — WYSOCKI

YR	NAME	LIMIT	ISSUE	TREND
79	BUTTERNUT FARMS	1000	75.00	1100.00
79	FAIRHAVEN BY THE SEA	1000	75.00	1100.00
79	FOX RUN	1000	75.00	1400.00
79	SHALL WE?	1000	75.00	1150.00
80	CALEB'S BUGGY BARN	1000	80.00	500.00
80	DERBY SQUARE	1000	90.00	1000.00
80	JOLLY HILL FARMS	1000	75.00	850.00
81	CARVER COGGINS	1000	145.00	1100.00
81	OLDE AMERICA	1500	125.00	550.00
81	PAGE'S BAKE SHOPPE	1000	115.00	325.00
81	PRAIRIE WIND FLOWERS	1000	125.00	1550.00
82	CARNIVAL CAPERS	620	200.00	460.00
82	CHRISTMAS PRINT, 1982	2000	80.00	850.00
82	NANTUCKET, THE	1000	145.00	300.00
82	SLEEPY TOWN WEST	1500	150.00	700.00
82	SUNSET HILLS, TEXAS WILDCATTERS	1000	125.00	175.00
83	AMISH NEIGHBORS	1000	150.00	1600.00
83	APPLE BUTTER MAKERS	1000	135.00	1150.00
83	COMMEMORATIVE PRINT	2000	55.00	100.00
83	COUNTRY RACE	1000	150.00	300.00
83	TEA BY THE SEA	1000	145.00	1300.00
84	A WARM CHRISTMAS LOVE	3951	80.00	400.00
84	BIRD HOUSE	1000	85.00	300.00
84	CAPE COD COLD FISH PARTY	1000	150.00	150.00
84	CHUMBUDDIES	1000	55.00	60.00
84	COMMEMORATIVE PRINT	2000	55.00	65.00
84	COTTON COUNTRY	1000	150.00	250.00
84	FOXY FOX OUTFOXES THE FOX HUNTERS, THE	1500	150.00	475.00
84	GANG'S ALL HERE, THE W/REM	250	90.00	175.00
84	GANG'S ALL HERE, THE/TEDDY BEAR	OP	65.00	65.00
84	STORIN' UP	450	325.00	1000.00
84	SWEETHEART CHESSMATE	1000	95.00	600.00
84	WARM CHRISTMAS LOVE	3950	80.00	350.00
84	YANKEE WINK HOLLOW	1000	95.00	1450.00
85	BIRDS OF A FEATHER	1250	145.00	900.00
85	CLAMMERS AT HODGE'S HORN	1000	150.00	1500.00
85	COMMEMORATIVE PRINT	2000	55.00	60.00
85	DEVILSTONE HARBOR/AN AMERICAN CELEB.	3500	195.00	400.00
85	I LOVE AMERICA	2000	20.00	20.00
85	MERRYMAKERS SERENADE	1250	135.00	170.00
85	SALTY WITCH BAY	475	350.00	2800.00
86	COMMEMORATIVE PRINT	2000	55.00	80.00
86	DADDY'S COMING HOME	1250	150.00	1400.00
86	DANCING PHEASANT FARMS	1750	165.00	575.00
86	DEVILBELLY BAY	1000	145.00	350.00
86	HICKORY HAVEN CANAL	1500	165.00	950.00
86	LADY LIBERTY INDEPENDENCE DAY	1500	140.00	300.00
86	MR. SWALLOBARK	2000	145.00	1750.00
87	BACH'S MAGNIFICAT IN D MINOR	2250	150.00	800.00
87	DAHALIA DINALHAVEN MAKES A DORY DEAL	2250	150.00	400.00
87	TWAS THE TWILIGHT BEFORE CHRISTMAS	7500	95.00	150.00
87	YEARNING FOR MY CAPTAIN	2000	150.00	300.00
87	YOU'VE BEEN SO LONG AT SEA, HORATIO	2500	150.00	300.00
88	AMERICANA BOWL, THE	3500	295.00	300.00
88	FEATHERED CRITICS	2500	150.00	150.00
88	HOME IS MY SAILOR	2500	150.00	150.00
89	ANOTHER YEAR AT SEA	2500	175.00	1150.00
89	BOSTONIANS AND BEANS	6711	225.00	750.00
89	CHRISTMAS GREETING	11000	125.00	125.00
89	DREAMERS	3000	175.00	400.00
89	FUN LOVIN' SILLY FOLKS	3000	185.00	525.00
89	MEMORY MAKER, THE	2500	165.00	165.00
90	BELLY WARMERS	2500	150.00	200.00

YR	NAME	LIMIT	ISSUE	TREND
90	JINGLE BELL TEDDY AND FRIENDS	5000	125.00	140.00
90	ROBIN HOOD	2000	165.00	165.00
90	WEDNESDAY NIGHT CHECKERS	2500	175.00	190.00
90	WHERE THE BUOYS ARE	2750	175.00	180.00
91	BEAUTY AND THE BEAST	2000	125.00	125.00
91	ROCKLAND BREAKWATER LIGHT	2500	165.00	350.00
91	SEA CAPTAIN'S WIFE ABIDING	1500	150.00	175.00
91	WEST QUODDY HEAD LIGHT	2500	165.00	180.00
91	WHISTLE STOP CHRISTMAS	5000	125.00	150.00
92	ETHEL THE GOURMET-CAT	10180	150.00	650.00
92	FREDERICK THE LITERATE-CAT	6500	150.00	2250.00
92	GAY HEAD LIGHT/LIGHTHOUSE	2500	165.00	165.00
92	LOVE LETTER FROM LARAMIE	1500	150.00	150.00
92	PROUD LITTLE ANGLER	2750	150.00	175.00
93	THREE SISTERS OF NAUSET/LIGHTHOUSE	2500	165.00	190.00
94	HOME SWEET HOME	*	25.00	25.00
94	LOST IN THE WOODIES	*	195.00	275.00
94	OLDE BUCKS COUNTY	*	250.00	500.00
94	REMINGTON THE HORTICULTWIST	*	195.00	250.00
95	MABEL THE STOWAWAY	*	175.00	250.00
95	MABEL THE STOWAWAY/CANVAS	*	*	900.00
95	MABEL THE STOWAWAY/FRAMED	*	*	1100.00
95	ROOT BEAR BREAK/BUTTERFIELD	*	160.00	200.00
95	SMALL TOWN CHRISTMAS	*	145.00	175.00

GUILDHALL INC.
W. BAIZE
88	BEST OF FRIENDS	575	85.00	175.00
88	WINTER ARRIVAL	575	85.00	180.00

C. DEHAAN
75	THREE OF A KIND	1000	30.00	140.00
79	FOGGY MORNIN' WAIT	650	75.00	2000.00
80	CIRCLE, THE	1000	30.00	140.00
80	TEXAS PANHANDLE	650	75.00	1250.00
81	FORGIN' THE KEECHI	85	650.00	325.00
81	MAC TAVISH	650	65.00	830.00
81	SURPRISE ENCOUNTER	750	85.00	170.00
82	O' THAT STRAWBERRY ROAN	750	85.00	200.00
83	CROSSIN' HORSE CREEK	650	100.00	320.00
83	KEEP A MOVIN' DAN	750	85.00	150.00
83	RIDIN' OL' PAINT	750	85.00	600.00
83	TWO OLD RENEGADES	150	150.00	2050.00
84	JAKE	650	100.00	330.00
84	SPOOKED	650	95.00	1400.00
85	HORSEMEN OF THE WEST (SUITE OF 3)	650	145.00	525.00
85	KEECHI COUNTRY	750	100.00	120.00
85	OKLAHOMA PAINTS	750	100.00	245.00
85	UP THE CHISHOLM	750	85.00	160.00
86	LONER, THE (W/BELT BUCKLE)	750	145.00	440.00
86	MOON DANCERS	750	100.00	145.00
86	MUSTANGERS, THE	750	100.00	190.00
86	SEARCHERS, THE	650	100.00	240.00
87	CROW CEREMONIAL DRESS	750	100.00	200.00
87	MURPHY'S LAW	750	100.00	275.00
87	SNOW BIRDS	750	100.00	325.00
87	SUPREMECY	750	100.00	200.00
87	WINTER SONGSINGER	750	95.00	190.00
88	MORNIN' GATHER	750	100.00	300.00
88	STAGE TO DEADWOOD	750	100.00	215.00
88	WATER BREAKIN'	750	125.00	550.00
89	CROWS	800	135.00	550.00
89	KENTUCKY BLUE	750	125.00	650.00
89	QUARTER HORSE, THE	800	125.00	130.00
89	VILLAGE MARKERS	750	125.00	200.00
90	CROW AUTUMN	925	135.00	135.00
90	ESCAPE	925	135.00	135.00
90	HIGH PLAINS DRIFTERS	925	140.00	150.00
90	WAR CRY	750	125.00	150.00
91	ENCOUNTER, THE	925	140.00	140.00
91	PIPE CARRIER, THE	925	140.00	140.00
91	PRIDEFUL ONES, THE	925	150.00	165.00
91	SUNDANCE	925	140.00	140.00
92	73 DEGREES IN AMARILLO...YESTERDAY	925	140.00	225.00
92	CROSSING AT THE BIG TREES	925	140.00	140.00
92	SILENT TRAIL TALK	925	140.00	160.00

B. MOLINE
88	COMPANIONS	575	85.00	150.00
88	PORTRAYING HIS HERITAGE	575	85.00	140.00

GUND INC.
H.D. MICHAEL

			FLIGHTS OF FANTASY	
95	A NEW DAY	1500	89.00	89.00
95	KAPUT!	1500	89.00	89.00
95	TALLY HO!	1500	89.00	89.00

HADLEY COMPANIES
A. AGNEW
95	BOY'S CLUB, THE	999	125.00	125.00
95	CHILD'S PLAY	999	100.00	130.00

YR	NAME	LIMIT	ISSUE	TREND
J. BANOVICH				
95	FOLLOWING THE TRACKS	999	125.00	150.00
95	PATRIARCH, THE	750	125.00	185.00
95	RETURN, THE	999	125.00	175.00
D. BARNHOUSE				
95	AMERICAN MADE	1250	125.00	300.00
95	BRAGGING RIGHTS	1250	125.00	625.00
95	FRIDAY EVENING	999	100.00	175.00
95	LAST CHORE OF THE DAY	1250	150.00	250.00
95	PERFECT TREE, THE	1250	150.00	175.00
95	SHOP TALK	*	30.00	60.00
95	SMALL TOWN SERVICE	1250	150.00	275.00
95	WINTER CAN BE FUN	999	125.00	150.00
96	TALES OF THE DAY	1500	150.00	225.00
B. BENGER				
96	BEDTIME STORY, THE	999	125.00	200.00
D. BUSH				
95	CRESCENT MOON BAY	999	125.00	400.00
95	MOONDANCE	999	125.00	425.00
95	WARMTH OF WINTER III	*	30.00	30.00
95	WINTER TRACKS	999	100.00	125.00
96	MOON SHADOWS	999	125.00	175.00
M. CAPSER				
95	A MOMENT IN TIME	999	120.00	120.00
95	ENCHANTED WATERS	999	100.00	175.00
95	GRAPEVINE ESTATES	999	100.00	175.00
95	MARINER'S POINT	999	100.00	180.00
95	ON GENTLE WINDS	999	100.00	135.00
95	SPRING CREEK FEVER	999	100.00	460.00
95	WINTER HAVEN	999	100.00	100.00
96	ACROSS THE CALM	999	100.00	100.00
L. DIDIER				
95	EARLY SNOW	999	125.00	75.00
95	ON SILENT WINGS	999	45.00	175.00
H. EDWARDS				
95	A BREATH OF SPRING	*	30.00	30.00
95	ART OF WINE, THE	750	40.00	40.00
95	CIRCA 1850	*	60.00	60.00
95	HOMESPUN	*	60.00	60.00
95	SUMMER'S RETREAT	*	30.00	30.00
95	YESTERYEAR	*	60.00	60.00
96	HEART OF SPRING	*	30.00	30.00
O. FRANCA				
90	WINDSONG	RT	100.00	250.00
91	LOVERS, THE	RT	125.00	1075.00
S. HAMRICK				
95	A FRIEND IN THE FIELDS	999	75.00	75.00
95	ALWAYS ALERT	999	75.00	160.00
95	COLD WATER, WARM HEART	1500	75.00	375.00
95	FIELD COMPANIONS: BLACK LAB	4000	35.00	35.00
95	FIELD COMPANIONS: GOLDEN RETRIEVER	4000	35.00	35.00
95	FIELD COMPANIONS: SPRINGER SPANIEL	4000	35.00	35.00
95	FIELD COMPANIONS: YELLOW LAB	4000	35.00	35.00
95	GETTING WARM	999	75.00	115.00
S. HANKS				
95	A CAPTIVE AUDIENCE	1500	150.00	225.00
95	COUNTRY COMFORT	999	100.00	325.00
95	DRIP CASTLE	4000	30.00	170.00
95	PACIFIC SANCTUARY	1500	150.00	225.00
95	ROOM TO THINK	999	125.00	200.00
95	SMALL MIRACLE	1500	125.00	160.00
95	STANDING ON THEIR OWN TWO FEET	1500	150.00	200.00
96	BIG SHOES TO FILL	1500	150.00	175.00
L. HARRISON				
95	INTRIGUED	*	30.00	30.00
95	MAKING WAVES	999	75.00	75.00
95	RURAL ROUTE #2	*	30.00	30.00
95	SEA SPIRIT	999	125.00	125.00
95	WINTER NAP	999	100.00	180.00
G. HOFF				
95	GOLDEN TREASURES	999	100.00	90.00
N. HOWE				
95	CYGNATURE	750	125.00	175.00
95	LITTLE MELODY POSTER	*	30.00	30.00
95	SUN DANCE	750	100.00	100.00
L. KAATZ				
95	LEFT BEHIND	*	30.00	30.00
T. LIESS				
95	WINTER SILENCE	*	30.00	30.00
T. MANGELSON				
96	BAD BOYS OF THE ARCTIC POSTER	*	25.00	25.00
96	CATCH OF THE DAY POSTER	*	25.00	25.00
B. MOON				
95	SIGNING OF THE PEACE TREATY	*	30.00	30.00
D. PLASSCHAERT				
95	OUR LEGACY	999	75.00	115.00

YR	NAME	LIMIT	ISSUE	TREND
T. REDLIN				
77	APPLE RIVER MALLARDS	RT	100.00	1300.00
77	OVER THE BLOWDOWN	RT	20.00	625.00
77	WINTER SNOWS	RT	20.00	625.00
78	BACK FROM THE FIELDS	720	40.00	500.00
78	BACKWATER MALLARDS	720	40.00	1200.00
78	OLD LOGGERS TRAIL	720	40.00	1250.00
78	OVER THE RUSHES	720	40.00	425.00
78	QUIET AFTERNOON	720	40.00	600.00
78	STARTLED	720	30.00	1150.00
79	AGING SHORELINE	960	40.00	400.00
79	COLORFUL TRIO	960	40.00	450.00
79	FIGHTING A HEADWIND	960	30.00	440.00
79	LONER, THE	960	40.00	350.00
79	MORNING CHORES	960	40.00	1425.00
79	WHITECAPS	960	40.00	440.00
80	AUTUMN RUN	960	60.00	620.00
80	BREAKING AWAY	960	60.00	725.00
80	CLEARING THE RAIL	960	60.00	900.00
80	COUNTRY ROAD	960	60.00	600.00
80	DRIFTING	960	60.00	400.00
80	HOMESTEAD, THE	960	60.00	600.00
80	INTRUDERS	960	60.00	385.00
80	NIGHT WATCH	2400	60.00	800.00
80	RUSTY REFUGE	960	60.00	475.00
80	SECLUDED POND	960	60.00	300.00
80	SILENT SUNSET	960	60.00	1000.00
80	SPRING THAW	960	60.00	600.00
80	SQUALL LINE	960	60.00	380.00
81	1981 MINNESOTA DUCK STAMP	7800	125.00	185.00
81	ALL CLEAR	960	150.00	430.00
81	APRIL SNOW	960	100.00	650.00
81	BROKEN COVEY	960	100.00	575.00
81	HIGH COUNTRY	960	100.00	525.00
81	HIGHTAILING	960	75.00	400.00
81	LANDMARK, THE	960	100.00	400.00
81	MORNING RETREAT	240	400.00	3000.00
81	PASSING THROUGH	960	100.00	400.00
81	RUSTY REFUGE II	960	100.00	560.00
81	SHARING THE BOUNTY	960	100.00	1450.00
81	SOFT SHADOWS	960	100.00	365.00
81	SPRING RUN-OFF	1700	100.00	650.00
82	1982 MINNESOTA TROUT STAMP	960	125.00	650.00
82	BIRCH LINE, THE	960	100.00	1100.00
82	EVENING RETREAT A/P	300	400.00	2300.00
82	LANDING, THE	RT	30.00	325.00
82	OCTOBER EVENING	960	100.00	875.00
82	REFLECTIONS	960	100.00	850.00
82	SEED HUNTERS	960	100.00	800.00
82	SPRING MAPLING	960	100.00	900.00
82	WHITEWATER	960	100.00	725.00
82	WINTER HAVEN	500	85.00	950.00
83	1983 NORTH DAKOTA DUCK STAMP	3438	135.00	190.00
83	AUTUMN SHORELINE	RT	50.00	675.00
83	BACKWOODS CABIN	960	100.00	1150.00
83	EVENING GLOW	960	150.00	1850.00
83	EVENING SURPRISE	960	150.00	2600.00
83	HIDDEN POINT	960	150.00	1000.00
83	ON THE ALERT	960	125.00	400.00
83	PEACEFUL EVENING	960	100.00	1400.00
83	PRAIRIE SPRINGS	960	150.00	600.00
83	RUSHING RAPIDS	960	125.00	850.00
84	1984 QUAIL CONSERVATION	1500	135.00	135.00
84	BLUEBILL POINT A/P	240	300.00	900.00
84	CHANGING SEASONS-SUMMER	960	150.00	1800.00
84	CLOSED FOR THE SEASON	960	150.00	475.00
84	LEAVING THE SANCTUARY	960	150.00	1200.00
84	MORNING GLOW	960	150.00	1350.00
84	NIGHT HARVEST	960	150.00	1550.00
84	NIGHTFLIGHT	360	600.00	1050.00
84	PRAIRIE SKYLINE	960	150.00	2100.00
84	RURAL ROUTE	960	150.00	600.00
84	RUSTY REFUGE III	960	150.00	1450.00
84	SILENT WINGS SUITE (SET OF 4)	960	200.00	1150.00
84	SUNDOWN	960	300.00	850.00
84	SUNNY AFTERNOON	960	150.00	950.00
84	WINTER WINDBREAK	960	150.00	800.00
85	1985 MINNESOTA DUCK STAMP	4385	135.00	175.00
85	AFTERNOON GLOW	960	150.00	1450.00
85	BREAKING COVER	960	150.00	550.00
85	BROWSING	960	150.00	775.00
85	CLEAR VIEW	1500	300.00	1250.00
85	DELAYED DEPARTURE	1500	150.00	1150.00
85	EVENING COMPANY	960	150.00	1150.00
85	NIGHT LIGHT	1500	300.00	1050.00
85	RIVERSIDE POND	960	150.00	950.00
85	RUSTY REFUGE IV	960	150.00	620.00
85	SHARING SEASON, THE	RT	60.00	200.00
85	WHISTLE STOP	960	150.00	850.00

Beginning Friends *by Paul Calle reflects upon the days when the white man and the Indian were at peace with one another. Mill Pond Press is the publisher.*

In Harmony, *by the late artist Alan Maley, captures the quiet feeling of comfort felt by this family. Published by Past Impressions.*

The tranquil grounds revealed in Gardens Beyond Autumn Gate, *produced by Lightpost Publishing, are typical of Thomas Kinkade's evocative style.*

Thomas Kinkade lends his own golden touch to the Golden Gate Bridge, San Francisco, *a print released in 1995 by Lightpost Publishing.*

YR	NAME	LIMIT	ISSUE	TREND
86	BACK TO THE SANCTUARY	960	150.00	400.00
86	CHANGING SEASONS-AUTUMN	960	150.00	600.00
86	CHANGING SEASONS-WINTER	960	200.00	925.00
86	COMING HOME	2400	100.00	1350.00
86	HAZY AFTERNOON	2560	200.00	1200.00
86	NIGHT MAPLING	2560	200.00	1825.00
86	PRAIRIE MONUMENTS	2560	200.00	650.00
86	SHARING SEASON II, THE	RT	60.00	190.00
86	SILENT FLIGHT	960	150.00	500.00
86	STORMY WEATHER	1500	200.00	700.00
86	SUNLIT TRAIL	960	150.00	440.00
86	TWILIGHT GLOW	960	200.00	1600.00
87	AUTUMN AFTERNOON	4800	100.00	725.00
87	CHANGING SEASONS-SPRING	960	200.00	725.00
87	DEER CROSSING	2400	200.00	1100.00
87	EVENING CHORES (PRINT/BOOK)	2400	400.00	1000.00
87	EVENING HARVEST	960	200.00	1900.00
87	GOLDEN RETREAT	500	800.00	2000.00
87	PREPARED FOR THE SEASON	RT	70.00	200.00
87	SHARING THE SOLITUDE	2400	125.00	1150.00
87	THAT SPECIAL TIME	2400	125.00	1150.00
87	TOGETHER FOR THE SEASON	CL	70.00	120.00
88	BOULDER RIDGE	4800	150.00	175.00
88	CATCHING THE SCENT	2400	200.00	200.00
88	COUNTRY NEIGHBORS	4800	150.00	500.00
88	HOUSE CALL	6800	175.00	1450.00
88	LIGHTS OF HOME	9500	125.00	1000.00
88	MASTER'S DOMAIN, THE	2400	225.00	1350.00
88	MOONLIGHT RETREAT	530	1,000.00	1050.00
88	PRAIRIE MORNING	4800	150.00	400.00
88	QUIET OF THE EVENING	4800	150.00	700.00
88	WEDNESDAY AFTERNOON	6800	175.00	900.00
89	AROMA OF FALL	6800	200.00	1400.00
89	HOMEWARD BOUND	RT	80.00	300.00
89	INDIAN SUMMER	4800	200.00	850.00
89	MORNING ROUNDS	6800	175.00	600.00
89	OFFICE HOURS	6800	175.00	1000.00
89	SPECIAL MEMORIES	570	1,000.00	1250.00
90	BEST FRIENDS	570	1,000.00	2400.00
90	EVENING SOLITUDE	RT	200.00	975.00
90	EVENING WITH FRIENDS	19500	225.00	1650.00
90	FAMILY TRADITIONS	RT	80.00	260.00
90	HEADING HOME	CL	80.00	500.00
90	MASTER OF THE VALLEY	RT	200.00	250.00
90	PURE CONTENTMENT	9500	150.00	690.00
90	WELCOME TO PARADISE	14500	150.00	950.00
91	COMFORTS OF HOME, THE	22900	175.00	400.00
91	FLYING FREE	14500	200.00	200.00
91	HUNTER'S HAVEN	*	1,000.00	1000.00
91	MORNING SOLITUDE	12107	250.00	625.00
91	PLEASURES OF WINTER, THE	24500	150.00	325.00
92	SUMMERTIME	24900	225.00	230.00
95	FROM SEA TO SHINING SEA	29500	250.00	350.00
95	HARVEST MOON BALL	9500	275.00	450.00
95	NIGHT ON THE TOWN	29500	150.00	200.00
95	TOTAL COMFORT	9500	275.00	350.00
96	EVENING REHEARSALS	9500	275.00	300.00

J. VAN ZYLE

YR	NAME	LIMIT	ISSUE	TREND
95	CAT PUCCINO	1250	50.00	50.00
95	LAST NIGHT, LONG NIGHT	580	125.00	125.00
95	SUSHI BAR	999	100.00	100.00
96	CATCH ME IF YOU CAN	580	125.00	125.00

O. WIEGHORST

YR	NAME	LIMIT	ISSUE	TREND
*	BEEF HERD	*	500.00	550.00
*	HIS SPOTTED PONY	*	500.00	500.00
*	LONESOME TRAIL W/ COMPANION PRINT	*	500.00	500.00
*	NOMADS OF THE PLAINS	*	500.00	525.00
73	CORRALLING THE CAVEY	1000	200.00	325.00
74	BUFFALO SCOUT	1000	150.00	1050.00
74	CALIFORNIA WRANGLER	1000	150.00	450.00
74	MISSING IN THE ROUNDUP	1000	100.00	375.00
74	NAVAJO PORTRAIT	1000	75.00	300.00
74	PACKING IN	1000	150.00	200.00
77	BOYS IN THE BUNKHOUSE	1000	150.00	625.00

HAROLD RIGSBY
H. RIGSBY

YR	NAME	LIMIT	ISSUE	RIGSBY TREND
78	AFRICAN LION I	500	20.00	200.00
78	CHEETAH	500	20.00	150.00
78	RACCOON	500	15.00	40.00
78	SIBERIAN TIGER	500	20.00	400.00
79	BOBCAT	500	15.00	75.00
79	SNOW LEOPARD	500	25.00	125.00
79	SNOW TIGER	500	25.00	250.00
80	AFRICAN LION II	200	50.00	250.00
80	BENGAL TIGER II	200	50.00	90.00
80	GIRAFFE	500	25.00	125.00
80	KOALA	500	25.00	100.00
80	RED FOX I	950	30.00	200.00

YR	NAME	LIMIT	ISSUE	TREND
80	RED FOX II	950	30.00	200.00
80	TIGER CUB	500	20.00	400.00
80	WHITE TIGER CUB	500	20.00	400.00
81	AFRICAN LION CUB	950	30.00	100.00
81	COTTONTAIL RABBIT	950	15.00	75.00
81	ZEBRA FOAL	500	50.00	400.00
82	COUGAR	500	50.00	425.00
82	GREY SQUIRREL	950	15.00	50.00
82	TIGER IV	950	20.00	75.00
83	BABY HARP SEAL	950	25.00	275.00
83	BALD EAGLE	950	15.00	100.00
83	BENGAL TIGER CUB	500	50.00	75.00
83	PANDA	950	35.00	90.00
83	WHITE BENGAL TIGER	950	20.00	125.00
84	BENGAL TIGER V	975	40.00	275.00
85	BLACK LEOPARD	975	50.00	350.00
85	GRAY WOLF	975	35.00	50.00

HELEN PAUL WATERCOLORS
H. PAUL

YR	NAME	LIMIT	ISSUE	TREND
95	GREEN PLANTER BOX	350	55.00	55.00
95	SPECIAL OCCASION	350	50.00	50.00
95	SUNFLOWER PATCH	350	75.00	75.00
96	CORNER OF THE GARDEN	350	75.00	75.00
96	SUNFLOWER BASKET	350	75.00	75.00

HENNING PUBLISHING
R. HENNING

YR	NAME	LIMIT	ISSUE	TREND
93	...AND BABY MAKES FOUR	300	25.00	25.00
93	A FAMILY AFFAIR	600	80.00	80.00
93	LION AND THE LAMB	200	80.00	80.00
95	BIG OLD JO	300	25.00	25.00
95	PATH TO GRANDMA'S, THE	450	60.00	60.00
96	DASHING THRU THE SNOW	950	100.00	100.00
96	FIRST RECITAL	600	70.00	70.00
96	LION AND THE LAMB (SHOWCASE)	200	60.00	60.00

R. HENNING
WINTER WORK HORSE

YR	NAME	LIMIT	ISSUE	TREND
93	HOME...AT LAST	350	80.00	80.00
93	HOME...AT LAST (SHOWCASE)	SO	60.00	60.00
93	STORM, THE	SO	75.00	200.00
93	STORM, THE (SHOWCASE)	200	60.00	60.00
94	HOMEWARD BOUND	350	80.00	80.00
94	HOMEWARD BOUND (SHOWCASE)	200	60.00	60.00
95	LIGHTS OF HOME, THE	350	80.00	80.00
95	LIGHTS OF HOME, THE (SHOWCASE)	200	60.00	60.00

HISTORICAL ART PRINTS LTD.
D. TROIANI

YR	NAME	LIMIT	ISSUE	TREND
82	CONFEDERATE STANDARD BEARER	600	75.00	2300.00
82	CPL. WHEAT'S FIRST SPEC. BAT.	600	40.00	675.00
83	BEFORE THE STORM (T.J. JACKSON)	600	75.00	2300.00
83	FORWARD THE COLORS	750	85.00	1150.00
83	UNION STANDARD BEARER	600	75.00	700.00
84	CONFEDERATE DRUMMER	625	75.00	900.00
84	J.E.B. STUART	850	95.00	775.00
84	LEE'S TEXANS	950	95.00	1000.00
84	UNION DRUMMER	625	75.00	525.00
85	FIGHT FOR THE COLORS, THE	950	95.00	1400.00
85	GRAY WALL, THE	950	95.00	775.00
85	REBEL YELL	950	95.00	1000.00
85	SOUTHERN STEEL (N.B. FOREST)	950	95.00	1900.00
86	BRONZE GUNS & IRON MEN	950	95.00	825.00
86	LAST ROUNDS, THE	950	95.00	580.00
86	MEN MUST SEE US TODAY, THE	950	95.00	800.00
86	OLD JACK	950	95.00	550.00
87	114TH PA/COLLIS ZOUAVES	750	65.00	350.00
87	2ND MD INFANTRY	750	65.00	330.00
87	8TH TEXAS CAVALRY	750	65.00	450.00
87	CLEAR THE WAY	950	125.00	2600.00
87	CO.D 2ND U.S. SHARP SHOOTER	750	65.00	400.00
87	GIVE THEM COLD STEEL...	950	95.00	2250.00
87	STARS & BARS	950	125.00	330.00
88	BAYONET	1000	100.00	500.00
88	BOY COLONEL, THE	1000	125.00	550.00
88	EAGLE OF THE 8TH	1000	125.00	600.00
88	GENERAL ROBERT E. LEE	950	125.00	425.00
88	LAST SALUTE, THE	1000	125.00	1300.00
88	SAVING THE FLAG	1000	125.00	785.00
89	12TH VIRGINIA CAVALRY, 1864	750	75.00	225.00
89	2ND U.S. CAVALRY, 1861	750	75.00	175.00
89	EMBLEMS OF VALOR	1000	125.00	625.00
89	FORLORN HOPE, THE	1000	150.00	460.00
89	THUNDER ON LITTLE KENNESAW	1000	150.00	800.00
89	UNITED STATES MARINES 1861-1865	750	65.00	275.00
90	BONNIE BLUE FLAG, THE	1000	150.00	475.00
90	CHARGE	1000	200.00	600.00
90	GRAY COMANCHES, THE	1000	175.00	825.00
90	OPDYCKE'S TIGERS	1000	200.00	550.00
91	1ST S.C. RIFLES, 1861	950	75.00	175.00

YR	NAME	LIMIT	ISSUE	TREND
91	DIEHARDS, THE	1000	200.00	750.00
91	MEN OF ARKANSAS	1000	200.00	450.00
91	RED DEVILS, THE	1000	200.00	650.00
91	WASHINGTON ARTILLERY OF NEW ORLEANS	950	75.00	250.00
92	RANGER MOSBY	1000	250.00	445.00
92	RETREAT BY RECOIL	1000	250.00	525.00
92	UNTIL SUNDOWN	1000	200.00	750.00

IMPERIAL GRAPHICS LTD.

L. LIU

YR	NAME	LIMIT	ISSUE	TREND
*	OLD STONE HOUSE	SO	50.00	50.00
*	PANSIES W/BLUE STARDRIFT	SO	25.00	25.00
*	ROSE FAIRIES	SO	80.00	140.00
*	VIOLET CROWNED HUMMINGBIRD W/MORNING GLORIES	SO	30.00	65.00
95	BURGUNDY IRISES W/FOXGLOVES	5500	60.00	100.00
95	BUTTERFLY GARDEN I	5500	50.00	90.00
95	BUTTERFLY GARDEN II	5500	50.00	90.00
95	MAGNOLIAS & DAY LILIES	5500	80.00	125.00
95	MAGNOLIAS & HYDRANGEAS	5500	80.00	125.00
95	PURPLE IRISES W/FOXGLOVES	5500	60.00	110.00
95	RUBY THROATED HUMMINGBIRD W/HIBISCUS	5800	40.00	75.00
95	WHITE EARED HUMMINGBIRD W/HYDRANGEA	5800	40.00	75.00
95	WREATH OF LILIES	5800	55.00	95.00
95	WREATH OF PANSIES	5500	55.00	85.00
96	MESSENGERS OF LOVE	5500	60.00	75.00
96	PROTECTORS OF PEACE	5500	60.00	75.00

L. LIU — CANVAS EDITION

YR	NAME	LIMIT	ISSUE	TREND
93	BASKET OF MAGNOLIAS	SO	195.00	195.00
94	MERMAID CALLAS	SO	295.00	295.00
95	LILAC BREEZES	300	295.00	295.00
95	MAGNOLIA PATH	300	395.00	395.00
95	NATURE'S RETREAT	300	395.00	395.00
95	SPRING GARDEN	300	395.00	395.00
95	SWEET BOUNTY	300	295.00	295.00
96	ANGEL W/HARP	300	145.00	145.00
96	ANGEL W/TRUMPET	300	145.00	145.00
96	GUARDIAN ANGEL	300	395.00	395.00

L. LIU — CELESTIAL SYMPHONY - CANVAS EDITION

YR	NAME	LIMIT	ISSUE	TREND
95	FLUTE INTERLUDE	300	145.00	70.00
95	FRENCH HORN MELODY	300	145.00	70.00
95	PIANO SONATA	300	145.00	70.00
95	VIOLIN CONCERTO	300	145.00	75.00

L. LIU — CELESTIAL SYMPHONY - PAPER EDITION

YR	NAME	LIMIT	ISSUE	TREND
95	FLUTE INTERLUDE	5500	40.00	40.00
95	FRENCH HORN MELODY	5500	40.00	40.00
95	PIANO SONATA	5500	40.00	40.00
95	VIOLIN CONCERTO	5500	40.00	40.00

L. LIU — LENA Y. LIU LIMITED EDITION IMAGES

YR	NAME	LIMIT	ISSUE	TREND
*	BASKET OF PANSIES	2500	40.00	100.00
*	FLORAL SYMPHONY	1950	95.00	100.00
*	HUMMINGBIRDS & IRIS	1950	40.00	50.00
*	IRIS GARDEN	1950	45.00	200.00
*	MIXED IRISES I	2500	50.00	200.00
*	MIXED IRISES II	2500	50.00	200.00
*	MOONLIGHT SPLENDOR	1950	60.00	75.00
*	MORNING GLORIES & HUMMER	1950	45.00	55.00
*	MORNING ROOM, THE	2500	95.00	375.00
*	ORIENTAL SCREEN	2500	95.00	375.00
*	PARENTHOOD	1950	45.00	100.00
*	PEONIES & AZALEAS	1950	35.00	70.00
*	PEONIES & FORSYTHIA	1950	35.00	70.00
*	PEONIES & WATERFALL	1950	65.00	100.00
*	ROMANTIC ABUNDANCE	1950	95.00	200.00
*	SOLITUDE	1950	60.00	300.00
*	SPRING DUET	1950	60.00	150.00
*	TWO WHITE IRISES	2500	40.00	75.00
88	CHICKADEES	950	35.00	50.00
89	SWANS & CALLAS	1950	65.00	100.00
89	WATERFALL W/BLOSSOMS	1950	65.00	225.00

L. LIU — MUSIC ROOM IV - CANVAS EDITION

YR	NAME	LIMIT	ISSUE	TREND
95	SWAN MELODY	300	425.00	425.00

L. LIU — MUSIC ROOM IV - PAPER EDITION

YR	NAME	LIMIT	ISSUE	TREND
95	SWAN MELODY	6500	150.00	150.00

L. LIU — PAPER EDITION

YR	NAME	LIMIT	ISSUE	TREND
90	POTTED BEAUTIES	SO	105.00	105.00
91	GARDEN PEONIES	SO	60.00	60.00
91	WILDFLOWERS WITH SINGLE BUTTERFLY	SO	50.00	50.00
94	SWEET DELIGHT	SO	50.00	50.00
95	LILAC BREEZES	5500	80.00	135.00
95	MAGNOLIA PATH	5500	135.00	135.00
95	NATURE'S RETREAT	5500	145.00	200.00
95	SPRING GARDEN	5500	125.00	325.00
95	SWEET BOUNTY	5500	80.00	175.00
96	ANGEL W/HARP	5500	40.00	40.00
96	ANGEL W/TRUMPET	5500	40.00	40.00
96	GUARDIAN ANGEL	5500	125.00	125.00

YR	NAME	LIMIT	ISSUE	TREND

J.S. PERRY ORIGINALS
J.S. PERRY

YR	NAME	LIMIT	ISSUE	TREND
84	MEW'S MIX	SO	38.00	500.00
84	MIDWESTERN SKY	*	38.00	48.00
84	PUSSYWILLOWS	800	38.00	72.00
84	STILL LIFE WITH CUPCATS	800	38.00	96.00
85	CALL OF THE WILD	800	95.00	220.00
85	CATTAILS	SO	38.00	500.00
85	CITY KITTY	CL	23.00	23.00
85	FRIENDS IN HIGH PLACES	800	95.00	165.00
85	HOMEWARD BOUND	*	38.00	48.00
85	PAPA WAS A ROLLING STONE	800	38.00	96.00
85	PURPLE CHESHIRE	CL	23.00	23.00
85	THREE SCOOPS	800	48.00	72.00
85	WAFTING AWAY	*	65.00	65.00
86	HOME SWEET HOME	800	48.00	96.00
86	SUMMER TALES	800	48.00	72.00
87	BACKYARD JUNGLE GYM, THE	800	48.00	96.00
87	BOXING MATCH, THE	800	65.00	100.00
87	PEEKABOO	800	65.00	130.00
87	YOGA YOU CAN DO AT HOME	SO	35.00	70.00
88	A WALK ON THE WILD SIDE	*	65.00	98.00
88	HOT PINK BIKINI, THE	800	35.00	70.00
88	KATMANDU	*	45.00	45.00
88	LOVE AT FIRST WHIFF	*	48.00	48.00
88	PICK OF THE LITTER	*	35.00	53.00
88	PUSS	*	35.00	35.00
89	SUNBATHERS, THE	375	395.00	395.00
90	GIRL'S NIGHT OUT	800	48.00	96.00
90	QUE PASTA?	*	35.00	53.00
90	STOWAWAYS	*	48.00	72.00
91	NIGHT GAMES	*	110.00	110.00
91	PEEPING TOMS	*	48.00	48.00
92	HAPPY HOUR	*	125.00	125.00
92	SHOPPING SPREE	*	56.00	56.00
92	SIMPLE PLEASURES	*	35.00	35.00
92	WELCOME HOME	*	56.00	56.00
93	POSITIVELY CATTAILS	*	125.00	125.00
93	SNUGGLERS	*	125.00	125.00

J.S. PERRY

YR	NAME	LIMIT	PUSSONALITIES	TREND
90	OFFICIAL FELINERS TEAM PORTRAIT,THE	800	48.00	72.00
90	OFFICIAL FELINERS TEAM PORTRAIT,THE- AP	80	48.00	48.00
92	HEY, KID!	800	65.00	98.00
92	HEY, KID! AP	80	65.00	65.00
93	STILL LIFE WITH CUPCATS	800	38.00	500.00
94	STAR BRIGHT	800	35.00	53.00
94	STAR BRIGHT AP	80	35.00	35.00
96	ASPARAGUS TIPSY!	800	35.00	35.00
96	ASPARAGUS TIPSY! AP	80	105.00	105.00
96	FORE?	800	35.00	35.00
96	FORE? AP	80	105.00	105.00
96	GILDA LOVES GARLIC!	800	56.00	56.00
96	GILDA LOVES GARLIC! AP	80	168.00	168.00
96	HIGHLAND FLING	800	35.00	35.00
96	HIGHLAND FLING AP	80	105.00	105.00
96	POWDER PUFFS	800	65.00	65.00
96	POWDER PUFFS AP	80	195.00	195.00
96	RAINY DAY	800	65.00	65.00
96	RAINY DAY AP	80	195.00	195.00

JACK TERRY FINE ART
J. TERRY

YR	NAME	LIMIT	FRAMED CANVAS EDITION	TREND
90	HOME FROM THE FAIR	250	495.00	515.00
91	AFTER THE CENTENNIAL PARADE	*	595.00	615.00
91	IF IT WEREN'T FOR BAD LUCK	SO	595.00	1200.00
91	PAY'S THE SAME, RAIN OR SHINE	SO	595.00	1100.00
91	SLOW AND EASY	SO	595.00	2000.00
91	TOO COLD TO SIT AND WAIT	SO	595.00	815.00
92	BIG NIGHT IN A SMALL TOWN	250	595.00	615.00
92	LADY IN RED	*	395.00	415.00
93	CHASE, THE	SO	295.00	650.00
93	CROSSING THE NUECES	SO	295.00	600.00
93	FAITHFUL EVENING	250	595.00	800.00
94	A SEASON TO REMEMBER	500	615.00	615.00
94	CLEARWATER CROSSING	500	615.00	715.00
94	HEADING HOME	500	595.00	715.00
95	A COWBOY'S TIME TO REFLECT	750	350.00	350.00
95	BAGGAGE, BULLION, AND BRAVE MEN	750	615.00	615.00
95	FAST AND FURIOUS	750	350.00	350.00
95	MISERY LOVES COMPANY	750	615.00	615.00
95	MORNING ON THE MERCED	250	615.00	615.00
95	PADRE'S GARDEN, THE	750	350.00	350.00
95	RUSTLING MUSTANGS	750	615.00	615.00
95	SAN FRANCISCO--THE 1880S	750	615.00	615.00
95	SEASONS OF CHANGE	750	350.00	350.00
95	SLEIGHBELLS AND MOONLIGHT	750	515.00	515.00
95	SOUTHERN CHARM	700	615.00	615.00
95	WHISPER VALLEY ROUNDUP	750	775.00	775.00

YR	NAME	LIMIT	ISSUE	TREND
J. TERRY				**PAPER EDITION**
90	HOME FROM THE FAIR	*	35.00	35.00
91	AFTER THE CENTENNIAL PARADE	SO	150.00	350.00
91	FRENCH REVOLUTION/PALETTE OF PARIS	*	125.00	125.00
91	IF IT WEREN'T FOR BAD LUCK	SO	150.00	400.00
91	PAY'S THE SAME, RAIN OR SHINE	*	150.00	350.00
91	SLOW AND EASY	SO	150.00	690.00
91	TOO COLD TO SIT AND WAIT	SO	150.00	300.00
92	BIG NIGHT IN A SMALL TOWN	*	125.00	125.00
92	LADY IN RED	*	125.00	125.00
93	CHASE, THE	SO	65.00	150.00
93	CROSSING THE NUECES	SO	65.00	200.00
93	FAITHFUL EVENING	950	125.00	175.00
94	A SEASON TO REMEMBER	500	150.00	150.00
94	CLEARWATER CROSSING	500	150.00	150.00
94	HEADING HOME	500	150.00	150.00
95	A COWBOY'S TIME TO REFLECT	250	75.00	75.00
95	BAGGAGE, BULLION, AND BRAVE MEN	250	150.00	150.00
95	FAST AND FURIOUS	250	75.00	75.00
95	MISERY LOVES COMPANY	250	150.00	150.00
95	MORNING ON THE MERCED	750	150.00	150.00
95	PADRE'S GARDEN, THE	250	75.00	75.00
95	RUSTLING MUSTANGS	*	150.00	150.00
95	SAN FRANCISCO--THE 1880S	*	150.00	150.00
95	SEASONS OF CHANGE	250	75.00	75.00
95	SLEIGHBELLS AND MOONLIGHT	250	150.00	150.00
95	SOUTHERN CHARM	250	150.00	150.00
95	WHISPER VALLEY ROUNDUP	250	200.00	200.00

JAN HAGARA COLLECTABLES

	NAME	LIMIT	ISSUE	TREND
J. HAGARA				**VICTORIAN CHILDREN**
*	BONNIE	*	*	65.00
*	HANNAH	*	*	150.00
75	TRINA	600	7.00	500.00
76	CHRIS	2000	5.00	75.00
77	SPRING & LANCE	2000	12.00	175.00
78	JUMEAU DOLL	1200	20.00	50.00
78	OLIVIA	600	55.00	800.00
79	DAISIES FROM MARYBETH	900	20.00	100.00
80	BETSY	750	45.00	400.00
80	JIMMY	750	45.00	300.00
80	LYDIA	650	65.00	350.00
81	JENNY	2000	45.00	300.00
81	STORYTIME	450	125.00	600.00
82	CAROL	2000	25.00	175.00
82	IN LINE	1000	65.00	1200.00
82	MANDY	500	60.00	400.00
83	JENNIFER	700	60.00	250.00
83	PAIGE	2000	47.50	200.00
85	CYNTHIA	600	50.00	175.00
85	GOLDIE	1200	47.50	125.00
85	NOEL	2000	30.00	95.00
86	PHILLIP'S COUSINS	1000	60.00	1050.00
86	SOPHIE	1200	50.00	125.00
87	CATHY	2000	30.00	150.00
87	NIKKI	2000	30.00	95.00
87	RENNY & BLUEBEARY	950	125.00	550.00
88	ADDIE	2000	65.00	175.00
88	MATTIE-FIRST COLLECTOR'S CLUB PRINT	YR	55.00	250.00

JIM HARRISON

	NAME	LIMIT	ISSUE	TREND
J. HARRISON				
*	C&S BANK	OP	45.00	45.00
*	CHURCH	OP	30.00	30.00
*	COKE BOTTLE THERMOMETER	OP	30.00	30.00
*	FISH HOUSE	OP	45.00	45.00
*	GEESE OVER MARSH	OP	45.00	45.00
*	GROCERY STORE	OP	30.00	30.00
*	HAMMER GALLERIES I	OP	45.00	45.00
*	HAMMER GALLERIES II	OP	*	N/A
*	HIS WORLD REMEMBERED	OP	45.00	45.00
*	J.J. CORN- 4TH	OP	45.00	45.00
*	LEE OVERALLS	OP	30.00	30.00
*	MAYTAG	OP	45.00	45.00
*	NICKEL COCA-COLA	OP	45.00	45.00
*	OAK TREE	OP	45.00	45.00
*	ROUND COCA-COLA	OP	30.00	30.00
*	SAND DUNES	OP	45.00	45.00
*	SOUTH CAROLINA POSTER	OP	45.00	45.00
*	SWEET SNUFF	OP	45.00	45.00
*	VINTAGE HOUSE	OP	45.00	45.00
73	COASTAL DUNES	1500	30.00	450.00
73	COASTAL MARSHES	1500	30.00	450.00
74	ABANDONED BOAT	1800	25.00	200.00
74	HOUSE IN COUNTRY	1500	25.00	200.00
74	RURAL AMERICANA/MAIL POUCH	1500	40.00	360.00
75	AMERICAN BYWAYS	1500	40.00	325.00
75	COUNTRY SEASONIN' - MORTON SALT	1500	40.00	300.00
75	DISAPPEARING AMERICA	1500	40.00	1400.00

YR	NAME	LIMIT	ISSUE	TREND
76	RURAL DELIVER/MAIL BOX	1500	40.00	425.00
76	YESTERYEAR/WAGON	1500	50.00	200.00
77	BURMAN SHAVE	1500	50.00	300.00
77	COMMUNITY CHURCH	1500	50.00	225.00
77	DR. PEPPER	1500	50.00	300.00
77	FALLOW & FORGOTTEN/PLOW	1500	50.00	200.00
78	666 COLA TABLETS	1500	50.00	275.00
78	PHILIP MORRIS	1500	50.00	275.00
78	RED COVERED BRIDGE	1500	50.00	310.00
78	WOOD PILE	1500	75.00	135.00
79	CLABBER GIRL	1500	75.00	325.00
79	GOLD DUST TWINS	1500	55.00	175.00
79	GOODY'S	1500	50.00	145.00
79	LUCKY STRIKE	1500	50.00	175.00
80	PEPSI & PLANTERS PEANUTS/PAIR	1500	60.00	250.00
80	TONIC & LINIMENT	1500	85.00	225.00
80	TUBE ROSE SNUFF	1500	60.00	175.00
80	UNPAINTED COVERED BRIDGE	1500	60.00	200.00
81	7-UP & BLACK EYED SUSANS	1500	75.00	225.00
81	HOUSE & BARN/PAIR	1500	50.00	225.00
81	OLD DUTCH CLEANSER	1500	75.00	155.00
82	BULL OF THE WOODS	1500	75.00	200.00
82	RAILROAD CROSSING	1500	75.00	300.00
82	WINDMILL	1500	75.00	150.00
83	FILLIN' STATION	1500	80.00	275.00
83	FRESH GRITS	1500	80.00	850.00
83	MOUNTAIN BRIDGE	1500	80.00	275.00
83	SHRINE CIRCUS	1500	80.00	160.00
84	MEMORIES I	750	90.00	200.00
84	MORTON SALT	1500	135.00	250.00
84	RED GOOSE SHOES	1500	90.00	160.00
84	SIGN OF THE TIMES	3000	45.00	135.00
85	MEMORIES II	750	90.00	200.00
85	OLD STONE BARN	1500	90.00	165.00
85	SAND DUNES/INLET MARSH/PAIR	1500	75.00	175.00
85	SPRING CLOUDS	1500	90.00	175.00
85	WIRE	500	45.00	175.00
86	FISHING VILLAGE	975	135.00	165.00
86	LIGHTHOUSE	975	135.00	325.00
87	COCA-COLA BRIDGE	975	135.00	475.00
87	JEFFERSON ISLAND SALT	975	135.00	135.00
87	ROYAL CROWN COLA	975	315.00	175.00
87	UNCLE JOHN'S SYRUP	975	135.00	175.00
88	COCA-COLA BARN	500	275.00	325.00
88	GULLS OVER BEACH	1500	75.00	175.00
88	HERSHEY BAR	975	135.00	200.00
88	RED BOAT	975	135.00	275.00
89	BABY RUTH	1000	45.00	120.00
89	BROWN'S MULE	975	135.00	135.00
89	FALL - RC COLA	975	95.00	180.00
89	VICKS VAPORUB	975	135.00	135.00
90	SANDPIPER	500	185.00	200.00
90	SODA POP SERIES	975	380.00	380.00
90	SPRING - 7-UP	975	95.00	160.00
90	SUMMER - COCA-COLA	975	95.00	225.00
90	WINTER - PEPSI	975	95.00	160.00
91	SINCLAIR STATION	500	135.00	550.00
91	TWELVE CENT GAS	975	200.00	175.00
92	CHURCH IN THE WOODS	975	185.00	225.00
93	TREES	975	185.00	185.00
94	WIND IN THE MARSH	975	185.00	185.00
95	RED BRIDGE IN SNOW	975	65.00	65.00
95	SUMMER COCA-COLA BRIDGE	975	185.00	225.00

J. HARRISON — ARTIST PROOF

YR	NAME	LIMIT	ISSUE	TREND
78	TOOLS	50	325.00	500.00
80	BRUSH AND BUCKET	50	350.00	400.00
91	TWELVE CENT GAS	50	250.00	250.00
92	CHURCH IN THE WOODS	50	235.00	235.00

J. HARRISON — REMARQUE

YR	NAME	LIMIT	ISSUE	TREND
91	TWELVE CENT GAS	25	350.00	350.00

J. HARRISON — SERIGRAPH

YR	NAME	LIMIT	ISSUE	TREND
78	TOOLS	300	275.00	450.00
80	BRUSH AND BUCKET	300	300.00	350.00

KRAPF IMAGES
P. KRAPF

YR	NAME	LIMIT	ISSUE	TREND
89	ANOTHER SEASON	*	90.00	90.00
89	CLOSE TO COVER	*	60.00	60.00
89	GRIZZLY COUNTRY	*	85.00	85.00
89	HUNTER'S REST	*	95.00	95.00
89	SURPRISED	*	55.00	55.00
90	AMERICAN ORIGINAL	*	80.00	80.00
90	CHIPPY ON THE ROCKS	*	50.00	65.00
90	DISTANT BUGLE	*	95.00	95.00
90	EDGE OF THE BURN	*	80.00	110.00
90	OCTOBER MORNING, CANYON DE CHELLY	*	85.00	85.00
90	ON HIS WAY	*	75.00	75.00
90	ON THE EDGE	*	90.00	90.00

YR	NAME	LIMIT	ISSUE	TREND
90	READY	*	95.00	150.00
90	YELLOWSTONE CANYON	*	80.00	80.00
91	ABOVE AND BEYOND	*	95.00	95.00
91	CAUGHT NAPPING	*	65.00	70.00

LANDMARK GALLERIES
C. KETCHIE

YR	NAME	LIMIT	ISSUE	TREND
79	HOWARD'S CREEK MILL	500	50.00	1200.00
83	AUTUMN'S BEST	750	35.00	135.00
83	NOVEMBER MORNING 1865	750	50.00	225.00
84	AUNT NETTIES PORCH	750	55.00	465.00
84	CHURNING TIME	750	55.00	465.00
85	HATTERAS DORY	750	35.00	150.00
85	WILLIAMSBURG VIGNETTE	750	35.00	50.00
85	WILLIAMSBURG WELLS	750	75.00	100.00
86	MURRAY'S MILL	750	85.00	400.00
87	QUIET COVE	750	75.00	500.00
89	CAROLINA COUNTRY	750	45.00	250.00
89	WINTERTIME IN WATAUGA	750	35.00	50.00
90	CAPE HATTERAS LIGHT	750	75.00	175.00
91	PILOT MOUNTAIN PINES	750	40.00	55.00
92	BALDHEAD LIGHT	750	35.00	70.00
92	CAPE LOOKOUT LIGHT	750	35.00	70.00
93	CAPE HATTERAS LIGHTHOUSE	750	35.00	70.00
93	OCRACOLE LIGHTHOUSE	750	35.00	70.00
93	WINTER SOLITUDE	750	25.00	75.00
94	BLUE RIDGE BLANKET	750	25.00	60.00

LIGHTPOST PUBLISHING
T. KINKADE

CANVAS EDITION

YR	NAME	LIMIT	ISSUE	TREND
85	MOONLIGHT ON THE WATERFRONT	260	795.00	700.00
86	ROOM WITH A VIEW	260	710.00	950.00
89	CARMEL, OCEAN AVENUE	CL	595.00	4500.00
89	ENTRANCE TO THE MANOR HOUSE	CL	565.00	2750.00
89	EVENING AT MERRITT'S COTTAGE	CL	595.00	1175.00
90	CHANDLER'S COTTAGE	CL	495.00	2000.00
90	CHRISTMAS COTTAGE	CL	295.00	1100.00
90	MORNING LIGHT A/P	CL	695.00	800.00
90	ROSE ARBOR	CL	495.00	1100.00
90	SPRING AT STONEGATE	550	345.00	600.00
91	AUTUMN GATE, THE	980	595.00	3200.00
91	BOSTON	550	435.00	1575.00
91	CARMEL, TUCK BOX TEA ROOM	980	595.00	2600.00
91	CEDAR NOOK COTTAGE	1960	315.00	625.00
91	CHRISTMAS EVE	980	395.00	795.00
91	FLAGS OVER THE CAPITOL	980	565.00	725.00
91	HOME FOR THE EVENING	980	215.00	450.00
91	HOME FOR THE HOLIDAYS	CL	595.00	2175.00
91	LIT PATH, THE	1960	215.00	450.00
91	MCKENNA'S COTTAGE	980	495.00	500.00
91	OLD PORTERFIELD TEA ROOM	980	495.00	1025.00
91	OPEN GATE, SUSSEX	980	195.00	450.00
91	PYE CORNER COTTAGE	1960	165.00	450.00
91	VICTORIAN EVENING	RT	595.00	1700.00
91	WOODMAN'S THATCH	1960	215.00	475.00
92	AMBER AFTERNOON	980	615.00	1450.00
92	BESIDE STILL WATERS	1250	515.00	2400.00
92	BLOSSOM HILL CHURCH	980	495.00	750.00
92	CHRISTMAS AT AHWAHNEE	980	495.00	650.00
92	COTTAGE-BY-THE-SEA	980	615.00	1450.00
92	COUNTRY MEMORIES	980	395.00	1200.00
92	EVENING CAROLERS	1960	315.00	415.00
92	GARDEN PARTY	980	515.00	650.00
92	JULIANNE'S COTTAGE	980	345.00	1550.00
92	MOONLIT SLEIGHRIDE	1960	315.00	500.00
92	OLD PORTERFIELD GIFT SHOPPE	980	515.00	750.00
92	SAN FRANCISCO, CALIFORNIA STREET	980	645.00	2500.00
92	SUNDAY AT APPLE HILL	980	515.00	1250.00
92	SWANBROOKE COTTAGE	980	595.00	2300.00
92	WEATHERVANE HUTCH	1960	315.00	375.00
92	YOSEMITE	980	615.00	765.00
93	BEYOND AUTUMN GATE	1650	815.00	2700.00
93	BLESSINGS OF AUTUMN, THE	1250	615.00	1150.00
93	END OF A PERFECT DAY	1250	515.00	1600.00
93	FISHERMAN'S WHARF, SAN FRANCISCO	2750	965.00	1300.00
93	HEATHER'S HUTCH	1250	395.00	550.00
93	HOMESTEAD HOUSE	1250	615.00	850.00
93	ST. NICHOLAS CIRCLE	1750	615.00	815.00
93	STUDIO IN THE GARDEN	1480	415.00	750.00
93	WINTER'S END	1450	615.00	750.00
94	BEACON OF HOPE	2750	615.00	995.00
94	BLESSINGS OF SPRING, THE	2750	515.00	650.00
94	CHRISTMAS MEMORIES	3450	515.00	650.00
94	CHRISTMAS TREE COTTAGE	2950	440.00	550.00
94	EMERALD ISLE COTTAGE	2750	515.00	700.00
94	END OF A PERFECT DAY II	2750	815.00	1500.00
94	GUARDIAN CASTLE	4750	865.00	1000.00
94	PARIS, EIFFEL TOWER	2750	795.00	950.00
94	POWER & THE MAJESTY, THE	2750	650.00	750.00

YR	NAME	LIMIT	ISSUE	TREND
94	VICTORIAN CHRISTMAS IV	CL	695.00	750.00
94	WARMTH OF HOME, THE	3450	440.00	550.00
95	AUTUMN LANE	2950	650.00	750.00
95	BLESSINGS OF SUMMER, THE	4950	865.00	1000.00
95	END OF A PERFECT DAY III	4950	995.00	1325.00
95	GOLDEN GATE BRIDGE, SAN FRANCISCO	3950	1,090.00	1325.00
95	HOMETOWN MEMORIES I	4950	865.00	1400.00
95	MAIN STREET TROLLEY	1250	650.00	750.00
95	MORNING DOGWOOD	4950	495.00	565.00
95	MORNING GLORY COTTAGE	4950	545.00	900.00
95	PETALS OF HOPE	3950	580.00	650.00
96	COBBLESTONE LANE	2950	975.00	1575.00
96	MEADOWOOD COTTAGE	4950	375.00	375.00
97	BEYONG SPRING GATE	3450	1,200.00	3200.00
97	BRIDGE OF FAITH	3950	1,150.00	1400.00
97	CLEARING STORM 24X36	2950	1,200.00	1400.00
97	CLEARING THE STORMS	2950	750.00	750.00
97	COBBLESTONE BROOKE	4950	1,200.00	1300.00
97	HOMETOWN EVENING	2950	*	1700.00
97	HOMETOWN LAKE	4950	*	1600.00
97	NEW DAY DAWNING	3950	*	1400.00
97	SPRING GATE	3450	1,200.00	1400.00
97	TEACUP COTTAGE	2950	750.00	800.00
97	VALLEY OF PEACE	3950	*	1400.00
T. KINKADE			**CANVAS EDITION AP**	
96	END OF A PERFECT DAY	295	1,300.00	1150.00
T. KINKADE			**CANVAS EDITION/AUTUMN GATE**	
94	GARDENS BEYOND AUTUMN GATE	CL	875.00	1350.00
97	BEYOND SPRING GATE	1750	815.00	2700.00
T. KINKADE			**CANVAS EDITION/BEAUTY OF THE FOREST**	
95	EVENING IN THE FOREST	OP	580.00	625.00
T. KINKADE			**CANVAS EDITION/BLOSSOM LANE**	
95	BLOSSOM BRIDGE	2950	580.00	650.00
T. KINKADE			**CANVAS EDITION/CHRISTMAS COTTAGE**	
92	SILENT NIGHT	980	395.00	900.00
93	STONEHEARTH HUTCH	1650	415.00	825.00
95	DEER CREEK COTTAGE	OP	390.00	550.00
T. KINKADE			**CANVAS EDITION/CLUB ITEM**	
94	COLLECTORS COTTAGE I	*	315.00	450.00
T. KINKADE			**CANVAS EDITION/COBBLESTONE LANE**	
97	COBBLESTONE BROOKE	3450	1,150.00	1100.00
T. KINKADE			**CANVAS EDITION/COUNTRY MEMORIES**	
93	VILLAGE INN, THE	1200	515.00	2000.00
T. KINKADE			**CANVAS EDITION/DOGWOOD GARDENS**	
91	AFTERNOON LIGHT, DOGWOODS	980	435.00	2100.00
T. KINKADE			**CANVAS EDITION/FAMILY TRADITIONS**	
93	SUNDAY OUTING	1250	515.00	1200.00
T. KINKADE			**CANVAS EDITION/GARDEN OF PROMISE**	
93	GARDEN OF PROMISE	1250	615.00	615.00
T. KINKADE			**CANVAS EDITION/HIDDEN COTTAGE**	
90	HIDDEN COTTAGE	CL	495.00	2000.00
93	HIDDEN COTTAGE II	1980	515.00	800.00
T. KINKADE			**CANVAS EDITION/HOME IS WHERE THE HEART IS**	
92	HOME IS WHERE THE HEART IS	980	615.00	2400.00
97	HOME IS WHERE THE HEART IS II	CL	725.00	900.00
T. KINKADE			**CANVAS EDITION/HOMETOWN MEMORIES**	
95	HOMETOWN CHAPEL	4950	895.00	1000.00
96	HOMETOWN EVENING	2950	975.00	1000.00
97	HOMETOWN LAKE	2950	1,000.00	1000.00
T. KINKADE			**CANVAS EDITION/LAMPLIGHT LANE**	
93	LAMPLIGHT BROOKE	1650	615.00	1200.00
93	LAMPLIGHT LANE	980	595.00	2700.00
94	LAMPLIGHT INN	2750	615.00	900.00
95	LAMPLIGHT VILLAGE	4950	650.00	1375.00
96	LAMPLIGHT BRIDGE	2950	*	700.00
T. KINKADE			**CANVAS EDITION/MAIN STREET MEMORIES**	
95	MAIN STREET CELEBRATION	1250	650.00	750.00
95	MAIN STREET MATINEE	1250	650.00	750.00
T. KINKADE			**CANVAS EDITION/MOMENTS OF GLORY**	
*	GLORY OF THE EVENING	*	485.00	550.00
*	GLORY OF THE MORNING	*	315.00	550.00
93	GLORY OF WINTER	1250	615.00	750.00
T. KINKADE			**CANVAS EDITION/MOONLIT LANE**	
94	MOONLIT LANE I	2400	515.00	675.00
T. KINKADE			**CANVAS EDITION/MOONLIT VILLAGE**	
96	SUNDAY EVENING SLEIGHRIDE	2950	725.00	750.00
T. KINKADE			**CANVAS EDITION/PARIS, CITY OF LIGHTS**	
93	PARIS, CITY OF LIGHTS	1980	695.00	1550.00
T. KINKADE			**CANVAS EDITION/SAN FRANCISCO**	
91	SAN FRANCISCO, UNION SQUARE	CL	695.00	4000.00
93	SAN FRANCISCO, FISHERMAN'S WHARF	2750	965.00	1200.00
94	SAN FRANCISCO, MARKET ST.	7500	795.00	725.00
95	SAN FRANCISCO, GOLDEN GATE BRIDGE	3950	1,090.00	1090.00
96	SAN FRANCISCO, HYDE ST.	3750	975.00	1140.00

YR	NAME	LIMIT	ISSUE	TREND
T. KINKADE		**CANVAS EDITION/SEASIDE MEMORIES**		
95	A LIGHT IN THE STORM	3950	650.00	800.00
96	LIGHT OF PEACE	2950	1,150.00	1425.00
T. KINKADE		**CANVAS EDITION/SECRET GARDEN**		
93	HIDDEN GAZEBO	2400	515.00	700.00
94	HIDDEN ARBOR	3750	515.00	650.00
T. KINKADE		**CANVAS EDITION/SIMPLER TIMES**		
95	SIMPLER TIMES I	OP	550.00	750.00
T. KINKADE		**CANVAS EDITION/SP**		
96	END OF A PERFECT DAY	95	3,650.00	3250.00
T. KINKADE		**CANVAS EDITION/SUGAR & SPICE COTTAGES**		
94	AUTUMN AT ASHLEY'S COTTAGE	395	675.00	795.00
T. KINKADE		**CANVAS EDITION/SWEETHEART COTTAGE**		
92	SWEETHEART COTTAGE	980	495.00	1000.00
93	SWEETHEART COTTAGE II	980	495.00	925.00
94	SWEETHEART COTTAGE III	1650	615.00	800.00
T. KINKADE		**CANVAS EDITION/SWEETHEART HIDEAWAYS**		
95	BROOKSIDE HIDEAWAY	CL	545.00	800.00
95	STEPPING STONE COTTAGE	2950	650.00	900.00
T. KINKADE		**CANVAS EDITION/THOMASHIRE**		
92	BROADWATER BRIDGE	980	495.00	400.00
92	EVENING AT SWANBROOK COTTAGE	980	595.00	1850.00
92	MILLER'S COTTAGE	CL	495.00	1200.00
T. KINKADE		**CANVAS EDITION/VICTORIAN CHRISTMAS**		
92	VICTORIAN CHRISTMAS	CL	595.00	3100.00
93	VICTORIAN CHRISTMAS II	1650	615.00	1745.00
94	VICTORIAN CHRISTMAS III	CL	615.00	815.00
T. KINKADE		**CANVAS EDITION/VICTORIAN GARDEN**		
92	VICTORIAN GARDEN	980	695.00	2650.00
T. KINKADE		**PAPER EDITION**		
*	MORNING LIGHT	*	*	500.00
84	DAWSON	CL	150.00	550.00
84	PLACERVILLE, 1916	CL	90.00	1100.00
85	BIRTH OF A CITY	CL	150.00	250.00
85	EVENING SERVICE	CL	90.00	340.00
85	MOONLIGHT ON THE WATERFRONT	CL	150.00	300.00
86	ROOM WITH A VIEW	CL	150.00	600.00
89	CARMEL, OCEAN AVENUE	CL	225.00	1475.00
89	ENTRANCE TO THE MANOR HOUSE	CL	125.00	900.00
89	EVENING AT MERRITT'S COTTAGE	CL	125.00	750.00
90	CHANDLER'S COTTAGE	CL	125.00	750.00
90	NEW YORK, 1932	935	225.00	1400.00
90	ROSE ARBOR	CL	125.00	300.00
90	SPRING AT STONEGATE	550	185.00	200.00
91	AUTUMN GATE, THE	OP	225.00	1250.00
91	BOSTON	550	175.00	500.00
91	CARMEL, DELORES ST.	980	285.00	500.00
91	CARMEL, TUCK BOX TEA ROOM	980	235.00	875.00
91	CHRISTMAS EVE	980	185.00	350.00
91	FLAGS OVER THE CAPITOL	980	235.00	250.00
91	HOME FOR THE EVENING	980	100.00	450.00
91	HOME FOR THE HOLIDAYS	980	225.00	675.00
91	MCKENNA'S COTTAGE	980	205.00	225.00
91	OLD PORTERFIELD TEA ROOM	980	205.00	350.00
91	OPEN GATE, SUSSEX	980	110.00	110.00
91	VICTORIAN EVENING	RT	150.00	250.00
92	AFTERNOON LIGHT, DOGWOODS	980	185.00	575.00
92	AMBER AFTERNOON	980	235.00	350.00
92	CHRISTMAS AT AHWAHNEE	980	205.00	225.00
92	COTTAGE-BY-THE-SEA	980	235.00	500.00
92	GARDEN PARTY	980	185.00	225.00
92	JULIANNE'S COTTAGE	980	185.00	750.00
92	OLD PORTERFIELD GIFT SHOPPE	980	195.00	205.00
92	SUNDAY AT APPLE HILL	980	175.00	400.00
92	SWANBROOKE COTTAGE	980	225.00	900.00
92	YOSEMITE	980	235.00	250.00
93	ST. NICHOLAS CIRCLE	1750	250.00	250.00
93	STUDIO IN THE GARDEN	980	175.00	200.00
93	WINTER'S END	875	250.00	250.00
94	CHRISTMAS MEMORIES	2450	205.00	225.00
94	EMERALD ISLE COTTAGE	2750	205.00	225.00
94	GUARDIAN CASTLE	2750	300.00	325.00
94	POWER & THE MAJESTY, THE	2750	250.00	250.00
94	WARMTH OF HOME, THE	2450	185.00	200.00
95	AUTUMN LANE	2850	235.00	275.00
95	BLOSSOM BRIDGE	2850	205.00	225.00
95	DEER CREEK COTTAGE	2850	185.00	205.00
95	END OF A PERFECT DAY III	4850	325.00	350.00
95	GOLDEN GATE BRIDGE, SAN FRANCISCO	3850	325.00	350.00
95	LIGHTS OF HOME, THE	250	225.00	225.00
95	SIMPLER TIMES I	3350	250.00	250.00
96	COBBLESTONE LANE	2850	300.00	300.00
96	MEADOWOOD COTTAGE	950	150.00	150.00
T. KINKADE		**PAPER EDITION/AUTUMN GATE**		
93	BEYOND AUTUMN GATE	1750	250.00	550.00
94	GARDENS BEYOND AUTUMN GATE	CL	325.00	600.00

YR NAME	LIMIT	ISSUE	TREND
T. KINKADE	**PAPER EDITION/BEAUTY OF THE FOREST**		
95 EVENING IN THE FOREST	4850	205.00	450.00
T. KINKADE	**PAPER EDITION/BLESSINGS OF THE SEASON**		
93 BLESSINGS OF AUTUMN, THE	1250	250.00	275.00
94 BLESSINGS OF SPRING, THE	2750	205.00	225.00
95 BLESSINGS OF SUMMER, THE	4850	300.00	300.00
T. KINKADE	**PAPER EDITION/CANVAS**		
90 BLUE COTTAGE	RT	125.00	250.00
90 SKATING IN THE PARK	750	275.00	2000.00
T. KINKADE	**PAPER EDITION/CANVAS/COUNTRY CHURCH**		
91 MOONLIT VILLAGE	935	225.00	1975.00
T. KINKADE	**PAPER EDITION/CHRISTMAS COTTAGE**		
90 CHRISTMAS COTTAGE	CL	95.00	500.00
92 SILENT NIGHT	980	185.00	375.00
93 STONEHEARTH HUTCH	1650	185.00	200.00
94 CHRISTMAS TREE COTTAGE	2950	185.00	200.00
T. KINKADE	**PAPER EDITION/COUNTRY CHURCH**		
92 BLOSSOM HILL CHURCH	OP	250.00	250.00
T. KINKADE	**PAPER EDITION/COUNTRY MEMORIES**		
92 COUNTRY MEMORIES	980	185.00	205.00
93 VILLAGE INN, THE	1200	195.00	205.00
T. KINKADE	**PAPER EDITION/DOGWOOD GARDENS**		
95 MORNING DOGWOOD	4850	195.00	200.00
T. KINKADE	**PAPER EDITION/END OF A PERFECT DAY**		
93 END OF A PERFECT DAY	CL	185.00	500.00
94 END OF A PERFECT DAY II	CL	300.00	450.00
T. KINKADE	**PAPER EDITION/FAMILY TRADITIONS**		
93 SUNDAY OUTING	980	205.00	300.00
T. KINKADE	**PAPER EDITION/FLOWER COTTAGES OF CARMEL**		
95 MORNING GLORY COTTAGE	4850	205.00	235.00
T. KINKADE	**PAPER EDITION/GARDEN OF PROMISE**		
93 GARDEN OF PROMISE	1250	235.00	450.00
95 PETALS OF HOPE	3850	205.00	225.00
T. KINKADE	**PAPER EDITION/GREAT MANSIONS OF AMERICA**		
93 HOMESTEAD HOUSE	1250	235.00	250.00
T. KINKADE	**PAPER EDITION/HIDDEN COTTAGE**		
90 HIDDEN COTTAGE	CL	125.00	800.00
93 HIDDEN COTTAGE II	1480	205.00	225.00
T. KINKADE	**PAPER EDITION/HOME IS WHERE THE HEART IS**		
92 HOME IS WHERE THE HEART IS	980	225.00	625.00
T. KINKADE	**PAPER EDITION/HOMETOWN MEMORIES**		
95 HOMETOWN CHAPEL	OP	75.00	75.00
95 HOMETOWN MEMORIES I	4850	300.00	300.00
T. KINKADE	**PAPER EDITION/LAMPLIGHT LANE**		
93 LAMPLIGHT BROOKE	1650	235.00	400.00
93 LAMPLIGHT LANE	980	235.00	750.00
94 LAMPLIGHT INN	2750	235.00	250.00
95 LAMPLIGHT VILLAGE	4850	235.00	250.00
96 LAMPLIGHT BRIDGE	2950	205.00	235.00
T. KINKADE	**PAPER EDITION/MAIN STREET MEMORIES**		
95 MAIN STREET CELEBRATION	1950	250.00	250.00
95 MAIN STREET MATINEE	OP	250.00	250.00
95 MAIN STREET TROLLEY	OP	250.00	250.00
T. KINKADE	**PAPER EDITION/MOMENTS OF GLORY**		
93 GLORY OF WINTER	1250	235.00	250.00
T. KINKADE	**PAPER EDITION/MOONLIGHT LANE**		
94 MOONLIT LANE I	2400	205.00	225.00
T. KINKADE	**PAPER EDITION/NEW YORK**		
86 NEW YORK, 6TH AVENUE	CL	150.00	1300.00
T. KINKADE	**PAPER EDITION/PARIS, CITY OF LIGHTS**		
93 PARIS, CITY OF LIGHTS	1980	285.00	250.00
94 PARIS, EIFFEL TOWER	OP	295.00	250.00
T. KINKADE	**PAPER EDITION/PLEIN-AIR COLLECTION**		
95 BIARRITZ	1200	95.00	95.00
95 BLOOMSBURY CAFE	1200	145.00	145.00
95 LUXEMBOURG GARDENS	1200	95.00	95.00
95 PACIFIC GROVE	1200	125.00	125.00
95 PARIS, ST. MICHEL	1200	125.00	125.00
95 PUERTA VALLARTA BEACH	1200	125.00	125.00
95 SAN FRANCISCO, ALCATRAZ	1200	145.00	145.00
95 VENICE CANAL	1200	95.00	95.00
95 WISTERIA ARBOR	1200	125.00	125.00
96 CHINATOWN, SAN FRANCISCO	950	95.00	95.00
T. KINKADE	**PAPER EDITION/SAN FRANCISCO**		
90 SAN FRANCISCO, 1909	CL	150.00	1300.00
91 SAN FRANCISCO, UNION SQUARE	CL	225.00	1750.00
92 SAN FRANCISCO, CALIFORNIA STREET	980	235.00	2050.00
93 SAN FRANCISCO, FISHERMAN'S WHARF	2750	300.00	325.00
94 SAN FRANCISCO, MARKET ST.	7500	375.00	325.00
96 SAN FRANCISCO, HYDE ST.	3850	300.00	300.00
T. KINKADE	**PAPER EDITION/SEASIDE MEMORIES**		
94 BEACON OF HOPE	OP	235.00	275.00
95 A LIGHT IN THE STORM	OP	235.00	275.00
96 LIGHT OF PEACE	2950	325.00	325.00

YR	NAME	LIMIT	ISSUE	TREND
	T. KINKADE	**PAPER EDITION/SECRET GARDEN**		
94	HIDDEN ARBOR	2750	195.00	225.00
94	HIDDEN GAZEBO	2400	185.00	250.00
	T. KINKADE	**PAPER EDITION/SOCIETY MEMBERS ONLY PIECE**		
95	LOCHAVEN COTTAGE, COLLECTOR COTTAGE II	CL	315.00	525.00
95	LOCHAVEN COTTAGE, COLLECTOR COTTAGE II	CL	95.00	95.00
	T. KINKADE	**PAPER EDITION/SPRING GATE**		
97	BEYOND SPRING GATE	3350	285.00	500.00
	T. KINKADE	**PAPER EDITION/STREAMS OF LIVING WATERS**		
92	BESIDE STILL WATERS	1250	195.00	825.00
	T. KINKADE	**PAPER EDITION/SUGAR & SPICE COTTAGES**		
93	HEATHER'S HUTCH	1250	185.00	200.00
94	AUTUMN AT ASHLEY'S COTTAGE	2450	185.00	205.00
	T. KINKADE	**PAPER EDITION/SWEETHEART COTTAGE**		
*	SWEETHEART COTTAGE II	980	185.00	500.00
92	SWEETHEART COTTAGE	CL	150.00	363.00
94	SWEETHEART COTTAGE III, HAVENCREST	CL	250.00	250.00
	T. KINKADE	**PAPER EDITION/SWEETHEART HIDEAWAYS**		
95	BROOKSIDE HIDEAWAY	OP	205.00	225.00
95	STEPPING STONE COTTAGE	2850	250.00	250.00
	T. KINKADE	**PAPER EDITION/THOMASHIRE**		
92	BROADWATER BRIDGE	CL	225.00	400.00
92	EVENING AT SWAVBROOK COTTAGE	980	250.00	600.00
92	MILLER'S COTTAGE	980	175.00	350.00
	T. KINKADE	**PAPER EDITION/VICTORIAN CHRISTMAS**		
92	VICTORIAN CHRISTMAS	980	225.00	1025.00
93	VICTORIAN CHRISTMAS II	CL	235.00	375.00
94	VICTORIAN CHRISTMAS III	CL	250.00	325.00
95	VICTORIAN CHRISTMAS IV	702	250.00	250.00
	T. KINKADE	**PAPER EDITION/VICTORIAN GARDEN**		
92	VICTORIAN GARDEN	980	275.00	700.00
	T. KINKADE	**TENTH ANNIVERSARY ARCHIVE COLLECTION**		
94	CREEKSIDE TRAIL	CL	690.00	725.00
94	CREEKSIDE TRAIL	1980	275.00	300.00
94	DAYS OF PEACE	1984	275.00	300.00
94	DAYS OF PEACE	CL	690.00	725.00
94	DUSK IN THE VALLEY	1984	275.00	300.00
94	DUSK IN THE VALLEY	CL	590.00	725.00
94	SPRING IN THE ALPS	CL	225.00	225.00
	T. KINKADE	**TENTH ANNIVERSARY ARCHIVE COLLECTION/CANVAS**		
94	SPRING IN THE ALPS	1984	575.00	575.00

LITTLE ANGEL PUBLISHING

YR	NAME	LIMIT	ISSUE	TREND
	D. GELSINGER			**CANVAS**
94	FLOWER FOR BABY A/P	25	585.00	585.00
94	FLOWER FOR BABY S/N	250	510.00	510.00
94	TOY BOX, THE A/P	25	525.00	525.00
94	TOY BOX, THE S/N	250	450.00	450.00
95	ALEXANDRIA'S TEDDY A/P	25	352.50	353.00
95	ALEXANDRIA'S TEDDY S/N	250	295.00	295.00
95	FIRELIGHT	300	520.00	520.00
95	FIRELIGHT A/P	SO	595.00	595.00
95	GOLDEN GATE A/P	20	795.00	795.00
95	GOLDEN GATE S/N	200	695.00	695.00
95	LIFE'S LITTLE TANGLES A/P	SO	595.00	595.00
95	LIFE'S LITTLE TANGLES S/N	350	520.00	520.00
95	MOTHERLY LOVE A/P	30	525.00	525.00
95	MOTHERLY LOVE S/N	300	450.00	450.00
95	PERFECT TREE, THE A/P	25	352.50	353.00
95	PERFECT TREE, THE S/N	250	295.00	295.00
96	LIGHTHOUSE KEEPER, THE A/P	CL	625.00	625.00
96	SUGAR & SPICE A/P	20	352.50	353.00
96	SUGAR & SPICE S/N	200	295.00	295.00
97	FAREWELL BEND S/N	40	575.00	575.00
97	JOYOUS FEAST, A S/N	54	290.00	290.00
	D. GELSINGER			**CANVAS GICLEE**
96	LIGHTHOUSE KEEPER, THE	CL	525.00	525.00
97	BOARDWALK, THE S/N	45	575.00	575.00
	D. GELSINGER	**CLASSIC MOMENTS IN OIL CANVAS EDITION**		
97	AN ANGEL'S TOUCH S/N	500	88.00	88.00
97	GENTLE GUIDANCE S/N	500	88.00	88.00
	D. GELSINGER			**PAPER**
94	FLOWER FOR BABY A/P	15	190.00	190.00
94	FLOWER FOR BABY S/N	150	140.00	140.00
94	TOY BOX, THE A/P	15	170.00	170.00
94	TOY BOX, THE S/N	150	120.00	120.00
95	ALEXANDRIA'S TEDDY A/P	15	120.00	120.00
95	ALEXANDRIA'S TEDDY S/N	150	80.00	80.00
95	FIRE LIGHT A/P	15	200.00	200.00
95	FIRE LIGHT S/N	150	150.00	150.00
95	GOLDEN GATE A/P	CL	230.00	230.00
95	GOLDEN GATE S/N	100	180.00	180.00
95	LIFE'S LITTLE TANGLES A/P	CL	200.00	200.00
95	LIFE'S LITTLE TANGLES S/N	150	150.00	150.00
95	MOTHERLY LOVE A/P	15	170.00	170.00
95	MOTHERLY LOVE S/N	150	120.00	120.00
95	PERFECT TREE, THE A/P	15	120.00	120.00

A bundle of cats hides in the cattails in Positively Cattails, *a print by J.S. Perry for J.S. Perry Originals.*

Sacred Circle, *a print by artist Bev Doolittle for The Greenwich Workshop, has increased in value since its 1991 release.*

Released in 1981 by Jan Hagara Collectables, Storytime *by Jan Hagara is a lithograph produced on 100% cotton rag paper. The limited edition of 450 was issued at $125 and currently lists for $600.*

YR	NAME	LIMIT	ISSUE	TREND
95	PERFECT TREE, THE S/N	150	80.00	80.00
96	SUGAR & SPICE A/P	5	120.00	120.00
96	SUGAR & SPICE S/N	50	80.00	80.00

D. GELSINGER — THE SEASONS OF ANGELS CANVAS

YR	NAME	LIMIT	ISSUE	TREND
96	SPRING ANGEL A/P	12	234.00	234.00
96	SPRING ANGEL S/N	125	184.00	184.00
96	WINTER ANGEL A/P	12	234.00	234.00
96	WINTER ANGEL S/N	125	184.00	184.00

D. GELSINGER — THE SEASONS OF ANGELS PAPER

YR	NAME	LIMIT	ISSUE	TREND
96	SPRING ANGEL A/P	12	87.00	87.00
96	SPRING ANGEL S/N	125	57.00	57.00
96	WINTER ANGEL S/N	125	57.00	57.00
96	WINTER ANGLE A/P	12	87.00	87.00

LYNN'S PRINTS
L. GRAEBNER

YR	NAME	LIMIT	ISSUE	TREND
87	BACKFIRE	750	40.00	170.00
87	BREAD AND MILK	*	40.00	150.00
87	FIRST LOVE	*	40.00	40.00
87	HORSEY'S TREAT	750	40.00	135.00
87	LITTLE APPLE PICKER	*	40.00	100.00
87	SUNDAY MEETING	750	25.00	65.00
88	AUCTION, THE	*	25.00	25.00
88	BACK PORCH QUILT FIXIN	750	25.00	95.00
88	BARN RAISING LUNCH	*	25.00	25.00
88	BARNYARD FRIENDS	*	25.00	25.00
88	CART FULL OF APPLES	750	25.00	100.00
88	MOTHERS SPECIAL DAY '88	750	20.00	130.00
88	ROADSIDE BERRY PICKIN	750	25.00	100.00
88	SHARING	*	15.00	45.00
88	SHARING THE LOAD	750	25.00	85.00
88	SWEET SMELLS	750	15.00	75.00
88	TALKING WITH DOLLY	750	15.00	70.00
89	AUTUMN PLAYTIME	*	85.00	85.00
89	CART FOR DOLLIES	*	25.00	25.00
89	COME A COURTIN	*	20.00	20.00
89	FALL AFTERNOON	*	30.00	30.00
89	FEEDING TIME BEFORE SCHOOL	*	30.00	30.00
89	FISHERMAN'S HELPER	*	30.00	30.00
89	IN TOWN CHRISTMAS	*	100.00	225.00
89	WILD GOOSE CHASE	*	30.00	30.00
89	YOU CAN'T HAVE MY DOLLY	*	20.00	20.00
90	AFTERNOON AT THE POND	*	65.00	65.00
90	AIRING THE QUILTS	*	30.00	30.00
90	BE GOOD TO EACH OTHER	50	100.00	250.00
90	CHRISTMASTIME IN THE COUNTRY	*	65.00	85.00
90	DOLLY'S QUILT	*	20.00	20.00
90	FETCH	*	20.00	20.00
90	FIRST QUILT	*	20.00	20.00
90	FIRST ROSE OF SUMMER	*	30.00	30.00
90	FOREVER YOURS DAD	*	20.00	40.00
90	FRIENDS	*	30.00	30.00
90	FRONT PORCH TEA PARTY	*	30.00	30.00
90	GRAPE PICKIN	*	30.00	30.00
90	LET'S BE FRIENDS	*	30.00	30.00
90	MMM GOOD	*	20.00	20.00
90	SUMMER SCENTS	*	20.00	20.00
90	SUNDAY MEETING HOOKY	*	65.00	65.00
91	CLOAK ROOM	*	150.00	150.00
91	COME DOWN AND HAVE A TREAT	*	25.00	25.00
91	HITCHIN A RIDE	*	25.00	25.00
91	KNIT PICKIN	*	25.00	25.00
91	MOTHER'S DAY SPECIAL 1991	*	25.00	25.00
91	ROUNDING UP THE PIGS	*	25.00	25.00
91	SEEDS FOR YOU MR. CARDINAL	*	25.00	85.00

MAFEKING COLLECTION
M. GREEN — MAN'S BEST FRIEND

YR	NAME	LIMIT	ISSUE	TREND
94	DEREK (THE LABRADOR RETRIEVER)	1500	17.39	25.00
94	MICKEY (SPANIEL CROSS)	1500	17.39	25.00
94	PEPPER (THE AIREDALE)	1500	17.39	25.00

MARTY BELL FINE ART
M. BELL — AMERICA THE BEAUTIFUL

YR	NAME	LIMIT	ISSUE	TREND
95	BLUEBIRD VICTORIAN, THE	YR	320.00	340.00
95	GRETEL'S COTTAGE	750	225.00	225.00
95	HANSEL'S HOUSE	750	225.00	225.00
95	MENDOCINO TWILIGHT	750	400.00	375.00
95	MORNING GLORY/TRIPLE	500	650.00	650.00
95	TELEGRAPH HILL	750	150.00	150.00
95	TUCK BOX CHRISTMAS	750	250.00	N/A
95	TUCK BOX, THE-TEA ROOM, CARMEL	500	456.00	1200.00
95	TUCK BOX, THE-TEA ROOM, CARMEL	OP	200.00	200.00

M. BELL — AMERICA THE BEAUTIFUL/GIFT

YR	NAME	LIMIT	ISSUE	TREND
95	BLUEBIRD, THE	YR	*	N/A

M. BELL — ENGLAND

YR	NAME	LIMIT	ISSUE	TREND
95	BLYTON COTTAGE	750	100.00	100.00
95	BURTON COTTAGE	750	100.00	100.00

YR	NAME	LIMIT	ISSUE	TREND
95	HOLLY COTTAGE	750	100.00	100.00
95	HONEYCOMB COTTAGE	750	100.00	100.00
95	MILL HAY MANOR	750	850.00	850.00
95	MRS. BROWNS FOR TEA	750	100.00	100.00
95	ROSE BOWER COTTAGE/TRIPLE	500	520.00	520.00
95	SISSINGHURST GARDEN	750	488.00	385.00
95	TULIP TIME	500	456.00	456.00
M. BELL			**GARDENS OF THE HEART**	
95	CLOISTER GARDEN	250	488.00	400.00
95	MAJESTY	500	700.00	742.00
95	SWEETHEART'S GATE	750	225.00	225.00
M. BELL			**HUGGA BELLS**	
95	LUV BOAT, THE	350	110.00	116.00
95	MOTHERLOVE	350	116.00	116.00
95	STORYTIME	350	110.00	115.00
95	WEDDED BLISS	350	116.00	116.00
M. BELL			**LIMITED EDITION LITHOGRAPHS**	
82	BIBURY COTTAGE	550	290.00	1400.00
82	BIG DADDY'S SHOE	950	64.00	300.00
82	CASTLE COMBE COTTAGE	550	264.00	1200.00
82	CROSSROADS COTTAGE	950	38.00	310.00
83	NESTLEWOOD	550	300.00	4900.00
84	PENHURST TEA ROOMS (ARCHIVAL)	1000	335.00	2750.00
84	PENHURST TEA ROOMS (CANVAS)	550	335.00	3600.00
84	WEST KINGTON DELL	550	240.00	1000.00
85	LITTLE BOXFORD	550	78.00	900.00
85	MEADOWLARK COTTAGE	550	78.00	700.00
85	SUMMER'S GLOW	550	98.00	1000.00
85	SURREY GARDEN HOUSE	550	98.00	1500.00
85	SWEET PINE COTTAGE	550	78.00	1500.00
85	WINDSONG COTTAGE	550	78.00	800.00
86	BURFORD VILLAGE STORE	550	120.00	1000.00
86	COTSWOLD PARISH CHURCH	1850	98.00	2000.00
86	HOUSEWIVES CHOICE	550	98.00	1000.00
86	LORNA DOONE COTTAGE	550	380.00	9000.00
86	YORK GARDEN SHOP	550	110.00	1000.00
87	ALDERTON VILLAGE	550	264.00	900.00
87	BROUGHTON VILLAGE	950	128.00	500.00
87	CHAPLAIN'S GARDEN, THE	550	264.00	2250.00
87	CHIPPENHAM FARM	550	120.00	900.00
87	DOVE COTTAGE GARDEN	950	272.00	500.00
87	DRIFTSONE MANOR	550	440.00	4000.00
87	DUCKSBRIDGE COTTAGE	550	430.00	2500.00
87	EASHING COTTAGE	950	128.00	350.00
87	FIDDLEFORD COTTAGE	550	78.00	1950.00
87	HALFWAY COTTAGE	950	272.00	800.00
87	LITTLE TULIP THATCH	550	120.00	600.00
87	MAY COTTAGE	950	128.00	620.00
87	MILLPOND STOCKBRIDGE, THE	550	120.00	1800.00
87	MORNING GLORY COTTAGE	550	120.00	600.00
87	SUNRISE THATCH	950	128.00	350.00
87	VICAR'S GATE, THE	550	110.00	900.00
87	WAKEHURST PLACE	950	520.00	2700.00
87	WELL COTTAGE, SANDY LANE	550	440.00	1600.00
87	WHITE LILAC THATCH	950	272.00	700.00
88	BISHOP'S ROSES, THE	2450	220.00	500.00
88	CLOVE COTTAGE	950	128.00	800.00
88	CLOVER LANE COTTAGE	1850	272.00	1100.00
88	COTSWOLD TWILIGHT	950	128.00	500.00
88	GINGER COTTAGE	1850	320.00	800.00
88	ICOMB VILLAGE GARDEN	RT	620.00	1800.00
88	JASMINE THATCH	950	272.00	700.00
88	LULLABYE COTTAGE	RT	220.00	525.00
88	MORNING'S GLOW	1850	280.00	650.00
88	MURRLE COTTAGE	1850	320.00	1000.00
88	RODWAY COTTAGE	RT	620.00	2000.00
88	SHERE VILLAGE ANTIQUES	950	272.00	825.00
88	SWEET TWILIGHT	RT	220.00	600.00
89	BLUSH OF SPRING	1250	96.00	225.00
89	FIRESIDE CHRISTMAS	550	136.00	800.00
89	GAMEKEEPER'S COTTAGE, THE	950	560.00	2000.00
89	LARKSPUR COTTAGE	2450	220.00	450.00
89	OLD BEAMS COTTAGE	950	368.00	700.00
89	PRIDE OF SPRING	1250	96.00	225.00
89	PRIMROSE COTTAGE	2450	88.00	88.00
90	ARBOR COTTAGE	950	130.00	250.00
90	BRYANTS PUDDLE THATCH	950	130.00	250.00
90	GOMSHALL FLOWER SHOP	950	396.00	2050.00
90	LITTLE WELL THATCH	950	130.00	250.00
90	LONGSTOCK LANE	950	130.00	250.00
90	LOWER BROCKHAMPTON MANOR	950	730.00	1825.00
90	OLD HERTFORDSHIRE COTTAGE	950	396.00	1500.00
90	READY FOR CHRISTMAS	550	148.00	1050.00
91	DEVON ROSES	1200	96.00	200.00
91	DORSET ROSES	1200	96.00	200.00
91	TEA TIME	900	130.00	200.00
91	WINDWARD COTTAGE, RYE	1100	228.00	625.00

YR	NAME	LIMIT	ISSUE	TREND
M. BELL		MEMBERS ONLY COLLECTORS CLUB		
91	LITTLE THATCH TWILIGHT	CL	288.00	380.00
92	BLOSSOM LANE	CL	288.00	288.00
92	CANDLE AT EVENTIDE	CL	*	N/A

MAZE CREEK STUDIO
A. THOMAS

YR	NAME	LIMIT	ISSUE	TREND
92	BATTLE OF CARTHAGE, THE	CL	35.00	80.00
95	CROSSING BUCK BRANCH	400	35.00	35.00
95	DELPHUS THEATER	400	19.00	19.00
95	GOOD EARTH, THE	400	50.00	50.00
95	SHAMANS SPIRIT	400	40.00	40.00
96	MAIN ST. JOPLIN 1900	400	45.00	45.00
96	PETTICOAT FLAG	400	35.00	35.00
A. THOMAS		TRANS-MISSISSIPPI SERIES		
98	SHELBY AND HIS MEN AT WESTPURT-BATTLE OF WESTPURT	900	50.00	50.00

MILITARY GALLERY
N. TRUDGIAN

YR	NAME	LIMIT	ISSUE	TREND
N. TRUDGIAN		AIR COMBAT LEGEND		
95	BLACK CAT RESCUE	800	65.00	65.00
95	MYNARSKI'S LANC	800	65.00	65.00
95	TRAINBUSTERS	800	65.00	65.00
N. TRUDGIAN		NICOLAS TRUDGIAN		
95	BOMBER FORCE	500	150.00	275.00
95	COMBAT OVER BEACHY HEAD	800	65.00	65.00
95	COMBAT OVER NEW GUINEA	800	65.00	65.00
95	INVASION FORCE	800	65.00	65.00
95	KIWI STRIKE	800	65.00	65.00
95	LAST MAN HOME	1000	150.00	250.00
95	LIGHTNING ENCOUNTER	1000	150.00	180.00
95	RETURN OF THE HUNTERS	1000	150.00	200.00
95	SQUADRON SCRAMBLE	800	65.00	65.00
95	TWILIGHT CONQUEST	600	150.00	150.00
R. TAYLOR		ROBERT TAYLOR		
95	AIR APACHES ON THE WARPATH	600	295.00	350.00
95	EAGLES OVER THE RHINE	1250	295.00	410.00
95	OUT OF FUEL AND SAFELY HOME	1250	295.00	340.00
95	RANGERS ON THE RAMPAGE	850	295.00	400.00
95	SIGNED BY ONE PILOT VICTORY FLYOVER	500	75.00	75.00
95	STEINHOFF TRIBUTE	1250	350.00	440.00
95	VALOR IN THE PACIFIC	1250	295.00	500.00
95	VICTORY FLYOVER	1200	295.00	560.00
95	WIDE HORIZONS	1250	100.00	100.00
R. TAYLOR		ROBERT TAYLOR POSTER		
95	VICTORY FLYOVER	OP	35.00	35.00
N. TRUDGIAN		WORLD WAR II INSIGNIA		
95	ALPINE MUSTANG	OP	65.00	65.00
95	FLYING FORTRESS	OP	65.00	65.00
95	FLYING TIGER	OP	65.00	65.00
95	KLINGS CLIFFE LIGHTNING	OP	65.00	65.00
95	MITCHELL OVER THE RIVIERA	OP	65.00	65.00
95	PACIFIC PIRATE	OP	65.00	65.00

MILL POND PRESS
R. BATEMAN

YR	NAME	LIMIT	ISSUE	TREND
*	AFRICAN FISH EAGLE	*	265.00	265.00
*	ARKANSAS DUCK STAMP 1987-WOOD DUCK	*	200.00	200.00
*	BUFFALO AT AMBOSELI-CAPE BUFFALO	*	400.00	600.00
*	CANADA DUCK PRINT W/S 1988-PINTAILS	*	175.00	175.00
*	CANADA DUCK STAMP-1985 W/2 MALLARD DUCKS	*	200.00	200.00
*	CANADA GEESE IN WINTER	*	*	2500.00
*	CHEETAH SIESTA	*	*	2500.00
*	CHICKADEE ON PINECONE-ETCHING	*	*	2000.00
*	COUGAR AND KIT	*	*	600.00
*	COUGAR IN THE SNOW	*	*	325.00
*	DESCENDING SHADOWS-WOLVES	*	*	325.00
*	DIK-DIKS	*	*	640.00
*	FOX-ETCHING	*	*	2200.00
*	GIANT PANDA IN THE WILD	*	295.00	310.00
*	GRIZZLY BEAR-ETCHING	*	*	2200.00
*	HOODED MERGANSER-DUCK	*	*	450.00
*	LION CUBS B/W	*	*	1000.00
*	LION-ETCHING	*	*	2200.00
*	LIONESS-ETCHING	*	*	2200.00
*	LOON PAIR AND YOUNG	*	*	425.00
*	MERGANSER DUCK-BRONZE	*	*	695.00
*	MEXICAN WOLF	*	*	285.00
*	MOOSE	*	*	1200.00
*	NEW YORK DUCK STAMP W/2 S	*	175.00	175.00
*	NO. AMERICAN WILD SHEEP STAMP	*	300.00	300.00
*	PEREGRINE AND YOUNG	*	*	395.00
*	PEREGRINE IN FLIGHT-BRONZE	*	*	1500.00
*	PREDATOR PORTFOLIO-WOLVERINE	*	275.00	275.00
*	RED-TAILED HAWK STUDY-BRONZE	*	*	1750.00
*	SAP BUCKET-MYRTLE WARBLER	*	195.00	175.00
*	SHADOW OF RAINFOREST-JAGUAR	*	*	650.00
*	SUMMER GARDEN - YOUNG ROBIN	*	235.00	235.00
*	SYMBOL OF RAINFOREST - JAGUAR	*	235.00	380.00

YR	NAME	LIMIT	ISSUE	TREND
*	TEXAS DUCK STAMP 1990-AMERICAN WIGEON	*	135.00	135.00
*	VIGILANCE - PREMIER	*	650.00	1000.00
*	WASHINGTON DUCK STAMP	*	150.00	150.00
*	WILDEBEEST AT SUNSET	*	400.00	400.00
*	WINTER TRACKERS COYOTE	*	335.00	335.00
*	WOLF SKETCH	*	250.00	440.00
78	BY THE TRACKS-KILLDEER	950	75.00	900.00
78	CHEETAH WITH CUBS	950	95.00	560.00
78	DOWNY WOODPECKER ON GOLDENROD	950	50.00	1100.00
78	LION CUBS	950	125.00	275.00
78	MAJESTY ON THE WING-BALD EAGLE	950	150.00	2100.00
78	YOUNG BARN SWALLOW	950	75.00	700.00
79	AFTERNOON GLOW-SNOWY OWL	950	125.00	625.00
79	AMONG THE LEAVES-COTTONTAIL RABBIT	950	75.00	2000.00
79	BULL MOOSE	950	125.00	1225.00
79	COUNTRY LANE-PHEASANTS	950	85.00	700.00
79	EVENING SNOWFALL-AMERICAN ELK	950	150.00	960.00
79	GOLDEN EAGLE	950	150.00	350.00
79	GREAT BLUE HERON	950	125.00	950.00
79	HIGH COUNTRY-STONE SHEEP	950	125.00	700.00
79	KING OF THE REALM-LION	950	125.00	650.00
79	MASTER OF THE HERD-AMERICAN BUFFALO	950	150.00	1900.00
79	SURF AND SANDERLINGS	950	65.00	1650.00
79	UP IN THE PINE-GREAT HORNED OWL	950	150.00	950.00
79	WILY AND WARY-RED FOX	950	125.00	1300.00
79	WINTER CARDINAL	950	75.00	2350.00
79	WINTER-SNOWSHOE HARE	950	95.00	2300.00
79	WOLF PACK IN MOONLIGHT	950	95.00	2300.00
79	YELLOW-RUMPED WARBLER	950	50.00	500.00
80	AFRICAN AMBER-LIONESS PAIR	950	175.00	525.00
80	ANTARCTIC ELEMENTS-SEA GULL	950	125.00	200.00
80	ARCTIC FAMILY-POLAR BEARS	950	150.00	1375.00
80	ASLEEP ON THE HEMLOCK-SCREECH OWL	950	125.00	700.00
80	AUTUMN OVERTURE-MOOSE	950	245.00	2000.00
80	AWESOME LAND-AMERICAN ELK	950	245.00	2250.00
80	BARN OWL IN THE CHURCHYARD	950	125.00	1000.00
80	BLUFFING BULL-AFRICAN ELEPHANT	950	135.00	1450.00
80	BROWN PELICAN AND PILINGS	950	165.00	950.00
80	CHAPEL DOORS	950	135.00	1000.00
80	COYOTE IN WINTER SAGE	950	245.00	2450.00
80	CURIOUS GLANCE-RED FOX	950	135.00	1300.00
80	EVENING GROSBEAK	950	125.00	950.00
80	FALLEN WILLOW-SNOWY OWL	950	200.00	620.00
80	FLYING HIGH-GOLDEN EAGLE	950	150.00	775.00
80	HERON ON THE ROCKS	950	75.00	1050.00
80	KINGFISHER IN WINTER	950	175.00	1500.00
80	KITTIWAKES GREETING	950	75.00	400.00
80	LEOPARD IN A SAUSAGE TREE	950	150.00	2400.00
80	LION AT TSAVO	950	150.00	400.00
80	MISCHIEF ON THE PROWL-RACCOON	950	85.00	200.00
80	MISTY COAST-GULLS	950	135.00	450.00
80	ON THE ALERT-CHIPMUNK	950	60.00	400.00
80	PRAIRIE EVENING-SHORT-EARED OWL	950	150.00	300.00
80	ROCKY WILDERNESS-COUGAR	950	175.00	1150.00
80	SPRING CARDINAL	950	125.00	475.00
80	SPRING THAW-KILLDEER	950	85.00	150.00
80	VANTAGE POINT-BALD EAGLE	950	245.00	1000.00
80	WHITE ENCOUNTER-POLAR BEAR	950	245.00	2500.00
80	WHITE FOOTED MOUSE IN WINTERGREEN	RT	60.00	350.00
80	WINTER ELM-AMERICAN KESTREL	950	135.00	1400.00
80	WINTER SONG-CHICKADEES	950	95.00	650.00
81	ARTIST AND HIS DOG	950	150.00	725.00
81	BRIGHT DAY-ATLANTIC PUFFINS	950	175.00	700.00
81	CANADA GEESE-NESTING	950	295.00	1750.00
81	CLEAR NIGHT-WOLVES	950	245.00	4200.00
81	COURTING PAIR-WHISTLING SWAN	950	245.00	300.00
81	COURTSHIP DISPLAY-WILD TURKEY	950	175.00	210.00
81	EDGE OF THE ICE-ERMINE	950	175.00	525.00
81	EVENING LIGHT-WHITE GYRFALCON	950	245.00	1000.00
81	GALLOPING HERD-GIRAFFES	950	175.00	1200.00
81	GRAY SQUIRREL	950	180.00	900.00
81	HIGH CAMP AT DUSK-HORSE	950	245.00	450.00
81	IN FOR THE EVENING-SHEEP	950	150.00	2000.00
81	KINGFISHER AND ASPENS	950	225.00	1200.00
81	LAST LOOK-BIGHORN SHEEP	950	195.00	200.00
81	LAUGHING GULL AND HORSESHOE CRAB	950	125.00	125.00
81	LITTLE BLUE HERON	950	95.00	300.00
81	MISTY MORNING-LOONS	950	150.00	2000.00
81	OSPREY FAMILY	950	245.00	250.00
81	PAIR OF SKIMMERS	950	150.00	200.00
81	RED-TAILED HAWK BY THE CLIFF	950	245.00	550.00
81	RED-WINGED BLACKBIRD AND RAIL FENCE	950	195.00	225.00
81	ROUGH-LEGGED HAWK IN THE ELM	950	175.00	185.00
81	ROYAL FAMILY-MUTE SWANS	950	245.00	950.00
81	SARAH E. WITH GULLS	950	245.00	3000.00
81	SHEER DROP-MOUNTAIN GOATS	950	245.00	2100.00
81	SWIFT FOX	950	175.00	1700.00
81	WATCHFUL REPOSE-BLACK BEAR	950	245.00	600.00
81	WINTER MIST-GREAT HORNED OWL	950	245.00	800.00

YR	NAME	LIMIT	ISSUE	TREND
81	WINTER WREN	950	135.00	500.00
81	WRANGLER'S CAMPSITE-GRAY JAY	950	195.00	900.00
82	ABOVE THE RIVER-TRUMPETER SWANS	950	200.00	950.00
82	ARCTIC EVENING-WHITE WOLF	950	185.00	1250.00
82	ARCTIC PORTRAIT-WHITE GYRFALCON	950	175.00	400.00
82	AT THE ROADSIDE-RED TAILED HAWK	950	185.00	1075.00
82	BAOBAB TREE AND IMPALA	950	245.00	400.00
82	BARN SWALLOWS IN AUGUST	950	245.00	425.00
82	CHEETAH PROFILE	950	245.00	400.00
82	DIPPER BY THE WATERFALL	950	165.00	600.00
82	EDGE OF THE WOODS-WHITETAIL DEER/BOOK	950	745.00	1400.00
82	FOX AT THE GRANARY	950	165.00	375.00
82	FROSTY MORNING-BLUE JAY	950	185.00	960.00
82	GALLINULE FAMILY	950	135.00	135.00
82	GENTOO PENGUINS AND WHALE BONES	950	205.00	750.00
82	GOLDEN CROWNED KINGLET W/RHODODENDRON	950	150.00	1900.00
82	LEOPARD AMBUSH	950	150.00	525.00
82	LIVELY PAIR-CHICKADEES	950	160.00	300.00
82	MEADOW'S EDGE-MALLARD	950	175.00	750.00
82	MERGANSER FAMILY IN HIDING	950	200.00	750.00
82	PILEATED WOODPECKER ON BEECH TREE	950	175.00	925.00
82	PIONEER MEMORIES-MAGPIE PAIR	950	175.00	180.00
82	POLAR BEAR PROFILE	950	210.00	2200.00
82	POLAR BEARS AT BAFFIN ISLAND	950	245.00	1200.00
82	QUEEN ANNE'S LACE/AMERICAN GOLDFINCH	950	150.00	875.00
82	READY FOR THE HUNT-SNOWY OWL	950	245.00	1000.00
82	RED SQUIRREL	950	245.00	325.00
82	RED WOLF	950	175.00	260.00
82	SPRING MARSH-PINTAIL PAIR	950	200.00	350.00
82	STILL MORNING-HERRING GULLS	950	200.00	250.00
82	WHITE WORLD-DALL SHEEP	950	200.00	650.00
82	WHITE-FOOTED MOUSE ON ASPEN	950	90.00	350.00
82	WILLET ON THE SHORE	950	125.00	175.00
83	BALD EAGLE PORTRAIT	950	185.00	400.00
83	CALL OF THE WILD-BALD EAGLE	950	200.00	200.00
83	EARLY SNOWFALL-RUFFED GROUSE	950	195.00	195.00
83	EARLY SPRING-BLUEBIRD	950	185.00	1100.00
83	EVENING IDYLL-MUTE SWANS	950	245.00	800.00
83	GHOST OF THE NORTH-GREAT GREY OWL	950	200.00	2400.00
83	GOSHAWK AND RUFFED GROUSE	950	185.00	580.00
83	GREAT HORNED OWL IN THE WHITE PINE	950	225.00	480.00
83	LOON FAMILY	950	200.00	1100.00
83	MORNING ON THE FLATS-BISON	950	200.00	400.00
83	MULE DEER IN WINTER	950	200.00	275.00
83	NEW SEASON-AMERICAN ROBIN	950	200.00	400.00
83	OSPREY IN THE RAIN	950	110.00	600.00
83	PHEASANT IN CORNFIELD	950	200.00	325.00
83	RUBY-THROAT AND COLUMBINE-HUMMINGBIRD	950	150.00	2500.00
83	SNOWY OWL ON DRIFTWOOD	950	170.00	700.00
83	SPIRITS OF THE FOREST-WOODTHRUSH	950	170.00	2200.00
83	TIGER PORTRAIT	950	130.00	500.00
83	WINTER BARN-SHEEP	950	170.00	450.00
83	WINTER LADY-CARDINAL	950	200.00	1250.00
83	WOLVES ON THE TRAIL	950	225.00	480.00
83	WOODLAND DRUMMER-RUFFED GROUSE	950	185.00	215.00
83	YOUNG ELF OWL-OLD SAGUARO	950	95.00	400.00
84	ACROSS THE SKY-SNOW GOOSE	950	220.00	950.00
84	ALONG THE RIDGE-GRIZZLY BEARS	950	200.00	980.00
84	AMERICAN GOLDFINCH-WINTER DRESS	950	75.00	135.00
84	BIG COUNTRY-PRONGHORN ANTELOPE	RT	185.00	200.00
84	COUGAR PORTRAIT	950	95.00	200.00
84	DOWN FOR A DRINK-MOURNING DOVE	950	135.00	250.00
84	HOODED MERGANSERS IN WINTER	950	210.00	450.00
84	HOUSE FINCH AND YUCCA	950	95.00	135.00
84	IN THE BRIER PATCH-COTTONTAIL	950	165.00	375.00
84	LILY PADS AND LOON	950	200.00	1400.00
84	MAY MAPLE-SCARLET TANAGER	950	175.00	725.00
84	MISTY LAKE-OSPREY	950	95.00	250.00
84	MORNING ON THE RIVER-TRUMPETER SWANS	950	185.00	350.00
84	PEREGRINE AND RUDDY TURNSTONES	950	200.00	660.00
84	READY FOR FLIGHT-PEREGRINE FALCON	950	185.00	500.00
84	RED FOX ON THE PROWL	RT	245.00	925.00
84	REEDS- STILLIFE	950	185.00	475.00
84	SMALLWOOD-LABRADOR DOG	950	200.00	500.00
84	STRETCHING-CANADA GOOSE	950	225.00	2650.00
84	SUMMER MORNING-LOON	950	185.00	1200.00
84	TADPOLE TIME	950	135.00	700.00
84	TIGER AT DAWN	950	225.00	1675.00
84	WHITE-THROATED SPARROW AND PUSSY WILLOW	950	150.00	700.00
84	WINDOW INTO ONTARIO	950	265.00	1600.00
84	WINTER SUNSET-MOOSE	950	245.00	2150.00
85	ARCTIC TERN PAIR	950	175.00	200.00
85	BEAVER POND REFLECTIONS	RT	185.00	260.00
85	CANADA GEESE FAMILY (STONE LITHO)	260	350.00	975.00
85	CANADA GEESE OVER THE ESCARPMENT	950	135.00	275.00
85	ENTERING THE WATER-COMMON GULLS	950	195.00	200.00
85	GAMBEL'S QUAIL PAIR	950	95.00	350.00
85	GIANT PANDA	*	245.00	725.00
85	GOLDEN EAGLE PORTRAIT	950	115.00	175.00

YR	NAME	LIMIT	ISSUE	TREND
85	IN THE HIGHLANDS-GOLDEN EAGLE	950	235.00	375.00
85	IN THE MOUNTAINS-OSPREY	950	95.00	180.00
85	IRISH COTTAGE AND WAGTAIL	950	175.00	325.00
85	LEOPARD AT SERONERA	950	175.00	360.00
85	LIONS IN THE GRASS	950	265.00	950.00
85	MORNING DEW-ROE DEER	950	175.00	175.00
85	OLD WHALING BASE AND FUR SEALS	950	195.00	275.00
85	ON THE GARDEN WALL-CHAFFINCH	950	115.00	275.00
85	ORCA PROCESSION	950	245.00	2525.00
85	PEREGRINE FALCON & WHITE-THROATED SWIFTS	950	245.00	950.00
85	SNOWY HEMLOCK-BARRED OWL	950	245.00	250.00
85	STREAM BANK-JUNE-BIRD	950	160.00	175.00
85	STRUTTING-RING-NECKED PHEASANT	950	225.00	500.00
85	SUDDEN BLIZZARD-RED-TAILED HAWK	950	245.00	550.00
85	TRUMPETER SWANS AND ASPEN	950	245.00	470.00
85	WEATHERED BRANCH-BALD EAGLE	950	115.00	300.00
85	WHITE-BREASTED NUTHATCH ON A BEECH TREE	950	175.00	200.00
85	WINGED SPIRIT - 2 PC. SNOWY OWL	*	*	425.00
85	WINTER COMPANION-YELLOW LAB. DOG	950	175.00	775.00
85	WOOD BISON PORTRAIT	950	165.00	250.00
86	A RESTING PLACE-CAPE BUFFALO	950	265.00	265.00
86	BLACK EAGLE	RT	200.00	200.00
86	BLACK-TAILED DEER IN THE OLYMPICS	RT	245.00	225.00
86	BLACKSMITH PLOVER	RT	185.00	185.00
86	CANADA GEESE WITH YOUNG	950	195.00	275.00
86	CHARGING RHINO	950	325.00	850.00
86	DARK GYRFALCON	950	225.00	300.00
86	DRIFTWOOD PERCH-STRIPED SWALLOWS	950	195.00	200.00
86	ELEPHANT HERD AND SANDGROUSE	950	235.00	375.00
86	EUROPEAN ROBIN AND HYDRANGEAS	950	130.00	350.00
86	FENCE POST AND BURDOCK	950	130.00	275.00
86	HOUSE SPARROW	950	125.00	180.00
86	HUMMINGBIRD PAIR (DIPTYCH)	950	330.00	700.00
86	IN THE GRASS-LIONESS	950	245.00	245.00
86	MALLARD FAMILY-MISTY MARSH	950	130.00	175.00
86	MALLARD PAIR-EARLY WINTER	41740	135.00	200.00
86	MALLARD PAIR-EARLY WINTER (24K GOLD)	950	1,650.00	2000.00
86	MALLARD PAIR-EARLY WINTER (GOLD)	7691	250.00	375.00
86	MARGINAL MEADOW-LANDSCAPE	950	220.00	220.00
86	MOOSE AT WATER'S EDGE	950	130.00	250.00
86	MULE DEER IN ASPEN	950	175.00	175.00
86	NORTHERN REFLECTIONS-LOON FAMILY	8631	255.00	1790.00
86	PROUD SWIMMER-SNOW GOOSE	950	185.00	185.00
86	RESTING PLACE-CAPE BUFFALO	950	265.00	265.00
86	ROBINS AT THE NEST	950	185.00	225.00
86	SPLIT RAILS-SNOW BUNTINGS	950	220.00	220.00
86	SUMMERTIME-POLAR BEARS	950	225.00	300.00
86	SWIFT FOX STUDY	950	115.00	250.00
86	WILDEBEEST	950	185.00	185.00
86	WINTER IN THE MOUNTAINS-RAVEN	950	200.00	200.00
87	AT THE NEST-SECRETARY BIRDS	950	290.00	290.00
87	CONTINUING GENERATIONS-SPOTTED OWLS	950	525.00	700.00
87	END OF SEASON-GRIZZLY	950	325.00	700.00
87	EVERGLADES-EGRET	950	360.00	350.00
87	FARM LANE AND BLUE JAYS	950	225.00	400.00
87	GOLDFINCH WITH MULLEIN	*	225.00	225.00
87	GREAT BLUE HERON IN FLIGHT	950	295.00	950.00
87	GREAT EGRET PREENING	950	315.00	800.00
87	GREATER KUDU BULL	950	145.00	145.00
87	HIGH KINGDOM-SNOW LEOPARD	950	325.00	725.00
87	HOUSE SPARROWS AND BITTERSWEET	950	220.00	425.00
87	HURRICANE LAKE-WOOD DUCKS	950	135.00	200.00
87	KING PENGUINS	950	130.00	225.00
87	LATE WINTER-BLACK SQUIRREL	950	165.00	175.00
87	LION AND WILDEBEEST	950	265.00	265.00
87	LIONESS AT SERENGETI	950	325.00	325.00
87	OLD WILLOW AND MALLARDS	950	325.00	350.00
87	OTTER STUDY	950	235.00	400.00
87	PEREGRINE FALCON/CLIFF (STONE LITHO)	525	350.00	730.00
87	PICNIC TABLE	*	250.00	250.00
87	PLOWED FIELD-SNOWY OWL	290	145.00	300.00
87	PRIDE OF AUTUMN	RT	135.00	500.00
87	PRIDE OF AUTUMN-CANADA GOOSE	950	135.00	200.00
87	RHINO AT NGORO NGORO	950	325.00	325.00
87	ROCKY POINT-OCTOBER-BOAT	950	195.00	450.00
87	RUDDY TURNSTONES	950	175.00	175.00
87	SNOWY OWL AND MILKWEED	950	235.00	700.00
87	STONE SHEEP RAM	950	175.00	175.00
87	SYLVAN STREAM-MUTE SWANS	950	125.00	175.00
87	VERMILION FLYCATCHER	*	95.00	115.00
87	WISE ONE, THE-ELEPHANT	950	325.00	750.00
88	CARDINAL AND WILD APPLES	950	235.00	240.00
88	CATTAILS, FIREWEED,YELLOWTHROAT WARBLER	950	235.00	290.00
88	CHALLENGE, THE-BULL MOOSE	10671	325.00	350.00
88	CHERRYWOOD WITH JUNCOS	950	245.00	250.00
88	COLONIAL GARDEN-LANDSCAPE	950	245.00	600.00
88	DOZING LYNX	950	335.00	1500.00
88	FIRST ARRIVAL-KILLDEER	*	265.00	265.00
88	GRASSY BANK-GREAT BLUE HERON	950	285.00	285.00

YR	NAME	LIMIT	ISSUE	TREND
88	GREAT CRESTED GREBE	950	135.00	135.00
88	HARDWOOD FOREST-WHITE TAILED BUCK	950	345.00	1700.00
88	HARLEQUIN DUCK-BULL KELP (EXEC.)	950	550.00	550.00
88	HARLEQUIN DUCK-BULL KELP (GOLD)	950	300.00	300.00
88	LEOPARD AND THOMSON GAZELLE KILL	950	275.00	275.00
88	MALLARD FAMILY AT SUNSET	950	235.00	235.00
88	MUSKOKA LAKE-COMMON LOONS	950	265.00	325.00
88	PANDAS AT PLAY (STONE LITHO)	160	400.00	1225.00
88	PHEASANTS AT DUSK	950	325.00	575.00
88	PREENING PAIR-CANADA GEESE	950	235.00	240.00
88	RED CROSSBILLS	950	125.00	130.00
88	SHELTER-RURAL LANDSCAPE	950	325.00	1075.00
88	TAWNY OWL IN BEECH	950	325.00	325.00
88	TREE SWALLOW OVER POND	950	290.00	290.00
88	YOUNG SANDHILL CRANES	950	325.00	325.00
89	BACKLIGHT-MUTE SWAN	950	275.00	510.00
89	BARN SWALLOW AND HORSE COLLAR	950	225.00	225.00
89	BROAD-TAILED HUMMINGBIRD PAIR	950	225.00	225.00
89	CATCHING THE LIGHT-BARN OWL	RT	295.00	295.00
89	CENTENNIAL FARM	950	295.00	300.00
89	DISPUTE OVER PREY	950	325.00	325.00
89	DISTANT DANGER-RACCOON	1600	225.00	225.00
89	EVENING CALL-COMMON LOON	950	235.00	500.00
89	GOLDFINCH IN THE MEADOW	1600	150.00	160.00
89	MANGROVE MORNING-ROSEATE SPOONBILLS	2000	325.00	400.00
89	MIDNIGHT-BLACK WOLF	25352	325.00	2000.00
89	NEAR GLENBURNIE-ROCK	950	265.00	265.00
89	PUMPKIN TIME	950	195.00	270.00
89	VULTURE AND WILDEBEEST	550	295.00	295.00
89	YOUNG KITTIWAKE-BIRD	950	195.00	195.00
89	YOUNG SNOWY OWL	950	195.00	195.00
90	AIR, THE FOREST & THE WATCH	42500	325.00	335.00
90	CHINSTRAP PENGUIN	810	150.00	175.00
90	HOMAGE TO AHMED-ELEPHANT	290	3,300.00	3300.00
90	IRELAND HOUSE-LANDSCAPE	950	265.00	345.00
90	KEEPER OF THE LAND-GRIZZLY	290	3,300.00	3300.00
90	LUNGING HERON	1250	225.00	225.00
90	MORNING COVE-COMMON LOON	950	165.00	200.00
90	MOSSY BRANCHES-SPOTTED OWL	4500	300.00	475.00
90	MOWED MEADOW	950	190.00	190.00
90	PEACEFUL FLOCK-AMERICAN WIGEON	*	225.00	325.00
90	PINTAILS IN SPRING	9651	135.00	400.00
90	POLAR BEAR	290	3,300.00	3300.00
90	POWERPLAY-RHINOCEROS	950	320.00	390.00
90	ROLLING WAVES-LESSER SCAUP	3330	125.00	125.00
90	SNOW LEOPARD	290	2,500.00	2500.00
90	SUMMER MORNING PASTURE-COWS	290	175.00	175.00
90	WHITE ON WHITE-SNOWSHOE HARE	290	195.00	500.00
91	ARCTIC CLIFF-WHITE WOLVES	13000	184.00	1300.00
91	ARCTIC CLIFF-WHITE WOLVES (CONSERV.)	13000	325.00	440.00
91	ARCTIC CLIFF-WHITE WOLVES (PREMIER ED.)	*	625.00	625.00
91	AT THE CLIFF-BOBCAT	RT	325.00	325.00
91	AT THE CLIFF-BOBCAT (SIGNATURE ED.)	*	400.00	400.00
91	BLUEBIRD AND BLOSSOMS	4500	235.00	275.00
91	BLUEBIRD AND BLOSSOMS (PRESTIGE ED.)	450	625.00	625.00
91	CEREMONIAL POSE-JAPANESE CRANE	*	*	3300.00
91	COTTAGE LANE-RED FOX	950	285.00	285.00
91	ELEPHANT COW AND CALF	950	300.00	600.00
91	ENCOUNTER IN THE BUSH-AFRICAN LIONS	950	295.00	350.00
91	ENDANGERED SPACES-GRIZZLY	4008	325.00	330.00
91	ENDANGERED SPACES-ROYAL-BEAR	*	925.00	2250.00
91	FLUID POWER-ORCA	290	2,500.00	2500.00
91	GULLS ON PILINGS	1950	265.00	325.00
91	MANGROVE SHADOW-COMMON EGRET	1250	285.00	285.00
91	SCOLDING, THE-CHICKADEES AND SCREECH OWL	*	235.00	400.00
91	SEA OTTER STUDY	*	150.00	225.00
91	TRUMPETER SWAN FAMILY	290	2,500.00	2500.00
91	WHISTLING SWAN-LAKE ERIE	1950	325.00	325.00
91	WIDE HORIZON-TUNDRA SWANS	2862	325.00	325.00
91	WIDE HORIZON-TUNDRA SWANS COMPANION	2862	325.00	325.00
91	YOUNG GIRAFFE	290	850.00	2000.00
92	ARCTIC LANDSCAPE-POLAR BEAR	5000	345.00	380.00
92	ARCTIC LANDSCAPE-POLAR BEAR, PREM. ED.	450	800.00	800.00
92	AT THE FEEDER-CARDINAL	950	125.00	200.00
92	BEACH GRASS & TREE FROG	1250	345.00	345.00
92	CANADA GOOSE	*	450.00	500.00
92	CLAN OF THE RAVEN	950	235.00	535.00
92	CRIES OF COURTSHIP-CRANE	950	350.00	690.00
92	INTRUSION-MOUNTAIN GORILLA	2250	325.00	400.00
92	JUNCO IN WINTER	1250	185.00	225.00
92	PREDATOR PORTFOLIO-COUGAR	950	465.00	1400.00
92	SIBERIAN TIGER	4500	325.00	325.00
92	SIBERIAN TIGER - PRESTIGE	*	625.00	625.00
92	TEMBO-ELEPHANT	1550	350.00	450.00
92	WHITE TAILED DEER THROUGH BIRCH	10000	335.00	335.00
92	WINTER COAT-LANDSCAPE	1250	245.00	245.00
93	CARDINAL & SUMAC	2500	235.00	235.00
93	DAY LILIES AND DRAGONFLIES	1250	345.00	345.00
93	GOLDEN-HEADED LION TAMARIN	*	350.00	350.00

YR	NAME	LIMIT	ISSUE	TREND
93	GRIZZLY AND CUBS	2250	335.00	350.00
93	KESTREL AND GRASSHOPPER	1250	335.00	335.00
93	MARBLED MURRELET-DUCK	55	1,200.00	1200.00
93	ON THE BRINK-RIVER OTTERS	1250	345.00	500.00
93	PREDATOR PORTFOLIO-GRIZZLY	950	475.00	475.00
93	PREDATOR PORTFOLIO-POLAR BEAR	950	485.00	485.00
93	PREDATOR PORTFOLIO-WOLF	950	475.00	475.00
93	RECLINING SNOW LEOPARD	1250	335.00	600.00
93	RIVER OTTER	290	1,500.00	1500.00
93	ROSE-BREASTED GROSBEAK	290	450.00	450.00
93	SAW WHET OWL & WILD GRAPES	950	185.00	185.00
93	SHADOWS OF THE RAINFOREST	RT	345.00	600.00
93	VIGILANCE	9500	330.00	330.00
94	IN HIS PRIME-MALLARD DUCK	950	195.00	325.00
94	MERU DUCK - LESSER KUDUS	950	135.00	135.00
94	PATH OF THE PANTHER	1950	295.00	295.00
94	PREDATOR PORTFOLIO-BLACK BEAR	950	475.00	475.00
94	SALT SPRING SHEEP	1250	235.00	275.00
94	SIERRA EVENING-MEXICAN WOLF	*	285.00	285.00
94	SNOWY NAP-TIGER	RT	185.00	1400.00
94	SNOWY OWL	150	265.00	700.00
94	WINTER PINE- G/H OWL		265.00	265.00
94	WINTER RUN-BULL MOOSE	*	295.00	295.00
94	WOLF PAIR IN THE SNOW	290	795.00	1400.00
95	SPARRING ELEPHANTS	*	325.00	325.00

A. BRACKENBURY

YR	NAME	LIMIT	ISSUE	TREND
83	GREAT EXPECTATIONS	950	40.00	350.00
83	UNDER THE RED TWIGS-COTTONTAIL	950	40.00	150.00
84	CATTAILS	950	60.00	100.00
84	COTTONTAIL FAMILY-RABBIT	*	40.00	50.00
84	FIRST EXCURSION-CHICKEN	*	*	75.00
84	GRIZZLY IN CHOKEBERRIES	*	60.00	100.00
85	CRAB APPLE CRAVING-SQUIRREL	*	60.00	75.00
85	PROWLING BANDITS-RACCOONS	*	50.00	75.00
85	SLED DOGS	950	50.00	175.00
85	TOADALLY CAPTIVATED-DOG	950	60.00	135.00
86	CHILLY DOG-YELLOW LAB	*	75.00	75.00
87	STONE LYIN'-CAT	*	85.00	125.00
88	CAT IN THE MAIZE	*	80.00	100.00
88	CHOCOLATE CLUSTER-CHOCOLATE LAB	*	80.00	125.00
88	CORN DOGS-LAB. DOG	*	85.00	85.00
88	FEATHERBRAIN-LAB. DOG	*	80.00	225.00
88	POLE CAT	*	85.00	100.00
89	BASKET CASE-PUPPIES	950	95.00	95.00
89	BUREAUCATS-KITTENS	*	95.00	95.00
89	RED TAPE-LAB. DOG	950	95.00	95.00
89	WINTER COAT-GOLDEN RETRIEVER	*	85.00	110.00
90	PUPULATION EXPLOSION-BLK VARI.-COCKER	950	95.00	125.00
90	PUPULATION EXPLOSION-GLD VARI.-COCKER	950	95.00	125.00
90	WAGGIN' TAILS-PUPPIES	950	95.00	95.00
91	DAWN ON THE BEACH-SNOWY EGRET	*	95.00	95.00

C. BRENDERS

YR	NAME	LIMIT	ISSUE	TREND
*	BROKEN SILENCE-FAWNS	*	195.00	225.00
*	BUTTERFLY COLLECTION - 2ND	*	375.00	375.00
*	BUTTERFLY COLLECTION - 3RD	*	375.00	375.00
*	CLOSE-UP, JAGUAR	*	110.00	110.00
*	DEN MOTHER - MOTHER WOLF	*	135.00	135.00
*	DEN MOTHER-PREMIER-WOLF	*	700.00	775.00
*	FULL HOUSE-PREMIER ED.- FOXES	*	900.00	900.00
*	GOSLING STUDY	*	35.00	35.00
*	HUNTER'S DREAM-ELK	*	950.00	1400.00
*	MONARCH IS ALIVE-PREMIER-EAGLE	*	900.00	900.00
*	POLAR BEAR CUB STUDY	*	35.00	35.00
*	WREN STUDY	*	35.00	35.00
84	ON THE ALERT-RED FOX	950	95.00	400.00
84	PLAYFUL PAIR-CHIPMUNKS	950	40.00	525.00
84	SILENT HUNTER-GREAT HORNED OWL	950	95.00	550.00
84	SILENT PASSAGE-COUGAR	950	150.00	500.00
84	WATERSIDE ENCOUNTER-RACCOON	950	95.00	1400.00
85	MIGHTY INTRUDER-BLACK BEAR	950	95.00	325.00
86	ACROBATS MEAL, THE-RED SQUIRREL	950	65.00	440.00
86	BLACK-CAPPED CHICKADEES	950	40.00	700.00
86	BLUEBIRDS	950	40.00	240.00
86	COLORFUL PLAYGROUND-COTTONTAILS	950	75.00	1000.00
86	DISTURBED DAYDREAMS	950	95.00	420.00
86	GOLDEN SEASON-GRAY SQUIRREL	950	85.00	850.00
86	HARVEST TIME-CHIPMUNK	950	65.00	400.00
86	LATE SNOW-GREAT BLUE HERON	*	90.00	125.00
86	MEADOWLARK	1250	165.00	300.00
86	ROBINS	950	40.00	125.00
87	AUTUMN LADY-DEER	950	150.00	975.00
87	CLOSE TO MOM-BEAR	950	150.00	1600.00
87	DOUBLE TROUBLE-RACCOONS	950	120.00	800.00
87	IVORY BILLED WOODPECKER	RT	95.00	1050.00
87	MIGRATION FEVER-BARN SWALLOWS	950	150.00	475.00
87	MYSTERIOUS VISITOR-BARN OWL	950	150.00	700.00
87	SILENT PASSAGE-LION	*	400.00	500.00
87	UNDER THE PINE TREES-CHIPMUNKS	*	65.00	180.00
87	WHITE ELEGANCE-TRUMPETER SWANS	950	115.00	575.00

YR	NAME	LIMIT	ISSUE	TREND
87	YELLOW-BELLIED MARMOT	950	95.00	500.00
88	A HUNTER'S DREAM	950	165.00	1400.00
88	APPLE HARVEST	950	115.00	440.00
88	CALIFORNIA QUAIL	*	95.00	400.00
88	FOREST SENTINEL-BOBCAT	950	135.00	600.00
88	HIDDEN IN THE PINES-GREAT HORNED OWL	950	175.00	1250.00
88	HIGH ADVENTURE-BLACK BEAR CUBS	950	105.00	380.00
88	LONG DISTANCE HUNTERS-WOLF	1250	175.00	1500.00
88	ROAMING THE PLAINS-PRONGHORNS	*	150.00	250.00
88	TALK ON THE OLD FENCE	950	165.00	1000.00
88	WITNESS OF A PAST-BISON	*	110.00	110.00
89	A YOUNG GENERATION-RABBIT	1250	165.00	225.00
89	APPLE LOVER, THE-ROBIN	1500	125.00	600.00
89	COMPANIONS, THE-WOLF	18036	200.00	675.00
89	FORAGER'S REWARD-RED SQUIRREL	*	135.00	140.00
89	LORD OF THE MARSHES-BLUE HERON	950	40.00	175.00
89	MERLINS AT THE NEST	1250	165.00	400.00
89	NORTHERN COUSINS-BLACK SQUIRREL	950	95.00	250.00
89	PREDATORS WALK, THE-COUGAR	*	150.00	300.00
89	RED-WINGED BLACKBIRDS	*	40.00	150.00
89	STELLER'S JAY	1250	135.00	160.00
89	SURVIVORS, THE-CANADA GEESE	*	225.00	560.00
90	A THREATENED SYMBOL-BALD EAGLE	1950	145.00	300.00
90	BLOND BEAUTY-HORSE	RT	185.00	185.00
90	FULL HOUSE-FOX FAMILY	20106	235.00	275.00
90	GHOSTLY QUIET-SPANISH LYNX	RT	200.00	200.00
90	MONARCH IS ALIVE,THE-EAGLE	RT	265.00	325.00
90	MOUNTAIN BABY-BIGHORN SHEEP	1950	165.00	165.00
90	ON THE OLD FARM DOOR-BLUEBIRD	1500	225.00	225.00
90	SHORELINE QUARTET-WHITE IBIS	1950	265.00	265.00
90	SMALL TALK	1500	125.00	150.00
90	SPRING FAWN	1500	125.00	225.00
90	SQUIRREL'S DISH	1950	110.00	110.00
91	BALANCE OF NATURE, THE-HAWK & RABBIT	1950	225.00	275.00
91	CALM BEFORE THE CHALLENGE-MOOSE	RT	225.00	225.00
91	NESTING SEASON, THE-HOUSE SPARROW	1950	195.00	200.00
91	ONE TO ONE - GRAY WOLF STUDY	*	120.00	275.00
91	ONE TO ONE-GRAY WOLF	10000	245.00	500.00
91	SHADOWS IN THE GRASS (PRESTIGE ED.)	*	*	450.00
91	SHADOWS IN THE GRASS-YOUNG COUGARS	*	*	235.00
91	WOLF STUDY	RT	125.00	125.00
92	DEN MOTHER - WOLF FAMILY	2500	250.00	325.00
92	ISLAND SHORES - SNOWY EGRET	2500	250.00	275.00
92	PATHFINDER - RED FOX	5000	245.00	250.00
92	RED FOX STUDY	1250	125.00	125.00
92	ROCKY KINGDOM - BIGHORN SHEEP	1750	255.00	255.00
92	SNOW LEOPARD PORTRAIT	1750	150.00	150.00
92	WOLF SCOUT #1-WOLF CUB	2500	105.00	105.00
92	WOLF SCOUT #2-WOLF CUB	2500	105.00	135.00
93	BLACK SPHINX	950	235.00	235.00
93	BUTTERFLY COLLECTION, THE	*	375.00	375.00
93	IN THE NORTHERN HUNTING GROUNDS	1750	375.00	375.00
93	MOTHER OF PEARLS-POLAR BEAR	5000	275.00	350.00
93	NARROW ESCAPE - CHIPMUNK	1750	150.00	150.00
93	ROCKY CAMP - COUGAR (GICLEE)	*	500.00	500.00
93	ROCKY CAMP - COUGAR FAMILY	5000	275.00	430.00
93	ROCKY CAMP CUBS	950	225.00	225.00
93	SUMMER ROSES - WINTER WREN	*	425.00	750.00
94	DALL SHEEP PORTRAIT	950	115.00	130.00
94	FOREST CARPENTER-PILEATED-WOODPECKER	*	195.00	195.00
94	POWER AND GRACE-DEER	*	525.00	900.00
94	RIVERBANK KESTREL	*	325.00	615.00
94	TAKE FIVE - CANADA LYNX	*	340.00	525.00
94	TUNDRA SUMMIT-ARCTIC WOLVES	*	340.00	400.00
95	FAMILY TREE, THE-OWLS	*	225.00	300.00

P. CALLE

YR	NAME	LIMIT	ISSUE	TREND
*	EARLY ARRIVALS	*	245.00	245.00
*	LONELY WATCH	*	100.00	150.00
*	PAUSE FOR A DRINK	*	100.00	100.00
*	THEY CALL ME WILLIAM	*	265.00	265.00
*	TRAIL BOSS	*	100.00	150.00
80	CARING FOR THE HERD	RT	110.00	110.00
80	CHIEF HIGH PIPE (PENCIL)	950	75.00	200.00
80	CHIEF JOSEPH-MAN OF PEACE	950	135.00	160.00
80	LANDMARK TREE	950	125.00	275.00
80	PRAYER TO THE GREAT MYSTERY	950	245.00	250.00
80	SIOUX CHIEF	RT	85.00	130.00
80	SOMETHING FOR THE POT	950	175.00	1650.00
80	VIEW FROM THE HEIGHTS	950	245.00	250.00
80	WHEN SNOW CAME EARLY	950	85.00	625.00
80	WINTER HUNTER, THE (PENCIL)	950	65.00	360.00
81	ALMOST HOME	950	150.00	150.00
81	AND STILL MILES TO GO	950	245.00	480.00
81	ANDREW AT THE FALLS	950	150.00	150.00
81	CHIEF HIGH PIPE (COLOR)	950	265.00	400.00
81	END OF A LONG DAY	RT	150.00	200.00
81	FRESH TRACKS	RT	150.00	165.00
81	FRIENDS	RT	150.00	150.00
81	JUST OVER THE RIDGE	950	245.00	245.00

The setting sun reflected in the water, the warm light of a cozy room and the smoke from the chimney represent the Comforts of Home by Terry Redlin. The 1991 Hadley House release was issued at $175 and is currently valued at $570.

A 1994 release by V.F. Fine Arts, Dear Santa by Sandra Kuck captures the innocence of a child at Christmastime.

YR	NAME	LIMIT	ISSUE	TREND
81	ONE WITH THE LAND	950	245.00	250.00
81	PAUSE AT THE LOWER FALLS	950	110.00	275.00
81	TETON FRIENDS	950	150.00	240.00
81	WINTER HUNTER, THE (COLOR)	950	245.00	975.00
82	BREATH OF FRIENDSHIP, THE	950	225.00	275.00
82	EMERGING FROM THE WOODS	RT	110.00	110.00
82	GENERATIONS IN THE VALLEY	RT	245.00	245.00
82	RETURN TO CAMP	950	245.00	540.00
82	TWO FROM THE FLOCK	950	245.00	700.00
83	A WINTER'S SURPRISE	950	195.00	700.00
83	COMPANIONS	*	150.00	200.00
83	FREE SPIRITS	950	195.00	480.00
83	IN SEARCH OF BEAVER	950	225.00	950.00
83	STRAYS FROM THE FLYWAY	950	195.00	275.00
84	BRACE FOR THE SPIT	950	110.00	850.00
84	CHANCE ENCOUNTER	950	225.00	360.00
84	FATE OF THE LATE MIGRANT	950	110.00	550.00
84	HEAR ME O' GREAT SPIRIT	*	175.00	275.00
84	MOUNTAIN MAN, THE	950	95.00	200.00
84	TRAPPER, THE	*	95.00	140.00
84	WHEN TRAILS CROSS	950	245.00	1500.00
85	CARRYING PLACE, THE	RT	195.00	330.00
85	GRANDMOTHER, THE	950	150.00	200.00
85	STORYTELLER OF THE MOUNTAINS	950	225.00	1150.00
86	FUR TRAPPER, THE	*	75.00	150.00
86	SNOW HUNTER, THE	950	150.00	250.00
87	IN THE LAND OF THE GIANTS	950	245.00	1115.00
87	INTO THE GREAT ALONE	950	245.00	1050.00
88	NEW DAY, A	950	150.00	200.00
88	VOYAGEURS & WATERFOWL	RT	265.00	975.00
89	AND A GOOD BOOK FOR COMPANY	950	135.00	620.00
89	BEAVER MEN, THE	950	125.00	175.00
89	GREAT MOMENT, THE	950	350.00	350.00
89	MOUNTAIN MEN, THE (LITHO)	RT	400.00	400.00
89	NAVAJO MADONNA	650	95.00	95.00
89	WHERE EAGLES FLY	*	265.00	475.00
89	WINTER FEAST	1250	265.00	440.00
90	CHILDREN OF WALPI	350	160.00	160.00
90	DOLL MAKER, THE	950	95.00	95.00
90	INTERRUPTED JOURNEY	1750	265.00	350.00
90	INTERRUPTED JOURNEY (PRESTIGE ED.)	RT	465.00	465.00
90	SON OF SITTING BULL	950	95.00	95.00
91	ALMOST THERE	RT	165.00	325.00
91	IN THE BEGINNING...FRIENDS	RT	250.00	360.00
91	MAN OF THE FUR TRADE	550	110.00	115.00
91	SILENCED HONKERS, THE	1250	250.00	265.00
91	THEY CALL ME MATTHEW	950	125.00	140.00
91	WHEN TRAILS GROW COLD	2500	265.00	275.00
91	WHEN TRAILS GROW COLD (PRESTIGE ED.)	RT	465.00	465.00
94	WHEN TRAPPERS MEET (PENCIL)	750	165.00	225.00

J. DALY

YR	NAME	LIMIT	ISSUE	TREND
*	A GIFT OF TIME-SCHOOL TEACHER	*	145.00	200.00
*	ANNIE'S RAGGEDY	*	75.00	350.00
*	MARSHALL, THE	*	150.00	150.00
*	MY BEST FRIENDS	*	140.00	140.00
*	SATURDAY MORNING	*	150.00	150.00
80	SUNDAY MORNING		350.00	160.00
82	SPRING FEVER	950	85.00	675.00
83	SATURDAY NIGHT	950	85.00	1450.00
86	FLYING HIGH-CHILDREN	950	50.00	450.00
87	FAVORITE READER-BOY	RT	85.00	350.00
87	ODD MAN OUT-BOY	RT	85.00	425.00
88	ON THIN ICE-BOY ICE SKATING	RT	95.00	275.00
88	TERRITORIAL RIGHTS-BOY	950	85.00	425.00
88	TIE BREAKER-CHECKERS	950	95.00	320.00
88	WIPED OUT-MARBLES	1250	125.00	500.00
89	IN THE DOGHOUSE-BOY/DOG	1500	75.00	380.00
89	LET'S PLAY BALL-BOY/DOG	1500	75.00	200.00
89	THIEF, THE-BOY/DOG	1500	95.00	400.00
89	THORN, THE	1500	125.00	450.00
90	BIG MOMENT, THE-CLOWN W/CHILD	1500	125.00	130.00
90	CONFRONTATION	1500	85.00	90.00
90	CONTENTMENT	1500	95.00	400.00
90	HONOR AND ALLEGIANCE	1500	110.00	160.00
90	ICE MAN, THE-BOY	1500	125.00	375.00
90	IT'S THAT TIME AGAIN	1500	120.00	120.00
90	MAKE BELIEVE-LITTLE GIRLS	RT	75.00	400.00
90	RADIO DAZE	1500	150.00	150.00
90	SCHOLAR, THE	1500	110.00	130.00
91	A NEW BEGINNING	5000	125.00	125.00
91	CAT'S CRADLE	950	450.00	450.00
91	HOME TEAM: ZERO-BASEBALL	1500	150.00	165.00
91	HOMEMADE	1500	125.00	200.00
91	PILLARS OF A NATION-ELLIS ISLAND	20000	175.00	175.00
91	TIME-OUT-CHILDREN	RT	125.00	125.00
92	WALKING THE RAILS	1500	175.00	175.00
93	TO ALL A GOOD NIGHT	1500	160.00	160.00
94	CATCH OF MY DREAMS	4500	45.00	50.00
94	MUD MATES	950	150.00	150.00

YR	NAME	LIMIT	ISSUE	TREND
94	SLUGGER	950	75.00	85.00
94	WIND-UP, THE	950	75.00	85.00
95	A GIFT OF TIME	*	145.00	200.00
N. ENGLE				
81	HOUSE BY THE SEA	950	75.00	1000.00
81	WILDERNESS MARSH	950	75.00	330.00
83	MORNING ON THE YELLOWDOG RIVER	950	75.00	700.00
83	QUIET WATERS	950	75.00	100.00
83	SUMMER RIVER	950	75.00	600.00
83	WILD OCTOBER	*	75.00	400.00
83	WINTER BROOK	*	75.00	75.00
84	APRIL LIGHT	*	*	125.00
84	AUTUMN BLUEBERRIES	950	75.00	125.00
84	EVENING HARBOR	950	75.00	150.00
84	ISLAND HOME	*	75.00	140.00
84	ISLAND LAKE	950	95.00	150.00
84	LOST CREEK	*	15.00	125.00
84	MARCH THAW	*	95.00	175.00
84	MELTING INTO SPRING	*	95.00	100.00
84	MIDDLE ISLAND POINT	*	115.00	195.00
84	PEACEFUL MORNING-CANADAS	*	50.00	50.00
85	AUTUMN GOLD	*	85.00	160.00
85	AUTUMN RIVER	*	50.00	120.00
85	GREAT PASSAGE	*	175.00	225.00
85	GROUSE COUNTRY	950	85.00	100.00
85	HEMLOCK MARSH	*	115.00	230.00
85	MISTY ISLE	*	150.00	180.00
85	MOUNTAIN COVE	*	125.00	160.00
85	SALTY DOG	*	95.00	170.00
85	WILD ROSE MARSH	950	95.00	800.00
86	SUNSET SWAMP	*	75.00	75.00
87	FISHERMAN AT DAWN	*	95.00	135.00
87	MOUNTAIN MEADOW	*	95.00	620.00
87	SAFE HARBOR	*	95.00	100.00
88	DEEP WOODS WINTER	*	95.00	125.00
88	EDGE OF WINTER-LAKE SUPERIOR	*	150.00	180.00
88	FOREST POOL	*	110.00	180.00
88	LIGHT IN THE WILLOWS-GREAT WHITE HERON	*	145.00	145.00
88	VICTORIAN SPRING-GRAND HOTEL	*	150.00	170.00
89	BRIGHT RIVER	950	150.00	150.00
89	CARRIAGE WAITING	950	75.00	135.00
89	DAISY BAY	*	150.00	900.00
89	FIRST COLOR	*	135.00	180.00
89	GOLDEN BEACH	*	110.00	160.00
90	AFTERNOON VISITOR	950	75.00	150.00
90	FEEDER STREAM	950	150.00	195.00
90	WILD ROSES BY THE SEA	*	150.00	650.00
F. MACHETANZ				
78	FACE TO FACE	950	150.00	2100.00
78	HUNTER'S DAWN	950	125.00	580.00
78	INTO THE HOME STRETCH	950	175.00	700.00
79	BEGINNINGS	950	175.00	400.00
79	DECISIONS ON THE ICE FIELD	950	150.00	475.00
79	PICK OF THE LITTER	950	165.00	250.00
79	REACHING THE CAMPSITE	950	200.00	400.00
80	KING OF THE MOUNTAIN	950	200.00	330.00
80	NELCHINA TRAIL	950	245.00	350.00
80	SOURDOUGH	950	245.00	1100.00
80	WHEN THREE'S A CROWD	950	225.00	850.00
81	GOLDEN YEARS	950	245.00	625.00
81	MIDDAY MOONLIGHT	950	265.00	425.00
81	WHAT EVERY HUNTER FEARS	950	245.00	1300.00
81	WHERE MEN AND DOGS SEEM SMALL	950	245.00	700.00
81	WINTER HARVEST	950	265.00	1000.00
82	MIGHTY HUNTER	950	265.00	775.00
82	MOONLIGHT STAKEOUT	950	265.00	650.00
82	MOOSE TRACKS	950	265.00	475.00
82	TENDER ARCTIC, THE	950	295.00	775.00
83	NANOOK	950	295.00	295.00
83	THEY OPENED THE NORTH COUNTRY	950	245.00	300.00
84	END OF A LONG DAY-POLAR BEAR	950	200.00	400.00
84	MANY MILES TOGETHER-ESKIMO	950	245.00	245.00
84	MIDNIGHT WATCH	950	250.00	250.00
84	SMOKE DREAMS	950	250.00	400.00
84	STORY OF THE BEADS	950	245.00	300.00
85	END OF THE HUNT-ESKIMO	950	245.00	325.00
85	LAND OF THE MIDNIGHT SUN-POLAR BEAR	950	245.00	300.00
85	LANGUAGE OF THE SNOW-ESKIMO	950	195.00	275.00
85	REACHING THE PASS-DOG SLED	950	265.00	975.00
86	KYROK-ESKIMO SEAMSTRESS	950	225.00	225.00
86	LEAVING THE NEST-POLAR BEAR	950	245.00	300.00
86	LONE MUSHER-ALASKA	950	245.00	245.00
86	MT. BLACKBURN-SOVEREIGN OF THE WRANGELLS	950	245.00	330.00
86	SON OF THE NORTH-ESKIMO	*	175.00	400.00
87	SPRING FEVER-POLAR BEAR	950	225.00	225.00
87	START OF THE DAY-ALASKA	*	200.00	200.00
87	TRAIL THROUGH THE PRESSURE ICE-ALASKA	*	*	225.00
88	CHANGE OF DIRECTION W/MEDAL	950	320.00	350.00
88	TENSE MOMENT-POLAR BEAR	*	200.00	325.00

YR	NAME	LIMIT	ISSUE	TREND
88	VETERAN OF THE TRAIL-DOG SLED	*	175.00	200.00
88	WHALING LOOKOUT-ESKIMO WHALING	*	*	195.00
89	CHIEF DANCES, THE-ESKIMO	950	235.00	235.00
89	INVADERS, THE-POLAR BEAR	*	235.00	235.00
89	TWO OF MY FAVORITE SUBJECTS	*	*	225.00
90	GLORY OF THE TRAIL-DOG MUSHING	950	225.00	225.00
90	GRASS IS ALWAYS GREENER, THE-DOG	950	*	200.00
90	QUALITY TIME-POLAR BEAR	950	200.00	620.00
91	KAYAK MAN	950	215.00	330.00
91	SEARCH FOR GOLD, THE	*	225.00	225.00
91	TUNDRA FLOWER	950	235.00	235.00
92	FIRST DAY IN HARNESS	*	225.00	300.00
93	FISHING RIGHTS-BROWN BEAR	*	195.00	195.00
93	RARIN' TO GO DOG SLED	*	225.00	300.00
94	SEARCH ON THE PRESSURE ICE	*	245.00	245.00

B. MOORE, JR.

YR	NAME	LIMIT	ISSUE	TREND
79	HARRY SHOURDES REDHEAD	950	65.00	110.00
79	LEE DUDLEY-CANVASBACK	950	65.00	300.00
79	WARD BROTHERS-CANADAS	950	85.00	155.00
80	WARD BROTHERS-CANVASBACKS	*	85.00	100.00
81	JOSEPH LINCOLN PINTAIL ON THE SANTEE	*	85.00	90.00
81	WAITING, THE	950	85.00	330.00
81	WIND CALLED HIS NAME, THE	950	85.00	400.00
82	GOLDEN DAWN	950	85.00	110.00
82	POINT AND HONOR	*	115.00	195.00
83	BECKY	*	75.00	300.00
86	THIS PLACE NOT FOR SALE	*	85.00	160.00

R. PARKER

YR	NAME	LIMIT	ISSUE	TREND
*	BLUE SHADOWS-ARCTIC FOX	*	175.00	185.00
*	BREAK IN THE ICE-CANADA GOOSE	*	150.00	175.00
*	EVENING SILHOUETTE-COYOTES	*	225.00	225.00
*	EVENING SOLITUDE-WOLF	*	195.00	195.00
*	FALLEN TOTEM-EAGLE	*	245.00	250.00
*	FOREST FLIGHT-EAGLE	*	195.00	195.00
*	FROSTY ALDER-EVENING GROSBEAK	*	125.00	125.00
*	GRIZZLIES AT THE FALLS	*	225.00	225.00
*	ICY CREEK-MINK	*	105.00	105.00
*	LAST LIGHT-COUGAR	*	235.00	235.00
*	WAPITI PORTRAIT-AMERICAN ELK	*	105.00	105.00
*	WARY GLANCE - CHIPMUNK	*	70.00	70.00
82	RACCOON PAIR	950	95.00	300.00
82	RAIDING THE CACHE	*	95.00	115.00
82	SNOW ON THE PINE-CHICKADEES	950	95.00	125.00
82	SPRING MIST-GRAY WOLF	950	155.00	325.00
82	WEATHERED WOOD-BLUEBIRDS	950	75.00	175.00
83	MALLARD FAMILY	950	95.00	110.00
83	MOUNTAIN BLOOMS-GROUND SQUIRREL	*	50.00	90.00
83	RED SQUIRREL	*	65.00	150.00
83	RIVERSIDE PAUSE-RIVER OTTER	950	95.00	540.00
83	YELLOW DAWN-AMERICAN ELK	950	130.00	130.00
84	CHICKADEES IN AUTUMN	950	75.00	75.00
84	FACE OF THE NORTH-WOLF	950	95.00	250.00
84	FAT AND SASSY-ROBIN	*	95.00	100.00
84	GRAY WOLF PORTRAIT	950	115.00	250.00
84	SILENT STEPS-LYNX	950	145.00	325.00
84	WHEN PATHS CROSS	950	185.00	300.00
84	WINTER JAY-BLUE JAY	950	95.00	200.00
85	AFTERNOON SHADOWS-MULE DEER	*	105.00	105.00
85	MISTY MORN-LOON	950	120.00	400.00
85	REFLECTIONS-MALLARD DUCK	*	175.00	400.00
85	SPRING ARRIVALS-CANADA GEESE	950	120.00	150.00
85	WAITING OUT THE STORM-WOLF	950	105.00	500.00
85	WINGS OVER WINTER-BALD EAGLE	950	135.00	325.00
85	WINTER CLOAK-ERMINE	*	105.00	125.00
86	ABOVE THE BREAKERS-OSPREY	950	150.00	175.00
86	AT END OF DAY-WOLVES	950	235.00	235.00
86	AUTUMN FIELDS-RED FOX	*	220.00	220.00
86	AUTUMN FORAGING-MOOSE	950	175.00	300.00
86	AUTUMN LEAVES-RED FOX	950	95.00	100.00
86	AUTUMN MEADOW-ELK	950	195.00	230.00
86	BEHIND THE HEMLOCK-LYNX	*	105.00	115.00
86	CARDINAL IN BLUE SPRUCE	950	125.00	135.00
86	CARDINAL IN BRAMBLES	950	125.00	125.00
86	CREEKSIDE-COUGAR	950	225.00	250.00
86	FOLLOWING MAMA-MUTE SWANS	950	165.00	600.00
86	JUST RESTING-SEA OTTER	950	85.00	400.00
86	MORNING ON THE LAGOON-MUTE SWAN	950	95.00	100.00
86	NORTHERN MORNING-ARCTIC FOX	950	125.00	125.00
86	RED-COCKADED WOODPECKER	*	120.00	120.00
86	RIMROCK-COUGAR	950	200.00	1000.00
86	STILL WATER - MALLARD DUCK	*	105.00	105.00
86	WHITETAIL AND WOLVES	950	180.00	265.00
86	WINTER CREEK-COYOTE	950	130.00	250.00
87	A BREAK IN THE ICE-CANADA GEESE	*	150.00	150.00
87	ABOVE THE WAVES-COMMON TERNS	*	95.00	95.00
87	ARCTIC SPRING-WHITE GYRFALCON	*	185.00	185.00
87	ARCTIC WOLF PORTRAIT	*	105.00	105.00
87	AUTUMN MORNING-GRIZZLY	*	200.00	200.00
87	BARN SWALLOWS ON FENCE POST	*	105.00	105.00

YR	NAME	LIMIT	ISSUE	TREND
87	DESERT RESPITE-KIT FOX	*	125.00	125.00
87	EVENING GLOW-WOLF PACK	950	245.00	250.00
87	EVENING REFLECTIONS-TRUMPETER SWAN	*	115.00	150.00
87	FREEZE UP-CANADA GEESE	950	85.00	85.00
87	GOLDEN GRASSES-CALIFORNIA QUAIL	*	95.00	95.00
87	LOW WATER-RACCOON	*	125.00	125.00
87	ON THE RUN-WOLF PACK	950	245.00	245.00
87	RAIL FENCE-BLUEBIRDS	950	105.00	105.00
87	RAMPARTS-MOUNTAIN GOATS	*	200.00	200.00
87	SHELTERED SPOT-LYNX	*	150.00	150.00
87	WALKING THE RIDGE-PRONGHORN	*	185.00	185.00
87	WHITE-CROWNED SPARROW ON DRIFTWOOD	*	125.00	160.00
87	WINTER CREEK AND WHITETAILS	950	185.00	185.00
87	WINTER ENCOUNTER-WOLF	950	235.00	500.00
87	WINTER PINE-DOWNY WOODPECKER	*	110.00	110.00
87	WINTER SAGE-COYOTE	950	225.00	225.00
87	WINTER STORM-COYOTES	950	245.00	245.00
88	EAGLES IN THE PINES	*	200.00	200.00
88	FIRST SNOW-ARCTIC WOLVES	*	175.00	175.00
88	FOX PUP AT THE DEN ENTRANCE	*	115.00	120.00
88	OLD MAN OF THE MOUNTAIN-BLACK BEAR	*	185.00	225.00
88	RED-BREASTED NUTHATCH ON PI	*	95.00	95.00
88	SEARCHING THE STREAM-RACCOON	*	125.00	200.00
88	SILENT PASSAGE-ORCAS WHALE	950	175.00	175.00
88	SNOW PALACE-MULE DEER	*	225.00	225.00
88	SUMMER-LOON	*	125.00	125.00
88	WHITE-TAILED TROPICBIRDS	*	130.00	130.00
88	WINTER VALLEY-ELK	*	150.00	150.00
88	WINTER WREN ON IVY	*	95.00	95.00
89	AUTUMN ASPEN-WHITE-TAILED DEER	*	175.00	175.00
89	AUTUMN CORNFIELD-CARDINAL	*	115.00	115.00
89	AUTUMN MAPLES-WOLVES	950	195.00	195.00
89	DEEP WATER-ORCAS WHALE	1250	195.00	195.00
89	EARLY SNOWFALL-ELK	950	185.00	185.00
89	EARLY SPRING-GREAT BLUE HERON	*	135.00	135.00
89	EUCALYPTUS CLIMBER-KOALA BEAR	*	110.00	110.00
89	EVENING AMBER-TRUMPETER SWAN	*	125.00	125.00
89	FLYING REDTAIL HAWK-ORIGINAL	290	295.00	295.00
90	BREAKING THE SILENCE-WOLVES	1250	195.00	200.00
90	ICY MORNING-RED FOX	950	150.00	150.00
90	INSIDE PASSAGE-ORCAS WHALE	1500	195.00	195.00
90	LIONESS AND CUBS	150	295.00	295.00
90	MOOSE IN THE BRUSH	950	195.00	195.00
90	WINTER LOOKOUT-COUGAR	950	175.00	175.00
91	DEEP SNOW-WHITETAIL DEER	950	175.00	275.00
91	FOREST TREK-GRAY WOLF	950	185.00	185.00
91	GILA WOODPECKER	950	135.00	135.00
91	MOONLIT TRACKS-WOLF	1500	200.00	250.00
91	MOTHER AND SON-ORCAS	950	185.00	225.00
91	THROUGH THE FIRS-EAGLE	*	500.00	700.00
91	WINTER'S FURY-MOUNTAIN GOATS	*	195.00	195.00
92	CROSSING THE RIDGE-WOLVES	*	265.00	400.00
92	SEA OTTER WITH URCHIN	*	150.00	150.00
95	COASTAL MORNING-GRIZZLY	*	195.00	155.00
M. REECE				
*	FLIGHT- CANADA GEESE - BRONZE	*	4,000.00	4000.00
*	MADISON COUNTY BRIDGE-PHEASANTS	*	135.00	150.00
*	QUIET LANDING-MALLARD-BRONZE	*	3,000.00	3000.00
*	ROSEMAN BRIDGE-MADISON CITY	*	135.00	150.00
*	SHALLOW RIVER-AMERICAN WIGEON	*	195.00	195.00
*	SUNSET-CANADA GEESE	*	195.00	195.00
*	TWIN FAWNS-WHITE-TAILED DEER	*	235.00	235.00
*	WASHINGTON DUCK 1989 - AMERICAN WIGEON	*	135.00	135.00
*	WATERFOWL ART OF MAYNARD	*	650.00	650.00
48	FEDERAL DUCK STAMP-BUFFLEHEADS	200	15.00	1200.00
51	FEDERAL DUCK STAMP-GADWALLS	250	15.00	1200.00
59	FEDERAL DUCK STAMP-RETRIEVER	400	15.00	4000.00
64	BOBWHITES (STONE LITHO)	950	20.00	650.00
64	MALLARDS (STONE LITHO)	950	20.00	20.00
69	FEDERAL DUCK STAMP-WHITE-WINGED SCOTERS	750	50.00	1000.00
69	MALLARDS-PITCHING IN	500	40.00	50.00
70	EDGE OF THE HEDGEROW-BOBWHITES	950	60.00	550.00
71	FEDERAL DUCK STAMP-CINNAMON TEAL	950	75.00	5000.00
72	AGAINST THE WIND-CANVASBACKS	950	60.00	400.00
73	FEEDING TIME-CANADA GEESE	550	75.00	200.00
73	LATE AFTERNOON-MALLARD	450	150.00	175.00
73	MARSHLANDER MALLARDS	600	60.00	60.00
73	PHEASANT COUNTRY	550	60.00	275.00
73	WOOD DUCKS	550	125.00	225.00
74	A BURST OF COLOR-RING-NECKED PHEASANTS	950	75.00	250.00
74	COURTSHIP FLIGHT-PINTAILS	950	75.00	150.00
74	EARLY ARRIVALS-MALLARDS	950	50.00	200.00
74	FLOODED OAKS-MALLARDS	850	150.00	350.00
74	MALLARDS-DROPPING IN	950	75.00	200.00
74	PASSING STORM, THE-CANVASBACKS	950	50.00	250.00
74	QUAIL COVEY	750	150.00	550.00
74	SANDBAR, THE-CANADA GEESE	950	50.00	200.00
74	SNOW GEESE-BLUE GEESE	750	150.00	250.00
74	SNOWY CREEK-MALLARDS	950	75.00	180.00

YR	NAME	LIMIT	ISSUE	TREND
74	SOLITUDE-WHITETAIL DEER	950	85.00	125.00
74	WINGING SOUTH-CANADA GEESE	750	150.00	150.00
74	WOODED SECLUSION-TURKEY	950	75.00	110.00
75	AFTERNOON SHADOWS-BOBWHITES	950	100.00	400.00
76	AUTUMN TRIO-RING-NECKED PHEASANTS	950	85.00	250.00
76	CANADA GEESE-COMING IN	950	85.00	350.00
76	DARK SKY-MALLARDS	950	85.00	575.00
76	FLIGHT-CANADA GEESE	950	50.00	60.00
76	GENTOO-PENGUINS	260	125.00	125.00
76	GOOD FETCH-LABRADOR RETRIEVER	950	150.00	250.00
76	RAIL FENCE, THE-BOBWHITES	950	85.00	325.00
76	SHALLOW POND-MALLARDS	950	125.00	250.00
76	THUNDERHEAD-CANADA GEESE	260	125.00	1150.00
76	WEATHERED WOOD-BOBWHITES	950	50.00	170.00
77	COVEY RISE-BOBWHITES	950	150.00	400.00
77	DARK SHADOWS-WHITETAIL DEER	950	85.00	102.00
77	EASY LANDING-PINTAILS	950	95.00	225.00
77	GRACEFUL PAIR-RING-NECKED PHEASANTS	950	50.00	200.00
77	JUMPING GREENWINGS-GREEN-WINGED TEAL	950	85.00	120.00
77	NINE TRAVELERS-CANADA GEESE	950	95.00	200.00
77	QUIET POND-MALLARDS	950	95.00	130.00
77	RESTING-WOOD DUCKS	950	50.00	180.00
77	SENTINEL, THE-WHITETAIL DEER	950	150.00	250.00
77	STICK POND-MALLARDS	950	125.00	165.00
77	THROUGH THE TREES-WOOD DUCKS	950	95.00	300.00
78	CHINSTRAP PENGUINS	*	50.00	60.00
78	CRESCENT LAKE-MALLARDS	950	125.00	190.00
78	DARK SKY-CANADA GEESE	950	175.00	540.00
78	NEW SNOW-WHITE TAIL DEER	950	95.00	145.00
78	OAK FOREST-TURKEY	950	125.00	180.00
78	OUT OF THE PINES-BOBWHITES	950	245.00	250.00
78	OVER THE POINT-LESSER SCAUPS	950	125.00	250.00
78	ROUGH WATER-CANVASBACKS	950	150.00	150.00
78	WINTER COVEY-BOBWHITES	950	225.00	400.00
79	DARK SKY-BOBWHITES	950	225.00	525.00
79	MARSH, THE	950	75.00	125.00
79	PHEASANT COVER	950	175.00	175.00
79	REGAL FLIGHT-WHISTLING SWANS	950	125.00	130.00
79	RENDEZVOUS-WHITE-FRONTED GEESE	950	85.00	140.00
79	SUNRISE-GREEN WINGED TEAL	950	150.00	190.00
79	VALLEY, THE-PINTAILS	950	150.00	150.00
79	WINDY DAY-MALLARDS	950	150.00	200.00
79	WINTER-RING-NECKED PHEASANTS	950	125.00	125.00
80	ALONG THE SHORE-REDHEADS	*	160.00	200.00
80	COLD MORNING-MALLARDS	*	175.00	175.00
80	DARK SKY-CANVASBACKS	950	195.00	200.00
80	DIAMOND ISLAND-MALLARDS	950	195.00	350.00
80	LANDING-CANADA GEESE	950	125.00	130.00
80	MOUNTAIN SNOW	950	95.00	135.00
80	POINTERS AND BOBWHITES	950	245.00	250.00
80	QUAIL COUNTRY	950	250.00	700.00
80	QUIET PLACE, THE-CANADA GEESE	950	175.00	350.00
80	TIMBER-WOOD DUCKS	950	160.00	225.00
80	TUNDRA-BLACK BRANT	950	85.00	85.00
80	TWILIGHT-AMERICAN WIDGEON	950	75.00	100.00
80	WILLOW, THE-GREEN-WINGED TEAL	950	160.00	400.00
81	DARK SKY-RUFFED GROUSE	950	245.00	400.00
81	DARK SKY-SNOW GEESE	*	175.00	175.00
81	EARLY SPRING-WILD TURKEYS	950	220.00	330.00
81	ESCAPE-RING-NECKED PHEASANTS	950	195.00	195.00
81	FROSTY MORNING-CANADA GEESE	950	175.00	300.00
82	BREAKING AWAY-PINTAILS	*	150.00	150.00
82	FLOODED TIMBER-MALLARDS	950	150.00	330.00
82	HEAVY SNOW-RUFFED GROUSE	*	150.00	150.00
82	MINIATURE SERIES I-MALLARDS	950	75.00	75.00
82	MINIATURE SERIES II-WOOD DUCKS	950	75.00	150.00
82	QUAIL COVEY-BOBWHITES	950	245.00	245.00
82	SPLASH, THE-SMALLMOUTH BASS	950	95.00	375.00
82	STONY LAKE-MALLARDS	*	100.00	125.00
83	ALONG THE RIVER-TRUMPETER SWANS	*	50.00	50.00
83	COASTING DOWN-CANADA GEESE	*	40.00	40.00
83	DARK SKY-PHEASANTS	950	125.00	465.00
83	PASSING THROUGH-LESSER SCAUP	*	100.00	100.00
83	PREENING-BLUE WINGED TEAL	*	115.00	115.00
83	RUNNING BLUES-SCALED QUAILS	*	100.00	100.00
83	TRANQUIL MARSH MALLARDS	*	60.00	60.00
84	DARK SKY-PINTAILS	*	125.00	125.00
84	MINIATURE SERIES III-BOBWHITES	950	75.00	100.00
84	MINIATURE SERIES IV-PHEASANTS	*	75.00	100.00
84	SECLUSION-WOOD DUCKS	*	150.00	150.00
85	FLARING-MALLARDS	*	175.00	260.00
85	HAZY DAY-BOBWHITES	950	150.00	350.00
85	HIGH COUNTRY SKIER	*	125.00	200.00
85	MUSKRAT HOUSE, THE-CANVASBACKS	*	95.00	100.00
85	PAIR-TRUMPETER SWAN, THE	*	95.00	160.00
85	SNOWSTORM, THE-MALLARDS	950	95.00	460.00
85	STORM CLOUDS-CANADA GOOSE	950	125.00	175.00
85	WATER'S EDGE-CANADA GEESE	950	95.00	465.00
86	AUTUMN MARSH-MALLARDS	950	120.00	250.00

YR	NAME	LIMIT	ISSUE	TREND
86	FAMILY, THE - CANADA GEESE	*	95.00	95.00
86	NORTHERN LAKE-COMMON LOONS	*	125.00	175.00
86	QUAIL RIDGE-BOBWHITES	*	175.00	175.00
86	SNOW COVER-CARDINAL	*	95.00	125.00
87	BERRY FOOD-CEDAR WAXWINGS	*	85.00	170.00
87	BIRCH, THE-RUFFED GROUSE	*	85.00	100.00
87	CAREFUL LANDING-CANADA GEESE	*	175.00	190.00
87	OLD TREE-BOBWHITE QUAIL	*	195.00	225.00
87	RED PINE-BLACK-CAPPED CHICKADEES	*	95.00	110.00
87	WHITE PINE- BLUE JAY	*	85.00	225.00
87	WINTER SOLITUDE-MALLARDS	*	125.00	150.00
88	AUTUMN MARSH-MALLARDS	950	135.00	230.00
88	LEAPING-RAINBOW TROUT	*	110.00	150.00
88	OAK TIMBER-MALLARDS	*	165.00	210.00
88	SONORAN DESERT-GAMBEL'S QUAIL	*	150.00	250.00
89	FLYING LOW-CANADA GEESE	*	225.00	225.00
89	ICY WATER-MALLARDS	*	175.00	190.00
89	OVER THE MARSH-CANADA GEESE	*	165.00	165.00
89	UPLAND SERIES I-BOBWHITES	950	125.00	150.00
89	WEEDY DRAW-RING-NECKED PHEASANTS	*	150.00	200.00
90	AMERICAN WIGEON-WASHINGTON CENTENNIAL	1058	*	135.00
90	GREENHEAD-MALLARD	150	245.00	425.00
90	UPLAND SERIES II-WILD TURKEYS & REDBUD	950	125.00	200.00
90	UPLAND SERIES III-RING-NECKED PHEASANT	*	125.00	200.00
91	CHASE, THE-WOLF PACK	550	150.00	150.00
91	OFFSHORE LUNCH-COMMON LOONS	550	195.00	195.00
91	UPLAND SERIES IV-RUFFED GOOSE	950	125.00	175.00
92	ALERT-WHITETAILED DEER	*	175.00	200.00
93	MISTY FLIGHT-CANADA GEESE	*	150.00	150.00

J. SEEREY-LESTER

YR	NAME	LIMIT	ISSUE	TREND
*	CANADA D.U. DUCK STAMP PRINT	*	135.00	135.00
*	CANADA D.U. DUCK STAMP-EXEC.	*	375.00	375.00
*	EARLY SNOW-RED FOX	*	200.00	170.00
*	ICE COMPANIONS-HARP SEAL-SEAL PUPS	*	175.00	175.00
*	IMPRESSION, OF INDIA/NEPAL-W/C WILDLIFE	*	550.00	550.00
*	KEEPING PACE-GRIZZLY W/CUBS	*	200.00	200.00
*	LEAVING THE NEST-WOOD DUCK	*	150.00	330.00
*	SNOWBOUNDING-GRIZZLY	*	225.00	275.00
*	YOUNG PREDATOR-LEOPARD CUB	*	200.00	200.00
83	COOL RETREAT-LYNX	950	85.00	230.00
83	EARLY WINDFALL-GRAY SQUIRRELS	950	85.00	100.00
83	FIRST SNOW-GRIZZLY BEARS	950	95.00	400.00
83	LONE FISHERMAN-GREAT BLUE HERON	950	85.00	500.00
83	REFUGE, THE-RACCOONS	950	85.00	300.00
83	RIVER WATCH-PEREGRINE FALCON	950	85.00	150.00
83	WINTER LOOKOUT-COUGAR	950	85.00	775.00
84	AMONG THE CATTAILS-CANADA GEESE	950	130.00	225.00
84	ARCTIC PROCESSION-WILLOW PTARMIGAN	950	220.00	775.00
84	BASKING-BROWN PELICANS	950	115.00	300.00
84	BREAKING COVER-BLACK BEAR	950	130.00	190.00
84	CLOSE ENCOUNTER-BOBCAT	950	130.00	130.00
84	HIGH GROUND-WOLVES	950	130.00	260.00
84	ICY OUTCROP-WHITE GYRFALCON	950	115.00	500.00
84	LYING LOW-COUGAR	950	85.00	700.00
84	MORNING MIST-SNOWY OWL	RT	95.00	275.00
84	PLAINS HUNTER-PRAIRIE FALCON	950	95.00	100.00
84	SPIRIT OF THE NORTH-WHITE WOLF	950	130.00	180.00
85	AWAKENING MEADOW-COTTONTAIL	950	50.00	125.00
85	CHILDREN OF THE FOREST-RED FOX KITS	950	110.00	400.00
85	CHILDREN OF THE TUNDRA-ARCTIC WOLF PUP	950	110.00	400.00
85	COUGAR HEAD STUDY	950	60.00	60.00
85	DAYBREAK-MOOSE	950	135.00	135.00
85	FALLEN BIRCH-CHIPMUNK	950	60.00	450.00
85	FIRST LIGHT-GRAY JAYS	950	130.00	170.00
85	GATHERING, THE-GRAY WOLVES	950	165.00	265.00
85	ISLAND SANCTUARY-MALLARDS	950	95.00	135.00
85	RED FOX KIT STUDY	*	60.00	125.00
85	RETURN TO WINTER-PINTAILS	RT	135.00	220.00
85	SUNDOWN REFLECTIONS-WOOD DUCK	950	85.00	100.00
85	UNDER THE PINES-BOBCAT	950	95.00	300.00
85	WINTER RENDEZVOUS-COYOTES	950	140.00	175.00
86	ABOVE THE TREELINE-COUGAR	950	130.00	150.00
86	AFTER THE FIRE-GRIZZLY BEAR	RT	95.00	105.00
86	ALONG THE ICE FLOW-POLAR BEARS	950	200.00	200.00
86	CONFLICT AT DAWN-HERON AND OSPREY	950	130.00	375.00
86	COTTONWOOD GOLD-BALTIMORE ORIOLE	950	85.00	85.00
86	EARLY ARRIVALS-SNOW BUNTINGS	950	75.00	75.00
86	HIDDEN ADMIRER-MOOSE	950	165.00	400.00
86	HIGH COUNTRY CHAMPION-GRIZZLY	950	175.00	525.00
86	KENYAN FAMILY-CHEETAHS	950	130.00	130.00
86	LAKESIDE FAMILY-CANADA GEESE	950	75.00	100.00
86	LOW TIDE-BALD EAGLES	950	130.00	155.00
86	MORNING FORAGE-GROUND SQUIRREL	RT	75.00	75.00
86	RACING THE STORM-ARCTIC WOLVES	950	200.00	350.00
86	SNOWY EXCURSION-RED SQUIRREL	950	75.00	175.00
86	SPRING MIST-CHICKADEES	950	105.00	175.00
86	TREADING THIN ICE-CHIPMUNK	950	75.00	100.00
86	WINTER HIDING-COTTONTAIL	950	75.00	75.00
86	WINTER PERCH-CARDINAL	950	85.00	150.00

YR	NAME	LIMIT	ISSUE	TREND
86	YOUNG EXPLORER, THE-RED FOX KIT	950	75.00	85.00
87	ALPENGLOW-ARCTIC WOLF	950	200.00	210.00
87	AMBOSELI CHILD-AF/ELEPHANT	950	160.00	200.00
87	AUTUMN MIST-BARRED OWL	950	160.00	175.00
87	AUTUMN THUNDER-MUSK OXEN	950	150.00	150.00
87	BATHING-MUTE SWAN	RT	175.00	275.00
87	CANYON CREEK-COUGAR	950	195.00	600.00
87	DAWN ON THE MARSH-COYOTE	950	200.00	200.00
87	FIRST TRACKS-COUGAR	950	150.00	175.00
87	HIGH REFUGE-RED SQUIRREL	950	120.00	120.00
87	IN DEEP-BLACK BEAR CUB	950	135.00	225.00
87	LYING IN WAIT-ARCTIC FOX	950	175.00	175.00
87	OUT OF THE BLIZZARD-TIMBER WOLVES	950	215.00	600.00
87	OUT OF THE MIST-GRIZZLY	950	200.00	450.00
87	RAIN WATCH-BELTED KINGFISHER	950	125.00	200.00
87	SUNDOWN ALERT-BOBCAT	950	150.00	175.00
87	WINTER VIGIL-GREAT HORNED OWL	RT	175.00	175.00
88	BATHING-BLUE JAY	950	95.00	95.00
88	CLIFF HANGER-BOBCAT	950	200.00	200.00
88	COASTAL CLIQUE-HARBOR SEALS	950	160.00	160.00
88	EDGE OF THE FOREST-TIMBER WOLVES	950	500.00	825.00
88	EVENING MEADOW-AMERICAN GOLDFINCH	950	150.00	150.00
88	HIDING PLACE-SAW-WHET OWL	950	95.00	100.00
88	LAST SANCTUARY-FLORIDA PANTHER	RT	175.00	440.00
88	MOONLIGHT FISHERMAN-RACCOON	RT	175.00	250.00
88	MOOSE HAIR	950	165.00	300.00
88	MORNING DISPLAY-COMMON LOONS	950	135.00	145.00
88	NIGHT MOVES-AFRICAN ELEPHANTS	950	150.00	150.00
88	NORTHWOODS FAMILY-MOOSE	950	75.00	75.00
88	SAVANNA SIESTA-AFRICAN LIONS	950	165.00	165.00
88	SNOWY WATCH-GREAT GRAY OWL	950	175.00	175.00
88	SPANISH MIST-YOUNG BARRED OWL	950	175.00	175.00
88	TUNDRA FAMILY-ARCTIC WOLVES	950	200.00	200.00
88	WINTER GRAZING-BISON	950	185.00	185.00
88	WINTER SPIRIT-GRAY WOLF	950	200.00	200.00
89	BEFORE THE FREEZE-BEAVER	950	165.00	225.00
89	COUGAR RUN	950	185.00	250.00
89	EVENING DUET-SNOWY EGRETS	1250	185.00	220.00
89	FLUKE SIGHTING-HUMPBACK WHALES	RT	185.00	200.00
89	GORILLA	290	400.00	530.00
89	HEAVY GOING-GRIZZLY	RT	175.00	240.00
89	HIGH AND MIGHTY-GORILLA	950	185.00	185.00
89	SNEAK PEEK-CHICKEN	950	950.00	225.00
89	SOFTLY, SOFTLY-WHITE TIGER	950	220.00	440.00
89	SPRING FLURRY-ADELIE PENGUINS	950	185.00	185.00
89	WATER SPORT-BOBCAT	RT	185.00	215.00
90	ARCTIC WOLF PUPS	290	500.00	500.00
90	BITTERSWEET WINTER-CARDINAL	1250	150.00	175.00
90	DAWN MAJESTY-WHITE TIGER	RT	185.00	190.00
90	GRIZZLY-ORIGINAL	290	400.00	400.00
90	IN THEIR PRESENCE-ORCAS	1250	200.00	200.00
90	MARKER 221-CANVASBACKS NEW YORK	*	*	135.00
90	MOUNTAIN CRADLE-GORILLA	1250	200.00	200.00
90	N.Y. DUCK STAMP	*	300.00	300.00
90	N.Y. DUCK STAMP -1990 W/MEDAL	*	550.00	550.00
90	NEW YORK DUCK STAMP 1990 RE	*	*	135.00
90	NIGHT RUN-ARCTIC WOLVES	1250	200.00	300.00
90	PLUNGE-NORTHERN SEA LIONS	1250	200.00	200.00
90	SEASONAL GREETING-CARDINAL	1250	150.00	200.00
90	SPOUT-WHALES	290	500.00	475.00
90	SUITORS, THE-WOOD DUCKS	3313	135.00	185.00
90	SUMMER RAIN-COMMON LOONS	RT	200.00	200.00
90	SUMMER RAIN-COMMON LOONS (SPECIAL)	450	425.00	425.00
90	THEIR FIRST SEASON-GRIZZLY BEAR	RT	200.00	200.00
90	TOGETHERNESS-LION	1250	125.00	125.00
90	WHITETAIL SPRING-WHITETAIL DEER	RT	185.00	185.00
91	DENALI FAMILY-GRIZZLY BEAR	950	195.00	250.00
91	EVENING ENCOUNTER-GRIZZLY & WOLF	1250	185.00	185.00
91	FACE TO FACE	1250	200.00	250.00
91	MONSOON-WHITE TIGER	RT	195.00	195.00
91	MOONLIGHT CHASE-COUGAR	250	195.00	195.00
91	OUT ON A LIMB-YOUNG BARRED OWL	950	185.00	225.00
91	PANDA TRILOGY	950	375.00	375.00
91	SISTERS-ARCTIC WOLVES	1250	185.00	185.00
91	SOMETHING STIRRED-BENGAL TIGER	950	195.00	195.00
92	BANYAN AMBUSH-BLACK PANTHER	RT	235.00	235.00
92	BLACK JADE-WOLVES	*	550.00	525.00
92	BLACK MAGIC-PANTHER	*	475.00	335.00
92	CHASE-SNOW LEOPARD, THE	950	200.00	200.00
92	OUT OF THE DARKNESS-BLACK PANTHER	290	200.00	200.00
92	RANTHAMBHORE RUSH-TIGER	950	225.00	225.00
92	REGAL MAJESTY-BLACK PANTHER	290	200.00	200.00
93	DARK ENCOUNTER-BLACK WOLF	*	200.00	250.00
93	FREEDOM I -HARPY EAGLE	350	500.00	500.00
93	FROZEN MOONLIGHT-ARCTIC WOLVES	2500	225.00	300.00
93	GRIZZLY IMPACT	950	225.00	400.00
93	LOONLIGHT-LOON	1500	225.00	225.00
93	MORNING GLORY-BALD EAGLE	1250	225.00	225.00
93	NIGHT SPECTER- BLACK JAGUAR	1250	195.00	195.00

YR	NAME	LIMIT	ISSUE	TREND
93	PHANTOMS OF THE TUNDRA-WOLVES	950	235.00	235.00
93	RAINS-TIGER, THE	950	225.00	225.00
93	SEEKING ATTENTION-GRIZZLY	950	200.00	200.00
93	WOLONG WHITEOUT-PANDA	950	225.00	225.00
94	ABANDONED-WOLF PUPS	*	175.00	175.00
94	CHILD OF THE OUTBACK-KOALA	950	175.00	185.00
94	COURTSHIP, THE-EGERTS	950	175.00	175.00
94	FOREST GLOW-JAGUAR	*	225.00	225.00
94	NIGHT PROWLER-WOLF	*	225.00	225.00
94	SQUIRREL MONKEY STUDY	*	145.00	145.00
95	ICE FISHING-POLAR BEAR	*	225.00	500.00
95	QINLING PANDA	*	225.00	260.00
95	RETURN TO YELLOWSTONE-WOLVES	*	235.00	235.00
95	SILENT WATERS-MOOSE	*	175.00	325.00

M. SOLBERG

YR	NAME	LIMIT	ISSUE	TREND
*	ANTELOPE RIDGE	*	150.00	150.00
*	DARK WATERS-HERON	*	70.00	70.00
*	FEMALE TIMBER WOLF	*	100.00	100.00
*	MALE TIMBER WOLF	*	100.00	100.00
79	BENGAL TIGER	*	65.00	200.00
80	CHALLENGE OF THE WILD	*	225.00	225.00
82	ACCEPT MY FATHERS SPIRIT	*	95.00	210.00
83	BANDITS, THE	*	125.00	125.00
84	BUFFALO BROTHERS	*	175.00	215.00
84	TOMORROW MAY BE COOLER-LION	*	135.00	135.00
85	ACROSS THE TUNDRA	*	135.00	310.00
85	MCNEIL RIVER FISHERMAN-BROWN BEAR	*	150.00	150.00
86	CHECKING FOR STRAYS	*	85.00	85.00
86	EARLY MORNING CHALLENGE-ELK	*	150.00	175.00
86	EDGE OF NIGHT-BARN OWL	*	150.00	260.00
86	LONG CAST, THE-FISHERMAN	*	95.00	95.00
86	MORNING MIST-CANADA GEESE	*	95.00	'50.00
86	MOUNTAIN VISTA-LANDSCAPE	950	95.00	690.00
86	ON SCENT-GERMAN SHORTHAIRS	*	115.00	95.00
86	SUNLIT MIST-ELK	*	85.00	85.00
86	VIRGIN WATERS-LANDSCAPE	*	150.00	250.00
86	WHERE THE TRAIL ENDS-SNOW LEOPARD	*	150.00	150.00
86	WINGS OF WONDER-BALD EAGLE	950	150.00	400.00
86	WINTER REFLECTION-BEAR	*	150.00	150.00
87	ALERT-DOE AND FAWN	*	125.00	200.00
87	BAD WATER BEAR	*	150.00	250.00
87	FROM NORTH THEY CAME-WOLF	*	85.00	85.00
87	GRAND DUKE, THE-OWL	*	150.00	150.00
87	HANDSOME HUNTER-AMERICAN KESTREL	950	115.00	500.00
87	HIGH COUNTRY MORNING-BIGHORN SHEEP	*	125.00	175.00
87	MONARCH OF THE SKY-GOLDEN EAGLE	950	200.00	200.00
87	MOUNTAIN SENTINEL-LION	*	125.00	150.00
87	ON THE HIGH SIDE-MOUNTAIN GOAT	*	95.00	100.00
87	SOMETHING MOVED-BOBCAT	*	125.00	125.00
87	YELLOWSTONE OSPREY	*	75.00	75.00
88	ARCTIC NOMADS	950	150.00	260.00
88	BLACK-CAPPED CHICKADEE	*	95.00	125.00
88	FATEFUL MOMENT-EAGLE	*	150.00	160.00
88	INTO THE STORM-CARIBOU	*	140.00	140.00
88	MORNING MEMORIES	*	135.00	220.00
88	ON SILENT WINGS-BALD EAGLE	*	150.00	330.00
88	RIVER OF DREAMS-FISHING	*	150.00	175.00
89	DECEPTIVE CALM-GOSHAWK	950	95.00	140.00
89	REFLECTION-WOLF	950	150.00	150.00
89	WHEN WINTER WARMS-POLAR BEAR	950	115.00	180.00
89	WHISPERING WINGS-TRUMPETER SWAN	*	135.00	330.00
89	WINTER WHITE-SNOWY OWL	*	95.00	95.00
90	BY FIRELIGHT-MOUNTAIN LION	*	160.00	125.00
90	NOMAD OF THE ICE-POLAR BEAR	1250	165.00	170.00
90	ON WATCH	950	150.00	150.00
90	OUT OF THE FOG-GRIZZLY BEAR	*	150.00	150.00
90	SERENE SETTING-AMERICAN KESTRELS	1250	150.00	150.00
90	SIGNS OF SPRING-HORSE	*	150.00	250.00
90	SMALL WONDER-CHIPMUNK	*	110.00	110.00
90	THISTLEDOWN-KESTREL	*	150.00	150.00
91	AFTERNOON SHADOWS-MULE DEER	*	145.00	200.00
91	AUTUMN CHALLENGE-ELK	*	150.00	200.00
91	KORBEL GARDENS-FLORAL	*	150.00	225.00
91	MOUSE TRACKS-COYOTE	*	150.00	165.00
91	TIMBER WOLF STUDY COMPANION	*	185.00	200.00
92	GARDEN VISITOR-RED FOX	*	210.00	280.00
92	ICE BEAR	*	210.00	210.00
94	TIMBER WOLF STUDY	*	75.00	190.00
94	WHITE WOLF STUDY	*	75.00	120.00

R. TORY PETERSON

YR	NAME	LIMIT	ISSUE	TREND
*	VOLUNTEERS	*	255.00	255.00
73	BALTIMORE ORIOLE	450	150.00	400.00
73	CARDINAL	450	150.00	775.00
73	FLICKER	450	150.00	700.00
73	WOOD THRUSH	450	150.00	370.00
74	BALD EAGLE	950	150.00	500.00
74	BARN SWALLOW	750	150.00	225.00
74	BLUE JAYS	950	150.00	510.00
74	BOBOLINK	750	150.00	600.00

YR	NAME	LIMIT	ISSUE	TREND
74	GREAT HORNED OWL	950	150.00	950.00
75	BOBWHITES	950	150.00	400.00
75	FUR SEALS	*	25.00	25.00
75	JAYS-COLOR PLATE #30-BLUE JAY	*	150.00	150.00
75	OWLS-COLOR PLATE #16	*	150.00	275.00
75	RUFFED GROUSE	950	150.00	400.00
75	SEA OTTERS	*	25.00	200.00
76	ADELIE PENGUINS	950	35.00	200.00
76	BARN OWL	950	225.00	460.00
76	GOLDEN EAGLE	950	200.00	460.00
76	QUAILS-COLOR PLATE #9	*	150.00	275.00
76	ROADRUNNER	*	25.00	175.00
76	SNOWY OWL	950	175.00	925.00
77	BLUEBIRD	950	75.00	300.00
77	PEREGRINE FALCON	950	175.00	1350.00
77	SCARLET TANAGER	950	125.00	225.00
77	SOOTY TERNS	450	50.00	200.00
77	WILD ORCHIDS AND TRILLIUMS	*	75.00	75.00
77	WILLETS	450	50.00	75.00
78	MOCKINGBIRD	950	125.00	560.00
78	RING-NECKED PHEASANT	950	200.00	700.00
78	ROBIN	950	125.00	775.00
78	ROSE-BREASTED GROSBEAK	950	125.00	450.00
78	SHOWY WAYSIDE FLOWERS	*	75.00	75.00
79	GYRFALCON	950	225.00	450.00
79	PUFFIN	*	175.00	175.00
81	WILD TURKEYS	*	195.00	400.00
83	ARCTIC GLOW-SNOWY OWL	*	200.00	250.00
86	LORD OF THE AIR-PEREGRINE FALCON	*	120.00	120.00

F. MACHETANZ — ALASKAN

YR	NAME	LIMIT	ISSUE	TREND
92	HARPOONER'S MOMENT-ALASKA	*	225.00	225.00
92	TRAIL OF GREAT WHITE BEAR-ALASKA	*	225.00	225.00

J. DALY — BOY

YR	NAME	LIMIT	ISSUE	TREND
87	FAVORITE READER	*	425.00	350.00

R. PARKER — BRONZE

YR	NAME	LIMIT	ISSUE	TREND
*	COYOTE	*	950.00	950.00
86	RIMROCK - BRONZE	*	1,450.00	1450.00

P. CALLE — INDIAN

YR	NAME	LIMIT	ISSUE	TREND
*	BUFFALO SKULL BUCKLE - BRONZE	*	95.00	95.00
*	BUFFALO SKULL BUCKLE - SILVER	*	750.00	750.00
*	ONE STAR	*	125.00	200.00

P. CALLE — MOUNTAIN MAN

YR	NAME	LIMIT	ISSUE	TREND
*	FREE TRAPPER, THE - BRONZE	*	*	N/A
*	I CALL HIM FRIEND - B/W	*	375.00	375.00
81	FRIEND OR FOE	950	125.00	175.00
83	FREE TRAPPER STUDY	*	125.00	325.00
84	MOUNTAIN MAN, THE (PENCIL)	*	95.00	425.00
85	FRONTIER BLACKSMITH	950	245.00	245.00
88	TRAPPER AT REST	550	95.00	175.00
89	WINTER FEAST, A PREMIER ED.	290	465.00	425.00
92	HUNTER OF GEESE	950	125.00	125.00
92	OUT OF THE SILENCE	2500	265.00	275.00
92	OUT OF THE SILENCE - PRESTIGE	290	465.00	465.00
92	THROUGH THE TALL GRASS	950	175.00	175.00
93	AND A GRIZZLY CLAW NECKLACE	750	150.00	175.00
93	I CALL HIM FRIEND - PRESTIGE	950	235.00	250.00
94	NEAR JOURNEY'S END	*	245.00	245.00
95	FIRESIDE COMPANIONS	*	150.00	150.00

P. CALLE — PORTRAIT

YR	NAME	LIMIT	ISSUE	TREND
92	JIMMY DOOLITTLE PORTRAIT	*	425.00	425.00

J. DALY — PORTRAIT

YR	NAME	LIMIT	ISSUE	TREND
*	WINNING CATCH	*	75.00	85.00
92	DOMINOES	1500	155.00	155.00
92	FAVORITE GIFT	RT	175.00	180.00
92	FLYING HORSES, THE	950	325.00	325.00
92	HER SECRET PLACE	*	275.00	335.00
92	IMMIGRANT SPIRIT, THE	5000	125.00	135.00
92	PLAYMATES	*	355.00	365.00
93	GOOD COMPANY	1500	155.00	155.00
93	LEFT OUT	1500	110.00	125.00
93	NEW CITIZEN, THE	5000	125.00	135.00
93	SECRET ADMIRER	1500	150.00	150.00
93	SUNDAY AFTERNOON	*	350.00	350.00
93	WHEN I GROW UP	1500	175.00	175.00
94	ALL ABOARD	*	145.00	145.00
94	CHILDHOOD FRIENDS	950	110.00	115.00
94	EYE TO EYE	*	95.00	230.00
95	SLIDING HOME	*	75.00	100.00

T. UTZ — UTZ

YR	NAME	LIMIT	ISSUE	TREND
81	GREENHOUSE NUDE, THE	550	95.00	135.00
81	LAVENDER LACE	950	75.00	75.00
81	MELANIE	450	85.00	120.00
81	PICNIC	550	110.00	115.00
81	PINK LADY	450	85.00	135.00
81	SOFT WIND, THE	950	75.00	75.00
83	INTERLUDE	*	40.00	40.00
86	MORNING MELODY	*	90.00	90.00
86	STRAND OF PEARLS	*	90.00	90.00

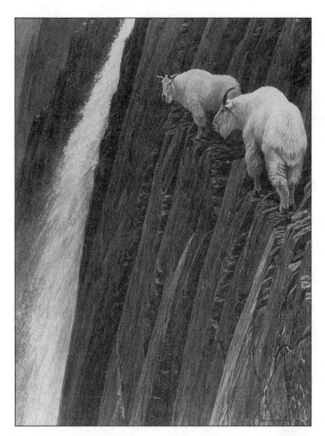

Sheer Drop—Mountain Goats *by Terry Redlin, released in 1981 for $245 by Mill Pond Press, is now worth over $2,000.*

Panda Trilogy–China Song *by John Seerey-Lester was limited to 950 in 1991 when Mill Pond Press issued the print for $375.*

YR	NAME	LIMIT	ISSUE	TREND
87	ANGELICA	*	85.00	85.00
87	GABRIELLA	*	85.00	85.00
88	GRANNY'S BOOTS	*	95.00	150.00
88	SOLITUDE	*	95.00	125.00
90	CONTEMPLATION	*	150.00	150.00
90	DRAGON SLAYER, THE	*	95.00	95.00
90	EARLY LIGHT	*	110.00	250.00
90	END OF THE RAINBOW	*	95.00	125.00
90	GOSSAMER	*	150.00	250.00
M. WARREN				**WARREN**
74	TOP HAND OF THE CONCHO	950	150.00	2000.00
81	A COLD DAY	950	245.00	775.00
81	APPROACHING STORM	*	195.00	300.00
81	WHEN COWBOYS GET EDGY	*	245.00	330.00
82	NIGHT IN CHIMAYO	*	125.00	225.00
J. ZEMSKY				**ZEMSKY**
79	COME AND SEE THE NEW COLT	950	65.00	70.00
79	JORDAN AT THE WEDDING	950	65.00	160.00
79	JORDAN'S DOLLY	950	65.00	225.00
79	LOVE AT FIRST SIGHT	950	75.00	75.00
79	WHEN THE THEN AND THE NOW HOLD HANDS	950	65.00	200.00
80	JORDAN'S SPRING	*	65.00	350.00
84	JENNY IN THE ATTIC	*	75.00	250.00
84	THEY'LL BE SORRY WHEN WE'RE GONE	*	75.00	135.00

MOSS PORTFOLIO
P. BUCKLEY MOSS

YR	NAME	LIMIT	ISSUE	TREND
*	APPLE PICKER	1000	30.00	125.00
*	BARELIMBED REFLECTIONS	1000	25.00	70.00
*	BLUE BOUQUET	1000	16.00	32.00
*	CENTRAL PARK	1000	80.00	200.00
*	EMILY	1000	30.00	100.00
*	FLAG BOY	1000	16.00	40.00
*	GINNY	1000	16.00	45.00
*	GRANDMOTHER	1000	60.00	120.00
*	JOHN	1000	16.00	45.00
*	LANDSCAPE W/GEESE (GOLD)	1000	500.00	1000.00
*	LESSON IN PATIENCE	1000	150.00	300.00
*	LITTLE GIRL IN BLUE	1000	16.00	40.00
*	LORDS OF THE REALM	1000	80.00	210.00
*	MARY AND MAGNOLIA	1000	15.00	42.00
*	SHENANDOAH SILHOUETTE	1000	25.00	60.00
*	STACK OF GIRLS	1000	25.00	125.00
*	STONE HOUSE	99	600.00	1250.00
78	BECKY AND TOM	1000	10.00	100.00
78	CANADA GEESE	1000	60.00	140.00
78	DAILY CHORES	1000	16.00	100.00
78	EVENING RUN	1000	55.00	155.00
78	FAMILY OUTING	1000	65.00	300.00
78	FOUR LITTLE GIRLS	1000	30.00	150.00
78	FRESH BOUQUET	1000	15.00	160.00
78	FRIENDLY STEED	1000	50.00	150.00
78	FRIENDS	1000	35.00	160.00
78	FROSTY FROLIC	1000	75.00	400.00
78	GINNY AND CHRIS WITH LAMBS	1000	35.00	150.00
78	GOLDEN WINTER	1000	150.00	430.00
78	GOSSIP	1000	45.00	130.00
78	HELPERS	1000	35.00	125.00
78	HUNGRY BABY BIRD	1000	15.00	100.00
78	LITTLE APPLES IN A ROW	1000	100.00	310.00
78	LITTLE FELLOW	1000	57.00	150.00
78	MILK LAD	1000	15.00	125.00
78	MILK MAID	1000	15.00	125.00
78	MOMMA APPLE (BLUE)	1000	10.00	125.00
78	MOMMA APPLE (GOLD)	1000	16.00	125.00
78	MOONLIT SKATERS I (LARGE)	1000	75.00	300.00
78	MOONLIT SKATERS II (SMALL)	1000	40.00	140.00
78	MUFFET BOY I	1000	10.00	75.00
78	MUFFET GIRL I	1000	10.00	75.00
78	NINE MENNONITES GIRLS	1000	40.00	180.00
78	PERFECT PET	1000	15.00	90.00
78	POPPA APPLE (BLUE)	1000	10.00	100.00
78	POPPA APPLE (GOLD)	1000	15.00	100.00
78	QUILTING BEE	1000	55.00	200.00
78	QUILTING LADIES	1000	40.00	200.00
78	RACHEL & JACOB	1000	150.00	610.00
78	RELUCTANT BALLERINA	1000	16.00	100.00
78	SEASON'S OVER	1000	35.00	150.00
78	SERENITY IN BLACK AND WHITE	1000	120.00	360.00
78	SHOWALTER'S FARM	1000	100.00	310.00
78	SKATING AWAY I	1000	70.00	200.00
78	SKATING LESSON	1000	150.00	500.00
78	SNOW GOOSE	1000	50.00	200.00
78	SNOWY BIRCHES	1000	60.00	200.00
78	SOLITARY SKATER	1000	35.00	200.00
78	SPIRIT OF EQUUS	1000	100.00	300.00
78	TENDING HER FLOCK	1000	80.00	250.00
78	WINTER CAMEO	1000	30.00	150.00
78	WINTER VISITOR	1000	80.00	180.00

YR	NAME	LIMIT	ISSUE	TREND
78	WORKDAY'S O'ER	1000	110.00	410.00
79	A WELCOME	1000	45.00	155.00
79	APPLE HARVEST	1000	75.00	225.00
79	AWAKE, O EARTH	1000	50.00	150.00
79	BEHOLD	1000	35.00	100.00
79	DEAR LORD (LONG)	1000	30.00	100.00
79	EVERY BLESSING	1000	50.00	150.00
79	FANEUIL HALL	1000	40.00	100.00
79	GRANNY'S FAVORITE	1000	40.00	160.00
79	HAIL THE DAY, SOLACE	1000	75.00	215.00
79	HARK	1000	40.00	160.00
79	HE LIVES	1000	25.00	95.00
79	HOW CALM THE MORN	1000	75.00	245.00
79	JOY	1000	16.00	80.00
79	LOVE	1000	10.00	105.00
79	MARY'S LAMB (LARGE)	1000	75.00	180.00
79	MARY'S LAMB (SMALL)	1000	40.00	100.00
79	MY HANDS TO THEE	1000	75.00	300.00
79	NEVER ALONE	1000	35.00	130.00
79	O GENTLE FRIEND	1000	40.00	175.00
79	OH LIFE	1000	40.00	150.00
79	PAVILION AT WOLFEBORO	1000	40.00	100.00
79	PROMISED	1000	40.00	150.00
79	PUBLIC GARDENS AND BEACON STREET	1000	50.00	260.00
79	TARRY NOT	1000	35.00	160.00
79	TIS GRACE	1000	20.00	120.00
79	TWO LITTLE HANDS	1000	35.00	150.00
79	WOMAN TALK	1000	35.00	150.00
80	CAPITOL SKATERS	1000	80.00	200.00
80	ON THE CANAL	1000	60.00	200.00
80	PEACH HARVEST	1000	150.00	500.00
80	RING AROUND A ROSIE	1000	40.00	200.00
80	STREET BY THE PARK	1000	200.00	600.00
80	WAYSIDE INN	1000	65.00	500.00
80	WAYSIDE INN (ETCHING)	99	1,800.00	3250.00
80	WINTER'S HOUSE	1000	350.00	750.00
81	BLACK CAT	1000	50.00	100.00
81	BLACK CAT ON PINK CUSHION	1000	40.00	130.00
81	QUILTING DREAMS	1000	40.00	150.00
81	SAM	1000	16.00	95.00
81	SARAH	1000	16.00	155.00
81	SKATING JOY	1000	200.00	610.00
81	SOLITARY SKATER II	1000	35.00	160.00
81	SOLO	1000	15.00	150.00
81	SPRING LOVE	1000	25.00	140.00
81	STREET BY THE PARK II	1000	125.00	290.00
81	SUNDAY MORNING	1000	60.00	270.00
81	SUNDAY'S RIDE	1000	60.00	200.00
81	TOGETHER	99	450.00	2000.00
81	WAITING FOR TOM	1000	40.00	525.00
81	WINTER AT THE MILL	1000	80.00	290.00
82	APPLE DAY	1000	80.00	210.00
82	APPLE GIRL	1000	30.00	145.00
82	AUTUMN RIDE	1000	80.00	200.00
82	BALLOON RIDE	1000	100.00	220.00
82	BLUE WINTER	1000	100.00	310.00
82	CAMEO GEESE	1000	40.00	180.00
82	CHRIS	1000	25.00	100.00
82	DANIEL	1000	20.00	180.00
82	DASHING AWAY	1000	100.00	325.00
82	DONKEY BOY	1000	40.00	105.00
82	EBONY'S JET	1000	150.00	340.00
82	FLAG GIRL	1000	10.00	75.00
82	FLOWER GIRL	1000	20.00	75.00
82	FRUIT OF THE VALLEY	1000	80.00	300.00
82	GAGGLE OF GEESE	1000	125.00	290.00
82	GRANDPA'S HOUSE	1000	40.00	110.00
82	HAND IN HAND	1000	40.00	130.00
82	HAYRIDE	1000	50.00	175.00
82	HURRAH!	1000	20.00	80.00
82	LISA AND TIGER	1000	30.00	120.00
82	LITTLE GIRL'S PRAYER	1000	35.00	140.00
82	MY PLACE	1000	30.00	150.00
82	MY SISTERS	1000	40.00	150.00
82	ON THE SWING	1000	40.00	190.00
82	OUR LITTLE BROTHER	1000	50.00	180.00
82	OUR LITTLE SISTER	1000	50.00	180.00
82	PALS	1000	25.00	100.00
82	PINK BALLERINA	1000	25.00	105.00
82	PLEASE GOD	1000	50.00	190.00
82	PLEASE!	1000	35.00	130.00
82	ROCKING	1000	40.00	130.00
82	SHENANDOAH HARVEST	1000	60.00	200.00
82	SKATING DUET	1000	40.00	155.00
82	SLEIGH RIDE	1000	50.00	170.00
82	STACK OF BOYS	1000	30.00	125.00
82	TAKING TURNS	1000	50.00	180.00
82	TOGETHER IN THE PARK	1000	80.00	190.00
82	TWO ON A BARREL	1000	25.00	130.00

YR	NAME	LIMIT	ISSUE	TREND
82	TWO ON A SWING	1000	50.00	150.00
82	WEDDING	1000	80.00	300.00
82	WEDDING DAY	1000	160.00	380.00
82	WEDDING II	1000	90.00	220.00
82	WINTER DUET	1000	90.00	260.00
82	WINTER'S GLIMPSE	1000	40.00	145.00
83	ADAM	1000	20.00	150.00
83	AMY	1000	20.00	160.00
83	BECKY	1000	20.00	160.00
83	BROTHERS	1000	35.00	150.00
83	CARRIE	1000	30.00	100.00
83	CHERISHED	1000	35.00	150.00
83	CHICKEN FARMERS	1000	40.00	140.00
83	CHRISTMAS CAROL	1000	60.00	580.00
83	COLONIAL SLEIGH RIDE	1000	125.00	310.00
83	COUNTRY CHURCH	1000	80.00	200.00
83	EVENING GUESTS	1000	60.00	145.00
83	EVENING WELCOME	1000	60.00	210.00
83	FAMILY, THE	1000	125.00	300.00
83	FINISHING TOUCHES	1000	60.00	130.00
83	FIRST LOVE	1000	60.00	150.00
83	GAGGLE OF GEESE (SILKSCREEN)	99	600.00	2000.00
83	GINGER	1000	40.00	125.00
83	GIRLS IN GREEN	1000	40.00	125.00
83	GOLDEN AUTUMN	1000	110.00	250.00
83	GOVERNOR'S PALACE	1000	50.00	240.00
83	GRANNY'S GIRL	1000	50.00	180.00
83	JOSHUA	1000	25.00	150.00
83	KATIE	1000	25.00	150.00
83	LONG GROVE CHURCH	1000	100.00	275.00
83	LORDS OF THE VALLEY	1000	175.00	390.00
83	MARY ANN	1000	20.00	110.00
83	MONARCH	1000	35.00	120.00
83	MY GIRLS	1000	60.00	300.00
83	NOTRE DAME	1000	90.00	180.00
83	OLD MILL HOUSE	1000	125.00	280.00
83	ORCHARD GIRL	1000	40.00	200.00
83	ORCHARD HELPERS	1000	75.00	310.00
83	OUR BIG BROTHER	1000	35.00	120.00
83	QUILT, THE	1000	90.00	260.00
83	RED BIKE	1000	35.00	120.00
83	RED HOUSE	1000	100.00	300.00
83	ROTHENBURG	1000	40.00	135.00
83	SISTERS FOUR	1000	60.00	240.00
83	SPRING BOUQUET	1000	40.00	150.00
83	SPRING SHEPHERDS	1000	40.00	145.00
83	SUMMER LOVE	1000	50.00	200.00
83	SUNDAY'S APPLES	1000	50.00	210.00
83	TENDER SHEPHERD	1000	50.00	180.00
83	TERRACE HILL	1000	110.00	425.00
83	TIMOTHY	1000	30.00	125.00
83	TOGETHER ON SUNDAY (SILKSCREEN)	99	600.00	2050.00
83	WEDDING III	1000	90.00	180.00
83	WHITE CHURCH, THE	1000	80.00	250.00
83	WINTER RIDE	1000	60.00	145.00
83	WINTER SKATER	1000	40.00	145.00
83	WINTER'S DAY	1000	50.00	200.00
83	WINTER'S JOY (SILKSCREEN)	99	500.00	1150.00
84	AUTUMN TRIPTYCH	1000	150.00	340.00
84	BALLOON GIRL	1000	20.00	65.00
84	BLESSING, THE	1000	60.00	260.00
84	BROWER HOMESTEAD	1000	100.00	240.00
84	CRAZY QUILT	1000	50.00	155.00
84	ENGAGEMENT, THE	1000	40.00	125.00
84	EVENING HOUR, THE	1000	70.00	145.00
84	FIRST BORN	1000	50.00	140.00
84	FROSTY RIDE	1000	70.00	265.00
84	GRANDMA'S BED	1000	60.00	235.00
84	HITCHING A RIDE	1000	60.00	150.00
84	HOMEWARD BOUND	1000	90.00	250.00
84	LOUDMOUTHS	1000	125.00	310.00
84	MAGGIE	1000	30.00	115.00
84	MARY JEN	1000	20.00	115.00
84	MIKE AND JESSIE	1000	60.00	180.00
84	MOLLY	1000	30.00	120.00
84	NEWBORN, THE	1000	55.00	200.00
84	OHIO STAR	1000	60.00	180.00
84	PRINCELY PAIR	1000	60.00	180.00
84	RED WAGON	1000	50.00	180.00
84	SCHOOL YARD, THE	1000	60.00	180.00
84	SECRET, THE	1000	50.00	150.00
84	SUNDAY'S PRAYER	1000	50.00	210.00
84	SWAN HOUSE	1000	80.00	170.00
84	TO GRANDMOTHER'S HOUSE WE GO	1000	80.00	210.00
84	VICTORIAN LEGACY	1000	150.00	390.00
84	WEDDING RIDE, THE	1000	130.00	350.00
84	WEDDING RING	1000	75.00	200.00
84	WINTER'S GLORY	1000	200.00	425.00
85	A VISIT TO THE CAPITOL	1000	30.00	120.00

YR	NAME	LIMIT	ISSUE	TREND
85	BILLY	1000	25.00	100.00
85	CATHY	1000	20.00	150.00
85	CHILDREN'S MUSEUM CAROUSEL, THE	1000	80.00	250.00
85	CINDY	1000	40.00	125.00
85	COUNTRY ROAD	1000	160.00	700.00
85	DANIEL HARRISON HOUSE, THE	1000	100.00	240.00
85	DAREDEVIL SKATERS	1000	100.00	220.00
85	ERIN	1000	25.00	100.00
85	EVENING HOUR IN LONG GROVE	1000	70.00	200.00
85	EVERYTHING NICE	1000	65.00	140.00
85	FAMILY HEIRLOOM	1000	80.00	260.00
85	HEARTLAND, THE	1000	80.00	200.00
85	HEATHER	1000	25.00	200.00
85	IMPERIAL MAJESTY (SILKSCREEN)	99	600.00	1450.00
85	JAKE	1000	25.00	100.00
85	KENTUCKY	1000	70.00	325.00
85	LANCASTER MORN	1000	275.00	850.00
85	LITTLE SISTER	1000	35.00	100.00
85	MARY'S WEDDING	1000	65.00	250.00
85	MIKE	1000	25.00	125.00
85	MINNESOTA	1000	70.00	195.00
85	MY LITTLE BROTHERS	1000	50.00	195.00
85	NANCY	1000	40.00	145.00
85	NIGHT BEFORE CHRISTMAS, THE	1000	65.00	260.00
85	NURSES, THE	1000	70.00	190.00
85	NURSING TEAM	1000	70.00	215.00
85	OUR GIRLS	1000	60.00	175.00
85	PAT	1000	25.00	100.00
85	PICKET FENCE	1000	60.00	180.00
85	PIE MAKERS, THE	1000	80.00	200.00
85	PLAYMATES	1000	70.00	180.00
85	PLEASE MA'AM	1000	50.00	150.00
85	RED CARRIAGE	1000	65.00	190.00
85	ROBBIE	1000	20.00	100.00
85	SCREECH OWL TWINS	1000	75.00	200.00
85	SENATORS, THE	1000	275.00	600.00
85	SENTINELS, THE	1000	65.00	140.00
85	SUMMER'S BLESSING	1000	65.00	210.00
85	THREE SISTERS	1000	70.00	190.00
85	TO EACH OTHER	1000	40.00	125.00
85	TWILIGHT RIDE	1000	80.00	160.00
85	WATCH, THE	1000	30.00	180.00
85	WEDDING BOUQUET	1000	75.00	180.00
85	WEDDING JOY	5000	200.00	625.00
85	WEDDING MORN	1000	70.00	300.00
85	WINTER'S TRAVELERS	1000	60.00	180.00
86	ALLELUIA!	1000	70.00	180.00
86	ALLISON	1000	20.00	150.00
86	AMY'S FLOWERS	1000	50.00	150.00
86	ANDREW	1000	20.00	150.00
86	ANNIE & TEDDY	1000	20.00	100.00
86	BRANDON	1000	20.00	100.00
86	BRIAN	1000	20.00	150.00
86	CANADA GEESE (ETCHING)	99	600.00	1500.00
86	CAROLINE	1000	30.00	95.00
86	DEAR LORD (SHORT)	1000	30.00	75.00
86	DIANA	1000	25.00	100.00
86	EVELYN	1000	40.00	115.00
86	FIRST PROMISE	1000	70.00	175.00
86	GENTLE SWING	1000	50.00	140.00
86	HOMESTEADERS	99	1,200.00	2300.00
86	JACK	1000	25.00	120.00
86	KIM	1000	20.00	150.00
86	MAID MARION	1000	50.00	145.00
86	PROFESSOR, THE	1000	40.00	150.00
86	SCHOOL DAYS	1000	70.00	160.00
86	SKATING WALTZ	1000	60.00	150.00
86	SPRING WEDDING	1000	70.00	200.00
86	STEPHANIE	1000	35.00	140.00
86	SUNDAY STROLL	1000	50.00	250.00
86	WINTER WEDDING	1000	80.00	195.00
86	WINTER'S EVE	1000	100.00	240.00
86	WINTER'S MATES	1000	50.00	180.00
87	BETTY	1000	20.00	80.00
87	BILL	1000	20.00	80.00
87	CHAMPIONS	1000	80.00	160.00
87	CHRISTMAS DANCE	1000	70.00	85.00
87	CONTEMPLATION	1000	75.00	155.00
87	SITTING PRETTY	1000	60.00	145.00
87	THREE LITTLE SISTERS	1000	70.00	180.00
87	YOUNG MAESTRO	1000	60.00	135.00
88	ANGEL'S PRAYER	1000	70.00	130.00
88	ANGELS TWO	1000	40.00	100.00
88	CAROL	1000	25.00	100.00
88	CHELSEA	1000	30.00	100.00
88	GEORGETOWN (ETCHING)	1000	1,000.00	2000.00
88	GRANDAD'S BUDDY	1000	45.00	105.00
88	LITTLE BROWN CHURCH	1000	100.00	250.00
89	A MOTHER'S LOVE	1000	45.00	120.00

YR	NAME	LIMIT	ISSUE	TREND
89	FOREVER YOURS	1000	125.00	350.00
89	KATIE'S FLOWERS	1000	30.00	150.00
89	MY BIG SISTER	1000	50.00	125.00
89	OUR BEDROOM	1000	70.00	160.00
89	PARTNERS	1000	40.00	110.00
89	WINTER GEESE (ETCHING)	99	400.00	1550.00
90	BABY BOY	1000	25.00	90.00
90	BABY GIRL	1000	25.00	75.00
90	CALLING ON FRIENDS	1000	110.00	200.00
90	SHADOWS OF ETERNITY	1000	50.00	125.00
90	SISTER LOVE	1000	40.00	155.00
90	SISTERS	1000	20.00	120.00
90	SPRING MORN	1000	125.00	250.00
90	TAMMY	1000	30.00	100.00
95	ACROSS THE SILENT SNOW	226	200.00	200.00
95	AMERICAN APPLES	1000	65.00	65.00
95	APPLE BARN	1000	80.00	140.00
95	APPLE BLOSSOM TIME	1000	75.00	75.00
95	ASHLEY'S DELIGHT	1000	45.00	45.00
95	AUSTIN	1000	45.00	45.00
95	BARN DANCE AT THE WHITE BARN	1000	95.00	95.00
95	BEAUTIES IN BLUE	1000	160.00	260.00
95	BEAUTY AT THE STAR BARN	1000	75.00	75.00
95	BIRDS OF PEACE	1000	60.00	60.00
95	BOO!	1000	60.00	60.00
95	BROTHERS TOGETHER	1000	55.00	160.00
95	CAROUSEL QUEEN	1000	80.00	80.00
95	CARRIE'S TREE	1200	75.00	75.00
95	CAT DREAMS	1000	75.00	75.00
95	COLLEGE MEMORIES	1000	100.00	100.00
95	CONTENTMENT	1000	70.00	70.00
95	COOL KRIS KRINGLE	1989	45.00	45.00
95	DANNY'S BEAR	1000	45.00	45.00
95	DASHING THROUGH THE SNOW	1000	130.00	130.00
95	DAVID'S CAT	1000	35.00	65.00
95	DIANE'S CAT	1000	35.00	35.00
95	DID YOU KNOW?	1000	45.00	80.00
95	DON'T LET GO!	1000	45.00	45.00
95	DOWN TOWN	1000	75.00	75.00
95	DUTCH DREAMS	1000	70.00	70.00
95	EARLY MORNING RIDE	1000	55.00	85.00
95	EASTER FRIENDS	1000	50.00	50.00
95	ELEMENTARY SCHOOL	1000	75.00	135.00
95	EMORY & HENRY	1000	100.00	100.00
95	EVENING LIGHT	1000	65.00	65.00
95	EVENING SURPRISE	1000	50.00	50.00
95	EXCHANGE PLACE	1000	145.00	440.00
95	FEED ME	1000	25.00	25.00
95	FIDDLE DANCE	1000	50.00	50.00
95	FISHING AT HUMPBACK BRIDGE	1000	100.00	100.00
95	FREE AS THE WIND	1000	175.00	175.00
95	FT. MYER MARRIAGE CARRIAGE	1000	100.00	100.00
95	GENTLE GIANT	1000	35.00	35.00
95	GIRLS IN A ROW	1000	60.00	60.00
95	GOLDEN LOVE	1000	75.00	75.00
95	GRANDMA'S BUREAU	1000	50.00	50.00
95	GRANDMA'S REDHEAD	1000	50.00	50.00
95	GREENBRIER, THE	1000	125.00	125.00
95	HEAVENLY BABE	2000	60.00	60.00
95	HEAVENLY GRACE	1000	75.00	75.00
95	HER FLOCK	1000	55.00	55.00
95	HOTEL ROANOKE	1000	225.00	225.00
95	IOWA HAY RIDE	1000	150.00	150.00
95	IOWA MORN	1000	100.00	100.00
95	IT'S A BOY	1000	45.00	45.00
95	IT'S A GIRL	1000	45.00	45.00
95	JEFFERSON'S GENTLEMEN	1000	50.00	50.00
95	JOHN DEERE GIRL, THE	1000	75.00	75.00
95	JOHNNY SHILOH	2000	115.00	115.00
95	JUST FOR NANA	1000	45.00	45.00
95	LAKE RIDE	1000	110.00	110.00
95	LET IT RAIN	1000	50.00	50.00
95	LET'S BE PALS	1000	45.00	45.00
95	LITTLE BROWN CHURCH REVISITED	1000	125.00	125.00
95	LITTLE RASCALS	1000	45.00	45.00
95	LOTS OF LOVE	1000	45.00	45.00
95	LOVE IN BLOOM	1000	65.00	65.00
95	LOVE'S WINTER RIDE	3000	45.00	45.00
95	MAGIC MOMENT	1000	45.00	45.00
95	MANSION, THE	1000	70.00	70.00
95	MARCHING W/OUR PIG	1000	55.00	55.00
95	MARK'S TRAIN	1000	40.00	40.00
95	MATTHEW'S TRAIN	1000	40.00	40.00
95	MEGHAN'S LAMB	1000	50.00	50.00
95	MILL HOUSE, THE	1000	60.00	60.00
95	MIRROR MIRROR ON THE WALL	1000	50.00	50.00
95	MONTICELLO	1000	125.00	125.00
95	MORNING GLORY	1000	35.00	35.00
95	MOTHER IS LOVE	1000	45.00	45.00

YR	NAME	LIMIT	ISSUE	TREND
95	MOTHER'S DAY	2000	50.00	50.00
95	MOVING IN	1000	75.00	75.00
95	MT. ZION	1000	75.00	75.00
95	MY TWO GIRLS	1000	50.00	50.00
95	NEVER ENDING LOVE	1000	60.00	60.00
95	OLD SLED, THE	1000	75.00	75.00
95	ONE MORE STAR	1500	100.00	100.00
95	OUR AMERICAN GOTHICS	1000	150.00	150.00
95	OUR FAMILY HERITAGE	1000	225.00	225.00
95	OUR GIRL SCOUT	1000	55.00	55.00
95	OUR WINTER DAY	1000	45.00	45.00
95	OUT ON A LIMB	1000	40.00	40.00
95	PAT'S PEACHES	1000	55.00	55.00
95	PEACE	1000	175.00	175.00
95	PRECIOUS FRIENDS	1000	65.00	65.00
95	PRECIOUS SISTERS	1000	50.00	50.00
95	READING, 'RITING & 'RITHMETIC	1000	100.00	100.00
95	RED BARN, THE	1000	45.00	45.00
95	ROYAL PAIR	1000	80.00	80.00
95	SALES BARN, THE	1000	135.00	135.00
95	SERVING OUR NEEDS	1000	100.00	100.00
95	SHADOWY RIDE	1000	175.00	175.00
95	SING ALONG, THE	1000	70.00	70.00
95	SNOWY MORNING ON THE FARM	8933	100.00	100.00
95	SOCIETY QUILT, THE	585	50.00	50.00
95	SPIRIT OF THE MIDWEST	1000	200.00	200.00
95	ST. JOHN'S CEMETARY	1000	225.00	225.00
95	STATE FAIR	1000	90.00	90.00
95	STAY TOGETHER	1000	50.00	50.00
95	STITCHED WITH LOVE	1000	275.00	275.00
95	STITCHING NURSE	1000	65.00	65.00
95	STITCHING SISTERS	1000	80.00	80.00
95	SUNDAY AT GRANDMA'S	1000	75.00	75.00
95	TEXAS STAR	1000	75.00	75.00
95	THREE YOUNG MEN	1000	60.00	60.00
95	TRACTORS ON PARADE	1000	135.00	135.00
95	TRAIN MAN	1000	65.00	65.00
95	TREES IN HARMONY	1000	120.00	120.00
95	TRICK OR TREAT	1000	40.00	40.00
95	TRIO, THE	1000	250.00	250.00
95	TULLIE SMITH HOUSE	1000	60.00	60.00
95	TWILIGHT FISHERMAN	1000	40.00	40.00
95	TWIN BOUQUETS	1000	45.00	45.00
95	UNDER THE MISTLETOE	7532	70.00	70.00
95	UNITED WE STAND	1000	70.00	70.00
95	VIOLET BANK	1000	75.00	75.00
95	VISIT TO THE RED SCHOOLHOUSE	1000	70.00	70.00
95	VISIT TO THE VILLAGE, A	1000	100.00	100.00
95	WATER TOWER, THE	1000	80.00	80.00
95	WATERLOO COUNTY HOMESTEAD	1000	100.00	100.00
95	WE THREE	1000	90.00	90.00
95	WEDDING IN WHITE	1000	75.00	75.00
95	WEDDING IN WINTER	1000	50.00	50.00
95	WELCOME	1000	60.00	60.00
95	WHICH ONE?	1000	60.00	60.00
95	WHITE BARN, THE	1000	55.00	55.00
95	WINFREE MEMORIAL, THE	500	100.00	100.00
95	WINTER HARMONY	1000	750.00	750.00
95	WINTER PRINCE	1000	75.00	75.00
95	WINTER'S GENTLE EVE	1000	115.00	115.00
95	WREN'S NEST REVISITED	1000	100.00	100.00
95	YATES CIDER MILL	1000	100.00	100.00
96	ALL DRESSED UP	1000	60.00	60.00
96	APPLE BLOSSOM LOVE	1000	80.00	80.00
96	DANCING JOY	1000	50.00	50.00
96	DELIVERY TEAM, THE	1000	75.00	75.00
96	FARM LIFE	1000	85.00	85.00
96	FISHERMAN, THE	1000	70.00	70.00
96	FOR THE GIRLS	1000	80.00	80.00
96	GIRL SERIES IV	1000	40.00	40.00
96	GUARDIAN ANGELS	1000	80.00	80.00
96	HAIRCUT, THE	1000	65.00	65.00
96	HERE I GO!	1000	35.00	35.00
96	JUST PURRFECT	1000	50.00	50.00
96	LIBERTY	1000	115.00	115.00
96	MOTHER'S HEART	1000	75.00	75.00
96	QUILTED CATS	1000	75.00	75.00
96	WE'RE ALWAYS TOGETHER	1000	70.00	70.00

P. BUCKLEY MOSS

SILKSCREEN

YR	NAME	LIMIT	ISSUE	TREND
95	HORSES FOUR	500	115.00	115.00
95	NURSES THREE	250	250.00	250.00

N. ROCKWELL GALLERY

N. ROCKWELL

YR	NAME	LIMIT	ISSUE	TREND
97	30TH ANNIVERSARY MAIN STREET CANVAS	5000	195.00	195.00

NAME THAT TOON

CHARACTER SHOP

ANHEUSER-BUSCH BUD FROGS

YR	NAME	LIMIT	ISSUE	TREND
96	CLYDESDALE- FOOTBALL	2000	198.00	202.00

YR	NAME	LIMIT	ISSUE	TREND
96	JAMMIN'	2000	198.00	202.00
96	SPEEDBOAT	2000	198.00	202.00
R. LAZZARINI				
		ANHEUSER-BUSCH BUD FROGS		
95	BUD FROGS II	2000	198.00	202.00
96	BUD FROGS/ ALLIGATOR	2000	198.00	198.00
S. WINSTON				
		ANHEUSER-BUSCH BUD FROGS		
95	BUD FROGS	2000	198.00	300.00
ATHERTON				
		ANHEUSER-BUSCH BUD ICE PENGUIN		
96	CHASE, THE	2000	198.00	202.00
PARK VILLAGE				
		ANHEUSER-BUSCH BUD ICE PENGUIN		
96	DOOBIE DOOBIE DOO	OP	38.00	38.00
*				
		CAMPBELL SOUP		
96	HOW WE MAKE TOMATO SOUP	2000	198.00	202.00
96	SOUP TIME	OP	38.00	38.00
AARDMAN				
		CHEVRON TECHRON CARS		
95	WASH ME	2000	198.00	202.00
S. WINSTON				
		COCA-COLA GORILLA		
96	CHOICE, THE	2000	198.00	202.00
A. CLOBEY				
		COCA-COLA GUMBY		
95	ALWAYS FRIENDS	2000	198.00	225.00
*				
		COCA-COLA NBA LIMELIGHT		
95	ALWAYS JAMMIN'	2000	198.00	202.00
*				
		COCA-COLA POLAR BEARS RHYTHM & HUES		
94	ALWAYS COOL	SO	198.00	500.00
94	PAUSE THAT REFRESHES	2000	198.00	300.00
95	CUBS DAY OUT	2000	198.00	250.00
95	ENCHANTED EVENING	2000	198.00	250.00
96	COCA-COLA SEAL	2000	198.00	202.00
96	GOOD FRIENDS	2000	198.00	250.00
96	LATE NIGHT LUGE	2000	198.00	250.00
96	YES!	OP	38.00	38.00
*				
		COCA-COLA SUN COLOSSAL PICTURES		
94	REFRESHMENT	2000	198.00	202.00
95	SUN-DAY AT THE BEACH	2000	198.00	202.00
*				
		HERSHEY'S KISSES COLOSSAL PICTURES		
95	BUNNY HOP	2000	198.00	202.00
*				
		HERSHEY'S NOSTALGIA		
96	CLUB COCOA	OP	38.00	38.00
96	HERSHEY COW	OP	38.00	38.00
96	HERSHEY KISSES	OP	38.00	38.00
96	MEAL IN ITSELF, A	OP	38.00	38.00
W. VINTON				
		M&M MARS		
96	JUST YOUR FRIENDLY NEIGHBORHOOD M&M'S	2000	198.00	202.00
96	SO, IS IT LOVE?	OP	38.00	38.00
*				
		NABISCO LIFESAVER		
97	BALLOONS	OP	38.00	38.00
*				
		NABISCO MR. PEANUT		
97	CHORUS LINE	OP	38.00	38.00
ATHERTON				
		NABISCO MR. PEANUT		
97	EVERYBODY LOVES A NUT	2000	198.00	202.00
*				
		NABISCO OREO		
97	OREO DESSERT	OP	38.00	38.00
*				
		NABISCO RITZ		
97	SIMPLY MARVELOUS	OP	38.00	38.00
*				
		PILLSBURY DOUGHBOY		
95	POPPIN' FRESH	2000	198.00	202.00
96	DOUGHBOY DELIGHT	OP	38.00	38.00

NEW MASTERS PUBLISHING

P. BANNISTER

YR	NAME	LIMIT	ISSUE	TREND
78	BANDSTAND	250	75.00	550.00
80	DUST OF AUTUMN	200	200.00	1200.00
80	FADED GLORY	200	200.00	1200.00
80	GIFT OF HAPPINESS	200	200.00	2000.00
80	GIRL ON THE BEACH	200	200.00	1300.00
80	SEA HAVEN	SO	285.00	850.00
80	SILVER BELL, THE	200	200.00	2000.00
80	TITANIA	SO	300.00	1200.00
81	CRYSTAL	300	300.00	450.00
81	EASTER	SO	300.00	950.00
81	JULIET	SO	300.00	3400.00
81	MY SPECIAL PLACE	SO	300.00	620.00
81	PORCELAIN ROSE	SO	300.00	2000.00
81	REHEARSAL	SO	300.00	1600.00
82	AMARYLLIS	SO	285.00	1950.00
82	APRIL	SO	200.00	1300.00
82	CINDERELLA	500	285.00	550.00
82	EMILY	SO	285.00	775.00
82	IVY	SO	285.00	700.00
82	JASMINE	SO	235.00	470.00
82	LILY	500	235.00	400.00
82	MAIL ORDER BRIDES	SO	325.00	2350.00
82	MEMORIES	SO	235.00	500.00
82	NUANCE	SO	235.00	525.00
82	PARASOLS	500	235.00	250.00
82	PRESENT, THE	SO	285.00	1000.00

YR	NAME	LIMIT	ISSUE	TREND
83	DUCHESS, THE	SO	250.00	2500.00
83	MEMENTOS	SO	150.00	1350.00
83	OPHELIA	SO	150.00	480.00
83	WINDOW SEAT	SO	150.00	700.00
84	APRIL LIGHT	SO	150.00	600.00
84	FAN WINDOW, THE	SO	195.00	580.00
84	MAKE BELIEVE	SO	150.00	375.00
84	SCARLET RIBBONS	SO	150.00	350.00
86	PRIDE & JOY	SO	150.00	290.00
86	SOIREE	950	150.00	300.00
87	AUTUMN FIELDS	950	150.00	400.00
87	FIRST PRIZE	950	115.00	225.00
87	QUIET CORNER	SO	115.00	600.00
87	SEPTEMBER HARVEST	SO	150.00	375.00
88	APPLES AND ORANGES	SO	265.00	460.00
88	FLORIBUNDA	SO	265.00	650.00
88	GUINEVERE	485	265.00	1450.00
88	LOVE SEAT	SO	230.00	375.00
88	SUMMER CHOICES	300	250.00	760.00
89	CHAPTER ONE	SO	265.00	1600.00
89	DAYDREAMS	SO	265.00	590.00
89	LOW TIDE	SO	265.00	600.00
89	MARCH WINDS	SO	265.00	540.00
89	PEACE	SO	265.00	850.00
89	QUILT, THE	SO	265.00	1400.00
90	GOOD FRIENDS	SO	265.00	525.00
90	LAVENDER HILL	SO	265.00	725.00
90	RENDEZVOUS	SO	265.00	550.00
90	SEASCAPES	SO	265.00	380.00
90	SISTERS	SO	265.00	1200.00
90	SONGBIRD	SO	265.00	330.00
90	STRING OF PEARLS	SO	265.00	620.00
91	CELEBRATION	SO	350.00	900.00
91	CROSSROADS	SO	295.00	575.00
91	PUDDINGS & PIES	SO	265.00	365.00
91	TEATIME	SO	295.00	750.00
91	WILDFLOWERS	SO	295.00	380.00
92	BED OF ROSES	663	265.00	410.00
92	CRYSTAL BOWL	485	265.00	265.00
92	HEIRLOOM, THE	*	265.00	475.00
92	LOVE LETTERS	485	265.00	485.00
92	MORNING MIST	485	265.00	415.00
92	PERFECTION	*	85.00	85.00
93	CROWNING GLORY	485	265.00	550.00
93	DEJA VU	663	265.00	1475.00
93	IN THE WINGS	*	265.00	240.00
93	INTO THE WOODS	485	265.00	410.00
93	LILIES IN THE FIELD	*	265.00	415.00
93	RAMBLING ROSE	485	265.00	650.00
94	ANGELS	*	265.00	500.00
94	CUCKOO CLOCK	*	265.00	265.00
94	FOUNTAIN	485	265.00	410.00
94	FROM RUSSIA W/LOVE	950	165.00	275.00
94	ONCE UPON A TIME	950	265.00	600.00
95	MAGNOLIAS	950	265.00	1250.00
95	NOW AND THEN	*	265.00	265.00

NEWMARK PUBLISHING USA
P. VAUGHAN

YR	NAME	LIMIT	ISSUE	TREND
95	AWAY IN A MANGER	570	95.00	150.00
95	BEAUTIFUL DREAMER	750	95.00	1000.00
95	FAMILY TREE	1200	95.00	95.00
95	FOREVER FRIENDS	1200	95.00	150.00
95	HEIRLOOMS	2500	95.00	140.00
95	HER LITTLE RED SHOES	1200	95.00	200.00
95	OLE TIME RELIGION	1200	95.00	220.00
95	PEACEFUL AFTERNOON	1200	95.00	155.00

NORTHWOODS CRAFTSMAN
J. GADAMUS

YR	NAME	LIMIT	ISSUE	TREND
95	ANGEL OF LIGHT	850	110.00	190.00
95	ANGEL OF PEACE	850	110.00	110.00
95	CHANGING THE GUARD	750	135.00	225.00
96	ABE	850	135.00	200.00
96	SPRING ROSE	850	50.00	50.00

G. KOVACH

YR	NAME	LIMIT	ISSUE	TREND
95	BOYS OF SUMMER	950	150.00	215.00
95	EVENING AT HOLY HILL	2000	150.00	200.00
95	SANTA'S TREAT	1995	90.00	90.00
95	STAR SPANGLED NIGHT	950	150.00	180.00
96	HOME TOWN HEROES	1000	150.00	150.00
96	THOUGHTS OF HOME	950	150.00	245.00

T. SCHULTZ

YR	NAME	LIMIT	ISSUE	TREND
96	AUTUMN CRIMSON	600	50.00	50.00
96	HOMECOMING	600	90.00	90.00
96	SUMMERTIME GOLD	600	50.00	50.00

M. SINGLETON

YR	NAME	LIMIT	ISSUE	TREND
95	CIRCUS PARADE	600	50.00	90.00

YR	NAME	LIMIT	ISSUE	TREND
95	COTTAGE BY THE SHORE	600	75.00	135.00
95	SPRING CLEANING	600	50.00	90.00
96	NOAH'S ARK	600	80.00	145.00
96	SATURDAY NIGHT DOWNTOWN	600	75.00	75.00

M. SOLBERG

95	TO TOUCH THE SKY	950	150.00	150.00

J. GADAMUS   **CANVAS**

95	ANGEL OF LIGHT	100	300.00	300.00
95	ANGEL OF PEACE	100	300.00	300.00

G. KOVACH   **CANVAS**

95	BOYS OF SUMMER	200	350.00	350.00
95	EVENING AT HOLY HILL	200	400.00	400.00
95	SANTA'S TREAT	200	300.00	300.00
95	STAR SPANGLED NIGHT	200	350.00	350.00
96	HOME TOWN HEROES	200	375.00	375.00
96	THOUGHTS OF HOME	200	375.00	375.00

M. SINGLETON   **CANVAS**

95	CIRCUS PARADE	50	150.00	150.00
95	COTTAGE BY THE SHORE	50	250.00	250.00
95	SPRING CLEANING	50	150.00	150.00
96	NOAH'S ARK	50	275.00	250.00
96	SATURDAY NIGHT DOWNTOWN	50	250.00	250.00

M. SOLBERG   **CANVAS**

95	TO TOUCH THE SKY	100	350.00	350.00

ON THE WILD SIDE

J. MEGER   **MEGER**

*	SILHOUETTE-TIMBER WOLF	*	95.00	250.00
79	WILDSIDE I-CANVASBACKS	*	100.00	800.00
80	MANITOBA MEMORIES-CANVASBACKS	*	100.00	275.00
80	SPLIT DECISION-CANVASBACKS	*	100.00	325.00
81	STACK OF BILLS-LESSER SCAUP	*	75.00	250.00
81	WINGS IN THE WILLOWS	*	100.00	180.00
82	PRAIRIE POTHOLES-CANVASBACKS	*	60.00	150.00
82	STOP ON RED-REDHEADS	100	100.00	190.00
83	RISKY BUSINESS	75	75.00	100.00
84	BLUE BANDITS	60	60.00	120.00
84	GOOD MORNING	45	45.00	70.00
84	LEADING LADY	*	60.00	70.00
84	LEGACY-LOON	60	85.00	1320.00
85	BURNING THROUGH	*	100.00	275.00
85	FIELDSTONES-PHEASANTS	125	125.00	680.00
85	LEGACY-EAGLE	85	85.00	400.00
85	LEGACY-MOOSE	85	85.00	115.00
85	WINDSONG-CANADA GEESE	225	225.00	400.00
86	FIRST LIGHT-LOONS	95	95.00	125.00
86	SUNDANCE-SNOWY OWL	125	125.00	125.00
86	UNINVITED GUESTS	60	60.00	60.00
87	COMING HOME	125	125.00	185.00
87	HEARTLAND-PHEASANTS	100	100.00	350.00
87	INTERLUDE	75	75.00	135.00
87	ONE MORE PASS	60	60.00	60.00
87	OUTBACK-PHEASANTS	*	75.00	225.00
87	UP AT THE LAKE	95	95.00	125.00
88	FAST MOVING GAME	60	60.00	150.00
88	HERITAGE CARDINAL	*	85.00	250.00
88	LEGACY-TIMBERWOLVES (AP)	125	85.00	375.00
88	SEPTEMBER PASSAGE	*	125.00	225.00
88	SNOWY COURTSHIP-SNOWY OWLS	125	125.00	190.00
89	EDGE OF TOWN	95	95.00	95.00
89	HOMESTEAD-PHEASANTS (AP)	125	125.00	315.00
89	MOONRIDE-LOONS	95	95.00	825.00
89	PRAIRIE DANCEHALL-PHEASANTS	95	75.00	100.00
89	THREE'S A CROWD	60	60.00	95.00
90	ALPHA-TIMBER WOLF	*	150.00	280.00
90	ALPHA-TIMBER WOLF (AP)	225	225.00	330.00
90	ALPHA-TIMBER WOLF (COLLECTOR'S EDITION)	225	275.00	475.00
90	BREEZING UP-WOOD DUCKS (AP)	*	145.00	180.00
90	FANFARE-TRUMPETER SWANS	150	150.00	185.00
90	FIRST OUTING	60	60.00	300.00
90	HIDDEN GAME-TIMBER WOLF (AP)	75	75.00	80.00
90	MOON SHADOWS-WHITE-TAILED DEER	95	95.00	425.00
90	STORM WARNING-PHEASANTS	95	95.00	410.00
91	PROMISE, THE	*	150.00	175.00
91	PROMISE, THE (COLLECTOR'S EDITION)	295	295.00	350.00
91	SNOWY PURSUIT	*	125.00	240.00

PAST IMPRESSIONS

A. MALEY   **CANVAS**

87	LOVE LETTER	CL	445.00	700.00
87	PROMISE, THE	500	625.00	625.00
89	WINTER IMPRESSIONS	CL	595.00	925.00
90	CAFE ROYALE	CL	665.00	725.00
90	FESTIVE OCCASION	CL	595.00	595.00
90	GRACIOUS ERA	CL	645.00	645.00
90	ROMANTIC ENGAGEMENT	CL	445.00	445.00
91	SUMMER CAROUSEL	CL	345.00	725.00
92	CIRCLE OF LOVE	CL	445.00	1075.00

YR	NAME	LIMIT	ISSUE	TREND
92	ELEGANT AFFAIR	CL	595.00	1400.00
92	EVENING PERFORMANCE	CL	295.00	295.00
92	WALK IN THE PARK	CL	595.00	920.00
93	RAGS AND RICHES	CL	445.00	775.00
93	RECITAL, THE	CL	595.00	1100.00
93	SLEIGH BELLS	CL	595.00	1225.00
93	VISITING THE NURSERY	CL	445.00	1700.00
94	NEW YEAR'S EVE	CL	445.00	825.00
94	PARISIAN BEAUTIES	CL	645.00	1125.00
94	SUMMER ELEGANCE	CL	595.00	595.00
95	GRAND ENTRANCE	250	615.00	775.00
95	LETTER, THE	CL	465.00	810.00
95	NEW CARRIAGE	250	265.00	300.00
95	SLEIGH RACE	250	615.00	715.00
95	SOUTHERN BELLES	250	615.00	640.00
95	SUMMER ROMANCE	CL	465.00	640.00
96	BOATING PARTY, THE	350	665.00	720.00
96	PRIVATE CONVERSATION	350	615.00	615.00

A. MALEY   **PAPER PRINT**

YR	NAME	LIMIT	ISSUE	TREND
84	GLORIOUS SUMMER	CL	150.00	675.00
84	SECLUDED GARDEN	CL	150.00	950.00
85	PASSING ELEGANCE	CL	150.00	700.00
85	SECRET THOUGHTS	CL	150.00	850.00
86	TELL ME	CL	150.00	800.00
86	WINTER ROMANCE	CL	150.00	750.00
87	DAY DREAMS	CL	200.00	315.00
87	LOVE LETTER	CL	200.00	700.00
87	LOVE LETTER A/P	450	300.00	1000.00
87	PROMISE, THE	CL	200.00	550.00
88	BOARDWALK, THE	CL	250.00	340.00
88	JOYS OF CHILDHOOD	CL	250.00	350.00
88	OPENING NIGHT	CL	250.00	1950.00
88	TRANQUIL MOMENT	CL	250.00	330.00
88	VICTORIAN TRIO	CL	250.00	350.00
89	ENGLISH ROSE	CL	250.00	365.00
89	IN HARMONY	CL	250.00	350.00
89	WINTER IMPRESSIONS	750	250.00	615.00
90	CAFE ROYALE	750	275.00	400.00
90	FESTIVE OCCASION	CL	250.00	250.00
90	GRACIOUS ERA	750	275.00	390.00
90	ROMANTIC ENGAGEMENT	750	275.00	320.00
90	SUMMER PASTIME	CL	250.00	400.00
91	BETWEEN FRIENDS	750	275.00	400.00
91	EVENING PERFORMANCE	750	150.00	200.00
91	SUMMER CAROUSEL	750	200.00	200.00
91	SUNDAY AFTERNOON	750	275.00	445.00
91	WINTER CAROUSEL	750	200.00	200.00
92	AN ELEGANT AFFAIR	500	260.00	300.00
92	CIRCLE OF LOVE	500	250.00	515.00
92	INTIMATE MOMENT	750	250.00	345.00
92	WALK IN THE PARK	500	260.00	800.00
93	RAGS AND RICHES	500	250.00	250.00
93	RECITAL, THE	500	275.00	275.00
93	SLEIGH BELLS	500	260.00	400.00
93	VISITING THE NURSERY	500	250.00	300.00
94	NEW YEAR'S EVE	500	250.00	460.00
94	PARISIAN BEAUTIES	500	275.00	275.00
94	SUMMER ELEGANCE	500	275.00	550.00
95	GRAND ENTRANCE	500	250.00	550.00
95	LETTER, THE	500	250.00	400.00
95	NEW CARRIAGE	500	100.00	100.00
95	SLEIGH RACE	500	260.00	260.00
95	SOUTHERN BELLES	500	260.00	260.00
95	SUMMER ROMANCE	500	250.00	250.00
96	BOATING PARTY	400	275.00	275.00
96	PRIVATE CONVERSATION	400	260.00	550.00

A. MALEY   **WOMEN OF ELEGANCE/PAPER PRINT**

YR	NAME	LIMIT	ISSUE	TREND
89	ALEXANDRA	CL	125.00	200.00
89	BETH	CL	125.00	200.00
89	CATHERINE	CL	125.00	125.00
89	VICTORIA	CL	125.00	125.00

PEMBERTON & OAKES
D. ZOLAN

YR	NAME	LIMIT	ISSUE	TREND
84	SABINA IN THE GRASS	880	98.00	495.00
88	DAY DREAMER	1000	35.00	150.00
88	WAITING TO PLAY	1000	35.00	150.00
88	WINTER ANGEL	880	98.00	270.00
89	GRANDMA'S MIRROR	RT	98.00	170.00
89	RODEO GIRL	RT	98.00	180.00
89	SUMMER'S CHILD	RT	98.00	175.00
90	LAURIE AND THE CRECHE	RT	98.00	110.00
91	FLOWERS FOR MOTHER	RT	98.00	115.00

D. ZOLAN   **SINGLE ISSUE**

YR	NAME	LIMIT	ISSUE	TREND
82	BY MYSELF	880	98.00	210.00
82	ERIK AND DANDELION	880	98.00	225.00
86	TENDER MOMENT	880	98.00	212.00
87	TOUCHING THE SKY	880	98.00	245.00

YR	NAME	LIMIT	ISSUE	TREND
88	SMALL WONDER	880	98.00	160.00
88	TINY TREASURES	450	150.00	235.00
89	ALMOST HOME	880	98.00	198.00
89	BROTHERLY LOVE	880	98.00	280.00
89	CHRISTMAS PRAYER	880	98.00	225.00
89	DADDY'S HOME	880	98.00	294.00
89	MOTHER'S ANGELS	880	98.00	160.00
89	SNOWY ADVENTURE	880	98.00	129.00
90	COLORS OF SPRING	880	98.00	165.00
90	CRYSTAL'S CREEK	880	98.00	198.00
90	FIRST KISS	880	98.00	225.00
92	ENCHANTED FOREST	880	98.00	129.00
93	GRANDMA'S GARDEN	880	98.00	137.00

PINE RIDGE PRODUCTIONS
N.P. SANTOLERI

YR	NAME	LIMIT	ISSUE	TREND
86	DECEMBER DUSK	SO	50.00	175.00
86	PRISCILLA & PIGLETS	SO	50.00	100.00
86	WASHINGTON'S HEADQUARTERS	SO	50.00	150.00
87	DIAMOND ROCK SCHOOL HOUSE	SO	65.00	125.00
87	HERBAL BOUQUET	450	80.00	80.00
87	KNOX BRIDGE	SO	65.00	125.00
87	SQUARE, THE	SO	65.00	150.00
87	WE THE PEOPLE	SO	65.00	100.00
88	PORTRAIT OF A GOOSE	500	70.00	70.00
88	STARRY NIGHT	SO	80.00	200.00
89	POND'S EDGE	SO	100.00	150.00
89	VIEW OF THE HUNT, A	SO	95.00	400.00
90	BOATHOUSE ROW	SO	100.00	400.00
90	OLD TIMER	450	85.00	85.00
90	VALLEY GREEN	SO	100.00	275.00
90	WINTER RETREAT	SO	90.00	150.00
91	HARVARD'S BOATHOUSE	500	95.00	95.00
91	IN FOR THE EVENING	SO	100.00	300.00
91	LONGFELLOW HOUSE, THE	500	95.00	95.00
91	ON WALDEN POND	SO	100.00	200.00
91	REACHING FOR THE SKY	SO	100.00	400.00
92	AFTERNOON ON LAKE AFTON	500	50.00	50.00
92	CONTENTMENT FOUND	SO	100.00	200.00
92	EVENING AT EDGMONT	950	100.00	100.00
93	BOATHOUSE ROW III	SO	100.00	200.00
93	CHAPEL AT VILLANOVA	SO	100.00	150.00
93	WOODLAND VISITORS	2500	200.00	200.00
94	KIRBYS MILL	950	100.00	100.00
94	PHILA. MUSEUM OF ART	950	100.00	100.00
95	AFTER LABOR DAY	SO	100.00	500.00
95	BRANDYWINE CHRISTMAS	950	125.00	125.00
95	INDEPENDENCE HALL	950	100.00	100.00
96	BOATHOUSE ROW IV	1500	125.00	125.00
96	SNOW DAYS	950	100.00	100.00
96	ST. JOSEPH'S UNIVERSITY	950	100.00	100.00
96	ST. THOMAS OF VILLANOVA	950	100.00	100.00
96	VIEW OF COLUMBIA AVE, A	950	125.00	125.00
97	ANGEL OF THE SEA	950	125.00	125.00
97	VALLEY GREEN II	950	125.00	125.00
98	PENN STATE (OLD MAIN)	2500	100.00	100.00
98	PENN STATE (OLD MAIN)	1750	100.00	100.00

PORTERFIELD'S
R. ANDERS

YR	NAME	LIMIT	ISSUE	TREND
97	DIGGING IN	5000	26.60	27.00
97	SAFE HARBOR	5000	26.60	27.00
97	TIME OUT	5000	16.60	27.00
97	TWO BITES TO GO	5000	26.60	27.00

PRIZM
P. ULVILDEN

YR	NAME	LIMIT	ISSUE	TREND
98	KNOCK KNOCK SANTA	750	180.00	180.00

RECO INTERNATIONAL
J. MCCLELLAND

			FINE ART CANVAS REPRODUCTION	
90	BEACH PLAY	350	80.00	80.00
91	FLOWER SWING	350	100.00	100.00
91	SUMMER CONVERSATION	350	80.00	80.00

S. KUCK

			LIMITED EDITION PRINT	
84	JESSICA	500	60.00	400.00
85	HEATHER	500	75.00	145.00
86	ASHLEY	500	85.00	175.00

J. MCCLELLAND

			MCCLELLAND	
*	I LOVE TAMMY	500	75.00	100.00
*	JUST FOR YOU	300	155.00	160.00
*	OLIVIA	300	175.00	175.00
*	REVERIE	300	110.00	100.00
*	SWEET DREAMS	300	145.00	150.00

RIE MUNOZ LTD.
R. MUNOZ

YR	NAME	LIMIT	ISSUE	TREND
71	DANCE IN KASHIM	100	8.00	450.00
73	ESKIMO STORY TELLER	300	30.00	825.00

Charles Wysocki put Maggie the Messmaker right in the middle of a sewing project in this 1996 AMCAL Fine Arts print.

Jim Daly's Contentment from Mill Pond Press shows relaxation as only a cat can express it. The 1990 limited edition of 1,500 was originally priced at $95 and is currently valued at $550.

YR	NAME	LIMIT	ISSUE	TREND
74	KING ISLAND	300	30.00	1600.00
74	SCARY SEA	500	30.00	1500.00
75	CREATION OF MAN	500	30.00	2000.00
75	CROW IN A MOUNTAIN ASH	950	30.00	845.00
77	CANNERY WORKERS, NAKNEK	500	30.00	820.00
77	CRABBING	100	30.00	350.00
77	CRANE LEGEND	500	40.00	1900.00
77	GATHERING EGGS	500	30.00	1250.00
77	GOSSIPING WOMEN	500	27.00	200.00
77	KOTZEBU BREAKUP	500	36.00	990.00
77	WINTER SUN, GAMBELL	500	30.00	550.00
78	BERRY PICKERS	500	36.00	415.00
78	RAFT OF DUCKS	950	30.00	715.00
78	RIBBON SEALS	950	20.00	480.00
79	BUTCHERING CRABS, TENAKEE	500	36.00	775.00
79	FISHING FOR KING CRAB, UKIVOK	500	36.00	875.00
79	LADIES IN THE BATH	500	36.00	500.00
80	BLUEBERRIES, BLUEBIRDS	500	30.00	295.00
80	CATS CRADLE	500	27.00	225.00
80	DOUGLAS CRAB BOAT	500	60.00	895.00
80	HAPPY HOUR, NOME	500	40.00	795.00
80	KETCHIKAN ALASKA	500	12.00	365.00
80	LAST CARIBOU	500	35.00	860.00
80	LOOSE DOGS	500	32.00	490.00
80	MIDDLETON	500	36.00	645.00
80	OFF TO SUMMER CAMP	500	40.00	590.00
80	RECESS AUKE BAY SCHOOL	500	42.00	870.00
80	STRING GAME	250	75.00	895.00
80	TUNDRA	500	32.00	440.00
81	BERRY PICKERS	550	40.00	450.00
81	BOOM BOAT	750	45.00	980.00
81	CRAB BUTCHERING PARTY	500	40.00	645.00
81	DANCER IN MOTION	500	36.00	365.00
81	FISHERMAN, KETCHIKAN	500	40.00	645.00
81	FRIENDS, GAMBELL	500	30.00	390.00
81	GATHERING GRASS	500	30.00	265.00
81	GOING BERRY PICKING, HOONAH	500	40.00	750.00
81	HOPKINS ALLEY	750	45.00	595.00
81	INTERVIEWING THE WINNER	500	40.00	650.00
81	MONKEY TREE	500	40.00	665.00
81	REINDEER ROUNDUP	200	200.00	1000.00
81	SEALIONS AT UNALASKA	750	50.00	685.00
81	STARRING	500	36.00	595.00
82	DRYING LAUNDRY & FISH	750	40.00	415.00
82	EVERGREEN BOWL	750	45.00	850.00
82	HAULING IN CRABS	750	40.00	540.00
82	ICE FISHING	750	32.00	720.00
82	IDITAROD RACE HEADQUARTERS	750	40.00	610.00
82	NOAH	750	36.00	685.00
82	RIE MUNOZ IN TAPESTRY	OP	20.00	40.00
82	SIGNS OF SPRING	750	30.00	465.00
82	SOME ALASKA BIRDS	175	45.00	565.00
82	SUMMER CAMP	750	45.00	125.00
82	SUMMER STORM, BUCKLAND	750	45.00	425.00
82	TESTING A SEAL SKIN FLOAT	750	28.00	325.00
83	CHASING MOULTING GEESE	750	32.00	645.00
83	ELFIN COVE	750	32.00	495.00
83	FISH BUYER, ELFIN COVE	750	40.00	440.00
83	IN THE PARK, FRANCE	500	15.00	550.00
83	PACKING FISH	500	28.00	220.00
83	POKER GAME	750	20.00	590.00
83	PRIEST, UNALASKA	750	36.00	595.00
83	ROOSTING BIRDS	200	85.00	530.00
83	SEAGULL STORY	750	32.00	355.00
83	SNOW BUNTINGS, GAMBELL	750	45.00	730.00
83	WHISTLING AT NORTHERN LIGHTS	500	36.00	670.00
83	WRANGELL WATER FRONT	750	40.00	465.00
84	BERRY PICKER	750	28.00	480.00
84	CHAPEL, ROCHE HARBOR	750	35.00	525.00
84	COMING HOME	750	45.00	695.00
84	CRABBER, UNALASKA	750	60.00	1175.00
84	DANCERS IN SEALGUT PARKAS	OP	20.00	20.00
84	FISH CAMP	750	48.00	300.00
84	GROCERIES NOME	750	38.00	475.00
84	IDITAROD, SHATOOLOK	750	64.00	600.00
84	ISTKA SUMMER FESTIVAL	OP	20.00	40.00
84	PACKING FISH	750	40.00	400.00
84	PAINT JOB THOMAS BASIN	750	36.00	335.00
84	POTLATCH BAR, KETCHIKAN	750	30.00	395.00
84	SANDHILL CRANES	750	50.00	695.00
84	ST. NICHOLAS, JUNEAU	750	38.00	695.00
84	STEAMBATH LAKE, ILIAMNA	750	30.00	900.00
84	STORY KNIFE	750	20.00	445.00
84	SWING, THE	750	20.00	430.00
84	TANGLED TRACES	750	20.00	385.00
84	WAITING FOR FERRY, TENAKEE	750	40.00	525.00
85	CLEANING FISH	750	40.00	245.00
85	CRAB POTS, SITKA	750	36.00	455.00
85	HALIBUT $1	750	60.00	1100.00

YR	NAME	LIMIT	ISSUE	TREND
85	JUNEAU CANNERY	750	45.00	525.00
85	NORTH STAR COMING	750	50.00	400.00
85	SPRING SUNDAY	750	38.00	395.00
85	WOMAN BEAR LEGEND	750	60.00	1000.00
86	BLUEBERRIES	750	45.00	435.00
86	CACHE	750	36.00	230.00
86	CATHEDRAL, SITKA	750	48.00	500.00
86	CLEANING SALMON	750	48.00	235.00
86	DINNER, NOME	750	40.00	355.00
86	FALL MIGRATION	750	65.00	565.00
86	GREY POUPON	750	20.00	465.00
86	INNER HARBOR	750	45.00	390.00
86	JESSIE'S FLOWERS	750	45.00	450.00
86	LATE BOAT	750	48.00	425.00
86	LOOKING FOR HALLEY'S COMET	750	30.00	600.00
86	PACKING DUNGENESS	750	25.00	375.00
86	RASPBERRY PATCH	750	20.00	255.00
86	STORM AT FISH CAMP	750	50.00	190.00
86	UNLOADING WALRUS MEAT	750	50.00	295.00
86	WHALE	750	50.00	375.00
87	ABANDONED CABIN	950	35.00	90.00
87	CASH BUYER, KOTZEBUE	750	40.00	165.00
87	DOWNHILL SKIERS, EAGLECREST	750	60.00	795.00
87	FIRST SNOW, STARR HILL	750	30.00	600.00
87	FIRST SNOW, TENAKEE	750	48.00	240.00
87	FISHERMAN'S FAMILY, EAGEGIK	750	35.00	165.00
87	GREENHOUSE	750	45.00	400.00
87	HAULING WATER, TENAKEE	750	28.00	28.00
87	MUG UP, METLAKATLA	750	45.00	105.00
87	PUNTING OVER TO THE MIDNIGHT SUN	750	42.00	220.00
87	RUSSIAN CHURCH, UNALASKA	750	30.00	180.00
87	SPRING FLOWERS	750	25.00	145.00
87	TEKAKEE CABIN	750	55.00	295.00
87	UNLOADING FREIGHT, GAMBRELL	750	65.00	950.00
88	CANNERY COOK, CRAIG	750	30.00	180.00
88	COMING INTO TENAKEE INLET	750	55.00	295.00
88	FEEDING THE SWANS CORNWALL	750	55.00	475.00
88	FOLLOWING THE LEADER	750	45.00	370.00
88	GOING FISHING	750	32.00	380.00
88	LONDON PUB	750	25.00	225.00
88	NOATAK	750	48.00	320.00
88	RUNAWAY MITTENS	750	50.00	485.00
88	SELF PORTRAIT, 4TH ST. STAIRS	750	50.00	340.00
88	WINTER VILLAGE, NOATAK	750	55.00	315.00
89	BLUE MOON CAFE	750	55.00	300.00
89	EDDIE BAUER'S IDITAROD RACER	950	60.00	525.00
89	FALL COLORS	750	55.00	370.00
89	HOLY ASSUMPTION CHURCH	750	60.00	295.00
89	MUSHER	750	40.00	185.00
89	NIGHT SLEDDING, JUNEAU	750	60.00	395.00
89	PTARMIGAN LIFT	750	60.00	700.00
89	SEABIRDS OF ALEUTIANS	750	65.00	215.00
89	WINTER, JUNEAU	750	65.00	440.00
90	ARK IN ALASKA	750	70.00	810.00
90	CREEK STREET, KETCHIKAN	750	72.00	700.00
90	EMBRACE, THE	750	35.00	750.00
90	LAUNDRY, EGEGIK	750	45.00	45.00
90	LOADING CRAB POTS	750	65.00	285.00
90	OFF TO THE BATH, TENAKEE	750	48.00	185.00
90	RUSSIAN CHURCH, JUNEAU	750	68.00	400.00
91	ANDY	950	45.00	190.00
91	MARRY ME, MY DEAR	950	40.00	85.00
91	NUMBER 27	950	45.00	95.00
91	SHADE TREE	950	65.00	65.00
91	SHARPENING AN ULU	950	68.00	200.00
91	SLIDING AT UNALAKLEET	950	90.00	250.00
91	SPRING MIGRATION	950	60.00	375.00
91	STAR PRINCESS	950	75.00	275.00
91	SWING, TENAKEE	750	55.00	215.00
91	TULIPS $2	950	50.00	125.00
91	WHALE LEGEND	950	60.00	60.00
91	WHALE WATCH	750	60.00	100.00
91	WINTER CABIN, TENAKEE	950	55.00	325.00
91	WINTER GAMES	950	65.00	195.00
92	MOLLY-O	950	100.00	340.00
92	NORTHERN LIGHTS, JUNEAU	950	125.00	825.00

R. MUNOZ | | | | **SERIGRAPH** |

YR	NAME	LIMIT	ISSUE	TREND
74	CATS CRADLE	105	27.00	760.00
75	BELUGA WHALE & CALF	950	25.00	845.00
75	HONKERS	100	21.00	300.00
75	REINDEER HERD	*	27.00	325.00
75	SPLITTING WALRUS HIDE	100	27.00	215.00
76	CRESTED AUKLET	95	21.00	450.00
76	ICE FISHING	120	30.00	395.00
77	CANNERY WORKER	105	36.00	425.00
77	COMMERCIAL CRABBER	95	30.00	400.00
78	SEINER	350	25.00	1400.00
79	CARIBOU HUNTER	190	36.00	850.00
79	DANCER	250	50.00	795.00

YR	NAME	LIMIT	ISSUE	TREND
79	NORTHERN LIGHTS, JUNEAU	250	75.00	775.00
79	RAVEN HAD TWO WIVES	90	50.00	1325.00
80	ADRIFT	250	60.00	1130.00
80	DRUMMER & DANCER	350	36.00	475.00
80	FISH GRADER	250	50.00	1500.00
80	SUMMER VOYAGE	250	75.00	900.00
81	INVITATION	250	65.00	856.00
81	RAVEN LEGEND	77	60.00	1295.00
82	SPRING ICE FISHING	200	85.00	1300.00
83	ESKIMO GAME	200	124.00	1200.00
84	ARK IN ALASKA	200	125.00	1635.00
84	MERMAID	220	45.00	410.00
85	WOMAN BEAR LEGEND	183	60.00	1100.00
86	THROAT CHANTERS	750	110.00	1325.00

R. MUNOZ — STONE LITHO

YR	NAME	LIMIT	ISSUE	TREND
74	BUTCHERING AT GAMBELL	125	85.00	690.00
75	SEATED DANCER	125	50.00	175.00
81	WHALE DANCE	100	225.00	450.00
82	ESKIMO MOTHER	100	185.00	1700.00

ROMAN INC.
A. WILLIAMS — ABBIE WILLIAMS

YR	NAME	LIMIT	ISSUE	TREND
88	MARY, MOTHER OF THE CARPENTER	TL	100.00	100.00

F. HOOK — HOOK

YR	NAME	LIMIT	ISSUE	TREND
81	CARPENTER, THE	YR	100.00	1000.00
81	CARPENTER, THE (REMARQUE)	YR	100.00	3000.00
82	BOUQUET	1200	70.00	375.00
82	FROLICKING	1200	60.00	375.00
82	GATHERING	1200	60.00	350.00
82	LITTLE CHILDREN, COME TO ME	1950	50.00	525.00
82	LITTLE CHILDREN, COME TO ME (REMARQUE)	50	100.00	525.00
82	POSING	1200	70.00	375.00
82	POULETS	1200	60.00	375.00
82	SURPRISE	1200	50.00	375.00

F. HOOK — PORTRAITS OF LOVE

YR	NAME	LIMIT	ISSUE	TREND
88	EXPECTATION	2500	25.00	25.00
88	IN MOTHER'S ARMS	2500	25.00	25.00
88	MY KITTY	2500	25.00	25.00
88	REMEMBER WHEN...	2500	25.00	25.00
88	SHARING	2500	25.00	25.00
88	SUNKISSED AFTERNOON	2500	25.00	25.00

R.J. ZOLAN — RICHARD JUDSON ZOLAN COLLECTION

YR	NAME	LIMIT	ISSUE	TREND
95	BLESSING, THE	500	100.00	100.00
95	CHILDREN OF GOD	500	100.00	100.00
95	EVENING PRAYER	500	100.00	100.00
95	KNOCKING AT THE DOOR	500	100.00	100.00
95	PORTRAIT OF CHRIST	500	100.00	100.00
95	WAY TO EMMAUS, THE	500	100.00	100.00
97	COME UNTO ME	500	100.00	100.00
97	LOVE ONE ANOTHER	500	100.00	100.00

ROYALHAUS PUBLISHING
D. ROTTINGHAUS

YR	NAME	LIMIT	ISSUE	TREND
95	IDES OF AUTUMN, THE	950	125.00	170.00
95	SAINT NICHOLAS CHRISTMAS BREAK	550	65.00	65.00
95	SUMMER DAYS	999	125.00	125.00
96	SANCTUARY	950	125.00	170.00

S & V ENTERPRISES
S. LYONS

YR	NAME	LIMIT	ISSUE	TREND
87	BLUES HORNET	200	45.00	700.00
87	LEAD SOLO	200	45.00	650.00
88	GEORGIA EAGLE	200	45.00	650.00
89	FLYIN' TIME	325	45.00	895.00
90	GAS'IN UP	450	450.00	750.00
91	MORNING REFLECTIONS	600	75.00	250.00
97	MACON' A LIVING	200	95.00	95.00
97	ST. GEORGE LIGHTHOUSE	200	95.00	95.00
98	FLYING IS THE PITTS	OP	20.00	20.00
98	FLYING IS THE PITTS	*	125.00	125.00
98	PIEDMONT PACEMAKER-THE BEGINNING	OP	20.00	20.00
98	PIEDMONT PACEMAKER-THE BEGINNING	*	125.00	125.00

S. LYONS — CUB SERIES

YR	NAME	LIMIT	ISSUE	TREND
88	MAD DOG AT THE FOUR OAKS	300	45.00	1625.00
93	SITTIN' PRETTY	600	95.00	1500.00

SAN MARTIN FINE ART
ANNE-LAN

YR	NAME	LIMIT	ISSUE	TREND
88	LA NAISSANCE DU PRINTEMPS	175	250.00	1350.00
88	MATERNITE	225	250.00	1150.00
88	PERSEPHONE	385	600.00	800.00
88	SETTING SUN	495	950.00	1250.00
89	EYES OF THE NIGHT	385	350.00	750.00
89	FEMME FLEUR	385	250.00	500.00
89	REVE DE CHAT	262	250.00	800.00
90	HEURE BLEUE	262	500.00	500.00
90	L'AURORE	262	500.00	500.00
90	LA GRANDE CASCADE	230	200.00	240.00

YR	NAME	LIMIT	ISSUE	TREND
90	PLUME	385	500.00	550.00
90	PUPUCE	230	200.00	240.00
91	EGLANTINE	450	60.00	60.00
91	INVITATION AU VOYAGE	262	500.00	500.00
91	LE CHATEAU FLEURI	300	450.00	450.00
91	LOVE STORY	450	60.00	60.00

SANDY CLOUGH STUDIO
S. CLOUGH

YR	NAME	LIMIT	ISSUE	TREND
95	GOD BLESS OUR HOME	1500	70.00	80.00
95	IN THE GARDEN	2500	75.00	75.00
95	TEA PARTY II	3500	55.00	55.00
96	SERENITY	3500	50.00	50.00
96	SUNDAY STROLL	3500	40.00	40.00
97	BLESSED ARE THE PURE IN HEART	3900	80.00	80.00
98	HIS EYE IS ON THE SPARROW	3900	80.00	80.00
98	REMEMBER ME	3900	60.00	60.00
98	SEWING WITH MAMA	3900	60.00	60.00

SARAH'S ATTIC
S. SCHULTZ

YR	NAME	LIMIT	ISSUE	TREND
97	ADORA ANGEL- WOOD	1000	14.00	14.00
97	ANGELS ON EARTH- GOLD	1000	24.00	24.00
97	ANGELS ON EARTH- WOOD	1000	15.00	15.00
97	CHILLY/BURLEY- GOLD	1000	24.00	24.00
97	CHILLY/BURLEY- WOOD	1000	15.00	15.00
97	ENOS ANGEL- WOOD	1000	14.00	14.00
97	FLITTER ANGEL- WOOD	1000	14.00	14.00
97	FLUTTER ANGEL- WOOD	1000	14.00	14.00
97	GINGERBREAD- WOOD	RT	14.00	14.00
97	KATIE PRAYING- WOOD	1000	14.00	14.00
97	MAGGIE- GOLD	1000	24.00	24.00
97	MAGGIE- WOOD	1000	15.00	15.00
97	MATT- GOLD	1000	24.00	24.00
97	MATT- WOOD	1000	15.00	15.00
97	MISSY/MIKEY- GOLD	1000	24.00	24.00
97	MISSY/MIKEY- WOOD	1000	15.00	15.00
97	NAT- GOLD	1000	24.00	24.00
97	NAT- WOOD	1000	15.00	15.00
97	NETTIE- GOLD	1000	24.00	24.00
97	NETTIE- WOOD	1000	15.00	15.00
97	NOAH'S ANGEL- GOLD	1000	24.00	24.00
97	NOAH'S ANGEL- WOOD	1000	15.00	15.00
97	SANTA OF WOODS- GOLD	1000	24.00	24.00
97	SANTA OF WOODS- WOOD	1000	15.00	15.00
97	SARAH'S GANG- WOOD	1000	24.00	24.00
97	TILLIE	1000	14.00	14.00
97	WILLIE & TILLIE- GOLD	1000	34.00	34.00

SCHMID
J. FERRANDIZ
FERRANDIZ LITHOGRAPHS

YR	NAME	LIMIT	ISSUE	TREND
80	MOST PRECIOUS GIFT	425	125.00	1300.00
80	MOST PRECIOUS GIFT (REMARQUE)	50	225.00	2900.00
80	MY STAR	675	100.00	700.00
80	MY STAR (REMARQUE)	75	175.00	1900.00
81	HEART OF SEVEN COLORS	600	100.00	400.00
81	HEART OF SEVEN COLORS (REMARQUE)	75	175.00	660.00
82	HE SEEMS TO SLEEP	450	150.00	800.00
82	HE SEEMS TO SLEEP (REMARQUE)	25	300.00	3250.00
82	MIRROR OF THE SOUL	225	150.00	500.00
82	MIRROR OF THE SOUL (REMARQUE)	35	250.00	2450.00
82	OH SMALL CHILD	450	125.00	500.00
82	OH SMALL CHILD (REMARQUE)	50	225.00	1500.00
82	ON THE THRESHOLD OF LIFE	425	150.00	500.00
82	ON THE THRESHOLD OF LIFE (REMARQUE)	50	275.00	1400.00
82	RIDING THROUGH THE RAIN	900	165.00	400.00
82	RIDING THROUGH THE RAIN (REMARQUE)	100	300.00	775.00
82	SPREADING THE WORD	675	125.00	300.00
82	SPREADING THE WORD (REMARQUE)	75	225.00	1100.00
83	FRIENDSHIP	460	165.00	500.00
83	FRIENDSHIP (REMARQUE)	15	1,200.00	2350.00
84	STAR IN THE TEAPOT	410	165.00	175.00
84	STAR IN THE TEAPOT (REMARQUE)	15	1,200.00	2100.00

L. DAVIS
LOWELL DAVIS LITHOGRAPHS

YR	NAME	LIMIT	ISSUE	TREND
81	DUKE'S MIXTURE	899	75.00	130.00
81	DUKE'S MIXTURE (REMARQUE)	101	150.00	375.00
81	PLUM TUCKERED OUT	899	75.00	390.00
81	PLUM TUCKERED OUT (REMARQUE)	101	100.00	350.00
81	SURPRISE IN THE CELLAR	899	75.00	553.00
81	SURPRISE IN THE CELLAR (REMARQUE)	101	100.00	400.00
82	BIRTH OF A BLOSSOM	400	125.00	420.00
82	BIRTH OF A BLOSSOM (REMARQUE)	50	200.00	450.00
82	BUSTIN' WITH PRIDE	899	75.00	125.00
82	BUSTIN' WITH PRIDE (REMARQUE)	101	150.00	250.00
82	FOXFIRE FARM	800	125.00	125.00
82	FOXFIRE FARM (REMARQUE)	100	200.00	250.00
82	SUPPERTIME	400	125.00	300.00
82	SUPPERTIME (REMARQUE)	50	200.00	450.00
85	SELF PORTRAIT	450	75.00	160.00

YR	NAME	LIMIT	ISSUE	TREND
87	BLOSSOM'S GIFT	450	75.00	195.00
89	SUN WORSHIPPERS	750	100.00	145.00
90	SUNDAY AFTERNOON TREAT	750	100.00	100.00
91	WARM MILK	750	100.00	100.00
92	CAT AND JENNY WREN	750	100.00	100.00

M.I. HUMMEL   **M.I. HUMMEL LITHOGRAPHS**

YR	NAME	LIMIT	ISSUE	TREND
80	MOONLIGHT RETURN	900	150.00	850.00
81	A TIME TO REMEMBER	720	150.00	300.00
82	POPPIES	450	150.00	650.00
83	ANGELIC MESSENGER (75TH ANNIV. ED.)	195	375.00	700.00
83	ANGELIC MESSENGER, CHRISTMAS MESSENGER	400	275.00	330.00
85	BIRTHDAY BOUQUET I	195	450.00	550.00
85	BIRTHDAY BOUQUET II	225	375.00	375.00
85	BIRTHDAY BOUQUET III	100	195.00	395.00

SERENDIPITY TRADING CO.
B. RABBIT

YR	NAME	LIMIT	ISSUE	TREND
87	ELDERS, THE	950	45.00	200.00
87	FROM EARTH MAN CAME	950	65.00	200.00
88	FAITHFUL, THE	350	90.00	275.00
88	YESTERDAY, TODAY AND TOMORROW	1500	35.00	200.00
89	AFTER THE RAINS	650	65.00	135.00
89	PROMISES, DREAMS AND HOPE	650	65.00	175.00
90	ANCESTORS	350	125.00	375.00
90	COMING OF WINTER	200	250.00	750.00
90	FEAST DAY	350	125.00	375.00
90	PRICE OF PEPPERS, THE	650	75.00	90.00
90	PROPOSAL, THE	350	125.00	375.00
90	STRENGTH TOGETHER	350	125.00	375.00
90	WARMTH OF YOUR TOUCH	350	125.00	130.00

SIMON ART
C. BLACK

YR	NAME	LIMIT	ISSUE	TREND
84	BLUE LADY	290	85.00	100.00
85	SUMMER DAY/CHARLES STREET	350	60.00	75.00
86	CHRISTMAS MORNING	225	125.00	1200.00
86	HALTON HOMESTEAD	125	100.00	850.00
86	MAITLAND HALL	125	85.00	500.00
86	NANA'S BACK DOOR	125	85.00	650.00
86	SILENT VISITOR	125	50.00	130.00
86	SNOW & THUNDER	125	125.00	275.00
86	WELCOME HOME	125	100.00	150.00
87	CENTURY FARM	395	125.00	450.00
87	FIRST CHRISTMAS	395	125.00	175.00
87	HOME FOR CHRISTMAS	395	125.00	650.00
87	JOURNEY'S END	395	125.00	700.00
87	OLD APPLE TREE, THE	395	125.00	175.00
87	SNOWED IN	395	125.00	500.00
88	CAROLE'S GARDEN	395	170.00	200.00
88	DADDY'S GIRL	395	170.00	350.00
88	MORNING ON MAIN STREET	395	200.00	500.00
89	AUNT MARTHA'S	390	170.00	175.00
89	HIGH HOUSE	390	170.00	175.00
89	SILENT NIGHT	390	170.00	170.00
90	A NIGHT'S LODGING	390	210.00	210.00
90	HOME FOR THE HOLIDAYS	450	170.00	170.00
90	MARY'S KITCHEN	490	170.00	170.00
91	SATURDAY MORNING	*	130.00	130.00
91	SPRING PLANTING	*	130.00	130.00

A. KINGSLAND

YR	NAME	LIMIT	ISSUE	TREND
86	BROKEN FENCE	390	50.00	50.00
86	LONER, THE	560	30.00	40.00
86	MAIL BOX, THE	450	120.00	200.00
86	OLD GOLD	560	30.00	60.00
86	OLD RED	390	50.00	50.00
86	ROUNDHOUSE, THE	200	120.00	150.00
86	SEA SCAVENGERS	450	120.00	120.00
86	SILENT MIST	390	80.00	80.00
86	SNOW TRACKS	450	120.00	120.00
86	WAITING OUT WINTER	560	30.00	30.00
86	WINTER BIRCH	560	30.00	60.00
87	CALM WATERS	450	150.00	150.00
87	COUNTRY FOLK	450	150.00	150.00
87	FISHING BOATS	450	150.00	150.00
87	GIANT, THE	200	180.00	225.00
87	HOMESTEAD & RURAL ROUTE, THE (SET OF 2)	450	250.00	250.00
87	OCTOBER	450	150.00	150.00
87	WINTER DRESS	450	150.00	150.00
88	BOYS OF SUMMER	450	90.00	90.00
88	COUNTRY AUTUMN	450	150.00	150.00
88	HOME TEAM, THE	450	90.00	178.00
88	JUST A GAME	450	90.00	90.00
88	LASER FUN	450	150.00	150.00
88	SHINNY	450	150.00	400.00
88	SNOWBALLS	450	150.00	150.00
88	TADPOLES	450	150.00	150.00
89	CROSSING THE 16TH	200	180.00	180.00
89	MILL POND, THE	490	110.00	110.00
89	PLAYOFF, THE	450	180.00	270.00

YR	NAME	LIMIT	ISSUE	TREND
89	SKATERS, THE	490	180.00	180.00
89	SNOWMAN, THE	450	180.00	180.00
89	TEMPESTUOUS SKY	450	180.00	180.00
90	A WINTER VISIT	490	200.00	200.00
90	COLLECTIBLES	490	110.00	110.00
90	MY HOME TOWN	490	180.00	180.00
90	SHADY LADY	490	190.00	190.00
90	SKI TRAIN	390	200.00	200.00
90	WHERE DREAMS BEGIN	490	190.00	250.00
91	CLEAR THE TRACK	*	180.00	180.00
91	DEDICATED	790	216.00	216.00
91	WINTER VIGIL	790	140.00	140.00

L. LESPERANCE

YR	NAME	LIMIT	ISSUE	TREND
83	WATERS EDGE	350	115.00	230.00
85	COOL INTERLUDE	390	115.00	250.00
85	WATCHFUL GUARDIAN	390	115.00	170.00
86	AMBUSH!	690	95.00	400.00
86	MAY BRINGS FLOWERS	690	90.00	110.00
86	SILENT REFLECTIONS	350	115.00	800.00
87	MYSTICAL SHADOWS	790	140.00	230.00
87	SUMMER'S END-COYOTES	*	110.00	110.00
87	WINGING WESTWARD	790	160.00	800.00
88	MARCH FLURRIES	790	150.00	275.00
88	MORNING PATROL	790	150.00	155.00
89	GREAT ESCAPE, THE	590	225.00	260.00
89	THOSE EYES	590	150.00	150.00
90	DELICATE BALANCE	790	200.00	200.00
90	OLD TIRE SWING, THE	790	200.00	300.00
90	PHANTOM OF THE MARSH	950	225.00	225.00
90	SILENT WINGS	790	225.00	225.00
90	SPOOKING THE HERD	590	225.00	225.00
91	PLAYTIME	790	190.00	240.00
91	SIBLINGS	*	200.00	200.00

J. LUMBERS

YR	NAME	LIMIT	ISSUE	TREND
85	MR. EMMET'S FISHIN' HOLE	200	200.00	5250.00
85	SATURDAY MORNING	200	250.00	2000.00
86	ADRIFT	390	200.00	1400.00
86	BEYOND THE SHORE	390	200.00	1250.00
86	CHANGING SEASONS	390	200.00	550.00
86	COUNTRY KITCHEN	390	200.00	975.00
86	DEJA VU	390	200.00	580.00
86	DUNROWAN	450	160.00	1400.00
86	GONE FISHIN'	390	200.00	2000.00
86	JOY RIDE	390	200.00	400.00
86	KITE, THE	390	200.00	980.00
86	SECRET OF THE WELL	450	160.00	770.00
87	BIG CATCH, THE	390	250.00	1200.00
87	CATS	390	250.00	2775.00
87	INHERITANCE, THE	390	250.00	1210.00
87	MEMORIES FOR SALE	390	250.00	475.00
87	SUNSET MEMORIES	390	250.00	490.00
88	BILLY NINE FINGERS	590	250.00	415.00
88	CHERRY HILL ROAD COLLECTION (SET OF 4)	490	500.00	950.00
88	DOUBLE TROUBLE	490	250.00	275.00
88	FIRESIDE SHADOWS	590	250.00	850.00
88	JUST FOR YOU	590	250.00	775.00
88	LUCKY STRIKE	790	250.00	775.00
88	MISCHIEF	590	250.00	775.00
88	OUT ON A LIMB	490	250.00	475.00
89	A WINTER'S GLOW	790	250.00	475.00
89	ABANDONED HERITAGE	790	280.00	1050.00
89	LONE PINE	950	280.00	1150.00
89	MORNING REFLECTIONS	950	280.00	285.00
89	SHADES OF SUMMER	790	280.00	660.00
89	SIDE BY SIDE	2183	350.00	1000.00
89	STIRRING MEMORIES	790	280.00	1075.00
89	SUMMERS PAST	790	280.00	360.00
90	AN ENCHANTED EVENING	1500	280.00	430.00
90	CAT NAPPING	1500	280.00	325.00
90	DAYS GONE BY	950	280.00	650.00
90	DIFFERENT TIMES	1500	280.00	280.00
90	PLAYING THROUGH	950	280.00	865.00
90	SHOPPING	1500	280.00	230.00
91	A BOY AND HIS DREAM	*	275.00	360.00
91	A BOY AND HIS DREAM (CS)	*	1,250.00	2250.00
91	MR. HOCKEY	*	275.00	240.00
91	MR. HOCKEY (CS)	*	1,250.00	1250.00
91	SUN NEVER SETS, THE	*	280.00	225.00

J. REID

YR	NAME	LIMIT	ISSUE	TREND
*	AT BAT	650	200.00	300.00
*	O.K., BLUE JAYS!	390	150.00	200.00
*	QUEEN & SPADINA	390	150.00	950.00
*	WHERE THE WORLD COMES TO PLAY	521	300.00	350.00
85	CAT TAILS	450	125.00	125.00
85	FLOWER HOUSE	450	125.00	600.00
85	NEAR ELORA	450	125.00	200.00
85	SNOW PODS	450	125.00	125.00
86	GEORGIAN BAY SKY	450	125.00	125.00

YR	NAME	LIMIT	ISSUE	TREND
86	NORTHERN STREAM	450	125.00	125.00
87	RAIL FENCE	450	150.00	150.00
87	SNOW BANKS	450	180.00	180.00
87	SUGAR SHACK	450	150.00	150.00
88	BEDFORD MILLS	450	170.00	170.00
88	MORNING MAIL	450	125.00	125.00
88	MURPHY'S PLACE	450	125.00	125.00
88	SILENT STREAM AND STANDING BY (SET OF 2)	450	210.00	210.00
89	CHRISTMAS HOUSE	450	170.00	170.00
89	HURON COUNTRY	450	170.00	170.00
90	DAYBREAK	450	170.00	170.00
90	SHORELINE TRILOGY (SET OF 3)	450	125.00	125.00

J. TRINIDAD

YR	NAME	LIMIT	ISSUE	TREND
88	A COUNTRY SCENE	590	210.00	260.00
88	A SUMMER PLACE	590	210.00	260.00
88	BACKYARD SETTING	590	210.00	260.00
88	FLOWER GIRL	590	210.00	210.00
88	LITTLE GARDENERS	450	210.00	650.00
89	CATHERINE	450	170.00	245.00
89	COUNTRY WALK	450	125.00	400.00
89	MARKET, THE	450	170.00	170.00
89	PLAYTIME	450	125.00	125.00
89	SUMMER RESORT	450	170.00	170.00
89	TEA TIME	450	210.00	210.00
90	FLOWER LOVER	590	145.00	145.00
90	GUARDIAN OF THE ROSES	590	210.00	210.00
90	SHARING	450	170.00	170.00
90	WINTER WARMTH	450	170.00	170.00

SMITH & SCHOEN

R. TEJADA **M.I. HUMMEL**

YR	NAME	LIMIT	ISSUE	TREND
89	CHILD WITH BLUE BELLS	5000	125.00	125.00
89	SIEGLINDE'S FIRST TREE	5000	125.00	125.00

SOMERSET HOUSE PUBLISHING

G. HARVEY

YR	NAME	LIMIT	ISSUE	TREND
74	POKER PALS	500	50.00	75.00
76	BOSS' NEW RIG	1500	60.00	175.00
76	CAREFREE COWHANDS	500	50.00	100.00
78	CROSSING THE CANYON	2000	50.00	700.00
78	DRIFTING COWHANDS	2000	60.00	500.00
78	LEAVIN' THE LINE SHACK	2000	50.00	350.00
79	CHANGING OF THE RANGELAND	250	150.00	2650.00
79	WHEN BANKERS WORE BOOTS	1000	75.00	840.00
80	COMING HOME, THE	1000	75.00	140.00
80	EARLY RUN	1000	75.00	265.00
80	GOOD LORD WILLIN/CREEK DON'T RISE	1000	90.00	165.00
80	IN THE LAND OF THE ROCKIES	1000	90.00	200.00
80	IN THE LAND OF THE WALKIN' RAIN	1000	75.00	190.00
80	RANCHING-PUMP JACK STYLE	1000	90.00	1400.00
80	RIDING THE SALT RIVER CANYON	1000	75.00	180.00
80	RIDING WITH GRANDPA	1000	90.00	375.00
80	SATURDAY NIGHT POKER PALACE	1000	75.00	175.00
80	SILENT HUNTER, THE	1000	75.00	130.00
80	SPRING PALETTE	1000	90.00	200.00
80	TEXAS FROM HIDE AND HORN	1000	90.00	275.00
80	TIMES REMEMBERED	2250	100.00	150.00
81	BOOMTOWN DRIFTERS	2250	150.00	400.00
81	OIL PATCH	1000	150.00	600.00
81	ON THE STREETS OF NEW ORLEANS	1000	150.00	280.00
81	WALL STREET	SO	150.00	1725.00
81	WITH NO INTENTION OF CHARGING	1000	150.00	400.00
82	BOOT TOP DEEP	1000	150.00	1875.00
82	COWBOYS' CHRISTMAS BALL	1000	150.00	235.00
82	COWTOWN 1880	1000	150.00	1750.00
82	DALLAS 1908	1200	150.00	800.00
82	INDEPENDENT OILMEN	1000	150.00	400.00
82	LEAVING THE OIL PATCH	1000	150.00	425.00
82	PLAZA, NEW YORK, THE	1000	150.00	300.00
82	SUPPLIES FOR THE MISSION	1000	150.00	175.00
83	COUNTRY POST OFFICE	1000	150.00	415.00
83	FAMILY CHRISTMAS	1250	150.00	300.00
83	FRESH SNOW FIRST LIGHT	1250	150.00	230.00
83	STREETCARS ALONG THE AVENUE	2500	90.00	750.00
84	AMERICAN WEST	1250	150.00	300.00
84	EARLY DOWNTOWN HOUSTON	1250	150.00	420.00
84	GRAND OPENING	1250	150.00	170.00
84	ME, GRANDPA, AND LITTLE SIS	1250	150.00	180.00
84	TOO WET TO PLOW	1000	*	520.00
84	TRADING AT THE GENERAL STORE	1250	150.00	175.00
85	A NEW LEASE	1250	150.00	420.00
85	CHESTNUT VENDOR	1250	150.00	180.00
85	DALLAS REMEMBERED	1250	150.00	450.00
85	ONLY WORKING HORSEBACK	1250	150.00	375.00
85	SANTA FE PLAZA	1250	150.00	225.00
86	INDEPENDENT TEXANS	1250	150.00	390.00
86	REFLECTIONS OF YESTERDAY (W/BOOK)	1250	275.00	1500.00
86	ROYAL STREET	1250	160.00	275.00
86	TEXAS RANCHER	1250	150.00	150.00

YR	NAME	LIMIT	ISSUE	TREND
86	TIES OF HOME, THE	1250	150.00	150.00
87	EVENING ALONG THE AVENUE	1250	150.00	380.00
87	FIFTH AVENUE	1250	150.00	300.00
88	FLOWER CART, THE	1250	150.00	380.00
88	MEN OF THE AMERICAN WEST	1250	150.00	700.00
88	PENNSYLVANIA AVENUE	2575	150.00	1350.00
88	SATURDAY NIGHT CONTRACT	1250	150.00	515.00
89	COWBOY'S PAYDAY	1250	165.00	500.00
89	EARLY RIDERS	*	150.00	230.00
89	JEB STUART'S RETURN	1800	165.00	700.00
89	WALL STREET-NEW YORK	4378	165.00	550.00
90	AN EVENING WITH THE PRESIDENT	*	165.00	1000.00
90	CITY BY THE BAY	*	165.00	800.00
90	HORSE TROLLEY ON PARK ROW	*	165.00	175.00
90	PICKET'S REPORT	1800	165.00	500.00
90	REMEMBERING THE GOOD TIMES	*	165.00	325.00
90	THINKING OF SPRING	*	165.00	240.00
90	THOUGHTS OF HOME	*	165.00	185.00
91	CATHEDRAL OF ST. BASIL, THE-RED SQUARE	*	165.00	375.00
91	GENTEEL NATION	*	165.00	175.00
91	WIND RIVER RANGE	*	165.00	200.00

V. HOLLAN SWAIN

YR	NAME	LIMIT	ISSUE	TREND
86	BRIDGES AND BLOSSOMS	950	80.00	300.00
86	WHISPERING LIGHT	950	80.00	135.00
87	CASCADE OF COLOR	950	80.00	140.00
87	COURTYARD, THE	950	80.00	165.00
87	ENCHANTED POND, THE	950	80.00	135.00
87	QUIET VILLAGE, THE	950	80.00	400.00
88	MORNING LIGHT-DEVON	950	80.00	130.00
88	RIVERWALK	950	80.00	130.00

P. VAUGHAN

YR	NAME	LIMIT	ISSUE	TREND
84	REFLECTIONS OF THE PAST	1000	40.00	250.00
84	TIMELESS ELEGANCE	1000	40.00	180.00
85	AUNT VERDI'S PORCH	1000	45.00	235.00
85	FRIENDSHIP QUILTS	1000	50.00	775.00
85	PRESERVED IN TIME	1000	50.00	100.00
85	SISTERS THREE	1000	50.00	180.00
85	SUMMERS REMEMBERED (PAIR)	5000	50.00	150.00
85	UPSTAIRS SEWING ROOM, THE	1000	45.00	380.00
85	YESTERDAY'S DREAMS	1000	45.00	110.00
86	A BOUQUET FOR ELIZABETH	1000	50.00	300.00
86	A CAMEO OF THE PAST	1000	50.00	115.00
86	FABRIC OF DREAMS, THE	1000	50.00	90.00
86	FOREVER YOURS (SET OF 3)	1500	90.00	135.00
86	IN THE GARRET	1000	50.00	70.00
86	VICTORIAN BOUQUET	1000	50.00	90.00
87	A BREATH OF SPRING	1000	50.00	135.00
87	COTILLION	1000	50.00	90.00
87	FIDDLER AND THE QUILT MAKER	1000	50.00	90.00
87	LITTLE WOMEN	1000	50.00	125.00
87	TEA, ROSES AND ROMANCE	1675	60.00	380.00
88	CHERISHED MOMENTS	1000	55.00	95.00
88	LOVE SONGS	1000	55.00	150.00
88	ROSE OF SHARON	1000	55.00	200.00
88	SOMETHING OLD, SOMETHING NEW	1000	55.00	540.00

SOUDERS FINE ART

R. SOUDERS

YR	NAME	LIMIT	ISSUE	TREND
80	COUNTRY GROCERY	750	30.00	255.00
80	SANTA FE LINE	750	30.00	225.00
80	VICTORIAN REFLECTIONS	500	25.00	500.00
81	AUTUMN YEARS	750	40.00	1200.00
81	COUNTRY MUSIC	750	25.00	125.00
81	FLOYD'S SUPER SERVICE	750	50.00	475.00
81	MORNING GLORY	750	25.00	125.00
81	RED'S CAFE	750	50.00	450.00
82	DAYBREAK	750	65.00	400.00
83	AMAZING GRACE	750	60.00	475.00
83	COUNTY SEAT	750	70.00	375.00
84	INDEPENDENCE DAY	750	75.00	365.00
84	PENN STREET	750	70.00	785.00
85	CATTLE BARON'S BALL	750	70.00	775.00
85	HARVEST TIME	750	70.00	185.00
85	WEST TEXAS GOLD	1100	50.00	385.00
86	BISHOP'S PALACE	950	80.00	225.00
88	SOUTHERN LIVING	950	90.00	110.00
89	SINGING IN THE RAIN	950	100.00	175.00
90	LOST AT SEA	950	85.00	100.00
92	GOLDEN GATE	950	60.00	75.00
92	SHEPHERD'S PRAYER	950	60.00	75.00

SPORTS COLLECTORS WAREHOUSE

C. PALUSO

YR	NAME	LIMIT	ISSUE	TREND
86	CARL YASTRZEMSKI	452	95.00	275.00
86	DON DRYSDALE	465	95.00	240.00
86	DON SUTTON	310	95.00	200.00
86	MICKEY MANTLE	250	175.00	2250.00
86	SPARKY ANDERSON	574	75.00	140.00
87	CARL HUBBELL	800	75.00	185.00

YR	NAME	LIMIT	ISSUE	TREND
87	SANDY KOUFAX	950	100.00	325.00
88	BILL DICKEY	800	75.00	425.00
88	CHARLES GEHRINGER	800	75.00	185.00
88	LEFTY GOMEZ	800	75.00	185.00
88	MUHAMMAD ALI	300	250.00	1395.00
88	NOLAN RYAN	383	125.00	600.00
88	TED WILLIAMS	406	185.00	950.00
89	BILLY HERMAN	800	110.00	140.00
89	BOB FELLER	500	125.00	140.00
89	JOE SEWELL	800	110.00	200.00
89	JOHNNY MIZE	500	125.00	140.00
89	LOU BOUDREAU	500	125.00	145.00
89	MONTE IRVIN	500	125.00	140.00
89	RALPH KINER	500	125.00	145.00
89	RICK FERRELL	800	110.00	145.00
89	ROY CAMPANELLA	250	600.00	1490.00
89	STAN MUSIAL	475	185.00	625.00
89	WILLIE MAYS	500	185.00	325.00
90	GORDIE HOWE	500	125.00	350.00
90	JOE MONTANA	400	400.00	790.00
90	JOHNNY UNITAS	500	150.00	280.00
90	MAURICE RICHARD	500	125.00	200.00
90	PEE WEE REESE	500	175.00	185.00
90	YOGI BERRA	500	185.00	225.00

D. SMITH

YR	NAME	LIMIT	ISSUE	TREND
*	ROGER CRAIG	1060	65.00	345.00
86	HUDDLE, THE	1000	60.00	400.00
88	SWEETNESS: WALTER PAYTON	1000	200.00	300.00
89	JERRY RICE	1060	60.00	525.00
89	NATURAL, THE: WILL CLARK	1060	65.00	640.00
90	BO JACKSON	*	80.00	175.00
90	MONEY: M. JORDAN	1990	80.00	215.00
90	MVP: JOE MONTANA	950	325.00	800.00
90	SPECIAL TEAMS	1000	80.00	300.00
90	STEVE LARGENT	1060	120.00	425.00
90	TOP GUN: DAN MARINO	950	120.00	345.00

SPORTS IMPRESSIONS

YR	NAME	LIMIT	ISSUE	TREND
*	ARTFUL DODGERS, THE	1000	95.00	395.00

J. CATALANO

YR	NAME	LIMIT	ISSUE	TREND
*	MICK, THE: MANTLE	750	125.00	295.00
*	YANKEE GREATS	750	95.00	245.00

B. JOHNSON

YR	NAME	LIMIT	ISSUE	TREND
*	DON MATTINGLY H/S	950	125.00	200.00
*	DON MATTINGLY PLAYER OF THE YEAR H/S	950	125.00	350.00
*	DON MATTINGLY PLAYER OF THE YEAR U/S	950	95.00	200.00

R. SIMON

YR	NAME	LIMIT	ISSUE	TREND
*	DON MATTINGLY ROOKIE H/S	950	125.00	295.00
*	LIVING TRIPLE CROWN	950	195.00	450.00
*	MANTLE ALL STAR	750	125.00	375.00
*	MANTLE HALL OF FAME	750	125.00	375.00
*	MANTLE ROOKIE H/S	750	125.00	375.00
*	MANTLE TRIPLE CROWN	750	125.00	375.00
*	MICKEY AT NIGHT	750	125.00	450.00
*	STARS AND STRIPES	500	125.00	225.00
*	TED WILLIAMS G/E	950	125.00	250.00
91	BOYS OF SUMMER	500	335.00	350.00

STEINER PRINTS

R. STEINER

YR	NAME	LIMIT	ISSUE	TREND
81	1981 CALIFORNIA DUCK STAMP	1150	115.00	400.00
82	UNEXPECTED SPRIG	200	45.00	80.00
83	BULL SPRIG AT BUTTE SINK	450	85.00	90.00
83	FLUSHED WOODIES	450	45.00	80.00
83	STORMY MORNING MALLARDS	450	85.00	300.00
84	1984 NEVADA DUCK STAMP	1990	135.00	250.00
84	BLACK LAB WITH PINTAIL	950	25.00	150.00
85	1985 MICHIGAN DUCK STAMP	980	135.00	200.00
85	EARLY LIGHT A/P	175	135.00	275.00
85	HONKERS AT DAWN	350	85.00	350.00
86	1986 FLORIDA DUCK STAMP	1000	135.00	250.00
86	CALIFORNIA PHEASANT (CIRCLE)	100	99.00	100.00
86	REFLECTIVE SPRIG	350	45.00	50.00
86	SILENT PARTNER	780	65.00	70.00
87	1987 CALIFORNIA DUCK STAMP	750	135.00	400.00
87	1987 CALIFORNIA DUCK STAMP (MED.)	50	300.00	900.00
87	1987 NEW HAMPSHIRE DUCK STAMP	5507	135.00	500.00
87	1987 NEW HAMPSHIRE DUCK STAMP (GOV.)	50	850.00	3500.00
87	1987 NEW HAMPSHIRE DUCK STAMP (MED.)	50	300.00	1000.00
87	CALIFORNIA QUAIL W/POPPIES	450	65.00	65.00
87	EMPERORS OVER THE ALEUTIANS	350	85.00	85.00
87	OPENING DAY	350	65.00	100.00
87	PINTAILS AT THE COLORADO	450	85.00	90.00
88	1988 CALIFORNIA DUCK STAMP	750	135.00	300.00
88	1988 CALIFORNIA DUCK STAMP (MED.)	300	300.00	700.00
88	1988 NEW HAMPSHIRE DUCK STAMP	5507	135.00	300.00
88	1988 NEW HAMPSHIRE DUCK STAMP (GOV.)	100	500.00	300.00

YR	NAME	LIMIT	ISSUE	TREND
88	1988 NEW HAMPSHIRE DUCK STAMP (MED.)	50	300.00	600.00
89	1989 ARIZONA DUCK STAMP	900	135.00	200.00
89	1989 ARIZONA DUCK STAMP (GOV.)	200	500.00	1200.00
89	1989 ARIZONA DUCK STAMP (MED.)	100	300.00	400.00
89	1989 CALIFORNIA DUCK STAMP	750	145.00	200.00
89	1989 CALIFORNIA DUCK STAMP (MED.)	300	300.00	500.00
89	1989 NEW HAMPSHIRE DUCK STAMP	5507	135.00	300.00
89	LATE SNOW WOOD DUCKS	100	65.00	70.00
90	1990 COLORADO GOVERNOR'S ED STAMP	4980	58.00	65.00
90	1990 COLORADO PRINT	14500	169.00	250.00
90	1990 COLORADO PRINT (GOV)	400	619.00	1500.00
90	1990 COLORADO PRINT (MED)	2000	319.00	500.00
90	1990 NEW HAMPSHIRE GOVERNOR'S ED STAMP	1380	54.00	65.00
90	1990 NEW HAMPSHIRE PRINT	5507	140.00	300.00
90	1990 NEW HAMPSHIRE PRINT (GOV)	135	505.00	2000.00
90	1990 NEW HAMPSHIRE PRINT (MED)	50	305.00	600.00
90	1990 RHODE ISLAND GOVERNOR'S ED STAMP	1800	57.50	65.00
90	1990 RHODE ISLAND PRINT	3000	153.50	250.00
90	1990 RHODE ISLAND PRINT (GOV)	200	558.00	1500.00
90	1990 RHODE ISLAND PRINT (MED)	300	308.50	500.00
90	GRACEFUL ASCENT	1850	45.00	80.00
91	1991 COLORADO GOVERNOR'S ED STAMP	1380	55.00	65.00
91	1991 COLORADO PRINT	8000	169.00	200.00
91	1991 COLORADO PRINT (GOV)	200	619.00	1200.00
91	1991 COLORADO PRINT (MED)	1000	319.00	400.00
91	1991 NEW HAMPSHIRE GOVERNOR'S ED STAMP	990	54.00	65.00
91	1991 NEW HAMPSHIRE PRINT	5507	154.00	200.00
91	1991 NEW HAMPSHIRE PRINT (GOV)	130	519.00	1200.00
91	1991 NEW HAMPSHIRE PRINT (MED)	50	319.00	400.00
91	1991 NEW MEXICO GOVERNOR'S ED STAMP	3990	57.50	65.00
91	1991 NEW MEXICO PRINT	12000	179.00	250.00
91	1991 NEW MEXICO PRINT (GOV)	500	649.00	1200.00
91	1991 NEW MEXICO PRINT (MED)	1000	339.00	500.00
91	1991 RHODE ISLAND GOVERNOR'S ED STAMP	1200	57.50	65.00
91	1991 RHODE ISLAND PRINT	8000	169.00	200.00
91	1991 RHODE ISLAND PRINT (GOV)	130	574.00	1200.00
91	1991 RHODE ISLAND PRINT (MED)	200	319.00	400.00
91	1991 UTAH PRINT	14028	163.00	200.00
91	1991 UTAH PRINT (GOV)	75	618.00	1800.00
91	1991 UTAH PRINT (MED)	1600	318.00	400.00
92	1992 NEW MEXICO PRINT (GOV)	95	505.00	649.00
92	1992 NEW MEXICO PRINT (MED)	600	305.00	339.00

T.S.M. & COMPANY
A. MANOCCHIA

MANOCCHIA

YR	NAME	LIMIT	ISSUE	TREND
84	COYOTE	150	45.00	85.00
84	SKIRMISH IN THE TALL GRASS	500	65.00	150.00
85	ROOM FOR ONLY ONE	600	60.00	120.00
85	SOARING	600	65.00	150.00
87	ALONE AT HOME	500	85.00	250.00
87	EVENING HUNT	500	70.00	200.00
87	SAVE THE SOUND	OP	20.00	75.00
88	HARRIS HAWK	350	60.00	75.00
89	EARLY MORNING AUSABLE	350	45.00	100.00
89	FALL FISHING	350	40.00	85.00
89	FALL WHITETAIL COUNTRY	*	35.00	80.00
89	FIRST CATCH	150	60.00	60.00
89	FISHING THE EAST BRANCH	350	40.00	80.00
89	FROM HIGH ABOVE	OP	25.00	80.00
89	MOUNT KATAHDIN-MOOSE	*	135.00	135.00
89	SPARROW	350	50.00	50.00
90	A WAITING GAME	*	85.00	85.00
90	BAY BRANT	*	200.00	300.00
90	IT DOESN'T GET BETTER THAN THIS...	*	75.00	75.00
90	JUSTIES SET	*	75.00	135.00
90	MOUNT KATAHDIN-WHITETAIL	*	135.00	135.00
90	TEAMWORK	*	80.00	80.00
91	AFTER THE LIMIT	*	270.00	270.00
91	EARLY MORNING WORKOUT	*	10.00	25.00
91	HONORS COURSE-9TH HOLE USGA	*	195.00	195.00
91	MOUNT KATAHDIN-BLACK BEAR	*	135.00	135.00
91	ROCK HOLE, THE	*	90.00	165.00
91	TODAY'S WATER TEMPERATURE IS...	*	45.00	45.00
91	TOO LATE FOR LUNCH	*	60.00	60.00
91	YELLOWSTONE MAGIC	*	75.00	75.00

THE ART OF GLYNDA TURLEY
G. TURLEY

YR	NAME	LIMIT	ISSUE	TREND
97	KEEPING WATCH	7500	77.00	77.00
97	WREATH OF SPRING	7500	64.00	64.00

G. TURLEY

ARTIST PROOF

YR	NAME	LIMIT	ISSUE	TREND
95	ABUNDANCE III	50	109.50	110.00
95	ALMOST AN ANGEL	50	84.00	84.00
95	GLYNDA'S GARDEN	50	109.50	110.00
95	GRAND GLORY III	50	97.50	98.00
95	GRAND GLORY IV	50	97.50	98.00
95	HOLLYHOCKS III	50	103.50	104.00
95	IN FULL BLOOM III	50	96.00	96.00
95	LITTLE RED RIVER	50	109.50	110.00

YR	NAME	LIMIT	ISSUE	TREND
95	MABRY IN SPRING	50	97.50	98.00
95	REMEMBER WHEN	50	109.50	110.00
95	SOUTHERN SUNDAY II	50	109.50	110.00
95	SUMMER IN VICTORIA	50	79.50	80.00
96	A SOUTHERN TRADITION I	50	109.50	110.00
96	SECRET GARDEN III	50	97.50	98.00

G. TURLEY   **CANVAS REPLICA**

YR	NAME	LIMIT	ISSUE	TREND
95	ABUNDANCE III	350	380.00	380.00
95	ALMOST AN ANGEL	350	260.00	260.00
95	GLYNDA'S GARDEN	350	380.00	380.00
95	GRAND GLORY III	350	320.00	320.00
95	GRAND GLORY IV	350	320.00	320.00
95	HOLLYHOCKS III	350	320.00	320.00
95	IN FULL BLOOM III	350	280.00	280.00
95	LITTLE RED RIVER	350	380.00	380.00
95	MOBRY IN SPRING	350	320.00	320.00
95	REMEMBER WHEN	350	380.00	380.00
95	SOUTHERN SUNDAY II	350	380.00	380.00
95	SUMMER IN VICTORIA	350	260.00	260.00
96	A SOUTHERN TRADITION V	350	380.00	380.00
96	SECRET GARDEN III	350	320.00	320.00

G. TURLEY   **GLYNDA TURLEY COLLECTION**

YR	NAME	LIMIT	ISSUE	TREND
95	CIRCLE OF FRIENDS	4800	67.00	67.00
95	COURTYARD II	4800	99.00	99.00
95	FLOWERS FOR MOMMY	4800	85.00	85.00
95	PAST TIMES	4800	78.00	78.00
95	PLAYING HOOKIE AGAIN	4800	83.00	83.00
95	SECRET GARDEN II	RT	95.00	95.00

G. TURLEY   **MEANINGFUL HARVEST**

YR	NAME	LIMIT	ISSUE	TREND
97	CHRYSANTHEMUMS & APPLES	7500	64.00	64.00
97	PEARS & ROSES	7500	64.00	64.00

G. TURLEY   **OLD MILL STREAM**

YR	NAME	LIMIT	ISSUE	TREND
97	OLD MILL STREAM IV	7500	73.00	73.00

G. TURLEY   **PAPER EDITION**

YR	NAME	LIMIT	ISSUE	TREND
95	ABUNDANCE III	7500	73.00	73.00
95	ALMOST AN ANGEL	7500	56.00	56.00
95	GLYNDA'S GARDEN	7500	73.00	73.00
95	GRAND GLORY III	7500	65.00	65.00
95	GRAND GLORY IV	7500	65.00	65.00
95	HOLLYHOCKS III	7500	69.00	69.00
95	IN FULL BLOOM III	7500	64.00	64.00
95	LITTLE RED RIVER	7500	73.00	73.00
95	MABRY IN SPRING	7500	65.00	65.00
95	REMEMBER WHEN	7500	73.00	73.00
95	SOUTHERN SUNDAY II	7500	73.00	73.00
95	SUMMER IN VICTORIA	7500	53.00	53.00
96	A SOUTHERN TRADITION V	7500	73.00	73.00
96	SECRET GARDEN III	7500	65.00	65.00

V.F. FINE ARTS
S. KUCK

YR	NAME	LIMIT	ISSUE	TREND
86	SILHOUETTE	250	60.00	245.00
86	SUMMER REFLECTIONS	900	60.00	250.00
86	TENDER MOMENTS	500	70.00	250.00
87	A QUIET TIME	900	40.00	170.00
87	DAISY, THE	900	30.00	145.00
87	FLOWER GIRL, THE	900	40.00	125.00
87	LE PAPILLION	350	90.00	150.00
87	LOVESEAT, THE	900	30.00	160.00
87	MOTHER'S LOVE	150	195.00	550.00
87	READING LESSON, THE	900	60.00	215.00
88	FIRST RECITAL	150	200.00	800.00
88	KITTEN, THE	350	120.00	1200.00
88	LITTLE BALLERINA	150	110.00	300.00
88	MY DEAREST	350	160.00	775.00
88	WILD FLOWERS	350	160.00	220.00
89	BUNDLE OF JOY	1000	125.00	250.00
89	DAY DREAMING	900	150.00	200.00
89	INNOCENCE	900	150.00	200.00
89	PUPPY	500	120.00	615.00
89	ROSE GARDEN	500	95.00	230.00
89	SISTERS	900	95.00	275.00
89	SONATINA	900	150.00	230.00
90	CHOPSTICKS	1500	80.00	130.00
90	FIRST SNOW	500	95.00	250.00
90	LE BEAU	1500	80.00	125.00
90	LE BELLE	1500	80.00	125.00
90	LILLY POND	750	150.00	235.00
91	GOD'S GIFT	1500	95.00	250.00
91	MEMORIES	5000	195.00	235.00
92	DUET	950	125.00	185.00
92	JOYOUS DAY	1200	125.00	130.00
92	YESTERDAY	950	95.00	175.00
93	BEST FRIENDS	2500	145.00	160.00
93	GARDEN MEMORIES	2500	145.00	150.00
93	GOOD MORNING	2500	145.00	150.00
93	THINKING OF YOU	2500	145.00	150.00

P. Buckley Moss' To Grandmother's House We Go *has almost tripled in value since its 1984 release.*

Hitching A Ride *by P. Buckley Moss, produced by Moss Portfolio, has more than doubled in value.*

Ole Time Religion, *a print by Paula Vaughan for Newmark Publishing U.S.A., has increased in value since its 1995 release.*

YR	NAME	LIMIT	ISSUE	TREND
94	DEAR SANTA	*	495.00	495.00
94	READING TO THEODORE	*	145.00	150.00

VISUAL DELITES
P. RASHFORD
HAND PAINTED PHOTO PRINT

YR	NAME	LIMIT	ISSUE	TREND
93	CASTLES MADE OF SAND	1000	375.00	375.00

P. RASHFORD
PRINT

YR	NAME	LIMIT	ISSUE	TREND
91	PASSAGEWAY	500	72.00	72.00
92	TWO TREES ON A HILL	850	72.00	72.00
93	MOMENT OF SECLUSION	*	30.00	30.00
94	PATHS NOT TAKEN	500	30.00	30.00
94	PLACID AFTERNOON	500	30.00	30.00
94	PUPPY	500	22.00	22.00

P. RASHFORD
SERIGRAPH

YR	NAME	LIMIT	ISSUE	TREND
89	MOUNTAIN LAKE	CL	850.00	850.00
89	NO BLUE HORIZONS	CL	285.00	285.00
90	CARAVANSERAI	465	90.00	90.00
90	WISE LIKENESS	RT	30.00	30.00

VOYAGEUR ART
K. DANIEL

YR	NAME	LIMIT	ISSUE	TREND
*	ADORNMENT OF WINTER	*	85.00	100.00
*	CONSEQUENCE OF FIRE	*	225.00	260.00
*	FIRST RECITAL	*	125.00	175.00
*	LOST DECOY II	*	85.00	170.00
*	SEARCH FOR SURVIVAL	*	145.00	150.00
*	WINTER SILENCE	*	155.00	155.00
80	WETLAND AND WIKIS	*	120.00	140.00
81	BARNYARD TUSSLE	*	85.00	85.00
81	OUT ON A LIMB	*	85.00	125.00
81	PINE RIDGE	*	85.00	200.00
82	A TOUCH OF ORANGE	*	85.00	180.00
82	BEWILDERED	*	85.00	150.00
82	BLUE HERONS	*	85.00	150.00
82	CHICKADEE	*	50.00	50.00
82	SAFE AND SOUND	*	50.00	100.00
82	SILENT SENTINEL	*	85.00	175.00
83	PRIDE OF THE LAKES	*	85.00	325.00
84	BREAK IN THE STORM	*	85.00	125.00
84	LOST DECOY	*	85.00	150.00
85	ON THE RUN	*	85.00	110.00
85	RUFFED GROUSE SPRING CREEK	*	85.00	125.00
85	SUMMER BLUE JAY	*	85.00	100.00
85	WINGS OF THE NORTH	*	85.00	150.00
86	BOUNDARY WATER SOLITUDE	*	85.00	100.00
86	MAJESTIC VIEW	*	85.00	150.00
90	CONSEQUENCE OF TIME	*	225.00	230.00
90	MISTY WATERS	*	155.00	230.00
90	STALKING THE BLUFFS	*	150.00	225.00
90	SWEET DREAMS	*	185.00	200.00
91	RHAPSODY IN BLOOM	*	185.00	185.00

WHITE DOOR PUBLISHING
G. ALEXANDER

YR	NAME	LIMIT	ISSUE	TREND
95	A PLACE IN THE SUN	380	125.00	175.00

D.E. KUCERA

YR	NAME	LIMIT	ISSUE	TREND
95	SHADOW OF A DREAM	680	150.00	150.00
96	RENEZVOUS AT TRAILS END	680	125.00	125.00

D. MIEDUCH

YR	NAME	LIMIT	ISSUE	TREND
95	LORD HELPS THOSE...., THE	750	150.00	150.00

C.L. PETERSON

YR	NAME	LIMIT	ISSUE	TREND
89	STALL,THE	950	95.00	950.00
89	SUNDAY HITCH	950	95.00	1450.00
90	ALL ABOARD	950	125.00	1950.00
90	ANDERSON'S STORE	950	125.00	1400.00
90	CONCERT, THE	950	150.00	2500.00
91	FAMILY REUNION	950	125.00	2650.00
91	POTLUCK AT JUDDVILLE	1250	150.00	1100.00
91	SWING YOUR PARTNER	950	150.00	975.00
92	AT THE MILL	1250	175.00	400.00
92	EVENING LEMONADE	1250	165.00	1150.00
92	ON VALENTINE LANE	1250	175.00	950.00
92	RECITATION	1500	175.00	1000.00
93	COUNTRY DOCTOR	1750	175.00	375.00
93	NEIGHBORS	1500	185.00	1100.00
93	VOLUNTEERS	1500	185.00	500.00
94	FIRST HAIRCUT	2000	175.00	300.00
94	FIRST SNOW	2000	185.00	500.00
94	HARMONY	2000	185.00	500.00
94	R.F.D.	1850	185.00	300.00
95	AND APPLE PIE	2500	195.00	500.00
95	GRANDMA'S QUILT	2000	195.00	700.00
95	HAYRIDE	2600	195.00	260.00
95	HOME GROWN	2000	195.00	460.00
96	AUCTION DAY	2800	225.00	400.00
96	SKATERS ICE	2800	195.00	300.00
96	SUGAR TIME	2500	195.00	210.00

YR NAME	LIMIT	ISSUE	TREND
96 TALK OF SPRING	2500	195.00	225.00
97 STITCH IN TIME	2800	195.00	180.00
J. SLOANE			
95 CHRISTMAS MAGIC	650	65.00	90.00
		CANVAS EDITION	
B.J. PARRISH			
95 NORTH POLE EXPRESS	250	395.00	275.00
		MEMORIES COLLECTION	
R. SALTER			
95 WALKING IN A WINTER WONDERLAND	680	115.00	130.00
		PAPER EDITION	
B.J. PARRISH			
95 NORTH POLE EXPRESS	1500	175.00	260.00

WILD WINGS INC.

YR NAME	LIMIT	ISSUE	TREND
R. ABBETT			
96 ON THE WILLOWEMOC	850	145.00	145.00
S. BOURDET			
96 SEPTEMBER MORNING-CARDINAL	750	125.00	125.00
98 MOUNTAIN MEMORIES	750	85.00	85.00
J. BRANDENBURG			
96 AUTUMN WOLF	9500	85.00	85.00
R. BURNS			
96 STODDARD'S LANE	850	125.00	125.00
98 ARCTIC ECHOES-ARCTIC WOLVES	850	125.00	125.00
C. CUMMINGS			
96 EVENING IN SPRING	750	125.00	125.00
98 HIGH SPIRITS	850	95.00	95.00
M. HANSON			
96 GOLDEN GLORIES-GOLDFINCHES	*	50.00	50.00
J. HAUTMAN			
96 1996 MN DSP	2000	145.00	145.00
96 ROCKY SHALLOWS-LOONS	950	125.00	125.00
J. KASPER			
96 SPRING FEVER-EASTERN WILD TURKEYS	950	145.00	145.00
98 SOUTHERN CHARMS-OSCEOLA TURKEYS	950	125.00	125.00
J. KILLEN			
96 GREAT HUNTING DOGS-LABRADORS	980	125.00	125.00
98 GREAT HUNTING DOGS II-LABS	1200	125.00	125.00
S. KOZAR			
96 LATE SUMMER REFLECTIONS	850	145.00	145.00
L. KROMSCHROEDER			
96 FLANK SPEED-ORCAS	950	175.00	175.00
98 BICYCLE BUILT FOR TWO-CARDINALS	1200	95.00	95.00
98 PEEPING TOMS, THE	1200	145.00	145.00
D. MAASS			
96 BREAKING SKIES-CANVASBACKS	850	175.00	175.00
96 THREE BIRDS UP-RUFFED GROUSE	950	175.00	175.00
98 EVENING FLIGHT-PHEASANTS	1200	175.00	175.00
R. MILLETTE			
96 BACKWATER PASSAGE-WHITETAIL DEER	950	145.00	145.00
96 BACKWATER PASSAGE-WILD TURKEYS	950	145.00	145.00
97 MEADOW MIST-PHEASANTS	CL	145.00	145.00
97 MEADOW MIST-WHITETAIL DEER	CL	145.00	145.00
98 AFTER THE STORM-PHEASANTS	1200	145.00	145.00
98 PRAIRIE MONARCHS-BISON	950	95.00	95.00
P. SCHOLER			
98 TWILIGHT PATROL-LOONS	950	95.00	95.00
R. SCOTT			
96 SILENT GUNS	850	145.00	145.00
98 SILVER AND GOLD TRIPTYCH	950	195.00	195.00
M. SIEVE			
96 A DAY IN THE SUN-DALL SHEEP	950	145.00	145.00
96 MISTY FOREST-BALD EAGLE	1500	145.00	145.00
96 SCRAPELINE BUCK	1500	145.00	145.00
98 1998 MINNESOTA WILD TURKEY	*	*	N/A
98 BOSSIES 'N BLUEBELLS	950	145.00	145.00
98 RULE NUMBER SIX-GET LUCKY	*	*	N/A
M. SUSINNO			
96 DUPED-BROWN TROLT	850	125.00	125.00
98 MATCHING THE HATCH-BROOK TROUT	950	85.00	85.00
98 MATCHING THE HATCH-BROWN TROUT	950	85.00	85.00
98 MATCHING THE HATCH-CUTTHROAT TROUT	950	85.00	85.00
98 MATCHING THE HATCH-RAINBOW TROUT	950	85.00	85.00
S. TIMM			
96 1996 WI DSP	1500	145.00	145.00
96 STARLIGHT NIGHT	950	125.00	125.00
R. VAN GILDER			
96 PINNACLE BOONE & CROCKETT, THE	1200	175.00	175.00
98 WHEN SPRING CALLS	950	95.00	95.00
P.C. WEIRS			
96 DREAM TEAM-WHITETAIL DEER	1900	145.00	145.00
96 FROSTY MORNING	950	145.00	145.00
96 LONESOME BULL-ELK	950	145.00	145.00
98 COFFEE AND CHOCOLATE IN THE MORNING	850	85.00	85.00
98 MOONRISE-WOLVES	950	95.00	95.00
N. YOUNG			
96 BENEATH SPRING BLOSSOMS	750	125.00	125.00

YR NAME	LIMIT	ISSUE	TREND
M. SIEVE		**SURVIVAL SERIES**	
98 RULE NUMBER FIVE-HOLD TIGHT	6327	125.00	125.00

WILDLIFE INTERNATIONALE
J. RUTHVEN

	LIMIT	ISSUE	RUTHVEN
* ALGONQUIN	750	75.00	200.00
* ALLEN'S HUMMINGBIRD	750	75.00	125.00
* AMERICAN WIDGEON	950	65.00	100.00
* ANNA'S HUMMINGBIRD	750	75.00	125.00
* BALD EAGLE-INITIAL	1000	30.00	900.00
* BATELEUR EAGLE	750	110.00	250.00
* BENGAL TIGER-COMMISSION, IDAHO	1000	100.00	675.00
* BENGAL TIGER-REGAL	1000	80.00	2000.00
* BENGAL TIGER-SAFARI	5000	65.00	1000.00
* BLACK MANED LION	5000	65.00	120.00
* BLUE WINGED TEAL	500	75.00	190.00
* BLUEBIRDS-INITIAL	1000	30.00	700.00
* BLUEBIRDS-SPRING, COMMISSION	200	*	250.00
* BOBWHITE QUAIL-AMERICANA	1000	80.00	500.00
* BOBWHITE QUAIL-INITIAL	1000	360.00	400.00
* BOBWHITE QUAIL-KNOB CREEK	750	75.00	425.00
* BROADBILLED HUMMINGBIRD	500	75.00	125.00
* BROWN PELICAN	500	125.00	400.00
* CALIFORNIA VALLEY QUAIL	950	50.00	180.00
* CANADA GOOSE	1000	95.00	400.00
* CANVASBACKS-DU COMMISSION	150	425.00	750.00
* CANVASBACKS-NORTH AMERICAN	1000	50.00	650.00
* CARDINAL-INITIAL	1000	30.00	900.00
* CARDINAL-MARIEMONT	500	75.00	225.00
* CARDINAL-SONGBIRD	950	75.00	650.00
* CAROLINA PARAQUET	500	300.00	1200.00
* CAROLINA WREN	950	50.00	100.00
* CEDAR WAXWING	950	50.00	225.00
* CHICKADEES	950	50.00	150.00
* CHIPMUNK	750	50.00	450.00
* CHIPPEWA BRAVE	950	50.00	175.00
* CINNAMON TEAL	2000	30.00	285.00
* COMMON ELDERS-DU CANADA COMMISSION	100	125.00	200.00
* DECOY	750	125.00	1100.00
* DOUBLE TIME	750	85.00	200.00
* DOWNY WOODPECKER	600	55.00	425.00
* DUSTY	950	150.00	680.00
* EAGLE TO THE MOON	500	150.00	1590.00
* EASTERN WILD TURKEY-INITIAL	1000	30.00	600.00
* EASTERN WILD TURKEY-KNOB CREEK	750	75.00	500.00
* ELEPHANTS	5000	65.00	200.00
* FLICKERS	950	65.00	275.00
* FLYING SNOWY OWL	950	125.00	400.00
* FOX MASQUE I	1000	30.00	175.00
* FOX MASQUE II	1000	30.00	165.00
* FRIENDS-INDIAN CHILDREN	500	75.00	150.00
* GIANT PANDA	5000	65.00	700.00
* GOLDFINCH-COMMISSION	600	55.00	375.00
* GRANT'S ZEBRA	3500	75.00	100.00
* GRAY FOX FAMILY	950	150.00	200.00
* GRAY FOX-MASTERPIECE	950	125.00	1300.00
* GRAY FOX-WOODLAND	1500	200.00	275.00
* GREAT HORNED OWL	1000	90.00	330.00
* GREEN WINGED TEAL	500	75.00	200.00
* GREY SQUIRREL	600	55.00	325.00
* HERRING GULLS	1000	50.00	175.00
* HOODED MERGANSER	750	75.00	190.00
* HOODED MERGANSER (SM.)	1000	50.00	100.00
* INDIGO BUNTING	950	50.00	50.00
* IVORY BILLED WOODPECKERS	5000	350.00	500.00
* JAGUAR	950	65.00	550.00
* KIRTLAND WARBLER	1000	100.00	175.00
* KIT FOX	500	100.00	400.00
* LABRADOR DUCK	500	350.00	350.00
* LEOPARD	3500	75.00	200.00
* MALLARD-INITIAL	1000	50.00	500.00
* MALLARD/WOOD DUCK (PR.)	99	750.00	1850.00
* MISTY-REDHEAD DUCKS	100	125.00	300.00
* N.Y. STATE BLUEBIRD	1000	50.00	250.00
* NATURE CENTER CARDINAL	1000	50.00	225.00
* OAKGROVE PINTAIL (SM.)	3000	50.00	100.00
* ON THE HUNT	1000	90.00	120.00
* PASSENGER PIGEON-AQUATINT	500	350.00	500.00
* PASSENGER PIGEON-MARTHA	500	100.00	400.00
* PEREGRINE FALCON	600	65.00	65.00
* PHEASANT (PAIR)	99	850.00	1750.00
* PHEASANT-INITIAL	1000	30.00	100.00
* RED FOX FAMILY	1000	90.00	1200.00
* RED FOX-COMMISSION	1000	100.00	600.00
* RED FOX-REGAL	1000	90.00	1700.00
* RED FOX-WOODLAND	950	150.00	330.00
* REDHEAD DUCKS	450	350.00	425.00
* REDHEADED WOODPECKERS	1000	50.00	180.00
* RIVOLI'S HUMMINGBIRD	750	75.00	125.00

YR	NAME	LIMIT	ISSUE	TREND
*	ROADRUNNER	1000	50.00	190.00
*	ROBIN FAMILY	600	55.00	350.00
*	ROBINS	1000	50.00	360.00
*	RUBY-THROATED HUMMINGBIRD	750	75.00	125.00
*	RUDDY DUCKS-COMMISSION	650	55.00	500.00
*	RUDDY DUCKS-GEORGETOWN	1000	50.00	100.00
*	RUDDY DUCKS-NORTH AMERICAN	1000	50.00	650.00
*	RUFFED GROUSE (PAIR)	99	750.00	1200.00
*	RUFFED GROUSE-INITIAL	1000	40.00	450.00
*	RUFOUS HUMMINGBIRD	750	75.00	125.00
*	RUMMY	950	150.00	700.00
*	SAND HILL CRANE	950	150.00	150.00
*	SAW WHET OWLS	950	50.00	100.00
*	SCARLET IRISH SETTER	950	150.00	180.00
*	SCREECH OWL-HOMESTEAD	950	50.00	400.00
*	SCREECH OWLS-INITIAL	1000	30.00	600.00
*	SNOWY OWL	1000	50.00	135.00
*	TERNS	750	150.00	425.00
*	TIMBER WOLF	950	150.00	150.00
*	TOWHEES	950	75.00	250.00
*	WANDERING BRAVE	1000	90.00	900.00
*	WHITE TIGERS	1000	150.00	600.00
*	WHITE-TAILED DEER-KNOB CREEK	750	150.00	700.00
*	WHITE-TAILED DEER-OHIO DIV. WILDLIFE	500	125.00	300.00
*	WILD BOAR	200	100.00	200.00
*	WILSON'S PLOVER	500	75.00	175.00
*	WINSTON-SPRINGER SPANIEL	950	150.00	300.00
*	WOOD DUCKS-INITIAL	1000	40.00	215.00
*	WOOD DUCKS-NORTH AMERICAN	1000	90.00	650.00
*	WOOD DUCKS-OHIO DUCK STAMP (PRINT ONLY)	10000	125.00	450.00
*	WOOD DUCKS-OHIO DUCK STAMP (STAMP ONLY)	10000	5.75	60.00
76	BALD EAGLE-BICENTENNIAL	776	350.00	765.00
76	EASTERN WILD TURKEY-BICENTENNIAL	776	350.00	300.00
80	WINGS IN THE WIND	750	200.00	180.00
81	BLUEBIRDS-1981	950	75.00	500.00
81	CARDINAL-1981	950	75.00	500.00
81	MALLARD-1981	500	75.00	175.00
81	OSPREY	750	175.00	175.00
81	PHEASANT-1981	950	75.00	175.00
81	SWALLOW-TAILED KITES	500	100.00	90.00
82	KESTREL AND MOUSE	950	150.00	175.00
82	KINGLET	950	75.00	150.00
82	NUTHATCH	950	75.00	150.00
83	ARCTIC FOX	350	350.00	380.00
83	GOLDFINCH-1983	950	75.00	175.00
83	PAPAW BANDIT	600	125.00	175.00
83	PILEATED WOODPECKER	350	350.00	550.00
83	QUAIL WITH YOUNG	950	50.00	100.00
84	BENGAL TIGER	950	200.00	250.00
84	RIVER OTTERS	500	125.00	300.00
84	SPRING FLOWERS	600	125.00	400.00
85	BLACK DUCK FAMILY	600	125.00	125.00
85	EASTERN FOX SQUIRREL	600	75.00	150.00
85	RACCOONS (FAMILY)	1000	125.00	250.00
85	WINTER REFLECTION	500	225.00	270.00
86	BLUEBIRDS-EASTERN	500	30.00	275.00
86	FROSTY MORNING	400	75.00	250.00
86	STONY RUN-RED FOX	750	225.00	400.00
87	WINTER QUARTET	400	75.00	200.00

WILLITTS DESIGNS

C. PYLE

HISTORY OF ANGELS COLLECTION BY BILL DALE

95	ANGEL GABRIEL, THE	2500	30.00	30.00
95	ARCHANGEL MICHAEL, THE	2500	30.00	30.00
95	ASCENSION OF THE SOUL, THE	2500	30.00	30.00
95	GARDEN OF GETHSEMANE, THE	2500	30.00	30.00

MAJOR LEAGUE BASEBALL FILM CEL

*		*	25.00	25.00
98	BABE RUTH EDITION	*	25.00	25.00
98	BABE RUTH SPECIAL EDITION	*	25.00	25.00
98	HANK AARON EDITION	*	25.00	25.00
98	LOU GEHRIG EDITION	*	25.00	25.00
98	TED WILLIAMS EDITION	*	25.00	25.00

MAJOR LEAGUE BASEBALL MOTION CEL

*		*	25.00	25.00
98	BABE RUTH EDITION	*	25.00	25.00
98	HANK AARON EDITION	*	25.00	25.00
98	JACKIE ROBINSON EDITION	*	25.00	25.00
98	STAN MUSIAL EDITION	*	25.00	25.00
98	TED WILLIAMS EDITION	*	25.00	25.00

MAJOR LEAGUE BASEBALL PRINT W/LIGHTED FILM CEL

*		*	150.00	150.00
98	BABE RUTH & LOU GEHRIG EDITION	*	125.00	125.00
98	HANK AARON EDITION	*	125.00	125.00
98	JACKIE ROBINSON EDITION	*	125.00	125.00
98	TED WILLIAMS EDITION	*	125.00	125.00

STAR WARS: A NEW HOPE FILM CEL

*		*	12.50	13.00
98	BEN KENOBI	*	12.50	13.00
98	C-3PO	*	12.50	13.00
98	CHEWBACCA	*	12.50	13.00
98	CREATURES			

YR	NAME	LIMIT	ISSUE	TREND
98	DARTH VADER	*	12.50	13.00
98	GALACTIC EMPIRE	*	12.50	13.00
98	HAN SOLO	*	12.50	13.00
98	LUKE SKYWALKER	*	12.50	13.00
98	PRINCESS LEIA	*	12.50	13.00
98	R2-D2	*	12.50	13.00
98	REBEL ALLIANCE	*	12.50	13.00
98	STORMTROOPER	*	12.50	13.00

R. MCQUARRIE STAR WARS: A NEW HOPE PRINT W/LIGHTED FILM CEL

YR	NAME	LIMIT	ISSUE	TREND
98	CANTINA ON MOS EISLEY	*	200.00	200.00
98	MILLENNIUM FALCON	*	200.00	200.00
98	REBEL ATTACK ON THE DEATH STAR	*	200.00	200.00
98	REBEL CEREMONY	*	200.00	200.00

STAR WARS: ESB II FILM CEL

YR	NAME	LIMIT	ISSUE	TREND
98	DARTH VADER	*	12.50	13.00
98	HAN SOLO & PRINCESS LEIA	*	12.50	13.00
98	JEDI MASTER YODA	*	12.50	13.00
98	JEDI TRAINING	*	12.50	13.00
98	LANDO CALRISSIAN	*	12.50	13.00
98	LIGHTSABER DUEL SPECIAL EDITION	*	12.50	13.00
98	LUKE SKYWALKER/CLOUD CITY	*	12.50	13.00
98	REBEL ESCAPE	*	12.50	13.00

R. MCQUARRIE STAR WARS: ESB PRINT W/LIGHTED FILM CEL

YR	NAME	LIMIT	ISSUE	TREND
98	CLOUD CITY OF BESPIN	*	200.00	200.00
98	ICE PLANET HOTH BATTLE	*	200.00	200.00
98	LUKE & DARTH DUEL	*	200.00	200.00
98	LUKE & TAUNTAUN ON PATROL	*	200.00	200.00
98	LUKE & TAUNTAUN ON PATROL SIGNED BY MARK HAMILL	*	250.00	250.00

STAR WARS: ESBI FILM CEL

YR	NAME	LIMIT	ISSUE	TREND
98	IMPERIAL ATTACK	*	12.50	13.00
98	LUKE SKYWALKER ON HOTH	*	12.50	13.00
98	MILLENNIUM FALCON	*	12.50	13.00
98	REBEL ALLIANCE	*	12.50	13.00
98	YODA SPECIAL EDITION	*	12.50	13.00

STAR WARS: RETURN OF THE JEDI FILM CEL

YR	NAME	LIMIT	ISSUE	TREND
98	ALIENS OF JABBA'S PALACE	*	12.50	13.00
98	DARTH VADER	*	12.50	13.00
98	DROIDS	*	12.50	13.00
98	EMPEROR PALPATINE	*	12.50	13.00
98	EWOKS	*	12.50	13.00
98	FINAL CONFRONTATION	*	12.50	13.00
98	GENERAL HAN SOLO	*	12.50	13.00
98	IMPERIAL FORCES	*	12.50	13.00
98	JABBA THE HUTT SPECIAL EDITION	*	12.50	13.00
98	JEDI	*	12.50	13.00
98	PRINCESS LEIA	*	12.50	13.00
98	THE JEDI EMERGES	*	12.50	13.00
98	THE REBELLION	*	12.50	13.00
98	TURNING POINTS	*	12.50	13.00

R. MCQUARRIE STAR WARS: RETURN OF THE JEDI PRINT W/LIGHTED FILM CEL

YR	NAME	LIMIT	ISSUE	TREND
98	DEATH STAR MAIN REACTOR	*	200.00	200.00
98	JABBA THE HUTT	*	200.00	200.00
98	RANCORE PIT, THE	*	200.00	200.00
98	SPEEDER BIKE CHASE	*	200.00	200.00

WALT DISNEY SHOWCASE COLLECTION FILM CEL

YR	NAME	LIMIT	ISSUE	TREND
98	COMMEMORATIVE EDITION	*	25.00	25.00
98	EVIL QUEEN	*	25.00	25.00
98	MENAGERIE EDITION	*	25.00	25.00
98	ROYALS EDITION	*	25.00	25.00
98	SEVEN DWARFS	*	25.00	25.00
98	SNOW WHITE EDITION	*	25.00	25.00
98	STEP FAMILY EDITION	*	25.00	25.00

WALT DISNEY SHOWCASE COLLECTION MOTION CEL

YR	NAME	LIMIT	ISSUE	TREND
98	SHOW WHITE SERIES	*	25.00	25.00

WALT DISNEY SHOWCASE COLLECTION PRINT W/LIGHTED FILM CEL

YR	NAME	LIMIT	ISSUE	TREND
98	CINDERELLA LITHOGRAPH	2500	250.00	250.00
98	SNOW WHITE LITHOGRAPH	2500	250.00	250.00

WINDBERG ENTERPRISES
D. WINDBERG

YR	NAME	LIMIT	ISSUE	TREND
68	PELICAN	OP	*	650.00
70	ONE SUMMER DAY 12X16	OP	10.00	200.00
70	ONE SUMMER DAY 18X24	OP	20.00	300.00
70	ONE SUMMER DAY 8X10	OP	5.00	50.00
71	BIG TREE 12X16 AMERICAN MASTERS	OP	100.00	100.00
71	BIG TREE 24X36 NEW YORK GRAPHICS	OP	200.00	200.00
71	BIG TREE 8X10 AMERICAN MASTERS	OP	50.00	50.00
71	LBJ LIBRARY & SCHOOL OF PUBLIC AFFAIRS, THE	OP	3.00	330.00
71	MOONGLOW	OP	1,200.00	1200.00
71	SAND DUNES 12X16 W.E.I.	OP	10.00	100.00
71	SAND DUNES 18X24 W.E.I.	OP	20.00	150.00
71	SAND DUNES 24X36 NEW YORK GRAPHICS	OP	*	175.00
71	SAND DUNES 8X10 W.E.I.	OP	*	50.00
71	TRANQUILITY 12X16	OP	10.00	75.00
71	TRANQUILITY 8X10	OP	5.00	45.00
71	WOODLAND REFLECTIONS 12X16 AM. MASTERS	OP	10.00	100.00
71	WOODLAND REFLECTIONS 18X24 AM. MASTERS	OP	*	200.00

YR	NAME	LIMIT	ISSUE	TREND
71	WOODLAND REFLECTIONS 8X10 AM. MASTERS	OP	5.00	50.00
71	YESTERYEAR 12X16	OP	10.00	100.00
71	YESTERYEAR 18X24	OP	20.00	200.00
71	YESTERYEAR 8X10	OP	5.00	50.00
72	AUTUMN MEMORIES	*	40.00	600.00
73	BLUE SPRINGTIME	*	50.00	200.00
73	COUNTRY HUES 12X16	OP	10.00	60.00
73	COUNTRY HUES 18X24	*	20.00	100.00
73	CYPRESS MIST 12X16	OP	100.00	100.00
73	CYPRESS MIST 18X24	OP	200.00	200.00
73	CYPRESS MIST 8X10	OP	50.00	50.00
73	HIDDEN COVE 12X16	OP	10.00	200.00
73	HIDDEN COVE 8X10	OP	5.00	40.00
73	OBSCURITY 12X16	OP	10.00	75.00
73	OBSCURITY 18X27	OP	20.00	150.00
73	OBSCURITY 8X10	OP	5.00	50.00
73	WINTER'S REPOSE	OP	*	250.00
74	AUTUMN'S GOLD	*	40.00	175.00
74	GLOW OF LOVE	*	50.00	1000.00
74	GOIN' COURTIN'	*	35.00	550.00
74	HILL COUNTRY	*	50.00	500.00
74	LOVE'S REFLECTION	*	50.00	1250.00
74	MORNING MIST	*	*	350.00
74	OLD HOME PLACE	*	50.00	450.00
74	SAFE PASSAGE	*	50.00	100.00
74	SECLUSION	*	50.00	750.00
74	SUNDAY OUTING	*	30.00	500.00
74	WINTRY PASTORAL	*	40.00	125.00
75	AUTUMN'S WAY 1 OF SET OF 4	*	325.00	325.00
75	BAYOU COUNTRY	*	220.00	220.00
75	FROM SEA TO SEA 1 OF 4	*	300.00	300.00
75	MOUNTAIN'S MAJESTY, THE 1 OF 4	*	*	300.00
75	OUR DESERT'S BOUNTY 1 OF 4	*	*	300.00
75	SECLUDED FALLS	*	60.00	375.00
75	SPRING'S WAY	*	50.00	375.00
75	SUMMER'S WAY	*	50.00	350.00
75	TRANQUIL TIMES	*	80.00	850.00
75	UNDISTURBED	*	50.00	400.00
75	WINTER'S WAY	*	50.00	130.00
76	CONTENTMENT	*	80.00	2300.00
76	DAWN'S SERENITY 12X16	OP	100.00	75.00
76	DAWN'S SERENITY 18X24	OP	150.00	150.00
76	DAWN'S SERENITY 8X10	OP	40.00	40.00
76	FLEETING SPLENDOR	*	60.00	200.00
76	NATURE'S INNER GLOW	*	50.00	600.00
76	PELICAN'S WHARF	*	40.00	725.00
76	SNOW-CLAD RELICS	*	45.00	480.00
77	EVENING RADIANCE	*	65.00	90.00
77	GLADSOM SOLITUDE	*	60.00	180.00
77	HARMONY IN THE HIGHLANDS	*	55.00	90.00
77	LAST STAND	*	70.00	2500.00
77	MEMORABLE SPRINGTIDE 12X16 AM. MASTERS	OP	100.00	70.00
77	MEMORABLE SPRINGTIDE 18X24 AM. MASTERS	OP	150.00	110.00
77	MEMORABLE SPRINGTIDE 8X10 AM. MASTERS	OP	50.00	50.00
77	NIGHTLONG SENTINELS	*	375.00	480.00
78	BLACKSMITH SHOP, THE	OP	10.00	300.00
78	IN SEASONAL ATTIRE	*	70.00	125.00
78	PERPETUAL HAVEN	*	60.00	100.00
78	REFLECTIVE ELEGANCE	OP	80.00	150.00
78	ROSEATE SHORELINE	*	65.00	70.00
78	SPANNING THE STREAM OF TIME	*	70.00	45.00
79	NOCTURNAL HARMONY	*	80.00	340.00
79	SEASON OF RENEWAL	*	80.00	300.00
79	SNOW-CROWNED SILENCE	*	70.00	300.00
79	THUNDERING SPLENDOR 16X12, THE	OP	24.00	75.00
80	EMBRACED BY MOONLIGHT 12X16	OP	24.00	24.00
80	EMBRACED BY MOONLIGHT 18X24	OP	35.00	60.00
80	FLOURISH OF NATURE'S HUES 12X16, THE	OP	20.00	75.00
80	GIFT OF LOVE	*	120.00	250.00
80	MELODY OF THE MAROON BELLS 12X16	OP	24.00	43.00
80	MELODY OF THE MAROON BELLS 18X24	OP	35.00	35.00
80	MEMORABLE SPRINGTIDE 12X16 W.E.I.	OP	24.00	24.00
80	MEMORABLE SPRINGTIDE 18X24 W.E.I.	OP	35.00	35.00
80	MOTHER EARTH-FATHER SKY	*	90.00	450.00
80	OPALESCENT IMAGES 12X16	OP	24.00	135.00
80	TIMEWORN SHELFERS	*	90.00	100.00
80	WOODLAND REFLECTIONS 12X16 W.E.I.	OP	24.00	24.00
81	A MISTY COUNTRY MORN 12X16	OP	24.00	24.00
81	A MISTY COUNTRY MORN 18X24	OP	35.00	35.00
81	COMPANIONS IN NATURE 12X16	OP	24.00	90.00
81	COMPANIONS IN NATURE 18X24	*	80.00	125.00
81	DELIGHTFUL RETREAT	*	120.00	80.00
81	ENDURING REFUGE	OP	24.00	125.00
81	MOONLIT COVE 12X16	OP	24.00	43.00
81	QUIET GRANDEUR 16X12	*	80.00	55.00
81	SLUMBEROUSE INTERLUDE	*	120.00	90.00
82	A REFRESHING PAUSE	OP	12.00	875.00
82	COMPANIONS IN NATURE 8X10	OP	24.00	45.00
82	HEARTFELT MEMORIES 12X16			43.00

YR	NAME	LIMIT	ISSUE	TREND
82	TRANQUIL CROSSING	*	120.00	120.00
82	WINTER'S VELVET MANTLE	*	150.00	180.00
83	1983 DEER UNLIMITED STAMP & PRINT	*	125.00	450.00
83	BLOOMS AMID THORNS	OP	25.00	70.00
83	DAWNLIGHT	*	160.00	260.00
83	OLD FRIENDS	*	90.00	90.00
83	SPRING VELVET	*	150.00	150.00
83	TIMELESS SENTINELS 12X16	OP	24.00	75.00
84	A TIME OF MEMORIES	*	175.00	420.00
84	CANYON GOLD 10X20	OP	24.00	90.00
84	NIGHTIME REPOSE	*	150.00	150.00
84	SUMMER LIGHT 16X12	OP	24.00	75.00
84	SUMMER OF INNOCENCE	*	300.00	500.00
85	A MISTY COUNTRY MORN 8X10	OP	12.00	12.00
85	CLASSIC ELEGANCE	*	300.00	600.00
85	COUNTRY MORN	*	90.00	90.00
85	EMBRACED BY MOONLIGHT 8X10	OP	12.00	35.00
85	ENCHANTING DOMAIN 12X16	OP	24.00	43.00
85	ENCHANTING DOMAIN 8X10	OP	12.00	20.00
85	HARMONY OF NATURE, THE	*	150.00	200.00
85	HEARTFELT MEMORIES 8X10	OP	12.00	12.00
85	MELODY OF THE MAROON BELLS 8X10	OP	12.00	12.00
85	MEMORABLE SPRINGTIDE 8X10 W.E.I.	OP	12.00	35.00
85	MOONLIT COVE 8X10	OP	12.00	12.00
85	NEW DAY BREAKING	*	150.00	150.00
85	OPALESCENT IMAGES 8X10	OP	12.00	135.00
85	ROUTINE MAINTENANCE	*	225.00	440.00
85	SUMMER LIGHT 8X10	OP	12.00	40.00
85	TIMELESS SENTINELS 8X10	OP	12.00	40.00
86	EQUINE PARADISE	*	150.00	150.00
86	EVENING QUIESCENCE	OP	24.00	24.00
86	EVERLASTING SANCTUARY 12X16	OP	24.00	140.00
86	FROSTY HOMECOMING	*	195.00	550.00
86	NEPTUNE'S LACE	*	95.00	325.00
86	PASTORAL COLOURS	OP	35.00	35.00
86	PRESIDIO LA BAHIA 8X10	OP	12.00	50.00
87	A MOMENT FOR MEMORIES	*	125.00	400.00
87	ENLIGHTENED PATHWAY	*	125.00	125.00
87	MISSION ESPIRITU SANTO 8X10	OP	12.00	90.00
87	NATURE'S WINTER BLANKET	*	195.00	300.00
87	SEASIDE TREASURY 18X24	OP	35.00	100.00
88	A LAZY DAY IN THE MEADOW	*	150.00	200.00
88	AGELESS MONARCH	*	195.00	200.00
88	COACH TO EL PASO	OP	24.00	24.00
88	ONE SERENE AND MOONLIT NIGHT	*	195.00	475.00
88	SYMPHONY OF THE WILDERNESS	*	195.00	250.00
89	A CUSTOM OF GENERATIONS	OP	24.00	155.00
89	A FAMILIAR EARTHLY TASK	*	150.00	190.00
89	A JAUNT ACROSS THE DIVIDE	*	195.00	450.00
89	PEACE BE UNTO YOU	*	225.00	1100.00
89	SEASONABLE RETURN	*	150.00	650.00
90	CELEBRATION OF THE WOODLANDS	*	125.00	165.00
90	CELESTIAL GLORY	*	225.00	1000.00
90	MOONLIGHTIN'	OP	225.00	390.00
90	ROARING ONWARD	*	225.00	375.00
90	SLUMBERING HOMEPLACE	OP	35.00	35.00
90	SPRINGTIME TRILOGY - TRIPTYCH	*	150.00	200.00
91	A COZY MOUNTAIN RETREAT	*	225.00	225.00
91	AMBIANCE OF AUTUMN	OP	45.00	80.00
91	BENEVOLENT PROVIDER, THE	*	225.00	225.00
91	HILL COUNTRY FLORESCENCE	OP	45.00	460.00
91	SILENT PINNACLES	OP	45.00	85.00
91	STROLLING WITH AN OLD FRIEND	*	225.00	375.00
91	TEXAS OAK	*	*	400.00
92	AFTERGLOW OF SPRING SHOWERS	*	225.00	350.00
92	AMID TRANQUILITY OF THE MORNING	*	225.00	225.00
92	FORAGING ON A WINTER EVENING	*	250.00	250.00
93	ANTICIPATION	*	250.00	375.00
93	ROMANTIC TRADITIONS	*	150.00	540.00
93	TAKING A BREAK	*	260.00	215.00
93	TEA TIME REFLECTIONS	*	150.00	150.00
94	COURT'N BY MOONLIGHT	*	150.00	1800.00
94	FIRST LIGHT ON A WINTRY DAY	*	250.00	245.00
94	HOME AT LAST	*	250.00	400.00
94	INNOCENCE OF SPRING	*	150.00	215.00
94	LAKESIDE HIDEAWAY	OP	24.00	225.00
94	MAKING OF A MEMORY	*	250.00	275.00
94	NIGHTWATCH	OP	24.00	24.00
94	ONE SUMMER NIGHT	OP	24.00	90.00
94	RETIRED	OP	24.00	150.00
95	JOYOUS EVENSONG	*	250.00	250.00
95	MORNING DELIGHT/EVENING TREAT	*	150.00	300.00
95	PERFECT SERENITY	*	150.00	150.00
96	OUR SPECTACULAR SURROUNDINGS	*	195.00	195.00

D. WINDBERG   **CANVAS EDITION**

YR	NAME	LIMIT	ISSUE	TREND
72	ANTICIPATION	*	350.00	1000.00
93	AMID TRANQUILITY OF THE MORNING	*	350.00	350.00
93	TAKING A BREAK	*	350.00	350.00
94	FIRST LIGHT ON A WINTRY DAY	*	350.00	350.00

YR	NAME	LIMIT	ISSUE	TREND
94	HOME AT LAST	*	350.00	350.00
94	INNOCENCE OF SPRING	*	350.00	350.00
94	MAKING OF A MEMORY	*	350.00	325.00
95	A GLIMPSE OF UPLAND GRANDEUR	250	350.00	350.00
95	AN ENCHANTING VIEW OF THE NIGHT	250	350.00	350.00
95	HILLTOP GARDENS	250	350.00	350.00
95	JOYOUS EVENSONG	*	350.00	350.00
95	MORNING DELIGHT/EVENING TREAT		350.00	350.00
D. WINDBERG				**FIESTA POSTER**
91	REFLECTIONS OF THE NIGHT	OP	45.00	45.00
D. WINDBERG				**NATIONAL PARK**
79	THUNDERING SPLENDOR	SO	50.00	250.00
80	FLOURISH OF NATURE'S HUES, THE	*	50.00	175.00
81	QUIET GRANDEUR	SO	50.00	150.00
86	EVERLASTING SANCTUARY	*	140.00	300.00
D. WINDBERG				**NATURAL PARK**
84	CANYON GOLD	SO	50.00	200.00
D. WINDBERG				**PAPER EDITION**
95	A GLIMPSE OF UPLAND GRANDEUR	1000	250.00	250.00
95	AN ENCHANTING VIEW OF THE NIGHT	1000	250.00	350.00
95	HILLTOP GARDENS	1000	250.00	250.00
D. WINDBERG				**POSTER**
88	AMERICAN IMPRESSIONS	OP	35.00	35.00
88	GALLERY AMERICANA	*	35.00	35.00
88	VISIONS OF AMERICA	OP	35.00	35.00
88	WILDERNESS	OP	35.00	75.00
D. WINDBERG				**SPECIAL EDITION**
86	PRESIDIO LA BAHIA	*	80.00	900.00
87	MISSION ESPIRITU SANTO	*	80.00	90.00

WINN DEVON

YR	NAME	LIMIT	ISSUE	TREND
T. BERG				
97	THE COVE AT DUSK	375	750.00	750.00
J. COLOMER				
97	AT THE STREAM	375	750.00	750.00
97	BESIDE THE STILL WATERS	375	750.00	750.00
97	NOBLE NATURE	375	825.00	825.00
97	TALL REFLECTIONS	375	750.00	750.00
97	WATER'S EDGE	375	775.00	775.00
C. GLADSON				
97	ARBORETUM PATHWAY	950	95.00	95.00
97	ARBORETUM VISTA	950	95.00	95.00
97	REFLECTIONS ON LAKE MELANCHOLY	950	95.00	95.00
E. GUNN				
97	FLORAL SENSATION	375	300.00	300.00
97	PLEASANT VIEW	375	300.00	300.00
97	STILL LIFE WITH LILIES I	375	550.00	550.00
97	STILL LIFE WITH LILIES II	375	550.00	550.00
K. HAINES DENCH				
97	ANGEL TRUMPETS I	250	550.00	550.00
97	ANGEL TRUMPETS II	250	550.00	550.00
97	PERSIMMON STILL LIFE	175	550.00	550.00
97	POMEGRANATE STILL LIFE	175	550.00	550.00
M. HAYSLETTE				
97	CRANBERRY DELIGHT I	950	95.00	95.00
97	CRANBERRY DELIGHT II	950	95.00	95.00
97	LAPIS MOON I	950	95.00	95.00
97	LAPIS MOON II	950	95.00	95.00
97	MEMORIES OF THE NIGHT	950	95.00	95.00
97	MOON ASCENDING #1	950	95.00	95.00
97	MOON ASCENDING #2	950	95.00	95.00
97	SONG OF THE SAMURAI	950	95.00	95.00
L. LI				
97	BROOK, THE	950	95.00	95.00
97	FLOWERING VINE BY THE STREAM	950	95.00	95.00
97	SPRING BLOOMS ALONG THE RAVINE	950	95.00	95.00
E. RODRIGUEZ				
97	CORTE CANALE	275	235.00	235.00
97	DE L'APRES MIDI	275	235.00	235.00
97	FEVRIER	275	235.00	235.00
97	LA VISITE	275	235.00	235.00
97	PROVENCE	275	235.00	235.00
97	RIALTO	275	235.00	235.00
97	SAN CROCE	275	235.00	235.00
97	SAN PAULO	275	235.00	235.00
SARINA				
97	CASA BONITA	200	550.00	550.00
97	CASA DORADO	200	550.00	550.00
97	CASA TORTUGA	200	550.00	550.00
G. SINGLEY				
97	ARBOR ROSES	375	375.00	375.00
97	BLUE GATE	375	375.00	375.00
97	CASCADING ROSES	375	375.00	375.00
97	EUROPEAN GARDEN I	375	375.00	375.00
97	EUROPEAN GARDEN II	375	375.00	375.00
97	SPRING MEDLEY REVISITED I	375	425.00	425.00

YR	NAME	LIMIT	ISSUE	TREND
97	SPRING MEDLEY REVISITED II	375	425.00	425.00
97	WHITE ROSE ARBOR	375	375.00	375.00

R. STRIFFOLINO

YR	NAME	LIMIT	ISSUE	TREND
97	LAKESIDE TREES	375	750.00	750.00
97	RIVER BEND	375	750.00	750.00

WORLD ART EDITIONS

MAGO

MAGO

YR	NAME	LIMIT	ISSUE	TREND
82	DEPOSITION	300	325.00	325.00
82	SIPARIO	300	325.00	325.00

F. MASSERIA

MASSERIA

YR	NAME	LIMIT	ISSUE	TREND
80	EDUARDO	300	275.00	2700.00
80	FIRST KISS	300	375.00	2200.00
80	NINA	300	325.00	1950.00
80	ROSANNA	300	257.00	3200.00
81	ELEANOR	300	375.00	775.00
81	ELISA WITH FLOWER	300	325.00	775.00
81	FIRST FLOWER	300	325.00	2200.00
81	JESSICA	300	375.00	2300.00
81	JULIE	300	375.00	950.00
81	SELENE	300	325.00	2200.00
81	SOLANGE	300	325.00	2200.00
81	SUSAN SEWING	300	375.00	2500.00
82	AMY	300	425.00	775.00
82	JAMIE	300	425.00	750.00
82	JILL	300	425.00	775.00
82	JODIE	300	425.00	775.00
82	JUDITH	300	425.00	750.00
82	ROBIN	300	425.00	775.00
82	YASMIN	300	425.00	720.00
82	YVETTE	300	425.00	775.00
83	ANTONIO	300	450.00	1100.00
83	TARA	300	450.00	775.00
84	BETTINA	250	550.00	775.00
84	CHRISTOPHER	300	450.00	700.00
84	MEMOIRS	300	450.00	775.00
84	PETER	950	395.00	495.00
84	REGINA	950	395.00	495.00
84	VINCENTE	360	550.00	775.00
85	CHRISTINA	300	500.00	775.00
85	JORGITO	300	500.00	700.00
85	MARGUERITA	950	495.00	495.00
85	TO CATCH A BUTTERFLY	950	495.00	495.00

WREN'S NEST GALLERY INC.

L. MARTIN

YR	NAME	LIMIT	ISSUE	TREND
95	MAGNOLIAS & GREEK REVIVAL	950	65.00	65.00
95	ROYAL FLUSH	950	85.00	180.00
95	SPRING GARDEN	950	75.00	75.00
95	TREDAWAY HOME, THE	950	28.00	28.00
96	MOLTEN GOLD	950	65.00	65.00
96	NEW GEMS	950	38.00	38.00
96	TRAIL BOSS	950	110.00	110.00

L. MARTIN

AMERICA THE BEAUTIFUL

YR	NAME	LIMIT	ISSUE	TREND
95	SPACIOUS SKIES I	500	100.00	175.00
95	SPACIOUS SKIES II	500	28.00	65.00
96	AMERICA, AMERICA I	500	85.00	85.00
96	AMERICA, AMERICA II	500	65.00	65.00
96	GOD SHED HIS GRACE ON THEE	950	100.00	100.00
96	PURPLE MOUNTAIN MAJESTIES	950	100.00	100.00

ZOLAN FINE ARTS/WINSTON ROLAND

D. ZOLAN

YR	NAME	LIMIT	ISSUE	TREND
96	RAINED OUT	CL	35.00	47.00

D. ZOLAN

SYMPHONY OF SEASONS

YR	NAME	LIMIT	ISSUE	TREND
98	COUNTRY PUMPKINS	400	220.00	220.00
98	SUMMERTIME FRIENDS	400	220.00	220.00

Steins

Ken Armke

Beer steins, more than nearly any other component of today's collectibles market, bridge the gap between authentic antiques and contemporary limited editions.

After all, some of the most popular lines of today's collectibles are not yet 20 years old. Even M.I. Hummel figurines have been around for just over 60 years.

Steins, on the other hand, have been going strong for more than 400 years. Even if one discounts the early utilitarian steins that were used for centuries, these drinking vessels emerged as an artistic collectible popular in the United States during the late 1800s.

It's no wonder then that steins are often thought of as a "traditional" aspect of the collectibles secondary market. With the exception of some of the Anheuser-Busch issues, they tend to perform with less volatility—fewer wondrous jumps in value and correspondingly fewer disastrous plunges—than do most other collectibles.

For this reason, steins—for those who enjoy them and the artwork they represent—should be looked upon with favor by those collectors seeking a longer-term commitment to their collectibles. Traditional art has always shown a strong tendency to grow in value over time to at least match inflation.

KEN ARMKE SR., president of OHI Exchange, initiated one of the first comprehensive secondary market exchanges covering architectural miniatures. His company has since become a primary source for cottages available on the secondary market.

STEINS

YR	NAME	LIMIT	ISSUE	TREND
	ANHEUSER-BUSCH INC.			
	J.C. LEYENDECKER			
96	SATURDAY EVENING POST FOURTH OF JULY	5000	180.00	180.00
*				**A&EAGLE**
75	A&EAGLE CSL2	RT	*	250.00
76	A&EAGLE CS2	RT	*	215.00
76	A&EAGLE CS26	RT	*	156.00
76	A&EAGLE CS28	RT	*	228.00
93	A&E EAGEL TRADEMARK II W/TIN CS218	*	*	N/A
94	A&EAGLE TRADEMARK II CS219	RT	24.00	35.00
94	A&EAGLE TRADEMARK III W/TIN CS238	*	*	35.00
95	A&E EAGEL TRADEMARK IV W/TIN CS255	*	*	27.00
95	A&EAGLE TRADEMARK III CS240	OP	25.00	22.00
96	A&EAGLE TRADEMARK IV CS271	OP	*	25.00
96	TRADEMARK IV STEIN	30000	27.00	27.00
*				**ANIMAL/WILDLIFE**
88	BUDWEISER FIELD & STREAM SET CS95	RT	70.00	N/A
89	BALD EAGLE CS106	RT	25.00	585.00
90	ASIAN TIGER CS126	RT	27.50	130.00
91	AFRICAN ELEPHANT CS135	RT	29.00	65.00
91	AMERICAN BALD EAGLE CS164	RT	125.00	140.00
92	DOLPHIN CS187	RT	90.00	50.00
92	GIANT PANDA CS173	RT	29.00	65.00
92	KILLER WHALE CS186	RT	100.00	60.00
92	PEREGRINE FALCON CS183	OP	125.00	137.00
93	GRIZZLY BEAR CS199	OP	29.50	30.00
93	LABRADOR CS195	RT	32.50	98.00
94	GRAY WOLF CS226	OP	29.50	30.00
94	MANATEE CS203	OP	33.50	35.00
94	OSPREY STEIN CS212	RT	135.00	700.00
94	SETTER CS205	OP	32.50	30.00
95	COUGAR CS253	OP	*	30.00
95	GOLDEN RETRIEVER CS248	OP	*	30.00
95	GREAT HORNED OWL CS264	OP	137.00	130.00
95	GREAT WHITE SHARK STEIN CS247	OP	*	35.00
96	BEAGLE CS272	OP	*	30.00
*				**ANIMALS/WILDLIFE**
96	DOLPHIN STEIN CS284	*		36.00
*				**BREWERY SPECIFIC**
*	ADOLPHUS BUSCH	RT	*	N/A
85	LIMITED EDITION I CS64	RT	30.00	176.00
86	BREW HOUSE CS67	RT	20.00	46.00
86	LIMITED EDITION II CS65	RT	30.00	52.00
87	BUDWEISER STABLES CS73	RT	20.00	78.00
87	LIMITED EDITION III CS71	RT	30.00	50.00
88	CLASSIC I CS93	RT	35.00	175.00
88	GRANT'S CABIN CS83	RT	*	30.00
88	LIMITED EDITION IV CS75	RT	30.00	50.00
88	OLD SCHOOL HOUSE CS84	RT	20.00	46.00
89	CLASSIC II CS104	RT	55.00	130.00
89	LIMITED EDITION V CS98	RT	35.00	50.00
90	CLASSIC III CS113	RT	65.00	98.00
91	AFTER THE HUNT CS155	RT	100.00	90.00
91	CLASSIC IV CS130	RT	75.00	51.00
92	BERNINGHAUS CS105	RT	75.00	90.00
92	CHERUB CS182	RT	100.00	70.00
92	COLUMBIAN EXPOSITION CS169	RT	35.00	46.00
93	A&EAGLE TRADEMARK I CS191	RT	22.00	45.00
93	A&EAGLE TRADEMARK I CS201	RT	31.00	98.00
93	ADOLPHUS BUSCH CS216	OP	180.00	165.00
93	GANYMEDE CS190	RT	35.00	35.00
94	A&EAGLE TM III CS238	RT	28.00	45.00
94	AUGUST A. BUSCH ST. CS229	RT	220.00	254.00
94	BUDWEISER GREATEST TRIUMPH CS222	RT	35.00	30.00
94	SIX-PACK II MINI STEINS N4571	OP	*	19.00
95	ADOLPHUS BUSCH III CS265	OP	*	215.00
95	BUD-WEIS-ER FROG MUG N5402-5	*	*	23.00
95	MIRROR OF TRUCH CS252	OP	*	30.00
96	AUGUST A. BUSCH JR. CS286	*	*	200.00
96	BUD-WEIS-ER FROG CS289	OP	*	25.00
96	BUDWEISER LABEL CS282	OP	*	19.00
*				**BUSCH GARDENS**
90	EXTINCTION IS FOREVER II BG1	10000	*	N/A
92	EXTINCTION IS FOREVER III BG2	10000	*	N/A
*				**CLYDESDALES**
76	CLYDESDALE DECANTER CS33	RT	*	N/A
76	CLYDESDALES CS15	RT	*	325.00
76	CLYDESDALES CS15/II	RT	*	433.00
76	CLYDESDALES CSL15	RT	*	N/A
76	CLYDESDALES CSL29	RT	*	295.00
76	CLYDESDALES CSL9	RT	*	176.00

YR	NAME	LIMIT	ISSUE	TREND
83	BUD LIGHT BARON CS61	RT	*	35.00
86	HORSESHOE CS68	RT	15.00	52.00
87	HORSEHEAD CS76	RT	16.00	35.00
87	HORSEHEAD CS78	RT	15.00	72.00
87	HORSESHOE CS77	RT	16.00	35.00
87	WORLD FAMOUS CLYDESDALE CS74	RT	9.95	39.00
88	CLYDESDALE MARE & FOAL CS90	RT	*	52.00
88	HORSE HARNESS CS94	RT	16.00	60.00
89	PARADE DRESS CS99	RT	11.50	24.00
91	CLYDESDALES TRAINING HITCH CS131	RT	13.00	33.00
94	PROUD AND FREE CS223	OP	17.00	17.00
*			**COLLECTOR CLUB**	
95	BREWHOUSE CLOCK TOWER CB2	RT	*	650.00
95	CLYDESDALES AT BAUERNHF CB1	RT	*	140.00
*			**EARLY YEARS**	
*	SENIOR GRANDE CS6	RT	*	590.00
75	GERMAN PILIQUE CS5	RT	*	325.00
75	GERMAN TAVERN SCENE CSL6	RT	*	180.00
75	SENIOR GRANDE CSL4	RT	*	N/A
76	BUDWEISER CENT. HOFBRAU ST. CS22	RT	*	325.00
76	BUDWEISER CENTENNIAL CS13	RT	*	375.00
76	BUDWEISER CENTENNIAL CSL7	RT	*	395.00
76	CORACAO DECANTER SET 5 PC SET CS31	RT	*	485.00
76	GERMAN PILIQUE CSL5	RT	*	N/A
76	GERMAN TAVERN SCENE CS4	RT	*	85.00
76	KATAKOMBE CS3	RT	*	200.00
76	KATAKOMBE CSL3	RT	*	277.00
76	ST. LOUIS DECANTER SET CS37	RT	*	433.00
76	ST. LOUIS DECANTER SET CS38	RT	*	1018.00
76	U.S. BICENTENNIAL CS14	RT	*	488.00
76	U.S. BICENTENNIAL CSL8	RT	*	515.00
76	WURZBURGER CS39	RT	*	275.00
P. FORD				**FIRST HUNT**
96	LABRADOR STEIN	10000	190.00	194.00
*			**GERZ MEISTERWERKE**	
*	WINCHESTER GL2	RT	*	163.00
92	SANTA'S MAILBAG GM1	RT	*	310.00
93	GOLDEN RETRIEVER GM2	OP	*	170.00
93	JOHN F. KENNEDY GM4	OP	*	180.00
94	MALLARD GM7	OP	*	190.00
94	ROSIE THE RIVETER GM9	OP	*	150.00
94	SPRINGER SPANIEL GM5	OP	*	170.00
94	WINCHESTER MODEL 94 GM10	OP	*	150.00
95	GIANT PANDA GM8	OP	*	190.00
95	POINTER GM16	OP	*	170.00
96	FOURTH OF JULY GM15	OP	*	165.00
N. ROCKWELL				**GERZ MEISTERWERKE**
93	DUGOUT, THE GL1	RT	*	150.00
93	SANTA'S HELPER GM3	OP	*	180.00
94	ALL I WANT FOR CHRISTMAS GM13	OP	*	190.00
94	TRIPLE SELF-PORTRAIT GM6	OP	*	225.00
*			**HOLIDAY**	
76	BUDWEISER CHAM. CLYDESDALE CS19	RT	9.95	83.00
80	BUDWEISER CHAM. CLYDESDALES CS19/II	RT	*	124.00
81	SNOWY WOODLAND CS50	RT	9.95	255.00
82	50TH ANNIV. CELEBRATION CS57	RT	9.95	130.00
83	CAMEO WHEATLAND CS58	RT	9.95	140.00
84	COVERED BRIDGE CS62	RT	9.95	78.00
85	SNOW CAPPED MTNS. CS63	RT	9.95	20.00
86	TRADITIONAL HOUSES CS66	RT	9.95	39.00
87	GRANT'S FARM GATES CS70	RT	9.95	39.00
88	COBBLESTONE PASSAGE CS88	RT	13.00	20.00
89	WINTER EVENING CS89	RT	13.50	34.00
90	AN AMERICAN TRADITION CS112	RT	*	46.00
90	AN AMERICAN TRADITION GOLD CS112	RT	50.00	152.00
90	AN AMERICAN TRADITION SIG. ED. CS112SE	RT	14.50	40.00
91	SEASON'S BEST CS133	RT	*	34.00
91	SEASON'S BEST, GOLD CS133	RT	50.00	152.00
91	SEASON'S BEST, SIG. ED. CS133SE	RT	14.50	65.00
92	A PERFECT CHRISTMAS CS167	RT	*	34.00
92	A PERFECT CHRISTMAS, GOLD CS167	RT	50.00	152.00
92	A PERFECT CHRISTMAS, SIG. ED. CS167SE	RT	15.00	65.00
93	SPECIAL DELIVERY CS192	RT	60.00	20.00
93	SPECIAL DELIVERY, GOLD CS192	RT	*	135.00
93	SPECIAL DELIVERY, SIG. ED. CS192	RT	65.00	100.00
94	'94 HOLIDAY SG. ED.	OP	14.00	116.00
94	1994 HOLIDAY CS211	OP	*	20.00
95	'95 HOLIDAY, SG. ED.	OP	*	116.00
95	CHRISTMAS-SATURDAY EVENING POST GL5	*	*	116.00
96	HOLIDAY SIGNATURE CS273SE			143.00
S. RYAN				**HUNTER'S COMPANION**
96	BEAGLE STEIN	50000	35.00	35.00
*			**RARITIES**	
*	AMERICANA CS17	RT	*	415.00

YR	NAME	LIMIT	ISSUE	TREND
*	CLYDESDALE HOFBRAU CS29	RT	*	173.00
*	DAS FESTHAUS CS41	RT	*	182.00
*	HAMBURG CS16	RT	*	375.00
*	MINI MUGS SET OF 4 CS8	RT	*	1250.00
75	MINIATURE BAVARIAN MUG CS7	RT	*	560.00
76	CANTEEN DECANTER SET 7 PC FLORAL CS036	RT	*	N/A
76	CLYDESDALES CS12/VERSION OF CSL9	RT	*	250.00
76	DELFT, ASST. DESIGNS CS11	RT	*	462.00
76	GERMAN WINE SET 7 PC CS32	RT	*	625.00
76	HOLANDA DECANTER SET 7 PC BRN CS34	RT	*	N/A
76	HOLANDA DECANTER SET 7 PC CO. BLU CS35	RT	*	N/A
77	A&EAGLE, BAVARIAN SHAPE CS24	RT	*	880.00
80	BUSCH HOFBRAU STYLE CS44	RT	*	212.00
80	MICHELOB HOFBRAU ST. CS45	RT	*	98.00
80	NATURAL LIGHT HOFBRAU CS43	RT	*	212.00
81	BUDWEISER HOFBRAU ST. CS46	RT	*	65.00
*				**SPECIAL EVENT**
80	BUDWEISER CHICAGO SKYLINE CS40	RT	*	78.00
81	BUDWEISER CALIFORNIA CS56	RT	*	30.00
81	BUDWEISER CHICAGOLAND CS51	RT	*	46.00
81	BUDWEISER TEXAS CS52	RT	*	59.00
83	BUDWEISER SAN FRANCISCO CS29	RT	*	228.00
83	SAN FRANCISCO CS59	*	*	175.00
89	NORTH/SOUTH DAKOTA SO42268	*	*	33.00
90	DAYTONA BUD BIKE WK. N/A-2	*	*	33.00
90	DAYTONA BUD SPEED W N/A-3	*	*	33.00
90	IDAHO: CENTENNIAL SO49804	*	*	25.00
90	INTRO. TO WI WILDLIFE DUCK N/A-4	*	*	N/A
90	MICHIGAN DUCKS UNLIMITED SO42208	*	*	25.00
90	SEATTLE: GOOD WILL GMS. SO47627	*	*	33.00
90	WISCONSIN WILDLIFE: DEER SO49700	*	*	25.00
90	WISCONSIN WILDLIFE: DUCK SO48249	*	*	25.00
90	WYOMING: CENTENNIAL N SP50138	*	*	33.00
91	ARKANSAS: RICE/DUCK SO51582	*	*	33.00
91	CA: BIG BEAR OKTOBERFEST SO53954	*	*	46.00
91	COLORADO: AND NO... SP52848	*	*	33.00
91	DODGE CITY DAYS SO53465	*	*	100.00
91	FORT LEWIS, WASHINGTON SO54147	*	*	25.00
91	GEORGIA FISHING: ON... SO53834	*	*	25.00
91	GEORGIA HUNTING: ON... SO54141	*	*	25.00
91	HOUSTON RODEO N/A-5	*	*	N/A
91	ILLINOIS STATE SO54808	*	*	33.00
91	KANSAS: GOOD TO KNOW SO53618	*	*	33.00
91	KENTUCKY: THE CELEB. SO54022	*	*	25.00
91	MARDI GRAS: NOTHING... SO50500	*	*	46.00
91	MICHIGAN DU. LOON SO54807	*	*	25.00
91	MINNESOTA WILDLIFE: LOON SO53143	*	*	25.00
91	MISSISSIPPI BASS: ALWAY SO54822	*	*	25.00
91	MISSISSIPPI DEER: ALWAY SO54806	*	*	25.00
91	MISSOURI WAKE UP... SO54149	*	*	25.00
91	NEBRASKA: TRADITIONS SO50512	*	*	33.00
91	NEW YORK: A STATE OF... SO54214	*	*	25.00
91	OHIO: THE HEART OF... SO55446	*	*	25.00
91	OKLAHOMA: BETTER SOON SO53689	*	*	33.00
91	OKLAHOMA: FESTIVAL OF... SO55447	*	*	25.00
91	OKTOBERFEST SO54077	*	*	25.00
91	PENNSYLVANIA: A STATE... SO54215	*	*	25.00
91	REDLANDS: CHILI COOK-OFF SO53757	*	*	25.00
91	SAN ANTONIO: FIESTA SO52190	*	*	33.00
91	SAVE LAKE PONTC'TRAIN SO54240	*	*	25.00
91	SAVE THE BAY I SO52286	*	*	25.00
91	TEMECULA: TRACTOR RACE SO53847	*	*	25.00
91	UTAH: NATURALLY SO52847	*	*	33.00
91	VERMONT: BICENTENNIAL SO53758	*	*	25.00
91	WISCONSIN WILDLIFE: BEST S055713	*	*	150.00
92	ADVERTISING THROUGH... N3989	*	*	85.00
92	ALABAMA STATE SO64282	*	*	33.00
92	ATHENS, NY FIREFIGHTERS SO64209	*	*	25.00
92	BUDWEISER BURNS COAL SO64374	*	*	33.00
92	BUDWEISER RACING N3553	*	*	N/A
92	CARDINALS: 100TH ANNIV. N3767	*	*	59.00
92	CINCINNATI: TALLSTACKS N3942	*	*	N/A
92	DU QUOIN: STATE FAIR N3941	*	*	78.00
92	GEORGIA: BASS SO63840	*	*	39.00
92	GEORGIA: DEER SO64054	*	*	39.00
92	INDIANA: CROSSROADS... SO68206	*	*	33.00
92	IOWA: THE TIME IS... SO67816	*	*	33.00
92	IT'S A BUD THING N3645	*	*	N/A
92	LOUISIANA: WE'RE REALLY SO67814	*	*	33.00
92	MARDI GRAS 1992: BUD SO56219	*	*	33.00
92	MICHIGAN DU SO64169	*	*	25.00
92	MICHIGAN DUCKS UNLIMITED N3828	*	*	N/A
92	MINNESOTA WILDLIFE: MALLARD SO67817	*	*	33.00
92	NC: CAROLINA ON MY... SO64215	*	*	33.00
92	NEW YORK STATE II SO67691	*	*	25.00

The 1992 U.S. Olympic Team is honored in this stein by Anheuser-Busch.

The thrill of victory is celebrated in this 1992 Summer Olympics stein by Anheuser-Busch.

Anheuser-Busch reminds collectors that the Giant Panda is one of many endangered species.

Anheuser-Busch commemorates the 1893 Columbian Exposition.

YR	NAME	LIMIT	ISSUE	TREND
92	O'DOUL'S: WHAT BEER..N3522	*	*	35.00
92	PUERTO RICO: QUINTO... SO65691	*	*	33.00
92	TENNESSEE: WE'RE PLAY SO63887	*	*	33.00
92	TEXAS: LIVING FREE... N3648	*	*	N/A
92	WEST TEXAS: CENTENNIAL N3943	*	*	N/A
93	ARKANSAS: BREWED.. N3940	*	*	N/A
93	MARDI GRAS 1993 N4073	*	*	N/A
93	MISSOURI: ALWAYS IN... N4118	*	*	N/A
93	NEBRASKA WILDLIFE N4117	*	*	N/A
93	OHIO JAYCEES: PARTNES N4119	*	*	N/A
93	PHOENIX: ONE MILLION... N4105	*	*	N/A
93	SAVE THE BAY II N4120	*	*	N/A
96	1996 ST. PATRICK'S DAY CS269	OP	*	24.00
96	OCTOBERFEST STEIN CS291	*	*	25.00
97	ST. PATRICK'S DAY	OP	*	25.00
*				**SPECIALTY**
75	BUD MAN CS1	RT	*	450.00
75	BUD MAN CS1/II	RT	*	485.00
76	BUDWEISER LABEL CS18	RT	*	550.00
76	MICHELOB CS27	RT	*	165.00
77	NATURAL LIGHT CS9	RT	*	245.00
80	OKTOBERFEST BUSCH GAR. CS42	RT	*	170.00
82	POST CONV.-OLYMPIC CS53	RT	*	336.00
82	POST CONV.-OLYMPIC CS54	RT	*	336.00
82	POST CONV.-OLYMPIC CS55	RT	*	336.00
87	KING COBRA CS80	RT	*	270.00
87	ST. NICK CS79	RT	*	65.00
88	ADOLPHUS BUSCH CS87	RT	*	142.00
88	AUGUST BUSCH SR. CS102	RT	*	125.00
89	ADOLPHUS BUSCH III CS114	RT	*	60.00
89	BUD MAN, 1989 STYLE CS100	RT	30.00	111.00
89	BUDWEISER LABEL CS101	RT	14.00	15.00
89	ST. LOUIS CARDINALS CS125	RT	30.00	35.00
90	A&EAGLE LOGO CS148	RT	16.00	18.00
90	AUGUST BUSCH JR. CS141	RT	*	50.00
90	BUD LIGHT LOGO CS144	RT	16.00	18.00
90	BUDWEISER ANTIQUE LABEL CS127	RT	14.00	15.00
90	BUDWEISER LOGO CS143	RT	16.00	18.00
90	BUSCH LOGO CS147	RT	16.00	18.00
90	MICHELOB DRY LOGO CS146	RT	16.00	18.00
90	MICHELOB LOGO CS145	RT	16.00	18.00
90	NINA CS107	RT	40.00	59.00
91	AUGUST BUCSH III CS174	*	35.00	35.00
91	BEVO FOX CS160	RT	250.00	350.00
91	BEVO FOX GERZ/CS160	RT	*	225.00
91	BOTTLED BEER W/TIN N3292	*	*	N/A
91	BUD DRY LOGO CS156	RT	16.00	18.00
91	BUDWEISER BOTTLED BEER CS136	RT	15.00	15.00
91	BUDWEISER PEWTER N2755	*	*	125.00
91	ERIN GO BUD CS109	RT	15.00	78.00
91	GEN. ULYSSES S. GRANT CS181	RT	150.00	195.00
91	MICHELOB DRY PEWTER N2371	*	*	125.00
91	MICHELOB PEWTER CS158	RT	*	125.00
91	PINTA CS129	RT	40.00	59.00
92	1993 BUDWEISER OKTOBERFEST CS202	RT	18.00	33.00
92	BUDWEISER OKTOBERFEST CS185	OP	16.00	33.00
92	BUDWEISER RODEO CS184	RT	18.00	20.00
92	CLYDESDALES ON PARADE CS161	RT	16.00	15.00
92	GEN. ROBERT E. LEE CS188	RT	150.00	195.00
92	MINI STEINS SET OF 6 N3289	*	*	N/A
92	POT OF GOLD CS166	OP	15.00	20.00
92	SANTA MARIA CS138	RT	40.00	59.00
93	ABRAHAM LINCOLN CS189	RT	*	195.00
93	BOTTLED TREASURE CS193	RT	15.30	52.00
93	BUD MAN, 1993 STYLE CS213	RT	45.00	98.00
94	AIR FORCE CS228	OP	19.00	20.00
94	BUDWEISER SALUTES THE ARMY CS224	OP	19.00	18.00
94	LUCK O' THE IRISH CS210	OP	18.00	18.00
94	WALKING TALL BOOT CS251	OP	17.50	18.00
95	1995 ST. PATRICK'S DAY CS242	OP	19.00	17.00
95	BUDWEISER SALUTES THE NAVY CS243	OP	19.50	20.00
95	MARINES CS256	OP	*	20.00
96	A&EAGLE LOGO IV CS255	OP	*	27.00
*				**SPORTS**
84	1984 BUDWEISER OLYMPIC GAMES CS60	RT	*	25.00
87	1988 WINTER OLYMPICS CS81	RT	50.00	60.00
87	BUDWEISER WINTER OLYMPICS CS85	RT	25.00	25.00
88	BUDWEISER SUMMER OLYMPICS CS91	RT	55.00	45.00
88	BUDWEISER SUMMER OLYMPICS CS92	RT	55.00	25.00
90	AM. FAVORITE PASTIME CS124	RT	20.00	39.00
91	1992 WINTER OLYMPICS CS162	RT	85.00	50.00
91	BABE RUTH CS142	RT	85.00	78.00
91	BUDWEISER 1992 OLYMPICS CS168	RT	16.00	15.00
91	CHASING CHECKERED FLAG CS132	RT	22.00	39.00
91	GRIDIRON LEGACY CS128	RT	20.00	33.00

YR	NAME	LIMIT	ISSUE	TREND
91	HEROES OF HARDWOOD CS134	OP	*	24.00
92	1992 SUMMER OLYMPICS CS163	RT	85.00	50.00
92	JIM THORPE CS171	RT	85.00	117.00
92	PAR FOR THE COURSE CS165	RT	*	46.00
93	BILL ELLIOTT CS196	RT	150.00	115.00
93	BILL ELLIOTT, SIG. ED. CS196SE	RT	295.00	243.00
93	CENTER ICE CS209	OP	22.00	33.00
93	JOU LOUIS CS206	RT	85.00	116.00
93	RACING TEAM CS194	RT	19.00	25.00
94	1994 WORLD CUP COMMN CS230	RT	40.00	45.00
94	FORE! GOLF BAG CS225	OP	16.00	16.00
95	'96 OLYMPICS, CENTENNIAL	OP	*	45.00
95	'96 OLYMPICS, GYMNASTICS	OP	*	75.00
95	'96 OLYMPICS, TRACK	OP	*	75.00
95	BASEBALL MIT STEIN CS244	OP	*	18.00
95	CHIP MANAUER MUG N5511	OP	*	22.00
95	KEN SCHRADER MUG B5510	OP	*	22.00
95	KENNY BERNSTEIN MUG N5512	*	*	22.00
96	BILLIARDS CS278	OP	*	22.00
96	BOWLING CS288	*	*	23.00
96	CENTENNIAL OLYMPIC GAMES CS267	YR	*	525.00
96	OLYMPIC GAMES CS249	*	*	N/A

FENTON ART GLASS

CONNOISSEUR COLLECTION

YR	NAME	LIMIT	ISSUE	TREND
*				
83	CRAFTSMEN STEIN 9640WI	1500	35.00	75.00

HADLEY COMPANIES

T. REDLIN

YR	NAME	LIMIT	ISSUE	TREND
95	WINTER WONDERLAND	45 DAYS	40.00	40.00
96	PLEASURES OF WINTER	2000	60.00	60.00

LONGTON CROWN

* — **ALL-STAR SLUGGERS**

YR	NAME	LIMIT	ISSUE	TREND
96	MICKEY MANTLE		40.00	40.00

L. MARTIN — **AMERICA THE BEAUTIFUL**

96	GOD'S GRACE ON THEE	OP	32.95	33.00

* — **BABE RUTH**

97	THE 60TH HOME RUN, 1927		40.00	40.00

* — **CINEMA SWEETHEART**

97	SEVEN YEAR ITCH		45.00	45.00

L. KAATZ — **CLASSIC WATERFOWL**

96	MALLARDS AT SUNRISE		40.00	40.00

H. SUNDBLOM — **COCA-COLA CHRISTMAS**

97	SEASON'S GREETINGS		45.00	45.00
97	THINGS GO BETTER WITH COKE		45.00	45.00

K. DANIELS — **CRY OF THE WOLFPACK**

96	SCOUTING THE BLUFFS		40.00	40.00

T. KINKADE — **EMERALD ISLE**

97	EMERALD ISLE COTTAGE		45.00	45.00

* — **FACES OF HOPE**

97	NOBLE GRIZZLY		45.00	45.00

* — **GOLDEN AGE OF ELVIS COLLECTION**

97	TEDDY BEAR		45.00	45.00

* — **GREAT BATTLES OF THE CIVIL WAR**

97	GETTYSBURG		42.00	42.00

T. KINKADE — **HOME FOR THE HOLIDAYS**

97	VICTORIAN CHRISTMAS		48.00	48.00

* — **LEGENDS OF BASEBALL SIGNATURE**

96	JIMMIE FOXX: THE BEAST	OP	34.95	35.00
96	WALTER JOHNSON: BIG TRAIN	OP	34.95	35.00

* — **NASA MISSIONS OF HONOR**

97	EAGLE HAS LANDED, THE		40.00	40.00

* — **NATIONAL FRESHWATER FISHING HALL OF FAME**

97	LARGE MOUTH BASS 22 LB. 4 OZ.		50.00	50.00

C. COOLIDGE — **ORIGINAL POKER DOGS**

97	THE LAST HAND		30.00	30.00

* — **PORTRAITS OF THE WILD**

97	WHITE TAILED DEER		40.00	40.00

N. ROCKWELL — **ROCKWELL'S ANNUAL CHRISTMAS COLLECTION**

97	SANTA'S WORKSHOP		50.00	50.00

* — **STAR TREK: THESE ARE THE VOYAGES**

97	THE DOOMSDAY MACHINE		45.00	45.00

* — **SUPERBOWL CHAMPIONS**

97	GREEN BAY PACKERS		50.00	50.00
97	MIAMI DOLPHINS, THE		50.00	50.00
97	SAN FRANCISCO 49ERS		50.00	50.00

L.K. MARTIN — **THE SPORTING BREEDS**

97	BLACK LABORADOR		35.00	35.00
97	CHOCOLATE LABORADOR		35.00	35.00

K. DANIELS — **TIMBERWOLF: LORD OF THE WILDERNESS**

96	FIRST OUTING	OP	42.95	43.00

YR	NAME	LIMIT	ISSUE	TREND
*		**UNDER THE LIGHT OF DANCING SKIES**		
97	NEW MOON'S LIGHT	*	50.00	50.00
*		**UNDER THE LIGHT OF DANCING SKIES COLLECTION**		
97	ECHOES IN THE NIGHT	*	50.00	50.00
	T. KINKADE		**WOODLAND RETREAT**	
97	AUTUMN'S GLORY	*	40.00	40.00
97	SIMPLER TIMES	*	40.00	40.00
	T. KINKADE	**WOODLAND RETREAT COLLECTION**		
97	BEGINNING OF A PERFECT DAY	*	40.00	40.00
	C. FRACE	**WORLD'S MOST MAGNIFICENT CATS**		
97	NOBLE CONFINES	*	40.00	40.00

M. CORNELL IMPORTERS

YR	NAME	LIMIT	ISSUE	TREND
*			**CORNELL STEINS**	
86	JOIN US! GEMUETLICHKEIT 3766	10000	30.00	40.00
87	A TOAST 3963	10000	88.00	113.00
87	ALPINE FLOWER 4047	5000	90.00	100.00
87	BEERWAGON 6280	4000	110.00	133.00
87	BERLIN CITY 3788	5000	130.00	159.00
87	BERLIN CITY UNLIDDED 3789	5000	88.00	113.00
87	CLUB HUNT 4402	8000	87.00	106.00
87	ELK 6340	5000	100.00	120.00
87	ELK UNLIDDED 6342	5000	30.00	38.00
87	FARMER & PLOW 3423	10000	88.00	113.00
87	FARMER & PLOW UNLIDDED 3424	10000	35.00	49.00
87	GOLDEN HOPS & MALT 6279	4000	159.00	219.00
87	GRIZZLY BEAR 6331	5000	100.00	120.00
87	GRIZZLY BEAR UNLIDDED 6333	5000	30.00	38.00
87	HAPPY DWARF 6282	4000	106.00	137.00
87	HEIDELBERG 6278	4000	100.00	125.00
87	HOT AIR BALLOON	5000	100.00	130.00
87	JOIN US! GEMUETLICHKEIT 3767	10000	78.00	100.00
87	JOIN US! GEMUETLICHKEIT 3768	10000	125.00	150.00
87	MAY STROLL 3770	10000	79.00	100.00
87	MAY STROLL UNLIDDED 3769	10000	30.00	40.00
87	MOOSE 6337	5000	100.00	120.00
87	MOOSE UNLIDDED 6339	5000	100.00	120.00
87	WEDDING PARADE 3776	10000	85.00	104.00
87	WEDDING PARADE UNLIDDED 3775	10000	35.00	48.00
87	WHITE TAIL DEER 6343	5000	100.00	120.00
87	WHITE TAIL DEER UNLIDDED 6345	5000	30.00	38.00
87	ZITHER PLAYER 3773	10000	85.00	106.00
87	ZITHER PLAYER UNLIDDED 3772	10000	35.00	48.00
88	BEER BARREL 6285	4000	130.00	137.00
88	FATHER & SON 6291	4000	115.00	135.00
88	PROLETARIAN 3970	5000	100.00	118.00
88	ROYAL KING LUDWIG 6287	4000	194.00	200.00
88	SUMMER 6286	4000	80.00	89.00
88	TYROLEAN 4413	9000	80.00	84.00
89	AHRENS-FOX FIRE ENGINE 3719	10000	119.00	158.00
89	AHRENS-FOX FIRE ENGINE UNLIDDED 3720	10000	35.00	44.00
89	APOSTLE 6298	2000	239.00	290.00
89	BICYCLIST 4723	5000	68.00	86.00
89	CAROUSEL 6467	5000	159.00	190.00
89	CAROUSEL MUSICAL 6468	5000	184.00	220.00
89	COOPER (BARREL MAKER)	2000	110.00	135.00
89	FIREFIGHTER 4765	5000	68.00	86.00
89	GAMBRINUS 3792	10000	125.00	130.00
89	GAMBRINUS UNLIDDED 3793	10000	40.00	50.00
89	MUNICH 3790	10000	115.00	190.00
89	PROLETARIAN UNLIDDED 3972	5000	45.00	60.00
89	RED BARON 6295	4000	100.00	130.00
89	SINGER 4768	5000	68.00	86.00
89	SINGER UNLIDDED 4767	5000	38.00	45.00
89	ST. GEORGE 4409	6000	150.00	165.00
89	VILLAGE BLACKSMITH 6308	2000	110.00	135.00
89	WEDDING DANCE JUG 4048	1500	239.00	299.00
89	WEIHNACHTEN 3716	10000	150.00	185.00
89	WEIHNACHTEN UNLIDDED 3717	10000	110.00	139.00
90	BERLIN WALL 6320	2000	100.00	110.00
90	BICYCLIST 6325	4000	120.00	130.00
90	CLIPPER 3814	10000	168.00	185.00
90	CLIPPER UNLIDDED 3811	10000	47.00	50.00
90	FIREFIGHTER 6327	4000	120.00	135.00
90	FRIEDOLIN 3785	10000	99.00	110.00
90	FRIEDOLIN UNLIDDED 3784	10000	47.00	50.00
90	GOLFER 3820	10000	168.00	185.00
90	GOLFER UNLIDDED 3816	10000	47.00	50.00
90	GRENZAU CASTLE 4590	12000	119.50	132.00
90	LORELEY 3782	10000	95.00	104.00
90	LORELEY UNLIDDED 3781	10000	43.00	47.00
90	MUNICH BIER-WAGON 6326	4000	150.00	165.00
90	NAS GRIZZLY BEAR 4451	20000	175.00	193.00
90	NAS HUMPBACK WHALE	20000	175.00	193.00
90	NAS PEREGRINE FALCON 4452	20000	175.00	193.00

Wolves take center stage in the Scouting the Bluffs stein available from Longton Crown in 1996. It was based on artwork by Kevin Daniels.

Limited to 50,000, Anheuser-Busch's Beagle stein is part of the company's "Hunters Companion Series."

This open edition St. Patrick's Day stein from Anheuser-Busch celebrates the Irish holiday.

Mallards at Sunrise was offered in the "Classic Waterfowl" series from Longton Crown. It was based on art by Lynn Kaatz.

YR	NAME	LIMIT	ISSUE	TREND
90	NAS WOOD DUCK 4453	20000	175.00	193.00
90	NOAH'S ARK 6469	5000	129.00	150.00
90	SEPPL 3779	10000	95.00	104.00
90	SEPPL UNLIDDED 3778	10000	43.00	47.00
90	STONEWARE NUTCRACKER 6473	5000	139.00	150.00
90	TURNVATER JAHN 3797	10000	137.50	150.00
90	TURNVATER JAHN UNLIDDED 3796	10000	95.00	104.00
90	WIESBADEN 3794	2000	125.00	140.00
90	WIESBADEN UNLIDDED 3795	2000	100.00	115.00
E. BREIDEN			**CORNELL STEINS**	
87	MALLARD 4041	4000	100.00	130.00
87	WILD BOAR 4044	4000	100.00	130.00
P. DUEMLER			**CORNELL STEINS**	
87	BIBLE 3870	10000	80.00	99.00
87	BIBLE UNLIDDED 3869	10000	30.00	42.00
87	BICYCLISTS UNLIDDED, THE 3857	10000	30.00	42.00
87	BICYCLISTS, THE 3858	10000	80.00	100.00
87	CARDPLAYER UNLIDDED, THE 3868	10000	35.00	47.00
87	CARDPLAYER, THE 3867	10000	190.00	220.00
87	CENTURIO 3861	10000	74.00	88.00
87	CENTURIO UNLIDDED 3860	10000	30.00	42.00
87	CHERUSKAN 3873	10000	109.00	148.00
87	CHERUSKAN UNLIDDED 3872	10000	40.00	55.00
87	DR. FAUST 3851	10000	80.00	98.00
87	DR. FAUST 3852	10000	30.00	40.00
87	MINUET 3876	10000	79.00	108.00
87	MINUET UNLIDDED 3875	10000	30.00	42.00
87	PATRIZIER 3864	10000	75.00	88.00
87	PATRIZIER UNLIDDED 3863	10000	30.00	42.00
88	DRAGON SLAYER 3980	10000	165.00	200.00
88	DRAGON SLAYER BEER CHALICE 3982	10000	79.00	105.00
88	ROYALTY 3878	10000	80.00	88.00
88	ROYALTY 3880	10000	110.00	130.00
89	CRUSADER 3883	10000	145.00	180.00
89	GENERAL TILLY TANKARD 3715	5000	379.50	440.00
89	ROYALTY 3887	10000	65.00	75.00
89	ROYALTY UNLIDDED 3888	10000	35.00	47.00
W. GOSSEL			**CORNELL STEINS**	
90	BABA YAGA 4993	5000	238.00	249.00
J. LIM			**CORNELL STEINS**	
89	BALD EAGLE 3721	10000	150.00	175.00
89	BALD EAGLE 3722	10000	110.00	139.00
89	BALD EAGLE UNLIDDED 3723	10000	40.00	48.00
89	DRAGON REGIMENTAL 4992	5000	199.00	249.00

CATEGORY INDEX

COMPANY INDEX

A

3-Dimensional Editions, 784
Adolf Sehring Studio, 194
Adrian Taron & Sons, 194, 509
Amazee Gifts, 22
AMCAL Fine Arts, 784
American Artists, 194, 640, 784
American Greetings, 509
American Legacy, 785
American Masters, 785
American Rails & Highways, 640
American Rose Society, 641
Americast Inc., 194
Anheuser-Busch Inc., 195, 510, 641, 880
Annalee Mobilitee, 82, 510
Anna-Perenna, 195, 510, 642, 788
ANRI, 10, 107, 195, 511, 642
Applejack Ltd., 788
Arabia Annual, 643
Ardleigh-Elliott, 206
Armani, 206, 511
Armstrong's, 211, 644, 788
Art Impressions West, 788
Art of Glynda Turley, The, 867
Art World of Bourgeault, 644, 788
Artaffects, 10, 108, 211, 511, 645, 788
Arthur Court Designs, 512
Artists of the World, 10, 214, 512, 650, 789
Ashton-Drake Galleries, 108, 215, 512
Attic Babies, 118
Aviation Art Museum, 789
Avonlea Traditions Inc., 119, 215

B

B. Bourgeau Richards Collection, 789
Banberry Designs Inc., 215
Band Creations, 22, 215, 512
Barber Gallery, 790
Bareuther, 651
Bartz Studios, 791
Belleek, 651
Benson Fine Art Prints, 791
Berlin Design, 651
Biedermann & Sons, 513, 652
Bill Vernon Studios, 217
Bing & Grondahl, 10, 218, 513, 652
Bishop Fine Art Ltd., 792
Boehm Studios, 218, 656
Boyds Collection Ltd., 119, 223, 513
Bradford Editions, 11, 121, 225, 514
Bradford Exchange, 121, 656
Brandywine Woodcrafts, 23, 514
Briercroft, 225, 514, 681, 792
Brighter Image Publishing, 792
Buccellati, 514
Byers' Choice Ltd., 226
Byliny's Porcelain, 681

C

C.U.I./Carolina Collection, 11, 682
Cairn Studio Ltd., 228
Caney Creek Publishing, 792
Carriage House Studio Inc., 514
Cast Art, 232
Cat Corcilius, 792
Cavanagh Group, 24, 121, 233, 514, 682
Cazenovia Abroad, 516

Charles Sadek Import Co., 235
Charming Tails, 235, 517
Christian Ulbricht USA, 237
Christina's World, 518
Christopher Paluso Art Works, 792
Christopher Radko, 520
Chust Country, 238, 792
Circle Fine Art, 792
Clarissa's Creations, 682
Cole Fine Art, 796
Collectables, The, 186
Competitive Images, 796
Constance Collection, 238
Country Artists, 240
Creart, 242
Creative Craftsmen, 25
Crestley Collection, 682
Cross Gallery, 797
Crown & Rose, 11
Crown Parian, 683
Crystal World, 243
Cybis, 250, 532

D

D'arceau Limoges, 684
Daddy's Long Legs, 121, 254
Danbury Mint, 11, 254, 686
Dave Grossman Creations, 11, 25, 254, 532, 687, 797
David Winter Cottages/Enesco Corp., 25
David Winter Cottages/John Hine Studios, 26
Deborah Robinson, 797
Delgado Studio, 798
Delphi, 688
Dennis P. Lewan Fine Art Studios, 798
Department 56, 11, 31, 123, 258, 533, 690
Diana Art, 691
Diane Phalen Watercolors, 798
Dianna Effner Porcelain Dolls, 123
Different Drummer Studios, 42
Dimensional Aesthetics, 799
Dolls by Jerri, 123
Duncan Royale, 264, 691
Dynasty Doll, 124

E

Eagle Editions Ltd., 799
Edna Hibel Studios, 126, 691, 799
Edwin M. Knowles, 126, 692
Eggspressions, 267
Eighth Avenue Graphics, 800
Elke's Originals, 127
Emi, 269
Enchantica, 702
Endurance, 269
Enesco Corp., 11, 43, 127, 270, 534, 702
Ertl Collectibles, 43, 127, 299, 554

F

Fairmont, 704
Fantastic Art, 800
Faraway, 802
Fenton Art Glass, 12, 128, 299, 554, 704, 885
Figi Collections Inc., 318, 554

Fitz & Floyd, 128, 705
FJ Designs/Cat's Meow, 43, 319, 554
Flambro, 320, 555, 706, 803
For Arts Sake, 803
Forma Vitrum, 53
Fountainhead, 706, 803
Frame House, 803
Franklin Mint, 325, 706

G

Ganz, 128, 325, 555
Gartlan USA, 328, 706, 805
Genesis Designs, 54, 330
Geo. Zoltan Lefton Co., 330
Georgetown Collection Inc., 128, 708
Ghent Collection, 708
Glass Eye, 331, 556
Goebel Inc., 15, 54, 129, 331, 556, 708
Goebel Miniatures, 345
Good-Kruger Dolls, 134
Gorham, 15, 135, 348, 558, 709
Grande Copenhagen, 712
Granget, 350
Greenwich Workshop, 16, 351, 805
Guildhall Inc., 810
Gund Inc., 138, 351, 810

H

H & G Studios, 138, 712
Hackett American, 712
Hadley Companies, 54, 558, 713, 810, 885
Hallmark, 16, 139, 351, 559, 713
Hamilton Collection, 139, 352, 714
Hamilton Gifts, 16, 355, 608
Hamilton/Boehm, 356, 729
Hampshire Pewter Co., 16
Hand & Hammer, 610
Hanford's, 357
Harbour Lights, 54, 613
Harmony Kingdom, 357
Harold Rigsby, 814
Haviland & Parlon, 730
Haviland, 730
Hawthorne, 56, 358, 613
Helen Paul Watercolors, 815
Helen Sabatte Designs Inc., 358
Henning Publishing, 815
Historical Art Prints Ltd., 815
Hutschenreuther, 360, 730

I

Imperial Ching-te Chen, 731
Imperial Graphics Ltd., 816
Incolay, 731
International Silver, 732
Iris Arc, 360
Ispanky, 360

J

J.H. Boone, 363
J.S. Perry Originals, 817
Jack Terry Fine Art, 817
Jan Hagara Collectables, 16, 143, 364, 614, 732, 818
Jan McLean Originals, 143
Jan's Originals, 62, 364
Jeffrey Scott Co., 62, 365

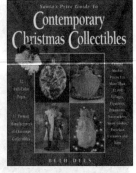